August 24–27, 2014
New York, NY, USA

Association for Computing Machinery

Advancing Computing as a Science & Profession

KDD

KDD'14

Proceedings of the 20th ACM SIGKDD International Conference on Knowledge Discovery and Data Mining

Sponsored by:

ACM SIGKDD
ACM SIGMOD

Supported by:

Bloomberg, Bosch, Facebook, Microsoft, Rapidminer, Amazon, AT&T, Baidu, Booking.com, Criteo, Goldman Sachs, Google, Huawei, IBM Research, IBM Watson, SAS, Siemens, Verizon, Yahoo! Labs, eBay, Flipkart.com, Stanford, Collective, Technicolor, Leidos, Zementis, Knime, dstillery, KDnuggets, Big Data Journal, Kaggle, NYU Stern, Donors Choose.org, NSF, American Airlines, Oracle Labs

Association for Computing Machinery

Advancing Computing as a Science & Profession

The Association for Computing Machinery
2 Penn Plaza, Suite 701
New York, New York 10121-0701

ISBN: 978-1-4503-2956-9 (Digital)

ISBN: 978-1-4503-3270-5 (Print)

Additional copies may be ordered prepaid from:

ACM Order Department
PO Box 30777
New York, NY 10087-0777, USA

Phone: 1-800-342-6626 (USA and Canada)
+1-212-626-0500 (Global)
Fax: +1-212-944-1318
E-mail: acmhelp@acm.org
Hours of Operation: 8:30 am – 4:30 pm ET

ACM Order Number: 618142

Printed in the USA

General Chairs' Welcome

This Year's Theme: Data Science for Social Good

It is our great pleasure to welcome you to the 20th ACM SIGKDD Conference on Knowledge Discovery and Data Mining (KDD). The annual ACM SIGKDD conference is the premier international forum for data science, data mining, knowledge discovery and big data. It brings together researchers and practitioners from academia, industry, and government to share their ideas, research results and experiences. KDD-2014 features plenary presentations, paper presentations, poster sessions, workshops, tutorials, exhibits, and the KDD Cup competition. We are happy to announce that this year we are partnering with Bloomberg to emphasize our theme of Data Science for Social Good. To this end, part of our workshop and tutorial program will be held at the Bloomberg facilities together with Bloomberg-specific events, all focusing on issues pertaining to social good.

Today, you hear a lot about data science, big data and data intensive computing. The core of this work is extracting knowledge and useful information from data, which for science leads to beautiful insights, and for applications leads to actions, alerts and decisions. The KDD community has always been at the center of this activity and it is clear from this conference that it will continue to drive this broader field of data science.

This year we had a record number of submissions. There were 1036 submissions to the Research Track, and 151 papers were accepted. There were 197 submissions to the Industry and Government Track, and 44 papers were accepted.

KDD also has a history of inviting talks that are of broad interest to the KDD community. This year we chose to have 4 plenary talks. A program committee also selected 8 talks to present at the Industry and Government track.

A strength of the KDD conference is the number of workshops and tutorials that are co-located with it. This year there were 9 full-day workshops, 16 half-day workshops, and 12 tutorials. As part of our partnership with Bloomberg on the theme of social good, Bloomberg will have 3 workshops jointly located with our workshops at their New York Office.

Our community is a unique blend of industry and academia, ranging from people starting their career to leaders in their respective fields. This year, we are piloting programs to facilitate networking amongst these groups. Specifically, we have a networking lounge for industry and job-seekers to meet and we helped find good matches. We also have a networking event focused on defining what a data science career looks like and have senior members meet young people to help them understand the skills needed and what a job in this discipline might entail.

We would like to thank all sponsors, who are a very important part of the conference, and the members of the Organizing Committee and our other colleagues who volunteered their time during the past year to make this conference a success. Special thanks goes to the Research Track Co-Chairs and the Industry and Government Track Co-Chairs. Also special thanks are due to the Workshops Co-Chairs, the Sponsorship Chair, the Treasurer, the Publications Co-Chairs, and the KDD Cup Committee.

We are grateful to the several program committees that provided the advice necessary to put together a quality program – the Research Track Program Committee, the Research Track Senior Program Committee, the Industry and Government Track Program Committee, the Industry Practice Expo Program Committee, the Workshop Program Committee, and the Tutorial Program Committee.

Please join us for KDD-2014 to gain new knowledge and to exchange exciting new research results, leading practices, high impact applications, and to increase your social network. We hope that you will find this program interesting and thought-provoking and that the conference will provide you with a valuable opportunity to share ideas with other researchers and practitioners from institutions around the world.

Sofus A. Macskassy
KDD 2014 General Co-Chair
Facebook, USA

Claudia Perlich
KDD 2014 General Co-Chair
Dstillery, USA

Research Track Program Chairs' Welcome

The KDD conference has seen remarkable growth since its origins as an IJCAI workshop in Detroit in 1989, evolving into a full-fledged research conference in 1995, underscoring the important role that data mining as a field has played in extracting knowledge and actionable insights from vast troves of data that are being generated in the digital world as well as in the physical world around us. This year, we received a record-high number of 1,036 submissions to the research program, out of which 151 papers were accepted. Overall, the number of submissions has increased 42% over the last year (KDD '13), while the acceptance rate dropped from 17.2% last year to 14.6% this year. This makes KDD 2014 by far the biggest and the most competitive KDD in its 20-year history.

Among academic conferences, the KDD conference typically has more of an emphasis on research motivated by real-world applications. It is important to keep in mind that it is this synergy of research in areas such as algorithms, computational geometry, database, graph theory, machine learning, natural language processing, statistics, visualization, and many others when applied to problems arising in diverse fields, such as the Web, medicine, biology, and marketing, driving our field forward and making it vibrant and fun.

The breadth of topics covered in this year's research program is truly comprehensive and nicely balanced among social and information networks (6.58% of papers), data mining for social good (5.26%), graph mining (5.26%), statistical techniques for big data (5.26%), recommender systems (4.61%), data streams (3.95%), scalable methods (3.95%), Web mining (3.29%), clustering (3.29%), feature selection (3.29%), applications to health care and medicine (3.29%), mining rich data types (2.63%), and many more. In particular, we are happy to observe an increase in the number of papers related to data mining for social good, as well as works on scaling up algorithms to deal with big data. It is extremely encouraging to see that data mining is branching out to many application areas of societal importance: public policy, education, healthcare, medicine, smart cities, the Internet of things, and many others. We hope that this trend of data mining affecting all aspects of our society will definitely continue in the future.

We are also very fortunate to have four world-class keynote speakers this year spanning industry and academia, providing inspirational talks on cutting-edge techniques and issues in big data, automatic knowledge discovery, and decision making in medicine, science, and understanding human behavior.

The process of whittling down the initial 1,036 submissions to the final set of 151 accepted papers required the coordination and time of a large number of willing volunteers. The program committee (PC) consisted of 376 reviewers (PC members) and 46 senior PC members. The selection of the PC members involved quantitative constraints to achieve a well-balanced coverage of expertise matching the expected distribution of the submissions' subject areas, as well as requiring seniority and freshness in the field. In the first review phase, each submitted paper was automatically assigned to three reviewers (after a bidding process). After the first round of reviewing was complete, the papers were assigned to the senior PC members based on their bids. The senior PC members then initiated discussions on many of the papers, e.g., if there was significant divergence in scores among reviewers or if a paper was on the borderline of being accepted. Following the discussion phase, the senior PC members provided a recommendation score and a meta-review for each paper. In the final phase, we (the program chairs) normalized and analyzed all of this information, starting with the obvious accept and reject decisions, and then we gradually focused in more detail on the papers near the borderline, seeking additional reviews and input from the PC and senior PC members where appropriate. The top-rated papers were provided to an awards committee, chaired by Thorsten Joachims and Sunita Sarawagi, who chose the best paper and best student paper award winners.

We conclude with some well-deserved words of thanks to the large supporting cast. We thank all authors for submitting their research to KDD 2014. We are extremely grateful to the PC members and senior PC members for volunteering their time to help in the review process. Diligent peer review is an essential cornerstone for research progress, and we thank you all for the many detailed and conscientious reviews that were generated. Last year's program chairs, Inderjit Dhillon and Yehuda Koren, were generous in providing us with advice and expertise based on lessons learned in 2013. We would also like to convey our sincere thanks to the staff who run the Microsoft CMT system—they were more than willing to answer questions and help us at all times during the submission, review, and decision process. Finally, we would like to thank all of our colleagues on the KDD 2014 organization committee, who were a pleasure to work with and without whom we would not have such a wonderful conference. Let the 20th ACM SIGKDD conference begin—we hope you enjoy it!

Jure Leskovec and Wei Wang
ACM SIGKDD 2014 Program Chairs

Industry & Government Track Program Chairs' Welcome

The 2014 Industry & Government Track continues the focus on real applications of KDD technologies that provide measurable and documented benefits to Industry and Government. One of the changes implemented this year is the merger of the previous years' Industry Practice Expo (IPE) with the Industry & Government Track, to be presented as the Industry Government Track Invited Talk series. We have done this in an effort to better align scheduling and content.

Overall, the Industry & Government Track is focused on highlighting the contributions that KDD researchers and practitioners have made towards solving problems in industry and government organizations, as well as increasing awareness and understanding of practical issues regarding the deployment and use of KDD technologies. We solicited papers in three areas:

(1) Deployed papers that describe the implementation, deployment, and evaluation of KDD systems in industry and government.
(2) Emerging papers that are not about deployed systems but solve a real problem in industry and government using real data, solid evaluation and a clear path to deployment. The expectation is that these applications will be deployed in the future and these papers are reporting on early work.
(3) Discovery papers that describe discoveries of new knowledge that is valuable to an industry or government organization. These papers are typically very rare and the discoveries need to be evaluated by domain experts.

There were several classes of technically sound papers that were not a good fit to the Industry and Government track and were thus rejected. Papers that asserted the existence of a potential problem that could be solved by KDD technologies but provided no evidence of interest from potential users of that problem, and papers that used real data but did not attempt to deal with real-world complexities were rejected. Papers that proposed and applied a novel algorithm to a real dataset that achieved better performance according to some metric, but did not have any evidence of external validation or interest from potential users, were also rejected from this track. Those papers are valuable for the KDD community but not a good fit for the Industry & Government Track which is focused on real, deployed (or on the path to deployment) applications as opposed to applying an algorithm to a data set. As one PC member stated in a review "Using real data is not the same as solving real problems in a real operational setting."

On the other hand, papers that discussed enabling infrastructure or issues of general interest regarding the real-world use of KDD technologies were viewed favorably, even when they did not discuss a specific case study or application. These infrastructure and issue papers were included in the "emerging" category.

The application areas of accepted papers cover a broad range, including the theme this year of social good, public safety, advertising, social analytics, personalization, workforce analytics, health, and others, showing the wide range of fields to which KDD is being applied and adding value.

The track received **193** papers and accepted **44**, for an overall acceptance rate of **22.7%**. All submitted papers received at least three reviews from separate PC members. For papers with divergent recommendations, a discussion among reviewers was held to reach consensus. The Senior PC member assigned to the paper then performed a meta-review of all papers whose ratings and reviews were sufficiently positive that there was a possibility of acceptance. We then made our final decisions based on paper quality, initial reviews, meta-review, and fit to the track's goals as evidenced by the paper's ranking on all of the review criteria.

We would like to thank all our PC and Senior PC members whose reviews were critical in helping us select the best possible program for this year's Industry and Government track.

The Industry & Government Track Invited Talk series features presentations from leading experts who have developed and deployed large-scale data mining applications and systems in their respective fields that have generated measurable and meaningful impact. We trust that this opportunity for the KDD community to hear directly from industry and government practitioners will inspire new advances and broader interdisciplinary collaboration between researchers, industry and government counterparts and organizations leveraging data for social good.

Following in the steps of three previous Industry Practice Expo (IPE) sessions, we have worked hard to live up to the high bar set by previous speakers and to strive for the right balance between business context and technical depth in this year's invited talks.

This year, we present to you world-renowned experts whose talks will help you learn and take key ideas back to your respective professional endeavors. Featured topics include applications in medicine, crime, data collection and compensation in emerging markets, personalization, using unstructured text and imaging data from natural disasters, real-world predictive modeling infrastructure and examples of data science work from the New York Mayor's Office. Attendees will also learn about the new science of Information Environment Security. We're excited that a number of talks align with the conference theme of "Data Science for Social Good". Jake Porway (of DataKind) will host an "ignite"-style session where NGOs and other non-profits will present their applications, goals and issues related to their data assets to further inspire attendees in the area of social good.

It has been a great pleasure to work with our invited talk advisory committee comprising Misha Bilenko, Eric Bloedorn, Usama Fayyad, Johannes Gehrke, Ronny Kohavi, Ying Li, Gabor Melli, Rajesh Parekh, Jian Pei, Gregory Piatetsky, Ramasamy Uthurusamy and Mohammed Zaki. We thank them and the other members of the organizing committee for advice and support throughout the search for candidate speakers.

We warmly welcome you to the KDD 2014 Industry & Government Track, and hope you find these papers and invited talks interesting and insightful. Your suggestions and comments are much appreciated.

Best Regards,
Rayid Ghani, Prem Melville, Brian Dalessandro, and Paul Bradley

Bloomberg Welcome

On behalf of Bloomberg, and particularly the technology and design organizations within Bloomberg, we are pleased to welcome you to "KDD at Bloomberg."

Bloomberg sits at the intersection of technology, data and finance. We recognize that we have a unique opportunity to leverage our strengths to drive meaningful change, while we also create competitive advantage and value for our customers. It is why we are so excited to be a part of the SIGKDD's annual flagship KDD 2014 conference, which has a special focus on applying data science to improve civic and social outcomes.

Data scientists have a tremendous opportunity to contribute to the most pressing problems faced by policy makers today. Since the inception of our company, we've shown that data is crucial to making informed decisions, and that it can also have a broader societal impact. This event presents an excellent opportunity to help bring together communities that are ideally positioned to help address society's greatest challenges.

Through our event researchers and participants will be able to engage with practitioners, policy makers and activists engaged in NGO's. We hope that together they will discover opportunities to utilize data science in socially relevant application domains like public health, medicine, urbanization and geopolitical disparity. Our motivation is to explore how technical innovation around data-driven analytics can identify new opportunities and accelerate solutions to pressing societal issues like climate change or the spread of disease.

We hope that by partnering with KDD, we are creating a platform so that industry and academic research can come together to generate not just a conversation but more importantly concrete, measurable actions that will help make the world a better place.

Vlad K.
Bloomberg Head of R&D

Shawn E.
Bloomberg CTO

Table of Contents

Research Session 3: Applications to Healthcare and Medicine II

Research Session 4: Recommender Systems

Research Session 5: Clustering

Research Session 6: Supervised Learning I

Research Session 7: Supervised Learning II

Research Session 8: Trend, Anomaly and Novelty Detection

Research Session 9: Data Streams

Research Session 10: Active Learning

Research Session 11: Feature Selection

Research Session 12: Statistical Techniques for Big Data

Research Session 13: Scaling-up Methods for Big Data

Research Session 14: Large-scale Optimization and Learning

Research Session 15: Web Mining

Research Session 16: Transfer Learning

Research Session 17: Recommendations and Ratings

Research Session 18: Topic Modeling

Research Session 19: Security and Privacy

Volume 1 - Author Index 961

Research Session 20: Dimensionality Reduction

Research Session 21: Novel Applications

Research Session 22: Crowds and Markets

Research Session 23: Text Mining

Research Session 24: Dynamic Graph Analysis

Research Session 25: Diffusion in Social and Information Networks

Research Session 26: Social and Information Networks

Research Session 27: Graph Mining and Modeling

Research Session 28: Network Community Detection

Research Session 29: Scaling-up Graph Algorithms

Research Session 30: Social Network Analysis

Industry & Government Invited Talks

Industry & Government

Panel

Tutorials

KDD'14 Conference on Knowledge Discovery & Data Mining Organization

General Chairs: Sofus Macskassy (Facebook)
Claudia Perlich (Dstillery)

Research Track Program Chairs: Jure Leskovec (Stanford University)
Wei Wang (UCLA)

Industry & Government Track Program Chairs: Rayid Ghani (University of Chicago & Edgeflip)
Prem Melville (Social Alpha)

Industry & Government Track Invited Talks Chairs: Paul Bradley (MethodCare)
Brian Dalessandro (Dstillery)

Workshop Chairs: Alejandro Jaimes (Yahoo!)
Dragos Margineantu (Boeing)

Tutorial Chairs: Ying Li (EV Analysis Corporation)
Jian Pei (Simon Fraser University)

Poster and Spotlight Chairs: Aris Gionis (Aalto University)
Jie Tang (Tsinghua University)

Local Arrangements Chair: Shannon Cunningham (Executive Events)

Exhibits and Demo Chair: Shannon Cunningham (Executive Events)

SIGKDD 2014 Awards Chair: Gabor Melli (VigLink)

KDD Cup Chairs: William Cukierski (Kaggle)
Ben Hamner (Kaggle)

Media and Publicity Chairs: Kaitlin Atkinson (PeekAnalytics)
Polo Chau (Georgia Tech)
Ankur Teredesai (University of Washington)

Panel Chairs: Raghu Ramakrishnan (Microsoft)
Geoff Webb (Monash University)

Publications Chairs: Jing Gao (University at Buffalo)
Xiang Zhang (Case Western Reserve University)

Sponsorship Chair: Balaji Krishnapuram (Siemens)

Treasurer: Ted Senator (Leidos)

Best Paper Chairs: Thorsten Joachims (Cornell University)
Sunita Sarawagi (IIT Bombay)

Student Award Chairs: Tanya Berger-Wolf (University of Illinois at Chicago)
Bart Goethals (University of Antwerp)

Webmaster & Web Designers: Andrej Krevl (Stanford University)
Sébastien Robaszkiewicz (Stanford University)

Registration Chair: Brooke Daley (Executivevents, Inc.)

KDD'14 Research Track Senior Program Committee

Naoki Abe (IBM T. J. Watson Research Center)
Deepak Agarwal (LinkedIn)
Charu C. Aggarwal (IBM T. J. Watson Research Center)
James Bailey (The University of Melbourne)
Arindam Banerjee (University of Minnesota)
Paul Bennett (Microsoft Research)
Francesco Bonchi (Yahoo! Labs)
Deepayan Chakrabarti (Facebook)
Hong Cheng (Chinese University of Hong Kong)
Diane Cook (Washington State University)
W. Bruce Croft (University of Massachusetts)
Ian Davidson (University of California, Davis)
Inderjit Dhillon (University of Texas at Austin)
Tina Eliassi-Rad (Rutgers University)
Martin Ester (Simon Fraser University)
Christos Faloutsos (Carnegie Mellon University)
Evgeniy Gabrilovich (Google)
Lise Getoor (University of California, Santa Cruz)
Aristides Gionis (Aalto University)
Bart Goethals (University of Antwerp)
Dimitrios Gunopulos (University of Athens)
Jiawei Han (University of Illinois at Urbana-Champaign)
Thorsten Joachims (Cornell University)
Eamonn Keogh (University of California, Riverside)
Yehuda Koren (Google)
Ravi Kumar (Google)
Shou-de Lin (National Taiwan University)
Chih-Jen Lin (National Taiwan University)
Christopher Meek (Microsoft Research)
Srinivasan Parthasarathy (Ohio State University)
Jian Pei (Simon Fraser University)
Saharon Rosset (Tel Aviv University)
Sunita Sarawagi (IIT Bombay)
Jimeng Sun (Georgia Tech)
Jie Tang (Tsinghua University)
Evimaria Terzi (Boston University)
Andrew Tomkins (Google)
S. V. N. Vishwanathan (Purdue University)
Geoff Webb (Monash University)
Stefan Wrobel (University of Bonn and Fraunhofer IAIS)
Hui Xiong (Rutgers, the State University of New Jersey)
Kenji Yamanishi (University of Tokyo)
Xifeng Yan (University of California, Santa Barbara)
Qiang Yang (Hong Kong University of Science and Technology)
Philip S. Yu (University of Illinois at Chicago)
Jeffrey Yu (Chinese University of Hong Kong)

KDD'14 Research Track Program Committee

Bruno Abrahao (Cornell University)
Leman Akoglu (Stony Brook University)
Aijun An (York University)
Annalisa Appice (Università degli Studi di Bari)
Ira Assent (Aarhus University)
Tony Bagnall (University of East Anglia)
Fabricio Benevenuto (Federal University of Minas Gerais)
Tanya Berger-Wolf (University of Illinois at Chicago)
Michele Berlingerio (IBM Research Dublin)
Michael Berthold (KNIME)
Smriti Bhagat (Technicolor Palo Alto)
Jinbo Bi (University of Connecticut)
Klemens Bohm (Karlsruhe Institute of Technology (KIT))
Mario Boley (University of Bonn)
Christian Borgelt (European Centre for Soft Computing)
Henrik Bostrom (University of Stockholm)
Christos Boutsidis (IBM)
Pavel Brazdil (University of Porto)
Ulf Brefeld (Technische Universität Darmstadt)
David Buttler (Lawrence Livermore National Laboratory)
Deng Cai (Zhejiang University)
Rui Cai (Microsoft Research)
Berkant Barla Cambazoglu (Yahoo! Research)
Longbing Cao (University of Technology Sydney)
Yunbo Cao (Microsoft Research Asia)
Licia Capra (University College of London)
Lawrence Carin (Duke University)
Carlos Castillo (Qatar Computing Research Institute)
Edward Chang (HTC)
Kai-Wei Chang (University of Illinois)
Duen Horng Chau (Georgia Tech)
Nitesh Chawla (University of Notre Dame)
Sanjay Chawla (University of Sydney)
Bee-Chung Chen (LinkedIn)
Enhong Chen (University of Science and Technology of China)
Haifeng Chen (NEC Research Lab)
Ji Chen (eBay Inc.)
Ming-Syan Chen (Academic Sinica)
Songqing Chen (George Mason University)
Wei Chen (Microsoft Research)
Weizhu Chen (Microsoft)
Ye Chen (Microsoft)
Yixin Chen (Washington University in St Louis)
James Cheng (Chinese Univ. of Hong Kong)
Reynold Cheng (University of Hong Kong)
Wei Cheng (University of North Carolina at Chapel Hill)
Junghoo Cho (University of California)
Peter Christen (The Australian National University)
Wei Chu (Microsoft Research)
Tyson Condie (University of California)
Gao Cong (Nanyang Technological University)
Bin Cui (Institute of Network Computing and Information Systems)
Peng Cui (Tsinghua University)
Mahashweta Das (University of Texas)
Atish Das Sarma (eBay Research Labs)
Anirban Dasgupta (Indian Institute of Technology at Gandhinagar)
Chris Ding (University of Texas at Arlington)
Nan Ding (Google)
Wei Ding (University of Massachusetts Boston)
Carlotta Domeniconi (George Mason University)
Debora Donato (Yahoo! Research)
Anlei Dong (Yahoo! Labs)
Pinar Donmez (Salesforce)
Gideon Dror (Yahoo! Labs)
Saso Dzeroski (J. Stefan Institute)
Dora Erdos (Boston University)
Hui Fang (University of Delaware)
Elena Ferrari (University of Insubria)
Marcus Fontoura (Google)
Ada Fu (The Chinese University of Hong Kong)
Ryohei Fujimaki (NEC Laboratories America)
Benjamin C. M. Fung (McGill University)
Glenn Fung (University of Wisconsin at Madison)
Joao Gama (University of Porto)
Jing Gao (University at Buffalo)
Minos Garofalakis (Technical University of Crete)
Yong Ge (University of North Carolina at Charlotte)
David Gleich (Purdue University)
Manuel Gomez Rodriguez (Max Planck Institute for Intelligent Systems)

Francesco Gullo (Yahoo! Labs)
Asela Gunawardana (Microsoft Research)
Stephan Gunnemann (Carnegie Mellon University)
Rahul Gupta (Google)
Wook-Shin Han (POSTECH)
Jingrui He (Stevens Institute of Technology)
Qi He (LinkedIn)
Steven Hoi (Nanyang Technological University)
Geoff Holmes (The University of Waikato)
Andreas Hotho (University of Kassel)
Vagelis Hristidis (University of California)
Cho-Jui Hsieh (UT Austin)
Chun-Nan Hsu (University of California)
Jun Huan (Information and Telecommunication Technology Center)
Heng Huang (University of Texas)
Ling Huang (Intel Labs)
Seung-won Hwang (POSTECH)
Tomoharu Iwata (NTT Communication Science Laboratories)
Arun Iyer (IIT Bombay)
Prateek Jain (Microsoft Research)
Szymon Jaroszewicz (Polish Academy of Sciences)
Shuiwang Ji (Old Dominion University)
Hongxia Jin (IBM Research)
Ruoming Jin (Kent State University)
Wen Jin (Simon Fraser University)
Xiaoming Jin (Tsinghua University)
Panos Kalnis (KAUST)
Jaap Kamps (University of Amsterdam)
U Kang (KAIST)
Murat Kantarcioglu (University of Texas at Dallas)
Hisashi Kashima (The University of Tokyo)
Kristian Kersting (University of Bonn)
Myunghwan Kim (LinkedIn)
Ron Kohavi (Microsoft)
George Kollios (Boston University)
Christian Konig (Microsoft Research)
Nick Koudas (University of Toronto)
Stefan Kramer (Johannes Gutenberg - Universität Mainz)
Andreas Krause (ETH Zurich)
Peer Kroger (Ludwig-Maximilians-Universität München)
Wai Lam (The Chinese University of Hong Kong)
Theodoros Lappas (Stevens Institute of Technology)
Quoc Le (Google/CMU)
Dongwon Lee (Penn State University)
Mong-Li Lee (National University of Singapore)
Victor Lee (Kent State University)
Kristina Lerman (The University of Southern California)
Cheng-Te Li (National Taiwan University)
Guoliang Li (Tsinghua University)
Hang Li (Huawei Technologies)
Juanzi Li (Tsinghua University)
Ninghui Li (Purdue University)
Xiaoli Li (Institute for Infocomm Research)
Yuefeng Li (Queensland University of Technology)
Zhenhui Li (Penn State University)
Bangyong Liang (Microsoft Incorporation)
Ee-Peng Lim (Singapore Management University)
Hsuan-Tien Lin (National Taiwan University)
Charles Ling (Western University)
Chao Liu (Sogou Inc.)
Fei Liu (Carnegie Mellon University)
Guimei Liu (National University of Singapore)
Nathan Nan Liu (Yahoo! Labs)
Shixia Liu (Microsoft Research)
Tie-Yan Liu (Microsoft Research)
Yan Liu (University of Southern California)
David Lo (Singapore Management University)
Hung-Yi Lo (Shih-Chien University)
Yue Lu (Twitter, Inc.)
Chang-Tien Lu (Virginia Tech)
Dijun Luo (RetailMeNot)
Jiebo Luo (Rochester University)
Ping Luo (HP Lab)
Ashwin Machanavajjhala (Duke University)
Donato Malerba (University of Bari)
Hiroshi Mamitsuka (Kyoto University)
Nikos Mamoulis (University of Hong Kong)
Julian McAuley (Stanford University)
Qiaozhu Mei (University of Michigan)
Wagner Meira Jr (Universidade Federal de Minas Gerais)
Weiyi Meng (Binghamton University)
Vahab Mirrokni (Google Research)
Dunja Mladenic (J. Stefan Institute)
Katharina Morik (University of Dortmund)
Klaus-Robert Muller (TU Berlin)
Emmanuel Muller (Karlsruhe Institute of Technology (KIT))
Mirco Nanni (Istituto I.S.T.I.)

Alexandros Nanopoulos (University of Eichstätt-Ingolstadt)
Vivek Narasayya (Microsoft Research)
Franco Nardini (Information Science and Technologies Institute)
Olfa Nasraoui (University of Louisville)
Jennifer Neville (Purdue University)
Raymond Ng (University of British Columbia)
See-Kiong Ng (Institute for Infocomm Research)
Wilfred Ng (The Hong Kong University of Science and Technology)
Zaiqing Nie (Microsoft Research Asia)
Siegfried Nijssen (Leiden University)
Tim Oates (University of Maryland Baltimore County)
Zoran Obradovic (Temple University)
Iadh Ounis (University of Glasgow)
Gerhard Paass (Fraunhofer IAIS)
Rong Pan (Sun Yat-Sen University)
Spiros Papadimitriou (IBM)
Laurence Park (Univ. of Western Sydney)
Douglass Parker (University of California)
Vladimir Pavlovic (Rutgers University)
Dino Pedreschi (University of Pisa)
Wen-Chih Peng (National Chiao Tung University)
Chang-Shing Perng (IBM Research)
Bernhard Pfahringer (The University of Waikato)
Claudia Plant (The Florida State University)
Aditya Prakash (Virginia Tech)
Kunal Punera (Yahoo! Research)
Weining Qian (East China Normal University)
Kira Radinsky (Sales Predict)
Troy Raeder (Media6Degrees)
Ganesh Ramakrishnan (IIT Bombay)
Sujith Ravi (Google)
Chandan Reddy (Wayne State University)
Steffen Rendle (University of Konstanz)
Matthias Renz (Ludwig-Maximilians-Universität München)
Lior Rokach (Ben-Gurion University of the Negev)
Stefan Ruping (Fraunhofer IAIS)
Ankan Saha (LinkedIn)
Lorenza Saitta (University of Torino)
Yasushi Sakurai (Kumamoto University)
Jorg Sander (University of Alberta)
Maria Sapino (University of Torino)
Tamas Sarlos (Google)
Shin'ichi Satoh (National Institute of Informatics)
Ralf Schenkel (Max-Planck-Institut für Informatik)
Lars Schmidt-Thieme (Stiftung Universität Hildesheim)
Jeff Schneider (Carnegie Mellon University)
Dou Shen (CityGrid Media)
Heng Shen (The University of Queensland)
Jialie Shen (Singapore Management University)
Yelong Shen (Kent State University)
Yi-Dong Shen (Chinese Academy of Sciences)
Kyuseok Shim (Seoul National University)
Fabrizio Silvestri (Yahoo! Labs)
Vikas Sindhwani (IBM T.J.Watson Research Center)
Parag Singla (IIT Delhi)
Le Song (Georgia Institute of Technology)
Yangqiu Song (University of Illinois at Urbana-Champaign)
Myra Spiliopoulou (Otto-von-Guericke-Universitaet Magdeburg)
Rohini Srihari (University at Buffalo)
Gerd Stumme (University of Kassel)
Karthik Subbian (IBM T.J. Watson Labs)
L Subramaniam (IBM Research - India)
Torsten Suel (Polytechnic Institute of NYU)
Masashi Sugiyama (Tokyo Institute of Technology)
Aixin Sun (Nanyang Technological University)
Jian-Tao Sun (Microsoft Research)
Yizhou Sun (Northeastern Univ)
Einoshin Suzuki (Kyushu University)
Partha Talukdar (Carnegie Mellon University)
Ah-Hwee Tan (Nanyang Technological University)
Dacheng Tao (The University of Technology)
Yufei Tao (Chinese University of Hong Kong)
Nikolaj Tatti (Aalto University)
Alex Thomo (University of Victoria)
YongHong Tian (Peking University)
Hanghang Tong (IBM Research)
Agma Traina (University of São Paulo at São Carlos)
Volker Tresp (Ludwig Maximilian University of Munich/Siemens)
Panayiotis Tsaparas (University of Ioannina)
Vincent Tseng (National Cheng Kung University)
Jaideep Vaidya (Rutgers University)
Sergei Vassilvitskii (Google)
Michalis Vazirgiannis (Athens University of Economics and Business)
Suresh Venkatasubramanian (University of Utah)
Michail Vlachos (IBM Zurich Research Laboratory)

Jilles Vreeken (Max-Planck Institute for Informatics and Saarland University)
Slobodan Vucetic (Temple University)
Bai Wang (Bejing University of Posts and Telecommunications)
Fei Wang (IBM T. J. Watson Research Lab)
Hua Wang (Colorado School of Mines)
Jian Wang (LinkedIn)
Jianyong Wang (Tsinghua University)
Ke Wang (Simon Fraser University)
Shaojun Wang (Kno.e.sis)
Shengrui Wang (University of Sherbrooke)
Takashi Washio (Osaka University)
Ingmar Weber (Qatar Computing Research Institute)
Zhen Wen (IBM Research)
Tim Weninger (University of Notre Dame)
Robert West (Stanford University)
Raymond Wong (Hong Kong University of Science and Technology)
Junjie Wu (Beihang University)
Teresa Wu (Arizona State University)
Xintao Wu (University of North Carolina at Charlotte)
Evan Xiang (Baidu)
Xiaokui Xiao (Nanyang Technological University)
Yanghua Xiao (Fudan University)
Xing Xie (Microsoft Research Asia)
Takeshi Yamada (NTT Communication Science Laboratories)
Feng Yan (Facebook)
Rong Yan (Facebook)
De-Nian Yang (Academic Sinica)
Jaewon Yang (LinkedIn)
Jieping Ye (Arizona State University)
Mi-Yen Yeh (Academic Sinica)
Ainur Yesenalina (Amazon)
Dit-Yan Yeung (Hong Kong University of Science and Technology)
Emine Yilmaz (Microsoft Research)
Jie Yin (CSIRO ICT)
Hwanjo Yu (POSTECH)
Lei Yu (Binghamton University)
Shipeng Yu (Siemens Medical Solutions)
Xiao Yu (University of Illinois)
Yang Yu (Nanjing University)
Jing Yuan (Microsoft Research Asia)
Hyokun Yun (Purdue University)
Carlo Zaniolo (University of California)
Gerson Zaverucha (Federal University of Rio de Janeiro)
Dan Zhang (Facebook)
Kun Zhang (Max Planck Institute for Intelligent Systems)
Nan Zhang (The George Washington University)
Peng Zhang (Chinese Academy of Sciences)
Shichao Zhang (University of Technology)
Xiang Zhang (Case Western Reserve University)
Xiangliang Zhang (KAUST)
Xiaodan Zhang (Vertex Pharmaceuticals Inc.)
Xinhua Zhang (NICTA)
Zhaojun Zhang (UNC)
Zhenjie Zhang (ADSC)
Zhongfei Zhang (Binghamton University)
Peng Zhang (Chinese Academy of Science)
Bo Zhao (Microsoft Research)
Yuchen Zhao (Sumo Logic)
Zheng Zhao (SAS)
Yu Zheng (Microsoft)
Wenjun Zhou (University of Tennessee)
Feida Zhu (Singapore Management University)
Jun Zhu (Tsinghua University)
Xingquan Zhu (University of Technology)
Arthur Zimek (Ludwig-Maximilians-Universität München)

KDD'14 Industry & Government Track Senior Program Committee

Sugato Basu (Google)
Roberto Bayardo (Google)
Misha Bilenko (Microsoft)
Eric Bloedorn (MITRE)
Nancy Grady (SAIC)
Ronny Kohavi (Microsoft)
Jimmy Lin (University of Maryland)
Gabor Melli (VigLink)
Foster Provost (NYU)
Matthew Richardson (Microsoft Research)
D Sculley (Google)
Ted Senator (Leidos)
Vikas Sindhwani (IBM)

KDD'14 Industry & Government Track Program Committee

Dean Abbott (Abbott Analytics)
Naoki Abe (IBM T.J. Watson Research Center)
Kareem Aggour (GE Global Research)
Kamal Ali (Grokker)
Ricardo Baeze-Yates (UPF)
Michele Berlingerio (IBM Research Dublin)
Michael Berthold (KNIME)
Kanishka Bhaduri (NASA)
Christos Boutsidis (IBM)
Tilmann Bruckhaus (Outright)
Rui Cai (Microsoft Research)
Berkant Barla Cambazoglu (Yahoo! Research, Barcelona)
Longbing Cao (University of Technology Sydney)
Yunbo Cao (Microsoft Research Asia)
Charlie Catlett (University of Chicago)
Haifeng Chen (NEC Research Lab)
Wei Chen (Microsoft Research)
Weizhu Chen (Microsoft)
Ye Chen (Microsoft)
Ira Cohen (HP)
Rob Cooley (Optimine)
Chad Cumby (PNT Financial)
Michelandgelo D'Agostino (BrainTree)
Brian Dalessandro (Dstillery)
Kamalika Das (NASA Ames Research Center)
Atish Das Sarma (eBay Research Labs)
Wei Ding (University of Massachusetts Boston)
Anlei Dong (Yahoo! Labs)
Pinar Donmez (Salesforce)
Seymour Douglas (Deloitte)
Gideon Dror (Yahoo! Labs)
Wei Fan (IBM Research)
Andrew Fano (Accenture)
Marcus Fontoura (Google)
Dayne Freitag (SRI)
Ryohei Fujimaki (NEC Laboratories America)
Shalini Ghosh (SRI)
David Hardcastle (GCHQ, UK)
Michael Hart (Google)
Qi He (LinkedIn)
Shawndra Hill (U Penn Wharton)
Jianying Hu (IBM T.J. Watson Research Center)
Ling Huang (Intel Labs)
Mario Inchiosa (IBM)
Sergei Izrailev (Collective)
Alex Jaimes (Yahoo!)
Prateek Jain (Microsoft Research - India)
Bin Jiang (Facebook)
Daxin Jiang (Microsoft)
Hongxia Jin (IBM Research)
George John (Rocket Fuel Inc.)
Vanja Josifovski (Google)
Christian Konig (Microsoft Research)
Georgia Koutrika (HP Labs)
Rui Kuang (University of Minnesota)
Mohit Kumar (Accenture)
Mounia Lalmas (Yahoo! Labs Barcelona)
Ming-Long Lam (SAS)
Richard Lawrence (IBM Research)
Aleksandar Lazarevic (Travelers)
Bangyong Liang (Microsoft Incorporation)
Nathan Nan Liu (Yahoo! Labs)
Shixia Liu (Microsoft Research)
Tie-Yan Liu (Microsoft Research)
Yue Lu (Twitter, Inc.)
Jiebo Luo (University of Rochester)
Ping Luo (HP Lab)
Mohammad Mahdian (Google)
Arun Maiya (Institute for Defense Analyses)
Manish Marwah (HP Labs)
Sameep Mehta (IBM Research - India)
Vahab Mirrokni (Google Research)
Thomas Montgomery (Ford Motor Company)
Vivek Narasayya (Microsoft Research)
Suman Nath (Microsoft Research)
Zaiqing Nie (Microsoft Research Asia)
Feng Pan (Microsoft)
Gaurav Pandey (Mount Sinai School of Medicine)
Rina Panigrahy (Microsoft Research)
Spiros Papadimitriou (IBM)
Jan Pedersen (Microsoft)
Ana-Maria Popescu (Consultant)
Ned Porter (Census)

Troy Raeder (Media6Degrees)
Matthew Rattigan (Edgeflip)
Karl Rexer (Rexer Analytics)
Romer Rosales (LinkedIn)
Ramendra Sahoo (Citi)
Krishna Sankar (TCS)
Mohak Shah (GE Global Research)
Jimi Shanahan (Consultant)
Abhishek Sharma (NEC Research Lab)
Dou Shen (CityGrid Media)
Amy Shi-Nash (SingTel)
Alexander Smola (Carnegie Mellon University)
Ramakrishnan Srikant (Google)
L Subramaniam (IBM Research - India)
Gordon Guo-zheng Sun (Sun Tencent Technology)
Jian-Tao Sun (Microsoft Research)
Jimeng Sun (Georgia Tech)
Neel Sundaresan (eBay Research)
Shu Tao (IBM Research)
Wayne Thompson (SAS)
Hanghang Tong (IBM Research)
Volker Tresp (Ludwig Maximilian University of Munich/Siemens)
Ranga Vatsavai (Oak Ridge National Labs)
Darren Vengroff (Rich Relevance)
Michail Vlachos (IBM Zurich Research Laboratory)
Fei Wang (IBM T.J. Watson Research Lab)
Zhen Wen (IBM Research)
Graham Williams (Togaware)
Michael Witbrock (Cyc)
Xing Xie (Microsoft Research Asia)
Oksana Yakhnenko (Google)
Rong Yan (Facebook)
Jiangang Yu (Microsoft)
Shipeng Yu (Siemens Medical Solutions)
Kun Zhang (Max Planck Institute for Intelligent Systems)
Bo Zhao (Microsoft Research)
Zheng Zhao (SAS)
Yu Zheng (Microsoft Research)
Scott Zoldi (FICO)
Peter van der Putten (Pegasystems & Leiden University)

KDD'14 Research Track Additional Reviewers

Sofiane Abbar (Qatar Computing Research Institute)
Ibrahim Abdelaziz (KAUST)
Ehab Abdelhamid (KAUST)
Ameeta Agrawal (York University)
Zahra Ahmadi (University of Mainz)
Cuneyt Gurcan Akcora (Qatar Computing Research Institute)
Shahid Alam (University of Victoria)
Darko Aleksovski (JSI, Ljubljana)
Razen Al-Harbi (KAUST)
Khalil Al-Hussaeni (Concordia University)
Sarah Alkhodair (Concordia University)
Vania Almeida (LIAAD-INESC TEC)
Stefanos Antaris (Aristotle University of Thessaloniki)
Shuang Ao (Western University)
Karim Awara (KAUST)
Yukino Baba (National Institute of Informatics)
Ahmet Bakan (Kabbage Inc.)
Anu Banerjee (Siemens Medical Solutions)
Gabor Bartok (ETH Zurich)
Daniel Bartz (TU Berlin)
Daniel Bengs (DIPF Frankfurt/Main)
Hendrik Blom (TU Dortmund University)
Kenneth Sejdenfaden Bøgh (Aarhus University)
Mohamed Bouguessa (Universite du Quebec at Montreal)
Panagiotis Bouros (Humboldt University Berlin)
Janez Brank (Jozef Stefan Institute)
Mikio Braun (TU Berlin)
Ivan Brugere (University of Illinois at Chicago)
Yilin Cai (University of Hong Kong)
K. Selcuk Candan (Arizona State University)
Xi hang Cao (Temple University)
AlexanFaria de Carvalho (INESC TEC)
Diego Ceccarelli (IMT Institute for Advanced Studies, Lucca)
Janathan Chang (Facebook)
Changyou Chen (National ICT Australia)
Chun-Hao Chen (Tamkang University Taipei)
Danqi Chen (Stanford University)
Lifei Chen (Fujian Normal University)
Ning Chen (SCE, NTU)
Ting Chen (NEU)
Yuxin Chen (ETH Zurich)
Dehua Cheng (USC)
Shiwen Cheng (University of California, Riverside)
Sean Chester (Aarhus University)
Flavio Chierichetti (Sapienza University of Rome)
Belkacem Chikhaoui (University of Toronto)
Freddy Chong-Tat (CHUA)
Maria Christoforaki (NYU Poly)
Paolo Cintia (University of Pisa)
Yang Cong (Chinese Academy of Sciences)
João Paulo Cordeiro (University of Beira Interior / INESC-TEC)
Mario Cordeiro (LIAAD-INESC TEC)
Robson L. F. Cordeiro (University of São Paulo)
Michele Coscia (Harvard University)
Alceu Ferraz Costa (University of Sao Paulo)
Gaby Dagher (Concordia University)
Pradipto Das (University at Buffalo)
Wei-Yen Day (Purdue University)
Elnaz Delpisheh (York University)
Vasil Denchev (Google Inc.)
Hongbo Deng (Yahoo Labs)
Martin Dimkovski (York University)
Costas Dimopoulos (NYU)
Steven H. H. Ding (McGill University)
Huang Dong (Institute for Infocomm Research)
Xiaowen Dong (Ecole Polytechnique Fédérale de Lausanne (EPFL))
João Duarte (LIAAD-INESC)
Wouter Duivesteijn (TU Dortmund)
Ahmed El-Kishky
Nuno Escudeiro (ISEP, Porto)
Cristobal Esteban (Siemens)
Meng Fang (University of Technology, Sydney)
Yuan Fang (University of Illinois at Urbana Champaign)
Zheng Fang (Zhejiang University)
Elaine Faria (University of Uberlandia)
Jing Feng (University of Munich)
Wei Feng (Tsinghua University)
Carlos Ferreira (Liaad-Inesc Tec)

Ricky Fok (York University)
Manoel Vitor Macedo França (City University London)
Alberto De Francesco (ISTI-CNR)
Hao Fu (Microsoft Reserach)
Hao Fu (University of Science and Technology of China)
Fabio Fumarola (Università degli Studi di Bari "Aldo Moro")
Bin Gao (Microsoft Research)
Shi Gao (University of California, Los Angeles)
Tianshi Gao (Facebook)
Michael Geilke (University of Mainz)
Bluma Gelley (NYU)
Djordje Gligorijevic (Temple University)
Jean-Pierre Glouzon (University of Sherbrooke, Canada)
Nico Goernitz (Technical University Berlin)
Neil Zhenqiang Gong (University of California, Berkeley)
Alkis Gotovos (ETH Zurich)
Josif Grabocka (University of Hildesheim)
Yupeng Gu (NEU)
Huan Gui (University of Illinois at Urbana Champaign)
Riccardo Guidotti (University of Pisa)
Hongchen Guo (Tsinghua University)
Nima Haghpanah
Chao Han (Temple University)
Chunhui Han (Tsinghua University)
Melinda Han (Dstillery)
Xiantian Hao (HKUST)
Xiao He (University of Munich)
Zhouzhou He (Zhejiang University)
Shohei Hido (Preferred Infrastructure, Inc.)
Linmei HU (Tsinghua University)
Xiaocheng Hu (Chinese University of Hong Kong)
Shengyu Huang (Arizona State University)
Silu Huang (Chinese University of Hong Kong)
Yi-Hung Huang
Nina Hubig (Helmholtz Zentrum München)
Fuad Jamour (KAUST)
Zongcheng JI (Huawei Technologies)
Lili Jiang (Max Planck Institute for Informatics)
Xueyan Jiang (Ludwig-Maximilian University of Munich)
Ulf Johansson (University of Boras)
Aditya Johri (George Mason University)
Alipio Jorge (Universidade do Porto)
Shafiq Joty (Qatar Research)
Minsuk Kahng (Georgia Institute of Technology)
Hiroshi Kajino (The University of Tokyo)
David Kale (USC)
Michael Kamp (Fraunhofer IAIS)
Lakesh Kansakar (Temple University)
Alex Kantchelian (University of California, Berkeley)
Komal Kapoor (University of Minnesota)
Hima P Karanam (IBM Research-India)
Masayuki Karasuyama (Kyoto University)
Amin Karbasi (ETH Zurich)
Rasoul Karimi (University of Hildeshiem)
Isak Karlsson (Stockholm University)
Andreas Karwath (University of Mainz)
Gilad Katz (Ben Gurion University)
Fabian Keller (Karlsruhe Institute of Technology)
Zuhair Khayyat (KAUST)
Mark Kibanov (University of Kassel)
Doo Soon Kim (Bosch Research and Technology Center)
Mijung Kim (Arizona State University)
Dragi Kocev (Jozef Stefan Institute)
Giorgos Kollias
Xiangnan Kong (University of Illinois at Chicago)
Denis Krompass (Ludwig-Maximilian University of Munich)
Guo-Cheng Lan (National Cheng Kung University)
Ni Lao (Google)
Sangkyun Lee (TU Dortmund University)
Jurica Levatic (JSI, Ljubljana)
Qi Li (University at Buffalo)
Qing Li (University of Sherbrooke, Canada)
Rui Li (PRIME Research)
Xiang Li (University of Western University)
Xiaoyi Li (University at Buffalo)
Xinsheng Li (Arizona State University)
Yaliang Li (University at Buffalo)
Yan Li (Wayne State University)
Yingming Li (Zhejiang University)
Yuemeng Li (University of North Carolina at Charlotte)
Zhixing Li (Tsinghua University)

Defu Lian (University of Science and Technology of China & Microsoft Research)
Jianxun Lian (University of Science and Technology of China)
Hongwei Liang
Hongyu Liang (Facebook)
Yu Liang (Institute for Infocomm Research)
Thomas Liebig (TU Dortmund)
Luiz Alberto Lima (Petrobras)
Kawuu W. Lin (National Kaohsiung University of Applied Sciences)
Tian Lin (Tsinghua University)
Wenqing Lin (Nanyang Technological University)
Bo Liu (quare)
Jing Liu (Harbin Institute of Technology)
Lu Liu (Northwestern University)
Xiang Liu (NYU)
Yandong Liu (Yahoo! Labs)
Tuve Lofstrom (University of Boras)
Corrado Loglisci (University of Bari Aldo Moro)
Nikhil Londhe (University at Buffalo)
Eric Hsueh-Chan Lu (National Taitung University)
Yi Lu (Chinese University of Hong Kong)
Minh Luan (Nguyen Institute for Infocomm Research)
Yan Luo (Western University)
Lin Ma (Noah's Ark Lab, Huawei Technologies)
Zongyang Ma (Nanyang Technological University)
Craig Macdonald (University of Glasgow)
Björn Elmar Macek (University of Kassel)
Gjorgji Madjarov (University Ss. Cyril and Methodius, Skopje)
Hamid Mahini
Son T. Mai (University of Munich)
Silviu Maniu (University of Hong Kong)
Andreas Maunz (Oncotest)
Sam Maurus (Helmholtz-Zentrum München)
Giuseppe M. Mazzeo (University of California, Los Angeles)
Richard McCreadie (University of Glasgow)
Yashar Mehdad (UBC)
Rishabh Mehrotra (University College London)
Yelena Mejova (Qatar Computing Research Institute)
Lei Meng (Nanyang Technological University)
Barbora Micenkova (Aarhus University)
Letizia Milli (University of Pisa)
Luyi Mo (University of Hong Kong)
John Moeller (University of Utah)
Noman Mohammed (McGill University)
Anna Monreale (University of Pisa)
Grégoire Montavon (TU Berlin)
C. Moore (Santa Fe Institute)
Michael Lind Mortensen (Aarhus University)
Benjamin Moseley (TTI Institute)
Shinichi Nakajima (Nikon)
Benjamin Negrevergne (KU Leuven)
Ido Nevat (Institute for Infocomm Research)
M. E. J. Newman (University of Michigan)
Hoang Vu Nguyen (Karlsruhe Institute of Technology)
Rad Niazadeh (Cornell University)
Thomas Niebler
Yung-Kyun Noh (KAIST)
Nozomi Nori (Kyoto University)
Inna Novalija
Alja Osojnik (Josef Stefan Institute)
Panagiotis Papapetrou (Stockholm University)
Peng Peng (The Hong Kong University of Science and Technology)
Ruggero G. Pensa (University of Torino)
Antonio Penta (University of Turin)
Te Pi (Zhejiang University)
Nico Piatkowski (TU Dortmund University)
Gianvito Pio (University of Bari Aldo Moro)
Francesca Pratesi (University of Pisa)
Fang Qiong (HKUST)
Ahsanur Rahman (CS, VT)
Rajiur Rahman (Wayne State University)
Piyush Rai (Duke University)
Karthik Raman (Cornell University)
Dusan Ramljak (Temple University)
Xiang Ren (University of Illinois at Urbana Champaign)
Yazhou Ren (South China University of Technology)
Matt Revelle (George Mason University)
Marcela Xavier Ribeiro (Federal University of Sao Carlos)
Rita Ribeiro (LIAAD-INESC TEC)
Salvatore Rinzivillo (KDDLab-ISTI-CNR)
Jose Fernando Rodrigues (University of Sao Paulo)
Shoumik Roychoudhury
Delia Rusu (Jozef Stefan Institute)

Mrinmaya Sachan (Carnegie Mellon University)
Shouq Sadah (University of California, Riverside)
Tanwistha Saha (George Mason University)
Hiroaki Sasaki (Tokyo Institute of Technology)
Claudio Schifanella (Joint Research Centre - European Commission Ispra)
Nicolas Schilling (University of Hildesheim)
Jana Schmidt (TU München)
Erich Schubert (LMU Munich)
Lena Schwemmlein
Madeleine Seeland (TU München)
Moloud Shahbazi (University of California, Riverside)
Lifeng Shang (Noah's Ark Lab, Huawei Technologies)
Junming Shao (University of Mainz)
Wei Shen (Tsinghua University)
Jieming Shi (University of Hong Kong)
Yanchen Shi
Motoki Shiga (Gifu University)
Zhang Shitao (Tsinghua University)
Alexander Shkapsky
Sergio F. Silva (Federal University of Goias)
Adish Singla (ETH Zurich)
Ng Wee Siong (Institute for Infocomm Research)
George Skoumas
Vinícius M. A. de Souza (Instituto de Ciências Matemáticas e de Computação - ICMC/USP)
Ivan Stojkovic (Temple University)
Marco Stolpe (TU Dortmund University)
Dong Su (Purdue University)
Ja-Hwung Su (Kainan University)
Amar Subramanya (Google Research)
Umar Syed
Andrea Tagarelli (University of Calabria)
Tadej Tajner (Jožef Stefan Institute)
Ben Tan (HKUST)
Jovan Tanevski (JSI, Ljubljana)
Jun Tang (The Hong Kong University of Science and Technology)
Youze Tang (Nanyang Technological University)
Maryam Tavakol (TU Darmstadt)
Teck-Hou Teng (Nanyang Technological University)
Pavel Tokmakov (University of Bonn)
Daniel Trabold (Fraunhofer IAIS)
Caetano Traina, Jr. (University of Sao Paulo)
Mitja Trampus (Jozef Stefan Institute)
Emmanouil Tzouridis (TU Darmstadt)
Alexey Uversky (Temple University)
Hastagiri Vanchinathan (ETH Zurich)
Celine Vens (UGent)
Manisha Verma (University College London)
Sarah Vieweg (Qatar Computing Research Institute)
Bhanukiran Vinzamuri (Wayne State University)
Jan Vosecky (HKUST)
Dawei Wang (University of Massachusetts)
Hao Wang (University of Hong Kong)
Quan Wang (Chinese Academy of Sciences)
Yue Wang (University of North Carolina at Charlotte)
Zhigang WANG (Tsinghua University)
Chen Wei (Institute for Infocomm Research)
Steven Whang (Google Research)
Joerg Wicker (University of Mainz)
Matthew Wiley (University of California, Riverside)
Martin Wistuba (University of Hildesheim)
Dingming Wu (University of Hong Kong)
Huanhuan WU (The Chinese University of Hong Kong)
Le Wu (University of Science and Technology of China)
Wei Wu (Facebook)
Zhiang Wu (Nanjing University of Finance and Economices)
Daniel Xia (University of Victoria)
Houping Xiao (University at Buffalo)
Min Xie (The Hong Kong University of Science and Technology)
Jun Xu (Noah's Ark Lab, Huawei Technologies)
Tianbing Xu (Facebook)
Yanyan Xu (Chinese University of Hong Kong)
Zenglin Xu (Purdue University)
Yang Xuan (The University of Hong Kong)
Makoto Yamada (Yahoo Labs)
Da Yan (HKUST)
Ming Yang (Zhejiang University)
Mohan Yang
Jianhua Yin (Tsinghua University)
Josh Jia-Ching Ying (National Cheng-Kung University)
Jane You (Amazon.com)
Chung-Hsien Yu

Yaoliang Yu (Carnegie Mellon University)
Quan Yuan (Nanyang Technological University)
Kai Zeng
Kay Zeng
Bernard Zenko (Jozef Stefan Institute)
Chenyi Zhang
Fuzheng Zhang (University of Science and Technology of China)
Fuzheng Zhang (Microsoft Research)
Jianfei Zhang (University of Sherbrooke)
Jun Zhang (Nanyang Technological University)
Miao Zhang (University of Texas Arlington)
Ning Zhang (University of California, Berkeley)
Shanshan Zhang (Temple University)
Shaonan Zhang (Amazon.com)
Wangda Zhang (University of Hong Kong)
Wei Zhang (Tsinghua University)
Xian Zhang (Microsoft)
Yao Zhang (CS VT)
Jing Zhao (Stockholm University)
Kaiqi Zhao (Nanyang Technological University)
Kunsheng Zhao
Xueyi Zhao (Zhejiang University)
Vincent Zheng (Advanced Digital Sciences Center (ADSC))
Wen Zhong (Microsoft Research)
Yuan Zhong (Microsoft Research)
Linfei Zhou (University of Munich)
Yan Zhou (University of Texas at Dallas)
Zhao Zhou (HKUST)
Zhuojie Zhou (George Washington University)
Diwen Zhu (Nanyang Technological University)
Haohan Zhu (Boston University)
Linhong ZHU (University of Southern California)
Yin Zhu (Hong Kong University of Science and Technology)
Morteza Zihayat (York University)
Anastasios Zouzias (IBM Research)
Andreas Züfle (Ludwig-Maximilians-Universität München)

KDD'14 Sponsors & Supporters

Sponsors:

Supporter: Platinum

Supporters: Gold

Supporters: Silver

Supporters: Silver (continued)

Supporters: Bronze

Supporter: Research Paper Award

Supporter: Best Industry & Government Paper Award

Supporter: Best Test of Time Paper Award

Supporter: Lanyard Sponsor

Supporters: Media

Supporter: WiFi

Supporter: Mobile App

Supporters:
KDD CUP

Supporter:
Student
Travel
Awards

Supporter:
Travel

Supporter:
Program Ad

Exhibitors:

The Battle for the Future of Data Mining

Oren Etzioni
Allen Institute for AI
2157 N. Northlake Way, Suite 110
Seattle, WA 98103 1-206-548-5600
OrenE@allenai.org

ABSTRACT
Deep learning has catapulted to the front page of the New York Times, formed the core of the so-called "Google brain", and achieved impressive results in vision, speech recognition, and elsewhere. Yet researchers have offered simple conundrums that deep learning doesn't address. For example, consider the sentence: "The large ball crashed right through the table because it was made of Styrofoam." What was made of Styrofoam? The large ball? Or the table? The answer is obviously "the table", but if we change the word "Styrofoam" to "steel", the answer is clearly "the large ball". To automatically answer this type of question, our computers require an extensive body of knowledge. We believe that text mining can provide the requisite body of knowledge. My talk will describe work at the new Allen Institute for AI towards building the next-generation of text-mining systems.

Categories and Subject Descriptors
K.0 [**Computing Milieux**]: General

Keywords: data mining; deep learning; text-mining

BIO
Dr. Oren Etzioni is Chief Executive Officer of the Allen Institute for AI. He was a Professor at the University of Washington's Computer Science department starting in 1991, receiving several awards including GeekWire's Hire of the Year (2014), Seattle's Geek of the Year (2013), the Robert Engelmore Memorial Award (2007), the IJCAI Distinguished Paper Award (2005), AAAI Fellow (2003), and a National Young Investigator Award (1993). He was also the founder or co-founder of several companies including Farecast (sold to Microsoft in 2008) and Decide (sold to eBay in 2013), and the author of over 100 technical papers that have garnered roughly 20,000 citations. The goal of Oren's research is to solve fundamental problems in AI, particularly the automatic learning of knowledge from text. Oren received his Ph.D. from Carnegie Mellon University in 1991, and his B.A. from Harvard in 1986.

KDD'14, Aug 24–27, 2014, New York, NY, USA
ACM 978-1-4503-2956-9/14/08.
http://dx.doi.org/10.1145/2623330.2630816

Data, Predictions, and Decisions in Support of People and Society

Eric Horvitz
Microsoft Research
Redmond, WA 98052
+1 425-706-8080
horvitz@microsoft.com

ABSTRACT

Deep societal benefits will spring from advances in data availability and in computational procedures for mining insights and inferences from large data sets. I will describe efforts to harness data for making predictions and guiding decisions, touching on work in transportation, healthcare, online services, and interactive systems. I will start with efforts to learn and field predictive models that forecast flows of traffic in greater city regions. Moving from the ground to the air, I will discuss fusing data from aircraft to make inferences about atmospheric conditions and using these results to enhance air transport. I will then focus on experiences with building and fielding predictive models in clinical medicine. I will show how inferences about outcomes and interventions can provide insights and guide decision making. Moving beyond data captured by hospitals, I will discuss the promise of transforming anonymized behavioral data drawn from web services into large-scale sensor networks for public health, including efforts to identify adverse effects of medications and to understand illness in populations. I will conclude by describing how we can use machine learning to leverage the complementarity of human and machine intellect to solve challenging problems in science and society.

Categories and Subject Descriptors

I.2.6 [**Computing Methodologies**]: Learning—*Induction*

Keywords: Machine learning; probabilistic inference; decision analysis; probabilistic graphical models; transportation; healthcare

BIO

Eric Horvitz is distinguished scientist and director of Microsoft Research at Redmond. His interests span theoretical and practical challenges with machine learning, inference, and decision making. His efforts have helped to bring multiple systems and services into the world, including innovations in healthcare, ecommerce, aerospace, systems & networking, human-computer interaction, and privacy. He has been elected fellow of Association for the Advancement of Artificial Intelligence (AAAI), the American Association for the Advancement of Science (AAAS), the American Academy of Arts and Sciences, and the National Academy of Engineering, and has been inducted into the CHI Academy. He has served as president of AAAI, chair of the AAAS Section on Information, Computing, and Communications, and on the advisory committees for the National Science Foundation's (NSF) Directorate for Computer & Information Science & Engineering (CISE), the Computing Community Consortium (CCC), and the Information and Science Study Group (ISAT) of the Defense Advanced Research Projects Agency (DARPA). Information on publications, collaborations, and activities can be found at http://research.microsoft.com/~horvitz.

KDD'14, Aug 24–27, 2014, New York, NY, USA
ACM 978-1-4503-2956-9/14/08.
http://dx.doi.org/10.1145/2623330.2630817

A Data Driven Approach to Diagnosing and Treating Disease

Eric Schadt
Icahn School of Medicine at Mount Sinai, New York
212-659-6790, USA
eric.schadt@mssm.edu

ABSTRACT

Throughout the biomedical and life sciences research community, advanced integrative biology algorithms are employed to integrate large scale data across many different high-dimensional datatypes to construct predictive network models of disease. The causal inference approaches we employ for this purpose well complement the types of natural artificial intelligence/machine learning approaches that have become nearly standard in the life and biomedical sciences for building classifiers for a range of problems, from disease classification and subtype stratification, to the identification of responders and non-responders for a given treatment strategy. By building a causal network model that spans multiple scales (from the molecular to the cellular, to the tissue/organ, to the organism and community) we can understand the flow of information and how best to modulate that flow to improve human wellbeing, whether better diagnosing and treating disease or improving overall health(*1-4*). More specifically, we have constructed predictive network models for Alzheimer's disease, along with other common human diseases such as obesity, diabetes, heart disease, and inflammatory bowel disease, and cancer, and demonstrated a causal network common across all of these diseases(*3, 5-10*). Not only do we demonstrate that our predictive models uncover important mechanisms of disease and mechanistic connections among different diseases, but that they have led to a natural way to prioritize therapeutic points of intervention and provide optimal molecular phenotypes for high throughput screening. Our application of these models in a number of disease areas has led to the identification of novel genes that are causal for disease and that may serve as efficacious points of therapeutic intervention, as well as to personalized treatment strategies that provide a more quantitative and accurate approach to tailoring treatments to specific forms of disease.

Categories and Subject Descriptors

J.3 [**Computer Applications**]: Life and medical sciences, Biology and Genetics.

Keywords

Systems biology; multiscale biology; causal network inference; predictive network modeling; drug discovery

REFERENCES

1. A. Califano, A. J. Butte, S. Friend, T. Ideker, E. Schadt, Leveraging models of cell regulation and GWAS data in integrative network-based association studies. *Nature genetics* 44, 841 (Aug, 2012).
2. E. Schadt, R. Chang, Genetics. A GPS for navigating DNA. *Science* 337, 1179 (Sep 7, 2012).
3. B. Zhang *et al.*, Integrated systems approach identifies genetic nodes and networks in late-onset Alzheimer's disease. *Cell* 153, 707 (Apr 25, 2013).
4. B. A. Kidd, L. A. Peters, E. E. Schadt, J. T. Dudley, Unifying immunology with informatics and multiscale biology. *Nature immunology* 15, 118 (Jan 21, 2014).
5. Y. Chen *et al.*, Variations in DNA elucidate molecular networks that cause disease. *Nature* 452, 429 (Mar 27, 2008).
6. V. Emilsson *et al.*, Genetics of gene expression and its effect on disease. *Nature* 452, 423 (Mar 27, 2008).
7. L. Jostins *et al.*, Host-microbe interactions have shaped the genetic architecture of inflammatory bowel disease. *Nature* 491, 119 (Nov 1, 2012).
8. X. Yang *et al.*, Validation of candidate causal genes for obesity that affect shared metabolic pathways and networks. *Nature genetics*, (Mar 8, 2009).
9. H. Zhong *et al.*, Liver and adipose expression associated SNPs are enriched for association to type 2 diabetes. *PLoS genetics* 6, e1000932 (2010).
10. H. Zhong, X. Yang, L. M. Kaplan, C. Molony, E. E. Schadt, Integrating pathway analysis and genetics of gene expression for genome-wide association studies. *American journal of human genetics* 86, 581 (Apr 9, 2010).

KDD'14, August 24–27, 2014, New York, NY, USA.
ACM 978-1-4503-2956-9/14/08.
http://dx.doi.org/10.1145/2623330.2630817

Short Bibliography

Dr. Eric Schadt joined Mount Sinai Medical School as Chairman and Professor, Department of Genetics and Genomic Sciences and is the founding Director of the Icahn Institute for Genomics and Multiscale Biology in 2011. Previously, Dr. Schadt had been the Chief Scientific Officer at Pacific Biosciences, overseeing the scientific strategy for the company, including creating the vision for next-generation sequencing applications of the company's technology. Dr. Schadt is also a founding member of Sage Bionetworks, an open access genomics initiative designed to build and support databases and an accessible platform for creating innovative, dynamic models of disease. Dr. Schadt's current efforts at Mount Sinai to generate and integrate large-scale, high-dimension molecular, cellular, and clinical data to build more predictive models of disease so that we may better diagnose and treat disease, were motivated by the genomics and systems biology research he led at Merck to elucidate common human diseases and drug response using novel computational approaches applied to genetic and molecular profiling data. His research helped revolution a field in statistical genetics (the genetics of gene expression), has energized the systems biology field, and has led to a number of discoveries relating to the causes of common human diseases. Dr. Schadt received his B.S. in applied mathematics from California Polytechnic State University, his M.S. in pure mathematics from UCD, and his Ph.D. in biomathematics from UCLA.

Bugbears or Legitimate Threats? (Social) Scientists' Criticisms of Machine Learning?

Sendhil Mullainathan
Harvard University
1805 Cambridge St
Cambridge, MA 02138
1 617-496-2720
mullain@fas.harvard.edu

ABSTRACT

Social scientists increasingly criticize the use of machine learning techniques to understand human behavior. Criticisms include: (1) They are atheoretical and hence of limited scientific value; (2) They do not address causality and are hence of limited policy value; and (3) They are uninterpretable and hence of limited generalizability value (outside contexts very narrowly similar to the training dataset). These criticisms, I argue, miss the enormous opportunity offered by ML techniques to fundamentally improve the practice of empirical social science. Yet each criticism does contain a grain of truth and overcoming them will require innovations to existing methodologies. Some of these innovations are being developed today and some are yet to be tackled. I will in this talk sketch (1) what these innovations look like or should look like; (2) why they are needed; and (3) the technical challenges they raise. I will illustrate my points using a set of applications that range from financial markets to social policy problems to computational models of basic psychological processes. This talk describes joint work with Jon Kleinberg and individual projects with Himabindu Lakkaraju, Jure Leskovec, Jens Ludwig, Anuj Shah, Chenhao Tan, Mike Yeomans and Tom Zimmerman.

Biography

Sendhil Mullainathan is a Professor of Economics at Harvard University and a Cornell Tech Fellow. His real passion is behavioral economics. His work runs a wide gamut: the impact of poverty on mental bandwidth; whether CEO pay is excessive; using fictitious resumes to measure discrimination; showing that higher cigarette taxes makes smokers happier; modeling how competition affects media bias; and a model of coarse thinking. His latest research focuses on using machine learning and data mining techniques to better understand human behavior.

He enjoys writing, having recently co-authored Scarcity: Why Having too Little Means so Much and writes regularly for the New York Times.

He also occasionally enjoys doing. He helped co-found a non-profit to apply behavioral science (ideas42), co-founded a center to promote the use of randomized control trials in development (the Abdul Latif Jameel Poverty Action Lab), serves on the board of the MacArthur Foundation, and has worked in government in various roles, including most recently as Assistant Director of Research at the Consumer Financial Protection Bureau.

Much to the surprise of those who know him, he is a recipient of the MacArthur "genius" Award, was designated a "Young Global Leader" by the World Economic Forum, labeled a "Top 100 Thinker" by Foreign Policy Magazine, and named to the "Smart List: 50 people who will change the world" by Wired Magazine (UK). His hobbies include basketball, board games, googling and fixing-up classic espresso machines. He also enjoys speaking about himself in the third person, which works well for bios but less well in daily life.

Prediction of Human Emergency Behavior and their Mobility following Large-scale Disaster

Xuan Song, Quanshi Zhang, Yoshihide Sekimoto and Ryosuke Shibasaki
Center for Spatial Information Science, The University of Tokyo, Japan
songxuan@csis.u-tokyo.ac.jp

ABSTRACT

The frequency and intensity of natural disasters has significantly increased over the past decades and this trend is predicted to continue. Facing these possible and unexpected disasters, accurately predicting human emergency behavior and their mobility will become the critical issue for planning effective humanitarian relief, disaster management, and long-term societal reconstruction. In this paper, we build up a large human mobility database (GPS records of 1.6 million users over one year) and several different datasets to capture and analyze human emergency behavior and their mobility following the Great East Japan Earthquake and Fukushima nuclear accident. Based on our empirical analysis through these data, we find that human behavior and their mobility following large-scale disaster sometimes correlate with their mobility patterns during normal times, and are also highly impacted by their social relationship, intensity of disaster, damage level, government appointed shelters, news reporting, large population flow and etc. On the basis of these findings, we develop a model of human behavior that takes into account these factors for accurately predicting human emergency behavior and their mobility following large-scale disaster. The experimental results and validations demonstrate the efficiency of our behavior model, and suggest that human behavior and their movements during disasters may be significantly more predictable than previously thought.

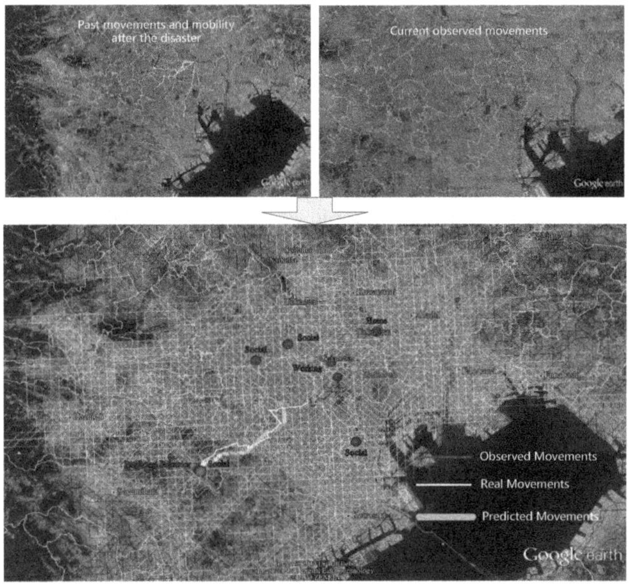

Figure 1: Prediction of human emergency behavior and their mobility following large-scale disaster. Can we predict human emergency behavior and its movements by modeling its past movements during disaster? If some future disaster occur, given person's current observed movements, which place will it go next time period? How about its traveling routes?

Categories and Subject Descriptors

H.2 [**Database Management**]: Spatial databases and GIS; H.2 [**Database Management**]: Data mining; H.4 [**Information Systems Applications**]: Decision support (e.g., MIS)

Keywords

human mobility, disaster informatics, spatio-temporal data mining

1. INTRODUCTION

Most severe disasters cause large population movements and evacuations. Predicting these movements are critical for planning effective humanitarian relief, disaster management, and long-term societal reconstruction. Even though human movement and behavior patterns have a high degree of freedom and variation, they also exhibit structural patterns due to geographic and social constraints [1]. In particular, after large-scale disasters, population mobility pattern seem to be highly influenced by several disaster states and various factors, such as intensity of disaster, damage level, government declarations, news reports and etc [2]. Lu *et al.* [3] found that population mobility patterns following the 2010 Haitian earthquake disaster were highly correlated with their daily movements prior to the event, and concluded that population movements after large-scale disasters may be significantly more predictable than previously thought. Song *et al.* [2] found that: after the Great East Japan Earthquake and Fukushima nuclear accident, in regions that were instantaneously impacted by the earthquake and tsunami, large numbers of people sought immediate refuge in nearby cities or government shelters. However, in regions more impacted by the release of nuclear materials, evacuation patterns were highly influenced by government declarations and news reports.

KDD'14, August 24–27, 2014, New York, NY, USA.

ACM 978-1-4503-2956-9/14/08 ...$15.00.
http://dx.doi.org/10.1145/2623330.2623628.

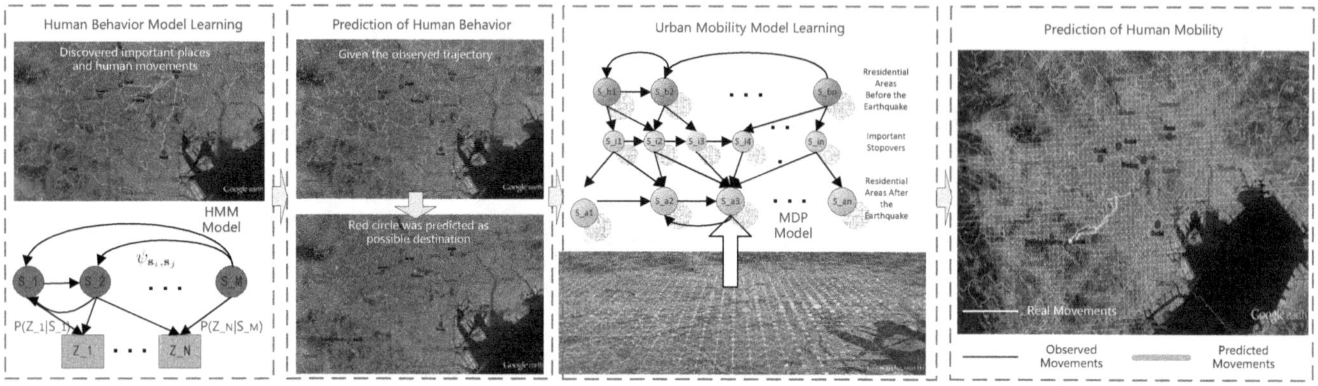

Figure 2: Overview of the approach. Our approach decomposes the predicting problem into two sub-problems: (1) Firstly, we use people's past movements during disasters, and its important places to train a HMM-based human behavior model. Then, given person's current observed movements and disaster states, our model predicts its possible behavior at next time period. (2) Secondly, we use the whole collected population movements of a specific urban areas to train the urban mobility model. Then, our model predicts person's possible movements given its predicted behavior at next time period.

Even though the above are some of the fundamental questions and hypotheses about human behavior and mobility after large-scale disasters, answers to them remain largely unknown mostly due to the lack of supported data or a powerful human behavior model that is able to fully depict how these factors will influence population mobility patterns. Therefore, in this paper, we built up a large population mobility database that stored and managed daily GPS records from approximately 1.6 million individuals throughout Japan over one year (from 1 August 2010 to 31 July 2011), and several different dataset to capture and analyze population behavior and their mobility following the Great East Japan Earthquake and Fukushima nuclear accident. On the basis of empirical analysis of population mobility patterns through these databases, we found that population behavior and their mobility after this unprecedented composite disaster sometimes correlated with their mobility patterns during normal times, and were also highly impacted by their social relationship, intensity of disaster, damage level, government appointed shelters, government declarations, movements of large population flow and etc (as shown in Figure 1). Based on these findings, we tried to model the relationship between human emergency behavior and these influenced factors, and developed a model of human behavior for predicting population movements following large-scale disaster. In our work, we decomposed the predicting problem into two sub-problems (as illustrated in Figure 2): (1) given the current state of disasters or other influenced factors, and observed human movements, predicting its possible behavior at next step; and then (2) predicting its possible movements given the estimated behavior distribution. *To the best of our knowledge, this work is the first to model human emergency behavior under various disaster states, and is able to accurately predict population movements following large-scale disasters.*

The remainder of this paper is structured as follows: Section 2 introduces the databases and the empirical analysis of population mobility patterns following the Great East Japan Earthquake and Fukushima nuclear accident. Section 3 describes the human behavior model based on our empirical analysis, and the prediction of human behavior after disasters. Section 4 provides the details about urban mobility model learning, and the prediction of human movements. Experimental results are presented in Section 5. Related work is briefly reviewed in Section 6, and the paper is finally summarized in Section 7.

2. DATABASE AND EMPIRICAL ANALYSIS

2.1 Database

In this study, we built up a large human mobility database and several different dataset to capture and analyze population emergency behavior and their mobility following large-scale disaster, and they were able to be summarized as follows:

Human mobility database: This mobility database stored and managed GPS records of approximately 1.6 million anonymized users throughout Japan from 1 August 2010 to 31 July 2011, which contained approximately 9.2 billion GPS records, more than 600GB csv files. We utilized five computer (Xeon 2.6GHz CPU, 8GB memory, and 2x2TB disk.) to build up a Hadoop cluster, which contained 32 cores, 32GB memory, 16TB storages, and was able to run 28 tasks at the same time. Furthermore, we utilized Hive on top of Hadoop to make the whole system support SQL-like spatial query. The visualization of human mobility in the Greater Tokyo Area during the earthquake is shown in Figure 3. From this figure, we can clearly see that the transportation of Tokyo before the earthquake was very busy (Fig.3-A,B). In contrast, after the earthquake, the transportation network of whole Greater Tokyo Area was almost stalled (Fig.3-C,D).

Disaster intensity data: We collected various kinds of disaster information about the Great East Japan Earthquake and Fukushima nuclear accident from Japan Government statistical reports, and built up a disaster intensity dataset. This dataset contained seismic scale of the earthquake and damage level (1-4) of this composite disaster (e.g. destroyed buildings by the earthquake and tsunami) in the whole East Japan.

Disaster reporting data: Serious radioactive releases (e.g. Fuku shima Daiichi nuclear accident) were quite different from the traditional natural diaster, because its real affection was still uncertain to human society, and will last for a very long time [2]. Facing such kind of unfamiliar disaster, people did not have direct feeling of its destructiveness, and their mobility were usually influenced and caused by government declarations or various kinds of news reporting [2]. To capture this influence, we collected government declarations [4] as well as news reports from mainstream medias in Japan and all over the world [5] from 11th March, 15:00 to 31 March, 24:00, and built up a disaster reporting dataset. Based on these information, we empirically divided these reporting and dec-

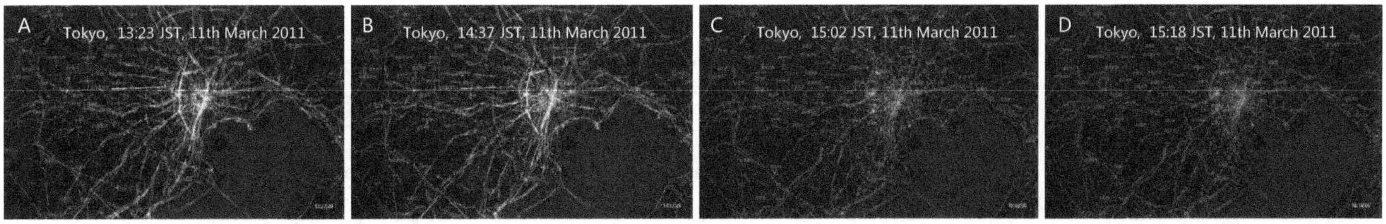

Figure 3: Visualization of human mobility during the earthquake. This figure shows population mobility of the Greater Tokyo Area during the earthquake. The color denotes the directions of population mobility. Figure A and B show population mobility before the earthquake, and Figure C and D show the ones after the earthquake. We can clearly see that the whole transportation of the Greater Tokyo Area was stopped suddenly during the earthquake (Fig.C,D). For more details, please see our supplementary video.

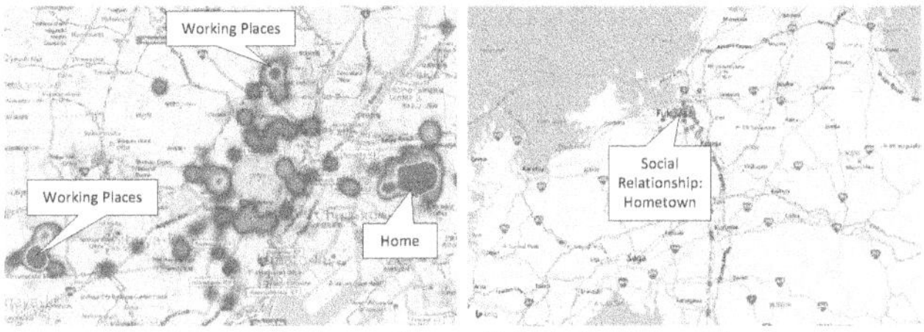

(a) Distribution of geographic location on woking days (b) Distribution of geographic location on important holidays

Figure 4: Distribution of geographic location for individual people. This figure shows the distribution of geographic location for specific person (one of the authors) during normal times. The color denotes the probability of staying location of an individual person at a specific time period; warmer ones indicate higher probability. Figure (a) shows this distribution on working days, and Figure (b) shows the cases on some important holidays (e.g. national holiday, New Year Festival, Christmas day).

larations into four levels to measure this event (e.g. one level means not serious from the reporting, and four level means extremely serious), and performed the time series analysis.

2.2 Empirical Analysis of Human Disaster Behavior

Important places discovery: While people travel further and faster than ever before, it is still the case that they spend much of their time at a few important places. To perform the analysis of population emergency behavior, we need to discover and recognize important places in people's lives, e.g. home, working places, and places of important social relationships (e.g. hometown, parents, relatives and good friends). In this study, we utilized GPS data in several months before the earthquake (1st, August 2010 to 11st, March 2011) to compute distribution of geographic location [2, 6] for individual people (as shown in Figure 4). Based on the analysis of this distribution with time, it is easy for us to find and recognize some important places of individual people. For example, the highest frequency staying place by daylight on working day is usually people's working place, and the one in night is usually people's home (as shown in Figure 4-a). Meanwhile, some high frequency visited places on the weekend and some important holiday (e.g. national holiday, New Year Festival, Christmas day) are recognized as the people's important social relationships (as shown in Figure 4-b). Furthermore, we also computed people's geographic location distribution after the Great East Japan Earthquake and Fukushima nuclear accident in a specific time period, and discover some high frequency staying places to analyze human disaster behavior. The example is shown in Figure 5.

Empirical Analysis: On the basis of seismic scale of the earthquake and damage level of this composite disaster, we focused on analyzing population behaviors in Fukushima, Miyagi, Iwate prefectures and the Greater Tokyo Area (the largest metropolitan area in the world with more than 1/3 GDP of Japan). In most areas of Fukushima, Miyagi, Iwate prefectures, the damage level were the highest ones, and seismic scale of the earthquake were above five. In contrast, the damage level and seismic scale of the Greater Tokyo Area were relatively low, most of which were with one damage level, three to four seismic scale. Although the Greater Tokyo Area were not highly destroyed by this composite disaster, its public transportation systems were completely disrupted (almost the whole metro or railway services). On the other hand, we found that: on the first 24 hours after the earthquake, population behaviors or evacuations were mainly responded to the huge earthquake and tsunami themselves. In contrast, on the next several days, Japan people understood the seriousness of the Fukushima nuclear accident, and large number of evacuations or long distance movements were discovered. Hence, we performed the empirical analysis of population behavior in the two separated time periods.

Figure 6 shows the statistics of various kinds of human behaviors after the disasters in Fukushima, Miyagi, Iwate prefectures and the Greater Tokyo Area, as well as some important news reporting related to this event. During the first 24 hours after this disaster, most behaviors of people in the Greater Tokyo Area (Fig.6-a) were similar to the normal times, but at the night (8 to 16 hours after the earthquake), many people had to stay at unknown places (e.g. metro station, hotel, restaurant and etc.) or stayed with their social relationship (e.g. friends and colleagues) due to the disruption of the public transportation systems. In contrast, at most areas of Fukushima, Miyagi, Iwate prefectures, people chose to stop their work while the earthquake occurred, and seek refuge at once to some safe and unknown places (Fig.6-b) due to the huge earthquake and tsunami.

On the other hand, during the 19 days after the earthquake, the majority of people in Fukushima, Miyagi, Iwate prefectures (Fig.6-d) chose to leave their home and stop working due to the high damage level of this disaster as well as extensive release of radioactivity, they usually went to stay with their social relationship or stayed at some unknown places (e.g. government appointed shelters, hotels of large neighboring cities and etc.). In contrast, the situation of the Greater Tokyo Area was a bit different (Fig.6-c). Although most areas in the Greater Tokyo Area were not severely damaged, when people began to more fully understand the seriousness of the Fukushima nuclear accident from the mainstream worldwide media, they stopped working and chose to leave far away from the East Japan (from 3/15 to 3/27).

Figure 5: Discovery of people's important places before and after the earthquake. The first two figures show people's geographic location distribution before and after the earthquake. The size of the circles indicates the probability of staying location of an individual person at a specific time; larger circles indicate higher probability that persons stay or live there. Blue and orange circles indicate this distribution before and after the earthquake respectively. Based on the analysis of this distribution with time, we discover the important places of this person (as shown in the third figure).

3. PREDICTION OF HUMAN DISASTER BEHAVIOR

Based on our empirical analysis of human behavior above, we concluded that human emergency behavior and mobility following the Great East Japan Earthquake and Fukushima nuclear accident sometimes correlated with their mobility patterns during normal times, and were also highly impacted by their social relationship, intensity of disaster, damage level, government appointed shelters, government declarations, news reporting and etc. Hence, in this section, we study how to model human disaster behavior by considering these influenced factors, and predict their possible behavior at next time period.

3.1 Preliminaries

Consider a set of individual people's GPS trajectories $Tra = \{tra_1, tra_2, ..., tra_n\}$ after the disasters, and each trajectories $tra_i = \mathbf{r}_1\mathbf{r}_2...\mathbf{r}_m$ consists of a series of m GPS records and disaster information. Each record $\mathbf{r}$ is a tuple in the form of $\mathbf{r} =< uid, time, latitude, longtitude, distance, intensity, damage, reporting, behavior >$, where uid is the id of people, $time$ is the time of record, $latitude$ and $longtitude$ specify the geographic position of the record. $distance$ is the distance from the event (e.g. Fukushima Daiichi nuclear power plant), $intensity$ is the seismic scale of the earthquake at this position, $damage$ is the damage level of this position, and $reporting$ is the government declarations and news reporting level. Here, $behavior$ specify the people's behavior related to the discovered important places before and after the earthquake (as shown in Figure 5), e.g., stay at home, work in office, go to important social relationships, evacuate to nearby cities, evacuate to government appointed shelters, etc., and it is a label of discovered important places as described in the last section.

Therefore, our goal is to learn a prediction model from Tra. Given a individual people's GPS trajectory $tra_{ob} = \mathbf{r}_1\mathbf{r}_2...\mathbf{r}_t$ from time 1 to time t, we want to predict its behavior next specific time period p at time $t + p$.

3.2 Disaster Behavior Model

HMM based Behavior Model: In this study, we use hidden Markov model (HMM) [7, 8] to model dependency between disaster behaviors. In our problem, we define a set of hidden states $\mathbf{S} = \{\mathbf{s}_1, \mathbf{s}_2, ..., \mathbf{s}_M\}$ which correspond to the human behavior states, and a set of observations $\mathbf{Z} = \{\mathbf{z}_1, \mathbf{z}_2, ...\mathbf{z}_N\}$ which correspond to the people's GPS records and its related disaster states. The overall behavior model with its graphical representation is shown in Figure 7. In our study, the following three key parameter components of HMM model need to be learned: (1) initial state probability $\phi_{\mathbf{s}_i}$ for each hidden states $\mathbf{s}_i \in \mathbf{S}$; (2) state transition probability $\psi_{\mathbf{s}_i,\mathbf{s}_j}$ from the hidden states $\mathbf{s}_i$ to $\mathbf{s}_j$; and (3) state-dependent output probability $P(\mathbf{z}_j|\mathbf{s}_i)$, which determines the probability of the people's mobility $\mathbf{z}_j \in \mathbf{Z}$ given the hidden behavior state $\mathbf{s}_i \in \mathbf{S}$.

We abstract people's mobility within a specific time period as a sequence of length T, i.e., $tra = \mathbf{Z}_1\mathbf{Z}_2...\mathbf{Z}_T$ (abbreviated as $tra = \mathbf{Z}_{1:T}$), and use these observed sequences to train the HMM. Here, $\mathbf{Z}_t \in \mathbf{Z}$ represents the observed people's mobility at time t, $1 \leq t \leq T$. Each $\mathbf{Z}_t$ is associated with a random variable $\mathbf{S}_t \in \mathbf{S}$, representing the unknown behavior state at time t. In the following, we will present details on HMM model learning.

Model Learning: To learn the overall behavior model, we need to estimate the key parameters of HMM as the discussion above, and a suitable solution is to use EM approach which aims at maximizing the likelihood of the observation sequences. In our study, the overall likelihood should be summed over all possible routes through the underlying hidden states, and is able to be computed by:

$$P(\mathbf{Z}_{1:T}) = \sum_{\mathbf{S}_1=\mathbf{s}_1}^{\mathbf{s}_M} ... \sum_{\mathbf{S}_T=\mathbf{s}_1}^{\mathbf{s}_M} \phi_{\mathbf{S}_1} \prod_{t=2}^{T} \psi_{\mathbf{S}_{t-1},\mathbf{S}_t} \prod_{t=1}^{T} P(\mathbf{Z}_t|\mathbf{S}_t). \quad (1)$$

Here, we assume the HMM is time-homogeneous, and state transition probabilities and state-dependent output probabilities do not change with time t.

According to [8], we reformulate Equation (1) as:

$$P(\mathbf{Z}_{1:T}) = \Phi\mathcal{P}_{\mathbf{Z}_1}\Psi\mathcal{P}_{\mathbf{Z}_2}...\Psi\mathcal{P}_{\mathbf{Z}_T}\mathbf{1}^\top, \quad (2)$$

which is expressed by matrix multiplications to reduce the computational cost. Here, Φ is a $1 \times M$ initial state distribution vector, Ψ is a $M \times M$ hidden state transition matrix where $\Psi_{ij} = \psi_{\mathbf{s}_i,\mathbf{s}_j}$, and $\mathcal{P}_{\mathbf{Z}_T}$ is a $M \times M$ diagonal matrix with $P(\mathbf{Z}_t|\mathbf{s}_i)$ on the diagonal and other entries as 0. Then we can use Baum-Welch algorithm [9] to estimate the hidden state transition probabilities and the state-dependent output probabilities.

To decide the right number of hidden states M in learning the HMM, we use *Bayesian Information Criterion* (BIC) [10] to evaluate the HMM with different state numbers, and a smaller BIC value always leads to better model fitness.

3.3 Prediction of Disaster Behavior

When given a length-t observed GPS records and its related disaster states $\mathbf{Z}_{1:t}$, we can predict people's behavior $\mathbf{S}_{t+1}$ at time $t + 1$ with the learnt HMM. This prediction is able to be achieved

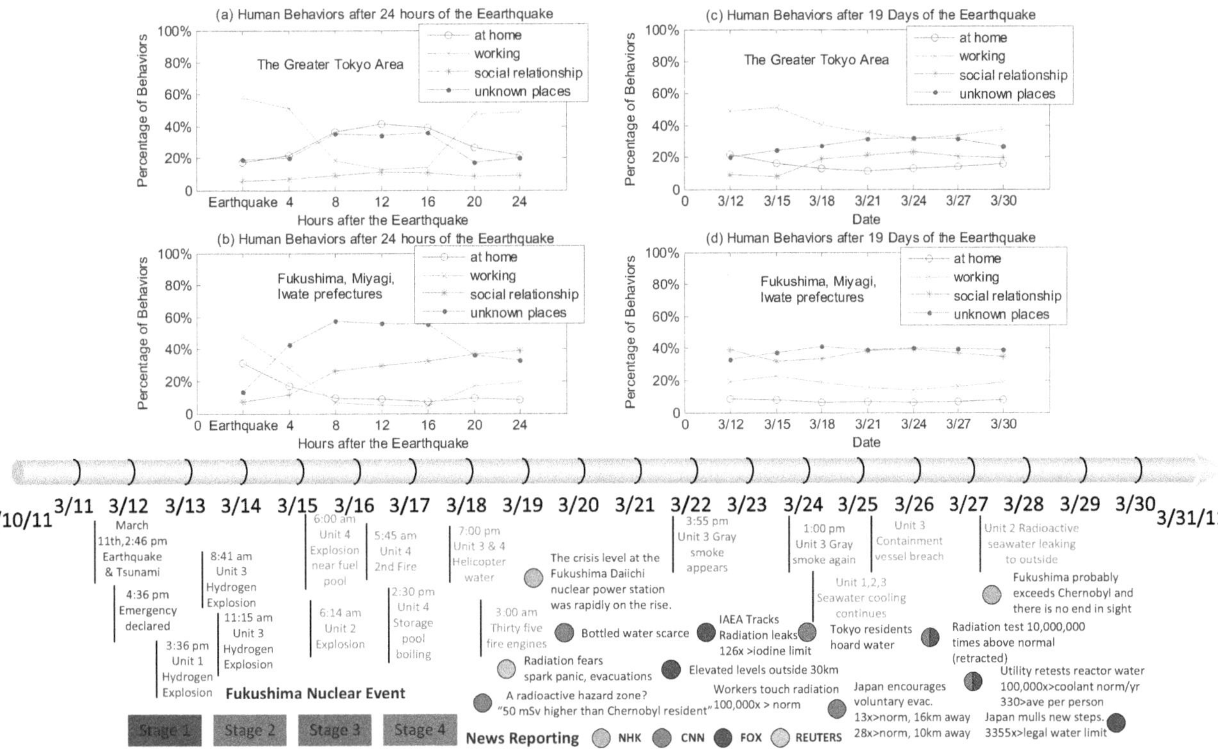

Figure 6: Empirical analysis of human behaviors after the Great East Japan Earthquake and Fukushima nuclear accident. This figure shows percentage of different human behaviors after this disaster with some important news reporting. Figure (a) and (b) show analysis of human behaviors at first 24 hours after this disaster in the Greater Tokyo Area and Fukushima, Miyagi, Iwate prefectures. Figure (c) and (d) show the cases during 19 days after this disaster.

by maximizing the probability as:

$$\mathbf{S}_{t+1} = \arg\max_{\mathbf{s}_i \in \mathbf{S}} P(\mathbf{S}_{t+1}|\mathbf{Z}_{1:t}), \tag{3}$$

where $P(\mathbf{S}_{t+1}|\mathbf{Z}_{1:t})$ is able to be computed from learnt $\psi_{\mathbf{s}_t,\mathbf{s}_{t+1}}$ and $P(\mathbf{S}_t|\mathbf{Z}_{1:t})$ according to the law of total probability as:

$$P(\mathbf{S}_{t+1}|\mathbf{Z}_{1:t}) = \sum \psi_{\mathbf{s}_t,\mathbf{s}_{t+1}} P(\mathbf{S}_t|\mathbf{Z}_{1:t}), \tag{4}$$

where $P(\mathbf{S}_t|\mathbf{Z}_{1:t})$ is able to be computed by a Bayesian recursion:

$$P(\mathbf{S}_t|\mathbf{Z}_{1:t}) = \gamma P(\mathbf{Z}_{1:t}|\mathbf{S}_t) \sum \psi_{\mathbf{s}_t,\mathbf{s}_{t-1}} P(\mathbf{S}_{t-1}|\mathbf{Z}_{1:t-1}), \tag{5}$$

where γ is the normalization constant, $P(\mathbf{Z}_{1:t}|\mathbf{S}_t)$ is the learnt observation model of HMM, which corresponds to the observed human mobility and disaster states.

To perform the efficient behavior prediction, we utilize particle filter [11] approach to compute Equation (3)-(5). The basic idea behind a particle filter is very simple. Starting with a weighted set of samples $\{w_t^{(k)}, \mathbf{s}_t^{(k)}\}_{k=1}^K$ approximately distributed according to $p(\mathbf{s}_{t-1}|\mathbf{z}_{t-1})$, new samples are generated from a suitably designed proposal distribution $q(\mathbf{s}_t|\mathbf{s}_{t-1}, \mathbf{z}_t)$. To maintain a consistent sample, the new importance weights are set to

$$w_t^{(k)} \propto w_{t-1}^{(k)} \frac{p(\mathbf{z}_t|\mathbf{s}_t^{(k)})\psi_{\mathbf{s}_t^{(k)},\mathbf{s}_{t-1}^{(k)}}}{q(\mathbf{s}_t^{(k)}|\mathbf{s}_{t-1}^{(k)}, \mathbf{z}_t)}, \sum_{k=1}^{K} w_t^{(k)} = 1. \tag{6}$$

More details on the particle filter technique can be found in [11]. In our study, the overall filtering process is present as follows:

1. Initialization:
Generate K weighted set of samples $\{w_t^{(k)}, \mathbf{s}_t^{(k)}\}_{k=1}^K$ from the learnt initial state probability $\phi_{\mathbf{s}_i}$ of HMM.
2. Resampling:
Resample K particles from the particle set $\mathbf{S}_t$ using weights of respective particles.
3. Prediction:
Predict the next state of the particle set $\mathbf{S}_t$ with the learnt transition probability $\psi_{\mathbf{s}_i,\mathbf{s}_j}$ of HMM.
4. Weighting:
Recalculate the weight of $\mathbf{S}_t$ by using Equation (6). Here, we utilize the learnt observation model $P(\mathbf{Z}_{1:t}|\mathbf{S}_t)$ of HMM as the proposal distribution in Equation (6).
5. States Estimation:
Estimate people's behavior states by calculating the expectation of the particle set $\mathbf{S}_t$.
6. Iteration:
Iterate Steps 2, 3, 4, and 5 until convergence.

During the particle filtering process, we can easily obtain people's current behavior state $\mathbf{S}_t$ in stage 5, and predict people's behavior $\mathbf{S}_{t+1}$ at next time period in stage 3.

4. PREDICTION OF HUMAN MOBILITY AFTER DISASTER

Given the predicted behavior of individual person after the disasters, we also need to predict its possible mobility or evacuation routes, which will play a vital role on effective humanitarian relief and disaster management. In our study, people's predicted behavior is usually corresponding to an important places, e.g., home, work-

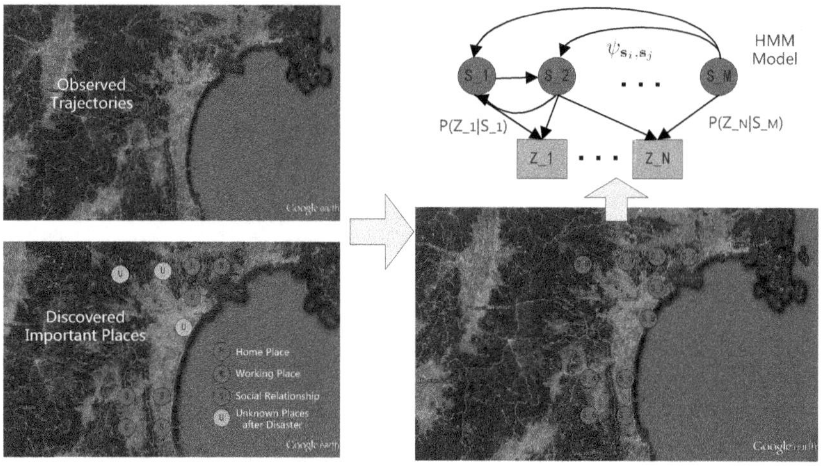

Figure 7: HMM-based human behavior model. Given person's important places, we use its past movements under various kinds of diaster states to train a HMM-based human behavior model.

ing places, parents or relatives' home, government appointed shelters and etc., given a predicted place and its current location, it is not difficult to find a possible route for a specific person. *However, human's mobility following large-scale disaster is usually different from the ones under normal circumstances.* During the disaster, human's mobility usually will be impacted by other people, and they usually tend to find a much safer routes for evacuations [2]. Furthermore, in most cases, the common transportation network is usually unavailable following large-scale disasters (as shown in Figure 3). Hence, in this section, we will present details on how to predict human mobility or their evacuation routes after disasters.

4.1 Mobility Graph Construction

Given the predicted places where individual person will go and its current location after the disasters, it is easy to think of using transportation networks to plan and predict its possible movements. However, most public transportation systems are usually not available after the earthquake occurred. Furthermore, based on our previous research, we found that population mobility after large-scale disaster would highly impacted by other people, and sometimes became a large population flow [2, 12, 13, 15]. Therefore, modeling large population movements after the disasters will play a vital role on prediction of individual person's mobility. In this study, we utilize a large number of population trajectories following the Great East Japan Earthquake and Fukushima nuclear accident to construct population mobility graph to model their mobility through collaborative learning [14]. The creation of this type of model is possible because social interactions and political responses in some urban areas are typically stable through time, and large population movements (which are often influenced by these conditions) are likely to remain the same following different emergency situations (e.g. the public transportation systems are unavailable again).

Region Construction: To construct the population mobility graph, we firstly need to discover connected urban areas after earthquake with the population movements. We divide the geographical range into disjoint cells by a given cell length l. Thus, the specific position of the persons is able to be mapped into a cell, and overall population trajectories are transformed into a sequence of cells. Then, we computed connection support of these cells, and explored the connected geographical regions. After cell merging process, we can build up the region of the population mobility graph. For more technical detail about it, please refer [14, 15].

Edge Inference: Once the regions in the population mobility graph are generated, we then need to infer edges and derive some edge information, such as travel frequency, travel time and etc. In this study, the mobility graph is a directed graph $G = (V, E)$, where V is a set of vertices and E is a set of edges. Each vertex v represents a geographical area, and the directed edge e indicates a transition relationship, including travel frequency and travel time.

Given the constructed regions R, and the population trajectories, we utilize these population movements traversing the regions to derive edge connections and information within regions. For each trajectory traversing the region, we infer the shortest path between any two consecutive points of the trajectory by virtual bidirected edges in the region, and the travel time of each edge is estimated by the median of all the travel times of the edge. In addition, the travel frequency of each edge is able to be estimated by recording the number of traversing trajectories. Similarly, we can also generate edges between regions: if some trajectories traversers from one region to another region, the edges is constructed between the two regions, and its edge information is estimated by the same methods as previous discussions.

4.2 Urban Mobility Model Learning

Based on the constructed urban mobility graph, the prediction model is able to be developed by using the Markov Decision Process (MDPs) [16]. MDPs provide a natural framework for representing sequential decision making, such as movements through various of urban areas. In MDP theory, the agent takes as sequence of *actions* ($a \in A$), which transition between *states* ($s \in S$) and incur and action-based *cost* ($c(a) \in \Re$). The agent is trying to minimize the sum of costs while reaching some destination, and the sequence of action is called a *path* ζ. For MDPs, a set of *features* ($\mathbf{f}_a \in \Re$) characterize each action, and the cost of the action is a linear function of these features parameterized by a *cost weight* vector ($\phi \in \Re$). Path feature, $\mathbf{f}_\zeta$ are the sum of the features of actions in the path: $\sum_{a \in \zeta} \mathbf{f}_a$. Thus, the cost weight applied to the path features is:

$$cost(\zeta|\phi) = \sum_{a \in \zeta} \phi^\top \mathbf{f}_a = \phi^\top \mathbf{f}_\zeta \quad (7)$$

In our problem, the population mobility graph provide us a deterministic MDP, the urban region (nodes) is able to be seem as *state*, the edge is the *action*, and the *path* is the people's movements after the earthquake. These movements are parameterized by their path feature $\mathbf{f}_\zeta$. For instance, a person's movements can be described by: travel through region A ($dens = 0.37$, $type = residential$) to region B ($dens = 0.58$, $type = commercial$), and finally stayed in region C ($dens = 0.75$, $type = administrative$) with route 1 ($frq = 0.37$, $time = 0.58$) ($A \rightarrow B$) and route 2 ($frq = 0.29$, $time = 0.62$)($B \rightarrow C$), where $dens$ is the region population density, $type$ the region types (e.g. residential, commercial and etc.), frq the travel frequency of the route, $time$ is the travel time of the route, and etc. Hence, we need to utilize all the population trajectories to train a MDPs model that is able to optimally demonstrate these people's behavior after the earthquake. Obviously, this is an *Inverse Reinforcement Learning* problem. In this study, we utilize the *Maximum Entropy Inverse Reinforcement Learning* algorithm [17, 18] to train the overall predictive model. With this training model, the people's movement or behaviors during some future emergency situations is able to be easily simulated or predicted [2, 15].

4.3 Prediction of Human Mobility

Given the predicted places where individual person will go, its current location after the disasters and the learnt urban mobility models, we can easily predict human movements by performing the Markov model route planning. In our study, we assume that people usually will find a safe and fast route (e.g. high frequency visited route and low travel time) for evacuation after the disasters. Hence, we employ the route planning using the destination-conditioned Markov Model [19]. This model recommends the most probable route satisfying origin and destination constraints. Lastly, we can obtain predicted route for a specific person (as shown in Figure 8-c,f).

5. EXPERIMENTAL RESULTS

In this section, we present extensive experimental results and evaluation of our approach for prediction of human behavior and their mobility.

5.1 Data Pre-processing and Experimental Setup

In our experiments, we focused on predicting population behaviors and their movements in Fukushima, Miyagi, Iwate prefectures and the Greater Tokyo Area. The three prefectures are the major disaster areas of the Great East Japan Earthquake and Fukushima nuclear accident, and the Greater Tokyo Area is the largest metropolitan area in the world which is as well highly impacted by this event. We selected the person who had more than 3,000 GPS records during 20 days after the earthquake for evaluation, and the total number of analyzed persons was more than 130,000. We utilized the GPS records of these persons in several months before the earthquake (1st, August 2010 to 11st, March 2011) and 20 days data after the earthquake to compute distribution of geographic location for individual people, and discovered their important places. Meanwhile, we randomly selected 80% of their GPS trajectories after the earthquake to train the behavior model for individual people, and the urban mobility graph as well as MDP model for the whole urban areas. We used the remaining 20% data for testing and evaluation.

5.2 Visualization of Results

Figure 8 shows the visualization of our prediction results. Given the persons' current observed movements (blue lines), and its important places, our approach predicted its possible destination as the red circle (Fig.8-a,d). Meanwhile, given the learnt urban mobility graph (Fig.8-b,e), persons' possible movements were predicted as the bold and colorful lines (Fig.8-c,f), and its actual movements were shown in the white lines. The first row shows the example results of a person in the Greater Tokyo Area, our approach predicted its possible movements at next four hours. The second row shows the person's case in Fukushima prefecture, and our model predicted its possible movements at next one day.

5.3 Evaluation of Behavior Prediction

Evaluation metrics: To evaluate the performance of different predictive model, we followed the work [1], and used the following evaluation metrics. (1) Predictive accuracy: This metric measures the overall accuracy of different predictive models, i.e., given the time of day of GPS trajectories in the test set, how accurately can each model predict the exact place where the people will go. For instance, accuracy of 0.7 means that 70% of the time the model correctly predicts the exactly places where people will go. (2) Log-likelihood: This metric measures the average log-likelihood of the GPS trajectories in the test set, which is able to measure how well the test set fits the model. (3) Expected distance error: This metric can be considered a soft version of predictive accuracy in that it does not insist on predicting the exact places, and it takes into account the spatial proximity of predictions to actual destination. For more details and definition on this metric, please refer [1].

Baseline models: We considered three non-trivial baseline models for comparison. (1) *Most Frequented Location Model (MF)*: For every hour of the day, this model predicts the most likely (most frequent visited) place of a particular people. Despite its simplicity, this model is very strong baseline. Lu *et al.* [3] also used this model to predict population mobility after the 2010 Haitian earthquake. (2) *Gaussian Model (GM):* This model has been proposed by Gonzales *et al.* [20], and it models human movements as a stochastic process centered around a single point. This model is static in time and captures the scale of a person's movements more than anything else. (3) *Periodic Mobility Model (PMM):* This model is built on the intuition that the majority of human movement is based on periodic movement between a small set of locations. As the state-of-the-art methods, it has been proposed by Cho *et al.* [1], which is able to predict the locations and dynamics of future human movements.

Performance evaluation: We compared the performance of our model with the performance of the baselines, and Figure 9 shows their performance. From this figure, we can see that our approach obtained a much better performance than the other competing methods on our dataset. In addition, we can see that: on the first 3 days after the earthquake, the performance of PMM for people in the Greater Tokyo Area is approximate to ours (Fig.9-a), but our method outperforms PMM much at other time. A possible explanation is that: on the first 3 days after the earthquake, many people's mobility in the Greater Tokyo Area was same to their mobility during normal times (e.g. working at daytime and go home at night). But at the following days, people began to more fully understand the seriousness of the Fukushima nuclear accident, and many of them chose to evacuate to other places. Obviously, our approach is powerful for predicting human disaster behaviors and emergency mobility than these competing methods that are used for predicting human mobility during normal times.

5.4 Evaluation of Mobility Prediction

To evaluate the accuracy of the predictive paths of people, we used three different metrics discussed in [18]. The first compares the model's most likely path estimate with the actual demonstrated path and evaluates the amount of route distance shared. The second shows what percentage of the testing paths match at least 90%

(a) Prediction of human behavior (b) Human mobility graph of the Greater Tokyo Area (c) Prediction of human mobility

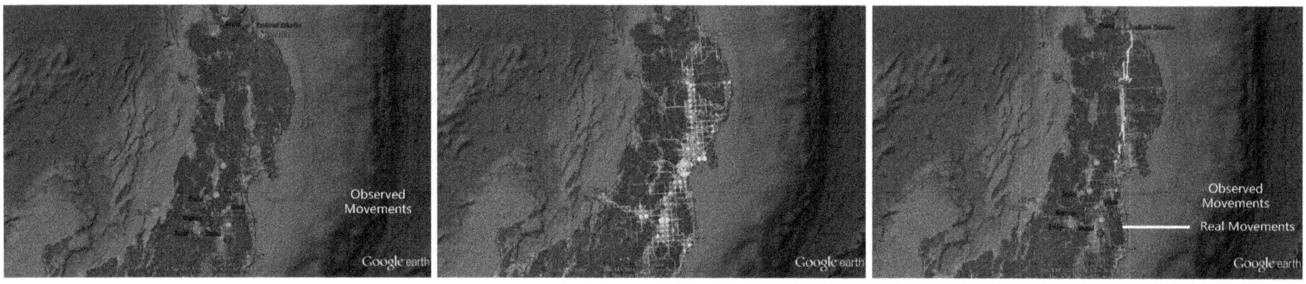

(d) Prediction of human behavior (e) Human mobility graph of Fukushima, Miyagi and Iwate prefectures (f) Prediction of human mobility

Figure 8: Visualization of the results. This figure shows our prediction results of human behaviors and their possible movements. Given the persons' current observed movements (blue lines in Fig.a,d), and its important places (blue and orange circles), the possible destinations are predicted as the red circle (Fig.a,d). Meanwhile, given the learnt urban mobility graph (Fig.b,e), persons' possible movements are predicted as the bold and colorful lines (Fig.c,f), and its actual movements are shown in the white lines (Fig.c,f). The first row shows the example results of a person in the Greater Tokyo Area, and our approach predicted its possible movements at next four hours. The second row shows the person's case in Fukushima prefecture, and our model predicted its possible movements at next one day. Note that the edge color in (Fig.b,e) indicates the edge parameters of urban human mobility graph. Here, it shows the travel frequency after the earthquake, the warmer one means the higher travel frequency; and this value is normalized from 0 to 1. In addition, the color of predicted trajectories (c,f) shows the probability which is normalized from 0 to 1. The warmer one means the higher probability.

(distance) with the model's predicted path. The final metric measures the average log probability of paths in the training set under the given model. Meanwhile, we chose the approach developed by Song *et al.* [15] as the baseline model. This approach also uses the population mobility graph to predict possible population movements after large-scale disaster, but it does not take into account the important places of people and some important disaster states.

Table 1 shows the performance of our method and method of Song *et al.* [15]. From this table, we can see that our method outperforms method of Song *et al.* [15] by 7.46% to 11.08%.

6. RELATED WORK

Recently, a number of studies on human mobility patterns during disasters have been proposed [21, 22], mainly focusing on small-scale and short-term emergencies (e.g. crowd panics and fires). However, research on the dynamics of population movements on a national scale during large-scale disasters (e.g. earthquakes, tsunamis, and hurricanes) is very limited [3], likely the result of difficulties in collecting representative longitudinal data in places where infrastructure and social order have collapsed [23, 24] and where study populations are moving across vast geographical areas [3]. In contrast, auto-mobile sensor data offer a new way to circumvent methodological problems of earlier research because they offer high temporal and spatial resolution are instantaneously available, have no interview bias, and provide longitudinal data for very large populations [25, 20, 3, 23, 26, 27]. Meanwhile, human mobility or trajectory data mining [28, 29, 30, 31, 32, 33, 34, 35, 36, 37, 38, 39, 40, 41, 42] have become a very hot topic in various research fields. Zheng *et al.* [38] aim to mine interesting locations and travel sequences from GPS trajectories. Cho *et al.* [1] propose a periodic mobility model (PMM) for predicting dynamics of future human movements by using check-in data. Ye *et al.* [7] propose a HMM-based human behavior model to predict human activity from check-in data. Yuan *et al.* [42] propose a graph-based model for population mobility summarization.

More Recently, Lu *et al.* [3] collected data from 1.9 million mobile users in Haiti to analyze population displacement after the 2010 Haitian earthquake, and concluded that population movements during disasters may be significantly more predictable than previously thought. Song *et al.* [2] collected data from 1.6 million GPS users in Japan to mine and modeling population evacuations during the 2011 Great East Japan Earthquake and Fukushima nuclear accident, and demonstrated that the prediction of large population movements after large-scale disaster was very possible. However, due to the lack of a powerful human behavior model that is able to fully depict how different disaster factors will influence population mobility patterns, they are difficult to accurately predict behavior or mobility of individual person. Thus, in this study, we firstly try to develop a concise human behavior model for accurately predicting human mobility after large-scale disaster.

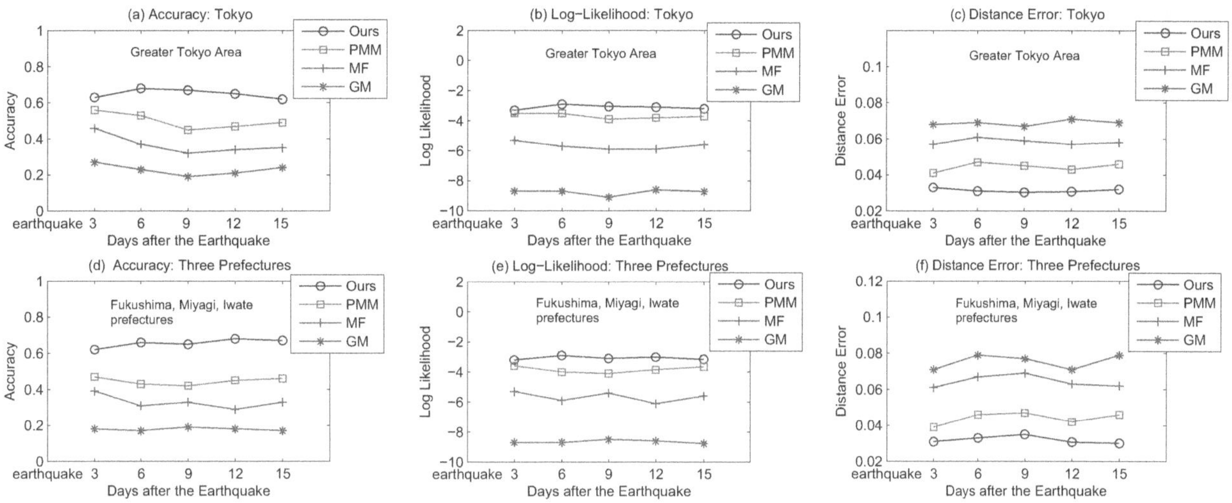

Figure 9: Evaluation of behavior prediction. This figure shows the performance evaluation of four methods with three different evaluation metrics. The first row shows the evaluation of people in the Greater Tokyo Area, and the second row shows the case of people in Fukushima, Miyagi, Iwate prefectures.

Table 1: Evaluation of Mobility Prediction

Algorithm	Matching	90% Matching	Log-Prob
Our Method (the Greater Tokyo Area)	80.68%	58.73%	-6.53
Method [15] (the Greater Tokyo Area)	72.76%	51.27%	-7.15
Our Method (Other three prefectures)	83.39%	63.36%	-5.97
Method [15] (Other three prefectures)	73.28%	52.28%	-7.33

7. CONCLUSION

In this paper, we build up a large human mobility database and several different datasets to capture and analyze human behavior and their mobility after the Great East Japan Earthquake and Fukushima nuclear accident. In addition, we develop a model of human behavior that takes into account different disaster factors for accurately predicting their behavior and mobility. The experimental results and validations demonstrate the efficiency of our behavior model, and it obtains a much better performance than previous approaches.

We note several limitations within our study. The population mobility database used is constructed from mobile devices and does not incorporate data from some representative portions of the population (i.e. people who do not own mobile devices or do not register for GPS service can not be incorporated into this study). Additionally, data are slightly biased towards younger age groups who are more likely to own GPS-based equipment than older age groups. However, we are confident that the data, which offers movement behaviors for the approximately 1.6 million people included in the database, are reflective of general movement patterns in the country following the composite disaster. A second limitation of our study is related to the difficulty in extrapolating movement patterns predicted by our predictive model for use in places outside of Japan or non-affected places by this disaster.

For future work, this research can be extended and improved in the followings: at present, the learnt behavior model is only able to applied to a specific person (learnt with its movements after disaster). In the future, we try to extend our behavior model into a general one by using transfer learning technology.

8. ACKNOWLEDGEMENTS

This work was partially supported by Grant-in-Aid for Young Scientists (26730113) of Japan's Ministry of Education, Culture, Sports, Science, and Technology (MEXT), Grant of Microsoft Research, Grant of Japan's Ministry of Land, Infrastructure, Transport and Tourism (MLIT), and DIAS/GRENE project of MEXT. We specially thank ZENRIN DataCom CO., LTD for their supporting.

9. REFERENCES

[1] E. Cho, S. A. Myers, and J. Leskovec. Friendship and mobility: User movement in location-based social networks, *Proc. of ACM SIGKDD*, (2011), pp. 1082-1090.

[2] X. Song, Q. Zhang, Y. Sekimoto, T. Horanont, S. Ueyama, and R. Shibasaki. Modeling and Probabilistic Reasoning of Population Evacuation During Large-scale Disaster, *Proc. of ACM SIGKDD*, (2013), pp. 1231-1239.

[3] X. Lu, L. Bengtssona, and P. Holme. Predictability of population displacement after the 2010 Haiti earthquake, *Proc. of the National Academy of Sciences of USA (PNAS)*, 109 (2012), pp. 11576-11581.

[4] Japanese Cabinet Secretariat, http://www.cas.go.jp/.

[5] R. Hoetzlein. Visual communication in Times of crisis: the Fukushima Nuclear Accident, *Leonardo Journal of Arts, Science and Technology*, 45 (2012), pp. 113-118.

[6] P. Tan, M. Steinbach, and V. Kumar, *Introduction to Data Mining*, Addison Wesley, (2005).

[7] J. Ye, Z. Zhu, and H. Cheng. What's Your Next Move: User Activity Prediction in Location-based Social Networks,

Proc. of SIAM International Conference on Data Mining (SDM), (2013).
[8] W. Zucchini, and I. L. MacDonald. Hidden Markov models for time series: an introduction using R, Chapman and Hall, London, (2009).
[9] L. E. Baum, T. Petrie, G. Soules, and N. Weiss. A maximization technique occurring in the statistical analysis of probabilistic functions of markov chains, *The Annals of Mathematical Statistics*, (1970), pp. 164-171.
[10] G. Schwarz. Estimating the dimension of a model, *The Annals of Statistics*, (1978), pp. 461-464.
[11] A. Doucet, S.J. Godsill, and C. Andrieu.On sequential Monte Carlo sampling methods for Bayesian filtering, *Statistics and Computing*, (2000), pp. 197-208.
[12] X. Song, Q. Zhang, Y. Sekimoto, T. Horanont, S. Ueyama, and R. Shibasaki. An Intelligent System for Large-scale Disaster Behavior Analysis and Reasoning, *IEEE Intelligent Systems*, 28 (2013), pp. 35-42.
[13] Y. Sekimoto, R. Shibasaki, H. Kanasugi, T. Usui and Y. Shimazaki. Reconstructing People Flow Recycling Large-Scale Social Survey Data, *IEEE Pervasive Computing*, (2011), pp. 27-35.
[14] L. Wei, Y. Zheng, and W. Peng. Constructing Popular Routes from Uncertain Trajectories, *Proc. of ACM SIGKDD*, (2012), pp. 195-203.
[15] X. Song, Q. Zhang, Y. Sekimoto, and R. Shibasaki. Intelligent System for Urban Emergency Management During Large-scale Disaster, *Proc. of AAAI Conference on Artificial Intelligence (AAAI)*, (2014).
[16] M. L. Puterman. *Markov Decision Processes: Discrete Stochastic Dynamic Programming*, Wiley-Interscience, (1994).
[17] B. D. Ziebart, A. Maas, J.A. Bagnell, and A. K. Dey. Navigate Like a Cabbie: Probabilistic Reasoning from Observed Context-Aware Behavior, *Proc. of Ubicomp.*, (2008), pp. 322-331.
[18] B. D. Ziebart, A. Maas, J.A. Bagnell, and A. K. Dey. Maximum Entropy Inverse Reinforcement Learning, *Proc. of AAAI Conference on Artificial Intelligence (AAAI)*, (2008), pp. 1433-1438.
[19] R. Simmons, B. Browning, Y. Zhang, and V. Sadekar. Learning to predict driver route and destination intent, *Proc. Intelligent Transportation Systems Conference*, (2006), pp. 127-132.
[20] MC. Gonzalez, CA. Hidalgo, and AL. Barabasi. Understanding individual human mobility patterns, *Nature*, 453 (2008), pp. 779-782.
[21] M. Moussaid, S. Garnier, G. Theraulaz, and D. Helbing. Collective information processing and pattern formation in swarms, flocks, and crowds, *Top Cogn. Sci.*, 1 (2009), pp. 469-497.
[22] J. Hahm and JH. Lee. Human errors in evacuation behavior during a traumatic emergency using a virtual fire, *Cyberpsychol Behavior*, 12 (2009), pp. 98-98.
[23] JP. Bagrow, DS. Wang, and AL Barabasi. Collective response of human populations to large-scale emergencies, *Plos ONE*, 6 (2011).
[24] L. Bengtsson, X. Lu, A. Thorson, R. Garfield, J. von Schreeb. Improved response to disasters and outbreaks by tracking population movements with mobile phone network data: A post-earthquake geospatial study in Haiti, *PLoS Medical*, 8 (2011).
[25] CM. Song, ZH. Qu, N. Blumm, and AL. Barabasi. Limits of predictability in human mobility, *Science*, 327 (2010), pp. 1018-1021.
[26] C. Song, T. Koren, P. Wang, and AL. Barabasi, Modelling the scaling properties of human mobility, *Nature Physics*, 6 (2010), pp. 818-823.
[27] N. Eagle, A. Pentland, and D. Lazer. Inferring friendship network structure by using mobile phone data, *Proc. of the National Academy of Sciences of USA (PNAS)*, 106 (2009), pp. 15274-15278.
[28] Z. Chen, H. T. Shen and X. Zhou. Discovering Popular Routes from Trajectories, *Proc. of IEEE ICDE*, (2011), pp. 900-911.
[29] Z. Chen, H.T. Shen, X. Zhou, Y. Zheng and X. Xie. Searching Trajectories by Locations - An Efficiency Study, *Proc. of ACM SIGMOD*, (2010), pp. 255-266.
[30] F. Giannotti, M. Nanni, D. Pedreschi, F. Pinelli, C. Renso, S. Rinzivillo and R. Trasarti. Unveiling the complexity of human mobility by querying and mining massive trajectory data, *The VLDB Journal*, 20 (2011), pp. 695-719.
[31] Z. Li, M. Ji, J. Lee, L. Tang, Y. Yu, J. Han, R. Kays. MoveMine: mining moving object databases, *Proc. of ACM SIGMOD*, (2010), pp. 1203-1206.
[32] J. Yuan, Y. Zheng abd X. Xie. Discovering regions of different functions in a city using human mobility and POIs, *Proc. of ACM SIGKDD*, (2012), pp. 186-194.
[33] L. Backstrom, E. Sun, and C. Marlow. Find me if you can: improving geographical prediction with social and spatial proximity, *Proc. of WWW*, (2010), pp. 61-70.
[34] F. Giannotti, M. Nanni, F. Pinelli, and D. Pedreschi. Trajectory pattern mining, *Proc. of ACM SIGKDD*, (2007), pp. 330-339.
[35] Z. Li, B. Ding, J. Han, R. Kays, and P. Nye. Mining periodic behaviors for moving objects, *Proc. of ACM SIGKDD*, (2010), pp. 1099-1108.
[36] S. Scellato, A. Noulas, and C. Mascolo. Exploiting place features in link prediction on location-based social networks, *Proc. of ACM SIGKDD*, (2011), pp. 1046-1054.
[37] Y. Ye, Y. Zheng, Y. Chen, J. Feng, and X. Xie, Mining individual life pattern based on location history, *Proc. of MDM*, (2009), pp. 1-10.
[38] Y. Zheng, L. Zhang, X. Xie, and W. Y. Ma. Mining interesting locations and travel sequences from GPS trajectories, *Proc. of WWW*, (2009), pp. 791-800.
[39] Z. Li, B. , J. Han, and R. Kays. Swarm: Mining Relaxed Temporal Moving Object Clusters, *Proc. of VLDB*, (2010), pp. 723-734.
[40] Y. Xue, R. Zhang, Y. Zheng, X. Xie, J. Huang, Z. Xu. Destination Prediction by Sub-Trajectory Synthesis and Privacy Protection Against Such Prediction, *Proc. of IEEE ICDE*, (2013), pp. 254-265.
[41] H. Su, K. Zheng, H. Wang, J. Huang and X. Zhou. Calibrating Trajectory Data for Similarity-based Analysis, *Proc. of ACM SIGMOD*, (2013), pp. 833-844.
[42] J. Yuan, Y. Zheng, X. Xie, G. Sun. T-Drive: Enhancing driving directions with taxi drivers' intelligence, *IEEE Transactions on Knowledge and Data Engineering*, 25(2013), pp. 220-232.

Inferring User Demographics and Social Strategies in Mobile Social Networks

Yuxiao Dong†, Yang Yang‡, Jie Tang‡, Yang Yang†, Nitesh V. Chawla†
†Department of Computer Science and Engineering, University of Notre Dame
†Interdisciplinary Center for Network Science and Applications, University of Notre Dame
‡Department of Computer Science and Technology, Tsinghua University
ydong1@nd.edu, yyang.thu@gmail.com, jietang@tsinghua.edu.cn, yyang1@nd.edu, nchawla@nd.edu

ABSTRACT

Demographics are widely used in marketing to characterize different types of customers. However, in practice, demographic information such as age, gender, and location is usually unavailable due to privacy and other reasons. In this paper, we aim to harness the power of big data to automatically infer users' demographics based on their daily mobile communication patterns.

Our study is based on a real-world large mobile network of more than 7,000,000 users and over 1,000,000,000 communication records (CALL and SMS). We discover several interesting *social strategies* that mobile users frequently use to maintain their social connections. First, young people are very active in broadening their social circles, while seniors tend to keep close but more stable connections. Second, female users put more attention on cross-generation interactions than male users, though interactions between male and female users are frequent. Third, a persistent same-gender triadic pattern over one's lifetime is discovered for the first time, while more complex opposite-gender triadic patterns are only exhibited among young people.

We further study to what extent users' demographics can be inferred from their mobile communications. As a special case, we formalize a problem of double dependent-variable prediction—inferring user gender and age simultaneously. We propose the *WhoAmI* method, a Double Dependent-Variable Factor Graph Model, to address this problem by considering not only the effects of features on gender/age, but also the interrelation between gender and age. Our experiments show that the proposed WhoAmI method significantly improves the prediction accuracy by up to 10% compared with several alternative methods.

Categories and Subject Descriptors

J.4 [**Social and Behavioral Sciences**]: Sociology; H.2.8 [**Database Management**]: Database Applications

Keywords

Demographic prediction, Social strategy, Mobile social network, Human communication

KDD'14, August 24–27, 2014, New York, NY, USA.

http://dx.doi.org/10.1145/2623330.2623703.

1. INTRODUCTION

From a recent report by the International Telecommunications Union (ITU) at the 2013 Mobile World Congress, the number of mobile-phone subscriptions reached 6.8 billion, corresponding to a global penetration of 96%. As of 2014, the number of mobile subscriptions across the globe has exceeded the world population. These mobile devices record huge amounts of user behavioral data, in particular users' daily communications with others. This provides us with an unprecedented opportunity to study how people behave differently and form different groups.

Previous work on mobile social networks mainly focuses on macro-level models, like network formation [26], scale free [5], duration distribution [4, 29], and mobility modeling [30, 33]. Recently, however, researchers have started to pay more attention to the micro-level analysis of the mobile networks. For example, Eagle et al. [6] studied the friendship network of 100 specific mobile users (students or faculties at MIT). They investigated human interactions (what people do, where they go, and with whom they communicate) based on the machine-sensed environmental data collected by mobile devices. However, they do not consider the user demographics. More recently, Nokia Research organized the 2012 Mobile Data Challenge to infer mobile user demographics by using communication records of 200 users [21, 35]. However, the scale of the network is very limited. In this paper, we aim to leverage a large-scale mobile network to study how users' communication behaviors correlate with their demographic information.

Demographic information is often available in the telecommunication industry. For example, a *postpaid* mobile user[1] is required to create an account by providing detailed demographic information (e.g., name, age, gender, etc.). However, a recent report[2] indicates that there is still a large portion of *prepaid* users[3] (also commonly referred to as pay-as-you-go) who are required to purchase credit in advance of service use. Statistics show that 95% of mobile users in India are prepaid, 80% in Latin America, 70% in China, 65% in Europe, and 33% in the United States. Even in the U.S., the switch to prepaid plans is accelerating during the economic recession from 2008. Prepaid services allow the users to be anonymous—no need to provide any user-specific information. However, building demographic profiles for all customers is critical to mobile service providers. This can help them make better marketing strategies (e.g., identify potential customers and prevent customer churns). Moreover, by using demographic information, service providers can supply users with more personalized services and focus on enhancing the communication experience. Therefore, one interesting but challenging question is the extent to which user demographic

[1] http://en.wikipedia.org/wiki/Postpaid_mobile_phone
[2] http://www.itu.int/
[3] http://en.wikipedia.org/wiki/Prepaid_mobile_phone

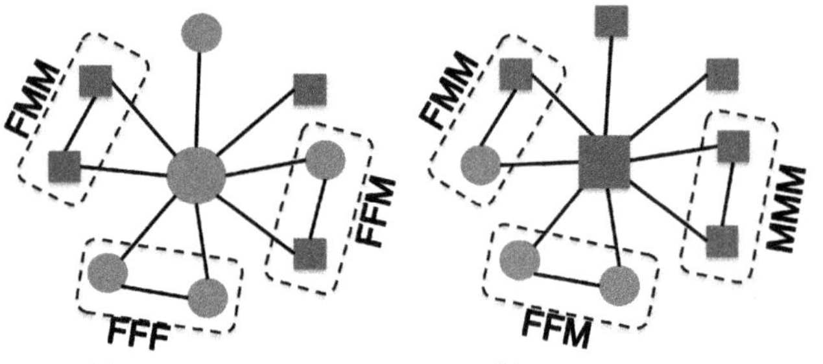

(a) Female Ego Network (b) Male Ego Network.

Figure 1: Ego Network. Red circle: female; blue square: male; MMM: Male-Male-Male; FFF: Female-Female-Female.

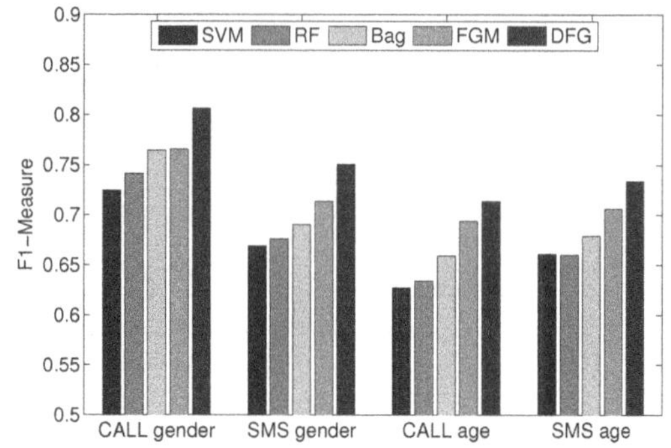

Figure 2: Demographic prediction performance of comparison methods (Cf. §5 for details of the comparison methods).

profiles can be inferred from their mobile communication interactions.

In this paper, we employ a real-world large mobile network comprised of more than 7,000,000 users and over 1,000,000,000 communication records (CALL and SMS) as the basis of our study, which we use to systematically investigate the interplay of user communication behaviors and demographic information. Through the study, we first reveal several intriguing *social strategies* that users of different ages and genders use to maintain their social connections. Based on the discoveries, we then develop a unified probabilistic model to predict users' demographics based on their communication behaviors. To the best of our knowledge, we are the first to study the problem of inferring user demographics and social strategies in such a real-large mobile network.

To highlight several of our key findings, we discovered that young people are very active in broadening their social circles, while seniors have the tendency to maintain small but close connections. We found that male users maintain broader social connections than female users when they are young. We also found that cross-gender communications are more frequent than those between same-gender users. We also observed frequent cross-generation interactions that are essential for bridging age gaps in family, workplace, education, and human society as a whole [20]. We discovered significant gender differences in human interactions throughout their lives, which reflects dynamic gender-biased social strategies. Figure 1 shows examples of both female and male ego networks. Human social behaviors reveal both same-gender relationships—'FFF' (Female-Female-Female) and 'MMM' (Male-Male-Male) triads—and opposite-gender social groups ('FMM' and 'FFM' triads) during the dating and reproductively active period (18-34 years old). Upon entering into middle-age, people's attention to opposite-gender triads quickly disappears. However, the insistence and social investment on same-gender social groups ('FFF' and 'MMM') lasts for a lifetime. Finally, our analysis shows strong interrelations between users' age and gender. For example, a 20-year-old female's behaviors are distinct from not only a 20-year-old male's, but also from a 50-year-old female's.

Based on these interesting discoveries, we further study to what extent users' demographic information can be inferred by mobile social networks. We formally define a double dependent-variable classification problem. The objective is to infer users' gender and age simultaneously by leveraging their interrelations. This problem is very different from traditional classification problems, where only the correlations between the dependent variable Y and feature vector $\mathbf{X}$ are considered. In this problem, we are given two dependent variables Y (gender) and Z (age), and feature vector $\mathbf{X}$. We aim to capture the correlations between $\mathbf{X}$ and Y, $\mathbf{X}$ and Z, and the interrelations between Y and Z to infer Y and Z simultaneously. To address this problem, we present the *WhoAmI* method, whereby the interrelations between two dependent variables are modeled. The WhoAmI method is able to infer user gender and age simultaneously. On both the CALL and SMS networks, the proposed method can achieve an accuracy of 80% for predicting users' age and gender according to their daily mobile communication patterns, significantly outperforming (by up to 10% in terms of F1-Measure shown in Figure 2) several alternative methods (Cf. §5 for details of the comparison methods). To scale up the proposed method to handle large-scale networks, we further develop a distributed learning algorithm, which can reduce the computational time to sub-linear speedup (9–10× with 16 cores) by leveraging parallel computing.

Organization. We introduce the mobile networks in Section 2. Followed by the interesting discoveries in Section 3, we formalize the double dependent-variable demographic classification problem and present our solution in Section 4. Prediction results are shown in Section 5. Finally, we summarize the related work in Section 6 and conclude this work in Section 7.

2. MOBILE NETWORK

Data. The dataset used in this paper is extracted from a collection of more than 1 billion (1,000,229,603) call and text-message events from an anonymous country [26, 17], which spans from Aug. 2008 to Sep. 2008. We construct two undirected and weighted mobile communication networks from the deidentified and anonymous data: call network (referred to as CALL) and messaging network (referred to as SMS). Specifically, we view each user as a node v_i and create an edge e_{ij} between two users v_i and v_j if and only if they made reciprocal calls (v_i called v_j and also v_j called v_i for at least one time during the observation period) or messages between each other. The strength w_{ij} of the edge is defined as the number of communications between v_i and v_j. Then we extract the largest connected components from each network as our experimental networks: CALL and SMS. The resultant CALL network consists of 7,440,123 nodes and 32,445,941 edges and the SMS network is composed of 4,505,958 nodes and 10,913,601 edges. The data also does not contain any communication content.

Demographics. In this dataset, around 45% of the users are female and 55% are male. We compare the demographic population distribution of mobile users in the dataset with the 2008 global population distribution. We found that both female and male users between the ages of 20 and 55 are strongly overrepresented in the mobile population compared to the global population. This is reasonable, because teenagers (under 18 years old) and the elderly (aged 80 or over) use mobile phones less frequently. Thus in our study, we focus on users aged between 18 and 80 years old. To simplify the notations, we use F and M to respectively denote the female and male users. Following [10, 3], we also split users into four groups according to ages: Young (18-24), Young-Adult (25-34), Middle-Age (35-49), and Senior (> 49).

Network Characteristics. We present a basic correlation analysis between network characteristics and user demographics to see how people of different gender and age maintain their mobile social networks. In particular, we consider the following network metrics:

- *Degree Centrality*: the number of edges incident upon a node in the network;
- *Neighbor Connectivity*: the average degree of neighbors of a specific user [37];
- *Triadic Closure*: the local clustering coefficient (cc) of each user [15];
- *Embeddedness*: the degree that people are enmeshed in networks [9]. More accurately, a user u's embeddedness is defined as

$$\frac{1}{|N_u|}\sum_{v\in N_u}\frac{|N_u\cap N_v|}{|N_u\cup N_v|} \tag{1}$$

where N_u is the neighbors of u.

Figure 3 plots the correlations between the four network metrics and the user age. From sub-figures 3(a)-3(b), we observe that the degree and neighbor connectivity of both female and male users achieve peak values around 22 years old, then decrease with valleys around 38-40 years old. An interesting phenomenon is that before this valley, the males have clearly higher scores on both metrics (degree and neighbor connectivity), while the situation is reversed after this point.

From sub-figures 3(c)-3(d), we see that both triadic closure and embeddedness increase when users become older. Similar to the first two metrics, there is also a reversion phenomenon at age 38-40. The difference lies in that the male's triadic closure and embeddedness are at first smaller than the female's, and then become larger after the reversion point. All four network metrics are observed at a 95% confidence interval.

Social Strategies. From a sociological perspective, the analysis that results in Figure 3 can be also explained by different social strategies that people use to maintain their social connections. It seems that young people (who have higher degree scores) are very active in broadening their social circles, while seniors (who have higher triadic closure scores cc) tend to keep small but more stable connections.

3. COMMUNICATION DEMOGRAPHICS

Human communications form the structural backbone of human societies, in the shape of networks [26]. The mobile data provides rich information for understanding human communications in real-world daily life. In this section, we focus on the individual level to study how a user communicates with others in her/his *ego network*. To be precise, one's ego network is defined by viewing herself/himself as the central node and her/his directed friends as surrounding nodes. Clearly, the ego network is a sub-network of the original network. Figure 1 gives two examples of ego networks. Herein, we investigate the interplay of human communication interactions and demographic characteristics in ego networks. Three social strategies are revealed from the data, including homophily

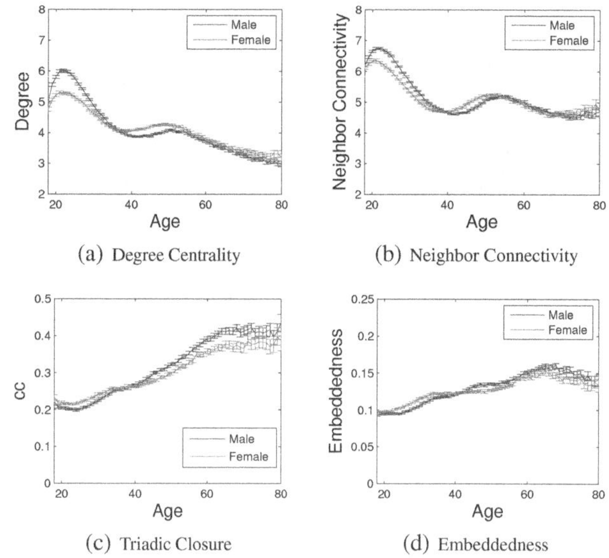

(a) Degree Centrality (b) Neighbor Connectivity (c) Triadic Closure (d) Embeddedness

Figure 3: Correlations between demographics and network characteristics.

on gender and age, cross-generation communication, and demographic dynamics of social relationships. We present the discoveries in the CALL network due to the page limit, and the SMS network shows the similar results.

Homophily on Gender and Age. The principle of homophily suggests that people tend to be connected with those who are similar to them [14]. It has been extensively studied and verified in online social networks [16, 19] and mobile networks [4, 12]. With the ego network of each user, we study the demographic homophily on both gender and age. Figure 4 shows friends' demographic distribution for female and male users of different ages. The X-axis represents central users' age from 18 to 80 years old and the Y-axis represents the demographic distribution of users' friends, in which positive numbers denote female friends' ages and negative numbers denote male friends'. The spectrum color, which extends from dark blue (low) to red (high), represents the probability of one's friends belonging to the corresponding age (Y-axis) and gender (positive or negative). Interestingly, there exists a highlighted diagonal line in each figure, which suggests that people tend to communicate with others of similar age. In particular, the age homophily is much stronger for people aged between 35 to 55 years old. Simultaneously, the highlighted diagonals appear in the same gender range, i.e. females appear in the positive Y range (F) and males in the negative Y range (M), which shows the existence of a high degree of gender homophily.

Cross-generation Communication. The analysis above confirms the existence of demographic homophily in mobile social networks. But what are the patterns underlying cross-generational communication, e.g., parents and kids? In fact, the cross-generational communication is a fundamental issue in sociology. The bulk of research [20, 28] has been conducted toward bridging age gaps in human society at large.

In Figure 5, we use heat maps to visualize the communication frequencies for different demographics. Figure 5(a) reports the average number of calls per month between people. Figures 5(b)-5(d) detail the analysis by reporting the average numbers of calls between two male users, two female users, and one male and one

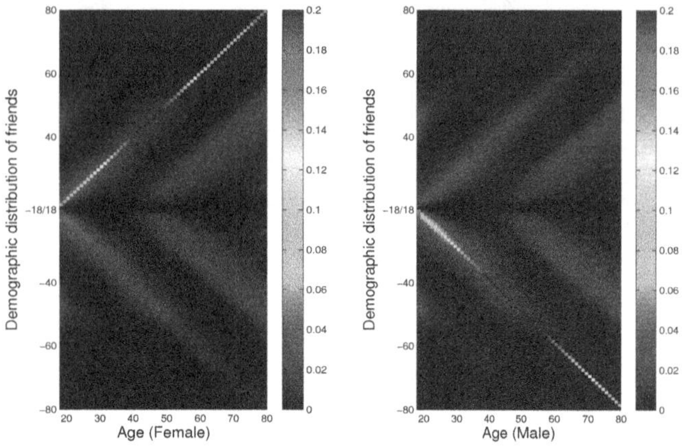

(a) Demog. dist. of Female's friends (b) Demog. dist. of Male's friends

Figure 4: Friends' demographic distribution. X-axis: (a) female age; (b) male age. Y-axis: age of friends (positive: female friends, negative: male friends). The spectrum color represents the friends' demographic distribution.

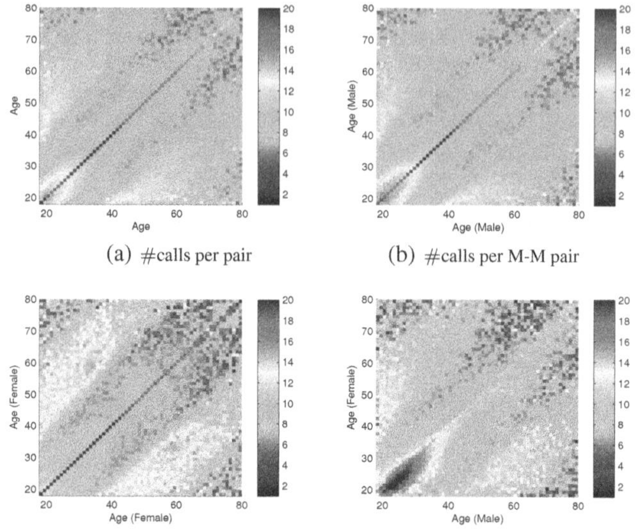

(a) #calls per pair (b) #calls per M-M pair

(c) #calls per F-F pair (d) #calls per M-F pair

Figure 5: Strength of social tie. XY-axis: age of users with specific gender. The spectrum color represents the number of calls per month. (a), (b), and (c) are symmetric.

female user, respectively. Again, we discover highlighted diagonal lines in Figures 5(a)-5(c), which correspond to the gender and age homophily. We also notice that there are highlighted areas corresponding to cross-generational communications. In Figure 5(a), the color of cross-generation areas that extends from green to yellow indicates that on average 13 calls per month have been made between people aged 20-30 and those aged 40-50 years old. This corresponds to communications between parents and children, managers and subordinates, advisors and advisees, etc.

In addition, we observe that the communications between female users seem to be much more frequent than those between male users (Cf. Figures 5(b) and 5(c)). This is possibly because communications between mothers and daughters are more frequent than those between fathers and sons. Moreover, we find a "brothers" phenomenon among male users. In Figure 5(b), the diagonal highlights from 18 to 34 years (Young and Young-Adult) are much larger and denser than the corresponding area in Figure 5(c). This indicates that male users tend to maintain broader social connections than female users when they are young. Finally, from Figure 5(d), we observe a highlighted red area between people aged 18-34 years old, which means that cross-gender communications are more frequent than those between users of the same gender. A similar observation has also been reported in [16].

Demographic Dynamics. Human interactions between demographics reveal homophily or cross-generation phenomena not only in topologically but also in their dynamics. Evolutionary theory suggests that one's social strategy on her/his ego network vary and evolve across her/his lifetime as a function of the tradeoff between different social needs [27]. Herein, we focus our attention on the demographic dynamics in ego networks.

In Figure 6, we first report the friends' demographic distribution in one's ego network as a function of the central user's age. The X-axis denotes the central user's age x, and the Y-axis denotes the proportion of the age-groups her/his friends belong to, including the same generation ($x-5$ to $x+5$), older generation ($x+20$ to $x+30$), and younger generation ($x-30$ to $x-20$). From this, it is apparent that strong demographic dynamics exist in human interactions. First, the young and young-adult put increasing focus on the same generation ('blue' and 'red' lines) and maintain decreasing interactions with the older generation ('green' and 'pink' lines). Second, the middle-aged and seniors start to devote more attention to the new generation ('black' and 'cyanine' lines) even despite the sacrifice of homophily (the decreasing of 'blue' and 'red' lines). Third, during middle-age, the connections with the age-matched opposite-gender in ego networks ('blue' in Figure 6(a), 'red' in Figure 6(b)) decrease, and the proportion of same-gender friends ('red' in Figure 6(a) and 'blue' in Figure 6(b)) stay relatively stable.

In Figure 7, the heat map visualizes the distribution of minimum age (X-axis) and maximum age (Y-axis) of three users in a close social triad structure. Figures 7(a) and 7(d) show the same-gender triads: 'FFF' and 'MMM', and Figures 7(b) and 7(c) present the age distribution for users in opposite-gender triads: 'FFM' and 'FMM'. When people are young, the strong triadic relationships are revealed in all four kinds of gender-triads: 'FFF', 'MMM', 'FFM' and 'FMM' by highlighted red areas at the left-bottom corners. More excitingly, when entering middle-age, people only maintain the same-gender triadic relationships, which is revealed by the red diagonal lines in Figure 7(a) and Figure 7(d). However, the opposite-gender triadic relationships vanish when people pass 34 years old in Figure 7(b) and 7(c). The instability of opposite-gender triadic relationships and the persistence of same-gender triadic relationships across one's lifetime are novel discoveries and reveal human social strategy dynamics that are more complex and crucial than can be revealed by a static view.

Social Strategies. First, Figure 4 confirms that people have the tendency to interact with others with similar gender and age. Second, Figure 5 shows that the cross-generation interactions are maintained to pass the torch of family, workforce, and human knowledge from generation to generation in social society. Third, human interactions reveal striking gender differences in social triadic relationships across one's lifespan, which reflects dynamic gender-bias of human behaviors from young to old. Figure 7 shows that people tend to expand their social connections with both females and

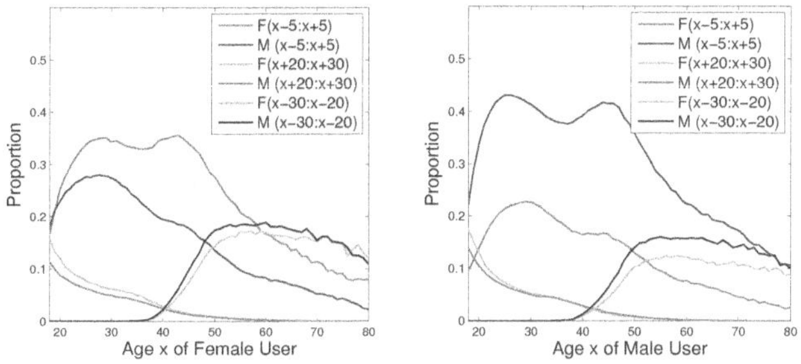

(a) Proportion of Female's friends' age (b) Proportion of Male's friends' age

Figure 6: Dynamics of friends' demographic distribution in ego networks. X-axis: (a) female age; (b) male age. Y-axis: Proportion of friends' age groups.

males during the dating and reproductively active period, and put more social investment on maintaining same-gender social groups after entering into middle-age.

4. DEMOGRAPHIC PREDICTION

All the observations above clearly demonstrate the strong demographic interrelations between users' gender and age. For example, a 20-year-old female's behaviors are distinct from not only a 20-year-old male's, but also from a 50-year-old female's. Based on this, we formalize the demographic prediction as a double dependent-variable classification problem, i.e., we infer gender and age simultaneously. The *WhoAmI* method, a Double Dependent-Variable Factor Graph Model, is proposed to solve this problem by leveraging not only the correlations between features and gender/age, but also the interrelations between gender and age.

4.1 Problem Definition

Let $G = (V, E, Y, Z)$ denote the undirected and weighted mobile network, where V is a set of $|V| = N$ users and $E \subseteq V \times V$ is a set of communication edges (CALL or SMS) between users. Each user $v_i \in V$ is associated with demographic information, i.e., Gender $y_i \in Y$ and Age $z_i \in Z$. $\mathbf{X}$ is the attribute matrix, where each row $\mathbf{x}_i$ represents an $|\mathbf{x}_i|$ dimensional feature vector for user v_i. Given this, we define our problem below.

Problem 1. **Demographic Prediction:** Given a partially labeled network $G = (V^L, V^U, E, Y^L, Z^L)$ and the attribute matrix $\mathbf{X}$, where V^L is a set of users with labeled demographic information Y^L and Z^L, and V^U is a set of unlabeled users, the objective is to learn a function

$$f : G = (V^L, V^U, E, Y^L, Z^L), \mathbf{X} \rightarrow (Y^U, Z^U)$$

to predict users' gender and age simultaneously, where Y^U, Z^U are the demographic information for the unlabeled users V^U.

Different from previous work on demographic prediction [3, 10], where users' gender and age are inferred by modeling $P(Y|G, \mathbf{X})$ and $P(Z|G, \mathbf{X})$ separately, our problem here is to model $P(Y, Z|G, \mathbf{X})$ and predict users' gender and age simultaneously. We leverage not only the correlation between $\mathbf{X}$ and Y/Z but also the interrelations between gender Y and age Z. The motivation here comes from the fact that Section 3 reveals strong demographic interrelations in human communication behaviors.

In this work, we infer gender as a binary classification problem, i.e., Female or Male, and infer age as a four-class classification

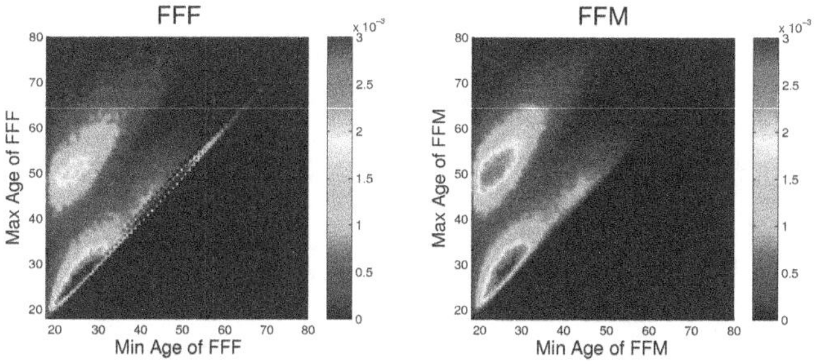

(a) Triad FFF demog. dist. (b) Triad FFM demog. dist.

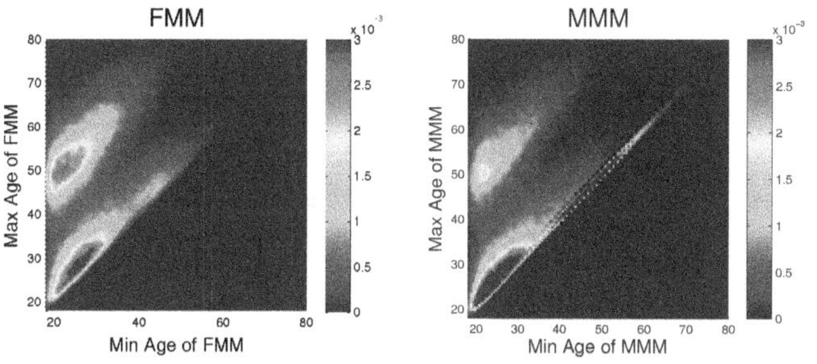

(c) Triad FMM demog. dist. (d) Triad MMM demog. dist.

Figure 7: Demographic distribution in social triad. X-axis: minimum age of three users in a triad. Y-axis: maximum age of three users. The spectrum color represents the distributions.

problem by splitting users' age into four groups: Young (18-24), Young-Adult (25-34), Middle-Age (35-49), and Senior (> 49).

4.2 The WhoAmI Framework

Our goal is to design a unified model to capture not only users' attributes on demographics but also the interrelations between users' gender and age. We propose the WhoAmI method, a Double Dependent-Variable Factor Graph Model. To handle large-scale networks, we further develop a distributed learning algorithm.

4.2.1 Double Dependent-Variable Factor Graph

We define an objective function by maximizing the conditional probability of users' gender Y and age Z given their corresponding attributes and the input network structure, i.e., $P_\theta(Y, Z|G, \mathbf{X})$. The factor graph [13] provides a way to factorize the "global" probability as a product of "local" factor functions, which makes the maximization simple, i.e.,

$$P(Y, Z|G, \mathbf{X}) = \frac{P(\mathbf{X}, G|Y, Z)P(Y, Z)}{P(\mathbf{X}, G)} \propto P(Y, Z|G)P(\mathbf{X}|Y, Z)$$
$$\propto \prod_{v_i \in V} P(\mathbf{x}_i|y_i, z_i) \prod_{c \in G} P(Y_c, Z_c) \quad (2)$$

where $P(Y_c, Z_c)$ denotes the probability of labels given the structure c of the network and $P(\mathbf{x}_i|y_i, z_i)$ is the probability of generating attributes $\mathbf{x}_i$ given the label y_i and z_i.

In this model, we design three kinds of factors. The first is an attribute factor $f(y_i, z_i, \mathbf{x}_i)$ for capturing correlations between users' demographics and communication attributes. The second is a dyadic factor $g(\mathbf{y}_e, \mathbf{z}_e)$ for modeling correlations between users' demographics and their direct relationships in ego networks, where Y_c in Eq. 2 is represented as $\mathbf{y}_e$ (y_i, y_j), and Z_c is denoted by $\mathbf{z}_e$ (z_i and z_j) iff $e_{ij} \in E$. The third is a triadic factor $h(\mathbf{y}_c, \mathbf{z}_c)$ for correlating users' demographics and triadic relationships in their ego

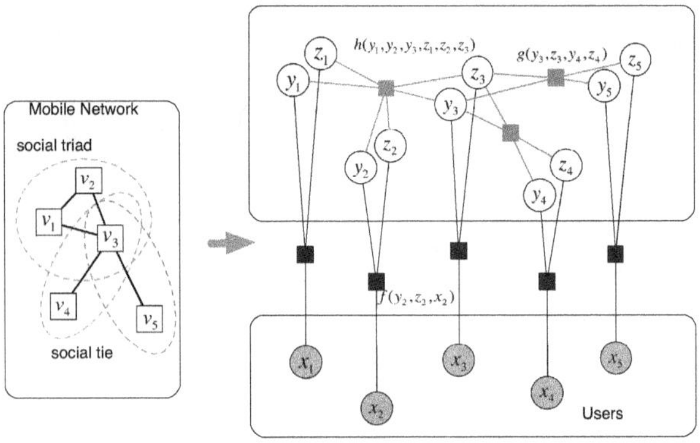

Figure 8: An illustration of the proposed model. y_i **and** z_i **indicate the gender and age of the user** v_i**.** x_i **denotes communication attributes of the user** v_i **extracted from the mobile network** G**.** $f(y_i, z_i, \mathbf{x}_i)$**,** $g(\mathbf{y}_e, \mathbf{z}_e)$**, and** $h(\mathbf{y}_c, \mathbf{z}_c)$ **respectively represent attribute factor, dyadic factor, and triadic factor in the proposed model.**

networks. Similarly, $\mathbf{y}_c$ means y_i, y_j, y_k and $\mathbf{z}_c$ is z_i, z_j, z_k when three users v_i, v_j, v_k form a close triangle structure.

Therefore, the joint distribution can be further factorized as:

$$P(Y, Z|G, \mathbf{X}) = \prod_{v_i \in V} f(y_i, z_i, \mathbf{x}_i) \times \prod_{e_{ij} \in E} [g(\mathbf{y}_e, \mathbf{z}_e)] \prod_{c_{ijk} \in G} [h(\mathbf{y}_c, \mathbf{z}_c)] \tag{3}$$

Figure 8 shows an illustration of our proposed model, which consists of two layers of nodes. The bottom layer contains random variables and the upper layer contains the three kinds of factors introduced above. The joint distribution over the whole set of random variables can be factorized as the product of all factors. Specifically, we instantiate the three factors as follows.

Attribute factor. We use this factor $f(y_i, z_i, \mathbf{x}_i)$ to represent the correlation between user v_i's demographics and her/his network characteristics $\mathbf{x}_i$. More specifically, we instantiate the factor by an exponential-linear function:

$$f(y_i, z_i, \mathbf{x}_i) = \frac{1}{W_v} \exp\{\alpha_{y_i z_i} \cdot \mathbf{x}_i\} \tag{4}$$

where α is one parameter of the proposed model, and W_v is a normalization term. For each pair of (y_i, z_i), $\alpha_{y_i z_i}$ is an $|\mathbf{x}|$-length vector, where the k-th dimension indicates how x_{ik} distributes over (y_i, z_i). For example, let's say x_{ik} represents the degree of user v_i. This factor can capture the fact that people with different gender and age have the different network properties shown in Figure 3. Traditional probabilistic graphical models can only model the correlations between features and one single type of dependent variable, while our proposed model captures how the features distribute over two types of dependent variables jointly.

Dyadic factor. We next define the dyadic factor $g(\mathbf{y}_e, \mathbf{z}_e)$, where $e_{ij} \in E$, to represent the correlation between user v_i and v_j's demographic information. Specifically, we have

$$g(\mathbf{y}_e, \mathbf{z}_e) = \begin{cases} \frac{1}{W_{e_1}} \exp\{\beta_1 \cdot g'_1(y_i, y_j)\} \\ \frac{1}{W_{e_2}} \exp\{\beta_2 \cdot g'_3(y_i, z_i)\} \\ \cdots \\ \frac{1}{W_{e_6}} \exp\{\beta_6 \cdot g'_6(z_i, z_j)\} \end{cases} \tag{5}$$

where β_p is the model parameters for this type of factor, $g'_p(\cdot)$ is defined as a vector of indicator functions, and W_{e_p} is the normalization term. We can enumerate in total 6 different combinations of each pair of demographic variables from (y_i, y_j, z_i, z_j). The intuition behind is that v_i's friends' demographics distribute differently by varying either v_i's own age or gender, as Figure 6 suggests.

Triadic factor. We finally define the triadic factor $h(\mathbf{y}_c, \mathbf{z}_c)$ to represent the correlation among the demographics of social triads, where $c = \{v_i, v_j, v_k | e_{ij}, e_{jk}, e_{ik} \in E\}$ indicates the triangle structure in G. More specifically, we have

$$h(\mathbf{y}_c, \mathbf{z}_c) = \begin{cases} \frac{1}{W_{c_1}} \exp\{\gamma_1 \cdot h'_1(y_i, y_j, y_k)\} \\ \frac{1}{W_{c_2}} \exp\{\gamma_2 \cdot h'_2(y_i, y_j, z_i)\} \\ \cdots \\ \frac{1}{W_{c_{20}}} \exp\{\gamma_{20} \cdot h'_{20}(z_i, z_j, z_k)\} \end{cases} \tag{6}$$

where $h'_q(\cdot)$ is the vector of indicator functions and W_{c_q} is the normalization term similar with W_{e_p}. There are 20 different kinds of three-variable enumerations from $(y_i, y_j, y_k, z_i, z_j, z_k)$. We use these triadic factors to model the distributions of users' age and gender within a social triangle. See details in Figure 7.

Finally, combing Eq. 4, 5, 6 into Eq. 3, we define the objective function as the log-likelihood of the proposed model as:

$$\mathcal{O}(\alpha, \beta, \gamma) = \sum_{v_i \in V} \alpha_{y_i z_i} \mathbf{x}_i + \sum_{e_{ij} \in E} \sum_{p=1}^{6} \beta_p g'_p(\cdot) + \sum_{c_{ijk} \in G} \sum_{q=1}^{20} \gamma_q h'_q(\cdot) - \log W \tag{7}$$

where $W = W_v W_e W_c$ is the global normalization term, $W_e = \prod_{e_p=1}^{6} W_{e_p=1}$, and $W_c = \prod_{c_q=1}^{20} W_{c_q}$.

The technical novelty of the proposed model is that it considers two types of labels in a unified framework, which differentiates our model from traditional classification models. By considering two types of labels, the main advantage is that our model can characterize the correlations between gender/age and features more precisely.

4.2.2 Feature Definition

Given a network with labeled and unlabeled users, the goal is to infer unlabeled users' demographic information. This scenario satisfies a real-world application for mobile operators. There are three kinds of features designed in our experiments, namely attribute features, friend features, and circle features. Specifically, given an ego network with one central user v and her/his direct friends, we extract three kinds of features for this central user v as follows:

Individual feature. Characteristic attributes are extracted based on the network topological properties discussed in Section 2. It includes the degree, neighbor connectivity, clustering coefficient, embeddedness, and weighted degree (#calls or #messages).

Friend feature. There are two types of friend features, including friend attributes and dyadic factor. First, friend attributes are used to model the demographic distribution of v's direct friends in her/his ego network, including the number of connections to female, male, young, young-adult, middle-age, and senior friends. In the prediction scenario, not all friends of the central user v are labeled with gender or age information, so we extract the friend attributes only based on her/his labeled friends. Second, to further model the distribution of unlabeled and labeled friends together, dyadic factor is used as the other type of friend feature (Cf. Eq. 5).

Circle feature. Similarly, it also contains two kinds of features: circle attributes and triadic factor. First, circle attributes refer to the triadic demographic distribution of v's ego network. Because we aim to infer the central user v's demographics, we count the numbers of different gender triads, i.e., 'FF-v', 'FM-v', 'MM-v', and different age-group triads. Let A/B/C/D denote the young/young-adult/middle-age/senior age-groups, respectively. There are in total ten kinds of triads based on age-groups: 'AA-v', 'AB-v', 'AC-v', 'AD-v', 'BB-v' ,'BC-v' ,'BD-v', 'CC-v', 'CD-v', 'DD-v'. Second, triadic factor is used to model the demographic distributions over triangles with both unlabeled and labeled users (Cf. Eq. 6).

The individual, friend, and circle attributes are captured by the attribute factor in our DFG (Cf. Eq. 4). There are in total 24 attribute features used in our models.

4.2.3 DFG Learning and Inference

The goal of learning the DFG model is to find a configuration for the free parameters $\theta = \{\alpha, \beta, \gamma\}$ that maximize the log-likelihood of the objective function $\mathcal{O}(\theta)$ in Eq. 7 given by the training set, i.e.,

$$\theta^{\star} = \arg\max \mathcal{O}(\theta)$$

Learning. We first introduce how we learn the model in a single-processor configuration, and then explain how to extend the learning algorithm to a distributed one for handling large-scale networks.

To solve the optimization problem, we adopt a gradient decent method (or a Newton-Raphson method). Specifically, we derive the objective function with respect to each parameter with regard to our objective function in Eq. 7.

$$\begin{aligned}
\frac{\partial \mathcal{O}(\theta)}{\partial \alpha} &= \boldsymbol{E}[\sum_{v_i \in V} f(y_i, z_i, \mathbf{x}_i)] - \boldsymbol{E}_{P_\alpha(Y,Z|X)}[\sum_{v_i \in V} f(y_i, z_i, \mathbf{x}_i)] \\
\frac{\partial \mathcal{O}(\theta)}{\partial \beta} &= \boldsymbol{E}[\sum_{e_{ij} \in E} g(\mathbf{y}_e, \mathbf{z}_e)] - \boldsymbol{E}_{P_\beta(Y,Z|\mathbf{X},G)}[\sum_{e_{ij} \in E} g(\mathbf{y}_e, \mathbf{z}_e)] \\
\frac{\partial \mathcal{O}(\theta)}{\partial \gamma} &= \boldsymbol{E}[\sum_{c_{ijk} \in G} h(\mathbf{y}_c, \mathbf{z}_c)] - \boldsymbol{E}_{P_\gamma(Y,Z|\mathbf{X},G)}[\sum_{c_{ijk} \in G} h(\mathbf{y}_c, \mathbf{z}_c)]
\end{aligned} \tag{8}$$

where in the first Equation of Eq. 8, $\boldsymbol{E}[\sum_{v_i \in V} f(y_i, z_i, \mathbf{x}_i)]$ is the expectation of the summation of the attribute factor functions given the data distribution over Y, Z, and X in the training set, and $\boldsymbol{E}_{P_\alpha(Y,Z|X)}[\sum_{v_i \in V} f(y_i, z_i, \mathbf{x}_i)]$ is the expectation of the summation of the attribute factor functions given by the estimated model. The other expectation terms have similar meanings in the other two equations. As the network structure in the real-world may contain cycles, it is intractable to estimate the marginal probability in the second terms of Eq. 8. In this work, we adopt Loopy Belief Propagation (LBP) [23] to calculate the marginal probability of $P(Y, Z)$ and compute the expectation terms.

The learning process then can be described as an iterative algorithm. Each iteration contains two steps: First, we call LBP to calculate marginal distributions of unknown variables $P_\alpha(Y, Z|X)$. Second, we update α, β, and γ with the learning rate η by Eq. 9. The learning algorithm terminates when it reaches convergence.

$$\theta_{new} = \theta_{old} + \eta \cdot \frac{\partial \mathcal{O}(\theta)}{\partial \theta} \tag{9}$$

Distributed learning. We further develop a distributed algorithm to scale up our model to handle these large-scale networks. Our distributed learning algorithm utilizes a Message Passing Interface (MPI) framework, by which we can split the network into small parts and learn the parameters on different processors. As most computing time is consumed in the first step of our learning algorithm introduced above, we speed up this learning processes by distributing multiple 'slave' computing processors for this step. The second step is calculated in the 'master' processor by collecting the results from all 'slave' processors on the first step.

Specifically, our distributed learning algorithm based on the master-slave framework can be described in two phases. At the first phase, the large-scale network G is partitioned into K sub-networks $G_1, \cdots, G_k, \cdots, G_K$, and the K sub-networks are distributed to K 'slave' processors. At the second phase, we iteratively learn the parameters in two steps. First, each processor can compute the local marginal probability on its sub-network G_k. Second, the 'master' processor collects all gradients obtained from different subgraphs and updates all parameters. The second phase is repeated until convergence.

There are two notes for our model implementation. At the first phase, different from partitioning the large network based on communities in previous work [31], we partition the country-wide mobile network based on different administrative regions, i.e., provinces or states. The mobile operator can obtain this information when its users first register their mobile phones. The other one is that we first extract all features for each user from the original large network. We then split it into sub-networks that are handled by each 'slave' processor.

Prediction. With the estimated parameter θ, we can now assign the value of unknown labels Y, Z by looking for a label configuration that will maximize the objective function, i.e.

$$(Y^*, Z^*) = \arg\max \mathcal{O}(Y, Z|G, \mathbf{X}, \theta)$$

In this paper, we use the max-sum algorithm [18] to solve the above problem.

5. EXPERIMENTS

We present the effectiveness and efficiency of our proposed DFG model on demographic prediction by various experiments. The code used in the experiment is publicly available.[4]

5.1 Experiment Setup

Data and Evaluation. We use two large-scale mobile networks, CALL and SMS, to infer users' gender and age. Detailed data information is introduced in Section 2. To infer user demographics effectively for mobile operators, we only consider active users who have at least five contacts in two months. After filtering, there are 1.09 million and 304,000 active users in CALL and SMS networks, respectively. We repeat the prediction experiments ten times, and report the average performance in terms of weighted Precision, Recall, and F1-Measure. We consider weighted evaluation metrics because every class in female/male or young/young-adult/middle-age/senior is as important as each other. It is worth noting that the weighted Recall has the same score as Accuracy.

All code is implemented in C++, and experiments are performed in a server with four 16-core 2.4 GHz AMD Opteron processors with 256GB RAM. We use the speedup metric with different numbers of computing cores (1-16) to evaluate the scalability of our distributed learning algorithm.

Comparison methods. We compare our proposed DFG model that can capture the interrelation between two dependent variables

[4]http://arnetminer.org/demographic

(gender and age) with different classification algorithms, including Logistic Regression (**LRC**), Support Vector Machine (**SVM**), Naive Bayes (**NB**), Random Forest (**RF**), Bagging (**Bag**), Gaussian Radial Basis Function Neural Network (**RBF**), and Factor Graph Model (**FGM**). For LRC, NB, RF, Bag, RBF, we employ Weka[5] and use the default setting and parameters. For SVM, we use liblinear[6]. For FGM, the model proposed in [19] is used. Note that our proposed DFG model is equal to FGM if we do not consider the interrelations between gender and age.

For all comparison methods, we use the same unstructured features (characteristic, friend, and circle attributes) introduced in Section 4.2.2. For the graphical models, FGM and DFG , the structure features (dyadic and triadic factors) are further used to model user demographics on network structure. The major difference between our DFG and FGM model is that DFG can capture not only the correlation between different users, but also the interrelation between two dependent variables of each user, i.e., gender and age.

5.2 Experiment Results

We report the demographic prediction performance for different methods in the CALL and SMS networks as follows. In prediction experiments, we use 50% of the labeled data in each network as a training set and the remaining 50% for testing.

Predictive performance. Table 1 shows the prediction results of different algorithms on the four prediction cases, i.e., gender and age predictions in the CALL and SMS networks, respectively. Clearly our DFG model yields better performance than the other alternative methods in the four cases. The Bag algorithm achieves the best prediction results among all non-graphical methods. The FGM model outperforms a series of non-graphical algorithms by modeling the correlations among structured nodes via dyadic and triadic factors. The DFG model outperforms FGM by further leveraging the interrelations between user gender and age. In terms of weighted Precision, Recall, and F1-Measure, DFG achieves up to 10% improvements compared with the baselines for the prediction of users' gender and age. As for Accuracy, the DFG model can infer 80% of the users' gender in the CALL network and 73% of the users' age in the SMS network correctly. Finally, we observe that the CALL network can reveal more users' gender information than the SMS network, as the overall performance of gender prediction in CALL is about 5% higher than that in SMS. However, predicting age from SMS behaviors is relatively easier than predicting it from CALL communications.

Effects of demographic interrelation. We evaluate the effects of demographic interrelation on the predictions. Without modeling the interrelation between gender and age, our proposed DFG model degenerates to a basic factor graph model (FGM/DFG-d). From Table 1, we clearly observe the 2% to 4% improvements achieved by DFG to FGM on weighted F1-Measure. We further analyze feature contributions for demographic prediction. Recall that in Section 4.2.2, besides the individual features, we introduced the friend features (friend attributes and edge factor) and circle features (circle attributes and triad factor). By removing either friend or circle features, we evaluate the decrease in predictive performance in terms of weighted F1-Measure, plotted in Figure 9. DFG-df, DFG-dc and DFG-dfc stand for the removing of friend features, circle features, and both, conditioned on DFG-d without modeling gender and age interrelations. Clearly, we can see that for inferring gender, the performance when removing circle features drops more than when

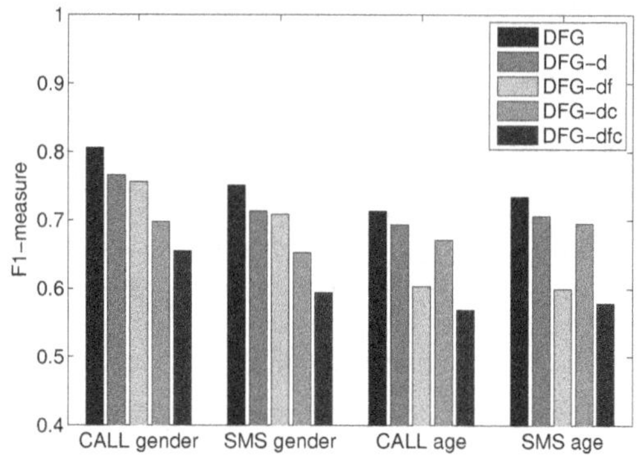

Figure 9: Feature Contribution Analysis. DFG is the proposed model. TFG-d is the basic version of DFG without modeling the correlation between gender and age. DFG-df stands for further ignoring friend features. DFG-dc stands for further ignoring circle features. DFG-dcf stands for ignoring both friend and circle features.

removing friend features, which indicates a stronger contribution of circle features to gender prediction than friend features. However, for inferring user age, friend features contribute more than circle features. The feature contribution analysis further validates our observations of demographic-based social strategies, and demonstrates that the proposed model works well by capturing the observed phenomena.

Training/test ratio. We provide further analysis on the effects of training ratio on predictive performance. Figure 10 shows the prediction results when varying the percentage of labeled users in the training set. Clearly, we can see rising trends as the training set increases in Figure 10(a) and 10(b). This indicates the positive effects of training data size on predicting the gender of mobile users. The smooth lines in Figure 10(c) and 10(d) reveal the limited contributions of training data size on predicting age. We can see that in all cases, obvious improvements can be obtained by our proposed DFG model with different sizes of training data.

Scalability. We verify the distributed learning algorithm by partitioning the original large-scale network into multiple sub-networks based on different administrative areas. We determine users' areas by their postal code information during registration. Each subnetwork in one area is used as the input for a given core. By utilizing MPI, our distributed algorithm can achieve 9-10× speedup with 16 cores with <2% drop in performance. Basically, our learning algorithm can converge in 100 iterations, and each iteration costs about 2-5 minutes for one single processor. By leveraging a distributed learning algorithm, our DFG model is efficient even for large-scale networks with millions of nodes.

6. RELATED WORK

The availability of mobile phone communication records has offered researchers many ways to analyze mobile networks, greatly enhancing our understanding of human mobile behaviors.

To better model the macro properties of mobile communication networks, Onnela [26] and Nanavati et al. [24] examine the local and global structure of a society-wide mobile communication network. Faloutsos et al. [29] first propose the double pareto-lognormal distribution to model the macro properties in call networks, which is beyond power-law and lognormal distributions. They further discover that not only the node properties but also

[5]http://www.cs.waikato.ac.nz/ml/weka/

[6]http://www.csie.ntu.edu.tw/ cjlin/liblinear/

Table 1: Demographic Prediction performance by weighted Precision, Recall, and F1-Measure. The weighted Recall score is equal to the Accuracy score. The number in parentheses is the standard deviation.

Network	Method	Gender			Age		
		wPrecision	wRecall/Accu	wF1-Measure	wPrecision	wRecall/Accu	wF1-Measure
CALL	LRC	0.7327 (0.0003)	0.7289 (0.0003)	0.7245 (0.0005)	0.6350 (0.0005)	0.6466 (0.0003)	0.6337 (0.0005)
	SVM	0.7327 (0.0004)	0.7287 (0.0003)	0.7242 (0.0003)	0.6369 (0.0004)	0.6463 (0.0005)	0.6273 (0.0005)
	NB	0.7222 (0.0004)	0.7227 (0.0003)	0.7222 (0.0004)	0.6246 (0.0011)	0.6224 (0.0002)	0.6223 (0.0002)
	RF	0.7437 (0.0003)	0.7310 (0.0002)	0.7415 (0.0003)	0.6382 (0.0010)	0.6482 (0.0008)	0.6388 (0.0009)
	Bag	0.7644 (0.0005)	0.7648 (0.0004)	0.7643 (0.0005)	0.6607 (0.0010)	0.6688 (0.0004)	0.6592 (0.0005)
	RBF	0.7283 (0.0015)	0.7275 (0.0005)	0.7252 (0.0017)	0.6194 (0.0062)	0.6272 (0.0068)	0.6218 (0.0068)
	FGM	0.7658 (0.0096)	0.7662 (0.0115)	0.7659 (0.0113)	0.6998 (0.0094)	0.6989 (0.0087)	0.6935 (0.0089)
	DFG	0.8088 (0.0139)	0.8076 (0.0148)	0.8063 (0.0131)	0.7266 (0.0097)	0.7140 (0.0094)	0.7132 (0.0091)
SMS	LRC	0.6766 (0.0013)	0.6758 (0.0006)	0.6689 (0.0014)	0.6702 (0.0011)	0.6890 (0.0008)	0.6630 (0.0008)
	SVM	0.6749 (0.0006)	0.6750 (0.0005)	0.6690 (0.0007)	0.6654 (0.0163)	0.6884 (0.0006)	0.6607 (0.0006)
	NB	0.6231 (0.0003)	0.6655 (0.0011)	0.6603 (0.0021)	0.6563 (0.0014)	0.6588 (0.0015)	0.6570 (0.0012)
	RF	0.6399 (0.0009)	0.6749 (0.0009)	0.6757 (0.0009)	0.6623 (0.0013)	0.6775 (0.0008)	0.6598 (0.0011)
	Bag	0.6905 (0.0005)	0.6918 (0.0009)	0.6901 (0.0009)	0.6907 (0.0008)	0.6987 (0.0009)	0.6791 (0.0009)
	RBF	0.6712 (0.0006)	0.6592 (0.0131)	0.6468 (0.0139)	0.6295 (0.0062)	0.6640 (0.0051)	0.6356 (0.0042)
	FGM	0.7132 (0.0040)	0.7138 (0.0050)	0.7133 (0.0057)	0.7154 (0.0046)	0.7154 (0.0046)	0.7059 (0.0058)
	DFG	0.7589 (0.0187)	0.7549 (0.0159)	0.7507 (0.0178)	0.7409 (0.0199)	0.7303 (0.0208)	0.7337 (0.0198)

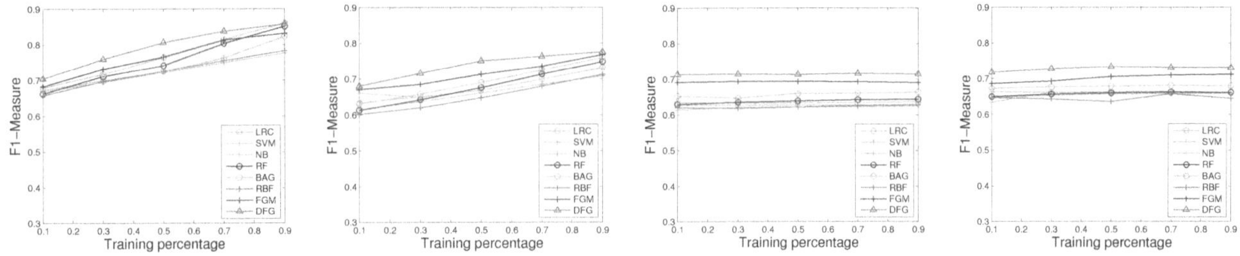

(a) CALL Gender Prediction (b) SMS Gender Prediction (c) CALL Age Prediction (d) SMS Age Prediction

Figure 10: Performance of demographic prediction with different percentages of labeled data.

clique structures follow the power-law distribution in mobile networks [5]. Dong et al. [4] investigate the mobile call duration behaviors in mobile social networks and find that people who are familiar with each other tend to make short calls. Recently, the emergence of work on mobility [30, 33, 8, 36] and location-based mobile networks [7, 2, 1], where human movements or locations are tracked by mobile phones, provides us a means of understanding and predicting mobile social behaviors. Eagle et al. [6] try to infer the friendship network in mobile phone data. As for mobility applications, mobile patterns are applied to predict the future location of users in [22, 25, 34]. However, most previous work focuses on scaling the macroscopic properties of mobile networks, while our work incorporates the micro-network structure to model human communication behaviors in mobile networks.

Furthermore, there are several works on user demographic and profile modeling. Existing works try to infer user demographics based on their online browsing [10] and search [3] behaviors. Leskovec and Horvitz [16] examine the interplay of the MSN network and user demographic attributes. Tang et al. extract and model the researcher profiles in large-scale collaboration networks [32]. Additionally, researchers have used network information to identify user status differences in email [11] and LinkedIn networks [37]. Nokia research organized the 2012 Mobile Data Challenge to infer mobile user demographics by using 200 individual communication records without network information [21, 35]. Kovanen et al. [12] utilize temporal motifs to reveal demographic homophily in dynamic communication networks. The main difference between existing work and our efforts lies in that existing work mainly analyzes demographics (gender, age, status, etc.) separately, while our analysis and model consider the correlation among different demographic attributes.

7. CONCLUSION

In this paper, we study human interactions on demographics by investigating a country-wide mobile communication network. From this, we discover a set of social strategies stemming from human communications. First, young people put more focus on enlarging their social circles; as they age, they have the tendency to maintain small but close social relationships. Second, we observe a strong homophily of human interactions on gender and age simultaneously. Third, beyond these observations, we find that the frequent cross-generation interactions are maintained to pass the torch of family, workforce, and human knowledge from generation to generation in social society. Finally, we observe striking gender differences in social triadic relationships across individuals' lifespans, which reflects dynamic gender-bias of human behaviors from young to old.

Through these observations, we engage in answering the question of to what extent individual demographic can be revealed from mobile communication interactions. We formalize a demographic prediction problem to infer user gender and age simultaneously, and further propose the WhoAmI method to solve this problem by modeling not only the correlations between gender/age and features, but also the interrelations between gender and age. Experimental results in the CALL and SMS networks demonstrate the effectiveness and efficiency of our proposed model.

Detecting user demographics makes social networks more colorful and closer to our real human networks. For future work, some other social theories and strategies can be explored and validated for modeling human mobile social interactions. In addition, examining how the inferred demographic can help other topics in social network analysis, such as influence propagation, community detection, and network evolution, would also be very meaningful.

Acknowledgements. We sincerely thank Dr. Albert-*László* Barab*á*si for sharing the mobile phone data with the University of Notre Dame. We also thank anonymous reviewers for their useful comments, and Reid Johnson at Notre Dame for his insightful discussion. Jie Tang and Yang Yang are supported by the National High-Tech R&D Program of China (No. 2014AA015103), Natural Science Foundation of China (No. 61222212, 61073073), and National Basic Research Program of China (2013CB329603) and a research fund supported by Huawei Inc. Nitesh V. Chawla, Yuxiao Dong, and Yang Yang are supported by the Army Research Laboratory under Cooperative Agreement Number W911NF-09-2-0053, and the U.S. Air Force Office of Scientific Research (AFOSR) and the Defense Advanced Research Projects Agency (DARPA) grant #FA9550-12-1-0405.

8. REFERENCES

[1] J. Bao, Y. Zheng, D. Wilkie, and M. Mokbel. A survey on recommendations in location-based social networks. *ACM TIST*, 2014.

[2] M. Berlingerio, F. Calabrese, G. D. Lorenzo, R. Nair, F. Pinelli, and M. L. Sbodio. Allaboard: A system for exploring urban mobility and optimizing public transport using cellphone data. In *ECML/PKDD (3)*, pages 663–666. Springer, 2013.

[3] B. Bi, M. Shokouhi, M. Kosinski, and T. Graepel. Inferring the demographics of search users: Social data meets search queries. In *WWW '13*, pages 131–140, 2013.

[4] Y. Dong, J. Tang, T. Lou, B. Wu, and N. V. Chawla. How long will she call me? distribution, social theory and duration prediction. In *ECML/PKDD (2)*, pages 16–31, 2013.

[5] N. Du, C. Faloutsos, B. Wang, and L. Akoglu. Large human communication networks: Patterns and a utility-driven generator. In *KDD '09*, pages 269–278. ACM, 2009.

[6] N. Eagle, A. S. Pentland, and D. Lazer. Inferring social network structure using mobile phone data. *PNAS*, 106(36), 2009.

[7] H. Gao, J. Tang, X. Hu, and H. Liu. Modeling temporal effects of human mobile behavior on location-based social networks. In *CIKM '13*, pages 1673–1678, 2013.

[8] F. Giannotti and D. Pedreschi. *Mobility, data mining and privacy: Geographic knowledge discovery*. Springer, 2008.

[9] M. Granovetter. Economic action and social structure: The problem of embeddedness. *The American Journal of Sociology*, 1985.

[10] J. Hu, H.-J. Zeng, H. Li, C. Niu, and Z. Chen. Demographic prediction based on user's browsing behavior. In *WWW '07*, pages 151–160, 2007.

[11] X. Hu and H. Liu. Social status and role analysis of Palin's email network. In *WWW '12 Companion*, pages 531–532. ACM, 2012.

[12] L. Kovanen, K. Kaski, J. Kertész, and J. Saramäki. Temporal motifs reveal homophily, gender-specific patterns, and group talk in call sequences. *PNAS*, 2013.

[13] F. R. Kschischang, B. J. Frey, and H. A. Loeliger. Factor graphs and the sum-product algorithm. *IEEE TOIT*, 47:498–519, 2001.

[14] P. F. Lazarsfeld and R. K. Merton. Friendship as a social process: A substantive and methodological analysis. *Freedom and control in modern society, New York: Van Nostrand*, pages 8–66, 1954.

[15] J. Leskovec, L. Backstrom, R. Kumar, and A. Tomkins. Microscopic evolution of social networks. In *KDD '08*, pages 462–470, 2008.

[16] J. Leskovec and E. Horvitz. Planetary-scale views on a large instant-messaging network. In *WWW '08*, pages 915–924. ACM, 2008.

[17] R. N. Lichtenwalter, J. T. Lussier, and N. V. Chawla. New perspectives and methods in link prediction. In *KDD '10*, pages 243–252. ACM, 2010.

[18] H.-A. Loeliger. An introduction to factor graphs. *Signal Processing Magazine, IEEE*, 21(1):28–41, 2004.

[19] T. Lou, J. Tang, J. Hopcroft, Z. Fang, and X. Ding. Learning to predict reciprocity and triadic closure in social networks. *ACM TKDD*, 7(2):5:1–5:25, 2013.

[20] M. Mead. *Culture and commitment: a study of the generation gap*. Natural History Press, 1970.

[21] K. Mo, B. Tan, E. Zhong, and Q. Yang. Your phone understands you. In *Nokia MDC '12*, 2012.

[22] A. Monreale, F. Pinelli, R. Trasarti, and F. Giannotti. Wherenext: A location predictor on trajectory pattern mining. In *KDD '09*, pages 637–646, 2009.

[23] K. P. Murphy, Y. Weiss, and M. I. Jordan. Loopy belief propagation for approximate inference: An empirical study. In *UAI '99*, pages 467–475, 1999.

[24] A. A. Nanavati, S. Gurumurthy, G. Das, D. Chakraborty, K. Dasgupta, S. Mukherjea, and A. Joshi. On the structural properties of massive telecom call graphs: Findings and implications. In *CIKM '06*, pages 435–444, 2006.

[25] A. Noulas, S. Scellato, N. Lathia, and C. Mascolo. Mining user mobility features for next place prediction in location-based services. In *ICDM '12*, pages 1038–1043, 2012.

[26] J. P. Onnela, J. Saramäki, J. Hyvönen, G. Szabó, D. Lazer, K. Kaski, J. Kertész, and A.-L. Barabási. Structure and tie strengths in mobile communication networks. *PNAS*, 2007.

[27] V. Palchykov, K. Kaski, J. Kertész, A.-L. Barabási, and R. I. M. Dunbar. Sex differences in intimate relationships. *Scientific Reports*, 2:370, 2012.

[28] R. Prasad. *Generation Gap: A study of intergenerational sociological conflict*. Mittal Publications, 1992.

[29] M. Seshadri, S. Machiraju, A. Sridharan, J. Bolot, C. Faloutsos, and J. Leskovec. Mobile call graphs: beyond power-law and lognormal distributions. In *KDD '08*, pages 596–604. ACM, 2008.

[30] C. Song, Z. Qu, N. Blumm, and A.-L. Barabási. Limits of predictability in human mobility. *Science*, 2010.

[31] J. Tang, S. Wu, and J. Sun. Confluence: Conformity influence in large social networks. In *KDD '13*, pages 347–355. ACM, 2013.

[32] J. Tang, J. Zhang, L. Yao, J. Li, L. Zhang, and Z. Su. Arnetminer: Extraction and mining of academic social networks. In *KDD '08*, pages 990–998, 2008.

[33] D. Wang, D. Pedreschi, C. Song, F. Giannotti, and A.-L. Barabasi. Human mobility, social ties, and link prediction. In *KDD '11*, pages 1100–1108. ACM, 2011.

[34] A. Y. Xue, R. Zhang, Y. Zheng, X. Xie, J. Huang, and Z. Xu. Destination prediction by sub-trajectory synthesis and privacy protection against such prediction. In *ICDE '13*, pages 254–265, 2013.

[35] J. Ying, Y.-J. Chang, C.-M. Huang, and V. S. Tseng. Demographic prediction based on user's mobile behaviors. In *Nokia MDC '12*, 2012.

[36] N. J. Yuan, Y. Wang, F. Zhang, X. Xie, and G. Sun. Reconstructing individual mobility from smart card transactions: A space alignment approach. In *ICDM'13*, pages 877–886, 2013.

[37] Y. Zhao, G. Wang, P. S. Yu, S. Liu, and S. Zhang. Inferring social roles and statuses in social networks. In *KDD '13*, pages 695–703, 2013.

Travel Time Estimation of a Path using Sparse Trajectories

Yilun Wang[1,2,*], Yu Zheng[1,+], Yexiang Xue[1,3,*]
[1]Microsoft Research, No.5 Danling Street, Haidian District, Beijing 100080, China
[2]College of Computer Science, Zhejiang University
[3]Department of Computer Science, Cornell University
{v-yilwan, yuzheng}@microsoft.com, yexiang@cs.cornell.edu

ABSTRACT

In this paper, we propose a citywide and real-time model for estimating the travel time of any path (represented as a sequence of connected road segments) in real time in a city, based on the GPS trajectories of vehicles received in current time slots and over a period of history as well as map data sources. Though this is a strategically important task in many traffic monitoring and routing systems, the problem has not been well solved yet given the following three challenges. The first is the data sparsity problem, i.e., many road segments may not be traveled by any GPS-equipped vehicles in present time slot. In most cases, we cannot find a trajectory exactly traversing a query path either. Second, for the fragment of a path with trajectories, they are multiple ways of using (or combining) the trajectories to estimate the corresponding travel time. Finding an optimal combination is a challenging problem, subject to a tradeoff between the length of a path and the number of trajectories traversing the path (i.e., support). Third, we need to instantly answer users' queries which may occur in any part of a given city. This calls for an efficient, scalable and effective solution that can enable a citywide and real-time travel time estimation. To address these challenges, we model different drivers' travel times on different road segments in different time slots with a three dimension tensor. Combined with geospatial, temporal and historical contexts learned from trajectories and map data, we fill in the tensor's missing values through a context-aware tensor decomposition approach. We then devise and prove an object function to model the aforementioned tradeoff, with which we find the most optimal concatenation of trajectories for an estimate through a dynamic programming solution. In addition, we propose using frequent trajectory patterns (mined from historical trajectories) to scale down the candidates of concatenation and a suffix-tree-based index to manage the trajectories received in the present time slot. We evaluate our method based on extensive experiments, using GPS trajectories generated by more than 32,000 taxis over a period of two months. The results demonstrate the effectiveness, efficiency and scalability of our method beyond baseline approaches.

Categories and Subject Descriptors

H.2.8 [Database Management]: Database Applications - data mining, Spatial databases and GIS;

Keywords

Travel time estimation; tensor; trajectories; urban computing;

**The paper was done when the first and third authors were interns in Microsoft Research under the supervision of the second author who contributed the main idea and algorithms of this paper.*

KDD'14, August 24–27, 2014, New York, New York, USA.
Copyright © 2014 ACM 978-1-4503-2956-9/14/08…$15.00
http://dx.doi.org/10.1145/2623330.2623656

1. INTRODUCTION

Real-time estimation of the travel time of a path, which is represented by a sequence of connected road segments, is of great importance for traffic monitoring [1], finding driving directions [20], ridesharing [13] and taxi dispatching [22]. Existing solutions, e.g., using loop sensors, usually tell people the travel speed of an individual road segment rather than the travel time of an entire path. The latter's value is not a simple summation of the travel time of each individual road segment, as a path also contains road intersections (sometimes with traffic lights) where a driver needs to slow down or wait for a while. Explicitly modeling the time delay at an intersection is not easy [8]. In addition, these methods have limited coverage, as many streets do not have a loop sensor embedded.

An alternative method is to use floating car data (e.g., GPS trajectories of vehicles) to estimate the travel time of a path. For example, as shown in Figure 1, we estimate the travel time of path $r_1 \rightarrow r_2 \rightarrow r_3 \rightarrow r_4$, using four trajectories Tr_1, Tr_2, Tr_3, and Tr_4. Unfortunately, there are three major issues remaining unsolved in existing methods. They are as follows:

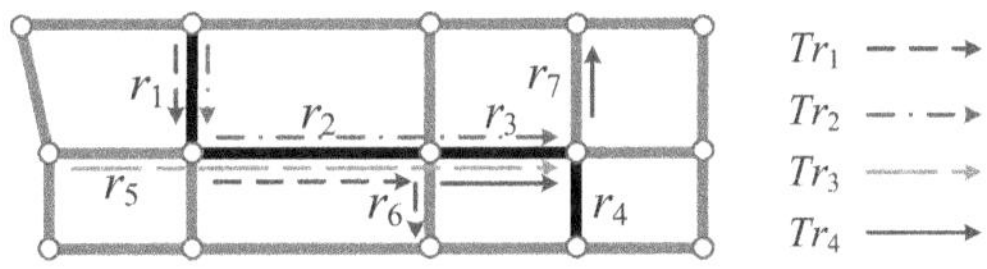

Figure 1. Problem demonstration

1) Data sparsity: For example, r_4 is not traversed by any trajectory in the previous 30 minutes. Using an average of r_4's historical travel times is not accurate enough (since its traffic conditions change over time of day and day of the week). Sometimes, the road may never be traversed by any trajectories (even in history) in our dataset, as in practice we only have the data of a sample of vehicles.

2) Trajectory concatenation: For the sub-path (e.g., $r_1 \rightarrow r_2 \rightarrow r_3$) with trajectories, how to combine these trajectories effectively to achieve an accurate estimate is still a challenging problem. Clearly, there are multiple ways of using the four trajectories shown in Figure 1. For instance, we can calculate the travel time of $r_1 \rightarrow r_2 \rightarrow r_3$ solely based on Tr_2. Or, we can compute the travel time for r_1 (based on Tr_1 and Tr_2), r_2 (based on Tr_1, Tr_2 and Tr_3), and r_3 (using Tr_2, Tr_3 and Tr_4), separately. Later, the travel time of $r_1 \rightarrow r_2 \rightarrow r_3$ can be obtained by summing the travel times of each road segment. We can also use Tr_2 and Tr_3 to estimate the travel time of $r_2 \rightarrow r_3$, then concatenating it with that of r_1; or, do $r_1 \rightarrow r_2$ first based on Tr_1 and Tr_2, then concatenating it with r_3.

Different concatenations have their own advantages and disadvantages, subject to a trade-off between their support and length. The ideal situation is to estimate the travel time of $r_1 \rightarrow r_2 \rightarrow r_3$ using many trajectories like Tr_2 covering the entire path. Such trajectories reflect the traffic conditions of an entire path, including intersections, traffic lights and direction turns, hence, no need to model these complex factors separately and

+ *Yu Zheng is the correspondence author of this paper.*

explicitly. However, as the length of a path increases, the number of trajectories (i.e., the support) traveling on the path decreases (refer to Figure 10 A) for details). Consequently, the confidence of the travel time (derived from few drivers) decreases. For example, what if Tr_2 is generated by an uncommon driver or in an unusual situation like pedestrians crossing a street? Furthermore, in many cases, we cannot even find a trajectory passing an entire path. On the other hand, using the concatenation of shorter sub-paths can have more occurrences of trajectories on each sub-path (i.e., having a high confidence in the derived travel time for each sub-path). But this results in more fragments, across which the aforementioned complex factors are difficult to model. The more fragments a concatenation contains, the more inaccuracy a path's travel time could involve.

3) *Tradeoff among Scalability, effectiveness and efficiency*: As users can query any path in a city, we need to model the traffic conditions with a city scale, which usually contains tens of thousands of road segments. In the meantime, we have to answer users' query instantly. So, a good solution should be scalable, effective and efficient, all simultaneously. This requirement fails some complex models that work well on a particular road.

In this paper, we propose a model for instant Path Travel Time Estimation (PTTE), based on sparse trajectories generated by a sample of vehicles (e.g., some GPS equipped taxicabs) in the recent time slots as well as in history. Our model is comprised of two major components. One is to estimate the travel time for road segments without being traversed by trajectories through a context-aware tensor decomposition (CATD) approach. The second is to find the most optimal concatenation (OC) of trajectories to estimate a path's travel time using a dynamic programing solution. Our work has three primary contributions:

- *Dealing with the missing values*: We model different drivers' travel times on different road segments in different time slots with a three dimensional tensor. Combined with geospatial, temporal and historical contexts learned from other data sources, we fill in the tensor's missing values through a context-aware tensor decomposition approach. To expedite the inference, we partition a city into disjoint geo-regions and carry out the decomposition for each region in parallel.
- *Optimal concatenation*: We devise and prove an object function that can model the tradeoff between the support and length of a concatenation. Using a dynamic programming solution, we find the most optimal concatenation of trajectories for estimating a path's travel time. In addition, we use frequent trajectory patterns mined in advance to scale down the candidates of concatenation and propose a suffix-tree-based index to manage the recently received trajectories, improving the efficiency of our model.
- *Evaluation*: We evaluate our model with the real trajectories generated by over 32,000 taxis over a period of 2 month on Beijing's road network. The results of extensive experiments demonstrate the advantages of our model. A sample of the data has been released at [25].

The rest of the paper is organized as follows: Section 2 overviews our model. Section 3 elaborates on the method for inferring the travel time of road segments without trajectories. Section 3 introduces the method that searches for the most optimal concatenation. Section 4 presents the experiments and Section 5 summarizes related work. We conclude the paper in Section 6.

2. OVERVIEW

Definition 1: Road Network. A road network RN is comprised of a set of road segments $\{r\}$ connected among each other in a graph format. Each road segment r is a directed edge with two terminal points, a list of intermediate points describing the segment, a length $r.len$, a level $r.lev$ (e.g. a highway or a street), a direction $r.dir$ (e.g. one-way or bi-directional) and the number of lanes $r.n$.

Definition 2: Trajectory. A spatial *trajectory* Tr is a sequence of time-ordered points, $Tr: p_1 \rightarrow p_2 \rightarrow \cdots \rightarrow p_n$, where each point has a geospatial coordinate set and a timestamp, $p = (x, y, t)$.

Definition 3: Path. A path P is represented by a sequence of connected road segments, e.g., $P: r_1 \rightarrow r_2 \rightarrow \cdots \rightarrow r_n$, in an RN.

Definition 4: Trajectory pattern. A trajectory pattern TP is a sequential pattern of road segments with a support over a threshold, calculated by the number of trajectories traversing these road segments. If we set support as 2, $r_1 \rightarrow r_2$ and $r_2 \rightarrow r_3$ in Figure 1 are trajectory patterns, while $r_1 \rightarrow r_2 \rightarrow r_3$ is not eligible.

Definition 5: Concatenation. A path $\boldsymbol{P}$ can be decomposed into different concatenations ($||$) of its sub-paths, $\boldsymbol{P} = P_1 || \ldots || P_i \ldots || P_j \ldots || P_n, \forall 1 \leq i, j \leq n, i \neq j, P_i \cap P_j = \emptyset$. For instance, $r_1 \rightarrow r_2 \rightarrow r_3 \rightarrow r_4$ can be formed by $(r_1 \rightarrow r_2 \rightarrow r_3) || r_4$, or $(r_1 \rightarrow r_2) || (r_3 \rightarrow r_4)$, or $r_1 || (r_2 \rightarrow r_3 \rightarrow r_4)$. Thus, the travel time of $\boldsymbol{P}$ can be obtained via the summation of different concatenations, e.g., $t_{\boldsymbol{P}} = t_{r_1 \rightarrow r_2 \rightarrow r_3} + t_{r_4}$, or $t_{\boldsymbol{P}} = t_{r_1 \rightarrow r_2} + t_{r_3 \rightarrow r_4}$, or $t_{\boldsymbol{P}} = t_{r_1} + t_{r_2 \rightarrow r_3 \rightarrow r_4}$.

Definition 6: Travel Time. A driver u's travel time on a road segment r in time slot k is defined as $t_{r,u,k}$. Likewise, $t_{P,u,k}$ denotes u's travel time on path P in time slot k.

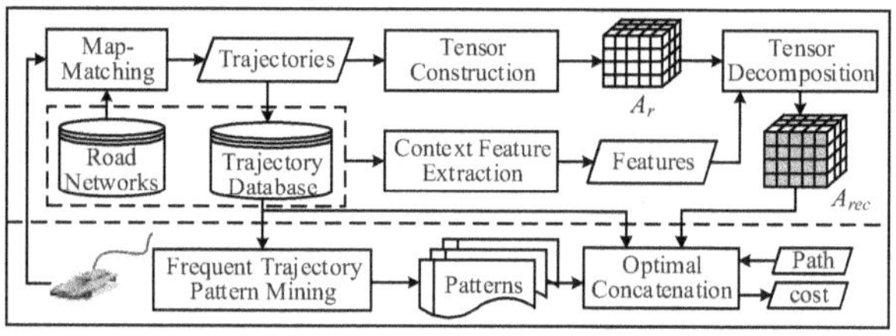

Figure 2. Framework of our model

Figure 2 presents the framework of our model which is comprised of two major parts. In the above part, we project each trajectory received in a current time slot onto a road network, using a map-matching algorithm [21]. The trajectories (combined with road network data) are then used to construct a 3D tensor $\mathcal{A}_r$ where the three dimensions stand for road segments, time slots and drivers, respectively. Each entry is the travel time of a particular driver on a particular road segment in a specific time slot. We partition a day into several time slots based on a certain time interval (e.g., we divide a day into 48 time slots with 30 minutes each in the experiments). Clearly, the tensor is very sparse (i.e., having many entries without values), as a driver can only travel a few road segments in a time slot. To deal with the data sparsity problem, we extract three categories of features, consisting of geospatial, temporal, and historical contexts, from the road network data and trajectories. The first two feature sets are stored in two matrices, respectively, and the historical context is represented by another tensor $\mathcal{A}_h$. The two matrices and $\mathcal{A}_h$ are then factorized with $\mathcal{A}_r$ collaboratively, helping fill $\mathcal{A}_r$'s missing entries in a current time slot (i.e., inferring the travel time of road segments without being traveled by trajectories in the current time slot). The general idea is that road segments with similar contexts could have a similar travel time. The context matrices and tensor reveal the similarity and with a more proportion of non-zero entries than $\mathcal{A}_r$, thereby reducing the factorization error and improving the inference accuracy. After filling the missing entries in $\mathcal{A}_r$, we obtain the travel time of any driver on any road segment in current time slot (stored in $\mathcal{A}_{rec}$).

In the bottom part, given a query path P, we estimate its travel time in the current time slot, based on $\mathcal{A}_{rec}$, the trajectories received in the time slot and trajectory patterns. Specifically, we devise and prove an objective function that can represent the tradeoff between the length and support of a trajectory pattern. Based on the objective function, we find the most optimal concatenation of trajectories for a path, using a dynamic programing approach. In practice, it is not necessary to try every possible concatenation of a path, as some sub-paths have never been traversed by any trajectory. So, we mine frequent trajectory patterns from historical trajectories in advance and study the concatenation of these existing patterns to estimate the travel time of a path. This reduces the online computational loads significantly, while guaranteeing accuracy in travel time estimation. Note that we are not using the historical travel time of a trajectory pattern. The patterns just provide us with candidate schemes of subpaths for finding an optimal concatenation of a path. Each trajectory pattern's travel time in current time slot is mainly calculated based on the trajectories received in the time slot. If a pattern contains road segments without being traversed by trajectories in the current time slot, we retrieve the inferred time from $\mathcal{A}_{rec}$, according to the driver, road segment and time slot. For instance, two drivers (u_1, u_2) travelled $r_1 \to r_2$, but nobody traveled r_3 in a pattern $r_1 \to r_2 \to r_3$, in current time slot k. That is, $t_{r_1 \to r_2, u_1, k}$, and $t_{r_1 \to r_2, u_2, k}$ can be calculated from the present trajectory data, while $t_{r_3, u_1, k}$ and $t_{r_3, u_2, k}$ are unknown. In this case, we retrieve the latter two from $\mathcal{A}_{rec}$, calculating

$$t_{r_1 \to r_2 \to r_3, u_1, k} = t_{r_1 \to r_2, u_1, k} + t_{r_3, u_1, k} \text{, and}$$

$$t_{r_1 \to r_2 \to r_3, u_2, k} = t_{r_1 \to r_2, u_2, k} + t_{r_3, u_2, k}.$$

With $\mathcal{A}_{rec}$, we can estimate a driver's travel time on a trajectory pattern even if the recently received data is incomplete. The dimension of drivers in $\mathcal{A}_{rec}$ enables us to calculate the variance among different drivers' travel times on a road segment or a sub-path. Intrinsically, different drivers travel the same road segment with different times, majorly depending on the different traffic conditions they experience. Thus, the variance implies the complexity of traffic conditions on a road segment or a sub-path, helping estimate a more accurate travel time of a path (elaborated in Section 4.1). Finally, the travel time of a path is calculated as:

$$T = \sum_{TP \in \Psi} \frac{\sum_{u \in U} t_{TP,u,k}}{|U|}; \qquad (1)$$

Where Ψ is the concatenation of path P, represented by a set of trajectory pattern TPs; U is a collection of drivers traversing (or partially traversing) a TP; k is the current time slot.

3. DEALING WITH MISSING VALUES

3.1 Tensor Building and Feature Extraction

To model the traffic conditions of the current time slot, we construct a tensor $\mathcal{A}_r \in \mathbb{R}^{N \times M \times L}$, with the three dimensions standing for road segments, drivers and time slots, respectively, based on the GPS trajectories received in the most recent L time slots and the road network data. As shown in Figure 3, an entry $\mathcal{A}_r(i, j, k) = c$ denotes the ith road segment is traveled by the jth driver with a time cost c in time slot k (e.g., 2-2:30pm). The last time slot denotes the present time slot, combined with the L-1 time slots right before it to formulate the tensor. Clearly, the tensor is very sparse as a driver can only travel a few road segments in a short time period. If we were able to fill in the missing entries in terms of the values of non-zero entries, we can know the travel time of any driver on any road segment in the present time slot.

A common approach to this problem is to decompose a tensor into the multiplication of a few (low-rank) matrices and a core tensor (or just a few vectors), based on the tensor's non-zero entries. For example, we can decompose $\mathcal{A}_r$ into the multiplication of a core tensor $S \in \mathbb{R}^{d_R \times d_U \times d_T}$ and three matrices, $R \in \mathbb{R}^{N \times d_R}$, $U \in \mathbb{R}^{M \times d_U}$, $T \in \mathbb{R}^{L \times d_T}$, if using a tucker decomposition model. An objective function is defined as Equation 2 to control the errors.

$$\mathcal{L}(S, R, U, T) = \frac{1}{2} \|\mathcal{A}_r - S \times_R R \times_U U \times_T T\|^2 + \frac{\lambda}{2} (\|S\|^2 + \|R\|^2 + \|U\|^2 + \|T\|^2), \qquad (2)$$

where $\|\cdot\|^2$ denotes the l_2 norm and $\frac{\lambda}{2} (\|S\|^2 + \|R\|^2 + \|U\|^2 + \|T\|^2)$ is a regularization of penalties to avoid over-fitting; d_R, d_U, and d_T are usually very small, denoting the number of latent factors. λ is a parameter controlling the contributions of the regularization. Afterwards, we can recover the missing values in $\mathcal{A}_r$ by multiplying decomposed factors as $\mathcal{A}_{rec} = S \times_R R \times_U U \times_T T$.

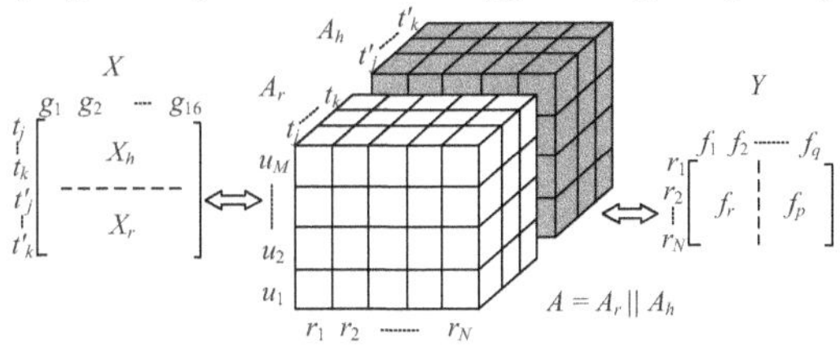

Figure 3. The model dealing with data sparsity

In our problem, however, the tensor is over sparse. For example, if setting 30 minutes as a time slot, only 0.03% entries of $\mathcal{A}_r$ have values. Decomposing $\mathcal{A}_r$ solely based on its own non-zero entries is not accurate enough. To this end, we build another tensor $\mathcal{A}_h$ based on the historical trajectories over a long period of time (e.g. one month). As shown in Figure 3, $\mathcal{A}_h$ has the same structure as $\mathcal{A}_r$, while an entry $\mathcal{A}_h(i, j, k) = c'$ denotes the jth driver's average travel time on the ith road segment in time slot k in the history. Intrinsically, $\mathcal{A}_h$ is much denser than $\mathcal{A}_r$, denoting the historical traffic patterns and drivers' behavior on an entire road network. For instance, using one-month trajectories and setting 30 minutes as a time slot, the non-zero entries of $\mathcal{A}_h$ is about 0.4%. Decomposing $\mathcal{A}_r$ and $\mathcal{A}_h$ together reduces the error of supplementing $\mathcal{A}_r$.

Besides $\mathcal{A}_h$, we also construct another two matrices X and Y to help the decomposition of $\mathcal{A}_r$. Specifically, as illustrated in Figure 4 A), Y stores the geographical features f_r of each road segment, such as $r.len$, $r.lev$, $r.dir$, $r.n$, the number of neighbors (e.g., r_1 has 2 and 3 neighbors) at its terminals, and a tortuosity ratio τ (e.g. $r_1.\tau = r_1.len/d_1$), as well as the distribution of Point of Interests (POIs) f_p around r's terminals. While Y captures the similarity between different road segments in geographic spaces, matrix X (consisting of X_r and X_h) represents the correlation between different time slots in terms of the coarse-grained traffic conditions. More specifically, we partition a city into disjoint and uniform grids (e.g., 4×4 in Figure 4 B), each of which is comprised of many road segments. X_r is built based on the recent trajectory data received from t_i to t_j (e.g., 1pm-3pm), reflecting the present traffic conditions on a road network. An entry of X_r denotes the number of vehicles traversing a particular grid in a particular time slot. A row of X_r represents coarse-grained traffic conditions in a city of a particular time slot. Consequently, the similarity of two different rows indicates the correlation of traffic flows between two time slots. Additionally, in contrast to using the traffic flow on each individual road segment in $\mathcal{A}_r$, X_r can be filled densely, therefore can help reduce the error of decomposing $\mathcal{A}_r$. X_h has the same structure as X_r, storing the historical average number of vehicles traversing a grid from t_i to t_j. In other words, X_r and X_h

respectively correspond to the coarse-grained current and historical traffic conditions in the same span of time of day. In the implementation, we build A_h and X_h of an entire day in advance and retrieve the entries according to current time (and the number of time slots L needed) when constructing X and A. For example, as shown in Figure 4 C), the rows from t_i to t_j will be retrieved from the prebuilt X_h to construct X with X_r.

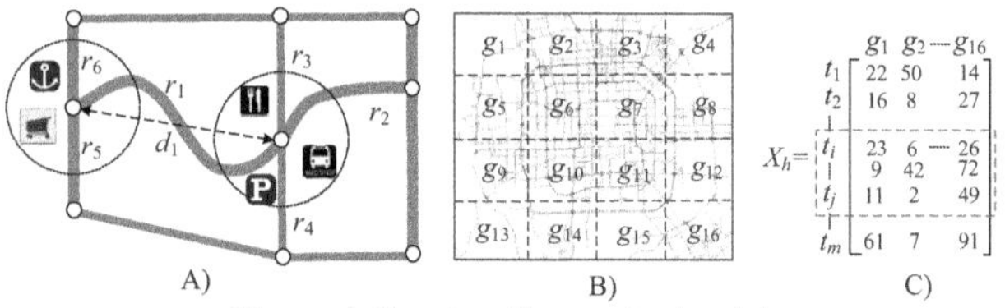

Figure 4. Constructing context matrices

3.2 Tensor Decomposition

To achieve a high accuracy of decomposition, we put together $\mathcal{A}_r$ and $\mathcal{A}_h$(i.e., $\mathcal{A} = \mathcal{A}_r || \mathcal{A}_h$, as shown in Figure 3), decomposing $\mathcal{A}$ with context matrices X and Y collaboratively. The objective function is defined as Equation 3,

$$\mathcal{L}(S,R,U,T,F,G) = \frac{1}{2}\|\mathcal{A}_r - S \times_R R \times_U U \times_T T\|^2 + \frac{\lambda_1}{2}\|X - TG\|^2 + \frac{\lambda_2}{2}\|Y - RF\|^2 + \frac{\lambda_3}{2}(\|S\|^2 + \|R\|^2 + \|U\|^2 + \|T\|^2 + \|F\|^2 + \|G\|^2), \quad (3)$$

where $\mathcal{A} \in \mathbb{R}^{N \times M \times 2L}$ and $X \in \mathbb{R}^{2L \times P}$, P denotes the number of grids; $Y \in \mathbb{R}^{N \times Q}$, Q denotes the dimension of geographical features; $T \in \mathbb{R}^{2L \times d_T}$, $G \in \mathbb{R}^{d_T \times P}$, $R \in \mathbb{R}^{N \times d_R}$ and $F \in \mathbb{R}^{d_R \times Q}$ are low rank latent factor matrices for time slots, grids, roads and geographical features. Later, we can recover $\mathcal{A}$ according to $\mathcal{A}_{rec} = S \times_R R \times_U U \times_T T$. λ_1, λ_2, and λ_3 are parameters controlling the contribution of different parts.

In our model, $\mathcal{A}$ and X shares matrix T, and $\mathcal{A}$ and Y share matrix R. The dense representation of X and Y helps generate a relatively accurate T and R, which reduce the decomposition error of $\mathcal{A}$ in turn. Additionally, the combination of X_r and X_h reveals how current coarse-grained traffic condition deviates from its historical patterns. The information of the deviation is then propagated to $\mathcal{A}$, helping figure out the fine-grained deviation between current traffic conditions and historical traffic patterns on each road segment. So, our model considers both geospatial and temporal correlations. It also incorporates the knowledge from present and historical traffic data. As there is no closed-form solution for finding the most optimal result of Equation 3, we use a numeric method, gradient descent, to find a local optimization, as presented in Figure 5.

Algorithm 1: Tensor Decomposition

Input: tensor $\mathcal{A}$, matrix X, and matrix Y, an error threshold ε
Output: R, U, T, S

Initialize $S \in \mathbb{R}^{d_R \times d_U \times d_T}$, $R \in \mathbb{R}^{N \times d_R}$, $U \in \mathbb{R}^{M \times d_U}$, $T \in \mathbb{R}^{2L \times d_T}$, $G \in \mathbb{R}^{d_T \times P}$, $F \in \mathbb{R}^{d_R \times Q}$ with small random values
Set η as step size
While $L_t - L_{t+1} > \varepsilon$
  Foreach $\mathcal{A}_{ijk} \neq 0$
    $Y_{ijk} = S \times_R R_{i*} \times_U U_{j*} \times_T T_{k*}$;
    $R_{i*} \leftarrow R_{i*} - \eta\lambda_3 R_{i*} - \eta(Y_{ijk} - \mathcal{A}_{ijk}) \times S \times_U U_{j*} \times_T T_{k*} - \eta\lambda_2(R_{i*} \times F - Y_{i*}) \times F$;
    $U_{j*} \leftarrow U_{j*} - \eta\lambda_3 U_{j*} - \eta(Y_{ijk} - \mathcal{A}_{ijk}) \times S \times_R R_{i*} \times_T T_{k*}$;
    $T_{k*} \leftarrow T_{k*} - \eta\lambda_3 T_{k*} - \eta(Y_{ijk} - \mathcal{A}_{ijk}) \times S \times_R R_{i*} \times_U U_{j*} - \eta\lambda_1(T_{k*} \times G - X_{k*}) \times G$;
    $S \leftarrow S - \eta\lambda_3 S - \eta(Y_{ijk} - \mathcal{A}_{ijk}) \times R_{i*} \otimes U_{j*} \otimes T_{k*}$;
    $G \leftarrow G - \eta\lambda_3 G - \eta\lambda_1(T_{k*} \times G - X_{k*}) \times T_{k*}$;
    $F \leftarrow F - \eta\lambda_3 F - \eta\lambda_2(R_{i*} \times F - Y_{i*}) \times R_{i*}$;
Return R, U, T, S

Figure 5. Algorithm for decomposing a tensor

The Symbol "×" denotes the matrix multiplication; $\times_R$ stands for the tensor-matrix multiplication, where the subscript R stands for the direction, e.g., $H = S \times_R R$ is $H_{ijk} = \sum_{i=1}^{d_R} S_{ijk} \times R_{ij}$; $\otimes$ is the tensor outer product (also called Kronecker product); the entries of the i th row of matrix R are represented as R_{i*}. More specifically, we use an element-wise optimization algorithm (instead of batch decomposition) [10], which updates the factors independently (meaning they can be performed in parallel).

In reality, tensor $\mathcal{A}$ is very large, given hundreds of thousands of road segments and tens of thousands of drivers. Decomposing such a big tensor is very time consuming, therefore reducing the feasibility of our method in providing online services. To address this issue, as illustrated in Figure 6, we partition a city into several disjoint regions, building a tensor for each region based on the data of the region. The matrices X and Y are built in each smaller region accordingly. By setting a proper splitting boundary, we try to keep these small tensors a similar size. As a result, $\mathcal{A}$ is replaced by a few small tensors, which will be factorized in parallel and more efficiently. We validate (in later experiments) that the partition does not compromise the accuracy of the original decomposition when choosing a proper number of partitions.

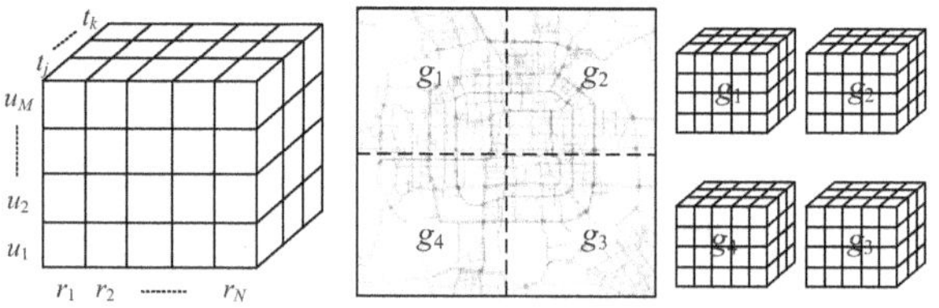
Figure 6. Spatial partition for expediting the tensor decomposition

4. OPTIMAL CONCATENATION (OC)

4.1 Objective Function

Given a path $\boldsymbol{P}$ covered by trajectories, we need to find the best concatenation that results in an accurate travel time estimation. Intuitively, the best decomposition is the one that achieves the lowest empirical risk between the estimate and true travel time $\mu_{\boldsymbol{P}}$. Suppose $\boldsymbol{P}$ is decomposed as $P_1||P_2||\cdots||P_k$, where the estimated travel time is $\bar{t}_{P_1} + \bar{t}_{P_2} + \cdots + \bar{t}_{P_k}$, the squared empirical risk is then wrote as,

$$LSE_{\boldsymbol{P},P_1,P_2,\cdots,P_k} \triangleq E(\mu_{\boldsymbol{P}} - \bar{t}_{P_1} - \bar{t}_{P_2} - \cdots - \bar{t}_{P_k})^2, \quad (4)$$

Hence, our problem is to search for the best concatenation which yields the least empirical risk, formally defined as,

$$\operatorname{argmin}_{P_1,P_2,\cdots,P_k} LSE_{\boldsymbol{P},P_1,P_2,\cdots,P_k},$$
$$\text{subject to } P_1||P_2||\cdots||P_k = \boldsymbol{P}. \quad (5)$$

To come up with a computable form of $LSE_{\boldsymbol{P},P_1,P_2,\cdots,P_k}$, we relate $LSE_{\boldsymbol{P},P_1,P_2,\cdots,P_k}$ with $E(\mu_{P_i} - \bar{t}_{P_i})^2$, where μ_{P_i} is the true travel time of sub-path P_i. It is fair to assume if $\boldsymbol{P} = P_1||P_2||\cdots||P_k$, then $\mu_{\boldsymbol{P}} = u_{P_1} + u_{P_2} + \cdots + u_{P_k}$. Hence we have,

$$LSE_{\boldsymbol{P},P_1,P_2,\cdots,P_k} = E(\mu_{\boldsymbol{P}} - \bar{t}_{P_1} - \bar{t}_{P_2} - \cdots - \bar{t}_{P_k})^2$$
$$= E(\mu_{P_1} + \mu_{P_2} + \cdots \mu_{P_k} - \bar{t}_{P_1} - \bar{t}_{P_2} - \cdots - \bar{t}_{P_k})^2$$
$$= E\left(\sum_{i=1}^{k}(\mu_{P_i} - \bar{t}_{P_i})^2 + \sum_{i=1}^{k}\sum_{j=1}^{k}(\mu_{P_i} - \bar{t}_{P_i})(\mu_{P_j} - \bar{t}_{P_j})\right)$$
$$= \sum_{i=1}^{k} E(\mu_{P_i} - \bar{t}_{P_i})^2 + \sum_{i=1}^{k}\sum_{j=1}^{k} E\left((\mu_{P_i} - \bar{t}_{P_i})(\mu_{P_j} - \bar{t}_{P_j})\right)$$

If assuming $\bar{t}_{P_i}$ and $\bar{t}_{P_j}$ are independent, we have $E\left((\mu_{P_i} - \bar{t}_{P_i})(\mu_{P_j} - \bar{t}_{P_j})\right) = E(\mu_{P_i} - \bar{t}_{P_i})E(\mu_{P_j} - \bar{t}_{P_j})$=0, Therefore,

$$LSE_{\boldsymbol{P},P_1,P_2,\cdots,P_k} = \sum_{i=1}^{k} E(\mu_{P_i} - \bar{t}_{P_i})^2. \quad (6)$$

Further, $E(\mu_{P_i} - \bar{t}_{P_i})^2 = E(\mu_{P_i} - \frac{1}{n_{P_i}}\sum_{j=1}^{n_{P_i}} t_{P_i,j})^2$

$$= \frac{1}{n_{P_i}^2} E \sum_{j=1}^{n_{P_i}} (\mu_{P_i} - t_{P_i,j})^2 = \frac{1}{n_{P_i}^2} \sum_{j=1}^{n_{P_i}} E(\mu_{P_i} - t_{P_i,j})^2$$

$$= \frac{1}{n_{P_i}} Var(t_{P_i,j}), \quad (7)$$

where n_{P_i} is the number of drivers passing P_i, and $t_{P_i,j}$ denotes the jth driver's travel time on P_i; $Var(t_{P_i,j})$ is the variance of these drivers' travel times. Then, Equation 5 can be represented as:

$$\text{argmin}_{P_1,P_2,\cdots,P_k} \ \sum_{i=1}^{k} \frac{1}{n_{P_i}} Var(t_{P_i,j})$$
$$\text{subject to } \ P_1||P_2||\cdots||P_k = \boldsymbol{P} \quad (8)$$

Equation 8 well reflects the aforementioned tradeoff between the support and length of a concatenation. On one hand, it is easier to find more drivers traveling a shorter sub-path. The more the drivers pass a sub-path (i.e. support is higher, n_{P_i} is bigger), the smaller the error of the inferred travel time is. On the other hand, the shorter a sub-path is, the bigger the variance in travel time would be. There are a lot of uncertainties of traveling a short path. E.g., if only traveling one road segment, the travel time will be significantly influenced by a traffic light. As a result, different drivers' travel times could be dramatically different.

4.2 Dynamic Programing Solution

To solve the optimization problem shown in Equation 8, we propose a dynamic programing solution. Suppose a path $\boldsymbol{P}: r_1 \to r_2 \to \cdots \to r_n$, $P' = r_1 \to r_2 \to \cdots \to r_i$, $i < n$, denote $g(P_i) = \frac{1}{n_{P_i}} Var(t_{P_i,j})$, then the optimization problem of P' can be represented as Equation 9.

$$\text{argmin}_{P_1,P_2,\cdots,P_l} \ \sum_{j=1}^{l} g(P_j)$$
$$\text{subject to } \ P_1||P_2||\cdots||P_l = P'. \quad (9)$$

Let opt_i be the minimal value of P' to the above problem, then the minimal value of the squared empirical risk function of $\boldsymbol{P}$ is opt_n. Additionally, we have a state transition function as Equation 10.

$$opt_n = \min_{1 \le i < n}(opt_i + g(P_{r_{i+1}||r_{i+2}\cdots||r_n})). \quad (10)$$

Algorithm 2: Query path decomposition

Input: a query path $\boldsymbol{P} = r_1 \to r_2 \to \cdots \to r_n$, a collection of trajectory pattern TPs, a time slot k, trajectories received in k, and tensor $\mathcal{A}_{rec}$
Output: Ψ_n, the most optimal concatenation of path $\boldsymbol{P}$

```
1. opt_0 ← 0, Ψ_0 ← ∅;
2. For i = 1 to n do
3.     opt_i ← +∞; Ψ_i = ∅;
4.     For j = i down to 1 do
5.         P' = r_j → r_{j+1} → ··· → r_i; t_{P',u,k} ←0;
6.         U ← retrieve the drivers traversing (or partially traversing)
               P' from the trajectory database
7.         Foreach u ∈ U do
8.             t_{P',u,k} ← 0;
9.             Foreach r_e ∈ P' not traversed by u's trajectory Tr
10.                t_{P',u,k} += (A_rec)_{r_e,u,k};
11.            t_{P_s',u,k} ←Calculate the time for the rest of P' based on Tr;
12.            t_{P',u,k} += t_{P_s',u,k};
13.        g(P') = 1/|U| Var_{u∈U}(t_{P',u,k});
14.        If opt_{j-1} + g(P') < opt_i
15.            opt_i ← opt_{j-1} + g(P');
16.            Ψ_i ← Ψ_{j-1}||P';
17. Return Ψ_n;
```

Figure 7. Algorithm for finding the most optimal concatenation

Using Algorithm 2 shown in Figure 7, we solve this problem with a complexity of $O(n^2 \times m)$, where n is the number of road segments in $\boldsymbol{P}$ and m is the number of drivers passing a segment.

In practice, it is not necessary to check every concatenation of a path, as many sub-paths may not be traversed by any trajectory in the current time slot. To further improve the efficiency of our solution, we mine frequent trajectory patterns from historical trajectories in advance. Then, we just need to check the concatenation of the trajectories patterns. Specifically, we can stop the iteration at Line 4 in algorithm 2 if P' is not a trajectory pattern.

We use a suffix-tree-based algorithm [18] to find the frequent trajectory patterns. Specifically, after being map-matched, a trajectory can be regarded as a string of road segment IDs. By building a suffix tree, where a node denotes a road segment ID, a trajectory is then represented as a path on the tree. For example, the four trajectories shown in Figure 1 can be represented as the tree depicted in Figure 8 A), where $r_1 \to r_2 \to r_3$ is the most left path of the tree. $r_2 \to r_3$ and r_3 are suffixes of $r_1 \to r_2 \to r_3$. The number associated with each link stands for the number of the trajectories passing the path (i.e., the support). If setting 2 as a support, we find $r_1 \to r_2$, $r_2 \to r_3$, and r_3 are patterns. In reality, the suffix-tree is built based on historical trajectories over a long period of time. As long trajectory patterns are very rare, we set the maximum length of a pattern to 20 road segments.

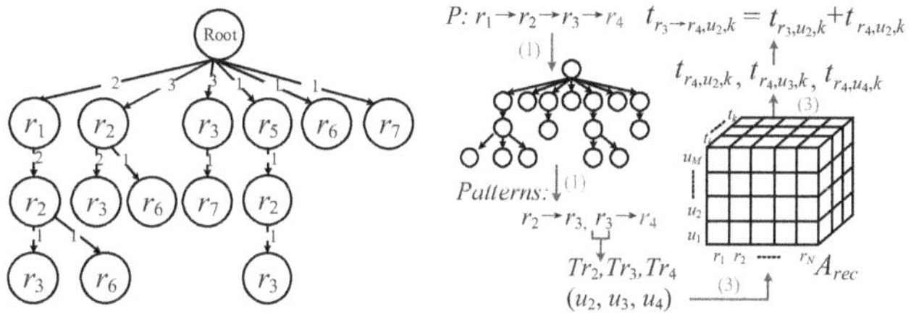

A) An example of suffix-tree B) Filling in the missing time for a pattern

Figure 8. Mining frequent trajectory patterns and used with tensor

4.3 Working with Tensor $\mathcal{A}_{rec}$

Note that a query path may have some road segments that are not traversed by any trajectory in the current time slot, though these segments may belong to a trajectory pattern (in history). Following the example shown in Figure 1, we demonstrate in Figure 8 B) how $\mathcal{A}_{rec}$ is used with trajectory patterns to help the decomposition of a query path. To estimate the travel time of a query path $P: r_1 \to r_2 \to r_3 \to r_4$ in time slot k, we first search the suffix tree, which was built based on the trajectory data over a long history (not the one shown in the left part of Figure 8 A), for the trajectory patterns that P contains, e.g., $r_2 \to r_3$ and $r_3 \to r_4$. To calculate $g(r_3 \to r_4)$ defined in Equation 9, we need to know the travel time of each driver passing $r_3 \to r_4$. However, r_4 is not traversed by any trajectory in time slot k. That is $t_{r_3\to r_4,u,k}$ is unknown for every driver, though $t_{r_3,u,k}$ can be calculated based on the recently received trajectories, i.e. Tr_2, Tr_3 and Tr_4. To address this issue, we retrieve $t_{r_4,u_2,k}$, $t_{r_4,u_3,k}$, and $t_{r_4,u_4,k}$ from $\mathcal{A}_{rec}$ and calculate $t_{r_3\to r_4,u,k}$ for $u = (u_2, u_3, u_4)$, respectively, by Equation 11.

$$t_{r_3\to r_4,u,k} = t_{r_3,u,k} + t_{r_4,u,k}, \quad (11)$$

Having $t_{r_3\to r_4,u,k}$, we can calculate the most optimal concatenation according to Equation 9, 10 and Algorithm 2. When the supplement of an entry is negative, we resort to the historical average travel time. The dimension of users in tensor $\mathcal{A}_r$ enables us to retrieve a more accurate travel time for a particular driver, resulting in a better estimate of the variance of travel times (as Equation 8). We validate that this is more accurate than just using a historical average of travel times. After finding the most optimal concatenation, we calculate the travel time of path P by Equation 1, setting Ψ_n as Ψ.

In the implementation, if not building an effective indexing structure, we need to scan a trajectory when calculating the travel time of a path based on the trajectory (i.e., Line 11 of Algorithm 2). This becomes very time consuming if we need to repeat the process many times. To address this issue, we propose an indexing structure to maintain the trajectories received in the current time slot, as shown in Figure 9. The structure looks like the suffix tree we build for mining trajectory patterns. However, each node in the tree stores the ID of the trajectory that traverses the path from the root to the node and the corresponding travel time. For example, Tr_1 and Tr_2 shown in Figure 1 are stored in the index demonstrated in Figure 9, where $t_{r_1 \to r_2 \to r_3}$ stands for the time for traveling path $r_1 \to r_2 \to r_3$.

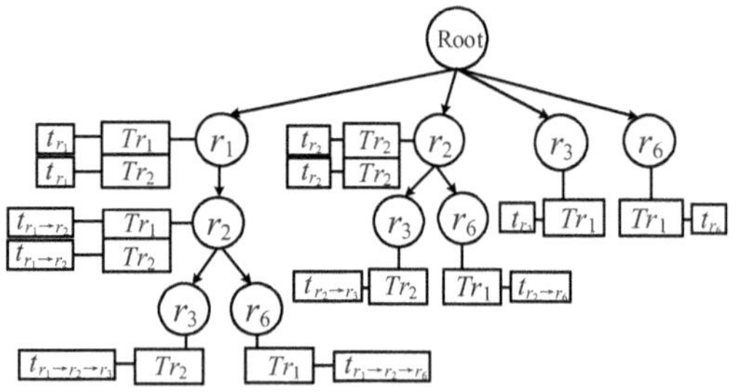

Figure 9. Indexing structure for maintaining recent trajectories

5. EXPERIMENTS

In this section, we evaluate the effectiveness and efficiency of the two major parts of PTTE, i.e., CATD and OC, respectively.

5.1 Settings

5.1.1 Datasets

Taxi Trajectories. We use a GPS trajectory dataset generated by 32,670 taxicabs in Beijing from Sept. 1 to Oct. 31, 2013. The number of GPS points reaches 673,469,757, and the total length of the trajectories is over 26,218,407km. The average sampling rate is 96 seconds per point.

Road networks: We use the road network of Beijing, which is comprised of 148,110 nodes and 196,307 edges. The road network covers a 40×50km spatial range, with a total length (of road segments) of 21,985km.

POIs: The dataset consists of 273,165 POIs of Beijing, which are classified into 195 tier two categories. We only chose the top 10 categories that occur around road segments most frequently.

After projecting the trajectories onto the road network, we build $\mathcal{A}_r$ and $\mathcal{A}_h$ to model the recent and historical traffic conditions, respectively. We set four time slots (each time slot is 30 minutes) in the two tensors, as we find 4 have a good tradeoff between effectiveness and efficiency (see Figure 12 A). In the implementation, we remove the road segments that are traveled less than 50 times in two months (i.e., less than 1 time per entire day). The GPS points on such road segments may be noises, or due to the imperfect map-matching algorithm or such places cannot be traveled by vehicles (such as pedestrian streets), and therefore may not be really queried by drivers. Finally, 118,401 road segments are used in our models. We also build geographic and temporal contexts X and Y based on the above mentioned datasets. Table 1 shows the statistics of these tensors and matrices, where the third row means $\mathcal{A}_r$ is partitioned into 25 sub-tensors.

As shown in Figure 10 A), the maximum number of trajectories traversing a path (per day) decreases quickly as the length of the path increases. For instance, a path with 10 road segments is traversed by less than 245 trajectories per day. Figure 10 B) presents the number road segments traveled by taxis with different times. For example, from 8am to 9am, about 25,000 roads segments are traversed by taxis 1-2 times and 8,000 segments (about 4% of Beijing road network) are traveled 3-4 times.

Table 1. Statistics on the data models

	Size	Average non-zero entries
$\mathcal{A}_r$	118,401×32,670×4	0.035%
$\mathcal{A}_h$	118,401×32,670×4	0.4%
$\mathcal{A}_r$/(5×5)	4,736×12,674×4	0.09%
X	8×16	1
Y	118,401×18	1

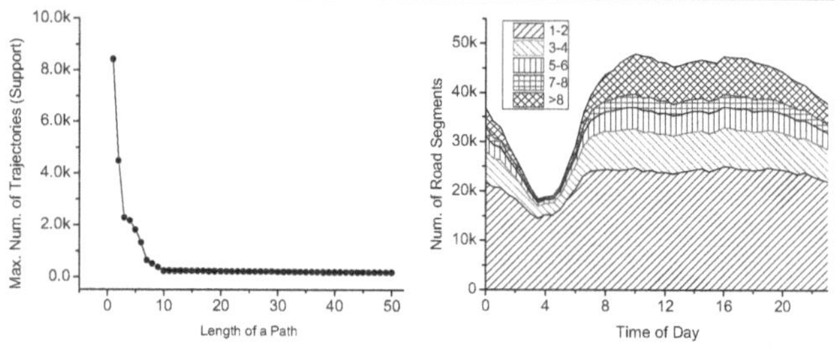

A) Support of Path W.r.t. it length B) Road segments traversed

Figure 10. Statistics on the trajectory data set

5.1.2 Baseline Methods

We compare PTTE with the following four baseline methods.

1) *Speed-Constraint-based* (SC) method. The travel time of each road segment is computed by the length of a road segment and its speed constraint. The travel time of a path is then a summation of that of each road segment.

2) *Trajectory-based Simple Concatenation* (TSC) method. TSC estimates the travel time of each road segment individually based on the trajectories passing the road segment in the most recent time slot. If a road segment is not covered by any recent trajectory, TSC uses the average historical travel time instead. The travel time of a path is then a summation of that of each road segment.

3) *Optimal Concatenation with Historical Travel Time* (OC+H) method. OC+H uses Algorithm 2 proposed in this paper to find the most optimal concatenation of trajectories to estimate the travel time of a path. For a road segment not covered by any trajectories, this method uses an average historical travel time of the road segment.

4) *Optimal Concatenation with Nonnegative Matrix Factorization* (OC+MF). This method is similar to OC+H, except for using MF (rather than historical average) to infer the travel time of segments without trajectories. MF is applied to the road-time matrix, which is degraded from tensor $\mathcal{A}$ by averaging the driver dimensions.

Comparing PTTE with the first baseline, we can demonstrate the advantages of using the trajectory data. The second baseline method can reveal the contribution of the proposed optimal concatenation algorithm. Through comparing it with the third and fourth baselines, we can justify why a tensor with the driver dimension is needed in PTTE. Regarding CATD, the first step of PTTE, we study the contribution of using context matrices and historical data, respectively, in filling the missing values of $\mathcal{A}_r$.

5.1.3 Query Paths and Ground Truth

We randomly pick out 50 paths, each of which has been fully traversed by at least two drivers, in each hour of a day, from the taxi trajectory data. We then use these paths as queries and the average travel time of these trajectories as the ground truth. Once a trajectory is selected as a ground truth, we remove them from the training data. In total, we generate 12,384 queries, whose length ranges from 2KM to 16KM following the distribution as shown in Figure 11 B) and time span follows the distribution depicted in Figure 11 C). The total length of these query paths is 76,412.6km with an effective total time span of 2733.9hours. The queries selected in this way cover different times of day (from 6am to 11pm) and follow the distance distribution of people's true travel patterns in a city's road network. In the experiments, we do not study the query after 11pm and earlier than 6am, as there is almost no traffic at those times. In other words, people can travel as fast as the speed constraint of a road. According to Figure 11 A), these query paths (denoted as blue road segments) also cover the majority of the Beijing road network.

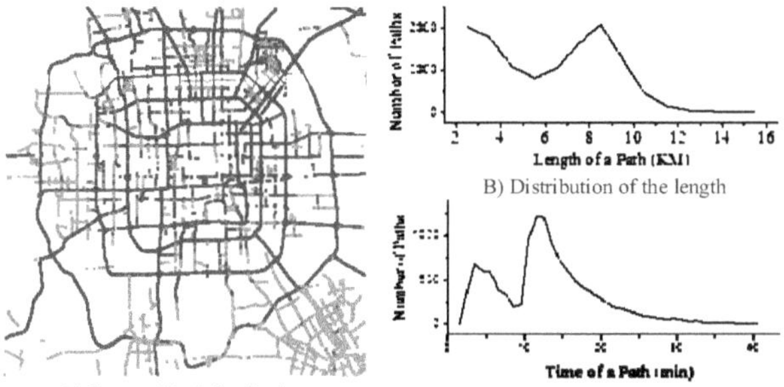

A) Geographical distribution B) Distribution of the length C) Distribution of time length

Figure 11. Distributions of the query paths

We study the mean absolute error (MAE) and mean relative error (MRE) of an estimate according to Equation 12 and 13, respectively, where y_i is an estimate and $\hat{y}_i$ is the ground truth.

$$MAE = \frac{\sum_i |y_i - \hat{y}_i|}{n}, \quad (12)$$

$$MRE = \frac{\sum_i |y_i - \hat{y}_i|}{\sum_i \hat{y}_i}, \quad (13)$$

5.2 Results

5.2.1 Performance of CATD

To test the accuracy of estimating the travel time of road segments absent of trajectories, we randomly remove 30% of non-zero entries from the last time slice of tensor $\mathcal{A}_r$. We then infer these entries with our method, using their original values as a ground truth to calculate MAE and RMSE, as shown in Table 2 (λ_1=λ_2=λ_3= 0.01). RMSE is widely used to measure the error of a tensor decomposition, defined as Equation 14.

$$RMSE = \sqrt{\frac{\sum_i (y_i - \hat{y}_i)^2}{n}}; \quad (14)$$

Adding historical trajectories (i.e.., $\mathcal{A}_h$) and context matrices gradually into the tensor decomposition, denoted as TD+H and TD+H+C, respectively, we achieve a clear increase of performance in estimating the missing values.

Table 2. The performance of CATD

	MAE (min)	RMSE
TD	0.747	1.646
$TD + H$	0.732	1.629
$CATD\ (TD + H + C)$	0.714	1.613

We further study the effectiveness and efficiency of CATD changing over the number of time slices in Figure 12 A). Adding more time slices into $\mathcal{A}_r$ and $\mathcal{A}_h$ achieves a more accurate estimate of missing values (i.e., the travel time of road segments without trajectories), as we have richer information of previous traffic conditions. On the other hand, more time slices consume a longer time. We find that formulating a tensor with 4 time slices is a relatively strong tradeoff between effectiveness and efficiency.

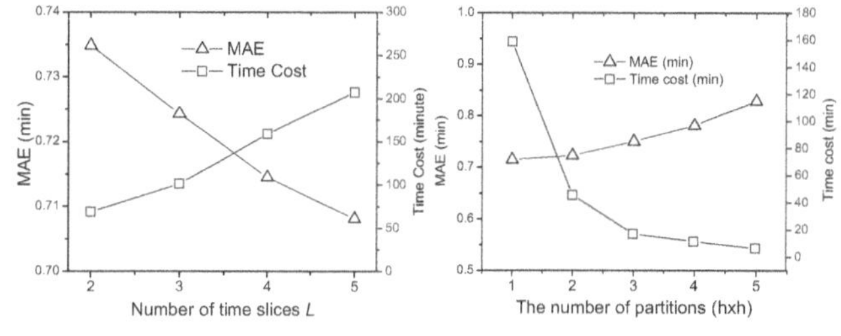

A) W.r.t. time slices B) w.r.t. partitions

Figure 12. Performance of CATD

However, the time cost for decomposing such big tensors and matrices (see Table 1) makes our method impractical for answering instant queries. As a consequence, we partition a city into disjointed regions, building individual tensors and matrices, separately and in parallel. Figure 12 B) shows the performance changing over the number of partitions. When dividing Beijing into 5×5 regions, we can finish CATD for each region in 6 minutes. The partition does not compromise the accuracy (only a 0.1min gap) as compared to decomposing the original tensors. Additionally, the tensor decomposition method we adopt can be performed in parallel, further reducing the time cost of CATD.

5.2.2 Overall Performance

Table 3 presents the overall performance of our model PTTE (i.e., CATD+OC) and baseline methods. Besides MAE and MRE, we also present the average error of travel time per km (MAE/L). For example, the average error of PTTE in estimating the travel time of a path is about 0.412min (25 seconds) per kilometer. Clearly, PTTE outperforms all the baselines in terms of the three metrics. Given the queries introduced in Section 5.1.3, on average, the absolute error of the estimated travel time is about 2 minutes per path, which is about 19% of the true travel time. From the results, we can draw the following conclusions. First, using trajectory data (TSC) is much better than that only based on speed constraints of roads. But, simply concatenating the travel time of each individual road segment (TSC) is not an optimal solution. As we mentioned before, the more fragments involved in a concatenation, the more uncertain of travel time for crossing two consecutive fragments occurs is. Second, regarding estimating the travel time of road segments without covered by trajectories, using the historical average travel time (OC+H) is significantly better than using its speed constraint. Using a collaborative filtering model (OC+MF) is slightly better than using an historical average. The PTTE considering the driver dimension is even better than OC+MF.

Table 3. Comparison of different methods

	MAE (min)	MRE	MAE/L (min/km)
SC	8.808	0.665	1.428
TSC	5.244	0.396	0.850
$OC + H$	3.245	0.245	0.526
$OC + MF$	3.061	0.231	0.496
PTTE	**2.545**	**0.192**	**0.412**

Figures 13 and 14 present the performance of SC, TSC, and PTTE changing over time of day, on weekdays and weekends. We do not show that of OC+H and OC+MF, as they almost follow the same trend as (but worse than) PTTE. As depicted in Figure 11, the error of SC increases tremendously during peak traffic hours, around 8-9am and 6-7pm. The complex traffic conditions on roads at these moments deviate the true travel speed far from their speed constraints. When time goes to late night (i.e., no complex traffic conditions anymore), the error decreases and approaches our PTTE method. This is also the reason that we do not need to perform PTTE on late night time sets, especially after 12am and before 6am. Simply estimating the travel time for each individual road segment and then doing a summation (TSC) is not accurate enough. When there are not enough taxis traveling on Beijing's road network, e.g., after 9pm and before 8am, MAE of TSC is higher than other time slots. With the help of CATD, the MAE of our method only increases slightly after 9am. This demonstrates the value of inferring the missing values.

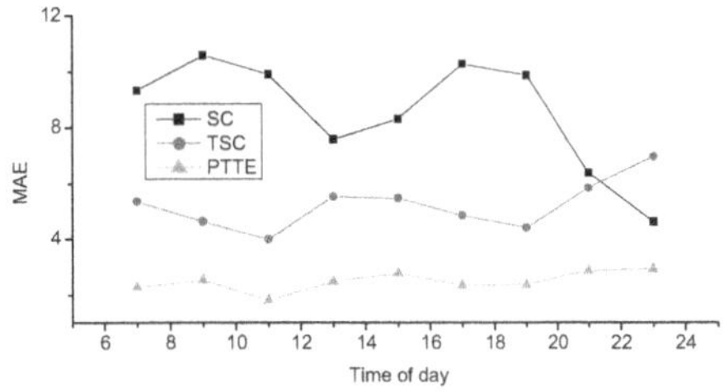

Figure 13. Performance changing over time of day (Weekday)

As most people do not drive to work on weekends, we observe different trends of the performance in Figure 14, in contrast to Figure 13. SC's MAE reaches its peak around 6pm which is the weekend rush hour. The reason why PTTE has the biggest error around 9am on weekends is a tradeoff between the number of taxis and the complexity of traffic conditions in a road network. On weekends, the number of taxis traveling in Beijing's road network is still very small at 9am, while the traffic conditions start becoming complex. As time goes by, more taxis are present on Beijing's road network, alleviating the data sparsity problem and decreasing the MAE. Conversely, before 8am, the traffic condition is still very simple to predict on roads. The travel speed is almost close to the speed limit.

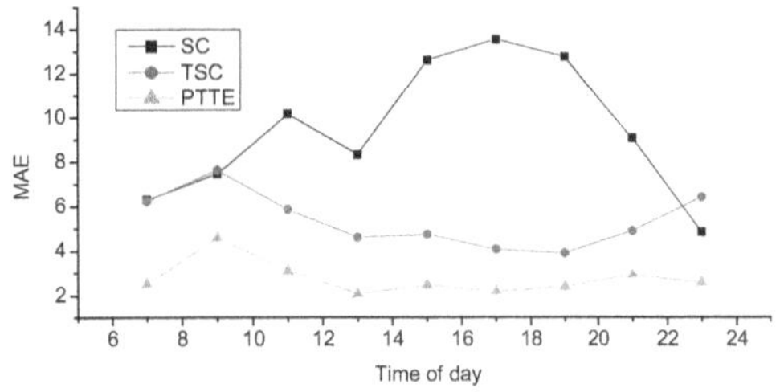

Figure 14. Performance changing over time of day (Weekend)

Figure 15 shows the performance of PTTE changing over the length of a query path. As the length increases, both MAE and MRE decrease. A longer path is more likely to contain more trajectory patterns, which provide more choices for an optimal concatenation. This also echoes the assumption we proposed in the introduction. The shorter a sub-path is the more unstable its travel time could be. In an extreme case, the travel time of a single road segment is terrifically impacted by traffic lights and pedestrians crossing it. So, the travel time varies in time quickly and tremendously, becoming hard to predict.

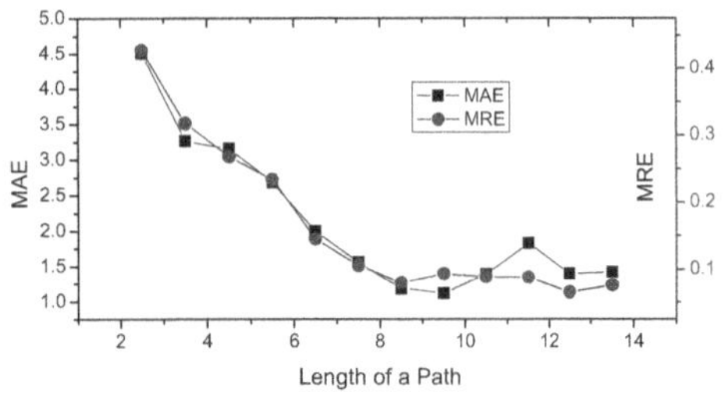

Figure 15. Performance of PTTE changing over the length of a path

Table 4 presents the time and space cost of PTTE's two major components for processing the trajectories received in recent 30 minutes. The first component CATD is only performed once for the entire dataset, while OC is conducted for each query path. All numbers are obtained by only using a single core of a server with 2.80GHz Xeon CPU and 24GB RAM. For example, if we partition a city into 25 regions, building $\mathcal{A}_r$ and $\mathcal{A}_h$ for an individual region needs 44 and 233 seconds, respectively, costing 4.4MB and 14.6 MB of memory, respectively (each tensor contains 4 time slices). Using Algorithm 1 to decompose these tensors with context matrices X and Y needs about 6.31min for each region. We do not list the time for building matrix Y, as it is static and can be built offline. In total, we can infer the travel time on each road segment for each particular driver within 6.4min if using 25 cores in a server. Note that Algorithm 1 is based on an entry-wised decomposition approach, which can be performed in parallel further. If using six 25-core servers, we can finish CATD in about 1 minute. In the optimal concatenation, we can process a query path in 2.3ms. However, the time is much longer if the trajectory patterns and the real-time indexing structure proposed in Figure 9 are not used.

Table 4. Time and memory cost for each step of PTTE

	Components		Time	Memory (MB)
Deal with missing values (*CATD*)	Building matrix X, Y		34ms	9
	Tensor construction	$\mathcal{A}_r$	44ms	4.4
		$\mathcal{A}_h$	233ms	14.6
	Decomposition	5×5	6.31min	116
	Total		6.4min	144
Optimal Concatenation (OC)	Best OC		**2.3ms**	**995**
	w/o trajectory patterns		8.6ms	877
	w/o index		12.2s	714

Figure 16 A) shows the tradeoff between effectiveness (measured by MAE) and efficiency (by time cost) of using trajectory patterns in optimal concatenations, where the horizontal axis denotes the threshold of support. For example, if setting 400 as a threshold, we regard a path as a trajectory pattern if the path has been covered by over 400 trajectories in the two-month dataset. The bigger threshold is the smaller number of trajectory patterns we can obtain. So, the time cost decreases and the MAE increases, as the support increases. Additionally, as depicted in Figure 16 B), setting a smaller support threshold leads to a bigger size of the suffix-tree-based index for trajectory pattern mining. In the implementation, we find 500 is a good tradeoff among MAE, time cost, and index size. Note that without using the indexing structure proposed in Section 4.3, we need about 12 seconds to find the most optimal concatenation for a query path (see Table 4).

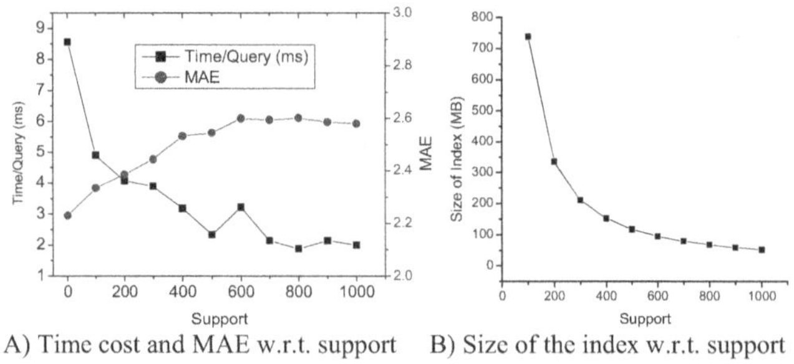

A) Time cost and MAE w.r.t. support B) Size of the index w.r.t. support

Figure 16. Performance of OC w.r.t. support of a trajectory pattern

The recovered tensor $\mathcal{A}_{rec}$ helps the optimal concatenation significantly. In the experiments, we test our model with 12,384 query paths, which are comprised of 217,326 road segments in total. When processing the query paths, we access tensor $\mathcal{A}_{rec}$ 1,706,648 times (i.e., 137.8 times per query) to retrieve the missing travel time of a road segment in a trajectory pattern. The travel times of 58,223 road segments (about 26.8% of the road segments in the query paths) are finally retrieved from $\mathcal{A}_{rec}$ for constructing the most optimal concatenation, i.e., 4.7 road segments per path.

We study the performance of PTTE changing over different number of vehicles in Figure 17, aiming to figure out how many GPS equipped vehicles are needed to have accurate results. For example, using 30,000 GPS-equipped vehicles in Beijing is enough to achieving a MRE smaller than 0.23. In other words, if having 1.36 vehicles on every kilometer road in a city, we can achieve a relative error of estimation smaller than 0.23.

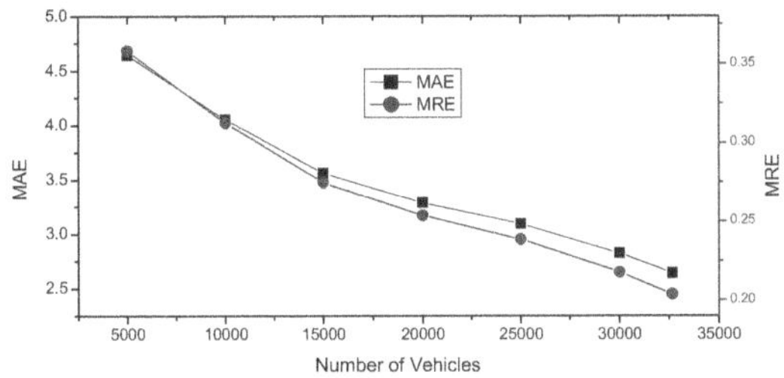

Figure 17. Performance w.r.t the number of taxis

5.2.3 Field Study

Besides using GPS trajectories from taxi drivers, we also send two drivers carrying a GPS logger to test the accuracy of our method from Sept. 1 to Oct. 30. Finally, we collect 114 driving paths with a total length of 999.4km and an effective total time period of 61.6hours. The sampling rate of these GPS trajectories is 5 seconds per point. Table 5 shows the performance of the study, where we observe a better MRE than using taxi drivers' trajectories as a ground truth. The major reason is the length of a path collected in the study is usually long (on average 8.78KM each), where our model has a better accuracy than a shorter path. Additionally, the map-matching for high sampling rate trajectories is more accurate than low sampling rate taxi trajectories, resulting in a more accurate estimation of the ground truth.

Table 5. Performance of the in-the field study

	MAE (min)	MRE	MAE/L (min/km)
SC	18.193	0.561	2.075
TSC	11.300	0.349	1.289
$OC+H$	4.990	0.154	0.569
$OC+MF$	4.052	0.125	0.462
PTTE	**3.771**	**0.116**	**0.430**

6. RELATED WORK

6.1 Road Segment-Based Travel Time

Approaches using Loop Detectors: Estimating travel time based on loop detectors installed on both endpoints of a road segment has been studied intensively over the past few decades. When a vehicle passes through, the time interval for crossing two adjacent loop detectors is recorded, based on which the speed of the vehicle is inferred. [9, 14, 16] use various models to estimate the travel speed on an individual road segment based on the sensor readings from loop detectors, and then convert the speed into a travel time. [19] predicts the travel time of a road segment by applying support vector regression to its historical travel times. As many roads do not have a loop detector buried, this category of research mainly focuses on individual road segments, and therefore is difficult to scale up to an entire city.

Floating-Car-Data Approaches: Learning city transportation using floating car data has gained more attention recently [1, 5, 17, 23, 24]. In these approaches, cars driven in a city serve as dynamic sensors to probe traffic conditions, and their GPS trajectories are used to compute the speed and travel time on road segments. Most methods infer the travel time of an individual road segment without considering the correlation between the traffic conditions on different roads. This reduces the accuracy of an inference in an urban environment where traffic conditions are inter-related.

Some models [2] predict the travel speed of a road segment by considering the traffic patterns of other road segments connected to it. Unfortunately, when scaling up to an entire city, these methods often result in a model with high complexities. Additionally, they do not tackle the data sparsity problem, i.e. many road segments are not traveled by trajectories in the current time slot, which is quite common in reality. The neighboring segments' traffic patterns can be regarded as the local correlation between road segments. However, the correlation between road segments that are not geospatially connected is not considered in these modes. [8] aims to estimate the travel time between two points on a road network using low sampling rate trajectory data. It considers the correlation between different road segments in terms of their historical traffic patterns to infer the travel time on a road segment and the delay at intersections. The model is trained using a Maximum Likelihood Estimation over the collected data in an urban road network.

However, these methods still follow the idea of first estimating the travel time of individual road segments and then summing up the travel times of the road segments belonging to a path. As we mentioned before, it is difficult to explicitly model the complex factors for crossing two road segments, e.g., intersections, direction turns, and traffic lights. Though we also infer the travel time for individual segments, the time is combined with trajectory patterns to formulate a sub-path rather than simply concatenating them one by one. The variance of different users' travel times also captures the complexity of traffic conditions on a road segment or a sub-path. In the meantime, when inferring the travel time of a road segment, we incorporate both spatial correlation between different road segments and the temporal correlation between the traffic conditions of different time slots, as well as the deviation between current traffic conditions and historical traffic patterns.

6.2 Path-Based Travel Time

A possible approach to deal with the weakness of the individual road segment-based methods is to estimate the travel time of a path as a whole based on frequent trajectory patterns. For example, we can mine frequent patterns from historical trajectories [6, 7, 12] in advance, and then use the average travel time of a pattern to represent the travel of the path corresponding to the pattern. Some models can also be built based on the historical data of a path [15] to estimate the future travel time of the path. This approach needs a balance between the coverage of queries that it can answer and the accuracy of the inferred travel time. To be able to answer various query paths, these methods need to select more trajectory patterns by using a small support. However, the travel time derived from a small support is not accurate. Additionally, a path's travel time of current time slot may deviate from its historical average significantly, depending on the real-time traffic conditions. Moreover, many query paths may not be traversed by any trajectories in current time slot as well in the history.

Recent research has started finding more optimal concatenations of road segments to estimate the travel time of a path. A series of research attempts to explicitly calculate the time spent on intersections using an interpolation method [11], or a joint probability model [3], or a dynamic Bayesian network [4]. This could result in a more accurate summation of individual road segments' travel times. However, these methods do not study how to leverage sub-trajectories to construct an optimal estimation of a path. As we mentioned before, the accuracy of estimating a sub-path's travel time is subject to the tradeoff between its length and the number of trajectories passing the sub-path. In our model, we propose and prove an objective function that can represent the tradeoff. We also consider the variance of different drivers' travel times, resulting in a more accurate travel time estimation of a path.

Based on the trajectories generated by a large number of taxis, [20] builds a landmark graph, where a node (entitled a landmark) is a road segment frequently traveled by taxis and an edge denotes the aggregation of taxis' commutes between two landmarks. The travel time of a path is then approximated by the summation of the travel times between landmarks. Though the proposed landmark graph can also deal with the data sparsity problem, the main goal of [20] is to find the quickest driving path between an origin and a destination; this is different from our problem. Knowing the shortest time for traveling between two points does not mean we can obtain the travel time of any path traversing the two points.

7. CONCLUSION

In this paper, we propose a real-time and citywide model, called PTTE, to estimate the travel time of a path in current time slot in a city's road network, using the GPS trajectories from a sample of vehicles (e.g. taxicabs). Though this is a very important foundation for many traffic monitoring and routing systems, the problem has not been well solved given three challenges: 1) data sparsity, 2) finding an optimal combination of trajectories (i.e., the tradeoff between the length of a sub-path and the number of trajectories passing the sub-path), and 3) the tradeoff between scalability, effectiveness and efficiency. PTTE is comprised of two major components, CATD and OC. The former infers the travel time of a road segment without being traversed by trajectories in the current time slot through a context-aware tensor decomposition approach. The latter searches for the most optimal concatenation of trajectories for a query path using a dynamic programing solution. We evaluate PTTE with extensive experiments based on GPS trajectories generated by over 32,000 taxicabs over a period of two months in Beijing. We test the effectiveness and efficiency of CATD and OC, respectively. First, the results demonstrate the advantages of CATD in accurately filling in the missing values beyond baseline methods, such as using speed constraints, or using a historical average travel time, or using a matrix factorization-based approach. The driver dimension in tensor $\mathcal{A}_r$ helps us calculate the variance of different drivers' travel times on a road segment. The variance indicates the complexity of a road's traffic condition, helping us find the most optimal concatenation for a path. In addition, the geospatial/temporal contexts and historical traffic patterns increase the accuracy of estimating the missing values. Regarding the most optimal concatenation, we devise an objective function which has been proved to be able to model the tradeoff between a sub-path's length and the number of trajectories passing it. Tested by 12,384 query paths, PTTE achieves a mean absolute error of 0.4min per km, which is about 19% of the truth travel time. The results of the in-the-field study have an even smaller estimation error (11.6%). Using the suffix-tree-based indexing structure to manage the trajectories received currently and the trajectory patterns (mined in advance) to scale down the concatenation candidates, on average, we are able to infer the travel time of a path in 2.3ms. The codes and a sample of the data used here have been released at [25].

In the future, we plan to infer the travel time of a path for a particular driver. In addition, we would like to study the impact of other factors, such as weather conditions and air quality, on the travel time estimation of a path.

8. REFERENCES

[1] S. Chawla, Y. Zheng, J. Hu. 2012. Inferring the Root Cause in Road Traffic Anomalies. In *Proc. of IEEE ICDM 2012*.

[2] C. De Fabritiis, R. Ragona, G. Valenti. 2008. Traffic estimation and prediction based on real time floating car data. In *Proc. of IEEE ITSC 2008*.

[3] A. Hofleitner, A. Bayen. 2011. Optimal decomposition of travel times measured by probe vehicles using a statistical traffic flow model. In *Proc. of IEEE ITSC 2011*.

[4] A. Hofleitner, R. Herring, P. Abbeel, A. Bayen. 2012. Learning the dynamics of arterial traffic from probe data using a dynamic Bayesian network. *IEEE Trans. on Intelligent Transportation Systems*, 13(4), 1679-1693.

[5] B. Hull, V. Bychkovsky, Y. Zhang, K. Chen, M. Goraczko, A. Miu, E. Shih, H. Balakrishnan, S. Madden. 2006. CarTel: a distributed mobile sensor computing system. In *Proc. of ACM Sensys 2006*.

[6] J. Han, M. Kamber, J. Pei. 2006. Data mining: concepts and techniques. *Morgan kaufmann*.

[7] J. Han, J. Pei, Y. Yin. 2000. Mining frequent patterns without candidate generation. *ACM SIGMOD Record*, 29(2), 1-12.

[8] E. Jenelius, H. N. Koutsopoulos. 2013. Travel time estimation for urban road networks using low frequency probe vehicle data. *Transportation Research Part B: Methodological*, 53, 64-81.

[9] Z. Jia, C. Chen, B. Coifman, P. Varaiya. 2001. The PeMS algorithms for accurate, real-time estimates of g-factors and speeds from single-loop detectors. *IEEE Trans. on Intelligent Transportation Systems*.

[10] A. Karatzoglou, X. Amatriain, L. Baltrunas, N. Oliver. 2010. Multiverse recommendation: n-dimensional tensor factorization for context-aware collaborative filtering. In *Proc. of ACM Recsys 2010*.

[11] T. V. Larsen. Travel-Time Estimation in Road Networks Using GPS Data. White paper.

[12] W. Luo, H. Tan, L. Chen, L. M. Ni. 2013. Finding time period-based most frequent path in big trajectory data. In *Proc. of ACM SIGMOD 2013*.

[13] S. Ma, Y. Zheng, O. Wolfson. 2013. T-share: A large-scale dynamic taxi ridesharing service. In *Proc. of IEEE ICDE 2013*.

[14] K. F. Pettya, P. Bickelb, J. Jiangc, M. Ostlandb, J. Riceb, Y. Ritovd, F. Schoenbergb. 1998. Accurate estimation of travel times from single-loop detectors. *Transportation Research Part A: Policy and Practice*, 32(1), 1-17.

[15] M. Rahmani, E. Jenelius, H. N. Koutsopoulos. 2013. Route travel time estimation using low-frequency floating car data. In *Proc. of IEEE ITSC 2013*.

[16] J. Rice, E. Van Zwet. 2004. A simple and effective method for predicting travel times on freeways. *IEEE Trans. on Intelligent Transportation Systems*, 5(3), 200-207.

[17] R. Sevlian, R. Rajagopal. 2010. Travel Time Estimation Using Floating Car Data. arXiv preprint arXiv:1012.4249.

[18] R. Song, W. Sun, B. Zheng, Y. Zheng, C. Tu, S. Li. 2014. PRESS: A Novel Framework of Trajectory Compression in Road Networks. In *Proc. of VLDB 2014*.

[19] C. H. Wu, J. M. Ho, D. T. Lee. 2004. Travel-time prediction with support vector regression. *IEEE Trans. on Intelligent Transportation Systems*, 5(4), 276-281.

[20] J. Yuan, Y. Zheng, C. Zhang, W. Xie, X. Xie, G. Sun, Y. Huang. 2010. T-Drive: Driving Directions Based on Taxi Trajectories. In *Proc. of ACM SIGSPATIAL 2010*.

[21] J. Yuan, Y. Zheng, C. Zhang, X. Xie, G. Sun. 2010. An interactive-voting based map matching algorithm. In *Proc. of IEEE MDM 2010*.

[22] N. J. Yuan, Y. Zheng, L. Zhang, X. Xie. 2013. T-finder: A recommender system for finding passengers and vacant taxis. *IEEE Trans. on Knowledge and Data Engineering*, 25(10), 2390-2403.

[23] Y. Zheng, Y. Chen, Q. Li, X. Xie, W. Y. Ma. 2010. Understanding transportation modes based on GPS data for web applications. *ACM Trans. on the Web*, 4(1), 1.

[24] Zheng, Y., Capra, Li, Wolfson, O., Yang, H. 2014. Urban computing: concepts, methodologies, and applications. *ACM Trans. on Intelligent systems and Technology*, 5(3).

[25] Data released: http://research.microsoft.com/apps/pubs/?id=217493

Modeling Human Location Data with Mixtures of Kernel Densities

Moshe Lichman
Department of Computer Science
University of California, Irvine
mlichman@ics.uci.edu

Padhraic Smyth
Department of Computer Science
University of California, Irvine
smyth@ics.uci.edu

ABSTRACT

Location-based data is increasingly prevalent with the rapid increase and adoption of mobile devices. In this paper we address the problem of learning spatial density models, focusing specifically on individual-level data. Modeling and predicting a spatial distribution for an individual is a challenging problem given both (a) the typical sparsity of data at the individual level and (b) the heterogeneity of spatial mobility patterns across individuals. We investigate the application of kernel density estimation (KDE) to this problem using a mixture model approach that can interpolate between an individual's data and broader patterns in the population as a whole. The mixture-KDE approach is evaluated on two large geolocation/check-in data sets, from Twitter and Gowalla, with comparisons to non-KDE baselines, using both log-likelihood and detection of simulated identity theft as evaluation metrics. Our experimental results indicate that the mixture-KDE method provides a useful and accurate methodology for capturing and predicting individual-level spatial patterns in the presence of noisy and sparse data.

Categories and Subject Descriptors

H.2.8 [**Database Management**]: Database Application—*Data Mining, Spatial databases and GIS*

Keywords

spatial; kernel density estimation; anomaly/novelty detection; probabilistic methods; social media; user modeling

1. INTRODUCTION

Human location data is increasingly available in the modern mobile world, often in the form of geolocation tags attached to human behavioral data such as phone calls, text messages, social media activities, and more. With the widespread availability of this data there is increasing interest

KDD'14, August 24–27, 2014, New York, NY, USA.

ACM 978-1-4503-2956-9/14/08 ...$15.00.
http://dx.doi.org/10.1145/2623330.2623681.

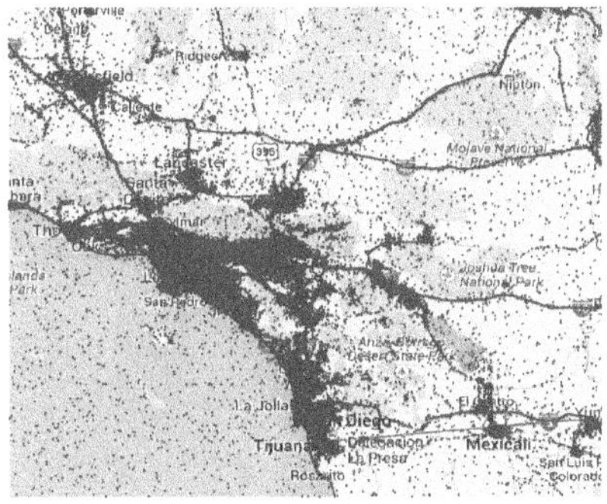

Figure 1: Geolocated Twitter tweets in southern California. Points over the ocean and sparsly populated areas are largely a result of noise in the geolocation data rather than actual locations.

across a variety of fields of study in creating accurate models to characterize the spatial distributions of populations and individuals. For example, Sadilek et al. [23] analyze the spread of infectious diseases through geolocation data from Twitter, opening up potential new approaches for real-time computational epidemiology. Cranshaw et al. [9] use Foursquare check-in data to identify local spatial clusters within urban areas, with potential applications in urban planning to economic development and resource allocation. From a commercial perspective, location-based services and personalization are becoming increasingly important to individual mobile device users, with an increasing number of applications that are location-aware, including maps, localized search results, recommender systems, and advertising [28].

In this paper we focus on the problem of developing accurate individual-level models of spatial location based on geolocated event data. The term "event" here can be interpreted in a broad context—examples include communication events such as phone calls or text messages, check-in events, social media actions, and so on. The goal is to be able to accurately characterize and predict the spatial pattern of an individual's events. The problem is challenging for two main reasons. Firstly, there is often relatively little data for many of the individuals making it difficult to build accurate models at the individual level. Secondly, there is often considerable variety and heterogeneity in the spatial pattern of events of individual users, rendering techniques such as clustering less than ideal for individual-level modeling.

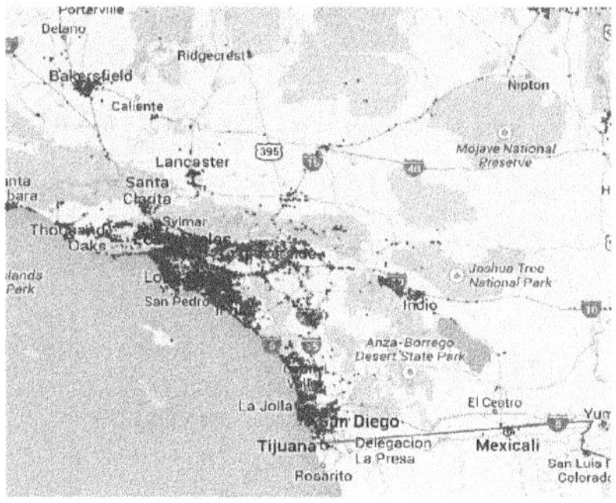

Figure 2: Gowalla checkins in southern California.

The primary contribution of our paper is a systematic approach for individual-level modeling of geolocation data based on kernel density estimates. Kernel density approaches have been relatively unexplored to date in the context of spatial modeling of geolocation data. While in principle they provide a flexible and general framework for spatial density estimation, direct application at the level of individual event data will tend to lead to significant over-fitting (because of the sparsity of data at the individual level). We propose a hierarchical extension of the traditional kernel approach that can avoid the over-fitting problem by systematically smoothing an individual's data towards the population data. We demonstrate how adaptive bandwidth techniques provide better quality density estimates compared to fixed bandwidths. Using two large geolocation data sets from Twitter and Gowalla (see Figures 1 and 2) we show that the proposed kernel method is significantly more accurate than baselines such as Gaussian mixtures for such data, in terms of the quality of predictions on out-of-sample data.

This paper is organized as follows. Section 2 provides an overview of existing approaches for modeling human location data and elaborates on the challenges of developing spatial models in practice. In section 3 we review kernel density estimation and discuss the use of adaptive bandwidth methods and in section 4 we describe our proposed mixture-KDE approach for modeling and predicting individuals' locations. In section 5 we present empirical experiments using two different geospatial/check-in data sets and using both test log-likelihood and accuracy in detection of simulated identity theft. Section 6 discusses scalability and online algorithms for the proposed approach and we conclude with a brief discussion in Section 7.

2. BACKGROUND AND RELATED WORK

2.1 Notation and Problem Definition

In this paper we consider data available in the form of individual-level geotagged events, $\mathbf{E} = \{E_1, \dots, E_N\}$ where $E_i = \{e_i^1, \dots, e_i^{n_i}\}$ and e_i^j is the jth event for the ith individual, $1 \leq i \leq N$. Each event e_i^j consists of a tuple $< i, x, y, t >$, where x and y are longitude and latitude respectively and t is a time-stamp, e.g., geotagged tweets based on GPS location.

One approach in analyzing such data is to focus on the problem of sequentially predicting a user's behavior in terms of their short-term trajectory, e.g., predicting where a user i's next event e_i^{j+1} is likely to occur in terms of location $< x, y >$ given their event history $\{e_i^1, \dots, e_i^j\}$, where events may be minutes or hours apart (e.g., Song et al. [27] and Scellato et al. [24]). In this paper we focus on a different problem, that of modeling a user's spatial patterns over a longer time-period in a more aggregate sense. Specifically, we focus on learning probability density models of the form $f_i(x, y)$ that represent the spatial density of user i's events. Given an event has occurred for individual i, the probability that it lies in any area A is $\int\int f_i(x, y)dxdy$ where the integral is over the region defined by A (see also [16]). In this context we focus in this paper on modeling $f_i(x, y)$ rather than $f_i(x, y, t)$, and only use the time dimension t to order the data. e.g. for online training and prediction. In principle it should be possible to extend the 2-dimensional spatial modeling methods proposed in this paper to include the temporal dimension, allowing for inclusion of circadian and calendar-dependent aspects of an individual's behavior.

2.2 Modeling of Discretized Locations

A widely-used approach in location modeling is to restrict attention to a finite set of known fixed locations, effectively discretizing space and turning the problem into a multivariate data analysis problem where each location represents a single dimension. One can use such representations to generate a sparse matrix consisting of individuals as rows and locations as columns, where each cell i, j contains the count of the number of events for individual i that occurred at location j. The locations (columns) can be defined in different ways. For example, one can define the columns by identifying a set of specific locations such as shops, restaurants, and so forth (e.g., see [5, 6, 9]). An alternative approach is to discretize the spatial domain into disjoint cells (e.g., via clustering), and then associate a discrete set of venues with each cell (as in Cranshaw et al. [10] who used Foursquare check-in venues) or to aggregate the counts of geolocated events within each cell (as in Lee et al. [20] and Frias-Martinez et al. [15]). The advantage of these discretized representations is that they allow the application of broad set of multivariate data analysis tools, such as clustering techniques or matrix decomposition methods. However, they do not explicitly encode spatial semantics and, as such, do not provide the ability to make predictions in continuous space, which is a primary aim in our work.

2.3 Continuous Spatial Models

In the context of continuous models, a number of authors have explored such models for individual location data in prior work. For example, Gonzalez et al. [16] and Brockmann et al. [4] explored general distributional patterns of human mobility from location data. Eagle and Pentland [12], Li et al. [21], and Cho et al. [7] demonstrated how different aspects of individuals' daily routines can be effectively extracted from traces of location data.

A simple approach to modeling an individual's spatial density $f_i(x, y)$ is to use a single Gaussian density function, i.e.,

$$\begin{aligned} f_G(x, y|\underline{\mu}_i, \Sigma_i) &= f_G(e_i|\underline{\mu}_i, \Sigma_i) \\ &= \frac{1}{(2\pi)\,|\Sigma_i|^{\frac{1}{2}}} e^{-\frac{1}{2}(e_i-\underline{\mu}_i)'\Sigma_i^{-1}(e_i-\underline{\mu}_i)} \quad (1) \end{aligned}$$

where $e_i = (x, y)$ is a 2-dimensional longitude-latitude pair, $\underline{\mu}_i$ is a 2-dimensional mean vector, and Σ_i is a 2×2 covariance matrix. The unimodal and elliptical density contours

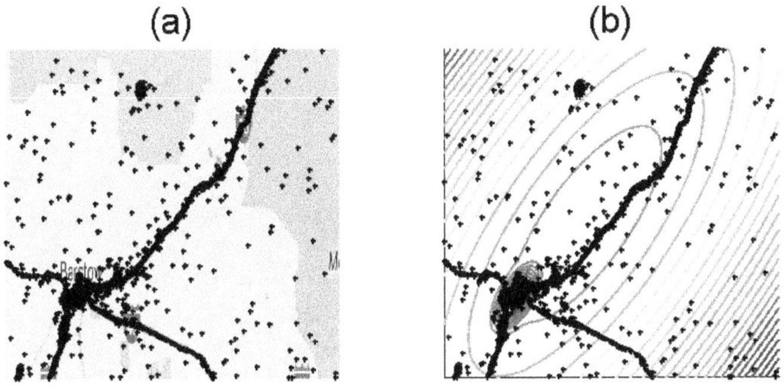

Figure 3: On the left (a): Geotagged events in the area between Los Angeles and Las Vegas near the city of Barstow, CA. (b): The contour lines of a Gaussian mixture model with 2 components. Figure best viewed in color.

of a single Gaussian are too simple to accurately represent human location data in practice. With this in mind, a finite mixture of C Gaussian densities can provide additional flexibility, defined as

$$f_{MG}(e_i|\theta_i) = \sum_{c=1}^{C} \pi_{ic} f_G(e|\underline{\mu}_{ic}, \Sigma_{ic}) \quad (2)$$

with parameters θ_i consisting of the C mixing weights $\pi_1, \ldots, \pi_C$, $\sum_c \pi_c = 1$, and means $\underline{\mu}_{ic}$ and covariance matrices Σ_{ic}, $1 \leq c \leq C$. For example, as described in Cho et al. [7], a two-component ($C = 2$) spatial model may be a useful model for capturing the bimodal variation due to "home" and "work" components in an individual's spatial data.

While the mixture model can provide additional modeling power beyond that of a single Gaussian, it has a number of practical limitations. Firstly, the number of components C required for an accurate density model may vary considerably across different individuals, and automatically and reliably determining the number of components is a non-trivial problem. Secondly, the number of data points per individual is usually skewed towards small counts. For example, in our Twitter data set 60% of the individuals have associated with them 5 or fewer events over a 2 month period (July and August 2013). This makes it challenging, if not impossible, to fit mixture models, even if the number of components C for each individual is known and fixed. A third limitation of the Gaussian mixture approach is a more pragmatic one. Human mobility is constrained by our environment resulting in sharp transitions in spatial densities, due both to natural topography (mountains, oceans) and man-made artifacts (roads, city centers, etc.). Figure 3(a) shows Twitter data for a region near Barstow, California. The spatial density of the data shows significant local variation, including regions of high density for the town of Barstow (bottom left), for the military base (top center), and along the various major roads, with very low density in the surrounding desert. Figure 3(b) shows a fitted mixture density model with two components: it is unable to capture many of the high density patterns and "wastes" considerable probability mass over sparsely populated desert regions.

3. KERNEL DENSITY ESTIMATION FOR SPATIAL LOCATION DATA

To address these limitations, we investigate the use of kernel density estimation (KDE) methods as outlined in detail in the next section. There has been limited prior work investigating the application of KDE methods in the context of human location data. Zhang and Chow [29] illustrated the advantages of KDE techniques (over Gaussian mixture models) for data from location-based social networks, but used 1-dimensional kernel densities on distances rather than 2-dimensional spatial models, and Hasan et al. [18] illustrated the use of 2-dimensional spatial KDE models for exploratory analysis of check-in data. KDE methods have also been used in application areas such as epidemiology [2], ecology [14], and marketing [11], for modeling spatial densities of *populations* of individual entities, but not for modeling spatial densities of individuals themselves.

3.1 Kernel Density Estimation

Kernel density estimation is a non-parametric method for estimating a density function from a random sample of data [25]. Let $E = \{e^1, \ldots, e^n\}$ be a set of historical events where $e^j = < x, y >$ is a two-dimensional location, $1 \leq j \leq n$, and where we have suppressed any dependence on individual i for the moment and dropped dependence on time t. We will refer to E as the training data set. A simple approach for estimating a bivariate density function from such data is to use a single fixed bandwidth h for both spatial dimensions and a Gaussian kernel function $K(\cdot)$. This results in a bivariate KDE of the following form:

$$f_{KD}(e|E, h) = \frac{1}{n} \sum_{j=1}^{n} K_h(e, e^j) \quad (3)$$

$$K_h(e, e^j) = \frac{1}{2\pi h} \exp\left(-\frac{1}{2}(e - e^j)^t \Sigma_h^{-1} (e - e^j)\right) \quad (4)$$

$$\Sigma_h = \begin{pmatrix} h & 0 \\ 0 & h \end{pmatrix}$$

where e is the location for which we wish to compute the density and $h > 0$ is a fixed scalar bandwidth parameter for all events in E. It is well known that the resulting density estimate f_{KD} can be highly sensitive to the value of the bandwidth h, producing densities that are sharply peaked around the training data points e^j when h is too small, and producing an overly smooth estimate that may omit important structure in the data (such as multiple modes) when h is too large [25].

There are a number of techniques that can be used to evaluate the quality of a particular value for the bandwidth h. One straightforward data-driven option is to measure the log-probability (or log-likelihood) of a set of test data points not used in constructing the density estimate, i.e.,

$$L(h) = \frac{1}{n_t} \sum_{r=1}^{n_t} \log f_{KD}(e^r|E, h) \quad (5)$$

where the n_t events e^r are data points not included in the training data E (e.g., a validation set). Larger values of $L(h)$ are preferred since it means that higher probability is being assigned to new unseen data. Hence, a simple approach to

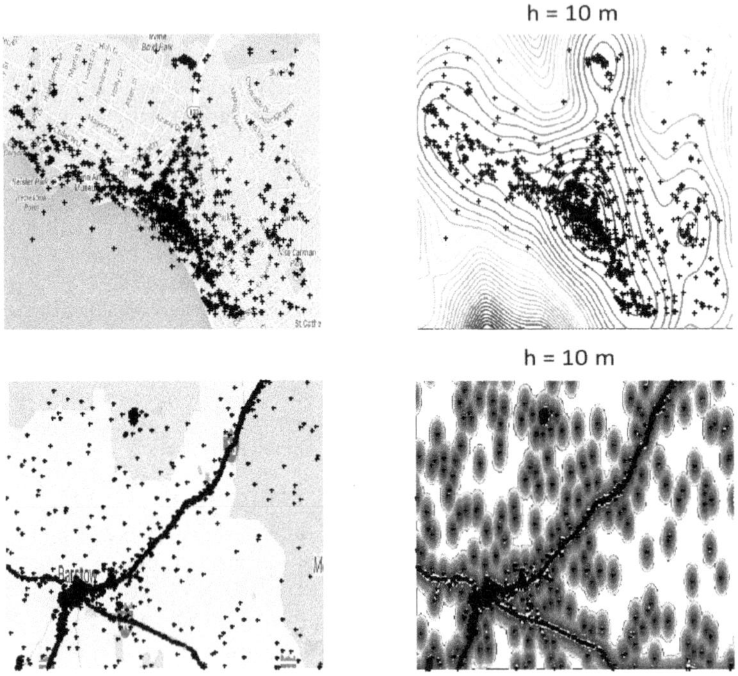

Figure 4: Left plots: Events in the city of Laguna Beach in southern California (top row) and in an area between Los Angeles and Las Vegas (bottom row). Points on the map represent observed events. Middle plots: Contour of the log-probability of a KDE model with fixed $h = 10$ meters. Right Plots: Contour of the log-probability of a KDE model with fixed $h = 400$ meters. Best viewed in color.

bandwidth selection (at least for a single bandwidth parameter h) is to perform a grid-search on h using a validation set. We will use the above out-of-sample log-probability score function $L(h)$ later in the paper for both bandwidth selection and for comparing different types of density models.

One could also use various "plug-in" estimates for h, such as that of Silverman [25, pages 86-88]. These estimates are optimal (e.g. in a mean integrated squared error sense) if the true underlying density being estimated is Gaussian, and can work well in practice for other related smooth non-Gaussian densities. However, for spatial location data we found that "plug-in" estimates for h were much too large and significantly oversmoothed the KDE results in a very poor fit due to the highly multimodal nature of location data.

At this point in the discussion it is worth noting that, in addition to its advantages in terms of flexibility, kernel density estimation has some well known drawbacks that have tended to limit its use in practice in the past, particularly in machine learning and data mining. The first drawback is that it is particularly susceptible to the curse of dimensionality, essentially requiring an exponential number of data points as a function of data dimensionality d. This is not an issue for location-data modeling since we are in the low-dimensional regime of $d = 2$. A second drawback of kernel densities (as with related "neighbor-based" methods) is the need to store all of the training data in memory at prediction time. This was arguably a relevant point 10 years or more ago when memory was relatively expensive, but in current times it is relatively inexpensive (both computationally and financially) to keep millions (or even hundreds of millions) of points accessible in main memory at prediction time. We will return to this point in more detail later in the paper—here it is sufficient to note that kernel density estimation is practical for 2-dimensional problems with millions of data points.

3.2 The Adaptive Bandwidth Method

A limitation of the approach described above is that the smoothing is homogeneous, i.e., the amount of smoothing is constant through the 2-dimensional region since the bandwidth h is fixed for all events. This does not reflect the realities of human-location data where dense urban areas will tend to have high event density and sparsely-populated rural areas will have low event density. This limitation is clearly visible in Figure 4. The two plots in the center use the same small fixed bandwidth of $h = 10$ meters, which works well for the relatively dense area of Laguna Beach (upper plot), but works poorly (overfits) for the rural area near Barstow, CA in the lower plot. If the bandwidth is increased to $h = 400$ meters, as in the two plots to the right, we find that this produces a more acceptable result in the lower plot (the rural area) but is vastly oversmoothing in the upper plot.

One approach to address this issue is to use an adaptive kernel bandwidth, several methods of which have been proposed in the literature, that relaxes the assumption of a constant fixed bandwidth parameter. Breiman et al. [3] suggested adapting the kernel bandwidth h^j *to each data point* e^j. Using this idea, we let h^j be the Euclidean distance to the kth nearest neighbor to e^j in the training data. Hence

	Bandwidth	AvgLogL
Fixed	$h = 10^{-2}$	−0.592
	$h = 10^{-3}$	−0.157
	$h = 10^{-4}$	0.139
	$h = 10^{-5}$	−0.326
Adaptive	$k = 2$	0.046
	$k = 5$	1.275
	$k = 10$	1.196
	$k = 20$	0.354

Table 1: Average log-probability scores on held-out events, comparing the fixed and the adaptive approaches for kernel density estimation for Twitter geolocation data.

we can define an adaptive bandwidth kernel density estimate as:

$$f_{KD}(e|E) = \frac{1}{n}\sum_{j=1}^{n} K_{h^j}(e, e^j) \qquad (6)$$

where K_{h^j} is defined as in Equation 4 replacing h with h^j.

Table 1 shows the results from a series of tests on a validation data set, comparing the fixed and adaptive bandwidth approaches using different values for (a) the fixed bandwidth h, and (b) the number of neighbors k (for the adaptive method). We trained the models using 100,000 randomly selected events from our Twitter data set (described in more detail later in the paper) and then computed the log-probability score (Equation 5) using a set of $n_t = 100,000$ randomly selected held-out events. From the results, we can see that the adaptive bandwidth models dominate the performance of the fixed bandwidth methods. As a sidenote, the "plug-in" methods performed significantly worse (results not shown).

4. MODELING AN INDIVIDUAL'S LOCATION DATA

So far, our predictive model $f_{KD}(e|E, h)$, does not depend on the identity of an individual i. However, our primary goal in this work is to be able to build accurate predictive spatial density models at the individual level.

4.1 Mixtures of Kernel Density Models

To address this task, we could apply the adaptive kernel density methods described above at the level of an individual (rather than for aggregations of events across a population of individuals), computing $f_{KD}(e|E_i)$ in Equation 6 where we now condition on just the individual's event data E_i rather than the events for the population E.

A significant challenge with building individual-level models in this manner is the "cold-start" problem, given that we typically have very little data for many of the individuals for whom we wish to make predictions. To address this data sparsity problem we propose a multi-scale kernel model where we use a mixture of (a) an individual's potentially noisy kernel density estimate with (b) more robust coarse-scale models[1] . More specifically we define a mixture-KDE for individual i as

$$P_{MKD}(e|E) = \sum_{c=1}^{C} \alpha_c f_{KD}(e|E^c) \qquad (7)$$

where $\alpha_1, \ldots, \ldots, \alpha_C$ are non-negative mixing weights with $\sum_c \alpha_c = 1$, and $f_{KD}(e|E^c)$ is the cth component of the mixture. Here component c is a kernel density estimate computed as a function only of a subset of points (or events) E^c. The component density estimates, f_{KD}, can be any density model, including fixed or adaptive bandwidth KDEs. We use adaptive bandwidth KDEs, with $k = 5$ (following Table 1), for all of the components in the mixture-KDEs used in this paper.

As a specific example consider a model for individual i where $C = 2$, with the first component being the individual-level kernel density with $E^1 = E_i$, and the second component being a population-level kernel density estimate with $E^2 = E$. This mixture will have the effect of smoothing the individual's density towards the population density, with more or less smoothing depending on the relative size of the α weights. Note that this mixture is significantly different in nature to the use of a Gaussian mixture for an individual's data (e.g., as in [7]). In that approach, each component typically represents a different spatial location around which an individual's activity is centered (such as "home" and "work"), whereas in the mixture-KDE each mixture component is responsible for a broader spatial scale of activity.

For C components, where $C > 2$, we can have the first component be an individual level density, and the Cth component be the population density, where the intermediate components $c = 2, \ldots, C-1$ can represent different spatial scales (such as neighborhoods, cities, states, and even countries). Given that the data sets we are using in this paper are from the Southern California region, we chose to use a 3-level model ($C = 3$), with the first and last components being the individual and population level models respectively, and the $c = 2$ model representing (approximately) the "home city" for an individual (more details on this intermediate scale component are provided later in the paper). This process of selecting additional spatial components, that are "between" the individual and the full population, is somewhat arbitrary—we chose a single intermediate component in the work below, but other choices could be explored for other applications.

From a generative perspective, one interpretation of Equation 7 above for the mixture-KDE is as follows. Assuming that the first component is based only on individual i's data, individual i has a probability α_1 of generating events in the future in a manner similar to his/her past behavior, and a probability α_c ($c = 2, \ldots, C$) of generating events in accordance with the larger "subpopulations" defined by events E^c. In this paper, in the absence of additional metadata about the individuals, we defined the larger subpopulations solely on spatial characteristics (component 2 being roughly a city, and component 3 being the whole southern California region). However, one could also define the larger subpop-

[1]A potential alternative option would be a Bayesian hierarchical model—however Bayesian modeling with kernel densities is not straightforward given that kernels don't have parameters that can be "shrunk" as in the usual Bayesian approach.

ulations based on metadata (if it were available), such as demographics, social ties, and so forth.

Another way to interpret the mixture-KDE model is that it provides a relatively simple weighting mechanism to allow us to upweight data points from individual i in the kernel density estimate and downweight points that don't belong to the individual. Given that kernel densities are defined as weighted sums over all points, the mixture-KDE can be thought of as a form of kernel density estimate where the points are given an additional level of weighting depending on what component they belong to. As a sidenote, in the results presented here we allow data points to belong to multiple sets E^c, e.g., a data point for individual i can be included in the kernel density estimate for all C components. The other option would be to only allow points to belong to a single component. Either option is fine in theory: from the weighted kernel perspective it only changes (in effect) the manner in which we are assigning weights to each point in the overall weighted sum.

4.2 Training the Model

Given a set of components $f_{KD}(e|E^c), c = 1 \ldots C$, the next step is to compute the mixing weights $\alpha_1, \ldots, \alpha_C$ in Equation 7. To do so, we randomly sample a validation set, disjoint from the training set, and use it to learn the weights as follows. For each event in the validation set, its density value under each component c is computed (using the training set for the KDE computation). This results in a fixed set of component density values on the validation data points and we can optimize over the convex set of mixing weights α_c to find the highest-likelihood combination. We used the Expectation-Maximization (EM) algorithm since it is easy to implement and converges quickly (one could use other optimization techniques such as gradient descent)—this is in essence the same as using EM for learning finite mixtures (such as Gaussian mixtures) but where the parameters of the component densities are known and fixed and one is just learning the mixture weights (see also Smyth and Wolpert [26]). An alternative to using fixed α's would be to allow the weights to vary by individual, in particular as a function of the number of data points for each individual. Preliminary exploration of this idea suggested that any additional predictive power that might be attained would likely not be justified by the additional complexity.

5. EXPERIMENTS AND RESULTS

5.1 Data Sets

For our experiments, we use two geolocation/check-in data sets: **Twitter** and **Gowalla**. Twitter is a popular microblogging service that allows the posting of short texts (up to 140 characters) and pictures. Using the Twitter API [1] we collected over 4 million public tweets from 230,450 unique individuals in the Southern California area over the period of July-August 2013. In the experiments in this paper we use data only from weekdays, i.e. Monday trough Friday. To remove repeated and bursty events we replaced tweets occurring with the same hour and within 50 meters of each other with a single effective tweet. Figure 1 shows the spatial distribution of our data set. The Gowalla data is the same data used by Cho et al. [7], containing $145,558$ events from $7,653$ unique individuals on weekdays between January and October, 2010, in the southern California area as shown in Figure 2. Training, validation, and test sets were extracted from both data sets for our experiments (details provided later).

5.2 Models Evaluated

We evaluated each of the following individual-level models in our experiments. By an "individual-level model" we mean a model that is fit to each individual i using only their data E_i, and then used for predicting future events for that individual i.

Gaussian: A Gaussian density model. We used maximum likelihood estimates for the mean and maximum a posteriori (MAP) estimates for the covariance matrices (e.g., see [22], chapter 4.6.2):

$$\mu = \hat{\mu}_{MLE}, \quad \Sigma = \lambda\Sigma_0 + (1-\lambda)\hat{\Sigma}_{MLE}, \quad \lambda = \frac{n_0}{n_0 + n_i}$$

where the prior parameters were set to $n_0 = 3$ and $\sigma = 5$ kilometers (for the diagonal on the prior covariance) via a grid search over the log-likelihood on a validation set across all individuals.

Gaussian Mixture Model (GMM): Two different Gaussian mixture models with $C = 2$ and $C = 4$ components. The models were fit using the EM algorithm. Again, we used maximum likelihood to estimate the μ_c and MAP estimates for the Σ_c. Parameters for the priors were also determined on a validation set.

Fixed KDE: A fixed bandwidth kernel density estimate using Equation 3. The validation set was used to determine a single fixed bandwidth, $h = 5.3$ kilometers, for all users.

Adaptive KDE: An adaptive kernel density estimate using Equation 6. The validation set was used to determine a nearest-neighbor value of $k = 5$ for all users.

In addition, for our log-likelihood experiments we evaluated a single "global" population model (Population KDE) using an adaptive kernel density estimate ($k = 5$) based on **all** data points in the training set (i.e., not an individual-level model).

For our mixture-KDE model we used 3 components, the first and last corresponding to individual i and to the full population, respectively. Each component is an adaptive bandwidth KDE with $k = 5$ neighbors. For the middle component we divided the southern Calfornia area into 81 regions corresponding to a 9×9 array of equal-sized grid boxes. Each individual i was associated with the region that contains the majority of their individual events—thus, the $c = 2$ component in the model represents the scale of a local region or city. A similar approach was used in prior work for finding the "home" location of an individual [7]. Using EM to determine the mixture weights resulted in the following values for the α's: 0.85 for α_1 (the individual level), 0.12 for α_2 (the region level), and 0.03 for α_3 (the population level) for the Twitter data set, and $\alpha_1 = 0.5$, $\alpha_2 = 0.3$ and $\alpha_3 = 0.2$ for the Gowalla data set.

5.3 Evaluation using Log-Likelihood

The training set for the Twitter data consists of all events recorded for the month of July, 2013. The test set for Twit-

Model	Individual		Event	
	Mean	Median	Mean	Median
Gaussian	-0.586	0.151	-0.242	1.357
GMM (C = 2)	-0.469	0.221	0.001	1.676
GMM (C = 4)	-0.474	0.279	-0.015	1.712
Fixed KDE	-1.025	-0.714	-0.869	-0.688
Adaptive KDE	-7.154	0.446	(*)	-4.908
Population KDE	2.014	0.563	0.784	0.237
Mixture-KDE	**4.279**	**4.312**	**5.293**	**6.302**

Table 2: Average log-probabilities on the test data for individuals and events from the Twitter data set.

Model	Individual		Event	
	Mean	Median	Mean	Median
Gaussian	-1.513	0.008	-1.133	1.027
GMM (C = 2)	-1.532	0.308	-0.956	1.412
GMM (C = 4)	-1.522	-0.479	-0.958	1.471
Fixed KDE	-1.136	-0.749	-1.092	-0.742
Adaptive KDE	(*)	-0.247	-3.288	1.355
Population KDE	3.388	1.237	4.021	0.923
Mixture-KDE	**6.599**	**6.296**	**6.568**	**2.619**

Table 3: Average log-probabilities on the test data for individuals and events from the Gowalla data set.

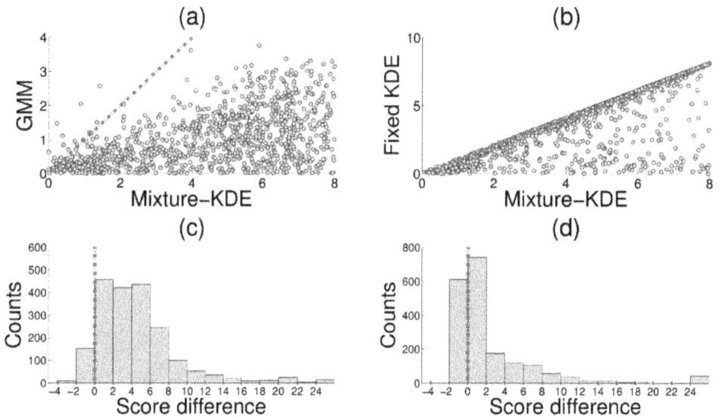

Figure 5: Upper plots (a) and (b): scatter plots for a sample of test set log-probability scores for Twitter individuals with (a) individual Gaussian mixtures ($C = 4$) versus the mixture-KDE, and (b) individual fixed-KDE versus the mixture-KDE. Lower plots (c) and (d): histograms of the score differences per event for the mixture-KDE minus the score of the corresponding model on the y-axis in the upper plot.

ter is all of the events in August 2013 for a randomly selected set of 2000 individuals, selected from the individuals that have at least 2 events in July. To create the Gowalla training set we used the data from the months of January to June, 2010. The test set for Gowalla is all of the events from the months of July to October, 2010 for a randomly selected set of 1000 individuals, selected from the individuals that have at least 2 events in the months of January to June, 2010. A validation set was generated for each of the Twitter and Gowalla data sets by setting aside approximately 37,000 and 25,000 randomly selected events from each training data set.

We built models on the data from our training data set and computed the test set log-probability score of the events in the test set, under each model. We report results both in terms of the mean and median log-likelihood per event, and the mean and median log-likelihood per individual (the latter giving equal weight to individuals, the former to events). The mean and median scores, for both individual and event-level scores, are shown in Tables 2 and 3 for the Twitter and Gowalla data sets respectively. A (*) indicates that the test log-likelihood was not computed due to numerical underflow. The mixture-KDE model clearly outperforms all other methods, on both data sets, for all metrics, assigning significantly higher log-probability to the test events than any of the other modeling approaches. Figures 5 and 6 show the comparison between the mixture-KDE approach and the GMM (on the left) and fixed KDE (on the right) when looking at each individual separately, again clearly showing the improvement of the mixture-KDE approach over the other methods.

5.4 Evaluation using Simulated Identity Theft

We now compare the different models by using a simulated real-world application based on identity theft. Over 8 million people are victims of identity theft every year in the United States alone, with an annual cost exceeding 4 billion dollars and over 32 million hours spent by individuals to resolve the problem [8]. To simulate identify theft we replaced the geolocation events for an individual over a specific time-window with the geolocation events of a *different individual* and then tested the ability of our models to detect the resulting anomalous spatial patterns of events.

We used the Twitter data set for our experiment since the Gowalla data set did not show any significant differences for this problem between the different models (single Gaussian, mixtures of Gaussians, various forms of KDEs). We believe this may be due to the fact that our data set for Gowalla has fewer individuals than Twitter, and that these individuals use many of the same checkins, limiting the effectiveness of Gowalla data for detecting "identity switching".

Focusing on the Twitter data set, we defined the training set to be all events in the month of July, 2013. The test set consists of two types of event streams in August, 2013: events for normal "control" individuals and events with simulated identity theft. The control individuals are a randomly selected set of 950 individuals that have at least 2 events in July and at least 10 events in August. The individuals with simulated identity theft correspond to a set of 50 randomly selected individuals with at least 2 events in July. For each of these 50, we then replaced their real test data events in August, with the set of events from a different randomly selected individual, among individuals who have at least 10 events in August. In this manner, our test data has 50 event sets where the spatial distribution for each sets will in general look different (in a realistic manner, as if a different individual were using the Twitter account), compared to the event sets for the "true" individual in the training data from July.

To evaluate the different models we computed a surprise index S_i for each individual i, defined as the negative log-probability of individual i's events in the test data set rela-

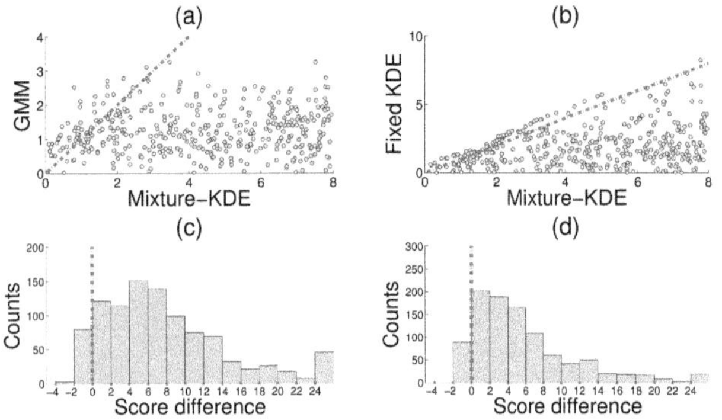

Figure 6: Upper plots (a) and (b): scatter plots for a sample of test set log-probability scores for Gowalla individuals with (a) individual Gaussian mixtures ($C = 4$) versus the mixture-KDE, and (b) individual fixed-KDE versus the mixture-KDE. Lower plots (c) and (d): histograms of the score differences per event for the mixture-KDE minus the score of the corresponding model on the y-axis in the upper plot.

tive to a model constructed on historical data:

$$S_i = -\frac{1}{n_i}\sum_{r=1}^{n_i}\log \hat{f}_i(e_i^r) \qquad (8)$$

where e_i^r is the rth event in the test data set for individual i, and $\hat{f}_i$ is the density estimate for individual i constructed using the training data. The larger the surprise score S_i, then the more anomalous the events e_i^r are relative to the model $\hat{f}_i$. In these experiments we used all of the models that we used in the log-likelihood experiments as described earlier in the paper, except for the population model which is unable to generate rankings at the individual level.

We used a grid search on the validation set (defined in a similar manner to the training-test setup above) to determine various parameters of the models, where the parameter values were selected to optimize precision on the identity theft task. In general, optimizing for precision results in different parameter values for the various models compared to optimizing for likelihood. The priors of the Gaussian mixture model resulted in $n_0 = 0.1$ and $\sigma = 5$ kilometers. The optimal parameters for the individual KDE were estimated to be a fixed bandwidth of $h = 3$ kilometers and $k = 5$ for the adaptive method. The optimal mixture weights for the mixture-KDE model were $\alpha_1 = 0.9$ (the individual level), $\alpha_2 = 0.08$ (the region level), and $\alpha_3 = 0.02$ for the population model.

For each model, we then ranked all of the individuals in the test data by their surprise index S_i and computed precision relative to the known ground truth in terms of which individuals correspond to simulated identity theft and which to the controls. Table 4 shows the precision at 20, the fraction of simulated identity theft cases correctly detected in the top 20 ranked individuals. These precision numbers are the result of averaging over 50 different randomly generated test sets, using the methodology described earlier. The rows correspond to different models and the columns correspond to 3 different scenarios: computing the surprise-index per individual based on their first n events (in time) for each individual in the test set, with $n = 1, n = 5, n = 10$. Table 5 shows the same information for a "cold-start" scenario, where now test sets are generated for simulated identity theft and normal individuals (using the same general procedure as before) who are constrained to have between 2 and 5 events in their training data (compared to any number greater than or equal to 2 for the general case).

	$n = 1$	$n = 5$	$n = 10$
Gaussian	**0.612**	0.470	0.325
GMM (C=2)	0.320	0.240	0.160
GMM (C=4)	0.240	0.170	0.130
Fixed KDE	0.500	0.500	0.460
Adaptive KDE	0.432	0.309	0.274
Mixture-KDE	0.531	**0.747**	**0.816**

Table 4: Average precision (over 50 runs) for the top 20 ranked individuals in the test data, as a function of the number of observed test events n_t per individual.

	$n = 1$	$n = 5$	$n = 10$
Gaussian	0.379	0.341	0.240
GMM (C=2)	0.260	0.220	0.150
GMM (C=4)	0.240	0.190	0.150
Fixed KDE	0.330	0.370	0.320
Adaptive KDE	0.296	0.188	0.142
Mixture-KDE	**0.459**	**0.589**	**0.644**

Table 5: Average precision (over 50 runs) for the top 20 ranked individuals in the test data, as a function of the number of observed test events per individual, for "cold-start" individuals (as defined in the text).

The results in the two tables show that the mixture-KDE model dominates all of the other methods, with a Wilcoxon signed rank p-value of $p < 0.02$, except for the Gaussian model in the non-cold-case situation for $n = 1$. This may be due to the fact that for a simulated identity theft case, a sampled new event has a high probability of coming from a popular area.

The mixture-KDE model improves as it sees more events in the test set (as n increases from left to right in the table). However, the other methods all decrease in precision as n increases. On closer inspection we found that this was being caused by their sensitivity to false alarms, i.e., with more data points per individual there is a higher chance that a control individual (a false alarm) will have an event in the test data that is not close spatially to the individual's events in the training data, resulting in a high-surprise score and a high rank for that individual. The mixture-KDE is more robust to this type of variation, consistent with results earlier in the paper in terms of log-likelihood.

6. SCALABILITY AND ONLINE COMPUTATION

6.1 Scalability

Our experience suggests that kernel density models are quite scalable for two-dimensional data, and can likely be scaled to millions of individuals and hundreds of millions of events relatively easily. To compute the density of a new

	Individual		Event	
Model	Mean	Median	Mean	Median
Mixture-KDE	4.279	4.321	5.293	6.302
Online	**4.892**	**4.913**	**5.788**	**6.531**

	Individual		Event	
Model	Mean	Median	Mean	Median
Mixture-KDE	6.599	6.296	6.568	2.619
OnLine	**6.987**	**6.742**	**7.432**	**3.022**

Table 6: Predictive log-probability scores, averaged over individuals and events for a) Twitter (top table) and b) Gowalla (bottom table). "Online" is the online version of the Mixture-KDE model as described in the text.

point e, given a training data set E, we need to compute the contribution of each training point to e's density, as shown in Equation 3. In general, storing the N training data points requires $O(N)$ space and computing the density for a new event will result in time complexity $O(dN)$ where d is the dimension of the data (here $d = 2$). In our implementation of the KDE models for the results in this paper we used k-d trees, as described in [17], to further speedup our KDE implementation. This effectively computes only contributions from nearby points to e, based on a k-d tree partition of the 2-dimensional space, resulting in a significant reduction in computation time. We coded our algorithm for kernel density estimation in Java[2] and ran the code on an 8-core 2.4GHz Intel Xeon CPU with 8 hyper threads and 48 GB of RAM memory. Using one million events as training data points, the average time for computing the density of a new event is 8 milliseconds, making the model tractable for large data sets. Additional speed-ups could be achieved for example by distributed computation since the density contribution from different subsets of points are independent from one another. Hence, one can "split" the training data set into disjoint groups and aggregate the density contributions in parallel.

6.2 Online Prediction

The results presented up to this point in the paper have used a batch approach to training and testing. A useful feature of the kernel density approach, including the mixture-KDE, is that it is quite easy to implement an *online* version that can sequentially be updated as new events arrive in streaming fashion. When a new event e arrives we simply add it to the training set. For the adaptive bandwidth approach, every time the training set changes, we need to find the k neighbors of the new point, as well as potentially needing to find new neighbors for all N existing points. In practice, however, only a very small fraction of existing points will need to have their neighbors updated. Other parameters of the mixture-KDE model, such as mixture weights for the components, are likely to change relatively slowly over time, and can be periodically updated on validation subsets.

Tables 6(a) and 6(b) show predictive log-probability scores for the same training and test data used earlier for likelihood experiments, but now, each sequential test event is included in the training data in an online fashion before computing the log-probability of the next event. The online model shows a significant systematic improvement in predictive scores compared to the batch model, suggesting that online adaptation is beneficial with human location data. This certainly makes intuitive sense, as we expect individual behavior to be non-stationary and changing over time. In a practical application of an online model one would likely incorporate some downweighting (e.g., via exponential weighting) or windowing of events that are further back in time, allowing the model to adapt to changes in individual behavior.

7. CONCLUSIONS

In this paper we proposed and investigated a systematic framework for modeling human location data at an individual level using kernel density estimation methods. We found that adaptive bandwidth methods had distinct advantages for this type of data over fixed bandwidth methods. To address the problem of data sparsity at the individual level we introduced the idea of mixtures of kernel density estimates at different spatial scales. This allows smoothing of an individual's model towards the aggregate population model, motivated by the desire for better generalization to new data. Experimental results on both Twitter and Gowalla data sets systematically illustrated the benefits of our approach in terms of predictive power: kernel methods were systematically better than mixture models, adaptive bandwidth methods were systematically better than fixed bandwidth methods, and mixing individual and population estimates via the multi-scale mixture-KDE model outperformed all other approaches.

There are a number of extensions that could be further explored. One example is the discrete-location effect in data sets such as Twitter and Gowalla, namely that certain specific longitude-latitude locations are over-represented in the data. This suggests that additional gains in accuracy could be gained by modeling such locations as discrete delta-functions (with probability weights) in the kernel model, rather than using the simpler standard kernel approach. Another aspect we did not pursue in this paper is including time in our models—for many applications (such as identity theft detection) it would beneficial to have a distribution over time as well as space for individual events. Initial experiments in this direction suggestion that including time is not as straightforward as simply extending the spatial kernel densities from 2 to 3 dimensions—the temporal dimension, not surprisingly, has distinctly different characteristics than the spatial dimensions. Nonetheless we anticipate that spatio-temporal kernel density models can be developed in a relatively straightforward manner.

Acknowledgements

This work was supported by a gift from the University Affairs Committee at Xerox Corporation, by the National Science Foundation under award IIS-1320527, and by Office of Naval Research under MURI grant N00014-08-1-1015.

[2]The code is available for download at http://www.datalab.uci.edu/resources/

8. REFERENCES

[1] Twitter streaming api. *https://dev.twitter.com/docs/using-search.*

[2] J. Bithell. An application of density estimation to geographical epidemiology. *Statistics in Medicine*, 9(6):691–701, 1990.

[3] L. Breiman, W. Meisel, and E. Purcell. Variable kernel estimates of multivariate densities. *Technometrics*, 19(2):135–144, 1977.

[4] D. Brockmann, L. Hufnagel, and T. Geisel. The scaling laws of human travel. *Nature*, 439(7075):462–465, 2006.

[5] J. Chang and E. Sun. Location 3: How users share and respond to location-based data on social networking sites. In *Proceedings of the Fifth International AAAI Conference on Weblogs and Social Media*, pages 74–80, 2011.

[6] C. Cheng, H. Yang, I. King, and M. R. Lyu. Fused matrix factorization with geographical and social influence in location-based social networks. In Proceedings of the 26th *AAAI*, pages 17-23, 2012.

[7] E. Cho, S. A. Myers, and J. Leskovec. Friendship and mobility: user movement in location-based social networks. In *Proceedings of the 17th ACM SIGKDD International Conference on Knowledge Discovery and Data Mining*, pages 1082–1090, ACM, 2011.

[8] Federal Trade Commission Identity theft survey report, 2006. *URL http://www.ftc.gov/reports/federal-trade-commission-2006-identity-theft-survey-report-prepared-commission-synovate*

[9] J. Cranshaw, R. Schwartz, J. I. Hong, and N. M. Sadeh. The livehoods project: Utilizing social media to understand the dynamics of a city. In Proceedings of the Sixth *ICWSM*, pages 58-65, 2012.

[10] J. Cranshaw and T. Yano. Seeing a home away from the home: Distilling proto-neighborhoods from incidental data with latent topic modeling. In *CSSWC Workshop at NIPS*, 2010.

[11] N. Donthu and R. T. Rust. Estimating geographic customer densities using kernel density estimation. *Marketing Science*, 8(2):191–203, 1989.

[12] N. Eagle and A. S. Pentland. Eigenbehaviors: Identifying structure in routine. *Behavioral Ecology and Sociobiology*, 63(7):1057–1066, 2009.

[13] M. D. Escobar and M. West. Bayesian density estimation and inference using mixtures. *Journal of the American Statistical Association*, 90(430):577–588, 1995.

[14] J. Fieberg. Kernel density estimators of home range: smoothing and the autocorrelation red herring. *Ecology*, 88(4):1059–1066, 2007.

[15] V. Frias-Martinez, V. Soto, H. Hohwald, and E. Frias-Martinez. Characterizing urban landscapes using geolocated tweets. In *Privacy, Security, Risk and Trust (PASSAT), 2012 International Conference on and 2012 International Confernece on Social Computing (SocialCom)*, pages 239–248. IEEE, 2012.

[16] M. C. Gonzalez, C. A. Hidalgo, and A.-L. Barabasi. Understanding individual human mobility patterns. *Nature*, 453(7196):779–782, 2008.

[17] A. G. Gray and A. W. Moore. Nonparametric density estimation: Toward computational tractability. In Proceeding of the 2003 SIAM International Conference of Data Mining, pages 203-211, 2003.

[18] S. Hasan, X. Zhan, and S. V. Ukkusuri. Understanding urban human activity and mobility patterns using large-scale location-based data from online social media. In *Proceedings of the 2nd ACM SIGKDD International Workshop on Urban Computing*, ACM, 2013.

[19] K. Joseph, C. H. Tan, and K. M. Carley. Beyond local, categories and friends: clustering foursquare users with latent topics. In *Proceedings of the 2012 ACM Conference on Ubiquitous Computing*, pages 919–926. ACM, 2012.

[20] R. Lee, S. Wakamiya, and K. Sumiya. Urban area characterization based on crowd behavioral lifelogs over twitter. *Personal and Ubiquitous Computing*, 17(4):605–620, 2013.

[21] Z. Li, B. Ding, J. Han, R. Kays, and P. Nye. Mining periodic behaviors for moving objects. In *Proceedings of the 16th ACM SIGKDD International Conference on Knowledge Discovery and Data Mining*, pages 1099–1108. ACM, 2010.

[22] K. P. Murphy. *Machine Learning: A Probabilistic Perspective.* MIT Press, 2012.

[23] A. Sadilek, H. A. Kautz, and V. Silenzio. Modeling spread of disease from social interactions. In *Proceedings of the Sixth AAAI International Conference on Weblogs and Social Media (ICWSM)*, pages 322-329, 2012.

[24] S. Scellato, M. Musolesi, C. Mascolo, V. Latora, and A. T. Campbell. Nextplace: a spatio-temporal prediction framework for pervasive systems. In *Pervasive Computing*, pages 152–169. Springer, 2011.

[25] B. W. Silverman. *Density Estimation for Statistics and Data Analysis.* CRC press, 1986.

[26] P. Smyth and D. Wolpert. Linearly combining density estimators via stacking. *Machine Learning*, 36(1-2):59–83, 1999.

[27] L. Song, D. Kotz, R. Jain, and X. He. Evaluating next-cell predictors with extensive wi-fi mobility data. *Mobile Computing, IEEE Transactions on*, 5(12):1633–1649, 2006.

[28] S. J. Vaughan-Nichols. Will mobile computing's future be location, location, location? *Computer*, 42(2):14–17, 2009.

[29] J.-D. Zhang and C.-Y. Chow. igslr: personalized geo-social location recommendation: a kernel density estimation approach. In *Proceedings of the 21st ACM SIGSPATIAL International Conference on Advances in Geographic Information Systems*, pages 324–333. ACM, 2013.

A Cost-Effective Recommender System for Taxi Drivers

Meng Qu
Rutgers Business School
daisymengqu@hotmail.com

Hengshu Zhu
University of Science and Technology of China
zhuhengshu@gmail.com

Junming Liu
Rutgers, the State University of New Jersey
jl1433@scarletmail.rutgers.edu

Guannan Liu
Tsinghua University
guannliu@gmail.com

Hui Xiong*
Rutgers Business School
Rutgers University
hxiong@rutgers.edu

ABSTRACT

The GPS technology and new forms of urban geography have changed the paradigm for mobile services. As such, the abundant availability of GPS traces has enabled new ways of doing taxi business. Indeed, recent efforts have been made on developing mobile recommender systems for taxi drivers using Taxi GPS traces. These systems can recommend a sequence of pick-up points for the purpose of maximizing the probability of identifying a customer with the shortest driving distance. However, in the real world, the income of taxi drivers is strongly correlated with the effective driving hours. In other words, it is more critical for taxi drivers to know the actual driving routes to minimize the driving time before finding a customer. To this end, in this paper, we propose to develop a cost-effective recommender system for taxi drivers. The design goal is to maximize their profits when following the recommended routes for finding passengers. Specifically, we first design a net profit objective function for evaluating the potential profits of the driving routes. Then, we develop a graph representation of road networks by mining the historical taxi GPS traces and provide a Brute-Force strategy to generate optimal driving route for recommendation. However, a critical challenge along this line is the high computational cost of the graph based approach. Therefore, we develop a novel recursion strategy based on the special form of the net profit function for searching optimal candidate routes efficiently. Particularly, instead of recommending a sequence of pick-up points and letting the driver decide how to get to those points, our recommender system is capable of providing an entire driving route, and the drivers are able to find a customer for the largest potential profit by following the recommendations. This makes our recommender system more practical and profitable than other existing recommender systems. Finally, we carry out extensive experiments on a real-world data set collected from the San Francisco Bay area and the experimental results clearly validate the effectiveness of the proposed recommender system.

*Contact author.

KDD'14, August 24–27, 2014, New York, NY, USA.

http://dx.doi.org/10.1145/2623330.2623668.

Categories and Subject Descriptors

H.2.8.d [**Information Technology and Systems**]: Database Applications - Data Mining

General Terms

Algorithms, Experimentation

Keywords

Cost-Effective, Mobile Recommender Systems, Taxi Drivers

1. INTRODUCTION

Recent years have witnessed the rapid development of wireless sensor technologies in mobile environments, such as GPS, Wi-Fi and RFID. The advances of such technologies indicate the possibility to change radically the existing methods of doing taxi business. Indeed, recent efforts have been made on providing personalized mobile services to taxi drivers through the analysis of Taxi GPS traces. In general, there are three existing ways to provide such services. The first way is to focus on the development of the fastest driving route [25, 26, 28, 27, 14], which shows the fastest driving route from the current location to the destination. The second way is to provide a sequence of pick-up points for taxi drivers. The goal is to allow the taxi driver to find a customer within the shortest driving distance [8]. Finally, an alternative service is to strike a balance between the needs of taxi drivers and passengers [24].

Indeed, most of the existing mobile recommender systems for taxi business are focused on extracting energy-efficient transportation patterns from historical location traces and recommending a sequence of potential pick-up points for taxi drivers [25, 26, 8]. However, in the real world, the income of taxi drivers is strongly correlated with the effective driving hours which may not necessarily lead to energy-efficiency. In other words, it is more critical for taxi drivers to know the actual driving routes to minimize the driving time before finding a customer. Taxi drivers usually rent their cabs from taxi companies for a fixed time period. There is a fixed per-hour cost associated with gas usage and the rental fee. The profit of a taxi driver really depends on how much money the driver can make per hour; that is, how effectively the drivers can make use of their driving time.

To that end, in this paper, we propose to develop a cost-effective recommender system for taxi drivers. The design goal is to maximize their profits when following the recommended routes for finding passages. In particular, the proposed system can provide an entire driving route rather than just recommending a sequence of discrete pick-up points and letting the driver decide how to get to those points, and the drivers are able to find a customer with the largest potential profit by following the recommended route. This makes our recommender system more practical and profitable than other existing mobile recommender systems [8].

To achieve the design goal and recommend an entire driving route which allows the taxi drivers to maximize their profits by following the recommended route, there are several factors to be considered. First, it is necessary to know the pick-up probabilities along the route. Second, it should be able to compute the profit that drivers can make after picking up a customer somewhere on the route. Third, the potential driving time on the route should be estimated. Indeed, all these issues can be solved by mining the historical Taxi GPS traces. However, a key challenge is how to combine the impact of all these factors. Indeed, in this paper, we develop a net profit objective function to collectively integrate the impact of the above factors. The net profit objective function can be used for evaluating the potential profit of the driving routes. Then, we develop a graph representation of road networks and provide a Brute-Force strategy to generate optimal driving route for finding passengers. In addition, the search for candidate driving routes is essential a combinatorial search problem. The computational cost is prohibited. Therefore, we further develop a pruning strategy to reduce the search space and improve the computational performances. In particular, we first change the graph representation of road networks to a new structure, namely a recursion tree, based on the special form of the net profit function. Then, we design a novel recursion strategy based on the recursion tree for searching optimal candidate routes in an efficient way.

When recommending the driving routes to the taxi drivers, we also provide a strategy for making a better load balance for the recommendations happening at the same location. Specifically, we exploit a minimum redundant strategy. For each target location, we transform each candidate route in the recommended list associated with this location into a direction vector. Then, we are able to calculate the correlations among this candidate route in terms of their directions. If there are several requests happening at the same location within a short time period, this minimum redundant strategy can provide recommendations in a load balanced way.

Finally, we carry out extensive experiments on a real-world data set collected from the San Francisco Bay area and the experimental results clearly validate both the effectiveness and efficiency of the proposed recommender system.

Overview. The remainder of this paper is organized as follows. Section 2 shows the related works of this paper. In Section 3, we formulate the problem of cost-effective recommendations for taxi drivers and introduce some preliminaries. Section 4 provides a detailed description of our recommender system. In Section 5, we report the experimental results. Finally, Section 6 concludes this work.

2. RELATED WORK

In the literature, many efforts have been devoted to building personalized recommender systems, such as content-based recommendation [13], collaborative filtering based recommendation [17] as well as the hybrid recommendation [15]. Furthermore, some recommender systems [2] also aim to address the information overloaded problem by identifying user interests and providing personalized suggestions. However, those traditional recommender systems [4, 7, 11] are more focused on recommendation of online information, such as online movie, article, book or webpage. In most of the cases, the research data are based on user ratings, which are very different from the data collected in mobile environment.

The development of personalized recommender systems in mobile and pervasive environments is much more challenging than developing recommender systems from traditional domains due to the complexity of spatial data and intrinsic spatio-temporal relationships, the unclear roles of context-aware information [30], and the increasing availability of environment sensing capabilities. Those unique challenges are actually inherit in the mobile data we have. Indeed, recommender systems in the mobile environments have been studied before [1, 3, 5, 6, 12, 19, 20]. For instance, the works in [1, 5] target at the development of mobile tourist guides. Zhu *et al.* proposed a uniform framework of personalized context-aware recommendation for mobile users. The framework can discover users' personal context-aware preferences by mining the context logs of many mobile users. Heijden *et al.* [30] have discussed some technological opportunities associated with mobile recommendation systems [20]. Averjanova *et al.* have developed a map-based mobile recommender system that can provide users with some personalized recommendations [3]. However, the above prior works are mostly based on user ratings or interactions, and corresponding recommender systems are developed for smart mobile devices, such as mobile phones. Indeed, the problem of building mobile recommender systems for taxi business remains pretty much open.

Recently, the abundant availability of Taxi GPS traces has enabled new ways of doing taxi business. Plenty efforts have been made on developing mobile recommender systems for taxi drivers by using Taxi GPS traces. These systems can extract energy-efficient transportation patterns from historical location traces and recommending potential pick-up points for taxi drivers. For example, Ge *et al.* [8] defined a novel problem of mobile sequential recommendation by leveraging the historical GPS data from taxi drivers. By solving this problem, a novel energy-efficient mobile recommender system has been developed. This system can provide a optimal sequence of pick-up points for taxi drivers. Also, Powell *et al.* [16] proposed a grid-based method to suggest the profit locations for taxi drivers by constructing a spatio-temporal profitability map. In addition, Yuan *et al.* [24, 25, 26] have carried out a series of studies on mobile intelligence by leveraging taxi trajectories, such as pick-up points detection based on probabilistic models, and location recommendation for both the taxi drivers and customers. Different from the above studies, in this paper, we propose to develop a novel recommender system that is capable of providing an entire driving route instead of discrete pick-up points, and the drivers are able to find a customer for the largest potential profit by following the recommendations.

3. PROBLEM FORMULATION

In this section, we first introduce some preliminaries, and

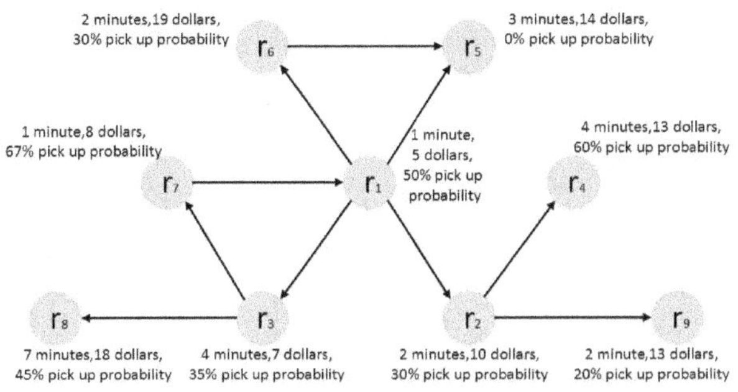

Figure 1: An example of a route segment network.

then formally define the problem of Maximum Net Profit (MNP) recommendation for taxi drivers.

3.1 Preliminaries

Here, we first introduce some basic concepts used throughout this paper.

3.1.1 Road Network Formulation

DEFINITION 1 (ROAD SEGMENT). *A long street can be separated into several road segments r by its crossroads. Specifically, each segment r is associated with a start point $r.s$ and an end point $r.e$. Moreover, each segment r also has several adjacent segments forming a set $r.next[]$, which satisfies $\forall r_i \in r.next[]$ iff. $r.e = r_i.s$.*

DEFINITION 2 (ROUTE). *A route R is a sequence of connected road segments, i.e., $R = (r_1 \to r_2 \to \cdots \to r_M)$, where $r_{k+1}.s = r_k.e$ $(1 \le k < M)$. The start point and the end point of a route R can be represented as $R.s = r_1.s$ and $R.e = r_n.e$.*

DEFINITION 3 (ROAD SEGMENT NETWORK). *The road segment network G can be represented by a graph $G =< V, E >$, where $V = \{r_i\}$ is the node set that consists of all road segments and E is the edge set, which satisfies $\exists e_{ij} \in E$ iff. $r_j \in r_i.next[]$.*

Figure 1 demonstrates an example of the road segment network. In this graph, each node represents for a road segment. Note that, each edge only has one direction. This is because we do not allow taxi drivers to drive back and forth in the same single road segment, which is not recommended in real life and has a high potential to result in traffic jam and accidents. However, taxi drivers can take a loop through three road segments, such as nodes r_1, r_3 and r_7, which can form a loop for drivers.

3.1.2 Calculation of Net Profit

For each segment r, the net profit $g(r)$ consists of two components, namely *potential earning* and *potential cost*. Specifically, we define the potential earnings of segment r as $e(r)$, which can be computed by

$$e(r) = \frac{\sum_{i=1}^{N_r} Fee(i;r)}{N_r} P(r), \qquad (1)$$

where N_r is the number of picking-up passengers in segment r during a given time period, $Fee(i;r)$ is the earning from the i-th pick-up passenger and $P(r)$ is the pick-up possibility in segment r, which will be introduced in Section 4. Meanwhile, the potential cost of segment r, i.e., $c(r)$, can be computed by

$$c(r) = (1 - P(r))(L(r) \cdot Gas + T(r) \cdot CompanyFee), \qquad (2)$$

where $L(r)$ is the length of segment r, Gas is the price of Gas per unite distance (e.g., per mile), $T(r)$ is the traveling time through segment r and $CompanyFee$ is the opportunity cost per unit time (e.g., per minute). Indeed, $T(r)$ is sensitive to the real-time traffic conditions. For example, a traffic jam will result in a high $T(r)$, and thus bring a high cost of $T(r) \cdot CompanyFee$. In this case, the segment will not recommended by our model. Therefore, the net profit of segment r, i.e., $g(r)$, can be computed by

$$g(r) = e(r) - c(r). \qquad (3)$$

Based on the above, we can further define the net profit for each route R. Specifically, given a route $R = (r_1 \to r_2 \to \cdots \to r_M)$ starting from r_1, its total net profit can be computed by

$$G(R, r_1, M) = g(r_1) + \sum_{i=2}^{M} g(r_i) \prod_{j=1}^{i-1} (1 - P(r_j)). \qquad (4)$$

Intuitively, the net profit of route R is the sum of the net profit of road segments $\{r_i\}$ contained in R, which is weighted by the possibility of not picking up any passenger in previous segments (i.e., r_1 to r_{i-1}).

Indeed, with the possibility weights in net profit, the taxi driver will not consider the segments which are far away from her current location because the expected profit there is very low. To be more specific, we can define the average increasing rate of net profit as $\tau = \frac{<G(R,r_i,M+1)>-<G(R,r_i,M)>}{<G(R,r_i,M+1)>}$ to indicate the profit increase when increasing one more road segment in the route. Figure 2 shows the trend of the increasing rate with respect to different numbers of increased road segments and different pick-up possibilities. We can observe that the increasing rate is less than 10% after increasing more than 5 road segments. Indeed, the average pick-up probability of each road segment in our experiments is always less than 0.1, therefore it is possible for us to set an upper bound Λ for route length M in Equation 4. Based on the above definitions, we can formally define the MNP recommendation problem as follows.

DEFINITION 4 (PROBLEM STATEMENT). *Given the current location $LCab \in r$ of a taxi driver, a fixed cruising length M, and a set of route candidates $\mathbb{R}$, where $\forall R \in \mathbb{R}$ satisfies R starts from r. The MNP recommendation problem is to recommend a route $R^* \in \mathbb{R}$, which has the maximum net profit, i.e.,*

$$R^* = \arg\max_{R \in \mathbb{R}} \{G(R, r, M)\}. \qquad (5)$$

Different from other existing recommender systems for taxi drivers, which mainly focus on extracting energy-efficient transportation patterns based on traveling time/length and recommending a sequence of potential pick-up points for taxi drivers [25, 26, 8], the MNP recommendation problem focuses on providing an entire driving route with maximum net profits for a taxi driver. Along this line, there are two major challenges for solving the MNP recommendation problem. First, how to calculate the parameters $g(r)$, $P(r)$ of

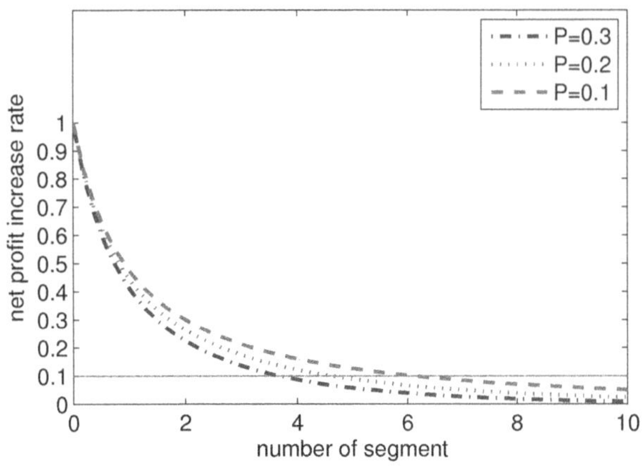

Figure 2: The average increase rate of net profit with respect to different number of increased road segment and the different fixed pick up possibility (i.e., $P(r) = 0.1$, $P(r) = 0.2$, $P(r) = 0.3$).

each segment r from the historical pick-up data. Second, how to efficiently search an optimal route from the complex directed-cyclic route segmentation network. In the following section, we will introduce our solutions for the above two challenges, respectively.

4. MAXIMUM NET PROFIT (MNP) RECOMMENDATION

In this section, we introduce the technical details of our solutions for the MNP recommendation problem.

4.1 Parameter Estimation with Road Buffer

To accurately obtain the taxi driver's current location and the parameters for estimating net profit, i.e., $P(r)$ and $g(r)$, we exploit the *road buffer* estimation for each road segment. Specifically, in geographic information systems, a buffer is a zone of specified distance around the spatial object. The boundary of the buffer is the solid line of equal distance to the edge of the object. Figure 3(a) is an illustration of different buffer operations, such as buffers on a point, three line segments and a polygon [21]. Intuitively, people would like to wait for taxis at road side instead of in the middle of road, and the pick-up points of taxis are always around the road side. Therefore, when calculating for the number of historical pick-up events, we need to build a buffer around each road segment for obtaining the new boundaries of the road. This road buffer usually looks like a rectangle surrounding the road, which is similar with the buffer operation of three line segments. Particularly, the size of the buffer depends on the demands of different real-world problems.

To build the road buffer, we need to define the vertical road and the horizontal road first. To be specific, by using the longitude and the latitude of the starting and the ending points of each road segment, we can calculate the tangent value of this road segment. If the absolute value of the tangent is greater than 1, then we regard the corresponding road as vertical road, otherwise it is a horizontal road. For each vertical road, we keep the longitudes of its starting and ending points and extend the corresponding latitudes to west and east. For each horizontal road, we keep the latitudes of

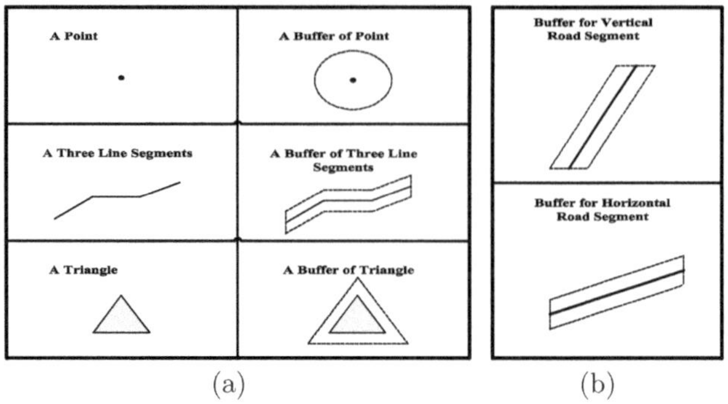

Figure 3: (a) Different buffer operations; (b) Buffer operations on vertical and horizontal roads.

its starting and ending points and extend the corresponding longitudes to north and south. The above buffer operation results in new boundaries formed by four vertex coordinates. For example, Figure 3(b) shows the buffer operations on vertical road and horizontal road.

Given the historical pick-up data and the road buffers, we are able to calculate the total number of pick-up events in each road segment r, which indicates how frequently a pick-up event can happen when cabs travel across each road segment. Let N_r^0 denote the number of times that taxis are vacant in the buffer of road segment r, and N_r^* denote the number of times that taxis had pick-up events in the buffer of segment r. Thus, the probability of pick-up event for each road segment r, i.e., $P(r)$, can be estimated as

$$P(r) = \frac{N_r^*}{N_r^0 + N_r^*}. \quad (6)$$

From the i-th historical pick-up event in segment r, we can also obtain the earnings $Fee(i;r)$ in Equation 1. Furthermore, the road length $L(r)$ and real-time traveling time $T(r)$ can be estimated from the historical data or some external resources, such as Google Map. Therefore, the net profit of $g(r)$ can be calculated by Equation 3. Particularly, the value $T(r)$, $g(r)$ and $P(r)$ of each road segment r can be pre-stored in corresponding node of the road segment network (e.g., Figure 1).

4.2 MNP Route Recommendation

In this subsection, we introduce how to solve the problem of NMP recommendation by different strategies.

4.2.1 *Brute-Force Recommendation Strategy*

After obtaining the road segment network, we can leverage it for generating route candidates can MNP recommendation. To this end, we first propose a Brute-Force strategy for this task based on the Breadth-First search. Specifically, the recommendation algorithm is shown in Algorithm 1. In this algorithm, we keep a route queue Q for generating a set of route candidates C, and the function $MNP(C)$ in Step 5 is used for finding the optimal route with maximum net profit in candidate set C. However, such Brute-Force method for searching the MNP route is not efficient, since it has to check all possible routes with length M in G.

LEMMA 1. *Given a fixed cruising length M and the road segment network $G = \{V, E\}$, where $|V| = N$, the compu-*

Algorithm 1 Brute-Force based MNP Recommendation

Input 1: road segment network $G = \{V, E\}$;
Input 2: the cruising length M;
Input 3: taxi driver's current segment r_1;
Output: the MNP route R^*;
Initialization: A route queue $Q = \{R_0\}$, where $R_0 = \{r_1\}$;
1: $C = \emptyset$;
2: //get route from queue Q;
3: $R = Q.del()$;
4: **if** $(R = \emptyset)$ **do**
5: **return** $R^* = MNP(C)$;
6: **else if** $(|R| == M)$ **do**
7: $C = C \cup R$;
8: **else if** $(|R| < M)$ **do**
9: $//r_k$ is the last road segment in R;
10: **for each** $(r_i \in V, \exists e_{ki} \in E)$ **do**
11: //add route from queue Q;
12: $Q.add(R \cup \{r_i\})$;
13: **go to Step 3;**

tational complexity of searching an optimal MNP route by Brute-Force algorithm is $\mathcal{O}(MN^{M-1})$

PROOF. Obviously, the total number of route candidates in road segment network G is $\leq N^{M-1}$, and computing the net profit for each route needs M operations. Thus, the complexity of searching optimal MNP route is $\mathcal{O}(MN^{M-1})$ □

Intuitively, the computational complexity of the Brute-Force algorithm is too high to satisfy the needs of real-world applications. There are some algorithm can save the reaching time of freeway travel in real world. To this end, we further propose another recommendation strategy based on the recursive characteristic of the net profit function.

4.2.2 Recursive Recommendation Strategy

By observing the form of the net profit of routes, we can re-write the Equation 4 as follows.

$$G(R, r_1, M) = g(r_1) + \big(1 - P(r_1)\big)G(R - r_1, r_2, M - 1), \quad (7)$$

where $R = (r_1 \rightarrow r_2 \rightarrow \cdots \rightarrow r_M)$. Indeed, the special form of total net profit can be realized by a recursion algorithm. To this end, for each road segment r_1, we can denote all the route candidates starting from r_1 as a *recursion tree* structure. Specifically, the recursion tree of a road segment can be defined as follows.

DEFINITION 5 (RECURSION TREE). *The recursion tree Υ_{r_1} of a road segment r_1 is a tree, where each node represents a road segment and the root node is r_1. Moreover, for each node r_i in the recursion tree, it has a children node set that equals to $r_i.next[]$.*

For example, Figure 4 shows an example of the recursion tree of road segment A. In this paper, we propose a method $RTree(r, M)$ for building a M-depth recursion tree Υ_r for r, which is shown in Algorithm 2. Particularly, the tree Υ_r obtained by our algorithm will hold M node sets $\Upsilon_r.level[i]$ $(1 \leq i \leq M)$, which represents the nodes in the i-th level of the tree. With this structure, the MNP recommendation from segment r_1 can be separated into several simpler MNP recommendation tasks recursively. Take Figure 4 as an example, we can develop a bottom-up method to compute the MNP route with length 3, of which the net profit is denoted as $G(A, 3)$. Specifically, according to the definition of net profit, we can obtain $G(A, 3) = g(A) + (1 - P(A)) \times max\{G(B; 2), G(C; 2), G(F; 2); G(E; 2)\}$, where the net profit of each MNP route with length 2 can also be computed by the profit of their sub-routes. For example, we have $G(B; 2) = g(B) + (1 - P(B)) \times max\{G(D; 1), G(I; 1)\}$, and the profit of each individual segment (i.e., leaf nodes of the tree) can be directly computed by its profit, e.g., $g(D)$. Therefore, given a recursion tree of r, we can obtain the MNP route with length M by recursing $M - 1$ times. Specifically, in this paper we develop a recursion algorithm $rNMP(r, K)$ for MNP recommendation, which is shown in Algorithm 3. By implementing our algorithm with parameters $r = r_1$ and $K = M$, the MNP route starting from road segment r_1 with length M and corresponding MNP value will be obtained.

Algorithm 2 RTree(r,M)

Input 1: road segment r_1 as root node;
Input 2: the depth M of recursion tree;
Output: a M-depth recursion tree Υ_r;
Initialization: $Depth = 1$; $\Upsilon_r.level[i] = \emptyset$ $(1 \leq i \leq M)$;
1: $\Upsilon_r.root = r$; $\Upsilon_r.level[1] = \{r\}$;
2: **if** $(Depth \geq M)$ **do**
3: **return** Υ_r;
4: **else**
5: **for each** $(r_{cur} \in \Upsilon.r.level[Depth])$ **do**
6: $\Upsilon_r.level[Depth + 1] \cup = r_{cur}.next[]$;
7: $Depth += 1$;
8: **go to Step 2;**

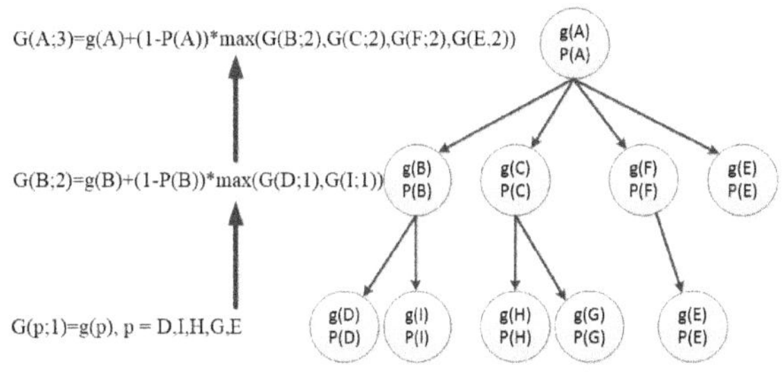

Figure 4: The recursion tree representation of route network. We can calculate the MNP $G(R, A, 3)$ from the leaf nodes of the tree.

Algorithm 3 rMNP(r,K)

Input 1: recursion tree of Υ_r;
Input 2: the depth M of recursion tree;
Output: the MNP value and route stating from r;
1: $Depth = M - K + 1$;
2: **if** $(Depth == M)$ **do**
3: $Profit = \emptyset$;
4: $Route = \emptyset$;
5: **for each** $(r_i \in \Upsilon_r.level[Depth])$ **do**
6: $Profit[i] = g(r)$;
7: $Route[i] = r_i$;
8: **return** $(Max(Profit), Max(Route))$;
9: **else**
10: $Profit = \emptyset$;
11: $Route = \emptyset$;
12: **for each** $(r_i \in \Upsilon_r.level[Depth])$ **do**
13: $(Profit^*, Route^*) = rMNP(r_i, K - 1)$;
14: $New_route[i] = r_i \cup Route^*$
15: $Profit[i] = g(r_i) + (1 - p(r_i)) \cdot Profit^*$;
16: **return** $(Max(Profit), Max(Route))$;

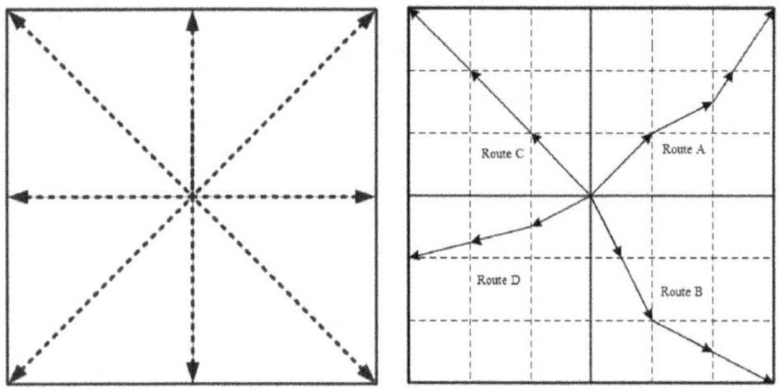

(a) (b)

Figure 5: (a) Direction-based clustering; (b) Top-K route Recommendation.

LEMMA 2. *Given a M-depth recursion tree Υ, where $\forall r \in \Upsilon$, $|r.next[]| \leq N$, the complexity of searching an optimal MNP route by the recursion method is $\mathcal{O}(N^{M-1})$*

PROOF. Assume that the computational cost of finding $G(R, r_1, M)$ is $T(M)$, obviously we have $T(M) \leq NT(M-1)+1$. Moreover $\forall r$ satisfies $|r.next[]| = N$, the computation can be separated into N sub-problems. Particularly, for route with only one segment, we have $T(1) = 1$. Meanwhile, after recursing $M-1$ times, we have $T(M) \leq N^{M-1}T(1) + \frac{N^{M-1}}{N-1}$. Therefore, the computational complexity of searching optimal MNP route by recursing tree is $\mathcal{O}(N^{M-1})$ □

Although the recursion tree can achieve more efficient recommendation than the Brute-Force method, the computational cost increases significantly as M becomes larger. According to the discussion in Section 3, we can set an upper bond Λ for M, since the average increasing rate of the net profit is very low after $M > 5$. Therefore, we set $\Lambda = 5$ in our experiments.

4.3 Top-K Route Recommendation

Based on the above algorithms, our recommender system can recommend an optimal MNP route for a single taxi driver. However, in real life, an ideal recommender system must be capable of recommending multiple taxi drivers in the same area simultaneously. In this section, we address this problem and introduce a minimum redundant strategy for the recommendation process in the real world.

Intuitively, a straightforward recommendation strategy is to recommend the optimal driving route to all available drivers. However, if we recommend the same route to too many drivers at the same time, it will cause an overloaded problem and degrade the performance of the recommender system. The overloaded problem is a classic problem which has been widely studied. For example, the load balancing mechanism distributes requests among web servers in order to minimize the execution time [22, 10]. In our problem, we can treat multiple empty cabs as jobs and multiple optimal drive routes as computers. Instead of solving this overloaded problem by exploiting existing load balancing algorithm, we want to focus on the direction characteristics in the mobile recommender system and exploit a direction-based clustering (DEN) method [29] to distribute the empty cabs by following the top-K optimal drive routes [9, 23].

Before recommending driving routes to taxi drivers, we first rank all the route candidates according to their net profits and obtain the top-K driving routes. After recommending the top ranked route to the first taxi driver, we need to calculate the correlation between this route and all other $K-1$ candidate routes, and then recommend the route with the lowest correlationship [18] to the second driver.

In order to calculate the correlation between those candidate routes, we first partition the space into grids and turn the movement statistics in each grid into a vector which represents the probabilities of moving directions within the grid. Then, we transform the direction information of the taxis' movement into the same data format, and further partition each small grid into 8 direction bins. For example, in Figure 5(a) the angle of each bin has a range of $\pi/4$. Next, we transform each grid into a direction vector $g = (p_1, p_2, p_3, ..., p_8)$, where each p_i is the probability of moving towards direction i within this grid and $p_i = f_i / \sum_{k=1}^{8} f_k$, where f_i is the frequency of moving objects that have passed this grid and has the direction along the direction i.

For instance, as shown in Figure 5(b), we first recommend route A to the first taxi driver, route B,C and D are other candidate routes at the same time and same location. Then we divide the space into small grids and get the direction vectors for each grid. A driving route candidate which has lowest correlation with the previous recommending route is usually the one with a different driving direction in the beginning. Therefore, we only need to analyze the first n grids to decide the driving directions. We combine the direction vectors in n grids together and get a vector with $8n$ elements for each candidate route. For example, the vector for route A is $g(A) = (p_{11}, p_{12}, ...p_{n7}, p_{n8})$. Then, we calculate the correlation of those vectors for each pair of candidate routes. Thus, the correlation between route A and B can be computed by $\rho(A, B) = Cov(g(A), g(B))/\sigma_g(A)\sigma_(g(B)$. If route B has the lowest correlation with route A, we will recommend route B for next coming empty cab.

5. EXPERIMENTAL RESULTS

To validate the efficiency and effectiveness of the proposed recommender system, extensive experiments are performed on real world data sets collected in the San Francisco Bay Area in 30 days.

5.1 Experimental Data

Taxi GPS Traces. In the experiments, we use the real-world taxi GPS traces collected by the Exploratorium-the museum of science, art and human perception through the cabspotting project. The mobility traces are the records of the cabs' driving states in consecutive time, with each be represented as a tuple, (*latitude, longitude, fare identifier, time stamp*). By cleaning the dataset, we obtained 89,897 pick-up and drop-off activities in total. Generally, we assume that most drivers would follow the suggested driving route provided by the Google Map, thus we can get the fare related to the specific trip and the fare information can also be used to calculate the profits concerning the trip. The following Figure 6 is an example of one hundred taxi drivers' pick-up points in 30 days in the San Francisco Bay Area, with each red point representing one pick-up activity. Figure 7 is an heat map illustration of pick-up probabilities. Here, different color and area of circles represent different pick-up probabilities. This map shows there are lots of pick-up activities around the Market Street of San Francisco, which is a very busy street with lots of shopping places and

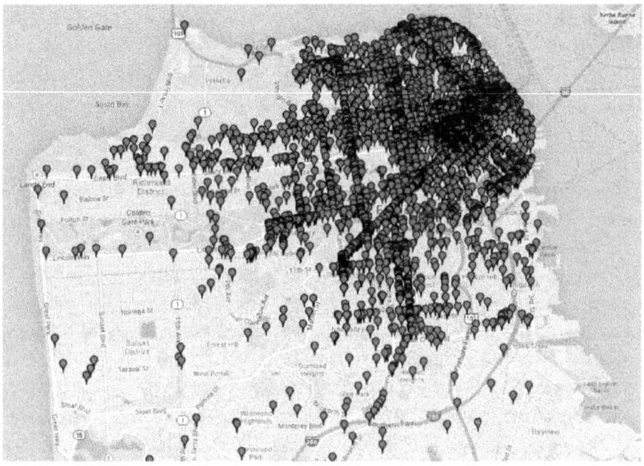

Figure 6: A Demonstration of pick-up points in the dataset.

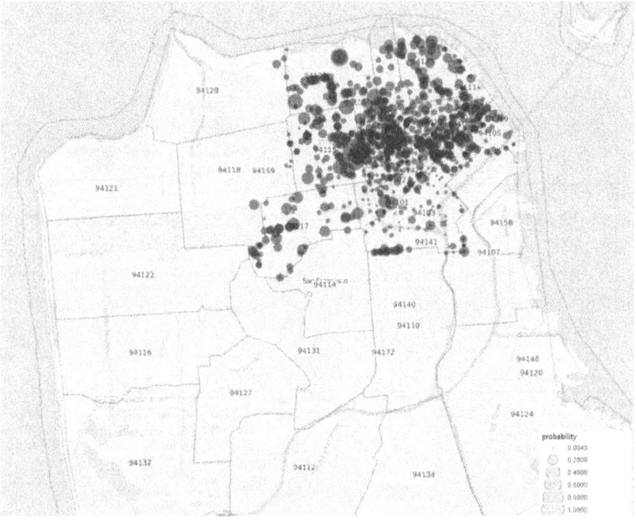

Figure 7: The heat map of pick-up probabilities in the San Francisco bay area.

museums. Other pick-up hot spots including Fisherman's Wharf, Divisadero St, Cathedral Hill and Western Addition.

Road Network Data. Because the quality of existing road networks in San Francisco is not sufficient. We build the road network dataset of San Francisco by using google API. First, we searched for all the street names in San Francisco. Second, we run the google API to find out if there is an intersection between two streets. We keep a record of each intersection point. Figure 8(a) is an illustration of our intersection points. Then, we use each intersection point to search the nearest points in four different directions and connect those 5 points together. Therefore, we can obtain four different connected road segments with starting points and ending points. However, as the yellow line in Figure 8(b), we may accidentally connect two intersections with no road between them. To solve this problem, we calculate the distance of those two intersections by using coordinates and compare it with the driving distance measured by the Google map. If there is a road between those two points, those two distances should be very close to each other. If the distances are not close to each other, it means there is no road between those two intersections and we delete this road segment from the road network dataset.

(a)

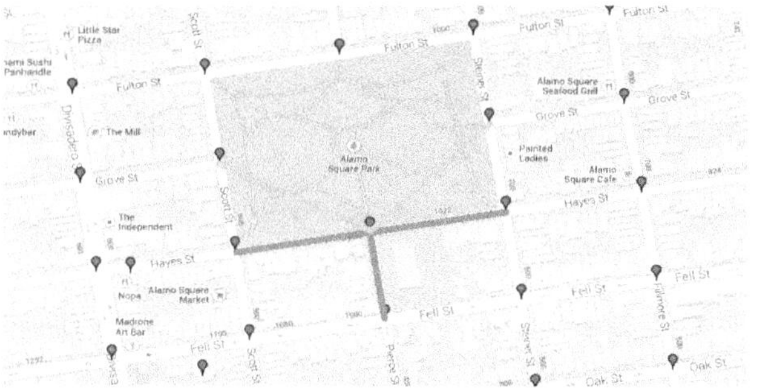

(b)

Figure 8: (a) Intersections; (b) Connected Road Segments.

The road network dataset contains 5391 roads in the San Francisco Bay Area, with each consisting of the ID, starting points, ending points and we also calculate the historical pick-up probability and net profit associate with each road segment. For each road, several coordinates of the intermediate points may be recorded and there are also some noise points. After removing the noise points, we selected 2,149 roads with high pick-up probability for our experiment. Then, we can build road buffer with the starting points and the ending points in those road segments.

By matching the pick-up coordinates of the Road Network Dataset with the Taxi Dataset, we are able to get 87,688 valid pick-up activities which can be located in the road segments, therefore the two data sets are combined together with each pick-up point mapped to the constructed road buffer. To implement the proposed algorithm, we also need to calculate the pick-up probability and the net profit for each road segment in those road segments. This has already been presented in Section 4.

Finally, we get the coordinates of the starting and the ending points for each road segment, along with the pick-up probability, the net profit and the average driving time in this road segment. Note that the average driving time is estimated as the distance of each road segment divided by the average driving speed in the San Francisco Bay Area.

5.2 Empirical Studies on Recommendations

Here, we provide two case studies. One case study is on cost effective route recommendations. Another case study is on top-k recommendations.

5.2.1 A Case Study on Cost-Effective Route Recommendations

Here, we show two examples of MNP route recommended by our approach and compare it with the suggested route by the Google map. Specifically, in Figure 9 and Figure 10, we plot the optimal driving route suggested by our rec-

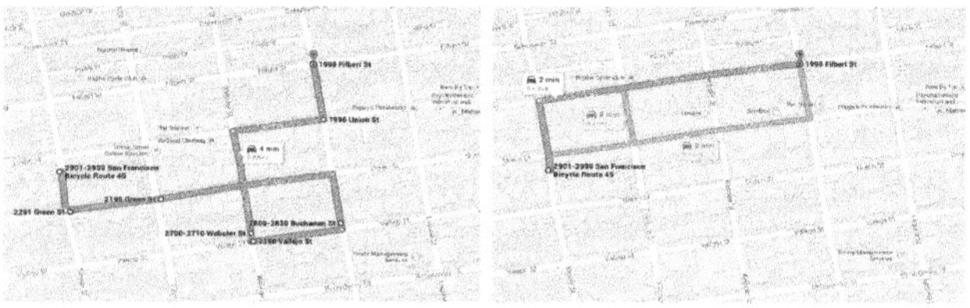

Figure 9: Case Study (a)

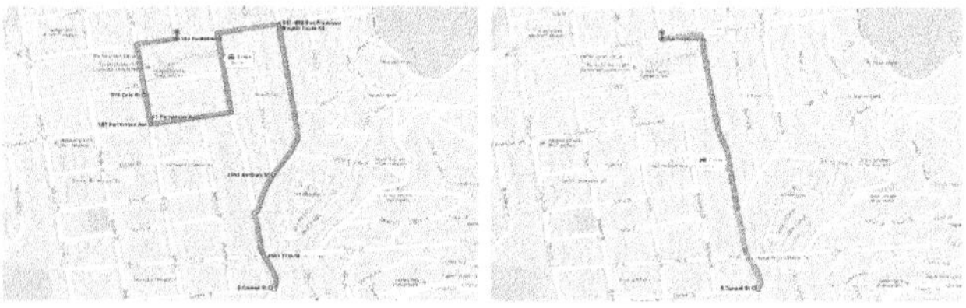

Figure 10: Case Study (b)

ommender system at a randomly selected initial location of the target cab. We also assumed that the driver's expected cruising length is 5, and after every 5 road segments, the system will use the current location as the new starting point for search and restart the recommendation process. In order to do the comparison, we calculate the real driving time of each trip of taxi drivers and restart our recommendation system until the total driving time in those MNP routes is equal to the real driving time of each trip. Then, we connect those MNP routes together and this is the entire driving route that should be recommended to the drivers. In those Figures, the left figures are the driving route recommended by the MNP recommender system and the right figures are the route suggested by the Google Map based on the shortest driving distance. However, this driving route suggested by the Google map cannot maximize taxi drivers' net profit.

Recently, most recommender system can only suggest a sequence of hot spots to taxi drivers. There is no such recommendation system that can suggest an entire driving route. If taxi drivers do not know how to drive to the nearest hot spot, he or she has to follow the driving route provided by the Google map. However, both the pick-up probability and the potential net profit may be very low along those routes. The drivers have a high probability of losing money until they reach the next hot spot. Our recommender system can improve potential net profits for taxi drivers compared to the routes suggested by the Google map.

5.2.2 A Case Study on Top-K Recommendations

In Section 4, we introduced a minimum redundant strategy to recommend the Top-K driving routes and solved the overloaded problem. In figure 11, we demonstrate the Top K driving routes starting from the same location, where K equals to 4 in this case. The figure shows that each route has different driving directions and the correlations between those driving distances are very small. Therefore, the minimum redundant strategy can improve the performance of our recommender system.

5.3 Route Recommendation for Inexperienced Taxi Drivers

Given one specific location, our proposed algorithm can recommend several routes with high expected utility for drivers. The algorithm is especially applicable for inexperienced drivers, since they lack of knowledge about the roadmap and the local driving routes that can make profits. To validate the effectiveness of the proposed algorithm, we firstly divide all the drivers into two categories based on their average net profits. The top 10% drivers in the dataset are treated as 'experienced' drivers, while the others are 'inexperienced'. Therefore, the driving routes of the experienced drivers are used as training set and we recommend driving routes for the inexperienced drivers.

We define driver's event $\mathbf{e}$ as a consecutive sequence of 'roam $\rightarrow$ pick up $\rightarrow$ drop off', by extracting the pick-up and drop-off activities of each user, we can reconstruct each event. For each driver, we define the location where the driver starts to search for potential pick-ups as l_0, and after roaming in Δt time, the driver picks up passengers at location l_1 and drive for $\Delta t'$ and drop off at l_2. Let $r_{i,j}$ denotes the road segment between location l_i and l_j, then event e can be represented with $(r_{0,1}, \Delta t, r_{1,2}, \Delta t')$, and the unit time profit of the event can be calculated as $p_e = \frac{pr_{12}}{\Delta t + \Delta t'}$. Thus, the proposed algorithm starts with the location l' which is neareset to l_0, and return a sequence of recommended potential pick-up points and road segments.

The performance of the recommended driving route is measured by the average net profit per unit time p_r, and it is compared with the average unit net profit of the inexperienced drivers, i.e., $p_d = \frac{\sum p_e}{|\mathbf{e}|}$.

The statistical experiment results for recommended driving routes for inexperienced drivers are shown in Table 1, the average net profits per unit time outperforms the real profit of the inexperienced drivers.

Table 1: Net Profits per Unit Time

	Recommender System	Inexperienced Drivers
Mean	0.038148	0.024162
SD	0.017815	0.018455

We first plot the distribution for the net profit per unit time, i.e., the number of events for specific profit values, as shown in Figure 12. The net profit per unit time of our recommended route is compared with the inexperienced taxi drivers' performance based on statistical histogram. The blue bar of the histogram shows the net profits from our recommendation results and the red bar shows the profits from the inexperienced taxi drivers. As we can see from the figure, the recommendation events mostly positioned on bigger values. This indicates that our recommender systems provide higher profit routes than the real routes by inexperienced drivers.

To further investigate the performance of the recommender system, we also study the difference of net profit per unit time between the recommended routes and the drivers' real routes for each event, i.e. $p_r - p_e$. As shown in Figure 13, the X axis is the difference between the profits of the recommended results and the inexperienced taxi drivers' profits. We can see that most of dot points are positioned to the right of $X = 0$, meaning that the profits of our recommended routes outperform the profits of the routes by the inexperienced drivers.

Then, we evaluated the performance of the Brute-Force recommendation strategy and the performance of the recursive recommendation strategy. This experiment was conducted across 1000 randomly picked starting points. We

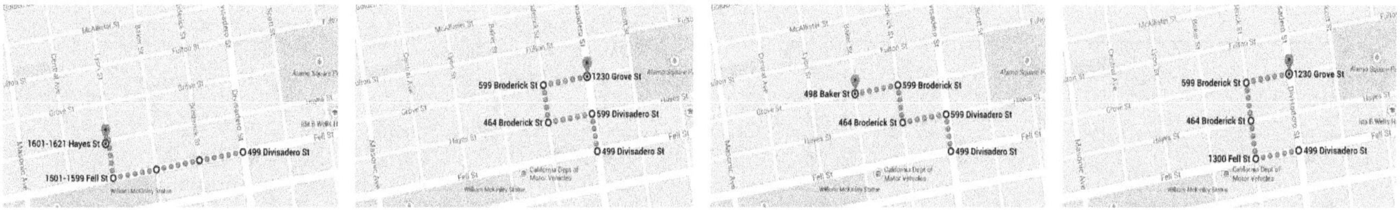

(a) (b) (c) (d)

Figure 11: The Top 4 driving routes starting from the same location (longitude: 37.77407074 and latitude:-122.4376221)

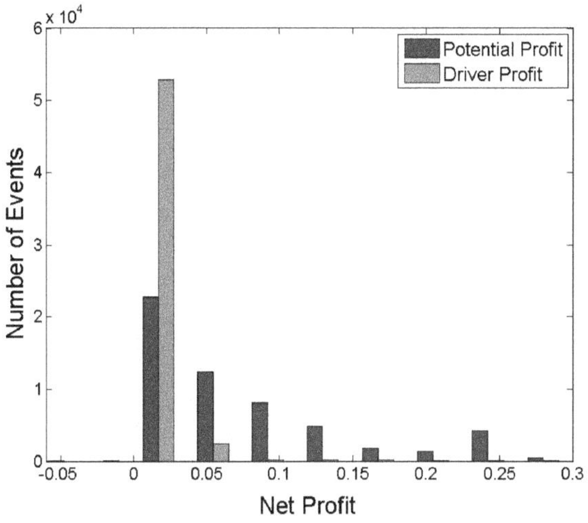

Figure 12: Net Profit Statistics. The blue bar represents the potential profits of our optimized routes and the orange bar represents the profits of taxi drivers' traditional routes ranked below top 10%

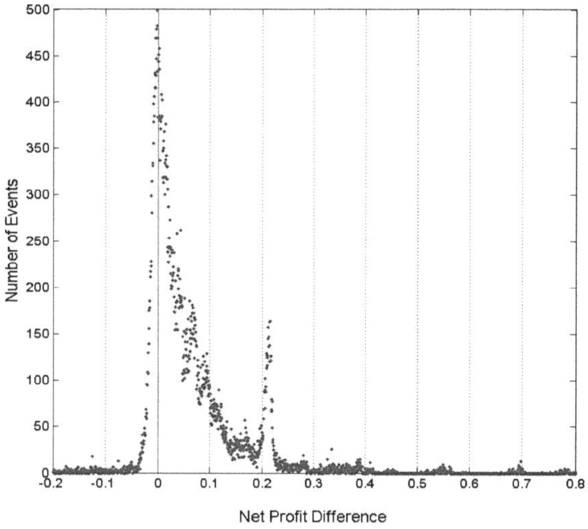

Figure 13: Profit Difference. X axis is Net Profit Difference between our optimized routes and taxi drivers' traditional routes ranked below top 10%. Y axis is the number of events

only compared the running time for five road segments, because the increasing rate of pick-up probability in Equation 4 is less than 10% after increasing more than 5 road segments. As shown in Figure 14, the red line is the running time for the Brute-Force recommendation strategy and the black line is the running time of the recursive Strategy. We can see that the recursive strategy can lead to better efficiency compared to the Brute-Force strategy. Note that all the experiments were conducted on a Windows 7 with Intel(R) Core(TM)i5-3210 CPU and 6.0 GB RAM.

To sum up, the experiments showed that the cost-effective recommender system could help inexperienced taxi drivers find better routes so as to maximize their potential profits. Also, the recursive strategy can help to efficiently identify the recommended optimal routes.

6. CONCLUDING REMARKS

In this paper, we proposed a cost-effective recommender system for taxi drivers to maximize their profits by providing profitable driving routes. To be specific, we first provided a net profit objective function for evaluating the driving routes before finding a customer. Then, we proposed a graph based approach to efficiently generate candidate driving routes for finding passengers. As a result, we can use the net profit objective function to rank each candidate route and make recommendations to taxi drivers in a cost-effective way. An unique perspective of our recommender system is that it can recommend an entire driving route instead of only recommending a sequence of discrete pick-up points. Also, the drivers are able to maximize their profits within the fixed time period by following the recommended driving routes. Finally, the extensive experiments on a real-world data set collected from the San Francisco Bay area clearly validated the effectiveness of the proposed recommender system.

Acknowledgement

This research was partially supported by National Science Foundation (NSF) via grant numbers CCF-1018151 and IIS-1256016. Also, it was supported in part by Natural Science Foundation of China (71329201)

7. REFERENCES

[1] G. Abowd, C. Atkeson, and et al. Cyber-guide: A mobile context-aware tour guide. *Wireless Networks*, 3(5):421–433, 1997.

[2] G. Adomavicius and A. Tuzhilin. Towards the next generation of recommender systems: A survey of the state-of-the art and possible extensions. *TKDE*, 2005.

[3] O. Averjanova, F. Ricci, and Q. N. Nguyen. Map-based interaction with a conversational mobile

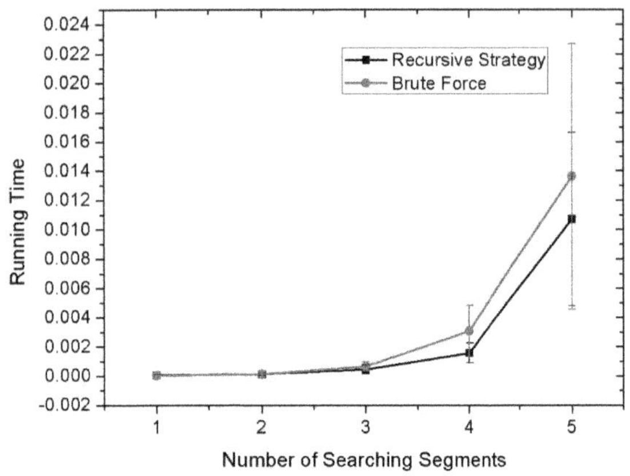

Figure 14: A Comparison of the Running Time. The red line represents the running time of the Brute-Force strategy and the black line represents the running time of the Recursive strategy

recommender system. In *The 2nd Int'l Conf on Mobile Ubiquitous Computing, Systems, Services and Technologies*, 2008.

[4] R. M. Bell and Y. Koren. Scalable collaborative filtering with jointly derived neighborhood interpolation weights. In *Data Mining, 2007. ICDM 2007. Seventh IEEE International Conference on*, pages 43–52. IEEE, 2007.

[5] F. Cena, L. Console, and et al. Integrating heterogeneous adaptation techniques to build a flexible and usable mobile tourist guide. *AI Communications*, 19(4):369–384, 2006.

[6] K. Cheverst, N. Davies, and et al. Developing a context-aware electronic tourist guide: some issues and experiences. In *the SIGCHI Conference on Human Factors in Computing Systems*, pages 17–24, 2000.

[7] M. Deshpande and G. Karypis. Item-based top-n recommendation algorithms. *ACM Transactions on Information Systems (TOIS)*, 22(1):143–177, 2004.

[8] Y. Ge, H. Xiong, A. Tuzhilin, K. Xiao, M. Gruteser, and M. Pazzani. An energy-efficient mobile recommender system. In *Proceedings of the 16th ACM SIGKDD international conference on Knowledge discovery and data mining*, pages 899–908. ACM, 2010.

[9] Y. Ge, H. Xiong, Z.-H. Zhou, H. Ozdemir, J. Yu, and K. Lee. Top-eye: Top-k evolving trajectory outlier detection. In *CIKM'10*.

[10] D. Grosu and A. T. Chronopoulos. Algorithmic mechanism design for load balancing in distributed systems. *IEEE TSMC-B*, 34(1):77–84, 2004.

[11] Y. Koren. Factorization meets the neighborhood: a multifaceted collaborative filtering model. In *Proceedings of the 14th ACM SIGKDD international conference on Knowledge discovery and data mining*, pages 426–434. ACM, 2008.

[12] B. N. Miller, I. Albert, and et al. Movielens unplugged: Experiences with a recommender system on four mobile devices. In *international conference on Intelligent user interfaces*, 2003.

[13] R. J. Mooney and L. Roy. Content-based book recommendation using learning for text categorization. In *Workshop Recommender Systems: Algorithms and Evaluation*, 1999.

[14] G. Nagy and S. Salhi. Heuristic algorithms for single and multiple depot vehicle routing problems with pickups and deliveries. *European Journal of Operational Research*, 162(1):126–141, 2005.

[15] M. Pazzani. A framework for collaborative, content-based, and demographic filtering. *Artificial Intelligence Review*, 1999.

[16] J. W. Powell, Y. Huang, F. Bastani, and M. Ji. Towards reducing taxicab cruising time using spatio-temporal profitability maps. In *Proceedings of the 12th International Conference on Advances in Spatial and Temporal Databases*, SSTD'11, pages 242–260, Berlin, Heidelberg, 2011. Springer-Verlag.

[17] X. Su and T. M. Khoshgoftaar. A survey of collaborative filtering techniques. *Adv. in Artif. Intell.*, 2009:4:2–4:2, Jan. 2009.

[18] L.-A. Tang, Y. Zheng, X. Xie, J. Yuan, X. Yu, and J. Han. Retrieving k-nearest neighboring trajectories by a set of point locations. In *Advances in Spatial and Temporal Databases*, pages 223–241. Springer, 2011.

[19] A. Tveit. Peer-to-peer based recommendations for mobile commerce. In *the 1st international workshop on Mobile commerce*, 2001.

[20] H. van der Heijden, G. Kotsis, and R. Kronsteiner. Mobile recommendation systems for decision making 'on the go'. In *ICMB*, 2005.

[21] H. Xiong, S. Shekhar, Y. Huang, V. Kumar, X. Ma, and J. S. Yoo. A framework for discovering co-location patterns in data sets with extended spatial objects. In *SDM*. SIAM, 2004.

[22] Z. Xu and R. Huang. Performance study of load balancing algorithms in distributed web server systems. In *TR*, CS213 Univ. of California,Riverside.

[23] J. Yuan, G.-Z. Sun, Y. Tian, G. Chen, and Z. Liu. Selective-nra algorithms for top-k queries. In *Advances in Data and Web Management*, pages 15–26. Springer, 2009.

[24] J. Yuan, Y. Zheng, X. Xie, and G. Sun. T-drive: Enhancing driving directions with taxi drivers' intelligence. *Knowledge and Data Engineering, IEEE Transactions on*, 25(1):220–232, 2013.

[25] J. Yuan, Y. Zheng, C. Zhang, W. Xie, X. Xie, G. Sun, and Y. Huang. T-drive: driving directions based on taxi trajectories. In *Proceedings of the 18th SIGSPATIAL International Conference on Advances in Geographic Information Systems*, pages 99–108. ACM, 2010.

[26] J. Yuan, Y. Zheng, L. Zhang, X. Xie, and G. Sun. Where to find my next passenger. In *Proceedings of the 13th international conference on Ubiquitous computing*, pages 109–118. ACM, 2011.

[27] Y. Zheng, Y. Liu, J. Yuan, and X. Xie. Urban computing with taxicabs. In *Proceedings of the 13th international conference on Ubiquitous computing*, pages 89–98. ACM, 2011.

[28] Y. Zheng, J. Yuan, W. Xie, X. Xie, and G. Sun. Drive smartly as a taxi driver. In *Ubiquitous Intelligence & Computing and 7th International Conference on Autonomic & Trusted Computing (UIC/ATC), 2010 7th International Conference on*, pages 484–486. IEEE, 2010.

[29] W. Zhou, H. Xiong, Y. Ge, J. Yu, H. Ozdemir, and K. C. Lee. Direction clustering for characterizing movement patterns. In *Information Reuse and Integration (IRI), 2010 IEEE International Conference on*, pages 165–170. IEEE, 2010.

[30] H. Zhu, E. Chen, K. Yu, H. Cao, H. Xiong, and J. Tian. Mining personal context-aware preferences for mobile users. In *Proceedings of the IEEE 12th International Conference on Data Mining*, ICDM'12, pages 1212–1217, 2012.

LUDIA: An Aggregate-Constrained Low-Rank Reconstruction Algorithm to Leverage Publicly Released Health Data

Yubin Park
The University of Texas at Austin
yubin.park@utexas.edu

Joydeep Ghosh
The University of Texas at Austin
ghosh@ece.utexas.edu

ABSTRACT

In the past few years, the government and other agencies have publicly released a prodigious amount of data that can be potentially mined to benefit the society at large. However, data such as health records are typically only provided at aggregated levels (e.g. per State, per Hospital Referral Region, etc.) to protect privacy. Unfortunately aggregation can severely diminish the utility of such data when modeling or analysis is desired at a per-individual basis. So, not surprisingly, despite the increasing abundance of aggregate data, there have been very few successful attempts in exploiting them for individual-level analyses. This paper introduces LUDIA, a novel low-rank approximation algorithm that utilizes aggregation constraints in addition to auxiliary information in order to estimate or "reconstruct" the original individual-level values from aggregate data. If the reconstructed data are statistically similar to the original individual-level data, off-the-shelf individual-level models can be readily and reliably applied for subsequent predictive or descriptive analytics. LUDIA is more robust to nonlinear estimates and random effects than other reconstruction algorithms. It solves a Sylvester equation and leverages multi-level (also known as hierarchical or mixed-effect) modeling approaches efficiently. A novel graphical model is also introduced to provide a probabilistic viewpoint of LUDIA. Experimental results using a Texas inpatient dataset show that individual-level data can be reasonably reconstructed from county-, hospital-, and zip code-level aggregate data. Several factors affecting the reconstruction quality are discussed, along with the implications of this work for current aggregation guidelines.

Categories and Subject Descriptors

H.4 [**Information Systems Applications**]: Miscellaneous

Keywords

Data aggregation, Low rank approximation, Multi-level model

KDD'14, August 24–27, 2014, New York, NY, USA.
Copyright 2014 ACM 978-1-4503-2956-9/14/08 ...$15.00.
http://dx.doi.org/10.1145/2623330.2623659 .

1. INTRODUCTION

Individual-level datasets that contain one or more records per person are rich sources for data mining applications. In the healthcare domain, the application of advanced data mining methods on individual level records across large populations can enable major breakthroughs in both personalized and population-level healthcare, leading to much improved, more cost-effective and timely diagnoses and interventions [33]. However, such data often contain a substantial amount of privacy-sensitive attributes. In practice, privacy concerns are typically addressed through multiple Statistical Disclosure Limitation (SDL) techniques [10], such as data aggregation [1], data swapping [8, 13], top-coding, feature generalization such as k-anonymity [36] or l-diversity [28], and additive random noise with measurement error [17]. Each method has distinct utility and risk aspects. Often an appropriate mix of disclosure limitation techniques is carefully chosen by domain experts and statisticians. For example, Centers for Medicare and Medicaid Services applied six different SDL techniques when publishing synthetic public use files[1]: variable reduction, suppression, substitution, imputation, data perturbation, and coarsening.

Among various SDL approaches, data aggregation is currently the most widely used. Data aggregation is a process of summarizing individual-level data into a small set of representative values such as mean and median statistics computed over groups that are typically geographically or administratively defined (such as county, hospital group, state, etc). This process is straightforward to apply on diverse datasets: wireless sensor networks [22], regional healthcare statistics [7], and government data [9]. Moreover, such aggregate data can be efficiently and effortlessly generated in RDBMS [29] and statistical programming languages [37]. Data collecting agencies publish various aggregate datasets at different levels of aggregation (including individual-level for non-sensitive information). In particular, the U.S. government's open data project, data.gov has recently released a substantial amount of regional and topic-based aggregate data regarding agriculture, education, and energy. Centers for Disease Control and Prevention annually publishes various regional statistics related to aging, cancer, and diabetes. Other notable sources of aggregated health data are dartmouthatlas.org and healthdata.gov.

The use of aggregate data is typically limited to group-level studies, often referred to as ecological studies for his-

[1] http://www.cms.gov/Research-Statistics-Data-and-Systems/Statistics-Trends-and-Reports/SynPUFs/DE_Syn_PUF.html

Table 1: Illustrative health data files: artificial individual-level data (left) and aggregate-level summary (right) [24].

ID	Age	Length	State
1	19	1 day	TX
2	35	2 days	CA
3	3	10 days	FL
6	68	100 days	FL
⋮	⋮	⋮	⋮

State	Avg. Hospital Charge
CA	$ 2,706
FL	$ 1,809
NY	$ 1,954
TX	$ 2,001
⋮	⋮

toric reasons. Applying the result from aggregate data to individual-level inference often results in the classic problem of ecological fallacy [35]. Ecological fallacy occurs when aggregate-level statistics are misinterpreted as individual-level inferences. For example, the high correlation between "per capita consumption of dietary fat" and "breast cancer" in different countries [6] does not imply that dietary fat causes breast cancer.

There have been many attempts to circumvent the ecological fallacy while analyzing aggregate data. This is because individual-level data acquisition is usually expensive, and it is sometimes legally and ethically implausible. Duncan [11] developed the method of bounds that uses the constraints of contingency tables, but the bounds are often uninformative in real applications [14]. The constancy assumption, suggested by Goodman [21], allows an individual-level interpretation of ecological regression. Suppose that we want to check the relationship between Length of Stay (LoS) and Hospital Charge (HC) variables from state-level aggregate data:

$$\mathrm{HC}_{\mathrm{state}} \sim c_{\mathrm{state}} + \beta_{\mathrm{state}}\mathrm{LoS}_{\mathrm{state}}$$

The constancy assumption states that daily hospital charge rates are the same across different states i.e. $\beta_{\mathrm{state}} = \beta$ and $c_{\mathrm{state}} = c$. Of course, this assumption is rarely true in real datasets; for this example, it is more natural to assume that each state has a different daily charge rate, thereby indicating that multi-level modeling can be used [19]. Such an approach, however, is under-identified and can't be solved using aggregate data, since we have more parameters than observations. King [25, 26] proposed a Bayesian prior-based multi-level approach to overcome the limitation of Goodman's assumption, but Freedman [15] criticized that King's method cannot be validated on the basis of aggregate data.

We provide a novel approach for addressing the ecological fallacy dilemma by leveraging available sources of individual-level data for which the values of the partitioning or aggregation variable is known. For example, an aggregation variable can indicate state, county, or zip codes, that can be used to link to aggregate-level dataset that is aggregated along such geographical regions. In practice, it is not difficult to collect multiple datasets with different levels of aggregations from multiple agencies, so little added data-collection expense is involved.

Table 1 shows a simple, illustrative example of two health datasets. Non-sensitive fields are published at individual-level, while a sensitive field (hospital charge) is aggregated over the partition variable "state". Our approach is substantially different from previous ecological fallacy solutions where only aggregate data were considered.

We use a two-stage approach to avoid the ecological fallacy. We first reconstruct the masked individual-level variables from aggregate data, then apply multi-level regression models to the reconstructed data. In other words, we first synthesize "pseudo individual-level" data that are statistically similar to the original (unseen) individual-level data. Not only multi-level regression models, but also numerous off-the-shelf data mining algorithms can be easily applied to such pseudo individual-level data. Our reconstruction algorithm is based on two key observations:

- Aggregation is a linear transformation, thus it preserves several algebraic properties including the associative property.
- Using a proper data model, additional individual-level data can provide statistical clues for the reconstruction of the masked columns. From the previous hospital charge example, if we know *a priori* that hospital charge (aggregate-level) is a function of length of stay (individual-level), we roughly expect that a person with a longer stay may have paid more than a person who stayed only a day. We demonstrate that such clues can be captured using a low rank model.

We demonstrate our reconstruction algorithm on both simulated and real datasets. Many factors contribute to the reconstruction quality, for example, the number of data points per aggregation and correlation strength with other columns. These factors will be illustrated in Section 6 using Texas Inpatient Public Use Files. The main contributions of this paper are:

- We formulate a data model, LUDIA, that reconstructs individual values from aggregate values.
- We derive efficient algorithms for solving optimization problems associated with LUDIA.
- We show that our reconstructed data can capture aggregate-level random effects, thus the reconstructed data can be used for multi-level analyses as well as more sophisticated data mining applications.

The first two contributions will be illustrated in Section 3, the last contribution will be explained in Section 4. Experimental results are provided in Section 6, followed by discussions in Section 7.

2. PRELIMINARIES & RELATED WORK

This section starts by setting up the notation of this paper, and visiting two key existing approaches for tackling aggregate data. We extend these approaches to reconstruct the original individual-level data, and briefly discuss their modeling assumptions and limitations.

Aggregation is a compressive linear transformation, which we denote as $\mathbf{A}$. For example, suppose that there are five individuals from two different groups: the first two from Group A and the last three from Group B. Individual-level observations, say $\mathbf{y} = \begin{bmatrix}1 & 2 & 3 & 4 & 5\end{bmatrix}^\top$, can be aggregated into two groups by multiplying an aggregation matrix defined as follows:

$$\mathbf{s} = \begin{bmatrix}1.5\\ 4\end{bmatrix} = \mathbf{A}\mathbf{y} = \begin{bmatrix}1/2 & 1/2 & 0 & 0 & 0\\ 0 & 0 & 1/3 & 1/3 & 1/3\end{bmatrix}\mathbf{y}$$

Table 2 summarizes the notation of this paper.

Table 2: Notation. For simplicity but without loss of generality, we use $d = 1$ in this paper.

Symbol	Explanation
$\mathbf{X}$	$n \times m$, individual-level matrix
$\mathbf{x}_i$	$1 \times m$, ith row of $\mathbf{X}$
$\mathbf{y}$	$n \times d$, masked individual-level vector
$\mathbf{A}$	$p \times n$, aggregation matrix
$\mathbf{s}$	$p \times d$, aggregate-level vector i.e. $\mathbf{Ay}$
$\mathbf{U}, \mathbf{V}$	$n \times r$, $m \times r$ low-rank matrices

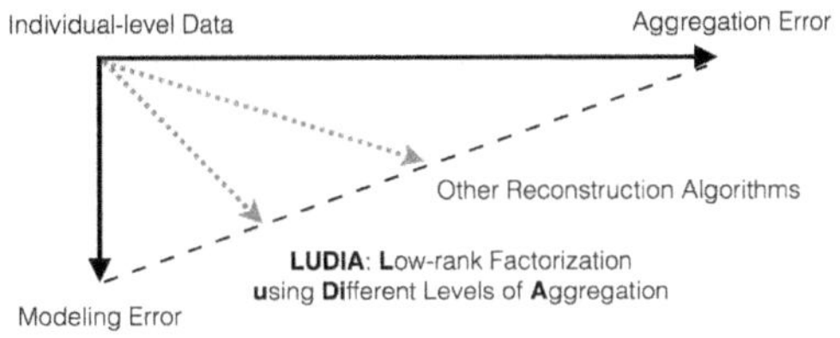

Figure 1: Reconstruction triangle and LUDIA.

The processes of aggregation and reconstruction can be illustrated as follows:

$$\text{(Compression)} \qquad \mathbf{Ay} \xrightarrow{\text{compressive linear}} \mathbf{s}$$

$$\text{(Reconstruction)} \qquad \hat{\mathbf{y}} \xleftarrow{\text{low-rank modeling}} \text{Recon}(\mathbf{s}, \mathbf{A}, \mathbf{X})$$

where $\mathbf{X}$ represents individual-level data, and Recon is a reconstruction algorithm. To give a brief overview, our reconstruction algorithm, LUDIA (**L**ow-rank factorization **U**sing **Di**fferent levels of **A**ggregation), is a constrained low-rank factorization algorithm that can capture multi-level effects. Figure 1 illustrates the overall idea of LUDIA and other reconstruction algorithms. We have two sources of errors that construct our reconstruction triangle: aggregation and modeling errors. LUDIA reduces the aggregation error using a low-rank model, but the LUDIA error is lower-bounded by the modeling error.

To illustrate existing approaches for aggregate data, let us consider the previous "hospital charge vs. length of stay" example. When using aggregate data, three approaches have been popular:

- The neighborhood model [16], proposed by Freedman, will imply that hospital charges are more influenced by geographical attributes rather than the length of stay variable, since each geographical partition is assumed to contain a homogeneous population group.
- Ecological regression [20], suggested by Goodman, will assume that the effect size of length of stay is the same across different states, based on the constancy assumption. According to the constancy assumption, geographical partitions are treated as different batches of i.i.d. experiments.
- Ecological inference, also known as King's method [26], combines the method of bounds and Goodman's ecological regression. King's method is a multi-level approach that models different effect sizes for different states. The multi-level parameters are first characterized by their acceptable regions using the method of bounds, then their joint distributions are modeled under three assumptions [27]: uni-modal joint distribution, absence of spatial correlation, and independence between multi-level coefficients and dependent variables. However, these assumptions are not verifiable on the basis of aggregate-level data [15], and this method requires manual tuning of the parameter distributions. In short, ecological inference is a method with many knobs and unverifiable assumptions, and we do not include this method in our baseline methods.

These previous approaches have been developed to tackle aggregate data, and need to be slightly modified to synthesize individual-level data. Imagine that we now obtained individual-level length of stay data[2] $\mathbf{X}$ and each individual's location information $\mathbf{A}$. To reconstruct the masked hospital charge data $\mathbf{y}$, two direct extensions from the previous approaches can be considered:

- Moore-Penrose (MP) solution is an extension of the neighborhood model. As the neighborhood model only focuses on the aggregation matrix $\mathbf{A}$, the reconstructed values are obtained by applying the Moore-Penrose pseudo-inverse of $\mathbf{A}$ to the aggregate data:

  $$\hat{\mathbf{y}}_{\text{MP}} = \mathbf{A}^{+}\mathbf{s}$$

  where $\mathbf{A}^{+} = \mathbf{A}(\mathbf{A}\mathbf{A}^{\top})^{-1}$.
- Ecological Regression (ER) solution is an extension of Goodman's ecological regression. Assuming that the effect sizes are the same across different states, we obtain the regression parameter $\boldsymbol{\beta}$ from the aggregate data, then apply to the individual-level covariate:

  $$\hat{\mathbf{y}}_{\text{ER}} = \boldsymbol{\beta}_{\text{ER}}\mathbf{X}$$

  where $\boldsymbol{\beta}_{\text{ER}} = (\mathbf{Z}^{\top}\mathbf{Z})^{-1}\mathbf{Z}^{\top}\mathbf{s}$ and $\mathbf{Z}$ is the aggregate-level representation of $\mathbf{X}$ i.e. $\mathbf{AX}$.

MP and ER exhibit different failure modes. MP ignores the effects of individual-level covariates, which may substantially leverage the utility of aggregate data. On the other hand, ER relies on the constancy assumption, which is rarely true in real settings.

For our hospital charge example, daily charge rates are significantly different across city and rural areas (see Section 6). This geographical variation on daily charge rates can be expressed as follows:

$$\begin{aligned} y_i &= \mathbf{x}_i\boldsymbol{\beta}_{\text{state}} + \zeta_{\text{state}} + e_i & e_i &\sim \text{N}(0, \sigma_e^2) \\ \boldsymbol{\beta}_{\text{state}} &= \boldsymbol{\beta}_{\text{global}} + \boldsymbol{\eta}_{\text{state}} & \boldsymbol{\eta}_{\text{state}} &\sim \text{N}(0, \sigma_\eta^2\mathbf{D}) \\ \zeta_{\text{state}} &\sim \text{N}(0, \sigma_\zeta^2) \end{aligned}$$

where ζ_{state} and $\boldsymbol{\eta}_{\text{state}}$ represent state-level biases for the intercept and slope; they are called random intercept and random slope, respectively. Assuming that we have two states A and B, and individuals listed by state, this multi-level approach [18] can be written in a matrix form:

$$\begin{bmatrix} y_1 \\ y_2 \\ \vdots \\ y_{n-1} \\ y_n \end{bmatrix} = \begin{bmatrix} \mathbf{x}_1 \\ \mathbf{x}_2 \\ \vdots \\ \mathbf{x}_{n-1} \\ \mathbf{x}_n \end{bmatrix} \boldsymbol{\beta}_{\text{global}} + \begin{bmatrix} \mathbf{x}_1 & \mathbf{0} & 1 & 0 \\ \mathbf{x}_2 & \mathbf{0} & 1 & 0 \\ \vdots & \vdots & \vdots & \vdots \\ \mathbf{0} & \mathbf{x}_{n-1} & 0 & 1 \\ \mathbf{0} & \mathbf{x}_n & 0 & 1 \end{bmatrix} \begin{bmatrix} \boldsymbol{\eta}_A \\ \boldsymbol{\eta}_B \\ \zeta_A \\ \zeta_B \end{bmatrix} + \mathbf{E}$$

[2] **Note**: This simple example has only one individual level (LoS) and one aggregated (HC) feature, and one level of aggregation, called "State", so as to convey the concepts most easily. Our approach readily generalizes to multiple individual and aggregate variables as well as multiple levels of aggregations, as will be seen later

We define new matrices $\boldsymbol{\gamma}$ (random effects) and $\mathbf{G}$ (covariates for random effects) to obtain a compact form:

$$\mathbf{y} = \mathbf{X}\boldsymbol{\beta}_{\text{global}} + \mathbf{G}\boldsymbol{\gamma} + \mathbf{E} \tag{1}$$

Aggregate data are obtained through the aggregation operation as follows:

$$\begin{aligned} \mathbf{A}\mathbf{y} &= \mathbf{A}\mathbf{X}\boldsymbol{\beta}_{\text{global}} + \mathbf{A}\mathbf{G}\boldsymbol{\gamma} + \mathbf{A}\mathbf{E} \\ \Rightarrow \quad \mathbf{s} &= \mathbf{Z}\boldsymbol{\beta}_{\text{global}} + \mathbf{A}\mathbf{G}\boldsymbol{\gamma} + \mathbf{A}\mathbf{E} \end{aligned}$$

As can be seen, the ER solution is valid only if

- $\boldsymbol{\gamma} = 0$ (no random effect)
- $((\mathbf{A}\mathbf{X})^\top \mathbf{A}\mathbf{X})^{-1}(\mathbf{A}\mathbf{X})^\top \mathbf{A}\mathbf{y} = (\mathbf{X}^\top\mathbf{X})^{-1}\mathbf{X}^\top\mathbf{y}$

These two conditions are rarely realistic in real applications.

MP and ER are formulated based on two orthogonal assumptions. MP assumes that only geographical partitions affect the dependent variable, while ER posits that geographical partitions are merely random groupings. These assumptions are necessary to obtain some meaningful results from aggregate data, as the ecological fallacy is, in fact, the problem of statistical under-identification [34]. However, the direct extensions from the previous approaches do not utilize the full potential of auxiliary individual-level data.

A recent breakthrough in the use of aggregate data to augment individual-level models was made by Park and Ghosh [30, 32, 31]. The suggested model, CUDIA, is a probabilistic clustering algorithm that utilizes both aggregated and individual-level data. CUDIA models the data points as being generated from a mixture of exponential family distributions. The parameters of CUDIA are estimated using a Monte-Carlo Expectation Maximization (MCEM) algorithm. Although CUDIA can reasonably reconstruct the data based on the estimated cluster centers, the primary objective of CUDIA is still clustering rather than reconstruction. Furthermore, the presented MCEM algorithm is not scalable to large-scale data. We show that CUDIA is, in fact, a special case of LUDIA with a non-negative constraint on $\mathbf{U}$ (see Section 5). LUDIA generalizes CUDIA with a more flexible representation of $\mathbf{U}$. This generalization provides an efficient optimization algorithm that is suitable for large-scale data.

3. LUDIA

LUDIA is a low-rank factorization algorithm using aggregate data. We first describe the underlying data model of LUDIA, then formulate LUDIA's objective function. Because of the non-trivial aggregation constraint, we derive a customized minimization approach that uses the Sylvester equation.

3.1 Low-rank Data Model

LUDIA employs a bottom-up approach starting from individual level data. We first design a data model for a complete matrix $\mathbf{D} = [\mathbf{X} \quad \mathbf{y}]$, then formulate an objective function when $\mathbf{y}$ is masked and only $\mathbf{s} = \mathbf{A}\mathbf{y}$ is provided. The data model for LUDIA is based on the low-rank approximation theory as follows:

$$[\mathbf{X} \quad \mathbf{y}] = \mathbf{U}\mathbf{V}^\top + \mathbf{E} = \mathbf{U}\left[\mathbf{V}_x^\top \quad \mathbf{v}_y^\top\right] + \mathbf{E} \tag{2}$$

where $\mathbf{U} \in \mathbb{R}^{n\times r}$, $\mathbf{V} \in \mathbb{R}^{m\times r}$, $\mathbf{E} \in \mathbb{R}^{n\times m}$, and $r \le \min(n, m)$. Note that we divided $\mathbf{V}$ into two block matrices: $\mathbf{V}_x$ and $\mathbf{v}_y$, so that $\mathbf{X} \approx \mathbf{U}\mathbf{V}_x$ and $\mathbf{y} \approx \mathbf{U}\mathbf{v}_y$.

The main objective of this paper is to reconstruct the masked values, $\mathbf{y}$. In theory, under certain assumptions such as an underlying low-rank structure and a uniform missing mechanism, missing values in a matrix can be reconstructed. Candes and Recht [5] showed that, for matrix entries that are missing at random, they can be exactly recovered if the number of observations exceed a certain threshold value. However, the settings for the matrix completion problem are not suitable for our problem, since we consider a situation wherein one or more columns of a matrix is entirely missing, but its aggregated statistics are given.

We approximate the original matrix using two low-rank matrices. This problem is different from the matrix completion problem [23]. Low-rank approximation is typically posed as a minimization problem as follows:

$$\min \|\hat{\mathbf{D}} - \mathbf{D}\|_F^2 \quad \text{s.t.} \quad \text{rank}(\hat{\mathbf{D}}) \le r$$

where $\mathbf{D}$ and $\hat{\mathbf{D}}$ are both $n\times m$ matrices, and $r \le \min(n, m)$. The Eckart-Young-Mirsky theorem [12] says that rank r approximation of the data matrix $\mathbf{D}$ is given as follows:

$$\hat{\mathbf{D}} = \mathbf{U}\boldsymbol{\Gamma}\mathbf{V}^\top = (\mathbf{U}\boldsymbol{\Gamma}^{1/2})(\boldsymbol{\Gamma}^{1/2}\mathbf{V}^\top) = \tilde{\mathbf{U}}\tilde{\mathbf{V}}^\top$$

where $\mathbf{U}$, $\boldsymbol{\Gamma}$, $\mathbf{V}$ are $n\times r$, $r\times r$, $m\times r$ truncated Singular Vector Decomposition matrices, respectively. The data model in Equation 2 is, however, inapplicable to our reconstruction application. The model should instead reflect the constraint that $\mathbf{y}$ is masked and only $\mathbf{s} = \mathbf{A}\mathbf{y}$ is provided.

3.2 Aggregation Constraint

A novel optimization problem for three latent matrices $\mathbf{y}$, $\mathbf{U}$, and $\mathbf{V}$ is proposed as follows:

$$\begin{aligned} \min_{\mathbf{y},\mathbf{U},\mathbf{V}} \quad & \|[\mathbf{X} \quad \mathbf{y}] - \mathbf{U}\mathbf{V}^\top\|_F^2 \\ \text{subject to} \quad & \mathbf{A}\mathbf{y} = \mathbf{s} \end{aligned} \tag{3}$$

A simultaneous minimization over $\mathbf{y}$, $\mathbf{U}$, and $\mathbf{V}$ is a difficult non-convex optimization problem. However, minimization over one set of variables alone is a convex problem.

We tackle this problem by removing the equality constraint. The equality constraint on $\mathbf{y}$ can be eliminated if we fix the other two variables. Given that $\mathbf{U}$ and $\mathbf{V}$ are fixed, the optimality condition [4] is given as:

$$\mathbf{A}\mathbf{y}^* = \mathbf{s} \quad \text{and} \quad \nabla f(\mathbf{y}^*) + \mathbf{A}^\top\boldsymbol{\Psi}^* = 0$$

where $f(\mathbf{Y}) = \|\mathbf{X} - \mathbf{U}\mathbf{V}_x^\top\|_F^2 + \|\mathbf{y} - \mathbf{U}\mathbf{v}_y^\top\|_2^2$ and $\boldsymbol{\Psi}^* \in \mathbb{R}^p$ is a dual variable. $\mathbf{Y}^*$ is optimal if and only if there exists $\boldsymbol{\Psi}^*$ satisfying the optimality conditions. It turns out that, for this system, $\mathbf{y}^*$ can be solved in a closed form.

To eliminate the constraint, we solve Karush-Kuhn-Tucker (KKT) equations as follows:

$$\nabla f(\mathbf{y}^*) + \mathbf{A}^\top\boldsymbol{\Psi}^* = 2\mathbf{y}^* - 2\mathbf{U}\mathbf{v}_y^\top + \mathbf{A}^\top\boldsymbol{\Psi}^* = 0$$

We multiply $\mathbf{A}$ on both sides of the second KKT equation, and solve for $\boldsymbol{\Psi}^*$:

$$\begin{aligned} 2\mathbf{A}\mathbf{y}^* - 2\mathbf{A}\mathbf{U}\mathbf{v}_y^\top + \mathbf{A}\mathbf{A}^\top\boldsymbol{\Psi}^* &= 0 \\ \boldsymbol{\Psi}^* &= -2(\mathbf{A}\mathbf{A}^\top)^{-1}(\mathbf{s} - \mathbf{A}\mathbf{U}\mathbf{v}_y) \end{aligned}$$

Thus, the optimal $\mathbf{y}^*$ is:

$$\mathbf{y}^* = \mathbf{U}\mathbf{v}_y^\top + \mathbf{A}^\top(\mathbf{A}\mathbf{A}^\top)^{-1}(\mathbf{s} - \mathbf{A}\mathbf{U}\mathbf{v}_y^\top) \tag{4}$$

We plug the optimal $\mathbf{y}^*$ into the original objective function to obtain:

$$\min_{\mathbf{U},\mathbf{V}} \|\mathbf{X} - \mathbf{U}\mathbf{V}_x\|_F^2 + (\mathbf{s} - \mathbf{A}\mathbf{U}\mathbf{v}_y)^\top(\mathbf{A}\mathbf{A}^\top)^{-1}(\mathbf{s} - \mathbf{A}\mathbf{U}\mathbf{v}_y) \tag{5}$$

We have thus transformed the original objective function with three variables and an equality constraint into a simpler unconstrained objective function with two variables.

3.3 Objective Function

Although we simplified the constrained optimization problem to the non-constrained optimization problem in Equation 5, solving the objective function poses another challenge. Intuitively, one can approach the problem using an alternating minimization approach over $\mathbf{U}$ and $\mathbf{V}$. Solving for $\mathbf{U}$, however, does not have a closed form solution, because the low rank matrix $\mathbf{U}$ is surrounded by $\mathbf{A}$ and $\mathbf{v}_y$. Using a divide-and-conquer approach, we can solve for one row $\mathbf{u}_i$ of $\mathbf{U}$, and iterate over the entire rows. This divide-and-conquer approach is, however, susceptible to the sequence of rows, and cannot be generalized to an arbitrary aggregation matrix.

We propose a simple and efficient optimization solution by introducing an auxiliary variable $\mathbf{\Pi} = \mathbf{A}\mathbf{U}$ where we treat $\mathbf{\Pi}$ as an independent variable. We also relax the hard relationship between $\mathbf{\Pi}$ and $\mathbf{U}$ as a penalty term.

Combining these two tricks, our new objective function is written as follows:

$$\min_{\mathbf{U},\mathbf{V},\mathbf{\Pi}} \|\mathbf{X} - \mathbf{U}\mathbf{V}_x^\top\|_F^2 + \|\sqrt{\mathbf{W}}(\mathbf{s} - \mathbf{\Pi}\mathbf{v}_y^\top)\|_2^2 + \|\mathbf{A}\mathbf{U} - \mathbf{\Pi}\|_F^2 \tag{6}$$

where $\mathbf{W} = (\mathbf{A}\mathbf{A}^\top)^{-1}$. This objective function is LUDIA's objective function, and denote as $\mathcal{L}(\mathbf{U},\mathbf{V},\mathbf{\Pi})$. We now apply our alternating minimization technique to Equation 6.

3.3.1 *Solving for* U

First, we derive the partial derivative of the LUDIA objective function with respect to $\mathbf{U}$:

$$\frac{\partial\mathcal{L}(\mathbf{U},\mathbf{V},\mathbf{\Pi})}{\partial\mathbf{U}} = -\mathbf{X}\mathbf{V}_x + \mathbf{U}\mathbf{V}_x^\top\mathbf{V}_x + \mathbf{A}^\top\mathbf{A}\mathbf{U} - \mathbf{A}^\top\mathbf{\Pi} = 0$$

Rearranging the terms, we obtain:

$$\mathbf{U}\mathbf{V}_x^\top\mathbf{V}_x + \mathbf{A}^\top\mathbf{A}\mathbf{U} = \mathbf{X}\mathbf{V}_x + \mathbf{A}^\top\mathbf{\Pi}$$

This is a type of a Sylvester equation [2]. This form of equation widely appears in the field of control theory [3], and the continuous Lyapanov equation is a special case of the Sylvester equation. If $\mathbf{V}_x^\top\mathbf{V}_x$ and $\mathbf{A}^\top\mathbf{A}$ have no common eigenvalues, a unique solution exists and it is given as:

$$\text{vec}(\mathbf{U}) = (\mathbf{V}_x^\top\mathbf{V}_x \otimes \mathbf{I}_n + \mathbf{I}_r \otimes \mathbf{A}^\top\mathbf{A})^{-1}\text{vec}(\mathbf{X}\mathbf{V}_x + \mathbf{A}^\top\mathbf{\Pi})$$

where vec is a vectorization operator, and $\otimes$ represents the Kronecker product. For example, vec($\mathbf{U}$) is defined as:

$$\text{vec}(\mathbf{U}) = \begin{bmatrix} u_{1,1} & \dots & u_{n,1} & u_{1,2} & \dots & u_{1,r}, \dots u_{n,r} \end{bmatrix}^\top$$

3.3.2 *Solving for* Π

Next, we derive a partial derivative of the LUDIA objective function with respect to $\mathbf{\Pi}$:

$$\frac{\partial\mathcal{L}(\mathbf{U},\mathbf{V},\mathbf{\Pi})}{\partial\mathbf{\Pi}} = -\mathbf{W}(\mathbf{s} - \mathbf{\Pi}\mathbf{v}_y^\top)\mathbf{v}_y - \mathbf{A}\mathbf{U} + \mathbf{\Pi} = 0$$

Rearranging the terms, we obtain another Sylvester equation:

$$\mathbf{W}\mathbf{\Pi}\mathbf{v}_y^\top\mathbf{v}_y + \mathbf{\Pi} = \mathbf{W}\mathbf{s}\mathbf{v}_y + \mathbf{A}\mathbf{U}$$

The solution is given as:

$$\text{vec}(\mathbf{\Pi}) = (\mathbf{I}_r \otimes \mathbf{I}_p + \mathbf{v}_y^\top\mathbf{v}_y \otimes \mathbf{W})^{-1}\text{vec}(\mathbf{W}\mathbf{s}\mathbf{v}_y + \mathbf{A}\mathbf{U})$$

3.3.3 *Solving for* V

Finally, we derive closed form update equations for two block matrices $\mathbf{V}_x$ and $\mathbf{v}_y$. The partial derivative with respect to $\mathbf{V}_x$ is given as:

$$\frac{\partial\mathcal{L}(\mathbf{U},\mathbf{V},\mathbf{\Pi})}{\partial\mathbf{V}_x} = -\mathbf{U}^\top(\mathbf{X} - \mathbf{U}\mathbf{V}_x) = 0$$

Rearranging the terms, we obtain:

$$\mathbf{V}_x = (\mathbf{U}^\top\mathbf{U})^{-1}\mathbf{U}^\top\mathbf{X}$$

Similarly, the partial derivative with respect to $\mathbf{v}_y$ is:

$$\frac{\partial\mathcal{L}(\mathbf{U},\mathbf{V},\mathbf{\Pi})}{\partial\mathbf{v}_y} = -\mathbf{\Pi}^\top\mathbf{W}(\mathbf{s} - \mathbf{\Pi}\mathbf{v}_y^\top) = 0$$

Thus, the update form is:

$$\mathbf{v}_y^\top = (\mathbf{\Pi}^\top\mathbf{W}\mathbf{\Pi})^{-1}\mathbf{\Pi}^\top\mathbf{W}\mathbf{s}$$

3.4 Algorithm

Algorithm 1 summarizes our alternating minimization approach combining three different minimization equations for $\mathbf{U}$, $\mathbf{\Pi}$, and $\mathbf{V}$. The algorithm takes three input matrices: individual-level matrix $\mathbf{X}$, aggregation matrix $\mathbf{A}$, and aggregate-level matrix $\mathbf{s}$. The output of the algorithm is the reconstructed individual-level data $\hat{\mathbf{y}}$. The algorithm does not require any other parameters.

Algorithm 1: LUDIA Estimation Algorithm

Data: $\mathbf{X}, \mathbf{A}, \mathbf{s}$
Result: $\hat{\mathbf{y}}$
$r = \text{rank}(\mathbf{X}))$;
$\bar{\mathbf{y}} = \mathbf{A}^+\mathbf{s}$;
$\mathbf{U}, \mathbf{V} = \text{SVD}(\begin{bmatrix}\mathbf{X} & \bar{\mathbf{y}}\end{bmatrix}, \text{rank} = r)$;
$\mathbf{\Pi} = \mathbf{A}\mathbf{U}$;
while *not converged* **do**
  $\text{vec}(\mathbf{U}) = (\mathbf{V}_x^\top\mathbf{V}_x \otimes \mathbf{I}_n + \mathbf{I}_r \otimes \mathbf{A}^\top\mathbf{A})^{-1}\text{vec}(\mathbf{X}\mathbf{V}_x + \mathbf{A}^\top\mathbf{\Pi})$;
  $\text{vec}(\mathbf{\Pi}) = (\mathbf{I}_r \otimes \mathbf{I}_p + \mathbf{v}_y^\top\mathbf{v}_y \otimes \mathbf{W})^{-1}\text{vec}(\mathbf{W}\mathbf{s}\mathbf{v}_y + \mathbf{A}\mathbf{U})$;
  $\mathbf{V}_x = (\mathbf{U}^\top\mathbf{U})^{-1}\mathbf{U}^\top\mathbf{X}$;
  $\mathbf{v}_y^\top = (\mathbf{\Pi}^\top\mathbf{A}\mathbf{A}^\top\mathbf{\Pi})^{-1}\mathbf{\Pi}^\top\mathbf{A}\mathbf{A}^\top\mathbf{s}$;
end
$\hat{\mathbf{y}} = \mathbf{U}\mathbf{v}_y^\top$;
// correction equation;
$\hat{\mathbf{y}} = \hat{\mathbf{y}} + \mathbf{A}^+(\mathbf{s} - \mathbf{A}\hat{\mathbf{y}})$

The initialization of $\mathbf{U}$ and $\mathbf{V}$ is based on the MP solution. We first pseudo-reconstruct the masked individual-level data using MP, then run SVD on the pseudo-complete matrix. The rank parameter of the SVD algorithm is given as the rank of $\mathbf{X}$. This setting captures both our low-rank data model and a linear model defined as $\mathbf{y} = \mathbf{X}\boldsymbol{\beta}$. If this linear model is the true underlying data model for the data, then the rank of the complete matrix is the same as the rank of $\mathbf{X}$.

The last line of the algorithm calibrates the final output. Recall that the optimal $\mathbf{y}^*$ was given in Equation 4. This correction equation ensures that the aggregation of the reconstructed values are the same as the given aggregate data i.e. $\mathbf{s} = \mathbf{A}\hat{\mathbf{y}}$. However, if the aggregate values do not necessarily need to match the reconstructed values (possibly from noise or sub-sampling), we can ignore the last line of the algorithm.

4. EXTENSIONS

We illustrate two extensions of the LUDIA algorithm. The first extension shows that LUDIA can directly incorporate multi-level data models. This extended reconstruction method can capture group-level effects, which were not possible in classical frameworks. The second extension explores whether we can improve the reconstruction quality if we have multiple levels of aggregate data.

4.1 Multi-level Modeling

The ecological fallacy problem is essentially "statistical under-identification" [34]. For aggregate data analyses, the maximum degrees of freedom are limited by the number of partitions. Individual-level analyses, such as multi-level models [19], often require more parameters than the number of partitions. This under-identification problem is traditionally approached by more assumptions; Goodman's and King's assumptions are two extreme cases. These assumptions are usually unrealistic, and they are almost impossible to verify on the basis of aggregate data.

Smartly utilizing auxiliary individual-level data can provide higher degrees of freedom than the number of partitions. The key observation comes from the connection between the degrees of freedom and the rank of a full matrix. Suppose that a target $\mathbf{y}$ is a function of r degrees of freedom. Then the rank of the full matrix $\begin{bmatrix}\mathbf{X} & \mathbf{y}\end{bmatrix}$ is r, since $\mathbf{y}$ can be expressed by a linear combination of $\mathbf{X}$. Analogously, if a target is a multi-level function of r variables and p levels, then the degrees of freedom for this model is given by $(r \times p)$. To capture the variability of the target, the corresponding full matrix needs to have the rank of $(r \times p)$. In this section, we show that this rank augmentation can be seamlessly integrated with the LUDIA framework.

As illustrated in Equation 1, a multi-level model can be compactly written as:

$$\mathbf{y} = \mathbf{X}\boldsymbol{\beta} + \mathbf{G}\boldsymbol{\gamma} + \mathbf{E} \approx \begin{bmatrix}\mathbf{X} & \mathbf{G}\end{bmatrix}\begin{bmatrix}\boldsymbol{\beta}\\ \boldsymbol{\gamma}\end{bmatrix}$$

where $\boldsymbol{\gamma} \in \mathbb{R}^{l\times 1}$ is a random effect vector, and $\mathbf{G} \in \mathbb{R}^{n\times l}$ represents encoded covariates according to $\boldsymbol{\gamma}$. For this model, the degrees of freedom are given as $(r+l)$ where $r = \text{rank}(\mathbf{X})$. The full matrix has $(r+l+1)$ columns, and this matrix can be written as a product of two rank $(r+l)$ matrices.

To fully reconstruct the masked individual-level data, the rank of our low-rank model should be at least $(r+l)$. This can be achieved by augmenting the data by l:

$$\begin{bmatrix}\mathbf{X} & \mathbf{G} & \mathbf{y}\end{bmatrix} \approx \begin{bmatrix}\mathbf{U} & \tilde{\mathbf{U}}\end{bmatrix}\begin{bmatrix}\mathbf{V}_x^\top & \tilde{\mathbf{V}}_{x1} & \mathbf{v}_y^\top\\ \tilde{\mathbf{V}}_{x2} & \tilde{\mathbf{V}}_{x3} & \mathbf{v}_a^\top\end{bmatrix}$$

where $\tilde{\mathbf{U}} \in \mathbb{R}^{n\times l}$, $\tilde{\mathbf{V}}_{x\cdot} \in \mathbb{R}^{l\times l}$, and $\mathbf{v}_a \in \mathbb{R}^{1\times l}$.

Although one can run LUDIA with these augmented terms, we show that a simple post-processing approach can mimic the result from this augmentation. The block matrix $\tilde{\mathbf{V}}_x$ can be treated as a nuance parameter, since it does not directly affect the reconstruction of $\mathbf{y}$. The trick is to specify our low-rank matrices to be of a specific form as follows:

$$\begin{bmatrix}\mathbf{X} & \mathbf{G} & \mathbf{y}\end{bmatrix} \approx \begin{bmatrix}\mathbf{U} & \mathbf{G}\end{bmatrix}\begin{bmatrix}\mathbf{V}_x^\top & \mathbf{0} & \mathbf{v}_y^\top\\ \mathbf{0} & \mathbf{I}_l & \mathbf{v}_a^\top\end{bmatrix}$$

Then we do not need to estimate $\tilde{\mathbf{U}}$ and $\tilde{\mathbf{V}}_x$, but only $\mathbf{v}_a$. The augmented term $\mathbf{v}_a$ needs to minimize the second term of Equation 6:

$$\min_{\mathbf{v}_a} \|\sqrt{\mathbf{W}}(\mathbf{s} - \mathbf{A}\begin{bmatrix}\mathbf{U} & \mathbf{G}\end{bmatrix}\begin{bmatrix}\mathbf{v}_y^\top\\ \mathbf{v}_a^\top\end{bmatrix})\|_2^2$$

The solution for this minimization problem is given as follows:

$$\hat{\mathbf{v}}_a^\top = ((\mathbf{AG})^\top\mathbf{WAG})^{-1}(\mathbf{AG})^\top\mathbf{W}(\mathbf{s} - \mathbf{AU}\mathbf{v}_y^\top)$$

Using this $\mathbf{v}_a$, we calibrate the reconstruction of $\mathbf{y}$:

$$\hat{\mathbf{y}} = \mathbf{U}\mathbf{v}_y^\top + \mathbf{G}\hat{\mathbf{v}}_a^\top$$

This adjustment equation mimics the original augmentation.

This data augmentation technique for multi-level modeling is not suitable for the MP and ER frameworks. MP only focuses on the aggregation matrix, and does not involve individual-level covariates. Adding the augmented block matrix $\mathbf{G}$ requires a different approach. The number of covariates in ER is upper-bounded by the number of partitions. The simplest multi-level model, a random intercept model, requires the number of covariates to be the same as the number of partitions. LUDIA utilizes the full potential of individual-level covariates, and thus it can be easily extended to more complex models.

4.2 Aggregation Stacking

Thus far, we have considered only one source of aggregate data. There can be many levels of groupings based on geography, administration, or other factors. This section answers how one can further improve the reconstruction quality with additional aggregate data.

The key trick is to stack two aggregate-level datasets and create a new aggregate dataset. Algorithm 2 illustrates this approach. In the algorithm, we have two sources of aggregate data: $(\mathbf{A}_1, \mathbf{s}_1)$ and $(\mathbf{A}_2, \mathbf{s}_2)$. For example, there can be county-level and state-level aggregate data, respectively. This kind of augmentation can further improve the reconstruction accuracy. This is because we have more constraints on $\mathbf{y}$, and the degrees of freedom for $\mathbf{y}$ decrease accordingly.

Algorithm 2: LUDIA with Aggregation Stacking

Data: $\mathbf{X}, \mathbf{A}_1, \mathbf{s}_1, \mathbf{A}_2, \mathbf{s}_2$
Result: $\hat{\mathbf{y}}$
$\mathbf{A} = \begin{bmatrix}\mathbf{A}_1\\ \mathbf{A}_2\end{bmatrix}$ and $\mathbf{s} = \begin{bmatrix}\mathbf{s}_1\\ \mathbf{s}_2\end{bmatrix}$;
$\hat{\mathbf{y}} = \text{LUDIA}(\mathbf{X}, \mathbf{A}, \mathbf{s})$;

5. PROBABILISTIC INTERPRETATION

This section presents a probabilistic interpretation of the proposed LUDIA objective function. Figure 2a shows our low-rank model for the complete data. Note that the node for y is not shaded, since the variable is masked. To incorporate the aggregation constraint, we draw another plate that represents groupings. Figure 2b illustrates the graphical model for LUDIA. Each $\mathbf{u}_i$ in a group is assumed to be

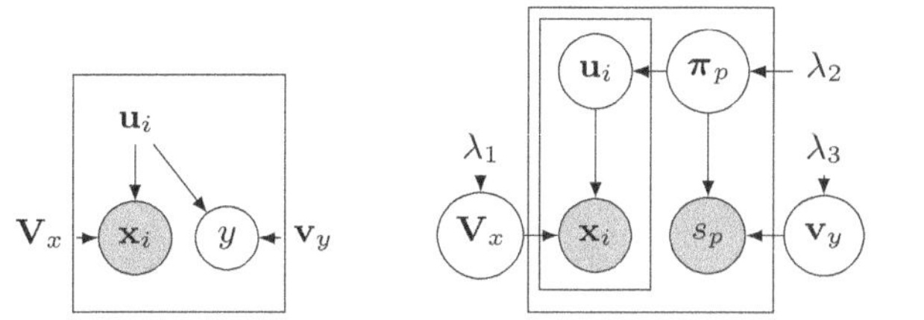

(a) Low-rank model for complete data. (b) Low-rank model with the aggregation constraint.

Figure 2: Probabilistic Models for LUDIA.

drawn from a multivariate Gaussian centered at $\boldsymbol{\pi}_p$. Thus, the log-likelihood $\log p(\mathbf{U}, \mathbf{V}, \mathbf{\Pi} \mid \mathbf{X}, \mathbf{s})$ of LUDIA is written as:

$$\begin{aligned} &-(\mathbf{X}-\mathbf{U}\mathbf{V}_x^\top)^\top \mathbf{\Sigma}_x^{-1}(\mathbf{X}-\mathbf{U}\mathbf{V}_x^\top)\\ &-(\mathbf{s}-\mathbf{\Pi}\mathbf{v}_y^\top)^\top \mathbf{\Sigma}_y^{-1}(\mathbf{s}-\mathbf{\Pi}\mathbf{v}_y^\top)\\ &-(\mathbf{\Pi}-\mathbf{A}\mathbf{U})^\top \mathbf{\Sigma}_\pi^{-1}(\mathbf{\Pi}-\mathbf{A}\mathbf{U}) + \text{const.} \end{aligned}$$

In our setting, each row of $\mathbf{X}$ is i.i.d., thus $\mathbf{\Sigma}_x$ can be modeled as an identity matrix $\mathbf{I}_n$. Before characterizing $\mathbf{\Sigma}_y$, we first show that $\mathbf{A}\mathbf{A}^\top$ is invertible and positive-semidefinite. This property can be shown from the fact that $\text{rank}(\mathbf{A}) = p$ and $\mathbf{A}\mathbf{A}^\top \in \mathbb{R}^{p\times p}$. Moreover, the (p,p)th diagonal component of $(\mathbf{A}\mathbf{A}^\top)^{-1}$ is the same as n_p, the number of data points in group p. Thus, $\mathbf{A}\mathbf{A}^\top$ can replace $\mathbf{\Sigma}_y$. Finally, if we assume that $\mathbf{\Sigma}_\pi = \mathbf{I}_p$, then this log-likehood is actually a negative of the LUDIA objective function.

To show the connection to CUDIA, let us assume that we restrict the shape of $\mathbf{U}$ to be as follows:

$$\mathbf{U}_C \quad \text{s.t.} \quad u_{ij} \in \{0,1\} \quad \text{and} \quad \sum_j u_{ij} = 1$$

In other words, each column of $\mathbf{U}$ becomes an indicator column for clusters. The rank parameter r of LUDIA is now interpreted as r different clusters, and $\mathbf{V}$ represents cluster centers. If we plug in this constraint to the LUDIA's log-likelihood function, we obtain the log-likelihood of CUDIA. Although this formulation may provide a different perspective on combining multiple sources of data, the minimization of the CUDIA objective function is more complicated to solve because of the non-negative constraint. Thus, CUDIA requires a computationally heavy MCEM algorithm, or greedy deterministic algorithm [31]. As the non-negative case is a special case of $\mathbf{U}$, we also have:

$$\|\mathbf{D}-\mathbf{U}\mathbf{V}^\top\|_F^2 \le \|\mathbf{D}-\mathbf{U}_C\mathbf{V}^\top\|_F^2$$

This is why the CUDIA imputation is not so suitable for complex modeling such as multi-level modeling and non-linear estimates, while the LUDIA reconstruction provides valid inferences in such situations (see Section 6).

6. EXPERIMENTAL RESULTS

We provide experimental results using simulated data and Texas Inpatient Discharge data. A simulated dataset is used to illustrate the differences between ER, MP, and LUDIA. Next, we illustrate reconstruction tasks using actual health data. In this set of experiments, we mask sensitive columns, then show how well LUDIA can reconstruct the masked original values for different analytical tasks including non-linear estimates and multi-level modeling.

6.1 Simulated Data

We generate four different simulated datasets as follows:

- Low-Rank (LR) model emulates the model assumption of LUDIA. The parameters are given as $r = 2$ and $m = 4$. The equation for simulated data is as follows:

  $$[\mathbf{X} \quad \mathbf{y}] = \mathbf{U}\mathbf{V}^\top + \mathbf{E}$$

  where $\mathbf{U}$ and $\mathbf{V}$ are drawn from the standard normal distribution, and the noise matrix $\mathbf{E}$ is drawn from a normal distribution with 0.4 standard deviation.

- Fixed Effect (FE) model emulates the model assumption of ER. We generate individual-level matrices with $m = 2$ from the standard normal distribution. The model equation is:

  $$\mathbf{y} = \mathbf{c} + \mathbf{X}\boldsymbol{\beta} + \mathbf{E}$$

  where $\mathbf{E}$ is drawn from a normal distribution with 0.2 standard deviation.

- Random Intercept (RE1) and Random Slope (RE2) model check whether the LUDIA's multi-level argument is valid. The model equation is:

  $$\mathbf{y} = \mathbf{c} + \mathbf{X}\boldsymbol{\beta} + \mathbf{G}\boldsymbol{\gamma} + \mathbf{E}$$

  where $\boldsymbol{\gamma}$ is drawn from a normal distribution with 0.2 standard deviation.

We fix the number of partitions to be five, and vary the number of total data points. Aggregation matrices are generated using random assignment of partitions.

Figure 3 shows the reconstruction errors for different simulated data and reconstruction methods. Each cell represents a different simulated dataset, and the horizontal axes represent the number of data points per partition. The lower the curve is, the better the reconstruction quality is. MP is not affected by the number of data points per partition, but its performance is the worst from the experiments. The performance of ER is comparable with that of LUDIA for the FE dataset, but it does not capture the low-rank structure and random effects. For the random effect datasets, ER is largely affected by the number of data points per partition. LUDIA shows robust and stable performances over different datasets.

Figure 4 shows the reconstructed values compared to the original values from the RE1 dataset. The leftmost first two cells show the reconstructed values from MP and ER, respectively. In this figure, we show three different initialization methods for LUDIA: MP, ER, and random initialization methods. The alternating minimization approach of LUDIA does not guarantee the convergence to the global optimum, and the algorithm is susceptible to initial points. All three initialization methods provide comparable performances, and it would be worthwhile to investigate the better choice of initialization methods. The rest of the experiments use the MP initialization to maintain the consistency of our algorithm.

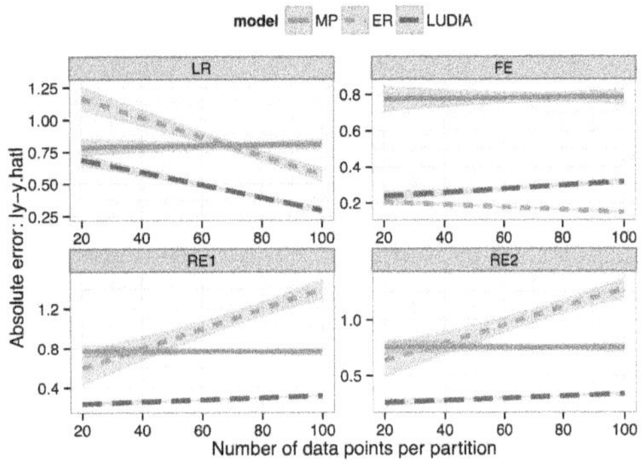

Figure 3: Reconstruction error vs. number of data points per partition. Except the FE case, the LUDIA reconstruction shows the least absolute errors.

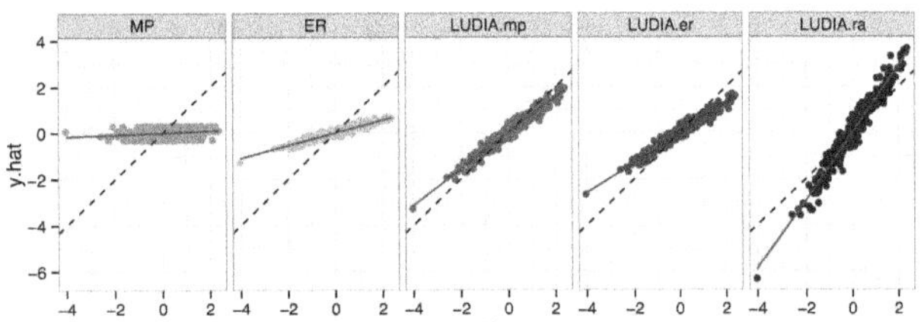

Figure 4: Reconstructed vs. original. We show three different initializations for LUDIA: MP, ER, and random initializations. All these three LUDIA reconstructions are closer to the original values, and the MP initialization performs the best.

6.2 Texas Inpatient Data

We use Texas Inpatient Public Use Data File [38] from the Texas Department of State Health Services (DSHS). Hospital billing records collected from 1999 to 2007 are publicly available through their website. Each yearly dataset contains about 2.8 millions events with more than 250 features including hospital name, county, patient ZIP codes, etc. Specifically, we use the inpatient records from Central Texas in the fourth quarter of 2006. Except for a few exempt hospitals, all the hospitals in Texas reported inpatient discharge events to DSHS. The public use data file we use is a subset of the DSHS's hospital discharge database. Our primary interest is the hospital charge for normal delivery. We aggregate the individual-level hospital charges at county-, hospital-, and ZIP code-levels. We assume that some of the individual-level covariates are available such race, specialty unit, length of stay variables.

Hospital charge is primarily a function of length of stay, but it is substantially different across regions and is also affected by many other factors:

$$\mathrm{HC} = \beta_{\mathrm{hospital}}\mathrm{LoS}^{\alpha} + \mathrm{unit} + \mathrm{severity} + \ldots + \mathrm{error}$$

where HC and LoS represent Hospital Charge and Length of Stay, respectively. Note that the coefficient for LoS is indexed by hospital, since daily charge rate is a function of hospital. The distribution of HC is, in fact, similar to a log-normal distribution. It is a better practice to log-transform the data, before applying a linear model:

$$\log \mathrm{HC} = \log \beta_{\mathrm{hospital}} + \alpha \log \mathrm{LoS} + \ldots + \mathrm{Error}'$$

Table 3: Reconstruction Accuracy of the Texas dataset

Level	Model	MAE	MSE
County	MR	0.648 (± 0.75)	0.976 (± 3.28)
	ER	**0.466** (± 0.45)	**0.422** (± 0.87)
	LUDIA	0.514 (± 0.48)	0.497 (± 1.14)
Hospital	MR	0.609 (± 0.69)	0.851 (± 2.92)
	ER	0.513 (± 0.49)	0.501 (± 1.10)
	LUDIA	**0.435** (± 0.40)	**0.348** (± 0.68)
Patient ZIP	MR	0.589 (± 0.69)	0.824 (± 2.92)
	ER	0.319 (± 0.28)	0.184 (± 0.38)
	LUDIA	**0.289** (± 0.26)	**0.152** (± 0.34)

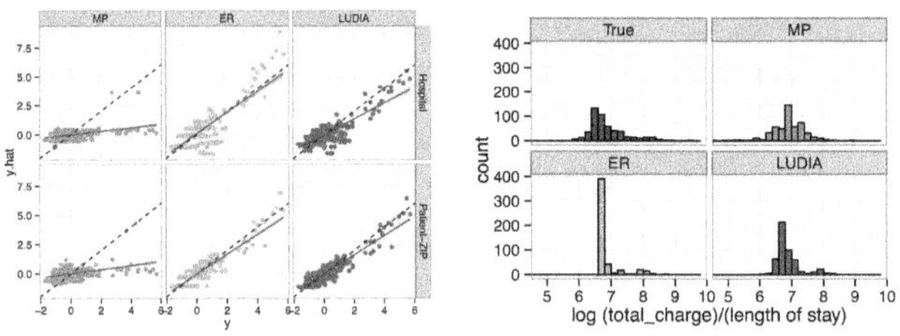

(a) (b)

Figure 5: (a) Reconstructed vs. original for the 3 models. (b) Estimated histograms of daily hospital charges. LUDIA histogram is the closest to the original.

This log-transformed linear model turns out to be a simple random intercept model.

Table 3 shows the reconstruction errors from three different levels of aggregation. Except for the county-level case, the LUDIA-reconstructed values are the closest to the original values with smallest variances. ER performs slightly better than LUDIA for the county-level aggregate data. This is because the multi-level effects at county-level are not distinctive enough i.e. the constancy assumption can be applied. Figure 5a illustrates the reconstructed values compared to the original values. If reconstruction is perfect, points should lie on the dotted diagonal lines. As can be seen, the MP reconstructions do not capture the tails. This is because, when the HC values are averaged, those tail values are typically cancelled out, and MP cannot infer beyond the provided average statistics. The ER reconstructions perform reasonably well, but does not capture the multi-level bias. LUDIA provides better estimates for the original values in terms of Mean Absolute Error (MAE).

The advantages of LUDIA are even more highlighted when calculating non-linear estimates. As an illustrative example, suppose that we want to estimate average daily charges. To calculate this value, we first need to reconstruct individual-level hospital charges, and then divide the reconstructed charges by the individual-level length of stay variable. In other words, average daily charges are calculated as follows:

$$\text{Average Daily Charge} = \frac{1}{n}\sum_i \frac{\hat{\mathrm{HC}}_i}{\mathrm{LoS}_i}$$

Figure 5b show the histograms of the estimated average daily charges. As can be seen, the histogram from LUDIA captures the asymmetrical shape of the original histogram.

As shown in Section 4, multi-level modeling can be directly integrated with LUDIA. We extract rural counties of

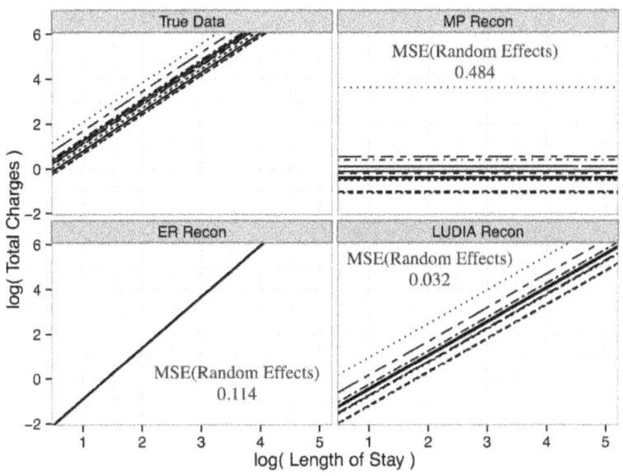

Figure 6: Multi-level modeling and the mean squared errors, shown as "MSE(Random Effects)", between the original random effects and estimated random effects. LUDIA's random effects are almost the same as the original.

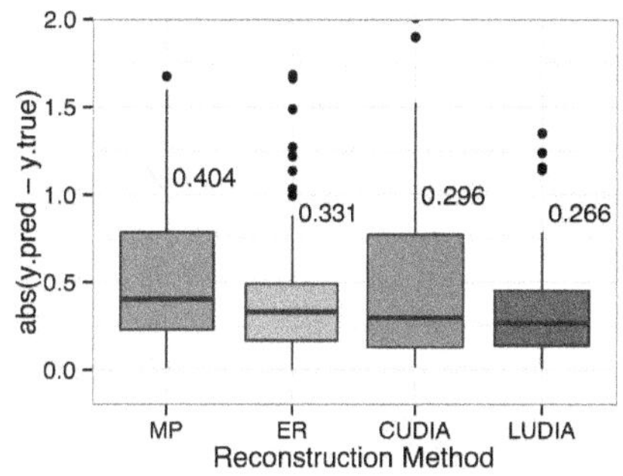

Figure 7: Predictive performance of the Lasso (`glmnet`) models trained on the reconstructed data. Absolute errors are measured using a hold-out dataset.

Central Texas, and compare the hospital charges by applying a random intercept model. Figure 6 shows the fitted lines from the multi-level models. As can be seen, the original data clearly show the random intercept terms. It was impossible to estimate the slope term from the MP reconstructed values. For the ER reconstructed values, although the global model was similar to the original data, we cannot visually check the random intercepts. This is because ER ignores the information from the aggregation matrix. On the other hand, LUDIA provides almost the exact same random effect coefficients.

Reconstructed values from aggregate data can be used in various data mining applications. In this paper, we show a simple predictive analysis when a target column is provided in an aggregate form. By reconstructing the individual-level target values from the aggregate data, we can train a model, and then apply the model to test data as follows:

1. Combine the aggregate and individual-level data, then reconstruct the masked column
2. Train a predictive model using the pseudo complete data
3. For new data points, predict the target values using the trained model

We first divided the Texas inpatient dataset into a training (80%) and a hold-out (test, 20%) set. Assuming the total charges (target) are provided in only an aggregate form, we reconstruct the target using three different algorithms. We trained a Lasso regression model, and then measured the predictive accuracies of the target. Figure 7 shows the results from the test set. As can be seen, the LUDIA-reconstructed training dataset provides the best Lasso model in terms of MAEs. In this example, we included the performance of a model that is trained on CUDIA-reconstructed data. The CUDIA-reconstructed dataset provides better predictive accuracies than the MP- and ER-reconstructed training datasets. However, CUDIA is still a clustering algorithm, and the reconstruction from CUDIA is based on estimated cluster centers. Although CUDIA provides homogenous cluster centers, it does not generate fine-grained reconstruction like LUDIA. The predictive Lasso model trained on the CUDIA-reconstructed dataset exhibits higher MAE and variances than the model trained on the LUDIA-reconstructed dataset.

7. DISCUSSION

The implication of our research can be viewed from two perspectives.

Utility perspective. Our method allows aggregated data to be effectively utilized in individual-level inferential tasks. This is particularly important since standard imputation techniques do not make use of the summary statistics provided by aggregated data that are widely available for social good. Many machine learning algorithms that require completely observed data can now be directly applied to the LUDIA-reconstructed data.

Privacy perspective. Although the reconstructed values are not guaranteed to be identical to the true values, it is clear that the estimated values are correlated with the actual values. If additional theoretical guarantees are developed, data aggregation may be no longer perfectly safe from privacy attacks. With enough auxiliary information, it is possible that private information gets revealed using techniques similar to LUDIA. This implies that, in the future, reconstruction performance will need to be considered prior to data aggregation, to guarantee that privacy requirements are met.

The proposed LUDIA framework can be extended to more complex data models. It is also worthwhile to investigate more efficient solutions for the Sylvester equation. One can also explore theoretical reconstruction guarantees that depend on the characteristics of the datasets and of the aggregation matrices.

Acknowledgements

This work is supported by NSF IIS-1016614 and by TATP grant 01829.

8. REFERENCES

[1] M. P. Armstrong, G. Rushton, and D. L. Zimmerman. Geographically masking health data to preserve confidentiality. *Statistics in Medicine*, 18:497–525, 1999.

[2] R. H. Bartels and G. W. Stewart. Solution of the matrix equation $ax + xb = c$. *Communications of the ACM*, 15(9):820–826, 1972.

[3] R. Bhatia and P. Rosenthal. How and why to solve the operater equation $ax - xb = y$. *Bulletin of the London Mathematical Society*, 29(1):1–21, 1997.

[4] S. Boyd and L. Vandenberghe. *Convex Optimization.* Cambridge University Press, 2004.

[5] E. J. Candes and B. Recht. Exact Matrix Completion via Convex Optimization. *Foundations of Computational Mathematics*, 2008.

[6] K. Carroll. Experimental evidence of dietary factors and hormone-dependent cancers. *Cancer Research*, 35:3374–3383, 1975.

[7] Centers for Disease Control and Prevension (CDC). Data and statistics. `http://www.cdc.gov/datastatistics/`, 2014.

[8] T. Dalenius and S. P. Reiss. Data-swapping: A technique for disclosure control (exteded abstract). In *Proceedings of the Section on Survey Research Methods*, 1978.

[9] Data.CMS.gov. Inpatient prospective payment system. `https://data.cms.gov/Medicare/Inpatient-Prospective-Payment-System-IPPS-Provider/97k6-zzx3`, 2014.

[10] G. T. Duncan, M. Elliot, and J.-J. Salazar-Gonzalez. *Statistical Confidentiality: Principles and Practice.* Springer, 2011.

[11] O. D. Duncan and B. Davis. An alternative to ecological correlation. *American Sociological Review*, 18:665–666, 1953.

[12] C. Eckart and G. Young. The approximation of one matrix by another lower rank. *Psychometrika*, 1936.

[13] S. E. Fienberg and J. McIntyre. Data swapping: Variations on a theme by Dalenius and Reiss. *Journal of Official Statistics*, 21:309–323, 2005.

[14] D. A. Freedman. Ecological inference and the ecological fallacy. Technical Report 549, Department of Statistics, University of California Berkeley, CA 94720, October 1999.

[15] D. A. Freedman, S. P. Klein, M. Ostland, and M. Roberts. On "solutions" to the ecological inference probelm. *Journal of the American Statistical Association*, 93:1518–22, 1999.

[16] D. A. Freedman, S. P. Klein, J. Sacks, C. A. Smyth, and C. G. Everett. Ecological regression and voting rights. *Evaluation Review*, (673-816), 15.

[17] W. A. Fuller. Masking procedures for microdata disclosure limitation. *Journal of Official Statistics*, 9(2):383–406, 1993.

[18] A. Gelman and J. Hill. *Data Analysis using Regression and Multilevel/Hierarchical Models.* Cambridge University Press, 2007.

[19] H. Goldstein. *Multilevel Statistical Models.* Wiley, 4th edition, 2010.

[20] L. Goodman. Ecological regression and the behavior of individuals. *American Sociological Review*, 18:663–664, 1953.

[21] L. Goodman. Some alternatives to ecological correlation. *American Journal of Socialogy*, 64:610–625, 1959.

[22] W. He, X. Liu, H. Nguyen, K. Nahrstedt, and T. Abdelzaher. PDA: Privacy-preserving data aggregation in wireless sensor netoworks. *IEEE International Conference on Computer Communications*, pages 2045–2053, 2007.

[23] C. R. Johnson. Matrix completion problems: a survey. *Proceedings of Symposia in Applied Mathematics*, 1990.

[24] Kaiser Family Foundation. Hospital adjusted expenses per inpatient day. `http://kff.org/other/state-indicator/expenses-per-inpatient-day/`, 2011.

[25] G. King. *A Solution to the ecological inference problem: reconstructing individual behavior from aggregate data.* Princeton University Press, 1997.

[26] G. King, O. Rosen, and M. A. Tanner. Binomial-beta hierarchical models for ecological inference. *Sociological Methods and Research*, 28:61–90, 1999.

[27] G. King, O. Rosen, and M. A. Tanner. *Ecological Inference.* Cambridge University Press, 2004.

[28] A. Machanavajjhala, D. Kifer, J. Gehrke, and M. Venkitasubramanian. l-diversity: Privacy beyond k-anonymity. *Transactions on Knowledge Discovery from Data*, 1, 2007.

[29] C. Ordonez and Z. Chen. Horizontal aggregations in sql to prepare data sets for data mining analysis. *IEEE Transactions on Knowledge and Data Engineering*, pages 678–691, 2012.

[30] Y. Park and J. Ghosh. A generative framework for predictive modeling using variably aggregated, multi-source healthcare data. In *Proceedings of the 17th ACM SIGKDD International Conference on Knowledge Discovery and Data Mining Workshop on Medicine and Healthcare*, pages 27–32, 2011.

[31] Y. Park and J. Ghosh. Cudia: Probabilistic cross-level imputation using individual auxiliary information. *ACM Transactions on Intelligent Systems and Technology*, 2012.

[32] Y. Park and J. Ghosh. A probabilistic imputation framework for predictive analysis using variably aggregated, multi-source healthcare data. In *Proceedings of the 2nd ACM SIGHIT International Health Informatics Symposium*, 2012.

[33] President's Concil of Advisors on Science and Technology. Report to the president realizing the full potential of health information technology to improve healthcare for americans: the path forward. Technical report, Office of Science and Technology Policy, the White House, December 2010.

[34] J. Richmond. Aggregation and identification. *International Economic Review*, 17:47–56, 1976.

[35] W. S. Robinson. Ecological correlations and the behavior of individuals. *American Sociological Review*, 15:351–357, 1950.

[36] L. Sweeney. k-anonymity: a model for protecting privacy. *Int. J. Uncertain. Fuzziness Knowl.-Based Syst.*, 10:557–570, October 2002.

[37] M. Templ. Statistical disclosure control for microdata using the r-package sdcMicro. *Transactions on Data Privacy*, pages 67–85, 2008.

[38] Texas Department of State Health Services. Texas Inpatient Public Use Data File. `https://www.dshs.state.tx.us/thcic/hospitals/Inpatientpudf.shtm`, 2014.

People on Drugs: Credibility of User Statements in Health Communities

Subhabrata Mukherjee[†] Gerhard Weikum[†] Cristian Danescu-Niculescu-Mizil[‡]
[†]Max Planck Institute for Informatics, [‡]Max Planck Institute for Software Systems
smukherjee@mpi-inf.mpg.de, weikum@mpi-inf.mpg.de, cristian@mpi-sws.org

Abstract

Online health communities are a valuable source of information for patients and physicians. However, such user-generated resources are often plagued by inaccuracies and misinformation. In this work we propose a method for automatically establishing the credibility of user-generated medical statements and the trustworthiness of their authors by exploiting linguistic cues and distant supervision from expert sources. To this end we introduce a probabilistic graphical model that jointly learns user trustworthiness, statement credibility, and language objectivity.

We apply this methodology to the task of extracting rare or unknown side-effects of medical drugs—this being one of the problems where large scale non-expert data has the potential to complement expert medical knowledge. We show that our method can reliably extract side-effects and filter out false statements, while identifying trustworthy users that are likely to contribute valuable medical information.

Categories and Subject Descriptors

H.3.3 [**Information Storage and Retrieval**]: Information Search and Retrieval - *Information Filtering*; I.2.7 [**Computing Methodologies**]: Artificial Intelligence - *Natural Language Processing*

General Terms

Design, Algorithms, Measurement, Experimentation

Keywords

Credibility; Trustworthiness; Objectivity; Veracity; Probabilistic Graphical Models

1. INTRODUCTION

Online social media includes a wealth of topic-specific communities and discussion forums about politics, music, health, and many other domains. User-generated content in such communities offer a great potential for distilling and analyzing facts and opinions. In particular, online health communities constitute an important source of information for patients and doctors alike, with 59% of the adult U. S. population consulting online health resources [13], and nearly half of U. S. physicians relying on online resources for professional use [17].

One of the major hurdles preventing the full exploitation of information from online health communities is the widespread concern regarding the quality and credibility of user-generated content [37, 48]. To address this issue, this work proposes a model that can automatically assess the credibility of medical statements made by users of online health communities. In particular, we focus on extracting rare or unknown side-effects of drugs—this being one of the problems where large scale non-expert data has the potential to complement expert medical knowledge [47], but where misinformation can have hazardous consequences [7].

The main intuition behind the proposed model is that there is an important interaction between the credibility of a statement, the trustworthiness of the user making that statement and the language used in the post containing that statement. Therefore, we consider the mutual interaction between the following factors:

- *Users:* the overall *trustworthiness* (or authority) of a user, corresponding to her status and engagement in the community.
- *Language:* the *objectivity*, rationality (as opposed to emotionality), and general quality of the language in the users' posts. Objectivity is the quality of the post to be free from preference, emotion, bias and prejudice of the author.
- *Statements:* the *credibility* (or truthfulness) of medical statements contained within the posts. Identifying accurate drug side-effect statements is a goal of the model.

These factors have a strong influence on each other. Intuitively, a statement is more credible if it is posted by a trustworthy user and expressed using confident and objective language. As an example, consider the following review about the drug Depo-Provera by a senior member of `healthboards.com`, one of the largest online health communities:

"...Depo is very dangerous as a birth control and has too many long term side-effects like reducing bone density ..."

This post contains a credible statement that a side-effect of Depo-Provera is to reduce bone density. Conversely, highly subjective and emotional language suggests lower credibility of the user's statements. A negative example along these lines is:

KDD'14, August 24–27, 2014, New York, NY, USA.
Copyright 2014 ACM 978-1-4503-2956-9/14/08 ...$15.00.
http://dx.doi.org/10.1145/2623330.2623714.

"I have been on the same cocktail of meds (10 mgs. Elavil at bedtime/60-90 mgs. of Oxycodone during the day/1/1/2 mgs. Xanax a day....once in a while I have really bad hallucination type dreams. I can actually "feel" someone pulling me of the bed and throwing me around. I know this sounds crazy but at the time it fels somewhat demonic."

Although this post suggests that taking Xanax can lead to hallucination, the style in which it is written renders the credibility of this statement doubtful. These examples support the intuition that to identify credible medical statements, we also need to assess the trustworthiness of users and the objectivity of their language. In this work we leverage this intuition through a *joint analysis of statements, users, and language* in online health communities.

Although information extraction methods using probabilistic graphical models [39, 21] have been previously employed to extract statements from user generated content, they do not account for the inherent bias, subjectivity and misinformation prevalent in health forums. Unlike standard information extraction techniques [23, 5, 41], our method considers the role language can have in assessing the credibility of the extracted statements. Stylistic features—such as the use of modals and inferential conjunctions—help identify accurate statements, while affective features help determine the emotional state of the user making those statements (e.g., anxiety, confidence).

The main technical contribution of this paper is a probabilistic graphical model which is tailored to the problem setting as to facilitate joint inference over users, language, and statements. We devise a Markov Random Field (MRF) with individual users, posts, and statements as nodes, as summarized in Figure 1. The quality of these nodes—trustworthiness, objectivity, and credibility—is modeled as binary random variables. The model is semi-supervised with a subset of training side-effect statements derived from expert medical databases, labeled as true or false. In addition, the model relies on linguistic and user features that can be directly observed in online communities. Inference and parameter estimation is done via an EM (Expectation-Maximization) framework, where MCMC sampling is used in the *E-step* for estimating the label of unknown statements and the Trust Region Newton method [27] is used in the *M-step* to compute feature weights.

We apply our method to 2.8 million posts contributed by 15,000 users of one of the largest online health community `healthboards.com`. Our model achieves an overall accuracy of 82% in identifying drug side-effects, bringing an improvement of 13% over an SVM baseline using the same features and an improvement of 4% over a stronger SVM classifier which uses distant supervision to account for feature sparsity. We further evaluate how the proposed model performs in two realistic use cases: discovering rare side-effects of drugs and identifying trustworthy users in a community.

To summarize, this paper brings the following main contributions:

- *Model:* It proposes a model that captures the interactions between user trustworthiness, language objectivity, and statement credibility in social media (Section 2), and devises a comprehensive feature set to this end (Section 3);
- *Method:* It introduces a method for joint inference over users, language, and statements (Section 4) through a probabilistic graphical model;
- *Application:* It applies this methodology to the problem of extracting side-effects of medical drugs from online health forums (Section 5);
- *Use-cases:* It evaluates the performance of the model in the context of two realistic practical tasks (Section 6).

2. OVERVIEW OF THE MODEL

Our approach leverages the intuition that there is an important interaction between statement credibility, linguistic objectivity, and user trustworthiness. We therefore model these factors jointly through a probabilistic graphical model, more specifically a Markov Random Field (MRF), where each statement, post and user is associated with a binary random variable. Figure 1 provides an overview of our model. For a given statement, the corresponding variable should have value 1 if the statement is credible, and 0 otherwise. Likewise, the values of post and user variables reflect the objectivity and trustworthiness of posts and users.

Nodes, Features and Labels Nodes associated with users and posts have observable features, which can be extracted from the online community. For users, we derive engagement features (number of questions and answers posted), interaction features (e.g., replies, giving thanks), and demographic information (e.g., age, gender). For posts, we extract linguistic features in the form of discourse markers and affective phrases. Our features are presented in details in Section 3. While for statements there are no observable features, we can derive distant training labels for a subset of statements from expert databases, like the Mayo Clinic,[1] which list typical as well as rare side-effects of widely used drugs.

Edges The primary goal of the proposed system is to retrieve the credibility label of unobserved statements given *some* expert labeled statements and the observed features by leveraging the mutual influence between the model's variables. To this end, the MRF's nodes are connected by the following (undirected) edges:

- each user is connected to all her posts;
- each statement is connected to all posts from which it can be extracted (by state of the art information extraction methods);
- each user is connected to statements that appear in at least one of her posts.

Configured this way, the model has the capacity to capture important interactions between statements, posts, and users — for example, credible statements can boost a user's trustworthiness, whereas some false statements may bring it down. Furthermore, since the inference (detailed in Section 4) is centered around the cliques in the graph (factors) and multiple cliques can share nodes, more complex "cross-talk" is also captured. For instance, when several highly trustworthy users agree on a statement and one user disagrees, this reduces the trustworthiness of the disagreeing user.

In addition to establishing the credibility of statements, the proposed system also computes individual likelihoods as a by-product of the inference process, and therefore can output rankings for all statements, users, and posts, in descending order of credibility, trustworthiness, and objectivity.

[1] `mayoclinic.org/drugs-supplements/`

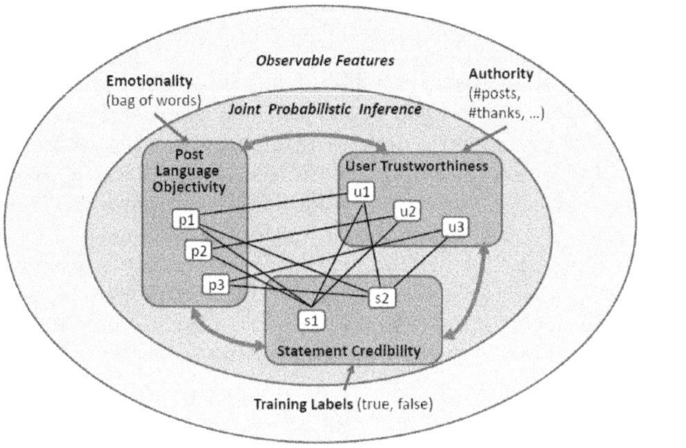

Figure 1: Overview of the proposed model, which captures the interactions between statement credibility, post objectivity, and user trustworthiness.

Feature types	Example values
Strong modals	might, could, can, would, may
Weak modals	should, ought, need, shall, will
Conditionals	if
Negation	no, not, neither, nor, never
Inferential conj.	therefore, thus, furthermore
Contrasting conj.	until, despite, in spite, though
Following conj.	but, however, otherwise, yet
Definite det.	the, this, that, those, these
First person	I, we, me, my, mine, us, our
Second person	you, your, yours
Third person	he, she, him, her, his, it, its
Question particles	why, what, when, which, who
Adjectives	correct, extreme, long, visible
Adverbs	maybe, about, probably, much
Proper nouns	Xanax, Zoloft, Depo-Provera

Table 1: Stylistic features.

3. FEATURES

3.1 Linguistic Features

The linguistic characteristics of a post can convey the author's attitude towards her statements as well as her emotional state [8]. In our model we use *stylistic* and *affective* features to assess a post's objectivity and quality.

Stylistic Features Consider the following user post:

"I heard Xanax can have pretty bad side-effects. You may have peeling of skin, and apparently some friend of mine told me you can develop ulcers in the lips also. If you take this medicine for a long time then you would probably develop a lot of other physical problems. Which of these did you experience ?"

This post evokes a lot of uncertainty, and does not specifically point to the occurrence of any side effect from a first-hand experience. Note the usage of strong modals (depicting a high degree of uncertainty) "can", "may", "would", the indefinite determiner "some", the conditional "if", the adverb of possibility "probably" and the question particle "which". Even the usage of too many named entities for drug and disease names can impact the credibility of a statement (refer the introductory example).

Contrast the above post with the following one :

"Depo is very dangerous as a birth control and has too many long term side-effects like reducing bone density. Hence, I will never recommend anyone using this as a birth control. Some women tolerate it well but those are the minority. Most women have horrible long lasting side-effects from it."

This post uses the inferential conjunction "hence" to draw conclusions from a previous argument, the definite determiners "this", "those", "the" and "most" to pinpoint entities and the highly certain weak modal "will".

Table 1 shows a set of linguistic features which we deem suitable for discriminating between these two kinds of posts. Many of the features related to epistemic modality have been discussed in prior linguistic literature [8, 46] and features related to discourse coherence have also been employed in earlier computational work (e.g., [31, 51]).

For each stylistic feature type f_i shown in Table 1 and each post p_j, we compute the relative frequency of words of type f_i occurring in p_j, thus constructing a feature vector $F^L(p_j) = \langle freq_{ij} = \#(words\ in\ f_i)\ /\ length(p_j)\rangle$. We further aggregate these vectors over all posts p_j by a user u_k into

$$F^L(u_k) = \langle \sum_{p_j\ by\ u_k} \#(words\ in\ f_i)\ /\ \sum_{p_j\ by\ u_k} length(p_j)\rangle. \tag{1}$$

Affective Features Each user has an *affective state* that depicts her attitude and emotions that are reflected in her posts. Note that a user's affective state may change over time; so it is a property of posts, not of users per se. As an example, consider the following post:

"I've had chronic depression off and on since adolescence. In the past I've taken Paxil (made me anxious) and Zoloft (caused insomnia and stomach problems, but at least I was mellow). I have been taking St. John's Wort for a few months now, and it helps, but not enough. I wake up almost every morning feeling very sad and hopeless. As afternoon approaches I start to feel better, but there's almost always at least a low level of depression throughout the day."

The high level of depression and negativity in the post makes one wonder if the statements on drug side-effects are really credible. Contrast this post to the following one:

"A diagnosis of GAD (Generalized Anxiety Disorder) is made if you suffer from excessive anxiety or worry and have at least three symptoms including...If the symptoms above, touch a chord with you, do speak to your GP. There are effective treatments for GAD, and Cognitive Behavioural Therapy in particular can help you ..."

where the user objectivity and positivity in the post make it much more credible.

We use the WordNet-Affect lexicon [40], where each word sense (WordNet synset) is mapped to one of 285 attributes of the affective feature space, like *confusion, ambiguity, hope, anticipation, hate.* We do not perform word sense disambiguation (WSD), and instead simply take the most common sense of a word (which is generally a good heuristics for WSD). For each post, we create an affective feature vector $\langle F^E(p_j)\rangle$ using these features, analogous to the stylistic vectors $\langle F^L(p_j)\rangle$. Table 2 shows a sample of the affective features used in this work.

Preliminary Feature Exploration To test whether the linguistic features introduced so far are sufficiently informative of how helpful a user is in the context of health forums, we conduct a preliminary experimental study. In

Sample Affective Features
affection, antipathy, anxiousness, approval, compunction, confidence, contentment, coolness, creeps, depression, devotion, distress, downheartedness, eagerness, edginess, embarrassment, encouragement, favor, fit, fondness, guilt, harassment, humility, hysteria, ingratitude, insecurity, jitteriness, levity, levitygaiety, malice, misery, resignation, selfesteem, stupefaction, surprise, sympathy, togetherness, triumph, weight, wonder

Table 2: Examples of affective features.

the `healthboards.com` forum, community members have the option of expressing their gratitude to a user if they find one of her posts helpful by giving "thanks" votes. Solely for the purpose of this preliminary experiment, we use the *total number of "thanks" votes* that a user received from all her posts as a weak proxy measure for user helpfulness.

We train a regression model on the per-user stylistic feature vectors $F^L(u_k)$ with #thanks normalized by #posts for each user u_k as response variable. We repeat the same experiment using only the per-user affective feature vectors $F^E(u_k)$ to identify the most important affective features.

Figure 2 shows the relative weight of various stylistic and affective linguistic features in determining user *helpfulness*, with positive weights being indicative of features contributing to a user being considered helpful by the community. Figure 2a shows that user confidence, pride, affection and positivity in statements are correlated with user helpfulness, in contrast to misery, depression and negativity in attitude. Figure 2b shows that inferential statements about definite entities have a positive impact, as opposed to the use of hypothetical statements, contrasting sentences, doubts and queries.

This experiment confirms that linguistic features can be informative in the context of online health communities. Although we use "thanks" votes as a proxy for user helpfulness, there is no guarantee that the information provided by helpful users is actually correct. A user can receive "thanks" for a multitude of reasons (e.g. being compassionate or supportive), and yet provide incorrect information. Hence, while the features described here are part of our final model, the feature weights learned in this preliminary experiment are not going to be used; instead, partially provided expert information is used to train our probabilistic model (refer to Section 4).

3.2 User Features

User demographics like age, gender and location, as well as engagement in the community reflected by the number of posts, questions, replies, or thanks received, are expected to correlate with user authority in social networks. Also, users who write long posts tend to deviate from the topic, often with highly emotional digression. On the other hand, short posts can be regarded as being crisp, objective and on topic. We attempt to capture these intuitive aspects as additional per-user features $< F^U(u_k) >$.[2]

4. PROBABILISTIC INFERENCE

As outlined in Section 2, we model our learning task as a Markov Random Field (MRF), where the random variables are the users $U = \{u_1, u_2, ...u_{|U|}\}$, their posts $P = \{p_1, p_2...p_{|P|}\}$, and the distinct statements $S = \{s_1, s_2...s_{|S|}\}$ about drug side-effects extracted from all posts. Our model is semi-supervised in that we harness ground-truth labels for a subset of statements, derived from the expert databases. Let S^L be the set of statements labeled by an expert as true or false, and let S^U be the set of unlabeled statements. Our goal is to infer labels for the statements in S^U.

The cliques in our MRF are triangles consisting of a statement s_i, a post p_j that contains that statement, and a user u_k who wrote this post. As the same statement can be made in different posts by the same or other users, there are more cliques than statements. For convenient notation, let S^* denote the set of statement instances that correspond to the set of cliques, with statements "repeated" when necessary.

Let $\phi_i(S_i^*, p_j, u_k)$ be a potential function for clique i. Each clique has a set of associated feature functions F_i with a weight vector W. We denote the individual features and their weights as f_{il} and w_l. The features are constituted by the stylistic, affective, and user features explained in Section 3: $F_i = F^L(p_j) \cup F^E(p_j) \cup F^U(u_k)$.

Instead of computing the joint probability distribution $Pr(S, P, U; W)$ like in a standard MRF, we adopt the paradigm of Conditional Random Fields (CRF's) and settle for the simpler task of estimating the conditional distribution:

$$Pr(S|P, U; W) = \frac{1}{Z(P, U)} \prod_i \phi_i(S_i^*, p_j, u_k; W), \quad (2)$$

with normalization constant $Z(P, U)$; or with features and weights made explicit:

$$Pr(S|P, U; W) = \frac{1}{Z(P, U)} \prod_i \exp(\sum_l w_l \times f_{il}(S_i^*, p_j, u_k)). \quad (3)$$

CRF parameter learning usually works on fully observed training data. However, in our setting, only a subset of the S variables have labels and we need to consider the partitioning of S into S^L and S^U:

$$Pr(S^U, S^L|P, U; W) = \frac{1}{Z(P, U)} \prod_i \exp(\sum_l w_l \times f_{il}(S_i^*, p_j, u_k)). \quad (4)$$

For parameter estimation, we need to maximize the marginal log-likelihood:

$$LL(W) = \log Pr(S^L|P, U; W) = \log \sum_{S^U} Pr(S^L, S^U|P, U; W). \quad (5)$$

We can clamp the values of S^L to their observed values in the training data [42, 54] and compute the distribution over S^U as:

$$Pr(S^U|S^L, P, U; W) = \frac{1}{Z(S^L, P, U)} \prod_i \exp(\sum_l w_l \times f_{il}(S_i^*, p_j, u_k)). \quad (6)$$

There are different ways of addressing the optimization problem for finding the argmax of $LL(W)$. In this work, we choose the Expectation-Maximization (EM) approach [29]. We first estimate the labels of the variables S^U from the posterior distribution using Gibbs sampling, and then maximize

[2]For verbosity, we compute the first three moments of each user's post-length distribution (#sentences and #words).

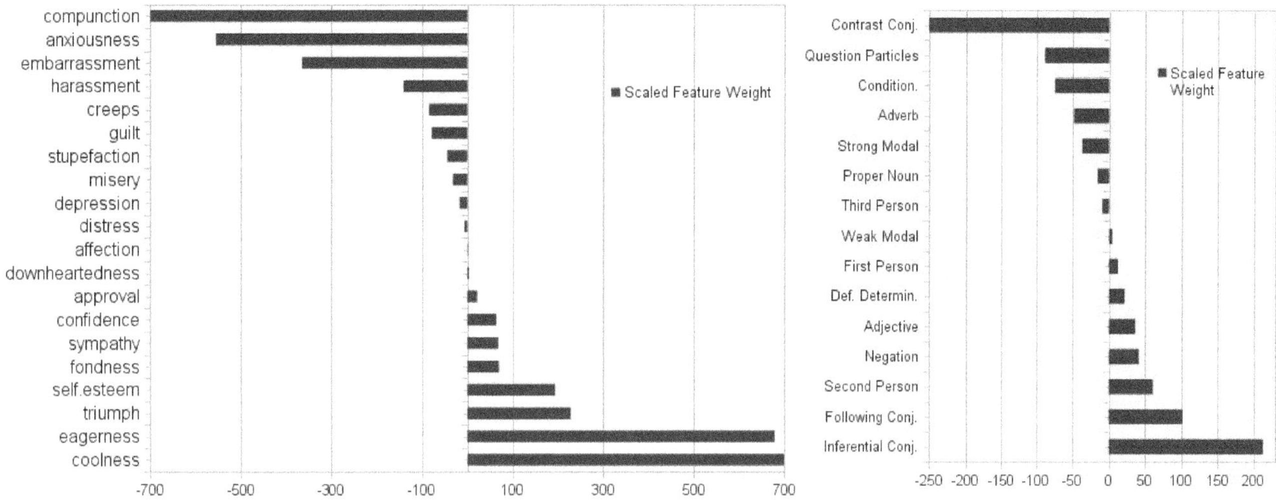

(a) Weight of top 20 affective features.

(b) Weight of stylistic features.

Figure 2: Relative importance of linguistic features for predicting user helpfulness in a preliminary experiment.

the log-likelihood to estimate the feature weights:

$$E-Step: q(S^U) = Pr(S^U|S^L, P, U; W^{(\nu)}) \quad (7a)$$

$$M-Step: W^{(\nu+1)} = argmax_{W'} \sum_{S^U} q(S^U) \log Pr(S^L, S^U|P, U; W'). \quad (7b)$$

The update step to sample the labels of S^U variables by Gibbs sampling is given by:

$$Pr(S_i^U|P, U, S^L; W) \propto \prod_{\nu \in C} \phi_\nu(S_\nu^*, p_j, u_k; W), \quad (8)$$

where C denotes the set of cliques containing statement S_i^U.

For the M-step in Equation 7b, we use an L_2-regularized Trust Region Newton Method [27], suited for large-scale unconstrained optimization, where many feature values may be zero. For this we use an implementation of LibLinear [12].

The above approach captures user trustworthiness implicitly via the weights of the feature vectors. However, we may want to model user trustworthiness in a way that explicitly aggregates over all the statements made by a user. Let t_k denote the trustworthiness of user u_k, measured as the fraction of her statements that were considered true in the previous EM iteration:

$$t_k = \frac{\sum_i \mathbb{1}_{S_{i,k}=\text{True}}}{|S_k|}, \quad (9)$$

where $S_{i,k}$ is the label assigned to u_k's statement S_i in the previous EM iteration. Equation 8 can then be modified into:

$$Pr(S_i^U|P, U, S^L; W) \propto \prod_{\nu \in C} t_k \times \phi_\nu(S_\nu^*, p_j, u_k; W) \quad (10)$$

Therefore, the random variable for trustworthiness depends on the proportion of *true* statements made by the user. The *label* of a statement, in turn, is determined by the language objectivity of the posts and trustworthiness of all the users in the community that make the statement.

The inference is an iterative process consisting of the following 3 main steps:

1. Estimate user trustworthiness t_k using Equation 9.
2. Apply the E-Step to estimate $q(S^U; W^{(\nu)})$
   For each i, sample S_i^U from Equation 7a and 10.
3. Apply the M-Step to estimate $W^{(\nu+1)}$ using Equation 7b.

5. EXPERIMENTAL EVALUATION

In this section, we study the predictive power of our probabilistic model and compare it to three baselines.

5.1 Data

We use data from the `healthboards.com`, one of the largest online health communities, with 850,000 registered members and over 4.5 million posted messages. We extracted 15,000 users and all of their posts, 2.8 million posts in total. Users are sampled based on their post frequency; Table 3 shows the user categorization in terms of their community engagement.[3] We employ an IE tool [11] to extract side-effect statements from the posts. Details of the experimental setting are available on our website.[4]

As ground truth for drug side-effects, we rely on data from the Mayo Clinic portal,[5] which contains curated expert information about drugs, with side-effects being listed as *more common, less common and rare* for each drug. We extracted 2,172 drugs which are categorized into 837 drug families. For our experiments, we select 6 widely used drug families (based on `webmd.com`). Table 4 provides information on this sample and its coverage on `healthboards.com`. Table 5 shows the number of common, less common, and rare side-effects for the six drug families as given by the Mayo Clinic portal.

[3]Overall, 77.7% of the active contributors are female.
[4]`http://www.mpi-inf.mpg.de/impact/peopleondrugs/`
[5]`mayoclinic.org/drugs-supplements/`

Member Type	Members	Posts	Average Qs.	Average Replies
Administrator	1	-	363	934
Moderator	4	-	76	1276
Facilitator	16	> 4700	83	2339
Senior veteran	966	> 500	68	571
Veteran	916	> 300	41	176
Senior member	4321	> 100	24	71
Member	5846	> 50	13	28
Junior member	1423	> 40	9	18
Inactive	1433	-	-	-
Registered user	70	-	-	-

Table 3: User statistics.

Drugs	Description	Users	Posts
alprazolam, niravam, xanax	relieve symptoms of anxiety, depression, panic disorder	2785	21112
ibuprofen, advil, genpril, motrin, midol, nuprin	relieve pain, symptoms of arthritis, such as inflammation, swelling, stiffness, joint pain	5657	15573
omeprazole, prilosec	treat acidity in stomach, gastric and duodenal ulcers, ...	1061	3884
metformin, glucophage, glumetza, sulfonylurea	treat high blood sugar levels, sugar diabetes	779	3562
levothyroxine, tirosint	treat hypothyroidism: insufficient hormone production by thyroid gland	432	2393
metronidazole, flagyl	treat bacterial infections in different body parts	492	1559

Table 4: Information on sample drug families: number of posts and number of users reporting at least one side effect.

5.2 Baselines

We compare our probabilistic model against the following baseline methods, using the same features as our model and classifying the same set of side-effect candidates.

Frequency Baseline For each statement on a drug side-effect, we consider how frequently the statement has been made in community. This gives us a ranking of side-effects.

SVM Baseline For each drug and possible side-effect we determine all posts where it is mentioned and aggregate the features F^L, F^E, F^U, described in Section 3 over all these posts, thus creating a single feature vector for each side-effect.

We use the ground-truth labels from the Mayo Clinic portal to train a Support Vector Machine (SVM) classifier with a linear kernel, L_2 loss, and L_1 or L_2 regularization, for classifying unlabeled statements.

Drug family	Common	Less common	Rare
alprazolam	35	91	45
ibuprofen	30	1	94
omeprazole	-	15	20
metformin	24	37	5
levothyroxine	-	51	7
metronidazole	35	25	14

Table 5: Number of common, less common, and rare side-effects listed by experts on Mayo Clinic.

SVM Baseline with Distant Supervision As the number of common side-effects for any drug is typically small, the above approach to create a single feature vector for each side-effect results in a very small training set. Hence, we use the notion of *distant supervision* to create a rich, expanded training set.

A feature vector is created for *every mention* or instance of a side-effect in different user posts. The feature vector $< S_i, p_j, u_k >$ has the label of the side-effect, and represents the set of cliques in Equation 2. The semi-supervised CRF formulation in our approach further allows for information sharing between the cliques to estimate the labels of the unobserved statements from the expert-provided ones.

This process creates a noisy training set, as a post may contain multiple side-effects, positive and negative. This results in multiple similar feature vectors with different labels. During testing, the same side-effect may get different labels from its different instances. We take a majority voting of the labels obtained by a side-effect, across predictions over its different instances, and assign a unique label to it.

5.3 Experiments and Quality Measures

We conduct two lines of experiments, with different settings on what is considered ground-truth.

Experimental Setting I We consider only *most common side-effects* listed by the Mayo Clinic portal as positive ground-truth, whereas all other side-effects (less common, rare and unobserved) are considered to be negative instances (i.e., so unlikely that they should be considered as false statements, if reported by a user). The training set is constructed in the same way. This setting aims to study the predictive power of our model in determining the common side-effects of a drug, in comparison to the baselines.

Experimental Setting II Here we address our original motivation: discovering less common and rare side-effects. During training, as positive ground-truth we consider common and less common side-effects (as stated by the experts on the Mayo Clinic site), whereas all rare and unobserved side-effects are considered negative instances. Our goal here is to test how well the model can identify *less known* and *rare* side-effects as true statements.

We purposely do not consider rare side-effects as positive training examples, as users frequently talk about experiencing all possible side-effects. Instead we aim to evaluate the model's ability to retrieve such statements starting only from very reliable positive instances. We measure performance on rare side-effects as the recall for such statements being labeled as true statements, in spite of considering *only* common and less common side-effects as positive instances during training.

Train-Test Data Split For each drug family, we create multiple random splits of 80% training data and 20% test data. All results reported below are averaged over 200 such splits. All baselines and our CRF model use same test sets.

Evaluation Metrics The standard measure for the quality of a binary classifier is *accuracy*: $\frac{tp+tn}{tp+fn+tn+fp}$. We also report the *specificity* ($\frac{tn}{tn+fp}$) and *sensitivity* ($\frac{tp}{tp+fn}$). Sensitivity measures the true positive rate or the model's ability to identify positive side-effects, whereas specificity measures true negative rate.

Drugs	Post Freq.	SVM			CRF
		w/o DS	DS		
			L_1	L_2	
Alprazolam	57.8	70.2	73.3	73.1	79.4
Metronidazole	55.8	68.8	79.8	78.5	82.6
Omeprazole	60.6	71.1	76.8	79.2	83.2
Levothyroxine	57.5	76.8	69.0	76.3	80.5
Metformin	55.7	53.2	79.3	81.6	84.7
Ibuprofen	58.4	74.2	77.8	80.3	82.8

Table 6: Accuracy comparison in setting I.

Drugs	Sensi-tivity	Speci-ficity	Rare SE Recall	Acc-uracy
Metformin	79.8	91.2	99.0	86.1
Levothyroxine	89.5	74.5	98.5	83.4
Omeprazole	80.8	88.8	89.5	85.9
Metronidazole	75.1	93.8	71.0	84.2
Ibuprofen	76.6	83.1	69.9	80.9
Alprazolam	94.3	68.8	61.3	74.7

Table 7: CRF performance in setting II.

5.4 Results and Discussions

Table 6 shows the accuracy comparison of our system (CRF) with the baselines for different drug families in the first setting. The first naive baseline, which simply considers the frequency of posts containing the side-effect by different users, has an average accuracy of 57.6% across different drug families.

Incorporating supervision in the classifier as the first SVM baseline (SVM w/o DS), along with a rich set of features for users, posts and language, achieves an average accuracy improvement of 11.4%. In the second SVM baseline (SVM DS), we represent each post reporting a side-effect as a separate feature vector. This not only expands the training set leading to better parameter estimation, but also represents the set of cliques in Equation 2 (we therefore consider this to be a strong baseline). This brings an average accuracy improvement of 7% when using L_1 regularization and 9% when using L_2 regularization. Our model (CRF), by further considering the coupling between users, posts and statements, allows information to flow between the cliques in a feedback loop bringing a further accuracy improvement of 4% over the strong SVM DS L_2 baseline.

Figure 3 shows the sensitivity and specificity comparison of the baselines with the CRF model. Our approach has an overall 5% increase in sensitivity and 3% increase in specificity over the SVM L_2 baseline.

The specificity increase over the SVM L_2 baseline is maximum for the Alprazolam drug family at 8.3%. Users taking such anti-depressants often suffer from anxiety disorder, panic attacks or depression and report a large number of side-effects; also there are a large number of expert-reported side-effects for this drug family (refer Table 5). Hence, the task of discarding certain side-effects is harder for this particular drug, but our linguistic features help our model overcome this and perform well.

The drugs Metronidazole, Metformin and Omeprazole treat some serious physical conditions, have less number of expert and user-reported side-effects. Consequently, our model captures user statement corroboration well to attain a sensitivity improvement of 7.8%, 6.5% and 6.3% respectively. Overall, our classifier performs best for these drug categories.

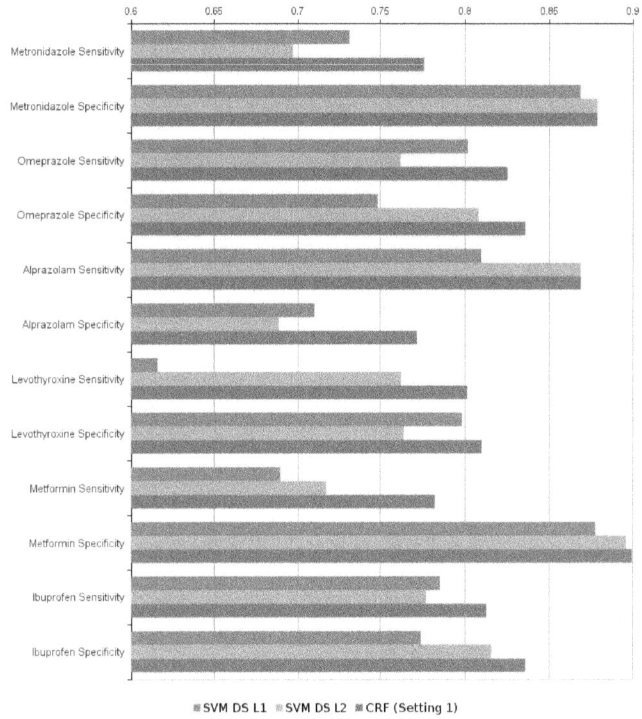

Figure 3: Specificity and sensitivity comparison of models.

Table 7 shows the overall model performance, as well as the recall for identifying rare side-effects of each drug in the second setting. The drugs Metformin, Levothyroxine and Omeprazole have much fewer side-effects, and the classifier does an almost perfect job in identifying all of them.

Feature Informativeness In order to find the *predictive power* of individual feature classes, tests are performed using L_2-loss and L_2-regularized SVM over a split of the test data. Affective features are found to be the most informative, followed by document length statistics, which are more informative than user and stylistic features. The importance of the document length features support our intuition that objective posts tend to be crisp, whereas longer ones often indulge in emotional digressions.

Among user features, the most informative is the ratio of number of replies to number of questions, followed by gender, number of posts and, finally, the number of thanks received from fellow users.

When considered independently, user, affective and stylistic features achieve F_1 scores between 51% and 55% for Alprazolam; whereas the combination of all features yield 70% F_1 score.

6. USE-CASE EXPERIMENTS

The previous section has focused on evaluating the predictive power of our model and inference method. Now we shift the focus to two application-oriented use-cases: discovering side-effects that are not covered by expert databases, and identifying the most trustworthy users that are worth following.

6.1 Discovering Rare Side Effects

Members of an online community may report side-effects that are either flagged as very rare in an expert knowledge base (KB) or not listed at all. We call the latter *out-of-KB* statements. As before, we use the data from the Mayo Clinic portal as our KB, and focus on the following two drugs representing different kinds of medical conditions and patient-reporting styles: Alprazolam and Levothyroxine. For each of these drugs, we perform an experiment as follows.

For each drug X, we identify all side-effects S that are reported for X by members of the health community; here we consider all side-effects listed for *any* drug in the KB as a potential result. For example, if "hallucination" is listed for some drug but not for the drug Xanax, we capture mentions of hallucination in posts about Xanax. We use our probabilistic model to compute credibility scores for these out-of-KB side-effects, and compile a ranked list of 10 highest-scoring side-effects for each drug. This ranked list is further extended by 10 randomly chosen out-of-KB side-effects (if reported at least once for the given drug).

The ranked list of out-of-KB side-effects is shown to two annotators[6] who manually assess their credibility, by reading the complete discussion thread (including expert replies to patient posts) and other threads that involve the users who reported the side-effect. The assessment is binary: the side-effect is considered either true (1) or false (0); we choose the final label via majority voting, breaking ties using other expert databases (`patient.co.uk` and `webmd.com`). This way, we can compute the quality of the ranked list in terms of the NDCG (Normalized Discounted Cumulative Gain) measure [18] $NDCG_p = \frac{DCG_p}{IDCG_p}$, where

$$DCG_p = rel_1 + \sum_{i=2}^{p} \frac{rel_i}{\log_2 i}. \tag{11}$$

Here, rel_i is the graded relevance of a result (0 or 1 in our case) at position i. DCG penalizes relevant items appearing lower in the rank list, where the graded relevance score is reduced logarithmically proportional to the position of the result. As the length of lists may vary for different queries, DCG scores are normalized using the ideal score, IDCG where the results of a rank list are sorted by relevance giving the maximum possible DCG score. We also report the Cohen's Kappa inter-annotator agreement measure.

Table 8 shows the Kappa and NDCG score comparison between the baseline and our CRF model. The baseline here is to rank side-effects by frequency, i.e., how often are they reported in the posts of different users on the given drug. The strength of Kappa is considered "moderate" (but significant), which depicts the difficulty in identifying the side-effects of a drug just by looking at user posts in a community. The baseline performs very poorly for the anti-depressant Alprazolam, as users suffering from anxiety disorders report a large number of side-effects most of which are not credible. On the other hand, for Levothyroxine (a drug for hypothyroidism) the baseline model performs quite well, as users report more serious symptoms and conditions associated with the drug (which also has much less expert-stated side-effects compared to Alprazolam, as shown in Table 4). The CRF model performs perfectly for both drugs.

[6]None of authors were among the annotators.

Drug	Kappa	Model NDCG Scores	
		Frequency	CRF
Alprazolam, Xanax	0.47	0.31	1
Levothyroxine, Tirosint	0.41	0.94	1

Table 8: Use-case experiment on discovering rare side-effects.

Drug	Kappa	Model NDCG Scores	
		Most-thanked	CRF
Alprazolam, Xanax	0.78	0.82	1
Levothyroxine, Tirosint	0.80	0.57	0.81

Table 9: Use-case experiment on identifying trustworthy users.

6.2 Following Trustworthy Users

In the second use-case experiment, we evaluate how well our model can identify trustworthy users in a community. We find the top-ranked users in the community given by their trustworthiness scores (t_k, as defined in Section 4), for each of the drugs Alprazolam and Levothyroxine. The baseline model selects the most-thanked contributors in the community. The moderators and facilitators of the community, listed by both models as top users, are removed from the ranked lists, in order to focus on the interesting, non-obvious cases. Two annotators are asked to annotate the top-ranked users listed by each model as trustworthy or not, based on the users' posts on the target drug. The judges are asked to mark a user as trustworthy if they would consider following the respective user in the community. Judgements were aggregated via majority voting, with ties being considered as not trustworthy. Although this task may seem highly subjective, the Cohen's Kappa scores show high inter-annotator agreement (Table 9). The strength of agreement is considered to be "very good" for the user posts on Levothyroxine, and "good" for the Alprazolam users. Also in this use-case, our model performs well and outperforms the baseline for both drug families.

7. RELATED WORK

Subject-Predicate-Object statement extraction There is ample work on extracting Subject-Predicate-Object (SPO) statements from natural-language text [39, 23, 5, 41]. State-of-the-art methods combine pattern matching with extraction rules and consistency reasoning. This can be done either in a shallow manner, over sequences of text tokens, or in combination with deep parsing and other linguistic analyses. The resulting SPO triples often have highly varying confidence, as to whether they are really expressed in the text or picked up spuriously. Judging the credibility of statements is out of the scope of classic SPO extraction methods.

Biomedical Information Extraction Customized IE techniques have been developed to tap biomedical publications like PubMed articles for extracting facts about diseases, symptoms, and drugs. Emphasis has been on the molecular level, i.e. proteins, genes, and regulatory pathways (e.g., [6, 22, 4]), and to a lesser extent on biological or medical events from scientific articles and from clinical narratives [19, 52]. LDA-style models have been used for summarizing drug-experience reports [36] and for building large knowledge bases for life science and health [11]. More recently, search engine query logs were shown to be a valuable source for identifying unknown drug side-effects [47]. Our work is complementing these approaches, by emphasizing the role of user generated content on social media.

Truth Finding Our work relates to a research direction that aims to assess the truth of a given statement that is frequently observed on the Web—a typical example being "Obama is a Muslim" [53, 33, 35]. Information-retrieval techniques are used to systematically generate alternative hypotheses for a given statement—"Obama is a Christian"—and assess the evidence for each alternative [25]. Similar approaches have been developed for structured data such as flight times or stock quotes, where different Web sources often yield contradictory values [24]. Recently, an LDA-style latent-topic model was used for discriminating true from false claims, with various ways of generating incorrect statements (guesses, mistakes, lies) [34]. None of this prior work considered online discussion forums. Truth assessment for medical claims about diseases and their treatments (including drugs and general phrases such as "surgery") was casted as an information retrieval style evidence-aggregation and ranking method over curated health portals [45]. Although these are elaborate models, they are not geared for our setting where the credibility of statements is intertwined with user trustworthiness and the linguistic properties of user posts.

Language Analysis for Social Media Social media is an important setting for linguistic tasks that relate to our work, such as sentiment analysis (e.g., [43, 32, 28, 31, 30]), identifying bias [14, 38] and, more broadly, characterizing subjective language [49, 26]. Particularly relevant to our research direction is the link between subjectivity analysis and information extraction [50].

Trust and Reputation Management A lot of work has been dedicated to building trust and reputation management systems in social media, mostly motivated by the need to filter and organize customer product reviews, but also in the context of social networks. One type of approach has been to model the propagation of trust within a network of users [20, 15]. TrustRank [20] has become a popular measure of trustworthiness, based on random walks on (or spectral decomposition of) the user graph. Reputation management has been studied in multiple contexts, such as peer-to-peer systems, blogs, and online interactions [1, 2, 9, 3, 16]. Most of this work focused on explicit relationships between users to infer authority and trust levels, and make little or no use of the content. An exception is a model for trust propagation which devises a HITS-style algorithm for propagating trust scores in a heterogeneous network of claims, news sources, and news articles [44], building on an intuition similar to that behind our proposed approach. Evidence for a claim is collected from related news articles using generic IR-style word-level measures. In contrast, our work considers user-generated content which is represented by rich linguistic features and employs a CRF to model the complex interaction characteristic of online communities.

8. CONCLUSION

Discussions in online communities are often plagued by inaccuracies and misinformation. This hinders the exploitation of these rich and valuable resources as information sources. In this work we focus on establishing the credibility of side-effect statements in health communities. To this end, we propose a probabilistic graphical model to jointly learn the interactions between user trustworthiness, statement credibility and language use. We apply the model to extract side-effects of drugs from health communities, where we leverage the user interactions, stylistic and affective features of language use, and user properties to learn the credibility of user statements. We show that our approach is effective in reliably extracting side-effects of drugs and filtering out false information prevalent in online health communities.

In addition to validating our system's performance against expert knowledge, we show it can be successfully used in two application oriented use-cases: identifying unknown side-effects of drugs, a scenario where large-scale non-expert data has the potential to complement expert knowledge, and selecting trustworthy users that are deemed worth following.

Although our model achieves high accuracy in most of the test cases, it relies on a relatively simple information extraction machinery to identify candidate side-effect statements, which is prone to errors. The tool misses out on certain kinds of paraphrases (e.g. "nightmares" and "unusual dream" for Xanax) resulting in a drop in recall. We believe that a more sophisticated information extraction approach can further improve our approach.

Acknowledgements We thank the anonymous reviewers for their helpful (and credible) comments. We also thank Patrick Ernst for helping setting up the statement extraction tool and Amy Siu for helping in the annotation task.

9. REFERENCES

[1] B.T. Adler, L. Alfaro. A content-driven reputation system for the Wikipedia. WWW, 2007.

[2] N. Agarwal, H. Liu. Trust in Blogosphere. Encyclopedia of Database Systems, 2009.

[3] L. Alfaro, A. Kulshreshtha, I. Pye, B.T. Adler. Reputation systems for open collaboration. Commun. ACM, 2011.

[4] J. Björne, F. Ginter, S. Pyysalo, J. Tsujii, T. Salakoski. Complex event extraction at PubMed scale. Bioinformatics [ISMB], 2010.

[5] P. Bohannon, N. Dalvi, Y. Filmus, N. Jacoby, S. Keerthi, A. Kirpal. Automatic web-scale information extraction. SIGMOD, 2012.

[6] M. Bundschus, M. Dejori, M. Stetter, V. Tresp, H.P. Kriegel. Extraction of semantic biomedical relations from text using conditional random fields. BMC Bioinformatics, 2008.

[7] R.J.W. Cline, K.M. Haynes. Consumer health information seeking on the Internet: the state of the art. Health education research, 2001.

[8] J. Coates. Epistemic Modality and Spoken Discourse. Transactions of the Philological Society, 1987.

[9] Z. Despotovic. Trust and Reputation in Peer-to-Peer Systems. Encyclopedia of Database Systems, 2009.

[10] X. Dong, L. Berti-Equille, Y. Hu, D. Srivastava. SOLOMON: Seeking the Truth Via Copying Detection. PVLDB, 2010.

[11] P. Ernst, C. Meng, A. Siu, G. Weikum. KnowLife: a Knowledge Graph for Health and Life Sciences. ICDE, 2014.

[12] R.E. Fan, K.W. Chang, C.J. Hsieh, X.R. Wang, C.J. Lin. LIBLINEAR: A library for large linear classification. JMLR, 2008.

[13] S. Fox, M. Duggan. Health online 2013. Pew Internet and American Life Project, 2013.

[14] S. Greene, P. Resnik. More than Words: Syntactic Packaging and Implicit Sentiment. HLT-NAACL, 2009.

[15] R.V. Guha, R. Kumar, P. Raghavan, A. Tomkins. Propagation of trust and distrust. WWW, 2004.

[16] C. Hang, Z. Zhang, M.P. Singh. Shin: Generalized Trust Propagation with Limited Evidence. IEEE Computer, 2013.

[17] IMS Institute for Healthcare Informatics. Engaging Patients through Social Media. Report, 2014, http://www.theimsinstitute.org/.

[18] K. Järvelin. J. Kekäläinen. Cumulated gain-based evaluation of IR techniques. ACM Trans. Inf. Syst., 2002.

[19] P. Jindal, D. Roth. End-to-End Coreference Resolution for Clinical Narratives. IJCAI, 2013.

[20] S.D. Kamvar, M.T. Schlosser, H. Garcia-Molina. The Eigentrust algorithm for reputation management in P2P networks. WWW, 2003.

[21] D. Koller, N. Friedman. Probabilistic Graphical Models: Principles and Techniques. MIT Press, 2009.

[22] M. Krallinger, A. Valencia, L. Hirschman. Linking Genes to Literature: Text Mining, Information Extraction, and Retrieval Applications for Biology. Genome Biology, 2008.

[23] R. Krishnamurthy, Y. Li, S. Raghavan, F. Reiss, S. Vaithyanathan. Web Information Extraction. Encyclopedia of Database Systems, 2009.

[24] X. Li, X.L. Dong, K. Lyons, W. Meng, D. Srivastava. Truth Finding on the Deep Web: Is the Problem Solved? PVLDB, 2012.

[25] X. Li, W. Meng, C.T. Yu. T-verifier: Verifying truthfulness of fact statements. ICDE, 2011.

[26] C. Lin, Y. He, R. Everson. Sentence Subjectivity Detection with Weakly-Supervised Learning. IJCNLP, 2011.

[27] C. Lin, R.C. Weng, S.S Keerthi. Trust Region Newton Method for Logistic Regression. JMLR, 2008.

[28] B. Liu. Sentiment Analysis and Opinion Mining. Synthesis Lectures on Human Language Technologies, Morgan & Claypool Publishers, 2012.

[29] A. McCallum, K. Bellare, F. Pereira. A conditional random field for discriminatively-trained finite-state string edit distance. UAI, 2005.

[30] S. Mukherjee, G. Basu, S. Joshi. Joint Author Sentiment Topic Model. SDM, 2014.

[31] S. Mukherjee, P. Bhattacharyya. Sentiment Analysis in Twitter with Lightweight Discourse Analysis. COLING, 2012.

[32] B. Pang, L. Lee. Opinion Mining and Sentiment Analysis. Foundations and Trends in Information Retrieval, 2007.

[33] J. Pasternack, D. Roth. Knowing What to Believe (when you already know something). COLING, 2010.

[34] J. Pasternack, D. Roth. Latent credibility analysis. WWW, 2013.

[35] J. Pasternack, D. Roth. Making Better Informed Trust Decisions with Generalized Fact-Finding. IJCAI, 2011.

[36] M.J. Paul, M. Dredze. Drug Extraction from the Web: Summarizing Drug Experiences with Multi-Dimensional Topic Models. HLT-NAACL, 2013.

[37] G. Peterson, P Aslani, K.A. Williams. How do consumers search for and appraise information on medicines on the Internet? A qualitative study using focus groups. Journal of Medical Internet Research, 2003.

[38] M. Recasens, C. Danescu-Niculescu-Mizil, D. Jurafsky. Linguistic Models for Analyzing and Detecting Biased Language. ACL, 2013.

[39] S. Sarawagi. Information Extraction. Foundations and Trends in Databases, 2008.

[40] C. Strapparava, A. Valitutti. Wordnet-affect: an affective extension of Wordnet. LREC, 2004.

[41] F.M. Suchanek, G. Weikum. Knowledge harvesting from text and Web sources. ICDE, 2013.

[42] C.A. Sutton, A. McCallum. An Introduction to Conditional Random Fields. Foundations and Trends in Machine Learning, 2012.

[43] P.D. Turney. Thumbs Up or Thumbs Down? Semantic Orientation Applied to Unsupervised Classification of Reviews. ACL, 2002.

[44] V.G.V. Vydiswaran, C. Zhai, D. Roth. Content-driven Trust Propagation Framework. KDD, 2011.

[45] V.G.V. Vydiswaran, C. Zhai, D. Roth. Gauging the Internet Doctor: Ranking Medical Claims based on Community Knowledge. KDD Workshop on Data Mining for Healthcare, 2011.

[46] P. Westney. How to Be More-or-Less Certain in English - Scalarity in Epistemic Modality. IRAL, 1986.

[47] R.W. White, R. Harpaz, N.H. Shah, W. DuMouchel, E. Horvitz. Toward Enhanced Pharmacovigilance using Patient-Generated Data on the Internet. Nature CPT, 2014.

[48] R.W. White, E. Horvitz. From health search to healthcare: explorations of intention and utilization via query logs and user surveys. JAMIA, 2014.

[49] J. Wiebe, E. Riloff. Creating Subjective and Objective Sentence Classifiers from Unannotated Texts. CICLing, 2005.

[50] J. Wiebe, E. Riloff. Finding Mutual Benefit between Subjectivity Analysis and Information Extraction. Trans. Affective Computing, 2011.

[51] F. Wolf, E. Gibson, T. Desmet. Discourse coherence and pronoun resolution. Language and Cognitive Processes, 2004.

[52] Y. Xu, K. Hong, J. Tsujii, E.C. Chang. Feature engineering combined with machine learning and rule-based methods for structured information extraction from narrative clinical discharge summaries. JAMIA, 2012.

[53] X. Yin, J. Han, P.S. Yu. Truth discovery with multiple conflicting information providers on the Web. KDD, 2007.

[54] X. Zhu, Z. Ghahramani, J. Lafferty. Semi-supervised learning using gaussian fields and harmonic functions. ICML, 2003.

Unfolding Physiological State: Mortality Modelling in Intensive Care Units

Marzyeh Ghassemi
Massachusetts Institute of Technology
77 Massachusetts Ave.
Cambridge, MA 02139 USA
mghassem@mit.edu

Tristan Naumann
Massachusetts Institute of Technology
77 Massachusetts Ave.
Cambridge, MA 02139 USA
tjn@mit.edu

Finale Doshi-Velez
Harvard
10 Shattuck Street
Boston, MA 02115 USA
finale@alum.mit.edu

Nicole Brimmer
Massachusetts Institute of Technology
77 Massachusetts Ave.
Cambridge, MA 02139 USA
nbrimmer@mit.edu

Rohit Joshi
Massachusetts Institute of Technology
77 Massachusetts Ave.
Cambridge, MA 02139 USA
rjoshi@mit.edu

Anna Rumshisky
University of Massachusetts Lowell
One University Ave.
Lowell, MA 01854 USA
arum@cs.uml.edu

Peter Szolovits
Massachusetts Institute of Technology
77 Massachusetts Ave.
Cambridge, MA 02139 USA
psz@mit.edu

ABSTRACT

Accurate knowledge of a patient's disease state and trajectory is critical in a clinical setting. Modern electronic healthcare records contain an increasingly large amount of data, and the ability to automatically identify the factors that influence patient outcomes stand to greatly improve the efficiency and quality of care.

We examined the use of latent variable models (viz. Latent Dirichlet Allocation) to decompose free-text hospital notes into meaningful features, and the predictive power of these features for patient mortality. We considered three prediction regimes: (1) baseline prediction, (2) dynamic (time-varying) outcome prediction, and (3) retrospective outcome prediction. In each, our prediction task differs from the familiar time-varying situation whereby data accumulates; since fewer patients have long ICU stays, as we move forward in time fewer patients are available and the prediction task becomes increasingly difficult.

We found that latent topic-derived features were effective in determining patient mortality under three timelines: in-hospital, 30 day post-discharge, and 1 year post-discharge mortality. Our results demonstrated that the latent topic features important in predicting hospital mortality are very different from those that are important in post-discharge mortality. In general, latent topic features were more predictive than structured features, and a combination of the two performed best.

The time-varying models that combined latent topic features and baseline features had AUCs that reached 0.85, 0.80, and 0.77 for in-hospital, 30 day post-discharge and 1 year post-discharge mortality respectively. Our results agreed with other work suggesting that the first 24 hours of patient information are often the most predictive of hospital mortality. Retrospective models that used a combination of latent topic features and structured features achieved AUCs of 0.96, 0.82, and 0.81 for in-hospital, 30 day, and 1-year mortality prediction.

Our work focuses on the dynamic (time-varying) setting because models from this regime could facilitate an on-going severity stratification system that helps direct care-staff resources and inform treatment strategies.

KDD'14, August 24–27, 2014, New York, NY, USA.

ACM 978-1-4503-2956-9/14/08 ...$15.00.
http://dx.doi.org/10.1145/2623330.2623742.

General Terms

Primary: Data mining for social good.
Secondary: Healthcare and medicine; Topic, graphical and latent variable models; Text; Support vector machines.

1. INTRODUCTION

In a fragmented healthcare system of patients, doctors, caregivers, and specialists, an accurate knowledge of a patient's disease state is critical. Electronic monitoring systems and health records facilitate the flow of information among these parties to effectively manage patient health. However, information is not knowledge, and often only some of the information will be relevant in the context of providing care. Expert physicians want to sift through these extensive records to discover the data most relevant to a patient's current condition. As such, systems that can identify these patterns of relevant characteristics stand to improve the efficiency and quality of care.

This work focused on the task of on-going mortality prediction in the intensive care unit (ICU). The ICU is a particularly challenging environment because each patient's severity of illness is constantly evolving. Further, modern ICUs are equipped with many independent measurement devices that often produce conflicting (and even false) alarms, adversely affecting the quality of care. Consequently, much recent work in ICU mortality models [8, 10, 17] has aimed to consolidate data from these devices (primarily structured data and physiological waveforms) and transform these information streams into knowledge. However, these works omit perhaps the most descriptive sources of medical information: free-text clinical notes and reports.

The narrative in the clinical notes, recorded by expert care staff, is designed to provide trained professionals a quick glance into the most important aspects of a patient's physiology. Combining features extracted from these notations with standard physiological measurements results in a more complete representation of patients' physiological states, thus affording improved outcome prediction. Unfortunately, free-text data are often more difficult to include in predictive models because they lack the structure required by most machine learning methods. To overcome the obstacles inherent in clinical text, latent variable models such as topic models [1, 2] may be used to infer intermediary representations that can in turn be used as structured features for a prediction task.

We demonstrate the value of incorporating information from clinical notes, via latent topic features, in the task of in-hospital mortality prediction as well as 30 day and 1 year post-discharge mortality prediction. Specifically, we evaluated mortality prediction under three prediction regimes: (1) baseline regime, which used structured data available on admission (2) time-varying regime, which used baseline features together with dynamically accumulated clinical text using increasigly large subsets of the patient's narrative record, and (3) retrospective regime, which used all clinical text generated from a hospital stay to supplement the baseline features. In all targeted outcomes, we demonstrate that adding information from clinical notes improves predictions of mortality.

2. RELATED WORK

Mortality models for acute (i.e. ICU) settings constitute a broad area of research. Siontis et al. [16] reviewed 94 studies with 240 assessments of 118 mortality prediction tools from 2009 alone. Many of these studies evaluated established clinical decision rules for predicting mortality, such as APACHE [9], SAPS-II [10], and SOFA [17] (with median reported AUCs of 0.77, 0.77, and 0.84, respectively). Sionitis et al. also noted a large variability of these measures across various diseases and population subgroups. Other acuity scores have also been proposed, including the recent OASIS score [8] which uses machine-learning algorithms to identify the minimal set of variables capable of yielding an accurate severity of illness score (AUC 0.88).

Work by Hug et al. [7] used several hundred structured clinical variables to create a real-time ICU acuity score that reported an AUC of 0.88-0.89 for in-hospital mortality prediction. Notably, most of the predictive power of their models was from data gathered within the first 24 hours of the ICU stay. For example, their computed acuity score reported an AUC of 0.809 for in-hospital mortality prediction based on information during the first 24 hours of ICU stays in 1,954 patients.

Several recent works have used information from clinical notes in their model formulations. Saria et al. [15] combined structured physiological data with concepts from the discharge summaries to achieve a patient outcome classification F1 score of 88.3 with a corresponding reduction in error of 23.52%. Similarly, [5] described preliminary results indicating that topic models extracted from clinical text in a subgroup of ICU patients were valuable in the prediction of per-admission mortality. They found that common topics from the unlabeled clinical notes were predictive of mortality, and an RBF SVM achieved a retrospective AUC of 0.855 for in-hospital mortality prediction using only learned topics. Finally, Lehman et al. [11] applied Hierarchical Dirichlet Processes to nursing notes from the first 24 hours for ICU patient risk stratification. They demonstrated that unstructured nursing notes were enriched with clinically meaningful information, and this information could be used for clinical support. Using topic proportions, the average AUC for hospital mortality prediction was 0.78 ($\pm$ 0.01). In combination with the SAPS-I variable, their average AUC for hospital mortality prediction was 0.82 ($\pm$ 0.003).

3. METHODS

Figure 1 gives a general overview of our experimental process. First, we extract clinical baseline features, including age, sex, and SAPS-II score, from the database for every patient. We also extract each patient's de-identified clinical notes. We use these notes as the observed data in an LDA topic model, and infer a total of 50 topics. We normalize the word counts associated with each note, so that each note is represented by a 50-dimension vector, summing to 1. These per-note topic distributions are then aggregated on a 12 hour semi-continuous timescale (e.g. notes within 0-12 hours, notes within 0-24 hours, etc.). A linear kernel SVM is trained to create classification boundaries with combinations of the structured clinical features and latent topic features to predict in-hospital mortality, 30 day post-discharge mortality, and 1 year post-discharge mortality.

3.1 Data and Pre-Processing

We used ICU data from the MIMIC II 2.6 database [13], a publicly-available, de-identified medical corpus which includes electronic medical records (EMRs) for 26,870 ICU patients at the Beth Israel Deaconess Medical Center (BIDMC) collected from 2001 to 2008. Patient age, sex, SAPS-II scores, International Classification of Diseases-Ninth Revision (ICD-9) diagnoses, and Disease-Related Group were extracted. Medical co-morbidities were represented by the Elixhauser scores (EH) for 30 co-morbidities as calculated from the ICD-9 codes. Patient mortality outcomes were also queried to determine which patients died in-hospital, or lived past the most recent query of Social Security records.

We extracted all clinical notes recorded prior to the patient's first discharge, including notes from nursing, physicians, labs, and radiology. The discharge summaries themselves were excluded because they typically stated the patient's outcome explicitly. Vocabularies for each note were generated by first tokenizing the free text and then removing

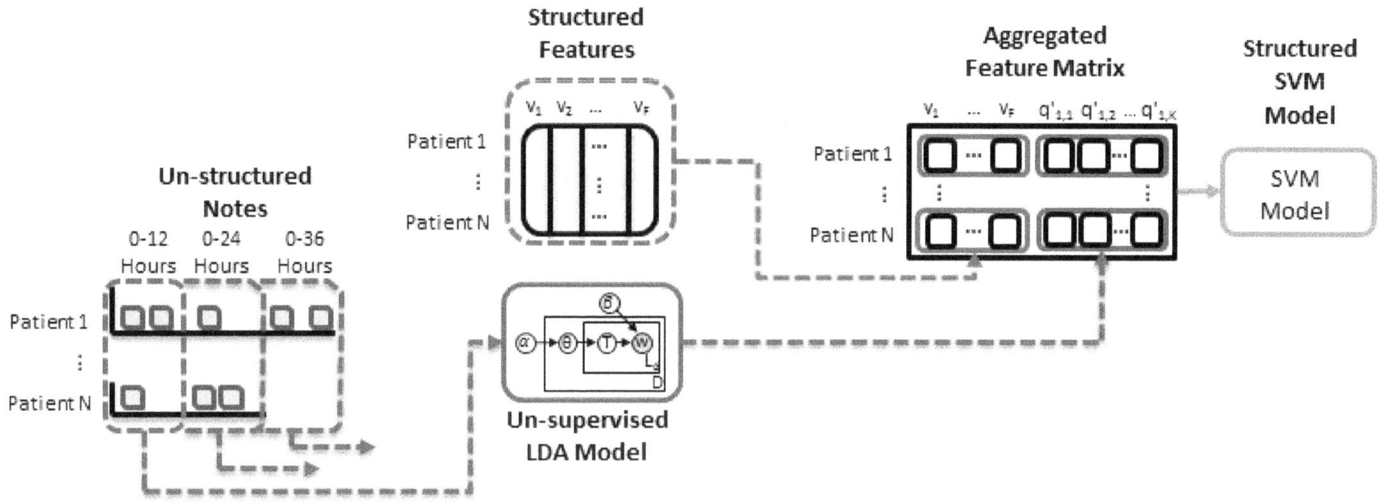

Figure 1: Overall flow of experiment. 1) Clinical baseline features are extracted from the database for every patient (e.g. age, sex, admitting SAPS-II score) and derived features are computed (e.g. maximum/minimum SAPS-II score) to form the *Structured Features* matrix v ($v_{p,f}$ is the value of feature f in the pth patient). 2) Each patient's de-identified clinical notes are used as the observed data in an LDA topic model (i.e., *Un-supervisted LDA Model*), and a total of 50 topics are inferred to create the per-note topic proportion matrix q. 3) Per-note latent topic features are aggregated in extending 12 hour windows (e.g. notes within 0-12 hours, notes within 0-24 hours, etc.) and used to form matrix q' where $q'_{m,k}$ is the overall proportion of topic k in time-window m. 4) Depending on the model and time window being evaluated, subsets of the feature matrix v and matrix q' are combined into an *Aggregated Feature Matrix.* 5) A linear kernel SVM is trained to create classification boundaries for three clinical outcomes: in-hospital mortality, 30 day post-discharge mortality, and 1 year post-discharge mortality (i.e. *Structured SVM Model*).

Table 1: Cohort Composition

	Train	Test	Total
Patients	13,524	5,784	19,308
Notes	331,635	142,129	473,764

stopwords using the Onix stopword list [1]. A TF-IDF metric [14] was applied to determine the 500 most informative words in each patient's notes, and we then limited our overall vocabulary to the union of the most informative words per-patient. This pre-processing step reduced the overall vocabulary down to 285,840 words from over 1 million terms while maintaining the most distinctive features of each patient.[2]

Patients were excluded if they had fewer than 100 non-stop words or were under the age of 18. Specific notes were excluded if they occurred after the the end of the day in which a patient died or was discharged (e.g. radiology or lab reports whose results were reported afterwards). The resulting cohort consisted of 19,308 patients with 473,764 notes. We held out a random 30% of the patients as a test set. The remaining 70% of patients were used to train our topic models and mortality predictors. Table 1 summarizes the number of notes and patients in the training and test sets.

3.2 Structured and Derived Features

In total, we extracted and derived 36 structured clinical variables for each patient: the age, gender, SAPS II score on admission, minimum SAPS II score, maximum SAPS II score, final SAPS II score, and the 30 EH comorbidities. Data were scaled to avoid the range of a feature impacting its classification importance. This formed a feature matrix v, where the element $v_{p,f}$ was the value of feature f in the pth patient.

3.3 Topic Inference

Instead of considering each note separately, we used the set of all of notes that occurred in a particular time period as features for that period. We examined the distribution of note times, and found three peaks in note entry for any given day in a patient's stay (e.g. day 1, day 2, etc.): around 06:00, 18:00 and 24:00.[3] Given this distribution, we used 12-hour windows for our time windows.

Topics were generated for each note using Latent Dirichlet Allocation [2,6]. Our initial experiments found no significant difference in held-out prediction accuracy across a range of 20 to 100 topics. We set hyperparameters on the Dirichlet priors for the topic distributions (α) and the topic-word distributions (β) as $\alpha = \frac{50}{numberTopics}, \beta = \frac{200}{numberWordsInVocab}$. We used 50 topics in our final experiments, and topic distributions were sampled from an MCMC chain after 2,500 iterations. This topic-modeling step resulted in a 50-dimensional vector of topic proportions for each patient for each note.

[1]Onix Text Retrieval Toolkit, API Reference, http://www.lextek.com/manuals/onix

[2]Some medical term canonicalization parsers were also examined, but we found their outputs to be fairly unreliable for this task.

[3]The increases in note submission at 06:00 and 18:00 were likely due to the current 12 hour nursing shift cycle. The large number of notes submitted at end-of-day were likely due to a previously common 14:00 - midnight nursing shift.

We concatenated the topic vectors into a matrix q where the element $q_{n,k}$ was the proportion of topic k in the nth note. Of particular interest was whether certain topics were enriched for in-hospital mortality and long-term survival. We used an enrichment measure defined by Marlin et al [12], where the probability of mortality for each topic is calculated as $\theta_k = \frac{\sum_{n=1}^{N} q_{n,k} * y_k}{\sum_{n=1}^{N} q_{n,k}}$, where y_n is the noted mortality outcome (0 for a patient that lives, and 1 for a patient that dies). These enrichment measures are reported in section 4.1.

The time windows were used to construct feature vectors for each prediction task, where (at each step) we extended the period of consideration forward by 12 hours. From the previously constructed per-note matrix q that describes the distribution over topics in each note, we collapse into another matrix q' where $q'_{m,k}$ describes the overall proportion of topic k in time-window m. The element $q'_{m,k}$ is given by the mean of that topic's proportions of all the notes in time-window m: $\text{mean}_{n \in m} q_{n,k}$.

3.4 Prediction

We considered three prediction regimes with the inferred topic distributions: baseline prediction, dynamic (time-varying) outcome prediction and retrospective outcome prediction for the outcomes of in-hospital, 30-day, and 1-year mortality.

A separate linear SVM [4] was trained for each of the three outcomes, and each set of model features evaluated. The loss and class weight parameters for the SVM were selected using five-fold cross-validation on the training data to determine the optimal values with AUC as an objective. The learned parameters were then used to construct a model for the entire training set, and make predictions on the test data.

All outcomes had large class-imbalance (mortality rates of 10.9% in-hospital, 3.7% 30 day post-discharge, and 13.7% 1 year post-discharge[4]). To address this issue, we randomly sub-sampled the negative class in the training set to produce a minimum 70%/30% ratio between the negative and positive classes. Test set distributions were not modified to reflect the reality of class imbalance during prediction, and reported performance reflects those distributions.

First, we established a static baseline model using only structured features present at admission (i.e. clinical baseline features and derived features thereof). We then ran dynamic outcome prediction in intervals of 12 hours at each step by including larger sets of patient notes in a step-wise manner. We finally performed retrospective outcome predictions, where we included structured features and all notes written during the stay as a static entity for prediction. Significantly, predictions of mortality with this type of feature set are a retrospective exercise only: it is not possible to first select all notes that occur before a patient's death, and then predict in-hospital mortality, because the time of mortality is not known a-priori. The observer would have to "know" that the patient's hospital record was about to finish (either by death or discharge). The following settings were evaluated:

- *Admission Baseline Model*: A baseline model using the structured features of age, gender, and the SAPS II score at admission. These baseline features are extracted from the data present at patient admission only. (3 features total)
- *Time-varying Topic Model 1 - 20*: Outcome prediction performed by including notes in a step-wise fashion, extending the period of consideration forward by 12 hours at each step. For example, Time-varying Topic Model 1 includes topic features derived from all notes written during the first 12 hours of a patient's stay in the ICU, while Time-varying Topic Model 20 includes those derived from the first 240 hours. (50 features total)
- *Combined Time-varying Model 1 - 20*: Outcome prediction using the same setup as Time-varying Topic Model 1 - 20, but with the static structured features from Admission Baseline Model (gender, age, admitting SAPS score) included. (53 features total)
- *Retrospective Derived Features Model*: A retrospective model using the structured features of age, gender, admitting SAPS II score, the minimum SAPS II score, the maximum SAPS II score, the final SAPS II score, and all EH comorbidities. (36 features total)
- *Retrospective Topic Model*: A retrospective model using topics derived from all notes written during a patient's stay in the ICU. (50 features total)
- *Retrospective Topic + Admission Model*: A retrospective model combining structured features from Admission Baseline Model (gender, age, admitting SAPS scores) with latent topic features from Retrospective Topic Model. (53 features total)
- *Retrospective Topic + Derived Features Model*: A retrospective model combining structured features from Retrospective Derived Features Model (gender, age, admitting/min/max/final SAPS scores, EH comorbidities) with latent topic features from Retrospective Topic Model. (86 features total)

We compare the prediction results for all models on each of the outcomes in Figure 3 and Table A.2. We again emphasize that retrospective models are retrospective exercises only to establish the isolated and combined prediction ability of clinical notes and features. We also note that our *Time-varying Topic Model* is time-varying only in its application. We do not use other possible latent variable models such as "Dynamic topic models" [3], because we do not want to model the time evolution of topics, but rather the time evolution of membership to a given set of topics.

4. RESULTS

4.1 Qualitative Enrichment

Table 2 lists the top words for the topics which had the largest enrichment ($\theta_k = \frac{\sum_{n=1}^{N} q_{n,k} * y_k}{\sum_{n=1}^{N} q_{n,k}}$) for in-hospital mortality, the smallest enrichment for in-hospital mortality, and the highest enrichment for 1 year mortality. The relative distributions of the in-hospital mortality probabilities for each of the 50 topics are shown in Figure 2. There were a wide variation in the in-hospital mortality concentration for the different topics, ranging from 3% - 30%. (See Table A.3 for a listing of top ten words for all topics.)

[4]This includes those who die within the first 30-days post-discharge, so two of the prediction targets have overlap.

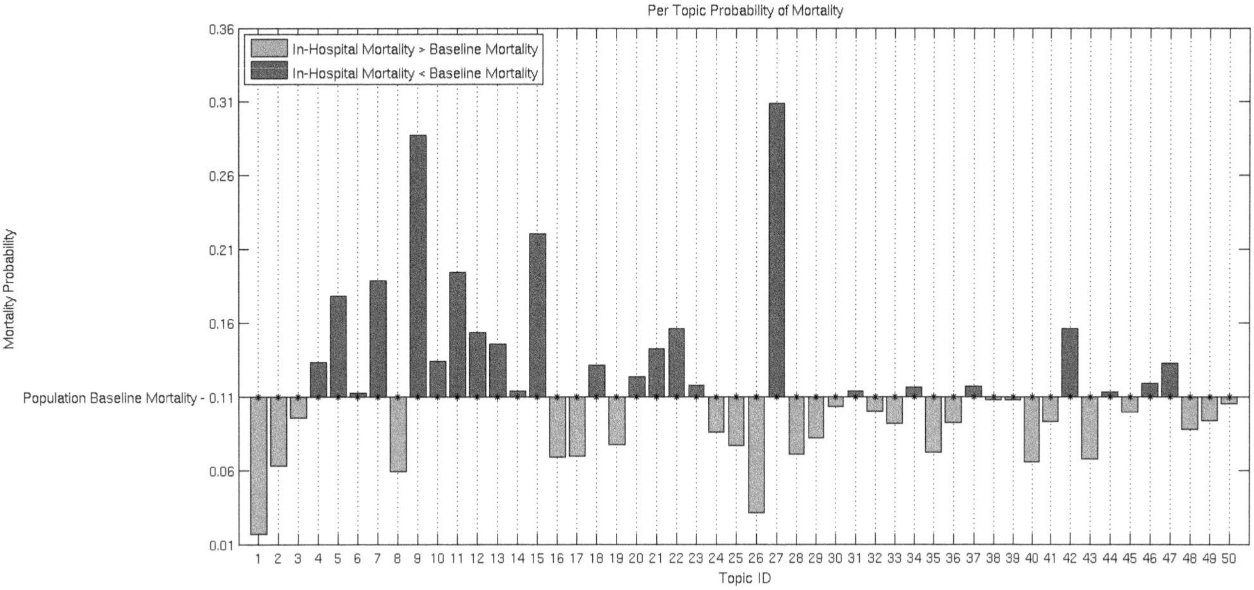

Figure 2: The probability of in-hospital mortality for each topic, indicating that topics represent differences in outcome. Probabilities are calculated as $\theta_k = \frac{\sum_{n=1}^{N} q_{n,k} * y_n}{\sum_{n=1}^{N} q_{n,k}}$ (see section 3.3). Each bar shows the prevalence of a given topic k in the mortality category, as compared to the set of all patients. Bars are shown as above (in red) or below (in green) the baseline in-hospital mortality based on the value of θ_k for each topic k.

The topics enriched for in-hospital mortality presented a detailed view of the possible causes of death in the ICU. For example, patients in a modern ICU rarely die suddenly. Often patient life is sustained for some time in order for their family to express their wishes regarding terminal care and death. This could be one interpretation for Topic 27, which pertains to the discussion of end-of-life care options. Other topics with in-hospital mortality enrichment pertained to top causes of ICU mortality: respiratory infection (Topic 7), respiratory failure (Topic 15), and renal failure (Topic 5).

Hospital survival was also marked by topics which seem relevant to factors tied closely to the ability to recover from physiological insults: patients who are admitted for cardiovascular surgery (Topic 1) are often not allowed as surgical candidates until they are in very good health; patients who are able to respond to their care staff and the ICU environment (Topic 26, Table A.3) are adequately dealing with the known stress of ICU admission; patients with trauma-based injuries such as fracture and pneumothorax (Topics 8, 40); and patients with chronic conditions like diabetes (Topic 16).

The topics enriched for 1 year post-discharge mortality suggested that patients who are discharged but die within a year have conditions with a low chance of long-term survival. For example, cancer (Topic 4), the need for long-term IV access while in the ICU (Topic 3), and the use of coronary catheterization (Topic 45) to diagnose activity in coronary arteries or other valvular/cardiac issues.

4.2 Prediction

We evaluated the predictive power of each model and outcome pair. Figure 3 shows the AUCs achieved by each model for the three targeted outcomes. Table A.2 lists a more complete set of the SVM classification metrics.

As shown in Table A.2, the prevalent class imbalance resulted in a bias toward low specificities in the *Admission Baseline Model*. The balance between sensitivity and specificity generally leaned towards favoring higher specificities for in-hospital and 30 day mortality prediction as time moved forward in the *Time-varying* models, but this was not uniformaly true in all cases. In general, the *Retrospective Derived Features Model* had a high sensitivity and low specificity, the *Retrospective Topic Model* had good specificity, and the combined models tended to have a more even set of both measures.

For 30 day and 1 year post-discharge mortality prediction, the *Admission Baseline Model* was very steady, averaging an AUC of 0.68 over all time windows for both outcomes. The *Combined Time-varying Model* achieved an average/best performance of 0.77/0.8 for 30 day mortality and 0.75/0.77 for 1 year mortality. In both outcomes the *Time-varying Topic Model* performed strictly better than the *Admission Baseline Model* until the available patient subset became minimal (the 204 -216 hour windows), and the *Combined Time-varying Model* was always better than either alone.

As expected, the four *Retrospective* models were generally more predictive than any of the *Time-varying* models. *Retrospective* models tended to increase performance as more features were added. For in-hospital and 30 day mortality prediction, the *Retrospective Topic Model* performed better than the *Retrospective Derived Features Model* (AUCs increased from 0.90 to 0.94 and 0.75 to 0.78 respectively). For 1 year mortality this was reversed (AUC decreased from 0.78 to 0.76).

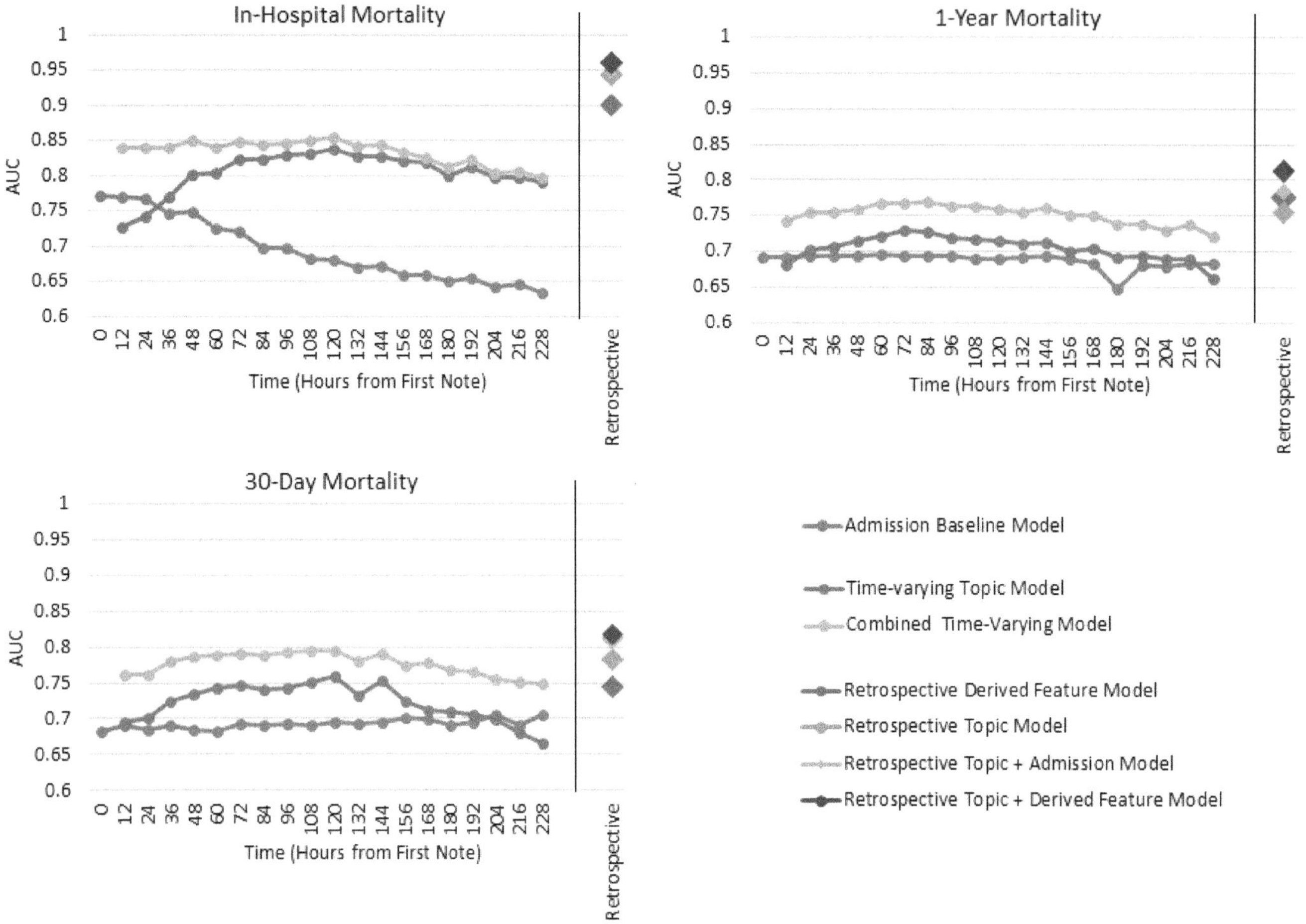

Figure 3: Linear SVM model performance measured via AUC on three outcomes: in-hospital mortality, 30 day post-discharge mortality, and 1 year post-discharge mortality. In each case, the features used are described in detail in Section 3.4. Our prediction task is different from the usual situation where data is accumulated over time. Since fewer patients have long ICU stays, in this case, we actually lose data points as time goes on, making the prediction task harder. For example, at time 0 there are 5,784 patients (5,157 controls/627 positives for in-hospital mortality) in the test set. By 72 hours, this had dropped to 5,084 patients (4,591 controls/493 positives for in-hospital mortality) and at 144 hours to 3,496 patients (3,141 controls/355 positives for in-hospital mortality). (Table A.1)

In the in-hospital mortality setting, it seemed that admission features were not needed once latent topic features are known, but the derived features did provide extra information[6]. However, in the 30 day setting, latent topic features were similarly improved by either the admission features or the derived features[7]. This is likely because the derived features included EH comorbidities derived from the ICD-9 codes, and the ICD-9 codes themselves are often transcribed after a patient's discharge with the most actionable (or billable) conditions a patient presented. It is possible that these features are most relevant to in-hospital mortality risks (e.g. EH scores for myocardial infarction, congestive heart failures, etc.).

[6]Adding the admission features did not improve the *Retrospective Topic Model*, but adding the derived features boosted AUC slightly to 0.96.

[7]Adding the admission features to the *Retrospective Topic Model* improved AUC to 0.81 but adding the derived features did not improve AUC further.

5. DISCUSSION

Models that incorporated latent topic features were generally more predictive than those using only structured features, and a combination of the two feature types performed best. Notably, the combination provides a robustness that is able to perform well initially, leveraging primarily the structured information, and then continue to improve over the first 24 hours by incorporating the latent topic features. This resilience is particularly important since we observed that the first 24 hours of clinical notes appear to be the most meaningful toward predicting in-hospital mortality, while the baseline begins to steadily decrease.

Our observation of the importance of early data agrees with other reported results. Recall that, using topics derived from the first 24 hours of notes only, Lehman et al obtained an average AUC for in-hospital mortality prediction of 0.78 ($\pm$ 0.01), and this was increased to 0.82 ($\pm$ 0.003) with the SAPS-I variable. Further, Hug et al. obtained an AUC of 0.809 for in-hospital mortality prediction based on information during the first 24 hours of ICU. As such, we

Table 2: Top ten words in topics enriched for in-hospital mortality, hospital survival (any number of days post-discharge), and 1 year post-discharge mortality.

	Topic	Top Ten Words	Possible Topic
In-hospital Mortality	27	name, family, neuro, care, noted, status, plan, stitle, dr, remains	Discussion of end-of-life care
	15	intubated, vent, ett, secretions, propofol, abg, respiratory, resp, care, sedated	Respiratory failure
	7	thick, secretions, vent, trach, resp, tf, tube, coarse, cont, suctioned	Respiratory infection
	5	liver, renal, hepatic, ascites, dialysis, failure, flow, transplant, portal, ultrasound	Renal Failure
Hospital Survival	1	cabg, pain, ct, artery, coronary, valve, post, wires, chest, sp	Cardiovascular surgery
	40	left, fracture, ap, views, reason, clip, hip, distal, lat, report	Fracture
	16	gtt, insulin, bs, lasix, endo, monitor, mg, am, plan, iv	Chronic diabetes
1 Year Mortality	3	picc, line, name, procedure, catheter, vein, tip, placement, clip, access	PICC[5] line insertion
	4	biliary, mass, duct, metastatic, bile, cancer, left, ca, tumor, clip	Cancer treatment
	45	catheter, name, procedure, contrast, wire, french, placed, needle, advanced, clip	Coronary catheterization

examined our results for in-hospital mortality when using topics derived from the first 24 hours of notes only (prediction time of 36 hours in Figure 3), and obtained corresponding AUCs of 0.77 for the *Time-varying Topic Model*, and 0.841 for the *Combined Time-varying Model*. Compared to Lehman et al's result, this implies that (with enough data) neither the extra hierarchical machinery added with HDPs nor the knowledge-based cleansing of medical terms before modeling improve prediction results (i.e. an AUC of 0.78 vs. 0.77). Compared to Hug et al's results, this implies that the addition of clinical text provides reasonable performance boosts to the power of gold-standard structured information like SAPS-II score (i.e. an AUC of 0.809 vs. 0.841).

Further, when predicting in-hospital mortality, we observed that the *Admission Baseline Model*'s predictive power (i.e. information acquired on admission) becomes much less valuable to predicting mortality as patients stay longer. This is likely because those who are not discharged within the first day of hospital admission are significantly sicker than those who are. Note that the average ICU stay time in the MIMIC II database is 3 days, and Figure 3 shows that after this time there was no additional predictive power gained by adding the structured admission information to the latent topic features (i.e., the *Time-varying Topic Model* and the *Combined Time-varying Model* converge).

This convergence draws attention to another interesting observation. Namely, both of the *Time-varying* models trended up in their ability to predict in-hospital mortality until 120 hours, and then trended down until the end of prediction. While initially counterintuitive, this is likely due to the loss of a significant number of patients (from both death and discharge) in the available patient cohort. For example, the test set population goes from 4,030 patients (3,626 control/404 positive for in-hospital mortality) to 3570 patients at this point (3,210 control/360 positive for in-hospital mortality).

Additionally, the predictive power of each topic changed depending on the target outcome. This appeals to intuition asIn a modern ICU, conditions that lead to in-hospital mortality are very different from those that would allow for a live discharge leading to a 30 day or 1 year mortality. As such, information about which topics tend to bias a patient towards any set of outcomes in useful for clinicians, when compared to the typical "black-box" approach to feature selection.

Finally, much work focuses on retrospective prediction of mortality outcomes. We also performed these predictions to compare the relative predictive power of different feature types and were able to achieve retrospective AUCs of 0.9, 0.94 and 0.96 for in-hospital mortality prediction using the *Retrospective Derived Feature Model*, *Retrospective Topic Model*, and combined *Retrospective Topic + Dervied Features Model*. However, we re-emphasize that predictions of mortality with retrospective feature sets are not helpful or relevant for clinical staff because statistical functions of signals or features (e.g. min/max) and other structured data (such as ICD-9 codes and EH comorbidities) are not known a-priori.

6. CONCLUSIONS

Modern electronic healthcare records contain an increasingly large amount of data including high-frequency signals from biomedical instrumentation, intermittent results from lab tests, and text from notes. Such voluminous records can make it difficult for care-staff to identify the information relevant to diagnose a patient's condition and stratify patients with similar characteristics.

Standard approaches to hospital mortality prediction use features such as gender, age, SAPS and SOFA score. In this work, we examined the utility of augmenting these standard features with textual information—specifically in the form of topic-based features—for predicting mortality in the ICU. Features extracted by latent variable models are attractive in this clinical application because scientific understanding is as important as clinical utility.

Qualitatively, the discovered topics correlated with known causes of in-hospital and post-discharge death. Further, adding latent topic features to structured clincal features increased classification performance in a variety of prediction scenarios: in-hospital mortality, 30-day mortality, and 1-year mortality.

The models and results explored in this work could ultimately be useful for interpretable models of disease and mortality.

7. ACKNOWLEDGMENTS

This research was funded in part by the Intel Science and Technology Center for Big Data and the National Library of Medicine Biomedical Informatics Research Training grant (NIH/NLM 2T15 LM007092-22) which supported Marzyeh Ghassemi and Tristan Naumann.

The authors would like to thank Abbas Benjamin Munson-Ghassemi for many nights of heartburn and kick-fueled writing.

8. REFERENCES

[1] C. Arnold et al. Clinical case-based retrieval using latent topic analysis. In *AMIA Annual Symposium Proceedings*, volume 2010, page 26. AMIA, 2010.

[2] D. Blei, A. Ng, and M. Jordan. Latent dirichlet allocation. *JMLR*, 3(5):993–1022, 2003.

[3] D. M. Blei and J. D. Lafferty. Dynamic topic models. In *Proceedings of the 23rd international conference on Machine learning*, pages 113–120. ACM, 2006.

[4] C.-C. Chang and C.-J. Lin. LIBSVM: A library for support vector machines. *ACM TIST*, 2:27:1–27:27, 2011.

[5] M. Ghassemi, T. Naumann, R. Joshi, and A. Rumshisky. Topic models for mortality modeling in intensive care units. In *Proceedings of ICML 2012 (Machine Learning for Clinical Data Analysis Workshop), Poster Presentation*, Edinburgh, UK, June 2012.

[6] T. Griffiths and M. Steyvers. Finding scientific topics. In *PNAS*, volume 101, pages 5228–5235, 2004.

[7] C. W. Hug and P. Szolovits. Icu acuity: real-time models versus daily models. In *AMIA Annual Symposium Proceedings*, volume 2009, page 260. American Medical Informatics Association, 2009.

[8] A. E. Johnson, A. A. Kramer, and G. D. Clifford. A new severity of illness scale using a subset of acute physiology and chronic health evaluation data elements shows comparable predictive accuracy*. *Critical care medicine*, 41(7):1711–1718, 2013.

[9] W. A. Knaus, D. Wagner, E. e. a. Draper, J. Zimmerman, M. Bergner, P. G. Bastos, C. Sirio, D. Murphy, T. Lotring, and A. Damiano. The apache iii prognostic system. risk prediction of hospital mortality for critically ill hospitalized adults. *CHEST Journal*, 100(6):1619–1636, 1991.

[10] J. Le Gall, S. Lemeshow, and F. Saulnier. A new simplified acute physiology score (saps ii) based on a european/north american multicenter study. *JAMA*, 270(24):2957–2963, 1993.

[11] L.-w. Lehman, M. Saeed, W. Long, J. Lee, and R. Mark. Risk stratification of icu patients using topic models inferred from unstructured progress notes. In *AMIA Annual Symposium Proceedings*, volume 2012, page 505. American Medical Informatics Association, 2012.

[12] B. M. Marlin, D. C. Kale, R. G. Khemani, and R. C. Wetzel. Unsupervised pattern discovery in electronic health care data using probabilistic clustering models. In *Proceedings of the 2nd ACM SIGHIT International Health Informatics Symposium*, pages 389–398. ACM, 2012.

[13] M. Saeed et al. Multiparameter Intelligent Monitoring in Intensive Care II: A public-access intensive care unit database. *Critical Care Medicine*, 39(5):952–960, May 2011.

[14] G. Salton and C. S. Yang. On the specification of term values in automatic indexing. *Journal of Documentation*, 29(4):351–372, 1973.

[15] S. Saria, G. McElvain, A. K. Rajani, A. A. Penn, and D. L. Koller. Combining structured and free-text data for automatic coding of patient outcomes. In *AMIA Annual Symposium Proceedings*, volume 2010, page 712. American Medical Informatics Association, 2010.

[16] G. Siontis, I. Tzoulaki, and J. Ioannidis. Predicting death: an empirical evaluation of predictive tools for mortality. *Archives of internal medicine*, pages archinternmed–2011, 2011.

[17] J.-L. Vincent, R. Moreno, J. Takala, S. Willatts, A. De Mendonça, H. Bruining, C. Reinhart, P. Suter, and L. Thijs. The sofa (sepsis-related organ failure assessment) score to describe organ dysfunction/failure. *Intensive care medicine*, 22(7):707–710, 1996.

APPENDIX

A. PATIENT COHORT SIZES

Table A.1.

Table A.1: Patient cohort size at each time tested by time-varying models. Note that patients are removed from a prediction time if they are discharged or die prior to that time.

Time (Hours)	Total	Cohort Size (Control, Positive)		
		In-Hospital	30 Day	1 Year
0	5784	5157, 627	5597, 187	5058, 726
12	5784	5157, 627	5597, 187	5058, 726
24	5749	5128, 621	5563, 186	5026, 723
36	5563	4998, 565	5382, 181	4855, 708
48	5497	4937, 560	5318, 179	4795, 702
60	5161	4664, 497	4986, 175	4480, 681
72	5084	4591, 493	4911, 173	4407, 677
84	4691	4241, 450	4524, 167	4043, 648
96	4587	4140, 447	4421, 166	3945, 642
108	4116	3710, 406	3963, 153	3530, 586
120	4030	3626, 404	3877, 153	3448, 582
132	3570	3210, 360	3427, 143	3023, 547
144	3496	3141, 355	3354, 142	2956, 540
156	3026	2707, 319	2898, 128	2533, 493
168	2967	2652, 315	2840, 127	2479, 488
180	2580	2291, 289	2468, 112	2138, 442
192	2541	2254, 287	2431, 110	2109, 432
204	2215	1953, 262	2117, 98	1825, 390
216	2186	1925, 261	2090, 96	1802, 384
228	1925	1681, 244	1837, 88	1575, 350

B. MODEL PERFORMANCE RESULTS

Table A.2.

C. LIST OF INFERRED TOPICS

Table A.3.

Table A.2: Detailed model prediction results for three outcomes: in-hospital mortality, 30 day post-discharge mortality, and 1 year post-discharge mortality. This also appears in Figure 3.

Outcome Predicted	Model Used	AUC	Sens.	Spec.
In-Hospital Mortality	Admission Baseline Model	0.771	0.999	0.010
	Time-varying Topic Model 1	0.728	0.858	0.471
	...		...	
	Time-varying Topic Model 10	0.838	0.686	0.829
	...		...	
	Time-varying Topic Model 20	0.791	0.525	0.853
	Combined Time-varying Model 1	0.840	0.638	0.85
	...		...	
	Combined Time-varying Model 10	0.854	0.666	0.844
	...		...	
	Combined Time-varying Model 20	0.798	0.299	0.950
	Retrospective Derived Features Model	0.901	0.997	0.108
	Retrospective Topic Model	0.944	0.856	0.892
	Retrospective Topic + Admission Model	0.944	0.821	0.910
	Retrospective Topic + Derived Features Model	0.961	0.915	0.870
30 Day Mortality	Admission Baseline Model	0.683	0.995	0.075
	Time-varying Topic Model 1	0.695	0.150	0.944
	...		...	
	Time-varying Topic Model 10	0.759	0.817	0.551
	...		...	
	Time-varying Topic Model 20	0.665	0.602	0.579
	Combined Time-varying Model 1	0.761	0.348	0.885
	...		...	
	Combined Time-varying Model 10	0.796	0.641	0.770
	...		...	
	Combined Time-varying Model 20	0.75	0.011	0.991
	Retrospective Derived Features Model	0.745	0.941	0.220
	Retrospective Topic Model	0.783	0.342	0.909
	Retrospective Topic + Admission Model	0.813	0.872	0.633
	Retrospective Topic + Derived Features Model	0.818	0.096	0.985
1 Year Mortality	Admission Baseline Model	0.692	0.997	0.021
	Time-varying Topic Model 1	0.681	0.218	0.907
	...		...	
	Time-varying Topic Model 10	0.715	0.321	0.870
	...		...	
	Time-varying Topic Model 20	0.662	0.834	0.379
	Combined Time-varying Model 1	0.743	0.705	0.665
	...		...	
	Combined Time-varying Model 10	0.760	0.512	0.812
	...		...	
	Combined Time-varying Model 20	0.722	0.451	0.804
	Retrospective Derived Features Model	0.776	0.999	0.045
	Retrospective Topic Model	0.755	0.358	0.890
	Retrospective Topic + Admission Model	0.784	0.314	0.919
	Retrospective Topic + Derived Features Model	0.813	0.464	0.887

Table A.3: Top ten most probable words for all topics.

Topic Number	Top Ten Words
1	cabg, pain, ct, artery, coronary, valve, post, wires, chest, sp
2	ccu, cath, mg, am, sp, groin, bp, cardiac, hr, cont
3	picc, line, name, procedure, catheter, vein, tip, placement, clip, access
4	biliary, mass, duct, metastatic, bile, cancer, left, ca, tumor, clip
5	liver, renal, hepatic, ascites, dialysis, failure, flow, transplant, portal, ultrasound
6	ct, contrast, pelvis, abdomen, fluid, bowel, clip, free, wcontrast, iv
7	thick, secretions, vent, trach, resp, tf, tube, coarse, cont, suctioned
8	chest, pneumothorax, tube, reason, clip, sp, ap, left, portable, ptx
9	remains, family, gtt, line, map, cont, levophed, cvp, bp, levo
10	name, neo, gtt, stitle, dr, sbp, resp, cont, wean, aware
11	remains, increased, temp, hr, pt, cc, ativan, cont, mg, continues
12	micu, code, stool, hr, bp, social, note, id, received, cchr
13	chest, pulmonary, bilateral, edema, portable, clip, reason, ap, pleural, effusions
14	resp, cough, sats, mask, sob, wheezes, nc, status, mg, neb
15	intubated, vent, ett, secretions, propofol, abg, respiratory, resp, care, sedated
16	gtt, insulin, bs, lasix, endo, monitor, mg, am, plan, iv
17	drainage, pain, abd, fluid, draining, drain, incision, sp, intact, pt
18	heparin, afib, ptt, am, gtt, mg, rate, hr, pvcs, iv
19	name, pacer, namepattern, placement, heart, pacemaker, ventricular, av, rate, chest
20	left, lung, effusion, lobe, pleural, lower, chest, upper, ct, opacity
21	skin, noted, care, left, applied, changed, draining, coccyx, wound, edema
22	tube, placement, tip, line, portable, ap, reason, position, chest, ng
23	noted, shift, name, pt, patent, patient, foley, agitated, soft, mg
24	hct, pt, gi, blood, bleeding, am, stable, unit, bleed, noted
25	name, am, mg, able, bp, time, night, times, doctor, confused
26	pain, co, denies, oriented, neuro, plan, diet, po, pt, floor
27	name, family, neuro, care, noted, status, plan, stitle, dr, remains
28	clip, reason, ro, medical, examination, evidence, impression, underlying, condition, normal
29	neuro, sbp, bp, commands, iv, cough, soft, status, lopressor, swallow
30	skin, stable, social, family, intact, tsicu, id, note, support, endo
31	woman, female, husband, name, pain, patient, pm, am, hospital, noted
32	diagnosis, admitting, name, reason, please, examination, yearold, eval, findings, underlying
33	name, neck, soft, patient, noted, anterior, epidural, level, posterior, namepattern
34	ct, contrast, chest, lymph, optiray, images, lesions, iv, nodes, lobe
35	left, stenosis, disease, clip, reason, carotid, severe, report, radiology, final
36	femoral, foot, left, leg, iliac, groin, lower, patent, graft, extremity
37	acute, reason, head, clip, evidence, eval, name, wo, status, ct
38	aortic, aorta, cta, wwo, dissection, recons, contrast, left, aneurysm, chest
39	left, ivc, filter, vein, pulmonary, veins, dvt, clip, inferior, upper
40	left, fracture, ap, views, reason, clip, hip, distal, lat, report
41	spine, cervical, spinal, clip, thoracic, fall, lumbar, vertebral, contrast, reason
42	hemorrhage, head, ct, left, frontal, contrast, subdural, hematoma, clip, bleed
43	ct, trauma, contrast, injury, fracture, fractures, pelvis, clip, wcontrast, sp
44	contrast, brain, head, left, mri, images, mra, stroke, clip, cerebral
45	catheter, name, procedure, contrast, wire, french, placed, needle, advanced, clip
46	artery, left, common, distal, catheter, internal, branches, flow, name, middle
47	vein, stent, catheter, name, mm, portal, tips, balloon, venous, sheath
48	service, distinct, procedural, artery, sel, carotid, left, cath, name, clip
49	catheter, name, performed, embolization, contrast, bleeding, procedure, mesenteric, extravasation, clip
50	artery, carotid, left, aneurysm, injection, vertebral, internal, evidence, clip, cerebral

Unsupervised Learning of Disease Progression Models

Xiang Wang
IBM Research
Yorktown Heights, NY
wangxi@us.ibm.com

David Sontag
New York University
New York, NY
dsontag@cs.nyu.edu

Fei Wang
IBM Research
Yorktown Heights, NY
fwang@us.ibm.com

ABSTRACT

Chronic diseases, such as Alzheimer's Disease, Diabetes, and Chronic Obstructive Pulmonary Disease, usually progress slowly over a long period of time, causing increasing burden to the patients, their families, and the healthcare system. A better understanding of their progression is instrumental in early diagnosis and personalized care. Modeling disease progression based on real-world evidence is a very challenging task due to the incompleteness and irregularity of the observations, as well as the heterogeneity of the patient conditions. In this paper, we propose a probabilistic disease progression model that address these challenges. As compared to existing disease progression models, the advantage of our model is three-fold: 1) it learns a continuous-time progression model from discrete-time observations with non-equal intervals; 2) it learns the full progression trajectory from a set of incomplete records that only cover short segments of the progression; 3) it learns a compact set of medical concepts as the bridge between the hidden progression process and the observed medical evidence, which are usually extremely sparse and noisy. We demonstrate the capabilities of our model by applying it to a real-world COPD patient cohort and deriving some interesting clinical insights.

Categories and Subject Descriptors

H.2.8 [**Database Management**]: Database Applications-Data mining

Keywords

Bayesian network, Markov jump process, disease progression modeling, medical informatics

1. INTRODUCTION

Chronic diseases usually progress slowly over time. For example, Chronic Obstructive Pulmonary Disease (COPD) can take well over 10 years to evolve from (according to the GOLD criteria [6]) Stage I (mild) to Stage IV (very severe).

KDD'14, August 24–27, 2014, New York, NY, USA.

http://dx.doi.org/10.1145/2623330.2623754.

It may also take 10 years for Congestive Heart Failure (CHF) to progress from Stage I (mild) to Stage IV (severe). Late detection and intervention for such chronic diseases significantly increases the burden on both the patients and the healthcare system. Being able to detect the development of chronic diseases at an early stage is instrumental to preventive care and personalized medicine.

Disease Progression Modeling (DPM) [11], the modeling of the progression of a target disease with computational methods, is an important technique that can help with the early detection and management of chronic diseases. By characterizing the entire disease progression trajectory, DPM also facilitates disease prognosis improvement, drug development, and clinical trial design. There have been a few existing work on DPM that targets a specific domain. For example, Jackson et al. [9] presented a general Hidden Markov Model for simultaneously estimating the transition rates and the probabilities of stage misclassification. Ito et al. [8] conducted a meta analysis to model the longitudinal changes of patients with mild to moderate Alzheimer's disease. Zhou et al. [17] proposed a fused group lasso approach for disease progression modeling with known biomarkers. Exarchos et al. [5] developed a dynamic Bayesian network based technique to model the progression of Coronary Atherosclerosis. Some difficulties of applying these existing methods to general-purpose evidence-based disease progression modeling include:

- ***Multiple Covariates.*** The progression of disease usually involves the evolution of many different types of hidden covariates. Identifying these covariates with limited or no supervision is a very challenging task.
- ***Progression Heterogeneity.*** Different patients may have different progression trajectories. For instance, a COPD patient who had lung infection could progress rapidly, whereas another COPD patient who quit smoking could remain stable. There is no natural alignment between different records with varied progression rates.
- ***Incomplete Records.*** The patient records are not complete, meaning that in most of the cases it only covers a segment of the entire progression trajectory.
- ***Discrete Observation.*** Although the disease progression is a continuous-time process, the patient conditions are only observed at discrete timestamps with varied intervals.
- ***Irregular Visits.*** The patients will only have medical records when they visit a medical facility. There-

fore the time granularity of patient records vary significantly across different patients, and for the same patient over different time periods.

- ***Limited Supervision.*** For some diseases we have very limited yet crucial domain knowledge available, e.g. the known symptoms of a particular disease. Incorporating the available domain knowledge into the progression model is a nontrivial task.

To address these challenges, we propose an *unsupervised* disease progression model. As show in Figure 1, our model is composed of three layers: The top layer is a Markov Jump Process which captures the continuous-time diseases state transitions. The middle layer is a set of Markov chains capturing the relationship between the hidden state transitions and the onset pattern of a set of comorbid conditions (comorbidities). The third layer is a noisy-or network [14] (Figure 2) capturing the relationship between those comorbidities and the observed clinical evidence. Note that instead of linking the clinical observations directly to the disease progression states, we "group" them into comorbidities, which tend to evolve coherently with the progression of disease. This abstraction also makes the learned DPM more robust and interpretable. An Expectation-Maximization (EM) based algorithm is presented to estimate the parameters as well as the hidden variables. We apply our model to a real-world COPD patient cohort to demonstrate its capabilities.

It is worthwhile to highlight the following aspects of the proposed model:

- Our model is unsupervised. We learn the entire disease progression trajectory from the observed patient records without any training labels on the ground truth stages that a patient was in.
- Our model learns the continuous-time disease progression trajectory even though the medical records were only observed at discrete timestamps with irregular intervals.
- Our model can "stitch together" partial disease trajectories (i.e., incomplete records from individual patients) into a global path of disease progression.
- Our model can learn meaningful comorbidities associated with different disease stages. We allow the injection of *anchor findings*, which are clinical features that distinctly signifies the presence of a certain comorbidity, to improve the interpretability and medical validity of our model.

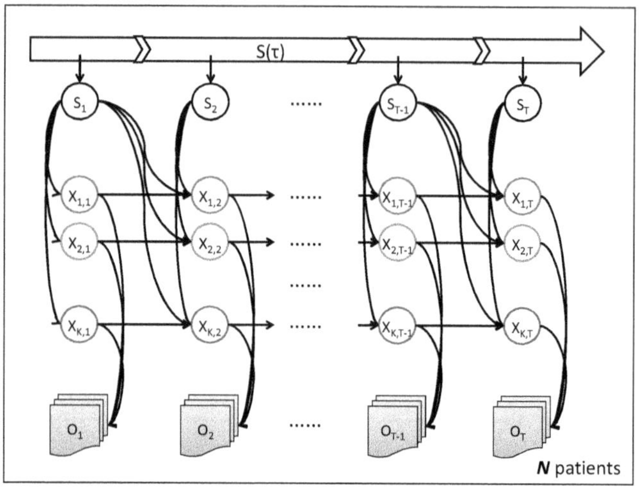

Figure 1: The outline of our model: S are progression state variables, X are comorbidity variables, and O are observed clinical findings.

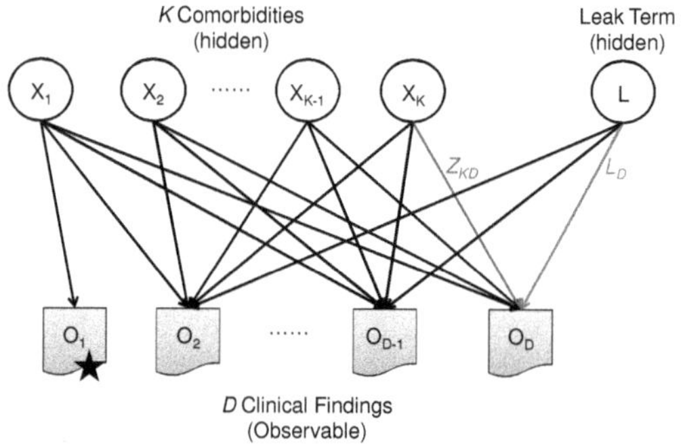

Figure 2: The noisy-or Bayesian network (also known as QMR-DT network). The clinical findings can be activated by a present comorbidity, or by the always-on leak term. The starred finding (O_1) is an anchor, which means it can only be activated by a specific comorbidity (X_1 in this case).

2. RELATED WORK

Disease progression modeling is an important topic in medical informatics [11]. Existing work on disease progression models have been proved effective for drug development and early intervention. For example, Post et al. [12] proposed a family of models to describe the progression of degenerative diseases (such as type 2 diabetes and Parkinson's disease) as a function of disease process and treatment effects. De Winter et al. [3] developed a mechanism based technique for modeling the progression of diabetes mellitus by tracking the interaction between several key indicators. Ito et al. [8] presented a model based on literature meta-analysis to describe the longitudinal changes of patients with mild to moderate Alzheimer's disease. These papers from the medical field tend to be specific to a single target disease. They require substantial domain knowledge on the progression, mechanism, and key indicators/measurements for the target disease. This is not the case for our model because we aim to learn a general-purpose model for any chronic disease based on a general input data type: Electronic Health Records. We do not assume prior knowledge of either the ground truth progression stages or the key indicators that signify the stage transitions.

Another line of efforts, to which our approach belongs, model the progression of disease using machine learning and statistical techniques based on observational data, also referred to as evidence based modeling. For example, Jackson et al. [9] developed a multistage Hidden Markov Model and applied it to an aneurysm screening study. Sukkar et al. [15] applied Hidden Markov Model to Alzheimer's disease. Cohen et al. [2] performed hierarchical clustering of 45 physiological, clinical, and treatment variables collected every minute in an intensive care unit to identify patient states. They used these clusters to visualize individual patient states over time, with each state obtained by assigning the corresponding data point to a cluster. Zhou et al. [17] proposed a fused group lasso formulation for disease progression modeling with known biomarkers. Zhou et al. modeled disease progression using a multi-task learning framework [18]. As pointed out by Yang et al. [16], if we model patient records as time sequences, disease progression stages can also be captured by joint time sequence segmentation. The difference between these existing techniques and our approach includes: 1) Unlike the discrete-time HMM based models, our model is continuous-time, which is a more natural way to handle the irregular time intervals between patient visits; 2) Some existing work were dealing with synchronous time sequences, i.e. there are explicit or implicit correspondence between the timestamps of different patients. This assumption is not true for our model where a patient record could start and end at any point of the progression path.

3. MODEL

We model the progression of a target disease based on the longitudinal clinical findings of a cohort of patients who have developed, or are at risk developing, such disease. First of all, we use a Markov Jump Process to model the transition of disease stages/states, which implies 1) the progression is continuous-time; 2) the transition probability to the future state only relies the current state and the time span.

Second, we use the onset pattern of comorbidities to drive the transitions of the Markov Jump Process. Generally speaking, a comorbidity is a disease or syndrome that co-occurs with the target disease. For example, hypertension is a common comorbidity of diabetes and osteoporosis is a common comorbidity of COPD. Since the onset of a new comorbidity often signifies the exacerbation of the target disease, we use the onset pattern of multiple comorbidities to collectively capture the state transitions of the target disease. We assume the comorbidities are conditionally independent given the state of the target disease. This is a mild assumption in our case because medically meaningful comorbidities are by definition mutually independent diseases.

Finally, in order to infer the presence of the comorbidities from the observed clinical findings, we use a bipartite noisy-or Bayesian network [7, 14] (Figure 2). Simply speaking, given a set of comorbidities and a set of clinical findings, we assume an observed clinical finding was "activated" by the presence of any of the comorbidities with a certain *activation probability*; it is also possible that none of the comorbidities is present and the finding was activated by an always-on hidden cause with a *leak probability*. Such structure is especially well suited to our setting due to its flexibility in modeling sparse and noisy observations.

Our overall model is illustrated in Figure 1. Some notations that are used throughout the rest of the paper are listed in Table 1.

3.1 Variables

We assume that there are K different comorbidities underpinning the progression of the target disease, D different clinical findings, and M different progression states. We have N different patients and each patient n has T_n visits, with timestamps $\tau_1, \ldots, \tau_{T_n}$. We introduce the following

Table 1: Notations and Meanings

N	Number of patients
M	Number of progression states
K	Number of comorbidities
D	Number of clinical findings
t/τ	Discrete/continuous timestamp
$\mathbf{S}$	Disease states
$\mathbf{X}$	Cormorbidities
$\mathbf{O}$	Clinical findings
π	Initial state distribution
Q	Transition generator matrix
$A(\Delta)$	Transition probability matrix over time span Δ
B	Onset probability for comorbidities
Z	Activation probability for clinical findings
L	Leak probability for clinical findings

variables for our model:

$$\text{Disease States (hidden):} \quad S_{n,t} \in \{1, \ldots, M\}$$
$$\text{Comorbidities (hidden):} \quad X_{k,n,t} \in \{0, 1\}$$
$$\text{Clinical Findings (observable):} \quad O_{d,n,t} \in \{0, 1\}$$

The underlying patient state is assumed to evolve according to a continuous-time Markov process. However, we only observe evidence about the patient at specific times $\tau_1, \ldots, \tau_{T_n}$ when the patient interacts with the healthcare system (e.g. visits a doctor or fills a prescription). The random variables $S_{n,t}$ and $X_{k,n,t}$ for $t = 1, \ldots, T_n$ denote the patient's disease state and comorbidities, respectively, at these discrete times. $X_{k,n,t} = 1$ means patient n has comorbidity k at visit t, and is 0 otherwise. In our generative model, the presence or absence of comorbidity k at time t, i.e. $X_{k,n,t}$, depends on whether the patient had the comorbidity in the previous time step, $X_{k,n,t-1}$ as well as the patient's progression state. Associated with each visit is a set of observed clinical findings, $O_{d,n,t}$, which we assume to be conditionally independent given the disease's current state of progression and the comorbidities. We model these using a noisy-or bipartite network, shown in Figure 2 and discussed further in Section 3.4.

3.2 Markov Model of Disease Progression

The continuous-time Markov process is parameterized by an $M \times M$ **transition generator matrix** Q that drives the transition between M states. The transition probability from state i to j with a time span Δ is defined as:

$$\begin{aligned} A_{ij}(\Delta) &\triangleq P(S_t = j | S_{t-1} = i, \tau_t - \tau_{t-1} = \Delta; Q) \\ &= \mathrm{expm}(\Delta Q)_{ij}, \end{aligned} \tag{1}$$

where expm$(\cdot)$ is the matrix exponential.

The $M \times 1$ **initial state probability** π is defined as:

$$\pi_i \triangleq p(S_0 = i), \; i = 1, \ldots, M. \tag{2}$$

3.3 Model of Comorbidities

The disease progression is manifested through a number of comorbidities, which we model as binary random variables. The state of each comorbidity variable at time t, $X_{k,n,t}$, is decided by the current disease state $S_{n,t}$ as well as the state of the same comorbidity variable at the previous time step, $X_{k,n,t-1}$. We further constrain that a comorbidity onset can only happen when there is a state transition from $S_{n,t-1}$ to

$S_{n,t}$ (which means the overall condition of the patient has changed). This conditional distribution is parameterized by a $K \times M \times 2$ **comorbidity onset probability** B:

$$B_{k,m,a} \triangleq p(X_{k,n,t} = 1 | S_{n,t} = m, S_{n,t-1} \neq m, X_{k,n,t-1} = a), \tag{3}$$

$a \in \{0, 1\}$. We assume that B is homogeneous with time t and independent of the particular patient n. For what follows, we define the shorthand:

$$\begin{aligned} &\Psi(X_{k,n,t} | S_{n,t}, X_{k,n,t-1}) \\ &\triangleq B_{k,S_{n,t},X_{k,n,t-1}}^{X_{k,n,t}} (1 - B_{k,S_{n,t},X_{k,n,t-1}})^{1-X_{k,n,t}}. \end{aligned} \tag{4}$$

At $t = 0$, the initial onset probability B^0 is defined as:

$$B_{k,m}^0 \triangleq p(X_{k,n,0} = 1 | S_{n,0} = m). \tag{5}$$

3.4 Model of Clinical Findings

What remains is to describe how we generate the observed findings (e.g., the diagnosis codes) given the disease and comorbidity states. For this part of the model we use a bipartite noisy-or Bayesian network. Such networks have been previously used for medical diagnosis, a prominent example being the Quick Medical Reference (QMR-DT) [14]. However, rather than having a single diagnosis model per patient, we use a new one for each visit, tying them together by having the prior distribution for the comorbidities (the top-level in Figure 2) depend on the state of the comorbidities in the previous visit and on the overall disease state.

We have one parameter $Z_{k,d}$ for the **activation probability** of comorbidity k and finding d. The larger $Z_{k,d}$ is, the more likely observation $O_{d,n,t}$ is to be 1 whenever $X_{k,n,t}$ is 1. If none of the comorbidity variables are active, an observation $O_{d,n,t}$ still has the chance to be activated by an unknown cause, assumed to always be on, with the **leak probability** $L_d \triangleq p(O_{d,n,t} = 1 | \sum_{k=1}^{K} X_{k,n,t} = 0)$. Overall, $O_{d,n,t}$ follows a noisy-or distribution. We define $\Phi(O_{d,n,t}|\mathbf{X})$ as a shorthand for:

$$\Phi(O_{d,n,t}|\mathbf{X}) \triangleq \left(1 - (1 - L_d) \prod_{k=1}^{K} (1 - X_{k,n,t} Z_{k,d})\right)^{O_{d,n,t}}$$
$$\left((1 - L_d) \prod_{k=1}^{K} (1 - X_{k,n,t} Z_{k,d})\right)^{1-O_{d,n,t}}$$

Only $\mathbf{O}$ is observable. $\mathbf{X}$ and $\mathbf{S}$ are hidden, and π, Q, B, L, Z are parameters to estimate.

4. INFERENCE

We give the progression model parameters B, L and Z Beta priors and perform marginal inference over both the latent variables and the model parameters using Gibbs sampling. Estimation of the Markov Jump Process is challenging in our setting due to incomplete observations nonequidistant in time [10], and for computational reasons it is preferable to perform Maximum Likelihood Estimation of the parameters of the continuous-time Markov chain, i.e. $\max_{\pi,Q} p(\mathbf{O}; \pi, Q)$. We use Expectation-Maximization to find a local optimum of the likelihood. The overall learning algorithm is summarized in Algorithm 1.

We omit details of the Gibbs sampling and EM algorithm that are standard, instead focusing our description on estimation of the continuous-time Markov model and on other aspects that are special to our setting.

Algorithm 1: Our Algorithm

Input: Clinical findings $\mathbf{O}$
Output: Transition generator matrix Q, initial state probability π, activation probability Z, leak probability L, onset probability B

```
Initialize S, X, Q, π, B, Z, L;
repeat
    // E-step
    repeat
        Gibbs sampling from p(S, X, B, L, Z | O; π, Q);
    until Convergence;
    Use samples to estimate p(S_{n,0} = i | O; π, Q) and
      p(S_{n,t-1} = i, S_{n,t} = j | O; π, Q);
    Compute C_ij(Δ) = Σ_{n=1}^{N} Σ_{t=1}^{T_n} p(S_{n,t-1} = i, S_{n,t} =
      j | O; π, Q) 1_{τ_t − τ_{t−1} = Δ}, ∀Δ;
    // M-step
    Update π_i ← Σ_{n=1}^{N} p(S_{n,0}=i|O;π,Q) / Σ_{n=1}^{N} Σ_{i=1}^{M} p(S_{n,0}=i|O;π,Q);
    repeat
        Compute E[N_ij(Δ)|k, l, Q] and E[R_i(Δ)|k, l, Q]
          (see Section 4);
        Update Q ← Σ_Δ Σ_{k,l∈[M]} E[N_ij(Δ)|k,l,Q] C_{k,l}(Δ) / Σ_Δ Σ_{k,l∈[M]} E[R_i(Δ)|k,l,Q] C_{k,l}(Δ);
    until Convergence;
until Convergence;
```

4.1 E-Step

The complete log-likelihood is $\log p(\mathbf{O}, \mathbf{S}, S(\tau); \pi, Q)$. Both the discrete states $\mathbf{S}$ and the continuous process $S(\tau)$ are hidden, so in the E-step we take their expectation with respect to the posterior distribution over $\mathbf{S}$ and $S(\tau)$ using the current parameter setting π', Q':

$$\begin{aligned} &\mathbb{E}_{p(\mathbf{S},S(\tau)|\mathbf{O};\pi',Q')}[\log p(\mathbf{O}, \mathbf{S}, S(\tau); \pi, Q)] \\ &= \mathbb{E}_{p(\mathbf{S}|\mathbf{O};\pi',Q')}[\log \pi + \log p(\mathbf{O}|\mathbf{S})] \\ &+ \mathbb{E}_{p(\mathbf{S},S(\tau)|\mathbf{O};\pi',Q')}[\log p(\mathbf{S}, S(\tau); \pi, Q)]. \end{aligned} \tag{6}$$

The second term in Eq. (6) can be written as (see [10] for detailed derivation):

$$\mathbb{E}_{p(\mathbf{S},S(\tau)|\mathbf{O};\pi',Q')}[\log p(\mathbf{S}, S(\tau); \pi, Q)] = \sum_{\Delta} \sum_{i,j \in [M]} C_{ij}(\Delta)$$
$$\left(\sum_{k,l \in [M], k \neq l} (\log Q_{kl}) \mathbb{E}[\mathcal{N}_{kl}(\Delta)|\mathbf{S}; Q'] - Q_{kl} \mathbb{E}[\mathcal{R}_k(\Delta)|\mathbf{S}; Q'] \right)$$

where we define

$$C_{ij}(\Delta) \triangleq \sum_{n=1}^{N} \sum_{t=1}^{T_n} p(\mathbf{O}, S_{n,t-1} = i, S_{n,t} = j; \pi', Q') \mathbf{1}_{\tau_t - \tau_{t-1} = \Delta}$$

and for which we need to compute

$$p(\mathbf{O}, S_{n,t-1} = i, S_{n,t} = j; \pi', Q'), \forall n, t, i, j. \tag{7}$$

$\mathcal{N}_{kl}(\Delta)$ is defined as the number of transitions from state k to l during the time interval Δ. $\mathcal{R}_k(\Delta)$ is the amount of time spent in state k during the time interval Δ. Note that these are auxiliary latent variables that we introduce to help us learn the continuous-time Markov process. We will later describe how to estimate their expectations.

Gibbs Sampling

The posterior distribution for B, Z, and L can be obtained in closed-form since the Beta distribution is conjugate for the Bernoulli. To perform Gibbs sampling of these continuous parameters (with range [0,1]), we use a fixed set of discrete values. For instance, we can sample from 0.01 to 0.99 with 0.01 increment; finer sampling granularity can be chosen at the cost of longer runtime (the complexity is linear to the number of values).

We perform block sampling of both $\mathbf{X}$ and $\mathbf{S}$, substantially improving the mixing time of Gibbs sampling at the cost of only double the running time per iteration. For fixed n and k, we sample $X_{k,n,t}, t = 1, \ldots, T_n$ from the joint distribution:

$$\begin{aligned} &p(X_{k,n,0}, \ldots, X_{k,n,T_n}|\Theta, \mathbf{O}) \\ &= p(X_{k,n,0}|\Theta, \mathbf{O}) \prod_{t=1}^{T_n} p(X_{k,n,t}|\Theta, \mathbf{O}, X_{k,n,t-1}) \\ &= p(X_{k,n,0}|\Theta, \mathbf{O}) \prod_{t=1}^{T_n} \frac{p(X_{k,n,t}, X_{k,n,t-1}|\Theta, \mathbf{O})}{p(X_{k,n,t-1}|\Theta, \mathbf{O})}, \end{aligned} \tag{8}$$

in which $p(X_{k,n,t} = i|\Theta, \mathbf{O})$ and $p(X_{k,n,t} = j, X_{k,n,t-1} = i|\Theta, \mathbf{O}), i, j \in \{0, 1\}, \forall t$ need to be estimated. Here $\Theta = (\mathbf{X}_{-k}, \mathbf{S}, B, Z, L)$.

Define $\alpha_i(t) \triangleq p(O_{d,n,0}, \ldots, O_{d,n,t}, X_{k,n,t} = i|\Theta)$. It can be updated sequentially as

$$\begin{aligned} &\alpha_i(0) \leftarrow \Psi(X_{k,n,0} = i|S_{n,0}) \\ &\quad \prod_{d=1}^{D} \Phi(O_{d,n,0}|\{X_{k',n,0}\}_{k' \neq k}, X_{k,n,0} = i) \\ &\alpha_i(t+1) \leftarrow \\ &\left(\sum_{j=0,1} \alpha_j(t)\Psi(X_{k,n,t+1} = i|S_{n,t+1}, X_{k,n,t} = j)\right) \\ &\quad \prod_{d=1}^{D} \Phi(O_{d,n,t+1}|\{X_{k',n,t+1}\}_{k' \neq k}, X_{k,n,t+1} = i) \end{aligned} \tag{9}$$

Also define $\beta_i(t) \triangleq p(O_{d,n,t+1}, \ldots, O_{d,n,T_n}|X_{k,n,t} = i, \Theta)$. It can be updated sequentially as $\beta_i(T_n) \leftarrow 1$ and

$$\begin{aligned} &\beta_i(t-1) \leftarrow \sum_{j=0,1} (\beta_j(t)\Psi(X_{k,n,t} = j|S_{n,t}, X_{k,n,t-1} = i) \\ &\quad \prod_{d=1}^{D} \Phi(O_{d,n,t}|\{X_{k',n,t}\}_{k' \neq k}, X_{k,n,t} = j)) \end{aligned}$$

Then it is easy to show [13] that:

$$\begin{aligned} &p(X_{k,n,t} = i|\Theta, \mathbf{O}) \propto \alpha_i(t)\beta_i(t), \\ &p(X_{k,n,t+1} = j, X_{k,n,t} = i|\Theta, \mathbf{O}) \\ &\propto \alpha_i(t)\beta_j(t+1)\Psi(X_{k,n,t+1} = j|S_{n,t+1}, X_{k,n,t} = i) \\ &\quad \prod_{d=1}^{D} \Phi(O_{d,n,t+1}|\{X_{k',n,t+1}\}_{k' \neq k}, X_{k,n,t+1} = j)). \end{aligned}$$

Therefore the forward sampling probability for $X_{k,n,t}$ is:

$$\begin{aligned} &p(X_{k,n,t+1} = j|X_{k,n,t} = i, \Theta, \mathbf{O}) \\ &\propto \frac{\beta_j(t+1)}{\beta_i(t)} \Psi(X_{k,n,t+1} = j|S_{n,t+1}, X_{k,n,t} = i) \\ &\quad \prod_{d=1}^{D} \Phi(O_{d,n,t+1}|\{X_{k',n,t+1}\}_{k' \neq k}, X_{k,n,t+1} = j)). \end{aligned} \tag{10}$$

The α's cancel out in Eq. (10), so we do not actually need to compute them (other than $\alpha_i(0)$). A similar forward sampling procedure can be derived for $S_{n,t}$, $t = 0, \ldots, T_n$. The details are omitted due to space limitations.

4.2 M-Step

In the M-step we update two parameters: π and Q. Updating π_i is straightforward:

$$\pi_i \leftarrow \frac{\sum_{n=1}^{N} p(\mathbf{O}, S_{n,0} = i; \pi', Q')}{\sum_{n=1}^{N} \sum_{i=1}^{M} p(\mathbf{O}, S_{n,0} = i; \pi', Q')}. \tag{11}$$

We update Q using the closed-form solution based on eigendecomposition introduced in [10]:

$$\begin{aligned} &Q_{ij} \leftarrow \frac{\sum_\Delta \sum_{k,l \in [M]} \mathbb{E}[\mathcal{N}_{ij}(\Delta)|S(\Delta) = l, S(0) = k; Q']C_{k,l}(\Delta)}{\sum_\Delta \sum_{k,l \in [M]} \mathbb{E}[\mathcal{R}_i(\Delta)|S(\Delta) = l, S(0) = k; Q']C_{k,l}(\Delta)} \\ &U\Lambda U^{-1} \leftarrow Q \text{ (eigendecomposition)} \\ &\chi_{pq}(\Delta) \leftarrow \begin{cases} \Delta \exp(\Delta\Lambda_p) & \Lambda_p = \Lambda_q \\ \frac{\exp(\Delta\Lambda_p) - \exp(\Delta\Lambda_q)}{\Lambda_p - \Lambda_q} & \Lambda_p \neq \Lambda_q \end{cases} \\ &\mathbb{E}[\mathcal{R}_i(\Delta)|S(\Delta) = l, S(0) = k; Q'] \\ &\quad \leftarrow \frac{1}{A_{kl}(\Delta)} \sum_{p=1}^{M} U_{kp}U_{pi}^{-1} \sum_{q=1}^{M} U_{iq}U_{ql}^{-1}\chi_{pq}(\Delta) \\ &\mathbb{E}[\mathcal{N}_{ij}(\Delta)|S(\Delta) = l, S(0) = k; Q'] \\ &\quad \leftarrow \frac{Q_{ij}}{A_{kl}(\Delta)} \sum_{p=1}^{M} U_{kp}U_{pi}^{-1} \sum_{q=1}^{M} U_{jq}U_{ql}^{-1}\chi_{pq}(\Delta) \end{aligned}$$

Recall that $A_{kl}(\Delta)$ is the transition probability from state k to l given the time span Δ (Eq. 1).

In our implementation, instead of returning to Gibbs sampling over $\mathbf{S}$ immediately after Q is updated, we first repeat the above procedure until Q converges (i.e., only recomputing expectations of $S(\tau)$ with respect to the new parameters), and then go back to the Gibbs sampling step. This is an approximation based on the assumption that a small change in Q will not lead to a significant change in the marginal distribution of $\mathbf{S}$.

4.3 Fast Evaluation of the Noisy-Or Network

In the Gibbs sampling step, we need to repeatedly evaluate the likelihood of the noisy-or network given the current parameter and variable assignments:

$$\prod_{d=1}^{D} \Phi(O_{d,n,t}|\{X_{k',n,t}\}_{k' \neq k}, X_{k,n,t} = i)),$$

$i \in \{0, 1\}$, for a given n and t.

To compute this likelihood in its original form, the complexity is proportional to D, the total number of findings, which is typically very large (tens of thousands for EHR data). However, notice that we do not need to evaluate this over all possible findings:

$$
\begin{aligned}
&\prod_{d=1}^{D} \Phi(O_{d,n,t}|\{X_{k',n,t}\}_{k'\neq k}, X_{k,n,t}=i)) \\
&= \prod_{d=1}^{D} \left(1-(1-L_d)\prod_{k=1}^{K}(1-X_{k,n,t}Z_{k,d})\right)^{O_{d,n,t}} \\
&\quad \left((1-L_d)\prod_{k=1}^{K}(1-X_{k,n,t}Z_{k,d})\right)^{1-O_{d,n,t}} \qquad (12)\\
&= \prod_{d:O_{d,n,t}=1} \left(1-(1-L_d)\prod_{k=1}^{K}(1-X_{k,n,t}Z_{k,d})\right) \\
&\quad \prod_{d:O_{d,n,t}=0} \left((1-L_d)\prod_{k=1}^{K}(1-X_{k,n,t}Z_{k,d})\right)
\end{aligned}
$$

When we sample a specific $X_{k,n,t}$, most terms in the last line of the above equation, corresponding to the negative findings, cancel out. Consequently the ratio between the two likelihoods can be simplified to:

$$
\begin{aligned}
&\frac{\prod_{d=1}^{D} \Phi(O_{d,n,t}|\{X_{k',n,t}\}_{k'\neq k}, X_{k,n,t}=1))}{\prod_{d=1}^{D} \Phi(O_{d,n,t}|\{X_{k',n,t}\}_{k'\neq k}, X_{k,n,t}=0))} \\
&= \prod_{d:O_{d,n,t}=0} (1-Z_{k,d}) \\
&\frac{\prod_{d:O_{d,n,t}=1}\left(1-(1-L_d)(1-Z_{k,d})\prod_{k'\neq k}(1-X_{k',n,t}Z_{k',d})\right)}{\prod_{d:O_{d,n,t}=1}\left(1-(1-L_d)\prod_{k'\neq k}(1-X_{k',n,t}Z_{k',d})\right)}
\end{aligned} \qquad (13)
$$

With this improvement, the complexity of evaluating Φ is only proportional to the number of **positive** findings, which is far smaller than the total number of findings. More specifically, let N be the number of patients, M the number of progression states, T the number of visits (assuming each patient has the same number of visits), K the number of Comorbidities, and D the number of clinical findings. The cost of sampling $\mathbf{X}$ is reduced from $\mathcal{O}(NTK^2D)$ to $\mathcal{O}(NTK^2D^+)$, where $D^+ \ll D$ is the number of positive findings for an individual patient. The cost of sampling L, which benefits from the same optimization, is reduced from $\mathcal{O}(NTKD+NTMD)$ to $\mathcal{O}(NTKD^+ + NTMD)$; the cost of sampling Z is reduced from $\mathcal{O}(K^2D^2NT)$ to $\mathcal{O}(K^2D^+DNT)$. The cost of sampling B remains $\mathcal{O}(KMNT)$.

5. EMPIRICAL STUDY

In this section we apply our model to COPD, one of most prevalent chronic diseases worldwide. It is a particularly interesting target for a disease progression study because it has a prolonged progression path and is associated with a range of well-studied comorbidities [1,4]. Understanding the progression trajectory of COPD is crucial for early intervention and personalized care plan management.

We tested our model on a real COPD cohort to demonstrate that our model can automatically discover medically meaningful comorbidities among COPD patients. We present the COPD progression stages as identified by our model, which help explain the medical characteristics of COPD at different stages and the key medical events that trigger exacerbation. We showcase a typical application of the learned model, which is to infer the progression trajectories of individual patients based on their clinical observations. We also demonstrate the convergence behavior of our model and the importance of incorporating anchor findings.

Note that there are some existing clinical evaluation criteria for the progression/severity of COPD, such as GOLD and BODE index [6]. The progression trajectories defined by these criteria, which are mainly focused on the deterioration of respiratory function, are fundamentally different from the progression trajectories defined by our model, which are the onset patterns of various comorbidities. In practice our model is complementary to these existing standards in offering the medical practitioners a comprehensive characterization of the patients' condition.

5.1 Data Description

Our data came from a real-world longitudinal Electronic Medical Record (EMR) database of over 300,000 patients over the course of 4 years. For each patient encounter, a set of International Classification of Diseases - Version 9 (ICD-9) codes were recorded to indicate what medical conditions that patient had at that time point. Other information, such as drug prescription, lab test results, were also recorded. Note that in our database we did not have the lab measurements needed by either the GOLD or BODE criteria.

We first consulted our medical experts to identify the patients who were confirmed of having COPD at any time point during the record. The criteria we developed were the occurrence of at least one ICD-9 code that is related to COPD *and* the prescription of at least one COPD-related medication. Based on this selection criteria, we were able to identify 3,705 confirmed COPD patients from the database. For these patients, we extract their records in terms of ICD-9 codes. In total we had 5,263 unique ICD-9 codes associated with these patients. We removed infrequent ICD-9 codes that appeared for fewer than 200 patients, leaving us with 264 distinct codes (our findings). Considering the relative slow progression of COPD, we further decrease the time granularity of the original record. We segmented the time dimension into disjoint 90-day windows and combined all the observations within each window, viewing it as one encounter. In the end we had 34,976 encounters with 189,815 positive observations. Notice that the observations were very sparse: on average each patient had 10 encounters and 5.4 positive observations (ICD-9 code assignment) per encounter. The average record span of a patient was 816 days and the largest span was 1,094 days. Notice that this time span is significantly shorter than the span of regular COPD progression, which makes our setting very challenging.

5.2 Model Customization

Setting Anchors for Comorbidities: Our model infers the disease progression through the onsets of the comorbidities. Therefore the validity and relevance of the comorbidities have a great impact on the interpretability of our model. On the one hand, our model can be fully unsupervised and learn the comorbidities from the clinical findings. On the other hand, if we already have some domain knowledge on the important comorbidities, our model can incorporate such knowledge via setting anchor findings and produce comorbidities in alignment with the domain

Table 2: COPD comorbidities, associated medical conditions, and anchor ICD-9 diagnosis codes used.

Comorbidity	Representative Conditions (Anchor ICD-9 Codes)
COPD	Chronic Bronchitis (491), Emphysema (492, 518), Chronic Airway Obstruction (496)
Asthma	Asthma (493)
Cardiovascular	Hypertension (401), Congestive Heart Failure (428), Arrhythmia (427), Ischemic Heart Disease (414)
Lung Infection	Pneumonia (481, 485, 486)
Lung Cancer	Malignant Neoplasm of Upper/Lower Lobe, Bronchus or Lung (162)
Diabetes	Diabetes with Different Types and Complications (250)
Musculoskeletal	Spinal Disorders (724), Soft Tissue Disorders (729), Osteoporosis (733)
Kidney	Acute Kidney Failure (584), Chronic Kidney Disease (585), Renal Failure (586)
Psychological	Anxiety (300), Depression (296, 311)
Obesity	Morbid Obesity (278)

Table 3: Top-5 ICD-9 codes with highest activation probability of each comorbidity group as identified by our model. * means anchor findings.

COPD	Asthma
.45 Chronic Airway Obstruction*	.40 Asthma*
.05 Chronic Bronchitis with Exacerbation*	.07 Allergic Rhinitis
.04 Emphysema*	.05 Cough
.04 Chronic Bronchitis without Exacerbation*	.04 Acute Bronchitis
.03 Respiratory Abnormalities	.03 Acute Upper Respiratory Infections
Cardiovascular	**Lung Infection**
.30 Benign Essential Hypertension*	.30 Pneumonia*
.25 Unspecified Essential Hypertension*	.10 Shortness of Breath
.15 Atrial Fibrillation*	.10 Respiratory Abnormalities
.10 Congestive Heart Failure*	.10 Cough
.10 Hyperlipidemia	.06 Abnormal Findings of Lung
Lung Cancer	**Diabetes**
.60 Cancer of Bronchus and Lung, Unspecified*	.60 Type II Diabetes without Complication*
.15 Other Diseases of Lung	.15 Type II Diabetes without Complication, Uncontrolled*
.15 Cancer of Other Parts of Bronchus or Lung*	.10 Hyperlipidemia
.15 Cancer of Upper Lobe, Bronchus or Lung*	.06 Pure Hypercholesterolemia
.15 Swelling, Mass, or Lump in Chest	.06 Type II Diabetes with Renal Manifestations*
Musculoskeletal	**Kidney**
.15 Lumbago*	.20 Chronic Kidney Disease, Moderate*
.15 Pain in Limb*	.15 Anemia
.10 Osteoporosis*	.10 Chronic Kidney Disease, Unspecified*
.06 Myalgia and Myositis*	.08 Urinary Tract Infection
.04 Acquired Hypothyroidism	.08 Chronic Kidney Disease, Severe*
Psychological	**Obesity**
.15 Depression, Unspecified*	.25 Obesity, Unspecified*
.15 Anxiety*	.10 Morbid Obesity*
.04 Other Malaise and Fatigue	.03 Pure Hypercholesterolemia
.04 Major Depression, Recurrent Episode*	.02 Edema
.03 Major Depression, Single Episode*	.02 Sleep Apnea

Leak Terms: Hyperlipidemia .07, Need for Flu Vaccine .05, Acute Bronchitis .04, Routine Medical Examination .04, Acquired Hypothyroidism .04, Mammogram Screening .03, Actinic Keratosis .03, Urinary Tract Infection .03, Cough .03, Pure Hypercholesterolemia .03

knowledge. The study of COPD belongs to the latter case since COPD has some well-studied comorbidities, and discovering the progression of these designated comorbidities in terms of the progression of COPD is of great practical significance. We reviewed the literature with our medical experts and identified nine important COPD comorbidities (or comorbidity groups): asthma, cardiovascular diseases, lung infection, lung cancer, diabetes, musculoskeletal disorders, kidney diseases, psychological disorders, and obesity. In Table 2 we list these comorbidities along with the ICD-9 codes we used to anchor them. We also created an additional comorbidity to track the target disease itself, which was anchored by the ICD-9 codes we used to confirm COPD. Following the notions introduced in [7], if feature d is anchor of comorbidity k, we set $Z_{k',d}$ to $1e-6$ for any $k' \neq k$ (we chose this small value instead of 0 to avoid numerical underflow).

Constraining Progression Trajectory: For the results in the next section, we add a constraint to the transition generator matrix Q enforcing that we learn a linear pro-

Table 4: An example comorbidity identified without anchors. Although important conditions were identified, they were mixed together with no coherent medical interpretation (comparing to Table 3).

.35 Benign Essential Hypertension
.30 Type II Diabetes without Complication
.25 Mixed Hyperlipidemia
.20 Coronary Atherosclerosis Of Native Coronary Artery
.20 Pure Hypercholesterolemia
.15 Type II Diabetes without Complication, Uncontrolled
.08 Coronary Atherosclerosis Of Unspecified Type
.08 Chest Pain
.06 Anemia
.06 Chronic Ischemic Heart Disease, Unspecified

gression trajectory: we disallowed transitions from a later state to an earlier state by setting $Q_{ij} = 0, \forall j < i$. This constraint could be relaxed in many different ways, allowing us to learn a non-linear progression trajectory and/or multiple progression trajectories simultaneously. Such extensions will be discussed at the end of the paper.

Setting the Parameters: In order to learn a more sparse noisy-or network (thus better interpretability), we set the priors for Z to Beta(0.1, 1). Thus our model will suppress the influence of findings that are loosely connected to the underlying comorbidities. We did not impose any such preference on L and B and set their priors to Beta(1, 1). We sample Z from 0.01 to 0.1 with 0.01 increment and from 0.1 to 0.95 with 0.05 increment; we sample B and L from 0.01 to 0.99 with 0.01 increment. Since most of our model's comorbidities are chronic and their presence is expected to be persistent, we fix $B_{k,m,1} \triangleq p(X_{k,n,t} = 1|S_{n,t} = m, X_{k,n,t-1} = 1) = 1$. This implies that once a comorbidity is turned on, it cannot be turned off in the future. We also introduce a monotonicity constraint on B^0 enforcing that the initial probability of comorbidity onset is higher for patients who at $t = 0$ are at a later progression stage than those at an earlier progression stage. After introducing this constraint, we update B^0 in the outer EM loop (together with π and Q) using a standard convex optimization procedure to maximize the likelihood subject to the monotonicity constraint. Finally, we set the number of states to $M = 6$ and the number of comorbidities to $K = 10$.

5.3 Results and Analysis

5.3.1 Comorbidities Identified

First we present the comorbidities as well as the leak term learned by our model (Table 3). For each comorbidity we list the top-5 ICD-9 codes in terms of activation/leak probability ($Z_{k,d}$ and L_d). All the comorbidities have clear and coherent clinical interpretations: the top findings either describe the main conditions corresponding to the comorbidity (e.g. Diabetes and Kidney), or are the common symptoms caused by those conditions (e.g., Lung Infection).

We contribute such interpretability to the anchor findings (starred entries in Table 3). As a comparison, we trained our model using the exact same settings but without the anchors. As a result, conditions from different comorbidities were mixed into one (see Table 4). This is natural from the model's perspective because these conditions frequently co-occur (thus the name comorbid) and no extra knowledge indicates they should be separated into different groups.

It is important to point out that our model was guided, but not fixed, by the anchor findings. For instance, there were anchor ICD-9 codes that did not appear in the top findings because the model did not consider them indicative enough; there were also some ICD-9 codes that were not anchored but ranked highly in relevant comorbidities (e.g. 'Lump in Chest' for Lung Cancer and 'Urinary Tract Infection' for Kidney). Rhinitis and Acute Bronchitis showed up in the Asthma group because they are among the top burdens of asthma patients.

5.3.2 Progression Trajectories Identified

Next we characterize the progression trajectories learned by our model from the COPD patient cohort. Given the generative nature of our model, we used it to generate 10,000 "virtual patients". We chose virtual patients over real patients because the patient records we had were only 4 years long and cannot cover the entire progression path of COPD. To generate a virtual patient, we assume the patient comes in at timestamp 0 in State 1. Then we used the learned model to generate the patient's subsequent states and the comorbidity onsets corresponding to those states until the patient reached State 6 (the last state). We averaged over the 10,000 records we generated and computed the average holding time for each state as well as the prevalence of different comorbidities at each state, as summarized in Figure 3.

Figure 3 gives us an intuitive view of how our trained model depicts the average progression trajectories of confirmed COPD patients. First, comparing different comorbidity groups across all progression stages, COPD has the highest prevalence (this is expected because we had a COPD case cohort); other highly prevalent comorbidities include cardiovascular diseases and musculoskeletal disorders; lung cancer is the rarest comorbidity. Next, we can observe that State 1 is the "healthy" state where the prevalence of all comorbidities are low. The transition from State 1 to 2 is driven by the onset of COPD, cardiovascular diseases, and musculoskeletal disorders. Starting from State 3, the prevalence of COPD is already 100% while the prevalence of other comorbidities rise steadily. The sudden increase in the onset rate of diabetes, kidney diseases, and lung infections at later stages of COPD conform well to previous studies in the medical literature. The onset rates of lung cancer, asthma, psychological disorders, and obesity are relatively stable across all progression stages.

5.3.3 Evidence Based Inference of Progression Trajectories

Next we showcase how to use our model to infer the progression trajectory of an individual patient based on the existing medical evidence. We picked two representative patients from our cohort and used MAP inference to infer their most likely progression stages and comorbidity onsets at each timestamp, respectively. Specifically, given the trained model, we repeatedly sample $\mathbf{X}$ and $\mathbf{S}$ conditioned on the observations from the query patient 1,000 times initialized by 10 different random seeds. We illustrated the results with maximum posterior probability in Figure 4.

We can see that patient (a) was correctly diagnosed by our model with musculoskeletal disorder and psychological disorder at the beginning and was assigned to the least se-

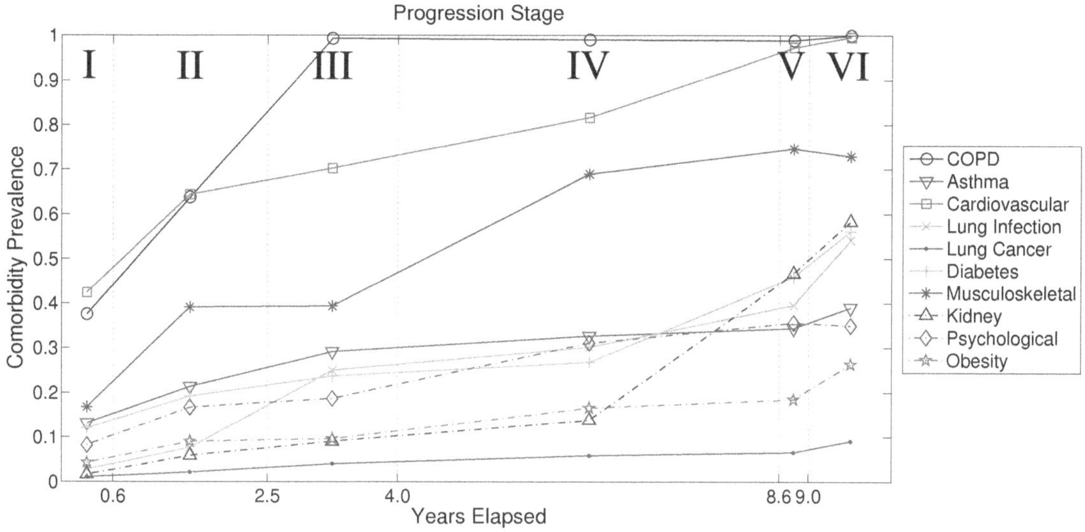

Figure 3: The change in comorbidity prevalence vs. the progression state transitions averaged over 10,000 virtual patients generated by our model.

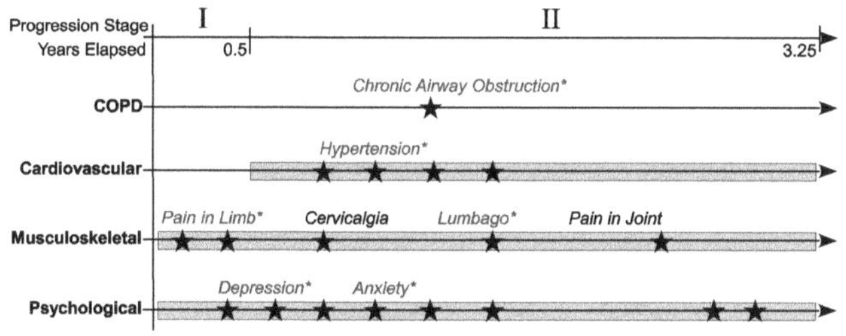

(a) A Stable Trajectory

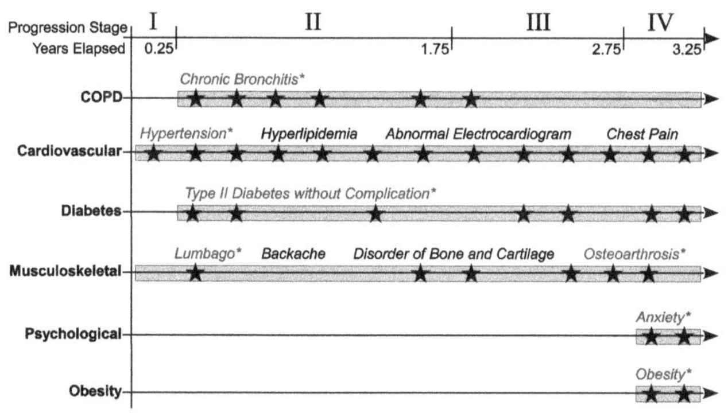

(b) A Progressive Trajectory

Figure 4: Inference of the progression trajectory and comorbidity onset of individual patients. Predicted stages are at the top of each plot; gray bars indicate predicted comorbidity onset; and stars denote the occurrence of relevant ICD-9 codes in the data (descriptions are on top of the timeline).

vere stage. After 6 months, our model diagnosed this patient with cardiovascular disease. The patient was subsequently moved into Stage 2 and stayed there throughout the record span. Note that the patient had a single occurrence of COPD related diagnosis code in the record. However,

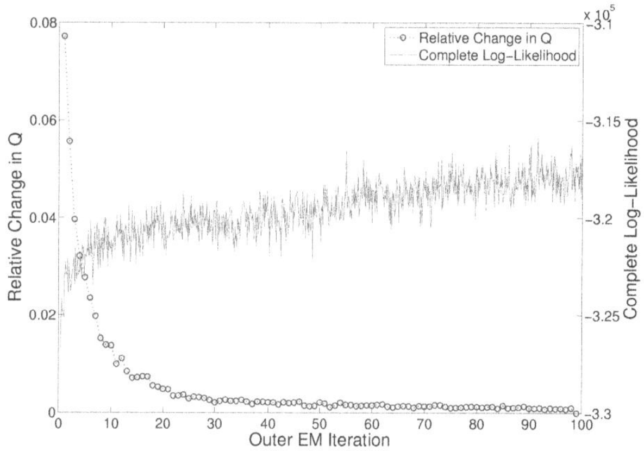

Figure 5: The convergence of our algorithm.

our model decided this was not enough evidence to turn on the COPD comorbidity; as a result, it was explained by the leak term (for all anchor findings we assigned a fixed leak probability of 10^{-6}). In contrast to patient (a), patient (b) exhibited a quick exacerbation of COPD. The patient started with cardiovascular disease and musculoskeletal disorder (Stage 1), followed by COPD and diabetes onset soon afterward (Stages 2 and 3), then eventually developed psychological disorder and obesity (Stage 4). We use these two representative patients to demonstrate the potential of incorporating our model into clinical decision support systems to provide medical practitioners with evidence based prediction and recommendation.

5.3.4 Model Convergence and Runtime

In Figure 5 we show the convergence behavior of the learning algorithm in terms of the relative change in Q as well as the complete data log-likelihood. We did 10 Gibbs sampling updates before first updating Q and π. We repeated the outer EM iterations 100 times. Despite the small number of Gibbs sampling updates, our model converged quickly thanks to the use of anchors. We implemented our algorithm in Python. With parallelization and aforementioned optimizations, each full Gibbs sampling update took about 3 minutes on a 24-core 2.6 GHz machine.

6. DISCUSSION

The techniques presented in this paper open the door to many new applications of disease progression modeling. When paired with visualization tools, clinicians could use these models to better understand the evolution of chronic illnesses, optimize treatments, and design clinical guidelines.

Our empirical study focused on the problem of discovering a single disease progression model for COPD. Thus, we constrained the continuous-time Markov model to allow only forward transitions. However, for many diseases it is unlikely that there is a single disease trajectory that most patients follow, but rather a set of common trajectories. We can modify our algorithm to learn a *mixture* of disease trajectories simply by partitioning the state space and enforcing forward transitions within each partition.

Our proposed approach for learning disease progression models is flexible and can easily accommodate new sources of data and/or domain knowledge. For example, we could include lists of medications prescribed or procedures performed in the set of clinical findings to complement diagnosis codes. Because we use a generative model, it is trivial to marginalize over clinical findings that are unobserved on a specific visit. We could also introduce patient-specific global variables, either latent or observed. For example, the distribution over the initial disease state could be parameterized to be a function of age, gender, and family history. The rate matrix for the continuous-time Markov process could depend on factors such as whether the patient has stopped smoking, which might decrease the rate of progression. Going a step further, each specialist (e.g., endocrinologist versus a gynecologist) is likely to have a different distribution of diagnosis codes that they are likely to assign. Thus, if the specialist is provided in the data, the model could make the activation probabilities for clinical findings be different for each specialist.

An interesting question for follow-up work is whether it is possible to use non-case patients to learn disease progression models. In our experimental results we used only patients that were diagnosed with COPD. However, this limits the amount of training data. At a minimum, it may be possible to use the non-case patients to initialize the distribution of clinical findings for each comorbidity.

7. REFERENCES

[1] F. Baty, P. M. Putora, B. Isenring, T. Blum, and M. Brutsche. Comorbidities and burden of COPD: a population based case-control study. *PLoS ONE*, 8(5):e63285, 2013.

[2] M. Cohen, A. Grossman, D. Morabito, M. M. Knudson, A. Butte, and G. Manley. Identification of complex metabolic states in critically injured patients using bioinformatic cluster analysis. *Critical Care*, 14(1):R10, 2010.

[3] W. De Winter, J. DeJongh, T. Post, B. Ploeger, R. Urquhart, I. Moules, D. Eckland, and M. Danhof. A mechanism-based disease progression model for comparison of long-term effects of pioglitazone, metformin and gliclazide on disease processes underlying type 2 diabetes mellitus. *Journal of pharmacokinetics and pharmacodynamics*, 33(3):313–343, 2006.

[4] M. Decramer, W. Janssens, and M. Miravitlles. Chronic obstructive pulmonary disease. *Lancet*, 379(9823):1341–1351, Apr 2012.

[5] K. Exarchos, T. Exarchos, C. Bourantas, M. Papafaklis, K. Naka, L. Michalis, O. Parodi, and D. Fotiadis. Prediction of coronary atherosclerosis progression using dynamic bayesian networks. In *EMBC*, pages 3889–3892, 2013.

[6] G. I. for Chronic Obstructive Lung Disease. Global strategy for the diagnosis, management, and prevention of copd, January 2014.

[7] Y. Halpern and D. Sontag. Unsupervised learning of noisy-or bayesian networks. In *UAI*, pages 272–281, 2013.

[8] K. Ito, S. Ahadieh, B. Corrigan, J. French, T. Fullerton, and T. Tensfeldt. Disease progression meta-analysis model in alzheimer's disease. *Alzheimer's & Dementia*, 6(1):39–53, 2010.

[9] C. H. Jackson, L. D. Sharples, S. G. Thompson, S. W. Duffy, and E. Couto. Multistate markov models for disease progression with classification error. *Journal of the Royal Statistical Society: Series D (The Statistician)*, 52(2):193–209, 2003.

[10] P. Metzner, I. Horenko, and C. Schütte. Generator estimation of markov jump processes based on incomplete observations nonequidistant in time. *Physical Review E*, 76(6):066702, 2007.

[11] D. Mould. Models for disease progression: new approaches and uses. *Clinical Pharmacology & Therapeutics*, 92(1):125–131, 2012.

[12] T. M. Post, J. I. Freijer, J. DeJongh, and M. Danhof. Disease system analysis: basic disease progression models in degenerative disease. *Pharmaceutical research*, 22(7):1038–1049, 2005.

[13] L. Rabiner. A tutorial on hidden markov models and selected applications in speech recognition. *Proceedings of the IEEE*, 77(2):257–286, 1989.

[14] M. A. Shwe, B. Middleton, D. Heckerman, M. Henrion, E. Horvitz, H. Lehmann, and G. Cooper. Probabilistic diagnosis using a reformulation of the internist-1/qmr knowledge base. *Meth. Inform. Med*, 30:241–255, 1991.

[15] R. Sukkar, E. Katz, Y. Zhang, D. Raunig, and B. T. Wyman. Disease progression modeling using hidden markov models. In *EMBC*, pages 2845–2848. IEEE, 2012.

[16] J. Yang, J. J. McAuley, J. Leskovec, P. LePendu, and N. Shah. Finding progression stages in time-evolving event sequences. In *WWW*, pages 783–794, 2014.

[17] J. Zhou, J. Liu, V. A. Narayan, and J. Ye. Modeling disease progression via fused sparse group lasso. In *KDD*, pages 1095–1103. ACM, 2012.

[18] J. Zhou, J. Liu, V. A. Narayan, and J. Ye. Modeling disease progression via multi-task learning. *NeuroImage*, 78(0):233 – 248, 2013.

Good-Enough Brain Model: Challenges, Algorithms and Discoveries in Multi-Subject Experiments

Evangelos E. Papalexakis
Carnegie Mellon University
epapalex@cs.cmu.edu

Alona Fyshe
Carnegie Mellon University
afyshe@cs.cmu.edu

Nicholas D. Sidiropoulos
University of Minnesota
nikos@ece.umn.edu

Partha Pratim Talukdar
Carnegie Mellon University
partha.talukdar@cs.cmu.edu

Tom M. Mitchell
Carnegie Mellon University
tom.mitchell@cmu.edu

Christos Faloutsos
Carnegie Mellon University
christos@cs.cmu.edu

ABSTRACT

Given a simple noun such as *apple*, and a question such as *is it edible?*, what processes take place in the human brain? More specifically, given the stimulus, what are the interactions between (groups of) neurons (also known as *functional connectivity*) and how can we automatically infer those interactions, given measurements of the brain activity? Furthermore, how does this connectivity differ across different human subjects?

In this work we present a simple, novel *good-enough* brain model, or GEBM in short, and a novel algorithm SPARSE-SYSID, which are able to effectively model the dynamics of the neuron interactions and infer the functional connectivity. Moreover, GEBM is able to simulate basic psychological phenomena such as *habituation* and *priming* (whose definition we provide in the main text).

We evaluate GEBM by using both synthetic and real brain data. Using the real data, GEBM produces brain activity patterns that are strikingly similar to the real ones, and the inferred functional connectivity is able to provide neuroscientific insights towards a better understanding of the way that neurons interact with each other, as well as detect regularities and outliers in multi-subject brain activity measurements.

Categories and Subject Descriptors

H.2.8 [**Database Management**]: Database Applications—*Data mining*; G.3 [**Mathematics of Computing**]: Probability and Statistics—*Time series analysis*; J.3 [**Computer Applications**]: Life and Medical Sciences—*Biology and genetics*; J.4 [**Computer Applications**]: Social and Behavioral Sciences—*Psychology*

Keywords

Brain Activity Analysis; System Identification; Brain Functional Connectivity; Control Theory; Neuroscience

KDD'14, August 24–27, 2014, New York, NY, USA.

http://dx.doi.org/10.1145/2623330.2623639.

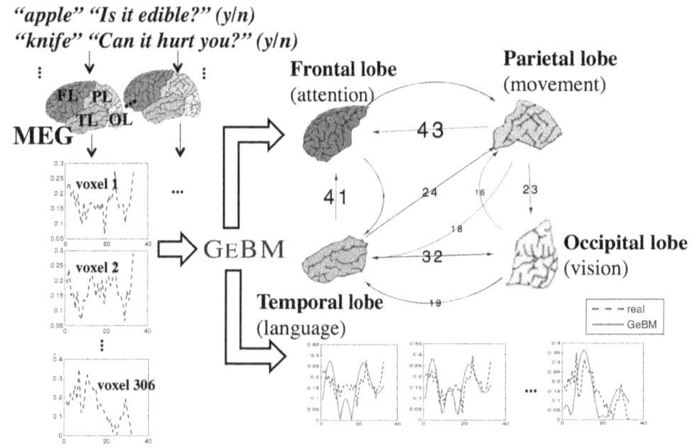

Figure 1: Big picture: our GEBM estimates the hidden functional connectivity (top right, weighted arrows indicating number of inferred connections), when given multiple human subjects (left) that respond to yes/no questions (e.g., *edible?*) for typed words (e.g., *apple*). Bottom right: GEBM also produces brain activity (in solid-red), that matches reality (in dashed-blue).

1. INTRODUCTION

Can we infer the brain activity for subject 'Alice', when she is shown the typed noun *apple* and has to answer a yes/no question, like *is it edible*? Can we infer the connectivity of brain regions, given numerous brain activity data of subjects in such experiments? These are the first two goals of this work: single-subject, and multi-subject analysis of brain activity.

The third and final goal is to develop a brain connectivity model, that can also generate activity that agrees with psychological phenomena, like *priming*[1] and *habituation*[2]

Here we tackle all these challenges. We are given *Magnetoencephalography* (MEG) brain scans for nine subjects, shown several typed nouns (*apple*, *hammer*, etc), and being requested to answer a yes/no question (*is it edible?*, *is it dangerous?*, and so on), by pressing one of two buttons.

Our approach: Discovering the multi-billion connections among

[1] *Priming* illustrates the power of context: a person hearing the word *iPod*, and then *apple*, will think of *Apple-inc*, as opposed to the fruit *apple*

[2] *Habituation* illustrates compensation: a person hearing the same word all the time, will eventually stop paying attention.

the tens of billions [23, 2] of neurons would be the holy grail, and clearly outside the current technological capabilities. How close can we approach this ideal? We propose to use a *good-enough* approach, and try to explain as much as we can, by assuming a small, manageable count of neuron-regions and their interconnections, and trying to guess the connectivity from the available MEG data. In more detail, we propose to formulate the problem as 'system identification' from control theory, and we develop novel algorithms to find *sparse* solutions.

We show that our *good-enough* approach is a very good first step, leading to a tractable, yet effective model (GEBM), that can answer the above questions. Figure 1 gives the high-level overview: at the bottom-right, the blue, dashed-line time sequences correspond to measured brain activity; the red lines correspond to the guess of our GEBM model. Notice the qualitative goodness of fit. At the top-right, the arrows indicate interaction between brain regions that our analysis learned, with the weight being the strength of interaction. Thus we see that the vision cortex ('occipital lobe') is well connected to the language-processing part ('temporal lobe'), which agrees with neuroscience, since all our experiments involved typed words.

Our **contributions** are as follows:

- *Novel analytical model*: We propose the GEBM model (see Section 3, and Eq (2)-(3)).
- *Algorithm*: we introduce SPARSE-SYSID, a novel, sparse, system-identification algorithm (see Section 3).
- *Effectiveness*: Our model can explain psychological phenomena, such as habituation and priming (see Section 5.4); it also gives results that agree with experts' intuition (see Section 5.1)
- *Validation*: GEBM indeed matches the given activity patterns, both on synthetic, as well as real data (see Section 4 and 5.3, resp.).
- *Multi-subject analysis*: Our SPARSE-SYSID, applied on 9 human subjects (Section 5.2), showed that (a) 8 of them had very consistent brain-connectivity patterns while (b) the outlier was due to exogenous factors (excessive road-traffic noise during his experiment).

Additionally, our GEBM highlights connections between multiple, mostly disparate areas: 1) Neuroscience, 2) Control Theory & System Identification, and 3) Psychology.

Reproducibility: Our implementation is open sourced and publicly available [3]. Due to privacy reasons, we are not able to release the MEG data, however, in the online version of the code we include the synthetic benchmarks, as well as the simulation of psychological phenomena using GEBM.

2. PROBLEM DEFINITION

As mentioned earlier, our goal is to infer the brain connectivity, given measurements of brain activity on multiple *yes/no tasks*, of multiple subjects. We define as **yes/no task** the experiment where the subject is given a yes/no question (like, *'is it edible?', 'is it alive?'*), and a typed English word (like, *apple, chair*), and has to decide the answer.

Throughout the entire process, we attach m sensors that record brain activity of a human subject. Here we are using Magnetoencephalography (MEG) data, although our GEBM model could be applied to any type of measurement (fMRI, etc). In Section 5.4 we provide a more formal definition of the measurement technique.

Thus, in a given experiment, at every time-tick t we have m measurements, which we arrange in an $m \times 1$ vector $\mathbf{y}(t)$. Additionally, we represent the stimulus (e.g. *apple*) and the task (e.g. *is it edible?*) in a time-dependent vector $\mathbf{s}(t)$, by using feature representation of the stimuli; a detailed description of how the stimulus vector is formed can be found in Section 5.4. For the rest of the paper, we shall use interchangeably the terms *sensor, voxel* and neuron-region.

We are interested in two problems: the first is to understand how the brain works, given a single subject. The second problem is to do cross-subject analysis, to find commonalities (and deviations) in a group of several human subjects. Informally, we have:

INFORMAL PROBLEM 1 (SINGLE SUBJECT). *Definition:*

- **Given**: *The input stimulus; and a sequence of $m \times T$ brain activity measurements for the m voxels, for all timeticks $t = 1 \cdots T$*
- **Estimate**: *the functional connectivity of the brain, i.e. the strength and direction of interaction, between pairs of the m voxels, such that*
    1. *we understand how the brain-regions collaborate, and*
    2. *we can effectively simulate brain activity.*

For the second problem, informally we have:

INFORMAL PROBLEM 2 (MULTI-SUBJECT). *Definition:*

- **Given**: *Multi-subject experimental data (brain activity for 'yes/no tasks')*
- **Detect**: *Regularities, commonalities, clusters of subjects (if any), outlier subjects (if any).*

For the particular experimental setting, prior work [15] has only considered transformations from the space of noun features to the voxel space and vice versa, as well as word-concept specific prediction based on estimating the covariance between the voxels [7].

Next we formalize the problems, we show some straightforward (but unsuccessful) solutions, and finally we give the proposed model GEBM, and the estimation algorithm.

3. PROBLEM FORMULATION AND PROPOSED METHOD

There are two over-arching assumptions:

- linearity: linear models are good-enough
- stationarity: the connectivity of the brain does not change, at least for the time-scales of our experiments.

Non-linear/sigmoid models is a natural direction for future work; and so is the study of neuroplasticity, where the connectivity changes. However, as we show later, linear, static, models are "*good-enough*" to answer the problems we listed, and thus we stay with them.

However, we have to be careful. Next we list some natural, but unsuccessful models, to illustrate that we did do 'due dilligence', and to highlight the need for our slightly more complicated, GEBM model. The conclusion is that the hasty, Model$_0$, below, leads to poor behavior, as we show in Figure 2 (red, and black, lines), completely missing all the trends and oscillations of the real signal (in dotted-blue line). In fact, the next subsection may be skipped, at a first reading.

3.1 First (unsuccessful) approach: Model$_0$

Given the linearity and static-connectivity assumptions above, a natural additional assumption is to postulate that the $m \times 1$ brain activity vector $\mathbf{y}(t+1)$ depends *linearly*, on the activities of the previous time-tick $\mathbf{y}(t)$, and, of course, the input stimulus, that is, the $s \times 1$ vector $\mathbf{s}(t)$.

[3] http://www.cs.cmu.edu/~epapalex/src/GeBM.zip

Formally, in the absence of input stimulus, we expect that

$$\mathbf{y}(t+1) = \mathbf{A}\mathbf{y}(t).$$

where $\mathbf{A}$ is the $m \times m$ connectivity matrix of the m brain regions. Including the (linear) influence of the input stimulus $\mathbf{s}(t)$, we reach the MODEL$_0$:

$$\mathbf{y}(t+1) \quad = \quad \mathbf{A}_{[m\times m]} \times \mathbf{y}(t) \; + \; \mathbf{B}_{[m\times s]} \times \mathbf{s}(t) \qquad (1)$$

The $\mathbf{B}_{[m\times s]}$ matrix shows how the s input signals affect the m brain-regions.

To solve for $\mathbf{A}, \mathbf{B}$, notice that: $\mathbf{y}(t+1) = \begin{bmatrix}\mathbf{A} & \mathbf{B}\end{bmatrix} \begin{bmatrix}\mathbf{y}(t) \\ \mathbf{s}(t)\end{bmatrix}$ which eventually becomes $\mathbf{Y}' = \begin{bmatrix}\mathbf{A} & \mathbf{B}\end{bmatrix} \begin{bmatrix}\mathbf{Y} \\ \mathbf{S}\end{bmatrix}$

In the above equation, we arranged all the measurement vectors $\mathbf{y}(t)$ in matrices: $\mathbf{Y} = \begin{bmatrix}\mathbf{y}(1) & \cdots & \mathbf{y}(T-1)\end{bmatrix}$,
$\mathbf{Y}' = \begin{bmatrix}\mathbf{y}(2) & \cdots & \mathbf{y}(T)\end{bmatrix}$, and $\mathbf{S} = \begin{bmatrix}\mathbf{s}(1) & \cdots & \mathbf{s}(T-1)\end{bmatrix}$

This is a well-known, least squares problem. We can solve it 'as is'; we can ask for a low-rank solution; or for a sparse solution - none yields a good result, but we briefly describe each, next.

- **Least Squares (LS)**: The solution is unique, using the Moore-Penrose pseudo-inverse, i.e. $\begin{bmatrix}\mathbf{A} & \mathbf{B}\end{bmatrix}_{LS} = \mathbf{Y}' \times \begin{bmatrix}\mathbf{Y} \\ \mathbf{S}\end{bmatrix}^{\dagger}$.
- **Canonical Correlation Analysis (CCA)**: The reader may be wondering: *what if we have over-fitting here - why not ask for a low-rank solution.* This is exactly what CCA does [14]. It solves for the same objective function as in LS, further requesting low rank r for $\begin{bmatrix}\mathbf{A} & \mathbf{B}\end{bmatrix}$
- Sparse solution: what if we solve the least squares problem, further requesting a sparse solution? We tried that, too, with ℓ_1 norm regularization.

None of the above worked. Fig. 2 shows the real brain activity (dotted-blue line) and predicted activity, using LS (pink) and CCA (black), for a particular voxel. The solutions completely fail to match the trends and oscillations. The results for the ℓ_1 regularization, and for several other voxels, are similar to the one shown, and omitted for brevity.

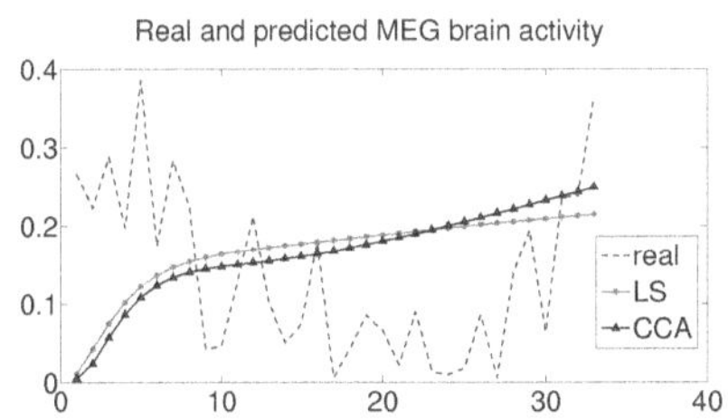

Figure 2: MODEL$_0$ fails: True brain activity (dotted blue) and the model estimate (pink, and black, resp., for the least squares, and for the CCA variation).

The conclusion of this subsection is that we need a more complicated model, which leads us to GEBM, next.

3.2 Proposed approach: GeBM

Before we introduce our proposed model, we should introduce our notation, which is succinctly shown in Table 1.

Formulating the problem as MODEL$_0$ is not able to meet the requirements for our desired solution. However, we have not exhausted the space of possible formulations that live within our set of simplifying assumptions. In this section, we describe GEBM, our proposed approach which, under the assumptions that we have already made in Section 2, is able to meet our requirements remarkably well.

Symbol	Definition
n	number of hidden neuron-regions
m	number of MEG sensors/voxels we observe (306)
s	number of input signals (40 questions)
T	time-ticks of each experiment (340 ticks, of 5msec each)
$\mathbf{x}(t)$	vector of neuron activities at time t
$\mathbf{y}(t)$	vector of voxel activities at time t
$\mathbf{s}(t)$	vector of input-sensor activities at time t
$\mathbf{A}_{[n\times n]}$	connectivity matrix between neurons (or neuron regions)
$\mathbf{C}_{[m\times n]}$	summarization matrix (neurons to voxels)
$\mathbf{B}_{[n\times s]}$	perception matrix (sensors to neurons)
$\mathbf{A}_v$	connectivity matrix between voxels
REAL	real part of a complex number
IMAG	imaginary part of a complex number
$\mathbf{A}^{\dagger}$	Moore-Penrose Pseudoinverse of $\mathbf{A}$

Table 1: Table of symbols

In order to come up with a more accurate model, it is useful to look more carefully at the actual system that we are attempting to model. In particular, the brain activity vector $\mathbf{y}$ that we observe is simply the collection of values recorded by the m sensors, placed on a person's scalp. In MODEL$_0$, we attempt to model the dynamics of the sensor measurements directly. However, by doing so, we are directing our attention to an *observable proxy* of the process that we are trying to estimate (i.e. the functional connectivity). Instead, it is more beneficial to model the direct outcome of that process. Ideally, we would like to capture the dynamics of the internal state of the person's brain, which, in turn, cause the effect that we are measuring with our MEG sensors.

Let us assume that there are n *hidden* (hyper-)regions of the brain, which interact with each other, causing the activity that we observe in $\mathbf{y}$. We denote the vector of the hidden brain activity as $\mathbf{x}$ of size $n \times 1$. Then, by using the same idea as in MODEL$_0$, we may formulate the temporal evolution of the hidden brain activity as:

$$\mathbf{x}(t+1) = \mathbf{A}_{[n\times n]} \times \mathbf{x}(t) \; + \; \mathbf{B}_{[n\times s]} \times \mathbf{s}(t)$$

A subtle issue that we have yet to address is the fact that $\mathbf{x}$ is *not observed* and we have no means of measuring it. We propose to resolve this issue by modelling the measurement procedure itself, i.e. model the transformation of a hidden brain activity vector to its observed counterpart. We assume that this transformation is linear, thus we are able to write

$$\mathbf{y}(t) = \mathbf{C}_{[m\times n]}\mathbf{x}(t)$$

Putting everything together, we end up with the following set of equations, which constitute our proposed model GEBM:

$$\boxed{\begin{aligned} \mathbf{x}(t+1) &= \mathbf{A}_{[n\times n]} \times \mathbf{x}(t) \; + \; \mathbf{B}_{[n\times s]} \times \mathbf{s}(t) \qquad (2) \\ \mathbf{y}(t) &= \mathbf{C}_{[m\times n]} \times \mathbf{x}(t) \qquad (3) \end{aligned}}$$

The key concepts behind GEBM are:

- **(Latent) Connectivity Matrix**: We assume that there are n regions, each containing 1 or more neurons, and they are connected with an $n \times n$ adjacency matrix $\mathbf{A}_{[n\times n]}$. We only observe m voxels, each containing multiple regions, and we record the activity (eg., magnetic activity) in each of them; this is the total activity in the constituent regions

- **Measurement Matrix**: Matrix $\mathbf{C}_{[m \times n]}$ is an $m \times n$ matrix, with $c_{i,j}$ =1 if voxel i contains region j
- **Perception Matrix**: Matrix $\mathbf{B}_{[n \times s]}$ shows the influence of each sensor to each neuron-region. The input is denoted as $\mathbf{s}$, with s input signals
- **Sparsity**: We require that our model's matrices are *sparse*; only few sensors are responsible for a specific brain region. Additionally, the interactions between regions should not form a complete graph, and finally, the perception matrix should map only few activated sensors to neuron regions at every given time.

3.3 Algorithm

Our solution is inspired by control theory, and more specifically by a sub-field of control theory, called *system identification.* In the appendix, we provide an overview of how this can be accomplished. However, the matrices we obtain through this process are usually dense, counter to GEBM's specifications. We, thus, need to refine the solution until we obtain the desired level of sparsity. In the next few lines, we show why this sparsification has to be done carefully, and we present our approach.

Crucial to GEBM's behavior is the spectrum of its matrices; in other words, any operation that we apply on any of GEBM's matrices needs to preserve the eigevnalue profile (for matrix $\mathbf{A}$) or the singular values (for matrices $\mathbf{B}, \mathbf{C}$). Alterations thereof may lead GEBM to instabilities. From a control theoretic and stability perspective, we are mostly interested in the eigenvalues of $\mathbf{A}$, since they drive the behavior of the system. Thus, in our experiments, we heavily rely on assessing how well we estimate these eigenvalues.

Sparsifying a matrix while preserving its spectrum can be seen as a similarity transformation of the matrix to a sparse subspace. The following lemma sheds more light towards this direction.

LEMMA 1. *System identification is able to recover matrices* $\mathbf{A}$, $\mathbf{B}$, $\mathbf{C}$ *of* GEBM *up to rotational/similarity transformations.*

PROOF. See the appendix. □

An important corollary of the above lemma (also proved in the appendix) is the fact that pursuing sparsity only on, say, matrix $\mathbf{A}$ is not well defined. Therefore, since all three matrices share the same similarity transformation freedom, we have to sparsify all three.

In SPARSE-SYSID, we propose a fast, greedy sparsification scheme which can be seen as approximately applying the aforementioned similarity transformation to $\mathbf{A}, \mathbf{B}, \mathbf{C}$, without calculating or applying the transformation itself. Iteratively, for all three matrices, we delete small values, while maintaining ther spectrum within ϵ from the one obtained through system identification. Additionally, for $\mathbf{A}$, we also do not allow eigenvalues to switch from complex to real and vice versa. This scheme works very well in practice, providing very sparse matrices, while respecting their spectrum. In Algorithm 1, we provide an outline of the algorithm.

So far, GEBM as we have described it, is able to give us the hidden functional connectivity and the measurement matrix, but does not directly offer the voxel-to-voxel connectivity, unlike MODEL$_0$, which models it explicitly. However, this is by no means a weakness of GEBM, since there is a simple way to obtain the voxel-to-voxel connectivity (henceforth referred to as $\mathbf{A}_v$) from GEBM's matrices.

LEMMA 2. *Assuming that* $m > n$, *the voxel-to-voxel functional connectivity matrix* $\mathbf{A}_v$ *can be defined and is equal to* $\mathbf{A}_v = \mathbf{CAC}^\dagger$

Algorithm 1: SPARSE-SYSID: Sparse System Identification of GEBM

Input: Training data in the form $\{\mathbf{y}(t), \mathbf{s}(t)\}_{t=1}^{T}$, number of hidden states n.
Output: GEBM matrices $\mathbf{A}$ (hidden connectivity matrix), $\mathbf{B}$ (perception matrix), $\mathbf{C}$ (measurement matrix), and $\mathbf{A}_v$ (voxel-to-voxel matrix).

$\{\mathbf{A}^{(0)}, \mathbf{B}^{(0)}, \mathbf{C}^{(0)}\} = \text{SYSID}\left(\{\mathbf{y}(t), \mathbf{s}(t)\}_{t=1}^{T}, n\right)$
$\mathbf{A} = \text{EIGENSPARSIFY}(\mathbf{A}^{(0)})$
$\mathbf{B} = \text{SINGULARSPARSIFY}(\mathbf{B}^{(0)})$
$\mathbf{C} = \text{SINGULARSPARSIFY}(\mathbf{C}^{(0)})$
$\mathbf{A}_v = \mathbf{CAC}^\dagger$

Algorithm 2: EIGENSPARSIFY: Eigenvalue Preserving Sparsification of System Matrix $\mathbf{A}$.

Input: Square matrix $\mathbf{A}^{(0)}$.
Output: Sparsified matrix $\mathbf{A}$.

$\boldsymbol{\lambda}^{(0)} = \text{EIGENVALUES}(\mathbf{A}^{(0)})$
Initialize $\mathbf{d}_R^{(0)} = \mathbf{0}$, $\mathbf{d}_I^{(0)} = \mathbf{0}$. Vector $\mathbf{d}_R^{(i)}$ holds the element-wise difference of the real part of the eigenvalues of $\mathbf{A}^{(i)}$. Similarly for $\mathbf{d}_I^{(i)}$ and the imaginary part.
Set vector $\mathbf{c}$ as a boolean vector that indicates whether the j-th eigenvalue in $\boldsymbol{\lambda}^{(0)}$ is complex or not. One way to do it is to evaluate element-wise the following boolean expression: $\mathbf{c} = \left(\text{IMAG}(\boldsymbol{\lambda}^{(0)}) \neq 0\right)$.
Initialize $i = 0$
while $\mathbf{d}_R^{(i)} \leq \epsilon$ **and** $\mathbf{d}_I^{(i)} \leq \epsilon$ **and** $\left(\text{IMAG}(\boldsymbol{\lambda}^{(i)}) \neq 0\right) == \mathbf{c}$ **do**
  Initialize $\mathbf{A}^{(i)} = \mathbf{A}^{(i-1)}$
  $\{v_i^*, v_j^*\} = \arg\min_{v_i, v_j} |\mathbf{A}^{(i-1)}(v_i, v_j)|$ s.t. $\mathbf{A}^{(i-1)}(v_i, v_j) \neq 0$.
  Set $\mathbf{A}^{(i)}(v_i^*, v_j^*) = 0$
  $\boldsymbol{\lambda}^{(i)} = \text{EIGENVALUES}(\mathbf{A}^{(i)})$
  $\mathbf{d}_R^{(i)} = |\text{REAL}(\boldsymbol{\lambda}^{(i)}) - \text{REAL}(\boldsymbol{\lambda}^{(i-1)})|$
  $\mathbf{d}_I^{(i)} = |\text{IMAG}(\boldsymbol{\lambda}^{(i)}) - \text{IMAG}(\boldsymbol{\lambda}^{(i-1)})|$
end while
$\mathbf{A} = \mathbf{A}^{(i-1)}$

Algorithm 3: SINGULARSPARSIFY: Singular Value Preserving Sparsification

Input: Matrix $\mathbf{M}^{(0)}$.
Output: Sparsified matrix $\mathbf{M}$

$\boldsymbol{\lambda}^{(0)} = \text{SINGULARVALUES}(\mathbf{A}^{(0)})$
Initialize $\mathbf{d}_R^{(0)} = \mathbf{0}$ which holds the element-wise difference of the singular values of $\mathbf{A}^{(i)}$.
Initialize $i = 0$
while $\mathbf{d}_R^{(i)} \leq \epsilon$ **do**
  Initialize $\mathbf{M}^{(i)} = \mathbf{M}^{(i-1)}$
  $\{v_i^*, v_j^*\} = \arg\min_{v_i, v_j} |\mathbf{M}^{(i-1)}(v_i, v_j)|$ s.t. $\mathbf{M}^{(i-1)}(v_i, v_j) \neq 0$.
  Set $\mathbf{M}^{(i)}(v_i^*, v_j^*) = 0$
  $\boldsymbol{\lambda}^{(i)} = \text{SINGULARVALUES}(\mathbf{M}^{(i)})$
  $\mathbf{d}_R^{(i)} = |\boldsymbol{\lambda}^{(i)} - \boldsymbol{\lambda}^{(i-1)}|$
end while
$\mathbf{M} = \mathbf{M}^{(i-1)}$

PROOF. The observed voxel vector can be written as

$$\mathbf{y}(t+1) = \mathbf{Cx}(t+1) = \mathbf{CAx}(t) + \mathbf{CBs}(t)$$

Matrix $\mathbf{C}$ is tall (i.e. $m > n$), thus we can write: $\mathbf{y}(t) = \mathbf{Cx}(t) \Leftrightarrow \mathbf{x}(t) = \mathbf{C}^{\dagger}\mathbf{y}(t)$ Consequently, $\mathbf{y}(t+1) = \mathbf{CAC}^{\dagger}\mathbf{y}(t) + \mathbf{CBs}(t)$ Therefore, it follows that $\mathbf{CAC}^{\dagger}$ is the voxel-to-voxel matrix $\mathbf{A}_v$. □

Finally, an interesting aspect of our proposed model GEBM is the fact that if we ignore the notion of the summarization, i.e. matrix $\mathbf{C} = \mathbf{I}$, then our model is reduced to the simple model MODEL$_0$. In other words, GEBM contains MODEL$_0$ as a special case. This observation demonstrates the importance of hidden states in GEBM.

4. EVALUATION

4.1 Implementation Details

The code for SPARSE-SYSID has been written in Matlab. For the system identification part, initially we experimented with Matlab's System Identification Toolbox and the algorithms in [10]. These algorithms worked well for smaller to medium scales, but were unable to perform on our full dataset. Thus, in our final implementation, we use the algorithms of [20]. Our code is publicly available at `http://www.cs.cmu.edu/~epapalex/src/GeBM.zip`.

4.2 Evaluation on synthetic data

In lieu of ground truth in our real data, we generated synthetic data to measure the performance of SPARSE-SYSID.

The way we generate the ground truth system is as follows: First, given fixed n, we generate a matrix $\mathbf{A}$ that has 0.25 on the main diagonal, 0.1 on the first upper diagonal (i.e. the $(i, i+1)$ elements), -0.15 on the first lower diagonal (i.e., the $(i-1, i)$ elements), and 0 everywhere else. We then create randomly generated sparse matrices $\mathbf{B}$ and $\mathbf{C}$, varying s and m respectively.

After we generate a synthetic ground truth model, we generate Gaussian random input data to the system, and we obtain the system's response to that data. Consequently, we use the input/output pairs with SPARSE-SYSID, and we assess our algorithm's ability to recover the ground truth. Here, we show the *noiseless* case due to space restrictions. In the noisy case, estimation performance is slowly degrading when n increases, however this is expected from estimation theory.

We evaluate SPARSE-SYSID's accuracy with respect to the following aspects:

Q1: How well can SPARSE-SYSID recover the true hidden connectivity matrix $\mathbf{A}$?

Q2: How well can SPARSE-SYSID recover the voxel-to-voxel connectivity matrix $\mathbf{A}_v$?

Q3: Given that we know the the true number of hidden states n, how does SPARSE-SYSID behave as we vary the n used for GEBM?

In order to answer **Q1**, we measure how well (in terms of RMSE) SPARSE-SYSID recovers the eigenvalues of $\mathbf{A}$. We are mostly interested in recovering perfectly the real part of the eigenvalues, since even small errors could lead to instabilities. Figure 4(a) shows our results: We observe that the estimation of the real part of the eigenvalues of $\mathbf{A}$ is excellent. We are omitting the estimation results for the imaginary parts, however they are within the ϵ we selected in our sparsification scheme of SPARSE-SYSID. Overall, SPARSE-SYSID is able to recover the true GEBM, for various values of m and n.

With respect to **Q2**, it suffices to measure the RMSE of the true $\mathbf{A}_v$ and the estimated one, since we have thoroughly tested the system's behavior in **Q1**. Figure 4(b) shows that the estimation of the voxel-to-voxel connectivity matrix using SPARSE-SYSID is highly accurate. Additionally, for ease of exposition, in Figure 3 we show an example a true matrix $\mathbf{A}_v$, and its estimation through SPARSE-SYSID; it is impossible to tell the difference between the two matrices, a fact also corroborated by the RMSE results.

The third dimension of SPARSE-SYSID's performance is its sensitivity to the selection of the parameter n; In order to test this, we generated a ground truth GEBM with a known n, and we varied our selection of n for SPARSE-SYSID. The result of the experiment is shown in Fig. 4(c). We observe that for values of n smaller than the real one, SPARSE-SYSID's performance is increasingly good, and still, for small values of n the estimation quality is good. When n exceeds the value of the real n, the performance starts to degrade, due to *overfitting*. This provides an insight on how to choose n for SPARSE-SYSID in order to fit GEBM: it is better to under-estimate n rather than over-estimate it, thus, it is better to start with a small n and possibly increase it as soon as performance (e.g. qualitative assessment of how well the estimated model predicts brain activity) starts to degrade.

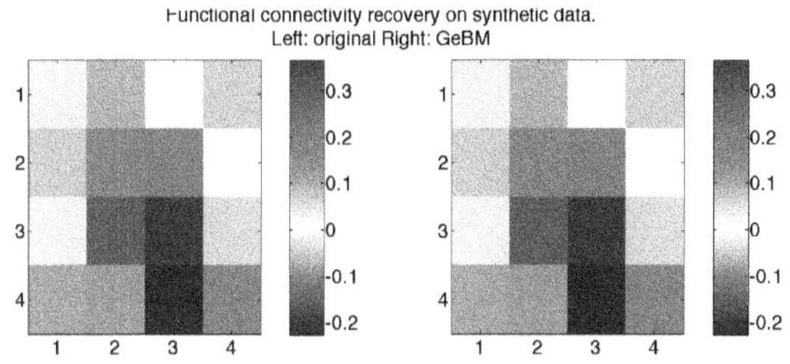

Figure 3: Q2: Perfect estimation of $\mathbf{A}_v$:Comparison of true and estimated $\mathbf{A}_v$, for $n = 3$ and $m = 4$. We can see, qualitatively, that GEBM is able to recover the true voxel-to-voxel functional connectivity.

5. GeBM AT WORK

This section is focused on showing different aspects of GEBM at work. In particular, we present the following discoveries:

D1: We provide insights on the obtained functional connectivity from a Neuroscientific point of view.

D2: Given multiple human subjects, we discover regularities and outliers, with respect to functional connectivity.

D3: We demonstrate GEBM's ability to simulate brain activity.

D4: We show how GEBM is able to capture two basic psychological phenomena.

Dataset Description & Formulation.

We are using real brain activity data, measured using MEG. MEG (Magnetoencephalography) measures the magnetic field caused by many thousands of neurons firing together, and has good time resolution (1000 Hz) but poor spatial resolution. fMRI (functional Magnetic Resonance Imaging) measures the change in blood oxygenation that results from changes in neural activity, and has good spatial resolution but poor time resolution (0.5-1 Hz). Since we are interested in the temporal dynamics of the brain, we choose to operate on MEG data.

All experiments were conducted at the University of Pittsburgh Medical Center (UPMC) Brain Mapping Center. The MEG machine consists of $m = 306$ sensors, placed uniformly across the subject's scalp. The temporal granularity of the measurements is 5ms, resulting in $T = 340$ time points; after experimenting with different aggregations in the temporal dimension, we decided to use

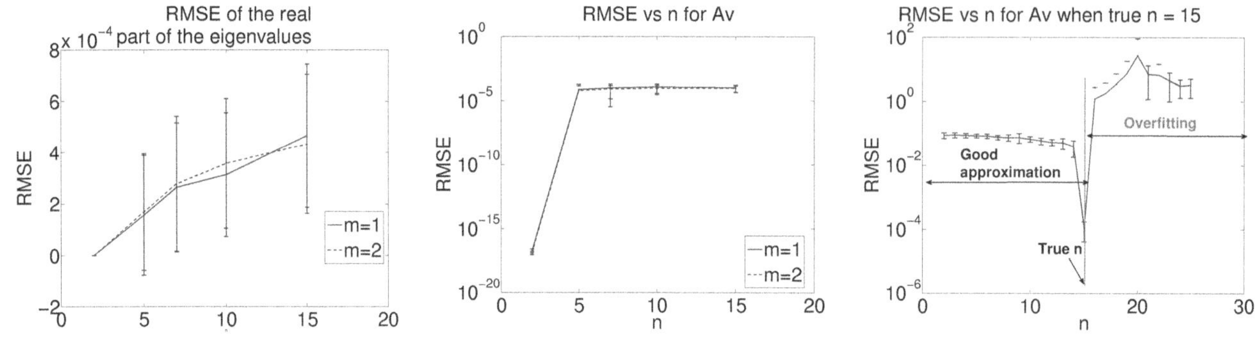

(a) **Q1**: RMSE of REAL(eigenvalues) of $\mathbf{A}$ vs. n.

(b) **Q2**: Estimation RMSE for $\mathbf{A}_v$ vs. n.

(c) **Q3**: Estimation RMSE for $\mathbf{A}_v$ vs. n, where the true n is fixed and equal to 15.

Figure 4: Sub-figure (a) refers to **Q1**, and show sthat SPARSE-SYSID is able to estimate matrix $\mathbf{A}$ with high accuracy, in control-theoretic terms. Sub-figure (b) illustrates SPARSE-SYSID's ability to accurately estimate the voxel-to-voxel functional connectivity matrix $\mathbf{A}_v$. Finally, sub-figure (c) shows the behavior of SPARSE-SYSID with respect to parameter n, when the true value of this parameter is known; the message from this graph is that as long as n is under-estimated, SPARSE-SYSID's performance is steadily good and is not greatly influenced by the particular choice of n.

50ms of time resolution, because this yielded the most interpretable results.

For the experiments, nine right handed human subjects were shown a set of 60 concrete English nouns (*apple, knife* etc), and for each noun 20 simple yes/no questions (*Is it edible? Can you buy it?* etc). The subject were asked to press the right button if their answer to each question was 'yes', or the left button if the answer was 'no'. After the subject pressed the button, the stimulus (i.e. the noun) would disappear from the screen. We also record the exact time that the subject pressed the button, relative to the appearance of the stimulus on the screen. A more detailed description of the data can be found in [15].

In order to bring the above data to the format that our model expects, we make the following design choices: In lack of sensors that measure the response of the eyes to the shown stimuli, we represent each stimulus by a set of semantic features for that specific noun. This set of features is a superset of the 20 questions that we have already mentioned; the value for each feature comes from the answers given by Amazon Mechanical Turk workers. Thus, from time-tick 1 (when the stimulus starts showing), until the button is pressed, all the features that are active for the particular stimulus are set to 1 on our stimulus vector $\mathbf{s}$, and all the rest features are equal to 0; when the button is pressed, all features are zeroed out. On top of the stimulus features, we also have to incorporate the task information in $\mathbf{s}$, i.e. the particular question shown on the screen. In order to do that, we add 20 more rows to the stimulus vector $\mathbf{s}$, each one corresponding to every question/task. At each given experiment, only one of those rows is set to 1 for all time ticks, and all other rows are set to 0. Thus, the number of input sensors in our formulation is $s = 40$ (i.e. 20 neurons for the noun/stimulus and 20 neurons for the task).

As a last step, we have to incorporate the button pressing information to our model; to that end, we add two more voxels to our observed vector $\mathbf{y}$, corresponding to left and right button pressing; initially, those values are set to 0 and as soon as the button is pressed, they are set to 1.

Finally, we choose $n = 15$ for all the results we show in the following lines; particular choice of n did not incur qualitative changes in the results, however, as we highlight in the previous section, it is better to under-estimate n, and therefore we chose $n = 15$ as an adequately small choice which, at the same time, produces interpretable results.

5.1 D1: Functional Connectivity Graphs

The primary focus of this work is to estimate the functional connectivity of the human brain, i.e. the interaction pattern of groups of neurons. In the next few lines, we present our findings in a concise way and provide Neuroscientific insights regarding the interaction patterns that GEBM was able to infer.

In order to present our findings, we post-process the results obtained through GEBM in the following way: The data we collect come from 306 sensors, placed on the human scalp in a uniform fashion. Each of those 306 sensors is measuring activity from one of the four main regions of the brain, i.e.

- **Frontal Lobe**, associated with attention, short memory, and planning.
- **Parietal Lobe**, associated with movement.
- **Occipital Lobe**, associated with vision.
- **Temporal Lobe**, associated with sensory input processing, language comprehension, and visual memory retention.

Even though our sensors offer within-region resolution, for exposition purposes, we chose to aggregate our findings per region; by doing so, we are still able to provide useful neuroscientific insights.

Figure 5 shows the functional connectivity graph obtained using GEBM. The weights indicate the strength of the interaction, measured by the number of distinct connections we identified. These results are consistent with current research regarding the nature of language processing in the brain. For example, Hickock and Poeppel [9] have proposed a model of language comprehension that includes a "dorsal" and "ventral" pathway. The ventral pathway takes the input stimuli (spoken language in the case of Hickock and Poeppel, images and words in ours) and sends the information to the temporal lobe for semantic processing. Because the occipital cortex is responsible for the low level processing of visual stimuli (including words) it is reasonable to see a strong set of connections between the occipital and temporal lobes. The dorsal pathway sends processed sensory input through the parietal and frontal lobes where they are processed for planning and action purposes. The task performed during the collection of our MEG data required that subjects consider the meaning of the word in the context of a semantic question. This task would require the recruitment of the dorsal pathway (occipital-parietal and parietal-frontal connections). In addition, frontal involvement is indicated when the task performed by the subject requires the selection of semantic information [3], as in our question answering paradigm. It is interesting that the number of connections from parietal to occipital cortex is larger than from occipital to parietal, considering the flow of information is likely occipital to parietal. This could, however, be indicative of what is termed "top down" processing, wherein higher level cognitive processes can work to focus upstream sensory processes. Perhaps the semantic task causes the subjects to focus in anticipation of the upcoming word while keeping the semantic question in mind.

5.2 D2: Cross-subject Analysis

In our experiments, we have 9 participants, all of whom have undergone the same procedure, being presented with the same stimuli, and asked to carry out the same tasks. Availability of such a rich, multi-subject dataset inevitably begs the following question: are there any differences across people's functional connectivity? Or is everyone, more or less, wired equally, at least with respect to the stimuli and tasks at hand?

By using GEBM, we are able (to the extent that our model is able to explain) to answer the above question. We trained GEBM for each of the 9 human subjects, using the entire data from all stimuli and tasks, and obtained matrices $\mathbf{A}, \mathbf{B}, \mathbf{C}$ for each person. For the purposes of answering the above question, it suffices to look at matrix $\mathbf{A}$ (which is the hidden functional connectivity), since it dictates the temporal dynamics of the brain activity. At this point, we have to note that the exact location of each sensor can differ between human subjects, however, we assume that this difference is negligible, given the current voxel granularity dictated by the number of sensors.

In this multi-subject study we have two very important findings:

- **Regularities**: For 8 out of 9 human subjects, we identified almost identical GEBM instances, both with respect to RMSE and to spectrum. In other words, for 8 out of 9 subjects in our study, the inferred functional connectivity behaves almost identically. This fact most likely implies that for the particular set of stimuli and assorted tasks, the human brain behaves similarly across people.
- **Anomaly**: One of our human subjects (#3) deviates from the aforementioned regular behavior.

In Fig. 6(a) & (b) we show the real and imaginary parts of the eigenvalues of $\mathbf{A}$. We can see that for 8 human subjects, the eigenvalues are almost identical. This finding agrees with neuroscientific results on different experimental settings [18], further demonstrating GEBM's ability to provide useful insights on multi-subject experiments. For subject #3 there is a deviation on the real part of the first eigenvalue, as well as a slightly deviating pattern on the imaginary parts of its eigenvalues. Figures 6(c) & (d) compare matrix $\mathbf{A}$ for subjects 1 and 3. Subject 3 negative value on the diagonal (blue square at the $(8, 8)$ entry), a fact unique to this specific person's connectivity.

Moreover, according to the person responsible for the data collection of Subject #3:

> *There was a big demonstration outside the UPMC building during the scan, and I remember the subject complaining during one of the breaks that he could hear the crowd shouting through the walls.*

This is a plausible explanation for the deviation of GEBM for Subject #3.

5.3 D3: Brain Activity Simulation

An additional way to gain confidence on our model is to assess its ability to simulate/predict brain activity, given the inferred functional connectivity. In order to do so, we trained GEBM using data from all but one of the words, and then we simulated brain activity time-series for the left-out word. In lieu of competing methods, we compare our proposed method GEBM against our initial approach (whose unsuitability we have argued for in Section 3, but we use here in order to further solidify our case). As an initial state for GEBM, we use $\mathbf{C}^{\dagger}\mathbf{y}(0)$, and for MODEL$_0$, we simply use $\mathbf{y}(0)$. The final time-series we show, both for the real data and the estimated ones are normalized to unit norm, and plotted in absolute values. For exposition purposes, we sorted the voxels according to the ℓ_2 norm of their time series vector, and we are displaying the high ranking ones (however, the same pattern holds for all voxels)

In Fig. 7 we illustrate the simulated brain activity of GEBM (solid red), compared against the ones of MODEL$_0$ (using LS (dash-dot magenta) and CCA (dashed black)), as well as the original brain activity time series (dashed blue) for the four highest ranking voxels. Clearly, the activity generated using GEBM is far more realistic than the results of MODEL$_0$.

5.4 D4: Explanation of Psychological Phenomena

As we briefly mentioned in the Introduction, we would like our proposed method to be able to capture some of the psychological phenomena that the human brain exhibits. We, by no means, claim that GEBM is able to capture convoluted and still under heavy investigation psychological phenomena, however, in this section we demonstrate GEBM's ability to simulate two very basic phenomena, *habituation* and *priming*. Unlike the previous discoveries, the following experiments are on synthetic data and their purpose is to showcase GEBM's additional strengths.

Habituation In our simplified version of habituation, we observe the demand behaviour: Given a repeated stimulus, the neurons initially get activated, but their activation levels decline ($t = 60$ in Fig. 8) if the stimulus persists for a long time ($t = 80$ in Fig. 8). In Fig. 8, we show that GEBM is able to capture such behavior. In particular, we show the desired input and output for a few (observed) voxels, and we show, given the functional connectivity obtained according to GEBM, the simulated output, which exhibits the same, desired behavior.

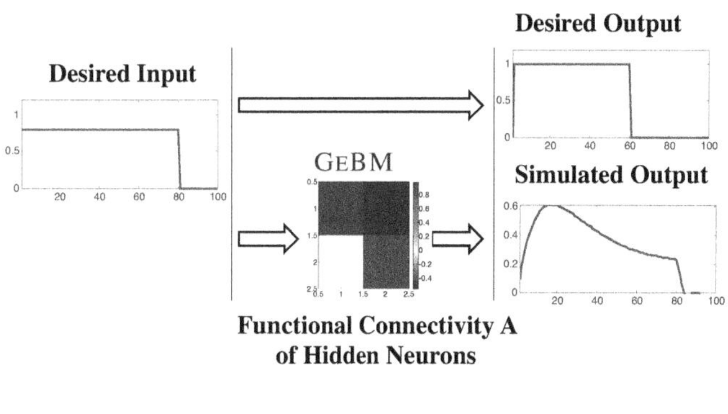

Figure 8: GEBM captures *Habituation*: Given repeated exposure to a stimulus, the brain activity starts to fade.

Priming In our simplified model on priming, first we give the stim-

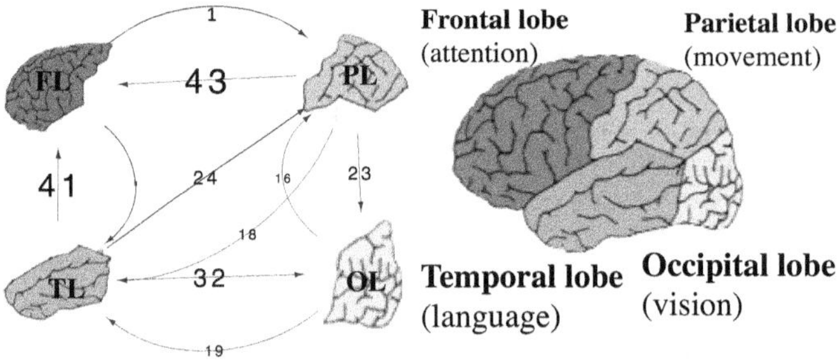

Figure 5: The functional connectivity derived from GEBM. The weights on the edges indicate the number of inferred connections. Our results are consistent with research that investigates natural language processing in the brain.

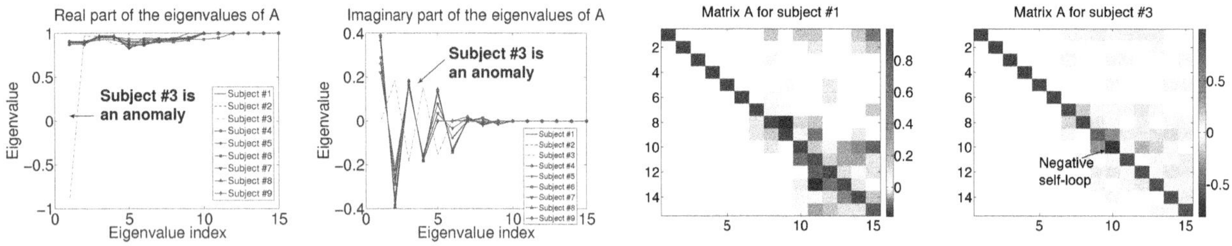

(a) Real part of eigenvalues (b) Imaginary part of eigenvalues (c) Subject #1 (d) Subject #3

Figure 6: Multi-subject analysis: Sub-figures (a) and (b), show the real and imaginary parts of the eigenvalues of matrix $\mathbf{A}$ for each subject. For all subjects but one (subject #3) the eigenvalues are almost identical, implying that the GEBM that captures their brain activity behaves more or less in the same way. Subject #3 on the other hand is an outlier; indeed, during the experiment, the subject complained that he was able to hear a demonstration happening outside of the laboratory, rendering the experimental task assigned to the subject more difficult than it was supposed to be. Sub-figures (c) and (d) show matrices $\mathbf{A}$ for subject #1 and #3. Subject #3's matrix seems sparser and most importantly, we can see that there is a negative entry on the diagonal, a fact unique to subject #3.

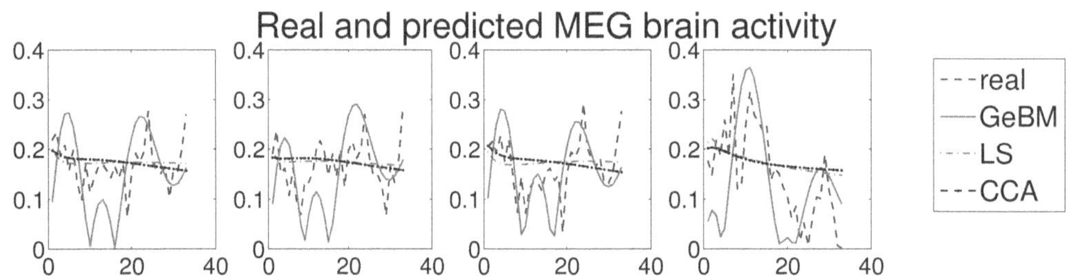

Figure 7: Effective brain activity simulation: Comparison of he real brain activity and the simulated ones using GEBM and MODEL$_0$, for the first four high ranking voxels (in the ℓ_2 norm sense).

ulus *apple*, which sets off neurons that are associated with the fruit 'apple', as well as neurons that are associated with Apple inc. Consequently, we are showing a stimulus such as *iPod*; this predisposes the regions of the brain that are associated with Apple inc. to display some small level of activation, whereas suppressing the regions of the brain that are associate with apple (the fruit). Later on, the stimulus *apple* is repeated, which, given the aforementioned predisposition, activates the voxels associated with Apple (company) and suppresses the ones associated with the homonymous fruit.

Figure 9 displays is a pictorial description of the above example of priming; given desired input/output pairs, we derive a model that obeys GEBM, such that we match the priming behavior.

6. RELATED WORK

Brain Functional Connectivity Estimating the brain's functional connectivity is an active field of study of computational neuroscience. Examples of works can be found in [13, 8, 7]. There have been a few works in the data mining community as well: In [16], the authors derive the brain region connections for Alzheimer's patients, and recently [5] that leverages tensor decomposition in order to discover the underlying network of the human brain. Most related to the present work is the work of Valdes et al [19], wherein the authors propose an autoregressive model (similar to MODEL$_0$) and solve it using regularized regression. However, to the best of our knowledge, this work is the first to apply system identification concepts to this problem.

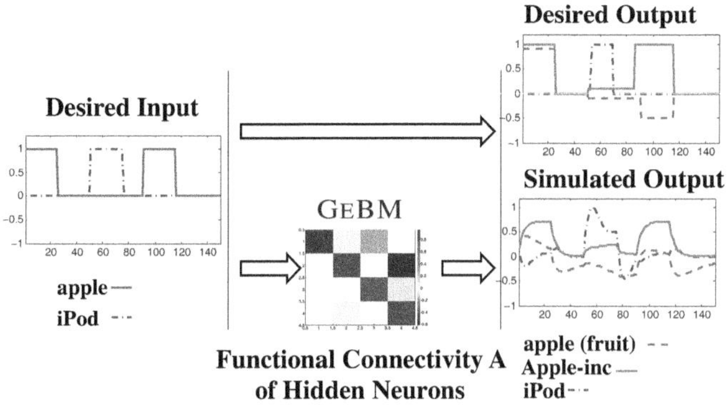

Figure 9: GeBM captures *Priming*: When first shown the stimulus *apple*, both neurons associated with the fruit 'apple' and Apple inc. get activated. When showing the stimulus *iPod* and then *apple*, *iPod* predisposes the neurons associated with Apple inc. to get activated more quickly, while suppressing the ones associated with the fruit.

Psychological Phenomena A concise overview of literature pertaining to habitutation can be found in [17]. A more recent study on habitutation can be found in [12]. The definition of priming, as we describe it in the lines above concurs with the definition found in [6]. Additionally, in [11], the authors conduct a study on the effects of priming when the human subjects were asked to write sentences. The above concepts of priming and habituation have been also studied in the context of spreading activation [1, 4] which is a model of the cognitive process of memory.
Control Theory & System Identification System Identification is a field of control theory. In the appendix we provide more theoretical details on subspace system identification, however, [10] and [21] are the most prominent sources for system identification algorithms.
Network Discovery from Time Series Our work touches upon discovering underlying network structures from time series data; an exemplary work related to the present paper is [22] where the authors derive a who-calls-whom network from VoIP packet transmission time series.

7. CONCLUSIONS

The list of our contributions is:

- **Analytical model** : We propose GeBM, a novel model of the human brain functional connectivity.
- **Algorithm**: We introduce Sparse-SysId, a novel sparse system identification algorithm that estimates GeBM
- **Effectiveness**: GeBM simulates psychological phenomena (such as habituation and priming), as well as provides valuable neuroscientific insights.
- **Validation**: We validate our approach on synthetic data (where the ground truth is known), and on real data, where our model produces brain activity patterns, remarkably similar to the true ones.
- **Multi-subject analysis**: We analyze measurements from 9 human subjects, identifying a consistent connectivity among 8 of them; we successfully identify an outlier, whose experimental procedure was compromised.

Acknowledgements

Research was supported by grants NSF IIS-1247489, NSF IIS-1247632, NSF CDI 0835797, NIH/NICHD 12165321, DARPA FA87501320005, IARPA FA865013C7360, and by Google. This work was also supported in part by a fellowship to Alona Fyshe from the Multimodal Neuroimaging Training Program funded by NIH grants T90DA022761 and R90DA023420. Any opinions, findings, and conclusions or recommendations expressed in this material are those of the authors and do not necessarily reflect the views of the funding parties. We would also like to thank Erika Laing and the UPMC Brain Mapping Center for their help with the data and visualization of our results. Finally, we would like to thank Gustavo Sudre for collecting and sharing the data, and Dr. Brian Murphy for valuable conversations.

8. REFERENCES

[1] J.R. Anderson. A spreading activation theory of memory. *Journal of verbal learning and verbal behavior*, 22(3):261–95, 1983.

[2] Frederico AC Azevedo, Ludmila RB Carvalho, Lea T Grinberg, José Marcelo Farfel, Renata EL Ferretti, Renata EP Leite, Roberto Lent, Suzana Herculano-Houzel, et al. Equal numbers of neuronal and nonneuronal cells make the human brain an isometrically scaled-up primate brain. *Journal of Comparative Neurology*, 513(5):532–541, 2009.

[3] Jeffrey R Binder and Rutvik H Desai. The neurobiology of semantic memory. *Trends in cognitive sciences*, 15(11):527–36, November 2011.

[4] Allan M. Collins and Elizabeth F. Loftus. A spreading-activation theory of semantic processing. *Psychological Review*, 82(6):407–428, 1975.

[5] Ian Davidson, Sean Gilpin, Owen Carmichael, and Peter Walker. Network discovery via constrained tensor analysis of fmri data. In *ACM SIGKDD*, pages 194–202. ACM, 2013.

[6] Angela D Friederici, Karsten Steinhauer, and Stefan Frisch. Lexical integration: Sequential effects of syntactic and semantic information. *Memory & Cognition*, 27(3):438–453, 1999.

[7] Alona Fyshe, Emily B Fox, David B Dunson, and Tom M Mitchell. Hierarchical latent dictionaries for models of brain activation. In *AISTATS*, pages 409–421, 2012.

[8] Michael D Greicius, Ben Krasnow, Allan L Reiss, and Vinod Menon. Functional connectivity in the resting brain: a network analysis of the default mode hypothesis. *PNAS*, 100(1):253–258, 2003.

[9] Gregory Hickok and David Poeppel. Dorsal and ventral streams: a framework for understanding aspects of the functional anatomy of language. *Cognition*, 92(1-2):67–99, 2004.

[10] Lennart Ljung. *System identification*. Wiley Online Library, 1999.

[11] Martin J Pickering and Holly P Branigan. The representation of verbs: Evidence from syntactic priming in language production. *Journal of Memory and Language*, 39(4):633–651, 1998.

[12] Catharine H Rankin, Thomas Abrams, Robert J Barry, Seema Bhatnagar, David F Clayton, John Colombo, Gianluca Coppola, Mark A Geyer, David L Glanzman, Stephen Marsland, et al. Habituation revisited: an updated and revised description of the behavioral characteristics of habituation. *Neurobiology of learning and memory*, 92(2):135–138, 2009.

[13] Vangelis Sakkalis. Review of advanced techniques for the estimation of brain connectivity measured with eeg/meg.

Computers in biology and medicine, 41(12):1110–1117, 2011.

[14] Ioannis D Schizas, Georgios B Giannakis, and Zhi-Quan Luo. Distributed estimation using reduced-dimensionality sensor observations. *IEEE TSP*, 55(8):4284–4299, 2007.

[15] G. Sudre, D. Pomerleau, M. Palatucci, L. Wehbe, A. Fyshe, R. Salmelin, and T. Mitchell. Tracking neural coding of perceptual and semantic features of concrete nouns. *NeuroImage*, 2012.

[16] Liang Sun, Rinkal Patel, Jun Liu, Kewei Chen, Teresa Wu, Jing Li, Eric Reiman, and Jieping Ye. Mining brain region connectivity for alzheimer's disease study via sparse inverse covariance estimation. In *ACM SIGKDD*, pages 1335–1344. ACM, 2009.

[17] Richard F Thompson and William A Spencer. Habituation: a model phenomenon for the study of neuronal substrates of behavior. *Psychological review*, 73(1):16, 1966.

[18] Dardo Tomasi and Nora D Volkow. Resting functional connectivity of language networks: characterization and reproducibility. *Molecular psychiatry*, 17(8):841–854, 2012.

[19] Pedro A Valdés-Sosa, Jose M Sánchez-Bornot, Agustín Lage-Castellanos, Mayrim Vega-Hernández, Jorge Bosch-Bayard, Lester Melie-García, and Erick Canales-Rodríguez. Estimating brain functional connectivity with sparse multivariate autoregression. *Philosophical Transactions of the Royal Society B: Biological Sciences*, 360(1457):969–981, 2005.

[20] Michel Verhaegen. Identification of the deterministic part of mimo state space models given in innovations form from input-output data. *Automatica*, 30(1):61–74, 1994.

[21] Michel Verhaegen and Vincent Verdult. *Filtering and system identification: a least squares approach*. Cambridge university press, 2007.

[22] Olivier Verscheure, Michail Vlachos, Aris Anagnostopoulos, Pascal Frossard, Eric Bouillet, and Philip S Yu. Finding "who is talking to whom" in voip networks via progressive stream clustering. In *IEEE ICDM*, pages 667–677. IEEE, 2006.

[23] Robert W Williams and Karl Herrup. The control of neuron number. *Annual review of neuroscience*, 11(1):423–453, 1988.

APPENDIX

A. SYSTEM IDENTIFICATION FOR GeBM

Consider again the linear state-space model of GEBM

$$\mathbf{x}(t+1) = \mathbf{A}\mathbf{x}(t) + \mathbf{B}\mathbf{u}(t), \ \ \mathbf{y}(t) = \mathbf{C}\mathbf{x}(t).$$

Assuming $\mathbf{x}(0) = \mathbf{0}$, for simplicity, it is easy to see that

$$\mathbf{x}(t) = \sum_{i=0}^{t-1} \mathbf{A}^{t-1-i}\mathbf{B}\mathbf{u}(i),$$

and therefore $\mathbf{y}(t) = \sum_{i=0}^{t-1} \mathbf{C}\mathbf{A}^{t-1-i}\mathbf{B}\mathbf{u}(i)$, from which we can read out the *impulse response matrix* $\mathbf{H}(t) = \mathbf{C}\mathbf{A}^{t-1}\mathbf{B}$.

As we mentioned in Section 3, matrices $\mathbf{A}, \mathbf{B}, \mathbf{C}$ can be identified up to a similarity transformation. In order to show this, suppose that we have access to the system's inputs $\{\mathbf{u}(t)\}_{t=0}^{T-1}$ and outputs $\{\mathbf{y}(t)\}_{t=1}^{T}$, and we wish to identify the system matrices $(\mathbf{A}, \mathbf{B}, \mathbf{C})$. A first important observation is the following. From $\mathbf{x}(t+1) = \mathbf{A}\mathbf{x}(t) + \mathbf{B}\mathbf{u}(t)$ we obtain

$$\mathbf{M}\mathbf{x}(t+1) = \mathbf{M}\mathbf{A}\mathbf{x}(t) + \mathbf{M}\mathbf{B}\mathbf{u}(t) =$$

$$\mathbf{M}\mathbf{A}\mathbf{M}^{-1}\mathbf{M}\mathbf{x}(t) + \mathbf{M}\mathbf{B}\mathbf{u}(t).$$

Defining $\mathbf{z}(t) := \mathbf{M}\mathbf{x}(t)$, $\tilde{\mathbf{A}} := \mathbf{M}\mathbf{A}\mathbf{M}^{-1}$, and $\tilde{\mathbf{B}} := \mathbf{M}\mathbf{B}$, we obtain

$$\mathbf{z}(t+1) = \tilde{\mathbf{A}}\mathbf{z}(t) + \tilde{\mathbf{B}}\mathbf{u}(t),$$

and with $\tilde{\mathbf{C}} := \mathbf{C}\mathbf{M}^{-1}$, we also have

$$\mathbf{y}(t) = \mathbf{C}\mathbf{x}(t) = \mathbf{C}\mathbf{M}^{-1}\mathbf{M}\mathbf{x}(t) = \tilde{\mathbf{C}}\mathbf{z}(t).$$

It follows that $(\mathbf{A}, \mathbf{B}, \mathbf{C})$ and $(\tilde{\mathbf{A}}, \tilde{\mathbf{B}}, \tilde{\mathbf{C}}) = (\mathbf{M}\mathbf{A}\mathbf{M}^{-1}, \mathbf{M}\mathbf{B}, \mathbf{C}\mathbf{M}^{-1})$ are indistinguishable from input-output data alone. Thus, the sought parameters can only be (possibly) identified up to a basis (similarity) transformation, in the absence of any other prior or side information.

Under what conditions can $(\mathbf{A}, \mathbf{B}, \mathbf{C})$ be identified up to such similarity transformation? It has been shown by Kalman that if the so-called *controlability* matrix

$$\mathcal{C} := \left[\mathbf{B}, \mathbf{A}\mathbf{B}, \mathbf{A}^2\mathbf{B}, \cdots, \mathbf{A}^{n-1}\mathbf{B}\right]$$

is full row rank n, and the *observability matrix*

$$\mathcal{O} := \left[\mathbf{C} \ \ \mathbf{C}\mathbf{A} \ \ \mathbf{C}\mathbf{A}^2 \ \ \cdots \ \ \mathbf{C}\mathbf{A}^{n-1}\right]^T$$

is full column rank n, then it is possible to identify $(\mathbf{A}, \mathbf{B}, \mathbf{C})$ up to such similarity transformation from (sufficiently 'diverse') input-output data, and the impulse response in particular. This can be accomplished by forming a block Hankel matrix out of the impulse response, as follows,

$$\begin{bmatrix} \mathbf{H}(1) & \mathbf{H}(2) & \mathbf{H}(3) & \cdots & \mathbf{H}(n) \\ \mathbf{H}(2) & \mathbf{H}(3) & \cdots & & \\ \vdots & & & & \\ \mathbf{H}(n) & & & & \mathbf{H}(2n+1) \end{bmatrix} =$$

$$\begin{bmatrix} \mathbf{C}\mathbf{B} & \mathbf{C}\mathbf{A}\mathbf{B} & \mathbf{C}\mathbf{A}^2\mathbf{B} & \cdots & \mathbf{C}\mathbf{A}^{n-1}\mathbf{B} \\ \mathbf{C}\mathbf{A}\mathbf{B} & \mathbf{C}\mathbf{A}^2\mathbf{B} & \cdots & & \\ \vdots & & & & \\ \mathbf{C}\mathbf{A}^{n-1}\mathbf{B} & & & & \mathbf{C}\mathbf{A}^{2n-1}\mathbf{B} \end{bmatrix}.$$

This matrix can be factored into $\mathcal{O}\mathbf{M}\mathbf{M}^{-1}\mathcal{C}$, i.e., the 'true' $\mathcal{O}$ and $\mathcal{C}$ up to similarity transformation, using the singular value decomposition of the above Hankel matrix. It is then easy to recover $\tilde{\mathbf{A}}, \tilde{\mathbf{B}}, \tilde{\mathbf{C}}$ from $\mathcal{O}\mathbf{M}$ and $\mathbf{M}^{-1}\mathcal{C}$. This is the core of the Kalman-Ho algorithm for Hankel subspace-based identification [10].

This procedure enables us to identify $\tilde{\mathbf{A}}, \tilde{\mathbf{B}}, \tilde{\mathbf{C}}$, but, in our context, we are ultimately also interested in the true latent $(\mathbf{A}, \mathbf{B}, \mathbf{C})$.

PROPOSITION 1. *We can always, without loss of generality, transform $\tilde{\mathbf{A}}$ to maximal sparsity while keeping $\tilde{\mathbf{B}}$ and $\tilde{\mathbf{C}}$ dense - that is, sparsity of $\mathbf{A}$ alone does not help in terms of identification.*

PROOF. Suppose that we are interested in estimating a sparse $\mathbf{A}$, while preserving the eigenvalues of of $\tilde{\mathbf{A}}$. We therefore seek a similarity transformation (a matrix $\mathbf{M}$) that will render $\mathbf{A} = \mathbf{M}\tilde{\mathbf{A}}\mathbf{M}^{-1}$ as sparse as possible. Towards this end, assume that $\tilde{\mathbf{A}}$ has a full set of linearly independent eigenvectors, collected in matrix $\mathbf{E}$, and let Λ be the corresponding diagonal matrix of eigenvalues. Then, clearly, $\tilde{\mathbf{A}}\mathbf{E} = \mathbf{E}\Lambda$, and therefore $\mathbf{E}^{-1}\tilde{\mathbf{A}}\mathbf{E} = \Lambda$ - a diagonal matrix. Hence choosing $\mathbf{M} = \mathbf{E}^{-1}$ we make $\mathbf{A} = \mathbf{M}\tilde{\mathbf{A}}\mathbf{M}^{-1}$ maximally sparse. Note that $\mathbf{A}$ must have the same rank as $\tilde{\mathbf{A}}$, and if it has less nonzero elements it will also have lower rank. Finally, it is easy to see that if we apply this similarity transformation, the eigenvalues of $\tilde{\mathbf{A}}$ do not change. $\square$

FUNNEL: Automatic Mining of Spatially Coevolving Epidemics

Yasuko Matsubara[†], Yasushi Sakurai[†], Willem G. van Panhuis[§], Christos Faloutsos[‡]
[†] Dept. of Computer Science and Electrical Engineering, Kumamoto University,
[§] Dept. of Epidemiology, University of Pittsburgh, [‡] Dept. of Computer Science, Carnegie Mellon University
{yasuko,yasushi}@cs.kumamoto-u.ac.jp, wav10@pitt.edu, christos@cs.cmu.edu

ABSTRACT

Given a large collection of epidemiological data consisting of the count of d contagious diseases for l locations of duration n, how can we find patterns, rules and outliers? For example, the Project Tycho provides open access to the count infections for U.S. states from 1888 to 2013, for 56 contagious diseases (e.g., measles, influenza), which include missing values, possible recording errors, sudden spikes (or dives) of infections, etc. So how can we find a combined model, for all these diseases, locations, and time-ticks?

In this paper, we present FUNNEL, a unifying analytical model for large scale epidemiological data, as well as a novel fitting algorithm, FUNNELFIT, which solves the above problem. Our method has the following properties: (a) *Sense-making*: it detects important patterns of epidemics, such as periodicities, the appearance of vaccines, external shock events, and more; (b) *Parameter-free*: our modeling framework frees the user from providing parameter values; (c) *Scalable*: FUNNELFIT is carefully designed to be linear on the input size; (d) *General*: our model is general and practical, which can be applied to various types of epidemics, including computer-virus propagation, as well as human diseases.

Extensive experiments on real data demonstrate that FUNNELFIT does indeed discover important properties of epidemics: (P1) disease seasonality, e.g., influenza spikes in January, Lyme disease spikes in July and the absence of yearly periodicity for gonorrhea; (P2) disease reduction effect, e.g., the appearance of vaccines; (P3) local/state-level sensitivity, e.g., many measles cases in NY; (P4) external shock events, e.g., historical flu pandemics; (P5) detect incongruous values, i.e., data reporting errors.

Categories and Subject Descriptors: H.2.8 [**Database management**]: Database applications–*Data mining*

Keywords: Epidemics; Time-series; Automatic mining

1. INTRODUCTION

Given a huge collection of co-evolving epidemic time-series, such as measles and influenza, how can we find typical patterns or anomalies, and statistically summarize all the epidemic sequences? In this paper, we present a unifying model, namely FUNNEL, which provides a good description of large collections of epidemiological data. [1] Intuitively, the problem we wish to solve is as follows:

INFORMAL PROBLEM 1. *Given a large collection of epidemiological data, which consists of d diseases in l locations of duration n, with missing values and recording errors, we want to*

- *find basic patterns of diseases (e.g., seasonality)*
- *find extra patterns (e.g., outbreaks, sudden drops)*
- *detect anomalies (i.e., possible errors)*

Uncovering the mechanisms and patterns of contagious diseases is an important and challenging task for public health scientists and policy makers. In this paper, we study a publicly available resource of epidemiological data: *Tycho* [32], which contains the count of infections of 56 diseases in the U.S, covering over 125 years on a weekly basis. [2]

Preview of our results. Figure 1 (a) shows the number of measles cases in the United States from 1928 to 1982, as gray circles, and our fitted model, as a solid red line. The sequence has a clear yearly periodicity, but also characteristic bi- and triennial patterns resulting in alternating large (1941, 1958) and small (1940, 1947) epidemic years [22], which is known as "skip" phenomena [29]. It should also be noted that the number of cases suddenly dropped in 1965. This was achieved because of the vaccination program that started in 1963. Figure 1 (b) shows the potential population of susceptibles for measles for each state in the U.S. The top three states in this respect are, NY, PA, and CA.

Figure 1 (c) shows a scatter plot of the seasonality strength vs. the peak season for each disease. We determined four categories of diseases in terms of (1) the strength of annual periodicity (radius) and (2) their phase difference, i.e., the month in which they peak (angle). For example, we found previously characterized epidemic peaks for influenza in January-February and for respiratory childhood diseases (e.g., measles) in the spring [27], and for tick-borne diseases (e.g., Lyme disease) peaks in the summer [28]; There is no periodicity for sexually transmitted diseases, (e.g., gonorrhea).

We can capture these important patterns in epidemic data with our proposed model, simply by changing its parameters. More importantly, our method is *fully-automatic*, that is, it provides a good description of a large collection of epidemiological data, without user intervention, prior training, or parameter tuning.

Contrast with competitors. Table 1 illustrates the relative advantages of our method. Only our approach has checks against all entries, while,

- The SI model (and SIR, SIRS, etc.) can compress the data into a fixed number of parameters, and capture the dynamics of epidemiological data, however, it cannot describe periodic patterns, and is incapable of forecasting.

KDD'14, August 24–27, 2014, New York, NY, USA.
Copyright 2014 ACM 978-1-4503-2956-9/14/08 ...$15.00.
http://dx.doi.org/10.1145/2623330.2623624.

[1] Available at http://www.cs.kumamoto-u.ac.jp/~yasuko/software.html

[2] Project Tycho at University of Pittsburgh: http://www.tycho.pitt.edu/

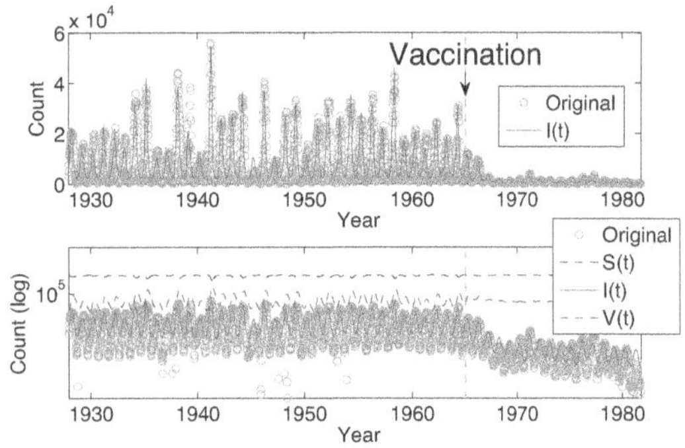

(a) Fitting result of FUNNELFIT (measles)

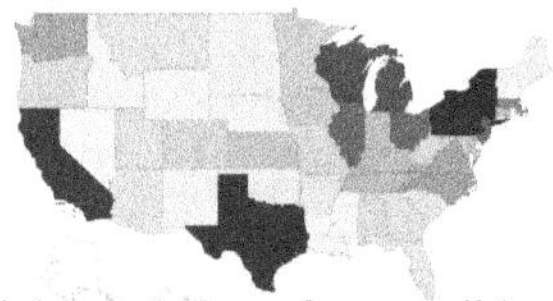

(b) Potential population of susceptibles (measles)

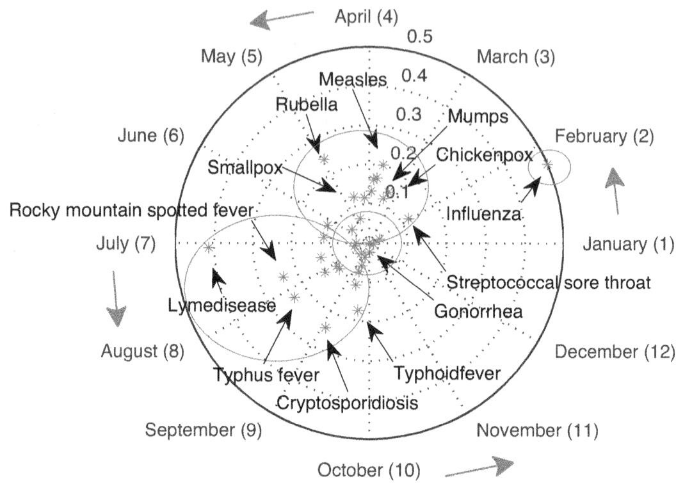

(c) Seasonality strength (radius) vs. peak season (angle)

Figure 1: Modeling power of FUNNELFIT: (a) the original number of measles cases (gray dots), and our model (red lines). It captures the yearly cycle, external spikes, and vaccination starting in 1963, as well as (b) the local sensitivity (e.g., many patients in NY, PA, CA, TX); (c) the scatter plot of the seasonality strength vs. the peak season - (angle): the peak month for each disease and (radius): the strength of the fluctuation, e.g., influenza peaks every winter, measles in the spring, and no periodicity for gonorrhea.

Table 1: Capabilities of approaches. Only our approach meets all specifications.

	SIRS	AR/*PLiF*	PARAFAC	FUNNELFIT
Compression	√	√	√	√
Domain knowledge	√			√
Missing values	√			√
Periodicity		√		√
Forecasting		√		√
Parameter free				√

- The auto regression (AR) model and *PLiF* [15] have the ability to compress and forecast sequences, but they are fundamentally unsuitable for epidemic data, and cannot capture the non-linear patterns of virus propagation.
- Our epidemic data can be turned into a tensor. PARAFAC is capable of compression, but it cannot handle missing values, periodicity, or forecasting.

Most importantly, none of above are parameter-free methods.

Contributions. Our method has the following desirable properties:

1. **Sense-making**: thanks to our modeling framework, our method can provide an intuitive explanation for epidemics, such as the seasonality of diseases, vaccination, and external shocks. It matches the behavior of various types of contagious diseases, such as measles, influenza, and smallpox.
2. **Automatic**: it is fully automatic, requiring no human intervention. Our algorithm is theoretically founded on the idea of minimizing the cost of the resulting modeling.
3. **Scalable**: it scales linearly with the input size.
4. **Generality**: it includes earlier patterns and models as special cases (e.g., SIRS), and it can be applied to various types of epidemic data including computer virus infections.

Outline. The rest of the paper is organized in the conventional way: Next we describe related work, followed by our proposed model and algorithms, experiments, discussion and conclusions.

2. RELATED WORK

We provide a survey of the related literature, which falls broadly into two categories: (1) epidemiology, and (2) pattern discovery in time series.

Epidemiology. The canonical textbook for epidemiological models including SI/SIR is Anderson and May [2]. Grenfell et al. [9] studied the recurrent travelling waves for measles, while the work in [8] explained the complex dynamical transitions in epidemics. Stone et al. [29] studied the seasonal dynamics of recurrent epidemics including measles, and identified a new threshold for predicting the occurrence of either a future epidemic, or a 'skip' (i.e., a year in which an epidemic fails to initiate). Van Panhuis et al. [32] digitized the entire history of weekly Nationally Notifiable Disease Surveillance Reports for the U.S. from 1888 to 2013.

Pattern discovery in time series. In recent years, there has been an explosion of interest in mining time series [4, 6, 21, 16]. Traditional approaches applied to data mining include auto-regression (AR), linear dynamical systems (LDS), Kalman filters (KF) and their variants [10, 15, 31]. Similarity search and pattern discovery in time sequences have also attracted huge interest [33, 13, 30, 26, 7]. Regarding large-scale time-series mining, TriMine [18] is a scalable method for forecasting co-evolving multiple (thousands of) sequences, while, [17] developed a fully-automatic mining algorithm for co-evolving time sequences. Rakthanmanon et al. [25] proposed a similarity search algorithm for "trillions of time series" under the DTW distance. Recently, analyses of epidemics, social media, propagation and the cascades they create have attracted much interest [24, 12, 14, 23, 19].

However, none of these methods specifically focused on automatic mining of non-linear dynamics in coevolving epidemics.

3. PROPOSED MODEL

In this section we present our proposed model.

3.1 Design philosophy of FUNNEL

Data description. The Project Tycho [32] covers more than a century of weekly surveillance reports of nationally notifiable diseases (56 diseases in total) for all 50 states in the U.S, from 1888 to the present, with 87,950,807 reported individual cases for diseases.

This dataset consists of tuples of the form: *(disease, location, timestamp)*. We then have a collection of entries with d unique diseases, and l states, with duration n (on a weekly basis). We can

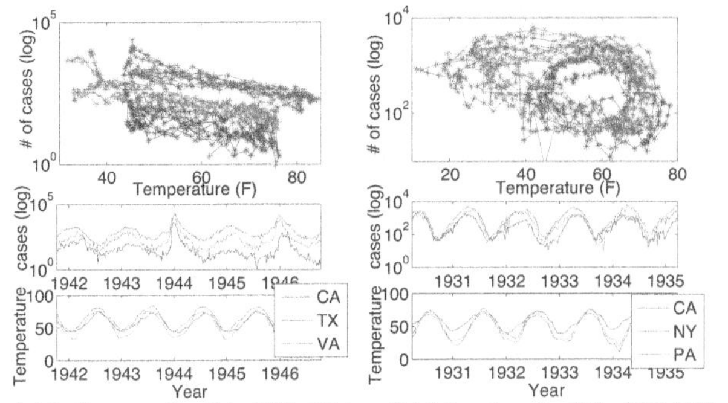

(a) Influenza (in CA, TX, VA)   (b) Measles (in CA, NY, PA)

Figure 2: The air temperature vs. # of cases: (a) influenza is completely anti-correlated with the air temperature (i.e., peaking in the winter), while, (b) measles also has strong periodicity, but it peaks in the spring (i.e., with a phase shift).

treat this set of $d \times l$ epidemic sequences as a 3rd-order tensor, i.e., $\mathcal{X} \in \mathbb{N}^{d \times l \times n}$, where the element $x_{ij}(t)$ of $\mathcal{X}$ shows the total number of entries of the i-th disease in the j-th state at time-tick t.

For example, ('measles', 'PA', 'April 1-7, 1931'; 4740), means that the number of cases due to 'measles' in 'PA' on 'April 1-7 in 1931' is '4740'.

We refer to each sequence of the i-th disease in the j-th state: $\boldsymbol{x}_{ij} = \{x_{ij}(t)\}_{t=1}^{n}$, as a "local/state"-level epidemic sequence. Similarly, we can turn these local sequences into "global/country"-level epidemics: $\bar{\boldsymbol{x}}_i = \{\bar{x}_i(t)\}_{t=1}^{n}$, where $\bar{x}_i(t)$ shows the total count of the i-th disease at time-tick t, i.e., $\bar{x}_i(t) = \sum_{j=1}^{l} x_{ij}(t)$.

Preliminary observations. Here, we provide the reader with several important observations. Figure 2 shows the scatter plots (top) and sequence plots (bottom) of the original local-level sequences of influenza and measles counts in three states, versus the average air temperature for five years. [3] In Figure 2 (a), influenza cases are strongly anti-correlated with the air temperature, corresponding to influenza epidemics in colder seasons. On the other hand, for measles (Figure 2 (b)), the scatter plot exhibits characteristic loop shapes, which indicates that there is a phase shift of measles vs. temperature - actually, measles peaks in the spring. As shown in Figure 1 (c), there are several groups of infectious diseases with specific seasonal patterns, including children's diseases (e.g., measles, mumps) in the spring, and tick-borne diseases (e.g., Lyme disease) in the summer. Consequently we have:

OBSERVATION 1 (DISEASE SEASONALITY). *Many diseases have yearly cycles with different phases, that is, they are correlated with air temperature and the seasons.*

The next observation refers to the abrupt decline of several diseases. Luckily, many diseases have been eradicated or significantly reduced over the last century, through various factors including vaccination, sanitation and antibiotics. For example, in Figure 1 (a), the number of measles cases has been decreasing since the vaccination program was introduced in 1963. We will collectively refer to such abrupt declines as *disease reduction* effects.

OBSERVATION 2 (DISEASE REDUCTION EFFECT). *Many infectious diseases have been reduced or eliminated through vaccination programs, antibiotics, sanitation, etc.*

Next, let us look at the topic from a local point of view. In Figure 2, three local sequences are correlated with each other, but with different fractions of patients, which correspond to the number of susceptible people in each state. For example, measles mainly affects children, and so, the more children there are, the more cases of measles there will be (see, NY, PA, CA, TX, in Figure 1 (b)).

[3] National climate data center: http://www.ncdc.noaa.gov/cag/

Table 2: Symbols and definitions

Symbol	Definition
d	Number of diseases
l	Number of states (i.e., locations)
n	Duration of sequences
$\mathcal{X}$	3rd-order tensor ($\mathcal{X} \in \mathbb{N}^{d \times l \times n}$)
$\boldsymbol{x}_{ij}$	Local-level epidemic sequence of disease i in state j
$\bar{\boldsymbol{x}}_i$	Global-level epidemic sequence of disease i
$S_{ij}(t)$	Count of susceptibles of disease i in state j at time t
$I_{ij}(t)$	Count of infectives of disease i in state j at time t
$V_{ij}(t)$	Count of vigilants of disease i in state j at time t
$\mathbf{B}$	Base matrix ($d \times 6$) i.e., $\mathbf{B} = \{\boldsymbol{b}_1, \dots, \boldsymbol{b}_d\}$
$\mathbf{R}$	Disease reduction matrix ($d \times 2$) i.e., $\mathbf{R} = \{\boldsymbol{r}_1, \dots, \boldsymbol{r}_d\}$
$\mathbf{N}$	Geo-disease matrix ($d \times l$) i.e., $\mathbf{N} = \{N_{ij}\}_{i,j=1}^{d,l}$
$\mathcal{E}$	External shock tensor i.e., $\mathcal{E} = \{\mathbf{E}^{(\mathbf{D})}, \mathbf{E}^{(\mathbf{T})}, \mathbf{E}^{(\mathbf{S})}\}$
$\mathcal{M}$	Mistake tensor i.e., $\mathcal{M} = \{m_{ij}(t)\}_{i,j,t=1}^{d,l,n}$
$\mathcal{F}$	Complete set of FUNNEL i.e., $\mathcal{F} = \{\mathbf{B}, \mathbf{R}, \mathbf{N}, \mathcal{E}, \mathcal{M}\}$

OBSERVATION 3 (AREA SPECIFICITY AND SENSITIVITY). *For each disease, neighbors are correlated with different sensitivity.*

The last two observations are the extra properties of epidemics. Figure 1 (a) shows large outbreaks of measles in 1941 and 1958, while Figure 2 (a) shows two large flu pandemics in 1944 and 1946.

OBSERVATION 4 (EXTERNAL SHOCK EVENTS). *There are some extreme spikes, representing major events such as historical flu pandemics.*

Basically, real-world datasets are subject to quality constraints such as typing errors and incorrect reports (we refer to them as "mistakes").

OBSERVATION 5 (MISTAKES). *There are some implausible spikes, which are completely independent of the dynamics of epidemic patterns.*

Summary. In this paper, we propose a new model, namely, FUNNEL, which tries to incorporate all the above important properties that we observed in the real epidemic data. Consequently, we would like to capture the following properties:

- **(P1)**: yearly periodicity
- **(P2)**: disease reduction effects
- **(P3)**: area specificity and sensitivity
- **(P4)**: external shock events
- **(P5)**: mistakes, incorrect values

For simplicity, let's focus on a simple step first, where (a) we assume that we are given a single epidemic sequence, say, the number of measles cases in NY. We then (b) extend our model to multiple co-evolving epidemics, that is, to capture the individual patterns of d diseases in l states.

3.2 FUNNEL - with a single epidemic

We begin with the simplest case, where we assume that we are given a single epidemic sequence.

3.2.1 *Base model* - FUNNEL-BASE

The model we propose has nodes (=people) of three classes:

- Susceptible: nodes in this class can get infected by any neighboring node who is infectious.
- Infected: nodes who have been infected and are capable of transmitting the infection to those in the susceptible class.
- Vigilant (i.e., recovered/immune): nodes in this class cannot get infected nor can they cause infections.

Figure 3 (a) shows a diagram of our base model, where, $\beta(t)$ represents the rate of effective contacts between infected and susceptible individuals; δ is the rate at which infected individuals recovered; γ is the immunization loss probability for a recovered or

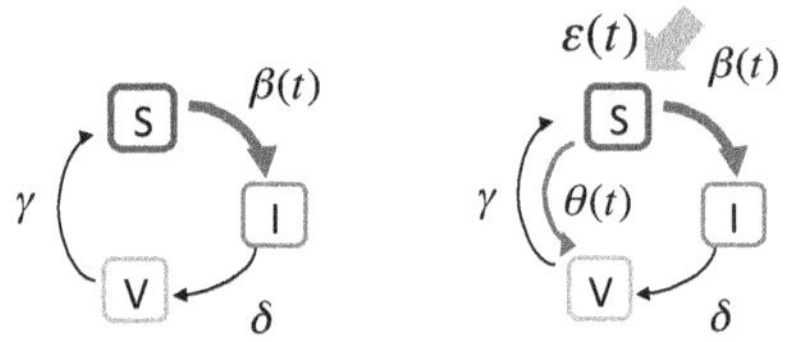

(a) FUNNEL-BASE (b) FUNNEL-RE

Figure 3: FUNNEL diagrams: there are three classes - susceptible (i.e., healthy, but can get infected), infected (i.e., capable of transmission), vigilant (i.e., healthy, and cannot get infected).

vigilant individual. [4] More importantly, to handle the first property of epidemics: **(P1)**, we assume that the infection rate $\beta(t)$ is a periodic function of time t. We refer to it as FUNNEL-BASE.

MODEL 1 (FUNNEL-BASE). *Let $S(t)$, $I(t)$, $V(t)$ be the number of susceptible, infected, vigilant people at time-tick t. Our base model is governed by the following equations:*

$$\begin{aligned} S(t+1) &= S(t) - \beta(t)S(t)I(t) + \gamma V(t) \\ I(t+1) &= I(t) + \beta(t)S(t)I(t) - \delta I(t) \\ V(t+1) &= V(t) + \delta I(t) - \gamma V(t) \end{aligned} \quad (1)$$

where $\beta(t) = \beta_0 \cdot \left(1 + P_a \cdot cos\left(\frac{2\pi}{P_p}(t + P_s)\right)\right)$, $P_p = 52$, [5] *and, we have the invariant* $N = S(t) + I(t) + V(t)$, *with initial conditions* $S(1) = N - 1$, $I(1) = 1$, $V(1) = 0$.

Consequently, FUNNEL-BASE consists of a set of the following parameters: $\boldsymbol{b} = \{N, \beta_0, \delta, \gamma, P_a, P_s\}$, specifically,

- N: Potential population of the disease. N is composed of susceptible, infected and vigilant individuals.
- β_0: Rate of effective contacts between infected and susceptible individuals averaged over the year.
- δ: Healing rate of the disease.
- γ: Forgetting rate of the diseases.
- P_a: Amplitude of the fluctuation, specifically, it gives the relative value of the peak/off-season.
- P_s: Phase shift of the seasonal cycle.

3.2.2 *With disease reduction* - FUNNEL-R

With respect to the second property: **(P2)**, we also introduce an essential concept, namely, the "disease reduction" effect.

MODEL 2 (FUNNEL-R). *We add a disease reduction rate: $\theta(t)$, to capture the effect of the disease reduction program, that is,*

$$\begin{aligned} S(t+1) &= S(t) - \beta(t)S(t)I(t) + \gamma V(t) - \theta(t)S(t) \\ I(t+1) &= I(t) + \beta(t)S(t)I(t) - \delta I(t) \\ V(t+1) &= V(t) + \delta I(t) - \gamma V(t) + \theta(t)S(t) \end{aligned} \quad (2)$$

where, the disease reduction program started at time t_θ and $\theta(t)$ is defined as: $\theta(t) = \begin{cases} 0 & (t < t_\theta) \\ \theta_0 & (t \geq t_\theta) \end{cases}$

The model is identical to FUNNEL-BASE, with the addition of the disease reduction factor, $\theta(t)$, which corresponds to the direct immunization probability when susceptible (see Figure 3 (b)). Note that this effect is due to vaccination, antibiotics and any other anti-disease factors. Hereafter, we simply say the "disease reduction effect", unless otherwise specified.

In addition to the base parameters $\boldsymbol{b}$, FUNNEL-R requires a set of two parameters, $\boldsymbol{r} = \{t_\theta, \theta_0\}$, where,

- t_θ: Starting time of the disease reduction effect.
- θ_0: Diffusion rate of the disease reduction effect.

[4] This factor also incorporates the birth and mortality rate.

[5] We have 52 time-ticks (weeks) in one year.

3.2.3 *With external shocks* - FUNNEL-RE

Next, with respect to the property: **(P4)**, we assume that there are external shock events, such as flu pandemics. So how do we go about capturing such unexpected patterns? Assume that there is a swine flu pandemic. In this situation, many more people in the susceptible class would become infected than in previous years.

An elementary concept we need to introduce is the *temporal susceptible rate*: $\epsilon(t)$. Figure 3 (b) describes how this is done. The idea is that the number of susceptibles $S(t)$ is the count of victims available for infection, and if there is an external shock event at time-tick t, the virus attacks are much stronger than usual, and, each victim-attack pair would lead to a new victim, and will eventually cause a major pandemic.

MODEL 3 (FUNNEL-RE). *Our full model can be described as the following equations:*

$$\boxed{\begin{aligned} S(t+1) &= S(t) - \beta(t)\epsilon(t)S(t)I(t) + \gamma V(t) - \theta(t)S(t) \\ I(t+1) &= I(t) + \beta(t)\epsilon(t)S(t)I(t) - \delta I(t) \\ V(t+1) &= V(t) + \delta I(t) - \gamma V(t) + \theta(t)S(t) \end{aligned} \quad (3)}$$

In addition, we introduce the temporal susceptible rate, $\epsilon(t)$, which is defined as follows:

$$\epsilon(t) = 1 + \sum_{i=1}^{k} f(t; \boldsymbol{e}_i^{(T)}), \; f(t; \boldsymbol{e}^{(T)}) = \begin{cases} \epsilon_0 & (t_\mu - t_\sigma < t < t_\mu + t_\sigma) \\ 0 & (else) \end{cases}$$

where, k is the number of shocks, and if $k = 0$, then $\epsilon(t) = 1$.
Here, each external shock consists of $\boldsymbol{e}^{(T)} = \{t_\mu, t_\sigma, \epsilon_0\}$, i.e.,

- t_μ: Central time point of the external shock event.
- t_σ: Duration of the event.
- ϵ_0: Strength of the external shock effect.

3.3 FUNNEL - with multi-evolving epidemics

So far we have seen how FUNNEL captures the dynamics of a single epidemic sequence. The next question is, "how can we apply FUNNEL to multiple co-evolving epidemics in $\mathcal{X}$, and capture the individual behavior of d diseases in l states?"

We want to estimate the parameter set of FUNNEL, for each individual epidemic sequence in $\mathcal{X}$. The straightforward solution would be that we consider a set of $(d \times l)$ sequences of length n generated from $\mathcal{X}$: $\{\boldsymbol{x}_{ij}\}_{i,j=1}^{d,l}$, (i.e, "local-level" epidemic sequences), and estimate parameter set: $\{\boldsymbol{b}, \boldsymbol{r}, \boldsymbol{e}^{(T)}\}$ for each sequence. However, some of the *(disease, state)* pairs have very sparse sequences (e.g., Lyme disease in Alaska), which derails the fitting result. Also, we are interested in capturing global/country-level patterns, as well as local/state-level trends. So how can we deal with this issue? We thus propose "sharing" the global-level parameters for all l states, to achieve much better modeling.

FUNNEL - full model parameter set. Our goal is to extract the main trends and external patterns of co-evolving epidemics $\mathcal{X} \in \mathbb{N}^{d \times l \times n}$, and make a good representation of $\mathcal{X}$. Figure 4 shows our modeling framework. Given epidemic data $\mathcal{X}$, we try to find important patterns with respect to the following five aspects, **(P1)** **B**: base properties of diseases, **(P2)** **R**: disease reduction effects, **(P3)** **N**: locations vs. diseases, **(P4)** $\mathcal{E}$: external shock events, and **(P5)** $\mathcal{M}$: mistake values. The first two are global/country-level parameter sets, and the third is a local/state-level parameter set, and the last two are used for describing extra trends in $\mathcal{X}$.

DEFINITION 1 (COMPLETE SET OF FUNNEL). *Let $\mathcal{F}$ be a complete set of parameters (namely, $\mathcal{F} = \{\mathbf{B}, \mathbf{R}, \mathbf{N}, \mathcal{E}, \mathcal{M}\}$) that describe the global/local/extra patterns of epidemics in $\mathcal{X}$.*

Next, we will see each property in detail.

(P1), (P2) Global/country view. Basically, we assume that the following parameters are the same for all l states.

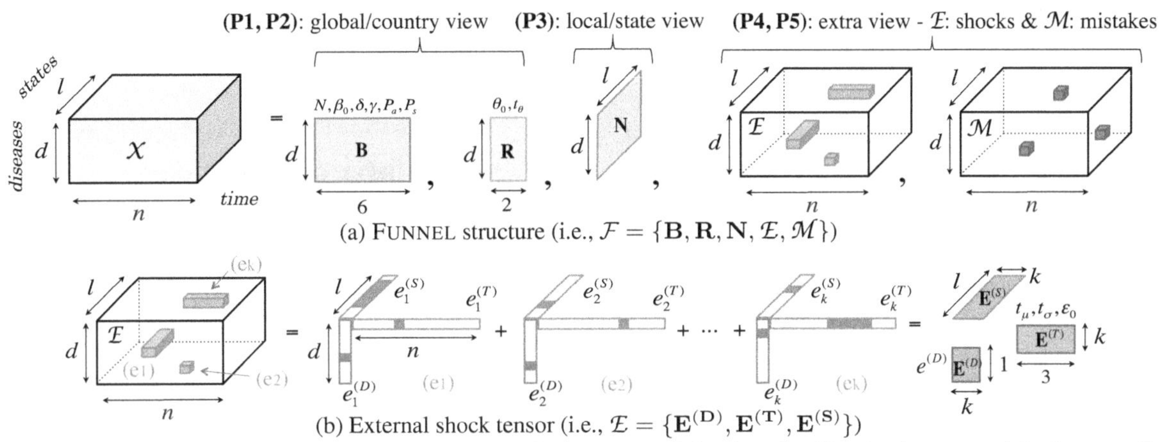

(a) FUNNEL structure (i.e., $\mathcal{F} = \{\mathbf{B}, \mathbf{R}, \mathbf{N}, \mathcal{E}, \mathcal{M}\}$)

(b) External shock tensor (i.e., $\mathcal{E} = \{\mathbf{E^{(D)}}, \mathbf{E^{(T)}}, \mathbf{E^{(S)}}\}$)

Figure 4: Illustration of FUNNEL structure: (a) we extract the important behavior of epidemics from an original tensor $\mathcal{X}$, (i.e., the base matrix B, disease reduction matrix R, geo-disease matrix N, external shock tensor $\mathcal{E}$, and mistake tensor $\mathcal{M}$); Also, (b) the external shock tensor $\mathcal{E}$ can be described as a set of matrices i.e., $\{\mathbf{E^{(D)}}, \mathbf{E^{(T)}}, \mathbf{E^{(S)}}\}$, for *disease, state, time*.

DEFINITION 2 (BASE MATRIX $\mathbf{B}$ ($d \times 6$)). *Let* $\mathbf{B}$ *be a set of base parameters of d diseases, i.e.,* $\mathbf{B} = \{\boldsymbol{b}_1, \ldots, \boldsymbol{b}_d\}$ *where* $\boldsymbol{b}_i$ *is the parameter set of the i-th disease.*

For example, the infection/healing rate of measles should be the same for NY and FL. Similarly, once the measles vaccine has been introduced, (i.e., the disease reduction effect), it could be immediately spread all over the country, that is, the starting time of the disease reduction effect would be the same for all locations.

DEFINITION 3 (DISEASE REDUCTION MATRIX $\mathbf{R}$ ($d \times 2$)). *Let* $\mathbf{R}$ *be a parameter set of the reduction of d diseases, i.e.,* $\mathbf{R} = \{\boldsymbol{r}_1, \ldots, \boldsymbol{r}_d\}$ *where* $\boldsymbol{r}_i$ *is the parameter set of the i-th disease.*

(P3) Local/state view. We also want to analyze and explain local-specific patterns and trends in $\mathcal{X}$. So, what is the difference between measles *in NY* and *in FL*? Our answer is: they are exactly the same, except for the "local sensitivity" of the disease. The idea is that we share the parameters of the global-level matrices for all l states with but one exception, local sensitivity, N_{ij}, which describes the potential population of the disease i in the j-th state. Specifically, we set the invariant, $N_{ij} = S_{ij}(t) + I_{ij}(t) + V_{ij}(t)$ in Model 3. This parameter corresponds to the fraction of individuals who are likely to be infected by the disease. For example, NY has more measles patients than FL, because it mainly affects children (i.e., there were more children in NY than FL, in the last century).

DEFINITION 4 (GEO-DISEASE MATRIX $\mathbf{N}$ ($d \times l$)). *Let* $\mathbf{N}$ *be a parameter set of the potential population of d diseases and l states, i.e.,* $\mathbf{N} = \{N_{ij}\}_{i,j=1}^{d,l}$, *where* N_{ij} *is the potential population of susceptibles of the i-th disease in the j-th state.*

(P4) Extra view - external shocks. Consider that in 1946 a serious flu pandemic spread throughout the country. We want to describe this external shock event in terms of three aspects, *(disease, state, time)*, e.g., (e1) "influenza, country-wide, 1946". Similarly, there was a community-wide outbreak of cryptosporidiosis in Utah, in 2007. i.e., (e2) "cryptosporidiosis, Utah, 2007". To describe these external shock events, we create a new parameter set, namely external shock tensor $\mathcal{E}$, which consists of a set of k external shock events, as described in Figure 4 (b).

The external shock tensor $\mathcal{E}$ can be also decomposed into three-aspect matrices, $\{\mathbf{E^{(D)}}, \mathbf{E^{(S)}}, \mathbf{E^{(T)}}\}$, each of which shows the patterns in terms of *disease, state, time*. A single external shock event can be described as triplet vectors $\{\boldsymbol{e}^{(D)}, \boldsymbol{e}^{(S)}, \boldsymbol{e}^{(T)}\}$, where,

- The shock (disease) vector $\boldsymbol{e}^{(D)}$ shows the assignment of the external shock to the disease ID (i.e., $1 \leq \boldsymbol{e}^{(D)} \leq d$).

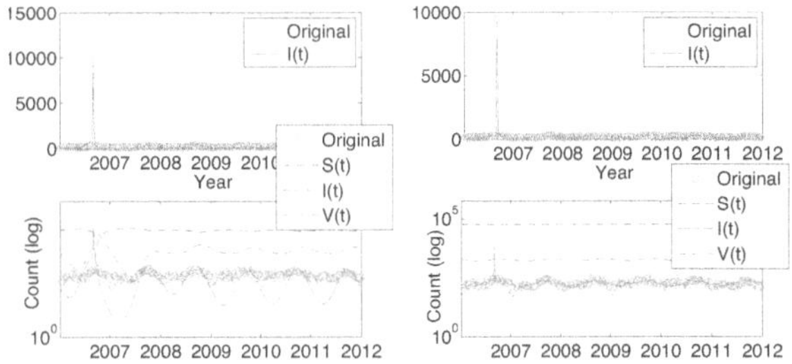

(a) External shock fitting (b) Mistake fitting

Figure 5: External shock vs. mistake for giardiasis in 2007: (a) the model (i.e., red line) is greatly influenced by the large distance of the outlier from the original sequence, while (b) it filters out the mistake point, and fits the sequence very well.

- The shock (state) vector $\boldsymbol{e}^{(S)}$ describes the participation strength of each state for each external shock event.
- The shock (time) vector $\boldsymbol{e}^{(T)}$ shows the temporal pattern of the external shock event.

Specifically, $\boldsymbol{e}^{(T)}$ is the global-level parameters, as described in subsubsection 3.2.3, and $\boldsymbol{e}^{(S)}$ is the local-level parameters, i.e., $\boldsymbol{e}^{(S)} = \{e_j^{(S)}\}_{j=1}^{l}$, where, we change ϵ_0 in Model 3 to describe the strength of the external shock for l individual locations. That is, the strength of the shock effect in the j-th state is, $\epsilon_0 \cdot e_j^{(S)}$. Consequently, we have the following:

DEFINITION 5 (EXTERNAL SHOCK TENSOR $\mathcal{E}$). *Let* $\mathcal{E}$ *be a 3rd-order tensor of k external shock events, i.e.,* $\mathcal{E} = \{\mathbf{E^{(D)}}, \mathbf{E^{(S)}}, \mathbf{E^{(T)}}\}$, *where triplet matrices show the parameters in terms of three aspects, namely, "disease", "state", and "time".*

(P5) Extra view - Mistakes. Basically, real datasets contain many errors such as incorrect reports. FUNNEL should detect and filter them out as outliers. We thus introduce an additional concept.

DEFINITION 6 (MISTAKE TENSOR $\mathcal{M}$). *Let* $\mathcal{M}$ *be a 3rd-order tensor of mistake data points, where, the element* $m_{ij}(t)$ *of* $\mathcal{M}$ *shows the entry of the i-th disease in the j-th state at time-tick t.*

Note that $\mathcal{M}$ is very sparse, and very often $m_{ij}(t) = 0$.

Figure 5 compares the fitting results of the external shock vs. mistake for the giardiasis cases, which contains an incongruous point in 2006 (approximately, 10,000). In this case, the point should be treated as (b) a mistake value, instead of (a) an external shock event; in figure (a), the model (red line) is strongly influenced by the extreme point, while in (b), it successfully captures the real patterns of the original sequence.

4. OPTIMIZATION ALGORITHM

In this section, we describe our fitting algorithm, FUNNELFIT. Our goal is to extract the important patterns of epidemics from $\mathcal{X}$. More specifically, the problem that we want to solve is as follows:

PROBLEM 1. **Given** *a tensor* $\mathcal{X}$ *of* $(disease, state, time)$ *triplets,* **Find** *a compact description that best summarizes* $\mathcal{X}$*, that is,* $\mathcal{F} = \{\mathbf{B}, \mathbf{R}, \mathbf{N}, \mathcal{E}, \mathcal{M}\}$.

We want to find a good representation $\mathcal{F}$ to solve the problem. The essential questions are: (a) How can we estimate the parameter set that best captures the dynamics and patterns in $\mathcal{X}$? (b) How should we decide the number of external shocks k? (c) How can we ignore mistake (i.e., outlier) values in $\mathcal{X}$?

4.1 Model quality and data compression

We provide a new intuitive coding scheme, which is based on the minimum description length (MDL) principle. In short, it follows the assumption that the more we can compress the data, the more we can learn about its underlying patterns.

Model description cost. The description complexity of model parameter set consists of the following terms,

- The number of diseases d, states l, and time-ticks n require $\log^*(d) + \log^*(l) + \log^*(n)$ bits. [6]
- The model parameter set of the base ($\mathbf{B}$), reduction ($\mathbf{R}$), geo-disease ($\mathbf{N}$) matrices require $d \times 6$, $d \times 2$, $d \times l$ parameters, respectively, i.e., $Cost_M(\mathbf{B}) + Cost_M(\mathbf{R}) + Cost_M(\mathbf{N}) = c_F \cdot d(6 + 2 + l)$, where c_F is the floating point cost[7].

Similarly, the model description cost of the external shock tensor $\mathcal{E} = \{\mathbf{E}^{(\mathbf{D})}, \mathbf{E}^{(\mathbf{S})}, \mathbf{E}^{(\mathbf{T})}\})$ consists of the following:

- The number of external shocks k requires $\log^*(k)$ bits.
- The shock-disease matrix $\mathbf{E}^{(\mathbf{D})}$ requires $k \log(d)$.
- The shock-time parameter set $\boldsymbol{e}^{(\boldsymbol{T})} = \{t_\mu, t_\sigma, \epsilon_0\}$ in $\mathbf{E}^{(\mathbf{T})}$ requires $\log(n)$, $\log(n)$, c_F, respectively.
- The shock-state matrix $\mathbf{E}^{(\mathbf{S})}$ requires $c_F \cdot kl$.

Consequently, the model cost of the external shock tensor $\mathcal{E}$ is $Cost_M(\mathcal{E}) = \log^*(k) + k\big(\log(d) + 2\log(n) + c_F \cdot (1 + l)\big)$. The model cost of mistake tensor $\mathcal{M}$ consists of

- The number of non-zero elements in $\mathcal{M}$ requires $\log^*(|\mathcal{M}|)$
- The location of each non-zero element and its value, $m_{ij}(t)$ require $\log(d)$,$\log(l)$,$\log(n)$, $\log^*(m_{ij}(t))$, respectively.

Thus, $Cost_M(\mathcal{M}) = \log^*(|\mathcal{M}|) + \sum_{m_{ij}(t)>0}^{|\mathcal{M}|}(\log(d) + \log(l) + \log(n) + \log^*(m_{ij}(t)))$, where, $|\mathcal{M}|$ is the number of non-zero elements in $\mathcal{M}$.

Data coding cost. Once we have decided the full parameter set $\mathcal{F}$, we can encode the data $\mathcal{X}$ using Huffman coding [3], i.e., a number of bits is assigned to each value in $\mathcal{X}$, which is the logarithm of the inverse of the probability of the values (here, we use a Gaussian distribution). The encoding cost of $\mathcal{X}$ given $\mathcal{F}$ is: $Cost_C(\mathcal{X}|\mathcal{F}) = \sum_{i,j,t=1}^{d,l,n} \log_2 p_{Gauss(\mu,\sigma)}^{-1}(x_{ij}(t) - m_{ij}(t) - I_{ij}(t))$, where, $x_{ij}(t)$, $m_{ij}(t)$ are the elements in $\mathcal{X}$ and the mistake tensor $\mathcal{M}$, respectively, and $I_{ij}(t)$ is the estimated count of infections (i.e., Model 3). Also, μ and σ are the mean and variance of the distance between the original and estimated values. [8]

Putting it all together. Consequently, the total code length for $\mathcal{X}$ with respect to a given parameter set $\mathcal{F}$ can be described as follows:

$$\begin{aligned} Cost_T(\mathcal{X}; \mathcal{F}) &= \log^*(d) + \log^*(l) + \log^*(n) \\ &+ Cost_M(\mathbf{B}) + Cost_M(\mathbf{R}) + Cost_M(\mathbf{N}) \\ &+ Cost_M(\mathcal{E}) + Cost_M(\mathcal{M}) + Cost_C(\mathcal{X}|\mathcal{F}) \end{aligned} \quad (4)$$

Thus our next goal is to minimize the above function.

4.2 Multi-layer optimization

Until now, we have seen how we can measure the goodness of the representation of $\mathcal{X}$, if we are given a candidate parameter set $\mathcal{F}$. The next question is, how to find an optimal solution of the full parameter set: $\mathcal{F} = \{\mathbf{B}, \mathbf{R}, \mathbf{N}, \mathcal{E}, \mathcal{M}\}$.

As described in subsection 3.3, our FUNNEL model consists of multiple parameter sets, each of which explains either the local or global pattern of epidemics in $\mathcal{X}$. For example, the base and reduction matrices $\mathbf{B}$, $\mathbf{R}$ explain the global-level behavior of each disease, while the geo-disease matrix $\mathbf{N}$ describes the local-level trends. Also, the extra tensors $\mathcal{E}$, $\mathcal{M}$ consist of both the global and local-level parameters. More specifically, the external shocks consists of $\mathcal{E} = \{\mathbf{E}^{(\mathbf{D})}, \mathbf{E}^{(\mathbf{S})}, \mathbf{E}^{(\mathbf{T})}\})$, where, the first two are the global-level, and the last one is the local-level. Similarly, the mistake tensor can also be describes by the triplet matrix $\mathcal{M} = \{\mathbf{M}^{(\mathbf{D})}, \mathbf{M}^{(\mathbf{S})}, \mathbf{M}^{(\mathbf{T})}\})$, each of which describes the location of the mistake values in terms of *disease, state, time*. So, how can we efficiently estimate these model parameters?

We propose a multi-layer optimization algorithm, to search for the optimal solution in terms of both the global and local-level parameters. The idea is that we split parameter set $\mathcal{F}$ into two subsets, i.e., $\mathcal{F}_\mathcal{G}$ and $\mathcal{F}_\mathcal{L}$, each of which corresponds to a global/local-level parameter set, and try to fit the parameter sets separately. Our algorithm consists of the following two phases:

- GLOBALFIT: find good global-level parameters for $\{\bar{\boldsymbol{x}}_i\}_{i=1}^d$, i.e., $\mathcal{F}_\mathcal{G} = \{\mathbf{B}, \mathbf{R}, \mathbf{E}^{(\mathbf{D})}, \mathbf{E}^{(\mathbf{T})}, \mathbf{M}^{(\mathbf{D})}, \mathbf{M}^{(\mathbf{T})}\}$
- LOCALFIT: find good local-level parameters: for $\{\boldsymbol{x}_{ij}\}_{i,j=1}^{d,l}$, i.e., $\mathcal{F}_\mathcal{L} = \{\mathbf{N}, \mathbf{E}^{(\mathbf{S})}, \mathbf{M}^{(\mathbf{S})}\}$

Here, the global epidemic sequence of the i-th disease: $\bar{\boldsymbol{x}}_i$ can be described as the sum of the l local sequences, i.e., $\bar{\boldsymbol{x}}_i(t) = \sum_{j=1}^{l} \boldsymbol{x}_{ij}(t)$. Algorithm 1 shows an overview of FUNNELFIT. Given a tensor $\mathcal{X}$, it finds the full set of FUNNEL parameters.

Algorithm 1 FUNNELFIT ($\mathcal{X}$)

1: **Input:** Tensor $\mathcal{X}$ ($d \times l \times n$)
2: **Output:** Complete set of parameters, i.e., $\mathcal{F} = \{\mathbf{B}, \mathbf{R}, \mathbf{N}, \mathcal{E}, \mathcal{M}\}$
3: /* Parameter fitting for global-level sequences */
4: $\{\mathcal{F}_\mathcal{G}\}$ =GLOBALFIT ($\mathcal{X}$);
5: /* Parameter fitting for local-level sequences */
6: $\{\mathcal{F}_\mathcal{L}\}$ =LOCALFIT ($\mathcal{X}, \mathcal{F}_\mathcal{G}$);
7: **return** $\mathcal{F} = \{\mathcal{F}_\mathcal{G}, \mathcal{F}_\mathcal{L}\}$;

4.2.1 *Global-level parameter fitting*

Given a tensor $\mathcal{X}$, our sub-goal is to find the optimal global-level parameter set: $\mathcal{F}_\mathcal{G}$, to minimize the cost function (i.e., Equation 4). We want to fit the basic parameters of each disease (i.e., the base and reduction matrices), and estimate the appropriate number of external shocks and mistake values, simultaneously. Finding the appropriate number of external-shocks/mistakes is a particular issue here, because the parameter fittings are very sensitive to outliers, as described in Figure 5 (a). To find a good basic parameter set for $\mathcal{X}$, we have to filter out the external shocks and mistakes appropriately. Simultaneously, a good external-shock/mistake filter requires a well estimated base model. We escape this circular dependency by applying an iterative method that employs external-shocks/mistakes detection and filtering, and basic model fitting in an alternating way until the cost function reaches a minimum value.

[6]Here, $\log^*$ is the universal code length for integers.

[7]We used 4×8 bits in our setting.

[8] Here, μ, σ need $2c_F$ bits, but we can eliminate them because they are constant values and independent of our modeling.

Algorithm 2 GLOBALFIT ($\mathcal{X}$)

Input: Tensor $\mathcal{X}$
Output: Set of global-level parameters $\mathcal{F_G}$
for $i = 1 : d$ **do**
  Create $\bar{\boldsymbol{x}}_i$ from $\mathcal{X}$; /* Global sequence $\bar{\boldsymbol{x}}_i$ of i-th disease */
  /* Initialize external shocks and mistake values for disease i */
  $\mathbf{E}_i^{(\mathbf{D})} = \mathbf{E}_i^{(\mathbf{T})} = \mathbf{M}_i^{(\mathbf{D})} = \mathbf{M}_i^{(\mathbf{T})} = \emptyset$;
  while improving the cost **do**
    $\boldsymbol{b}_i = \arg\min_{\boldsymbol{b}'_i} Cost_C(\bar{\boldsymbol{x}}_i | \boldsymbol{b}'_i, \boldsymbol{r}_i, \mathbf{E}_i^{(\mathbf{T})}, \mathbf{M}_i^{(\mathbf{T})})$; /* Base */
    $\boldsymbol{r}_i = \arg\min_{\boldsymbol{r}'_i} Cost_C(\bar{\boldsymbol{x}}_i | \boldsymbol{b}_i, \boldsymbol{r}'_i, \mathbf{E}_i^{(\mathbf{T})}, \mathbf{M}_i^{(\mathbf{T})})$; /* Reduction */
    $\mathbf{E}_i^{(\mathbf{D})} = \mathbf{E}_i^{(\mathbf{T})} = \mathbf{M}_i^{(\mathbf{D})} = \mathbf{M}_i^{(\mathbf{T})} = \emptyset$; /* Initialize values */
    /* Find external shocks and mistakes for disease i */
    while improving the cost **do**
      $\boldsymbol{e}^{(T)} = \arg\min_{\boldsymbol{e}'^{(T)}} Cost_C(\bar{\boldsymbol{x}}_i | \boldsymbol{b}_i, \boldsymbol{r}_i, \{\mathbf{E}_i^{(\mathbf{T})} \cup \boldsymbol{e}'^{(T)}\}, \mathbf{M}_i^{(\mathbf{T})})$;
      $\boldsymbol{m}^{(T)} = \arg\min_{\boldsymbol{m}'^{(T)}} Cost_C(\bar{\boldsymbol{x}}_i | \boldsymbol{b}_i, \boldsymbol{r}_i, \mathbf{E}_i^{(\mathbf{T})}, \{\mathbf{M}_i^{(\mathbf{T})} \cup \boldsymbol{m}'^{(T)}\})$;
      /* Compare external shock vs. mistake */
      if $Cost_T(\bar{\boldsymbol{x}}_i; \boldsymbol{e}^{(T)}) < Cost_T(\bar{\boldsymbol{x}}_i; \boldsymbol{m}^{(T)})$ **then**
        /* External shock wins - treat as an external shock */
        $\mathbf{E}_i^{(\mathbf{D})} = \{\mathbf{E}_i^{(\mathbf{D})} \cup i\}$; $\mathbf{E}_i^{(\mathbf{T})} = \{\mathbf{E}_i^{(\mathbf{T})} \cup \boldsymbol{e}^{(T)}\}$;
      else
        /* Mistake wins - treat as a mistake value */
        $\mathbf{M}_i^{(\mathbf{D})} = \{\mathbf{M}_i^{(\mathbf{D})} \cup i\}$; $\mathbf{M}_i^{(\mathbf{T})} = \{\mathbf{M}_i^{(\mathbf{T})} \cup \boldsymbol{m}^{(T)}\}$;
      end if
    end while
  end while
  /* Update parameter set of i-th disease */
  $\mathbf{B} = \mathbf{B} \cup \boldsymbol{b}_i$; $\mathbf{R} = \mathbf{R} \cup \boldsymbol{r}_i$;
  $\mathbf{E}^{(\mathbf{D})} = \mathbf{E}^{(\mathbf{D})} \cup \mathbf{E}_i^{(\mathbf{D})}$; $\mathbf{E}^{(\mathbf{T})} = \mathbf{E}^{(\mathbf{T})} \cup \mathbf{E}_i^{(\mathbf{T})}$;
  $\mathbf{M}^{(\mathbf{D})} = \mathbf{M}^{(\mathbf{D})} \cup \mathbf{M}_i^{(\mathbf{D})}$; $\mathbf{M}^{(\mathbf{T})} = \mathbf{M}^{(\mathbf{T})} \cup \mathbf{M}_i^{(\mathbf{T})}$;
end for
return $\mathcal{F_G} = \{\mathbf{B}, \mathbf{R}, \mathbf{E}^{(\mathbf{D})}, \mathbf{E}^{(\mathbf{T})}, \mathbf{M}^{(\mathbf{D})}, \mathbf{M}^{(\mathbf{T})}\}$;

External shock vs. mistake. There is also an important issue regarding the external shock vs. the mistake value. We want to distinguish automatically between an external shock event and a typing error. For example, in Figure 5, there is a clear "typo", rather than an external shock event. Our coding scheme enables us to provide the answer. The idea is that we try to fit the parameters by treating the data as both an external shock event and a mistake value, and then compare the cost of the two alternatives. For Figure 5, the cost of (b) is less than (a), thus the algorithm determines that there is a mistake value in 2007.

Algorithm. Algorithm 2 is a detailed algorithm of the global-level fitting. Given a tensor $\mathcal{X}$, it creates a set of d global sequences: $\{\bar{\boldsymbol{x}}_i\}_{i=1}^{d}$. It tries to fit the global-level parameter set, as well as find the appropriate number of external-shocks/mistakes. We use the *Levenberg-Marquardt (LM)* algorithm to minimize the cost function. Note that the extra tensors $\mathcal{E}$ and $\mathcal{M}$ consist of an entry $(disease, state, time)$, but this algorithm can find only the global-level entry, which consists of $(disease, time)$. The local-level entries $\mathbf{E}^{(\mathbf{S})}$ and $\mathbf{M}^{(\mathbf{S})}$ can be computed by local-level parameter fitting, as shown next in Algorithm 3. Also, the cost function (Equation 4) includes the cost of local-level parameters such as $\mathbf{N}$, but these terms are independent of the global model fitting. Hence, we can simply consider them to be constant.

4.2.2 *Local-level parameter fitting*

Given a set of $d \times l$ local-level sequences, $\{\boldsymbol{x}_{ij}\}_{i,j=1}^{d,l} \in \mathcal{X}$, and a set of global-level parameters, $\mathcal{F_G}$, our next goal is to fit the individual parameters of each disease in each state, that is, $\mathcal{F_L} = \{\mathbf{N}, \mathbf{E}^{(\mathbf{S})}, \mathbf{M}^{(\mathbf{S})}\}$. We propose an iterative optimization algorithm (see Algorithm 3). Our algorithm searches for the optimal solution with respect to (a) the geo-disease matrix $\mathbf{N}$, (b) the local-level external shocks $\mathbf{E}^{(\mathbf{S})}$, and (c) the local-level mistake values $\mathbf{M}^{(\mathbf{S})}$, so that the total coding cost is minimized.

Algorithm 3 LOCALFIT ($\mathcal{X}, \mathbf{B}, \mathbf{R}, \mathbf{E}^{(\mathbf{D})}, \mathbf{E}^{(\mathbf{T})}, \mathbf{M}^{(\mathbf{D})}, \mathbf{M}^{(\mathbf{T})}$)

Input: (a) Tensor $\mathcal{X}$, (b) global-level parameter set $\mathcal{F_G}$
Output: Set of local-level parameters, i.e., $\mathcal{F_L}$
while improving the cost **do**
  /* For each local sequence $\boldsymbol{x}_{ij}$ of i-th disease in j-th state */
  for $i = 1 : d$ **do**
    for $j = 1 : l$ **do**
      $N_{ij} = \arg\min_{N'_{ij}} Cost_C(\boldsymbol{x}_{ij} | \mathbf{B}, \mathbf{R}, N'_{ij}, \mathcal{E}, \mathcal{M})$;
    end for
  end for
  for each external shock $(\boldsymbol{e}^{(D)}, \boldsymbol{e}^{(S)}, \boldsymbol{e}^{(T)}) \in \mathcal{E}$ **do**
    Update $\boldsymbol{e}^{(S)}$ to minimize the cost /* Local participation rate */
  end for
  for each mistake $(\boldsymbol{m}^{(D)}, \boldsymbol{m}^{(S)}, \boldsymbol{m}^{(T)}) \in \mathcal{M}$ **do**
    Update $\boldsymbol{m}^{(S)}$ to minimize the cost /* Mistake value */
  end for
end while
return $\mathcal{F_L} = \{\mathbf{N}, \mathbf{E}^{(\mathbf{S})}, \mathbf{M}^{(\mathbf{S})}\}$;

LEMMA 1. *The computation time of* FUNNELFIT *is* $O(dln)$.

PROOF. To create the global-level sequences from $\mathcal{X}$, the algorithm requires $O(dln)$ time. For global-level parameter fitting, it needs $O(\#iter \cdot (k + |\mathcal{M}|) \cdot dn)$ time, where $\#iter$ is the number of iterations, k and $|\mathcal{M}|$ show the number of external shocks and non-zero values in $\mathcal{M}$, respectively. Similarly, for the local-level parameter fitting, it needs $O(\#iter \cdot (k + |\mathcal{M}|) \cdot dln)$ time to fit the parameters. Note that $\#iter$, k and $|\mathcal{M}|$ are small constant values that are negligible. Thus, the complexity is $O(dln)$. □

5. EXPERIMENTS

In this section we demonstrate the effectiveness of FUNNEL with real epidemic data. The experiments were designed to answer the following questions:

- Q1 *Sense-making*: Can our method help us understand the given input epidemic data?
- Q2 *Accuracy*: How well does our method match the data?
- Q3 *Scalability*: How does our method scale in terms of computational time?

5.1 Matching co-evolving epidemic patterns

We demonstrate how effectively FUNNEL can learn important patterns given a large collection of epidemics. Figure 6 shows the results of model fitting on 15 typical diseases. We show the original sequences (i.e., black dots) and estimated sequences: $I(t)$ (i.e., red line) in linear-linear (top) and linear-log (bottom) scales. In the log-log scale, we also show the susceptible $S(t)$ and vigilant $V(t)$ counts. We made several important observations, which correspond to the five properties of the epidemic sequences.

(P1) Disease seasonality. As we have already seen in the introduction section (Figure 1(c)), we identified four categories i.e.,

- Influenza has very strong periodic spikes, in January-February.
- Children's diseases (e.g., measles, mumps, chickenpox) also have strong periodicity, but they peak in spring [27].
- Tick-borne diseases (e.g., Lyme disease), and cryptosporidiosis (i.e., water-borne disease) have strong periodicity, peaking in the summer, related to vector and human behavior and climate factors [28].
- Gonorrhea, i.e., sexually transmitted disease (STD) has no periodicity.

(P2) Disease reduction effects. FUNNEL is capable of automatically detecting the disease reduction impact. For example, in Figure 6

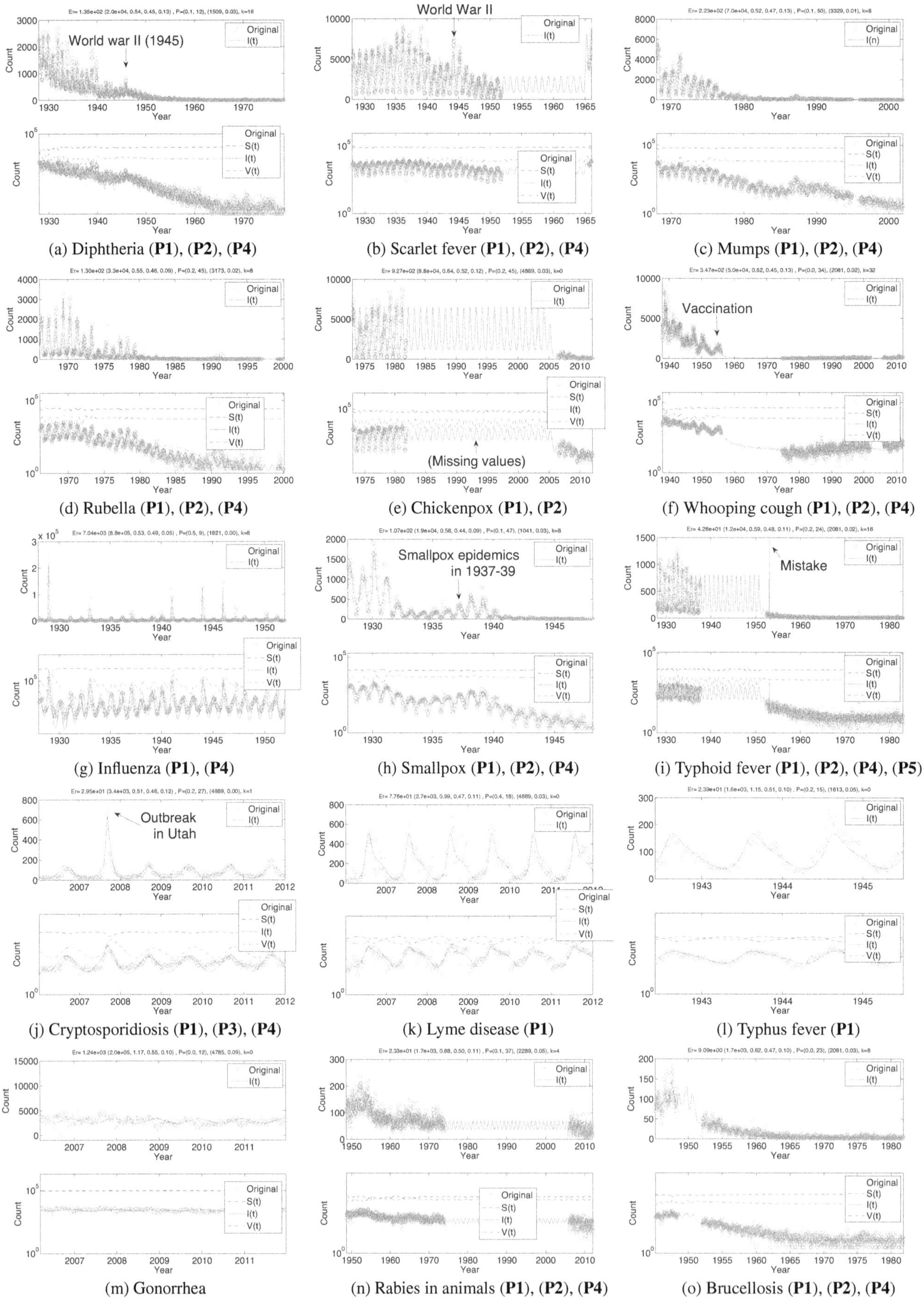

(a) Diphtheria (**P1**), (**P2**), (**P4**)
(b) Scarlet fever (**P1**), (**P2**), (**P4**)
(c) Mumps (**P1**), (**P2**), (**P4**)
(d) Rubella (**P1**), (**P2**), (**P4**)
(e) Chickenpox (**P1**), (**P2**)
(f) Whooping cough (**P1**), (**P2**), (**P4**)
(g) Influenza (**P1**), (**P4**)
(h) Smallpox (**P1**), (**P2**), (**P4**)
(i) Typhoid fever (**P1**), (**P2**), (**P4**), (**P5**)
(j) Cryptosporidiosis (**P1**), (**P3**), (**P4**)
(k) Lyme disease (**P1**)
(l) Typhus fever (**P1**)
(m) Gonorrhea
(n) Rabies in animals (**P1**), (**P2**), (**P4**)
(o) Brucellosis (**P1**), (**P2**), (**P4**)

Figure 6: Fitting results of FUNNEL for 15 diseases (global-level counts), shown in 'lin-lin'(top) and 'lin-log'(bottom) scales.

Figure 7: The year of vaccine licensure [32] vs. detection.

Disease	licensure	detected
Measles	1963	**1965**
Mumps	1967	**1975**
Whooping cough (pertussis)	1948	**1951**
Rubella	1969	**1972**

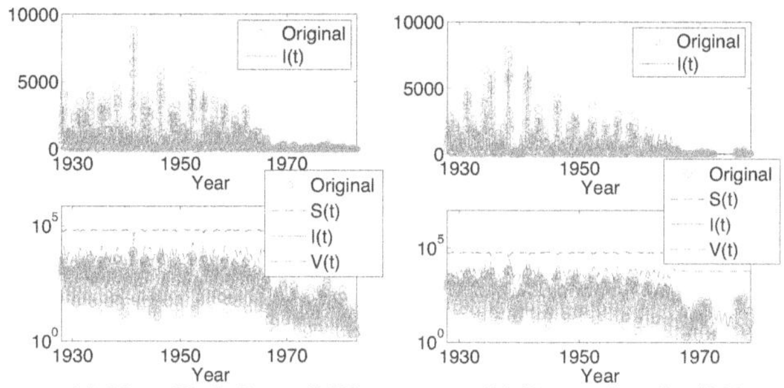

(a) New York State (NY) (b) Pennsylvania (PA)

Figure 8: Local-level fittings for measles: as with the global fitting shown in Figure 1, FUNNEL fits very well.

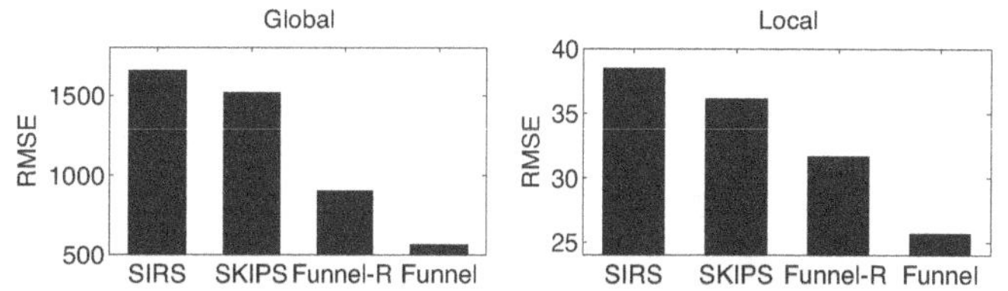

(a) Global fitting (b) Local fitting

Figure 9: Fitting accuracy for the (a) global sequences: $\{\bar{\boldsymbol{x}}_i(t)\}_{i,t}^{d,n}$ and (b) local sequences: $\{\boldsymbol{x}_{ij}(t)\}_{i,j,t}^{d,l,n}$. FUNNEL consistently outperforms the previous models w.r.t. ther RMSE between real and estimated values (lower is better).

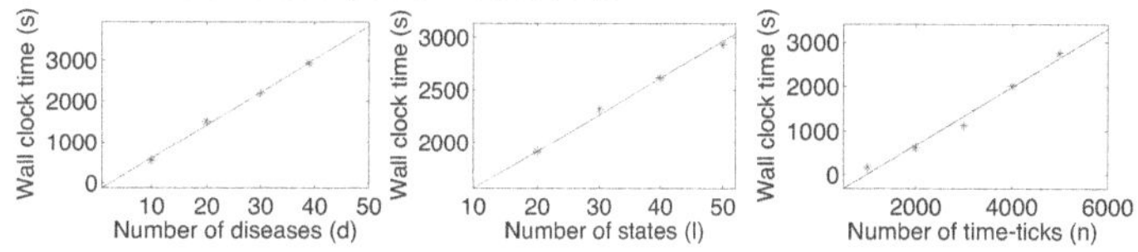

(a) Diseases (d) (b) States (l) (c) Duration (n)

Figure 10: FUNNELFIT scales linearly: wall clock time vs. dataset size ($d \times l \times n$). Our method is linear on the data size.

(a-f), most children's diseases include the reduction patterns. Figure 7 shows the year the first vaccine was licensed vs. the year detected as the starting point of the disease reduction effect. Basically, there is a lag of 2-3 years between the licensure and the detected point, which could be related to the diffusion rate of a vaccination program. Note that FUNNEL does not detect any disease reduction effect for influenza; This is because influenza epidemics continue to occur due to high mutation rates in influenza virus that limit protective immunity.

(P3) Area specificity. FUNNEL can find the local dynamics of each disease, as well as the global-level pattern of epidemics. For example, as described in Figure 1 (b), there are many measles patients in NY and PA. Specifically, Figure 8 shows the original local-level epidemic sequences of measles in (a) NY and (b) PA, and the results of our fittings. FUNNEL successfully captures yearly-periodic patterns, the disease reduction effects, and, *also*, the local spikes of each location (i.e., notice that the strengths of the external shock effects differ state to state).

(P4) External shock events. Figure 6 shows that FUNNELFIT automatically detects some important external shock events, e.g.,

- (a) Diphtheria and (b) scarlet fever (i.e., children's diseases) have multiple external shocks, e.g., during World War II.
- (g) Flu has several major pandemics in 1929, 1941 etc., due to immune dynamics and antigenic changes in the virus [20].
- (h) Epidemics of a milder form of smallpox occurred in Northwestern states in 1937-39 due to low vaccination rates [5].
- (j) A major outbreak of Cryptosporidiosis, (i.e., water-borne disease), was detected in Utah due to contaminated public pools in 2007 [1].

(P5) Mistakes. One of the strong points of FUNNELFIT is its robustness against noise. It can handle "mistake" points as well as missing values (e.g., Figure 6 (i) typhoid fever, which contains missing values in the 1940s, and a mistake value in 1953).

5.2 Model quality and scalability

Next, we discuss the quality of FUNNEL in terms of fitting accuracy. We compared FUNNEL with the standard *SIRS* model and *SKIPS* [29]. To evaluate the effect of the disease reduction parameters, we also compared with FUNNEL-R, (i.e., removing external shocks and mistakes). Figure 9 (a) shows the root mean square error between the original and predicted counts of the global sequences $\{\bar{\boldsymbol{x}}_i(t)\}_{i,t}^{d,n}$. Similarly, Figure 9 (b) shows the results of the local counts $\{\boldsymbol{x}_{ij}(t)\}_{i,j,t}^{d,l,n}$. A lower value indicates a better fitting accuracy. Note that the *SIRS* model cannot capture seasonal dynamics, while *SKIPS* has the ability to capture periodic patterns. Moreover, they are not intended to detect disease reductions, or external shocks. As shown in the figures, the *SIRS* model and *SKIPS* failed to capture the complicated patterns of epidemics, while our method achieved high fitting accuracy.

We also evaluated the scalability of FUNNELFIT, and verified the complexity of our method, which we discussed in Lemma 1, in section 4. Figure 10 shows the computational cost of FUNNELFIT in terms of the dataset size. We varied the dataset size with respect to (a) diseases d, (b) states l, and (c) duration n. As shown in Figure 10, FUNNELFIT is linear with respect to data size.

6. DISCUSSION

Here, we describe important applications and potential directions for our method.

FUNNEL at work - forecasting. Since FUNNEL has a very high fitting accuracy on real epidemic data, the most practical application would be forecasting. Figure 11 shows results of our forecasting in relation to three different diseases. We trained the model parameters by using the $2/3$ values for each sequence (solid black lines in the figure), and then forecasted the following years (solid red lines). Note that the vertical axis uses a logarithmic scale.

We compared FUNNEL with the auto regressive (AR) model, where we used the regression coefficients: $r = 52$ (i.e., one year), 26 (i.e., half year), and 8 (i.e., the same size as our base (6) + reduction (2) parameters). Also, since the original sequences are bursty we took their logarithm for the AR forecast.

Our method achieves high forecasting accuracy while AR failed. Specifically, for (a) influenza, and (b) cryptosporidiosis, FUNNEL captured the future trend correctly, while AR was strongly affected by multiple extreme spikes (e.g., in figure (b), there is a spike in 2007). Similarly, for (c) typhoid fever, which includes the disease reduction pattern, missing/mistake values, FUNNEL successfully forecasted the periodic patterns after the disease reduction effect.

Generality - epidemics on computer networks. Another promising step for FUNNEL would be its generalization to other domains such as modeling computer viruses. Computer viruses have similar characteristics to biological viruses [11]. For example, Figure 12 shows the fitting result of FUNNEL on publicly available reports

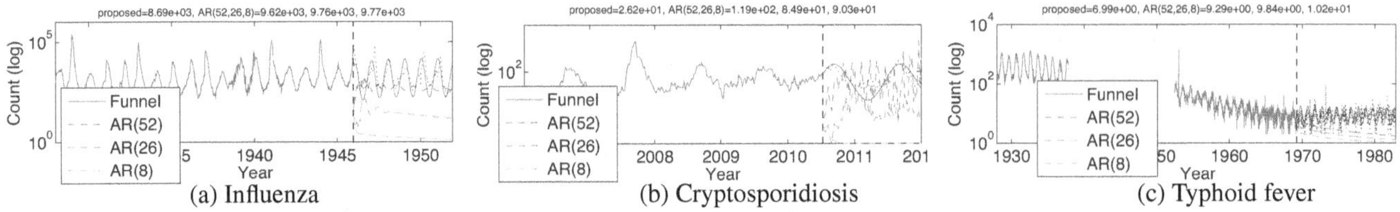

(a) Influenza (b) Cryptosporidiosis (c) Typhoid fever

Figure 11: Forecasting result: we train the model parameters using $2/3$ of each sequence (i.e., solid black lines). We then start forecasting (at the vertical dotted line). Note that the vertical axis uses a logarithmic scale.

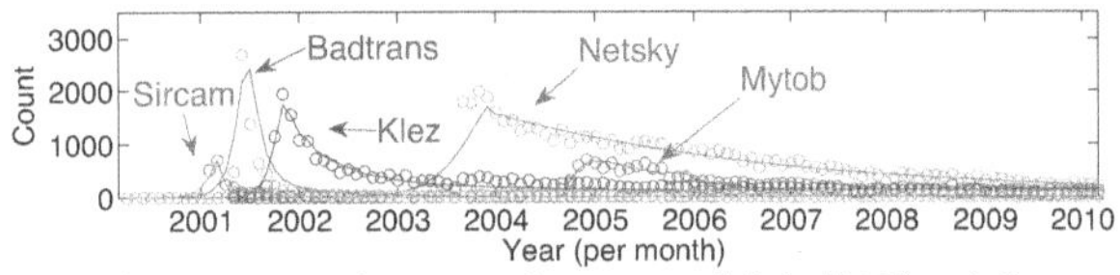

Figure 12: FUNNEL is general: our model (solid lines) fits computer virus data (in circles) very well. It captures rising spikes and viruse reduction effects (i.e., anti-virus software). Note that it shows the reported case count for each virus.

published by IPA, [9] which consists of annual reports on computer virus infections in Japan (e.g., private companies and public schools) covering more than ten years. The figure shows the original counts for the top five viruses (circles) and our fittings (solid lines) from 2000 to 2010. Here are some interesting observations: (a) "Badtrans" and "Klez" spread in 2001-2002 by exploiting a security hole in Microsoft Outlook. It spread very quickly due to the strong infection effect, but it also decayed very quick thanks to anti-virus software (i.e., the virus reduction effect); (b) "Netsky", which spreads via email attachment: there were huge infections in 2004, and it gradually decreased over the next 10 years, but still remains. Also, there is a weekly periodicity (i.e., less infection at weekends); (c) "Mytob", which spreads through corporate networks: there are some local-level (i.e., intra-office) infections. Very recently, there have been several worms (e.g., "Koobface", "Fbphotofake") that spread quickly through social networking sites including Facebook and Twitter, where they have a high potential population (# of users).

7. CONCLUSIONS

Our proposed method has the following appealing advantages:

1. It is **sense-making**: FUNNEL captures all essential aspects, i.e., yearly periodicity, discontinuities, local sensitivities. It can lead to disease clustering, find disease reduction effects (e.g., vaccines) and external shocks, and perform forecasting.
2. It is **automatic**: FUNNELFIT requires no training set and no hint regarding the number of parameters. Thanks to our coding scheme, it determines all of the above automatically.
3. It is **scalable**: FUNNELFIT scales very well, being linear on the database size, (i.e., $O(dln)$).
4. It is **general**: We demonstrated the generality of FUNNEL, by applying it to real epidemic datasets, including computer virus infections, as well as human diseases.

Acknowledgement. We thank Dr. Donald S. Burke, Dean of the Graduate School of Public Health, University of Pittsburgh for his support and expert opinion during this study. This work was supported by JSPS KAKENHI Grant-in-Aid for Scientific Research Number 24500138, 26730060, 26280112, 25·7946. This material is based upon work supported by the National Science Foundation under Grant No. CNS-1314632. Any opinions, findings, and conclusions or recommendations expressed in this material are those of the author(s) and do not necessarily reflect the views of the National Science Foundation.

8. REFERENCES

[1] Promotion of healthy swimming after a statewide outbreak of cryptosporidiosis associated with recreational water venues–utah, 2008-2009. *MMWR Morb Mortal Wkly Rep*, 61(19):348–52, 2012.
[2] R. M. Anderson and R. M. May. *Infectious Diseases of Humans Dynamics and Control*. Oxford University Press, 1992.
[3] C. Böhm, C. Faloutsos, J.-Y. Pan, and C. Plant. Ric: Parameter-free noise-robust clustering. *TKDD*, 1(3), 2007.
[4] G. E. Box, G. M. Jenkins, and G. C. Reinsel. *Time Series Analysis: Forecasting and Control*. Prentice Hall, Englewood Cliffs, NJ, 3rd edition, 1994.
[5] D. CC. Smallpox in the united states: It's decline and geographic distribution. *Public Health Reports*, 55(50):2303–2312, 1940.
[6] L. Chen and R. T. Ng. On the marriage of lp-norms and edit distance. In *VLDB*, pages 792–803, 2004.
[7] I. N. Davidson, S. Gilpin, O. T. Carmichael, and P. B. Walker. Network discovery via constrained tensor analysis of fmri data. In *KDD*, pages 194–202, 2013.
[8] D. J. Earn, P. Rohani, B. M. Bolker, and B. T. Grenfell. A simple model for complex dynamical transitions in epidemics. *Science*, 287(5453):667–70, 2000.
[9] B. T. Grenfell, O. N. Bjornstad, and J. Kappey. Travelling waves and spatial hierarchies in measles epidemics. *Nature*, 414:716, 2001.
[10] A. Jain, E. Y. Chang, and Y.-F. Wang. Adaptive stream resource management using kalman filters. In *SIGMOD*, pages 11–22, 2004.
[11] J. Kephart and S. White. Directed-graph epidemiological models of computer viruses. In *Research in Security and Privacy, 1991. Proceedings., 1991 IEEE Computer Society Symposium on*, pages 343–359, May 1991.
[12] R. Kumar, M. Mahdian, and M. McGlohon. Dynamics of conversations. In *KDD*, pages 553–562, 2010.
[13] J.-G. Lee, J. Han, and K.-Y. Whang. Trajectory clustering: a partition-and-group framework. In *SIGMOD*, pages 593–604, 2007.
[14] J. Leskovec, L. Backstrom, R. Kumar, and A. Tomkins. Microscopic evolution of social networks. In *KDD*, pages 462–470, 2008.
[15] L. Li, B. A. Prakash, and C. Faloutsos. Parsimonious linear fingerprinting for time series. *PVLDB*, 3(1):385–396, 2010.
[16] Y. Matsubara, L. Li, E. E. Papalexakis, D. Lo, Y. Sakurai, and C. Faloutsos. F-trail: Finding patterns in taxi trajectories. In *PAKDD (1)*, pages 86–98, 2013.
[17] Y. Matsubara, Y. Sakurai, and C. Faloutsos. Autoplait: Automatic mining of co-evolving time sequences. In *SIGMOD*, 2014.
[18] Y. Matsubara, Y. Sakurai, C. Faloutsos, T. Iwata, and M. Yoshikawa. Fast mining and forecasting of complex time-stamped events. In *KDD*, pages 271–279, 2012.
[19] Y. Matsubara, Y. Sakurai, B. A. Prakash, L. Li, and C. Faloutsos. Rise and fall patterns of information diffusion: model and implications. In *KDD*, pages 6–14, 2012.
[20] F. NM, G. AP, and B. RM. Ecological and immunological determinants of influenza evolution. *Nature*, 422(6930):428–33, 2003.
[21] S. Papadimitriou and P. S. Yu. Optimal multi-scale patterns in time series streams. In *SIGMOD Conference*, pages 647–658, 2006.
[22] F. PE and C. JA. Measles in england and wales–i: An analysis of factors underlying seasonal patterns. *Epidemiol*, 11(1):5–14, 1982.
[23] B. A. Prakash, A. Beutel, R. Rosenfeld, and C. Faloutsos. Winner takes all: competing viruses or ideas on fair-play networks. In *WWW*, pages 1037–1046, 2012.
[24] B. A. Prakash, D. Chakrabarti, M. Faloutsos, N. Valler, and C. Faloutsos. Threshold conditions for arbitrary cascade models on arbitrary networks. In *ICDM*, pages 537–546, 2011.
[25] T. Rakthanmanon, B. J. L. Campana, A. Mueen, G. E. A. P. A. Batista, M. B. Westover, Q. Zhu, J. Zakaria, and E. J. Keogh. Searching and mining trillions of time series subsequences under dynamic time warping. In *KDD*, pages 262–270, 2012.
[26] Y. Sakurai, S. Papadimitriou, and C. Faloutsos. Braid: Stream mining through group lag correlations. In *SIGMOD*, pages 599–610, 2005.
[27] D. SF. Seasonal variation in host susceptibility and cycles of certain infectious diseases. *Emerg Infect Dis.*, 7(3):369–74, 2001.
[28] M. SM, E. RJ, M. A, and M. P. Seasonality in six enterically transmitted diseases and ambient temperature. *Am J Trop Med Hyg.*, 2014.
[29] L. Stone, R. Olinky, and A. Huppert. Seasonal dynamics of recurrent epidemics. *Nature*, 446:533–536, March 2007.
[30] J. Sun, D. Tao, and C. Faloutsos. Beyond streams and graphs: dynamic tensor analysis. In *KDD*, pages 374–383, 2006.
[31] Y. Tao, C. Faloutsos, D. Papadias, and B. Liu. Prediction and indexing of moving objects with unknown motion patterns. In *SIGMOD*, pages 611–622, 2004.
[32] W. G. van Panhuis, J. Grefenstette, S. Y. Jung, N. S. Chok, A. Cross, H. Eng, B. Y. Lee, V. Zadorozhny, S. Brown, D. Cummings, and D. S. Burke. Contagious diseases in the united states from 1888 to the present. *NEJM*, 369(22):2152–2158, 2013.
[33] M. Vlachos, D. Gunopulos, and G. Kollios. Discovering similar multidimensional trajectories. In *ICDE*, pages 673–684, 2002.

[9] IPA - IT security center: https://www.ipa.go.jp/security/english/index.html

Marble: High-throughput Phenotyping from Electronic Health Records via Sparse Nonnegative Tensor Factorization

Joyce Ho
University of Texas at Austin
joyceho@utexas.edu

Joydeep Ghosh
University of Texas at Austin
ghosh@ece.utexas.edu

Jimeng Sun
Georgia Institute of Technology
jsun@cc.gatech.edu

ABSTRACT

The rapidly increasing availability of electronic health records (EHRs) from multiple heterogeneous sources has spearheaded the adoption of data-driven approaches for improved clinical research, decision making, prognosis, and patient management. Unfortunately, EHR data do not always directly and reliably map to phenotypes, or medical concepts, that clinical researchers need or use. Existing phenotyping approaches typically require labor intensive supervision from medical experts.

We propose Marble, a novel sparse non-negative tensor factorization method to derive phenotype candidates with virtually no human supervision. Marble decomposes the observed tensor into two terms, a bias tensor and an interaction tensor. The bias tensor represents the baseline characteristics common amongst the overall population and the interaction tensor defines the phenotypes. We demonstrate the capability of our proposed model on both simulated and patient data from a publicly available clinical database. Our results show that Marble derived phenotypes provide at least a 42.8% reduction in the number of non-zero element and also retains predictive power for classification purposes. Furthermore, the resulting phenotypes and baseline characteristics from real EHR data are consistent with known characteristics of the patient population. Thus it can potentially be used to rapidly characterize, predict, and manage a large number of diseases, thereby promising a novel, data-driven solution that can benefit very large segments of the population.

Categories and Subject Descriptors

H.2.8 [**Database Applications**]: Data mining

Keywords

Tensor; Dimensionality reduction; EHR phenotyping; Application

KDD'14, August 24–27, 2014, New York, NY, USA.

http://dx.doi.org/10.1145/2623330.2623658 .

1. INTRODUCTION

Electronic health records (EHRs) are becoming an increasingly important source of detailed patient information. Effective integration and efficient analysis of EHRs can aid in solving many of the healthcare problems: making informed clinical decisions, improving patient safety, and facilitating investigations and knowledge discovery. However, several formidable challenges arise from the application of EHR data to clinical research, including diverse populations, heterogeneous and noisy information, and interpretability constraints. Medical professionals are accustomed to reasoning based on concise and meaningful medical concepts, or phenotypes. EHR-based phenotyping is a process to map raw EHR data into meaningful medical concepts, learning medically relevant characteristics of the data [15], and is important for supporting genome-wide association studies [10]. An example is the severe early childhood obesity phenotype[1], which identifies children with increased risk of adult obesity and a potential lifetime of complications.

State of the art phenotype development, such as the eMerge Network[2], relies primarily on approaches that are heuristic, rule, and iterative based, and is a collaborative team effort between clinicians and IT experts [15, 22]. Recent work has focused on high-throughput phenotyping, efficient and automated phenotype extractions to reduce manual development. Although data mining tools have been utilized to automate the phenotype process, current high-throughput methodologies cannot generate large amounts of candidate phenotypes and achieve good performance without human annotated samples [5]. Therefore, a major limitation of existing phenotype efforts is the need for human annotation of case and control samples, which require substantial time, effort, and expert knowledge to develop.

The "ideal" phenotype (i) represents complex interactions between several sources, (ii) is concise and easily understood by a medical professional, and (iii) maps to domain knowledge. Thus, phenotyping can be viewed as a form of dimensionality reduction, where each phenotype forms a latent space [15]. Matrix factorization, a common dimensionality reduction approach, is insufficient as it cannot concisely capture structured EHR source interactions, such as multiple medications prescribed to treat a single disease. A more natural transformation is tensor factorization, which utilizes

[1]The phenotype definition can be found in Phenotype KnowledgeBase.

[2]The eMerge network explores the use of EHR to obtain phenotypic information at multiple medical institutions.

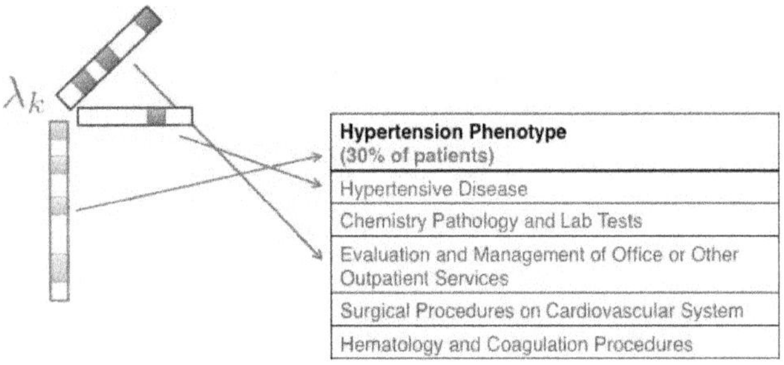

Figure 1: Example of a Marble-derived phenotype from CMS data.

Table 1: List of notations used in this paper

Symbol	Definition
α, γ	scalar
$\boldsymbol{\lambda}, \mathbf{u}, \mathbf{a}$	vector
$\mathbf{A}, \mathbf{B}, \mathbf{Z}, \mathbf{\Lambda}, \mathbf{\Pi}, \mathbf{\Phi}, \mathbf{\Psi}$	matrix
$\boldsymbol{\mathcal{X}}, \boldsymbol{\mathcal{M}}, \boldsymbol{\mathcal{C}}, \boldsymbol{\mathcal{V}}$	tensor
$\vec{i}$	tensor element index $(i_1, i_2, \cdots, i_N)$
$x_{\vec{i}}$	tensor element at index $\vec{i}$
$\mathbf{X}_{(n)}, \mathbf{M}_{(n)}, \mathbf{C}_{(n)}$	mode-n matricization of tensor
$*$	element-wise multiplication
$\oslash$	element-wise division
$\circ$	outer product
$\odot$	Khatri-Rao product
$< \mathbf{x}, \mathbf{y} >$	inner product of $\mathbf{x}, \mathbf{y}$

the multiway structure to produce concise and potentially more interpretable results. We conducted a pilot study to evaluate tensor-derived phenotypes using EHR data from the Geisinger Health System [14]. A medical expert evaluated 50 tensor-derived phenotypes and found that 82% generally mapped to a medical concept. However, the domain expert's comments primarily revolved around the lack of conciseness and the presence of "unnecessary" diagnoses and medications. Therefore, a sparse non-negative tensor factorization of count data is desired to simultaneously generate multiple concise phenotypes. An efficient and automated high-throughput phenotyping process can help identify existing, as well as novel, medical concepts from large-scale EHR data, and increase our ability to create personalized applications to improve the health and well-being of the general population.

This paper presents *Marble*, a novel sparse non-negative tensor factorization model to fit count data. Analogous to the geology domain, where marble rock is used to produce monuments, buildings, and sculptures, our algorithm can serve as the basis of automated high-throughput phenotyping tools. Our model extends the non-negative CANDECOMP/PARAFAC (CP) Poisson tensor decomposition [6] from two aspects: (i) constraints on the factor matrices to minimize the number of non-zero elements, and (ii) augmentation of the tensor approximation. Marble decomposes an observed tensor into two terms, a bias (or offset) tensor and an interaction (or signal) tensor. The bias tensor represents the baseline characteristics common amongst the overall population and also provides computational stability. The interaction term is compromised of concise, intuitive, and interpretable phenotypes in the data, illustrated in Figure 1. This paper details the tensor factorization model and presents the algorithm to solve the problem formulation using both an alternating minimization and sequential unconstrained minimization approach. We corroborate our model on simulation data as well as real EHR data. Our results demonstrate that Marble achieves at least a 42.8% reduction in the number of non-zero elements compared to CP-APR without sacrificing the quality of the tensor decomposition. Furthermore, the phenotypes and the baseline characteristics derived from the real EHR data are consistent with existing studies on the population.

The remainder of the paper is structured as follows. Section 2 presents preliminaries of matrix and tensor factorization and related work. Next, we detail our model in Section 3. Section 4 demonstrates and evaluates our model on simulation data and real EHR data. Finally, we summarize our work in Section 5.

2. PRELIMINARIES AND RELATED WORK

This section describes the preliminaries of matrix and tensor decomposition and related tensor factorization work. Table 1 provides a key for the symbols used in the paper. For indexing of matrix $\mathbf{A}$, we denote the (i,j)th element as a_{ij}, the jth column as $\mathbf{a}_{:j}$, and the ith column as $\mathbf{a}_{i:}$.

Matrix decomposition. Matrix factorization (MF) is a common dimensionality reduction approach, which represents the original data using a lower dimensional latent space. Standard MF approaches find two lower dimensional matrices that when multiplied together approximately produce the original matrix, $\mathbf{X} \approx \mathbf{WH}$. Although many matrix decomposition techniques exist, singular value decomposition and nonnegative matrix factorization (NMF) are two common algorithms used to reduce the feature dimension.

Notation Details. Definitions for algebraic operations used in the paper are provided below.

Definition 1. *The outer product of N vectors, $\mathbf{a}^{(1)} \circ \mathbf{a}^{(2)} \circ \cdots \circ \mathbf{a}^{(N)}$, produces a Nth order tensor $\boldsymbol{\mathcal{X}}$ where each element $x_{\vec{i}} = x_{i_1,i_2,\cdots,i_N} = a_{i_1}^{(1)} a_{i_2}^{(2)} \cdots a_{i_N}^{(N)}$.*

Definition 2. *The element-wise multiplication (and division) of two same-sized matrices $\mathbf{A} * \mathbf{B}$ ($\mathbf{A} \oslash \mathbf{B}$) produces a matrix $\mathbf{Z}$ of the same size such that the element $c_{\vec{i}} = a_{\vec{i}} b_{\vec{i}}$ ($c_{\vec{i}} = a_{\vec{i}} / b_{\vec{i}}$) for all $\vec{i}$.*

Definition 3. *The Khatri-Rao product of two matrices $\mathbf{A} \odot \mathbf{B}$ of sizes $I_A \times R$ and $I_B \times R$ respectively, produces a matrix $\mathbf{Z}$ of size $I_A I_B \times R$ such that $Z = \begin{bmatrix} \mathbf{a}_1 \otimes \mathbf{b}_1 & \cdots & \mathbf{a}_R \otimes \mathbf{b}_R \end{bmatrix}$, where $\otimes$ represents the Kronecker product. The Kronecker product of two vectors* $\mathbf{a} \otimes \mathbf{b} = \begin{bmatrix} a_1 \mathbf{b} \\ a_2 \mathbf{b} \\ \vdots \\ a_{I_A} \mathbf{b} \end{bmatrix}$.

Tensor Decomposition. A tensor is a generalization of matrices to higher dimensions. Thus, tensor factorization (decomposition) is a natural extension of matrix factorization and utilizes information from the multiway structure that is lost when modes are collapsed to use matrix factorization algorithms [21, 23]. The CANDECOMP / PARAFAC

(CP) [3, 13] model is a common tensor decomposition and can be viewed as a higher-order generalization of singular value decomposition [17]. The CP model approximates the original tensor $\boldsymbol{\mathcal{X}}$ as a sum of R rank-one tensors and can be expressed as

$$\begin{aligned}\boldsymbol{\mathcal{X}} &\approx \sum_{r=1}^{R} \lambda_r \mathbf{a}_r^{(1)} \circ \ldots \circ \mathbf{a}_r^{(N)} \\ &= [\![\boldsymbol{\lambda}; \mathbf{A}^{(1)}; \ldots; \mathbf{A}^{(N)}]\!].\end{aligned}$$

Note that $[\![\boldsymbol{\lambda}; \mathbf{A}^{(1)}; \ldots; \mathbf{A}^{(N)}]\!]$ is shorthand notation to describe the CP decomposition, where $\boldsymbol{\lambda}$ is a vector of the weights λ_r and $\mathbf{a}_r^{(n)}$ is the rth column of $\mathbf{A}^{(n)}$. The CP tensor decomposition has been used for concept discovery [16], network analysis of fMRI data [9], and community discovery [20]. The details of computing the CP decomposition and other tensor decomposition models can be found in [17].

Some domain applications may desire non-negative components, a higher-order generalization of NMF. Non-negative tensor factorization (NTF) requires the elements of the factor matrices and the weights to be non-negative. A broad survey of practical and useful NMF and NTF algorithms can be found in [8]. Our paper will focus on the nonnegative CP alternating Poisson regression (CP-APR) model to fit sparse count data [6]. Details of the algorithm and model are presented in the paper by Chi and Kolda [6].

NTF and NMF algorithms generally produce sparse representations. However, additional sparsity may be desired for the factor matrices. Traditional sparsity-inducing penalties such as ℓ_1 and ℓ_2 regularization [23] only deal with the standard least-squares minimization. Non-parametric Bayesian approaches to sparse Tucker decomposition have been recently proposed [24]. Nonetheless, there is a paucity of existing work regarding sparse factor representations using KL divergence as an objective function. A multi-layer NTF has been proposed to achieve sparse representations for various cost functions including KL divergence using a nonlinearly transformed gradient descent approach [7]. Yet, the approach is computationally expensive because multiple tensor factorization stages are required and sparsity constraints are achieved via an exponential update (i.e. $s \leftarrow s^{1+\gamma}$, for small γ). Sparse factor representation using KL divergence is difficult because (1) an incorrect zero in the factor representation causes the objective function to be ill-defined as $\lim_{i\to 0} \log i = -\infty$, and (2) data centering, a technique commonly used to remove the bias in continuous data prior to matrix/tensor factorization, is not feasible as the objective function (KL divergence) is defined on the non-negative orthant. Both challenges will be addressed in Section 3.3.

3. MARBLE

Marble is a sparse non-negative tensor factorization for count data. Marble decomposes an observed tensor into two terms, a bias (or offset) tensor and an interaction (or signal) tensor. The bias tensor represents the baseline characteristics common amongst the overall population and also provides computational stability. The interaction term is compromised of the R most prevalent phenotypes in the data (or medical concepts that are observed). Our model imposes sparsity constraints by reducing the "probabilistically unlikely" mode elements. Figure 2 illustrates the factorization of the patient by diagnosis by procedure tensor into R phenotypes and the bias vectors. We will first formulate the problem and provide a general overview of the algorithm. Next, we introduce the sparse factor representation and the augmented bias tensor. Then, we present the algorithm to solve the problem formulation. Finally, we illustrate how Marble can be used to perform high-throughput phenotyping in EHR data.

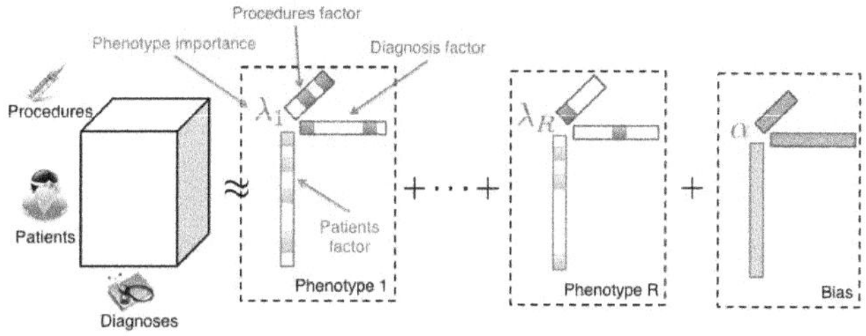

Figure 2: Deriving candidate phenotypes using Marble.

3.1 Problem Formulation and Overview

Let $\boldsymbol{\mathcal{X}}$ denote an observed tensor constructed from count data with size $I_1 \times I_2 \times \cdots \times I_N$ and $\boldsymbol{\mathcal{M}}$ represent a same-sized tensor of Poisson parameters for $\boldsymbol{\mathcal{X}}$. $\boldsymbol{\mathcal{M}}$ is split into two terms, a rank one bias tensor $\boldsymbol{\mathcal{C}}$ and a rank R interaction tensor $\boldsymbol{\mathcal{V}}$. The bias term, or baseline characteristics of the population, is composed of N positive vectors $\mathbf{u}^{(1)}, \cdots, \mathbf{u}^{(N)}$ and a positive scalar α. The interaction term is similar to the Poisson decomposition tensor, where each rank one tensor is comprised of N stochastic vectors (elements sum to 1 and non-negative) with a non-negative weight λ_r. However, Marble constrains the feasible space of the vectors to either be zero or above some threshold value γ_n. The optimization problem is defined as

$$\min f(\boldsymbol{\mathcal{M}}) \equiv \sum_{\vec{i}} (m_{\vec{i}} - x_i \log m_{\vec{i}}) \tag{1}$$

$$\begin{aligned}\text{s.t } \boldsymbol{\mathcal{M}} &= \boldsymbol{\mathcal{C}} + \boldsymbol{\mathcal{V}} \\ \boldsymbol{\mathcal{C}} &= [\![\alpha; \mathbf{u}^{(1)}; \cdots; \mathbf{u}^{(N)}]\!] \in \Omega_C \qquad (2) \\ \boldsymbol{\mathcal{V}} &= [\![\boldsymbol{\lambda}; \mathbf{A}^{(1)}; \cdots; \mathbf{A}^{(N)}]\!] \in \Omega_V \\ \Omega_C &= \Omega_\alpha \times \Omega_{u1} \times \cdots \times \Omega_{uN} \\ \Omega_\alpha &= (0, +\infty) \qquad (3) \\ \Omega_{un} &= \{\mathbf{u} \in (0,1]^{I_n \times 1} \mid ||\mathbf{u}||_1 = 1\} \qquad (4) \\ \Omega_V &= \Omega_\lambda \times \Omega_{A1} \times \cdots \times \Omega_{AN} \\ \Omega_\lambda &= [0, +\infty)^R \\ \Omega_{An} &= \{\mathbf{A} \in \{0, [\gamma_n, 1]\}^{I_n \times R} \mid ||\mathbf{a}_{:r}||_1 = 1 \ \forall r\}. \qquad (5)\end{aligned}$$

We solve the problem using an alternating minimization approach, cycling through each mode while fixing all other modes. For each mode, the algorithm first calculates the factor matrix associated with the interaction tensor. The matrix is then gradually projected onto the feasible space, described in Section 3.2, using a penalty method approach detailed in Section 3.4.2. Once the interaction factor matrix is computed, the bias vector is computed. After an iteration (where the algorithm has cycled through all the modes), the projection penalty is updated and the whole process is repeated until convergence occurs. A high-level view of the Marble algorithm is illustrated in Algorithm 1, with details described in Section 3.4.

Algorithm 1: Overview of Marble algorithm

while *not converged* **do**
  foreach *mode n* **do**
    Solve the nth interaction factor matrix (Section 3.2);
    Project onto sparse factors (Section 3.4.2);
    Solve nth bias vector (Section 3.3);
  end
  Calculate gradual projection penalty (Section 3.4.2);
end

3.2 Sparse Factor Representation

Sparse factor representations are desired to improve interpretability and address the problem where the CP-APR tensor factorization model produced "probabilistically unlikely" diagnoses and medications. The CP-APR model imposes a stochastic constraint on the columns of the factor matrices. For the rth rank one tensor, each non-zero element along the nth vector $\mathbf{a}_r^{(n)}$ represents a probabilistic estimate of the element's membership (e.g. probability the diagnosis diabetes belongs to this phenotype). Therefore, our model removes small non-zero elements to achieve sparse factor matrices, while also guaranteeing convergence to a local minimum. Marble modifies the stochastic constraints of CP-APR such that each nth factor matrix, $\mathbf{A}^{(n)}$, will have non-zero components that range from γ_n to 1 and the elements of each column sum to 1. Equation (5) captures the sparse factor representation constraint. Each mode can have a different threshold, γ_n, as the desired level of sparsity may depend both on domain constraints and the mode size.

3.3 Bias Tensor

Marble introduces a rank one bias tensor to capture baseline characteristics common amongst the overall population. Traditional tensor (or matrix) factorization approaches, which use a least squares loss, center the data by subtracting the feature mean from all the observations. Thus, the decomposition is only performed on the "signal" (or "interaction") aspects of the data. Unfortunately, the data centering technique is not feasible for Marble as the KL divergence is only defined for non-negative $x_{\bar{i}}$.

The bias tensor also provides computational stability for the "inadmissible zeros" resulting from the sparse factor representation. Under the assumption that γ_n in Equation (5) is set to be non-zero, the sparse factor representation will produce a limited number of non-zero elements. Given that R is not over-specified, the probability an element $m_{\bar{i}}$ is zero is high. If the corresponding observed tensor element is zero ($x_{\bar{i}} = 0$), then $m_{\bar{i}} - x_i \log m_{\bar{i}} = 0$. However, for a non-zero $x_{\bar{i}}$, the objective function is ill-defined as $\lim_{i \to 0} \log i = -\infty$, leading to an "inadmissible zero". Several works have dealt with this problem by either avoiding zeros [11], altering the updates [19], or shifting elements into the interior [6]. However, all these methods adversely effect the sparsity of the resulting factors.

We *augment* the Poisson tensor decomposition with an additional rank-one tensor, shown in Equation (2). The scalar constant α and the factor vectors $\mathbf{u}^{(1)}, \mathbf{u}^{(2)}, \cdots, \mathbf{u}^{(N)}$ must be *strictly positive*, which are captured in Equations (3) and (4). Although similar in nature to an additional clinical phenotype, the bias tensor is not equivalent to increasing the rank of the original decomposition $\boldsymbol{\mathcal{V}}$ to $R+1$. Each factor vector ($\mathbf{u}^{(1)}$ where $n > 1$) represents the common baseline characteristics amongst the *entire* population (e.g., the overall likelihood of developing diabetes, getting a chest x-ray, etc) and captures the data bias, or offset, of the observed tensor. Furthermore, the positive augmented tensor stabilizes the optimization problem by avoiding inadmissible zeros in $\boldsymbol{\mathcal{M}}$ and allows sparse factor matrices in the interaction tensor, $\mathbf{A}^{(n)}$.

3.4 Algorithm

3.4.1 Alternating Minimization Updates

The optimization problem presented in Section 3.1 is solved via an alternating minimization approach, where all factor vectors/matrices are fixed except for the one being updated. For each mode, we compute the subproblem solution using an approach similar to CP-APR [6]. For the nth mode, we express the mode-n matricization $\mathbf{V}_{(n)} = \mathbf{B}^{(n)} \mathbf{\Pi}^{(n)}$, where

$$\mathbf{B}^{(n)} = \mathbf{A}^{(n)} \mathbf{\Lambda}, \text{ where } \mathbf{\Lambda} = \text{diag}(\boldsymbol{\lambda}) \tag{6}$$

$$\mathbf{\Pi}^{(n)} = \left(\mathbf{A}^{(N)} \odot \cdots \odot \mathbf{A}^{(n+1)} \odot \mathbf{A}^{(n-1)} \odot \cdots \odot \mathbf{A}^{(1)}\right)^{\mathsf{T}}. \tag{7}$$

The weights ($\boldsymbol{\lambda}$) are absorbed into the nth factor matrix $\mathbf{B}^{(n)}$ in Equation (6) and we use the matrix $\mathbf{\Pi}^{(n)}$ to denote the fixed parts in Equation (7). Note that the size of matrix $\mathbf{B}^{(n)}$ is $I_n \times R$ while the size of matrix $\mathbf{\Pi}^{(n)}$ is $R \times \prod_{j=1, j \neq n}^{N} I_j$. Using the notation above, we can rewrite the objective function, Equation (1) as follows:

$$\mathbf{e}^{\mathsf{T}} \left[\mathbf{C}_{(n)} + \mathbf{B}^{(n)} \mathbf{\Pi}^{(n)} - \mathbf{X}_{(n)} * \log\left(\mathbf{C}_{(n)} + \mathbf{B}^{(n)} \mathbf{\Pi}^{(n)}\right)\right] \mathbf{e},$$

where $\mathbf{e}$ is a vector of all ones, $\mathbf{C}_{(n)}$ is the mode-n matricization of the bias tensor and $\mathbf{X}_{(n)}$ is the mode-n matricization of the observed tensor.

The multiplicative update derivation for the weighted factor matrix $\mathbf{B}^{(n)}$ can be computed by taking the partial derivative of the objective function respect to a single element b_{gh}.

$$\frac{\partial f}{\partial b_{gh}} = \sum_{\ell} \pi_{h\ell} - \sum_{\ell} x_{g\ell} \frac{\pi_{h\ell}}{c_{g\ell} + \sum_r b_{gr} \pi_{r\ell}}.$$

Setting the gradient descent step size set to $\frac{b_{gh}}{\sum_{\ell} \pi_{h\ell}}$ yields the multiplicative update:

$$b_{gh} = b_{gh} \left[\sum_{\ell} x_{g\ell} \frac{\pi_{h\ell}}{c_{g\ell} + \sum_r b_{gr} \pi_{r\ell}}\right].$$

The non-negative factor matrix constraints are satisfied using the multiplicative update. Generalizing for the entire factor matrix, the update equation is as follows:

$$\mathbf{B}^{(n)} = \mathbf{B}^{(n)} * \left[\mathbf{X} \oslash (\mathbf{C}_{(n)} + \mathbf{B}^{(n)} \mathbf{\Pi}^{(n)})\right] \mathbf{\Pi}^{(n)\mathsf{T}}. \tag{8}$$

We adopt the same alternating update strategy for the bias tensor $\boldsymbol{\mathcal{C}}$. In particular, we update the mode n bias vector $\mathbf{u}^{(n)}$ holding other modes constant, with the fixed parts denoted as $\mathbf{\Psi}^{(n)}$.

$$\mathbf{C}_{(n)} = \alpha \mathbf{u}^{(n)} \mathbf{\Psi}^{(n)}$$

$$\mathbf{\Psi}^{(n)} = \left(\mathbf{u}^{(N)} \odot \cdots \odot \mathbf{u}^{(n+1)} \odot \mathbf{u}^{(n-1)} \odot \cdots \odot \mathbf{u}^{(1)}\right)^{\mathsf{T}} \tag{9}$$

The update for the augmented bias vector follows a similar derivation as $\mathbf{B}^{(n)}$.

$$\mathbf{u}^{(n)} = \mathbf{u}^{(n)} * \left[\mathbf{X}_{(n)} \oslash (\alpha \mathbf{u}^{(n)} \mathbf{\Psi}^{(n)} + \mathbf{V}_{(n)})\right] \mathbf{\Psi}^{(n)\mathsf{T}}. \quad (10)$$

3.4.2 Gradual Projection

The alternating minimization updates satisfy the non-negative constraints of the weights ($\boldsymbol{\lambda}$), factor matrices $\mathbf{A}^{(n)}$, and basis vectors $\mathbf{u}^{(n)}$. However, the factor matrices will not satisfy the modified stochastic constraints in Equation (5). The projected gradient descent method can be used to threshold the factor matrices after each alternating minimization update. Experimental results (shown in Section 4) show that zeroing out components too early in the iterative process negatively impacts the quality of the factor representation. Instead, Marble uses a penalty method approach [2] to gradually adjust the projection threshold at each iteration. During the early iterations, when the factor representations are changing drastically, the "feasible set" is closer to the $[0, 1]$ range. As the factor representations start to stabilize (difference in objective function starts to approach zero), the projection occurs on the feasible set described in Equation (5). A new scalar ξ is introduced to calculate the gradual projection, where each iteration uses the threshold $\xi\gamma_n$. The range of ξ is [0,1], where zero represents no projection and 1 represents the full projection. After each iteration k where all the modes have been cycled through, we update ξ as follows:

$$\begin{aligned} \kappa^{(k)} &= 1 - \frac{|f(\boldsymbol{\mathcal{M}}^{(k-1)}) - f(\boldsymbol{\mathcal{M}}^{(k)})|}{|f(\boldsymbol{\mathcal{M}}^{(k-1)})|} \\ \xi^{(k+1)} &= \max(\xi^{(k)}, \frac{1}{2}\xi^{(k)} + \frac{1}{2}\kappa^{(k)}). \end{aligned} \quad (11)$$

Marble uses a moving average of the ξ to minimize drastic changes and also ensures that the penalty is non-decreasing at each iteration.

3.4.3 Algorithm Details

Subproblem Convergence. Marble performs several subproblem iterations (user-defined maximum L) at each mode n for both the factor matrix $\mathbf{A}^{(n)}$ and the bias vector $\mathbf{u}^{(n)}$. Empirical evidence suggests extra inner iterations can accelerate the convergence [6]. The benefit of subproblem iterations on simulation data is presented in Section 4. The exit criterion (Karush-Kuhn-Tucker (KKT) conditions) for the subproblem iterates is similar to the CP-APR algorithm [6]. For convenience, we introduce the following to matrices:

$$\mathbf{\Phi}^{(n)} = \left[\mathbf{X}_{(n)} \oslash (\alpha \mathbf{u}^{(n)} \mathbf{\Psi}^{(n)} + \mathbf{B}^{(n)} \mathbf{\Pi}^{(n)})\right] \mathbf{\Pi}^{(n)\mathsf{T}} \quad (12)$$

$$\mathbf{Z}^{(n)} = \left[\mathbf{X}_{(n)} \oslash (\alpha \mathbf{u}^{(n)} \mathbf{\Psi}^{(n)} + \mathbf{B}^{(n)} \mathbf{\Pi}^{(n)})\right] \mathbf{\Psi}^{(n)\mathsf{T}}, \quad (13)$$

which capture the multiplicative terms in Equations (8) and (10) respectively. These matrices are used to check convergence of the subproblem, with the algorithm exiting under the following conditions:

$$\min(\mathbf{A}^{(n)}, \mathbf{E} - \mathbf{\Phi}^{(n)}) = \mathbf{0}$$
$$\min(\mathbf{u}^{(n)}, \mathbf{E} - \mathbf{Z}^{(n)}) = \mathbf{0},$$

where $\mathbf{E}$ represents a matrix of all ones. Note that min is the element-wise minimum of the two matrices, and the result should be a matrix of all zeros. We relax the zero equality for practical purposes and check for convergence within a certain tolerance, e.g. $\min(\mathbf{u}^{(n)}, \mathbf{E} - \mathbf{Z}^{(n)}) \leq \mathsf{kktTol}$. The detailed Marble algorithm is presented in Algorithm 2.

Algorithm 2: Detailed Marble algorithm

```
Data: 𝓧, R, α, γ
Result: 𝓥, 𝓒
for k = 1,2,··· ,K do
    lastObj ← 0
    ξ ← 0
    //For each mode n
    for n = 1,··· ,N do
        Ω̂_n ← {0, [ξγ_n, 1]}^{I_n × R}
        Set Ψ^(n) using Equation (9)
        Set B^(n) using Equation (6)
        Set Π^(n) using Equation (7)
        //Solve nth interaction factor matrix
        for ℓ = 1,··· ,L do
            Calculate Φ^(n) using Equation (12)
            if min(B^(n), E − Φ^(n)) ≤ kktTol then break
            B^(n) ← B^(n) * Φ^(n)
        end
        //Project onto sparse factors
        B^(n) ← P_{Ω̂_n}(B^(n))
        λ ← e^T B^(n)
        A^(n) ← B^(n) Λ^{-1}
        //Solve nth bias vector
        for ℓ = 1,··· ,L do
            Calculate Z^(n) using Equation (13)
            if min(u^(n), E − Z^(n)) ≤ kktTol then break
            u^(n) ← u^(n) * Z^(n)
        end
        u^(n) ← u^(n) / ||u^(n)||_1
    end
    obj ← f(𝓜)
    if |obj − lastObj| < convergenceTol then break
    //Calculate projection penalty
    Update ξ using Equation (11)
    lastObj ← obj
end
```

Sparse Implementation. When $\boldsymbol{\mathcal{X}}$ is a sparse tensor, we construct $\boldsymbol{\mathcal{V}}$ and $\boldsymbol{\mathcal{C}}$ using the non-zero elements of the observed tensor and avoid constructing $\boldsymbol{\mathcal{V}}$ and $\boldsymbol{\mathcal{C}}$ explicitly. Our algorithm adopts the sparse tensor implementation approach presented in [1, 6]. The only calculations necessary are the ones that correspond to the non-zero elements in $\boldsymbol{\mathcal{X}}$. We can store $\boldsymbol{\mathcal{X}}$ as a set of values and indices (v^q, c), where Q are the non-zero elements of the tensor. We then form Q rows of $\mathbf{\Pi}$ and $\mathbf{Z}$ that correspond to each non-zero element of $\boldsymbol{\mathcal{X}}$. The qth vector of $\mathbf{\Pi}$ and $\mathbf{Z}$ are:

$$\begin{aligned} w^{(q)} &= \mathbf{a}^{(1)}_{(\vec{i}^{(q)}_1 :)} * \cdots * \mathbf{a}^{(n+1)}_{(\vec{i}^{(q)}_{n+1} :)} * \mathbf{a}^{(n-1)}_{(\vec{i}^{(q)}_{n-1} :)} * \cdots * \mathbf{a}^{(N)}_{(\vec{i}^{(q)}_N :)} \\ y^{(q)} &= \mathbf{u}^{(1)}_{(\vec{i}^{(q)}_1 :)} * \cdots * \mathbf{u}^{(n+1)}_{(\vec{i}^{(q)}_{n+1} :)} * \mathbf{u}^{(n-1)}_{(\vec{i}^{(q)}_{n-1} :)} * \cdots * \mathbf{u}^{(N)}_{(\vec{i}^{(q)}_N :)}, \end{aligned}$$

where $\mathbf{a}^{(1)}_{(\bar{i}_1^{(q)}:)}$ is the $\bar{i}_1^{(q)}$ row of $\mathbf{A}^{(1)}$. Thus, we can calculate element (i, r) of $\mathbf{\Pi}$ and $\mathbf{Z}$ as:

$$v^{(q)} = x^{(q)}/(<\mathbf{y}^{(q)}, \alpha\mathbf{u}^{(n)}_{(i_n^{(q)}:)}> + <\mathbf{w}^{(q)}, \mathbf{B}^{(n)}_{(i_n^{(q)}:)}>)$$

$$\Phi_{jr} = \sum_{q:i_n^{(q)}=j} v^{(q)}\mathbf{w}^{(q)}$$

$$z_{jr} = \sum_{q:i_n^{(q)}=j} v^{(q)}\mathbf{y}^{(q)}$$

Note that we require storage for the augmented tensor, which entails storing $\mathbf{y}^{(q)}$. Thus, we require Q additional storage compared to CP-APR.

Computational Complexity. Note that the subproblem iterates in the CP-APR model is the computational bottleneck of the algorithm. In particular, calculating $\mathbf{\Phi}$ requires on the order of the decomposition rank R times the product of the dimension of each tensor mode I_n. If we denote the size of the largest mode as D, then CP-APR has the computational complexity of $\mathcal{O}(D^N)$. Although our algorithm has to compute the additional augmented vector, the computational complexity remains the same as CP-APR.

3.5 Application to EHR-Phenotyping

While Marble is a general non-negative sparse tensor factorization model to fit count data, we motivated the problem to simultaneously derive multiple EHR phenotypes with minimal human intervention. We briefly describe the construction of an EHR count tensor and the resulting candidate phenotypes using our algorithm. Figure 3 provides a conceptual illustration of the high-throughput phenotyping process. Each patient is anchored using an index date (i.e. hospital admit date) and the observation window can be defined as a fixed time window either before or after the index date depending on the application. Any data that occurs during the observation window is used during the construction process. The EHR tensor is then constructed using the count of the co-occurrences between the various modes. In Figure 2, each tensor element represents the number of times either a normal or abnormal clinical measurement occurred.

Once the tensor is constructed, we can use Marble to fit a non-negative Poisson tensor decomposition to the data. The resultant tensor $\boldsymbol{\mathcal{V}}$ is then used to define R candidate phenotypes, similar to Figure 1. Thus, the rth candidate phenotype is defined using the non-zero elements of the rth column from all N factor matrices.

New patients can be projected onto the tensor-derived phenotypes to obtain a *phenotype membership* vector. We define the phenotype membership vector as the convex combination of the tensor-derived phenotypes, where the rth element denotes the probability the patient exhibits characteristics consist with the rth phenotype. For notation purpose, we will assume the patient mode is the first mode of the tensor. Thus given a new patient's tensor $\hat{\boldsymbol{\mathcal{X}}}$, we want to find $\hat{\boldsymbol{\lambda}}$ and $\hat{\mathbf{a}}^{(1)}$ that provides that best approximates the new patient's tensor. Our projection also needs to determine $\hat{\alpha}$, the strength of the bias in $\hat{\boldsymbol{\mathcal{X}}}$. We observe that this is equivalent to the optimization subproblem for the first mode with several noticeable differences: (1) the phenotype membership vector is obtained by normalizing the entries of $\hat{\mathbf{b}}^{(1)}$ across all R phenotypes instead of the standard column normalization for each phenotype, (2) setting the augmented vector ($\hat{u}^{(1)}$) to 1 and absorbing the weight into $\hat{\alpha}$, and (3) ignoring the projection onto the feasible set defined in the optimization problem.

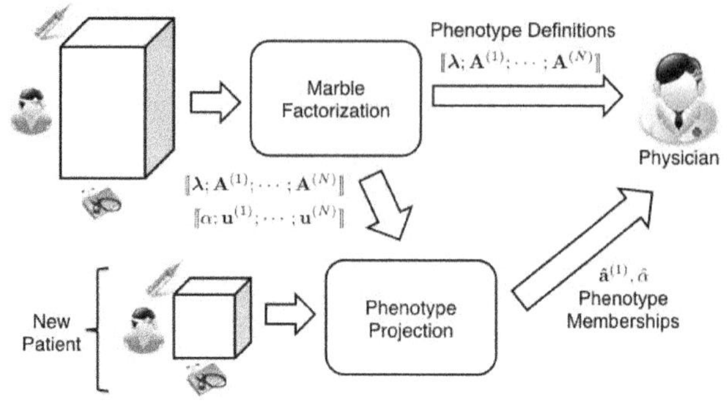

Figure 3: A high-level depiction of using Marble to generate high-throughput phenotypes.

4. EXPERIMENTS

In this section, we will first evaluate the algorithmic performance using a simulated dataset where the actual tensor factors are known. Then, we evaluate the phenotyping performance using a realistic EHR dataset.

Evaluation Metric Details. Definitions for the evaluation metrics are provided below.

$$\text{Non-zero Ratio} = \frac{\#\text{ Non-zeros in Computed Solution}}{\#\text{ Non-zeros in Actual Solution}}$$

$$\text{Similarity}(\mathbf{a}, \mathbf{b}) = \frac{\mathbf{a}^\intercal\mathbf{b}}{||\mathbf{a}||||\mathbf{b}||}$$

Similarity is calculated using the cosine similarity, a component of the factor match score (FMS), to quantify the similarity between the computed solution and the actual factor representation. FMS is commonly used to quantify the closeness of the computed solution and provides a single number between $[0, 1]$ [6]. However, FMS is an aggregate measure and can mask the mode-specific similarity results. For our analysis, we pair the computed rank-one tensors with the true rank-one tensors using a greedy algorithm, providing a lower bound on the similarity scores.

4.1 Simulation

First, we analyze simulated data where the underlying factor representation is known. Specifically, we consider a third-order tensor of size $100 \times 80 \times 60$ with rank of 10 ($R = 10$). We generate the model $\boldsymbol{\mathcal{M}} = \boldsymbol{\mathcal{C}} + \boldsymbol{\mathcal{V}}$, where $\boldsymbol{\mathcal{C}} = [\![\alpha; \mathbf{u}^{(1)}; \cdots; \mathbf{u}^{(N)}]\!]$ and $\boldsymbol{\mathcal{V}} = [\![\boldsymbol{\lambda}; \mathbf{A}^{(1)}; \cdots; \mathbf{A}^{(N)}]\!]$. Each factor matrix $\mathbf{A}^{(n)}$ is generated as follows: (1) Sample the non-zero element indices for each column according to the sparsity pattern for the mode; (2) From the sampled indices, randomly select 10% of the entries (or minimum of one) to sample uniformly from the interval $[0, 10]$ to mirror real EHR characteristics (e.g. one or two diagnosis contribute heavily to a phenotype); (3) For the remaining indices, sample uniformly from $[0, 1]$; and (4) Normalize the column so the elements sum to 1, and absorb the weight into $\boldsymbol{\lambda}$. Each augmented vector is chosen in a similar fashion except the weight is set to $\alpha = 2$. The full tensor $\boldsymbol{\mathcal{M}}$ is calculated from the factor matrices and the augmented vectors. Then each tensor element x_{ijk} is sampled from the Poisson distribution

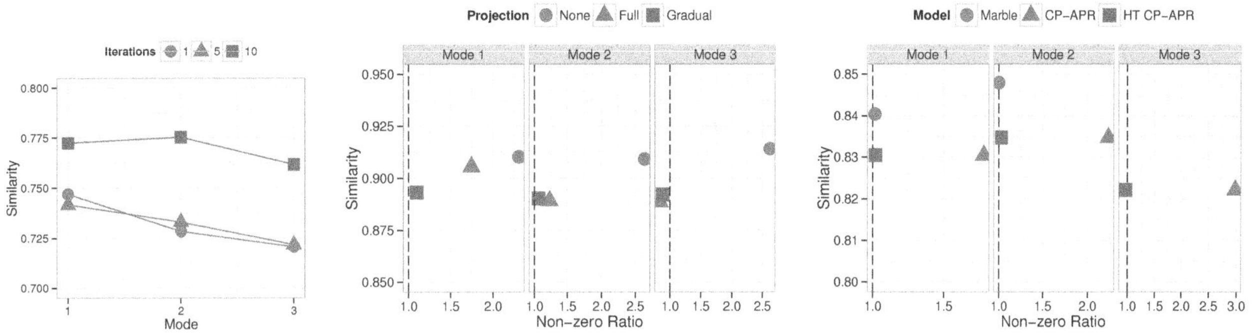

(a) Inner Iterations (b) Projection Type (c) Comparing Marble and CP-APR.

Figure 4: Simulation results on a third-order tensor

with the parameter set to m_{ijk}. Ten observation tensors are generated from the tensor $\mathcal{M}$.

4.1.1 *Inner iteration benefits*

The number of maximum subproblem iterations (L) represents the "closeness" to the subproblem solution. Thus, a single subproblem iteration (equivalent to the Lee-Seung multiplicative update [18]) only takes a step towards the subproblem solution as observed by [6]. For the simulated data, the average computation time (in seconds) for 1, 5, and 10 subproblem iterations was 37.6, 89.4, and 92.56 respectively. Additional inner iterations do not accelerate convergence, as the computational time increase with the number of iterations. However, Figure 4a illustrates the benefit of extra subproblem iterations on the similarity scores from the true solution. The similarity score at 10 inner iterations is the highest across all the modes. Therefore, more subproblem iterations improves the quality of the resulting tensor decomposition.

4.1.2 *Gradual projection benefits*

Empirical evidence for the gradual projection approach is presented in Figure 4b. We compare the gradual projection described in Section 3.4.2 to (i) no projection where $\xi = 0$ for all iterations, and (ii) full projection where $\xi = 1$ for all iterations. No projection yields the best similarity score across all three modes. However, the gradual projection approach results in tensor factors that are near the ideal non-zero ratio of 1. It also has higher similarity scores on two of the modes compared to full projection. Even though the observation matrix was generated from sparse factor representations with a relatively small bias effect ($\alpha = 2$), without any projection yields factor representations that on average contain at least $2\times$ more non-zero elements in each column. The results demonstrate that the gradual projection approach can reproduce the same sparsity ratio (number of non-zero elements / size of mode) as the true solution but sacrifices in terms of similarity to the true solution.

4.1.3 *CP-APR comparison*

Next, we perform a comparison with the CP-APR model. The multi-layer sparse NTF model [7] is omitted due to the added computational complexity of their model. Using a sparser underlying factor representation further highlights the differences between Marble and CP-APR. Marble is slower than CP-APR, primarily due to the computation of the augmented tensor decomposition. On the simulated data, Marble takes about 58 seconds to converge to a local optimal, while CP-APR obtains a solution in 45 seconds. However, in comparison to current phenotyping approaches, the 15 second difference is negligible given that a single disease phenotype can take months to develop.

Figure 4c displays a plot of the two algorithms based on the non-zero ratio used in Figure 4b. Marble's sparse factor representation results in a higher similarity score for the first and second mode. All the Marble modes are close to the ideal non-zero ratio of 1. Furthermore, Marble achieves a 42.8%, 55.1%, and 68.4% reduction on the non-zero ratio. Thus, the non-zero pattern across all three modes is better captured by our model, whereas CP-APR results in a higher number of non-zero elements.

4.2 CMS Claim Records

The Centers for Medicare and Medicaid Services (CMS) provides the *CMS Linkable 2008-2010 Medicare Data Entrepreneurs' Synthetic Public Use File (DE-SynPUF)*, a publicly available dataset that spans 3 years and contains inpatient, outpatient, carrier, and prescription drug event claims in addition to the beneficiary summary files[3]. The claims records have been synthesized from 5% of the 2008 Medicare population to protect the privacy of the beneficiaries. Although the relationships between some of the variables have been altered to minimize re-identification risk, the sheer volume of patients can still provide interesting and insightful phenotypes.

Our experiments focus on a random subset of 10,000 patients from Sample 1 (CMS released the data in 20 separate samples). We construct the tensor from the carrier claims records using the diagnosis and procedure codes. Individual International Classification of Diseases (ICD-9) diagnosis codes and Healthcare Common Procedure Coding System (HCPCS) procedure codes capture information at a fine-grained level. Thus, similar diagnosis codes (procedure codes) were grouped using the Unified Medical Language System[4] to aggregate the individual ICD-9 codes and HCPCS codes to higher level medical hierarchies. Therefore,

[3]A detailed description can be found on their website.

[4]The Metathesaurus contains the source vocabularies for 150 sources, including ICD-9-CM and HCPCS.

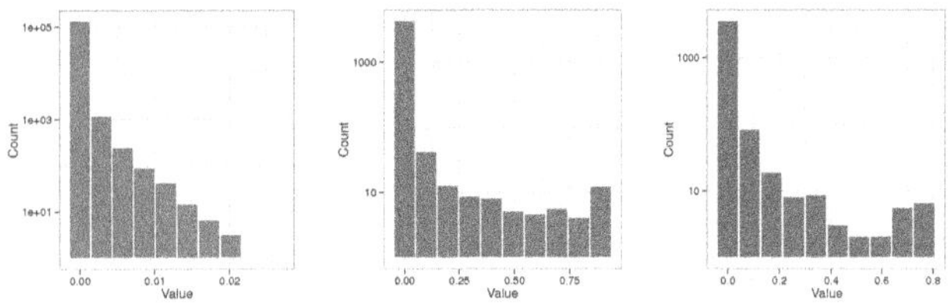

(a) Patient (b) Diagnosis (c) Procedure

Figure 5: The distribution of factor elements along the three CMS tensor modes. Zeros entries are omitted from the plot.

the constructed tensor is 10,000 patients by 129 diagnoses by 115 procedures.

4.2.1 Threshold selection

The Marble algorithm computes the sparse factor representation using predefined thresholds γ_n. These thresholds provide a tunable knob to adjust the sparsity of the candidate phenotypes. Domain constraints can be used to determine the threshold value (e.g. a phenotype should only contain a maximum of 3 unique diagnoses). However, given the absence of domain knowledge, the Marble algorithm can be used with $\gamma_n = 0$ for all n. A plot of the non-zero elements distribution along each mode can be used to determine the thresholds. Figure 5 shows the mean histogram of the CP-APR non-zero factor values along the three modes using $R = 50$ using the 10 subsamples. For all three plots, there is a noticeable difference in size (the y-axis uses a log scale) between the first two bins, which suggests the threshold occur at the start of the second bin. Thus, for the remainder of the paper, the thresholds used are $\boldsymbol{\gamma} = [0.0001, 0.01, 0.01]$.

4.2.2 Predictive performance

The phenotypes are evaluated on a classification task of predicting high cost (above 75th percentile) beneficiaries. Our algorithm is compared against (i) CP-APR derived phenotypes and (ii) the raw feature matrix with 129 × 115 columns, where each column represents a diagnosis-procedure combination. 10 random subsamples are obtained via stratified sampling with a 50-50 train test split, and the phenotypes are derived from the training dataset only. An ℓ_1 regularized logistic regression model is trained separately on each of the three feature sets (the phenotype membership matrix is the feature matrix for both Marble and CP-APR) and the predictive performance is evaluated on the test set.

Figure 6 displays a plot of the area under the receiver operating characteristic curve (AUC) as a function of the number of phenotypes (R). The predictive performance of both tensor factorization models using 50 phenotypes is similar to baseline, providing a 300× feature reduction from the original raw feature matrix. Beyond 50 phenotypes, the accuracy gradually increases with the number of phenotypes. Marble takes approximately 3.5 hours[5] to factor the data using 50 phenotypes. For the remainder of this paper, we use $R = 50$ to provide detailed analysis of the individual phenotypes.

Marble and CP-APR perform similarly in terms of predictive power. Table 2 illustrates a comparison between the

[5]A computer with an Intel® Xeon® Processor X5660 and 8 GB RAM.

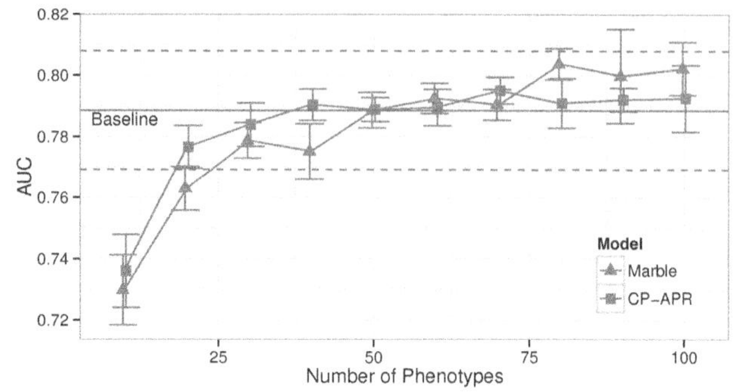

Figure 6: Area under the receiver operating characteristic curve for the three feature sets as a function of the number of phenotypes. The error bars display the 95% confidence interval.

first, or highest λ_r, Marble-derived phenotype and a "similar" CP-APR derived phenotype, where FMS is used to quantify overall closeness of the phenotypes. The CP-APR phenotype contains 10× more diagnosis and procedure elements because there is no sparsity constraint on the factorization. In contrast, a medical professional can easily digest the contents of the phenotype resulting from the Marble algorithm. Marble yields concise phenotypes without losing predictive power.

4.2.3 Data Bias

An added benefit of Marble is that it captures the baseline characteristics that exist in the overall population via the rank-one bias tensor. Table 3 shows the 10 highest valued elements from the diagnosis and procedure mode, in decreasing magnitude. The diagnosis bias vector shows that Medicare patients generally visit clinics because of various symptoms and complications. Furthermore, the diagnosis vector contains several chronic diseases common in the elderly population, such as hypertension, arthritis (arthropathies), heart disease, and diabetes (disease of other endocrine glands). Centers for Disease Control and Prevention (CDC) estimate that 80% of older adults suffer from at least one chronic condition and 50% have two or more chronic conditions [4]. The procedure basis vector also contains procedure codes relevant to the treatment of patients with chronic conditions. We verified the results in Table 3 with chronic disease reports provided by CDC[6].

4.2.4 Chronic disease performance

The United States spends more than 2.1 trillion dollars (75% of medical care) on the treatment of chronic diseases [4]. Thus, obtaining phenotypes related to chronic disease such as heart failure, diabetes, and cancer can help medical professionals tailor treatment options based on the patient's phenotypes. The CMS dataset provides chronic disease indicators[7] that we will use to identify phenotypes associated with specific chronic diseases.

Table 4 illustrates two of the heart-failure related phenotypes, which maps to varying degrees of disease severity. Pa-

[6]The latest disease reports are located at `http://www.cdc.gov/chronicdisease/resources/publications/aag.htm`

[7]A patient's chronic condition flag cannot be perfectly reproduced due to the synthetic claim process used.

Table 2: Comparison of two tensor-derived phenotypes (blue and red text correspond to non-zero elements in the diagnosis and procedure factors, respectively)

Marble Phenotype
Other metabolic and immunity disorders
Hypertensive disease
Complications of surgical and medical care
Chemistry Pathology and Laboratory Tests
Organ or Disease Oriented Panels
Hematology and Coagulation Procedures
Surgical Procedures on the Cardiovascular System

CP-APR Phenotype
Diseases of the blood and blood-forming organs
Nonspecific abnormal findings
Other diseases of digestive system
··· 24 total diagnoses
Chemistry Pathology and Laboratory Tests
Hematology and Coagulation Procedures
Organ or Disease Oriented Panels
Surgical Procedures on the Cardiovascular System
··· 63 total procedures

Table 3: Top 10 elements for the augmented bias tensor

Diagnosis Mode
Symptoms
Complications of surgical and medical care
Arthropathies and related disorders
Other forms of heart disease
Dorsopathies
Disorders of the human eye
Diseases of other endocrine glands
Hypertensive disease
Other metabolic and immunity disorder
Other diseases of urinary system

Procedure Mode
Evaluation and Management of Other Outpatient Services
Diagnostic Radiology Procedures
Hospital Inpatient Services
Chemistry Pathology and Laboratory Tests
Physical Medicine and Rehabilitation Procedures
Surgical Procedures on the Cardiovascular System
Cardiovascular Procedures
Emergency Department Services
Nursing Facility Services
Hematology and Coagulation Procedures

tients with the second phenotype (titled severe heart failure) require hospital stays (inpatient services) and have added complications from lung disease. Table 5 depicts two other chronic disease phenotypes. The diabetes phenotype describes patients with complications resulting from diabetes, as the procedures include organ or disease oriented panels. The second phenotype, associated with arthritis, suggests that patients belong to this phenotype are undergoing rehabilitation to strengthen their joints. Furthermore, all four phenotypes shown are concise, easily interpretable, and map to known characteristics of the chronic disease.

5. CONCLUSION

This paper presented Marble, a novel sparse non-negative tensor factorization model to fit EHR count data. Our algorithm offers a data-driven solution to simultaneously generate multiple phenotypes from a diverse EHR population without expert supervision. The resulting phenotypes are concise, intuitive, and interpretable; and automatically reveal patient clusters on specific diagnoses and procedures. Furthermore, Marble captures the baseline characteristics of the overall population via an augmented bias tensor.

The experimental results on simulated data and 10,000 patient records from the CMS De-SYNPUF dataset demonstrate the conciseness, interpretability, and predictive power of Marble-derived phenotypes. They underscore the promise of Marble for high-throughput phenotyping with minimal human intervention. Marble can potentially be used to rapidly characterize, predict, and manage a large number of diseases, thereby promising a novel, data-driven solution that can benefit very large segments of the population. Future work will focus on generalizing the sparse non-negative tensor factorization to multi-relational tensors [20] to incorporate multiple EHR data sources and examine quasi-Newton methods to improve computational speed of the algorithm [12].

Acknowledgements

We would like to thank Yubin Park and Suriya Gunasekar for their comments. This research is supported by the Schlumberger Centennial Chair in Engineering; Army Research Office under grant W911NF-11-1-0258; and Department of Defense award under award number 60036907.

6. REFERENCES

[1] B. W. Bader and T. G. Kolda. Efficient MATLAB computations with sparse and factored tensors. *SIAM Journal on Scientific Computing*, 2007.

[2] C. L. Byrne. Alternating Minimization as Sequential Unconstrained Minimization: A Survey. *Journal of Optimization Theory and Applications*, 156(3):554–566, Mar. 2013.

[3] J. D. Carroll and J.-J. Chang. Analysis of individual differences in multidimensional scaling via an N-way generalization of "Eckart-Young" decomposition. *Psychometrika*, 35(3):283–319, 1970.

[4] Centers for Disease Control and Prevention (CDC). Chronic diseases at a glance 2009. Technical report, CDC, Feb. 2009.

[5] Y. Chen, R. J. Carroll, E. R. M. Hinz, A. Shah, A. E. Eyler, J. C. Denny, and H. Xu. Applying active learning to high-throughput phenotyping algorithms for electronic health records data. *JAMIA*, 20(e2):e253–e259, Dec. 2013.

Table 4: Two heart failure related phenotypes

Heart Failure Phenotype
Other forms of heart disease Complications of surgical and medical care Symptoms
Cardiovascular Procedures Hematology and Coagulation Procedures Evaluation and Management of Other Outpatient Services Surgical Procedures on the Cardiovascular System Chemistry Pathology and Laboratory Tests

Severe Heart Failure Phenotype
Other forms of heart disease Pneumoconioses and other lung diseases Ill-defined and unknown causes of morbidity and mortality
Hospital Inpatient Services Cardiovascular Procedures

Table 5: Two chronic disease related phenotypes

Diabetes Phenotype
Diseases of other endocrine glands Complications of surgical and medical care
Chemistry Pathology and Laboratory Tests Organ or Disease Oriented Panels Hematology and Coagulation Procedures Surgical Procedures on the Cardiovascular System

Arthritis Phenotype
Arthropathies and related disorders
Physical Medicine and Rehabilitation Procedures Evaluation and Management of Other Outpatient Services Surgical Procedures on the Musculoskeletal System Diagnostic Radiology Procedures

[6] E. C. Chi and T. G. Kolda. On tensors, sparsity, and nonnegative factorizations. *SIAM Journal on Matrix Analysis and Applications*, 33(4):1272–1299, 2012.

[7] A. Cichocki, R. Zdunek, S. Choi, R. Plemmons, and S.-I. Amari. Novel multi-layer non-negative tensor factorization with sparsity constraints. In *ICANNGA 2007*, pages 271–280. Springer, 2007.

[8] A. Cichocki, R. Zdunek, A. H. Phan, and S.-I. Amari. *Nonnegative matrix and tensor factorizations: Applications to exploratory multi-way data analysis and blind source separation.* Wiley, 2009.

[9] I. Davidson, S. Gilpin, O. Carmichael, and P. Walker. Network discovery via constrained tensor analysis of fMRI data. In *KDD 2013*, Aug. 2013.

[10] J. C. Denny. Mining electronic health records in the genomics era. *PLoS Computational Biology*, 8(12):e1002823–e1002823, Dec. 2012.

[11] N. Gillis and F. Glineur. Accelerated multiplicative updates and hierarchical als algorithms for nonnegative matrix factorization. *Neural Computation*, 24(4), Apr. 2012.

[12] S. Hansen, T. Plantenga, and T. G. Kolda. Newton-Based Optimization for Nonnegative Tensor Factorizations. *arXiv*, Apr. 2013.

[13] R. A. Harshman. Foundations of the PARAFAC procedure: Models and conditions for an "explanatory" multimodal factor analysis. *UCLA Working Papers in Phonetics*, 16:1–84, 1970.

[14] J. C. Ho, J. Ghosh, S. Steinhubl, W. Stewart, J. C. Denny, B. A. Malin, and J. Sun. Limestone: High-throughput candidate phenotype generation via tensor factorization. *Journal of Biomedical Informatics*, accepted.

[15] G. Hripcsak and D. J. Albers. Next-generation phenotyping of electronic health records. *JAMIA*, 20(1):117–121, Dec. 2012.

[16] U. Kang, E. Papalexakis, A. Harpale, and C. Faloutsos. Gigatensor: Scaling tensor analysis up by 100 times-algorithms and discoveries. In *KDD 2012*, pages 316–324, 2012.

[17] T. G. Kolda and B. W. Bader. Tensor decompositions and applications. *SIAM Review*, 51(3):455–500, 2009.

[18] D. D. Lee and H. S. Seung. Learning the parts of objects by non-negative matrix factorization. *Nature*, 401(6755):788–791, Oct. 1999.

[19] C.-J. Lin. On the convergence of multiplicative update algorithms for nonnegative matrix factorization. *IEEE Transactions on Neural Networks*, 18(6):1589–1596, Nov. 2007.

[20] Y.-R. Lin, J. Sun, H. Sundaram, A. Kelliher, P. Castro, and R. Konuru. Community discovery via metagraph factorization. *ACM Transactions on Knowledge Discovery from Data*, 5(3), Aug. 2011.

[21] M. Mørup. Applications of tensor (multiway array) factorizations and decompositions in data mining. *Wiley Interdisciplinary Reviews: Data Mining and Knowledge Discovery*, 1(1):24–40, 2011.

[22] K. M. Newton, P. L. Peissig, A. N. Kho, S. J. Bielinski, R. L. Berg, V. Choudhary, M. Basford, C. G. Chute, I. J. Kullo, R. Li, J. A. Pacheco, L. V. Rasmussen, L. Spangler, and J. C. Denny. Validation of electronic medical record-based phenotyping algorithms: results and lessons learned from the eMERGE network. *JAMIA*, 20(e1):e147–e154, June 2013.

[23] D. Wang and S. Kong. Feature selection from high-order tensorial data via sparse decomposition. *Pattern Recognition Letters*, 33(13):1695–1702, 2012.

[24] Z. Xu, F. Yan, Yuan, and Qi. Infinite Tucker Decomposition: Nonparametric Bayesian Models for Multiway Data Analysis. In *ICML 2012*, pages 1023–1030. Alan, 2012.

Scalable Noise Mining in Long-Term Electrocardiographic Time-Series to Predict Death Following Heart Attacks

Chih-Chun Chia, Zeeshan Syed
University of Michigan
2260 Hayward St.
Ann Arbor, MI, U.S.A
{jazzchia,zhs}@eecs.umich.edu

ABSTRACT

Cardiac disease is the leading cause of death around the world; with ischemic heart disease alone claiming 7 million lives in 2011. This burden can be attributed, in part, to the absence of biomarkers that can reliably identify high risk patients and match them to treatments that are appropriate for them. In recent clinical studies, we have demonstrated the ability of computation to extract information with substantial prognostic utility that is typically disregarded in time-series data collected from cardiac patients. Of particular interest are subtle variations in long-term electrocardiographic (ECG) data that are usually overlooked as noise but provide a useful assessment of myocardial instability. In multiple clinical cohorts, we have developed the pathophysiological basis for studying probabilistic variations in long-term ECG and demonstrated the ability of this information to effectively risk stratify patients at risk of dying following heart attacks. In this paper, we extend this work and focus on the question of how to reduce its computational complexity for scalable use in large datasets or energy constrained embedded devices. Our basic approach to uncovering pathological structure within the ECG focuses on characterizing beat-to-beat time-warped shape deformations of the ECG using a modified dynamic time-warping (DTW) and Lomb-Scargle periodogram-based algorithm. As part of our efforts to scale this work up, we explore a novel approach to address the quadratic runtime of DTW. We achieve this by developing the idea of adaptive downsampling to reduce the size of the inputs presented to DTW, and describe changes to the dynamic programming problem underlying DTW to exploit adaptively downsampled ECG signals. When evaluated on data from 765 patients in the DISPERSE2-TIMI33 trial, our results show that high morphologic variability is associated with an 8- to 9-fold increased risk of death within 90 days of a heart attack. Moreover, the use of adaptive downsampling with a modified DTW formulation achieves a 7- to almost 20-fold reduction in runtime relative to DTW, without a significant change in biomarker discrimination.

KDD'14, August 24–27, 2014, New York, NY, USA.

ACM 978-1-4503-2956-9/14/08 ...$15.00.
http://dx.doi.org/10.1145/2623330.2623702.

Categories and Subject Descriptors

J.3 [**Computer Applications**]: Life and Medical Sciences; H.4 [**Information Systems**]: Information System Applications; I.2.1 [**Computing Methodologies**]: Applications and Expert SystemsMedicine and science

Keywords

cardiovascular disease; electrocardiogram; adaptive downsampling; time-warping; noise mining

1. INTRODUCTION

Heart disease is the leading cause of death around the world. The burden of ischemic heart disease alone in 2011 was 7 million lives [23]. In the United States, heart disease claims 830,000 lives each year (34% of all deaths, or one death every 38 seconds) [14]. Nearly 151,000 of these deaths take place in patients under the age of 65, and a third occur before the age of 75 [14]. Much of the difficulty in reducing this burden follows from an inability to match cardiac patients to treatments that are most appropriate for their individual risk. As one example of this, devices such as implantable cardioverter defibrillators (ICDs) can be life-saving for patients who experience fatal arrhythmias (over 300,000 sudden cardiac deaths in the U.S. each year among patients with diagnosed coronary disease) [16]. In most of these cases, the effects of the arrhythmia can be reversed if the victim is treated with an electrical shock within the first few minutes. However, existing decision-making methods fail to prescribe ICDs to the majority of patients who die [4]. Conversely, most of the patients who do presently receive an ICD do not receive any benefit from their device [4], resulting in an unnecessary risk to patients and unnecessary costs to the healthcare system.

Physicians use a variety of biomarkers to estimate patient risk and to match patients to treatments. In the setting of heart disease, these biomarkers are typically limited to information available through blood-based measurements of biochemical substrates (e.g., troponin I, C-reactive protein, and brain natriuretic peptide), or through imaging (e.g., left ventricular ejection fraction obtained through echocardiography) [12, 10]. In both these cases, the focus is on studying information that is present in instantaneous (i.e., 'snapshot') data, and where this information can be directly measured with limited or no computational aid. Despite these efforts, however, finding biomarkers that can accurately assess patient risk remains a challenge. For instance, while depressed left ventricular ejection fraction is commonly used to identify high risk patients following heart attacks, the absolute number of deaths is far greater among patients with relatively preserved left ventricular function [8].

Our recent research aims to address this situation through novel biomarkers that are computationally derived from physiological time-series, and that are designed to offer complementary information to existing blood- or imaging-based markers. Of particular interest is information potentially available in long-term electrocardiographic (ECG) signals. The ECG provides a continuous assessment of the electrical activity of the heart, and is routinely collected from patients during hospitalization to determine heart rate and detect arrhythmias. ECG has the advantage of being easy to acquire; the electrical activity of the heart can be measured on the surface of the body in an inexpensive and noninvasive manner over long periods. In an in-patient setting, the ECG is typically captured by bedside monitors. In an out-patient setting, a Holter monitor (a portable ECG device worn by patients) can record data continuously over multiple days. Since the ECG is routinely collected from patients in a wide variety of clinical settings, computational biomarkers deriving from long-term ECG time-series can be incorporated broadly into clinical practice without the need for any new hardware or without creating any additional burden on patients or caregivers.

In this paper, we focus on the question of how we can leverage long-term recordings of ECG activity (over days) to discover information that is unrecognized in previous studies centered on small snippets of data (over seconds). Our recent experiments, reported in the clinical literature [21], have approached this question by exploring the hypothesis that much of what is commonly perceived as noise in ECG signals may contain subtle but useful information about the health of the heart. The theory underlying this work is that increased variability in the morphology of ECG time-series is likely associated with a lack of consistency and repeatability in the electrical function of the heart. In other words, persistent fluctuations in the shape of the ECG waveform may suggest electrical instability in the heart muscle predisposing patients to fatal arrhythmias. The challenge in detecting this variability, however, is in being able to distinguish between shape deformations associated with pathological phenomena reflecting the health of the underlying heart muscle, and changes associated with artifacts that represent true noise. Making this distinction is difficult in short ECG recordings, but with the availability of long-term ECG time-series, pathological variations can be distinguished from true noise as structure that is persistent over long periods of time.

In preliminary clinical studies, we have developed the computationally generated ECG biomarker of pathological morphologic variability (which we subsequently refer to only as morphologic variability or MV) in long-term ECG to predict death following heart attacks. As a first step, our approach to measuring MV makes use of a modified dynamic time-warping (DTW)-based algorithm to quantify time-warped shape deformations in ECG time-series over long periods of time. As a second step, we draw upon a Lomb-Scargle periodogram approach to analyze the resulting non-uniformly sampled time-series representation of aggregate noise in the ECG for pathological structure. While the use of this methodology has shown promise in clinical cohorts [21] and provides information that is complementary to existing markers based on patient history and physical exam findings, echocardiography, and blood-based laboratory reports, our prior work has demonstrated the clinical utility of MV and not focused on the question of how to scale this basic approach to large databases of long-term ECG time-series or use in embedded devices (e.g., pacemakers and ICDs). To achieve this, we investigate here a novel approach that reduces the computational runtime of DTW through an adaptive downsampling of time-series inputs. The use of adaptive downsampling significantly reduces the ECG data presented to DTW while preserving rapidly changing waves (e.g., the QRS complex) smoothed out by existing downsampling approaches. However, due to adaptively downsampling rapidly changing parts of the ECG time-series less than more slowly changing parts of the signals, this approach also requires changes to the dynamic programming problem underlying DTW. In this paper, we present solutions for both the goal of adaptively downsampling ECG time-series, and for modifying the DTW dynamic programming formulation to leverage adaptively downsampled inputs.

We evaluate our ideas on data from 765 patients presenting with acute coronary syndrome in the DISPERSE2-TIMI33 trial. Our results show that high MV is associated with an 8- to 9-fold increased risk of death within 90 days of a heart attack. Moreover, the use of adaptive downsampling with a modified DTW formulation achieves an almost 4-fold reduction in runtime relative to DTW, without a significant change in biomarker discrimination. In contrast, existing downsampling approaches obtain a similar reduction in runtime but with noticeably worse performance for risk prediction.

The remainder of this paper is organized as follows. Section 2 presents background on ECG time-series and the pathophysiological basis for our efforts to mine noise in ECG time-series for information relevant to cardiac risk prediction. Section 3 describes the methodology for measuring MV using a modified DTW- and Lomb-Scargle periodogram-based approach. Section 4 proposes the concept of adaptive downsampling, and details how adaptive downsampling can be incorporated within the measurement of MV to scale it up to large amount of long-term time-series data. Section 5 presents the datasets and evaluation methodology for our study. Section 6 discusses the results of our experiments. Section 7 offers a summary and conclusions.

2. BACKGROUND

We begin with a brief background on ECG time-series and on the pathophysiological basis for mining noise in ECG time-series for information useful in predicting future cardiac risk.

2.1 Electrocardiogram

The ECG is a continuous recording of the electrical activity of the heart muscle or myocardium[13]. At rest, each cardiac muscle cell maintains a voltage difference across its cell membrane. During depolarization (i.e., the 'firing' of the heart muscle), this voltage increases. Consequently, when depolarization is propagating through a cell, there exists a potential difference on the membrane between the part of the cell that has been depolarized and the part of the cell at resting potential. After the cell is completely depolarized, its membrane is uniformly charged again, but at a more positive voltage than initially. The reverse situation takes place during repolarization, which returns the cell to base-

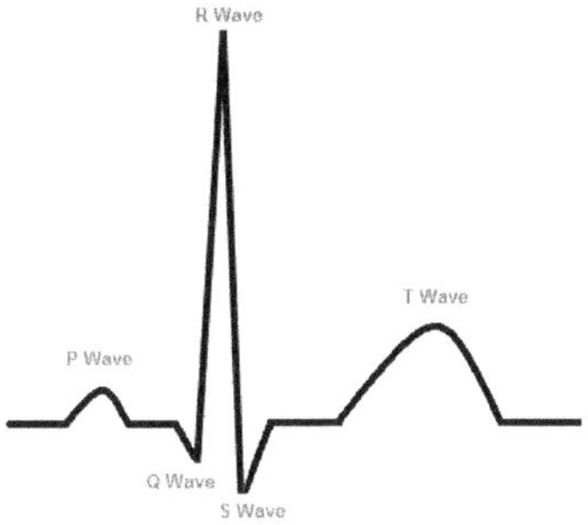

(a) Single ECG beat

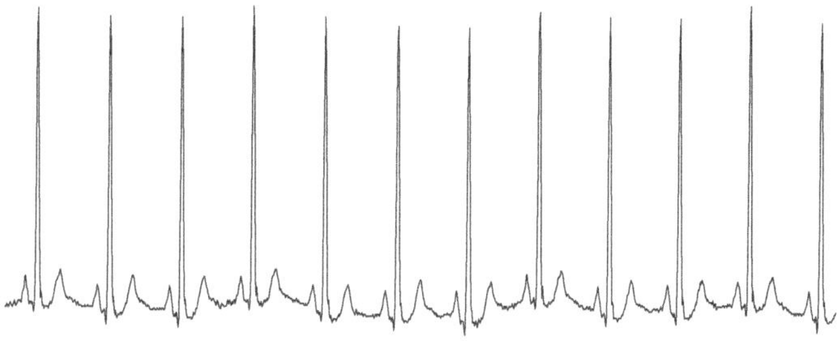

(b) Continuous ECG tracing

Figure 1: (a) Schematic representation of the normal ECG for a single heart beat, and (b) example recording of ECG waveform.

line. These changes in potential, summed over many cells, can be measured by electrodes placed on the surface of the body, leading to the ECG time-series.

The ECG is a quasi-periodic signal (i.e., corresponding to the quasi-periodic nature of cardiac activity). Three major segments can be identified in a normal ECG. The P wave is associated with depolarization of cardiac cells in the upper two chambers of the heart (i.e., the atria). The QRS complex (comprising the Q, R and S waves) is associated with depolarization of cardiac cells in the lower two chambers of the heart (i.e., the ventricles). The T wave is associated with repolarization of the cardiac cells in the ventricles. The QRS complex is larger than the P wave because the ventricles are much larger than the atria. The QRS complex also coincides with the repolarization of the atria, which is therefore usually not seen on the ECG. The T wave has a larger width and smaller amplitude than the QRS complex because repolarization takes longer than depolarization[13]. Figure 1(a) presents a schematic representation of the normal ECG, while Figure 1(b) shows an example tracing of a continuous ECG time-series over a few seconds.

2.2 Pathophysiology

In a healthy myocardium, the pathways of depolarization through excitable cells are usually similar for consecutive heart beats. However, in the presence of abnormalities, the conducting system has multiple irregular islands of severely depressed and unexcitable myocardium [7] (Figure 2). These lead to discontinuous electrical characteristics of the heart muscle, and create a situation analogous to the presence of race conditions within the heart. The presence of several possible adjacent pathways (e.g., the pathways shown in red and blue in Figure 2) that can potentially invade the non-functioning area leads to variations in the spatial direction of the invading vector [2]. Measured electrical activity in this setting is best described in a highly variable form, stemming from subtle unstable conduction bifurcations. Furthermore, the propagation of a beat may be dependent on the route of propagation of the previous beat. The overall effect of such minor conduction inhomogeneities is not well understood, but it is believed that they correlate with myocardial electrical instability and have potentially predictive value for ventricular arrhythmias [2] or other adverse events.

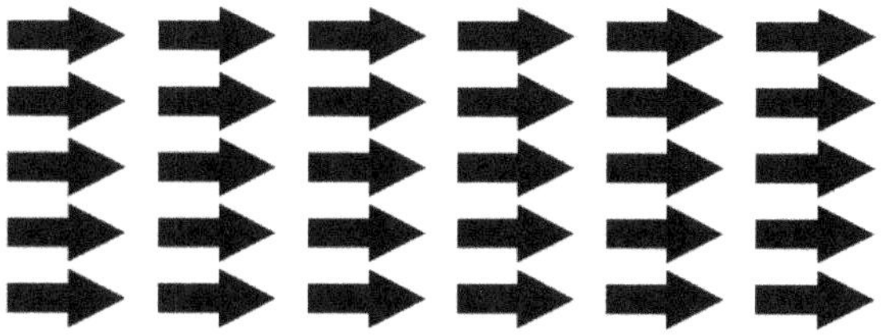

(a) Healthy myocardium

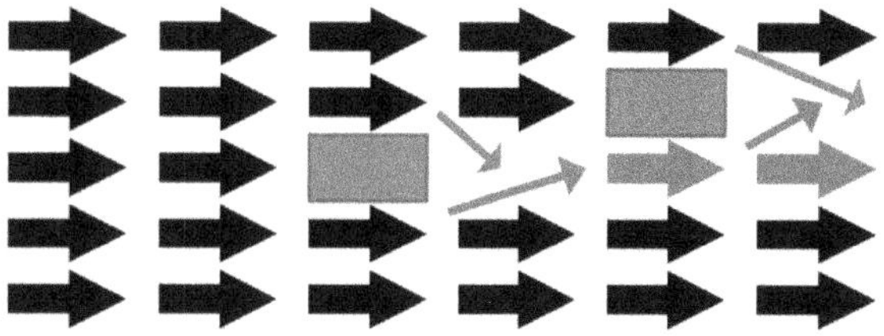

(b) Unhealthy myocardium

Figure 2: Illustration of process underlying noise-like pathological variability in ECG time-series. In healthy myocardium, electrical impulses are conducted smoothly through the heart muscle. In unhealthy myocardium (e.g., due to the presence of ischemia), unstable conduction bifurcations result in the path of impulse propagation, and consequently the ECG morphology, changing from beat to beat.

3. MORPHOLOGIC VARIABILITY (MV)

In this section, we describe our basic approach to measure MV in ECG time-series. In developing this methodology, we note that key challenges to measuring pathological variability that is often overlooked as noise in ECG signals include dealing with the presence of true noise and time-skew in these data, and addressing the need to discover potentially low amplitude disease signatures in the presence of high amplitude baseline activity. Section 4 describes how this basic approach can be scaled to very large volumes of ECG time-series through the use of adaptive downsampling.

For every pair of consecutively occurring beats in an ECG time-series, we quantify how the shapes of the beats dif-

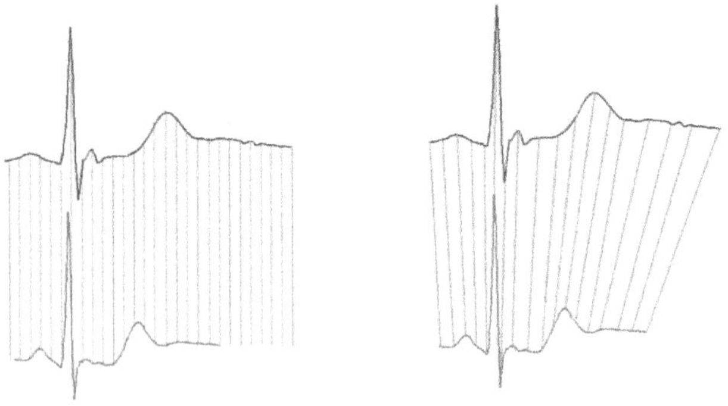

Figure 3: Comparison of time-warped shape deformations in ECG beats using DTW. In contrast to comparing activity that is time-aligned but not physiologically aligned (left), we use DTW in our study to relate similar parts of the ECG waveforms across beats in the presence of time skew.

fer using a variant of DTW (Figure 3). Given time-series $Q = q_1, \ldots, q_n$ and $C = c_1, \ldots, c_m$, DTW first constructs an n-by-m distance matrix where each entry (i, j) represents the distance $d(q_i, c_j)$. The l_2 norm is typically used to measure $d(q_i, c_j)$. DTW then finds the minimum cost path $W = w_1, \ldots, w_k, \ldots, w_K$ through this distance matrix where $w_k = (i_k, j_k)$ relates the i_k-th sample of Q to the j_k-th sample of C. The minimum cost path has the cost:

$$\sum_{k=1}^{K} d(q_{i_k}, c_{j_k})$$

and is subject to several constraints, including boundary conditions, continuity, and monotonicity[3]. This optimal path can be found efficiently using dynamic programming with the following recurrence:

$$\gamma(i,j) = d(q_i, c_j) + \min \begin{cases} \gamma(i-1, j-1) \\ \gamma(i-1, j) \\ \gamma(i, j-1) \end{cases}$$

where $\gamma(i, j)$ is the cumulative distance of the path from the start to cells (i, j). From simple observation, $DTW(Q, C) = \gamma(n, m)$ and the time and space complexity of this method is $O(nm)$.

We restrict the local range of the alignment path in the vicinity of a point to prevent biologically implausible alignments of large parts of one beat with small parts of another. For example, for an entry (i, j) in the distance matrix, we only allow valid paths passing through $(i-1, j-1)$, $(i-1, j-2)$, $(i-2, j-1)$, $(i-1, j-3)$ and $(i-3, j-1)$. This is an adaptation of the Type III and Type IV local continuity constraints proposed by Myers et al. [17] and ensures that there are no long horizontal or vertical edges along the optimal path through the distance matrix, corresponding to a large number of different samples in one beat being aligned with a single sample in the other. This leads to the following recurrence relation (also shown graphically in Figure 4):

$$\gamma(i,j) = d(q_i, c_j) + \min \begin{cases} \gamma(i-1, j-1) \\ d(q_{i-1}, c_j) + \gamma(i-2, j-1) \\ d(q_{i-1}, c_j) + d(q_{i-2}, c_j) + \gamma(i-3, j-1) \\ d(q_i, c_{j-1}) + \gamma(i-1, j-2) \\ d(q_i, c_{j-1}) + d(q_i, c_{j-2} + \gamma(i-1, j-3) \end{cases}$$

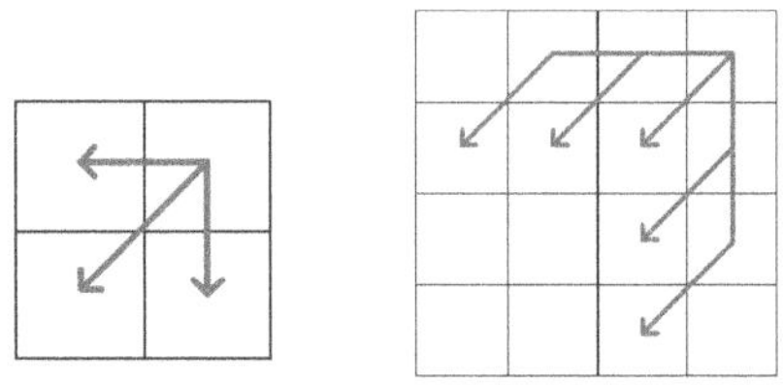

(a) Original DTW (b) Constrained DTW

Figure 4: Illustration of possible path alignments.

The process described here transforms the original ECG time-series into a sequence of time-warped morphology differences between consecutive beats. To characterize pathological structure within this sequence, we study its spectral characteristics. Since the activity of the heart is quasi-periodic (i.e., since the heart does not beat at an exact rate), the time gap between the samples of the sequence constructed through DTW is not uniform. We address this issue by estimating the power spectral density of the morphology differences time-series using the Lomb-Scargle periodogram [15]. For a time series where the value $m[n]$ is sampled at time $t[n]$, the Lomb-Scargle periodogram estimates the energy at frequency ω as:

$$P(\omega) = \frac{1}{2\sigma^2}\Big(\frac{\sum_n [(m[n] - \mu)\cos\omega(t[n] - \tau)]^2}{\sum_n \cos^2 \omega(t[n] - \tau)} + \frac{\sum_n [(m[n] - \mu)\sin\omega(t[n] - \tau)]^2}{\sum_n \sin^2 \omega(t[n] - \tau)}\Big)$$

where μ and σ are the mean and variance of the $m[n]$, and τ is defined as :

$$\tan(2\omega\tau) = \frac{\sum_n \sin(2\omega t[n])}{\sum_n \cos(2\omega t[n])}$$

We define our computationally generated biomarker, MV, as energy between 0.30 and 0.55 Hz (as estimated from the Lomb-Scargle periodogram) in the time-series of aggregate morphology changes constructed using DTW. The range of 0.30 to 0.55 Hz is based on theoretical and empirical observations suggesting that the discriminative ability of MV for predicting death following heart attacks is maximized over this range [22]. A flow chart of the whole process for generating MV is shown in Figure 5.

4. SCALING TO LARGE DATASETS

The basic methodology described in Section 3 parallels the approach investigated in our earlier clinical experiments [21]. Here, we focus on the question of how this methodology can be scaled for use with very large volumes of ECG data.

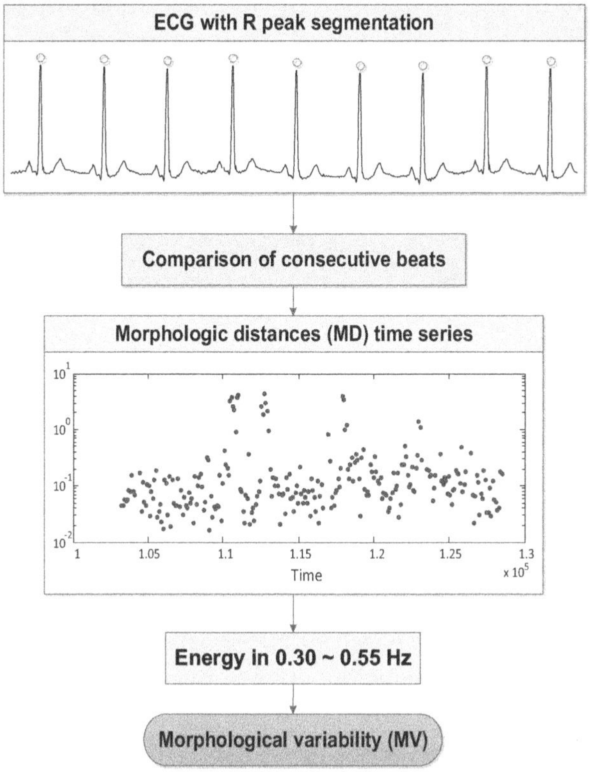

Figure 5: Flow chart of the process for generating Morphological Variability (MV).

The runtime of measuring MV is dominated by the time taken to quantify time-warped morphology differences between consecutive beats. For a total of p beats in an ECG time-series of length less than n, the computational complexity of this step is $O(pn^2)$. While reducing the number of consecutive pairs of beats to be examined (i.e., reducing p) offers one approach to reduce the overall runtime of MV, this approach is made challenging by multiple factors (e.g., poorer estimation of spectral energy, less data available to distinguish between persistent pathological variations and true noise, increased latency for real-time decision-making etc.). As a result, our efforts largely center on addressing the quadratic runtime of DTW (i.e., reducing the n^2 term above). We achieve this by exploring the idea of adaptively downsampling the time-series inputs to DTW, and describe how the dynamic programming problem inherent in DTW can be evolved to handle adaptively downsampled signals.

4.1 Adaptive Down-sampling (ADAP)

Our work builds upon the use of downsampling to improve the efficiency of the basic DTW algorithm.The general idea underlying this approach is to reduce the $O(n^2)$ runtime of DTW by reducing the sizes of its inputs. Popular existing approaches such as aggregate approximation (PAA) [9] and FastDTW [19] achieve this by downsampling signals uniformly, i.e., by a constant factor across time. We note that while the use of downsampling improves the runtime and space efficiency of DTW, the decision to carry out this downsampling by a constant factor over time causes both rapidly and slowly changing parts of a signal to be treated similarly. Downsampling in this case may be associated with the loss of important information.

We believe that this process can be improved by exploiting slowly changing parts of a signal by downsampling them at a higher rate than rapidly changing regions. In contrast to PAA and FastDTW, we therefore propose the idea of adaptive downsampling where the rate of reduction of time series varies according to the rate of changes taking place locally. This allows for the reduction of time series, while retaining sharp changes that would otherwise be smeared if downsampling were applied uniformly to the entire signal.

We achieve adaptive downsampling using trace segmentation [11]. While we describe this approach in more detail subsequently, the basic idea underlying trace segmentation is to divide the signal into regions with equal cumulative derivative activity. This places a higher number of boundaries for downsampling in regions that are rapidly changing (i.e., have higher cumulative derivative activity).

More formally, given a signal $Q = q_1, \ldots, q_n$ and a number of frames θ to downsample this signal to, we first calculate the cumulative difference $D_Q[k]$ for $k = 2, \ldots, n$ between each neighboring pair of samples:

$$D_Q[k] = \sum_{i=2}^{k} \mid q_i - q_{i-1} \mid \tag{1}$$

with $D_Q[1] = 0$. The sum of the total differences in Q is given by $D_Q[n]$. The cumulative difference in each adaptive downsampling bin is then set to $d_Q = \frac{D_Q[n]}{\theta}$. Using this, downsampling proceeds by finding the sample numbers t_i for $i = 0, \ldots, \theta$ such that for all values of i we have:

$$t_i = \min\{k \mid D_Q[k] \geq d_Q \cdot i\} \tag{2}$$

The corresponding amplitudes of Q at samples t_i are given by $x_i = q_{t_i}$. We can then use interpolation to approximate the fractional sample numbers $\hat{t}_i$ where we would expect $D_Q[\hat{t}_i] = d_Q \cdot i$. For $i = 0, \ldots, \theta$ using the notation:

$$\beta_i = \frac{D_Q[t_i] - d_Q \cdot i}{D_Q[t_i] - D_Q[t_i - 1]} \tag{3}$$

we have:

$$\begin{aligned} \hat{t}_i &= t_i - \beta_i \\ \hat{x}_i &= q_{t_i} - \beta_i(q_{t_i} - q_{t_i - 1}) \end{aligned} \tag{4}$$

The resulting adaptively downsampled representation of the original signal Q is given by two series corresponding to time and amplitude:

$$\begin{aligned} T^Q &= \hat{t}_0, \hat{t}_1, \ldots, \hat{t}_i, \ldots, \hat{t}_\theta \\ X^Q &= \hat{x}_0, \hat{x}_1, \ldots, \hat{x}_i, \ldots, \hat{x}_\theta \end{aligned} \tag{5}$$

This process can be carried out in time that is linear in the size of the input. Figure 6 presents the trace segmentation approach for downsampling graphically.

For ECG time-series, trace segmentation can preserve important information related to sharply changing parts of the signal (e.g., the QRS complex). This is illustrated in Figure 7. In contrast to PAA, a similar number of adaptively

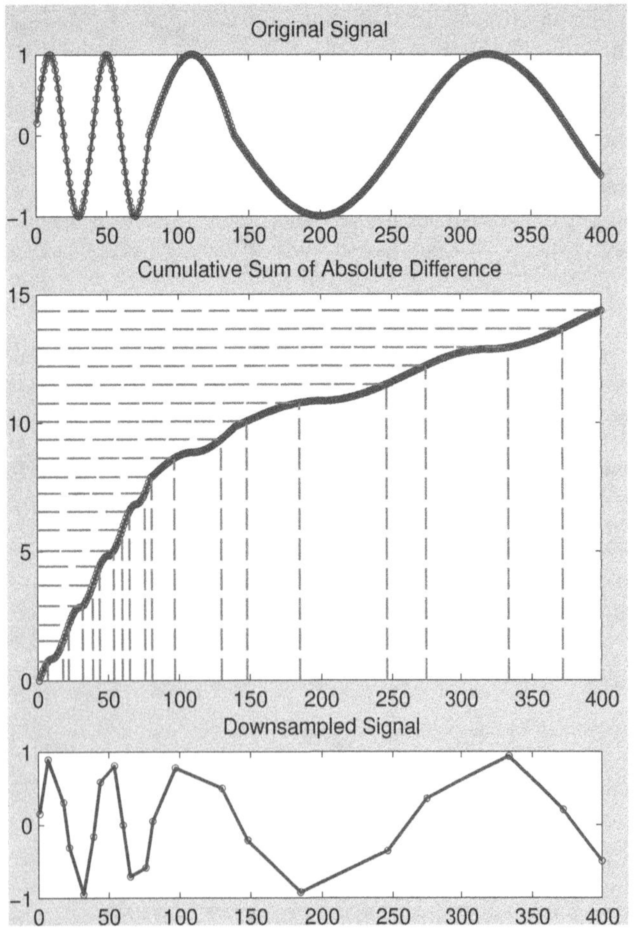

Figure 6: An illustration of the trace segmentation process.

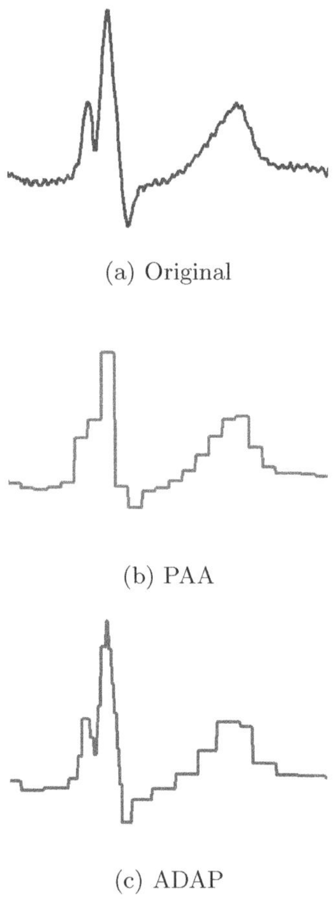

Figure 7: Adaptive downsampling of ECG signals.

downsampled segments provide a better characterization of notching within the R wave and also the sharpness of the S wave. While PAA achieves good results in a variety of real-world application domains, we believe the distinctions retained by adaptively downsampling are relevant to the specific goal here of measuring MV to predict death following heart attacks.

4.2 DTW with ADAP

DTW searches for the optimal alignment between two sequences in an efficient manner using dynamic programming. For uniformly downsampled signals, the dynamic programming process is essentially unchanged, although it is applied to reduced representations of the original signals. For adaptively downsampled signals, however, the cost of alignment cannot be calculated in a similarly simple manner from the Euclidean distance between the samples of the downsampled representations. Since the original signal is now divided into segments of variable lengths, this length information needs to be factored into consideration when deriving the distances for the DTW dynamic programming recurrence.

We represent two adaptively downsampled signals Q and C as comprised of segments $s_q(1),...,s_q(\theta)$ and $s_c(1),...,s_c(\theta)$ respectively, with θ corresponding to the number of downsampled segments. The amplitude of each segment $s_q(i)$ is represented by $x_q(i)$ and the duration by $l_q(i)$ (similar notation is used for the amplitude and duration of each segment $s_c(i)$). Using this notation, we describe the process through which the dynamic programming of DTW can be modified to handle adaptively downsampled segments.

Figure 8 shows, from left to right, three separate possibilities when aligning adaptively downsampled segments. In each case, the alignments of the adaptively downsampled segments are illustrated at the top, and the alignments of the original signals are illustrated below. The leftmost subfigure shows the situation where the adaptively downsampled segments are diagonally aligned, i.e. segment $s_q(i)$ is aligned with segment $s_c(j)$, while $s_q(i+1)$ is aligned with segment $s_c(j+1)$. Intuitively, we expect the warping path between the samples comprising the segments $s_q(i)$ and $s_c(j)$ in the original signals to be close to the diagonal. Without solving for the optimal path of alignment between these original samples, we approximate the cost of alignment between the segments $s_q(i)$ and $s_c(j)$ as the product of $d(s_q(i), s_c(j))$ (i.e., the Euclidean distance of $x_q(i)$ and $x_c(j)$) and $\max(l_q(i), l_c(j))$ (i.e., an estimate for the length of a diagonal path). We adopt a similar approach for the subfigure shown in the middle of Figure 8. In this case, the adaptively downsampled segment $s_q(i)$ is aligned with both $s_c(j)$ and $s_c(j+1)$. Again, without solving for the optimal path of alignment between the original samples for these segments, we expect the path of alignment for the

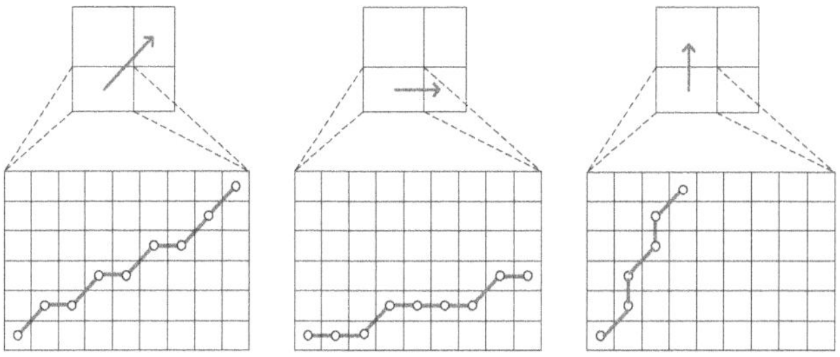

Figure 8: Illustration of derivation for adaptive recurrence equation. Left subfigure shows the diagonal case, the middle shows the horizontal case, while the right subfigure shows the vertical case.

samples comprising $s_q(i)$ and $s_c(i)$ to be roughly horizontal. We therefore approximate the length of this path to be the product of $d(s_q(i), s_c(j))$ and $l_q(i)$. The situation shown in the rightmost subfigure (i.e., a roughly vertical path of alignment for the samples comprising $s_q(i)$ and $s_c(j)$) is treated analogously.

We note that our approach of modifying the dynamic programming of DTW for use with adaptive downsampling approximates the path length in each case, and this approximation may not be optimal. However, this approach provides a simple way to augment the dynamic programming of DTW. In particular, in this setting, the recurrence relation for the cumulative path distance $\gamma(i,j)$ till the adaptively downsampled segments i and j can be represented as:

$$\gamma(i,j) = \min \begin{cases} \gamma(i,j,\mathbf{d}) \\ \gamma(i,j,\mathbf{h}) \\ \gamma(i,j,\mathbf{v}) \end{cases}$$

where the cumulative path distance $\gamma(i,j)$ depends on the direction in which the path proceeds next (i.e., diagonal $\mathbf{d}$, horizontal $\mathbf{h}$, or vertical $\mathbf{v}$) and:

$$\gamma(i,j,\mathbf{d}) = d(s_q(i), s_c(j)) \max(l_q(i), l_c(j)) + \min \begin{cases} \gamma(i-1,j-1,\mathbf{d}) \\ \gamma(i-1,j,\mathbf{h}) \\ \gamma(i,j-1,\mathbf{v}) \end{cases}$$

$$\gamma(i,j,\mathbf{h}) = d(s_q(i), s_c(j)) l_q(i) + \min \begin{cases} \gamma(i-1,j-1,\mathbf{d}) \\ \gamma(i-1,j,\mathbf{h}) \\ \gamma(i,j-1,\mathbf{v}) \end{cases}$$

$$\gamma(i,j,\mathbf{v}) = d(s_q(i), s_c(j)) l_c(j) + \min \begin{cases} \gamma(i-1,j-1,\mathbf{d}) \\ \gamma(i-1,j,\mathbf{h}) \\ \gamma(i,j-1,\mathbf{v}) \end{cases}$$

4.3 Path Constraints

In Section 3 we described a modification to the basic DTW recurrence relation to find more biologically plausible alignments (i.e., the situation shown in Figure 4). In this case, we made use of the recurrence relation:

$$\gamma(i,j) = d(q_i, c_j) + \min \begin{cases} \gamma(i-1,j-1) \\ d(q_{i-1}, c_j) + \gamma(i-2,j-1) \\ d(q_{i-1}, c_j) + d(q_{i-2}, c_j) + \gamma(i-3,j-1) \\ d(q_i, c_{j-1}) + \gamma(i-1,j-2) \\ d(q_i, c_{j-1}) + d(q_i, c_{j-2}) + \gamma(i-1,j-3) \end{cases}$$

We adopt an analogous approach to constrain DTW with adaptive downsampling for more meaningful alignments. Since the original signal is divided into unequally sized segments, we note that the above recurrence would not be directly applicable. Instead of restricting valid paths to pass through no more than 3 consecutive horizontal or vertical steps, we therefore restrict the path to traverse through at most k steps such that no such implausible alignment would occur. In other words, a segment $s_q(i)$ is only allowed to align with segments of s_c such that the total length of those k segments is no greater than three times the length of $s_q(i)$, which can be expressed as $3 \cdot l_q(i) \leq \sum_{n=1}^{k} l_c(j-n)$.

5. EVALUATION

We evaluated our research on ECG data from patients in the DISPERSE2-TIMI33 trial [5]. Patients in the DISPERSE2-TIMI33 trial were enrolled if they experienced ischemic symptoms at rest for a duration exceeding 10 minutes with either biochemical marker evidence of myocardial infarction (defined as Tronponin-T, -I, or creatinine kinase-MB elevation greater than the local myocardial infarction decision limit) or ECG evidence of ischemia (defined as the presence of new or presumably new ST-segment depression $\geq$0.05 mV, transient ST-segment elevation $\geq$0.1 mV, or T-wave inversion $\geq$0.1 mV in 2 or more contiguous leads). As part of this study, continuous electrocardiographic (ECG) data were recorded for a median duration of 4 days. Three-lead Life-Card CF Holter monitors were placed within 48 hours of the initial event, and the data were sampled at 128 Hz. Patients were followed up for a period of 90 days for cardiovascular death. In our study, we used data from the first 24 hours of ECG recording during hospitalization to predict the risk of death following heart attacks. There were a total of 765 patients in the DISPERSE2-TIMI33 trial with available ECG signals used in this analyses, with 14 deaths during follow-up. On average, each 24 hour recording contained 103,180 instantaneous heart rate measurements.

We evaluated MV, MV measured with downsampling using PAA, and MV measured with adaptive downsampling for cardiovascular risk stratification in multiple ways. First, we measured the areas under the receiver operating characteristic curves (AUROCs), which reflects the ability of the different MV approaches to discriminate between patients who died during follow up and those that remained event free. The AUROC is widely used in medicine, and is generally considered the standard for evaluating risk stratification methods [1]. As part of this evaluation, we compared the AUROC values for the downsampled MV approaches to the basic MV algorithm without downsampling using the method proposed by DeLong et al. [6] to assess whether the changes are statistically significant. Second, we also assessed the MV models with downsampling relative to the basic MV algorithm without downsampling by measuring the integrated discrimination improvement (IDI) proposed

Table 1: Univariate association of MV and other clinical variables with death following heart attacks.

Parameter	Hazard Ratio	P-value
Age>65	3.72	0.024
Women	2.76	0.054
Smoker	0.53	0.225
Hypertension	6.66	0.067
Diabetes	2.77	0.049
Hyperlipidemia	0.66	0.422
Previous Heart Attack	1.94	0.210
Previous Angina	2.86	0.103
ST depression>0.5mm	2.69	0.091
MV	5.16	0.002

by Pęncina et al. [18]. This was done by translating the MV values obtained through each approach into regression-based probabilistic risk estimates, and then measuring the difference between the mean predicted probabilities of events and non-events.

In addition to evaluating the predictive accuracy of MV measured through each approach, we also evaluated the runtime of the algorithms as the average time taken across ten runs to compute MV for all patients. These experiments were performed on a machine with quad-core Intel Xeon X3450 processors (2.67 GHz, 8MB Cache) and 8 GB RAM. The distance metrics were uniformly implemented in C++ on the Red Hat Enterprise Linux Server release 5.6 (Tikanga).

Finally, we also assessed how the relative ranking of patients between the different MV approaches changed with adaptive and non-adaptive downsampling. This metric was used to study how downsampling moves patients relative to each other while measuring MV. To measure this information, we computed the average absolute difference in the ranking of each patient by MV across different approaches.

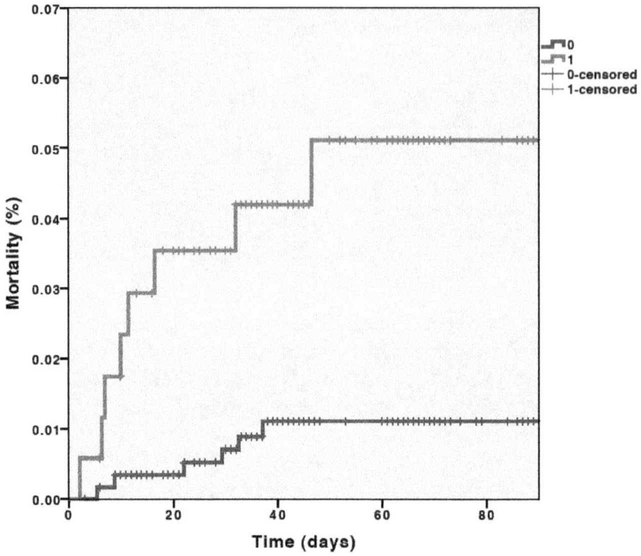

Figure 9: Kaplan-Meier mortality curve for patients in high MV (MV>50; shown in red) and low MV (MV≤50; shown in blue) groups. Patients with high MV were at a consistently elevated risk of death over the 90 day period following a heart attack.

Table 2: Comparison of AUROCs between DTW, PAA-DTW, and ADAP-DTW

Methods	AUROC	P-value
DTW	0.748	Referent
PAA_{30}	0.658	0.331
PAA_{50}	0.669	0.345
PAA_{70}	0.693	0.384
$ADAP_{30}$	0.718	0.345
$ADAP_{50}$	0.737	0.729
$ADAP_{70}$	0.736	0.721

6. RESULTS

6.1 Association of MV and death

The basic MV algorithm achieved an AUROC of 0.75 for discriminating between high and low risk patients following heart attacks. When the MV predictions were dichotomized at a simple threshold (MV>50 vs. MV≤50), patients with high MV were found to be at a significantly increased risk of death following heart attacks (Figure 9). For comparison, we show the relative increase in risk between patients with high and low MV, as well as the relative increases in risk for a variety of existing clinical variables in Table 1. In the DISPERSE2-TIMI33 dataset, MV identified a group of patients at a higher relative risk than any of these other metrics. These results are consistent with our earlier findings reported in the clinical literature [20].

6.2 Scaling up MV to Large Datasets

Table 2 compares the AUROC for the basic MV algorithm with the AUROCs obtained for MV measured with downsampling using PAA and MV measured with adaptive downsampling. For both the downsampling approaches, we experimented with downsampling the original heart beat signals to down to 30, 50 and 70 samples.

In general, downsampling the original signal led to a reduction in the discriminative ability of MV (although this difference was not significant at the 5% level given the sample size). In all of our experiments, however, MV with adaptive downsampling achieved a higher AUROC than downsampling with PAA for a similar factor of reduction. These results suggest that our use of adaptive downsampling retained more information that was relevant to the task of distinguishing between high and low risk patients than the use of PAA for this application.

We also assessed changes in the clinical utility of MV with downsampling by computing the IDI for each downsampled approaches relative to the basic MV algorithm. These results are presented in Table 3. In this case, the data from our experiments show that (consistent with the AUROC case) the use of downsampling with PAA led to a small decrease in performance. Conversely, the use of adaptive downsampling actually resulted in an increase in discriminative performance relative to the basic DTW algorithm as measured by the IDI. The differences for both downsampling with PAA and with adaptive downsampling relative to the basic DTW algorithm was not significant at the 5% level given the sample size.

Table 3: IDI comparing DTW with PAA-DTW and ADAP-DTW

Methods	IDI	P-value
PAA_{30}	-0.009	0.164
PAA_{50}	-0.009	0.178
PAA_{70}	-0.007	0.209
$ADAP_{30}$	0.017	0.160
$ADAP_{50}$	0.014	0.204
$ADAP_{70}$	0.020	0.160

Table 4: Average change in patient ranks relative to the basic DTW algorithm (shown as percentages of the DISPERSE2-TIMI33 population).

Methods	Change
PAA_{30}	20.3%
PAA_{50}	21.2%
PAA_{70}	20.9%
$ADAP_{30}$	18.3%
$ADAP_{50}$	18.8%
$ADAP_{70}$	18.4%

Table 5: Timing of the different MV algorithms.

Methods	Time (sec)
DTW	146,940
PAA_{30}	5,663
PAA_{50}	7,311
PAA_{70}	9,207
$ADAP_{30}$	7,831
$ADAP_{50}$	13,292
$ADAP_{70}$	20,782

The relative changes in ranks of patients between the basic DTW algorithm and the DTW approaches with downsampling are shown in Table 4. Consistent with the AUROC and IDI results, DTW with adaptive downsampling resulted in a smaller relative change in rank within the DISPERSE2-TIMI33 population relative to the basic DTW algorithm.

Finally, the timing results for the different methods are shown in Table 5. While downsampling reduced the runtime of the basic DTW algorithm substantially in each case, this reduction was greater for PAA than with the use of adaptive downsampling. This result can be attributed to the additional work that needs to be done to solve the modified dynamic programming problem for adaptively downsampled DTW. Comparing the PAA and adaptively downsampled approaches based on time rather than downsampling factor, however, still showed a higher level of performance with adaptive downsampling than with the use of PAA (e.g., for PAA_{70} AUROC: 0.693, IDI: -0.007, average rank change: 20.9% and time: 9,207 vs. for $ADAP_{30}$ AUROC: 0.718, IDI: 0.017, average rank change: 18.3% and time: 7,831)

7. CONCLUSION

In this paper, we studied the question of mining noise-like variations in long-term ECG time-series to identify patients at an increased risk of death following heart attacks. To achieve this, we made use of a modified DTW- and Lomb-Scargle periodogram-based approach that first transforms ECG time-series into sequences of beat-to-beat time-aligned morphology differences, and then relates properties of these sequences to patient risk. While the ideas underlying this work derive from our earlier experiments reported in the clinical literature [21], we focused here on the question of how this basic approach can be scaled to very large ECG time-series databases and for use in embedded devices. As part of this work, we investigated a novel approach to address the quadratic runtime of DTW. In particular, we proposed the idea of adaptive downsampling, i.e., downsampling slowly changing parts of a signal much more than rapidly changing parts of the same signal, to reduce the size of the inputs presented to DTW while retaining a good representation of the original time-series being compared. We also described changes to the dynamic programming underlying DTW to exploit such adaptively downsampled signals, where the downsampled segments may be of varying lengths.

We evaluated our ideas on real-world data from patients within the DISPERSE2-TIMI33 trial. Our experiments suggest that measuring MV with adaptive donwsampling substantially reduces runtime while providing similar performance to the basic MV algorithm that is not optimized for large volumes of data. In addition, the use of adaptive downsampling leads to more accurate performance than downsampling through the commonly used approach of PAA. We believe that these ideas may have additional merit in clinical applications where physiological time-warping is an issue during stratification.

8. ACKNOWLEDGEMENT

We thank Dr. Benjamin Scirica and the TIMI Study Group at the Brigham and Women's Hospital for the data used in our experiments. We are also grateful to Profs. John Guttag and Collin Stultz at MIT for their input on improving this work. This research was supported, in part, by the National Science Foundation and the American Heart Association.

9. REFERENCES

[1] D. Altman. *Practical statistics for medical research.* Chapman & Hall/CRC, 1991.

[2] S. Ben-Haim, B. Becker, Y. Edoute, M. Kochanovski, and O. Azaria. Beat-to-beat electrocardiographic morphology variation in healed myocardial infarction. *The American journal of cardiology*, 68(8):725–728, 1991.

[3] D. Berndt and J. Clifford. Using dynamic time warping to find patterns in time series. In *AAAI94 workshop on knowledge discovery in databases*, pages 359–370, 1994.

[4] F. BJ. Defibrillators are lifesaver, but risks give pause. *New York Times*, 2008.

[5] C. Cannon, S. Husted, R. Harrington, B. Scirica, H. Emanuelsson, G. Peters, R. Storey, et al. Safety, tolerability, and initial efficacy of azd6140, the first reversible oral adenosine diphosphate receptor antagonist, compared with clopidogrel, in patients with non-st-segment elevation acute coronary syndrome:: Primary results of the disperse-2 trial. *Journal of the American College of Cardiology*, 50(19):1844–1851, 2007.

[6] E. DeLong, D. DeLong, and D. Clarke-Pearson. Comparing the areas under two or more correlated receiver operating characteristic curves: a nonparametric approach. *Biometrics*, pages 837–845, 1988.

[7] N. El-Sherif, B. Scherlag, R. Lazzara, and R. Hope. Re-entrant ventricular arrhythmias in the late myocardial infarction period. *Circulation*, 55(5):686–702, 1977.

[8] J. Goldberger, M. Cain, S. Hohnloser, A. Kadish, B. Knight, M. Lauer, B. Maron, R. Page, R. Passman, D. Siscovick, et al. American heart association/american college of cardiology foundation/heart rhythm society scientific statement on noninvasive risk stratification techniques for identifying patients at risk for sudden cardiac death. *Circulation*, 118(14):1497–1518, 2008.

[9] E. Keogh, K. Chakrabarti, M. Pazzani, and S. Mehrotra. Dimensionality reduction for fast similarity search in large time series databases. *Knowledge and Information Systems*, 3(3):263–286, 2001.

[10] H. Krumholz, P. Douglas, L. Goldman, and C. Waksmonski. Clinical utility of transthoracic two-dimensional and doppler echocardiography. *Journal of the American College of Cardiology*, 24(1):125–131, 1994.

[11] M. Kuhn, H. Tomaschewski, and H. Ney. Fast nonlinear time alignment for isolated word recognition. In *Acoustics, Speech, and Signal Processing, IEEE International Conference on ICASSP'81.*, volume 6, pages 736–740. IEEE, 1981.

[12] L. Lilly. *Pathophysiology of heart disease.* Lippincott, Williams & Wilkins, 2003.

[13] L. Lilly. *Pathophysiology of Heart Disease:: A Collaborative Project of Medical Students and Faculty.* Lippincott Williams & Wilkins, 2010.

[14] D. Lloyd-Jones, R. Adams, T. Brown, M. Carnethon, S. Dai, G. De Simone, T. Ferguson, E. Ford, K. Furie, C. Gillespie, et al. Heart disease and stroke statistics - 2010 update. *Circulation*, 121(7):e46–e215, 2010.

[15] N. Lomb. Least-squares frequency analysis of unequally spaced data. *Astrophysics and space science*, 39(2):447–462, 1976.

[16] R. Myerburg. Sudden cardiac death: exploring the limits of our knowledge. *Journal of Cardiovascular Electrophysiology*, 12(3):369–381, 2001.

[17] C. Myers, L. Rabiner, and A. Rosenberg. Performance tradeoffs in dynamic time warping algorithms for isolated word recognition. *Acoustics, Speech and Signal Processing, IEEE Transactions on*, 28(6):623–635, 1980.

[18] M. Pencina, R. D'Agostino Sr, R. D'Agostino Jr, and R. Vasan. Evaluating the added predictive ability of a new marker: from area under the roc curve to reclassification and beyond. *Statistics in medicine*, 27(2):157–172, 2008.

[19] S. Salvador and P. Chan. Fastdtw: Toward accurate dynamic time warping in linear time and space. In *KDD Workshop on Mining Temporal and Sequential Data*, pages 70–80, 2004.

[20] Z. Syed, B. Scirica, S. Mohanavelu, P. Sung, E. Michelson, C. Cannon, P. Stone, C. Stultz, and J. Guttag. Relation of death within 90 days of non-st-elevation acute coronary syndromes to variability in electrocardiographic morphology. *The American Journal of Cardiology*, 103(3):307–311, 2009.

[21] Z. Syed, B. Scirica, C. Stultz, and J. Guttag. Computationally generated cardiac biomarkers for risk stratification after acute coronary syndrome. *Science Translational Medicine*, 4(131):131ra49, 2011.

[22] Z. Syed, P. Sung, B. Scirica, D. Morrow, C. Stultz, and J. Guttag. Spectral energy of ecg morphologic differences to predict death. *Cardiovascular Engineering*, 9(1):18–26, 2009.

[23] WHO. The top 10 causes of death. *http://www.who.int/mediacentre/factsheets/fs310*, 2011.

From Micro to Macro: Data Driven Phenotyping by Densification of Longitudinal Electronic Medical Records

Jiayu Zhou[1,2], Fei Wang[3], Jianying Hu[3], Jieping Ye[1,2]
[1]Center for Evolutionary Medicine and Informatics, The Biodesign Institute, ASU, Tempe, AZ
[2]Department of Computer Science and Engineering, ASU, Tempe, AZ
[3]Healthcare Analytics, IBM T.J. Watson Research Center, Yorktown Heights, NY

ABSTRACT

Inferring phenotypic patterns from population-scale clinical data is a core computational task in the development of personalized medicine. One important source of data on which to conduct this type of research is patient Electronic Medical Records (EMR). However, the patient EMRs are typically sparse and noisy, which creates significant challenges if we use them directly to represent patient phenotypes. In this paper, we propose a data driven phenotyping framework called PACIFIER (PAtient reCord densIFIER), where we interpret the longitudinal EMR data of each patient as a sparse matrix with a feature dimension and a time dimension, and derive more robust patient phenotypes by exploring the latent structure of those matrices. Specifically, we assume that each derived phenotype is composed of a subset of the medical features contained in original patient EMR, whose value evolves smoothly over time. We propose two formulations to achieve such goal. One is Individual Basis Approach (IBA), which assumes the phenotypes are different for every patient. The other is Shared Basis Approach (SBA), which assumes the patient population shares a common set of phenotypes. We develop an efficient optimization algorithm that is capable of resolving both problems efficiently. Finally we validate PACIFIER on two real world EMR cohorts for the tasks of early prediction of Congestive Heart Failure (CHF) and End Stage Renal Disease (ESRD). Our results show that the predictive performance in both tasks can be improved significantly by the proposed algorithms (average AUC score improved from 0.689 to 0.816 on CHF, and from 0.756 to 0.838 on ESRD respectively, on diagnosis group granularity). We also illustrate some interesting phenotypes derived from our data.

Categories and Subject Descriptors

H.2.8 [**Database Management**]: Database Applications—*Data Mining*; J.3 [**Life and Medical Sciences**]: Health, Medical information systems

KDD'14, August 24–27, 2014, New York, NY, USA.

http://dx.doi.org/10.1145/2623330.2623711.

Keywords

Medical informatics; phenotyping; sparse learning; matrix completion; densification

1. INTRODUCTION

Patient *Electronic Medical Records* (EMR) are systematic collections of longitudinal patient health information generated from one or more encounters in any care delivery setting. Typical information contained in EMR includes patient demographics, encounter records, progress notes, problems, medications, vital signs, immunizations, laboratory data and radiology reports, and etc. Effective utilization of EMR is the key to many medical informatics research problems, such as predictive modeling [36], disease early detection [30], comparative effectiveness research [17] and risk stratification [19].

Working directly with raw EMR is very challenging because it is usually sparse, noisy and irregular. Deriving better and more robust representation of the patients, or phenotyping, is very important in many medical informatics applications [13, 35]. One significant challenge for phenotyping with longitudinal EMR is *data sparsity*. To illustrate this, we show the EMR of a Congestive Heart Failure (CHF) patient in Fig.1, which is represented as a matrix. The horizontal axis is time with the granularity of days. The vertical axis is a set of medical events, which in this example is a set of diagnosis codes. Each dot in a matrix indicates that the corresponding diagnosis is observed for this patient at the corresponding day. From the figure we can see that there are only 37 nonzero entries within a 90-day window.

With those sparse matrices, many existing works just treat those zero values as actual zeros [30, 27, 25], and construct feature vectors from them with some summary statistics, then feed those feature vectors into computational models (e.g., classification, regression and clustering) for specific tasks. However, this may not be appropriate because many of those zero entries are not actual zeros but missing (the patient did not pay a visit and thus there is no corresponding record). Thus, the feature vectors constructed in this way are not accurate. As a consequence, the performance of the computational models will be compromised.

To handle the sparsity problem, we propose a general framework, PACIFIER (PAtient reCord densIFIER), for phenotyping patients with their EMRs, which imputes the values of those missing entries by exploring the latent structures on both feature and time dimensions. Specifically, we assume those observed medical features in EMR (microphenotypes) can be mapped to some latent medical con-

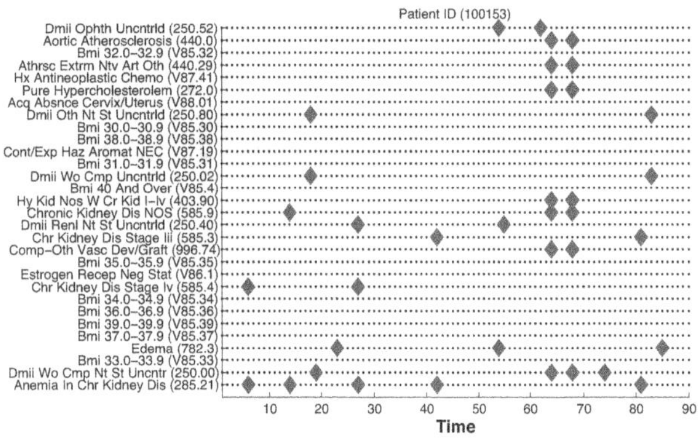

Figure 1: An example of the patient's EMR. The horizontal axis represents the number of days since the patient has records. The vertical axis corresponds to different diagnosis codes. A green diamond indicates the corresponding code is diagnosed for this patient at the corresponding day.

cept space with a much lower dimensionality, such that each medical concept can be viewed as a combination of several observed medical features (macro-phenotypes). In this way, we expect to discover a much denser representation of the patient EMR in the latent space, and the values of those medical concepts evolve smoothly over time. We develop the following two specific formulations to achieve such goal:

- *Individual Basis Approach* (IBA), which approximates each individual EMR matrix as the product of two latent matrices. One is the mapping from those observed medical features to the latent medical concepts, the other describes how the values of those medical concepts evolve over time.
- *Shared Basis Approach* (SBA), which also approximates the EMR matrix for each patient as the product of two latent matrices, but the mapping matrix from those observed medical features to the latent medical concepts is shared over the entire patient population.

When formulating PACIFIER, we enforce sparsity on the latent medical concept mapping matrix to encourage representative and interpretable medical concepts. We also enforce temporal smoothness on the concept value evolution matrix that captures the continuous nature of the patients. We develop an efficient *Block Coordinate Descent* (BCD) scheme for both formulations, that has the capability of processing large-scale datasets. We validate the effectiveness of our method in two real world case studies on predicting the onset risk of Congestive Heart Failure (CHF) patients and End State Renal Disease (ESRD) patients. Our results show that the average prediction AUC in both tasks can be improved significantly (from 0.689 to 0.816 on CHF prediction, and from 0.756 to 0.838 on ESRD respectively) with PACIFIER.

The rest of this paper is organized as follows: Section 2 presents the general representation of EMR and the problem of patient risk prediction which is one important problem that patient phenotyping will be applied to. In Section 3 we introduce the details of PACIFIER. The experimental results are presented in Section 4. In Section 5 we discuss the connection of the proposed approaches to related work and insights for future works. Section 6 concludes the paper.

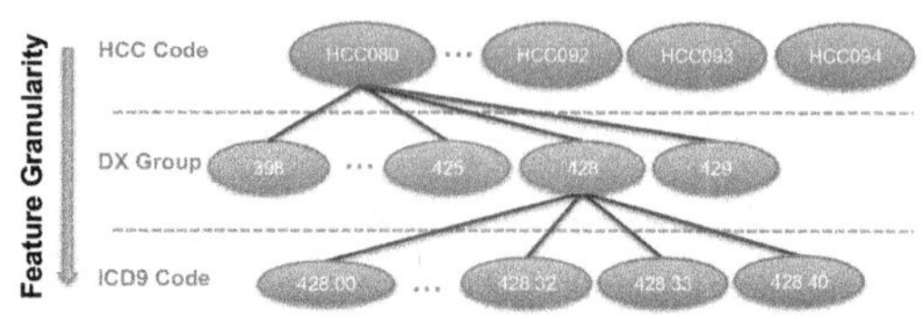

Figure 2: Granularity of medical features. For diagnosis events, features can be constructed at different levels of granularity: ICD9 code, diagnosis code (DxGroup) and HCC code.

2. PATIENT RISK PREDICTION WITH ELECTRONIC MEDICAL RECORDS

Risk prediction is among the most important applications in clinical decision support systems and care management systems, where it often requires building predictive models for a specific disease condition. As Electronic Medical Records (EMR) data becomes widely available, informative features for risk prediction can be constructed from EMR. Based on the EMR data, for example, care providers usually want to assess the risk scores of a patient developing different disease conditions, such as congestive heart failure [30, 6], diabetes [24], and end stage renal disease [1]. Once the risk of a patient is predicted, proper intervention and care plan can be designed accordingly.

The detailed EMR data documents the patient events in time, which typically includes diagnosis, medication, and clinical notes. The diagnosis events are among the most structured, feasible and informative events, and are prime candidates for constructing features for risk prediction [20, 26]. The diagnosis events, often in the form of International Classification of Diseases 9 (ICD9) codes, also come with well-defined feature groups at various levels of granularity such as diagnosis group (DxGroup) and higher-level hierarchical condition categories (HCC). For example, the code 401.1 *Benign Hypertension* belongs to DxGroup 401 *Essential Hypertension*, which is a subcategory in HCC 091 *Hypertension*.

One of the key steps of risk prediction from EMR is to construct features vectors from EMR events, which are used as inputs for classifiers. The goal of feature construction is to capture sufficient clinical nuances that are informative to a specific risk prediction task. Traditionally the feature vectors are directly derived from the raw EMR records [30, 27, 25]. In this paper for each patient we first construct a *longitudinal patient matrix*, with a feature dimension and a time dimension [27]. Maintaining the time dimension enables us to leverage the temporal information of the patients during feature construction. We present the procedure of constructing feature vectors via longitudinal patient matrices as follows.

In a cohort for a disease study, each patient is also associated with a disease status date called *operation criteria date* (OCD), on which the disease is diagnosed. A typical risk prediction task is to predict the disease status of the patients at a certain time point in the future (e.g., half a year). We call this period as the *prediction window*. To build useful predictive models, a prediction window before the OCD is usually specified, and the records before the prediction window are used to train the models, i.e., all records within the prediction window before the OCD are considered to be

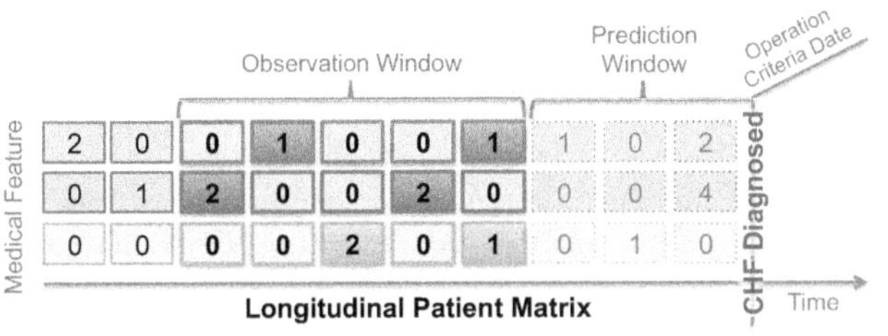

Figure 3: Construction of the longitudinal patient matrix [27] from Electronic Medical Records (EMR). The goal is to predict disease status of a patient at the operation criteria date (OCD), given the past medical information before the prediction window. For each patient, we construct a longitudinal patient matrix, using medical features at a specific granularity. For each patient, the feature vector for classification/regression is finally generated by extracting summary statistics from the longitudinal matrix within the observation window.

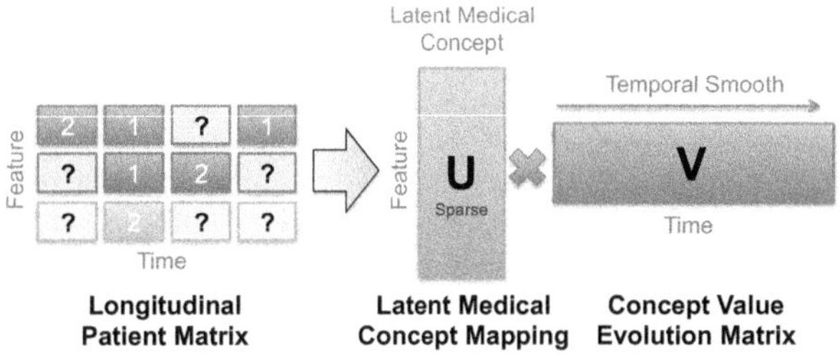

Figure 4: Illustration of the Pacifier framework. We treat a longitudinal patient matrix as a partially observed matrix from a *complete patient matrix*. We assume the medical features can be mapped to some latent medical concepts with a much lower dimensionality such that each medical concept can be viewed as a combination of several observed medical features. For each patient, the values of those medical concepts evolve smoothly over time. Thus the complete patient matrix for each patient can be factorized into a latent medical concept mapping matrix and a concept value evolution matrix.

invisible. Figure 3 illustrates the raw EMR data, OCD, and prediction window.

The next step is to construct a longitudinal patient matrix for each patient from the available EMR events, which consists of two dimensions: the feature dimension and the time dimension. One straightforward way to construct such matrices is to use the finest granularity in both dimensions: use the types of medical events as the feature space for the feature dimension and use *day* as the basic unit for time dimension. Unfortunately the patient matrices constructed in this way are too sparse to be useful. As a remedy, we use *weekly* aggregated time, and the value of each medical feature at one time point is given by the counts of the corresponding medical events within that week. Recall that the medical features can be retrieved at different levels of granularity, which also moderately reduces some sparsity in the data. The choice of feature granularity should not be too coarse, otherwise predictive information within features at a finer level may be lost during the retrieval, as we will show in the experiments. Note that after these preprocessing steps, the constructed patient matrices are still very sparse.

Finally we need to extract summary statistics from the longitudinal patient matrices as the feature vectors for classifiers. Since patients have different lengths of records, typically an *observation window* of interest is defined and the summary statistics (e.g., mean, standard deviation) are extracted within the observation window for all patients. The overall process is given in Figure 3.

3. TEMPORAL DENSIFICATION VIA PACIFIER

During the aforementioned feature construction process, there are many zeros in the longitudinal patient matrices due to the extreme sparsity in the raw EMR data. However, many of these zeros are not real zeros and instead, they indicate missing information (i.e, no visit). Treated as informative values in the feature extraction process, these values are likely to bias the training of classifiers and yield suboptimal performance. In this paper we propose to treat the zeros in the longitudinal patient matrices as missing values, and we densify the sparse matrices before extracting features to reduce the bias introduced by the sparsity, in hopes of that, the densified matrices provide better phenotyping of patients. We propose novel frameworks of densifying the partially observed longitudinal patient matrices, leveraging their observed medical histories. The proposed framework explores the latent structures on both feature and time dimensions and encourages the temporal smoothness of each patient.

Let there be n patients with EMR records available in the cohort, and there be in total p medical features. After the feature construction process we obtain n longitudinal patient matrices with missing entries, one for each patient. For the ith patient, its time dimension is denoted by t_i, i.e., there are medical event records covering a time span of t_i before the prediction window. We denote the ground truth matrix of the ith patient as $X_{(i)} \in \mathbb{R}^{p \times t_i}$, and in our medical records we only have a partial observation of the matrix at some locations, whose indices are given by a set $\Omega_{(i)}$. According to the macro phenotype assumption, we assume the medical features can be mapped to some latent medical concepts space with a much lower *latent dimension* of size k, such that each medical concept can be viewed as a combination of several observed medical features.

Specifically, we assume that the full longitudinal patient matrix can be approximated by a low rank matrix $X_{(i)} \approx U_{(i)}V_{(i)}$, which can be factorized into a sparse matrix $U_{(i)} \in \mathbb{R}^{p \times k}$ whose columns provide mappings from medical features to medical concepts, and a dense matrix $V_{(i)} \in \mathbb{R}^{k \times t_i}$ whose rows indicates the temporal evolution of these medical concepts acting on the patient over time. We call $U_{(i)}$ the *latent medical concept mapping matrix* (abbr. *latent mapping matrix*) and $V_{(i)}$ the *concept value evolution matrix* (abbr. *evolution matrix*). For each patient we assume that the values of those medical concepts evolve smoothly over time. Given the values and locations of observed elements in the longitudinal patient matrices, our proposed densification method learns their latent mapping matrices and evolution matrices. We call this densification framework

PACIFIER, which stands for PAtient reCord densIFIER. The idea of PACIFIER is illustrated in Figure 4.

Based on different natures of the medical cohorts, homogeneous or heterogeneous, we propose two densification formulations: an individual basis approach for heterogeneous patients and a shared basis approach for homogeneous patients, and then we provide an efficient optimization algorithm for PACIFIER that can be used to solve large-scale problems. Here and later we abuse the word *basis* to denote the columns of a concept mapping matrix, while we don't require them to be orthonormal. Note that the *real basis* of the space spanned by the columns of the latent mapping matrix can always be obtained by performing QR factorization on this basis matrix U_i.

3.1 Individual Basis Approach for Heterogeneous Cohort

In the heterogeneous cohort where patients are very different from each other in nature, the medical concepts for each patient may also be different from one patient to another. In the individual basis approach (PACIFIER-IBA), we allow patients to have different latent medical concepts.

Let $\Omega^c_{(i)}$ denote the complement of $\Omega_{(i)}$. We adopt the projection operator $\mathcal{P}_{\Omega_{(i)}}(X_{(i)})$ used in matrix completion [2]: $\mathcal{P}_{\Omega_{(i)}}(X_{(i)}) = X_{(i)}(j,k)$ if $(j,k) \in \Omega_{(i)}$ and $\mathcal{P}_{\Omega_{(i)}}(X_{(i)}) = 0$ otherwise. An intuitive approach for formulating PACIFIER-IBA is to solve the following problem for each patient:

$$\min_{U_{(i)}\geq 0, V_{(i)}} \frac{1}{2t_i}\|\mathcal{P}_{\Omega_{(i)}}(U_{(i)}V_{(i)} - X_{(i)})\|_F^2 + \mathcal{R}(U_{(i)}, V_{(i)}) \quad (1)$$

where $\mathcal{R}(U_{(i)}, V_{(i)})$ denotes the regularization terms that encode our assumptions and prevent overfitting. We also impose a non-negative constraint on the medical concept $U_{(i)}$ because most medical events and measurements in EMR are non-negative, and meaningful medical concepts consist of these medical events should also be non-negative. We now discuss how to design proper terms in $\mathcal{R}(U_{(i)}, V_{(i)})$ that lead to some desired properties:

1) Sparsity. We want only a few significant medical features to be involved in each medical concept so that the concepts can be interpretable. Therefore, we introduce sparsity in the latent mapping matrix $U_{(i)}$ via sparse inducing ℓ_1-norm on $U_{(i)}$. Indeed the non-negativity constraint may have already brought a certain amount of sparsity, and it has been shown that for non-negative matrix factorization, the sparsity regularization can further improve the decomposition [10].

2) Overfitting. To overcome overfitting we introduce an ℓ_2 regularization on the concept value evolution matrix $V_{(i)}$. It can be shown that this term also improves the numerical condition of computing a matrix inversion in our algorithm.

3) Temporal smoothness. A patient matrix describes the continuous evolution of medical features for a patient over time. Thus, along the time dimension it makes intuitive sense to impose the temporal smoothness, such that the value of one column of a longitudinal patient matrix is close to those of its previous and next columns. To this end, we introduce the temporal smoothness regularization on the columns of the concept value evolution, which describes the smooth evolution on the medical concepts. One commonly used strategy to enforce temporal smoothness is via penalizing pairwise difference [37, 34]:

$$\|V_{(i)}R_{(i)}\|_F^2 = \sum\nolimits_{j=1}^{t_i-1}(V_{(i)}(:,j) - V_{(i)}(:,j+1))^2$$

where $R_{(i)} \in \mathbb{R}^{t_i \times t_i+1}$ is the temporal smoothness coupling matrix defined as follows: $R_{(i)}(j,k) = 1$ if $i = j$, $R_{(i)}(j,k) = -1$ if $i = j+1$, and $R_{(i)}(j,k) = 0$ otherwise.

In the loss function of Eq. (1) we want the values of the low-rank matrix to be close to $X_{(i)}$ at the observed locations, directly solving which may lead to complex algorithms. An alternative way is to introduce an intermediate matrix S_i such that $\mathcal{P}_{\Omega_i}(S_i) = \mathcal{P}_{\Omega_i}(X_i)$, and we want $U_{(i)}V_{(i)}$ to be close to $S_{(i)}$. An immediate advantage of propagating the observed information from $X_{(i)}$ to $U_{(i)}V_{(i)}$ indirectly is that we can derive very efficient algorithms and data structures, which give the capability of solving large-scale problems, as we will show later. To this end, we propose the following PACIFIER-IBA learning model for each patient:

$$\begin{aligned}\min_{S_{(i)},U_{(i)},V_{(i)}} & \tfrac{1}{2t_i}\|S_{(i)} - U_{(i)}V_{(i)}\|_F^2 + \lambda_1\|U_{(i)}\|_1 \quad (2)\\ & +\lambda_2\tfrac{1}{2t_i}\|V_{(i)}\|_F^2 + \lambda_3\tfrac{1}{2t_i}\|V_{(i)}R_{(i)}\|_F^2,\\ \text{subject to:} \quad & \mathcal{P}_{\Omega_{(i)}}(S_{(i)}) = \mathcal{P}_{\Omega_{(i)}}(X_{(i)}), U_{(i)} \geq 0\end{aligned}$$

3.2 Shared Basis Approach for Homogeneous Cohort

In homogeneous cohorts where the medical concepts of patients are very similar to each other, we can assume that all patients share the same medical concept mapping $U \in \mathbb{R}^{p\times k}$. We propose the following PACIFIER-SBA formulation:

$$\begin{aligned}\min_{\{S_{(i)}\},U,\{V_{(i)}\}} & \sum\nolimits_{i=1}^{n}\tfrac{1}{2t_i}\|S_{(i)} - UV_{(i)}\|_F^2 + \lambda_1\|U\|_1 \quad (3)\\ & +\lambda_2\sum\nolimits_{i=1}^{n}\tfrac{1}{2t_i}\|V_{(i)}\|_F^2 + \lambda_3\sum\nolimits_{i=1}^{n}\tfrac{1}{2t_i}\|V_{(i)}R_{(i)}\|_F^2\\ \text{subject to:} \quad & \mathcal{P}_{\Omega_{(i)}}(S_{(i)}) = \mathcal{P}_{\Omega_{(i)}}(X_{(i)}), U \geq 0\end{aligned}$$

Since the densification of all patients are now coupled via the shared concept mapping, an immediate benefit of the PACIFIER-SBA formulation is that, we can transfer some knowledge among the patients, which is attractive especially when the available information for each patient is very limited and the patients are homogeneous in nature. We demonstrate in the experiments that the PACIFIER-SBA performs better than IBA when patients are homogeneous.

On a separate note, considering densification of each patient as a learning task, the SBA approach performs inductive transfer learning among the tasks via a shared representation of U and thus belongs to the multi-task learning paradigm [7, 8]. As such, the SBA in nature is a multi-task matrix completion problem.

3.3 Optimization Algorithm

The formulations of PACIFIER are non-convex and we present a block coordinate descent (BCD) optimization algorithm to obtain a local solution. Note that for each patient the subproblem of PACIFIER-IBA in Eq. (2) is a special case of the problem of PACIFIER-SBA in Eq. (3) given $n = 1$. Therefore in this section we present the algorithm for Eq. (3).

1) Solve U^+ given $V^-_{(i)}$ and $S^-_{(i)}$:

$$U^+ = \operatorname*{argmin}_{U\geq 0}\sum\nolimits_{i=1}^{n}\tfrac{1}{2t_i}\|S^-_{(i)} - UV^-_{(i)}\|_F^2 + \lambda_1\|U\|_1. \quad (4)$$

This is a standard non-negative ℓ_1-norm regularized problem and can be solved efficiently using scalable first order methods such as spectral projected gradient [29] and proximal Quasi-Newton method [14].

2) Solve $V^+_{(i)}$ given U^+ and $S^-_{(i)}$:

$$\{V^+_{(i)}\} = \underset{\{V_{(i)}\}}{\text{argmin}} \sum_{i=1}^{n} \tfrac{1}{2t_i}\|S^-_{(i)} - U^+V_{(i)}\|_F^2 \quad (5)$$
$$+ \lambda_2 \sum_{i=1}^{n} \tfrac{1}{2t_i}\|V_{(i)}\|_F^2 + \lambda_3 \sum_{i=1}^{n} \tfrac{1}{2t_i}\|V_{(i)}R_{(i)}\|_F^2$$

Note that the terms are decoupled for each patient, resulting in a set of minimization problems:

$$V^+_{(i)} = \underset{V_{(i)}}{\text{argmin}} \tfrac{1}{2}\|S^-_{(i)} - U^-V_{(i)}\|_F^2 \quad (6)$$
$$+ \tfrac{\lambda_2}{2}\|V_{(i)}\|_F^2 + \tfrac{\lambda_3}{2}\|V_{(i)}R_{(i)}\|_F^2,$$

The problem in (6) can be solved using existing optimization solvers. Moreover, since the problem is smooth, it admits a simple analytical solution [37].

LEMMA 1. *Let $Q_1\Lambda_1Q_1^T = U^TU + \lambda_2 I$ and $Q_2\Lambda_2Q_2^T = \lambda_3 R_{(i)}R_{(i)}^T$ be eigen-decompositions, and let $D = Q_1^TU^TS_{(i)}Q_2$, the problem (6) admits an analytical solution:*

$$V^*_{(i)} = Q_1\hat{V}Q_2, \quad \textit{where } \hat{V}_{j,k} = \frac{D_{j,k}}{\Lambda_1(j,j)+\Lambda_2(k,k)}. \quad (7)$$

Note that the parameter λ_2 improves the stability of the 'inversion' in $V_{j,k}$ so that the denominator is guaranteed to be a positive number. Excluding the time of the two QR factorizations, the cost of computing the analytical form solution for each sample is given by $O(k^2pt)$. The computation can be greatly accelerated as shown in the next section. Including the time of QR factorizations, obtaining the results from the analytical form is typically 100 times faster than that of solving (5) using optimization solvers.

3) Solve $S^+_{(i)}$ given U^+ and $V^+_{(i)}$:

$$\{S^+_{(i)}\} = \underset{\{S_{(i)}\}}{\text{argmin}} \sum_{i=1}^{n} \tfrac{1}{2t_i}\|S_{(i)} - U^+V^+_{(i)}\|_F^2. \quad (8)$$
$$\text{subject to: } \mathcal{P}_{\Omega_{(i)}}(S_{(i)}) = \mathcal{P}_{\Omega_{(i)}}(X_{(i)})$$

The problem is a constrained Euclidean projection, and is decoupled for each $S^+_{(i)}$. The subproblem for each one admits a closed-form solution: $S^+_{(i)} = \mathcal{P}_{\Omega^c_{(i)}}(U^+V^+_{(i)}) + \mathcal{P}_{\Omega_{(i)}}(X_{(i)})$.

Algorithm 1 The BCD algorithm for solving the PACIFIER-SBA in formulation (3). Given $n = 1$, the algorithm also solves the PACIFIER-IBA for each patient in the formulation (2).

Input: Observed locations $\{\Omega_{(i)}\}_1^n$, values of the observed entries for each patient $\{\mathcal{P}_{\Omega_{(i)}}(X_{(i)})\}_1^n$, initial solutions $\{V^0_{(i)}\}_1^n$, sparse parameter λ_1, parameter λ_2, smooth parameter λ_3, latent factor k.
Output: U^+, $\{V^+_{(i)}\}_1^n$, $\{S^+_{(i)}\}_1^n$.

```
Set V⁻(i) = V⁰(i), S⁻(i) = P_Ω(i)(X(i)) for all i.
while true do
  Update U⁺ by solving (4) via ℓ1 solvers (e.g. [14, 29]).
  Update V⁺(i) by computing (7).
  Update S⁺(i) = P_Ωc(i)(U⁺V⁺(i)) + P_Ω(X(i))
  if U⁺ and {V⁺(i)}₁ⁿ converge then
    return U⁺ and {V⁺(i)}₁ⁿ
  end if
  Set V⁻(i) = V⁺(i) and S⁻(i) = S⁺(i) for all i.
end while
```

We summarize the BCD algorithm of PACIFIER-SBA in Algorithm 1. In our implementation, we randomly generate the initial concept evolution matrix $V^0_{(i)}$, and set $U^0_{(i)} =$ (0). Therefore the initial value of $S^-_{(i)}$ is given by $S^-_{(i)} = \mathcal{P}_{\Omega_{(i)}}(X_{(i)}) + \mathcal{P}_{\Omega^c_{(i)}}(\mathbf{0}V^0_{(i)}) = \mathcal{P}_{\Omega_{(i)}}(X_{(i)})$. Since the problem of PACIFIER is non-convex, and thus it is easy to fall into a local minimum. One way to escape from local minimum is to 'restart' the algorithm by slightly perturbing V_i after the algorithm converges, and compute a new solution. Among the many solutions, we use the one with the lowest function value. In the following section we discuss how to accelerate the algorithm to solve large-scale problems.

3.4 Efficient Computation for Large Scale Problems

For large scale problems, the storage of the matrix S_i and $O(d^2)$-level computations are prohibitive. However, we notice that in each iteration, we have that $S^+_{(i)} = \mathcal{P}_{\Omega_i^c}(U^+V^+_{(i)}) + \mathcal{P}_{\Omega_i}(X_{(i)}) = U^+V^+_{(i)} + \mathcal{P}_{\Omega_i}(X_{(i)} - U^+V^+_{(i)})$. The "low rank + sparse" structure of $S^+_{(i)}$ indicates that there is no need to store the full matrices. Instead we only need to store two smaller matrices depending on k and a sparse residual matrix $\mathcal{P}_{\Omega_i}(X_{(i)} - U^+V^+_{(i)})$. This structure can be used to greatly accelerate the computation of Eqs. (4) and (5). In the following discussion we denote $S_{(i)} = U_{S_{(i)}}V_{S_{(i)}} + S_{S_{(i)}}$.

1) Solve U. The major computational cost of Eq. (4) lies on the evaluation of the loss function and the gradient of the smooth part. Taking advantage of the structure of S_i. We show that all prohibitive $O(d^2)$ level operations can be avoided given the special structures of $S^+_{(i)}$.

Gradient Evaluation:

$$\nabla_U\left(\sum_{i=1}^{n} \tfrac{1}{2t_i}\|S_{(i)} - UV_{(i)}\|_F^2\right)$$
$$= \nabla_U\left(\sum_{i=1}^{n} \tfrac{1}{2t_i}\|(U_{S_{(i)}}V_{S_{(i)}} + S_{S_{(i)}}) - UV_{(i)}\|_F^2\right)$$
$$= \sum_{i=1}^{n} \tfrac{1}{t_i}\left(U(V_{(i)}V_{(i)}^T) - U_{S_{(i)}}(V_{S_{(i)}}V_{(i)}^T) - S_{S_{(i)}}V_{(i)}^T\right)$$

Objective Evaluation:

$$\sum_{i=1}^{n} \tfrac{1}{2t_i}\|S_{(i)} - UV_{(i)}\|_F^2$$
$$= \sum_{i=1}^{n} \tfrac{1}{2t_i}\operatorname{tr}(S_{(i)}^TS_{(i)} - 2S_{(i)}^TUV_{(i)} + V_{(i)}^TU^TUV_{(i)})$$
$$= \sum_{i=1}^{n} \tfrac{1}{2t_i}\Big(\operatorname{tr}\left(V_{S_{(i)}}^T(U_{S_{(i)}}^TU_{S_{(i)}}V_{S_{(i)}})\right) + \operatorname{tr}\left(S_{S_{(i)}}^TS_{S_{(i)}}\right)$$
$$+ 2\operatorname{tr}\left((S_{S_{(i)}}^TU_{S_{(i)}})V_{S_{(i)}}\right) + \operatorname{tr}\left(V_{(i)}^T(U^TUV_{(i)})\right)$$
$$- 2\operatorname{tr}\left(V_{S_{(i)}}^T(U_{S_{(i)}}^TUV_{(i)})\right) - 2\operatorname{tr}\left((S_{S_{(i)}}^TU)V_{(i)}\right)\Big)$$

For the evaluation of the loss function, it can be shown that the complexity is $O(k^2npt)$ if all patients have t time slices. Similarly the complexity of computing the gradient is also given by $O(k^2npt)$. Therefore in the optimization, the computational cost in each iteration is linear with respect to n, p and t. Thus the algorithm is scalable to large data.

2) Solve V. The term $U^TS_{(i)}$ can again be computed efficiently using the similar strategy as above. Recall that in solving $V^+_{(i)}$ we need to perform eigen-decomposition on two matrices: a $\mathbb{R}^{k\times k}$ matrix U^TU and a $\mathbb{R}^{t\times t}$ tridiagonal matrix $R_{(i)}R_{(i)}^T$. The two matrices are equipped with special structures: the matrix U^TU is a low-rank matrix, and the matrix $R_{(i)}R_{(i)}^T$ is a tridiagonal matrix (a very sparse matrix), whose eigen-decomposition can be solved efficiently.

Note that the complexity of time dimension is less critical, because that in most EMR cohorts, the time dimension of the patients are often less than 1000. Recall that the finest time unit of the EMR records is day. Using weekly granularity, 1000 time dimension covers up to 20 years of records. In our implementation we use the built-in eigen-decomposition of Matlab, which typically takes less than 1 sec for a matrix with a time dimension of 1000 on regular desktop computers.

3.5 Latent Dimension Estimation

In the formulations in Eq. (2) and Eq. (3), we need to estimate the latent dimension of the patient matrices. Indeed, we can choose the latent dimension via validation methods, as done for other regularization parameters. As an alternative, we can use the rank estimation heuristic to adaptively set the latent dimension of the matrices by inspecting the information in the QR decomposition of the latent concept mapping matrix U, assuming that the latent dimension information of all patients is collectively accumulated in U after a few iterations of updates. The idea was originally proposed in [28, 23] to estimate the rank during the matrix completion of a single matrix.

In order to be self-contained we briefly summarize the algorithm as follows. After a specified iterations of updates, we perform the economic QR factorization on $UE = Q_U R_U$, where E is a permutation matrix such that $|\operatorname{diag}(R_U)| := [r_1 \ldots r_k]$ is non-increasing after the permutation. Denote $\mathcal{Q}_p = r_p/r_{p+1}$, and $\mathcal{Q}_{\max} = \max(\mathcal{Q}_p)$, and the location is given by $p_{\max}$. We compute the following ratio:

$$\tau = \frac{(K-1)\mathcal{Q}_{\max}}{\sum_{\{p \neq p_{\max}\}} \mathcal{Q}_i}.$$

A large τ indicates a large drop in the magnitude of $\mathcal{Q}_i$ after $p_{\max}$ elements, and we thus reduce the latent factor k to $p_{\max}$, retaining only the first $p_{\max}$ columns of U and the corresponding rows of the evolution matrices $\{V_{(i)}\}$. In our implementation we only perform the estimation once. Empirically as shown in Section 4.2, the latent dimension estimation works well when the PACIFIER-SBA works, i.e., patients are homogeneous, sharing a few latent concepts.

In the IBA approach the completion of patients are independent. If we apply latent dimension estimation on each patient, then each patient matrix may have a latent dimension different from others. This imposes difficulties when it comes to analyze the patients, and thus the estimation is not used in IBA.

4. EMPIRICAL STUDY

In this section we present the experimental results to demonstrate the performance of the proposed PACIFIER methods IBA and SBA. We then study the scalability of the proposed algorithm with varying feature dimensions, time dimensions, sample sizes, latent dimensions, and ratios of the observed entries. We then apply the proposed PACIFIER framework on two real clinical cohorts to demonstrate the improvement on predictive performance achieved by our approaches. The code for the proposed algorithm is available in [33].

4.1 Scalability

In this section we study the scalability of the proposed algorithm using synthetic datasets. In each of the following studies, we generate random datasets with a specified sample n, feature dimension p, average time dimension t, latent dimension k, and observation density $\|\Omega_i\|$. For simplicity we let all samples have the same time dimension. We report the average time cost over 50 iterations. For the two algorithms we set all parameters to be $1e-8$ in all studies.

Sample Size. We fix $p = 100$, $t = 100$, $r = 10$, $\|\Omega_i\| = 0.01$, and vary the sample size $n = 200 : 200 : 1800$. The results are given in Figure 5(a). We observe that for both methods the time costs increase linearly with respect to the sample size. The cost of IBA grows faster than the SBA version, which is expected because in IBA the computation costs of the loss and the gradients are more than those of SBA.

Feature Dimension. We fix $n = 100$, $t = 100$, $r = 10$, use $\|\Omega_i\| = 0.01$, and vary the feature dimension $p = 200 : 200 : 1800$. The results are given in Figure 5(b). We see that the time costs for both methods increase linearly with respect to feature dimension, which is consistent with our complexity analysis. The linear complexity of feature dimension is desired in clinical applications, since one might want to use as much information available as possible, resulting in a large feature space.

Time Dimension. We fix $n = 100$, $p = 100$, $r = 10$, $\|\Omega_i\| = 0.01$, and vary the time dimension $t = 100 : 100 : 900$. The results are given in Figure 5(c). We find superlinear complexity on the time dimension for both methods, which mainly comes from the eigen decomposition. The complexity on time dimension is less critical in the sense that for most medical records and longitudinal study, the time dimension is very limited. For example, if the time granularity is weekly, then we have 52 time dimensions each year. If 20-year records are available for one patient, then it yields only 1040 time dimensions. Besides, the eigen decomposition can be implemented in the way that utilizes the extreme sparsity of the temporal smoothness coupling matrix.

Latent Dimension. We fix $n = 100$, $p = 500$, $t = 500$, $\|\Omega_i\| = 0.01$, and vary the latent dimension input of the algorithms $r = 20 : 20 : 160$. The results are given in Figure 5(d). We find that the time costs increase superlinearly with respect to latent dimension for both methods, and the complexity of SBA is close to be linear.

Observed Entries. We fix $n = 100$, $p = 1000$, $t = 500$, $r = 10$, and vary the percentage of the observed entries $\|\Omega_i\| = 0.05 : 0.05 : 0.45$. The results are given in Figure 5(d). We see that the time costs increase only sublinearly with respect to the set of observed entries.

We note that the complexity of PACIFIER-IBA is of the same order as that of SBA. The difference between the two methods comes from the computation of the objective value and gradient in the U step. It is obvious that the IBA methods can be parallelized because the computation of all samples are decoupled. Similarly, the major computational complexity of SBA comes from the computation of U in the optimization and eigen-decomposition of $V_{(i)}$, which can also be parallelized by segmenting the computation of each patient.

4.2 Predictive Performance on Real Clinical Cohorts

To gauge the performance of the proposed PACIFIER framework we apply the two formulations on two real EMR cohorts from one of our clinical partners. In one cohort we

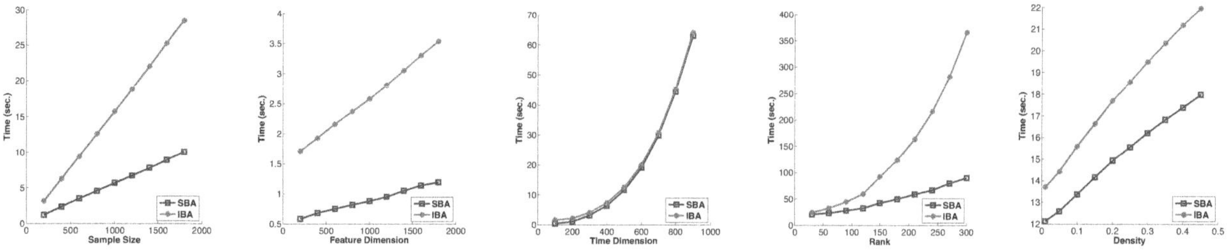

(a) Sample Size (b) Feature Dimension (c) Time Dimension (d) Latent Dimension (e) Observed Entries

Figure 5: Studies of scalability of Pacifier-Iba and Pacifier-Sba. In each study we vary one of the scale factors while fix other factors, and record the time costs. Both methods have the same complexity: linear with respect to samples size and feature dimension; superlinear with respect to time dimension and latent dimension; sublinear with respect to the number of observed entries.

study the predictive modeling of congestive heart failure (CHF), and in the other cohort we study end stage renal disease (ESRD). In both EMR cohorts we are given a set of patients associated with their outpatient diagnosis events in ICD9 codes and the corresponding timestamps. In our experiments we use the prediction windows lengths suggested by physicians (180 days for CHF and 90 days for ESRD), and we remove all events within the prediction window before the operation criteria date.

To construct the longitudinal patient matrices to be imputed, we use EMR data at the weekly granularity as discussed in Section 2. We select the patients with more than 100 events. Note that we are working on a large feature dimension, and thus for a patient with 100 EMR events the longitudinal patient matrix is still extremely sparse. Note that in our cohorts the number of case patients is much smaller than control patients, which is very common in most clinical studies. To avoid the effects of biased samples, we perform random under-sampling on the control patients so that we have the equal number of case and control patients in our datasets. To this end, we have constructed two datasets: 1) CHF dataset with 249 patients in each class; 2) ESRD dataset with 187 patients in each class.

The raw feature space in the low-level ICD9 codes is 14313. Because the matrix constructed using the low-level ICD9 codes is too sparse, we retrieve the medical features at coarser granularities. In order to study the effects of features at different granularities, we compare the medical features at ICD9 diagnosis group level (DxGroup) and HCC level. At DxGroup level there are 1368 features and at HCC level there are 252 features. In the two studies we consider the following commonly-used baselines methods:

- Zero Imputation (RAW). An intuitive way to impute missing values, which is equivalent to mean value imputation when the data set is first normalized (zero mean and unit standard deviation). This method is standard in the current medical literature for clinical studies [25, 27, 30].
- Row Average (AVG). In this baseline approach we fill the missing value using the average value of the observed values of the feature over time.
- Interpolation (INT) [5]. We use the next observation and previous observation along the timeline to interpolate the missing elements.
- Next Observation Carry Backward (NOCB) [5]. Missing values are filled using the next observation of this medical feature along the timeline.
- Last Observation Carry Forward (LOCF) [5]. Missing values are filled using the previous observation of this medical feature along the timeline.

We compare the baseline methods with the following competing methods:

- Individual Basis PACIFIER (IBA). Each patient is densified using Algorithm 1.
- IBA without temporal smoothness (IBA-NT). This variant of PACIFIER-IBA sets the temporal regularization λ_3 to 0.
- Shared Basis PACIFIER (SBA) using Algorithm 1.
- SBA without temporal smoothness (SBANT). This variant of PACIFIER-SBA sets the temporal regularization λ_3 to 0.
- SBA with Latent Dimension Estimation (SBA-E). The latent dimension estimation is described in Section 3.5, and only used once during the algorithm.
- SBA without Temporal Smoothness and with Latent Dimension Estimation (SBANT-E). This variant of PACIFIER-SBA sets the temporal regularization λ_3 to 0 and uses latent dimension estimation once.

Note that for the extremely sparse matrix as the clinical data in our studies, classical imputation methods such as those based on k-nearest neighbor [9] and expectation maximization [22] do not work. The methods IBANT and SBANT are included in the study to explore the effectiveness of the proposed temporal smoothness. For the parameter estimation we have separated an independent set of samples for validation, and we select the parameters that give the lowest recovery error on the validation set. In IBA, SBA, and SBANT, the latent dimension k is also determined via the validation set.

We finally test the predictive performance on the completed datasets using sparse logistic regression classifier (we use the SLEP implementation [15]). From the completed datasets, we derive features by averaging the features along the time dimension within a given observation window (52 weeks). To this end, each patient is represented as a vector of the same dimension as the feature dimension. We then randomly split the samples into 90% training and 10% testing, and train the classifier on the training data. The classifier parameter is tuned using standard 10 fold cross validation. We repeat the random splitting for 20 iterations, and report the average performance over all iterations. In order to be comparable, the splitting is the same for all methods in each iteration.

CHF Cohort. The predictive performance of competing methods is presented in Table 1. We find that in the CHF cohort: 1) most of the proposed PACIFIER approaches and their variants significantly improve the predictive performance as

Table 1: Predictive performance on the CHF cohort using DxGroup and HCC features.

DxGroup Features			
Method	AUC	Sensitivity	Specificity
RAW	0.689 ± 0.058	0.747 ± 0.046	0.528 ± 0.115
AVG	0.671 ± 0.051	0.744 ± 0.064	0.482 ± 0.083
INT	0.644 ± 0.066	0.803 ± 0.062	0.468 ± 0.110
NOCB	0.658 ± 0.048	0.845 ± 0.073	0.443 ± 0.096
LOCF	0.689 ± 0.055	0.866 ± 0.082	0.456 ± 0.087
IBA	**0.816 ± 0.040**	**0.843 ± 0.054**	**0.657 ± 0.078**
IBANT	0.754 ± 0.056	0.762 ± 0.089	0.597 ± 0.097
SBA	0.750 ± 0.062	0.776 ± 0.067	0.640 ± 0.106
SBANT	0.706 ± 0.054	0.672 ± 0.079	0.631 ± 0.066
SBA-E	0.730 ± 0.064	0.695 ± 0.074	0.653 ± 0.095
SBANT-E	0.661 ± 0.073	0.678 ± 0.090	0.588 ± 0.095

HCC Features			
Method	AUC	Sensitivity	Specificity
RAW	0.645 ± 0.089	0.672 ± 0.086	0.529 ± 0.072
AVG	0.660 ± 0.053	0.683 ± 0.063	0.526 ± 0.089
INT	0.596 ± 0.072	0.768 ± 0.093	0.489 ± 0.082
NOCB	0.602 ± 0.081	0.694 ± 0.088	0.511 ± 0.093
LOCF	0.625 ± 0.067	0.852 ± 0.079	0.480 ± 0.083
IBA	**0.755 ± 0.071**	0.747 ± 0.085	**0.641 ± 0.084**
IBANT	0.727 ± 0.060	0.740 ± 0.087	0.614 ± 0.070
SBA	0.736 ± 0.066	**0.753 ± 0.089**	0.629 ± 0.074
SBANT	0.645 ± 0.070	0.686 ± 0.087	0.550 ± 0.095
SBA-E	0.702 ± 0.079	0.688 ± 0.106	0.616 ± 0.067
SBANT-E	0.669 ± 0.062	0.702 ± 0.082	0.538 ± 0.079

compared to the baseline RAW approach. The best AUC obtained by PACIFIER-IBA dataset is 0.816 while the baseline is only 0.689 (a gain of 0.127); 2) the individual basis approaches outperform shared based ones; 3) temporal regularization significantly improves the predictive performance for all methods; 4) the methods with latent dimension estimation perform worse than those that do not use latent dimension estimation on this cohorts; 5) the features at DxGroup level outperform HCC level, which might be due to that in this predictive task, a fine granularity is likely to maintain more predictive information, than a coarse one.

ESRD Cohort. The predictive performance on ESRD cohort is given in Table 2. For the DxGroup features we observe similar patterns that is, IBA outperforms all other methods, which achieves an AUC of 0.828, compared to the baseline RAW method that achieves 0.756 (a gain of 0.072). The variants with temporal smoothness perform much better than the ones without temporal smoothness. For the HCC features we see that: 1) the shared basis approaches perform as well as the independent basis, where SBA-E achieves an AUC of 0.827. 2) again the temporal smoothness significantly improves the performance. 3) latent dimension estimation works well and outperforms the ones without latent dimension estimation.

As a summary, the experimental results have demonstrated the effectiveness of the proposed methods on real clinical data, and the temporal smoothness regularization brings significant improvements on predictive performance. In real clinical data, the samples tend to be heterogeneous and therefore the independent basis approaches perform better. However, using the HCC features of the two datasets, shared basis approaches perform better than using the DxGroup features. One potential explanation is that, using HCC features where the features space is smaller and features themselves are coarser (in terms of clinical concepts), the patients tend to be more homogeneous. We also notice that the latent dimension estimation only works well when shared basis works well. Recall that the idea of latent dimension estimation is to detect the jumps in the diagonal elements from the R_U factor of QR factorization. This is expected because

Table 2: Predictive performance on the ESRD cohort with DxGroup and HCC features.

DxGroup Features			
Method	AUC	Sensitivity	Specificity
RAW	0.756 ± 0.086	0.831 ± 0.113	0.581 ± 0.077
AVG	0.775 ± 0.079	0.821 ± 0.093	0.592 ± 0.084
INT	0.747 ± 0.083	0.919 ± 0.104	0.568 ± 0.110
NOCB	0.766 ± 0.092	0.914 ± 0.099	0.556 ± 0.103
LOCF	0.787 ± 0.085	0.958 ± 0.107	0.577 ± 0.079
IBA	**0.838 ± 0.072**	**0.842 ± 0.099**	0.658 ± 0.106
IBANT	0.796 ± 0.066	0.806 ± 0.101	0.600 ± 0.095
SBA	0.811 ± 0.065	0.769 ± 0.091	**0.722 ± 0.097**
SBANT	0.763 ± 0.068	0.719 ± 0.109	0.697 ± 0.075
SBA-E	0.803 ± 0.056	0.753 ± 0.098	0.681 ± 0.090
SBANT-E	0.770 ± 0.082	0.689 ± 0.099	0.700 ± 0.110

HCC Features			
Method	AUC	Sensitivity	Specificity
RAW	0.758 ± 0.058	0.747 ± 0.085	0.656 ± 0.093
AVG	0.778 ± 0.055	0.789 ± 0.088	0.660 ± 0.088
INT	0.729 ± 0.067	0.752 ± 0.091	0.652 ± 0.094
NOCB	0.752 ± 0.079	0.775 ± 0.089	0.658 ± 0.095
LOCF	0.771 ± 0.068	0.808 ± 0.082	0.665 ± 0.081
IBA	0.826 ± 0.051	0.800 ± 0.085	0.708 ± 0.080
IBANT	0.802 ± 0.064	0.775 ± 0.094	0.714 ± 0.089
SBA	0.820 ± 0.064	0.789 ± 0.091	**0.722 ± 0.092**
SBANT	0.771 ± 0.082	0.733 ± 0.084	0.681 ± 0.102
SBA-E	**0.827 ± 0.067**	**0.814 ± 0.077**	0.706 ± 0.096
SBANT-E	0.785 ± 0.060	0.736 ± 0.065	0.717 ± 0.092

if the patients are homogeneous and share only a few basis, then obviously there are such natural jumps.

4.3 Macro Phenotypes Learned from Data

In this section we show some meaningful medical concepts learned by the proposed PACIFIER-SBA method. In the latent medical concept mapping matrix U, we are able to obtain feature groups from data, because of the sparsity on the matrix. We first normalize weights of the columns such that the sum of each column is equal to 1. The normalized weights indicate the percentages of medical features contributing to the medical concept. We rank the medical features according to their contributions and find that in most of the medical concepts the top medical features are typically related and are comorbidities of a certain disease. In Figure 3, we show a list of medical concepts obtained from our CHF cohort. For example, in the first medical concept, the highly ranked diagnosis groups are all related to *Cardiovascular Disease*, e.g., Heart failure (428), Hypertension (401) and Dysrhythmias (427), and the second medical concepts include features that are typical related to *Diabetes* and its related comorbidities such as Hypertension (401), Chronic renal failure (585). In the CHF cohort, we have also found very similar medical concepts.

5. RELATED WORKS AND DISCUSSION

In this paper we treat the zeros in the longitudinal patient matrices as missing values, and proposed a novel framework PACIFIER to perform temporal matrix completion via low-rank factorization. To the best of our knowledge, there are no prior work that applies matrix completion techniques to solve the data sparsity in EMR data. The proposed PACIFIER framework aims at densifying the extremely sparse EMR data by performing factorization based matrix completion. The differences between the proposed completion method and existing works are that: instead of treating each patient as vectors and forming a single matrix, we treat each patient as a matrix with missing entries and consider a set of related matrix completion problems. We further propose to

Table 3: Medical concepts discovered by the Pacifier-Sba in our CHF cohort. In each medical concept, we firstly normalize the weights of the medical features in the medical concepts learned and rank the features. For each medical concept we list top 10 medical features and their diagnosis group codes.

Weight	DxGrp	Description
Medical Concept: Cardiovascular Diseases		
0.164	428	Heart failure
0.121	401	Essential hypertension
0.113	427	Cardiac dysrhythmias
0.108	780	General sympt.
0.141	414	Other form of chronic ischemic heart disease
0.053	785	Symp. inv. cardiovascular sys.
0.052	786	Symp. inv. respir. sys. and other chest sympt.
0.046	402	Hypertensive heart disease
0.042	272	Diso. of lipoid metabolism
Medical Concept: Diabetes		
Weight	DxGrp	Description
0.211	250	Diabetes mellitus
0.129	272	Diso. of lipoid metabolism
0.115	278	Obesity and other hyperalign.
0.095	593	Other diso. of kidney and ureter
0.093	585	Chronic renal failure
0.068	599	Other diso. of urethra and urinary tract
0.065	790	Nonspe. find on exam of blood
0.058	401	Essential hypertension
0.023	366	Cataract
0.019	285	Other and unspecified anemias
Medical Concept: Lung Diseases		
Weight	DxGrp	Description
0.117	518	Other diseases of lung
0.112	496	Chronic airways obstruction
0.110	786	Sympt. inv. respir. sys. and other chest symp.
0.098	V72	Special investigations and exam
0.089	493	Asthma
0.087	599	Other diso. of urethra and urinary tract
0.086	466	Acute bronchitis and bronch.
0.078	780	General symp.
0.067	787	Symp. inv. digestive sys.
0.057	793	Nonspec. ab. find on radio. and other exam of body structure
Medical Concept: Osteoarthrosis		
Weight	DxGrp	Description
0.185	729	Other diso. of soft tissues
0.123	715	Osteoarthrosis and allied diso.
0.120	726	Peripheral enthesopathies and allied syndr.
0.118	401	Essential hypertension
0.082	733	Other diso. of bone and cartilage
0.081	366	Cataract
0.069	719	Other and unspec. diso. of joint
0.066	272	Diso. of lipoid metabolism
0.065	780	General symp.
0.008	244	Acquired hypothyroidism
Medical Concept: Disorder of joints and softtissues		
Weight	DxGrp	Description
0.103	719	Other and unspec. diso. of joint
0.096	729	Other diso. of soft tissues
0.081	789	Other symp. involving abdomen and pelvis
0.078	722	Intervertebral disc diso.
0.058	724	Other and unspec. diso. of back
0.056	780	General symp.
0.055	721	Spondylosis and allied diso.
0.053	728	Diso. of muscle, ligament, and fascia
0.048	733	Other diso. of bone and cartilage
0.048	723	Other diso. of cervical region

incorporate the temporal smoothness to utilize the hidden temporal information of each patient.

The problem of imputation via matrix completion problem is one of the hottest topics in data mining and machine learning. In many areas such as information retrieval and social network, the data matrix is so sparse that classical imputation methods does not work well. The basic problem setting of the matrix completion is to recover the unknown data from only a few observed entries, imposing certain types of assumptions on the matrix to be recovered. The most popular assumption is to assume that the matrix has a low rank structure [2, 18, 28, 31]. There are two types of matrix completion in terms of the assumption on the observed entries: The first type assumes that the observation has no noise, and the goal is to find a low rank matrix whose values at the observed locations are exactly the same as the given ones [2, 3, 11]. In real world applications, however, noise is ubiquitous and thus the rigid constraint on the observed locations may result in overfitting. In contrast, the noisy matrix completion methods only require the values at the observed locations to be close to the given data [18, 28]. Directly dealing with the rank function in objectives are shown to be NP-Hard. Therefore many approaches seek to use the trace norm which is the convex envelope of the rank function [2, 11, 18]. Most of these approaches, however, require singular value decomposition (SVD) on large matrices, the complexity of which is prohibitive for large scale problems. Recent years have witnessed surging interests on the local search methods, which seek a local solution with extremely efficient algorithms [21, 28]. The PACIFIER framework is among these efficient local approaches, which does not require SVD and can be applied to solving large scale problems.

The completed data for each patient has the factorization form of $X_{(i)} = U_{(i)}V_{(i)}$, and for SBA all patients have the same $U_{(i)}$. Clearly, one advantage of SBA is that we have simultaneously learned a shared low-dimensional feature space for all patients, and their coordinates that can be used as new (and reduced) features. To see this, let $U = Q_U R_U$ be the QR factorization of U, then for each patient we have that $X_{(i)} = UV_{(i)} = Q_U(R_U V_{(i)})$, indicating that rows of $(RV_{(i)})$ can be considered as coordinates on the low dimensional space whose bases are given by columns of Q_U. One issue brought by the shared mapping is that the latent dimension is limited by the lowest time dimension of the patient, i.e., $\min_i t_i > k$. One solution is that we can extend the time dimension of the patients with non-informative time dimensions of all zeros.

We have shown in the experiments that a shared concept mapping works better on homogeneous samples while individual mappings work better on heterogeneous samples. In reality the samples may form some groups such that within the groups the patients are homogeneous and patients from different groups may be heterogeneous. The degree of homogeneous/heterogeneous is also affected by feature granularity as shown in our real clinical experiments, where in finer feature level the patients appear to be more heterogeneous. It is thus interesting to explore how to simultaneously identify feature groups and patient groups to further improve the quality of matrix completion. To do so, we can incorporate group learning into the objective as done in [32]:

$$\min_{\mathcal{G},\{S_i,U_j,V_i\}} \frac{1}{g}\Sigma_{j=1}^{g}\frac{1}{|\mathcal{G}_j|}\Sigma_{i\in\mathcal{G}_j}\|S_i - U_jV_i\|_F^2 + \mathcal{R}(\{U\},\{V\})$$

where $\mathcal{G}$ is the patient group assignment matrix, and patients within each group $\mathcal{G}_j$ share the same basis U_j. We leave this interesting study to our future works. One final note – the proposed PACIFIER framework proposed in this paper is not limited to healthcare domain, they can also be applied to temporal collaborative filtering [12, 16, 31], where each user has a rating preference that changes overtime.

6. CONCLUSION

In this paper, we propose a data driven phenotyping framework called PACIFIER (PAtient reCord densIFIER) to densify the sparse EMR data. The PACIFIER interprets the longitudinal EMR of each patient as a sparse matrix with a feature dimension and a time dimension, and estimates the missing entries in those matrices by leveraging the latent structures on both time and feature dimensions. We propose two formulations: Individual Basis Approach (IBA), which densifies the matrices patient by patient, and Shared Basis Approach (SBA), which densifies the matrices of a group of patients jointly. We develop an efficient optimization algorithm to solve the framework, which scales to large-size datasets. We have performed extensive empirical evaluations on both synthetic and real datasets, including two real world clinical datasets. Our results show that the predictive performance in both tasks can be improved significantly after the densification by the proposed methods.

Acknowledgment

The authors would like to thank the anonymous reviewers for their helpful comments. This work was supported in part by NIH R01 LM010730, NSF IIS-0953662, MCB-1026710, and CCF-1025177.

7. REFERENCES

[1] J. Blacher, A. P. Guerin, B. Pannier, S. J. Marchais, and G. M. London. Arterial calcifications, arterial stiffness, and cardiovascular risk in end-stage renal disease. *Hypertension*, 38(4):938–942, 2001.

[2] J.-F. Cai, E. J. Candès, and Z. Shen. A singular value thresholding algorithm for matrix completion. *SIAM J. on Opt.*, 20(4):1956–1982, 2010.

[3] E. J. Candès and B. Recht. Exact matrix completion via convex optimization. *Found. of Comp. Math.*, 9(6):717–772, 2009.

[4] S. Chang, G.-J. Qi, J. Tang, Q. Tian, Y. Rui, and T. S. Huang. Multimedia lego: Learning structured model by probabilistic logic ontology tree. In *ICDM*, pages 979–984. IEEE, 2013.

[5] J. M. Engels and P. Diehr. Imputation of missing longitudinal data: a comparison of methods. *Journal of clinical epidemiology*, 56(10):968–976, 2003.

[6] G. C. Fonarow, K. F. Adams Jr, W. T. Abraham, C. W. Yancy, W. J. Boscardin, et al. Risk stratification for in-hospital mortality in acutely decompensated heart failure. *JAMA*, 293(5):572–580, 2005.

[7] P. Gong, J. Ye, and C. Zhang. Multi-stage multi-task feature learning. In *NIPS*, pages 1997–2005, 2012.

[8] P. Gong, J. Ye, and C. Zhang. Robust multi-task feature learning. In *KDD*, pages 895–903. ACM, 2012.

[9] T. Hastie, R. Tibshirani, G. Sherlock, M. Eisen, P. Brown, and D. Botstein. Imputing missing data for gene expression arrays. *Tech. Report*, 1999.

[10] P. O. Hoyer. Non-negative matrix factorization with sparseness constraints. *JMLR*, 5:1457–1469, 2004.

[11] P. Jain, R. Meka, and I. Dhillon. Guaranteed rank minimization via singular value projection. In *NIPS*, pages 937–945. 2010.

[12] Y. Koren. Collaborative filtering with temporal dynamics. In *KDD*, pages 447–456, 2009.

[13] T. A. Lasko, J. C. Denny, and M. A. Levy. Computational phenotype discovery using unsupervised feature learning over noisy, sparse, and irregular clinical data. *PloS one*, 8(6):e66341, 2013.

[14] J. Lee, Y. Sun, and M. Saunders. Proximal newton-type methods for convex optimization. In *NIPS*, volume 25, pages 836–844. 2012.

[15] J. Liu, S. Ji, and J. Ye. *SLEP: Sparse Learning with Efficient Projections.* Arizona State University, 2009.

[16] Z. Lu, D. Agarwal, and I. S. Dhillon. A spatio-temporal approach to collaborative filtering. In *Proc. of the 3rd ACM Conf. on Rec. Sys.*, pages 13–20, 2009.

[17] M. Markatou, P. K. Don, J. Hu, F. Wang, J. Sun, R. Sorrentino, and S. Ebadollahi. Case-based reasoning in comparative effectiveness research. *IBM J. of Res. and Dev.*, (5):4, 2012.

[18] R. Mazumder, T. Hastie, and R. Tibshirani. Spectral regularization algorithms for learning large incomplete matrices. *The J. of Mach. Learn. Res.*, 99:2287–2322, 2010.

[19] S. D. Persell, A. P. Dunne, D. M. Lloyd-Jones, and D. W. Baker. Electronic health record-based cardiac risk assessment and identification of unmet preventive needs. *Med. Care*, 47(4):418–424, 2009.

[20] E. F. Philbin and T. G. DiSalvo. Prediction of hospital readmission for heart failure: development of a simple risk score based on administrative data. *J. of the Am. Co. of Card.*, 33(6):1560–1566, 1999.

[21] R. Salakhutdinov and A. Mnih. Probabilistic matrix factorization. *NIPS*, 20:1257–1264, 2008.

[22] T. Schneider. Analysis of incomplete climate data: Estimation of mean values and covariance matrices and imputation of missing values. *J. of Climate*, 14(5):853–871, 2001.

[23] Y. Shen, Z. Wen, and Y. Zhang. Augmented lagrangian alternating direction method for matrix separation based on low-rank factorization. *Opti. Met. and Soft.*, 0(0):1–25, 2012.

[24] M. Stern, K. Williams, D. Eddy, and R. Kahn. Validation of prediction of diabetes by the archimedes model and comparison with other predicting models. *Diab. Care*, 31(8):1670–1671, 2008.

[25] J. Sun, F. Wang, J. Hu, and S. Edabollahi. Supervised patient similarity measure of heterogeneous patient records. *SIGKDD Explorations*, (1):16–24, 2012.

[26] T. Van Staa, H. Leufkens, and C. Cooper. Utility of medical and drug history in fracture risk prediction among men and women. *Bone*, 31(4):508–514, 2002.

[27] F. Wang, N. Lee, J. Hu, J. Sun, and S. Ebadollahi. Towards heterogeneous temporal clinical event pattern discovery: a convolutional approach. In *KDD*, pages 453–461, 2012.

[28] Z. Wen, W. Yin, and Y. Zhang. Solving a low-rank factorization model for matrix completion by a nonlinear successive over-relaxation algorithm. *Math. Prog. Comp.*, 4(4):333–361, 2012.

[29] S. J. Wright, R. D. Nowak, and M. A. Figueiredo. Sparse reconstruction by separable approximation. *IEEE Trans. on Sig. Proc.*, 57(7):2479–2493, 2009.

[30] J. Wu, J. Roy, and W. F. Stewart. Prediction modeling using ehr data: challenges, strategies, and a comparison of machine learning approaches. *Med. Care*, 48(6):S106, 2010.

[31] L. Xiong, X. Chen, T.-K. Huang, J. Schneider, and J. G. Carbonell. Temporal collaborative filtering with bayesian probabilistic tensor factorization. In *SDM*, 2010.

[32] J. Zhou, J. Chen, and J. Ye. Clustered multi-task learning via alternating structure optimization. In *NIPS*, pages 702–710. 2011.

[33] J. Zhou, J. Chen, and J. Ye. *MALSAR: Multi-tAsk Learning via StructurAl Regularization.* Arizona State University, 2011. http://www.MALSAR.org.

[34] J. Zhou, J. Liu, V. A. Narayan, and J. Ye. Modeling disease progression via multi-task learning. *NeuroImage*, 78:233–248, 2013.

[35] J. Zhou, Z. Lu, J. Sun, L. Yuan, F. Wang, and J. Ye. Feafiner: biomarker identification from medical data through feature generalization and selection. In *KDD*, pages 1034–1042. ACM, 2013.

[36] J. Zhou, J. Sun, Y. Liu, J. Hu, and J. Ye. Patient risk prediction model via top-k stability selection. In *SDM*. SIAM, 2012.

[37] J. Zhou, L. Yuan, J. Liu, and J. Ye. A multi-task learning formulation for predicting disease progression. In *KDD*, pages 814–822. ACM, 2011.

Clinical Risk Prediction with Multilinear Sparse Logistic Regression

Fei Wang[1], Ping Zhang[1], Buyue Qian[1], Xiang Wang[1], Ian Davidson[2]
[1]IBM T. J. Watson Research Center. Yorktown Heights, NY
[2]Department of Computer Science. University of California, Davis.
{fwang,pzhang,bqian,wangxi}@us.ibm.com, davidson@cs.ucdavis.edu

ABSTRACT

Logistic regression is one core predictive modeling technique that has been used extensively in health and biomedical problems. Recently a lot of research has been focusing on enforcing sparsity on the learned model to enhance its effectiveness and interpretability, which results in sparse logistic regression model. However, no matter the original or sparse logistic regression, they require the inputs to be in vector form. This limits the applicability of logistic regression in the problems when the data cannot be naturally represented vectors (e.g., functional magnetic resonance imaging and electroencephalography signals). To handle the cases when the data are in the form of multi-dimensional arrays, we propose *MulSLR*: Multilinear Sparse Logistic Regression. *MulSLR* can be viewed as a high order extension of sparse logistic regression. Instead of solving one classification vector as in conventional logistic regression, we solve for K classification vectors in *MulSLR* (K is the number of modes in the data). We propose a block proximal descent approach to solve the problem and prove its convergence. The convergence rate of the proposed algorithm is also analyzed. Finally we validate the efficiency and effectiveness of *MulSLR* on predicting the onset risk of patients with Alzheimer's disease and heart failure.

Categories and Subject Descriptors

J.3 [**Life and Medical Sciences**]: Health; G.3 [**Probability and Statistics**]: Correlation and Regression Analysis

Keywords

Logistic Regression; Multilinear; Proximal Gradient; Healthcare

1. INTRODUCTION

Clinical risk prediction, such as predicting the onset [27] or hospitalization [19] risk of patients with chronic diseases, is an important problem in health informatics. Accurate risk prediction can greatly help reduce the unnecessary costs in hospitals as well as provide the right service at point-of-care.

There has been quite a few existing works in both data mining and health informatics domains on clinical risk prediction. For example, Sun *et al.* [27] developed a LASSO type of method for identifying important risk factors for predicting the onset risk of heart failure patients. Xiang *et al.* [30] proposed a multi-source learning approach for predicting the risk measured by cognitive score of patients with Alzheimer's disease. Miravitlles *et al.* [18] analyzed the factors associated with increased risk of exacerbation and hospital admission for patients with Chronic Obstructive Pulmonary Disease (COPD). In most of those works, logistic regression is at the heart of the predictive modeling process. Because of the large number of potentially related factors in different scenarios, a sparsity constraint is usually added on the learned model coefficients. The resultant model is referred to as sparse logistic regression, which can do both prediction and feature selection simultaneously. Depending on the different sparsity structures the model wants to explore, we can construct different sparsity-induced regularization terms. By adding them to the objective of conventional logistic regression we can get different types of sparse logistic regression models [13][17][26].

Until now most of the existing sparse logistic regression type of approaches assume their inputs are a set of data vectors. This means that we need to have a vector based representation for each patient if we want to adopt logistic regression type of methods to evaluate their risk. However, many patient medical data are not naturally in vector form. For example, X-Ray images are two-dimensional; Electroencephalography (EEG) is two dimensional if you stack all signals captured from different poles; functional Magnetic Resonance Imaging (fMRI) is three-dimensional. Even in patient Electronic Health Records (EHRs), there could be multiple diagnosis/symptoms accompanied with several drugs on the same claim. Therefore it is natural to represent a patient with a diagnosis by drug co-occurrence matrix if we want to consider the correlation between diagnosis and drugs when predicting the patient risk. We can also represent the patients with high order tensors if we want to consider more than two factors that are inter-correlated with each other. In these cases, if we still want to apply logistic regression one straightforward way is to stretch those matrices and tensors into vectors as people did in image processing, but this will lose the correlation information among different dimensions. Moreover, after stretching the dimensionality of

KDD'14, August 24–27, 2014, New York, New York, USA.

http://dx.doi.org/10.1145/2623330.2623754 .

the data objects will become very high, which will make traditional logistic regression inefficient.

Based on the above considerations, many researches on extending traditional vector based approaches to two (matrix based) or high order (tensor based) approaches have been becoming more and more popular. For example, two-dimensional Principal Component Analysis (PCA) [32] and Linear Discriminant Analysis [33] have been found to be more effective on face recognition task compared to traditional vector based PCA and LDA. Cai *et al.* [4] also extend Support Vector Machine to multidimensional data and got better results on document classification. Recently, Huang and Wang [9] developed a matrix variate logistic regression model and applied it in electroencephalography data analysis. Tan *et al.* [28] further extended logistic regression to tensor inputs and achieved good performance in a video classification task.

In this paper, we propose *MulSLR*, a multi-linear sparse logistic regression method that can directly take matrices or tensors as inputs and perform prediction. Because of the added L1 sparsity regularization terms, we developed a *Block Proximal Gradient* (BPG) method to solve the problem iteratively. We theoretically prove the convergence of the proposed algorithm and analyze the convergence rate based on the Kurdyka–Lojasiewicz inequality [3]. Finally we validate the effectiveness of our algorithm on both synthetic and real world data sets.

It is worthwhile to highlight the following aspects of *MulSLR*.

- *MulSLR* is able to directly take matrices and tensors as inputs, thus the resultant model can encode the correlation structure of the different types of data features.
- *MulSLR* does not need to stretch the data into vectors for model training, thus it avoids the curse of dimensionality and as a result the model can be more efficiently trained.
- The BPG method we developed to train *MulSLR* is theoretically guaranteed to converge. We also analyze the converge rate of *MulSLR*.
- We apply *MulSLR* to evaluate the onset risk of Alzheimer's disease and congestive heart failure on real world data sets and show some interesting results.

The rest of this paper is organized as follows. Section 2 reviews some related works. The details along with the convergence analysis of *MulSLR* is introduced in Section 3. Section 4 presents the experimental results, followed by the conclusions in Section 5.

2. RELATED WORK

Logistic regression [8] is a statistical classification method that has widely been used in many application areas, such as computer vision [23], information retrieval [6] and health informatics [18][30]. Suppose we have a training data matrix $\mathbf{X} = [\mathbf{x}_1, \mathbf{x}_2, \cdots, \mathbf{x}_n] \in \mathbb{R}^{d\times n}$, where $\mathbf{x}_i \in \mathbb{R}^d$ $(1 \leqslant i \leqslant n)$ is the i-th training data vector. Associated with each $\mathbf{x}_i$ we also have its corresponding label $y_i \in \{0, 1\}$. The goal of logistic regression is to train a linear classification function $f(\mathbf{x}) = \mathbf{w}^\top \mathbf{x} + b$ to discriminate the data in class 1 from the data in class 0 by minimizing the following logistic loss

$$\ell_{org}(\mathbf{w}, b) = \frac{1}{n}\sum_{i=1}^{n} \log\left[1 + \exp(-y_i(\mathbf{w}^\top \mathbf{x}_i + b))\right] \quad (1)$$

where $\mathbf{w} \in \mathbb{R}^d$ is the classification vector and b is the bias. They can be learned with gradient descent type of approaches.

In many real world applications, the data vectors $\{\mathbf{x}_i\}_{i=1}^n$ are usually sparse and high-dimensional (e.g., each patient could be a tens of thousands dimensional vector with bag-of-feature representation [27]). To enhance the interpretability of the model in these scenarios, we can add a sparsity regularization term on $\mathbf{w}$ and minimize the following ℓ_1-regularized logistic loss

$$\ell_{sp}(\mathbf{w}, b) = \frac{1}{n}\sum_{i=1}^{n} \log\left[1 + \exp(-y_i(\mathbf{w}^\top \mathbf{x}_i + b))\right] + \lambda\|\mathbf{w}\|_1 \quad (2)$$

where $\|\cdot\|_1$ is the vector $\ell 1$ norm and $\lambda > 0$ is a factor trading off the prediction accuracy and model sparsity. The resultant model is usually referred to as sparse logistic regression model [12]. Compared with the conventional logistic regression model obtained by minimizing $\mathcal{J}_{org}$, the $\mathbf{w}$ obtained by minimizing $\mathcal{J}_{sp}$ is sparse. In this way, we can not only get a predictor, but also know what are the feature dimensions that are important to the prediction, and these are the features with nonzero classification coefficients. Zou and Hastie [34] pointed out that there are some limitations if we only adopt 1 norm regularization, and they proposed a regularization term called *elastic net*, which is a mixture of 1 and 2 norm regularizers.

Sparse logistic regression has widely been used in health informatics because the applications in this field usually not only want a good prediction performance but also need the reason why. Basically what are the key factors that will affect the prediction performance. For example, sparse logistic regression has been used in the prediction of Leukemia [15], Alzheimer's disease [22] and cancers [10]. In recent years people also designed different regularization terms [13][17][26] to a enforce more complex sparsity patterns on the learned model. However, all these works require a vector based representation of the data. Fig.1 provides a graphical illustration on the difference of traditional vector based logistic regression and multilinear logistic regression when working on multi-dimensional data. Those traditional approaches need to stretch the data into an ultra-high dimensional vector first before they can be applied. This may suffer from the curse of dimensionality.

3. METHODOLOGY

We introduce the details of *MulSLR* in this section. First we will formally define the problem.

3.1 Problem Statement

Without the loss of generality, we assume each observation is a tensor $\mathcal{X}^i \in \mathbb{R}^{d_1\times d_2\times\cdots d_K}$, suppose its corresponding response is $y^i \in \{0, 1\}$, then *MulSLR* assumes

$$y^i \leftarrow \mathcal{X}^i \times_1 \mathbf{w}^1 \times_2 \mathbf{w}^2 \cdots \times_K \mathbf{w}^K + b \quad (3)$$

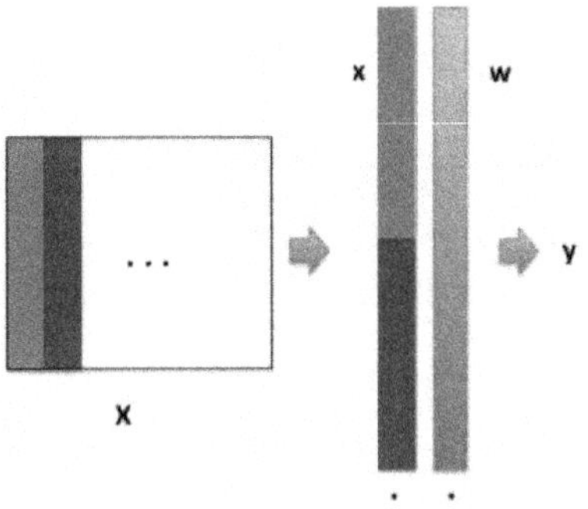

(a) Vector based logistic regression

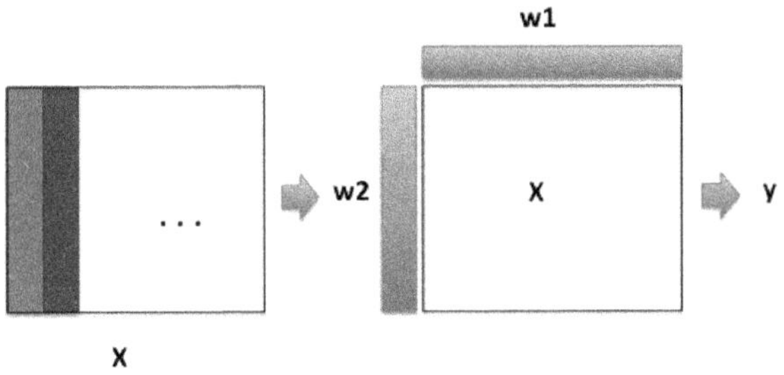

(b) Multilinear logistic regression

Figure 1: Traditional vector based logistic regression and multilinear logistic regression work on multi-dimensional data.

where $\times_k$ is the mode-k product, and $\mathbf{w}^k \in \mathbb{R}^{d_k \times 1}$ is the prediction coefficients on the k-th dimension. Then

$$\begin{aligned} & \mathcal{X}^i \times_1 \mathbf{w}^1 \times_2 \mathbf{w}^2 \cdots \times_K \mathbf{w}^K \\ &= \sum_{i_1=1}^{d_1} \sum_{i_2=1}^{d_2} \cdots \sum_{i_K=1}^{d_K} w^1_{i_1} w^2_{i_2} \cdots w^K_{i_K} X^i_{i_1 i_2 \cdots i_K} \end{aligned} \tag{4}$$

Let $\mathcal{W} = \{\mathbf{w}_1, \mathbf{w}_2, \cdots, \mathbf{w}_K\}$ be the set of prediction coefficient vectors. The loss we want to minimize is

$$\begin{aligned} \ell(\mathcal{W}, b) &= \frac{1}{n} \sum_{i=1}^{n} \ell(\mathcal{X}_i, y_i, \mathcal{W}) \qquad (5) \\ &= \frac{1}{n} \sum_{i=1}^{n} \ell(y_i, \mathcal{X}^i \times_1 \mathbf{w}^1 \times_2 \mathbf{w}^2 \cdots \times_K \mathbf{w}^K + b) \\ &= \frac{1}{n} \sum_{i=1}^{n} \ell(y_i, f_{(\mathcal{W},b)}(\mathcal{X}^i)) \end{aligned}$$

where for notational convince, we denote

$$f_{(\mathcal{W},b)}(\mathcal{X}^i) = \mathcal{X}^i \times_1 \mathbf{w}^1 \times_2 \mathbf{w}^2 \cdots \times_K \mathbf{w}^K + b \tag{6}$$

The loss function we considered in this paper is *Logistic Loss*:

$$\ell_l(\mathcal{W}, b) = \log[1 + \exp(-y_i f_{(\mathcal{W},b)}(\mathcal{X}^i))] \tag{7}$$

We adopt the following elastic net regularization term [34]

$$\begin{aligned} \mathcal{R}(\mathcal{W}) &= \mathcal{R}_1(\mathcal{W}) + \mathcal{R}_2(\mathcal{W}) \qquad (8) \\ &= \sum_{k=1}^{K} \lambda_k \|\mathbf{w}^k\|_1 + \frac{1}{2} \sum_{k=1}^{K} \mu_k \|\mathbf{w}^k\|_2^2 \qquad (9) \end{aligned}$$

Then the optimization problem we want to solve is

$$\min_{\mathcal{W}} \mathcal{J}(\mathcal{W}, b) = \ell(\mathcal{W}, b) + \mathcal{R}(\mathcal{W}) \tag{10}$$

We adopt a *Block Coordinate Descent* (BCD) procedure to solve the problem. Starting from some initialization $(\mathcal{W}_{(0)}, b_{(0)})$, at the i-th step of the t-th round of updates, we update $(\mathbf{w}^k_{(t)}, b_{(t)})$ by

$$\begin{aligned} & (\mathbf{w}^k_{(t)}, b_{(t)}) \qquad (11) \\ &= \arg\min_{(\mathbf{w},b)} \left[\ell(\mathcal{W}^{1\sim(k-1)}_{(t)}, \mathbf{w}, \mathcal{W}^{(k+1)\sim K}_{(t-1)}, b) + \lambda_k \|\mathbf{w}\|_1 + \frac{\mu_k}{2} \|\mathbf{w}\|_2^2 \right] \end{aligned}$$

where

$$\begin{aligned} \mathcal{W}^{1\sim(k-1)}_{(t)} &= \left\{ \mathbf{w}^1_{(t)}, \mathbf{w}^2_{(t)}, \cdots, \mathbf{w}^{k-1}_{(t)} \right\} \\ \mathcal{W}^{(k+1)\sim K}_{(t-1)} &= \left\{ \mathbf{w}^{k+1}_{(t-1)}, \mathbf{w}^{k+2}_{(t-1)}, \cdots, \mathbf{w}^{K}_{(t-1)} \right\} \end{aligned}$$

Algorithm 1 Block Coordinate Descent Procedure

Require: Data set $\{\mathcal{X}_i, y_i\}_{i=1}^n$, Regularization parameters $\{\lambda_k, \mu_k\}_{k=1}^K$

Initialization: $(\mathcal{W}_{(0)}, b_{(0)})$, $t = 0$
while Not Converge **do**
  for $k = 1 : K$ **do**
    Update $(\mathbf{w}^k_{(t)}, b_{(t,k)})$ by solving problem (11)
    $t = t + 1$
  end for
end while

3.2 Proximal Gradient Descent

The proximal descent procedure for updating $(\mathbf{w}^i_{(t)}, b_{(t,k)})$ is

$$\begin{aligned} & \mathbf{w}^k_{(t)} = \qquad (12) \\ & \arg\min_{\mathbf{w}} \Big[(\mathbf{w} - \widetilde{\mathbf{w}}^k_{(t)})^\top \nabla_{\mathbf{w}^k} \ell(\mathcal{W}^{1\sim(k-1)}_{(t)}, \widetilde{\mathbf{w}}^k_{(t)} \mathcal{W}^{(k+1)\sim K}_{(t-1)}, b_{(t,k-1)}) \\ & + \frac{\tau^k_{(t)}}{2} \|\mathbf{w} - \widetilde{\mathbf{w}}^k_{(t)}\|_2^2 + \lambda_k \|\mathbf{w}\|_1 + \frac{\mu_k}{2} \|\mathbf{w}\|_2^2 \Big] \end{aligned}$$

where

$$\begin{aligned} & \nabla_{\mathbf{w}^k} \ell(\mathcal{W}, b) = \frac{1}{n} \sum_{i=1}^{n} \nabla_{\mathbf{w}^k} \log[1 + \exp(-y_i f_{(\mathcal{W},b)}(\mathcal{X}^i))] \\ &= \frac{1}{n} \sum_{i=1}^{n} -y_i \frac{\exp(-y_i f_{(\mathcal{W},b)}(\mathcal{X}^i))}{1 + \exp(-y_i f_{(\mathcal{W},b)}(\mathcal{X}^i))} \nabla_{\mathbf{w}^k} f_{(\mathcal{W},b)}(\mathcal{X}^i) \\ &= -\frac{1}{n} \sum_{i=1}^{n} \left[1 + \exp(y_i f_{(\mathcal{W},b)}(\mathcal{X}^i)) \right]^{-1} y_i \nabla_{\mathbf{w}^k} f_{(\mathcal{W},b)}(\mathcal{X}^i) \qquad (13) \end{aligned}$$

and

$$\begin{aligned} & \nabla_{\mathbf{w}^k} f_{(\mathcal{W},b)}(\mathcal{X}^i) \qquad (14) \\ &= \mathcal{X}^i \times_1 \mathbf{w}^1 \times_2 \mathbf{w}^2 \cdots \times_{(k-1)} \mathbf{w}^{(k-1)} \times_{(k+1)} \mathbf{w}^{(k+1)} \cdots \times_K \mathbf{w}^K \end{aligned}$$

$\widetilde{\mathbf{w}}^k_{(t)}$ is an extrapolated point defined as

$$\widetilde{\mathbf{w}}^k_{(t)} = \mathbf{w}^k_{(t-1)} + \omega^k_{(t)} (\mathbf{w}^k_{(t-1)} - \mathbf{w}^k_{(t-2)}) \tag{15}$$

The optimal solution to problem (12) can be obtained as

$$\mathbf{w}^k_{(t)} = \mathcal{S}_{\alpha^k_{(t)}} \left(\frac{\tau^k_{(t)} \widetilde{\mathbf{w}}^k_{(t)} - \nabla_{\mathbf{w}^k} \ell^k_{(t)}(\widetilde{\mathbf{w}}^k_{(t)}, b_{(t,k-1)})}{\tau^k_{(t)} + \mu_k} \right) \tag{16}$$

where $\alpha^k_{(t)} = \lambda_k/(\tau^k_{(t)} + \mu_k)$ and $\mathcal{S}_{\alpha^k_{(t)}}$ is the component-wise shrinkage operator defined as

$$\left(\mathcal{S}_{\alpha^k_{(t)}}(\mathbf{v})\right)_i = \begin{cases} v_i - \alpha^k_{(t)}, & \text{if } v_i > \alpha^k_{(t)} \\ v_i + \alpha^k_{(t)}, & \text{if } v_i < -\alpha^k_{(t)} \\ 0, & \text{if } |v_i| \leqslant |\alpha^k_{(t)}| \end{cases} \tag{17}$$

Similarly we can update $b_{(t,k)}$ as

$$\begin{aligned} b_{(t,k)} &= \arg\min_b \Big[(b - \widetilde{b}_{(t,k)})^\top \nabla_b \ell(\mathcal{W}^{1\sim k}_{(t)}, \mathcal{W}^{(k+1)\sim K}_{(t-1)}, \widetilde{b}_{(t,k)}) \\ &\quad + \frac{\tau^k_{(t)}}{2} |b - \widetilde{b}_{(t,k)}|_2^2 \Big] \end{aligned} \tag{18}$$

and

$$\begin{aligned} \nabla_b \ell(\mathcal{W}, b) &= \frac{1}{n} \sum_{i=1}^n \nabla_b \log[1 + \exp(-y_i f_{(\mathcal{W},b)}(\mathcal{X}^i))] \\ &= -\frac{1}{n} \sum_{i=1}^n \left[1 + \exp(y_i f_{(\mathcal{W},b)}(\mathcal{X}^i))\right]^{-1} y_i \end{aligned} \tag{19}$$

$\widetilde{b}_{(t,k)}$ is the extrapolated point defined as

$$\widetilde{b}_{(t,k)} = b_{(t,k-1)} + \omega^k_{(t)}(b_{(t,k-1)} - b_{(t,k-2)}) \tag{20}$$

The optimal solution of problem (18) can be obtained by simple gradient descent as

$$b_{(t,k)} = \widetilde{b}_{t,k} - \frac{1}{\tau^k_{(t)}} \nabla_b \ell^k_{(t)}(\mathbf{w}^k_{(t)}, \widetilde{b}_{(t,k)}) \tag{21}$$

Putting Eq.(14) and Eq.(19) together, we have the following theorem

THEOREM 3.1. *The partial gradient $\nabla_{(\mathbf{w}^k,b)}\ell(\mathcal{W}, b)$ is Lipschitz continuous with constant*

$$\tau^k = \frac{\sqrt{2}}{n} \sum_{i=1}^n \left(\|\nabla_{\mathbf{w}^k} f_{(\mathcal{W},b)}(\mathcal{X}^i)\|_2 + 1\right)^2 \tag{22}$$

PROOF. See Appendix I. □

$\tau^k_{(t)}$ in Eq.(16) and Eq.(21) can be set as the Lipschitz constant according to Theorem 3.1. For notational convenience, we first introduce

$$\begin{aligned} &\nabla^{(t,k)}_{\mathbf{w}^k} f_{(\mathcal{W},b)}(\mathcal{X}^i) \\ &= \mathcal{X}^i \times_1 \mathbf{w}^1_{(t)} \times_2 \mathbf{w}^2_{(t)} \cdots \times_{(k-1)} \mathbf{w}^{(k-1)}_{(t)} \\ &\quad \times_{(k+1)} \mathbf{w}^{(k+1)}_{(t-1)} \cdots \times_K \mathbf{w}^K_{(t-1)} \end{aligned} \tag{23}$$

Then $\tau^k_{(t)}$ can be set as

$$\tau^k_{(t)} = \frac{\sqrt{2}}{n} \sum_{i=1}^n \left(\left\|\nabla^{(t,k)}_{\mathbf{w}^k} f_{(\mathcal{W},b)}(\mathcal{X}^i)\right\|_2 + 1\right)^2 \tag{24}$$

$\omega^k_{(t)}$ can be set as

$$\omega^k_{(t)} = \min\left(\omega_{(t)}, \delta_\omega \sqrt{\frac{\tau^k_{(t-1)}}{\tau^k_{(t)}}}\right) \tag{25}$$

where $\omega_{(t)} = (\eta_{(t-1)} - 1)/\eta_{(t)}$ with $\eta_{(0)} = 1$ and $\eta_{(t)} = \frac{1}{2}\left(1 + \sqrt{1 + 4\eta^2_{(t-1)}}\right)$.

Algorithm 2 summarized the whole algorithmic flow of our algorithm. At each iteration the most time consuming part is evaluating the gradient, which takes $O(n \prod_{i=1}^K d_i)$ time, that is linear with respect to data set size and data dimension.

Algorithm 2 Block Proximal Gradient Descent for Multilinear Sparse Logistic Regression

Require: Data set $\{\mathcal{X}_i, y_i\}_{i=1}^n$, Regularization parameters $\{\lambda_k, \mu_k\}_{k=1}^K$, $r_0 = 1$, $\delta_\omega < 1$
Initialization: $(\mathcal{W}_{(0)}, b_{(0)})$, $t = 1$
while Not Converge **do**
  for $k = 1 : K$ **do**
    Compute $\tau^k_{(t)}, \omega^k_{(t)}$ with Eq.(24) and Eq.(25)
    Compute $\widetilde{\mathbf{w}}^k_{(t)}, \mathbf{w}^k_{(t)}$ with Eq.(15) and Eq.(16)
    Update $\widetilde{b}_{(t,k)}, b_{(t,k)}$ by and Eq.(20) and Eq.(21)
  end for
  if $\ell(\mathcal{W}_{(t-1)}, b_{(t-1,K)}) \leqslant \ell(\mathcal{W}_{(t)}, b_{(t,K)})$ **then**
    Reupdate $\mathbf{w}^k_{(t)}$ and $b_{(t,k)}$ using Eq.(16) and Eq.(21), with $\widetilde{\mathbf{w}}^k_{(t)} = \mathbf{w}^k_{(t-1)}$ and $\widetilde{b}_{(t,k)} = b_{(t,k-1)}$
  end if
  $t = t + 1$
end while

3.3 Convergence Analysis

THEOREM 3.2. *Let $\mathcal{W}_{(t)}$ be the sequence generated by Algorithm 1 with $0 \leqslant \omega^k_{(t)} \leqslant \delta_\omega \sqrt{\tau^k_{(t-1)}/\tau^k_{(t)}}$ for $\delta_\omega < 1$. Then when $t \to \infty$, the sequence of $(\mathcal{W}_{(t)}, b_{(t,k)})$ will converge to some point $(\bar{\mathcal{W}}, \bar{b})$.*

PROOF. See Appendix II. □

With Theorem 3.2, it is not hard to see that $(\bar{\mathcal{W}}, \bar{b})$ is also a stationary point. This is because when $\mathcal{W}_{(t)} \to \bar{\mathcal{W}}$, $b_{(t,k)} \to \bar{b}$, according to Eq.(24), $\tau^k_{(t)} \to \bar{\tau}^k$. Therefore

$$\begin{aligned} &\bar{\mathbf{w}}^k = \\ &\arg\min_{\mathbf{w}} \Big[(\mathbf{w} - \bar{\mathbf{w}}^k)^\top \nabla_{\mathbf{w}^k} \ell(\bar{\mathcal{W}}^{1\sim(k-1)}, \bar{\mathbf{w}}^k \bar{\mathcal{W}}^{(k+1)\sim K}, \bar{b}) \\ &+ \frac{\bar{\tau}^k}{2}\|\mathbf{w} - \bar{\mathbf{w}}^k\|_2^2 + \lambda_k \|\mathbf{w}\|_1 + \frac{\mu_k}{2}\|\mathbf{w}\|_2^2\Big] \end{aligned} \tag{26}$$

Let $r(\mathbf{w}^k) = \lambda_k \|\mathbf{w}^k\|_1 + \frac{\mu_k}{2}\|\mathbf{w}^k\|_2^2$, then Eq.(26) suggests $\mathbf{0} \in \nabla_{\mathbf{w}^k} \ell(\bar{\mathcal{W}}, \bar{b}) + \partial r(\mathbf{w}^k)$ $(1 \leqslant k \leqslant K)$. Similarly, we also have $\nabla_b \ell(\bar{\mathcal{W}}, \bar{b}) = 0$. Therefore $(\bar{\mathcal{W}}, \bar{b})$ is a stationary point. To establish the convergence rate estimation result, we first introduce the following K-L inequality.

DEFINITION 3.3. **(Kurdyka-Lojasiewicz (K-L) Inequality)** *[11] [14] A function f is said to satisfy the Kurdyka-Lojasiewica inequality at point $\bar{\mathbf{\Psi}}$, if there exists $\theta \in [0, 1)$ such that*

$$\frac{|f(\mathbf{\Psi}) - f(\bar{\mathbf{\Psi}})|^\theta}{dist(\mathbf{0}, \partial f(\mathbf{\Psi}))} \tag{27}$$

is bounded for any $\mathbf{\Psi}$ near $\bar{\mathbf{\Psi}}$, where $\partial f(\mathbf{\Psi})$ is the limiting subdifferential of f at $\mathbf{\Psi}$ [24], and

$$dist(\mathbf{0}, \partial f(\mathbf{\Psi})) \equiv \min\{\|\mathbf{\Phi}\|_F : \mathbf{\Phi} \in \partial f(\mathbf{\Psi})\} \tag{28}$$

The K-L inequality was first introduced by Lojasiewicz [14] on real analytic functions, for which Eq.(27) is bounded around any stationary point $\bar{\Psi}$ for $\theta \in [\frac{1}{2}, 1)$. Kurdyka later extended this property to the functions on the o-minimal structure, and recenttly Bolte *et al.* [3] further extended it to non smooth sub analytic functions, and loss function $\mathcal{J}(\mathcal{W}, b)$ is one function of such type. Then it satisfies the K-L inequality. According to [31], we have the following theorem stating the convergence rate of our BPG method.

THEOREM 3.4. *Let $(\bar{\mathcal{W}}, \bar{b})$ be a stationary point of the $(\mathcal{W}_{(t)}, b_{(t)})$ sequence, then depending on the θ in Eq.(27), we have the following convergence rate.*

- *If $\theta = 0$, then $(\mathcal{W}_{(t)}, b_{(t)})$ converges to $(\bar{\mathcal{W}}, \bar{b})$ in finite iterations.*
- *If $\theta \in (0, \frac{1}{2}]$, then $(\mathcal{W}_{(t)}, b_{(t)})$ converges to $(\bar{\mathcal{W}}, \bar{b})$ at least linearly, i.e., $\|(\mathcal{W}_{(t)}, b_{(t)}) - (\bar{\mathcal{W}}, \bar{b})\|_F \leqslant Cr^t$ for some constant C and $r < 1$.*
- *If $\theta \in (\frac{1}{2}, 1)$, then $(\mathcal{W}_{(t)}, b_{(t)})$ converges to $(\bar{\mathcal{W}}, \bar{b})$ at least sublinearly, i.e., $\|(\mathcal{W}_{(t)}, b_{(t)}) - (\bar{\mathcal{W}}, \bar{b})\|_F \leqslant Ct^{-\frac{1-\theta}{2\theta-1}}$ for some constant C.*

PROOF. The proof can easily be derived from the proof of Theorem 2.9 in [31], thus we neglect the details here. □

4. EXPERIMENTS

In this section we will present the results of a set of experiments we conducted to test the effectiveness and efficiency of our method, including both synthetic examples and real world examples.

4.1 Synthetic Examples

We constructed some synthetic data sets to investigate two types of questions:

1. Whether *MulSLR* can effectively discover the latent data structure or not?
2. What is the scalability behavior of *MulSLR* when it is implemented on data sets with different scales?

(a) Sample from class 1 (b) Sample from class 0

Figure 2: Two samples from the synthetic data set we generated. (a) is from class 1, (b) is from class 0. The intensities of the pixels indicates the values of the corresponding entries, where dark means small values and bright means large values.

In order to answer question 1, we constructed a data set with two different patterns. Each data object is a square matrix with size 100×100, where the elements in the data matrices are generated independently from $\mathcal{N}(0, 1)$, i.e., univariate Gaussian distribution with zero mean and unit variance. The upper-left 20×20 block was different for the data matrices in class 1 and class 0 in the following sense. We generate two vectors $\mathbf{w}_1 \in \mathbb{R}^{20}$ and $\mathbf{w}_2 \in \mathbb{R}^{20}$ whose elements are generated independently from uniform distribution between 0 and 1. For any data matrix $\mathbf{X}$ from class 1, we have $\mathbf{w}_1^\top \widehat{\mathbf{X}} \mathbf{w}_2 + 1 \geqslant 0.5$, where $\widehat{\mathbf{X}}$ is the upper-left 20×20 block of $\mathbf{X}$. For any data matrix $\mathbf{Y}$ from class 2, we have $\mathbf{w}_1^\top \widehat{\mathbf{X}} \mathbf{w}_2 + 1 \leqslant -0.5$, where $\widehat{\mathbf{Y}}$ is the upper-left 20×20 block of $\mathbf{Y}$. Therefore there is a special correlation structure on the two dimensions of those data matrices. Basically the data from those two classes can only be identified from a bilinear combination on their upper-left 20×20 blocks. We provide two sample data matrices on Fig.2, one from each class. From the figure we cannot judge whether there is any differences between them. We generated 1000 samples for each class and thus the entire data set has 2000 samples.

In our implementation, we initialize $\mathbf{w}_1 \in \mathbb{R}^{100}$, $\mathbf{w}_2 \in \mathbb{R}^{100}$ as uniform vectors, and we iterate the *MulSLR* until a certain termination condition is satisfied. Such termination condition could be either a maximum number of iteration steps or the absolute difference of objective function value between two consecutive steps is less than a certain tolerance value. For those free parameters we set $\lambda_1 = \lambda_2 = 0.01$, $\mu_1 = \mu_2 = 0.0001$, $\delta_\omega = 0.99$. We set the maximum number of iterations to be 100. We randomly select 80% of the data for training (the data in class 1 and 0 are evenly sampled), and the rest 20% data for testing. The objective function value convergence plot is shown in Fig.3 (a), from which we can see that with the iterations going on, the objective function value decreases very fast during the first 30 steps, and decreases slowly from 30 to 60 steps, and becomes almost stable from then on. We also evaluated the prediction performance on the testing data set in terms of *Area Under the receiver operating characteristic Curve* (AUC) value using $\mathbf{w}_1$ and $\mathbf{w}_2$ obtained from each iteration. The prediction AUC versus number of iterations plot is illustrated in Fig.3 (b), which shows that the prediction performance also increases very fast during the first 30 steps, and slowly increase to 1 from step 30 to step 60.

As illustrations, we also plotted the matrix of $\mathbf{W} = \mathbf{w}_1 \mathbf{w}_2^\top$ after 100 iterations with *MulSLR* in Fig.4 (b). This is interesting because *MulSLR* makes decisions with a linear function, and in two dimension case the weight, or importance of the (i, j)-th entry is W_{ij} (as $\mathbf{w}_1^\top \mathbf{X} \mathbf{w}_2 = vec(\mathbf{W})^\top vec(\mathbf{X})$, where vec is a function vectorizing a matrix). From the we can clearly observe a block structure on the upper left corner. This complies with the latent data structure and explains the reason why we can achieve a 1 AUC. For comparison purpose, we also plotted the matrix of $\mathbf{w}_1 \mathbf{w}_2^\top$ after 100 iterations with *MulSLR* with $\lambda_1 = \lambda_2 = 0$ in Fig.4 (a), in which case the sparsity ($\ell 1$) regularizations on $\mathbf{w}_1$ and $\mathbf{w}_2$ do not take effect. We can observe that in this case the matrix is dense, which is because $\mathbf{w}_1$ and $\mathbf{w}_2$ are dense vectors. We also checked the predicted AUC value this dense $\mathbf{w}_1$ and $\mathbf{w}_2$ can get, which is only 0.6525. This validates the superiority of sparse multilinear logistic regression over plain multilinear logistic regression in this case.

To answer the second question, we conducted two sets of experiments on Mac OS 10.7 with 2.2GHz CPU and 12GB main memory. In the first set of experiments, we randomly generated a set of 100×100 data matrices, and we record the

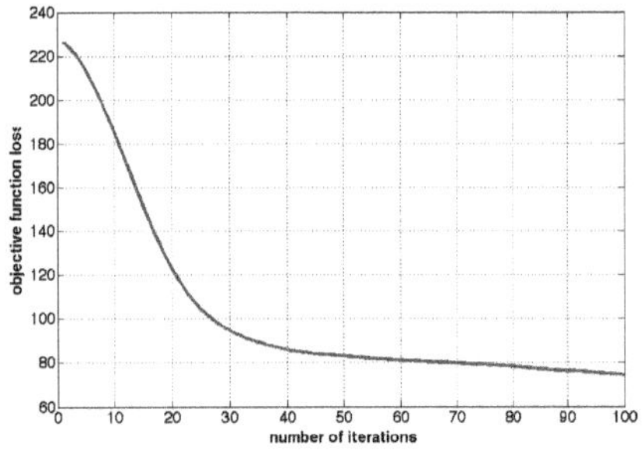

(a) Objective function loss vs. number of iterations

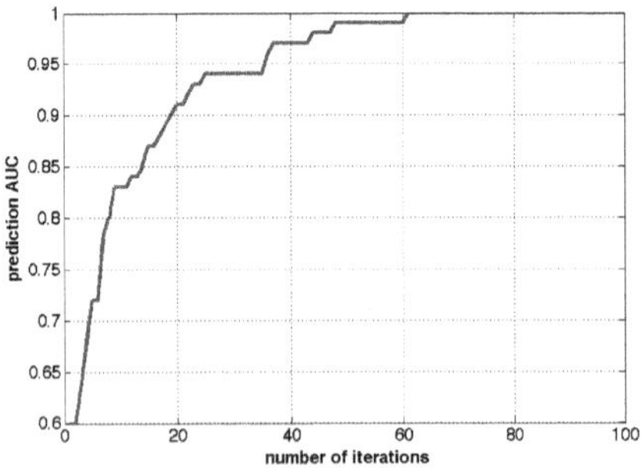

(b) Prediction AUC vs. number of iterations

Figure 3: Convergence plots on the synthetic data. (a) shows how the objective function value with respect to the number of iterations when training with 80% of the data. (b) shows how the corresponding testing AUC goes with number of iterations on the rest 20% data. From the figure we can see that in this case *MulSLR* converges in about 60 iterations

averaged running time per iteration for *MulSLR* with respect to different data set size. The result is shown in Fig.5(a), which shows a clear linear trend between the running time and data scale. In the second set of experiments, we fixed the data set size to be 100, but varying the data dimensionality from 50×50 to 2000×2000. The result is provided in Fig.5(b), which shows that the trend of that curve is slightly quadratic (as the entire data dimensionality is the square of the horizontal axis values). This is in accordance with our complexity analysis of Algorithm 2.

4.2 Experiments on fMRI Data

Functional magnetic resonance imaging or functional MRI (fMRI) is a functional neuroimaging procedure using MRI technology that measures brain activity by detecting associated changes in blood flow[1]. fMRI is an effective approach to investigate alterations in brain function related to the earliest symptoms of Alzheimer's disease, possibly before development of significant irreversible structural damage.

The raw fMRI scans used in our experiments were collected from real clinic cases of 1,005 patients [21], whose cognitive function scores (semantic, episodic, executive and spatial - ranges between -2.8258 and 2.5123) were also acquired at the same time using a cognitive function test.

[1] `http://en.wikipedia.org/wiki/Functional_magnetic_resonance_imaging`

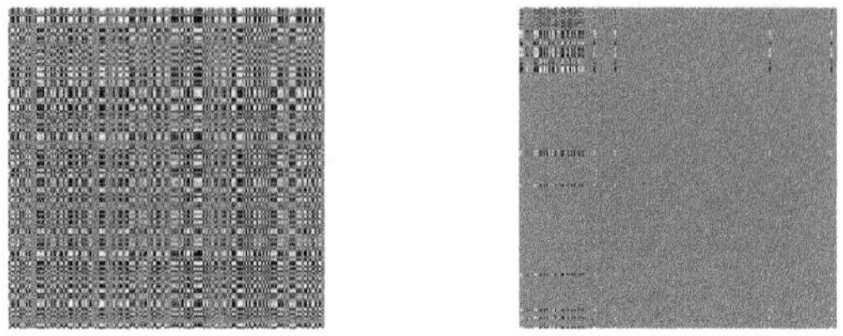

(a) No $\ell 1$ regularizations (b) With $\ell 1$ regularizations

Figure 4: The matrix of $\hat{\mathbf{w}}_1\hat{\mathbf{w}}_2^\top$, where $\hat{\mathbf{w}}_1, \hat{\mathbf{w}}_2$ are the converged solution over 100 iterations. (a) shows the result with $\lambda_1 = \lambda_2 = 0$, i.e., no $\ell 1$ regularizations. (b) shows the result of *MulSLR* with $\lambda_1 = \lambda_2 = 0.01$.

There are three types of MRI scans that were collected from the subjects: (1) FA, the fractional anisotropy MRI gives information about the shape of the diffusion tensor at each voxel, which reflects the differences between an isotropic diffusion and a linear diffusion; (2) FLAIR, Fluid attenuated inversion recovery is a pulse sequence used in MRI, which uncovers the white matter hyperintensity of the brain; (3) GRAY, gray MRI images revealing the gray matter of the brain. In the raw scans, each voxel has a value from 0 to 1, where 1 indicates that the structural integrity of the axon tracts at that location is perfect, while 0 implies either there are no axon tracts or they are shot (not working). The raw scans are preprocessed (including normalization, denoising and alignment) and then restructured to 3D tensors with a size of $134 \times 102 \times 134$. Fig.6 demonstrate a sample image for each of thee three types of scans. Another information we have for this data set is associated with each sample we have a label, which could be either *normal*, *Mild Cognitive Impairment* (MCI) or *demented*.

Because this is a three-class problem and logistic regression is for binary classification, we constructed three prediction tasks with one-versus-rest strategy, i.e., *normal* vs. *MCI* and *demented*, *MCI* vs. *normal* and *demented*, *demented* vs. *normal* and *MCI*. For *MulSLR*, we set the ℓ_1 term regularization parameters $\lambda_1 = \lambda_2 = \lambda_3$ and tune it from the grid $\{10^{-3}, 10^{-2}, 10^{-1}, 1, 10, 10^2, 10^3\}$ with five fold cross validation. The ℓ_2 term regularization parameters are set to $\mu_1 = \mu_2 = \mu_3 = 10^{-4}$. For comparison purpose, we also implemented the following baseline algorithms:

- **Nearest Neighbor** (NN). This is the one nearest neighbor classifier with standard Euclidean distance.
- **Support Vector Machine** (SVM). This is the regular vector based SVM method.
- **Logistic Regression** (LR). This is the traditional vector based logistic regression method.
- **Sparse Logistic Regression** (SLR). This is the vector based sparse logistic regression.
- **Multilinear Logistic Regression** (MLR). This is equivalent to *MulSLR* with all $\ell 1$ regularization parameters setting to 0.

We use *LIBLINEAR* [7] for the implementation of LR and SLR, and *LIBSVM* [5] for the implementation of SVM. Note

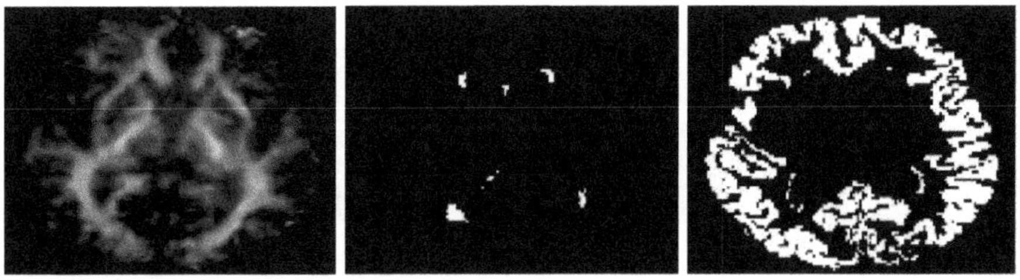

(a) FA (b) FLAIR (c) GRAY

Figure 6: Sample images of the three different types of scans.

Table 1: Prediction AUC Comparison for Different Methods and Different Tasks

method	*normal* vs. *MCI* and *demented*	*MCI* vs. *normal* and *demented*	*demented* vs. *normal* and *MCI*
NN	0.5052 ± 0.0555	0.5085 ± 0.0473	0.5106 ± 0.0487
SVM	0.6491 ± 0.1355	0.5230 ± 0.0567	0.5409 ± 0.0473
LR	0.6591 ± 0.1421	0.5860 ± 0.1007	0.6203 ± 0.1253
SLR	0.6595 ± 0.1396	0.5877 ± 0.0993	0.6220 ± 0.1243
MLR	0.6754 ± 0.0896	0.5994 ± 0.0627	0.6382 ± 0.1201
MulSLR	$\mathbf{0.6923 \pm 0.0706}$	$\mathbf{0.6015 \pm 0.0520}$	$\mathbf{0.6731 \pm 0.1054}$

that in order to test those vector based approaches, we need to stretch those fMRI tensors into very long vectors (with dimensionality 1,831,512).Table 1 summarized the average and standard deviation over 5-fold cross validation in terms of Areas Under the receiver operating characteristics Curve (AUC) values. The data we used are the FLAIR images. From the table we can observe that:

- The multilinear methods work better than traditional vector based approaches. One possible reason is because there is a clear spatial structure on fMRI images which those multilinear methods can take advantage of.
- The sparse methods work better than their non sparse counterparts. This can also be understood because the FLAIR images are sparse in nature.
- Discriminating MCI from normal and demented is more difficult compared with the other two tasks. This is because MCI is an intermediate state during the progression of Alzheimer's disease from normal to demented.

4.3 Experiments on CHF Onset Prediction

Congestive heart failure (CHF), which refers to a condition where the heart cannot pump enough blood to meet the body's needs, is a major chronic illness in the U.S., affecting more than five million patients. It is estimated CHF costs the nation an estimated $32 billion each year[2]. Effective prediction of the onset risk of potential CHF patients would help identify the patient at risk in time. Thus the decision makers can provide the proper treatment to the right patients. this can also help save unnecessary costs.

Electronic Health Records (EHR) are systematic collection of patient health information including diagnosis, medication, lab, procedure, demographics, etc. It has now been becoming one of the major information source for conducting healthcare analytics research. The data set we use in our experiments is from a real world EMR data warehouse including the longitudinal EHR of 319,650 patients over 4 years. On this data set, we identified 1,000 CHF case patients, i. e., the patients who are confirmed with CHF with the identification criterion in [29]. Then we did a group match according to patient demographics, comorbidities and primary care physicians similar as in [29] identifying 2,000 control patients. We use the medication orders of those patients within two years from their operational criteria date (for case patients, their operational criteria dates are just their CHF confirmation date. For control patients that date is just the date of their last records in the database). On each medication order we use the corresponding pharmacy class and the primary diagnosis in terms of Hierarchical Condition Category (HCC) codes [20] for the medication prescription. In total there are 92 unique pharmacy classes and 195 distinct HCC codes. Therefore each patient can be represented as a 92×195 matrix, where the (i, j)-th entry indicates the frequency that the i-th drug was prescribed during the two years with the j-th diagnosis code as primary diagnosis.

The parameters for *MulSLR* are set in the same manner as the experiments in last subsection. For comparison purpose, we also implemented NN, SVM, LR, SLR, MLR and reported the averaged AUC value over 5-fold cross validation along with their standard deviations on Fig.7. From the figure we can clearly observe that multilinear methods still work better than vector based methods (in order to implement vector based methods, we still need to stretch the patient matrices into vectors). *MulSLR* performs better than MLR, which is the regular ridged bilinear logistic regression, because the patient matrices formed are typically very sparse. However, in this case the vector based SLR works slightly worse than LR, this could be due to the sparsity structures of the patient matrices get lost when stretching them into vectors.

One interesting thing to check is the product of $\mathbf{w}_{med}$, which is the classification vector on the medication side, and $\mathbf{w}_{diag}^{\top}$, which is the classification vector on the diagnosis side. Just like what we examined on the toy data. In this way we

[2] `http://www.cdc.gov/dhdsp/data_statistics/fact_sheets/docs/fs_heart_failure.pdf`

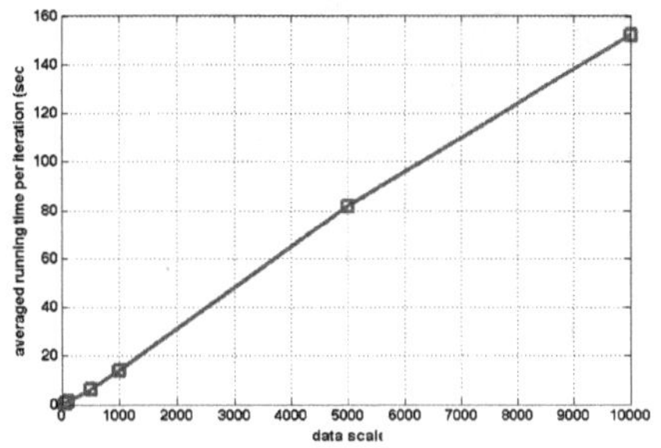

(a) Running time per iteration vs. data set size

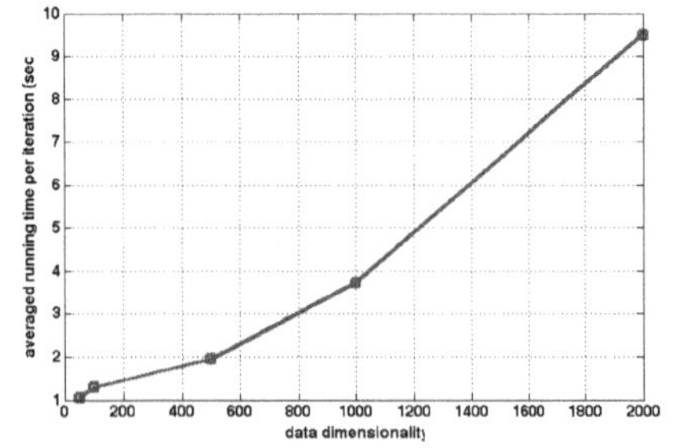

(b) Running time per iteration vs. data dimensionality

Figure 5: Averaged running time per iteration of *MulSLR*. (a) shows the running time per iteration vs. data set size plot, where the data dimensionality is fixed to 100. (b) shows the running time per iteration vs. one-side data dimensionality plot, where the data set size is fixed to 500.

can find some strongly correlated medications and diagnosis that could be highly predictive for CHF onset risk. To achieve this goal, we use all the data to train the $\mathbf{w}_{med}$ and $\mathbf{w}_{diag}$ and plot their outer-product as in Fig.8 (where we just show a submatrix due to space limitation), where warm color indicate high values and cold color indicates small values. From the image we can observe that:

- **Cardiac disease and their corresponding treatment drugs are highly correlated and predictive**. For example, *Antihypertensive, Antihyperlipidemic, Calcium Blocker, Beta Blockers, Cardiotonic* drugs with *CHF* (HCC080), *Acute Myocardial Infarction* (HCC081), *Hypertensive Heart Disease* (HCC090), *Hypertension* (HCC091) diagnosis.
- **CHF commorbidities and their corresponding treatment drugs are predictive**. For example, *Chronic Obstructive Pulmonary Disease* (COPD) (HCC108) [25] with *Corticosteroids*, and also *Chronic Kidney Disease* (CKD) (HCC436 and HCC439) [1].
- **CHF related symptoms and their corresponding treatment drugs are predictive**, such as Gout, which is a well-known Framingham symptom [16] for CHF patients.

Actually all those findings are also clinically validated in those references we cited. We also provide the detailed description of all HCC codes at `https://www.dropbox.com/s/6e1qbjf1ce7yi6x/hcc_codes.pdf`.

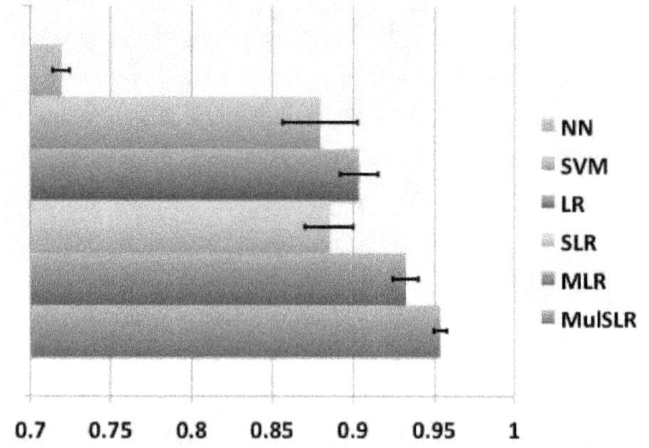

Figure 7: Prediction performance for different methods on the CHF onset prediction task in terms of averaged AUC value with 5-fold cross validation along with their standard deviations.

5. CONCLUSIONS

We propose a multilinear sparse logistic regression method called *MulSLR* in this paper, which can directly take data matrices or tensors as inputs and do prediction on that. *MulSLR* is formulated as an optimization problem and we propose an effective BCD strategy to solve it. We proved the convergence and analyzed the convergence rate theoretically. Finally we validate the effectiveness and efficiency of *MulSLR* on both synthetic and real world data sets. We demonstrate that *MulSLR* can not only achieve good performance, but also discover interesting predictive patterns.

Appendix I: Proof of Theorem 3.1

Let

$$\mathcal{W}_{\backslash k} = (\mathbf{w}^1, \mathbf{w}^2, \cdots, \mathbf{w}^{(k-1)}, \mathbf{w}^{(k+1)}, \cdots, \mathbf{w}^K) \tag{29}$$

Then for any $(\mathcal{W}_{\backslash k}, \mathbf{w}^k, b)$ and $(\mathcal{W}_{\backslash k}, \widehat{\mathbf{w}}^k, \widehat{b})$, we have

$$\begin{aligned}
& \left\| \nabla_{(\mathbf{w}^k,b)} \ell(\mathcal{W}_{\backslash k}, \mathbf{w}^k, b) - \nabla_{(\mathbf{w}^k,b)} \ell(\mathcal{W}_{\backslash k}, \widehat{\mathbf{w}}^k, \widehat{b}) \right\|_2 \\
\leqslant\ & \frac{1}{n} \sum_{i=1}^{n} \left| \left[1 + \exp\left(y_i f_{(\mathcal{W}_{\backslash k}, \mathbf{w}^k, b)}(\mathcal{X}^i)\right)\right]^{-1} \right. \\
& \left. - \left[1 + \exp\left(y_i f_{(\mathcal{W}_{\backslash k}, \widehat{\mathbf{w}}^k, \widehat{b})}(\mathcal{X}^i)\right)\right]^{-1} \right| \left(\|\nabla_{\mathbf{w}^k} f_{(\mathcal{W},b)}(\mathcal{X}^i)\|_2 + 1 \right) \\
\leqslant\ & \frac{1}{n} \sum_{i=1}^{n} \left(\|\nabla_{\mathbf{w}^k} f_{(\mathcal{W},b)}(\mathcal{X}^i)\|_2 + 1 \right)^2 \left(\left\| \mathbf{w}^k - \widehat{\mathbf{w}}^k \right\|_2 + |b - \widehat{b}| \right) \\
\leqslant\ & \frac{\sqrt{2}}{n} \sum_{i=1}^{n} \left(\|\nabla_{\mathbf{w}^k} f_{(\mathcal{W},b)}(\mathcal{X}^i)\|_2 + 1 \right)^2 \left\| \left(\mathbf{w}^k, b\right) - \left(\widehat{\mathbf{w}}^k, \widehat{b}\right) \right\|_2
\end{aligned}$$

This completes the proof.

Appendix II: Proof of Theorem 3.2

For notational convenience, we define

$$\ell_{(t)}^k(\mathbf{w}^k, b) = \ell(\mathcal{W}_{(t)}^{1\sim(k-1)}, \mathbf{w}^k, \mathcal{W}_{(t-1)}^{(k+1)\sim K}, b) \tag{30}$$

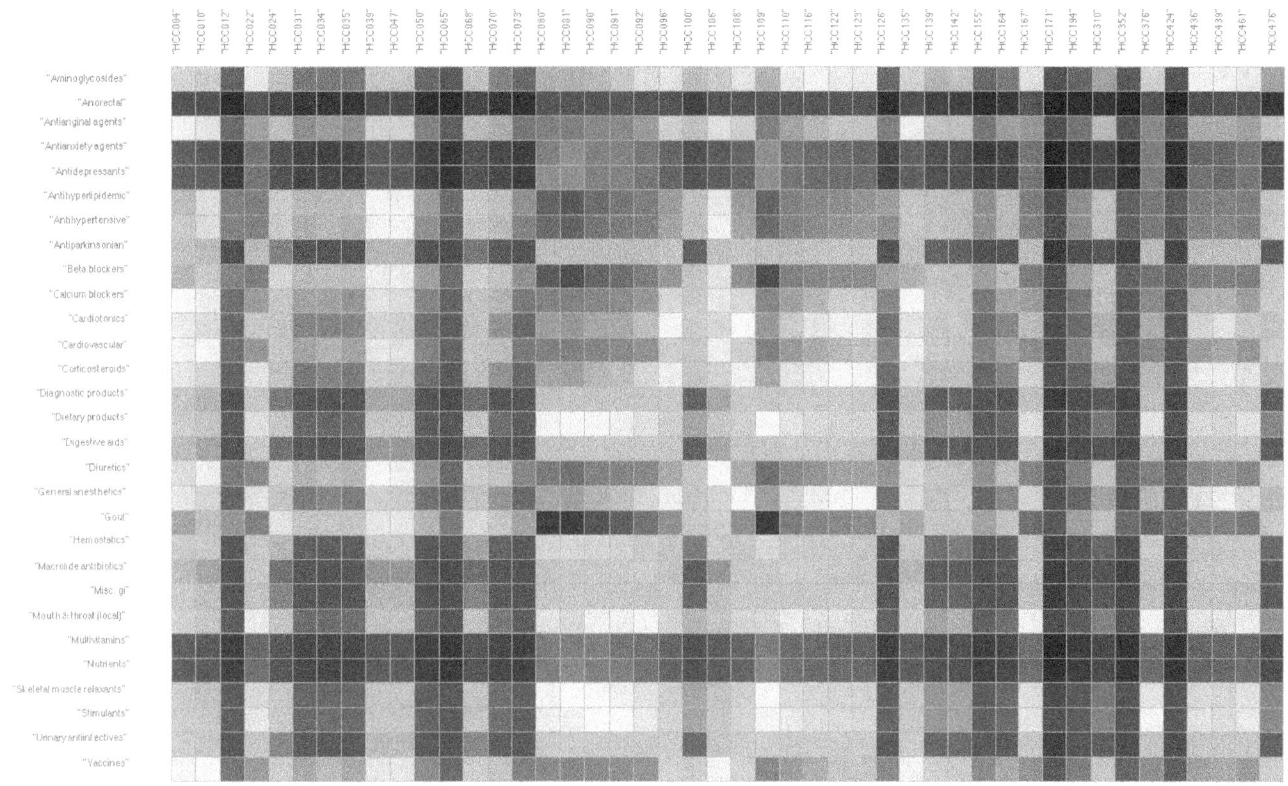

Figure 8: A sub matrix from the matrix of $\mathbf{w}_{med}\mathbf{w}_{diag}^{\top}$. Warm color indicates large value, and cold color indicates small value. Thus warm color indicates *MulSLR* gives larger weights to the corresponding entry when making a decision. There are some interesting red blocks in the image. For example, *Antihypertensive, Antihyperlipidemic, Calcium Blocker, Beta Blockers, Cardiotonic* drugs with *CHF* (HCC080), *Acute Myocardial Infarction* (HCC081), *Hypertensive Heart Disease* (HCC090), *Hypertension* (HCC091) diagnosis. Those are all cardiac disease and their corresponding treatment drugs. The row of drug *Corticosteroids* is also warm because it is used for treating pulmonary disease such as COPD, which is a common commorbidity of CHF. For similar reason, the column of diagnosis COPD (HCC108) is warm.

With Lemma 2.3 in [2], we have

$$\begin{aligned}
&\ell_{(t)}^k(\mathbf{w}_{(t-1)}^k, b_{(t,k-1)}) - \ell_{(t)}^k(\mathbf{w}_{(t)}^k, b_{(t,k)}) \\
&\geqslant \frac{\tau_{t-1}^k}{2}\|\widetilde{\mathbf{w}}_{(t-1)}^k - \mathbf{w}_{(t)}^k\|_2^2 + \frac{\tau_{t-1}^k}{2}|\widetilde{b}_{(t,k-1)} - b_{(t,k)}|^2 \\
&\quad + \tau_{(t-1)}^k(\widetilde{\mathbf{w}}_{(t-1)}^k - \mathbf{w}_{(t-1)}^k)^\top(\mathbf{w}_{(t)}^k - \widetilde{\mathbf{w}}_{(t-1)}^k) \\
&\quad + \tau_{(t-1)}^k(\widetilde{b}_{(t,k-1)} - b_{(t,k-1)}) \cdot (b_{(t,k)} - \widetilde{b}_{(t,k-1)}) \\
&= \frac{\tau_{t-1}^k}{2}\|\mathbf{w}_{(t-1)}^k - \mathbf{w}_{(t)}^k\|_2^2 + \frac{\tau_{t-1}^k}{2}|b_{(t,k-1)} - b_{(t,k)}|^2 \\
&\quad - \frac{\tau_{t-1}^k}{2}(\omega_{(t-1)}^k)^2[\|\mathbf{w}_{(t-2)}^k - \mathbf{w}_{(t-1)}^k\|^2 + |b_{(t,k-2)} - b_{(t,k-1)}|^2] \\
&\geqslant \frac{\tau_{t-1}^k}{2}\|\mathbf{w}_{(t-1)}^k - \mathbf{w}_{(t)}^k\|_2^2 + \frac{\tau_{t-1}^k}{2}|b_{(t,k-1)} - b_{(t,k)}|^2 \\
&\quad - \frac{\tau_{t-2}^k}{2}(\delta_\omega)^2[\|\mathbf{w}_{(t-2)}^k - \mathbf{w}_{(t-1)}^k\|^2 + |b_{(t,k-2)} - b_{(t,k-1)}|^2]
\end{aligned} \tag{31}$$

Then

$$\begin{aligned}
&\ell(\mathcal{W}_{(t-1)}, b_{(t-1,K)}) - \ell(\mathcal{W}_{(t)}, b_{(t,K)}) \\
&= \sum_{k=1}^K \left(\ell_{(t)}^k\left(\mathbf{w}_{(t-1)}^k, b_{(t,k-1)}\right) - \ell_{(t)}^k\left(\mathbf{w}_{(t)}^k, b_{(t,k)}\right)\right) \\
&\geqslant \sum_{k=1}^K \left(\frac{\tau_{t-1}^k}{2}\|\mathbf{w}_{(t-1)}^k - \mathbf{w}_{(t)}^k\|_2^2 + \frac{\tau_{t-1}^k}{2}|b_{(t,k-1)} - b_{(t,k)}|^2\right. \\
&\quad \left. - \frac{\tau_{t-2}^k}{2}(\delta_\omega)^2\|\mathbf{w}_{(t-2)}^k - \mathbf{w}_{(t-1)}^k\|^2 - \frac{\tau_{t-2}^k}{2}(\delta_\omega)^2|b_{(t,k-2)} - b_{(t,k-1)}|^2\right)
\end{aligned} \tag{32}$$

Therefore

$$\begin{aligned}
&\ell(\mathcal{W}_{(0)}, b_{(0,0)}) - \ell(\mathcal{W}_{(t)}, b_{(t,K)}) \\
&\geqslant \sum_{k=1}^K\sum_{t=1}^T \left(\frac{\tau_{t-1}^k}{2}\|\mathbf{w}_{(t-1)}^k - \mathbf{w}_{(t)}^k\|_2^2 + \frac{\tau_{t-1}^k}{2}|b_{(t,k-1)} - b_{(t,k)}|^2\right. \\
&\quad \left. - \frac{\tau_{t-2}^k}{2}(\delta_\omega)^2\|\mathbf{w}_{(t-2)}^k - \mathbf{w}_{(t-1)}^k\|^2 \frac{\tau_{t-2}^k}{2}(\delta_\omega)^2|b_{(t,k-2)} - b_{(t,k-1)}|^2\right) \\
&\geqslant \sum_{k=1}^K\sum_{t=1}^T \left(\frac{\tau_{t-1}^k(1-\delta_\omega^2)}{2}[\|\mathbf{w}_{(t-1)}^k - \mathbf{w}_{(t)}^k\|_2^2 + |b_{(t,k-1)} - b_{(t,k)}|^2]\right)
\end{aligned} \tag{33}$$

As $\ell(\mathcal{W}, b)$ is lower bounded, when $T \to \infty$, we have

$$\sum_{t=0}^{\infty} \|(\mathcal{W}_{(t)}, b_{(t,k)}) - (\mathcal{W}_{(t+1)}, b_{(t+1,k)})\|_2^2 < \infty$$

and $\|(\mathcal{W}_{(t-1)}, b_{(t-1,k)}) - (\mathcal{W}_{(t)}, b_{(t,k)})\|_F^2 \rightarrow 0$. This completes the proof.

6. REFERENCES

[1] A. Ahmed, M. W. Rich, P. W. Sanders, G. J. Perry, G. L. Bakris, M. R. Zile, T. E. Love, I. B. Aban, and M. G. Shlipak. Chronic kidney disease associated mortality in diastolic versus systolic heart failure: a propensity matched study. *The American journal of cardiology*, 99(3):393–398, 2007.

[2] A. Beck and M. Teboulle. A fast iterative shrinkage-thresholding algorithm for linear inverse problems. *SIAM Journal on Imaging Sciences*, 2(1):183–202, 2009.

[3] J. Bolte, A. Daniilidis, and A. Lewis. The lojasiewicz inequality for nonsmooth subanalytic functions with applications to subgradient dynamical systems. *SIAM Journal on Optimization*, 17(4):1205–1223, 2007.

[4] D. Cai, X. He, J.-R. Wen, J. Han, and W.-Y. Ma. Support tensor machines for text categorization. *Department of Computer Science Technical Report No. 2714, University of Illinois at Urbana-Champaign (UIUCDCS-R-2006-2714)*, 2006.

[5] C.-C. Chang and C.-J. Lin. Libsvm: a library for support vector machines. *ACM Transactions on Intelligent Systems and Technology (TIST)*, 2(3):27, 2011.

[6] W. S. Cooper, F. C. Gey, and D. P. Dabney. Probabilistic retrieval based on staged logistic regression. In *Proceedings of the 15th annual international ACM SIGIR conference on Research and development in information retrieval*, pages 198–210. ACM, 1992.

[7] R.-E. Fan, K.-W. Chang, C.-J. Hsieh, X.-R. Wang, and C.-J. Lin. Liblinear: A library for large linear classification. *The Journal of Machine Learning Research*, 9:1871–1874, 2008.

[8] D. W. Hosmer Jr and S. Lemeshow. *Applied logistic regression*. John Wiley & Sons, 2004.

[9] H. Hung and C.-C. Wang. Matrix variate logistic regression model with application to eeg data. *Biostatistics*, 14(1):189–202, 2013.

[10] Y. Kim, S. Kwon, and S. Heun Song. Multiclass sparse logistic regression for classification of multiple cancer types using gene expression data. *Computational Statistics & Data Analysis*, 51(3):1643–1655, 2006.

[11] K. Kurdyka. On gradients of functions definable in o-minimal structures. In *Annales de l'institut Fourier*, volume 48, pages 769–783. Institut Fourier, 1998.

[12] J. Liu, J. Chen, and J. Ye. Large-scale sparse logistic regression. In *Proceedings of the 15th ACM SIGKDD international conference on Knowledge discovery and data mining*, pages 547–556. ACM, 2009.

[13] Z. Liu, F. Jiang, G. Tian, S. Wang, F. Sato, S. J. Meltzer, and M. Tan. Sparse logistic regression with lp penalty for biomarker identification. *Statistical Applications in Genetics and Molecular Biology*, 6(1), 2007.

[14] S. Łojasiewicz. Sur la géométrie semi-et sous-analytique. In *Annales de l'institut Fourier*, volume 43, pages 1575–1595. Institut Fourier, 1993.

[15] T. Manninen, H. Huttunen, P. Ruusuvuori, and M. Nykter. Leukemia prediction using sparse logistic regression. *PloS one*, 8(8), 2013.

[16] P. A. McKee, W. P. Castelli, P. M. McNamara, and W. B. Kannel. The natural history of congestive heart failure: the framingham study. *New England Journal of Medicine*, 285(26):1441–1446, 1971.

[17] L. Meier, S. Van De Geer, and P. Bühlmann. The group lasso for logistic regression. *Journal of the Royal Statistical Society: Series B (Statistical Methodology)*, 70(1):53–71, 2008.

[18] M. Miravitlles, T. Guerrero, C. Mayordomo, L. Sánchez-Agudo, F. Nicolau, and J. L. Segú. Factors associated with increased risk of exacerbation and hospital admission in a cohort of ambulatory copd patients: a multiple logistic regression analysis. *Respiration*, 67(5):495–501, 2000.

[19] E. F. Philbin and T. G. DiSalvo. Prediction of hospital readmission for heart failure: development of a simple risk score based on administrative data. *Journal of the American College of Cardiology*, 33(6):1560–1566, 1999.

[20] G. C. Pope, R. P. Ellis, A. S. Ash, J. Ayanian, D. Bates, H. Burstin, L. Iezzoni, E. Marcantonio, and B. Wu. Diagnostic cost group hierarchical condition category models for medicare risk adjustment. *Health Economics Research, Inc. Waltham, MA*, 2000.

[21] B. Qian, X. Wang, F. Wang, H. Li, J. Ye, and I. Davidson. Active learning from relative queries. In *Proceedings of the Twenty-Third international joint conference on Artificial Intelligence*, pages 1614–1620. AAAI Press, 2013.

[22] A. Rao, Y. Lee, A. Gass, and A. Monsch. Classification of alzheimer's disease from structural mri using sparse logistic regression with optional spatial regularization. In *Engineering in Medicine and Biology Society, EMBC, 2011 Annual International Conference of the IEEE*, pages 4499–4502. IEEE, 2011.

[23] X. Ren and J. Malik. Learning a classification model for segmentation. In *Computer Vision, 2003. Proceedings. Ninth IEEE International Conference on*, pages 10–17. IEEE, 2003.

[24] R. T. Rockafellar, R. J.-B. Wets, and M. Wets. *Variational analysis*, volume 317. Springer, 1998.

[25] F. H. Rutten, M.-J. M. Cramer, J.-W. J. Lammers, D. E. Grobbee, and A. W. Hoes. Heart failure and chronic obstructive pulmonary disease: an ignored combination? *European journal of heart failure*, 8(7):706–711, 2006.

[26] S. Ryali, K. Supekar, D. A. Abrams, and V. Menon. Sparse logistic regression for whole-brain classification of fmri data. *NeuroImage*, 51(2):752–764, 2010.

[27] J. Sun, J. Hu, D. Luo, M. Markatou, F. Wang, S. Edabollahi, S. E. Steinhubl, Z. Daar, and W. F. Stewart. Combining knowledge and data driven insights for identifying risk factors using electronic health records. In *AMIA Annual Symposium Proceedings*, volume 2012, page 901. American Medical Informatics Association, 2012.

[28] X. Tan, Y. Zhang, S. Tang, J. Shao, F. Wu, and Y. Zhuang. Logistic tensor regression for classification. In *Intelligent Science and Intelligent Data Engineering*, pages 573–581. Springer, 2013.

[29] J. Wu, J. Roy, and W. F. Stewart. Prediction modeling using ehr data: challenges, strategies, and a comparison of machine learning approaches. *Medical care*, 48(6):S106–S113, 2010.

[30] S. Xiang, L. Yuan, W. Fan, Y. Wang, P. M. Thompson, and J. Ye. Multi-source learning with block-wise missing data for alzheimer's disease prediction. In *Proceedings of the 19th ACM SIGKDD international conference on Knowledge discovery and data mining*, pages 185–193. ACM, 2013.

[31] Y. Xu and W. Yin. A block coordinate descent method for multi-convex optimization with applications to nonnegative tensor factorization and completion. *SIAM Journal on imaging sciences*, 6(3), 2013.

[32] J. Yang, D. Zhang, A. F. Frangi, and J.-y. Yang. Two-dimensional pca: a new approach to appearance-based face representation and recognition. *Pattern Analysis and Machine Intelligence, IEEE Transactions on*, 26(1):131–137, 2004.

[33] J. Ye, R. Janardan, Q. Li, et al. Two-dimensional linear discriminant analysis. In *NIPS*, volume 4, page 4, 2004.

[34] H. Zou and T. Hastie. Regularization and variable selection via the elastic net. *Journal of the Royal Statistical Society: Series B (Statistical Methodology)*, 67(2):301–320, 2005.

Dual Beta Process Priors for Latent Cluster Discovery in Chronic Obstructive Pulmonary Disease

James C. Ross
Brigham and Women's Hospital, Harvard Medical School
jross@bwh.harvard.edu

Peter J. Castaldi
Brigham and Women's Hospital, Harvard Medical School
repjc@channing.harvard.edu

Michael H. Cho
Brigham and Women's Hospital, Harvard Medical School
remhc@channing.harvard.edu

Jennifer G. Dy
Department of Electrical and Computer Engineering, Northeastern University
jdy@ece.neu.edu

ABSTRACT

Chronic obstructive pulmonary disease (COPD) is a lung disease characterized by airflow limitation usually associated with an inflammatory response to noxious particles, such as cigarette smoke. COPD is currently the third leading cause of death in the United States and is the only leading cause of death that is increasing in prevalence [15]. It also represents an enormous financial burden to society, costing tens of billions of dollars annually in the U.S. It is widely accepted by the medical community that COPD is a heterogeneous disease, with substantial evidence indicating that genetic variation contributes to varying levels of disease susceptibility. This heterogeneity makes it difficult to predict health decline and develop targeted treatments for better patient care. Although researchers have made several attempts to discover disease subtypes, results have been inconclusive, in part because standard clustering methods have not properly dealt with disease manifestations that may worsen with increased exposure. In this paper we introduce a transformative way of looking at the COPD subtyping task. Specifically, we model the relationship between risk factors (such as age and smoke exposure) and manifestations of disease severity using Gaussian Processes, which allow us to represent so-called "disease trajectories". We also posit that individuals can be associated with multiple disease types (latent clusters), which we assume are influenced by genetics. Furthermore, we predict that only subsets of the numerous disease-related quantitative features are useful for describing each latent subtype. We model these associations using two separate beta process priors, and we describe a variational inference approach to discover the most probable latent cluster assignments. Results are validated with associations to genetic markers.

KDD'14, August 24–27, 2014, New York, NY, USA.

ACM 978-1-4503-2956-9/14/08 ...$15.00.
http://dx.doi.org/10.1145/2623330.2623750.

Categories and Subject Descriptors

G.3 [**Mathematics of Computing**]: Probability and Statistics—*Correlation and regression analysis, stochastic processes, nonparametric statistics*

Keywords

Gaussian processes; beta processes; Bayesian nonparametrics; latent clusters; disease trajectories

1. INTRODUCTION

COPD is a major cause of chronic morbidity and mortality throughout the world, being the fourth leading cause of death worldwide [7]. By 2030 it is estimated that approximately 9 million people will die annually from the disease in the U.S. [15, 14]. COPD also imposes an enormous financial burden on society, with an estimated cost of $2.1 trillion in 2010 globally.

COPD is characterized by airflow limitation resulting from chronic inflammatory responses in the airways and lungs to noxious particles or gases. There are two basic components of COPD: emphysema (destruction and loss of lung tissue) and small airways disease (inflammation and thickening of airway walls). Both of these processes result in breathing difficulty. Patients often undergo high resolution computed tomography (CT) scanning, which enables the direct evaluation of the lungs and airways (Figure 1). Additionally, COPD severity is assessed in the clinic using spirometry, a technique in which patients blow into a device that measures lung function.

Tobacco smoke is the most common environmental risk factor of COPD, but it is known to be a heterogeneous disease, with genetic factors predisposing individuals to varying levels of disease severity as a function of exposure. An improved understanding of the interplay between genetics and exposure should lead to better stratification of patients for prognosis and personalization of therapies. There have been several large clinical projects to better understand this complicated disease, one of the largest being COPDGene [17] (http://www.copdgene.org). A number of authors have also applied established machine learning approachs in an effort to identify distinct disease subtypes. [2] applied principal component analysis (PCA) followed by cluster analysis using the VARCLUS procedure on eight measures of disease severity. The authors in [6] used factor analysis to select a subset of features and followed this with K-means clustering to identify population subgroups which they then

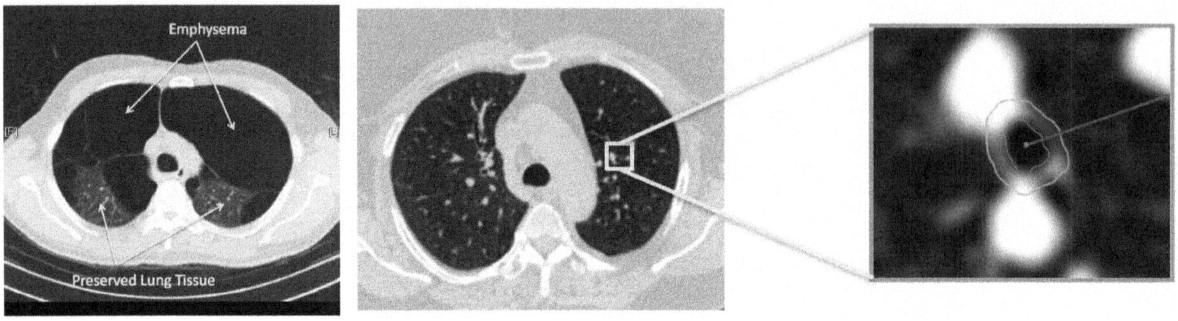

Figure 1: Left: CT scan illustrating a patient with advanced emphysema. Note that only a fraction of the lung cavity contains viable lung tissue; the remainder is empty space (emphysema). Right: the zoomed region depicts automatic detection of an airway's inner and outer walls, a step in evaluating airway thickening resulting from chronic inflammation.

investigated with genetic analysis. Recently our group performed a similar analysis in the COPDGene study cohort to identify four subgroups of subjects that associated with known genetic variants [4].

Although COPD clustering efforts to date have shed light on the disease, they have been limited by the application of approaches that do not specifically model the interplay of the available features. In particular, they pool together groups of people with different levels of disease severity, though these group differences may be partly explained by different levels of smoke exposure and age differences. Here we claim that individuals should be grouped according to biological and/or genetic similarity regardless of their level of disease severity; therefore, we seek associations of individuals to *disease trajectories* (i.e., grouping individuals based on their similarity in response to environmental and/or disease causing variables). We introduced this concept in a previous paper in which we described a clustering with constraints method using a Dirichlet process mixture of Gaussian processes in a variational Bayesian nonparametric framework [18]. This model assumes that each individual is a member of a single cluster (disease subtype), and it assumes that each feature is important for describing each of these clusters.

Here we introduce a more general framework that 1) permits both instances and features to belong to more than one cluster, 2) allows for overlapping clusters, and 3) identifies subsets of features associated with each cluster. We are again principally motivated by the concept of *disease trajectories*, but we allow for the possibility that a given individual may be suffering from multiple disease subtypes concurrently. Furthermore, it is likely the case that only a subset of features are needed to describe a particular subtype. Because the number of subtypes is unknown, we again turn to Bayesian nonparametric methods: we will describe a model that continues to use Gaussian Processes to represent trajectories and also builds on dual beta processes for instance and feature assignment to the latent subtype variables.

The rest of the paper is layed out as follows. In section 2 we provide an overview of the theory behind our model, focusing on Gaussin processes in section 2.1 and Beta processes in section 2.2. In section 3 we describe our probabilistic model; we define both the structure and the constituent probability distributions. The update equations used for variational inference are given in section 4. We demonstrate algorithm performance on both synthetic and clinical datasets in section 5 and conclude in section 6.

2. BACKGROUND

The model we propose is an instance of nonparametric overlapping subspace clustering. There are a number of related works in this context. [11] introduced the Infinite Overlapping Mixture Model (IOMM), a nonparametric clustering method that allows an unbounded number of potentially overlapping clusters. Assignments of points to (multiple) clusters is modeled using an Indian Buffet Process (IBP) and realized with a multiplicative mixture model likelihood function. This mixture model can be seen as a nonparametric generalization of the products-of-experts model indroduced by [12]. While they assume an unknown number of clusters and that all features are relevant for each cluster, [8] assume that the number of clusters is known but that features are local to a particular cluster. Their Bayesian Overlapping Subspace Clustering (BOSC) model is a hierarchical generative model for matrices with potentially overlapping sub-block structures.

While [8] used a pair of Beta-Bernoulli distributions with an assumed known number of clusters as priors for the latent row and column membership vectors, we adopt nonparametric priors based on dual beta processes: one prior for the association of data instances to latent clusters, and another for the association of observed features to latent clusters. This allows our model to discover the number of latent clusters best supported by our data, the associations of instances to those clusters, and the observed features that best describe them. We continue to use a Gaussian process likelihood function as described in [18], but we extend it using a multiplicative mixture model as [11], which permits both instances and features to be assigned to multiple clusters / subtypes. Importantly, we perform inference using a variational approach which further distinguishes our method from both [8] and [11]. In the remainder of this section we describe two elements central to our model: Gaussian and beta processes.

2.1 Gaussian Processes

Gaussian Processes (GPs) have been used extensively for Bayesian nonlinear regression. We cover the key concepts here as they pertain to our framework and refer the reader to [16] for details.

Gaussian Processes can be interpreted as a nonparametric prior over functions. They have the property that given a finite sampling of the domain, the corresponding vector of function values, $\mathbf{f}$, are distributed according to a multivariate Gaussian with mean $\mathbf{m}$ (typically set to $\mathbf{0}$ in standard practice) and covariance matrix $\mathbf{K}$:

$$\mathbf{f} \sim \mathcal{N}(\mathbf{f}|\mathbf{m}, \mathbf{K}) \tag{1}$$

The elements of $\mathbf{K}$ are determined by the kernel function, k: $[\mathbf{K}]_{n,n'} = k(\mathbf{x}_n, \mathbf{x}_{n'})$. The choice of kernel function and selection of its pa-

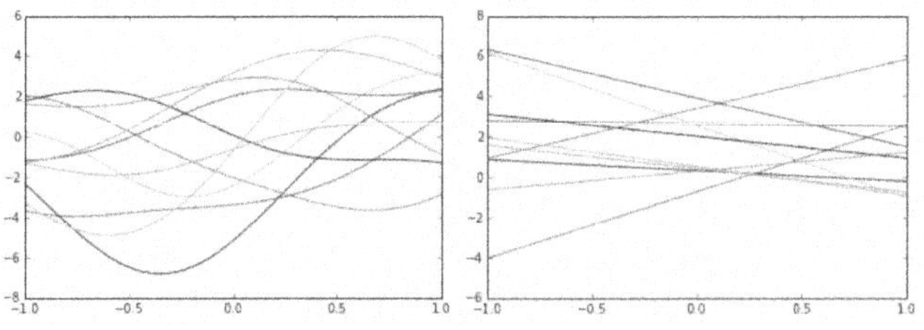

Figure 2: Ten random draws from Gaussian processes with a squared exponential kernel (left) and a linear kernel (right).

rameter values controls the behavior of the GP. One popular kernel function is the squared exponential (SE) given by

$$k(\mathbf{x}_n, \mathbf{x}_{n'}) = \theta_0 \exp\left(-\frac{\theta_1}{2} \| \mathbf{x}_n - \mathbf{x}_{n'} \|^2\right) \quad (2)$$

and another, more restrictive kernel function is the linear kernel:

$$k(\mathbf{x}_n, \mathbf{x}_{n'}) = \theta_0 + \theta_1 \sum_{d=1}^{D} (x_{n,d} - \theta_2)(x'_{n,d} - \theta_2) \quad (3)$$

where D is the vector dimension. A collection of random draws from each of these two kernels is illustrated in Figure 2.

In order to perform GP regression, we assume an observed dataset of inputs and corresponding (noisy) targets, $\mathcal{D} \equiv \{\mathbf{x}_n, y_n\}_{n=1}^{N}$, where we model the targets as $p(\mathbf{y}|\mathbf{f}) = \mathcal{N}(\mathbf{y}|\mathbf{f}, \sigma^2 \mathbf{I}_N)$. Here, σ^2 is the variance on the target variables. It can then be shown that the predicted mean and variance of target value y_* at some new input $\mathbf{x}_*$ are given by

$$\mu_* = \mathbf{k}_*^\top (\mathbf{K} + \sigma^2 \mathbf{I}_N)^{-1} \mathbf{y} \quad (4)$$

$$\sigma_*^2 = \sigma^2 + k_{**} - \mathbf{k}_*^\top (\mathbf{K} + \sigma^2 \mathbf{I}_N)^{-1} \mathbf{y} \quad (5)$$

where $k_{**} = k(\mathbf{x}_*, \mathbf{x}_*)$ and $[\mathbf{k}_*]_n = k(\mathbf{x}_n, \mathbf{x}_*)$.

2.2 Beta Processes

The beta process can be used as a Bayesian nonparametric prior for sparse latent feature models [9], i.e. as a prior over infinite binary matrices that indicate associations between instances (rows) to a potentially infinite number of latent features (columns). Beta processes are closely related to the Indian Buffet Process (IBP) introduced by [10], which has seen wide applicability to a number of problems. One limitation of the IBP, however, is that the distribution on the number of features per object and on the total number of latent features is coupled through a single parameter. This limits the expressivity of the prior. [9] later introduced a two-parameter version of the IBP which enables the amount of sharing between instances and latent features to be controlled. This is an attractive feature, but the authors did not describe how to realize this construction in a variational inference framework (which we note has computational benefits over sampling based inference methods as used in [9]).

More recently, [3] described a two-parameter, stick-breaking construction for beta process priors specifically for variational inference approaches. Their prior can be represented in the following manner

$$p(\mathbf{Z}|\mathbf{V}, \mathbf{T}, \mathbf{d})\, p(\mathbf{d}|\gamma)\, p(\mathbf{V}|\alpha)\, p(\mathbf{T}|\mathbf{d}, \alpha) \quad (6)$$

where $\mathbf{Z}$ is the infinite binary matrix and $\mathbf{V}$, $\mathbf{T}$, and $\mathbf{d}$ are latent features in their model. γ and α are the model parameters that control the amount of latent feature sharing between instances. We refer the reader to [3] for a detailed description of this construction.

3. FORMULATION

The desiderata of the model we propose in this section are a) the ability to identify the most probable number of latent disease subtypes, b) the flexibility to assign multiple subtypes to a given data instance (patient), and c) the capability to identify the subsets of features that best describe a given subtype.

In the remainder of this section we formalize the elements of our framework. Let $\mathbf{X} = [\mathbf{x}_1 \cdots \mathbf{x}_Q]$ be the $N \times Q$ matrix of observed inputs where N is the number of instances and Q is the dimension of the inputs. Let $\mathbf{Y} = [\mathbf{y}_1 \cdots \mathbf{y}_D]$ be the $N \times D$ matrix of corresponding target values, where D represents the dimension of the target variables. We designate the set of latent functions as $\left\{ f_d^{(k)}(\mathbf{x}) \right\}_{k=1,d=1}^{\infty,D}$. We collect all latent functions of trajectory k in the matrix $\mathbf{F}^{(k)} = \left[\mathbf{f}_1^{(k)} \cdots \mathbf{f}_D^{(k)}\right]$, and we designate the complete set of latent functions as $\left\{\mathbf{F}^{(k)}\right\}$. We introduce two latent binary indicator matrices, $\mathbf{Z}^r$ and $\mathbf{Z}^c$ (where the superscripts refer to the original $N \times D$ data matrix: r referring to the rows of that matrix, and c the columns). $\mathbf{Z}^r$ is an N row by infinite column matrix where each row represents a data instance and each column represents a latent cluster (subtype). Similarly, $\mathbf{Z}^c$ is a D row by infinite column matrix corresponding to the target features. We place beta process priors on each of these binary matrices using the stick-breaking construction introduced in [3].

The probabilistic graphical model describing our formulation can be seen in Figure 3, and the corresponding joint distribution is given by

$$\begin{aligned} &p(\mathbf{Y}, \{\mathbf{F}^{(k)}\}, \mathbf{d}^r, \mathbf{V}^r, \mathbf{T}^r, \mathbf{Z}^r, \mathbf{d}^c, \mathbf{V}^c, \mathbf{T}^c, \mathbf{Z}^c) = \\ &\quad p\left(\mathbf{Y}|\{\mathbf{F}^{(k)}\}, \mathbf{Z}^r, \mathbf{Z}^c\right) p\left(\{\mathbf{F}^{(k)}\}|\mathbf{X}\right) \times \\ &\quad p(\mathbf{d}^r|\gamma_r)\, p(\mathbf{V}^r|\alpha_r)\, p(\mathbf{T}^r|\mathbf{d}^r, \alpha_r)\, p(\mathbf{Z}^r|\mathbf{V}^r, \mathbf{T}^r, \mathbf{d}^r) \times \\ &\quad p(\mathbf{d}^c|\gamma_c)\, p(\mathbf{V}^c|\alpha_c)\, p(\mathbf{T}^c|\mathbf{d}^c, \alpha_c)\, p(\mathbf{Z}^c|\mathbf{V}^c, \mathbf{T}^c, \mathbf{d}^c) \end{aligned} \quad (7)$$

where we use two beta process priors – one for representing the association of instances to the latent clusters (indicated with the r superscript), and one for representing the association of observed features to latent clusters (indicated with the c superscript). (See section 2.2 above and [3] for details about the beta process prior).

The prior placed over the GPs representing each disease trajectory are given by

$$p\left(\{\mathbf{F}^{(k)}\}|\mathbf{X}\right) = \prod_{k=1}^{\infty} \prod_{d=1}^{D} \mathcal{N}\left(\mathbf{f}_d^{(k)}|\mathbf{m}_d, \mathbf{K}_d^{(k)}\right) \quad (8)$$

Note that we specify distinct kernel matrices and mean vectors for each target feature dimension d.

The likelihood term is given by

$$p\left(\mathbf{Y}_{n,d}|\{\mathbf{F}^{(k)}\}, \mathbf{Z}^r, \mathbf{Z}^c\right) = \begin{cases} \frac{1}{c(\mathbf{z})} \prod_{k=1}^{\infty} \mathcal{N}\left(\mathbf{Y}_{n,d}|\mathbf{F}_{n,d}^{(k)}, \sigma_d^2\right)^{\mathbf{z}_k}, & \text{if } \mathbf{z} \neq \mathbf{0} \\ \mathcal{N}\left(\mathbf{Y}_{n,d}|\hat{\mu}_d, \hat{\sigma}_d^2\right), & \text{Otherwise} \end{cases} \quad (9)$$

where $\mathbf{z}_k$ is the kth element of the vector $\mathbf{z} \equiv \mathbf{Z}^r{}_{n,\cdot} \odot \mathbf{Z}^c{}_{d,\cdot}$, the element-wise (Hadamard) product between vectors $\mathbf{Z}^r{}_{n,\cdot}$ and $\mathbf{Z}^c{}_{d,\cdot}$, and $c(\mathbf{z})$ is the normalization factor. If every element of $\mathbf{z}_k$ is 0, then $\mathbf{Y}_{n,d}$ is assumed to be generated from the noise component, $\mathcal{N}(\mathbf{Y}_{n,d}|\hat{\mu}_d, \hat{\sigma}_d^2)$.

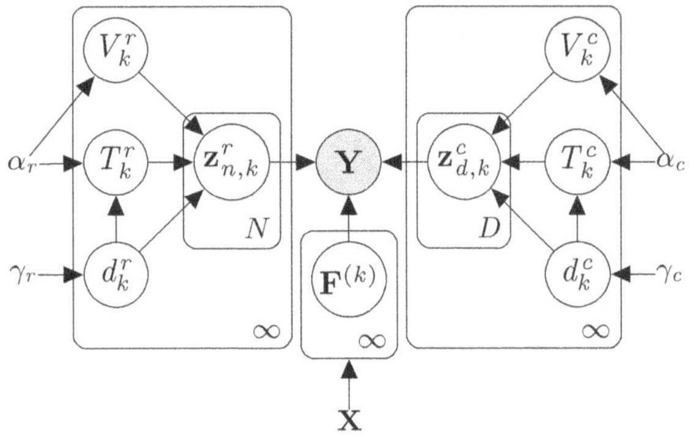

Figure 3: Probabilistic graphical model for our formulation.

4. INFERENCE

In this section we give the variational inference update equations that are specific to our model. Variational inference is a method of approximate inference that makes assumptions (typically a factorization) over the distribution of interest, and it turns an inference problem into an optimization problem [13]. Additionally, whereas approximate inference methods based on sampling (such as Monte Carlo Markov Chain) can be slow to converge, variational inference enjoys a greater computational advantage in this regard.

For our application, we are interested in the distribution over the latent variables in our model given our observations:

$$p\left(\{\mathbf{F}^{(k)}\}, \mathbf{Z}^r, \mathbf{Z}^c, \mathbf{d}^r, \mathbf{V}^r, \mathbf{T}^r, \mathbf{d}^c, \mathbf{V}^c, \mathbf{T}^c, | \mathbf{X}, \mathbf{Y}\right) \tag{10}$$

Direct evaluation of this posterior is intractable, so we approximate the posterior with a factorized distribution:

$$p^*\left(\{\mathbf{F}^{(k)}\}\right) p^*(\mathbf{Z}^r) p^*(\mathbf{Z}^c) p^*(\mathbf{d}^r) p^*(\mathbf{V}^r) p^*(\mathbf{T}^r) \times \\ p^*(\mathbf{d}^c) p^*(\mathbf{V}^c) p^*(\mathbf{T}^c) \tag{11}$$

As described in [3] we have

$$p^*(\mathbf{d}_k^r) = \text{Mult}(\mathbf{d}_k^r | \varphi_k) \tag{12}$$
$$p^*(\mathbf{V}^r) = \text{Beta}(\mathbf{V}_k^r | a_k^r, b_k^r) \tag{13}$$
$$p^*(\mathbf{T}^r) = \text{Gam}(\mathbf{T}_k^r | u_k^r, v_k^r) \tag{14}$$
$$p^*(\mathbf{Z}_{n,k}^r) = \text{Bern}(\mathbf{Z}_{n,k}^r | \phi_{n,k}) \tag{15}$$

and similarly for $p^*(\mathbf{d}^r)$, $p^*(\mathbf{V}^r)$, $p^*(\mathbf{T}^r)$, and $p^*(\mathbf{Z}_{d,k}^c)$. Parameter updates for the variational distributions over $\mathbf{d}_k^r$, $\mathbf{V}^r$, and $\mathbf{T}^r$ (similarly for $\mathbf{d}_k^c$, $\mathbf{V}^c$, and $\mathbf{T}^c$) can be found in [3]. In the remainder of this section we provide updates for $p^*\left(\{\mathbf{F}^{(k)}\}\right)$, $p^*(\mathbf{Z}^r)$, and $p^*(\mathbf{Z}^c)$.

To derive update expressions for the factors in the variational distribution, we compute the expectation of the log joint distribution with respect to the other factors in the variational distribution. In the case of $p^*\left(\{\mathbf{F}^{(k)}\}\right)$ this is

$$\ln p^*\left(\{\mathbf{F}^{(k)}\}\right) = \mathbb{E}\{\ln p(\cdot)\} + \text{const} \tag{16}$$

where $p(\cdot)$ abbreviates the joint distribution given in Equation 7 and the expectation is with respect to every variable in the the variational distribution other than $\{\mathbf{F}^{(k)}\}$. This leads to the variational distribution over $\{\mathbf{F}^{(k)}\}$

$$p^*\left(\{\mathbf{F}^{(k)}\}\right) = \prod_{k=1}^{K}\prod_{d=1}^{D} \mathcal{N}\left(\mathbf{f}_d^{(k)} | \mu_d^{(k)}, \mathbf{C}_d^{(k)}\right) \tag{17}$$

where

$$\mathbf{C}_d^{(k)} = \left(\mathbf{K}_d^{(k)\text{-}1} + \mathbf{R}_d^{(k)}\right)^{-1} \tag{18}$$
$$\mu_d^{(k)} = \mathbf{C}_d^{(k)}\left(\mathbf{K}_d^{(k)\text{-}1}\mathbf{m}_d + \mathbf{R}_d^{(k)}\mathbf{y}_d\right) \tag{19}$$

and

$$\mathbf{R}_d^{(k)} = \frac{\phi_{d,k}}{\sigma_d^2}\begin{pmatrix} \xi_{1,d}\phi_{1,k} & 0 & \cdots \\ 0 & \ddots & \\ \vdots & & \xi_{N,d}\phi_{N,k} \end{pmatrix} \tag{20}$$

where $\xi_{n,d}$ is the probability that instance n is associated with *any* latent feature that observed feature d can describe and is given by

$$\xi_{n,k} = 1 - \prod_{k=1}^{K}(1\text{-}\phi_{n,k}\phi_{d,k}) \tag{21}$$

Unfortunately, there is no closed form update expression for the parameters of $\mathbf{Z}^r$ and $\mathbf{Z}^c$. It can be shown that the difference between the factorized approximation and the true posterior is minimized when a quantity known as the variational lower bound is maximized. Therefore, we must turn to the variational lower bound and directly optimize those terms that depend on these parameters. We proceed by describing updates for $\mathbf{Z}^r$; updates for $\mathbf{Z}^c$ are obtained analogously. First we note that there are four terms in the lower bound that directly depend on $\mathbf{Z}^r$:

$$\sum_{n=1}^{N}\sum_{k=1}^{K}\varphi_k(1)\,\mathbb{E}\left\{\ln p\left(\mathbf{Z}_{n,k}^r|\mathbf{V}_k\right)\right\} + \\ \sum_{n=1}^{N}\sum_{k=1}^{K}\varphi_k(r>1)\,\mathbb{E}\left\{\ln p\left(\mathbf{Z}_{n,k}^r|\mathbf{V}_k, \mathbf{T}_k\right)\right\} - \\ \mathbb{E}\{\ln p^*(\mathbf{Z}^r)\} + \mathbb{E}\left\{\ln p\left(\mathbf{Y}|\{\mathbf{F}^{(k)}\}, \mathbf{Z}^r, \mathbf{Z}^c\right)\right\} \tag{22}$$

Variables φ_k and r appear in the stick-breaking construction of the beta process described in [3].

Expansion of the first term in Equation 22 gives

$$\phi_{n,k}\varphi_k(1)\left(\psi(a_k^r)\text{-}\psi(b_k^r)\right) \tag{23}$$

where $\psi(\cdot)$ is the digamma function. The second term in Equation 22 expands to

$$\phi_{n,k}\varphi_k(r>1)\left(\psi(a_k) - \psi(a_k+b_k) - \frac{u_k}{v_k} + \sum_{m=1}^{M}\Delta_k(m)\right) \tag{24}$$

where $\Delta_k(m)$ is given by

$$\frac{1}{m}\frac{\Gamma(a_k+b_k)}{\Gamma(a_k+b_k+m)}\frac{\Gamma(a_k+m)}{\Gamma(a_k)}\left(\frac{v_k}{v_k+m}\right)^{u_k} \tag{25}$$

and M is set to $1,000$ as in [3]. Expansion of the third term in 22 gives

$$-\phi_{n,k}\ln\phi_{n,k} - (1-\phi_{n,k})\ln(1-\phi_{n,k}) \tag{26}$$

Finally, the last term in 22 expands as

$$\sum_{d=1}^{D}\left(\xi_{n,d}\left[\sum_{k=1}^{K}\phi_{n,k}\phi_{d,k}\, g_{n,d}^{(k)} - h_{n,d} - \frac{1}{2} + \frac{1}{2}\ln\frac{1}{2\pi\sigma_d^2} - \Xi_{n,d}\right]\right) \tag{27}$$

where we use the following definitions

$$g_{n,d}^{(k)} \equiv \frac{1}{2}\left(\frac{\ln K}{K-1}\right) - \frac{\mathbf{Y}_{n,d}^2}{2\sigma_d^2} + \frac{\mathbf{Y}_{n,d}\mu_{n,d}^{(k)}}{\sigma_d^2} \tag{28}$$

$$h_{n,d} \equiv \frac{1}{2}\ln\left(\frac{1}{2\pi\hat{\sigma}_d^2}\right) - \frac{1}{2\hat{\sigma}_d^2}\left(\mathbf{Y}_{n,d} - \hat{\mu}_d\right)^2 \tag{29}$$

$$\Xi_{n,d} \equiv \frac{1}{2\sigma_d^2}\mathbb{E}\left\{\left(\sum_{k=1}^{K}\mathbf{Z}_{n,k}^r\mathbf{Z}_{d,k}^c\mathbf{F}_{n,d}^{(k)}\right)^2\right\} \tag{30}$$

and we note that the expression in Equation 30 can be evaluated in a straightforward manner by expanding the terms.

Together Equations 23, 24, 26, and 27 constitute an objective function for $\phi_{n,k}$ that we optimize using Brent's method on the interval $[0,1]$. Brent's method is a derivative-free optimization algorithm that uses inverse parabolic interpolation when possible to speed up convergence of the golden section method [1]. An analogous procedure is applied to update each $\phi_{d,k}$ using a similar objective function, except the outer sum in Equation 27 is from $n=1$ to N.

There are two terms in the updates for $\phi_{n,k}$ and $\phi_{d,k}$ that deserve special attention. The expectation in Equation 30 is an approximation the term

$$\mathbb{E}\left\{\left(\sum_{k=1}^{K}\mathbf{Z}_{n,k}^r\mathbf{Z}_{d,k}^c\mathbf{F}_{n,d}^{(k)}\right)^2 \Big/ \sum_{k=1}^{K}\mathbf{Z}_{n,k}^r\mathbf{Z}_{d,k}^c\right\} \tag{31}$$

This term emerges as a consequence of using the multiplicative mixture model, and the sum in the denominator makes this expectation intractable. However, we note that the expression we use in 30 is an upper bound of the original term given that the denominator in 31 will always be greater than or equal to 1 (recall that the likelihood given in Equation 9 is only active when $\mathbf{z} \neq 0$). Since it is the negative of Equation 31 that shows up in the lower bound, our approximation is in fact a lower bound of the original term. Hence we are gauranteed to be optimizing a lower bound of the original lower bound.

The second term of interest also comes from expanding the last term in Equation 22:

$$\mathbb{E}\left\{\ln\left(\sum_{k}^{K}\mathbf{Z}_{n,k}^r\mathbf{Z}_{d,k}^c\right)\right\} \tag{32}$$

which we again note is intractrable. However, noting that the sum will always be between 1 and K and that the natural log is a concave function, we can substitute Equation 33 with

$$\frac{\ln K}{K-1}\mathbb{E}\left\{\sum_{k}^{K}\mathbf{Z}_{n,k}^r\mathbf{Z}_{d,k}^c\right\} - 1 \tag{33}$$

which is easy to evaluate.

5. EXPERIMENTS

In this section we describe experimental results. We begin by illustrating our approach on a synthetic dataset and then describe the application of our algorithm to data taken from the COPDGene cohort [17].

5.1 Synthetic Example

Our algorithm is designed to identify not only the number of latent clusters, but also which data instances and which observed features associate with them. We demonstrate this with a synthetic example consisting of 120 samples and four observed features. The first two observed features are designed to be redundant: they both describe the same two latent clusters, represented by two lines; half of the samples belong to one line in both features, and the other half belong to the other. The third observed feature is a noise feature. Here all samples are drawn from the same normal distribution. The fourth observed feature contains three line segments that are distinct from the groupings present in the first two observed features (each of the three line segments consists of a third of the samples from each of the two lines described by observed features one and two).

We ran our algorithm with $K=20$, $\sigma^2=\hat{\sigma}^2=0.2$, $\alpha^r=3.5$, and $\gamma^r=\alpha^c=\gamma^c=1.5$. We used a linear kernel for each of the Gaussian processes with $\theta_0=2.0$ and $\theta_1=1.5$. Except for the variances, no special attention was given to the parameter settings; these were the first values selected and they produced the reported results. The variances provided to the algorithm were the same values used to generate the samples.

Figure 5.1 illustrates the results. Each latent feature is color-coded, so it can be seen that the first two observed features both describe the same two latent clusters. Observed feature three was correctly identified as a noise feature, i.e. not capable of describing any of the five latent clusters present in the data set. The algorithm also found the three latent clusters described by observed feature four.

5.2 Clinical Experiments

Here we report results from an experiment performed on clinical data from the COPDGene study, a large epidemiologic and genetic study of over 10,000 current and former smokers with and without COPD [17]. All subjects had blood collected for genetic analysis, and they completed spirometry and chest computed tomography (CT) scans, resulting in a large collection of features. The set of observed features we consider consists of seven lung function measures: functional residual capacity (FRC), pre- and post-bronchodilator forced expiratory volume in one second (FEV1), pre- and post-bronchodilator forced vital capacity (FVC), and pre- and post-bronchodilator FEV1/FVC. We also consider four CT-based measures of emphysema: total percent emphysema, the fifteenth percentile level of the intensity histogram in the lungs (Perc 15), and percent emphysema in the upper and lower lung lobes. We also include three airway disease measures: the wall area percent (WA%), percent gas trapping, and the predicted WA% of an airway with a $10mm$ perimeter (Pi10).

The predictors of our model are age, height, and pack years, which is a measure of life-long smoke exposure defined as the number of packs per day times the number of years of cigarette smoking. These constitute the inputs to the GP covariance matrices, and are meant to capture the factors that are causative of COPD severity. The use of height as a predictor of disease may seem odd, but it is known to influence lung function given that it affects lung mechanics, so we opted to include it in our model. We again choose to use the linear kernel for our experiments. This amounts to a form of nonparametric polynomial regression, and there are less computationally heavy ways to do this than with a Gaussian process framework. However, we emphasize that using GPs provide a much more flexible representation of possible disease trajectories. But in the absence of constraints between instances or observed features, we choose a more restrictive class of kernel function so as

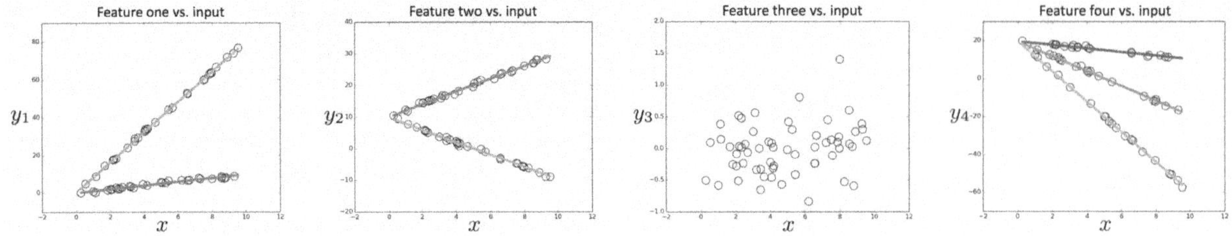

Figure 4: Synthetic example in which five latent clusters (color-coded) are discovered in a data set with four observed features. Left and left-middle: observed features y_1 and y_2 are redundant: both are useful for describing the red and green latent clusters. Right-middle: observed feature y_3 is determined to be a noise feature and is not useful for describing any of the five latent clusters. Right: observed feature y_4 describes three latent clusters, distinct from those described by observed features y_1 and y_2.

Table 1: Inputs and linear kernel parameters used for each GP in the clinical experiment

Feature	Inputs	θ_0	θ_0
Pre FEV1/FVC	Age, Pack Yrs	1.0	3.5
Post FEV1/FVC	Age, Pack Yrs	2.0	3.5
Pre FEV1	Age, Pack Yrs, Height	2.0	3.5
Post FEV1	Age, Pack Yrs, Height	2.0	3.5
Pre FVC	Age, Pack Yrs, Height	50.0	3.5
Post FVC	Age, Pack Yrs, Height	50.0	3.5
Total % Emph.	Age, Pack Yrs	50.0	3.5
Perc 15	Age, Pack Yrs	2e5	3.5
FRC	Age, Pack Yrs, Height	5.0	3.5
% Gas Trapping	Age, Pack Yrs	500.0	3.5
% Emph. Upper Lobes	Age, Pack Yrs	2.0	3.5
% Emph. Lower Lobes	Age, Pack Yrs	50.0	3.5
Pi10	Age, Height	2.0	3.5
WA%	Pack Yrs, Height	5e3	3.5

Feature	Red	Blue	Green	Magenta
Pre FEV1/FVC	1.00	1.00	1.00	1.00
Post FEV1/FVC	1.00	1.00	1.00	1.00
Pre FEV1	1.00	1.00	1.00	1.00
Post FEV1	1.00	1.00	1.00	1.00
Pre FVC	1.00	0.87	0.84	0.40
Post FVC	1.00	1.00	0.59	0.38
Total % Emph.	1.00	1.00	0.92	1.00
Perc 15	0.00	0.20	0.00	1.00
FRC	0.96	1.00	0.88	0.31
% Gas Trapping	1.00	1.00	1.00	1.00
% Emph. Upper Lobes	1.00	1.00	0.49	0.54
% Emph. Lower Lobes	1.00	1.00	0.98	0.65
Pi10	0.00	0.16	0.14	0.13
WA%	0.27	0.218	0.28	0.20

Table 2: Inputs and probability of association to each of four latent features, labeled by color for easy comparison to other figures.

to mitigate the effect of local minima during variational inference. Note that in our previous work we were able to apply more general kernel functions in the presence of data constraints [18]. We hope to extend the current approach once such constraints are available.

The inputs and kernel parameters for each of the observed features are given in Table 1. In order to guide the selection of inputs and kernel parameters, we performed standard multi-variate linear regression on each of the observed features using each of the three inputs as predictors. For a given observed feature, we only used as kernel inputs those predictors that had a significant association in the linear regression model. The slope intercept generated by the model informed the selection of the θ_0 parameter, which controls the intercept range over which a draw from the GP is likely to come from. For all fourteen observed features, we noticed only modest slope values for each of the regression coefficients. Therefore, we selected a θ_1 value of 3.5 for all kernel functions; we observed empirically from repeated draws of GPs using this value that slopes tend to be modest.

We chose σ_d^2 for each of the observed features by taking one tenth of the variance of the residuals from the multi-variate regression stage. This was an ad hoc selection, but the measurement variances for each of the observed features is as yet unknown. The selected values were chosen to be significantly lower than the residual variances in order to explore subgroups within the data. By comparison, simply using the residual variances would likely have caused the algorithm to simply recapitulate the multi-variate regression result, although we did not attempt this experiment. The noise means and variances, $\hat{\mu}_d$ and $\hat{\sigma}_d^2$, were simply chosen to be the mean and variance of each observed feature.

For the beta process priors, we set $K = 20$, $\alpha^r = 3.5$, and $\gamma^r = \alpha^c = \gamma^c = 1.5$ as in the synthetic experiments. We considered the first $1,000$ subjects to have enrolled in the COPDGene study, keeping only those that have complete data for all inputs and observed features, resulting in a collection of 851 subjects. We deployed our algorithm on our institution's computer cluster, and ran 200 jobs in parallel, executing 15 iterations for each job. Using this dataset with these parameters, each job took approximately 10 hours to complete. For each job we recorded the final variational lower bound value, and report results for the job that gave the largest lower bound.

Our algorithm identified four latent clusters in this data set, and assigned approximately half of the samples to the noise model. For each of the observed features, we give the probability of each being associated with each of the latent clusters in Table 2. We see that both Pi10 and WA% poorly describe the latent clusters; that is to say, those observed features are better described by the noise model. This is not unexpected, given that they both rely on direct measurements of airway wall thickness on CT images. Given that airways are small structures and difficult to measure accurately, these measurements are known to be noisy. On the other hand, the lung function measurements tend to do a much better job at describing the latent clusters.

Figure 5 provides scatter plots for several of the observed features, where we have again color-coded the latent clusters. We include a plot of Pi10, one of the variables that poorly describes the latent clusters, to illustrate the lack of structure in the data. It is also interesting to note that Perc 15 is only useful for describing two of these latent clusters. Summarizing these data we can identify two groups of individuals who have preserved lung function and lung tissue despite increasing age and smoke exposure (red and blue groups). The magenta and green groups appear to represent those individuals that are more susceptible to COPD: they show increased levels of emphysema and gas trapping as well as lower levels of lung function given increasing age and smoke exposure, with the magenta group being more susceptible than the green group.

Finally, we evaluate our clustering results by performing genetic association analysis using several single nucleotide polymorphisms (SNPs) known to associate with COPD [5]. As a comparison, we apply the same methodology we used in [4]: K-means clustering (with $K = 4$) on a feature set determined by factor analysis. We note however that our previous analysis was conducted on the entire COPDGene cohort, and here we only consider the 851 subjects analyzed by our algorithm. Table 3 shows the resulting odds ratios and associated confidence intervals. The odds ratio represents the effect size of the genetic variant; it is the odds of having the variant in one subtype divided by the odds of having the variant in another subtype – values further from 1.0 indicate greater effect of the genetic variant on membership in that subtype. Odds ratios are computed with respect to the healthiest group in each clustering result (the "red" group in the case of our algorithm). In the genome-wide analyses of COPD, effect sizes for the previously described genetic variants were approximately less than or equal to 1.4, suggesting that our approach can identify a more genetically susceptible subgroup.

6. CONCLUSION

We have introduced a nonparametric overlapping subspace clustering algorithm that relies on dual beta process priors in order to identify latent cluster structure. Our model finds associations between data instances and latent clusters, allowing for a given instance to belong to multiple clusters. Additionally, our algorithm identifies the observed features that best describe the latent clusters and thus serves as a form of feature selection. The likelihood term in our model is specifically chosen to address the challenges of disease subtype discovery in COPD: by using Gaussian processes to represent the dependence between observed features that measure levels of disease severity and inputs that are causative agents of disease progression, we can flexibly represent so-called "disease trajectories". We believe our contribution represents a step forward towards a better understanding of a complicated disease that will hopefully lead to better patient care.

We have made an implementation of our algorithm available on GitHub here, and the COPDGene data can be obtained from dbGaP here.

7. ACKNOWLEDGMENTS

This work was supported by NSF grant IIS-0915910, and by the US National Heart, Lung, and Blood Institute grants R01HL089856, R01HL089897 (COPDGene), K08HL102265, K08HL097029 and R01HL113264. The COPDGene study is also supported by the COPD Foundation through contributions made to an Industry Advisory Board comprised of AstraZeneca, Boehringer Ingelheim, Novartis, Pfizer, Siemens, and Sunovion.

References

[1] R. P. Brent. *Algorithms for minimization without derivatives.* Courier Dover Publications, 2013.

[2] P. R. Burgel, J. Paillasseur, D. Caillaud, I. Tillie-Leblond, P. Chanez, R. Escamilla, T. Perez, P. Carré, N. Roche, et al. Clinical copd phenotypes: a novel approach using principal component and cluster analyses. *European Respiratory Journal*, 36(3):531–539, 2010.

[3] L. Carin, D. M. Blei, and J. W. Paisley. Variational inference for stick-breaking beta process priors. In *Proceedings of the 28th International Conference on Machine Learning (ICML-11)*, pages 889–896, 2011.

[4] P. J. Castaldi, J. Dy, J. Ross, Y. Chang, G. R. Washko, D. Curran-Everett, A. Williams, D. A. Lynch, B. J. Make, J. D. Crapo, et al. Cluster analysis in the copdgene study identifies subtypes of smokers with distinct patterns of airway disease and emphysema. *Thorax*, 69(5):416–423, 2014.

[5] M. H. Cho, P. J. Castaldi, E. S. Wan, M. Siedlinski, C. P. Hersh, D. L. Demeo, B. E. Himes, J. S. Sylvia, B. J. Klanderman, J. P. Ziniti, et al. A genome-wide association study of copd identifies a susceptibility locus on chromosome 19q13. *Human molecular genetics*, 21(4):947–957, 2012.

[6] M. H. Cho, G. R. Washko, T. J. Hoffmann, G. J. Criner, E. A. Hoffman, F. J. Martinez, N. Laird, J. J. Reilly, and E. K. Silverman. Cluster analysis in severe emphysema subjects using phenotype and genotype data: an exploratory investigation. *Respir Res*, 11:30, 2010.

[7] M. Decramer, W. Janssens, and M. Miravitlles. Chronic obstructive pulmonary disease. *The Lancet Respiratory Medicine*, 379(9823), 2012.

[8] Q. Fu and A. Banerjee. Bayesian overlapping subspace clustering. In *Data Mining, 2009. ICDM'09. Ninth IEEE International Conference on*, pages 776–781. IEEE, 2009.

[9] Z. Ghahramani, T. L. Griffiths, and P. Sollich. Bayesian nonparametric latent feature models. 2007.

[10] T. Griffiths and Z. Ghahramani. Infinite latent feature models and the indian buffet process. 2005.

[11] K. A. Heller and Z. Ghahramani. A nonparametric bayesian approach to modeling overlapping clusters. In *International Conference on Artificial Intelligence and Statistics*, pages 187–194, 2007.

[12] G. E. Hinton. Training products of experts by minimizing contrastive divergence. *Neural computation*, 14(8):1771–1800, 2002.

[13] M. Jordan, Z. Ghahramani, T. Jaakkola, and L. Saul. An introduction to variational methods for graphical models. *Machine learning*, 37(2):183–233, 1999.

[14] C. D. Mathers and D. Loncar. Projections of global mortality and burden of disease from 2002 to 2030. *PLoS Med*, 3(11):e442, 11 2006.

[15] S. L. Murphy, J. Xu, and K. D. Kochanek. Deaths: final data for 2010. *National vital statistics reports*, 61(4), 2013.

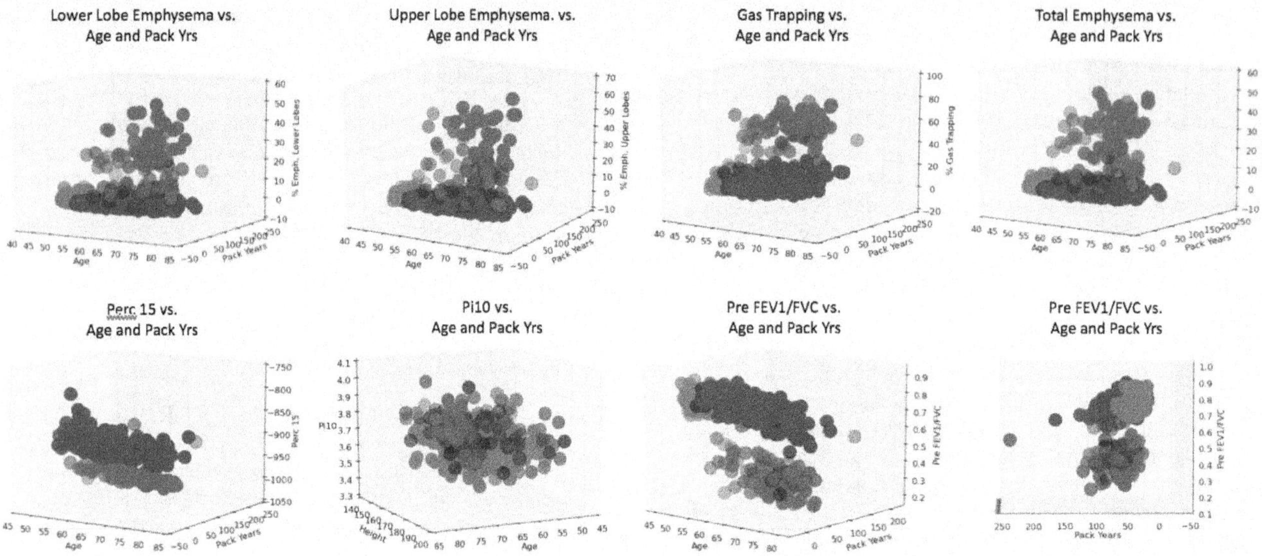

Figure 5: Scatter plots of COPDGene subjects color-coded by association to discovered latent clusters. The red and blue groups correspond to healthier individuals while the green and magenta groups represent those more susceptible to disease. The scatter plot of Pi10 illustrates a noisy feature. The Pre FEV1/FVC plot in the lower right is rotated to better illustrate that each group exhibits a decline in lung function with increasing smoke exposure.

Table 3: Odds ratios and associated confidence intervals (in parentheses) for three SNPs known to associate with COPD. All reported values are statistically significant at the $p < 0.05$ confidence level; a dash indicates that no significant association was found. Our dual beta-process, Gaussian process algorithm is abbreviated DBP-GP. For the K-means result we abbreviate the two cluster groups found to have significant genetic associations as C1 and C2. For the DBP-GP groups, we indicate cluster groups using the color-coding scheme described above. Next to each cluster identifier is the number of samples in that group.

	K-means		DBP-GP		
SNP	C1 (197)	C2 (328)	Blue (206)	Green (26)	Magenta (60)
rs13180	-	1.44 (1.26-1.64)	-	0.46 (0.33 - 0.65)	0.63 (0.50 - 0.80)
rs8034191	-	0.74 (0.65 - 0.84)	1.76 (1.43 - 2.17)	3.19 (2.18 - 4.66)	1.72 (1.33 - 2.23)
rs7937	1.38 (1.20 - 1.59)	-	-	-	-

[16] C. Rasmussen and C. Williams. *Gaussian processes for machine learning*, volume 1. MIT press Cambridge, MA, 2006.

[17] E. A. Regan, J. E. Hokanson, J. R. Murphy, B. Make, D. A. Lynch, T. H. Beaty, D. Curran-Everett, E. K. Silverman, and J. D. Crapo. Genetic epidemiology of copd (copdgene) study design. *COPD: Journal of Chronic Obstructive Pulmonary Disease*, 7(1):32–43, 2011.

[18] J. Ross and J. Dy. Nonparametric mixture of gaussian processes with constraints. In *Proceedings of the 30th International Conference on Machine Learning (ICML-13)*, pages 1346–1354, 2013.

COM: a Generative Model for Group Recommendation

Quan Yuan†*, Gao Cong†, Chin-Yew Lin‡
†School of Computer Engineering, Nanyang Technological University, Singapore 639798
{qyuan1@e., gaocong@}ntu.edu.sg
‡Microsoft Research, Beijing, China 100080
cyl@microsoft.com

ABSTRACT

With the rapid development of online social networks, a growing number of people are willing to share their group activities, *e.g.,* having dinners with colleagues, and watching movies with spouses. This motivates the studies on group recommendation, which aims to recommend items for a group of users. Group recommendation is a challenging problem because different group members have different preferences, and how to make a trade-off among their preferences for recommendation is still an open problem.

In this paper, we propose a probabilistic model named COM (COnsensus Model) to model the generative process of group activities, and make group recommendations. Intuitively, users in a group may have different influences, and those who are expert in topics relevant to the group are usually more influential. In addition, users in a group may behave differently as group members from as individuals. COM is designed based on these intuitions, and is able to incorporate both users' selection history and personal considerations of content factors. When making recommendations, COM estimates the preference of a group to an item by aggregating the preferences of the group members with different weights. We conduct extensive experiments on four datasets, and the results show that the proposed model is effective in making group recommendations, and outperforms baseline methods significantly.

Categories and Subject Descriptors

H.3.3 [**Information Search and Retrieval**]: Information Filtering

Keywords

Group Recommendation; Collaborative Filtering; Topic Models

1. INTRODUCTION

Recommender systems (RS) aim to suggest items for users based on their preferences, and they have been widely deployed to assist users to select items in various fields, such as movies (Netflix), products (Amazon), restaurants (Yelp), etc. A number of recommendation techniques have been proposed, such as user/item-based collaborative filtering (CF) [17, 21], clustering CF [24], matrix factorization [11], etc., and most of them focus on producing recommendations for individual users. However, people often participate in activities together with others, *e.g.,* having dinners with colleagues, watching movies with spouses, and having picnics with friends. This calls for recommendation techniques for a group. Unfortunately, recommender systems designed for individuals are not effective in making recommendations for a group of people. Furthermore, an increasing number of group event records are becoming available on the web, since users often share their group activities on social networks, such as Facebook, Meetup, and Foursquare. For example, the Foursquare check-in in Figure 1 shows that user *Angele D.*, together with her husband, visited the Outback steakhouse. The availability of group event data promotes the research interest on how to make effective recommendations for a group of users [3, 4, 6, 8, 13, 26], which not only facilitates groups making decisions, but also helps web services improve user engagement.

*Part of this work was done when the first author was on an internship at Microsoft Research.

KDD'14, August 24–27, 2014, New York, NY, USA.
Copyright 2014 ACM 978-1-4503-2956-9/14/08 ...$15.00.
http://dx.doi.org/10.1145/2623330.2623616.

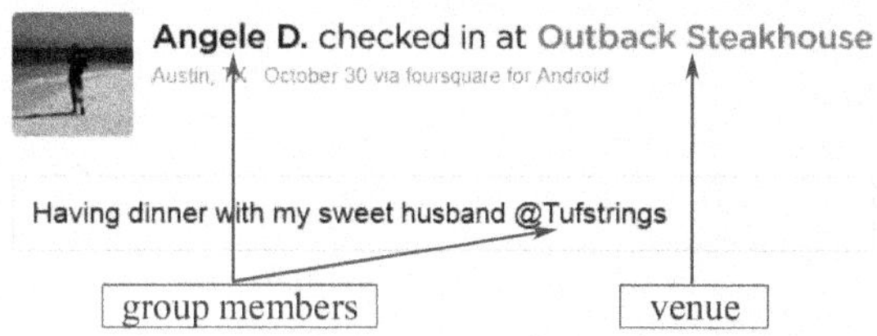

Figure 1: An Example of Group Check-in

However, making accurate recommendations for groups is not an easy task, because a group consists of multiple users who have different preferences. How to make a trade-off among their preferences to recommend items for a group is challenging. Previous solutions to group recommendation can be divided into two types: memory-based and model-based approaches. Memory-based approaches further fall in two categories based on the aggregation strategy: *preference aggregation* strategy first aggregates the profiles of group members into a new profile, and then employs recommendation techniques designed for individuals to make group recommendations [15, 28]; *score aggregation* strategy first calculates a recommendation list for each group member, and then aggregates these lists for group recommendation [4, 7, 14, 18, 20]. However, both strategies overlook the interactions between group members, and use trivial methods to aggregate members' preferences. Different from memory-based approaches, model-based methods exploit the interactions among members by modeling the generative process of a group [13, 26]. However, as to be detailed in Section 2, the assumptions of these models may not hold in real life.

To achieve better accuracy, we propose a latent Dirichlet allocation (LDA) [5] based generative model, named COnsensus Model (COM), to make group recommendations. COM is novel since it is built based on the following three considerations that have not been exploited by previous work:

1. Each group is relevant to several topics, *e.g.,* a picnic group is relevant to hiking and dining topics, and a movie watching group consisting of families may be relevant to the romance and comedy topics. The item selection of a group is influenced by both these relevant topics and group members' personal considerations of content factors, such as the geographical distance to venues for venue recommendation, and casts of movies for movie recommendation.
2. Users in a group may behave differently as group members from as individuals, *e.g.,* a user may prefer horror movies when he is alone, but will select romantic movies when watching with his wife.
3. Different users have different influences in making decisions in a group, and the influence degree of a user in a group is topic-dependent: a movie fan is probably influential in making decisions for a movie watching group, but is less influential in a dining group, because the dining group is less relevant to the movie topic.

Based on the three considerations, we model the generative process of a group as follows: each group has a multinomial distribution over latent topics, and these topics attract a set of users to join. The item selection of a user is influenced by both the group topic that attracted her, and her personal considerations of content factors (Consideration 1). Note that it is the topic of the group, instead of the user's, that account for her item selection (Consideration 2). The final decision of a group is made by aggregating the selections of all users in the group: if a user is an expert in the relevant topics of the group, her selections will have a larger weight (Consideration 3). Based on the generative model, we propose a recommendation method to suggest items for a target group.

In summary, the contributions of this paper are three-fold:

- We propose a generative model COM for modeling the process of item selection of a group, which considers members' topic-dependent influences and members' group behaviors.
- We develop a recommendation method to make group recommendations based on COM, which is able to exploit both users' selection history and users' personal considerations of content factors.
- We evaluate the effectiveness of the proposed method by extensive experiments on four datasets for event venue recommendation and movie recommendation. The experimental results show that our proposed method outperforms five baselines significantly by various evaluation metrics.

The rest of this paper is organized as follows. In Section 2, we review related work. Section 3 introduces the proposed COM model and the recommendation method. We present experimental results in Section 4. Finally, Section 5 concludes this paper.

2. RELATED WORK

We first briefly review recommendation systems in general, and then focus on techniques for group recommendation.

2.1 Recommender Systems

Recommender systems can be classified into three categories: content-based, collaborative filtering (CF), and hybrid recommendation approaches [1]. The content-based approaches make recommendations based on the content features of users (*e.g.,* age, gender, etc.) and items (*e.g.,* price, category, etc.), but do not exploit users' rating/selection history. Thus, when content features are not sufficient, the content-based techniques will fail to produce accurate recommendations. In contrast, CF approaches rely on rating/selection history, but do not make use of content features. Consequently, they suffer from the sparsity problem, *i.e.,* when the number of users' ratings is not enough for finding similar users, the performance of CF techniques will be bad. The hybrid approaches combine the content-based and CF methods to avoid their limitations. Our proposed model exploits both users' selection history and content information, and thus it belongs to the hybrid approaches. In addition, when the content information is not available, our model will be reduced as a CF model that makes recommendations based on users' selection history only.

CF approaches have been extensively studied and can be further divided into two categories, namely, *memory-based CF* and *model-based CF* [23]. Memory-based CF approaches employ rating/selection history to find similar users of the target user, and then compute a recommendation score for a candidate item by a weighted combination of historical ratings on the item from these similar users. In contrast, model-based CF builds recommendation models using data mining techniques, such as clustering [19], matrix factorization [11], probabilistic topic model [2, 25], etc. Our model exploits users' selection history in the model-based manner.

2.2 Group recommendation

Group recommendation techniques have been proposed for various domains, such as web/news pages [20], tourism [16], restaurants [14], music [7], TV programs [28], and movies [18]. Group recommendation methods in the earlier studies fall into two categories [3]: the *preference aggregation* approaches first aggregate the profiles of the group members into one profile, and makes recommendations based on the aggregated profile [15, 28]. The *score aggregation* approaches, in contrast, first produce recommendations for each group member respectively, and then aggregate their recommendation results for the group [4, 7, 14, 18, 20].

Compared with preference aggregation, score aggregation typically enjoys better flexibility [3, 10, 18], and thus receives more research attention. The score aggregation approaches usually employ either average (AVG) or least misery (LM) strategy to aggregate the recommendations of individuals. The AVG strategy averages the recommendation scores of all group members as the final score, aiming to maximize the overall satisfactions of a group [15, 28]; the LM strategy takes the smallest recommendation score of group members as the final score, and tries to make everyone happy [4]. For LM, the recommendation score of an item is largely influenced by the user who dislikes it most, even if all the others like it very much. For AVG, an item's relevance to different users might be diverse, and the recommendation results might be unfair to some users. Baltrunas *et al.* [4] compare different aggregation approaches, and find that there is no clear winner, and the effectiveness of an approach depends on the group size and inner group similarity. Amer-Yahia *et al.* [3] go one step further, and argue that an item is a good recommendation for a group if the group members have small disagreements on the item, where the disagreement is defined as the difference among relevance of the item to different group members.

Recently, several model-based approaches have been proposed. Seko *et al.* [22] develop a content-based group recommendation method based on the assumption that the choice made by a group is influenced by item genres. However, this approach can be only applied to pre-defined groups, *e.g.,* couples, while in real-life, groups are often ad-hoc. Carvalho *et al.* [6] introduce game theory into group recommendation by treating a group event as a noncooperative game among members, and transform the recommendation problem into finding the Nash equilibrium. However, this method cannot suggest a specific item, since the equilibrium contains a set of items.

The model-based approaches proposed in [8, 13, 26] adopt the same setting as ours. Ye *et al.* [26] assume that when selecting items, a group member will follow her friends' opinions. They propose a probabilistic generative model to produce group recommendations by aggregating the preferences of pairwise friends in the group, where one influences the other. However, the strong assumption of pairwise influence in a group may not be true, especially when the group is large. In addition, a group does not always consist of friends. Liu *et al.* [13] propose a topic model approach based on the assumption that the influential users will become the representatives of all groups to make item selections, irrespective of the group topics and the influential users' expertise. However, users' influences should be topic-dependent: a user may be influential in a group because of her expertise on the group's topics, but may not be in another group. Gorla *et al.* [8] assume that the recommendation score for an item depends on its relevance to each group member and its relevance to the group as a whole. They propose an information-matching based framework to make group recommendations. However, this framework has a high time complexity, which is $O(|U|^2|I|^2)$ for each target group, where $|U|$ and $|I|$ are the sizes of user and item sets, respectively. We implemented and ran this method, but it could not finish on our datasets after 5 days and we stopped it. It can only finish on very small data we tried.

In our experiments, we will report comparison results with the approaches in the three proposals [3,13,26]. In the existing studies, these approaches have not been empirically compared with each other.

Finally note that the "group recommendation" defined in [31] concentrate on personalized recommendation of event-based groups to a user, which is a totally different task.

3. CONSENSUS MODEL

We first define the group recommendation problem in Section 3.1, and then introduce the proposed COnsensus Model (COM) in Section 3.2. After that, the inference algorithm and the recommendation method are presented in Section 3.3 and 3.4, respectively. Finally, we present how to incorporate content information into the model in Section 3.5. All the notations used in this paper are listed in Table 1.

3.1 Problem Statement

Let U, I, G be the user, item and group sets, respectively. A *group* $g \in G$ consists of a set of users (group members) $\boldsymbol{u}_g = \{u_{g,1}, u_{g,2}, ..., u_{g,|g|}\}$, where $u_{g,i} \in U$, and $|g|$ is the size of the group, *i.e.,* the number of users in g. In addition, a group g is associated with an item $i_g \in I$, if i_g is selected by group g. We define a *group event* by $<\boldsymbol{u}_g, i_g>$, *i.e.,* the item selection event of the group members as a whole. For example, the members of a picnic group selecting a venue for picnic is a group event, and a family selecting a movie to watch is also a group event.

Then, given a target group g_t, the problem of group recommendation is defined as recommending a list of items that users in g_t may be interested in.

3.2 COnsensus Model for Group Recommendation

We model the generative process of a group event based on the following intuitions:

Table 1: Symbols

Symbol	Description
U, I, G	user set, item set, group set
K	the number of latent topics
N	the size of recommendation list
g, $\|g\|$	the group g, the size of group g
$\boldsymbol{u}_g$	the members in group g
i_g	the item selected by group g
u	user $u \in U$
z_j, c_j	the topic and switch of the user-item pair j
$\boldsymbol{i}^{(\cdot)}$	the set of items that are generated when $c = (\cdot)$
$\boldsymbol{\theta}_g$	distribution of topics specific to group g
ϕ_z^{ZU}	distribution of users specific to topic z
ϕ_z^{ZI}	distribution of items specific to topic z
ϕ_u^{UI}	distribution of items specific to user u
λ_u	the parameter of Bernoulli distribution specific to user u for sampling the binary switch c
$\boldsymbol{\alpha}, \boldsymbol{\beta}, \boldsymbol{\rho}, \boldsymbol{\eta}$	Dirichlet prior vector for $\boldsymbol{\theta}$, ϕ^{ZU}, ϕ^{UI} and ϕ^{ZI}
$\boldsymbol{\gamma}$	Beta prior for λ, where $\boldsymbol{\gamma} = \{\gamma, \gamma_t\}$
$n_{g,z,\neg j}^{GZ}$	number of times topic z is assigned to group g, excluding the jth user-item pair
$n_{z,u,\neg j}^{ZU}$	number of times user u is drawn from topic z, excluding the jth user-item pair
$n_{z,i,\neg j}^{ZI}$	number of times item i is drawn from topic z, excluding the jth user-item pair
$n_{u,i,\neg j}^{UI}$	number of times item i is drawn from user u, excluding the jth user-item pair
$n_{u,c,\neg j}^{UC}$	number of times switch c is drawn for user u, excluding the jth user-item pair

- **Intuition 1**: Each group is relevant to several topics with different degrees of match, *e.g.,* a picnic group is more relevant to the hiking and dining topics than to the body-building topic. The topics of a group attract users to join the group.
- **Intuition 2**: When selecting an item, users in a group have two considerations. The first is topics, *i.e.,* a user tends to select the items that are related to the group topic, which attracted her to join the group. The second is users' personal considerations of content factors, such as the geographical distance for venue recommendation, cast lists of movies for movie recommendation, etc. Most of these factors are user-specific, and cannot be captured by topics. In addition, different users make different trade-offs between group topics and personal considerations of content factors: some users tend to select the items that match the group topics best, while some may treat the personal considerations more important.
- **Intuition 3**: Users behave differently when selecting items as members in a specific group and when selecting items as individuals. In a group, a user tends to match her preference to the topics of the group.
- **Intuition 4**: The preference of a group to a candidate item is determined by the preferences of the group members [3, 8]. In addition to this, we exploit the following new intuition: the influence of each member on the item selection of the group is topic-dependent.

Specifically, we use a multinomial distribution $\boldsymbol{\theta}_g$ over latent topics to model the topic preferences of group g (**Intuition 1**). In addition, each latent topic z has a multinomial distribution ϕ_z^{ZU} over user set, which represents the relevance of users to the topic z, and a multinomial distribution ϕ_z^{ZI} over item set, which represents the relevance of items to the topic z. Here $\phi_{z,i}^{ZI}$ reflects given a topic z, how likely the item i is selected; $\phi^{ZU}_{z,u}$ reveals the appealing degree of topic z to the user u, or the user u's expertise on topic z. To model **Intuition 1** that users join a group because of different topics, for each member in group g, a latent topic z is sampled from its topic distribution $\boldsymbol{\theta}_g$, and then a user u is drawn according to ϕ^{ZU}_z.

A user in a group selects items either based on the group topics that attracted her to join the group, or her personal considerations of content factors (**Intuition 2**). We use a switch c to decide which one accounts for the item selection of a user, *i.e.,* if $c = 1$, the item is sampled based on the topic-specific multinomial distribution over items ϕ^{ZI}; if $c = 0$, the item is drawn from the user-specific multinomial distribution of items ϕ^{UI}. Since different users will make different trade-offs between group topics and personal considerations of content factors (**Intuition 2**), in our model, the switch c is drawn from a user-specific Bernoulli distribution with parameter λ_u. In other words, user u is influenced by group topics with probability λ_u, and is influenced by her personal considerations with probability $1 - \lambda_u$. Note that the Bernoulli distribution for λ_u has a Beta prior $\boldsymbol{\gamma} = \{\gamma, \gamma_t\}$.

Next we illustrate the model using an example. Suppose a picnic group is more relevant to both hiking and dining topics than body-building topic. The three topics are sampled from the topic distribution of the picnic group, which attract users u_1, u_2 and u_3, respectively. Then, these three users determine which venue to visit based on the group topics and their personal considerations of content factors such as traveling distance. Suppose u_1 does not mind traveling, and the topic "hiking" has a more significant influence to his selection. Then she may select a distant venue that matches the hiking topic best. Thus, the switch c for u_1 is more likely to be 1. u_2 and u_3 will also make trade-offs between group topics and their personal considerations to select the venue for picnic.

Different from COM, previous topic model based approaches [13, 26] assume that when selecting items, a group member only considers her own topic preference. The assumption may not hold, because users in a group may behave differently as group members from that when they make choices as individuals (**Intuition 3**). For example, suppose u_1 is interested in both hiking and movie topics. In previous approaches, u_1 may select a theater for the picnic group because of her interest in movie topic. In contrast, in our model, u_1 join the picnic group because of the hiking topic, and thus her selection will be related to hiking rather than movie.

In summary, the generative process of a collection of group events is as follows:

- For each topic z_k, $k = 1, ..., K$
  - Draw $\phi^{ZU}_k \sim Dirichlet(\boldsymbol{\beta})$;
  - Draw $\phi^{ZI}_k \sim Dirichlet(\boldsymbol{\eta})$;
- For each user u_v, $v = 1, ..., |U|$
  - Draw $\phi^{UI}_v \sim Dirichlet(\boldsymbol{\rho})$;
  - Draw $\lambda_v \sim Beta(\boldsymbol{\gamma})$;
- For each group g
  - Draw $\boldsymbol{\theta}_g \sim Dirichlet(\boldsymbol{\alpha})$;
  - For each group member
    * Draw $z \sim Multinomial(\boldsymbol{\theta}_g)$;
    * Draw $u \sim Multinomial(\phi^{ZU}_z)$;
    * Draw switch $c \sim Bernoulli(\lambda_u)$;
    * If $c = 0$
      · Draw $i \sim Multinomial(\phi^{UI}_u)$;
    * If $c = 1$
      · Draw $i \sim Multinomial(\phi^{ZI}_z)$;

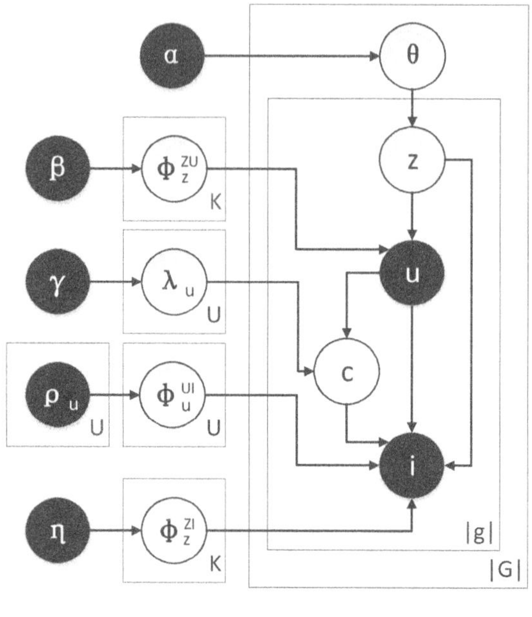

Figure 2: The Graphical Model of COM

The graphical model is shown in Figure 2.

Note that different users in a group will sample different items in the model, which is in accordance with our experience: users may have different preferences over items, and thus are likely to make different choices. In fact, the item selection of a group is often made by two steps: group members express their own opinions on item selections first, and then these selections are weighted and a consensus is reached. As to be detailed in Section 3.4, we propose a recommendation method that can aggregate the selections of group members based on their topic-dependent influences, and produce a single recommendation for the target group.

We remark that the aforementioned generative process is also applicable to the groups with pre-defined members, since these groups also have topic distributions. Consider some students plan to form a club group and the topics of the group are dining, hiking, etc. The group is formed because its topics attract the members. If someone is not interested in any of the group topics, she will not join the group. Thus, the generative process of the club can also be explained by the proposed model, where the group members are sampled from the students.

3.3 Parameter Estimation

The total likelihood of the group event corpus is:

$$\begin{aligned} & P(\mathbf{z}, \mathbf{u}, \mathbf{c}, \mathbf{i} | \boldsymbol{\alpha}, \boldsymbol{\beta}, \boldsymbol{\rho}, \boldsymbol{\eta}, \boldsymbol{\gamma}) \\ = & \int P(\mathbf{c}|\boldsymbol{\lambda}) P(\boldsymbol{\lambda}|\gamma, \gamma_t) d\boldsymbol{\lambda} \cdot \int P(\boldsymbol{z}|\boldsymbol{\theta}) P(\boldsymbol{\theta}|\boldsymbol{\alpha}) d\boldsymbol{\theta} \cdot \\ & \int P(\boldsymbol{u}|\boldsymbol{z}, \phi^{ZU}) P(\phi^{ZU}|\boldsymbol{\beta}) d\phi^{ZU} \cdot \\ & \int\int P(\boldsymbol{i}|\boldsymbol{u}, \boldsymbol{z}, \boldsymbol{c}, \phi^{UI}, \phi^{ZI}) P(\phi^{UI}|\boldsymbol{\rho}) P(\phi^{ZI}|\boldsymbol{\eta}) d\phi^{UI} d\phi^{ZI} \quad (1) \end{aligned}$$

We employ collapsed Gibbs sampling to obtain samples of the hidden variable assignment, and to estimate the unknown parameters $\{\boldsymbol{\lambda}, \phi^{ZU}, \phi^{UI}, \phi^{ZI}\}$. For ease of presentation, we define a user u together with the item i selected by u as a user-item pair $j = (u, i)$, where the user of j is $u \in U$, and the item of j is $i \in I$.

Since there are two latent variables in the model, namely z and c, we employ two-step Gibbs sampling method. We first sample topics z_j for all user-item pairs j, and then sample switches c_j for all j. For each latent variable (*e.g.*, z_j), a Gibbs sampling method computes the full conditional probability for the assignment of the variable conditioned on all the other assignments (*e.g.*, $\boldsymbol{z}_{\neg j}$). However, it is challenging to get the full conditional probability because of the complex interdependencies between user u, topic z, switch c and item i: u is sampled based on z, which influences the sampling of c, while i is sampled based on either z or u depending on c.

To solve this problem, we separate the items generated based on topics, and the items generated based on users' personal considerations of content factors. Then, the last part of Equation 1 becomes:

$$\begin{aligned}&\int\int P(\boldsymbol{i}|\boldsymbol{u},\boldsymbol{z},\boldsymbol{c},\boldsymbol{\phi}^{UI},\boldsymbol{\phi}^{ZI})P(\boldsymbol{\phi}^{UI}|\boldsymbol{\rho})P(\boldsymbol{\phi}^{ZI}|\boldsymbol{\eta})d\boldsymbol{\phi}^{UI}d\boldsymbol{\phi}^{ZI}\\ =&\int P(\boldsymbol{i}^{(0)}|\boldsymbol{u},\boldsymbol{c},\boldsymbol{\phi}^{UI})P(\boldsymbol{\phi}^{UI}|\boldsymbol{\rho})d\boldsymbol{\phi}^{UI}\cdot\\ &\int P(\boldsymbol{i}^{(1)}|\boldsymbol{z},\boldsymbol{c},\boldsymbol{\phi}^{ZI})P(\boldsymbol{\phi}^{ZI}|\boldsymbol{\eta})d\boldsymbol{\phi}^{ZI}\end{aligned}\tag{2}$$

where $\boldsymbol{i}^{(0)}$ is the set of items that are sampled based on users' personal considerations of content factors (*i.e.*, $c = 0$), and $\boldsymbol{i}^{(1)}$ is the set of items that are sampled based on topics (*i.e.*, $c = 1$).

Based on the new equation of total likelihood, we can derive the full conditional distribution of topic z_j and switch c_j assignments for each user-item pair j. If the item of j is drawn based on topics, *i.e.*, $c_j = 1$, we sample z_j according to the following probability:

$$\begin{aligned}&P(z_j=k|\boldsymbol{z}_{\neg j},\boldsymbol{u},\boldsymbol{i}^{(1)})\\ =&\frac{\int P(\boldsymbol{z}|\boldsymbol{\theta})P(\boldsymbol{\theta}|\boldsymbol{\alpha})d\boldsymbol{\theta}}{\int P(\boldsymbol{z}_{\neg j}|\boldsymbol{\theta})P(\boldsymbol{\theta}|\boldsymbol{\alpha})d\boldsymbol{\theta}}\cdot\frac{\int P(\boldsymbol{u}|\boldsymbol{z},\boldsymbol{\phi}^{ZU})P(\boldsymbol{\phi}^{ZU}|\boldsymbol{\beta})d\boldsymbol{\phi}^{ZU}}{\int P(\boldsymbol{u}|\boldsymbol{z}_{\neg j},\boldsymbol{\phi}^{ZU})P(\boldsymbol{\phi}^{ZU}|\boldsymbol{\beta})d\boldsymbol{\phi}^{ZU}}\cdot\\ &\frac{\int P(\boldsymbol{i}^{(1)}|\boldsymbol{z},\boldsymbol{c},\boldsymbol{\phi}^{ZI})P(\boldsymbol{\phi}^{ZI}|\boldsymbol{\eta})d\boldsymbol{\phi}^{ZI}}{\int P(\boldsymbol{i}^{(1)}|\boldsymbol{z}_{\neg j},\boldsymbol{c},\boldsymbol{\phi}^{ZI})P(\boldsymbol{\phi}^{ZI}|\boldsymbol{\eta})d\boldsymbol{\phi}^{ZI}}\\ \propto&\frac{n^{GZ}_{g_j,k,\neg j}+\alpha_k}{\sum\limits_{k'\in Z}(n^{GZ}_{g_j,k',\neg j}+\alpha_{k'})}\cdot\frac{n^{ZU}_{k,u,\neg j}+\beta_u}{\sum\limits_{u'\in U}(n^{ZU}_{k,u',\neg j}+\beta_{u'})}\cdot\frac{n^{ZI}_{k,i,\neg j}+\eta_i}{\sum\limits_{i'\in I}(n^{ZI}_{k,i',\neg j}+\eta_{i'})}\end{aligned}\tag{3}$$

where g_j is the group of j. If the item of j is drawn based on user's personal considerations of content factors, *i.e.*, $c_j = 0$, we have:

$$\begin{aligned}&P(z_j=k|\boldsymbol{z}_{\neg j},\boldsymbol{u},\boldsymbol{i}^{(0)})\\ \propto&\frac{n^{GZ}_{g_j,k,\neg j}+\alpha_k}{\sum_{k'\in Z}(n^{GZ}_{g_j,k',\neg j}+\alpha_{k'})}\cdot\frac{n^{ZU}_{k,u,\neg j}+\beta_u}{\sum_{u'\in U}(n^{ZU}_{k,u',\neg j}+\beta_{u'})}\end{aligned}\tag{4}$$

After sampling topics for all user-item pairs, we draw a switch c_j for each j according to the following posterior probability. When $c_j = 1$, we have:

$$\begin{aligned}&P(c_j=1|\boldsymbol{c}_{\neg j},\boldsymbol{z},\boldsymbol{u},\boldsymbol{i})\\ =&\frac{\int P(\boldsymbol{c}|\boldsymbol{\lambda})P(\boldsymbol{\lambda}|\gamma,\gamma_t)d\boldsymbol{\lambda}}{\int P(\boldsymbol{c}_{\neg j}|\boldsymbol{\lambda})P(\boldsymbol{\lambda}|\gamma,\gamma_t)d\boldsymbol{\lambda}}\cdot\frac{\int P(\boldsymbol{i}^{(0)}|\boldsymbol{u},\boldsymbol{c},\boldsymbol{\phi}^{UI})P(\boldsymbol{\phi}^{UI}|\boldsymbol{\rho})d\boldsymbol{\phi}^{UI}}{\int P(\boldsymbol{i}^{(0)}|\boldsymbol{u},\boldsymbol{c}_{\neg j},\boldsymbol{\phi}^{UI})P(\boldsymbol{\phi}^{UI}|\boldsymbol{\rho})d\boldsymbol{\phi}^{UI}}\cdot\\ &\frac{\int P(\boldsymbol{i}^{(1)}|\boldsymbol{z},\boldsymbol{c},\boldsymbol{\phi}^{ZI})P(\boldsymbol{\phi}^{ZI}|\boldsymbol{\eta})d\boldsymbol{\phi}^{ZI}}{\int P(\boldsymbol{i}^{(1)}|\boldsymbol{z},\boldsymbol{c}_{\neg j},\boldsymbol{\phi}^{ZI})P(\boldsymbol{\phi}^{ZI}|\boldsymbol{\eta})d\boldsymbol{\phi}^{ZI}}\end{aligned}\tag{5}$$

Note that since $c_j = 1$, the second term in the right hand side of Equation 5 is 1. Thus, we cancel this part, and get:

$$\begin{aligned}&P(c_j=1|\boldsymbol{c}_{\neg j},\boldsymbol{z},\boldsymbol{u},\boldsymbol{i})\\ \propto&\frac{n^{UC}_{u,(1),\neg j}+\gamma}{n^{UC}_{u,(0),\neg j}+n^{UC}_{u,(1),\neg j}+\gamma+\gamma_t}\cdot\frac{n^{ZI}_{z_j,i,\neg j}+\eta_i}{\sum_{i'\in I}(n^{ZI}_{z_j,i',\neg j}+\eta_{i'})}\end{aligned}\tag{6}$$

Similarly, we calculate the sampling probability for $c_j = 0$:

$$\begin{aligned}&P(c_j=0|\boldsymbol{c}_{\neg j},\boldsymbol{z},\boldsymbol{u},\boldsymbol{i})\\ \propto&\frac{n^{UC}_{u,(0),\neg j}+\gamma_t}{n^{UC}_{u,(0),\neg j}+n^{UC}_{u,(1),\neg j}+\gamma+\gamma_t}\cdot\frac{n^{UI}_{u,i,\neg j}+\rho_i}{\sum_{i'\in I}(n^{UI}_{u,i',\neg j}+\rho_{i'})}\end{aligned}\tag{7}$$

After sampling a sufficient number of iterations, we calculate the parameters $\boldsymbol{\phi}^{ZU}$, $\boldsymbol{\phi}^{UI}$, $\boldsymbol{\phi}^{ZI}$ and $\boldsymbol{\lambda}$ as follows:

$$\widehat{\phi^{ZU}_{z,u}}=\widehat{P}(u|z)=\frac{n^{ZU}_{z,u}+\beta_u}{\sum_{u'\in U}(n^{ZU}_{z,u'}+\beta_{u'})}\tag{8}$$

$$\widehat{\phi^{UI}_{u,i}}=\widehat{P}(i|u)=\frac{n^{UI}_{u,i}+\rho_i}{\sum_{i'\in I}(n^{UI}_{u,i'}+\rho_{i'})}\tag{9}$$

$$\widehat{\phi^{ZI}_{z,i}}=\widehat{P}(i|z)=\frac{n^{ZI}_{z,i}+\eta_i}{\sum_{i'\in I}(n^{ZI}_{z,i'}+\eta_{i'})}\tag{10}$$

$$\widehat{\lambda_u}=\widehat{P}(c=1|u)=\frac{n^{UC}_{u,(1)}+\gamma}{n^{UC}_{u,(0)}+n^{UC}_{u,(1)}+\gamma+\gamma_t}\tag{11}$$

3.4 Recommendation

When making recommendations for a target group g_t, we first discover its topic distribution based on the group members $\boldsymbol{u}_{g_t}$. The distribution, denoted by $\boldsymbol{\theta}_{g_t}$, can be learnt by performing Gibbs sampling on $\boldsymbol{u}_{g_t}$ according to the following equation:

$$P(z_j=k|\boldsymbol{z}_{\neg j},u_j=v,\boldsymbol{u}_{\neg j})\propto\widehat{\phi^{ZU}_{k,v}}(n^{GZ}_{g_t,k,\neg j}+\alpha_k)\tag{12}$$

Since the recommendations should match the topic distribution $\boldsymbol{\theta}_{g_t}$, based on the generative model, we define the recommendation score for candidate item i as follows:

$$P(i|\boldsymbol{u}_{g_t},\boldsymbol{\theta}_{g_t})\triangleq\prod_{u\in\boldsymbol{u}_{g_t}}\sum_{z\in Z}\theta_{g_t,z}\cdot\widehat{\phi^{ZU}_{z,u}}(\widehat{\lambda_u}\cdot\widehat{\phi^{ZI}_{z,i}}+(1-\widehat{\lambda_u})\cdot\widehat{\phi^{UI}_{u,i}})\tag{13}$$

Equation 13 embeds **Intuition 4** (when selecting items, different users in a group have different influence scores, and the influence scores are topic dependent) as follows: if the topic z is more relevant to group g_t, and a user u is an expert in z, then u will be more influential in item selection. Recall that the expertise of a user u on topic z is modeled by $\phi^{ZU}_{z,u}$. In Equation 13, $\theta_{g_t,z}\cdot\phi^{ZU}_{z,u}$ is the influence score of user u in group g_t for a given topic z, and $\lambda_u\cdot\phi^{ZI}_{z,i}+(1-\lambda_u)\cdot\phi^{UI}_{u,i}$ is u's preference to a candidate item i given topic z. We margin out the topics, and get the overall preference of u to i. Then the preferences of all members to i are multiplied as the group preference to i. The rationale is three-fold: 1) the preference of a group to an item depends on the preferences of all individuals; 2) ranking an item based on the product of preferences is equal to the geometric mean of these individuals' preferences. Compared with the traditional strategies that calculate the arithmetic mean of preferences (averaging) or concentrate on the smallest preference (least-misery), the aggregated preference score by geometric mean is less sensitive to extreme values; 3) this definition matches the proposed model well.

3.5 Incorporation of Content Information

The Dirichlet prior ρ to ϕ_u^{UI} allows us to incorporate different content information into the model. We illustrate the incorporation using two recommendation tasks, namely, venue recommendation and movie recommendation.

Venue recommendation for groups: People often visit venues together with others for shopping, dining, etc. Venue recommendation for a group aims to recommend the venues that the group members are interested in. For venue recommendation, geographical distance is an important factor to consider [27, 30]. Previous studies reported that users tend to visit nearby venues, and the willingness of visiting a venue decreases with the increase of distance from their current locations. Here, we adopt a power-law function of distance to model the willingness of a user moving from one venue to another as [29] does. More specifically, the willingness of a user to visit a d-km far away venue is defined by Equation 14.

$$\mathrm{wi}(d) = \omega \cdot d^{\kappa} \tag{14}$$

where ω and κ are parameters of the power law function, which can be learned by maximum likelihood estimation.

Then, given a user u, the set of venues that she has visited I_u, we calculate $P(i|I_u)$ for each candidate venue i according to the geographical distance, and use this value for $\rho_{u,i}$. Based on the Bayes rule, $P(i|I_u)$ is calculated as follows:

$$\begin{aligned}\rho_{u,i} = P(i|I_u) \propto & \quad P(i)P(I_u|i) \\ = & \quad P(i)\prod_{i' \in I_u} P(i'|i)\end{aligned} \tag{15}$$

where $P(i'|i)$ is proportional to the willingness value in Equation 14, in which d is the distance between venues i' and i. □

Movie recommendation for groups: When selecting a movie to watch, a user may consider several factors, such as genre, cast, etc. We take the cast as an example to illustrate how to exploit content information. Intuitively, users tend to watch the movies stared by their favorite actors or actresses. We incorporate user u's cast-based considerations to a movie i by modifying the prior $\rho_{u,i}$ as follows:

$$\rho_{u,i} \propto \sum_{s \in S_i} P(s|u) \tag{16}$$

where s is a movie star, and S_i is the cast list of movie i. $P(s|u)$ is estimated based on the occurrences of s in u's watching history. □

Note that the $|U| \times |I|$ dimensional matrix ϕ^{UI} requires a large amount of space, in which each value of $\phi_{u,i}^{UI}$ is determined by both the count $n_{u,i}^{UI}$ and the prior ρ_i (Equation 9). Since for each user u, the values of most items in ϕ^{UI} are 0 ($n_{u,i}^{UI} = 0$ and $\rho_{u,i} = 0$), we can use sparse matrix to store ϕ^{UI} to reduce the space complexity.

4. EXPERIMENTS

We first introduce the setup of the experiments in Section 4.1, and then present the experimental results in Section 4.2, in which we compare the recommendation accuracy of our model with five baselines on four datasets. After that, we analyze which factor influences group members' choices more significantly in Section 4.3. In the end, we show some sample topics discovered by the proposed model to examine their semantics in Section 4.4.

4.1 Experimental Setup

4.1.1 Datasets

Four real-world datasets are used in our experiments. The first dataset is used in previous work [12], which is collected from Plancast[1], an event-based social network (EBSN). In Plancast, a user can follow others' calendars, and join different events. An event involves a group of members, and is held at a venue. A venue is associated with a geographical coordinate. We treat an event as a group, where the users involved in the event are the group members, and the venue of the event is the item selected by them.

Table 2: Statistics of the Datasets

Dataset	Plancast	Jiepang	MovieLens -Simi	MovieLens -Rand
#Users	41,705	28,888	891	3,689
#Group Events	13,885	23,621	3,000	3,000
#Items	8,016	9,746	441	1,518
Avg. Group Size	20.30	4.68	5	5
Avg. #Items for a Group	1.00	1.01	14.97	3.73
Avg. #Records for a User	6.76	3.83	16.83	4.06
Avg. #Friends for a User	43.29	13.00	N/A	N/A
Avg. #Records for an Item	1.73	2.42	100.06	7.37

Second, we collect 45 million check-ins from Jiapang[2], a location-based social network (LBSN). As shown in Figure 1, LBSNs allow users to share their geographical information by check-ins, where a check-in has a user, time and venue, indicating the user visited the venue at that time. Each a venue in Jiepang is associated with its geographical coordinate. However, Jiepang does not contain explicit group information, and we extract implicit group check-ins as follows: we assume if a set of friends visit the same venue at the same time, they are the members of a group. Specifically, the set of individual check-ins made by friends within 0.5 hour is regarded as a group check-in. For both Jiepang and Plancast datasets, we aim to recommend venues for given groups.

The last two datasets are extracted from 1M MovieLens dataset[3] by following the approach in [4]. MovieLens allows users to rate the movies they have watched by stars ranging from 0 to 5. Two kinds of groups are considered in the experiments: similar and random, denoted by MovieLens-Simi and MovieLens-Rand, respectively. Groups in MovieLens-Simi have larger inner similarities between members, while groups in MovieLens-Rand are randomly formed. The two datasets simulate two kinds of groups in real-life: the groups formed by people who have similar preferences, and the groups that happen to be formed by a set of people. For each dataset, we randomly select 3000 groups with 5-members. We also evaluated groups of size 3 and 8, and obtained similar results. The details for generating the datasets can be found in [4]. Given a group, if every member gives 4 stars or above to a movie, we assume that the movie is adopted by the group. We also collect the cast list of each movie from IMDB[4] as content information.

The information of the four datasets is shown in Table 2. For each dataset, we randomly mark off 20% of group events as the test set to evaluate the recommendation accuracy of different methods.

4.1.2 Evaluation Metrics

Following previous work [3,4,8,13], we evaluate the accuracy of different methods with three metrics, namely average *precision@N* (*Pre@N*), average *recall@N* (*Rec@N*) and normalized discounted

[1]http://plancast.com/

[2]http://jiepang.com/

[3]http://grouplens.org/datasets/movielens/

[4]http://www.imdb.com/interfaces/

cumulative gain (*nDCG*), where *N* is the number of recommendations. We consider three values of *N* (*i.e.*, 5, 10, 20), where 5 is the default value.

Precision@N is the fraction of the top *N* recommendations that are adopted by a group, while *recall@N* is the fraction of items adopted by a group (true items) that are contained in the top *N* recommendations. Formally, given a group, the *precision@N* and *recall@N* are calculated as:

$$precision@N = \frac{|\{\text{top } N \text{ recommendations}\} \cap \{\text{true items}\}|}{|\{\text{top } N \text{ recommendations}\}|} \quad (17)$$

$$recall@N = \frac{|\{\text{top } N \text{ recommendations}\} \cap \{\text{true items}\}|}{|\{\text{true items}\}|} \quad (18)$$

We average the *precision@N* and *recall@N* of all testing groups as the *Pre@N* and *Rec@N*, respectively. Note that the average number of true items of a group in Plancast and Jiepang is close to 1 (Table 2). In this case, *Pre@N* is proportional to *Rec@N*, since |{top *N* recommendations}| is *N* times greater than |{true items}|. Thus, to save space, we only report *Rec@5* for the two datasets.

nDCG measures how well a method can rank the true item higher in the recommendation list. It is calculated as follows:

$$DCG = rel_1 + \sum_{i=2}^{N} \frac{rel_i}{log_2(i)} \quad (19)$$

$$nDCG = \frac{DCG}{IDCG} \quad (20)$$

where $rel_i = 1$ if the ith item in the recommendation list is adopted by the group, and $rel_i = 0$ otherwise. *IDCG* is the maximum possible discounted cumulative gain (*DCG*) with optimal top *N* recommendations. We average the *nDCG* values of all groups as the final result. In the experiments, *N* is fixed at 10.

For all metrics, larger value indicates better recommendation performance.

4.1.3 Recommendation Methods

We evaluate 7 methods in our experiments, namely CF-AVG, CF-LM, CF-RD [3], SIG [26], PIT [13], and the proposed methods COMP and COM. To the best of our knowledge, these state-of-the-art group recommendation methods have not been compared with each other in previous work, and our evaluation is the first experimental studies on them.

User-based CF with averaging strategy (CF-AVG): Given a candidate item *i*, CF-AVG first estimates the recommendation score of each user in the target group by user-based CF, and then uses the average of these scores as the recommendation score for the group.

User-based CF with least-misery strategy (CF-LM): Given a candidate item *i*, CF-LM first estimates the recommendation score of each user in the target group by user-based CF, and then uses the smallest score as the recommendation score for the group.

User-based CF with relevance and disagreement (CF-RD) [3]: This model calculates the recommendation score for a candidate item *i* based on the relevance and disagreement of the group, where the relevance is calculated based on either CF-AVG or CF-LM, and the disagreement can be either the average difference of recommendation scores of pair-wise group members, or the variance of members' recommendation scores.

Social influence based group recommendation (SIG) [26]: SIG is a topic model based approach, which has been introduced in Section 2. Since the MovieLens-Simi and MovieLens-Rand datasets have no friendship information, we do not report the results of SIG for them.

Personal impact topic model (PIT) [13]: PIT model assumes that different users have different impact scores, and in a group, the user who has a larger impact score is more likely to be selected as the representative. Given a group of users $\boldsymbol{u}_{g_t}$, PIT model first samples a representative user *r* from $\boldsymbol{u}_{g_t}$ based on users' impact scores, and then *r* selects a topic based on her topic preference, and finally the topic generates an item for the group.

COnsensus Model Plain (COMP): To make a fair comparison with these baselines which do not exploit users' considerations of content factors, we use a symmetric Dirichlet prior for ϕ^{UI} to disregard the effect of content information.

COnsensus Model (COM): The proposed model incorporated with users' considerations of content factors.

All baselines are evaluated under the optimal settings. For the hyperparameters in COMP and COM, we take fixed values ($\alpha = 50/K$, $\beta = \eta = 0.01$, $\gamma = \gamma_t = 0.5$ and $\rho = 0.01$ for COMP). The prior ρ in COM encodes the content-based knowledge, and needs to be set empirically. Previous work fixes its value as 0.01 [9], and thus the sum of the prior is $0.01 \times |I|$. In this paper, we normalize the value of ρ of each user to a fix value $0.01 \times p \times |I|$, where the parameter *p* is used to tune the confidence in the prior knowledge.

4.2 Experimental Results

Precision and Recall Under Different *N*

We first fix the number of topics *K* at 250, and vary the number of recommendations *N*. The *Pre@N* and *Rec@N* values on the four datasets are plotted in Figure 3. Please note that the MovieLens-Simi/Rand datasets do not contain social relations, and thus the baseline SIG cannot be applied to them.

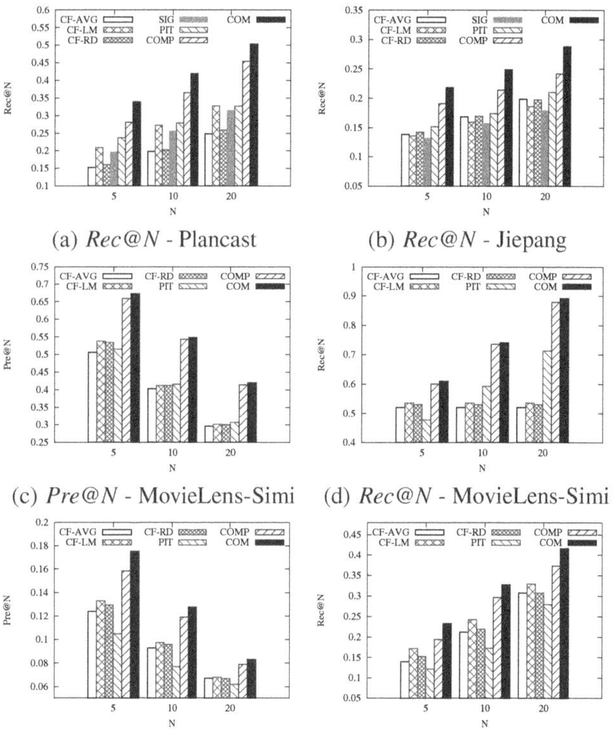

Figure 3: *Pre&Rec* under #recommendations made (*N*)

From Figure 3(a) and 3(b), we can see that the CF-based approaches, namely, CF-AVG, CF-LM and CF-RD, do not perform well on the Plancast and Jiepang datasets. This is because the three methods exploit neither the difference of individuals, nor the interactions among group members. They assume that users in a group make choices independently, and aggregate their choices for recommendations. The performance of SIG is not satisfactory, either. The reason is that SIG makes group recommendations based on the social relations between users in a group, and it requires tags of candidate items. However, in the groups of Plancast, only several or even none of the members are friends to each other, and neither of the two datasets has tag information. The lack of social relations and tags brings down its recommendation accuracy.

In contrast, PIT performs better than the CF based approaches on the Plancast and Jiepang datasets because PIT utilizes the interactions in a group by differentiating influences of users, and assumes that a user with a larger impact score will be influential in every group of the user. However, PIT ignores the fact that the influence of a user will be different across different topics. The performance of PIT on the two MovieLens datasets is not as good as on the Plancast and Jiepang datasets. This is because groups in the two datasets are loosely organized, and users select movie independently. Since no representative member exists to make item selections for a group, the basic assumption of PIT does not hold any more, which results in its bad recommendation accuracy.

Compared with the five baselines, our proposed method COMP always archives superior recommendation accuracy. For example, it outperforms CF-AVG, CF-LM, CF-RD, SIG and PIT by 84%, 34%, 76%, 43% and 19%, respectively, for *Rec*@5 on Plancast. The reasons are two-fold: on the one hand, COMP considers the behavior changes of users in a group; on the other hand, it estimates the topic-dependent influences of users in a group. Compared with COMP, COM further improves *Rec*@5 by more than 15% on Plancast, Jiepang and MovieLens-Rand, showing that COM is effective in incorporating the content information (geographical distance for Plancast and Jiepang, and cast list for MovieLens-Rand). The improvement on MovieLens-Simi is marginal, since its user-item selection matrix has a high density (about 4%). As a result, COMP, which only utilizes users' selection history, already achieves very good accuracy(*e.g., Rec*@5 is 67.3%), and thus the value of relative improvement is small.

Precision and Recall Under Different *K*

We fix the number of recommendations at 5, and vary the number of topics K from 50 to 400. The *Pre*@5 and *Rec*@5 values on the four datasets are plotted in Figure 4. Since CF-AVG, CF-LM and CF-RD do not involve topics, their *Pre*@5 and *Rec*@5 values do not vary with K.

For the topic model based approaches, namely, SIG, PIT, COMP and COM, their *Pre*@5 and *Rec*@5 values do not change much with varying the number of topics. In addition, we notice that SIG performs worse than CF-AVG, CF-LM and CF-RD on Plancast, but better than these CF-based approaches on Jiepang when $K \geq 250$. This is because the group events of Jiepang are extracted based on friendships, and thus they fit well with the assumption of the SIG. PIT's *Rec*@5 value is the best among the baselines on the Plancast and Jiepang datasets, but is worse than that of CF-AVG, CF-LM and CF-RD on MovieLens-Simi and MovieLens-Rand. Potential reason is the generative process of groups in the MovieLens datasets is different from that of PIT model. Our proposed method COMP outperforms the best baselines by about 20% on the four datasets. After incorporating users' personal considerations of content factors, COM further improve the *Rec*@5 values by more than 15% on the Plancast, Jiepang and MovieLens-Rand datasets, demonstrating the effectiveness of the proposed model.

nDCG* Under Different *K

Next, we vary the number of topics K, and examine the *nDCG* results of different approaches to see how well they can rank the true items higher. The results are plotted in Figure 5. We can see that the results display a similar trend with the previous experimental results based on *Pre*@5 and *Rec*@5: PIT performs the best among the baseline methods on Plancast and Jiepang, but the worst on MovieLens-Simi and MovieLens-Rand. However, our method COMP consistently outperforms the best baseline under different number of topics by more than 15% on the four datasets. COM achieves the best results, which are at least 16% greater than that of COMP on Plancast, Jiepang and MovieLens-Rand.

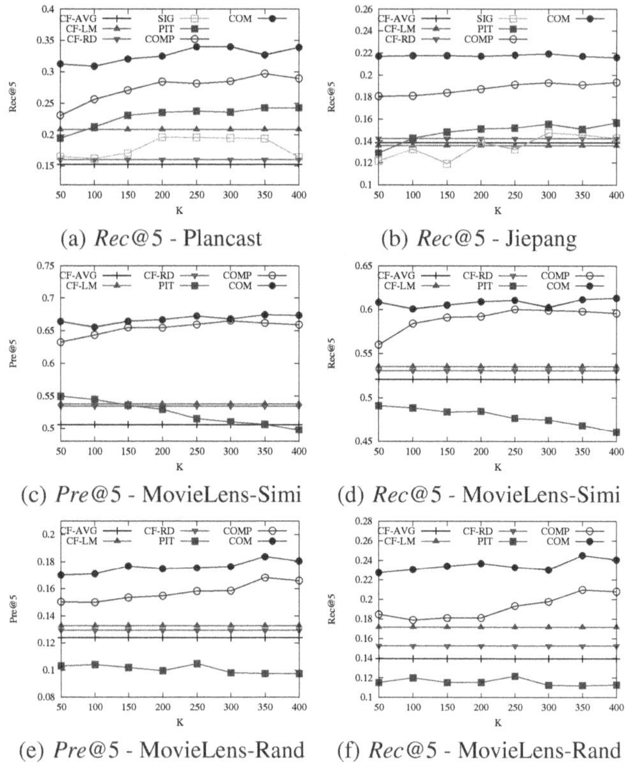

(a) *Rec*@5 - Plancast (b) *Rec*@5 - Jiepang
(c) *Pre*@5 - MovieLens-Simi (d) *Rec*@5 - MovieLens-Simi
(e) *Pre*@5 - MovieLens-Rand (f) *Rec*@5 - MovieLens-Rand

Figure 4: *Pre*@5&*Rec*@5 under #topics (*K*)

Effect of p

We next examine the effect of p on the recommendation accuracy of COM. Recall that after incorporating the users' personal considerations of content factors into the prior, we normalize the prior of each user to $p \cdot 0.01 \cdot |I|$. Parameter p is set to adjust the effect of the prior, *i.e.,* larger p implies that the distribution ϕ_u^{UI} is more influenced by the content information. We examine the recommendation accuracy of COM under different value of p ranging from 0.001 to 1000. The *Rec*@5 and *nDCG* on four datasets are plotted in Figure 6. We can see that the recommendation performance remains relatively stable when varying the value of p. The *Pre*@5 follows a similar trend with *Rec*@5, and we omit it due to the space limitation.

Performance for Different Size of Groups

This set of experiments is to study the performance of each recommendation method for groups of different sizes. We group the Plancast groups into bins based on group size, and plot the *Rec*@5 and *nDCG* curves of each method in Figure 7. The number of topics is fixed at 250. Due to the space limitation, the results on the other datasets are not given here. Figure 7 shows that the proposed methods COMP and COM outperform the baselines for groups of different sizes. Among the baselines, CF-AVG, CF-LM and CF-RD perform the worst, followed by SIG and PIT. Compared with that of other methods, the performance of CF-based approaches is

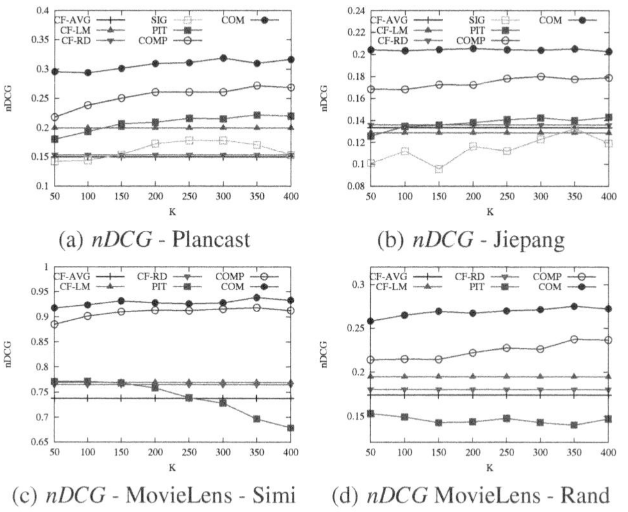

(a) *nDCG* - Plancast (b) *nDCG* - Jiepang

(c) *nDCG* - MovieLens - Simi (d) *nDCG* MovieLens - Rand

Figure 5: *nDCG* under #topics (*K*)

better for groups of small size, because their group organizations are simple, and thus these simple aggregating strategies are good for making recommendations.

4.3 Weight of Topics in Item Selection

In this section, we study the weight of topics in users' item selections by investigating parameter λ_u, the probability that a user selects an item according to group topics.

We first study the effect of the number of topics K on the value of λ_u. Specifically, for each dataset, we plot the average λ_u of all users as a function of K. The curves of COMP and COM on the four datasets are shown in Figure 8. We can see that for COMP which does not exploit the content information, the average λ_u is almost not affected by the value of K, and its value is between 0.75 to 0.9. The results reveal that most of items are selected according to topics, but there is still a set of items that are selected based on users' personal considerations of content factors. Compared with the average λ_u of COMP, that of COM is much smaller, since additional content information is incorporated. The value of λ_u on Plancast (around 0.5) is larger than that on Jiepang (around 0.2) for COM, indicating that topics have larger weight in venue selections of Plancast users. In addition, the λ_u values of both COMP and COM on MovieLens-Simi are larger than those on MovieLens-Rand, because groups in MovieLens-Simi consist of people with high similarities, and thus topic is a very important consideration.

Then, we fix the number of topics at 250, and plot the distribution of λ_u of COM on the four datasets in Figure 9. We notice that on all datasets, the λ_u value of the majority of users is smaller than 0.4, showing that the personal considerations of content information is important for most of people. In addition, we see that the curve

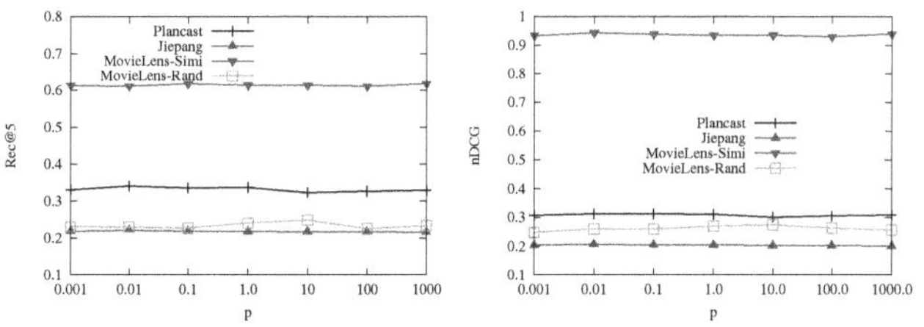

(a) *Rec*@5 (b) *nDCG*

Figure 6: *Rec*@5 and *nDCG* under different *p*

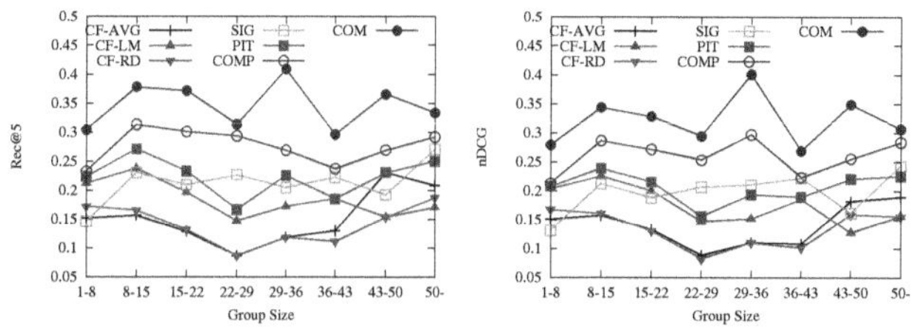

(a) *Rec*@5 (b) *nDCG*

Figure 7: *Rec*@5 and *nDCG* for Different Size of Groups

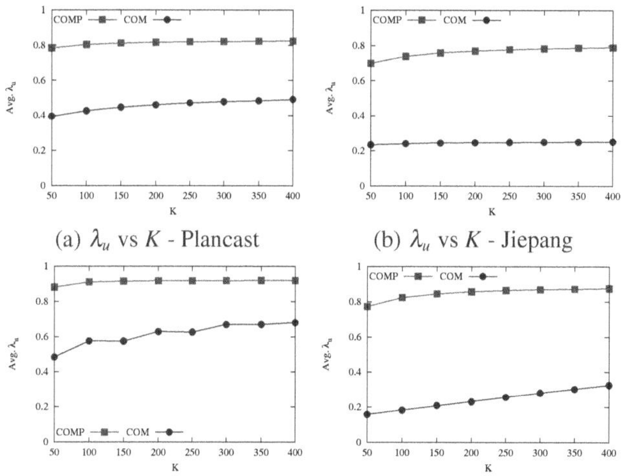

(a) λ_u vs *K* - Plancast (b) λ_u vs *K* - Jiepang

(c) λ_u vs *K* - MovieLens-Simi (d) λ_u vs *K* - MovieLens-Rand

Figure 8: Avg. λ_u under #topics (*K*)

of Plancast has a long tail, indicating that a considerable portion of users treat topics important. In addition, λ_u on MovieLens-Simi reaches another peak at $\lambda_u = 1$, showing that in a group with high inner-similarity, a considerable portion of people select items based on topics.

4.4 Topic Analysis

We first investigate the venue distribution of each topic generated by COM on Plancast and Jiepang datasets, where the number of topics is set to 250. For each topic z, we rank the venues i based on $\phi^{ZI}_{z,i}$. The top 5 venues of 5 randomly selected topics on the two datasets are plotted in Figure 10. We observe that for each topic, the top ranked venues are close to each other. This is because topics are estimated based on users' group participation history. Since users tend to join groups held at their nearby venues due to the spatial constraint, the venues visited by each user fall in a small geographical region, and thus the top ranked venues of each topic are close to each other.

Then, we examine the movie distributions of topics of COM on the MovieLens-Rand dataset. Specifically, we set the number of topics at 50 for COM, and randomly select 5 topics. For each topic z, we rank the movies i based on the learnt $\phi^{ZI}_{z,i}$. The top 3 movies of the 5 topics are listed in Table 3. The name of each topic is generated from the top 10 movies' genres in IMDB by majority vote. We can find that the discovered topics are semantically meaningful.

5. CONCLUSION

Recommender systems have been studied for decades, but most of them are designed for individuals. How to make accurate recommendations for groups is still an open problem. In this paper, we propose a probabilistic model COM to simulate the generative

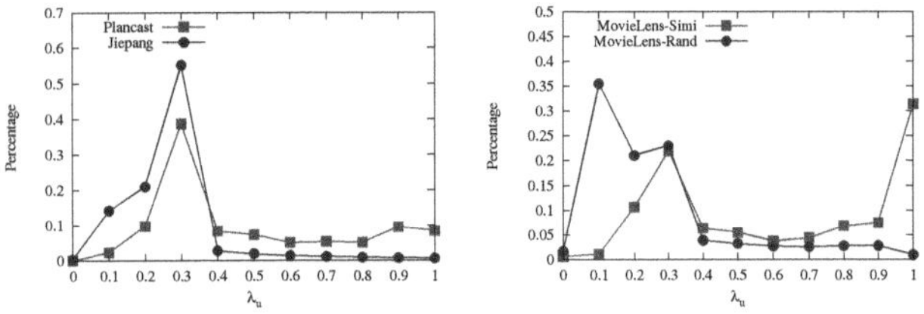

(a) Plancast/Jiepang (b) MovieLens Simi/Rand

Figure 9: Distribution of λ_u

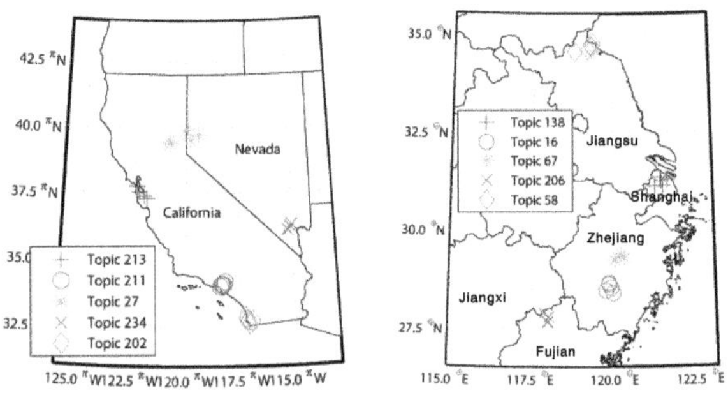

(a) Plancast (b) Jiepang

Figure 10: Venue Distribution of Topics

process of group events and make recommendations for a group of users. Since users' item selections are not only influenced by topics, but also by users' personal considerations of content factors, we incorporate the content information into the model. In addition, the proposed model considers the change of users' behaviors in a group from as individuals, and differentiates the influences of users in a group according to topics. Experimental results on four real-world datasets show that the proposed method outperforms five baselines significantly.

For the future work, it would be interesting to exploit social relations to make group recommendations, since the friendships in a group may influence the group's choices. In addition, several content factors are difficult to be incorporated into the our model, *e.g.*, time. We will investigate how to model such content factors.

6. ACKNOWLEDGEMENTS

This work is supported in part by a grant awarded by a Singapore MOE AcRF Tier 2 Grant (ARC30/12), a Singapore MOE AcRF Tier 1 Grant (RG66/12), and a grant awarded by Microsoft Research Asia. Quan Yuan would like to acknowledge the Ph.D. grant from the Institute for Media Innovation, Nanyang Technological University, Singapore.

Table 3: Representative Movies for COM Topics

Topic	Movies
Comedy	Big (1988), Romancing the Stone (1984), Four Weddings and a Funeral (1994)
Action	Raiders of the Lost Ark (1981) Star Wars: Episode V - The Empire Strikes Back (1980), Full Metal Jacket (1987)
Drama	Fight Club (1999), Trainspotting (1996), Magnolia (1999)
Thriller	Reservoir Dogs (1992), Gattaca (1997), Heavenly Creatures (1994)
Animation	Toy Story 2 (1999), Mulan (1998), Peter Pan (1953)

7. REFERENCES

[1] G. Adomavicius and A. Tuzhilin. Toward the next generation of recommender systems: A survey of the state-of-the-art and possible extensions. *IEEE Trans. Knowl. Data Eng.*, 17(6):734–749, 2005.

[2] D. Agarwal and B.-C. Chen. flda: matrix factorization through latent dirichlet allocation. In *WSDM*, pages 91–100, 2010.

[3] S. Amer-Yahia, S. B. Roy, A. Chawla, G. Das, and C. Yu. Group recommendation: Semantics and efficiency. *PVLDB*, 2(1):754–765, 2009.

[4] L. Baltrunas, T. Makcinskas, and F. Ricci. Group recommendations with rank aggregation and collaborative filtering. In *RecSys*, pages 119–126, 2010.

[5] D. M. Blei, A. Y. Ng, and M. I. Jordan. Latent dirichlet allocation. *Journal of Machine Learning Research*, 3:993–1022, 2003.

[6] L. A. M. C. Carvalho and H. T. Macedo. Users' satisfaction in recommendation systems for groups: an approach based on noncooperative games. In *WWW (Companion Volume)*, pages 951–958, 2013.

[7] A. Crossen, J. Budzik, and K. J. Hammond. Flytrap: intelligent group music recommendation. In *IUI*, pages 184–185, 2002.

[8] J. Gorla, N. Lathia, S. Robertson, and J. Wang. Probabilistic group recommendation via information matching. In *WWW*, pages 495–504, 2013.

[9] T. L. Griffiths and M. Steyvers. Finding scientific topics. *Proceedings of the National academy of Sciences of the United States of America*, 101(Suppl 1):5228–5235, 2004.

[10] A. Jameson and B. Smyth. Recommendation to groups. In *The adaptive web*, pages 596–627. Springer, 2007.

[11] Y. Koren, R. M. Bell, and C. Volinsky. Matrix factorization techniques for recommender systems. *IEEE Computer*, 42(8):30–37, 2009.

[12] X. Liu, Q. He, Y. Tian, W.-C. Lee, J. McPherson, and J. Han. Event-based social networks: linking the online and offline social worlds. In *KDD*, pages 1032–1040, 2012.

[13] X. Liu, Y. Tian, M. Ye, and W.-C. Lee. Exploring personal impact for group recommendation. In *CIKM*, pages 674–683, 2012.

[14] J. F. McCarthy. Pocket restaurant finder: A situated recommender systems for groups. In *Proceeding of Workshop on Mobile Ad-Hoc Communication at the 2002 ACM Conference on Human Factors in Computer Systems*, 2002.

[15] J. F. McCarthy and T. D. Anagnost. Musicfx: An arbiter of group preferences for computer aupported collaborative workouts. In *CSCW*, pages 363–372, 1998.

[16] K. McCarthy, M. Salamó, L. Coyle, L. McGinty, B. Smyth, and P. Nixon. Cats: A synchronous approach to collaborative group recommendation. In *FLAIRS Conference*, volume 2006, pages 86–91, 2006.

[17] M. R. McLaughlin and J. L. Herlocker. A collaborative filtering algorithm and evaluation metric that accurately model the user experience. In *SIGIR*, pages 329–336, 2004.

[18] M. O'Connor, D. Cosley, J. A. Konstan, and J. Riedl. Polylens: A recommender system for groups of user. In *ECSCW*, pages 199–218, 2001.

[19] M. O'Connor and J. Herlocker. Clustering items for collaborative filtering. In *Proceedings of the ACM SIGIR workshop on recommender systems*, volume 128. UC Berkeley, 1999.

[20] S. Pizzutilo, B. De Carolis, G. Cozzolongo, and F. Ambruoso. Group modeling in a public space: methods, techniques, experiences. In *Proceedings of the 5th WSEAS International Conference on Applied Informatics and Communications*, pages 175–180, 2005.

[21] B. M. Sarwar, G. Karypis, J. A. Konstan, and J. Riedl. Item-based collaborative filtering recommendation algorithms. In *WWW*, pages 285–295, 2001.

[22] S. Seko, T. Yagi, M. Motegi, and S. yo Muto. Group recommendation using feature space representing behavioral tendency and power balance among members. In *RecSys*, pages 101–108, 2011.

[23] X. Su and T. M. Khoshgoftaar. A survey of collaborative filtering techniques. *Adv. Artificial Intellegence*, 2009, 2009.

[24] L. H. Ungar and D. P. Foster. Clustering methods for collaborative filtering. In *AAAI Workshop on Recommendation Systems*, number 1, 1998.

[25] C. Wang and D. M. Blei. Collaborative topic modeling for recommending scientific articles. In *KDD*, pages 448–456, 2011.

[26] M. Ye, X. Liu, and W.-C. Lee. Exploring social influence for recommendation: a generative model approach. In *SIGIR*, pages 671–680, 2012.

[27] M. Ye, P. Yin, W.-C. Lee, and D. L. Lee. Exploiting geographical influence for collaborative point-of-interest recommendation. In *SIGIR*, pages 325–334, 2011.

[28] Z. Yu, X. Zhou, Y. Hao, and J. Gu. Tv program recommendation for multiple viewers based on user profile merging. *User Model. User-Adapt. Interact.*, 16(1):63–82, 2006.

[29] Q. Yuan, G. Cong, Z. Ma, A. Sun, and N. Magnenat-Thalmann. Time-aware point-of-interest recommendation. In *SIGIR*, pages 363–372, 2013.

[30] Q. Yuan, G. Cong, Z. Ma, A. Sun, and N. Magnenat-Thalmann. Who, where, when and what: discover spatio-temporal topics for twitter users. In *KDD*, pages 605–613, 2013.

[31] W. Zhang, J. Wang, and W. Feng. Combining latent factor model with location features for event-based group recommendation. In *KDD*, pages 910–918, 2013.

Leveraging User Libraries to Bootstrap Collaborative Filtering

Laurent Charlin*
Princeton University
Dept of Computer Science
Princeton, NJ, USA
lcharlin@cs.princeton.edu

Richard S. Zemel
University of Toronto
Dept of Computer Science
Toronto, ON, Canada
zemel@cs.toronto.edu

Hugo Larochelle
Université de Sherbrooke
Département d'informatique
Sherbrooke, QC, Canada
hugo.larochelle@usherbrooke.ca

ABSTRACT

We introduce a novel graphical model, the collaborative score topic model (CSTM), for personal recommendations of textual documents. CSTM's chief novelty lies in its learned model of individual libraries, or sets of documents, associated with each user. Overall, CSTM is a joint directed probabilistic model of user-item scores (ratings), and the textual side information in the user libraries and the items. Creating a generative description of scores and the text allows CSTM to perform well in a wide variety of data regimes, smoothly combining the side information with observed ratings as the number of ratings available for a given user ranges from none to many. Experiments on real-world datasets demonstrate CSTM's performance. We further demonstrate its utility in an application for personal recommendations of posters which we deployed at the NIPS 2013 conference.

1. INTRODUCTION

With the advent of online services and the wealth of information made accessible through them systems with the ability to filter the relevant from the irrelevant, such as recommendation systems, are becoming ubiquitous. Collaborative filtering (CF) models have rapidly established themselves as the *de facto* standard for many recommendation tasks where user-item preferences, scores or ratings, are available. In addition to such preferences, *side information* about users or items, for example other information that may be collected by an online service, is often available. Side-information has been particularly useful to address the *cold-start* problem that plagues collaborative filtering systems. Cold-start refers to a regime where scores for a set of users or items are unavailable or scarce. In some cases side information has also been shown to improve on the performance of collaborative filtering models in non-cold start (*warm-start*) data regimes [7, 20].

*Work done primarily while author was at the University of Toronto.

KDD'14, August 24–27, 2014, New York, NY, USA.

ACM 978-1-4503-2956-9/14/08 ...$15.00.
http://dx.doi.org/10.1145/2623330.2623663.

In this paper we are interested in the task of document recommendation using both user-item preferences and side information. The primary novelty of our work lies in leveraging a particular form of side information: the content of documents associated with users, which we call *user libraries*. A typical scenario that can be modelled in this way is scientific-paper recommendation for researchers; for example, Google Scholar recommends papers based on an individual's profile. A second scenario is paper-reviewer assignment, where each reviewer's previously published papers can be used to assess the match between their expertise and each submitted paper. Another relevant application domain is book recommendation, as online book merchants typically allow users to collect items in a virtual container akin to a personal library.[1] In each case a user's library, or side information, consists of documents which are not necessarily explicitly rated but nonetheless likely contain information about a user's preferences.

To model user-item scores as well as user and item content we introduce a novel directed graphical model. This model uses twin topic models, with shared topics, to model the side information. User and item topic proportions are then used as features to predict user-item scores with a collaborative filtering model. The collaborative filtering component allows the model to effectively make use of the side information with varying amounts of observed scores. We demonstrate empirically that the model outperforms several others on three datasets in both cold and warm-start data regimes. We further show that the model automatically learns to gradually trade off the use of side information in favor of information learned from user-item scores as the amount of user preference-data increases.

2. MODEL

Our approach to document recommendation relies on having: a) a set of observed user-item preferences ($\{r_{ud}\}$); b) contents of the items ($\{\mathbf{w}^s_d\}$); and c) the content of user-libraries ($\{\mathbf{w}^a_u\}$). The model's aim is to utilize the content in its user-item score predictions (which can then be used to recommend items to users). This contrasts with standard CF, which is not content-based.

Our content-based model is mediated by topics: we learn a shared topic model from the words of the documents and user libraries. We represent topic proportions with a normal

[1]For example., Amazon's Kindle and Kobo's tablets have an option for users to populate their libraries, while Barnes and Nobles' Nook gives users an *active shelf*.

distribution and realized topics $\mathbf{z}^u$ and $\mathbf{z}^d$ using the logistic normal [5]. User and item topic proportions offer a compact representation of user and item side information. We use these representations as covariates in a regression model to predict user-item preferences. The regression has two sets of parameters. The first are user-specific parameters on the item-topics covariates ($\boldsymbol{\gamma}_u$). The second are *compatibility parameters*, which are shared across users and items, and are based on the compatibility between the item topics and the topics of the user library ($\boldsymbol{\theta}$).

We now introduce the complete graphical model for this *collaborative score topic model (CSTM)*. A graphical representation of the model is given in Figure 1. The associated generative model is:

- Draw compatibility parameters: $\boldsymbol{\theta} \sim \mathcal{N}(\mathbf{0}, \lambda_\theta I)$
- Draw shared-user parameters: $\boldsymbol{\gamma}_0 \sim \mathcal{N}(\mathbf{0}, \lambda_{\gamma 0} I)$
- For each user $u = 1 \ldots U$:
  - Draw individual-user parameters: $\boldsymbol{\gamma}_u \sim \mathcal{N}(\mathbf{0}, \lambda_\gamma I)$
  - Draw user-topic proportions: $\mathbf{a}_u \sim \mathcal{N}(\mathbf{0}, \lambda_a I)$
- For each document $d = 1 \ldots D$:
  - Draw document-topic proportions: $\mathbf{s}_d \sim \mathcal{N}(\mathbf{0}, \lambda_s I)$
- For all of user u's user-library words, $n = 1 \ldots N$:[2]
  - Draw $z^a_{un} \sim \text{Mult}(\text{softmax}(\mathbf{a}_u))$
  - Draw $w^a_{un} \sim \text{Mult}(\beta_{z^a_{un}})$
- Repeat the above for all of document d's M words
- For each user-document pair (u, d), draw scores: $r_{ud} \sim \mathcal{N}((\mathbf{a}_u \otimes \mathbf{s}_d)^T \boldsymbol{\theta} + \mathbf{s}_d^T(\boldsymbol{\gamma}_0 + \boldsymbol{\gamma}_u), \sigma)$

where $\mathcal{N}(\mu, \sigma^2)$ represents a normal distribution with mean μ and variance σ^2, $\otimes$ stands for the elementwise product, $\text{softmax}(\mathbf{v}) = \frac{\exp(\mathbf{v})}{\sum_{k'} \exp(v_{k'})}$, and I is the identity matrix.

The specific parametrization of the preference regression is important. Our model is designed to perform well in both cold-start and warm-start data regimes. In cold-start settings the model needs the user's side information to predict user-item preferences. When the amount of observed preferences increases the model can gradually leverage that information, smoothly combining it with information gleaned from the side information to refine its model of missing preferences. To accomplish this, the regression model is separated in two parts: one part that exploits user side information ($(\mathbf{a}_u \otimes \mathbf{s}_d)^T \theta$) and another that does not ($\mathbf{s}_d^T(\boldsymbol{\gamma}_0 + \boldsymbol{\gamma}_u)$).

Item side information is incorporated by modulating the user information through an element-wise product. The weights $\boldsymbol{\theta}$ then serve several purposes: 1) they can act to amplify or reduce the effect of certain topics (for example diminish the influence of topics bearing little preference information); 2) they allow the model to more easily calibrate its output to the range of observed preference values; 3) changing the magnitude of $\boldsymbol{\theta}$ allows the model to control how much it uses the side information for preference prediction.

When user-item preferences are more abundant, the model can use them to learn a user-specific model, $\boldsymbol{\gamma}_u$, over item features. Note that these user-specific parameters are combined with a shared set of parameters, $\boldsymbol{\gamma}_0$, which allows for

[2]For simplicity, we'll assume in the notation that all user-libraries contain N words and all item documents contains M words.

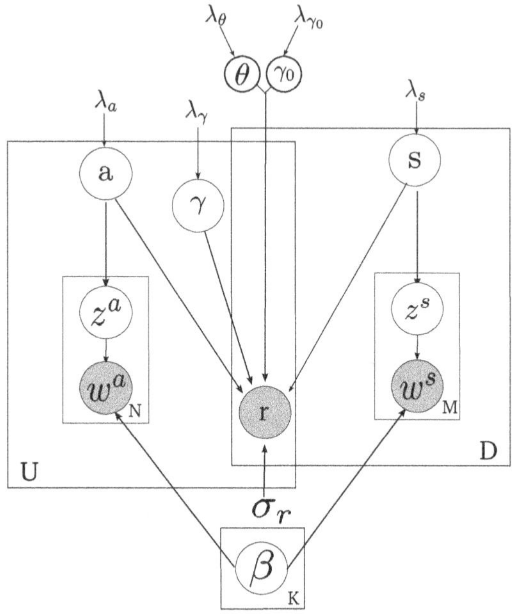

Figure 1: Graphical model for CSTM.

some transfer across users. The individual's $\boldsymbol{\gamma}_u$ can be used to increase that user's reliance on user-item preferences at the possible expense of item side information, as the joint magnitude of the $\boldsymbol{\gamma}$'s defines the weights associated with this part of the model.

Our model learns a single set of topics to model user and item content. Sharing topics ensures that the user and item representations ($\mathbf{a}_u$ and $\mathbf{s}_d$ $\forall u, \forall d$) are aligned and render their element-wise product meaningful.

2.1 The relationship between CSTM and standard models

Simplifying the proposed CSTM model in various ways produces other models that have been used for similar tasks. First, setting $\boldsymbol{\gamma}_0$ and $\boldsymbol{\gamma}_u$ $\forall u$ to zero and $\boldsymbol{\theta}$'s to a vector of ones we obtain a version of a language model (LM) first used by [12] for a similar task.[3] [12] and [7] used the LM in a preference prediction task and found its performance particularly strong in low-data regimes.

Further, setting $\boldsymbol{\theta}$ and $\boldsymbol{\gamma}_0$ to zero we obtain an individual user regression model (LR), which was shown to outperform purely collaborative filtering models in a similar preference prediction task with textual side information [7].

By modelling preferences as a combination of user features and item features, our model can also be seen as an instance of collaborative filtering. Collaborative filtering models have proven to be extremely powerful for missing preference prediction problems [15, 14, 3].

Finally, we have opted to represent topic proportions using a normal distribution instead of the more standard simplex representation used in latent Dirichlet allocation (LDA) [6]. This parametrization was proposed for correlated topic mod-

[3]One difference with our model is that since we represent users and items in topic space we do not have to handle normalization nor smoothing issues which are typical of word-space models.

els [5]; in our case we utilize the logistic normal due to its representational form, and not as a means of learning topic correlations.[4] Compared to a multinomial the normal distribution adds a level of flexibility that may be useful to better calibrate CSTM's preference predictions; the drawback is additional complexity in model inference.

3. LEARNING AND INFERENCE

For learning we use a version of the EM algorithm where we alternate between updates of the user-item specific variables ($\mathcal{H} = \{\{\boldsymbol{\gamma}_u\}, \{\mathbf{a}_u\}, \{\mathbf{s}_d\}, \{\mathbf{z}^a\}, \{\mathbf{z}^s\}\}$) in the E-step and updates of the parameters or shared variables ($\Theta = \{\boldsymbol{\gamma}_0, \boldsymbol{\theta}, \boldsymbol{\beta}\}$) in the M-step. The inference and learning procedures are similar to those proposed for nonconjugate LDA models in [20]. The general EM algorithm is shown in Algorithm 1.

E-Step

Inference in this model being intractable, we must rely on approximations when manipulating the posterior over the user-item specific varaibles. The log-posterior over user-item variables, given the fixed model parameters and the data, is

$$\begin{aligned}\mathcal{L} :=& -\frac{1}{2\lambda_a^2}\sum_u^U \mathbf{a}_u^T\mathbf{a}_u - \frac{1}{2\lambda_s^2}\sum_d^D \mathbf{s}_d^T\mathbf{s}_d - \frac{1}{2\lambda_\gamma^2}\sum_u^U \boldsymbol{\gamma}_u^T\boldsymbol{\gamma}_u \\ & - \frac{1}{2\sigma_r^2}\sum_{(u,d)\in\mathcal{O}}\left(r_{ud} - ((\mathbf{a}_u\otimes\mathbf{s}_d)^T\boldsymbol{\theta} + (\boldsymbol{\gamma}_0+\boldsymbol{\gamma}_u)^T\mathbf{s}_d)\right)^2 \\ & + \sum_{u,n}^{U,N}\log\frac{\exp(a_{uz^a_{un}})}{\sum_j \exp(a_{uj})} + \sum_{d,m}^{D,M}\log\frac{\exp(s_{dz^s_{dm}})}{\sum_j\exp(s_{dj})} \\ & + \sum_{u,n}^{U,N}\log\beta_{z^a_{un},w^a_{un}} + \sum_{d,m}^{D,M}\log\beta_{z^s_{dm},w^s_{dm}} - \log Z(\Theta) \qquad (1)\end{aligned}$$

where $\mathcal{O}$ stands for the set of observed preferences and $Z(\Theta)$ is an intractable normalizing constant of the posterior, in part because $\mathbf{a}_u$ and $\mathbf{s}_d$ cannot be analytically integrated out since they are not conjugate to the distribution over topic assignments [5].

We address this computational issue by employing variational approximate inference [11]. For the topic-proportion and regression variables $\{\mathbf{a}_u\}, \{\mathbf{s}_d\}, \{\boldsymbol{\gamma}_u\}$, we use a Dirac delta posterior parameterized by its mode $\{\widehat{\mathbf{a}}_u\}, \{\widehat{\mathbf{s}}_d\}, \{\widehat{\boldsymbol{\gamma}}_u\}$. For the topic-assignment variables $\{\mathbf{z}^a\}, \{\mathbf{z}^s\}$, we instead utilize a mean-field posterior. The full approximate posterior is thus:

$$\begin{aligned}q(\{\mathbf{a}_u\}, \{\mathbf{s}_d\}, \{\boldsymbol{\gamma}_u\}, \{\mathbf{z}^a_u\}, \{\mathbf{z}^s_d\}) = \left(\prod_u^U \delta_{\widehat{\boldsymbol{\gamma}}_u}(\boldsymbol{\gamma}_u)\right) \\ \left(\prod_u^U \delta_{\widehat{\mathbf{a}}_u}(\mathbf{a}_u)\prod_n^N \phi^a_{unz^a_u}\right)\left(\prod_d^D \delta_{\widehat{\mathbf{s}}_d}(\mathbf{s}_d)\prod_m^M \phi^s_{dmz^s_d}\right)\end{aligned}$$

where $\delta_\mu(x)$ is the delta function with mode μ and $\{\boldsymbol{\phi}^a_u\}$,$\{\boldsymbol{\phi}^s_d\}$ are the mean-field parameters (e.g., $\boldsymbol{\phi}^a_u$ is a matrix whose entries ϕ^a_{unj} are the probabilities that the nth word in user u's library belongs to topic j).

Approximate inference entails finding the variational parameters $\{\widehat{\mathbf{a}}_u\}, \{\widehat{\mathbf{s}}_d\}, \{\widehat{\boldsymbol{\gamma}}_u\}, \{\boldsymbol{\phi}^a_u\}, \{\boldsymbol{\phi}^s_d\}$ that minimize the KL-divergence with the true posterior

$$\begin{aligned}\mathrm{KL} :=& -\mathrm{E}_q\left[\mathcal{L}\right] - \mathrm{H}(q) \\ =& \frac{1}{2\lambda_a^2}\sum_u^U \widehat{\mathbf{a}}_u^T\widehat{\mathbf{a}}_u + \frac{1}{2\lambda_s^2}\sum_d^D \widehat{\mathbf{s}}_d^T\widehat{\mathbf{s}}_d + \frac{1}{2\lambda_\gamma^2}\sum_u^U \widehat{\boldsymbol{\gamma}}_u^T\widehat{\boldsymbol{\gamma}}_u \\ & + \frac{1}{2\sigma_r^2}\sum_{(u,d)\in\mathcal{O}}\left(r_{ud} - ((\widehat{\mathbf{a}}_u\otimes\widehat{\mathbf{s}}_d)^T\boldsymbol{\theta} + (\boldsymbol{\gamma}_0+\widehat{\boldsymbol{\gamma}}_u)^T\widehat{\mathbf{s}}_d)\right)^2 \\ & - \sum_{u,n,k}^{U,N,K}\phi^a_{unk}\left(\log\frac{\exp(\widehat{a}_{uk})}{\sum_j\exp(\widehat{a}_{uj})} + \log\beta_{k,w^a_{un}} - \log\phi^a_{unk}\right) \\ & - \sum_{d,m,k}^{D,M,K}\phi^s_{dmk}\left(\log\frac{\exp(\widehat{s}_{dk})}{\sum_j\exp(\widehat{s}_{dj})} + \log\beta_{k,w^s_{dm}} - \log\phi^s_{dmk}\right) \\ & + \text{constant}. \qquad (2)\end{aligned}$$

Our strategy is to perform one pass of coordinate descent, optimizing each set of variational parameters given the others.[5]

For $\widehat{\boldsymbol{\gamma}}_u$, we obtain a closed-form update by differentiating the above equation and setting the result to 0:

$$\begin{aligned}\widehat{\boldsymbol{\gamma}}_u =& \frac{1}{\sigma_r}\sum_{d\in\mathcal{O}(u)}(r_{ud} - (\widehat{\mathbf{s}}_d\otimes\widehat{\mathbf{a}}_u)^T\boldsymbol{\theta} - \widehat{\mathbf{s}}_d^T\boldsymbol{\gamma}_0)\widehat{\mathbf{s}}_d^T \\ & \left(\sum_{d\in\mathcal{O}(u)}\widehat{\mathbf{s}}_d\widehat{\mathbf{s}}_d^T/\sigma_r + \lambda_\gamma I/2\right)^{-1}\end{aligned}$$

where $\mathcal{O}(u)$ is the set of indices for documents that user u has rated. The $\{\widehat{\mathbf{a}}_u\}, \{\widehat{\mathbf{s}}_d\}$ parameters do not have closed-form solutions, hence we resort to optimization using conjugate gradient descent. We report the derivatives with respect to the posterior KL:

$$\begin{aligned}\frac{\partial\mathrm{KL}}{\partial\widehat{\mathbf{a}}_u} =& \lambda_a\mathbf{a}_u - \frac{1}{\sigma_r}\sum_{d\in\mathcal{O}(u)}(r_{ud} - \hat{r}_{ud})(\widehat{\mathbf{s}}_d\otimes\boldsymbol{\theta}) \\ & + N\frac{\exp(\widehat{\mathbf{a}}_u)}{\sum_j\exp(\widehat{a}_{uj})} - \sum_n \boldsymbol{\phi}^a_{un} \\ \frac{\partial\mathrm{KL}}{\partial\widehat{\mathbf{s}}_d} =& \lambda_s s_d - \frac{1}{\sigma_r}\sum_{u\in\mathcal{O}(d)}(r_{ud} - \hat{r}_{ud})(\widehat{\mathbf{a}}_u\otimes\boldsymbol{\theta} + \boldsymbol{\gamma}_0 + \widehat{\boldsymbol{\gamma}}_u) \\ & + M\frac{\exp(\widehat{\mathbf{s}}_d)}{\sum_j\exp(\widehat{s}_{dj})} - \sum_n \boldsymbol{\phi}^s_{dn}\end{aligned}$$

where, $\hat{r}_{ud} = (\widehat{\mathbf{a}}_u\otimes\widehat{\mathbf{s}}_d)^T\boldsymbol{\theta} + \widehat{\mathbf{s}}_d^T(\boldsymbol{\gamma}_0 + \widehat{\boldsymbol{\gamma}}_u)$.

For the mean-field parameters $\{\boldsymbol{\phi}^a_u\}$,$\{\boldsymbol{\phi}^s_d\}$, minimizing the KL while enforcing normalization leads to the following solutions:

$$\begin{aligned}\phi^a_{unk} &= \frac{\beta_{k,w^a_{un}}\exp(\widehat{a}_{uk})}{\sum_j\beta_{j,w^a_{un}}\exp(\widehat{a}_{uj})} \\ \phi^s_{dmk} &= \frac{\beta_{k,w^s_{dm}}\exp(\widehat{s}_{dk})}{\sum_j\beta_{j,w^s_{dm}}\exp(\widehat{s}_{dj})}.\end{aligned}$$

We update the variational parameters of all users and subsequently of all documents (see Algorithm 1).

[4]Since learning topic correlations has been found to improve on standard LDA, it is possible that learning the topic correlations could also improve our model.

[5]While we could cycle through all variational parameters until convergence before beginning the M-step, we've found a single pass of updates per E-step to work well in practice.

Algorithm 1 EM for the CSTM

Input: $\{\mathbf{w}_u^a\}, \{\mathbf{w}_d^s\}, \{r_{ud}\} \in \mathcal{O}$.

while Convergence criteria not met **do**
  # E-Step
  for all $d \in D$ **do**
    Update $\widehat{\mathbf{s}}_d, \boldsymbol{\phi}_d^s$
  end for
  for all $u = 1 \ldots U$ **do**
    Update $\widehat{\mathbf{a}}_u, \widehat{\gamma}_u, \boldsymbol{\phi}_u^a$
  end for

  # M-Step
  Update $\theta, \gamma_0, \boldsymbol{\beta}$
end while

M-Step

The M-step aims to maximize the expectation of the complete likelihood under the variational posterior (taking into account the prior over the parameters $\boldsymbol{\gamma}_0, \boldsymbol{\theta}$):

$$\begin{aligned}
&\mathrm{E}_q[\mathcal{L}] + \log p(\boldsymbol{\gamma}_0) + \log p(\boldsymbol{\theta}) = \\
&\quad \frac{1}{2\sigma_r^2} \sum_{(u,d)\in\mathcal{O}} \left(r_{ud} - ((\widehat{\mathbf{a}}_u \otimes \widehat{\mathbf{s}}_d)^T \boldsymbol{\theta} + (\boldsymbol{\gamma}_0 + \widehat{\boldsymbol{\gamma}}_u)^T \widehat{\mathbf{s}}_d) \right)^2 \\
&\quad + \sum_{u,n,k}^{U,N,K} \phi_{unk}^a \log \beta_{k,w_{un}^a} + \sum_{d,m,k}^{D,M,K} \phi_{dmk}^s \log \beta_{k,w_{dm}^s} \\
&\quad - \frac{1}{2\lambda_{\gamma_0}^2} \boldsymbol{\gamma}_0^T \boldsymbol{\gamma}_0 - \frac{1}{2\lambda_\theta^2} \boldsymbol{\theta}^T \boldsymbol{\theta} + \text{constant} . \qquad (3)
\end{aligned}$$

Setting derivatives to zero (and satisfying the β_{jw} parameters' normalization constraint), we obtain the following updates:

$$\begin{aligned}
\boldsymbol{\theta} &= -\frac{1}{\sigma_r} \Big(\sum_{(u,d)\in\mathcal{O}} (r_{ud} - \mathbf{s}_d^T(\boldsymbol{\gamma}_0 + \boldsymbol{\gamma}_u))(-s_d \otimes a_u)^T \Big) \\
&\quad \left(\sum_{(u,d)\in\mathcal{O}} (s_d \otimes a_u)^2/\sigma_r + \lambda_\theta I/2 \right)^{-1} \\
\gamma_0 &= -\frac{1}{\sigma_r} \Big(\sum_{(u,d)\in\mathcal{O}} (r_{ud} - (s_d \otimes a_u)^T \theta - (\gamma_u^T s_d)) s_d \Big) \\
&\quad \left(\sum_{(u,d)\in\mathcal{O}} \mathbf{s}_d \mathbf{s}_d^T / \sigma_r + \lambda_{\gamma_0} I/2 \right)^{-1} \\
\beta_{jk} &= \frac{\sum_{u,n} \phi_{unj}^a 1_{\{w_{un}^a = k\}} + \sum_{d,m} \phi_{dmj}^s 1_{\{w_{dm}^s = k\}}}{\sum_{k',u,n} \phi_{unj}^a 1_{\{w_{un}^a = k'\}} + \sum_{d,m} \phi_{dmj}^s 1_{\{w_{dm}^s = k'\}}} .
\end{aligned}$$

At test time, prediction of missing preferences is made using $\hat{r}_{ud}$, which is readily available. That is we use the expectation of the variational variables to form estimates of $\hat{r}$

4. RELATED WORK

Previous work includes a few models that have combined item-only topic and regression models for user-item preference prediction. We are not aware of any earlier work that develops a text-based model of a user, nor one that combines user and item side information as in CSTM.

In [2] the authors model several sources of side information including item textual side information using LDA. The topic assignment proportions of documents ($\sum_m z_{dm}^s/M \ \forall d$) are used as item features and combined multiplicatively with user-demographic and behavioural features. The result is linearly combined with the other sources of side information to generate preferences.

In [20] the authors also combine LDA with a regression model for the task of recommending scientific articles. Here the item topic proportions are used as a prior mean on normally-distributed item (regression) latent variables. User latent variables are also normally distributed from a zero-mean prior. A specific user-item score is then generated as the inner product of item and user latent variables: $r_{ud} = \mathbf{a}_u^T(\mathbf{s}_d + \boldsymbol{\epsilon}_d)$, where $\boldsymbol{\epsilon}_d$ is drawn from a zero-mean normal. The preference prediction model is the same as the one used in probabilistic matrix factorization [15]. [20] also report that on their data a modified version of their model which is analogous to the model of [2] performed worse. [16] proposed a similar model without ϵ and used CTM [5]. For a similar application, [18] propose an approach based on link-prediction in a user-item graph based on user and item similarity as well as user (binary) preferences.

The fact that we model an additional type of information (user textual side information) makes it difficult to directly compare our model to the ones above. In addition, the parametrization we use to predict preferences is very different from previous models. We initially experimented with a parametrization similar to [20], albeit modified to also model user side information, and found it did not perform as well as CSTM (see Section 5 for an experimental comparison).

Finally, [1] propose a collaborative filtering model with side information. Although the form of the side information is not amenable to using topic models, the authors utilize a combination of linear models to obtain good performance in both cold and warm-start data regimes.

5. EXPERIMENTS

We first describe the three datasets used for experiments. We then introduce a set of methods for empirical comparisons, ranging from pure CF methods to pure side information methods. We report three separate sets of experiments. In the first we focus on cold-start users and examine the effect of including user libraries. In the second we study how the methods perform on users with varying amounts of observed scores. Finally, we design a synthetic paper recommendation experiment and simulate incoming users in order to test the value of both the user library and the user-provided item scores.

5.1 Datasets

We evaluate the models using these three datasets:

Conf-1: A dataset from the 2010 edition of the neural information procession systems (NIPS) conference. Users are conference reviewers while documents are the set of papers submitted to the conference. The dataset consists of 48 users and 1251 documents. Each user's library consists of his/her own previously published papers. Users have an average of 31 documents which are concatenated into one. After some basic preprocessing the length of the joint vocabulary was slightly over 18,000 words. In this dataset all users have expressed scores (integers between 0 and 3) for an average of 143 papers (std. 14).

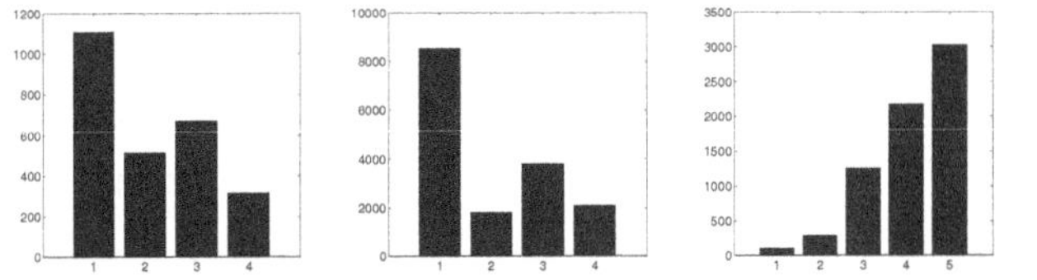

Figure 2: Number of each rating values for the three datasets, from left to right: Conf-1, Conf-2, Books-1.

	User side-info.	Document side-info.	Shared Params
LM-I	✓	✓	
LM-II	✓	✓	
LR		✓	
PMF			✓
CTR		✓	✓
CSTM	✓	✓	✓

Table 1: A comparison of the modelling capabilities of each model. "Shared Params" stands for models that share information in-between users and/or items (in other words those which use some form of CF).

Conf-2: A second dataset is from the international conference on machine learning (ICML 2012). This dataset consists of 433 users (reviewers) and 861 documents (submissions). Users have an average of 25 documents (std. 29) each and the length of the joint vocabulary is 16,201 words. In this dataset the average number of expressed scores per user is 48 (std. 25).

Books-1: The third dataset is from a large North American online book retailer.[6] It contains 316 users and 2601 documents (books). Users average 81 documents (std. 100). We removed very-infrequent and very-frequent words (those appearing in less than 1% or more than 95% of all documents). The resulting vocabulary contains 6,440 words. Users have a minimum of 15 expressed scores (mean 22, std. 6).

For each dataset the number of available preference values is shown in Figure 2. We note that the size of our datasets, and not the computational cost of learning in our model, limits our ability to scale up. In fact, learning CSTM on our largest dataset takes on the order of 2 hours on a modern machine using our *Matlab* implementation.

5.2 Competing models

We introduce several models which will serve as comparison to CSTM. Each model has particular characteristics (Table 1) which will help in understanding CSTM's performance.

Note that we use topic representations of documents for all competing models that use side information. Such representations were learned using a correlated topic model offline [5]. We re-use some of our previous notation to describe these models. Namely A_u and S_d are K-length vectors which designate a user's and a document's (topic) representation respectively.

[6]Kobo: `http://www.kobo.com`

Constant: Model predicts the average observed preferences for all missing preferences. Comparison to this baseline is useful to evaluate the value of learning.

LM-I: This model is meant to be a supervised version of the language model (LM[12]): $\hat{r}_{ud} := (A_u^T \theta_A)(S_d^T \theta_S)^T$ where, the parameters, θ_A, θ_S are $K \times F$ matrices. F is a hyper-parameter determined using a validation set (ranges from 5 to 30).

LM-II: Uses *isotonic regression* (see for example [4]) to calibrate the LM. The idea is to learn a regression model that satisfies the implicit ranking established by the LM:

$$\text{minimize}_{\hat{\mathbf{r}}_u, \forall u} \sum_{(ud)\in\mathcal{O}} (\hat{r}_{ud} - r_{ud})^2$$
$$\text{s.t. } \hat{r}_{ud} \leq \hat{r}_{u(d+1)}, \ \forall d.$$

where the constraints enforce a, user-specific, document ordering specified by the output of the LM. Once learned $\{\hat{r}\}$ are used as the model's predictions. To obtain predictions for an unobserved document we have found that using the average score given to the two (observed) documents ranked directly above and below the new document works well. The performed regression is user-specific and thus cannot be used for users with no observed preferences. For such users we simply re-use the learned parameters of its closest user (based on users' topic representations). A more principled approach, for example a collaborative one, lies outside of the scope of this paper.

LR: This is a user-specific regression model (see Section 2.1 for details) where predictions are given by: $r_{ud} = \gamma_u^T S_d$.

PMF [15]: PMF is a state-of-the-art collaborative filtering approach. PMF's generative model postulates that users and documents live in a low-dimensional latent space, represented respectively by U_u and V_d. A user-item preference is generated by taking the dot product between the corresponding user and item representations: $r_{ud} = U_u^T V_d$. The size of the latent space is determined using a validation set (range from 1 to 30).

Collaborative topic regression (CTR-CTM): CTR, is matrix factorization with document-content model introduced in [20]. CTR was briefly reviewed in Section 4. We use a slightly different version than the one introduced by its authors. Namely, we have replaced LDA by CTM. Also, in our application since all user-item scores are given we use a single variance value over scores (σ).

For *LM-I*, *LR* and *PMF* learning is performed using MAP by assuming a Gaussian likelihood model and zero-mean Gaussian priors over the model's parameters. The priors' variance are determined using a validation set.

We investigated a few other models which we do not fully describe here. Of note: instead of modeling user libraries as side-information we used the documents of user libraries as explicitly (highly-)scored items. We experimented with various scoring schemes but none lead to consistent improvements over baselines. We also experimented with replacing directed topic models with an supervised extension of an undirected topic model [13]. Further we experimented with replacing both topic models by (unconstrained) probabilistic matrix factorization [17]. However, in both cases, initial experiments were not as promising.

5.3 Results

To run CSTM on the above datasets we first concatenated user documents (for example a researcher's previously published papers) into a single document. To get user and item topic proportions we learned a CTM topic model [5] using the content of the items and then projected user documents into that (learned) topic space to obtain user topic proportions. We directly used these topics in LM-1,LM-II,LR. Further we used these topics as initialization in models which jointly learn topics and scores (CSTM,CTR). In all experiments we use 30 topics.

For training we create 5 folds from the available scores. Each fold is split into 80 percent observed and 20 percent test. We used the first fold to determine the hyper-parameters of the model. We report the average results over the five folds as well as the variance of this estimator.

We want to evaluate the performance of CSTM in settings where some users have no observed scores. The cold-start setting is of particular practical importance and one that should allow a good model to leverage the user's side-information. Accordingly, in our datasets we randomly selected one fourth of all users and removed all of their observed scores but kept their test scores. Further, for Conf-1 and Books-1, whose users have a more uniform number of ratings, we binned the remaining users (three quarters) uniformly into three *categories*. For Conf-1, users in each category had 15, 30 and 55 observed scores respectively. In each of the three categories 5 ratings per user were kept for validation. For Books-1 users in the first two categories had 8 and 10 scores while the scores of users in the last category were left untouched (5 scores per user were kept for validation). For Conf-2 since users are already naturally distributed into categories, we split the observed data into 25 percent validation and 75 percent train.

For the next two experiments, for each dataset, we train each model on all of the data but we divide our discussion into two parts. First we discuss cold-start users and after we examine the (other) user categories.

5.3.1 Cold-Start Data Regime

We first report the results for the completely cold-start data regime. For the cold-start users, it is difficult to calibrate the output of the model to the correct score range since only the users' side-information is available. The hope is that the models can use the side-information to get a better understanding of users preferences and discriminate between items of interest and other items. Accordingly we report results using *NDCG*. Normalized DCG (NDCG) is a well-established ranking measure, where a value of 1 indicates a perfect ranking and 0 a reverse-ordered perfect ranking [10]. NDCG@T considers exclusively the top T items. Table 2 reports results for the three datasets using NDCG@5 (note that other values of NDCG gave similar results). We can only report results for the methods that have the ability to predict scores for cold-start users. PMF, LR and CTR do not use any user side-information and hence do not have that ability.

In this challenging setting CSTM significantly outperforms the other methods. Further we see that methods using side-information typically outperform the constant baseline. This demonstrates that the useful information about user preferences can be leveraged from the user libraries. Further, the good performance of CSTM in this setting shows that the model is able to leverage that information.

	Conf-1	Conf-2	Books-1
Constant	$0.4378 \pm 2e^{-3}$	$0.6386 \pm 4e^{-5}$	$0.6882 \pm 5e^{-4}$
LM-I	$0.4684 \pm 2e^{-3}$	$0.7903 \pm 4e^{-5}$	$0.6873 \pm 1e^{-3}$
LM-II	$0.4696 \pm 3e^{-4}$	$0.7752 \pm 1e^{-4}$	$0.6926 \pm 6e^{-4}$
CSTM	$\mathbf{0.4846 \pm 1}e^{-3}$	$\mathbf{0.8096 \pm 1}e^{-4}$	$\mathbf{0.7360 \pm 2}e^{-4}$

Table 2: Comparisons between CSTM and competitors for cold-start users using NDCG@5.

5.3.2 Warm-start data regimes

The goal of CSTM is to perform well across different data regimes. In the previous section we examined models' performance on cold start users, we now focus on users with observed scores. For each dataset we report the performance of the various methods for each user category. For Conf-2 we separated users into roughly equal sized bins according to their number of observed scores. Results for our three datasets are provided in Figure 3. First we note that as the number of observed scores is increased the performance of the different methods also increases. CSTM outperforms all other methods on lower data-regimes. On users with more observed scores CSTM is competitive with both CTR-CTM and LR.

We notice that overall in this task, and even when many observed preferences are available, PMF is not competitive with most of the methods that have access to the side information. This highlights the value of content side-information on both user and item sides. This is further made clear by the relatively strong performance of both LM-I and LM-II.

Overall user libraries do not seem to help as much on the Books-1 dataset. There are several explanations for this. First, in Books-1 the distribution over scores is very skewed toward high scores. Thus a constant baseline does quite well. Further, bag-of-words representations are particularly well suited for academic papers where the presence (absence) of specific words are very good indications of the documents field and hence it's targeted audience. However, in (non-technical) books user preferences also rely on other aspects such as the document's prose which is harder to capture with a bag-of-words assumption.

5.3.3 Document Recommendations

We explore a different scenario which is meant to be closer to what would happen when a model is deployed in a complete recommendation system, for example to guide users to posters of interest in an academic conference. Specifically, we evaluate the performance of CTR and CSTM as new users arrive into the system and gradually provide information about themselves. We postulate that users first provide the system with their library. Then users gradually express their preferences for certain (user-chosen) items.

We trained CTR-CTM and CSTM on all but 50 randomly-chosen Conf-2 users with enough observed preferences (min. 15). We then simulated these users entering the system one by one. Since this experiment is about recommendations we report the results using NDCG.[7] Figure 4 presents the performance of CSTM and CTR-CTM as a function of the amount of data available in the system. When a user first

[7]In the absence of a recommendation objective and constraints it is reasonable to recommend the top-ranked items to each user

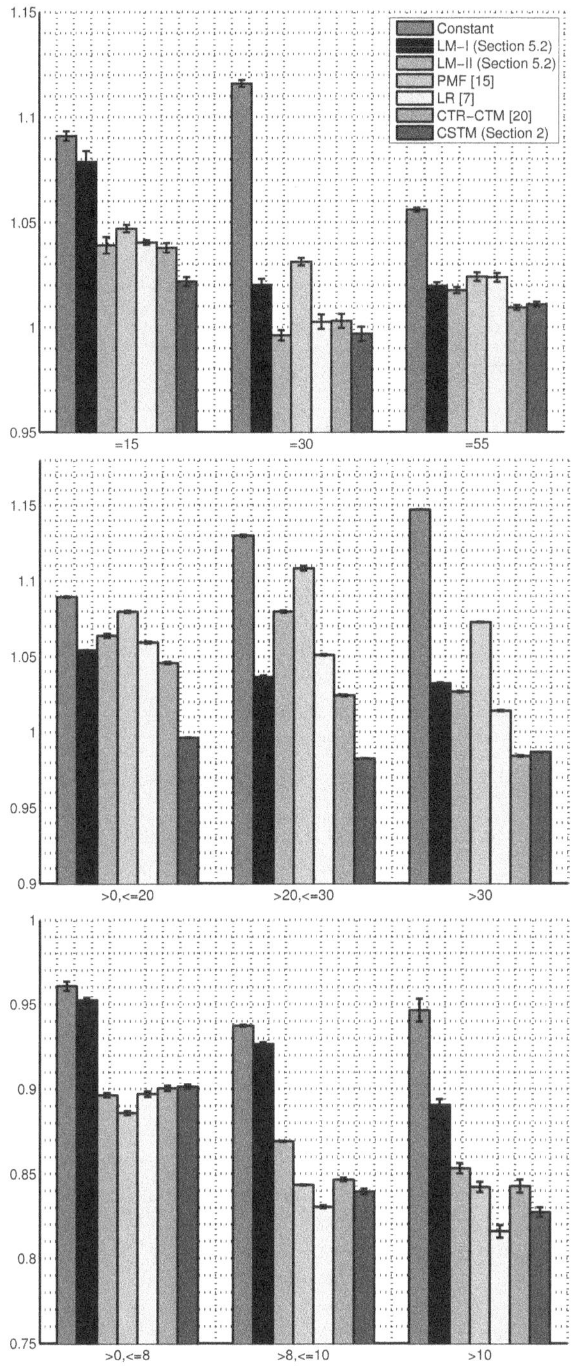

Figure 3: Test RMSE of the different methods across Conf-1, Conf-2, Books-1. In each figure each group of bars reports results for different subsets of users. Each user is part of a single subset. The x-axis indicates the number of training observations per users of a given subset. The subsets correspond to users with the least observed preferences (left) to the most (right). Figures better seen in color (however the ordering in the legends corresponds to the ordering of the bars in each group).

enters the system no data is available about her (indicated by "0" in the figure). The methods revert to using a constant predictor which predicts the mean of the previously observed scores across all users. Once a user provides a library (Lib.) we see that CSTM's performance increases very significantly. CTR cannot leverage that side information. Then once users provide scores, the performance of both methods increases and the performance of CTR eventually reaches the performance of CSTM.

Figure 4 demonstrates the advantage of having access to user side-information, namely, the system can quickly give good recommendations to new users. Further, in absolute terms the system performs relatively well without having access to any scores. It is also interesting to note that, in this experiment, as far as NDCG goes, the performance of CSTM only modestly improves as the number observed scores increases. This may be a consequence of our fairly primitive *online* learning procedure. As far as modelling goes this experiment is also a demonstration that our model of user libraries is effective at extracting features ($\mathbf{a}_u$ for all users) indicative of preferences and that the regression model then successfully combines the user and item side information.

As a practical experiment we deployed a system based on CSTM to a subset of the attendees of the most recent NIPS conference (NIPS-2013). NIPS is one of the most important machine learning conferences. We had previously gathered a dataset containing a few hundred of attendees' libraries and ratings. We also obtained text representations of the conference papers. Both sources of information were used to train CSTM. We used 20% of the observed ratings as a validation set used to determine the value of the hyper-parameters. Using the trained model we then generated predictions for each user using the same conditional inference procedure as above. We used each user's highest (predicted) ratings as their personalized recommendations. Furthermore, since NIPS 2013 had four daily poster sessions we allowed users to obtain independent paper recommendations for each day. A screen capture of the online user interface is provided in Figure 5.

We did not have a formal method of evaluating the quality or usefulness of the system beyond using the metrics we discussed in previous sections. Anecdotally, over 200 NIPS attendees accessed their recommendations and user feedback was almost unanimously positive. Furthermore we can explore the learned representations of the model as a way to assess its quality. Figure 6, shows the two-dimensional embeddings of user representations ($\mathbf{a}_u$) obtained using a popular (non-linear) dimensionality reduction technique for visualizing high-dimensional data [19]. We notice that, even in this low-dimensional representation, users cluster into different groups according to their areas of research. The model has discovered these groups using the similarities in user libraries and in their rating profiles. Similar results were obtained for paper representations.

6. CONCLUSION & FUTURE WORK

We have introduced a novel graphical model to leverage user libraries for preference prediction tasks. We showed experimentally that CSTM overall outperforms competing methods and can leverage the information of other users and of user libraries to perform particularly well in cold-start regimes. We also explored a paper recommendation

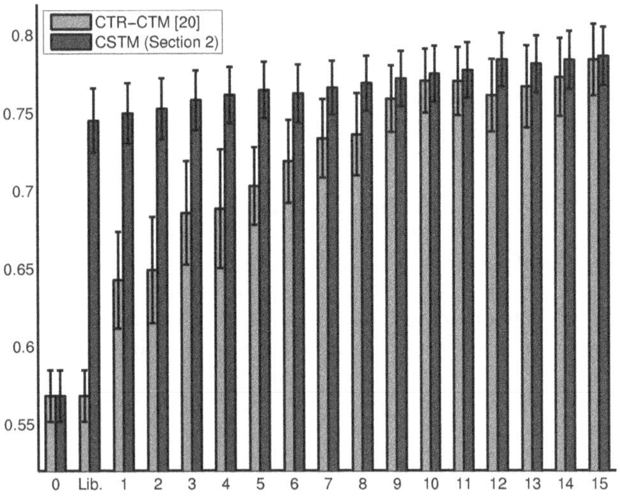

Figure 4: Comparison of CSTM and CTR's NDCG@10 performance on new users as a function of the amount of data provided by users. Without any user data (0) methods revert to a constant predictor. Then CSTM takes advantage of user libraries (Lib.). Finally, scores are added one by one. Error bars indicate the variance across users.

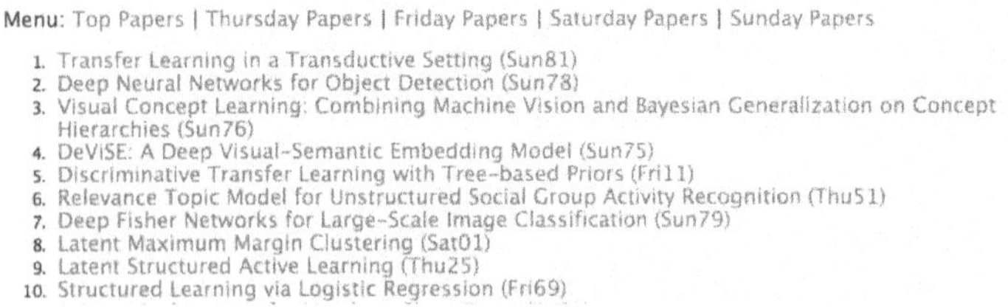

Figure 5: User interface of the NIPS-13 poster recommendations. The menu on the top of the page allows users of the system to obtain recommendations for one of the four daily poster sessions. Below the menu are the top-10 recommendations for a given user. Each recommendation links to the paper and contains the paper title and its unique conference identifier.

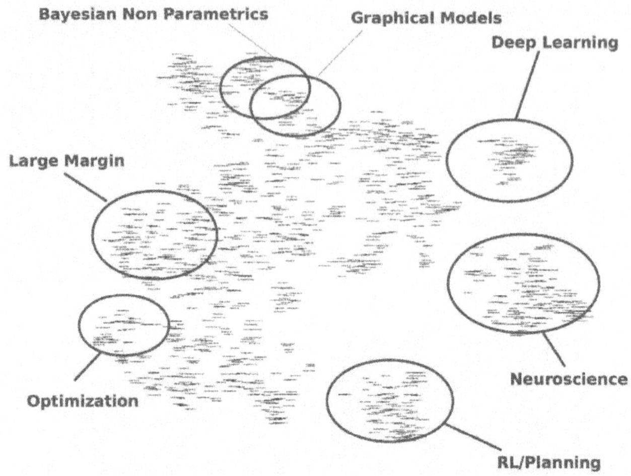

Figure 6: We used t-SNE to obtain a two-dimensional representation of users. Each user is denoted using his or her email address. We note that users cluster according to easily identifiable subject areas some of which we have highlighted. A fully vectorized map is available at `http://www.cs.toronto.edu/~lcharlin/tmp/n13_tsne.pdf`.

task and demonstrated the benefits of having access to user libraries.

Future work offers several possibilities. On one side we could refine the inference procedure used in training our model such as by using a fully variational approach or by leveraging the latest inference procedures of CTM [21]. Furthermore, it would also be straightforward to implement stochastic variational inference [9] for example by sampling users and updating relevant document and global parameters using a natural gradient. Stochastic inference is likely to be especially useful as we scale CSTM to very large datasets. On the other side we are examining extensions that enable the modelling of other types of side-information, such as book genres or academic-paper subject areas.

Another aspect of practical importance is that once we move to online recommendation, models must also be able to adapt to new data, including novel items and users, updates to user libraries, and new user-item scores. In the poster recommendations experiment we have seen that a simple *conditional inference* method works relatively well for novel users. However, one would also like to use the information from novel users to learn better representations of all users. In other words, we would need a mechanism which updates model parameters once a sufficient amount of new data is available. Furthermore, we could refine such a method *inter alia* to allow the system to adapt to the evolving preferences of users over time. For example, [1] propose a decaying mechanism to emphasize more recent scores over older ones. A similar mechanism could be use to weight the different documents in a user's library (for example based on date of publication for research papers or purchase date for books).

There is also the question of other potential applications for which CSTM could be useful. In addition to modelling text, topic models have also been shown to model images [8]. CSTM could then be used as an image recommendation tool (for example to photographers). In that case, much like for the books of the Books-1 dataset, it remains to be seen whether topic models can capture features of images which are indicative of preferences.

Acknowledgments: We thank the NIPS'10 and ICML'12 program chairs for allowing us to use their data as well as Kobo for providing us with a useful dataset and support. We also acknowledge the support of CIFAR and NSERC.

7. REFERENCES

[1] D. Agarwal and B.-C. Chen. Regression-based latent factor models. In *Proceedings of the 15th ACM SIGKDD international conference on Knowledge discovery and data mining*, KDD '09, pages 19–28, New York, NY, USA, 2009. ACM.

[2] D. Agarwal and B.-C. Chen. flda: matrix factorization through latent dirichlet allocation. In *Proceedings of the third ACM international conference on Web search and data mining*, WSDM '10, pages 91–100, New York, NY, USA, 2010. ACM.

[3] R. M. Bell and Y. Koren. Lessons from the netflix prize challenge. *SIGKDD Explorations*, 9(2):75–79, 2007.

[4] M. J. Best and N. Chakravarti. Active set algorithms for isotonic regression; a unifying framework. *Math. Program.*, 47:425–439, 1990.

[5] D. M. Blei and J. D. Lafferty. A correlated topic model of science. *AAS*, 1(1):17–35, 2007.

[6] D. M. Blei, A. Y. Ng, M. I. Jordan, and J. Lafferty. Latent Dirichlet allocation. *Journal of Machine Learning Research*, 3:993–1022, 2003.

[7] L. Charlin, R. Zemel, and C. Boutilier. A framework for optimizing paper matching. In *Proceedings of the Proceedings of the Twenty-Seventh Conference Annual Conference on Uncertainty in Artificial Intelligence (UAI-11)*, pages 86–95, Corvallis, Oregon, 2011. AUAI Press.

[8] P. P. E. Bart, M. Welling. Unsupervised organization of image collections: Taxonomies and beyond. *IEEE Transactions of Pattern Analysis and Machine Intelligence*, 2011.

[9] M. D. Hoffman, D. M. Blei, C. Wang, and J. Paisley. Stochastic variational inference. *J. Mach. Learn. Res.*, 14(1):1303–1347, May 2013.

[10] K. Järvelin and J. Kekäläinen. Ir evaluation methods for retrieving highly relevant documents. In *Proceedings of the 23rd annual international ACM SIGIR conference on Research and development in information retrieval*, SIGIR '00, pages 41–48, New York, NY, USA, 2000. ACM.

[11] M. I. Jordan, Z. Ghahramani, T. S. Jaakkola, and L. K. Saul. An introduction to variational methods for graphical models. *Mach. Learn.*, 37(2):183–233, Nov. 1999.

[12] D. M. Mimno and A. McCallum. Expertise modeling for matching papers with reviewers. In P. Berkhin, R. Caruana, and X. Wu, editors, *Proceedings of the 13th ACM SIGKDD International Conference on Knowledge Discovery and Data Mining (KDD)*, pages 500–509, San Jose, California, 2007. ACM.

[13] R. Salakhutdinov and G. Hinton. Replicated softmax: an undirected topic model. In Y. Bengio, D. Schuurmans, J. Lafferty, C. K. I. Williams, and A. Culotta, editors, *Advances in Neural Information Processing Systems 22 (NIPS)*, pages 1607–1614. 2009.

[14] R. Salakhutdinov and A. Mnih. Bayesian probabilistic matrix factorization using Markov chain Monte Carlo. In *Proceedings of the 25th International Conference on Machine Learning (ICML)*, volume 25, pages 880–887, Helsinki, Finland, 2008.

[15] R. Salakhutdinov and A. Mnih. Probabilistic matrix factorization. In J. Platt, D. Koller, Y. Singer, and S. Roweis, editors, *Advances in Neural Information Processing Systems 20 (NIPS)*, pages 1257–1264. MIT Press, Cambridge, MA, 2008.

[16] H. Shan and A. Banerjee. Generalized probabilistic matrix factorizations for collaborative filtering. In *Proceedings of the 2010 IEEE International Conference on Data Mining*, ICDM '10, pages 1025–1030, Washington, DC, USA, 2010. IEEE Computer Society.

[17] A. P. Singh and G. J. Gordon. Relational learning via collective matrix factorization. In *Proceedings of the 14th ACM SIGKDD International Conference on Knowledge Discovery and Data Mining*, KDD '08, pages 650–658, New York, NY, USA, 2008. ACM.

[18] G. Tian and L. Jing. Recommending scientific articles using bi-relational graph-based iterative rwr. In *Proceedings of the 7th ACM Conference on Recommender Systems*, RecSys '13, 2013.

[19] L. van der Maaten and G. Hinton. Visualizing Data using t-SNE. *Journal of Machine Learning Research*, 9:2579–2605, Nov. 2008.

[20] C. Wang and D. M. Blei. Collaborative topic modeling for recommending scientific articles. In *Proceedings of the 17th ACM SIGKDD international conference on Knowledge discovery and data mining*, KDD '11, pages 448–456, New York, NY, USA, 2011. ACM.

[21] C. Wang and D. M. Blei. Variational inference in nonconjugate models. *Journal of Machine Learning Research*, 14(1):1005–1031, Apr. 2013.

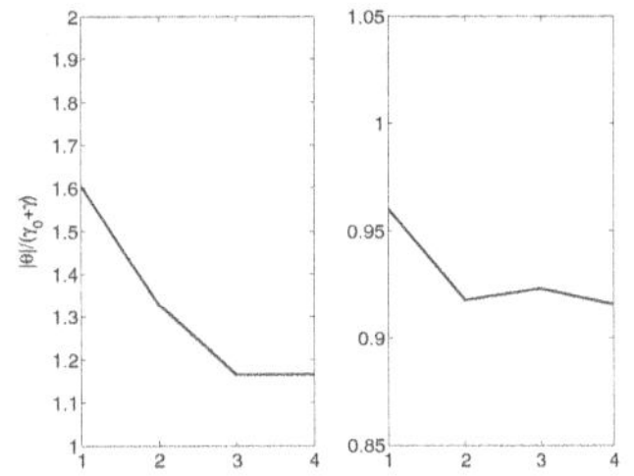

Figure 7: Averaged norm of parameters under users with varying number of scores (left Conf-1, right Conf-2).

	Conf-2
Constant	$0.8950 \pm 5e^{-4}$
LM-I	$0.9301 \pm 2e^{-4}$
LM-II	$0.9308 \pm 4e^{-4}$
PMF	$0.9100 \pm 3e^{-4}$
LR	$0.9288 \pm 2e^{-4}$
CTR	$0.9375 \pm 3e^{-4}$
CSTM	$\mathbf{0.9409 \pm 3}e^{-4}$

Table 3: For the un-modified Conf-2 dataset, comparisons between CSTM and competitors for cold-start users using NDCG@5.

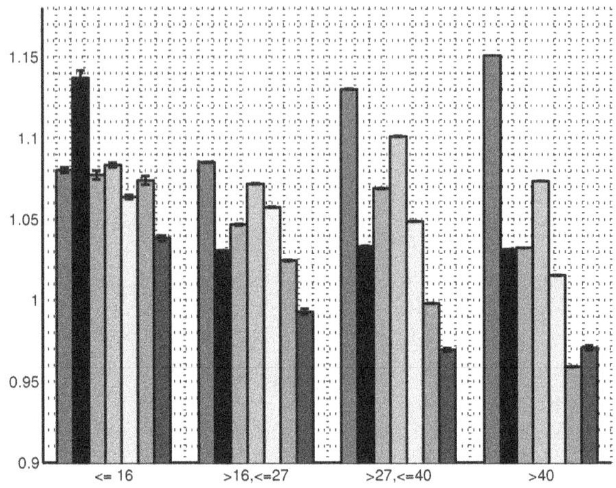

Figure 8: RMSE results on the un-modified Conf-2 dataset.

APPENDIX

A. ADDITIONAL RESULTS

A.1 Model's Tradeoff

In Section 2 we motivated the specific parametrization of CSTM by its ability to trade off the influence of the user library side information versus that of the user-item scores. Here we show that learning in our model performs as expected. Figure 7 reports the relative norm of $\boldsymbol{\theta}$ versus $(\boldsymbol{\gamma}_0 + \boldsymbol{\gamma})$ as a function of the number of observed scores. As hypothesized as the number of scores increases the relative weight of the user library side information decreases.

A.2 Variations of CSTM

We also experimented with variations of CSTM to better understand the roles played by the different aspects of the model and its training.

CSTM fixed topics (CSTM-FT): This model uses the exact preference regression model used by CSTM but it uses fixed topic user and document topic representations. That is it predicts preferences with: $r_{ud} = (\mathbf{a}_u \otimes \mathbf{s}_d)\theta^T + \mathbf{s}_d(\boldsymbol{\gamma}_0 + \boldsymbol{\gamma})^T$ where A and S are previously learned offline.

CSTM no user side information (CSTM-NUSI): To evaluate the gain of using user side information we experimented with a version of our model that does not model user side information (i.e., as if a user did not have any documents). Specifically, in this model $a_u \equiv \mathbf{0}\ \forall u$.

We provide some results comparing CSTM with its variations in table 4.

A.3 Results on original Conf-2 dataset

In Figure 8 and Table 3 we provide comparisons of the different methods on the original version of Conf-2.

	Conf-1	Books-1
CSTM-NUSI	$0.4941 \pm 4e^{-4}$	$0.7997 \pm 8e^{-5}$
CSTM-FT	$0.4984 \pm 2e^{-4}$	$0.8026 \pm 8e^{-5}$
CSTM	$\mathbf{0.5016 \pm 2}e^{-4}$	$\mathbf{0.8037} \pm 2e^{-5}$

	Conf-2	Conf-2(un-modified)
CSTM-NUSI	$0.7765 \pm 9e^{-5}$	$0.8048 \pm 9e^{-4}$
CSTM-FT	$0.8036 \pm 5e^{-5}$	$0.8066 \pm 8e^{-5}$
CSTM	$\mathbf{0.8217 \pm 2e^{-5}}$	$\mathbf{0.8322 \pm 2}e^{-4}$

Table 4: Comparisons between CSTM and two variations. Results report NDCG@5 over all users.

Topic-Factorized Ideal Point Estimation Model for Legislative Voting Network*

Yupeng Gu
Northeastern University
Boston, MA
ypgu@ccs.neu.edu

Yizhou Sun
Northeastern University
Boston, MA
yzsun@ccs.neu.edu

Ning Jiang
University of Illinois at Urbana-Champaign
Urbana, IL
jiang20@illinois.edu

Bingyu Wang
Northeastern University
Boston, MA
wang.bin@husky.neu.edu

Ting Chen
Northeastern University
Boston, MA
tingchen@ccs.neu.edu

ABSTRACT

Ideal point estimation that estimates legislators' ideological positions and understands their voting behavior has attracted studies from political science and computer science. Typically, a legislator is assigned a global ideal point based on her voting or other social behavior. However, it is quite normal that people may have different positions on different policy dimensions. For example, some people may be more liberal on economic issues while more conservative on cultural issues.

In this paper, we propose a novel topic-factorized ideal point estimation model for a legislative voting network in a unified framework. First, we model the ideal points of legislators and bills for each topic instead of assigning them to a global one. Second, the generation of topics are guided by the voting matrix in addition to the text information contained in bills. A unified model that combines voting behavior modeling and topic modeling is presented, and an iterative learning algorithm is proposed to learn the topics of bills as well as the topic-factorized ideal points of legislators and bills. By comparing with the state-of-the-art ideal point estimation models, our method has a much better explanation power in terms of held-out log-likelihood and other measures. Besides, case studies show that the topic-factorized ideal points coincide with human intuition. Finally, we illustrate how to use these topic-factorized ideal points to predict voting results for unseen bills.

Keywords

Ideal point estimation, legislative voting network, topic model, voting prediction

*The work was supported in part by the Yahoo ACE (Academic Career Enhancement) Award funding. The views and conclusions contained in this paper are those of the authors and should not be interpreted as representing any funding agencies.

KDD'14, August 24–27, 2014, New York, NY, USA.
Copyright 2014 ACM 978-1-4503-2956-9/14/08 $15.00.
http://dx.doi.org/10.1145/2623330.2623700 .

1. INTRODUCTION

Estimating voters' ideological positions is an important task, which can help us understand and predict their voting or other social behavior. For example, once we know a voter is more conservative, we can expect she is more likely to vote for republican candidates or vote against the bills that are very liberal. Ideal point estimation that estimates legislators' ideological positions has attracted studies from political science [4, 5, 8, 20] and computer science [6, 7], thanks to the widely available online voting records and other social behavior embedded in networks.

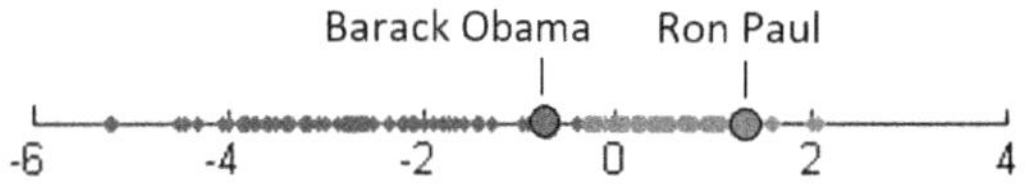

Figure 1: Illustration of standard one-dimensional ideal point model for sample Democrats (blue) and Republicans (red). B. Obama and R. Paul are highlighted.

In standard one-dimensional ideal point estimation models, a legislator is usually assigned a global ideal point based on her legislative voting records [4]. For example, in Fig. 1 we can see the ideal points of B. Obama and R. Paul according to their voting records when they were senator and house representative, respectively. From the figure, it is quite clear that Obama is liberal and Paul is conservative. The figure can also help to explain why Obama garnered support from some moderate republicans and conservatives during the 2008 election, and why Paul is regarded as one of the most conservative republicans in congress [17].

However, one-dimensional ideal point could be rather coarse to capture the whole picture of ideology, as it is quite normal that people may have different positions on different policy dimensions. For example, some people may be more liberal on economic issues while more conservative on cultural issues. From Fig. 2 we can see that the ideal points of Obama and Paul are rather different across a wide range of topics. In particular, the figure confirms the notion that Paul is the most conservative on the role of government on economy but not on social issues and foreign policy matters, especially as an opponent of war. Our goal of this paper is to estimate the ideal points of US House representatives and Senators in different topics, based on the roll call voting data from the 101st congress until now.

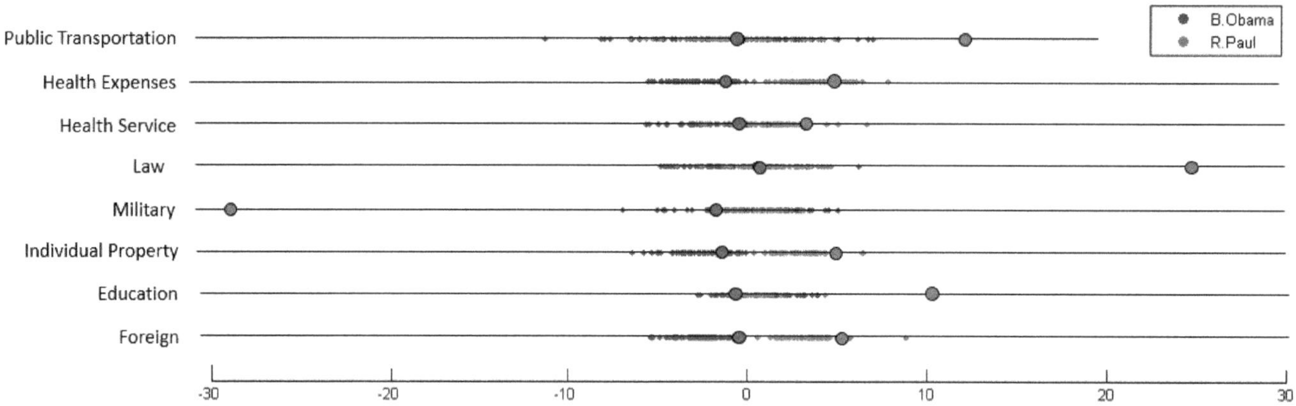

Figure 2: Illustration of topic-factorized ideal point model for sample Democrats (blue) and Republicans (red). B. Obama and R. Paul are highlighted.

A recent study [7] has shown that by incorporating the separately predetermined topic information of bills and modeling issue-adjusted ideal point for voters, the model has a much higher explanation power of the voting behavior. However, in this study, the topics are learned in advance, topic modeling and voting behavior modeling are two separate steps; and there is only a relative ideal point score in each topic. In this paper, we propose a novel topic-factorized ideal point estimation model by utilizing the legislative voting network data that contains (1) voting records between voters and bills, and (2) text information of the bills. The key idea is, on one hand, using topic and text information from the topic model can help enhance the voting link modeling; on the other hand, using voting data can help us gain a better understanding about the latent topics, therefore build a better latent topic distribution over text. Our approach enhances the issue-adjusted ideal point model in two-folds. First, we model the ideal point of voters and bills for each topic such that they can be comparable in different topic dimensions. Second, the generation of topics are guided by the voting matrix in addition to the text information in bills. A unified probabilistic model that combines voting behavior modeling and topic modeling is proposed. An iterative learning algorithm is proposed to learn the topics as well as the topic-factorized ideal points alternatively.

By comparing with the state-of-the-art ideal point models, our method has a much better explanation power in terms of held-out predictive accuracy. Besides, case studies show that the topic-factorized ideal points coincide with human intuition. Finally, we illustrate how to use these topic-factorized ideal points to make voting predictions for unseen bills.

The main contributions of our method can be summarized below.

- We propose a novel topic-factorized ideal point model based on text-rich legislative voting network, which simultaneously identifies the topics as well as the ideal points of voters and bills in a wide range of topics.
- An efficient algorithm is proposed to learn the model, which alternatively updates the topic distribution of each bill and ideal points for each voter and bill.
- The experiments are preformed on real-world US legislative roll call data. The results show that our model is superior to the state-of-the-art methods in several aspects.

The rest of this paper is organized as follows. In Section 2 we introduce the preliminaries and define the problem. In Section 3 we discuss our model in detail and introduce the learning algorithm. In Section 4 we show the experimental results. We summarize the related work in Section 5 and draw a conclusion of the paper in Section 6.

2. PRELIMINARY AND PROBLEM DEFINITION

In this section, we introduce the legislative voting network in our problem setting, the preliminary related to ideal point model (IPM), and define our problem formally.

2.1 Legislative Voting Network

A text-rich legislative voting network can be extracted from roll call voting data, which is comprised of three different types of objects: voters, bills, and words. Voters (u) and bills(d) are linked together according to the voting behavior, and the weight of links (v_{ud}) is either 1 ("YEA") or -1 ("NAY"). Bills and words are linked together if the word appears in the bill, and the weight is determined by the number of occurrences of the word. An example of such legislative voting network that is extracted from US roll call voting data is shown in Fig. 3. It is worth noting that the value of v_{ud} between user u and bill d can also be 0, which means the link between u and d is missing. We do not model missing links in this paper.

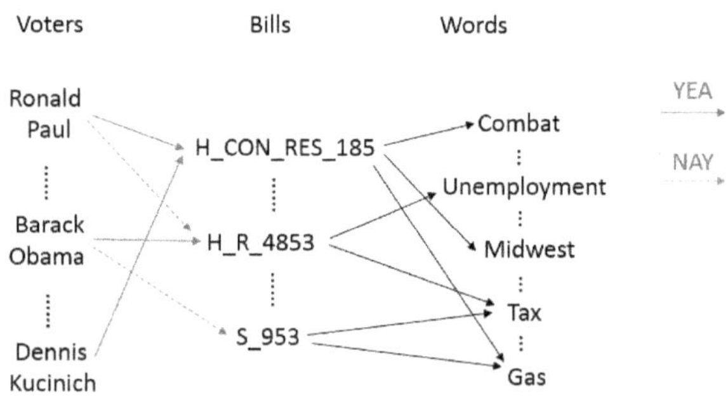

Figure 3: An illustration of legislative voting network.

2.2 Ideal Point Models

The goal of ideal point model is to estimate the policy positions of voters and bills that can explain the voting or other social behavior. Poole and Rosenthal [18] proposed a seminal one-dimensional ideal point model for understanding legislative behavior. In [20], Poole and Rosenthal studied a similar model in a higher-dimensional setting. Alternative higher-dimensional ideal point models have been developed by Clinton et al. [4], Heckman and Snyder [8], and Londregan [12]. We first briefly introduce one-dimensional and higher-dimensional ideal point models, then the closely-related issue-adjusted ideal point model by Blei and Gerrish [7] that utilized text information in bills to make topics as explicit dimensions.

One-dimensional ideal point model.

In one-dimensional ideal point model, each legislator u is associated with an ideal point x_u, which represents her position. Each bill d has a polarity a_d and a popularity offset b_d as well. The probability of voting "YEA" is given by $p(v_{ud} = 1) = \sigma(x_u \cdot a_d + b_d)$, where σ denotes the logistic or probit function. All the parameters are estimated by maximizing the likelihood of observing the voting matrix under this model.

Higher-dimensional ideal point model.

Due to the limitation that one-dimensional ideal point cannot capture the different behavior of legislators for different topics, some researches extend the above model to higher dimensions. For example, Clinton et al. [4] proposed to map each voter and bill into a K-dimensional space, and model the probability of a voter voting "YEA" for a bill with the probability $\sigma(\mathbf{x}_u \cdot \mathbf{a}_d + b_d)$, where $\mathbf{x}_u$ and $\mathbf{a}_d$ are in the space of $\mathbb{R}^K$ and " $\cdot$ " denotes dot product.

Issue-adjusted ideal point model.

The latent space derived in the higher-dimensional ideal point model, however, is very difficult to interpret. Thus, an issue-adjusted ideal point model [7] is proposed very recently to estimate the adjusted ideal points in some separately predetermined issues (topics). In this model, every legislator u has an adjusted issue preference vector $\mathbf{z}_u \in \mathbb{R}^K$ (K is the number of topics) beyond the global ideal point x_u. The probability of voting "YEA" is determined by her global ideal point as well as the adjusted ideal point in each topic, weighted by the conditional expectation of a bill's topic distribution: $p(v_{ud} = 1) = \sigma((\mathbf{z}_u^T \mathbb{E}[\boldsymbol{\theta}_d | \mathbf{w}_d] + x_u) a_d + b_d)$, where $\boldsymbol{\theta}_d$ is the topic distribution of a bill d and $\mathbf{w}_d$ is the observed word vector for bill d.

In this model, however, the topics are predetermined, and there is no impact from voting records which in fact can effectively enhance the topic generation. Besides, since ideal points for all topics are adjusted based on the same global point, the model puts constraints on how a voter can change her positions in different topics. We thus propose a new ideal point model that can overcome the two limitations, and the problem is defined formally in the following.

2.3 Problem Definition

Given a legislative voting network G, which contains N_U voters, N_D bills and N_W terms, and the number K of topics, our goal is to learn the topic models ($\boldsymbol{\Theta} = \{\boldsymbol{\theta}_d\}_{d=1}^{N_D}$, $\boldsymbol{\beta} = \{\beta_k\}_{k=1}^{K}$) and estimate topic-factorized ideal points for voters ($\mathbf{X} = \{x_{uk}\}$) and bills ($\mathbf{A} = \{a_{dk}\}$), which can best explain the observed network. Here, we use x_{uk} to denote the ideal point of voter u in topic k, and a_{dk} to denote the ideal point of bill d in topic k.

The detailed topic-factorized ideal point model that can solve this problem is introduced in next section, and all notations used can be found in Table 1.

Table 1: Table of Notation

Symbol	Description
N_U	Total number of voters
N_D	Total number of bills
N_W	Total number of terms
N_V	Total number of votes
K	Total number of topics
$\boldsymbol{\theta}_d$	Topic distribution for bill d
$\boldsymbol{\beta}_k$	Word distribution for topic k
x_{uk}	Ideal point for voter u in topic k
a_{dk}	Ideal point for bill d in topic k
$n(d, w)$	Frequency of word w appearing in bill d
v_{ud}	Voting from voter u to bill d
b_d	Constant offset of bill d
$\mathbf{V}$	The observed voting matrix $\{v_{ud}\}$
$\mathbf{W}$	The observed document-word matrix $\{n(d, w)\}$
$\boldsymbol{\Theta}$	The parameter matrix $\{\theta_{dk}\}$
$\mathbf{X}$	The parameter matrix $\{x_{dk}\}$
$\mathbf{A}$	The parameter matrix $\{a_{dk}\}$

3. OUR APPROACH

In this section, we first introduce the topic-factorized ideal point model (TF-IPM) in detail, and then propose the learning algorithm that can learn the parameters in the model given the observed legislative voting network.

3.1 The Topic-Factorized Ideal Point Model

The idea of our model is to build a probabilistic model for the legislative voting network, which contains two parts: (1) the probability modeling for observing the whole corpus of bills given the topic models, and (2) the probability modeling for the voting record given the topic distribution of bills as well as the ideal points for bills and voters in each topic. The goal is then to learn the parameters including the topic distributions and ideal points that can maximize the combined likelihood function.

The topic-factorized ideal point model is illustrated by a graphical model as shown in Figure 4. We now introduce the two parts separately in the following.

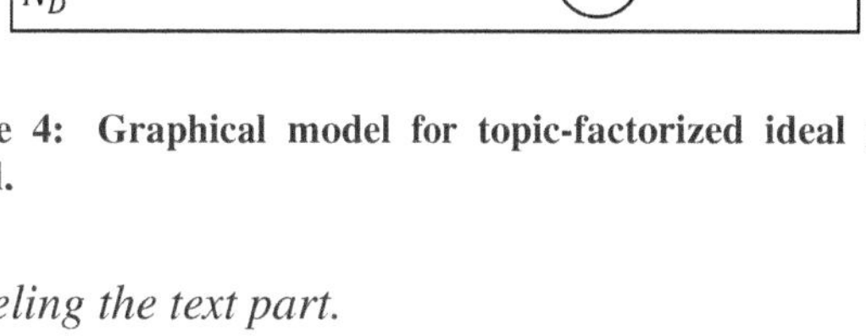

Figure 4: Graphical model for topic-factorized ideal point model.

Modeling the text part.

Following the idea of traditional topic models PLSA [10] and LDA [3], we can model the probability of each word in each document as a mixture of multinomial distributions. Let $n(d,w)$ be the frequency of term w appearing in bill d, $\theta_{dk} = p(k|d)$ be the probability of document d belonging to topic k, and $\beta_{kw} = p(w|k)$ be the probability that topic k generates word w, then the probability of word w appearing in document d with $n(d,w)$ occurrences can be defined as $(\sum_k \theta_{dk}\beta_{kw})^{n(d,w)}$. The probability of observing the word count vector $\mathbf{w}_d = (n(d,1), n(d,2), \ldots, n(d,N_W))$ for document d is then $p(\mathbf{w}_d|\mathbf{\Theta},\boldsymbol{\beta}) = \prod_w (\sum_k \theta_{dk}\beta_{kw})^{n(d,w)}$, and the probability of observing the whole corpus is then:

$$p(\mathbf{W}|\mathbf{\Theta},\boldsymbol{\beta}) = \prod_d \prod_w (\sum_k \theta_{dk}\beta_{kw})^{n(d,w)} \quad (1)$$

where $\mathbf{W}$ is the observed document-word count matrix.

Modeling voting links.

Now we introduce how the voting links can be modeled. Intuitively, legislator (u) are associated with different ideal points in different topics, which are represented using a K-dimensional vector $\mathbf{x}_u$; and bills (d) are also associated with different ideal points if they belong to different topics, which are represented using another K-dimensional vector $\mathbf{a}_d$. For each vote issued from a user u to a bill d, the probability of whether the $vote$ is an "YEA" or "NAY" is determined by the ideal points for u and d in each topic. For example, if the bill is a combination of "business" and "healthcare", we need to see whether the ideal points of u and d agree with each other in both topics.

Let v_{ud} be the vote score from voter u to bill d, we use $v_{ud} = 1$ to denote "YEA", i.e., u voted for d, and use $v_{ud} = -1$ to denote "NAY", i.e., u voted against d. The probabilities of the two values of v_{ud} are defined by:

$$\begin{aligned} p(v_{ud} = 1) &= \sigma(\sum_k \theta_{dk} x_{uk} a_{dk} + b_d) \\ p(v_{ud} = -1) &= 1 - \sigma(\sum_k \theta_{dk} x_{uk} a_{dk} + b_d) \end{aligned} \quad (2)$$

where θ_{dk} is the topic proportion for bill d in topic k, x_{uk} denotes the ideal point of voter u in topic k, a_{dk} denotes the ideal point of bill d in topic k, b_d denotes the constant offset, and σ denotes the logistic function. Since $\sum_k \theta_{dk} = 1$, the summation $\sum_k \theta_{dk} x_{uk} a_{dk}$ can be regarded as the weighted average of the agreement between legislator u and bill d in K topics. Note that, we only model the observed links from voters to bills, i.e., for the pairs (u,v) that $v_{ud} \neq 0$. In other words, whether a voter u votes a bill d is not modeled, as in reality legislators cast their votes for almost all bills in her term.

The overall likelihood of observed votes can be modeled as:

$$p(\mathbf{V}|\mathbf{\Theta},\mathbf{X},\mathbf{A},\mathbf{b}) = \prod_{(u,d):v_{ud}\neq 0} \left(p(v_{ud} = 1)^{\frac{1+v_{ud}}{2}} p(v_{ud} = -1)^{\frac{1-v_{ud}}{2}} \right) \quad (3)$$

where $\mathbf{V}$ is observed voting matrix, $\mathbf{\Theta}, \mathbf{X}, \mathbf{A}, \mathbf{b}$ are parameters in matrix/vector form for topic distribution, ideal points, and constant factors. $\frac{1+v_{ud}}{2}$ and $\frac{1-v_{ud}}{2}$ transforms the original votes to 1 or 0, which plays a role as an indicator function.

Putting it together.

We now combine the two parts together, and the final objective function is a linear combination of the two average log likelihood functions over the word links and voting links. In addition, we also add an l_2 regularization term to $\mathbf{A}$ and $\mathbf{X}$ to reduce the effect of over-fitting, equivalently by assuming they are from a Gaussian prior with mean as 0, and standard deviation as σ:

$$\begin{aligned} J(\boldsymbol{\theta},\boldsymbol{\beta},\boldsymbol{X},\boldsymbol{A},\mathbf{b}) = (1-\lambda)\frac{\sum_{d,w} n(d,w)\log\left(\sum_k \theta_{dk}\beta_{kw}\right)}{\sum_{d,w} n(d,w)} + \\ \lambda\frac{\sum_{(u,d):v_{ud}\neq 0}\left(\frac{1+v_{ud}}{2}\log p(v_{ud}=1) + \frac{1-v_{ud}}{2}\log p(v_{ud}=-1)\right)}{N_V} \\ -\frac{1}{2\sigma^2}\cdot\left(\sum_k x_{uk}^2 + \sum_k a_{dk}^2\right) \end{aligned} \quad (4)$$

s.t.

$$0 \le \theta_{dk} \le 1, \qquad \sum_k \theta_{dk} = 1$$

and

$$0 \le \beta_{kw} \le 1, \qquad \sum_w \beta_{kw} = 1$$

where $\sum_{d,w} n(d,w)$ denotes the total number of word occurrences in the bills, N_V denotes the total number of votes, and $\lambda \in (0,1)$ is the tradeoff weight over the two average log-likelihood functions. The goal is now to find the best parameters $\mathbf{\Theta}, \boldsymbol{\beta}, \mathbf{X}, \mathbf{A}, \mathbf{b}$ that maximize the objective function.

Discussions.

The Advantage of Modeling $\mathbf{\Theta}$

In issue-adjusted IPM, a pre-calculated $\mathbf{\Theta}$ has been used as an auxiliary parameter in the voting part. In practice, however, voting behaviors can also help to guide the topics generation. From our experiments, we can see that the held-out predictive accuracy can be significantly enhanced when topics are further adjusted according to voting behaviors.

Topic Model with Background

In [24], a background model is proposed to help improve the PLSA model. This background model can detect topics that are more distinctive. As there are many background words in the bills, we find that by including a background model in the topic modeling part, the performance of our model can be further enhanced. Considering to compare with issue-adjusted model more fairly, we do not introduce the results in the experiment section.

Adding Priors to TF-IPM

In issue-adjusted IPM, priors are added on the parameters. For example, $\boldsymbol{X}$ is assumed from a Gaussian distribution. Similar priors are put on the parameters of our model via the regularization term. In the experiment section, in order to compare all the models fairly, we put the same regularization term for all the baselines.

3.2 The Learning Algorithm

In this section, we introduce the learning algorithm to estimate the parameters, which is an iterative algorithm containing two steps. In the first step, we update the ideal points related parameters ($\mathbf{X}$, $\mathbf{A}$, and $\mathbf{b}$) when topics related parameters ($\mathbf{\Theta}$ and $\boldsymbol{\beta}$) are fixed; and in the second step, we update the topic models ($\mathbf{\Theta}$ and $\boldsymbol{\beta}$) when fixing ideal points related parameters ($\mathbf{X}$, $\mathbf{A}$, and $\mathbf{b}$).

The first step: updating $\mathbf{X}$, $\mathbf{A}$, $\mathbf{b}$.

We estimate $\mathbf{X}$, $\mathbf{A}$, $\mathbf{b}$ using gradient descent algorithm, which involves derivative calculation in the objective function. They are updated using the following rule:

$$
\begin{aligned}
x_{uk} &= x_{uk} + \eta \frac{\partial J}{\partial x_{uk}} \\
a_{dk} &= a_{dk} + \eta \frac{\partial J}{\partial a_{dk}} \\
b_d &= b_d + \eta \frac{\partial J}{\partial b_d}
\end{aligned} \tag{5}
$$

where η is the learning rate (we initialize η to be 10^{-5}, and use line search strategy to adjust η automatically), and

$$
\begin{aligned}
\frac{\partial J}{\partial x_{uk}} &= \lambda \frac{\sum_{d:v_{ud}\neq 0} a_{dk} x_{uk} \left(\frac{1+v_{ud}}{2} - p(v_{ud}=1)\right)}{N_V} - \frac{x_{uk}}{\sigma^2} \\
\frac{\partial J}{\partial a_{dk}} &= \lambda \frac{\sum_{u:v_{ud}\neq 0} \theta_{dk} x_{uk} \left(\frac{1+v_{ud}}{2} - p(v_{ud}=1)\right)}{N_V} - \frac{a_{dk}}{\sigma^2} \\
\frac{\partial J}{\partial b_d} &= \lambda \frac{\sum_{u:v_{ud}\neq 0} \left(\frac{1+v_{ud}}{2} - p(v_{ud}=1)\right)}{N_V}
\end{aligned} \tag{6}
$$

The second step: updating $\mathbf{\Theta}$ *and* $\boldsymbol{\beta}$*.*

Since the summation of θ is inside log function, the derivative is not easy to compute. Here we follow the idea of expectation-maximization (EM) algorithm and maximize a lower bound of the original objective function. We have noted that

$$
\begin{aligned}
&\sum_{d,w} n(d,w) \log \left(\sum_k \theta_{dk}\beta_{kw}\right) \\
=&\sum_{d,w} n(d,w) \log \left(\sum_k p(k|d,w) \frac{\theta_{dk}\beta_{kw}}{p(k|d,w)}\right) \\
\geq&\sum_{d,w} n(d,w) \sum_k p(k|d,w) \log \frac{\theta_{dk}\beta_{kw}}{p(k|d,w)} \\
=&\sum_{d,w} n(d,w) \sum_k p(k|d,w) \log \theta_{dk}\beta_{kw} - c
\end{aligned} \tag{7}
$$

where $c = \sum_{d,w} n(d,w) \sum_k p(k|d,w) \log p(k|d,w)$ is a constant with respect to θ and β. The inequality holds because of the Jensen's inequality of the concave function $\log(x)$. We denote this lower bound as:

$$
\begin{aligned}
&J_1(\mathbf{\Theta}, \boldsymbol{\beta}) = (1-\lambda) \sum_{d,w} n(d,w) \sum_k p(k|d,w) \log \theta_{dk}\beta_{kw} + \\
&\lambda \sum_{u,d} \left(\frac{1+v_{ud}}{2} \log p(v_{ud}=1) + \frac{1-v_{ud}}{2} \log p(v_{ud}=-1)\right) \\
&- \frac{1}{2\sigma^2} \cdot \left(\sum_k x_{uk}^2 + \sum_k a_{dk}^2\right)
\end{aligned} \tag{8}
$$

and now we seek to maximize it w.r.t $\mathbf{\Theta}$ and $\boldsymbol{\beta}$.

Updating $\mathbf{\Theta}$ given other parameters is a nonlinear constrained optimization problem. We could use the method of Lagrange multipliers to remove the constraints, but it involves to solve a complicated function of Lagrange multipliers. Here we use another method to remove the constraints. We regard θ_{dk} as a function of a new set of parameters μ_{dk} so that there is no constraints on $\boldsymbol{\mu}$. We define the logistic function-based transformation as

$$
\theta_{dk} = \begin{cases} \dfrac{e^{\mu_{dk}}}{1+\sum_{k'=1}^{K-1} e^{\mu_{dk'}}} & if\ 1 \leq k \leq K-1 \\[2ex] \dfrac{1}{1+\sum_{k'=1}^{K-1} e^{\mu_{dk'}}} & if\ k = K \end{cases} \tag{9}
$$

The new set of parameters $\mu_{dk} (1 \leq k \leq K-1)$ are real numbers and they have no constraints, therefore we can update μ_{dk} using gradient descent and recover θ_{dk} using the formula above.

The derivative w.r.t $\boldsymbol{\mu}$ is

$$
\frac{\partial J_1}{\partial \mu_{dk}} = \sum_{k'=1}^{K} \frac{\partial J_1}{\partial \theta_{dk'}} \frac{\partial \theta_{dk'}}{\partial \mu_{dk}} \tag{10}
$$

where

$$
\begin{aligned}
\frac{\partial J_1}{\partial \theta_{dk'}} &= -\frac{\sum_w n(d,w) p(k'|d,w)}{\theta_{dk'}} \\
&+ \sum_u a_{dk'} x_{uk'} \left(\frac{1+v_{ud}}{2} - p(v_{ud}=1)\right)
\end{aligned} \tag{11}
$$

and

$$
\frac{\partial \theta_{dk'}}{\partial \mu_{dk}} = \begin{cases} \theta_{dk}(1-\theta_{dk}) & if\ k' = k \\ -\theta_{dk'}\theta_{dk} & if\ k' \neq k \end{cases} \tag{12}
$$

We observe that $\boldsymbol{\beta}$ only appears in the topic model part. So we update $\boldsymbol{\beta}$ using the EM algorithm as Hofmann proposed [24]. The update rule of $\boldsymbol{\beta}$ is

$$
\beta_{kw}^{new} = \frac{\sum_d n(d,w) p(k|d,w)}{\sum_{d,w} n(d,w) p(k|d,w)} \tag{13}
$$

where

$$
p(k|d,w) = \frac{\theta_{dk}\beta_{kw}^{old}}{\sum_{k'} \theta_{dk'}\beta_{k'w}^{old}} \tag{14}
$$

4. EXPERIMENTS

In this section, we show the experimental results of our model on the legislative voting network extracted from U.S. House and Senate roll call data.

4.1 Data Description

We collect the U.S. House and Senate roll call data in the years between 1990 and 2013 from THOMAS[1], a public website providing federal legislative voting information. Votes and text information for bills are downloaded. We only select the bills where the text information is available, and keep the latest version of a bill if there are multiple versions. For each bill, we first remove stop words, and then choose 10,000 distinct words with highest frequency as the dictionary. 1299 House representatives and 241 senators are collected. Legislators from House have voted 6479 bills, while legislators from Senate have voted 1247 bills. There are 564 bills that are voted by both House and Senate.

In total, there are 1540 legislators, 7162 bills, and 2780453 votes. Some interesting statistics of the data set are shown in Fig. 5 and 6.

[1] `http://thomas.loc.gov/home/rollcallvotes.html`

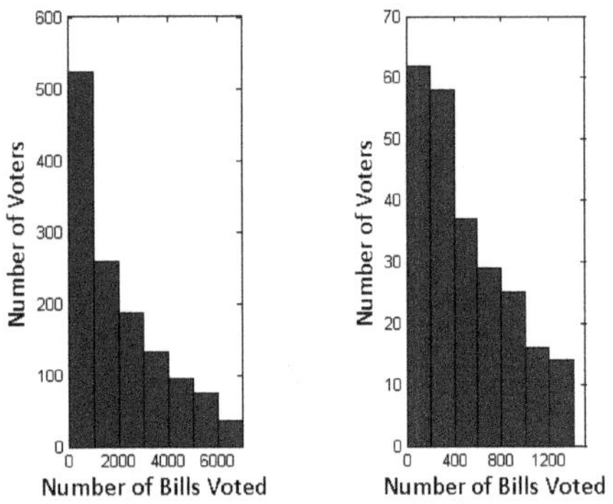

(a) House (b) Senate

Figure 5: Statistics of number of votes for legislators in House and Senate.

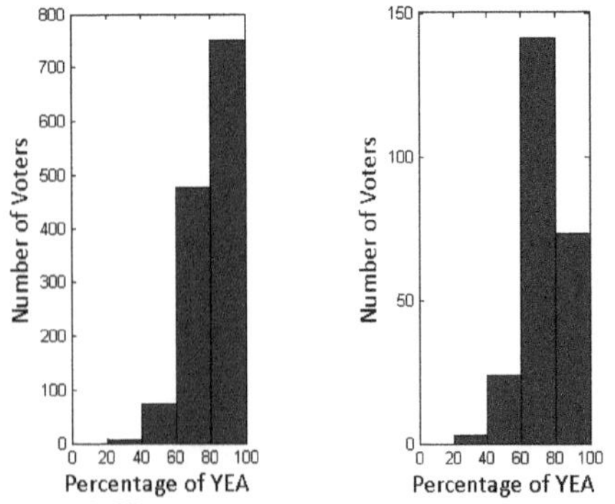

(a) House (b) Senate

Figure 6: Statistics of percentage of "YEA" for legislators in House and Senate.

4.2 Performance Evaluation

We now compare our TP-IPM model with several baseline methods in several aspects to demonstrate the power of the proposed model.

4.2.1 Baseline Methods

We compare our methods with three baseline methods.

1. One-dimensional ideal point model described in Section 2.2, denoted as 1-IPM.
2. High-dimensional ideal point model described in Section 2.2, denoted as H-IPM.
3. Issue-adjusted ideal point model described in Section 2.2, denoted as IA-IPM.

We use the same number of K for H-IPM, IA-IPM, and TF-IPM, to make sure that the dimensionality of idea points is the same.

4.2.2 Evaluation Measures

In order to see whether our model has good explanation power of the legislative network, we compare our model to others in terms of the following measures for both training and testing dataset, where we randomly select 90% of the votes as training and 10% of the votes as testing.

- Root-mean-square error (RMSE) between the predicted vote score and the ground truth vote score: $RMSE = \sqrt{\frac{\sum_{(u,d):v_{ud}\neq 0}\left(\frac{1+v_{ud}}{2} - p(v_{ud}=1)\right)^2}{N_V}}$.
- Accuracy of correctly predicted votes (using 0.5 as threshold for the predicted probability) among all the votes: $Accuracy = \frac{\sum(sgn(p(v_{ud}=1)-0.5)==v_{ud})}{N_V}$, where sgn is the sign function.
- Average log-likelihood of the voting link: $avglogL = \frac{\sum_{(u,d):v_{ud}\neq 0}\left(\frac{1+v_{ud}}{2}\log p(v_{ud}=1) + \frac{1-v_{ud}}{2}\log p(v_{ud}=-1)\right)}{N_V}$.

The total number of topics is set to be 10, and λ is set to be 0.8 in TF-IPM. The regularization parameter σ is chosen to be 22.4 in all methods so as to make the regularization coefficient $\frac{1}{2\sigma^2}$ around 0.001.

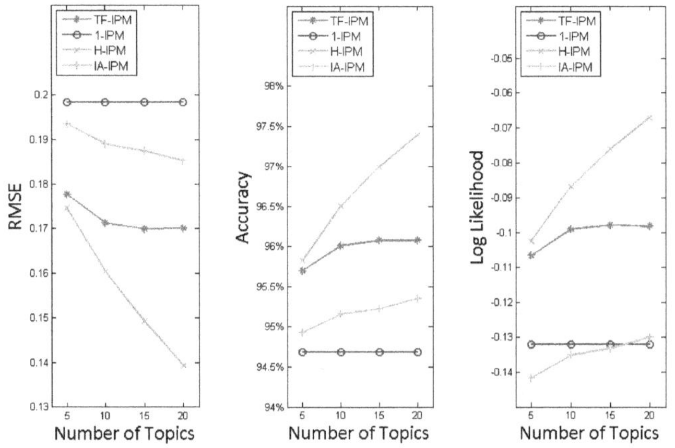

(a) RMSE (b) Accuracy (c) Average log-likelihood

Figure 7: Comparison on training data set.

From the Figure 7, we can see that high-dimensional IPM (H-IPM) has the best explanation power over the training dataset in terms of all three measures, due to its flexibility in choosing any possible latent factors. TF-IPM has the second best training accuracy. However, in Figure 8, we can see that, TF-IPM can overcome the overfitting issue of H-IPM when number of topics increases and has the better testing performance in terms of all three measures than all the other two baselines. Considering the interpretability of topic-factorized ideal points, we can see TF-IPM is a better choice.

Most of the models suffer from over-fitting problems when the total number of topics increases. We keep using 10 topics in the remaining part of the paper.

4.2.3 Parameter Study

In our model we have used the parameter λ that links the likelihood of topic model part and voting part as well as the regularization parameter σ. Intuitively, a larger λ means we pose more emphasis on the voting part. We evaluate the effect of λ and show it in Fig. 9. By varying the value of λ in the range of $(0, 1)$, we can derive different parameter estimations, and calculate the average log-likelihood and RMSE on testing data. From the result, we can clearly see that voting part indeed plays a more important role than the text part, but when λ is too big, the performance of our

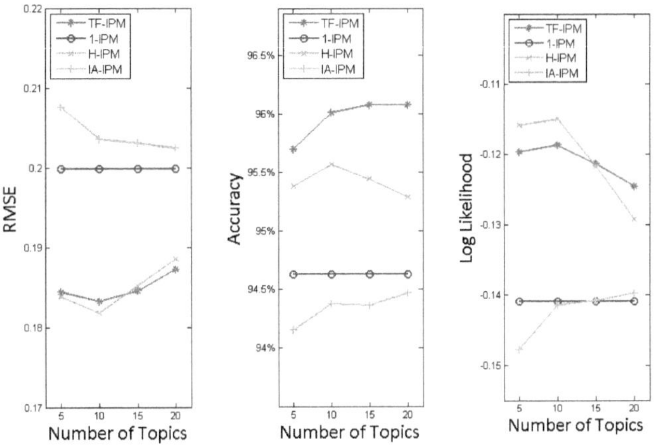

(a) RMSE (b) Accuracy (c) Average log-likelihood

Figure 8: Comparison on testing data set.

model will become worse due to overfitting. We set $\lambda = 0.8$ in all other experiments.

We also study the effect of the regularization term on the performance of our model. We try different values of σ and evaluate average log-likelihood and RMSE on testing dataset. The results are shown in Fig. 10, and we can see that the performance becomes less sensitive when σ becomes larger. We set $\sigma = 22.4$ in all other experiments.

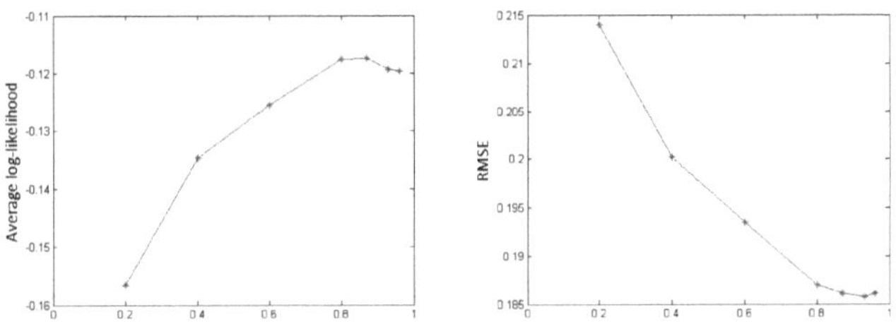

(a) Average log-likelihood (b) RMSE

Figure 9: Parameter study on λ.

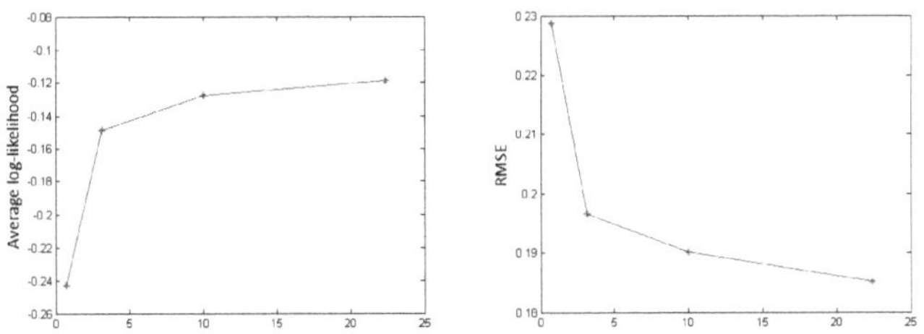

(a) Average log-likelihood (b) RMSE

Figure 10: Parameter study on σ.

4.2.4 *Convergence of Our Learning Algorithm*

In order to get a better idea of our iterative learning algorithm, we study the convergence of the learning algorithm here. Fig. 11 shows that our learning algorithm converges. Along with the iterations, the objective function is increasing, while training and testing errors are decreasing.

Table 2: Selected top words in each topic

#	Post-label	Top words
1	Foreign	Foreign, Government, International
2	Education	Education, School, Students
3	Individual property	Individual, Property, Fiscal
4	Financial	Institution, Financial, Agency, Bank
5	Military	Military, Defense, Duty
6	Law	Law, Authority, Provision
7	Health service	Health, Service, Assistance
8	Health expenses	Health, Fiscal, Expenses
9	Funds	Funds, Fiscal, Amounts
10	Public transportation	Public, Transportation, Motor

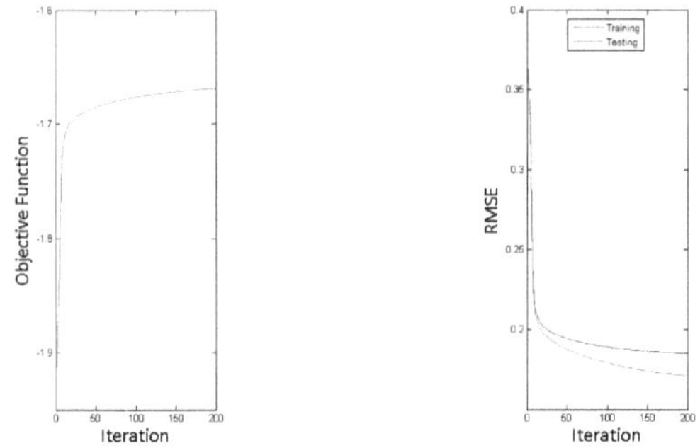

(a) Objective Function (b) RMSE

Figure 11: Convergence Study

4.3 Case Studies

We now show some case studies to demonstrate ideal points detected by our model. By setting topic number $K = 10$ and $\lambda = 0.8$, we get topics as shown in Table 2.

We study the voting behaviors for three famous legislators: Ronald Paul, Republican House representative from Texas (in office: 1976-1977, 1979-1985, and 1997-2013); Barack Obama, Democratic Senator from Illinois (in office: 2005 - 2008); and Joe Lieberman, Democratic representative from Connecticut (in office: 1989 - 2013). Their ideal points are shown in Fig. 12, 13, and 14, respectively. We also show the ideal points for some other people in order to understand their relative position and make the scale more meaningful. We can see that: (1) Obama is in general in the middle and moderately left in almost all the topics; (2) Paul is regarded as one of the most conservative republicans in congress, and is most conservative on the role of government on economy but not on social issues and especially is an opponent of war; and (3) Lieberman is regarded as a Democrat who is conservative in social goods (e.g., transportation) and military issues.

We also select one bill that Ronald Paul has voted. It is a bill in 2006 and its number is H.RES.578. It mainly covers supporting the government of Romania to improve the standard health care and well-being of children in Romania. We can find the positions a_{dk} as well as the topic distribution θ_{dk} of this bill in Fig. 15. We can clearly see that the most notable topics the bill belongs to are "Health Service" and "Funds." We can also infer from the ideal points of Ronald Paul and the ideal points for H.RES.578 that R.Paul is in favor of this bill.

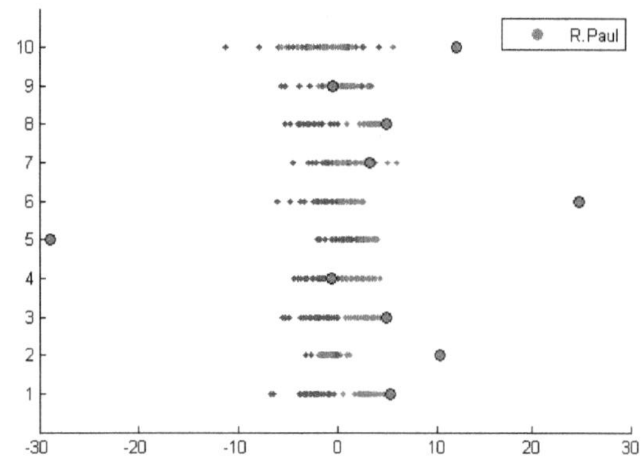

Figure 12: Estimated Ideal Points for Ronald Paul

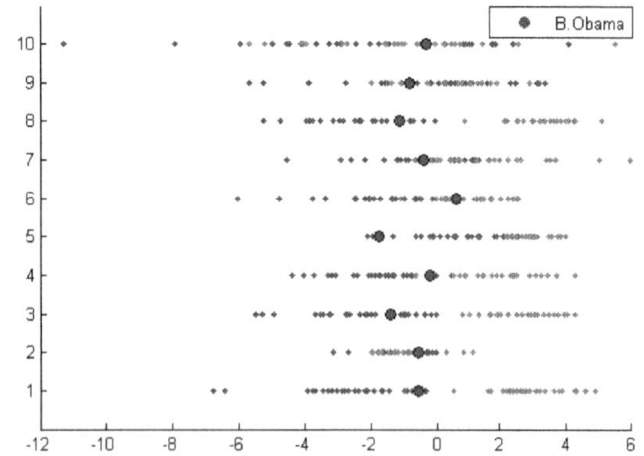

Figure 13: Estimated Ideal Points for Barack Obama

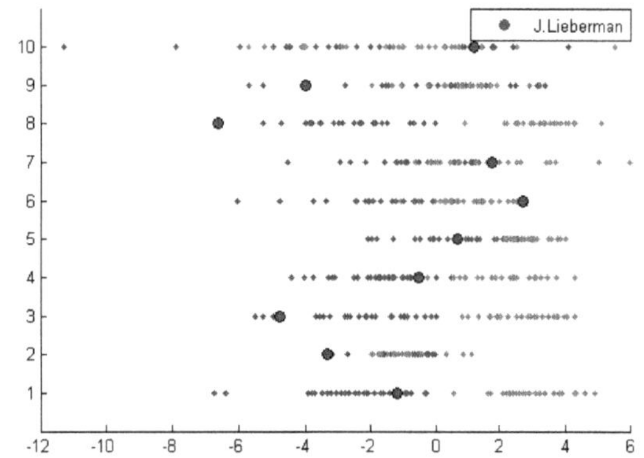

Figure 14: Estimated Ideal Points for Joe Lieberman

In addition, we select three topics, foreign issues, education and financial institution, and draw scatter plots for all the legislators in every two of these three topics. Democratic people are represented as blue dots, while Republican people are represented as red ones. Especially, Ronald Paul is represented as a yellow circle, Barack Obama as a green circle, and Joe Lieberman as a pink circle. We can see clearly from Fig. 16, 17 and 18 that legislators in different parties lie on different sides of each plane. It can be seen that, by such analysis it is easy to figure out how close two legislators are in terms of certain topic dimensions. We can also easily detect outliers from such visualization.

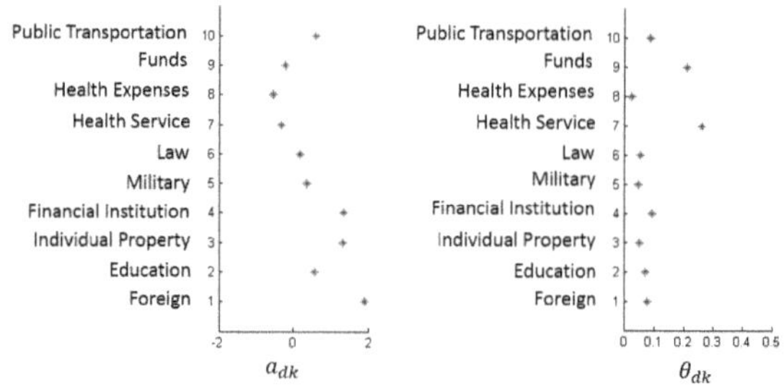

(a) Bill Positions (b) Topic Distributions

Figure 15: Bill H_RES_578

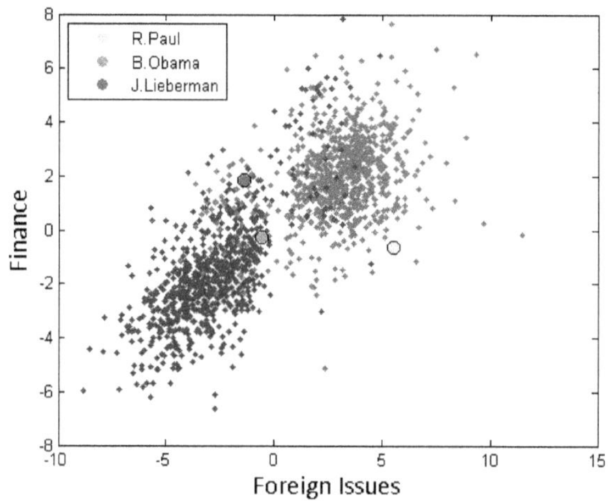

Figure 16: Scatter plot between "foreign issue" and "finance".

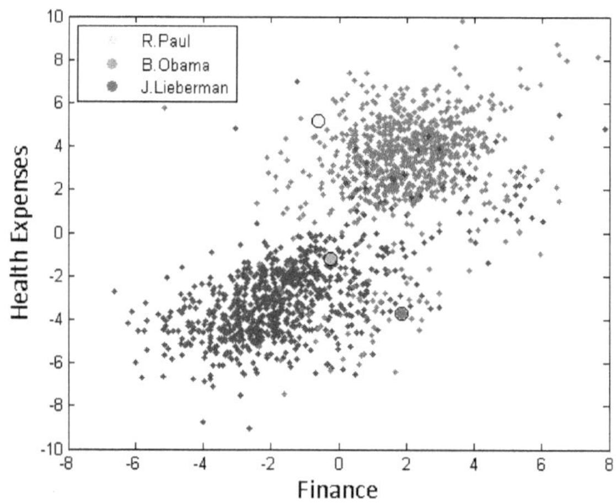

Figure 17: Scatter plot between "finance" and "health expenses".

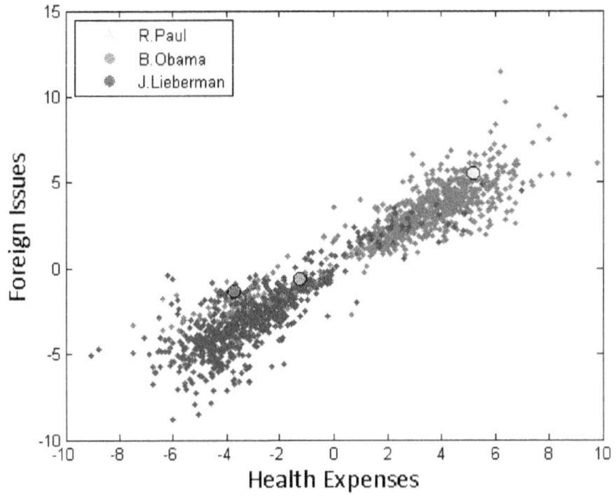

Figure 18: Scatter plot between "health expenses" and "foreign issue".

4.4 Application: Predicting Votes for Unseen Bills

An interesting application of our model is to make voting predictions for an unseen bill d with just text information. Note that, for 1-IPM and H-IPM, there is no way for us to predict votes related to an unseen bill, as it is impossible to get the latent feature for an unseen bill.

We perform our study in the following three steps:

- First, we estimate the topic distribution for the bill $\boldsymbol{\theta}_d$ according to current topic models, i.e., the $\boldsymbol{\beta}$, using simple language models.
- Second, we train a linear regression model to predict $\boldsymbol{a}_d$ and b_d, utilizing the text information (bag-of-word representation) as features. Note that, once we have learned the ideal points and popularity for the observed bills, we can then use these bills as training samples to learn the weights associated with the linear model. Using text to analyze data actually belongs to a broader study of opinion mining [16]. Here, we just use a simple approach to demonstrate our TF-IPM model.
- Finally for each legislator u, we can predict whether she favors this unseen bill by plugging in her ideal points in each topic: $p(v_{ud} = 1) = \sigma(\sum_k \theta_{dk} x_{uk} a_{dk} + b_d)$.

We find that by using 90% of the bills as training dataset and hide all the voting information for the remaining 10% bills as testing dataset, we can still achieve a 80.8% accuracy in predicting votes from voters to them. More studies along this line will be performed in future work.

5. RELATED WORK

In this section, we introduce other related work to our study.

5.1 Ideal Point Models

Poole and Rosenthal ([18], [19], [20]) make seminal contributions and launched a massive literature of ideal point models. Alternative methods of ideal point estimation are developed by political scientists include Clinton et al. [4], Heckman and Snyder [8], and Londregan [12]. In [7], an issue-adjusted ideal point model is developed in order to evaluate a legislator's position for each explicit topic in her voting behavior. Apart from a global position, legislators have adjusted positions for different topics. They try to explain legislators' voting behavior by their affinity to topics that a bill covers. A network-based method is proposed to estimate ideal points for Twitter users in [2]. The key idea is that Twitter users prefer to follow politicians whose political positions are similar to theirs. People's political positions are then inferred by those whom they follow in social network.

5.2 Recommendation System

Ideal point estimation model is closely related to recommendation tasks in computer science domain. Given a user-item rating matrix, where the entry at i^{th} row and j^{th} column denotes the rating score from user i to item j, the recommendation task is to predict the rating score of items for users. Traditional recommendation algorithms include collaborative filtering (CF) [9] and latent factor models [11, 15].

In latent factor models, people try to explain ratings by characterizing users and items to several latent topics. This idea is natural in that, people usually rate an item based on several aspects, and items also have the corresponding properties. One of the most well known latent factor models is matrix factorization [11]. In matrix factorization models, each user i is represented by a vector $\mathbf{u}_i$ and item by a vector $\mathbf{v}_j$ in the K-dimensional latent space. The rating of user i to item j can be seen as the inner-product of the user feature vector and the item feature vector: $\hat{r}_{ij} = \mathbf{u}_i \mathbf{v}_j^T$. It naturally leads to the decomposition of the rating matrix R into the product of two matrices $R = UV^T$, where U is an $N \times K$ user-factor matrix, and V is an $M \times K$ item-factor matrix.

In this paper, we focus on the modeling of the voting prediction on a legislative voting network, where legislators do not have freedom to choose bills to vote. Also, we want to include the text information to enhance the prediction accuracy.

5.3 Topic Modeling, Link-Enhanced Topic Modeling, and Text-Enhanced Recommendation

Topic model is a type of statistic model for discovering the abstract topics that occur in a collection of documents. In topic models, each document is represented as a bag of words. The basic idea is, a latent topic is drawn conditionally to the document, and each word is then generated from that topic. The classical topic models include PLSA [10] and LDA [3].

In addition to the text information in documents, the links between documents can be exploited to further enhance the result of topic models. [21] proposes a unified information network-enhanced topic model that integrates the structural information and text information in a document network, and [14] proposes a solution to the problem of topic modeling with network structure regularization. Both of the two studies can significantly enhance the original topics model quality. In this paper, the topic model part is enhanced from the voting link part, which is different from the two papers where links exist between the documents.

Topic model can be used to enhance recommendation as well [7, 1, 23]. A collaborative topic regression model is proposed to recommend scientific articles [22]. The recommendation algorithm is based on both content of articles and users' ratings, and topic distributions are converted into feature vectors for users. Different from these methods, we use topic distribution as a explicit dimension for ideal points analysis, while existing methods directly use topic distribution as feature vector for users or items. In [13], a topic model is built on the reviews from users to products to help the rating prediction. However, the text information exists directly on the links from users to items, while in our case, text information is only linked to bills (items).

6. CONCLUSION

In this paper, we propose a novel topic-factorized ideal point estimation model (TF-IPM) that uses text information and voting behavior collectively in a legislative voting network. First, we model the ideal points of legislators and bills for each topic instead of assigning them to a global one. Second, the generation of topics are guided by the voting matrix in addition to the text information contained in bills. A unified model that combines voting behavior modeling and topic modeling is presented, and an iterative learning algorithm is proposed to learn the topics of bills as well as the topic-factorized ideal points of legislators and bills. By comparing with the state-of-the-art ideal point estimation models, our method has a much better explanation power in terms of held-out log-likelihood and other measures. Besides, case studies show that the topic-factorized ideal points coincide with human intuition. Finally, we illustrate how to use these topic-factorized ideal points to predict voting results for unseen bills.

7. REFERENCES

[1] D. Agarwal and B.-C. Chen. flda: matrix factorization through latent dirichlet allocation. In *Proc. of the third ACM Int. Conf. on Web Search and Data Mining (WSDM'10)*, pages 91–100, 2010.

[2] P. Barberá. Birds of the same feather tweet together. bayesian ideal point estimation using twitter data. *Unpublished manuscript, New York University*, 2013.

[3] D. M. Blei, A. Y. Ng, and M. I. Jordan. Latent dirichlet allocation. *the Journal of Machine Learning Research (JMLR'03)*, 3:993–1022, 2003.

[4] J. Clinton, S. Jackman, and D. Rivers. The statistical analysis of roll call data. *American Political Science Review*, 98(02):355–370, 2004.

[5] S. Feldman and C. Johnston. Understanding the determinants of political ideology: Implications of structural complexity. *Political Psychology*, 2013.

[6] S. Gerrish and D. M. Blei. Predicting legislative roll calls from text. In *Proc. of the 28th Int. Conf. on Machine Learning (ICML'11)*, pages 489–496, 2011.

[7] S. Gerrish and D. M. Blei. How they vote: Issue-adjusted models of legislative behavior. In *Advances in Neural Information Processing Systems (NIPS'12)*, pages 2762–2770, 2012.

[8] J. J. Heckman and J. M. S. Jr. Linear probability models of the demand for attributes with an empirical application to estimating the preferences of legislators. *The RAND Journal of Economics*, 28:pp. S142–S189, 1997.

[9] J. L. Herlocker, J. A. Konstan, A. Borchers, and J. Riedl. An algorithmic framework for performing collaborative filtering. In *Proc. of the 22nd Annual Int. ACM SIGIR Conf. on Research and Development in Information Retrieval*, pages 230–237, 1999.

[10] T. Hofmann. Probabilistic latent semantic analysis. In *Proc. of the Fifteenth Conf. on Uncertainty in Artificial Intelligence (UAI'99)*, pages 289–296, 1999.

[11] Y. Koren, R. Bell, and C. Volinsky. Matrix factorization techniques for recommender systems. *Computer*, 42(8):30–37, 2009.

[12] J. Londregan. Estimating legislators' preferred points. *Political Analysis*, 8(1):35–56, 1999.

[13] J. McAuley and J. Leskovec. Hidden factors and hidden topics: understanding rating dimensions with review text. In *Proc. of the 7th ACM Conf. on Recommender Systems (RecSys'13)*, pages 165–172, 2013.

[14] Q. Mei, D. Cai, D. Zhang, and C. Zhai. Topic modeling with network regularization. In *Proc. of the 17th Int. Conf. on World Wide Web (WWW'08)*, pages 101–110, 2008.

[15] A. Mnih and R. Salakhutdinov. Probabilistic matrix factorization. In *Advances in Neural Information Processing Systems (NIPS'07)*, pages 1257–1264, 2007.

[16] B. Pang and L. Lee. Opinion mining and sentiment analysis. *Foundations and Trends in Information Retrieval*, 2(1-2):1–135, 2008.

[17] K. T. Poole. Recovering a basic space from a set of issue scales. *American Journal of Political Science*, 42(3):954–993, 1998.

[18] K. T. Poole and H. Rosenthal. A spatial model for legislative roll call analysis. *American Journal of Political Science*, 29(2):pp. 357–384, 1985.

[19] K. T. Poole and H. Rosenthal. Patterns of congressional voting. *American Journal of Political Science*, 35(1):pp. 228–278, 1991.

[20] K. T. Poole and H. Rosenthal. *Congress: A Political-Economic History of Roll Call Voting*. Oxford University Press, 1997.

[21] Y. Sun, J. Han, J. Gao, and Y. Yu. iTopicModel: Information network-integrated topic modeling. In *Proc. 2009 Int. Conf. Data Mining (ICDM'09)*, Miami, FL, 2009.

[22] C. Wang and D. M. Blei. Collaborative topic modeling for recommending scientific articles. In *Proc. of the 17th ACM SIGKDD Int. Conf. on Knowledge Discovery and Data Mining (KDD'11)*, pages 448–456, 2011.

[23] E. Wang, D. Liu, J. Silva, L. Carin, and D. B. Dunson. Joint analysis of time-evolving binary matrices and associated documents. In *Advances in Neural Information Processing Systems (NIPS'10)*, pages 2370–2378, 2010.

[24] C. Zhai, A. Velivelli, and B. Yu. A cross-collection mixture model for comparative text mining. In *Proc. of the tenth ACM SIGKDD Int. Conf. on Knowledge Discovery and Data Mining (KDD'04)*, pages 743–748, 2004.

Jointly Modeling Aspects, Ratings and Sentiments for Movie Recommendation (JMARS)

Qiming Diao
Singapore Mgt. University
qiming.ustc@gmail.com

Minghui Qiu*
Singapore Mgt. University
minghuiqiu@gmail.com

Chao-Yuan Wu*
Carnegie Mellon University
cywu@cmu.edu

Alexander J. Smola
CMU and Google
alex@smola.org

Jing Jiang
Singapore Mgt. University
jingjiang@smu.edu.sg

Chong Wang
Carnegie Mellon University
chongw@cs.cmu.edu

ABSTRACT

Recommendation and review sites offer a wealth of information beyond ratings. For instance, on IMDb users leave reviews, commenting on different aspects of a movie (e.g. actors, plot, visual effects), and expressing their sentiments (positive or negative) on these aspects in their reviews. This suggests that uncovering aspects and sentiments will allow us to gain a better understanding of users, movies, and the process involved in generating ratings.

The ability to answer questions such as *"Does this user care more about the plot or about the special effects?"* or *"What is the quality of the movie in terms of acting?"* helps us to understand *why* certain ratings are generated. This can be used to provide more meaningful recommendations.

In this work we propose a probabilistic model based on collaborative filtering and topic modeling. It allows us to capture the interest distribution of users and the content distribution for movies; it provides a link between interest and relevance on a per-aspect basis and it allows us to differentiate between positive and negative sentiments on a per-aspect basis. Unlike prior work our approach is entirely unsupervised and does not require knowledge of the aspect specific ratings or genres for inference.

We evaluate our model on a live copy crawled from IMDb. Our model offers superior performance by joint modeling. Moreover, we are able to address the *cold start* problem — by utilizing the information inherent in reviews our model demonstrates improvement for new users and movies.

Keywords

Collaborative Filtering; Topic Models; Integrated Modeling; Sentiment Analysis

*Equal contribution

KDD'14, August 24–27, 2014, New York, NY, USA.

http://dx.doi.org/10.1145/2623330.2623758.

1. INTRODUCTION

Collaborative filtering is a staple to many business in the internet economy. Data to build good content recommender systems essentially comes in three guises: interactions, ratings, and reviews. First and foremost there is information whether a recommended item was consumed (i.e. viewed, clicked-on, purchased). This is the key source of information in search, ranking and advertising systems [4]. A common approach to processing this data is to try to estimate the probability that a user will interact with a given item, using past interactions as training data. Second, there is rating information regarding whether the user enjoyed the recommended item. This is the traditional domain of collaborative filtering. Its use was popularized through the Netflix contest [3] and it aims to reconstruct a choice set of matrix entries [17] or the entire matrix altogether [5]. Third, there are *reviews*, as provided by the users. This is arguably the most valuable user generated content since in it users not only *rate* items but they also *explain why* they liked or disliked an item. Hence, a system capable of extracting this information automatically should be able to generate more relevant information, and, as a side effect, also allow us to obtain meaningful profiles of the users and objects involved [12]. Our system belongs to the family of *integrated* models that use ratings and reviews to extract a wealth of information. We provide a statistical model and we demonstrate in experiments that our approach excels at recommending movies while simultaneously providing meaningful analysis of the interests and aspects relevant for users and movies.

We begin with an example of the type of analysis we are able to obtain for reviews. In it, positive sentiments are annotated as green, negative ones as red, and blue terms are movie-specific. Below we omit information regarding the *specific* aspect for visualization purposes (see Table 6).

I enjoyed this DVD from the library very much. Daniel Craig plays a believable James Bond. There are some of the older 007 action scenes and similar gimmicks with updates thanks to the younger Quartermaster. Eve plays well with grit and feminism including a surprise revelation at the end. It's touching as well with the final scenes in the mansion and the old Caretaker. Adele's award for best song is well deserved. But the plot was pretty weak and the film dragged on and on and on, probably being 30 minutes too long. The filming is it's usual high quality, but still overall both my wife and I found this boring, something you can't usually level against a Bond film.

1.1 Integrated Modeling

The motivation for our work arises from the task of serving the *right* items to users. This involves a number of challenges ranging from designing an effective user interface to user personalization to solving the cold-start challenge of initializing a recommendation system with meaningful content. Given the wealth of information inherent in review sites, such as IMDb, Netflix and Amazon Prime, it is tempting to extract more than just ratings from the data. After all, we want to understand *why* a user liked a particular movie, what his *preferences* are when it comes to selecting a movie (visual effects, plot, choice of subject matter).

Conventionally, in factorization approaches to recommendation [9] one uses exclusively the information inherent in the ratings. Consequently the latent factors have a certain degree of ambiguity — for instance, if we capture user and movie attributes with vectors v_u and v_m to predict a score $r_{um} \sim \langle v_u, v_m \rangle$, then the parameters are invariant under rotation. That is, replacing v_u with Uv_u and v_m with Uv_m for some rotation U will leave the outcome unchanged, yet it may considerably alter the interpretation of coordinate-wise attributes in v_u and v_m. This is undesirable in several respects: It leads to hard-to-understand factors; The factors may change considerably while leaving the underlying statistical model unchanged.

However, these factors represented as a vector of numbers are usually hard to interpret. For instance, did the movie have good acting but bad story, did the user prefer the director but dislike the genre? At the same time many review sites have textual content *in addition* to the numerical scores. For instance, IMDb is primarily a review site, Netflix allows for comments, YouTube is comments-only, Yelp contains comments and reviews but is lacking in terms of recommendation, and Zagat primarily focuses on curated content. This allows us to solve the above problem. For example, the word "predictable" in a movie review tells us that the user is talking about the "plot" aspect with a "negative sentiment"; likewise, a word "hilarious" tell us that the movie is a comedy and that the user probably likes it.

It is therefore tempting to try extracting additional meaning from textual data. This is valuable, e.g. when building a search and retrieval system since it allows us to identify attractive (and undesirable) aspects. For example, if a user always likes to write reviews talking about the special effects, we should recommend movies with great special effects to her if we can identify these movies. Moreover, we can learn from aspect related specialization which terms are associated with aspect specific sentiments.

1.2 An Overview of the Model

Our model provides a principled extension of the factorization models commonly used for recommendation. That is, we retain the notion that reviews are generated by incorporating user and movie specific features. However, unlike simple vectorial rating models, we use a structured representation to capture the interaction between movie and user. In this sense our model borrows from the tensorial factorization approach of [16] and it extends it from scalars to documents.

More specifically, we assume that each user (and each movie) has an aspect distribution of interest. Reviews are generated by drawing from the product of movie and user aspects. For instance, a review text will likely contain details about special effects, but only if the user is actually interested in them *and* if the movie has special effects worth discussing. Hence, reviews inform both about the content of a movie and also about the interests of a user.

This differentiation allows us to attribute partial scores to interests, i.e. we assume that the review scores arise from the process of combining partial scores associated with different aspects of the movie. Not only does this improve rating accuracy, it also allows us to attach *sentiments* to aspects. In other words, we can model which terms associate with positive, negative, and neutral aspect specific words within an aspect. We model the following five groups of words:

Background That is, words uniformly distributed in every review are considered background words. For example, in the case of movie reviews, these words include "characters", "movies", etc.

Movie-specific Words such as the name of the characters in a movie, or any term that appears only in the movie are considered movie-specific. These two types of words provide less information about movie quality.

Aspect These are words associated with specific aspects. For example, "music", "sound", and "singing" are all aspect words related to the "music" aspect.

Aspect-Sentiment These words usually come with a specific aspect to express positive or negative sentiments. For example, words such as "bored", "predictable" usually appear with a discussion of the "plot".

General sentiment For example, words such as "great", "bad", or "worse" do not really convey any aspect specific content. We call them general sentiment words.

1.3 Contributions

The key contribution of our model is that it integrates all available data sources, that is, it provides a joint model of user activity, movie content, ratings, reviews, and a detailed language model of the reviews. We show the following:

- Our model outperforms state-of-the-art recommender systems such as matrix factorization [15].
- We obtain an aspect representation of user interests and movie properties.
- We are able to uncover aspect-specific sentiment words.
- We provide an efficient inference algorithm.
- Our experiments are carried out on a real-world snapshot of reviews crawled from IMDb.

In summary, this is the first model tackling the problem set as a whole rather than piecemeal. We begin with an overview of related work in Section 2. This is followed by a description of the model in Section 3. Inference algorithms are provided in Section 4. We then present experimental results in Section 5 and a conclusion in Section 7.

2. RELATED WORK

Collaborative filtering is a fertile area of research and there exists a multitude of techniques which can readily be applied to *subsets* of the problem that we tackle. See e.g. [18, 9] for a review. Specifically, probabilistic matrix factorization methods [15, 17] have proven successful in real world problems [3, 8, 11, 25, 22].

However, probabilistic matrix factorization techniques struggle to generalize to new items, i.e. they fail at the cold-start problem. Regression based latent factor models (RLFM) [1] use attribute features to solve this problem by incorporating observable features into latent factors. Recent research [22, 16] incorporates Latent Dirichlet Allocation (LDA) and uses the topic as features, e.g. for recommending scientific articles. In terms of ratings, [19] use a statistically more appropriate model for capturing the discrete nature of the reviews by formulating an exponential families approach.

Moreover, there is rich literature analyzing reviews, e.g. using LDA [14, 26, 23] to uncover topics and sentiments. These works provide a more fine-grained analysis of review texts by separating sentiment words from neutral aspect words. In light of this, we build a language model component in our integrated model to capture aspects and sentiments in reviews. Different from a semi-supervised component or opinion lexicon used in [14, 26], our sentiments are learnt by building a linkage between user ratings and sentiments.

A recent line of work aims to model multi-aspect ratings from reviews, e.g. [20, 13, 10, 13, 12]. However, it often relies on having aspects readily available, often with aspect-specific ratings. The work of [20] uses LDA based model to identify 'topics' that are correlated with user ratings. Similarly, [13] uses multi-aspect ratings to infer sentiments for predefined aspects. With respect to the importance of mining ratable aspects that contribute to user ratings, as shown in these works, our model also seeks to profile a user's aspect preference when it comes to selecting a movie.

The key difference in our model is that it provides an *integrated* approach to this broad range of problems. Probably Hidden Factors as Topics (HFT) [12] is the closest to our work. HFT jointly models review texts and user ratings by associating each topic dimension with a hidden factor. However, unlike HFT we do *not* have such constraint. This increases the range of applicability. As shown in experiments, our model discovers a more meaningful low-rank representations of aspects, sentiments and movies, and a better recommendation results.

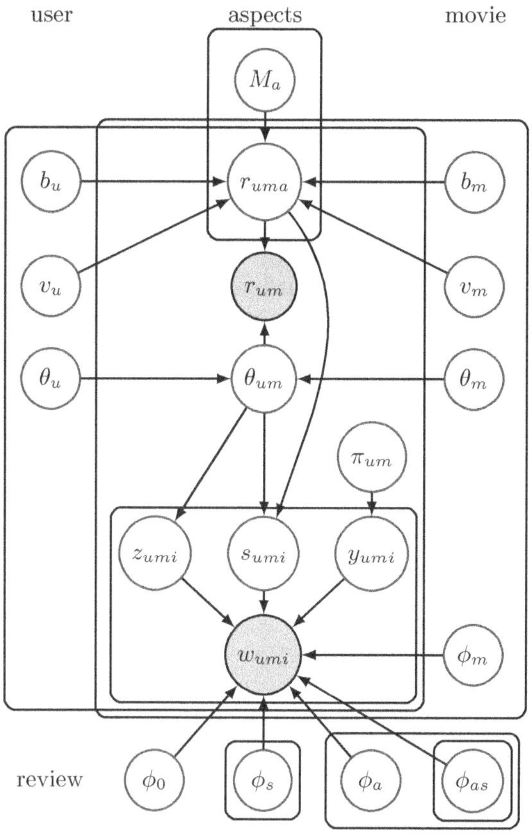

Figure 1: Factorized rating and review model. Note the symmetry between users and movies. The model contains four major plates: aspects, users, movies, and the words within a given review. They are nested and partially overlapping. For convenience we represent the aspect plate as two separate plates (language model and aspect review model are contained in the same plate).

3. MODEL

3.1 Modeling Assumptions

Our task is to predict for a given user u and a movie m both the observed rating r_{um} and also the review w_{um}, as given by a collection of words w_{umi}. In contrast to previous work we model both aspects jointly, using a multitude of observed and latent variables.

The most intuitive way of understanding the model of Figure 1 is to consider how a review is written. Users are assumed to have a given interest distribution θ_u in terms of aspects they write and care about. Moreover, they are also assumed to have biases b_u regarding what can be considered to be a reasonable baseline with regard to their choice. Likewise, movies contain a number of aspects, as indicated by θ_m and a bias b_m.

Whether a user likes a particular movie depends on a number of things. First, it helps if the movie contains aspects the user cares about. Secondly, it is also important that the user's expectations v_u match the movie's properties v_m, when viewed under the angle of a specific aspect, as captured by M_a. These aspect-specific ratings of a movie by a user r_{uma} are then aggregated, based on the user's priorities to obtain an aggregate rating r_{um}.

As for the actual review text, we assume the following: reviews contain words drawn from a baseline language model of words typically occurring in reviews ϕ_0. Moreover, there are positive and negative sentiment words, as indexed by ϕ_s, where $s \in \{\text{positive}, \text{negative}\}$. Finally, we assume that there are aspect specific word distributions ϕ_a, again colored by sentiment s, i.e. ϕ_{as}. Depending on whether a user appreciates a particular aspect of a movie, as indicated by r_{uma}, he will generate positive or negative sentiment words (or simply neutral ones). Finally, there are also movie-specific words, such as the name of the main protagonists, the title, and other named entities that are bound to occur in a review, regardless of the user. This approach of mixing between five different components summarizes our strategy. Probably most closely related is the model of [2] who use a similar switch construction to distinguish between positive and negative sentiment. The key difference is that we do not have any explicit information regarding attitude and aspects. Instead, we need to extract this from the reviews.

We employ a conventional bag of words representation, paired with a Dirichlet-Multinomial to capture the word distribution of the reviews. Aspect-specific ratings are generated by matrix factorization, i.e. a Gaussian inner-product model. The twist here is that we capture aspect specific preferences via a scaling matrix M_a. This is a strict generalization of regular factorization approaches. Finally, the mixing between these aspects occurs by an exponential linear model which also governs review combination.

3.2 Matrix Factorization with Aspects

As is common in collaborative filtering, only a tiny fraction of matrix entries are present — our dataset contained less than 0.03% observed entries. To infer the missing entries collaborative filtering relies on the assumption that the underlying matrix has fairly low rank and thus, a small number of terms suffice to determine the remainder of the results.

One may argue that this is only part of a solution, since the relative values of the entries matter more than their absolute value [25, 24]. That said, for the purpose of comparison to existing results we adopt the strategy of measuring the least mean square deviation. The matching probabilistic model is that of additive noise relative to an estimated relevance score. We build on the probabilistic matrix factorization (PMF) approach of [17].

As in PMF, we assume that users u and movies m are characterized by latent factor vectors v_u and v_m respectively, that are drawn from zero-mean spherical Gaussian priors

$$v_u \sim \mathcal{N}(0, \sigma_u^2 \mathbf{I}) \text{ and } v_m \sim \mathcal{N}(0, \sigma_m^2 \mathbf{I}). \quad (1)$$

The hyperparameters σ_u^2 and σ_m^2 are user-related and movie-related variances, respectively. In a conventional recommender model one would then assume that

$$r_{um}^{\text{conventional}} \sim \mathcal{N}(v_u^\top v_m + b_u + b_m, \sigma^2)$$

That is, given biases b_u and b_m, we observe a noisy variant of the compatibility. Different from PMF [15], we assume an aspect-specific rating of movie m by user u.

$$r_{uma} = v_u^\top M_a v_m + b_u + b_m + b_0. \quad (2)$$

Here b_u and b_m are biases for users and movies respectively and b_0 is a common bias. The idea is that while v_u and v_m encode the general profile, the matrix M_a emphasizes the aspect specific properties. That is, while movies may be overall good, they may or may not excel quite as much in specific aspects.

We assume Gaussian priors with fixed mean and precision on real-valued parameters. Specifically, we assume that each element of M_a, v_u, v_m, b_u, b_m follows a Gaussian distribution with zero mean and a fixed precision.

3.3 Two Factor Model

One of the challenges in combining user and movie attributes is in the task to *fuse* the respective attributes into a joint model. Our approach borrows from [7] by designing an exponential additive model in terms of θ_u and θ_m. The latter are user and movie specific aspect parameters which jointly generate the aspect distribution of a review. Our assumptions are as follows:

$$\theta_u \sim \mathcal{N}(0, \sigma_{\text{useraspect}}^2 \mathbf{1}) \text{ and } \theta_m \sim \mathcal{N}(0, \sigma_{\text{movieaspect}}^2 \mathbf{1}) \quad (3)$$

Moreover, the joint aspect distribution is given by

$$\theta_{um} \propto \exp(\theta_u + \theta_m) \text{ i.e. } p(a|\theta_u, \theta_m) = \frac{e^{\theta_{ua} + \theta_{ma}}}{\sum_{a'} e^{\theta_{ua'} + \theta_{ma'}}} \quad (4)$$

We also make the (slightly controversial) modeling assumption that the extent of discussion in a review and the relative importance of a aspect coincide. That is, aspects that are discussed at twice the length will contribute twice as much to the aggregate score for a review. This yields

$$\hat{r}_{um} = \mathbf{E}_{a|\theta_u, \theta_m} \left[v_u^\top M_a v_m + b_u + b_m + b_0 \right] \quad (5)$$

$$= v_u^\top \left[\sum_a p(a|\theta_u, \theta_m) M_a \right] v_m + b_0 + b_u + b_m \quad (6)$$

Here $\hat{r}_{um}$ is the predicted review rating, and the observed rating r_{um} is generated using $\mathcal{N}(\hat{r}_{um}, \epsilon^{-2})$. This is a strict generalization of the PMF model. The key difference is that the aspect weighting for a given (user,movie) combination is dependent on the aspects they excel in. In other words, the metric is variable in accordance with the content of the movie and the interest of the user. The idea is that, if a movie is a SciFi movie with correspondingly high value of $\theta_{m,\text{SciFi}}$, then the user's review of the movie will likely contain SciFi-related content and moreover, the SciFi quality of the movie will matter in terms of the overall rating. That is, $\theta_{um,\text{SciFi}}$ will likely be large.

A few comments regarding M_a are in order. First and foremost, it does not increase the total number of parameters dramatically, since we only require k terms for each diagonal matrix. In turn it allows us retain *one* joint latent attribute model in v_u and v_m while simultaneously being able to identify individual aspects as needed via $v_u^\top M_a v_m$.

3.4 A Language Model for Reviews

A key in our reasoning is the integration between ratings and reviews. We already established the link between general attributes, aspect-specific ratings and posited a model for the aspect distribution of the a review.

As shown in the sample review in the introduction, when writing a movie review, the user will express his opinions through a set of sentiment words, such as *best*, *weak* or *boring*. Close examination also shows that the user has different opinions on different aspects of the movie. For instance, the user might like the *music* of a movie but dislike the *plot*. This motivates us to model an aspect-specific sentiment for a movie. Overall, we assume that the review language model is given by a convex combination of five components.

- A background language model covering the default word distribution ϕ_0.
- A background sentiment distribution addressing positive and negative sentiments, i.e. ϕ_{s+} and ϕ_{s-}. They are not document specific.
- A movie-specific word distribution ϕ_m. This is employed to capture the names of actors, movie title, and primarily salient entities in the review.
- An aspect-specific word distribution ϕ_a.
- An aspect-specific sentiment distribution ϕ_{as+} and ϕ_{as-} capturing positive and negative sentiments. Note that the use of words can be highly context specific. For instance, while *brutal* tends to carry a negative connotation, it is associated with positive reviews in the context of war movies. We detect this automatically.

Crucial to the mixture between these models is the use of a switch variable which chooses between the above types. We accomplish this via π, the switching distribution. From it we draw the selector variable y_{umi} for each word and depending on its value we pick one of the above five components. We now go through each of the terms in detail:

Switching distribution π_{um}**:** We draw it from a Dirichlet prior. Subsequently draw y_{umi} from π_{um}, that is

$$\pi_{um} \sim \text{Dir}(\gamma) \text{ for } \pi_{um} \in \mathcal{P}_5 \quad (7)$$

$$y_{umi} \sim \text{Mult}(\pi_{um}) \quad (8)$$

In other words, we infer on a per-review basis what the mixture of generic and specific terms is.

Aspect z_{umi}**:** Whenever we draw an aspect-specific word, we need to decided the aspect. This is accomplished by sampling from θ_{um}, i.e.

$$z_{umi} \sim \text{Mult}(\theta_{um}). \quad (9)$$

Aspect sentiment s_{umi}**:** When s_{umi} is an aspect-specific sentiment, its sentiment is determined by the aspect-specific rating via a logistic link function.

$$p(s_{umi}|r_{uma}, z_{umi} = a) = \frac{1}{1 + e^{-s_{umi}(cr_{uma}-b)}}. \quad (10)$$

In other words, the propensity of picking a positive or a negative sentiment word are related to the aspect specific rating r_{uma}. Note that we identify $s_{umi} = 1$ with positive and -1 with negative sentiment.

Aggregate sentiment s_{umi}**:** When s_{umi} is an general sentiment, this is entirely analogous to above. The only difference is that we draw s_{umi} from the aggregate rating $\hat{r}_{um} = \sum_a \theta_{uma} r_{uma}$. In other words, as before, we use a logistic model to infer general sentiments, employing the predicted review rating $\hat{r}_{um}$.

Language models $\phi_0, \phi_s, \phi_a, \phi_{as}, \phi_m$**:** Each of the language models is a multinomial distribution with a Dirichlet as a conjugate. That is, we assume that

$$\phi_0 \sim \text{Dir}(\eta_0), \qquad \phi_s, \phi_{as} \sim \text{Dir}(\eta_{\text{sentiment}}),$$
$$\phi_a \sim \text{Dir}(\eta_{\text{aspect}}), \qquad \phi_m \sim \text{Dir}(\eta_{\text{movie}})$$

where the value of each element in $\eta_.$ depends the part-of-speech tag of the corresponding word. Adding hierarchy to language models is an obvious direction for improvement, albeit at the expense of a rather more expensive inference problem.

Emission model: The final piece in our approach is to model how the actual words are being generated.

- Based on y_{umi} decide which of the five model types to pick.
- If y_{umi} is aspect specific, select ϕ from the aspect models using aspect z_{umi}.
- If y_{umi} is aspect-sentiment specific, inspect s_{umi} for a matching sentiment for aspect z_{umi}.
- If y_{umi} is sentiment specific, inspect s_{umi} for the corresponding sentiment.

Likewise, we choose the baseline model ϕ_0 or the movie specific model ϕ_m as needed.

By default we choose Gaussian priors for real-valued parameters and Dirichlet conjugate priors for the multinomial distributions. This completes the model specification.

3.5 Properties

Before we delve into details of the inference algorithm, a brief discussion of some properties of the model is in order. The coupling between aspect specific sentiments and ratings allows us to infer such terms without the need for detailed reviews. In fact, it overcomes the problem arising in [19]: there the recommender model could not take advantage of aspect specific ratings to obtain a more refined user model. Moreover, it overcomes the limitation of having only a small number of aspects, such as in [12] since it does not require an explicit formulation of categories. To the best of our knowledge, this is the first integrated model for recommendation.

As byproduct we obtain aspect preferences for both movie and user. Furthermore, we are able to extract movie-specific terms via ϕ_m. This is useful for search and retrieval.

4. INFERENCE AND LEARNING

Our goal is to learn the hidden factor vectors, aspects, and sentiments of the textual content to accurately model user ratings and maximize the probability of generating the textual content. Hence our objective is the negative log posterior, defined as

$$\mathcal{L} := -\log p(\mathcal{R}, \mathcal{W}|\Upsilon, \Omega). \quad (11)$$

where $\mathcal{R}, \mathcal{W}$ denote the ratings and words respectively and Υ and Ω are the Gaussian and Dirichlet hyperparameters.

Unfortunately, inference in this problem is intractable in its direct formulation. Instead, we resort to a hybrid inference procedure combining sampling and variational optimization. That is, we use Gibbs-EM [21], an inference method that alternates between collapsed Gibbs sampling [6] and gradient descent, to estimate parameters in the model. After collapsing out the parameters pertaining to the language model, terms cease to be conditionally exchangeable, hence we cannot decompose $\mathcal{L}$ further. That said, all relevant terms decompose for the purpose of the inference algorithm and we have:

$$\mathcal{L} \text{ “=” } \sum_{r_{um} \in \mathcal{R}} \left[\epsilon^{-2}(r_{um} - \hat{r}_{um})^2 - \log p(w_{um}|\Upsilon, \Omega)\right]. \quad (12)$$

The first term denotes the prediction error on user ratings. The second term denotes the probability of observing the text conditioned on priors. Note that this is *not* a formal equality since each review and score depends on its annotation and, indirectly, on the annotations of all remaining documents. This is simply to convey the intuition of the inference approach that we will pursue.

In the E-step, we perform Gibbs sampling to learn the hidden variables by fixing the values of θ_{um} and $\{r_{uma}\}_{a=1}^A$. In the M-step, we perform gradient descent to learn hidden factor vectors by fixing the values of $\{y, z, s\}_{umi}$.

4.1 E-step

In the E-step, we perform Gibbs sampling to learn the hidden variables $\{y, z, s\}_{umi}$ by fixing the values of θ_{um} and all $\{r_{uma}\}_{a=1}^A$ updated in the gradient descent step. Dirichlet-Multinomial conjugacy allows Gibbs sampling to work by sampling on the individual tuple of $\{y, z, s\}_{umi}$, collapsing out all the language models ϕ. As this is a conventional step, we omit the detailed derivations and present the derived Gibbs sampling update rules. Interested readers are referred to [6] for more details.

For the word in the i-th position of the review written by user u for movie m, we jointly sample its switching variable y_{umi}, topic z_{umi} and sentiment s_{umi}, conditioned on its Markov blanket. Let $w = w_{umi}$ and d denote the set of variables $\{umi\}$.

$$p(y_d = y, z_d = z, s_d = s | y_{\neg d}, w, \theta_{um}, \Omega) \quad (13)$$

$$\propto \frac{C^y_{\neg d} + \gamma}{\sum_{y'=1}^{5} C^{y'}_{\neg d} + 5\gamma} \cdot \left[\frac{C^w_{y,\neg d} + \eta^w_0}{\sum_{w'=1}^{V} C^{w'}_{y,\neg d} + \eta^{(\cdot)}_0} \right]^{\mathbb{I}(y=0)}$$

$$\cdot \left[\frac{C^w_{y,\neg d,s} + \eta^w_{\text{sentiment}}}{\sum_{w'=1}^{V} C^{w'}_{y,\neg d,s} + \eta^{(\cdot)}_{\text{sentiment}}} p(s|\hat{r}_{um}) \right]^{\mathbb{I}(y=1)}$$

$$\cdot \left[\frac{C^w_{y,\neg d,z} + \eta^w_{\text{sentiment}}}{\sum_{w'=1}^{V} C^{w'}_{y,\neg d,z} + \eta^{(\cdot)}_{\text{sentiment}}} \cdot \theta_{umz} \cdot p(s|r_{umz}) \right]^{\mathbb{I}(y=2)}$$

$$\cdot \left[\frac{C^w_{y,\neg d,z} + \eta^w_{\text{aspect}}}{\sum_{w'=1}^{V} C^{w'}_{y,\neg d,z} + \eta^{(\cdot)}_{\text{aspect}}} \cdot \theta_{umz} \right]^{\mathbb{I}(y=3)}$$

$$\cdot \left[\frac{C^w_{y,\neg d,m} + \eta^w_{\text{movie}}}{\sum_{w'=1}^{V} C^{w'}_{y,\neg d,m} + \eta^{(\cdot)}_{\text{movie}}} \right]^{\mathbb{I}(y=4)}$$

Here $C^w_{y=4,\neg d,m}$ denotes the number of times that w is sampled as a movie-specific word in movie m excluding the current word assignment; all the other Cs are defined in the same way. $\mathbb{I}(\cdot)$ is a indicator function that returns 1 if the statement is true and 0 otherwise. In other words, we effectively have a big switch statement distinguishing 5 cases.

Note that when $y = 3$, the word is an aspect word, and we need to sample an aspect label from θ_{um}, which is a deterministic softmax transformation of the sum of θ_u and θ_m given by (4). The aspect sentiment probability $p(s|r_{umz})$ is based on (10) and the aggregate sentiment $p(s_d = s|\hat{r}_{um})$ uses an analogous logistic function for the predicted general rating $\hat{r}_{um}$ of the movie.

4.2 M-Step

In this step, we use gradient descent to learn the set of parameters $\Theta = [\{v_u, b_u, \theta_u\}_{u=1}^{U}, \{v_m, b_m, \theta_m\}_{m=1}^{M}, \{M_a\}_{a=1}^{A}]$ by fixing the values of $\{y, z, s\}_{umi}$. In this case, our objective function is further modified as follows:

$$\mathcal{L}' = \sum_{r_{um} \in \mathcal{R}} \left[\epsilon^{-2}(r_{um} - \hat{r}_{um})^2 - \log p(\{w, y, z, s\}_{um}|\Theta) \right] - \log p(\Theta|\Upsilon). \quad (14)$$

The first term remains unchanged from (12). The second goal is to maximize the likelihood of generating all the observed $\{y, z, s, w\}_{u,m}$ variables obtained from Gibbs sampling. The final term is the Gaussian prior of all the parameters. We then seek to minimize the following objective function, decomposed from (14).

Let $\mathcal{L}'_{um}$ be the objective for a single rating and review texts, i.e.: $\mathcal{L}' = \sum_{r_{um} \in \mathcal{R}} \mathcal{L}'_{um} - \log p(\Theta|\Upsilon)$. We expand the likelihood contribution of a given (user,movie) pair $\mathcal{L}'_{um}$ as follows:

$$\begin{aligned} \mathcal{L}'_{um} =& \epsilon^{-2}(r_{u,m} - \hat{r}_{u,m})^2 \\ & - \log p(\{w, z, s\}_{um} \mid \theta_u, v_u, b_u, \theta_m, v_m, b_m, M_a) \\ =& \epsilon^{-2}(r_{u,m} - \hat{r}_{u,m})^2 - \sum_s N^{y=1}_{u,m,s} \log p(s \mid \hat{r}_{um}) \\ & - \sum_a \sum_s N^{y=2}_{u,m,a,s} \log p(s|r_{uma}) - \sum_a N^{y=3}_{u,m,a} \log \theta_{uma}. \end{aligned}$$

where $N^{y=1}_{u,m,s}$ is the number of times general sentiment s appears in user u's review in movie m, and $N^{y=2}_{u,m,a,s}$ is the number of times the aspect sentiment s appears under aspect a, and $N^{y=3}_{u,m,a}$ is the number of times aspect a appears in the review. We then compute the first derivatives of $\mathcal{L}'$ with respect to the variables. We optimize $\mathcal{L}'$ using L-BFGS.

4.3 Implementation

We perform 500 runs of Gibbs EM. In each run, we run one iteration for the Gibbs sampling stage and another 10 iterations of gradient descent. We fixed the number of topics and the dimension of the latent factors. For our models and competing baseline models, we use grid search on a development set to select the model hyperparameters. For grid search, we choose latent factor size from $\{5, 10\}$. As our data is sparse, a fairly low rank of factor vectors is sufficient; we also choose a relatively small aspect size from $\{5, 10, 20\}$, so as to leave space for the model to learn a much larger number of movie words. In the following experiments, the regression parameter ϵ^{-2} is set to be 5.0. Aspect distributions θ_u, θ_m have Gaussian priors, with variances being 0.1 and 1.0 respectively. To reflect the fact that more sentiment words should be adjectives, adverbs, or verbs, η_0, η_{movie}, and η_{aspect} is 0.001 on adjectives, adverbs, and verbs, and 0.01 for other words. On the other hand, $\eta_{\text{sentiment}}$ is 0.01 on adjectives, adverbs, and verbs, and 0.001 for other words.

5. QUANTITATIVE EVALUATION

Having defined our model mathematically we now proceed to evaluating it. We begin with a quantitative evaluation in the present section. A qualitative discussion of the results follows. Our experiments show that:

- Our model outperforms state-of-the-art methods in terms of MSE on recommendation.
- Our model has better predictive power in terms of perplexity on new reviews.
- Our model is able to model review texts effectively and distinguish between words associated with aspects and sentiments.

5.1 Protocol

We use a dataset compiled from IMDb. We randomly select 50k movies and crawl all their reviews. We only keep those reviews with user ratings (scaled from 0 to 10). We remove users who have less than two reviews and then remove movies with less than two reviews. Note that despite this simple cleaning, our data is much more sparse with only 0.03% entries present, than, say Netflix [3] or the datasets studied in HFT [12]. Table 1 displays some statistics.

# users	54,671
# movies	22,380
# user reviews	348,415 (density 0.03%)
# unigram (after pruning)	118,616

Table 1: IMDb data set. Unigrams containing stop words or punctuations, as well as infrequent unigrams that appear less than five times in the corpus are removed during pruning.

We present histograms over different numbers of reviews for movies and user in Figure 2. Clearly, the majority of users only write a small number of reviews and the majority of movies only receive a few reviews. This is not too surprising, given that IMDb aims to catalogue all movies, including obscure works dating from the 19th century. This

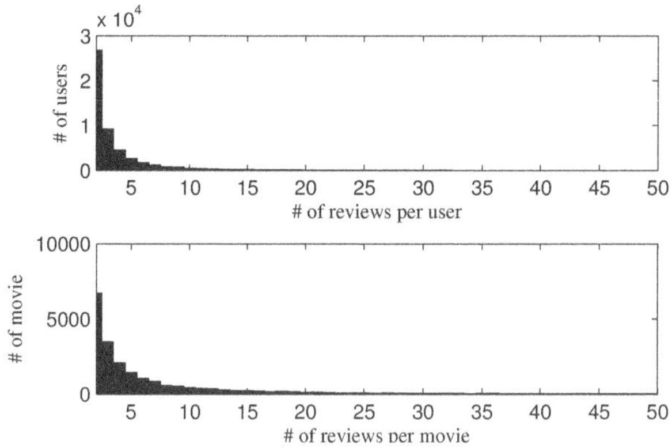

Figure 2: Histograms for reviews for movie and user.

sparsity underscores the importance of a method that can handle 'cold-start' for users or movies with few reviews.

We randomly split our data set into training, validation and test sets. Similar to [12], we use 80% of our dataset as training data, 10% for validation, and 10% for testing. We evaluate the following competing models for comparison: offset only, two state-of-the-art methods, and our model.

Offset only Predict the rating as the average of past ratings. This is the best constant predictor we can get.

PMF Probabilistic matrix factorization [15]. This model is designed for numerical ratings while ignoring all the review texts. By comparing to it, we evaluate the importance of jointly modeling ratings and reviews.

HFT Hidden factors with topics [12]. This work also models both review texts and ratings. It shows state-of-the-art performance on a variety of review data sets. By comparing with HFT, we examine which of them provides a better modeling of movie reviews.

JMARS Jointly modeling aspects, ratings and sentiments. This is the full model discussed in Section 3.

5.2 Perplexity

We analyze the perplexity of all the competing models. Perplexity is a standard measure to evaluate the quality of probabilistic models. The performance in terms of perplexity shows the prediction power of the model on unseen reviews, where a lower perplexity means a better performance.

Since PMF does not use review texts, it is not considered in this evaluation. For HFT and our model, we define perplexity as follows:

$$\log \mathrm{PPX}(D_{\text{test}}) = -\frac{1}{N_w} \sum_{\substack{u,m \\ d_{um} \in D_{test}}} \sum_{i} \log p(w_{umi}). \quad (15)$$

Here $p(w_{umi})$ denotes the likelihood of generating the i-th word in the review written by user u for movie m in D_{test}, and N_w is the total number of words in the test data. In the following formulas, we use w and y to refer to w_{umi} and y_{umi} whenever indices are obvious.

In HFT, the word likelihood $p(w_{umi})$ is defined as:

$$p(w) = \sum_{a} \hat{\phi}_{a,w} \hat{\theta}_{m,a}. \quad (16)$$

where $\hat{\phi}_{a,w}$ is the estimated word distribution of topic a, and $\hat{\theta}_{m,a}$ is the estimated topic distribution of the movie m.

In our model, $p(w_{umi})$ is defined as:

$$\begin{aligned} p(w) &= p(y=0 \mid \pi_{um})\hat{\phi}_0^w + p(y=1 \mid \pi_{um}) \sum_s p(s \mid \hat{r}_{um})\hat{\phi}_s^w \\ &+ p(y=2 \mid \pi_{um}) \sum_a \sum_s p(s \mid r_{uma})\hat{\theta}_{uma}\hat{\phi}_{as}^w \\ &+ p(y=3 \mid \pi_{um}) \sum_a \hat{\theta}_{uma}\hat{\phi}_a^w + p(y=4 \mid \pi_{um})\hat{\phi}_m^w. \end{aligned} \quad (17)$$

Here we use the word distributions ϕ, user parameters $\{v_u, b_u, \theta_u\}$, movie parameters $\{v_m, b_m, \theta_m\}$ and M_a learned in the training step. In this case, we can calculate all terms in Eqn. 17 except π_{um}. Then we run Gibbs sampling on the testing data for 50 iterations to estimate π_{um}.

We vary aspect size and latent factor size to test model performance. Note that HFT enforces topics and latent factors with the same dimension, but our model allows them to have different dimensions. To evaluate the sensitivity of model performance in terms of aspect size, we vary aspect size for each latent factor size. Results are shown in Table 2.

Factor size	HFT	JMARS		
		A=20	A=10	A=5
5	8,247	**3,348**	3,369	3,399
10	7,459	**3,335**	3,359	3,379

Table 2: Comparison of models in terms of perplexity on held-out data in terms of different topic and latent factor size.

Consistently, our model achieves better performance than HFT in terms of different factor size. The main difference between our model and HFT lies in the way of modeling review texts, where our model uncovers underlying rich information, e.g.: aspect, sentiment and movie-specific contents. This shows a carefully designed language model for review texts could have better predictive power for unseen data. Furthermore, our model's performance varies more in terms of different aspect size A instead of factor size K. This shows that the latent factor dimension in probabilistic matrix factorization has minor effect, compared to the aspect dimension in topic modeling.

5.3 Movie recommendation

Factor size	Offset	PMF	HFT	JMARS		
				A=20	A=10	A=5
5	7.07	5.99	5.21‡	**4.97**†	5.11	5.23
10		5.92	5.14‡	**5.05**†	5.18	5.28

Table 3: Comparison of models in terms of MSE on held-out data. † and ‡ mean the result is better than the method in the previous columns at 1% and 0.1% significance level, measured by McNemar's test.

We compare our model with baseline models on the movie recommendation task, measured by Mean-Square-Error (MSE) on the held-out test data. Results are shown in Table 3. Similarly we vary topic size and latent factor size to test model performance. Our observations as follows:

- The offset baseline does not perform well compared to all other methods, which shows that our rating data has a relatively large variance.
- HFT significantly outperforms PMF at 0.1% significance level. Hence adding review texts can significantly improve the matrix factorization model.
- Our model achieves the best performance in terms of different factor size when the size of aspect is 20.
- Different from HFT where each topic is associated with a hidden factor dimension in matrix factorization, our model learns aspect-specific ratings and use aspect preference of reviews to aggregate these ratings to account for the final rating. This allows us to diverge aspect size from hidden factor size. For example, in our data set, the ratings are sparse (density 0.03%) but with rich user generated textual contents. Therefore, with small factor size and relatively large aspect size, our model can better fit the data and achieve better results in terms of MSE.
- Our results also suggest that a lower size of aspects may not be sufficient to capture distinct aspects and aspect sentiments in our data, which is an important premise for modeling aspect-specific ratings in our model. A relatively large aspect size has better performance and clean aspect words. We will present detailed aspect words in Section 6. We have also tried a larger size of aspect, but the improvement is minor.

5.4 'Cold-start' recommendation

Making recommendations for new users or items which do not have enough rating data is a common issue in recommendation systems. For our model and HFT, although the training data for an item is scarce, the review associated with it can still provide important textual information. HFT clusters the review words into topics, which are tied with item factor vector. Our model identifies aspect distribution and aspect sentiment within the review, and associates the sentiment words with matrix factorization. Therefore, both models can potentially help to better deal with 'cold-start' users and items.

We compare the performance of our model with HFT in terms of relatively improvement over PMF. Performance is evaluated on movies/users with different amount of reviews in training data, as shown in Figure 3. Our findings are as follows:

- In the comparison of different numbers of training ratings for movies, both our model and the HFT consistently outperform PMF, ranging from 10% to 34% relative improvement over PMF. This shows the benefit of modeling review texts for recommendation. Compared with HFT, our model's performance is similar when the number of reviews for movie is small, which suggests that it is difficult to learn the user's aspect taste and movie's aspect property given a few reviews. However, our model outperforms HFT when the number of reviews for movie is relatively large. It suggests that our model can better utilize the textual information (e.g. aspects, sentiments, aspect-sentiments) within user reviews, while the HFT only cluster review contents as topics.
- Both our model and HFT consistently outperform PMF under different numbers of training ratings for users. Similarly, we also observe that our model outperforms HFT when the numbers of training ratings for users is relatively large, which suggest that our model can better fit the textual information.

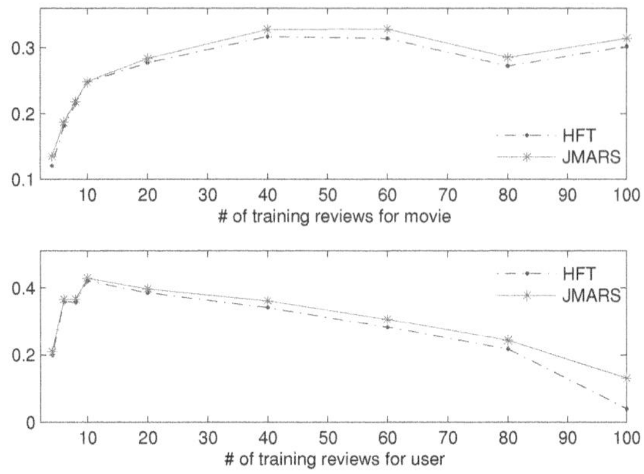

Figure 3: Improvement in MSE compared to PMF for 'cold-start' movies and users.

6. QUALITATIVE EVALUATION

6.1 Aspect rating

Aspect	Director	History	War	Life	Character
Rating	9.36	8.55	8.51	9.20	9.50
Prob	0.12	0.10	0.09	0.09	0.08

. . . what an excellent piece of cinema . . . the actors are great and directing incredible . . . in 300, Gerard Butler dominates the screen . . . battle scenes are incredible . . .

Table 4: The learnt aspect-specific ratings and latent sentiment identified by our model for a review.

To evaluate whether our model is capable of interpreting the reviews correctly, we examine the learned aspect ratings of our model. We present one review in our training set along with the learned aspect ratings and sentiments of the top 5 aspects in the table above. As we can see, the high aspect probability in 'director' aspect reflects the fact that positive sentiment has been expressed towards the director, e.g.: "directing incredible" in the review. Commonly one would assume that the *War* topic would dominate in anything written about the movie *300*, whereas here we are able to infer that it is the directing that is being reviewed.

6.2 Background and sentiment words

Background-word and sentiment-word distributions, ϕ_0 and ϕ_S, are presented in Table 5.

Not surprisingly, the top three background words are 'film', 'story', and 'character', all of which provide little information about aspects or sentiments. Positive sentiment words such as 'great' and 'good', and negative sentiment words such as 'bad' and 'boring', are all sentiment words which are not aspect-specific. Note that we do not handle negation, hence "not good" will be split into "not" and "good", which makes "good" appear in negative word distribution.

Type	Words
Background	film, story, character, films, characters, movies, scenes, scene, real, good
Positive	great, good, love, acting, fun, funny, excellent, lot, thought, perfect
Negative	bad, good, pretty, acting, plot, boring, worst, watching, minutes, stupid

Table 5: Top background words from ϕ_0 and sentiment words from ϕ_s.

6.3 Aspect and sentiment

Aspect words and aspect-sentiment words from three popular aspects are shown in Table 6. These words are easily interpretable. For example, for the aspect 'Adventure', the top words are "earth," "human" and "space". Aspect-sentiments contain sentiment words specific to aspects, e.g. "spectacular" of "Adventure" aspect, "sharp" of "Social" aspect, and "nasty" of "Violence" aspect. These words emphasize the importance of discriminating sentiment words for different aspects. Note that the word 'nasty' is classified as both positive and negative in the context of 'Violence'. In our opinion, this is not a mistake, as the word 'nasty' can indeed convey positive or negative connotations for different users at the same time.

6.4 Movie specific words

We present movie-specific words in Table 7. These are words that do not convey sentiment or genre information and are particular to the movie. They typically correspond to names of places, actors, and other entities. For example, character names like "Bond" and "James" pertaining to the movie "Casino Royale" and words like "Neo" to the movie "The Matrix Reloaded" . These words also provide a list of interpretable keywords specific to the movies.

Movie	Words
Casino Royale	bond, craig, james, casino, royale
Batman Begins	batman, bruce, wayne, bale, begins
The Matrix Reloaded	matrix, neo, reloaded, action, flight
American Beauty	beauty, american, spacey, lester, kevin

Table 7: Top movie-specific words from ϕ_m.

In summary, our model performs well at distinguishing different types of words: background, aspect, sentiment, aspect-sentiment and movie specific words. The resulting word distributions provide a low-rank representations of aspects, sentiments and movies, which give a great insight to understand them.

6.5 Failure Modes

After examining the cases which have higher prediction error rates, we find that one source of errors is the inconsistency of ratings and review words in reviews.

> Score: 1/10
>
> *I am a teenager, and I never thought of finding The Godfather so interesting! It shows a vivid and perfect example of the words Classic and Timeless in a movie...*

The reviewer expresses clearly positive opinions in the review yet gives a low rating. This is an observation that most systems would like to rule out since it may harm the whole system. One possible solution is to perform database cleaning by examining the inconsistency between sentiment words and ratings and rule out such cases. Our system can detect this case by observing the inconsistency between word probability and rating accuracy. This technique can then be applied to anomaly detection or database cleaning, which removes reviews with less meaningful information.

7. CONCLUSION

In this paper we proposed JMARS which provides superior recommendations by exploiting all the available data sources. Towards this end, we involve information from review and ratings. In fact our model is able to capture the sentiment in each aspect of a review, and predict partial scores under different aspects. Additionally the user interests and movie topics can also be inferred with the integrated model. We showed that our model outperforms state-of-the-art systems in terms of prediction accuracy and the language model for reviews is accurate. Future work includes capturing the hierarchical nature of movie topics and incorporating non-parametric models to increase flexibility. Moreover, a fast inference algorithm is required to further increase the scalability of this model.

8. ACKNOWLEDGEMENTS

This research is supported by the Singapore National Research Foundation under its International Research Centre @ Singapore Funding Initiative and administered by the IDM Programme Office, Media Development Authority (MDA).

9. REFERENCES

[1] D. Agarwal and B.-C. Chen. Regression-based latent factor models. In J. Elder, F. Fogelman-Soulié, P. Flach, and M. Zaki, editors, *ACM SIGKDD International Conference on Knowledge Discovery and Data Mining*, pages 19–28. ACM, 2009.

[2] A. Ahmed and E. P. Xing. Staying informed: supervised and semi-supervised multi-view topical analysis of ideological perspective. In *Conference on Empirical Methods in Natural Language Processing*, pages 1140–1150. ACL, 2010.

[3] R. M. Bell and Y. Koren. Lessons from the Netflix prize challenge. *SIGKDD Explorations*, 9(2):75–79, 2007.

[4] A. Z. Broder. Computational advertising and recommender systems. In P. Pu, D. G. Bridge, B. Mobasher, and F. Ricci, editors, *Conference on Recommender Systems*, pages 1–2. ACM, 2008.

[5] J.-F. Cai, E. J. Candès, and Z. Shen. A singular value thresholding algorithm for matrix completion. *SIAM Journal on Optimization*, 20(4):1956–1982, 2010.

[6] T. Griffiths and M. Steyvers. Finding scientific topics. *Proceedings of the National Academy of Sciences*, 101:5228–5235, 2004.

[7] L. Hong, A. Ahmed, S. Gurumurthy, A. Smola, and K. Tsioutsiouliklis. Discovering geographical topics in the twitter stream. In *International Conference on World Wide Web*, 2012.

"Adventure"			"Violence"			"Social"		
Aspect	Negative	Positive	Aspect	Negative	Positive	Aspect	Negative	Positive
earth	effects	effects	murder	nudity	violence	social	attempts	ultimately
human	special	visual	police	exploitation	cinematography	moral	result	level
space	cgi	adventure	killer	female	genre	society	sense	dramatic
world	sci-fi	exciting	crime	pace	solid	point	material	intelligent
planet	mess	sci-fi	cop	violent	gritty	question	superficial	contemporary
fight	monsters	human	mystery	tension	stylish	human	shallow	strength
action	science	impressive	detective	nasty	highly	god	fails	essentially
alien	lack	sets	case	gratuitous	sinister	act	trite	complexity
science	cg	epic	death	naked	inspired	nature	ugly	sympathetic
humans	effort	spectacular	dead	sleazy	engaging	issues	one-dimensional	genuinely
save	giant	cool	thriller	brutal	macabre	men	grotesque	compelling
kill	mindless	evil	victim	hilarious	blood	personal	banal	understated
battle	silly	elements	murdered	murderous	vicious	culture	awkward	sharp
crew	fairly	set	murders	low-budget	nasty	behavior	satirical	equally
attack	sci	created	criminal	trashy	compelling	conflict	excessive	thoughtful

Table 6: Top topic words from ϕ_a for three topics measure by aggregating all $\theta_{u,m}$ across reviews. The aspect labels (adventure, violence, social) are manually assigned.

[8] Y. Koren. Collaborative filtering with temporal dynamics. In *ACM SIGKDD International Conference on Knowledge Discovery and Data Mining*, pages 447–456, 2009.

[9] Y. Koren, R. Bell, and C. Volinsky. Matrix factorization techniques for recommender systems. *IEEE Computer*, 42(8):30–37, 2009.

[10] A. Lazaridou, I. Titov, and C. Sporleder. A bayesian model for joint unsupervised induction of sentiment, aspect and discourse representations. In *Annual Meeting of the Association for Computational Linguistics*, pages 1630–1639, 2013.

[11] H. Ma, H. Yang, M. R. Lyu, and I. King. SoRec: Social Recommendation Using Probabilistic Matrix Factorization. In *Conference on Information and Knowledge Management*, pages 931–940, 2008.

[12] J. McAuley and J. Leskovec. Hidden Factors and Hidden Topics: Understanding Rating Dimensions with Review Text. In *Conference on Recommender Systems*, pages 165–172, 2013.

[13] J. J. McAuley, J. Leskovec, and D. Jurafsky. Learning attitudes and attributes from multi-aspect reviews. In *International Conference on Data Mining*, pages 1020–1025, 2012.

[14] Q. Mei, X. Ling, M. Wondra, H. Su, and C. Zhai. Topic sentiment mixture: Modeling facets and opinions in weblogs. In *International Conference on World Wide Web*, pages 171–180, 2007.

[15] A. Mnih and R. Salakhutdinov. Probabilistic matrix factorization. In *Neural Information Processing Systems Conference*, pages 1257–1264, 2007.

[16] I. Porteous, E. Bart, and M. Welling. Multi-HDP: A non parametric bayesian model for tensor factorization. In D. Fox and C. Gomes, editors, *Conference on Artificial Intelligence*, pg. 1487–1490. 2008.

[17] R. Salakhutdinov and A. Mnih. Bayesian probabilistic matrix factorization using markov chain monte carlo. In W. Cohen, A. McCallum, and S. Roweis, editors, *International Conference on Machine Learning*, volume 307, pages 880–887. ACM, 2008.

[18] X. Su and T. M. Khoshgoftaar. A survey of collaborative filtering techniques. *Advances in Artificial Intelligence*, 2009 4:2, Jan. 2009.

[19] C. Tan, E. H. Chi, D. Huffaker, G. Kossinets, and A. J. Smola. Instant foodie: Predicting expert ratings from grassroots. In *Conference on Information and Knowledge Management*, 2013.

[20] I. Titov and R. Mcdonald. A Joint Model of Text and Aspect Ratings for Sentiment Summarization. In *Annual Meeting of the Association for Computational Linguistics*, pages 308–316, Columbus, Ohio, 2008.

[21] H. M. Wallach. Topic Modeling: Beyond Bag-of-words. In *International Conference on Machine Learning*, pages 977–984, 2006.

[22] C. Wang and D. M. Blei. Collaborative Topic Modeling for Recommending Scientific Articles. In *ACM SIGKDD International Conference on Knowledge Discovery and Data Mining*, pages 448–456, 2011.

[23] H. Wang, Y. Lu, and C. Zhai. Latent aspect rating analysis without aspect keyword supervision. In *ACM SIGKDD International Conference on Knowledge Discovery and Data Mining*, pages 618–626, 2011.

[24] M. Weimer, A. Karatzoglou, Q. Le, and A. J. Smola. Cofi rank - maximum margin matrix factorization for collaborative ranking. In J. Platt, D. Koller, Y. Singer, and S. Roweis, editors, *Advances in Neural Information Processing Systems 20*, 2008.

[25] S.-H. Yang, B. Long, A. Smola, H. Zha, and Z. Zheng. Collaborative competitive filtering: learning recommender using context of user choice. In W.-Y. Ma, J.-Y. Nie, R. A. Baeza-Yates, T.-S. Chua, and W. B. Croft, editors, *Research and Development in Information Retrieval*, pages 295–304. ACM, 2011.

[26] X. Zhao, J. Jiang, H. Yan, and X. Li. Jointly modeling aspects and opinions with a MaxEnt-LDA hybrid. In *Conference on Empirical Methods in Natural Language Processing*, pages 56–65, 2010.

User Effort Minimization Through Adaptive Diversification

Mahbub Hasan Abhijith Kashyap Vagelis Hristidis Vassilis Tsotras
Computer Science and Engineering, UC Riverside
{hasanm, akash001, vagelis, tsotras}@cs.ucr.edu

ABSTRACT

Ambiguous queries, which are typical on search engines and recommendation systems, often return a large number of results from multiple interpretations. Given that many users often perform their searches on limited size screens (e.g. mobile phones), an important problem is which results to display first. Recent work has suggested displaying a set of results (Top-k) based on their relevance score with respect to the query and their diversity with respect to each other. However, previous works balance relevance and diversity mostly by a predefined fixed way. In this paper, we show that for different search tasks there is a different ideal balance of relevance and diversity. We propose a principled method for adaptive diversification of query results that minimizes the user effort to find the desired results, by dynamically balancing the relevance and diversity at each query step (e.g. when refining the query or viewing the next page of results). We introduce a navigation cost model as a means to estimate the effort required to navigate the query-results, and show that the problem of estimating the ideal amount of diversification at each step is NP-Hard. We propose an efficient approximate algorithm to select a near-optimal subset of the query results that minimizes the expected user effort. Finally we demonstrate the efficacy and efficiency of our solution in minimizing user effort, compared to state-of-the-art ranking methods, by means of an extensive experimental evaluation and a comprehensive user study on Amazon Mechanical Turk.

Categories and Subject Descriptors

H.2.m [**Database Management**]: Miscellaneous

Keywords

Diversity; User Effort Minimization; Mobile Applications

1. INTRODUCTION

Now-a-days mobile devices have become increasingly popular for searching. The majority of ecommerce sales are currently performed through smartphones or tablets, and specifically about 35% exclusively through smartphones [27]. Keyword-based interfaces have been widely adopted as the preferred query method because they are simple and intuitive. Nevertheless, keyword queries are often *ambiguous*, that is, they have multiple interpretations, and consequently generate many results. As an example, consider the query "memory" which might refer to computer memory (RAM, ROM, Flash etc.) or the song Memory from the acclaimed musical Cats. For such ambiguous queries, a ranking that considers only relevance (e.g., [8]) might return a large number of similar results from just one interpretation of the query, e.g. DDR3 RAM, and a user with different search intent (say music) might not find any result that is relevant to her in the first page (Top-k) of the results.

To deal with query ambiguity, recently several search applications have incorporated diversification while ranking results to improve the user experience. Examples of such applications include web search [4][6], recommendation systems [9][18][19][20], semi-structured databases [23], graph search [2], and document summarization [15]. A diversified ranking includes not only relevant (as judged by the underlying ranking function) results, but also results that may be less relevant and are diverse with respect to other results in the ranked list. By covering results from multiple interpretations of a query, diversified ranking thereby increases the probability of the user finding desired results based on her query intent [1]. Of course, just focusing on diversity and displaying the set of most diverse results is ineffective since some of these results may have low relevance. In its most general form, the problem of query result diversification is modeled as a bi-criteria optimization problem [1][5], which uses a trade-off parameter (λ) to tune the relative effect of relevance and diversity factors during ranking. Using λ, the impact of the diversity factor can be increased for highly ambiguous queries so as to include more diverse elements in the result set; whereas for very specific (non-ambiguous) queries, this factor can be decreased to prevent inclusion of results of lesser relevance.

As an example, consider Figure 1a which depicts the result set returned for the query 'Camera' (on a structured dataset like Amazon.com). As seen in the figure, the result set includes products from several categories including DSLR, Compact cameras and Accessories. Each result has a set of features (e.g. Brand, Megapixel, Zoom etc.). Note that the Lenses of DSLR cameras are considered in the Accessory category, therefore DSLR cameras do not have a Zoom feature. Since there is a limited paginated interface available to the user for displaying the results (mobile screen size etc.), Figures 1b-1d show the Top-3 results (first page) selected by varying the trade-off parameter between diversity and relevance. Note that the relevance ranking in this example assigns a higher score to DSLRs. For a user shopping for DSLR cameras, the ranking shown in Figure 1b, which prefers relevance over diversity, might be sufficient. However, a user looking for a camera Lens would prefer the highly diversified ranking shown in Figure 1d, where she could click on the Lens attribute value for attribute Type in the Accessory category to see more camera lenses.

KDD '14, August 24–27, 2014, New York, NY, USA.
Copyright 2014 ACM 978-1-4503-2956-9/14/08…$15.00.
http://dx.doi.org/10.1145/2623330.2623610

ID	Product	Category	Features		Rel
1	Camera	DSLR	Brand: Canon	Megapixel: 18.0	0.9
2	Camera	DSLR	Brand: Nikon	Megapixel: 16.0	0.8
3	Camera	DSLR	Brand: Canon	Megapixel: 14.0	0.7
4	Camera	DSLR	Brand: Nikon	Megapixel: 12.0	0.6
5	Camera	DSLR	Brand: Sony	Megapixel: 12.0	0.6
6	Camera	Compact	Brand: Panasonic Megapixel: 14.0	Zoom: 7x	0.6
7	Camera	Compact	Brand: Panasonic Megapixel: 16.0	Zoom: 5x	0.6
8	Camera	Compact	Brand: Fujifilm Megapixel: 12.2	Zoom: 5x	0.4
9	Camera	Compact	Brand: Kodak Megapixel: 10.0	Zoom: 3x	0.2
10	Camera	Accessory	Type: Lens	Focal Length: 18 – 55 mm	0.3
11	Camera	Accessory	Type: Lens	Focal Length: 55 – 300 mm	0.2

(a) Result Set

ID	Product	Category	Features		Rel
1	Camera	DSLR	Brand: Canon	Megapixel: 18.0	0.9
2	Camera	DSLR	Brand: Nikon	Megapixel: 16.0	0.8
3	Camera	DSLR	Brand: Canon	Megapixel: 14.0	0.7

(b) High Relevance and Low Diversity

ID	Product	Category	Features		Rel
1	Camera	DSLR	Brand: Canon	Megapixel: 18.0	0.9
2	Camera	DSLR	Brand: Nikon	Megapixel: 16.0	0.8
6	Camera	Compact	Brand: Panasonic Megapixel: 14.0	Zoom: 7x	0.6

(c) Moderate Relevance and Moderate Diversity

ID	Product	Category	Features		Rel
1	Camera	DSLR	Brand: Canon	Megapixel: 18.0	0.9
6	Camera	Compact	Brand: Panasonic Megapixel: 14.0	Zoom: 7x	0.6
10	Camera	Accessory	Type: Lens	Focal Length: 18 – 55 mm	0.3

(d) Low Relevance and High Diversity

Figure 1: A subset of results of the query *Camera* and associated ranked list of results

Note that, for a given query, the user navigation cost (the user "effort" or actions required to find the desired results) varies for different choices of the trade-off parameter (see Figure 2, for the query "Camera" using the *MMR* algorithm [10] to implement diversified ranking). Moreover, in Section 5 (Figure 7), we show experimentally, that the best value of the trade-off parameter λ varies for different queries. However, no previous work addresses the problem of computing a trade-off parameter that will minimize the user effort. Instead, many hard-code it to a reasonable value (fixing the relative weight between relevance and diversity). Recently, several methods have been proposed [4][16] to learn the trade-off parameter λ. Unfortunately, these methods depend on training data provided by the experts which are expensive to collect or might not be available. Further, they compute a single trade-off parameter for a query, whereas we show how this trade-off changes as the query refinement or results viewing progress.

Because of the display interface, finding the desired result to a particular query might involve several steps. If the user does not find her desired result on the first page, then she might take additional actions to find the result, such as: (a) scan additional pages looking for the results of interest, or, (b) refine the query by clicking on a displayed attribute value to focus on a subset of the original results. Our goal in this paper is to compute at each step a set of k results (corresponding to a page in the user's interface) that dynamically balances diversity and relevance such that the expected user navigation cost is minimized.

Figure 2: Navigation Cost vs. λ for Query *Camera*

What makes the problem difficult is that when the query is posed, neither the target result nor the sequence of actions the user will execute to find it, are known. Therefore, to compute the best set of results to display at each step, we must probabilistically consider all the unknown future user actions, which is a key challenge of our solution. For example, if the user poses the (highly ambiguous) query Camera while her target object is Lens, she will need further actions if we provide the results in Figure 1b (high relevance) in the first page. A higher diversified result set (like the one in Figure 1d) would have been more appropriate. If instead, a more specific query is posed, like DSLR Camera, then higher relevance and lower diversity is preferable, because the user may (with high probability) satisfy her search with just one page. Note that this dynamic balancing of relevance versus diversity can also occur, within the subsequent navigation steps of the same query, as it is progressively refined by the user (e.g. after posing the Camera query and getting the results in Figure 1d, a user interested in lens might refine by selecting the condition Type: Lens).

To this end, we propose a user navigation model that considers factors such as the characteristics of the query result, the user's familiarity with various refine conditions, the number of pages the user would have to navigate and the expected number of navigation steps required to reach a result of interest. The resulting model is adaptive to user actions and constructs a diversified result that minimizes the expected user effort. This is in contrast to the fixed diversity vs. relevance trade-off achieved by previous techniques, which leads to a much higher navigation cost, as shown in our experiments. In summary, we make the following contributions:

1. A user navigation cost model that captures the actions of a user navigating a result set (Section 2).
2. The cost model is necessarily probabilistic since it computes the cost based on possible future actions taken by the user while navigating a result set. We propose ways of estimating the expected cost in Section 3.
3. We show that the problem of computing the best set of results to minimize the expected user effort is NP-hard and propose efficient approximate algorithms to compute an appropriately balanced diversified result-set that minimizes the expected user navigation cost (Section 4).
4. We present the results of an extensive experimental evaluation of the proposed techniques compared to state-of-the-art ranking methods using two real datasets (Section 5).
5. We validate our cost model and measure user navigation time with a user study at Amazon Mechanical Turk, which

shows that our methods outperform the state-of-the-art (Section 6).

Related work is discussed in Section 7 and we conclude in Section 8.

2. PROBLEM DEFINITION

We proceed with the problem setting (Section 2.1), and describe our navigation cost model (Section 2.2), which mimics the actions of a user navigating query results and quantifies the user effort, that is, assigns cost to the user actions. We then conclude with a formal problem definition (Section 2.3).

2.1 Preliminaries

Database: Let $D = \{r_1, \ldots, r_n\}$ be a database consisting of n tuples and $\mathcal{A} = \{A_1, \ldots, A_m\}$ be a set of attributes. Each attribute has an associated domain $ADom(A_i)$ consisting of uninterpreted constants. The database D is heterogeneous and each tuple $r_i \in D$ has a value for a subset $A^i \subseteq \mathcal{A}$ of attributes and a *null* (ϵ) value for the rest.

Query: The user exploring D, navigates the results $R_Q \subseteq D$ of a query Q which could be a keyword query. Each attribute-value combination in the results of R_Q, denoted by $c: A_i = v_i$, is a *condition* and can be used to *refine* the query. We denote the set of all conditions of R_Q by $C(R_Q)$.

Example: Figure 1a shows a result-set R_Q for *Q: Camera*, where the user could refine the query by selecting condition c_i : *Brand = Canon,* which would return the two Canon cameras (#1, #3).

Paginated Result Subset S_k: Typically, the result set R_Q is too large to fit into a single page on the user interface. These results are therefore *paginated* and only a small subset $S_k \subseteq R_Q$ of size k is presented to the user at a time. The size k of the result subset depends on the display size of the device. For example, e-commerce and web-search interfaces typically show 10-15 results at a time on desktop browsers and 5 on mobile devices. The latter are the key focus of this paper, which are even more challenging because the screen size does not allow displaying other result information like facets (see discussion in Section 7).

Example: Figures 1b-d show examples of various paginated result subsets (with $k = 3$) for the query results in Figure 1a.

The choice of the subset S_k is critical in determining the effectiveness of a search interface. In particular, S_k should contain relevant and a diverse set of results.

Let $rel(r, Q)$ be the relevance score of a result $r \in R_Q$, where a higher score means the result r is more relevant to query Q. Existing object relevance ranking functions like [8] can be used to compute $rel(r, Q)$. Also, let $dist(r_i, r_j)$ be the distance between two results $r_i, r_j \in R_Q$. For instance, $dist(r_i, r_j)$ can be the Euclidean distance between the vectors representing r_i and r_j. Currently, most systems model search result diversification as a bi-criteria optimization problem that balances the effect of relevance and diversity using a trade-off parameter ($\lambda \in [0,1]$) as follows:

$$S_k = argmax_{S \subseteq R_Q, |S|=k} \left(\begin{array}{c} (k-1)(1-\lambda) \sum_{r_i \in S} rel(r_i, Q) + \\ 2\lambda \sum_{r_i, r_j \in S} dist(r_i, r_j) \end{array} \right) \quad (1)$$

In Section 1, we described several scenarios where this bi-criteria optimization is problematic. The primary reason is the difficulty in selecting a value of λ for a given navigation step of a query.

Instead of fixing the trade-off between relevance and diversity, we model the diversification problem in terms of the user navigation effort. We do this by designing a holistic model of the user navigating a list of paginated results that considers all the actions taken by a user, discussed next.

2.2 Navigation Cost Model

Users execute queries on a search interface to satisfy a certain information need, which may be satisfied by a certain objects in the query result. Given a user query Q and corresponding result set R_Q, the query interface presents the first page of results $S_k \subseteq R_Q$ of size k to the user. Each result consists of a set of attribute-value conditions. These conditions are *selectable* (e.g. by clicking on the associated link), thereby refining the query. Note that the search interface does not provide any facet conditions to refine the results, but the results serve this dual purpose. Such an arrangement is desirable especially in mobile devices where there is not enough space to show both results and facet conditions.

```
NAVIGATE (Q, R_Q)
1. S_k = COMPUTE-PAGE(Q, R_Q)
2. READ-RESULT(S_k)
3. If search need satisfied by S_k
4.     TERMINATE
5. Choose one of the following:
6.  (a): Select a condition c ∈ C(S_k) to refine;
          REFINE(Q, c): Q ← Q ∧ c
    (b): NEXT-PAGE(R_Q, S_k): R_Q ← R_Q\S_k
7. NAVIGATE(Q, R_Q)
```

Figure 3: Diversification Navigation Model

In particular, the user chooses among the following possible actions at each step:

1. $TERMINATE$: If the user's search need is satisfied on the current page, the search is terminated.
2. $NEXT-PAGE(R_Q, S_k)$: The user can navigate to the next page of the result set in the hope of satisfying her search need there. In this case, the search interface computes the next page of results and presents these results to the user.
3. $REFINE(Q, c)$: Typically, a user has a notion of the properties or conditions that a target (desired) object must have. If one of these conditions is found in one of the displayed results, then the user can refine her query by selecting (clicking) this condition c. The query is then refined to $Q \wedge c$. For example, if a user is looking for *Compact* cameras while reading through the result subset in Figure 1d, she could click on the *Compact* attribute value. This user repeatedly executes REFINE and NEXT-PAGE actions until the target object is found, at which point the user TERMINATEs the navigation. This iterative result navigation process is captured by the recursive navigation model presented in Figure 3. At the beginning of each step (line 1), the system computes a page of k results to be presented to the user. The user reads all the results, represented by READ-RESULT(S_k) and the rest of the navigation repeats recursively.

In our model, the user executes an action based on the displayed result set. Such navigation models, where the user only selects actions proposed by the system, have been used extensively in the navigation of keyword-based query results [12][21][22]. Each user action (REFINE, READ-RESULT, NEXT-PAGE) is an effort on the part of the user. The total effort of the user to satisfy her search need is the *navigation cost*.

As an example, consider the user navigating the result set in Figure 1a using the initial pagination in Figure 1d. Further assume that the user is interested in *Lenses* with *55-300 mm Focal Length* (#11). As a first step, the user would read (READ-RESULT) the first page of 3 results. Next, the user REFINEs by *Type: Lens* to see only the *Lens* results, since she is interested in *Lenses*. Up to this point the navigation cost consists of 3 READ-RESULT actions and 1 REFINE. Upon REFINE, the interface presents the 2 lens results (#10,#11), which the user reads and finds the desired object, thereby TERMINATING the navigation. The overall navigation cost is 5 · READ-RESULT + 1 · REFINE.

If we assume that reading a result incurs unit cost (as was assumed in [12]), and the cost of REFINE (click) action is a constant greater than one (say $\alpha = 3$), the total cost is 5·1 + 1·3 = 8. This assumption about the constant α reflects our belief that REFINE incurs more user effort than reading a result, since the user has to consider all the conditions and then decide on a condition to click on. Similarly, the user could do NEXT-PAGE instead of REFINE if she does not find any useful condition to refine on. The cost of NEXT-PAGE is β.

2.3 Problem Statement

The overall navigation cost depends on the result subset S_k that is presented to the user at each step. For example, if the user in the example above is presented with a paginated result subset containing the Camera *Lens* with *55-300 Focal Length* (#11), then she would find the desired *target* object on the first page and TERMINATE the search. In this case, the total navigation cost is 3 (3 READ-RESULTs).

Therefore, we need to compute a paginated result subset $S_k \subseteq R_Q$, that will minimize the expected navigation cost, by appropriately balancing relevance and diversity. Let $cost(Q, R_Q, S_k)$ denote the cost of navigating the result set R_Q of a query Q, using the paginated result subset S_k. Then the minimal cost of navigation, $cost(Q, R_Q, k)$, is the cost of the paginated result set S_k^{opt}, amongst the $\binom{|R_Q|}{k}$ k-subsets, that has the minimum cost. Formally,

Problem 1: Minimum Cost Diversification(R_Q, Q, k): Given a query Q and its result set $R_Q(|R_Q| \geq k)$, compute the result subset S_k^{opt} of size k $(|S_k^{opt}| = k)$ such that the expected navigation cost incurred to satisfy the user's search need is minimized.

$$cost(Q, R_Q, k) = min_{S_k \subseteq R_Q} cost(Q, R_Q, S_k) \quad (2)$$

Next, we show how to estimate $cost(Q, R_Q, S_k)$, the cost of a result subset S_k for a result set R_Q.

3. NAVIGATION COST ESTIMATION

The navigation cost of a result set R_Q, computed as discussed in Section 2.2, depends on the actions taken by the user in reaching a target object and can be exactly determined after the navigation is complete. However, solution to the minimum cost diversification problem (Problem 1) requires the selection of result subset S_k before knowing what sequence of actions the user will perform after viewing S_k. In this section, we propose a way to estimate the cost of navigating a result subset S_k by means of a probabilistic cost model that assigns uncertainty measures to each possible action a user can take and computes the expected navigation cost for a given S_k.

We begin by introducing the probability measures that capture the uncertainty in user action. In the user navigation model in Figure 3, the user, at each navigation step, has three choices – (1) TERMINATE the navigation (line 3) (2) REFINE by a condition (line 6a) and (3) to go to the NEXT-PAGE of results (line 6b), and we introduce probability measures for each of these actions.

- **P_T (TERMINATE Probability):** This is the probability that the user finds the result she is looking for in S_k, and therefore terminates the navigation process.
- **P_R (REFINE Probability):** This is the probability that the user chooses to refine the result set R_Q by adding a condition c to the query Q. On the other hand, the user could instead choose to see the next page of the results. Since these are the only two choices supported by the navigation model, the probability that the user chooses the NEXT-PAGE action is $1 - P_R$.
- **P_c (REFINE by condition c Probability):** If the user chooses to REFINE, then she also has to select a condition $c \in C(S_k)$ to refine by. The probability P_c captures the probability that the user selects a condition c.

Given the probabilities defined above, the entire navigation process, which contains several iterations, can be expressed by the following recursive cost equation (*cost(.,..,.)* is overloaded):

$$cost(Q, R_Q, S_k) = |S_k| + (1 - P_T) \cdot \left[P_R \left\{ \alpha + \sum_{c \in C(S_k)} P_c \, cost(Q \wedge c, R_{Q \wedge c}, k) \right\} + (1 - P_R)\left(\beta + cost(Q, R_Q \setminus S_k, k)\right) \right] \quad (3)$$

This cost equation can be described as follows:

1. The user reads the results in S_k, and decides about her next action. The cost for reading the results is $|S_k|$ (assuming unit cost for the READ-RESULT action). If the user finds the target object then she terminates the navigation.
2. Otherwise, with probability $(1 - P_T)$, she can either refine the query or go to the next page,
   a. The user decides to refine the query with probability P_R. Let α be the cost for a REFINE action. As the user can select any condition $c \in C(S_k)$,we consider the cost associated with each selection candidate c (shown as $cost(Q \wedge c, R_{Q \wedge c}, k)$) weighted by the P_c value.
   b. With probability P_N the user decides to go to the next page. β is the cost of a NEXT-PAGE action, and the cost entailed by the NEXT-PAGE action and the cost of the rest navigation is $cost(Q, R_Q \setminus S_k, k)$.

The cost equation (Equation 3) depends on the key probability terms P_T, P_R and P_c. We present specific and reasonable methods to compute the probabilities used in our cost model. Depending on the specific application, other computation methods may more closely model the user. The computation of these probabilities is orthogonal to the algorithms presented in Section 4, which are the key contributions of this paper.

Computing P_T: This is the probability that the user finds the target object in S_k and therefore terminates the navigation. Since the target object is not known before navigation, a reasonable assumption is the probability of a potential target object is proportional to its *relevance* score $rel(r, Q)$. If the user finds the target object amongst the result subset S_k, then she can terminate the navigation. Therefore, we estimate the probability of termination as being proportional to the sum of relevance scores in the paginated result subset S_k and normalize it with sum of relevance scores of all the results in R_Q as $P_T = \sum_{r \in S_k} rel(r, Q) / \sum_{r \in R_Q} rel(r, Q)$. The choice of the relevance function is orthogonal to this paper and can be computed in various ways such as TF-IDF [13] for keyword queries or by using Probabilistic Information Retrieval models [8].

Computing P_R : The key assumption we make is that the user has a high likelihood of refining the query when the results in S_k are diverse. This is because a diverse S_k covers multiple aspects of the query by containing results from different interpretations [7], [24]. For example, the result subset in Figure 1d contains results from different categories and also contains a variety of attribute values, and hence offers many refinement opportunities, which translated to a high P_R. In contrast, the result subset of Figure 1b would translate to a low P_R.

To compute the diversity of a result subset S_k, we need to compute the distance between all pairs of results $r_i, r_j \in S_k$ [5]. Distance measures like Euclidean distance, Cosine Similarity can be used for this purpose and again the choice is orthogonal to this paper. The diversity of S_k can be defined as $div(S_k) = \sum_{r_i, r_j \in S_k} dist(r_i, r_j)$. Hence, P_R can be computed as $P_R = \frac{\sum_{r_i, r_j \in S_k} dist(r_i, r_j)}{max_{S \subseteq R_Q, |S| = k} \sum_{r_i, r_j \in S} dist(r_i, r_j)}$, where the denominator is used for normalization and is equal to the maximum possible diversity of a k-result set from R_Q. Finding the maximum diversity in the denominator is similar to the maximum clique problem, and therefore known to be NP-Complete [5]. We use *MMR* [10] to compute the maximum diversity for our experiments (in Section 5).

Computing P_c: This probability shows how likely the user will refine the query by selecting condition $c \in S_k$, which depends on the user's preferences or her familiarity to this condition. A reasonable choice is that P_c is proportional to the frequency of condition c in the result set as described in [12].

4. ADAPTIVE DIVERSIFICATION

Exact Algorithm: To compute the paginated result set such that cost of navigating R_Q is minimized, it is necessary to compute the cost, using Equation 3, of each subset $S_k \subseteq R_Q$ of size k and selecting the subset S_k^{opt} that has the minimum cost. We show that this problem (Problem 1) is NP-hard [28], by reducing Set Cover to a simplified version of this problem. There are two sources of complexity that make the exact algorithm computationally expensive:

1. Computing the navigation cost of each subset $S_k \subseteq R_Q$ of size k requires evaluating Equation 3 for $O\left(|R_Q|^k\right)$ subsets.
2. Since Equation 3 is recursive, to solve it we must compute for each condition c in S_k (more formally $c \in C(S_k)$), the minimum cost (according to Equation 2), which in turn requires computing the minimum cost over all subsets of R_Q (Figure 4(a)). This process continues recursively for deeper levels of the recursion tree. The depth of the recursion is $|R_Q|$ in the worst case, since each refinement may eliminate just one result in R_Q. The width of each recursive step, i.e., the cardinality of the summation, can be up to $m \cdot k$, which is the number of attribute values displayed at each step.

Approach overview: We attack the problem by proposing efficient techniques to approximate both sources of complexity. We first show how to effectively eliminate the recursion from Equation 3 using a sequence of two relaxations. Then we show how to avoid evaluating the simplified equation for every combination of result subsets using a greedy algorithm.

Our approach starts by eliminating recursion from Equation 3 using two relaxations. Figure 4 shows the recursive tree to compute Equation 3 and the simplifications achieved through the two relaxation steps.

Relaxation 1 (Eliminate Conditions from Recursion Tree): The navigation cost function (Equation 3) has two recursive calls – one each for REFINE and NEXT-PAGE actions, respectively to compute the navigation cost for subsequent navigation steps.

Intuitively, the navigation cost of a result-set R_Q is proportional to its size $|R_Q|$, since for a larger result-set the user must explore more results to reach the results of interest. This assumption is backed by our experiments in Section 5 (specifically Figure 6) and we use this observation to simplify the cost equation. Formally,

$$cost(Q, R_Q, k) \propto |R_Q| \qquad (o1)$$

The cost associated with REFINE actions, denoted by $cost(Q \wedge c, R_{Q \wedge c}, k)$, is the navigation cost incurred to reach the target results from the refined result set $R_{Q \wedge c}$. Based on the observation above, this cost is proportional to size of $R_{Q \wedge c}$, i.e.

$$cost(Q \wedge c, R_{Q \wedge c}, k) \propto |R_{Q \wedge c}| \qquad (o2)$$

Based on observations $o1$ and $o2$ and ignoring the constants of proportionality, the cost of the REFINE by a condition c can be estimated as:

$$cost(Q \wedge c, R_{Q \wedge c}, k) = \left(|R_{Q \wedge c}| / |R_Q|\right) cost(Q, R_Q, k)$$

Analogously, the cost of NEXT-PAGE action $\left(cost(Q, R_Q \setminus S_k, k)\right)$ can be approximated as $\frac{|R_Q \setminus S_k|}{|R_Q|} cost(Q, R_Q, k)$, since the user is left with $R_Q \setminus S_k$ of the original result-set R_Q after a NEXT_PAGE action.

By plugging in these approximations and rearranging terms, our cost equation can be rewritten as:

$$cost(Q, R_Q, S_k) = |S_k| + (1 - P_T) \cdot \left\{ \begin{array}{c} \alpha P_R + \beta(1 - P_R) + \\ cost(Q, R_Q, k) \left[P_R \sum_{c \in C(S_k)} P_c \frac{|R_{Q \wedge c}|}{|R_Q|} + (1 - P_R) \frac{|R_Q \setminus S_k|}{|R_Q|} \right] \end{array} \right\} \qquad (4)$$

Equation 4 replaces the recursive calls of REFINE and NEXT-PAGE actions (in Equation 3) with $cost(Q, R_Q, k)$(Figure 4(b)). However, it still requires evaluation of all possible k-subsets of R_Q to compute $cost(Q, R_Q, k)$ according to Equation 2. We address this by the next relaxation.

Relaxation 2 (Eliminate Result Subsets from Recursion Tree): Our goal is to find the result subset S_k that minimizes Equation 4. But note that this same optimal S_k is used to compute $cost(Q, R_Q, k)$ according to Equation 2. Hence, we can replace $cost(Q, R_Q, k)$ by $cost(Q, R_Q, S_k)$ in Equation 4.

Then, by solving for $cost(Q, R_Q, S_k)$, Equation 4 can be further simplified as:

$$cost(Q, R_Q, S_k) = \frac{|S_k| + (1 - P_T).\{P_R.\alpha + P_N.\beta\}}{1 - (1 - P_T).\{P_R.\sum_{c \in C(S_k)} P_c.\frac{|R_{Q \wedge c}|}{|R_Q|} + P_N.\frac{|R_Q \backslash S_k|}{|R_Q|}\}} \quad (5)$$

Equation 5 has no recursion, and can be easily computed for a given S_k. Note that Relaxation 2 does not incur any approximation error, in contrast to Relaxation 1.

Given the relaxed cost Equation 5, we still need to compute the cost of all possible k-result subsets S_k of R_Q to find the optimal S_k^{opt} with minimum cost.

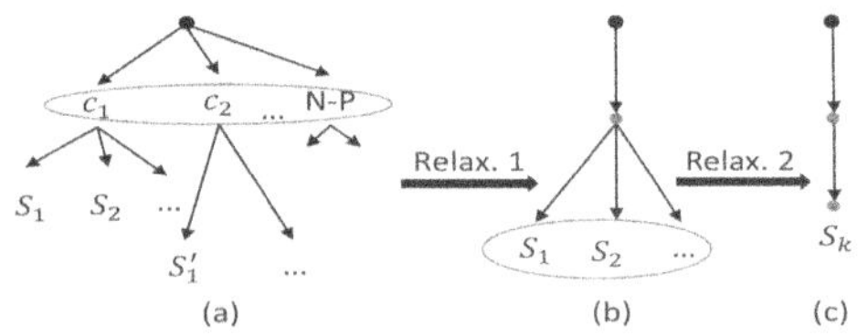

Figure 4: Elimination of Recursion Using Relaxations 1&2

Algorithm: $ADA(Q, R_Q)$
Input: Query Q and Result Set R_Q
Output: Set of k results, $S_k \subseteq R_Q$

1. $S_0 \leftarrow \emptyset$
2. $E \leftarrow R_Q$
3. $r \leftarrow argmax_{r_i \in R_Q} rel(r_i, Q)$
4. $S_1 \leftarrow S_0 \cup r$
5. $E \leftarrow E \backslash r$
6. for p $\leftarrow$ 2 to k do
7. $r \leftarrow argmin_{r_i \in E} cost(Q, R_Q, S_{p-1} \cup r)$
8. $S_p \leftarrow S_{p-1} \cup r$
9. $E \leftarrow E \backslash r$
10. return S_k

Figure 5: Adaptive Diversification Algorithm

For that, we present an efficient greedy algorithm, called *Adaptive Diversification Algorithm (ADA)*, which incrementally builds the result set S_k by adding at each step the result with minimum incremental navigation cost. At each iteration p $(0 \leq p \leq k)$, ADA makes use of two sets: the set of remaining results E and the set of selected results S_p, with $|S_p| = p$. Note that $E \cup S_p = R_Q$, the set of all the results. Initially $E = R_Q$ and $S_0 = \emptyset$. At each iteration, ADA computes $cost(Q, R_Q, S_{p-1} \cup r)$ (using Equation 5) for each result $r \in E$ and moves the result with minimum navigation cost to S_p. This process continues until we select k results (i.e. $p = k$).

Figure 5 shows the pseudo-code of our diversification algorithm ADA. The first result is chosen as the object with highest relevance score (line 3) since we want to provide to the user the most relevant object. After that, in each iteration, ADA ranks the results in E according to Equation 5 with S_k replaced by $S_{p-1} \cup r$, removes the result with minimum navigation cost from E, and adds it in the selected result set (line 6-9). The algorithm terminates when we select k results.

Complexity: The running time of ADA depends on the cost computation time in line 7, which is invoked up to $O(k \cdot |R_Q|)$ times. To compute $cost(Q, R_Q, S_{p-1} \cup r)$ using Equation 5, we need to calculate P_T, P_R, P_N, the cost of all possible REFINEments $(\sum_{c \in C(S_k)} P_c \cdot \frac{|R_{Q \wedge c}|}{|R_Q|})$ and of NEXT-PAGE action $(\frac{|R_Q \backslash S_k|}{|R_Q|})$. Computation of P_T and P_R (Section 3) is dominated by their denominators, which depend on the result set R_Q and k. However, in ADA we only need to compute these probabilities for the original result-set R_Q, which takes time $O(|R_Q|)$ and $O(k \cdot |R_Q|)$(using MMR [10]), respectively. The computation of all REFINEments cost $(\sum_{c \in C(S_k)} P_c . \frac{|R_{Q \wedge c}|}{|R_Q|})$ requires $O(k \cdot m + |R_Q|)$ time. The cost of NEXT-PAGE and P_N can be computed in $O(1)$ time. Therefore, the total running time of ADA is $O(k \cdot |R_Q|^2)$ (assuming $|R_Q| > k.m$). In practice, the execution time is much faster than this worst case bound (Section 5).

Example: Let us apply ADA to the result set in Figure 1a. We are interested to find the 3 results returned by ADA. But before that we analyze Equation 5 more closely to infer the implication of the cost equation. The cost of a result set S_k is minimized when the denominator of the right hand side in Equation 5 is maximized, which implies having higher P_T value. But when the result set size $|R_Q|$ is high, we have smaller P_T value (since the denominator part of P_T in Section 3 is high). Therefore, the navigation cost depends on the cost of REFINE and NEXT-PAGE actions. Since the NEXT-PAGE cost (denoted as $\frac{|R_Q \backslash S_k|}{|R_Q|}$) is the same for all result sets, the navigation cost is minimized for the result set S_k containing highly diverse results with popular selective conditions (i.e., with high P_c). As $|R_Q|$ becomes smaller, P_T dominates cost equation, therefore cost is minimized for highly relevant results.

The conclusion of the above discussion is that, initially when $|R_Q|$ is large (small P_T), ADA prefers diversity over relevance. As $|R_Q|$ becomes smaller (higher P_T) in the next iterations, ADA increases preference to relevance, and provides highly relevant results.

Returning to the running example, ADA initially prefers diversity over relevance in Figure 1a since $|R_Q|$ is relatively large. The first result is the result #1 as it has the highest relevance score (diversity is not a factor when selecting the first result, which is always selected by relevance). The second result would be from *Compact* or *Accessory* categories. Assuming all the conditions in *Compact* and *Accessory* categories have similar selectivity (similar P_c and similar diversity with respect to #1), the second result is #6 because of its high relevance score. The third result would be from the *Accessory* category to increase diversity, and specifically #10 since it has higher relevance score than #11. Thus ADA would return result set in Figure 1d. In the next iteration, as R_Q becomes smaller, ADA will return more relevant result-set snippets like the one in Figure 1c, and in the last iterations like the ones in Figure 1b.

5. EXPERIMENTAL EVALUATION

In this section, we describe the results of an extensive experimental evaluation of our approach. The setup, including methodology, datasets, baselines and metrics used, is described in Section 5.1. Sections 5.2 and 5.3 demonstrate the quality and performance of diversification algorithms in terms of user navigation cost and CPU time. All experiments were performed on a 2.5GHz Intel Core i5 CPU, 8GB RAM machine running Windows 7. We used MySQL as our database and all algorithms were implemented in Java.

5.1 Setup

Datasets: We evaluated our approach on two datasets:

1. **UsedCars:** This dataset consists of a listing of 15,191 used cars, extracted from a popular car-trade website. Each tuple has 10 attributes, 4 categorical and the rest numeric.
2. **Electronics:** This dataset consists of 65K products from the *Electronics* product catalog of a popular e-commerce website. The products were sampled from various *Electronics* categories, such as *Laptops, Desktops, Cameras, Printers* etc. and therefore the dataset is highly heterogeneous in nature. The dataset has a total of 86 (51 categorical and 35 numeric) attributes, but each product has values for a small subset (avg. 12) of these attributes and *null* for the rest.

Queries: We selected 8 queries each from the two datasets. These queries are shown in Table 1 along with result-set sizes. Note that we are interested optimizing the navigation of diverse result sets, and therefore these queries were selected to be deliberately ambiguous so as to include results from a variety of categories. For that, we use single-keyword queries, although our methods support any number of keywords or query conditions; more keywords could be used if larger e-commerce datasets were available. For each query, we select a target object, which we assume the user is looking for, i.e. the navigation terminates when the user locates this target object.

Table 1: Query Set

Electronics			UsedCars		
Query ID	Query	# Results	Query ID	Query	# Results
Q_1	Kodak	193	Q_9	Honda	789
Q_2	Dell	125	Q_{10}	BMW	730
Q_3	Canon	1097	Q_{11}	2001	2034
Q_4	Nikon	511	Q_{12}	2005	920
Q_5	Camcorder	789	Q_{13}	Dallas	2932
Q_6	Speaker	737	Q_{14}	Irving	1064
Q_7	Desktop	394	Q_{15}	Black	2163
Q_8	Laptop	518	Q_{16}	Blue	1183

State-of-the-art: Current approaches to diversification use a fixed *relevance-vs.-diversity* trade-off parameter (λ in Equation 1) to diversify rankings. However, as we argued in Section 1, setting this parameter is not always obvious and depends on the characteristics of the result set. In Section 5.2, we provide evidence to further support this claim. We compare with two commonly used approaches for ranking results:

1. **Baseline 1 (REL):** In this approach, the results were ranked solely based on relevance, i.e. by setting $\lambda = 0$ in Equation 1.
2. **Baseline 2 (MMR-$\lambda = 0.5$):** As a second baseline, we choose the Maximal Marginal Relevance (*MMR*) diversification algorithm [10]. *MMR* computes a diversified result-set by balancing relevance and diversity based on Equation 1. *MMR* is an approximation algorithm since computing a diversified set based on Equation 1 is NP-Complete [5]. In our experiments, we set $\lambda = 0.5$ giving equal weight to diversity and relevance factors.

Note that, for a fair comparison, we used *MMR* both as a baseline and to compute P_R in *ADA* algorithm. We chose *MMR* since it outperforms other algorithms in terms of time and generates quality results [5]. However, our use of *MMR* does not preclude the use of other diversification algorithms, e.g. GMC, GNE [5], which may produce better quality results but take more time compared to *MMR* [10].

Next, we describe the relevance (rel) and diversity ($dist$) measures used in our experimental evaluation. We reemphasize that computing these measures is orthogonal to our problem and any suitable rel and $dist$ versions can be plugged in to our approach. Due to space limitations we omit experiments with additional measures.

Computing $dist$: Computing diversity involves computing distance ($dist$) between two results. We use the sum of distances between the attribute values $dist(r_i, r_j) = \sqrt{\sum_{A_k \in \mathcal{A}} \left(r_i(A_k) - r_j(A_k)\right)^2}$. For numeric attributes, we used the Manhattan distance and for categorical attributes, the Kronecker delta function was used between the values of attribute.

Computing rel: In a structured result-set, the relevance of a result depends on relevance of its attribute values. We estimated the relevance of each attribute value by computing the Google Trends scores (see [8] for more details). The rationale for using Google Trends is based on the idea that the relevance of a term can be based on its frequency in a query workload [8].

Since results in R_Q satisfy all conditions in Q, the relevance scorewas computed using the unspecified attributes in $\mathcal{A}$ by Q, as was proposed by [8], where unspecified refers to an attribute that does not match any query condition. For example in Figure 1a, all the records satisfy the query condition *"Camera"* with their *Product* attribute. Therefore, we compute the relevance score using the unspecified attributes (e.g. *Category, Brand*).

Methodology: For each query in Table 1, we picked a result $t \in R_Q$ as the target object. The chance of selecting a result as the target object is proportional to its relevance score, which means the results with high relevance scores have a higher chance to be selected as the target object. We then simulated the user navigation until target t is reached. Since multiple navigation paths can lead to the target object t, we used a *randomized simulation* [12] to select navigation paths. Note that, given a set of displayed results S_k, the set of conditions that can lead to t is $C(S_k) \cap C(t)$. We assumed that the user will select one of these conditions, or go to next page, according to the navigation probabilities (Section 3). For example in Figure 1a, if the target object is #4, and we select Figure 1c as the displayed result subset, the conditions that lead to #4 are "Product=Camera", "Category = DSLR" and "Brand = Nikon". The user would go to the next page if she does not like or know these three conditions. Therefore, in our simulation, we computed P_N as $\prod_{c \in C(S_k) \cap C(t)}(1 - P_c)$ (the probability that the user would not like any condition in $C(S_k) \cap C(t)$) and P_R as $(1 - P_N)$. In case of refinement, the user could refine the query by selecting any condition in $C(S_k) \cap C(t)$. The choice of selecting a condition $c \in C(S_k) \cap C(t)$ is proportional to P_c.

We used $k = 10$ in the experiments in Section 5.2, 5.3, and showed the findings averaged over 1000 runs (50 random target objects, and 20 runs per target object) for each query.

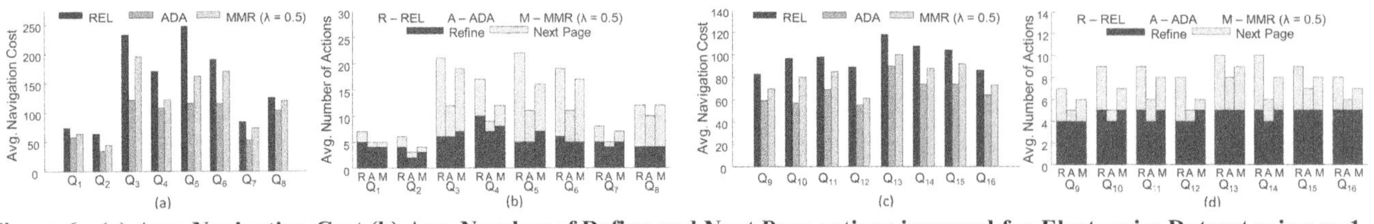

Figure 6: (a) Avg. Navigation Cost (b) Avg. Number of Refine and Next Page actions incurred for Electronics Dataset using α=1, β=1. (c), (d) show the same figures respectively for UsedCars Dataset

5.2 Qualitative Analysis

In this section, we present the experimental results of the qualitative evaluation of the three different algorithms (*REL*, *MMR* and our algorithm *ADA*). Figures 6(a), 6(b) show the average navigation cost and average number of $REFINE$ and $NEXT\ PAGE$ actions incurred respectively by each algorithm to reach the target object for the queries of *Electronics* dataset. Note that, all algorithms require similar number of *REFINE* actions (i.e. selection of target object conditions) to filter out enough undesired objects (Figure 6b). Since *REL* displays results from popular categories, it requires a larger number of $NEXT\ PAGE$ actions to display the conditions of the less relevant target objects. MMR has a fixed ratio of relevance and diversity, which happens to work well for some queries with small number of results like Q_1, Q_2 and Q_4, but is ineffective for other queries like Q_3, Q_6, where more *NEXT PAGE* actions are required to find the target object conditions.

ADA outperforms the other two algorithms, because of its adaptive nature. As discussed in Section 4, when $|R_Q|$ is high, *ADA* prefers diversity over relevance to pick the Top-k results. As R_Q becomes more selective over iterations, *ADA* switches to preferring relevance. Therefore, by balancing diversity and relevance based on the result set at hand, ADA displays the target object conditions much earlier compared to the other two algorithms. This results in fewer $NEXT\ PAGE$ actions, and thus reduces the navigation cost of *ADA* algorithm (Figure 6a). The improvement of *ADA* over the other two algorithms is more pronounced for the queries that have large number of results (e.g. Q_3, Q_5, Q_6).

Figures 6(c), 6(d) show the average cost and actions respectively for the queries of $UsedCars$ dataset. Similar to the *Electronics* dataset, *ADA* outperforms the other two algorithms for all the queries of $UsedCars$. Since the $UsedCars$ dataset is homogeneous, *REL* and *MMR* perform slightly better as compared to *Electronics* dataset, due to less variability in attribute conditions.

Table 2: Average Navigation Cost for the Datasets

Datasets	Average Navigation Cost (α=1, β=1)			
	REL	ADA	MMR (λ = 0.5)	Expected Optimal
Electronics	48.25	30.625	38.75	28.525
UsedCars	30.5	19.15	24.375	18.512

We also compare the average navigation cost incurred by the three algorithms, *REL*, *MMR* and *ADA*, with the expected *optimal* navigation cost computed by solving Equations 2 and 3. Due to the exponential complexity, we compute the expected optimal cost for smaller sizes of initial result sets (R_Q) and query parameter (k). Table 2 shows the average navigation costs for $|R_Q|$ = 100 and k = 5 across all queries for the two datasets *Electronics* and $Usedcars$. We see that our algorithm *ADA* is only 1.07 and 1.03 times worse than the optimal for the *Electronics* and $Usedcars$ datasets respectively. For *MMR* and *REL*, these factors are 1.36 (1.32) and 1.69 (1.65) respectively for the *Electronics* ($Usedcars$) dataset.

Figure 7 shows average navigation cost of MMR with increasing trade-off (λ) values (high λ value implies preference to diversity over relevance) for four queries from Table 1. The results of the other queries are shown in [28]. Since *ADA* is independent of λ value, therefore the cost of *ADA* is shown as a straight line. We skipped *REL* since it incurs higher cost compared to *ADA* and *MMR*. As seen from Figure 7, there is no value for λ that is optimal for a given dataset or even for a particular query. Intuitively λ should change adaptively, at each navigation step, depending on the characteristics of the result set. By balancing the relative importance of relevance and diversity adaptively at each step, *ADA* shows better performance (on average) compared to MMR with a fixed λ.

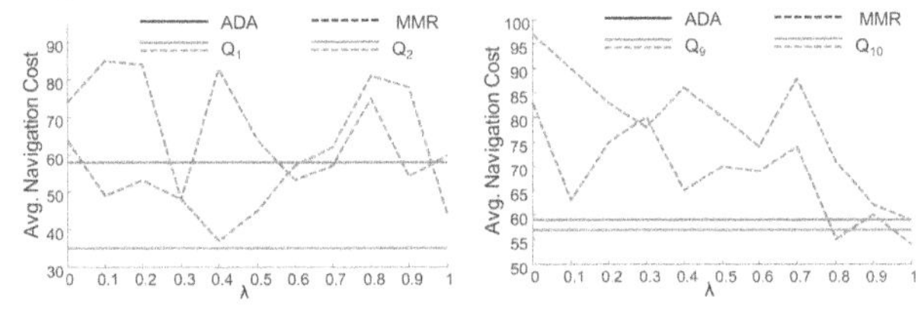

Figure 7: Average Navigation Cost vs. Tradeoff (λ) values

We also perform experiments while varying the model parameters (α, β). The results depict that the overall cost of *ADA* increases at a slower rate with the model parameters compared to REL and MMR [28].

5.3 Performance Analysis

We now present the performance results of *REL*, *MMR* and our *ADA* algorithms. Table 3 shows the average (across all queries) *computation* (CPU) times taken by each of these algorithms to reach the target object. As expected, the relevance-only algorithm (*REL*) takes the shortest time among all the algorithms. Computing diversity is a costly operation since it involves computation of distance between all pairs of results. As a result any algorithm that incorporates diversity is much slower as compared to *REL*; our implementation of *MMR* is *three times* slower as *REL*. Our algorithm (*ADA*) performs this distance computation over all future navigations and therefore is slower than *MMR* by a factor of 1.6. While *ADA* takes more time to compute the set of paginated results, it is very effective in reducing the time or effort incurred by users to navigate such diverse result sets (discussed in Section 6).

Table 3: Avg. CPU Time for the Datasets

Datasets	CPU Time (sec)		
	REL	ADA	MMR (λ = 0.5)
Electronics	0.02	0.106	0.066
UsedCars	0.058	0.156	0.107

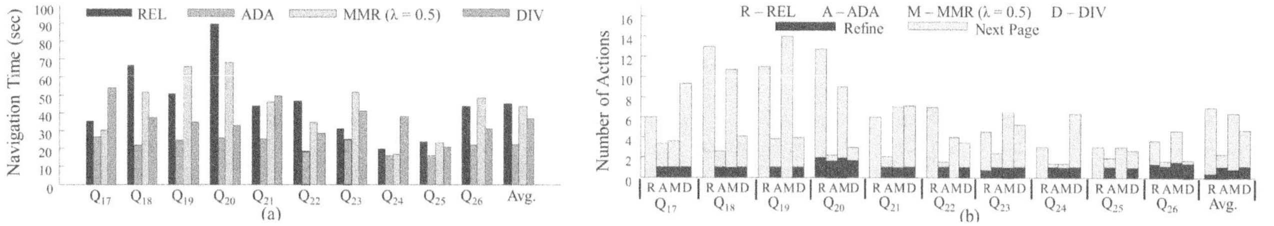

Figure 8. (a) Avg. User Navigation Time, (b) Avg. number of Refine and Next Page Actions incurred by the users for 10 different queries using UsedCars dataset (for α=1, β=1)

We also examine the scalability of our algorithm (*ADA*) by applying it to large result set and find that our algorithm scales almost linearly with result set size [28].

6. USER STUDY

In this section, we present the results of a user study that we conducted at Amazon Mechanical Turk (*MTurk*) [26] using the *UsedCars* dataset. We selected three keyword queries (e.g., *'Ford'*), and for each query we created a set of search tasks; each search task specifies a set of target conditions (e.g., find a car with Color = Green). We asked the users, starting from the results of the initial keyword query, to find the best car (according to the relevance score defined in Section 5.1) that satisfies all the target conditions.

Table 4: Query Set for User Study

Query ID	Initial Query	Initial Result Set Size	Target Conditions	# of Results contain all Target Conditions
Q_{17}	Toyota	1470	Color = Green	86
Q_{18}	Ford	2747	City = Grand Prairie	133
Q_{19}	Ford	2747	Model = F150 Regular CAB, State = MD, Color = Maroon	1
Q_{20}	Ford	2747	Color = Maroon	42
Q_{21}	Ford	2747	City = Ashland	75
Q_{22}	Ford	2747	Color = Beige	40
Q_{23}	Toyota	1470	City = Richmond	88
Q_{24}	Toyota	1470	Color = Red;	79
Q_{25}	Ford	2747	Color = Gold;	116
Q_{26}	BMW	730	Model = Convertible, City = Fairfax, Color = Grey;	1

We repeated the experiment for the four different ranking algorithms: *REL* ($\lambda = 0$), *MMR* ($\lambda = 0.5$), *ADA* (λ-independent) and a diversity-only baseline, *DIV*, which constructs the *k*-result subset greedily at each step by maximizing the score function (Equation 1); i.e. with $\lambda = 1$. The reason that we asked users to find the best and not any result is to avoid giving an unfair advantage to methods biased towards diversity like *DIV* which may help the user to find a satisfying result, but this result may have low relevance. Table 4 shows the list of initial queries, their results' cardinality, the target conditions, and the cardinality of results that satisfy all the target conditions. The page size (k) is set to 10. Each task was completed by 36 MTurk users; we present the average results.

Figures 8(a) and 8(b) show the average time taken and average number of actions executed respectively, by users to find the best target object. As seen in Figure 8(b), if we have more target conditions (e.g. Q_{19}, Q_{26}), using *DIV* (diversity-only), the chances of getting a desired target condition on a given page increases. This increases the probability of *REFINE* action and, therefore, *DIV* performs better (Figure 8(b)) than the other two baselines *REL*, *MMR*, and slightly worse that our algorithm *ADA*, which prefers diversity over relevance during the initial steps. If we decrease the number of target conditions, the performance of *DIV* degrades, especially if multiple results satisfy all target conditions (as seen for the other queries), since the user needs to find the best and not any object. For Q_{17} and Q_{24}, *MMR* ($\lambda = 0.5$) and *ADA* perform similarly, which intuitively shows that 0.5 happens to be the ideal balance between relevance and diversity for these two queries. This is clearly not that case for other queries such as Q_{23}, where *MMR* takes longer time even compared to the relevance-based *REL*.

As shown by the average values in Figure 8(a), *ADA* reduces the navigation time significantly compared to all other algorithms. On average, *ADA* is faster by a factor of 2.04 (p-value 0.004), 1.97 (p-value 0.001) and 1.66 (p-value 0.0002) over *REL*, *MMR* and *DIV*, respectively. This significant improvement is because of the smaller number of actions incurred by *ADA* compared to the other three algorithms (Figure 8(b)).

Figure 9 shows the actual user navigation time vs. the estimated cost (using our cost model in Section 3) for the 10 different queries using the four different algorithms, where for each query we average over all users. The figure and the trend line show a clear correlation, and specifically a linear relationship, which confirms the validity of the cost model.

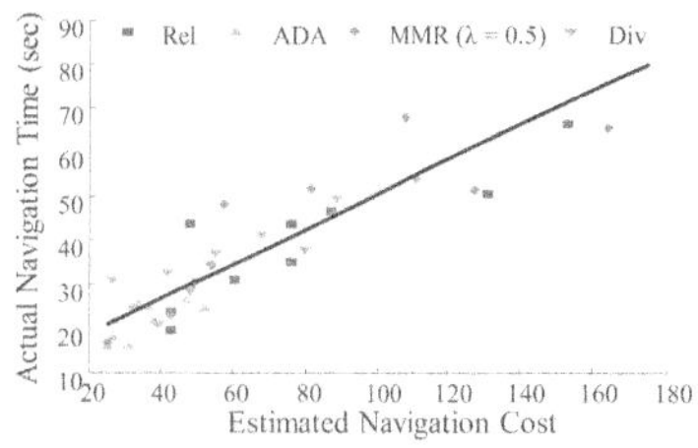

Figure 9. Estimated Cost vs. Actual Time

7. RELATED WORK

Diversification has recently been introduced in search engines and recommendation systems to increase user satisfaction. [6][17] use coverage approaches to cover diverse aspects of search space. [17] expresses the degree of diversification by a setting a parameter which also determines the size of final result set. [6] operates on Web documents and selects diverse documents to cover many different interpretations of the query. [18] provides diversity using the content of the recommendations and the past history of the user. [19] presents a method based on medoids clustering to select a set of diverse and highly-ranked items to recommend to a user. However, none of these approaches considers the problem of how to minimize the total navigation cost incurred by the user to find the target object by considering subsequent navigation steps. In this paper, we have addressed this concern by introducing a navigation cost model (Section 2).

Diversification is being used along with *relevance* in [1][3][5][10]. Most of these approaches (e.g. [5]) consider diversification as a bi-criteria optimization, which uses a fixed trade-off value for relevance and diversity. In Section 5, we have shown that different search tasks require different ideal trade-off value. Some learning methods [4][16] have been proposed to learn the trade-off value. However, these methods rely on training data provided by the experts which is expensive and difficult to obtain in all cases. [25] proposes a dynamic ranking model for interactive user feedback. The ranking is based on the history of other users. In contrast, our ranking function aims to minimize the expected user effort. Threshold based techniques, a variant of the optimization problem, have been proposed in [11] to solve the diversification problem. These approaches consider a threshold value of relevance and maximize the diversity between results (or vice versa). Setting a threshold value is hard, and depends on the domains. Moreover, [5] shows a comparison between several diversification approaches where *MMR* (the baseline used in this paper) clearly outperforms the threshold based approach in both quality and time. Our approach does not require the threshold value, and can adaptively set the balance between relevance and diversity for different tasks.

Faceted Search has been shown to be effective in reducing the user effort and time required to navigate large result sets of structured databases. For a given query, these approaches compute the best facet conditions and matching results to display to the user [12][21][22]. However, this model is not suitable for our setting of limited screen size, where we cannot display separately faceted conditions and results. Instead, our results serve a dual purpose, since a user can click on results' conditions to refine her navigation.

8. CONCLUSIONS

We described a novel framework for adaptive diversification of query results that dynamically adjusts the relevance and diversity of displayed results with the aim to minimize the total expected user navigation cost to reach the desired target objects. Based on this framework, we prove that the problem is NP-hard and we present an efficient approximate algorithm (*ADA*) that computes the best set results to display, by dynamically balancing relevance and diversity at each query step. We experimentally evaluate the performance of our proposed algorithm and show that it outperforms state-of-the-art algorithms. A Mechanical Turk user study confirms our findings and validates our navigation model. As a future work, we plan to extend our navigation model where the user can update/delete the selected conditions during the navigation process.

9. ACKNOWLEDGMENTS

This project was partially supported by NSF grants IIS-1161997, IIS-1216007, and a Samsung GRO grant.

10. REFERENCES

[1] C. Clarke, M. Kolla, G. Cormack, O. Vechtomova, A. Ashkan, S. Buttcher, I. MacKinnon. Novelty and Diversity in Information Retrieval Evaluation. In *SIGIR 2008*.

[2] H. Tong, J. He, Z. Wen, R. Konuru, and C. Lin. Diversified Ranking on Large Graphs: An Optimization Viewpoint.In *KDD 2011*.

[3] E. Demidova, P. Fankhauser, X. Zhou, and W. Nejdl. DivQ: Diversification for Keyword Search over Structured Databases. In *SIGIR 2010*.

[4] R. Santos, C. Macdonald, and I. Ounis. Selectively Diversifying Web Search Results. In *CIKM 2010*.

[5] M. Vieira, H. Razente, M. Barioni, M. Hadjieleftheriou, D. Srivastava, C. Traina, and V. Tsotras. On Query Result Diversification. In *ICDE 2011*.

[6] R. Agrawal, S. Gollapudi, A. Halverson, and S. Ieong. Diversifying Search Results. In *WSDM 2009*.

[7] F. Radlinski, P. Bennett, B. Carterette, and T. Joachims. Redundancy, Diversity and Interdependent Document Relevance. In *SIGIR Forum*, 43(2):46-52, *2009*.

[8] S. Chaudhuri, G. Das, V. Hristidis, G. Weikum. Probabilistic Ranking of Database Query Results. In *VLDB 2004*.

[9] K. Raman, P. Shivaswamy,and T. Joachims. Online Learning to Diversity from Implicit Feedback. In *KDD 2012*.

[10] J. Carbonell and J. Goldstein. The Use of MMR, Diversity-Based Reranking for Reordering Documents and Producing Summaries. In *SIGIR 1998*.

[11] L. Qin, J. X. Yu, and L. Chang: Diversifying Top-K Results, In *VLDB 2012*.

[12] A. Kashyap, V. Hristidis, and M. Petropoulos. FACeTOR: Cost-Driven Exploration of Faceted Query Results. In *CIKM 2010*.

[13] M. J. McGill, G. Salton. Introduction to Modern Information Retrieval. McGraw-Hill, 1986.

[14] E. Vee, U. Srivastava, J. Shanmugasundaram, P. Bhat, and S. A. Yahia. Efficient Computation of Diverse Query Results. In *ICDE 2008*.

[15] K. Liu, E. Terzi, and T. Grandison. Highlighting Diverse Concepts in Documents. In *SDM 2009*.

[16] Y. Yue, and T. Joachims. Predicting Diverse Subsets Using Structural SVMs. In *ICML 2008*.

[17] M. Drosou, E. Pitoura: DisC Diversity: Result Diversification based on Dissimilarity and Coverage, In *VLDB 2013*.

[18] C. Yu, L. Lakshmanan, and S. A.Yahia. It Takes Variety to Make a World: Diversification in Recommender Systems. In *EDBT 2009*.

[19] R. Boim, T. Milo, S. Novgorodov. Diversification and Refinement in Collaborative Filtering Recommender. In *CIKM 2011*.

[20] C.-N. Ziegler, S. McNee, J. Konstan, G. Lausen: Improving Recommendation Lists through Topic Diversification, in *WWW 2005*.

[21] S. B. Roy, H. Wang, G. Das, U. Nambiar, and M. Mohania. Minimum-Effort Driven Dynamic Faceted Search in Structured Databases. In *CIKM 2008*.

[22] K. Chakrabarti, S. Chaudhuri, and S. Hwang. Automatic Categorization of Query Results. In *SIGMOD 2004*.

[23] M. Hasan, A. Mueen, V. Tsotras and E. Keogh. Diversifying Query Results on Semi-Structured Data. In *CIKM 2012*.

[24] M. Hasan, A. Mueen and V. Tsotras. Distributed Diversification of Large Datasets. In *IC2E 2014*.

[25] C. Brandt, T. Joachims, Y. Yue and J. Bank. Dynamic Ranked Retrieval. In *WSDM 2011*.

[26] Amazon Mechanical Turk. https://www.mturk.com

[27] eMarketer Report http://www.emarketer.com/Article/Smartphones-Tablets-Drive-Faster-Growth-Ecommerce-Sales/1009835, 2013

[28] Extended Version of the paper appears at: http://www.cs.ucr.edu/~hasanm/adadiv.pdf

Relevant Overlapping Subspace Clusters on Categorical Data

Xiao He[1], Jing Feng[1], Bettina Konte[1], Son T.Mai[1], Claudia Plant[2]
[1]: University of Munich, [2]: Helmholtz Zentrum München, Technische Universität München
{he, feng, konte, mtson}@dbs.ifi.lmu.de, claudia.plant@helmholtz-muenchen.de

ABSTRACT

Clustering categorical data poses some unique challenges: Due to missing order and spacing among the categories, selecting a suitable similarity measure is a difficult task. Many existing techniques require the user to specify input parameters which are difficult to estimate. Moreover, many techniques are limited to detect clusters in the full-dimensional data space. Only few methods exist for subspace clustering and they produce highly redundant results. Therefore, we propose ROCAT (**R**elevant **O**verlapping Subspace Clusters on **Cat**egorical Data), a novel technique based on the idea of data compression. Following the Minimum Description Length principle, ROCAT automatically detects the most relevant subspace clusters without any input parameter. The relevance of each cluster is validated by its contribution to compress the data. Optimizing the trade-off between goodness-of-fit and model complexity, ROCAT automatically determines a meaningful number of clusters to represent the data. ROCAT is especially designed to detect subspace clusters on categorical data which may overlap in objects and/or attributes; i.e. objects can be assigned to different clusters in different subspaces and attributes may contribute to different subspaces containing clusters. ROCAT naturally avoids undesired redundancy in clusters and subspaces by allowing overlap only if it improves the compression rate. Extensive experiments demonstrate the effectiveness and efficiency of our approach.

Categories and Subject Descriptors

H.2.8 [**Database applications**]: Data Mining

Keywords

Relevant Subspace Clustering; Categorical Data; Minimum Description Length

KDD'14, August 24–27, 2014, New York, NY, USA.

ACM 978-1-4503-2956-9/14/08 ...$15.00.
http://dx.doi.org/10.1145/2623330.2623652.

1. INTRODUCTION

In many applications, ranging from social media to biomedicine, large categorical data sets are collected. The unique characteristic of categorical data is that the values of an attribute do not have any order. For example the attribute *genotype* having four values AA, Aa, aA and aa, where capital A represents the dominant normal variant of a gene and lowercase a the recessive version. There is no implicit order or quantitative spacing between the different categories.

To explore a large categorical data set, clustering is in principle very promising. Among the most successful approaches to unsupervised data mining, clustering aims at finding a natural partitioning of a data set into groups called clusters which represent the major patterns in the data. However, there are several special challenges associated with clustering moderate to high-dimensional categorical data:

1) Many existing algorithms require the user to choose a similarity metric and/or input parameters which are difficult to estimate, e.g. k-Modes [14], COOLCAT [5] and ROCK [13]. In comparison to numerical data where Minkowski distances are wide-spread and well-explored, the choice of a suitable similarity measure for categorical data is much more difficult: In a comparative survey [6], Boriah et al. studied the properties of 14 similarity measures and concluded that a suitable choice requires deep knowledge on the envisaged data mining task and the special characteristics of the data set to be analyzed. The same holds for input parameters like the number of clusters k in k-Modes [14], COOLCAT [5], SUBCAD [9], or the similarity threshold in ROCK [13].

2) Most techniques for clustering categorical data are limited to detect clusters in the full-dimensional space. For numerical data, the effects of the so-called *curse of dimensionality* have been extensively studied and many specialized techniques for clustering moderate to high-dimensional data have been proposed, for a survey see e.g. [16]. For categorical data, fewer approaches have been proposed, e.g. CACTUS [10], SUBCAD [9], and CLICKS [26], most of them associated with the problems mentioned above.

3) These methods are either partition-based (e.g. SUBCAD) or producing large redundancies (e.g. CLICKS). STATPC [19] and RESCU [20] are proposed to find relevant non-redundant subspace clusters but are applicable to numerical data only. Detecting relevant overlapping subspace clusters on categorical data is an open research question.

To address these challenges, we propose a novel approach ROCAT (<u>R</u>elevant <u>O</u>verlapping Subspace Clusters on <u>CAT</u>egorical data) combining the following benefits:

1. **Data compression as an intuitive notion of similarity.** Relating clustering to data compression, ROCAT considers the co-compressibility of the objects inside a cluster as one major aspect to evaluate the cluster quality. Thereby, ROCAT does not require the user to choose a similarity measure to quantify the pair-wise similarity among categorical data objects.

2. **Parameter-free detection of clusters.** Following the Minimum Description Length principle [22], co-compressibility is not the only aspect of cluster quality in ROCAT. We additionally consider the code length specifying the complexity of the clustering model and aim at minimizing both parts. Therefore, ROCAT is fully-automatic without requiring any parameters.

3. **Relevant overlapping subspace clusters.** The coding scheme of ROCAT allows overlapping in both objects and attributes set, but punishes redundancies. Therefore ROCAT finds the most relevant overlapping subspace clusters in the sense that they contribute to an effective compression of the data.

4. **Flexibly handling outliers.** ROCAT supports noise objects and noise attributes which are flexibly identified during the clustering process.

5. **Efficiency.** ROCAT scales linearly in data size.

The remainder of this paper is organized as follows: In the following section, we elaborate our optimization goal. Section 3 presents the algorithm in detail. Section 4 contains an extensive experimental evaluation. Section 5 briefly discusses related work and Section 6 concludes the paper.

2. OPTIMIZATION GOAL COMPRESSION

In this section, we elaborate how a subspace clustering can be used to effectively compress a categorical data set. The basic idea is that objects inside a cluster can be compactly represented by joint coding in the corresponding subspace. Since subspace clusters may overlap, we validate the relevance of each cluster by its contribution to compress the data. Following the Minimum Description Length (MDL) principle [22], the clustering is regarded as a model for compression. The better the data fits to the model, the better is the compression rate since we only need to encode the deviations of the data from the model. In addition to the data, we also need to encode the model itself, which avoids overly complex models and naturally balances goodness-of-fit.

Figure 1 depicts an example of how we use compression to evaluate a clustering of categorical data. The data is represented by a matrix with 10 rows and 8 columns, each row represents 40 data objects and each column is an attribute. Figure 1(a) indicates a subspace clustering with 4 subspace clusters marked as colored squares. The clusters share the homogeneous data in the corresponding subspace, while the white area represents heterogeneous data, i.e. objects have arbitrary categories of the corresponding attributes. It costs 6076.5 bits to compress the data with the proposed coding scheme. Figure 1(b) and 1(c) depict a full-dimensional clustering and no clustering, where we need 6147.1 bits and 6670.9 bits to represent the whole data sets.

In the following, we firstly provide the necessary definitions and then propose a MDL-based coding scheme, which is specially designed for clustering categorical data.

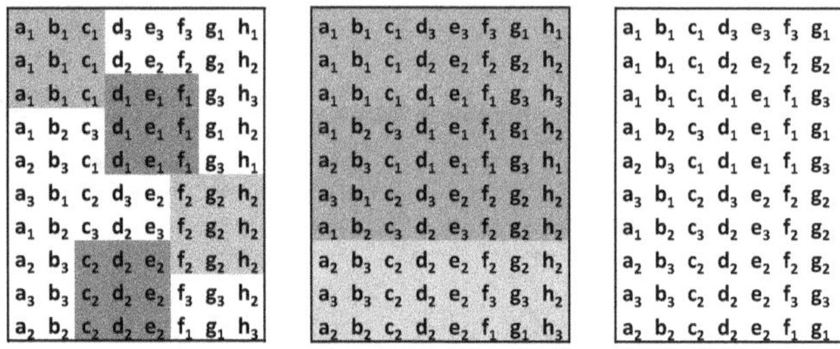

(a)Subspace Clustering (b)Full-D Clustering (c)No Clustering

Figure 1: Using compression to evaluate clustering.

2.1 Notations

DEFINITION 1. *A **Categorical Data Set** is defined as $D = (X, V)$ with N objects and M attributes. $A_1, ..., A_M$ denote a set of categorical attributes and $V_1, ..., V_M$ a set of domains, where $V_j = \{V_{j1}, ..., V_{jm}\}$ is the domain for attribute A_j. $X \in N \times M$ is a matrix storing the categorical value $X(i,j)$ of object i in attribute A_j.*

DEFINITION 2. *A **Subspace Cluster** $C_i = (X_i, V_i)$ is a subset of the data set $D = (X, V)$, where X_i is a sub-matrix of X and V_i is a subset of V.*

DEFINITION 3. *A **Pure Subspace Cluster** is a Subspace Cluster where the objects share the same value in all its attributes.*

DEFINITION 4. *A **Non-Clustered Area** S of data D modeled by subspace clusters $C_1, C_2, ..., C_K$ contains all the entries in matrix X that are not in any sub-matrix X_i, the white area in Figure 1(a).*

2.2 Coding Scheme

Following the concept of MDL principle, the quality of a model is provided by Eq. (1), where $L(H)$ denotes the cost for coding the model and $L(D|H)$ represents the cost of describing the data D under the model H.

$$L(D, H) = L(D|H) + L(H). \tag{1}$$

The model H contains K subspace clusters $C_1, C_2, ..., C_K$ and the non-clustered area S. According to our definition of a Subspace Cluster, $C_1, C_2, ..., C_K$ might overlap in both points and attributes set. The description of data D under the model H is provided by describing $C_1, C_2, ..., C_K$ and S separately. Therefore, $L(D|H)$ consists of two parts: the costs for the clusters and the non-clustered area.

$$L(D|H) = \sum_{i=1}^{K} CC_v(C_i) + CC_v(S). \tag{2}$$

In order to quantify the description length of a subspace cluster C_i or the non-clustered area S, we need to agree on an encoding scheme for C_i and S. For each cluster C_i, we encode the corresponding data sub-matrix X_i of C_i column by column. Specifically, for each assigned attribute A_j of cluster C_i, we calculate the probabilities for all categories in attribute A_j. Then any lossless coding method can be used to compress the column of attribute A_j in matrix X_i, i.e. Huffman coding. Practically we only need the coding length for evaluation, but not the true bits stream. Besides, lossless coding methods are lower bounded by the Shannon entropy.

Therefore, we suggest to calculate the coding length of an attribute A_j in cluster C_i with categories $V_j = \{V_{j1}, ..., V_{jm}\}$ by the Shannon Entropy, which is defined as:

$$Entropy(P) = -\sum_{k=V_{j1}}^{V_{jm}} \cdot P_k \cdot log_2 P_k, \quad (3)$$

$P = P_{V_{j1}}, ...P_{V_{jm}}$ are the probabilities of the categories in attribute A_j and cluster C_i, where $P_k = \frac{|X_i(:,j)==k|}{|C_i.obj|}$ and $|\cdot|$ is the number of entries in a set.

Then the coding cost for cluster C_i is provided as:

$$CC_v(C_i) = \sum_j |C_i.obj| \cdot Entropy(P). \quad (4)$$

The coding cost for the non-clustered area $CC_v(S)$ is calculated analogously to Eq. (4).

In addition to the data, we also need to describe the model itself $L(H)$. The model H contains the clustering assignments and probabilities that are used to encode C_i and S in Eq. (4). We need to describe both the object assignments CC_o and the attribute assignments CC_a to encode the clustering assignments for each subspace cluster C_i. In addition, we need to encode the probabilities used to describe data $L(D|H)$ since they are essential for lossless decoding. These probabilities are encoded as parameters CC_r.

$$L(H) = \sum_{i=1}^{K}(CC_o(C_i)+CC_a(C_i)+CC_r(C_i))+CC_r(S). \quad (5)$$

Specifically, we describe the clustering assignments with object ID tables and attribute ID tables. The object ID table for a subspace cluster is a length N binary table. Objects are assigned 1 if they belong to the cluster, and 0 otherwise. As before, we suggest to encode the tables using an optimal Shannon code. The coding cost for an object ID table of C_i is calculated by its Shannon entropy:

$$CC_o(i) = -N \cdot (p(i) \cdot log_2 p(i) + n(i) \cdot log_2 n(i)), \quad (6)$$

where $p(i) = \frac{|C_i.obj|}{N}$ is the percentage of 1s, $n(i) = 1 - p(i)$ is the percentage of 0s. The coding cost for the attribute ID table is derived analogously to Eq. (6).

We encode the probabilities used in Eq. (4) as parameters. Following [22], the cost for the probabilities can be approximated by:

$$CC_r(i) = 0.5 \cdot |Param| \cdot log_2|C_i.obj|, \quad (7)$$

where $|Param|$ is the number of parameters or probabilities. For each assigned attribute A_j of cluster C_i we need to encode $|V_j|$ probabilities. Therefore, $|Param| = \sum_j (|V_j|)$. The parameter cost for the non-clustered part $CC_r(S)$ is calculated analogously to Eq. (7).

The relevance of each cluster is validated by its contribution to compress the data. Thus the proposed coding scheme is perfectly suitable to evaluate relevant overlapping subspace clusters on categorical data. Firstly, it allows overlapping clusters in both objects and attributes set, but punishes those redundancies, since the overlapping parts will be encoded twice. Secondly, it avoids too complex models (too many small clusters) by encoding the model itself (clustering assignments and the probabilities), thus large informative clusters are preferred. In summary, clustering with the most relevant overlapping subspace clusters will achieve a lower coding cost under the proposed coding scheme.

3. ALGORITHM

In this section, we present an effective and efficient algorithm to identify the most relevant overlapping subspace clusters. Our optimization goal is to find the clustering model that best describes the categorical data set under the proposed coding scheme in Section 2.

3.1 Minimum Coding Problem

The proposed coding scheme does not specify how to find a good clustering; it can only say which of two clusterings is better. The problem, which we call the Minimum Coding Problem in the following, can be modeled as finding sub-matrices (Subspace Cluster) that allow the highest compression with respect to the proposed coding scheme. Given a data set D with N objects and M attributes, there are $I = (\sum_i^N \binom{N}{i}) \cdot (\sum_j^M \binom{M}{j})$ possible sub-matrices, further there are $\sum_i^I \binom{I}{i}$ possible clusterings with different combinations of sub-matrices. Obviously, an naive exhaustive search for the optimal result is infeasible even for a small data set, since the number of candidates $|I|$ is exponential to M and N. Even for the case that $|I|$ is polynomial to M and N, the Minimum Coding Problem is a NP-hard problem.

Minimum Coding Problem is NP-hard. The Set Covering Problem is known to be NP-hard [11]. Given a set of elements U and a set E of n sets, the Set Covering Problem finds smallest subsets of E whose union cover all the elements in U. The Minimum Coding Problem aims at finding sub-matrices of a data matrix X that cover all the entries of X, but uses a different kind of cost function, i.e. the proposed coding scheme. In the case that $|I|$ is polynomial and except of using a different cost function, the Minimum Coding Problem is equivalent to the Set Covering Problem or the Weighted Set Covering Problem. Since the proposed coding function can be calculated in polynomial time, the Minimum Coding Problem is NP-hard as well.

In summary, the Minimum Coding Problem is so difficult that we need an efficient and effective heuristic algorithm to achieve a local optimal result.

3.2 Algorithm ROCAT

The best-possible polynomial time approximation algorithm for the Set Cover Problem is the greedy algorithm [17]. At each stage, the set that contains the largest number of uncovered elements is selected. However, the greedy algorithm can not be used directly to solve the Minimum Coding Problem due to the following reasons. Firstly, the Minimum Coding Problem uses a different cost function, thus including the set that contains the largest number of uncovered elements may not reduce the proposed coding function. Secondly, the number of candidates $|I|$ is exponential to M and N, which makes the greedy algorithm exponential as well.

The proposed algorithm ROCAT is based on the greedy idea as well, but some essential modifications are made to solve the above two problems. Firstly, we need to iteratively include the Subspace Cluster that reduces the overall cost under the proposed coding function. Secondly, we need to reduce the number of candidate Subspace Clusters for greedy selection. Eq. (4) shows that including large Pure Subspace Clusters will lead to a reduction of the coding cost. Additionally, searching for large Pure Subspace Clusters will reduce the candidate space to polynomial as well. Therefore, we focus on selecting the Pure Subspace Clusters at first, then post-process them to get the final Subspace Clusters.

Algorithm 1 ROCAT

```
Input: Data set D = (X, V)
Output: Subspace clusters list SubClus

//Searching phase
SubClus = ∅; Queue queue = ∅; queue.Push(D);
while queue ≠ ∅ do
  Curr = queue.Pop;
  C = FindBestPure(Curr, SubClus);
  if Eq. (1) decreases with SubClus ∪ C then
    SubClus.Add(C);
    queue.PushAll(SplitSpace(Curr, C));
  end if
end while

//Combining phase
Priority queue Pairs = ∅;
for Each pair of clusters C_i, C_j ∈ SubClus do
  Overlap = |C_i.obj ∩ C_j.obj| · |C_i.att ∩ C_j.att|;
  If Overlap > 0, Pairs.Push(C_i, C_j);
end for
while Pairs ≠ ∅ do
  Process Pairs.Pop as shown in Figure 3;
  Choose one process with minimum Eq. (1);
end while

//Reassigning phase
while Convergence do
  for Each cluster C_i ∈ SubClus do
    Find all objects set O with same value in C_i.att;
    Assign or Remove O to C_i.obj based on Eq.(1);
  end for
  for Each cluster C_i ∈ SubClus do
    If C_i.obj changed, Re-select C_i.att based on Eq.(1);
  end for
end while

return SubClus
```

The found Pure Subspace Clusters can overlap and exhibit redundancies. Therefore, during post-processing we firstly combine or split them to remove redundancies, then refine the results by locally modifying clustering assignments.

More precisely, there are three phases in ROCAT: Searching, Combining and Reassigning. Firstly, we iteratively include large Pure Subspace Clusters if the coding cost can be reduced in the Searching phase. Then we merge or split these candidates to remove redundancies in the Combining phase. The candidates with higher redundancy will be processed first. Finally, a reassignment step refines the result by reassigning objects and re-selecting the attributes to the candidate clusters. All phases are guided by the proposed coding scheme, and so every step guaranties decreasing coding cost, which finally leads to reaching a local minimum. The pseudocode of ROCAT is provided in Algorithm 1.

Searching Phase. We iteratively search for the best relevant Pure Subspace Cluster that reduces the coding cost most. The baseline coding cost is determined from a clustering model where all data points belong to the non-clustered area. Eq. (4) shows that large Pure Subspace Cluster will reduce the coding cost most, since the entropy of such clusters is 0. For a given searching matrix we find m large Pure Subspace Clusters, where m is the number of columns of the matrix. The pseudocode for this procedure called **FindBestPure** is depicted in Algorithm 2. The first cluster only contains attribute a with minimum entropy (see Eq. (3)) and objects with largest probability with respect

Algorithm 2 FindBestPure

```
Input: Matrix, SubClus
Output: C

PureClus = ∅; Att' = ∅;
Obj = Matrix.obj; Att = Matrix.att;
while PureClus.Size < |Matrix.att| do
  Find a ∈ Att with min Entropy regarding Obj;
  Obj' = {o ∈ Obj, X_oa = v, |o ∈ Obj| is max};
  Att'.Add(a); Form cluster C with Obj' and Att';
  PureClus.Add(C); Att.Remove(a); Obj = Obj';
end while
C = {C_i ∈ PureClus, Eq.(1) is min for (SubClus ∪ C_i)};

return C;
```

to a. The second cluster is searched in the sub-matrix that contains the objects in the first cluster only. We expand the attribute set of the first cluster by the attribute that has the minimum entropy within the reduced data objects. This procedure is repeated until m Pure Subspace Clusters are found (see Figure 2a). Finally, the one that leads to minimum coding cost is returned as the best Pure Subspace Cluster. The first searching matrix is the value matrix X of data set D, in which we search for the best Pure Subspace Cluster C. If including C decreases the coding cost, we split the current searching matrix by C into two new ones (see Figure 2b) and add both to the searching matrix queue. We continue to search for best Pure Subspace Clusters until the searching queue is empty.

Combining phase. The Pure Subspace Clusters found in the Searching phase can overlap. We remove the redundancies in the Combining phase. The redundancy of each pair of clusters is modeled by their mutual information, which can be approximated by the overlapping entries between them. We firstly choose the two clusters C_i and C_j with the largest redundancy. Then we calculate the value of Eq. (1) for 4 different processing steps that are illustrated in Figure 3. We can preserve both clusters, combine the two clusters into one, preserve C_j and split C_i or preserve C_i and split C_j. Finally, we choose the step that yields the minimum coding cost. The phase is terminated when every pair of overlapped clusters has been processed.

Reassigning phase. The described Combining phase removes the redundancies by combining or splitting pairs of clusters only, thus redundancies may still exist among clusters. Besides, some objects may not be assigned to any cluster yet. Therefore we post-process the clusters in this phase to refine the result. Firstly, for each cluster C_i we

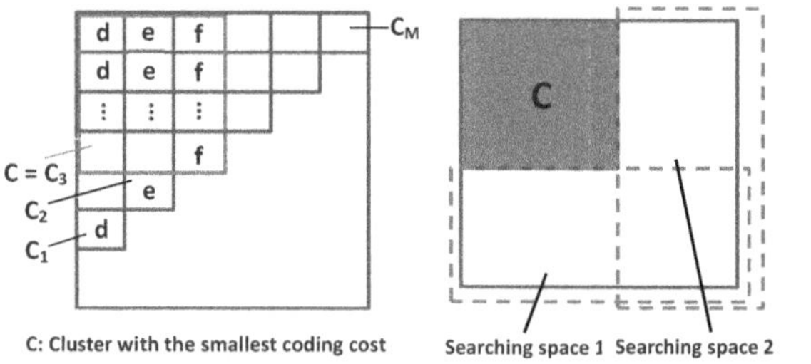

(a) Search the best C. (b) Split the search Space.

Figure 2: Searching Phase.

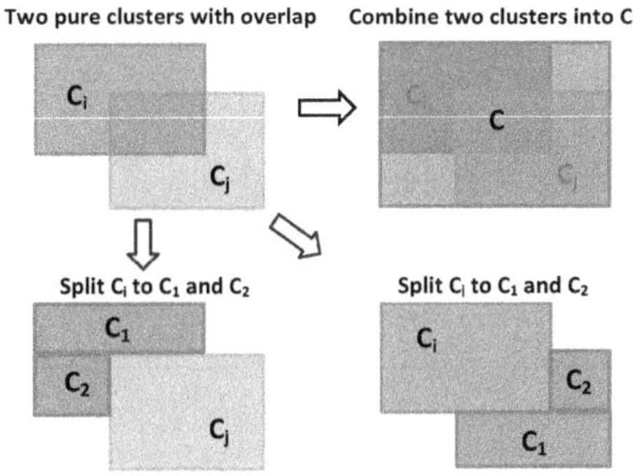

Figure 3: 4 processing candidates in Combining phase.

fix the attributes set and adjust the objects set. In detail, objects set $O \subset D.obj$ with identical value in $C_i.att$ is assigned to C_i or removed from it if this decreases the coding cost. Secondly, we fix the objects set and try to improve the subspace of each cluster. Intuitively, data objects should be compact in the subspace of C_i and sparse in the remaining attributes. Therefore, we rank the attributes according to their entropy (see Eq. (3)), since a compact attributes set leads to a lower entropy while a sparse attributes set causes a higher entropy. Finally, we compare the coding cost for the top-ranked attributes sets and keep the best one if it yields an improvement over the old attributes set. We iteratively do the two steps until no attributes or objects set changes. Those objects that still can not be assigned to any cluster are naturally regarded as outliers.

Runtime Complexity. The runtime complexity of ROCAT for a data set with N objects and M attributes can also be divided into 3 parts. In the Searching phase, we need to go through β objects α times for each dimension, where $\beta \leq N$ and $\alpha \leq M$. Suppose we find γ clusters, controlled by MDL normally $\gamma \ll N, M$. Therefore the runtime complexity in this phase is $O(\alpha \cdot \beta \cdot \gamma \cdot M)$, which is equal to $O(M^2 \cdot N)$. In the Combining phase we need to go through all pairs of clusters, so the runtime complexity in this phase is $O(\gamma^2 \cdot \kappa \cdot \iota)$, where $\kappa < N$ and $\iota < M$ are the average number of objects and attributes in each pure cluster. The runtime complexity in the Combining phase is equal to $O(M \cdot N)$. In the Reassigning phase, in each iteration for each cluster we need to go through its objects set and attributes set once. Therefore the runtime complexity in this phase is $O(i \cdot (N \cdot M))$, which is equal to $O(M \cdot N)$ since the Reassigning phase normally converges very fast. The overall runtime complexity of ROCAT therefore is $O(M^2 \cdot N)$.

4. EXPERIMENTS

In this section, we compare the performance of ROCAT to 8 methods from different areas which are related to this work. Firstly, we compare ROCAT to SUBCAD [9], CLICKS [26] and CLIQUE [2], 3 algorithms for subspace clustering on high-dimensional categorical data. CLIQUE is designed for numerical data but can be easily extended for categorical data. Moreover, we compare our work to two parameter-free algorithms for categorical data, DHCC [25] and AT-DC [7]. Due to space limitations, we do not compare to classical categorical clustering methods, i.e. K-modes [14], ROCK [13], COOLCAT [5]. These methods are not designed to find subspace clusters anyway and in addition DHCC [25] and AT-DC [7] have shown to yield better clustering models. Finally, we compare to 3 algorithms for informative itemset mining, Tiling [12], MTV [18] and Hyper+ [24], which try to find the most important itemsets. The itemset mining methods can be treated as categorical subspace clustering, since the detected itemsets can be regarded as the attributes sets of subspace clusters, while the objects that support the itemset forms the corresponding clusters. CLICKS and CLIQUE are based on the idea of itemset mining as well.

We implement ROCAT and SUBCAD in Java and use CLIQUE from the ELKI package [1]. The codes for all the other methods are provided by the authors. ROCAT, DHCC, AT-DC are parameter-free methods. SUBCAD and Tiling need the number of clusters K, where we set the true number for synthetic data and try different K for real data and output the best results. Besides, the performance of SUBCAD depends on its initialization, thus we report the average results of 10 runs. MTV is proposed as a parameter-free method, but as the execution time is too long and it allows the user to set the number of desired itemsets, we set it as for SUBCAD and Tiling. Two parameters are required for CLICKS (α and min_{sup}) and Hyper+ (false tolerant ratio f and min_{sup}) all from $[0, 1]$. We vary these parameters from 0.1 to 0.9 with a step of 0.1 for all data sets and report the best results. CLIQUE requires to pass grid size ξ and density τ as input parameters. We fix $\xi = 2 * W$ to fit categorical data, where W is the maximal number of categories. Then we vary τ from 0.1 to 0.9 with step 0.1 and report the best results. For Tiling, MTV and Hyper+, the points sets that support the detected itemsets might not cover all the points, thus we regard the rest as outliers like ROCAT.

To evaluate the cluster and subspace quality, we compare pairwise Precision, Recall and F-Measure as introduced in overlapping clustering literature [4, 8] for all data sets. A pair of points sharing at least one cluster is regarded as test outcome positive in clustering results or condition positive in golden standard. Precision is calculated as $\frac{t_p}{t_p+f_p}$ and Recall is obtained by $\frac{t_p}{t_p+f_n}$, where t_p, f_p and f_n are the numbers of true positives, false positives and false negatives respectively. F-Measure is the harmonic mean of Precision and Recall. In addition, we use the confusion matrix and the cluster content to evaluate the quality of all clusters and subspaces for the used real world data.

All experiments are performed on a workstation with 2.9 GHz Intel Core i7 CPU and 8.0 GB RAM.

4.1 Synthetic Data

We generate 4 synthetic data sets with different characteristics as depicted in Figure 4. *Syn*1 contains only overlapping attributes sets, whereas *Syn*2 contains only overlapping points sets. *Syn*3 adheres both kinds of overlapping, while *Syn*4 provides a more difficult scenario. The data sets are generated by first creating Pure Subspace Clusters and then randomly choosing 10% entries of each sub-matrix and randomly changing their values. Afterwards we randomly generate values for the remaining non-clustered area. The number of categories for each attribute is randomly chosen where the average number is 4. For each scenario we generate 5 data sets and report the average performance.

Cluster Quality. Table 1 summarizes the results. Due to space limitations, the following part presents the F-Measure results only. ROCAT is the only algorithm performing very well on all the synthetic data sets with a F-Measure above

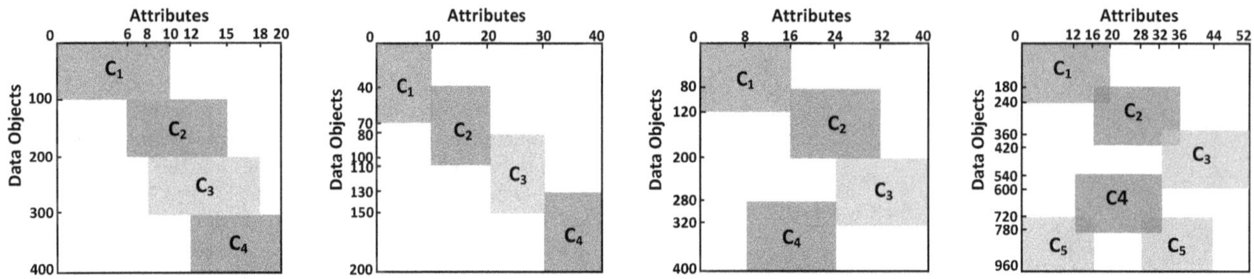

(a) Syn1. (b) Syn2. (c) Syn3. (d) Syn4.

Figure 4: Synthetic Data.

Table 1: Cluster Quality for Synthetic Data (F-Measure).

	Syn1	Syn2	Syn3	Syn4
ROCAT	**0.982**	**0.985**	**0.998**	**0.997**
SUBCAD	0.953	0.603	0.798	0.761
CLICKS	0.499	0.604	0.508	0.489
CLIQUE	0.414	0.604	0.507	0.516
DHCC	0.794	0.826	0.856	0.768
AT-DC	0.895	0.794	0.818	0.704
Tiling	0.542	0.532	-	-
MTV	0.509	0.496	0.439	0.526
Hyper+	0.565	0.634	0.565	0.491

Table 2: Subspace Quality for Synthetic Data (F-Measure).

	Syn1	Syn2	Syn3	Syn4
ROCAT	**1**	**1**	**1**	**1**
SUBCAD	0.975	0.524	0.967	0.949
CLICKS	0.742	0.375	0.375	0.528
CLIQUE	0.414	0	0	0
Tiling	0.808	0.849	-	-
MTV	0.831	0.777	0.638	0.621
Hyper+	0.565	0.469	0.744	0.853

0.982. Note that these results are obtained without requiring any input parameters from the user. Designed for categorical subspace clustering, with suitable parametrization SUBCAD performs well on data set *Syn*1 containing clusters overlapping in the attributes (F-Measure 0.95). However, the performance of SUBCAD severely degrades if clusters overlap in the objects (*Syn*2, F-Measure 0.6). CLICKS and CLIQUE perform worse than ROCAT with a F-Measure of about 0.5, since they output too many redundant clusters (thousands or tens of thousands clusters). DHCC and AT-DC perform fairly well on all the data sets with a F-Measure of about 0.8. However, DHCC and AT-DC are limited to find full-dimensional clusters and therefore do not provide any information about the subspaces in which clusters are contained. Besides, they only find partitioned clusters without any overlapping information. The three informative itemset mining methods Tiling, MTV and Hyper+ do not perform well on our synthetic data sets either and yield F-Measures of about 0.5. The results of Tiling on *Syn*3 and *Syn*4 are discarded since the running time is over 1 hour.

Subspace Quality. In contrast to traditional clustering, subspace clustering does not only aim at finding clusters but also at identifying the subspaces containing clusters with high accuracy. Table 2 shows that ROCAT is the only technique correctly identifying the subspaces in all cases with a F-measure of 1. We discard DHCC and AT-DC, since they do not support subspace clustering. SUBCAD performs well only if there is some overlap in the attributes (*Syn*1, *Syn*3 and *Syn*4), but the performance severely degrades on *Syn*2 where we only have overlap in terms of objects with an F-Measure of only 0.52. CLICKS and CLIQUE perform worst because they output too many redundant clusters. CLIQUE yields results with pairwise F-Measure values of 0 on *Syn*2, *Syn*3 and *Syn*4 because it outputs subspaces with a single attribute only. Tiling and MTV perform fairly well in terms of detecting subspaces with a F-Measure of 0.82 and 0.72 respectively. However, they only find the subsets of golden standard attributes sets. Hyper+ performs better with the more difficult scenarios *Syn*3 and *Syn*4 (F-Measure of about 0.8), but worse with the easier scenarios *Syn*1 and *Syn*2 (F-Measure of about 0.5). Since *Syn*1 and *Syn*2 are relative sparse, Hyper+ outputs more redundant clusters.

Robustness against outliers. We add different amounts of noisy objects to each synthetic data set. Particularly, we add 10% new records with random values in all attributes to *Syn*1 forming the noisy data $Syn1 - 10\%$ and analogously obtain other noisy data with different amounts. The pairwise F-Measure results are shown in Figure 5. We use the same settings for each scenario and for all the algorithms. Obviously ROCAT is extremely robust against noises. We cannot observe any decline in performance on *Syn*3 and *Syn*4. Moreover the decline is also negligible on the other two data sets yielding F-Measures above 0.96 on all examples even in the presence of 40% outliers. All the other algorithms severely degrade in performance in the presence of outliers, since they do not support the detection of noisy objects during the clustering process.

Scalability. To evaluate the scalability of ROCAT with respect to data size and dimensionality, we generate data sets using scenario 4 in Figure 4. For data size, each data set contains 52 attributes and the number of objects is varied from 10000 to 50000. For dimensionality, each data set contains 960 points and the dimensionality is varied from 50 to 200. The parameter settings are the same as for *Syn*4. Figure 6 summarizes the results. Some results are discarded if the running time is longer than 1 hour, i.e. SUBCAD and Tiling regarding data size and CLICKS and Tiling in terms of dimensionality. Figure 6 depicts that all the methods scale linearly in terms of number of objects. ROCAT performs similarly as DHCC and Hyper+, which is faster than MTV and slower than AT-DC, CLIQUE and CLICKS. With respect to dimensionality, ROCAT scales similar as DHCC, faster than SUBCAD and slower than AT-DC. CLIQUE, MTV and Hyper+ scale worst for dimensionality, where the

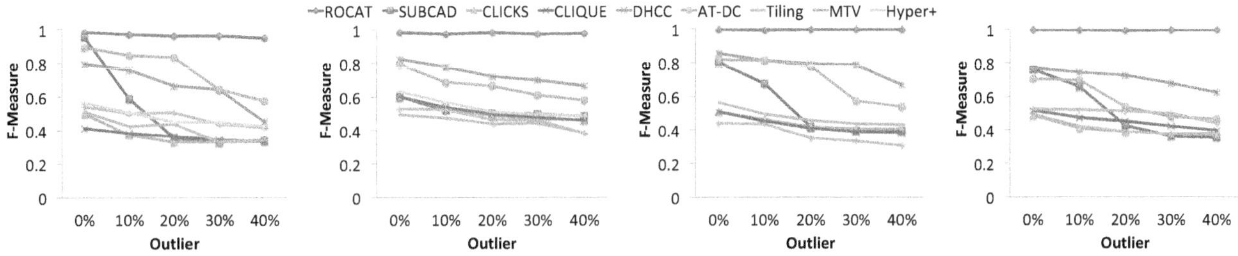

Figure 5: Robustness against outliers, *syn*1 to *syn*4 with outliers from left to right.

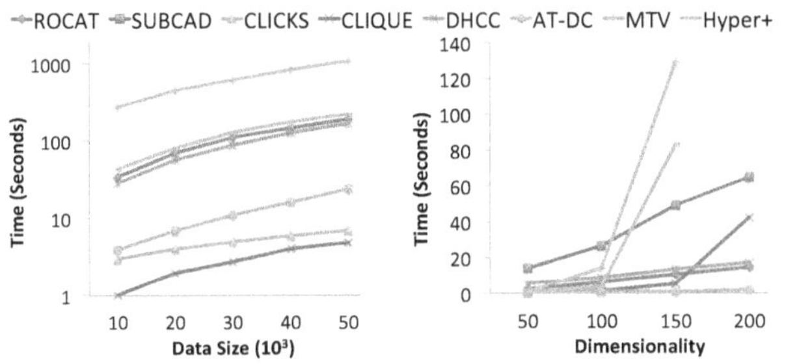

Figure 6: Scalability of ROCAT and comparisons.

running time severely increases when the dimensionality is added to 150 or 200.

4.2 Real World Data

In this section, we evaluate the performance of ROCAT and comparison methods on three real-world data sets: Congressional Votes, Mushroom and Molecular Biology (Splice-junction Gene Sequences) Data Set, which are publicly available at the UCI machine learning repository [1]. For these data sets, only non-overlapping class labels are available and there are only 2 or 3 classes. Moreover, most of the algorithms output many subspace clusters, which are normally the subsets of golden clusters. Therefore, Recall can not manifest the cluster quality anymore and we only use Precision for evaluation. We try different settings for all required parameters and choose the one with the best Precision as it is done for synthetic data sets. The results for real data sets are depicted in Table 3.

Table 3: Cluster Quality for Real Data (Precision).

	Vote	Mushroom	Splice
ROCAT	**0.812**	**0.999**	**0.861**
SUBCAD	**0.845**	0.501	0.378
CLICKS	0.525	0.508	0.343
CLIQUE	0.545	0.501	0.384
DHCC	0.793	0.766	**0.875**
AT-DC	0.521	0.612	0.497
Tiling	0.681	-	-
MTV	0.626	**0.943**	0.754
Hyper+	0.753	0.624	0.384

Congressional Votes. The data set consists of 435 instances, represented by 16 categorical attributes. There are 2 classes: democrat and republican. ROCAT and DHCC automatically output 2 clusters, while AT-DC finds 5 clusters. SUBCAD, Tiling and MTV output 2 clusters. Additionally, ROCAT, Tiling and MTV find an outlier cluster. CLICKS outputs 39 clusters, CLIQUE gives 12 clusters and Hyper+ provides 114 clusters. From Table 3 we can see that ROCAT outputs better clusters than most of the other methods with a Precision of 0.812. The confusion matrices are depicted in Table 4. Due to space limitation, we only show the results of the top 6 methods and clusters with large number of points for those with too many clusters. Clusters with high purity are highlighted in bold.

ROCAT yields two clusters with very high purity, see. Table 4a. Regarding subspace quality, the clusters found by ROCAT are more compact in the detected subspace ($Cp = 0.194$) than in the whole space ($Cp = 0.254$) and the whole data set ($Cp = 0.531$). The compactness value $Cp \in [0, 1]$ is defined in [9], and 0 means that all data values in the corresponding features are the same. Specifically, let us take a look at cluster 0 in Table 4a, which is a pure democrat cluster. ROCAT outputs 12 attributes as the subspace for this cluster. More than 95% of voters in this cluster have the same opinion in 5 of the 12 subspace attributes, they voted *yes* to *aid to nicaraguan contras*, *yes* to *adoption of the budget resolution*, *no* to *physician fee freeze*, *no* to *el salvador aid*, and *yes* to *anti satellite test ban*. Further, at least 80% of the people vote for the same in the other 5 attributes, while more than 70% of them have the same vote in the final two attributes. We get similar statistics for the other cluster. Therefore, ROCAT does find meaningful subspaces for the detected clusters. Since SUBCAD also performs very well on this data set, let us take a look at its democrat cluster as well (cluster 1 in Table 4e). The corresponding subspace consists of 3 attributes only, which represents much less information. ROCAT is able to detect higher dimensional subspace clusters due to the ability to label objects as outliers. In detail, the votes of the instances labeled as outliers are nearly averagely distributed in these 10 attributes. Therefore the properties of the outlier points are very different from those of the subspace clusters and thus it makes sense that ROCAT considers them as outliers. Tiling and MTV found outlier clusters as well. However, they can only find smaller Pure Subspace Clusters, which results in too many outliers. Some of the outliers that share similar subspaces as clusters are not detected.

Mushroom. The Mushroom data set contains 8124 records and 22 categorical attributes. Each record describes a mushroom specimen regarding 22 properties (e.g. shape, color, size) and is identified as definitely edible (4208 records) or poisonous (3916 records). ROCAT, DHCC and AT-DC automatically output 21, 10 and 6 clusters respectively. SUBCAD and MTV output 10 clusters. CLICKS outputs 260 clusters, CLIQUE gives 151 clusters and Hyper+ provides 183 clusters. Table 3 shows that ROCAT greatly outper-

[1]http://archive.ics.uci.edu/ml

Table 4: Results on Congressional Votes.

(a) ROCAT.

Cluster	Democrat	Repub.
0	**148**	**0**
1	**20**	**136**
Noise	99	32

(b) DHCC.

Cluster	Democrat	Repub.
0	49	159
1	**218**	**9**

(c) Hyper+.

Cluster	Democrat	Repub.
0	**9**	**106**
1	**107**	**2**
92	28	20

(d) MTV.

Cluster	Democrat	Repub.
0	**1**	**79**
1	**89**	**0**
Noise	177	80

(e) SUBCAD.

Cluster	Democrat	Repub.
0	**27**	**154**
1	**240**	**14**

(f) Tiling.

Cluster	Democrat	Repub.
0	**2**	**87**
1	**124**	**0**
Noise	141	81

forms the other methods with a Precision of 0.999. The confusion matrices of the top 6 methods are shown in Table 5. Not class-pure clusters are highlighted in bold.

Table 5a clearly shows that nearly all clusters detected by ROCAT are of high purity, which is much better than the other methods. Cluster 15 is the only one that contains several differently labeled records. However, DHCC, AT-DC and Hyper+ output clusters with hundreds of misclassified objects, like Cluster 0 in Table 5b, cluster 1 in Table 5d and cluster 5 in Table 5f. MTV is the second best algorithm on Mushroom data regarding Precision, because most of the clusters are Pure Subspace Clusters. However, there are still many clusters with hundreds of misclassified objects, like cluster 9 in Table 5e. CLICKS outputs many high purity clusters, however, some clusters contain 50 percent misclassified records, like cluster 210 in Table 5c. Besides, cluster 210 shows that the overlapping clusters provided by CLICKS are highly redundant. Cluster 210 contains nearly all the points and only one attribute as the subspace. In contrast ROCAT also finds overlapping clusters in the searching phase, however the redundancy is removed during the Combining and Reassigning phase. Finally, ROCAT outputs the most relevant subspace clusters without any redundancy.

In terms of subspace quality, the compactnesses Cp of the clusters found by ROCAT are 0.126 in the detected subspace, 0.171 in the whole space and 0.518 in the whole data set. Let us take Cluster 2 in Table 5a as an example. The 1296 mushrooms in this cluster are all poisonous. The subspace that this cluster exists in is composed of 14 attributes. Specifically, the cluster consists of specimen *without bruises* and *foul odor*, *free close broad gill*, with identical *shape*, *root* and *surface* of stalk, *partial white veil*, *one large ring* and the color of spore is *chocolate*. Mushrooms with these features are all poisonous. To validate the relevance of this subspace attributes, we calculate the category distribution of the remaining 8 attributes. The result indicates that the mushrooms in these attributes have different category values. For example, the *cap-shape* attribute, contains one half *bell* shaped and the other half *flat* records. Moreover, the *gill-color* attribute exhibits *buff*, *chocolate* and *green* mushrooms. Similar statistics can also be found on other clusters. Consequently, ROCAT can not only detect clusters, but can find the subspaces as well.

Splice. This data set consists of 3190 instances and 60 categorical attributes. The instances are gene sequences and attributes are the positions on the sequences. The value of each attribute is a DNA base (A, T, G, C). Splice contains class labels designating instances as either EI (767 records),

Table 5: Results on Mushroom.

(a) ROCAT.

Cluster	Edible	Poisonous
0	1728	0
1	0	1728
2	0	1296
3	512	0
4	192	0
5	0	256
6	768	0
7	96	0
8	0	192
9	0	288
10	192	0
11	288	0
12	192	0
13	96	0
14	0	72
15	**48**	**32**
16	48	0
17	48	0
18	0	8
19	0	8
20	0	36

(b) DHCC.

Cluster	Edible	Poisonous
0	**2880**	**736**
1	**808**	**72**
2	0	1296
3	216	0
4	0	1728
5	**32**	**24**
6	**64**	**16**
7	192	0
8	0	44
9	16	0

(c) CLICKS.

Cluster	Edible	Poisonous
43	1728	0
56	0	1728
201	**2516**	**80**
210	**4016**	**3856**
230	**2016**	**8**

(d) AT-DC.

Cluster	Edible	Poisonous
0	0	192
1	**798**	**1223**
2	**62**	**1065**
3	1296	0
4	1760	0
5	0	1728

(e) MTV.

Cluster	Edible	Poisonous
0	0	1728
1	1	1296
2	1728	0
3	768	0
4	**288**	**192**
5	512	0
6	480	0
7	528	0
8	**384**	**48**
9	**496**	**224**
Noise	**192**	**524**

(f) Hyper+.

Cluster	Edible	Poisonous
1	1152	0
2	16	1296
3	0	1152
5	**855**	**353**
10	**1056**	**240**

IE (768 records) or Neither (1655 records). EI and IE denote that exon/intron boundaries and intron/exon boundaries can be recognized in the sequence, respectively. Neither states that there are neither EI nor IE sites.

ROCAT, DHCC and AT-DC automatically output 8, 6, and 3 clusters respectively. Besides, ROCAT identifies 1,766 points as outliers. SUBCAD and MTV output 5 clusters. CLICKS, CLIQUE and Hyper+ output 256, 241 and 399 clusters respectively. From Table 3 we can see that ROCAT outperforms most of the other methods with a Precision of 0.861. The confusion matrices of top 6 methods are shown in Table 6. Clusters with good quality regarding the number of contained points and purity are highlighted in bold.

Table 6a clearly illustrates that the clusters found by ROCAT are of very high purity. Cluster 0 and Cluster 1 contain the majority of all data points and are very pure. Cluster 0 is composed of 92% objects from class *IE* and Cluster 1 contains 97% objects from class *EI*. Besides, the outliers detected by ROCAT are mainly composed of records in the *Neither* class. DHCC and MTV also perform well on Spice. The resulting clusters are very pure as well, like clusters 1 and 4 in Table 6f and cluster 0 and the noise cluster in Table 6d. Although DHCC finds many clusters that mainly contain records of the *Neither* class, it cannot label them as outliers. On the other hand, MTV is able to find noisy cluster, but also finds clusters of lower purity compared to ROCAT. The other methods do not perform well on Splice.

The compactnesses Cp of the clusters found by ROCAT are 0.249 in the detected subspace, 0.371 in the whole space and 0.741 in the whole data set, which indicates the good quality of detected subspaces. Particularly, we choose clus-

Table 6: Results on Splice.

(a) ROCAT.

Cluster	EI	IE	Neth.
0	**45**	**703**	**16**
1	**629**	**16**	**10**
2	1	17	0
3	0	8	0
4	15	0	0
5	9	0	0
6	8	0	0
7	10	0	0
Noise	**101**	**36**	**1629**

(b) AT-DC.

Cluster	EI	IE	Neth.
0	55	78	513
1	151	644	1058
2	**561**	**46**	**84**

(c) Hyper+.

Cluster	EI	IE	Neth.
0	**374**	**8**	**3**
52	153	75	127
197	300	302	709
349	130	4	442

(d) MTV.

Cluster	EI	IE	Neth.
0	**489**	**7**	**1**
1	175	605	38
2	294	50	10
3	28	170	6
4	35	142	5
Noise	**130**	**96**	**1601**

(e) CLIQUE.

Cluster	EI	IE	Neth.
0	174	158	380
95	161	197	378
179	227	123	402
240	136	153	393

(f) DHCC.

Cluster	EI	IE	Neth.
0	15	10	419
1	**668**	**19**	**28**
2	40	3	393
3	11	0	369
4	**28**	**728**	**34**
5	5	8	412

ter 0 of ROCAT in Table 6a as an example to show the effectiveness of ROCAT on detecting subspaces. The subspace is made up of 25 out of the 60 original attributes. Among the detected 25 attributes, there are 2 positions (28 and 29) with the same values (A and G) for all sequences. Moreover 90 percent of the genes include C on position 27. Besides, there are 10 and 12 positions where more than 80 and 60 percent of all genes only take 2 different base values, respectively. On the other hand, the 4 categories $\{A, T, G, C\}$ are averagely distributed in the remaining 35 positions by nearly all the gene sequences in Cluster 0. Therefore, ROCAT outputs reasonable subspaces for the Splice data set.

CLICKS, CLIQUE and Hyper+ output overlapping clusters on Splice data set. However, there are too many clusters with a large amount of redundancies. It is hard for users to interpret such results directly. The other methods all provide partition-based results. In contrast, ROCAT finds relevant overlapping subspace clusters on Splice data set. There are 63 objects with multiple labels and 5 pairs of clusters sharing objects. Cluster 1 and 4 in Table 6a for example, share 15 records. However, they are detected in different subspaces: 6 attributes for cluster 1 and the other 52 attributes for cluster 4. Cluster 1 is very compact in the 6 detected attributes, while the 15 instances in cluster 4 are also very similar in further 52 attributes. Therefore, the overlapping clusters provide additional information over other partition-based algorithms. Further, ROCAT only provides the most relevant clusters without any redundancy, which facilitates the interpretation of the clustering results.

5. RELATED WORK AND DISCUSSION

Compared to the large body of literature on clustering numerical data only relatively few papers focus on clustering categorical data. Some prominent approaches include the basic algorithm K-modes [14] extending the famous k-means algorithm to categorical data, ROCK [13] and COOLCAT [5], to mention a few. It is often difficult to find clusters in the full dimensional space even in moderate-dimensional data sets, and a problem that is known as the *curse of dimensionality* has been extensively studied. For an comprehensive survey on clustering high-dimensional numerical data see [16]. One of the most prominent technique is CLIQUE [2]. This grid-based approach actually discretized the numerical data and therefore is also applicable to categorical data. However, it enumerates all the possible subspace clusters which produces large redundancies.

Less algorithms have been designed for categorical subspace clustering. Ganti et al. [10] proposed the categorical clustering method CACTUS, which builds a summary information from the data set first and then projects the cluster onto each attribute. It can be extended to find subspace clusters, however though introduced in the paper, it was not implemented by the authors [26]. Gan and Wu [9] proposed the categorical subspace clustering algorithm SUBCAD. They define a cost function based on the idea that data points in relevant subspaces are compact while being sparse in irrelevant ones. LIMBO [3] is a hierarchical algorithm based on an information bottleneck framework. They try to maximise the mutual information between the clusters and attribute values. A good cluster accurately predicts the attribute values associated with objects of the cluster. Although LIMBO is based on information theories it does - in contrast to ROACT - not take into account the model complexity. Furthermore, CACTUS, SUBCAD and LIMBO are all partition-based method, which cannot find overlapping clusters, and need input parameters. CLICKS [26] is a subspace algorithm which constructs a k-partite graph based on all the values of all attributes and then searches for maximum cliques. CLICKS supports overlapping clustering, however, it often includes too many redundant clusters. Besides, the input parameters are hard to determine without having deeper knowledge of the data.

Subspace clustering methods are either partition-based or produce too many redundant clusters. To solve the redundant problem, STATPC [19] and RESCU [20] are proposed to find relevant non-redundant subspace clusters in high-dimensional numerical data. However, they are not applicable for categorical data. Moreover, they need many parameters to bound the searching space.

Pattern mining is another area related to the problem of categorical subspace clustering. For instance, the frequent itemsets found by pattern mining methods could be regarded as the subspaces of clusters, while the objects that support the itemsets can be seen as clusters. Among these pattern mining algorithms, informative itemset mining, which finds the most informative itemsets or ranks the importance of the itemsets, is the most relative one. For instance, Tiling [12] defines a tile as a region in the 0/1 database where all values are 1 (Subspace Cluster), which aims at finding a tiling consisting of at most K tiles covering the largest possible area. Tiling can only find tiles without fault-tolerance, besides it needs the number of tiles as input parameter. NoisyTile [15] uses the maximum entropy distribution to measure the informativeness of a tile or tiling and it supports noisy tiles. However, it needs a fault-tolerant itemset mining algorithm, i.e. [21], to generate the candidate noisy tiles. Moreover it only gives a rank of informativeness on itemsets. Similarly Hyper+ [24] tries to find overlapped hyper-rectangles (noisy tiles) from candidates that are generated by an itemset mining method with a different cost function. KRIMP [23] and MTV [18] are designed for informative itemset mining based on compression. KRIMP needs a minimum support value as input parameter while MTV is parameter-free. However, they do not support fault-tolerant itemsets thereby performing worse than ROCAT in our experiments. The cost function of ROCAT is different and thus their searching or ranking methods cannot be directly applied. Besides, ROCAT is fully automatic while most of these algorithms need input parameters. Furthermore, ROCAT scales better than these algorithms in terms of both data size and dimensionality.

Only very few algorithms support parameter-free clustering of categorical data. Xiong et al. [25] proposes a divisive hierarchical algorithm DHCC, which iteratively splits the higher level cluster by Multiple Correspondence Analysis (MCA) and then refines the result. Cesario et al. [7] proposes a top-down algorithm AT-DC, which iteratively generates and stabilizes clusters to achieve best quality. DHCC and AT-DC are both parameter-free methods based on a top-down splitting framework, thus they can only find partitioning clusters but not overlapping clusters. Besides, DHCC and AT-DC are greatly affected by outliers, where ROCAT can handle them very well.

6. CONCLUSION

In this paper, we introduced ROCAT, an effective and efficient algorithm for detecting the most relevant overlapping subspace clusters on categorical data. Combining a compression-based view on clustering with an effective search algorithm, ROCAT identifies the most relevant subspace clusters which may overlap in terms of the assigned objects and/or the constituting attributes. The compression-based approach of ROCAT naturally avoids undesired redundancy of the result and guarantees that each detected cluster is relevant since it contributes to compress the data.

Acknowledgments

Xiao He and Jing Feng are supported by the China Scholarship Council (CSC). Claudia Plant is funded by the Helmholtz Young Investigators Groups Program.

7. REFERENCES

[1] E. Achtert, H.-P. Kriegel, and A. Zimek. Elki: A software system for evaluation of subspace clustering algorithms. In *SSDBM*, pages 580–585, 2008.

[2] R. Agrawal, J. Gehrke, D. Gunopulos, and P. Raghavan. Automatic subspace clustering of high dimensional data for data mining applications. In *SIGMOD Conference*, pages 94–105, 1998.

[3] P. Andritsos, P. Tsaparas, R. J. Miller, and K. C. Sevcik. Limbo: Scalable clustering of categorical data. In *EDBT*, pages 123–146, 2004.

[4] A. Banerjee, C. Krumpelman, J. Ghosh, S. Basu, and R. J. Mooney. Model-based overlapping clustering. In *KDD*, pages 532–537, 2005.

[5] D. Barbará, Y. Li, and J. Couto. Coolcat: an entropy-based algorithm for categorical clustering. In *CIKM*, pages 582–589, 2002.

[6] S. Boriah, V. Chandola, and V. Kumar. Similarity measures for categorical data: A comparative evaluation. In *SDM*, pages 243–254, 2008.

[7] E. Cesario, G. Manco, and R. Ortale. Top-down parameter-free clustering of high-dimensional categorical data. *IEEE Trans. Knowl. Data Eng.*, 19(12):1607–1624, 2007.

[8] Q. Fu and A. Banerjee. Bayesian overlapping subspace clustering. In *ICDM*, pages 776–781, 2009.

[9] G. Gan and J. Wu. Subspace clustering for high dimensional categorical data. *SIGKDD Explorations*, 6(2):87–94, 2004.

[10] V. Ganti, J. Gehrke, and R. Ramakrishnan. Cactus - clustering categorical data using summaries. In *KDD*, pages 73–83, 1999.

[11] M. R. Garey and D. S. Johnson. *Computers and Intractability: A Guide to the Theory of NP-Completeness.* W. H. Freeman & Co., New York, NY, USA, 1990.

[12] F. Geerts, B. Goethals, and T. Mielikäinen. Tiling databases. In *Discovery Science*, pages 278–289, 2004.

[13] S. Guha, R. Rastogi, and K. Shim. Rock: A robust clustering algorithm for categorical attributes. In *ICDE*, pages 512–521, 1999.

[14] Z. Huang. A fast clustering algorithm to cluster very large categorical data sets in data mining. In *SIGMOD Workshop on Research Issues on Data Mining and Knowledge Discoery*, 1997.

[15] K.-N. Kontonasios and T. D. Bie. An information-theoretic approach to finding informative noisy tiles in binary databases. In *SDM*, pages 153–164, 2010.

[16] H.-P. Kriegel, P. Kröger, and A. Zimek. Clustering high-dimensional data: A survey on subspace clustering, pattern-based clustering, and correlation clustering. *TKDD*, 3(1), 2009.

[17] C. Lund and M. Yannakakis. On the hardness of approximating minimization problems. *J. ACM*, 41(5):960–981, 1994.

[18] M. Mampaey, N. Tatti, and J. Vreeken. Tell me what i need to know: succinctly summarizing data with itemsets. In *KDD*, pages 573–581, 2011.

[19] G. Moise and J. Sander. Finding non-redundant, statistically significant regions in high dimensional data: a novel approach to projected and subspace clustering. In *KDD*, pages 533–541, 2008.

[20] E. Müller, I. Assent, S. Günnemann, R. Krieger, and T. Seidl. Relevant subspace clustering: Mining the most interesting non-redundant concepts in high dimensional data. In *ICDM*, pages 377–386, 2009.

[21] A. K. Poernomo and V. Gopalkrishnan. Towards efficient mining of proportional fault-tolerant frequent itemsets. In *KDD*, pages 697–706, 2009.

[22] J. Rissanen. *Information and Complexity in Statistical Modeling.* Springer, 2007.

[23] J. Vreeken, M. van Leeuwen, and A. Siebes. Krimp: mining itemsets that compress. *Data Min. Knowl. Discov.*, 23(1):169–214, 2011.

[24] Y. Xiang, R. Jin, D. Fuhry, and F. F. Dragan. Summarizing transactional databases with overlapped hyperrectangles. *Data Min. Knowl. Discov.*, 23(2):215–251, 2011.

[25] T. Xiong, S. Wang, A. Mayers, and E. Monga. A new mca-based divisive hierarchical algorithm for clustering categorical data. In *ICDM*, pages 1058–1063, 2009.

[26] M. J. Zaki, M. Peters, I. Assent, and T. Seidl. Clicks: an effective algorithm for mining subspace clusters in categorical datasets. In *KDD*, pages 736–742, 2005.

Batch Discovery of Recurring Rare Classes toward Identifying Anomalous Samples

Murat Dundar*
Computer Science Department
IUPUI
723 W. Michigan St.
Indianapolis, IN 46202
dundar@cs.iupui.edu

Halid Ziya Yerebakan
Computer Science Department
IUPUI
723 W. Michigan St.
Indianapolis, IN 46202
hzyereba@cs.iupui.edu

Bartek Rajwa
Bindley Bioscience Center
Purdue University
1203 W. State Street
W. Lafayette, IN 47907
rajwa@cyto.purdue.edu

ABSTRACT

We present a clustering algorithm for discovering rare yet significant recurring classes across a batch of samples in the presence of random effects. We model each sample data by an infinite mixture of Dirichlet-process Gaussian-mixture models (DPMs) with each DPM representing the noisy realization of its corresponding class distribution in a given sample. We introduce dependencies across multiple samples by placing a global Dirichlet process prior over individual DPMs. This hierarchical prior introduces a sharing mechanism across samples and allows for identifying local realizations of classes across samples. We use collapsed Gibbs sampler for inference to recover local DPMs and identify their class associations. We demonstrate the utility of the proposed algorithm, processing a flow cytometry data set containing two extremely rare cell populations, and report results that significantly outperform competing techniques.

The source code of the proposed algorithm is available on the web via the link: `http://cs.iupui.edu/~dundar/aspire.htm`.

Categories and Subject Descriptors

I.5.3 [**Pattern recognition**]: Clustering—*algorithms*

Keywords

hierarchical Dirichlet process, random effects, batch clustering, recurring classes, rare classes, anomaly detection

*Corresponding author.

KDD'14, August 24–27, 2014, New York, NY, USA.
Copyright 2014 ACM 978-1-4503-2956-9/14/08 ...$15.00.
http://dx.doi.org/10.1145/2623330.2623695.

1. INTRODUCTION

Rare-class discovery is a difficult machine-learning problem that occurs in various practical settings, including visual surveillance and monitoring, quality control, astronomy, physics, and – last but certainly not least – life sciences. A solution to the detection of rare classes is essential for rapid identification of samples with anomalous patterns of data. In this context a normal sample can be considered to be a composition of data points each originating from a *predefined*, i.e., known, class. Unlike normal samples, anomalous samples contain data points originating from classes not known beforehand and thus are considered *undefined*. An anomalous sample may contain data points from both defined and undefined classes; however, the points belonging to undefined classes are usually far less frequent than those originating from predefined ones, hence the term *rare* classes. Predefined classes are recurring and form reproducible patterns (in terms of class membership proportions) across all normal samples, whereas rare classes do not necessarily recur, and when they do, they may form varying patterns of class proportions in each anomalous sample. Therefore, anomalous samples can be as different from each other as they are from normal samples, in terms of the specific subset of rare classes present and their membership proportions.

We assume that data for each sample are generated by local distributions of classes present in that sample. The total number of classes across all samples is not known. The number and the specific subset of classes locally realized in each sample are also not known. Ideally, local distributions of a given class across all samples should be identical, as they are snapshots of the same underlying model. However, random effects that arise from various sources affecting sample-to-sample heterogeneity cause local distributions of the same class to vary significantly from one sample to other. This makes automated matching of local distributions across samples an arduous task, which is further complicated when some classes are represented by only a small number of data points. As a result, identifying the subset of classes present in each sample and recovering true class distributions become impractical without modeling random effects. Thus, the main objective of this study reaches beyond clustering on a per-sample basis, but addresses the issue of grouping local clusters across multiple samples to identify subsets of classes present in each sample. This goal is achieved under the severe constraint imposing the model in which some classes are rare, local class distributions vary from sample to sample owing to random effects, and classes may disappear altogether from some samples.

1.1 Motivation

Our research has been motivated mainly by a practical problem related to automated clinical diagnostics, involving flow cytometry (FC) data analysis.

FC is a single-cell screening, analysis, and sorting technology that plays a crucial role in research and clinical immunology, hematology, and oncology. The power of FC lies in its ability to quantify phenotypic characteristics of individual cells in a high-throughput manner. This unique capability allows FC to study complex inter-cellular networks, such as the immune system as it responds to various external perturbants, including pathogens, chemical compounds (drugs), or vaccination. The cellular phenotypes are defined in FC by combinations of morphological features (measured by elastic light scatter) and abundances of surface and intracellular markers. Each biological sample contains multiple, functionally distinct cell types, or "cell populations" in FC vernacular. These populations form multidimensional clusters in the space defined by measured biological features. Although the characteristics of cell populations present in normal samples are generally known, the number of populations and the proportions of cells present in them could be substantially different in anomalous (often diagnostically relevant) samples.

Given the rapid increase in FC data abundance and the unsatisfactory level of engagement from the machine-learning community, FC researchers have been organizing the annual FlowCAP (Flow Cytometry Critical Assessment of Population Identification Methods) competition in order to increase awareness and elicit help from data scientists. The problem that our study tackles is related to the rare-class classification challenge introduced in FlowCAP 2012 [2]. The data set used in this challenge was produced by multiple laboratories participating in the External Quality Assurance Program Oversight Laboratory (EQAPOL) project [1].

The data sets containing two biologically important rare-cell populations represent samples that were subject to several potential sources of variation, including natural biological variability, different stimulation levels, and data acquisition in different laboratories. The challenge provided several data sets representing three biological samples, at three levels of stimulation, collected in fifteen FC laboratories across the US. For the purpose of method verification the data points (individual cells analyzed by FC) belonging to two rare classes were manually labeled by experts. The remaining data points, considered "normal" (and hence not interesting from the perspective of rare-class discovery), were all labeled as a single predefined abundant class. A typical sample contained about three hundred thousand data points of which only less than one percent belonged to one of the two rare classes.

The FlowCAP challenge framed this problem in a standard supervised classification setting in which the contestants were provided with half the samples as training data and were required to build classifier models subsequently assessed by the organizers using the remaining test data.

Although we appreciate the complexity and the difficulty of the challenge, we believe it represented the best-case scenario and a relatively easy problem setting. Therefore, our problem formulation presented in this report differs significantly from the FlowCAP challenge description. We recognize that biologically the rare classes may emerge as a result of various external perturbants, some of which may be unknown *a priori*. Thus, defining rare classes in an exhaustive fashion may not be realistic. In other words, defining rare classes on the basis of a small available subset present in the training data inevitably leads to classifiers that are biased towards those particular types of rare classes. Such models may not generalize well when applied to future samples in which rare classes may originate owing to other biological mechanisms. Therefore, our problem formulation requires that rare class discovery be performed in the absence of labeled data points representing these classes in the training sets. Herein, we present a non-parametric Bayesian algorithm called ASPIRE (anomalous sample phenotype identification with random effects) that identifies biologically significant phenotypes across a batch of samples in the presence of random effects.

1.2 Proposed Approach

We model each sample data by a mixture of potentially infinitely many Dirichlet-process Gaussian-mixture models (DPMs) with each individual DPM modeling the local distribution of a single class. Under fairly weak assumptions and given enough components, finite mixtures of Gaussian distributions can model a given density arbitrarily closely [9]. The DPM itself is a mixture of potentially infinitely many Gaussian distributions with the actual number of mixture components determined directly from the data during inference. Thus, modeling local class distributions by DPMs offers the flexibility needed to accommodate class data that may arise in samples subjected to significant sources of variations.

As local distributions of a given class are noisy realizations of the true class distribution we introduce a sharing mechanism to create dependencies across DPMs associated with the same class. This is achieved by centering the base distributions of DPMs associated with the same class on a unique global parameter, which itself is distributed according to a higher level DPM. This global DPM not only associates local distributions of a given class with one another but also models the number and proportions of classes in each sample.

We use a collapsed Gibbs sampler to perform inference. Model learning, which is performed in a single unified process, involves three main tasks: recovering DPMs in each sample, finding class associations of DPMs, and identifying the total number of classes and their proportions in each sample.

ASPIRE is capable of identifying recurring classes (both normal and rare) in a completely unsupervised way across a batch of samples that are significantly perturbed by random effects and can characterize normal as well as anomalous states given only very weak assumptions regarding sample characteristics and origin.

1.3 Related Work

Existing lines of work that can be adapted to solve the described problem can be broadly grouped into three categories.

The first approach involves pooling data from all samples and applying a standard clustering algorithm to cluster pooled data. Such an approach will have limited success with most real biological data sets because in the presence of random effects, local distributions belonging to one class may significantly overlap with local distributions of another class. The degree of overlap will be more severe in the presence of rare classes. As a result, clusters recovered this way are unlikely to have any meaningful correspondence with the true class distributions.

The second approach involves identifying clusters on a per-sample basis and then matching local clusters across samples to recover actual class distributions. Although this technique may perform better than the first solution operating with pooled data, the cluster-matching part will remain a big challenge in the presence of random effects and rare classes. As a result, local distributions corresponding to larger classes may not be recovered as a whole and clusters corresponding to rare classes may be incorrectly matched with the distributions of other dominant classes, failing to indicate rare classes. FLAME (flow analysis with automated multivariate estimation) [11] is a well-known specialized FC algorithm that can be considered an example belonging to this category. FLAME fits a mixture model into each sample data with four possible choices of density functions (Gaussian, skewed-Gaussian, t-distribution, skewed-t-distribution) available for individual mixture components. Local modes are pooled and then clustered to obtain a global template of meta-clusters. Local clusters are then assigned to these meta-clusters using graph-matching techniques. FLAME is somewhat similar to ASPIRE in the narrow sense that both techniques model individual sample data by a mixture model. However, there are significant differences in model learning. FLAME divides model learning into three tasks: clustering data in individual samples, finding the optimal number of local clusters in each sample, and matching local clusters across samples to recover classes. These three tasks are performed by FLAME independently in a sequential manner. Unlike FLAME, the model learning by ASPIRE is performed as a single unified process. Thus, ASPIRE can take advantage of recurring patterns of similarities across samples. For example, groups of isolated data points forming rare classes that would be ignored as outliers by clustering followed by cluster matching can be successfully identified as a rare class when these two tasks are performed simultaneously.

The third approach involves performing sample clustering jointly with cluster matching. The proposed ASPIRE model, the hierarchical Dirichlet-process Gaussian-mixture model (HDPM) [5], and HDPM with random effects (HDPM-RE) [8] all belong to this category. Thanks to their nonparametric nature, the number of local clusters and classes can arbitrarily grow in all three models to better accommodate data as needed. Both HDPM and HDPM-RE model individual sample data by a single DPM. HDPM uses the standard hierarchical Dirichlet process prior [13], assuming exact sharing of class parameters across all samples and ignoring the presence of random effects. In the presence of random effects this assumption leads to the creation of several extraneous classes. HDPM tackles this problem by post-processing the results to combine local clusters sharing a common mode. However, such a post-processing technique may have limited success, as local clusters of a given class may not necessarily share the same mode. Unlike HDPM, HDPM-RE assumes that local clusters are noisy realizations of true class distributions and probabilistically models the deviations of the local cluster means from the mean of the corresponding class distribution.

One key limitation of HDPM-RE is the assumption that local class distributions can be effectively captured using a single Gaussian distribution. This assumption is often violated in many real-world settings because different sources of variation introduced at different stages of the data collection and processing pipeline create class data that may not be closely approximated by a single Gaussian distribution. In the case of HDPM-RE, additional local clusters of a given class are treated as if they belong to another class, thereby splitting a single class into multiple subclasses. Unlike HDPM-RE, which uses a single Gaussian distribution for each local distribution of a class, ASPIRE uses a single DPM for each local distribution, allowing for an arbitrarily large number of Gaussian distributions for modeling of local class data. Individual DPMs across samples are linked through class-specific global parameters, which are in turn distributed according to a higher-level DPM model. In addition to modeling random effects, ASPIRE offers a more flexible data model that can recover class distributions with arbitrary shapes, avoiding the creation of artificial classes.

The rest of this report is organized as follows. In Section 2 we compare data models for DPM, HDPM, HDPM-RE, and ASPIRE. In Section 3 we discuss model inference for ASPIRE. In Section 4 we demonstrate the performance of ASPIRE with two experiments and compare results with three other competing techniques. In Section 5 we conclude by summarizing our contributions and offering future research directions.

2. ASPIRE GENERATIVE MODEL

We describe the technical details of our data model in four incremental stages. In the first stage we assume that each sample is modeled by a single DPM and that DPMs across multiple samples are independent. In the second stage we introduce dependencies across DPMs and impose exact sharing of mixture components corresponding to classes across samples. This is equivalent to the HDPM model. In the third stage we tackle random effects by relaxing the exact sharing of mixture components to allow local clusters to inherit noisy realizations of classes in individual samples. This is equivalent to the HDPM-RE model. In the fourth stage we describe the proposed data model for ASPIRE, which models each sample by a potentially infinite mixture of DPMs.

2.1 Independent Modeling of Samples by DPM

We denote point i in sample j by $\boldsymbol{x}_{ji} \in \Re^d$, where $i = \{1, \ldots, n_{j.}\}$ and $j = \{1, \ldots, J\}$, $n_{j.}$ is the number of points in sample j, and J is the total number of samples. In the DPM model $\boldsymbol{x}_{ji}$ is associated with a mixture component defined by $\theta_{ji} = \{\mu_{ji}, \Sigma_{ji}\}$, which in turn is generated i.i.d. from a DP as follows:

$$\begin{array}{rcl} \boldsymbol{x}_{ji} & \sim & p(\cdot|\theta_{ji}) \\ \theta_{ji} & \sim & G_j \end{array} \tag{1}$$

G_j are random probability measures distributed i.i.d. according to a DP with a base distribution G_0 and a precision parameter α.

$$G_j \sim DP(G_0, \alpha) \tag{2}$$

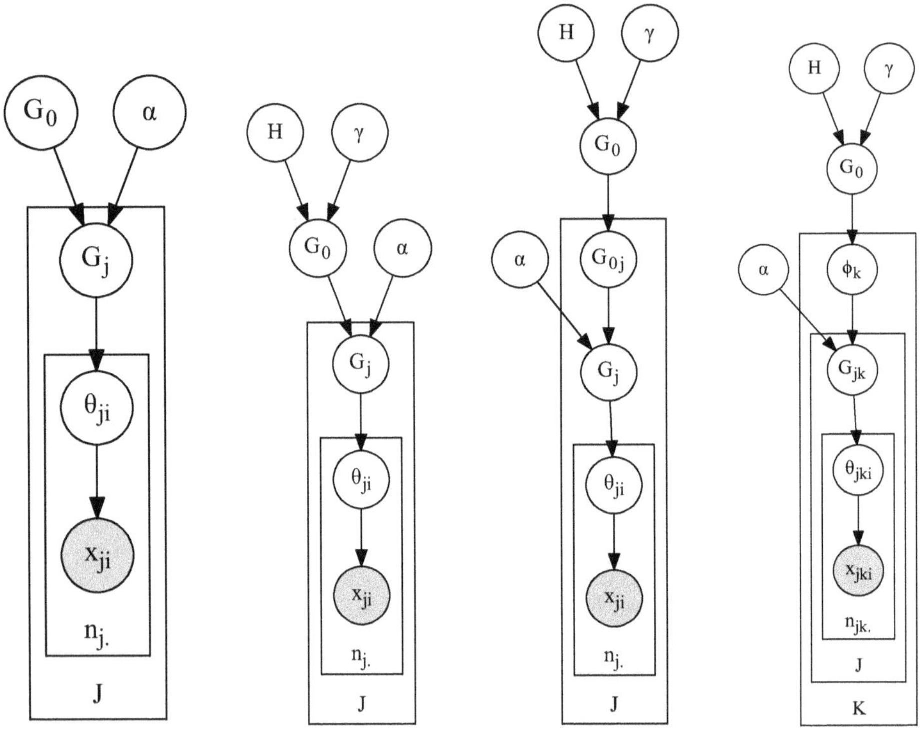

(a) DPM (b) HDPM (c) HDPM-RE (d) ASPIRE

Figure 1: Plate diagrams for DPM, HDPM, HDPM-RE, and ASPIRE.

Using the stick-breaking construction according to [7], we can express G_j as

$$G_j \;=\; \sum_{t=1}^{\infty} \beta_{jt}\delta_{\psi_{jt}} \tag{3}$$

where

$$\begin{array}{rcl} \beta_{jt} & = & \beta_{jt}^{'} \prod_{l=1}^{t-1}(1-\beta_{jl}^{'}) \\ \beta_{jt}^{'} & \sim & Beta(1,\alpha) \\ \psi_{jt} & \sim & G_0 \end{array}$$

The points ψ_{jt} are called the *atoms* of G_j. Note that unlike continuous distributions, the probability of sampling the same ψ_{jt} twice from G_j is not zero and is proportional to β_{jt}. Thus, G_j is considered a discrete distribution and offers a clustering property, as the same ψ_{jt} can be sampled for different θ_{ji}. In this model α is the parameter that controls the prior probability of assigning a point to a new cluster and thus plays a critical role in the number of clusters generated.

For the base distribution G_0, from which ψ_{jt} are drawn, we define a bivariate prior:

$$p(\boldsymbol{\mu},\Sigma) = N\left(\boldsymbol{\mu}|\boldsymbol{\mu}_0,\frac{\Sigma}{\kappa_0}\right)\times W^{-1}(\Sigma|\Sigma_0,m) \tag{4}$$

where $\boldsymbol{\mu}_0$ is the prior mean and κ_0 is a scaling constant that controls the deviation of the cluster means from the prior mean. The smaller the κ_0, the larger the separation will be between the cluster means. The parameter Σ_0 is a positive definite matrix that encodes our prior belief about the expected Σ, i.e., $E(\Sigma) = \frac{\Sigma_0}{m-d-1}$. The parameter m is a scalar that is negatively correlated with the degrees of freedom. In other words the larger the m, the less Σ will deviate from $E(\Sigma)$, and vice versa. The plate model for independent modeling of samples using one DPM for each sample is available in Figure 1a.

2.2 Introducing dependencies across samples by HDPM

In the previous section we introduced a clustering property across points in an individual sample by placing a DP prior over G_j as in (2). Since G_j is a discrete distribution, this prior enables sharing of the same cluster parameter by different points. When dealing with multiple samples, in addition to sharing of clusters by points formed within individual samples, a higher level of sharing occurs. Each local cluster in an individual sample is associated with a class. Thus, as we cluster points in each sample we also need to group local clusters into appropriate classes so that we can identify class associations of local clusters. This grouping can be achieved by introducing dependencies across individual DPMs by placing a hierarchical DP prior over G_0 [13]. The HDPM for joint clustering and cluster matching across multiple samples becomes

$$\begin{array}{rcl} \boldsymbol{x}_{ji} & \sim & p(\cdot|\theta_{ji}) \\ \theta_{ji} & \sim & G_j \\ G_j & \sim & DP(G_0,\alpha) \\ G_0 & \sim & DP(H,\gamma) \end{array} \tag{5}$$

where γ is the precision parameter for the higher-level DP prior and H is defined as in (4).

Using the stick-breaking construction we can express G_0 as

$$G_0 = \sum_{k=1}^{\infty} \beta_k \delta_{\phi_k} \quad (6)$$

where

$$\begin{aligned} \beta_k &= \beta_k' \prod_{l=1}^{k-1}(1-\beta_k') \\ \beta_k' &\sim Beta(1,\alpha) \\ \phi_k = \{\boldsymbol{\mu}_k, \Sigma_k\} &\sim H \end{aligned}$$

With this update, instead of letting G_0 be distributed according to (4) as in the independent modeling of samples we let H be distributed according to (4) and let the atoms of G_0 be distributed according to H. The distinct set of parameters ϕ_k corresponding to classes is sampled from H and local cluster parameters are sampled from G_j. Since G_j is a discrete distribution with its atoms sampled from G_0, and G_0 is a discrete distribution with its atoms sampled from H, each local cluster in turn inherits one of the ϕ_k, i.e., $\psi_{jt} \in \{\phi_k\}_{k=1}^{K}$ and $\theta_{ji} \in \{\psi_{jt}\}_{t=1}^{m_{j.}}$, where K is the number of classes and $m_{j.}$ is the number of local clusters in sample j.

Therefore, this model not only groups data points within each sample into clusters, but also groups local clusters across samples into classes. In other words, clustering and cluster matching are simultaneously addressed and depend on one another. The plate model for HDPM is available in Figure 1b.

2.3 Modeling random effects by HDPM-RE

In the standard HDPM the same parameters are inherited by all local realizations of a class. However, owing to the potential random effects this surmise may be unrealistic. Therefore, to account for random effects the HDPM-RE model [8] would be more suitable for the discovery of recurring classes. HDPM-RE presumes that sample data are generated by noisy versions of parameters defining classes. This change can be incorporated into the data model by updating the model in (5) as follows:

$$\begin{aligned} \boldsymbol{x}_{ji} &\sim p(\cdot|\theta_{ji}) \\ \theta_{ji} &\sim G_j \\ G_j &\sim DP(G_{0j}, \alpha) \\ G_0 &\sim DP(H, \gamma) \end{aligned} \quad (7)$$

where G_{0j} is a discrete distribution whose atoms are noisy versions of the corresponding atoms in G_0. With this change in the model each individual sample now inherits different noisy realizations of global parameters. The plate model for HDPM-RE is available in Figure 1c.

2.4 Modeling individual sample data with multiple DPMs

Both HDPM and HDPM-RE assumes that local distributions of classes can be closely approximated by a single Gaussian distribution. This assumption is often quite restrictive for many practical settings, as local class data, which are produced subject to random effects, may emerge in the form of skewed as well as multi-mode distributions. As a result, fitting a single Gaussian distribution for local class distributions creates artificial classes that may not be easily distinguished from other significant classes.

ASPIRE uses a potentially infinite mixture of DPMs to model each sample data where individual DPMs are linked together through a hierarchical DP prior. This hierarchical prior not only identifies local DPMs associated with the same class through sharing of a global parameter but also models the specific subset of classes present and their proportions in each sample.

We update our indexing notation from previous sections to introduce an additional subscript k to account for multiple DPMs in each sample. We denote point i of class k in sample j by $\boldsymbol{x}_{jki} \in \Re^d$, where $i = \{1, \ldots, n_{jk.}\}$, $k = \{1, \ldots, K\}$, and $j = \{1, \ldots, J\}$, $n_{jk.}$ is the number of points from class k in sample j, K is the total number of classes, and J is the total number of samples. The proposed ASPIRE data model is as follows.

$$\begin{aligned} \boldsymbol{x}_{jki} &\sim p(\cdot|\theta_{jki}) \\ \theta_{jki} &\sim G_{jk} \\ G_{jk} &\sim DP(F_{\phi_k}, \alpha) \\ \phi_k &\sim G_0 \\ G_0 &\sim DP(H, \gamma) \end{aligned} \quad (8)$$

where ϕ_k are global parameters each of which is associated with a different class. Individual DPMs associated with the same class inherit the same ϕ_k across samples. The notation F_{ϕ_k} indicates a distribution F centered at ϕ_k and defines class-specific base distributions of individual DPMs. Although F_{ϕ_k} is same for all DPMs associated with the same class, local clusters between samples are generated i.i.d. given ϕ_k of corresponding DPMs. Thus, each local realization of a given class is modeled by a different DPM, allowing for the modeling of sample-to-sample variations in a systematic manner. The plate model for ASPIRE is available in Figure 1d.

For the sake of simplicity and to preserve conjugacy we assume that the covariance matrices of all local clusters associated with the same class are identical and limit the susceptibility of local clusters to noise with their mean vectors. More specifically, $\mu_{jki} \sim G_{jk}$, $\Sigma_{jki} = \Sigma_k$, and F_{ϕ_k} is defined as follows.

$$F_{\phi_k = \{\boldsymbol{\mu}_k, \Sigma_k\}} = N(\boldsymbol{\mu}_k, \frac{\Sigma_k}{\kappa_1}) \quad (9)$$

Note that the covariance matrix of the base distribution F_{ϕ_k} is a function of Σ_k; hence conjugacy of the model is preserved. Conjugacy of the model is important as it enables us to implement a collapsed version of the Gibbs sampler as discussed in the next section. The scaling constant κ_1 adjusts the degree of deviation of local means from the corresponding global mean. A smaller κ_1 results in a situation where local realizations of global means deviate significantly from one sample to another, suggesting significant random effects. On the other hand, a larger κ_1 value limits these deviations, resulting in few to no random effects.

3. ASPIRE MODEL INFERENCE

Posterior inference for the proposed model in (8) can be performed by a Gibbs sampler by iteratively sampling local cluster indicator variables $\boldsymbol{t} = \left\{\left\{\{t_{jki}\}_{i=1}^{n_{jk.}}\right\}_{k=1}^{K}\right\}_{j=1}^{J}$, class indicator variables $\boldsymbol{c} = \left\{\left\{\{c_{jkt}\}_{t=1}^{m_{jk}}\right\}_{k=1}^{K}\right\}_{j=1}^{J}$, and local cluster parameters $\boldsymbol{\psi} = \left\{\left\{\{\psi_{jkt}\}_{t=1}^{m_{jk}}\right\}_{k=1}^{K}\right\}_{j=1}^{J}$ given the state of all other variables. Including $\boldsymbol{\psi}$ in the Gibbs sampler significantly increases the size of the state space and severely retards the convergence of the Gibbs sampler to the equilibrium distribution. Fortunately, our model uses a conjugate pair of H and $p(\cdot|\psi_{jkt})$, which allows us to integrate out ψ_{jkt} analytically. Thus, in the following we omit the discussion of sampling of $\boldsymbol{\psi}$ and describe sampling for only $\boldsymbol{t}$ and $\mathbf{c}$.

When sampling the local cluster indicator variable t_{jki} for $\boldsymbol{x}_{jki}$ we first remove $\boldsymbol{x}_{jki}$ from its current cluster and update the corresponding predictive distribution $p(\boldsymbol{x}_{jki}|D_{.c_{jkt}.}, D_{jkt})$. Then, we evaluate the likelihood of $\boldsymbol{x}_{jki}$'s belonging to an existing cluster by evaluating $p(\boldsymbol{x}_{jki}|D_{.c_{jkt}.}, D_{jkt})$ for all local clusters in sample j, and its likelihood of originating from a new cluster by evaluating the predictive distribution for an empty cluster, i.e., $p(\boldsymbol{x}_{jki})$. Finally, we sample t_{jki} based on the normalized values of the product of prior probabilities and the corresponding likelihood values. This can be expressed by the following equation:

$$p(t_{jki} = t|\boldsymbol{t}^{-jki}, \mathbf{c}, D_{...}) \propto \begin{cases} \alpha p(\boldsymbol{x}_{jki}) \\ \text{if} \quad t = m_{jk}+1 \\ n_{jkt}^{-jki} p(\boldsymbol{x}_{jki}|D_{.c_{jkt}.}, D_{jkt}^{-jki}) \\ \text{if} \quad t \leqslant m_{jk} \end{cases} \tag{10}$$

where $\boldsymbol{t}^{-jki}$ is the set of all cluster indicator variables, excluding the one for point i of class k in sample j, $D_{...}$ denotes the set of all points across all samples, $D_{.c_{jkt}.}$ denotes the subset of points sharing class c_{jkt} across all samples, D_{jkt}^{-jki} denotes the subset of points in sample j belonging to cluster t of class k, excluding point i, m_{jk} is the number of clusters associated with class k in sample j, and n_{jkt}^{-jki} is the number of data points in cluster t of class k in sample j, excluding point i.

As we model local clusters by Gaussian distributions with Gaussian and inverted Wishart priors defined over their mean vectors and covariance matrices, respectively, the predictive distribution $p(\boldsymbol{x}_{jki}|D_{.c_{jkt}.}, D_{jkt})$ turns out to be in the form of a Student-t distribution, the derivation of which is provided in Section 3.1.

When sampling the class indicator variable c_{jkt} for cluster t of class k in sample j we remove points D_{jkt} from $D_{.c_{jkt}.}$ and update the parameters of the predictive distribution for class c_{jkt}. Then, we evaluate the joint likelihood of cell data in D_{jkt} for existing classes as well as for a new class. Finally, we sample c_{jkt} based on the normalized values of the product of prior probabilities of classes and the corresponding joint likelihood values. This can be expressed by the following formula:

$$p(c_{jkt} = k|\boldsymbol{t}, \mathbf{c}^{-jkt}, D_{...}) \propto \begin{cases} \gamma \prod_{i:t_{jki}=t} p(\boldsymbol{x}_{jki}) \\ \text{if } k = K+1 \\ m_{.k}^{-jkt} \prod_{i:t_{jki}=t} p(\boldsymbol{x}_{jki}|D_{.k.}^{-jkt}) \\ \text{if } k \leq K \end{cases} \tag{11}$$

where $D_{.k.}^{-jkt}$ denotes the subset of points across all samples associated with class k, excluding points in cluster t in sample j. The predictive distribution $p(x|D_{.k.})$ is also obtained in the form of a Student-t distribution, and can be readily obtained from $p(\boldsymbol{x}_{jki}|D_{.c_{jkt}.}, D_{jkt})$ by setting D_{jkt} an empty set. The details are provided in Section 3.1.

Sampling both t_{jki} and c_{jkt} requires evaluating the predictive distribution for a new, i.e., an empty, cluster. The predictive distribution for a new cluster is denoted by $p(\boldsymbol{x}_{jki})$ in (10) and (11). This distribution can be obtained from $p(x|D_{.k.})$ by setting $D_{.k.}$ an empty set. The details are also provided in Section 3.1.

During a single run of the ASPIRE algorithm one sweep of the Gibbs sampler involves two main iterative loops. In the first loop t_{jki} are sampled for all points across all samples. In the second loop c_{jkt} are sampled for all local clusters across all samples. The Gibbs sampler is run for a thousand sweeps and the state with the maximum Gibbs likelihood is recorded for final evaluation.

3.1 Deriving predictive distributions

ASPIRE uses the following data model:

$$\begin{array}{lll} p(\boldsymbol{x}_{jki}|\boldsymbol{\mu}_{jkt}, \Sigma_k) & \sim & N(\boldsymbol{\mu}_{jkt}, \Sigma_k) \\ p(\boldsymbol{\mu}_k|\Sigma_k) & \sim & N(\boldsymbol{\mu}_0, \kappa_0^{-1}\Sigma_k) \\ p(\Sigma_k) & \sim & W^{-1}(\Sigma_0, m) \\ p(\boldsymbol{\mu}_{jkt}|\boldsymbol{\mu}_k, \Sigma_k) & \sim & N(\boldsymbol{\mu}_k, \kappa_1^{-1}\Sigma_k) \end{array} \tag{12}$$

For the above model the posterior predictive distribution of a local cluster can be derived by evaluating the following integral.

$$p(\boldsymbol{x}_{jki}|D_{.c_{jkt}.}, D_{jkt}) = \int\int p(\boldsymbol{x}_{jki}|\boldsymbol{\mu}_{jkt}, \Sigma_k) \, p(\boldsymbol{\mu}_{jkt}, \Sigma_k|D_{.c_{jkt}.}, D_{jkt}) \partial\boldsymbol{\mu}_{jkt} \partial\Sigma_k \tag{13}$$

To evaluate the integral in (13) we need the posterior distribution of the parameters $p(\boldsymbol{\mu}_{jkt}, \Sigma_k|D_{.c_{jkt}.}, D_{jkt})$, which can be expressed as follows using the Bayes theorem.

$$p(\boldsymbol{\mu}_{jkt}, \Sigma_k|D_{.c_{jkt}.}, D_{jkt}) \propto p(\boldsymbol{\mu}_{jkt}, \Sigma_k, \bar{\boldsymbol{x}}_{jkt}, A_{jkt}|\bar{\boldsymbol{x}}_{jkt:c_{jkt}=k}, A_k) \tag{14}$$

where $\bar{\boldsymbol{x}}_{jkt}$ and A_{jkt} are the sample mean and the scatter matrix for cluster t of class k in sample j, respectively and A_k is the scatter matrix of class k. These statistics are defined as in (15).

$$\begin{array}{lll} \bar{\boldsymbol{x}}_{jkt} & = & n_{jkt}^{-1} \sum_{jki:t_{jki}=t} \boldsymbol{x}_{jki} \\ A_{jkt} & = & \sum_{jki:t_{jki}=t} (\boldsymbol{x}_{jki} - \bar{\boldsymbol{x}}_{jkt})(\boldsymbol{x}_{jki} - \bar{\boldsymbol{x}}_{jkt})^T \\ A_k & = & \sum_{jkt:c_{jkt}=k} A_{jkt} \end{array} \tag{15}$$

In order to evaluate (14) we first need to obtain

$$\begin{array}{l} p(\boldsymbol{\mu}_{jkt}, \Sigma_k, \bar{\boldsymbol{x}}_{jkt}, A_{jkt}|\bar{\boldsymbol{x}}_{jkt:c_{jkt}=k}, A_k) = \\ p(\bar{\boldsymbol{x}}_{jkt}|\mu_{jkt}, \Sigma_k) p(A_{jkt}|\Sigma_k) \\ p(\boldsymbol{\mu}_{jkt}|\Sigma_k, \bar{x}_{jkt:c_{jkt}=k}) p(\Sigma_k|A_k) \end{array} \tag{16}$$

where

$$p(\bar{\boldsymbol{x}}_{jkt}|\Sigma_k) = N(\boldsymbol{\mu}_{jkt}, \boldsymbol{n}_{jkt}^{-1}\Sigma_k) \tag{17}$$

$$p(A_{jkt}|\Sigma_k) = W(\Sigma_k, n_{jkt}-1) \tag{18}$$

$$p(\boldsymbol{\mu}_{jkt}|\Sigma_k, \bar{\boldsymbol{x}}_{jkt:c_{jkt}=k}) = N(\bar{\boldsymbol{\mu}}, \bar{\kappa}^{-1}\Sigma_k) \tag{19}$$

$$p(\Sigma_k|A_k) = W^{-1}\left(\Sigma_0 + A_k, m + \sum_{jkt:c_{jkt}=k}(n_{jkt}-1)\right) \tag{20}$$

where

$$\bar{\boldsymbol{\mu}} = \frac{\sum_{jkt:c_{jkt}=k} \frac{n_{jkt}\kappa_1}{(n_{jkt}+\kappa_1)} \bar{\boldsymbol{x}}_{jkt} + \kappa_0\mu_0}{\sum_{jkt:c_{jkt}=k} \frac{n_{jkt}\kappa_1}{(n_{jkt}+\kappa_1)} + \kappa_0} \tag{21}$$

$$\bar{\kappa} = \frac{(\sum_{jkt:c_{jkt}=k} \frac{n_{jkt}\kappa_1}{(n_{jkt}+\kappa_1)} + \kappa_0)\kappa_1}{\sum_{jkt:c_{jkt}=k} \frac{n_{jt}\kappa_1}{(n_{jkt}+\kappa_1)} + \kappa_0 + \kappa_1} \quad (22)$$

Once the distributions in (17)-(20) are substituted into (14) a closed-form expression for $p(\boldsymbol{\mu}_{jkt}, \Sigma_k | D_{.c_{jkt}.}, D_{jkt})$ can be obtained. When we substitute this solution into (13) we obtain $p(\boldsymbol{x}_{jki}|D_{.c_{jkt}.}, D_{jkt})$ in the form of a multivariate Student-t distribution with three parameters.

$$p(\boldsymbol{x}_{jki}|D_{.c_{jkt}.}, D_{jkt}) = stu - t(\hat{\boldsymbol{\mu}}, \hat{\Sigma}, v) \quad (23)$$

The location vector ($\hat{\mu}$), the scale matrix ($\hat{\Sigma}$), and the degrees of freedom (v) are given below. Location vector:

$$\hat{\boldsymbol{\mu}} = \frac{n_{jkt}\bar{\boldsymbol{x}}_{jkt} + \bar{\kappa}\bar{\boldsymbol{\mu}}}{n_{jkt} + \bar{\kappa}} \quad (24)$$

Scale matrix:

$$\hat{\Sigma} = \frac{\Sigma_0 + A_k + A_{jkt} + \frac{n_{jkt}\bar{\kappa}}{n_{jkt}+\bar{\kappa}}(\bar{\boldsymbol{x}}_{jkt} - \bar{\boldsymbol{\mu}})(\bar{\boldsymbol{x}}_{jkt} - \bar{\boldsymbol{\mu}})^T}{\frac{(\bar{\kappa}+n_{jkt})\,v}{(\bar{\kappa}+n_{jkt}+1)}} \quad (25)$$

Degrees of freedom:

$$v = m + \sum_{jkt:c_{jkt}=k} (n_{jkt} - 1) + n_{jkt} - d + 1 \quad (26)$$

The predictive distribution of a class can be readily obtained from $p(\boldsymbol{x}_{jki}|D_{.c_{jkt}}, D_{jkt})$ by setting D_{jkt} an empty set. This is equivalent to dropping terms related to local clusters in equations (24), (25), and (26). Finally, the predictive distribution of an empty cluster can be obtained from $p(\boldsymbol{x}_{jki}|D_{.k.})$ by setting $D_{.k.}$ an empty set. This is equivalent to dropping terms in $p(\boldsymbol{x}_{jki}|D_{.k.})$ related to classes.

4. RESULTS AND DISCUSSIONS

We report results of experiments performed with two different data sets. The first experiment demonstrated the functionality of the algorithms tested using simulated data, while the second experiment utilized real FC data.

Aside from the proposed ASPIRE algorithm, three other techniques were considered: DPM, HDPM, and HDPM-RE. In Section 1.3 we described three different approaches to the clustering problem set forth in this study. The first method uses standard clustering algorithms applied to pooled data, the second approach performs clustering and cluster matching in a sequential way, and the third performs clustering jointly with cluster matching. Among the three benchmark techniques DPM belongs to the first category; HDPM and HDPM-RE along with ASPIRE belong to the third category. We chose the well-known FC algorithm FLAME to represent the second category. Unfortunately the implementation of FLAME available through GenePattern [12] produced errors during processing of many of the samples in the two data sets, so we were forced to exclude FLAME from this analysis. For HDPM we used the software provided by the authors in [5]. For the other three algorithms we used our own implementations. Each algorithm is run for a thousand sweeps, and the state with the best likelihood is recorded for subsequent analysis.

The F_1 score is used as the performance measure for comparing performances of these four techniques. As one-to-many matchings are expected between true and recovered classes, the F_1 score for each class is computed as the maximum of the F_1 scores for all recovered classes, similar to [3].

Table 1: F1 scores achieved and the number of classes recovered by each of the four techniques on the artificial data set.

	Class F1 Scores			
Method	1 (98.7%)	2 (0.3%)	3 (1%)	# Classes
DPM	1.00	0.75	0.56	5
HDPM	0.84	0.74	0.66	11
HDPM-RE	0.68	0.94	0.85	7
ASPIRE	1.00	1.00	0.90	3

Table 2: Number of points available from three classes in the FC data set before and after subsampling. Numbers in parentheses indicate percentage of the total number of points in the corresponding set.

	# points		
Method	Normal	Rare 1	Rare 2
Original	56.2M (99.94%)	10.2K (0.02%)	24.3K (0.04%)
Subsampled	1.9M (98.23%)	9.5K (0.50%)	24.1K (1.27%)

4.1 Experiment 1: Artificial Data Set

We generated twenty samples, each with five thousand data points in a two-dimensional feature space, using the model in (8) and the following values of the model parameters: $\kappa_0 = 0.01$, $\kappa_1 = 0.2$, $m = 20$, $\mu_0 = [0\ 0]^T$, $\Sigma_0 = I$, $\alpha = 0.2$, $\gamma = 0.2$, where I denotes the identity matrix. After all data points were sampled, three classes were produced by this model with overall class proportions of 0.987, 0.003, and 0.01, which indicates that two of the three recurring classes can be considered rare. For the pooled data, distributions of local clusters and the true values of the global parameters, i.e., ϕ_k, are shown in Fig. 2a by dashed and solid contours, respectively. The ellipses correspond to data distributions that are at most four standard deviations from the mean. Individual data points are shown by black dots.

We ran all four techniques (ASPIRE, DPM, HDPM, and HDPM-RE) on this data set and plotted contours representing recovered classes in Figures 2b, 2c, 2d, and 2e, respectively. F1 scores obtained for each class and numbers of classes recovered by all four techniques are included in Table 1. Results suggest that ASPIRE not only correctly predicts the true number of classes but also estimates global parameters with almost no bias, which in turn produces almost perfect F1 scores for each class. DPM produces a reasonable number of classes but estimates global parameters with a large bias. HDPM fails to consistently match local clusters across samples and substantially overpredicts the actual number of classes. HDPM-RE performs better compared to DPM and HDPM but generates several artificial classes, a direct result of modeling local class data by a single Gaussian distribution.

4.2 Experiment 2: Flow Cytometry Data Set with Two Rare Classes

We evaluated the performance of ASPIRE in discovering rare classes with a FC data set used in the FlowCAP 2012 competition [2]. The data set contained FC measurements of multiple aliquots of three biological samples exposed to three

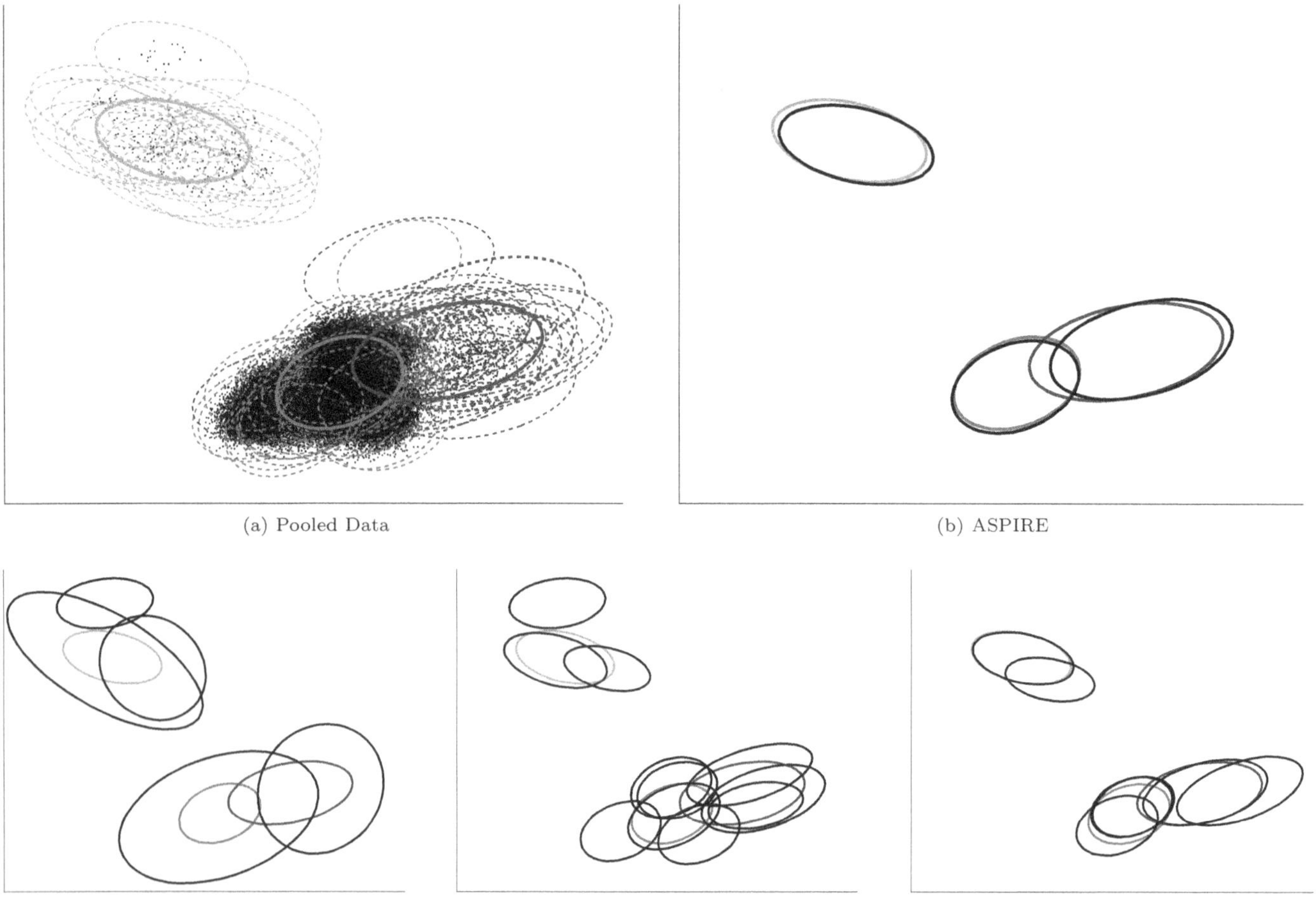

(a) Pooled Data (b) ASPIRE

(c) DPM (d) HDPM (e) HDPM-RE

Figure 2: An illustrative example showing the performance of DPM, HDPM, HDPM-RE, and ASPIRE algorithms in estimating global parameters corresponding to classes. Solid color contours plotted using true values of global parameters represent true classes. Dashed color contours indicate true distributions of local clusters with the color identifying the class origin. Solid black contours plotted using estimated values of the global parameters represent recovered classes. Black dots denote data points.

different stimulation levels. The samples were examined independently by fifteen FC laboratories. In this context the term "sample" denotes a tube containing white blood cells. Each cell is separately measured by a flow cytometer. The measurement provides the small-angle and large-angle light-scatter characteristics as well as four fluorescence intensity values. Thus, each cell is characterized by a six-dimensional feature vector. The goal is to recognize the cells belonging to two rare-cell populations, manually labeled by experts, without access to information about characteristics of these populations in the training data set. Cells not belonging to one of the two rare populations are considered "normal" and were all labeled as a single predefined abundant class. Thus, including the normal class there are three classes in this data set.

The original data set contained data points for about 60 million cells across 202 samples. To obtain a more manageable data-set size while preserving cells from rare classes we used a density-based subsampling technique and reduced the data size to 1.9 million points. The number of points available from each of the two rare classes as well as the normal class before and after subsampling and their percentages are shown in Table 2.

As in the previous experiment, we compare ASPIRE against DPM, HDPM, and HDPM-RE. The DPM model has five free parameters $(\alpha, \Sigma_0, m, \kappa_0, \mu_0)$, the HDPM model has one more parameter (γ) than DPM, and HDPM-RE and ASPIRE have one more parameter (κ_1) than HDPM. These parameters are selected using the following strategy.

Each feature is normalized to have zero mean and unit variance. As the sample batch may contain anomalous samples, prior information about the potential number of local clusters and global classes may not exist for most real-world FC data. Thus, for α and γ we use vague priors by fixing their value to one. We set m to the minimum feasible value, which is $d+2$, to achieve maximum degrees of freedom. By doing this we let the actual covariance matrices deviate significantly from the expected covariance matrix, which is $E(\Sigma) = \frac{\Sigma_0}{m-d-1}$. The prior mean μ_0 is set to the mean of the entire data. The scale matrix Σ_0 is set to I/s, where I is the identity matrix. This leaves the scaling constant s of Σ_0, κ_0, and κ_1 as the three free parameters that require

Table 3: F_1 scores achieved and the number of classes recovered by each of the four techniques on the entire FC data set. Results for ASPIRE are averages over ten repetitions. Numbers in parenthesis indicate standard deviations.

Method	Class F_1 Scores			# Classes
	Normal	Rare 1	Rare 2	
DPM	0.22	0.20	0.39	175
HDPM	0.23	0.01	0.02	75
HDPM-RE	0.22	0.46	0.63	91
ASPIRE	0.62 (0.02)	0.59 (0.03)	0.77 (0.01)	38.7 (3.20)

tuning. The parameter κ_1 models the deviation of cluster means from their corresponding class mean in the generative model. Thus, increasing κ_1 while κ_0 and s are fixed potentially increases the number of classes generated. The parameter κ_0 models the deviation of cluster means from the prior mean in the generative model. Thus, increasing κ_0 while κ_1 and s are fixed potentially increases the number of clusters generated. The parameter s models the expected size of clusters. Increasing s potentially increases the number of clusters generated. These three parameters were coarsely tuned using a generic 5-parameter peripheral-blood immunophenotyping data set previously collected and analyzed in our lab as part of an earlier study without retuning them for the FC data used in this experiment. The following values were used: $\kappa_0 = 0.05$, $\kappa_1 = 0.1$, $s = 10$.

F_1 scores computed for all three classes are shown in Table 3. Results for ASPIRE are averages of ten repetitions. As the run time for ten repetitions of the other algorithms would take on the order of weeks, we included results of a single run for these algorithms. Results in Table 3 favor methods modeling random effects (HDPM-RE and ASPIRE) over those that do not (DPM and HDPM) in terms of higher F_1 scores achieved for both rare classes. Between techniques that model random effects ASPIRE significantly outperforms HDPM-RE in terms of producing a more realistic number of classes and higher F_1 scores for all classes. ASPIRE models local realizations of classes by an infinite mixture of Gaussians, which allows for associating multiple clusters with individual classes during inference. The other three techniques use a single Gaussian distribution to model local realization of classes. If a local distribution of a class cannot be effectively modeled by a single Gaussian distribution, these techniques tend to produce multiple local clusters all of which are assigned to a distinct class. As a result ASPIRE tends to generate a fewer number of classes and achieves higher F_1 scores compared to the other three techniques.

We also compared ASPIRE with a supervised classifier to find out how F_1 scores would improve if a subset of the labeled data were to be used during training. We used all samples belonging to one of the biological samples for training and sequestered all samples for the other two biological samples for testing. The support vector machine toolbox in [6] was used to train and test a supervised classifier on this data. Parameters of this classifier are extensively tuned to optimize test performance. These results along with the results obtained by ASPIRE on the test data are shown in Table 4. Results suggest that ASPIRE can predict rare classes

Table 4: F_1 scores achieved by ASPIRE and SVM on the test portion of the FC data set. Results are averages over ten repetitions. Numbers in parenthesis indicate standard deviations.

Method	Class F_1 Scores		
	Normal	Rare 1	Rare 2
ASPIRE	0.62 (0.02)	0.54 (0.03)	0.75 (0.01)
Supervised	1.00 (0.00)	0.66 (0.01)	0.83 (0.01)

with F_1 scores comparable to those of a supervised classifier without using any labeled data. The F_1 score achieved by ASPIRE for the normal class is worse than that of the supervised classifier, mainly because the normal class is a combination of multiple uninteresting subclasses for which ASPIRE produces multiple classes to more effectively model the underlying class distribution. However, we do not believe this is a major limitation, as in most practical settings labeled data are present for normal classes as these are classes that are known and predefined. On the other hand, for rare classes, labeled data may not exist because rare classes are usually not known a priori and cannot be predefined. Under such circumstances training a supervised classifier that requires labeled data for all classes may not be very realistic. On the other hand, ASPIRE can cluster data in a fully unsupervised manner and with the help of a limited amount of labeled data from normal classes results can be post-processed to distinguish unknown classes from known ones.

For ASPIRE, one sweep of the Gibbs sampler involves two main iterative loops. In the first loop, cluster indicator variables are sampled for all data points across all samples. In the second loop, class indicator variables are sampled for all local clusters across all samples. As the first loop iterates over all points across all samples it is usually more computationally expensive than the second loop. Fortunately, during the sampling of the cluster indicator variables class parameters are fixed. This allows us to sample cluster indicator variables independently for each sample during a single sweep and leads to improvement in processing time on multi-processor machines. The actual run time for ASPIRE to process the FC data set containing 1.9 million points is about five and eleven hours with and without parallelization, respectively, on an eight-core workstation. The reduction in the overall computational time is not proportional to the number of processors, as the computational gain by parallelizing the first loop will be limited after a certain point by the computational time of the second loop.

5. CONCLUSIONS

We introduced ASPIRE as a new method for discovering recurring yet significant rare classes in the presence of random effects and showed experimental results that clearly favor ASPIRE over other benchmark techniques. We believe that ability to recover rare classes in FC data sets obtained in fifteen different laboratories convincingly demonstrates that automated identification of anomalous samples in research or diagnostic settings is indeed feasible.

Labeled information about normal, i.e., known classes, can be directly incorporated into the learning process by adopting a restricted Gibbs sampler scheme similar to the one introduced in [4]. Our research was mainly driven by a rare-class discovery problem in a clinical setting. However, ASPIRE is a general clustering technique that can be used in other disciplines to discover classes with recurring nature irrespective of whether they are rare or normal. ASPIRE can also be utilized for problems involving the detection of group anomalies [10, 14].

ASPIRE is implemented in C++. The source code is available on the web via the link `http://cs.iupui.edu/~dundar/aspire.htm`.

6. ACKNOWLEDGMENTS

This research was sponsored by the National Science Foundation (NSF) under Grant Number IIS-1252648 (CAREER), by the National Institute of Biomedical Imaging and Bioengineering (NIBIB) under Grant Number 5R21EB015707, and by the PhRMA Foundation (2012 Research Starter Grant in Informatics). The content is solely the responsibility of the authors and does not represent the official views of NSF, NIBIB or PhRMA.

7. REFERENCES

[1] External quality assurance program oversight laboratory (EQAPOL). `http://eqapol.dhvi.duke.edu/`.

[2] FlowCAP - flow cytometry: Critical assessment of population identification methods. `http://flowcap.flowsite.org/`.

[3] N. Aghaeepour, G. Finak, FlowCAP Consortium, DREAM Consortium, H. Hoos, T. R. Mosmann, R. Brinkman, R. Gottardo, and R. H. Scheuermann. Critical assessment of automated flow cytometry data analysis techniques. *Nature Methods*, 10(3):228–238, mar 2013.

[4] F. Akova, Y. Qi, B. Rajwa, and M. Dundar. Self-adjusting models for semi-supervised learning in partially-observed settings. In *IEEE International Conference on Data Mining (ICDM'12)*, 2012. under review.

[5] A. J. Cron, C. Gouttefangeas, J. Frelinger, L. Lin, S. K. Singh, C. M. Britten, M. J. P. Welters, S. H. van de Burg, M. West, and C. Chan. Hierarchical modeling for rare event detection and cell subset alignment across flow cytometry samples. *PLoS Computational Biology*, 9:e1003130, 2013.

[6] N. Djuric, L. Lan, S. Vucetic, and Z. Wang. Budgetedsvm: A toolbox for scalable svm approximations. *Journal of Machine Learning Research*, 14:3813–3817, 2013.

[7] H. Ishwaran and L. F. James. Gibbs sampling methods for stick-breaking priors. *Journal of the American Statistical Association*, 96(453):pp. 161–173, 2001.

[8] S. Kim and P. Smyth. Hierarchical Dirichlet processes with random effects. In B. Schölkopf, J. C. Platt, and T. Hoffman, editors, *Advances in Neural Information Processing Systems 19*, pages 697–704, Cambridge, MA, 2007. MIT Press.

[9] G. McLachlan and D. Peel. *Finite Mixture Models.* Wiley Series in Probability and Mathematical Statistics: Applied Probability and Statistics. John Wiley & Sons, 2001.

[10] K. Muandet and B. Schölkopf. One-class support measure machines for group anomaly detection. *CoRR*, abs/1303.0309, 2013.

[11] S. Pyne, X. Hu, K. Wang, E. Rossin, T.-I. Lin, L. M. Maier, C. Baecher-Allan, G. J. McLachlan, P. Tamayo, D. A. Hafler, P. L. De Jager, and J. P. Mesirov. Automated high-dimensional flow cytometric data analysis. *Proc Natl Acad Sci U S A*, 106(21):8519–24, 2009.

[12] M. Reich, T. Liefeld, J. Gould, J. Lerner, T. P., and M. J.P. Genepattern 2.0. *Nature Genetics*, 38(5):500–1, 2006.

[13] Y. Teh, M. Jordan, M. Beal, and D. Blei. Hierarchical Dirichlet processes. *Journal of the American Statistical Association*, 101(476):1566–1581, 2006.

[14] L. Xiong, B. Poczos, and J. Schneider. Group anomaly detection using flexible genre models. In J. Shawe-Taylor, R. Zemel, P. Bartlett, F. Pereira, and K. Weinberger, editors, *Advances in Neural Information Processing Systems 24*, pages 1071–1079. 2011.

A Dirichlet Multinomial Mixture Model-based Approach for Short Text Clustering

Jianhua Yin Jianyong Wang
Tsinghua National Laboratory for Information Science and Technology (TNList),
Department of Computer Science and Technology, Tsinghua University, Beijing, China
jhyin12@gmail.com, jianyong@tsinghua.edu.cn

ABSTRACT

Short text clustering has become an increasingly important task with the popularity of social media like Twitter, Google+, and Facebook. It is a challenging problem due to its sparse, high-dimensional, and large-volume characteristics. In this paper, we proposed a collapsed Gibbs Sampling algorithm for the Dirichlet Multinomial Mixture model for short text clustering (abbr. to GSDMM). We found that GSDMM can infer the number of clusters automatically with a good balance between the completeness and homogeneity of the clustering results, and is fast to converge. GSDMM can also cope with the sparse and high-dimensional problem of short texts, and can obtain the representative words of each cluster. Our extensive experimental study shows that GSDMM can achieve significantly better performance than three other clustering models.

Categories and Subject Descriptors

I.5.3 [**PATTERN RECOGNITION**]: Clustering—*Algorithms*

Keywords

Short text clustering; Dirichlet Multinomial Mixture; Gibbs Sampling

1. INTRODUCTION

Berkhin [4] discussed several important issues of clustering: 1) Setting of the number of clusters; 2) Ability to work with high-dimensional data; 3) Interpretability of results; 4) Scalability to large datasets. Short text clustering has all the above challenges. Different from the normal text clustering, short text clustering also has the problem of sparsity [1]. Most words only occur once in each short text, as a result, the Term Frequency-Inverse Document Frequency (TF-IDF) measure cannot work well in the short text setting. Furthermore, if we use the Vector Space Model [25] to represent the short texts, the sparse and high-dimensional vectors will result in waste of both memory and computation time.

In this paper, we try to cope with the above challenges of short text clustering. Specifically, we proposed a collapsed Gibbs Sampling algorithm for the Dirichlet Multinomial Mixture model [20] for short text clustering (abbr. to GSDMM). We also proposed the Movie Group Process (MGP) as an analogy of GSDMM. We can imagine the documents as students in a movie discussion course, and the words of a document as the movies the student has watched. The short text clustering problem turns out to be clustering the students into groups so that students in the same group will share similar interests (similar movie lists), while students in different groups will share different interests. The intuition of MGP is that we can randomly assign the students to K tables, then we ask each student to re-choose a table in turn with two rules: 1) Choose a table with more students; 2) Choose a table whose students share similar interests with him. As this process goes on, some tables will grow larger and others will vanish. Finally, only a part of the tables will still have students and the students in each table will share similar interests. In other words, we can cluster the students into several groups in this way. With the help of MGP, we explored how and why GSDMM works as well as the meaning of its parameters.

We find that GSDMM has the following nice properties: 1) GSDMM can infer the number of clusters automatically; 2) GSDMM has a clear way to balance the completeness and homogeneity of the clustering results; 3) GSDMM is fast to converge; 4) Unlike the Vector Space Model (VSM)-based approaches, GSDMM can cope with the sparse and high-dimensional problem of short texts; 5) Like Topic Models (e.g., PLSA [10] and LDA [6]), GSDMM can also obtain the representative words of each cluster.

In the experimental study, we compared GSDMM with K-means [13], the Hierarchical Agglomerative Clustering (HAC) model [15], and DMAFP [11]. We did not choose other clustering methods like Gaussian Mixture Model [5], Affinity Propagation [8], and Spectral clustering [18], because they are not scalable with high-dimensional and large-volume data like texts. We conducted experiments on four datasets and evaluated the results with five metrics, and found that GSDMM can achieve significantly better performance than K-means, HAC, and DMAFP.

The contributions of this paper are summarized as follows.

- To the best of our knowledge, this is the first attempt to apply the Dirichlet Multinomial Mixture (DMM) model for short text clustering, and our experimental

KDD'14, August 24–27, 2014, New York, NY, USA.

http://dx.doi.org/10.1145/2623330.2623715 .

study has validated its effectiveness. We find it can cope with the sparse and high-dimensional problem of short texts, and can obtain the representative words of each cluster.

- We proposed a collapsed Gibbs Sampling algorithm for DMM (abbr. to GSDMM) which can achieve very good performance on short text clustering. Meanwhile, GSDMM can infer the number of clusters automatically with a good balance between the completeness and homogeneity of the clustering results, and is fast to converge.
- We proposed the Movie Group Process (MGP) as an analogy of GSDMM which can help us understand how and why GSDMM works as well as the meaning of its parameters.

The remainder of this paper is organized as follows. In Section 2, we first propose the Movie Group Process (MGP), then we introduce the DMM model and our GSDMM algorithm. We discuss several important aspects of GSDMM in Section 3. Section 4 describes the design of experiments to evaluate the performance of our algorithm. In Section 5, we review the related work of short text clustering. We finally present conclusions and future work in Section 6.

2. APPROACH

2.1 Movie Group Process

In this part, we introduce an analogy for the short text clustering problem. We will use this analogy in the whole paper, and it can help us understand both the short text clustering problem and our GSDMM algorithm.

We can imagine that the professor of a movie discussion course plans to divide the students into several groups. She expects the students in the same group have watched more movies of the same, so they would have more things to discuss. The professor asks the students to write down the movies they have watched within several minutes. (The list will not be too long because the students do not have enough time, and they will more likely write down movies they watched recently or movies they love much.) Now, each student can be represented with a list of movies. The professor needs to find a way to cluster the students into several groups. The goal is that students in the same group will share similar interests (similar movie lists), while students in different groups will share different interests.

Let us restate the Movie Group Problem more formally and point out its relationship with the short text clustering problem. The input is D students (documents) and each student (document) is represented by a short list of movies (words). The goal is to cluster the students (documents) into several groups, so that students (documents) in the same group are similar and students (documents) in different groups are dissimilar. We define the number of distinct movies (words) as V. The sparse characteristic of short text means that V is really large (often larger than 10^5), while the average number of words ($\bar{L}$) in each short text is small (often less than 10^2).

We first discuss the common similarity-based clustering models for this problem before introducing our approach. Common similarity-based models like K-means [13] and HAC [15] for text clustering usually represent the documents with the Vector Space Model (VSM) [25]. Each document (student) is represented with a vector of length V. Each element of the vector is the weight of the corresponding word (e.g., TF-IDF). Due to the sparse problem of short texts, most words of the documents have TF=1, which means TF is almost useless in the representation of short texts. Although each short document has only a small number of words, it is represented with a vector of size V (often larger than 10^5). This VSM representation of documents results in both high time complexity and high space complexity, and is related to the high-dimensional problem of the short texts.

We can imagine that the professor invites the students into a huge restaurant and randomly assigns the students to K tables. Then she asks the students to re-choose a table in turn. We can expect that a student will choose a table according to the following two rules:

- Rule 1: Choose a table with more students.
- Rule 2: Choose a table whose students share similar interests (i.e., watched more movies of the same) with him.

As this process goes on, some tables will grow larger and others will vanish. We can expect that finally only a part of the tables will still have students and the students in each table will share similar interests. In other words, the professor can cluster the students into several groups in this way.

We call the above process as the Movie Group Process (MGP). We can see that the above two natural rules are related to the two goals of clustering: Completeness and Homogeneity [24]. Completeness represents the objective that all members of a ground true group are assigned to the same cluster. Rule 1 of MGP tends to result in high completeness, as it leads popular tables to be more popular (larger clusters are more likely to get larger), and students in the same ground true group are more likely to be in the same table (cluster). This is also known as the "richer gets richer" property. Homogeneity represents the objective that each cluster contains only members of a single ground true group. Rule 2 of MGP tends to result in high homogeneity, because it leads the students in the same table to be more similar (more likely to be in the same ground true group).

To our surprise, the Movie Group Process (MGP) is equivalent to our collapsed Gibbs Sampling algorithm for the Dirichlet Multinomial Mixture model (abbr. to GSDMM). We will first introduce the Dirichlet Multinomial Mixture model in the next section, then we will introduce our GSDMM algorithm in Section 2.3 and Section 2.4.

2.2 Dirichlet Multinomial Mixture

In this section, we introduce the Dirichlet Multinomial Mixture (DMM) model used in Nigam et al. [20]. DMM is a probabilistic generative model for documents, and embodies two assumptions about the generative process: (1) the documents are generated by a mixture model [17], and (2) there is a one-to-one correspondence between mixture components and clusters. When generating document d, DMM first selects a mixture component (cluster) k according to the mixture weights (weights of clusters), $p(z = k)$. Then document d is generated by the selected mixture component (cluster) from distribution $p(d|z = k)$. Thus we can characterize the likelihood of document d with the sum of the total

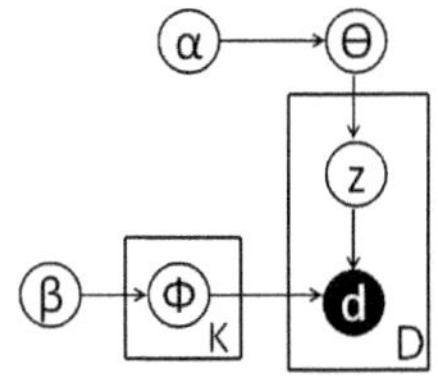

Figure 1: Graphical model of DMM.

V	number of words in the vocabulary
D	number of documents in the corpus
$\bar{L}$	average length of documents
$\vec{d}$	documents in the corpus
$\vec{z}$	cluster labels of each document
I	number of iterations
m_z	number of documents in cluster z
n_z	number of words in cluster z
n_z^w	number of occurrences of word w in cluster z
N_d	number of words in document d
N_d^w	number of occurrences of word w in document d

Table 1: Notations

probability over all mixture components:

$$p(d) = \sum_{k=1}^{K} p(d|z = k)p(z = k) \quad (1)$$

Here, K is the number of mixture components (clusters). Now, the problem becomes how to define $p(d|z = k)$ and $p(z = k)$. DMM makes the Naive Bayes assumption: that the words in a document are generated independently when the document's cluster label k is known, and the probability of a word is independent of its position within the document. Then the probability of document d generated by cluster k can be derived as follows:

$$p(d|z = k) = \prod_{w \in d} p(w|z = k) \quad (2)$$

Nigam et al. [20] assumes that each mixture component (cluster) is a multinomial distribution over words, such that $p(w|z = k) = p(w|z = k, \Phi) = \phi_{k,w}$, where $w = 1, ..., V$ and $\sum_w \phi_{k,w} = 1$. They assume a Dirichlet distribution as the prior for each mixture component (cluster), such that $p(\Phi|\vec{\beta}) = Dir(\vec{\phi}_k|\vec{\beta})$. They also assume that the weight of each mixture component (cluster) is sampled from a multinomial distribution, such that $p(z = k) = p(z = k|\Theta) = \theta_k$, where $k = 1, ..., K$ and $\sum_k \theta_k = 1$. In addition, they assume a Dirichlet prior for this multinomial distribution, such that $p(\Theta|\vec{\alpha}) = Dir(\vec{\theta}|\vec{\alpha})$.

The graphical model of DMM is shown in Figure 1. In our short text clustering problem, we need to estimate the mixture component (cluster) z for each document d. We will introduce our GSDMM algorithm with the help of the Movie Group Process (MGP) in the next section.

2.3 Gibbs Sampling for DMM

In this section, we introduce the collapsed Gibbs Sampling algorithm for the Dirichlet Multinomial Mixture model (abbr. to GSDMM), which is equivalent to the Movie Group Process (MGP) introduced in Section 2.1.

The detail of our GSDMM algorithm is shown in Algorithm 1, and the meaning of its variables is shown in Table 1. In the initialization step, we randomly assign the documents to K clusters, and record the following information: $\vec{z}$ (cluster labels of each document), m_z (number of documents in cluster z), n_z (number of words in cluster z), and n_z^w (number of occurrences of word w in cluster z). Then we traverse the documents for I iterations. (In Section 4.4, we found that GSDMM can achieve good and stable performance when I equals five.) In each iteration, we re-assign a cluster for each document d in turn according to the conditional distribution: $p(z_d = z|\vec{z}_{\neg d}, \vec{d})$, where $\neg d$ means the cluster label of document d is removed from $\vec{z}$. Each time we re-assign a cluster z to document d, the corresponding information in $\vec{z}$, m_z, n_z, and n_z^w are updated accordingly. Finally, only a part of the initial K clusters will remain non-empty, in other words, GSDMM can cluster the documents into several groups. Through experimental study in Section 4.5, we found that the number of non-empty clusters found by GSDMM can be near the true number of groups as long as K is larger than the true number. GSDMM is also a soft clustering model like Gaussian Mixture Model (GMM) [5], since we can get the probability of each document belonging to each cluster from $p(z_d = z|\vec{z}_{\neg d}, \vec{d})$.

Algorithm 1: GSDMM

```
Data: Documents in the input, d⃗.
Result: Cluster labels of each document, z⃗.
begin
    initialize m_z, n_z, and n_z^w as zero for each cluster z
    for each document d ∈ [1, D] do
        sample a cluster for d:
        z_d ← z ~ Multinomial(1/K)
        m_z ← m_z + 1 and n_z ← n_z + N_d
        for each word w ∈ d do
            n_z^w ← n_z^w + N_d^w
    for i ∈ [1, I] do
        for each document d ∈ [1, D] do
            record the current cluster of d: z = z_d
            m_z ← m_z − 1 and n_z ← n_z − N_d
            for each word w ∈ d do
                n_z^w ← n_z^w − N_d^w
            sample a cluster for d:
            z_d ← z ~ p(z_d = z|z⃗_¬d, d⃗) (Equation 4)
            m_z ← m_z + 1 and n_z ← n_z + N_d
            for each word w ∈ d do
                n_z^w ← n_z^w + N_d^w
```

We can derive $p(z_d = z|\vec{z}_{\neg d}, \vec{d})$ from the Dirichlet Multinomial Mixture (DMM) model, and find that it conforms to the two rules of MGP introduced in Section 2.1. We just introduce the results directly here, and will explain the derivation details in the next section.

If we assume each word can at most appear once in each document (In the movie group example, the assumption is that a movie can at most appear once in each student's list). We can derive a quite elegant form of the conditional distribution as follows:

$$p(z_d = z|\vec{z}_{\neg d}, \vec{d}) \propto \frac{m_{z,\neg d} + \alpha}{D - 1 + K\alpha} \frac{\prod_{w \in d}(n_{z,\neg d}^w + \beta)}{\prod_{i=1}^{N_d}(n_{z,\neg d} + V\beta + i - 1)} \quad (3)$$

where N_d is the number of words in document d. In short text setting, N_d is often less than 100.

The first part of Equation 3 relates to Rule 1 of MGP (Choose a table with more students). Here $m_{z,\neg d}$ is the number of students (documents) in table z without considering student d, and D is the total number of students. When table z has more students, the first part tends to be larger, and a student will tend to choose a table with more students. As a result, the first part of Equation 3 tends to result in large completeness, because it leads large tables (clusters) to be larger and students in the same ground true group are more likely to be in the same table (cluster). The second part of Equation 3 relates to Rule 2 of MGP (Choose a table whose students share similar interests with him). Here $n^w_{z,\neg d}$ and $n_{z,\neg d}$ are the number of occurrences of movie w in table z and the total number of movies in table z without considering student d, respectively. When table z has more students sharing similar interests with student d (i.e., watched more movies of the same), movies of student d will appear more often in table z (with larger $n^w_{z,\neg d}$), and the probability of student d choosing table z will be larger. As a result, the second part of Equation 3 tends to result in large homogeneity, because it can leads the students in the same table to be more similar (more likely to be in the same ground true group).

If we allow a word to appear multi-times in a document (A movie can appear multi-times in a student's list). We can derive the conditional probability as follows:

$$p(z_d = z|\vec{z}_{\neg d}, \vec{d}) \propto \frac{m_{z,\neg d} + \alpha}{D - 1 + K\alpha} \frac{\prod_{w\in d}\prod_{j=1}^{N_d^w}(n^w_{z,\neg d} + \beta + j - 1)}{\prod_{i=1}^{N_d}(n_{z,\neg d} + V\beta + i - 1)} \tag{4}$$

where N_d^w is the number of occurrences of word w in document d. We should note that the two parts of Equation 4 have similar relationship with MGP like that of Equation 3, and the complexity of Equation 4 is the same as Equation 3. The only difference between them is the numerator of their second part. We will try to derive Equation 3 and Equation 4 from the Dirichlet Multinomial Mixture (DMM) model in the next section.

2.4 Derivation of GSDMM

In this section, we try to formally derive the conditional distribution $p(z_d = z|\vec{z}_{\neg d}, \vec{d})$ used in our GSDMM algorithm as follows.

$$p(z_d = z|\vec{z}_{\neg d}, \vec{d}) = \frac{p(\vec{d}, \vec{z}|\vec{\alpha}, \vec{\beta})}{p(\vec{d}, \vec{z}_{\neg d}|\vec{\alpha}, \vec{\beta})} \propto \frac{p(\vec{d}, \vec{z}|\vec{\alpha}, \vec{\beta})}{p(\vec{d}_{\neg d}, \vec{z}_{\neg d}|\vec{\alpha}, \vec{\beta})} \tag{5}$$

where $\neg d$ means document d is excluded from $\vec{z}$ and $\vec{d}$. Now we need to derive the full distribution $p(\vec{d}, \vec{z}|\vec{\alpha}, \vec{\beta})$. From the graphical model of DMM in Figure 1, we can see $p(\vec{d}, \vec{z}|\vec{\alpha}, \vec{\beta}) = p(\vec{d}|\vec{z}, \vec{\beta})p(\vec{z}|\vec{\alpha})$. Then we need to derive $p(\vec{d}|\vec{z}, \vec{\beta})$ and $p(\vec{z}|\vec{\alpha})$.

Let us first investigate how to obtain $p(\vec{z}|\vec{\alpha})$. We can see that $p(\vec{z}|\vec{\alpha})$ can be obtained by integrating with respect to Θ as $p(\vec{z}|\vec{\alpha}) = \int p(\vec{z}|\Theta)p(\Theta|\vec{\alpha})d\Theta$. As mentioned in Section 2.2, $p(\Theta|\vec{\alpha})$ is a Dirichlet distribution and $p(\vec{z}|\Theta)$ is a multinomial distribution. With similar techniques of [9], we can get $p(\vec{z}|\vec{\alpha}) = \frac{\Delta(\vec{m}+\vec{\alpha})}{\Delta(\vec{\alpha})}$, where $\vec{m} = \{m_k\}_{k=1}^K$, and m_k is the number of documents (students) in the kth cluster (table). Here we adopt the Δ function in [9], and we have $\Delta(\vec{\alpha}) = \frac{\prod_{k=1}^K\Gamma(\alpha)}{\Gamma(\sum_{k=1}^K\alpha)}$ and $\Delta(\vec{m} + \vec{\alpha}) = \frac{\prod_{k=1}^K\Gamma(m_k+\alpha)}{\Gamma(\sum_{k=1}^K(m_k+\alpha))} = \frac{\prod_{k=1}^K\Gamma(m_k+\alpha)}{\Gamma(D+K\alpha)}$, where D is the number of documents in the dataset, $D = \sum_{k=1}^K m_k$.

Similarly, $p(\vec{d}|\vec{z}, \vec{\beta})$ can be obtained by integrating with respect to Φ as $p(\vec{d}|\vec{z}, \vec{\beta}) = \int p(\vec{d}|\vec{z}, \Phi)p(\Phi|\vec{\beta})d\Phi = \prod_{k=1}^K \frac{\Delta(\vec{n}_k+\vec{\beta})}{\Delta(\vec{\beta})}$, where $\vec{n}_k = \{n_k^w\}_{w=1}^V$, and n_k^w is the number of occurrences of word w in the kth cluster (table). Similarly, $\Delta(\vec{\beta}) = \frac{\prod_{w=1}^V\Gamma(\beta)}{\Gamma(\sum_{w=1}^V\beta)}$ and $\Delta(\vec{n}_k+\vec{\beta}) = \frac{\prod_{w=1}^V\Gamma(n_k^w+\beta)}{\Gamma(\sum_{w=1}^V(n_k^w+\beta))} = \frac{\prod_{w=1}^V\Gamma(n_k^w+\beta)}{\Gamma(n_k+V\beta)}$, where n_k is number of words (movies) in document (table) k, that is, $n_k = \sum_{w=1}^V n_k^w$.

Now the joint distribution becomes:

$$p(\vec{d}, \vec{z}|\vec{\alpha}, \vec{\beta}) = \frac{\Delta(\vec{m} + \vec{\alpha})}{\Delta(\vec{\alpha})} \prod_{k=1}^K \frac{\Delta(\vec{n}_k + \vec{\beta})}{\Delta(\vec{\beta})}$$

Then the conditional distribution in Equation 5 can be derived as follows:

$$\begin{aligned} p(z_d = z|\vec{z}_{\neg d}, \vec{d}) &\propto \frac{p(\vec{d}, \vec{z}|\vec{\alpha}, \vec{\beta})}{p(\vec{d}_{\neg d}, \vec{z}_{\neg d}|\vec{\alpha}, \vec{\beta})} \\ &\propto \frac{\Delta(\vec{m} + \vec{\alpha})}{\Delta(\vec{m}_{\neg d} + \vec{\alpha})} \frac{\Delta(\vec{n}_z + \vec{\beta})}{\Delta(\vec{n}_{z,\neg d} + \vec{\beta})} \\ &\propto \frac{\Gamma(m_z + \alpha)}{\Gamma(m_{z,\neg d} + \alpha)} \frac{\Gamma(D - 1 + K\alpha)}{\Gamma(D + K\alpha)} \\ &\quad \frac{\prod_{w\in d}\Gamma(n_z^w + \beta)}{\prod_{w\in d}\Gamma(n^w_{z,\neg d} + \beta)} \frac{\Gamma(n_{z,\neg d} + V\beta)}{\Gamma(n_z + V\beta)} \end{aligned} \tag{6}$$

where $m_z = m_{z,\neg d} + 1$ and $n_z = n_{z,\neg d} + N_d$. Because Γ function has the following property: $\frac{\Gamma(x+m)}{\Gamma(x)} = \prod_{i=1}^m(x+i-1)$. We can rewrite Equation 6 into the following form:

$$p(z_d = z|\vec{z}_{\neg d}, \vec{d}) \propto \frac{m_{z,\neg d} + \alpha}{D - 1 + K\alpha} \frac{\frac{\prod_{w\in d}\Gamma(n_z^w+\beta)}{\prod_{w\in d}\Gamma(n^w_{z,\neg d}+\beta)}}{\prod_{i=1}^{N_d}(n_{z,\neg d} + V\beta + i - 1)} \tag{7}$$

When we assume each word can at most appear once in each document (In the movie group example, the assumption is a movie can at most appear once in each student's list). We can get $\frac{\prod_{w\in d}\Gamma(n_z^w+\beta)}{\prod_{w\in d}\Gamma(n^w_{z,\neg d}+\beta)} = \prod_{w\in d}(n^w_{z,\neg d} + \beta)$ since $n_z^w = n^w_{z,\neg d} + 1$ holds, and Equation 7 turns out to be Equation 3.

When we allow a word to appear multi-times in each document (A movie can appear multi-times in each student's list).We can get $\frac{\prod_{w\in d}\Gamma(n_z^w+\beta)}{\prod_{w\in d}\Gamma(n^w_{z,\neg d}+\beta)} = \prod_{w\in d}\prod_{j=1}^{N_d^w}(n^w_{z,\neg d} + \beta + j - 1)$ since $n_z^w = n^w_{z,\neg d} + N_d^w$ holds, and Equation 7 turns out to be Equation 4.

3. DISCUSSION

3.1 Meaning of Alpha and Beta

In this part, we try to explore the meaning of α and β with the help of the Movie Group Process (MGP) as introduced in Section 2.1. From Equation 4, we can see that α relates to the prior probability of a student (document) choosing a table (cluster). If we set $\alpha = 0$, a table will never be chosen by the students once it gets empty, because the first part of Equation 4 is now zero. When α gets larger, the probability of a student choosing an empty table will also gets larger.

We can see β is in the second part of Equation 4 which relates to Rule 2 of MGP (Choose a table whose students share similar interests with him). If we set $\beta = 0$, a student will never choose a table when its movie lists do not contain a movie of the student. We can see this is not reasonable, because other movies of the student may appear many times in that table and he may share many similar interests with the students of that table.

DMM assumes symmetric priors for the Dirichlet distributions, in other words, it gives the same α's for all tables (clusters) and the same β's for all movies (words). The same α's for all tables implies that different tables (clusters) are equally important at start. This is consistent to our intuition. While the same β's for all movies implies that different movies (words) are equally important. This is not reasonable, for example, a movie watched by every student cannot give any positive information for clustering the students into groups, it actually will mislead the clustering algorithm. We should give less emphasis on too popular movies (words that appear in too many documents). Intuitively, we can achieve this goal by giving larger β's for these less important words. This means that GSDMM has potential to incorporate the global weighting metrics (e.g., IDF) for words which is a really important technique for document analysis. We plan to explore this in future.

3.2 Relationship with Naive Bayes Classifier

The conditional distribution $p(z_d = z|\vec{z}_{\neg d}, \vec{d})$ in Equation 3 is equivalent to the Naive Bayes Classifier (NBC) [16]. Intuitively, we can assign document d to a cluster z with the largest conditional probability $p(z_d = z|\vec{z}_{\neg d}, \vec{d})$ in Algorithm 1. However, in GSDMM we choose to sample cluster z from the conditional distribution $p(z_d = z|\vec{z}_{\neg d}, \vec{d})$. GSDMM can avoid falling into a local minimum which is a common problem of EM-based algorithms in this way.

We should note that GSDMM has potentially well performance for incremental clustering. We can first group a number of documents into clusters with GSDMM, and a Naive Bayes Classifier (NBC) is learned during this process. Then each time a new document arrives, we can classify it to one of the clusters with the Naive Bayes Classifier and update the classifier (update $\vec{z}$, m_z, n_z, and n_z^w). We plan to explore this in future.

The conditional distribution $p(z_d = z|\vec{z}_{\neg d}, \vec{d})$ in Equation 4 is equivalent to the Bayesian Naive Bayes Classifier (BNBC) [22]. Rennie [22] points out that BNBC performs worse in classification, because it over-emphasizes words that appear more than once in a test document. For example, if word (movie) w appears twice in a document (student) d, the contribution of w for Equation 3 is $(n_{z,\neg d}+\beta)^2$, while the contribution of w for Equation 4 is $(n_{z,\neg d}+\beta)(n_{z,\neg d}+\beta+1)$. The difference is greater when a word appears more frequently in a document. However, this is a good property in the text clustering problem, because words in a document tend to appear in bursts: if a word appears once, it is more likely to appear again [14],[23]. The conditional distribution $p(z_d = z|\vec{z}_{\neg d}, \vec{d})$ in Equation 4 can give words that appear multi-times in a document more emphasis, and allows GSDMM to capture the burstiness of words [7],[14].

3.3 Representation of Clusters

From Algorithm 1, we can see that GSDMM can assign each document to a cluster. With the fact that the Dirichlet distribution is conjugate to the multinomial distribution, we have:

$$p(\vec{\phi}_z|\vec{d}, \vec{z}, \vec{\beta}) = Dir(\vec{\phi}_z|\vec{n}_z + \vec{\beta}) \tag{8}$$

where $\vec{n}_z = \{n_z^w\}_{w=1}^V$, and n_z^w is the number of occurrences of word w in the zth cluster (table).

From Equation 8, we can obtain the posterior mean of Φ as follows:

$$\phi_{z,w} = \frac{n_z^w + \beta}{\sum_{w=1}^V n_z^w + V\beta} \tag{9}$$

where $\phi_{z,w}$ corresponds to the probability of word w being generated by cluster z, and can be regarded as the importance of word w to cluster z. As a result, GSDMM can obtain the representative words of each cluster like Topic Models (e.g., PLSA [10] and LDA [6]).

3.4 Complexity of GSDMM

In this part, we analyze the time and space complexity of GSDMM with a comparison of K-means [13]. The meaning of the notations is shown in Table 1.

First, we analyze the space complexity of GSDMM and K-means. From Algorithm 1, we can see GSDMM needs to store $\vec{z}$, m_z, n_z, and n_z^w. Their size are D, K, K, and KV, respectively. We can see none of them need much space. Actually, when dealing with huge datasets, GSDMM spends most space to store the words in each document with complexity $O(D\bar{L})$. Where $\bar{L}$ (often less than 10^2 in short text corpus) is the average length of the documents. K-means needs to represent the documents as vectors of size V (often larger than 10^5). Therefore, the space complexity of K-means is $O(DV)$. The vector space representation of short documents wastes much space, because most of the elements of the vectors are zero.

Next, we analyze the time complexity of each iteration of GSDMM and K-means. From Algorithm 1, we can see that for each iteration GSDMM needs to re-sample a cluster for the D documents in turn, and for each document d, it computes the conditional probability $p(z_d = z|\vec{z}_{\neg d}, \vec{d})$ for each cluster z. The complexity of $p(z_d = z|\vec{z}_{\neg d}, \vec{d})$ in Equation 4 is linear to the average length of documents, $\bar{L}$. Therefore, GSDMM's time complexity for each iteration is $O(KD\bar{L})$. The complexity of each iteration of K-means is $O(KDS)$, where S is the maximum number of non-zero elements in the vectors of centroids of the clusters [26]. We should note that the centroids of the clusters are not sparse, and S can be really large (even close to V).

4. EXPERIMENTAL STUDY

4.1 Data Sets

4.1.1 Google News

Similar to [2], we utilize Google News[1] as one of the labeled datasets to evaluate the clustering performance. In the Google News, the news articles are grouped into clusters (stories) automatically. We took a snapshot of the Google News on November 27, 2013, and crawled the titles and snippets of 11,109 news articles belonging to 152 clusters. We manually examined this dataset, and found that it is with really good quality (Almost all articles in the same

[1]http://news.google.com

cluster are about the same event, and articles in different clusters are about different events).

We further divided the dataset into three datasets: TitleSet (TSet), SnippetSet (SSet), and TitleSnippetSet (TSSet). The TitleSet and SnippetSet only contain the titles and snippets, respectively, while the TitleSnippetSet contains both the titles and snippets. We use these three datasets to test the performance of different clustering methods on short texts with different length.

4.1.2 TweetSet

In the 2011 and 2012 microblog tracks at Text REtrieval Conference (TREC)[2] , totally 109 queries were used. Using a standard polling strategy, the NIST assessors evaluated the tweets submitted for each query by the participants into: spam, not relevant, relevant, and highly-relevant. We regard the queries as clusters and the highly-relevant tweets of each query as documents in each cluster. After removing the queries with none highly-relevant tweets, we constructed a dataset with 89 clusters and totally 2,472 tweets. We refer this dataset as TweetSet.

4.1.3 PreProcessing

For all datasets, we conducted the following preprocessing: (1) Convert letters into lowercase; (2) Remove non-latin characters and stop words; (3) Perform stemming for words with the WordNet Lemmatizer of NLTK[3] ; (4) Remove words whose length are smaller than 2 or larger than 15; (5) Remove words with document frequency less than 2.

4.2 Evaluation Metrics

In this part, we introduce the evaluation metrics used in this paper: Homogeneity (H), Completeness (C), V-Measure, Adjusted Rand Index (ARI), Normalized Mutual Information (NMI), and Adjusted Mutual Information (AMI). We used the implementation of these metrics in sklearn[4] in the experimental study.

Homogeneity, Completeness, and V-Measure are used in [24]. Homogeneity represents the objective that each cluster contains only members of a ground true group and completeness represents the objective that all members of a ground true group are assigned to the same cluster. V-measure is an entropy-based measure which explicitly measures how successfully the criteria of homogeneity and completeness have been satisfied, and is actually equivalent to Normalized Mutual Information (NMI) that we will discuss later [3]. As a result, we will only report NMI in our experimental results.

We want to assign two documents to the same cluster if and only if they are similar, and clustering can be viewed as a series of pair-wise decisions. Rand index measures the percentage of decisions that are correct. Adjusted Rand Index (ARI) is the corrected-for-chance version of Rand index, whose expected value is zero [12].

Normalized Mutual Information (NMI) is often used in literature, which measures the amount of statistical information shared by the random variables representing the cluster assignments and the ground true groups of the documents. However, NMI is not adjusted for chance and will tend to increase as the number of different labels (clusters) increases. Adjusted Mutual Information(AMI) [19] corrects the effect of agreement solely due to chance between clusterings, similar to the way Adjusted Rand Index (ARI) corrects the Rand index.

[2]http://trec.nist.gov/data/microblog.html

[3]http://www.nltk.org

[4]http://scikit-learn.org

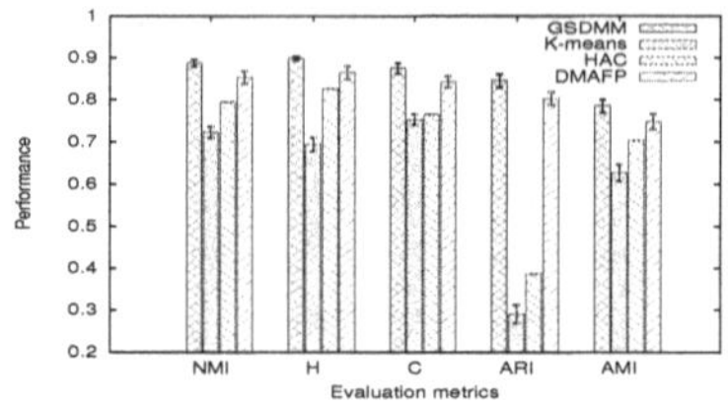

Figure 2: Performance of the models on the TweetSet.

		GSDMM	K-means	DMAFP
TSet	NMI	0.874 ± 0.007	0.732 ± 0.007	0.852 ± 0.009
	H	0.853 ± 0.010	0.692 ± 0.009	0.831 ± 0.010
	C	0.896 ± 0.006	0.775 ± 0.006	0.875 ± 0.007
	ARI	0.693 ± 0.043	0.133 ± 0.030	0.657 ± 0.051
	AMI	0.831 ± 0.012	0.639 ± 0.011	0.814 ± 0.015
SSet	NMI	0.896 ± 0.006	0.759 ± 0.008	0.868 ± 0.008
	H	0.871 ± 0.008	0.754 ± 0.009	0.846 ± 0.011
	C	0.921 ± 0.005	0.764 ± 0.009	0.892 ± 0.007
	ARI	0.746 ± 0.014	0.262 ± 0.017	0.703 ± 0.018
	AMI	0.853 ± 0.009	0.708 ± 0.008	0.819 ± 0.012
TSSet	NMI	0.928 ± 0.004	0.834 ± 0.005	0.901 ± 0.008
	H	0.911 ± 0.005	0.836 ± 0.005	0.889 ± 0.006
	C	0.945 ± 0.003	0.832 ± 0.005	0.912 ± 0.004
	ARI	0.789 ± 0.018	0.370 ± 0.029	0.736 ± 0.023
	AMI	0.897 ± 0.006	0.800 ± 0.006	0.847 ± 0.009

Table 2: Performance of GSDMM, K-means, and DMAFP on TitleSet, SnippetSet, and TitleSnippetSet.

4.3 Comparison of clustering models

In this part, we compare the performance of GSDMM with K-means [13], HAC [15], and DMAFP [11]. K-means and HAC are two popular similarity-based clustering models. DMAFP [11] is a state-of-the-art model-based clustering approach which can infer the number of clusters automatically.

For K-means and HAC, we set K at the true number of clusters of each dataset. For DMAFP and GSDMM, we set the initial number of clusters at 500 for all datasets. For K-means and DMAFP, we set the number of initializations at 20 to cope with their problem of falling into local maximum, and in each run we stop the algorithm when the relative change of the objective function or log marginal probability is less than $1e^{-7}$. For GSDMM, we set the number of iterations at 30, $\alpha = 0.1$, and $\beta = 0.1$ for all datasets. We run each model 20 times on each dataset, and report the mean and standard deviation of their performance measured by the five evaluation metrics introduced in Section 4.2.

Figure 2 shows the performance of GSDMM, K-means, HAC, and DMAFP on the TweetSet. First, we can see that GSDMM performs significantly better than K-means and HAC in terms of all the five metrics. This is because GSDMM can infer the number of clusters automatically with a good balance between the completeness and homogeneity of the clustering results. We will discuss this more deeply in Section 4.5. Second, GSDMM also performs better than DMAFP. This is because DMAFP is an EM-based algorithm which has the problem of falling into a local minimum, while GSDMM does not have the problem of falling into a local minimum as discussed in Section 3.2. We should note that

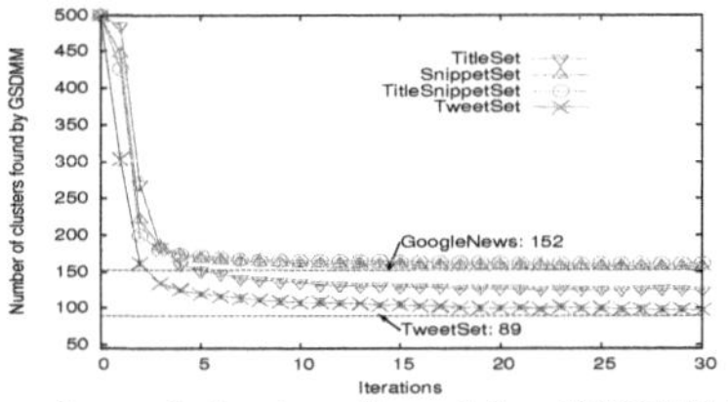

Figure 3: Number of clusters found by GSDMM with different number of iterations on the four datasets.

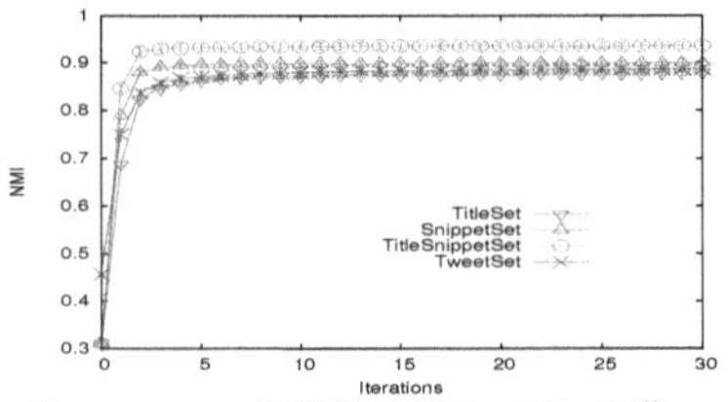

Figure 4: Performance of GSDMM with different number of iterations on the four datasets.

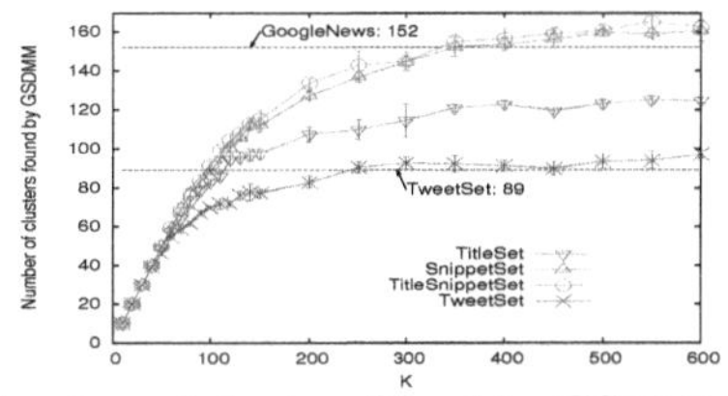

Figure 5: Number of clusters found by GSDMM with different values of K on the four datasets.

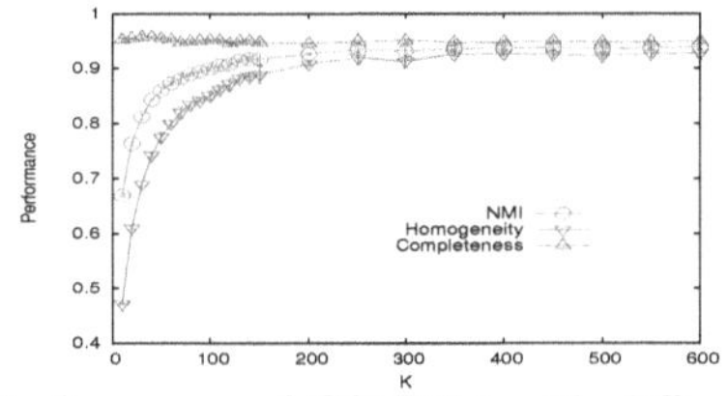

Figure 6: Performance of GSDMM with different values of K on the TitleSnippetSet.

GSDMM is much simpler than DMAFP, and we can understand how and why GSDMM works as well as the meaning of its parameters with the analogy of MGP. Third, GSDMM's ARI is significantly better than that of K-means and HAC. This means GSDMM's performance is much better than the random label assignments, while K-means and HAC are just a little better than the random case.

We find that HAC is not scalable with the Google News datasets. This is because the space complexity of HAC is quadratic in the number of documents. Therefore, we only report the performance of GSDMM, K-means, and DMAFP on the Google News datasets in Table 2. First, we can see GSDMM can achieve better performance than K-means and DMAFP on all the three datasets measured by all the five evaluation metrics. Second, we can see all the three models can achieve better performance on datasets with longer documents, which means we can improve the performance of short text clustering by enriching their representation with methods like [2]. Third, GSDMM can achieve relatively good performance on the TitleSet, even better than the performance of K-means on the TitleSnippetSet. This validates the effectiveness of GSDMM for short text clustering.

4.4 Influence of the number of iterations

In this part, we try to investigate the influence of the number of iterations to the number of clusters found by GSDMM and the performance of GSDMM. We set the initial number of clusters at 500, $\alpha = 0.1$, and $\beta = 0.1$ for all datasets.

Figure 3 shows the number of clusters found by GSDMM with different number of iterations. From Figure 3, we can see that the number of clusters drops quickly and almost gets stable within about ten iterations. We take the TweetSet as an example to explain this phenomenon. In the initialization step, GSDMM randomly assigns the 2,472 documents (students) of the TweetSet to 500 clusters (tables). For each iteration, GSDMM enumerates the students and lets them re-choose a table according to the two rules of MGP introduced in Section 2.1 in turn. In the beginning, some clusters get large quickly, because once they are chosen by a student, they are more likely to be chosen by other students that share similar interests with them. Similarly, some clusters vanish quickly. We can see that on the TweetSet, after one iteration the number of non-empty clusters drops to about 300 and after two iterations the number of non-empty clusters drops to about 160. With more iterations the allocation of documents will get stable.

Figure 4 shows the performance of GSDMM with different number of iterations measured by NMI on the four datasets. From Figure 4, we can see only after two iterations, GSDMM can achieve quite good performance, and can reach stable performance with about five iterations on all the four datasets. GSDMM can update the model every time it reassigns a document to a cluster which means it can update the model D times in each iteration (D is the number of documents in the corpus), as a result, GSDMM can converge really fast. We can also see the standard deviations of the 20 runs of GSDMM are almost zero which means the performance of GSDMM is highly stable.

4.5 Influence of K

In this part, we try to investigate the influence of K to the number of clusters found by GSDMM and the performance of GSDMM. We fix the number of iterations at 10, $\alpha = 0.1$, and $\beta = 0.1$ for all datasets.

Figure 5 shows the number of clusters found by GSDMM with different values of K on the four datasets. From Figure 5, we can see the number of clusters found by GSDMM grows when we enlarge K, and can finally get stable. The stable number of clusters found by GSDMM is near the ground true number of groups which means GSDMM can infer the number of clusters automatically when K is large enough.

Figure 6 shows the performance of GSDMM with different values of K on the TitleSnippetSet, and we have similar results on the other three datasets. Intuitively, we know a clustering algorithm will tend to have high completeness and low homogeneity when K is small. This is because when K is small, the algorithm can more easily assign the documents belonging to the same ground true group to the same cluster (high completeness), while more difficult to divide the documents in different ground true groups into different clusters (low homogeneity). Similarly, a clustering algorithm will tend to have high homogeneity and low completeness when K is large. From Figure 5, we can see the performance of GSDMM conforms to the above intuition when K is small. Different from the above intuition, GSDMM can achieve both high completeness and high homogeneity when K is

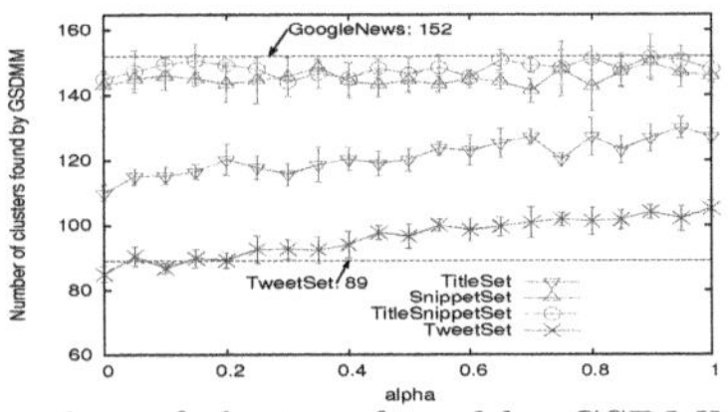

Figure 7: Number of clusters found by GSDMM with different values of α on the four datasets.

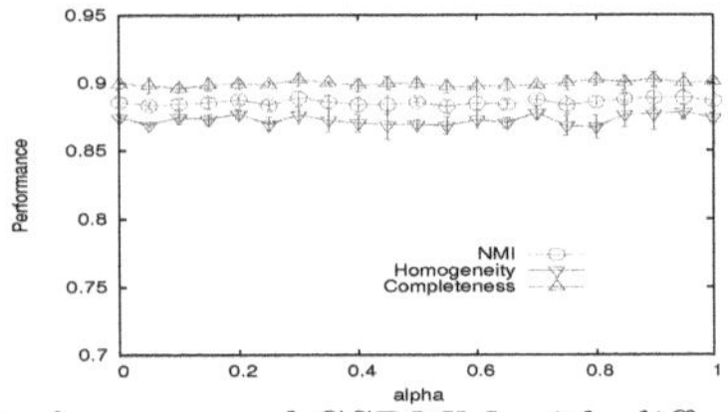

Figure 8: Performance of GSDMM with different values of α on the TweetSet.

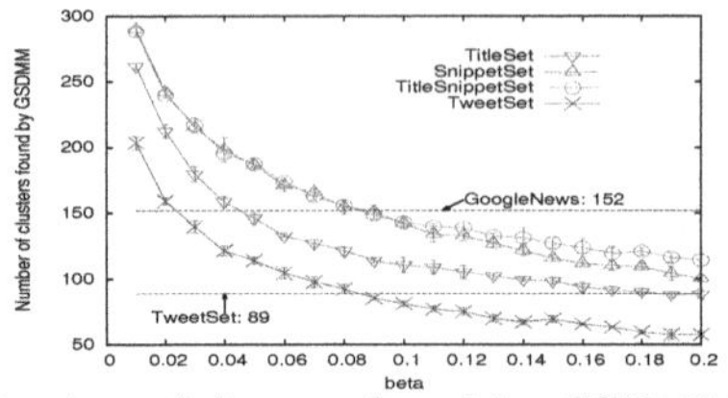

Figure 9: Number of clusters found by GSDMM with different values of β on the four datasets.

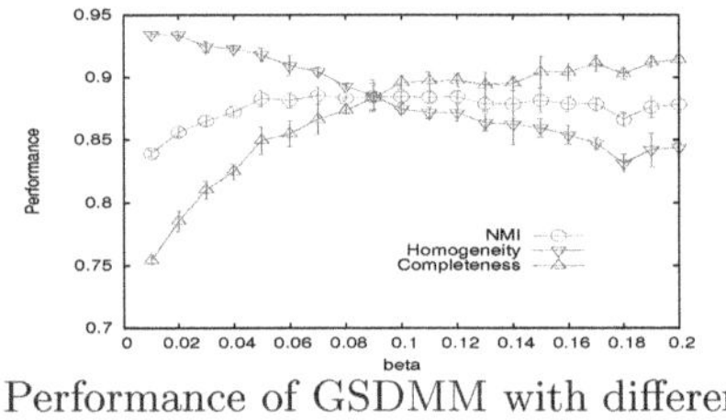

Figure 10: Performance of GSDMM with different values of β on the TweetSet.

larger than the true number of clusters. This is because GSDMM can balance the completeness and homogeneity of the clustering results with Equation 4 which relates to the two rules of MGP as discussed in Section 2.3.

4.6 Influence of Alpha

In this part, we try to investigate the influence of α to the number of clusters found by GSDMM and the performance of GSDMM. We fix the number of iterations at 10, the initial number of clusters at 300, and $\beta = 0.1$ for all datasets.

Figure 7 shows the number of clusters found by GSDMM with different values of α on the four datasets. We can see the number of non-empty clusters found by GSDMM grows slightly with the increase of α on the TweetSet and TitleSet. We investigate the clustering results of these two datasets, and find that larger α tends to result in clusters with only one document. We can explain this phenomenon with the Movie Group Process (MGP). In the extreme case, when we set $\alpha = 0$, a table will be discarded after it gets empty. Because the first part of Equation 4 is now zero for empty tables, and a student (document) will never choose an empty table (cluster). When α gets larger, a student will have a larger probability to choose an empty table. However, once a table gets empty, it will have a low probability of growing large because the "richer gets richer" property of MGP. As a result, the number of non-empty clusters found by GSDMM will get larger slightly with the increase of α, and GSDMM will result in more clusters with only one document. We can see that the number of non-empty clusters found by GSDMM tends to be stable in the SnippetSet and TitleSnippetSet. This is because the average length of the documents is larger in these two datasets, and the second part of Equation 4 plays a more important rule. The students are more likely to choose a table according to their interests, as a result, the empty tables have a lower probability of being chosen.

Figure 8 shows the performance of GSDMM with different values of α on the TweetSet, and we have similar results on the other three datasets. From Figure 8, we can see the performance of GSDMM is stable with different values of α. We also conducted experiments by ranging α from 1 to 10, and found that the performance of GSDMM drops slowly when α is larger than one. We conducted experiments to investigate the performance of GSDMM when $\alpha = 0$, and found that GSDMM almost does not result in clusters with only one document when $\alpha = 0$. We should note that we can also speed up GSDMM by setting α to zero. Because when $\alpha = 0$, we can just discard clusters (tables) that get empty as they will never be chosen again, which means K can decrease with the running of GSDMM. In Section 3.4, we analyzed the time complexity of GSDMM, which is $O(KD\bar{L})$. We can see that GSDMM can get faster with the decrease of K. We should note that Equation 4 cannot be derived from DMM when $\alpha = 0$, because α is the parameter of the Dirichlet distribution in DMM and must be larger than zero. This means the new algorithm should be related to another model, and we plan to investigate this more deeply in future.

4.7 Influence of Beta

In this part, we try to investigate the influence of β to the number of clusters found by GSDMM and the performance of GSDMM. We fix the number of iterations at 10, the initial number of clusters at 300, and $\alpha = 0.1$ for all datasets.

Figure 9 shows the number of clusters found by GSDMM with different values of β on the four datasets. From Figure 9, we can see the number of clusters found by GSDMM drops when we enlarge β. This is because β is in the second part of Equation 4 which relates to Rule 2 of MGP (Choose a table whose students share similar interests with him). When β is small, the probability of a student choosing a table is more sensitive to $n^w_{z,\neg d}$ (the number of occurrences of word w in cluster z). In other words, GSDMM gives more emphasis on the student's interests when β is small, and the students will have a larger probability to choose a table based on their interests rather than the popularity of tables. As a result, GSDMM will result in more non-empty tables (clusters) when β is small. Similarly, when β is large, GSDMM will result in fewer non-empty tables.

Figure 10 shows the performance of GSDMM with different values of β on the TweetSet, and we have similar results on the other three datasets. From Figure 10, we can see the completeness of GSDMM grows when we enlarge β. We can understand this phenomenon through Figure 9, where the number of clusters found by GSDMM drops when we enlarge β. As a result, students (documents) in the same ground true group are more likely to be in the same table (cluster), and GSDMM will result in larger completeness when we enlarge β. Similarly, we can understand why the homogeneity of GSDMM drops when we enlarge β. Therefore, β can be used for adjusting the performance of GSDMM. GSDMM can result in relatively more clusters and high homogeneity with small β, and relatively fewer clusters and high completeness with large β.

4.8 Scalability of GSDMM

In this part, we compare the scalability of GSDMM with DMAFP, K-means, and Mini-batch K-means [26]. Mini-batch K-means [26] is a variant of K-means which uses mini-batches to reduce the computation time. Different from K-means, every time Mini-batch K-means assigns a document to a cluster, it updates the centroid of that cluster. We should note that our GSDMM algorithm also updates the model every time it assigns a document to a cluster.

To the best of our knowledge, there is no large short text datasets that can be used to test the scalability of the clustering models. As a compromise, we copied the TitleSet 2 times, 4 times, 8 times,...,until 256 times. By this way, we obtained nine different datasets scaling from 11,109 documents to 2,843,904 documents. For GSDMM, we set $K = 300, \alpha = 0.1, \beta = 0.1$, and run 10 iterations for each dataset. For DMAFP, we set $K = 300$ and the maximum iteration number at 10. For K-means and Mini-batch K-means, we set $K = 152$ (the true number of clusters) and the maximum iteration number at 10. For Mini-batch K-means, we set the mini-batch size at one percent of the number of documents in each dataset. The experiments were conducted on a computer with 8G RAM and 3.4GHz Processor Speed.

Table 3 shows the time cost of GSDMM, DMAFP, K-means, and MiniBatch K-means on these nine datasets. First, we can see the running time of GSDMM, DMAFP, and K-means are both linear to the number of documents. Second, GSDMM and DMAFP can scale to the T256 set which contains 256 copies of the TitleSet with about 284 million titles. However, K-means and MiniBatch K-means cannot scale to the T256 set. Third, We can see that MiniBatch K-means is much faster than GSDMM, DMAFP, and K-means, especially on large datasets. We plan to explore how to speed up GSDMM in future. One promising direction is to utilize the incremental clustering approach discussed in Section 3.2. We can run GSDMM on a subset of the large dataset, then use the Naive Bayes Classifier (NBC) learned by GSDMM to classify other documents into the existing clusters. This approach has potential applications for texts like tweets and news that have many duplicates.

5. RELATED WORK

In this section, we review the related work from the following two perspectives: model-based clustering and short text clustering.

5.1 Model-based Clustering

Nigam et al. [20] used the Dirichlet Multinomial Mixture (DMM) model for classification with both labeled and unlabeled documents, when only unlabeled documents are provided, DMM turns out to be a clustering model. In [20], they proposed an EM-based algorithm for DMM (abbr. to EM-DMM). In this paper, we proposed a collapsed Gibbs Sampling algorithm for DMM (abbr. to GSDMM), and found that GSDMM can infer the number of clusters automatically with a good balance between the completeness and homogeneity of the clustering results, and is fast to converge. Yu et al. [30] proposed the DPMFS model for text clustering that can also infer the number of clusters automatically. However, DPMFS is slow to converge as discussed in [11]. In [11], they further proposed the DMAFP model as an approximation to the DMPFS model and a variational inference algorithm for DMAFP. They compared DMAFP with other four clustering models: EM-DMM [20], K-means [13], LDA [6], and EDCM [7]. They found that DMAFP can achieve better performance than these models especially when the number of clusters given for these models is imprecise. In the experimental study, we compared our GSDMM algorithm with DMAFP, and found that GSDMM can perform better than DMAFP on all the four datasets. In addition, We should note that GSDMM is much simpler than DMAFP, and we can understand how and why GSDMM works as well as the meaning of its parameters with the analogy of MGP.

5.2 Short Text Clustering

Rangrej et al. [21] compared three clustering algorithms for short text clustering: K-means, Singular Value Decomposition and Affinity Propagation on a small set of tweets, and found that Affinity Propagation [8] can achieve better performance than the other two algorithms. However, the complexity of Affinity Propagation is quadratic in the number of documents, which means Affinity Propagation cannot scale to huge datasets with millions of documents. Banerjee et al. [2] proposed a method of improving the accuracy of short text clustering by enriching their representation with additional features from Wikipedia. This method can be a complement for our GSDMM algorithm. Shou et al. [27], Tsur et al. [28], and Yin [29] focused on the problem of online clustering of a stream of tweets. They all utilized an incremental clustering framework that first groups a number of tweets into clusters, then assigns the newly arriving tweets to these clusters. In this paper, we primarily focus on clustering a static collection of short documents, however, we discussed how to use GSDMM for incremental clustering in Section 3.2. We plan to explore this in future.

6. CONCLUSION

In this paper, we proposed a collapsed Gibbs Sampling algorithm for the Dirichlet Multinomial Mixture model for short text clustering (abbr. to GSDMM). We also proposed the Movie Group Process (MGP) as an analogy of GSDMM which can help us understand how and why GSDMM works as well as the meaning of its parameters. We found that GSDMM can infer the number of clusters automatically with a good balance between the completeness and homogeneity of the clustering results, and is fast to converge. GSDMM can also cope with the sparse and high-dimensional problem of short texts, and obtain the representative words of each cluster. Thorough experimental study shows GSDMM can achieve significantly better performance than the baseline methods.

There are several future directions for us to explore. First, we plan to investigate how to incorporate the global weighting metrics (e.g., IDF) for words through β as discussed in Section 3.1. Second, as discussed in Section 4.6, GSDMM can achieve good performance and lower time complexity when we set $\alpha = 0$. However, now GSDMM cannot be de-

	Datasets	T1	T2	T4	T8	T16	T32	T64	T128	T256
	#Docs	11,109	22,218	44,436	88,872	177,744	355,488	710,976	1,421,952	2,843,904
Time	GSDMM	0.092	0.179	0.354	0.711	1.424	2.836	5.688	11.346	23.203
	DMAFP	1.346	2.565	5.090	9.947	19.447	38.991	77.503	154.275	308.651
	K-means	0.399	0.773	1.423	2.954	6.147	11.509	24.072	49.259	N/A
	MiniBatch	0.027	0.032	0.041	0.059	0.094	0.182	0.340	1.197	N/A

Table 3: Running time of the models on nine datasets (in minutes).

rived from DMM because α is the parameter of the Dirichlet distribution in DMM and must be larger than zero. We plan to explore which model this new algorithm is related to in future. Third, we also plan to study how to use GSDMM for incremental clustering as discussed in Section 3.2.

7. ACKNOWLEDGMENTS

This work was supported in part by National Natural Science Foundation of China under Grant No. 61272088, National Basic Research Program of China (973 Program) under Grant No. 2011CB302206, and Tsinghua University Initiative Scientific Research Program.

8. REFERENCES

[1] C. C. Aggarwal and C. Zhai. A survey of text clustering algorithms. In *Mining Text Data*, pages 77–128. 2012.

[2] S. Banerjee, K. Ramanathan, and A. Gupta. Clustering short texts using wikipedia. In *SIGIR*, pages 787–788, 2007.

[3] H. Becker. *Identification and Characterization of Events in Social Media*. PhD thesis, COLUMBIA UNIVERSITY, 2011.

[4] P. Berkhin. A survey of clustering data mining techniques. In *Grouping Multidimensional Data*. 2006.

[5] C. M. Bishop and N. M. Nasrabadi. *Pattern recognition and machine learning*, volume 1. springer New York, 2006.

[6] D. M. Blei, A. Y. Ng, and M. I. Jordan. Latent dirichlet allocation. *J. Mach. Learn. Res.*, 2003.

[7] C. Elkan. Clustering documents with an exponential-family approximation of the dirichlet compound multinomial distribution. In *ICML*, 2006.

[8] B. J. Frey and D. Dueck. Clustering by passing messages between data points. *science*, 315(5814):972–976, 2007.

[9] G. Heinrich. Parameter estimation for text analysis. Technical report version 2.9, vsonix GmbH and University of Leipzig, 2009.

[10] T. Hofmann. Probabilistic latent semantic indexing. In *SIGIR*, pages 50–57, 1999.

[11] R. Huang, G. Yu, Z. Wang, J. Zhang, and L. Shi. Dirichlet process mixture model for document clustering with feature partition. *IEEE Trans. Knowl. Data Eng.*, 25(8):1748–1759, 2013.

[12] L. Hubert and P. Arabie. Comparing partitions. *Journal of classification*, 2(1):193–218, 1985.

[13] A. K. Jain. Data clustering: 50 years beyond k-means. *Pattern Recognition Letters*, 31(8):651–666, 2010.

[14] R. E. Madsen, D. Kauchak, and C. Elkan. Modeling word burstiness using the dirichlet distribution. In *ICML*, pages 545–552, 2005.

[15] C. D. Manning, P. Raghavan, and H. Schütze. *Introduction to information retrieval*, volume 1. Cambridge University Press Cambridge, 2008.

[16] A. McCallum, K. Nigam, et al. A comparison of event models for naive bayes text classification. In *AAAI-98 workshop on learning for text categorization*, volume 752, pages 41–48. Citeseer, 1998.

[17] G. McLachlan and K. Basford. *Mixture Models: Inference and Applications to Clustering*. Marcel Dekker, New York, 1988.

[18] A. Y. Ng, M. I. Jordan, Y. Weiss, et al. On spectral clustering: Analysis and an algorithm. *Advances in neural information processing systems*, 2, 2002.

[19] X. V. Nguyen, J. Epps, and J. Bailey. Information theoretic measures for clusterings comparison: Variants, properties, normalization and correction for chance. *Journal of Machine Learning Research*, 11:2837–2854, 2010.

[20] K. Nigam, A. McCallum, S. Thrun, and T. M. Mitchell. Text classification from labeled and unlabeled documents using em. *Machine Learning*, 39(2/3):103–134, 2000.

[21] A. Rangrej, S. Kulkarni, and A. V. Tendulkar. Comparative study of clustering techniques for short text documents. In *WWW (Companion Volume)*, pages 111–112, 2011.

[22] J. D. Rennie. *Improving multi-class text classification with naive Bayes*. PhD thesis, Massachusetts Institute of Technology, 2001.

[23] J. D. Rennie, L. Shih, J. Teevan, and D. R. Karger. Tackling the poor assumptions of naive bayes text classifiers. In *ICML*, pages 616–623, 2003.

[24] A. Rosenberg and J. Hirschberg. V-measure: A conditional entropy-based external cluster evaluation measure. In *EMNLP-CoNLL*, pages 410–420, 2007.

[25] G. Salton, A. Wong, and C. S. Yang. A vector space model for automatic indexing. *Commun. ACM*, 18(11):613–620, 1975.

[26] D. Sculley. Web-scale k-means clustering. In *WWW*, pages 1177–1178, 2010.

[27] L. Shou, Z. Wang, K. Chen, and G. Chen. Sumblr: continuous summarization of evolving tweet streams. In *SIGIR*, pages 533–542, 2013.

[28] O. Tsur, A. Littman, and A. Rappoport. Efficient clustering of short messages into general domains. In *ICWSM*, 2013.

[29] J. Yin. Clustering microtext streams for event identification. In *IJCNLP*, pages 719–725, 2013.

[30] G. Yu, R. Huang, and Z. Wang. Document clustering via dirichlet process mixture model with feature selection. In *KDD*, pages 763–772, 2010.

Representative Clustering of Uncertain Data

Andreas Züfle* Tobias Emrich* Klaus Arthur Schmid* Nikos Mamoulis+
Arthur Zimek* Matthias Renz*
*Institute for Informatics, Ludwig-Maximilians-Universität München
{zuefle,emrich,schmid,zimek,renz}@dbs.ifi.lmu.de
+Department of Computer Science, University of Hong Kong
nikos@cs.hku.hk

ABSTRACT

This paper targets the problem of computing meaningful clusterings from uncertain data sets. Existing methods for clustering uncertain data compute a single clustering without any indication of its quality and reliability; thus, decisions based on their results are questionable. In this paper, we describe a framework, based on possible-worlds semantics; when applied on an uncertain dataset, it computes a set of representative clusterings, each of which has a probabilistic guarantee not to exceed some maximum distance to the ground truth clustering, i.e., the clustering of the actual (but unknown) data. Our framework can be combined with any existing clustering algorithm and it is the first to provide quality guarantees about its result. In addition, our experimental evaluation shows that our representative clusterings have a much smaller deviation from the ground truth clustering than existing approaches, thus reducing the effect of uncertainty.

1. INTRODUCTION

In a variety of application domains, our ability to unearth a wealth of new knowledge from a data set is impaired by unreliable, erroneous, obsolete, imprecise, and noisy data. Reasons and sources of such uncertainty are many. Sensing devices are inherently imprecise (e.g., due to signal noise, instrumental errors and transmission errors [15]). Moving objects can only be monitored sporadically, such that at a certain time the position of an object is not explicitly known [50]. Integration of data from heterogeneous sources may incur uncertainty, for example due to uncertain schema matchings between different data sources [3]. Uncertainty may also be injected to the data on purpose, for privacy preservation reasons [19].

Ignoring data uncertainty in a mining task (e.g., replacing any uncertain values by their expectations) may compromise the quality of the result. On the other hand, by considering the uncertainty directly in the mining process, we can assess the reliability of the result, giving the user a notion about its quality and giving an intuition of how likely it is identical, or at least similar, to the result of the mining task when applied to the true (but unknown) data values [48]. For instance, in association rule mining on uncertain data, confidence values of the probability that a given itemset is frequent are derived [5]. This notion of confidence allows the user to make a more educated judgement of the data, thus enhancing the underlying decision-making process.

This paper targets the problem of deriving a meaningful clustering from an uncertain dataset. For this purpose, our aim is not to develop a new clustering algorithm, but rather to allow clustering algorithms designed for certain data to return meaningful, reliable and correct results in the presence of uncertainty. To illustrate the challenge that arises by considering uncertain data, consider the work-flow depicted in Figure 1. Figure 1(a) shows a dataset containing six two-dimensional points, which correspond to the positions of moving objects at some point of time t. The shaded region in Figure 1(a) corresponds to a lake, which none of the moving objects may cross. To cluster the locations of these objects, a domain expert may opt to choose a clustering algorithm $\mathcal{C}$ from a suite of available options (e.g., a density-based algorithm [34], such as DBSCAN [17] or HDBSCAN [8], or one of the numerous variants from the k-means family [27]). Assuming that the true locations of the objects are known, $\mathcal{C}$ can compute the clustering shown in Figure 1(b). However, the true locations of the objects could be unknown and we may only have access to the last reported observations of these objects (e.g., by their GPS devices), shown as triangles in Figure 1(c). In such a scenario, an *uncertainty data model* is typically used to capture the distribution of the possible object locations. For instance, past observations as well as empirically learned moving patterns of an object can be used to obtain a probability function for the position at a time after the object's last observation [16]. Examples of *probability density functions* (PDFs) around the observations are shown in the Figure.

Object A, for instance, is likely to be moving around the lake (since movement inside the lake is impossible), while the movements of other objects are less constrained. If we follow a simplistic approach for clustering the data, by clustering the expected values of the objects according to the uncertain data model, then we may end up in deriving a clustering as shown in Figure 1(c) which arbitrarily deviates from the clustering of the actual (but unknown) locations of the objects shown in Figure 1(b). Therefore, approaches that aggregate the information given by the uncertain model to expected values and then apply clustering may yield results

KDD'14, August 24–27, 2014, New York, NY, USA.

http://dx.doi.org/10.1145/2623330.2623725.

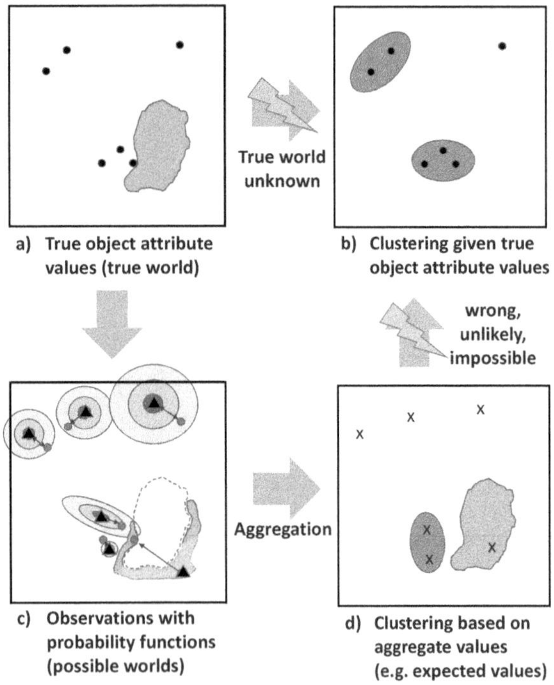

Figure 1: Uncertain Clustering Workflow.

of poor quality, due to information loss and potentially due to invalid input to the clustering process (e.g., the expected location of A after aggregating all its possible positions in Figure 1(d) is in the lake).

In this paper, our goal is neither the definition of new uncertain data models suited for clustering, nor the proposal of new clustering algorithms tailored for uncertain data. Instead, we aim at making possible the application of *any* existing clustering algorithm $\mathcal{C}$ on an uncertain database $\mathcal{DB}$, based on *any* given uncertain data model for $\mathcal{DB}$, assuming that $\mathcal{C}$ would be appropriate for $\mathcal{DB}$, if $\mathcal{DB}$ was certain. For example, we take that the clustering of Figure 1(b) by algorithm $\mathcal{C}$ is the ideal one, but infeasible to derive, given that we do not know the actual locations of the objects. The objective of our framework is to use the data of Figure 1(c) and algorithm $\mathcal{C}$ to derive a clustering that has a probabilistic guarantee (according to the uncertain data model used) to be very similar to that of Figure 1(b).

Our approach performs sampling and then represents the original uncertain database $\mathcal{DB}$ as a set of sample deterministic databases. We then run the clustering algorithm $\mathcal{C}$ on each of the sampled databases, to derive a set of possible clusterings PC. Our main contribution is to combine the resulting set PC into a concise set RPC of *representative clusterings*. Furthermore, using all clusterings in PC, we estimate a probability ϕ of each representative clustering in RPC, defined as the probability that this representative clustering does not exceed some maximum distance τ to the true clustering. Since ϕ has to be estimated from sampled databases, we obtain a lower bound of ϕ that is significant at a user specified level. We provide a methodology to derive an RPC for a given value of τ; and therefore impose quality constraints on the uncertain clustering results, unlike previous approaches on uncertain data clustering [41, 21, 23, 38, 32, 22, 31, 36, 37] which cannot provide quality guarantees.

In summary, our contributions are as follows.

- We propose a sampling-based solution to cluster uncertain data. This solution is generally applicable to all data domains and with any suitable uncertain data model, allowing the application of any existing clustering algorithm, originally designed for certain data. As opposed to previous work on uncertain clustering, our approach conforms to the possible worlds semantics and also considers any dependencies between objects.
- We present a methodology via which we can assess the quality of a clustering of a possible world compared to the true clustering of the data.
- We show how the confidence of clustering results on possible worlds can be improved by computing a set of multiple representative clusterings, each having a significant likelihood to resemble the true, unknown clustering.

The rest of the paper is organized as follows. Section 2 surveys existing methods for clustering uncertain data. Section 3 gives general definitions used in the remainder of this work. Section 4 shows how we can estimate the probability of the clustering result on a possible world to be the clustering of the true data values. Section 5 shows how, from a set of possible clusterings, we can find *representative clusterings* that are probabilistically guaranteed to be similar to the real clustering. Section 6 evaluates our framework experimentally. Section 7 concludes this work.

2. RELATED WORK

Clustering is undoubtedly one of the most important tools for unsupervised classification. A large number of clustering algorithms has been developed, as reflected in numerous surveys [28, 34, 45]. Although clustering has proved its applicability in many different domains and scenarios, the problem of clustering uncertain data has only gained little attention so far. Uncertain data clustering approaches either use expected distances between objects or assume that the distances between different pairs of objects are independent. In this work we review these methods and discuss their drawbacks.

Clustering Using Expected Distances. The main drawback of approaches based on expected distances [41, 21, 23] is the information loss incurred by describing a complex probability distance function by a single scalar. Considering additional moments of a probability distance function, such as deviation [23] works well in specific applications where objects have little uncertainty. Still, the quality of such approaches cannot be assessed, rendering them inappropriate for applications where decisions are to be made based on the computed clustering. As an example consider the setting of Figure 2, having two certain objects A and B, and an uncertain object U having two possible values U_1 and U_2. Now, assume a deterministic clustering algorithm $\mathcal{C}$ which clusters two objects only if there distance does not exceed $dist(A, U_1)$ $(= dist(B, U_2))$. Clearly, in the example of Figure 2, there are two possible clusterings, either the clustering having cluster $\{A, U\}$ and outlier B, or the clustering having cluster $\{U, B\}$ and outlier A. The probabilities of these possible clusterings equal the probabilities $0 < P(U_1) < 1$ and $P(U_2) = 1 - P(U_1)$ of alternatives U_1 and U_2 of U. However, using the expected distance between A and U given by

$$E(dist(A, U)) = P(U_1) \cdot dist(A, U_1) + P(U_2) \cdot dist(A, U_2),$$

Figure 2: Example of Uncertainty

objects A and U can never be located in the same cluster, since it holds that $E(dist(A,U)) > dist(A,U_1)$. The same holds for B and U. Thus, for the example of Figure 2, an approach using expected distance yields a clustering, which is strictly impossible. Summarizing, the use of expected distances is a heuristic to obtain a single clustering that represents the whole realm of possible clusterings, however, the derived result is not necessarily similar to any of them. Most clustering algorithms using expected distances focus on improving efficiency rather than addressing this drawback [38, 32, 41]. Gullo et al. [22] propose a method, called UK-medoids, for which they utilize the expected distance between two uncertain objects. Jiang et al. [31] propose to use the KL divergence between two uncertain objects which is often used to reflect similarity between two probabilistic density functions. They investigate the applicability to both K-means [40] and DBSCAN [17]. Since all these approaches are based on expected distances, their results are not in accordance with the possible worlds semantics and do not carry any quality guarantee.

Clustering Assuming Independent Distances. Kriegel and Pfeifle [36, 37] assume that pairwise distances between uncertain objects are mutually independent. This assumption may yield wrong results; in addition, the results are biased toward overestimating the size of clusters. In particular, they rely on the following assumption on distances between uncertain objects:

$$P(A \leftrightarrow_\epsilon B \wedge B \leftrightarrow_\epsilon C) = P(A \leftrightarrow_\epsilon B) \cdot P(B \leftrightarrow_\epsilon C).$$

$P(X \leftrightarrow_\epsilon Y)$ denotes the probability that the distance between the two uncertain objects X and Y is smaller than a threshold ϵ. However this assumption does not hold in the general case. For example, in Figure 2, the two random events $A \leftrightarrow_\epsilon U$ and $U \leftrightarrow_\epsilon B$ are negatively correlated: for the case where $dist(A,U_1) < \epsilon < dist(A,U_2)$, it even holds that both random events are mutually exclusive. That is, if U is close to A then it cannot be close to B and vice versa. Relaxing this assumption of independent distances yields a computationally hard problem, as a distance value may depend on a large number of uncertain objects.

Discussion. To our knowledge, there is no previous work on uncertain data clustering that conforms to the possible worlds semantics. A likely reason for this that general induction on uncertain data is a #P-hard problem [13]. In order to avoid the exponential run-time cost of considering all possible worlds, a common approach to handle uncertain data, in general, is sampling [30]. Given a sample of instances of the database (each corresponding to a possible world), a query or data mining task can be performed on each of them, and common results can be returned, associated with confidences of these results to be equal (or sufficiently similar) to the result on the true (but unknown) data. This is exactly the approach that we are following in this paper. We provide a small number of representative clusterings that have high confidence values to be similar to the true (but unknown) clustering.

3. DEFINITIONS

This section gives definitions for uncertain databases and clustering, which generalize all previous models and definitions. While existing works [37, 36, 38, 9, 23] generally assume that objects are points in a multi-dimensional feature space, we allow objects to have any abstract type $\mathcal{O}$, where $\mathcal{O}$ is an object space, such as a multi-dimensional feature space, the set of all strings, the set of all images, etc. Each *uncertain object* is then represented by a set of values in $\mathcal{O}$, each associated with a non-zero probability. This probability distribution can be a continuous *probability density function* (PDF) or a discrete *probability mass function* (PMF). To model the uncertainty of an object in a general way that captures both continuous [36, 42] and discrete [49, 42] models, we use the following general definition.

Definition 1 (Multivariate Uncertain Object). *A multivariate uncertain object o is defined by two functions* $\mathrm{pdf}_o : \mathcal{O} \to \mathbb{R}_0^+$ *and* $\mathrm{pmf}_o : \mathcal{O} \cup \perp \to [0,1]$ *such that*

$$\int_{\mathcal{O}} \mathrm{pdf}_o(x)dx + \sum_{\mathcal{O}\cup\perp} \mathrm{pmf}_o(x) = 1$$

Value $\perp$ is used to model existentially uncertainty, i.e., with a probability of $\mathrm{pmf}_o(\perp)$ object o does not exist at all in the database. By setting either $\mathrm{pdf}_o(x)$ or $\mathrm{pmf}_o(x)$ to the zero function, which maps any value to zero, the above definition can simulate discrete and continuous models, while also allowing mixed models.[1]

Consequently, if there is at least one uncertain object in a database, the state of the database becomes a random variable. To model the semantics of a database being a random variable, the concept of *possible worlds* is commonly used [43, 46, 54, 39]: an uncertain database is defined by a (potentially infinite) set of possible database states, called *possible worlds*. Each possible world is associated with its corresponding probability to be the true database state.

Definition 2 (Uncertain Database). *An uncertain database $\mathcal{DB}$ is defined by a set of uncertain objects $\mathcal{DB} = \{o_1, ..., o_{|\mathcal{DB}|}\}$ spanning a (potentially infinite) set of possible worlds $\mathcal{W}$ and a constructive generation rule $\mathcal{G}$ to draw possible worlds from $\mathcal{W}$ in an unbiased way. The probability to draw a world w equals the probability $P(w)$ of this world being the true (but unknown) world* oracle($\mathcal{DB}$).

Wherever independence is assumed between objects [25, 6, 10], the generation rule $\mathcal{G}$ is implicitly given by drawing samples from each object individually. In scenarios with interdependencies between uncertain objects (for example, expressed by a Bayesian network [44], or by lineage of relations [2]), a possible world can be drawn by using the factorized representation of the Bayesian network, and iteratively drawing objects conditioned to previously drawn objects.[2] To the best of our knowledge, our assumption of having a generation rule $\mathcal{G}$ is met in all state-of-the-art uncertain database management systems. The task of clustering can be defined as follows.

[1]Note that this definition avoids the (wrong) claim that a discrete distribution can be seen as a special case of a continuous distribution without any form of continuity correction.

[2]The factorized representation guarantees that at each iteration there must be one random variable for which the required conditions are met.

DEFINITION 3 (CLUSTERING). *A clustering $\mathcal{C}(S)$ of a set $S = \{a_1, ..., a_N\}$ of deterministic objects is a partitioning of S into pairwise disjoint subsets $C_1, ..., C_k \subseteq S$, such that $\bigcup_{1 \le i \le k} C_i = S$. Each subset $C_i, 1 \le i \le k$ is called a cluster.*

This abstract definition of clustering intentionally omits any objective rules toward a "good clustering", such as the requirement that similar objects should be in the same cluster. The reason is that our approach should be used in conjunction with any clustering algorithm $\mathcal{C}$, independently to the algorithm's objective. Due to the theoretical result that general query processing (or mining) on uncertain data is $\#P$-complete [13], coupled with the fact that an uncertain database may yield a number of possible clusterings exponential in the size of the database, we now explore the possibility of using a Monte-Carlo approach to perform clustering over uncertain data.

4. CLUSTERING SAMPLED WORLDS

Let $\mathcal{DB}$ be an uncertain database and let $\mathcal{C}$ be a clustering algorithm. Let $X = \{X_1, ..., X_{|X|}\}$ be a multiset[3] of possible worlds of $\mathcal{DB}$ generated from $\mathcal{DB}$ using generation rule $\mathcal{G}$ and let $\mathcal{C}(X)$ denote the multiset of clusterings obtained by clustering each sample world in X. We denote the set of distinct clusterings in $\mathcal{C}(X)$ as the set PC of *possible clusterings* obtained from sample X. For any clustering C in PC, the *support* $C.supp$ of C is defined as $\sum_{i=1}^{|X|} I(\mathcal{C}(X_i) = C)$, where $I(\cdot)$ is an indicator function that returns 1 if its operand is true and 0, otherwise. Simply speaking, $C.supp$ is the number of occurrences of clustering C in the multiset $\mathcal{C}(X)$.

LEMMA 1 (APPROXIMATION OF THE TRUE CLUSTERING). *For any possible clustering $C \in PC$, the probability $\hat{P}(C) = \frac{C.supp}{|X|}$ is an unbiased estimator the probability $P(C)$ that C is the true clustering $\mathcal{C}(\text{oracle}(\mathcal{DB}))$ of $\mathcal{DB}$; i.e., $E(\hat{P}(C)) = P(C)$.*

PROOF.

$$E(\hat{P}(C)) = E\left(\frac{C.supp}{|X|}\right) = E\left(\frac{\sum_{X_i \in X} I(X_i = C)}{|X|}\right),$$

Since the expectation of a non-random variable is the identity, we obtain

$$E(\hat{P}(C)) = \frac{E\left(\sum_{X_i \in X} I(X_i = C)\right)}{|X|},$$

Since all sample databases X_i are drawn independently, and since the expectation of a sum of independent random variables is the sum of their expectations, we get:

$$E(\hat{P}(C)) = \frac{\sum_{X_i \in X} E(I(X_i = C))}{|X|}$$

Due to the assumption that each sample X_i is drawn unbiased from the distribution of all worlds of $\mathcal{DB}$, which implies that $E(I(X_i = C)) = P(X_i)$, we obtain

$$\frac{\sum_{X_i \in X} P(X_i)}{|X|} = P(X_i)$$

□

[3]Due to independent sampling, the same sample may be drawn multiple times.

Such a straightforward sampling approach works well for small databases, including the running example depicted in Figure 2, where the number of possible clusterings C is reasonably small. In a large database setting, where the probability of finding exactly the same clustering on two samples in X approaches zero, this approach becomes inapplicable. The reason is twofold. First, the probabilities $P(C)$ of a clustering C being the true clustering of $\mathcal{DB}$, become very small. Due to independent samplings $X_i, 1 \le i \le |X|$, the number of samples where $\mathcal{C}(X_i) = C$ follows a binomial $B(\pi = P(C), n = |X|)$ distribution. Estimating the probability parameter π of a binomial distribution given a sample, requires a very large sample size n if π is small. A rule of thumb is that $n \cdot \pi \ge 5$ [11, 52]. Second, the large number of possible clusterings combined with small probabilities makes the exact results meaningless for a user. A huge set of possible clusterings, potentially exponentially large in the number of uncertain objects, where many may be very similar, yet different between each other, is of little use.

5. REPRESENTATIVE CLUSTERINGS

Our goal is to reduce the (potentially huge) set of clusterings produced by the Monte-Carlo approach to a small set of possible clusterings, which are diverse and at the same time guaranteed to be similar to the clustering on the real (but unknown) database. In Section 5.1, we discuss a general concept for determining one representative from a set, the medoid approach [47]. In Section 5.2, we generalize this approach to select a set of multiple representative clusterings and show how we can estimate how well they can approximate the real clustering.

It is a common trend in the clustering community to provide several, different ("alternative" [20, 18, 14]) results rather than just one. On the other hand, it is also consensus to avoid an abundance of redundant results [35, 55]. The eminent question is then, how many solutions to provide and how representative these solutions are. For the problem of clustering uncertain data, we therefore present, in Section 5.3, a methodology for selecting a set of representative clusterings of guaranteed quality.

5.1 Sample Medoid

Let PC denote the set of possible clusterings derived from sampled worlds $X = \{X_1, ..., X_n\}$. Let D be the *distance* $|PC| \times |PC|$ matrix such that

$$D_{i,j} := \text{dist}(PC_i, PC_j).$$

Here, dist denotes a distance measure between two clusterings, such as, e.g., the Adjusted Rand Index (ARI) [26]. Similarity usually takes a value between 0 (no agreement) and 1 (identical partitionings) and can be converted to a distance after subtraction from 1.

The *median* of PC can be defined as

$$\text{Median}(PC) = \text{Median}_{X_i \in X}(\mathcal{C}(X_i)) =$$

$$\arg\min_i \sum_{j=1}^{n} \text{dist}(\mathcal{C}(X_i), \mathcal{C}(X_j)) =$$

$$\arg\min_i \sum_{j=1}^{n} D_{i,j} \cdot PC_i.supp$$

Arguably, the median clustering can be the most representative clustering out of all sampled clusterings $\mathcal{C}(X_i)$. However, we do not have confidence information for Median(PC), i.e., the deviation of the true clustering $\mathcal{C}(\text{oracle}(\mathcal{DB}))$ from Median(PC) is impossible to assess.

It is important to note that Median(PC), albeit derived using expected distances between clusterings, does not suffer from the same drawbacks as existing works on clustering uncertain data using expected object positions and expected distances (cf. Section 2). The main difference is that Median(PC) is a clustering derived from a possible database instance that was generated consistently to the uncertainty data model, i.e., considering the value distributions and stochastic dependencies between objects.

5.2 Multiple Representatives

The possible clusterings of an uncertain database may be very heterogeneous; depending on object attribute values of a world, an individual cluster may become noise, may shatter into multiple clusters, or may be absorbed by another cluster in some worlds, but not in others. Such large changes in the overall clustering may be caused by minimal changes in the underlying dataset: the density of a critical region may drop below the threshold of a density-based clustering algorithm; a partition-based cluster representative may change slightly, yielding a new data partitioning and leading into a spiral of changes. Keeping this potential heterogeneity of possible clusterings in mind, a single sample medoid clustering could be insufficient: it may be an unlikely pivot between a number of likely clusterings and it may not even be similar to the most likely possible worlds. Instead, a user may be more interested in a smaller set of clusterings, all having a significantly high probability to be similar (but not necessarily equal) to the true clustering, i.e., being representative. We define a representative clustering as follows:

DEFINITION 4 (REPRESENTATIVE CLUSTERING). *Let $\mathcal{DB}$ be an uncertain database and let $\mathcal{C}$ be a clustering algorithm. We call a clustering $\mathcal{C}(X_i)$ a τ-ϕ-representative clustering, if the probability*

$$P(X_i, \tau) := P(\text{dist}(\mathcal{C}(X_i), \mathcal{C}(\text{oracle}(\mathcal{DB}))) \leq \tau)$$

that the true clustering $\mathcal{C}(\text{oracle}(\mathcal{DB}))$ of $\mathcal{DB}$ has a distance $\text{dist}(\mathcal{C}(X_i), \mathcal{C}(\text{oracle}(\mathcal{DB})))$ of at most τ is at least ϕ.

LEMMA 2 (APPROXIMATION OF REPRESENTATIVES). *Let $X = \{X_1, ..., X_{|X|}\}$ be a set of possible worlds of $\mathcal{DB}$ generated from $\mathcal{DB}$ using generation rule $\mathcal{G}$ and let dist be a distance measure on clusterings. Let PC be the set of clusterings obtained from X associated with their supports. The probability*

$$\hat{P}(X_i, \tau) := \frac{\sum_{j=1}^{|X|} I(\text{dist}(\mathcal{C}(X_i), \mathcal{C}(X_j)) \leq \tau)}{|X|}$$

is an unbiased estimator of the probability

$$P(X_i, \tau) := P(\text{dist}(\mathcal{C}(X_i), \mathcal{C}(\text{oracle}(\mathcal{DB}))) \leq \tau)$$

that cluster representative X_i has a distance of at most τ to the true clustering of $\mathcal{DB}$.

PROOF. Analogous to Lemma 1, by substituting the predicate $(\text{dist}(\mathcal{C}(X_i), \mathcal{C}(X_j)) \leq \tau)$ for $(C = X_i)$. □

Albeit unbiased, the probability $\hat{P}(X_i, \tau)$ cannot be used directly to assess the probability $P(X_i, \tau)$ of cluster X_i having a distance of at most τ to the true clustering $\mathcal{C}(\text{oracle}(\mathcal{DB}))$. Thus, X_i can not simply be returned as a τ-$\phi = \hat{P}(X_i, \tau)$-representative according to Definition 4, because the estimator $\hat{P}(X_i, \tau)$ may overestimate the true probability $P(X_i, \tau)$. To return τ-ϕ representative clusters to the user, our aim is to find a lower bound $\hat{P}(X_i, \tau, \alpha)$ such that we can guarantee that $P(X_i, \tau) \geq \hat{P}(X_i, \tau, \alpha)$ with a probability of α, where α is a domain specific level of significance (typically, $\alpha = 0.95$).

To derive such a significant lower bound of $P(X_i, \tau)$ we may exploit the fact that sampled possible worlds were drawn independently. Therefore, the absolute number $\hat{P} \cdot |X|$ of sampled worlds which are represented by X_i follows a binomial $B(P(X_i, \tau), |X|)$ distribution. To estimate the true probability $P(X_i, \tau)$, given realization $\hat{P} \cdot |X|$, we borrow techniques from statistics to obtain a one sided $1 - \alpha$ confidence interval of the true probability $P(X_i, \tau)$. A simple way of obtaining such confidence interval is by applying the central limit theorem to approximate a binomial distribution by a normal distribution.

DEFINITION 5 (α-CONFIDENCE PROBABILITIES). *Let $\mathcal{DB}$ be an uncertain database. For a set of drawn database instances X, and for a possible clustering $\mathcal{C}(X_i), X_i \in X$, a distance threshold τ and a level of significance α, the probability*

$$\hat{P}(X_i, \tau, \alpha) = \hat{P}(X_i, \tau) - z \cdot \sqrt{\frac{1}{|X|} \hat{P}(X_i, \tau) \left(1 - \hat{P}(X_i, \tau)\right)},$$

is called α-confidence probability of τ-representative X_i, where z is the $100 \cdot (1 - \alpha)$ percentile of the standard normal distribution.

The α-confidence probability $\hat{P}(X_i, \tau, \alpha)$ can be used to return the clustering $\mathcal{C}(X_i)$ as a τ-ϕ-representative clustering to the user, as it guarantees, that by a user specified level of confidence α, the true probability $P(X_i, \tau)$ is guaranteed to be larger than $\hat{P}(X_i, \tau, \alpha)$. To compute $\hat{P}(X_i, \tau, \alpha)$ as in Definition 5 we argue that in our setting the central limit theorem is applicable, since the sample size $|X|$ should be sufficiently large (≥ 30 as a rule of thumb [7]). Furthermore, the probability $P(X_i, \tau)$ should not be extremely small, since a cluster representative having an extremely small value of $P(X_i, \tau)$ is meaningless and should not be returned to the user in the first place. In the case where all cluster representatives have an extremely small $P(X_i, \tau)$ value, the parameter τ should be increased to obtain meaningful representatives. Yet, we note that more accurate approximations can be obtained using Wilson Score Intervals [53] or using exact binomial confidence intervals [11].

5.3 Selection of Representative Worlds

Using the techniques of Section 5.2 we can estimate, for a given τ the probability of any drawn possible world to be a τ-representative. In this section, we show how good representatives having a high confidence and low τ can be extracted automatically from a set of sampled worlds. Furthermore, when more than a single representative world is returned, a requirement is to minimize redundancy between sets of worlds represented by each representative [12, 29, 55]. This requirement is important in order to avoid overly similar clustering representatives. To solve this challenge, we propose a general approach to first derive a clustering of the set of clusterings PC that have been obtained by applying the domain specific clustering algorithm $\mathcal{C}$ to sampled possible worlds X. Then, a single representative clustering R is chosen from each cluster of PC such that τ is minimized while the fraction of drawn possible clusterings is maximized. Formally:

DEFINITION 6 (REPRESENTATIVE WORLDS CLUSTERING). *Let PC denote the set of possible clusterings derived from sampled worlds* $X = \{X_1, ..., X_n\}$. *Let* D *be a* $|X| \times |X|$ *matrix such that*

$$D_{i,j} := \text{dist}\,(X_i, X_j)\,.$$

Let $\mathcal{C}'$ *be a metric clustering algorithm based on* dist *and let* $\mathcal{C}'(PC)$ *denote the meta-clustering returned by applying* $\mathcal{C}'$ *to the set PC of possible clusters. For each meta-cluster* $Y \in \mathcal{C}'(PC)$, *a* Representative Worlds Clustering *returns a triple* $(R, \tau, \hat{P}(R, \tau, \alpha))$, *where* $R \in Y$ *is the clustering chosen to represent* Y, *and* R *is an* α*-significant representative (cf. Definition 5) with a probability* ϕ *of at least* $\hat{P}(R, \tau, \alpha)$.

In Definition 6, two parameters are undefined, the choice of the clustering algorithm $\mathcal{C}'(PC)$ and a heuristic to obtain a representative from each meta-cluster in $\mathcal{C}'(PC)$. For the choice of clustering algorithm $\mathcal{C}'$, any clustering algorithm which is appropriate for general metric spaces could be used [33, 28, 34]. For the problem of defining a representative for each a meta-cluster Y, we propose the following two heuristics. Our first heuristic requires all possible clusterings in a meta-cluster $Y \in \mathcal{C}'(PC)$ to be represented.

DEFINITION 7 (COMPLETE REPRESENTATIVE). *For a meta-cluster* $Y \in \mathcal{C}'(PC)$, *the* complete representative *is the clustering*

$$R_{complete} := \arg\min_{R \in Y} \left(\max_{R' \in R} \left(\text{dist}(R, R')\right)\right)$$

which has the minimum maximum distance

$$\tau = \max_{R' \in R} \left(\text{dist}(R, R')\right)$$

to all other clusterings in Y.

This representative R_{complete} can be returned as a τ-ϕ-representative with confidence probability $\phi = \hat{P}(R_{\text{complete}}, \tau, \alpha)$ using a user specified level of confidence α as described in Section 5.2.

A drawback of the complete representative approach is that the value of τ may grow arbitrarily large, being at least half of the corresponding clusters diameter. A τ-representative having an overly large τ value, such as an ARI-distance [26] value greater than 0.2, may have no semantic meaning to the user, as the space of clusterings represented by this τ-representative grows too large to allow meaningful decision making. Furthermore, a large value of τ yields overlapping clusters. For instance, for a pair of complete representatives R_i and $R_j, i \neq j$, where R_i is an τ_i-representative and R_j is an τ_j representative, it may hold that for a single sampled clustering $X_k \in X$ that $\mathcal{D}(X_k, R_i) \leq \tau_i$ and $\mathcal{D}(X_k, R_j) \leq \tau_j$. This drawback of complete representatives can be particularly bad, if the underlying clustering algorithm $\mathcal{C}$ allows clusters to have a large diameter (e.g., $\mathcal{C}$ is k-means). In contrast, complete representatives may yield good results in settings where density-based clustering algorithms such as DBSCAN are used.

Table 1: Datasets [4] and Parameters

Dataset	Tuples	Dim	ϵ	MinPts
abalone	4177	8	.08	5
ecoli	336	8	.12	4
glass	214	10	.3	4
iris	150	4	.4	4
letter	20000	16	.04	5
segmentation	2310	19	.3	4
wine	178	13	.6	4
yeast	1484	8	.08	5

For the general case, we propose a different approach, where a maximum threshold for τ is provided. This parameter, which is specific to the chosen distance function dist, should be chosen in a way that a user should treat two clusterings, having a distance of no more than τ as similar.

DEFINITION 8 (τ_{max}-CLUSTERING). *Given a* $\tau_{\max}$ *threshold, for a cluster* $C \in \mathcal{C}'(PC)$ *a* $\tau_{\max}$ representative *is a* τ-ϕ*-representative, such that* $\tau \leq \tau_{\max}$ *given by*

$$R_{\tau_{\max}} := \arg\max_{R \in Y} \left(\sum_{C_i \in Y} I\left(\text{dist}(R, C_i) \leq \tau_{\max}\right) \right) \cdot C_i.supp.$$

Again, this representative $R_{\tau_{\max}}$ can be returned as a τ-ϕ-representative by computing a confidence probability $\phi = \hat{P}(R_{\tau_{\max}}, \tau_{\max}, \alpha)$ with a user specified level of confidence α as described in Section 5.2.

The main drawback of τ_{max} clusterings is that large fractions of possible clusterings may not be assigned to any τ-representative. The semantics of such result, however, may be useful, indicating that a large fraction of possible clusterings deviate too much from other clusterings. This indication of high heterogeneity of possible clusterings has to be considered when making decisions based on the uncertain data set $\mathcal{DB}$.

6. EXPERIMENTS

6.1 Experimental Setup

The focus of this paper is to mitigate the effect of uncertainty by obtaining an uncertain clustering that is similar to applying algorithm $\mathcal{C}$ on the real, unknown data set oracle($\mathcal{DB}$), independent of the choice of $\mathcal{C}$.

Datasets and Ground Truth. Evaluations have been run on synthetic data as well as on the datasets summarized in Table 1. For reasons of comparability, we normalized all datsets to [0,1] in each dimension. In a preparation step, we apply a traditional (certain) clustering algorithm, DBSCAN [17], to obtain the ground-truth clustering $\mathcal{C}$(oracle($\mathcal{DB}$)). We then tuned the parameters ϵ and MinPts in order to yield a high F-measure for predicting the class labels of each database object. Those parameters are specified along with the datasets in Table 1.

Then, we discarded the class-information from the datasets, and treated the result of $\mathcal{C}$ as the ground truth $\mathcal{C}$(oracle($\mathcal{DB}$)). Recall that our goal is to compute clustering results on an uncertain version of each dataset similar to $\mathcal{C}(\text{oracle}(\mathcal{DB}))$, independent of the quality of $\mathcal{C}$ in terms of its F-measure. Yet, the parameters of $\mathcal{C}$ should have meaningful values in our setting, to avoid effects such as having only a single cluster or no clusters at all.

Uncertainty Generation. In an uncertain setting we do not have access to the certain database oracle($\mathcal{DB}$) and are rather given an uncertain database $\mathcal{DB}$. Thus, for each object $o \in \mathcal{DB}$, we draw a new object using a multivariate Gaussian or multivariate uniform distribution. In both cases, we use a parameter ext to describe the uncertainty. In the Gaussian case we uniformly chose a standard deviation $\sigma \in [0; ext/4]$ in each dimension and generated a center of a generating probability distribution by drawing one sample point g from the Gaussian PDF with $\mu = o$. Using g as observation of o, we generate $i-1$ additional points from the normal distribution $\mu = g$. The resulting i points correspond to samples of an uncertain object observed at location g.

In case of uniform distribution, a rectangle r was constructed having an extent chosen uniformly in the interval $[0, ext]$ in each dimension. The resulting new object u is chosen uniformly from this interval. Then, the rectangle r is centered at u and $i-1$ more points are drawn uniformly from r. In addition to o, which is guaranteed to be inside r by construction we generated $i-1$ additional points uniformly distributed in r. All generated uncertain objects form the uncertain database $\mathcal{DB}$.

For our experiments, we used $ext = 0.04$ and $i = 10$. Our approach sampled $|X| = 100$ possible worlds, assuming mutual independence of objects.

Algorithms. In our experiments we set the parameters of our framework to $\mathcal{C}$ = DBSCAN [17] and $\mathcal{C}'$ = PAM [33], a k-medoid variant, and dist $= 1 -$ ARI, i.e., a distance between clusterings, based on the Adjusted Rand Index [26].

As baseline, we use a *Median Clustering* (MC) of the data set, which performs DBSCAN on the uncertain objects by reducing each uncertain object to one single possible alternative which corresponds to the median of its alternatives. This approach is a representative of naïve approaches [41, 21, 23] which reduce the uncertainty information of an uncertain object to a single point (the median in this case). A comparison partner from the literature is FDBSCAN [36]. The parameters were chosen identically for MC, FDBSCAN, and our approach.

All algorithms were obtained from or implemented in the ELKI-Framework [1] and executed on a 64-Bit Linux Computer with eight cores at 3.40GHz and 32GB RAM.

6.2 Experiments on Synthetic Data

Before evaluating the proposed approach in a broad experimental setting, we first demonstrate the difference regarding the result of the clustering task between our technique and previous work on clustering uncertain objects (represented by MC). For this purpose, we generated a toy example consisting of three Gaussian distributed point clouds $\{A, B, C\}$ which represent our ground truth data. After adding Gaussian uncertainty, as described in the previous section, all objects consist of several sample points which can be covered by a minimum bounding rectangle; these rectangles are shown in Figures 3 and 4.

Figure 3(a) illustrates the clustering of the original data set without uncertainty. Objects belonging to the same cluster are plotted using the same color. Outliers are plotted in a different color. Figure 3(b) shows the result of MC, which yields a different clustering compared to the original one, since the lower two point clouds are merged to a single cluster.

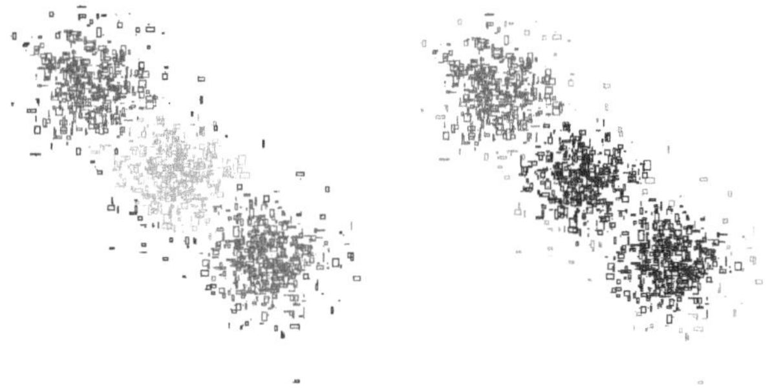

(a) Clustering of original data (b) Median Clustering (MC)

Figure 3: Clustering results of sample dataset

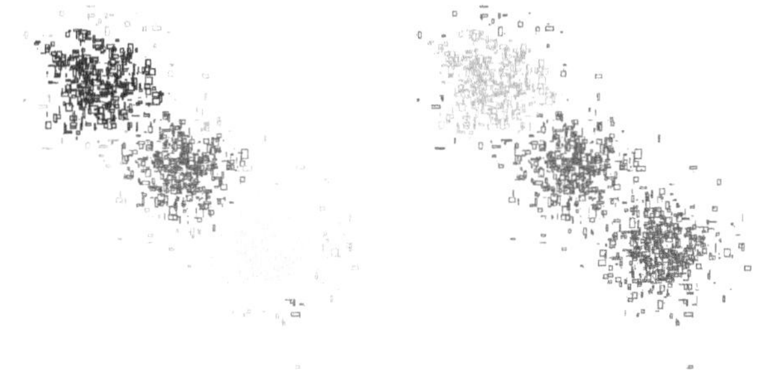

(a)$\hat{P}(X_1, 0.075, 0.95) = 0.36$ (b)$\hat{P}(X_2, 0.094, 0.95) = 0.25$

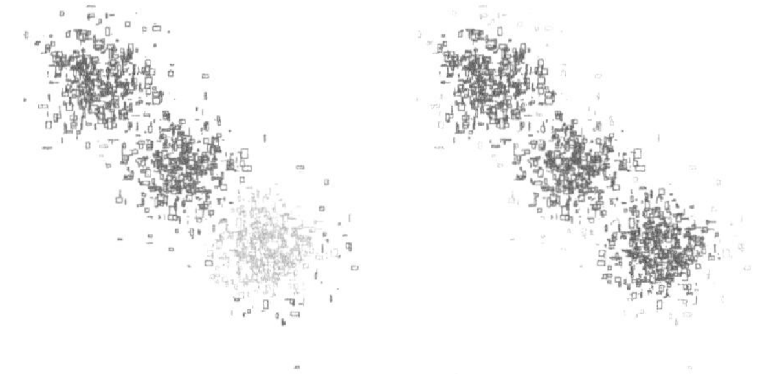

(c)$\hat{P}(X_3, 0.075, 0.95) = 0.19$ (d)$\hat{P}(X_4, 0.22, 0.95) = 0.12$

Figure 4: Four representative clusterings

Next consider the results of our approach when generating four representative clusterings $\{X_1, ..., X_4\}$ in Figure 4. First, note that the four results coarsely reflect the four expected possible results of a density based clustering approach ({A}, {B}, {C}), ({A, B}, {C}), ({A}, {B, C}) and ({A, B, C}). The corresponding confidence probabilities $\hat{P}(X_i, \tau, \alpha)$ (cf. Definition 5) are shown for each representative. For instance, representative X_1, shown in Figure 4(a), is an $\alpha = 0.95$-significant representative having a probability of 0.38 to have an ARI-distance of at most $\tau = 0.075$ to the ground-truth clustering $\mathcal{C}(\text{oracle}(\mathcal{DB}))$.

The real ARI-distances of the four representatives to $\mathcal{C}(\text{oracle}(\mathcal{DB}))$ are 0.038, 0.400, 0.404, and 0.851, respectively. In this toy example, the clustering with the smallest ARI to the base clustering has the highest probability. This

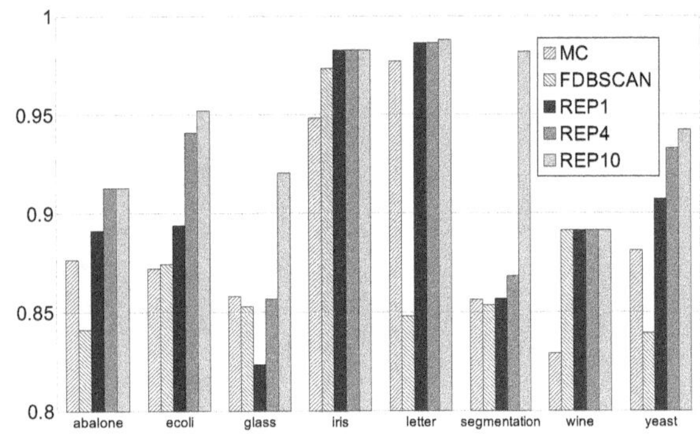

Figure 5: ARI on all datasets.

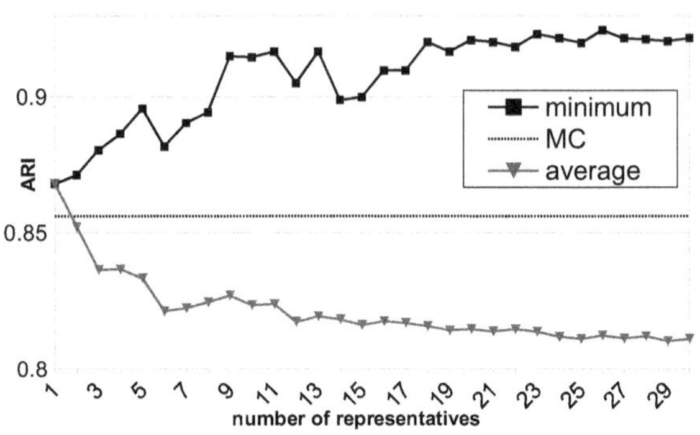

Figure 6: ARI vs. the number of representatives.

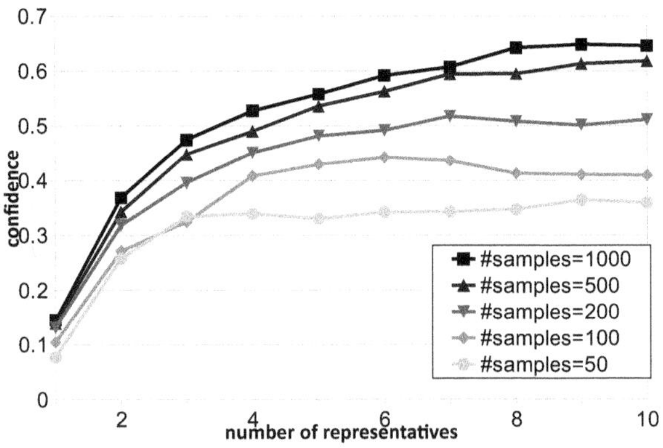

Figure 7: Confidence depending on samples.

is not always the case and our approach might also return a result having a large distance with the highest probability. Yet, our approach usually returns at least one possible clustering having a very high similarity with the true clustering. However, more importantly, unlike existing approaches, our approach is able to assess the probabilistic quality of its results and can provide multiple representative clusterings for the user to choose from.

6.3 Experiments on Real Data

Clustering Quality. Figure 5 illustrates the results under the default values on all tested datasets. Shown is the Adjusted Rand Index (ARI) [26] to the certain clustering on the original dataset. Thus, a value of one means that the method produces the same clustering result on the uncertain data than on the certain data, whereas a value closer to zero means that the two clusterings differ drastically. As observed, in several cases the rather simple MC performs better than the more sophisticated FDBSCAN. This might be because of the shortcomings of FDBSCAN regarding the consideration of possible worlds semantics as discussed in Section 2. Yet still, although the MC approach returns a clustering of a possible world, it cannot assign any measure of confidence to it, possibly resulting in a highly unlikely world. This becomes obvious when revisiting the results in Figure 5. Even for the case were only one representative is returned by our method (REP1), this representative resembles the original clustering better and in addition it also carries a confidence about its similarity to the true clustering. For instances of our method with multiple representatives, the figure shows the ARI of the representative with the minimum distance. Thus, increasing the number of representatives (REP4, REP10) ensures that at least one representative resembles the original clustering very closely.
Number of Representatives. An important question is how many representatives should be presented to the user. Presenting the user too few representatives may yield an insufficient understanding of the possible outcomes and the result may not contain a clustering which is close to the "true" clustering at all, while presenting too many representatives may overwhelm the user. In Figure 6, we show the averaged ARI over all considered datasets when increasing the number of representatives. Observe that the average ARI of all our representatives (weighted by the confidence of the representatives) decreases in comparison to the MC approach (we exclude the FDBSCAN in this graph due to its larger deviation). This can be explained by the diversity that increases with a higher number of representatives. On the other hand, the closest representative to the original clustering yields a higher score when increasing the number of representatives – as a larger number of representatives increases the likelihood of having a representative close to the ground truth clustering. Summarizing, our experiments show that the quality of our result gains only up to about ten representatives returned, after which no significant improval can be seen anymore. Furthermore, if becomes apparent that a set of four cluster representatives already yields fair results in most cases, while it can still be considered as concise enough to be represented to an average user.
Number of Samples. In our next experiment, we investigate how many samples $|X|$ are required in order to obtain significant results on the D31 data set [51] using the same parameter setting as for *yeast* (cf. Table 1). For this purpose, we aggregated the $\hat{P}(X_i, \tau, \alpha)$ of all cluster representatives X_i for $\tau = 0.1$, $\alpha = 0.95$ for different values of $|X|$. The result is shown in Figure 7, where it can be observed that a larger sample size $|X|$ increases the lower probability bounds obtained by Definition 5. More information on obtaining confidence intervals for a binomial probability function such as $P(X_i, \tau)$ can be found in the literature [24].
Runtime. The runtime of our approach directly corresponds to the number of samples we utilize. Thus our approach will always be slower in terms of runtime than other approaches like MC for the exchange of more valuable information and insights into the dataset, which is normal for data mining tasks such as clustering. Thus we present, in Figure 8, which modules of the process effect runtime the

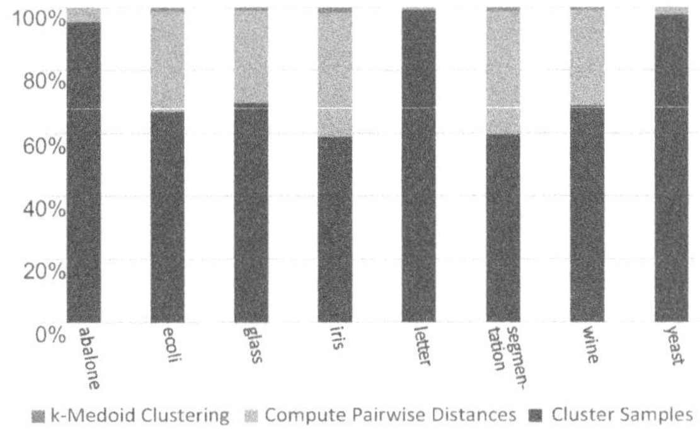

Figure 8: Relative Runtime.

most. We divided the procedure of finding cluster representatives into three steps:

- Cluster Samples: This step includes drawing possible instances of the database and clustering them using DBSCAN. This process is repeated until $|X| = 100$ instances have been processed.
- Compute Pairwise Distances: During the last step, ARI-distances between clustered database instances are required several times, thus we precomputed the $\frac{100 \cdot 99}{2}$ pairwise distances.
- k-Medoid Clustering: In this step, we perform k-medoid clustering of the sampled (certain) clusterings.

The first two steps of the overall procedure are the computational bottleneck. Obviously, applying $\mathcal{C}$ a large number of times is computationally expensive. The second step of computing the pairwise distances of the clustering results usually takes less time. This step strongly depends on the characteristics of the outcome of the first step. Specifically, computing the ARI-distance between two clusterings becomes more expensive if the clusterings contain more clusters. ARI is based on the pre-computation of the cluster contingency table which counts the number of objects in each pair of clusters of two clusterings. The number of clusters in a clustering is of course dependent on the dataset and the parameter settings.

7. CONCLUSIONS

We presented a general solution for clustering of uncertain objects. Our challenge was to develop a framework making any clustering that has been developed for certain data applicable for the case of uncertain data. We approached this challenge by employing a sampling approach to obtain a number of possible database instances from the uncertain database. Applying a domain specific clustering algorithm to each obtained database instance yields a (possibly large) set of different clusterings. Therefore, the challenge is to find a representative solution for all these possible clusterings. For this purpose, we defined the notion of τ-ϕ-representative clusterings: a τ-ϕ-representative clustering is a clustering having probability at least ϕ to have a distance of at most τ to the actual clustering of the data if the data were certain. Our solution follows a sampling approach, which returns clusterings that are guaranteed to be τ-ϕ-representative clusterings at a user specified level of significance. To the best of our knowledge, our approach is the first to yield clusterings associated with confidences, allowing the user to assess the quality of the clustering result, and conforming to the possible worlds semantics. Furthermore, by returning multiple representative clusterings to the user, we can improve the quality (and therefore usefulness) of results, as shown by our experimental study.

8. REFERENCES

[1] E. Achtert, H.-P. Kriegel, E. Schubert, and A. Zimek. Interactive data mining with 3D-Parallel-Coordinate-Trees. In *Proc. SIGMOD*, pages 1009–1012, 2013.

[2] P. Agrawal, O. Benjelloun, A. D. Sarma, C. Hayworth, S. Nabar, T. Sugihara, and J. Widom. Trio: A system for data, uncertainty, and lineage. In *Proc. VLDB*, 2006.

[3] P. Agrawal, A. D. Sarma, J. Ullman, and J. Widom. Foundations of uncertain-data integration. *PVLDB*, 3(1-2):1080–1090, 2010.

[4] K. Bache and M. Lichman. UCI machine learning repository, 2013.

[5] T. Bernecker, H.-P. Kriegel, M. Renz, F. Verhein, and A. Züfle. Probabilistic frequent itemset mining in uncertain databases. In *Proc. KDD*, pages 119–128, 2009.

[6] J. Boulos, N. Dalvi, B. Mandhani, S. Mathur, C. Re, and D. Suciu. Mystiq: a system for finding more answers by using probabilities. In *Proc. SIGMOD*, pages 891–893, 2005.

[7] L. D. Brown, T. Cai, and A. DasGupta. Interval estimation for a binomial proportion. *Stat. Sci.*, 16(2):101–133, 2001.

[8] R. J. G. B. Campello, D. Moulavi, and J. Sander. Density-based clustering based on hierarchical density estimates. In *Proc. PAKDD*, pages 160–172. 2013.

[9] M. Chau, R. Cheng, B. Kao, and J. Ng. Uncertain data mining: An example in clustering location data. In *Proc. PAKDD*, pages 199–204, 2006.

[10] R. Cheng, S. Singh, and S. Prabhakar. U-DBMS: a database system for managing constantly-evolving data. In *Proc. VLDB*, 2005.

[11] C. Clopper and E. S. Pearson. Probable inference, the law of succession, and statistical inference. *Biometrika*, 26:404–413, 1934.

[12] Y. Cui, X. Z. Fern, and J. G. Dy. Non-redundant multi-view clustering via orthogonalization. In *Proc. ICDM*, pages 133–142, 2007.

[13] N. Dalvi and D. Suciu. Efficient query evaluation on probabilistic databases. *VLDB J.*, 16(4):523–544, 2007.

[14] X. H. Dang, I. Assent, and J. Bailey. Multiple clustering views via constrained projections. In *Proc. SIAM DM Workshop MultiClust*, 2012.

[15] A. Deshpande, C. Guestrin, S. R. Madden, J. M. Hellerstein, and W. Hong. Model-based approximate querying in sensor networks. *VLDB J.*, 14(4):417–443, 2005.

[16] T. Emrich, H.-P. Kriegel, N. Mamoulis, M. Renz, and A. Züfle. Querying uncertain spatio-temporal data. In *Proc. ICDE*, 2012.

[17] M. Ester, H.-P. Kriegel, J. Sander, and X. Xu. A density-based algorithm for discovering clusters in large spatial databases with noise. In *Proc. KDD*, pages 226–231, 1996.

[18] I. Färber, S. Günnemann, H.-P. Kriegel, P. Kröger, E. Müller, E. Schubert, T. Seidl, and A. Zimek. On using class-labels in evaluation of clusterings. In *Proc. ACM SIGKDD Workshop MultiClust*, 2010.

[19] G. Ghinita, P. Karras, P. Kalnis, and N. Mamoulis. Fast data anonymization with low information loss. In *VLDB*, pages 758–769, 2007.

[20] D. Gondek and T. Hofmann. Non-redundant clustering with conditional ensembles. In *Proc. KDD*, pages 70–77, 2005.

[21] F. Gullo, G. Ponti, and A. Tagarelli. Clustering uncertain data via k-medoids. In *Scalable Uncertainty Management*, pages 229–242, 2008.

[22] F. Gullo, G. Ponti, and A. Tagarelli. Minimizing the variance of cluster mixture models for clustering uncertain objects. *Stat. Anal. Data Min.*, 6(2):116–135, 2013.

[23] F. Gullo and A. Tagarelli. Uncertain centroid based partitional clustering of uncertain data. *PVLDB*, 5(7):610–621, 2012.

[24] W. Hoeffding. Probability inequalities for sums of bounded random variables. *JASA*, 58(301):13–30, 1963.

[25] J. Huang, L. Antova, C. Koch, and D. Olteanu. Maybms: A probabilistic database management system. In *Proc. SIGMOD*, pages 1071–1074, 2009.

[26] L. Hubert and P. Arabie. Comparing partitions. *J. Classif.*, 2(1):193–218, 1985.

[27] A. K. Jain. Data clustering: 50 years beyond k-means. *Pattern Recognition Lett.*, 31(8):651–666, 2010.

[28] A. K. Jain, M. N. Murty, and P. J. Flynn. Data clustering: A review. *ACM CSUR*, 31(3):264–323, 1999.

[29] P. Jain, R. Meka, and I. S. Dhillon. Simultaneous unsupervised learning of disparate clusterings. *Stat. Anal. Data Min.*, 1(3):195–210, 2008.

[30] R. Jampani, F. Xu, M. Wu, L. Perez, C. Jermaine, and P. J. Haas. The monte carlo database system: Stochastic analysis close to the data. *ACM Trans. Database Syst.*, 36(3):18:1–18:41, 2011.

[31] B. Jiang, J. Pei, Y. Tao, and X. Lin. Clustering uncertain data based on probability distribution similarity. *IEEE TKDE*, 25(4):751–763, 2013.

[32] B. Kao, S. D. Lee, D. W. Cheung, W. S. Ho, and K. F. Chan. Clustering uncertain data using voronoi diagrams. In *Proc. ICDM*, pages 333–342, 2008.

[33] L. Kaufman and P. J. Rousseeuw. *Finding Groups in Data: An Introduction to Cluster Analyis.* John Wiley&Sons, 1990.

[34] H.-P. Kriegel, P. Kröger, J. Sander, and A. Zimek. Density-based clustering. *WIREs DMKD*, 1(3):231–240, 2011.

[35] H.-P. Kriegel, P. Kröger, and A. Zimek. Subspace clustering. *WIREs DMKD*, 2(4):351–364, 2012.

[36] H.-P. Kriegel and M. Pfeifle. Density-based clustering of uncertain data. In *Proc. KDD*, pages 672–677, 2005.

[37] H.-P. Kriegel and M. Pfeifle. Hierarchical density-based clustering of uncertain data. In *Proc. ICDM*, pages 689–692, 2005.

[38] S. D. Lee, B. Kao, and R. Cheng. Reducing uk-means to k-means. In *ICDM Workshops*, pages 483–488, 2007.

[39] J. Li, B. Saha, and A. Deshpande. A unified approach to ranking in probabilistic databases. *PVLDB*, 2(1):502–513, 2009.

[40] J. MacQueen. Some methods for classification and analysis of multivariate observations. In *5th Berkeley Symposium on Mathematics, Statistics, and Probabilistics*, volume 1, pages 281–297, 1967.

[41] W. K. Ngai, B. Kao, C. K. Chui, R. Cheng, M. Chau, and K. Y. Yip. Efficient clustering of uncertain data. In *Proc. ICDM*, pages 436–445, 2006.

[42] J. Pei, M. Hua, Y. Tao, and X. Lin. Query answering techniques on uncertain and probabilistic data: tutorial summary. In *Proc. SIGMOD*, pages 1357–1364, 2008.

[43] A. D. Sarma, O. Benjelloun, A. Halevy, and J. Widom. Working models for uncertain data. In *Proc. ICDE*, 2006.

[44] P. Sen, A. Deshpande, and L. Getoor. Prdb: Managing and exploiting rich correlations in probabilistic databases. *VLDB J.*, 18(5):1065–1090, 2009.

[45] K. Sim, V. Gopalkrishnan, A. Zimek, and G. Cong. A survey on enhanced subspace clustering. *Data Min. Knowl. Disc.*, 26(2):332–397, 2013.

[46] M. A. Soliman, I. F. Ilyas, and K. C.-C. Chang. Top-k query processing in uncertain databases. In *Proc. ICDE*, pages 896–905, 2007.

[47] A. Struyf, M. Hubert, and P. Rousseeuw. Clustering in an object-oriented environment. *Journal of Statistical Software*, 1(4):1–30, 1997.

[48] L. Sun, R. Cheng, D. W. Cheung, and J. Cheng. Mining uncertain data with probabilistic guarantees. In *Proc. KDD*, pages 273–282, 2010.

[49] Y. Tao, R. Cheng, X. Xiao, W. K. Ngai, B. Kao, and S. Prabhakar. Indexing multi-dimensional uncertain data with arbitrary probability density functions. In *Proc. VLDB*, pages 922–933, 2005.

[50] G. Trajcevski, R. Tamassia, P. Scheuermann, D. Hartglass, and C. Zamierowski. Ranking continuous nearest neighbors for uncertain trajectories. *VLDB J.*, 20(5):767–791, 2011.

[51] C. J. Veenman, M. J. T. Reinders, and E. Backer. A maximum variance cluster algorithm. *IEEE TPAMI*, 24(9):1273–1280, 2002.

[52] S. Wallis. Binomial confidence intervals and contingency tests: Mathematical fundamentals and the evaluation of alternative methods. *Journal of Quantitative Linguistics*, 20(3):178–208, 2013.

[53] E. B. Wilson. Probable inference, the law of succession, and statistical inference. *JASA*, 22:209–212, 1927.

[54] K. Yi, F. Li, G. Kollios, and D. Srivastava. Efficient processing of top-k queries in uncertain databases. In *Proc. ICDE*, 2008.

[55] A. Zimek and J. Vreeken. The blind men and the elephant: On meeting the problem of multiple truths in data from clustering and pattern mining perspectives. *Mach. Learn.*, 2013.

SMVC: Semi-Supervised Multi-View Clustering in Subspace Projections

Stephan Günnemann
Carnegie Mellon University, USA
sguennem@cs.cmu.edu

Ines Färber Matthias Rüdiger Thomas Seidl
RWTH Aachen University, Germany
{faerber, ruediger, seidl}@cs.rwth-aachen.de

ABSTRACT

Since data is often multi-faceted in its very nature, it might not adequately be summarized by just a single clustering. To better capture the data's complexity, methods aiming at the detection of *multiple, alternative clusterings* have been proposed. Independent of this research area, semi-supervised clustering techniques have shown to substantially improve clustering results for *single-view clustering* by integrating prior knowledge. In this paper, we join both research areas and present a solution for integrating prior knowledge in the process of detecting multiple clusterings.

We propose a Bayesian framework modeling multiple clusterings of the data by multiple mixture distributions, each responsible for an individual set of relevant dimensions. In addition, our model is able to handle prior knowledge in the form of instance-level constraints indicating which objects should or should not be grouped together. Since a priori the assignment of constraints to specific views is not necessarily known, our technique automatically determines their membership. For efficient learning, we propose the algorithm SMVC using variational Bayesian methods. With experiments on various real-world data, we demonstrate SMVC's potential to detect multiple clustering views and its capability to improve the result by exploiting prior knowledge.

Categories and Subject Descriptors

H.2.8 [**Database Management**]: Database Applications —*Data mining*; I.2.6 [**Artificial Intelligence**]: Learning

Keywords

semi-supervised learning; subspace clustering; constraints

1. INTRODUCTION

Clustering aims at grouping data instances based on their similarity. For complex data, however, the similarity often depends on the point of view. In a customer database, for example, users might be grouped according to their demographic profile or according to their buying patterns. In a document database, different groups might reflect the documents' subjects or their writing style. Thus, depending on the application and the user's preferences, a single grouping does not capture all aspects but *multiple, alternative clustering solutions* are required. The emerging research field of multi-view or alternative clustering [27] addresses this challenge by finding multiple high quality clusterings.

On the other hand, semi-supervised clustering techniques [8] try to incorporate the user's preferences by exploiting prior knowledge during the clustering process. For traditional single-view clustering, these techniques have shown to substantially increase the clustering results. Motivated by the success of both research areas, we propose a semi-supervised multi-view clustering technique. Our goal is to exploit user provided prior knowledge to enhance the results of multiple, alternative clusterings.

For semi-supervised clustering, it is crucial that the user can provide supervision in an easy and understandable way. While cluster level constraints, such as the clusters' sizes, positions, or distributions, usually require an abstract understanding of the desired clustering structure, instance level constraints which, e.g., indicate partial information about cluster memberships, are much more intuitive. A popular way of modeling such prior information is via equivalence constraints, which indicate for pairs of instances whether they should belong to the same cluster (must-link constraint) or to different clusters (cannot-link). Even though lacking a full understanding of the clustering structure, this allows the user to partly specify her intuition by indicating for selected object pairs their pairwise cluster relation. Since in many cases these user constraints express a belief rather than certainty, we use the concept of soft constraints, where mistakes are possible and a complete fulfillment is not enforced.

The transfer of the semi-supervised clustering principle to the multi-view case poses a severe challenge, particularly regarding the multi-faceted nature of the data. One user might for example see the similarity of two movies based on their cast, while another user might foreground their dissimilarity based on differing genres. It, therefore, might remain unclear to which view specific constraints refer to. In particular, when naively assigning all constraints to a single view, a large proportion of the constraints might be conflicting such that even a relaxation to soft constraints will not be sufficient anymore. Therefore, the challenge in semi-supervised multi-view clustering is not only to optimize the clustering such that constraints are optimally fulfilled but also to *learn the affiliation of constraints to views*.

It has to be highlighted that some of the *sequentially* working multi-view clustering approaches (which iteratively find

KDD'14, August 24–27, 2014, New York, NY, USA.
Copyright 2014 ACM 978-1-4503-2956-9/14/08 ...$15.00.
http://dx.doi.org/10.1145/2623330.2623734.

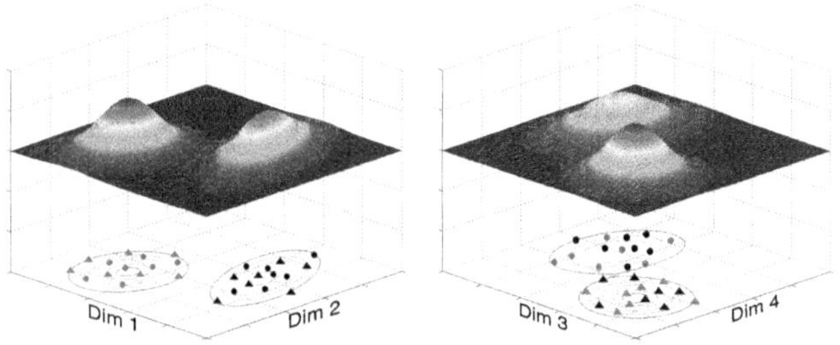

Fig. 1: Example for the multi-view scenario

one clustering at a time) (e.g. [4, 30]) already work based on instance level constraints to incorporate the feedback of rejected prior clusterings via cannot-link constraints. These constraints, however, are used for a different goal: they guide the clustering method to find *a single* new clustering. Thus, all constraints need to refer to this single clustering, and none of the previous clusterings can be affected by these constraints. In contrast, our aim is to incorporate instance level constraints which might improve the *overall* result of all clusterings. It becomes apparent, that in this case we have to rely on a multi-view clustering technique which detects all clusterings *simultaneously*.

Only few approaches for simultaneous multi-view clustering have been proposed (e.g. [28, 23, 22, 21]). Here, the inevitable connection of multi-view clustering and subspace clustering has been observed first [28, 22, 21], which later also influenced sequentially working approaches like [15]. Subspace clustering assumes each cluster to have an individual set of relevant data attributes, which corresponds well with the motivation of multi-view clustering that different views on the data (i.e. considering different characteristics of the data) might reveal different clustering structures.

In this work we join the three paradigms of simultaneous multi-view clustering, subspace clustering, and constraint-based clustering. We present a Bayesian framework that models the different clustering views via several multivariate mixture distributions located in subspace projections (cf. Figure 1). Each object follows multiple components, each in a different mixture model, each defining a distribution only for a certain view (i.e. subspace) of the data, and each representing a different role of the object. We integrate the optimal fulfillment of user provided instance level constraints into the Bayesian learning process, where we tackle the challenge of automatically learning the responsibility of views for specific constraints. Our contributions are:

- *Multiple clusterings:* We propose a sound Bayesian model which represents multiple clusterings via individual mixture models, each representing a distinct view.
- *Semi-supervision:* Our model incorporates prior knowledge in form of (soft) must-link and cannot-link instance level constraints. Our method automatically learns the assignment of these constraints to specific views if their responsibility is not explicitly specified.
- *Algorithm design:* We present an efficient algorithm based on the principle of variational inference for learning our model.
- *Effectiveness:* We analyze the effectiveness of our method on various datasets and show its potential to increase the clustering result by using prior knowledge.

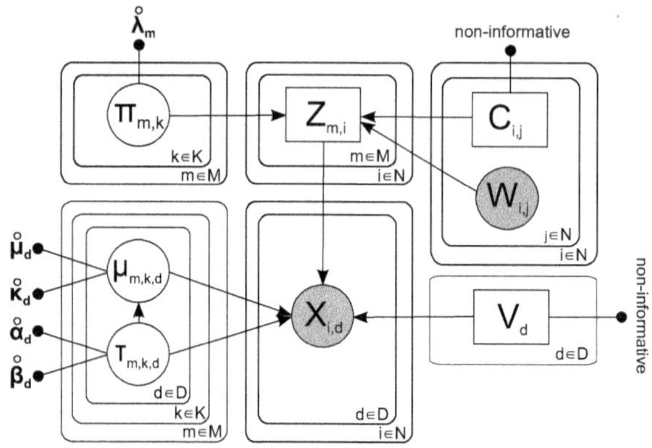

Fig. 2: Graphical model of our method. Rectangles denote discrete random variables, circles continuous random variables, and black dots (deterministic) hyperparameters of the prior distributions.

2. BAYESIAN FRAMEWORK

In this section, we introduce a Bayesian framework for semi-supervised multi-view clustering. An overview of our framework is given by the graphical model depicted in Fig. 2. While this section introduces the generative process of our model, we describe in Section 3 how to learn the model's parameters given a set of observations. Following convention, we do not distinguish between a random variable x and its realization $x = \mathbf{x}$ if it is clear from the context. As an abbreviation, we denote sets of random variables with the index $*$, e.g. $y_{*,d}$ is the set of random variables $\{y_{i,d}\}$ with i in the corresponding index domain, and Y is an abbreviation for the set $y_{*,*}$.

The number of objects is denoted with N, the number of dimensions with D, the number of clusters/components with K, and the number of alternative views/clusterings with M. We write $k \in K$, as a shortcut for $k \in \{1, \ldots, K\}$.

Multiple Mixture Models. The general idea of our method is to represent the multiple clusterings of the data by multiple mixture models, each located in a different subspace projection (cf. Figure 1). In this work, we focus on Gaussian mixture models; extensions to other distributions are straightforward. Following standard principles, each of the M mixture models is based on K components, where each of these components is associated with a mean and a covariance/precision matrix. To reduce the number of parameters to be estimated, we focus on diagonal precision matrices. Thus, for a Bayesian treatment, we introduce the random variables

$$(\mu_{m,k,d}, \tau_{m,k,d}) \sim \mathcal{NG}(\mathring{\mu}_d, \mathring{\kappa}_d, \mathring{\alpha}_d, \mathring{\beta}_d) \tag{1}$$

where $\mu_{m,k,d}$ is the mean of component k in dimensions d for clustering m, and $\tau_{m,k,d}$ the corresponding precision. We select the normal-gamma distribution $\mathcal{NG}$ as a prior since it represents the variables' conjugate prior. The hyperparameters denoted by $\mathring{*}$ can be used to control the mixture models' components if some prior knowledge is available. Per default, we choose least informative priors by selecting $\mathring{\kappa}_d, \mathring{\alpha}_d \to 0$ and setting $\mathring{\mu}_d/\mathring{\beta}_d$ to be the sample mean/sum of squared deviations in dimension d.

Besides the components parameters, each mixture model is associated with a corresponding random variable representing the mixture weights. Obviously, since we want to find multiple different clusterings, these weights can be different for each view. We use the random variable

$$\vec{\pi}_m \sim Dir(\mathring{\lambda}) \quad (2)$$

where $\pi_{m,k}$ is the weight of component k in clustering m. Due to conjugate properties, we use a Dirichlet distribution as its prior. Again, in our study, we use a non-informative prior by selecting $\mathring{\lambda} = 1$ since a priori no knowledge about the cluster sizes is given.

Integrating Subspaces. To detect the data's multiple views, we refer to the principle of subspace clustering. Our goal is to assign each mixture model to a specific subspace projection, which it describes well. Since the relevant dimensions of the mixtures are a priori not known, we learn them with our method. Therefore, we introduce the random variable

$$v_d \sim Categorical(\vec{r}_d) \quad (3)$$

to indicate which of the M clusterings is responsible for a specific dimension d. The vector $\vec{r}_d \in [0 \ldots 1]^M$ (with $\sum r_{k,m} = 1$) can be used to give some prior knowledge which dimension belongs to which view. Again, we use a constant non-informative prior, i.e. $r_{k,m} = 1/M$.

Knowing about the subspaces as well as the mixture models' parameters, we are now able to generate observations which show multiple clustering structures: We denote with $z_{m,i}$ the random variable indicating to which cluster an object i belongs to in clustering m, i.e.

$$z_{m,i} \sim Categorical(\vec{\pi}_m) \quad (4)$$

Note that for each view m, the object might follow a different cluster, i.e. $z_{m,i} \neq z_{m',i}$ is possible. Thus, in each view the object might be grouped together with different objects. This idea is illustrated in Figure 1: the grouping on the left differs from the one on the right. Given $z_{m,i}$, the attribute value of object i in dimension d is drawn according to

$$x_{i,d} \sim \mathcal{N}(\mu_{m,k,d}, \tau_{m,k,d}^{-1}) \text{ with } m = v_d \text{ and } k = z_{m,i} \quad (5)$$

That is, we use the clustering m which is responsible for dimensions d and the corresponding component k the object belongs to in this view.

Integrating User Constraints. So far, our model corresponds to a completely unsupervised technique for finding multiple clusterings. As a major advancement, we now integrate user provided prior-knowledge. As discussed, we aim to support the concept of instance level constraints. More precisely, we support the idea of soft constraints between pairs of objects that indicate whether the objects should or should not be grouped together. We selected this type of semi-supervision since it reflects an intuitive understanding of clustering and is easy to specify for the user.

The user can provide a constraint between the objects i and j via a weight $w_{i,j}$. If the weight is positive, the user indicates that there should exist a clustering where the objects are grouped together. If the weight is negative, the user indicates that there should exist a clustering where i and j are not grouped together. Different magnitudes of the weights can be used to indicate the different importance or relevance of the constraints.

At this point it is crucial to keep in mind that we are interested in finding multiple, alternative clusterings: A constraint between i and j means that *there exists a view* where the constraint is fulfilled. We do not require that i and j are grouped together in *all views*, which actually would contradict the fundamental assumption for multi-view scenarios that clusterings of different views differ and contain alternative knowledge. Forcing constraints to be valid for all views would be too restrictive. Furthermore, we argue that the user is generally not aware of the details of all possible groupings. Thus, the user should not define constraints restricting views that he does not understand. Accordingly, for each constraint, we are interested in finding (at least) one clustering fulfilling this constraint.

Resulting from this principle, another challenge of our method becomes apparent: we have to determine the clustering which is responsible for a specific constraint. In the following, we show how to model all these aspects.

As mentioned, the constraints are modeled via weights. In our model, we represent them via a symmetric matrix W of size $N \times N$, where entries with weight zero indicate no prior knowledge about the corresponding pairs of objects. In practice, we can use a *sparse representation* of the matrix which only encodes the given constraints and allows for an efficient processing. Interesting to note is that the (observed) matrix W appears in our grapical model as one of the root nodes (cf. Figure 2), and not as a leaf like X. As shown, the weights influence the grouping Z of the objects.

Additionally, we introduce the categorical random variables $c_{i,j}$ (due to the symmetry of the weights, we only need to consider $i < j$). These variables indicate which view is responsible for a specific constraint. That is, we have

$$c_{i,j} \sim Categorical(\vec{h}^{(i,j)}) \quad (6)$$

where $\vec{h}^{(i,j)} \in [0...1]^M$ with $\sum_{m \in M} h_m^{(i,j)} = 1$. The user can use $\vec{h}^{(i,j)}$ to express some further prior knowledge about the constraint between object i and j. If the user, for example, knows that a set of constraints should most likely belong to one view, the h vectors can be selected accordingly. Per default, we assume that no knowledge about the assignment of constraints to views is known, i.e. we use $h_m^{(i,j)} = 1/M$.

Given W and C, how can we use their values to influence the clustering structure of the data? Our idea is to add a bias to the probability distribution of the $z_{m,j}$. The probability of generating a clustering that matches the constraints should be higher than the probability of a clustering which violates the constraints. Particularly, this results in a dependency between the variables $z_{m,*}$ which is guided by the constraints. We define

$$p(z_{m,*} \mid \vec{\pi}_m, W, C) \propto \prod_{i=1}^{N} \pi_{m,z_{m,i}} \cdot \prod_{i=1}^{N} \prod_{\substack{j>i \\ c_{i,j}=m}}^{N} e^{w_{i,j} \cdot \delta(z_{m,i}, z_{m,j})} \quad (7)$$

Here, $\delta(z_{m,i}, z_{m,j})$ denotes the Kronecker delta, which evaluates to 1 if both objects are located in the same cluster (in view m), and 0 otherwise. Please note that Equation 7 is the joint distribution for all $z_{m,*}$.

The first part of the equation corresponds to the mixture weights as used in standard mixture models. If all $w_{i,j} = 0$, Equation 4 and 7 are equivalent. The second part models the bias to specific groupings: As one can see, if $w_{i,j}$ is positive and the objects are located in the same cluster, the probability of selecting this grouping increases. Accordingly, if $w_{i,j}$ is negative, one would decrease the probability of clusterings where i and j are grouped together. A similar principle was used in [25, 7] for single-view clustering.

Important to mention is that the second part of the equation incorporates the automatic assignment of constraints to views. The constraint between i and j adds a bias to the clustering structure in view $c_{i,j} = m$ only. In accordance to our discussion above, the other views are not affected.

Given the new definition for the distribution of Z, the actual observations are, as before, generated according to Equation 5. Overall, our model combines the principle of multiple clusterings in subspace projections with the paradigm of semi-supervised clustering and automatically assigns constraints to their responsible views.

3. THE SMVC ALGORITHM

While the previous section has focused on the model's generative process, we now present our learning technique. That is, *given* a set of observations X and a set of constraints W, we infer the model's parameters. Our method is called SMVC (Semi-Supervised Multi-View Clustering).

3.1 Variational Inference

The general inference problem we have to solve is to determine the distribution $p(Y|X, W)$, where $Y=\{V, Z, C, \vec{\pi}, \mu, \tau\}$ is the set of all latent variables. Based on this distribution, we can, e.g., pick the realizations of the latent variables leading to the highest likelihood given the data. Since computing $p(Y|X, W)$ is intractable, we compute an approximation based on the principle of variational inference [10]: we approximate $p(Y|X, W)$ by a tractable family of parametrized distributions $q(Y|\Psi)$. The parameters Ψ are the free variational parameters. These parameters are optimized such that the best approximation between q and p is obtained. Technically, one minimizes the Kullback-Leibler divergence between q and p by optimizing Ψ. Using Jensen's inequality, minimizing the KL divergence is equivalent to maximizing the following lower bound on the log marginal likelihood [10]:

$$\mathcal{L}(X, W; \Psi) = \mathbb{E}_q[\ln p(X, W, Y)] - \mathbb{E}_q[\ln q(Y|\Psi)] \quad (8)$$

where $\mathbb{E}_q[.]$ denotes the expectation w.r.t. the q distribution.

Following primarily the idea of mean field approximation, we assume the function q to factorize in

$$p(Y \mid X, W) \approx q(Y|\Psi) := \prod_d q_1(v_d) \cdot \prod_m \prod_i q_2(z_{m,i})$$

$$\cdot \prod_i \prod_{j>i} q_3(c_{i,j}) \cdot \prod_m q_4(\vec{\pi}_m) \cdot \prod_m \prod_k \prod_d q_5(\mu_{m,k,d}, \tau_{m,k,d})$$

As we will later see, assuming the above factorization, the optimal variational distributions have the form

$$\begin{aligned} q_1(v_d) &= Categorical(v_d \mid \phi_{d,1}, ..., \phi_{d,M}) \\ q_2(z_{m,i}) &= Categorical(z_{m,i} \mid \psi_{m,i,1}, ..., \psi_{m,i,K}) \\ q_3(c_{i,j}) &= Categorical(c_{i,j} \mid \xi_{i,j,1}, ..., \xi_{i,j,M}) \\ q_4(\vec{\pi}_m) &= Dir(z_{m,i} \mid \vec{\lambda}_m) \\ q_5(\mu_{m,k,d}, \tau_{m,k,d}) &= \mathcal{NG}(\mu_{m,k,d}, \tau_{m,k,d} \mid \\ &\qquad \tilde{\mu}_{m,k,d}, \tilde{\kappa}_{m,k,d}, \tilde{\alpha}_{m,k,d}, \tilde{\beta}_{m,k,d}) \end{aligned}$$

where $\Psi = \{\phi, \psi, \xi, \vec{\lambda}, \tilde{\mu}, \tilde{\kappa}, \tilde{\alpha}, \tilde{\beta}\}$ are the variational parameters to be optimized. Note that each distribution has its own variational parameters [10]. Thus, e.g. the functions $q_1(v_d)$ and $q_1(v_{d'})$, are not necessarily identical. This extra degree of freedom allows to find a good approximation between q and p. As discussed in Section 2, for $c_{i,j}$, i.e. the function q_3, we only need to consider pairs i, j with $w_{i,j} \neq 0$.

General Processing Scheme. We use an iterative coordinate ascent method to maximize Equation 8 w.r.t. the parameters Ψ (the update equations follow in Section 3.2). The processing scheme is as follows:

while *not converged* **do**
  for $i, j \in N : j > i \wedge w_{i,j} \neq 0$ **do** update $\xi_{i,j,*}$ — Eq. 10
  for $d \in D$ **do** update $\phi_{d,*}$ — Eq. 11
  for $m \in M, i \in N$ **do** update $\psi_{m,i,*}$ — Eq. 12
  for $i \in N, m \in M$ **do** update $\vec{\lambda}_m$ — Eq. 13
  for $m \in M, k \in K, d \in D$ **do** — Eq. 14
    update $\tilde{\mu}_{m,k,d}, \tilde{\kappa}_{m,k,d}, \tilde{\alpha}_{m,k,d}, \tilde{\beta}_{m,k,d}$

Note that due to the properties of variational inference [10], it is guaranteed that the method converges. In practice, we assume convergence if the change in the lower bound on the marginal likelihood is below than 0.01. Additionally, to avoid the problem of local minima, we enhance the processing scheme by gradually increasing the importance of the constraints. That is, starting with low weights, we linearly increase the values $w_{i,j}$ until they reach the user specified scores. For initializing our method, we exploit the same principle as described in [21]. The random variable C/q_3 is initialized randomly based on its prior distribution.

3.2 Update Equations

We briefly present the update equations required for the coordinate ascent method. We primarily follow the principle of [10]: The optimal distribution for $q_x(B)$ can be determined by

$$\ln q_x^*(B) = \mathbb{E}_{q \setminus B}[\ln p(X, Y, W)] + \mathcal{C} \quad (9)$$

Here, the constant $\mathcal{C}$ absorbs all terms which are independent of B and, thus, do not affected the optimal distribution of q_x. $\mathbb{E}_{q\setminus B}[.]$ denotes the expectation w.r.t. the distribution q taken over all variables Y except of B. To avoid cluttering the notation, we simply write $\mathbb{E}_q$ in the following (it is clear from the context which variable is excluded).

Updating the constraint responsibility. Let $[\![.]\!]$ denote the Iverson bracket. We can rewrite Equation 7 as follows

$$\prod_{i=1}^{N} \prod_{k=1}^{K} \pi_{m,k}^{[\![z_{m,i}=k]\!]} \cdot \prod_{i=1}^{N} \prod_{j>i}^{N} \prod_{k=1}^{K} e^{w_{i,j} [\![z_{m,i}=k]\!] [\![z_{m,j}=k]\!] [\![c_{i,j}=m]\!]}$$

This formulation makes it easier to derive the following results. Accordingly, we can rewrite the remaining equations.

The optimal distribution for $q_3(c_{a,b})$ (with $a < b$) can be obtained via Eq. 9. Removing all terms which are independent of $c_{a,b}$ and using the above reformulation, we get

$$\begin{aligned} &\log q_3^*(c_{a,b} = y) \\ &= \mathbb{E}_q[\log (P(c_{i,j}) P(Z|\pi, C, W))] + \mathcal{C} \\ &= \mathbb{E}_q[\log \frac{1}{M}] + \mathbb{E}_q[\log \prod_{m=1}^{M} \Big(\prod_{i=1}^{N} \prod_{k=1}^{K} \pi_{m,k}^{[\![z_{m,i}=k]\!]} \cdot \prod_{i=1}^{N} \prod_{j>i}^{N} \\ &\qquad \cdot \prod_{k=1}^{K} e^{w_{i,j} [\![z_{m,i}=k]\!] [\![z_{m,j}=k]\!] [\![c_{i,j}=m]\!]} \Big)] + \mathcal{C} \\ &= \mathbb{E}_q[\sum_{m=1}^{M} \sum_{k=1}^{K} \log e^{w_{a,b} [\![z_{m,a}=k]\!] [\![z_{m,b}=k]\!] [\![c_{a,b}=m]\!]}] + \mathcal{C} \\ &= w_{a,b} \sum_{k=1}^{K} \mathbb{E}_q [\![z_{y,a} = k]\!] \cdot \mathbb{E}_q [\![z_{y,b} = k]\!] + \mathcal{C} \end{aligned}$$

Since $c_{a,b}$ has a finite domain, the distribution q_3 is a categorical distribution. Renaming the variables, the optimal hyperparameters of the distribution $q_3(c_{i,j})$ are given by

$$\xi_{i,j,m} \propto exp^{\left(w_{i,j} \sum_{k=1}^{K} \mathbb{E}_q [\![z_{m,i}=k]\!] \cdot \mathbb{E}_q [\![z_{m,j}=k]\!]\right)} \quad (10)$$

where $\sum_m \xi_{i,j,m} = 1$. The occurring expectations can be replaced by the known expectations of the variational distributions (cf. appendix). Intuitively, the parameter $\xi_{i,j,m}$ shows the probability of assigning the constraint between i and j to the view m.

Updating the views. Computing Eq. 9 for $q_1(v_d)$ and removing all terms which are independent of v_d leads to

$$
\begin{aligned}
&\ln q_1^*(v_d = y)\\
&= \mathbb{E}_q[\log (P(x_{*,d}|v_d, Z, \mu, \tau)P(v_d))] + \mathcal{C}\\
&= \mathbb{E}_q[\log \prod_{m=1}^{M}\prod_{i=1}^{N}\prod_{k=1}^{K} \mathcal{N}(x_{i,d}|\mu_{m,k,d}, \tau_{m,k,d}^{-1})^{[\![v_d=m]\!][\![z_{m,i}=k]\!]}]\\
&\qquad + \mathbb{E}_q[\log \frac{1}{M}] + \mathcal{C}\\
&= \mathbb{E}_q[\log \prod_{i=1}^{N}\prod_{k=1}^{K} \mathcal{N}(x_{i,d}|\mu_{y,k,d}, \tau_{y,k,d}^{-1})^{[\![z_{y,i}=k]\!]}] + \mathcal{C}\\
&= \sum_{i=1}^{N}\sum_{k=1}^{K} \mathbb{E}_q[\![z_{y,i} = k]\!] \cdot f(y,k,d,i) + \mathcal{C}
\end{aligned}
$$

Here, we used the definition

$$
\begin{aligned}
&f(m,k,d,i) := \mathbb{E}_q[\mathcal{N}(x_{i,d}|\mu_{m,k,d}, \tau_{m,k,d}^{-1})]\\
&= \mathbb{E}_q[\log \sqrt{\frac{\tau_{y,k,d}}{2\pi}} e^{\frac{-(x_{i,d}-\mu_{y,k,d})^2\tau_{y,k,d}}{2}}]\\
&= \frac{1}{2}\mathbb{E}_q[\log \frac{\tau_{y,k,d}}{2\pi}] + \frac{1}{2}\mathbb{E}_q[-(x_{i,d}-\mu_{y,k,d})^2\tau_{y,k,d}]\\
&= \frac{1}{2}\cdot(\mathbb{E}_q[\log \tau_{y,k,d}] - x_{i,d}^2 \cdot \mathbb{E}_q[\tau_{y,k,d}] + 2\cdot x_{i,d}\cdot \mathbb{E}_q[\mu_{y,k,d}\cdot\tau_{y,k,d}]\\
&\qquad - \mathbb{E}_q[\mu_{y,k,d}^2 \cdot \tau_{y,k,d}] - \mathbb{E}_q[\log 2\pi])
\end{aligned}
$$

Thus, q_1 is a categorical distribution and the optimal hyperparameters for $q_1(v_d)$ are given by

$$\phi_{d,m} \propto exp^{\sum_{i=1}^{N}\sum_{k=1}^{K} \mathbb{E}_q[\![z_{m,i}=k]\!]\cdot f(m,k,d,i)} \tag{11}$$

where $\sum_m \phi_{d,m} = 1$.

Updating the cluster indicator. The same principle can be applied for the cluster indicator variable. We obtain:

$$
\begin{aligned}
&\log q_2^*(z_{m,a} = y)\\
&= \mathbb{E}_q[\log (P(x_{a,*}|V, Z, \mu, \tau)P(Z|\pi, C, W))] + \mathcal{C}\\
&= \mathbb{E}_q[\log \prod_{d=1}^{D}\prod_{k=1}^{K} \mathcal{N}(x_{a,d}|\mu_{m,k,d}, \tau_{m,k,d}^{-1})^{[\![v_d=m]\!][\![z_{m,a}=k]\!]}] +\\
&\quad \mathbb{E}_q[\log \prod_{k=1}^{K}\prod_{i=1}^{N} \pi_{m,k}^{[\![z_{m,i}=k]\!]} \prod_{i=1}^{N}\prod_{j>i}^{N} e^{w_{i,j}[\![z_{m,i}=k]\!][\![z_{m,j}=k]\!][\![c_{i,j}=m]\!]}]\\
&= \sum_{d=1}^{D} \mathbb{E}_q[\![v_d = m]\!]\, \mathbb{E}_q[\log \mathcal{N}(x_{a,d}|\mu_{m,y,d}, \tau_{m,y,d}^{-1})] + \mathbb{E}_q[\log \pi_{m,y}]\\
&\quad + \sum_{i=1}^{N}\sum_{j>i}^{N} w_{i,j}\, \mathbb{E}_q[\![z_{m,i} = y]\!]\, \mathbb{E}_q[\![z_{m,j} = y]\!]\, \mathbb{E}_q[\![c_{i,j} = m]\!] + \mathcal{C}\\
&= \sum_{d=1}^{D} \mathbb{E}_q[\![v_d = m]\!] \cdot f(m,y,d,a) +\\
&\qquad \mathbb{E}_q[\log \pi_{m,y}] + \sum_{j\neq a}^{N} w_{a,j}\, \mathbb{E}_q[\![z_{m,j} = y]\!]\, \mathbb{E}_q[\![c_{a,j} = m]\!] + \mathcal{C}
\end{aligned}
$$

Here, we exploit the symmetry of $w_{i,j}$ and the definition of f as given above. Note again, that we do not actually need to sum over all $j \neq a$ when using a sparse encoding of the matrix W. It is sufficient to iterate over those j for which a constraint with a is given. Similar as before, the optimal hyperparameters for $q_2(z_{m,i})$ are given by

$$
\begin{aligned}
\psi_{m,i,k} \propto exp\Big(&\sum_{d=1}^{D} \mathbb{E}_q[\![v_d = m]\!] \cdot f(m,k,d,i)\\
&+ \mathbb{E}_q[\log \pi_{m,k}] + \sum_{j\neq i}^{N} w_{i,j}\, \mathbb{E}_q[\![z_{m,j} = k]\!]\, \mathbb{E}_q[\![c_{i,j} = m]\!]\Big)
\end{aligned} \tag{12}
$$

with $\sum_k \psi_{m,i,k} = 1$.

Updating the mixing weights. The mixing weights are continuous. Since we selected a conjugate prior in our model, it follows:

$$
\begin{aligned}
&\log q_4^*(\vec{\pi}_m)\\
&= \mathbb{E}_q[\log (P(\pi_m)P(z_{m,*}|\pi, C, W))] + \mathcal{C}\\
&= \mathbb{E}_q[\log \left(\frac{\Gamma(\mathring{\lambda}K)}{\Gamma(\mathring{\lambda})^K} \prod_{k=1}^{K} \pi_{m,k}^{\mathring{\lambda}-1}\right)] + \mathbb{E}_q[\log \Big(\prod_{i=1}^{N}\prod_{k=1}^{K} \pi_{m,k}^{[\![z_{m,i}=k]\!]} \prod_{i=1}^{N}\\
&\qquad \cdot \prod_{j>i}^{N}\prod_{k=1}^{K} e^{w_{i,j}[\![z_{m,i}=k]\!][\![z_{m,j}=k]\!][\![c_{i,j}=m]\!]}\Big)] + \mathcal{C}\\
&= \sum_{k=1}^{K} (\mathring{\lambda} - 1)\mathbb{E}_q[\log \pi_{m,k}] + \sum_{i=1}^{N}\sum_{k=1}^{K} \mathbb{E}_q[\![z_{m,i} = k]\!]\mathbb{E}_q[\log \pi_{m,k}] + \mathcal{C}\\
&= \sum_{k=1}^{K} \left((\mathring{\lambda} - 1) + \sum_{i=1}^{N} \mathbb{E}_q[\![z_{m,i} = k]\!]\right) \cdot \mathbb{E}_q[\log \pi_{m,k}] + \mathcal{C}
\end{aligned}
$$

As seen, the optimal distribution for q_4 is a Dirichlet distribution, where the hyperparameters are given by

$$\tilde{\lambda}_m[k] = \mathring{\lambda} + \sum_{i=1}^{N} \mathbb{E}_q[\![z_{m,i} = k]\!] \tag{13}$$

Updating the mixture components. Updating the mean and precision of each mixture component follows the standard principle of variational inference in a conjugate setting. Let $u_{m,k} = \sum_{i=1}^{N} \mathbb{E}_q[\![z_{m,i} = k]\!]$ be the unnormalized weight of a cluster and $\bar{x}_{m,k,d} = \frac{1}{u_{m,k}} \sum_{i=1}^{N} x_{i,d}\mathbb{E}_q[\![z_{m,i} = k]\!]$ its weighted mean in dimension d (when considering the expectation w.r.t. q). Using conjugacy, it follows that the optimal hyperparameters of the distribution q_5 are given by

$$
\begin{aligned}
&\tilde{\mu}_{m,k,d} = \frac{\mathring{\kappa}_d\, \mathring{\mu}_d + u_{m,k}\, \bar{x}_{m,k,d}}{\mathring{\kappa}_d + u_{m,k}} \qquad \tilde{\kappa}_{m,k,d} = \mathring{\kappa}_d + u_{m,k}\\
&\tilde{\alpha}_{m,k,d} = \mathring{\alpha}_d + \frac{u_{m,k}}{2}\\
&\tilde{\beta}_{m,k,d} = \mathring{\beta}_d + \frac{1}{2}\sum_{i=1}^{N} (x_{i,d} - \bar{x}_{m,k,d})^2 + \frac{\mathring{\kappa}_d\, u_{m,k}}{\mathring{\kappa}_d + u_{m,k}} \frac{(\bar{x}_{m,k,d} - \mathring{\mu}_d)^2}{2}
\end{aligned} \tag{14}
$$

3.3 Complexity and Summary

Inspecting the individual update equations, it becomes apparent that each iteration of our algorithm runs in time $\mathcal{O}(M \cdot N \cdot K \cdot (D + W))$, where W denotes the number of constraints. Thus, we obtain a *linear complexity* in all important parameters.

Overall, our method efficiently computes an approximation of the posterior distribution $p(Y|X, W)$ which shows us the multiple clustering structures, their relevant subspaces, and the assignment of constraints to views.

4. RELATED WORK

Our approach is related to four main paradigms in the field of cluster analysis, as we will discuss in the following. Table 1 shows on overview of the related works and their corresponding properties.

Subspace clustering. For traditional full-space clustering, a large proportion of irrelevant attributes can cause an obfuscation of the clustering structure. The underlying assumption of subspace clustering (co-clustering/bi-clustering) [24, 2, 26] is that the set of irrelevant attributes might differ for each cluster. These locally irrelevant attributes hinder a meaningful global dimensionality reduction [29] and make traditional, full-space approaches futile. The consideration of attribute subsets is highly related to our multi-view scenario, since different views of the data are most likely attributable to different characteristics. However, subspace clustering does not realize a grouping of clusters to represent alternative views as required for multi-view clustering.

Multi-view clustering. The paradigm of multi-view or alternative clustering can be categorized in three types [27]: Approaches of the first category, e.g. [23, 4, 13, 14], operate in the full-space and, therefore, suffer from similar problems as traditional clustering. Furthermore, they usually aim at finding just two alternative clusterings. The second category's representatives iteratively determine an alternative clustering based on the previous one via space transformations such as PCA [11, 15] or distortion of the distance function [30]. They do not globally/simultaneously optimize the whole set of all clusterings. Since previous clustering solutions serve as guidance for the discovery of new clustering structures, these approaches can partially be categorized as semi-supervised. However, the constraints affect only the solution of the single, next clustering and, thus, already detected solutions cannot benefit from them. Additionally, distortions of the original space usually hinder an intuitive interpretation of the clustering result. Contrarily, axis-parallel projections of the data as used in our approach allow an easy interpretation. The third category, which is mostly related to our approach, represents methods that *simultaneously* reveal all clusterings by analyzing axis-parallel subspace projections [28, 22, 21]. These approaches do not incorporate any user knowledge. With our SMVC approach, we want to examine the usefulness of instance level constraints for the process of simultaneous multi-view clustering.

Model-based clustering. This general paradigm assumes the considered data to be sampled from a statistical model. Several approaches for estimating the parameters of the underlying probability distributions, e.g., to maximize the log-likelihood of the data, were proposed including the EM or variational inference [10]. Model-based clustering is very flexible as the modeled distributions can be arbitrarily complex. Traditionally, such approaches use a *single* mixture distribution (which spans across all dimensions of the data space). Even though each observation might be associated with a membership degree (e.g. the likelihood of belonging to a cluster), this principle does not capture the idea of generating objects through multiple components as required for the multi-view scenario. To overcome this issue, a few models [17, 5, 19] try to represent such multi-component membership (i.e. overlapping clusters). Although, these models lead to results where an object might take multiple roles within a single view, they do not account for the principle of multiple views. So far, MVGen [21] is the only approach

	Multi-View	Simultaneous processing	Subspace projections	Semi-supervised	Constraint responsibility
Subspace clustering	–	✓	✓	–	–
Multi-view clustering					
↪ iterative	✓	–	–	○	fixed
↪ simultaneous	✓	✓	✓	–	–
Semi-supervised clust.	–	✓	–	✓	fixed
Our method	✓	✓	✓	✓	learned

Table 1: Overview of related paradigms

assuming a statistical model where each data point is drawn from multiple components each within a different view. It has proven to successfully detect the multi-view clustering structure on various data sets.

Semi-supervised clustering. As already argued, the detection of multiple clustering solutions strongly depends on the user's preferences. Semi-supervised clustering [8] provides a possibility to accommodate these preferences as additional information or domain knowledge into the clustering process. For traditional single view, full-space clustering (e.g. k-Means) a popular solution is to use instance level constraints: the objective function is extended by penalizing violated constraints [6] or one learns a distance metric that best represents the constraints [9]. For model-based clustering few extensions for equivalence constraints exist. [31] introduces a closed form EM based on the transitive closure of must-link constraints and proposes a Markov network for handling cannot-link constraints. Since it neither can incorporate both constraint types simultaneously nor cope with conflicting constraints, [25, 7] propose to integrate negative and positive pairwise constraints as priors into Gaussian mixture models, which allows for modeling soft as well as hard constraints. These approaches have shown to substantially improve the clustering result in the single view case. Since in the multi-view case we are uncertain which constraints refer to which view, these existing solutions cannot easily be transferred.

Methods such as [1] use supervision (e.g. human interaction) to enhance the clustering in a single given subspace. In contrast, we exploit supervision to enhance the clustering result across all views simultaneously. Works such as [18] combine subspace clustering with graph clustering. The underlying graph might be regarded as a certain type of supervision. These methods do not focus on finding alternative groupings in the attribute space.

Overall, none of the existing approaches is able to incorporate prior information for a multi-view clustering solution, where constraints may refer to different clustering views. Our new statistical model handles different clustering views in different attribute subspaces and learns responsibilities of views for the provided equivalence constraints.

5. EXPERIMENTAL ANALYSIS

Setup. We compare SMVC with representatives from all three paradigms: multi-view clustering, subspace clustering, and semi-supervised clustering. For multi-view clustering we choose the four approaches *Multi-View 1* and *Multi-View 2* proposed in [11], the *Alternative Clustering* method proposed in [30], and our *MVGen* [21] approach. These approaches best reflect the demands for multi-view clustering

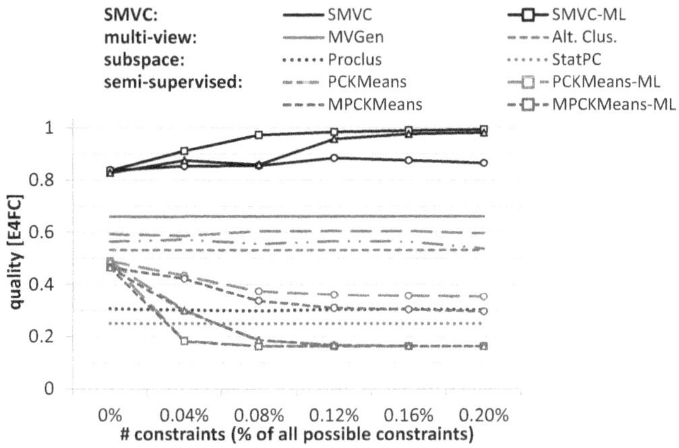

Fig. 3: Quality for a varying number of constraints

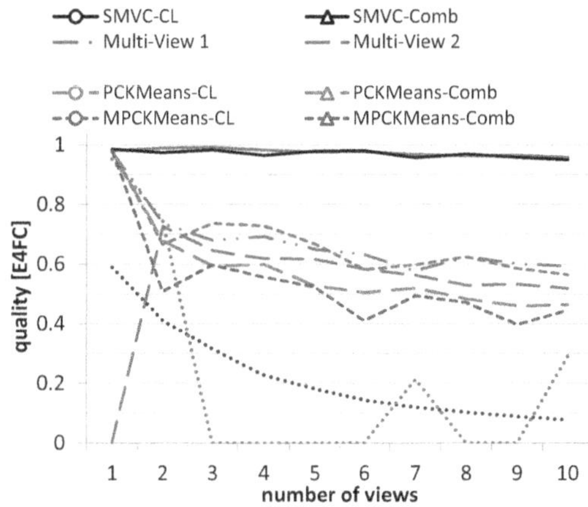

Fig. 4: Quality for a varying number of views

as discussed in Sec. 4. As subspace clustering approaches we choose the partitioning approach *Proclus* and *StatPC*, which allows for overlapping clusters. Furthermore, we compare against the two semi-supervised approaches *PCKMeans* [6] and *MPCKMeans* [9], both using instance level constraints.

For case studies on real world data we use the CMU-Faces, Iris, and Wine data (all from the UCI repository [3]), and drawn stick figures. Synthetic data containing multiple views is generated based on our generative model. The default data set contains 2 disjoint views, each with 4 clusters, 20 dimensions, and 5000 objects.

Each method is provided with the number m_{max} of views and the number k_{max} of clusters per view. If the algorithm does not allow for setting these parameters, we choose the default parameter setting.

Runtime is measured on 4GHz AMD FX-8350 CPU with 16 GB main memory. Quality is assessed based on the *E4SC* measure [20], which is a symmetric and subspace aware variant of the popular F1 measure. Since most of the competing approaches do not determine axis parallel subspaces, we refrain from evaluating the subspaces and just concentrate on the object groupings (for clarity we rename the measure to 'E4FC'). For all quality experiments, we average the results over ten executions.

5.1 Evaluation on Synthetic Data

Varying number of constraints. We start our evaluation by examining the influence of a varying number of constraints in Figure 3. Here, we tested three different variants of the semi-supervised clustering approaches: We either used only must-link constraints (SMVC-ML), only cannot-link constraints (SMVC-CL), or a combination of 50% from both (SMVC-Comb). Note that in this experiment, we randomly generated constraints based on the ground truth clusters known for synthetic data. These constraints might not help to improve the clustering and, thus, represent only very weak supervision. In practice, the user might provide better constraints, e.g. via the principles of active learning [6].

Figure 3 shows the results for an increasing number of constraints: Here, we generated a challenging dataset with a large variance to study the benefit of semi-supervision. Most approaches fail to identify a meaningful clustering structure for this difficult clustering scenario. SMVC is not only the approach showing the best clustering results without the help of prior knowledge, it is also the only approach able to improve its clustering based on additional constraints. For the two other semi-supervised approaches PCKMeans and MPCKMeans, we even observe a decreasing clustering quality with increasing amount of prior knowledge! This indicates, that they cannot deal with the potentially disagreeing constraints of the two views.

We furthermore can see the varying influence of the different constraints (100% must-link constraints, 100% cannot-link constraints, or 50%must-link + 50% cannot-link). The higher the proportion of must-link constraints, the higher is the influence. The reason is that cannot-link constraints a priori have a higher possibility to be fulfilled than must-link constraints (for m views, each with k clusters, the probability to fulfill a cannot-link constraint is $m \cdot \binom{k}{2}$, whereas for must-link constraints it is $m \cdot k$). Therefore, we will focus on must-link constraints in the following experiments.

Another interesting observation, also stated in [16], is that more constraints do not necessarily result in a better quality. They can even decrease the clustering quality. In Figure 3 we can observe this slightly for cannot-link constraints (SMVC-CL); other experiments showed similar effects for must-link constraints. We kindly refer to [16] for a discussion about these effects. Unfortunately the principles discussed in [16] for wisely choosing the set of constraints are not easily transferable to our scenario.

Varying number of views. In the next experiment, we study the potential of using SMVC as an unsupervised technique in a multi-view setting. In Figure 4, we vary the number of hidden views in the data. The dimensionality of each view is 5, i.e. with increasing number of views, the data's overall dimensionality increases as well. As depicted, SMVC and MVGen are the only approaches able to detect the clustering structure in the case of a large number of views. Their clustering quality is very high and proves to be robust against a varying number of views. The competing methods behave differently: while for single-view data the quality is relatively high, their quality heavily decreases with an increasing number of views.

Scalability. Even though the focus for SMVC lies on its clustering quality, we briefly analyze its efficiency. As already discussed in Section 3, SMVC scales linearly in the number of objects (Figure 5), linearly in the number of dimensions (Figure 6), and linearly in the number of constraints (Figure 7). Please note the logarithmic scaling of both axes in all three plots. For a varying database size

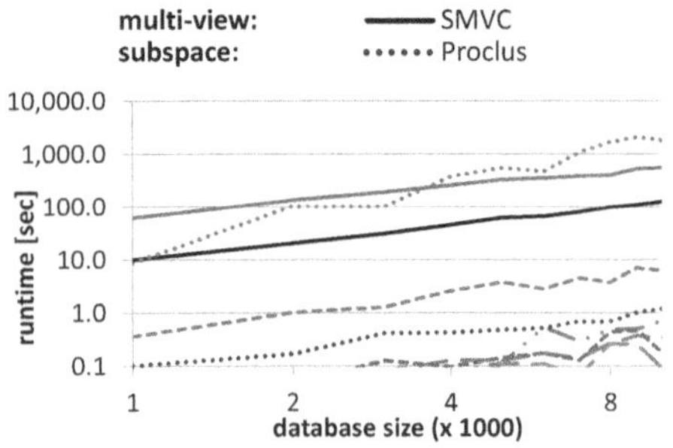

Fig. 5: Runtime vs. database size

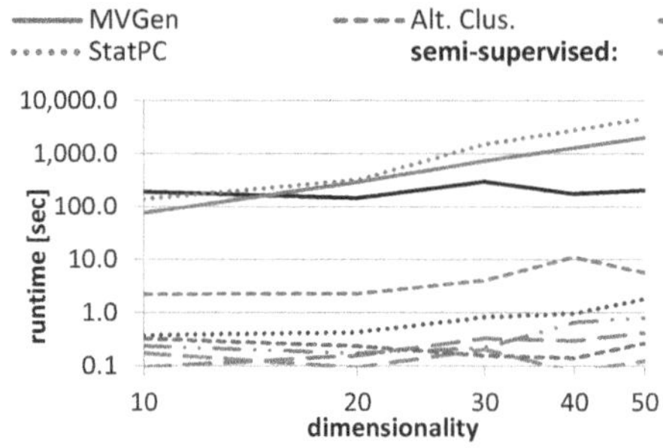

Fig. 6: Runtime vs. dimensionality

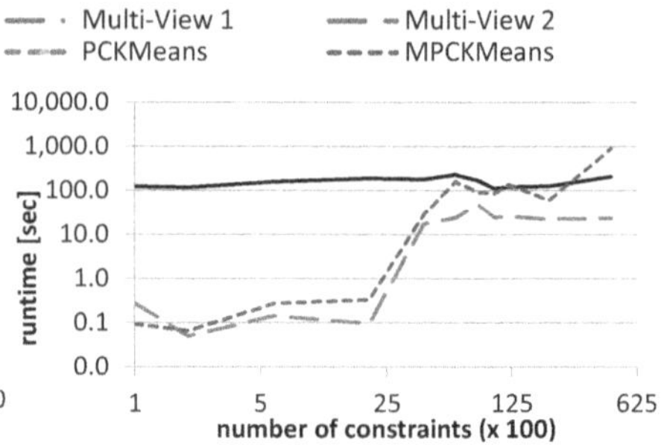

Fig. 7: Runtime vs. # constraints

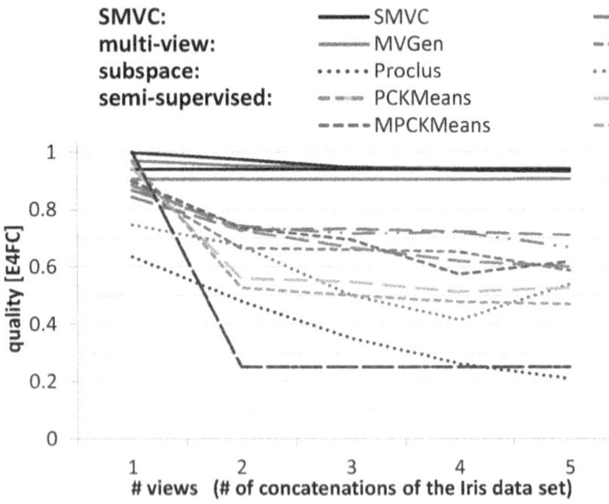

Fig. 8: Quality on iris data

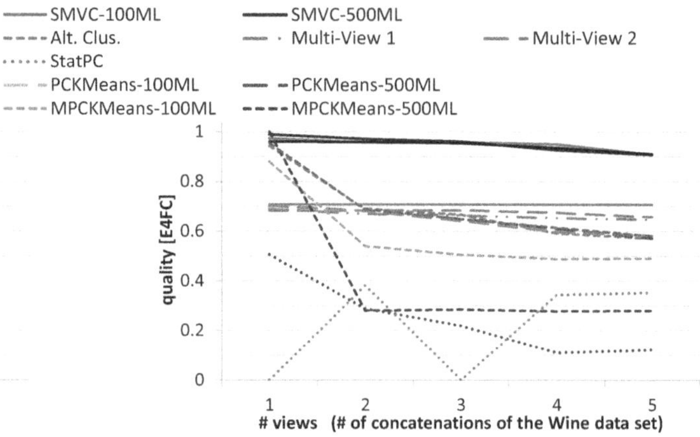

Fig. 9: Quality on wine data

(Figure 5), all algorithms show an increasing runtime. The approaches that represent adaptations of the simple and efficient KMeans algorithm (which also includes Proclus) clearly show the lowest runtimes. The runtime of SMVC is comparable to the other algorithms analyzing subspace projections (MVGen, StatPC) and even manages to outperform them thanks to the efficient variational inference techniques.

The benefit of SMVC becomes apparent for a high data dimensionality (Figure 6). Due to the exponential number of subspaces, most subspace clustering algorithms (e.g. StatPC) suffer from a tremendously increasing runtime for an increasing number of dimensions. Also MVGen cannot compete with our SMVC due to the complex model selection process. Contrarily, for SMVC, we observe a moderate increase in runtime. This enables us to apply SMVC also on high-dimensional data, as we will see in the experiments on real world data.

Figure 7 shows the runtime results of the semi-supervised methods for a varying number of constraints. Here, it is hard to verify the linear runtime of SMVC because constraints support the clustering procedure and, thus, help decreasing the number of iterations. For a small number of constraints, the two KMeans-based approaches can maintain a low runtime. For an increasing number of constraints, however, their runtime eventually even meets the one of SMVC. Of course, such a high number of constraints might not be realistic for most applications.

5.2 Evaluation on Real World Data

For evaluation on real world data we use different evaluation principles, all focusing on the multi-view aspect.

Case study A. In Figures 8 and 9, we extend the data sets Iris and Wine to data containing multiple views: for this, we randomly concatenate the attribute values of different objects up to five times to a higher dimensional space. The original data sets have dimensionalities of 4 and 13, respectively, while the extension to multi-view data leads to dimensionalities up to $5 \cdot 4 = 20$ (Iris) and $5 \cdot 13 = 65$ (Wine).

For just one view, the quality of some competing approaches is similar to the one of SMVC. However, for an increasing number of views the clustering quality for almost all competing approaches decreases. Only MVGen and SMVC are nearly not affected by an increasing number of views but detect the different object groupings even for multiple views.

To study the effects of semi-supervision, we additionally provided for both datasets 100 and 500 constraints. For just a single view SMVC is able to improve the cluster quality. On iris, for example, the quality increases from 0.94 over 0.97 to 1.0. The full potential of our approach, however, can bee seen in the case of multiple views: While it is still able to benefit from prior knowledge, the clustering quality of the competing approaches dramatically decreases.

It is noticeable, that with increasing number of views, the constraints seem to have less positive effect on the result of SMVC. This phenomenon can, however, easily be explained by the fact that the constraints have to be distributed among the views, i.e. the proportion of prior knowledge decreases with increasing number of views.

Summarizing, the results for real world data are consistent with the observations made for the synthetic data.

Case study B. For our next study, we created a data set consisting of 900 20x20 images of 'dancing stick figures'. This dataset allows an easy visual interpretation of the clustering results. We drew 9 basic stick figures (Figure 10(a)) and built 900 samples by randomly introducing noise. Since the subspace clustering and single-view clus-

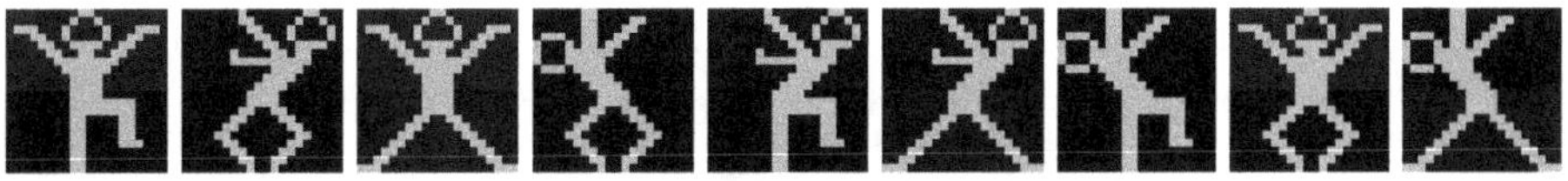

(a) Samples of the stick figures data

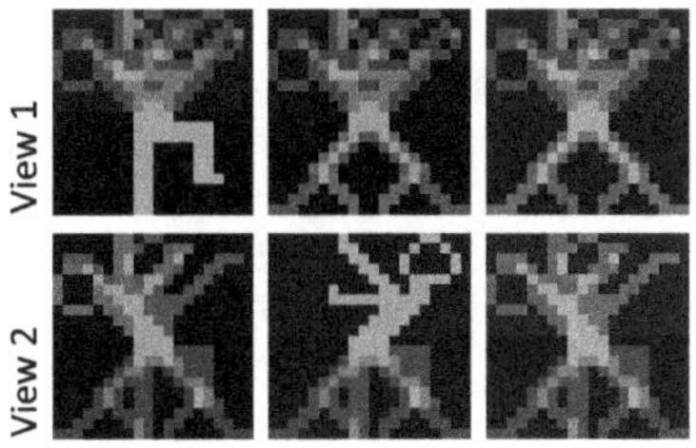

(b) SMVC result with 0 constraints

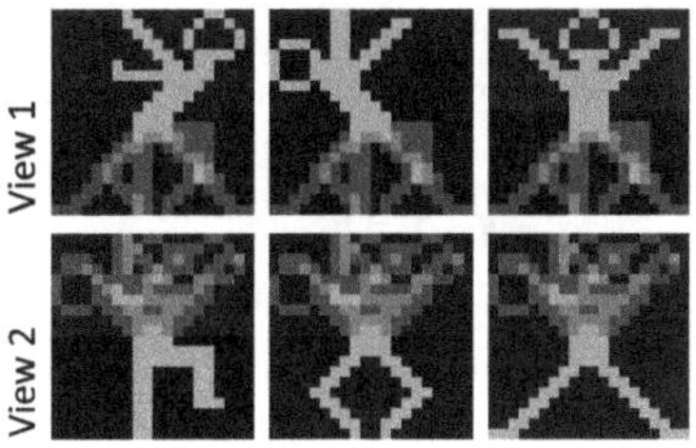

(c) SMVC with 100 constraints

Algorithm	E4FC
SMVC 0 constraints	0.700
SMVC 100 constraints	**1**
MVGen	0.760
Alt. Clus.	0.585
Multi-View 1	0.735
Multi-View 2	0.781

(d) Multi-view algorithm results

Fig. 10: Evaluation of multi-view clustering algorithms on the stick figures dataset

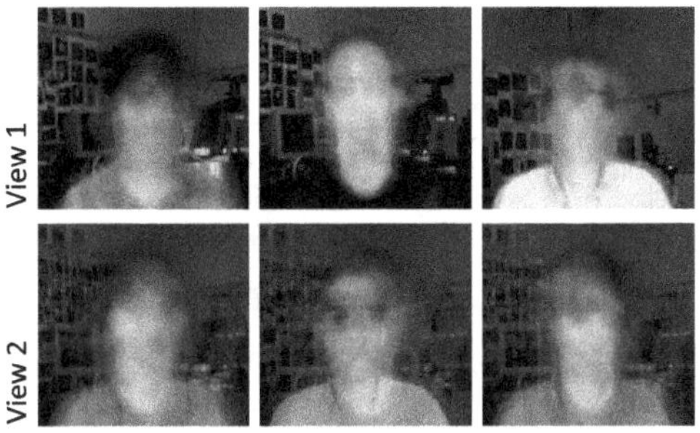

(a) SMVC result with 0 constraints

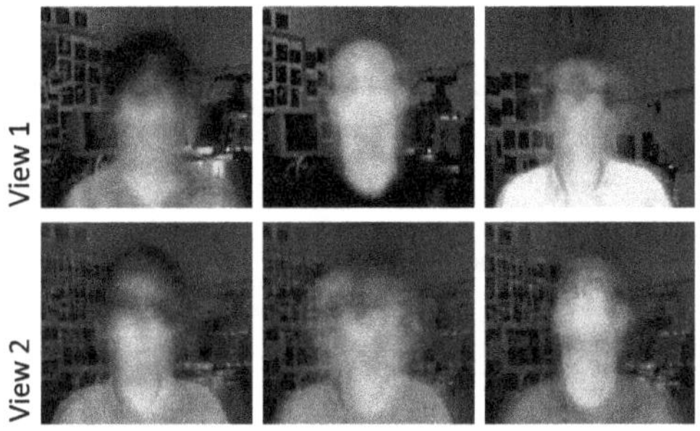

(b) SMVC with 100 constraints

Algorithm	E4FC
SMVC 0 constraints	0.691
SMVC 100 constraints	**0.780**
MVGen	0.720
Alt. Clus.	0.667
Multi-View 1	0.623
Multi-View 2	0.666

(c) Multi-view algorithm results

Fig. 11: Evaluation of multi-view clustering algorithms on the faces data set

tering approaches have proven to be not applicable for the multi-view scenario, we applied only the multi-view clustering approaches in this experiment. We provide this data set on our website[1]

Although this data does not seem to be very complex, all approaches are challenged in identifying two meaningful views as shown by their clustering results (cf. Figure 10(d)). Even the initial result of our SMVC approach is not convincing as it produces the clustering depicted in Figure 10(b), which is very similar to those of the other approaches. The illustrated images correspond to the means of each detected cluster. In contrast, if we provide SMVC with 100 must-link constraints, it is able to perfectly identify the two clustering views as depicted in Figure 10(c). These two views differentiate between the stick figures' top position (view 1) and their leg position (view 2). Please note that we only choose 100 random constraints out of the 269,100 ($= 2 \cdot (3 \cdot \binom{300}{2})$) possible constraints. By exploiting this small amount of prior knowledge, our SMVC approach clearly outperforms all competing methods.

Case study C. To show that the findings of the stick figures data also apply to more complex scenarios, we next analyze the clustering result of all multi-view approaches on the CMUFace data. This data is interesting for multi-view clustering since it consists of images taken from persons showing varying characteristics such as their facial expressions (neutral, happy, sad, angry), head positions (left, right, straight, up), and eye states (open, sunglasses). As also done in [12], we randomly select 3 persons with all their images and applied PCA retaining at least 90% of the data's variance as a pre-processing.

[1] http://www.dme.rwth-aachen.de/SMVC

The result of SMVC without prior knowledge for two views each with three clusters is illustrated in Figure 11(a). The images correspond again to the clusters' means. By visual inspection, we can easily identify that the first view partitions the images based on the 3 different persons. The second view, in contrast, cannot be explained easily.

If we provide 100 constraints in order to find one view for partitioning w.r.t. the persons and another view to partition w.r.t. the head position (in total 2,592 ($= 3 \cdot \binom{32}{2} + 4 \cdot \binom{24}{2}$) possible constraints), SMVC gets the result depicted in Figure 11(b). Here we can easily identify the different head positions straight, side (left and right), and up (note that we have four head positions but only search for 3 clusters). Using the original labels provided by the dataset as ground truth, i.e. the groupings based on the different persons and the grouping based on different head positions, we obtain the clustering results of Figure 11(c). We can see, that the unsupervised multi-view approaches all yield similar clustering qualities. They were only able to identify the first view. For SMVC, we can observe a noticeable quality improvement if we integrate prior knowledge into the clustering process.

Overall, our experiments show that SMVC is able to detect the multi-view clustering structure on a variety of data sets. It successfully solves the challenge to learn the assignment of user constraints to views such that it is able to improve its clustering results based on this prior knowledge.

6. CONCLUSION

We have presented the semi-supervised clustering method SMVC that detects multiple clustering solutions in subspace projections and that exploits prior knowledge by incorporating instance level constraints. Our method is based on a sound Bayesian framework which models the data via multiple mixture distributions. The model uses the instance level constraints to guide the clustering of objects, and it automatically determines which views are responsible for which constraints. For learning the clustering, we use the principle of variational inference. Our experimental study has shown the high potential of SMVC to detect multiple clustering views and its capability to use the prior knowledge for improving the clustering results.

Acknowledgments. This work has been partly funded by the SteerSCiVA DFG-664/11 project (part of SPP 1335). Stephan Günnemann has been supported by a fellowship within the postdoc-program of the German Academic Exchange Service (DAAD).

7. REFERENCES

[1] C. C. Aggarwal. A human-computer interactive method for projected clustering. *IEEE Trans. Knowl. Data Eng.*, 16(4):448–460, 2004.

[2] C. C. Aggarwal, J. L. Wolf, P. S. Yu, C. Procopiuc, and J. S. Park. Fast algorithms for projected clustering. In *SIGMOD*, pages 61–72, 1999.

[3] A. Asuncion and D. Newman. UCI machine learning repository, http://archive.ics.uci.edu/ml, 2010.

[4] E. Bae and J. Bailey. Coala: A novel approach for the extraction of an alternate clustering of high quality and high dissimilarity. In *ICDM*, pages 53–62, 2006.

[5] A. Banerjee, C. Krumpelman, J. Ghosh, S. Basu, and R. J. Mooney. Model-based overlapping clustering. In *KDD*, pages 532–537, 2005.

[6] S. Basu, A. Banerjee, and R. J. Mooney. Active semi-supervision for pairwise constrained clustering. In *SDM*, pages 333–344, 2004.

[7] S. Basu, M. Bilenko, and R. J. Mooney. A probabilistic framework for semi-supervised clustering. In *KDD*, pages 59–68, 2004.

[8] S. Basu, I. Davidson, and K. Wagstaff. *Constrained Clustering: Advances in Algorithms, Theory, and Applications.* Chapman & Hall/CRC, 2008.

[9] M. Bilenko, S. Basu, and R. J. Mooney. Integrating constraints and metric learning in semi-supervised clustering. In *ICML*, pages 81–88, 2004.

[10] C. Bishop. *Pattern recognition and machine learning.* Springer, 2006.

[11] Y. Cui, X. Z. Fern, and J. G. Dy. Non-redundant multi-view clustering via orthogonalization. In *ICDM*, pages 133–142, 2007.

[12] X. H. Dang and J. Bailey. Generation of alternative clusterings using the cami approach. In *SDM*, pages 118–129, 2010.

[13] X. H. Dang and J. Bailey. A hierarchical information theoretic technique for the discovery of non linear alternative clusterings. In *KDD*, pages 573–582, 2010.

[14] X. H. Dang and J. Bailey. A framework to uncover multiple alternative clusterings. *Machine Learning*, pages 1–24, 2013.

[15] X. H. Dang and J. Bailey. Generating multiple alternative clusterings via globally optimal subspaces. *DMKD*, 28(3):569–592, 2013.

[16] I. Davidson. Two approaches to understanding when constraints help clustering. In *KDD*, pages 1312–1320, 2012.

[17] Q. Fu and A. Banerjee. Multiplicative mixture models for overlapping clustering. In *ICDM*, pages 791–796, 2008.

[18] S. Günnemann, B. Boden, and T. Seidl. Finding density-based subspace clusters in graphs with feature vectors. *DAMI*, 25(2):243–269, 2012.

[19] S. Günnemann and C. Faloutsos. Mixed membership subspace clustering. In *ICDM*, pages 221–230, 2013.

[20] S. Günnemann, I. Färber, E. Müller, I. Assent, and T. Seidl. External evaluation measures for subspace clustering. In *CIKM*, pages 1363–1372, 2011.

[21] S. Günnemann, I. Färber, and T. Seidl. Multi-view clustering using mixture models in subspace projections. In *KDD*, pages 132–140, 2012.

[22] S. Günnemann, E. Müller, I. Färber, and T. Seidl. Detection of orthogonal concepts in subspaces of high dimensional data. In *CIKM*, pages 1317–1326, 2009.

[23] P. Jain, R. Meka, and I. S. Dhillon. Simultaneous unsupervised learning of disparate clusterings. *SADM*, 1(3):195–210, 2008.

[24] H.-P. Kriegel, P. Kröger, and A. Zimek. Clustering high-dimensional data: A survey on subspace clustering, pattern-based clustering, and correlation clustering. *TKDD*, 3(1), 2009.

[25] Z. Lu and T. K. Leen. Semi-supervised learning with penalized probabilistic clustering. In *NIPS*, pages 849–856, 2004.

[26] G. Moise and J. Sander. Finding non-redundant, statistically significant regions in high dimensional data: a novel approach to projected and subspace clustering. In *KDD*, pages 533–541, 2008.

[27] E. Müller, S. Günnemann, I. Färber, and T. Seidl. Discovering multiple clustering solutions: Grouping objects in different views of the data. In *ICDM*, 2010.

[28] D. Niu, J. G. Dy, and M. I. Jordan. Multiple non-redundant spectral clustering views. In *ICML*, pages 831–838, 2010.

[29] L. K. M. Poon, N. L. Zhang, T. Chen, and Y. Wang. Variable selection in model-based clustering: To do or to facilitate. In *ICML*, pages 887–894, 2010.

[30] Z. Qi and I. Davidson. A principled and flexible framework for finding alternative clusterings. In *KDD*, pages 717–726, 2009.

[31] N. Shental, A. Bar-Hillel, T. Hertz, and D. Weinshall. Computing gaussian mixture models with em using equivalence constraints. In *NIPS*, 2003.

APPENDIX

For the variational distributions, the following holds:

$$\mathbb{E}_q[\![z_{m,i} = k]\!] = \psi_{m,i,k} \qquad \mathbb{E}_q[\![c_{i,j} = m]\!] = \xi_{i,j,m}$$

$$\mathbb{E}_q[\![v_d = m]\!] = \phi_{d,m} \qquad \mathbb{E}_q[\pi_{m,k}] = \frac{\tilde{\lambda}_m[k]}{\sum_{i=1}^{K} \tilde{\lambda}_m[i]}$$

$$\mathbb{E}_q[\log \pi_{m,k}] = \psi(\tilde{\lambda}_m[k]) - \psi(\sum_{i=1}^{K} \tilde{\lambda}_m[i])$$

$$\mathbb{E}_q[\mu_{m,k,d}] = \tilde{\mu}_{m,k,d} \qquad \mathbb{E}_q[\mu_{m,k,d} \cdot \tau_{m,k,d}] = \tilde{\mu}_{m,k,d} \cdot \frac{\tilde{\alpha}}{\tilde{\beta}}$$

$$\mathbb{E}_q[\tau_{m,k,d}] = \frac{\tilde{\alpha}}{\tilde{\beta}} \qquad \mathbb{E}_q[\log \tau_{m,k,d}] = \psi(\tilde{\alpha}) - \log(\tilde{\beta})$$

$$\mathbb{E}_q[\mu_{m,k,d}^2 \cdot \tau_{m,k,d}] = \frac{1}{\tilde{\kappa}_{m,k,d}} + \tilde{\mu}_{m,k,d}^2 \cdot \frac{\tilde{\alpha}}{\tilde{\beta}}$$

FastXML: A Fast, Accurate and Stable Tree-classifier for eXtreme Multi-label Learning

Yashoteja Prabhu
Indian Institute of Technology - Delhi
yashoteja.prabhu@gmail.com

Manik Varma
Microsoft Research
manik@microsoft.com

ABSTRACT

The objective in extreme multi-label classification is to learn a classifier that can automatically tag a data point with the most relevant *subset* of labels from a large label set. Extreme multi-label classification is an important research problem since not only does it enable the tackling of applications with many labels but it also allows the reformulation of ranking problems with certain advantages over existing formulations.

Our objective, in this paper, is to develop an extreme multi-label classifier that is faster to train and more accurate at prediction than the state-of-the-art Multi-label Random Forest (MLRF) algorithm [2] and the Label Partitioning for Sub-linear Ranking (LPSR) algorithm [35]. MLRF and LPSR learn a hierarchy to deal with the large number of labels but optimize task independent measures, such as the Gini index or clustering error, in order to learn the hierarchy. Our proposed FastXML algorithm achieves significantly higher accuracies by directly optimizing an nDCG based ranking loss function. We also develop an alternating minimization algorithm for efficiently optimizing the proposed formulation. Experiments reveal that FastXML can be trained on problems with more than a million labels on a standard desktop in eight hours using a single core and in an hour using multiple cores.

Categories and Subject Descriptors

I.2.6 [**Artificial Intelligence**]: Learning

General Terms

Algorithms, Performance, Machine Learning, Optimization

Keywords

Multi-label Learning; Ranking; Extreme Classification

1. INTRODUCTION

The objective in extreme multi-label classification is to learn a classifier that can automatically tag a data point with the most relevant *subset* of labels from a large label set. For instance, there are more than a million categories on Wikipedia and one might wish to build a classifier that annotates a novel web page with the subset of most relevant Wikipedia categories. It should be emphasized that multi-label learning is distinct from multi-class classification which aims to predict a single mutually exclusive label.

KDD'14, August 24–27, 2014, New York, NY, USA.

ACM 978-1-4503-2956-9/14/08 ...$15.00.
http://dx.doi.org/10.1145/2623330.2623651.

Extreme classification is an important research problem not just because modern day applications have many categories but also because it allows the reformulation of core learning problems such as recommendation and ranking. For instance, [2] treated search engine queries as labels and built an extreme classifier which, given a novel web page, returned a ranking of queries in decreasing order of relevance. Similarly, [35] treated YouTube videos as distinct labels in an extreme classifier so as to recommend a ranked list of videos to users. Both methods provided a fresh way of thinking about ranking and recommendation problems that led to significant improvements over the state-of-the-art.

Extreme classification is also a challenging research problem as one needs to simultaneously deal with a large number of labels, dimensions and training points. An obvious baseline is provided by the 1-vs-All technique where an independent classifier is learnt per label. Such a baseline has at least two major limitations. First, training millions of high dimensional classifiers might be computationally expensive. Second, the cost of prediction might be high since all the classifiers would need to be evaluated every time a prediction needed to be made. These problems could be ameliorated if a label hierarchy was provided. Unfortunately, such a hierarchy is unavailable in many applications [2, 35].

State-of-the-art methods therefore learn a hierarchy from training data as follows: The root node is initialized to contain the entire label set. A node partitioning formulation is then optimized to determine which labels should be assigned to the left child and which to the right. Nodes are recursively partitioned till each leaf contains only a small number of labels. During prediction, a novel data point is passed down the tree until it reaches a leaf node. A base multi-label classifier of choice can then be applied to the data point focusing exclusively on the leaf node label distribution. This leads to prediction costs that are sub-linear or even logarithmic if the tree is balanced.

Tree based methods can often outperform the 1-vs-All baseline in terms of prediction accuracy at a fraction of the prediction cost. However, such methods can also be expensive to train. In particular, the Label Partitioning by Sublinear Ranking (LPSR) algorithm of [35] can have even higher training costs than the 1-vs-All baseline since it needs to learn the hierarchy in addition to the base classifier. Similarly, the Multi-label Random Forest (MLRF) approach of [2] required a cluster of a thousand nodes as random forest training was found to be expensive in high dimensional spaces. Such expensive approaches not only increase the cost of deploying extreme classification models and the cost of daily experimentation but also put such models beyond the reach of most practitioners.

Our objective, in this paper, is to tackle this problem and build a tree based extreme multi-label classifier, referred to as FastXML, that is faster to train as well as more accurate than the state-of-the-art MLRF and LPSR. Our key technical contributions are a novel node partitioning formulation and an algorithm for its efficient optimization. In terms of training time, FastXML can be significantly faster than MLRF since the proposed node partitioning formulation can be optimized more efficiently than the entropy or Gini index based formulations in random forests. At the same time, FastXML can be faster to train than LPSR which has to first learn computationally expensive base classifiers for accurate prediction. In terms of prediction accuracy, almost all extreme classification applications deal with scenarios where the number of relevant positive labels for a data point is orders of magnitude smaller than the number of irrelevant negative ones. Prediction accuracy is therefore not measured using traditional multi-label metrics, such as the Hamming loss, which give equal weightage to all labels whether positive or negative. Instead, most applications prefer employing ranking based measures such as precision at k which focuses exclusively on the positive labels by counting the number of correct predictions in the top k positive predictions. FastXML's proposed node partitioning formulation therefore directly optimizes a rank sensitive loss function which can lead to more accurate predictions over MLRF's Gini index or LPSR's clustering error.

Experiments indicated that FastXML could be significantly more accurate at prediction (by as much as 5% in some cases) on benchmark data sets with thousands of labels where accurate models for MLRF, LPSR and the 1-vs-All baseline could be learnt. Furthermore, FastXML could efficiently scale to problems involving a million labels where accurate training of MLRF, LPSR and 1-vs-ALL models would require a very large cluster. For instance, using a single core on a standard desktop, a single FastXML tree could be trained in under 10 minutes on a data set with about 4 M training points, 160 K features and 1 M labels. The entire ensemble could be trained in 8 hours using a single core and in 1 hour using multiple cores. MLRF and 1-vs-All could not be trained on such extreme multi-label data sets on a standard desktop. LPSR training could be made tractable by replacing the computationally expensive 1-vs-All base classifier by the cheaper Naïve Bayes but then its classification accuracy was found to lag behind by more than 20% on data sets such as Wikipedia.

Our contributions are: (a) We formulate a novel node partitioning objective which directly optimizes an nDCG based ranking loss and which implicitly learns balanced partitions; (b) We propose an efficient optimization algorithm for the novel formulation; and (c) we combine these in a tree algorithm which can train on problems with a million labels on a standard desktop while increasing prediction accuracy. Code for FastXML can be downloaded by clicking here.

2. RELATED WORK

There has been much recent progress in extreme multi-label classification [2,4,8,10,12,15,19,20,22,29,34–36,38] and most approaches are either based on trees or on embeddings.

To clarify the discussion, it is assumed that the training set can be represented as $\{(\mathbf{x}_i, \mathbf{y}_i)_{i=1}^N\}$ with D dimensional real-valued feature vectors $\mathbf{x}_i \in \mathcal{R}^D$ with sparsity $O(\hat{D})$, and L dimensional binary label vectors $\mathbf{y}_i \in \{0,1\}^L$ with $\mathbf{y}_{il} = 1$ if label l is relevant for point i and 0 otherwise. If one further assumes that the cost of training a linear binary classifier is $O(N\hat{D})$, then the training cost of the linear 1-vs-All baseline is $O(LN\hat{D})$ and the prediction cost is $O(L\hat{D})$. This is infeasible when L and N are in the range 10^5 – 10^6. One can mitigate the training cost by sub-sampling the negative class for each binary classifier but the prediction cost would still be high.

Embedding methods [4,8,10,12,15,19,20,22,29,34,36,38] exploit label correlations and sparsity to compress the number of labels from L to $\hat{L}$. A low-dimensional embedding of the label space is found typically through a linear projection $\hat{\mathbf{y}} = \mathbf{P}\mathbf{y}$ where $\mathbf{P}$ is a $\hat{L} \times L$ projection matrix. The 1-vs-All strategy can now be applied and the cost of training and prediction in the compressed space reduces to $O(\hat{L}N\hat{D})$ and $O(\hat{L}\hat{D})$ respectively. The compressed label predictions also need to be uncompressed at an additional cost of $O(\hat{L}L)$ or higher. Methods mainly differ in the choice of compression and decompression techniques such as compressed sensing [19, 22], Bloom filters [12], SVD [29], landmark labels [4, 8], output codes [38], *etc.* An interesting variant can be obtained by compressing the features $\hat{\mathbf{x}} = \mathbf{R}\mathbf{x}$ to the same $\hat{L}$ dimensional space as the labels [34]. Predictions can then be efficiently made in the embedding space via nearest neighbour techniques and no decompression is required.

Embedding methods have many advantages including simplicity, ease of implementation, strong theoretical foundations, the ability to handle label correlations, the ability to adapt to online and incremental scenarios, *etc.* Unfortunately, embedding methods can also pay a heavy price in terms of prediction accuracy due to the loss of information during the compression phase. For instance, none of the embedding methods developed so far have been able to consistently outperform the 1-vs-All baseline when $\hat{L} \approx \log(L)$.

Tree methods that learn a hierarchy enjoy many of the same advantages as the embedding methods. In addition, they can outperform the 1-vs-All baseline even when the prediction costs are $O(\hat{D}\log L)$. Our primary comparison is therefore with tree-based methods.

The Label Partitioning by Sub-linear Ranking (LPSR) method of [35] focussed on reducing the prediction time by learning a hierarchy over a base classifier or ranker. First, a base multi-label classifier was learnt for the entire label set. This step governs the overall training complexity and prediction accuracy. Generative classifiers such as Naïve Bayes are quick to train but have low accuracy whereas discriminative classifiers such as 1-vs-All with linear SVMs [18], deep nets or Wsabie [34] are expensive to train but have higher accuracy. Next, a hierarchy was learnt in terms of a single binary tree. Nodes in the tree were grown by partitioning the node's data points into 2 clusters, corresponding to the left and the right child, using a variant of k-means over the feature vectors. The tree was grown until each leaf node had a small number of data points and corresponding labels. Finally, a relaxed integer program was optimized at each leaf node via gradient descent to activate a subset of the labels present at the node. During prediction, a novel point was passed down the tree until it reached a leaf node. Predictions were then made using the base classifier restricted to the set of active leaf node labels.

The Multi-label Random Forest (MLRF) approach of [2] did not need to learn a base classifier. Instead, an ensemble of randomized trees was learnt. Nodes were partitioned into a left and a right child by brute force optimization of a multi-label variant of the Gini index defined over the set of positive labels in the node. Trees were grown until each leaf node had only a few labels present. During testing, a novel point was passed down each tree and predictions were made by aggregating all the leaf node label distributions.

Both LPSR and MLRF have high training costs. LPSR needs to train an accurate base multi-label classifier, perform hierarchical k-means clustering and solve a label assignment problem at each leaf node. MLRF needs to learn an ensemble of trees where the cost of growing each node is high. In particular, while training in high dimensional spaces, random forests need to sample a large number of features at each node in order to achieve a good quality, balanced split (extremely random trees [17] and other variants do not work in extreme classification scenarios as they learn imbalanced splits). Furthermore, brute force optimization of the Gini index or entropy over each feature is expensive when there are a large number of training points and labels. All in all, accurate LPSR and MLRF training can require large clusters – with up to a thousand nodes in the case of MLRF.

Finally, care should be taken to note that our objective of learning a multi-label hierarchy is very different from the objective of learning a multi-class hierarchy [5, 11, 13, 16] or exploiting a pre-existing multi-label hierarchy [7, 9, 27].

3. FASTXML

Our primary objective, in developing FastXML, is to enable training on a single desktop or a small cluster. At the same time, we aim to achieve greater prediction accuracy by optimizing a more suitable rank sensitive loss function as compared to MLRF's Gini index and LPSR's clustering error. We start this Section by presenting an overview of the FastXML algorithm, then go into the details of optimizing a loss function to learn a node partition and finally analyze FastXML's cost of prediction.

3.1 FastXML overview

FastXML learns a hierarchy, not over the label space as is traditionally done in the multi-class setting [5, 13, 16], but rather over the feature space. The intuition is similar to LPSR and MLRF's and comes from the observation that only a small number of labels are present, or active, in each region of feature space. Efficient prediction can therefore be carried out by determining the region in which a novel point lies by traversing the learnt feature space hierarchy and then focusing exclusively on the set of labels active in the region. Like MLRF, and unlike LPSR, FastXML defines the set of labels active in a region to be the union of the labels of all training points present in that region. This speeds up training as FastXML does not need to solve the label assignment integer program in each region. Furthermore, like MLRF, and unlike LPSR, FastXML learns an ensemble of trees and does not need to rely on base classifiers.

Algorithm 1 FastXML($\{\mathbf{x}_i, \mathbf{y}_i\}_{i=1}^N, T$)

```
parallel-for i = 1,..,T do
    n^root ← new node
    n^root.Id ← {1,..,N}                  # Root contains all instances
    GROW-NODE-RECURSIVE(n^root)
    T_i ← new tree
    T_i.root ← n^root
end parallel-for
return T_1,..,T_T

procedure GROW-NODE-RECURSIVE(n)
    if |n.Id| ≤ MaxLeaf then              # Make n a leaf
        n.P ← PROCESS-LEAF({x_i, y_i}_{i=1}^N, n)
    else          # Split node and grow child nodes recursively
        {n.w, n.left_child, n.right_child}
                          ← SPLIT-NODE({x_i, y_i}_{i=1}^N, n)
        GROW-NODE-RECURSIVE(n.left_child)
        GROW-NODE-RECURSIVE(n.right_child)
    end if
end procedure

procedure PROCESS-LEAF({x_i, y_i}_{i=1}^N, n)
    P ← top-k( (Σ_{i∈n.Id} y_i) / |n.Id| )
return P                     # Return scores for top k labels
end procedure
```

Predictions are made by returning the ranked list of most frequently occurring active labels in all the leaf nodes in the ensemble containing the novel point. Algorithms 1 and 3 present pseudo-code for FastXML training and prediction respectively.

3.2 Learning to partition a node

Training FastXML consists of recursively partitioning a parent's feature space between its children. Such a node partition should ideally be learnt by optimizing a global measure of performance such as the ranking predictions induced by the leaf nodes, Unfortunately, optimizing global measures can be expensive as all nodes in the tree would need to be learnt jointly [21]. Existing approaches therefore optimize local measures of performance which depend solely on predictions made by the current node being partitioned. This allows the hierarchy to be learnt node by node starting from the root and going down to the leaves and is more efficient than learning all the nodes jointly.

MLRF and LPSR optimize the Gini index and clustering error as their local measure of performance. Unfortunately, neither measure is particularly well suited for ranking or extreme multi-label applications where correctly predicting the few positive relevant labels is much more important than predicting the vast number of irrelevant ones.

FastXML therefore proposes to learn the hierarchy by directly optimizing a ranking loss function. In particular, it optimizes the normalized Discounted Cumulative Gain (nDCG) [33]. This results in learning superior partitions due to two main reasons. First, nDCG is a measure which is sensitive to both ranking and relevance and therefore ensures that the relevant positive labels are predicted with ranks that are as high as possible. This cannot be guaranteed by rank insensitive measures such as the Gini index or the clustering error. Second, by being rank sensitive, nDCG

Algorithm 2 SPLIT-NODE($\{\mathbf{x}_i, \mathbf{y}_i\}_{i=1}^N, n$)

$Id \leftarrow n.Id$
$\delta_i[0] \sim \{-1, 1\}, \forall i \in Id$ # Random coin tosses
$\mathbf{w}[0] \leftarrow \mathbf{0}, t \leftarrow 0, t_{\mathbf{w}} \leftarrow 0, \mathcal{W}_0 \leftarrow 0$ # Various counters
repeat
  $\mathbf{r}^{\pm}[t+1] \leftarrow \text{rank}_L\left(\sum_{i \in Id} \frac{1}{2}(1 \pm \delta_i[t]) I_L(\mathbf{y}_i)\mathbf{y}_i\right)$
  for $i \in Id$ **do**
    $v^{\pm} \leftarrow C_\delta(\pm 1)\log(1 + e^{\mp \mathbf{w}[t]^\top \mathbf{x}_i})$
    $\quad - C_r I_L(\mathbf{y}_i) \sum_{l=1}^{L} \left(\frac{y_{i r_l^{\pm}[t+1]}}{\log(1+l)}\right)$
    # Refer to (5)
    if $v^+ = v^-$ **then**
      $\delta_i[t+1] = \delta_i[t]$
    else
      $\delta_i[t+1] = \text{sign}(v^- - v^+)$
    end if
  end for
  if $\boldsymbol{\delta}[t+1] = \boldsymbol{\delta}[t]$ **then** # Update $\mathbf{w}$
    $\mathbf{w}[t+1] \leftarrow \underset{\mathbf{w}}{\text{argmin}} \|\mathbf{w}\|_1 + C_\delta(\delta_i[t]) \sum_{i \in Id} \log(1 + e^{-\delta_i[t]\mathbf{w}^\top \mathbf{x}_i})$
    $\mathcal{W}_{t_{\mathbf{w}}+1} \leftarrow t+1$ # Store time step of the update
    $t_{\mathbf{w}} \leftarrow t_{\mathbf{w}} + 1$ # We made one more update to $\mathbf{w}$
  else
    $\mathbf{w}[t+1] \leftarrow \mathbf{w}[t]$
  end if
  $t \leftarrow t+1$
until $\boldsymbol{\delta}[\mathcal{W}_{t_{\mathbf{w}}}] = \boldsymbol{\delta}[\mathcal{W}_{t_{\mathbf{w}}-1}]$ # Convergence
$n^+ \leftarrow$ new node, $n^- \leftarrow$ new node
$n^+.Id \leftarrow \{i \in Id : \mathbf{w}[t]^\top \mathbf{x}_i > 0\}$
$n^-.Id \leftarrow \{i \in Id : \mathbf{w}[t]^\top \mathbf{x}_i \leq 0\}$
return $\mathbf{w}[t], n^+, n^-$

can be optimized across all L labels at the current node thereby ensuring that the local optimization is not myopic.

We stick to the notation introduced in the previous Section. it is assumed that the training set can be represented as $\{(\mathbf{x}_i, \mathbf{y}_i)_{i=1}^N\}$ with D dimensional real-valued feature vectors $\mathbf{x}_i \in \mathcal{R}^D$ and L dimensional binary label vectors $\mathbf{y}_i \in \{0,1\}^L$ with $\mathbf{y}_{il} = 1$ if label l is relevant for point i and 0 otherwise. Permutation indices $i_1^{\text{desc}}, \ldots, i_L^{\text{desc}}$ that sort a real-valued vector $\mathbf{y} \in \mathcal{R}^L$ in descending order are defined such that if $j > k$ then $y_{i_j^{\text{desc}}} \geq y_{i_k^{\text{desc}}}$. The $\text{rank}_k(\mathbf{y})$ operator, which returns the indices of the k largest elements of $\mathbf{y}$ ranked in descending order (with ties broken randomly), can then be defined as

$$\text{rank}_k(\mathbf{y}) = [i_1^{\text{desc}}, \ldots, i_k^{\text{desc}}]^\top \tag{1}$$

Let $\Pi(1, L)$ denote the set of all permutations of $\{1, 2, \ldots, L\}$. The Discounted Cumulative Gain (DCG) at k of a ranking $\mathbf{r} \in \Pi(1, L)$ given a ground truth label vector $\mathbf{y}$ with binary levels of relevance is

$$\mathcal{L}_{\text{DCG@}k}(\mathbf{r}, \mathbf{y}) = \sum_{l=1}^{k} \frac{y_{r_l}}{\log(1+l)} \tag{2}$$

Note that the $\log(1+l)$ term ensures that it is beneficial to predict the positive labels with high ranks. Thus, unlike precision (which would have been obtained had the $\log(1+l)$ term been absent), DCG is sensitive to both the ranking and the relevance of predictions. The normalized DCG, or

Algorithm 3 PREDICT($\{\mathcal{T}_1, ..\mathcal{T}_T\}, \mathbf{x}$)

for $i = 1, .., T$ **do**
  $n \leftarrow \mathcal{T}_i$.root
  while n is not a leaf **do**
    $\mathbf{w} \leftarrow n.\mathbf{w}$
    if $\mathbf{w}^\top \mathbf{x} > 0$ **then**
      $n \leftarrow n$.left_child
    else
      $n \leftarrow n$.right_child
    end if
  end while
  $\mathbf{P}_i^{\text{leaf}}(\mathbf{x}) \leftarrow n.\mathbf{P}$
end for
$\mathbf{r}(\mathbf{x}) = \text{rank}_k\left(\frac{1}{T}\sum_{i=1}^{T} \mathbf{P}_i^{\text{leaf}}(\mathbf{x})\right)$
return $\mathbf{r}(\mathbf{x})$

nDCG, is then defined as

$$\mathcal{L}_{\text{nDCG@}k}(\mathbf{r}, \mathbf{y}) = I_k(\mathbf{y}) \sum_{l=1}^{k} \frac{y_{r_l}}{\log(1+l)} \tag{3}$$

$$\text{where } I_k(\mathbf{y}) = \frac{1}{\sum_{l=1}^{\min(k, \mathbf{1}^\top \mathbf{y})} \frac{1}{\log(1+l)}} \tag{4}$$

where $I_k(\mathbf{y})$ is the inverse of the DCG@k of the ideal ranking for $\mathbf{y}$ obtained by predicting the ranks of all of $\mathbf{y}$'s positive labels to be higher than any of its negative ones. This normalizes $\mathcal{L}_{\text{nDCG@}k}$ to lie between 0 and 1 with larger values being better and ensures that nDCG can be used to compare rankings across label vectors with different numbers of positive labels.

FastXML partitions the current node's feature space by learning a linear separator $\mathbf{w}$ such that

$$\begin{aligned} \min \quad & \|\mathbf{w}\|_1 + \sum_i C_\delta(\delta_i)\log(1 + e^{-\delta_i \mathbf{w}^\top \mathbf{x}_i}) \\ & - C_r \sum_i \tfrac{1}{2}(1 + \delta_i)\mathcal{L}_{\text{nDCG@}L}(\mathbf{r}^+, \mathbf{y}_i) \\ & - C_r \sum_i \tfrac{1}{2}(1 - \delta_i)\mathcal{L}_{\text{nDCG@}L}(\mathbf{r}^-, \mathbf{y}_i) \\ \text{w.r.t.} \quad & \mathbf{w} \in \mathcal{R}^D, \boldsymbol{\delta} \in \{-1, +1\}^L, \mathbf{r}^+, \mathbf{r}^- \in \Pi(1, L) \end{aligned} \tag{5}$$

where i indexes all the training points present at the node being partitioned, $\delta_i \in \{-1, +1\}$ indicates whether point i was assigned to the negative or positive partition and $\mathbf{r}^+$ and $\mathbf{r}^-$ represent the predicted label rankings for the positive and negative partition respectively. C_δ and C_r are user defined parameters which determine the relative importance of the three terms.

The first term in (5) is an ℓ_1 regularizer on $\mathbf{w}$ which ensures that a sparse linear separator is used to define the partition. Given a novel point $\mathbf{x}$, the FastXML trees can therefore be traversed efficiently during prediction depending on the sign of $\mathbf{w}^\top \mathbf{x}$ at each node. The second term is the log loss of $\delta_i \mathbf{w}^\top \mathbf{x}_i$. This term couples $\boldsymbol{\delta}$ and $\mathbf{w}$ as the optimal solution of this term alone is $\delta_i^* = \text{sign}(\mathbf{w}^{*\top} \mathbf{x}_i)$. This makes it likely that points assigned to the positive (negative) partition, i.e. points for which $\delta_i = +1$ ($\delta_i = -1$), will have positive (negative) values of $\mathbf{w}^\top \mathbf{x}_i$. C_δ is relaxed to be a function of δ_i so as to allow different misclassification penalties for the positive and negative points. The third and fourth term in (5) maximize the nDCG@L of the rankings predicted for the positive and negative partitions, $\mathbf{r}^+$ and $\mathbf{r}^-$ respectively, given the ground truth label vectors $\mathbf{y}_i$ assigned to these partitions. These terms couple $\mathbf{r}^\pm$ to $\boldsymbol{\delta}$ and thus to $\mathbf{w}$. As discussed, maximizing nDCG makes it likely that the relevant positive labels for each point are predicted with ranks as high as possible. As a result, points within a partition are likely to have similar labels whereas points across partitions are likely to have different labels.

Furthermore, it is beneficial to maximize nDCG@L at each node even though the ultimate leaf node rankings will be evaluated at $k \ll L$. This leads to non-myopic decisions at the root and internal nodes. For example, optimizing nDCG at $k = 5$ at the root node of the Wikipedia data set would be equivalent to finding a separator such that all the hundreds of thousands of Wikipedia articles assigned to the positive partition could be accurately labeled with just the five most frequently occurring Wikipedia categories in the positive partition and similarly for the negative partition. Clearly this will not lead to good results at the root node and superior partitions can be learnt by considering all the Wikipedia categories rather than just the top five. Of course, as already pointed out, rank insensitive measures such as precision cannot be optimized at $k = L$ as they become more and more uninformative with increasing k and $\mathcal{L}_{\text{precision@}L}(\mathbf{r}^\pm, \mathbf{y}_i) = 0$ for all points irrespective of the partitioning.

It is also worth noting that (5) allows a label to be assigned to both partitions if some of the points containing the label are assigned to the positive partition and some to the negative. This makes the FastXML trees somewhat robust as the child nodes can potentially recover from mistakes made by the parents [2,13,16,35].

Finally, note that $\boldsymbol{\delta}$ and $\mathbf{r}^\pm$ were deliberately chosen to be independent variables for efficient optimization rather than functions dependent on $\mathbf{w}$. In particular, (5) could have been formulated as an optimization problem in just $\mathbf{w}$ by discarding the log loss term and defining $\delta_i(\mathbf{w}) = \text{sign}(\mathbf{w}^\top \mathbf{x}_i)$ and $\mathbf{r}^\pm(\mathbf{w}) = \text{rank}_L\left(\sum_i \frac{1}{2}(1 \pm \delta_i(\mathbf{w}))I_L(\mathbf{y}_i)\mathbf{y}_i\right)$. Such a formulation would also have been natural but intractable at scale. Direct optimization via efficient techniques such as stochastic sub-gradient descent would not be possible due to the sharp discontinuities in $\boldsymbol{\delta}(\mathbf{w})$ and $\mathbf{r}^\pm(\mathbf{w})$. Furthermore, updates to $\mathbf{w}$ would necessitate expensive updates to $\boldsymbol{\delta}$ and $\mathbf{r}^\pm$. We therefore decouple $\boldsymbol{\delta}$ and $\mathbf{r}$ from $\mathbf{w}$ by treating them as variables for efficient optimization but then couple their optimal values through the objective function. We develop the optimization algorithm for (5) in Section 4.

3.3 Prediction

The objective function defined in (5) can be optimized efficiently and can lead to accurate predictions. A good objective function should, in addition, also lead to balanced partitions in order to ensure efficient prediction.

Given a novel point $\mathbf{x} \in \mathcal{R}^D$, FastXML's top ranked k predictions are given by

$$\mathbf{r}(\mathbf{x}) = \text{rank}_k\left(\frac{1}{T}\sum_{t=1}^{T}\mathbf{P}_t^{\text{leaf}}(\mathbf{x})\right) \tag{6}$$

where T is the number of trees in the FastXML ensemble and $\mathbf{P}_t^{\text{leaf}}(\mathbf{x}) \propto \sum_{i \in S_t^{\text{leaf}}(\mathbf{x})} \mathbf{y}_i$ and $S_t^{\text{leaf}}(\mathbf{x})$ are the label distribution and set of points respectively of the leaf node containing $\mathbf{x}$ in tree t. The average cost of prediction is upper bounded by $O(TDH + T\hat{L} + \hat{L}\log\hat{L})$ where H is the average length of the path traversed by $\mathbf{x}$ in order to reach the leaf nodes in the T trees and $\hat{L}$ is the number of non-zero elements in the vector $\sum_{t=1}^{T}\mathbf{P}_t^{\text{leaf}}(\mathbf{x})$. The cost is dominated by $O(TDH)$ as $\hat{L} \ll DH$. If the FastXML trees are balanced then $H = \log N \approx \log L$ and the overall cost of prediction becomes $O(TD\log L)$ which is logarithmic in the total number of labels.

One might therefore be tempted to add a balancing term to (5) so as to get H as close to $\log N$ as possible. However, this comes at the cost of reduced prediction accuracy as the objective function trades-off accuracy for balance. As it empirically turns out, our proposed nDCG based objective function learns highly balanced trees and a balancing term does not need to be added to (5). Thus, FastXML's predictions can be made accurately in logarithmic time.

4. OPTIMIZING FASTXML

It is well recognized in the learning to rank literature that nDCG is a difficult function to optimize [25,26,31,32] since it is sharply discontinuous with respect to $\mathbf{w}$ and hence standard stochastic sub-gradient descent techniques cannot be applied. FastXML therefore employs an alternate strategy and optimizes (5) using an iterative alternating minimization algorithm. The algorithm is initialized by setting $\mathbf{w} = \mathbf{0}$ and δ_i to be -1 or $+1$ uniformly at random. Each iteration, then, consists of taking three steps. First, $\mathbf{r}^+$ and $\mathbf{r}^-$ are optimized while keeping $\mathbf{w}$ and $\boldsymbol{\delta}$ fixed. This step determines the ranked list of labels that will be predicted by the positive and negative partitions respectively. Second, $\boldsymbol{\delta}$ is optimized while keeping $\mathbf{w}$ and $\mathbf{r}^\pm$ fixed. This step assigns training points in the node to the positive or negative partition. The third step of optimizing $\mathbf{w}$ while keeping $\boldsymbol{\delta}$ and $\mathbf{r}^\pm$ fixed is taken only if the first two steps did not lead to a decrease in the objective function. This is done to speed up training since optimizing with respect to $\boldsymbol{\delta}$ and $\mathbf{r}^\pm$ takes only seconds while optimizing with respect to $\mathbf{w}$ can take minutes. This is the primary reason why (5) was formulated as a function of $\mathbf{w}$, $\boldsymbol{\delta}$ and $\mathbf{r}^\pm$ rather than just $\mathbf{w}$. The algorithm terminates when $\mathbf{r}^\pm$, $\boldsymbol{\delta}$ and $\mathbf{w}$ do not change from one iteration to the next. We prove that the objective decreases strictly in each iteration and that the proposed algorithm terminates in a finite number of iterations. In practice, it was observed on all data sets that the algorithm made rapid progress and yielded state-of-the-art results as soon as a single update to $\mathbf{w}$ had been made. We now detail the steps in each iteration.

4.1 Optimizing with respect to $\mathbf{r}^\pm$

Given $\mathbf{w}$ and $\boldsymbol{\delta}$, the first step in each iteration is to find the optimal rankings $\mathbf{r}^+$ and $\mathbf{r}^-$ that will be predicted by the positive and negative partition respectively. Fixing $\mathbf{w}$ and $\boldsymbol{\delta}$ simplifies (5) to

$$\max_{\mathbf{r}^\pm \in \Pi(1,L)} C_r \sum_i \tfrac{1}{2}(1+\delta_i)\mathcal{L}_{\text{nDCG@}L}(\mathbf{r}^+, \mathbf{y}_i) + C_r \sum_i \tfrac{1}{2}(1-\delta_i)\mathcal{L}_{\text{nDCG@}L}(\mathbf{r}^-, \mathbf{y}_i) \tag{7}$$

which can be compactly expressed as two independent optimization problems

$$\max_{\mathbf{r}^\pm \in \Pi(1,L)} \sum_{i:\delta_i=\pm 1} I_L(\mathbf{y}_i) \sum_{l=1}^{L} \frac{y_{i r_l^\pm}}{\log(1+l)} \tag{8}$$

$$\equiv \max_{\mathbf{r}^{\pm}\in\Pi(1,L)} \sum_{l=1}^{L} \sum_{i:\delta_i=\pm 1} \frac{I_L(\mathbf{y}_i) y_{il}}{\log(1+r_l^{\pm})} \quad (9)$$

$$\equiv \max_{\mathbf{r}^{\pm}\in\Pi(1,L)} \left(\sum_{i:\delta_i=\pm 1} I_L(\mathbf{y}_i)\mathbf{y}_i \right)^\top \mathbf{d}^{\pm} \quad (10)$$

where $\mathbf{d}^{\pm}$ is an L-vector such that $d_l^{\pm} = 1/\log(1+r_l^{\pm})$. Since $\mathbf{r}^+$ and $\mathbf{r}^-$ are permutations of $1, 2, \ldots, L$ it is clear that (10) will be maximized if $r_l^{\pm}$ is chosen as the index of the lth largest value in the vector $\sum_{i:\delta_i=\pm 1} I_L(\mathbf{y}_i)\mathbf{y}_i$. Thus

$$\mathbf{r}^{\pm^*} = \text{rank}_L \left(\sum_{i:\delta_i=\pm 1} I_L(\mathbf{y}_i)\mathbf{y}_i \right). \quad (11)$$

Note that the optimal values of $\mathbf{r}^{\pm}$ can be computed efficiently in time $O(n \log L + \hat{L} \log \hat{L})$ where n is the number of training points present in the node being partitioned, $\hat{L}$ is the sparsity of the vector $\sum_i I_L(\mathbf{y}_i)\mathbf{y}_i$ and it is assumed that $\mathbf{y}_i$ is $\log L$-sparse.

4.2 Optimizing with respect to δ

The next step in an iteration is to optimize (5) with respect to $\boldsymbol{\delta}$ while keeping $\mathbf{w}$ and $\mathbf{r}^{\pm}$ fixed. This reduces to

$$\begin{aligned} \min_{\delta\in\{-1,+1\}^L} \quad & \sum_i C_\delta(\delta_i) \log(1+e^{-\delta_i \mathbf{w}^\top \mathbf{x}_i}) \\ & - C_r \sum_i \tfrac{1}{2}(1+\delta_i)\mathcal{L}_{\text{nDCG@}L}(\mathbf{r}^+, \mathbf{y}_i) \quad (12) \\ & - C_r \sum_i \tfrac{1}{2}(1-\delta_i)\mathcal{L}_{\text{nDCG@}L}(\mathbf{r}^-, \mathbf{y}_i) \end{aligned}$$

which decomposes over i. Thus, each δ_i can be optimized independently by seeing whether (12) is optimized by $\delta_i^* = +1$ or -1. This yields

$$\delta_i^* = \text{sign}(v_i^- - v_i^+) \quad \text{where} \quad (13)$$

$$v_i^{\pm} = C_\delta(\pm 1) \log(1+e^{\mp \mathbf{w}^\top \mathbf{x}_i}) - C_r I_L(\mathbf{y}_i) \sum_{l=1}^{L} \frac{y_{ir_l^{\pm}}}{\log(1+l)}$$

The time complexity of obtaining $\boldsymbol{\delta}^*$ is $O(n\hat{D} + n\log L)$ assuming that the feature vectors are $\hat{D}$-sparse and the label vectors are $\log L$-sparse. This reduces to $O(n \log L)$ since $\mathbf{w} = \mathbf{0}$ in the first iteration and $\mathbf{w}^\top \mathbf{x}_i$ can be cached for all points in subsequent updates of $\mathbf{w}$.

4.3 Optimizing with respect to w

The final step of optimizing (5) with respect to $\mathbf{w}$ while keeping $\boldsymbol{\delta}$ and $\mathbf{r}^{\pm}$ fixed is carried out only if the first two steps did not make any progress in decreasing the objective function. This can be efficiently determined in time $O(n)$ by checking that $\boldsymbol{\delta}$ has remained unchanged. Optimizing (5) with respect to $\mathbf{w}$ while keeping $\boldsymbol{\delta}$ and $\mathbf{r}^{\pm}$ fixed is equivalent to solving the standard ℓ_1 regularized logistic regression problem with the labels given by $\boldsymbol{\delta}$

$$\min_{\mathbf{w}\in\mathcal{R}^D} \quad \|\mathbf{w}\|_1 + \sum_i C_\delta(\delta_i) \log(1+e^{-\delta_i \mathbf{w}^\top \mathbf{x}_i}) \quad (14)$$

This problem has been extensively studied in the literature [3,24,37]. FastXML optimizes (14) using the newGLMNET algorithm [37] as implemented in the Liblinear package [14]. No tuning of the learning rate parameter is required since (14) is optimized in the dual. The algorithm is terminated after 10 passes over the training set in case it hasn't converged already. The overall time complexity of the method is $O(n\hat{D})$ where n is the number of training points in the node being partitioned and $\hat{D}$ is the average number of non-zero entries in a feature vector. This is the most time consuming of the three steps.

4.4 Finite termination

The formulation in (5) is non-convex, non-smooth and has a mix of discrete and continuous variables. Furthermore, even the sub-problems obtained by optimizing with respect to only one block of variables might not be convex or smooth. It is well recognized that alternating minimization based techniques can fail to converge for such hard problems in general [6]. However, in our case, it is straightforward to show that FastXML's alternating minimization algorithm for optimizing (5) will not oscillate and will converge in a finite number of iterations.

THEOREM 1. *Suppose Algorithm 2 has not yet terminated and let* $\mathcal{W} = \langle \mathcal{W}_1, \mathcal{W}_2, \ldots, \mathcal{W}_i, \ldots \rangle$ *be the sequence of iterations at which* $\mathbf{w}$ *is updated. Let* $\overline{\mathcal{W}_i} = \mathcal{W} - \mathcal{W}_i$ *be the sequence obtained by removing* $\mathcal{W}_i$ *from* $\mathcal{W}$. *Furthermore, let* $\mathcal{W}_i \leq t < \mathcal{W}_{i+1}$. *Then (a)* $\boldsymbol{\delta}[\mathcal{W}_i] \notin \{\boldsymbol{\delta}[\mathcal{W}_j] | \mathcal{W}_j \in \overline{\mathcal{W}_i}\}$; *and (b)* $\boldsymbol{\delta}[t] \notin \{\boldsymbol{\delta}[j] | \mathcal{W}_i \leq j \neq t < \mathcal{W}_{i+1}\}$.

PROOF. Let the objective value in (5), after iteration i, be $O[i]$. The individual sub-problems (10,12,14), that comprise a single iteration of 2, are all minimization problems, which minimize (5) w.r.t a single block of variables, and hence can never increase the objective value. In addition, algorithm 2 also ensures that any change in $\boldsymbol{\delta}$ is accompanied by a non-zero decrease in the objective.

(a) Let $\mathcal{W}_i$ be the iteration at which $\mathbf{w}$ is updated for the ith time. The algorithm ensures that, when $\boldsymbol{\delta} = \boldsymbol{\delta}[\mathcal{W}_i]$, $\mathbf{w}[\mathcal{W}_i]$ is the minimizer of (14), and $\mathbf{r}^{\pm}[\mathcal{W}_i]$ is the minimizer of (10), which together imply that $O[\mathcal{W}_i]$ is the unique minimum value of (5) when optimized over $\mathbf{w}, \mathbf{r}^{\pm}$, while fixing $\boldsymbol{\delta} = \boldsymbol{\delta}[\mathcal{W}_i]$.
Hence, for a given $\mathcal{W}_i$ and a $\mathcal{W}_j \in \overline{\mathcal{W}_i}$

$$(\boldsymbol{\delta}[\mathcal{W}_i] = \boldsymbol{\delta}[\mathcal{W}_j]) \implies (O[\mathcal{W}_i] = O[\mathcal{W}_j]) \quad (15)$$

Without loss of generality, let $\mathcal{W}_i < \mathcal{W}_j$. Since by assumption, the algorithm has not yet terminated, $\boldsymbol{\delta}[\mathcal{W}_i] \neq \boldsymbol{\delta}[\mathcal{W}_{(i+1)}]$. But, since there has been an update to $\boldsymbol{\delta}$, $O[\mathcal{W}_i] > O[\mathcal{W}_{(i+1)}] \geq O[\mathcal{W}_j]$. This, combined with (15) gives us $\boldsymbol{\delta}[\mathcal{W}_i] \neq \boldsymbol{\delta}[\mathcal{W}_j]$.

(b) Let $u \in \{j : \mathcal{W}_i \leq j \neq t \leq \mathcal{W}_{i+1}\}$. Without loss of generality, assume $t < u$. Since we are between two $\mathbf{w}$ updates, $\mathbf{w}[t] = \mathbf{w}[u]$. If $\boldsymbol{\delta}[t] = \boldsymbol{\delta}[u]$, then using $\mathbf{w}[t] = \mathbf{w}[u]$, we essentially solve the same optimization w.r.t $\mathbf{r}^{\pm}$ and $\boldsymbol{\delta}$ in steps $t+1$ and $u+1$. Hence, $O[t+1] = O[u+1]$. But, absence of $\mathbf{w}$ updates imply that $\boldsymbol{\delta}[t+1] \neq \boldsymbol{\delta}[t+2]$, which further implies $O[t+1] > O[t+2] \geq O[u+1]$, contradicting the earlier equality. Hence, $\boldsymbol{\delta}[t] \neq \boldsymbol{\delta}[u]$. □

Theorem 1 (b) states that $\boldsymbol{\delta}$ cannot repeat between two consecutive updates to $\mathbf{w}$ (in iterations $\mathcal{W}_i$ and $\mathcal{W}_{i+1}$). Since $\boldsymbol{\delta}$ can only take a finite number of values, this implies the number of iterations between $\mathcal{W}_i$ and $\mathcal{W}_{i+1}$ is bounded. Similarly, Theorem 1(a) states that $\boldsymbol{\delta}[\mathcal{W}_i]$ can never repeat for values $\mathcal{W}_j \in \mathcal{W}$. By a similar argument as above and Theorem 1(b), we conclude that $\mathcal{W}_i$ is bounded for all i. Thus, the proposed alternating minimization algorithm cannot oscillate and terminates in a finite number of iterations.

Table 1: Data set statistics

Data set	Train N	Features D	Labels L	Test M	Avg. labels per pt.	Avg. pts per label
BibTeX	4880	1836	159	2515	2.40	111.71
Delicious	12920	500	983	3185	19.02	311.61
MediaMill	30993	120	101	12914	4.38	1902.16
RCV1-X	781265	47236	2456	23149	4.61	1510.13
WikiLSHTC	1892600	1617899	325056	472835	3.26	23.74
Ads-430K	1118084	87890	434594	502926	2.10	7.86
Ads-1M	3917928	164592	1082898	1563137	1.96	7.07

Table 2: Results on small and medium data sets. FastXML was run with default hyper-parameter settings on all data sets. FastXML-T presents results when the parameters were tuned.

(a) BibTeX $N = 4.8K, D = 1.8K, L = 159$

Algorithm	P1 (%)	P3 (%)	P5 (%)
FastXML-T	**64.53 ± 0.72**	**40.17 ± 0.63**	**29.27 ± 0.53**
FastXML	63.26 ± 0.84	39.19 ± 0.66	28.72 ± 0.48
MLRF	62.81 ± 0.84	38.74 ± 0.69	28.45 ± 0.43
LPSR	62.95 ± 0.70	39.16 ± 0.64	28.75 ± 0.45
1-vs-All	63.39 ± 0.64	39.55 ± 0.65	29.13 ± 0.45

(b) Delicious $N = 13K, D = 500K, L = 983$

Algorithm	P1 (%)	P3 (%)	P5 (%)
FastXML	**69.65 ± 0.82**	**63.93 ± 0.50**	**59.36 ± 0.57**
MLRF	67.86 ± 0.70	62.02 ± 0.55	57.59 ± 0.43
LPSR	65.55 ± 0.99	59.39 ± 0.48	53.99 ± 0.31
1-vs-All	65.42 ± 1.05	59.34 ± 0.56	53.72 ± 0.50

(c) MediaMill $N = 30K, D = 120, L = 101$

Algorithm	P1 (%)	P3 (%)	P5 (%)
FastXML	**87.35 ± 0.27**	**72.14 ± 0.20**	**58.15 ± 0.15**
MLRF	86.83 ± 0.18	71.18 ± 0.19	57.09 ± 0.16
LPSR	82.33 ± 2.15	66.37 ± 0.35	50.00 ± 0.20
1-vs-All	82.31 ± 2.19	66.17 ± 0.43	50.32 ± 0.56

(d) RCV1-X $N = 781K, D = 47K, L = 2.5K$

Algorithm	P1 (%)	P3 (%)	P5 (%)
FastXML	**91.23 ± 0.22**	**73.51 ± 0.25**	**53.31 ± 0.65**
MLRF	87.66 ± 0.46	69.89 ± 0.43	50.36 ± 0.74
LPSR	90.04 ± 0.19	72.27 ± 0.20	52.34 ± 0.61
1-vs-All	90.18 ± 0.18	72.55 ± 0.16	52.68 ± 0.57

Table 3: Results on large data sets comparing the performance of FastXML to LPSR trained with Naïve Bayes as the base classifier.

(a) WikiLSHTC $N = 1.78M, D = 1.62M, L = 325K$

Algorithm	P1 (%)	P3 (%)	P5 (%)	Train Time (hr)	Test Time (min)
FastXML	**49.78**	**33.06**	**24.40**	9.14	5.10
LPSR-NB	27.91	16.04	11.57	**1.59**	**3.52**

(b) Ads-430K $N = 1.12M, D = 88K, L = 0.43M$

Algorithm	P1 (%)	P3 (%)	P5 (%)	Train Time (hr)	Test Time (min)
FastXML	**27.24**	**16.28**	**11.91**	1.81	**1.68**
LPSR-NB	19.69	12.71	9.70	**0.84**	3.95

(c) Ads-1M $N = 3.91M, D = 165K, L = 1.08M$

Algorithm	P1 (%)	P3 (%)	P5 (%)	Train Time (hr)	Test Time (min)
FastXML	**23.45**	**14.21**	**10.41**	8.09	**6.26**
LPSR-NB	17.08	11.38	8.83	**3.78**	19.32

Table 4: FastXML's wall clock training time (in hours) vs the number of cores used on a single machine.

Cores	WikiLSHTC (hr)	Ads-430K (hr)	Ads-1M (hr)
1	16.80 (1.00×)	2.46 (1.00×)	12.34 (1.00×)
2	8.62 (1.94×)	1.24 (1.98×)	7.09 (1.74×)
4	4.53 (3.71×)	0.62 (3.97×)	3.93 (3.13×)
8	2.21 (7.60×)	0.33 (7.45×)	2.09 (5.90×)
16	1.27 (13.22×)	0.19 (12.95×)	1.02 (12.10×)

Table 5: The variation in FastXML's performance with the number of training iterations. $\mathcal{W}_i$ denotes the iteration at which $\mathbf{w}$ is updated for the ith time at the root node on the Ads-430K data set. Precision values and training times are reported for the full ensemble.

i	$\mathcal{W}_i$	Objective value	Train time (hr)	P1 (%)	P3 (%)	P5 (%)
1	15	403419.87	1.88	27.21	16.28	11.89
2	21	237151.20	3.79	27.01	16.39	12.09
3	24	183542.04	5.60	26.95	16.37	12.10
4	26	163416.65	7.33	26.98	16.38	12.11
5	29	153592.21	8.99	26.93	16.38	12.11

5. EXPERIMENTS

This Section compares the performance of FastXML to MLRF, LPSR and the 1-vs-All baseline on some of the largest multi-label classification data sets.

Data sets: Experiments were carried out on data sets with label set sizes ranging from a hundred to a million to benchmark the performance of FastXML in various regimes. The data sets include two small scale data sets with hundreds of labels, BibTeX [23] and MediaMill [28], two medium scale data sets with thousands of labels, Delicious [30] and RCV1-X, and three large scale data sets with up to a million labels, WikiLSHTC [1], Ads430K and Ads1M. Table 1 lists the statistics of these data sets.

Features and labels are publically available for all the data sets, apart from the two proprietary Ads data sets, and were used in the experiments. WikiLSHTC is a challenge data set for which the test set has not been released and we therefore partitioned the data provided into 75% for training and 25% for testing. The RCV1-X data set has the same features as the original RCV1 data set but its label set has been expanded by forming new labels from pairs of original labels. The two proprietary Ads data sets comprise of bag of words TF-IDF features extracted from expansions of queries from the Bing query logs. Other queries similar to a given query are used as labels for that query.

Table 6: FastXML learns more stable and balanced trees than MLRF and LPSR leading to both faster training as well as faster prediction. Tree balance is measured as $H/\log(N/\text{MaxLeaf})$, where H is the average length of the path traversed by a point in that tree and $\log(N/\text{MaxLeaf})$ is the average length of a path traversed in a perfectly balanced tree with at most MaxLeaf points at each leaf node. Smaller values of tree balance are better with a balance of 1 indicating a perfectly balanced tree.

Data set	Tree Balance: $\frac{H}{log(N/MaxLeaf)}$ FastXML	MLRF	LPSR	Avg. labels per leaf for FastXML
BibTeX	**1.02 ± 0.01**	3.45 ± 0.01	1.56 ± 0.11	6.15
Delicious	**1.03 ± 0.01**	4.95 ± 0.01	3.14 ± 0.71	69.12
MediaMill	**1.01 ± 0.01**	1.59 ± 0.01	1.06 ± 0.01	10.26
RCV1-X	**1.02 ± 0.01**	5.62 ± 0.15	1.32 ± 0.02	18.73
WikiLSHTC	**1.01 ± 0.01**	-	3.69 ± 0.01	13.36
Ads-430K	**1.00 ± 0.01**	-	94.71 ± 0.01	10.97
Ads-1M	**1.00 ± 0.01**	-	105.83 ± 0.01	11.03

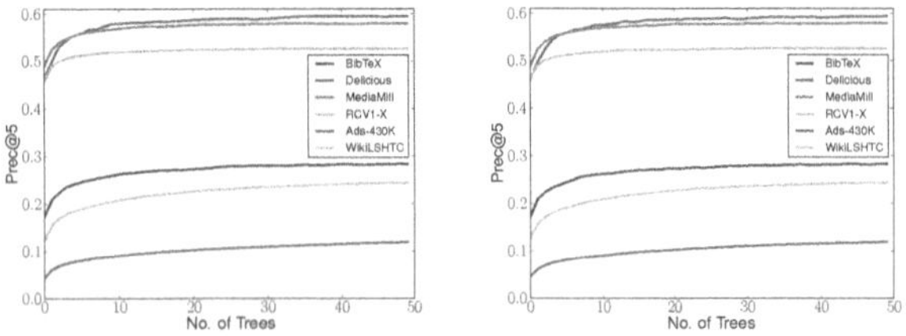

(a) Random order (b) Forward sequential

Figure 1: The variation in FastXML's precision at 5 with the number of trees selected according to (1a) random order; and (1b) highest individual prediction accuracy on the training set. The training time can be halved on most data sets with a minimal decrease in prediction accuracy by training only 25 trees in random order.

Results are reported by averaging over ten random train and test splits for the small and medium data sets apart from RCV1-X for which only 3 splits were used. A single split was used for the large data sets.

Baseline algorithms: FastXML was compared to state-of-the-art tree based extreme multi-label methods such as MLRF and LPSR (see Section 2 for details) as well as the 1-vs-All baseline as implemented in M3L [18]. The 1-vs-All strategy was also used to learn the base classifier for LPSR on the small and medium data sets as it offered better performance as compared to other base classifiers such as Wsabie [34]. Unfortunately, M3L and Wsabie cannot be trained on the large data sets on a single desktop in a day. Naïve Bayes was therefore used as a base classifier for LPSR on these data sets.

Finally, note that we do not compare explicitly to embedding methods [4, 8, 10, 12, 15, 19, 20, 22, 29, 34, 36, 38] since none of these have been shown to consistently outperform the 1-vs-All base classifier.

Parameters: The following hyper-parameters settings were used for FastXML across all data sets: (a) Co-efficient of logistic-loss: $C_\delta = 1.0$; (b) Co-efficient of negative-nDCG loss: $C_r = 1.0$; (c) Number of trees: $T = 50$; (d) Maximum number of instances allowed in a leaf node: MaxLeaf = 10; (e) Number of labels in a leaf node whose probability scores are retained: $k = 20$; (f) Bias multiplier for Liblinear: 1.0; (g) Number of training iterations in Algorithm 2: 1; and (h) Maximum number of (outer,inner) iterations of Liblinear before termination: $(10, 10)$. Using these default settings, it was observed that FastXML could outperform LPSR, MLRF and the 1-vs-All M3L. Tuning the hyper-parameters for each data set would lead to even superior prediction accuracies. The hyper-parameters for MLRF, LPSR and M3L were set

Table 7: Results obtained by replacing the nDCG@L loss function in FastXML with others such as nDCG@5 (FastXML-nDCG5) or precision at 5 (FastXML-P5) and by replacing the Gini index in MLRF with the proposed nDCG@L loss function.

(a) BibTeX $N = 4.8K, D = 1.8K, L = 159$

Algorithm	P1 (%)	P3 (%)	P5 (%)
FastXML	**63.26 ± 0.84**	**39.19 ± 0.66**	**28.72 ± 0.48**
FastXML-P5	39.95 ± 1.09	23.01 ± 0.46	17.42 ± 0.36
FastXML-nDCG5	51.75 ± 1.28	30.87 ± 0.63	22.70 ± 0.42
MLRF-nDCG	58.41 ± 1.20	36.45 ± 0.65	26.95 ± 0.49

(b) Delicious $N = 13K, D = 500K, L = 983$

Algorithm	P1 (%)	P3 (%)	P5 (%)
FastXML	**69.65 ± 0.82**	**63.93 ± 0.50**	**59.36 ± 0.57**
FastXML-P5	60.11 ± 0.91	53.97 ± 0.53	49.81 ± 0.58
FastXML-nDCG5	64.96 ± 0.83	59.28 ± 0.69	54.70 ± 0.56
MLRF-nDCG	66.70 ± 0.75	61.08 ± 0.44	56.72 ± 0.44

(c) MediaMill $N = 30K, D = 120, L = 101$

Algorithm	P1 (%)	P3 (%)	P5 (%)
FastXML	**87.35 ± 0.27**	**72.14 ± 0.20**	**58.15 ± 0.15**
FastXML-P5	80.73 ± 0.29	67.48 ± 0.22	54.11 ± 0.20
FastXML-nDCG5	86.66 ± 0.27	70.81 ± 0.21	56.51 ± 0.20
MLRF-nDCG	86.67 ± 0.26	71.13 ± 0.22	57.24 ± 0.21

(d) RCV1-X $N = 781K, D = 47K, L = 2.5K$

Algorithm	P1 (%)	P3 (%)	P5 (%)
FastXML	**91.23 ± 0.22**	**73.51 ± 0.25**	**53.31 ± 0.65**
FastXML-P5	66.62 ± 0.23	56.41 ± 0.40	40.83 ± 0.14
FastXML-nDCG5	75.60 ± 0.39	60.85 ± 0.43	43.98 ± 0.16
MLRF-nDCG	87.19 ± 0.41	69.69 ± 0.46	50.25 ± 0.56

(e) WikiLSHTC $N = 1.78M, D = 1.62M, L = 325K$

Algorithm	P1 (%)	P3 (%)	P5 (%)
FastXML	**49.78**	**33.06**	**24.40**
FastXML-P5	18.74	12.33	8.71
FastXML-nDCG5	20.50	12.51	8.80

(f) Ads-430K $N = 1.12M, D = 88K, L = 0.43M$

Algorithm	P1 (%)	P3 (%)	P5 (%)
FastXML	**27.24**	**16.28**	**11.91**
FastXML-P5	25.06	14.36	10.27
FastXML-nDCG5	24.93	14.34	10.29

(g) Ads-1M $N = 3.91M, D = 165K, L = 1.08M$

Algorithm	P1 (%)	P3 (%)	P5 (%)
FastXML	**23.45**	**14.21**	**10.41**
FastXML-P5	21.09	12.32	8.87
FastXML-nDCG5	21.25	12.47	9.01

using fine grained validation on each data set so as to achieve the highest possible prediction accuracy for each method.

Evaluation Metrics: Extreme multi-label classification data sets exhibit positive label sparsity in that each data point has only a few positive labels associated with it. It therefore becomes important to focus on the accurate prediction of the few positive labels per data point than on the vast number of negative ones. As such, most papers [2, 19, 22, 34–36] evaluate prediction accuracy using precision at k which counts the number of correct predictions in the top k positive predictions. More formally, the precision at k for a prediction $\hat{\mathbf{y}} \in \mathcal{R}^L$ given the ground truth label vector $\mathbf{y} \in \{0,1\}^L$ is defined as

$$\mathrm{P}k(\hat{\mathbf{y}}, \mathbf{y}) = \frac{1}{k} \sum_{i \in \mathrm{rank}_k(\hat{\mathbf{y}})} \mathbf{y}_i. \quad (16)$$

All experiments were carried out on a single core of an Intel Core 2 Duo machine running at 3.3 GHz with 8 Gb of RAM. Training times were measured using the `clock` function available in C++. Parallelization experiments in Table 4 were carried out on multiple cores of Intel Xeon processors running at 2.1 GHz.

Results on small and medium data sets: Table 2 benchmarks the performance of FastXML on the small and medium data sets where accurate MLRF, LPSR and 1-vs-All models could be learnt. The focus is on prediction accuracy as neither training nor prediction present any challenge on these data sets – even the expensive MLRF, LPSR and 1-vs-All can be trained in seconds on BibTeX and Delicious, in minutes on MediaMill and in two hours on RCV1-X.

As compared to LPSR and 1-vs-All, FastXML could be up to 5% more accurate in terms of precision at 1 and up to 8% in terms of precision at 5. Large improvements were obtained on both Delicious and MediaMill. The smallest improvements were obtained on BibTeX which had less than five thousand training points. FastXML with default parameter settings gave more or less the same P1 as LPSR and 1-vs-All on BibTeX. A marginal improvement of 1% over the other methods could be obtained by tuning FastXML's hyper-parameters (referred to as FastXML-T in Table 2). FastXML's gains over MLRF were smaller as compared to the gains over LPSR and 1-vs-All but could still go up to 3% in terms of both precision at 1 and at 5 (on RCV1-X). All in all, these results indicate that FastXML could be significantly more accurate at prediction than highly tuned MLRF, LPSR and 1-vs-All classifiers.

Results on large data sets: Extreme classification is most concerned with large scale data sets having hundreds of thousands or even millions of labels. Training MLRF and 1-vs-All on such data sets was found to be infeasible without using a large cluster. LPSR training could be made tractable on a single core by replacing the 1-vs-All base classifier with Naïve Bayes. Table 3 compares the performance of FastXML to LPSR-NB. FastXML's improvements over LPSR-NB in terms of P1 ranged from 5% on Ads-1M to almost 22% on WikiLSHTC and in terms of P5 ranged from approximately 1.5% on Ads-1M to almost 13% on WikiLSHTC. FastXML could train in 1.81 hours on Ads-430K using a single core and in 8 to 9 hours on Ads-1M and WikiLSHTC with individual trees being grown in about 10 minutes. This opens up the possibility of practitioners training accurate extreme classification models on commodity hardware. Finally, FastXML could be almost 1.5 to 3 times faster at prediction than LPSR-NB which could be a critical factor in certain applications.

Validating FastXML's hyper-parameter settings and design choices: Table 4 lists the reduction in wall clock training time obtained by growing FastXML's trees in parallel across multiple cores on a single machine. Training could be speeded up 12 to 13 times by utilizing 16 cores demonstrating that FastXML is trivially parallelizable. The entire ensemble could be trained in approximately an hour on Ads-1M and WikiLSHTC and in 12 minutes on Ads-430K.

All the FastXML results presented so far were obtained by terminating the proposed optimization algorithm after a single update to $\mathbf{w}$. Table 5 shows the effects of allowing multiple updates to $\mathbf{w}$ while training on the Ads-430K data set. High precisions were reached after the first update to $\mathbf{w}$ which occurred after 15 updates to $\boldsymbol{\delta}$ and $\mathbf{r}$. Subsequent updates to $\mathbf{w}$, $\boldsymbol{\delta}$ and $\mathbf{r}$ yielded a significant drop in the value of the objective function but little change in prediction accuracy. As such, it would appear that training time could be significantly reduced without much loss in precision by early termination.

Table 7 reports the effects of replacing the proposed nDCG@L loss function in FastXML with others such as precision at 5 (FastXML-P5) and nDCG@5 (FastXML-nDCG5). As is evident, both these loss functions were inferior to nDCG@L even when performance was measured using precision at 5. This demonstrates that rank sensitive loss functions such as nDCG are better suited to extreme multi-label classification as compared to rank insensitive ones such as precision. Furthermore, nDCG should be computed non-myopically over all labels rather than just the top few.

Finally, the key difference in FastXML's formulation as compared to MLRF's was the use of the nDCG based loss function and the use of a linear separator to partition each node. Table 7 demonstrates that both these ingredients were necessary as simply replacing the Gini index or entropy in MLRF with the nDCG based loss function (MLRF-nDCG) yielded significantly poorer results as compared to FastXML.

6. CONCLUSIONS

This paper developed the FastXML algorithm for multi-label learning with a large number of labels. FastXML learnt an ensemble of trees with prediction costs that were logarithmic in the number of labels. The key technical contribution in FastXML was a novel node partitioning formulation which optimized an nDCG based ranking loss over all the labels. Such a loss was found to be more suitable for extreme multi-label learning than the Gini index optimized by MLRF or the clustering error optimized by LPSR. nDCG is known to be a hard loss to optimize using gradient descent based techniques. FastXML therefore developed an efficient alternating minimization algorithm for its optimization. It was proved that the proposed alternating minimization algorithm would not oscillate and would converge in a finite number of iterations. Experiments revealed that FastXML could be significantly more accurate than MLRF and LPSR while efficiently scaling to problems with more than a million labels. The FastXML code is publically available and should enable practitioners to train accurate extreme multi-label models without needing large clusters.

Acknowledgments

We are very grateful to Purushottam Kar and Prateek Jain for helpful discussions. Yashoteja Prabhu is supported by a TCS PhD Fellowship at IIT Delhi.

7. REFERENCES

[1] Wikipedia dataset for the 4th large scale hierarchical text classification challenge. http://lshtc.iit.demokritos.gr/.

[2] R. Agrawal, A. Gupta, Y. Prabhu, and M. Varma. Multi-label learning with millions of labels: Recommending advertiser bid phrases for web pages. In *WWW*, pages 13–24, 2013.

[3] G. Andrew and J. Gao. Scalable training of L_1-regularized log-linear models. In *ICML*, pages 33–40, 2007.

[4] K. Balasubramanian and G. Lebanon. The landmark selection method for multiple output prediction. In *ICML*, 2012.

[5] S. Bengio, J. Weston, and D. Grangier. Label embedding trees for large multi-class tasks. In *NIPS*, 2010.

[6] D. Bertsekas. *Nonlinear Programming*. Athena Scientific, 1999.

[7] W. Bi and J. T.-Y. Kwok. Multilabel classification on tree- and dag-structured hierarchies. In *ICML*, 2011.

[8] W. Bi and J. T.-Y. Kwok. Efficient multi-label classification with many labels. In *ICML*, pages 405–413, 2013.

[9] N. Cesa-Bianchi, C. Gentile, and L. Zaniboni. Incremental algorithms for hierarchical classification. *JMLR*, 7, 2006.

[10] Y.-N. Chen and H.-T. Lin. Feature-aware label space dimension reduction for multi-label classification. In *NIPS*, pages 1538–1546, 2012.

[11] A. Choromanska and J. Langford. Logarithmic time online multiclass prediction. http://arxiv.org/abs/1406.1822, 2014.

[12] M. Cissé, N. Usunier, T. Artières, and P. Gallinari. Robust bloom filters for large multilabel classification tasks. In *NIPS*, pages 1851–1859, 2013.

[13] J. Deng, S. Satheesh, A. C. Berg, and F. Li. Fast and balanced: Efficient label tree learning for large scale object recognition. In *NIPS*, 2011.

[14] R.-E. Fan, K.-W. Chang, C.-J. Hsieh, X.-R. Wang, and C.-J. Lin. LIBLINEAR: A library for large linear classification. *JMLR*, 9:1871–1874, 2008.

[15] C.-S. Feng and H.-T. Lin. Multi-label classification with error-correcting codes. *JMLR*, pages 289–295, 2011.

[16] T. Gao and D. Koller. Discriminative learning of relaxed hierarchy for large-scale visual recognition. In *ICCV*, pages 2072–2079, 2011.

[17] P. Geurts, D. Ernst, and L. Wehenkel. Extremely randomized trees. *ML*, pages 3–42, 2006.

[18] B. Hariharan, S. V. N. Vishwanathan, and M. Varma. Efficient max-margin multi-label classification with applications to zero-shot learning. *ML*, 2012.

[19] D. Hsu, S. Kakade, J. Langford, and T. Zhang. Multi-label prediction via compressed sensing. In *NIPS*, 2009.

[20] S. Ji, L. Tang, S. Yu, and J. Ye. Extracting shared subspace for multi-label classification. In *KDD*, pages 381–389, 2008.

[21] C. Jose, P. Goyal, P. Aggrwal, and M. Varma. Local deep kernel learning for efficient non-linear svm prediction. In *ICML*, June 2013.

[22] A. Kapoor, R. Viswanathan, and P. Jain. Multilabel classification using bayesian compressed sensing. In *NIPS*, 2012.

[23] I. Katakis, G. Tsoumakas, and I. Vlahavas. Multilabel text classification for automated tag suggestion. In *ECML/PKDD Discovery Challenge*, 2008.

[24] K. Koh, S.-J. Kim, and S. Boyd. An interior-point method for large-scale l1-regularized logistic regression. *JMLR*, 8:1519–1555, 2007.

[25] A. Kustarev, Y. Ustinovsky, Y. Logachev, E. Grechnikov, I. Segalovich, and P. Serdyukov. Smoothing ndcg metrics using tied scores. In *CIKM*, pages 2053–2056, 2011.

[26] P. D. Ravikumar, A. Tewari, and E. Yang. On ndcg consistency of listwise ranking methods. In *AISTATS*, pages 618–626, 2011.

[27] J. Rousu, C. Saunders, S. Szedmak, and J. Shawe-Taylor. Kernel-based learning of hierarchical multilabel classification models. *JMLR*, 7, 2006.

[28] C. Snoek, M. Worring, J. van Gemert, J.-M. Geusebroek, and A. Smeulders. The challenge problem for automated detection of 101 semantic concepts in multimedia. In *ACM Multimedia*, pages 421–430, 2006.

[29] F. Tai and H.-T. Lin. Multi-label classification with principal label space transformation. In *Workshop proceedings of learning from multi-label data*, 2010.

[30] G. Tsoumakas, I. Katakis, and I. Vlahavas. Effective and efficient multilabel classification in domains with large number of labels. In *ECML/PKDD 2008 Workshop on Mining Multidimensional Data*, 2008.

[31] H. Valizadegan, R. Jin, R. Zhang, and J. Mao. Learning to rank by optimizing ndcg measure. In *SIGIR*, pages 41–48, 2000.

[32] M. N. Volkovs and R. S. Zemel. Boltzrank: Learning to maximize expected ranking gain. In *ICML*, pages 1089–1096, 2009.

[33] Y. Wang, L. Wang, Y. Li, D. He, and T.-Y. Liu. A theoretical analysis of nDCG type ranking measures. In *COLT*, pages 25–54, 2013.

[34] J. Weston, S. Bengio, and N. Usunier. Wsabie: Scaling up to large vocabulary image annotation. In *IJCAI*, 2011.

[35] J. Weston, A. Makadia, and H. Yee. Label partitioning for sublinear ranking. In *ICML*, volume 28, pages 181–189, 2013.

[36] H.-F. Yu, P. Jain, P. Kar, and I. S. Dhillon. Large-scale multi-label learning with missing labels. *ICML*, 2014.

[37] G.-X. Yuan, C.-H. Ho, and C.-J. Lin. An improved glmnet for l1-regularized logistic regression. *JMLR*, 13:1999–2030, 2012.

[38] Y. Zhang and J. G. Schneider. Multi-label output codes using canonical correlation analysis. In *AISTATS*, pages 873–882, 2011.

A Multi-class Boosting Method with Direct Optimization

Shaodan Zhai, Tian Xia, and Shaojun Wang
Kno.e.sis Center
Department of Computer Science and Engineering
Wright State University
{zhai.6,xia.7,shaojun.wang}@wright.edu

ABSTRACT

We present a direct multi-class boosting (DMCBoost) method for classification with the following properties: (i) instead of reducing the multi-class classification task to a set of binary classification tasks, DMCBoost *directly* solves the multi-class classification problem, and only requires very weak base classifiers; (ii) DMCBoost builds an ensemble classifier by *directly* optimizing the non-convex performance measures, including the empirical classification error and margin functions, without resorting to any upper bounds or approximations. As a non-convex optimization method, DMCBoost shows competitive or better results than state-of-the-art convex relaxation boosting methods, and it performs especially well on the noisy cases.

Categories and Subject Descriptors

I.2 [**Artificial Intelligence**]: Learning

Keywords

Classification; supervised learning; boosting; direct optimization; noise tolerance

1. INTRODUCTION

Boosting is a machine learning and data mining approach [34] that combines a set of weak classifiers to produce a single strong classifier. Most boosting methods were designed for binary classification tasks, while many real-world applications involve multiple classes, such as handwritten digit recognition, image segmentation, and automatic speech recognition. To effectively extend well-studied binary boosting algorithms to solve multi-class problems is still an ongoing research topic.

Multi-class boosting methods can be roughly divided into two categories. The first is to reduce the multi-class problem to multiple binary classification problems. Methods in this category include "one-vs-all", "all-vs-all", and other general output coding based approaches [2, 8, 10, 12, 13, 17, 18, 27]. Binary classification is well-studied, but there are some problems with the binary reduction, including (i) it may produce imbalanced data distributions, which are known to have a negative effect on the classifier performance [30, 16], (ii) a lack of guarantees of an optimal joint predictor [25], or (iii) using binary boosting scores that do not represent true class probabilities [21].

The second category is to build a multi-class classifier directly by using multi-class base classifiers, such as decision trees. Boosting methods of this category include AdaBoost.M1, SAMME, AdaBoost.MM, GD-MCBoost, et al. [10, 22, 25, 36, 37]. Usually, these methods require strong base classifiers which substantially increase complexity and have a high potential for overfitting [25]. Moreover, all of these methods formulate multi-class tasks as a convex optimization problem by using surrogates, and it has been shown that all boosting algorithms based on convex optimization are susceptible to random classification noise [19]. In addition, none are designed to directly maximize the multi-class margin, although some of them have the effects of margin enforcing.

In this paper, we introduce a new direct multi-class boosting algorithm named DMCBoost that extends the work of DirectBoost in [35] from binary classification to multi-class classification. DMCBoost uses multi-class decision trees as base classifiers to build an ensemble classifier by directly optimizing the performance measures, without reducing them to binary classification problems. The process of DMCBoost includes two phases: it first directly minimizes the empirical classification error by iteratively adding base classifiers to the ensemble classifier. Once the classification error reaches a coordinatewise local minimum[1], it continuously adds base classifiers by directly maximizing the average margin of a certain set of bottom samples.

Both DMCBoost and DirectBoost [35] can be viewed as a coordinate optimization in the hypothesis space, and in each iteration only one coordinate is chosen and the corresponding parameter is computed by line search approaches. However, DMCBoost is a non-trivial extension of DirectBoost in [35] to multi-class classification, where we have to mathematically re-formulate the multi-class classification problem and identify the scenarios that lead to efficient computation of the empirical error of a weak classifier in the first phase, and identify the scenarios that lead to efficient computation of the margin curve of a weak classifier in the second phase. Thus DMCBoost uses very different optimization

[1]See the definition of coordinatewise minimum/maximum on page 479 in [31].

KDD'14, August 24–27, 2014, New York, NY, USA.

http://dx.doi.org/10.1145/2623330.2623689.

techniques: since the objectives are more complex and more difficult to optimize, we propose new efficient line search algorithms that can find the parameter with the optimal objective value along one coordinate; moreover, constructing decision trees for DMCBoost is more challenging, while it is straightforward in [35].

DMCBoost is a non-convex optimization method. In general, non-convex problems are very difficult to solve. However, for the special 0-1 loss minimization and margin maximization problems, we propose efficient algorithms to find a local optima. In many real applications, it is possible that the local optima of non-convex optimization is less serious than the inconsistencies [20]. The computational cost of DMCBoost is K times larger than the computational cost of AdaBoost.M1 and SAMME, where K is the number of classes. Nevertheless, we will show that DMCBoost performs better than the convex relaxation algorithms such as AdaBoost.M1, SAMME, AdaBoost.MH, and GD-MCBoost in terms of accuracy under a bearable time limitation on a number of UCI datasets and it is more robust in noisy cases. Furthemore, DMCBoost only requires very weak base classifiers, and it is more efficient in driving down the empirical classification error than other multi-class boosting algorithms when the same depth trees are used as weak learners, as shown in our experimental results.

2. DMCBOOST ALGORITHM

In a multi-class classification, we want to predict the labels of examples lying in an instance space $\mathcal{X}$. Let $\mathcal{D}$ denote a distribution over $\mathcal{X} \times \mathcal{Y}$, where $\mathcal{Y} = \{1, \cdots, K\}$ be the set of all the labels. We are provided a training set of labeled examples $\mathcal{S} = \{(x_1, y_1), \cdots, (x_n, y_n)\}$, where each example $x_i \in \mathcal{X}$ has a unique label y_i in the set $\mathcal{Y}$. Denoting $\mathcal{H} = \{h_1, ..., h_{|\mathcal{H}|}\}$ as the set of all possible weak classifiers that can be produced by the weak learning algorithm, where a weak classifier $h_j \in \mathcal{H}$ is a mapping from an instance space $\mathcal{X}$ to $\mathcal{Y}$.

Boosting combines weak classifiers to form a highly accurate ensemble classifier for multi-class classification by making a prediction according to the weighted plurality vote of the classifiers:

$$F(x) \quad = \quad \arg\max_{y \in \{1, \cdots, K\}} f(x, y), \tag{1}$$

where $f(x, y) = \sum_{h \in \mathcal{H}} \alpha_h 1(h(x) = y), \alpha_h \in \mathbb{R}$ is the inference function which is used to infer the predicted label, and $1(\cdot)$ is the indicator function. Our goal is to find an ensemble classifier F that generalizes well on any unseen dataset in $\mathcal{X}$. To this end, we design a boosting approach through the following two phases: we first directly minimize the 0-1 loss on training data, and then directly maximize the average margin of a certain set of bottom samples. Phase I, which is very efficient in minimizing the empirical 0-1 loss, serves as an initialization method of phase II. The motivation is that phase II often performs better when it starts with a low training error. In phase II, a margin objective is optimized, which leads to a further improvement of generalization.

2.1 Phase I: Minimizing Multi-class Classification Errors

In multi-class classification, the empirical error is given by

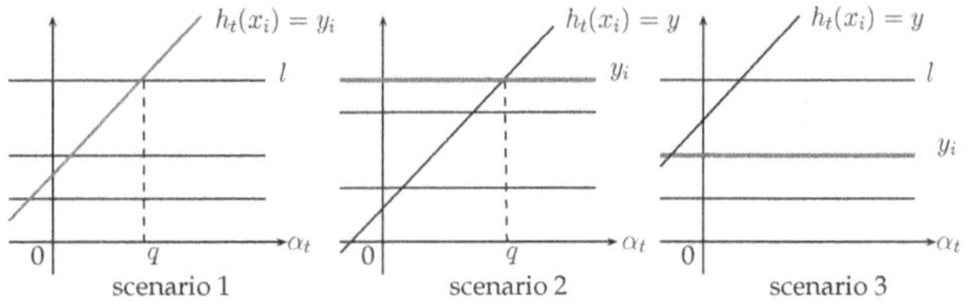

Figure 1: Three scenarios to compute the empirical error of a weak learner h_t over an example pair (x_i, y_i), where l denotes the incorrect label with the highest score, and q denotes the intersection point that results in an empirical error change. The red bold line for each scenario represents the inference function of example x_i and its true label y_i.

Algorithm 1 0-1 loss minimization algorithm.

1: **Initialize:** $t = 0$
2: **repeat**
3: $\quad t \leftarrow t + 1$.
4: $\quad$Select a weak classifier h_t by Algorithm 1.2.
5: $\quad$Get the interval that has the minimum classification error by calling Algorithm 1.1 with h_t, and let α_t be the value within this interval.
6: $\quad$Update: $f_t(x_i, y) = f_{t-1}(x_i, y) + \alpha_t 1(h_t(x_i) = y)$.
7: **until** the training error reaches the local coordinatewise minimum.
8: **Output:** $f_t(x_i, y)$.

$$\text{error}(F, \mathcal{S}) = \frac{1}{n} \sum_{i=1}^{n} 1(F(x_i) \neq y_i) \tag{2}$$

Due to the nonconvexity, nondifferentiability, and discontinuity of the classification error function (2), many previous multi-class boosting algorithms optimize the convex upper bounds of (2). While the convex surrogate losses are computationally efficient to globally optimize [3], they are sensitive to outliers [19, 23] and inconsistent under some conditions [20]. In contrast, our approach is to directly optimize 0-1 loss (2).

We use a greedy coordinate descent algorithm to directly minimize the empirical error (2) by constructing an ensemble classifier. Consider the tth iteration, the inference function is $f_t(x, y) = \sum_{k=1}^{t} \alpha_k 1(h_k(x) = y)$, $\forall y \in \mathcal{Y}$, where previous $t-1$ weak classifiers $h_k(x)$ and corresponding weights α_k, $k = 1, \cdots, t-1$ have been selected and determined, and our goal is to select a weak classifier h_t and its weight α_t such that (2) is minimized. Algorithm 1 outlines the greedy coordinate descent algorithm that sequentially minimizes 0-1 loss of (2), we will introduce the line search algorithm and the weak learning algorithm later. On each round, we first select a weak classifier h_t by Algorithm 1.2 (line 4), then the 0-1 loss (2) is a stepwise function w.r.t α_t. Next we can compute the interval that has the minimum classification error by using the line search algorithm (Algorithm 1.1) along the h_t coordinate. Since any value of α_t within this interval will lead to the largest error reduction, we can simply choose the middle point of the interval (line 5). In the end of each iteration, the inference function is updated (line 6). We repeat this procedure until the training error reaches a local coordinatewise minimum (line 7).

Algorithm 1.1 Line search algorithm to find the interval with the minimum 0-1 loss.

1: **Input:** a weak classifier $h_t \in \mathcal{H}$.
2: Let $\mathbf{e} : \mathbb{R} \to \mathbb{Q}$. ▷ $\mathbf{e}$ map intersection points to error updates.
3: **for** $i = 1, \cdots, n$ **do**
4:   **if** $h_t(x_i) = y_i$ **then** ▷ scenario 1
5:     $q = a(x_i, l) - a(x_i, y_i)$.
6:     $error\_update = -1$.
7:   **else if** $h_t(x_i) = y$, $y \neq y_i$, and $a(x_i, y_i) > a(x_i, y)$ **then** ▷ scenario 2
8:     $q = a(x_i, y) - a(x_i, y_i)$.
9:     $error\_update = 1$.
10:   **end if**
11:   $\mathbf{e}[q] = \mathbf{e}[q] + error\_update$. ▷ $\mathbf{e}[q] = 0$ if q is not in $\mathbf{e}$
12: **end for**
13: Sort $\mathbf{e}$ by the *keys* in an increasing order.
14: Incrementally calculate classification error on each interval.
15: **Output:** the interval with minimum 0-1 loss.

Algorithm 1.2 Constructing tree algorithm.

1: **Input:** a training set $\mathcal{S}$, current tree depth dep.
2: Let $dep \leftarrow dep + 1$.
3: **if** $dep \leq max\_dep$ **then**
4:   **for** a binary split **do**
5:     Split $\mathcal{S}$ into $\mathcal{S}_{left}$ and $\mathcal{S}_{right}$.
6:     **if** $|\mathcal{S}_{left}| = 0$ or $|\mathcal{S}_{right}| = 0$ **then** continue.
7:     $\ell_{left} = \arg\min_{\ell \in 1, \cdots, K} \{$0-1 loss that compute by Algorithm 1.1, while setting the input $h_t(x) = \ell$ if $x \in \mathcal{S}_{left}\}$.
8:     Let $h_t(x) = \ell_{left}$ if $x \in \mathcal{S}_{left}$.
9:     $\ell_{right} = \arg\min_{\ell \in 1, \cdots, K} \{$0-1 loss that compute by Algorithm 1.1, while setting the input $h_t(x) = \ell$ if $x \in \mathcal{S}_{right}\}$.
10:     Let $h_t(x) = \ell_{right}$ if $x \in \mathcal{S}_{right}$.
11:   **end for**
12: **end if**
13: Choose the optimal binary split which splits $\mathcal{S}$ into $\mathcal{S}^*_{left}$ and $\mathcal{S}^*_{right}$ with the corresponding ℓ^*_{left} and ℓ^*_{right}.
14: Let $h_t(x) = \ell^*_{left}$ if $x \in \mathcal{S}^*_{left}$, and $h_t(x) = \ell^*_{right}$ if $x \in \mathcal{S}^*_{right}$.
15: Call constructing tree algorithm with input $\mathcal{S}^*_{left}$ and $dep + 1$.
16: Call constructing tree algorithm with input $\mathcal{S}^*_{right}$ and $dep + 1$.
17: **Output:** a weak classifier $h_t \in \mathcal{H}$.

The line search algorithm describes how to find the optimal value of α for any given hypothesis $h \in \mathcal{H}$ such that (2) is minimized. The key idea is how to find the points that lead the 0-1 loss changes efficiently. Let $a(x_i, y) = \sum_{k=1}^{t-1} \alpha_k 1(h_k(x) = y)$, then let the inference functions for example x_i be

$$f_t(x_i, y) = a(x_i, y) + \alpha_t 1(h_t(x) = y), \qquad (3)$$

which is a linear function of α_t with intercept $a(x_i, y)$ and slope $1(h_k(x) = y)$. Obviously, the inference function is either a line with slope 1 or a horizontal line. The inference functions are used to compute the empirical error (2). More specifically, given a weak learner $h_t \in \mathcal{H}$, for each example pair (x_i, y_i), there are 3 scenarios to compute the empirical error, see Figure 1. Scenario 1 is the case that $h_t(x_i) = y_i$. $f_t(x_i, y_i)$ is a line with slope 1, and assume that $l = \arg\max_{y \in \mathcal{Y}, y \neq y_i} a(x_i, y)$, then $f_t(x_i, l)$ is a line with slope 0. The intersection of $f_t(x_i, y_i)$ and $f_t(x_i, l)$ is at $\alpha_t = a(x_i, l) - a(x_i, y_i)$. Thus when α_t is set on the left side of the intersection point, there is an error for example x_i, otherwise there is no error. Scenario 2 is the case that $h_t(x_i) = y$, $y \neq y_i$, and $a(x_i, y_i) > a(x_i, y)$ $\forall y \in \mathcal{Y}$, $y \neq y_i$. Then $f_t(x_i, y)$ is a line with slope 1, and $f_t(x_i, y_i)$ is a line with slope 0. The intersection point of $f_t(x_i, y)$ and $f_t(x_i, y_i)$ is at $\alpha_t = a(x_i, y) - a(x_i, y_i)$. Thus when α_t is set on the right side of the intersection point, there is an error for example x_i, otherwise there is no error. Scenario 3 is the case that $h_t(x_i) = y$, and $y \neq y_i$, and $\exists l \in \mathcal{Y}$, $l \neq y_i$ such that $a(x_i, l) > a(x_i, y_i)$, in this case there is always an error no matter what value α_t has.

Formally, Algorithm 1.1 describes the line search procedure. We use $\mathbf{e}$ (bold letter denotes a vector valued function or variable) to record all the intersection points and their corresponding error updates on the right-hand side (line 2). More specifically, for each training example, we first categorize it into the three scenarios. For an example in Scenario 1, the intersection point is at $q = a(x_i, l) - a(x_i, y_i)$, and the error update on the right-hand side of q is -1 (line 4-6). In Scenario 2, the intersection point is at $q = a(x_i, y) - a(x_i, y_i)$ and the error update on the right-hand side of q is 1 (line 7-9). We add the intersection points as the *keys* and their corresponding error updates as the *values* into $\mathbf{e}$ (line 11). We only care about the examples in Scenario 1 and 2 since the examples in Scenario 3 do not lead to an error update no matter what value α_t has. Once all the intersection points are added into $\mathbf{e}$, we sort $\mathbf{e}$ by the *keys* in an increasing order (line 13). These intersections divide the coordinate to (at most) $|\mathbf{e}| + 1$ intervals, the classification error on each interval can be incrementally calculated by the *values* of $\mathbf{e}$ (line 14), and hence the interval which gives the minimum error is easy to obtain.

The weak learning algorithm is described in Algorithm 1.2. Here we only consider the decision trees algorithm with binary splits. The binary splits are preferred [15] since (i) multiway splits fragment the data too quickly, leaving insufficient data at the next level down; and (ii) multiway splits can be achieved by a series of binary splits. For a binary splitting node that splits the training examples into two subsets, we denote them as $\mathcal{S}_{left}$ and $\mathcal{S}_{right}$ (line 5). We first enumerate all the possible labels from 1 to K on $\mathcal{S}_{left}$, that produce K hypotheses that belong to $\mathcal{H}$. We choose the optimal label which leads to the minimum value of (2) by running the line search algorithm (Algorithm 1.1) with these K hypotheses (line 7). We then fix the selected label for $\mathcal{S}_{left}$ (line 8), and apply the same process on $\mathcal{S}_{right}$ (line 9). We simply choose the attribute to split by minimizing the 0-1 loss (line 13), and use a top-down, greedy search approach to build trees. If the problem involves real-valued variables, they are first binned into intervals, each interval being treated as an ordinal attribute. Note that since the historical information $f_{t-1}(x_i, y_i)$ is used in Algorithm 1.1 through building trees, Algorithm 1.2 will not end up with the same tree on each iteration t though DMCBoost does not maintain a distribution over training samples.

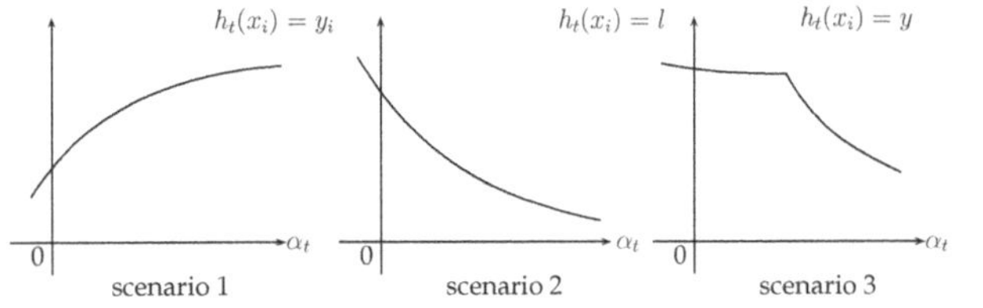

Figure 2: Three scenarios of margin curve of a weak learner h_t over an example pair (x_i, y_i), where l denotes the incorrect label with the highest score.

The computational cost of Algorithm 1 is $O(nMK)$ on each round when decision stumps[2] are used as weak learners, where M is the number of binary splits. It has the same computational cost as AdaBoost.MH, and is K times larger than the computational costs of AdaBoost.M1 and SAMME. Algorithm 1 may trap a coordinatewise local minimum of 0-1 loss. Nevertheless, we switch to the algorithm that directly maximizes various margins.

2.2 Phase II: Maximizing a Margin Objective

For boosting, the minimization of the training error is only one side of the story. To explain why boosting works, Schapire et al. [26] introduced the margin theory, which suggested that boosting is especially effective at maximizing the margins of training data. In multi-class classification, the most direct generalization of the margin is simply the difference between the score (weighted fraction of votes) obtained by the correct label and the score of the highest scoring incorrect label. We denote the (normalized) margin of an example (x_i, y_i) with respect to an inference function $f_t(x_i, y) = \sum_{k=1}^{t} \alpha_k 1(h_k(x_i) = y)$, $\forall y \in \mathcal{Y}$ by $\mathcal{M}_i$. Formally,

$$\mathcal{M}_i = \frac{f_t(x_i, y_i)}{\sum_{k=1}^{t} |\alpha_k|} - \max_{y \in \mathcal{Y}, y \neq y_i} \frac{f_t(x_i, y)}{\sum_{k=1}^{t} |\alpha_k|} \tag{4}$$

This definition of margin (4) is given in some earlier studies [2, 26]. A large margin implies the ensemble classifier confidently classifies the corresponding training sample.

While boosting's success can be ascribed to maximizing the margins, most boosting methods were not designed to specially optimize any margin functions [28]. Some exceptions, such as LPBoost [7], SoftBoost [33], and DirectBoost [35], explicitly maximize a relaxed minimum margin objective, but they are designed for binary classification problems. For the well-known multi-class boosting algorithms AdaBoost.M1 [10], SAMME [36], and AdaBoost.MM [22], none of them has been shown to maximize the multi-class margin [25]. The recently proposed algorithms CD-MCBoost and GD-MCBoost [25] optimize a margin enforcing loss function, but actually this objective is not related to the margin in the sense that one can minimize the loss function while simultaneously achieving a bad margin even for binary problems [24]. In this section, we introduce a coordinate ascent algorithm that directly maximizes the predefined margin objective functions for multi-class classification.

[2]Decision stumps are the special decision trees with a depth of 1. When more powerful trees are used, the complexity of Algorithm 1 has the same increasing rate as other boosting algorithms.

We first introduce the objective function that we are working on in this section. We can sort $\mathcal{M}_i$ in an increasing order, and consider n' worst training examples $n' \leq n$ that have smaller margins, then define the average margin over those n' labeled examples by $g_{avg\ n'}$. Formally,

$$g_{avg\ n'} = \frac{1}{n'} \sum_{i \in B_{n'}} \mathcal{M}_i \tag{5}$$

where $B_{n'}$ denotes the set of n' labeled examples having the smallest margins. The minimum margin (hard margin) $g_{min} = \min_{i \in \{1,\cdots,n\}} \mathcal{M}_i$ and average margin $g_{avg} = \frac{1}{n} \sum_{i=1}^{n} \mathcal{M}_i$ are special cases for $n' = 1$ and $n' = n$ respectively. The parameter n' indicates how much we relax the hard margin on training examples, and we set n' based on knowledge of the number of noise examples in training data. The higher the noise rate, the larger the n' that should be used.

The following theorem shows the objective function (5) is equivalent to the soft margin, this conclusion is also given in [29] for binary classification, here we propose a general proof for multi-class classification and use different proof skills.

THEOREM 1. *Maximizing the average margin of the bottom n' examples (5) is equivalent to solving the soft margin maximization problem*

$$\max_{\alpha \in \mathbb{R}^+, \boldsymbol{\xi} \in \mathbb{R}^+, \rho \in \mathbb{R}} \rho - \frac{1}{n'} \sum_{i=1}^{n} \xi_i \tag{6}$$
$$s.t. \quad \mathcal{M}_i + \xi_i \geq \rho, \ i = 1, \cdots, n$$

where $\boldsymbol{\xi}$ are slack variables.

Due to the max operator in the definition of margin (4), the soft margin optimization problem (6) is very difficult to solve, unlike its binary counterpart. To the best of our knowledge, there is no multi-class boosting designed to solve this soft margin optimization problem. Thus, one of the reasons for using (5) as objective is to solve the soft margin problem but from another point of view.

Another motivation of optimizing (5) is that the average of the bottom n' margins can be used to measure the generalization performance of a combined classifier, as shown in the following theorem.

THEOREM 2. *If the set of possible base classifiers $\mathcal{H}$ is finite, and $\theta = \frac{1}{n'} \sum_{i \in \mathcal{B}_{\{n'|f\}}} \mathcal{M}_i > \frac{8}{|\mathcal{H}|}$, then for any $\delta > 0$ and $n' \in \{1, \cdots, n\}$, with the probability at least $1 - \delta$ over the random choice of the training set $\mathcal{S}$ with size n, each inference function $f \in \mathcal{C}(\mathcal{H})$ satisfies the following bound:*

$$\Pr_{\mathcal{D}}[\mathcal{M}(f, x, y) < 0] \leq (K-1)\frac{\log |\mathcal{H}|}{2n} + \sqrt{\frac{\log |\mathcal{H}|}{2n^2}} + D^{-1}\left(\frac{n'-1}{n}, \frac{1}{n}u\right)$$

where $\Pr_{\mathcal{D}}[\mathcal{M}(f, x, y) < 0]$ denotes the generalization error of the ensemble classifier F, $\mathcal{M}(f, x, y)$ denotes the margin of an example (x, y) associated with f, $D^{-1}(v_1, v_2)$ denotes the inverse of K-L divergence between v_1 and v_2 when v_1 is fixed [32], and

$$u = \frac{8}{\theta^2} \log \frac{2n^2}{\log |\mathcal{H}|} \log 2|\mathcal{H}| + \log |\mathcal{H}| + \log \frac{1}{\delta}$$

The outline of the greedy coordinate ascent algorithm that sequentially maximizes the average margin of bottom n' examples is described in Algorithm 2. Similar to the 0-1 loss minimization algorithm, we intend to select a weak classifier

Algorithm 2 Margin maximization algorithm.

1: **Initialize:** t and $\boldsymbol{\alpha}$ from 0-1 loss minimization algorithm.
2: **repeat**
3: $\quad t \leftarrow t+1$.
4: $\quad$ Select a weak learner h_t by weak learning algorithm.
5: $\quad$ Compute q^* by Algorithm 2.1 which maximizes (5) along the coordinate h_t. Set $\alpha_t = q^*$.
6: $\quad$ Update: $f_t(x_i, y) = f_{t-1}(x_i, y) + \alpha_t 1(h_t(x_i) = y)$
7: **until** the average margin of bottom n' examples reaches local coordinatewise maximum.
8: **Output:** $f_t(x_i, y)$.

h_t (line 4) and its weight α_t (line 5) on round t, but this time our target is maximizing (5). This procedure terminates if there is no increment in the average margin over the bottom n' examples over h_t (line 8). Its convergence can be proved in the same way as for the binary classification given in [35].

The key step is the line search algorithm which finds the value of α_t that maximizes (5) for a given weak classifier $h_t \in \mathcal{H}$. At tth iteration, let $c = \sum_{k=1}^{t-1} |\alpha_k|$, then the margin on the example (x_i, y_i) can be rewritten as,

$$\begin{aligned}\mathcal{M}_i &= \frac{a(x_i,y_i) + \alpha_t 1(h_t(x_i) = y_i)}{c + |\alpha_t|} \\ &\quad - \max_{y \in \mathcal{Y}, y \neq y_i} \frac{a(x_i, y) + \alpha_t 1(h_t(x_i) = y)}{c + |\alpha_t|} \end{aligned} \tag{7}$$

Consider the case that $\alpha_t \geq 0$. For each example pair (x_i, y_i), there are three scenarios of the margin (7) to consider, as shown in Figure 2. Scenario 1 is the case that $h_t(x_i) = y_i$, and assume that $l = \arg\max_{y \in \mathcal{Y}, y \neq y_i} a(x_i, y)$, then $\mathcal{M}_i = \frac{a(x_i,y_i) - a(x_i,l) + \alpha_t}{c + \alpha_t}$. This corresponds to the curve which is monotonically increasing in Figure 2. Scenario 2 is the case that $h_t(x_i) = l$, $y \neq y_i$, and $a(x_i, l) > a(x_i, y)$, $\forall y \in \mathcal{Y}$, $y \neq y_i$, then $\mathcal{M}_i = \frac{a(x_i,y_i) - a(x_i,l) - \alpha_t}{c+\alpha_t}$. This corresponds to the curve which is monotonically decreasing in Figure 2. Scenario 3 is the case that $h_t(x_i) = y$, and $y \neq y_i$, and $\exists l \in \mathcal{Y}$, $l \neq y_i$ such that $a(x_i, l) > a(x_i, y)$, in this case the margin curve of $\mathcal{M}_i$ has two pieces. When $\alpha_t < a(x_i, y) - a(x_i, l)$, $\mathcal{M}_i = \frac{a(x_i,y_i) - a(x_i,l)}{c+\alpha_t}$ and when $\alpha_t > a(x_i, y) - a(x_i, l)$, $\mathcal{M}_i = \frac{a(x_i,y_i) - a(x_i,y) - \alpha_t}{c+\alpha_t}$. The scenarios for the case that $\alpha_t < 0$ can be similarly identified.

Finding the exact solution of optimal α_t along the h_t coordinate is computationally difficult since the examples in Scenario 3 can either intersect with the examples in Scenario 1 or intersect with the examples in Scenario 2. Fortunately, we can prove that (5) is a quasi-concave function [4, 6], this property allows us to design an efficient line search algorithm.

THEOREM 3. *Denote the average margin of the bottom n' examples with respect to the set of weak classifiers $\mathcal{H}$ and their weights $\boldsymbol{\alpha}$ as*

$$\begin{aligned} g_{avg\ n'}(\boldsymbol{\alpha}) &= \frac{1}{n'} \sum_{i \in \{B_{n'}|\boldsymbol{\alpha}\}} \frac{\sum_{j=1}^{|\mathcal{H}|} \alpha_j 1(h_j(x_i) = y)}{\sum_{j=1}^{|\mathcal{H}|} |\alpha_j|} \\ &\quad - \max_{y \in \mathcal{Y}, y \neq y_i} \frac{\sum_{j=1}^{|\mathcal{H}|} \alpha_j 1(h_j(x_i) = y)}{\sum_{j=1}^{|\mathcal{H}|} |\alpha_j|} \end{aligned} \tag{8}$$

where $\{B_{n'}|\boldsymbol{\alpha}\}$ denotes the set of n' examples whose margins are at the bottom for fixed $\boldsymbol{\alpha}$. Then $g_{avg\ n'}(\boldsymbol{\alpha})$ is a quasi-concave function for any $\boldsymbol{\alpha}$.

Algorithm 2.1 Line search algorithm to find the solution q^* that maximizes (5).

1: **Input:** a weak classifier $h_t \in \mathcal{H}$, an interval $[begin, end]$, and a small number th.
2: **repeat**
3: $\quad$ Set $q = \frac{begin+end}{2}$, calculate the value of $\frac{\partial g_{avg\ n'}}{\partial q}$ as equation (9).
4: $\quad$ **if** $\frac{\partial \mathcal{M}_{avg\ n'}}{\partial q} > 0$ **then**
5: $\quad\quad begin = q$.
6: $\quad$ **else**
7: $\quad\quad end = q$.
8: $\quad$ **end if**
9: **until** $end - begin < th$.
10: **Output:** $q^* = \frac{begin+end}{2}$.

Therefore, we can design an algorithm that maximizes (5) efficiently by checking the derivative of (5) as

$$\frac{\partial g_{avg\ n'}}{\partial \alpha_t} = \frac{1}{n'} \sum_{i \in B_{n'}} \frac{\partial \mathcal{M}_i}{\partial \alpha_t}, \tag{9}$$

where $\frac{\partial \mathcal{M}_i}{\partial \alpha_t}$ denotes the derivative of $\mathcal{M}_i$ with respect to α_t, which is calculated as,

$$\frac{\partial \mathcal{M}_i}{\partial \alpha_t} = \begin{cases} \frac{c - (a(x_i,y_i) - a(x_i,l))}{(c+\alpha_t)^2} & \text{Scenario 1} \\ \frac{-c - (a(x_i,y_i) - a(x_i,l))}{(c+\alpha_t)^2} & \text{Scenario 2} \\ -\frac{a(x_i,y_i) - a(x_i,l)}{(c+\alpha_t)^2} & \text{Scenario 3} \end{cases} \tag{10}$$

Assume q^* is the optimal value of α_t that maximizes (5), then (5) is monotonically increasing at $\alpha_t < q^*$, otherwise it is monotonically decreasing. Thus, (9) is less than 0 at $\alpha_t < q^*$, and (9) is greater than 0 at $\alpha_t > q^*$. Formally, the line search algorithm to calculate the value of q^* with a small deviation threshold th is described in Algorithm 2.1.

To select the weak classifier, we use a similar procedure as in Algorithm 1.2 and replace the measure to the average margin of the bottom n' examples. Again, we only consider the decision trees algorithm with binary splits, and apply Algorithm 2.1 on the two subsets respectively. We choose the attributes to split by maximizing the average margin of the bottom n' examples, and use a top-down, greedy search approach to build trees. Same as Algorithm 1, the computational cost of Algorithm 2 is $O(nMK)$ on each round when decision stumps are used as weak learners, where M is the number of binary splits.

Since (5) is non-differentiable at turning points, the coordinate ascent algorithm may get stuck at a corner from which it is impossible to make progress along any coordinate direction. To overcome this difficulty, we use an ϵ-relaxation method [5], which allows a single coordinate to change even if this worsens the objective value. When a coordinate is changed, it is set to ϵ plus (or ϵ minus) the value that maximizes the objective function along that coordinate, where ϵ is a small positive number. If ϵ is small enough, the algorithm can eventually approach a small neighborhood of the optimal solution.

Table 1: Description of 13 UCI datasets

Data	# Examples	K	# Variables	Error Estimation
Abalone	4177	28	8	5-CV
Car	1728	4	6	5-CV
CNAE-9	1080	9	856	5-CV
Glass	214	6	10	5-CV
Krkopt	28056	18	6	5-CV
Letter	20000	26	16	5-CV
Nursery	12960	5	8	5-CV
Poker525k	525010/500000	10	11	test error
Segmentation	210/2100	7	19	test error
Vowel	990	11	10	5-CV
Waveform	5000	3	21	5-CV
Wine	178	3	13	5-CV
Yeast	1484	10	8	5-CV

Table 2: Test error (and standard deviation) of multi-class boosting methods AdaBoost.M1, SAMME, GD-MCBoost, and DMCBoost on 13 UCI datasets, using multi-class decision trees with a depth of 3.

Data	AdaBoost.M1	SAMME	GD-MCBoost	DMCBoost
Abalone	-	74.20(1.8)	74.62(1.5)	**74.03(2.0)**
Car	10.96(2.5)	4.75(1.0)	3.60(1.1)	**2.78(0.8)**
CNAE-9	-	14.91(2.4)	11.4(1.9)	**7.59(1.2)**
Glass	29.52(10.7)	31.9(8.0)	27.0(7.4)	**26.19(10.8)**
Krkopt	-	64.33(0.9)	26.55(0.4)	**22.76(0.7)**
Letter	-	24.94(0.9)	5.40(1.3)	**4.89(0.3)**
Nursery	9.70(1.5)	3.26(0.7)	0.2(0.0)	**0.02(0.0)**
Poker525k	49.16	69.09	-	**30.09**
Segmentation	8.29	6.43	6.0	**5.1**
Vowel	-	19.19(2.6)	9.2(2.6)	**5.66(1.9)**
Waveform	17.8(1.2)	16.96(1.2)	16.2(1.1)	**14.38(1.1)**
Wine	8.57(4.9)	7.43(4.8)	7.54(5.3)	**3.43(4.7)**
Yeast	43.65(2.6)	44.73(4.5)	43.6(3.5)	**42.43(2.8)**

3. EXPERIMENTS

To evaluate the performance of the DMCBoost algorithm, we first conduct experiments with 13 datasets from the UCI repository [9], then examine its noise robustness on two datasets with random label noise. For comparison, we also report the results of AdaBoost.M1 [11], AdaBoost.MH [27], SAMME [36], and GD-MCBoost [25]. All these algorithms use multi-class base classifiers except AdaBoost.MH, which essentially reduces the multi-class problem to a set of binary classification problems. The classification error is estimated either by a test error or five-fold cross-validation. The datasets which come with pre-specified training and testing sets are evaluated by the test error, where n' is set to $\frac{n}{4}$ for DMCBoost and the number of rounds is set to the maximum of 5000 for each method. For datasets which are evaluated by cross-validation, we partition them into five parts evenly for 5-fold. In each fold, we use three parts for training, one part for validation, and the remaining part for testing. We use the validation data to choose the optimal model for each algorithm. For AdaBoost.M1, AdaBoost.MH, SAMME, and GD-MCBoost the validation data is used to perform early stopping. We run these algorithms with a maximum of 5000 iterations, and then choose the ensemble classifier from the round with minimal error on the validation data. For DMCBoost, the parameter n' is chosen on the values $\{1, \frac{n}{10}, \frac{n}{5}, \frac{n}{4}, \frac{n}{3}, \frac{n}{2}, \frac{2n}{3}\}$ by the validation set. The stopping criterion of DMCBoost is defined as line 7 in Algorithm 2 where DMCBoost terminates at the margin maximization solution, thus we need not to apply early stopping. In all the experiments, the value of ϵ is set to be 0.01 and the value of th is set to be 1e-5.

An overview of these 13 UCI datasets is shown in Table 1. The datasets have different numbers of input variables (6-856), classes (3-26), and instances (178-1,025,010), and represent a wide area of types of problems. In the # Examples column, the number of training/test examples are listed for datasets coming with pre-specified training and testing sets, and the entire number of examples is given for the rest datasets. The original Poker dataset has 25,010 training examples and 1,000,000 examples for testing. Since the test data is very large, same as the way Li did in [17, 18], we randomly divide it equally into two parts, and add them to training and testing sets respectively, thus its training size becomes 525,010 and the test size becomes 500,000. Therefore, the datasets we selected include fairly large datasets (Poker525k) as well as datasets of moderate sizes (Krkopt, Letter and Nursery).

3.1 Experimental Results on UCI Datasets

We compare all multi-class boosting algorithms on 13 UCI datasets. First, we restrict the base classifiers to smaller trees to test the performance of each algorithm when the base classifiers are very weak. We exclude the results of AdaBoost.MH as all the rest algorithms use multi-class base classifiers, and we want to compare the performance of each algorithm with the same hypothesis space $\mathcal{H}$. Table 2 shows the results of different methods when multi-class decision trees with a depth of 3 are used as weak learners[3]. With small trees, DMCBoost gives the best results on all datasets indicating that DMCBoost only requires very weak base classifiers even if there is no exact weak learner condition for DMCBoost. GD-MCBoost achieves the second best accuracy, this algorithm also requires weaker base classifiers since it is able to boost any type of weak learners with non-zero directional derivatives [25]. We do not report its results on the Poker525k dataset since its one iteration takes more than 12 hours to run by the authors' matlab code. For SAMME, the weak learner conditions can be satisfied easily, but it couldn't drive down the training error when the base classifier is very weak, and its performance is much worse. AdaBoost.M1 gives the worst results, and it is not able to boost the base classifiers for 5 of 13 datasets, as shown in Table 2.

With the same hypothesis space $\mathcal{H}$ (trees with a depth of 3), 0-1 loss minimization algorithm (Algorithm 1) usually achieves a lower training classification error rate. The left panel of Figure 3 shows a typical training error curve on the

[3]Whether a base classifier is weak or not often depends on the properties of the datasets, such as number of classes, examples and input variables. For the most multi-class datasets in Table 1, decision trees with a depth of 3 is weak enough. The previous multi-class boosting [10, 22, 36] studies often use much larger trees in the experiments.

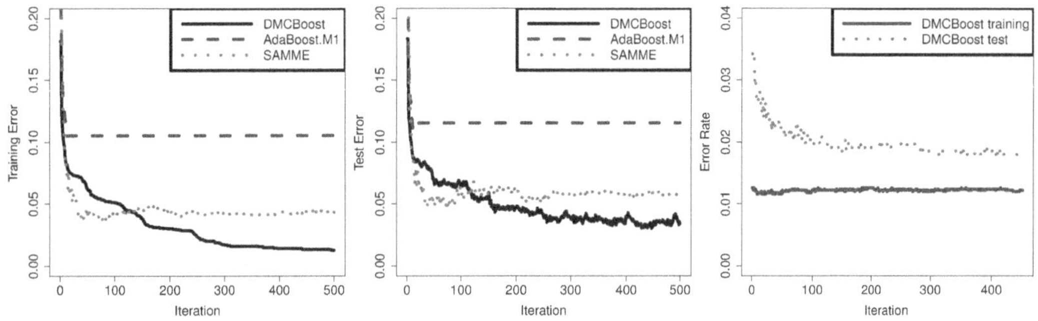

Figure 3: Left: Training errors of AdaBoost.M1, SAMME, and DMCBoost with 0-1 loss minimization algorithm on the Car dataset. Middle: Test errors of AdaBoost.M1, SAMME, and DMCBoost with 0-1 loss minimization algorithm on Car dataset. Right: Training and test error of DMCBoost when it switches to the margin maximization algorithm on the Car dataset.

Table 3: Test error (and standard deviation) of multi-class boosting methods AdaBoost.M1, AdaBoost.MH, SAMME, GD-MCBoost, and DMCBoost on 13 UCI datasets, using decision trees with a maximum depth of 12.

Data	AdaBoost.M1	AdaBoost.MH	SAMME	GD-MCBoost	DMCBoost
Abalone	76.41(1.4)	75.33(1.2)	73.70(1.7)	74.62(1.5)	**73.44(1.8)**
Car	3.36(0.8)	2.84(0.6)	3.65(0.9)	2.8(0.8)	**2.67(0.8)**
CNAE-9	20.9(2.7)	8.43(1.3)	13.43(1.3)	10.6(2.1)	**7.5(1.2)**
Glass	27.14(9.3)	29.52(9.2)	24.76(8.7)	**24.0(6.8)**	24.76(9.9)
Krkopt	14.3(0.3)	11.68(0.3)	12.71(0.2)	12.20(0.3)	**11.04(0.2)**
Letter	3.48(0.3)	**3.1(0.1)**	4.88(0.3)	3.37(0.2)	**3.1(0.2)**
Nursery	0.12(0.1)	0.03(0.0)	0.16(0.1)	**0.0(0.0)**	**0.0(0.0)**
Poker525k	30.19	**2.01**	18.74	-	2.77
Segmentation	4.86	6.14	5.1	6.0	**4.52**
Vowel	5.96(2.9)	7.68(1.8)	6.25(2.3)	**5.6(3.0)**	5.66(1.9)
Waveform	15.2(1.4)	14.56(1.4)	15.08(1.0)	15.2(0.8)	**14.26(1.1)**
Wine	8.57(4.9)	9.16(5.3)	7.43(4.8)	7.54(5.3)	**3.43(4.7)**
Yeast	41.69(1.8)	41.82(2.1)	41.22(3.1)	43.2(3.6)	**40.23(2.5)**

Car dataset, and the middle panel shows the corresponding test error curve. Once the 0-1 loss minimization algorithm terminates at a coordinatewise local minimum, DMCBoost switches to the margin maximization algorithm (Algorithm 2), and it can still drive down the test error even when the training error does not decrease, as shown in the right panel of Figure 3.

We now analyze the running time of AdaBoost.M1, SAMME, and DMCBoost on the Poker525k dataset, which has 525,000 training examples. We implemented each algorithm by C++, and test them on a PC with Core2 Duo 2.6GHz. We left GD-MCBoost out of the comparison since it is unfair to compare a matlab implementation with C++ implementations, and GD-MCBoost runs too slow to record the running time. AdaBoost.M1 and SAMME are very efficient in terms of running time, they take about 10s on each round. For DMCBoost, it takes about 90s on each round, which is slower than AdaBoost.M1 and SAMME but it is bearable on such a scale as the dataset.

We next investigate how these algorithms perform with more powerful base classifiers. We tried all tree depths in the candidate set {3,5,8,12} for each dataset. This time we compare the algorithms not restricted in the same hypothesis space $\mathcal{H}$, so we also add AdaBoost.MH in the comparison. As shown in Table 3, among all the methods, DMCBoost gives the most accurate results in 10 of the 13 datasets, and its results are close to the best results produced by the other methods for the remaining 3 datasets.

3.2 Evaluation of Noise Robustness

In many real-world applications, training samples are obtained through manual labeling and there will be unavoidable human errors that provoke wrong labels. Hence, it is desirable that the designed classification algorithm is robust to noise. In the experiments conducted below, we check the noise robustness of each boosting algorithm on Car and Nursery datasets with additional label noise. We randomly change the labels on training and validation data at the rates of 5% and 20% respectively, and keep the the test data clean. Again, the tree depths are chosen from the candidate set {3,5,8,12}. The results via 5-fold cross-validation (as described in the begining of section 3) are reported in Table 4. The affection of label noise to the performance of DMCBoost is very limited, especially for the Nursery dataset, the test error only increases from 0 to 1.6% when 20% of the training examples have wrong labels. Similar to AdaBoost in binary cases, AdaBoost.M1 and SAMME are quite sen-

Table 4: Test error (and standard deviation) of multi-class boosting methods AdaBoost.M1, AdaBoost.MH, SAMME, GD-MCBoost, and DMCBoost on the two UCI datasets with random noise, using decision trees with a maximum depth of 12.

Data	Noise rate	AdaBoost.M1	AdaBoost.MH	SAMME	GD-MCBoost	DMCBoost
Car	0	3.36(0.8)	2.84(0.6)	3.65(0.9)	3.6(1.1)	**2.67(0.8)**
	0.05	9.22(1.5)	6.09(1.0)	7.94(2.0)	5.8(1.1)	**3.54(1.2)**
	0.2	14.55(2.4)	9.1(1.0)	14.2(1.9)	9.6(1.1)	**6.55(1.6)**
Nursery	0	0.12(0.1)	0.03(0.0)	0.16(0.1)	**0.0(0.0)**	**0.0(0.0)**
	0.05	3.93(1.3)	1.82(0.5)	2.29(0.2)	2.4(0.5)	**0.37(0.2)**
	0.2	6.61(0.9)	3.47(0.6)	6.61(0.9)	4.4(0.9)	**1.61(0.5)**

sitive to noise, their performance is hurt badly even with a 5% noise rate.

DMCBoost achieves good performance by varying the parameter n', the higher the noise rate, the larger n' should be used. Consider the Car dataset as an example, for the case that the training set is clean (noise rate is 0), the optimal n' via cross-validation is $\frac{n}{10}$ and the training error is 1.5%, thus the algorithm focus on the difficult examples. For the case that the noise rate is 5%, the optimal n' is $\frac{n}{4}$ and the training error is 7.1%, indicating that DMCBoost allows some misclassification to achieve a better performance. For a noise rate of 20%, DMCBoost considers more examples in the bottom set, the optimal n' via cross-validation is $\frac{n}{2}$. In this case, DMCBoost further allows more misclassification (the training error is 22.2%), but its corresponding test error is only 6.55%.

4. CONCLUSION AND FUTURE WORKS

In this paper we have proposed a multi-class boosting approach that directly optimizes the 0-1 loss and the targeted margins. Experiments show that our method gives better results in the case of restricting the weak learning algorithm to small decision trees, and performs highly competitively with the existing boosting algorithms in the case of deeper decision trees. More importantly, our method is more robust on the noisy data.

In this study we restrict the weak learners to multi-class decision trees as the combination of boosting with a decision trees is the state-of-the-art classification method [1]. For future works, we will consider more weak learning algorithms and the case that $|\mathcal{H}|$ is infinite, such as k-Nearest Neighbors, Naive Bayes, and Neural Networks.

5. ACKNOWLEDGMENTS

This research is supported in part by AFOSR under grant FA9550-10-1-0335, NSF under grant IIS:RI-small 1218863, DoD under grant FA2386-13-1-3023, and a Google research award.

6. REFERENCES

[1] R. Appel, T. Fuchs, T. Dollar and P. Perona. Quickly boosting decision trees - Pruning underachieving features early. *International Conference on Machine Learning* (ICML), 2013.

[2] E. Allwein, R. Schapire and Y. Singer. Reducing multiclass to binary: A unifying approach for margin classifiers. *Journal of Machine Learning Research*, 1:113-141, 2000.

[3] P. Bartlett, M. Jordan and J. McAuliffe. Convexity, classification, and risk bounds. *Journal of the American Statistical Association*, 101(March):138-156, 2006.

[4] M. Bazaraa, H. Sherali and C. Shetty. *Nonlinear Programming: Theory and Algorithms*, 3rd Edition. Wiley-Interscience, 2006.

[5] D. Bertsekas. *Network Optimization: Continuous and Discrete Models*. Athena Scientific, 1998.

[6] S. Boyd and L. Vandenberghe. *Convex Optimization*. Cambridge University, 2004.

[7] A. Demiriz, K. Bennett and J. Shawe-Taylor. Linear programming boosting via column generation, *Machine Learning*, 46:225–254, 2002.

[8] T. Dietterich and G. Bakiri. Solving multiclass learning problems via error-correcting output codes. *Journal of Artificial Intelligence Research*, 2:263–286, 1995.

[9] A. Frank and A. Asuncion. UCI Machine Learning Repository. Irvine, CA: University of California, School of Information and Computer Science, 2010.

[10] Y. Freund and R. Schapire. Experiments with a new boosting algorithm. *The 13th International Conference in Machine Learning*, 148-156, 1996.

[11] Y. Freund and R. Schapire. A decision-theoretic generalization of on-line learning and an application to boosting. *Journal of Computer and System Sciences*, 55(1):119–139, 1997.

[12] J. Friedman, T. Hastie and R. Tibshirani. Additive logistic regression: A statistical view of boosting. *The Annals of Statistics*, 28(2):337–374, 2000.

[13] J. Friedman. Greedy function approximation: A gradient boosting machine. *The Annals of Statistics*, 28(2):1189–1232, 2001.

[14] W. Gao, Z. Zhou. On the doubt about margin explanation of boosting. *Artificial Intelligence*, 203:1–18, 2013.

[15] T. Hastie, R. Tibshirani, J. Friedman. *The Elements of Statistical Learning*, 2nd Edition. Springer, 2009.

[16] H. He, E.A. Garcia. *Learning from imbalanced data*. IEEE Trans. Knowl. Data Eng, 21(9):1263–1284, 2009.

[17] P. Li. ABC-Boost: Adaptive base class boost for multi-class classification. *International Conference on Machine Learning* (ICML), 2009.

[18] P. Li. Robust LogitBoost and adaptive base class (ABC) LogitBoost. *Uncertainty on Artificial Intelligence* (UAI), 2010.

[19] P. Long and R. Servedio. Random classification noise defeats all convex potential boosters. *Machine Learning*, 78:287-304, 2010.

[20] D. McAllester, T. Hazan and J. Keshet. Direct loss minimization for structured prediction. *Advances in Neural Information Processing Systems* (NIPS), 23:1594–1602, 2010.

[21] D. Mease and A. Wyner. Evidence contrary to the statistical view of boosting. *Journal of Machine Learning Research*, 9:131–156, 2008.

[22] I. Mukherjee and R. Schapire. A theory of multiclass boosting. *Journal of Machine Learning Research*, 14:437–497, 2013.
[23] T. Nguyen and S. Sanner. Algorithms for direct 0-1 loss optimization in binary classification. *International Conference on Machine Learning* (ICML), 2013.
[24] C. Rudin, I. Daubechies and R. Schapire. The dynamics of AdaBoost: Cyclic behavior and convergence of margins. *Journal of Machine Learning Research*, 5:1557-1595, 2004.
[25] M. Saberian and N. Vasconcelos. Multiclass boosting: Theory and algorithms. In Proc. *Neural Information Processing Systems* (NIPS), 2011.
[26] R. Schapire, Y. Freund, P. Bartlett and W. Lee. Boosting the margin: A new explanation for the effectiveness of voting methods. *The Annals of Statistics*, 26(5):1651–1686, 1998.
[27] R. Schapire and Y. Singer. Improved boosting algorithms using confidence-rated predictions. *Machine Learning*, 37(3):297–336, 1999.
[28] R. Schapire and Y. Freund. *Boosting: Foundations and Algorithms*. MIT Press, 2012.
[29] S. Shalev-Shwartz and Y. Singer. On the equivalence of weak learnability and linear separability: new relaxations and efficient boosting algorithms. *Machine Learning*, 80(2-3): 141-163, 2010.
[30] Y. Sun, M.S. kamel, A.K.C. Wong, Y. Wang. Cost-sensitive boosting for classification of imbalanced data. *Pattern Recognition*, 40(12): 3358-3378, 2007.
[31] P. Tseng. Convergence of block coordinate descent method for nondifferentiable minimization. *Journal of Optimization Theory and Applications*, 475–494, 2001.
[32] L. Wang, M. Sugiyama, Z. Jing, C. Yang, Z. Zhou and J. Feng. A refined margin analysis for boosting algorithms via equilibrium margin. *The Journal of Machine Learning Research*, 12:1835-1863, 2011.
[33] M. Warmuth, K. Glocer and G. Ratsch. Boosting algorithms for maximizing the soft margin. *Advances in Neural Information Processing Systems* (NIPS), 21, 2007.
[34] X. Wu, V. Kumar, J. Quinlan, J. Ghosh, Q. Yang, H. Motoda, G. McLachlan, A. Ng, B. Liu, P. Yu, Z. Zhou, M. Steinbach, D. Hand, and D. Steinberg. Top 10 algorithms in data mining. *Knowledge and Information System*, 14(1):1-37, 2008.
[35] S. Zhai, T. Xia, M. Tan and S. Wang. Direct 0-1 loss minimization and margin maximization with boosting. *Advances in Neural Information Processing Systems* (NIPS), 2013.
[36] J. Zhu, H. Zou, S. Rosset and T. Hastie. Multi-class AdaBoost. *Statistics and Its Interface*, 2:349–366, 2009.
[37] H. Zou, J. Zhu and T. Hastie. New multi-category boosting algorithms based on multicategory Fisher-consistent losses. *Annals of Applied Statistics*, 2(4): 1290-1306, 2008.

APPENDIX

A. PROOF OF THEOREM 1

PROOF. : (i) We first show that when the optimal solution of soft margin optimization is achieved, $\mathcal{M}_i + \xi_i = \rho$ always holds for those $\xi_i > 0$. Suppose when the optimal solution is achieved, there exists an example such that $\mathcal{M}_i + \xi_i > \rho$ and $\xi_i > 0$. The slack variable $\xi_i > 0$ indicates $\mathcal{M}_i < \rho$, then we can always find a $\xi_i' < \xi$ such that $\mathcal{M}_i + \xi_i' = \rho$, and therefore replace ξ to ξ' in objective function that produce a greater objective value, a contradiction.

(ii) We next prove under the optimal solution, there are at most n' examples that are allowed to lie below (or equal) ρ, that is, $|\{x_i|\mathcal{M}_i \leq \rho\}| \leq n'$. Suppose we arrived a optimal solution and $n' < |\{x_i|\mathcal{M}_i \leq \rho\}| \leq m'$, with the corresponding slack variable $\boldsymbol{\xi}$. Then we can always find a $\rho' < \rho$ such that $|\{x_i|\mathcal{M}_i \leq \rho'\}| \leq n'$, with the slack variable $\boldsymbol{\xi}'$. We denote $\delta = \rho - \rho'$, then by (i) $\xi_i' = \xi_i - \delta$ for the examples with $\xi_i' > 0$. We use $B_{m'}$ to denote the set of m' examples having the smallest margins, then $B_{n'} \subset B_{m'}$ and $B_{n'}^c \cap B_{m'} \neq \emptyset$. We have

$$\begin{aligned}\rho - \frac{1}{n'}\sum_{i=1}^{n}\xi_i &= \rho' - \frac{1}{n'}(\sum_{i\in B_{m'}}\xi_i - n'\delta)\\ &= \rho' - \frac{1}{n'}\sum_{i\in B_{n'}}\xi_i' - \frac{1}{n'}\sum_{i\in B_{n'}^c\cap B_{m'}}\xi_i\\ &\leq \rho' - \frac{1}{n'}\sum_{i\in B_{n'}}\xi_i'\end{aligned}$$

which is a contradiction.

(iii) We further show that $|\{x_i|\mathcal{M}_i \leq \rho\}| \geq n'$ under the optimal solution. Suppose there is an optimal solution with $|\{x_i|\mathcal{M}_i \leq \rho\}| \leq m' < n'$ and slack variable $\boldsymbol{\xi}$, then there must exist a $\rho' > \rho$ such that $m' < |\{x_i|\mathcal{M}_i \leq \rho\}| \leq n'$ and corresponding $\boldsymbol{\xi}'$. We denote $\delta = \rho' - \rho$ and we have

$$\begin{aligned}\rho - \frac{1}{n'}\sum_{i=1}^{n}\xi_i &= \rho' - \frac{1}{n'}(\sum_{i\in B_{m'}}\xi_i + n'\delta)\\ &\leq \rho' - \frac{1}{n'}(\sum_{i\in B_{m'}}\xi_i' + \sum_{i\in B_{m'}^c\cap B_{n'}}\xi_i')\\ &= \rho' - \frac{1}{n'}\sum_{i\in B_{n'}}\xi_i'\end{aligned}$$

where the inequation holds since $\xi_i' \leq \delta$ if $x_i \in B_{m'}^c \cap B_{n'}$. A contradiction.

(iv) Combine the results (ii) and (iii), we have $|\{x_i|\mathcal{M}_i \leq \rho\}| = n'$, and therefore $\sum_{i\in B_{n'}}(\mathcal{M}_i + \xi_i) = n'\rho$, it follows that $\sum_{i\in B_{n'}}\mathcal{M}_i = n'\rho - \sum_{i\in B_{n'}}\xi_i = n'\rho - \sum_{i=1}^{n}\xi_i$. Dividing by n' on both sides of the equation, we get $\frac{1}{n'}\sum_{i\in B_{n'}}\mathcal{M}_i = \rho - \frac{1}{n'}\sum_{i=1}^{n}\xi_i$. □

B. PROOF OF THEOREM 2

PROOF. : Our proof is inspired by the works in [14, 26, 32]. Let $\mathcal{C}(\mathcal{H})$ denote the convex hull of $\mathcal{H}$, and let $\mathcal{C}_N(\mathcal{H})$ denote the set of unweighted averages over N elements from $\mathcal{H}$. Formally,

$$\mathcal{C}(\mathcal{H}) = \{f : f = \sum_k \alpha_k \mathbf{1}(h_k(x) = y), \sum_k \alpha_k = 1, \alpha_k \geq 0, h_k \in \mathcal{H}\}$$

$$\mathcal{C}_N(\mathcal{H}) = \{g : g = \frac{1}{N}\sum_{j=1}^{N}\mathbf{1}(h_j(x) = y), h_j \in \mathcal{H}\}$$

We denote the distribution over $\mathcal{H}$ by the coefficients $\{\alpha_k\}$ to be $\mathcal{Q}(f)$. Let $B_{\{n'|f\}}$ be the set of n' examples having the smallest margins associate with the inference function f. By [26] we know that for any fixed $\beta > 0$

$$\Pr_{\mathcal{D}}[\mathcal{M}(f, x, y) < 0] \leq \Pr_{D, g\sim\mathcal{Q}(f)}[\mathcal{M}(g, x, y) < \beta] + \exp(\frac{-N\beta^2}{2}) \tag{11}$$

Let $\mathcal{M}(g, x_{(k)}, y_{(k)})$ denote the k-th smallest margin with respect to g. For any $n' \in \{1, \cdots, n\}$ and $\epsilon_N > 0$, we consider the following probability:

$$\begin{aligned}&\Pr_S[\Pr_{\mathcal{D}}[\mathcal{M}(g, x, y) < \beta] > \mathbf{1}(\mathcal{M}(g, x_{(n')}, y_{(n')}) \leq \beta) + \epsilon_N]\\ &\leq \sum_{i=0}^{n'-1}\binom{n}{i}\epsilon_N^i(1-\epsilon_N)^{n-i} \leq \exp(-nD(\frac{n'}{n}|\epsilon))\end{aligned}$$

by using the relative entropy Chernoff bound.

Let $\mathcal{Z} = \{i/|\mathcal{H}| : i = 1, \cdots, |\mathcal{H}|\}$, we only consider β at the values in $\mathcal{Z}$. By the fact that $|\mathcal{C}_N(\mathcal{H})| \leq |\mathcal{H}|^N$ and applying the union bound, for any $n' \in \{1, \cdots, n\}$,

$$\Pr_{S, g\sim\mathcal{Q}(f)}[\exists g \in \mathcal{C}_N(\mathcal{H}), \exists\beta \in \mathcal{Z}, \Pr_{\mathcal{D}}[\mathcal{M}(g, x, y) < \beta] > \mathbf{1}[\mathcal{M}(g, x_{(n')}, y_{(n')}) \leq \beta] + \epsilon_N] \leq |\mathcal{H}|^{N+1}\exp(-nD(\frac{n'}{n}|\epsilon))$$

Let $\delta_N = |\mathcal{H}|^{N+1}\exp(-nD(\frac{n'}{n}|\epsilon))$, then

$$\epsilon_N = D^{-1}(\frac{n'-1}{n}, \frac{1}{n}\log\frac{|\mathcal{H}|^{N+1}}{\delta_N})$$

Thus, with a probability at least $1 - \delta_N$ over the training sample S, for all $f \in \mathcal{C}(\mathcal{H})$, all $\beta \in \mathcal{Z}$, and all fixed n', we have

$$\Pr_{\mathcal{D}}[\mathcal{M}(g, x, y) < \beta] \leq \mathbf{1}[\mathcal{M}(g, x_{(n')}, y_{(n')}) \leq \beta] + D^{-1}(\frac{n'-1}{n}, \frac{1}{n}\log\frac{|\mathcal{H}|^{N+1}}{\delta_N})$$

Since

$$\Pr_{D, g\sim\mathcal{Q}(f)}[\mathcal{M}(g, x, y) \leq \beta] = E_{g\sim\mathcal{Q}(f)}[\Pr_{\mathcal{D}}[\mathcal{M}(g, x, y) < \beta]] \leq \Pr_{g\sim\mathcal{Q}(f)}[\mathcal{M}(g, x_{(n')}, y_{(n')}) \leq \beta] + D^{-1}(\frac{n'-1}{n}, \frac{1}{n}\log\frac{|\mathcal{H}|^{N+1}}{\delta_N})$$

And for any $\theta > \beta$,

$$\Pr_{g\sim\mathcal{Q}(f)}[\mathcal{M}(g, x_{(n')}, y_{(n')}) \leq \beta] \leq \mathbf{1}[\frac{1}{n'}\sum_{i\in B_{\{n'|f\}}}\mathcal{M}(f, x_i, y_i) < \theta] + \Pr_{g\sim\mathcal{Q}(f)}[\mathcal{M}(f, x_{(n')}, y_{(n')}) \geq \theta, \mathcal{M}(g, x_{(n')}, y_{(n')}) \leq \beta]$$

Thus, we have

$$\Pr_{D, g\sim\mathcal{Q}(f)}[\mathcal{M}(g, x, y) \leq \beta] \leq \mathbf{1}[\frac{1}{n'}\sum_{i\in B_{\{n'|f\}}}\mathcal{M}(f, x_i, y_i) < \theta] + D^{-1}(\frac{n'-1}{n}, \frac{1}{n}\log\frac{|\mathcal{H}|^{N+1}}{\delta_N}) + \Pr_{g\sim\mathcal{Q}(f)}[\mathcal{M}(f, x_{(n')}, y_{(n')}) \geq \theta, \mathcal{M}(g, x_{(n')}, y_{(n')}) \leq \beta] \quad (12)$$

We now prove if $\mathcal{M}(f, x_{(n')}, y_{(n')}) \geq \theta$ and $\mathcal{M}(g, x_{(n')}, y_{(n')}) \leq \beta$ with $\theta > \beta$, there always exists an example (x_i, y_i) such that $\mathcal{M}(f, x_i, y_i) \geq \theta$ and $\mathcal{M}(g, x_i, y_i) \leq \beta$. Since there exists a bijection between $\{\mathcal{M}(f, x_{(1)}, y_{(1)}), \cdots, \mathcal{M}(f, x_{(n)}, y_{(n)})\}$ and $\{\mathcal{M}(g, x_{(1)}, y_{(1)}), \cdots, \mathcal{M}(g, x_{(n)}, y_{(n)})\}$, we can assume $\mathcal{M}(f, x_{(n')}, y_{(n')})$ corresponding to $\mathcal{M}(g, x_{(\tilde{n})}, y_{(\tilde{n})})$ for some $\tilde{n} \leq n$. If $\tilde{n} \leq n'$, then $(x_{(n')}, y_{(n')})$ of $\mathcal{M}(f, x_{(n')}, y_{(n')})$ is desired. On the other hand, if $\tilde{n} > n'$, then there are at least $n - n'$ examples greater than or equal to θ in $\{\mathcal{M}(f, x_i, y_i) : i \neq n'\}$ but at most $n - n' - 1$ examples greater than β in $\{\mathcal{M}(g, x_i, y_i) : i \neq \tilde{n}\}$. Thus,

$$\begin{aligned}
&\Pr_{g\sim\mathcal{Q}(f)}[\mathcal{M}(f, x_{(n')}, y_{(n')}) \geq \theta, \mathcal{M}(g, x_{(n')}, y_{(n')}) \leq \beta] \\
\leq &\Pr_{g\sim\mathcal{Q}(f)}[\exists(x_i, y_i) : \mathcal{M}(f, x_i, y_i) \geq \theta, \mathcal{M}(g, x_i, y_i) \leq \beta] \\
\leq &\Pr_{g\sim\mathcal{Q}(f)}[\exists(x_i, y_i) : \forall\tilde{y} : f(x_i, y_i) - f(x_i, \tilde{y}) \geq \theta, \exists\tilde{y} : g(x_i, y_i) - g(x_i, \tilde{y}) \leq \beta] \\
\leq &n(K-1)\exp(\frac{-N(\theta-\beta)^2}{2})
\end{aligned}$$

By combining (11) and (12), we obtain that with probability at least $1 - \delta_N$ over the training sample S, for all $f \in \mathcal{C}(\mathcal{H})$, all $\beta \in \mathcal{Z}$ and all $\theta > \beta$ and all $n' = \{1, \cdots, n\}$, but fixed N,

$$\begin{aligned}
&\Pr_{\mathcal{D}}[\mathcal{M}(f, x, y) < 0] \\
\leq &\mathbf{1}[\frac{1}{n'}\sum_{i\in B_{\{n'|f\}}}\mathcal{M}(f, x_i, y_i) < \theta] + \exp(\frac{-N\beta^2}{2}) \\
&+ n(K-1)\exp(\frac{-N(\theta-\beta)^2}{2}) + D^{-1}(\frac{n'-1}{n}, \frac{1}{n}\log\frac{|\mathcal{H}|^{N+1}}{\delta_N})
\end{aligned}$$

To let β takes values only in $\mathcal{Z}$, we set $\beta = \frac{\theta}{2} - \frac{\eta}{|\mathcal{H}|}$ with $0 \leq \eta < 1$ and $N = \left\lceil \frac{8}{\theta^2}\log\frac{2n^2}{\log|\mathcal{H}|}\right\rceil$, the following inequality holds for $\theta \geq \frac{8}{|\mathcal{H}|}$

$$\exp(\frac{-N\beta^2}{2}) + n(K-1)\exp(\frac{-N(\theta-\beta)^2}{2}) \leq (K-1)\frac{\log|\mathcal{H}|}{2n} + \sqrt{\frac{\log|\mathcal{H}|}{2n^2}}$$

Setting $\delta = 2^N\delta_N$. Thus, with probability at least $1-\delta$ over the random choice of the training data S of n examples, for all $f \in \mathcal{C}(\mathcal{H})$ and all $n' = \{1, \cdots, n\}$, we obtain

$$\Pr_{\mathcal{D}}[\mathcal{M}(f, x, y) < 0] \leq \mathbf{1}[\frac{1}{n'}\sum_{i\in B_{\{n'|f\}}}\mathcal{M}(f, x_i, y_i) < \theta] + (K-1)\frac{\log|\mathcal{H}|}{2n} + \sqrt{\frac{\log|\mathcal{H}|}{2n^2}} + D^{-1}(\frac{n'-1}{n}, \frac{1}{n}u)$$

where

$$u = \frac{8}{\theta^2}\log\frac{2n^2}{\log|\mathcal{H}|}\log 2|\mathcal{H}| + \log|\mathcal{H}| + \log\frac{1}{\delta}$$

□

C. PROOF OF THEOREM 3

PROOF. : By definition of quasiconcave, $g_{avg\ n'}(\boldsymbol{\alpha})$ is quasiconcave if and only if its upper contour sets are convex sets. The γ-upper-contour set $\mathcal{S}_\gamma$ of $g_{avg\ n'}(\boldsymbol{\alpha})$ is denoted as

$$\mathcal{S}_\gamma = \left\{\boldsymbol{\alpha} : \sum_{i\in\{B_{n'}|\boldsymbol{\alpha}\}}\left(\sum_{j=1}^{|\mathcal{H}|}\alpha_j 1(h_j(x_i) = y_i) - \max_{y\in\mathcal{Y}, y\neq y_i}\sum_{j=1}^{|\mathcal{H}|}\alpha_j 1(h_j(x_i) = y)\right) \geq \gamma\sum_{j=1}^{|\mathcal{H}|}|\alpha_j|\right\}$$

We now prove that $\mathcal{S}_\gamma$ is a convex set. For $\forall\boldsymbol{\alpha}^{(1)}$, $\boldsymbol{\alpha}^{(2)} \in \mathcal{S}_\gamma$, $\forall\lambda \in [0, 1]$, we have

$$\begin{aligned}
&\sum_{i\in\{B_{n'}|(1-\lambda)\boldsymbol{\alpha}^{(1)}+\lambda\boldsymbol{\alpha}^{(2)}\}}(\sum_{j=1}^{|\mathcal{H}|}((1-\lambda)\alpha_j^{(1)} + \lambda\alpha_j^{(2)})1(h_j(x_i) = y_i) \\
&- \max_{y\in\mathcal{Y}, y\neq y_i}\sum_{j=1}^{|\mathcal{H}|}((1-\lambda)\alpha_j^{(1)} + \lambda\alpha_j^{(2)})1(h_j(x_i) = y)) \\
\geq &(1-\lambda)\sum_{i\in\{B_{n'}|\boldsymbol{\alpha}^{(1)}\}}(\sum_{j=1}^{|\mathcal{H}|}\alpha_j^{(1)}1(h_j(x_i) = y_i) - \max_{y\in\mathcal{Y}, y\neq y_i}\sum_{j=1}^{|\mathcal{H}|}\alpha_j^{(1)}1(h_j(x_i) = \\
&+ \lambda\sum_{i\in\{B_{n'}|\boldsymbol{\alpha}^{(2)}\}}(\sum_{j=1}^{|\mathcal{H}|}\alpha_j^{(2)}1(h_j(x_i) = y_i) - \max_{y\in\mathcal{Y}, y\neq y_i}\sum_{j=1}^{|\mathcal{H}|}\alpha_j^{(2)}1(h_j(x_i) = y)) \\
\geq &(1-\lambda)\gamma\sum_{j=1}^{|\mathcal{H}|}|\alpha_j^{(1)}| + \lambda\gamma\sum_{j=1}^{|\mathcal{H}|}|\alpha_j^{(2)}| \geq \gamma\sum_{j=1}^{|\mathcal{H}|}|(1-\lambda)\alpha_j^{(1)} + \lambda\alpha_j^{(2)}|
\end{aligned}$$

Therefore, $(1-\lambda)\boldsymbol{\alpha}^{(1)} + \lambda\boldsymbol{\alpha}^{(2)} \in \mathcal{S}_\gamma$. $g_{avg\ n'}(\boldsymbol{\alpha})$ is quasiconcave. □

An Efficient Algorithm For Weak Hierarchical Lasso

Yashu Liu
Arizona State University
Tempe, AZ 85287
Yashu.Liu@asu.edu

Jie Wang
Arizona State University
Tempe, AZ 85287
jie.wang.ustc@asu.edu

Jieping Ye
Arizona State University
Tempe, AZ 85287
Jieping.Ye@asu.edu

ABSTRACT

Linear regression is a widely used tool in data mining and machine learning. In many applications, fitting a regression model with only linear effects may not be sufficient for predictive or explanatory purposes. One strategy which has recently received increasing attention in statistics is to include feature interactions to capture the nonlinearity in the regression model. Such model has been applied successfully in many biomedical applications. One major challenge in the use of such model is that the data dimensionality is significantly higher than the original data, resulting in the small sample size large dimension problem. Recently, weak hierarchical Lasso, a sparse interaction regression model, is proposed that produces sparse and hierarchical structured estimator by exploiting the Lasso penalty and a set of hierarchical constraints. However, the hierarchical constraints make it a non-convex problem and the existing method finds the solution of its convex relaxation, which needs additional conditions to guarantee the hierarchical structure. In this paper, we propose to directly solve the non-convex weak hierarchical Lasso by making use of the GIST (General Iterative Shrinkage and Thresholding) optimization framework which has been shown to be efficient for solving non-convex sparse formulations. The key step in GIST is to compute a sequence of proximal operators. One of our key technical contributions is to show that the proximal operator associated with the non-convex weak hierarchical Lasso admits a closed form solution. However, a naive approach for solving each subproblem of the proximal operator leads to a quadratic time complexity, which is not desirable for large-size problems. To this end, we further develop an efficient algorithm for computing the subproblems with a linearithmic time complexity. We have conducted extensive experiments on both synthetic and real data sets. Results show that our proposed algorithm is much more efficient and effective than its convex relaxation.

KDD'14, August 24–27, 2014, New York, NY, USA.

http://dx.doi.org/10.1145/2623330.2623665.

Categories and Subject Descriptors

H.2.8 [**Database Management**]: Database Applications, Data Mining

General Terms

Algorithms

Keywords

Sparse learning; non-convex; weak hierarchical Lasso; proximal operator

1. INTRODUCTION

Consider a linear regression model with the outcome variable y and d predictors $x_1, \ldots, x_d$:

$$y = w_0 + \sum_{i=1}^{d} x_i w_i + \epsilon, \tag{1}$$

where w_0 is the bias term, $w_i, i = 1 \ldots, d$ is the coefficient and $\epsilon \sim N(0, \sigma^2)$ is the noise term. In many applications, a simple linear regression model is not sufficient for predictive or explanatory purposes. One strategy which has recently received increasing attention in statistics is to include interaction terms into the model to capture the nonlinearity of the data [17, 22]. For example, the linear model including terms of order-2 and lower has the following form:

$$y = w_0 + \sum_{i=1}^{d} x_i w_i + \frac{1}{2} \sum_{i=1}^{d} \sum_{j=1}^{d} x_i x_j Q_{i,j} + \epsilon, \tag{2}$$

where the cross-product term $x_i x_j$, $i \neq j$ refers to as the interaction variable (one may view x_i^2 as a special interaction variable), and $w_i's$ and $Q \in \mathbb{R}^{d \times d}$ are the main effect and interaction effect coefficients respectively. Applications with interaction regression models are omnipresent. For example, in psychological study, the effectiveness of using 3-way interactions was demonstrated in testing psychological hypothesis [9]; there are strong evidences found in [4] that genetic-environment interactions have significant effects on conduct disorders; the research in [11] found a couple of evidences of gene-environment interactions in predicting depression status; in [26], the interaction between continuance commitment and affective commitment was found significant in predicting job withdraw intentions and absenteeism; [13] discovered that brain-derived neurotrophic factor interacts with early life stress in predicting cognitive features of depression and anxiety.

However, the use of higher order terms leads to data of high dimensionality. For instance, for regression model (1), if one wants to add all terms of order-k and lower, then there will be a total of $\mathcal{O}(d^k)$ variables, which is computationally demanding for parameter estimation even when k and d are fairly small. Thus, an efficient approach that is able to deal with huge dimensionality is desired in such cases, and the sparse learning methodology is one promising approach for tackling such problem [27, 18, 7, 5, 32]. In this paper, we focus on the model (2) with pairwise interactions, *i.e.*, two-factor interactions. Note that the analysis can be extended to the model with higher-order interactions.

In general, not all of the main effects and interactions are of interest, thus it is critical to select the variables of great significance. One simple approach for high dimensional interaction regression is to directly apply the Lasso [27], also known as the "all-pairs Lasso" [2] in the case of two-factor interactions. However, the all-pairs Lasso estimator does not account for any structural information which has been shown to be important for prediction and interpretation of the high dimensional interaction regression model [2, 30, 25, 29, 6]. In statistics, a hierarchical structure between main effects and interaction effects has been shown to be very effective in constraining the search space and identifying important individual features and interactions [2, 30, 25, 29, 6]. Specifically, the hierarchical constraint requires that an interaction term $x_i x_j$ is selected in the model only if the main effects x_i and/or x_j are included. Strong theoretical properties have been established for such hierarchical model [29, 30]. The hierarchical structure is supported by the argument that large main effects may result in interaction of more importance, and it is desired in a wide range of applications in engineering and underlying science. Traditional approaches to fit such a model typically follow the following two-step procedures [22]:

(i) Fit a linear regression model that only includes the main effects and then select the significant features;

(ii) Fit the reformulated model with the identified individual features and the interactions constructed via domain knowledge.

Since even a small d may lead to a huge amount of interaction variables, the two-step procedure is still time-consuming in many applications. Recently, there have been growing research efforts on imposing the hierarchical structure on main effects and interactions in the regression model with novel sparse learning methods. In [2], in order to enable feature selection and impose heredity structures, the authors proposed strong hierarchical Lasso which adds a set of constraints to the Lasso formulation to achieve the *strong hierarchy* where the interaction effects are non-zero only if the corresponding main effects are non-zero. In [25], a Lasso-type penalized least square formulation called VANISH was proposed to achieve the strong hierarchy between the interaction effects and main effects. In [29], a type of non-negative garrote method was proposed to achieve the heredity structures. In [30], the Composite Absolute Penalties were proposed to achieve heredity structures for interaction models. In contrast to the above works which fulfill the hierarchical structure via solving convex problems, Choi *et al.* in [6] formulated a non-convex problem to achieve the strong hierarchy by assuming that the coefficient of an interaction term is a product of a scalar and main effect coefficients. Different from the strong hierarchy, the *weak hierarchy* between the main effects and the interaction effects requires that an interaction is included in the model only if at least one of the main effects is included in the model. In mathematical form, $Q_{i,j} \neq 0$ only if $w_i \neq 0$ OR $w_j \neq 0$. The weak hierarchy can be considered as a structure in between the strong hierarchy and no hierarchical structure [2, 29, 30]. Specifically, weak hierarchy allows those interactions with only one significant "parent" (main effect) to be included in the model. Several existing empirical studies have demonstrated the stronger predictive power of weak hierarchical model [19]. In our study, we mainly focus on the interaction regression model with weak hierarchical structure.

We follow the weak hierarchical Lasso approach recently proposed by [2] to fit the pairwise interaction regression model with the weak hierarchy. By imposing restrictions of the weak hierarchy and taking advantage of the Lasso penalty [27] that leads to sparse coefficients, the weak hierarchical Lasso is able to simultaneously attain a hierarchical solution and identify important main effects and interactions. However, the set of constraints restricting hierarchical constraints make the problem non-convex; the algorithm proposed in [2] aims to solve a convex relaxation. The convex relaxation, however, requires additional conditions to guarantee the weak hierarchy, which is not desirable.

In this paper, we propose to directly solve the weak hierarchical Lasso using the GIST (General Iterative Shrinkage and Thresholding) optimization framework recently proposed by [15]. The GIST framework has been shown to be highly efficient for solving large-scale non-convex problems. The most critical step in GIST is to compute a sequence of proximal operators [23]. In this paper, we first show that the proximal operator related to weak hierarchical Lasso admits an analytical form solution by factorizing unknown coefficients into sign matrices and non-negative coefficients. However, a naive method of computing the subproblem of the proximal operator leads to a quadratic time complexity, which is not desirable for large-size problems. To this end, we further develop an efficient algorithm for solving the subproblems, which achieves a linearithmic time complexity. We evaluate the efficiency and effectiveness of the proposed algorithm and compare it with the convex relaxation in [2] and other state-of-the-art methods using synthetic and real data sets. Our empirical study demonstrates the high efficiency of our algorithm and the superior predictive performance of weak hierarchical Lasso over the competing methods.

The remaining of the paper is organized as follows: we give a brief review of the weak hierarchical Lasso and its convex relaxation in Section 2. In Section 3, we derive the closed form solution to the proximal operator of the original weak hierarchical Lasso by decomposing the unknown coefficients into signs and the non-negative coefficients. Then, we show how the associated proximal operator can be computed efficiently. We report the experimental results in Section 4. We conclude this paper in Section 5.

2. THE WEAK HIERARCHICAL LASSO

In this section, we briefly review the weak hierarchical Lasso and its corresponding convex relaxed formulation [2]. Suppose we are given n pairs of data points $\{(x_i, y_i)\}_{i=1}^n \subset \mathbb{R}^d \times \mathbb{R}$. Let $Y \in \mathbb{R}^{n\times 1}$ be the vector of outcome and $X \in$

$\mathbb{R}^{n\times d}$ be the design matrix. Let $Z \in \mathbb{R}^{n\times(d\cdot d)}$ be the matrix of interactions where

$$Z = \left[Z^{(1)}, Z^{(2)}, \ldots, Z^{(d)}\right],$$

$Z^{(i)} \in \mathbb{R}^{n\times d}$ and each column of $Z^{(i)}, i = 1, \ldots d$ is an interaction, *i.e.*, $Z^{(i)}_{\cdot,j} = X_{\cdot,i} \odot X_{\cdot,j}$ ($\odot$ is the operator of element-wise product). Thus, $Z^{(i)}$ captures the pairwise interactions between the i-th feature and all d features. Note that, we include the quadratic terms x_i^2 in the interaction model for clearer presentation, however our analysis is still applicable if they are not included in the model. By assuming that Y is centered and X, Z are column-wise normalized to zero mean and unit standard deviation, we can set the bias term $w_0 = 0$. Thus, in matrix form, the pairwise interaction regression model can be expressed as

$$Y = Xw + \frac{1}{2}Z \cdot \text{vec}(Q) + \epsilon, \tag{3}$$

where $\epsilon \sim N(\mathbf{0}, \sigma^2\mathbf{I})$ and "vec" is the vectorization operator that transforms a matrix to a column vector by stacking the columns of the matrix. Thus, the least square loss function of (3) is given by:

$$\mathcal{L}(w, Q) = \frac{1}{2}\left\|Y - Xw - \frac{1}{2}Z \cdot \text{vec}(Q)\right\|_2^2. \tag{4}$$

Then, the weak hierarchical Lasso formulation takes the form of [2]:

$$\begin{aligned} &\min_{x,Q}\ \mathcal{L}(w, Q) + \lambda\|w\|_1 + \frac{\lambda}{2}\|Q\|_1 \\ &\text{s.t.}\quad \|Q_{\cdot,j}\|_1 \le |w_j| \quad \text{for} \quad j = 1, \ldots, d, \end{aligned} \tag{5}$$

where $\|Q\|_1 = \sum_{i,j}|Q_{i,j}|$ and λ is the Lasso penalty parameter.

Note that the constraints in (5) guarantee the weak hierarchical structure since the coefficient $Q_{i,j}$ of interaction $x_i x_j$ is non-zero only if at least one of its main effects is included in the model, *i.e.*, $w_i \neq 0$ or $w_j \neq 0$. However, the imposed hierarchical constraints make problem (5) non-convex. Instead of solving (5), Bien *et al.* in [2] proposed to solve the following relaxed version:

$$\begin{aligned} &\min_{w,Q}\ \mathcal{L}(w^+ - w^-, Q) + \lambda\mathbf{1}^T(w^+ + w^-) + \frac{\lambda}{2}\|Q\|_1 \\ &\left.\begin{aligned} \text{s.t.}\quad &\|Q_{\cdot,j}\|_1 \le w_j^+ + w_j^- \\ &w_j^+ \ge 0 \\ &w_j^- \ge 0 \end{aligned}\right\} \quad \text{for} \quad j = 1, \ldots, d, \end{aligned} \tag{6}$$

where $\mathbf{1}$ represents a column vector of all ones. In view of (6), we can see that $\|w\|_1$ is relaxed to $w^+ + w^-$. Problem (6) is convex and can be solved by many efficient solvers such as FISTA [1]. However, Bien *et al.* in [2] showed that problem (6) needs an additional ridge penalty to guarantee the weak hierarchical structure of the estimator. In this paper, we propose an efficient algorithm which directly solves the non-convex weak hierarchical Lasso formulation in (5).

3. THE PROPOSED ALGORITHM

In this section, we propose an efficient algorithm named "eWHL", which stands for "**e**fficient **W**eak **H**ierarchical **L**asso", to directly solve the weak hierarchical Lasso. eWHL makes use of the optimization framework of GIST (General Iterative Shrinkage and Thresholding) due to its high efficiency and effectiveness for solving non-convex sparse formulations. One of the critical steps in GIST is to compute the proximal operator associated with the penalty functions. As one of our major contributions, we first factorize the unknown coefficients into the product of their signs and magnitudes; and then show that the proximal operator of (5) admits a closed form solution in Section 3.1. Another major contribution is that we present an efficient algorithm for computing the proximal operator associated with the non-convex weak hierarchical Lasso in Section 3.2. The time complexity of solving each subproblem of the proximal operator can be reduced from quadratic to linearithmic. We then summarize our algorithm for computing the proximal operator in Section 3.2.

3.1 The Closed Form Solution to the Proximal Operator

In this section, we show how to derive the closed form solution of the proximal operator associated with (5) in detail. Let

$$\mathcal{P} = \left\{(a, B),\ a \in \mathbb{R}^d,\ B \in \mathbb{R}^{d\times d}\ \middle|\ \|B_{\cdot,j}\|_1 \le |a_j|,\ j = 1, \ldots, d\right\}$$

and the indicator function be defined by

$$\mathcal{R}(w, Q) = \begin{cases} \lambda\|w\|_1 + \frac{\lambda}{2}\|Q\|_1, & \text{if} \quad (w, Q) \in \mathcal{P} \\ +\infty, & \text{if} \quad (w, Q) \notin \mathcal{P} \end{cases}. \tag{7}$$

Given a sequence $\left\{\left(w^{(k)}, Q^{(k)}\right)\right\}$, the proximal operator associated with weak hierarchical Lasso is:

$$\begin{aligned} &\left(w^{(k+1)}, Q^{(k+1)}\right) \\ &= \arg\min_{w,\ Q}\ \mathcal{L}\left(w^{(k)}, Q^{(k)}\right) + \left\langle \nabla_w\mathcal{L}\left(w^{(k)}, Q^{(k)}\right),\ w - w^{(k)}\right\rangle \\ &+ \left\langle \nabla_Q\mathcal{L}\left(w^{(k)}, Q^{(k)}\right),\ Q - Q^{(k)}\right\rangle + \frac{t^{(k)}}{2}\left\|w - w^{(k)}\right\|_2^2 \\ &+ \frac{t^{(k)}}{2}\left\|Q - Q^{(k)}\right\|_F^2 + \mathcal{R}(w, Q), \end{aligned} \tag{8}$$

where $t^{(k)} > 0$.

Simple algebraic manipulation leads to

$$\begin{aligned} \left(w^{(k+1)}, Q^{(k+1)}\right) = \arg\min_{w,\ Q}\ &\frac{1}{2}\left\|w - v^{(k)}\right\|_2^2 + \frac{1}{2}\left\|Q - U^{(k)}\right\|_2^2 \\ &+ \frac{1}{t^{(k)}}\mathcal{R}(w, Q), \end{aligned} \tag{9}$$

where

$$\begin{aligned} v^{(k)} &= w^{(k)} - \nabla_w\mathcal{L}\left(w^{(k)}, Q^{(k)}\right)/t^{(k)}, \\ U^{(k)} &= U^{(k)} - \nabla_Q\mathcal{L}\left(w^{(k)}, Q^{(k)}\right)/t^{(k)}. \end{aligned}$$

Thus, problem (5) can be solved by iteratively solving the proximal operator in (9). Because $\mathcal{R}(w, Q)$ is an indicator function, we can rewrite the proximal operator (9) as

$$\begin{aligned}&\arg\min_{w,\,Q}\ \frac{1}{2}\|w-v\|_2^2+\frac{1}{2}\|Q-U\|_F^2+\frac{\lambda}{t}\|w\|_1+\frac{\lambda}{2t}\|Q\|_1\\ &\quad \text{s.t. } \|Q_{\cdot,j}\|_1\le |w_j| \quad \text{for} \quad j=1,\dots,d.\end{aligned} \tag{10}$$

We omit the superscripts for notational simplicity.

The vector of main effect coefficients can be written as

$$w = S^0\tilde{w},$$

where $\tilde{w}_j = |w_j|, j = 1,\dots,d$ and $S^0 \in \mathbb{R}^{d\times d}$ is a diagonal matrix whose j-th diagonal element is the sign of w_j, *i.e.*, $S^0_{j,j} = \text{sign}(w_j)$. We define

$$\text{sign}(w)=\begin{cases}1 & \text{if} \quad w>0\\ -1 & \text{if} \quad w<0\,,\\ 0 & \text{if} \quad w=0\end{cases} \tag{11}$$

and we assume in this paper that the sign operator is applied on vectors or matrices elementwise. Similarly, we factorize each column of the interaction coefficient matrix as $Q_{\cdot,j} = S^j\widetilde{Q}_{\cdot,j}$, $j = 1\dots,d$, where $\widetilde{Q}_{i,j} = |Q_{i,j}|$ and $S^j \in \mathbb{R}^{d\times d}$ is the diagonal sign matrix. Then, the proximal operator (10) is equivalent to

$$\begin{aligned}&\arg\min_{w,\,Q}\ \frac{1}{2}\|w-v\|_2^2+\frac{1}{2}\|Q-U\|_F^2+\frac{\lambda}{t}\|w\|_1+\frac{\lambda}{2t}\|Q\|_1\\ &\text{s.t. } \left.\begin{aligned}&\|Q_{\cdot,j}\|_1\le|w_j|\\ &w_j=S^0_{j,j}\tilde{w}_j\\ &Q_{\cdot,j}=S^j\widetilde{Q}_{\cdot,j}\\ &\tilde{w}_j\ge 0\\ &\widetilde{Q}_{\cdot,j}\succeq\mathbf{0}\end{aligned}\right\}\quad \text{for} \quad j=1,\dots,d,\end{aligned} \tag{12}$$

where $\widetilde{Q}$, $\tilde{w}$ and S^j, $j = 0,\dots,d$ are the unknown variables, $\succeq$ is defined as the element-wise "greater than or equal to" comparison operator, *i.e.*, for $V,\ U \in \mathbb{R}^{d\times 1}, V \succeq U \Leftrightarrow V_i \ge U_i, i = 1\dots,d$. Therefore, the solutions of the original weak hierarchical Lasso can be obtained by iteratively solving (12). Note that the amounts of l_1 penalties on w and Q can be different. Here we use the same penalty parameter λ for notational simplicity and consistency with the original formulation of weak hierarchical Lasso (5) studied in [2]. Though the factorization introduces more variables and constraints, we show that the resulting proximal operator admits a closed form solution. More importantly, we show that each sub-problem of the proximal operator can be solved by the proposed eWHL algorithm in linearithmic time. Indeed, the factorization of w and Q into their signs and magnitudes is the first key to directly solve the original weak hierarchical Lasso.

It is clear that the proximal operator in (12) can be decoupled into d subproblems:

$$\begin{aligned}&\arg\min_{\tilde{w}_j,S^0_{jj},\widetilde{Q}_{\cdot,j},S^j}\ \frac{1}{2}\left\|S^0_{jj}\tilde{w}_j-v_j\right\|_2^2+\frac{1}{2}\left\|S^j\widetilde{Q}_{\cdot,j}-U_{\cdot,j}\right\|_2^2\\ &\qquad+\frac{\lambda}{t}\tilde{w}_j+\frac{\lambda}{2t}\mathbf{1}^T\widetilde{Q}_{\cdot,j}\\ &\text{s.t.}\quad \left.\begin{aligned}&\mathbf{1}^T\widetilde{Q}_{\cdot,j}\le\tilde{w}_j\\ &\widetilde{Q}_{\cdot,j}\succeq\mathbf{0}\end{aligned}\right\},\quad \text{for } j=1,\dots,d.\end{aligned} \tag{13}$$

Next, we show that (13) has a closed form solution. Since

$$\begin{aligned}\frac{1}{2}(w_j-v_j)^2=&\frac{1}{2}\left(S^0_{jj}\tilde{w}_j-v_j\right)^2\\ =&\frac{1}{2}\left(S^0_{jj}\left(S^0_{jj}\tilde{w}_j-v_j\right)\right)^2=\frac{1}{2}\left(\tilde{w}_j-S^0_{jj}v_j\right)^2\end{aligned}$$

and $\tilde{w}_j \ge 0$, $S^0_{j,j}$ must have the same sign as v_j, that is, w_j has the same sign as v_j. Otherwise, the value of $\frac{1}{2}\left(\tilde{w}_j - S^0_{jj}v_j\right)^2$ will not achieve the minimum. Similarly, one can show that $S^j_{i,i}$, *i.e.*, the sign of $Q_{i,j}$, must be the same as the sign of $U_{i,j}$. Thus, the diagonal elements $\text{diag}(S^0) = \text{sign}(v)$, $\text{diag}(S^j) = \text{sign}(U_{\cdot,j})$, $j = 1,\dots,d$. Next, we show how to compute $\tilde{w}$ and $\widetilde{Q}$.

By letting $\tilde{v}_j = S^0_{jj}v_j$ and $\widetilde{U}_j = S^jU_{\cdot,j}$, each subproblem (13) is equivalent to

$$\begin{aligned}&\arg\min_{\tilde{w}_j,\widetilde{Q}_{\cdot,j}}\ \frac{1}{2}\|\tilde{w}_j-\tilde{v}_j\|_2^2+\frac{1}{2}\left\|\widetilde{Q}_{\cdot,j}-\widetilde{U}_{\cdot,j}\right\|_2^2+\frac{\lambda}{t}\tilde{w}_j+\frac{\lambda}{2t}\mathbf{1}^T\widetilde{Q}_{\cdot,j}\\ &\text{s.t.}\quad \begin{aligned}&\mathbf{1}^T\widetilde{Q}_{\cdot,j}\le\tilde{w}_j\\ &\widetilde{Q}_{\cdot,j}\succeq\mathbf{0}\end{aligned}\ .\end{aligned} \tag{14}$$

After rearrangement, problem (14) can be expressed as:

$$\begin{aligned}&\min_{\tilde{w}_j,\widetilde{Q}_{\cdot,j}}\ \frac{1}{2}\|\tilde{w}_j-\check{v}_j\|_2^2+\frac{1}{2}\left\|\widetilde{Q}_{\cdot,j}-\check{U}_{\cdot,j}\right\|_2^2\\ &\text{s.t.}\quad \begin{aligned}&\mathbf{1}^T\widetilde{Q}_{\cdot,j}\le\tilde{w}_j\\ &\widetilde{Q}_{\cdot,j}\succeq\mathbf{0}\end{aligned}\ ,\end{aligned} \tag{15}$$

where $\check{v}_j = \tilde{v}_j - \frac{\lambda}{t}\mathbf{1}$ and $\check{U}_{\cdot,j} = \widetilde{U}_{\cdot,j} - \frac{\lambda}{2t}\mathbf{1}$.

We solve (15) by deriving its dual problem. Let $\gamma \ge 0$ be the Lagrangian multiplier dual variable of the first inequality constraint. Define the Lagrangian function of (15) as:

$$l(\gamma,\tilde{w},\widetilde{Q})=\frac{1}{2}(\tilde{w}-\check{v})^2+\frac{1}{2}\left\|\widetilde{Q}-\check{U}\right\|_2^2+\gamma\left(\mathbf{1}^T\widetilde{Q}-\tilde{w}\right)$$

where we omit the subscripts for simplicity with a little abuse of notation. Since the constraint $\mathbf{1}^T\widetilde{Q} \le \tilde{w}$ is affine, the strong duality holds for the minimization problem (15). Thus, the dual problem of (15) is:

$$\max_{\gamma\ge 0}\ \min_{\tilde{w},\widetilde{Q}\succeq\mathbf{0}}\ \frac{1}{2}(\tilde{w}-\check{v})^2+\frac{1}{2}\left\|\widetilde{Q}-\check{U}\right\|_2^2+\gamma\left(\mathbf{1}^T\widetilde{Q}-\tilde{w}\right). \tag{16}$$

By rearranging the terms, (16) is equivalent to:

$$\max_{\gamma\ge 0}\ \min_{\tilde{w},\widetilde{Q}\succeq\mathbf{0}}\ \frac{1}{2}(\tilde{w}-(\check{v}+\gamma))^2+\frac{1}{2}\left\|\widetilde{Q}-\left(\check{U}-\gamma\mathbf{1}\right)\right\|_2^2+h(\gamma), \tag{17}$$

where $h(\gamma) = -\check{v}\gamma - \frac{1}{2}\gamma^2 + \gamma\mathbf{1}^T\check{U} - \frac{1}{2}\gamma^2\mathbf{1}^T\mathbf{1}$.

For fixed γ, in order to obtain the minimum of the objective function in (17), we conclude that

$$\begin{cases}\check{v}+\gamma\ge 0 & \Rightarrow \quad \tilde{w}=\check{v}+\gamma\\ \check{v}+\gamma<0 & \Rightarrow \quad \tilde{w}=0\\ \check{U}_i-\gamma\ge 0 & \Rightarrow \quad \widetilde{Q}_i=\check{U}_i-\gamma\\ \check{U}_i-\gamma<0 & \Rightarrow \quad \widetilde{Q}_i=0\end{cases} \tag{18}$$

due to the constraints $\tilde{w} \ge 0$ and $\widetilde{Q} \succeq \mathbf{0}$. Therefore, if we obtain a dual optimal solution γ^* that maximizes the dual problem (17), then we can readily compute the closed form solution to (13) and thus to (12). That is, $w^* =$

$S^0\tilde{w}^*$, $Q^*_{:,j} = S^j\widetilde{Q}^*_{:,j}$ where $\text{diag}(S^0) = \text{sign}(v_j)$, $\text{diag}(S^j) = \text{sign}(U_{:,j})$, $j = 1, \ldots, d$ and $\tilde{w}^*$, $\widetilde{Q}^*$ are obtained via (18) at the optimal dual solution γ^*.

3.2 The Dual Optimal Solution

Next, we show how to efficiently compute the dual optimal solution γ^*. First, we sort $-\breve{v}$ and $\breve{U}_i, i = 1, \ldots, d$ in ascending order. Without loss of generality, we assume:

$$\breve{U}_1 \leq \ldots \leq \breve{U}_L \leq -\breve{v} \leq \breve{U}_{L+1} \leq \ldots \leq \breve{U}_d. \tag{19}$$

There are four possible cases about the locations of γ. We discuss how to identify the optimal dual solution γ^* in each of the four cases.

Case 1 :
When $\ldots \leq \breve{U}_G \leq \gamma \leq \breve{U}_{G+1} \leq \ldots \leq -\breve{v} \leq \ldots$, the objective in (17) at γ^* becomes

$$\begin{aligned} &\frac{1}{2}\sum_{i=1}^{G}\left(\breve{U}_i - \gamma\right)^2 + \frac{1}{2}(\breve{v}+\gamma)^2 + h(\gamma) \\ =&\frac{1}{2}\sum_{i=1}^{G}\breve{U}_i^2 + \sum_{i=G+1}^{d}\gamma\breve{U}_i - \frac{d-G}{2}\gamma^2 + \frac{1}{2}\breve{v}^2. \end{aligned} \tag{20}$$

Function (20) is a quadratic function with respect to γ and the unconstrained maximum is achieved at the axis of symmetry point $\frac{\sum_{i=G+1}^{d}\breve{U}_i}{d-G} \geq \breve{U}_{G+1}$. Since γ falls in the interval $\left[\breve{U}_G, \breve{U}_{G+1}\right]$, we set

$$\gamma = \breve{U}_{G+1}$$

to achieve the maximum objective value of (17). It can be further concluded that, in **Case 1**, among all the intervals on the left of $-\breve{v}$, the maximum objective value of (17) is achieved at the $\breve{U}_G$.

Case 2:
When $\ldots \leq \breve{U}_L \leq \gamma \leq -\breve{v} \leq \breve{U}_{L+1} \leq \ldots$, it turns out that the objective value in (17) at γ is similar to (20):

$$\frac{1}{2}\sum_{i=1}^{L}\breve{U}_i^2 + \sum_{i=L+1}^{d}\gamma\breve{U}_i - \frac{d-L}{2}\gamma^2 + \frac{1}{2}\breve{v}^2. \tag{21}$$

By a similar argument, we can set $\gamma = -\breve{v}$ to achieve the maximum. Combining the results of **Case 1** and **Case 2**, we conclude that, we may only consider γ in the range $[\max(-\breve{v}, 0), +\infty]$. Note that when $L = d$, that is $\breve{U}_d \leq \gamma \leq -\breve{v}$, (21) is a constant $\frac{1}{2}\sum_{i=1}^{d}\breve{U}_i^2 + \frac{1}{2}\breve{v}^2$, and thus γ can be any value in the interval $\left[\breve{U}_d, -\breve{v}\right]$.

Case 3:
When $\ldots \leq \breve{U}_L \leq -\breve{v} \leq \gamma \leq \breve{U}_{L+1} \leq \ldots$, the value of the objective function in (17) at γ^* becomes

$$\begin{aligned} &\frac{1}{2}\sum_{i=1}^{L}\left(\breve{U}_i - \gamma\right)^2 + h(\gamma) \\ =&\frac{1}{2}\sum_{i=1}^{L}\breve{U}_i^2 + \gamma\left(\sum_{i=L+1}^{d}\breve{U}_i - \breve{v}\right) - \frac{d+1-L}{2}\gamma^2. \end{aligned} \tag{22}$$

Again, (22) is a quadratic function of γ and $\frac{\sum_{i=L+1}^{d}\breve{U}_i - \breve{v}}{d+1-L} \geq -\breve{v}$. If $\frac{\sum_{i=L+1}^{d}\breve{U}_i - \breve{v}}{d+1-L} \geq \breve{U}_{L+1}$, the maximum is achieved at

$$\gamma = \breve{U}_{L+1},$$

otherwise the maximum is achieved at

$$\gamma = \frac{\sum_{i=L+1}^{d}\breve{U}_i - \breve{v}}{d+1-L}.$$

Case 4:
When $\ldots \leq -\breve{v} \leq \ldots \leq \breve{U}_G \leq \gamma \leq \breve{U}_{G+1} \leq \ldots$, the objective value in (17) is similar to (22):

$$\frac{1}{2}\sum_{i=1}^{G}\breve{U}_i^2 + \gamma\left(\sum_{i=G+1}^{d}\breve{U}_i - \breve{v}\right) - \frac{p+1-G}{2}\gamma^2. \tag{23}$$

If $\frac{\sum_{i=G+1}^{d}\breve{U}_i - \breve{v}}{d+1-G} \geq \breve{U}_{G+1}$, then the maximum is achieved at

$$\gamma = \breve{U}_{G+1};$$

If $\frac{\sum_{i=G+1}^{d}\breve{U}_i - \breve{v}}{d+1-G} \leq \breve{U}_G$, then the maximum is achieved at

$$\gamma = \breve{U}_G;$$

If $\breve{U}_G \leq \frac{\sum_{i=G+1}^{d}\breve{U}_i - \breve{v}}{d+1-G} \leq \breve{U}_{G+1}$, the maximum is achieved at

$$\gamma = \frac{\sum_{i=G+1}^{d}\breve{U}_i - \breve{v}}{d+1-G}.$$

Since we know exactly the value of γ for all the four cases, one naive way to find the optimal γ^* is to enumerate all the possible locations and pick the one that maximizes the objective function value in (17). However, evaluating the objectives for all possible locations from $\max(-\breve{v}, 0)$ to $\breve{U}_d$ leads to a quadratic time algorithm for solving (17). Interestingly, we show below that the time complexity of solving (17) can be reduced to $\mathcal{O}(d\log(d))$.

Let us first list some useful properties as follows:
Given the ordered sequence (19):

- **Property 1:**
  The maximum objective value of (17) in Case 3 is larger than the one in Cases 1 & 2;
- **Property 2:**
  In Case 4, for a pair of adjacent intervals $\left[\breve{U}_{G-1}, \breve{U}_G\right]$ and $\left[\breve{U}_G, \breve{U}_{G+1}\right]$, if $\frac{\sum_{i=G+1}^{d}\breve{U}_i - \breve{v}}{d+1-G} \geq \breve{U}_{G+1}$ for $[\breve{U}_G, \breve{U}_{G+1}]$, then $\frac{\sum_{i=G}^{d}\breve{U}_i - \breve{v}}{d+1-(G-1)} \geq \breve{U}_G$ for $[\breve{U}_{G-1}, \breve{U}_G]$;
- **Property 3:**
  In Case 4, if $\frac{\sum_{i=G+1}^{d}\breve{U}_i - \breve{v}}{d+1-G} \geq \breve{U}_{G+1}$ for $\left[\breve{U}_G, \breve{U}_{G+1}\right]$, the maximum objective value of (17) in $\left[\breve{U}_G, \breve{U}_{G+1}\right]$ is larger than or equal to the one in $\left[\breve{U}_{G-1}, \breve{U}_G\right]$.
- **Property 4:**
  In Case 4, for a pair of adjacent intervals $\left[\breve{U}_{G-1}, \breve{U}_G\right]$ and $\left[\breve{U}_G, \breve{U}_{G+1}\right]$, if we have $\frac{\sum_{i=G}^{d}\breve{U}_i - \breve{v}}{d+1-(G-1)} \leq \breve{U}_{G-1}$ for $\left[\breve{U}_{G-1}, \breve{U}_G\right]$, then $\frac{\sum_{i=G+1}^{d}\breve{U}_i - \breve{v}}{d+1-G} \leq \breve{U}_G$ for $\left[\breve{U}_G, \breve{U}_{G+1}\right]$.

- **Property 5:**
  In Case 4, if $\frac{\sum_{i=G}^{d} \breve{U}_i - \breve{v}}{d+1-(G-1)} \leq \breve{U}_{G-1}$ for $\left[\breve{U}_{G-1}, \breve{U}_G\right]$, the maximum objective value of (17) in $\left[\breve{U}_{G-1}, \breve{U}_G\right]$, is larger than or equal to the one in $\left[\breve{U}_G, \breve{U}_{G+1}\right]$.

- **Property 6:**
  In Case 4, if $\breve{U}_G \leq \frac{\sum_{i=G+1}^{d} \breve{U}_i - \breve{v}}{d+1-G} \leq \breve{U}_{G+1}$ for $\left[\breve{U}_G, \breve{U}_{G+1}\right]$, then $\frac{\sum_{i=G}^{d} \breve{U}_i - \breve{v}}{d+1-(G-1)} \geq \breve{U}_G$ for $\left[\breve{U}_{G-1}, \breve{U}_G\right]$ and $\frac{\sum_{i=G+2}^{d} \breve{U}_i - \breve{v}}{d+1-(G+1)}$ $\leq \breve{U}_{G+1}$ for $\left[\breve{U}_{G+1}, \breve{U}_{G+2}\right]$, and the maximum value of (17) in the interval $\left[\breve{U}_G, \breve{U}_{G+1}\right]$ is larger than or equal to the ones in its neighbor intervals.

Properties 2-6 also apply for adjacent intervals $\left[-\breve{v}, \breve{U}_{L+1}\right]$ and $\left[\breve{U}_{L+1}, \breve{U}_{L+2}\right]$ in Case 3.

We omit the proof of Properties 1-6 since they are direct applications of 1-D quadratic optimization. Property 1 indicates that it is sufficient for the algorithm to start searching γ^* from Case 3. Properties 2 & 3 imply that, for some interval, if the axis of symmetry is on the right hand side of the interval, then one only needs to consider the intervals to the right. Similarly, Properties 4 & 5 indicate that, for some interval, if the axis of symmetry is on the left hand side of the interval, then one only needs to consider the intervals to the left. Property 6 combined with Properties 1-5 imply that, for certain interval, if it contains the axis of symmetry, then γ^* is the axis of symmetry point. Thus, we can draw the following conclusion: (1) if $\max\left(\breve{U}_d, -v\right) < 0$, then

$$\gamma^* = 0;$$

(2) if $-\breve{v} > \breve{U}_d$, then

$$\gamma^* = \max(-\breve{v}, 0);$$

(3) if $\breve{U}_G \leq \frac{\sum_{i=G+1}^{d} \breve{U}_i - \breve{v}}{d+1-G} \leq \breve{U}_{G+1}$ for a certain interval $\left[\breve{U}_G, \breve{U}_{G+1}\right]$, then

$$\gamma^* = \frac{\sum_{i=G+1}^{d} \breve{U}_i - \breve{v}}{d+1-G}.$$

At each move, the axis of symmetry $\frac{\sum_{i=G+1}^{d} \breve{U}_i - \breve{v}}{d+1-G}$ can be calculated by a constant operation based on the value from the last step, and the time complexity of searching γ^* reduces from quadratic to $\mathcal{O}(d\log(d))$ as the computation is dominated by the sorting operation. Once γ^* is determined, we can compute $\tilde{w}$ and $\widetilde{Q}$ by (18). Note that, the subproblem of the proximal operator associated with the convex relaxation in [2] is solved by searching for the dual variable in a different way with time complexity $\mathcal{O}(d^2)$.

In summary, we reformulate the proximal operator for the original weak hierarchical Lasso by factorizing the unknown coefficients. The reformulated proximal operator is shown to admit a closed form solution, which enables directly solving the weak hierarchical Lasso problem. Moreover, the subproblem of the proximal operator can be computed efficiently with a time complexity of $\mathcal{O}(d\log(d))$. The detailed algorithm for solving the proximal operator (12) is described in Algorithm 1. We give the details of eWHL algorithm in Algorithm 2. Following [15], we choose the step size $t^{(k)}$ by the Barzilai-Borwein (BB) Rule.

Algorithm 1 Computation of the Proximal Operator of Weak Hierarchical Lasso

Input: $v \in \mathbb{R}^{d\times 1}$, $U \in \mathbb{R}^{d\times d}$, $t \in \mathbb{R}_+$, $\lambda \in \mathbb{R}_+$
Output: $w \in \mathbb{R}^{d\times 1}$, $Q \in \mathbb{R}^{d\times d}$

```
v̆ = sign(v) ⊙ v − (λ/t) 1;
Ŭ = sign(U) ⊙ U − (λ/2t) 1 1^T;
for j = 1 : d do
  c = −v̆_j;
  Sort Ŭ_{·,j} to get a sequence S in ascending order where S_1 ≤ S_1 ≤ ... ≤ S_d;
  if S_d < 0 and c < 0 then
    w̃_j = 0;
    Q̃_{·,j} = 0;
  else
    if S_d < c then
      γ = max(c, 0);
    else
      k = d;
      while 1 do
        c = c + S_k;
        k = k − 1;
        if c/(d + 1 − k) ≥ S_k then
          γ = c;
          break;
        end if
      end while
    end if
    w̃_j = max(v̆_j + γ, 0);
    Q̃_{·,j} = max(Ŭ_{·,j} − γ, 0);
  end if
end for
w = sign(v) ⊙ w̃;
Q = sign(U) ⊙ Q̃;
```

4. EXPERIMENTS

In this section, we evaluate the efficiency and effectiveness of the proposed algorithm on both synthetic and real data sets. In our first experiment, we compare the efficiency of our proposed algorithm and the convex relaxation of weak hierarchical Lasso [2] on synthetic data sets where the weak hierarchical structure holds between main effects and interaction effects. In our second experiment, we compare the classification performance of the weak hierarchical Lasso with other classifiers and sparse learning techniques on the data collected from Alzheimer's Disease Neuroimaging Initiative (ADNI)[1].

4.1 Efficiency and Effectiveness Comparison on Synthetic Data Sets

In this experiment, we compare the efficiency of the proposed eWHL algorithm with the convex relaxation on synthetic data sets. Our algorithm is built upon the GIST framework which is available online [16]. The source code of the convex relaxed weak hierarchical Lasso (cvxWHL) was available in the R package "*hierNet*" [3] where the optimiza-

[1]http://www.adni-info.org/

Algorithm 2 The Efficient Weak Hierarchical Lasso Algorithm (eWHL)

Input: $X \in \mathbb{R}^{n \times d}$, $Z \in \mathbb{R}^{n \times (d \cdot d)}$, $\lambda \in \mathbb{R}_+$, $\eta > 1$
Output: $w \in \mathbb{R}^{d \times 1}$, $Q \in \mathbb{R}^{d \times d}$

Initialize $k \leftarrow 0$ and starting points $w^{(0)}$ and $Q^{(0)}$;
repeat
  Choose the step size $t^{(k)}$ by the BB Rule
  repeat
    $v^{(k)} = w^{(k)} - \nabla_w \mathcal{L}\left(w^{(k)}, Q^{(k)}\right)/t^{(k)}$;
    $U^{(k)} = U^{(k)} - \nabla_Q \mathcal{L}\left(w^{(k)}, Q^{(k)}\right)/t^{(k)}$;
    Solve $\left(w^{(k+1)}, Q^{(k+1)}\right)$ by Algorithm 1 with input $\left(v^{(k)}, U^{(k)}, t^{(k)}, \lambda\right)$;
    $t^{(k)} \leftarrow \eta t^{(k)}$;
  until line search criterion is satisfied
  $k \leftarrow k + 1$
until stop criterion is satisfied

tion procedure was implemented by C. Since the proposed algorithm in this paper directly solves the non-convex weak hierarchical Lasso (5), and the eventual goal of the convex relaxed weak hierarchical Lasso is also to find a good "relaxed" solution to the original problem, we compare the two algorithms in terms of the objective function in (5). In the experiment, entries of $X \in \mathbb{R}^{n \times d}$ are i.i.d generated from the standard normal distribution, *i.e.,* $X_{i,j} \sim N(0,1)$. The matrix of interactions, Z, is then generated via the normalized X where $Z = \left[Z^{(1)}, Z^{(2)}, \ldots, Z^{(d)}\right]$, $Z^{(i)} \in \mathbb{R}^{n \times d}$, $Z^{(i)}_{\cdot,j} = X_{\cdot,i} \odot X_{\cdot,j}$. The ground truths $w \in \mathbb{R}^{d \times 1}$ and $Q \in \mathbb{R}^{d \times d}$ are generated based on the weak hierarchical structure $\|Q_{\cdot,j}\|_1 \leq |w_j|, j = 1, \ldots, d$. In addition, we vary the ratio of coefficient sparsity, *i.e.,* the portion of zero entries in w and Q, from 30% to 85%. Then, the outcome vector Y is constructed as $Y = Xw + \frac{1}{2}Z \cdot \mathrm{vec}(Q) + \epsilon$ where X and Z are normalized to zero mean and unit standard deviation and $\epsilon \sim N(\mathbf{0}, 0.01 \cdot \mathbf{I})$. We use sample size $n = 100$ and 200 and we choose the number of main effects d from $\{100, 200, 300, 400, 500, 600\}$. The parameter of the l_1 penalty, λ, is chosen from $\{1, 3, 5, 10, 20\}$. All algorithms are executed on a 64-bit machine with Intel(R) Core(TM) quad-core processor (i7-3770 CPU @ 3.40 GHz) and 16.0 GB memory. We terminate the algorithm when the maximum relative difference of the coefficients between two consecutive iterations is less than $1e^{-5}$. We run 20 trials for each setting and report the average execution time. The detailed results are shown in Table 1.

From Table 1, we observe that eWHL is significantly faster than cvxWHL. Our algorithm is up to 25 times faster than the competing algorithm. As the dimension increases, the running time of cvxWHL increases much faster than our proposed algorithm. Specifically, when the number of individual features increases to 400 (corresponds to 80200 interactions), cvxWHL may take more than one thousand seconds, while the proposed eWHL is reasonably fast even when the number of total variables is around two hundred thousands.

To make further comparisons of efficiency, we randomly generate three synthetic data sets where the weak hierarchical structure between main effects and interactions holds. The three data sets are of the same sample size $n = 100$ and

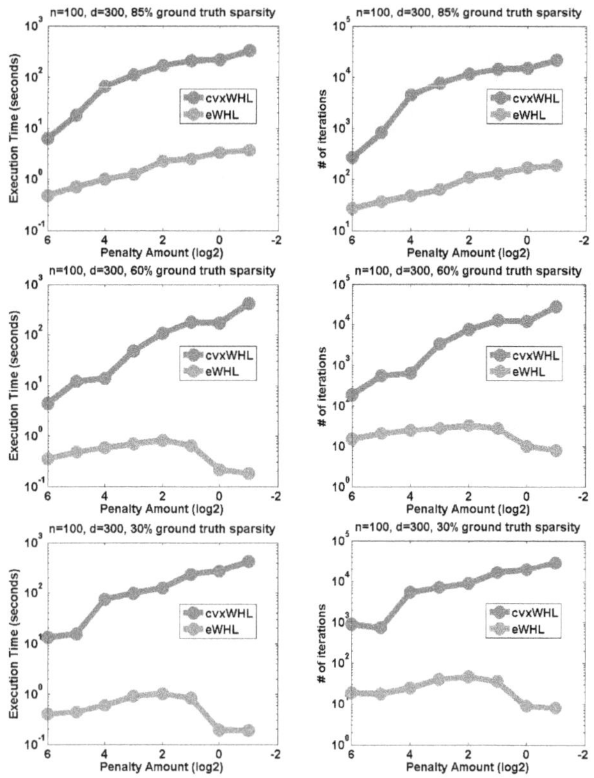

Figure 1: Comparison of the running time and the number of iterations by the two algorithms. Three synthetic data sets are generated where the portions of zeros in the ground truth are 85%, 60%, 30% respectively. The plots in the same row correspond to the same data set. The plots in the left column present the running time and those in the right column show the number of iterations.

the number of individual features is $d = 300$. The ratios of zero entries in the ground truth are 85%, 60% and 30% respectively. The regularization parameters are chosen from $\{0.5, 1, 2, 4, 6, 8, 16, 32, 64\}$. On each data set, we first run cvxWHL, and then the objective value of (5) in the final step is recorded. Then, we run the proposed eWHL and terminate the algorithm when the objective value of (5) is less than the one obtained by cvxWHL. The running time and the number of iterations needed to achieve the same objective value of both algorithms are reported in Figure 1. We can observe from Figure 1 that the proposed eWHL is much faster than cvxWHL.

Moreover, we also conduct an experiment to compare the recovery performance of eWHL and cvxWHL. We generate synthetic data sets with sample size $n = 100$ and the number of individual features is $d = 50$ (1225 cross interactions). The number of non-zero main effects varies from $\{3, 4, 5, 6, 7\}$ and the number of non-zero interaction effects is from $\{2, 4, 5, 8, 10\}$, respectively. For each setting, ten synthetic data sets are generated with noise $\epsilon \sim N(\mathbf{0}, 0.01 \cdot \mathbf{I})$. We run both eWHL and cvxWHL with parameter selected via 5-fold cross-validation. Then we compute the sensitivity and specificity of recovery (where non-zero entries are positive and zero entries are negative). The means of sensitivity and specificity are plotted in Figure 2. We can observe that

Table 1: Comparison of execution time (second) of the proposed algorithm for the non-convex weak hierarchical Lasso (eWHL) and the one for the convex relaxed formulation (cvxWHL) on synthetic data. The penalty parameters used in the experiment are from $\{1, 3, 5, 10, 20\}$. The data is generated under the weak hierarchical constraints where the portion of sparse coefficients is controlled to 85%, 60% and 30%. Two sample sizes, $n = 100$ and $n = 200$, are used and we vary the number of individual features from $\{200, 300, 400, 500, 600\}$ corresponding to $\{20100, 45150, 80200, 125250, 180300\}$ interactions (including the self product terms).

		n = 100					n = 200				
		85% Ground Truth Sparsity									
d	Methods	1	3	5	10	20	1	3	5	10	20
	cvxWHL	196.5536	54.8801	43.3018	27.2806	15.7909	116.8207	24.6601	17.8850	9.1765	4.7783
200	eWHL	15.9318	10.7613	7.2212	5.6287	2.6236	16.4134	9.5164	8.3827	5.4922	3.9255
	speedup	**12.3**	**5.1**	**6.0**	**4.8**	**6.0**	**7.1**	**2.6**	**2.1**	**1.7**	**1.2**
	cvxWHL	336.7086	213.7712	186.7997	109.7893	54.9521	319.6003	147.5044	112.5928	59.0820	36.2484
300	eWHL	35.6846	23.3044	17.9931	11.5569	10.8269	38.5045	20.0161	16.4566	10.3588	6.9153
	speedup	**9.4**	**9.2**	**10.4**	**9.5**	**5.1**	**8.3**	**7.4**	**6.8**	**5.7**	**5.2**
	cvxWHL	547.0450	280.6981	207.8486	170.4894	85.1425	921.7651	376.4949	256.8054	144.3066	81.4817
400	eWHL	52.8138	35.0482	29.5107	18.1944	13.8530	80.4882	54.1618	39.1673	26.6412	14.7667
	speedup	**10.4**	**8.0**	**7.0**	**9.4**	**6.1**	**11.5**	**7.0**	**6.6**	**5.4**	**5.5**
	cvxWHL	1018.9779	757.2096	524.9644	333.0070	204.2017	1405.9651	1142.2343	964.0598	286.2120	165.2558
500	eWHL	88.0526	66.0113	59.7805	42.2917	18.6453	127.0921	89.1293	70.0550	42.0014	29.0936
	speedup	**11.6**	**11.5**	**8.8**	**7.9**	**11.0**	**11.1**	**12.8**	**13.8**	**6.8**	**5.7**
	cvxWHL	2543.5021	1594.9729	1517.9605	887.8254	462.2604	2826.0083	1558.1431	1332.3515	873.6990	261.6806
600	eWHL	161.7944	100.3758	82.7961	71.1211	40.9529	197.5593	132.2163	107.5831	76.1834	45.0594
	speedup	**15.7**	**15.9**	**18.3**	**12.5**	**11.3**	**14.3**	**11.8**	**12.4**	**11.5**	**5.8**
		60% Ground Truth Sparsity									
	cvxWHL	106.6262	40.3105	29.1357	20.8624	10.3064	113.3342	44.1169	27.2844	18.7616	11.9756
200	eWHL	15.1405	9.6837	6.9516	5.4949	3.3569	18.3514	10.5571	8.1777	5.1257	4.1127
	speedup	**7.0**	**4.2**	**4.2**	**3.8**	**3.1**	**6.2**	**4.2**	**3.3**	**3.7**	**2.9**
	cvxWHL	187.7983	131.7578	106.2882	61.3653	38.3189	290.0877	155.0435	131.7942	85.8886	44.4029
300	eWHL	33.3861	22.2763	16.3251	12.3395	9.2993	47.8122	26.1554	21.9835	13.7322	10.5702
	speedup	**5.6**	**5.9**	**6.5**	**5.0**	**4.1**	**6.1**	**5.9**	**6.0**	**6.3**	**4.2**
	cvxWHL	418.9647	276.2089	169.4631	131.9086	84.4169	686.8900	297.7161	226.6632	166.2235	85.4570
400	eWHL	66.8376	43.0676	35.7516	20.5413	11.9166	69.1413	41.3634	37.3495	25.9975	16.0270
	speedup	**6.3**	**6.4**	**4.7**	**6.4**	**7.1**	**9.9**	**7.2**	**6.1**	**6.4**	**5.3**
	cvxWHL	1501.3934	801.0146	548.8402	362.7110	206.0816	1333.8803	861.6311	729.1297	310.6121	202.0412
500	eWHL	112.5519	80.5276	60.2488	38.6862	25.5497	114.5243	73.6990	63.4899	47.9597	31.5058
	speedup	**13.3**	**9.9**	**9.1**	**9.4**	**8.1**	**11.6**	**11.7**	**11.5**	**6.5**	**6.4**
	cvxWHL	1976.0945	1733.8494	1814.1974	815.4298	323.4841	1622.9061	1205.8489	987.4595	1063.2823	333.8406
600	eWHL	159.8307	112.8232	80.3703	50.8628	34.4373	175.9730	140.7086	96.3447	73.7633	52.2213
	speedup	**12.4**	**15.4**	**22.6**	**16.0**	**9.4**	**9.2**	**8.6**	**10.2**	**14.4**	**6.4**
		30% Ground Truth Sparsity									
	cvxWHL	139.4226	116.3866	85.1606	50.2425	23.8680	223.2468	165.9219	52.1613	40.8929	25.3084
200	eWHL	18.5023	13.6312	8.7261	7.1346	4.4546	20.8344	15.0214	9.7081	6.8616	4.0905
	speedup	**7.5**	**8.5**	**9.8**	**7.0**	**5.4**	**10.7**	**11.0**	**5.4**	**6.0**	**6.2**
	cvxWHL	275.4393	162.5627	139.4590	79.0609	41.2985	575.3758	223.1688	205.4368	142.9171	97.5106
300	eWHL	41.4815	27.6094	23.3748	14.2635	7.9047	52.3714	33.1059	25.5594	15.9962	10.6426
	speedup	**6.6**	**5.9**	**6.0**	**5.5**	**5.2**	**11.0**	**6.7**	**8.0**	**8.9**	**9.2**
	cvxWHL	916.5276	510.0533	342.0358	208.9260	104.5098	1688.7030	814.6646	560.1970	332.3118	204.4852
400	eWHL	75.6108	47.3789	38.8362	23.9130	17.6649	92.1627	60.4650	45.9561	34.6420	23.9751
	speedup	**12.1**	**10.8**	**8.8**	**8.7**	**5.9**	**18.3**	**13.5**	**12.2**	**9.6**	**8.5**
	cvxWHL	1460.8334	900.1424	767.7501	576.6498	242.9080	2003.7611	2040.7488	1632.3245	584.2366	313.8258
500	eWHL	114.9244	71.4278	58.4604	37.5124	25.9513	154.1934	102.7105	84.2729	63.9484	35.2531
	speedup	**12.7**	**12.6**	**13.1**	**15.4**	**9.4**	**13.0**	**19.9**	**19.4**	**9.1**	**8.9**
	cvxWHL	2799.5549	2842.9022	2076.6074	1148.0632	460.4660	4067.0519	2795.7589	2128.9981	1946.2750	1140.4244
600	eWHL	186.1483	119.8450	85.9816	65.2515	41.2607	165.9264	179.4403	146.7908	102.6978	71.8432
	speedup	**15.0**	**23.7**	**24.2**	**17.6**	**11.2**	**24.5**	**15.6**	**14.5**	**19.0**	**15.9**

both algorithms achieve high recovery rate while directly solving the original weak hierarchical Lasso leads to slightly better performance in recovering the non-zero effects.

4.2 Classification Comparison on ADNI Data

In this experiment, we compare the weak hierarchical Lasso with its convex relaxation as well as other classifiers on the Alzheimer's Disease Neuroimaging Initiative (ADNI) data set.

In Alzheimer's Disease (AD) research, Mild Cognitive Impairment (MCI) is an intermediate state between normal elderly people and AD patients [24]. The MCI patients are considered to be at high risk of progression to AD. Many recent work focus on how to accurately predict the MCI-AD conversion and identifying significant bio-markers for the prediction [8, 10, 12, 19, 21, 28, 31, 14].

In this experiment, we compare the classification performance of the proposed eWHL with the convex relaxation and other classifiers on the task of discriminating the MCI

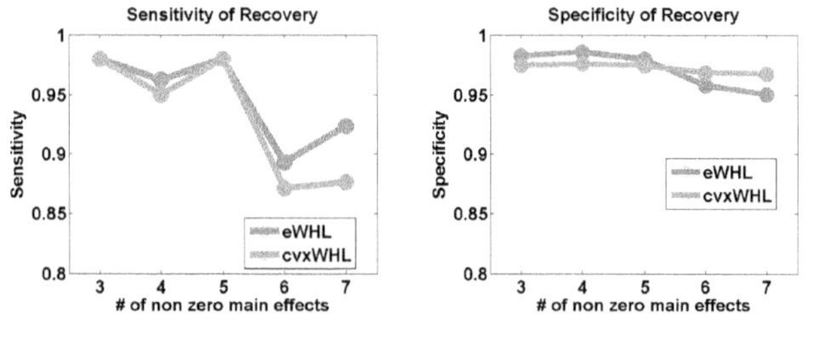

Figure 2: Comparison of eWHL and cvxWHL in terms of recovery on synthetic data sets.

Table 2: **The performance of MCI converter vs. MCI non-converter classification achieved by random forest (RF), Support Vector Machine (SVM), Sparse Logistic Regression (spsLog), the convex relaxed weak hierarchical Lasso (cvxWHL) and the proposed algorithm (eWHL). Classifiers are performed on main effects only (top) and on both the main effects and interactions (bottom). The average and standard deviation of accuracy, sensitivity and specificity obtained from 10-fold cross-validation are reported.**

Main Effects Only					
	RF	SVM	spsLog	cvxWHL	eWHL
Accuracy (%)	74.23 ± 8.67	75.22 ± 8.72	74.34 ± 9.56	NA	NA
Sensitivity (%)	78.75 ± 14.00	80.18 ± 13.89	80.18 ± 13.88	NA	NA
Specificity (%)	69.29 ± 11.63	69.76 ± 12.80	69.52 ± 13.74	NA	NA
Main Effects + Interactions					
	RF	SVM	spsLog	cvxWHL	eWHL
Accuracy (%)	71.26 ± 10.22	59.45 ± 14.43	73.57 ± 10.30	75.22 ± 11.02	77.42 ± 8.50
Sensitivity (%)	83.04 ± 13.18	59.29 ± 17.83	74.29 ± 16.22	75.71 ± 19.11	77.14 ± 12.05
Specificity (%)	58.10 ± 23.23	60.00 ± 15.42	72.86 ± 12.46	74.52 ± 16.84	77.62 ± 15.02

subjects who convert to dementia (*i.e.*, MCI converter) within a three-year period from the MCI subjects who remain at MCI (*i.e.*, MCI non-converter). The features used in the experiment (provided by our clinical collaborators) involve demographic information such as age, gender, years of education, clinical information such as scores of mini mental state examination (MMSE), Auditory Verbal Learning Test (A.V.L.T.), and the bio-markers including status of Apolipoprotein E, volume of hippocampus, thickness of Mid Temporal Gray Matter. There are 133 samples in total and the number of individual features is 36 (corresponds to 630 two way interactions). The interactions are generated by the normalized individual features and are normalized before entering the model. Since this is a classification task with binary labels, we replace the least square loss with logistic loss in the weak hierarchical Lasso. Besides the non-convex and convex weak hierarchical Lasso, we apply random forest (RF), Support Vector Machine (SVM) and sparse logistic regression on main effects, and on both main effects and interactions, respectively. We report the means and standard deviations of accuracy, sensitivity and specificity obtained from 10-fold cross-validation. The penalty parameters are tuned via 5-fold cross-validation in the training procedure. The sample statistics are shown in Table 3 and the classification performance is reported in Table 2.

Table 3: **The statistics of the ADNI data set used in our experiment. The MCI converters (MCI-cvt) are characterized as positive samples and the MCI non-converters (MCI non-cvt) are used as negative samples.**

	Total	(+) MCI-cvt	(-) MCI non-cvt
# of samples	133	71	62
# of main effects	36		
# of interactions	630		

From Table 2, we can observe that, if we only use individual features for classification, then all the classifiers are biased towards the positive class, *i.e.*, MCI converter. When interactions are included, we observe that the performances of random forest and SVM become worse. One possible reason is that the large number of variables brought by the interactions weakens their discriminative power. This is not the case for sparse logistic regression, which demonstrates the importance of feature selection. We can observe from the table that the convex relaxed weak hierarchical Lasso and the non-convex weak hierarchical Lasso achieve much better classification performance than the competitors. The improvement of the classification performance demonstrates the effectiveness of imposing hierarchical structures in interaction models. In addition, the superior classification performance (around 77% accuracy, sensitivity and specificity) of the proposed eWHL demonstrates that directly solving the non-convex weak hierarchical Lasso leads to solutions of higher quality than the convex relaxation.

5. CONCLUSIONS

In this paper, we propose an efficient algorithm, eWHL, to directly solve the non-convex weak hierarchical Lasso. One critical step in eWHL is to compute the proximal operator associated with the non-convex penalty functions. As one of our major contributions, we show that the proximal operator associated with the regularization function in weak hierarchical Lasso admits a closed form solution. Furthermore, we develop an efficient algorithm which computes each subproblem of the proximal operator with a time complexity of $\mathcal{O}(d \log d)$. Extensive experiments on both synthetic and real data sets demonstrate the superior performance of the proposed algorithm in terms of efficiency and accuracy.

In the future, we plan to apply the non-convex weak hierarchical Lasso to other important and challenging applications such as depression study [20]. In addition, we plan to extend the proposed techniques to solve the non-convex strong hierarchical Lasso formulation.

6. ACKNOWLEDGEMENT

This work was supported in part by NIH (R01 LM010730) and NSF (IIS-0953662, MCB-1026710, and CCF-1025177).

7. REFERENCES

[1] A. Beck and M. Teboulle. A fast iterative shrinkage-thresholding algorithm for linear inverse problems. *SIAM Journal on Imaging Sciences*, 2(1):183–202, 2009.

[2] J. Bien, J. Taylor, and R. Tibshirani. A lasso for hierarchical interactions. *The Annals of Statistics*, 41(3):1111–1141, 2013.

[3] J. Bien and R. Tibshirani. *hierNet: A Lasso for Hierarchical Interactions*, 2013. R package version 1.5.

[4] R. J. Cadoret, W. R. Yates, G. Woodworth, M. A. Stewart, et al. Genetic-environmental interaction in the genesis of aggressivity and conduct disorders. *Archives of General Psychiatry*, 52(11):916, 1995.

[5] E. J. Candes and J. Romberg. Quantitative robust uncertainty principles and optimally sparse decompositions. *Foundations of Computational Mathematics*, 6(2):227–254, 2006.

[6] N. H. Choi, W. Li, and J. Zhu. Variable selection with the strong heredity constraint and its oracle property. *Journal of the American Statistical Association*, 105(489):354–364, 2010.

[7] A. d'Aspremont, L. El Ghaoui, M. I. Jordan, and G. R. Lanckriet. A direct formulation for sparse pca using semidefinite programming. In *NIPS*, volume 16, pages 41–48, 2004.

[8] C. Davatzikos, P. Bhatt, L. M. Shaw, K. N. Batmanghelich, and J. Q. Trojanowski. Prediction of mci to ad conversion, via mri, csf biomarkers, and pattern classification. *Neurobiology of aging*, 32(12):2322–e19, 2011.

[9] J. F. Dawson and A. W. Richter. Probing three-way interactions in moderated multiple regression: development and application of a slope difference test. *Journal of Applied Psychology*, 91(4):917, 2006.

[10] D. Devanand, G. Pradhaban, X. Liu, A. Khandji, S. De Santi, S. Segal, H. Rusinek, G. Pelton, L. Honig, R. Mayeux, et al. Hippocampal and entorhinal atrophy in mild cognitive impairment prediction of alzheimer disease. *Neurology*, 68(11):828–836, 2007.

[11] T. C. Eley, K. Sugden, A. Corsico, A. M. Gregory, P. Sham, P. McGuffin, R. Plomin, and I. W. Craig. Gene–environment interaction analysis of serotonin system markers with adolescent depression. *Molecular psychiatry*, 9(10):908–915, 2004.

[12] C. Fennema-Notestine, D. J. Hagler, L. K. McEvoy, A. S. Fleisher, E. H. Wu, D. S. Karow, and A. M. Dale. Structural mri biomarkers for preclinical and mild alzheimer's disease. *Human brain mapping*, 30(10):3238–3253, 2009.

[13] J. Gatt, C. Nemeroff, C. Dobson-Stone, R. Paul, R. Bryant, P. Schofield, E. Gordon, A. Kemp, and L. Williams. Interactions between bdnf val66met polymorphism and early life stress predict brain and arousal pathways to syndromal depression and anxiety. *Molecular psychiatry*, 14(7):681–695, 2009.

[14] P. Gong, J. Ye, and C. Zhang. Multi-stage multi-task feature learning. In *NIPS*, pages 1997–2005, 2012.

[15] P. Gong, C. Zhang, Z. Lu, J. Huang, and J. Ye. A general iterative shrinkage and thresholding algorithm for non-convex regularized optimization problems. In *ICML*, 2013.

[16] P. Gong, C. Zhang, Z. Lu, J. Huang, and J. Ye. *GIST: General Iterative Shrinkage and Thresholding for Non-convex Sparse Learning.* Tsinghua University, 2013.

[17] T. Hastie, R. Tibshirani, J. Friedman, T. Hastie, J. Friedman, and R. Tibshirani. *The elements of statistical learning*, volume 2. Springer, 2009.

[18] K. Koh, S.-J. Kim, and S. Boyd. An interior-point method for large-scale 1-regularized logistic regression. *Journal of Machine learning research*, 8(7), 2007.

[19] H. Li, Y. Liu, P. Gong, C. Zhang, J. Ye, A. D. N. Initiative, et al. Hierarchical interactions model for predicting mild cognitive impairment (mci) to alzheimer's disease (ad) conversion. *PloS one*, 9(1):e82450, 2014.

[20] Y. Liu, Z. Nie, J. Zhou, M. Farnum, V. A. Narayan, G. Wittenberg, and J. Ye. Sparse generalized functional linear model for predicting remission status of depression patients. In *Pacific Symposium on Biocomputing. Pacific Symposium on Biocomputing*, volume 19, pages 364–375. World Scientific, 2013.

[21] D. A. Llano, G. Laforet, and V. Devanarayan. Derivation of a new adas-cog composite using tree-based multivariate analysis: prediction of conversion from mild cognitive impairment to alzheimer disease. *Alzheimer Disease & Associated Disorders*, 25(1):73–84, 2011.

[22] D. C. Montgomery, E. A. Peck, and G. G. Vining. *Introduction to linear regression analysis*, volume 821. Wiley, 2012.

[23] N. Parikh and S. Boyd. Proximal algorithms. *Foundations and Trends in optimization*, 1(3):123–231, 2013.

[24] R. C. Petersen. Mild cognitive impairment clinical trials. *Nature Reviews Drug Discovery*, 2(8):646–653, 2003.

[25] P. Radchenko and G. M. James. Variable selection using adaptive nonlinear interaction structures in high dimensions. *Journal of the American Statistical Association*, 105(492):1541–1553, 2010.

[26] M. J. Somers. Organizational commitment, turnover and absenteeism: An examination of direct and interaction effects. *Journal of Organizational Behavior*, 16(1):49–58, 1995.

[27] R. Tibshirani. Regression shrinkage and selection via the lasso. *Journal of the Royal Statistical Society. Series B (Methodological)*, pages 267–288, 1996.

[28] J. Ye, M. Farnum, E. Yang, R. Verbeeck, V. Lobanov, N. Raghavan, G. Novak, A. DiBernardo, V. A. Narayan, et al. Sparse learning and stability selection for predicting mci to ad conversion using baseline adni data. *BMC neurology*, 12(1):46, 2012.

[29] M. Yuan, V. R. Joseph, and H. Zou. Structured variable selection and estimation. *The Annals of Applied Statistics*, pages 1738–1757, 2009.

[30] P. Zhao, G. Rocha, and B. Yu. The composite absolute penalties family for grouped and hierarchical variable selection. *The Annals of Statistics*, 37(6A):3468–3497, 12 2009.

[31] J. Zhou, J. Liu, V. A. Narayan, and J. Ye. Modeling disease progression via multi-task learning. *NeuroImage*, 78:233–248, 2013.

[32] H. Zou, T. Hastie, and R. Tibshirani. Sparse principal component analysis. *Journal of computational and graphical statistics*, 15(2):265–286, 2006.

Online Multiple Kernel Regression

Doyen Sahoo
School of Information Systems
Singapore Management University
Singapore
doyensahoo@gmail.com

Steven C.H. Hoi
School of Information Systems
Singapore Management University
Singapore
stevenhoi@gmail.com

Bin Li
Economics and Management School
Wuhan University
P. R. China
binli.whu@whu.edu.cn

ABSTRACT

Kernel-based regression represents an important family of learning techniques for solving challenging regression tasks with non-linear patterns. Despite being studied extensively, most of the existing work suffers from two major drawbacks: (i) they are often designed for solving regression tasks in a batch learning setting, making them not only computationally inefficient and but also poorly scalable in real-world applications where data arrives sequentially; and (ii) they usually assume a fixed kernel function is given prior to the learning task, which could result in poor performance if the chosen kernel is inappropriate. To overcome these drawbacks, this paper presents a novel scheme of Online Multiple Kernel Regression (OMKR), which sequentially learns the kernel-based regressor in an online and scalable fashion, and dynamically explore a pool of multiple diverse kernels to avoid suffering from a single fixed poor kernel so as to remedy the drawback of manual/heuristic kernel selection. The OMKR problem is more challenging than regular kernel-based regression tasks since we have to on-the-fly determine both the optimal kernel-based regressor for each individual kernel and the best combination of the multiple kernel regressors. In this paper, we propose a family of OMKR algorithms for regression and discuss their application to time series prediction tasks. We also analyze the theoretical bounds of the proposed OMKR method and conduct extensive experiments to evaluate its empirical performance on both real-world regression and times series prediction tasks.

Categories and Subject Descriptors

I.2.6 [**Artificial Intelligence**]: Learning

General Terms

Theory, Algorithms, Experimentation

Keywords

Online Learning; Multiple Kernel Learning; Kernel Regression; Time Series Prediction

KDD'14, August 24–27, 2014, New York, NY, USA.
Copyright 2014 ACM 978-1-4503-2956-9/14/08 ...$15.00.
http://dx.doi.org/10.1145/2623330.2623712.

1. INTRODUCTION

Kernel methods have been extensively studied for regression tasks and found successes in many real-world applications [29, 28]. In contrast to linear regression methods, kernel-based regression methods are able to tackle challenging non-linear regression tasks using the kernel trick that implicitly maps data from the original space to a high or even infinite dimensional space by means of a kernel function. Although a variety of kernel methods have been proposed for regression tasks [28], most conventional kernel methods suffer from two major drawbacks. First of all, they are often designed for solving regression tasks in a batch learning setting. This often results in a high re-training cost when there is any new training data, making them poorly scalable in many real-world applications where data arrives sequentially. Second, they usually assume that prior to the learning task, a fixed kernel function is given either by manual selection or via cross validation. This could result in poor performance if the chosen kernel is inappropriate in a new environment, which happens commonly for some real-world applications, such as time series prediction where data observations can be non-stationary and the optimal kernel function may change over time.

To overcome the above drawbacks, this paper investigates a novel scheme of Online Multiple Kernel Regression (OMKR), which sequentially learns a kernel-based regressor with multiple kernels in an online fashion for regression tasks. On one hand, the proposed OMKR technique, as an online learning method that often makes simple incremental update for a new training data example, avoids the expensive re-training cost of conventional batch kernel methods, and thus significantly improves the efficiency and scalability, especially when handling data stream applications. On the other hand, OMKR explores a pool of multiple diverse kernels to remedy the drawback of using a single fixed kernel by existing kernel-based regression methods that often suffer considerably when the single kernel is inappropriate.

The proposed OMKR problem is however very challenging since we not only need to sequentially learn the optimal kernel-based regressor for each individual kernel in the pool, but also need to simultaneously decide the best way of combining the multiple kernel regressors on the fly at every learning round. We tackle the challenges by (i) exploring two online kernel regression algorithms, Widrow-Hoff learning [33] and NORMA learning [17], for online regression tasks with each individual kernel; and (ii) determining the best combination of the multiple kernel regressors by applying two online learning techniques: *Hedge* algorithm [9] that can track the best kernel regressor, and *Online Gradient Descent*(OGD)[38] that can find the optimal linear combination. We analyze the theoretical bound of OMKR, and also discuss a natural extension of OMKR for the prediction of Autoregressive (AR) time series. To validate the efficacy of the proposed method, we conduct extensive experiments by evaluating the proposed algorithms on both real-world regression and time series datasets, in which our empirical results show that OMKR significantly outperforms conventional single kernel online regression approaches for most cases, especially for time series prediction tasks.

The rest of the paper is organized as follows. Section 2 reviews the related work of both online learning and kernel methods. Section 3 gives the problem formulation of online learning with multiple kernels, and then presents the OMKR algorithms followed by theoretical analysis. Section 4 presents our experimental results and discussions, and finally Section 5 concludes this paper.

2. RELATED WORK

In this section, we review some of major related work in online learning and kernel learning in the context of OMKR.

2.1 Online Learning

Online learning algorithms have been extensively explored in different contexts and applications [6, 35, 22]. For more references please refer to [27, 5, 14]. Many online algorithms have been proposed for extending kernel methods in an online setting, in which several techniques have have been proposed for online kernel regression, such as Naive Online R_{reg} Minimization Algorithm (NORMA) [17], Online Passive Aggressive Regression [6], Sparse Implicit Online Learning with Kernels (ILK and SILK) [26] and Primal Online Algorithm (PRIONA) [3].

In addition, some kernel-based online learning studies focus on the budget issue [7, 4]. These help to speed up computation cost by bounding the number of support vectors. Some well-known example algorithms include Forgetron [8], Projectron [23], and the Bounded Online Gradient Descent (BOGD) [36]. Further, our work is also related to online prediction with expert advice [9, 20, 32]. One of the most well-known algorithms is the Hedge Algorithm [9], which was a direct generalization of Weighted Majority Algorithm [20].

2.2 Kernel Learning

Most kernel methods often assume that a predefined parametric kernel is given a priori, where the parameters are chosen either manually or via cross validation. Kernel learning aims to learn an effective kernel from data automatically. Some studies have attempted to learn kernel functions or matrices from labeled and unlabeled data. Examples include marginalized kernels [16], idealized kernel learning [18], graph-based spectral kernel learning [2, 13], and non-parametric kernel learning [11, 37]. These methods often follow a batch (and transductive) learning setting and thus are difficult to be applied in an online learning scenario.

Another prevalent kernel learning technique is Multiple Kernel Learning (MKL) [19], which aims to find the optimal combination of multiple kernels. Unlike most existing MKL techniques that are batch learning [19, 30, 10], our work focuses on online regression tasks, and is related to existing online MKL studies that focus on classification tasks [15, 12] and that addresses structured prediction [21].

3. ONLINE MULTIPLE KERNEL REGRESSION

3.1 Overview

In this section, we present the proposed Online Multiple Kernel Regression (OMKR) scheme. We will first motivate the problem by introducing the formulation of batch Multiple Kernel Learning (MKL). We then present our OMKR framework, the detailed algorithms for addressing different challenges, and finally theoretical analysis of OMKR.

Consider a set of training examples $\mathcal{D} = (\mathbf{x}_i, y_i), i = 1, \ldots, T$ where $\mathbf{x}_i \in \mathbb{R}^d$, $y_i \in \mathbb{R}$ and a collection of m kernel functions $\mathcal{K} = \{\kappa_i : \chi \times \chi \rightarrow \mathbb{R}, i = 1, \ldots, m\}$. Multiple Kernel Learning aims to learn a kernel-based prediction model by identifying the best linear combination of the m kernels, that is, a weighted combination $\theta = (\theta_1, \ldots, \theta_m)$. The learning task can be cast into the following optimization [19]:

$$\min_{\theta \in \Delta} \min_{f \in \mathcal{H}_{K(\theta)}} \frac{1}{2} |f|^2_{\mathcal{H}_{K(\theta)}} + C \sum_{i=1}^{n} \ell(f(\mathbf{x}_i), y_i) \quad (1)$$

where $\Delta = \{\theta \in \mathbb{R}^m_+ | \theta^T \mathbf{1}_m = 1\}$, $K(\theta)(\cdot, \cdot) = \sum_{i=1}^{T} \theta_i \kappa_i(\cdot, \cdot)$ and $\ell(f(\mathbf{x}_i), y_i)$ is a convex loss function.

The above convex optimization problem of regular batch MKL can be solved by different schemes [30, 34, 10]. Despite being studied extensively, it remains very challenging when solving the batch MKL for large-scale applications. Besides, similar to most batch kernel methods, regular MKL has some drawbacks: (i) the trained model, if it is not retrained with new data, may work poorly for non-stationary data in a new environment; but (ii) the re-training cost is extremely expensive for data streams, making it non-scalable.

3.2 OMKR Framework

To overcome the limitations of MKL for a regression task, we propose a new scheme of Online Multiple Kernel Regression (OMKR) by applying the emerging online multiple kernel learning principle [12] for tackling regression tasks, which attempts to sequentially learn the online multiple-kernel regressor given a new data example using a two-step updating scheme: (i) update the set of kernel-based regressors for each individual kernel; and (ii) update the weights for combining the multiple kernel regressors. In the following, we discuss the details of the proposed algorithms for tackling online regression tasks at each of the two steps.

3.2.1 *Learning Online Kernel-Based Regressors*

The goal of this task is to learn a regression function $f_t \in \mathcal{H}_\kappa$ in an online setting, where $\mathcal{H}_\kappa$ a reproducing kernel Hilbert space (RKHS) induced by a given specific kernel $\kappa \in \mathcal{K}$. We solve this task by exploring two online regression solutions: Kernel Widrow-Hoff [33] and NORMA [17], which follows the same principle of Online Gradient Descent (OGD) [38] for online convex optimization and but optimizes two slightly different objective functions.

Kernel Widrow-Hoff Learning. Given a sequence of data instances $\mathcal{D} = (\mathbf{x}_i, y_i), i = 1, \ldots, T$, the goal of kernelized Widrow-Hoff learning is to minimize the total cumulative loss over the whole regression task $\mathcal{L}$ defined as follows:

$$\mathcal{L} = \Sigma_{t=1}^{T} \ell(f_t(x_t), y_t) \triangleq \Sigma_{t=1}^{T} \mathcal{L}_t(f_t) \quad (2)$$

where $f_t(x_t)$ is the prediction made by a kernel regressor on the t-th instance, $\ell(f_t(\mathbf{x}_t), y_t)$ denoted by $\mathcal{L}_t(f_t)$ for short, is a convex loss function. Following OGD [38], we have the following online update rule given a data instance $(\mathbf{x}_t, y_t)$:

$$f_{t+1} \leftarrow f_t - \eta_t \nabla \mathcal{L}_t(f_t) \qquad (3)$$

where $\eta_t > 0$ is a learning rate parameter that can be either a small constant $\eta_t = \eta$ used in Widrow-Hoff [33] or a factor depending on t. When choosing the squared loss for ℓ:

$$\ell(f_t(\mathbf{x}_t), y_t) = (f_t(\mathbf{x}_t) - y_t)^2,$$

we have the online updating rule expressed explicitly as

$$f_{t+1}(\cdot) \leftarrow f_t(\cdot) - \eta_t(f_t(\mathbf{x}_t) - y_t)\kappa(\mathbf{x}_t, \cdot). \qquad (4)$$

NORMA. The above method has two potential drawbacks. First, it may lead to overfitting when dealing with noisy data. Second, due to the use of squared loss, almost every training instance will be added as support vectors (unless $f_t(x_t)$ is identical to y_t), making the prediction function computationally intensive when handling large-scale datasets. To overcome these drawbacks, we explore another online regression scheme by following the idea of NORMA [17], which replaces $\mathcal{L}_t(f_t)$ by the following regularized loss:

$$\mathcal{L}_t(f_t) = \frac{\lambda}{2}||f||^2_{\mathcal{H}_\kappa} + \ell(f_t(\mathbf{x}_t), y_t) \qquad (5)$$

By the OGD principle, we have the online updating rule as:

$$f_{t+1} \leftarrow (1 - \eta_t\lambda)f_t - \eta_t \nabla \ell(f_t(\mathbf{x}_t), y_t) \qquad (6)$$

where $\eta_t > 0$ is the learning rate parameter. Instead of using the square loss, we exploit the ϵ-insensitive loss function which is defined as

$$\ell(f_t(\mathbf{x}_t), y_t) = \max(0, |y_t - f_t(\mathbf{x}_t)| - \epsilon),$$

where ϵ represents the width of the insensitivity zone. We can further modify the loss function by making ϵ as a variable of the optimization:

$$\ell_t(f_t, \mathbf{x}_t) = \max(0, |y_t - f_t(\mathbf{x}_t)| - \epsilon) + \nu\epsilon_t \qquad (7)$$

where $\nu > 0$ is a parameter, and ϵ_t is a variable to be updated in online learning process. Using the above loss function, we can derive the online updating rule for NORMA:

$$f_{t+1} \leftarrow \begin{cases} (1-\eta_t\lambda)f_t + \eta_t * sgn(d)\kappa(\mathbf{x}_t, \cdot) & \text{if } |d| > \epsilon_t \\ (1-\eta_t\lambda)f_t & \text{otherwise} \end{cases} \qquad (8)$$

$$\epsilon_{t+1} \leftarrow \begin{cases} \epsilon_t + (1-\nu)\eta_t & \text{if } |d| > \epsilon_t \\ \epsilon_t - \eta_t\nu & \text{otherwise} \end{cases} \qquad (9)$$

where we denote $d = y_t - f(\mathbf{x}_t)$.

Remark. For both of the above methods, at the end of each online learning round, we can express the prediction function of the regressor as a kernel expansion [25]:

$$f_{t+1}(\mathbf{x}) = \Sigma_{i=1}^t \alpha_i \kappa(\mathbf{x}_i, \mathbf{x})$$

where the α_i coefficients are computed based on the updating rules in (4) or (8). When $\alpha_i \neq 0$, the i-th instance is often called as a Support Vector (SV). Thus, the time complexity for prediction is linear with respect to the number of SV's. When using the squared loss, we will have $\alpha_i \neq 0$ for almost every instance, leading to a large number of support vectors. By contrast, when using the ϵ-insensitive loss, whenever the difference between the prediction on the i-th instance $f_i(x_i)$ and y_i is small enough, i.e., within the ϵ tube, we have $\alpha_i = 0$, which thus generates a much smaller SV size and significantly improves the prediction efficiency.

3.2.2 *Learning the Best Kernel Combination*

The previous online kernel regression method allows us to learn a set of kernel regressors $f_t^i \in \mathcal{H}_{\kappa_i}, i = 1, \ldots, m$ with respect to the pool of multiple diverse kernels $\mathcal{K}$. The idea of OMKR is to learn an effective regressor $F_t(\mathbf{x})$ by combining the set of multiple kernel regressors:

$$F_t(\mathbf{x}) = \sum_{i=1}^m w_t^i \mathbf{f}_t^i(\mathbf{x}) \qquad (10)$$

where $w_t^i \in \mathbb{R}$ denotes the combination weight for the i-th kernel regressor. The remaining problem then is to determine the appropriate combination weights $\mathbf{w}_t$ for the set of kernels. We note that this is a very challenging task since we may not have prior knowledge for empirical performance of each kernel, and the optimal combination weights may even change over time in the online learning process especially when dealing with non-stationary data.

One naive solution is to simply adopt a uniform combination for all the kernels, i.e., $w_t^i = 1/m$, which does explore all the kernels, but often results in sub-optimal performance, as observed in our empirical studies. In this section, we attempt to learn the best kernel combination weights by exploring two different online learning algorithms: the Hedge algorithm [9] and the OGD algorithm [38]. We will first present each algorithm in detail and finally discuss their strengths and weaknesses for different scenarios.

Hedge Algorithm: The Hedge algorithm is the most popular online algorithm for solving the problem of decision-theoretic online learning or known as prediction with expert advice [32, 5]. Specifically, by treating each online kernel regressor as an expert, the Hedge algorithm aims to minimize the regret of the learner for the regression task, which is the difference between the learner's cumulative loss and the cumulative loss of the best kernel regressor. In theory, Hedge can achieve an optimal upper bound of regret $O(T \ln m)$ with T learning rounds and m kernel regressor experts. It is thus an ideal online learning algorithm for tracking the best online kernel regressor especially when there is some kernel regressor significantly dominates the rest.

Specifically, the Hedge algorithm runs in a fairly simple way. Consider the OMKR problem, at the beginning, the combination weights $\mathbf{w}_t$ are initialized as a uniform distribution, i.e., $w_1^i = 1/m, i = 1, \ldots, m$. At the end of each learning round, according to the performance of the multiple kernel regressors, the weights are updated by:

$$w_{t+1}^i = w_t^i \beta^{\ell_t^i}, i = 1, \ldots, m \qquad (11)$$

where $\beta \in (0, 1)$ is a discounting (learning rate) parameter, and ℓ_t^i denotes the loss suffered by the i-th kernel regressor at round t, i.e., $\ell_t^i = \ell(f_t^i(x_t), y_t)$. Finally, we normalize all w_{t+1}^i's to ensure the combination weights as a distribution.

We refer to the proposed OMKR algorithm that adopts the Hedge algorithm as the *Deterministic OMKR* (Hedge) algorithm, as shown in Algorithm 1. In the algorithm, we can update each kernel regressor f_{t+1}^i by adopting either the Widrow-Hoff learning in (4) or NORMA in (8).

Although Hedge is ideal for tracking the best kernel regressor, it is not always perfect for solving a practical OMKR problem since our goal is to learn the best combination of multiple kernels. In the following, we present an online gradient descent (OGD) based algorithm that attempts to learn the optimal linear combination of multiple kernel regressors.

Algorithm 1 Deterministic OMKR (Hedge)

INPUT:

- Kernels: $\kappa(\cdot,\cdot) : \chi \times \chi \rightarrow i = 1,\ldots,m$
- Discounting Parameter: $\beta \in (0,1)$
- Step size parameter for each kernel: η
- Regression parameters: λ and ν for OMKR(NORMA)

Initialization: $\mathbf{f}_1 = \mathbf{0}$, $\mathbf{w}_1 = \frac{1}{m}\mathbf{1}$

```
for t = 1,...,T do
  Receive instance: x_t
  Predict ŷ_t = Σ_{i=1}^{m} w_t^i f_t^i(x_t)
  Reveal true value y_t
  for i = 1,...,m do
    Set ℓ_t^i = ℓ(f_t^i(x_t), y_t);
    Update f_{t+1}^i = Eq. (4) OR (8)
    Update w_{t+1}^i = w_t^i β^{ℓ_t^{*i}} where ℓ_t^{*i} = (f_t^i(x_t) − y_t)^2;
  end for
  Set w_{t+1}^i = w_t^i / W_t where W_t = Σ_{i=1}^{m} w_t^i, i = 1,...,m
end for
```

OGD Algorithm: Our goal is to learn the optimal combination weight vector $\mathbf{w}_t \in \mathbb{R}^m$ for combining the multiple kernel regressors. It can be cast into the following online optimization

$$\mathbf{w}_{t+1} \leftarrow \arg\min_{\mathbf{w}} \ell(\mathbf{w}^\top \mathbf{f}_t(\mathbf{x}_t), y_t) \triangleq (\mathbf{w}^\top \mathbf{f}_t(\mathbf{x}_t) - y_t)^2 \quad (12)$$

where $\mathbf{f}_t(\mathbf{x}_t)$ is a vector representing the predictions made by all the kernel regressors on instance $\mathbf{x}_t$, and ℓ is a loss function denoting the loss suffered by the OMKR. We simply adopt the squared loss in our solution (though it may also include a regularizer). Following the OGD, we can derive the updating rule as follows:

$$\mathbf{w}_{t+1} \leftarrow \mathbf{w}_t - \eta_w(\hat{y}_t - y_t)\mathbf{f}_t(\mathbf{x}_t) \quad (13)$$

where η_w is a learning rate parameter, and $\hat{y}_t = \mathbf{w}^\top \mathbf{f}_t(\mathbf{x}_t)$.

Using the above OGD algorithm for learning the optimal combination weights, we propose another OMKR scheme, called *Deterministic OMKR*(OGD), as shown in Algorithm 2. Like in OMKR(Hedge), we can also update each kernel regressor by either Widrow-Hoff in (4) or NORMA in (8).

Algorithm 2 Deterministic OMKR (OGD)

INPUT:

- Kernels: $\kappa(\cdot,\cdot) : \chi \times \chi \rightarrow i = 1,\ldots,m$
- Learning rate parameter: η_w
- Step size parameter for each kernel: η
- Regression parameters: λ and ν for OMKR(NORMA)

Initialization: $\mathbf{f}_1 = \mathbf{0}$, $\mathbf{w}_1 = \mathbf{0}$

```
for t = 1,...,T do
  Receive instance: x_t
  Predict ŷ_t = Σ_{i=1}^{m} w_t^i f_t^i(x_t)
  Reveal true value y_t
  for i = 1,...,m do
    Set ℓ_t^i = ℓ(f_t^i(x_t), y_t);
    Update f_{t+1}^i = Eq. (4) OR (8)
  end for
  Update w_{t+1} = w_t − η_w(ŷ_t − y_t) f_t(x_t)
end for
```

Remark. In online MKL work related to classification [15, 12], Hedge algorithm was used to combine multiple predictions. In contrast, our proposed OGD approach interprets the kernel predictions as new rich features which can be combined linearly. In terms of update rules, Hedge makes multiplicative updates while OGD makes additive updates. Further, for the combination weight vector $\mathbf{w}_t$, Hedge always keep $\mathbf{w}_t$ a distribution ($w_t^i \geq 0$ and $\sum_i w_t^i = 1$) while OGD is able to learn any real-valued vector for $\mathbf{w}_t$. In general, both Hedge and OGD have their different merits. Hedge is good at tracking the best kernel regressor, while OGD is good at learning the optimal combination of multiple kernel regressors. However, OGD often suffers from slow convergence rate. In practice, the empirical performance of OMKR(Hedge) and OMKR(OGD) may vary a lot in different scenarios. Due to the nature of multiplicative update of Hedge, it converges quickly, and in an online setting, may tend to achieve better performance than OGD, if the dataset is small, or if the pattern changes due to non-stationarity. We conduct more in-depth analysis through our extensive experimental studies in Section 4.

3.3 Application to Time Series Prediction

OMKR can be applied a variety of online regression tasks, especially for mining data streams. A natural application of OMKR is Time Series Prediction, which is the task of predicting the future value based on given past values. Kernel methods have been commonly used for solving such problems [31, 24]. We first introduce the popular time series prediction model known as Autoregressive (AR) model, and then present a kernelized AR model, followed by showing the application of OMKR for time series prediction.

Autoregressive(AR) model is used for a univariate time series where the value of the series at a particular time is linearly dependent on its own previous values. An $AR(p)$ model denotes an autoregressive process of order p, i.e., y_t is described by a noisy linear combination of $[y_{t-1}y_{t-2}\ldots y_{t-p}]$:

$$y_t = c + \Sigma_{i=1}^{p}\zeta_i y_{t-i} + \epsilon_t \quad (14)$$

where c is a constant, ϵ_t is white noise, and ζ_i are the parameters describing the dependency. A simple $AR(p)$ model assumes linear dependency on the previous p values. This may not be true. We use kernels to explore nonlinear dependencies. The kernelized $AR(p)$ model is given by:

$$y_t = c + f(y_{t-1}, y_{t-2}, \ldots, y_{t-p}) + \epsilon_t = c + f(Y_{t-1}^p) + \epsilon_t$$

where $f(Y_{t-1}^p) \in \mathcal{H}_\kappa$ is the prediction of the regression function using a kernel κ. Here, a new challenge arises, i.e., to choose the appropriate kernel function. In addition, another issue is how to choose the appropriate parameter p.

To solve these two issues, we propose to construct a pool of multiple kernels for varying values of parameter p. For example, for $p \in [p_1, p_2, \ldots, p_k]$, and m kinds of diverse kernels, we can create the following pool of mk kernel functions:

$$\mathcal{K} = \left\{\kappa^i(Y_t^{p_1}, \cdot), \ldots, \kappa^i(Y_t^{p_k}, \cdot) \text{ for } i = 1, \ldots, m.\right\}$$

The above can now be directly plugged into the OMKR framework for solving time series prediction tasks. In comparison to existing kernel methods for times series prediction, the proposed OMKR solution enjoys the important advantages of avoiding tedious kernel selection and parameter selection (e.g., p) and exploiting the power of combining multiple kernels for more accurate prediction.

3.4 Theoretical Analysis

Without loss of generality we assume that $\forall\ i$, $\forall\ t$, $\kappa^i(x_t \cdot x_t) \leq 1$, and $\ell_t(f_t^i(\mathbf{x}_t), y_t) \leq 1$ We define the optimal kernel regressor with respect to the squared loss (Widrow-Hoff) as:

$$F(\kappa_i, \ell, \mathcal{D}) = \min_{f \in \mathcal{H}_\kappa} \left[\frac{\Sigma_{t=1}^T (f(x_t) - y_t)^2}{1-\eta} + \frac{||f||^2}{\eta} \right] \tag{15}$$

where $\mathcal{D}$ is a sequence of instances.

THEOREM 1. *After receiving a sequence of T instances, the cumulative loss suffered by OMKR (Hedge) using the Widrow-Hoff Algorithm is bounded as*

$$\mathcal{L}_{OMKR} \leq \frac{\ln(\frac{1}{\beta})}{1-\beta} \min_{1 \leq i \leq m} F(\kappa_i, \ell, \mathcal{D}) + \frac{\ln(m)}{1-\beta} \tag{16}$$

Here $\mathcal{L}_{OMKR}$ is the total loss suffered at each prediction, and due to the convexity of the loss function, we have

$$\mathcal{L}_{OMKR} = \Sigma_{t=1}^T \ell(\Sigma_{i=1}^m w_t^i f_t^i(x_t), y_t) \leq \Sigma_{t=1}^T \Sigma_{i=1}^m w_t^i \ell(f_t^i(x_t), y_t)$$

and by choosing $\beta = \frac{\sqrt{T}}{\sqrt{T} + \sqrt{\ln m}}$, we get:

$$\mathcal{L}_{OMKR} \leq (1 + \sqrt{\frac{\ln m}{T}} \min_{1 \leq i \leq m} F(\kappa_i, \ell, \mathcal{D}) + \ln m + \sqrt{T \ln m})$$

PROOF. The proof follows from combining the proof of Hedge Algorithm and the Widrow-Hoff Regression. Let $\phi_t^i = ||f_t^i - f||_2^2$ for any $f \in \mathcal{H}_{\kappa_i}$. Also, let Δ_t denote the change in f during each update, such that $\Delta_t = \eta(f_t(x_t) - y_t)\kappa(x_t, \cdot)$. We also define $\ell_t = f_t(x_t) - y_t$ as the signed error suffered by f_t, and $\ell_t^* = f(x_t) - y_t$ be the signed error suffered by f.

$$\begin{aligned} \phi_{t+1}^i - \phi_t^i &= ||f_{t+1}^i - f||_2^2 - ||f_t^i - f||_2^2 \\ &= ||\Delta_t||_2^2 - 2(f_t^i - f) \cdot \Delta_t \\ &= \eta^2 \ell_t^{i2} \kappa(x_t \cdot x_t) - 2\eta \ell_t \kappa(x_t, \cdot) \cdot (f_t^i - f) \\ &\leq \eta^2 \ell_t^{i2} - 2\eta \ell_t^2 + 2\eta \ell_t \ell_t^* \\ &= \eta^2 \ell_t^{i2} - 2\eta \ell_t^{i2} + 2\eta \left[(\ell_t^i \sqrt{1-\eta})(\frac{\ell_t^*}{\sqrt{1-\eta}}) \right] \end{aligned}$$

The inequality follows from the assumption $\kappa(x_t \cdot x_t) \leq 1$.

$$\begin{aligned} \phi_{t+1}^i - \phi_t^i &\leq \eta^2 \ell_t^{i2} - 2\eta \ell_t^{i2} + \eta(1-\eta)\ell_t^{i2} + \frac{\eta}{1-\eta} \ell_t^{*2} \\ &= -\eta \ell_t^{i2} + \frac{\eta}{1-\eta} \ell_t^{*2} \end{aligned} \tag{17}$$

In the above equation we use the algebraic inequality $ab \leq (a^2 + b^2)/2$. From this, by assuming $f_1 = \mathbf{0}$, and using a telescoping sum, it is very simple to prove that

$$\mathcal{L}_{WH}^i \leq \min_{f \in \mathcal{H}_\kappa} \left[\frac{\Sigma_{t=1}^T (f(x_t) - y_t)^2}{1-\eta} + \frac{||f||^2}{\eta} \right] \tag{18}$$

where $\mathcal{L}_{WH}^i$ is the cumulative loss suffered by the regression function learnt by the the Widrow-Hoff Algorithm in the RKHS by the ith kernel. Plugging this into the Hedge Algorithm gives us the bound. The choice of β maybe over-estimated because of the assumption that the loss suffered by the algorithm is T. □

Similarly, bounds can be derived for any generic convex loss function by using online gradient descent for learning each regression function. For a decaying $\eta_t = \frac{1}{\sqrt{t}}$, OGD can achieve a sublinear regret bound of $O(\sqrt{T})$ with respect to the best linear combination of multiple kernel predictions. For a fixed η, the bound is weaker and may indicate poor learning. However, a fixed η is more suitable in a non-stationary environment, as it can adapt to a changing pattern faster.

3.5 Stochastic and Budget OMKR

In the worst case, all the instances become support vectors for each kernel in the OMKR framework(which is invariably the case when using squared loss). For the tth instance, the time taken for a prediction to be made by a single kernel is in $O(t)$, and for m predictions to be made by m kernels is in $O(mt)$. However, not all kernels are good candidates for prediction, especially when their weights are low. In addition, not all the historical instances are good candidates for making the prediction, particularly in a non-stationary setting. With this motivation, we propose stochastic update and budget online kernel learning strategies.

3.5.1 Stochastic Update for OMKR

An update to a kernel regressor involves adding a new support vector. If SVs are not added to less important kernels, the time taken for prediction by these kernels is significantly reduced. The intuition is if there is only one good kernel or a small subset of good performing kernels, it is only these should be given more data to learn the function, and the poor kernels are still allowed to make predictions (but with limited data), which takes much lesser computational time. We define a probability sampling denoted by q_t^i, which determines the probability of a kernel being selected for updates.

$$q_t^i = \frac{|w_t^i|}{\max_{1 \leq j \leq m} |w_t^j|} \tag{19}$$

This indicates that higher the absolute weight, the higher is the probability, and the best kernel has a probability of 1. When OMKR(Hedge) is used the weights can never be negative. In case of OGD updates in weights, there is a theoretical possibility for the weights to become negative, and hence we take absolute values to compute q_t^i, so as to account for weights having the maximum impact on the prediction. To prevent kernels with low weights, that do not have a significant impact to the prediction, from completely losing out, we introduce a smoothing parameter $\delta \in (0, 1)$. The idea is to add a small component of uniform weights. The new probability of a kernel being selected for update is denoted by:

$$p_t^i = (1-\delta)q_t^i + \frac{\delta}{m} \tag{20}$$

Here δ is a small value. A similar idea was used in [1], to tradeoff between exploration and exploitation. Using p we sample a subset of kernels based on Bernoulli Sampling, i.e., $m_t^i = Bernoulli(p_t^i)$. Only those kernels that are selected will be chosen for an update. The steps are described in Algorithm 3.

THEOREM 2. *After receiving a sequence of T instances the expected loss of the Stochastic Update OMKR (Hedge) denoted by $\mathbb{E}[\mathcal{L}] = \mathbb{E}[\Sigma_{t=1}^T \ell(\Sigma_{i=1}^m \theta_t^i f_t^i(x_t), y_t)]$ is bounded as:*

$$\mathbb{E}[\mathcal{L}] \leq \frac{\ln(\frac{1}{\beta})}{\delta(1-\beta)} \min_{1 \leq i \leq m} F(\kappa_i, \ell, \mathcal{D}) + \frac{\ln(m)}{\delta(1-\beta)} \tag{21}$$

Algorithm 3 Stochastic OMKR scheme

INPUT:

- Kernels: $\kappa(\cdot,\cdot) : \chi \times \chi \rightarrow i = 1,\ldots,m$
- Update Parameter: $\beta \in (0,1)$ if Hedge or η_w for OGD
- Smoothing Parameter: $\delta \in (0,1)$
- Step Size Parameter for each kernel: η
- Regression parameters:λ, ν for OMKR(NORMA) NORMA)

Initialization: $f_1 = 0$, $\mathbf{w}_1 = \frac{1}{m}\mathbf{1}$

for t = 1,...,T **do**
  Receive instance: x_t
  Predict $\hat{y}_t$ based on Hedge or OGD combination
  Reveal true value y_t
  $q_t^i = \frac{|w_t^i|}{\max_{1\leq j\leq m} |w_t^j|}$, $i = 1,\ldots,m$
  $p_t^i = (1-\delta)q_t^i + \frac{\delta}{m}$, $i = 1,\ldots,m$
  Sample $m_t^i = BernoulliSampling(q_t^i)$, $i = 1,\ldots,m$
  for i = 1,...,m **do**
    Set $\ell_t^i = \ell(f_t^i(x_t), y_t)$
    if $m_t^i == 1$ **then**
      Update $f_{t+1}^i =$ Eq. (3) OR (6)
    end if
  end for
  Update $\mathbf{w}_{t+1}$ based on Hedge or OGD
end for

and by choosing $\beta = \frac{\sqrt{T}}{\sqrt{T}+\sqrt{\ln m}}$, *we get:*

$$\mathbb{E}[\mathcal{L}] \leq \frac{1}{\delta}(1+\sqrt{\frac{\ln m}{T}} \min_{1\leq i\leq m} F(\kappa_i, \ell, \mathcal{D}) + \ln m + \sqrt{T\ln m})$$

The proof is similar to the proof of OMKR(Hedge). We omit the details.

3.5.2 *Budget OMKR*

Often, a subset of instances can explain the data as well as the entire data. Further, in a non-stationary time series setting, it is common to introduce a sliding window so as to give importance to only the most recent instances. In our case, we have a sliding window of the most recent support vectors that explain the data. This is also particularly helpful in the case of NORMA, where in each iteration, the old support vectors get reduced by a factor of $(1-\eta\lambda)$. As t grows, the α values of the old support vectors get reduced to almost zero. Such support vectors can be ignored without any significant impact to the prediction. Therefore, we propose a parameter τ which restricts the total number of support vectors that are allowed to be stored by each regressor. The older support vectors are deleted.

3.5.3 *Comparison between Stochastic and Budget*

Stochastic OMKR improves efficiency by reducing the number of support vectors of poor performing kernels. However, if all kernels are equally good, there is no reduction in computational time. The budget strategy restricts the number of support vectors of each kernel, and has a worst case complexity of $O(m\tau)$ in each iteration to make the prediction. Both address non-stationarity in different ways. Stochastic approach trades off between exploration and exploitation to determine if another kernel has become more suitable for the changing pattern, and the budget approach gives more importance to the most recent data.

4. EXPERIMENTAL EVALUATION

In this section, we empirically evaluate the performance of all OMKR variants on regression data and time series data.

4.1 Experimental Setup

4.1.1 *Data*

We use five regular regression datasets and seven time series datasets. The data is from different applications, with a wide range of data size and dimensionality. All data attributes including the target were scaled to [0, 1]. The algorithms were run on ten random permutations of the regular regression datasets to establish robustness. Such permutations are not applicable in the case of time series. The details of the datasets used can be seen in Table 1.

Table 1: List of Datasets

ID	Name	# Instances	# Attributes
	Regression Datasets		
D1	Abalone	4177	8
D2	Parkinsons	5875	20
D3	Spacega	3107	6
D4	Cadata	20640	8
D5	Add10	9792	11
	Time Series Datasets		
D6	Laser	10073	20|10
D7	Physiological	17000	2
D8	Currency Exch. 1	3000	20|10
D9	Currency Exch. 2	3000	20|10
D10	Astrophysical	598	20|10
	Large Time Series Datasets		
D11	Santafe Computer	100000	20|10
D12	Twitter	583250	77

Datasets D1, D2 and D12 were taken from the UCI repository[1], D3-D4 from StatLib[2], D5 is a synthetic dataset obtained from Delve[3]. D6-D11 are datasets from the Santa Fe Time Series Competition Data[4]. D6 is stationary, D7 is non-stationary, and unlike other time series data, is not univariate, but is dependent on 2 attributes, D8 and D9's stationarity property is unknown, and D10 is characterized by noise. D11 is non-stationary with a slow drift. D12 is about predicting buzz in social media. For univariate time series data the attribute column having 20|10 indicates the choice of 2 kernelized $AR(p)$ process with $p = 10, 20$ each having its own m kernel functions.

4.1.2 *Kernels*

We evaluate the performance of OMKR by using a pool of 24 predefined kernels. These include 4 polynomial kernels $\kappa(x,y) = (x^T y)^p$ of degree parameter $p = 1,2,3,4$, 13 RBF kernels ($\kappa(x,y) = e^{(\frac{-||x-y||^2}{2\sigma^2})}$) of kernel width parameter σ in $[2^{-6}, 2^{-5}, \ldots, 2^6]$, 5 Cauchy kernels ($\kappa(x,y) = \frac{1}{1+\frac{||x-y||^2}{\sigma^2}}$) with parameter σ in $[2^{-2}, 2^{-1}, \ldots, 2^2]$, one sigmoid kernel($\kappa(x,y) = \tanh(xy)$) and a Chi-Square Kernel

[1]`http://archive.ics.uci.edu/ml/`
[2]`http://lib.stat.cmu.edu/`
[3]`http://www.cs.toronto.edu/~delve/data/datasets.html`
[4]`http://www-psych.stanford.edu/~andreas/Time-Series/SantaFe.html`

$(\kappa(x,y) = 1 - \Sigma_{i=1}^{n} \frac{(x_i - y_i)^2}{\frac{1}{2}(x_i + y_i)})$. Since all our data is scaled to $[0,1]$, we clip the kernel prediction to this range, i.e., $\hat{y_t} = \max(0, \min(1, \hat{y_t}))$.

4.1.3 Comparison and Performance Metrics

We compare the algorithms based on Mean Squared Error (MSE), time taken, and the weight distribution. The algorithms compared are - (i) *Regression(V)*: Best Kernel by validation; (ii) *Regression(H)*: Best Kernel in hindsight; (iii) *Uniform OMKR*: Uniform weight distribution over kernels (to see if this can eliminate the impact of a poor kernel choice); (iv) *Deterministic OMKR (Hedge)*; and (v) *Deterministic OMKR (OGD)*. We then analyze the performance of efficiency enhancing variants of OMKR and study the tradeoff between accuracy and efficiency. For the large datasets (D11 and D12), we compare only the budget versions of all algorithms.

4.1.4 Parameter Setting

All parameters for the regression tasks (if any), and the best kernel for Regression(V) were chosen by online validation technique. We performed a grid search and evaluated the performance of the parameters on the of first 100 instances or first 10% of the instances, whichever was lesser. The value of Hedge parameter β was fixed to 0.5 in all cases, and the learning rate η_w was fixed to 0.025 for OGD update of weights). We also conducted sensitivity analysis for the weight update parameters. The learning rate η for each kernel regression was fixed at 0.1. Since η is the same for both single kernel and multi kernel versions, its choice does not affect the comparison between Single Kernel Regression and OMKR. For budget strategies, we fixed the budget size $\tau = 500$ support vectors. In stochastic OMKR, the smoothing parameter δ was set to 0.05 in all cases.

4.2 Experimental Results and Analysis

4.2.1 Evaluation of Deterministic OMKR

The detailed results of single kernel regression against OMKR can be seen in Table 2. Columns Reg(V) and Reg(H) represent single kernel regression by validation and in hindsight. Columns Uniform, Hedge, OGD represent OMKR with uniform weights, weight updated by Hedge, and weight updated by OGD respectively.

With almost no exception both our proposed methods OMKR (Hedge and OGD) outperform Reg(V) very significantly, at times achieving as low as 1% of error of Reg(V). We should note that in a real world setting, it is hard to choose a better kernel for unseen data than by a validation method. Reg(H) is the best kernel in hindsight, and is not known prior to running the experiments. Despite this, OMKR algorithms significantly outperform Reg(H) in most cases. In cases, where it OMKR does not beat Reg(H), their performance is very closely matched. Thus, without any a priori knowledge, OMKR is able to outperform even the best kernel in hindsight. This is because OMKR is able to identify a linear combination of kernels, which provide complementary information to each other in order to give a weighted prediction which beats any single best kernel. Uniform OMKR is affected by the usage of certain poor kernels and its performance is very inconsistent across datasets. It never beats OMKR(OGD), and beats OMKR(Hedge) in only one case (D1-Norma). This however is probably an exception, in which the optimal linear combination is close to a uniform distribution, because of which uniform weights are probably just a lucky guess. The difference in performance by Reg(V) and Reg(H), and the poor performance by Uniform(OMKR) highlight the difficulty of choosing the best kernel function for a given task. In terms of efficiency, Deterministic OMKR takes roughly m times the amount of time take by single kernel regression.

Hedge and OGD are suitable in different scenarios. Due to a multiplicative update, Hedge converges very quickly, by identifying the single kernel that best represents the data, which is often the case. However, since Hedge only offers a linear combination of the best kernel(s), we expect the optimal linear combination determined by OGD to outperform Hedge. This does not happen if the the data is not large enough for OGD to converge to optimal linear combination, or the data is non-stationary such that the appropriate kernel function changes too frequently for OGD to be able to learn the optimal combination. We plot the cumulative mean squared error against time for some representative datasets in Figures 1 and 2. It can be seen, that in most cases, OMKR(Hedge) attains a very low MSE from the beginning and does not improve much further, whereas, OMKR(OGD) starts with a relatively higher MSE, but it is continuously improving its performance. Referring back to Table 2, it can be seen that in general that OMKR(OGD) has relative advantage in larger datasets, and OMKR(Hedge) in smaller ones. Additionally, we also look at the weight distribution attained by the algorithms, which is shown in Figure 3. The weight distribution by OMKR(Hedge) concentrates largely on the best kernel in hindsight, and otherwise has weights over certain reasonably good performing kernels. Unlike OMKR(Hedge), OMKR(OGD) does not have a concentrated distribution of weights over few kernels.

4.2.2 Evaluation of OMKR Efficiency Enhancers

The MSE and the time taken by Deterministic, Stochastic and Budget OMKR are detailed in Tables 3 and 4. Clearly the time taken by both stochastic and budget techniques is significantly lower than Deterministic OMKR. Despite this, in most cases, the efficiency enhancers give comparable MSEs with respect to Deterministic OMKR. In many cases, particularly time series, the variants are able to outperform the deterministic version. This shows their ability to retain important information from the data, and adapt to changes in the pattern. Stochastic is faster than budget in smaller datasets, but in larger datasets, the number of SVs in stochastic start dominating even if only for a few kernels, and hence Budget is faster.

Using Budget OMKR, we run the algorithm on two large datasets (D11 and D12). In this case, we use a budget for all 5 algorithms. The details are shown in Table 5. The results are consistent with our previous findings of OMKR outperforming single kernel regression.

4.2.3 Effect of weight update parameters β and η_w

OMKR(Hedge) is not very sensitive to the value of the discount rate parameter β. There is a reasonably large range of values of β in which OMKR(Hedge)'s relative performance to other algorithms remains the same. OMKR(OGD)'s sensitivity to the learning rate η_w shows a tradeoff between large and small learning rates. This behavior is typical of all gradient descent algorithms.

Table 2: Single Kernel Regression vs Multiple Kernel Regression:
Each field is the ratio $\frac{MSE_{algorithm}}{MSE_{Reg(V)}}$. Lower ratio implies lower MSE. Best ratios are in bold. The results for the regression datasets are averaged over 10 different permutations. The standard deviation is significantly lower in OMKR versions.

	Widrow Hoff					Norma				
ID	Reg(V)	Reg(H)	Uniform	Hedge	OGD	Reg(V)	Reg(H)	Uniform	Hedge	OGD
				Regression Datasets						
D1	1.00	**0.85**	1.06	0.89	0.98	1.00	0.36	0.29	0.31	**0.26**
D2	1.00	**0.39**	0.79	**0.39**	0.45	1.00	0.40	0.49	0.40	**0.39**
D3	1.00	**0.69**	3.90	**0.69**	0.82	1.00	0.87	1.55	**0.52**	0.60
D4	1.00	**0.79**	1.13	**0.79**	0.85	1.00	0.77	0.93	0.74	**0.67**
D5	1.00	**0.53**	2.85	0.56	0.62	1.00	**0.21**	0.53	**0.21**	0.22
				Time Series Datasets						
D6	1.00	**0.13**	0.50	**0.14**	**0.14**	1.00	0.96	1.68	0.70	**0.57**
D7	1.00	0.96	1.61	0.93	**0.37**	1.00	0.98	0.69	0.23	**0.15**
D8	1.00	**0.96**	12.40	1.65	1.67	1.00	0.73	0.30	**0.15**	0.18
D9	1.00	**0.01**	0.07	**0.01**	**0.01**	1.00	0.79	0.65	**0.18**	**0.17**
D10	1.00	0.83	2.90	0.84	**0.66**	1.00	0.67	1.60	**0.45**	0.54

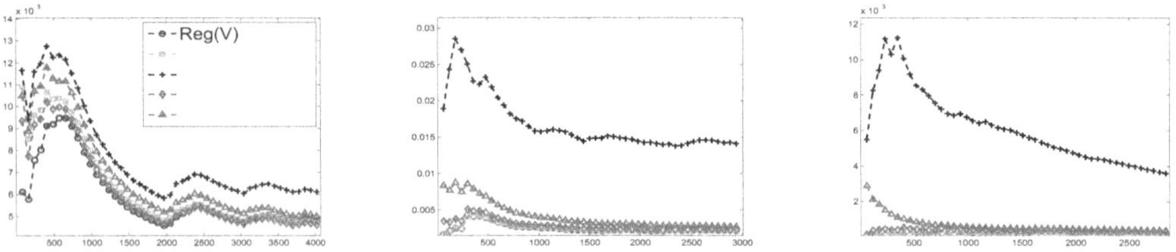

(a) D1 (b) D3 (c) D8

Figure 1: Cumulative Mean Squared Error with time (when Widrow-Hoff is used for regression):
All results are displayed for data after the validation stage during which the parameters were determined.

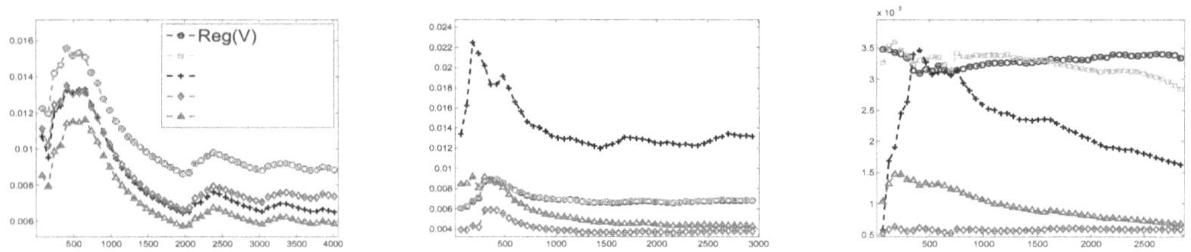

(a) D1 (b) D3 (c) D8

Figure 2: Cumulative Mean Squared Error with time (when Norma is used for regression):
All results are displayed for data after the validation stage during which the parameters were determined.

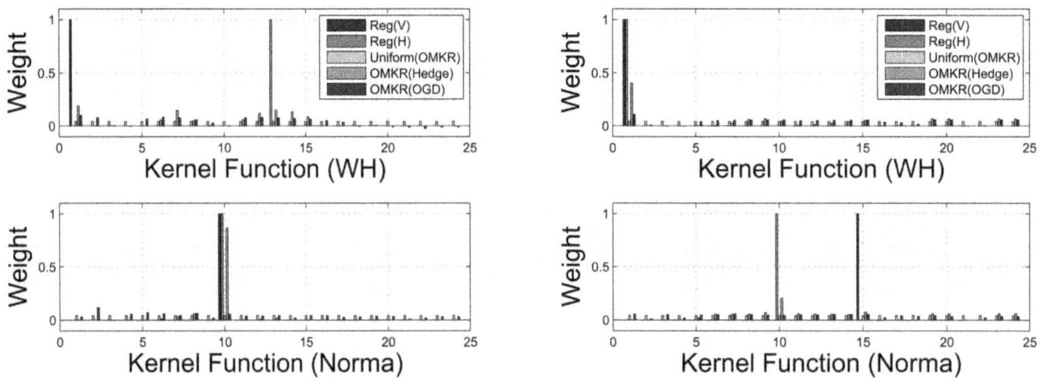

(a) D1 (b) D3

Figure 3: Weight distribution attained by all algorithms

Table 3: OMKR (Hedge) vs Stochastic and Budget Strategies:
Here again, the results of regression datasets are averaged over 10 random permutations. All times are in seconds.

	Widrow Hoff						Norma					
ID	**Determinisitc**		**Stochastic**		**Budget**		**Det OMKR**		**Stochastic**		**Budget**	
	MSE	Time	MSE	Time	MSE	Time	MSE	Time	MSE	Time	MSE	TIME
Regression Datasets												
D1	**0.0075**	348	0.0079	39	0.0096	74	0.0121	220	**0.0113**	45	0.0122	68
D2	**0.0209**	707	0.0488	32	0.0436	109	**0.0451**	537	0.0544	45	0.0467	102
D3	**0.0028**	193	0.0035	22	0.0058	54	**0.0049**	159	0.0050	37	**0.0049**	53
D4	**0.0245**	8496	**0.0243**	376	0.0354	385	0.0477	6397	**0.0416**	354	**0.0413**	388
D5	**0.0054**	1950	0.0096	64	0.0122	183	**0.0108**	1338	0.0151	112	0.0116	171
Time Series Datasets												
D6	**0.0022**	4062	0.0034	146	0.0066	427	0.0058	2611	**0.0034**	182	0.0059	413
D7	**0.0025**	5728	0.0030	831	0.0088	312	**0.0008**	5101	0.0017	1118	**0.0008**	322
D8	0.0003	346	**0.0002**	15	0.0007	117	0.0005	274	**0.0002**	136	0.0005	111
D9	**0.0009**	352	0.0010	56	0.0011	118	**0.0006**	280	0.0010	119	**0.0006**	114
D10	**0.0074**	16	0.0086	3	0.0089	15	**0.0047**	12	0.0086	6	**0.0047**	12

Table 4: OMKR (OGD) vs Stochastic and Budget Strategies:
Here again, the results of regression datasets are averaged over 10 random permutations. All times are in seconds.

	Widrow Hoff						Norma					
ID	**Determinisitc**		**Stochastic**		**Budget**		**Det OMKR**		**Stochastic**		**Budget**	
	MSE	Time	MSE	Time	MSE	Time	MSE	Time	MSE	Time	MSE	TIME
Regression Datasets												
D1	**0.0082**	348	0.0086	43	0.0097	76	0.0105	220	**0.0095**	48	0.0105	69
D2	**0.0230**	707	0.0488	35	0.0432	111	**0.0442**	537	0.0521	49	0.0466	105
D3	**0.0034**	193	0.0045	24	0.0043	55	0.0055	159	**0.0044**	40	0.0056	54
D4	**0.0261**	8496	**0.0260**	414	0.0311	393	**0.0006**	6397	0.0322	382	0.0363	396
D5	**0.0060**	1950	0.0109	70	0.0108	187	**0.0115**	1338	**0.0115**	121	0.0121	174
Time Series Datasets												
D6	**0.0021**	4062	0.0039	160	0.0055	427	**0.0048**	2611	**0.0048**	200	**0.0048**	413
D7	**0.0010**	5728	0.0011	914	0.0023	318	**0.0005**	5101	0.0008	1230	0.0006	328
D8	0.0003	346	**0.0002**	17	0.0004	117	0.0006	274	**0.0002**	149	0.0006	111
D9	**0.0004**	352	0.0005	62	0.0005	118	0.0006	280	**0.0004**	130	0.0006	114
D10	**0.0058**	16	0.0113	3	0.0066	15	**0.0056**	12	0.0063	6	**0.0056**	12

Table 5: Budget OMKR on large time series datasets:
The comparison is against the budget version of all algorithms. All values are MSE achieved by each algorithm. Runtime of D11 was 4000 seconds, and of D12 was 12000 seconds.

	Widrow Hoff					Norma				
ID	Reg(V)	Reg(H)	Uniform	Hedge	OGD	Reg(V)	Reg(H)	Uniform	Hedge	OGD
Large Time Series Datasets										
D11	0.074807	0.015779	0.040779	0.015709	**0.007766**	0.017452	0.012429	0.028378	0.011465	**0.006457**
D12	0.000327	**0.000026**	0.001580	**0.000027**	0.000028	0.000915	0.000637	0.020063	0.000605	**0.000031**

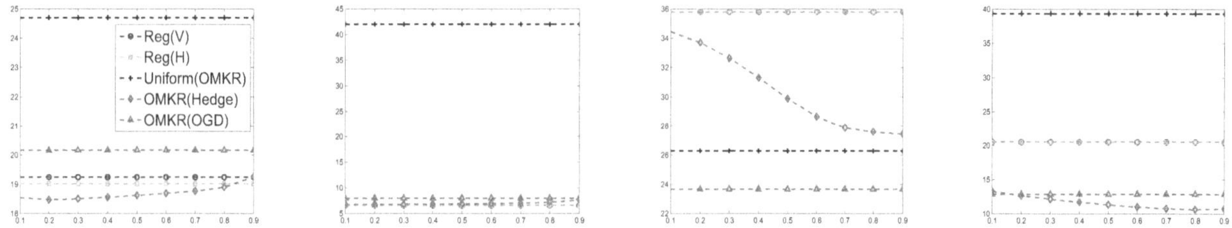

(a) D1 (WH) (b) D3 (WH) (c) D1 (Norma) (d) D3 (Norma)

Figure 4: Sensitivity of OMKR(Hedge) to discount rate parameter β:
We vary β keeping the performance of all other algorithms fixed.

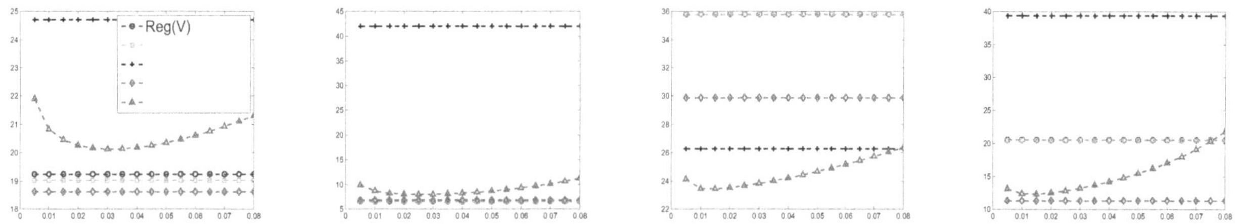

(a) D1 (WH) (b) D3 (WH) (c) D1 (Norma) (d) D3 (Norma)

Figure 5: Sensitivity of OMKR(OGD) to learning rate η_w:
We vary η_w keeping the performance of all other algorithms fixed.

5. CONCLUSION

This paper proposes a family of OMKR algorithms for kernel based regression using a pool of predefined kernels. They overcome the challenges of existing work which are largely designed for a batch setting and assume that the appropriate kernel function is known. OMKR sequentially learns the kernel based regressor in an online and scalable fashion, and dynamically explores a pool of multiple diverse kernels to avoid problems of poor kernel choice by manual or heuristic selection. Further, OMKR is particularly useful in a time series setting, where the appropriate window size p of an $AR(p)$ process is not known. Varying values of p, each with its own set of predefined kernels, are plugged into the OMKR framework, thus exploring and identifying the best kernel based regressor dynamically. We evaluate the performance of OMKR based on two types of loss functions. Any kernel based regression task can be plugged into the generic OMKR framework, and is likely to achieve a better result than any single kernel. We also propose stochastic and budget techniques to enhance efficiency. Our empirical evaluations show the excellent performance of OMKR, often beating the best prediction function determined in hindsight.

6. REFERENCES

[1] P. Auer, N. Cesa-Bianchi, Y. Freund, and R. E. Schapire. The nonstochastic multiarmed bandit problem. *SIAM Journal on Computing*, 32(1):48–77, 2002.

[2] O. Bousquet and D. J. Herrmann. On the complexity of learning the kernel matrix. *Advances in NIPS*, pages 415–422, 2003.

[3] D. Brugger, W. Rosenstiel, and M. Bogdan. Online svr training by solving the primal optimization problem. *Journal of Signal Processing Systems*, 65(3):391–402, 2011.

[4] G. Cavallanti, N. Cesa-Bianchi, and C. Gentile. Tracking the best hyperplane with a simple budget perceptron. *Machine Learning*, 69:143–167, 2007.

[5] N. Cesa-Bianchi and G. Lugosi. *Prediction, learning, and games.* Cambridge University Press, 2006.

[6] K. Crammer, O. Dekel, J. Keshet, S. Shalev-Shwartz, and Y. Singer. Online passive-aggressive algorithms. *JMLR*, 7:551–585, Dec. 2006.

[7] K. Crammer, J. Kandola, and Y. Singer. Online classification on a budget. In *Advances in NIPS 16.* MIT Press, Cambridge, MA, 2004.

[8] O. Dekel, S. Shalev-Shwartz, and Y. Singer. The forgetron: A kernel-based perceptron on a budget. *SIAM Journal on Computing*, 37(5):1342–1372, 2008.

[9] Y. Freund and R. E. Schapire. A desicion-theoretic generalization of on-line learning and an application to boosting. In *Computational Learning Theory*, volume 904, pages 23–37. Springer Berlin Heidelberg, 1995.

[10] M. Gönen and E. Alpaydın. Multiple kernel learning algorithms. *The Journal of Machine Learning Research*, 12:2211–2268, 2011.

[11] S. C. Hoi, R. Jin, and M. R. Lyu. Learning nonparametric kernel matrices from pairwise constraints. In *ICML*, pages 361–368. ACM, 2007.

[12] S. C. Hoi, R. Jin, P. Zhao, and T. Yang. Online multiple kernel classification. *Machine Learning*, 90(2):289–316, 2013.

[13] S. C. Hoi, M. R. Lyu, and E. Y. Chang. Learning the unified kernel machines for classification. In *KDD*, pages 187–196. ACM, 2006.

[14] S. C. Hoi, J. Wang, and P. Zhao. *LIBOL: A Library for Online Learning Algorithms.* Nanyang Technological University, 2012.

[15] R. Jin, S. Hoi, and T. Yang. Online multiple kernel learning: Algorithms and mistake bounds. In *Algorithmic Learning Theory*, volume 6331, pages 390–404. Springer Berlin Heidelberg, 2010.

[16] H. Kashima, K. Tsuda, and A. Inokuchi. Marginalized kernels between labeled graphs. In *ICML*, volume 3, pages 321–328, 2003.

[17] J. Kivinen, A. Smola, and R. Williamson. Online learning with kernels. *Signal Processing, IEEE Transactions on*, 52(8):2165–2176, 2004.

[18] J. T. Kwok and I. W. Tsang. Learning with idealized kernels. In *ICML*, pages 400–407, 2003.

[19] G. R. G. Lanckriet, N. Cristianini, P. Bartlett, L. E. Ghaoui, and M. I. Jordan. Learning the kernel matrix with semidefinite programming. *J. Mach. Learn. Res.*, 5:27–72, Dec. 2004.

[20] N. Littlestone and M. K. Warmuth. The weighted majority algorithm. In *Foundations of Computer Science, 1989., 30th Annual Symposium on*, pages 256–261. IEEE, 1989.

[21] A. F. Martins, M. A. Figueiredo, P. M. Aguiar, N. A. Smith, and E. P. Xing. Online multiple kernel learning for structured prediction. *arXiv preprint arXiv:1010.2770*, 2010.

[22] E. Moroshko and K. Crammer. A last-step regression algorithm for non-stationary online learning. *CoRR*, abs/1303.3754, 2013.

[23] F. Orabona, J. Keshet, and B. Caputo. The projectron: a bounded kernel-based perceptron. In *ICML*, pages 720–727. ACM, 2008.

[24] N. Sapankevych and R. Sankar. Time series prediction using support vector machines: a survey. *Computational Intelligence Magazine, IEEE*, 4(2):24–38, 2009.

[25] B. Schölkopf and A. J. Smola. *Learning with kernels.* ŞTheŤ MIT Press, 2002.

[26] L. C. S. V. D. Schuurmans and S. W. Caelli. Implicit online learning with kernels. In *NIPS*, volume 19, page 249. MIT Press, 2007.

[27] S. Shalev-Shwartz. Online learning: Theory, algorithms, and applications. 2007.

[28] J. Shawe-Taylor and N. Cristianini. *Kernel methods for pattern analysis.* Cambridge university press, 2004.

[29] A. J. Smola and B. Schölkopf. A tutorial on support vector regression. *Statistics and computing*, 14(3):199–222, 2004.

[30] S. Sonnenburg, G. Rätsch, C. Schäfer, and B. Schölkopf. Large scale multiple kernel learning. *JMLR*, 7:1531–1565, 2006.

[31] U. Thissen, R. Van Brakel, A. De Weijer, W. Melssen, and L. Buydens. Using support vector machines for time series prediction. *Chemometrics and intelligent laboratory systems*, 69(1):35–49, 2003.

[32] V. Vovk. A game of prediction with expert advice. In *COLT*, pages 51–60. ACM, 1995.

[33] B. WIDROW, M. E. HOFF, et al. Adaptive switching circuits. 1960.

[34] Z. Xu, R. Jin, I. King, and M. R. Lyu. An extended level method for efficient multiple kernel learning. In *NIPS*, pages 1825–1832, 2008.

[35] H. Yang, Z. Xu, I. King, and M. R. Lyu. Online learning for group lasso. In *Proceedings of the 27th ICML*, pages 1191–1198, 2010.

[36] P. Zhao, J. Wang, P. Wu, R. Jin, and S. C. Hoi. Fast bounded online gradient descent algorithms for scalable kernel-based online learning. 2012.

[37] J. Zhuang, I. W. Tsang, and S. C. Hoi. A family of simple non-parametric kernel learning algorithms. *JMLR*, 12:1313–1347, 2011.

[38] M. Zinkevich. Online convex programming and generalized infinitesimal gradient ascent. 2003.

Class-Distribution Regularized Consensus Maximization for Alleviating Overfitting in Model Combination

Sihong Xie† Jing Gao§ Wei Fan‡ Deepak Turaga¶ Philip S. Yu†
†Department of Computer Science, University of Illinois at Chicago, Chicago, IL, USA
§Department of Computer Science, University at Buffalo, Buffalo, NY, USA
¶IBM T.J Watson Research Yorktown Height, NY, USA
‡Huawei Noah's Ark Lab, Hong Kong

ABSTRACT

In data mining applications such as crowdsourcing and privacy-preserving data mining, one may wish to obtain consolidated predictions out of multiple models without access to features of the data. Besides, multiple models usually carry complementary predictive information, model combination can potentially provide more robust and accurate predictions by correcting independent errors from individual models. Various methods have been proposed to combine predictions such that the final predictions are maximally agreed upon by multiple base models. Though this maximum consensus principle has been shown to be successful, simply maximizing consensus can lead to less discriminative predictions and overfit the inevitable noise due to imperfect base models. We argue that proper regularization for model combination approaches is needed to alleviate such overfitting effect. Specifically, we analyze the hypothesis spaces of several model combination methods and identify the trade-off between model consensus and generalization ability. We propose a novel model called Regularized Consensus Maximization (RCM), which is formulated as an optimization problem to combine the maximum consensus and large margin principles. We theoretically show that RCM has a smaller upper bound on generalization error compared to the version without regularization. Experiments show that the proposed algorithm outperforms a wide spectrum of state-of-the-art model combination methods on 11 tasks.

Categories and Subject Descriptors

H.2.8 [**Database Applications**]: Data Mining

Keywords

Ensemble; Large Margin; Generalization Error

KDD'14, August 24–27, 2014, New York, NY, USA.
ACM 978-1-4503-2956-9/14/08 ...$15.00.
http://dx.doi.org/10.1145/2623330.2623676.

1. INTRODUCTION

Combining multiple supervised and unsupervised models can be desirable and beneficial, or sometimes even a must. For example, in crowdsourcing, privacy-preserving data mining or big data applications, there could be only predictions from multiple models available, with raw features of the data being withheld or discarded. One has to merge the output of these models to obtain the final classification or clustering results. On the one hand, there are various new consensus-based solutions, such as those proposed in [16, 34, 30, 13, 18, 27, 37]. One common idea that these algorithms share is to learn a model that has highest prediction consensus among base models. On the other hand, simple model combination algorithms, such as majority voting [15], that do not pursue model consensus are portrayed as baselines inferior to the algorithms seeking consensus. These comparisons give the illusion that the more consensus one can achieve, the more likely the consolidated predictions will be accurate. One might ask: are the consolidated predictions that achieve maximal consensus the best choice? Could these consensus-based methods overfit the noisy and limited *observed* data, leading to results inconsistent with the *true* data distribution? After all, the goal of classification/clustering is to produce discriminative predictions [4, 29].

In this paper, we study the above questions based on the Consensus Maximization framework [16] (CM for short in the sequel), due to its generality and effectiveness. We first present a running example of CM in Table 1 to demonstrate that solely maximizing the consensus can lead to undesirable results. Suppose we have 5 instances in 2 classes, whose ground truth labels are shown in the first column of the table. There are 2 supervised models (M_1 and M_2) and 2 unsupervised model (M_3 and M_4). A supervised (resp. unsupervised) model predicts the class (resp. cluster) labels of all instances. The predictions from a model are shown under the header with the model's name. Note that neither the correspondence between class labels and cluster labels, nor the correspondence between cluster labels from different clustering models is known. We describe the details of CM later and for the moment, one can think of CM as a black box that consolidates the predictions of base models and outputs predictive posteriors $p(y = 1|\mathbf{x})$ that achieve maximal consensus among base models. For majority voting (MV for short in the sequel), it simply averages the predictions from supervised models (predictions of unsupervised models cannot be used by MV because the correspondence between classes and cluster labels is unknown). The consolidated predictions produced by CM and MV are shown in the last two columns of the table.

From this running example, one can see that CM makes more correct predictions than MV does. However, the posteriors $p(y = 1|\mathbf{x})$ produced by CM tend to be closer to the decision boundary and the margins between $p(y = 1|\mathbf{x})$ and $p(y = 0|\mathbf{x})$ are quite small. We have two observations. First, according to the margin-based generalization error analysis [24], a smaller margin of posterior class distributions between different classes leads to a higher *empirical margin risk*, which contributes to the overall generalization error. If one can produce consolidated predictions with a large posterior margin, a tighter upper bound on the generalization error can be obtained. Second, if the hypothesis space for a model combination algorithm has large capacity (measured by VC-dimension, growth function or covering number, etc.), then the upper bound of generalization error is also higher. One may incorporate certain relevant prior knowledge of the data to shrink the size of the hypothesis space. For example, for multi-class single-label classification, desirable consensus predictions should be discriminative in the sense that an instance belongs to one and *only* one class. Our goal is to reduce empirical margin risk and the capacity of the hypothesis space of model combination methods such as CM, and obtain a smaller upper bound on the generalization error.

We propose a family of regularization objectives over class distribution to reduce generalization errors. As a solid instance, we add regularization objectives to CM to obtain Regularized Consensus Maximization (RCM). In terms of algorithmic effectiveness, though the regularization introduces many tuning parameters and makes the optimization problem not jointly convex, we develop a simple yet efficient approximation to the regularization term without introducing additional parameters. An alternative optimization procedure is developed to find a local minimum with reasonably good empirical results. In terms of theoretical effectiveness of learning, we give a detailed analysis of the algorithm and formally prove that, comparing to the original version, RCM achieves a smaller upper bound on generalization error. In summary, we make the following contributions:

- To the best of our knowledge, this is the first work to consider, address and theoretically analyze (Section 2.2 and 4) the overfitting issue in model combination methods.
- We propose a class distribution regularization framework and formulate it as an optimization problem to trade-off between maximal consensus and large margin principles. The optimization problem can be solved conveniently using gradient descent.
- We compare the performance of the proposed algorithm to a wide range of state-of-the-art model combination methods. Extensive experiments on 11 datesets demonstrate the theory and the effectiveness of the proposed framework.

2. OVERFITTED CONSENSUS MAXIMIZATION

In this section, we recapitulate some basic concepts used in the CM framework, which is followed by an analysis of why it tends to overfit the data.

Table 1: Running CM Example

y	Predictions				MV Results	CM Results
	M_1	M_2	M_3	M_4	$P(y=+\|\mathbf{x})$	$P(y=+\|\mathbf{x})$
+	+	+	C1	R0	1	0.5073
+	+	+	C0	R0	1	0.5097
+	−	+	C0	R0	.5	0.5024
−	+	−	C1	R1	.5	0.4946
−	−	−	C1	R1	0	0.4873

Table 2: Notations

$\mathbf{x}^i \in \mathcal{X} = \mathbb{R}^d$	An instance of data
$\mathcal{D} = \{\mathbf{x}^1, \ldots, \mathbf{x}^n\}$	Collection of instances
$Y = [y_1, \ldots, y_n]^\top$	Ground truth labels of $\mathcal{D}$
$U_{n\times c}$	Membership indicators of data
$Q_{v\times c}$	Membership indicators of groups
$A_{n\times v}$	Affinity matrix
c	Number of classes
$\mathbf{u}^i$	The i-th row of matrix U
$\mathbf{u}_j$	The j-th column of matrix U

2.1 Preliminaries

CM combines the output of multiple supervised and unsupervised base models (as shown in Table 1). Let the set of instances be $\mathcal{D} = \{\mathbf{x}^1, \ldots, \mathbf{x}^n\}$, each of which belongs to one of c classes $\{1, \ldots, c\}$. Suppose we have m models $\{M_1, \ldots, M_m\}$. Without loss of generality, we assume that the first $0 \le r \le m$ models are supervised models, and the rest are unsupervised models. A supervised model predicts the class label of each instance, while an unsupervised model predicts the cluster label and partitions $\mathcal{D}$ into c clusters. Given the predictions of m models, without access to the data $\mathcal{D}$, CM computes consolidated predictions to achieve maximal consensus among base models.

We use the example in Table 1 to demonstrate how CM constructs a bipartite graph and obtains consensus predictions. The bipartite graph contains group nodes and instance nodes, where a group node represent a class or cluster from a supervised or unsupervised model, and an instance node represent a data instance. Therefore, there are $c \times m$ group nodes and n instance nodes. We number the group nodes such that class/cluster ℓ from the j-th model is labeled as the $((j-1) \times c + \ell)$-th group. The bipartite graph constructed using the toy example is shown in Figure 1. An instance node is connected to a group node iff the corresponding instance is classified or clustered into the corresponding class or cluster of a model. A group node of a supervised model is also connected to an external node representing its ground truth label (the left-most nodes in the figure). As $\mathbf{x}^1$ is predicted to have label 1 by M_1, instance node $\mathbf{x}^1$ is linked to the group nodes g^1 representing class 1 of M_1. Similarly, $\mathbf{x}^5$ is linked to group node g_8 to indicate that the instance belongs to the second group (R_1) by M_4.

CM consolidates these base models into a single model whose predictions achieve maximal consensus among the predictions of base models. Formally, we denote the membership distribution of an instance node for $\mathbf{x}^i$ by a row probabilistic vector $\mathbf{u}^i = [u^i_1, \ldots, u^i_c]$. Similarly, the membership distribution of a group node is given by a row probabilistic vector $\mathbf{q}^j = [q^j_1, \ldots, q^j_c]$. These vectors can be collectively denoted by two matrices: $U = [\mathbf{u}^{1\top}, \ldots, \mathbf{u}^{n\top}]^\top$ and

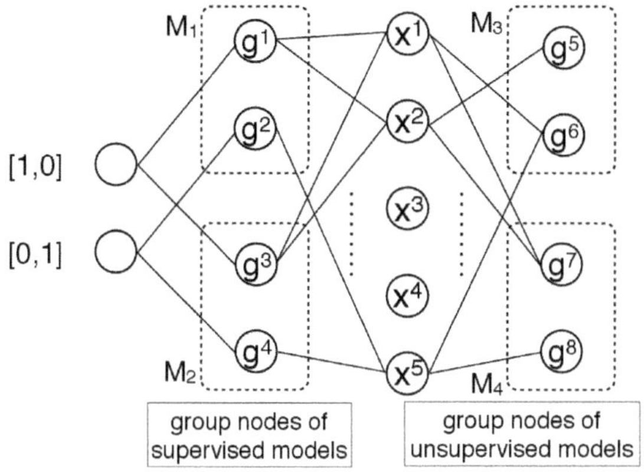

Figure 1: Bipartite graph representation in CM

$Q = [\mathbf{q}^{1\top}, \ldots, \mathbf{q}^{v\top}]^\top$ where $v = c \times m$. CM seeks smooth probability distributions U and Q, such that *any* connected nodes in the graph have similar probabilistic distributions. CM solves the following optimization problem:

$$\begin{aligned} \min_{U,Q} \quad & \sum_{i=1}^{n}\sum_{j=1}^{v} a_j^i \|\mathbf{u}^i - \mathbf{q}^j\|^2 + \alpha \sum_{j=1}^{v} b_j \|\mathbf{q}^j - \bar{\mathbf{y}}^j\|^2 \\ \text{s.t.} \quad & u_\ell^i \geq 0, \textstyle\sum_{\ell=1}^{c} u_\ell^i = 1, i = 1, \ldots, n \\ & q_\ell^j \geq 0, \textstyle\sum_{\ell=1}^{c} q_\ell^j = 1, j = 1, \ldots, v \end{aligned}$$

where $a_j^i = 1$ if the i-th instance node is connected to the j-th group nodes, and is equal to 0 otherwise. b_j indicates if the j-th group node is from a classification model ($b_j = 1$) or a clustering model ($b_j = 0$). $\bar{\mathbf{y}}^j$ is a vector indicating the class label of the j-th group node from a classification model. For example, $\bar{\mathbf{y}}^1 = [1, 0]$ and $\bar{\mathbf{y}}^2 = [0, 1]$ in the above running example. $\bar{\mathbf{y}}^j$ is an all zero vector if the corresponding group node is from a clustering model.

We denote the objective by $\mathcal{L}(U, Q)$ and is defined as **consensus loss**. It measures the level of disagreement between the consolidated predictions and the outputs of base models. By minimizing $\mathcal{L}(U, Q)$, consensus among base models is maximized. The second term accounts for the initial predictions of supervised models, and does not play a role if all base models are unsupervised. The whole optimization is solved via block coordinate descent:

$$Q = (D_v + \alpha K_v)^{-1}(A^\top U + \alpha K_v Y) \tag{1}$$

$$U = D_n^{-1} A Q \tag{2}$$

Here $A = (a_j^i)_{n \times v}$, $D_v = \text{diag}(A^\top \times \mathbb{1}_n)$ and $D_n = \text{diag}(A \times \mathbb{1}_v)$, $K_v = \text{diag}(\bar{\mathbf{Y}} \times \mathbb{1}_c)$. Here $\mathbb{1}_k$ is an all one column vector of length k. Upon convergence, the final posterior distributions are given in the rows of U and one can use Bayes' optimal decision rule to decide the most likely label.

2.2 CM overfits

The hypothesis space of a learning algorithm is the set of all feasible solutions of the algorithm. A larger hypothesis space has more expressive power comparing to a smaller one, leading to less training errors. However, models with a larger hypothesis space is more complicated and can lead to less generalization ability and more predicting errors [29]. Therefore, one needs to trade-off between minimizing training error and model complexity. We compare the hypothesis spaces of two model combination methods, MV and CM, leading to some insights into the overfitting issue of CM.

Suppose there are m base models (for ease of presentation, assume all models are supervised models). For each instance and each class, a model outputs 1 (a vote) or 0 (no vote). A model combination method is a function f that maps predictions of base models to posterior distributions on the probabilistic simplex:

$$f : X \to S \tag{3}$$

$$S = \{p \subset \mathbb{R}^\ell | p = \sum_{\ell=1}^{c} \theta_\ell \mathbf{e}_\ell = [\theta_1, \ldots, \theta_\ell], \sum_{\ell=1}^{c} \theta_\ell = 1, \theta_\ell \geq 0\}$$

where we abuse the notation X, such that X is the collection of base model predictions. $\mathbf{e}_\ell$ is the standard basis having 1 in its ℓ-th position and 0 anywhere else, representing the distribution of class ℓ, θ_ℓ is the probability that an instance belongs to class ℓ. When $c = 3$, an example of 2-simplex is shown in Figure 2(a). Various model combination methods can be seen as ways of searching a suitable mapping f in the hypothesis space $\mathcal{F}$ of all such mappings, to optimize certain objectives. Existing methods differ in their hypothesis spaces $\mathcal{F}$ and the way they searches, but the capacity of the hypothesis space is directly related to the generalization ability of a method. Note that the domain of all model combination methods are the same, so the capacities of their hypothesis spaces are completely determined by the images of the maps $f(X) \subset S$.

Majority voting simply sums up the number of votes for each class and assigns an instance to the class having the most votes. Formally, given the output of r models for an instance, say, $[\hat{y}_1, \ldots, \hat{y}_r]$, $\hat{y}_k \in \{1, \ldots, c\}$, the decision of majority voting is made based on the the vector:

$$\frac{1}{r}\left[\sum_{k=1}^{r} \mathbb{1}[\hat{y}_k = 1], \ldots, \sum_{k=1}^{r} \mathbb{1}[\hat{y}_k = c]\right] \in S \tag{4}$$

Note that majority voting maps the predictions of base models to rational vectors on the simplex, with denominators equal to the number of models. For example, if an instance receives two votes for class 1, one votes for class 2 and 0 vote for class 3, from a total of three classifiers, then the output of f is $[2/3, 1/3, 0]$, shown as the square with an arrow in Figure 2(b).

CM maps predictions of base models of an instance to a posterior distribution in S, and the image of the map is the whole simplex S. The relaxation from rational vectors to real vectors allows a larger hypothesis space such that CM can find an f to attain low consensus loss (see Section 5.2). However, it also allows CM to pick an f that outputs predictions close to uniform distribution with small margin (like the diamond in Figure 2(c)), leading to higher empirical margin risk (see Section 4) It is verified in Section 5 that CM does tend to output predictions that have small consensus losses and small margins. Here we define "overfitting" in model combination in a vague sense, and defer the formal analysis to Section 4.

DEFINITION 1 (OVERFITTING IN MODEL COMBINATION). *A model combination method consolidates predictions of base models to achieve a high degree of model consensus but with higher generalization error upper bound.*

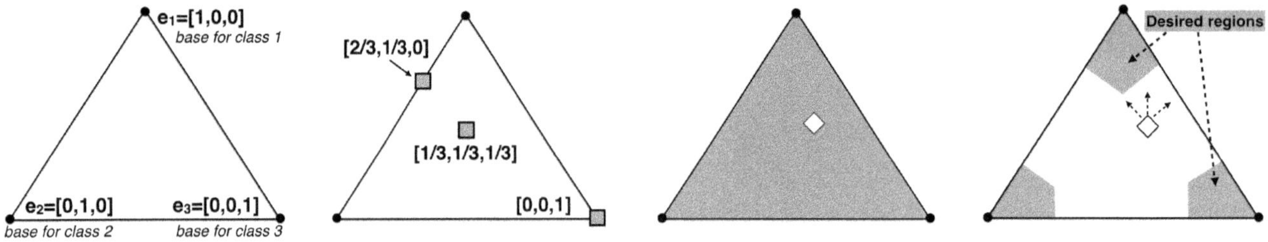

(a) 2-Simplex

(b) Hypothesis spaces of MV (only part of the output space is shown)

(c) Hypothesis space of CM

(d) Hypothesis space of RCM

Figure 2: Hypothesis space of various methods: the tips of the triangles represent the bases $\mathbf{e}_\ell$

3. CLASS-DISTRIBUTION REGULARIZED CONSENSUS MAXIMIZATION

3.1 Regularization over class distributions

According to the above analysis, if we adopt a reasonably small but rich enough hypothesis space for CM, then we could avoid over-fitting and achieve better performance. How can we specify a suitable hypothesis space for CM? Note that the predictions lying near the corners of the simplex (shadows in Figure 2(d)) have a more dominating component θ_{ℓ_0} for some class ℓ_0. On the one hand, when the difference between $p(y=\ell_0|\mathbf{x})$ and any other $p(y=\ell|\mathbf{x})$ is larger, the prediction is more discriminative to reflect the true class distribution. On the other hand, if the number of dominating entries in $p(y|\mathbf{x})$ is greater than 1, then those dominating classes are correlated since they co-occur, conflicting the multi-class distribution assumption. This observation indicates that when searching for solutions in the hypothesis space, CM should penalize solutions that lie too far away from any corner of the simplex and encourage solutions that lie close to the corners. For CM to reduce the penalized consensus loss $\mathcal{L}(U,Q)$, it must move its predictions towards one of the corners on the simplex, as shown by the arrows in Figure 2(d). The above intuition suggests that the consolidated predictions should exhibit some sort of independence between classes, given the problem is a multi-class single label problem.

Specifically, recall that U is the consolidated prediction, with the ℓ−th column being the posterior probabilities $p(y=\ell|\mathbf{x})$, we can compute the empirical class correlation matrix $\Sigma = U^\top U$. We want the matrix Σ to be close to a $c \times c$ matrix D, which represents the ideal class correlations. For example, to enforce independence between classes in multi-class classification problems, we can set the diagonal elements of D to a positive number whose scale is comparable to the empirical correlations, and set the off-diagonal elements to a positive number much smaller than the diagonal elements.

By adopting the Frobenius norm, we obtain the following regularization term

$$\Delta_F = \frac{1}{2}\|\Sigma - D\|_F \tag{5}$$

or by adopting the relative entropy [5]

$$\Delta_E = \frac{1}{2}\sum_{i,j=1}^{c} \Sigma_{ij} \log \frac{\Sigma_{ij}}{D_{ij}} \tag{6}$$

Adding any of the above regularization terms to the objective of CM, we obtain the following optimization problem:

$$\begin{aligned} \min_{U,Q} \quad & \sum_{i=1}^{n}\sum_{j=1}^{v} a_{ij}\|\mathbf{u}^i - \mathbf{q}^j\|^2 + \alpha\sum_{j=1}^{v} b_j\|\mathbf{q}^j - \bar{\mathbf{y}}^j\|^2 + \lambda\Delta \\ \text{s.t.} \quad & u^i_\ell \geq 0, \|\mathbf{u}^i\|_1 = 1, i = 1,\dots,n \\ & q^j_\ell \geq 0, \|\mathbf{q}^j\|_1 = 1, j = 1,\dots,v \end{aligned}$$

where $\Delta = \Delta_F$ or Δ_E. The parameter λ controls the trade-off between model consensus and class independence. We will see that the regularization helps reduce the capacity of hypothesis space and also the empirical margin risk.

3.2 Optimization of the Class-distribution Regularized Model

Our plan for solving the optimization problem Eq.(7) is to first ignore the constraints that $\mathbf{u}^i$ and $\mathbf{q}^j$ are probability distributions and solve the unconstrained optimization problem using gradient descent, then we address the probabilistic constraints on $\mathbf{u}^i$ and $\mathbf{q}^j$ in the next section. The gradient descent steps for the first two terms in the above objective function are given in Eq.(1) and Eq.(2), the gradients of the regularization term Δ with respect to column $\mathbf{u}_j$ are as follows:

$$\begin{aligned} \frac{\partial \Delta_F}{\partial \mathbf{u}_j} &= \sum_{i=1}^{c}(\Sigma_{ij} - D_{ij})\mathbf{u}_i \\ \frac{\partial \Delta_E}{\partial \mathbf{u}_j} &= \sum_{i=1}^{c}(1 + \log\frac{\Sigma_{ij}}{D_{ij}})\mathbf{u}_i \end{aligned}$$

Thus a gradient descent step for the regularization term with respect to column $\mathbf{u}_j$ are:

$$\mathbf{u}_j \leftarrow \mathbf{u}_j - \eta_t \sum_{i=1}^{c}(\Sigma_{ij} - D_{ij})\mathbf{u}_i \tag{7}$$

$$\mathbf{u}_j \leftarrow \mathbf{u}_j - \eta_t \sum_{i=1}^{c}(1 + \log\frac{\Sigma_{ij}}{D_{ij}})\mathbf{u}_i \tag{8}$$

where $\leftarrow$ indicates the assignment of an updated $\mathbf{u}_j$ to itself. η_t is the learning rate in the t-th iteration with $\eta_t = \eta_0/\sqrt{t}$ and η_0 is the initial learning rate. We let the trade-off parameter λ in the RCM objective be absorbed in η_0. Eq.(7) and Eq.(8) have a quite intuitive meaning: for each column $\mathbf{u}_i$ representing the i-th class, depending on whether the empirical class correlation Σ_{ij} exceeds the ideal class correlation D_{ij}, $\mathbf{u}_j$ is moved away from ($\Sigma_{ij} > D_{ij}$) or towards

$(\Sigma_{ij} < D_{ij})$ $\mathbf{u}_i$, and the amount of displacement is proportional to the distance between the empirical and ideal class correlation. In practice, it is not easy to specify the ideal class correlation matrix D, and the scaling parameters $\beta_{ij} = \Sigma_{ij} - D_{ij}$ (or $1 + \log \frac{\Sigma_{ij}}{D_{ij}}$) may be sensitive to the choice of D. Simply setting all the β_{ij} to be 1 will actually hurt the performance, as we ignore the information about the class correlations.

We propose an approximation of Eq.(7) and Eq.(8) to avoid specifying the parameters D and to maintain the effect of the regularization, namely, a large margin between class distributions. Note that in Eq.(8), for $i \neq j$, D_{ij} should be some small number and if$\Sigma_{ij} \gg D_{ij}$, the scaling parameter $1 + \log \frac{\Sigma_{ij}}{D_{ij}}$ will be large; on the other hand, ifΣ_{ij} is about the same as D_{ij}, $1 + \log \frac{\Sigma_{ij}}{D_{ij}}$ will be close to 1. According to this observation, when computing the gradient for the column $\mathbf{u}_j$, we can set β_{ij} as follows:

$$\beta_{ij} = \begin{cases} 1 & \text{if } i = \text{argmin}_{k \neq j} \|\mathbf{u}_k - \mathbf{u}_j\|_2 \\ -1 & \text{if } i = j \\ 0 & \text{otherwise} \end{cases} \tag{9}$$

The resulting regularization term is

$$\Delta_A = \frac{1}{2} \sum_{j=1}^{c} \|\mathbf{u}_j - \mathbf{u}_{d(j)}\|_2^2 \tag{10}$$

where

$$d(j) = \underset{k \neq j}{\text{argmin}} \|\mathbf{u}_j - \mathbf{u}_k\|_2 \tag{11}$$

Eq.(7) and Eq.(8) become

$$\mathbf{u}_j \leftarrow \mathbf{u}_j - \eta_t(\mathbf{u}_{d(j)} - \mathbf{u}_j) \tag{12}$$

So far we have specified all necessary gradient descent steps for RCM. Nonetheless, the original CM gradient descent steps involve the rows of the matrices U and Q, while to minimize the regularization term Δ, one has to work with the columns of U. It is non-trivial to derive gradient descent steps involving both rows and columns of a matrix. We adopt an alternative optimization procedure that first minimizes the consensus loss $\mathcal{L}(U, Q)$ through Eq.(1) and Eq.(2), then minimizesΔ_A through Eq.(12). These two steps are alternatively repeated until it converges.

3.3 Projection to the Probabilistic Simplex

The converted unconstrained optimization problem ignores the constraints:

$$\begin{aligned} u_\ell^i \geq 0, \|\mathbf{u}^i\|_1 = 1, i = 1, \ldots, n \\ q_\ell^j \geq 0, \|\mathbf{q}^j\|_1 = 1, j = 1, \ldots, v \end{aligned} \tag{13}$$

Although Eq.(1) and (2) maintain rows of U and Q as probability distributions, Eq.(12) might bring any entry of U to be greater than 1 or less than 0, and a row in U or Q might not sum up to 1. We propose to perform *probabilistic projection* for all $\mathbf{u}^i$ after all gradient descent steps in each iteration. More formally, the following optimization problem finds $\mathbf{v}$, the projection of $\mathbf{u}^i$ onto the probabilistic simplex

$$\begin{aligned} \min_{\mathbf{v}} \quad & \|\mathbf{v} - \mathbf{u}^i\|_2 \\ \text{s.t.} \quad & \|\mathbf{v}\|_1 = 1, v_\ell \geq 0, \ell = 1, \ldots, c \end{aligned}$$

The optimal solution $\mathbf{v}^*$ serves as the new $\mathbf{u}^i$ for the next iteration, with the probabilistic constraints satisfied. An efficient algorithm (in $O(cn)$) with implementation to solve the above problem can be found in [12]. The complete algorithm is described in Algorithm 1.

Algorithm 1 Regularized Consensus Maximization (RCM)

Input: Affinity matrix A, initial learning rate η_0
Set $\mathbf{u}^j$ to uniform distribution.
for $t = 1 \rightarrow$ MaxIterNum **do**
  $Q = (D_v + \alpha K_v)^{-1}(A^\top U + \alpha K_v Y)$
  $U = D_n^{-1} A Q$
  $\eta_t = \eta_0 / \sqrt{t}$
  for $j = 1 \rightarrow c$ **do**
    $d(j) = \arg\min_{k \neq j} \|\mathbf{u}_k - \mathbf{u}_j\|$
    $\mathbf{u}_j \leftarrow \mathbf{u}_j - \eta_t(\mathbf{u}_{d(j)} - \mathbf{u}_j)$
  end for
  Project $\mathbf{u}^i$ to the probabilistic simplex.
end for

4. GENERALIZATION ERROR OF RCM

In this section, we prove that, compared to CM, the proposed regularization leads to a smaller upper bound on generalization error. The generalization error bound consists of two terms: the empirical margin risk on training data and a term measuring the capacity of the hypothesis space explored by a learning algorithm. Regarding the empirical margin risk, we first define the multi-class margin [24].

DEFINITION 2 (CANONICAL FUNCTION). *Given a function $f \in \mathcal{F}$ that maps predictions of base models to posterior distribution (see Section 2.2). For the instance $\mathbf{x}$, $f(\mathbf{x}) = [f_1(\mathbf{x}), \ldots, f_c(\mathbf{x})] \in S$ where $f_\ell(\mathbf{x})$ is the probability that $\mathbf{x}$ belongs to class ℓ, according to f. Let M_1 be the smallest index ℓ such that $f_\ell(\mathbf{x}) = \max_k f_k(\mathbf{x})$, and M_2 be the smallest index ℓ such that $f_\ell(\mathbf{x}) = \max_{k \neq M_1} f_k(\mathbf{x})$. The canonical function $\Delta f : X \rightarrow [-1, 1]^c$, with the ℓ-th component being:*

$$\Delta f_\ell(\mathbf{x}) = \begin{cases} f_\ell(\mathbf{x}) - f_{M_2}(\mathbf{x}) & \text{if } \ell = M_1 \\ f_\ell(\mathbf{x}) - f_{M_1}(\mathbf{x}) & \text{otherwise} \end{cases} \tag{14}$$

M_1 is the label selected by Bayes decision rule and M_2 is the closest runner-up.Δ f_ℓ measures how far away the selected label is from the other competitors. Based on the canonical function, we define the multi-class empirical margin risk

DEFINITION 3 (EMPIRICAL MARGIN RISK). *For $\gamma > 0$ and training set $s = \{\mathbf{x}_i, \mathbf{y}_i\}_{i=1}^m$, the empirical margin risk $R_s^\gamma(f)$ of the function f is*

$$R_s^\gamma(f) = \frac{1}{m} |\{\mathbf{x}_i | \exists \ell \in \{1, \ldots, c\}, y_{i\ell} \cdot \Delta f_\ell(\mathbf{x}_i) < \gamma\}| \tag{15}$$

where $y_{i\ell}$ is the ℓ-th component of the true label vector $\mathbf{y}_i$.

Next we define necessary concepts to measure the capacity of hypothesis spaces.

DEFINITION 4 (SUPREMUM METRIC FOR FUNCTIONS). *[24, 3] Suppose $\mathcal{F}$ is the collection of functions mapping from X to S, and $s = \{\mathbf{x}_i\}_{i=1}^m \subset X$ is a given set of instances. Define the metric (distance measure) for functions $d(\cdot, \cdot) : \mathcal{F} \times \mathcal{F} \rightarrow [0, +\infty)$ on s by*

$$d_s(f, \tilde{f}) = \max_{\mathbf{x}_i \in s} \sum_{\ell=1}^{c} |f_\ell(\mathbf{x}_i) - \tilde{f}_\ell(\mathbf{x}_i)| \tag{16}$$

Note that the metric such defined depends on the set of instances s.

DEFINITION 5 (COVERING NUMBER). *Let $(\mathcal{F}, d_s)$ be the space of functions equipped with the supremum metric, where $s \subset X$ a finite set of instances. Define $B_s(f,r)$ the closed ball centered at f with radius r:*

$$B_s(f,r) = \{g \in \mathcal{F} | d_s(f,g) \leq r\} \tag{17}$$

The covering number $\mathcal{N}(\epsilon, \mathcal{H}, d_s)$ of a set $\mathcal{H} \subset \mathcal{F}$ is defined as

$$\mathcal{N}(\epsilon, \mathcal{H}, d_s) = \inf_T \{|T|\} \ s.t. \ \mathcal{H} \subset \cup_{f \in T} B_s(f, \epsilon) \tag{18}$$

The set T is called an ϵ-cover of the subset $\mathcal{H}$.

The following bound on generalization error for multi-class classification is given in [24]:

THEOREM 1. *Let $\mathcal{F}$ be a set of functions from X to S and $\Delta\mathcal{F}$ be the set of canonical functions Δf. Let s be a learning set of size m drawn iid. from a probability distribution P. Let $0 < \gamma < 1$. With probability $1 - \delta$, $\forall f \in \mathcal{F}$,*

$$R(f) \leq R_s^\gamma(f) + \sqrt{\frac{1}{2m} \ln\left(\frac{2\mathcal{N}_\infty(\gamma/2, \Delta\mathcal{F}^\gamma)}{\delta}\right)} \tag{19}$$

where

$$\mathcal{N}_\infty(\gamma, \mathcal{F}) = \sup_{s:|s|=2m} \mathcal{N}(\gamma, \mathcal{F}, d_s) \tag{20}$$

$\Delta\mathcal{F}^\gamma = \{\pi_\gamma \circ \Delta f : \Delta f \in \Delta\mathcal{F}\}$ where π_γ is the truncation function applied to each of the c components of Δf

$$\pi_\gamma(f_\ell(\mathbf{x})) = \begin{cases} \gamma \cdot sign(f_\ell(\mathbf{x})) & if \ |f_\ell(\mathbf{x})| \geq \gamma \\ f_\ell(\mathbf{x}) & otherwise \end{cases} \tag{21}$$

Given the bound in Eq.(19), we want to prove that both terms in the bound for the regularized CM are smaller than those for the original CM, and obtain the following theorem:

THEOREM 2. *RCM has a smaller upper bound on generalization error compared with that of CM.*

The above theorem is proved in two steps in the following two lemmas.

LEMMA 1. *RCM achieves a lower empirical margin risk if we use Δ_E as our regularization term and the matrix D is such set that the scaling parameters $\beta_{ij} = \beta_{ji}$ and $\beta_{ii} = 1$.*

PROOF. Given training data s, $0 < \gamma < 1$, $1 - R_s^\gamma(f)$ is the proportion of correctly classified instances with margin greater than γ. Suppose f is the prediction function found by CM and $\tilde{f}$ is that found by RCM. In other words, $\tilde{f}$ is obtained by applying Eq.(8) to f. Note that $R_s^\gamma(\tilde{f}) \leq R_s^\gamma(f) \iff 1 - R_s^\gamma(\tilde{f}) \geq 1 - R_s^\gamma(f)$, we need to prove, for any correctly classified instance with margin greater than γ, its margin under $\tilde{f}$ is not smaller than that under f.

Let $\mathbf{u} = [f_1, \ldots, f_c]$ and $\tilde{\mathbf{u}} = [\tilde{f}_1, \ldots, \tilde{f}_c]$ be the evaluations of f and $\tilde{f}$ at some point $\mathbf{x}$ that is correctly classified with margin larger than γ (we ignore the arguments of f and $\tilde{f}$). Assume $1 = \text{argmax}_\ell f_\ell$ and $2 = \text{argmax}_{\ell \neq 1} f_\ell$. Then $y_1 \cdot \Delta f_1 \geq \gamma$. But $y_1 = 1$, so $\Delta f_1 = f_1 - f_2 \geq \gamma$. The gradients Eq.(8) at $\mathbf{x}$ be

$$g_j = \eta_t \sum_{i=1}^{c} (1 + \log \frac{\Sigma_{ij}}{D_{ij}}) f_i > 0, j = 1, 2 \tag{22}$$

Assume that proper values are set to matrix D, such that $\Sigma_{ii} = D_{ii}$ but$\Sigma_{ij} \gg D_{ij}$ for $i \neq j$. Then the gradients are

$$g_j = \eta_t \sum_{i=1}^{c} \beta_{ij} f_i, j = 1, 2 \tag{23}$$

where $\beta_{ii} \ll \beta_{ij}, i \neq j$. That is, for a given j, f_i has a much larger weight than f_j in g_j for $i \neq j$. If $\beta_{ij} = \beta_{ji}$, then by $f_1 > f_2$, we have $g_2 > g_1$,

$$\Delta\tilde{f}_1 = \tilde{f}_1 - \tilde{f}_2 = (f_1 - g_1) - (f_2 - g_2) = \Delta f_1 - (g_1 - g_2) > \Delta f_1 \tag{24}$$

□

LEMMA 2. *The hypothesis space of RCM has smaller covering number than the hypothesis space of CM.*

PROOF. Let$\Delta\ \mathcal{F}^\gamma = \{\pi_\gamma \circ \Delta f : \Delta f \in \Delta\mathcal{F}\}$ and$\Delta\ \tilde{\mathcal{F}}^\gamma = \{\pi_\gamma \circ \Delta\tilde{f} : \Delta f \in \Delta\tilde{\mathcal{F}}\}$ where $\mathcal{F}$ is the collection of functions $f : X \to S$ and $\tilde{\mathcal{F}}$ are their large margin version as defined in Lemma 1,$\Delta\ f$ is the canonical function and π_γ is the truncation function Eq.(21). Then$\Delta\ \tilde{\mathcal{F}}^\gamma \subset \Delta\mathcal{F}$ since for any $f \in \mathcal{F}$, its large margin version $\tilde{f} \in \mathcal{F}$, thus we have $\Delta\tilde{\mathcal{F}} \subset \Delta\mathcal{F}$. After truncation, $\Delta\tilde{\mathcal{F}}^\gamma \subset \Delta\mathcal{F}^\gamma$.

Given any training data s of size $2m$, any $\gamma/2$-cover of $\Delta\mathcal{F}^\gamma$ is also a $\gamma/2$-cover of$\Delta\ \tilde{\mathcal{F}}^\gamma$. Therefore by definition Eq.(18),

$$\mathcal{N}(\gamma/2, \Delta\mathcal{F}^\gamma, s) = \inf\{|T|\} \geq \ \inf\{|T'|\} = \mathcal{N}(\gamma/2, \Delta\tilde{\mathcal{F}}^\gamma, s) \tag{25}$$

where $T \in \{\gamma/2\text{-covers of}\Delta\ \mathcal{F}^\gamma\}$ and $T' \in \{\gamma/2\text{-covers of}\Delta\ \tilde{\mathcal{F}}^\gamma\}$. By the definition Eq.(20), we conclude that

$$\begin{aligned} \mathcal{N}_\infty(\gamma/2, \Delta\mathcal{F}^\gamma) &= \sup_s \mathcal{N}(\gamma/2, \Delta\mathcal{F}^\gamma) \\ &\geq \sup_s \mathcal{N}(\gamma/2, \Delta\tilde{\mathcal{F}}^\gamma) = \mathcal{N}_\infty(\gamma/2, \Delta\tilde{\mathcal{F}}^\gamma) \end{aligned}$$

□

5. EXPERIMENTAL RESULTS

In this section, we first summarize the experimental settings, including evaluation benchmarks and model combination baselines. Then we demonstrate how CM overfits the data and how the proposed RCM resolves the issue.

5.1 Experimental Settings

Benchmarks A model consolidation method consolidates the predictions of multiple supervised and/or unsupervised models to come up with improved predictive performance. Therefore, to evaluate the performance, we need the predictions from multiple base models for the datasets, whose information are summarized in Table 3. The dataset[1] contains 11 text classification tasks. Each task contains the predictions given by the output of 2 classification and 2 clustering models. For details of how they processed the data, please refer to [16].

We compare RCM with CM in order to verify the effectiveness of the large margin constraint. CM and RCM share most of the parameters such as number of iterations, importance of supervised models, etc.. For the shared parameters, we adopt the parameter settings of CM [16]. In addition, we set the initial learning rate η_0 to be 0.1. We also compare RCM with other state-of-the-art cluster ensemble methods:

[1]available at `http://www.cse.buffalo.edu/~jing/`

Table 4: Overall Performance on Text Classification Tasks

Methods	Newsgroups 1	Newsgroups 2	Newsgroups 3	Newsgroups 4	Newsgroups 5	Newsgroups 6	Cora 1	Cora 2	Cora 3	Cora 4	DBLP 1
MCLA	0.7574	0.8345	0.7816	0.8225	0.8039	0.8332	0.8522	0.8009	0.8442	0.8262	0.8604
HBGF	0.721	0.636	0.7677	0.6885	0.6421	0.7482	0.7966	0.6574	0.7655	0.7912	0.8146
SNNMF	0.5980	0.6904	0.6384	0.5733	0.6245	0.6753	0.7407	0.6492	0.7051	0.6989	0.6307
BCE	0.6639	0.2544	0.7082	0.7230	0.7247	0.7474	0.6546	0.8915	0.5565	0.2482	0.2887
ECMC	0.5599	0.6215	0.6294	0.6759	0.6338	0.4530	0.5973	0.6428	0.5252	0.8513	0.7771
CM	**0.8131**	**0.9106**	0.8608	0.9117	0.8857	0.9094	0.8688	0.9151	0.8951	0.9036	0.9412
RCM	**0.8131**	0.9030	**0.8735**	**0.9232**	**0.8927**	**0.9134**	**0.8703**	**0.9222**	**0.9203**	**0.9128**	**0.9429**

Table 3: Datasets and Base Models

Datasets		# Instances	# Classes	Predictors
20NG	1	1568	4	Apply SVM, Logistic Regression, K-means and mini-cut to texts. 4 Predictors in total.
	2	1588	4	
	3	1573	4	
	4	1484	4	
	5	1584	4	
	6	1512	4	
Cora	1	663	3	Apply Logistic Regression K-means to citation/publication network and texts. 4 Predictors in total.
	2	977	4	
	3	1468	5	
	4	975	5	
DBLP		4236	4	

MCLA [27], HBGF [27], SNNMF [18], BCE [30] ECMC [37]. MCLA and HBGF are graph partition based approaches, which use spectral clustering [23, 11] to partition the bipartite or hyper graph constructed from the predictions of base models. There is no parameter to tune for these two methods. SNNMF is a matrix factorization based method, which derives clustering of instances using the similarity matrix constructed from base models' predictions. We run SNNMF to its convergence to obtain the final predictions. BCE is a Bayesian approach to consensus maximization. We set its parameters as follows: LDA parameters $\alpha = 0.5, \beta = 0.1$, number of iterations for Gibbs sampling is set to 50,000, the topic distributions of the words in documents are randomly initialized. We observe that performance the Gibbs sampling for BCE is sensitive to the initialization of the parameters and unstable, we run the BCE for 10 times and report its best performance. We also implemented BCE using variational inference, but the procedure did not converge after long runs, so we do not report the corresponding results. ECMC is a matrix factorization method with a de-noising step, we adopt the implementations of robust PCA and matrix completion packages[2], with $d_0 = 0.4, d_1 = 0.6$ and other parameters being the default values (see [37] for details).

5.2 Overfitting in Consensus Maximization

In Section 2.1 and 2.2 we theoretically showed that, CM produces predictions that minimize the consensus loss but overfit the data, and therefore might not generalize well, and in Section 3.1, we proposed RCM to solve the issues. By comparing CM and RCM in consensus loss, prediction margins and accuracy (next section), we verify that CM does have the overfitting issue and RCM can effectively mitigate overfitting.

On the one hand, one can see from Figure 3 that CM has a lower consensus loss than RCM does across all datasets.

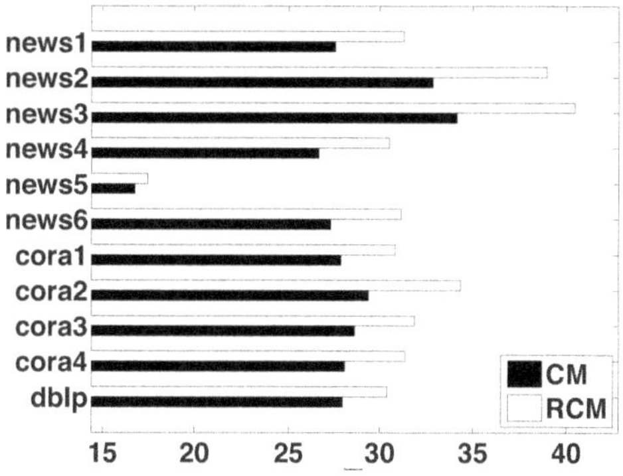

Figure 3: Consensus Loss

This is because CM solely minimizes the consensus loss while RCM minimizes a regularized consensus loss and has a smaller hypothesis space. On the other hand, we use entropy of $\mathbf{u}^i$ ($h^i = -\sum_{\ell=1}^{c} u_\ell^i \log u_\ell^i$) as a measure of prediction margin: the higher the entropy, the smaller the margin $\mathbf{u}^i$ has and the less discriminative $\mathbf{u}^i$ is. We show the averaged entropy $\frac{1}{n}\sum_{i=1}^{n} h^i$ for each dataset in Figure 4(a), 4(b), 4(c). From the figures, we can see that the entropy is higher in the predictions of CM across all datasets except on the *dblp* dataset. (the result on the *cora1* dataset is not shown due to the scale). Therefore on average, the predictions of CM have smaller margins than those of RCM. Since margin is used as an indicator of generalization performance of a learning algorithm [4], CM might overfit the data while RCM should improve the generalization ability and accuracy of CM.

5.3 Accuracy

In Table 4, we compare the accuracies of RCM and the baselines on 11 text classification tasks. From the table, we can see that BCE is very unstable and there are two main reasons for this. First, similar to LDA, BCE needs a lot of observed data to infer the consolidated labels, yet usually we have only a couple of base models. Second, Gibbs sampling is too sensitive to initial conditions while variational inference does not converge given only a handful of data. ECMC and SNNMF sometimes give reasonable performance, such as ECMC on the *cora4* task. However, their optimization are also sensitive to initialization, and their solutions are unstable. Both MCLA and HBGF in general have better performance than ECMC and SNNMF, though they are still outperformed by both CM and RCM.

The comparison between CM and RCM is more interesting. Using the proposed regularization over the class distributions, RCM controls the size of its hypothesis space and focuses on the more discriminative predictions. As we can see from the table, RCM outperforms CM on 10 out of 11

[2] `http://perception.csl.illinois.edu/matrix-rank/sample_code.html`

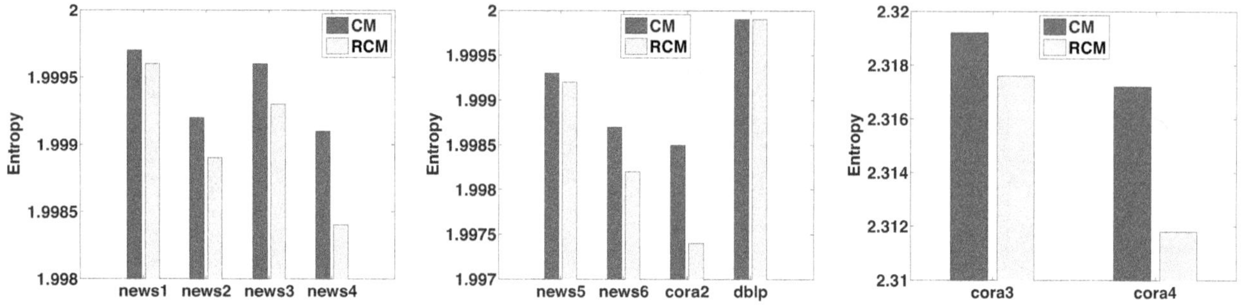

(a) Prediction Entropy (b) Prediction Entropy (c) Prediction Entropy

Figure 4: Consensus loss and entropy of CM and RCM

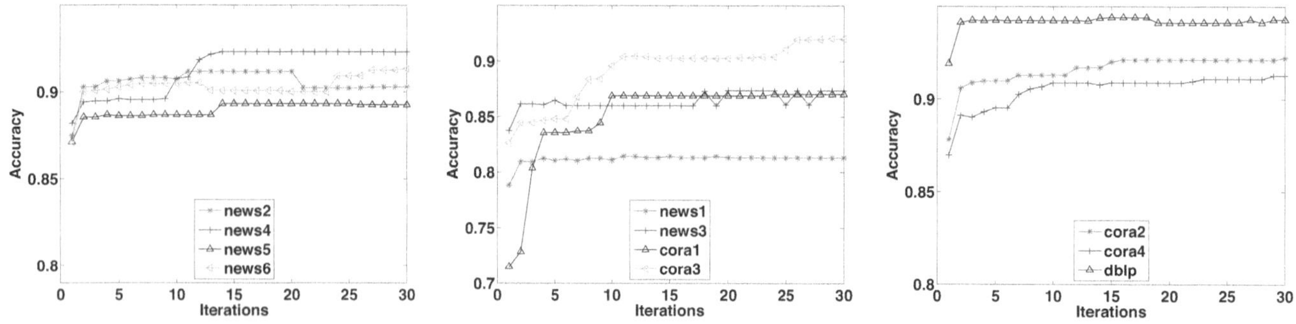

(a) (b) (c)

Figure 5: Convergence of RCM

datasets. These evidences, together with the comparisons of consensus loss and entropy in Section 5.2, clearly demonstrate that CM overfits the data to produce highly consensus predictions, while RCM is able to trade-off between two objectives and achieves better accuracy.

Statistical significance of the results We verify that the improvements brought by the proposed method is statistically significant. According to [10], one can compare the effectiveness of different algorithms based on their performance on multiple datasets. Since among all baselines, CM has the closest performance to RCM, we compare these two methods using the Wilcoxon signed-ranks test. For the details of how to carry out the test, please refer to [10]. The test shows that RCM is statistically significantly superior to CM with $\alpha = 0.05$, where α is the probability that RCM is *not* better than CM.

5.4 Convergence Study

For each of the text classification tasks, we record the accuracy at the end of each iteration of RCM. In Figure 5, we plot the accuracies against the number of iterations. From the figure, we can see that, except for the *news3* and *dblp* tasks, RCM converges to some fixed accuracies. Even for those two exceptions where there are some zigzag's at the tails of the curves, we notice that the lowest accuracies obtained after the 25th iteration are at least the same as the best baseline (CM in both cases). Therefore, we conclude that given a big enough number of iterations, the algorithm performs better than or comparable with the baselines.

6. RELATED WORK

Graph partition based methods [27, 14]. In the pioneering work of [27], they presented three methods for cluster ensemble. For example, HGPA in [27] constructs a hypergraph consisting of membership indicators from clustering models as hyperedges, then a hypergraph partition algorithm partitions the hypergraph. Another method in [27], MCLA, partitions the hypergraph into k subgraphs, each of which consists of membership indicators from clustering models. These subgraphs are then used to calculate the association strength of an instance with subgraphs. HBGF is proposed in [14]. HBGF constructs the same bipartite graph as that in [16], then it partitions the graph using spectral clustering or METIS. Since the graph contains both group nodes and instance nodes (See Section 2.1), the results is a partition of both types of nodes. The partition of instance nodes is taken as the aggregated clustering. All these methods do not take discriminative constraints into account in their optimization formula.

Matrix factorization methods [18, 19]. They solve the consensus clustering problem through symmetric nonnegative matrix factorization (SNNMF). Using the predictions of base models, a similarity matrix is derived and factorized into orthonormal cluster membership indicators. The indicator matrices play the role of the consolidated predictions in CM. The orthonormality constraint on the indicators acts as the large margin regularization. Note that the orthonormality and the non-negative constraint are more restrictive than the large margin regularization proposed in this paper, as the consolidated predictions can have only one entry as 1, with all the other entries being 0. We compare the proposed algorithm with the SNNMF formulation in Section 5.

Probabilistic methods [30, 1, 32, 20]. In [30], they solve the consensus clustering problem using a LDA like model. Predictions from base models are treated as documents in LDA, and the consolidated predictions as the latent topics of the documents. The method differs from LDA in that different models are assumed to have different topic-word distributions. In [1], they extend the above method in order to combine both supervised and unsupervised predictions in a transfer learning setting, which is different from the problem we are addressing here. In [32], they propose a non-parametric Bayesian method to select the number of clusters in consensus clustering. This algorithm is best employed as a parameter selection step before applying the method proposed in the paper.

In [2], they propose to combine supervised and unsupervised models as a way of knowledge transfer, where unsupervised models in the target domain serve as additional constraints while supervised models provide initial labeling. It might be important to give different weights to different base models, which might have different importance for the clustering task. In [34], they improve the performance of CM via functional space sampling. They impose weights on base models, where the weights are learned iteratively while seeking consensus results. In [18], weighted consensus ensemble is formulated as a sparse learning problem where the most important base models can be selected for consolidation. In [13], they provide a general framework for cluster ensemble called "Generalized Weighted Cluster Aggregation". Their goal is to find an affinity matrix that is close to all other affinity matrices derived from predictions of base models. Note that the proposed large margin formulation can be adopted by the above algorithms as a building block, and thus is not directly comparable.

Combining structural predictions has also been studied. For example, in multilabel classification, label correlations provide important information to achieve better classification performance. In [35], they propose a novel consensus classification algorithm to combine multi-label predictions from multiple base models, taking both label correlation and model consensus into account. Learning to rank is an important research problem in information retrieval, and recently, aggregating multiple ranking results is attracting more and more attention, due to its potential to improve ranking performance over single ranking model. The oldest ranking aggregation method called "Borda Couting", which can be traced back to 1770. The modern statistical ranking aggregation started with the Bradley-Terry (BT) model [7, 6], which infers the underlying ranking via maximum likelihood estimation. There are also many extensions of the BT model. For example, in [9], they extended the BT model by adding and learning weights on the base ranking models. In [33], they propose an online Bayesian learning algorithm for the BT model. In [25], they study the theoretical aspect of combining multiple ranking results into one ranking list. They present conditions under which certain popular ranking aggregation algorithms converge. Aggregating multiple ranking results has also found its place in gaming, such as XBox platform [17] In [31], they propose a Bayesian model to aggregate multiple visual trackers' output for reliable visual tracking. The proposed method in the paper focuses on combining flat predictions instead of structural predictions.

This work is also related to crowdsourcing, which aims at design mechanisms and algorithms to collect useful information from massive human population. Aggregating the data collected from multiple human beings is similar to combining the predictions given by multiple base models considered in this paper. In [26], they use crowdsourcing to obtain cheap annotations for NLP tasks, such as affect recognition, word similarity, etc. In [22], they propose to carry out multiple related crowdsourcing tasks simultaneously to alleviate data sparsity for a single crowdsourcing task. In [36], they propose to actively select annotator-instance pairs for human labeling. The idea is that by identifying the most uncertain instance and the corresponding most reliable annotator for the instance, one can learn underlying labels of the instances more effectively.

The algorithm proposed here is motivated by the maximum margin principle widely adopted in previous works [38, 28, 39]. In these works, to encourage discriminability, models are trained with the constraint that the prediction of a labeled instance should be closer to its true label than to other labels by some distance. However, these works focus on supervised learning, which is quite a different setting from the unsupervised setting here. There are a few works addressing overfitting in clustering [8, 21]. In [8], they analyze the issue from a learning theory perspective, and propose a general algorithm called "nearest neighbor clustering" to restrict the hypothesis space and avoid overfitting. The algorithm learns the similarity matrix for better spectral clustering results, and might be used to construct the affinity matrix in CM. These algorithms focus on clustering and do not address the model combination problem directly.

7. CONCLUSIONS

In this paper, we consider the overfitting issue in consensus maximization for model combination. The problem is analyzed by inspecting the hypothesis space and margin-based generalization error of CM. To solve the problem, we develop a model called class-distribution regularized CM that trades off two objectives, namely, consensus among base models and margins in predictions. The resulting optimization problem is challenging to solve since it involves many regularization parameters and is not jointly convex. We propose a simple and efficient approximation of the original problem, which can be solved using gradient descent. In the experiments, we compared the proposed method with CM and other baselines on 11 datasets, demonstrating the improvement due to the large margin regularization.

Acknowledgements

This work is supported in part by China 973 Fundamental R&D Program (No.2014CB340304), NSF grants (CNS-1115234, DBI-0960443, OISE-1129076, and IIS-1319973) and Huawei grant.

8. REFERENCES

[1] Acharya Ayan, Hruschka Eduardo, R., Ghosh Joydeep, Sarwar Badrul, and Ruvini Jean-David. Probabilistic combination of classifier and cluster ensembles for non-transductive learning. In *SDM*, 2013.

[2] Acharya Ayan, R. Hruschka Eduardo, Ghosh Joydeep, and Acharyya Sreangsu. An optimization framework for semi-supervised and transfer learning using multiple classifiers and clusterers. In *CoRR*, 2012.

[3] P. L. Bartlett. The sample complexity of pattern classification with neural networks: The size of the weights is more important than the size of the network. *IEEE Trans. Inf. Theor.*, 2006.

[4] Asa Ben-Hur, David Horn, Hava T. Siegelmann, and Vladimir Vapnik. Support vector clustering. *Journal of Machine Learning Research*, 2002.

[5] Stephen Boyd and Lieven Vandenberghe. *Convex Optimization*. Cambridge University Press, 2004.

[6] Ralph Allan Bradley. Rank analysis of incomplete block designs: Ii. additional tables for the method of paired comparisons. *Biometrika*, 41(3/4):pp. 502–537, 1954.

[7] Ralph Allan Bradley and Milton E. Terry. Rank analysis of incomplete block designs: I. the method of paired comparisons. *Biometrika*, 39(3/4):pp. 324–345, 1952.

[8] Sébastien Bubeck and Ulrike von Luxburg. Nearest neighbor clustering: A baseline method for consistent clustering with arbitrary objective functions. *Journal of Machine Learning Research*, 2009.

[9] Xi Chen, Paul N. Bennett, Kevyn Collins-Thompson, and Eric Horvitz. Pairwise ranking aggregation in a crowdsourced setting. WSDM, 2013.

[10] Janez Demšar. Statistical comparisons of classifiers over multiple data sets. *Journal of Machine Learning Research*, 2006.

[11] Inderjit S. Dhillon, Yuqiang Guan, and Brian Kulis. Kernel k-means: spectral clustering and normalized cuts. In *SIGKDD*, 2004.

[12] John Duchi, Shai Shalev-Shwartz, Yoram Singer, and Tushar Chandra. Efficient projections onto the l1-ball for learning in high dimensions. ICML, 2008.

[13] Wang Fei, Wang Xin, and Li Tao. Generalized cluster aggregation. In *IJCAI*, 2009.

[14] Xiaoli Zhang Fern and Carla E. Brodley. Solving cluster ensemble problems by bipartite graph partitioning. ICML, 2004.

[15] Jing Gao, Wei Fan, Deepak Turaga, Olivier Verscheure, Xiaoqiao Meng, Lu Su, and Jiawei Han. Consensus extraction from heterogeneous detectors to improve performance over network traffic anomaly detection. In *INFOCOM*, 2011.

[16] Jing Gao, Feng Liang, Wei Fan, Yizhou Sun, and Jiawei Han. Graph-based consensus maximization among multiple supervised and unsupervised models. In *NIPS*, 2009.

[17] Ralf Herbrich, Tom Minka, and Thore Graepel. Trueskill(tm): A bayesian skill rating system. NIPS.

[18] Tao Li and Chris Ding. Weighted Consensus Clustering. SDM, 2008.

[19] Tao Li, Chris Ding, and Michael I. Jordan. Solving consensus and semi-supervised clustering problems using nonnegative matrix factorization. ICDM, 2007.

[20] Xudong Ma, Ping Luo, Fuzhen Zhuang, Qing He, Zhongzhi Shi, and Zhiyong Shen. Combining supervised and unsupervised models via unconstrained probabilistic embedding. IJCAI, 2011.

[21] Meila Marina and Shortreed Susan. Regularized spectral learning. *Journal of Machine Learning Research*, 2006.

[22] Kaixiang Mo, Erheng Zhong, and Qiang Yang. Cross-task crowdsourcing. KDD, 2013.

[23] Andrew Y. Ng, Michael I. Jordan, and Yair Weiss. On spectral clustering: Analysis and an algorithm. In *NIPS*, 2001.

[24] H. Paugam-Moisy, A. Elisseeff, and Y. Guermeur. Generalization performance of multiclass discriminant models. In *Neural Networks, 2000. IJCNN 2000*, 2000.

[25] Arun Rajkumar and Shivani Agarwal. A statistical convergence perspective of algorithms for rank aggregation from pairwise data. In *ICML*, 2014.

[26] Rion Snow, Brendan O'Connor, Daniel Jurafsky, and Andrew Y. Ng. Cheap and fast—but is it good?: Evaluating non-expert annotations for natural language tasks. EMNLP, 2008.

[27] Alexander Strehl and Joydeep Ghosh. Cluster ensembles - a knowledge reuse framework for combining multiple partitions. *Journal of Machine Learning Research*, 2003.

[28] Ben Taskar, Carlos Guestrin, and Daphne Koller. Max-margin markov networks. In *NIPS*. 2004.

[29] Vladimir Vapnik. *Statistical learning theory*. Wiley, 1998.

[30] Hongjun Wang, Hanhuai Shan, and Arindam Banerjee. Bayesian cluster ensembles. In *SDM*, 2009.

[31] Naiyan Wang and Dit-Yan Yeung. Ensemble-based tracking: Aggregating crowdsourced structured time series data. In *ICML*, 2014.

[32] Pu Wang, Carlotta Domeniconi, and Kathryn Blackmond Laskey. Nonparametric bayesian clustering ensembles. In *ECML PKDD*, 2010.

[33] Ruby C. Weng and Chih-Jen Lin. A bayesian approximation method for online ranking. *J. Mach. Learn. Res.*, 12, 2011.

[34] Sihong Xie, Wei Fan, and Philip S. Yu. An iterative and re-weighting framework for rejection and uncertainty resolution in crowdsourcing. In *SDM*, 2012.

[35] Sihong Xie, Xiangnan Kong, Jing Gao, Wei Fan, and Philip S. Yu. Multilabel consensus classification. In *ICDM*, 2013.

[36] Yan Yan, Romer Rosales, Glenn Fung, and Jennifer Dy. Active learning from crowds. ICML, 2011.

[37] Jinfeng Yi, Tianbao Yang, Rong Jin, A.K. Jain, and M. Mahdavi. Robust ensemble clustering by matrix completion. ICDM, 2012.

[38] Yi Zhang and Jeff Schneider. Maximum margin output coding. ICML, 2012.

[39] Jun Zhu, Amr Ahmed, and Eric P. Xing. Medlda: maximum margin supervised topic models for regression and classification. ICML, 2009.

Large Margin Distribution Machine

Teng Zhang and Zhi-Hua Zhou
National Key Laboratory for Novel Software Technology
Nanjing University, Nanjing 210023, China
{zhangt, zhouzh}@lamda.nju.edu.cn

ABSTRACT

Support vector machine (SVM) has been one of the most popular learning algorithms, with the central idea of maximizing the *minimum margin*, i.e., the smallest distance from the instances to the classification boundary. Recent theoretical results, however, disclosed that maximizing the minimum margin does not necessarily lead to better generalization performances, and instead, the margin distribution has been proven to be more crucial. In this paper, we propose the Large margin Distribution Machine (LDM), which tries to achieve a better generalization performance by optimizing the margin distribution. We characterize the margin distribution by the first- and second-order statistics, i.e., the margin mean and variance. The LDM is a general learning approach which can be used in any place where SVM can be applied, and its superiority is verified both theoretically and empirically in this paper.

Categories and Subject Descriptors

I.2.6 [**Artificial Intelligence**]: Learning; I.5.2 [**Pattern Recognition**]: Design Methodology—*classifier design and evaluation*; H.2.8 [**Database Management**]: Database Applications—*Data mining*

Keywords

Margin distribution; minimum margin; classification

1. INTRODUCTION

Support Vector Machine (SVM) [5, 26] has always been one of the most successful learning algorithms. The basic idea is to identify a classification boundary having a large margin for all the training examples, and the resultant optimization can be accomplished by a quadratic programming (QP) problem. Although SVMs have a long history of literatures, there are still great efforts [16, 6, 25, 14, 8] on improving SVMs.

KDD'14, August 24–27, 2014, New York, NY, USA.

ACM 978-1-4503-2956-9/14/08...$15.00.
http://dx.doi.org/10.1145/2623330.2623710.

It is well known that SVM can be viewed as a learning approach trying to maximize over training examples the *minimum margin*, i.e., the smallest distance from the examples to the classification boundary, and the margin theory [26] provided a good support to the generalization performance of SVM. It is noteworthy that the margin theory not only plays an important role for SVMs, but also has been extended to interpret the good generalization of many other learning approaches, such as AdaBoost [10], a major representative of ensemble methods [31]. Specifically, Schapire et al. [21] first suggested margin theory to explain the phenomenon that AdaBoost seems resistant to overfitting; soon after, Breiman [4] indicated that the minimum margin is crucial and developed a boosting-style algorithm, Arc-gv, which is able to maximize the minimum margin but with a poor generalization performance. Later, Reyzin et al. [20] found that although Arc-gv tends to produce larger minimum margin, it suffers from a poor margin distribution; they conjectured that the margin distribution, rather than the minimum margin, is more crucial to the generalization performance. Such a conjecture has been theoretically studied [27, 11], and it was recently proven by Gao and Zhou [11]. Moreover, it was disclosed that rather than simply considering a single-point margin, both the margin mean and variance are important [11]. All these theoretical studies, however, focused on boosting-style algorithms, whereas the influence of the margin distribution for SVMs in practice has not been well exploited.

In this paper, we propose the Large margin Distribution Machine (LDM), which tries to achieve strong generalization performance by optimizing the margin distribution. Inspired by the recent theoretical result [11], we characterize the margin distribution by the first- and second-order statistics, and try to maximize the margin mean and minimize the margin variance simultaneously. For optimization, we propose a dual coordinate descent method for kernel LDM, and propose an averaged stochastic gradient descent (ASGD) method for large scale linear kernel LDM. Comprehensive experiments on twenty regular scale data sets and twelve large scale data sets show the superiority of LDM to SVM and many state-of-the-art methods, verifying that the margin distribution is more crucial for SVM-style learning approaches than minimum margin.

The rest of this paper is organized as follows. Section 2 introduces some preliminaries. Section 3 presents the LDM. Section 4 reports on our experiments. Section 5 discusses about some related works. Finally, Section 6 concludes.

2. PRELIMINARIES

We denote by $\mathcal{X} \in \mathbb{R}^d$ the instance space and $\mathcal{Y} = \{+1, -1\}$ the label set. Let $\mathcal{D}$ be an unknown (underlying) distribution over $\mathcal{X} \times \mathcal{Y}$. A training set of size m

$$S = \{(\boldsymbol{x}_1, y_1), (\boldsymbol{x}_2, y_2), \ldots, (\boldsymbol{x}_m, y_m)\},$$

is drawn identically and independently (i.i.d.) according to the distribution $\mathcal{D}$. Our goal is to learn a function which is used to predict the labels for future unseen instances.

For SVMs, f is regarded as a linear model, i.e., $f(\boldsymbol{x}) = \boldsymbol{w}^\top \phi(\boldsymbol{x})$ where $\boldsymbol{w}$ is a linear predictor, $\phi(\boldsymbol{x})$ is a feature mapping of $\boldsymbol{x}$ induced by a kernel k, i.e., $k(\boldsymbol{x}_i, \boldsymbol{x}_j) = \phi(\boldsymbol{x}_i)^\top \phi(\boldsymbol{x}_j)$. According to [5, 26], the margin of instance $(\boldsymbol{x}_i, y_i)$ is formulated as

$$\gamma_i = y_i \boldsymbol{w}^\top \phi(\boldsymbol{x}_i), \forall i = 1, \ldots, m. \tag{1}$$

From [7], it is shown that in separable cases where the training examples can be separated with the zero error, SVM with hard-margin (or Hard-margin SVM),

$$\begin{aligned} \min_{\boldsymbol{w}} \ & \frac{1}{2}\boldsymbol{w}^\top \boldsymbol{w} \\ \text{s.t.} \ & y_i \boldsymbol{w}^\top \phi(\boldsymbol{x}_i) \geq 1, \ i = 1, \ldots, m, \end{aligned}$$

is regarded as the maximization of the minimum margin $\{\min\{\gamma_i\}_{i=1}^m\}$.

In non-separable cases where the training examples cannot be separated with the zero error, SVM with soft-margin (or Soft-margin SVM) is posed,

$$\begin{aligned} \min_{\boldsymbol{w}, \boldsymbol{\xi}} \ & \frac{1}{2}\boldsymbol{w}^\top \boldsymbol{w} + C\sum_{i=1}^m \xi_i \\ \text{s.t.} \ & y_i \boldsymbol{w}^\top \phi(\boldsymbol{x}_i) \geq 1 - \xi_i, \\ & \xi_i \geq 0, \ i = 1, \ldots, m. \end{aligned} \tag{2}$$

where $\boldsymbol{\xi} = [\xi_1, \ldots, \xi_m]^\top$ measure the losses of instances, and C is a trading-off parameter. There exists a constant $\bar{C}$ such that (2) can be equivalently reformulated as,

$$\begin{aligned} \max_{\boldsymbol{w}} \ & \gamma_0 - \bar{C}\sum\nolimits_{i=1}^m \xi_i \\ \text{s.t.} \ & \gamma_i \geq \gamma_0 - \xi_i, \\ & \xi_i \geq 0, \ i = 1, \ldots, m, \end{aligned}$$

where γ_0 is a relaxed minimum margin, and $\bar{C}$ is the trading-off parameter. Note that γ_0 indeed characterizes the top-p minimum margin [11]; hence, SVMs (with both hard-margin and soft-margin) consider only a single-point margin and have not exploited the whole margin distribution.

3. LDM

In this section, we first formulate the margin distribution, and then present the optimization algorithms and the theoretical guarantee.

3.1 Formulation

The two most straightforward statistics for characterizing the margin distribution are the first- and second-order statistics, that is, the mean and the variance of the margin. Formally, denote $\boldsymbol{X}$ as the matrix whose i-th column is $\phi(\boldsymbol{x}_i)$, i.e., $\boldsymbol{X} = [\phi(\boldsymbol{x}_1) \ldots \phi(\boldsymbol{x}_m)]$, $\boldsymbol{y} = [y_1, \ldots, y_m]^\top$ is a column vector, and $\boldsymbol{Y}$ is a $m \times m$ diagonal matrix with $y_1, \ldots, y_m$ as the diagonal elements. According to the definition in (1), the margin mean is

$$\bar{\gamma} = \frac{1}{m}\sum_{i=1}^m y_i \boldsymbol{w}^\top \phi(\boldsymbol{x}_i) = \frac{1}{m}(\boldsymbol{X}\boldsymbol{y})^\top \boldsymbol{w}, \tag{3}$$

and the margin variance is

$$\begin{aligned} \hat{\gamma} &= \frac{1}{m^2}\sum_{i=1}^m\sum_{j=1}^m (y_i \boldsymbol{w}^\top \phi(\boldsymbol{x}_i) - y_j \boldsymbol{w}^\top \phi(\boldsymbol{x}_j))^2 \\ &= \frac{2}{m^2}(m\boldsymbol{w}^\top \boldsymbol{X}\boldsymbol{X}^\top \boldsymbol{w} - \boldsymbol{w}^\top \boldsymbol{X}\boldsymbol{y}\boldsymbol{y}^\top \boldsymbol{X}^\top \boldsymbol{w}). \end{aligned} \tag{4}$$

Inspired by the recent theoretical result [11], LDM attempts to maximize the margin mean and minimize the margin variance simultaneously.

We first consider a simpler scenario, i.e., the separable cases where the training examples can be separated with the zero error. In these cases, the maximization of the margin mean and the minimization of the margin variance leads to the following hard-margin LDM,

$$\begin{aligned} \min_{\boldsymbol{w}} \ & \frac{1}{2}\boldsymbol{w}^\top \boldsymbol{w} + \lambda_1 \hat{\gamma} - \lambda_2 \bar{\gamma} \\ \text{s.t.} \ & y_i \boldsymbol{w}^\top \phi(\boldsymbol{x}_i) \geq 1, \ i = 1, \ldots, m, \end{aligned}$$

where λ_1 and λ_2 are the parameters for trading-off the margin variance, the margin mean and the model complexity. It's evident that the hard-margin LDM subsumes the hard-margin SVM when λ_1 and λ_2 equal 0.

For the non-separable cases, similar to soft-margin SVM, the soft-margin LDM leads to

$$\begin{aligned} \min_{\boldsymbol{w}, \boldsymbol{\xi}} \ & \frac{1}{2}\boldsymbol{w}^\top \boldsymbol{w} + \lambda_1 \hat{\gamma} - \lambda_2 \bar{\gamma} + C\sum_{i=1}^m \xi_i \\ \text{s.t.} \ & y_i \boldsymbol{w}^\top \phi(\boldsymbol{x}_i) \geq 1 - \xi_i, \\ & \xi_i \geq 0, \ i = 1, \ldots, m. \end{aligned} \tag{5}$$

Similarly, soft-margin LDM subsumes the soft-margin SVM if λ_1 and λ_2 both equal 0. Because the soft-margin SVM often performs much better than the hard-margin one, in the following we will focus on soft-margin LDM and if without clarification, LDM is referred to the soft-margin LDM.

3.2 Optimization

We in this section first present a dual coordinate descent method for kernel LDM, and then present an average stochastic gradient descent (ASGD) method for large scale linear kernel LDM.

3.2.1 Kernel LDM

By substituting (3)-(4), (5) leads to the following quadratic programming problem,

$$\begin{aligned} \min_{\boldsymbol{w}, \boldsymbol{\xi}} \ & \frac{1}{2}\boldsymbol{w}^\top \boldsymbol{w} + \frac{2\lambda_1}{m^2}(m\boldsymbol{w}^\top \boldsymbol{X}\boldsymbol{X}^\top \boldsymbol{w} - \boldsymbol{w}^\top \boldsymbol{X}\boldsymbol{y}\boldsymbol{y}^\top \boldsymbol{X}^\top \boldsymbol{w}) \\ & - \lambda_2 \frac{1}{m}(\boldsymbol{X}\boldsymbol{y})^\top \boldsymbol{w} + C\sum_{i=1}^m \xi_i \\ \text{s.t.} \ & y_i \boldsymbol{w}^\top \phi(\boldsymbol{x}_i) \geq 1 - \xi_i, \\ & \xi_i \geq 0, \ i = 1, \ldots, m. \end{aligned} \tag{6}$$

(6) is often intractable due to the high or infinite dimensionality of $\phi(\cdot)$. Fortunately, inspired by the representer

theorem in [22], the following theorem states that the optimal solution for (6) can be spanned by $\{\phi(\boldsymbol{x}_i), 1 \le i \le m\}$.

THEOREM 1. *The optimal solution $\boldsymbol{w}^*$ for problem (6) admits a representation of the form*

$$\boldsymbol{w}^* = \sum_{i=1}^m \alpha_i \phi(\boldsymbol{x}_i) = \boldsymbol{X}\boldsymbol{\alpha}, \tag{7}$$

where $\boldsymbol{\alpha} = [\alpha_1, \ldots, \alpha_m]^\top$ are the coefficients.

PROOF. $\boldsymbol{w}^*$ can be decomposed into a part that lives in the span of $\phi(\boldsymbol{x}_i)$ and an orthogonal part, i.e.,

$$\boldsymbol{w} = \sum_{i=1}^m \alpha_i \phi(\boldsymbol{x}_i) + \boldsymbol{v} = \boldsymbol{X}\boldsymbol{\alpha} + \boldsymbol{v}$$

for some $\boldsymbol{\alpha} = [\alpha_1, \ldots, \alpha_m]^\top$ and $\boldsymbol{v}$ satisfying $\phi(\boldsymbol{x}_j)^\top \boldsymbol{v} = 0$ for all j, i.e., $\boldsymbol{X}^\top \boldsymbol{v} = \boldsymbol{0}$. Note that

$$\boldsymbol{X}^\top \boldsymbol{w} = \boldsymbol{X}^\top (\boldsymbol{X}\boldsymbol{\alpha} + \boldsymbol{v}) = \boldsymbol{X}^\top \boldsymbol{X}\boldsymbol{\alpha},$$

so the second and the third terms of (6) are independent of $\boldsymbol{v}$; further note that the constraint is also independent of $\boldsymbol{v}$, thus the last terms of (6) is also independent of $\boldsymbol{v}$.

As for the first term of (6), since $\boldsymbol{X}^\top \boldsymbol{v} = \boldsymbol{0}$, consequently we get

$$\begin{aligned}\boldsymbol{w}^\top \boldsymbol{w} &= (\boldsymbol{X}\boldsymbol{\alpha} + \boldsymbol{v})^\top (\boldsymbol{X}\boldsymbol{\alpha} + \boldsymbol{v}) = \boldsymbol{\alpha}^\top \boldsymbol{X}^\top \boldsymbol{X}\boldsymbol{\alpha} + \boldsymbol{v}^\top \boldsymbol{v} \\ &\ge \boldsymbol{\alpha}^\top \boldsymbol{X}^\top \boldsymbol{X}\boldsymbol{\alpha}\end{aligned}$$

with equality occurring if and only if $\boldsymbol{v} = \boldsymbol{0}$.

So, setting $\boldsymbol{v} = \boldsymbol{0}$ does not affect the second, the third and the last term while strictly reduces the first term of (6). Hence, $\boldsymbol{w}^*$ for problem (6) admits a representation of the form (7). □

According to Theorem 1, we have

$$\begin{aligned}\boldsymbol{X}^\top \boldsymbol{w} &= \boldsymbol{X}^\top \boldsymbol{X}\boldsymbol{\alpha} = \boldsymbol{G}\boldsymbol{\alpha}, \\ \boldsymbol{w}^\top \boldsymbol{w} &= \boldsymbol{\alpha}^\top \boldsymbol{X}^\top \boldsymbol{X}\boldsymbol{\alpha} = \boldsymbol{\alpha}^\top \boldsymbol{G}\boldsymbol{\alpha},\end{aligned}$$

where $\boldsymbol{G} = \boldsymbol{X}^\top \boldsymbol{X}$ is the kernel matrix. Let $\boldsymbol{G}_{:i}$ denote the i-th column of $\boldsymbol{G}$, then (6) can be cast as

$$\begin{aligned}\min_{\boldsymbol{\alpha},\boldsymbol{\xi}} \ & \frac{1}{2}\boldsymbol{\alpha}^\top \boldsymbol{Q}\boldsymbol{\alpha} + \boldsymbol{p}^\top \boldsymbol{\alpha} + C\sum_{i=1}^m \xi_i \\ \text{s.t.} \ & y_i \boldsymbol{\alpha}^\top \boldsymbol{G}_{:i} \ge 1 - \xi_i, \\ & \xi_i \ge 0, \ i = 1, \ldots, m,\end{aligned} \tag{8}$$

where $\boldsymbol{Q} = 4\lambda_1(m\boldsymbol{G}^\top \boldsymbol{G} - (\boldsymbol{G}\boldsymbol{y})(\boldsymbol{G}\boldsymbol{y})^\top)/m^2 + \boldsymbol{G}$ and $\boldsymbol{p} = -\lambda_2 \boldsymbol{G}\boldsymbol{y}/m$. By introducing the lagrange multipliers $\boldsymbol{\beta} = [\beta_1, \ldots, \beta_m]^\top$ and $\boldsymbol{\eta} = [\eta_1, \ldots, \eta_m]^\top$ for the first and the second constraints respectively, the Lagrangian of (8) leads to

$$\begin{aligned}L(\boldsymbol{\alpha}, \boldsymbol{\xi}, \boldsymbol{\beta}, \boldsymbol{\eta}) = & \frac{1}{2}\boldsymbol{\alpha}^\top \boldsymbol{Q}\boldsymbol{\alpha} + \boldsymbol{p}^\top \boldsymbol{\alpha} + C\sum_{i=1}^m \xi_i \\ & - \sum_{i=1}^m \beta_i (y_i \boldsymbol{\alpha}^\top \boldsymbol{G}_{:i} - 1 + \xi_i) - \sum_{i=1}^m \eta_i \xi_i.\end{aligned} \tag{9}$$

By setting the partial derivations of $\{\boldsymbol{\alpha}, \boldsymbol{\xi}\}$ to zero, we have

$$\frac{\partial L}{\partial \boldsymbol{\alpha}} = \boldsymbol{Q}\boldsymbol{\alpha} + \boldsymbol{p} - \sum_{i=1}^m \beta_i y_i \boldsymbol{G}_{:i}, \tag{10}$$

$$\frac{\partial L}{\partial \xi_i} = C - \beta_i - \eta_i = 0, \ i = 1, \ldots, m. \tag{11}$$

Algorithm 1 Kernel LDM

Input: Data set $\boldsymbol{X}$, λ_1, λ_2, C
Output: $\boldsymbol{\alpha}$
Initialize $\boldsymbol{\beta} = \boldsymbol{0}$, $\boldsymbol{\alpha} = \frac{\lambda_2}{m}\boldsymbol{Q}^{-1}\boldsymbol{G}\boldsymbol{y}$, $\boldsymbol{A} = \boldsymbol{Q}^{-1}\boldsymbol{G}\boldsymbol{Y}$, $h_{ii} = \boldsymbol{e}_i^\top \boldsymbol{Y}\boldsymbol{G}\boldsymbol{Q}^{-1}\boldsymbol{G}\boldsymbol{Y}\boldsymbol{e}_i$;
while $\boldsymbol{\beta}$ not converge **do**
  for $i = 1, \ldots m$ **do**
    $[\nabla f(\boldsymbol{\beta})]_i \leftarrow \boldsymbol{e}_i^\top \boldsymbol{Y}\boldsymbol{G}\boldsymbol{\alpha} - 1$;
    $\beta_i^{old} \leftarrow \beta_i$;
    $\beta_i \leftarrow \min\left(\max\left(\beta_i - \frac{[\nabla f(\boldsymbol{\beta})]_i}{h_{ii}}, 0\right), C\right)$;
    $\boldsymbol{\alpha} \leftarrow \boldsymbol{\alpha} + (\beta_i - \beta_i^{old})\boldsymbol{A}\boldsymbol{e}_i$;
  end for
end while

By substituting (10) and (11) into (9), the dual [1] of (8) can be cast as:

$$\begin{aligned}\min_{\boldsymbol{\beta}} \ & f(\boldsymbol{\beta}) = \frac{1}{2}\boldsymbol{\beta}^\top \boldsymbol{H}\boldsymbol{\beta} + \left(\frac{\lambda_2}{m}\boldsymbol{H}\boldsymbol{e} - \boldsymbol{e}\right)^\top \boldsymbol{\beta}, \\ \text{s.t.} \ & 0 \le \beta_i \le C, \ i = 1, \ldots, m.\end{aligned} \tag{12}$$

where $\boldsymbol{H} = \boldsymbol{Y}\boldsymbol{G}\boldsymbol{Q}^{-1}\boldsymbol{G}\boldsymbol{Y}$, $\boldsymbol{Q}^{-1}$ refers to the inverse matrix of $\boldsymbol{Q}$ and $\boldsymbol{e}$ stands for the all-one vector. Due to the simple decoupled box constraint and the convex quadratic objective function, as suggested by [29], (12) can be efficiently solved by the dual coordinate descent method. In dual coordinate descent method [13], one of the variables is selected to minimize while the other variables are kept as constants at each iteration, and a closed-form solution can be achieved at each iteration. Specifically, to minimize β_i by keeping the other $\beta_{j \ne i}$'s as constants, one needs to solve the following subproblem,

$$\begin{aligned}\min_t \ & f(\boldsymbol{\beta} + t\boldsymbol{e}_i) \\ \text{s.t.} \ & 0 \le \beta_i + t \le C,\end{aligned} \tag{13}$$

where $\boldsymbol{e}_i$ denotes the vector with 1 in the i-th coordinate and 0's elsewhere. Let $\boldsymbol{H} = [h_{ij}]_{i,j=1,\ldots,m}$, we have

$$f(\boldsymbol{\beta} + t\boldsymbol{e}_i) = \frac{1}{2}h_{ii}t^2 + [\nabla f(\boldsymbol{\beta})]_i t + f(\boldsymbol{\beta}),$$

where $[\nabla f(\boldsymbol{\beta})]_i$ is the i-th component of the gradient $\nabla f(\boldsymbol{\beta})$. Note that $f(\boldsymbol{\beta})$ is independent of t and thus can be dropped. Considering that $f(\boldsymbol{\beta} + t\boldsymbol{e}_i)$ is a simple quadratic function of t, and further note the box constraint $0 \le \alpha_i \le C$, the minimizer of (13) leads to a closed-form solution,

$$\beta_i^{new} = \min\left(\max\left(\beta_i - \frac{[\nabla f(\boldsymbol{\beta})]_i}{h_{ii}}, 0\right), C\right).$$

Algorithm 1 summarizes the pseudo-code of kernel LDM.

For prediction, according to (10), one can obtain the coefficients $\boldsymbol{\alpha}$ from the optimal $\boldsymbol{\beta}^*$ as

$$\begin{aligned}\boldsymbol{\alpha} &= \boldsymbol{Q}^{-1}(\boldsymbol{G}\boldsymbol{Y}\boldsymbol{\beta}^* - \boldsymbol{p}) = \boldsymbol{Q}^{-1}\left(\frac{\lambda_2}{m}\boldsymbol{G}\boldsymbol{Y}\boldsymbol{e} + \boldsymbol{G}\boldsymbol{Y}\boldsymbol{\beta}^*\right) \\ &= \boldsymbol{Q}^{-1}\boldsymbol{G}\boldsymbol{Y}\left(\frac{\lambda_2}{m}\boldsymbol{e} + \boldsymbol{\beta}^*\right).\end{aligned}$$

[1]Here we omit constants without influence on optimization.

Hence for testing instance $\boldsymbol{z}$, its label can be obtained by

$$sgn\left(\boldsymbol{w}^\top\phi(\boldsymbol{z})\right) = sgn\left(\sum_{i=1}^m \alpha_i k(\boldsymbol{x}_i, \boldsymbol{z})\right).$$

3.2.2 Large Scale Kernel LDM

In section 3.2.1, the proposed method can efficiently deal with kernel LDM. However, the inherent computational cost for the kernel matrix in kernel LDM takes $O(m^2)$ time, which might be computational prohibitive for large scale problems. To make LDM more useful, in the following, we present a fast linear kernel LDM for large scale problems by adopting the average stochastic gradient descent (ASGD) method [19].

For linear kernel LDM, (5) can be reformulated as the following form,

$$\begin{aligned}\min_{\boldsymbol{w}}\ g(\boldsymbol{w}) = &\frac{1}{2}\boldsymbol{w}^\top\boldsymbol{w} + \frac{2\lambda_1}{m^2}\boldsymbol{w}^\top(m\boldsymbol{X}\boldsymbol{X}^\top - \boldsymbol{X}\boldsymbol{y}\boldsymbol{y}^\top\boldsymbol{X}^\top)\boldsymbol{w}\\ &- \frac{\lambda_2}{m}(\boldsymbol{X}\boldsymbol{y})^\top\boldsymbol{w} + C\sum_{i=1}^m \max\{0, 1 - y_i\boldsymbol{w}^\top\boldsymbol{x}_i\}, \qquad (14)\end{aligned}$$

where $\boldsymbol{X} = [\boldsymbol{x}_1 \ldots \boldsymbol{x}_m]$, $\boldsymbol{y} = [y_1, \ldots, y_m]^\top$ is a column vector.

For large scale problems, computing the gradient of (14) is expensive because its computation involves all the training examples. Stochastic gradient descent (SGD) works by computing a noisy unbiased estimation of the gradient via sampling a subset of the training examples. Theoretically, when the objective is convex, it can be shown that in expectation, SGD converges to the global optimal solution [15, 3]. During the past decade, SGD has been applied to various machine learning problems and achieved promising performances [30, 23, 2, 24].

The following theorem presents an approach to obtain an unbiased estimation of the gradient $\nabla g(\boldsymbol{w})$.

THEOREM 2. *If two examples $(\boldsymbol{x}_i, y_i)$ and $(\boldsymbol{x}_j, y_j)$ are sampled from training set randomly, then*

$$\begin{aligned}\nabla g(\boldsymbol{w}, \boldsymbol{x}_i, \boldsymbol{x}_j) = &4\lambda_1\boldsymbol{x}_i\boldsymbol{x}_i^\top\boldsymbol{w} - 4\lambda_1 y_i\boldsymbol{x}_i y_j\boldsymbol{x}_j^\top\boldsymbol{w} + \boldsymbol{w}\\ &- \lambda_2 y_i\boldsymbol{x}_i - mC\begin{cases} y_i\boldsymbol{x}_i & i \in \boldsymbol{I},\\ 0 & otherwise,\end{cases} \qquad (15)\end{aligned}$$

where $\boldsymbol{I} \equiv \{i \mid y_i\boldsymbol{w}^\top\boldsymbol{x}_i < 1\}$ is an unbiased estimation of $\nabla g(\boldsymbol{w})$.

PROOF. Note that the gradient of $g(\boldsymbol{w})$ is

$$\nabla g(\boldsymbol{w}) = \boldsymbol{Q}\boldsymbol{w} + \boldsymbol{p} - C\sum_{i=1}^m y_i\boldsymbol{x}_i, i \in \boldsymbol{I},$$

where $\boldsymbol{Q} = 4\lambda_1(m\boldsymbol{X}\boldsymbol{X}^\top - \boldsymbol{X}\boldsymbol{y}(\boldsymbol{X}\boldsymbol{y})^\top)/m^2 + \boldsymbol{I}$ and $\boldsymbol{p} = -\lambda_2\boldsymbol{X}\boldsymbol{y}/m$. Further note that

$$\begin{aligned}E_{\boldsymbol{x}_i}[\boldsymbol{x}_i\boldsymbol{x}_i^\top] &= \frac{1}{m}\sum_{i=1}^m \boldsymbol{x}_i\boldsymbol{x}_i^\top = \frac{1}{m}\boldsymbol{X}\boldsymbol{X}^\top,\\ E_{\boldsymbol{x}_i}[y_i\boldsymbol{x}_i] &= \frac{1}{m}\sum_{i=1}^m y_i\boldsymbol{x}_i = \frac{1}{m}\boldsymbol{X}\boldsymbol{y}.\end{aligned} \qquad (16)$$

According to the linearity of expectation, the independence between $\boldsymbol{x}_i$ and $\boldsymbol{x}_j$, and with (16), we have

$$\begin{aligned}&E_{\boldsymbol{x}_i,\boldsymbol{x}_j}[\nabla g(\boldsymbol{w}, \boldsymbol{x}_i, \boldsymbol{x}_j)]\\ &= 4\lambda_1 E_{\boldsymbol{x}_i}[\boldsymbol{x}_i\boldsymbol{x}_i^\top]\boldsymbol{w} - 4\lambda_1 E_{\boldsymbol{x}_i}[y_i\boldsymbol{x}_i]E_{\boldsymbol{x}_j}[y_j\boldsymbol{x}_j]^\top\boldsymbol{w} + \boldsymbol{w}\\ &\quad - \lambda_2 E_{\boldsymbol{x}_i}[y_i\boldsymbol{x}_i] - mCE_{\boldsymbol{x}_i}[y_i\boldsymbol{x}_i \mid i \in \boldsymbol{I}]\\ &= 4\lambda_1\frac{1}{m}\boldsymbol{X}\boldsymbol{X}^\top\boldsymbol{w} - 4\lambda_1\frac{1}{m}\boldsymbol{X}\boldsymbol{y}\left(\frac{1}{m}\boldsymbol{X}\boldsymbol{y}\right)^\top\boldsymbol{w} + \boldsymbol{w}\\ &\quad - \lambda_2\frac{1}{m}\boldsymbol{X}\boldsymbol{y} - mC\frac{1}{m}\sum_{i=1}^m y_i\boldsymbol{x}_i, i \in \boldsymbol{I}\\ &= \boldsymbol{Q}\boldsymbol{w} + \boldsymbol{p} - C\sum_{i=1}^m y_i\boldsymbol{x}_i, i \in \boldsymbol{I}\\ &= \nabla g(\boldsymbol{w}).\end{aligned}$$

It is shown that $\nabla g(\boldsymbol{w}, \boldsymbol{x}_i, \boldsymbol{x}_j)$ is a noisy unbiased gradient of $g(\boldsymbol{w})$. □

With Theorem 2, the stochastic gradient update can be formed as

$$\boldsymbol{w}_{t+1} = \boldsymbol{w}_t - \eta_t\nabla g(\boldsymbol{w}, \boldsymbol{x}_i, \boldsymbol{x}_j), \qquad (17)$$

where η_t is a suitably chosen step-size parameter in the t-th iteration.

In practice, we use averaged stochastic gradient descent (ASGD) which is more robust than SGD [28]. At each iteration, besides performing the normal stochastic gradient update (17), we also compute

$$\bar{\boldsymbol{w}}_t = \frac{1}{t - t_0}\sum_{i=t_0+1}^t \boldsymbol{w}_i,$$

where t_0 determines when we engage the averaging process. This average can be computed efficiently using a recursive formula:

$$\bar{\boldsymbol{w}}_{t+1} = \bar{\boldsymbol{w}}_t + \mu_t(\boldsymbol{w}_{t+1} - \bar{\boldsymbol{w}}_t),$$

where $\mu_t = 1/\max\{1, t - t_0\}$.

Algorithm 2 summarizes the pseudo-code of large scale kernel LDM.

Algorithm 2 Large Scale Kernel LDM

Input: Data set $\boldsymbol{X}$, λ_1, λ_2, C
Output: $\bar{\boldsymbol{w}}$
Initialize $\boldsymbol{u} = \boldsymbol{0}$, $T = 5$;
for $t = 1, \ldots Tm$ **do**
  Randomly sample two training examples $(\boldsymbol{x}_i, y_i)$ and $(\boldsymbol{x}_j, y_j)$;
  Compute $\nabla g(\boldsymbol{w}, \boldsymbol{x}_i, \boldsymbol{x}_j)$ as in (15);
  $\boldsymbol{w} \leftarrow \boldsymbol{w} - \eta_t\nabla g(\boldsymbol{w}, \boldsymbol{x}_i, \boldsymbol{x}_j)$;
  $\bar{\boldsymbol{w}} \leftarrow \bar{\boldsymbol{w}} + \mu_t(\boldsymbol{w} - \bar{\boldsymbol{w}})$;
end for

3.3 Analysis

In this section, we study the statistical property of LDM. Specifically, we derive a bound on the expectation of error for LDM according to the leave-one-out cross-validation estimate, which is an unbiased estimate of the probability of test error.

Here we only consider the linear case (14) for simplicity, however, the results are also applicable to any other feature mapping ϕ. Following the same steps in Section 3.2.1, one can have the dual problem of (14), i.e.,

$$\min_{\boldsymbol{\alpha}} \ f(\boldsymbol{\alpha}) = \frac{1}{2}\boldsymbol{\alpha}^\top \boldsymbol{H}\boldsymbol{\alpha} + \left(\frac{\lambda_2}{m}\boldsymbol{H}\boldsymbol{e} - \boldsymbol{e}\right)^\top \boldsymbol{\alpha}, \quad \text{s.t. } 0 \le \alpha_i \le C, \ i = 1, \ldots, m. \tag{18}$$

where $\boldsymbol{H} = \boldsymbol{Y}\boldsymbol{X}^\top \boldsymbol{Q}^{-1}\boldsymbol{X}\boldsymbol{Y}$, $\boldsymbol{Q} = \frac{4\lambda_1}{m^2}(m\boldsymbol{X}\boldsymbol{X}^\top - \boldsymbol{X}\boldsymbol{y}(\boldsymbol{X}\boldsymbol{y})^\top) + \boldsymbol{I}$, $\boldsymbol{e}$ stands for the all-one vector and $\boldsymbol{Q}^{-1}$ refers to the inverse matrix of $\boldsymbol{Q}$.

THEOREM 3. *Let $\boldsymbol{\alpha}$ denote the optimal solution of (18), and $E[R(\boldsymbol{\alpha})]$ be the expectation of the probability of error, then we have*

$$E[R(\boldsymbol{\alpha})] \le \frac{E[h\sum_{i \in \boldsymbol{I}_1} \alpha_i + |\boldsymbol{I}_2|]}{m}, \tag{19}$$

where $\boldsymbol{I}_1 \equiv \{i \mid 0 < \alpha_i < C\}$, $\boldsymbol{I}_2 \equiv \{i \mid \alpha_i = C\}$ and $h = \max\{diag\{\boldsymbol{H}\}\}$.

PROOF. Suppose

$$\boldsymbol{\alpha}^* = \operatorname*{argmin}_{0 \le \boldsymbol{\alpha} \le C} f(\boldsymbol{\alpha}), \quad \boldsymbol{\alpha}^i = \operatorname*{argmin}_{0 \le \boldsymbol{\alpha} \le C, \alpha_i = 0} f(\boldsymbol{\alpha}), \ i = 1, \ldots, m, \tag{20}$$

and the corresponding solution for the linear kernel LDM are $\boldsymbol{w}^*$ and $\boldsymbol{w}^i$, respectively.

As shown in [17],

$$E[R(\boldsymbol{\alpha})] = \frac{E[\mathcal{L}((\boldsymbol{x}_1, y_1), \ldots, (\boldsymbol{x}_m, y_m))]}{m}, \tag{21}$$

where $\mathcal{L}((\boldsymbol{x}_1, y_1), \ldots, (\boldsymbol{x}_m, y_m))$ is the number of errors in the leave-one-out procedure. Note that if $\alpha_i^* = 0$, $(\boldsymbol{x}_i, y_i)$ will always be classified correctly in the leave-one-out procedure according to the KKT conditions. So for any misclassified example $(\boldsymbol{x}_i, y_i)$, we only need to consider the following two cases:

1) $0 < \alpha_i^* < C$, according to the definition in (20), we have

$$f(\boldsymbol{\alpha}^i) - \min_t f(\boldsymbol{\alpha}^i + t\boldsymbol{e}_i) \le f(\boldsymbol{\alpha}^i) - f(\boldsymbol{\alpha}^*), \tag{22}$$

$$f(\boldsymbol{\alpha}^i) - f(\boldsymbol{\alpha}^*) \le f(\boldsymbol{\alpha}^* - \alpha_i^* \boldsymbol{e}_i) - f(\boldsymbol{\alpha}^*), \tag{23}$$

where $\boldsymbol{e}_i$ denotes a vector with 1 in the i-th coordinate and 0's elsewhere. We can find that, the left-hand side of (22) is equal to $(1 - y_i \boldsymbol{x}_i^\top \boldsymbol{w}^i)^2/2h_{ii}$, and the right-hand side of (23) is equal to $\alpha_i^{*2} h_{ii}/2$. So by combining (22) and (23), we have

$$(1 - y_i \boldsymbol{x}_i^\top \boldsymbol{w}^i)^2/2h_{ii} \le \alpha_i^{*2} h_{ii}/2.$$

Further note that $y_i \boldsymbol{x}_i^\top \boldsymbol{w}^i < 0$, rearranging the above we can obtain $1 \le \alpha_i^* h_{ii}$.

2) $\alpha_i^* = C$, all these examples will be misclassified in the leave-one-out procedure.

So we have

$$\mathcal{L}((\boldsymbol{x}_1, y_1), \ldots, (\boldsymbol{x}_m, y_m)) \le h \sum_{i \in \boldsymbol{I}_1} \alpha_i^* + |\boldsymbol{I}_2|,$$

where $\boldsymbol{I}_1 \equiv \{i \mid 0 < \alpha_i^* < C\}$, $\boldsymbol{I}_2 \equiv \{i \mid \alpha_i^* = C\}$ and $h = \max\{h_{ii}, i = 1, \ldots, m\}$. Take expectation on both side and with (21), we get that (19) holds. □

4. EMPIRICAL STUDY

In this section, we empirically evaluate the effectiveness of LDM on a broad range of data sets. We first introduce the experimental settings in Section 4.1, and then compare LDM with SVM and three state-of-the-art approaches[2] in Section 4.2 and Section 4.3. In addition, we also study the cumulative margin distribution produced by LDM and SVM in Section 4.4. The computational cost and parameter influence are presented in Section 4.5 and Section 4.6, respectively.

4.1 Experimental Setup

We evaluate the effectiveness of our proposed LDMs on twenty regular scale data sets and twelve large scale data sets, including both UCI data sets and real-world data sets like KDD2010[3]. Table 1 summarizes the statistics of these data sets. The data set size is ranged from 106 to more than 8,000,000, and the dimensionality is ranged from 2 to more than 20,000,000, covering a broad range of properties. All features are normalized into the interval $[0, 1]$. For each data set, half of examples are randomly selected as the training data, and the remaining examples are used as the testing data. For regular scale data sets, both linear and RBF kernels are evaluated. Experiments are repeated for 30 times with random data partitions, and the average accuracies as well as the standard deviations are recorded. For large scale data sets, linear kernel is evaluated. Experiments are repeated for 10 times with random data partitions, and the average accuracies (with standard deviations) are recorded.

LDMs are compared with standard SVMs which ignore the margin distribution, and three state-of-the-art methods, that is, Margin Distribution Optimization (MDO) [12], Maximal Average Margin for Classifiers (MAMC) [18] and Kernel Method for the direct Optimization of the Margin Distribution (KM-OMD) [1]. For SVM, KM-OMD and LDM, the regularization parameter C is selected by 5-fold cross validation from $[10, 50, 100]$. For MDO, the parameters are set as the recommended parameters in [12]. For LDM, the regularization parameters λ_1, λ_2 are selected by 5-fold cross validation from the set of $[2^{-8}, \ldots, 2^{-2}]$, the parameters η_t and t_0 are set with the same setup in [28], and T is fixed to 5. The width of the RBF kernel for SVM, MAMC, KM-OMD and LDM are selected by 5-fold cross validation from the set of $[2^{-2}\delta, \ldots, 2^2\delta]$, where δ is the average distance between instances. All selections are performed on training sets.

4.2 Results on Regular Scale Data Sets

Tables 2 and 3 summarize the results on twenty regular scale data sets. As can be seen, the overall performance of LDM is superior or highly competitive to SVM and other compared methods. Specifically, for linear kernel, LDM performs significantly better than SVM, MDO, MAMC, KM-OMD on 12, 9, 17 and 10 over 20 data sets, respectively, and achieves the best accuracy on 13 data sets; for RBF kernel, LDM performs significantly better than SVM, MAMC, KM-OMD on 10, 18 and 15 over 20 data sets, respectively, and achieves the best accuracy on 15 data sets. MDO is not compared since it is specified for the linear kernel. In addition, as can be seen, in comparing with standard SVM which does not consider margin distribution,

[2] These approaches will be briefly introduced in Section 5.

[3] https://pslcdatashop.web.cmu.edu/KDDCup/downloads.jsp

Table 1: Characteristics of experimental data sets.

Scale	Dataset	#Instance	#Feature	Dataset	#Instance	#Feature
regular	*promoters*	106	57	*haberman*	306	14
	planning	182	12	*vehicle*	435	16
	colic	188	13	*clean1*	476	166
	parkinsons	195	22	*wdbc*	569	14
	colic.ORIG	205	17	*isolet*	600	51
	sonar	208	60	*credit-a*	653	15
	vote	232	16	*austra*	690	15
	house	232	16	*australian*	690	42
	heart	270	9	*fourclass*	862	2
	breast	277	9	*german*	1,000	59
large	*farm-ads*	4,143	54,877	*ijcnn1*	141,691	22
	news20	19,996	1,355,191	*skin*	245,057	3
	adult-a	32,561	123	*covtype*	581,012	54
	w8a	49,749	300	*rcv1*	697,641	47,236
	cod-rna	59,535	8	*url*	2,396,130	3,231,961
	real-sim	72,309	20,958	*kdd2010*	8,407,752	20,216,830

Table 2: Accuracy (mean±std.) comparison on regular scale data sets. Linear kernels are used. The best accuracy on each data set is bolded. •/○ indicates the performance is significantly better/worse than SVM (paired t-tests at 95% significance level). The win/tie/loss counts are summarized in the last row.

Dataset	SVM	MDO	MAMC	KM-OMD	LDM
promoters	0.723±0.071	0.713±0.067	0.520±0.096○	**0.736±0.061**	0.721±0.069
planning-relax	0.683±0.031	0.605±0.185○	**0.706±0.034•**	0.479±0.050○	**0.706±0.034•**
colic	0.814±0.035	0.781±0.154	0.661±0.062○	0.813±0.028	**0.832±0.026•**
parkinsons	0.846±0.038	0.732±0.270○	0.764±0.035○	0.814±0.024○	**0.865±0.030•**
colic.ORIG	0.618±0.027	0.624±0.040	0.623±0.027	**0.635±0.045•**	0.619±0.042
sonar	0.725±0.039	0.734±0.035	0.533±0.045○	**0.766±0.033•**	0.736±0.036
vote	0.934±0.022	0.587±0.435○	0.884±0.022○	0.957±0.013•	**0.970±0.014•**
house	0.942±0.015	0.943±0.015	0.883±0.029○	0.957±0.020•	**0.968±0.011•**
heart	0.799±0.029	0.826±0.026•	0.537±0.057○	**0.836±0.026•**	0.791±0.030
breast-cancer	0.717±0.033	0.710±0.031	0.706±0.027	0.696±0.031○	**0.725±0.027•**
haberman	0.734±0.030	0.728±0.029	**0.738±0.020**	0.667±0.040○	**0.738±0.020**
vehicle	0.959±0.012	0.956±0.012	0.566±0.160○	**0.960±0.010**	0.959±0.013
clean1	0.803±0.035	0.798±0.031	0.561±0.025○	**0.821±0.027•**	0.814±0.019•
wdbc	0.963±0.012	0.966±0.010	0.623±0.020○	0.968±0.009•	**0.968±0.011•**
isolet	0.995±0.003	0.501±0.503○	0.621±0.207○	0.995±0.003	**0.997±0.002•**
credit-a	0.861±0.014	0.862±0.013	0.596±0.063○	0.863±0.013	**0.864±0.013•**
austra	0.857±0.013	0.842±0.055	0.567±0.044○	0.858±0.013	**0.859±0.015**
australian	0.844±0.019	0.842±0.020	0.576±0.049○	0.858±0.016•	**0.866±0.014•**
fourclass	0.724±0.014	0.377±0.238○	0.641±0.020○	**0.736±0.014•**	0.723±0.014
german	0.711±0.030	0.737±0.014•	0.697±0.017○	0.729±0.017•	**0.738±0.016•**
Ave. accuracy	0.813	0.743	0.650	0.807	0.823
LDM: w/t/l	12/8/0	9/10/1	17/3/0	10/5/5	

the win/tie/loss counts show that LDM is always better or comparable, never worse than SVM.

4.3 Results on Large Scale Data Sets

Table 4 summarizes the results on twelve large scale data sets. KM-OMD did not return results on all data sets and MDO did not return results on KDD2010 in 48 hours due to the high computational cost. As can be seen, the overall performance of LDM is superior or highly competitive to SVM and other compared methods. Specifically, LDM performs significantly better than SVM, MDO, MAMC on 6, 7 and 12 over 12 data sets, respectively, and achieves the best accuracy on 8 data sets. In addition, the win/tie/loss counts show that LDM is always better or comparable, never worse than SVM.

4.4 Margin Distributions

Figure 1 plots the cumulative margin distribution of SVM and LDM on some representative regular scale data sets. The curves for other data sets are similar. The point where a curve and the x-axis crosses is the corresponding minimum margin. As can be seen, LDM usually has a little bit smaller minimum margin than SVM, whereas the LDM curve generally lies on the right side, showing that the

Table 3: Accuracy (mean±std.) comparison on regular scale data sets. RBF kernels are used. The best accuracy on each data set is bolded. •/∘ indicates the performance is significantly better/worse than SVM (paired t-tests at 95% significance level). The win/tie/loss counts are summarized in the last row. MDO does not have results since it is specified for the linear kernel.

Dataset	SVM	MDO	MAMC	KM-OMD	LDM
promoters	0.684±0.100	N/A	0.638±0.121∘	0.701±0.085	**0.715±0.074•**
planning-relax	**0.708±0.035**	N/A	0.706±0.034	0.683±0.031∘	0.707±0.034
colic	0.822±0.033	N/A	0.623±0.037∘	0.825±0.024	**0.841±0.018•**
parkinsons	**0.929±0.029**	N/A	0.852±0.036∘	0.906±0.033∘	0.927±0.029
colic.ORIG	0.638±0.043	N/A	0.623±0.027	0.621±0.039	**0.641±0.044**
sonar	0.842±0.034	N/A	0.753±0.052∘	0.821±0.051∘	**0.846±0.032**
vote	0.946±0.016	N/A	0.913±0.019∘	0.930±0.029∘	**0.968±0.013•**
house	0.953±0.020	N/A	0.561±0.139∘	0.938±0.022∘	**0.964±0.013•**
heart	0.808±0.025	N/A	0.540±0.043∘	0.805±0.048	**0.822±0.029•**
breast-cancer	0.729±0.030	N/A	0.706±0.027∘	0.691±0.024∘	**0.753±0.027•**
haberman	0.727±0.024	N/A	**0.742±0.021•**	0.676±0.042∘	0.731±0.027
vehicle	0.992±0.007	N/A	0.924±0.025∘	0.988±0.008∘	**0.993±0.006**
clean1	0.890±0.020	N/A	0.561±0.025∘	0.772±0.043∘	**0.891±0.024**
wdbc	0.951±0.011	N/A	0.740±0.042∘	0.941±0.040	**0.961±0.010•**
isolet	0.998±0.002	N/A	0.994±0.004∘	0.995±0.003∘	**0.998±0.002**
credit-a	0.858±0.014	N/A	0.542±0.032∘	0.845±0.029∘	**0.861±0.013**
austra	0.853±0.013	N/A	0.560±0.018∘	0.854±0.017	**0.857±0.014•**
australian	0.815±0.014	N/A	0.554±0.015∘	**0.860±0.014•**	0.854±0.016•
fourclass	**0.998±0.003**	N/A	0.791±0.014∘	0.838±0.014∘	0.998±0.003
german	0.731±0.019	N/A	0.697±0.017∘	0.742±0.017•	**0.743±0.016•**
Ave. accuracy	0.844	N/A	0.701	0.822	0.854
LDM: w/t/l	10/10/0	N/A	18/1/1	15/5/0	

Table 4: Accuracy (mean±std.) comparison on large scale data sets. Linear kernels are used. The best accuracy on each data set is bolded. •/∘ indicates the performance is significantly better/worse than SVM (paired t-tests at 95% significance level). The win/tie/loss counts are summarized in the last row. KM-OMD and MDO did not return results on some data sets in 48 hours.

Dataset	SVM	MDO	MAMC	KM-OMD	LDM
farm-ads	0.880±0.007	0.880±0.007	0.759±0.038∘	N/A	**0.890±0.008•**
news20	0.954±0.002	0.948±0.002∘	0.772±0.017∘	N/A	**0.960±0.001•**
adult-a	0.845±0.002	0.788±0.053∘	0.759±0.002∘	N/A	**0.846±0.003•**
w8a	0.983±0.001	**0.985±0.001•**	0.971±0.001∘	N/A	0.983±0.001
cod-rna	**0.899±0.001**	0.774±0.203	0.667±0.001∘	N/A	0.899±0.001
real-sim	0.961±0.001	0.955±0.002∘	0.744±0.004∘	N/A	**0.971±0.001•**
ijcnn1	0.921±0.003	**0.921±0.002**	0.904±0.001∘	N/A	0.921±0.002
skin	0.934±0.001	0.929±0.003∘	0.792±0.000∘	N/A	**0.934±0.001**
covtype	0.762±0.001	0.760±0.003∘	0.628±0.002∘	N/A	**0.763±0.001**
rcv1	0.969±0.000	0.959±0.000∘	0.913±0.000∘	N/A	**0.977±0.000•**
url	**0.993±0.006**	0.993±0.006	0.670±0.000∘	N/A	0.993±0.006
kdd2010	0.852±0.001	N/A	0.853±0.000•	N/A	**0.881±0.001•**
Ave. accuracy	0.913	0.899	0.786	N/A	0.919
LDM: w/t/l	6/6/0	7/3/1	12/0/0	N/A	

margin distribution of LDM is generally better than that of SVM. In other words, for most examples, LDM generally produce a larger margin than SVM.

4.5 Time Cost

We compare the time cost of LDM and SVM on the twelve large scale data sets. All the experiments are performed with MATLAB 2012b on a machine with 8×2.60 GHz CPUs and 16GB main memory. The average CPU time (in seconds) on each data set is shown in Figure 2. We denote SVM implemented by the LIBLINEAR [9] package as SVM_l and SVM implemented by ASGD[4] as SVM_a, respectively. It can be seen that, both SVM_a and LDM are much faster than SVM_l, owing to the use of ASGD. LDM is just slightly slower than SVM_a on three data sets (news20, real-sim and skin) but highly competitive with SVM_a on the other nine data sets. Note that both SVM_l and SVM_a are very fast implementa-

[4]http://leon.bottou.org/projects/sgd

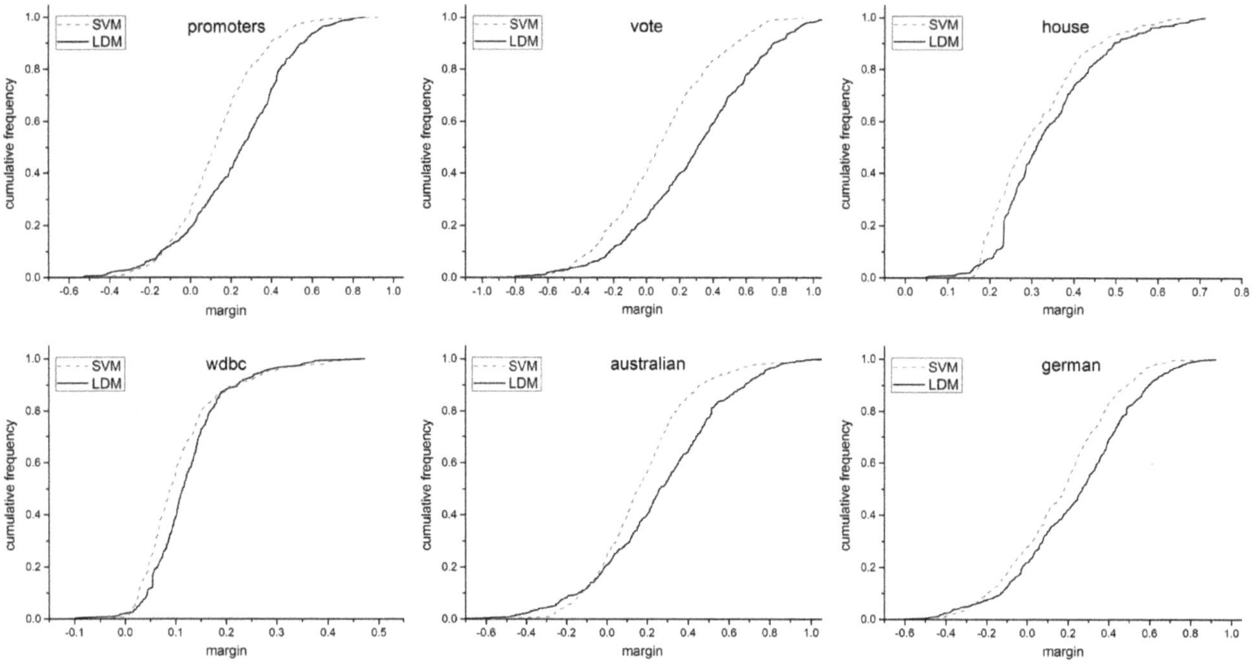

Figure 1: Cumulative frequency (y-axis) with respect to margin (x-axis) of SVM and LDM on some representative regular scale data sets. The more right the curve, the larger the accumulated margin.

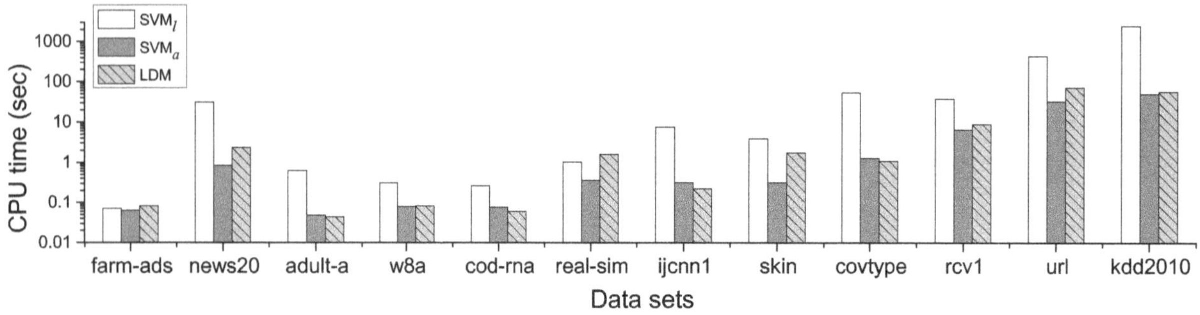

Figure 2: CPU time on the large scale data sets.

tions of SVMs; this shows that LDM is also computationally efficient.

4.6 Parameter Influence

LDM has three regularization parameters, i.e., λ_1, λ_2 and C. In previous empirical studies, they are set according to cross validation. Figure 3 further studies the influence of them on some representative regular scale data sets by fixing other parameters. Specifically, Figure 3(a) shows the influence of λ_1 on the accuracy by varying it from 2^{-8} to 2^{-2} while fixing λ_2 and C as the value suggested by the cross validation described in Section 4.1. Figure 3(b) and Figure 3(c) are obtained in the same way. It can be seen that, the performance of LDM is not very sensitive to the setting of the parameters, making LDM even more attractive in practice.

5. RELATED WORK

There are a few studies considered margin distribution in SVM-like algorithms [12, 18, 1]. Garg et al. [12] proposed the Margin Distribution Optimization (MDO) algorithm which minimizes the sum of the cost of each instance, where the cost is a function which assigns larger values to instances with smaller margins. MDO can be viewed as a method of optimizing weighted margin combination, where the weights are related to the margins. The objective function optimized by MDO, however, is non-convex, and thus, it may get stuck in local minima. In addition, MDO can only be used for linear kernel. As our experiments in Section 4 disclosed, the performance of MDO is inferior to LDM.

Pelckmans et al. [18] proposed the Maximal Average Margin for Classifiers (MAMC) and it can be viewed as a special case of LDM assuming that the margin variance is zero. MAMC has a closed-form solution, however, it will degenerate to a trivial solution when the classes are not with equal sizes. Our experiments in Section 4 showed that LDM is clearly superior to MAMC.

Aiolli et al. [1] proposed a Kernel Method for the direct Optimization of the Margin Distribution (KM-OMD) from a game theoretical perspective. Similar to MDO, this method

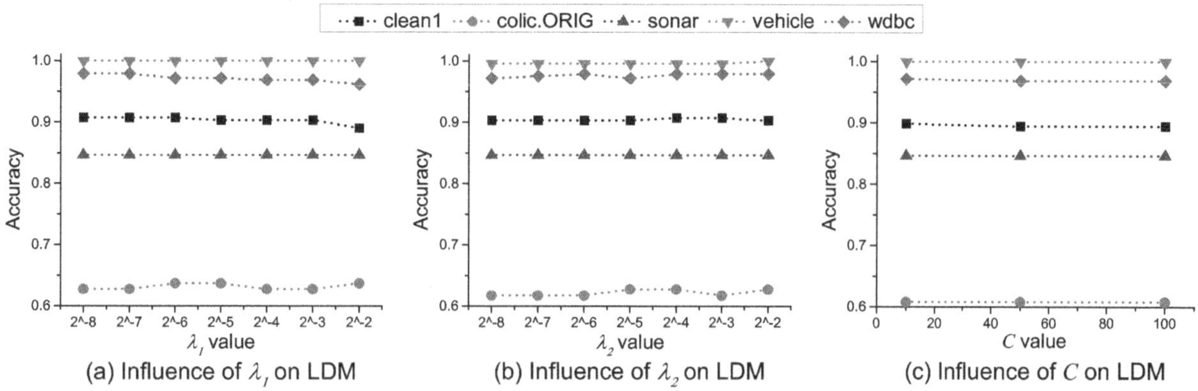

Figure 3: Parameter influence on some representative regular scale data sets.

also directly optimizes a weighted combination of margins over the training data, ignoring the influence of margin variances. Besides, this method considers hard-margin only, which may be another reason why it behaves worse than our method. It is noteworthy that the computational cost prohibits KM-OMD to be applied to large scale data, as shown in Table 4.

6. CONCLUSIONS

Support vector machines work by maximizing the minimum margin. Recent theoretical results suggested that the margin distribution, rather than a single-point margin such as the minimum margin, is more crucial to the generalization performance. In this paper, we propose the large margin distribution machine (LDM) which tries to optimize the margin distribution by maximizing the margin mean and minimizing the margin variance simultaneously. The LDM is a general learning approach which can be used in any place where SVM can be applied. Comprehensive experiments on twenty regular scale data sets and twelve large scale data sets validate the superiority of LDM to SVMs and many state-of-the-art methods. In the future it will be interesting to generalize the idea of LDM to regression and other learning settings.

7. ACKNOWLEDGMENTS

The authors want to thank anonymous reviewers for helpful comments and suggestions. This research was supported by the National Science Foundation of China (61333014) and the National Key Basic Research Program of China (2014CB340501).

8. REFERENCES

[1] F. Aiolli, G. San Martino, and A. Sperduti. A kernel method for the optimization of the margin distribution. In *Proceedings of the 18th International Conference on Artificial Neural Networks*, pages 305–314, Prague, Czech, 2008.

[2] A. Bordes, L. Bottou, and P. Gallinari. Sgd-qn: Careful quasi-newton stochastic gradient descent. *Journal of Machine Learning Research*, 10:1737–1754, 2009.

[3] L. Bottou. Large-scale machine learning with stochastic gradient descent. In *Proceedings of the 19th International Conference on Computational Statistics*, pages 177–186, Paris, France, 2010.

[4] L. Breiman. Prediction games and arcing classifiers. *Neural Computation*, 11(7):1493–1517, 1999.

[5] C. Cortes and V. Vapnik. Support-vector networks. *Machine Learning*, 20(3):273–297, 1995.

[6] A. Cotter, S. Shalev-shwartz, and N. Srebro. Learning optimally sparse support vector machines. In *Proceedings of the 30th International Conference on Machine Learning*, pages 266–274, Atlanta, GA, 2013.

[7] N. Cristianini and J. Shawe-Taylor. *An Introduction to Support Vector Machines and Other Kernel-based Learning Methods*. Cambridge University Press, Cambridge, UK, 2000.

[8] H. Do and K. Alexandre. Convex formulations of radius-margin based support vector machines. In *Proceedings of the 30th International Conference on Machine Learning*, pages 169–177, Atlanta, GA, 2013.

[9] R. E. Fan, K. W. Chang, C. J. Hsieh, X. R. Wang, and C. J. Lin. Liblinear: A library for large linear classification. *Journal of Machine Learning Research*, 9:1871–1874, 2008.

[10] Y. Freund and R. E. Schapire. A decision-theoretic generalization of on-line learning and an application to boosting. In *Proceedings of the 2nd European Conference on Computational Learning Theory*, pages 23–37, Barcelona, Spain, 1995.

[11] W. Gao and Z.-H. Zhou. On the doubt about margin explanation of boosting. *Artificial Intelligence*, 199–200:22–44, 2013.

[12] A. Garg and D. Roth. Margin distribution and learning algorithms. In *Proceedings of the 20th International Conference on Machine Learning*, pages 210–217, Washington, DC, 2003.

[13] C. J. Hsieh, K. W. Chang, C. J. Lin, S. S. Keerthi, and S. Sundararajan. A dual coordinate descent method for large-scale linear svm. In *Proceedings of the 25th International Conference on Machine Learning*, pages 408–415, Helsinki, Finland, 2008.

[14] C. Jose, P. Goyal, P. Aggrwal, and M. Varma. Local deep kernel learning for efficient non-linear svm prediction. In *Proceedings of the 30th International Conference on Machine Learning*, pages 486–494, Atlanta, GA, 2013.

[15] H. J. Kushner and G. G. Yin. *Stochastic approximation and recursive algorithms and applications; 2nd ed.* Springer, New York, 2003.

[16] S. Lacoste-julien, M. Jaggi, M. Schmidt, and P. Pletscher. Block-coordinate frank-wolfe optimization for structural svms. In *Proceedings of the 30th International Conference on Machine Learning*, pages 53–61, Atlanta, GA, 2013.

[17] A. Luntz and V. Brailovsky. On estimation of characters obtained in statistical procedure of recognition (in russian). *Technicheskaya Kibernetica*, 3, 1969.

[18] K. Pelckmans, J. Suykens, and B. D. Moor. A risk minimization principle for a class of parzen estimators. In J. Platt, D. Koller, Y. Singer, and S. Roweis, editors, *Advances in Neural Information Processing Systems 20*, pages 1137–1144. MIT Press, Cambridge, MA, 2008.

[19] B. T. Polyak and A. B. Juditsky. Acceleration of stochastic approximation by averaging. *SIAM Journal on Control and Optimization*, 30(4):838–855, 1992.

[20] L. Reyzin and R. E. Schapire. How boosting the margin can also boost classifier complexity. In *Proceedings of 23rd International Conference on Machine Learning*, pages 753–760, Pittsburgh, PA, 2006.

[21] R. E. Schapire, Y. Freund, P. L. Bartlett, and W. S. Lee. Boosting the margin: a new explanation for the effectives of voting methods. *Annuals of Statistics*, 26(5):1651–1686, 1998.

[22] B. Schölkopf and A. Smola. *Learning with kernels: support vector machines, regularization, optimization, and beyond.* MIT Press, Cambridge, MA, 2001.

[23] S. Shalev-Shwartz, Y. Singer, and N. Srebro. Pegasos: Primal estimated sub-gradient solver for svm. In *Proceedings of the 24th International Conference on Machine Learning*, pages 807–814, Helsinki, Finland, 2007.

[24] O. Shamir and T. Zhang. Stochastic gradient descent for non-smooth optimization: Convergence results and optimal averaging schemes. In *Proceedings of the 30th International Conference on Machine Learning*, pages 71–79, Atlanta, GA, 2013.

[25] M. Takac, A. Bijral, P. Richtarik, and N. Srebro. Mini-batch primal and dual methods for svms. In *Proceedings of the 30th International Conference on Machine Learning*, pages 1022–1030, Atlanta, GA, 2013.

[26] V. Vapnik. *The Nature of Statistical Learning Theory.* Springer-Verlag, New York, 1995.

[27] L. W. Wang, M. Sugiyama, C. Yang, Z.-H. Zhou, and J. Feng. A refined margin analysis for boosting algorithms via equilibrium margin. *Journal of Machine Learning Research*, 12:1835–1863, 2011.

[28] W. Xu. Towards optimal one pass large scale learning with averaged stochastic gradient descent. *CoRR, abs/1107.2490*, 2011.

[29] G. X. Yuan, C. H. Ho, and C. J. Lin. Recent advances of large-scale linear classification. *Proceedings of the IEEE*, 100(9):2584–2603, 2012.

[30] T. Zhang. Solving large scale linear prediction problems using stochastic gradient descent algorithms. In *Proceedings of the 21st International Conference on Machine learning*, pages 116–123, Banff, Canada, 2004.

[31] Z.-H. Zhou. *Ensemble Methods: Foundations and Algorithms.* CRC Press, Boca Raton, FL, 2012.

Distance Metric Learning Using Dropout: A Structured Regularization Approach

Qi Qian[†], Juhua Hu[‡], Rong Jin[†], Jian Pei[‡] and Shenghuo Zhu[⋆]
[†]Department of Computer Science and Engineering
Michigan State University, East Lansing, MI, 48824, USA
[‡]School of Computing Science
Simon Fraser University, 8888 University Drive, Burnaby, BC, V5A 1S6
[⋆]NEC Laboratories America, Cupertino, CA, 95014, USA
{qianqi, rongjin}@cse.msu.edu, juhuah@sfu.ca, jpei@cs.sfu.ca, zsh@nec-labs.com

ABSTRACT

Distance metric learning (DML) aims to learn a distance metric better than Euclidean distance. It has been successfully applied to various tasks, e.g., classification, clustering and information retrieval. Many DML algorithms suffer from the over-fitting problem because of a large number of parameters to be determined in DML. In this paper, we exploit the dropout technique, which has been successfully applied in deep learning to alleviate the over-fitting problem, for DML. Different from the previous studies that only apply dropout to training data, we apply dropout to both the learned metrics and the training data. We illustrate that application of dropout to DML is essentially equivalent to matrix norm based regularization. Compared with the standard regularization scheme in DML, dropout is advantageous in simulating the structured regularizers which have shown consistently better performance than non structured regularizers. We verify, both empirically and theoretically, that dropout is effective in regulating the learned metric to avoid the over-fitting problem. Last, we examine the idea of wrapping the dropout technique in the state-of-art DML methods and observe that the dropout technique can significantly improve the performance of the original DML methods.

Categories and Subject Descriptors

H.2.8 [**Database Management**]: Database Applications—*Data Mining*; I.2.6 [**Artificial Intelligence**]: Learning

General Terms

Algorithms, Experimentation

Keywords

Distance Metric Learning, Dropout

KDD'14, August 24–27, 2014, New York, NY, USA.

http://dx.doi.org/10.1145/2623330.2623678.

1. INTRODUCTION

Learning a good distance metric is essential to distance based algorithms and applications, e.g., k-nearest neighbors, k-means clustering, content-based image retrieval (CBIR), etc. Distance metric learning (DML) aims to learn a linear mapping such that in the mapped space, examples from the same class are closer to each other than those from different classes. Many methods have been developed for DML [6, 7, 16, 26, 27] in the past, and DML has been successfully applied in various domains, including information retrieval [13], ranking [6], supervised classification [26], clustering [27], semi-supervised clustering [5] and domain adaptation [20].

One problem with DML is that since the number of parameters to be determined in DML is quadratic in the dimension, it may overfit the training data [26], and lead to a suboptimal solution. Although several heuristics, such as early stopping, have been developed to alleviate the over-fitting problem [26], their performance is usually sensitive to the setting of parameters (e.g. stopping criterion in early stopping), making it difficult for practitioners. Another problem with many existing DML methods is their high computational cost since they have to project intermediate solutions onto the Positive Semi-Definite (PSD) cone at every iteration to ensure that the learned metric is PSD. In [6], the authors show that it is possible to avoid the high cost of PSD projection by an one-projection paradigm that only needs to project the learned metric onto the PSD cone once at the end of the optimization algorithm. We adopt the one-projection paradigm in this paper to alleviate the high computational cost.

Recently, dropout has been found to be helpful in alleviating the over-fitting problem in training deep neural networks [14]. It randomly omits half of the feature detectors to prevent the complex co-adaptation between those neurons. The main intuition behind dropout is that it improves the robustness of individual neurons in order to avoid the over-fitting problem. Theoretical analysis about the regularization role of dropout in neural network can be found in [1]. Besides the success in deep learning, dropout has been applied to regression [24] in order to obtain robust feature representations. Features with artificial noises has been a classic topic in machine learning and data mining, and has been examined by many studies [17, 19] with the focus on additive noise that usually leads to a L_2 regularizer [2]. Wager *et al.* [25] analyze dropout within the framework of regression and find that dropout is first-order equivalent to a L_2 regularizer for the dataset scaled by the inverse diagonal Fisher information matrix. Although dropout has received a lot of interests in machine learning and data mining community, to the best of our knowledge, this is the first study that exploits dropout for alleviating the over-fitting problem in DML.

In this paper, we, for the first time, introduce dropout to DML. Unlike previous studies on dropout that only apply dropout to training data, we apply dropout to both the learned metrics and the training data. By applying appropriate dropout probabilities to the learned metric, we show that dropout can be equivalent to Frobenius norm and L_p in expectation. In addition, we develop a structured regularizer using the dropout technique. Unlike the conventional regularizer that treats diagonal and off diagonal elements equivalently, the structured regularizer introduces different dropout probabilities for diagonal elements and off diagonal elements. To verify the effect of dropout in DML, we have conducted a comprehensive study that compares the dropout technique to other regularization techniques used in DML. Experimental results show that dropout significantly improves the classification performance on most datasets. In addition, we observe that dropout behaves like a trace norm based regularizer in DML when applied to training data: it controls the rank of the learned metric and leads to a skewed distribution of eigenvalues. This is in contrast to the previous studies that view dropout as a L_2 regularizer. Finally, we show that the dropout technique can be easily incorporated into the state-of-art DML methods and significantly improve their performance for most cases. The main contribution of this work is summarized as follows.

- We, for the first time, introduce dropout to DML and apply it to both the learned metric and the training data.
- We show that it is possible to construct structured regularizers using the dropout technique, and verify its performance, both theoretically and empirically.
- We apply the dropout to the state-of-art DML methods and show it can significantly enhance their performance.

The rest of the paper is organized as follows. Section 2 introduces the related DML methods and the analysis for dropout. Section 3 describes applying dropout to the learned metric and training data, respectively. Section 4 summarizes the results of the empirical study. Section 5 concludes this work and discusses the future directions.

2. RELATED WORK

Distance metric learning has been studied sufficiently during the past years [6, 7, 22, 26, 27] and detailed investigations could be found in the survey papers [15, 28]. The early works focus on optimizing pair-wise constraints [7, 27] to make sure the distance between examples from the same class is less than a pre-defined threshold while that from the different classes is larger than the other threshold. Nowadays, triplet constraints, where the distance of examples from the same class should be marginally smaller than that of examples from different classes, are preferred [6, 26] due to their superior performance compared with pair-wise constraints. More analysis shows that triplet constraints have the large margin property and could be explained as learning a set of local SVMs [8]. However, either taking pair-wise constraints or triplet constraints increases the number of training data exponentially, which significantly promotes the risk of over-fitting for DML. In fact, over-fitting phenomenon is reported by many DML methods [6, 26], and most of them try to alleviate it by PSD constraint. PSD constraint, on one hand, is the feasible set where the optimal metric should live in, and on the other hand, restricts the learned metric in the PSD cone to reduce the complexity of the model. Given a huge number of constraints, stochastic gradient descent (SGD) is widely used to learn the metric and PSD projection occurs at every iteration [23]. Unfortunately, the computational cost of PSD projection is cubic to the dimension of data, which significantly limits the application of DML in high dimensional datasets. Additionally, recent empirical study [6] demonstrates that one-projection paradigm, which only performs PSD projection once at the end of the algorithm, has the similar performance as projecting at every iteration. In this paper, we bring dropout to overcome over-fitting in DML. We adopt triplet constraints and one-projection paradigm setting, and show that dropout significantly improves the performance of existing DML methods.

Dropout is a technique developed for training deep neural networks [14]. Since deep neural network is a very complex model and is easy to overfit a small size of training data, dropout randomly omits half of neurons during training to limit the co-adaptation between neurons. Dropout makes sure that each learned neuron is robust. Besides deep learning, dropout has been introduced to more general regression task these years [24, 25]. Maaten *et al.* [24] use dropout to learn a robust feature representation for bag-of-words features, which significantly improves the performance over the original features. Although dropout belongs to the classic artificially corrupted features, it is better than other kinds of noises as reported in the work [24]. Recently, Wager *et al.* [25] analyze dropout within the framework of general regression task, and find that dropout is first-order equivalent to the L_2 regularizer on the rescaled data. The experiments in the study [25] demonstrate that dropout, as a data-dependent L_2 regularizer, outperforms the standard L_2 norm significantly. In this paper, we introduce dropout for DML. Unlike the previous works that focus on dropout in features [24, 25], we also apply dropout for the learned metric. We observe that dropout is equivalent to Frobenius norm, L_1 norm and trace norm with different dropout strategies. Empirical study validates the effectiveness of dropout in DML.

3. DML USING DROPOUT

Given the dataset $X = [\mathbf{x}_1, \cdots, \mathbf{x}_n] \in \mathbb{R}^{d\times n}$, distance metric learning is to learn a good Mahalanobis distance metric M, so that for each triplet constraint $(\mathbf{x}_i, \mathbf{x}_j, \mathbf{x}_k)$, where x_i and x_j are in the same class and x_k is from a different class, we have

$$\mathrm{dist}(\mathbf{x}_i, \mathbf{x}_k) - \mathrm{dist}(\mathbf{x}_i, \mathbf{x}_j) > 1$$

where $\mathrm{dist}(\mathbf{x}_i, \mathbf{x}_j)$ is the squared Mahalanobis distance between $\mathbf{x}_i$ and $\mathbf{x}_j$ and is measured by

$$\mathrm{dist}(\mathbf{x}_i, \mathbf{x}_j) = (\mathbf{x}_i - \mathbf{x}_j)^\top M(\mathbf{x}_i - \mathbf{x}_j)$$

Algorithm 1 SGD for DML

1: **Input:** Dataset $X \in \mathbb{R}^{d\times n}$, #Iterations T, Stepsize η
2: Initial M_0 as an identity matrix
3: **for** $t = 1, \cdots, T$ **do**
4: Randomly sample a triplet $\{\mathbf{x}_i^t, \mathbf{x}_j^t, \mathbf{x}_k^t\}$
5: $\boxed{M_t = M_{t-1} - \eta\nabla\ell}$
6: **end for**
7: **return** $\Pi_{psd}(\bar{M})$

Therefore, the objective optimization problem based on minimizing empirical risk could be written as

$$\min_{M\in S_+^d} \sum_t \ell(\langle A_t, M\rangle)$$

where S_+^d is the $d\times d$ symmetric PSD cone, $\ell(\cdot)$ is the convex loss function, and $A_t = (\mathbf{x}_i^t - \mathbf{x}_j^t)(\mathbf{x}_i^t - \mathbf{x}_j^t)^\top - (\mathbf{x}_i^t - \mathbf{x}_k^t)(\mathbf{x}_i^t - \mathbf{x}_k^t)^\top$. $\langle\cdot,\cdot\rangle$ denotes the dot product for matrix.

Since the number of triplets is very large (it can be as high as $\mathcal{O}(n^3)$), the optimization problem is usually solved by stochastic gradient descent (SGD) [7, 23]. Instead of projecting the learned metric onto PSD cone at every iteration, which can be an expensive operation, we adopt one-projection paradigm [6], which only projects the learned metric onto the PSD cone once at the end of iterations. Empirical studies have shown that one-projection-paradigm is significantly more efficient and yields the similar performance as SGD with PSD projection performed at every iteration. Therefore, in this work, we will focus on the following optimization problem without the PSD constraint.

$$\min_{M\in S^d} \sum_t \ell(\langle A_t, M\rangle)$$

Algorithm 1 gives the standard SGD algorithm for DML and dropout will be applied to perturb Step 5. We will discuss the details in the next section within this framework. In particular, we will discuss two different applications of dropout, i.e. application of dropout to the learned metric and application of dropout to the training data, in the following two subsections.

3.1 Applying Dropout to Distance Metric

In this section, we focus on applying dropout to the learned metric. Let M be the metric learned from the previous iteration. To apply the dropout technique, we introduce a Bernoulli random matrix $\delta = [\delta_{i,j}]_{i,j=1}^d$, where each $\delta_{i,j}$ is a Bernoulli random variable with $\delta_{i,j} = \delta_{j,i}$. Using the random matrix δ, we compute the dropped out distance metric, denoted by $\hat{M}$ as

$$\hat{M}_{i,j} = \delta_{i,j} M_{i,j}, \quad i,j = 1,\ldots,d$$

Note that by enforcing $\delta_{i,j} = \delta_{j,i}$, $\hat{M}$ is ensured to be a symmetric matrix. Below, we will discuss how to design the dropout probabilities for the Bernoulli random matrix δ to simulate the effect of Frobenius norm based regularization and L_1 norm based regularization, respectively.

3.1.1 Frobenius norm

Frobenius norm is the most widely used regularizer in DML [23, 26], and the standard DML problem with Frobenius norm is given by

$$\min_{M\in S^d} \frac{1}{T}\sum_{t=1}^T \ell(\langle A_t, M\rangle) + \frac{q}{2\eta}\|M\|_F^2 \quad (1)$$

The updating rule in SGD for Frobenius norm based regularization is

$$M_t = M_{t-1} - qM_{t-1} - \eta\nabla\ell_t(M_{t-1})$$

where $\ell_t(M) = \ell(\langle A_t, M\rangle)$.

Instead of using the regularizer directly, we could simulate the effect of Frobenius norm based regularization by applying dropout to the learned metric M_{t-1}. In particular, the Bernoulli random matrix δ is constructed by sampling each $\delta_{i,j:i\leq j}$ independently from a Bernoulli distribution with $\Pr[\delta = 0] = q$ and setting $\delta_{j,i} = \delta_{i,j}$ to ensure that δ is symmetric. It is easy to verify that

$$E[\hat{M}_{t-1}] = (1-q)M_{t-1}$$

and the updating rule becomes

$$M_t = \hat{M}_{t-1} - \eta\nabla\ell_t(M_{t-1})$$

THEOREM 1. *Let M_* be the optimal solution output by Algorithm 1. Let $\bar{M}$ be the solution output by Algorithm 1 with dropout in Step 5 and q be the probability that dropout occurs in each item of the learned metric. Assume $|\mathbf{x}|_2 \leq r$ and $q = 1/T$, we have*

$$E[\ell(\bar{M})] - \ell(M_*) \leq \frac{1}{\eta T}\|M_*\|_F^2 + 8\eta r^2(1 + \frac{1}{T})$$

The detailed proof can be found in appendix. By setting the stepsize η as

$$\eta = \frac{\|M_*\|_F}{r\sqrt{8+8T}}$$

we have

$$E[\ell(\bar{M})] - \ell(M_*) \leq \frac{4r\sqrt{2+2T}}{T}\|M_*\|_F = \mathcal{O}(1/\sqrt{T})$$

It is well known that $\mathcal{O}(1/\sqrt{T})$ is the minimax convergence rate for SGD, when the loss function is Lipschitz continuous [11, 12, 29]. As a result, with the appropriate choice of dropout probabilities, dropout will maintain the same convergence rate as the standard SGD method. We also notice that q is suggested to be set as $1/T$ in order to achieve $O(1/\sqrt{T})$ convergence. This result implies that dropout should not be taken too frequently, which is consistent with the analysis of other corrupted feature methods [2, 24]. Finally, since the derivation of convergence rates keep the same regardless of the sampling probabilities used in dropout, we thus will omit the analysis on convergence for the following cases.

3.1.2 L_1 norm

Besides Frobenius norm, L_1 norm also could be used in DML as

$$\min_{M\in S^d} \frac{1}{T}\sum_t \ell(\langle A_t, M\rangle) + \frac{q}{\eta}\|M\|_1$$

It is known as the composite optimization problem [18] and could be solved by iterative thresholding method

$$\begin{cases} M_t' = M_{t-1} - \eta\nabla\ell_t(M_{t-1}) \\ M_{t:i,j} = \text{sign}(M_{t:i,j}')\max\{0, |M_{t:i,j}'| - q\} \end{cases}$$

With different design of sampling probabilities, we can apply dropout to the learned metric to simulate the effect of L_1 regularization. In particular, we introduce a data-dependent dropout probability as

$$\Pr[\delta_{i,j}=0]=\min\{1,\frac{q}{|M_{i,j}|}\}$$

Now, instead of perturbing M_{t-1}, we apply dropout to M'_t, i.e. the matrix after the gradient mapping. It is easy to verify that the expectation of the perturbed matrix $\hat{M}'$ is given by

$$E\left[[\hat{M}'_t]_{i,j}\right]=\left\{\begin{array}{lcl}[M'_t]_{i,j}-\mathrm{sign}([M'_t]_{i,j})q & : & q\leq|[M'_t]_{i,j}| \\ 0 & : & q>|[M'_t]_{i,j}|\end{array}\right.$$

which is equivalent to the thresholding method stated above.

It is straightforward to extend the method to L_p norm

$$L_p(M)=(\sum_{i,j}|M_{i,j}|^p)^{1/p}$$

by setting the probability as

$$\Pr[\delta_{i,j}=0]=\min\{1,\frac{q|M_{i,j}|^{p-2}}{(\sum_{i,j}M_{i,j}^p)^{1-1/p}}\}$$

Note that when $p=1$, it is equivalent to the probability for L_1 norm.

3.1.3 *Structured regularizer*

Although these conventional regularizers have been applied for DML, they cannot exploit the structure of metrics sufficiently. Given a distance metric, the diagonal elements are more important than those from off diagonal. It is due to the fact that diagonal elements represent the importance of each feature (e.g., linear classifier) rather than the interactions between different features, and they also control the trace of the learned metric. Therefore, different regularizers should be assigned for diagonal and off diagonal elements, respectively. Fortunately, dropout can serve this purpose conveniently.

Given Q, which is a random matrix with each element from a uniform distribution in $[0,1]$, we investigate the matrix

$$R=(Q+Q^\top)/2 \tag{2}$$

It is obvious that the diagonal elements of R are still from the same uniform distribution, while elements in off diagonal are from a triangle distribution with cumulative distribution function as

$$F(q)=\left\{\begin{array}{rcl}2q^2 & : & 0\leq q<0.5 \\ 1-2(1-q)^2 & : & 0.5\leq q\leq 1\end{array}\right.$$

Figure 1 illustrates the cumulative distribution function for the diagonal elements of R and those living in off diagonal. The dropout probability based on the random matrix R is defined as

$$\Pr[\delta_{i,j}=0]=\Pr[R_{i,j}\leq q]$$

First, we consider dropout with the same probability for each item of the metric as for Frobenius norm. Then, the probability of δ is

$$\Pr[\delta_{i,j}=0]=\Pr[R_{i,j}\leq q]=\left\{\begin{array}{lcl}q & : & i=j \\ 2q^2 & : & i\neq j\end{array}\right. \tag{3}$$

Figure 1: Cumulative distribution function for diagonal elements and those in off diagonal.

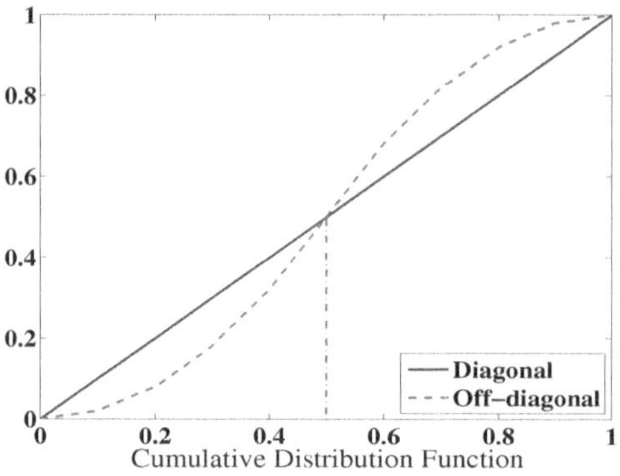

Algorithm 2 Dropout as Structured Frobenius Norm (SGD-M1)

Input: Dataset $X\in\mathbb{R}^{d\times n}$, #Iterations T, Stepsize η
Initial M_0 as an identity matrix
for $t=1,\cdots,T$ **do**
  Randomly sample a triplet $(\mathbf{x}_i^t,\mathbf{x}_j^t,\mathbf{x}_k^t)$
  Generate random matrix R as in Eqn. 2
  Generate dropout parameters δ by Eqn. 3
  Dropout: $\hat{M}_{t-1}=\delta M_{t-1}$
  $M_t=\hat{M}_{t-1}-\eta\nabla\ell$
end for
return $\Pi_{psd}(\bar{M})$

since $q=1/T\ll 0.5$ as indicated in Theorem 1.

Therefore, the expectation of $\hat{M}_{t-1}$ is

$$\hat{M}_{t-1}=\left\{\begin{array}{lcl}M_{i,j}^{t-1}-qM_{i,j}^{t-1} & : & i=j \\ M_{i,j}^{t-1}-2q^2M_{i,j}^{t-1} & : & i\neq j\end{array}\right.$$

which is equivalent to solving the following problem

$$\min_{M\in S^d}\frac{1}{T}\sum_t\ell(\langle A_t,M\rangle)+\frac{q}{2\eta}\sum_i^d M_{i,i}^2+\frac{q^2}{\eta}\sum_{i,j:i\neq j}M_{i,j}^2$$

It is obvious that the L_2 norm of diagonal elements in the metric is penalized quadratically more than those from off diagonal. This regularizer seems complex but the implementation by dropout is quite straightforward and Algorithm 2 summarizes the method.

Then, we consider dropout with the probability based on the elements as

$$\Pr[\delta_{i,j}=0]=\Pr[R_{i,j}\leq\min\{1,\frac{q}{|M_{i,j}|}\}] \tag{4}$$

$$=\left\{\begin{array}{rcl}\min\{1,q/|M_{i,j}|\} & : & i=j \\ 2(q/|M_{i,j}|)^2 & : & i\neq j,q<0.5|M_{i,j}| \\ 1-2(1-q/|M_{i,j}|)^2 & : & i\neq j,0.5\leq q/|M_{i,j}|\leq 1 \\ 1 & : & q>|M_{i,j}|\end{array}\right.$$

It seems too complicated to analyze at the first glance, but Figure 1 could help us to understand the dropout strategy clearly. For the diagonal elements, they are actually shrunk by q as the L_1 regularizer. For the off diagonal elements, if $|M_{i,j}|>2q$, the red dashed curve is under the blue solid one, which means the shrinkage is less than q. When $q\leq|M_{i,j}|\leq 2q$, the red dashed curve stands above the blue solid

Algorithm 3 Dropout as Structured L_1 Norm (SGD-M2)

Input: Dataset $X \in \mathbb{R}^{d \times n}$, #Iterations T, Stepsize η
Initial M_0 as an identity matrix
for $t = 1, \cdots, T$ **do**
  Randomly sample a triplet $(\mathbf{x}_i^t, \mathbf{x}_j^t, \mathbf{x}_k^t)$
  $M_t' = M_{t-1} - \eta \nabla \ell$
  Generate random matrix R as in Eqn. 2
  Generate dropout parameters δ by Eqn. 4
  Dropout: $M_t = \delta M_t'$
end for
return $\Pi_{psd}(\bar{M})$

one and the shrinkage on these elements is much faster than the standard L_1 norm. Since q is very small, most of the off diagonal elements have relatively larger values and will be shrunk slower than those with extremely small values. Algorithm 3 summarizes this method. Unlike Algorithm 2, dropout in Algorithm 3 is performed after updating with the current gradient.

3.2 Applying Dropout to Training Data

Besides dropout within the learned metric, in this section we apply dropout to the training data as many pervious studies [24, 25]. Since the analysis for data highly depends on the loss function, we take the hinge loss, which is the most widely used loss function in DML [6, 7, 23, 26], as an example.

Hinge loss is defined as $\ell(z) = [1+z]_+$, where $z = \langle A_t, M\rangle$ and

$$A_t = (\mathbf{x}_i^t - \mathbf{x}_j^t)(\mathbf{x}_i^t - \mathbf{x}_j^t)^\top - (\mathbf{x}_i^t - \mathbf{x}_k^t)(\mathbf{x}_i^t - \mathbf{x}_k^t)^\top$$

Obviously, the loss function penalizes A_t rather than the individual example, so dropout is taken according to the structure of A_t. To avoid affecting the decision of hinge loss, we perturb A_t after calculating the hinge loss.

We begin with additive noise as

$$\hat{A}_t = (\mathbf{x}_i^t - \mathbf{x}_j^t + \epsilon)(\mathbf{x}_i^t - \mathbf{x}_j^t + \epsilon)^\top - (\mathbf{x}_i^t - \mathbf{x}_k^t)(\mathbf{x}_i^t - \mathbf{x}_k^t)^\top \quad (5)$$

where $\epsilon \sim \mathcal{N}(0, qI_{d\times d})$. So the expectation of $\hat{A}_t$ is

$$\begin{aligned} E[\hat{A}_t] &= E[(\mathbf{x}_i^t - \mathbf{x}_j^t + \epsilon)(\mathbf{x}_i^t - \mathbf{x}_j^t + \epsilon)^\top] \\ &\quad -(\mathbf{x}_i^t - \mathbf{x}_k^t)(\mathbf{x}_i^t - \mathbf{x}_k^t)^\top \\ &= A_t + qI \end{aligned}$$

By replacing A_t in Prob. 1 with $\hat{A}_t$, the expectation of the problem becomes

$$\min_{M\in S^d} \sum_t \ell(\langle A_t, M\rangle) + \sum_{t:\ell_t>0} q\|M\|_{tr} \quad (6)$$

Note that the trace norm stands outside of the hinge loss, since the noise is added only after computing the hinge loss and only active constraints will contribute to the trace norm. We use the trace norm rather than the trace of the metric, because the final metric will be projected onto the PSD cone, where the trace of metric is equivalent to the trace norm. Algorithm 4 describes the details of the method.

Although the Guassian noise could perform as the trace norm, the external noise may affect the solution. Therefore, we consider dropout as

$$\hat{\mathbf{x}}_i^t = \delta_t \mathbf{x}_i^t, \quad \hat{\mathbf{x}}_j^t = \delta_t \mathbf{x}_j^t$$

Algorithm 4 Additive Noise as Trace Norm (SGD-D1)

Input: Dataset $X \in \mathbb{R}^{d \times n}$, #Iterations T, Stepsize η
Initial M_0 as an identity matrix
for $t = 1, \cdots, T$ **do**
  Randomly sample a triplet $(\mathbf{x}_i^t, \mathbf{x}_j^t, \mathbf{x}_k^t)$
  if $\ell(A_t, M_{t-1}) > 0$ **then**
    Generate a Guassian noise vector ϵ
    Add noise as in Eqn. 5
    $M_t = M_{t-1} - \eta \hat{A}_t$
  end if
end for
return $\Pi_{psd}(\bar{M})$

Algorithm 5 Dropout as Trace Norm (SGD-D2)

Input: Dataset $X \in \mathbb{R}^{d \times n}$, #Iterations T, Stepsize η
Initial M_0 as an identity matrix
for $t = 1, \cdots, T$ **do**
  Randomly sample a triplet $(\mathbf{x}_i^t, \mathbf{x}_j^t, \mathbf{x}_k^t)$
  if $\ell(A_t, M_{t-1}) > 0$ **then**
    Dropout as in Eqn. 7
    $M_t = M_{t-1} - \eta \hat{A}_t$
  end if
end for
return $\Pi_{psd}(\bar{M})$

where δ_t is a binary value random variable and

$$\Pr[\delta_t = 1 + q/(\mathbf{x}_i^t - \mathbf{x}_j^t)^2] = 1/(1 + q/(\mathbf{x}_i^t - \mathbf{x}_j^t)^2)$$

It is obvious that $E[\delta_t] = 1$ and $V[\delta_t] = 1 + q/(\mathbf{x}_i^t - \mathbf{x}_j^t)^2$. Similar to the additive noise, we only apply dropout for the first item of A_t as

$$\hat{A}_t = (\hat{\mathbf{x}}_i^t - \hat{\mathbf{x}}_j^t)(\hat{\mathbf{x}}_i^t - \hat{\mathbf{x}}_j^t)^\top - (\mathbf{x}_i^t - \mathbf{x}_k^t)(\mathbf{x}_i^t - \mathbf{x}_k^t)^\top$$

Note that when we perform dropout to the training data according to this strategy, we actually drop the rows and the corresponding columns in the first component $(\mathbf{x}_i^t - \mathbf{x}_j^t)(\mathbf{x}_i^t - \mathbf{x}_j^t)^\top$ of A_t. Since the expectation of random variables in diagonal is the variance and it is 1 in off diagonal, the expectation of $\hat{A}$ is

$$\begin{aligned} E[\hat{A}_t] &= E[(\hat{\mathbf{x}}_i^t - \hat{\mathbf{x}}_j^t)(\hat{\mathbf{x}}_i^t - \hat{\mathbf{x}}_j^t)^\top] - (\mathbf{x}_i^t - \mathbf{x}_k^t)(\mathbf{x}_i^t - \mathbf{x}_k^t)^\top \\ &= A_t + qI \end{aligned}$$

By taking $\hat{A}_t$ back to Prob. 1, we obtain the same problem as Prob. 6. Algorithm 5 summarizes this dropout strategy for training data.

THEOREM 2. *Let M_* be the optimal solution output by Algorithm 1. Let $\bar{M}$ be the solution output by Algorithm 5 and q be the probability that dropout occurs in each feature of the dataset. Assume $|\mathbf{x}|_2 \le r$ and $q = 1/T$, we have*

$$E[\ell(\bar{M})] - \ell(M_*) \le \frac{\|M_*\|_F^2}{2\eta T} + 8\eta r^2 + \frac{4\eta r^2}{T}(2d+1) + \frac{\|M_*\|_{tr}}{T}$$

The detailed proof is referred in appendix. If we set the stepsize η as

$$\eta = \frac{\|M_*\|_F}{2r\sqrt{4T + 4d + 2}}$$

we have

$$\ell(\bar{M}) - \ell(M_*) \leq \frac{1}{T}\left(2r\sqrt{(4T+4d+2)}\|M_*\|_F + \|M_*\|_{tr}\right)$$

where $\mathcal{O}(1/\sqrt{T})$ convergence rate, the well known result for standard SGD, is also observed as in Theorem 1.

According to Theorem 2, applying dropout to training data with the appropriate component and dropout probability does not hurt the convergence performance of standard SGD method too. Furthermore, q is required to be sufficiently small to avoid the suboptimal solution, which is also consistent with the analysis in Theorem 1.

4. EXPERIMENTS

4.1 Experiments Setting

Six datasets from different application scenarios are used to verify the effectiveness of the proposed method. Table 1 summarizes the information of these datasets. *ta* is a social network dataset with 6 different categories of terrorist attacks [21]. *semeion* is a handwritten digit dataset downloaded directly from the UCI repository [9]. *caltech10* is a subset of Caltech256 image dataset [10] with 10 most popular categories and we use the version pre-processed by the study [6], where each image is represented by an 1,000-dimension vector. The other datasets are directly downloaded from LIBSVM database [4]. For *dna*, *protein* and *sensit*, we use the standard training/testing split provided by the original dataset. For the rest datasets, we randomly select 70% of data for training and use the remaining 30% for testing. For each dataset, we randomly select $T = 100,000$ active triplets (e.g., incur the positive hinge loss by Euclidean distance) within the range of 3-nearest same class neighbors as suggested by the study [26]. K-Nearest Neighbor (k=3) classifier is applied after obtaining the metric, since we optimize the triplets from 3-nearest neighbors. All experiments are repeated by 5 trials on different randomly generated triplet sets and the average result with standard deviation is reported.

4.2 Comparison with SGD Methods

In the first experiment, we compare the standard SGD for DML to five SGD variants including our proposed methods (i.e., SGD-M1, SGD-M2, SGD-D1, and SGD-D2). The methods are summarized as follows.

- **SGD**: stochastic gradient descent method as described in Algorithm 1.
- **SGD-PSD**: SGD with PSD projection at every iteration.
- **SGD-M1**: SGD with dropout for the learned metric as structured Frobenius norm (Algorithm 2).
- **SGD-M2**: SGD with dropout for the learned metric as structured L_1 norm (Algorithm 3).
- **SGD-D1**: SGD with additive Guassian noise in training data as trace norm (Algorithm 4).
- **SGD-D2**: SGD with dropout for training data as trace norm (Algorithm 5).

Euclidean distance is also included as the baseline method and denoted as "**Euclid**".

All of these SGD methods are applied on the same triplet set and take one-projection paradigm except SGD-PSD that projects the learned metric onto the PSD cone at every iteration. We search the stepsize η in $\{0.1, 1, 10\}$ by cross validation and $\eta = 1$ shows the best performance, so we fix it for all experiments. The dropout probability parameter q for the proposed methods is searched in $\{10^{-i} : i = 1, \cdots, 5\}$. All SGD methods are started with an identity matrix in the experiment.

Table 1: Statistics for the datasets used in the empirical study. #C is the number of classes. #F is the number of features. #Train and #Test represent the number of training data and test data, respectively.

	# C	# F	#Train	#Test
ta	6	106	902	391
semeion	10	256	1,115	478
dna	3	180	2,000	1,186
caltech10	10	1,000	3,151	1,338
protein	3	357	17,766	6,621
sensit	3	100	78,823	19,705

Table 2 shows the classification accuracy of different SGD methods. First, it is not surprising to observe that all DML algorithms improve the performance compared to the Euclidean distance. Second, for all datasets, we observe that the proposed SGD methods with dropout (i.e., SGD-M1, SGD-M2, SGD-D1, and SGD-D2) significantly outperform the baseline SGD methods (i.e., SGD and SGD-PSD), which is also demonstrated by the statistical significance examined via pairwise t-tests at the 5% significance level. Concretely, on most datasets, the accuracy of SGD with dropout is about 2% improved compared with that of SGD and it is even 4% on *protein*.

Furthermore, we observe that SGD-M1 shows the best performance on *semeion*, *caltech10* and *protein*, while SGD-M2 outperforms other methods on *ta* and *dna*, and SGD-D2 is the best on *sensit*. It is because dropout in the learned metric and dropout in the training data represent different regularizers, and different dataset prefers different regularizer. SGD-D1 and SGD-D2 have the similar performance because they optimize the same trace norm. However, SGD-D2 is a little bit better than SGD-D1 due to the reason that no additional Guassian noise is introduced by SGD-D2. Finally, SGD-PSD performs same as if not worse than SGD, which is consistent with the observation in the study [6].

Then, we investigate if dropout can perform as the regularizers as we expected. Figure 2 compares the effect of different norms with different weights to that of SGD, where only the parameter q of dropout varies and the others are kept the same. First, since SGD-M1 puts more aggressive penalty on the diagonal, Figure 2(a) shows how L_2 norm of the diagonal elements in the metric learned by SGD-M1 varies as q decreases. We observe that the smaller the parameter is, the larger the L_2 norm is, and even when $q = 10^{-5}$, the L_2 norm is still less than that of SGD. It demonstrates that dropout as structured Frobenius norm restricts the size of diagonal elements well. Second, Figure 2(b) compares the sparsity of the learned metric, where sparsity is defined as

$$\text{Sparsity} = \frac{\#(M_{i,j} = 0)}{d^2}.$$

Without the constraint of L_1 norm, the sparsity of the metric learned by SGD is small as shown by the blue dashed line.

Table 2: **Comparison of classification accuracy (%) for different SGD methods, and the best result is bolded (statistical significance examined via pairwise t-tests at the 5% significance level between baselines and the proposed methods).**

	ta	*semeion*	*dna*	*caltech10*	*protein*	*sensit*
Euclid	80.15	91.63	80.10	62.36	50.05	72.72
SGD	83.14±0.39	94.14±0.36	92.58±0.39	65.29±0.29	60.19±0.16	74.92±0.09
SGD-PSD	82.94±0.56	94.27±0.11	92.61±0.35	64.88±0.39	58.15±0.47	74.54±0.08
SGD-M1	85.77±0.42	**96.03±0.39**	93.86±0.33	**67.32±0.29**	**64.05±0.31**	76.33±0.10
SGD-M2	**86.55±0.22**	95.61±0.42	**94.76±0.59**	66.04±0.24	62.76±0.47	76.10±0.08
SGD-D1	84.33±0.69	95.31±0.55	93.36±0.41	65.85±0.46	61.36±0.57	76.82±0.05
SGD-D2	84.74±0.50	95.40±0.39	93.66±0.39	66.07±0.37	62.86±0.46	**76.89±0.07**

Figure 2: Trend of effect for dropout as regularizers on dataset *caltech*. **Fig.(a) is the L_2 norm of the diagonal elements in the metric learned by SGD-M1. Fig.(b) is the sparsity of the metric learned by SGD-M2. Fig.(c) is the rank of the metric learned by SGD-D2.**

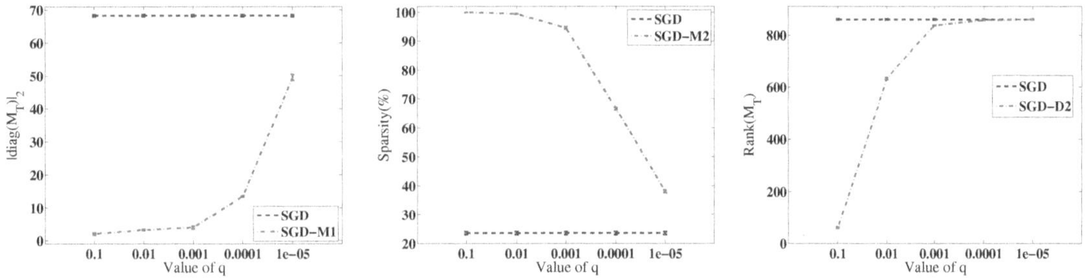

(a) *SGD-M1* (b) *SGD-M2* (c) *SGD-D2*

Figure 3: Comparison of training error and test error of different SGD methods with different size of triplets. There is no over-fitting observed for SGD method with dropout.

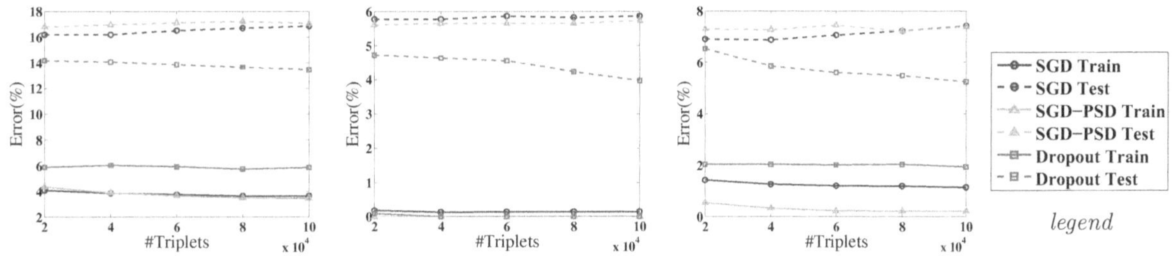

(a) *ta* (b) *semeion* (c) *dna* *legend*

However, in SGD-M2 as plotted by the red dash dotted line, with the increasing of the probability of dropout as the structured L_1 norm, the learned metric becomes more sparse, which confirms the effectiveness of SGD-M2. Finally, trace norm constraint usually leads to a low-rank metric [3], so we study the rank of the learned metric by SGD-D2 in Figure 2(c). As expected, when q becomes larger, more stress is put on the trace norm and the lower-rank metric is induced.

Since dropout is found to be helpful to overcome over-fitting in deep learning [10], we empirically study the role of dropout for alleviating over-fitting problem in DML. We fix all parameters as above except the number of sampled triplets, to study the changes of training error and test error on the training and test set, with the increasing of the number of triplets. Figure 3 shows the training error and test error of SGD, SGD-PSD and SGD with best dropout strategy on three small datasets (i.e., SGD-M1 on *semeion* and SGD-M2 on the others), while the number of sampled triplets increases from 20,000 to 100,000. First, we observe that the training error of SGD with dropout is similar to that of conventional SGD methods as we indicate in Theorem 1. However, over-fitting is observed for SGD and SGD-PSD when the number of triplets is up to 40,000, while there is no over-fitting phenomenon for SGD with dropout. It further demonstrates the overwhelming performance of dropout strategies in Table 2 and confirms that dropout is also helpful to overcome the over-fitting problem in DML.

4.3 Comparison with State-of-Art Methods

Besides the comparison with various SGD methods, we also compare our proposed dropout methods to three state-of-art DML algorithms as follows.

- **SPML** [23]: a mini-batch stochastic gradient descent algorithm for DML, which optimizes the hinge loss with Frobenius norm as the regularizer.

Table 3: **Comparison of classification accuracy (%) with state-of-art DML methods. "Dropout" refers to the best result of dropout from Table 2. Note that LMNN is a batch learning algorithm, and there is no limitation for the triplets it uses and the number of PSD projections. The best result is bolded (statistical significance examined via pairwise t-tests at the 5% significance level).**

	ta	*semeion*	*dna*	*caltech10*	*protein*	*sensit*
SPML	83.56±0.50	94.60±0.27	92.85±0.37	65.46±0.50	59.15±0.37	74.99±0.10
OASIS	83.20±0.95	94.06±0.19	88.57±0.28	65.06±0.40	58.83±0.38	73.50±0.15
LMNN	84.79±0.65	93.77±0.48	**95.13±0.26**	**67.17±0.49**	60.73±0.12	76.47±0.04
Dropout	**86.55±0.22**	**96.03±0.39**	**94.76±0.59**	**67.32±0.29**	**64.05±0.31**	**76.89±0.07**

Table 4: **Comparison of classification accuracy (%) for SPML and its variants by wrapping different dropout strategies in. The best result is bolded.**

	ta	*semeion*	*dna*	*caltech10*	*protein*	*sensit*
SPML	83.56±0.50	94.60±0.27	92.85±0.37	65.46±0.50	59.15±0.37	74.99±0.10
SPML-M1	84.59±0.38	**95.48±0.41**	93.27±0.16	**66.68±0.70**	61.38±0.36	75.63±0.08
SPML-M2	84.46±0.44	95.27±0.35	**93.91±0.32**	66.15±0.40	61.03±0.48	75.90±0.23
SPML-D	**84.74±0.56**	95.44±0.27	93.41±0.23	66.27±0.36	**62.14±0.68**	**76.84±0.13**

Table 5: **Comparison of classification accuracy (%) for OASIS and its variants by wrapping different dropout strategies in. The best result is bolded.**

	ta	*semeion*	*dna*	*caltech10*	*protein*	*sensit*
OASIS	83.20±0.95	94.06±0.19	88.57±0.28	65.06±0.40	58.83±0.38	73.50±0.15
OASIS-M1	84.74±0.86	**95.69±0.43**	93.35±0.33	**67.11±0.31**	62.44±0.55	75.47±0.15
OASIS-M2	**84.79±0.79**	94.73±0.38	**94.33±0.54**	66.12±0.49	62.61±0.60	75.47±0.12
OASIS-D	84.38±0.59	95.23±0.48	93.15±0.28	66.71±0.62	**63.06±0.55**	**76.56±0.15**

- **OASIS** [6]: an online learning approach for DML and the symmetric version is adopted in the comparison.
- **LMNN** [26]: a batch learning method with Frobenius norm for DML.

SPML and OASIS use the same triplet set as the proposed methods and also adopt one-projection paradigm. LMNN is a batch learning method, and thus there is no limitation for the type and the number of triplets that it could use for each iteration. Specifically, LMNN is not restricted to the set of triplets used by other methods. There is also no constraint for PSD projection in LMNN and it can perform PSD projection whenever it requires. All codes for these methods are from the authors and the recommended parameters are used. Since SPML is a stochastic method, it shares the same setting as the proposed methods, where the parameter for Frobenius norm is searched within the same range as q to obtain the best performance. SPML and OASIS are both initialized with an identity matrix, while LMNN starts with the matrix from PCA without dimension reduction, which usually has a better performance than the identity matrix for the method [26].

Table 3 summarizes the classification accuracy of different DML algorithms. "**Dropout**" denotes the best result of dropout methods adopted from Table 2. It can be easily observed that, although LMNN is a batch learning method and could utilize much more information than our methods, LMNN only has the similar performance on *dna* and *caltech10*, while SGD method with dropout significantly outperforms on all other datasets. It further demonstrates the effectiveness of the proposed methods. SPML and OASIS are slightly better than the standard SGD method, but significantly worse than SGD method with dropout technique. The performance of OASIS could be explained by the fact that it does not include any conventional regularizer and over-fitting could be easily induced. Although SPML combines the Frobenius norm as the regularizer, it is worse than SGD-M1 and SGD-M2 shown in Table 2, which implies that the proposed structured norm by dropout is more effective than the standard norm.

4.4 Wrap Dropout in Existing DML Methods

In this section, we demonstrate that dropout can be easily wrapped in the existing DML methods and help improve the performance. First, we wrap dropout in SPML, which is a state-of-art mini-batch SGD method for DML. Note that SPML has the Frobenius norm as the regularizer, so we drop it first to make sure that there is only one regularizer at one time. Since it is a SGD method, the dropout on M is the same as Algorithm 2 and Algorithm 3. We denote dropout as the structured Frobenius norm on SPML as "SPML-M1" and dropout as the structured L_1 norm as "SPML-M2". Instead of randomly selecting one triplet at each iteration, SPML samples b triplets at one time and updates according to the batch of the gradient. Therefore, when applying dropout to the training data, we simply perform the dropout on different matrix A in the mini-batch as in Algorithm 5 and the method is denoted as "SPML-D".

Table 4 summarizes the results for wrapped SPML methods. First, it is not surprising to observe that all dropout strategies improve the performance of SPML. On almost all datasets, the improvement on accuracy is more than 1% and it is even about 3% on *protein*, which is also consistent with the observation in the comparison for various SGD methods. Although SPML applies the standard Frobenius norm as the regularizer, SPML with different dropout strategies outperforms it significantly according to the statistical sig-

Figure 4: Procedure of wrapping dropout in OASIS.

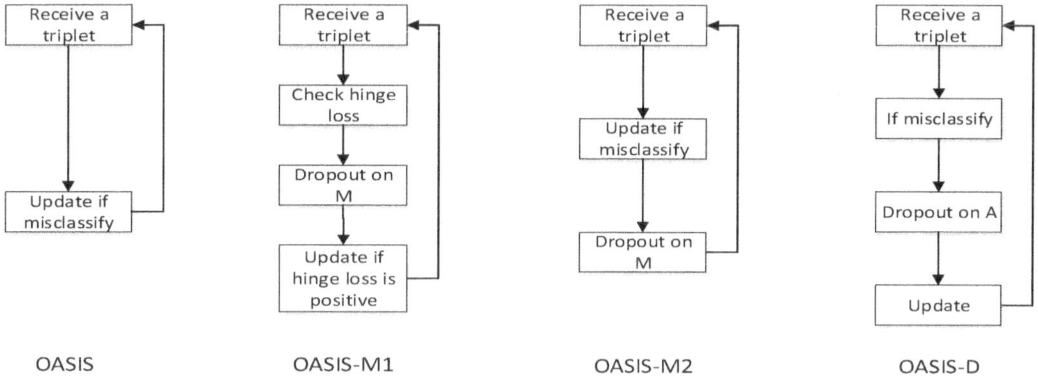

nificance examined via pairwise t-tests at the 5% significance level, which shows the superior performance of the proposed structured regularizers.

Then, we wrap dropout in OASIS, which is a state-of-art online learning method for DML. Since online learning has the similar process as stochastic gradient descent method, wrapping dropout in is pretty straightforward. Figure 4 illustrates the procedures of wrapping different dropout strategies in OASIS. Let "OASIS-M1", "OASIS-M2","OASIS-D" denote dropout as the structured Frobeniuse norm, the structured L_1 norm and the trace norm in OASIS, respectively. The comparison of classification accuracy applied by 3-NN is summarized in Table 5. The similar phenomenon as for SPML is observed, that dropout always helps to improve the performance of OASIS significantly according to pairwise t-test at the 5% significance level.

In summary, wrapping dropout in existing DML methods is not only convenient but also very helpful for performance improvement.

5. CONCLUSION

In this paper, we propose two strategies to perform dropout for DML, i.e., dropout in the learned metric and dropout in the training data. For dropout in the metric, we propose the structured regularizer, which is simulated with dropout by assigning different dropout probabilities for the diagonal elements and those living in off diagonal. For dropout in the training data, the data-dependent dropout probability is adopted to mimic the trace norm. We develop the theoretical guarantees for both dropout scenarios to show that dropout will not affect the convergence rate of SGD with the appropriate dropout probability. Furthermore, we demonstrate that the proposed strategies are very convenient to wrap in the existing DML methods. Our empirical study confirms that the proposed methods have the overwhelming performance compared with the baseline methods, and could significantly improve the classification accuracy for the state-of-art DML methods. Since we currently apply dropout to the learned metric and the training data separately, we plan to examine the performance of the combination in the near future.

Acknowledgment

Qian and Jin are supported by ARO (W911NF-11-1-0383), NSF (IIS-1251031) and ONR Award (N000141410631). Hu and Pei's research is supported in part by a NSERC Discovery Grant and a BCIC NRAS Team project. All opinions, findings, conclusions and recommendations in this paper are those of the authors and do not necessarily reflect the views of the funding agencies.

6. REFERENCES

[1] P. Baldi and P. J. Sadowski. Understanding dropout. In *NIPS*, pages 2814–2822, 2013.

[2] C. M. Bishop. Training with noise is equivalent to tikhonov regularization. *Neural computation*, 7(1):108–116, 1995.

[3] E. J. Candès and T. Tao. The power of convex relaxation: near-optimal matrix completion. *IEEE Transactions on Information Theory*, 56(5):2053–2080, 2010.

[4] C.-C. Chang and C.-J. Lin. Libsvm: A library for support vector machines. *ACM TIST*, 2(3):27, 2011.

[5] H. Chang and D.-Y. Yeung. Locally linear metric adaptation for semi-supervised clustering. In *ICML*, pages 153–160, 2004.

[6] G. Chechik, V. Sharma, U. Shalit, and S. Bengio. Large scale online learning of image similarity through ranking. *JMLR*, 11:1109–1135, 2010.

[7] J. V. Davis, B. Kulis, P. Jain, S. Sra, and I. S. Dhillon. Information-theoretic metric learning. In *ICML*, pages 209–216, 2007.

[8] H. Do, A. Kalousis, J. Wang, and A. Woznica. A metric learning perspective of svm: on the relation of lmnn and svm. In *AISTATS*, pages 308–317, 2012.

[9] A. Frank and A. Asuncion. UCI machine learning repository, 2010.

[10] G. Griffin, A. Holub, and P. Perona. Caltech-256 object category dataset, 2007.

[11] E. Hazan, A. Agarwal, and S. Kale. Logarithmic regret algorithms for online convex optimization. *Machine Learning*, 69(2-3):169–192, 2007.

[12] E. Hazan and S. Kale. Beyond the regret minimization barrier: an optimal algorithm for stochastic strongly-convex optimization. In *COLT*, pages 421–436, 2011.

[13] X. He, W.-Y. Ma, and H. Zhang. Learning an image manifold for retrieval. In *ACM Multimedia*, pages 17–23, 2004.

[14] G. E. Hinton, N. Srivastava, A. Krizhevsky, I. Sutskever, and R. Salakhutdinov. Improving neural networks by preventing co-adaptation of feature detectors. *CoRR*, abs/1207.0580, 2012.

[15] B. Kulis. Metric learning: A survey. *Foundations and Trends in Machine Learning*, 5(4):287–364, 2013.

[16] D. K. H. Lim, B. McFee, and G. Lanckriet. Robust structural metric learning. In *ICML*, 2013.

[17] K. Matsuoka. Noise injection into inputs in back-propagation learning. *IEEE Transactions on Systems, Man, and Cybernetics*, 22(3):436–440, 1992.

[18] Y. Nesterov et al. Gradient methods for minimizing composite objective function, 2007.

[19] S. Rifai, X. Glorot, Y. Bengio, and P. Vincent. Adding noise to the input of a model trained with a regularized objective. *CoRR*, abs/1104.3250, 2011.

[20] K. Saenko, B. Kulis, M. Fritz, and T. Darrell. Adapting visual category models to new domains. In *ECCV*, pages 213–226. Springer, 2010.

[21] P. Sen, G. Namata, M. Bilgic, L. Getoor, B. Gallagher, and T. Eliassi-Rad. Collective classification in network data. *AI Magazine*, 29(3):93–106, 2008.

[22] S. Shalev-Shwartz, Y. Singer, and A. Y. Ng. Online and batch learning of pseudo-metrics. In *ICML*, 2004.

[23] B. Shaw, B. C. Huang, and T. Jebara. Learning a distance metric from a network. In *NIPS*, pages 1899–1907, 2011.

[24] L. van der Maaten, M. Chen, S. Tyree, and K. Q. Weinberger. Learning with marginalized corrupted features. In *ICML*, pages 410–418, 2013.

[25] S. Wager, S. Wang, and P. Liang. Dropout training as adaptive regularization. In *NIPS*, pages 351–359, 2013.

[26] K. Q. Weinberger and L. K. Saul. Distance metric learning for large margin nearest neighbor classification. *JMLR*, 10:207–244, 2009.

[27] E. P. Xing, A. Y. Ng, M. I. Jordan, and S. J. Russell. Distance metric learning with application to clustering with side-information. In *NIPS*, pages 505–512, 2002.

[28] L. Yang and R. Jin. Distance metric learning: a comprehensive survery. 2006.

[29] M. Zinkevich. Online convex programming and generalized infinitesimal gradient ascent. In *ICML*, pages 928–936, 2003.

APPENDIX

A. PROOF OF THEOREM 1

PROOF.

$$\|M_t - M_*\|_F^2 = \|\hat{M}_{t-1} - \eta A_t - M_*\|_F^2$$
$$= \|\delta M_{t-1} - (1-q)M_{t-1} + M_{t-1} - \eta A_t - M_* - qM_{t-1}\|_F^2$$
$$= (\delta - (1-q))^2\|M_{t-1}\|_F^2 + \|M_{t-1} - M_*\|_F^2 + \eta^2\|A_t\|_F^2$$
$$+ q^2\|M_{t-1}\|_F^2 - 2\eta\langle A_t, M_{t-1} - M_*\rangle$$
$$+ 2(\delta - (1-q))\langle M_{t-1}, M_{t-1} - \eta A_t - M_* - qM_{t-1}\rangle$$
$$- 2q\langle M_{t-1}, M_{t-1} - \eta A_t - M_*\rangle$$

Since the loss function is convex, we have

$$\ell(M_{t-1}) - \ell(M_*) \le \frac{1}{2\eta}(\|M_{t-1} - M_*\|_F^2 - \|M_t - M_*\|_F^2)$$
$$+ \frac{\eta}{2}\|A_t\|_F^2 + \frac{1}{2\eta}\left((\delta - (1-q))^2\|M_{t-1}\|_F^2 + q^2\|M_{t-1}\|_F^2\right.$$
$$+ 2(\delta - (1-q))\langle M_{t-1}, M_{t-1} - \eta A_t - M_* - qM_{t-1}\rangle$$
$$\left.- 2q\langle M_{t-1}, M_{t-1} - \eta A_t - M_*\rangle\right)$$

Taking expectation on δ, we have

$$E[\ell(M_{t-1})] - \ell(M_*) \le \frac{1}{2\eta}(\|M_{t-1} - M_*\|_F^2 - \|M_t - M_*\|_F^2)$$
$$+ \frac{\eta}{2}\|A_t\|_F^2 + \frac{1}{2\eta}(q\|M_{t-1}\|_F^2 - 2q\langle M_{t-1}, M_{t-1} - \eta A_t - M_*\rangle)$$
$$\le \frac{1}{2\eta}(\|M_{t-1} - M_*\|_F^2 - \|M_t - M_*\|_F^2) + \frac{\eta}{2}\|A_t\|_F^2$$
$$+ \frac{q}{2\eta}(2\langle M_{t-1}, \eta A_t + M_*\rangle - \|M_{t-1}\|_F^2)$$
$$\le \frac{1}{2\eta}(\|M_{t-1} - M_*\|_F^2 - \|M_t - M_*\|_F^2) + \frac{\eta}{2}\|A_t\|_F^2$$
$$+ \frac{q}{2\eta}(\|\eta A_t + M_*\|_F^2)$$
$$\le \frac{1}{2\eta}(\|M_{t-1} - M_*\|_F^2 - \|M_t - M_*\|_F^2)$$
$$+ \frac{(1+q)\eta}{2}\|A_t\|_F^2 + \frac{q}{2\eta}\|M_*\|_F^2 + q\ell(M_*)$$

Since $|\mathbf{x}| \le r$, $\|A_t\|_F \le 4r$. Adding iterations from 1 to T and setting $q = 1/T$, we have

$$E[\ell(\bar{M})] - (1 - 1/T)\ell(M_*) \le \frac{1}{\eta T}\|M_*\|_F^2 + 8r^2(1 + 1/T)\eta$$

□

B. PROOF OF THEOREM 2

PROOF.

$$\|M_t - M_*\|_F^2 = \|M_{t-1} - \eta\hat{A}_t - M_*\|_F^2$$
$$= \|M_{t-1} - M_*\|_F^2 + \eta^2\|\hat{A}_t\|_F^2 - 2\eta\langle\hat{A}_t, M_{t-1} - M_*\rangle$$

Taking expectation on $\hat{A}_t$, we have

$$\|M_t - M_*\|_F^2$$
$$= \|M_{t-1} - M_*\|_F^2 + \eta^2 E[\|\hat{A}_t\|_F^2] - 2\eta\langle A_t + qI, M_{t-1} - M_*\rangle$$

Since the loss function is convex, it is

$$E[\ell(M_{t-1})] - \ell(M_*) \le \frac{1}{2\eta}(\|M_{t-1} - M_*\|_F^2 - \|M_t - M_*\|_F^2)$$
$$+ \frac{\eta}{2}E[\|\hat{A}_t\|_F^2] + q(\|M_*\|_{tr} - \|M_{t-1}\|_{tr})$$
$$\le \frac{1}{2\eta}(\|M_{t-1} - M_*\|_F^2 - \|M_t - M_*\|_F^2)$$
$$+ \frac{\eta r^2}{2}(16 + 16dq + 8q) + q\|M_*\|_{tr}$$

where q's high order items are omitted since q is a small number. Sum over the iteration from 1 to T, we have

$$E[\ell(\bar{M})] - \ell(M_*) \le \frac{\|M_*\|_F^2}{2\eta T} + \eta r^2(8 + 8dq + 4q) + q\|M_*\|_{tr}$$

The proof is finished by setting $q = 1/T$. □

Box Drawings for Learning with Imbalanced Data

Siong Thye Goh
Operations Research Center
Massachusetts Institute of Technology
Cambridge, MA02139, USA
stgoh@mit.edu

Cynthia Rudin
CSAIL and Sloan School of Management
Massachusetts Institute of Technology
Cambridge, MA02142, USA
rudin@mit.edu

ABSTRACT

The vast majority of real world classification problems are imbalanced, meaning there are far fewer data from the class of interest (the positive class) than from other classes. We propose two machine learning algorithms to handle highly imbalanced classification problems. The classifiers are disjunctions of conjunctions, and are created as unions of parallel axis rectangles around the positive examples, and thus have the benefit of being interpretable. The first algorithm uses mixed integer programming to optimize a weighted balance between positive and negative class accuracies. Regularization is introduced to improve generalization performance. The second method uses an approximation in order to assist with scalability. Specifically, it follows a *characterize then discriminate* approach, where the positive class is characterized first by boxes, and then each box boundary becomes a separate discriminative classifier. This method has the computational advantages that it can be easily parallelized, and considers only the relevant regions of feature space.

Categories and Subject Descriptors

I.2.6 [**Artificial Intelligence**]: Learning

Keywords

Classification; Imbalanced Data; Decision Trees

1. INTRODUCTION

Our interest is in deriving interpretable predictive classification models for use with imbalanced data. Data classification problems having imbalanced (also called "unbalanced") class distributions appear in many domains, ranging from mechanical failure detection or fault detection, to fraud detection, to text and image classification, to medical disease prediction or diagnosis. Imbalanced data cause typical machine learning methods to produce trivial results, that is, classifiers that only predict the majority class. One cannot optimize vanilla classification accuracy and use standard classification methods when working with imbalanced data. This is explained nicely by Chawla, Japkowicz, and Kolcz [7] who write: "*The class imbalance problem is pervasive and ubiquitous, causing trouble to a large segment of the data mining community.*"

KDD'14, August 24–27, 2014, New York, NY, USA.

ACM 978-1-4503-2956-9/14/08 ...$15.00.
http://dx.doi.org/10.1145/2623330.2623648.

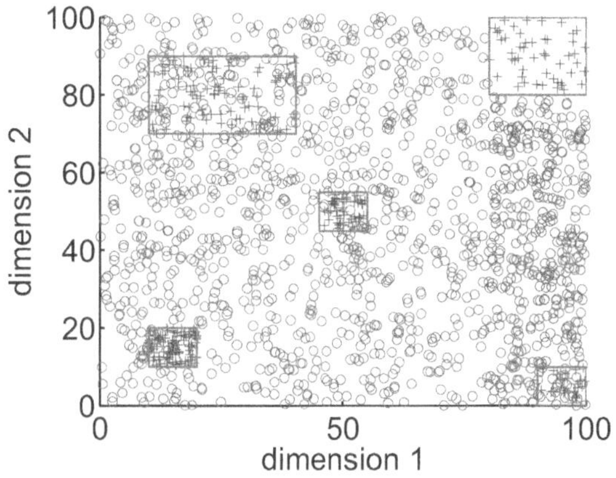

Figure 1: Example of box drawing classifier.

In order for the models we derive to be interpretable to human experts, our classifiers are formed as a union of axis parallel rectangles around the positive (minority class) examples, and we call such classifiers *box drawing classifiers*. These are "disjunctions of conjunctions" where each conjunction is a box. An example of a box drawing classifier we created is in Figure 1, exemplifying our goal to classify the positive examples correctly even if they are scattered within a sea of negative examples. Our classifiers are regularized in several ways, to prefer fewer boxes and larger boxes. We take two polar approaches to creating box drawing classifiers, where the first is an exact method, based on mixed integer programming (MIP). This method, called *Exact Boxes* can be used for small to medium sized datasets, and provides a gold standard to compare with. If we are able to make substantial approximations and still obtain performance close to that of the gold standard, our approximations would be justified. Our second method, *Fast Boxes* makes such an approximation.

Fast boxes takes the approach of *characterize then discriminate*, where we first characterize the positive (minority) class alone, and then bring in the negative examples to form decision boundaries around each clusters of positives. This approach has significant computational advantages, in that using just the minority class in the first step requires a small fraction of the data, assuming a high imbalance ratio. Also by creating decision boundaries locally in the second step, the number of examples involved in each classifier is smaller; further, creating each classifier separately allows computations to be made parallel, though since the computation for each decision boundary is analytical, that may not be necessary for many datasets. The computation is analytical because there is a closed form solution for the placement of the decision boundary. Thus, the discriminate step becomes many parallel local analytical calculations. This is much simpler and scalable than, for instance, a decision tree that chooses splits greedily and fails to scale with dimension and large number of observations.

We make several experimental observations, namely that: box drawing classifiers become more useful as data imbalance increases; the approximate method performs at the top level of its competitors, despite the fact that it is restricted to producing interpretable results; and performance can be improved on the same datasets by using the mixed integer programming method.

After related work just below, we describe the advantages of our approach in Section 2. In Section 3, we introduce our two algorithms. Experimental results will be presented in Section 4. Section 4 provides a vignette to show how box drawing models can be interpretable. In Section 5, theoretical generalization bounds will be presented for box drawing classifiers. Section 6 discusses possible approaches to make the MIP formulation more scalable.

2. RELATED WORKS

Overviews of work on handling class imbalance problems include those of He and Garcia [11], Chawla, Japkowiz and Kolcz [7] and Qi [19]. Many works discuss problems caused by class imbalance [22, 16]. There are many avenues of research that are not directly related to the goal of interpretable imbalanced classification, specifically kernel and active learning methods [20, 23], and work on sampling [1, 6] that includes undersampling, oversampling, and data generation, which can be used in conjunction with methods like the ones introduced here. We use a cost-sensitive learning approach in our methods, similar to Liu and Zhou [14] and McCarthy et al. [15]. We note that many papers on imbalanced data do not experimentally compare their work with the cost-sensitive versions of decision tree methods. We choose to compare with other cost-sensitive versions of decision trees as our method is a cost-sensitive method.

There is some evidence that more complex approaches that layer different learning methods seem to be helpful for learning [20, 23], though the results would not be interpretable in that case. This, however, is in contrast with other views (e.g., [12]) that for most common datasets, simple rules exists and we should explore them.

The works most similar to ours are that of the Patient Rule Induction Method (PRIM) [9] and decision tree methods for imbalanced classification (e.g., [13]), as they partition the input space like our work. Approaches that partition space tend to recover simple decision rules that are easier for people to understand. Decision tree methods are composed using greedy splitting criteria, unlike our methods. PRIM is also a greedy method that iteratively peels off parts of the input space, though unfortunately we found it to be extremely slow - as described by Sniadecki [21], "PRIM is eloquently coined as a patient method due to the slow, stepwise mechanism by which it processes the data." Neither our Exact Boxes nor Fast Boxes methods are greedy methods, though Fast Boxes makes a different type of approximation, which is to characterize before discriminating. As discussed by Raskutti [20], one-class learning can be useful for highly imbalanced datasets - our characterization step is a one-class learning approach.

3. NEW ALGORITHMS

We start with the mixed-integer programming formulation, which acts as our gold standard for creating box drawing classifiers when solved to optimality.

3.1 Exact Boxes

For box drawing classifiers, a minority class (positive) example is correctly classified only if it resides within at least one box. A majority class (negative) example is correctly classified if it does not reside in any box. We are given training examples $\{(\mathbf{x}_i, y_i)\}_{i=1}^m, \mathbf{x}_i \in \mathcal{R}^n, y_i \in \{-1,+1\}$. We introduce some notation in Table 1 that we will use throughout this subsection. We use this notation from here on.

Notation	Definitions
K	Number of parallel axes boxes
m	Number of examples
n	Number of features
i	Index for examples
j	Index for features
x_{ij}	j-th feature of example i
k	Index for box
l_{jk}	Lower boundary of feature j for box k
u_{jk}	Upper boundary of feature j for box k
v	Margin for decision boundary
$\widetilde{l}_{ijk}$	$\widetilde{l}_{ijk} = 1$ if $x_{ij} > l_{jk} + v$ and 0 otherwise
$\widetilde{u}_{ijk}$	$\widetilde{u}_{ijk} = 1$ if $x_{ij} < u_{jk} - v$ and 0 otherwise
w_{ik}	$w_{ik} = 1$ if example i is in box k and 0 otherwise
z_i	$z_i = 1$ if it is classified correctly.
S_+	Index set of example of minority class
S_-	Index set of example of majority class
c_e	A regularizer to encourage expansion of box
c_I	Weight for majority class, $c_I < 1$

Table 1: Notation for Box Drawings with Mixed Integer Programming

The *Exact Boxes* method solves the following, where the hypothesis space $\mathcal{F}$ is the set of box drawings (unions of axis parallel rectangles), where $f \in \mathcal{F}$ has $f : \mathcal{R}^n \to \{-1, 1\}$.

$$\max_{f\in\mathcal{F}} \sum_{i:y_i=1} \mathbf{1}_{[f(\mathbf{x}_i)=1]} + C_I \sum_{i:y_i=-1} \mathbf{1}_{[f(\mathbf{x}_i)=-1]} - C_E(\#\text{of boxes of } f).$$

The objective is a weighted accuracy of positives and negatives, regularized by the number of boxes. This way, the number of boxes is not fixed, and a smaller number of clusters is preferred (analogous to nonparametric Bayesian models where the number of clusters is not fixed). Our gold standard will be the minimizer of this objective. We now derive the MIP that computes this minimizer.

If $i \in S_+$, the definitions of $\widetilde{l}_{ijk}$, $\widetilde{u}_{ijk}$, w_{ik}, and z_i give rise to the following constraints:

$$l_{jk} + v < x_{ij} \text{ iff } \widetilde{l}_{ijk} = 1 \quad (1)$$

$$u_{jk} - v > x_{ij} \text{ iff } \widetilde{u}_{ijk} = 1, \quad (2)$$

which say that x_{ij} need to be at least margin v away from the lower (resp. upper) boundary of the box in order for $\widetilde{l}_{ijk} = 1$ (resp. $\widetilde{u}_{ijk} = 1$). Further, our definitions give rise also to

$$\sum_{j=1}^{n} \widetilde{u}_{ijk} + \widetilde{l}_{ijk} > 2n - 1 \text{ iff } w_{ik} = 1, \tag{3}$$

which says that for example i to be in box k, all of the $\widetilde{u}_{ijk}$ and $\widetilde{l}_{ijk}$ are 1 for box k. We also have, still for $i \in S_+$, that the example must be in one of the boxes in order to be classified correctly, that is:

$$\sum_{k=1}^{K} w_{ik} > 0 \text{ iff } z_i = 1. \tag{4}$$

Continuing this same type of reasoning for $i \in S_-$, the definitions of $\widetilde{l}_{ijk}$,$\widetilde{u}_{ijk}$, w_{ik}, and z_i give rise to the following constraints:

$$\begin{aligned} l_{jk} - v > x_{ij} &\quad \text{iff} \quad \widetilde{l}_{ijk} = 1 \\ u_{jk} + v < x_{ij} &\quad \text{iff} \quad \widetilde{u}_{ijk} = 1 \\ \sum_{j=1}^{n} \widetilde{u}_{ijk} + \widetilde{l}_{ijk} > 0 &\quad \text{iff} \quad w_{ik} = 0 \\ \sum_{k=1}^{K} w_{ik} > 0 &\quad \text{iff} \quad z_i = 0. \end{aligned}$$

By setting M to be a large positive constant and setting ϵ to be a small positive number (to act as a strict inequality), we now have the following formulation:

$$\max_{l,\widetilde{l},u,\widetilde{u},w,z} \left[-c_e K + \sum_{i \in S_+} z_i + c_I \sum_{i \in S_-} z_i \right] \text{subject to}$$

$$x_{ij} - l_{jk} - v \le M\widetilde{l}_{ijk}, \forall i \in S_+, \forall j, k \tag{5}$$

$$M(\widetilde{l}_{ijk} - 1) + \epsilon \le x_{ij} - l_{jk} - v, \forall i \in S_+, \forall j, k \tag{6}$$

$$u_{jk} - v - x_{ij} \le M\widetilde{u}_{ijk}, \forall i \in S_+, \forall j, k \tag{7}$$

$$M(\widetilde{u}_{ijk} - 1) + \epsilon \le u_{jk} - x_{ij} - v, \forall i \in S_+, \forall j, k \tag{8}$$

$$\sum_{j=1}^{n} \widetilde{l}_{ijk} + \sum_{j=1}^{n} \widetilde{u}_{ijk} - 2n + 1 \le w_{ik}, \forall i \in S_+, \forall j, k \tag{9}$$

$$2nw_{ik} \le \sum_{j=1}^{n} \widetilde{l}_{ijk} + \sum_{j=1}^{n} \widetilde{u}_{ijk}, \forall i \in S_+, \forall j, k \tag{10}$$

$$\sum_{k=1}^{K} w_{ik} \le Kz_i, \forall i \in S_+, \forall k \tag{11}$$

$$z_i \le \sum_{k=1}^{K} w_{ik}, \forall i \in S_+, \forall k \tag{12}$$

$$l_{jk} - v - x_{ij} \le M\widetilde{l}_{ijk}, \forall i \in S_-, \forall j, k \tag{13}$$

$$M(\widetilde{l}_{ijk} - 1) + \epsilon \le l_{jk} - v - x_{ij}, \forall i \in S_-, \forall j, k \tag{14}$$

$$x_{ij} - u_{jk} - v \le M\widetilde{u}_{ijk}, \forall i \in S_-, \forall j, k \tag{15}$$

$$M(\widetilde{u}_{ijk} - 1) + \epsilon \le x_{ij} - u_{jk} - v, \forall i \in S_-, \forall j, k \tag{16}$$

$$\sum_{j=1}^{n} \widetilde{l}_{ijk} + \sum_{j=1}^{n} \widetilde{u}_{ijk} - 2n + 1 \le 2n(1 - w_{ik}), \quad \forall i \in S_-, \forall j, k \tag{17}$$

$$1 - w_{ik} \le \sum_{j=1}^{n} \widetilde{l}_{ijk} + \sum_{j=1}^{n} \widetilde{u}_{ijk}, \forall i \in S_-, \forall j, k \tag{18}$$

$$\sum_{k=1}^{K} w_{ik} \le K(1 - z_i), \forall i \in S_-, \forall k \tag{19}$$

$$1 - z_i \le \sum_{k=1}^{K} w_{ik}, \forall i \in S_-, \forall k \tag{20}$$

$$l_{jk} \le u_{jk}, \forall j, k. \tag{21}$$

Here, (5) and (6) are derived from (1), (7) and (8) are derived from (2), (9) and (10) are derived from (3), (11) and (12) are derived from (4), equations (13)-(20) are derived analogously for S_-. The last constraint (21) is to make sure that the solution that we obtain is not degenerate, where the lower boundary is above the upper boundary. In practice, M should be chosen as a fixed large number and ϵ should be chosen as a fixed small number based on the representation of numbers in the computing environment.

In total, there are $O(mnK)$ equations and $O(mnK)$ variables, though the full matrix of variables corresponding to the mixed integer programming formulation is sparse since most boxes operate only on a small subset of the data. This formulation can be solved efficiently for small to medium sized datasets using MIP software, producing a gold standard box drawing classifier for any specific number of boxes (determined by the regularization constant). The fact that Exact Boxes produces the best possible function in the class of box drawing classifiers permits us to evaluate the quality of Fast Boxes, which operates in an approximate way on a much larger scale.

3.2 Fast Boxes

Fast Boxes uses the approach of *characterize then discriminate.* In particular, we hypothesize that the data distribution is such that the positive examples cluster together relative to the negative examples. This implies that a reasonable classifier might first cluster the positive examples and then afterwards discriminate positives from negatives. The discrimination is done by drawing a high dimensional axis-parallel box around each cluster and then adjusting each boundary locally for maximum discriminatory power. If the cluster assumption about the class distributions is not correct, then Fast Boxes could have problems, though it does not seem to for most real imbalanced datasets we have found, as we show in the experiments. Fast Boxes has three main stages as follows.

---

1. Clustering stage: Cluster the minority class data into K clusters, where K is an adjustable parameter. The decision boundaries are initially set as tight boxes around each of the clusters of positive examples.
2. Dividing space stage: The input space of the data is partitioned to determine which positive and negative examples will influence the placement of each decision boundary.
3. Boundary expansion stage: Each boundary is expanded by minimizing an exponential loss function. The solution for the decision boundary is analytical.

Details of each stage are provided below.

3.2.1 Clustering Stage

In the clustering stage, the minority class data are clustered into K clusters. Since this step involves only the minority class data, it can be performed efficiently, particularly if the data are highly imbalanced. Cross-validation or other techniques can be used to determine K. In our experiments, we used the basic k-means algorithm with Euclidean distance. Other clustering techniques or other distance metrics can be used.

After the minority class data are separated into small clusters, we construct the smallest enclosing parallel axes rectangle for each cluster. The smallest enclosing parallel axes rectangle can be computed by taking the minimum and maximum of the minority class data in each cluster and for each feature. Let $l_{s,j,k}$ and $u_{s,j,k}$ denote the lower boundary and upper boundary for the j-th dimension, for the k-th cluster. Here the subscript s is for "starting" boundary, and in the next part we will created a "revised" boundary which will be given subscript r. The "final" boundary will be given subscript f.

3.2.2 Dividing Space Stage

Define the set $X_{l,j,k}$ as follows:

$$\begin{aligned} X_{l,j,k} \quad := \quad & \{x : x_j \leq l_{s,j,k}\} \cup \left\{x : l_{s,j,k} \leq x_j \leq \frac{l_{s,j,k}+u_{s,j,k}}{2},\right. \\ & l_{s,p,k} \leq x_p \leq u_{s,p,k}, p \neq j\}, \end{aligned} \quad (22)$$

These are the data points that will be used to adjust the lower boundary of the j-th dimension of the k-th rectangle.

Similarly, we let

$$\begin{aligned} X_{u,j,k} \quad := \quad & \{x : x_j \geq u_{s,j,k}\} \cup \left\{x : \frac{l_{s,j,k}+u_{s,j,k}}{2} \leq x_j \leq u_{s,j,k},\right. \\ & l_{s,p,k} \leq x_p \leq u_{s,p,k}, p \neq j\}. \end{aligned} \quad (23)$$

These are the training examples that will be used to determine the upper boundary of the j-th dimension of the k-th rectangle.

Figure 2 illustrates the domain for $X_{u,j,k}$ to the right of the blue dashed line.

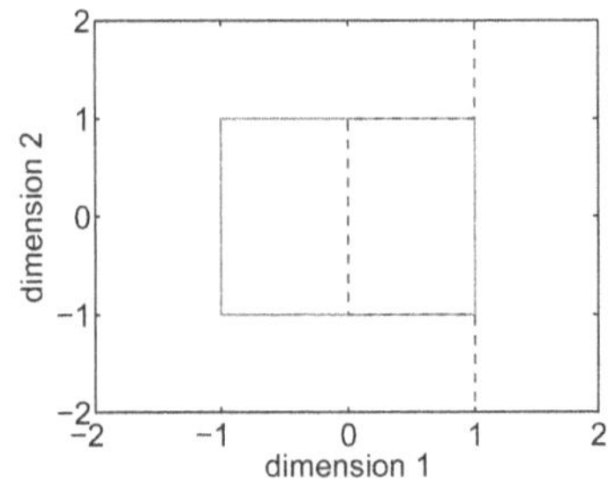

Figure 2: The examples used to determine the right vertical decision boundary are on the right side of the blue dotted line.

Note that this method is very parallelizable after the clustering stage. The dividing space stage computations can be done in parallel for each cluster, and for the boundary expansion stage discussed below, each boundary of each box can be determined in parallel.

3.2.3 Boundary Expansion Stage

In this stage we discriminate between positives and negatives by creating a 1-dimensional classifier for each boundary of each box. We use a regularized exponential loss. Specifically, for lower boundary j of box k, We minimize the following with respect to $l_{r,j,k}$ where $l_{r,j,k}$ refers to the lower boundary of the j-th dimension of k-th revised box being determined by the loss function:

$$\begin{aligned} & \sum_{x \in S_+^k \cap X_{l,j,k}} \exp[-(x_j - l_{r,j,k})] \\ & + \; c \sum_{x \in S_-^k \cap X_{l,j,k}} \exp\left[+\left(x_j - l_{r,j,k}\right.\right. \\ & + \left.\left.\sum_{p \neq j} (\lfloor x_p - u_{s,p,k} \rfloor_+ + \lfloor l_{s,p,k} - x_p \rfloor_+)\right)\right] + \beta l_{r,j,k}. \end{aligned}$$

where c is the weight for the majority class, $c < 1$, S_+^k is the set of positive examples in the k-th cluster, S_-^k is the set of examples not in the k-th cluster, β is a regularization parameter that tends to expand the box, and $\lfloor . \rfloor$ denotes max$(., 0)$. For simplicity, we use the same parameter to control the expansion for all the clusters and all the features. Note that the term $\sum_{p \neq j} (\lfloor x_p - u_{s,p,k} \rfloor_+ + \lfloor l_{s,p,k} - x_p \rfloor_+)$ is designed to give less weight to the points that are not directly opposite the box edges (the points that are diagonally away from the corners of the box). To explain these terms, recall that the exponential loss in classification usually operates on the term $y_i f(x_i)$, where the value of $f(x_i)$ can be thought of as a distance to the decision boundary. In our case, for the lower decision boundary we use the perpendicular distance to the decision boundary $|x_j - l_{r,j,k}|$, and include the additional distance in every other dimension p for the diagonal points. For the upper diagonal points we include the distance to the upper boundary $u_{s,p,k}$, namely $x_p - u_{s,p,k}$, and analogously for the points on the lower diagonal we include distance $l_{s,p,k} - x_p$. We perform an analogous calculation for the upper boundary.

Note that we perform a standard normalization of all features to be between -1 and 1 before any computation begins, which also mitigates numerical issues when dealing with the (steep) exponential loss. Another mechanism we use for avoiding numerical problems is by multiplying each term in the objective by exp(1) and dividing each term by the same factor. We will construct the derivation of the lower boundary as follows. We rewrite the objective to minimize:

$$\begin{aligned} & R_+^{l,j,k} \exp\left(-l_{s,j,k} + 1 + l_{r,j,k}\right) \\ & + c R_-^{l,j,k} \exp\left(l_{s,j,k} - 1 - l_{r,j,k}\right) + \beta l_{r,j,k}, \end{aligned} \quad (24)$$

where

$$R_+^{l,j,k} \quad := \quad \sum_{x \in S_+^k \cap X_{l,j,k}} \exp\left[-(x_j - l_{s,j,k} + 1)\right], \quad (25)$$

$$\begin{aligned} R_-^{l,j,k} \quad := \quad & \sum_{x \in S_-^k \cap X_{l,j,k}} \exp\left[x_j - l_{s,j,k} + 1\right. \\ & \left. + \sum_{p \neq j} (\lfloor x_p - u_{s,p,k} \rfloor_+ + \lfloor l_{s,p,k} - x_p \rfloor_+)\right] \end{aligned} \quad (26)$$

Because of the factors of 1 added and subtracted in the exponent, we ensure $R_+^{l,j,k}$ is at least $\exp(-1) > 0.3$, avoiding numerical problems. From there, we can solve for $l_{r,j,k}$ by taking the derivative of the objective and equating it to zero. Then we multiply both sides of the resulting equation by $\exp\left(l_{s,j,k} - 1 - l_{r,j,k}\right)$ and solve a quadratic equation. The the result is below. The details have been omitted due to space constraints.

PROPOSITION 1. *If $R_-^{l,j,k} > 0$, the solution to (24) is*

$$l_{r,j,k} = l_{s,j,k} - 1 + \log\left(\frac{-\beta + \sqrt{\beta^2 + 4cR_+^{l,j,k}R_-^{l,j,k}}}{2R_+^{l,j,k}}\right). \quad (27)$$

.

If $R_-^{l,j,k} = 0$ or close to zero, which can happen when there are no points outside the smallest enclosing box in direction j, we set $l_{r,j,k} = \overline{l_j}$ where $\overline{l_j}$ is the smallest value of feature j. In that case, the boundary effectively disappears from the description of the classifier, making it more interpretable.

The interpretation of the proposition is that the boundary has moved from its starting position $l_{s,j,k}$ by amount $1 - \log\left(\frac{-\beta+\sqrt{\beta^2+4cR_+^{l,j,k}R_-^{l,j,k}}}{2R_+^{l,j,k}}\right)$.

Similarly, we let $u_{r,j,k}$ be the revised upper boundary of the jth dimension for the k-th revised box and it can be computed as follows.

PROPOSITION 2. *If $R_-^{l,j,k} > 0$,*

$$u_{r,j,k} = u_{s,j,k} + 1 + \log\left(\frac{\beta + \sqrt{\beta^2 + 4cR_+^{u,j,k}R_-^{u,j,k}}}{2cR_-^{u,j,k}}\right) \quad (28)$$

where

$$R_+^{u,j,k} := \sum_{x \in S_+^k \cap X_{u,j,k}} \exp\left[-(u_{s,j,k} - x_j + 1)\right], \quad (29)$$

$$R_-^{u,j,k} := \sum_{x \in S_-^k \cap X_{u,j,k}} \exp\Bigg[u_{s,j,k} - x_j + 1 + \sum_{p \neq j}(\lfloor x_p - u_{s,p,k}\rfloor_+ + \lfloor l_{s,p,k} - x_p\rfloor_+)\Bigg] \quad (30)$$

The proof and interpretation are similar to Proposition 1.

If $R_-^{u,j,k} = 0$ or close to zero, we set $v = \overline{u_j}$ where $\overline{u_j}$ is the largest possible value for feature j.

After we learn each of the decision boundaries, we perform a final adjustment that accomplishes two tasks: (i) it ensures that the box always expands rather than contracts, (ii) further expands the box to ϵ away from the nearest negative example. This gives us final values $l_{f,j,k}$ and $u_{f,j,k}$, where subscript "f" is for final. Written out, this is:

$$\begin{aligned} l_{f,j,k} &:= \sup\{x_j | x \in S_-, x_j \\ &< \min(l_{r,j,k}, l_{s,j,k})\} + \epsilon, \forall j,k \quad (31) \\ u_{f,j,k} &:= \inf\{x_j | x \in S_-, x_j \\ &> \max(u_{r,j,k}, u_{s,j,k})\} - \epsilon, \forall j,k \quad (32) \end{aligned}$$

where ϵ is a small number. The boxes always expand for this algorithm, which implies that this algorithm is meant for applications where correct classification of the minority class data is crucial in practice. This expansion step can be omitted if desired, for instance if misclassifying the negative examples is too costly.

The algorithm is summarized as follows:

3.2.4 Overall Algorithm

Input: number of boxes K, tradeoffs c and β, Data $\{\mathbf{x}_i, y_i\}_i$.
Output: Boundaries of boxes.

1. Normalize the features to be between -1 and 1.
2. Cluster the minority class data into K clusters.
3. Construct the minimal enclosing box for each cluster, that is compute starting boundaries $l_{s,j,k}$ and $u_{s,j,k}$, the j-th dimension lower boundary and upper boundary respectively for the k'th cluster.
4. Construct data for local classifiers $X_{l,j,k}$ and $X_{u,j,k}$ based on equations (22) and (23) respectively.
5. Compute $R_+^{l,j,k}$, $R_-^{l,j,k}$, $R_+^{u,j,k}$, $R_-^{u,j,k}$, according to equations (25), (26), (29), and (30).
6. Compute $l_{r,j,k}$ based on equation (27) and $u_{r,j,k}$ based on equation (28) respectively.
7. Perform expansion based on equations (31) and (32).
8. Un-normalize by rescaling the features back to get meaningful values.

Note that after the clustering step on the minority class data, all the other steps are easily parallellizable.

4. PREDICTION QUALITY

Now that we have two very different algorithms for creating box drawing classifiers, we will compare their performances experimentally.

Evaluation Metric

We chose to use the area under the convex hull of the ROC curve (AUH) [18] as our evaluation metric; it is frequently used for imbalanced classification problems and considers the full ROC curve (Receiver Operator Characteristic) curve to evaluate performance. To compute the AUH, we compute classifiers for various settings of the tradeoff parameter c, which controls the relative importance of positive and negative classes. Each setting of c corresponds to a single point on the ROC curve, with a count of true and false positives. We compute the AUH formed by the points on the ROC curve, and normalize as usual by dividing it by the number of positive examples times the number of negative examples. The best possible result is an AUH of 1.

Baseline Algorithms

For comparison, we consider logistic regression, SVM with radial basis kernel, CART, C4.5, Random Forests, AdaBoost (with decision trees), C5.0, and Hellinger Distance Decision Tree (HDDT) [8]. Most of these algorithms are listed among the top 10 algorithms in data mining [24]. Among these algorithms, only CART, C4.5, C5.0, and HDDT yield potentially interpretable models. HDDT uses Hellinger distance as the splitting criterion, which is robust and skew-insensitive.

In addition to the baselines above, we implemented the Patient Rule Induction Method (PRIM) for "bump hunting" [9]. This method also partitions the input variable space into box shaped regions, but in a different way than our method. PRIM searches iteratively for sub-regions where the target variable has a maxima, and peels them off one at a time, whereas our clustering step finds maxima simultaneously.

The data sets we considered are listed in Table 2. Some data sets (castle, corner, diamond, square, flooded, castle3D, corner3D, diamond3D, flooded3D, flooded3D) are simulated data that are able to be visualized (made publicly available at [10]). The breast and pima data sets were obtained from the UCI Machine Learning Repository [3]. The data set fourclass was obtained from LIBSVM [4]. The remaining imbalanced data sets were obtained from the KEEL (Knowledge Extraction based on Evolutionary Learning) imbalanced data repository [2]. The Iris0 data set is an imbalanced version of the standard iris data set, where two of the classes (iris-versicolor and iris-virginica) have been combined to form the majority class.

Data	number of examples	feature size	imbalance ratio
pima	768	8	1.8657
castle	8716	2	22.2427
corner	10000	2	99
diamond	10000	2	24.9067
square	10000	2	11.2100
flooded	10000	2	31.1543
fourclass	862	2	1.8078
castle3D	545	3	7.2576
corner3D	1000	3	28.4118
diamond3D	1000	3	33.4828
square3D	1000	3	7
flooded3D	1000	3	26.7778
breast	569	30	1.6840
abalone19	4174	9	129.4375
yeast6	1484	8	41.4
yeast5	1484	8	32.7273
yeast1289	947	8	30.5667
yeast4	1484	8	28.0980
yeast28	482	8	23.1000
yeast1458	693	8	22.1000
abalone918	731	9	16.4048
pageblocks134	472	10	15.8571
ecoli4	336	7	15.8000
yeast17	459	7	14.3
shuttle04	1829	9	13.8699
glass2	214	9	11.5882
vehicle3	846	18	2.9906
vehicle1	846	18	2.8986
vehicle2	846	18	2.8807
haberman	306	3	2.7778
yeast1	1484	8	2.4592
glass0	214	9	2.0571
iris0	150	4	2
wisconsin	683	9	1.8577
ecoli01	220	7	1.8571
glass1	214	9	1.8158
breast tissue	106	9	3.8182

Table 2: Summary of datasets used for experiments

Performance analysis

Here we compare the performance of Fast Boxes with the baseline algorithms. For each algorithm (except C4.5) we set the imbalance weighting parameter to each value $[0.1, 0.2, 0.3, \ldots, 1]$. The other parameters were set in data-dependent way; for instance, for SVM with RBF kernel, the kernel width was chosen using the sigest function in the R programming language. The data were separated into 10 folds, where each fold was used in turn as the test set. We do not prune the decision trees beyond their built-in pruning as previous research shows that unpruned decision trees are more effective in their predictions on the minority class [17, 5], and because it would introduce more complexity that would be difficult to control for. Within the training set, for the Fast Boxes algorithm we used 3-fold cross-validation to select the cluster number and expansion parameter.

Table 5 shows the performances in terms of AUH means and standard deviations. The values that are bolded represent the algorithms whose results are not statistically significantly different from the best algorithm using a matched pairs sign test with significance level $\alpha = 0.05$. When there was more than one best-performing classifier, the one with the smaller standard deviation was chosen as the best performer for that data set. Fast Boxes was often (but not always) one of the best performers for each dataset. This brings up several questions, such as: *Under what conditions does Fast Boxes perform well? How do its parameters effect the result? Does it tend to produce trivial results? Can Exact Boxes improve upon Fast Boxes' results in cases where it does not perform well? Are the results interpretable?* These are questions we will address in the remainder of this section.

We start with a partial answer to the question of when Fast Boxes performs well - it is when the classes are more imbalanced. Figure 3 shows a scatter plot of the quality of Fast Boxes' performance versus the imbalance ratio of the dataset. The vertical axis represents our rank in performance among all of the algorithms we tested. The horizontal axis is the number of negatives divided by the number of positives. The performance of Fast Boxes changes from being among the worst performers when the data are not imbalanced (and the cluster assumption is false), to being among the best performers when the data are imbalanced.

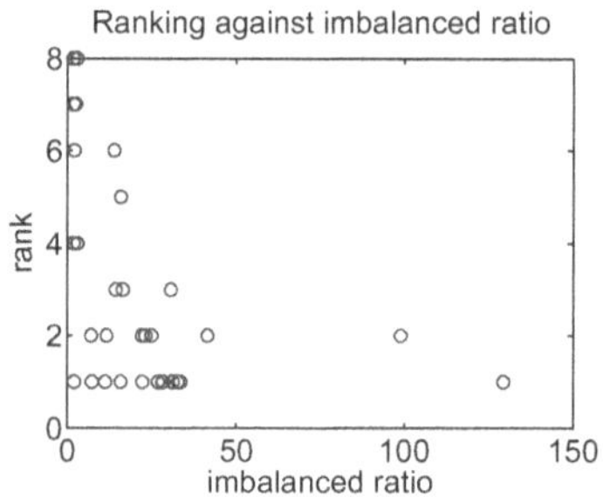

Figure 3: Ranking of Fast Boxes versus imbalance ratio of data

Below we provide some intuition about Fast Boxes' clusters and the expansion parameter before answering the questions posed just above.

Effect of Fast Boxes' parameter settings

We expect that if our main modeling assumption holds, which is that the positive examples naturally cluster, there should be a single best number of clusters. If we choose the number of clusters too small, we might underfit, and if we allow too many clusters, we could overfit. Figure 4 illustrates the cluster assumption on the diamond3D dataset, where this effect of overfitting and underfitting can be seen.

The expansion parameter is also designed to assist with generalization. We would like our boxes to be able to capture more of the positive cluster than is provided by the tightest box around the training examples, particularly since true positives are worth more than true negatives in our objective function. The exponential loss creates a discriminative classifier, but with a push outwards. Naturally, as we increase the expansion parameter, the training AUH will drop as more negative training examples are included within the box. On the other hand, the test AUH tends to increase

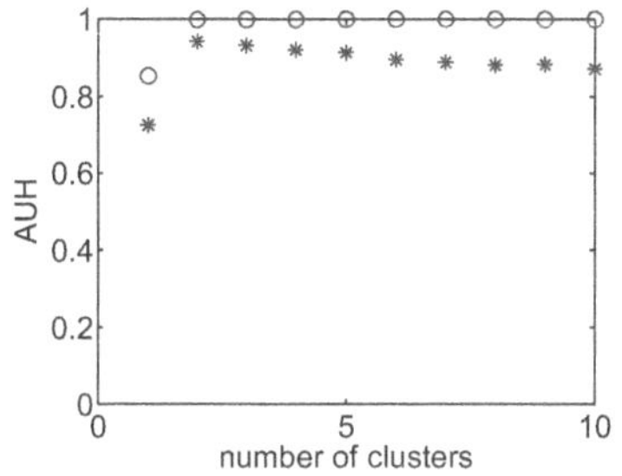

Figure 4: The effect of the number of clusters on AUH for the data set diamond3D. Fast Boxes was run once for each number of clusters. Training AUH is reported as circles, and testing AUH as stars.

before decreasing, as more positive examples are within the expanded box. This effect is illustrated in Figure 5.

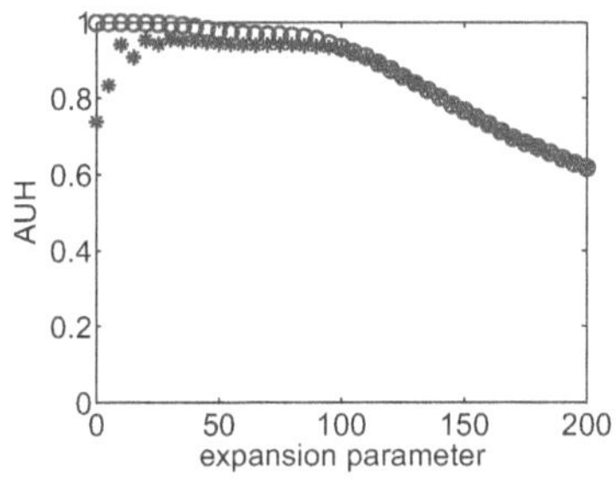

Figure 5: The effect of the expansion parameter on AUH for the diamond3D data set.

Considering the final expansion stage, Figure 6 illustrates why this stage is necessary. We visualize the iris0 dataset with dimension 1 and dimension 4, where if we had not expanded out to the nearest negative example, we would have missed a part of the positive distribution within the test set.

Production of trivial rules

When the data are highly imbalanced, we have found that some of the baseline algorithms for producing interpretable models often produce trivial models, that is, models that always predict a single class. This is true even when the weighting factor on the positive class is varied throughout its full range at a reasonably fine granularity. This means that either it is not possible to obtain a meaningful model for the dataset with that method, or it means one would need to work fairly hard in order to find a weighting factor that did not produce a trivial model; that is, the range for which nontrivial models are possible is very small. Figure 3 considers three interpretable methods we compare with, namely CART, C4.5, and C5.0. It shows the fraction of time these algorithms produce trivial models. For CART, C5.0, and Fast Boxes, the percentage was computed over 100 models computed over 10 splits and 10 options for the imbalance parameter. C4.5 does not have a built in imbalance parameter, so the percentage was computed over 10 splits.

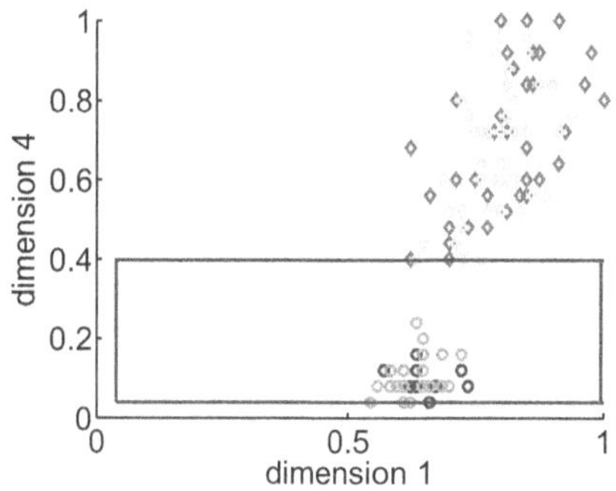

Figure 6: The red and yellow points are negative training points and testing point respectively, the blue and green points are positive training points and testing points respectively. If we had used the tightest decision boundary around the positive training examples, we would have missed part of the positive distribution.

Data	CART	C4.5	C5.0	Fast Boxes
pima	0.00	0.00	0.00	0.07
castle	0.00	0.00	0.00	0.10
corner	0.00	**0.60**	**0.70**	0.00
diamond	0.00	0.00	0.00	0.00
square	0.00	0.00	0.00	0.00
flooded	0.00	**0.70**	**0.80**	0.00
fourclass	0.00	0.00	0.00	0.03
castle3D	0.00	0.00	0.00	0.10
corner3D	0.00	**0.50**	**0.50**	0.07
diamond3D	0.00	**1.00**	**1.00**	0.06
square3D	0.00	**0.90**	**0.80**	0.10
flooded3D	0.05	**1.00**	**1.00**	0.09
breast	0.00	0.00	0.00	0.37
abalone19	0.43	**1.00**	**1.00**	0.35
yeast6	0.00	0.00	0.00	0.02
yeast5	0.00	0.00	0.00	0.36
yeast1289	0.16	**0.70**	**0.60**	0.35
yeast4	0.00	0.20	0.20	0.30
yeast28	0.39	**0.90**	**0.90**	0.00
yeast1458	0.24	**0.70**	**0.90**	0.19
abalone918	0.00	0.10	0.10	0.40
pageblocks134	0.00	0.00	0.00	0.39
ecoli4	0.00	0.00	0.00	0.32
yeast17	0.03	0.20	0.30	0.21
shuttle04	0.00	0.00	0.00	0.00
glass2	0.09	0.40	**0.70**	0.28
vehicle3	0.00	0.00	0.00	0.01
vehicle1	0.00	0.00	0.00	0.02
vehicle2	0.00	0.00	0.00	0.27
haberman	0.00	0.40	**0.70**	0.13
yeast1	0.00	0.00	0.00	0.08
glass0	0.00	0.00	0.00	0.08
iris0	0.00	0.00	0.00	0.03
wisconsin	0.00	0.00	0.00	0.34
ecoli01	0.00	0.00	0.00	0.21
glass1	0.00	0.00	0.00	0.16
breast tissue	0.00	0.00	0.00	0.08

Table 3: Fraction of the time we get a trivial model. Bold indicates values over 0.5.

Comparison of Fast Boxes and Exact Boxes

Since we know that Fast Boxes is competitive with other baselines for handling imbalanced data, we would like to know whether Exact Boxes has the potential to yield significant performance gains over Fast Boxes and other methods. We implemented the MIP using GUROBI on a quad core Intel i7 860 2.8 GHz, 8GB cache, processor with 4 cores with hyperthreading and 16GM of RAM. We first ran the Exact Boxes algorithm for 30 minutes, and if the AUH performance was not competitive and the optimality gap was above 1%, we ran it up to 90 minutes for each instance. We did not generally allow the MIP to solve to provable optimality. This has the potential to hinder performance, but as we were performing repeated experiments we needed to be able to solve the method repeatedly.

Table 4 shows results from Exact Boxes for several of the smaller data sets, along with the results from Fast Boxes for comparison. Bold font in this table summarizes results from the other baseline algorithms as well: if the entry is in bold, it means that the result is not statistically significantly different than the best out of *all* of the algorithms. Thus, for 5 out of 8 datasets we tried, the MIP was among the top performers. Further, the AUH value was substantially improved for some of the data sets. Thus, restricting the algorithm to produce a box drawing classifier does not generally seem to hinder performance.

Data	Best Performance	Fast Boxes	Exact Boxes	Exact Boxes ranking
vehicle2	0.9496 (0.015)	0.9191 (0.0242)	0.9496 (0.015)	1
haberman	0.6699 (0.0276)	0.5290 (0.0265)	**0.6632** (0.0303)	2
yeast1	0.7641 (0.0133)	0.5903 (0.0286)	0.7392 (0.0172)	2
glass0	0.8312 (0.0345)	0.7937 (0.0212)	0.7977 (0.0421)	2
iris0	1 (0)	**1** (0)	**1** (0)	1
wisconsin	0.9741 (0.0075)	0.8054 (0.1393)	**0.9726** (0.0079)	2
ecoli01	0.9840 (0.0105)	0.9433 (0.0300)	**0.9839** (0.0109)	2
glass1	0.7922 (0.0377)	0.6654 (0.0356)	**0.7922** (0.0337)	1

Table 4: Comparison of test data AUH of interpretable methods with Exact Boxes. Bold font includes results from non-interpretable methods.

Note that it is time-consuming to perform cross-validation on the MIP, so the cluster number that we found using cross-validation for Fast Boxes was used for Exact Boxes.

Interpretability demonstration

We provide a classifier we learned from the glass2 data set that predicts whether a particular glass is a building window that is non-float processed. The other types of glasses are building windows that are float processed, vehicle windows, containers, tableware, and headlamps. The attributes include the refraction index as well as various indices for metals. These metals include Sodium, Magnesium, Aluminum, Silicon, Potassium, Calcium, Barium, and Iron.

One of the predictive models from Fast Boxes is as follows. To be a particular glass of a building window that is non-float processed:

1) The refractive index should be above 1.5161.
2) Magnesium index must be above 3.3301.
3) Aluminum should be below 1.7897.
4) Silicon should be below 73.0199.
5) Potassium should be below 0.6199.
6) Calcium should be between 8.3101 and 2.3741.
7) Barium should be below 2.6646.
8) Sodium and iron are not important factors.

We believe that this simple form of model would appeal to practitioners because of the natural threshold structure of the box drawing classifiers.

5. THEORETICAL GUARANTEE ON PERFORMANCE

Statistical learning theory will allow us to provide a probabilistic guarantee on the performance of our algorithms. We will construct a uniform generalization bound, which holds over all box drawing classifiers with K boxes anchored at M_j different fixed values for each dimension, where K is fixed. We might choose M_j as the count of numbers with at most a certain number of decimal places (say 2 decimal places) in between the largest and smallest possible values for a particular feature. (Often in practice only 2 decimal places are used.) The main step in our proof is to count the number of possible box drawing classifiers. The set of all box drawing classifiers with up to K boxes, with l_j and u_j attaining the M_j values, will be called F.

Define the empirical risk to be the objective of Exact Boxes with no regularization,

$$R^{emp}(f) = \sum_{i:y_i=1} \mathbf{1}_{[f(\mathbf{x}_i)=1]} + C_I \sum_{i:y_i=-1} \mathbf{1}_{[f(\mathbf{x}_i)=-1]},$$

and let the true risk $R^{true}(f)$ be the expectation of this taken over the distribution that the data are drawn iid from.

Proposition 3. *For all $\delta > 0$ with probability at least $1-\delta, \forall f \in F$,*

$$R^{true}(f) \leq R^{emp}(f) + \sqrt{\frac{K\sum_{j=1}^{n}\log(\frac{M_j(M_j-1)}{2}) - logK! + \log\frac{1}{\delta}}{2m}}.$$

To outline the proof, there are $\prod_{j=1}^{n}\binom{M_j}{2}$ ways to construct a single box, since for each dimension, we select 2 values, namely the lower boundary l_j and upper boundary u_j. To construct multiple boxes, there are at most $\prod_{j=1}^{n}\binom{M_j}{2}^K$ ways if the order of construction of the boxes matter. Since the order does not matter, we need to divide the term by $K!$. Note that this is an upper bound which is not tight since some boxes can be a proper subset or equal to another box. Although we are considering the set of all box drawing classifiers up to K boxes, it suffices to consider box drawing classifiers with exactly K boxes. This can be seen by supposing we constructed a classifier with $l < K$ boxes, and noting the same classifier can be constructed using K boxes by duplicating some boxes. We apply Hoeffding's inequality and the union bound to complete the proof.

6. MAKING THE MIP MORE PRACTICAL

From the experimental outcome, it is clear that Exact Boxes is indeed a competitive solution. The main challenge lies in its computational complexity. There are several ways one might make the MIP more practical: first, one could limit computation to focus only a neighborhood of the positive data, and use the solution to this problem to warm start the MIP on the full problem. In that case we would consider only negative points that are close to the positive points in at least one dimension, which can be identified in a single pass through the negative examples. Alternatively, one can perform clustering first as in the Fast Boxes approach, and solve the MIP on each cluster. For each cluster, we would scan through each feature of the data in a single pass and keep only the data that are close to the mean of the cluster center to use in the MIP.

7. DISCUSSION AND CONCLUSION

We have presented two new approaches to designing interpretable predictive models for imbalanced data settings. Exact Boxes is formulated as a mixed integer program, and acts as a gold standard interpretable modeling technique to compare with. It can be used for small to moderately sized problems. Fast Boxes uses a characterize-then-discriminate approach, and tends to work well when the minority class is naturally clustered (for instance when the clusters represent different failure modes of mechanical equipment). We illuminated the benefits and limitations of our approaches, and hope that these types of models will be able to provide alternative explanations and insights into imbalanced problems. In comparing Fast Boxes with gold standard interpretable techniques like Exact Boxes, and with many other methods, we can now judge the power of the class of interpretable models: it is interesting that such simple approaches can achieve comparable performance with even the best state-of-the-art techniques.

Acknowledgements Funding for this work provided by Siemens.

8. REFERENCES

[1] N. Abe. Sampling approaches to learning from imbalanced datasets: Active learning, cost senstive learning and beyond, 2003. Proc. ICML, Workshop Learning from Imbalanced Data Sets II.

[2] J. Alcala-Fdez, A. Fernandez, J. Luengo, J. Derrac, and S. Garcia. Keel data-mining sofware tool: Data set repository, integration of algorithms and experimental analysis framework. 2011. `http://sci2s.urg.es/keel/imbalanced.php#sub3`.

[3] K. Bache and M. Lichman. UCI machine learning repository. 2013. `http://archive.ics.uci.edu/ml`.

[4] C.-C. Chang and C.-J. Lin. LIBSVM: A library for support vector machines. *ACM Transactions on Intelligent Systems and Technology*, 2:27:1–27:27, 2011. Software available at `http://www.csie.ntu.edu.tw/~cjlin/libsvm`.

[5] N. V. Chawla. C4.5 and imbalanced data sets: investigating the effect of sampling method, probabilistic estimate, and decision tree structure. In *In Proceedings of the ICMLo03 Workshop on Class Imbalances*, 2003.

[6] N. V. Chawla, K. W. Bowyer, L. O. Hall, and W. P. Kegelmeyer. Smote: Synthetic minority over-sampling technique. *Journal of Artificial Intelligence Research*, 16:321–357, 2002.

[7] N. V. Chawla, N. Japkowicz, and A. Kotcz. Editorial: Special issue on learning from imbalanced data sets. *SIGKDD Explor. Newsl.*, 6(1):1–6, June 2004.

[8] D. Cieslak, T. Hoens, N. Chawla, and W. Kegelmeyer. Hellinger distance decision trees are robust and skew-insensitive. *Data Mining and Knowledge Discovery*, 24(1):136–158, 2012.

[9] J. Friedman and N. Fisher. Bump hunting in high-dimensional data. *Statistics and Computing*, 9(2):123–143, 1999.

[10] S. T. Goh and C. Rudin. 2014. `http://web.mit.edu/stgoh/www/imbalanceddatafolder/`.

[11] H. He and E. Garcia. Learning from imbalanced data. *Knowledge and Data Engineering, IEEE Transactions on*, 21(9):1263–1284, Sept 2009.

[12] R. C. Holte. Very simple classification rules perform well on most commonly used datasets. In *Machine Learning*, pages 63–91, 1993.

[13] N. Japkowicz. Class imbalances: Are we focusing on the right issue? In *Notes from the ICML Workshop on Learning from Imbalanced Data Sets II*, 2003.

[14] X.-Y. Liu and Z.-H. Zhou. The influence of class imbalance on cost-sensitive learning: An empirical study. In *Data Mining, 2006. ICDM '06. Sixth International Conference on*, pages 970–974, Dec 2006.

[15] K. McCarthy, B. Zabar, and G. Weiss. Does cost-sensitive learning beat sampling for classifying rare classes? In *Proceedings of the 1st International Workshop on Utility-based Data Mining*, UBDM '05, pages 69–77, New York, NY, USA, 2005. ACM.

[16] R. Prati, G. Batista, and M. Monard. Class imbalances versus class overlapping: An analysis of a learning system behavior. In R. Monroy, G. Arroyo-Figueroa, L. Sucar, and H. Sossa, editors, *MICAI 2004: Advances in Artificial Intelligence*, volume 2972 of *Lecture Notes in Computer Science*, pages 312–321. Springer Berlin Heidelberg, 2004.

[17] F. Provost and P. Domingos. Tree induction for probability-based ranking, 2002.

[18] F. Provost and T. Fawcett. Robust classification for imprecise environments. *Machine Learning*, 42(3):203–231, 2001.

[19] Y. Qi. A brief literature review of class imbalanced problem. IR-Lab Project of Yanjun Qi, 2004.

[20] B. Raskutti and A. Kowalczyk. Extreme re-balancing for svms: A case study. *SIGKDD Explor. Newsl.*, 6(1):60–69, June 2004.

[21] J. Sniadecki. Bump hunting with sas: A macro approach to employing prim. SAS Global Forum 2011, Data Mining and Text Analytics, 2011.

[22] G. M. Weiss. Mining with rarity: A unifying framework. *SIGKDD Explor. Newsl.*, 6(1):7–19, June 2004.

[23] G. Wu and E. Y. Chang. Class-boundary alignment for imbalanced dataset learning. In *In ICML 2003 Workshop on Learning from Imbalanced Data Sets*, pages 49–56, 2003.

[24] X. Wu, V. Kumar, Ross, J. Ghosh, and et al. Top 10 algorithms in data mining. *Knowledge and Information Systems*, 14(1):1–37, 2008.

Data	Logistic	SVM	CART	C4.5	Ada-Boost	RF	C5.0	HDDT	Fast Boxes
pima	**0.8587** (0.0112)	**0.8468** (0.0126)	0.7738 (0.0123)	0.6579 (0.0347)	0.6810 (0.0218)	0.6942 (0.0126)	0.6574 (0.0353)	0.6642 (0.0274)	0.7298 (0.0241)
castle	0.5 (0)	**1** (0)	0.9941 (0.0068)	0.9947 (0.0060)	**0.9949** (0.0046)	**0.9922** (0.0079)	0.9941 (0.0060)	**0.9949** (0.0062)	**1** (0)
corner	**0.9871** (0.0129)	**0.9948** (0.0005)	0.9488 (0.2717)	0.5997 (0.1482)	0.6984 (0.0449)	0.6828 (0.0265)	0.5612 (0.1110)	0.6865 (0.0365)	0.9891 (0.0001)
diamond	0.5 (0)	**0.9980** (0.0004)	0.9585 (0.0129)	0.9328 (0.0181)	0.9460 (0.0117)	0.9433 (0.0121)	0.9311 (0.0208)	0.9364 (0.0180)	0.9744 (0.0062)
square	0.5404 (0.0718)	0.9944 (0.0001)	0.9949 (0.0051)	0.9949 (0.0043)	0.9939 (0.0033)	0.9947 (0.0033)	0.9949 (0.0043)	0.9949 (0.0027)	**0.9984** (0.0015)
flooded	0 (0)	**0.9831** (0.0010)	0.9466 (0.0157)	0.5488 (0.1074)	0.7017 (0.0231)	0.7036 (0.0252)	0.5482 (0.1077)	0.6992 (0.0208)	09638 (0.0091)
fourclass	0.8122 (0.0195)	**0.9957** (0.0176)	0.9688 (0.0176)	0.9916 (0.0296)	0.9670 (0.0265)	**0.9920** (0.0053)	0.9670 (0.0130)	0.9698 (0.0116)	0.9546 (0.0174)
castle3D	0.5449 (0.0324)	**1** (0)	0.9532 (0.0347)	0.9530 (0.0374)	0.9272 (0.0499)	**0.9455** (0.0563)	0.9439 (0.0615)	0.9530 (0.0374)	**1** (0)
corner3D	0.8448 (0.0316)	**0.9225** (0.0463)	0.8481 (0.0504)	0.5596 (0.0729)	0.6245 (0.03927)	0.5657 (0.0309)	0.5622 (0.0778)	0.6413 (0.0457)	**0.9736** (0.0091)
diamond3D	0.5449 (0.0324)	**0.7962** (0.0917)	0.7372 (0.0347)	0.5 (0.0374)	0.5492 (0.0499)	0.5957 (0.0309)	0.5622 (0.0778)	0.6883 (0.0542)	**0.9516** (0.0119)
square3D	0.5 (0)	**0.9626** (0.0156)	**0.9106** (0.0306)	0.5387 (0.1224)	0.8703 (0.01451)	0.8790 (0.0234)	0.5811 (0.1712)	0.9034 (0.0322)	**0.9578** (0.0090)
flooded3D	0.5 (0)	0.7912 (0.0781)	0.7724 (0.0902)	0.5 (0)	0.5471 (0.0329)	0.5489 (0.0440)	0.5 (0)	0.6422 (0.0749)	**0.9233** (0.0307)
breast	0.9297 (0.0230)	**0.9801** (0.0079)	0.9516 (0.0173)	0.9251 (0.0138)	0.9457 (0.0329)	0.9609 (0.0102)	0.9281 (0.0135)	0.9231 (0.0180)	0.8888 (0.0313)
abalone19	0.5188 (0.0182)	0.5 (0)	0.5382 (0.0261)	0.5 (0)	0.5 (0)	0.5 (0)	0.5 (0)	0.5116 (0.0164)	**0.6882** (0.0583)
yeast6	**0.8503** (0.0341)	**0.8649** (0.0246)	0.7995 (0.0624)	0.7129 (0.0829)	0.7126 (0.0536)	0.7277 (0.0581)	0.7129 (0.0853)	0.7064 (0.0772)	**0.8609** (0.0585)
yeast5	**0.9499** (0.0479)	0.9229 (0.0339)	**0.9197** (0.0575)	0.8280 (0.1159)	0.8305 (0.0859)	0.8061 (0.0616)	0.8241 (0.1157)	0.7931 (0.1126)	**0.9767** (0.0092)
yeast1289	**0.6319** (0.0433)	0.5618 (0.0332)	**0.7076** (0.0665)	0.5088 (0.0322)	0.5152 (0.0288)	0.5067 (0.0141)	0.5156 (0.0342)	0.5531 (0.0436)	0.5932 (0.0557)
yeast4	0.8001 (0.0309)	0.7836 (0.0480)	0.7595 (0.0410)	0.6115 (0.0902)	0.6131 (0.0326)	0.5922 (0.0326)	0.6210 (0.07899)	0.6289 (0.0471)	**0.8794** (0.0274)
yeast28	**0.7907** (0.0525)	0.6596 (0.0565)	0.6402 (0.0893)	0.5100 (0.0316)	0.5 (0)	0.6489 (0.0472)	0.5248 (0.0784)	0.6126 (0.0606)	**0.7366** (0.0467)
yeast1458	**0.6164** (0.0510)	0.5420 (0.0322)	**0.6032** (0.0281)	0.5 (0)	0.5023 (0.0088)	0.5095 (0.0154)	0.5 (0)	0.5340 (0.0467)	**0.6090** (0.0431)
abalone918	**0.8849** (0.0270)	0.6780 (0.0391)	0.7427 (0.0517)	0.5904 (0.0581)	0.6117 (0.0456)	0.5580 (0.03213)	0.5725 (0.0470)	0.6310 (0.0418)	0.7171 (0.0603)
pageblocks 134	0.9461 (0.0444)	0.7874 (0.1184)	**0.9945** (0.0109)	**0.9908** (0.0219)	**0.9908** (0.0449)	**0.9500** (0.0345)	**0.9908** (0.0219)	**0.9551** (0.0487)	0.9500 (0.0359)
ecoli4	**0.8926** (0.0615)	**0.9176** (0.0424)	**0.8809** (0.0593)	0.7759 (0.07756)	**0.7965** (0.0775)	**0.8494** (0.0775)	0.8471 (0.0532)	**0.8430** (0.0743)	**0.9202** (0.0622)
yeast17	**0.7534** (0.0611)	**0.6905** (0.0386)	**0.7481** (0.0713)	0.5841 (0.0698)	0.5382 (0.0225)	0.5529 (0.0359)	0.5721 (0.0699)	0.6070 (0.0509)	**0.7033** (0.0547)
shuttle04	**0.9965** (0.0045)	**0.9828** (0.0105)	**1** (0)	**0.9994** (0.0008)	**1** (0)	**1** (0)	**1** (0)	**0.9994** (0.0008)	**0.9967** (0.0042)
glass2	**0.7609** (0.0726)	0.6128 (0.0941)	**0.7112** (0.1090)	0.5541 (0.0640)	0.5324 (0.0417)	0.5479 (0.0597)	0.5200 (0.0415)	0.5892 (0.0573)	**0.7334** (0.0904)
vehicle3	**0.8397** (0.0079)	**0.8524** (0.0169)	0.7733 (0.0255)	0.6515 (0.0401)	0.6591 (0.0212)	0.6484 (0.0232)	0.6621 (0.02117)	0.6823 (0.0300)	0.7003 (0.0267)
vehicle1	**0.8587** (0.0112)	0.8468 (0.0126)	0.7738 (0.0123)	0.6579 (0.0347)	0.6810 (0.0218)	0.6942 (0.0126)	0.6574 (0.0353)	0.6719 (0.0265)	0.7298 (0.0241)
vehicle2	0.9632 (0.0134)	**0.9837** (0.0072)	0.9437 (0.01880)	0.9351 (0.0133)	0.9677 (0.0097)	**0.9775** (0.0106)	0.9365 (0.0129)	0.9248 (0.0243)	0.9191 (0.0242)
haberman	**0.6589** (0.1713)	**0.6898** (0.0427)	**0.6699** (0.0276)	**0.5733** (0.0748)	0.6004 (0.0323)	0.6130 (0.0318)	**0.5420** (0.6780)	0.5604 (0.0231)	0.5290 (0.0265)
yeast1	0.7836 (0.0184)	**0.7991** (0.0150)	0.7641 (0.0133)	0.6672 (0.0372)	0.6859 (0.0219)	0.6130 (0.0318)	0.5420 (0.0678)	0.6369 (0.0128)	0.5903 (0.0286)
glass0	0.7951 (0.0437)	**0.8636** (0.0336)	0.8312 (0.0345)	0.7687 (0.0619)	0.7998 (0.0381)	**0.8572** (0.0281)	0.7690 (0.0595)	0.7569 (0.0424)	0.7937 (0.0212)
iris0	**1** (0)	**0.998** (0.0063)	**1** (0)	**0.978** (0.0175)	**1** (0)	**1** (0)	**0.972** (0.0169)	**0.9880** (0.0193)	**1** (0)
wisconsin	**0.9746** (0.0093)	**0.9735** (0.0073)	**0.9741** (0.0075)	0.9455 (0.0124)	0.9611 (0.0122)	0.9672 (0.0072)	0.9416 (0.0121)	0.9249 (0.0203)	0.8054 (0.1393)
ecoli01	**0.9728** (0.0140)	**0.9850** (0.0091)	**0.9840** (0.0105)	**0.9806** (0.0107)	**0.9828** (0.0063)	**0.9855** (0.0097)	**0.9806** (0.0107)	0.9806 (0.0107)	0.9433 (0.0300)
glass1	0.7247 (0.0363)	**0.8057** (0.0340)	0.7598 (0.0490)	0.7050 (0.0358)	0.6997 (0.0478)	0.7833 (0.0274)	0.6822 (0.0320)	0.7189 (0.0586)	0.6654 (0.0356)
breast tissue	0.9411 (0.0394)	0.9908 (0.0064)	0.9417 (0.0747)	0.9450 (0.0602)	0.9632 (0.0297)	0.9531 (0.0505)	0.9630 (0.0403)	0.9314 (0.0550)	**0.9953** (0.0042)

Table 5: Comparison of test data AUH of Fast Boxes with other algorithms

Incremental and Decremental Training for Linear Classification

Cheng-Hao Tsai
Dept. of Computer Science
National Taiwan Univ., Taiwan
r01922025@csie.ntu.edu.tw

Chieh-Yen Lin
Dept. of Computer Science
National Taiwan Univ., Taiwan
r01944006@csie.ntu.edu.tw

Chih-Jen Lin
Dept. of Computer Science
National Taiwan Univ., Taiwan
cjlin@csie.ntu.edu.tw

ABSTRACT

In classification, if a small number of instances is added or removed, incremental and decremental techniques can be applied to quickly update the model. However, the design of incremental and decremental algorithms involves many considerations. In this paper, we focus on linear classifiers including logistic regression and linear SVM because of their simplicity over kernel or other methods. By applying a warm start strategy, we investigate issues such as using primal or dual formulation, choosing optimization methods, and creating practical implementations. Through theoretical analysis and practical experiments, we conclude that a warm start setting on a high-order optimization method for primal formulations is more suitable than others for incremental and decremental learning of linear classification.

Categories and Subject Descriptors

I.5.2 [**Pattern Recognition**]: Design Methodology—*Classifier design and evaluation*

Keywords

warm start; incremental learning; decremental learning; linear classification

1. INTRODUCTION

In supervised learning, when a small amount of data is added or removed, the classification model may not change much. Therefore, incremental and decremental algorithms are useful to update the model without re-training the problem from scratch. However, the design of good incremental and decremental learning algorithms is never easy. First, they are often extended from a standard learning method, but the resulting procedure may become very complicated. Second, applying incremental and decremental algorithms is not guaranteed to be faster than re-training the data from scratch. Third, the scenarios to use incremental and decremental learning may significantly vary according to applications, so designing software for general use is difficult.

In this paper, we study incremental and decremental algorithms for logistic regression (LR) and linear support vector machine (SVM). The decision to work on linear rather than kernel classifiers comes from a long journey of attempting to support incremental and decremental learning in our SVM software LIBSVM [4]. Although many users have requested this function and some studies have been conducted, we were hampered by two difficulties. First, extending the commonly used decomposition methods to flexibly enlarge or shrink the cached kernel elements during training is complicated. Note that adding or removing data causes a "two-dimensional" change of rows and columns of the kernel matrix. Second, existing extensions of decomposition methods for incremental or decremental learning may not effectively reduce the running time. Recently, in contrast to using kernels, linear classification has been shown to give comparable accuracy on some applications (see, e.g., a survey in [19]). The popularity of linear classification has motivated us to study incremental and decremental learning again. However, the goal becomes to support this functionality in another software LIBLINEAR [8] for large-scale linear classification.

We point out that the difficulties occurred in incremental and decremental learning for kernel classifiers may be alleviated for linear classifiers because more optimization algorithms are applicable. For kernel classifiers, it is rather restrictive to design optimization algorithms because the model is represented by a linear combination of training instances. Therefore, the optimization problem must be designed to find coefficients for this linear combination. In contrast, as we will explain in Section 2, there are more options in solving optimization problems for linear classifiers. We show that this difference between linear and kernel classifiers strongly affects their extensions to incremental and decremental training.

In Section 3, we apply a warm start strategy for incremental and decremental training of linear classification. The optimal solution of training past data is modified as an initial solution for solving the new problem after data addition or removal. We consider in Section 4 three representative optimization algorithms for linear classification. They differ in several aspects such as solving primal or dual formulation, and using first-order (i.e., gradient) or second-order information of the optimization problem. Our main findings are that the warm start setting is in general more effective to improve the primal initial solution than the dual and that the warm start setting more effectively speeds up

KDD'14, August 24–27, 2014, New York, NY, USA.

ACM 978-1-4503-2956-9/14/08 ...$15.00.
http://dx.doi.org/10.1145/2623330.2623661.

a high-order optimization method than a low-order one. After addressing some implementation issues, we have successfully finished an extension of the software LIBLINEAR for incremental and decremental learning. It is available at http://www.csie.ntu.edu.tw/~cjlin/papers/ws.

This paper is organized as follows. In Section 2, we show the formulations of SVM and LR, and discuss existing methods for incremental and decremental learning. In Section 3, we propose a warm start setting, followed by analyzing the difference between using primal and dual forms. The comparison between high-order and low-order optimization methods is described in Section 4. In Section 5, we discuss implementation issues for building a solid tool. Experiments are presented in Section 6. Section 7 concludes our work. Supplementary materials with additional results and programs for experiments are also available at the above-mentioned web site.

2. SVM, LR, AND THEIR INCREMENTAL AND DECREMENTAL TRAINING

Assume we are given (label, feature-vector) pairs of training data $(y_i, \boldsymbol{x}_i) \in \{-1, 1\} \times R^n, i = 1, \ldots, l$. Linear classification involves the following optimization problem.

$$\min_{\boldsymbol{w}} f(\boldsymbol{w}) \text{ where } f(\boldsymbol{w}) \equiv \frac{1}{2}\boldsymbol{w}^T\boldsymbol{w} + C\sum\nolimits_{i=1}^{l} \xi(\boldsymbol{w}; \boldsymbol{x}_i, y_i). \quad (1)$$

where $\xi(\boldsymbol{w}; \boldsymbol{x}_i, y_i)$ is the loss function and C is a user-specified parameter. Common loss functions include

$$\xi_{\text{L1}}(\boldsymbol{w}; \boldsymbol{x}_i, y_i) \equiv \max(0, 1 - y_i\boldsymbol{w}^T\boldsymbol{x}_i), \quad (2)$$

$$\xi_{\text{L2}}(\boldsymbol{w}; \boldsymbol{x}_i, y_i) \equiv \max(0, 1 - y_i\boldsymbol{w}^T\boldsymbol{x}_i)^2, \quad \text{and} \quad (3)$$

$$\xi_{\text{LR}}(\boldsymbol{w}; \boldsymbol{x}_i, y_i) \equiv \log(1 + e^{-y_i\boldsymbol{w}^T\boldsymbol{x}_i}). \quad (4)$$

If (2) or (3) is used, then problem (1) is SVM [1, 7]. If (4) is used, then we have logistic regression. The three loss functions in (2)-(4) have different differentiability.

L1 loss:	not differentiable
L2 loss:	differentiable but not twice differentiable
LR loss:	twice differentiable

Many convex optimization methods have been considered to find the optimal $\boldsymbol{w}$. Alternatively, from optimization theory or the representer theorem [12], the optimal $\boldsymbol{w}$ is a linear combination of training instances with coefficients $\boldsymbol{\alpha}$.

$$\boldsymbol{w} = \sum\nolimits_{i=1}^{l} y_i\alpha_i\boldsymbol{x}_i. \quad (5)$$

Then we can instead solve an optimization problem over $\boldsymbol{\alpha}$. A common way is to derive the dual problem of (1).

$$\max_{\boldsymbol{\alpha}} f^D(\boldsymbol{\alpha}) \equiv \sum_{i=1}^{l} h(\alpha_i, C) - \frac{1}{2}\sum_{i=1}^{l}\sum_{j=1}^{l}\alpha_i\alpha_j K(i,j) - \sum_{i=1}^{l}\frac{\alpha_i^2}{2}d$$

$$\text{subject to} \quad 0 \le \alpha_i \le U, \forall i = 1, \ldots, l, \quad (6)$$

where $K(i,j) = y_iy_j\boldsymbol{x}_i^T\boldsymbol{x}_j$ and

$$U = \begin{cases} C \\ \infty \end{cases} \quad d = \begin{cases} 0 & \text{for L1-loss SVM and LR,} \\ \frac{1}{2C} & \text{for L2-loss SVM.} \end{cases}$$

Further, $h(\alpha_i, C) =$

$$\begin{cases} \alpha_i & \text{for L1-loss and L2-loss SVM,} \\ C\log C - \alpha_i\log\alpha_i - (C - \alpha_i)\log(C - \alpha_i) & \text{for LR.} \end{cases}$$

We define $0 \log 0 = 0$, so

$$h(0, C) = 0 \quad (7)$$

for all three losses. Besides (6), the dual problem can also be represented by the following matrix form.

$$\max_{\boldsymbol{\alpha}} \quad \sum\nolimits_{i=1}^{l} h(\alpha_i, C) - \frac{1}{2}\boldsymbol{\alpha}^T\bar{Q}\boldsymbol{\alpha}$$

$$\text{subject to} \quad 0 \le \alpha_i \le U, \forall i = 1, \ldots, l, \quad (8)$$

where $\bar{Q} = Q + D \in R^{l \times l}$, $Q_{ij} = K(i,j)$, and D is diagonal with $D_{ii} = d, \forall i$. We refer to (1) as the primal problem.

We briefly discuss the difference between linear and kernel classifiers. A kernel classifier maps data to a high (maybe infinite) dimensional space, so problem (1) cannot be directly solved. Instead, by kernel tricks we solve an optimization problem of $\boldsymbol{\alpha}$ like (6).[1] In contrast, for linear classifiers, it is more flexible to design optimization algorithms because we can solve problems of $\boldsymbol{w}$ or $\boldsymbol{\alpha}$. We will show in Section 3 that this difference between linear and kernel classifiers has an impact on their incremental and decremental training.

2.1 Existing Methods

Most existing studies on incremental or decremental training focus on kernel rather than linear classifiers. By considering the dual problem of kernel SVM, [3] and subsequent works [9, 11, 13, 16] investigate how to maintain the optimality condition when data are slightly changed. Note that at an optimum, all $\alpha_i \in (0, U)$ correspond to the solution of a linear system. They propose methods to quickly identify these α_i's for the new data and efficiently solve the linear system. A kernel sub-matrix is required to be enlarged or shrunk. Careful implementations are essential as we can see that [13] wrote "incremental SVM may not be so easy to implement." The only work known to us that solves the primal problem is [14]. They propose a Newton method for both kernel and linear SVM. However, their method is not scalable because matrix inversions are needed.

3. INCREMENTAL AND DECREMENTAL LEARNING WITH WARM START

We consider a warm start setting by adjusting the optimal solution before data change as the initial solution of the new optimization problem. Because optimization algorithms are iterative procedures, we hope that a good initial solution can reduce the number of iterations to save the training time. Let

$$(y_i, \boldsymbol{x}_i), i = 1, \ldots, l$$

be the original training set, and $\boldsymbol{w}^*$ and $\boldsymbol{\alpha}^*$ be optimal solutions of the primal and the dual problems, respectively. For the primal problem with the variable $\boldsymbol{w}$, the number of variables is independent of data change because $\boldsymbol{w}$'s size is the same as the number of features. Therefore, $\boldsymbol{w}^*$ can be directly used such that

$$\bar{\boldsymbol{w}} \equiv \boldsymbol{w}^*$$

is the new initial solution. In contrast, if a dual problem is used, $\boldsymbol{\alpha}$'s size is changed after data addition or removal. For incremental learning, we assume

$$(y_i, \boldsymbol{x}_i), i = l + 1, \ldots, l + k$$

[1] Besides (6), other optimization problems over $\boldsymbol{\alpha}$ may be considered; see, for example, [6].

are instances being added, and the following $\bar{\boldsymbol{\alpha}}$ is considered as the initial dual solution.

$$\bar{\boldsymbol{\alpha}} = [\alpha_1^*, \ldots, \alpha_l^*, 0, \ldots, 0]^T \in R^{(l+k)\times 1}.$$

For $\bar{\alpha}_{l+1}, \ldots, \bar{\alpha}_{l+k}$, any value in $[0, U]$ can be chosen to ensure the feasibility. Because it is unclear which value is the best, we simply consider the zero value. For decremental learning, we assume instances

$$(y_i, \boldsymbol{x}_i), i = 1, \ldots, k$$

are removed, and consider the following feasible $\bar{\boldsymbol{\alpha}}$ as the initial dual solution.

$$\bar{\boldsymbol{\alpha}} = [\alpha_{k+1}^*, \ldots, \alpha_l^*]^T. \tag{9}$$

We hope that an initial solution closer to the optimum helps to reduce the running time. Subsequently, we check the initial objective values of solving the primal and the dual problems. A finding is that the primal initial point is closer to the optimal point if the change of data is not significant.

3.1 Initial Values for Incremental Learning

The optimization problem after considering new data is

$$\min_{\boldsymbol{w}} \quad \frac{1}{2}\boldsymbol{w}^T\boldsymbol{w} + C\sum\nolimits_{i=1}^{l+k} \xi(\boldsymbol{w}; \boldsymbol{x}_i, y_i). \tag{10}$$

The primal and dual initial values are, respectively,

$$\frac{1}{2}\bar{\boldsymbol{w}}^T\bar{\boldsymbol{w}} + C\sum\nolimits_{i=1}^{l} \xi(\bar{\boldsymbol{w}}; \boldsymbol{x}_i, y_i) + C\sum\nolimits_{i=l+1}^{l+k} \xi(\bar{\boldsymbol{w}}; \boldsymbol{x}_i, y_i) \tag{11}$$

and

$$\sum_{i=1}^{l} h(\alpha_i^*, C) + \sum_{i=l+1}^{l+k} h(0, C) - \frac{1}{2}\begin{bmatrix}\boldsymbol{\alpha}^{*T} & \boldsymbol{0}^T\end{bmatrix}\begin{bmatrix}\bar{Q} & \vdots \\ \cdots & \end{bmatrix}\begin{bmatrix}\boldsymbol{\alpha}^* \\ \boldsymbol{0}\end{bmatrix}$$
$$= \frac{1}{2}\bar{\boldsymbol{w}}^T\bar{\boldsymbol{w}} + C\sum\nolimits_{i=1}^{l} \xi(\bar{\boldsymbol{w}}; \boldsymbol{x}_i, y_i), \tag{12}$$

where (12) comes from (7), and the property of same primal and dual optimal values in training the original set. Then

$$\begin{aligned} \text{dual initial value} &\leq \text{new optimal objective value} \\ &\leq \text{primal initial value} \end{aligned}$$

because $\bar{\boldsymbol{w}}$ and $\bar{\boldsymbol{\alpha}}$ are feasible solutions of the new primal and dual problems, respectively.

We argue that the primal initial value is usually closer to the optimal objective value of the new problem than the dual. A scaled form of problem (1) is

$$\min_{\boldsymbol{w}} \quad \frac{1}{2Cl}\boldsymbol{w}^T\boldsymbol{w} + \frac{1}{l}\sum\nolimits_{i=1}^{l} \xi(\boldsymbol{w}; \boldsymbol{x}_i, y_i), \tag{13}$$

which minimizes the average loss with regularization. If the original and new data points follow a similar distribution, and the original optimal solution $\boldsymbol{w}^*$ describes the average loss well, then the optimal $\boldsymbol{w}$ of (10) should be similar to $\boldsymbol{w}^*$. Therefore, (11) may be a good approximation of the new optimal objective value.

For the dual initial objective value, from (10)-(12), we suspect that it may be far away from the new optimal value because of lacking the following term

$$C\sum\nolimits_{i=l+1}^{l+k} \xi(\bar{\boldsymbol{w}}; \boldsymbol{x}_i, y_i).$$

One may question the above conclusion on the superiority of the primal initial value by claiming that the regularization parameter C must be adjusted for a larger training set. That is, to keep the same amount of total training losses, the following optimization problem can be considered.

$$\min_{\boldsymbol{w}} \quad \frac{1}{2}\boldsymbol{w}^T\boldsymbol{w} + \Delta_I C\sum\nolimits_{i=1}^{l+k} \xi(\boldsymbol{w}; \boldsymbol{x}_i, y_i),$$

where $\Delta_I = l/(l+k)$. The corresponding dual problem is

$$\begin{aligned} \max_{\boldsymbol{\alpha}} \quad & \sum_{i=1}^{l+k} h(\alpha_i, \Delta_I C) - \frac{1}{2}\sum_{i=1}^{l+k}\sum_{j=1}^{l+k} \alpha_i\alpha_j K(i,j) - \sum_{i=1}^{l+k} \frac{\alpha_i^2}{2}\frac{d}{\Delta_I} \\ \text{subject to} \quad & 0 \leq \alpha_i \leq U, \forall i = 1, \ldots, l+k. \end{aligned} \tag{14}$$

For LR and L1-loss SVM, the upper bound U becomes

$$U = \Delta_I C. \tag{15}$$

We then consider the following initial solutions

$$\text{primal: } \bar{\boldsymbol{w}} \qquad \text{dual: } \Delta_I\bar{\boldsymbol{\alpha}}. \tag{16}$$

We must scale $\bar{\boldsymbol{\alpha}}$ because of the new upper bound in (15), but $\bar{\boldsymbol{w}}$ can still be used without modification. We have

$$\begin{aligned} & \text{new optimal objective value} \\ \leq\, & \text{primal initial value} \qquad (17) \\ =\, & \frac{1}{2}\bar{\boldsymbol{w}}^T\bar{\boldsymbol{w}} + \Delta_I C\sum\nolimits_{i=1}^{l} \xi(\bar{\boldsymbol{w}}; \boldsymbol{x}_i, y_i) + \Delta_I C\sum\nolimits_{i=l+1}^{l+k} \xi(\bar{\boldsymbol{w}}; \boldsymbol{x}_i, y_i). \end{aligned}$$

Further,

$$\begin{aligned} & \text{dual initial value} = \sum\nolimits_{i=1}^{l+k} h(\Delta_I\bar{\alpha}_i, \Delta_I C) \\ & - \frac{1}{2}\Big(\sum\nolimits_{i=1}^{l+k}\sum\nolimits_{j=1}^{l+k} \Delta_I\bar{\alpha}_i\Delta_I\bar{\alpha}_j K(i,j) + \sum\nolimits_{i=1}^{l+k} (\Delta_I\bar{\alpha}_i)^2\frac{d}{\Delta_I}\Big) \\ =\, & \Delta_I C\sum\nolimits_{i=1}^{l} \xi(\bar{\boldsymbol{w}}; \boldsymbol{x}_i, y_i) + \frac{l(l+2k)}{2(l+k)^2}\bar{\boldsymbol{w}}^T\bar{\boldsymbol{w}}, \end{aligned} \tag{18}$$

where details of deriving (18) are in Appendix. Because

$$\frac{l(l+2k)}{2(l+k)^2} \leq \frac{1}{2} \text{ and } \Delta_I C\sum_{i=l+1}^{l+k} \xi(\bar{\boldsymbol{w}}; \boldsymbol{x}_i, y_i) \text{ is lacked,} \tag{19}$$

(18) tends to be too small. Thus, even if the parameter C has been adjusted, the dual initial solution may still be farther away from the optimum than the primal. In Section 6, we will conduct experiments to confirm our findings.

3.2 Initial Values for Decremental Learning

The optimization problem after data removal is

$$\min_{\boldsymbol{w}} \quad \frac{1}{2}\boldsymbol{w}^T\boldsymbol{w} + C\sum\nolimits_{i=k+1}^{l} \xi(\boldsymbol{w}; \boldsymbol{x}_i, y_i). \tag{20}$$

The corresponding dual problem is

$$\begin{aligned} \max_{\boldsymbol{\alpha}} \quad & \sum_{i=k+1}^{l} h(\alpha_i, C) - \frac{1}{2}\sum_{i=k+1}^{l}\sum_{j=k+1}^{l} \alpha_i\alpha_j K(i,j) - \sum_{i=k+1}^{l} \frac{\alpha_i^2}{2}d \\ \text{subject to} \quad & 0 \leq \alpha_i \leq U, \forall i = k+1, \ldots, l. \end{aligned} \tag{21}$$

Using the initial points defined in (9), the primal and dual initial objective values are, respectively,

$$\frac{1}{2}\bar{\boldsymbol{w}}^T\bar{\boldsymbol{w}} + C\sum\nolimits_{i=k+1}^{l} \xi(\bar{\boldsymbol{w}}; \boldsymbol{x}_i, y_i) \tag{22}$$

and

$$\sum_{i=k+1}^{l} h(\alpha_i^*, C) - \frac{1}{2}(\sum_{i=k+1}^{l}\sum_{j=k+1}^{l} \alpha_i^*\alpha_j^* K(i,j) + \sum_{i=k+1}^{l} (\alpha_i^*)^2 d)$$

$$= \frac{1}{2}\bar{\boldsymbol{w}}^T\bar{\boldsymbol{w}} + C\sum\nolimits_{i=k+1}^{l} \xi(\bar{\boldsymbol{w}}; \boldsymbol{x}_i, y_i)$$

$$- \frac{1}{2}\sum\nolimits_{i=1}^{k}\sum\nolimits_{j=1}^{k} \alpha_i^*\alpha_j^* K(i,j). \tag{23}$$

Details are in Appendix. Similar to (10), we have

$$\text{dual initial value} \leq \text{new optimal objective value} \leq \text{primal initial value}$$

because $\bar{\boldsymbol{w}}$ and $\bar{\boldsymbol{\alpha}}$ are feasible solutions of the new primal and dual problems, respectively.

For decremental learning, we can also argue that the primal initial objective value is usually closer than the dual to the optimal objective value of the new problem. By (1), (20), and the same explanation for incremental learning, if not many data are removed, the optimal $\boldsymbol{w}$ should not change significantly. In contrast, because of the

$$-\frac{1}{2}\sum\nolimits_{i=1}^{k}\sum\nolimits_{j=1}^{k} \boldsymbol{\alpha}_i^*\boldsymbol{\alpha}_j^* K(i,j).$$

term in (23), the dual initial objective value should be less close to the new optimal value.

Like incremental learning, we discuss the situation of adjusting the parameter C to maintain a similar total training loss. The following optimization problem is considered.

$$\min_{\boldsymbol{w}} \quad \frac{1}{2}\boldsymbol{w}^T\boldsymbol{w} + \Delta_D C\sum\nolimits_{i=k+1}^{l} \xi(\boldsymbol{w}; \boldsymbol{x}_i, y_i),$$

where $\Delta_D = l/(l-k)$. The dual problem is the same as (21) except that C becomes $\Delta_D C$, d becomes d/Δ_D, and $U = \Delta_D C$ for L1-loss SVM and LR. Like (16), the following initial solutions can be used.

$$\text{primal: } \bar{\boldsymbol{w}} \qquad \text{dual: } \Delta_D\bar{\boldsymbol{\alpha}}.$$

For initial objective values, we have

$$\text{new optimal objective value} \tag{24}$$

$$\leq \text{primal initial value} = \frac{1}{2}\bar{\boldsymbol{w}}^T\bar{\boldsymbol{w}} + \Delta_D C\sum\nolimits_{i=k+1}^{l} \xi(\bar{\boldsymbol{w}}; \boldsymbol{x}_i, y_i)$$

and

$$\text{dual initial value} = \sum\nolimits_{i=k+1}^{l} h(\Delta_D\alpha_i^*, \Delta_D C) -$$

$$\frac{1}{2}\sum\nolimits_{i=k+1}^{l}\sum\nolimits_{j=k+1}^{l} \Delta_D^2\alpha_i^*\alpha_j^* K(i,j) - \sum\nolimits_{i=k+1}^{l} (\Delta_D\alpha_i^*)^2\frac{d}{2\Delta_D}$$

$$= \frac{1}{2}\bar{\boldsymbol{w}}^T\bar{\boldsymbol{w}} + \Delta_D C\sum_{i=k+1}^{l} \xi(\bar{\boldsymbol{w}}; \boldsymbol{x}_i, y_i) - \frac{\Delta_D}{2}\sum_{i=1}^{k}\sum_{j=1}^{k} \alpha_i^*\alpha_j^* K(i,j)$$

$$- \frac{\Delta_D^2 - \Delta_D}{2}\sum_{i=k+1}^{l}\sum_{j=k+1}^{l} \alpha_i^*\alpha_j^* K(i,j) + \frac{\Delta_D - 1}{2}\bar{\boldsymbol{w}}^T\bar{\boldsymbol{w}}, \tag{25}$$

where the details of (25) are in supplementary materials because of space limitation. If not many data are removed, $\Delta_D \approx 1$ and the last two terms in (25) are close to zero. Then the difference between (24) and (25) is similar to that between (22) and (23) without changing C. Therefore, even if the regularization parameter has been adjusted, the dual initial solution tends to be farther away from the optimum than the primal.

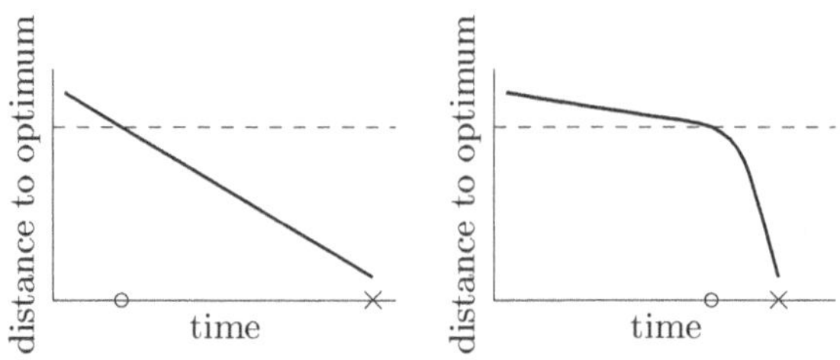

(a) Linear convergence (b) Superlinear or quadratic convergence

Figure 1: An illustration on how optimization methods may affect the effectiveness of a warm start setting. The y-axis is log-scaled. $\circ$: initial solution $\times$: optimum. The dashed horizontal line indicates the initial distance to the optimum.

4. OPTIMIZATION METHODS AND INCREMENTAL/DECREMENTAL LEARNING

The effectiveness of a warm start strategy may be strongly related to the optimization method. We use Figure 1 to illustrate this point. If an initial solution is close to the optimum, then a high-order optimization method may be advantageous because of the fast final convergence; see Figure 1(b). Therefore, higher-order methods such as quasi Newton or Newton may be preferred for incremental and decremental learning.

Interestingly, for linear classification, lower-order methods such as stochastic gradient (SG) or coordinate descent are more commonly used than high-order methods. The reason is that low-order methods can quickly return a useful model. On the contrary, a high-order method like Newton methods may take considerable time to finish the first few iterations for obtaining an approximate solution.

To investigate if high-order methods become useful for incremental and decremental learning, in the rest of this section, we briefly describe three methods that will be detailedly compared in Section 6.

- Newton method to solve the primal problem.
- Coordinate descent method to solve the primal problem.
- Coordinate descent method to solve the dual problem.

The Newton method uses second-order information, while the coordinate descent method considers only gradient (i.e., first order) information.

4.1 Solving Primal Problem by a Trust Region Newton Method

We consider the Newton method in LIBLINEAR to solve the primal problem (1). It is a trust region Newton (TRON) method developed in [15]. Because differentiability is required, this method is not applicable to L1-loss SVM.

At current iterate $\boldsymbol{w}$, TRON obtains an approximate Newton step $\boldsymbol{d}$ within the trust region by solving the following sub-problem.

$$\min_{\boldsymbol{d}} \quad q(\boldsymbol{d}) \quad \text{subject to} \quad \|\boldsymbol{d}\|_2 \leq \Delta, \tag{26}$$

where $\quad q(\boldsymbol{d}) \equiv \nabla f(\boldsymbol{w})^T\boldsymbol{d} + \frac{1}{2}\boldsymbol{d}^T\nabla^2 f(\boldsymbol{w})\boldsymbol{d}$

is an approximation of $f(\boldsymbol{w}+\boldsymbol{d}) - f(\boldsymbol{w})$ and Δ is the size of the trust region. Afterward by checking the ratio between real function value reduction $f(\boldsymbol{w}+\boldsymbol{d}) - f(\boldsymbol{w})$ and the estimated reduction $q(\boldsymbol{d})$, TRON decides if $\boldsymbol{w}$ should be updated and then adjusts the current trust region Δ. The sub-problem (26) is solved by the conjugate gradient method, so *matrix inversion is not needed.* For LR, whose objective function is twice differentiable, [15] shows that TRON has quadratic convergence.

4.2 Solving Primal Problem by a Coordinate Descent Method

We consider the coordinate descent method in [5] to solve the primal problem (1). This method updates one component w_i of $\boldsymbol{w}$ at a time.

$$w_i \leftarrow w_i + \arg\min_d f(\boldsymbol{w} + d\boldsymbol{e}_i), \tag{27}$$

where $\boldsymbol{e}_i \equiv [0, \ldots, 0, 1, 0, \ldots, 0]^T$ is zero except the ith element. The work [5] applies a Newton method to approximately solve the one-variable sub-problem in (27), which does not have a closed-form solution. Their approach, applicable to L2-loss SVM and LR, requires only $\nabla_i f(w)$ and $\nabla^2_{ii} f(w)$ at each step. Therefore, this method is a low-order one in compared with TRON that needs the whole Hessian matrix. The linear convergence is established in [5]. We refer to this method as PCD.

4.3 Solving Dual Problem by a Coordinate Descent Method

For solving dual problem (6), we consider the coordinate descent methods in [10, 18] that update α_i at a time by

$$\alpha_i \leftarrow \min\left(\max\left(\alpha_i + \arg\min_d f^D(\boldsymbol{\alpha} + d\boldsymbol{e}_i), 0\right), U\right), \tag{28}$$

where $f^D(\cdot)$ is the dual objective function. A difference between (28) and (27) is that in (28) we must ensure the new α_i is in $[0, U]$. The one-variable problem in (28) has a closed-form solution for L1-loss and L2-loss SVM, but for LR, we need an optimization procedure to obtain an approximate solution. It is shown in [10, 17] that this dual coordinate descent method linearly converges.

5. IMPLEMENTATION ISSUES

Although warm start is a simple strategy, its implementation may be complicated. Recall in Section 1 we mentioned that the need to maintain the kernel cache is the main obstacle for us to support incremental and decremental learning in the kernel SVM software LIBSVM. Now for linear classification, although the implementation is more straightforward, many issues still need to be addressed in this section.

We begin with checking if additional information must be maintained in the model after training. If the primal problem is considered, then $\bar{\boldsymbol{w}}$ is readily available because the previously obtained $\boldsymbol{w}$ must be stored for prediction. In contrast, the dual solution $\boldsymbol{\alpha}$ is not maintained in a linear classifier even if a dual-based solver is used. The reason is because we can generate and store $\boldsymbol{w}$ by (5) for prediction. Therefore, to employ a dual solver for incremental and decremental learning, $\boldsymbol{\alpha}$ must be additionally stored. Unfortunately, maintaining $\boldsymbol{\alpha}$ is a complicated task because of the following concerns on the correspondence between $\boldsymbol{\alpha}$ and data instances.

- If new instances are randomly inserted into the existing set, it is difficult to maintain the mapping between $\boldsymbol{\alpha}$ and instances. Similarly, for decremental learning, the indices of removed instances must be known, though in practice this information may not be available.
- The task of multi-class classification is often decomposed to several binary classification problems, so a set of $\boldsymbol{\alpha}$ vectors must be maintained. The storage cost can be high if both numbers of instances and classes are large. Further, if each binary problem involves a subset of data (e.g., the one-against-one approach for multi-class classification), the above-mentioned problem of mapping $\boldsymbol{\alpha}$ and data occurs.

Therefore, the implementation of dual solvers with warm start is more complicated than that of primal solvers.

Stopping conditions of optimization algorithms are another implementation issues because some relative conditions depend on the initial point. For example, the TRON implementation in LIBLINEAR employs the following condition.

$$\frac{\|\nabla f(\boldsymbol{w}^k)\|_2}{\|\nabla f(\boldsymbol{w}^0)\|_2} \le \epsilon \cdot \frac{\min(l^+, l^-)}{l}, \tag{29}$$

where $\boldsymbol{w}^0$ is the initial point, $\boldsymbol{w}^k$ is the current iterate, ϵ is the user-specified stopping tolerance, and l^+ and l^- are numbers of positive and negative data, respectively. For standard linear classification, in general $\boldsymbol{w}^0 = \boldsymbol{0}$ is used. However, with a warm start setting, the initial $\boldsymbol{w}^0$ is better than $\boldsymbol{0}$, so a smaller $\|\nabla f(\boldsymbol{w}^0)\|_2$ appears in the denominator in (29). Then the stopping condition becomes too strict under the same ϵ. To address this problem, in our implementation, $\|\nabla f(\boldsymbol{w}^0)\|_2$ in (29) is fixed to be $\|\nabla f(\boldsymbol{0})\|_2$.

Table 1: Data statistics: Density is the average ratio of non-zero features per instance.

Data set	l: #instances	n: #features	density
ijcnn	49,990	22	41.37%
webspam	350,000	254	33.51%
news20	19,996	1,355,191	0.03%
rcv1	20,242	47,236	0.16%
real-sim	72,309	20,958	0.24%
yahoo-japan	140,964	832,026	0.16%

6. EXPERIMENTS

In this section, we experimentally compare primal and dual solvers with the warm start strategy. We consider data sets ijcnn, webspam, news20, rcv1, real-sim and yahoo-japan, where details are shown in Table 1. All sets except yahoo-japan are available at LIBSVM data set.[2] All the experiments are conducted on a 2.50 GHz computer with 16 GB of RAM.

To evaluate methods for incremental learning, we randomly divide each data set to r parts so that

$r-1$ parts as original data, and
1 part as new data.

Therefore, the solution of training the $r-1$ parts is used to construct the initial point for training the whole set of r parts. We consider $r = 5, 50$ and 500 to investigate the effectiveness of the warm start method under different levels of data changes. Note that a larger r means a smaller increase of the data. Our setting ensures that the enlarged set remains the same regardless of different r values. We need

[2] `http://www.csie.ntu.edu.tw/~cjlin/libsvmtools/datasets/`

this property so in figures for comparison only one curve is drawn for the approach without a warm start setting. For decremental learning, we use the following setting to ensure that the reduced set is the same regardless of r. We split 1/5 data to r parts and have

4/5 data + 1 part of 1/5 data as the original data and

4/5 data as the reduced set.

Our evaluation is by the relative difference to the optimal function value:

$$|\frac{f(\boldsymbol{w}) - f(\boldsymbol{w}^*)}{f(\boldsymbol{w}^*)}| \text{ and } |\frac{f^D(\boldsymbol{\alpha}) - f^D(\boldsymbol{\alpha}^*)}{f^D(\boldsymbol{\alpha}^*)}| \tag{30}$$

for primal- and dual-based algorithms, respectively. Note that optimal $\boldsymbol{w}^*$ and $\boldsymbol{\alpha}^*$ are not available, so we obtain their approximations by running a huge number of iterations of optimization methods.

6.1 Analysis on Initial Values

In Sections 3.1 and 3.2, we discuss properties of primal and dual initial solutions. To confirm our analysis, Table 2 shows the relative difference between initial and optimal function values for incremental and decremental learning. We check two values of the regularization parameter: $C = 1$ and $C = 128$. Because of space limitation, we consider only logistic regression, although results for l2-loss SVM (in Tables III and IV of supplementary materials) are similar.[3] As a comparison, we include results without the warm start setting by using $\boldsymbol{w} = \mathbf{0}$ and $\boldsymbol{\alpha} = \mathbf{0}$ as initial points for primal- and dual-based methods, respectively. Note that $f_D(\mathbf{0}) = 0$, so

$$|\frac{f^D(\mathbf{0}) - f^D(\boldsymbol{\alpha}^*)}{f^D(\boldsymbol{\alpha}^*)}| = 1.$$

In contrast, primal $f(\mathbf{0})$ is larger. For example, for logistic loss, $f(\mathbf{0}) = Cl\log(2)$. Therefore, without a warm start setting, the primal initial point is far away from the optimal solution. This situation can be clearly seen in Table 2.

We further make the following observations. First, from results of each row of Table 2, the warm start setting significantly reduces the distance from the primal initial solution to the optimum. In contrast, the improvement on the dual initial solution is only modest.

Second, with the warm start setting, if $C = 1$, the distance of the primal initial solution to the optimum is smaller than that of the dual. In particular, for data with a small number of features (e.g., ijcnn), the primal initial solution is very close to the optimum. This result confirms the calculation in Sections 3.1 and 3.2. However, the difference becomes smaller for some sparse data (e.g., news20). An explanation is that because of more features, more instances are needed to have a stable optimal $\boldsymbol{w}$.

Third, if a larger $C = 128$ is used, the superiority of the primal initial solution becomes less clear. For sparse data, it is sometimes worse than the dual initial solution under the incremental learning scenario. This result is reasonable because a large C causes a better fitting of the original data. Then the solution $\boldsymbol{w}$ is sensitive to the increase of data. However, we notice that for these data sets, a large C is often not needed. Interestingly, for decremental learning with a large C, the primal initial point is competitive for sparse data. The reason might be that the remained data have been used in training the original set. In contrast, for incremental learning, some unseen instances are added to form the new training set.

Finally, we observe that under a larger r both primal and dual initial solutions are closer to the optimum. This result follows from our setting that a larger r implies a smaller change of the data. If the change of data is minor, then the initial solution $\bar{\boldsymbol{w}}$ or $\bar{\boldsymbol{\alpha}}$ is almost good enough to be a model for the modified problem. For example, even under $r = 5$, if $C = 1$ and the primal-based algorithm TRON is used for incremental learning, the default stopping condition of LIBLINEAR is reached within two Newton iterations for all data sets except webspam.

6.2 Comparison of Optimization Methods for Incremental and Decremental Learning

In Figures 2 and 3, we compare the three optimization methods discussed in Section 4. Each sub-figure shows the relationship between the training time and the relative difference to the optimal function value; see (30). Because of space limitation, we present results of only logistic regression and leave the results of L2-loss SVM in supplementary materials. We can make the following observations.

First, the warm start strategy is useful regardless of optimization methods. If data are not significantly changed (i.e., larger r), the improvement is dramatic.

If without applying warm start, DCD is the fastest among the three optimization methods. This situation has been know from earlier works such as [10]. However, with warm start settings TRON becomes competitive. Generally TRON benefits more from warm start than DCD. For example, in Figure 2(b), if $r = 500$, to reach 10^{-8} relative difference, the warm start strategy reduces the DCD's training time from 4.5 to 3 seconds, while TRON's training time from 40 to around 10 seconds. This result confirms our conjecture in Figure 1 that warm start strategies are more helpful for high-order optimization methods.

Although the warm start setting significantly improves the training speed of TRON for solving the primal problem, from Figures 2 and 3, DCD is still faster in general. Past works (e.g., [10]) have shown that DCD may become inferior to TRON if C is larger or feature values are in a large numerical range. In Figures I and II of supplementary materials, we present results of using $C = 128$. For data such as ijcnn, webspam, rcv1 and real-sim, we can clearly see that TRON is generally faster than DCD.

The two primal-based methods (PCD and TRON) share the same initial point. PCD quickly decreases the function value, but becomes slow in the end. In contrast, TRON is overall superior because of fast final convergence.

7. CONCLUSIONS

This research has lead to an extension of LIBLINEAR for incremental and decremental learning. Currently we choose TRON as the underlying solver because of the following results obtained in this research work.

- The warm start setting generally gives a better primal initial solution than the dual (Section 3).
- The warm start setting more effectively speeds up a high-order optimization method such as TRON (Section 4).
- For implementation, a primal-based method is more straightforward than a dual-based method (Section 5).

[3]We did not consider L1-loss SVM here because our primal-based optimization methods require the differentiability of the objective function.

Table 2: Relative objective value difference between the initial point and the optimal solution. Logistic regression is considered. wo-ws: without warm start. The better value between primal and dual is boldfaced.

Data set	Formulation	$C = 1$				$C = 128$			
		wo-ws	$r = 5$	$r = 50$	$r = 500$	wo-ws	$r = 5$	$r = 50$	$r = 500$
ijcnn	Primal	2.4e+00	**3.4e−04**	**2.2e−05**	**1.3e−06**	2.5e+00	**4.0e−04**	**2.5e−05**	**1.4e−06**
	Dual	**1.0e+00**	1.9e−01	1.8e−02	1.2e−03	**1.0e+00**	1.9e−01	1.9e−02	1.2e−03
webspam	Primal	2.1e+00	**1.2e−04**	**8.5e−06**	**1.4e−06**	2.4e+00	**2.7e−04**	**4.5e−05**	**2.9e−06**
	Dual	**1.0e+00**	1.9e−01	1.9e−02	2.1e−03	**1.0e+00**	2.0e−01	2.0e−02	2.3e−03
news20	Primal	1.3e+00	**1.7e−02**	**1.3e−03**	**1.3e−04**	2.5e+01	5.6e−01	4.6e−02	2.2e−03
	Dual	**1.0e+00**	1.6e−01	1.4e−02	1.4e−03	**1.0e+00**	**1.6e−01**	**1.3e−02**	**9.5e−04**
rcv1	Primal	2.4e+00	**1.4e−02**	**9.9e−04**	**1.5e−04**	3.4e+01	8.2e−01	5.8e−02	1.7e−02
	Dual	**1.0e+00**	1.5e−01	1.3e−02	1.7e−03	**1.0e+00**	**2.0e−01**	**1.5e−02**	**2.1e−03**
real-sim	Primal	3.8e+00	**1.2e−02**	**1.1e−03**	**1.4e−04**	3.4e+01	5.5e−01	5.9e−02	5.2e−03
	Dual	**1.0e+00**	1.5e−01	1.4e−02	1.7e−03	**1.0e+00**	**2.2e−01**	**2.2e−02**	**1.8e−03**
yahoo-japan	Primal	2.4e+00	**1.6e−02**	**1.3e−03**	**1.7e−04**	1.1e+01	6.7e−01	5.9e−02	8.3e−03
	Dual	**1.0e+00**	1.9e−01	1.8e−02	2.4e−03	**1.0e+00**	**2.4e−01**	**2.2e−02**	**3.5e−03**

(a) Incremental learning

Data set	Formulation	$C = 1$				$C = 128$			
		wo-ws	$r = 5$	$r = 50$	$r = 500$	wo-ws	$r = 5$	$r = 50$	$r = 500$
ijcnn	Primal	2.3e+00	**3.3e−04**	**3.2e−05**	**1.9e−06**	2.5e+00	**4.1e−04**	**3.8e−05**	**2.1e−06**
	Dual	**1.0e+00**	4.6e−02	5.0e−03	2.2e−04	**1.0e+00**	4.2e+00	6.5e−01	2.5e−02
webspam	Primal	2.0e+00	**1.1e−04**	**1.1e−05**	**1.9e−06**	2.4e+00	**2.6e−04**	**5.7e−05**	**4.5e−06**
	Dual	**1.0e+00**	1.0e−02	9.0e−04	9.1e−05	**1.0e+00**	3.5e−01	9.6e−02	9.3e−03
news20	Primal	1.2e+00	1.3e−02	1.5e−03	1.4e−04	2.3e+01	**7.2e−02**	**8.2e−03**	5.6e−04
	Dual	**1.0e+00**	**8.5e−03**	**8.2e−04**	**4.0e−05**	**1.0e+00**	2.8e−01	3.9e−02	**2.2e−04**
rcv1	Primal	2.2e+00	1.1e−02	1.1e−03	1.7e−04	3.3e+01	**1.1e−01**	**8.8e−03**	1.7e−03
	Dual	**1.0e+00**	**3.6e−03**	**3.4e−04**	**3.6e−05**	**1.0e+00**	4.6e−01	4.5e−02	**7.8e−04**
real-sim	Primal	3.5e+00	8.9e−03	1.1e−03	1.6e−04	3.4e+01	**1.1e−01**	**1.2e−02**	**1.7e−03**
	Dual	**1.0e+00**	**5.2e−03**	**6.3e−04**	**9.4e−05**	**1.0e+00**	9.9e−01	8.5e−02	5.8e−03
yahoo-japan	Primal	2.3e+00	1.3e−02	1.4e−03	2.0e−04	1.2e+01	**1.4e−01**	**1.4e−02**	**2.4e−03**
	Dual	**1.0e+00**	**1.0e−02**	**1.1e−03**	**1.9e−04**	**1.0e+00**	8.6e−01	1.1e−01	1.9e−02

(b) Decremental learning

With the release of the software, we hope feedbacks from real applications can lead us to refine the methods for incremental and decremental learning.

8. ACKNOWLEDGMENTS

This work was supported in part by the National Science Council of Taiwan via the grant 101-2221-E-002-199-MY3. The authors thank Chia-Hua Ho for fruitful discussion.

9. REFERENCES

[1] B. E. Boser, I. Guyon, and V. Vapnik. A training algorithm for optimal margin classifiers. In *COLT*, 1992.

[2] L. Bottou and C.-J. Lin. Support vector machine solvers. In *Large Scale Kernel Machines*. 2007.

[3] G. Cauwenberghs and T. Poggio. Incremental and decremental support vector machine learning. In *NIPS*. 2001.

[4] C.-C. Chang and C.-J. Lin. LIBSVM: A library for support vector machines. *ACM TIST*, 2:27:1–27:27, 2011.

[5] K.-W. Chang, C.-J. Hsieh, and C.-J. Lin. Coordinate descent method for large-scale L2-loss linear SVM. *JMLR*, 9:1369–1398, 2008.

[6] O. Chapelle. Training a support vector machine in the primal. *Neural Comput.*, 19:1155–1178, 2007.

[7] C. Cortes and V. Vapnik. Support-vector network. *MLJ*, 20:273–297, 1995.

[8] R.-E. Fan, K.-W. Chang, C.-J. Hsieh, X.-R. Wang, and C.-J. Lin. LIBLINEAR: A library for large linear classification. *JMLR*, 9:1871–1874, 2008.

[9] S. Fine and K. Scheinberg. Incremental learning and selective sampling via parametric optimization framework for SVM. In *NIPS*. 2001.

[10] C.-J. Hsieh, K.-W. Chang, C.-J. Lin, S. S. Keerthi, and S. Sundararajan. A dual coordinate descent method for large-scale linear SVM. In *ICML*, 2008.

[11] M. Karasuyama and I. Takeuchi. Multiple incremental decremental learning of support vector machines. *IEEE TNN*, 21:1048–1059, 2010.

[12] G. S. Kimeldorf and G. Wahba. A correspondence between Bayesian estimation on stochastic processes and smoothing by splines. *Ann. Math. Stat.*, 41:495–502, 1970.

[13] P. Laskov, C. Gehl, S. Krüger, and K.-R. Müller. Incremental support vector learning: Analysis, implementation and applications. *JMLR*, 7:1909–1936, 2006.

[14] Z. Liang and Y. Li. Incremental support vector machine learning in the primal and applications. *Neurocomputing*, 72(10):2249–2258, 2009.

[15] C.-J. Lin, R. C. Weng, and S. S. Keerthi. Trust region Newton method for large-scale logistic regression. *JMLR*, 9:627–650, 2008.

[16] A. Shilton, M. Palaniswami, D. Ralph, and A. C. Tsoi. Incremental training of support vector machines. *IEEE TNN*, 16:114–131, 2005.

[17] P.-W. Wang and C.-J. Lin. Iteration complexity of feasible descent methods for convex optimization. *JMLR*, 2014.

[18] H.-F. Yu, F.-L. Huang, and C.-J. Lin. Dual coordinate descent methods for logistic regression and maximum entropy models. *MLJ*, 85:41–75, 2011.

[19] G.-X. Yuan, C.-H. Ho, and C.-J. Lin. Recent advances of large-scale linear classification. *PIEEE*, 100:2584–2603, 2012.

APPENDIX

Details of Deriving (18)

To begin, we show that for any constant $\Delta > 0$,

$$h(\Delta\alpha, \Delta C) = \Delta h(\alpha, C). \tag{31}$$

For L1 and L2 losses, $h(\alpha, C) = \alpha$, so (31) obviously holds. For LR loss,

$$\begin{aligned}
&h(\Delta\alpha, \Delta C)\\
=&\Delta C \log \Delta C - \Delta\alpha \log \Delta\alpha - (\Delta C - \Delta\alpha)\log(\Delta C - \Delta\alpha)\\
=&\Delta C(\log\Delta + \log C) - \Delta\alpha(\log\Delta + \log\alpha)\\
&- \Delta(C-\alpha)(\log\Delta + \log(C-\alpha))\\
=&\Delta(C\log C - \alpha\log\alpha - (C-\alpha)\log(C-\alpha)) = \Delta h(\alpha, C).
\end{aligned}$$

With $\Delta_I = l/(l+k)$ defined in Section 3.1, we have

$$\begin{aligned}
&\frac{1}{2}\boldsymbol{\alpha}^{*T}\bar{Q}\boldsymbol{\alpha}^* - \frac{\Delta_I}{2}\boldsymbol{\alpha}^{*T}(Q + \frac{D}{\Delta_I})\boldsymbol{\alpha}^* \qquad (32)\\
=&\frac{1}{2}\boldsymbol{\alpha}^{*T}(Q+D)\boldsymbol{\alpha}^* - \frac{\Delta_I}{2}\boldsymbol{\alpha}^{*T}(Q + \frac{D}{\Delta_I})\boldsymbol{\alpha}^* = \frac{k}{2(l+k)}\boldsymbol{\alpha}^{*T}Q\boldsymbol{\alpha}^*.
\end{aligned}$$

Finally, we derive (18) in detail.

$$\begin{aligned}
&\text{dual initial value} = \sum_{i=1}^{l+k} h(\Delta_I\bar{\alpha}_i, \Delta_I C)\\
&\quad - \frac{1}{2}\left(\sum_{i=1}^{l+k}\sum_{j=1}^{l+k}\Delta_I\bar{\alpha}_i\Delta_I\bar{\alpha}_j K(i,j) + \sum_{i=1}^{l+k}(\Delta_I\bar{\alpha}_i)^2\frac{d}{\Delta_I}\right)\\
=&\Delta_I\left(\sum_{i=1}^{l+k} h(\bar{\alpha}_i, C) - \frac{\Delta_I}{2}\boldsymbol{\alpha}^{*T}(Q+\frac{D}{\Delta_I})\boldsymbol{\alpha}^*\right)\\
=&\Delta_I\left(\frac{1}{2}\bar{\boldsymbol{w}}^T\bar{\boldsymbol{w}} + C\sum_{i=1}^{l}\xi(\bar{\boldsymbol{w}};\boldsymbol{x}_i,y_i)\right.\\
&\left.+\frac{1}{2}\boldsymbol{\alpha}^{*T}\bar{Q}\boldsymbol{\alpha}^* - \frac{\Delta_I}{2}\boldsymbol{\alpha}^{*T}(Q+\frac{D}{\Delta_I})\boldsymbol{\alpha}^*\right)\\
=&\Delta_I C\sum_{i=1}^{l}\xi(\bar{\boldsymbol{w}};\boldsymbol{x}_i,y_i) + \frac{\Delta_I}{2}\bar{\boldsymbol{w}}^T\bar{\boldsymbol{w}} + \frac{\Delta_I k}{2(l+k)}\boldsymbol{\alpha}^{*T}Q\boldsymbol{\alpha}^*\\
=&\Delta_I C\sum_{i=1}^{l}\xi(\bar{\boldsymbol{w}};\boldsymbol{x}_i,y_i) + \frac{l(l+2k)}{2(l+k)^2}\bar{\boldsymbol{w}}^T\bar{\boldsymbol{w}}.
\end{aligned}$$

The second equality is from (31) and $\bar{\alpha}_{l+1} = \cdots = \bar{\alpha}_{l+k} = 0$. The third equality is from (7) and (12). The fourth equality is from (32). The last equality uses the property $\boldsymbol{w}^{*T}\boldsymbol{w}^* = \boldsymbol{\alpha}^{*T}Q\boldsymbol{\alpha}^*$ of optimal solutions.

Details of Deriving (23)

To begin, we show that

$$h(\alpha_i^*, C) - \frac{1}{2}d\alpha_i^{*2} - y_i\alpha_i^*\boldsymbol{w}^{*T}\boldsymbol{x}_i = C\xi(\boldsymbol{w}^*;\boldsymbol{x}_i,y_i) \tag{33}$$

holds for L1, L2 and LR losses. For L1-loss SVM,

$$\alpha_i^* - y_i\alpha_i^*\boldsymbol{w}^{*T}\boldsymbol{x}_i = \alpha_i^*(1 - y_i\boldsymbol{w}^{*T}\boldsymbol{x}_i) = C\max(1 - y_i\boldsymbol{w}^{*T}\boldsymbol{x}_i, 0)$$

by the following optimality condition (e.g., Eq. (17) in [2]).

$$\alpha_i^* = \begin{cases} C & \text{if } 1 - y_i\boldsymbol{w}^{*T}\boldsymbol{x}_i > 0,\\ 0 & \text{if } 1 - y_i\boldsymbol{w}^{*T}\boldsymbol{x}_i < 0.\end{cases}$$

For L2-loss SVM,

$$\begin{aligned}
\alpha_i^* - \frac{1}{4C}\alpha_i^{*2} - y_i\alpha_i^*\boldsymbol{w}^{*T}\boldsymbol{x}_i &= \alpha_i^*(1 - y_i\boldsymbol{w}^{*T}\boldsymbol{x}_i) - \frac{1}{4C}\alpha_i^{*2}\\
&= C\max(1 - y_i\boldsymbol{w}^{*T}\boldsymbol{x}_i, 0)^2.
\end{aligned}$$

The last equality is from the optimality condition

$$\alpha_i^* = 2C\max(1 - y_i\boldsymbol{w}^{*T}\boldsymbol{x}_i, 0).$$

For LR, consider the following optimality condition

$$\alpha_i^* = C\frac{e^{-y_i\boldsymbol{w}^{*T}\boldsymbol{x}_i}}{1 + e^{-y_i\boldsymbol{w}^{*T}\boldsymbol{x}_i}}$$

in Section 3.4 of [18]. Then we have (33) by

$$\begin{aligned}
&C\log C - \alpha_i^*\log\alpha_i^* - (C - \alpha_i^*)\log(C - \alpha_i^*) - y_i\alpha_i^*\boldsymbol{w}^{*T}\boldsymbol{x}_i\\
=&C\log\frac{C}{C - \alpha_i^*} + \alpha_i^*\log\frac{C - \alpha_i^*}{\alpha_i^*} - y_i\alpha_i^*\boldsymbol{w}^{*T}\boldsymbol{x}_i\\
=&C\log(1 + e^{-y_i\boldsymbol{w}^{*T}\boldsymbol{x}_i}).
\end{aligned}$$

Denote the optimal value of the original problem as V^*.

$$V^* = \sum_{i=1}^{l} h(\alpha_i^*, C) - \frac{1}{2}\left(\sum_{i=1}^{l}\sum_{j=1}^{l}\alpha_i^*\alpha_j^*K(i,j) + \sum_{i=1}^{l}d\alpha_i^{*2}\right).$$

Next, we denote the initial value of the decremented problem as V_{init} and extract the term V_{init} from V^* to have

$$\begin{aligned}
V^* =& V_{\text{init}} - \sum_{i=1}^{k}\sum_{j=1}^{l}\alpha_i^*\alpha_j^*K(i,j) + \frac{1}{2}\sum_{i=1}^{k}\sum_{j=1}^{k}\alpha_i^*\alpha_j^*K(i,j)\\
&- \frac{1}{2}\sum_{i=1}^{k}d\alpha_i^{*2} + \sum_{i=1}^{k}h(\alpha_i^*, C)\\
=& V_{\text{init}} - \sum_{i=1}^{k}y_i\alpha_i^*\boldsymbol{w}^{*T}\boldsymbol{x}_i + \sum_{i=1}^{k}h(\alpha_i^*, C) - \frac{1}{2}\sum_{i=1}^{k}d\alpha_i^{*2}\\
&+ \frac{1}{2}\sum_{i=1}^{k}\sum_{j=1}^{k}\alpha_i^*\alpha_j^*K(i,j)\\
=& V_{\text{init}} + C\sum_{i=1}^{k}\xi(\boldsymbol{w}^*;\boldsymbol{x}_i,y_i) + \frac{1}{2}\sum_{i=1}^{k}\sum_{j=1}^{k}\alpha_i^*\alpha_j^*K(i,j).
\end{aligned}$$

The second equality uses (5) and the last equality is from (33). By the definitions of $\bar{\boldsymbol{w}}$ and V^*, and (12),

$$\begin{aligned}
V_{\text{init}} &= V^* - C\sum_{i=1}^{k}\xi(\bar{\boldsymbol{w}};\boldsymbol{x}_i,y_i) - \frac{1}{2}\sum_{i=1}^{k}\sum_{j=1}^{k}\alpha_i^*\alpha_j^*K(i,j)\\
&= \frac{1}{2}\bar{\boldsymbol{w}}^T\bar{\boldsymbol{w}} + C\sum_{i=k+1}^{l}\xi(\bar{\boldsymbol{w}};\boldsymbol{x}_i,y_i) - \frac{1}{2}\sum_{i=1}^{k}\sum_{j=1}^{k}\alpha_i^*\alpha_j^*K(i,j).
\end{aligned}$$

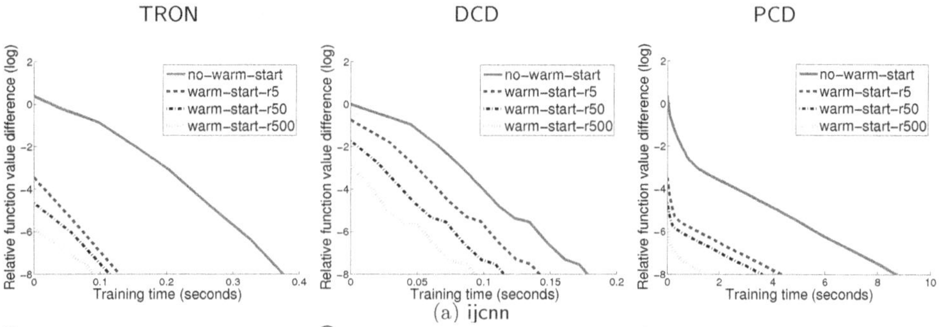

(a) ijcnn

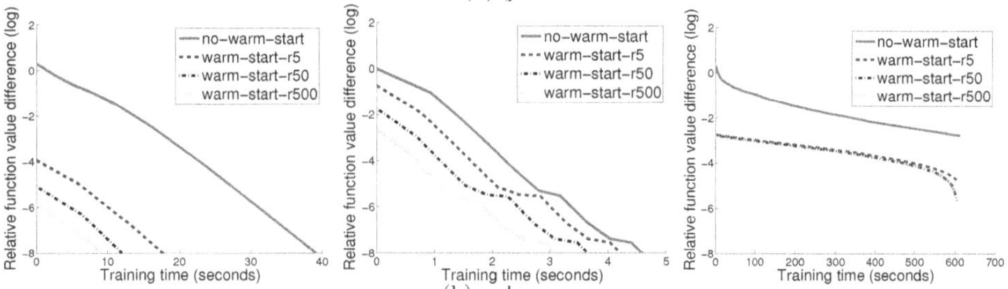

(b) webspam

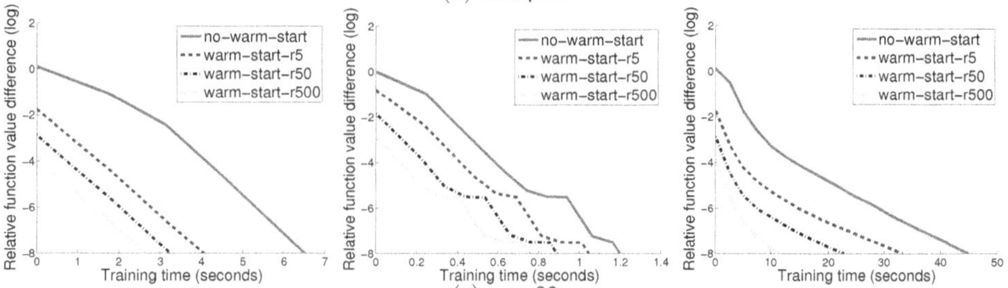

(c) news20

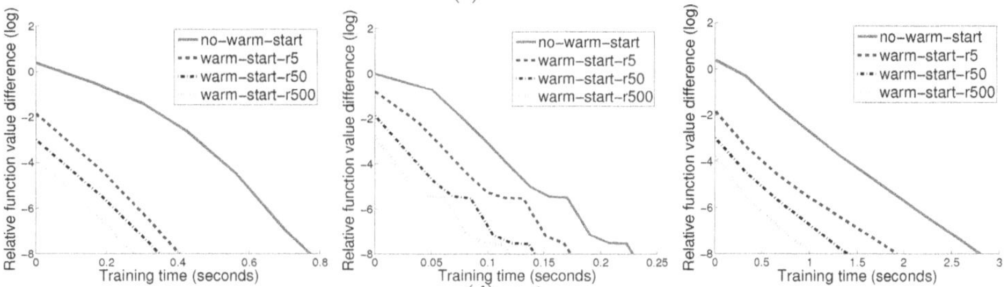

(d) rcv1

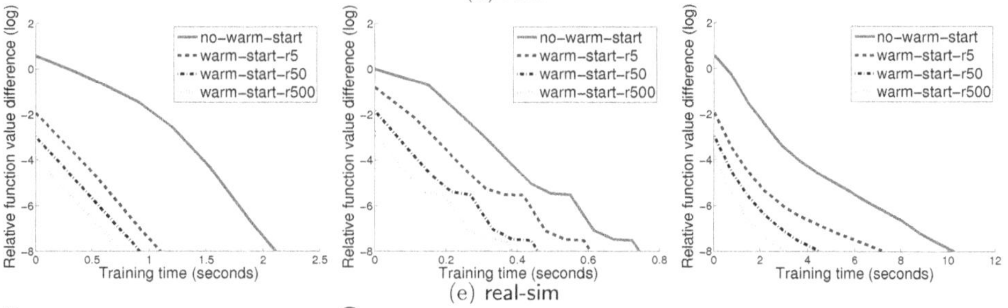

(e) real-sim

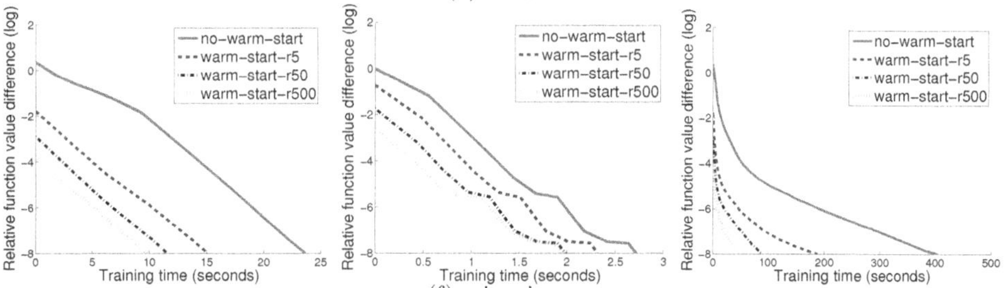

(f) yahoo-japan

Figure 2: Incremental learning: running time (in seconds) versus the relative objective value difference. Logistic regression with $C = 1$ is used.

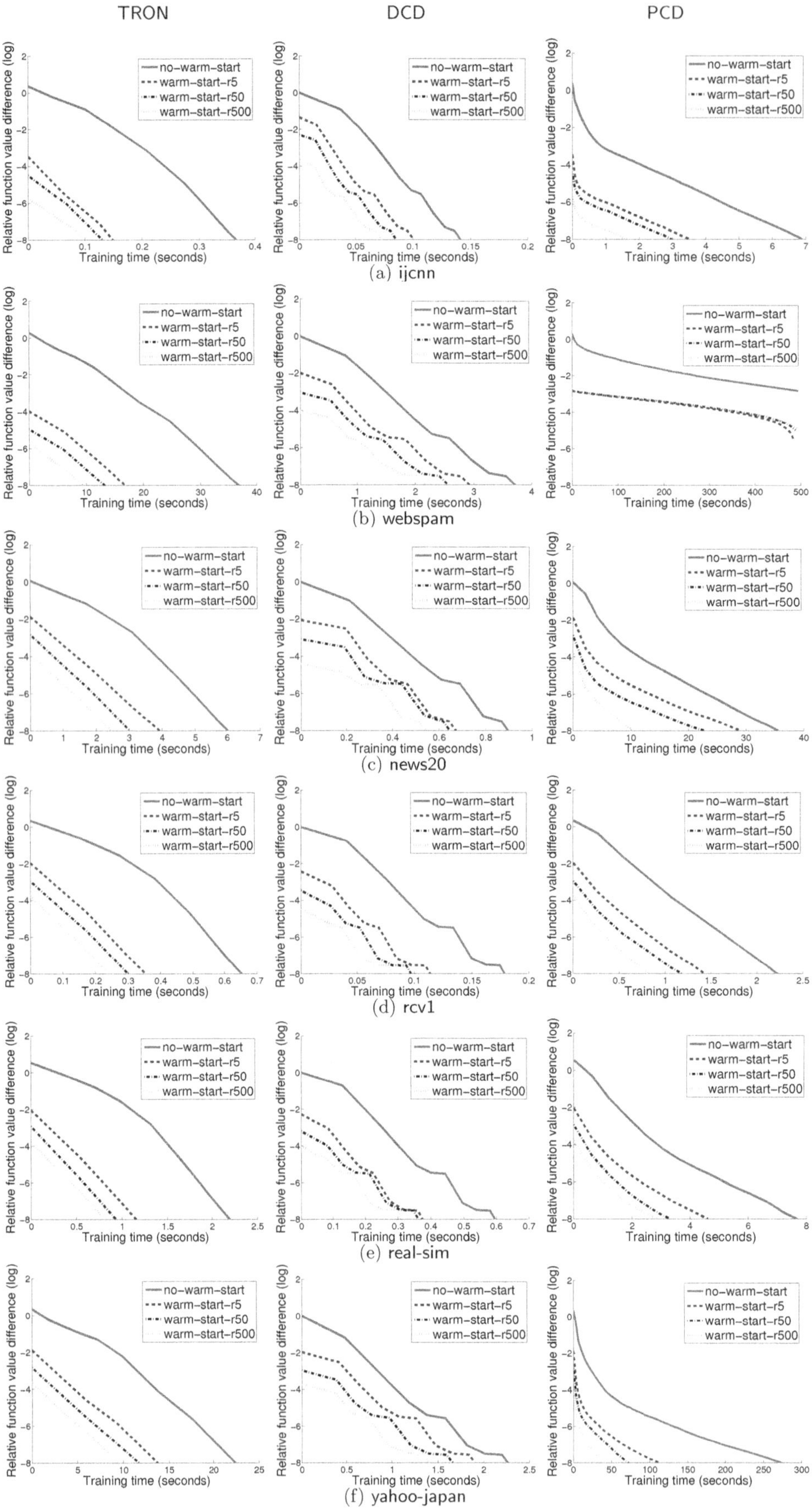

Figure 3: Decremental learning: running time (in seconds) versus the relative objective value difference. Logistic regression with $C = 1$ is used.

Supervised Deep Learning with Auxiliary Networks

Junbo Zhang[†,‡], Guangjian Tian[‡], Yadong Mu[‡], Wei Fan[‡]
[†]School of Information Science and Technology,
Southwest Jiaotong University, Chengdu 610031, China
[‡]Huawei Noah's Ark Lab, Hong Kong
jbzhang@my.swjtu.edu.cn, {tian.guangjian,mu.yadong,david.fanwei}@huawei.com

ABSTRACT

Deep learning well demonstrates its potential in learning latent feature representations. Recent years have witnessed an increasing enthusiasm for regularizing deep neural networks by incorporating various side information, such as user-provided labels or pairwise constraints. However, the effectiveness and parameter sensitivity of such algorithms have been major obstacles for putting them into practice. The major contribution of our work is the exposition of a novel supervised deep learning algorithm, which distinguishes from two unique traits. First, it regularizes the network construction by utilizing similarity or dissimilarity constraints between data pairs, rather than sample-specific annotations. Such kind of side information is more flexible and greatly mitigates the workload of annotators. Secondly, unlike prior works, our proposed algorithm decouples the supervision information and intrinsic data structure. We design two heterogeneous networks, each of which encodes either supervision or unsupervised data structure respectively. Specifically, we term the supervision-oriented network as "auxiliary network" since it is principally used for facilitating the parameter learning of the other one and will be removed when handling out-of-sample data. The two networks are complementary to each other and bridged by enforcing the correlation of their parameters. We name the proposed algorithm SUpervision-Guided AutoencodeR (SUGAR). Comparing prior works on unsupervised deep networks and supervised learning, SUGAR better balances numerical tractability and the flexible utilization of supervision information. The classification performance on MNIST digits and eight benchmark datasets demonstrates that SUGAR can effectively improve the performance by using the auxiliary networks, on both shallow and deep architectures. Particularly, when multiple SUGARs are stacked, the performance is significantly boosted. On the selected benchmarks, ours achieve up to 11.35% relative accuracy improvement compared to the state-of-the-art models.

Categories and Subject Descriptors

I.2.6 [**Artificial Intelligence**]: Learning

KDD'14, August 24–27, 2014, New York, NY, USA.

http://dx.doi.org/10.1145/2623330.2623618 .

Keywords

Deep Neural Networks; Supervision; Autoencoder

1. INTRODUCTION

In recent years, learning feature representations from deep neural networks has emerged as a prominent methodology in the machine learning and data mining communities. It has gained numerous success in the fields such as computer vision [14], speech recognition [8] and natural language processing [25]. Some comprehensive surveys of recent progress are provided by Bengio in [2, 3].

Many classic deep neural networks, such as Autoencoders and Restricted Boltzmann Machines (RBMs), operate in the unsupervised manner. For example, an autoencoder pursues the optimal network parameters piloted by the intuition of data self-reconstruction. Nevertheless the deep neural networks can be also trained in a supervised manner, such as Convolutional Neural Networks (CNN) developed by LeCun et al. [16]. However, most attempts before 2006 at training supervised deep architectures failed. It turns out that the deep supervised feedforward neural network tends to yield inferior performances in terms of prediction error than shallow ones (with 1 or 2 hidden layers). Hinton's revolutionary work on Deep Belief Networks (DBN) [12] in 2006 shed a light on effective supervised deep learning. Other multi-layered deep neural networks like Stacked Denoising Autoencoders (SDAE) [27] can be efficiently pre-trained in layer-wise manner, followed by supervised back-propagation in order to fine-tune the parameters [4].

However, existing schemes for incorporating side information into deep neural networks are far from being satisfactory. For example, though achieving striking empirical results on several real-world applications, the two-step procedure adopted by DBN (*i.e.*, unsupervised pre-training followed by supervised fine-tuning) does not effectively handle sparse side information (*e.g.*, sparse similarity or dissimilarity constraints on data pairs). Moreover, the methodology of separately performing unsupervised or supervised parameter optimization also tends to converge to non-optimal solutions. Our algorithm is proposed to address the above-mentioned issues, and motivated by the recent surge in weakly-supervised extensions of the autoencoder algorithm [4, 20, 24, 25, 32]. These extensions advance the original autoencoder algorithm by adding label-specific output besides the data reconstruction [4], using recursive structure [25] or non-parametric Gaussian process [24].

In this paper, we propose a novel deep learning model, whose architecture is illustrated in Figure 1. Each layer of the deep model includes a SUpervision-Guided AutoencodeR, which is referred to as "SUGAR". SUGAR is comprised of a main network, an auxiliary network, and a bridge that connects the two networks. The main network adopts the data self-reconstruction criteria as in the autoencoder algorithm, and enforces the solutions to be of moder-

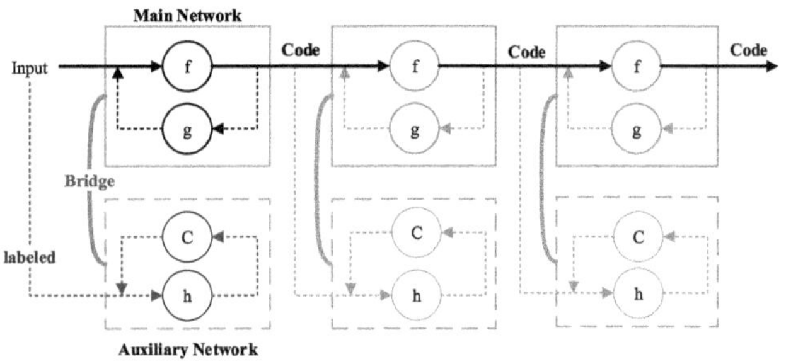

Figure 1: Deep Architecture. Each layer consists of three components: *Main Network* (solid box), *Auxiliary Network* (dotted box), and *Bridge*. f, h are two encoders, g is a decoder, C is a discernibility function. After training, the feedback decoding modules g and the encoder modules h with the corresponding classifier modules (all dashed lines) are discarded and the system is used to produce very compact representations by a feed-forward pass through the chain of encoders f.

ate sparsity in order to reduce the over-fitting risk. The auxiliary network encapsulates the supervision information. It is designed to ensure that both the similarity or dissimilarity pairwise constraints are satisfied. In the stage of parameter learning, these two networks are simultaneously optimized. The name "auxiliary networks" follows from the fact that the network will be removed when handling out-of-sample data. In other words, the auxiliary network mainly plays the role of regularizing the main network. Using the idea of auxiliary network, SUGAR is able to accomplish a seamless hybrid of unsupervised data structure discovery and sparsely-supervised learning.

Comparing to competing models, our proposed model has the following advantages:

- SUGAR employs a novel architecture to build deep networks, *i.e.*, "auxiliary networks" + "main networks" + "bridge". The auxiliary networks can be easily embedded into the conventional networks, and then provide a sparsely-supervised guidance. These two networks are complementary to each other, since the auxiliary network can learn discriminant features and the autoencoder-based main network can learn generative features. At the same time, the sparsity penalty is employed to make SUGAR more robust and efficient.

- SUGAR is very flexible and easily extendible. For example, one can replace the autoencoder (AE) term in SUGAR by many other autoencoder variants. In this paper, we tentatively explore two extensions, *i.e.*, the denoising autoencoder (DAE) [27] and the contractive autoencoder (CAE) [22].

- SUGAR can be also easily stacked as a deep learning model. After pre-training multiple hidden layers effectively, the deep stacked SUGARs can learn highly abstracted features and more meaningful representations.

2. METHODOLOGY

In this section we will elaborate on the details of the proposed algorithm.

Table 1: Mathematical notation

Symbol	Definition
N	number of data samples
N_l	number of labeled data samples
D	dimensionality of data sample
K	number of hidden units
$\mathbf{X} \in \mathbb{R}^{D \times N}$	data samples
$\mathbf{X}_l \in \mathbb{R}^{D \times N_l}$	labeled data samples
$\mathbf{x} \in \mathbb{R}^D$	data sample
$\widehat{\mathbf{x}} \in \mathbb{R}^D$	vector of reconstruction
$\mathbf{z} \in \mathbb{R}^K$	hidden representation
$\mathbf{h} \in \mathbb{R}^K$	hashing representation
$\mathbf{W} \in \mathbb{R}^{K \times D}$	weight matrix for autoencoder
$\mathbf{b} \in \mathbb{R}^K$	bias for encoder
$\mathbf{b}' \in \mathbb{R}^D$	bias for decoder
$\mathbf{P} \in \mathbb{R}^{K \times D}$	weight matrix for hashing
$\mathbf{t} \in \mathbb{R}^D$	bias for hashing
$\boldsymbol{\Omega} \in \mathbb{R}^{N_l \times N_l}$	indicator matrix
$\mathbf{I} \in \mathbb{R}^{K \times K}$	identity matrix
$\mathbb{H}^K = \{\pm 1\}^K$	K-dimensional Hamming space
$\mathcal{M}$	neighbor-pairs
$\mathcal{C}$	nonneighbor-pairs

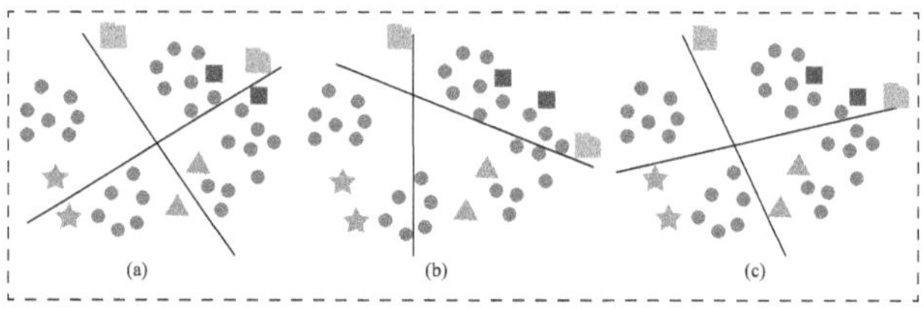

Figure 2: Illustration for the semi-supervised learning. (a) unsupervised; (b) supervised; (c) semi-supervised. Supervised learning in (b) generates reasonable solution yet does not ensure it is consistent to the underlying data distribution. The result by semi-supervised learning on (c) is more reasonable.

2.1 Problem Formulation

Suppose that there are N training samples $\mathbf{X} = \{\mathbf{x}_i\}_{i=1}^N \in \mathbb{R}^{D \times N}$ where each sample $\mathbf{x}_i \in \mathbb{R}^D$. Among them, N_l samples are labeled, noted as $\mathbf{X}_l \in \mathbb{R}^{D \times N_l}$ and its corresponding label $\mathbf{Y}$. Table 1 lists other mathematical notation used in the paper. The traditional deep learning model such as RBM and autoencoders are learnt in the unsupervised manner which has been demonstrated to be effective for learning the latent representations. The unsupervised pre-training methods are based on the hypothesis that the marginal probability distribution of the input $P(\mathbf{X})$ contains some relevant information about the conditional probability $P(\mathbf{Y}|\mathbf{X})$. Supervised learning can remarkably improve its performance when it comes to the specific tasks. Intuitively, the labeled data comes from the joint distribution of training data $\mathbf{X}$ and its corresponding label $\mathbf{Y}$, $P(\mathbf{X}, \mathbf{Y})$, while the unlabeled data comes the marginal distribution of $\mathbf{X}$, $P(\mathbf{X})$. The joint utilization of $P(\mathbf{X}, \mathbf{Y})$ and $P(\mathbf{X})$ is supposed to be able to extract more useful information from the unlabeled data. Figure 2 illustrates a simple case in the linear feature space, where latent representations are learnt from merely unlabeled data, supervision information, or both. In order to make unsupervised learning useful, there must be connection between the joint distribution $P(\mathbf{X}, \mathbf{Y})$ and marginal distribution

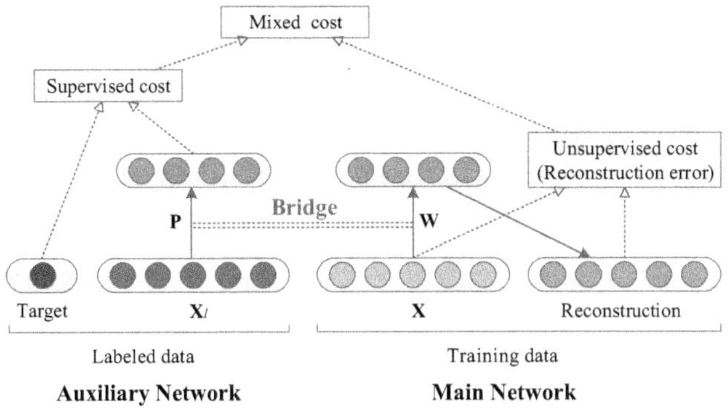

Figure 3: Architecture of SUGAR. It is trained on labeled data with the supervised learning on *Auxiliary Network* and unlabeled data with the unsupervised autoencoder on *Main Network*. They are bridged by enforcing the correlation of their parameters.

$P(\mathbf{X})$. The pure unsupervised autoencoder may not constrain this connection, so we applied an explicit sparsely-supervised model to the autoencoder to construct this connection. The flow chart of the proposed method is shown in Figure 3. The mixed model includes the following three components:

Main Network is used to reconstruct the input, *i.e.*, the unsupervised autoencoder;

Auxiliary Network is used to regularize the learnt network by pairwise similarity or dissimilarity constraints, *i.e.*, the supervised learning;

Bridge is used to connect *Main Network* and *Auxiliary Network* by enforcing the correlation of their parameters.

In the following part of this section, we first introduce the main network that is designed to capture the intrinsic data structure, then move to the auxiliary network that can regularize the main network by pairwise similarity or dissimilarity constraints among data. After that, the mixed model is introduced which involves a bridge. Finally, we describe how to learn higher level feature with deep networks.

2.2 Main Network

We propose a sparsity-encouraging variant of the classic autoencoder [23] to construct our main network. Autoencoder was introduced to address the problem of "backpropagation without a teacher", by using the input data as the teacher. It is a feed forward neural network conventionally used for reducing feature dimensionality and pre-training deep networks. For the consideration of being self-contained, we will first briefly review the key idea of autoencoder and afterwards highlight the significance of our proposed variant.

The standard autoencoder consists of two parts: an encoder and a decoder. It uses unlabeled training samples as both input and output of the neural network. The encoder is a function f that maps an input $\mathbf{x} \in \mathbb{R}^D$ to a hidden representation $\mathbf{z} \in \mathbb{R}^K$. It has the form as

$$\mathbf{z} = f(\mathbf{x}) = S_f(\mathbf{W}\mathbf{x} + \mathbf{b}), \tag{1}$$

where $\mathbf{W} \in \mathbb{R}^{K \times D}$ is a weight matrix, $\mathbf{b} \in \mathbb{R}^K$ is a hidden bias vector, and S_f is an activation function, typically a logistic sigmoid$(\tau) = \frac{1}{1+e^{-\tau}}$ or $\tanh(\tau) = \frac{e^{\tau}-e^{-\tau}}{e^{\tau}+e^{-\tau}}$. The decoder function g maps the hidden representation $\mathbf{z}$ back to a reconstruction $\widehat{\mathbf{x}}$:

$$\widehat{\mathbf{x}} = g(\mathbf{z}) = S_g(\mathbf{W}'\mathbf{z} + \mathbf{b}'), \tag{2}$$

where $\mathbf{W}' \in \mathbb{R}^{D \times K}$ is a weight matrix, $\mathbf{b}' \in \mathbb{R}^D$ is a bias vector, and S_g is a decoder's activation function, typically either the identity (yielding linear reconstruction) or a sigmoid.

The objective of a classic autoencoder is to minimize the reconstruction error on a training set $\mathbf{X}$, *i.e.*, $\arg\min_\phi \sum_{\mathbf{x}\in\mathbf{X}} \mathcal{L}(\mathbf{x}, \widehat{\mathbf{x}})$, with respect to the parameters $\phi = \{\mathbf{W}, \mathbf{W}', \mathbf{b}, \mathbf{b}'\}$. $\mathcal{L}$ is the loss function for the reconstruction residual. Typically it is set to be the squared error $\mathcal{L}(\mathbf{x}, \widehat{\mathbf{x}}) = \|\mathbf{x} - \widehat{\mathbf{x}}\|^2$ when S_g is the identity function and the cross-entropy loss $\mathcal{L}(\mathbf{x}, \widehat{\mathbf{x}}) = -(\sum_{i=1}^{D} x_i \log \widehat{x}_i + (1 - x_i)\log(1 - \widehat{x}_i))$ when S_g is the sigmoid function.

A critical downside of classic autoencoder is the over-fitting issue caused by the extremely many parameters. To attack this issue, we set $\mathbf{W}' = \mathbf{W}^T$ and enforce $\mathbf{W}$ to be sparse. Specifically, we add $\|\mathbf{W}\|_{\ell_1}$ to the objective function. In this way, we obtain

$$\arg\min_\phi \sum_{\mathbf{x}\in\mathbf{X}} \mathcal{L}(\mathbf{x}, \widehat{\mathbf{x}}) + \lambda\|\mathbf{W}\|_{\ell_1}, \tag{3}$$

where λ is a free parameter to control the sparsity of $\mathbf{W}$, and $\|\cdot\|_{\ell_1}$ denotes the sum of the absolute values of matrix entries, *i.e.*, $\|\mathbf{W}\|_{\ell_1} \triangleq \sum_{ij} |W_{ij}|$. In the experiments, we investigate the relationship between the solution sparsity and prediction accuracies, as depicted in Figure 5(c).

2.3 Auxiliary Network

We propose to use a data similarity-preserving criterion to construct our auxiliary network. Specifically, we generate binary code for each datum and optimize the model parameters, which is known as "supervised hashing" in the literature. The inner produce of two hash codes approximately reflects the corresponding data similarity in the original feature space. Hashing is known to be more suitable for approximate similarity search for high-dimensional data. Some related methods have been proposed for learning a compact representations for the discriminative tasks, such as locality sensitive hashing [1], spectral hashing [30], and semi-supervised hashing [19, 29].

Hashing aims to map the input data into a K-dimensional Hamming space to obtain its compact representation $\mathbb{H}^K = \{\pm 1\}^K$. Suppose that there are N_l labeled training samples, so the matrix is given by $\mathbf{X}_l = \{\mathbf{x}_i\}_{i=1}^{N_l} \in \mathbb{R}^{D \times N_l}$ where each sample $\mathbf{x}_i \in \mathbb{R}^D$. Given an input $\mathbf{x}$, one can learn K hash functions $\mathbf{H} = [h_1, \cdots, h_K]$ to produce a hashing representation $\mathbf{h} \in \mathbb{R}^K$ by the form

$$\mathbf{h} = \mathbf{H}(\mathbf{x}) = \operatorname{sgn}(\mathbf{P}\mathbf{x} + \mathbf{t}), \tag{4}$$

where $\operatorname{sgn}(\cdot)$ is the signum function, and $\mathbf{P} \in \mathbb{R}^{K \times D}$ is a projection matrix, each column $\mathbf{p}_k \in \mathbb{R}^D$ is a projection vector, $\mathbf{t} \in \mathbb{R}^K$ is a bias vector, each element $t_k = -\frac{1}{n}\sum_{i=1}^{n} \mathbf{p}_k^T \mathbf{x}_i$ is equal to the mean of the projected data and zero for centered data.

In the supervised hashing, the weight matrix $\mathbf{P}$ is determined by enforcing the output of the corresponding hash functions $\mathbf{H} = [h_1, \cdots, h_K]$ to be consistent to the pre-specified side information. Suppose the side information is provided in the form of either similarity or disimilarity constraints between data pairs, we propose to maximize the following objective function:

$$\mathcal{J}(\mathbf{P}) = \sum_{k=1}^{K} \left\{ \frac{1}{|\mathcal{M}|} \sum_{(\mathbf{x}_i, \mathbf{x}_j) \in \mathcal{M}} h_k(\mathbf{x}_i) h_k(\mathbf{x}_j) - \frac{1}{|\mathcal{C}|} \sum_{(\mathbf{x}_i, \mathbf{x}_j) \in \mathcal{C}} h_k(\mathbf{x}_i) h_k(\mathbf{x}_j) \right\}, \quad (5)$$

where any pair $(\mathbf{x}_i, \mathbf{x}_j)$ from set $\mathcal{M}$ denotes a neighbor-pair. $\mathbf{x}_i$ and $\mathbf{x}_j$ are either neighbors in a metric space or shared common class labels. Similarly, a pair $(\mathbf{x}_i, \mathbf{x}_j) \in \mathcal{C}$ reflects the fact that $\mathbf{x}_i$ and $\mathbf{x}_j$ are far away in a metric space or have different class labels. Such an idea has been well explored in the context of discriminative subspace learning [28]. Its effectiveness in supervised deep learning was proved in prior works on neural networks such as [6]. However, our adopted formulation supports sparse supervision and is significantly more tractable.

For notation simplicity, the above objective function can be expressed in a compact matrix. For this purpose, an indicator matrix $\mathbf{\Omega}$ incorporating the pairwise labeled information from $\mathbf{X}_l \in \mathbb{R}^{D \times N_l}$ as:

$$\Omega_{ij} = \begin{cases} 1 \times \frac{1}{|\mathcal{M}|}, & (\mathbf{x}_i, \mathbf{x}_j) \in \mathcal{M}, \\ -1 \times \frac{1}{|\mathcal{C}|}, & (\mathbf{x}_i, \mathbf{x}_j) \in \mathcal{C}, \\ 0, & \text{otherwise}. \end{cases} \quad (6)$$

With indicator matrix $\mathbf{\Omega}$, one can rewrite Eq. (5) as

$$\mathcal{J}(\mathbf{P}) = \frac{1}{2} \mathbf{tr}\{\mathbf{H}(\mathbf{X}_l) \mathbf{\Omega} \mathbf{H}(\mathbf{X}_l)^T\}. \quad (7)$$

Without loss of generality, data are assumed to be zero-centered. For numerical tractability, we relax the sign of the projection values to be the signed magnitude, *i.e.*, $\mathbf{H}(\mathbf{X}_l) = \text{sgn}(\mathbf{P}\mathbf{X}_l)$ is replaced by $\mathbf{P}\mathbf{X}_l$. As in spectral hashing [30] and semi-supervised hashing [29], one can use the balancing and pairwise decorrelation constraints that can help generate good hash codes in which bits are independent and each bit maximizes the information by generating a balanced partition of the data. These constraints are replaced by the orthogonality constraints $\mathbf{P}\mathbf{P}^T = \mathbf{I}$. In summary, we intend to learn the supervised hashing by maximizing the relaxed objective function with constraints as:

$$\begin{aligned} \arg\max_{\mathbf{P}} \quad & \frac{1}{2} \mathbf{tr}\{\mathbf{P}\mathbf{X}_l \mathbf{\Omega} \mathbf{X}_l^T \mathbf{P}^T\}, \\ \text{subject to} \quad & \mathbf{P}\mathbf{P}^T = \mathbf{I}. \end{aligned} \quad (8)$$

2.4 Bridge

The bridge is the most important component in our model. It connects the auxiliary network to the main network by enforcing the correlation of their parameters. According to the above introduction, the main network consists in finding the parameters that minimize the reconstruction error and the auxiliary network consists in finding the parameters that maximize the empirical accuracy. We require the mixed model to inherit these two models; in other words, the learnt features are expected to be generative, such that they can produce good reconstructions, and to be discriminative, such that they can obtain the high empirical accuracy on labeled data. At the same time, we also desire the features to be sparse, which can improve robustness and efficiency of the model. Under these requirements, we connect the unsupervised term and supervised term, see Figure 3. The features $\mathbf{W}$ learnt from the unsupervised autoencoder is majorly useful for data reconstruction rather than classifier. Therefore, a good connection can make the features $\mathbf{W}$ be as consistent to the features $\mathbf{P}$ as possible where $\mathbf{P}$ is discriminative. This process can be viewed as Guidance; therefore, our model is named SUpervision-Guided AutoencodeR (SUGAR). All of these yield the following mixed objective:

$$\begin{aligned} \arg\min_{\phi, \mathbf{P}} \quad & \alpha \mathcal{J}_{AE}(\phi) + (1-\alpha) \mathcal{J}_{SH}(\mathbf{P}) + \\ & \frac{\epsilon}{2} \|\mathbf{P} - \mathbf{W}\|_F^2 + \lambda \|\mathbf{W}\|_{\ell_1}, \\ \text{subject to} \quad & \mathbf{P}\mathbf{P}^T = \mathbf{I}. \end{aligned} \quad (9)$$

where ϵ is a correlation coefficient between $\mathbf{P}$ and $\mathbf{W}$, λ is sparsity penalty ratio, $\alpha \in [0, 1]$ is a guiding coefficient, and linearly blends the following two objectives:

$$\mathcal{J}_{AE}(\phi) = \sum_{\mathbf{x} \in \mathbf{X}} \mathcal{L}(\mathbf{x}, \widehat{\mathbf{x}}) = \frac{1}{2} \sum_{\mathbf{x} \in \mathbf{X}} \|\mathbf{x} - \widehat{\mathbf{x}}\|^2, \quad (10)$$

$$\mathcal{J}_{SH}(\mathbf{P}) = -\frac{1}{2} \mathbf{tr}\{\mathbf{P}\mathbf{X}_l \mathbf{\Omega} \mathbf{X}_l^T \mathbf{P}^T\}. \quad (11)$$

In the autoencoder term $\mathcal{J}_{AE}$, the encoder is a linear transformation followed by a fixed element-wise nonlinearity. And the squared reconstruction error is employed.

2.4.1 *Optimization Algorithm*

$\|\mathbf{W}\|_{\ell_1}$ in the objective function is not differentiable at 0, which poses a problem for gradient-based methods. Though other alternative optimization schemes exist, we resort to the following simple approximation for function smoothing,

$$\|\mathbf{W}\|_{\ell_1} \approx \sum_{ij} \sqrt{W_{ij}^2 + \varpi}, \quad (12)$$

where ϖ is a pre-specified positive scalar that is negligibly small. In this way, the gradient calculation is enabled.

Another complication is from the orthogonality constraints on $\mathbf{P}$, *i.e.*, $\mathbf{P}\mathbf{P}^T = \mathbf{I}$. The constraint is difficult since it is non-convex and of high computational complexity to preserve in each iteration. Though sophisticated update schemes (*e.g.*, Crank-Nicolson-like update scheme in [31]) have been proposed to preserve such constraint, we adopt the following operation in practice, which simply sets the singular values of $\mathbf{P}$ to be all ones [13],

$$\mathbf{P} \leftarrow (\mathbf{P}\mathbf{P}^T)^{-\frac{1}{2}} \mathbf{P}. \quad (13)$$

The above operation is conducted after every gradient descent step to keep the orthogonality. We here propose to take mini-batches to update each iteration, where the true gradient is approximated by a sum over a small number of randomly training samples. During each iteration, we alternate the optimization of $\mathbf{P}$ and $\phi = \{\mathbf{W}, \mathbf{b}, \mathbf{b}'\}$ while fixing the other one. The overall algorithm is described in Algorithm 1. We name the algorithm as MSGD-SUGAR, where MSGD stands for Mini-batch Stochastic Gradient Descent.

2.5 Extensions

Nowadays, autoencoders have been widely researched and have many variants, such as [7, 8, 21, 22, 26]. The autoencoder term in our proposed model can also be replaced by many other autoencoder variants, *e.g.*, the denoising autoencoder (DAE) [27] or the contractive autoencoder (CAE) [22]. DAE encourages robustness of reconstruction $g(f(\mathbf{x}))$, whereas CAE explicitly encourages robustness of latent representation $f(\mathbf{x})$. Both learn the robust features in the unsupervised scheme with different aspects, and that, our proposed model can also be learnt in supervised scheme. Therefore, we here extend our proposed model to guide DAE and CAE.

Algorithm 1: MSGD-SUGAR

Input: Learning rate η, mini-batch size m and m', guiding coefficient α, penalty coefficient ϵ, sparse coefficient λ. A set of training data $\mathbf{X}$ where labeled data is $\mathbf{X}_l$.

begin
- Initialize the parameters $\phi = \{\mathbf{W}, \mathbf{b}, \mathbf{b}'\}, \mathbf{P}$.
- **repeat**
  - `// Fix` ϕ`, Update` $\mathbf{P}$
  - Pick m samples $\mathbf{X}'_l$ from $\mathbf{X}_l$
  - Let $\mathcal{J}_1 = (1-\alpha)\mathcal{J}_{SH}(\mathbf{P}) + \frac{\epsilon}{2}\|\mathbf{P}-\mathbf{W}\|_F^2$ $= \frac{\alpha-1}{2m^2}\mathbf{tr}\{\mathbf{P}\mathbf{X}'_l\mathbf{\Omega}\mathbf{X}'^T_l\mathbf{P}^T\} + \frac{\epsilon}{2}\|\mathbf{P}-\mathbf{W}\|_F^2$
  - Update parameters $\mathbf{P}$ by $$\mathbf{P} \leftarrow \mathbf{P} - \eta\frac{\partial\mathcal{J}_1}{\partial\mathbf{P}}$$
  - Orthogonal projection by $$\mathbf{P} \leftarrow (\mathbf{P}\mathbf{P}^T)^{-\frac{1}{2}}\mathbf{P}$$
  - `// Fix` $\mathbf{P}$`, Update` ϕ
  - Pick m' samples $\mathbf{X}'$ from $\mathbf{X}$
  - Let $\mathcal{J}_2 = \alpha\mathcal{J}_{AE}(\phi) + \frac{\epsilon}{2}\|\mathbf{P}-\mathbf{W}\|_F^2 + \lambda\|\mathbf{W}\|_{\ell_1}$ $= \frac{\alpha}{2m'}\sum_{\mathbf{x}\in\mathbf{X}'}\|\mathbf{x}-\widehat{\mathbf{x}}\|^2 + \frac{\epsilon}{2}\|\mathbf{P}-\mathbf{W}\|_F^2 + \lambda\|\mathbf{W}\|_{\ell_1}$
  - Update parameters ϕ by $$\phi \leftarrow \phi - \eta\frac{\partial\mathcal{J}_2}{\partial\phi}$$
- **until** *stopping criteria is met*;

end

2.5.1 SUGAR with DAE

DAE can be used to learn robust representations through the additive binary making noise (some input components are randomly set as 0 in accordance with the corruption ratio ρ) or Gaussian noise with the form $\widetilde{x} = x + \zeta, \zeta \sim \mathcal{N}(0, \sigma^2 I)$, where ρ or σ are called the corruption ratio, and used to control the degree of regularization. Simply, we here use DAE to replace AE in our proposed model, then it generates a new model, *i.e.*, "SUGAR with DAE". This yields the following objective function:

$$\begin{aligned} \arg\min_{\phi,\mathbf{P}} \quad & \alpha\mathcal{J}_{DAE}(\phi) + (1-\alpha)\mathcal{J}_{SH}(\mathbf{P}) + \\ & \frac{\epsilon}{2}\|\mathbf{P}-\mathbf{W}\|_F^2 + \lambda\|\mathbf{W}\|_{\ell_1}, \qquad (14) \\ \text{subject to} \quad & \mathbf{P}\mathbf{P}^T = \mathbf{I}. \end{aligned}$$

where $\mathcal{J}_{DAE}(\phi) = \sum_{\mathbf{x}\in\mathbf{X}} \mathbb{E}_{\widetilde{\mathbf{x}}\sim q(\widetilde{\mathbf{x}}|\mathbf{x})}\left[\mathcal{L}(\mathbf{x}, \widehat{\widetilde{\mathbf{x}}})\right]$. Here, the expectation is over corrupted versions $\widetilde{\mathbf{x}}$ of the input $\mathbf{x}$ obtained from a corruption process $q(\widetilde{\mathbf{x}}|\mathbf{x})$ where $\widehat{\widetilde{\mathbf{x}}}$ is the reconstruction of $\widetilde{\mathbf{x}}$.

2.5.2 SUGAR with CAE

From the motivation of robustness to small perturbations around the training points, CAE is more strongly contracting at the training samples. Similarly, we use CAE to replace AE, and propose "SUGAR with CAE", which yields the following objective function:

$$\begin{aligned} \arg\min_{\phi,\mathbf{P}} \quad & \alpha\mathcal{J}_{CAE}(\phi) + (1-\alpha)\mathcal{J}_{SH}(\mathbf{P}) + \\ & \frac{\epsilon}{2}\|\mathbf{P}-\mathbf{W}\|_F^2 + \lambda\|\mathbf{W}\|_{\ell_1}, \qquad (15) \\ \text{subject to} \quad & \mathbf{P}\mathbf{P}^T = \mathbf{I}. \end{aligned}$$

where $\mathcal{J}_{CAE}(\phi) = \sum_{\mathbf{x}\in\mathbf{X}}\left(\mathcal{L}(\mathbf{x}, \widehat{\mathbf{x}}) + \mu\|J_f(\mathbf{x})\|_F^2\right)$. Here, μ is the contraction ratio and $\|J_f(\mathbf{x})\|_F^2 = \sum_{ij}\left(\frac{\partial z_j(x)}{\partial x_i}\right)^2$ is the Frobenius norm of the Jacobian. In the case of a sigmoid nonlinearity, this norm has a simple expression $\|J_f(\mathbf{x})\|_F^2 = \sum_{i=1}^{K}(z_i(1-z_i))^2\sum_{i=1}^{D}W_{ij}^2$ [22] where z denotes the hidden representation of the input.

2.6 Building Deep Neural Networks

Stacking SUGARs to initialize a deep neural network works in similar way as stacking RBMs in deep belief networks (DBN) [11, 12] or standard autoencoders [4, 27]. Stacked SUGARs always consists two stages: pre-training and fine-tuning. A greedy layer-wise strategy, by Hinton [11], has been proven to be very useful in pre-training [9]. It was originally used to train a DBN one layer at a time, and it also can train each layer as an autoencoder. Unlike unsupervised pre-training, in our model, we use the supervised method with the label information into the antoencoder, *i.e.*, SUGAR. In other words, we use SUGAR to replace the standard autoencoder. The difference between SUGAR and the standard autoencoder is that the standard autoencoder only transmit the unlabeled data to next layer but SUGAR also takes the labeled data. The labeled hidden representation is used to guide the next layer as well as the current layer. The complete procedure for pre-training is shown in Figure 1.

Once a stack of encoders are built, the top level hidden representation can be used as input to a stand-alone supervised learning algorithm, *e.g.*, a logistic regression or a support vector machine classifier. In our model, as same as the strategy of [27], we also add a logistic regression layer on top of the encoders to yield a deep neural network to supervised learning. Then, all parameters of the whole system can be fine-tuned using a backpropagation technique. This stage is called as fine-tuning.

3. EXPERIMENTS

We first show the ability of SUGAR from multiple perspectives. Then we evaluate SUGARs as a pre-training strategy deep networks, using the stacking procedure that we introduced in Section 2.6. We will mainly compare the classification performance of Stacked SUGARs versus some state-of-the-art models such as Stacked Autoencoders on a benchmark of classification problems.

3.1 Datasets

We used the well-known digit classification problem and eight deep learning benchmark datasets [15].

3.1.1 MNIST digits

The **MNIST digits**[1] is a well-known classification problem. The entire dataset is partitioned into three parts: a training set with 50000 samples, a validation set with 10000 samples, and a test set with 10000 samples.

3.1.2 Benchmark classification tasks

The benchmark classification tasks[2] include 8 different datasets. Each of which contains tens of thousands of gray-level images of size 28 × 28 pixels. Among them, the datasets **Rectangles**, **Rect**$_{Img}$ and **Convex** are two-class problems. The train set (validation set) sizes of these three datasets are 1000 (200), 10000 (2000) and 7000 (1000), respectively. The following five datasets are **MNIST digits** variants with ten-class problems. The train set and validation set sizes of these five variants are 10000 and 2000,

[1] http://yann.lecun.com/exdb/mnist.

[2] http://www.iro.umontreal.ca/~lisa/icml2007.

respectively. Each dataset has 50000 test examples. Details on the datasets are listed in Table 2 and a few example images are shown in Figure 4.

Table 2: Description of Datasets

Data Set	Train	Valid.	Test	Class
Rectangles	1000	200	50000	2
Rect$_{Img}$	10000	2000	50000	2
Convex	7000	1000	50000	2
MNIST$_{Basic}$	10000	2000	50000	10
MNIST$_{Rot}$	10000	2000	50000	10
MNIST$_{Rand}$	10000	2000	50000	10
MNIST$_{Img}$	10000	2000	50000	10
MNIST$_{RotImg}$	10000	2000	50000	10

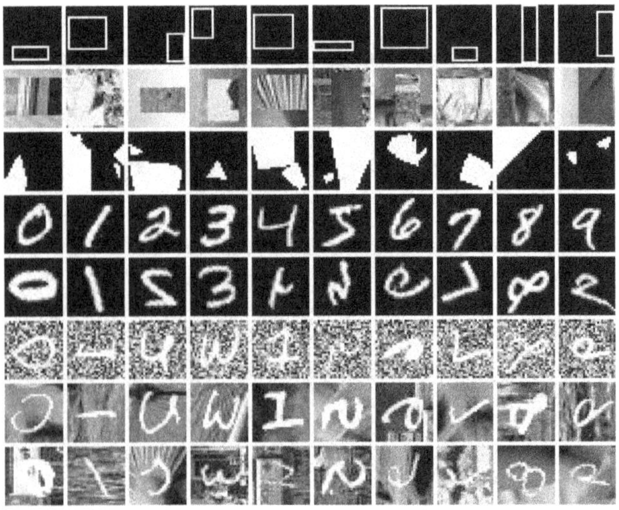

Figure 4: Samples from the various image benchmark datasets. From top row to bottom row: Rectangles, Rect$_{Img}$, Convex, MNIST$_{Basic}$, MNIST$_{Rot}$, MNIST$_{Rand}$, MNIST$_{Img}$, MNIST$_{RotImg}$.

3.2 Hyper-parameters Selection

It is non-trivial to find an optimal combination of the hyper-parameters (the number of hidden layers as well as that of hidden units in each layer, the pre-training learning rate and the fine-tuning learning rate, etc.). Fortunately, many researchers have devised various rules of thumb for choosing hyper-parameters in a neural network [17]. In our experiments, we mainly refer the strategies that used in [15]. Network parameters were trained from a random start[3], using mini-batch stochastic gradient descent[4] to perform all weight updates with a fixed learning rate (*e.g.*, 0.01 or 0.001).The guiding coefficient α shown in Eq. (9) allows us to adjust the relative contribution of the supervised guidance. We perform a grid search over the range of settings for α at intervals of 0.1. In all the datasets, we tried two values for the correlation coefficient between $\mathbf{W}$ and $\mathbf{P}$ (*i.e.*, $\epsilon = 0.000001$ or $\epsilon = 0.0000001$). The sparsity penalty ratio λ controls the sparsity of $\mathbf{W}$. We can observe the sparsity on each epoch using a small newtork architecture firstly, then empirically set a rough value and add the user-specified sparsity threshold to "stopping criteria", such as the sparsity $\geq 30\%$. We selected the value of hyper-parameters that yielded, after fine-tuning, the best classification performance on the validation set. Final classification error rate was then computed on the test set. The Python Theano Library[5] [5] is used for most of our experiments.

[3]Weights are sampled independently form a uniform in range $[-4 \times \frac{6}{\sqrt{nin+nout}}, 4 \times \frac{6}{\sqrt{nin+nout}}]$ for the sigmoid activation that is used in our experiments where nin, $nout$ in this case are the input and output dimensions, respectively [10].

[4]In most cases, the mini-batch size is equal to 10.

3.3 Performance Evaluation

3.3.1 Shallow Architecture

SUGAR with the shallow architecture (single hidden layer) is used to construct our experiments as well as the standard autoencoder on **MNIST**. We desired to know the effect by using the auxiliary network. Typically, the weight decay penalization is also used in the standard autoencoder.

1) *Effect of the guiding coefficient α*

We start to compare SUGAR and the standard autoencoder with the adjustment of the hyper-parameter α, which controls the relative importance of the supervised guidance. Both models have the same setup, *i.e.*, 500 hidden units, the sigmoid activation function. Figure 5(a) shows the classification error rates on three shallow neural network models, *i.e.* SUGAR, Autoencoder, and NNet (a standard single hidden layer feed-forward neural network). Obviously, SUGAR performs best in all cases. The best classification error rate of SUGAR is 1.50%. It improves 0.35% as compared with that of the standard autoencoder, whose classification error rate is 1.85%.

2) *Effect of labeled data*

In real applications, there are always fewer labeled data than unlabeled data. To assess the benefit of SUGAR on different sizes of the labeled data, we randomly sample $1000, 2000, \cdots, 10000$ labeled samples incrementally; at the same time, use all training data as unlabeled data. Concretely, taking 1000 for example, we use 1000 labeled samples and all 50000 training samples for pre-training and use 1000 labeled samples for fine-turning. We set the number of hidden layers as 100 and $\alpha = 0.2$. The same experiments were carried out in the unsupervised pre-training manner with the pure autoencoder. Figure 5(b) shows the results. We find that some supervised guidance is beneficial. And, it always performs better when increasing the labeled data.

3) *Effect of the sparsity penalty*

Here, we show the effect of the sparsity penalty. We use a subset of **MNIST** and select 1000 training samples. We here also set the number of hidden layer as 100, $\alpha = 0.2$, and fixed ϵ, but varying λ which controls the sparseness of $\mathbf{W}$. Figure 5(c) shows that the classification error firstly decreases and then increases as the sparsity increases. We also lists some related filters learnt by different sparsity, shown in Figure 6. It demonstrates our proposed model is more robust and efficient.

4) *Guidance to DAE and CAE*

We tried to construct the experiments to verify the guiding ability on different variants of autoencoder, *i.e.*, the denoising autoencoder and the contractive autoencoder. The autoencoder term in SUGAR can be replaced by DAE and CAE, see the details in Section 2.5. We use binary making noise in DAE and set the corruption ratio as 10%. In CAE, we set contraction ratio as 0.1. A group of subsets of **MNIST** are chosen with varying training samples. We also set

[5]`http://deeplearning.net/software/theano/`.

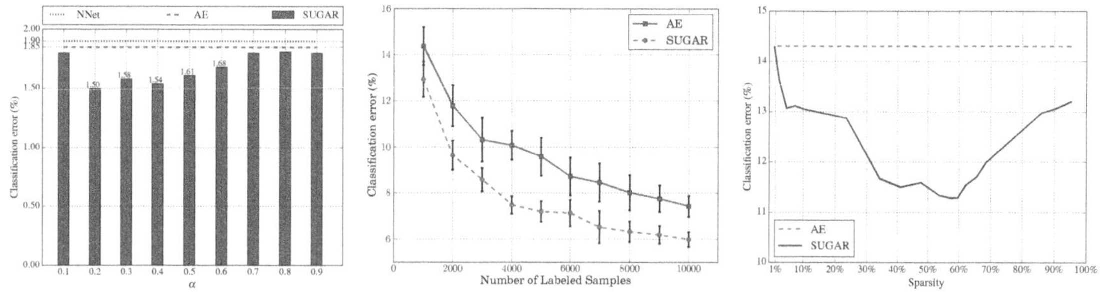

(a) (b) (c)

Figure 5: Experimental results on MNIST. (a) Classification error rates on the shallow neural network. NNet is a single layer neural network without pre-training and its result is taken from [4]. (b) A comparison of SUGAR ($\alpha = 0.2$) and the standard autoencoder versus the number of labeled samples. Error Bars show 95% confidence interval. (c) Classification error rates on the varying sparsity in SUGAR.

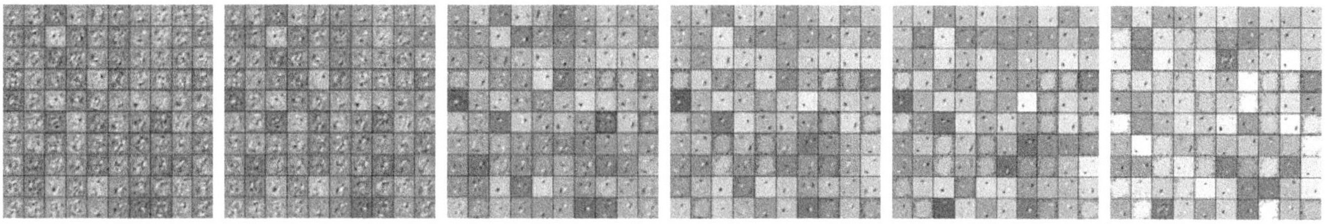

(a) 10% (b) 25% (c) 40% (d) 50% (e) 60% (f) 70%

Figure 6: Filters learnt by SUGAR from MNIST with various sparsity of W. Filters at the same position in all six images are related here, but only by the fact that SUGAR is started from the same random initialization point in the parameter space.

the number of hidden layer as 100 and $\alpha = 0.2$. As shown in Figure 7, it demonstrates that the auxiliary network can improve DAE and CAE effectively, and our proposed model is flexible and can be used with other autoencoder types.

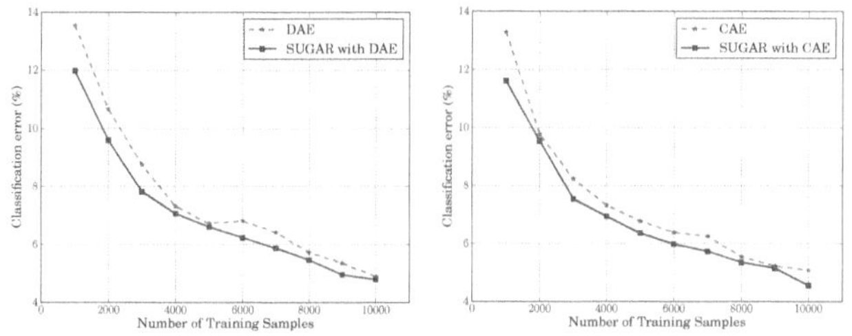

(a) DAE vs. SUGAR with DAE (b) CAE vs. SUGAR with CAE

Figure 7: Guiding ability on autoencoder variants

3.3.2 *Deep Architecture*

We stacked multiple SUGARs as deep neural networks and tested classification performances on the eight benchmark datasets. In detail, 1, 2, 3 hidden layers are noted as SUGAR-1, SUGAR-2 and SUGAR-3, respectively. We used a relatively small architecture (500 or 1000 units in the first and second hidden layer and 1000 hidden units in the third layer) in most of datasets. The guiding coefficient α is an important hyper-parameter and it controls the relative importance of supervised guidance. In Section 3.3.1, we have shown that different α almost can improve the classification accuracy of an autoencoder through the grid search on $[0, 1]$. However, a full grid search is always time-consuming and even infeasible. Here, we use bisection search to replace grid search to determine α. It needs only several times to find a near optimal α. For the sparsity, we start a smaller sparsity penalty ratio (such as $\lambda = 0.0001$), and observe the sparsity of $\mathbf{W}$ and adjust λ to the proper value. Then, we add the sparsity requirement to "stopping criteria" (the sparsity $\geq 50\%$).

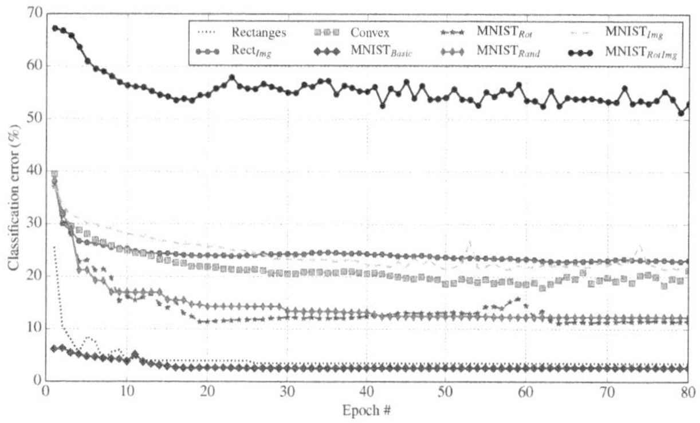

Figure 8: Validation error rates of SUGAR-3 on eight benchmark datasets. It needs only about 20 epochs to obtain almost the best validation error rate in most cases.

Figure 8 shows the error rates on validation sets in the stage of fine-tuning of SUGAR-3. It is easy to see that it needs only about 20 epochs to obtain almost the best validation error rate, which demonstrates our proposed model can provide an effective pre-training. Final classification error rate was we computed on the test set by selected parameters that yielded the best validation error rate. SUGARs with 1, 2 and 3 layers (SUGAR-1, SUGAR-2 and SUGAR-3) and SAA-3 (the deep autoencoders model) are compared in Figure 9. As the depth of the neural network increases, the classification accuracy also increases. It demonstrates our pro-

Table 3: **Classification error rates on the benchmark datasets (error rates are in %). Models: SVM-RBF: SVM with RBF kernels. SVM-Poly: SVM with polynomial kernels. NNet: (MLP) Feed-forward neural net. GSM: Gated softmax classifier. NonGSM: Non-factored gated softmax classifier. SAA-3: Three-layer stacked auto-associator. RBM: Restricted boltzmann machine. SUGAR-3: Three-layer stacked SUGAR. The results of SVM-RBF, SVM-Poly, NNet, SAA-3 and RBM are taken from [15], GSM and NonGSM results from [18]. The best results obtained by all these models are marked in bold.**

Dataset/Model:	SVM-RBF	SVM-Poly	NNet	GSM	NonGSM	SAA-3	RBM	SUGAR-3
Rectangles	02.15	02.15	07.16	0.83	**0.56**	02.41	04.71	03.49
Rect$_{Img}$	24.04	24.05	33.20	**22.51**	23.17	24.05	23.69	**22.55**
Convex	19.13	19.82	32.25	17.08	21.03	18.41	19.92	**17.00**
MNIST$_{Basic}$	**03.03**	03.69	04.69	03.70	03.98	03.46	03.94	03.47
MNIST$_{Rot}$	11.11	15.42	18.11	11.75	16.15	10.30	14.69	**9.53**
MNIST$_{Rand}$	14.58	16.62	20.04	10.48	11.89	11.28	**09.80**	11.40
MNIST$_{Img}$	22.61	24.01	27.41	23.65	22.07	23.00	**16.15**	20.65
MNIST$_{RotImg}$	55.18	56.41	62.16	55.82	55.16	51.93	52.21	**49.40**
Average	18.98	20.27	25.63	18.23	19.25	18.11	18.14	**17.19**

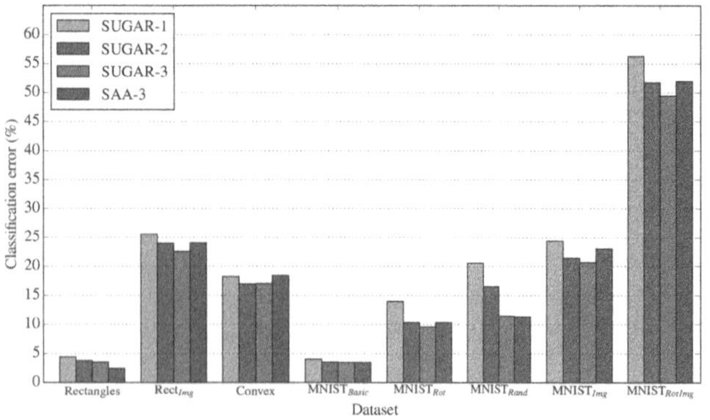

Figure 9: Classification error rates on eight benchmark classification tasks. SUGAR-3 appears to achieve performance superior or equivalent to SAA-3 on all problem except *Rectangles*. Notably, SUGAR-2 outperforms SAA-3 in three of the eight datasets.

posed model can learn more meaningful representations with deep neural networks. In most cases, stacking 3 layers of SUGAR seems to be better than stacking 3 layers of autoencoders in SAA-3.

Table 3 reports the classification perfomance obtained on eight deep learning benchmark datasets using SUGAR-3 as well as some state-of-the-art models. It indicates that SUGAR-3 performs well on all datasets. We see that SUGAR-3 outperforms the baseline SVM-RBF, as well as SVM-Poly in six out of 8 cases (except for Rectangles and MNIST$_{basic}$). The similar results can be found on the baseline GSM and NonGSM. It is among the best (within 0.04 tolerance), or the best performer, in four out of 8 cases. Intuitively, we also gave the average classification error rates of there models on all datasets. It is relatively from 1.12% up to 11.35% higher classification accuracy than these models, which demonstrates that the proposed model has a best classification ability in average.

4. CONCLUSIONS

To the best of our knowledge, most of the existing deep learning methods operate in the purely unsupervised manner or supervised manner. In this paper, we proposed a novel supervised deep learning model. Each layer includes a SUGAR, which is consisting of a main network, an auxiliary network, and a bridge. SUGAR regularizes the learnt networks by pairwise similarity or dissimilarity constraints among data. At the same time, the sparse regularization is employed, all of which make SUGAR produce good, sparse and robust representations, and therefore effectively improve deep networks with higher accuracy. The superiority of SUGAR is confirmed on MNIST digits and eight benchmark classification tasks. Further, SUGAR can be easily extended and used with the denoising autoencoder or the contractive autoencoder. It is demonstrated to provide a good guidance. Finally, the comprehensive experiments on the deep model show that it achieves performance superior to the existing state-of-the-art models on four out of eight datasets. All of these demonstrate that SUGAR can learn good feature representations for classification tasks.

Acknowledgments

The work is partly supported by a grant from China 973 Fundamental R&D Program (No.2014CB340304).

5. REFERENCES

[1] A. Andoni and P. Indyk. Near-optimal hashing algorithms for approximate nearest neighbor in high dimensions. *Commun. ACM*, 51(1):117–122, Jan. 2008.

[2] Y. Bengio. Learning deep architectures for AI. *Foundations and trends® in Machine Learning*, 2(1):1–127, 2009.

[3] Y. Bengio. Deep learning of representations: Looking forward. In A.-H. Dediu, C. Martín-Vidie, R. Mitkov, and B. Truthe, editors, *Statistical Language and Speech Processing*, volume 7978 of *Lecture Notes in Computer Science*, pages 1–37. Springer Berlin Heidelberg, 2013.

[4] Y. Bengio, P. Lamblin, D. Popovici, and H. Larochelle. Greedy layer-wise training of deep networks. *Advances in neural information processing systems*, 19:153, 2007.

[5] J. Bergstra, O. Breuleux, F. Bastien, P. Lamblin, R. Pascanu, G. Desjardins, J. Turian, D. Warde-Farley, and Y. Bengio. Theano: a CPU and GPU math expression compiler. In *Proceedings of the Python for Scientific Computing Conference (SciPy)*, June 2010. Oral Presentation.

[6] S. Chopra, R. Hadsell, and Y. LeCun. Learning a similarity metric discriminatively, with application to face verification. In *Computer Vision and Pattern Recognition, 2005. CVPR 2005. IEEE Computer Society Conference on*, volume 1, pages 539–546 vol. 1, June 2005.

[7] A. Coates, A. Y. Ng, and H. Lee. An analysis of single-layer networks in unsupervised feature learning. In *International Conference on Artificial Intelligence and Statistics*, pages 215–223, 2011.

[8] L. Deng, M. L. Seltzer, D. Yu, A. Acero, A.-r. Mohamed, and G. E. Hinton. Binary coding of speech spectrograms using a deep auto-encoder. In *INTERSPEECH*, pages 1692–1695. Citeseer, 2010.

[9] D. Erhan, Y. Bengio, A. Courville, P.-A. Manzagol, P. Vincent, and S. Bengio. Why does unsupervised pre-training help deep learning? *J. Mach. Learn. Res.*, 11:625–660, Mar. 2010.

[10] X. Glorot and Y. Bengio. Understanding the difficulty of training deep feedforward neural networks. In *International Conference on Artificial Intelligence and Statistics*, pages 249–256, 2010.

[11] G. E. Hinton, S. Osindero, and Y.-W. Teh. A fast learning algorithm for deep belief nets. *Neural computation*, 18(7):1527–1554, 2006.

[12] G. E. Hinton and R. R. Salakhutdinov. Reducing the dimensionality of data with neural networks. *Science*, 313(5786):504–507, 2006.

[13] A. Hyvärinen, P. O. Hoyer, and M. Inki. Topographic independent component analysis. *Neural computation*, 13(7):1527–1558, 2001.

[14] A. Krizhevsky, I. Sutskever, and G. E. Hinton. Imagenet classification with deep convolutional neural networks. In F. Pereira, C. Burges, L. Bottou, and K. Weinberger, editors, *Advances in Neural Information Processing Systems 25*, pages 1097–1105. Curran Associates, Inc., 2012.

[15] H. Larochelle, D. Erhan, A. Courville, J. Bergstra, and Y. Bengio. An empirical evaluation of deep architectures on problems with many factors of variation. In *Proceedings of the 24th international conference on Machine learning*, ICML '07, pages 473–480, New York, NY, USA, 2007. ACM.

[16] Y. LeCun, L. Bottou, Y. Bengio, and P. Haffner. Gradient-based learning applied to document recognition. *Proceedings of the IEEE*, 86(11):2278–2324, 1998.

[17] Y. LeCun, L. Bottou, G. B. Orr, and K.-R. Müller. Efficient backprop. In *Neural networks: Tricks of the trade*, pages 9–50. Springer, 1998.

[18] R. Memisevic, C. Zach, M. Pollefeys, and G. E. Hinton. Gated softmax classification. In *Advances in Neural Information Processing Systems*, pages 1603–1611, 2010.

[19] Y. Mu, J. Shen, and S. Yan. Weakly-supervised hashing in kernel space. In *Computer Vision and Pattern Recognition (CVPR), 2010 IEEE Conference on*, pages 3344–3351, June 2010.

[20] M. A. Ranzato and M. Szummer. Semi-supervised learning of compact document representations with deep networks. In *Proceedings of the 25th international conference on Machine learning*, ICML '08, pages 792–799, New York, NY, USA, 2008. ACM.

[21] S. Rifai, G. Mesnil, P. Vincent, X. Muller, Y. Bengio, Y. Dauphin, and X. Glorot. Higher order contractive auto-encoder. In *Proceedings of the 2011 European conference on Machine learning and knowledge discovery in databases - Volume Part II*, ECML PKDD'11, pages 645–660, Berlin, Heidelberg, 2011. Springer-Verlag.

[22] S. Rifai, P. Vincent, X. Muller, X. Glorot, and Y. Bengio. Contractive auto-encoders: Explicit invariance during feature extraction. In *Proceedings of the 28th International Conference on Machine Learning (ICML-11)*, pages 833–840, 2011.

[23] D. E. Rumelhart, G. E. Hinton, and R. J. Williams. Learning representations by back-propagating errors. *Nature*, 323(6088):533–536, Oct. 1986.

[24] J. Snoek, R. P. Adams, and H. Larochelle. Nonparametric guidance of autoencoder representations using label information. *J. Mach. Learn. Res.*, 13(1):2567–2588, Sept. 2012.

[25] R. Socher, J. Pennington, E. H. Huang, A. Y. Ng, and C. D. Manning. Semi-supervised recursive autoencoders for predicting sentiment distributions. In *Proceedings of the Conference on Empirical Methods in Natural Language Processing*, EMNLP '11, pages 151–161, Stroudsburg, PA, USA, 2011. Association for Computational Linguistics.

[26] P. Vincent, H. Larochelle, Y. Bengio, and P.-A. Manzagol. Extracting and composing robust features with denoising autoencoders. In *Proceedings of the 25th international conference on Machine learning*, ICML '08, pages 1096–1103, New York, NY, USA, 2008. ACM.

[27] P. Vincent, H. Larochelle, I. Lajoie, Y. Bengio, and P.-A. Manzagol. Stacked denoising autoencoders: Learning useful representations in a deep network with a local denoising criterion. *J. Mach. Learn. Res.*, 11:3371–3408, Dec. 2010.

[28] F. Wang and C. Zhang. Feature extraction by maximizing the average neighborhood margin. In *Computer Vision and Pattern Recognition, 2007. CVPR '07. IEEE Conference on*, pages 1–8, June 2007.

[29] J. Wang, S. Kumar, and S.-F. Chang. Semi-supervised hashing for scalable image retrieval. In *Computer Vision and Pattern Recognition (CVPR), 2010 IEEE Conference on*, pages 3424–3431, 2010.

[30] Y. Weiss, A. Torralba, and R. Fergus. Spectral hashing. In *Advances in neural information processing systems*, pages 1753–1760, 2008.

[31] Z. Wen and W. Yin. A feasible method for optimization with orthogonality constraints. *Mathematical Programming*, 142(1-2):397–434, 2013.

[32] Y. Yang, G. Shu, and M. Shah. Semi-supervised learning of feature hierarchies for object detection in a video. In *Computer Vision and Pattern Recognition (CVPR), 2013 IEEE Conference on*, pages 1650–1657. IEEE, 2013.

Sleep Analytics and Online Selective Anomaly Detection

Tahereh Babaie
University of Sydney & NICTA
Sydney, NSW, Australia
tahereh.babaie@sydney.edu.au

Sanjay Chawla
University of Sydney & NICTA
Sydney, NSW, Australia
sanjay.chawla@sydney.edu.au

Romesh Abeysuriya
University of Sydney
Sydney, NSW, Australia
r.abeysuria@physics.usyd.edu.au

ABSTRACT

We introduce a new problem, the Online Selective Anomaly Detection (OSAD), to model a specific scenario emerging from research in sleep science. Scientists have segmented sleep into several stages and stage two is characterized by two patterns (or anomalies) in the EEG time series recorded on sleep subjects. These two patterns are sleep spindle (SS) and K-complex. The OSAD problem was introduced to design a residual system, where all anomalies (known and unknown) are detected but the system only triggers an alarm when non-SS anomalies appear. The solution of the OSAD problem required us to combine techniques from both data mining and control theory. Experiments on data from real subjects attest to the effectiveness of our approach.

Keywords

Sleep EEG Anomalies, Dynamic Residue Model

1. INTRODUCTION

Research in human sleep condition has emerged as a rapidly growing area within medicine, biology and physics. A defining aspect of sleep research is the large amount of data that is generated in a typical sleep experiment. One of the key tools in sleep research experiments is polysomnography, which consists of overnight recordings of a range of measures,of a human subject, in a state of sleep. Polysomnography addresses a subject's eye movement, muscle tone, and neural activity recorded with electroencephalography (EEG) [20, 5]. A typical full night EEG time-series, recorded between 4-64 locations on the scalp, at 200 Hz, for eight hours, will generate approximately 300MB of data. A typical clinical study may use 10–50 subjects, which results in very large data sets. Surprisingly vast majority of sleep clinics still use a manual process to analyze the recorded EEG time-series. Hence there is considerable interest in automating the analysis of EEG generated from sleep experiments.

Scientists have segmented sleep into several stages based on the responsiveness of the subject and other physiological

KDD'14, August 24–27, 2014, New York, NY, USA.

http://dx.doi.org/10.1145/2623330.2623699.

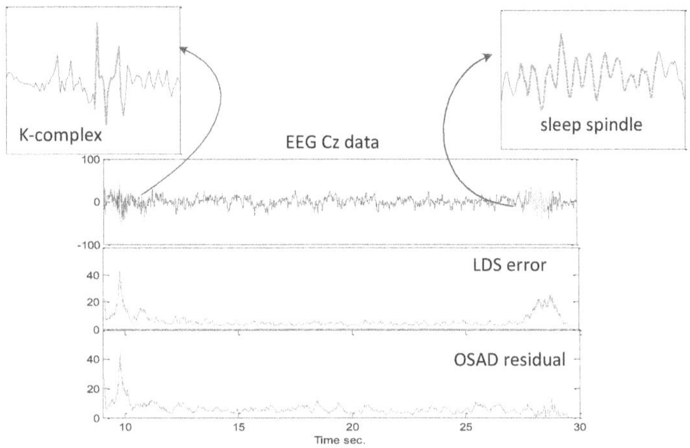

Figure 1: Sleep spindles (SS) along with K-complexes (KC) are defining characteristics of stage 2 sleep. Both SS and KC will show up as residuals in an LDS system. The OSAD problem will lead to a *new* residual time-series where SS will be automatically supressed but KC will remain unaffected.

features.(See Appendix B for more information regarding sleep stages). Of particular important is what is termed as stage 2 (moderately deep sleep). This stage is characterized by two phenomenon that occur in the EEG time series. These are *sleep spindles*, which are transient bursts of neural activity with a characteristic frequency of 12–14 Hz, and *K-Complexes*, which are short, large-amplitude voltage spikes. Both phenomena are implicated in memory consolidation and learning, but the physiology and mechanisms by which they occur are not yet fully understood, see [5, 10, 20, 9].

The physiological mechanisms and functional roles of K-complexes and sleep spindles is under investigation, but analyzing their properties requires identifying them in the EEG, which is a significant challenge for several reasons. Sleep spindles and K-complexes typically last less than 1 s, and there are only on the order of 100 of these events over the course of an entire night. Identification of these events is further complicated by the presence of artifacts in the data, which are often caused by movement of the subject, but which can also occur due to electrical noise or loose electrode connections. These artifacts must be ignored when attempting to identify sleep spindles and K-complexes. Because the electric fields produced by the brain are quite weak (the induced electrical potential is on the order of $50\,\mu$V), the signals also contain a significant noise component. Finally, a typical full-night EEG time-series consists of eight hours of data sampled at 200 Hz.

In this paper we introduce the Online Selective Anomaly Detection (OSAD) problem which captures a particular scenario in sleep research. As noted above, around 100 sleep spindles will occur during the course of a night. The number of K-Complexes is much fewer. For some experiments scientists are interested in identifying both sleep spindles and K-Complexes but only want to be notified with an alert when a non-spindle anomaly occurs (for example K-Complexes).

The solution of the OSAD problem combines techniques form both data mining and control theory. Data Mining is used to model and infer the normal EEG pattern per subject. Experiments have shown that model parameters do not transfer accurately across to other subjects. In our case we will use a Linear Dynamical System (LDS) to model the EEG time series. Then based on frequency analysis, we infer the sleep spindle (SS) pattern and integrate the pattern as a disturbance into the LDS. The control theory part is used to *design* a new residual which suppresses SS signals but faithfully represents other errors generated by the LDS model. Thus by selectively suppressing SS pattern, the objectives of the OSAD problem are achieved.

For example, consider Figure 1. The top frame shows a typical EEG time series with both the SS and KC highlighted. The middle frame shows a typical residual time series based on an LDS model. The bottom frame shows a new residual designed to solve the OSAD problem. Notice that the error due to the presence of SS is suppressed but the residual due to the appearance of KC remains unaffected.

The main contributions of the paper are:

- We introduce the Online Selective Anomaly Detection(OSAD) to address the requirement of selectively reporting sleep anomalies based on specifications by domain experts.
- In order to solve OSAD, we combine techniques from data mining and control theory. In particular we will use a Linear Dynamic System (LDS) to model the underlying data generating process and use control theory techniques to design an appropriate residual system.

The rest of the paper is as follows. In Section 2, we rigorously define the OSAD problem. In Section 3 we present our methodology to infer the parameters of the LDS and use control theory to design a new residual system. In Section 4, we apply our approach to real sleep data and evaluate our results. We overview related work in Section 5 and conclude in Section 6 with a summary and potential ideas for future research.

2. PROBLEM DEFINITION

In this section we present our problem statement for selective anomaly detection.

The starting point is an observed time series of N points $y = \{y_i\}_{i=1}^N$ where each $y_i \in \mathbb{R}^m$. Furthermore, we assume that the y measures the output of a system which is generated from a latent variable $x \in \mathbb{R}^n$. The relationship between x and y is governed by a standard Linear Dynamic system (LDS) model [27] which is specified as

$$\begin{aligned} x(t+1) &= \mathbf{A}x(t) \\ y(t) &= \mathbf{C}x(t) \end{aligned}$$

Here $\mathbf{A}$ is an $n \times n$ state matrix which governs the dynamics of the LDS while $\mathbf{C}$ is an $m \times n$ observation matrix. The modern convention is to represent the LDS as graphical model as shown in Figure 2. The state of the system, x, evolves according to LDS beginning at time $t = 0$, with value x_0. The standard learning problem is as follows.

PROBLEM 1 (LEARNING PROBLEM). *Given an observable time series $\{y_i\}_{i=1}^N$ and assuming that the observed y and the latent x are governed by an LDS, infer $\mathbf{A}$ and $\mathbf{C}$.*

The standard LDS inference problem has been extensively studied in both the machine learning and control theory literature. Several algorithms have been proposed including those based on gradient descent, Expectation Maximization, subspace identification and spectral approaches [28, 30, 17, 4]. Several extensions of LDS to include non-linear relationships as well as to include stochastic disturbances have been proposed. However, for sleep analysis, the above LDS will suffice. For the sake of completeness, in the Appendix we will describe a simple but effective approach for inferring $\mathbf{A}$ and $\mathbf{C}$ based on a spectral method [4].

The standard approach to detect outliers using an LDS is to use the inferred $\mathbf{A}$ and $\mathbf{C}$ matrices to compute the latent and observed error variables as:

$$\begin{aligned} \varepsilon(t) &:= x(t) - \hat{x}(t) \\ e(t) &:= y(t) - \hat{y}(t) \end{aligned}$$

where $\hat{x}$ and $\hat{y}$ are estimated using LDS. Then given a threshold parameter δ, an anomaly is reported whenever, $e(t) > \delta$. However, our objective is not to report all anomalies but suppress some known user-defined patterns or even known anomalous pattern. We now formalize the notion of pattern.

DEFINITION 1. *A* **pattern P** *is a user-defined matrix which operates in the latent space.*

In our context, we will design a specific matrix $\mathbf{P}$ for a sleep spindle. The matrix $\mathbf{P}$ is integrated into the LDS as

$$\begin{aligned} x(t+1) &= \mathbf{A}x(t) + \mathbf{P}\zeta(t) \\ y(t) &= \mathbf{C}x(t) \end{aligned}$$

We are now ready to define the design part of the OSAD problem.

PROBLEM 2 (DESIGN PROBLEM). *Given an LDS, a pattern $\mathbf{P}$ in the latent space, design a residual $r(t)$ such that*

$$r(t) = \begin{cases} 0 & \text{if } \epsilon(t) = \mathbf{P}\zeta(t) \\ \mathbf{S}e(t) & \text{otherwise} \end{cases}$$

Here $\mathbf{S}$ is suitably defined linear transformation on $e(t)$. Notice that the residual $r(t)$ depends both on the latent error $\epsilon(t)$ and the observed error $e(t)$. In practice, $r(t)$ will never be exactly zero when the pattern $\mathbf{P}$ is active but will have small absolute values.

3. THE OSAD METHOD

In this section we propose a method based on statistical inference and control theory to provide a solution of the

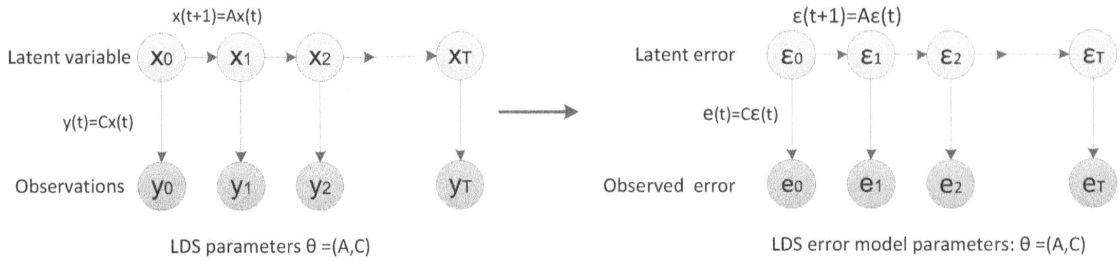

Figure 2: A linear dynamic system is a model which defines a linear relationship between the latent (or hidden) state of the model and observed outputs. The LDS parameters **A** and **C** need to be estimated from data. The LDS can also be used to model the relationship between the latent and the observed residuals (right figure).

OSAD problem. Using the LDS, we first develop a `Dynamic Residue Model` (DRM). Then we will show how to adjust the DRM parameters in order to design a residual $r(t)$ which will satisfy the constraints of the problem, i.e. the selected anomalous pattern will be canceled (or projected out) in the generated residual space.

3.1 DRM Formulation

Assume data is generated by an LDS. Any deviation of the state from its expected value can be captured by a structured error model. Intuitively, the discrepancy between the observed error $e(t)$ and latent error $\varepsilon(t)$ is modeled by the same LDS (because of linearity):

$$\begin{aligned} \varepsilon(t+1) &= \mathbf{A}\varepsilon(t) + \mathbf{P}\xi(t) \\ e(t) &= \mathbf{C}\varepsilon(t) \end{aligned}$$

The above error model can be used to detect changes occurring in the latent space.

We design a feedback loop (as shown in Figure 3) to effect the output of the error model. In particular a function of the residual will be used to manipulate the changes in the error. The design objective will be to map the anomalies generated by the **P** pattern into the null space of the new residual. The DRM based on this feedback design is developed as follows:

To design the feedback we define two transformation matrices **W** and **F** for error values to be weighted as:

$$\begin{aligned} r(t) &:= \mathbf{W}e(t) \\ u(t) &:= \mathbf{F}e(t) \end{aligned}$$

F will be used as the feedback gain matrix and maps the error to the feedback vector $u(t)$, and **W** is the residual weighting matrix that generates the new residual $r(t)$. Now feeding back $u(t)$ into the LDS (as shown in Figure 2), with $u(t)$, the residual dynamic model will be:

$$\begin{aligned} \hat{x}(t+1) &= \mathbf{A}\hat{x}(t) + u(t) \\ &= \mathbf{A}\hat{x}(t) + \mathbf{F}e(t) \\ &= \mathbf{A}\hat{x}(t) + \mathbf{F}(y(t) - \hat{y}(t)) \\ &= \mathbf{A}\hat{x}(t) + \mathbf{F}(\mathbf{C}x(t) - \mathbf{C}\hat{x}(t)) \\ &= \mathbf{A}\hat{x}(t) + \mathbf{FC}x(t) - \mathbf{FC}\hat{x}(t) \\ &= (\mathbf{A} - \mathbf{FC})\hat{x}(t) + \mathbf{FC}x(t) \\ &= (\mathbf{A} - \mathbf{FC})\hat{x}(t) + \mathbf{F}y(t) \end{aligned}$$

Notice that since the residual is a linear transformation of the error, its rank (suppose $r(t) \in \mathbb{R}^p$) can not be larger than the observation dimension, i.e., $p \leq m$.

We are now able to define the dynamic of the latent error as:

$$\begin{aligned} \varepsilon(t+1) &= x(t+1) - \hat{x}(t+1) \\ &= \mathbf{A}x(t) - (\mathbf{A} - \mathbf{FC})\hat{x}(t) - \mathbf{F}y(t) \\ &= \mathbf{A}x(t) - \mathbf{A}\hat{x}(t) - \mathbf{FC})\hat{x}(t) + \mathbf{FC}x(t) \\ &= (\mathbf{A} - \mathbf{FC})(x(t) - \hat{x}(t)) \\ &= (\mathbf{A} - \mathbf{FC})\varepsilon(t) \end{aligned}$$

and the residue $r(t)$ is obtained as:

$$\begin{aligned} r(t) &= \mathbf{W}(y(t) - \hat{y}(t)) \\ &= \mathbf{W}(\mathbf{C}x(t) - \mathbf{C}\hat{x}(t)) \\ &= \mathbf{WC}(x(t) - \hat{x}(t)) \\ &= \mathbf{WC}\varepsilon(t) \end{aligned}$$

We therefore have the following dynamic model for the latent error:

$$\begin{aligned} \varepsilon(t+1) &= (\mathbf{A} - \mathbf{FC})\varepsilon(t) \\ r(t) &= \mathbf{WC}\varepsilon(t) \end{aligned}$$

Notice that the observed residue $r(t)$ is governed by state error $\varepsilon(t)$ through matrix **WC** while it evolves in time through $\mathbf{A} - \mathbf{FC}$.

To simplify the notation, denote $\mathbf{C}_f = \mathbf{WC}$ and $\mathbf{A}_f = \mathbf{A} - \mathbf{FC}$. The DRM is then defined as:

$$\begin{aligned} \varepsilon(t+1) &= \mathbf{A}_f\varepsilon(t) \\ r(t) &= \mathbf{C}_f\varepsilon(t) \end{aligned}$$

The graphical diagram for this error model is shown in Figure 3.

3.2 OSAD Parameter Design

In this section we address the problem of designing the **F** and **W** matrix with objective of making the DRM insensitive to anomalies generated by **P**. The overarching design is shown in Figure 4 and is related to the use of control theory for fault diagnosis [23, 24, 6]. A typical LDS model will output the observed error $e(t)$. However, the OSAD model has a feedback loop which takes **W** and **F** matrices as input and return a variable $u(t)$ which is fed back into the model. The observed error is also transformed by a **W** matrix. The **F** and the **W** matrices satisfy the constraints which involve the **A**, **C** and the **P** matrices.

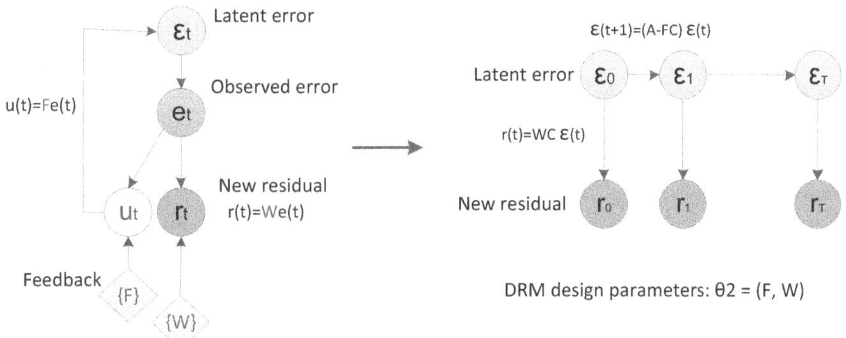

Figure 3: Using parameter $\mathbf{F}$ a virtual input $u(t)$ is generated to feed the error back to the latent space. The error $e(t)$ is is then calibrated by $\mathbf{W}$ to generate a new residual space $r(t)$.

Since the model is time-dependent, we follow a standard approach and map the model into the frequency domain using a $\mathcal{Z}$-transform to design the $\mathbf{W}$ and $\mathbf{F}$ matrices. In the frequency domain, it will be easier to design matrices $\mathbf{W}$ and $\mathbf{F}$ such that $\mathbf{WC}(\mathbf{A}-\mathbf{FC}) = 0$ and $\mathbf{WCP} = 0$.

DEFINITION 2. *The Z-transform of a discrete-time sequence $x(k)$ is the series $X(z)$ defined as*

$$X(z) = \mathcal{Z}\{x(k)\} = \sum_{0}^{\infty} x(k)z^{-k}.$$

OBSERVATION 1. *Two important (and well known) properties of the Z-transform are linearity and time shifting:*

$$ax(k) + by(t) \overset{Z}{\longleftrightarrow} aX(z) + bY(Z)$$

$$x(k+b) \overset{Z}{\longleftrightarrow} z^b X(z)$$

Applying Z-transform $\mathcal{Z}()$ to the DRM yields:

$$\begin{aligned} z\mathcal{E}(z) &= \mathbf{A}_f\mathcal{E}(z) + \mathbf{P}\boldsymbol{\xi}(z) \\ \mathcal{E}(z) &= (z\mathbf{I}-\mathbf{A}_f)^{-1}\mathbf{P}\boldsymbol{\xi}(z) \end{aligned}$$

and:

$$\begin{aligned} R(z) &= \mathbf{C}_f\mathcal{E}(z) \\ &= [\mathbf{C}_f(z\mathbf{I}-\mathbf{A}_f)^{-1}\mathbf{P}]\boldsymbol{\xi}(z) \end{aligned}$$

in which $\boldsymbol{\xi}(z) = \mathcal{Z}(\xi(t))$, $\boldsymbol{\vartheta} = \mathcal{Z}(\vartheta(t))$, $R(z) = \mathcal{Z}(r(t))$. The transfer gain between $\boldsymbol{\xi}$ and R:

$$\mathbf{G}_\xi(z) := \mathbf{C}_f(z\mathbf{I}-\mathbf{A}_f)^{-1}\mathbf{P}$$

Thus if $\mathbf{G}_\xi$ would be zero, the residual $R(z)$ is independent of the $\boldsymbol{\xi}(z)$. In the other word, to make $R(z)$ independent of $\boldsymbol{\xi}(z)$, one must null the space of $\mathbf{G}_\xi(z)$. Then whenever $\mathcal{P}$ occurs it is transferred by a zero gain to the residual space. To find the null space $\mathbf{G}_\xi(z) = 0$, we expand it as:

$$\begin{aligned} \mathbf{G}_\xi(z) &= z^{-1}\mathbf{C}_f(\mathbf{I}+\mathbf{A}_f z^{-1} + \mathbf{A}_f^2 z^{-2} + ...)\mathbf{P} \\ &= 0 \end{aligned}$$

The sufficient conditions for $\mathbf{G}_\xi(z)$ to be nulled are $\mathbf{C}_f\mathbf{P} = 0$ and either $\mathbf{C}_f\mathbf{A}_f = 0$ or $\mathbf{A}_f\mathbf{P} = 0$. Thus we have the following result.

THEOREM 1. *For a DRM, a sufficient condition for $\mathbf{G}_\xi(z) = 0$ is*

$$\mathbf{C}_f\mathbf{P} = 0 \textit{ and } \{\mathbf{C}_f\mathbf{A}_f = 0 \textit{ or } \mathbf{A}_f\mathbf{P} = 0\}$$

Now as $\mathbf{C}_f = \mathbf{WC}$, for $\mathbf{C}_f\mathbf{P} = 0$ it is sufficient that $\mathbf{WC}$ be orthogonal to $\mathbf{P}$. Furthermore for $\mathbf{C}_f\mathbf{A}_f = 0$, it is sufficient to design a matrix $\mathbf{A}_f$ such that its left eigenvectors corresponding to the zero eigenvalue are orthogonal to $\mathbf{P}$. Similarly, for $\mathbf{A}_f\mathbf{P} = 0$, it is sufficient to design a matrix $\mathbf{A}_f$, such that the right eigenvectors corresponding to the zero eigenvalues are orthogonal to $\mathbf{P}$. See Appendix A.

Now, it design a system which operates in an online fashion we proceed as follows. From the definition of residue:

$$r(t) = \mathbf{W}[y(t) - \hat{y}(t)]$$

Using the Z-transform, the computational form of the residual will be:

$$R(z) = [\mathbf{W} - \mathbf{C}_f(z\mathbf{I}-\mathbf{A}_f)^{-1}\mathbf{F}]Y(z)$$

Since $\mathbf{C}_f\mathbf{A}_f = 0$:

$$\mathbf{C}_f(z\mathbf{I}-\mathbf{A}_f)^{-1}\mathbf{F} = z^{-1}\mathbf{C}_f$$

Replacing this result to the above $R(z)$ equation:

$$R(z) = (\mathbf{W} - z^{-1}\mathbf{C}_f\mathbf{F})Y(z)$$

Applying the inverse Z-transform, the equation will be:

$$r(t) = [\mathbf{W} \quad -\mathbf{C}_f\mathbf{F}] \begin{bmatrix} y(t) \\ y(t-1) \end{bmatrix}$$

This clearly says that the residual can be represented directly in terms of the observations. This property is crucial to make the anomaly detection system operate in near real-time.

3.3 Eigenpair Assignment and the F Matrix

In this section we explain the eigenpair assignment problem and its solution which is used for designing the matrix $\mathbf{F}$. Recall from Theorem 1, that we require either $\mathbf{C}_f\mathbf{A}_f = 0$ or $\mathbf{A}_f\mathbf{P} = 0$.

PROBLEM 3. *Given a set of scalars $\{\lambda_i\}$ and a set of n-vectors $\{v_i\}$ (for $i = 1, 2, ..., n$), find a real matrix $\mathbf{A}_o$ ($m \times n$) such that the eigenvalues of $\mathbf{A}_o$ are precisely those of the set of scalars $\{\lambda_i\}$ with corresponding eigenvectors the set $\{v_i\}$.*

Given the residue model transition matrix $\mathbf{A}_f = \mathbf{A} - \mathbf{FC}$, the problem is to find a matrix $\mathbf{F}$ such that this matrix has the eigenvalues $\{\lambda_i\}$ corresponding to eigenvectors $\{v_i\}$,i.e.,:

$$(\mathbf{A} - \mathbf{FC})v_i = \lambda_i v_i$$

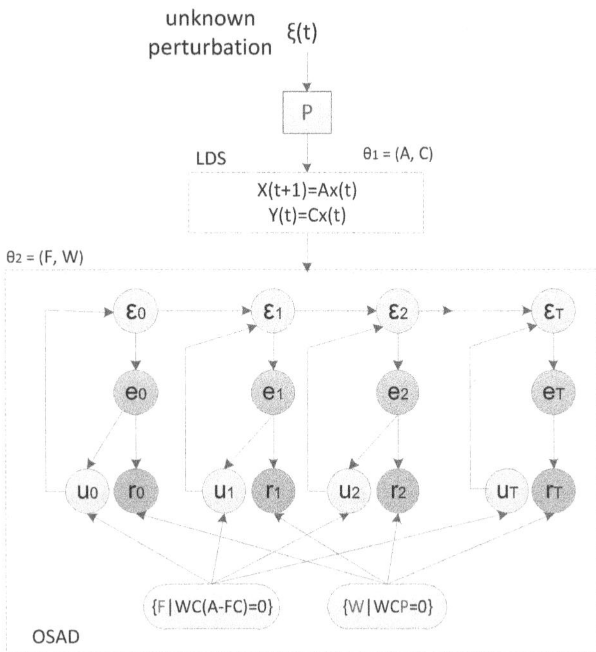

Figure 4: The complete diagram of OSAD. Using parameters $\mathbf{W}$ and $\mathbf{F}$ the residue space $r(t)$ is calibrated to cancel the impact of $\mathbf{P}\xi(t)$.

Algorithm 1 Find $\mathbf{F}$ such that the set $\{\lambda_i, v_i\}$ be the eigenpairs of $\mathbf{A}-\mathbf{FC}$

Input $\mathbf{A}$,$\mathbf{C}$, $\lambda_i = 0\ \forall i$ and $v_i = P(:,i)$.
Output $\mathbf{F}$ such that $(\mathbf{A}-\mathbf{FC})\mathbf{P} = \mathbf{0}$.
for $i = 1 : n$ **do**
  $\phi_i = null\begin{bmatrix}\mathbf{A}-\lambda_i\mathbf{I} & \mathbf{C}'\end{bmatrix}$
  Find an element $[v_i\ q_i]' \in \phi_i$
end for
$\mathbf{F} = -\begin{pmatrix}q_1 & q_2 & \dots & q_n\end{pmatrix}\begin{pmatrix}v_1 & v_2 & \dots & v_n\end{pmatrix}^+$

---

or:

$$\begin{bmatrix}\mathbf{A}-\lambda_i\mathbf{I} & \mathbf{C}'\end{bmatrix}\begin{bmatrix}v_i \\ -\mathbf{F}v_i\end{bmatrix} = 0$$

Define $q_i := -\mathbf{F}v_i$, then:

$$\begin{bmatrix}\mathbf{A}-\lambda_i\mathbf{I} & \mathbf{C}'\end{bmatrix}\begin{bmatrix}v_i \\ q_i\end{bmatrix} = 0$$

The implication of the above statement is of great importance: The vectors $\begin{bmatrix}v_i & q_i\end{bmatrix}'$ must be in the *kernel space* of $\begin{bmatrix}\mathbf{A}-\lambda_i\mathbf{I} & \mathbf{C}'\end{bmatrix}$, meaning, for $i = 1, 2, ..., n$:

$$\begin{bmatrix}q_1 & q_2 & \dots & q_n\end{bmatrix} = \begin{bmatrix}-\mathbf{F}v_1 & -\mathbf{F}v_2 & \dots & -\mathbf{F}v_n\end{bmatrix}$$

The matrix $\mathbf{F}$ now can be obtained as:

$$\mathbf{F} = -\begin{bmatrix}q_1 & q_2 & \dots & q_n\end{bmatrix}\begin{bmatrix}v_1 & v_2 & \dots & v_n\end{bmatrix}^+$$

where '+' stands for pseudoinverse. The whole procedure is summarized in Algorithm 1.

3.4 Degrees of Freedom of P

There is an an important constraint that the matrix $\mathbf{P}$ must satisfy for the DRM approach to be valid solution of the OSAD problem. As the $\mathbf{WCP} = 0$, a necessary condition is that

$$\text{rank}(\mathbf{P}) \leq \text{rank}(\mathbf{C})$$

In the other word, the effective number of independent perturbations generated by the matrix $\mathbf{P}$ is bounded by the effective number of independent measurements governed by the observation matrix $\mathbf{C}$, see [24]. For example, if $\mathbf{C}$ is the independent matrix on an LDS where the state vector has dimensionality n, then the rank of the $\mathbf{P}$ matrix must be less than $(n-1)$.

3.5 Inferring the Matrix P

The OSAD model is predicated on the existence of a $\mathbf{P}$ matrix. This matrix can be provided by a domain expert or can sometimes be inferred from data. For example, in the case of sleep spindle, frequency analysis shows that sleep spindles occur in the interval twelve to fourteen Hz. The exact frequency can change from one subject to another. The signature for K-Complexes is more a function of the amplitude of the signal rather than the frequency.

We now show how to construct a $\mathbf{P}$ matrix from data. For example, suppose there exists a frequency/peridicity $\mathcal{T} = f^{-1}$ in the EEG time series or:

$$x(t+\mathcal{T}) \quad = x(t)$$

Replace this in linear dynamics:

$$\begin{aligned} x(t+1) \quad &= \mathbf{A}x(t) \\ &= \mathbf{A}x(t+\mathcal{T}) \end{aligned}$$

Applying z-transform:

$$zX(z) \quad = \mathbf{A}z^{\mathcal{T}}X(z)$$

Using Tailor expansion we expand $z^{\mathcal{T}}$ around $z = 1$:

$$z^{\mathcal{T}} \approx 1 + \alpha + \beta z + \gamma z^2$$

where $\alpha = 0.5\mathcal{T}(\mathcal{T}-3)$, $\beta = 0.5\mathcal{T}(\mathcal{T}-1)$ and $\gamma = -\mathcal{T}(\mathcal{T}-2)$. An approximation by this expansion will be:

$$zX(z) \quad \approx \mathbf{A}X(z) + \alpha\mathbf{A}X(z) + \beta z\mathbf{A}X(z) + \gamma z^2 X(z)$$

Returning to the time-domain, we obtain

$$\begin{aligned} x(t+1) \quad &\approx \mathbf{A}x(t) + \alpha\mathbf{A}x(t) + \beta\mathbf{A}x(t+1) + \gamma\mathbf{A}x(t+2) \\ &\approx \mathbf{A}x(t) + [\alpha\mathbf{A} \quad \beta\mathbf{A} \quad \gamma\mathbf{A}][x(t) \quad x(t+1) \quad x(t+2)]' \end{aligned}$$

3.6 Summary Example

To summarize, the solution of the OSAD problem requires the availability of the following matrices:

Table 1: Parameters for learning and design

Matrix	Description	Source
A	The State Matrix	Inferred from data
C	The Observation Matrix	Inferred from data
P	The Pattern Matrix	Given by domain-expert
F	Feedback Gain Matrix	Designed using Theorem 1
W	Error Weighting Matrix	Designed using Theorem 1

We will now give a concrete example. Assume we have an LDS system given as

$$\begin{aligned}\varepsilon(t+1) &= \mathbf{A}\varepsilon(t) + \mathbf{P}\xi(t)\\ e(t) &= \mathbf{C}\varepsilon(t)\end{aligned}$$

Assume have identified the **A** and **C** matrices as

$$\mathbf{A} = \begin{pmatrix}0.5 & 0.3\\ 0.3 & 0.2\end{pmatrix} \text{ and } \mathbf{C} = \begin{pmatrix}1 & 0\\ 0 & 1\end{pmatrix} \text{ and } \mathbf{P} = \begin{pmatrix}1 & 1\\ 2 & 2\end{pmatrix}$$

Now, to form the OSAD model, we have to identify **W** and **F** such that:

1. **W** is in the null space of **CP** and
2. **A** − **FC** has its left eigenvectors (corresponding to the **0** eigenvalue), the rows of **WC**.

Since **C** is the identity matrix, an example of **W** is

$$\mathbf{W} = \begin{pmatrix}2 & -1\\ 2 & -1\end{pmatrix}$$

Similarly, an example of **F** matrix is

$$\mathbf{F} = \begin{pmatrix}0.0 & 0.2\\ -0.7 & 0\end{pmatrix}$$

As mentioned, the residual matrix is given by

$$r(t) = \begin{pmatrix}1.3 & -1.4\\ 1.3 & -1.4\end{pmatrix}\begin{pmatrix}y(t)\\ y(t-1)\end{pmatrix}$$

4. EXPERIMENTAL RESULT

We now report on the experiments that have been carried out to test the effective of the proposed OSAD solution on sleep data. Our particular focus will be determining if OSAD can recognize sleep spindle and K-Complex anomalies and selectively raise an alert for non-Spindle anomalies.

4.1 Sleep Data Set

Our data set consists of EEG time series from four health controls (age 25-36) as described in [12]. Recordings were made with an Alice-4 system (Respironics, Murraysville PA, USA) at the Woolcock Institute of Medical Research, at Sydney University, using 6 EEG channels with a sampling rate of 200 Hz, and electrodes positioned according to the International 10-20 system, see Figure 5. A notch filter at 50 Hz (as provided by the Alice-4 system) was used to remove mains voltage interference. No other hardware filters were used.

Sleep spindles were labeled for the Cz electrode during sleep stages 2–4 using a previously developed automated detection routine [1]. In summary, the spindles are detected by applying an 11–16 Hz bandpass filter to the EEG time series, then squaring and downsampling to 10 Hz. This processed signal is large when sleep spindles are present, and a threshold for spindle detection is determined based on this signal. In this limited data set, K-complexes were identified visually.

4.2 Inference of A and C Matrices

Our first task is to learn the **A** and **C** matrices from the LDS for each subject. Others have reported, and our experiments confirm, that EEG of each subject tends to different and separate models need to learnt per subject. For each subject we took a sample of size 2000 (10 seconds) of EEG

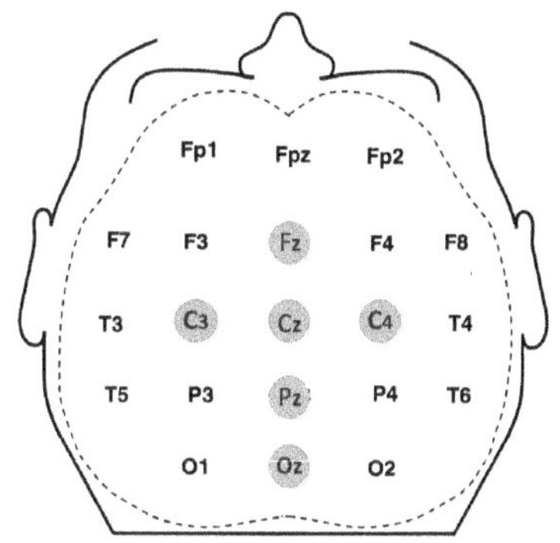

Figure 5: The position of scalp electrodes for EEG experiment follows the International 10-20 system [20, 5].

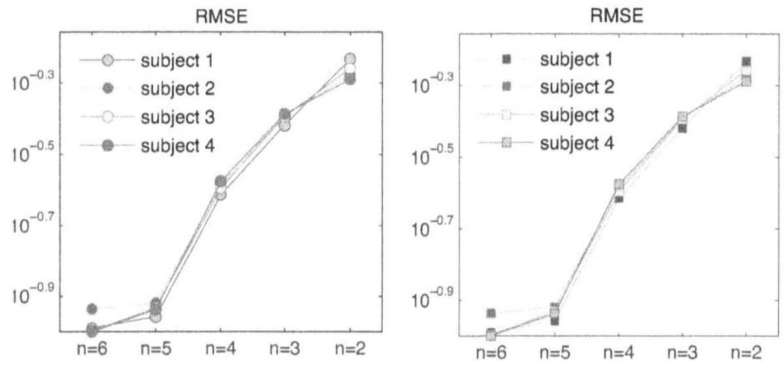

(a) Subspace method (b) Spectral method

Figure 6: The RMSE error obtained from both methods are comparable. Notice the RMSE increases as the rank of LDS is reduced.

time series which did not contain either sleep spindle or K-Complex. We then formed a 2000×6 data matrix, **O**. The columns of the **O** matrix are time series associated with the six channels of EEG. We used both subspace and spectral methods to infer the matrices **A** and **C**. Both these methods are based on SVD decomposition of the **O** matrix and require as input the rank required of the inferred matrices. We evaluated the inferred matrices using RMSE and the results are shown in Figure 6a and Figure 6b. Both the subspace and spectral methods have similar performance and RMSE goes up significantly when the rank falls below five. We selected a rank six matrix (maximum possible rank) for both **A** and **C**. In terms of running time, the two methods are comparable as we have to carry out an SVD of a relatively small 6×6 matrix.

4.3 Detection of SS and K-Complex

For each of the four subjects, statistics of the labeled sleep spindles and K-Complexes and those detected by the LDS are shown in Table 2. For LDS detection, we used a threshold derived from CUSUM which automatically adjusts for mean and standard deviation of the observed residual time series $e(t)$. To specify a CUSUM threshold we applied the alpha and beta approach in [18] and we set the probabilities of a false positive and a false negative to 10^{-4} and the change detection parameter to 1 sigma, in all subjects.

Table 2: Summary statistics of results. LDS is quite accurate but tends to over-predict the number of anomalies.

	No. of Labeled Anomalies		No. of Detected Anomalies	
	Spindle	K-Complex	Spindle	K-Complex
subject 1	170	277	164	251
subject 2	6	13	6	11
subject 3	23	38	21	37
subject 4	141	205	132	186

Table 3: Summary statistics for spindles. LDS has higher precision than recall and total length of predicted interval is higher than the length of labeled intervals.

	Total time of spindles		Performance	
	Labeled in min	Detected in min	Recall	Precision
subject 1	129.8	168.74	71.24%	95.53%
subject 2	3.45	3.55	97.18%	97.38%
subject 3	15.15	16.23	83.88%	95.66%
subject 4	93.5	103.2	79.15%	95.42%

In all four subjects, the LDS residual slightly under predicts the number of spindles and K-Complexes. Since each labeled and predicted SS and K-Complex spans a time-interval, we have modified the definitions of `precision` and `recall` to account for the intervals. For a given subject, let $\{[a_i, b_i]\}_{i=1}^{n}$ be the intervals of the labeled anomalies (spindles or K-Complex). Let $\{[a_j^{'}, b_j^{'}]\}_{j=1}^{m}$ be the predicted spindles. Then

$$\texttt{precision} = \frac{\sum_{i=1}^{n}\sum_{j=1}^{m} |[a_i, b_i] \cap [a_j^{'}, b_j^{'}]|}{\sum_{j=1}^{m} |[a_j^{'}, b_j^{'}]|}$$

and

$$\texttt{recall} = \frac{\sum_{i=1}^{n}\sum_{j=1}^{m} |[a_i, b_i] \cap [a_j^{'}, b_j^{'}]|}{\sum_{j=1}^{m} |[a_j, b_j]|}$$

Here, $|[a_i, b_i]|$, is the number of points in the time interval $[a_i, b_i]$. With these definitions in place, Table 3 and Table 4 show the precision and recall SS and K-Complex across alls the subjects. In general both precision and recall are high across subjects, but precision is significantly more higher than recall. For SS, the recall varies more than precision ranging for 71.24% to 97.18%. Also notice that the length of detection of both SS and K-Complex is higher compared to their labeled lengths.

4.4 Evaluation across Subjects

We now investigate the transfer properties of the inferred LDS across subjects. That is, we learn the **A** an **C** matrices on one subject and evaluate it against an another. We just focus on the anomaly. The `recall` and `precision` results are shown in Table 5 and Table 6 respectively. The diagonal of the table corresponds to the results in Table 3 and Table 4. It is clear that there is a substantial reduction in accuracy and that indeed the EEG of subjects varies substantially. We have also computed the "average" **A** and **C**

Table 4: Summary statistics for K-Complex. Both precision and recall are high. Total length of predicted interval is higher than labeled intervals.

	Total time of K-Complex		Performance	
	Labeled in min	Detected in min	Recall	Precision
subject 1	198.23	216.35	90.45%	93.43%
subject 2	11.48	11.25	92.76%	94.12%
subject 3	21.39	24.56	91.01%	92.06%
subject 4	147.68	160.49	91.28%	93.73%

Table 5: Recall across subjects. A substantial reduction in accuracy when model of one subject is evaluated against the EEG of another.

	A_1, C_1, W_1, F_1	A_2, C_2, W_2, F_2	A_3, C_3, W_3, F_3	A_4, C_4, W_4, F_4
subject 1	71.24%	38.13%	44.13%	41.29%
subject 2	41.32%	97.18%	35.26%	37.85%
subject 3	48.74%	43.21%	83.88%	44.43%
subject 4	51.26%	43.81%	35.36%	79.15%

Table 6: Precision across the subjects. Again, a substantial reduction in accuracy when model of one subjected is evaluated against another.

	A_1, C_1, W_1, F_1	A_2, C_2, W_2, F_2	A_3, C_3, W_3, F_3	A_4, C_4, W_4, F_4
subject 1	95.53%	41.11%	47.19%	43.67%
subject 2	39.54%	97.38%	37.82%	39.21%
subject 3	48.21%	41.29%	95.77%	41.83%
subject 4	51.77%	53.34%	33.49%	95.42%

Table 7: Recall and Precision on each subject evaluated against an averaged model. Again, a substantial reduction in accuracy compared to individual models.

	Recall	*Precision*
subject 1	69.35%	51.39%
subject 2	65.43%	57.22%
subject 3	61.77%	61.47%
subject 4	68.12%	53.92%

matrix and evaluated against all the four subjects. The results are shown in Table 7. While there is an improvement compared to results in Table 5 and Table 6, the absolute performance is still quite low compared to the situation where the learning was customized per individual subject.

4.5 Performance of Designed Residual

In this section we evaluate whether the new residual $r(t)$ satisfies the design criterion. Recall, $r(t)$ was designed to suppress the signal whenever a sleep spindle (SS) appears and behave like the observed error $\mathbf{e(t)}$ in otherwise. Figure 7 shows the distribution for $|r(t) - e(t)|_2$ for values of t when t is in (and not in) the predicted SS interval $[a_j^{'}, b_j^{'}]$ for some j. It is clear that the distribution when t is in a predicted SS interval is towards the right compared to when it is not in the interval. This is because in an SS interval, $r(t)$ will have a small absolute value (by design). In a non-SS in-

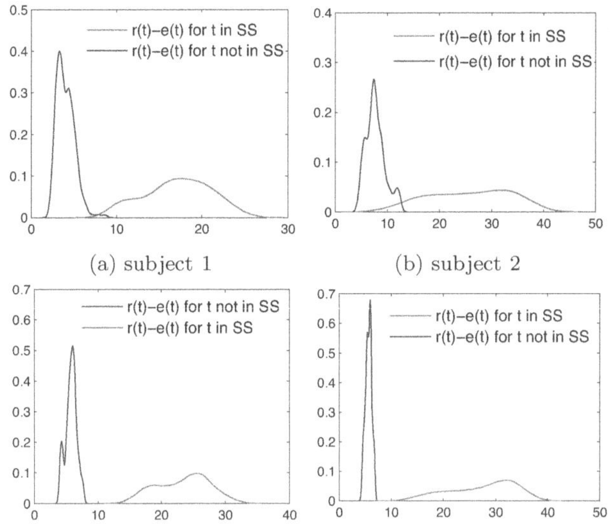

(a) subject 1 (b) subject 2

(c) subject 3 (d) subject 4

Figure 7: Comparison of the distribution of the norm of $r(t) - e(t)$ for SS and non-SS intervals. In all four subjects the designed residual suppresses spindles as designed as the norm is higher for SS intervals.

Table 8: Delay statistics. The lag between appearance and prediction of SS is, on average, a fraction of a second.

	Mean($a_i - a'_i$)	Mean($b_i - b'_i$)	Std($a_i - a'_i$)	Std($b_i - b'_i$)
subject 1	- 0.0678	- 0.0961	0.0589	0.0995
subject 2	0.0041	0.0016	0.0113	0.0089
subject 3	-0.0426	0.0663	0.0550	0.0478
subject 4	-0.0340	-0.0480	0.0474	0.0407

terval, $r(t)$ will be a linear function of $e(t)$, as $r(t) = \mathbf{W}e(t)$. This behavior is observed across subjects suggesting that in all cases that $r(t)$ is behaving as designed.

4.6 Delay in Detection of Anomalies

OSAD detects anomalies in near real time. We now discuss the lag between the appearance of a SS and before it is reported by the LDS. Figure 8 presents the delay distributions for subject 1 and subject 4 who experienced 164 and 132 labeled sleep spindles, respectively. In general, the predicted SS interval are longer and contain the actual intervals. This is confirmed in Figure 9 which shows one specific example of the location of the labeled sleep spindle and the predicted interval. In this case (which is typical), the prediction of SS begins before and ends later than the labeled spindle. Table 8 shows the results of the mean delay between matched intervals. Thus a mean of (a_i, a'_i) equal to -0.0678 implies that on average, there was a delay of 1/200 second before LDS reported an anomaly. On the other hand for subject 2 there the SS was, on average, reported before it showed up in the labeled sequence. As noted in [12], this is consistent with the observation (and confirmed by double-blind scoring) that the labeling of SS is more conservative i.e., SS are labeled for a shorter duration than what they should be.

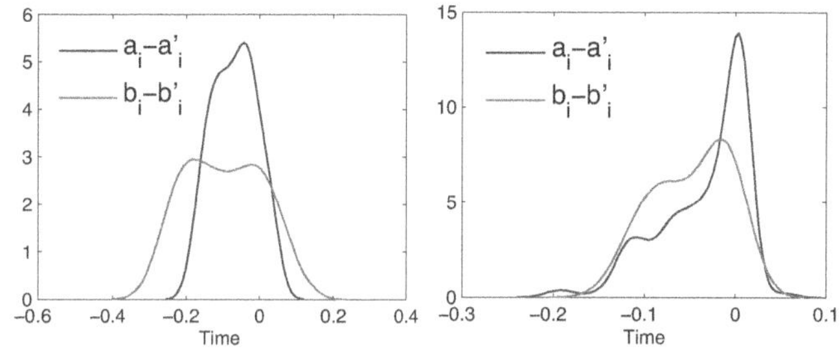

(a) subject 1 (b) subject 4

Figure 8: OSAD provides near real time detection. The delay between the actual appearance of a spindle and the predicted appearance is a fraction of a second. Similarly the lag between when the actual spindle disappears and it is reported to disappear is very small too. The x-axis is in seconds.

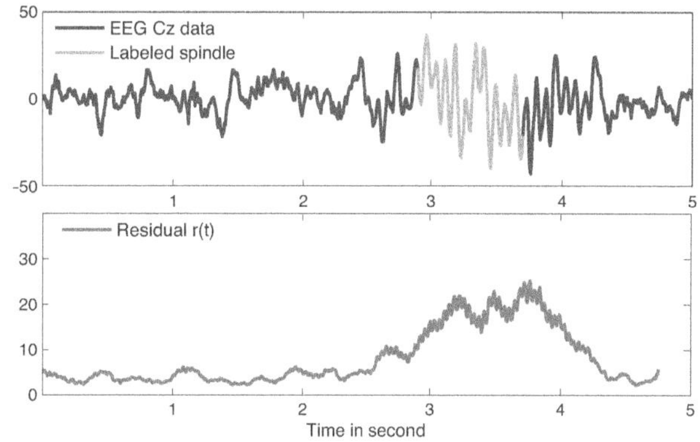

Figure 9: Top: Cz data and a typical sleep spindle labeled. Bottom: Residual and detected sleep spindle. In general the predicted spindle interval is longer than the labeled interval. The predicted interval tends to include the labeled interval, i.e., it begins earlier and finishes later. The EEG shows that the labeled intervals are actually quite conservative.

5. RELATED WORK

Automatic detection of sleep spindles is now an important topic in biomedical research. Different techniques including FFTs, wavelet analysis and autoregressive time series modeling have been applied for sleep spindle detection [25, 11, 14]. Attempts to integrate SVM to detect sleep spindles have also been explored [2]. There seems to be a large variability between sleep EEG across subjects. In our experiments we have also observed this phenomenon. This combined with the large amount of EEG noise has resulted in low level of agreement on the exact profile of sleep spindle [21].

The use of linear dynamical systems (LDS) to model time series is ubiquitous both in computer science [27] and control theory [30, 17, 19, 8, 16]. Expressing LDS in the language of graphical models and connections with HMM have been extensively examined in machine learning. The use of LDS for anomaly detection has also been investigated in network anomaly detection, among other areas [29]. The use of subspace identification methods for inferring the parameters of LDS have been discussed by Overschee [30]. Subspace methods estimate LDS parameters through a spectral decomposition of a matrix of observations to yield an estimate of the underlying state space. Subspace methods have low computational cost, are robust to perturbations and are relatively easy to implement. The recently introduced spectral learning methods are variations of the subspace method [4, 13]

The use of eigenstructure assignment to alter the residual of an LDS has been investigated in the control theory literature especially in the context of fault diagnosis [3].Our approach closely follows the work Patton et. al. [22] who have used eigenstructure assignment for altering the LDS model using feedback. Other variations of LDS and fault diagnosis are discussed in [7, 23, 6, 24].

6. CONCLUSION

In this paper we have introduced a new problem, the Online Selective Anomaly Detection (OSAD) to capture a specific scenario in sleep research. Scientists working on sleep EEG data required an alert system, which trigger alerts on selected anomalies. For example, sleep stage two is characterized by two known anomalies: sleep spindle and K-complex. The requirement was to design a system which detected both anomalies but only generated an alert when a non sleep spindle anomaly appeared. We combined methods from data mining, machine learning and control theory to design such a system. Experiments on real data set demonstrate that our approach is accurate and produces the required results and is potentially applicable to many other situations. We also note that data from sleep EEG provides a fertile ground to apply existing data mining methodologies and potentially design new computational problems and algorithms.

7. ACKNOWLEDGMENTS

This work is partially supported by NICTA[1]. NICTA is funded by the Australian Government as represented by the Department of Broadband, Communications and the Digital Economy and the Australian Research Council through the ICT Centre of Excellence program. Sanjay Chawla would also like to acknowledge CRC for Alertness, Safety and Productivity for access to the data set.

8. REFERENCES

[1] R. G. Abeysuriya, C. J. Rennie, P. A. Robinson, and J. W. Kim. Experimental observation of a theoretically predicted nonlinear sleep spindle harmonic in human EEG. *Journal of Clinical Neurophysiology*, 2014.

[2] N. Acır and C. Güzeliş. Automatic recognition of sleep spindles in eeg via radial basis support vector machine based on a modified feature selection algorithm. *Neural Computing & Applications*, 14(1):56–65, 2005.

[3] A. Andry, E. Shapiro, and J. C. Chung. Eigenstructure assignment for linear systems. *Aerospace and Electronic Systems, IEEE Transactions on*, AES-19(5):711–729, 1983.

[4] B. Boots, S. Siddiqi, and G. Gordon. Closing the learning-planning loop with predictive state representations. In *Proceedings of Robotics: Science and Systems*, Zaragoza, Spain, June 2010.

[5] G. Buzsaki. *Rhythms of the Brain*. Oxford University Press, 2006.

[1]http://nicta.com.au/

[6] C. Chen and R. Patton. *Robust Model-Based Fault Diagnosis For Dynamic Systems*. Kluwer International Series on Asian Studies in Computer and Information Science, 3. Kluwer, 1999.

[7] J. Chen and R. Patton. Optimal filtering and robust fault diagnosis of stochastic systems with unknown disturbances. *Control Theory and Applications, IEE Proceedings* -, 143(1):31–36, 1996.

[8] J. H. Cochrane. *Asset Pricing*. Princeton University Press, 2001.

[9] T. T. Dang-Vu, S. M. McKinney, O. M. Buxton, J. M. Solet, and J. M. Ellenbogen. Spontaneous brain rhythms predict sleep stability in the face of noise. *Current Biology*, 20(15):R626–R627, 2010.

[10] S. Diekelmann and J. Born. The memory function of sleep. *Nature Reviews Neuroscience*, 11(2):114–126, 2010.

[11] A. L. D́Rozario, J. W. Kim, K. K. Wong, D. J. Bartlett, N. S. Marshall, D.-J. Dijk, P. A. Robinson, and R. R. Grunstein. A new {EEG} biomarker of neurobehavioural impairment and sleepiness in sleep apnea patients and controls during extended wakefulness. *Clinical Neurophysiology*, 124(8):1605 – 1614, 2013.

[12] F. Duman, A. Erdamar, O. Erogul, Z. Telatar, and S. Yetkin. Efficient sleep spindle detection algorithm with decision tree. *Expert Systems with Applications*, 36(6):9980–9985, 2009.

[13] D. Hsu, S. M. Kakade, and T. Zhang. A spectral algorithm for learning hidden markov models. *CoRR*, abs/0811.4413, 2008.

[14] E. Huupponen, G. Gómez-Herrero, A. Saastamoinen, A. Värri, J. Hasan, and S.-L. Himanen. Development and comparison of four sleep spindle detection methods. *Artificial intelligence in medicine*, 40(3):157–170, 2007.

[15] C. Iber, S. Ancoli-Israel, A. Chesson, and S. F. Quan. *The AASM Manual for the Scoring of Sleep and Associated Events: Rules, Terminology and Technical Specification*. American Academy of Sleep Medicine, Winchester, Illinois, 1st edition, 2007.

[16] G. Kitagawa. Non-gaussian state space modeling of nonstationary time series. *Journal of the American statistical association*, 82(400):1032–1041, 1987.

[17] L. Ljung. *System Identification*. John Wiley & Sons, Inc., 2001.

[18] D. Montgomery. *Introduction to Statistical Quality Control*. Wiley, 2004.

[19] O. Nelles. *Nonlinear System Identification: From Classical Approaches to Neural Networks and Fuzzy Models*. Engineering Online Library. Springer, 2001.

[20] E. Niedermeyer and F. L. da Silva. *Electroencephalography: basic principles, clinical applications, and related fields*. Lippincott Williams & Wilkins, 2005.

[21] A. Nonclercq, C. Urbain, D. Verheulpen, C. Decaestecker, P. Van Bogaert, and P. Peigneux. Sleep spindle detection through amplitude–frequency normal modelling. *Journal of neuroscience methods*, 214(2):192–203, 2013.

[22] R. Patton and J. Chen. Robust fault detection using eigenstructure assignment: a tutorial consideration and some new results. In *Decision and Control, 1991., Proceedings of the 30th IEEE Conference on*, pages 2242–2247 vol.3, 1991.

[23] R. Patton and J. Chen. Observer-based fault detection and isolation: Robustness and applications. *Control Engineering Practice*, 5(5):671 – 682, 1997.

[24] R. J. Patton and J. Chen. On eigenstructure assignment for robust fault diagnosis. *International Journal of Robust and Nonlinear Control*, 10(14):1193–1208, 2000.

[25] L. B. Ray, S. M. Fogel, C. T. Smith, and K. R. Peters. Validating an automated sleep spindle detection algorithm using an individualized approach. *Journal of sleep research*, 19(2):374–378, 2010.

[26] A. Rechtschaffen and A. Kales. *A manual of standardized terminology, techniques and scoring system for sleep stages of human subjects.* US Government Printing Office, US Public Health Service, Washington DC, 1968.

[27] S. Roweis and Z. Ghahramani. A unifying review of linear gaussian models. *Neural Comput.*, 11(2):305–345, 1999.

[28] R. H. Shumway and D. S. Stoffer. An approach to time series smoothing and forecasting using the em algorithm. *Journal of Time Series Analysis*, 3(4):253–264, 1982.

[29] A. Soule, K. Salamatian, and N. Taft. Combining filtering and statistical methods for anomaly detection. In *IMC '05 Proceedings of the 5th ACM SIGCOMM conference on Internet Measurement*, IMC '05, pages 31–31, 2005.

[30] P. van Overschee and L. de Moor. *Subspace identification for linear systems: theory, implementation, applications.* Number v. 1. Kluwer Academic Publishers, 1996.

APPENDIX

A. PROOF OF THEOREM 1

Theorem 1. For a DRM, a sufficient condition for $\mathbf{G}_{\xi}(z)$ to be zero, is

$$\mathbf{C}_f\mathbf{P} = 0 \text{ and } \{\mathbf{C}_f\mathbf{A}_f = 0 \text{ or } \mathbf{A}_f\mathbf{P} = 0\}$$

Proof: Let the set $\{\lambda_i = 0, v_i\}$, for $i = 1 : n$, be the left eigenvectors and corresponding eigenvalues of $\mathbf{A}_f$, i.e.

$$\begin{aligned} v_i\mathbf{A}_f &= \lambda_i v_i \\ &= 0 \end{aligned}$$

If one chooses v_1 as the rows of matrix $[\mathbf{WC}]$, then:

$$[v_1 \;\; ... \;\; v_n]'\,\mathbf{A}_f = 0 \quad \Rightarrow \quad \mathbf{WCA}_f = 0$$

The matrix $\mathbf{A}_f = \mathbf{A} - \mathbf{FC}$, so it is sufficient to chose $\mathbf{F}$ so that the set $\{\lambda_i = 0, v_i = [\mathbf{CW}]'\}$ to be assigned as left eigenpairs of $(\mathbf{A} - \mathbf{FC})$.

In the other side, suppose If the columns of $\mathbf{P}$ are the right eigenvectors of $\mathbf{A}_f$ corresponding to zero-values eigenvectors, then

$$\mathbf{A}_f v_i = 0 \quad \Rightarrow \quad \mathbf{A}_f\mathbf{P} = 0$$

So it is sufficient to chose the matrix $\mathbf{F}$ so that the set $\{\lambda_i = 0, v_i = \mathbf{P}\}$ to be assigned as right eigenpairs of $(\mathbf{A} - \mathbf{FC})$.

B. SLEEP POLYSOMNOGRAPHY

To keep the paper self-contained we give a brief description to sleep segmentation. Sleep researchers often classify sleep into one of several sleep stages that provide a qualitative overview of subject responsiveness and sleep physiology at different points throughout the night [15, 26]. Broadly, sleep can be divided into REM sleep during which dreaming occurs, and non-REM sleep, which is further divided into sleep stages S1, S2, S3 and S4 that approximately correspond to how deeply asleep the subject is. A subject's arousal state is classified on the basis of some or all of the measures in the polysomnogram, and EEG plays a key role in this process.

In wake sate with eyes closed, the EEG signal is dominated by the alpha rhythm, an oscillation at approximately 8–12 Hz depending on the individual, which is superimposed on a background signal whose power approximately scales as $1/f$. Sleep typically begins with a short period of S1 sleep, which is a transition stage corresponding to very light sleep, during which time the alpha oscillation disappears. Sleep then deepens into stage 2, which is accompanied by an increase in low frequency activity and the appearance of two transient phenomena in the EEG time series, sleep spindles and K-complexes. Sleep spindles originate in the thalamus, and are believed to play a role in memory consolidation and learning. The K-complex is a short, high amplitude voltage spike that occurs spontaneously during sleep stages 2, 3 and 4, but can also be evoked by sensory stimulation such as an audio tone. The role played by K-complexes is a still under investigation, but recent work suggests that K-complexes help to suppress arousal due to sensory stimulus during sleep. Sleep stages 3 and 4 correspond to deep sleep, where the EEG is dominated by very low frequency oscillations (< 3 Hz), and the low frequency part of the power spectrum approximately scales as $1/f^2$ or even $1/f^3$. Sleep spindles and K-complexes may be present, although they typically occur less frequently than in S2 sleep.

Stage REM sleep is typically accompanied by EEG features similar to S1, but with the addition of eye movement, changes in muscle tone, and the presence of vertex waves, which are similar to K-complexes but are smaller in amplitude and shorter in duration. Normal sleep cycles between non-REM and REM sleep occur several times over the course of the night.

GLAD: Group Anomaly Detection in Social Media Analysis

Rose Yu
Department of Computer Science
University of Southern California
qiyu@usc.edu

Xinran He
Department of Computer Science
University of Southern California
xinranhe@usc.edu

Yan Liu
Department of Computer Science
University of Southern California
yanliu.cs@usc.edu

ABSTRACT

Traditional anomaly detection on social media mostly focuses on individual point anomalies while anomalous phenomena usually occur in groups. Therefore it is valuable to study the collective behavior of individuals and detect group anomalies. Existing group anomaly detection approaches rely on the assumption that the groups are known, which can hardly be true in real world social media applications. In this paper, we take a generative approach by proposing a hierarchical Bayes model: *Group Latent Anomaly Detection* (GLAD) model. GLAD takes both pair-wise and point-wise data as input, automatically infers the groups and detects group anomalies simultaneously. To account for the dynamic properties of the social media data, we further generalize GLAD to its dynamic extension d-GLAD. We conduct extensive experiments to evaluate our models on both synthetic and real world datasets. The empirical results demonstrate that our approach is effective and robust in discovering latent groups and detecting group anomalies.

Categories and Subject Descriptors

H.2.8 [**Database Applications**]: Data mining

Keywords

anomaly detection; social media analysis; hierarchical Bayes modeling

1. INTRODUCTION

Social media provide convenient platforms for people to share, communicate, and collaborate. While people enjoy the openness and convenience of social media, many malicious behaviors, such as bullying, terrorist attack planning, and fraud information dissemination, can happen. Therefore, it is extremely important that we can detect these abnormal activities as *accurately* and *early* as possible to prevent disasters and attacks.

KDD'14, August 24–27, 2014, New York, NY, USA.

http://dx.doi.org/10.1145/2623330.2623719 .

By definition, anomaly detection aims to find "an observation that deviates so much from other observations as to arouse suspicion that it was generated by a different mechanism" [8]. Several algorithms have been developed specifically for social media anomaly detection such as power-law models [2], spectral decomposition [18], scan statistics [15], and random walk [14, 17]. However, these algorithms only detect the individual *point anomaly*. For example, [2] proposes an "OddBall" algorithm to spot anomalous nodes in a graph. The algorithm extracts features from the egonet of the node and declares anomaly node whose features deviate from the power-law pattern.

In reality, anomaly may not only appear as an individual point, but also as a group. For instance, a group of people collude to create false product reviews or threat campaign in social media platforms; in large organizations, malfunctioning teams or insider groups closely coordinate with each other to achieve a malicious goal. Those appear as examples for another type of anomaly: *group anomaly*, which has not been thoroughly examined in social media analysis. In this work, we focus on group anomaly detection. We are interested in finding the groups which exhibit a pattern that does not conform to the majority of other groups. This problem has found its applications in galaxy identification [19], high energy particle physics [13], anomalous image detection and turbulence vorticity modeling [20].

We identify three major challenges in group anomaly detection: (i) Two forms of data coexist in social media: one is the point-wise data, which characterize the features of an individual person. The other is pair-wise relational data, which describe the properties of social ties. In social science, a fundamental axiom of social media analysis is the concept that structure matters. For example, teams with the same composition of member skills can perform very differently depending on the patterns of relationships among the members [5]. Therefore, it is important to take into account both point-wise and pair-wise data during anomaly detection. (ii) Group anomaly is usually more subtle than individual anomaly. At the individual level, the activities might appear to be normal [21]. Therefore, existing anomaly detection algorithms usually fail when the anomaly is related to a group rather than individuals. (iii) Empirical studies in social media analysis suggest the dynamic nature of individual network positions [12]. People's activities and communications change constantly over time and we can hardly know the groups beforehand. Thus developing a method that can be easily generalized to dynamic setting is critical to anomaly detection in evolving social media data.

In this paper, we take a graphical model approach to address those challenges. We propose a hierarchical model, i.e, *Group Latent Anomaly Detection* (GLAD) model, to connect two forms of data. To handle the dynamic characteristics of the social media data, we further develop a dynamic extension of GLAD: the d-GLAD model. We show that GLAD outperforms existing approaches in terms of group anomaly detection accuracy and robustness. When dealing with dynamic social networks, the dynamic extension of GLAD achieves lower false positive rate and better data fitting. The major contributions of this paper can be summarized as follows:

1. We formulate the problem of group anomaly detection in the context of social media analysis for both static and dynamic settings and articulate the three major challenges associated with the task.
2. We develop a graphical model called GLAD. GLAD can successfully discover the group structure of social media and detect group anomalies. We also generalize GLAD to its dynamic extension and provide tractable model inference algorithms.
3. We conduct thorough experiments on both synthetic and real world datasets using anomaly injections. We also construct a meaningful dataset from ACM publication dataset for rigorous evaluation. The dataset is accessible at `http://www-bcf.usc.edu/~liu32/data.html`.

2. RELATED WORK

We review the related models on group anomaly detection and illustrate the motivation behind our approach.

The Multinomial Genre Model (MGM) proposed in [19] first investigates the problem following the paradigm of Latent Dirichlet Allocation (LDA) [4]. As a text processing tool, LDA assumes that each word is associated with a topic and a document is a mixture of topics. Similarly, MGM models a group as a mixture of Gaussian distributed topics with certain mixture rate and assumes there exists "best" mixture rates, corresponding to the mixture rates of normal groups. Then it conducts group anomaly detection by scoring the mixture rate likelihood of each group. One drawback of MGM is that the set of candidate mixture rates is shared globally by groups. It might leads to poor performance when groups have different sets of mixture rates. [20] further extends MGM to Flexible Genre Model (FGM) with more flexibility in the generation of topics. Specifically, the model considers the set of topic mixture rates as random variables rather than model hyper-parameters, which would adapt to diverse "genres" in groups, each of which is a typical distribution of topic mixture rates.

Another line of work takes a discriminative approach. [13] uses the same definition of group anomaly from [19]. It considers kernel embedding of the probabilistic distributions and generalizes one-class support vector machine from point anomaly detection to group anomaly detection. The proposed support measure machine (SMM) algorithm maps the distributions to a probability measure space with kernel methods, which can handle the aggregate behavior of data points.

However, existing approaches separate the group anomaly detection task into two stages: group discovery and anomaly detection. They require the group information to be given before applying the anomaly detection algorithms. For example, in [19], the Sloan Digital Sky Survey (SDSS) dataset needs to be pre-processed before feeding into MGM. The authors first construct a neighborhood graph and then treat the connected components in the graph as groups. For the application on turbulence data, the FGM model [20] considers the vertices in a local cubic region as a group. In SMM [13], the authors treat the high energy particles generated from the same collision event as a group.

The two-stage approaches identify the groups from the pair-wise data and infer the anomalies based on the point-wise data. This strategy assumes that the point-wise and pair-wise data are marginally independent. However, such independence assumption might underestimate the mutual influence between the group structure and the feature attributes. The detected group anomalies can hardly reveal the joint effect of these two forms of data. These motivate us to build an alla prima that can account for both forms of data and accomplish the tasks of group discovery and anomaly detection all at once.

Additionally, existing work can only deal with static network and fixed size groups. This is not feasible for the time-evolving nature of social media data. For example, in corporate networks, employees may switch teams from one to the other. The organization structure of a team may also change. As the dynamic setting needs to take into account the flexible group size and the changing mixture rates, we further adapt our model to the dynamic setting and formulate the problem as a change point detection task.

Group anomaly detection in social media analysis may shed light on a wide range of real world problems such as corporate restructuring, team job-hopping and political inclination shift to which our approach can apply. In section 3, we provide a formal definition of group anomaly in social media analysis. With the definition, we develop the GLAD model in section 4 and present its learning and inference algorithm. In section 5, we describe the dynamic extension of the GLAD model: the d-GLAD model, which can handle the dynamic social networks. Section 6 shows the empirical evaluation results of GLAD and d-GLAD on synthetic and real world datasets compared with existing baseline models.

3. DEFINITION OF GROUP ANOMALY

The core of our group anomaly definition lies in the collective behavior of individuals. For example, a document is a mixture of various topics and a team is a mixture of different roles. Therefore, we model the node features of each group as a mixture of components. Each component could be an article topic, a social role or a job title. Specifically, we can describe a component as either a discrete variable such as multinomial distribution or a continues variable like Gaussian distribution, depending on the data type of features. Here we use the term *role* as a general notion for the component. We assume that there are a fixed number of roles and each of which denotes a particular distribution of node features. All groups share the same set of roles but possibly with different role mixture rates. Normal groups follow the same pattern with respect to their role mixture rates, but the anomalous group has a role mixture rate that deviates from the normal pattern.

For the static GLAD model, we are interested in the distribution of the role mixture rates across the groups. According to our assumption, the mixture rates of normal groups are more likely to appear. For groups with very rare role mixture rates, we treat them as group anomalies. One example of this type of group anomaly comes from particle physics. It is widely accepted that the dynamics of known particles are governed by the *Standard Model*, which corresponds to the normal pattern. Unknown particles would contaminate the distribution of the Standard Model. Detecting those anomalies could potentially lead to the discovery of new physical phenomenon. In practice, we first identify the normal mixture rates. Then for each learned group, we evaluate the likelihood of its observations being generated with the normal mixture rates. The lower the likelihood value is, the more anomalous the group would be.

For the dynamic d-GLAD model, we emphasize on the temporal aspect of the data and detect the change of the role mixture rate within the groups. For instance, in scientific area, it is valuable to study the evolution of research topics and detect the bursty time periods. In the dynamic setting, since the structure of groups change as well as their role mixture rates, detecting groups with rare mixture rate no long applies. Therefore, we think of the task as a change point detection problem and aim to detect the groups whose mixture rates change drastically from the previous time stamps. Compared with GLAD, we not only need to decide whether a group is anomaly or not, but also need to specify when the group appears anomalous.

Even though we use slightly different definitions of group anomaly for the GLAD model and the d-GLAD model, the key ideas behind our definitions are the same. Both definitions build upon the notion of role mixture rate, which essentially requires a precise inference of both the group membership and role identity for each individual in the group.

4. THE GLAD MODEL

Suppose that we are given a social network with N nodes. We observe node activities $\mathbf{X} = \{X_1, X_2, \ldots, X_N\}$ and their communications $\mathbf{Y} = \{Y_{1,1}, Y_{1,2}, \ldots, Y_{N,N}\}$. $X_p \in \mathbb{R}^V$ consists of V entries, denoting a feature vector of V dimensions. $Y_{p,q} \in \{0, 1\}$ is a binary valued variable, indicating the pairwise relationship of nodes. These two forms of data are our inputs. Our goal is to analyze these data jointly and declare the group that has irregular role mixture rate as anomaly. In the following sections, we first describe the motivation for our hierarchical Bayes model and provide its generative process and the plate notation. Then we derive the inference algorithm using the variational Bayesian approach.

4.1 Model Specification

We model a social network with N individuals. Assuming that each person p is associated with a group identity G_p and a role identity R_p. By groups, we mean the clusters that capture the similarity suggested by the pair-wise communications. By roles, we refer to the mixture components that categorize the point-wise feature values of the nodes. For simplification, we fix the number of groups as M and the number of roles as K. Figure 1 shows the plate notation for the GLAD model. The motivation for us to assume two identities for an individual comes from the controversial viewpoints of what is the right metric for a community. In community detection literature [7], some argue that a community is the one that has dense communications within clusters while others suggest that people in the same community should share common activity features. We get around the controversy by recognizing the arguments of both sides and assume two types of latent structures coexist in the data.

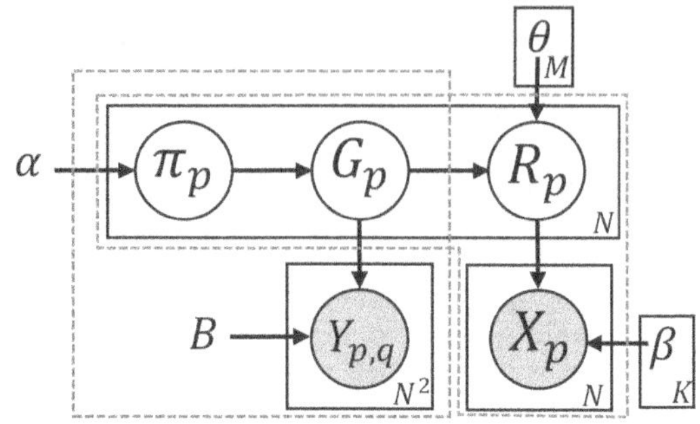

Figure 1: Plate notation for the Group Latent Anomaly Detection (GLAD) model. Shaded circles are observations, blank circles are latent variables and the variables without a circle are model parameters. The blue rectangular resembles MMSB. The red polygon integrates the generating process of LDA.

For each person p, he joins a group according to the membership probability distribution π_p. We impose a Dirichlet prior on the membership distribution. It is well known that the Dirichlet distribution is conjugate to the multinomial distribution. As we will show later, when dealing with latent variables, the Dirichlet prior facilitates the learning and inference of the model. We assume the pair-wise link $Y_{p,q}$ between person p and person q depends on the group identities of both p and q with the parameter B. Furthermore, we model the dependency between the group and the role using a multinomial distribution parameterized by a set of role mixture rate $\{\theta_{1:M}\}$. The role mixture rate characterizes the constitution of the group: the proportion of the population that plays the same role in the group. Finally, we model the activity feature vector of the individual X_p as the dependent variable of his role with parameter set $\{\beta_{1:K}\}$. Table 1 summarizes the notations used in our model.

We specify the generative process of the GLAD model in Algorithm 1. Our model unifies the ideas from both the Mixture Membership Stochastic Block (MMSB) model [1] and the Latent Dirichlet Allocation (LDA) model [4]. As shown in Figure 1, the blue dashed rectangular on the left side resembles MMSB which models the formation of groups using link information. The red dashed polygon integrates the generating process of LDA which is often used for topic extraction from documents. By assuming mixture of groups and roles, we allow each person to have multiple roles and multiple group memberships. Without loss of generality, we assume that the activity data have discrete values and choose to model X_p with a multinomial distribution. When the activity data are distributed in other forms, we can easily adapt GLAD to model other type of X_p.

4.2 Inference and Learning

Inference requires us to compute the posterior distributions of the latent variables given the data. The normalizing term of the posterior distribution involves the calculation of the marginal likelihood of the data for which we resort to variational EM algorithms [10].

Table 1: Notations of GLAD

Symbol	Description
α	Dirichlet prior parameter
π_p	membership distribution of person p
$Y_{p,q}$	pair-wise communication between p and q
B	global block probability among groups
G_p	group of p
R_p	role of p
$\theta_{1:M}$	role mixture rate for M groups
X_p	activity of p
$\beta_{1:K}$	activity distribution for K roles

Algorithm 1 Generative Process of GLAD

for individual $p = 1 \to N$ **do**
  Draw membership distribution $\pi_p \sim \text{Dir}(\alpha)$
  Draw $G_p \sim \text{Multinomial}(\pi_p)$
  for individual $q = 1 \to N$ **do**
    Sample $Y_{p,q} \sim \text{Bernoulli}\ (G_p^T B G_q)$
  end for
  Draw $R_p \sim \text{Multinomial}(R_p|\theta_{1:M}, G_p)$
  Draw $X_p \sim \text{Multinomial}(X_p|\beta_{1:K}, R_p)$
end for

Denote the set of model parameters as $\Theta = \{\alpha, B, \theta_{1:M}, \beta_{1:K}\}$, the set of observed variables as $v = \{X_{1:N}, Y_{1:N}\}$, and the set of the hidden variables as $h = \{\pi_{1;N}, G_{1:N}, R_{1:N}\}$. Our aim is to estimate the posterior distribution $p(h, \Theta|v)$. We can first write out the complete joint likelihood of observed and latent variables as follows:

$$\begin{aligned} p(v, h|\Theta) &= \prod_p p(\pi_p|\alpha) \times \prod_{p,q} p(Y_{p,q}|G_p, G_q, B) \\ &\times \prod_p p(X_p|R_p, \beta_{1:K}) p(R_p|G_p, \theta_{1:M}) p(G_p|\pi_p). \end{aligned}$$

Computing the maximizer for the marginal likelihood of the data $p(v|\Theta) = \int_h p(v, h|\Theta) dh$ requires the integration over all the latent variables in the equation above, which is intractable [1]. Therefore, we apply the variational Bayesian approach [10] to perform the inference approximately. The essence of the variational Bayesian approach is to choose a variational distribution $q(h)$ to approximate the actual posterior distribution, so that the Kullback-Leibler divergence (KL-divergence) between $p(h, \Theta|v)$ and its approximation $q(h)$ is minimized.

Rewriting the marginal log likelihood and plugging in the variational distribution, we have

$$\log p(v|\Theta) = D_{KL}(p||q) + \langle \log p(v, h|\Theta) \rangle_q - \langle \log q(h) \rangle_q,$$

where we use $\langle f \rangle_p$ to represent the expectation of the function f with respect to the distribution p. Since the marginal likelihood $\log p(v|\Theta)$ is invariant to the choice of q, minimizing the KL-divergence $D_{KL}(p||q)$ is equivalent to maximizing the last two terms $\langle \log p(v, h|\Theta) \rangle_q - \langle \log q(h) \rangle_q$. In practice, we choose $q(h)$ to be factorized over the latent variables with free parameters $\Delta = \{\gamma_{1:N}, \mu_{1:N}, \lambda_{1:N}\}$ as follows:

$$q(h|\Delta) = \prod_p q(\pi_p|\gamma_p) q(R_p|\mu_p) q(G_p|\lambda_p).$$

Our goal is to find the optimal set of free parameters that provides a variational distribution closest to the actual posterior. Then our problem is to maximize the objective function formulated as follows subject to probability constraints:

$$\begin{aligned} \Delta^* &= \arg\max_{\Delta} \langle \log p(v, h|\Theta) \rangle_q - \langle \log q(h|\Delta) \rangle_q \\ &= \arg\max_{\Delta} L(v, h, \Theta, \Delta). \end{aligned}$$

The objective function L, by plugging in the joint likelihood and the variational distribution and taking expectations, is given by

$$\begin{aligned} & L(v, h, \Theta, \Delta) \\ = & \sum_p \langle \log p(X_p|R_p, \beta_{1:K}) \rangle_q \\ + & \sum_p \langle \log p(R_p|G_p, \theta_{1:M}) \rangle_q + \sum_p \langle \log p(G_p|\pi_p) \rangle_q \\ + & \sum_{p,q} \langle \log p(Y_{p,q}|G_p, G_q, B) \rangle_q + \sum_p \langle \log p(\pi_p|\alpha) \rangle_q \\ - & \sum_p \langle \log q(\pi_p|\gamma_p) \rangle_q \\ - & \sum_p \langle \log q(R_p|\mu_p) \rangle_q - \sum_p \langle \log q(G_p|\lambda_p) \rangle_q. \end{aligned}$$

We follow a variational EM procedure in order to maximize $L(v, h, \Theta, \Delta)$ over Δ. Basically we iteratively update the free parameters by taking the derivative of the Lagrange function of the objective L over one parameter at a time given the value of others from the last iteration. Since $\{Y_{p,q}\}$ is symmetric, the objective function will result in a quadratic term with respect to λ_p. Taking the derivative over the variational parameter would not have a closed form solution. A simple workaround is by assuming constant probability for the generation of $\{Y_{p,p}\}$. We omit the tedious derivations and only present the final update formulas of each of the free parameters, as shown in Algorithm 2. For convenience, we denote $f(Y_{p,q}, B_{m,n}) = Y_{p,q} \log B_{m,n} + (1 - Y_{p,q}) \log(1 - B_{m,n})$.

Algorithm 2 Variational Inference for GLAD

initialize $\gamma_{p,m} := 1/M$
initialize $\mu_{p,k} := 1/K$
initialize $\lambda_{p,m} := 1/M$
repeat
  for $p = 1 \to N$, $m = 1 \to M$ $k = 1 \to K$ **do**
    $\gamma_{p,m} = \alpha_m + \lambda_{p,m}$
    $\lambda_{p,m} = \exp\{\sum_k \log \theta_{m,k} \mu_{p,k} + \psi(\gamma_{p,m}) - \psi(\sum_n \gamma_{p,n}) + \sum_{q \neq p} \sum_n \lambda_{q,n} \cdot f(Y_{p,q}, B_{m,n})\}$
    $\mu_{p,k} = \exp\{\sum_v \log \beta_{v,k} X_{p,v} + \sum_m \log \theta_{m,k} \lambda_{p,m}\}$
  end for
until convergence

For the parameter estimation, we apply the empirical Bayes method on the variational likelihood. We maximize the Lagrange function of $L(v, h, \Theta, \Delta)$ over model parameters $\Theta = \{\alpha, B, \theta_{1:M}, \beta_{1:K}\}$. Due to the compounding of Dirichlet distribution, there is no close form solution for the maximizer w.r.t α. We apply the Newton-Raphson method to reach a numerical solution. The resulting parameter updating functions for α and B are the same as those of MMSB [1] and the parameters β and θ can be estimated as follows:

$$\beta_{v,k} = \frac{\sum_p X_{p,v}\mu_{p,k}}{\sum_{v,p} X_{p,v}\mu_{p,k}} \quad \theta_{m,k} = \frac{\sum_p \mu_{p,k}\lambda_{p,m}}{\sum_{k,p} \mu_{p,k}\lambda_{p,m}}.$$

With our definition of group anomaly in section 3, we score the group anomalousness using $-\sum_{p\in G}\langle\log p(R_p|\Theta)\rangle_p$. The most anomalous group will have the highest anomaly score. We approximate the true log likelihood with the variational log likelihood to get $-\sum_{p\in G}\langle\log p(R_p|\Theta)\rangle_q$.

A limitation of GLAD is that it only models the static network. This might be restrictive if we want to further consider dynamic networks. Besides the anomaly group whose mixture rate deviates significantly from other groups, we are also interested to study how the mixture rate evolves over time. Fortunately, GLAD can be easily extended to account for this dynamics. This leads to the dynamic extension of the GLAD model, which will be discussed in the next section.

5. DYNAMIC EXTENSION OF GLAD

We now generalize the GLAD model to take into account the dynamics in the social media. We refer the dynamic extension of GLAD as the d-GLAD model. To be consistent with our description for GLAD in section 4, we start with the model specification and then provide the model inference algorithm using both the variational Bayesian method and the Monte Carlo sampling technique.

5.1 Model Specification

Generalization of GLAD to d-GLAD stems from the template models [23], which use the model for a particular time stamp as a template, duplicate it over time and connect temporal components sequentially. Similarly, we can adapt GLAD to the dynamic setting by making a copy of GLAD for each time point. To simplify the model, we assume that the latent factors including role R_p, group G_p and mixture rate $\{\theta_{1:M}\}$ change over time but the membership distribution $\{\pi_p\}$ and model parameters are fixed.

We model the temporal evolution of the role mixture rate for each group with a series of multivariate Gaussian distributions. At a particular time point, the Gaussian has its mean as the value of the mixture rate. And the mixture rate of the next time point is a normalized sample from this Gaussian distribution. Since we require the mixture rate to be the parameters of a multivariate distribution over features, we apply a soft-max function to normalize the sample drawn from the multivariate Gaussian. The soft-max function is defined as $S(\theta_m) = \frac{\exp\theta_m}{\sum_m \exp\theta_m}$. When the total time length T equals one, d-GLAD reduces to the GLAD model. Figure 2 depicts the probabilistic graphical model of d-GLAD and the meanings of notations used. We summarize the generative process of d-GLAD in Algorithm 3.

In d-GLAD model, since the mixture rate of next time stamp is drawn from a multivariate Gaussian centering around the mixture rate of its previous time stamp, it imposes smoothness on the mixture rates across time, preventing the mixture rate from having drastic changes. The soft-max function maps the samples from the multivariate Gaussian to the parameters for the multinomial distribution. Similar idea can be seen from the generalization of LDA to the dynamic topic model [3]. While it is true that d-GLAD model shares the constraints of GLAD on fixed group/role number and constant self-loop, it has certain intriguing advantages over static models. (i) d-GLAD captures the dynamics of the latent variables G_p and R_p, thus allows an individual to switch groups and roles over time.(ii) The smoothness of the mixture rate over time models the behavior of normal groups, so detecting groups whose mixture rates θ_m^t undergo substantial change becomes easier.

Algorithm 3 Generative Process of DGLAD

```
for t = 1 → T do
    for m = 1 → M do
        Draw θ_m^(t) ~ Gaussian(θ_m^(t-1), σ)
    end for
    for individual p = 1 → N do
        Draw membership distribution π_p^(t) ~ Dir(α)
        Draw G_p^(t) ~ Multinomial(π_p)^(t)
        for individual q = 1 → p − 1 and q = p + 1 → N
do
            Sample Y_(p,q)^(t) ~ Binomial ((G_p^(t))^T B G_q^(t))
        end for
        Draw R_p^(t) ~ Multinomial(R_p^(t) | S(θ_{G_p^(t)}^(t)))
        Draw X_p^(t) ~ Multinomial(X_p^(t) | β_{R_p^(t)})
    end for
end for
```

5.2 Inference and Learning

The variational inference of d-GLAD is similar to the GLAD model except for the longitudinal factor $\theta_{1:M}^{(1:T)}$. We add a variational distribution $p(\theta_m^{1:T}|\hat{\theta}^{1:T})$ to approximate the original posterior where $\{\hat{\theta}^{1:T}\}$ are variational parameters. Then we apply the variational Kalman Filter technique [3] to infer the sequential latent variables and learn the model parameters. The transition for the mixture rate of each group is Gaussian distributed:

$$\theta^{(t)}|\theta^{(t-1)} \sim \mathcal{N}(\theta^{(t-1)}, \sigma^2 I).$$

We can write the variational distribution for the transition as follows:

$$\hat{\theta}^{(t)}|\theta^{(t-1)} \sim \mathcal{N}(\theta^{(t-1)}, \hat{v}^2 I).$$

Then we can apply similar variational EM procedure incorporating the transitions to infer the variational parameters. Due to the numerical difficulty of variational Kalman filter method, we also implement a version of the Monte Carlo sampling for d-GLAD model, which is used in our empirical evaluations. The algorithm is elaborated in Algorithm 4. The inference of the transitional part $\{\theta^{1:T}\}$ is based on the Particle Filtering method [22]. The anomaly score of the d-GLAD model is measured by $\|\theta_m^{(t)} - \theta_m^{(t-1)}\|$.

6. EXPERIMENTS

To evaluate the effectiveness of our model, we conduct thorough experiments on synthetic datasets and real world datasets. We study the applications of our approach by analyzing scientific publications and senator voting records.

6.1 Baselines

To our knowledge, all existing algorithms are two-stages approaches: (i) identify groups, (ii) detect group anomalies.

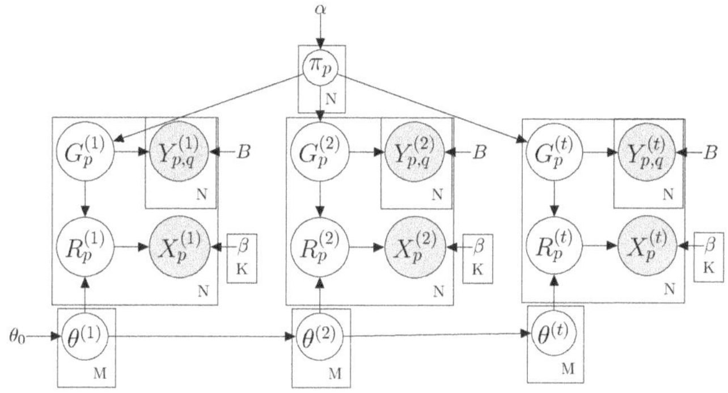

Notation	Description
α	Dirichlet parameter
π_p	membership distribution
$G_p^{(t)}$	group of p at time t
$Y_{p,q}^{(t)}$	pair-wise communication at time t
B	global block probability
$R_p^{(t)}$	role of p at time t
$\beta_{1:K}$	activity mixture rate
$X_p^{(t)}$	activity of p at time t
θ_0	initial Gaussian mean
$\theta_{1:M}^{(t)}$	role mixture rates at time t

Figure 2: Plate notation for the d-GLAD model and the meaning of notations. The subscript p denotes each person in the social network. The superscript t denotes the network snapshot at time stamp t.

Algorithm 4 Monte Carlo Sampling of DGLAD

Initialize $\alpha, \theta_0, \beta_{1:K}, B$
$R_{1:N}^{1:T} = 1/K$, $G_{1:N}^{1:T} = 1/M$, $\pi_{1:N} \sim \text{Dir}(\alpha)$
repeat
  for $p = 1 \to N$ **do**
    for $t = 1 \to T$ **do**
      Update $R_p^{(t)} \sim \text{Mul}(\mathcal{S}(\theta^{(t-1)}_{G_p^{(t-1)}}))\text{Mul}(X_p^{(t)})$
      Update $G_p^{(t)} \sim \text{Mul}(\pi_p^{(t-1)})\text{Mul}(\mathcal{S}(\theta^{(t-1)}_{G_p^{(t-1)}}))$
    end for
    Update $\pi_p \sim \text{Dir}(\alpha)$
  end for
  for $t = 1 \to T$ **do**
    Update $\theta^{(t)}$ using Particle Filtering
  end for
until Convergence

We summarize these algorithms in Table 2. We use following approaches as baseline methods in comparison to GLAD and d-GLAD:

1. **MMSB-LDA**:First use the MMSB model to learn a group membership distribution for each individual node, then assign the node to the group with the highest probability. Finally, for each group, train an LDA model and infer the role identity.

2. **MMSB-MGM**: Group is learned using the same method as MMSB-LDA. For the role inference, train an multi-modal MGM instead of LDA.

3. **Graph-LDA**: Run an off-the-shelf graph clustering algorithm Min-Cut to get group membership and then train a LDA model for each group.

4. **Graph-MGM**: Get group membership with the graph clustering algorithm Min-Cut and then train a MGM model for each group.

6.2 Synthetic Dataset

We experiment on two type of synthetic datasets. One is a synthetic dataset with injected group anomalies. The other is a benchmark dataset generated by a simulator with individual anomaly labels.

Table 2: Two stage models in existing work

Algorithm	Stage-1	Stage-2
Heard 2010 [9]	spectrum	Poisson process
Xiong 2011-a [19]	clustering	Mixture Genre Model
Xiong 2011-b [20]	clustering	Flexible Genre Model
Muandet 2013 [13]	simulator	One class SMM

6.2.1 *Synthetic Data with Anomaly Injection*

We generate a network with 500 nodes using GLAD in Algorithm 1. To evaluate the anomaly detection performance, we set the mixture rates of anomalous groups as $[0.9, 0.1]$ and normal groups as $[0.1, 0.9]$. We vary the number of groups from 5 to 50 and inject 20% anomalous groups. The rest 80% groups are normal. Since we know the normal and anomalous mixture rates, we calculate the anomaly score of each group by directly computing the differences between the inferred mixture rate and the ground truth normal mixture rate. During the testing procedure, we rank the groups with respect to their anomaly score and retrieve top 20% groups. For all methods, we set the number of groups and number of roles the same as the ground truth.

We compare the learned groups of three grouping approaches with the ground truth: GLAD, MMSB and Graph, for the case of 5 groups. The inferred group memberships are shown as adjacent matrices in Figure 3. For better visualization, we intentionally put the nodes that belong to the same group together. Ideally, we should observe dense links within groups and sparse links between groups. Therefore, the dark pixels in the plot would aggregate along the principal diagonal of the matrix. We use blue color to highlight the groups learned. The group discovery result of GLAD is the closest to the ground truth. The high connectivity in the graph and the lack of point-wise information could be the reasons for the poor performance of Graph and MMSB.

Figure 4 shows the anomaly detection performance with different number of groups for GLAD and four other baselines. GLAD achieves the highest detection accuracy. It is also more robust over 10 random runs. Note that the differences for the first stage of baselines are more obvious than the second stage. This is because the Bernoulli distribution limits the number of samples in the pair-wise data, making the first stage more difficult to learn.

We also report the simulation results on group anomaly detection for d-GLAD. The data is generated according to

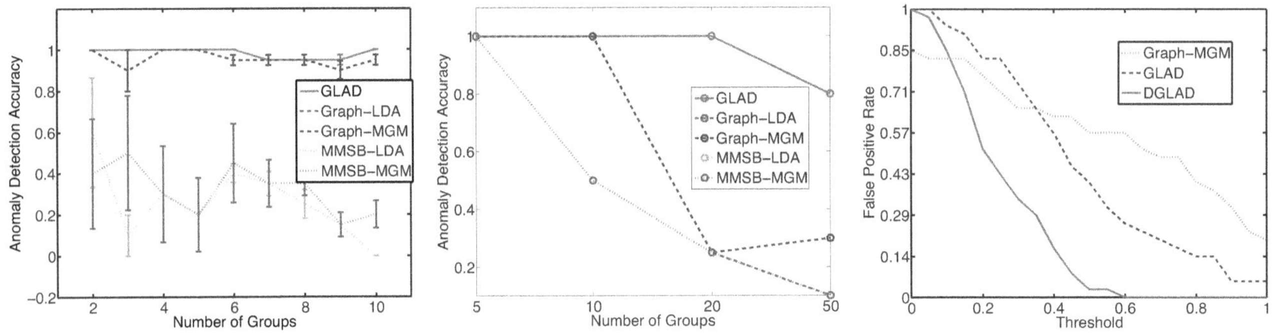

(a) Robustness (b) Accuracy (c) d-GLAD

Figure 4: Anomaly detection performance of GLAD and baseline methods on synthetic dataset of 500 samples, with 20% anomalous groups. (a): Detection accuracy error bar plot of five algorithms for detection accuracy with group number from 2 to 10. (b): Mean detection accuracy for different number of groups up to 50, averaged over 10 random runs. (c):False positive rate over different thresholds for d-GLAD, MMSB-MGM and GLAD for synthetic data. 10% group anomalies are injected.

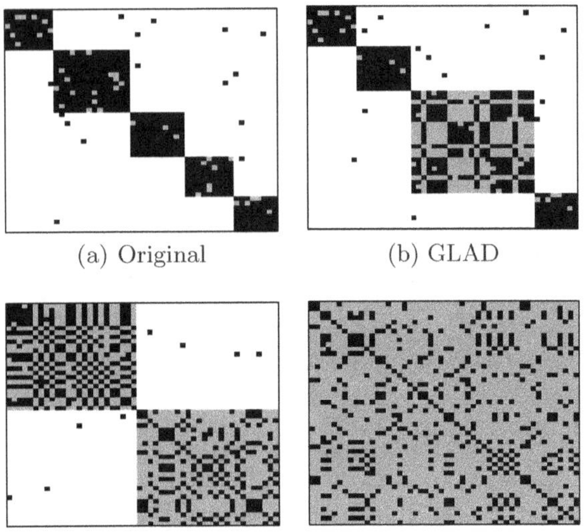

(a) Original (b) GLAD

(c) MMSB (d) Graph

Figure 3: The 50 × 50 adjacent matrix re-arranged by the group membership discovered by three grouping approaches on a subset of synthetic data of 5 groups. Dark pixels denote links and white pixels denote no links. Blue block highlights the learned group membership.

Algorithm 3 with 5 time stamps. We manipulate the mixture rate of 50% of the groups at time point 4 as injected anomalies. Then we raise alarms if the group's mixture rate deviates from the previous time by a certain threshold. In Figure 4(c), we display the false positive rate with different threshold values. For comparison, we train MMSB-MGM and GLAD at each time independently as baselines. It can be seen that d-GLAD achieves the lowest false positive rate, which demonstrates the gain of d-GLAD over static models on the dynamic dataset.

6.2.2 Benchmark Data with Anomaly Labels

The benchmark data set is generated by a simulator from a federal funded program. It contains email communication records and working activities from 258 company employees. Each employee is featured by 6 types of activities. The labeled dataset contains 39 individual anomalies and 5 of them cannot be detected by any existing algorithms. We set the number of groups as 20 as the optimal setting obtained from cross validation and calculate the anomaly score of each group by MCMC sampling. We treat all members in the most anomalous group as individual anomalies and compare them with the anomaly labels. Though the anomaly labels are point anomalies rather than group anomalies, the anomaly detection result reflects the potential of our approach to tackle other type of difficult anomaly detection problems. The precision, recall and F1 score over 20 runs on the benchmark dataset is shown in Figure 5.

We can see that the GLAD model achieves comparable precision and recall with low variances. In contrast, the detection performances of the two-stage models fluctuates significantly. In terms of the F1 scores in Figure 5(c), both GLAD and MMSB-MGM beat the other algorithms while GLAD has a lower variance than MMSB-MGM. One possible explanation is that the point-wise features prevent the size of the group to become either too large or too small, thus leading to more robust performance.

6.3 Real World Datasets

6.3.1 Scientific Publications

Researchers study the topics of papers seeking for concise representations of scientific publications, which contain both pair-wise data like co-authorship and point-wise data such as bag of words features. Detecting anomalous topic distributions in scientific publications can sharpen our understanding of the structure of research communities and possibly reveal unusual research trends. In order to quantify our method, we resort to anomaly injection and construct a dataset with group anomaly labels. One way to construct group anomalies is the scenario that a conference paper corpus is contaminated by group of papers from conferences in other domains.

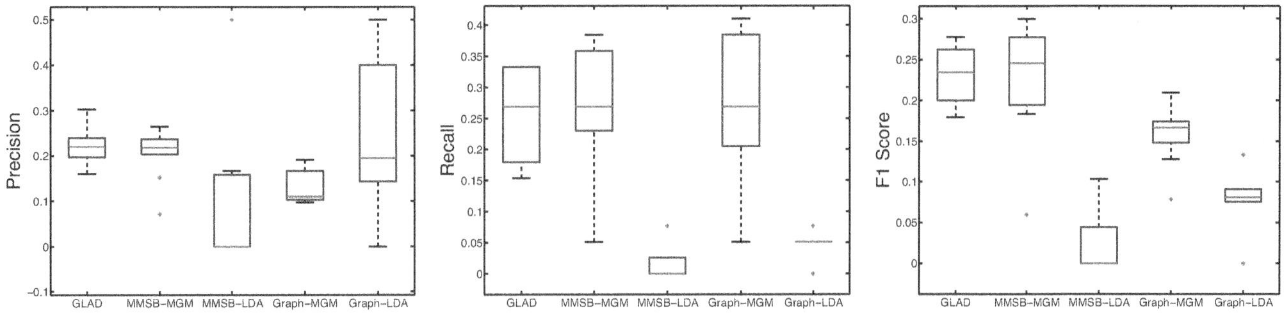

(a) Precision (b) Recall (c) F1 Score

Figure 5: (a): Precision (b): Recall (c): F1 score on the benchmark dataset of GLAD and four baseline methods over 20 runs. All members in the anomalous groups are treated as individual anomalies and compared with 39 true anomalies.

Table 3: Group Anomaly Accuracy of GLAD and four baselines on DBLP publications. With KDD papers treated as normal groups and other conferences are treated as group anomalies respectively.

Methods	GLAD	Graph-LDA	Graph-MGM	MMSB-LDA	MMSB-MGM
`DBLP:KDD/CVPR`	**0.4167**	0.3333	0.3333	0.2500	0.2500
`DBLP:KDD/ICML`	**0.2500**	0.0833	0.0833	0.1667	0.1667
`DBLP:KDD/SIGMOD`	**0.2875**	0.0750	0.0500	0.1625	0.1625
`DBLP:KDD/CIKM`	**0.4500**	0.4000	0.3625	0.2625	0.2625
`DBLP:KDD/EDBT`	**0.2625**	0.0500	0.0875	0.2000	0.2000

We create a dataset from a pre-processed Digital Bibliography and Library Project (DBLP) dataset from [6]. The dataset consists of conference papers from 20 conferences of four major area: database (DB), data mining (DM), information retrieval (IR) and artificial intelligence (AI). Each paper has a bag-of words feature vector with a vocabulary size of 11,771 and associated 28,702 authors information. The detailed statistics of the dataset are shown in the top half of Table 4. We set up the group anomaly detection scenario as follows: we randomly sample groups of papers from KDD and treat them as normal groups. Then we sample groups of papers from the other conferences (e.g, CVPR, ICML , SIGMOD) and inject them into KDD papers as group anomalies. If the two papers have at least one common author, we add a link between them.

Accordingly, all conferences share four topics. But different conferences might have difference point of emphasis, resulting in different mixture rates of topics. Our goal is to pick out the "anomalous" papers from the corpus. We sample 50 groups of papers and inject 20% group anomalies. We apply different models with 50 groups and 4 roles to the data for inference of the membership and role distributions. Then we rank 50 groups with respect to their anomaly scores. We treat the top 20% groups as the detected anomalies. Table 3 shows the anomaly detection accuracy by GLAD and four other baselines. GLAD is superior to all four baselines models for different combination of normal/abnormal settings. We also display the topics learned by the GLAD model. In Table 5, we show the top ten most representative words for the four topics, which well reproduce the topic results reported in [6].

Since the DBLP dataset does not contain time-specific information which is not suitable for the d-GLAD model, we process another ACM dataset downloaded from ArnetMiner

Table 4: Key statistics of the DBLP and ACM publication datasets

DBLP			
# of docs	28,569	# of authors	28,702
# of conf	20	# of words	11,771
# of links	104,962	# of area	4
ACM			
# of docs	31,574	# of authors	4,474
# of year	10	# of words	8,024

[16]. The dataset contains the publications from year 2000 to 2009 by 4,474 authors, mainly from the data mining community. In order to study the topic evolution for academic scholars, we extract the abstracts of all publications and group them by authors and publishing years. For each author, we construct a bag of words feature vector out of all the papers he/she has written in one year. And the communication networks we generate are based on the co-authorship of the papers. Whenever two authors have collaborations in a certain year, we create a link between them for the network snapshot in that year.

Due to the lack of labels, it is difficult to directly evaluate our model on anomaly detection task. As an alternative, we design a prediction task to compare the modeling performance of GLAD and d-GLAD on ACM publications. Specifically, we separate the papers into training and testing sets and measure the predictive model log-likelihood on the testing data. For d-GLAD, we train our model using a series of publications from previous years, and test on the year immediately after. For the GLAD model, as it is a static model, time independence assumption applies. We train the model using previous year and test on the next year. The model fitting results are shown in Table 6. Out

Table 6: Prediction negative log likelihood for GLAD and d-GLAD on ACM dataset over 9 years.

Year	2001	2002	2003	2004	2005	2006	2007	2008	2009
GLAD	28421.63	28023.68	**30184.66**	**32039.92**	28317.67	**30539.66**	26105.21	34340.53	25967.75
DGLAD	**34411.28**	**33411.14**	29935.87	31958.92	**30082.65**	29696.12	**30042.77**	**34395.68**	**31683.49**

Table 5: The most representative words learned by GLAD on DBLP dataset of four topics: database, data mining, information retrieval and artificial intelligence.

DB	DM	IR	AI
databases	data	web	query
object	mining	information	system
access	efficient	learning	management
database	query	search	processing
oriented	algorithm	retrieval	web
security	queries	clustering	efficient
based	clustering	query	performance
indexing	databases	text	infomation
systems	algorithms	model	distributed
privacy	large	classification	optimization

of 9 training-testing experiments, d-GLAD model achieves higher log-likelihood than GLAD model for 6 times, indicating d-GLAD as a better fit for the evolving publication modeling.

6.3.2 *US Senate Voting*

We collect the voting records from the government website of United States 109th Congress [1] using the New York Time Congress API [2]. The records of 109th Congress contain 100 senators' voting spanning two sessions from Jan 1st 2005 to Dec 31st 2006. We divide the 24 months records into 8 time slots, where each slot denotes a 3-month interval. Then we apply the method of [11] to construct a network from original yay/nay votes. For the nodes features, we collect the statistics of votes in six dimensions, namely House Joint Resolution(hjres), House of Representatives(hr), Presidential Nomination(pn), Simple Resolution(s), sconres(Senate Concurrent Resolution) and Senate Joint Resolution(sjres). We evaluate GLAD on single aggregated network and d-GLAD on the 8 time slots time-varying data.

We set the number of groups as 2 and number of roles as 3 as the Senate consists of two major parties and maintains three types of committees. Figure 6 shows the groups inferred by GLAD. The blue nodes denote Democratic party members and the red ones are Republican. Compared with known facts, the model correctly reveals the party affiliation except for two outliers: Ben Nelson (Democratic) and James Jeffords (Independent). The underlying reason is that the votes of these two senators are often at odds with the leadership of his party, leading to false grouping. We conduct an anecdotal investigation and find that the congressional vote rating from the National Journal placed Ben Nelson to the right of five Senate Republicans in 2006. For James Jeffords, he served as a Republican until 2001, when he left the party to become an Independent and began caucusing with the Democrats.

[1] http://www.senate.gov/

[2] http://developer.nytimes.com/docs/read/congress_api

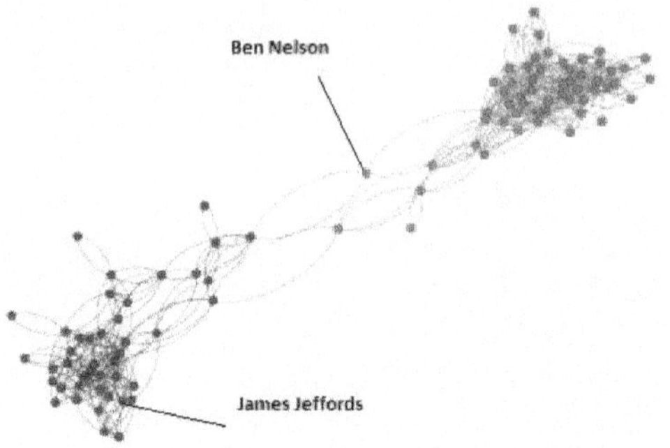

Figure 6: Common votes graph with party labels inferred by GLAD for 100 senators on the aggregated network. Compared with ground truth, two outliers are highlighted due to their anomalous voting behavior.

Since there are merely two groups, it is impetuous to say one party is more anomalous than the other. Instead, we use d-GLAD to detect time points when the role mixture rates change dramatically. In fact, d-GLAD raises an alarm at the 7th time-step for Democratic. A well known political event happened during this time is that Democratic senator Joseph Lieberman lost the Democratic Party primary election and became a independent Democratic in September 2006. Though it may be over-optimistic to draw the conclusion that this event causes the sudden change of role mixture rates, it serves as an evidence that the dynamics of the voting behavior is closely related to the party affiliation of members.

7. CONCLUSION

In this paper, we study the problem of group anomaly detection in social media analysis. We identify the group membership and the role for each individual and define the group anomaly with respect to the *role mixture rate*. We develop a hierarchical Bayes model: the GLAD model, for detecting the group anomaly. The GLAD model utilizes both the pair-wise and point-wise data and automatically infers the group membership and the role at the same time. To further account for the dynamic nature of social media, we generalize GLAD to the d-GLAD model as an extension for handling time series. We derive the variational Bayesian method as well as the Monte Carlo sampling for the model inference.

The superior performances of GLAD and d-GLAD are demonstrated on synthetic datasets and real world social media datasets. For example, GLAD successfully detects "anomalous" papers from the scientific publication corpus with injected anomalies. d-GLAD uncovers the party affiliation changes in the Senate which correspond to political events. The type of group anomaly that we define here has also been investigated in the applications of astronomy [19], particle physics [13] and fluid mechanics [20]. But our work is the first study in group anomaly detection that aims to identify groups and detect anomalies simultaneously. During this study, we mainly focus on the applications in social media analysis, but we believe that our model is capable of tackling similar problems in other domains.

Our current approach has a number of limitations. First, the lack of labeled data for group anomaly increases the difficulty in evaluation. Here we create a benchmark dataset using anomaly injection. But the injected anomaly cannot fully represent the naturally occurred anomaly in practice. Secondly, we do not fully address the problem of model selection for our approach. For the experiments on senator and publication datasets, we either manually choose the model hyper-parameters based on our prior knowledge or use cross-validation. Finally, given the complexity of the model and the particle filtering approach, the d-GLAD model is computational expensive. Thus it is not yet scalable to data with long time span.

For future directions, we will apply the variational Bayesian method for d-GLAD or parallel sampling procedure to achieve further speed-up for large-scale data. Furthermore, it would be interesting to build non-parametric models to automatically learn the number of groups and roles. Future research should also address better procedures and criteria for evaluating the group anomaly detection methods in real world social media applications.

8. ACKNOWLEDGMENTS

The research was sponsored by the U.S. Defense Advanced Research Projects Agency (DARPA) under the Anomaly Detection at Multiple Scales (ADAMS) program, Agreement Number W911NF-11-C-0200 and NSF research grants IIS-1134990. The views and conclusions are those of the authors and should not be interpreted as representing the official policies of the funding agency, or the U.S. Government.

9. REFERENCES

[1] E. M. Airoldi, D. M. Blei, S. E. Fienberg, and E. P. Xing. Mixed membership stochastic blockmodels. *Journal of Machine Learning Research*, 9(1981-2014):3, 2008.

[2] L. Akoglu, M. McGlohon, and C. Faloutsos. Anomaly detection in large graphs. In *In CMU-CS-09-173 Technical Report*. Citeseer, 2009.

[3] D. M. Blei and J. D. Lafferty. Dynamic topic models. In *Proceedings of the 23rd international conference on Machine learning*, pages 113–120. ACM, 2006.

[4] D. M. Blei, A. Y. Ng, and M. I. Jordan. Latent dirichlet allocation. *the Journal of machine Learning research*, 3:993–1022, 2003.

[5] S. P. Borgatti, A. Mehra, D. J. Brass, and G. Labianca. Network analysis in the social sciences. *science*, 323(5916):892–895, 2009.

[6] H. Deng, J. Han, B. Zhao, Y. Yu, and C. X. Lin. Probabilistic topic models with biased propagation on heterogeneous information networks. In *Proceedings of the 17th ACM SIGKDD international conference on Knowledge discovery and data mining*, pages 1271–1279. ACM, 2011.

[7] S. Fortunato. Community detection in graphs. June 2009. Physics Reports 486, 75-174 (2010).

[8] D. M. Hawkins. *Identification of outliers*. Chapman and Hall, 1980.

[9] N. A. Heard, D. J. Weston, K. Platanioti, and D. J. Hand. Bayesian anomaly detection methods for social networks. 2010.

[10] M. I. Jordan, Z. Ghahramani, T. S. Jaakkola, and L. K. Saul. An introduction to variational methods for graphical models. *Machine learning*, 37(2):183–233, 1999.

[11] M. Kolar, L. Song, A. Ahmed, E. P. Xing, et al. Estimating time-varying networks. *The Annals of Applied Statistics*, 4(1):94–123, 2010.

[12] G. Kossinets. Empirical analysis of an evolving social network. *Science*, 311(5757):88–90, Jan. 2006.

[13] K. Muandet and B. SchÃűlkopf. One-class support measure machines for group anomaly detection. Mar. 2013.

[14] J.-Y. Pan, H.-J. Yang, C. Faloutsos, and P. Duygulu. Automatic multimedia cross-modal correlation discovery. In *Proceedings of the tenth ACM SIGKDD international conference on Knowledge discovery and data mining*, pages 653–658. ACM, 2004.

[15] C. E. Priebe, J. M. Conroy, D. J. Marchette, and Y. Park. Scan statistics on enron graphs. *Computational & Mathematical Organization Theory*, 11(3):229–247, 2005.

[16] J. Tang, J. Zhang, L. Yao, J. Li, L. Zhang, and Z. Su. Arnetminer: Extraction and mining of academic social networks. In *KDD'08*, pages 990–998, 2008.

[17] H. Tong, C. Faloutsos, and J.-Y. Pan. Fast random walk with restart and its applications. 2006.

[18] U. Von Luxburg. A tutorial on spectral clustering. *Statistics and computing*, 17(4):395–416, 2007.

[19] L. Xiong, B. Poczos, J. Schneider, A. Connolly, and J. Vanderplas. Hierarchical probabilistic models for group anomaly detection. pages 789–797, 2011.

[20] L. Xiong, B. Póczos, and J. G. Schneider. Group anomaly detection using flexible genre models. In *NIPS*, pages 1071–1079, 2011.

[21] V. Chandola, A. Banerjee, and V. Kumar. Anomaly detection: A survey. *ACM Computing Surveys (CSUR)*, 41(3):15, 2009.

[22] A. Doucet and A. M. Johansen. A tutorial on particle filtering and smoothing: Fifteen years later.

[23] D. Koller and N. Friedman. Probabilistic graphical models: principles and techniques. MIT press, 2009.

FBLG: A Simple and Effective Approach for Temporal Dependence Discovery from Time Series Data

Dehua Cheng, Mohammad Taha Bahadori, Yan Liu
University of Southern California
Los Angeles, CA 90089
{dehua.cheng,mohammab,yanliu.cs}@usc.edu

ABSTRACT

Discovering temporal dependence structure from multivariate time series has established its importance in many applications. We observe that when we look in reversed order of time, the temporal dependence structure of the time series is usually preserved after switching the roles of *cause* and *effect*. Inspired by this observation, we create a *new* time series by reversing the time stamps of original time series and combine both time series to improve the performance of temporal dependence recovery. We also provide theoretical justification for the proposed algorithm for several existing time series models. We test our approach on both synthetic and real world datasets. The experimental results confirm that this surprisingly simple approach is indeed effective under various circumstances.

Categories and Subject Descriptors

G.3 [**Probability and Statistics**]: Time Series Analysis

Keywords

Time Series Analysis; Generalized Linear Model

1. INTRODUCTION

Discovering temporal dependence structures from multivariate time series is one of the central tasks in time series analysis. It easily finds applications in many domains. For example, in social networks, accurate identification of influence networks from users' time series activity records is of significant importance for advertising, marketing, and psychological studies. In biology, the gene regulatory networks recovered from time series microarray data reveals key information on gene functions.

Inferring dependency network structures from time series data has been extensively studied in the past. The *Granger causality* framework, which establishes temporal dependence structures based on regression techniques, has become popular due to its simplicity, robustness, and extendability [23, 7, 16, 3, 22]. Nowadays, as more and more large-scale time series data become available, traditional approaches for identifying Granger causality are confronted with a series of challenges, such as inconsistency, high computational complexity, and so on. To address these problems, penalized regression techniques (e.g. lasso or lasso-type regressions) have been applied, leading to major improvement for applications with *sparse* temporal dependence structures [29, 2, 27]. However, the overall performance of existing Granger causality techniques still leaves room for improvement. In this paper, we aim to explore a new direction by considering the procedure of reversing the time in time series data.

The inspiration for our work comes from classical mechanics where it is well-known that the basic equations of the classical physics remains valid when we look in reversed order of time, i.e., replacing time stamp t with $-t$. In a simple world, if time flows in the opposite direction, objects interact with each other under the same physical laws, and we will not notice the difference. Instead of explaining all phenomena from the underlying physical law, we usually apply simplified mathematical models to real world events. Since the underlying physics mechanism is time reversible, we would expect our model applies when the time is reversed. The question remains whether we can consolidate and enhance our estimation accuracy by utilizing the information from both directions.[1]

To fully utilize such an idea, we need to examine the effect of reversing the time on the temporal dependence structures. One important assumption of Granger causality is that *the cause occurs before the effect.* If an event A at time t causes an event B to happen at time $t+k$, we will see a correlation between events A and B with time lag k. By reversing time, the correlation between events A and B still exists, with the difference that B occurs before A. Granger causality-based algorithms should suggest that A causes B with time lag k from the original time series. Similarly, we expect that the same algorithm would also indicate that B causes A with time lag k from the reversed time series. Note that our argument is not limited to Granger causality, it also applies to other algorithms that rely on the correlation with time lags between time series, e.g., transfer entropy [26].

[1] It should be noted that, for a closed complex system, the trend of entropy eliminates the ambiguity on the time direction, as suggested by the second law of thermodynamics. But since the model only addresses a particular aspect of the system, the restriction usually does not apply.

KDD'14, August 24–27, 2014, New York, NY, USA.
Copyright 2014 ACM 978-1-4503-2956-9/14/08 ...$15.00.
http://dx.doi.org/10.1145/2623330.2623709 .

The link between the original time series and the reversed time series raises the possibility of combining these two directions for enhanced temporal dependence inference. This motivates us to propose a novel but simple approach, namely forward backward (FB) Granger causality, to infer the temporal dependence structures for multivariate time series. Firstly, we apply Granger causality-based algorithm on both the original time series and the time-reversed time series, then we combine the results by simple averaging. Note that similar approach has been applied in *Natural Language Processing*[21], where they estimate the transition kernel of the Markov chain from both directions. Performance improvement has been observed when the size of data is limited. We provide both theoretical analysis and empirical studies on the effectiveness of the proposed approach. The rest of the paper is organized as follows: we first review the preliminary and related works in Section 2. In Section 3, we describe our FB Granger causality algorithm and provide theoretical analysis on several existing models. Finally, we show experimental results in Section 4 and conclusion in Section 5.

2. PRELIMINARIES AND RELATED WORK

Notation.

We define the forward time series as the original multivariate time series $\{\mathbf{y}^{(t)}\}$, $t = \ldots, 0, 1, \ldots$, and the backward time series $\{\mathbf{z}^{(t)}\}$ is defined as $\mathbf{z}^{(t)} := \mathbf{y}^{(-t)}$. $\{\mathbf{y}^{(t)}\}$ and $\{\mathbf{z}^{(t)}\}$ both contain N time series; univariate time series are denoted by $\{y_i^{(t)}\}$ and $\{z_i^{(t)}\}$ for $i = 1, \ldots, N$. Both $\mathbf{y}^{(t)}$ and $\mathbf{z}^{(t)}$ are vectors of the values for each time series at time t, respectively. If the ith time series at time t is caused by the jth time series at time $t-k$, we say that i is caused by j with lag k. Moreover, we represent this temporal dependence relation by the ordered *temporal dependence triplet* (i, j, k). And the inverse of temporal dependence triplet (i, j, k) is defined as (j, i, k). In addition, $\mathcal{C}_y$ denotes the set of all *temporal dependence triplets* for time series $\{\mathbf{y}^{(t)}\}$.

Related Work.

Causal inference has consistently been an important task for researchers in various fields of science. There are two main tasks in causal inference: (1) How to cancel the confounding bias, e.g., [24] and (2) How to discover the causal structures among the given variables when a set of assumptions are satisfied [28]. In this paper, the second task is our concern and we intend to improve the existing causal discovery algorithms.

The causal discovery task is challenging and may require many assumptions with weak guarantees of finding the true causal structure, see for example the theoretical discussions in [25]. *Granger causality* is one of the most popular approaches to quantify temporal dependence structures for time series observations. It is based on two major principles: (i) The cause happens prior to the effect and (ii) The cause makes unique changes in the effect [14, 15]. In practice, Granger causality tests are carried out by fitting a *Vector Auto-regression* (VAR) model. Up to now, two major approaches based on VAR model have been developed to uncover Granger causality for multivariate time series. One approach is the *significance test* [20, ch. 3.6.1]: given multiple time series $\{\mathbf{y}^{(t)}\}$, we run a VAR model as follows,

$$\mathbf{y}^{(t)} = \sum_{\ell=1}^{P} \mathbf{A}_\ell^\top \mathbf{y}^{(t-\ell)} + \boldsymbol{\epsilon}^{(t)}, \tag{1}$$

where P is the maximal time lag. We can determine that time series $\{y_j^{(t)}\}$ Granger causes $\{y_i^{(t)}\}$ if at least one value in the coefficient vector $\{\mathbf{A}_\ell\}_{ij}$ for $\ell = 1, \ldots, P$ is nonzero by statistical significant tests. The second approach is the *Lasso-Granger approach* [29, 2, 27], which applies a lasso-type VAR model to obtain a sparse and robust estimate of the coefficient vectors for Granger causality tests. Specifically, the regression task in Eq. (1) can be achieved by solving the following optimization problem:

$$\min_{\mathbf{A}_\ell} \sum_{t=L+1}^{T} \left\| \mathbf{y}^{(t)} - \sum_{\ell=1}^{P} \mathbf{A}_\ell^\top \mathbf{y}^{(t-\ell)} \right\|_2^2 + \lambda \sum_{\ell=1}^{P} \|\mathbf{A}_\ell\|_1, \tag{2}$$

where λ is the penalty parameter, which determines the sparsity of the coefficients $\mathbf{A}_\ell$.

Several approaches have been proposed for identification of Granger causality for nonlinear time series; among the notable ones, kernelized regression [22], nonparametric techniques such as [16, 23, 26], non-Gaussian structural VAR [17], generalized linear autoregressive models [19, 5], and the Copula Granger [4].

The proposed method in this paper is similar to bootstrap aggregating (bagging) techniques [6] in the sense that it averages over the results from multiple datasets. But the fundamental difference between the two techniques stems from the way that the algorithms generate datasets: the bagging techniques sample the original dataset and create subsamples of the dataset and then average over the results of the algorithm on each new datasets. Here we do not subsample the original dataset; instead we create a new dataset by reversing time. Randomization techniques [12] constitute another wide class of dataset manipulation techniques. However, note that the our proposed method is purely deterministic.

3. MODEL ANALYSIS

In this section, we first describe our algorithms for exploiting the information in the backward time series, and then elaborate theoretical bases for the gain achieved by these algorithms.

3.1 Forward Backward Granger Causality

Given a specific temporal dependence inference algorithm, if it indicates the existence of the temporal dependence triplet (i, j, k) based on the forward time series $\{\mathbf{y}^{(t)}\}$, as argued in Section 1, intuitively we would expect the algorithm to find the triplet (j, i, k) based on the backward time series $\{\mathbf{z}^{(t)}\}$. This motivates our core design principle for utilizing this property: we can achieve more robust temporal dependence inference by appropriately combining the results from both the forward time series and the backward time series produced by the same temporal dependence inference algorithm.

The validity of such an approach depends on both the original temporal dependence inference algorithm and how we combine the results. We mainly focus on the Granger causality-based algorithms in this paper.

Algorithm 1 Naive Forward Backward Lasso Granger Causality

Input: Time series $\{\mathbf{y}^{(t)}\}$, lag P, penalty parameter λ.
Output: Coefficients $\mathbf{A}_\ell^{FB}$, $\ell = 1, 2, \ldots, P$.
Define the backward time series $\{\mathbf{z}^{(t)}\}$ by $\mathbf{z}^{(t)} = \mathbf{y}^{(-t)}$.
Get forward coefficients $\mathbf{A}_\ell$ via Lasso-Granger with $\{\mathbf{y}^{(t)}\}$, P, and λ.
Get backward coefficients $\mathbf{B}_\ell$ via Lasso-Granger with $\{\mathbf{z}^{(t)}\}$, P, and λ.
Return $\mathbf{A}_\ell^{FB} = \frac{1}{2}(\mathbf{A}_\ell + \mathbf{B}_\ell^\top)$, $\ell = 1, 2, \ldots, P$.

Algorithm 2 Naive Forward Backward Copula Lasso Granger Causality

Input: Time series $\{\mathbf{y}^{(t)}\}$, lag P, penalty parameter λ.
Output: Coefficients $\mathbf{A}_\ell^{FB}$, $\ell = 1, 2, \ldots, P$.
for each $i = 1, 2, \ldots, N$ **do**
  Transform $y_i^{(t)} \to w_i^{(t)}$ by equation 3.
end for
Get coefficients $\mathbf{A}_\ell^{FB}$ by calling algorithm 1 with $\{\mathbf{w}^{(t)}\}$, P, and λ.
Return $\mathbf{A}_\ell^{FB}$, $\ell = 1, 2, \ldots, P$.

In general, suppose that the assumptions for correctness of Granger causality are satisfied such that the coefficients estimated by Granger causality indicate the existence of temporal dependence relationships; such assumptions have been studied in [13, 4]. The simplest way to combine the results is to add the coefficients for (i, j, k) in the forward time series and (j, i, k) in the backward time series, which yields the *Naive Forward Backward Lasso Granger Causality Algorithm*, shown in Algorithm 1. It is important to note that since we only flipped the temporal order of the original dataset, the results from forward and backward time series are expected to be correlated. But the coefficients are not fully correlated for time series with finite length, which is supported by our experimental results.

However, Granger causality is designed for linear time series, which is not always the case for the data of interest. Given a time series $\{\mathbf{x}^{(t)}\}$, we can map the data using the empirical marginal distribution of time series to the Gaussian distribution by

$$y_i^{(t)} = s_i \Phi^{-1}(\hat{F}(x_i^{(t)})), \quad \text{for } i = 1, \ldots, N, \tag{3}$$

where $\hat{F}$ is the empirical *cumulative distribution function* (CDF) of the ith time series, Φ is the CDF for standard Gaussian distribution and s_i is the standard derivative of the ith time series, which helps to retain original information. $\{\mathbf{y}^{(t)}\}$ will be treated as a linear representation for the original time series, to which we can apply Granger causality based algorithms, e.g., the *Copula Lasso Granger Causality* [4], and similarly, *Naive Forward Backward Copula Lasso Granger Causality* as described in algorithm 2.

3.2 Analysis of Continuous Time Series

In this section[2], we show that for the time series generated from *Vector Autoregressive Model* (VAR), the backward time series is also a VAR under some conditions. To do so, we assume $\boldsymbol{\epsilon}^{(t)} \sim \mathcal{N}(0, \gamma I)$, where γ is a constant which governs the level of noise, and $\mathcal{N}(\mu, \sigma^2)$ denotes the Gaussian (normal) distribution. The VAR model with the Gaussian noise uniquely defines a multivariate Gaussian distribution on $(\mathbf{y}^{(t)}, \mathbf{y}^{(t-1)}, \ldots)$. This provides the foundation for us to derive the conditional distribution of the same form as equation (1) for *backward time series* $\{\mathbf{z}^{(t)} | \mathbf{z}^{(t)} \equiv \mathbf{y}^{(-t)}\}$. We show that the backward time series is also a VAR model only with different set of coefficients $\mathbf{B}_i$ and noise. However, for arbitrary VAR, the causation defined on the forward time series $\mathbf{y}^{(t)}$ is not the same as the inverse of the causation defined on the backward time series $\{\mathbf{z}^{(t)}\}$, i.e., the set of causation triplets of the backward time series $\mathcal{C}_z \neq \{(j, i, k) | (i, j, k) \in \mathcal{C}_y\}$ where $\mathcal{C}_y = \{(i, j, k)\}$ is the set of causation triplets of the forward time series. In the following theorem, we show that the temporal dependence triplets on the backward time series $\{\mathbf{z}^{(t)}\}$ is closely related to the inverse of the triplets on $\{\mathbf{y}^{(t)}\}$.

Theorem 3.1. *If the forward time series $\{\mathbf{y}^{(t)}\}$ is stable and there exists $\delta > 0$ and a matrix norm $|||\cdot|||$, e.g., the Frobenius norm, so that $|||\mathbf{A}_i||| < \delta, \forall i = 1, 2, \ldots, P$. Then the backward time series $\{\mathbf{z}^{(t)}\}$ is also a VAR, defined by*

$$\mathbf{z}^{(t)} = \sum_{i=1}^{P} \mathbf{B}_i \mathbf{z}^{(t-i)} + \boldsymbol{\omega}_t,$$

where $\boldsymbol{\omega}_t \sim \mathcal{N}(0, \gamma[\mathbf{I} + \Theta(\delta)])$ and $\mathbf{B}_i = \mathbf{A}_i^\top + o(\delta)$, $\forall\, i$.

Proof. By the definition of $\{\mathbf{y}^{(t)}\}$, we have

$$\mathbf{y}^{(t)} | \mathbf{y}^{(t-1)}, \ldots, \mathbf{y}^{(t-P)} \sim \mathcal{N}(\sum_{i=1}^{P} \mathbf{A}_i \mathbf{y}^{(t-i)}, \gamma \mathbf{I}).$$

Because time series $\{\mathbf{y}^{(t)}\}$ is stable, so it is also strictly stationary [20, Ch. 2.1.3] and the marginal distribution of the P consecutive time stamps has the following representation:

$$\mathbf{Y}^{(t)} = (\mathbf{y}^{(t+1)^\top}, \mathbf{y}^{(t+2)^\top}, \ldots, \mathbf{y}^{(t+P)^\top})^\top \sim N(0, \gamma\{\Lambda_{ij}\}^{-1}),$$

where the $\mathbf{Y}^{(t)}$ is an $NP \times 1$ vector, and the $\{\Lambda_{ij}\}$ is the precision matrix (represented in blocks), each block Λ_{ij} is an $N \times N$ matrix. Given the stationarity of the time series, we can set $t = 0$ without the loss of generality. The probability density function (PDF) of the marginal distribution of the $P + 1$ consecutive time stamps are proportional to

$$\begin{aligned} &\exp[-\frac{1}{2\gamma}(\sum_{i,j=1}^{P} \mathbf{y}^{(i)^\top} \Lambda_{ij} \mathbf{y}^{(j)} \\ &+ (\mathbf{y}^{(P+1)} - \sum_{i=1}^{P} \mathbf{A}_i \mathbf{y}^{(i)})^\top (\mathbf{y}^{(P+1)} - \sum_{i=1}^{P} \mathbf{A}_i \mathbf{y}^{(i)}))] \\ &= \exp[-\frac{1}{2\gamma}(\sum_{i,j=1}^{P+1} \mathbf{y}_i^\top (\Lambda_{ij} + \mathbf{A}_i^\top \mathbf{A}_j) y_j)], \end{aligned}$$

where $\mathbf{A}_{P+1} = -\mathbf{I}$, $\Lambda_{P+1,i} = \Lambda_{j,P+1} = \mathbf{0}$. The PDF of the conditional distribution of $\mathbf{y}^{(1)}$ given $\mathbf{y}^{(2)}, \ldots, \mathbf{y}^{(P+1)}$ is proportional to

$$\exp[-\frac{1}{2\gamma}(\mathbf{y}^{(1)^\top} (\Lambda_{11} + \mathbf{A}_1^\top \mathbf{A}_1) \mathbf{y}^{(1)} - 2 \sum_{i=2}^{P+1} \mathbf{y}^{(i)^\top} (\Lambda_{i1} + \mathbf{A}_i^\top \mathbf{A}_1) \mathbf{y}^{(1)})$$

$$\sim \mathcal{N}((\Lambda_{11} + \mathbf{A}_1^\top \mathbf{A}_1)^{-1}(-\sum_{i=2}^{P+1} (\Lambda_{1i} + \mathbf{A}_1^\top \mathbf{A}_i) \mathbf{y}^{(i)}), \gamma(\Lambda_{11} + \mathbf{A}_1^\top \mathbf{A}_1)^{-1}).$$

[2]Note that by continuous or discrete time series, we refer to whether the variables take on continuous or discrete values.

To study the structure of the covariance matrix $\{\Lambda_{ij}\}^{-1}$, we recall that the *Moving Average* representation of VAR model, which is

$$\mathbf{Y}^{(t)} \sim \sum_{i=1}^{+\infty} \mathbf{A}^i \mathbf{U}^{(t-i)},$$

where $\mathbf{U}^{(t)} = (0^\top, 0^\top, \dots, \epsilon^{(t)\top})^\top$, and

$$\mathbf{A} = \begin{bmatrix} 0 & \mathbf{I} & 0 & 0 \\ 0 & 0 & \mathbf{I} & \vdots \\ 0 & 0 & \ddots & \mathbf{I} \\ \mathbf{A}_P & \mathbf{A}_{P-1} & \dots & \mathbf{A}_1 \end{bmatrix}.$$

So we have that

$$\gamma\{\Lambda_{ij}\}^{-1} = \gamma \sum_{i=1}^{+\infty} \mathbf{A}^i \Sigma_{t-i} (\mathbf{A}^i)^T,$$

where the lower right block of $\mathbf{\Sigma}_{t-i}$ is $\mathbf{I}$, otherwise is $\mathbf{0}$.

By some derivations, we can show that

$$\{\Lambda_{ij}\}^{-1} = \mathbf{I} + \Theta(\delta),$$

where the diagonal blocks are $\mathbf{I}+\Theta(\delta)$ by setting all $\mathbf{A}_i = \mathbf{0}$. And the first row of blocks are $(\mathbf{I}+\Theta(\delta), \mathbf{A}_P^\top + o(\delta), \dots, \mathbf{A}_2^\top + o(\delta))$, which can be derived by studying the first $P+1$ terms in the series. So by inversion, we have that

$$\Lambda_{1i} = -\mathbf{A}_{P+2-i}^T + o(\delta), \forall i = \{2, \dots P\},$$

$$\Lambda_{11} = \mathbf{I} + o(1).$$

Together with $\mathbf{A}_1^T \mathbf{A}_i = o(\delta), \forall i = 1, 2, \dots, P$, we have

$$-(\Lambda_{1i} + \mathbf{A}_1^T \mathbf{A}_i) = \mathbf{A}_{P+2-i}^T + o(\delta),$$

$$(\Lambda_{11} + \mathbf{A}_1^T \mathbf{A}_1) = \mathbf{I} + o(1) = \mathbf{I} + \Theta(\delta).$$

By replacing $\mathbf{y}^{(t)}$ with $\mathbf{z}^{(-t)}$, we have

$$\mathbf{z}^{(t)} = \sum_{i=1}^{P} \mathbf{B}_i \mathbf{z}^{(t-i)} + \boldsymbol{\omega}_t = \sum_{i=1}^{P} [\mathbf{A}_i^\top + o(\delta)] \mathbf{z}^{(t-i)} + \boldsymbol{\omega}_t,$$

where $\boldsymbol{\omega}_t \sim \mathcal{N}(0, \gamma[\mathbf{I} + \Theta(\delta)])$. □

The assumption in Theorem 3.1 implies that the strength of the influence in time series $\{\mathbf{y}^{(t)}\}$ has an upper bound, which is sufficient but not necessary. It can be relaxed, since the proof only requires that the higher order product between $\mathbf{A}_i$ is negligible comparing with $\mathbf{A}_i$ itself. This assumption can be easily satisfied when the temporal dependence structure is sparse, which is usually true in real world applications.

Theorem 3.1 shows that the first order components of the influence on the backward VAR is exactly the inverse of the forward VAR, i.e., not only $(i, j, k) \in \mathcal{C}_y \Leftrightarrow (j, i, k) \in \mathcal{C}_z$, but they also share the same strength $\{\mathbf{A}_k\}_{ij}$, which indicates a much stronger link between the forward time series and the backward time series. The link also results in a simple form, which justifies our approach of combining the results from both directions, i.e., averaging on the corresponding coefficients. Moreover, Granger causality provides an unbiased estimation for both directions, and the results in [27] indicate that they have the same variance. Therefore the average of both directions is also unbiased with smaller variance, when the correlation of two estimations are strictly less than 1. Additionally, when we have sufficiently long time series, i.e., $T \gg N$, we would expect that the forward backward approach provides an estimation similar to the original Lasso Granger causality, since both forward and backward should provide accurate coefficients estimation, as suggested by the consistency of the penalized maximal likelihood estimation. This phenomenon has been observed in our experiments on synthetic datasets.

For nonlinear time series, we apply the copula transformation before Granger causality. In order to show similar theoretical results for this approach, we need the data to be generated from the *Granger Non-paranormal (G-NPN) model* as follows:

Definition.

Granger Non-paranormal (G-NPN) model We say a time series $\mathbf{x}^{(t)} = (x_1^{(t)}, \dots, x_N^{(t)})$ has Granger-Nonparanormal distribution $G - NPN(\mathbf{x}, \mathbf{A}, F)$ if there exist monotonically increasing functions $\{F_i\}_{i=1}^N$ such that $F_i(x_i^{(t)})$ for $i = 1, \dots, N$ are jointly Gaussian and can be factorized according to the VAR model with coefficients $\mathbf{A} = \{\mathbf{A}_k\}_{k=1}^P$. More specifically, the joint distribution for the transformed random variables $y_i^{(t)} \triangleq F_i(x_i^{(t)})$ can be factorized as follows

$$p_{\mathbf{y}^{(\mathbf{t})}}(\mathbf{y}^{(\mathbf{t})}) = \mathcal{N}(\mathbf{y}^{(1:P)}) \prod_{i=1}^{N} \prod_{t=P+1}^{T} p_{\mathcal{N}}(y_j^{(t)} | \sum_{k=1}^{P} \mathbf{A}_k \mathbf{y}^{(t-k)}, \sigma_j),$$

where $p_{\mathcal{N}}(y|\mu, \sigma)$ is the Gaussian density function with mean μ and variance σ^2.

Proposition 3.1. *Using the copula transformation on the data generated from G-NPN model, the forward and backward relationships in Theorem 3.1 hold for the transformed random processes.*

Proof. Our proof is mainly to show that the copula transformation recovers the original vector auto-regressive process. The key step to prove this result is to show that if $X \sim \mathcal{N}(0, 1)$ and $Y = F(X)$, where $F(\cdot)$ is a monotonically increasing function, then $\Phi^{-1}(F_Y(Y)) \sim \mathcal{N}(0, 1)$. Furthermore, the independence relationships will be preserved a the copula mapping, as the transformation $\Phi^{-1}(F_Y(\cdot))$ is a deterministic transformation. This is because $X \perp\!\!\!\perp Y$ if and only if $g(X) \perp\!\!\!\perp h(Y)$ for any arbitrary random variables X and Y and deterministic one-to-one transformation functions $g(\cdot)$ and $h(\cdot)$.

After applying the above result to each variable $x_i^{(t)}$, we can show [4] that by using the copula transformation we obtain $y_i^{(t)}$ which are multivariate Gaussian as defined in the definition of G-NPN. □

The definition of the Granger Non-paranormal (G-NPN) model indicates that the underlying mechanism of time series $\{\mathbf{x}^{(t)}\}$ is a linear time series, which subsumes numerous circumstances. When $\{\mathbf{x}^{(t)}\}$ is an observation of $\{\mathbf{y}^{(t)}\}$ with deterministic bias, the copula transformation helps to restore the original information as stated in Proposition 3.1. And then we can apply our argument for the VAR model.

3.3 Analysis of Discrete Time Series

Nowadays, social media provides a rich source for time series analysis because the interactions among individuals are naturally reflected in the time series of action logs. One way to analyze the social influence among users is to create time series of user activity by assigning 1 to a user at a particular time interval if she has at least one activity in that time interval and 0 otherwise [1]. For example, tweeting (i.e., posting on Twitter) activity naturally defines a time series, where $y_i^{(t)} = 1$ if user i posts at time interval t, and $y_i^{(t)} = 0$ otherwise. We can also recover influence relationship among users based on retweeting. For example, if user i retweets user j, we say that i has been influenced by j. Such social network time series pose a unique challenge for the temporal dependence inference algorithms.

In this section, we first define a general type of binary time series, which includes many existing models. Then, with additional Assumption 3.2, we prove that applying Granger causality to binary time series provides consistent temporal dependence structure recovery. Furthermore, by Assumption 3.2 and Lemma 3.4, we build the connection between the forward times series and the backward time series, which leads to the consistency results on temporal dependence structure recovery for the backward time series. By consistency we refer to that with appropriate thresholding on the estimated coefficients, we can correctly recover all temporal dependence triplets from the time series. Note that we are applying Granger causality on a misspecified model (i.e., the binary time series is not generated from VAR), the consistency results also justify our approach which applies Granger causality on certain non-VAR time series.

Given a binary multivariate time series $\{\mathbf{y}^{(t)}\}$, we say the ith series is activated at time t if and only if $y_i^{(t)} = 1$. In addition to the previous notations, we denote $\mathbf{y}^{(t-1:t-P)} = (\mathbf{y}^{(t-1)}, \mathbf{y}^{(t-2)}, \dots, \mathbf{y}^{(t-P)})$. $\Omega_{\mathbf{y}^{(t-1:t-P)}}$ is the set of activated variables in $\mathbf{y}^{(t-1:t-P)}$. We have the following assumptions:

Assumption 3.1.
Markov Assumption

The probability of activation for any variable at time t only depends on the states of the most recent P times $(t-1, t-2, \dots, t-P)$, which is

$$P(y_i^{(t)} = 1|\mathbf{y}^{(t-1)}, \mathbf{y}^{(t-2)}, \dots) = P(y_i^{(t)} = 1|\mathbf{y}^{(t-1:t-P)}) = P(y_i^{(t)} = 1|\Omega_{\mathbf{y}^{(t-1:t-P)}}).$$

The last equality is because of variables only take binary value, so the status of $\mathbf{y}^{(t-1:t-P)}$ is uniquely defined by $\Omega_{\mathbf{y}^{(t-1:t-P)}}$.
Activation Rate Monotonicity

$y_j^{(t-k)} \notin \Omega_{\mathbf{y}^{(t-1:t-P)}}$ implies

$$P(y_i^{(t)} = 1|\{y_j^{(t-k)}\}\cup\Omega_{\mathbf{y}^{(t-1:t-P)}}) \geq P(y_i^{(t)} = 1|\Omega_{\mathbf{y}^{(t-1:t-P)}}),$$

which means that there is no negative influence on the activation rate if more variables from the histories become activated.
Influcence Significance

If there exist a set $\Omega_{\mathbf{y}^{(t-1:t-P)}}$, such that $y_j^{(t-k)} \notin \Omega_{\mathbf{y}^{(t-1:t-P)}}$ and $P(y_i^{(t)} = 1|\Omega_{\mathbf{y}^{(t-1:t-P)}}\cup\{y_j^{(t-k)}\}) > P(y_i^{(t)} = 1|\Omega_{\mathbf{y}^{(t-1:t-P)}})$, then there exist $\delta_{ijk} > 0$, for any $\Omega_{\mathbf{y}^{(t-1:t-P)}}$, $y_j^{(t-k)} \notin \Omega_{\mathbf{y}^{(t-1:t-P)}}$ implies

$$P(y_i^{(t)} = 1|\Omega_{\mathbf{y}^{(t-1:t-P)}}\cup\{y_j^{(t-k)}\}) > P(y_i^{(t)} = 1|\Omega_{\mathbf{y}^{(t-1:t-P)}}) + \delta_{ijk}.$$

And we say j is a cause *for i with lag k*

The last term in Assumption 3.1 actually implies that the causation is significant under any circumstances, i.e. the activation of time series j at time $t-k$ will increase the activation rate of time series i at time t by at least δ_{ijk}, regardless of other variables in $\mathbf{y}^{(t-1:t-P)}$, or the status of $y_i^{(t)}$ does not depends on the status of $y_j^{(t-k)}$ at all. We stress that Assumption 3.1 can be easily satisfied in practical applications and many existing models fall in this category.

Example 3.1. ***Independent Cascade****[18] (IC) model is originally proposed for modeling the diffusion process in social networks. We modify it to model the activity on networks over time. IC model defined on a weighted directed graph $\{\mathcal{V}, \mathcal{E}\}$, with each vertex represents an individual in the network. If vertex v is activated at time t, it attempts to activate its neighbor s with probability $p_{v\to s}$ at time $t+1$ independently. If any neighbor of s activates s successfully, s will be marked as activated at time $t+1$. It can also activate itself by probability μ_s. The activation rate has the following representation*

$$P(s^{(t+1)} = 1) = 1 - (1-\mu_s) \prod_{\substack{v^{(t)}=1 \\ (v\to s)\in\mathcal{E}}} (1 - p_{v\to s}).$$

And the IC model satisfies Assumption 3.1.

Note that because we are applying Granger causality as a misspecified model, we need one more assumption to support the consistency results on binary time series.

Assumption 3.2. ***Diminishing Influcence*** *Let a binary time series $\{y_i^{(t)}\}i = 1, 2, \dots, N$ satisfy Assumption 3.1. Let's denote $\mathbf{y}^{(t-1:t-P)} - \{y_j^{(t-k)}\}$ by $\mathcal{S}_{jk}$, then we assume*

$$\frac{P(\mathcal{S}_{jk}|y_j^{(t-k)} = 1) - P(\mathcal{S}_{jk}|y_j^{(t-k)} = 0)}{P(\mathcal{S}_{jk}|y_j^{(t-k)} = 1) + P(\mathcal{S}_{jk}|y_j^{(t-k)} = 0)} = O(\frac{1}{N}),$$

for all possible values of $\mathcal{S}_{jk}$ as $N \to +\infty$.

And for any vector β_{jk} of the same size as $\mathcal{S}_{jk}$, we assume that $||\beta_{jk}||_\infty = O(1)$ and

$$E[\beta_{jk} \cdot \mathcal{S}_{jk}|y_j^{(t-k)} = 1] - E[\beta_{jk} \cdot \mathcal{S}_{jk}|y_j^{(t-k)} = 0] = O(\frac{1}{N}),$$

for all possible value of $\mathcal{S}_{jk}$ as $N \to +\infty$.

Assumption 3.2 shows that the influence of an individual on the entire network is diminishing as the size of the network increases. For example, the difference of joint distribution of $\mathcal{S}_{jk}$ given $y_j^{(t-k)} = 0$ or $y_j^{(t-k)} = 1$ represents the influence of $y_j^{(t-k)}$ on $\mathcal{S}_{jk}$, e.g., when there is no difference, $y_j^{(t-k)}$ and $\mathcal{S}_{jk}$ are independent. Moreover, note that, if Assumption 3.2 holds for $\{\mathbf{y}^{(t)}\}$, then $\{\mathbf{z}^{(t)}\}$ also satisfy the same assumption, since $\mathbf{z}^{(t-1:t-P)} = \mathbf{y}^{(1-t:P-t)}$.

Assumption 3.3. *Given a binary time series $\{y_i^{(t)}\}$, $i = 1, 2, \dots, N$, we have*

$$P(y_i^{(t)}|y_j^{(t-k)} = 1) - P(y_i^{(t)}|y_j^{(t-k)} = 0) \geq \Theta(\delta_{ijk}) > 0,$$

if j is a cause *for i with lag k. Otherwise,*

$$P(y_i^{(t)}|y_j^{(t-k)} = 1) - P(y_i^{(t)}|y_j^{(t-k)} = 0) = O(\frac{1}{N}),$$

as $N \to +\infty$.

Assumption 3.3 helps us to establish the connection between the forward time series and the backward time series, and it is important for the consistency result in Theorem 3.3. Furthermore, we have an important lemma connecting the Assumption 3.3 with 3.1 and 3.2.

Lemma 3.2. *Given a binary time series $\{y_i^{(t)}\}, i = 1, 2, \ldots, N$ satisfy Assumption 3.1 and 3.2, then it satisfies Assumption 3.3.*

Proof. Given the binary time series $\{y_i^{(t)}\}$, $i = 1, 2, \ldots, N$, we denote $y^{(t-1:t-P)} - \{y_j^{(t-k)}\}$ by $\mathcal{S}_{jk}$, and we have

$$P(y_i^{(t)}|y_j^{(t-k)}) = \sum_{\mathcal{S}_{jk}} P(y_i^{(t)}|y^{(t-1:t-P)})P(\mathcal{S}_{jk}|y_j^{(t-k)}).$$

By Assumption 3.1 and 3.2, if j is a *cause* for i with lag k, we have

$$\begin{aligned}P(y_i^{(t)}|y_j^{(t-k)} = 1) - &P(y_i^{(t)}|y_j^{(t-k)} = 0)\\ \geq &\sum_{\mathcal{S}_{jk}}(\Theta(\delta_{ijk}) + O(1/N))P(\mathcal{S}_{jk}|y_j^{(t-k)} = 0)\\ = &\Theta(\delta_{ijk}).\end{aligned}$$

Otherwise, we have

$$\begin{aligned}P(y_i^{(t)}|y_j^{(t-k)} = 1) - &P(y_i^{(t)}|y_j^{(t-k)} = 0)\\ = &\sum_{\mathcal{S}_{jk}} O(1/N)P(\mathcal{S}_{jk}|y_j^{(t-k)} = 0)\\ = &O(1/N),\end{aligned}$$

as $N \to +\infty$. □

We now state our main theorem in this section, which suggests the consistency of Granger causality on binary time series with appropriate thresholding.

Theorem 3.3. *Let a binary time series $\{y_i^{(t)}\}, i = 1, 2, \ldots, N$ satisfy Assumption 3.2 and 3.3. We denote the coefficients by $\mathbf{A}_k, k = 1, 2, \ldots, P$ as in VAR model, which are estimated by applying Granger causality on time series $\{\mathbf{y}^{(t)}\}$, we have*

$$\{\mathbf{A}_k\}_{ij} \geq \Theta(\delta_{ijk}) > 0,$$

if j is a cause *for i with lag k. Otherwise,*

$$\{\mathbf{A}_k\}_{ij} = O(\frac{1}{N}),$$

as $N \to +\infty$.

Proof. As $T \to +\infty$, we have the objective function of the regression as follows:

$$\sum_{\mathbf{y}^{(t-1:t-k)}} \sum_{i} \sum_{y_i^{(t)}} P(y_i^{(t)}, \mathbf{y}^{(t-1:t-k)})(y_i^{(t)} - b_i - \sum_{k=1}^{P} \mathbf{A}_k \mathbf{y}^{(t-k)})^2.$$

Note that we do not sum over t, since we weight the loss term by its own marginal distribution. Without loss of generality, we study the coefficient $\{\mathbf{A}_k\}_{ij}$ (denoted by β_{ijk}), which connecting $y_i^{(t)}$ and $y_j^{(t-k)}$. Let us denote $\mathbf{y}^{(t-1:t-P)} - \{y_j^{(t-1:t-P)}\}$ by $\mathcal{S}_{jk}$ and the associated coefficients by β_{jk}. By absorbing the constant into b, we can shift the value of $y_j^{(t-k)}$ from $\{0, 1\}$ to $\{-0.5, 0.5\}$. The related objective is as follows:

$$\sum_{\substack{\mathcal{S}_{jk}\\ \mathbf{y}^{(t-1:t-k)}}} P(y_i^{(t)}, \mathbf{y}^{(t-1:t-k)})(y_i^{(t)} - b_i - y_j^{(t-k)}\beta_{ijk} - \mathcal{S}_{jk} \cdot \beta_{jk})^2.$$

By taking the derivative w.r.t. β_{ijk}, we have

$$\begin{aligned}&P(y_i^{(t)} = 1|y_j^{(t-k)} = -0.5) - P(y_i^{(t)} = 1|y_j^{(t-k)} = 0.5) + \beta_{ijk}\\ &+E[\mathcal{S}_{jk} \cdot \beta_{jk}|y_j^{(t-k)} = 0.5] - E[\mathcal{S}_{jk} \cdot \beta_{jk}|y_j^{(t-k)} = -0.5] = 0.\end{aligned}$$

Recall that $\{\mathbf{y}^{(t)}\}$ satisfy Assumption 3.2, which indicates that

$$\beta_{ijk} \geq \Theta(\delta_{ijk}) > 0,$$

if j is a *cause* for i with lag k. Otherwise,

$$\beta_{ijk} = O(\frac{1}{N}),$$

as $N \to +\infty$. This proves the theorem. □

Theorem 3.3 indicates that by setting an appropriate threshold (on the order of $\min_{\{i,j,k\}}\{\delta_{ijk}\}$) on the coefficients, we can reconstruct the correct temporal dependence structure. We now explain the connection between the forward time series $\{\mathbf{y}^{(t)}\}$ and the backward time series $\{\mathbf{z}^{(t)}\}$.

Lemma 3.4. *Given a binary time series $\{y_i^{(t)}\} i = 1, 2, \ldots, N$ satisfy Assumption 3.3, we have*

$$P(y_j^{(t-k)}|y_i^{(t)} = 1) - P(y_j^{(t-k)}|y_i^{(t)} = 0) \geq \Theta(\delta_{ijk}) > 0,$$

if j is a cause *for i with lag k. Otherwise,*

$$P(y_j^{(t-k)}|y_i^{(t)} = 1) - P(y_j^{(t-k)}|y_i^{(t)} = 0) = O(\frac{1}{N}).$$

as $N \to +\infty$, if $P(y_i^{(t)}) = \Theta(1), \forall i, t$.

Proof. Let A and B be two binary random variables with $P(A, B) = \Theta(1)$. And for simplicity, we denote $P(A = i, B = j)$ by p_{ij}. We have

$$\begin{aligned}&P(A = 1|B = 1) > P(A = 1|B = 0) + \delta\\ \Leftrightarrow&\frac{p_{11}}{p_{01} + p_{11}} > \frac{p_{10}}{p_{00} + p_{10}} + \delta\\ \Leftrightarrow&\frac{p_{00}}{p_{10}} > \frac{p_{01}}{p_{11}} + \Theta(\delta)\\ \Leftrightarrow&\frac{p_{00}}{p_{01}} > \frac{p_{10}}{p_{11}} + \Theta(\delta)\\ \Leftrightarrow&\frac{p_{11}}{p_{10} + p_{11}} > \frac{p_{01}}{p_{00} + p_{01}} + \Theta(\delta).\\ \Leftrightarrow&P(B = 1|A = 1) > P(B = 1|A = 0) + \Theta(\delta).\end{aligned}$$

Replace $y_j^{(t-k)}$ and $y_i^{(t)}$ by A, B, we proved the Lemma. □

Note that $y_j^{(t-k)}$ and $y_i^{(t)}$ are switched, compared with Assumption 3.3. Simply combining Lemma 3.4 with Theorem 3.3, we have similar consistency results for the backward time series:

Theorem 3.5. *Let a binary time series $\{y_i^{(t)}\}, i = 1, 2, \ldots, N$ satisfy Assumptions 3.1 and 3.2. We define the backward time series by $\{z_i^{(t)}|z_i^{(t)} = y_i^{(-t)}\}$ and denote the coefficients* *by $\mathbf{B}_k, k = 1, 2, \ldots, P$ as in VAR model, which are estimated by applying Granger causality on time series $\{z^{(t)}\}$. We have*

$$\{\mathbf{B}_k\}_{ji} \geq \Theta(\delta_{ijk}) > 0,$$

if j is a cause *for i with lag k w.r.t. $\{y_i^{(t)}\}$. Otherwise,*

$$\{\mathbf{B}_k\}_{ji} = O(\frac{1}{N}),$$

as $N \to +\infty$, if $P(y_i^{(t)}) = \Theta(1), \forall i, t$.

Proof. We prove this theorem based on existing theorems and lemmas. Forward time series $\{y_i^{(t)}\}$, $i = 1, 2, \ldots, N$ satisfy Assumption 3.2, so does the backward time series since Assumption 3.2 is symmetric in time. Forward time series $\{y_i^{(t)}\}$, $i = 1, 2, \ldots, N$ satisfy Assumption 3.1 and 3.2, by Lemma 3.2, it also satisfies Assumption 3.3. Then by Lemma 3.4, the backward time series also satisfy Assumption 3.3. Then by Theorem 3.3, we prove Theorem 3.5. □

Theorem 3.5 indicates that applying Granger causality on the backward time series also provides consistent temporal dependence inference results. Note that we only assume 3.1 and 3.2 for the forward time series. In fact, the backward time series might not satisfy Assumption 3.1 at all.

3.4 Summary and Discussion

In Section 3.2 and 3.3, we investigate several well-known time series models and establish the connection between forward and backward time series in terms of temporal dependence structures. For VAR, the strength $\{\mathbf{A}_k\}_{ij}$ of triplet (i, j, k) in forward time series is approximately the same as that for $\{\mathbf{B}_k\}_{ji}$ of triplet (j, i, k) in backward time series. For binary time series models that satisfy Assumptions 3.1 and 3.2, the strength of triplets (i, j, k) and (j, i, k) for forward and backward time series, respectively, share the same order of magnitude. These connections justify our approach to combine the results from the forward and the backward time series for better temporal dependence inference.

Note that information inferred from the backward time series is not exactly the same as that inferred from the forward time series, but they indeed share considerable similarities, which can be utilized as suggested. Moreover, when applied to real world data, model misspecification should be considered, which is absent in our current analysis. In addition, one should be aware of the data preprocessing procedure, to make sure it is compatible with our assumptions, especially when the preprocessing relies on a specific order of time.

4. EXPERIMENT RESULTS

In the experiments, we evaluate the effectiveness of our proposed approach on several synthetic datasets and two real world datasets. Next, we describe the data collections, baseline methods, evaluation metric and experimental results.

4.1 Datasets

Synthetic Datasets Since we do not have the access to the true underlying temporal dependence structure in most applications, we generate synthetic datasets to evaluate the performance of temporal dependence structure recovery.

For discrete time series, we generate two synthetic datasets: one is generated from the IC model (as discussed in example 3.1), and the other is an instance of the generalized linear models (later referred to as LOG model), with a Bernoulli distribution and the link function $\sigma(\cdot)^{-1}$ as a logistic sigmoid function. Specifically, the distribution of $\mathbf{y}^{(t)}$ is a Bernoulli random vector with parameter

$$P(y_i^{(t)} = 1|\mathbf{y}^{(t-1:t-P)}) = E[y_i^{(t)}|\mathbf{y}^{(t-1:t-P)}], i = 1, \ldots, N,$$

defined as follows:

$$\sigma^{-1}(E[\mathbf{y}^{(t)}|\mathbf{y}^{(t-1:t-P)}]) = \mu + \sum_{k=1}^{P} \mathbf{A}_k \mathbf{y}^{(t-k)}.$$

If $\mathbf{A}_k$ are all nonnegative matrices, it satisfies Assumption 3.1.

For continuous time series, we also generate two synthetic datasets: one is linear time series generated according to VAR, and the other is nonlinear time series generated from generalized linear model with polynomial link function and Gaussian noises (POLY). Specifically, the distribution of $\mathbf{y}^{(t)}$ is a multivariate Gaussian, i.e.,

$$\mathbf{y}^{(t)}|\mathbf{y}^{t-1:t-P} \sim \mathcal{N}(f(\sum_{k=1}^{P} \mathbf{A}_k \mathbf{y}^{(t-k)}), \epsilon I),$$

where $f(\cdot)$ is defined by $f(x) = x + bx^3$. We vary b to change the level of nonlinearity.

For each model, we set the lag to 1 and generate a sparse temporal dependence structure $\mathbf{A}$ with 5% nonzero entries. For the IC, each nonzero entry in $\mathbf{A}$ is drawn from a uniform distribution Uniform(0, 1). For LOG, μ_i is drawn from $\mathcal{N}(0, 1)$, and each nonzero entry in $\mathbf{A}$ is drawn from $\mathcal{N}(0, 1)$. For VAR and POLY, each nonzero entry in $\mathbf{A}$ is drawn from $\mathcal{N}(0, 1)$, and then we normalize $\mathbf{A}$ by its Frobenius norm to ensure the stability of the time series. Moreover, for each model, we generate time series $\{y_i^{(t)}\}$, $i = 1, \ldots, N$, $t = 1, \ldots, T$ by setting N and T with two scenarios: (1) $N = 30, T = 2000$, which corresponds to the low-dimensional case, and (2) $N = 100, T = 150$, which mimics the high-dimensional case.

Twitter Datasets We collect the *Haiti* dataset[5] with all the tweets published between Oct 2009 and Jan 2010 on "Haiti earthquake". We choose this topic because it was one of the hot topics during that time period and many tweets have been generated around the event.

For the *Haiti* dataset, we collect the tweets by searching the keyword "Haiti" from Jan. 12, 2010 for 17 days. We then generate multivariate time series datasets by counting the number of tweets from the top 1000 users (who tweet most on the topics) over these 1000 intervals. For accurate modeling, we remove the users that are highly correlated with each other, most of which are operated by the same persons and tweet exactly the same contents. We also remove robot-like user-accounts who tweet on very regular intervals. Finally, we select a set of users with at least one interaction with another user, which results in a subset of 274 users.

Microarray Dataset Most multicellular organisms rely on their immune systems to defend against the infection from a multitude of pathogens. We collect the time series microarray data on macrophages from human immune cells from the supporting website of [9, 11]. It consists of 1651 genes with 9 time series observations. We apply the proposed model to this dataset in order to infer the temporal dependence networks for immune system genes. Due to the

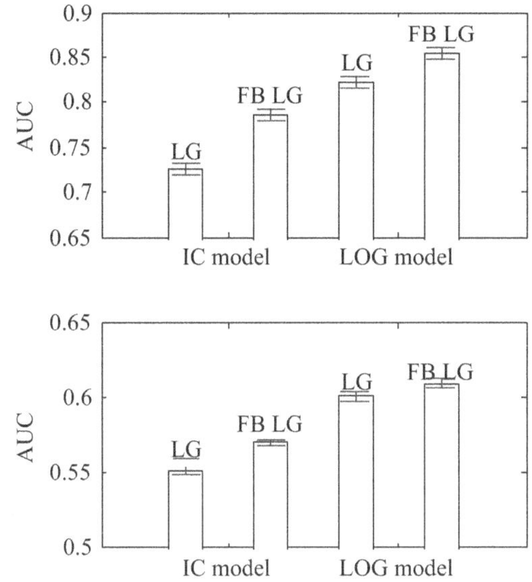

Figure 1: The performance of temporal dependence recovery on IC and LOG datasets. Top: $N = 30, T = 2000$; Down: $N = 100, T = 150$. Results suggest that LG benefits from the forward backward approach.

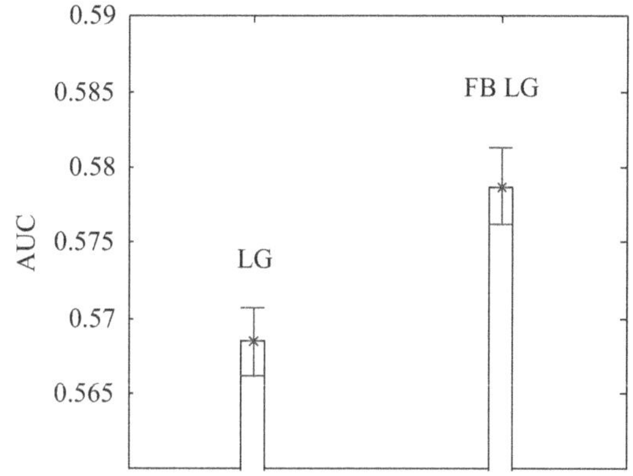

Figure 2: The performance of temporal dependence recovery on VAR dataset with $N = 100, T = 150$. Results suggest that LG benefits from the forward backward approach.

space limit, we only show the results of a subset of 6 genes, whose interactions have been well studied.

4.2 Baseline Algorithms

We use the following baselines for comparison analysis on the synthetic datasets:

- *Lasso Granger Causality* (LG) and *Naive Forward Backward Lasso Granger Causality*[1] (FB LG) as described in section 3.1.
- *Copula Lasso Granger Causality* (CLG) and *Naive Forward Backward Copula Lasso Granger Causality*[2] (FB CLG). For nonlinear time series, we apply the copula transformation for each time series first, and then apply the *Granger causality* based algorithms.

For *Lasso* based algorithm, we choose the penalty parameter λ to minimize the prediction error on the validation dataset.

For the Haiti dataset, we also test the *Transfer Entropy* (TE) algorithm [26]. Transfer entropy is another related technique which identifies the temporal dependence structure between two time series by measuring the decrease in uncertainty of one time series in the future, given the past information of the other time series. Namely, the transfer entropy is defined as

$$T_{\mathbf{y}_j \to \mathbf{y}_i} = \mathcal{H}(y_i^{(t)} | \mathbf{y}_i^{t-1:t-P}) - \mathcal{H}(y_i^{(t)} | \mathbf{y}_i^{t-1:t-P}, \mathbf{y}_j^{t-1:t-P}),$$

where $\mathcal{H}(x)$ is the Shannon entropy of the random variable x. We also test the *Naive Forward Backward Transfer Entropy* (FB TE), where we measure the influence from j to i by $T_{\mathbf{y}_j \to \mathbf{y}_i} + T_{\mathbf{z}_i \to \mathbf{z}_j}$.

4.3 Evaluation Measures

To evaluate the performance of different methods in recovering temporal dependence structures, we choose the Area Under the Curve (AUC) measure as it is a good performance measure for the ground truth with unbalanced ratio of positive and negative labels. The value of AUC is the probability that the algorithm will assign a higher value to a randomly chosen positive (existing) edge than a randomly chosen negative (non-existing) edge in the graph [10].

For synthetic datasets, we calculate AUC against the ground truth, i.e., the temporal dependence structure defined by $\mathbf{A}$. The reported results are averaged over 20 randomly generated datasets.

For the Twitter dataset, since we do not have access to the true underlying influence graph in the social network, we use the retweet information as indirect evaluation. It has been argued that the retweet graph in the future time can reflect the influence in social networks to a certain extent [8]. We first represent the retweet information by a weighted graph $\mathcal{G}_{RT}$, where the weight of an edge $(s \to t)$ denotes the number of tweets from user s retweeted by user t. The retweet graph $\mathcal{G}_{RT}$ on Haiti earthquake has 867 edges.

For the microarray dataset, we do not have the complete ground truth as well. We therefore compare our results with those reported interactions in the BioGRID database[3], a curated biological database of protein-protein and genetic interactions.

4.4 Experiment Results

In this section, we present the result of our experiments. We focus on the difference of performance between the original version of algorithm and the forward backward version.

Results on Synthetic Datasets We aim to test whether the forward and backward approach can improve the performance of LG on IC and LOG datasets. We report the AUC scores of LG and FB LG in Figure 1. We can see that FB LG consistently outperforms LG, which suggests that FB LG indeed benefits from combining estimates from forward and backward time series.

On the VAR dataset, we focus on the performance for linear continuous time series. We report the AUC scores of LG and FB LG in Figure 2. For high-dimensional time series, FB LG outperforms LG significantly, which indicates that combining two directions helps to improve the performance.

[3]www.thebiogrid.org

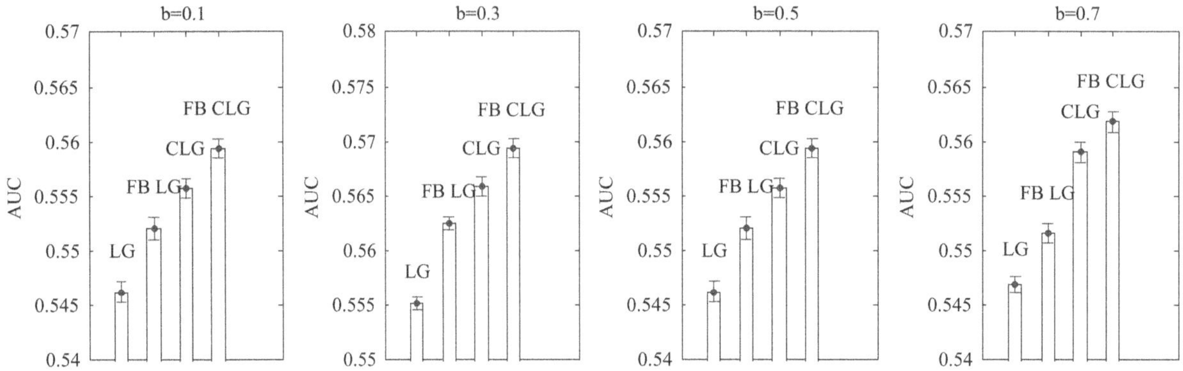

Figure 3: The performance of temporal dependence recovery on POLY dataset with different b and $N = 100, T = 150$. Results suggest that both LG and CLG benefit from the forward backward approach.

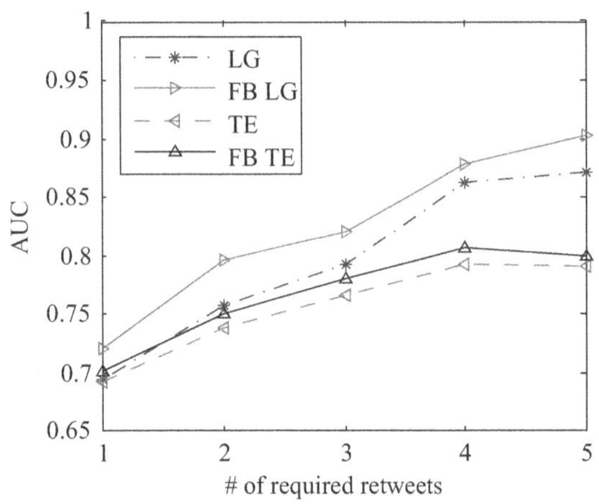

Figure 4: The performance of temporal dependence recovery on Haiti dataset. The performance of FB LG and FB TE outperform the LG and TE, respectively.

On the POLY dataset, we aim to test whether the forward and backward approach can further improve the performance of LG and CLG for nonlinear time series. We report the AUC scores of LG, FB LG, CLG, FB CLG on the POLY datset in Figure 3. As we can see CLG can improve LG thanks to the copula transformation. And FB CLG can further improve CLG for high-dimensional case. For both VAR and POLY datasets, when $N = 30, T = 2000$, we find that the performance of LG and FB LG are similar, as suggested in Section 3.2.

Results on Twitter Dataset We test LG, FB LG, TE, and FB TE on the Haiti dataset (see Figure 4 for results). We set the lag $P = 15$ for all algorithms for fair comparison, which corresponds to 6 hours approximately. The AUC is calculated against the retweet graph $\mathcal{G}_{RT}$, and we vary the required number of retweets, so that only if the retweets from j by i passes the required number n, we establish an edge from i to j. Intuitively, n screens the weak influence between users. As we can see, all algorithms perform better as we increase n. In addition, the forward backward approach improves the performance for both baseline algorithms.

Table 1: Top 20 predictions for gene interaction by LG and FB LG. Bold terms are ground truth suggested by BioGRID database.

Lasso Granger	F/B Lasso Granger
PCNA→CCNA2	CDC2→E2F1
E2F1→CCNA2	RFC4→E2F1
CDKN3→CDC2	CDKN3→CDC2
CDC2→RFC4	**PCNA→CCNA2**
CCNA2→RFC4	RFC4→CDKN3
CCNA2→CDC2	CCNA2→RFC4
RFC4→CDKN3	CCNA2→CDC2
CDC2→E2F1	**RFC4→PCNA**
CCNA2→CDKN3	PCNA→E2F1
E2F1→CDC2	**E2F1→CCNA2**
PCNA→RFC4	PCNA→RFC4
RFC4→PCNA	CDC2→RFC4
CDKN3→CCNA2	RFC4→CDC2
CDKN3→RFC4	CCNA2→CDKN3
RFC4→CCNA2	CDKN3→RFC4
RFC4→CDC2	**CCNA2→E2F1**
CDC2→CDKN3	CDC2→PCNA
E2F1→PCNA	CDKN3→E2F1
CCNA2→PCNA	E2F1→CDC2
RFC4→E2F1	CDKN3→PCNA

Results on Microarray Dataset We test LG and FB LG on the time series microarray dataset, and achieve AUCs of **0.6923** and **0.7308**, respectively. Moreover, we list the top edges identified by both algorithms in Table 1. The bold ones are the ground truth suggested by BioGRID database. LG correctly identified 3 interactions while FB LG identified all 4 known interactions.

5. CONCLUSION AND FUTURE WORK

Inspired by time-reversibility of physical laws and its effect on temporal dependency structure, we proposed the forward backward approach to improve the performance of Granger causality. We developed the forward and backward Lasso Granger causality algorithm, which combines the coefficients estimated from the forward time series and backward time series to provide better performance of temporal dependency structure recovery. We show that with the copula transformation, we can extend our algorithm for non-linear time series. Theoretical analysis on several existing times series models including VAR and IC model confirms our intuition. Our empirical results on both synthetic and real world datasets demonstrate that the forward backward approach can improve the performance of temporal dependence inference using forward time series only.

For future work, we will investigate other combination strategies for forward backward approach, other than simply averaging the coefficients. the performance. We will also examine more general types of time series models where the forward backward approach is applicable.

6. ACKNOWLEDGMENT

We thank Aram Galstyan, Greg Ver Steeg for discussions, and David C. Kale for helpful suggestions. This research was sponsored by the NSF research grants IIS-1254206, Okawa Foundation Research Award, and U.S. Defense Advanced Research Projects Agency (DARPA) under Social Media in Strategic Communication (SMISC) program, Agreement Number W911NF-12-1-0034. The views and conclusions are those of the authors and should not be interpreted as representing the official policies of the funding agency or the U.S. Government.

References

[1] A. Anagnostopoulos, R. Kumar, and M. Mahdian. Influence and correlation in social networks. In *KDD*, 2008.

[2] A. Arnold, Y. Liu, and N. Abe. Temporal causal modeling with graphical granger methods. In *KDD*, 2007.

[3] I. Asimakopoulos, D. Ayling, and W. M. Mahmood. Non-linear granger causality in the currency futures returns. *Econ. Letters*, 2000.

[4] M. T. Bahadori and Y. Liu. An examination of practical granger causality inference. In *SDM*, 2013.

[5] M. T. Bahadori, Y. Liu, and E. P. Xing. Fast structure learning in generalized stochastic processes with latent factors. In *KDD*, 2013.

[6] L. Breiman. Bagging predictors. *Mach. Learning*, 1996.

[7] A. Brovelli, M. Ding, A. Ledberg, Y. Chen, R. Nakamura, and S. L. Bressler. Beta oscillations in a large-scale sensorimotor cortical network: directional influences revealed by Granger causality. *PNAS*, 2004.

[8] M. Cha, H. Haddadi, F. Benevenuto, and P. K. Gummadi. Measuring user influence in twitter: The million follower fallacy. *ICWSM*, 2010.

[9] D. Chaussabel, R. T. Semnani, M. A. McDowell, D. Sacks, A. Sher, and T. B. Nutman. Unique gene expression profiles of human macrophages and dendritic cells to phylogenetically distinct parasites. *Blood*, 2003.

[10] C. Cortes and M. Mohri. Confidence intervals for the area under the roc curve. In *NIPS*, 2005.

[11] C. S. Detweiler, D. B. Cunanan, and S. Falkow. Host microarray analysis reveals a role for the salmonella response regulator phop in human macrophage cell death. *PNAS*, 2001.

[12] E. S. Edgington and P. Onghena. *Randomization Tests*. Chapman & Hall/CRC, 2007.

[13] M. Eichler. Graphical modelling of multivariate time series. *Probab. Theory Related Fields*, 2012.

[14] C. W. Granger. Investigating causal relations by econometric models and cross-spectral methods. *Econometrica*, 1969.

[15] C. W. Granger. Testing for causality: A personal viewpoint. *J. Econ. Dynam. Control*, 1980.

[16] C. Hiemstra and J. D. Jones. Testing for Linear and Nonlinear Granger Causality in the Stock Price-Volume Relation. *J. Finance*, 1994.

[17] A. Hyvärinen, K. Zhang, S. Shimizu, P. O. Hoyer, and P. Dayan. Estimation of a Structural Vector Autoregression Model Using Non-Gaussianity. *JMLR*, 2010.

[18] D. Kempe, J. Kleinberg, and É. Tardos. Maximizing the spread of influence through a social network. In *KDD*. ACM, 2003.

[19] Y.-H. Kim, H. H. Permuter, and T. Weissman. Directed information, causal estimation, and communication in continuous time. *IEEE Trans Inf Theory*, 2009.

[20] H. Lütkepohl. *New Introduction to Multiple Time Series Analysis*. Springer, 2005.

[21] C. D. Manning and H. Schütze. *Foundations of statistical natural language processing*. MIT press, 1999.

[22] D. Marinazzo, M. Pellicoro, and S. Stramaglia. Kernel Granger causality and the analysis of dynamical networks. *Phys. Rev. Lett. E*, 2008.

[23] C. D. Panchenko and Valentyn. Modified hiemstra-jones test for granger non-causality. Technical report, Society for Computational Economics, 2004.

[24] J. Pearl. *Causality: Models, Reasning and Inference*. Cambridge University Press, 2009.

[25] J. M. Robins, R. Scheines, P. Spirtes, and L. Wasserman. Uniform consistency in causal inference. *Biometrika*, 2003.

[26] T. Schreiber. Measuring Information Transfer. *Phys. Rev. Lett.*, 2000.

[27] S. Song and P. J. Bickel. Large Vector Auto Regressions. *arxiv:1106.3915*, 2011.

[28] P. Spirtes, C. Glymour, and R. Scheines. *Causation, Prediction, and Search, Second Edition*. The MIT Press, 2001.

[29] P. A. Valdés-Sosa, J. M. Sánchez-Bornot, A. Lage-Castellanos, M. Vega-Hernández, J. Bosch-Bayard, L. Melie-García, and E. Canales-Rodríguez. Estimating brain functional connectivity with sparse multivariate autoregression. *Phil. Trans. R. Soc. B*, 2005.

Learning Time-Series Shapelets

Josif Grabocka, Nicolas Schilling, Martin Wistuba, Lars Schmidt-Thieme
Information Systems and Machine Learning Lab
University of Hildesheim
Samelsonplatz 22, Hildesheim 31141, Germany
{ josif, schilling, wistuba, schmidt-thieme }@ismll.uni-hildesheim.de

ABSTRACT

Shapelets are discriminative sub-sequences of time series that best predict the target variable. For this reason, shapelet discovery has recently attracted considerable interest within the time-series research community. Currently shapelets are found by evaluating the prediction qualities of numerous candidates extracted from the series segments. In contrast to the state-of-the-art, this paper proposes a novel perspective in terms of learning shapelets. A new mathematical formalization of the task via a classification objective function is proposed and a tailored stochastic gradient learning algorithm is applied. The proposed method enables learning near-to-optimal shapelets directly without the need to try out lots of candidates. Furthermore, our method can learn true top-K shapelets by capturing their interaction. Extensive experimentation demonstrates statistically significant improvement in terms of wins and ranks against 13 baselines over 28 time-series datasets.

1. INTRODUCTION

Time-series research has attracted significant interest within the data mining community, due to the fact that series data are present in a wide range of real-life domains. Time-series data often exhibit inter-class differences in terms of small sub-sequencies rather than the full series structure [17]. A recently introduced concept, named *shapelet*, represents a maximally discriminative sub-sequence of time series data. Stated more directly, shapelets identify short discriminative series segments [17, 11]. Apart from their high prediction accuracy, shapelets also offer interpretable features to domain experts. Moreover, discovering shapelets has been a hot topic in the time-series domain during the last five years [17, 11, 10, 19, 8, 12, 9].

State-of-the-art methods discover shapelets by trying a pool of candidate sub-sequences from all possible series segments [17, 10] and then sorting the top performing segments according to their target prediction qualities. Distances between series and shapelets represent shapelet-transformed [10] classification features for a series of segregation metrics, such as information gain [17, 11], F-Stat [8] or Kruskall-Wallis [9]. The brute-force candidates search approach, based on an exhaustive search of candidates, suffers from a high runtime complexity, therefore several speed-up techniques have aimed at reducing the discovery time of shapelets [11, 12, 1]. In terms of classification performance, the shapelet-transformation method constructs qualitative predictors for standard classifiers and has recently shown improvements with respect to prediction accuracy [10, 8].

This paper proposes an entirely new perspective on time-series shapelets. For the first time, we propose a mathematical formulation of the shapelet learning task as an optimization of a classification objective function. Furthermore, we propose a learning method that *learns* (not searches for) the shapelets which optimize the objective function. Concretely, we learn shapelets whose distances to series can linearly separate the time series instances by their targets, as shown in Figure 1. In comparison to existing approaches, our method can learn near-to-optimal shapelets and **true** top-K shapelet interactions. In a large pool of 28 datasets we demonstrate that the proposed method yields a large and statistically significant improvement over 13 baselines.

2. RELATED WORK

Shapelets were first proposed by [17] as time-series segments that maximally predict the target variable. All possible segments were considered as potential candidates, while the minimum distances of a candidate to all training series were used as a predictor feature for ranking the information gain accuracy of that candidate on the target variable. Other quality metrics have been proposed for evaluating the prediction accuracy of a shapelet candidate such as F-Stats [10], Kruskall-Wallis or Mood's median [8]. In addition, the minimum distance of a set of shapelets to time series can be perceived as a data transformation [10], while standard classifiers have achieved high accuracy over the shapelet-transformed representation [8].

Due to the high number of candidates, the runtime of brute-force shapelet discovery is not feasible. Therefore, a series of speed-up techniques such as early abandoning of distance computations and entropy pruning of the information gain metric have been proposed [17]. Other speed-ups rely on the reuse of computations and pruning of the search space [11], as well as exploiting projections on the SAX representation [12]. Alternatively, the training time has been reduced by elaborating the usage of infrequent shapelet candidates [7]. Moreover, hardware-based optimization have assisted the discovery of shapelets using GPUs [1]. Shapelets have been applied in a series of real-life applications. Unsupervised shapelets have also been utilized for clustering time series [19]. Shapelets have been found useful for identifying humans through their gait data [13]. Gesture recognition is another application domain that has benefited from the discovery of shapelets [5, 6]. In the domain of

KDD'14, August 24–27, 2014, New York, NY, USA.

http://dx.doi.org/10.1145/2623330.2623613 .

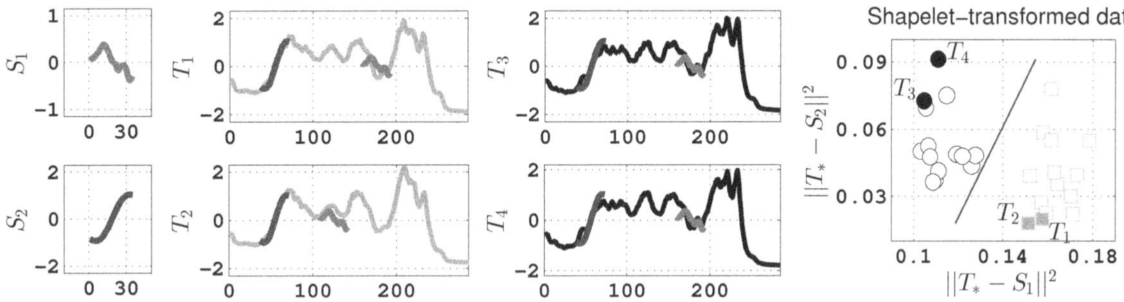

Figure 1: An illustration of two shapelets S_1, S_2 (leftmost plots) learned on the Coffee dataset. Series' distances to shapelets can optimally project the series into a 2-dimensional space, called the shapelet-transformed representation [10] (rightmost plot). The middle plots show the closest matches of the shapelets on series of two classes having light-blue and black colors.

medical and health informatics, interpretable shapelets have been used to enable efficient early classification of time-series [16, 15].

In comparison to the state-or-the-art methods, we propose a novel method that **learns** near-to-optimal shapelets directly, without the need to search exhaustively among a pool of candidates extracted from time-series segments.

3. PROPOSED METHOD

3.1 Definitions and Notations

3.1.1 Time-Series Dataset

A time-series dataset is composed of I training instances and for notation ease we assume that each series contains Q-many ordered values, even though our method can operate on variable series lengths. The dataset is defined as $T^{I\times Q}$, while the series target is a nominal variable $Y \in \{1,\dots,C\}^I$ having C categories.

3.1.2 Sliding Window Segment

A sliding window segment of length L is an ordered sub-sequence of a series. Concretely, the segment starting at time j inside the i-th series is defined as $(T_{i,j},\dots,T_{i,j+L-1})$. There are totally $J := Q - L + 1$ segments in a time series provided the starting index of the sliding window is incremented by one.

3.1.3 Shapelets

A shapelet of length L is simply an ordered sequence of values from a data structure perspective. Nevertheless, shapelets semantically represent intelligence on how to discriminate the target variable of a series dataset. The K-most informative shapelets are denoted as $S \in \mathbb{R}^{K\times L}$.

3.1.4 Distances Between Shapelets and Series

The distance between the i-th series T_i and the k-th shapelet S_k is defined as the minimum distance $M_{i,k}$ (shown in Equation 1) among the distances between the shapelet S_k and each segment j of T_i [17, 18]. Informally speaking, it is the distance of a shapelet to the most similar series segment, as shown in Figure 1.

$$M_{i,k} \quad = \quad \min_{j=1,\dots,J} \frac{1}{L}\sum_{l=1}^{L}\left(T_{i,j+l-1} - S_{k,l}\right)^2 \qquad (1)$$

3.1.5 Shapelet Transformation

Minimum distances to shapelets can be characterized as a transformation of the time-series data $T \in \mathbb{R}^{I\times Q}$ into a new representation $M \in \mathbb{R}^{I\times K}$ [10]. Such a transformation reduces the dimensionality of the original time-series, because typically $K < Q$. General purpose classifiers (e.g.: SVMs, Bayesian Network, ...) have been recently shown to achieve high prediction accuracy over the new representation M [8].

3.1.6 Logistic Sigmoid Function

The logistic sigmoid function is an S shaped instance of the logistic function and is defined as $\sigma(Y) = \left(1+e^{-Y}\right)^{-1}$. We are going to use the sigmoid function for the prediction of target variables via a logistic regression loss.

3.2 A Novel Principle

In this paper we propose a novel principle in learning time-series shapelets. Instead of searching among possible shapelet candidates from the series segments [17, 10], we propose a formal method that can directly learn optimal shapelets without needing to explore all possible candidates. Our principle can be summarized in two steps: (i) Start with rough initial guesses for the shapelets, (ii) Iteratively learn/optimize the shapelets by minimizing a classification loss function. In order to conduct the shapelet optimization, we define a novel classification model that is differentiable with respect to shapelets. Therefore, shapelets can be updated in a stochastic gradient descent optimization fashion, by taking steps towards the minimum of the classification loss function (i.e. towards maximal prediction accuracy).

3.3 Objective Function

For the sake of simplicity, the model introduced in this Section will be focused only on binary targets $Y \in \{0,1\}^I$ and a fixed shapelet length L. A general version of the model, with extended properties, is described Section 5.

3.3.1 Learning Model

Since the minimum distances M are the new predictors in the transformed shapelets space, a linear learning model can predict approximate target values $\hat{Y} \in \mathbb{R}^{I\times K}$ via the predictors M and linear weights $W \in \mathbb{R}^K$ (plus bias $W_0 \in \mathbb{R}$), as shown in Equation 2.

$$\hat{Y}_i \quad = \quad W_0 + \sum_{k=1}^{K} M_{i,k}W_k, \qquad \forall i \in \{1,\dots,I\} \qquad (2)$$

3.3.2 Loss Function

In this paper we are going to exploit the logistic regression classification model, because it provides an option to interpret predicted binary targets as probabilistic confidences. Such a probabilistic interpretation will ensure extending our approach to the multi-class case in Section 5. The logistic regression operates by minimizing the logistic loss, defined in Equation 3, between true targets Y and estimated ones $\hat{Y}$.

$$\mathcal{L}(Y, \hat{Y}) \;=\; -Y \ln \sigma(\hat{Y}) - (1-Y) \ln \left(1 - \sigma(\hat{Y})\right) \quad (3)$$

3.3.3 Regularized Objective Function

The logistic loss function together with regularization terms represent the regularized objective function, denoted as $\mathcal{F}$ in Equation 4. ***The idea of this paper is to jointly learn the optimal shapelets S and the optimal linear hyper-plane W that minimize the classification objective $\mathcal{F}$.***

$$\underset{S,W}{\operatorname{argmin}}\; \mathcal{F}(S,W) = \underset{S,W}{\operatorname{argmin}} \sum_{i=1}^{I} \mathcal{L}(Y_i, \hat{Y}_i) + \lambda_W ||W||^2 \quad (4)$$

3.4 Differentiable Soft-Minimum Function

In order to compute the derivative of the objective function, all the involved functions of the model need to be differentiable. Unfortunately, the minimum function of Equation 1 is not differentiable and the partial derivative $\frac{\partial M}{\partial S}$ is not defined. A differentiable approximation to the minimum function is introduced in this section.

For the sake of organizational clarity we will introduce the distance between the j-th segment of series i and the k-th shapelet as $D_{i,k,j}$ and define it in Equation 5.

$$D_{i,k,j} \;:=\; \frac{1}{L} \sum_{l=1}^{L} \left(T_{i,j+l-1} - S_{k,l}\right)^2 \quad (5)$$

A differentiable approximation of the minimum function is the popular *Soft Minimum* function that is depicted in Equation 6. A parameter α controls the *precision* of the function and the soft minimum approaches the true minimum for $\alpha \rightarrow -\infty$.

$$M_{i,k} \;\approx\; \hat{M}_{i,k} = \frac{\sum_{j=1}^{J} D_{i,k,j}\, e^{\alpha D_{i,k,j}}}{\sum_{j'=1}^{J} e^{\alpha D_{i,k,j'}}} \quad (6)$$

Please note that the soft minimum has the shapelets as the only varying input, which appear embedded inside the distance definition D. We would like to explain the operating principle of the soft minimum with the aid of Figure 2.

A series from the FaceFour dataset and a shapelet are depicted in the upper plot of Figure 2. The shapelet is a slightly distorted variant of the series segment starting at time index 51. If we slide the shapelet over all the series segments and record the distance of shapelets to segments (i.e. Equation 5), then the Euclidean distances' plot in blue is achieved. Two plots in red (bottommost) illustrate the operation of the soft minimum function. Each point j of the soft minimum plots correspond to $\frac{D_{i,k,j}\, e^{\alpha D_{i,k,j}}}{\sum_{j'=1}^{J} e^{\alpha D_{i,k,j'}}}$, while the **area** under the soft-minimum plots sums up to the true minimum distance between the shapelet and the series (i.e. Equation 1). It is important to realize in the third plot ($\alpha = -20$) that the amount by which a segment distance impacts the overall minimum is directly related to how small is that segment's distance compared to other segment distances. As can be seen in the bottom plot, if $\alpha = -100$, then only the true minimum segment distance is allowed to contribute to the grand total minimum. We found out that $\alpha = -100$ is small enough to make the soft minumum yield exactly the same results as the true minimum. Therefore, we kept this value fixed throughout all our experiments.

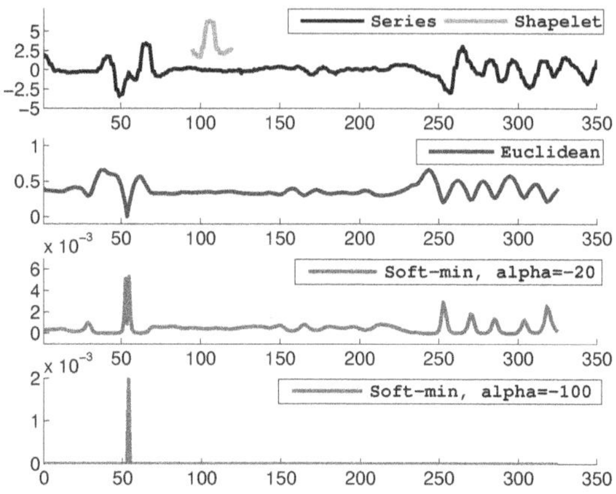

Figure 2: Illustration of the soft minimum between a shapelet (green) and all the segments of a series (black) from the FaceFour dataset

3.5 Per-Instance Objective

The optimization we will adopt in this paper is a stochastic gradient descent approach that remedies the classification error caused by one instance at a time. The Equation 7 demonstrates the decomposed objective function $\mathcal{F}_i$, which corresponds to a division of the objective of Equation 4 into per-instance losses for each time series.

$$\mathcal{F}_i \;=\; \mathcal{L}(Y_i, \hat{Y}_i) + \frac{\lambda_W}{I} \sum_{k=1}^{K} {W_k}^2 \quad (7)$$

3.6 Gradients for Shapelets

The learning algorithm requires the definition of the gradients of the objective function with respect to the shapelets. The gradient of point l in shapelet k with respect to the objective of the i-th time series is defined in Equation 8 and is derived through the chain rule of derivation.

$$\frac{\partial \mathcal{F}_i}{\partial S_{k,l}} \;=\; \frac{\partial \mathcal{L}(Y_i, \hat{Y}_i)}{\partial \hat{Y}_i} \frac{\partial \hat{Y}_i}{\partial \hat{M}_{i,k}} \sum_{j=1}^{J} \frac{\partial \hat{M}_{i,k}}{\partial D_{i,k,j}} \frac{\partial D_{i,k,j}}{\partial S_{k,l}} \quad (8)$$

Furthermore, the gradient of the loss with respect to the predicted target is defined in Equation 9, while the gradient of the minimum distances with respect to the estimated target is shown in Equation 10.

$$\frac{\partial \mathcal{L}(Y_i, \hat{Y}_i)}{\partial \hat{Y}_i} \;=\; -\left(Y_i - \sigma\left(\hat{Y}_i\right)\right) \quad (9)$$

$$\frac{\partial \hat{Y}_i}{\partial \hat{M}_{i,k}} \;=\; W_k \quad (10)$$

In addition, the gradient of the overall minimum distance with respect to a segment distance is presented in Equation 11 and the gradient of a segment distance with respect to a shapelet point is derived in Equation 12.

Algorithm 1 Learning Time-Series Shapelets

Require: $T \in \mathbb{R}^{I \times Q}$, Number of Shapelets K, Length of a shapelet L, Regularization λ_W, Learning Rate η, Number of iterations: maxIter
Ensure: Shapelets $S \in \mathbb{R}^{K \times L}$, Classification weights $W \in \mathbb{R}^K$, Bias $W_0 \in \mathbb{R}$

for iteration=$\mathbb{N}_1^{\text{maxIter}}$ **do**
  for $i = 1, \ldots, I$ **do**
    for $k = 1, \ldots, K$ **do**
      $W_k \leftarrow W_k - \eta \frac{\partial \mathcal{F}_i}{\partial W_k}$
      for $L = 1, \ldots, L$ **do**
        $S_{k,l} \leftarrow S_{k,l} - \eta \frac{\partial \mathcal{F}_i}{\partial S_{k,l}}$
      end for
    end for
    $W_0 \leftarrow W_0 - \eta \frac{\partial \mathcal{F}_i}{\partial W_0}$
  end for
end for
return S, W, W_0

$$\frac{\partial \hat{M}_{i,k}}{\partial D_{i,k,j}} = \frac{e^{\alpha D_{i,k,j}}\left(1+\alpha\left(D_{i,k,j}-\hat{M}_{i,k}\right)\right)}{\sum_{j'=1}^{J} e^{\alpha D_{i,k,j'}}} \quad (11)$$

$$\frac{\partial D_{i,k,j}}{\partial S_{k,l}} = \frac{2}{L}\left(S_{k,l} - T_{i,j+l-1}\right) \quad (12)$$

3.7 Gradients for Classification Weights

The hyper-plane weights W can also be learned to minimize the classification objective via stochastic gradient descent. Equation 13 shows the partial gradient of updating each weight W_k and Equation 14 presents the bias term W_0.

$$\frac{\partial \mathcal{F}_i}{\partial W_k} = -\left(Y_i - \sigma\left(\hat{Y}_i\right)\right)\hat{M}_{i,k} + \frac{2\lambda_W}{I} W_k \quad (13)$$

$$\frac{\partial \mathcal{F}_i}{\partial W_0} = -\left(Y_i - \sigma\left(\hat{Y}_i\right)\right) \quad (14)$$

3.8 Learning Algorithm

After having derived the gradients of the shapelets and the weights, we can introduce the overall learning algorithm. Our approach iterates in a series of epochs and updates the values of the shapelets and weights in the negative direction of the derivative with respect to the classification objective of each training instance.

The steps of the learning process are shown in Algorithm 1. The pseudo-code iterates over all training instances I and updates all K shapelets S and the weights W, W_0 by a learning rate η.

3.9 Convergence

The convergence of Algorithm 1 depends on two parameters, the learning rate η and the maximum number of iterations. High values for the learning rate can minimize the objective in less iterations, but pose the risk of divergence, while small learning rates require more iterations. Subsequently, the learning rate and the number of iterations should be learned via cross-validation from the training data.

For instance Figure 3 illustrates the convergence of the learning algorithm on the Coffee dataset for 57 shapelets. Both the training and the testing loss converge very smoothly for $\eta = 0.01$. As a consequence of optimizing the training loss, the train and test errors also decrease simultaneously. In addition, the regularization

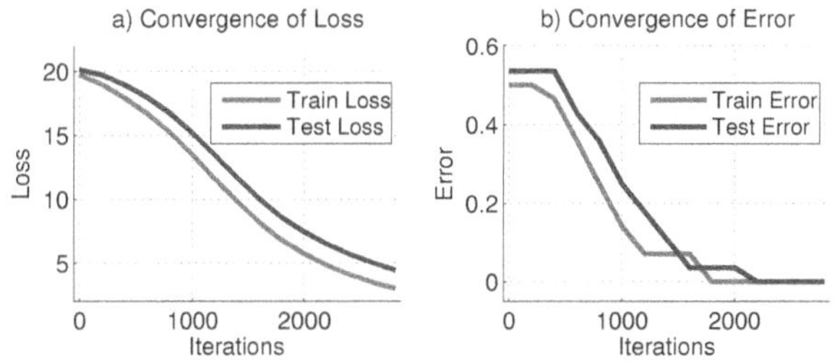

Figure 3: Convergence of the Coffee dataset, Parameters: $K = 57$, $L = 143$, $\eta = 0.01$, $\lambda_W = 0.001$, $\alpha = -100$

weight $\lambda_W = 0.001$ ensures that the train and test loss have small differences, which can be interpreted as a generalization quality without any over-fitting effect.

3.10 Model Initialization

Equation 4 is a non-convex function in terms of S and W because both are variables that need to be learned. Gradient descent techniques do not theoretically guarantee the discovery of global optima in non-linear functions. Unfortunately, non-convex optimization techniques are very slow for data mining problems, therefore gradient based approaches are often selected as a compromise between feasibility and optimality [14].

Gradient descent optimization requires a good initialization of the parameters when applied to non-convex functions. In other words, if the initialization starts the learning around a region where the global optimum is located, then the gradient can update the parameters to the exact location of the optimum.

Initialization can influence a gradient based technique significantly. We are going to illustrate the sensitivity of shapelets initialization through an experiment shown in Figure 4. For the sake of two-dimensional illustration, we initialized one shapelet (S) in the Gun-Point dataset using two values. The first 15 points of a 30 points long shapelet ($S_{1:15}$) were given a fixed initial value, while the other half points of the shapelet $S_{16:30}$ were initialized with another fixed value. Figure 4 demonstrate that different initial values of the shapelet can result in different loss values and error rates over the training instances.

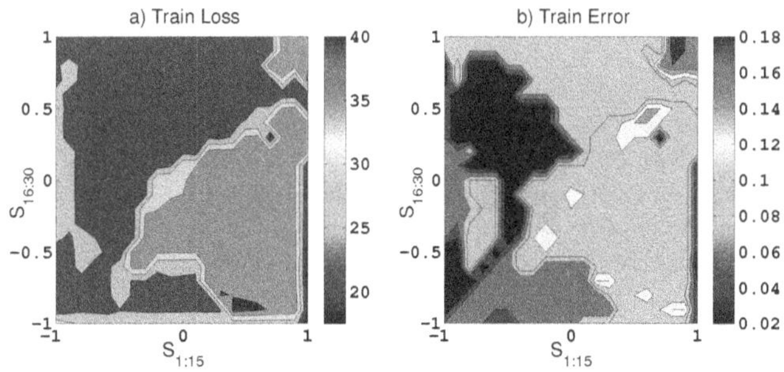

Figure 4: Sensitivity of Shapelet Initialization, Gun-Point dataset, Parameters: $L = 30$, $\eta = 0.01$, $\lambda_W = 0.01$, Iterations$= 3000$, $\alpha = -100$

In order to robustify the initialization guesses we use the K-Means centroids of all segments as initial values for the shapelets. Since centroids represent typical patterns of the data, they offer a good variety of shapes for initializing shapelets and help our method achieve high prediction accuracy. The initialization is conducted before Algorithm 1 starts, while W is also initialized randomly around 0.

3.11 Illustrating The Mechanism

An illustration of the learning algorithm is depicted in Figure 5. Two shapelets of length 40 are learned from the Gun-Point dataset. Sub-figure a) demonstrates the initialization values of the shapelets and the arrangement of the minimum values of the time series to shapelets. As can be seen, a linear hyper-plane W cannot easily separate the two classes. After 400 iterations of our method, the shapelets are updated as shown in sub-figure b). In addition, the shapelet transformed data representation M becomes almost linearly separable with few exceptions. Finally, the algorithm approaches convergence in sub-figure c) after 800 iterations. The linear hyper-plane W separates the shapelet-transformed instances of the binary dataset with just a single error (in red).

4. ANALYSIS OF OUR METHOD

4.1 Algorithmic Complexity

The baseline method which exhaustively tries candidates from series segments [17, 10] requires $\mathcal{O}(I^2Q^3)$ running time for discovering the best shapelet of a particular length Q. On the other hand, our method requires $\mathcal{O}(IQ^2 \times \text{maxIter})$, therefore our algorithm finds the best shapelet in a faster time, given that usually maxIter $<< IQ$.

4.2 Comparison to State of the Art

4.2.1 Learning Near-To-Optimal Shapelets

The optimal solution of Equation 4 gives the optimal shapelets, while a gradient descent approach can find a near-to-optimal minimum given an appropriate initialization.

The baseline approaches, on the other hand, provide no guarantee of optimal solutions for two primary reasons. First of all, the baselines are bound to shapelet candidates from the pool of series segments and cannot explore candidates which do not appear literally as segments. Secondly, minimizing the classification objective through candidate guesses has no guarantee of optimality, while a gradient-based optimization guarantees at least near-to-optimal minima.

4.2.2 Capturing Interactions Among Shapelets

The baselines find the score of each shapelet independently and then sort the individual quality of each shapelet, in order to select the top performers. However, such an approach does not take into account interactions among patterns. In other words, two shapelets can be individually sub-optimal, but when combined together they can improve the results. In fact, this problem is well known in data mining and referred to as variable subset selection [2].

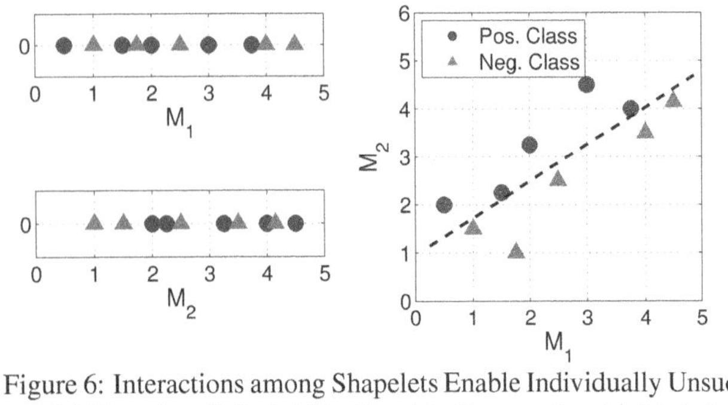

Figure 6: Interactions among Shapelets Enable Individually Unsuccessful Shapelets (left plots) to Excel in Cooperation (right plot)

For instance, Figure 6 demonstrates an example on how interactions among shapelets can become a game changing factor. On the left plots, we show the minimum distances of series to two shapelets. As can be observed, the individual discriminative quality of the shapelets is poor. On the other hand, a simple 2-dimensional interaction of exactly the **same** distances M_1, M_2 can yield drastically improved results, as shown on the right plot. When combined together, the distances to those shapelets can create a linearly separable discrimination, i.e. a perfect classification accuracy.

If the baseline's exhaustive discovery approach would attempt to select the **true** top-K interaction of shapelets out of $I(Q-L+1)$ candidates, then it will need to check the interaction of: $\binom{I(Q-L+1)}{K} = \frac{(I(Q-L+1))!}{K!(I(Q-L+1)-K)!}$ many combinations of candidates. For instance finding the **true** top 100 shapelets of length 30 from the Adiac dataset with $I = 390$ and $Q = 176$ requires checking 3.42×10^{317} combination trials using the baseline's approach. Clearly, the exhaustive search baseline cannot find **true** top-K shapelet interactions within a feasible time-frame. On the contrary, our method can find the interactions at a simple linear scale K, due to the property of jointly learning the shapelets and their interactions.

4.2.3 Weaker Aspects of Our Paper

Our method relies on more hyper-parameters than the baselines, such as the learning rate η, the number of iterations, the regularization parameter λ_W and the soft-min precision α. However, given the high prediction accuracy that will be demonstrated in Section 6, we argue that the very high accuracy by far out-weights the model's learning efforts.

The time needed for the baselines to compute the top-K shapelets is not significantly large with respect to the time needed to find a single shapelet. Such a behavior comes from the fact that the quality of each candidate is known and ready in the end of the discovery. On the other hand, our method needs K-many time units for K shapelets, w.r.t. learning one shapelet. However, such a disadvantage in time for large K is well spent in terms of accuracy, because our method can learn **true** top-K shapelet interactions and significantly improve the classification accuracy. Moreover, we believe that our method may yield to further improvements in efficiency by exploiting "early abandoning" and caching of partial results (as in [7]). For brevity we ignore such issues here and focus on forcefully demonstrating the improvements in accuracy.

5. LEARNING GENERAL SHAPELETS

The model presented in Section 3.3 can be generalized to multi-class labels and multi-size shapelets. Basically the model is extended to classify multi-class targets and capture interactions among shapelets of various sizes.

5.1 Decomposition of the Multi-Class Problem Into One-vs-all Subproblems

In order to learn from multi-class targets $Y \in \{1, \ldots, C\}^I$ with C categories, we will convert the problem into C-many one-vs-all sub-problems. Each sub-problem will discriminate one class against all the others. The one-vs-all binary targets $Y^b \in \{0,1\}^{I \times C}$ are defined in Equation 15.

$$Y^b_{i,c} = \begin{cases} 1 & Y_i = c \\ 0 & Y_i \neq c \end{cases}, \quad \forall i \in \{1, \ldots, N\}, \; \forall c \in \{1, \ldots, C\} \quad (15)$$

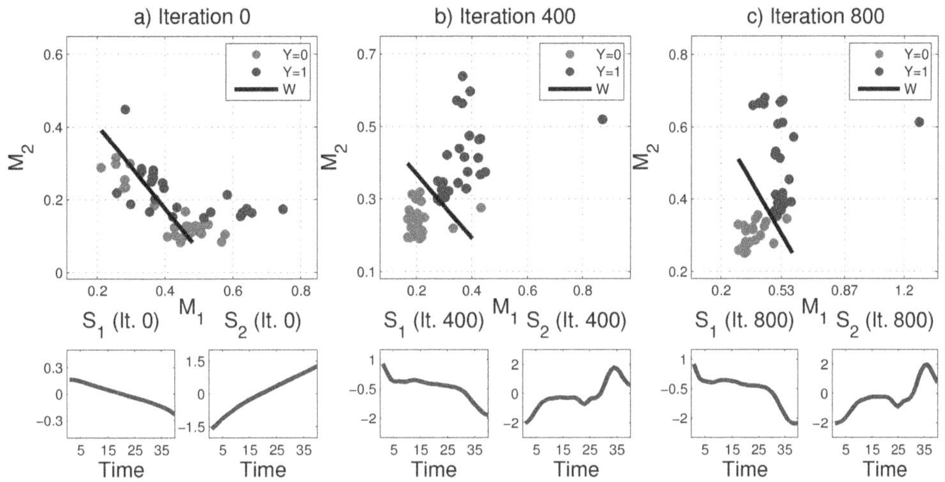

Figure 5: Learning Two Shapelets on the Gun-Point Dataset: Parameters $L = 40, \eta = 0.01, \lambda_W = 0.01, \alpha = -100$

In fact, the conversion to one-vs-all sub-problems will be useful for the operation of the logistic regression classifier. The output of the logistic regression for a binary problem can be perceived as a confidence probability. Therefore, the index of the most confident among the C-many classifiers is selected as the predicted categorical value of a test instance.

5.2 Interactions among Shapelets having Various Lengths

Capturing interactions among shapelets having various lengths is another aspect of the extended method. Our generalized model learns R different scales of shapelet lengths starting at a minimum L^{min} as $\{L^{\text{min}}, 2L^{\text{min}}, \dots, RL^{\text{min}}\}$. The shapelets therefore will be defined as $S \in \mathbb{R}^{R \times K \times *}$, where $S \in \bigcup_{r=1}^{R} \mathbb{R}^{K \times rL^{\text{min}}}$, and represent K-many shapelets for each scale R, i.e. totally KR shapelets. The length of a shapelet at scale $r \in \{1, \dots, R\}$ is $r \cdot L^{min}$. Consequently, the number of segments in a time series depends on the scale of the shapelet's length to be matched against and is $J(r) = Q - r \cdot L^{min} + 1$.

5.3 Generalized Objective Function

The objective function of the generalized model is presented in Equation 16, which is a regularized logistic regression loss between the true targets and the predicted ones shown in Equation 17. The notation $M_{r,i,k}$ identifies the minimum distance of the i-th series to the k-th shapelet of scale r, i.e. to $S_{r,k} \in \mathbb{R}^{r \cdot L^{min}}$. In addition, the weight $W_{c,r,k}$ identifies the class c classifier and the weight of the k-th shapelet at scale r.

$$\underset{S,W}{\text{argmin}} \ \mathcal{F} = \sum_{i=1}^{I} \sum_{c=1}^{C} \mathcal{L}(Y_{i,c}^b, \hat{Y}_{i,c}^b) + \lambda_W ||W||^2 \quad (16)$$

$$\hat{Y}_{i,c}^b = W_{c,0} + \sum_{r=1}^{R} \sum_{k=1}^{K} M_{r,i,k} W_{c,r,k} \quad (17)$$

5.4 Classification of Test Instances

Once the model is learned, a test instance indexed t is classified as the one-vs-all classifier which yields maximum confidence, as presented in Equation 18. The algorithmic complexity of classifying a test instance is $O(CRKJ(\cdot))$, but since C, R, K are asymptotically smaller values than $J(\cdot)$, the big-O notation complexity is $O(J(\cdot))$.

$$\hat{Y}_t \leftarrow \underset{c \in \{1,\dots,C\}}{\text{argmax}} \ \sigma\left(\hat{Y}_{t,c}^b\right), \quad \forall t \in \{1, \dots, I^{Test}\} \quad (18)$$

5.5 Generalized Soft-Minimum

The soft minimum function can be trivially generalized to include the notation for the scales r as shown in Equation 19. The distance between the k-th shapelet at scale r and the j-th segment of time series i is denoted as $D_{r,i,k,j}$ in Equation 20.

$$M_{r,i,k} \approx \hat{M}_{r,i,k} = \frac{\sum_{j=1}^{J(r)} D_{r,i,k,j} \, e^{\alpha D_{r,i,k,j}}}{\sum_{j'=1}^{J(r)} e^{\alpha D_{r,i,k,j'}}} \quad (19)$$

$$D_{r,i,k,j} = \frac{1}{r \cdot L^{\text{min}}} \sum_{l=1}^{r \cdot L^{\text{min}}} (T_{i,j+l-1} - S_{r,k,l})^2 \quad (20)$$

5.6 Gradients of Generalized Objective Function

The objective function can be split per each instance i and the loss of each one-vs-all classifier c and denoted in Equation 21 as $F_{i,c}$.

$$\mathcal{F}_{i,c} = \mathcal{L}(Y_{i,c}^b, \hat{Y}_{i,c}^b) + \frac{\lambda_W}{IC} \sum_{r=1}^{R} \sum_{k=1}^{K} W_{c,r,k}{}^2 \quad (21)$$

5.6.1 *Shapelet Gradients*

The derivative of the per-cell objective $F_{i,c}$ with respect to each shapelet $S_{r,k,l}$ is shown in Equation 22.

$$\frac{\partial \mathcal{F}_{i,c}}{\partial S_{r,k,l}} = -\left(Y_{i,c}^b - \sigma\left(\hat{Y}_{i,c}^b\right)\right) \frac{\partial \hat{M}_{r,i,k}}{\partial S_{r,k,l}} W_{c,r,k} \quad (22)$$

Moreover, the derivative of the minimum distances with respect to the generalized shapelets is defined in Equations 23-24.

$$\frac{\partial \hat{M}_{r,i,k}}{\partial D_{r,i,k,j}} = \frac{e^{\alpha D_{r,i,k,j}}\left(1+\alpha\left(D_{r,i,k,j}-\hat{M}_{r,i,k}\right)\right)}{\sum_{j'=1}^{J(r)} e^{\alpha D_{r,i,k,j'}}} \tag{23}$$

$$\frac{\partial D_{r,i,k,j}}{\partial S_{r,k,l}} = \frac{2\left(S_{r,k,l}-T_{i,j+l-1}\right)}{r\cdot L^{\min}} \tag{24}$$

5.6.2 *Classification Weights' Gradients*

The gradients of the per-cell objective with respect to the generalized weights and the bias terms are presented in Equations 25-26.

$$\frac{\partial \mathcal{F}_{i,c}}{\partial W_{c,r,k}} = -\left(Y^b_{i,c}-\sigma\left(\hat{Y}^b_{i,c}\right)\right)\hat{M}_{r,i,k} + \frac{\lambda_W W_{c,r,k}}{IC} \tag{25}$$

$$\frac{\partial \mathcal{F}_{i,c}}{\partial W_{c,0}} = -\left(Y^b_{i,c}-\sigma\left(\hat{Y}^b_{i,c}\right)\right) \tag{26}$$

5.6.3 *Optimized Learning Algorithm*

Algorithm 2 summarizes all the steps of the learning process. The first section of the procedure pre-computes terms which are used frequently in the gradients of the shapelets, such as ξ, D, ψ, ϑ. The pre-computations boost the learning time and avoid computing the same terms repeatedly. The second part of the algorithm updates the weights and the shapelets using the defined gradients and the precomputed terms.

Algorithm 2 Generalized Shapelets Learning

Require: Time series $T \in \mathbb{R}^{I\times Q}$, Binary labels $Y^b \in \mathbb{R}^{I\times C}$, Number of shapelets K, Learn Rate η, Regularization λ_W, Scales of shapelet lengths $R \in \mathbb{N}$, Minimum Shapelet Length $L^{\min}$, Number of Iterations: maxIter

Ensure: Shapelets $S \in \mathbb{R}^{R\times K\times *}$, Classification weights $W \in \mathbb{R}^{R\times C\times K}$, $W_0 \in \mathbb{R}^C$

Initialize S, W, W_0
for iteration=$\{1,\ldots,\text{maxIter}\}$ **do**
  for $i=\{1,\ldots,I\}$ **do**
    {Pre-compute Terms}
    for $r=\{1,\ldots,R\}$, $k=\{1,\ldots,K\}$ **do**
      for $j=\{1,\ldots,J(r)\}$ **do**
        $D_{r,i,k,j} := \frac{1}{r\cdot L^{\min}}\sum_{l=1}^{r\cdot L^{\min}}\left(T_{i,j+l-1}-S_{r,k,l}\right)^2$
        $\xi_{r,i,k,j} := e^{\alpha D_{r,i,k,j}}$
      end for
      $\psi_{r,i,k} := \sum_{j=1}^{J(r)}\xi_{r,i,k,j}$
      $\hat{M}_{r,i,k} := \frac{1}{\psi_{r,i,k}}\sum_{j=1}^{J(r)} D_{r,i,k,j}\,\xi_{r,i,k,j}$
    end for
    for $c=\{1,\ldots,C\}$ **do**
      $\sigma(\hat{Y}^b_{i,c}) := \left(1+e^{-\sum_{r=1}^{R}\sum_{k=1}^{K}\hat{M}_{r,i,k}W_{c,r,k}}\right)^{-1}$
      $\vartheta_{i,c} := Y^b_{i,c}-\sigma(\hat{Y}^b_{i,c})$
    end for
    {Learn Shapelets and Classification Weights}
    for $c=\{1,\ldots,C\}$ **do**
      for $r=\{1,\ldots,R\}$, $k=\{1,\ldots,K\}$ **do**
        $\mathbf{W}_{c,r,k} \mathrel{+}= \eta\left(\vartheta_{i,c}\hat{M}_{r,i,k}-\frac{2\lambda_W}{IC}\mathbf{W}_{c,r,k}\right)$
        for $j=\{1,\ldots,J(r)\}$ **do**
          $\phi_{r,i,k,j} := \frac{2\xi_{r,i,k,j}\left(1+\alpha\left(D_{r,i,k,j}-\hat{M}_{r,i,k}\right)\right)}{r\cdot L^{\min}\psi_{r,i,k}}$
          for $l=\{1,\ldots,r\cdot L^{\min}\}$ **do**
            $\mathbf{S}_{r,k,l} \mathrel{+}= \eta\,\vartheta_{i,c}\,\phi_{r,i,k,j}\times$
              $\left(\mathbf{S}_{r,k,l}-T_{i,j+l-1}\right)W_{c,r,k}$
          end for
        end for
      end for
      $\mathbf{W}_{c,0} \mathrel{+}= \eta\,\vartheta_{i,c}$
    end for
  end for
end for
return S, W, W_0

6. EXPERIMENTAL RESULTS

6.1 Setup And Reproducibility

6.1.1 *Datasets*

For the sake of equivalent comparison, we selected exactly the same set of datasets as the closest baselines [10, 8]. A large pool of 28 datasets consisting of time-series datasets having various numbers of instances, lengths and number of classes is selected and details are shown in Table 1. In order to ensure a fair comparison with the baselines, we used the default train and test data splits, **same** as the baselines [10, 8]. The datasets are available through the UCR[1] and UEA[2] websites.

6.1.2 *Reproducibility and Hyper-parameter Search*

Our method (hereafter denoted as LTS, for **L**earning **T**ime-Series **S**hapelets) requires the tuning of a series of hyper-parameters, which were found through a grid search approach using cross-validation over the training data. The number of shapelets was searched in a range of $K \in \{0.05, 0.15, 0.3\}$, which is a fraction of the series length, e.g. $K=0.3$ means 30% of Q. Similarly, $L^{\min} \in \{0.025, 0.075, 0.125, 0.175, 0.2\} \times 100\%$ of Q, while three scales of shapelet lengths were searched from $R \in \{1,2,3\}$. The regularization parameter was one of $\lambda_W \in \{0.01, 0.1, 1\}$. The learning rate was kept fixed at a small value of $\eta = 0.01$, while the number of iterations is selected from maxIter$\in \{2000, 5000, 10000\}$. All our method' parameters for all datasets are shown in Table 1. **The authors are devoted to promote reproducibility, therefore the source code, datasets and instructions are made publicly available**[3].

[1] http://www.cs.ucr.edu/~eamonn/time_series_data/

[2] http://www.uea.ac.uk/computing/machine-learning/shapelets/shapelet-data

[3] http://fs.ismll.de/publicspace/LearningShapelets/

6.1.3 *Baselines*

Thirteen different baselines were compared against, which are grouped into the following four clusters.

- **Shapelet Tree Methods**, constructed from shapelets whose qualities are measured using: *i)* Information gain quality criterion (IG) [17, 11], *ii)* Kruskall-Wallis quality criterion (KW) [8], *iii)* F-Stats quality criterion (FST) [10] and *iv)* the Mood's Median Criterion (MM) [8].

- **Basic Classifiers** [10], learned over shapelet-transformed data, such as: Nearest Neighbors (1NN), Naive Bayes (NB) and C4.5 tree (C4.5).

- **More Complex Classifiers** [8], learned over shapelet transformed data, such as: Bayesian Networks (BN), Random

Table 1: Dataset Information, Parameter Search Results and Running Time for The Best Shapelet [8]

Dataset Information				**Parameter Values (LTS)**					**Run-Time (Best Shap.)**	
Dataset	Train/Test	Length	Cls.	K	$L^{\min}$	R	λ_W	maxIter	F-Stat (Sec)	LTS (Sec)
Adiac	390/391	176	37	0.3	0.2	3	0.01	10000	4509.91	3017.23
Beef	30/30	470	5	0.15	0.125	3	0.01	10000	1251.21	293.68
Beetle/Fly	20/20	512	2	0.15	0.125	1	0.01	5000	21496.51	131.015
Bird/Chicken	20/20	512	2	0.3	0.075	1	0.1	10000	20465.63	81.405
Chlorine.	467/3840	166	3	0.3	0.2	3	0.01	10000	15681.39	558.51
Coffee	28/28	286	2	0.05	0.075	2	0.01	5000	258.15	90.96
Diatom.	16/306	345	4	0.3	0.175	2	0.01	10000	53.91	173.1
DP_Little	400/645	250	3	0.15	0.175	1	1	5000	78005.7	1525.595
DP_Middle	400/645	250	3	0.3	0.025	3	1	10000	91208.52	910.33
DP_Thumb	400/645	250	3	0.05	0.175	3	0.1	5000	123766.49	963.765
ECGFiveDays	23/861	136	2	0.05	0.125	2	0.01	5000	149.1	29.365
FaceFour	24/88	350	4	0.3	0.175	3	1	5000	4556.41	386.45
GunPoint	50/150	150	2	0.15	0.2	3	0.1	10000	569.42	46.69
ItalyPower.	67/1029	24	2	0.3	0.2	3	0.01	5000	1.75	10.285
Lighting7	70/73	319	7	0.05	0.075	3	1	5000	14912.74	394.44
MedicalImages	381/760	99	10	0.3	0.2	2	1	10000	7742.97	406.725
MoteStrain	20/1252	84	2	0.3	0.2	3	1	10000	10.76	16.875
MP_Little	400/645	250	3	0.3	0.2	3	0.01	5000	88071.5	965.27
MP_Middle	400/645	250	3	0.05	0.2	2	0.01	5000	134731.54	940.555
Otoliths	64/64	512	2	0.15	0.125	3	0.01	2000	55874.19	407.835
PP_Little	400/645	250	3	0.15	0.125	3	1	10000	79993.31	890.925
PP_Middle	400/645	250	3	0.15	0.175	2	0.01	10000	57815.02	1574.805
PP_Thumb	400/645	250	3	0.3	0.175	2	0.1	10000	91401.49	1449.36
SonyAIBO.	20/601	70	2	0.3	0.125	2	0.01	10000	6.73	11.415
Symbols	25/995	398	6	0.05	0.175	1	0.1	5000	8901.28	308.99
SyntheticControl	300/300	60	6	0.15	0.125	3	0.01	5000	984.36	219.97
Trace	100/100	275	4	0.15	0.125	2	0.1	10000	54128.53	275.375
TwoLeadECG	23/1139	82	2	0.3	0.075	1	0.1	10000	3.12	15.415

Forest (RAF), Rotation Forest (ROF) and Support Vector Machines (SVM).

- **Other Related Methods:** The Fast Shapelets (FSH) [12] exploits a fast random projection technique on the SAX representation, while the **Dynamic Time Warping** (DTW) classifier on the raw time-series data is also selected due to its reputation as a strong similarity metric [4].

6.2 Very High Prediction Accuracy

We compared our method of learning shapelets (denoted as LTS) against the selected baselines in terms of classification accuracy ratio (fraction of correct classifications) as shown in Table 2. The best method per dataset is highlighted in **bold**.

Our method LTS has a very large superiority in terms of Absolute Wins (17.28 absolute wins in 28 datasets against 13 baselines) and 1-to-1 wins, as indicated by the respected rows in the end of the table. Each dataset awards one point, which is split into fractions in case of draws. In addition, we compared the ranks of the classifiers and found out that LTS has a significantly better rank of 1.946 ± 0.536 against the closest baseline's (SVM) rank 4.554 ± 1.180. In order to bullet-proof our claim, we ran the well-known Wilcoxon signed ranks test [3] against all baselines and found out that all results are statistically significant at $p < 0.05$, as can be deduced by the p-values of the most bottom row.

6.3 Competitive Running Time

Since the idea of this paper is entirely novel, our first priority is to evaluate its prediction accuracy rather than elaborating on speed-up techniques, as in the fast shapelets approach [12]. Nevertheless, we would like to show that our method is indeed feasible and competitive in terms of running time and faster than the exhaustive candidate search approach [10, 8]. We compared the time needed to find the best shapelet of each dataset against the F-Stat metric, which is the fastest quality metric [10, 8]. The best shapelet run-time comparison is advocated by our baseline [8], in order to ensure that methods can process the same number of candidates. As can be seen from Table 1, our method can learn the shapelet within a faster time (57 times faster in average) compared to the baseline, which is an indication that our method is practically feasible in terms of running time. Each execution of our method searched over five different shapelet sizes $\{0.025, 0.075, 0.125, 0.175, 0.2\} \times Q$ and the other parameters were set to $\eta = 0.01$, maxIter= 3000 and $\lambda_W = 0.001$.

7. CONCLUSION

In this study we introduced a novel perspective into learning time-series shapelets. In contrast to related work which searches for top shapelets from a pool of candidates, we propose a novel mathematical formulation of the task via a classification objective function. In addition, we introduced a learning algorithm which *learns* near-to-optimal shapelets by exploring shapelet interactions. An extensive experimentation on 28 time-series datasets and 13 base-

Table 2: Accuracy Ratios involving 28 Time Series Datasets and 13 Baselines

#	Dataset	IG	KW	FST	MM	DTW	C4.5	1NN	NB	BN	RAF	ROF	SVM	FSH	LTS
1	Adiac	0.299	0.266	0.156	0.271	0.491	0.243	0.253	0.281	0.251	0.304	0.307	0.238	**0.558**	0.542
2	Beef	0.500	0.333	0.567	0.300	0.433	0.600	0.833	0.733	**0.900**	0.600	0.700	0.867	0.517	0.800
3	Beetle/Fly	0.775	0.700	0.900	0.800	0.650	0.750	**1.000**	0.925	0.975	0.900	0.950	0.975	0.742	0.950
4	Bird/Chicken	0.850	0.875	0.900	0.875	0.725	0.900	0.975	0.875	0.950	0.950	0.925	0.950	0.843	**1.000**
5	ChlorineConcentration	0.588	0.520	0.535	0.521	0.634	0.565	0.569	0.460	0.571	0.576	0.635	0.562	0.578	**0.743**
6	Coffee	0.964	0.857	**1.000**	0.857	0.464	0.857	**1.000**	0.929	0.964	**1.000**	0.893	**1.000**	0.925	**1.000**
7	DiatomSizeReduction	0.722	0.621	0.765	0.448	0.925	0.752	0.935	0.788	0.902	0.804	0.830	0.922	0.869	**0.951**
8	DP_Little	0.654	0.680	0.603	0.710	0.493	0.659	0.728	0.735	0.729	0.730	0.747	**0.752**	0.566	0.727
9	DP_Middle	0.705	0.693	0.619	0.737	0.546	0.712	0.737	0.740	0.747	0.755	0.768	**0.796**	0.581	0.758
10	DP_Thumb	0.581	0.720	0.560	0.703	0.530	0.580	0.607	0.630	0.639	0.641	0.671	0.698	0.580	**0.740**
11	ECGFiveDays	0.775	0.872	0.990	0.928	0.828	0.962	0.984	0.964	0.995	0.933	0.986	0.990	0.996	**1.000**
12	FaceFour	0.841	0.443	0.750	0.409	0.830	0.761	**1.000**	0.977	**1.000**	0.875	0.989	0.977	0.909	**1.000**
13	GunPoint	0.893	0.940	0.953	0.920	0.913	0.907	0.980	0.920	0.993	0.960	0.987	**1.000**	0.932	**1.000**
14	ItalyPowerDemand	0.892	0.910	0.931	0.911	0.961	0.910	0.921	0.925	0.924	0.930	0.920	0.921	0.921	**0.962**
15	Lighting7	0.493	0.480	0.411	0.274	0.726	0.534	0.493	0.575	0.658	0.644	0.658	0.699	0.601	**0.877**
16	MedicalImages	0.488	0.471	0.508	0.490	0.690	0.449	0.457	0.174	0.282	0.508	0.515	0.525	0.608	**0.734**
17	MoteStrain	0.825	0.840	0.840	0.840	0.816	0.844	0.903	0.888	0.891	0.846	0.870	0.887	0.785	**0.913**
18	MP_Little	0.664	0.697	0.578	0.703	0.558	0.634	0.685	0.688	0.695	0.714	0.752	0.750	0.565	**0.758**
19	MP_Middle	0.710	0.750	0.609	0.720	0.470	0.733	0.709	0.720	0.711	0.752	0.747	0.769	0.605	**0.780**
20	Otoliths	0.672	0.609	0.578	0.547	0.594	0.656	0.719	0.688	0.641	0.656	0.594	0.641	0.560	**0.766**
21	PP_Little	0.596	0.720	0.586	0.673	0.495	0.574	0.672	0.692	0.701	0.666	0.698	**0.721**	0.549	0.710
22	PP_Middle	0.614	0.683	0.581	0.697	0.499	0.625	0.685	0.698	0.714	0.705	0.754	0.759	0.580	**0.767**
23	PP_Thumb	0.608	0.713	0.591	0.730	0.526	0.595	0.677	0.694	0.695	0.678	0.728	**0.755**	0.536	0.715
24	SonyAIBORobotSurface	0.845	0.727	**0.953**	0.749	0.699	0.845	0.840	0.790	0.897	0.852	0.890	0.867	0.698	0.952
25	Symbols	0.780	0.557	0.801	0.574	0.934	0.471	0.856	0.780	0.923	0.846	0.844	0.846	0.930	**0.959**
26	SyntheticControl	0.943	0.900	0.957	0.857	0.973	0.903	0.930	0.780	0.767	0.890	0.920	0.873	0.917	**1.000**
27	Trace	0.980	0.940	0.980	**1.000**	0.990	0.980	0.980	0.980	**1.000**	0.980	0.980	0.980	**1.000**	**1.000**
28	TwoLeadECG	0.851	0.764	0.970	0.853	0.795	0.853	0.995	0.991	0.988	0.961	0.980	0.993	0.922	**1.000**
Absolute Wins		**0.00**	**0.00**	**1.20**	**0.25**	**0.00**	**0.00**	**1.53**	**0.00**	**1.58**	**0.20**	**0.00**	**4.70**	**1.25**	**17.28**
LTS 1-to-1 Wins		**28**	**27**	**26**	**26**	**28**	**28**	**23**	**27**	**23**	**26**	**24**	**20**	**26**	-
LTS 1-to-1 Draws		**0**	**0**	**1**	**1**	**0**	**0**	**2**	**0**	**2**	**1**	**1**	**2**	**1**	-
LTS 1-to-1 Losses		**0**	**1**	**1**	**1**	**0**	**0**	**3**	**1**	**3**	**1**	**3**	**6**	**1**	-
Rank Mean		**9.768**	**9.982**	**9.107**	**9.500**	**9.804**	**10.036**	**6.196**	**7.714**	**5.518**	**6.321**	**5.357**	**4.554**	**9.196**	**1.946**
Rank Confidence Interval		**1.016**	**1.259**	**1.318**	**1.273**	**1.867**	**0.781**	**1.195**	**1.091**	**1.150**	**0.743**	**0.898**	**1.180**	**1.519**	**0.536**
Rank Standard Deviation		**2.743**	**3.398**	**3.559**	**3.436**	**5.040**	**2.108**	**3.228**	**2.944**	**3.104**	**2.005**	**2.423**	**3.186**	**4.102**	**1.448**
Wilcoxon Test p-values		**0.000**	**0.000**	**0.000**	**0.000**	**0.000**	**0.000**	**0.000**	**0.000**	**0.000**	**0.000**	**0.000**	**0.003**	**0.000**	-

lines is conducted. Our method outperforms all the baselines with statistically significant margins in terms of both wins and ranks.

8. ACKNOWLEDGMENT

This study was partially co-funded by the Seventh Framework Programme (FP7) of the European Commission, through project REDUCTION[4] (#288254).

9. REFERENCES

[1] K.-W. Chang, B. Deka, W. mei W. Hwu, and D. Roth. Efficient pattern-based time series classification on gpu. In M. J. Zaki, A. Siebes, J. X. Yu, B. Goethals, G. I. Webb, and X. Wu, editors, *ICDM*, pages 131–140. IEEE Computer Society, 2012.

[2] A. Das and D. Kempe. Algorithms for subset selection in linear regression. In *Proceedings of the 40th Annual ACM Symposium on Theory of Computing*, STOC '08, pages 45–54, New York, NY, USA, 2008. ACM.

[3] J. Demšar. Statistical comparisons of classifiers over multiple data sets. *J. Mach. Learn. Res.*, 7:1–30, Dec. 2006.

[4] H. Ding, G. Trajcevski, P. Scheuermann, X. Wang, and E. J. Keogh. Querying and mining of time series data: experimental comparison of representations and distance measures. *PVLDB*, 1(2):1542–1552, 2008.

[5] B. Hartmann and N. Link. Gesture recognition with inertial sensors and optimized dtw prototypes. In *IEEE International Conference on Systems Man and Cybernetics*, 2010.

[6] B. Hartmann, I. Schwab, and N. Link. Prototype optimization for temporarily and spatially distorted time series. In *the AAAI Spring Symposia*, 2010.

[7] Q. He, F. Zhuang, T. Shang, Z. Shi, et al. Fast time series classification based on infrequent shapelets. In *11th IEEE International Conference on Machine Learning and Applications*, 2012.

[8] J. Hills, J. Lines, E. Baranauskas, J. Mapp, and A. Bagnall. Classification of time series by shapelet transformation. *Data Mining and Knowledge Discovery*, 2013.

[9] J. Lines and A. Bagnall. Alternative quality measures for time series shapelets. In *Intelligent Data Engineering and Automated Learning*, volume 7435 of *Lecture Notes in Computer Science*, pages 475–483. 2012.

[10] J. Lines, L. Davis, J. Hills, and A. Bagnall. A shapelet transform for time series classification. In *Proceedings of the 18th ACM SIGKDD International Conference on Knowledge Discovery and Data Mining*, 2012.

[11] A. Mueen, E. Keogh, and N. Young. Logical-shapelets: an expressive primitive for time series classification. In *Proceedings of the 17th ACM SIGKDD International Conference on Knowledge Discovery and Data Mining*, 2011.

[12] T. Rakthanmanon and E. Keogh. Fast shapelets: A scalable algorithm for discovering time series shapelets. *Proceedings of the 13th SIAM International Conference on Data Mining*, 2013.

[13] P. Sivakumar and T. Shajina. Human gait recognition and classification using time series shapelets. In *IEEE International Conference on Advances in Computing and Communications*, 2012.

[14] E. W. Wild. *Optimization-based Machine Learning and Data Mining*. ProQuest, 2008.

[15] Z. Xing, J. Pei, and P. Yu. Early classification on time series. *Knowledge and information systems*, 31(1):105–127, 2012.

[16] Z. Xing, J. Pei, P. Yu, and K. Wang. Extracting interpretable features for early classification on time series. *Proceedings of the 11th SIAM International Conference on Data Mining*, 2011.

[17] L. Ye and E. Keogh. Time series shapelets: a new primitive for data mining. In *Proceedings of the 15th ACM SIGKDD International Conference on Knowledge Discovery and Data Mining*, 2009.

[18] L. Ye and E. Keogh. Time series shapelets: a novel technique that allows accurate, interpretable and fast classification. *Data Mining and Knowledge Discovery*, 22(1):149–182, 2011.

[19] J. Zakaria, A. Mueen, and E. Keogh. Clustering time series using unsupervised-shapelets. In *Proceedings of the 12th IEEE International Conference on Data Mining*, 2012.

[4] `www.reduction-project.eu`

Utilizing Temporal Patterns for Estimating Uncertainty in Interpretable Early Decision Making

Mohamed F. Ghalwash*
Temple University
Philadelphia, PA
mohamed@temple.edu

Vladan Radosavljevic†
Yahoo Labs
Sunnyvale, CA
vladan@yahoo-inc.com

Zoran Obradovic
Temple University
Philadelphia, PA
zoran.obradovic@temple.edu

ABSTRACT

Early classification of time series is prevalent in many time-sensitive applications such as, but not limited to, early warning of disease outcome and early warning of crisis in stock market. For example, early diagnosis allows physicians to design appropriate therapeutic strategies at early stages of diseases. However, practical adaptation of early classification of time series requires an easy to understand explanation (interpretability) and a measure of confidence of the prediction results (uncertainty estimates). These two aspects were not jointly addressed in previous time series early classification studies, such that a difficult choice of selecting one of these aspects is required. In this study, we propose a simple and yet effective method to provide uncertainty estimates for an interpretable early classification method. The question we address here is "*how to provide estimates of uncertainty in regard to interpretable early prediction.*" In our extensive evaluation on twenty time series datasets we showed that the proposed method has several advantages over the state-of-the-art method that provides reliability estimates in early classification. Namely, the proposed method is more *effective* than the state-of-the-art method, is *simple* to implement, and provides *interpretable* results.

Categories and Subject Descriptors

H.2.8 [**Database Management**]: Database Applications—*Data mining*; I.5.2 [**Pattern Recognition**]: Design Methodology—*Classifier design and evaluation*

Keywords

Interpretability, earliness, uncertainty, time series, reliability

1. INTRODUCTION

Time series early classification models aim to predict the label of the entire time series by observing the phenomenon for very short time and as soon as enough data is available. If the available data is insufficient to make an accurate classification, more data, which might be expensive, is required.

The framework of time series early classification is illustrated in Figure 1. The model looks into a portion of l observations of the time series T of length L (where $l < L$) and determines the label of the entire time series without observing the rest of the time series. If the method can not classify the time series at time l, the observation segment is enlarged and the process is repeated with the aim of predicting the class label of the entire time series.

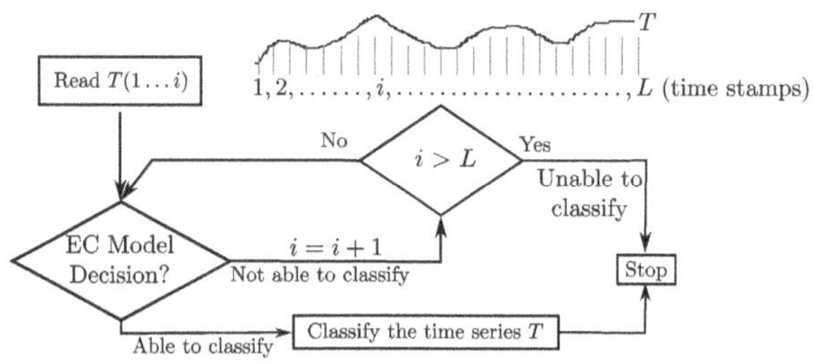

Figure 1: Framework of Early Classification (EC) of time series.

Early classification of time series is important in many applications. For example, early diagnosis could save patients' lives by allowing administration of treatment before the diseases are fully manifested [6, 3]. In such applications it is highly desirable to have easily interpretable results, as physicians aim to understand why a prediction is made. Moreover, in order to decide whether the available data is sufficient for the model to make an accurate prediction, uncertainty estimates of the predictions would be provided by the model. For example, in medical applications, providing uncertainty estimates would assist physicians in optimizing therapy. We illustrate the importance of providing uncertainty estimates using the following example.

Example 1. Time series from the red and blue classes from a medical dataset (ECG dataset) are shown in Figure 2a. The time series are very similar to each other such that it is hard to distinguish between the classes using human eyes. Using only the principle of early classification without the notion of uncertainty, the blue time series in Figure 2b could be incorrectly classified as the red class at time point 12 (this is done using the interpretable early classification method described later in Section 2). Since the method does not provide uncertainty estimates, there is no clue indicating how accurate the classification is. However, if the method provides high uncertainty estimates with that classification decision, then additional data would be required in order to provide a more confident decision.

*Ain Shams University, Cairo, Egypt.
†This study was conducted while the author was a postdoctoral associate at Prof. Obradovic's laboratory at Temple University.

KDD'14, August 24-27, 2014, New York, New York, USA.

ACM 978-1-4503-2956-9/14/08 ...$15.00.
http://dx.doi.org/10.1145/2623330.2623694.

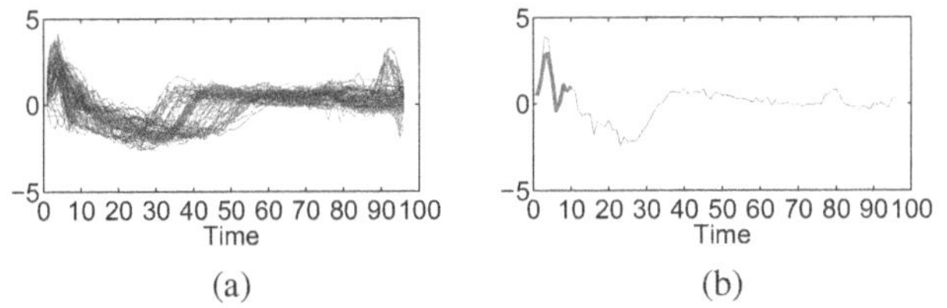

Figure 2: (a) Time series from the blue and red classes. (b) A blue time series is early incorrectly classified as a member of the red class. Additional time and data is needed to provide a more confident decision.

Table 1: Three properties are used to categorize time series classification methods: interpretability (I), earliness (E), and uncertainty estimate (U).

	LDS/SVM [1]	HMM [10]	Shapelet [16]	ECTS [14]	EDSC [15]	PR [12]	QDA [11]
I	X	X	✓	X	✓	X	X
E	X	X	X	✓	✓	✓	✓
U	X	X	X	X	X	✓	✓

Therefore, the early classification method is needed to provide uncertainty estimates with the classification decision such that confident results are obtained as early as possible. Although earliness, interpretability, and uncertainty estimates are highly desirable properties in many time series classification applications, to the best of our knowledge, existing methods are limited to addressing at most two of these aspects. Table 1 summarizes properties of several methods (discussed later in Section 2) that successfully addressed some of these aspects. There is not yet a time series classification method that simultaneously provides these three aspects.

In this study, we propose a *simple but effective* method that satisfies all three properties. This is achieved by extending a recently proposed interpretable early classification method, called early distinctive shapelet classification (EDSC), to estimate the temporal uncertainty associated with the prediction.

In Section 2, existing methods for time series classification that address some of the three aspects shown in Table 1 are reviewed. The EDSC method is summarized in Section 3 followed by a description of our proposed temporal uncertainty estimation method provided in Section 4. Extensive evaluation results on benchmark datasets (twenty time series datasets) are presented in Section 5. Finally, the conclusions and future work is given in Section 6.

2. RELATED WORK

In this section we discuss the existing time series classification methods that address some aspects of earliness, interpretability, and uncertainty estimates.

2.1 Adapting time series classification methods for early classification

Several time series classification methods are *adapted* for early classification by applying the method at each time point. Such methods are inflexible, as for methods trained on time series of length t, the prediction is always done at the tth time point, which limits the applicability of the model, e.g. in medical applications, patients may develop diseases at different times, which this type of methods can not handle appropriately.

Examples of methods in this category are [1] and [10]. In [1] a linear dynamical system and support vector machines are used to model time series for gene expression while in [10], a method that utilizes hidden Markov models with less states than the time points is proposed. These methods are evaluated at each time point and the best results were obtained when using the entire time series. These results provide evidence that there is a need for methods designed specifically for early classification.

Shapelets, which are subsequences of time series, have been used as features representing the characteristics of time series [16]. A perfect shapelet of a class is the one representing all time series in that class but not covering any time series in other classes. These shapelets are used for interpretable time series classification where they are able to handle challenges such as drifts and changes, which often occur in medical domain [8] and which are usually addressed by boosting algorithms [5]. Although the shapelet method provides interpretability, it provides neither uncertainty estimate nor early classification.

2.2 Early classification

The problem of early classification of time series is formulated recently [13, 14]. A novel concept of minimum prediction length is introduced in the early classification of time series (ECTS) method [13, 14]. ECTS makes early predictions and retains accuracy comparable with that of the 1-nearest neighbor classifier using the entire time series. However, ECTS does not extract patterns from the training data; thus, users may not be able to gain insights from the classification results.

The drawback of ECTS has been resolved in a method called early distinctive shapelet classification (EDSC) [15]. The EDSC method extracts local shapelets which distinctly manifest the target class locally, and are effective for early classification. However, the EDSC method does not provide uncertainty estimates.

2.3 Early classification with uncertainty estimate

A method is proposed to represent the patient risk (PR) as a time series and estimates the uncertainty as the distance between the evolving approximate daily risk of a patient and the hyperplane learned by SVM [12]. The PR model requires labels for each time point in the time series, not just a label for the entire time series, and therefore can not be compared to our method. The state-of-the-art method for early classification of signals using a quadratic discriminant analysis (QDA) classifier was developed recently [11]. QDA provides a reliability bound on the classifier's decision for every time point. The disadvantage of these methods is that they are not interpretable and can be used only as "black box" classifiers.

3. BACKGROUND: EDSC

In this section we briefly describe the early distinctive shapelet classification (EDSC) method for interpretable early classification and the details of EDSC are described in the subsequent subsections [1]. EDSC extracts discriminative shapelets for early classification. In this approach shapelets, which are subsequences of time series and thus are highly interpretable, have been used as features representing the characteristics of the time series [16].

Example 2. Suppose we have a dataset of time series for 3 unhealthy subjects (red) and 3 healthy subjects (blue) as illustrated in Figure 3. The extracted shapelet is the time series segment that represents the characteristics of the class (drawn as solid lines).

Given a time series dataset D where each time series is associated with a label, the task is to classify the time series as early as possible. The EDSC method addresses this problem in 4 steps:

[1] For more details about EDSC, the reader is referred to [15]

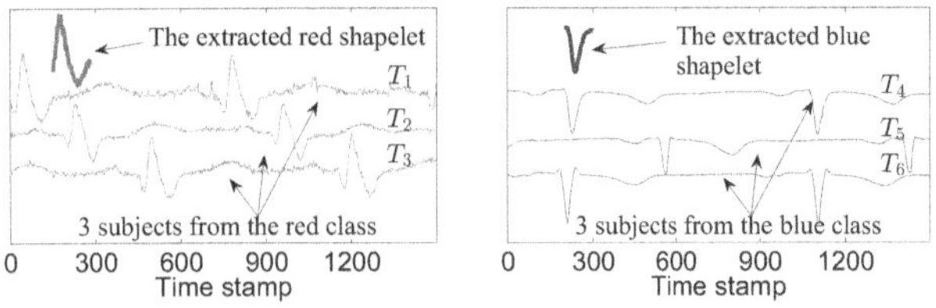

Figure 3: Three subjects from the red (blue) class are shown in the left (right) panel, respectively. The discriminative shapelet is represented as solid line. Clearly, the shapelet represents the characteristics of its class.

1. extracts all shapelets of different lengths, where for each shapelet a distance threshold is learned such that the shapelet discriminates between classes,

2. ranks the shapelets using a utility function that incorporates earliness and accuracy of the shapelet,

3. prunes the shapelets by selecting the top shapelets that cover the entire dataset,

4. classifies unknown time series based on the closest matching shapelet.

3.1 Extracting all shapelets

The shapelet is defined as $S = (s, l, \delta, c)$ where s is a time series subsequence of length l, c is the class label of the shapelet which is called the target class. The other classes ($\overline{c}$) are called the non-target classes. δ is a distance threshold which needs to be learned. To compute the distance threshold, we compute the distances between the subsequence s and all time series in the dataset.

To compute the distance between a subsequence s of length l and a time series T of length L (where $l < L$), we slide a window of length l over the time series T to extract all subsequences $\{h_1, h_2, \ldots h_{L-l+1}\}$ of length l (Figure 4a). Then, the distance is computed as

$$dist(s,T) = \min_{\forall i \in \{1,2,\ldots,L-l+1\}} dist(s, h_i). \quad (1)$$

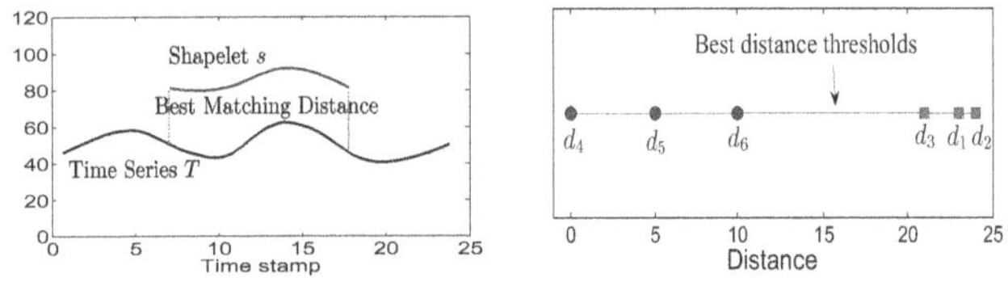

(a) (b)

Figure 4: (a) Best matching distance $dist(s, T)$ between the shapelet s and the time series T. (b) The distance between the shapelet and each blue/red time series is represented as a blue/red point on the order line, respectively. The distance threshold δ is computed such that the shapelet discriminates between the classes.

The distance between the shapelet S and each time series is represented as a point on the order line (Figure 4b). Then, the distance threshold δ is computed such that the shapelet discriminates between the classes[2].

Then, the EDSC method iterates over all time series in D to extract all subsequences of length l, where l is the length of the potential shapelets. The EDSC method varies l between $minL$ and $maxL$ which are user parameters.

[2]The details of the distance threshold computation are explained in [15].

3.2 Ranking the shapelets

The EDSC method extracts all possible shapelets and computes the distance threshold for each shapelet. The number of the extracted shapelets from the dataset is large. Therefore, to find the discriminative shapelets, EDSC assigns a score to each shapelet that incorporates both the earliness and the accuracy.

The earliness defines how early, on average, the shapelet matches the target time series (*the shapelet S **matches** the time series T if $dist(s,T) \leq \delta$*). Technically, the earliness between the shapelet $S = (s, l, \delta, c)$ and the time series T of length L is defined as

$$EML(S,T) = \min_{\forall i \in \{1,2,\ldots,L-l+1\}} dist(s, h_i) \leq \delta, \quad (2)$$

where h_i are all subsequences of the time series T of length l. Then, using the earliness, the weighted recall of the shapelet is computed as

$$WRecall(S) = \frac{1}{\|T_{\overline{c}}\|} \sum_{T \in D} \frac{1}{\sqrt[\alpha]{EML(S,T)}}, \quad (3)$$

where α is a user defined parameter that determines the importance of the earliness, and $\|T_{\overline{c}}\|$ is the number of non-target time series. Finally, the utility score of the shapelet is defined as

$$Utility(S) = \frac{2 \times Precision(S) \times WRecall(s)}{Precision(S) + WRecall(S)}, \quad (4)$$

where $Precision$ is the fraction of the matched time series that are relevant (target time series) and is computed as

$$Precision(S) = \frac{\|\{d_i \leq \delta \bigwedge Class(T_i) = c\}\|}{\|\{d_i \leq \delta\}\|}, \quad (5)$$

where $d_i = dist(s, T_i)$ and $Class(T_i)$ is the class of the ith time series T_i.

3.3 Pruning the shapelets

The EDSC method sorts the shapelets descending based on their utility scores (Equation 4). It starts with the highest ranked shapelet and removes all time series from the dataset that are covered by the shapelet. The shapelet $S = (s, l, \delta, c)$ ***covers*** the time series T if the shapelet matches the time series ($dist(s,T) \leq \delta$) and has the same class as the shapelet. Then, EDSC stores the shapelets and the next highest shapelet is considered. If the shapelet covers any of the remaining time series, the shapelet will be added to the list and all covered time series will be removed. The method iteratively does so until all time series in the dataset are covered. In this manner, the EDSC method ends up with a small list of shapelets that is used in the classification phase.

3.4 Classification phase

The EDSC method initially reads a portion of length $minL$ from the test time series (where $minL$ is the length of the shortest extracted shapelet). The highest-ranked shapelet is considered. If the shapelet matches the current segment of the time series then the time series is classified as the class of the shapelet and the prediction is made. Otherwise, the next shapelet from the ranked list is considered and the process of checking each shapelet is repeated. If none of the shapelets match the current portion of the test time series then the method reads one more time stamp and continues classifying the time series (Figure 1). If the method reaches the end of the time series and none of the shapelets match it, then EDSC marks the time series as a not-classified example.

4. THE PROPOSED METHOD FOR UNCERTAINTY ESTIMATION

4.1 Motivating example

We start by proposing a method to provide an uncertainty estimate to the interpretable EDSC method. Assume that we have a shapelet $S = (s, l, \delta, c)$ and a time series T. If the distance $dist(s, T)$ between T and S is less than or equal to δ, then T is classified as class c. In this scenario, we did not measure how confident the classification is.

Imagine that the shapelet S is represented as a point as in Figure 5a. The radius of the black colored circle around the shapelet represents the shapelet's distance threshold δ. Assume that we have two time series T_1 and T_2. If the distance between S and each time series T_1 and T_2 is less than δ then T_1 and T_2 are represented as points inside the circle and both are then classified as the shapelet's class. However, the distance between T_1 and S is less than the distance between T_2 and S which reflects the fact that the shapelet is more certain about the classification of T_1 than the classification of T_2.

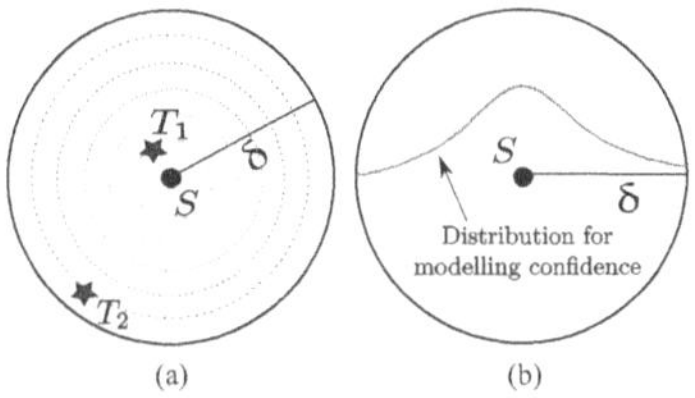

Figure 5: (a) The shapelet is represented as a point and the radius of the circle around S represents the shapelet's distance threshold δ. T_1 and T_2 are two time series that are less than δ-distant apart from the shapelet. (b) The confidence of the shapelet: the shapelet is more certain about closer time series than time series that are δ-distant apart.

In Figure 5a, different red dotted circles represent different levels of confidence. Intuitively, the shapelet is more certain about the time series in the most inner red circle than the time series in the bigger red circles. Therefore, the uncertainty reaches the highest level when the time series lies on the boundary of the black circle.

4.2 Uncertainty estimation

Instead of modeling the uncertainty directly, we model the confidence $C(c)$ of classifying a time series as class c. The uncertainty $U(c)$ of classifying a time series as class c can be computed as

$$U(c) = 1 - C(c). \tag{6}$$

4.2.1 Confidence of a single shapelet

We assume that we have a shapelet $S = (s, l, \delta, c)$ and a time series T. We also assume that the distance $dist(s, T)$ between T and S is less than or equal to δ, so we say that S matches T and then T is classified as class c.

Due to imperfections in sensors architecture, observed time series are often affected by measurement noise. Therefore, distance between time series T and shapelet S contains uncertainty in itself. To account for uncertainty in measurements, we define distance between T and S as a random variable d

$$d = dist(s, T) + \epsilon, \tag{7}$$

where ϵ is some random variable with mean equal to 0 and standard deviation equal to σ.

Knowing that shapelet S matches time series T, confidence $C_S(c)$ of classifying T as class c based on a shapelet S has two components: 1) confidence in the fact that d is less than a threshold δ and 2) confidence in the ability of shapelet S to accurately classify time series T. To take these two components into account, we define $C_S(c)$ as

$$\begin{aligned} C_S(c) =& C_S(d < \delta, class(T) = c | S \text{ matches } T) \\ =& C_S(d < \delta | S \text{ matches } T) C_s(class(T) = c | S \text{ matches } T), \end{aligned} \tag{8}$$

where the assumption of independence is considered. To calculate the first component $C_S(d < \delta | S \text{ matches } T)$ we use Equation 7

$$\begin{aligned} C_S(d < \delta | S \text{ matches } T) =& P(d < \delta | dist(s, T) < \delta) \\ =& P(dist(s, T) + \epsilon < \delta | dist(s, T) < \delta) \\ =& P(\epsilon < \delta - dist(s, T) | dist(s, T) < \delta). \end{aligned} \tag{9}$$

If we assume that ϵ follows some distribution with 0 mean and σ standard deviation (we do not assume any parametric form of the distribution), then we can calculate a lower bound for confidence using Cantelli's inequality (sharpened version of Chebyshev's inequality which is commonly used in medical domain [7])

$$\begin{aligned} C_S(d < \delta | S \text{ matches } T) =& P(\epsilon < \delta - dist(s, T) | dist(s, T) < \delta) \\ =& 1 - P(\epsilon > \delta - dist(s, T)) \\ \geq& 1 - \frac{\sigma^2}{\sigma^2 + (\delta - dist(s, T))^2} \\ =& \frac{(\delta - dist(s, T))^2}{\sigma^2 + (\delta - dist(s, T))^2}. \end{aligned} \tag{10}$$

The closer $dist(s, T)$ is to δ the lower the confidence is. Also, larger σ means lower confidence. Figure 5b demonstrates graphically this concept.

We calculate the second component of Equation 8 as

$$\begin{aligned} & C_S(class(T) = c | S \text{ matches } T) \\ =& P(class(T) = c | dist(s, T) < \delta) \\ =& \frac{P(class(T) = c, dist(s, T) < \delta)}{P(dist(s, T) < \delta)} = Precision(S), \end{aligned} \tag{11}$$

where we used $Precision$ from Equation 5. Then, the lower bound for confidence is calculated as

$$C_S(c) \geq \frac{(\delta - dist(s, T))^2}{\sigma^2 + (\delta - dist(s, T))^2} * Precision(S). \tag{12}$$

Since both terms in this product take value between 0 and 1, the highest value of the $C_S(c)$ is 1. Equation 12 incorporates two measures: how far is the time series from the shapelet and the performance of the shapelet in the training data.

Note that *each shapelet has its own threshold and hence its own confidence distribution. Therefore, for any time series, we compute the distance $dist(s, T)$ between the time series and the shapelet. If the distance is less than or equal to the threshold, then the confidence $C_S(c)$ is computed using Equation 12. If the distance is greater than the threshold, the confidence is not computed because the time series lies outside the region (circle) of the shapelet. Hence, the confidence is computed only when the shapelet matches the time series.*

4.2.2 Aggregated class confidence

If there is only one shapelet from the class c that matches the time series, then the confidence estimate for predicting the time series as class c is the same as the shapelet's confidence and is computed using Equation 12.

Now, we consider the case of computing the class confidence when multiple shapelets match the time series. Let us start with a simple case.

Simple Case.

Assume we have two shapelets S_1 and S_2 from class c that match the time series, then the class confidence $C(c)$ of classifying the time series as c is computed as

$$\begin{aligned} C(c) &= C_{S_1 \cup S_2}(c) \\ &= C_{S_1}(c) + C_{S_2}(c) - C_{S_1 \cap S_2}(c) \\ &= C_{S_1}(c) + C_{S_2}(c) - C_{S_1}(c) * C_{S_2}(c), \end{aligned} \quad (13)$$

where the assumption of the shapelets' independence is considered. The value of the class confidence $C(c)$ is greater than the confidence of any of the individual shapelets S_1 and S_2, which does make sense because our confidence for classifying the time series as class c is increased by having two matched shapelets.

General Case.

Assume that $S^c = \{S_1, S_2, \ldots, S_N\}$ is the set of all shapelets from class c that match the current time series. Then the classification confidence of the time series for class c is computed as

$$\begin{aligned} C(c) &= C_{S^c}(c) \\ &= C_{S_1 \cup S_2 \cup \ldots \cup S_N}(c) \\ &= \sum_{k=1}^{N} (-1)^{k+1} \sum_{\substack{I \subset \{1,2,\ldots,N\} \\ |I|=k}} C_{S_I}(c), \end{aligned} \quad (14)$$

where the last sum runs over all subsets I of the indices $\{1, \ldots, N\}$ which contain exactly k elements, and $S_I = \cap_{i \in I} S_i$. The value of the class confidence $C(c)$ is greater than the confidence of any of the individual shapelet $S_i; i = \{1, 2, \ldots, N\}$ because the confidence for classifying the time series as class c is increased by having multiple matched shapelets.

Now, the class confidence $C(c)$ satisfies all properties of the confidence measure, i.e. takes values on the range $[0, 1]$ and has value higher than any individual shapelet.

Moreover, the uncertainty estimate for classifying a time series should decrease as time evolves and more information about the time series becomes available. The uncertainty measure defined in Equation 6 satisfies this property. Assume that at time t there are k shapelets that match the time series and at time $t + 1$ two more shapelets match the time series. Since the k shapelets (at time t) are a subset of the $k + 2$ shapelets (at time $t + 1$) then the confidence of the $k + 2$ shapelets has to be greater than the confidence of the k shapelets (as in Equations 14), which means that the confidence at time $t + 1$ is greater than the confidence at time t. In other words, the uncertainty propagates over time and decreases as time evolves.

4.3 Modified EDSC with Uncertainty estimates (MEDSC-U)

Typically, the uncertainty generated by having only one matched shapelet is higher than the uncertainty generated by having multiple matched equal-performance shapelets. Therefore, in order to better capture a reliable uncertainty estimate, we modify the EDSC method to obtain more discriminative shapelets. In particular, the pruning and classification phases of EDSC are modified. We call our method MEDSC-U.

4.3.1 Pruning phase

The MEDSC-U method sorts the shapelets descending based on their utility scores and starts with the highest ranked shapelet S. The method removes all time series from the dataset that are covered by the shapelet and stores the shapelet S and ***all other shapelets that have the same utility score (Equation 4) as S, we call these shapelets as equal-performance shapelets***.

Then, the next ranked shapelet is considered. If the shapelet covers any of the remaining time series, the shapelet and all other equal-performance shapelets are added to the extracted list and all covered time series are removed. The method iteratively does so until all time series in the dataset are covered. In this manner, the MEDSC-U method ends up with a longer list of equal-performance shapelets that is used for classification purposes. The list of the shapelets extracted from the MEDSC-U method is longer than the extracted list from the EDSC method. However, the longer list does not contain shapelet with lower utility score (Equation 4) than the shorter list. The intuition is that *with the richer model, the uncertainty would be better estimated.*

4.3.2 Classification phase

To better use the uncertainty estimates generated by MEDSC-U, we change the classification process. When we have a time series with an unknown label, we compute the distance between the current stream of the time series and ***all*** discriminative shapelets extracted by MEDSC-U (we do not start with the highest one until a match is found as EDSC). Then we compute the uncertainty for each class based on ***all matched*** shapelets from that class. If we do not have any matched shapelet for a class then we do not have uncertainty associated with that class.

At each time point we compute the uncertainty for each class. The time series is classified based on the class that has minimum uncertainty. If the produced uncertainty is not satisfactory for the user, the method continues classifying the time series until a predefined level of uncertainty is obtained.

Note that if a shapelet matches the time series at time t, then, just by chance, there is a high probability that the same shapelet matches the time series at time $t+1$ and at consecutive time points. That will increase the confidence estimation while it happens just by chance. To prevent that, MEDSC-U does not allow the same shapelet to match the time series at consecutive time points. In other words, if the shapelet S has length l and matches the time series at time t, then MEDSC-U does allow S to match the time series at time points $t + 1$ up to $t + l/2$.

4.3.3 Recommending an uncertainty threshold

At each time point MEDSC-U classifies the time series as the class that has the minimum uncertainty at that time point. MEDSC-U continues classifying the time series as long as the produced uncertainty is not satisfactory for the user. However, the domain expert might have no clue about what the recommended uncertainty threshold would be. In addition, the uncertainty threshold may be different not only from one dataset to another but even from one class to another. Therefore, we provide a simple way to find a good uncertainty threshold to be used for each class in order to get confident results.

We apply the MEDSC-U method on a validation dataset which is different from the training dataset. Then, we compute the precision of each class at different values of uncertainty thresholds. Based on a desired value of precision, the user can choose the corresponding uncertainty threshold (we illustrate this on a case study in Section 5.2.1).

5. EXPERIMENTAL RESULTS

We evaluated our method on 20 time series datasets (Table 2) from the UCR time series archive [9]. To compare the proposed method to the original EDSC method, we use the same set of parameters as recommended in [15] ($\alpha = 3, minL = 5, maxL = L/2$, *and Chebyshev's inequality for computing distance threshold*). The code and all details about our experiments can be found at our website[3].

Table 2: Datasets description. The 20 datasets are sorted descending by the number of classes and time series length.

Dataset	Training Size	Test Size	Time Series Length	No. of Classes
SwedishLeaf	500	625	128	15
FacesUCR	200	2050	131	14
FaceAll	560	1690	131	14
MedicalImages	381	760	99	10
Fish	175	175	463	7
Lightning7	70	73	319	7
OSULeaf	200	242	427	6
SynCon	300	300	60	6
OliveOil	30	30	570	4
DiatomSizeReduction	16	306	345	4
TwoPatterns	1000	4000	128	4
CBF	30	900	128	3
GunPoint	50	150	150	2
ECGFiveDays	23	861	136	2
ECG200	100	100	96	2
MoteStrain	20	1252	84	2
TwoLeadECG	23	1139	82	2
SonyAIBORobotSurface	20	601	70	2
SonyAIBORobotSurfaceII	27	953	65	2
ItalyPowerDemand	67	1029	24	2

We used 4 evaluation measures:

1. **Coverage**: the percentage of time series out of the test time series dataset that are classified. For example, if 8 out of 10 time series are classified then the coverage is 80%.
2. **Relative Accuracy**: the average between sensitivity and specificity relative to the covered time series. For example, if the coverage is 80% and all covered time series are classified correctly then the relative accuracy is 100%.
3. **Accuracy**: the average between sensitivity and specificity relative to the total number of test time series. if one method has better accuracy and less coverage and the second method has better coverage and less accuracy, so it is not clear which one is better. Therefore, in order to obtain a fair comparison, the method classifies the not-covered examples according to the majority class and then the accuracy is computed.
4. **Earliness**: the fraction of the time points used for classification.

[3]http://www.dabi.temple.edu/~mohamed/uncertainty/.

5.1 MEDSC-U versus EDSC

MEDSC-U allows more equal-performance shapelets to be included in the final list in order to have reliable uncertainty estimates. We first evaluate the effect of including more shapelets on the accuracy and earliness performance of the MEDSC-U method without using the advantages of uncertainty estimates. Therefore, the MEDSC-U method classifies the test time series based on the closest matching shapelet even with high uncertainty estimates 1.

The accuracy (blue circles) and earliness (red squares) of both the MEDSC-U and EDSC methods on each dataset are shown in Figure 6. In the area under the diagonal, the EDSC method is better than the MEDSC-U method, while in the area above the diagonal the MEDSC-U method is better than the EDSC method. We plot 100-earliness instead of earliness to preserve "*the higher the better*" property.

As shown in Figure 6, most of the circles lie very close to the diagonal line which means that MEDSC-U method has comparable accuracy with the EDSC method. Therefore, including equal-performance shapelets into the model does not negatively affect the accuracy of the model. The reason for this is that: since the additionally included shapelets have the same accuracy performance on the training data, it would be better to include them to allow for variability among time series' patterns and that would slightly improve the earliness of the classification decision, as evident in the right panel of Figure 6.

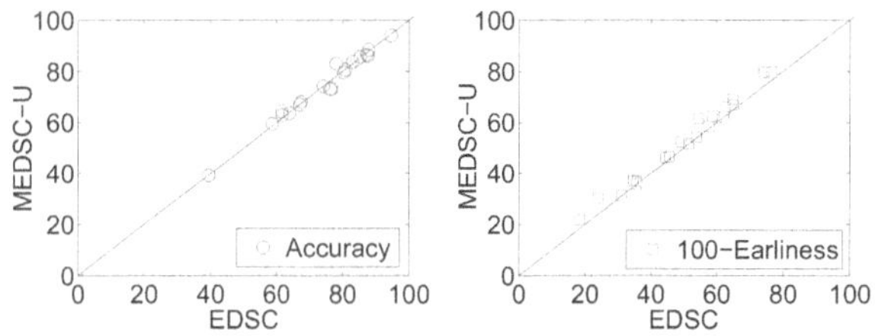

Figure 6: Comparison between MEDSC-U and ESDC with respect to the accuracy (left) and the earliness (right). The left (right) panel has 20 circles (squares) for the 20 datasets where each circle (square) represents the accuracy (100-earliness) of the two methods on exactly one dataset, respectively. The EDSC method is better on the lower triangle while the MEDSC-U method is better on the upper triangle. Points (datasets) on the diagonal indicate that the two methods have similar accuracy/earliness performance. For more details (per each dataset) about these experiments check the website.

5.2 Case studies

We show the effectiveness of our uncertainty method on real examples from different datasets. In particular, we show how the method provides *more confident class prediction by either having a shapelet that confidently matches the time series (Section 5.2.1) or having multiple shapelets match the time series (Section 5.2.2) as in Equation 14.* In addition, we explain how to appropriately choose an uncertainty threshold using CBF dataset as a case study.

5.2.1 Classification based on a confident shapelet: CBF case study

The CBF dataset has three classes, as shown in the first column of Figure 7. The EDSC method has extracted one shapelet from each class and has achieved 88% accuracy. However, the EDSC method incorrectly classified the cylinder (red) example shown in Figure 7d as funnel (black) example. The same case happened if we just used the MEDSC-U with uncertainty 1 as shown in panel (e).

This is because the shapelets extracted by EDSC or MEDSC-U from the funnel and the cylinder classes are similar to each other. Therefore, it might happen, as shown in the figure, that a cylinder example is classified incorrectly as funnel example or vice versa. To overcome this problem we need to measure the uncertainty for the classification decision, especially from these two classes, and therefore we use lower value of uncertainty in order to obtain more confident classification by the MEDSC-U method.

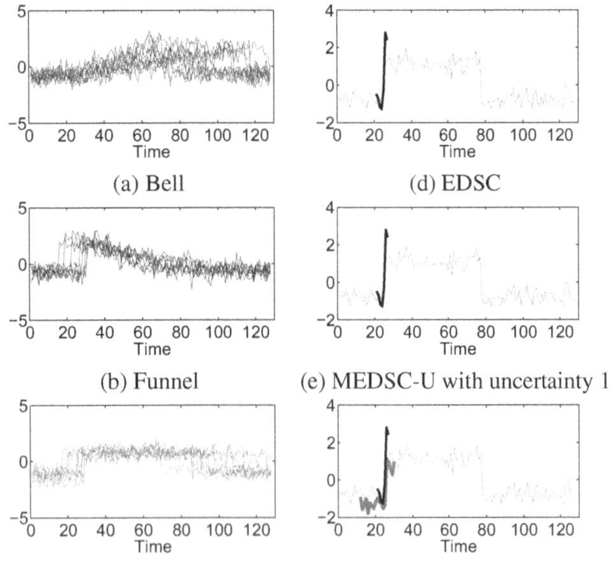

(a) Bell (d) EDSC (b) Funnel (e) MEDSC-U with uncertainty 1 (c) Cylinder (f) MEDSC-U

Figure 7: (a,b,c) Time series from the CBF datasets from the bell, funnel, and cylinder classes, respectively. (d,e) A cylinder time series which is incorrectly classified by the EDSC method (d) and the MEDSC-U method with uncertainty 1 ***(e), respectively. (f) The cylinder time series is correctly classified by MEDSC-U with lower uncertainty*** 0.13.

The uncertainty associated with the classification using the black shapelet at time point 27 is 0.49. If this value is not satisfactory (because we know that these two classes are similar to each other and as we show later that this uncertainty is not enough to classify a time series as black), we might wait and not provide classification at this point in the hope that the uncertainty reduces under a certain threshold. At time point 30 a cylinder shapelet matches the time series with uncertainty 0.13, so the method is more confident to '*correctly*' classify the time series as a cylinder class than to classify it as a funnel class.

Therefore, the user can decide if he/she is satisfied about the classification results using the uncertainty estimates provided by the method. That uncertainty threshold could be varied from one class to another class. For example, since we know that the shapelets from the funnel and cylinder classes are similar, then if the test time series is classified as one of these classes, the user may lower the value of the uncertainty threshold and delays the decision in order to obtain accurate results. On the other hand, if the test time series is classified as the bell class (completely different from the other two classes), then higher value of uncertainty threshold might be sufficient in order not to delay the results.

Recommending an uncertainty threshold.

As we just mentioned, the uncertainty threshold may be different from one class to another class. The domain expert might have no notion about the recommended threshold for each class. To find the recommended uncertainty threshold, MEDSC-U is applied on a validation dataset and the precision of each class is computed for each uncertainty threshold as shown in Figure 8.

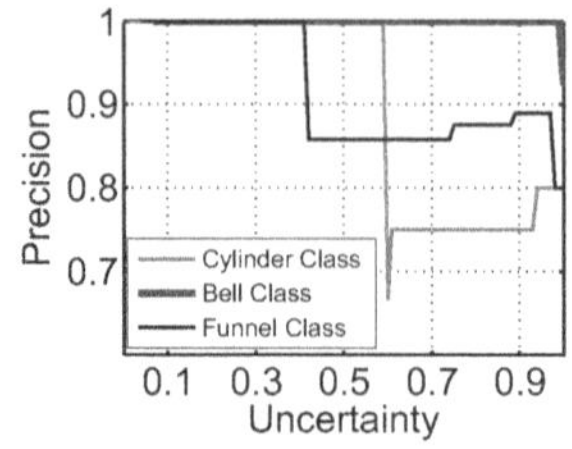

Figure 8: The precision of the MEDSC-U method on the CBF dataset for the three classes at different values of uncertainty threshold. The blue class (the blue curve along with the upper x-axis) is easy to classify by MEDSC-U even with high uncertainty, while the red and black classes are similar to each other which requires lower uncertainty threshold for each of them.

As shown in Figure 8, the blue class has 100% precision at each level of uncertainty and then the precision drops at high value of uncertainty (very close to uncertainty estimate 1), while the precision of the other two classes drop earlier. This illustrates that the blue class is dissimilar to the other classes and can be recognized by our method even with high value of uncertainty such as 0.9 (or even higher). However, the precision for the red (Cylinder) and black (Funnel) classes dropped at approximately 0.6 and 0.4, respectively. Therefore, 0.6 (0.4) would be a good estimate for the uncertainty thresholds for the red (black) class, respectively. Also, if the domain expert has a desired value of precision, say for example 0.9, then we draw a horizontal line at the precision 0.9 in Figure 8 and find the uncertainty thresholds corresponding to the intersection of that line and the three (classes) precision curves.

This is very consistent with the results reported in Figure 7. Since the test time series is classified initially as black class with uncertainty 0.49 and we know from Figure 8 that the recommended threshold for the black class is 0.4, we wait and do not classify the time series at that time point. The next matched shapelet classifies the time series as red class with uncertainty 0.13 and the recommended threshold for the red class is 0.6, therefore the classification is done at that time point which is the correct class.

To simplify the presentation of the paper, the remaining results are shown using a single threshold for all classes instead of showing results using class-specific and dataset-specific threshold.

Uncertainty versus performance measures.

This begs the question "*How does the uncertainty threshold affect the accuracy and earliness performance?*". We have shown that if we reduce the uncertainty threshold from 0.49 to 0.13 we get more accurate results, but it delays the decision for 3 time points. The results for varying different threshold versus the accuracy is shown in Figure 9a. *Note that we use the same uncertainty threshold for all classes.* It is clear from the figure that the accuracy increases when lowering the value of the uncertainty threshold. However, as shown in Figure 9b, the classification decisions is delayed as expected. For example, using the uncertainty threshold 0.9 delays the results until, on average, 40% of the time series length (at time point ~ 51) while the accuracy would be $\sim 95\%$ (the original EDSC method has achieved accuracy 88% and earliness 35%).

Now we have conveyed the message that if the uncertainty associated with the classification decision is high, then we wait until another shapelet with lower uncertainty to match the time series in order to provide more accurate results. However, this is not the only

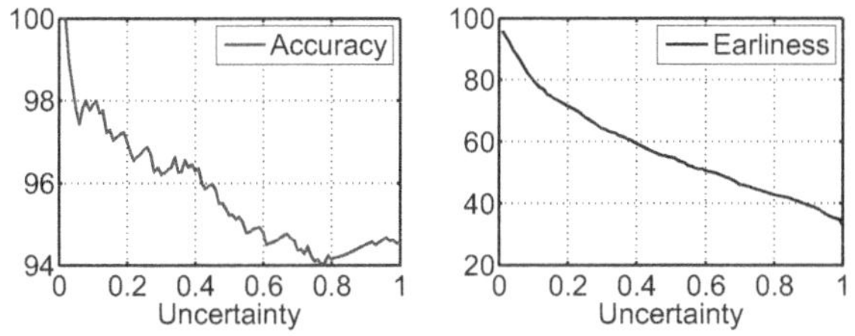

(a) (b)

Figure 9: The accuracy (a) and the earliness (b) of MEDSC-U for different uncertainty thresholds on CBF dataset. Lower value of uncertainty threshold gives more accurate results but delays the decision.

way to obtain more confident results. More confident results may be achieved when multiple shapelets from the same class match the time series. We illustrate this using the ECGFiveDays dataset in the next section.

5.2.2 Classification based on multiple shapelets: ECGFiveDays case study

The ECGFiveDays dataset has two classes (the red and the blue classes). A time series from the blue class is shown in Figure 10. The time series matches the first (red) shapelet at time 50 with uncertainty 0.98 which means that the uncertainty associated for the red class is 0.98 and no uncertainty associated for the blue class because no blue shapelet matches the time series up to that point. Then, at time 79, the time series matches a blue shapelet with uncertainty 0.97. Therefore, at that point the method classifies the time series as a red class with uncertainty 0.98 and as a blue class with uncertainty 0.97. These uncertainties propagate until time 83, where a new (blue) shapelet matches the time series. The uncertainties from the two matched blue shapelets are aggregated using Equation 14 to give total uncertainty 0.52 for the blue class, which reveals the fact that the method is now more certain to classify the time series as a blue class (correct classification). In other words, more confident results are obtained by having multiple shapelets matching the time series.

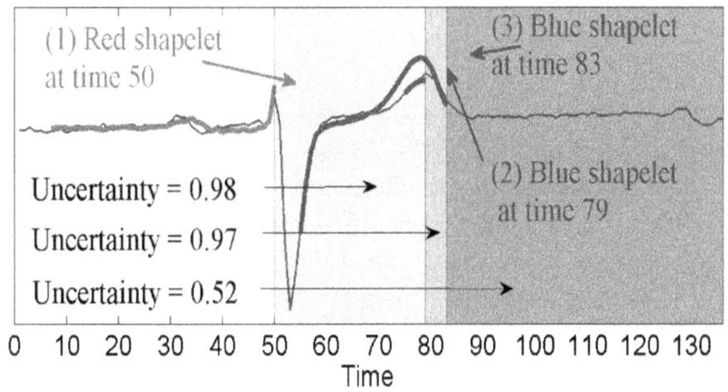

Figure 10: A time series from the blue class of the ECGFiveDays dataset is classified at the time point 83 ***with uncertainty*** 0.52. ***The yellow region denotes the region where the model is uncertain about the clasification. The green region represents the region where the model is confident about the classification.***

Therefore, the uncertainty of the classification decision is reduced by having multiple events (such as multiple shapelets appearing in the portion of the time series seen so far), and that uncertainty decreases overtime. The average uncertainty over all time series at each time point is shown in Figure 11. As shown in the figure, the uncertainty decreases over time, which emphasizes that the model becomes more and more certain about the classification as time evolves.

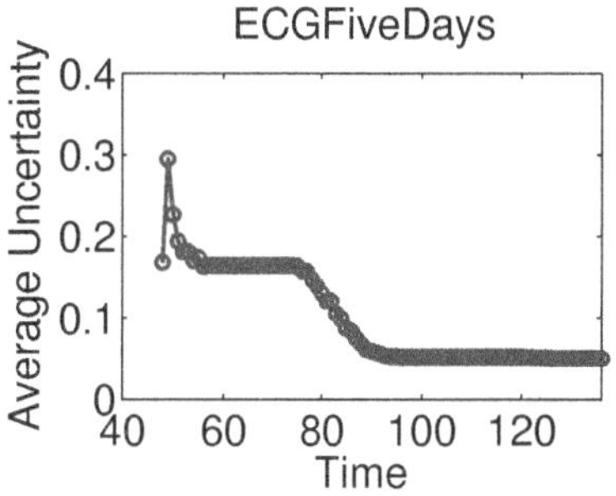

Figure 11: The average uncertainty over all patients at each time point for the ECGFiveDays dataset. The method starts with high uncertainty and then becomes certain about the classification as time evolves.

For Figure 11, it has to be pointed out that the average uncertainty increases sometimes and then decreases (for example, at time 48 is 0.17 and at time 49 is 0.29 and then it decreases over time). The reason behind the increase in the average of uncertainties is that the model covered more examples at time 49 than at time 48, therefore, the uncertainties of the new covered examples increase the value of the average uncertainty from time 48 to time 49. However, the uncertainty for each time series example does not increase over time.

In Figure 12a, we show the uncertainties for each time series over time. The MEDSC-U method classifies many time series using only the first 60-80 time points but with high uncertainty (yellow bars). These uncertainties decrease over time (yellow-to-green bars). For instance, in Figure 12b, some of the time series are shown where it is clear that the method becomes more certain about the classification between time 82 - 86.

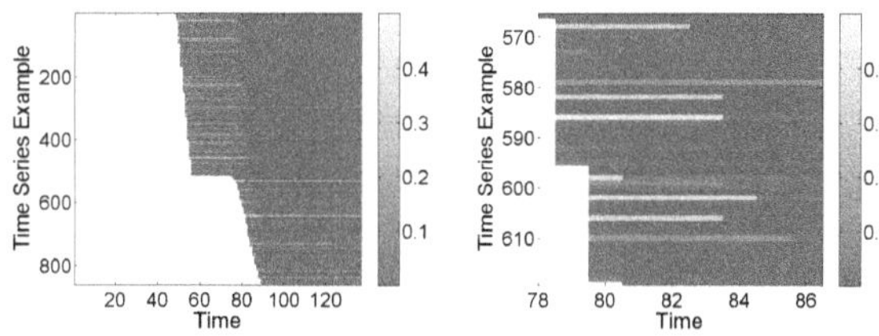

(a) (b)

Figure 12: The values of uncertainty over time for each time series from the ECG2FiveDays dataset. The white bar indicates that there is no classification at that point and hence there is no uncertainty.The MEDSC-U method provides more certain results as time evolves. The temporal uncertainty for each time series never increases.

Now we have shown that the proposed interpretable early classification MEDSC-U method that provides uncertainty estimates gives more accurate results over time than the EDSC method but that affects the earliness of the decision. Therefore, the uncertainty threshold controls the trade off between the accuracy and the earliness of the method. Moreover, that uncertainty threshold may differ from one dataset to another, and even from one class to another as we explained previously in Section 5.2.1.

In order to make the flow of the paper easy to follow and due to the lack of the page space, we have shown these aspects on two datasets: CBF and ECGFiveDays. However, the results for the other datasets are very consistent with what we have shown and therefore the remaining results are presented in the appendix. In addition, all details of these results are on our website. In the next section we compare our method to other methods that provide uncertainty estimates.

5.3 Comparison to localQDA

Two existing methods we have mentioned in the related work section that provide uncertainty for time series classification that could be used in the context of early classification. The PR method represents the patient risk as a time series and estimates the uncertainty as the distance between the evolving approximate daily risk of a patient and the hyperplane learned by SVM [12]. So, the uncertainty is measured as the distance between the measurement (value of the time series at a particular time point) and the hyperplane. The proposed uncertainty estimates could be used for the early classification context, i.e. the model proceeds over the time series until a confident results (furthest to the hyperplane) obtained. However, the PR model requires labels for each time point in the time series, not just a label for the entire time series, and therefore we can not compare MEDSC-U to the PR method.

The state-of-the-art method for early classification of signals using a quadratic discriminant analysis (localQDA) classifier was developed [11]. The localQDA method does not provide uncertainty but instead it provides a reliability bound on the classifier's decision for every time point. As noted by [11], "*With probability at least τ (reliability), will the classification decision from incomplete data be the same as that which would be made from the complete data?*" The reliability τ measures the probability that the early classification will be the same as the classification at the end of the time series. The uncertainty measure provided by our method is not directly comparable to the reliability measure provided by localQDA method, but they are correlated. Thereby, we assume that the $Uncertainty = 1 - \tau$.

For fair comparison between MEDSC-U and localQDA, we use the same set of parameters as they had recommended in [11]. We show the comparison between the two methods on the ECG200 datasets as a case study in Table 3. The remaining comparisons are in the appendix.

Table 3: Comparison of our proposed MEDSC-U method to the state-of-the-art localQDA method on the ECG200 dataset at different values of uncertainty $(1-\tau)$***. localQDA is accurate than MEDSC-U but MEDSC-U prvides classification decisions much ealier than localQDA.***

	τ	0.1	0.25	0.5	0.75	0.9
	Uncertainty	0.9	0.75	0.5	0.25	0.1
Accuracy	localQDA	**89**	**89**	**88**	**88**	**87**
	MEDSC-U	82	81	81	82	82
Earliness	localQDA	60.19	62.18	64.02	66.27	68.34
	MEDSC-U	**23.24**	**24.23**	**28.14**	**29.45**	**35.14**

As shown in Table 3, localQDA is more accurate than MEDSC-U but the classification decision is provided much later than the decision from the MEDSC-U method. We also compute F_β score for different values of $\beta = \{0.1, 1, 2\}$. F_β score is the weighted average of the accuracy and 100−earliness where $\beta = 2$ weights earliness higher than accuracy, $\beta = 0.1$ puts more emphasis on accuracy than earliness, and $\beta = 1$ is the balanced harmonic mean.

As shown in Figure 13, our method has comparable $F_{0.1}$ score with the state-of-the-art localQDA method, which weights accuracy more than earliness. For the other two measures F_1 and F_2, MEDSC-U clearly outperforms localQDA at every level of uncertainty.

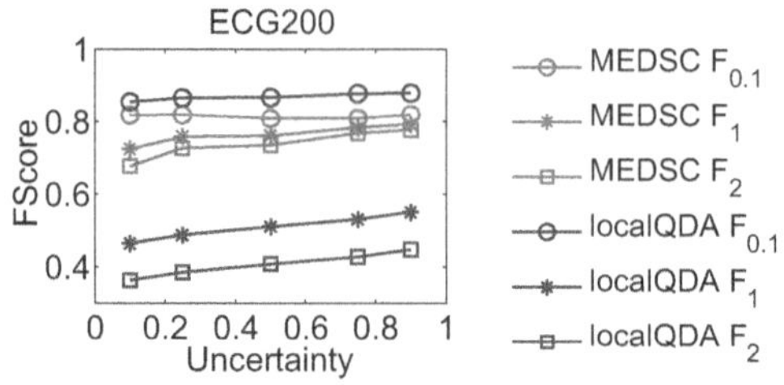

Figure 13: Comparison between the MEDSC-U method and localQDA on the ECG200 dataset for different values of uncertainty (1-tau).

To make a conclusion from all comparisons between MEDSC-U and localQDA, we plot the number of datasets where MEDSC-U has higher F_β score than the localQDA method (or vice versa) at each uncertainty threshold. The results are shown in Figure 14.

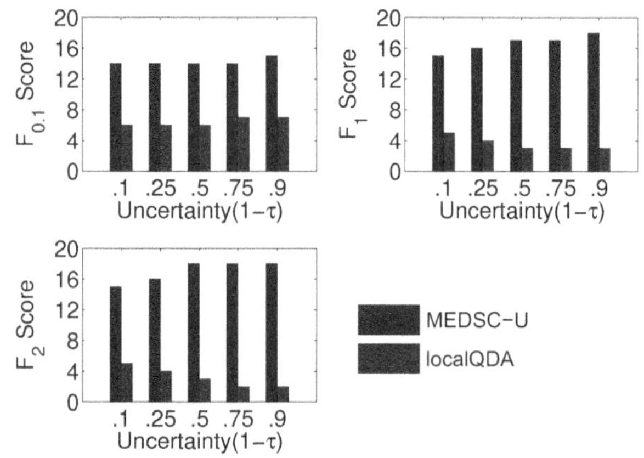

Figure 14: Number of datasest where MEDSC-U (blue bar) has better F_β ***score than the localQDA (red bar), or vice versa, at each uncertainty threshold. Clearly, MESDC-U ourperforms localQDA in most cases especially in*** F_1 ***and*** F_2 ***settings where the earliness is important.***

As shown in Figure 14, for $F_{0.1}$, MEDSC-U outperformed the localQDA method in 13 (or little bit more) datasets at each uncertainty estimate. For F_1 and F_2 scores, MEDSC-U clearly outperformed localQDA in most of the datasets at each level of uncertainty. These results show that our proposed MEDSC-U method is comparable to or even better than the state-of-the-art localQDA method in every F score, as shown by our experiments. In addition to that, MEDSC-U is very simple to implement and provides interpretable results (shapelets) convincing to the practitioners, which are not addressed by the state-of-the-art localQDA method.

6. CONCLUSION AND FUTURE WORK

Providing classification of time series as early as possible is vital in many domains including the medical domain, where early diagnosis can save patients' lives by providing early treatment. However, applications often require the method to be interpretable and have uncertainty estimates. We extended the interpretable early classification method (EDSC) and proposed the MEDSC-U method to measure the temporal uncertainty with the classification. The proposed uncertainty estimates meets the requirements of uncertainty where it has range $[0, 1]$ and propagates over time. The

MEDSC-U method is very simple to implement and provides interpretability for the classification results. In addition, it is more effective than the state-of-the-art method, as shown in our experiments on twenty datasets. The temporal uncertainty estimates provided by MEDSC-U can be extended to the multivariate case [2, 4] where uncertainties from shapelets from different variables could be integrated as in Equation 14.

Acknowledgment

This work was funded, in part, by DARPA grant [DARPAN66001-11-1-4183] negotiated by SSC Pacific grant.

7. REFERENCES

[1] K. M. Borgwardt, S. Vishwanathan, and H.-P. Kriegel. Class prediction from time series gene expression profiles using dynamical systems kernels. In *Pacific Symposium on Biocomputing*, volume 11, pages 547–558, 2006.

[2] M. F. Ghalwash and Z. Obradovic. Early classification of multivariate temporal observations by extraction of interpretable shapelets. *BMC Bioinformatics*, 13(195), August 2012.

[3] M. F. Ghalwash, V. Radosavljevic, and Z. Obradovic. Early diagnosis and its benefits in sepsis blood purification treatment. In *International Workshop on Data Mining for Healthcare*, Philadelphia, PA, Sep 2013.

[4] M. F. Ghalwash, V. Radosavljevic, and Z. Obradovic. Extraction of interpretable multivariate patterns for early diagnostics. In *IEEE International Conference on Data Mining (ICDM)*, Dallas, TX, Dec 2013.

[5] M. Grbovic and S. Vucetic. Tracking concept change with incremental boosting by minimization of the evolving exponential loss. In *Proceedings of the 2011 European Conference on Machine Learning and Knowledge Discovery in Databases, Part I, ECML/PKDD'11*, pages 516–532, 2011.

[6] M. P. Griffin and J. R. Moorman. Toward the early diagnosis of neonatal sepsis and sepsis-like illness using novel heart rate analysis. *PEDIATRICS*, 107(3):97–104, 2001.

[7] F. Ieva, R. Longhi, A. M. Paganoni, and M. P. Protti. Estimating point and interval frequency of antigen-specific CD4+ T cells based on short in vitro expansion and improved poisson distribution analysis. *PLoS ONE*, 7(8), 2012.

[8] E. Keogh and T. Rakthanmanon. Fast shapelets: A scalable algorithm for discovering time series shapelets. In *Proceedings of the 13th SIAM International Conference on Data Mining*, pages 668–676, 2013.

[9] E. Keogh, Q. Zhu, B. Hu, Y. Hao, X. Xi, L. Wei, and C. A. Ratanamahatana. The UCR time series classification and clustering homepage, 2011.

[10] T. Lin, N. Kaminski, and Z. Bar-Joseph. Alignment and classification of time series gene expression in clinical studies. *Bioinformatics*, 24:i147–i155, July 2008.

[11] N. Parrish, H. S. Anderson, M. R. Gupta, and D. Y. Hsiao. Classifying with confidence from incomplete information. *Journal of Machine Learning Research*, 14:3561–3589, 2014.

[12] J. Wiens, J. Guttag, and E. Horvitz. Patient risk stratification for hospital-associated c. diff as a time-series classification task. In *Neural Information Processing System (NIPS)*, 2012.

[13] Z. Xing, J. Pei, and P. S. Yu. Early prediction on time series: A nearest neighbor approach. In *Proceedings of the 21st international joint conference on Artifical intelligence*, pages 1297–1302, 2009.

[14] Z. Xing, J. Pei, and P. S. Yu. Early classification on time series. *Knowl Inf Syst*, 31:105–107, 2011.

[15] Z. Xing, J. Pei, P. S. Yu, and K. Wang. Extracting interpretable features for early classification on time series. In *Proceedings of 11th SIAM International Conference on Data Mining*, pages 439–451, 2011.

[16] L. Ye and E. Keogh. Time series shapelets: A new primitive for data mining. In *Proceesings of the 15th ACM SIGKDD Conference on Knolwedge Discovery and Data Mining (KDD)*, 2009.

APPENDIX

A. REMAINING RESULTS

The accuracy, earliness, and coverage performance for some of the datasets are shown in Figure 15, and the results for comparing the proposed MEDSC-U method with the localQDA method are shown in Figure 16, while, for the lack of page space, the remaining results are on our website.

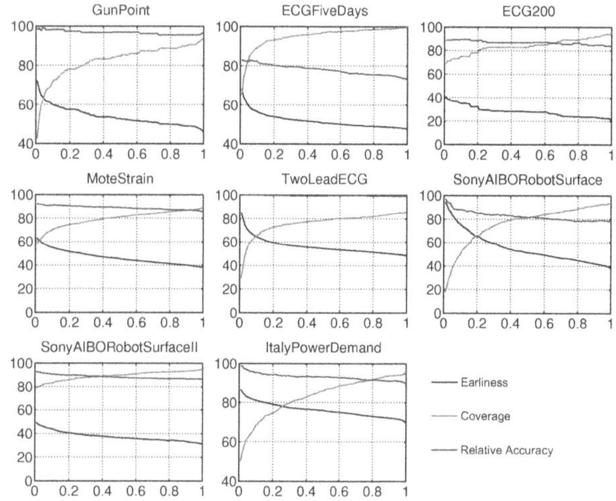

Figure 15: Uncertainty (x-axis) versus relative accuracy (blue), earliness (black), and coverage(red) for 5 datasets.

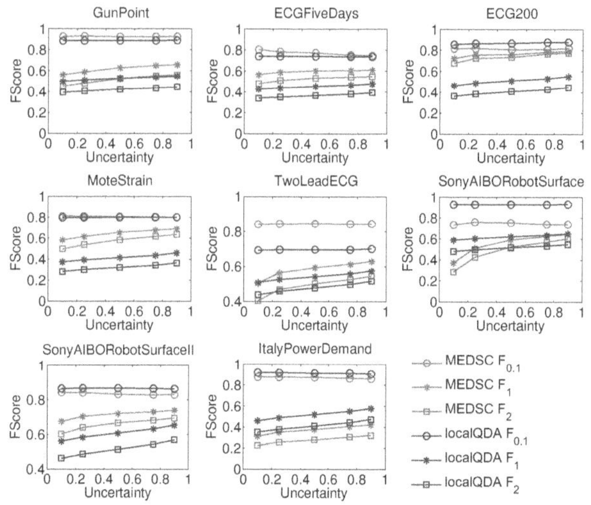

Figure 16: Comparison between MEDSC-U and localQDA for different values of uncertainty. X-axis is the uncertainty threshold $(1-\tau)$ and y-axis is the F_β score.

Prototype-based Learning on Concept-drifting Data Streams

Junming Sha[1,2], Zahra Ahmadi[1], Stefan Kramer[1]
[1]University of Mainz, 55128 Mainz, Germany
[2]University of Electronic Science and Technology of China , 611731 Chengdu, China
{junmshao, zaahmadi}@uni-mainz.de, kramer@informatik.uni-mainz.de

ABSTRACT

Data stream mining has gained growing attentions due to its wide emerging applications such as target marketing, email filtering and network intrusion detection.In this paper, we propose a prototype-based classification model for evolving data streams, called SyncStream, which dynamically models time-changing concepts and makes predictions in a local fashion. Instead of learning a single model on a sliding window or ensemble learning, SyncStream captures evolving concepts by dynamically maintaining a set of prototypes in a new data structure called the P-tree. The prototypes are obtained by error-driven representativeness learning and synchronization-inspired constrained clustering. To identify abrupt concept drift in data streams, PCA and statistics based heuristic approaches are employed. SyncStream has several attractive benefits: (a) It is capable of dynamically modeling evolving concepts from even a small set of prototypes and is robust against noisy examples. (b) Owing to synchronization-based constrained clustering and the P-Tree, it supports an efficient and effective data representation and maintenance. (c) Gradual and abrupt concept drift can be effectively detected. Empirical results shows that our method achieves good predictive performance compared to state-of-the-art algorithms and that it requires much less time than another instance-based stream mining algorithm.

Categories and Subject Descriptors

H.2.8 [**Database Management**]: Database Applications - Data Mining

Keywords

Data stream; Concept drift; Classification; Synchronization

1. INTRODUCTION

Data stream classification is a challenging data mining task because of two important properties: potentially infinite length and evolving nature. Currently, there are two main strategies to mine evolving data streams: single model learning and ensemble learning. Single model learning tries to learn and update a classification model by training on a fixed or adaptive window of recent incoming examples [9], [12]. The prediction performance of this type of learning usually suffers in the presence of concept drift. By contrast, ensemble learning partitions continuous data streams into smaller chunks and uses them to train a number of base classifiers to capture evolving concepts [16], [2]. Ensembles can scale up to large volumes of streaming data and adapt quickly to new concepts. However, two existing limitations of ensemble learning are considered only little. First, the performance of ensemble learning depends on the accuracy of each base classifier capturing the concept, where each base classifier is actually used in a black-box fashion. For illustration, let us take Fig. 1 as an example. If the size of data chunk is small (data arrived during $[t0, t1)$), the concept of the data stream for each base classifier cannot be sufficiently learned. On the other hand, if the size of a data chunk is too large (data arrived during $[t0, t2)$), base classifiers may learn more than one concept. Second, it is difficult to decide whether more recent or older examples are more relevant (e.g., the relatively old example P_1 is important for predicting the class label of P_2 in Fig. 1 (a)). Learning from recent examples, as in most established algorithms, is not always optimal. A more natural way is to dynamically select short-term and/or long-term representative examples to capture the trend of time-changing concepts, and use them to predict the test data (cf. Fig. 1 (b)).

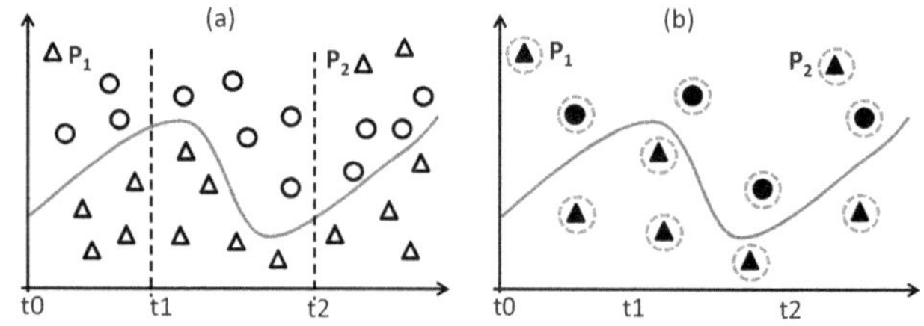

Figure 1: How to select suitable training examples for learning a classification model on an evolving data stream?

In this paper, we propose a new prototype-based learning method to mine evolving data streams. To dynamically identify prototypical examples, error-driven representativeness learning is used to compute the representativeness of examples over time. Noisy examples with low representativeness are discarded, and representative examples can

KDD'14, August 24–27, 2014, New York, NY, USA.
Copyright 2014 ACM 978-1-4503-2956-9/14/08 ...$15.00.
http://dx.doi.org/10.1145/2623330.2623609.

be further summarized by a smaller set of prototypes using synchronization-inspired constrained clustering. To dynamically represent the online training data, a new data structure, the P-Tree, is proposed to update the set of prototypes, to capture time-changing concepts and to support accurate predictions.

Contributions

Building upon the data representation of synchronization-inspired constrained clustering, SyncStream has several attractive benefits, most importantly:

- **Prototype-based Data Representation:** Due to the properties of synchronization-inspired constrained clustering, examples in data streams can be well summarized and represented as a set of prototypes, which allows preserving the data structure as well as the class distribution of the original examples.
- **Concept Modeling:** Instead of using a set of base classifiers or learning on a window of recent data, SyncStream provides an intuitive way to model evolving concepts by dynamically maintaining a small set of short-term and/or long-term prototypes based on *error-driven representativeness learning* (see Section 3.4.1).
- **High Performance:** Thanks to the efficient and effective online data maintenance relying on the proposed *P-Tree* data structure (see Section 3.4.2), SyncStream allows adapting to time-changing concepts quickly to make accurate predictions.

The remainder of this paper is organized as follows: In the following section, we briefly survey related work. Section 3 presents our algorithm in detail. Section 4 contains an extensive experimental evaluation. We finally conclude the paper in Section 5.

2. RELATED WORK

Data stream classification has received much attention in recent decades. Early algorithms focused on learning a single model from evolving data (e.g., [9]). But very soon they were replaced by ensemble models in order to obtain more accurate predictions. Ensemble models (e.g., [16, 2]) are of great interest, as each model can represent one possible distribution over the data, therefore current data can be generated from a mixture of distributions with changing weights over time. Also, if one of the previous concepts reappears, they can handle this case more effectively [8]. However, as explained in Section 1, ensemble models have some shortcomings in determining a suitable window size and useful instances. One efficient solution to address these shortcomings is the use of instance-based learning, which has been considered in some papers in recent years [10, 17, 13]. In instance-based learning, instead of taking time to build a global model, the target function is approximated locally by means of selected instances. The inherent incremental nature of instance-based learning algorithms and their simple and flexible adaptation mechanism makes this type of algorithm suitable for learning in complex dynamic environments. Nevertheless, instance-based learning algorithms have to face their own challenges, such as their space requirements and their sensitivity to noise. To manage memory consumption and accelerate nearest neighbor lookup, researchers usually use a tree based data structure such as the M-Tree [17, 13]. In this tree, instances of small neighborhoods are kept in the leaves; inner nodes combine their subnodes to form bigger spheres, and the root encompasses all the data. The number of subnodes is determined heuristically. In contrast, we provide an intuitive and effective strategy to summarize data, and dynamically maintain a small set of prototypes in the proposed P-Tree to support effective and efficient online data maintenance.

To handle concept drift in an evolving data stream, one strategy is to dynamically monitor the change of a distribution over time and set a flag whenever drift is detected. This type of method is referred to as explicit concept drift detection. In contrast to this strategy, implicit methods adapt to new concepts by updating a model continuously. The benefit of using explicit methods is the ability to react to sudden drift more quickly, while implicit methods are more suitable for data streams with gradual concept drift. Generally, methods for concept drift detection are categorised into statistical techniques (e.g., [5]) and those based on performance monitoring between two consecutive data chunks (e.g., [1]). If concept drift is detected, the model may be reconstructed from scratch (e.g., [7]) or only the affected parts of the model are updated (e.g., [9]). Locally updating a model has the benefit of maintaining useful knowledge from previous data and is especially useful in recognizing recurring concepts. In this paper, error-driven representativeness learning is introduced to identify the most important prototypes to capture the trend of time-changing concepts in an implicit and local way, while sudden concept drift is handled based on two heuristic strategies.

3. PROPOSED METHOD

In this section, we present the SyncStream algorithm for mining evolving data streams. Before that, we provide an overview of the algorithm and the intuition behind it.

3.1 Overview

As introduced in Section 1, the basic idea of our algorithm is to dynamically keep track of short-term and/or long-term representative examples to capture the trend of time-changing concepts, and use them for prediction in a local instance-based fashion. Specifically, a small set of data examples is first regarded as initial prototypes and inserted into a proposed hierarchical tree structure called the P-Tree, which is used to maintain prototypes and drifting concepts on two levels, respectively. For each new example, the nearest prototype in the P-Tree is used to predict its label. Meanwhile, during the classification process, an error-driven learning approach is employed to determine the representativeness of prototypes in the P-Tree. If the nearest prototype correctly predicts the new example, this indicates that the prototype is in line with the trend of the current concept of the new example. The representativeness of a prototype is thus increased (and decreased in the opposite case). However, due to restricted memory, we cannot store all prototypes in the P-Tree. To fit the P-Tree in an any-space memory framework and support efficient prediction, inappropriate or noisy examples with low representativeness are discarded. The representative examples are further summarized as a smaller set of prototypes based on synchronization-inspired constrained clustering, where each prototype solely belongs to one specific class (cf. Section 3.2). Relying on constrained clustering, historical data is summarized and, more importantly, the data structure of the original examples is well preserved. To further handle the evolving nature of data streams, PCA and statistics based methods are introduced to detect sudden concept drift, so that prototypes in the P-Tree can be updated quickly to capture a new concept. Once a new concept is emerging, the previous concept is modeled as a set of prototypes and stored on the concept level of the P-Tree. In the following, we will first elaborate on how to summarize historical data based on synchronization-inspired constrained clustering, before we move on to drift detection and the P-tree.

3.2 Prototype-based Data Representation

In the context of an evolving data stream, it is infeasible to keep track of the entire history of the data. To support effective and efficient online data maintenance, we first introduce a data summarization technique by adapting synchronization-inspired clustering [14], [3]. The key philosophy of synchronization-based clustering approaches (e.g., *Sync* [3] or *pSync* [14]) is to regard each example as a phase oscillator and simulate the dynamical behavior of the examples over time. Based on the non-linear local interactions among examples, similar examples will finally synchronize together and end up in the same common phase. The synchronized common phase represents the set of similar examples, and thus provides an intuitive way to summarize the data.

Typically, a synchronization-based clustering algorithm needs three definitions to simulate a dynamic clustering process. In the following, we give a short summary of all necessary definitions.

Definition 1 (ϵ-**Range Neighborhood**)

Given a $\epsilon \in \mathcal{R}$ and $x \in \mathcal{D}$, the ϵ-range neighborhood of an example x, denoted by $N_\epsilon(x)$, is defined as:

$$N_\epsilon(x) = \{y \in \mathcal{D} | dist(y, x) \le \epsilon\}, \qquad (1)$$

where $dist(y, x)$ is a metric distance function, and the Euclidean distance is used in this study.

Definition 2 (**Interaction Model**)

Let $x \in \mathcal{R}^d$ be an example in the data set $\mathcal{D}$ and x_i be the i-th dimension of the example x, respectively. Each example x is viewed as a phase oscillator. With an ϵ-range neighborhood interaction, the dynamics of each dimension x_i of the example x is defined by:

$$x_i(t+1) = x_i(t) + \frac{1}{|N_\epsilon(x(t))|} \cdot \sum_{y \in N_\epsilon(x(t))} \sin(y_i(t) - x_i(t)), \qquad (2)$$

where $sin(\cdot)$ is the coupling function. $x_i(t+1)$ describes the renewal phase value of the i-th dimension of example x at $t = (0, \ldots, T)$ during the dynamic clustering.

To characterize the level of synchronization between oscillators during the synchronization process, a cluster order parameter R_c is defined to measure the coherence of the local oscillator population.

Definition 3 (**Cluster Order Parameter**)

The cluster order parameter R_c is used to terminate the dynamic clustering by investigating the degree of local synchronization, which is defined as:

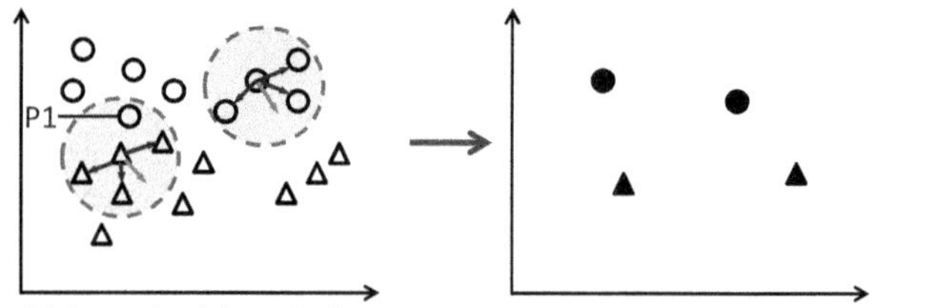

Figure 2: Illustration of synchronization-inspired constrained clustering.

$$R_c = \frac{1}{N} \sum_{i=1}^{N} \frac{1}{|N_\epsilon(x)|} \sum_{y \in N_\epsilon(x)} \mathbf{e}^{-||y-x||}. \qquad (3)$$

The dynamic clustering terminates when $R_c(t)$ converges, which indicates local phase coherence. At this moment, cluster examples have the same phase (common location in the feature vector space).

One of the most salient features of synchronization-based clustering is its dynamic property. During the process of clustering, each object moves in a non-linear way driven by the local data structure, and finally a set of examples with similar local structure will group together. The synchronized phase thus provides a natural way to summarize the local data. In contrast to computing the center of cluster examples or other summarized statistics, the synchronized phases represent the original data without losing the local structure of the data.

However, for data stream classification, clustering-based data summarization needs to be conducted in a supervised manner, i.e. it needs to take into account class information. Therefore, the interaction model needs to be extended to make sure the examples in a cluster solely belong to the same class. To achieve this goal, there are two strategies: active or passive. The active strategy is to exert the opposite interaction on two examples with different class labels. Although this strategy can push the examples with different class labels away from each other, the local structure cannot be maintained. The passive strategy is to impose a cannot-link constraint [15], where two examples with different class labels cannot interact with each other. Without interaction, the examples with distinct class labels cannot synchronize together. Thereby, we reformulate the interaction model using the cannot-link constraint as follows.

Definition 4 (**Interaction Model with Constraint**)

Let $x \in \mathcal{R}^d$ be an example in the data set $\mathcal{D}$ and x_i be the i-th dimension of the example x, respectively. $l_x \in L$ is the class label of example x. With an ϵ-range neighborhood interaction, the dynamics of each dimension x_i of the example x is defined by:

$$x_i(t+1) = x_i(t) + \frac{1}{|N_\epsilon(x(t))|} \cdot \qquad (4)$$

$$\sum_{y \in N_\epsilon(x(t)), eq(l_x, l_y)} \sin(y_i(t) - x_i(t)),$$

where l_x and l_y indicate the class labels of examples x and y, respectively. $eq(\cdot, \cdot)$ is the function to check whether two class labels are equal.

Based on the extended interaction model, Fig. 2 displays two snapshots of the simulated dynamical example movement for data synchronization. Specifically, there are two classes of examples with different shapes. Given an interaction range (Fig. 2 (a)), examples of the same class will interact together, while examples of different classes will not (e.g., example $P1$). Finally, due to the non-linear interaction driven by local structure, similar examples of the same label synchronize together (Fig. 2 (b)). In this paper, we define the synchronized phases as prototypes. Due to the benefits of synchronization-based constrained clustering, we obtain two desirable properties of a prototype-based data representation:

- **Data Structure Preservation**. Since a prototype is defined as a synchronized phase, it provides an intuitive way to summarize the set of synchronized examples and further envelops the local cluster structure (both data structure and class distribution are represented).
- **Multi-scale Representation**. As a prototype can be viewed as a regular example, it supports a multi-scale representation, which means a set of prototypes can be further summarized by clustering.

In Section 3.4, we will demonstrate that the two properties are useful for online data maintenance.

3.3 Concept Drift Detection

After the prototype-based data representation, we introduce two heuristic strategies to identify abruptly drifting concepts, so that the classification model allows quickly learning and adapting to emerging new concepts. Instead of only investigating the change of the data distribution (for details, see the review paper by Gama *et al.* [6]), we exactly examine the change of the target concepts (i.e., the class distributions).

Formally, let D_t and D_{t+1} be two given sequential data chunks in a data stream D, and $L = \{l_1, l_2, \cdots, l_{|L|}\}$ be the set of labels. The objective is to analyze whether or not the statistical properties of each target concept (class distribution) between D_t and D_{t+1} have changed over time.

3.3.1 Principal Component Analysis (PCA)

To identify concept drift, the first proposal is to analyze the change of each class distribution using principal component analysis (PCA):

- For each class label $l \in L$, the examples associated with class label l in two data sets (D_t and D_{t+1}) are collected, respectively, denoted as D_t^l and D_{t+1}^l (e.g., D_t^1 and D_{t+1}^1 in Fig. 3), if existing.
- PCA is used to decompose the covariance matrix Σ of examples of each individual collected data chunk, which is denoted by $\Sigma = VEV^T$. The orthogonal matrix V is called eigenvector matrix and the diagonal matrix E is eigenvalue matrix. The eigenvectors represent the principal directions of the data set, and the eigenvalues represent the variance along these directions. We sort the eigenvectors according to the corresponding eigenvalues in descending order. Finally, the major direction of the data set is obtained (e.g., $V_{D_t}^1(1)$ is the major direction of D_t^1 for class **1**).

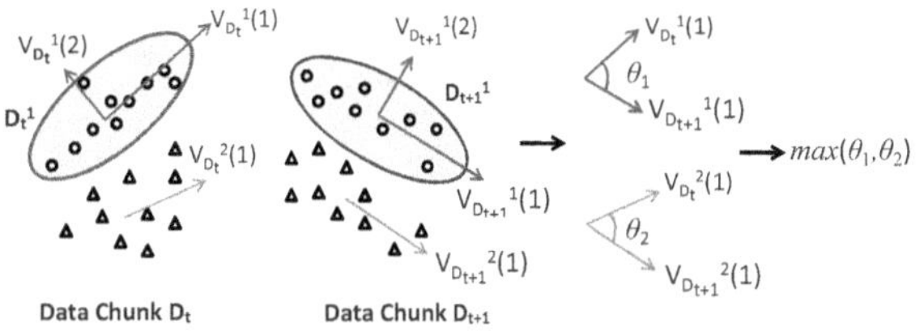

Figure 3: PCA-based concept drift analysis.

- We analyze the concept drift between two data sets (D_t and D_{t+1}) by investigating the variances of all class distributions. Specifically, let $V_{D_t}^l(1)$ and $V_{D_{t+1}}^l(1)$ be the major eigenvectors for class label l on the data set D_t and D_{t+1}, respectively, the degree of concept drift is finally defined as:

$$Angle(D_t, D_{t+1}) = \max_{l \in L} acos(V_{D_t}^l(1) \cdot V_{D_{t+1}}^l(1)), \quad (5)$$

where $\cdot$ denotes the inner product. For illustration, Fig. 3 describes the procedure of PCA-based concept drift analysis.

3.3.2 Statistical Analysis

The second strategy for concept drift detection is based on statistical analysis. The basic idea is to compute a suitable statistic, which is sensitive to class distribution changes between two sets of examples. The degree of concept drift is measured by the resulting p-value. Although statistical analysis is a straightforward solution to concept drift detection, computing statistics on multivariate data is usually complicated and time consuming. Here, we extend Brunner and Munzel's generalized Wilcoxon test statistic [4], [11] to compare the differences of class distributions of two data sets. In contrast to most existing statistics (e.g., Welch test, Mann-Whitney U test), this non-parametric statistical test allows for relaxation of the assumption of equality of variance and normal distributions simultaneously. More importantly, it allows an efficient computation. Formally, Brunner and Munzel's generalized Wilcoxon test statistic is calculated as follows.

Given each data pair (D_t^l and D_{t+1}^l), we investigate whether the sets of examples corresponding to class label l in the data sets D_t and D_{t+1} are significantly different. For this purpose, we define the intra- and inter-rank on both data sets as follows. Let $\Gamma^l = D_t^l \bigcup D_{t+1}^l$, $R_{D_t^l}^{ij}$, $R_{D_{t+1}^l}^{ij}$ and $R_{\Gamma^l}^{ij}$ are defined as the rank of examples $x \in D_t^l$, $y \in D_{t+1}^l$ and $z \in \Gamma^l$ on the jth dimension, respectively. In addition, we further calculate $\overline{R_{D_t^l}^{j}}$ and $\overline{R_{D_{t+1}^l}^{j}}$, which are the jth dimensional mean ranks of examples from D_t^l and D_{t+1}^l in the data set Γ^l. Formally, we compute the estimated variance σ_{BF}^2 as follows:

$$\sigma_{BF}^2 = \frac{(|D_t^l| + |D_{t+1}^l|)\nu_{D_t^l}^2}{|D_{t+1}|} + \frac{(|D_t^l| + |D_{t+1}^l|)\nu_{D_{t+1}^l}^2}{|D_t^l|}, \quad (6)$$

where

$$\nu_{D_t^l}^2 = \frac{1}{|D_t^l| - 1} \sum_{j=1}^{d} \sum_{i=1}^{|D_t^l|} (R_{\Gamma^l}^{ij} - R_{D_t^l}^{ij} - \overline{R_{D_t^l}^{j}} + \frac{|D_t^l| + 1}{2})^2, \quad (7)$$

$$\nu^2_{D^l_{t+1}} = \frac{1}{|D^l_{t+1}|-1}\sum_{j=1}^{d}\sum_{i=1}^{|D^l_{t+1}|}(R^{ij}_{\Gamma^l} - R^{ij}_{D^l_{t+1}} - \overline{R^j_{D^l_{t+1}}} + \frac{|D^l_{t+1}|+1}{2})^2. \tag{8}$$

Finally, the adapted Brunner and Munzel's generalized Wilcoxon test statistic, W^l_{BF}, is defined as:

$$W^l_{BF} = \sqrt{\frac{|D^l_t||D^l_{t+1}|}{|D^l_t| + |D^l_{t+1}|}} \cdot \frac{\sum_{j=1}^{d}(\overline{R^j_{D^l_t}} - \overline{R^j_{D^l_{t+1}}})}{\sigma_{BF}} \tag{9}$$

If both numbers of examples are large enough (>20), then the statistic W^l_{BF} is asymptotically standard normal. The test statistic is compared with a normal distribution of zero mean and unit standard deviation to obtain a p-value. The minimal value of all resulting p-values on the data pairs is used to measure the degree of concept drift between the two data chunks D_t and D_{t+1}.

3.4 Online Data Maintenance

In this section we will first demonstrate how to learn the representativeness of prototypes over time. Subsequently, a hierarchical tree structure, called P-Tree, is proposed to dynamically maintain the set of prototypes and evolving concepts building upon the prototype-based data representation and concept drift detection as introduced above.

3.4.1 Error-driven representativeness learning

In an evolving data stream, either short-term or long-term historical examples may be important for prediction. Traditional single model learning or ensemble learning approaches usually capture the current data concept by operating on a sliding window of data or a set of data chunks. However, how to decide the size of a window or horizon of the training data is a non-trivial task. In addition, for both traditional single model learning or ensemble learning, usually, not all examples in the window or in a data chunk are relevant for classification. Therefore, in this paper, we propose an error-driven approach to automatically learn the representativeness of data and dynamically identify the short-term or long-term prototypical examples to capture the data concepts.

The basic idea is to leverage the prediction performance of incoming examples to infer the representativeness of examples in the training data. Formally, given a new example x, let $\mathcal{C}$ be the current training data set (a set of prototypes), and $y \in \mathcal{C}$ the one prototype nearest to x. x_l and x_{pl} are the true label and the predicted label of x by y, respectively. The representativeness of the prototype y is updated as follows:

$$Rep(y) := Rep(y) + Sign(x_{pl}, x_l), \tag{10}$$

where the initial value of $Rep(y)$ is one and $Sign(x, y)$ is the sign function, and 1 if x equals y, -1 otherwise.

3.4.2 P-Tree

To support efficient and effective online data maintenance, we propose a tree structure called the P-Tree. The P-Tree is a hierarchical tree structure consisting of two levels, where the first level stores a set of time-changing prototypes capturing the current concept, and the second level stores drifting concepts over time (see Fig. 4). Except for the inclusion of new, incoming examples continuously, the P-Tree is also

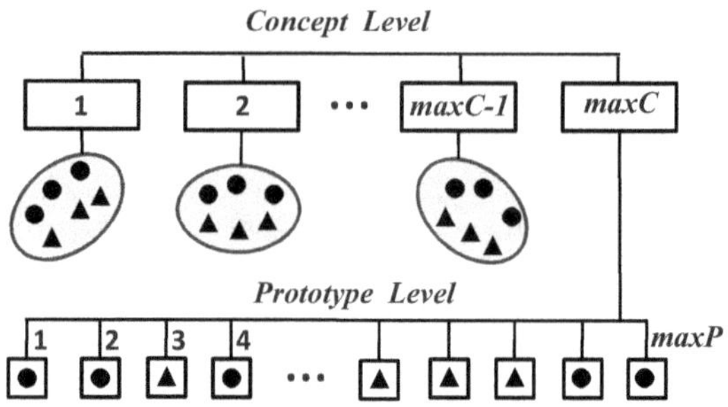

Figure 4: An illustration of the P-Tree structure.

required to be updated when the following two scenarios occur: (a) *maximum boundary*, or (b) *concept drift*.

Maximum boundary limits the number of prototypes and the number of concepts that can be stored in the P-Tree. This restriction allows us to perform data stream classification on any computer at hand in an any-space memory framework. The updating procedure is as follows: For each incoming example, if the size of the prototypes in the P-Tree does not exceed the maximum boundary (i.e., $maxP$), it is directly inserted into the entry on the first level of the P-Tree, and meanwhile the representativeness of existing prototypes in the P-Tree is computed based on error-driven learning (cf. Section 3.4.1). Once the size exceeds $maxP$, prototypes with different representativeness are handled separately. (a) Prototypes with low representativeness (e.g., a negative value) in the P-Tree are directly removed. (b) Prototypes with high representativeness (e.g., a positive value) in the P-Tree are kept, which indicates these prototypes can capture the current concept well. (c) Prototypes with unchanged representativeness are further summarized by a new and smaller set of prototypes based on synchronization-inspired constrained clustering (cf. Section 3.2). Due to the two desirable properties of prototype-based data representation (cf. Section 3.2), the newly generated prototypes preserve the original data structure well and can be summarized further on a higher level of abstraction. Moreover, to maintain the time-changing concepts on the second level, once the number of concepts is greater than $maxC$, the oldest concept is removed.

The second scenario occurs when a new concept is emerging, which can be detected by PCA or statistical analysis (cf. Section 3.3). In this case, we draw sample data from all prototypes representing a previous concept, and perform synchronization-inspired constrained clustering on it. The resulting set of new prototypes is inserted into one entry of the concept level of the P-Tree. Meanwhile, all prototypes representing the previous concept are removed from the first level of the P-Tree. Moreover, if there is no significant concept change over time (i.e., gradual concept drift or no concept drift), we also extract the concept based on the prototypes in the P-Tree by clustering after a specified time T; yet the prototypes are not removed. This strategy helps to give a summarization of data over time on the concept level.

3.5 SyncStream Algorithm

Building upon the proposed online data maintenance, finally instance-based learning in the form of the nearest neighbor classifier is used for data stream classification. In contrast to eager learning approaches, SyncStream only needs

Algorithm 1 SyncStream

```
Input: D, D_init, maxP, maxC, chunkSize, type, T

P-Tree.insert(D_init); //P-Tree initialization
while NoError do
  for each new example x ∈ D do
    //error-driven representativeness learning
    y := NN(P-Tree, x); x.prelabel := y.label;
    if x.prelabel == x.label then
      y.Rep++;
    else
      y.Rep--;
    end if
    measure := computAccuracy(x.prelabel);
    P-Tree.insert(x);

    //maximum boundary in prototype level
    if P-Tree.prototypeSize == maxP then
      S_n := P-Tree.getNegativePrototypes();
      P-Tree.remove(S_n);
      S_u := P-Tree.getUnchangedPrototypes();
      P := ConstrainedSync(S_u);
      P-Tree.remove(S_u); P-Tree.insert(P);
    end if

    //maximum boundary in concept level
    if P-Tree.conceptSize == maxC then
      P-Tree.removeOldestConcept();
    end if

    //concept drift detection
    if numObj==chunkSize then
      if type == PCA then
        θ := angle(curChunk, preChunk);
      else
        p := p-value(curChunk, preChunk);
      end if
      if θ ≥ 60° or p ≤ 0.01 or numInstance ≥ T then
        P_s := Sample(P-Tree.prototypes);
        C_s := ConstrainedSync(P_s);
        P-Tree.addConcept(C_s);
        if θ ≥ 60° or p ≤ 0.01 then
          P-Tree.prototypes.clear();
        end if
      end if
    end if
  end for
end while

Output: P-Tree, measure;
```

to maintain the online training data (represented by a small set of time-changing prototypes) in the P-Tree. Finally, the pseudocode of SyncStream is shown in Algorithm 1.

4. EXPERIMENTAL EVALUATION

In this section, we evaluate our proposed algorithm SyncStream on both synthetic and real-world data streams.

4.1 Experiment Setup

Data sets. We evaluate the proposed method on synthetic data and four different types of real-world data: Spam, Electricity, Covtype, and Sensor. Table 1 lists statistics of the four real-world data streams.

Synthetic Data was generated based on a moving hyperplane [16]. The hyperplane in 2-dimensional space was used to simulate different time-changing concepts by altering its orientation and position in a smooth or sudden manner. In this study, two synthetic data consisting of one million examples each were created to characterize the data stream with gradual and sudden concept drift, respectively (Fig. 5 and Fig. 6).

Spam Filtering Data is a collection of 9324 email messages derived from the Spam Assassin collection[1]. Each email is represented by 500 attributes using the Boolean bag-of-words approach.

Electricity Data contains 45,312 instances, which was collected from the Australian New South Wales Electricity Market for every five minutes. In this market, prices are not fixed and affected by demand and supply on the market.

Covtype Data containing 581,012 instances describes seven forest cover types on a 30×30 meter grid with 54 different geographic measurements.

Sensor Data collects information (temperature, humidity, light, and sensor voltage) from 54 sensors deployed in the Intel Berkeley Research Lab over a two months period (one reading per 1-3 minutes). It totally contains 2,219,803 instances belonging to 54 classes.

Evaluation Metrics. To quantitatively evaluate SyncStream, we consider the following performance metrics:

- *Prediction performance.* We evaluate the performance of SyncStream in terms of Accuracy, Precision, Recall and F1-Measure.
- *Efficiency.* We evaluate the computation time as efficiency metric.
- *Sensitivity.* We test how classification performance is sensitive against parameter variation.

Selection of comparison methods. To extensively evaluate the proposed algorithm SyncStream, we compare its performance to several representatives of data stream classification paradigms.

Adaptive Hoeffding Tree [9]: is an incremental, anytime decision tree induction algorithm capable of learning from massive evolving data streams, using ADWIN to monitor the performance of branches in the tree and to replace them by new branches if they turn out to be more accurate.

IBLStreams [13]: an instance-based learning algorithm for classification on data streams. A prediction for a new example is achieved by combining the outputs of the neighbors of this example in the training data.

Weighted Ensemble [16]: a general framework for mining concept-drifting data streams using weighted ensemble classifiers.

OzaBagAdwin [2]: is an online bagging method by Oza and Russell with the addition of the ADWIN algorithm as a change detector and an estimator for the weights of the boosting method. When a change is detected, the worst classifier of the ensemble of classifiers is removed and a new classifier is added to the ensemble.

PASC [8]: is a pool and accuracy based strategy to exploit the existence of recurring concepts in the learning process and improve the classification of data streams.

We have implemented SyncStream in Java. The source code of PASC was obtained from the authors, and the IBLStreams algorithm is available at: `http://www.uni-marburg.de/fb12/kebi/research/software/iblstreams`. Adaptive Hoeffding Tree, Weighted Ensemble and OzaBagAdwin have

[1] `http://spamassassin.apache.org/`

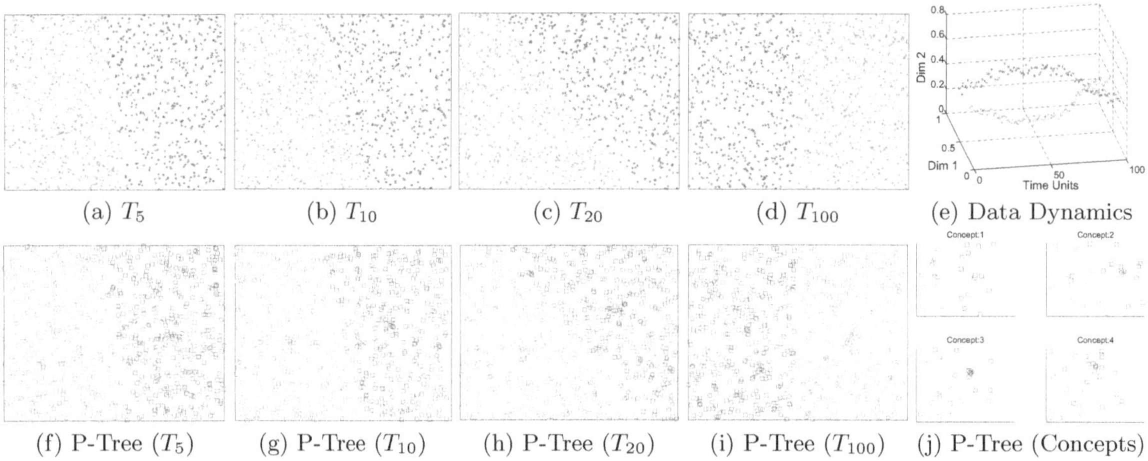

(a) T_5 (b) T_{10} (c) T_{20} (d) T_{100} (e) Data Dynamics

(f) P-Tree (T_5) (g) P-Tree (T_{10}) (h) P-Tree (T_{20}) (i) P-Tree (T_{100}) (j) P-Tree (Concepts)

Figure 5: Performance of SyncStream algorithm on synthetic data stream with gradual concept drift.

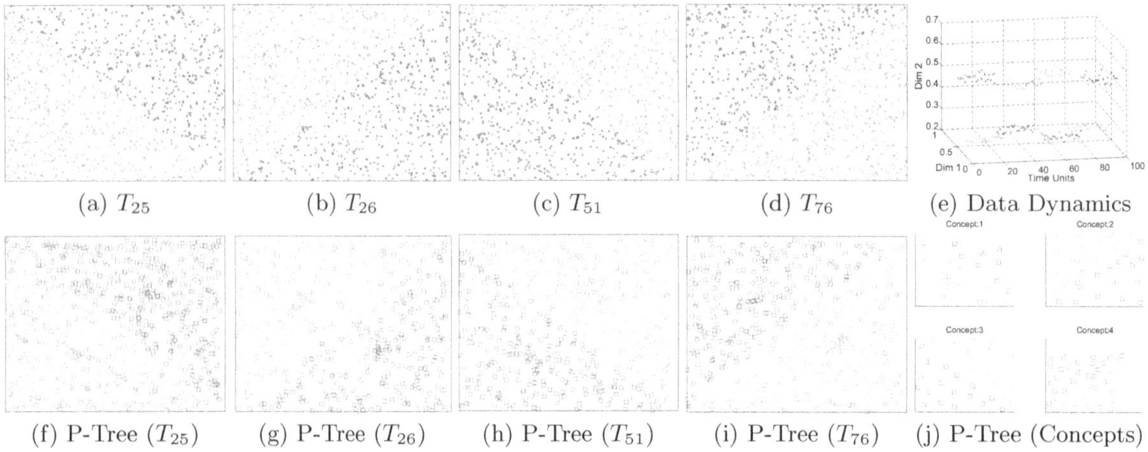

(a) T_{25} (b) T_{26} (c) T_{51} (d) T_{76} (e) Data Dynamics

(f) P-Tree (T_{25}) (g) P-Tree (T_{26}) (h) P-Tree (T_{51}) (i) P-Tree (T_{76}) (j) P-Tree (Concepts)

Figure 6: Performance of SyncStream algorithm on synthetic data stream with sudden concept drift.

been implemented in the MOA framework available at `http://moa.cms.waikato.ac.nz/`. All experiments have been performed on a workstation with 3.0 GHz CPU and 32 GB RAM.

4.2 Proof of Concept

We start the evaluation with two-dimensional synthetic data streams to facilitate presentation and demonstrate some properties of SyncStream.

Concept Modeling: We first evaluate whether or not SyncStream can capture the data concept with the proposed P-Tree. Fig. 5 (a) - (d) and Fig. 6 (a) - (d) show two synthetic data streams consisting of one million examples with gradual and sudden concept drift, respectively. The evolving mean values of the data for each class are plotted in Fig. 5 (e) and Fig. 6 (e), where each time unit (T) is composed of one thousand examples. It is interesting to note that the derived prototypes in the P-Tree at any time interval enable to capture the changing data concept regardless of the type of data stream (Fig. 5 (f) - (i) and Fig. 6 (f) - (i)). Instead of learning a recent window of historical data or learning a set of base classifiers as a black box, SyncStream well captures the trend of time-changing data concepts by maintaining a set of short-term or long-term prototypes dynamically. Fig. 6 (j) displays the four changing concepts, which are preserved in the concept level of the P-Tree. For the data stream with gradual concept drift, the concepts are also learned after a specified time window (e.g., 25,000 examples in this experiment) and inserted into the concept level of the P-Tree (see Fig. 5 (j)).

Concept Drift Detection: To investigate the performance of sudden concept drift detection, Fig. 7 shows the results based on the PCA and statistical analysis, respectively. For the data stream with gradual concept drift, we can observe that the PCA-resulting angles over time are relatively stable and lower than $10°$, and similarly, the derived p-values are high and no significant concept drift is detected (see Fig. 7 (a) and (c)). In contrast, for the sudden concept-drifting data stream, both the PCA and the statistical approach are capable of identifying the abruptly changing concept effectively (Fig. 7 (b) and (d)).

Prototype-based Data Representation: Based on the synchronization-inspired constrained clustering, important examples are further summarized as a set of prototypes. From Fig. 5 and Fig. 6, it is interesting to observe that the derived prototypes stored in the P-Tree preserve the data structure as well as the class distribution. Moreover,

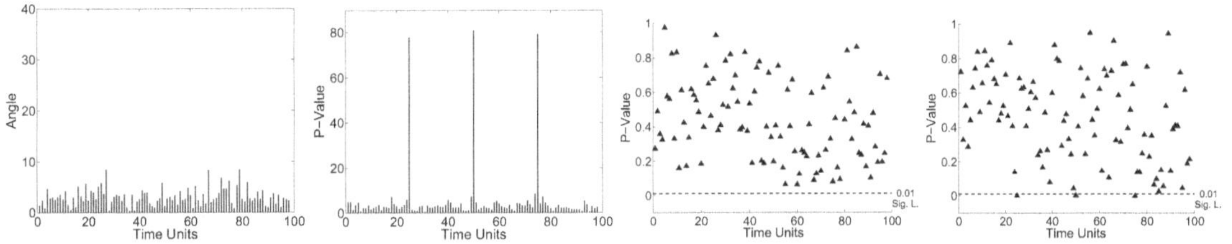

(a) PCA (G) (b) PCA (S) (c) Statistical Test (G) (d) Statistical Test (S)

Figure 7: Results of two strategies for concept drift detection, where "G" and "S" indicate gradual and sudden concept drift, respectively.

inappropriate examples can be handled even in the presence of noise by error-driven representativeness learning (Fig. 8). The proposed prototype-based data representation provides an effective and efficient strategy to handle a large amount of online training data.

(a) Data stream with noise (b) Prototypes in P-Tree

Figure 8: Effective prototype-based data representation in a data stream with noise.

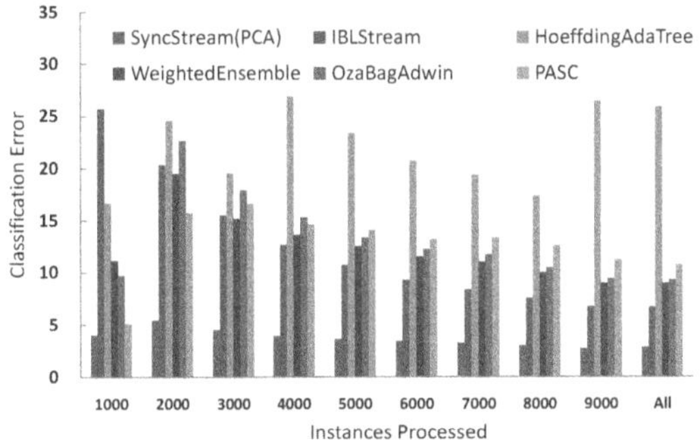

Figure 9: Performance of different data stream classification algorithms on spam data.

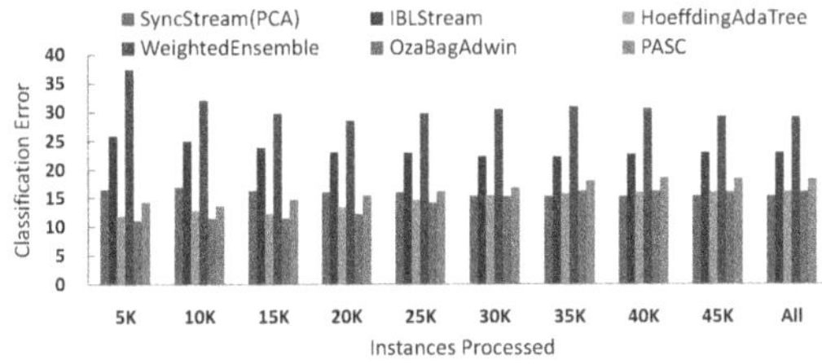

Figure 10: Performance of different data stream classification algorithms on electricity data.

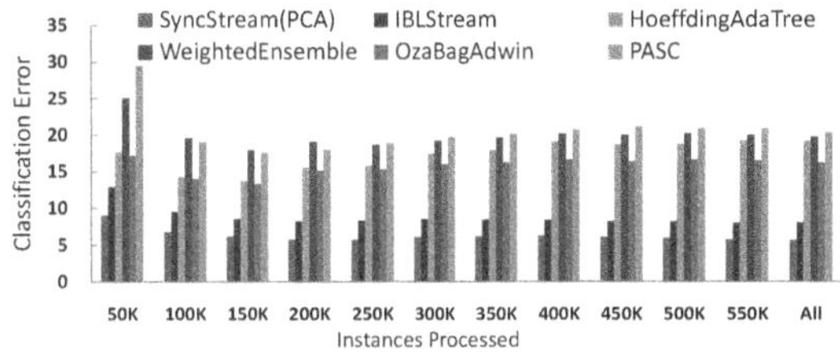

Figure 11: Performance of different data stream classification algorithms on covtype data.

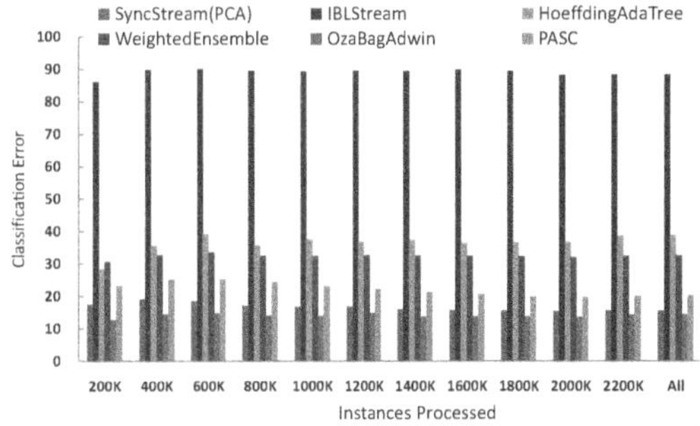

Figure 12: Performance of different data stream classification algorithms on sensor data.

4.3 Prediction Performance Analysis

In this section, we compare the performance of different stream classification algorithms on the mentioned four real data streams. For SyncStream, unless specified otherwise, the parameters were set to $maxP = 1000$, $maxC = 10$ and $chunkSize = 1000$. For all other algorithms, the default parameters suggested by the authors were used.

Fig. 9 - Fig. 12 plot the prediction performance against the number of processed instances. Generally, with an increasing number of processed examples, the prediction error of SyncStream is quite small and relatively stable. This is the result of modeling concepts by sets of dynamically adjusted prototypes. Instead of focusing on recent data or a set of data chunks, SyncStream can select the prototypes to capture the data concept on the instance level. Although IBLStream is similar to SyncStream in capturing local data characteristics by instance-based learning, it cannot adapt well to evolving concepts, and thus prediction performance fluctuates over time. HoeffdingAdaTree is a typical single model learner: due to the insufficient handling of time-changing concepts, it achieves the worst prediction performance in most cases. Although the ensemble learning ap-

Table 1: Performance of different data stream classification algorithms on real-world data sets.

Data	#Obj	#Dim	#Class	Methods	Acc.	Prec.	Rec.	F_1	Time (ms)
Spam	9324	500	2	**SyncStream (PCA)**	**0.9719**	**0.9590**	**0.9665**	**0.9627**	60410
				SyncStream (Stat.)	**0.9719**	**0.9590**	**0.9665**	**0.9627**	29780
				IBLStream	0.9370	0.9070	0.372	0.9218	702632
				HoeffdingAdaTree	0.9071	0.8717	0.8935	0.8824	2252
				WeightedEnsemble	0.8629	0.8139	0.8176	0.8158	13000
				OzaBagAdwin	0.9108	0.8765	0.8973	0.8868	10848
				PASC	0.8931	0.9178	0.9415	0.9295	**2142**
Electricity	45,312	8	2	**SyncStream (PCA)**	0.8457	0.8423	0.8420	0.8421	3118
				SyncStream (Stat.)	**0.8459**	**0.8425**	0.8419	0.8422	3280
				IBLStream	0.7688	0.7648	0.7584	0.7616	7512
				HoeffdingAdaTree	0.8398	0.8409	0.8296	0.8352	**750**
				WeightedEnsemble	0.7092	0.7024	0.7022	0.7023	3920
				OzaBagAdwin	0.8397	0.8399	0.8302	0.8350	3810
				PASC	0.8170	0.8316	**0.8552**	**0.8432**	1327
Covtype	581,012	54	7	**SyncStream (PCA)**	**0.9438**	**0.8915**	**0.8980**	**0.8947**	207176
				SyncStream (Stat.)	**0.9438**	**0.8915**	**0.8980**	**0.8947**	226331
				IBLStream	0.9197	0.8620	0.8573	0.8597	3005412
				HoeffdingAdaTree	0.8087	0.7085	0.7173	0.7129	**31692**
				WeightedEnsemble	0.8033	0.7476	0.6690	0.7061	365582
				OzaBagAdwin	0.8383	0.7848	0.7722	0.7784	176000
				PASC	0.7972	0.8291	0.8348	0.8319	125387
Sensor	2,219,803	5	54	**SyncStream (PCA)**	0.8453	0.8508	0.8460	0.8484	244110
				SyncStream (Stat.)	0.8453	0.8508	0.8460	0.8484	246492
				IBLStream	0.1173	0.1805	0.1397	0.1575	345930
				HoeffdingAdaTree	0.6121	0.6269	0.6282	0.6276	**166600**
				WeightedEnsemble	0.6752	0.7918	0.6805	0.7319	2105133
				OzaBagAdwin	**0.8563**	**0.8660**	**0.8639**	**0.8649**	1343065
				PASC	0.7968	0.8420	0.8150	0.8283	264161

proaches, Weighted Ensemble, OzaBagAdwin and PASC, allow adapting to changing concepts quickly according to previous studies, the classification accuracies are not promising, which may caused by the two limitations stated in Section 1. Table 1 further summarizes the performance of the algorithms in terms of different evaluation measures. Regarding the computation time, HoeffdingAdaTree is the fastest algorithm due to the Hoeffding bound, yet the classification accuracy suffers. SyncStream, Weighted Ensemble, OzaBagAdwin and PASC are comparable, while IBLStream is the most time-consuming algorithm. From the experiments, we can see that SyncStream not only allows making accurate classifications, but also working efficiently in terms of computation time (Table 1).

4.4 Sensitivity Analysis

In this section, we perform a sensitivity analysis of SyncStream on the cover type data.

Maximum Boundary: As stated in Section 3.4.2, the maximum number of prototypes $maxP$ needs to be specified to indicate how many prototypes can be dynamically maintained in the P-Tree according to the available computational resources. The higher the value of $maxP$, the more prototypes can be managed to model the concepts. In this experiment, we varied $maxP$ from 500 to 3000. Fig. 13 (a) plots the classification accuracies dependent on the numbers of prototypes, the corresponding computation time is shown in Fig. 13 (b). We observe that the classification performance is quite stable, while the computation time is gradually growing due to the increased effort needed for nearest neighbor search.

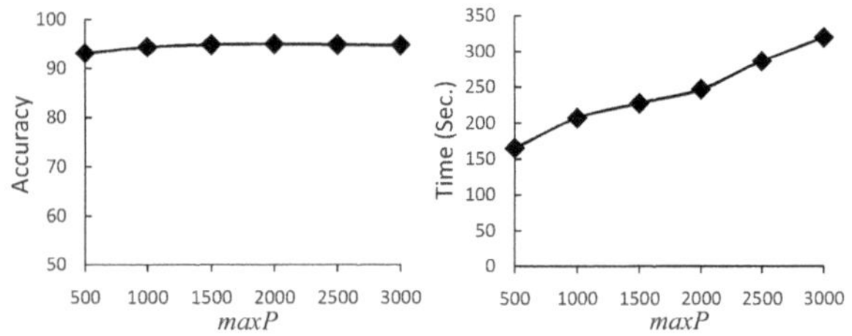

Figure 13: The sensitivity analysis with $maxP$.

Chunk Size: The chunk size determines how many examples have been used to examine whether the concept has changed across two consecutive data chunks. Fig. 14 (a) shows the classification performance with respect to different chunk sizes ranging from 500 to 3000. Similarly, the corresponding number of time-changing concepts is reported in Fig. 14 (b). With increasing chunk size, the number of detected concepts is gradually decreasing, as more data make the transition from one concept to another appear smoother. However, thanks to error-driven representativeness learning, the set of dynamical prototypes in the P-Tree has already learned the evolving concepts implicitly. By combining representativeness learning and concept drift detection, SyncStream allows adapting to both gradual and sudden concept drift quickly, which results in high classification accuracies in the experiments (Fig. 14 (a)).

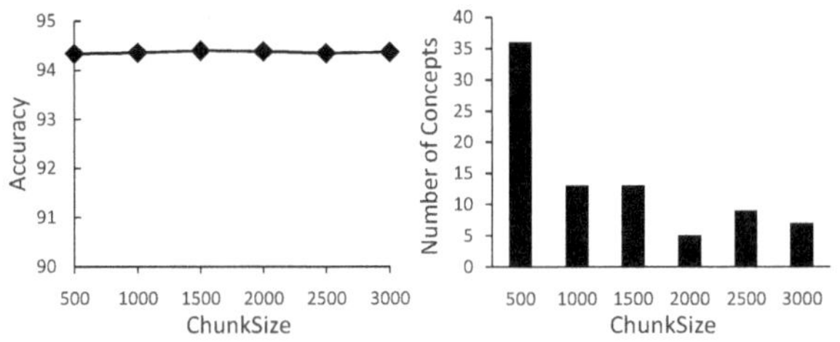

Figure 14: Sensitivity analysis with *chunkSize*.

5. DISCUSSION AND CONCLUSION

In this paper, we introduce a new prototype-based classification algorithm, SyncStream, to learn from evolving data streams. While existing approaches focus on learning a single model on a window of recent data or a set of base classifiers on recent data chunks, time-changing concepts may not be learned well in this way due to two factors: the difficulty of selecting a suitable horizon of the training data and the loss of relevant historical data. In the light of these problems, this paper proposes error-driven representativeness learning to determine the importance of training examples. Only representative examples, allowing to model the current concept, are kept and further summarized as a smaller set of prototypes by synchronization-inspired constrained clustering. With this strategy, SyncStream allows dynamically learning a set of prototypes to capture evolving concepts implicitly on the level of instances. Moreover, in order to adapt to abrupt concept drift quickly, two heuristic concept drift detection approaches are introduced. Equipped with both implicit and explicit concept drift handling, SyncStream allows modeling time-changing concepts (either gradual or sudden) effectively. One other attractive property of SyncStream is its any-memory property. Owing to the prototype-based data representation, a multi-scale representation of the data (a set of prototypes) is possible. Although SyncStream is an instance-based learning scheme, it largely differs from traditional instance-based learning such as IBLStreams. One main difference is that IBLStreams keeps track of recent instances, while SyncStream dynamically learns a set of prototypes and supports efficient data maintenance. In comprehensive experiments, we have shown that SyncStream outperforms several other state-of-the-art data stream classification methods.

6. REFERENCES

[1] A. Bifet and R. Gavalda. Learning from time-changing data with adaptive windowing. In *Proceedings of the 11th SIAM International Conference on Data Mining*, pages 443–448, 2007.

[2] A. Bifet, G. Holmes, B. Pfahringer, R. Kirkby, and R. Gavaldà. New ensemble methods for evolving data streams. In *Proceedings of the 15th ACM SIGKDD international conference on Knowledge discovery and data mining*, pages 139–148, 2009.

[3] C. Böhm, C. Plant, J. Shao, and Q. Yang. Clustering by synchronization. In *Proceedings of the 16th ACM SIGKDD international conference on Knowledge discovery and data mining*, pages 583–592, 2010.

[4] E. Brunner and U. Munzel. The nonparametric Behrens-Fisher problem: Asymptotic theory and a small-sample approximation. *Biometrical Journal*, 42(1):17–25, 2000.

[5] A. Dries and U. Rückert. Adaptive concept drift detection. *Statistical Analysis and Data Mining*, 2(5-6):311–327, 2009.

[6] J. Gama, A. Bifet, M. Pechenizkiy, and A. Bouchachia. A survey on concept drift adaptation. *ACM Computing Surveys*, (5-6):1–35, 2013.

[7] J. Gama, P. Medas, G. Castillo, and P. Rodrigues. Learning with drift detection. *Lecture notes in computer science*, pages 286–295, 2004.

[8] M. J. Hosseini, Z. Ahmadi, and H. Beigy. Using a classifier pool in accuracy based tracking of recurring concepts in data stream classification. *Evolving Systems*, 4(1):43–60, 2013.

[9] G. Hulten, L. Spencer, and P. Domingos. Mining time-changing data streams. In *Proceedings of the 7th ACM SIGKDD international conference on Knowledge discovery and data mining*, pages 97–106, 2001.

[10] L. I. Kuncheva and J. S. Sánchez. Nearest neighbour classifiers for streaming data with delayed labelling. In *IEEE 8th International Conference on Data Mining*, pages 869–874, 2008.

[11] M. Neuhäuser and G. D. Ruxton. Distribution-free two-sample comparisons in the case of heterogeneous variances. *Behavioral Ecology and Sociobiology*, 63(4):617–623, 2009.

[12] S. Papadimitriou, A. Brockwell, and C. Faloutsos. Adaptive, hands-off stream mining. In *Proceedings of the 29th international conference on Very large data bases-Volume 29*, pages 560–571, 2003.

[13] A. Shaker and E. Hüllermeier. IBLStreams: a system for instance-based classification and regression on data streams. *Evolving Systems*, 3(4):235–249, 2012.

[14] J. Shao, X. He, C. Böhm, Q. Yang, and C. Plant. Synchronization-inspired partitioning and hierarchical clustering. *IEEE Transaction on Knwoledge and Data Engineering*, 25(4):893–905, 2013.

[15] K. Wagstaff and C. Cardie. Clustering with instance-level constraints. In *Proceedings of the 7th International Conference on Machine Learning*, pages 1103–1110, 2000.

[16] H. Wang, W. Fan, P. S. Yu, and J. Han. Mining concept-drifting data streams using ensemble classifiers. In *Proceedings of the 9th ACM SIGKDD international conference on Knowledge discovery and data mining*, pages 226–235, 2003.

[17] P. Zhang, B. J. Gao, X. Zhu, and L. Guo. Enabling fast lazy learning for data streams. In *IEEE 11th International Conference on Data Mining*, pages 932–941, 2011.

Detecting Moving Object Outliers In Massive-Scale Trajectory Streams

Yanwei Yu *
Yantai University
Yantai, Shandong China
yuyanwei0530@126.com

Lei Cao *
Elke A. Rundensteiner
Worcester Polytechnic Institute
Worcester, MA U.S.A
lcao|rundenst@cs.wpi.edu

Qin Wang
University of Science and Technology Beijing
Beijing, China
wangqin@ies.ustb.edu.cn

ABSTRACT

The detection of abnormal moving objects over high-volume trajectory streams is critical for real time applications ranging from military surveillance to transportation management. Yet this problem remains largely unexplored. In this work, we first propose classes of novel trajectory outlier definitions that model the anomalous behavior of moving objects for a large range of real time applications. Our theoretical analysis and empirical study on the Beijing Taxi and GMTI (Ground Moving Target Indicator) datasets demonstrate its effectiveness in capturing abnormal moving objects. Furthermore we propose a general strategy for efficiently detecting the new outlier classes. It features three fundamental optimization principles designed to minimize the detection costs. Our comprehensive experimental studies demonstrate that our proposed strategy drives the detection costs 100-fold down into practical realm for applications producing high volume trajectory streams to utilize.

Categories and Subject Descriptors

H.2 [**Information Systems**]: Database Management

Keywords

Outlier, Moving Object, Trajectory Stream

1. INTRODUCTION

Motivation. In recent years, the location-acquisition devices like GPS, smart phone, and RFID have become prevalent. These devices, monitoring the motion of vehicles, people, goods, services, and animals, are producing massive-volume high-speed trajectory streams. Many applications from traffic management [5], security surveillance [2], scientific studies [13], to mobile social networks [18] rely on continuously discovering abnormal objects in such trajectory streams to deliver critical decisions within an actionable time.

*Authors contribute equally to this work. This work was done when Yanwei Yu visited Worcester Polytechnic Institute.

KDD'14, August 24–27, 2014, New York, NY, USA.
Copyright 2014 ACM 978-1-4503-2956-9/14/08 ...$15.00.
http://dx.doi.org/10.1145/2623330.2623735.

In security surveillance systems, a visitor at a miliary base will be considered as an outlier and thus a potential safety threat if he does not obey the strict order to stay together with his designated group members. In traffic management systems a taxi driver will be classified as an outlier in terms of his erratic behavior if he keeps changing lanes and switching his neighboring travel companions. Potentially this may help flag speeding, drunk driving, or other erratic behaviors of concern.

Similarly, if considering the price, volume, or gains of stocks at a particular time point as coordinates in a multi-dimensional space, then real time stock quotes can be modeled as a trajectory stream. Its analysts may reveal recent promising stocks by detecting the outlier stocks whose performance trajectories dramatically deviate from those of other stocks in the same industry.

Challenges. In all the applications described above, outliers can be characterized as moving objects that behave differently from the majority in trajectory streams. Despite the importance of continuously detecting such types of outliers, to the best of our knowledge, this problem has not previously been considered in the literature.

In the streaming context Bu et al. [2] defined when to consider a trajectory *segment* of a single moving object to be an outlier, while our work instead focuses on a much more complicated problem, namely locating outlier objects in the trajectory stream populated with massive scale moving objects. In [2] a given trajectory is divided into equal sized segments. A segment is said to be abnormal if it is not similar to a group of segments adjacent to it in time. The effectiveness of this definition is based on the *local continuity* observation. Namely one moving object usually is expected to behave consistently within a short time interval. However in our context whether one moving object is an outlier or not depends on its relationship with other objects. The moving patterns of a large set of objects are more complex and dynamic than one single object's path and hence cannot be modeled by the local continuity property. Therefore this definition cannot be applied to our problem.

In static spatio-temporal (time series) databases, a trajectory is said to be an outlier if it does not show the global characteristics of the majority of the trajectories in the overall database [8, 11]. Since all trajectories are known apriori, these techniques rely on expensive offline pre-processing. Normally they first mine all frequent patterns to build a model of global characteristics of the dataset. In the second phase the model is then used to classify each trajectory as being either an outlier or not. However in unbounded continuous trajectory streams where concept drift consistently arises, using one single (pre-computed) model to continuously detect outliers would inevitably lead to inaccurate results, while periodically rebuilding the global model can be prohibitively expensive for real time stream trajectory outlier detection due to the modeling costs.

Therefore to effectively identify abnormal objects in trajectory streams, new semantics have to be defined to satisfy the requirement of streaming trajectory outlier detection. First, lightweight metrics suitable to identify outliers in place of complicated statistical models are desirable. These metrics must capture the key characteristics of moving objects. Second, given the dynamic nature of stream trajectories this definition should be robust to concept drift and amenable to swiftly evicting obsolete models of outlierness.

Furthermore, if such a lightweight yet effective outlier definition could be found, we must be able to process this detection semantics to assure we can extract real time insights from *high volume* trajectory stream data, such as the streams of surveillance, stocks, or traffic. Thus strategies must be designed to efficiently discover the stream trajectory outliers online as stream data passes by.

Proposed Solution. In this paper, we propose new trajectory outlier definitions by introducing the notion of "trajectory neighbor" to measure the similarity among different trajectories. Unlike the traditional neighbor definition [8] which simply considers the physical distance among two objects at a given point of time, the trajectory neighbor concept captures the key properties of stream trajectories. Namely it not only considers the spatial proximity of trajectory objects, but also takes the duration of the spatial similarity across time into account.

Furthermore our analysis of realtime trajectory applications reveals that applications vary in their particular synchronization requirements with respect to the neighbor relationships among multiple trajectories. We thus propose two variants of the trajectory neighbor concept with different synchronization regulations that facilitate users to customize the semantics via controlled parameters. By measuring the *Precision* and *Recall* on the *GMTI* [3] and *Taxi* [16, 17] data, our empirical study confirms that the new definitions successfully model the deviating behavior that characterizes outliers in a rich variety of trajectory stream applications.

Moreover we design a comprehensive strategy to efficiently detect these new outlier types over high volume trajectory streams, called the *minimal examination* (MEX) framework.

The MEX framework integrates three fundamental optimization principles that apply to both neighbor-based outlier definitions. First, given a trajectory Tr_i, the *minimal support examination* principle guides MEX to always acquire only the minimal yet sufficient set of neighbor evidence called *minimal support*. The key insight is to stop immediately once the outlier status of Tr_i has been proven. Second, MEX leverages the temporal relationships among trajectory points to prioritize the processing order among points during the neighbor search process. This principle, called *time-aware examination*, guarantees that we find the relationships most useful for outlier detection. Furthermore MEX establishes the *lifetime* concept signaling the furthest window up to which we can predict the status of Tr_i based on current trajectory evidence. This enables MEX to transform the periodical per-window based outlier detection process into a *lifetime-triggered* detection process. Our experimental studies on the Taxi data show that MEX can successfully handle up to one million moving objects per second on a standard desktop, rendering trajectory outlier detection practical in massive-scale moving object streams.

Contributions. The main contributions of this paper include: 1) We propose novel neighbor-based trajectory outlier definitions which are theoretically shown to successfully model the abnormal behavior of moving objects in the trajectory stream. 2) We design incremental algorithms for trajectory outlier detection which leverage the overlap of sliding windows. Our complexity analysis highlights the need for more sophisticated techniques. 3) We thus propose the *minimal examination* (MEX) framework equipped with three core optimization principles. 4) We propose efficient algorithms for the new trajectory outlier definitions based on the MEX framework, successfully driving the detection costs 100-fold down. 5) Our empirical study using GMTI and Taxi datasets demonstrate the robust *Precision* and *Recall* of our new proposed definitions.

2. NEIGHBOR-BASED TRAJECTORY OUTLIER DETECTION

2.1 Notations

We denote the set of n moving objects as $MO = \{o_1, o_2, \ldots, o_n\}$, where o_i is the moving object with $id = i$. The multi-dimensional data point p_i^j produced by the moving object o_i at time t_j is called a trajectory point of Tr_i. We assume a minimal time interval at which objects produce events as trajectory points. We utilize the term "timebin" to refer to this smallest time granularity. The trajectory of a moving object o_i is thus an infinite sequence of trajectory points produced at timebins $\{t_1, t_2, \ldots, t_j, \ldots\}$, denoted as Tr_i=$\{p_i^1, p_i^2, \ldots p_i^j, \ldots\}$. In this work a moving object is not limited to an object equipped with location-acquisition device. Instead it is an abstraction of any object that continuously observes distinct events along time. Correspondingly the trajectory point is not necessarily only a spatial position, but could be any multi-dimensional coordinate where each dimension corresponds to one of the domains of the attributes of an object's observation.

We define a trajectory stream *S* of *n* moving objects in *MO* as an infinite sequence of trajectory points ordered by timebins *S* = $\{p_1^1 p_2^1 \ldots p_n^1,\ p_1^2 p_2^2 \ldots p_n^2,\ \ldots,\ p_1^i p_2^i \ldots p_n^i,\ \ldots\}$. Trajectory points $p_1^i p_2^i \ldots p_n^i$ are said to fall into the same timebin i in the stream *S*.

In this work, we use the periodic sliding window semantics as proposed by CQL [1] to define a finite sub-stream of an infinite trajectory data stream. In particular, a query Q specifies a fixed window size w and slide size s for time-based windows, while count-based windows can similarly be defined. Each window W has a starting time $W.T_{start}$ and an ending time $W.T_{end} = W.T_{start} + w - 1$. The population of the current window W_c of *S* consists of all points whose timebin falls into W_c. It is the finite subsequence of the trajectory stream *S*: $\{p_1^{t_c-w+1} p_2^{t_c-w+1} \ldots p_n^{t_c-w+1}, p_1^{t_c-w+2} p_2^{t_c-w+2} \ldots p_n^{t_c-w+2}, \ldots, p_1^{t_c} p_2^{t_c} \ldots p_n^{t_c}\}$, where t_c is the current timebin. Periodically the current window W_c slides, causing $W.T_{start}$ and $W.T_{end}$ to increase by *s* timebins. Henceforth a trajectory Tr_i refers to a set of trajectory points produced by one moving object o_i throughout a window W_j.

We use the function $dist(p_m^j, p_n^j)$ to denote the distance between two trajectory points p_m^j and p_n^j at the same timebin j. Without loss of generality, we utilize Euclidean distance as the distance measure, though any other distance measure could equally be plugged in.

Definition 1. ***(Point Neighbor).*** *For two trajectory points p_m^j and p_n^j in the same timebin t_j, if $dist(p_m^j, p_n^j) \leq d$, we say that p_m^j is a **point neighbor** of p_n^j, with d a given distance threshold.*

For point p_n^j, all point neighbors of p_n^j at timebin t_j w.r.t. the distance threshold d comprise the **Point Neighbor Set** of p_n^j, denoted as $PN(p_n^j, d)$.

Definition 2. ***(Trajectory Neighbor).*** *In window W, trajectory Tr_m is called a **trajectory neighbor** of Tr_n w.r.t. the given timebin count threshold thr_t, iff there exist at least thr_t timebins in W such that p_m is a point neighbor of p_n at each of these thr_t timebins with point neighbor as per Def. 1.*

The set of trajectory neighbors of a trajectory Tr_n in the window W_c, w.r.t. distance threshold d and timebin count threshold thr_t is denoted as $TN(Tr_n, d, thr_t)$.

2.2 Trajectory Outlier Definitions

2.2.1 Point-Neighbor Based Trajectory Outlier

Definition 3. *Given a distance threshold d, a neighbor count threshold k, and timebin count threshold* thr_t*, a trajectory* Tr_i *in the window W is called a* ***point-neighbor based trajectory outlier****, or in short,* ***PN-Outlier****, if* $|T| < thr_t$*, where* $T = \{t_j \mid |PN(Tr_i, t_j, d)| \geq k,\ t_j \in [W.T_{Start}, W.T_{End}]\}$*. Otherwise* Tr_i *is a* ***PN-Inlier****. Any timebin* t_j *with* $|PN(p_i^j, d)| \geq k$ *is called a neighboring timebin of* Tr_i*.*

This *PN-Outlier* is based on whether a trajectory has a sufficient number of neighboring timebins throughout the window. Intuitively, a normal inlier trajectory has a sufficient number of moving objects in its vicinity for most of the time, i.e., for at least thr_t timebins. That is, such inliers are in a crowd in at least thr_t timebins. On the other hand, a trajectory is said to be an *outlier* if most of the time it differs from other objects in a significant fashion.

Example 1. *See example of Def. 3 in Fig. 1. Suppose* $k = 2$*,* $thr_t = 4$*. The trajectory* Tr_3 *only has two neighboring timebins* $\{t_1, t_4\}$*, for which* Tr_3 *has more than k point neighbors. Thus* $|T| < 4$*. So* Tr_3 *is a PN-Outlier. All other trajectories have at least* thr_t *neighboring timebins, hence are PN-Inliers.*

Applications. *PN-Outlier* effectively models the notion of outliers prevalent in many real time applications. For example in the security surveillance, foreign personnel may be considered as potentially unsafe if he separates out from others for too much of the time during his visit. In a marathon race a runner who runs alone without any other competitors around him for long stretches of time might be considered as suffering from some physical discomfort and possibly needing medical assistance, or should be checked for possible cheating by taking shortcuts.

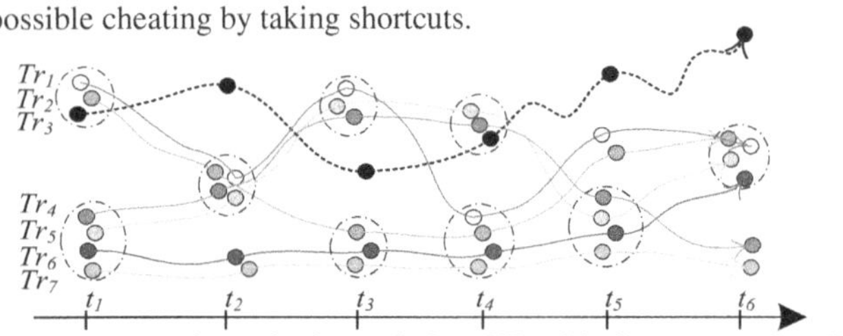

Figure 1: 7 trajectories in a window W_c with size $w = 6$. Small circle represents a trajectory point. Dashed oval indicates pairwise point neighbors. PN-$Outlier$: Tr_3. PN-$Inliers$: Tr_1, Tr_2, Tr_4, Tr_5, Tr_6, **and** Tr_7.

2.2.2 Trajectory-Neighbor Based Trajectory Outlier

Definition 4. *Given a distance threshold d, a neighbor count threshold k, and timebin count threshold* thr_t*, a trajectory* Tr_i *in the window W is a* ***trajectory-neighbor based trajectory outlier****, or in short,* ***TN-Outlier****, if* $|TN(Tr_i, d, thr_t)| < k$ *in W. Otherwise the trajectory* Tr_i *is a* ***TN-Inlier****.*

This *TN-Outlier* definition classifies a trajectory Tr_i as outlier if it does not have a sufficient number of trajectory neighbors throughout the window W. Put differently, there are not enough other objects in the dataset that consistently behave similarly to Tr_i within the observed time period W.

Example 2. *Consider the trajectories in Fig. 2. Suppose* $k = 2$*,* $thr_t = 4$*. Then* Tr_4 *is a TN-Outlier having no trajectory neighbor.* Tr_1 *and* Tr_2 *are trajectory neighbors of each other by Def. 2, because they are point neighbors at all 6 timebins.* Tr_1*,* Tr_2*, and* Tr_7 *are pairwise trajectory neighbors, because all three trajectories meet at at least 4 timebins. Since* Tr_1*,* Tr_2 *and* Tr_7 *each have* k *(2) trajectory neighbors, they are TN-Inliers.* Tr_3 *has two trajectory neighbors* Tr_5 *and* Tr_6*. Thus* Tr_3 *is a TN-Inlier.*

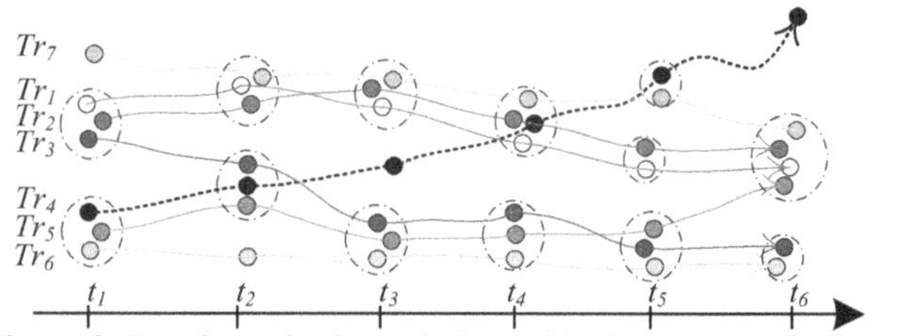

Figure 2: 7 trajectories in a window with size *w*=6, *k* = 2, thr_t = 4. *TN-Outlier*: Tr_4; ***TN-Inlier*:** $Tr_1, Tr_2, Tr_3, Tr_5, Tr_6, Tr_7$.

Unlike the *PN-Outlier* definition (Def. 3), *TN-Outlier* concept does not care about whether a given trajectory has a sufficient number of neighboring timebins, rather the granularity of similarity is instead at the level of complete trajectories and their relationship with Tr_i. Thus although Tr_4 has four neighboring timebins ($\geq thr_t$), it is still a *TN-Outlier* as we have shown above.

Applications. *TN-Outlier* definition fits many real life applications. Consider traffic management applications [15] where we expect most drivers to drive consistently in lockstep with neighboring cars on a highway, for instance in the same or in adjacent lanes. Deviating from the majority of other cars may indicate that the drivers change their neighbors frequently due to speeding (too fast) or drunk driving (too slow) and thus never stay long enough at similar speed with other cars. Similarly in the stock sticker stream, stocks in the same industry tend to exhibit similar trends. Therefore a stock whose performance consistently deviates from that of other stocks in the same industry will be considered as a *TN-Outlier*, even if at many timebins some stocks (each time different ones) happen to be its neighbors.

2.2.3 Effectiveness Analysis

Now we analyze the effectiveness of our proposed definitions. Due to space restriction in this work we only focus on *PN-Outlier*. A similar analysis could be applied to *TN-Outlier*.

Although no single outlier definition effectively models all real world scenarios, the general notion of what constitutes an outlier was first introduced by Hawkins in [7]. An observation is said to be outlier if it statistically deviates so much from other observations as to arouse suspicion that it was generated by a different mechanism.

Next we establish a statistical model for trajectory outliers. It relies on the strong assumption that the stream data consistently follows a particular distribution. In reality we may not know the distribution of a given stream. Worst yet it may change its distribution at any moment, while computing the statistical model periodically would be highly inefficient. However idealistically it still provides a solid baseline to contrast our definition that rests upon zero assumption.

To facilitate analysis, let us consider the scenario where each trajectory point set D_i composed of all trajectory points at any timebin t_i follows the *normal distribution* $N(\mu, \sigma^2)$. A trajectory point Tr_j^i is considered as an outlier point in D_i if it lies 3 or more standard deviation σ from the mean μ [4]. Correspondingly given a trajectory Tr_j with W trajectory points in a window, the probability of Tr_j having *m* of *W* outlier trajectory points will follow the binomial distribution $Bin(m|\,W, \mu')$ with μ' representing the probability of a given trajectory point Tr_j^i to be an outlier point in D_i. Then statistically trajectories can be considered as outliers if they contain more than $W\mu' + 3\sqrt{W\mu'(1-\mu')}$ outlier points. Here $W\mu'$ is the expectation of *Bin*, while $W\mu'(1-\mu')$ is the variance of *Bin*. We denote this definition as Def_{stat}.

Now we show the effectiveness of *PN-Outlier* by proving the following lemma.

Lemma 1. *Trajectory Tr_j is an outlier according to Def_{stat} iff Tr_j is a PN-Outlier with d* = 0.13σ, *k = 0.0012W, $thr_t = 0.9972W - 3\sqrt{0.0028(1-0.0028)W}$.*

Lemma 1 shows that our lightweight *PN-Outlier* definition will indeed produce the identical outliers that Def_{stat} had produced if the stream is normal distributed for a given set of statistical determined parameters.

PROOF. We use probabilities to represent the number of points lying in a d-neighborhood. Specifically, the probability p is $\frac{k}{W} = 0.0012$ that the distance between 2 randomly sampled points s_1 and s_2 from D_i is less than or equal to d. s_1 and s_2 can be considered to be random variables following normal distribution $N(\mu, \sigma^2)$. Then we define $z_1 = \frac{s_1-\mu}{\sigma}$ and $z_2 = \frac{s_2-\mu}{\sigma}$ as standard normal variables. That is, $z_1, z_2 \sim N(0, 1)$. Given d = 0.13σ, $p = 0.0012$, we get:

$Pr(|s_1 - s_2| \leq 0.13\sigma) \leq 0.0012 \Leftrightarrow Pr(s_1 - 0.13\sigma \leq s_2 \leq s_1 + 0.13\sigma) \leq 0.0012 \Leftrightarrow Pr(z_1 - 0.13 \leq z_2 \leq z_1 + 0.13) \leq 0.0012$.

Using the normal distribution table [4] we get $z_1 \leq -3.0$ or $z_1 \geq 3.0 \Leftrightarrow s_1 \leq \mu - 3\sigma$ or $s_1 \leq \mu + 3\sigma$. This proves that an outlier timebin t_i of trajectory Tr_j in *PN-Outlier* definition is an outlier point of D_i in Def_{stat}.

Next, by Def_{stat} the probability of s_1 being an outlier point will be $Pr(z_1 \leq -3.0)+ Pr(z_1 \geq 3.0) = 2Pr(z_1 \geq 3.0) = 2(1 - Pr(z_1 \leq 3.0)) = 0.0028$. In other words, the mean of *Bin* μ' = 0.0028. Therefore the expectation of *Bin* $E[m] = 0.0028W$. Its variance $var[m] = 0.0028(1-0.0028)W$. By Def_{stat} trajectory Tr_j will be an outlier if it has more than $E[m] + 3\sqrt{var[m]}$ outlier points. Since $E[m] + 3\sqrt{var[m]} = W - thr_t$, this is equivalent to the condition of *PN-Outlier* with thr_t as the minimum number of neighboring timebins for Tr_j to be an inlier. □

3. THE BASIC OUTLIER DETECTOR

Given a trajectory stream S and the semantics of *PN-Outlier* or *TN-Outlier*, we need to design algorithms to continuously detect and output the trajectory outliers in each window W_c. For this we now design the INC algorithm which detects both classes of outliers in a unified way. It first utilizes range queries to search for all point neighbors of each trajectory Tr_i at each timebin. Then the acquired point neighbors are used as evidence to validate the status of Tr_i. Furthermore INC leverages the fact that in sliding window streams adjacent windows overlap with each other. By cleverly maintaining the already known neighbor relationships, the INC algorithm successfully eliminates any redundant range query search at the previously examined timebins, resulting in saving in system resources.

We first introduce the data structures that enable the INC algorithm to extensively reuse the already recognized neighbor-related information. We use DB_{Tr} to denote the set of all trajectories in the current window W_c. To support *PN-Outlier* detection, each trajectory Tr_i maintains a list $Tr_i.tlist$, which stores the IDs of its neighboring timebins in W_c. For *TN-Outlier* detection, we need to track the trajectory neighbors of Tr_i to evaluate whether Tr_i has a sufficient number of trajectory neighbors. Therefore a neighbor table, denoted as $Tr_i.NT$, is maintained by each trajectory Tr_i, which records information about all trajectories having at least one point neighbor with Tr_i in the current window (see Fig. 4). Each record in the neighbor table $Tr_i.NT$ is a $< key, valueList >$ pair, where *key* denotes the identifier of Tr_i's neighboring trajectory Tr_j, and *valueList* corresponds to the list of timebins during which Tr_i and Tr_j are point neighbors.

Using an example-driven approach, we now describe how the INC algorithm detects the two outlier classes with the assistance of the just introduced $Tr_i.tlist$ and $Tr_i.NT$ structures. Fig. 3 shows 6 trajectories in two consecutive sliding windows with window size $w = 4$ and slide size $s = 1$. Given a query Q with $k = 2$ and $thr_t = 3$. Fig. 4 illustrates how the INC algorithm incrementally processes Tr_1 and Tr_5.

Data Structure Initialization. Given the trajectory dataset in the first window W_1, INC first utilizes a range query operation to search for point neighbors of Tr_1 at timebin t_1. The distance threshold d is used as the range. As shown in Fig. 3(a), Tr_1 does not have any point neighbor. So both $Tr_1.NT$ and $Tr_1.tlist$ are null. Tr_5 instead acquires one point neighbor p_2^1 at timebin 1. So the record $< Tr_2, [t_1] >$ is created for p_2^1 and inserted into $Tr_5.NT$ as shown in Fig. 10(a). Since only one point neighbor is acquired (<*k*), timebin t_1 is not a neighboring timebin of Tr_5. $Tr_5.tlist$ thus is null. Similarly INC proceeds to detect point neighbors using a range query and updates the data structures at each time bin. After timebin t_4 is processed, the final neighboring information for W_1 is established as shown in Fig. 4(c).

Trajectory Outlier Detection. Then using $Tr_i.tlist$ and $Tr_i.NT$ INC can quickly detect both classes of trajectory outliers. As shown in Fig. 3(a), Tr_1 and Tr_5 can be immediately identified as *PN-Outliers*, because the cardinality of $Tr_1.tlist$ and $Tr_5.tlist$ (♯ of neighboring timebins) is smaller than thr_t (3) respectively.

Similarly the *TN-Outliers* can be detected based on the neighbor table $Tr_i.NT$. Tr_1 is a *TN-Outlier* because it does not have any trajectory neighbor in $Tr_1.NT$. For that we only need to examine $Tr_i.NT$ to find the trajectories having no less than thr_t point neighbors with Tr_i. Tr_5 however is not a *TN-Outlier*, because it has two trajectory neighbors $\{Tr_2, Tr_6\}$ (k = 2) according to $Tr_5.NT$.

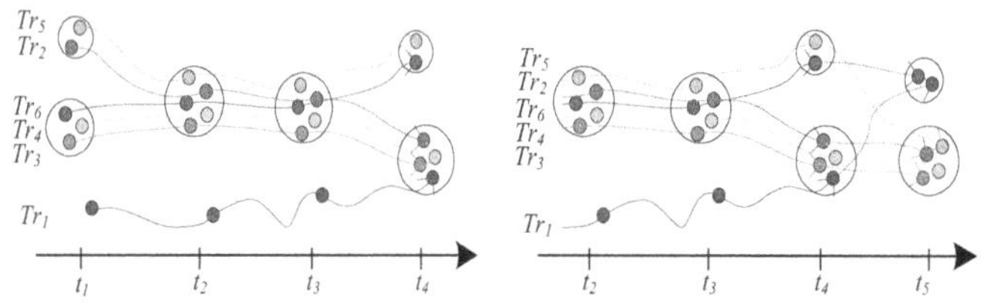

(a) Window $W1$ (b) Window $W2$

Figure 3: An example of two consecutive windows

Data Structure Update. After the new timebin t_5 arrives, the window slides from $W1$ to $W2$ (Fig. 3(b)). Since timebin t_1 has expired, all information of t_1 will be removed from $Tr_i.NT$ and $Tr_i.tlist$. The INC algorithm only needs to detect the point neighbors for each trajectory Tr_i at the new timebin t_5. This again is done by a range query search. The corresponding data structures are then updated (see Fig. 4(d)).

Outlier re-examination. Then the status of all the trajectories will be re-examined by again checking the $Tr_i.tlist$ and $Tr_i.NT$ structures. In the new window W_2, Tr_1 is still a *PN-Outlier*. However Tr_5 has evolved into a *PN-Inlier*, because Tr_5 acquires an new neighboring timebin at t_5. Thus now $|Tr_5.tlist| = thr_t$ (3).

$Tr_1.NT$

neighbors	Timebins
null	null

$Tr_5.NT$

neighbors	Timebins
Tr_2	t_1

$Tr_1.Tlist$: null

$Tr_5.Tlist$: null

(a) Timebin t_1

$Tr_1.NT$

neighbors	Timebins
null	null

$Tr_5.NT$

neighbors	Timebins
Tr_2	t_1, t_2
Tr_3	t_2
Tr_4	t_2
Tr_6	t_2

$Tr_1.Tlist$: null

$Tr_5.Tlist$: t_2

(b) Timebin t_2

$Tr_1.NT$

neighbors	Timebins
Tr_2	t_4
Tr_3	t_4
Tr_4	t_4

$Tr_5.NT$

neighbors	Timebins
Tr_2	t_1, t_2, t_3
Tr_3	t_2, t_3
Tr_4	t_2, t_3
Tr_6	t_2, t_3, t_4

$Tr_1.Tlist$: t_4

$Tr_5.Tlist$: t_2, t_3

(c) Timebin t_4

$Tr_1.NT$

neighbors	Timebins
Tr_2	t_4
Tr_3	t_4
Tr_4	t_4
Tr_6	t_5

$Tr_5.NT$

neighbors	Timebins
Tr_2	t_1, t_2, t_3, t_5
Tr_3	t_2, t_3, t_5
Tr_4	t_2, t_3, t_5
Tr_6	t_2, t_3, t_4

$Tr_1.Tlist$: t_4

$Tr_5.Tlist$: t_2, t_3, t_5

(d) Timebin t_5

Figure 4: Data structures of INC algorithm

Tr_1 is still reported as a *TN-Outlier* in W_2, because it still has no trajectory neighbor. Tr_5 remains a *TN-Inlier*, since it has four trajectory neighbors as shown in $Tr_5.NT$ of Fig. 4(d).

Complexity Analysis. The INC algorithm detects both types of outliers by first running a range query search for each trajectory at each new timebin. The complexity is $O(n^2)$. Then INC detects *PN-Outlier* by checking the cardinality of each $Tr_i.tlist$. The cost is $O(n)$. So the overall complexity of *PN-Outlier* detection is dominated by the range query whose complexity is $O(n^2)$.

TN-Outlier detection is much more expensive than *PN-Outlier* due to the extra cost of having to traverse the neighbor table $Tr_i.NT$ to discover trajectory neighbors. Its worst case complexity is $O(n^2)$. Therefore the overall complexity of *TN-Outlier* detection is determined by both the range query search and the lookup of the full neighbor relationship produced by range query.

4. OPTIMIZED DETECTION FRAMEWORK

Although the INC algorithm for the current window detection fully reuses the neighbor relationships collected in the previous window, it still incurs high computational costs when the number (n) of the trajectories is large. This performance bottleneck is driven due to the $O(n^2)$ complexity of the expensive neighbor range query search and the corresponding neighbor lookup operation as shown in the complexity analysis above. To further drive down the CPU and memory costs, we now present our *minimal examination* (MEX) optimized framework. By proposing three innovative optimization principles, namely *minimal support examination*, *time-aware examination*, and *lifetime-triggered detection*, the MEX framework thoroughly eliminates the performance bottleneck of the INC algorithm caused by its "range query search first, outlier examination next" strategy.

4.1 Key Observations

Each trajectory in a window *W* is eventually reported as either *outlier* or *inlier*. A trajectory will be labeled as inlier if sufficient neighbor evidence has been acquired for this object. This fact leads to an important observation. That is, to identify whether a trajectory is a neighbor-based inlier, we may not need to find out all its neighbor information. Instead a potentially small subset of the full *neighbor evidence* often can be sufficient to prove that it is an *inlier*. Similarly a small subset of the *non-neighbor evidence* might also in some cases found to be sufficient to classify a trajectory as an *outlier*. To characterize the least amount of information needed to prove Tr_i's status we define the concept of *Minimal Support*.

Definition 5. ***(Minimal Support).*** *Given a stream trajectory outlier detection query Q and a trajectory set DB_{Tr} in a window W_c, for a trajectory $Tr_i \in DB_{Tr}$, if the evidence pair (TR, T) composed of trajectory points and timebins with $(TR = \{Tr_1, \dots Tr_x, \dots Tr_m \mid Tr_x \in DB_{Tr}(1 \leq x \leq m)\}$, $T = \{t_1, \dots t_j \dots t_n \mid t_j \in [W_c.T_{Start}, W_c.T_{End}](1 \leq j \leq n)\})$ is sufficient to validate that Tr_i is either inlier or outlier, and for any subset $TR' \subseteq TR$ and $T' \subseteq T$, the pair (TR', T') is not sufficient to prove Tr_i's status, then (TR, T) is a minimal support of Tr_i in W_c.*

The above structure of *minimal support* provides the minimal amount of evidence for identifying both *inliers* and *outliers*. This minimal support concept guides us to propose the *minimal support examination* principle (Sec. 4.2.1) to optimize the trajectory outlier detection process, in particular to reduce the neighbor search and lookup costs related to the range queries.

We also observe that the *minimal support* is not unique for a trajectory in each window. That is, several distinct minimal support sets may exist because the definition of the outlier only imposes a constraint on the neighbor evidence count, but not on which particular neighbor evidence must be utilized.

Next we introduce the second optimization principle, namely *Predicted Support* in Lemma 2. This principle guide our MEX framework to discover the *best minimal support* for each trajectory.

Lemma 2. ***Predicted Support:*** *Given a stream trajectory outlier detection query Q, if the evidence pair (TR, T) is a minimal support of trajectory Tr_i in W_c as per Def. 5, then (TR, T) is also a minimal support of Tr_i in the subsequent windows from W_{c+1} to W_{c+x}, where $W_{c+x}.T_{start}$=$Min(T)$ and $Min(T)$ represents the minimal timebin in T.*

PROOF. By Defs. 3 and 4, the criteria we can use to determine the status of a trajectory Tr_i remains constant in each window. Therefore as the stream slides to a new window W_{c+1}, if no element of a minimal support set *MS* of Tr_i expires, *MS* is still sufficient to determine the status of Tr_i in W_{c+1}. Since W_{c+x} is the last window in which all elements of *MS* are guaranteed to survive, (TR, T) is still a minimal support for Tr_i in the windows from W_{c+1} to W_{c+x}. □

Lemma 2 reveals two promising opportunities for optimizing stream trajectory outlier detection.

First, the status of Tr_i can be predicted in certain future windows without first having to observe all data points of these windows. This insight inspires us to introduce the *lifetime-trigged detection optimization* principle in Sec. 4.2.3.

Second the more windows a minimal support of Tr_i covers, the less re-evaluation effort will be needed for Tr_i. Therefore acquiring the minimal support covering the longest window sequence with minimal CPU costs is critical for stream trajectory outlier detection. This observation guides us to propose the *time-aware examination optimization* as highlighted in Sec. 4.2.2.

4.2 Optimization Principles

Based on the above *minimal support* and *predicted support* observations, we now are ready to propose three fundamental principles for optimizing the stream trajectory outlier detection process.

4.2.1 Minimal Support Examination Optimization

Leveraging the minimal support observation (Def. 5) the *minimal support examination* (MSE) principle eliminates the complete and thus expensive point neighbor search for each trajectory adopted by the INC algorithm.

PRINCIPLE 1. *Given a trajectory outlier detection query Q and the trajectory set DB_{Tr} of window W_c, when evaluating a trajectory $Tr_i \in DB_{Tr}$, the* ***minimal support examination*** *principle suggests that the status determination process of Tr_i can be terminated as soon as k neighbors have been found.*

This principle aims to prove the status of a given trajectory Tr_i by only discovering a small subset of its neighbors instead of searching through its complete neighborhood to classify all points. As shown in Corollaries 1 and 2, this principle is equally applicable to both *PN-Outlier* and *TN-Outlier* detection, although they each have different concepts of neighbor respectively.

Corollary 1. *Given a PN-Outlier detection query Q in window W_c, a timebin t_j can be safely classified as a* ***neighboring timebin*** *of Tr_i if k point neighbors have been acquired for Tr_i at t_j.*

Corollary 2. *Given a TN-Outlier detection query Q in window W_c, a trajectory Tr_i can be safely classified as a* ***TN-Inlier*** *if k trajectory neighbors have been identified for Tr_i.*

The proof of Corollaries 1 and 2 directly follows the definition of neighboring timebin (Def. 3) and $TN\text{-}Inlier$ (Def. 4) respectively.

The MSE principle enables us to design a lightweight neighbor search operation called *Examining* to replace range query.

Definition 6. *Given a trajectory Tr_i in the window W_c, examining is an operation that evaluates the distance between the trajectory points of Tr_i and the corresponding points of other trajectories until either k neighbors (either point or trajectory neighbors) are acquired or Tr_i's entire neighborhood has been evaluated.*

Since the neighbor-count threshold k is much smaller than the average number of the neighbors we expect each trajectory may have, this examining operation is fundamentally more efficient than the full range query search.

4.2.2 Time-aware Examination Optimization

Our second optimization principle, called the *time-aware examination* (TAE) further optimizes the process of acquiring the timebin set *T* of the minimal support pair (TR, T).

PRINCIPLE 2. ***Time-aware Examination:*** *Given the detection query Q and a trajectory Tr_i in the current window W_c, the examining operation should identify the neighbor evidence for trajectory Tr_i from the most recent to the earlier un-evaluated timebins until either neighbor evidence is found at thr_t timebins or non-neighbor evidence are identified at $(w - thr_t + 1)$ timebins.*

The TAE principle has two implications. First, the examining operation should evaluate the un-evaluated timebins in the **latest time first order**. Second, TAE provides the criteria for the examining operation to *terminate the neighboring timebin search process*. Similar to the MSE principle, TAE can equally be applied to $PN\text{-}Outlier$ and $TN\text{-}Outlier$.

For a $PN\text{-}Outlier$ detection query w.r.t parameters (d, k, thr_t), the status of a trajectory Tr_i can be determined once either of the termination conditions shown in the following lemmas is reached.

Lemma 3. *Given a $PN\text{-}Outlier$ detection query Q, if a trajectory Tr_i has already acquired t neighboring timebins in the current window W_c, then Tr_i is an $PN\text{-}Inlier$ in W_c as well as in the subsequent (t_l-$W_c.T_{Start}$) windows, where t_l is the oldest neighboring timebin acquired by Tr_i.*

PROOF. First, by Def. 3, Tr_i is a $PN\text{-}Inlier$ in W_c. Second, $\forall$ timebin $t_j \in T$, $t_j \geq t_l$. Therefore the minimal timebin in T (*Min(T)*) equals to t_l. By Lemma 2, Tr_i thus is also a $PN\text{-}Inlier$ in the subsequent windows from W_{c+1} to W_{c+x}, where $W_{c+x}.T_{Start} = t_l$. Therefore, Tr_i is guaranteed to be a $PN\text{-}Inlier$ in the next (t_l-$W_c.T_{Start}$) windows. □

However, the status of Tr_i after window W_{c+x} (after t_l expires) is uncertain because the remaining evidence (k-1 neighboring timebins) is no longer sufficient to prove its status. Therefore, t_l is the furthest foreseeable timebin until which the status of Tr_i is guaranteed to be certain. We call t_l the **closed time** of Tr_i to be a *PN-Inlier*.

Similarly the TAE principle is effective on the $TN\text{-}Outlier$ (Lemma 4).

Lemma 4. *Given a $TN\text{-}Outlier$ detection query Q, if Tr_i has already acquired thr_t neighboring timebins with a given trajectory Tr_m in the current window W_c, then Tr_i and Tr_m are guaranteed to be trajectory neighbors in W_c and in the subsequent (t_l-$W_c.T_{start}$) windows, where t_l is their oldest neighboring timebins.*

For Lemma 4, timebin t_l is called the **closed time** of Tr_i to be trajectory neighbor of Tr_m. Due to space restriction, the proof is omitted here.

In summary, TAE aims to not only find the minimal timebin set sufficient to determine the trajectory's status, but also guarantees that the identified evidence is reused for the longest subsequent number of windows. Together the TAE and MSE principles guide the *examining operation* to effectively gather the optimal *minimal support* for each trajectory rather than conducting expensive and wasteful range query searches.

4.2.3 Lifetime-triggered Detection Optimization

The above two principles focus on how to optimize each single examining operation. To further reduce the computational costs, we now introduce another optimization principle regarding to the minimization of the examining frequency, termed *lifetime-triggered detection optimization* (LTD).

First, we define the *lifetime* concept of a trajectory.

Definition 7. ***(Lifetime).*** *Given a trajectory Tr_i in the current window W_c, if Tr_i is guaranteed to keep its status (being inlier or outlier) until timebin t_{life} ($W_c.T_{Start} \leq t_{life} \leq W_c.T_{End}$) expires according to the identified evidence, then t_{life} is called the* ***lifetime*** *of Tr_i in the current window W_c.*

In other words the lifetime of Tr_i indicates the duration of its current status (outlier or inlier).

Next we introduce a methodology for identifying the lifetime of a given trajectory for each of the two neighbor-based trajectory outlier definitions respectively.

Lemma 5. *Given a trajectory Tr_i, the lifetime of Tr_i to be a $PN\text{-}inlier$ is the closed time of Tr_i in W_c.*

PROOF. Lemma 5 can be easily proven by Lemmas 3. If Tr_i is a $PN\text{-}inlier$, Tr_i will remain to be inlier until its close time expires by Lemma 3. □

Lemma 6. *Given a trajectory Tr_i, the lifetime of Tr_i to be a $TN\text{-}inlier$ is $min\{Tr_j.closedTime | Tr_j \in TN\}$, where TN is the trajectory neighbor set of Tr_i in W_c.*

PROOF. Omitted due to space constrain. □

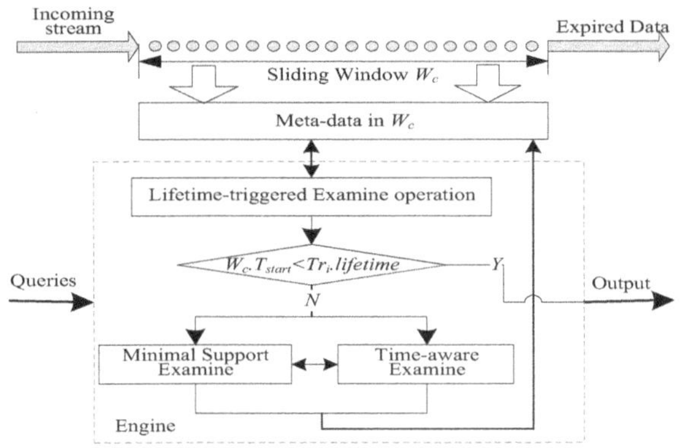

Figure 5: Architecture of MEX framework

Next we define the LTD optimization principle based on the above lifetime concept.

PRINCIPLE 3. ***Lifetime-triggered Detection:*** *Given a trajectory Tr_i, the examining operation will be triggered on Tr_i if and only if the lifetime of Tr_i holds with: $Tr_i.life \leq W_c.T_{start}$.*

By the LTD principle, the status of a trajectory is re-examined only when its lifetime expires. This effectively transforms the **continuous** query execution into **lifetime-triggered** execution. Whenever a trajectory is being re-examined, the examining operation which incorporates both MSE and TAE optimizations can be exploited to re-establish the minimal support in the new window. It does so by only acquiring enough new evidence rather than building a new minimal support from scratch. We call this enhanced examining operation *lifetime-aware examining* or in short LIFT.

4.3 Minimal Examination Framework

The high-level architecture of our MEX framework is depicted in Fig. 5. Similar to the INC algorithm, the MEX framework utilize the $Tr_i.tlist$ and $Tr_i.NT$ structures to store the meta-data. Therefore it also leverages the overlap of the adjacent windows in the sliding window stream.

Then the MEX framework continuously detects the trajectory outliers by conducting the LIFT operation on each trajectory. Given a trajectory Tr_i, the LIFT operation is not triggered if $W_c.T_{Start} < Tr_i.lifetime$. Once triggered, then LIFT employs both of the MSE and TAE principles to establish the new minimal support. The status and the lifetime of Tr_i are also updated based on the new minimal support. Finally it outputs the outliers of the current window. The detailed description of the algorithm specific to each of the trajectory outlier definitions is described in the following section.

5. MEX-BASED TRAJECTORY OUTLIER DETECTION ALGORITHMS

5.1 The Optimized PN-Outlier Algorithm

Alg. 1 shows the optimized $PN\text{-}Outlier$ detection algorithm as extension of the MEX framework, named *PN-Opt*. For each trajectory Tr_i, $Tr_i.untlist$ maintains the unchecked timebins in the current window, while $Tr_i.ntlist$ and $Tr_i.tlist$ correspond to the lists of non-neighboring and neighboring timebins of Tr_i respectively. The lifetime-triggered detection optimization is employed first (line 1). That is, only the trajectories whose lifetime has expired are re-examined in the current window. For these triggered

Algorithm 1 PN-Opt algorithm($PN\text{-}Outlier$ detection using MEX framework)

Input: Trajectory Set DB_{Tr}, the current window W_c, parameters: d, k and t.
Output: outliers

```
1: Get DB_lt ← (W_c.T_Start − 1).triggered;
2: for each Tr_i ∈ DB_lt do
3:    for each t_j ∈ Tr_i.untlist from W_c.T_End to head do
4:       if (true == Tr_i.LIFT.MSEInHistory(t_j)) then
5:          Tr_i.ntlist.add(t_j);
6:       end if
7:       if (true == Tr_i.LIFT.MSEInNewTrjaectory(t_j)) then
8:          Tr_i.tlist.add(t_j);
9:       else
10:         Tr_i.ntlist.add(t_j);
11:      end if
12:      Tr_i.LIFT.TAE()
13:   end for
14:   Tr_i.updateLifetime();
15:   Lifetime.triggered.add(Tr_i);
16: end for
```

trajectories that must be examined, *PN-Opt* utilizes the MSE optimization principle to acquire new neighboring timbins (line 4). More specifically *PN-Opt* first checks whether Tr_i can acquire k point neighbors in the new timebin by searching through the trajectories who have been neighbors with Tr_i in at least one other timebin. The other remaining trajectory points will be tested only if Tr_i still has not acquired k point neighbors (line 7). Then the TAE principle will be utilized to determine whether the neighboring timebin search process should be terminated, namely whether thr_t timebins have been acquired in the new window (lines 3, 12). Finally, the lifetime of Tr_i, utilized by the LTD principle to determine whether the status of Tr_i should be re-examined, is updated (lines 14,15).

5.2 The Optimized TN-Outlier Algorithm

Algorithm 2 TN-Opt algorithm ($TN\text{-}Outlier$ detection using MEX framework)

Input: Trajectory Set DB_{Tr}, the current window W_c, parameters: d, k and t.
Output: Outliers

```
1: Get DB_lt ← (W_c.T_Start − 1).triggered;
2: for each Tr_i ∈ DB_lt do
3:    for each Tr_m ∈ Tr.NT.keys do
4:       Tr_i.LIFT.TAE(Tr_m);
5:       Tr_i.LIFT.MSE();
6:    end for
7:    if (false == Tr_i.getkNeighbors()) then
8:       for each Tr_m ∈ (DB_Tr − Tr.NT.keys) do
9:          Tr_i.LIFT.TAE(Tr_m);
10:         Tr_i.LIFT.MSE();
11:      end for
12:      if (false == Tr_i.getkNeighbors()) then
13:         Tr_i.status='outlier';
14:      end if
15:   end if
16:   Tr_i.updateLifetime();
17:   Lifetime.triggered.add(Tr_i);
18: end for
```

Alg. 2 utilizes the MEX framework to solve the $TN\text{-}Outlier$ detection problem. Here, $Tr_i.NT$ denotes the neighbor table of Tr_i. Each element of $Tr_i.NT$ contains three parts: $tlist$, $ntlist$, $untlist$. $untlist$ maintains the unchecked timebins between Tr_i and some trajectory Tr_j, while $ntlist$ and $tlist$ are the lists of non-neighboring and neighboring timebins between Tr_i and Tr_j. Similar to Alg. 1, *TN-Opt* algorithm also employs the LTD first to check if the lifetime of Tr_i has expired (line 1). If so, then *TN-Opt* assesses the status of Tr_i again.

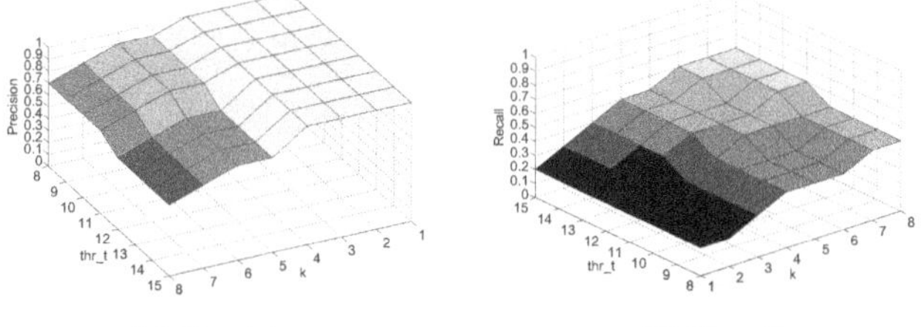

(a) Precision (b) Recall

Figure 6: PN-Outlier (Taxi data)

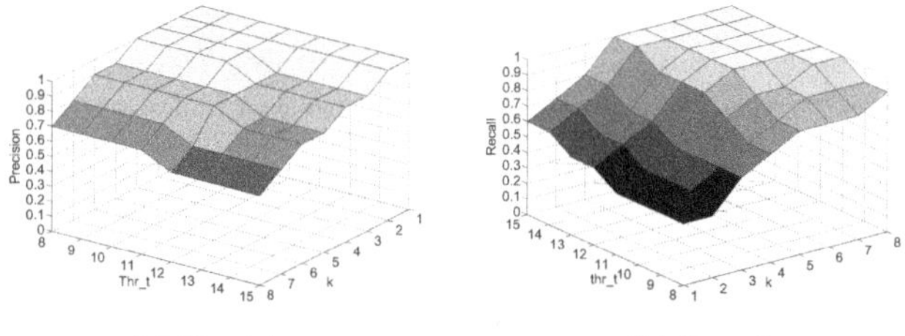

(a) Precision (b) Recall

Figure 7: TN-Outlier (GMTI data)

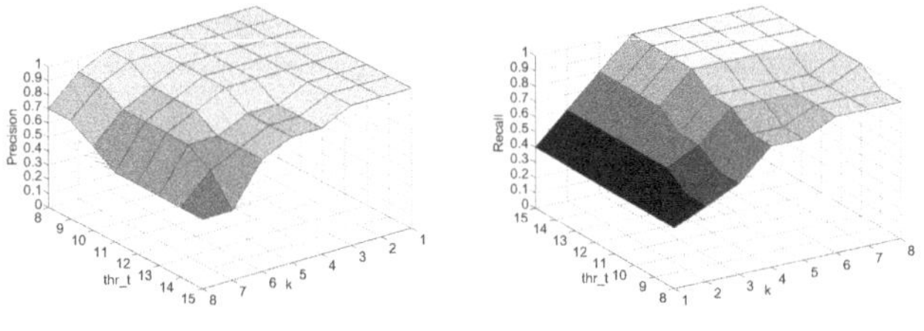

(a) Precision (b) Recall

Figure 8: PN-Outlier (Taxi data)

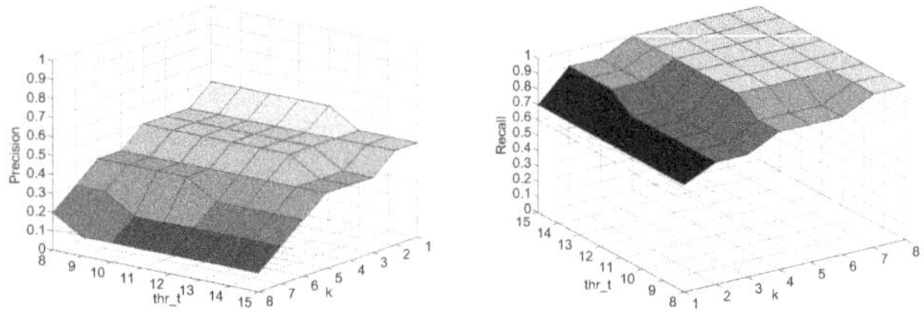

(a) Precision (b) Recall

Figure 9: TN-Outlier (Taxi data)

TN-Opt first applies the TAE optimization principle (lines 4,9) to test whether a given trajectory Tr_j is a trajectory neighbor of Tr_i. Starting from the latest timebin, *TN-Opt* keeps testing the trajectory points at the unchecked timebins in *untlist* between Tr_i and Tr_j until point neighbors at *t* timebins are found. By the MSE principle (lines 5, lines 10), the trajectory neighbor search process stops immediately after Tr_i acquires sufficient (*k*) trajectory neighbors or all the trajectories have been tested. Finally, the lifetime of Tr_i is updated (lines 16,17).

6. EXPERIMENTAL EVALUATION

6.1 Experimental Setup

All algorithms are implemented in JAVA on CHAOS stream engine [6]. Our experiments are performed on a PC with 3.4G Hz Intel i7 processor and 6GB memory, which runs Windows 7 OS.

Real Datasets. We used two real streaming datasets. The *Taxi Dataset* is the real GPS trajectory data generated by 10,357 taxis in a period from Feb. 2 to Feb. 8, 2008 in Beijing [16] [17]. The total number of points in this dataset is about 15 million. The average time interval between two points is around 177 seconds. To model timebins, we interpolate the time granularity to 1 minute per timebin. The **GMTI** (Ground Moving Target Indicator) dataset [3] records the real-time trajectories of 150 moving objects gathered by 24 different data ground stations or aircraft in 6 hours. It has around 100,000 records regarding the information of vehicles and helicopters moving in a certain geographic region. In our experiment, we used all 14 dimensions of GMTI while detecting outliers based on targets' latitude and longitude.

Metrics & Measurements. We evaluate both the effectiveness of our outlier definitions and the efficiency of our MEX outlier detection algorithms.

For the effectiveness evaluation, we measure the quality of reported outliers by *Precision* and *Recall* as follows:

$$Precision = \frac{|R_o \cap D_o|}{|D_o|},\ Recall = \frac{|R_o \cap D_o|}{|R_o|}$$

where R_o denotes the set of annotated outliers in a dataset, namely the real outliers and D_o the outliers detected by our algorithms.

For the efficiency evaluation, we measure two metrics common for stream systems, namely CPU resources and memory consumption. Experiments are conducted on 1,000 windows for the Taxi dataset. Both metrics are averaged over all windows.

6.2 Effectiveness Evaluation

We evaluate the effectiveness of the new proposed outlier definitions by measuring the *precision* and *recall* on the real GMTI and taxi datasets. For the GMTI dataset, we use the outlier set manually labeled by the experts familiar with the data as the ground truth R_o. For the Taxi dataset the ground truth outlier set R_o is instead produced by a user study. In this user study 100 sets of trajectories were selected from the taxi dataset. Each set contains 10 trajectories with 30 consecutive 6-minutes window. We invited 50 users from both WPI and USTB. The users were divided into 5 groups, with 10 trajectory sets assigned to each group. The users were asked to mark trajectories in each set that they believe are most likely to be outliers. Each trajectory marked by at least 5 users is labeled as a "real" outlier.

We vary the thresholds *k* and thr_t to investigate how *Precision* and *Recall* are impacted. The *d* threshold is fixed as 200 meter for GMTI data and 300 meter for Taxi data.

GMTI data. The results for GMTI data are shown in Figs. 6 and 7. From Figs. 6(a) and 7(a) the *Precision* of both *PN-Outlier* and *TN-Outlier* is nearly 100% once the parameters *k* and thr_t fall in a rather large range. Fig. 7(b) shows that the *Recall* of *TN-Outlier* is also good and robust. However the *Recall* of *PN-Outlier* (Fig. 6(b)) is much worse than *TN-Outlier*. In the GMTI dataset the moving objects (soldiers) are divided into 3 military units. The members of each unit are expected to operate in a team. If they do not continuously operate together, they will be labeled as outliers even if they happen to stay close to others at times. *TN-Outlier* perfectly covers this scenario. However sometimes *PN-Outlier* might fail to locate the soldier separated from his own unit, since *PN-Outlier* would not classify an object as outlier if there are a sufficient number of moving objects in its vicinity.

Taxi data. We also investigate the effectiveness of *PN-Outlier* and *TN-Outlier* for the Taxi data. As shown in Figs. 8(a) and 8(b) *PN-Outlier* shows nearly 100% *Precision* and *Recall* when the parameters *k* and thr_t varies in a large range. However the *Precision* of *TN-Outlier* is worse than *PN-Outlier* (Fig. 9(a)), although its *Recall* is as good as *PN-Outlier* (Fig. 9(b)). In the user study the users tend to classify a taxi as an outlier if it always moves alone. Intuitively taxis do not necessarily move together with others as a group. The behavior of a taxi driver will be considered as abnormal only if he always operates in areas that other drivers rarely visit. This scenario fits *PN-Outlier* better than *TN-Outlier*, since

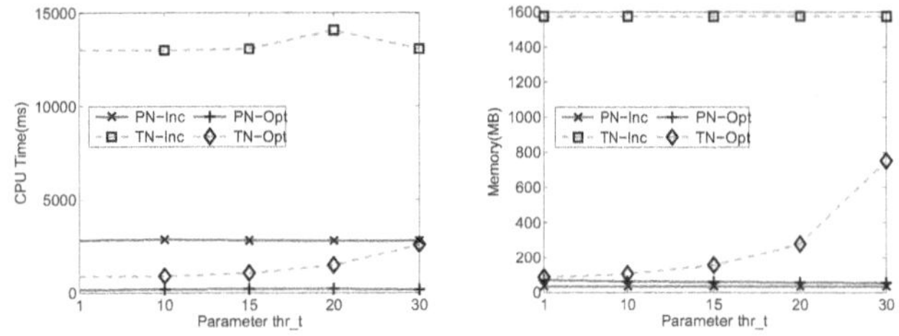

(a) CPU time (b) Memory

Figure 10: Varying thr_t on taxi data

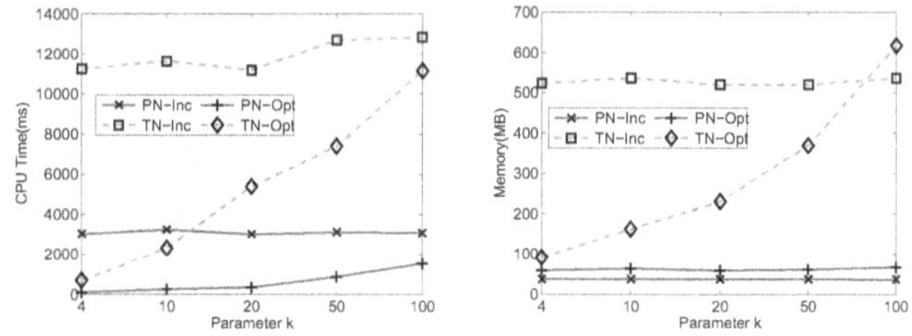

(a) CPU time (b) Memory

Figure 11: Varying k on taxi data

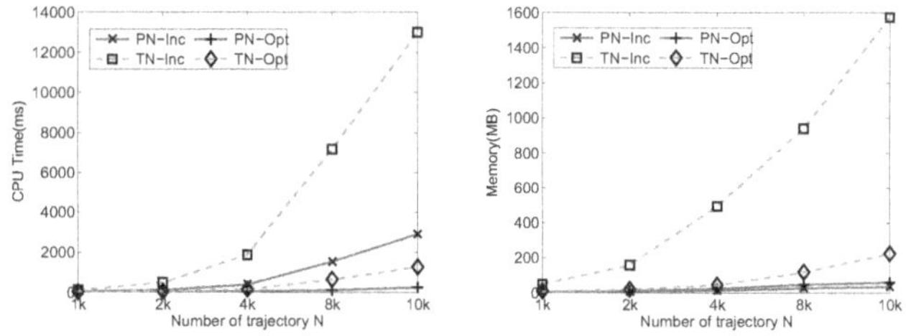

(a) CPU time (b) Memory

Figure 12: Varying number n of trajectories on taxi data

TN-Outlier tends to misclassify the taxis lack of consistent companions as outliers.

In summary the above empirical study confirms the effectiveness of our new proposed *PN-Outlier* and *TN-Outlier* definitions in capturing the moving object outliers with only a very loose parameter setting requirement. Furthermore it shows that *PN-Outlier* and *TN-Outlier* best cover distinct application categories with different similarity requirement to be neighbors.

6.3 Efficiency Evaluation

Next we evaluate the efficiency of our outlier detection algorithms using the Taxi data. The performance of MEX algorithms is compared with the INC algorithms. We denote the INC solution for $PN\text{-}Outlier$, $TN\text{-}Outlier$ detection as *PN-INC*, *TN-INC* and the *MEX*-based solution as *PN-Opt* and *TN-Opt* respectively. We vary the most important parameters, to (1) assess the impact of our *MEX* framework versus the INC baseline, (2) evaluate sensitivity of parameter variations on each method.

6.3.1 Varying Timebin Count Threshold thr_t

CPU Resources. First, we evaluate the effect of varying the timebin count threshold thr_t from 1 to the full window size. This varies the definition from very relaxed (that is, one trajectory Tr_i is inlier for instance if only in 1 of *w* timebins tr_i has the needed neighbors) to very strict (Tr_i must have k neighbors in all w timebins to be considered an inlier). We fix the window size to 30, k to 4, and d to 200 meters. As shown in Figs. 10, our MEX-based algorithms are superior to the corresponding basic INC-based solutions w.r.t the CPU time in all cases. In particular, *PN-Opt* is 117 times faster than *PN-INC* (Fig. 10(a)). When thr_t is equal to the full window, the outliers rates of the two definitions are at their highest, namely 5% and 20% respectively. However, even in these cases the optimized algorithms still outperform their corresponding counterparts 31 and 5 fold.

We also notice that INC algorithms are not very sensitive to thr_t, since INC always tests all timebins of each trajectory. Whereas by employing the TAE optimization principle (Sec. 4.2.2) MEX significantly reduces the distance calculation by only acquiring the minimal yet sufficient neighboring timebins.

Memory Resources. We see similar positive trends also for the memory usage. That is, *TN-Opt* uses on average 21% of the memory consumed by its counterpart *TN-INC* algorithm. This can be explained by the fact that the MEX framework only maintains k trajectory neighbors for $TN\text{-}Outlier$, while the INC solution aggressively stores all neighbor information. As expected, the memory consumption of *TN-Opt* increases as thr_t increases, because more neighboring timebins have to be maintained for each trajectory neighbor as the required neighbor count thr_t rises.

As shown in Fig. 10(b), the memory usage of both *PN-Opt* and *PN-INC* is very small. *PN-Opt* uses a little more memory than *PN-INC*. For each trajectory Tr_i, *PN-Opt* stores the trajectories which have point neighbors with Tr_i in the history to reduce the trajectory search scope for acquiring new neighboring timebins. However this extra memory leads to huge gains in CPU processing resources (at least 31 times faster than *PN-INC*).

6.3.2 Varying Neighbor Count Threshold k

Next we evaluate the performance of the four algorithms by varying the neighbor count threshold k from 4 to 100. To be classified as an inlier the number of neighbors that a trajectory Tr_i needs to discover increases from very few to a large number. That is, the inlier criteria for any trajectory Tr_i changes from very relaxed to strict. We fix the window size to 30, thr_t to 15, and d to 200.

CPU Resources. Fig. 11(a) shows both MEX-based algorithms clearly outperform their counterparts. The two MEX-based algorithms save on average 91% and 56% of CPU time compared to the corresponding INC solution. As k increases, the CPU time of the MEX-based solutions increases linearly since more neighbors have to be acquired to determine the status of a given trajectory. For the INC-based solutions instead we observe no sensitivity for varying k. This is because the INC-based solutions determine the status of Tr_i always by first acquiring all neighbors with expensive complete range query searches no matter how large k is. However, the MEX-based solutions still outperform INC-based algorithms even for the extreme case of $k = 100$. In this case the outlier rate is extremely high, namely 90%, and thus unrealistic.

Memory Resources. *TN-INC* only uses on average 55% of the memory compared to *TN-INC* (Fig. 11(b)). As k increases, they need to store more trajectory neighbors. Thus their memory consumption increases. As k increases to 100, *TN-Opt* uses more memory than *TN-INC*. Again this is an unrealistic setting we do not expect to see in practice, as surely 90% of all data would not be considered as "exceptions" (outliers) but rather as the norm.

6.3.3 Varying Number of Trajectories n

We evaluate the scalability of our algorithms in the number of trajectories they can simultaneously handle. In this experiment we randomly select from 1k up to 10k trajectories from the Taxi data. We fix the window size to 30, k to 4, thr_t to 15. To eliminate the effect of variations in the outlier rates, we stabilize the outlier rate in all cases to around 4% by slightly adjusting the distance threshold d from 200 to 300 meters.

CPU Resources. As shown in Fig. 12(a), the MEX algorithms exhibit much better scalability than their INC-based counterparts.

As the number of trajectories increases, as expected all algorithms require more time to process more trajectories. However, the MEX algorithms outperform the INC-based ones more and more as the number of trajectories increases, because unlike the INC solution MEX avoids expensive range queries for the needed searches.

CPU Resources. As shown in Fig. 12(b), the memory consumption of all algorithms also increases as the number of trajectories increases, because more trajectory information must be stored. However, *TN-Opt* saves more memory than *TN-INC* as n increases, while the memory usage of *PN-Opt* remains consistently small.

7. RELATED WORK

Trajectory Outlier Detection in Static Datasets. Knorr et al. [9] applied the distance-based outlier notion defined in [8] to spatio-temporal data. It first extracted features from the trajectories already located in the database and mapped the trajectories into a feature space. Then it relied on the distance in this feature space to determine the relationships among the trajectories. The status of each trajectory was evaluated and reported only once. This definition does not fit the requirement of streaming data. First the features of the stream trajectories keep evolving. Therefore no stable feature space exists. Furthermore the effect of the observed events keeps fading. Therefore the outliers have to be continuously reported in real time based on the latest events rather than reporting them only once based one the whole trajectory database.

Li et al. [12] proposed a classification-based trajectory outlier detection algorithm. In their algorithm, trajectories are represented using discrete pattern fragments called motifs. The set of motifs forms a feature space in which the trajectories are placed. Then a rule-based classifier is trained to classify the trajectories into either "normal" or "abnormal". This algorithm cannot be adapted to the streaming context since it requires an offline training stage and a labeled training dataset to train the classifier.

Lee et al. [11] proposed a two-step trajectory outlier detection approach. At the first step, each trajectory is partitioned into a sequence of t-partitions. Within this set of t-partitions, outlying t-partitions are determined based on distance or density based metrics. This work targets on a completely different problem, namely to discover unusual sub-trajectories within one single trajectory. Instead we aim to locate abnormal moving objects.

Outlier detection over trajectory data streams. Bu et al. [2] detected abnormal trajectory segments in the stream context with the assumption that a stream trajectory is locally continuous. That is, a trajectory is expected to behave consistently within a short time interval. They use a base window to constrain the part of a trajectory they are interested in into a trajectory segment. Then whether a given trajectory segment is said to be anomalous or not is based on the similarity to its own historical trajectory in a larger window. Thus this method, focusing on identifying an outlying trajectory segment of one particular moving object, cannot address our problem, namely identifying suspicious moving objects significantly deviating from other synchronously moving objects.

Liu et al. [14] studied causal interaction detection in traffic data streams. They first divide the city areas into regions. A graph is built by mapping each region to a vertex. The trajectories are then simplified into links connecting two corresponding regions. This much smaller dataset, i.e., a graph of regions, enables them to map their problem into frequent subgraph mining. That is, they determine the anomalous links in each time frame by comparing their load features of links in the graph (e.g., number of traversals) with those of their temporal neighbors. This method focuses on a totally different problem, namely discovering anomalous regions rather than abnormal moving objects.

Trajectory clustering and pattern mining. Other domains of mining moving object streams have been studied with clustering of trajectory the closest to outlier detection. Lee et al. [10] presented a clustering algorithm on discovering common sub-trajectories in static trajectory databases. Trajectories are first partitioned into a set of quasi-linear segments using the minimum description length principle. Then the line segments are grouped by a density-based clustering algorithm. Although this algorithm could potentially be applied in a reverse direction to detect *abnormal trajectory segment*, it cannot solve our problem. First, the trajectory segments falling in one cluster are not necessarily observed at the same time period, while in trajectory stream to online detect abnormal moving objects only the "concurrent" behavior of the objects should be considered. Second, our goal is to continuously detect abnormal *moving objects* at real time rather than locate the unusual *segments* of the trajectories known apriori.

8. CONCLUSIONS

In this work we focus on the detection of abnormal moving objects over massive-scale trajectory streams. After analyzing the requirements of stream trajectory applications, we propose novel neighbor-based trajectory outlier definitions. Our empirical study on the GMTI and Taxi data shows that our definitions can effectively capture moving object outliers in different scenarios. Furthermore we design an optimized MEX strategy scalable to big data trajectory streams to detect the new classes of outliers, rendering moving object outliers detection practical in real time applications.

9. REFERENCES

[1] A. Arasu, S. Babu, and J. Widom. The cql continuous query language: semantic foudations and query execution. The VLDB Journal, 15(2):121–142, July 2006.

[2] Y. Bu, L. Chen, A. W.-C. Fu, and D. Liu. Efficient anomaly monitoring over moving object trajectory streams. In Proceedings of SIGKDD 2009, pages 159–168. ACM, June 2009.

[3] J. N. Entzminger, C. A. Fowler, and W. J. Kenneally. Jointstars and gmti: Past, present and future. IEEE Trans. on Aerospace and Electronic Systems, 35(2):748–761, Apr 1999.

[4] D. Freedman, R. Pisani, and R. Purves. Statistics. W. W. Norton & Company, 2007.

[5] Y. Ge, H. Xiong, C. Liu, and Z.-H. Zhou. A taxi driving fraud detection system. In Proceedings of ICDM 2011, pages 181–190. IEEE, December 2011.

[6] C. Gupta, S. Wang, I. Ari, and M. Hao. Chaos: A data stream analysis architecture for enterprise applications. In Proceedings of CEC 2009, pages 33–40. IEEE, July 2009.

[7] D. M. Hawkins. Identification of Outliers. Springer, 1980.

[8] E. M. Knorr and R. T. Ng. Algorithms for mining distance-based outliers in large datasets. In Proceedings of VLDB 1998, pages 392–403, August 1998.

[9] E. M. Knorr, R. T. Ng, and V. Tucakov. Distance-based outliers: Algorithms and applications. The VLDB Journal, 8(3-4):237–253, March 2000.

[10] J.-G. Lee and J. Han. Trajectory clustering: A partition and group framework. In Proceedings of SIGMOD 2007, pages 593–604. ACM, June 2007.

[11] J.-G. Lee, J. Han, and X. Li. Trajectory outlier detection: A partition-and-detect framework. In In Proceedings of ICDE 2008, pages 140–149. IEEE, April 2008.

[12] X. Li, J. Han, S. Kim, and H. Gonzalez. Roam: Rule- and motif-based anomaly detection in massive moving object data sets. In Proceedings of SDM 2007, pages 273–284. SIAM, April 2007.

[13] Z. Li, B. Ding, J. Han, and R. Kays. Swarm: Mining relaxed temporal moving object clusters. In Proceedings of VLDB 2010, pages 723–734, August 2010.

[14] W. Liu, Y. Zheng, and S. Chawla. Discovering spatio-temporal causal interactions in traffic data streams. In Proceedings of SIGKDD 2011, pages 1010–1018. ACM, July 2011.

[15] J. Yuan, Y. Zheng, X. Xie, and G. Sun. Driving with knowledge from the physical world. In KDD, pages 316–324, 2011.

[16] J. Yuan, Y. Zheng, X. Xie, and G. Sun. T-drive: Enhancing driving directions with taxi drivers' intelligence. Transactions on Knowledge and Data Engineering, 25(1):220–232, January 2013.

[17] J. Yuan, Y. Zheng, C. Zhang, W. Xie, X. Xie, G. Sun, and Y. Huang. T-drive: driving directions based on taxi trajectories. In GIS, pages 99–108, 2010.

[18] Y. Zheng, X. Xie, and W.-Y. Ma. Geolife: A collaborative social networking service among user, location and trajectory. IEEE Data Engineering Bulletin, 33(2):32–40, June 2010.

The Setwise Stream Classification Problem

Charu C. Aggarwal
IBM T. J. Watson Research Center
1101 Kitchawan Road
Yorktown Heights, NY, USA
charu@us.ibm.com

ABSTRACT

In many applications, classification labels may not be associated with a single instance of records, but may be associated with a *data set* of records. The class behavior may not be possible to infer effectively from a single record, but may be only be inferred by an aggregate set of records. Therefore, in this problem, the class label is associated with a *set of instances both in the training and test data*. Therefore, the problem may be understood to be that of classifying a *set of data sets*. Typically, the classification behavior may only be inferred from the overall patterns of data distribution, and *very little information is embedded in any given record for classification purposes*. We refer to this problem as the *setwise classification problem*.

The problem can be extremely challenging in scenarios where the data is received in the form of a stream, and the records within any particular data set may not necessarily be received contiguously. In this paper, we present a first approach for real time and streaming classification of such data. We present experimental results illustrating the effectiveness of the approach.

Categories and Subject Descriptors

H.2.8 [**Database Management**]: Database Applications

Keywords

Data Streams; Data Classification

1. INTRODUCTION

In many applications, classification labels are not associated with individual records, but with *groups of records* in the underlying data. Thus, each group of records is treated as an indivisible entity, along with an associated class label. In most cases, the classification behavior can only be inferred from the *overall distribution pattern* of the records in this entity, and a given record typically provides very little information about classification behavior. This kind of problem can arise in the context of a wide variety of applications:

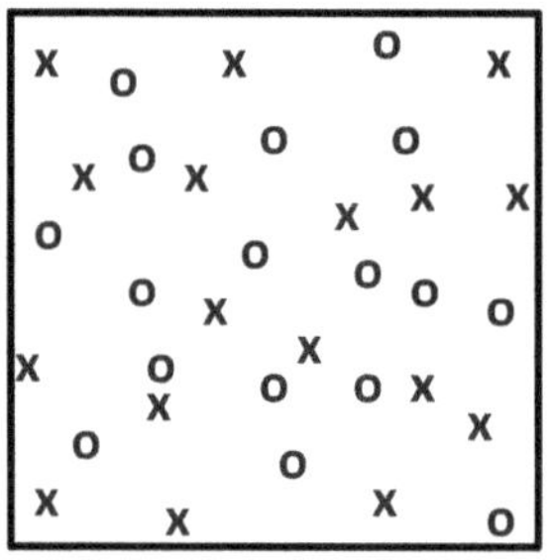

Figure 1: Setwise Classification Scenario

- In a sensor application, a single event of significance may cause a large number of data records, and the nature of the event can only be classified on the basis of the *aggregate* patterns of these different records. Any single record is unlikely to provide any useful understanding of the underlying causality.
- A large supermarket chain may have thousands of stores, each of which is associated with buying behavior of different customers. It may be very difficult to make any prediction of the geographical information of a particular buying pattern from a single transaction. It is much easier to make predictions from *aggregates*.
- In an environmental application, many large scale predictions can often be made only on the basis of multiple samples of the data from different geographical regions. In such cases, the overall pattern of the data is more relevant than the value on any specific record.

This problem is referred to as the *setwise classification problem*. We note that each set may contain tremendous variations in the feature values of the given records, and in many applications, it is by analyzing the specific *patterns of these variations*, that the setwise entities can be assigned a particular class. In many cases, individual records cannot be meaningfully assigned to classes, because many different classes may contain very similar data points. In order to illustrate this point, we have shown the distribution of the data records in a two such entities belonging to different classes in Figure 1, which are marked by 'x' and 'o' respectively. At first sight, it would seem that there is no difference

KDD'14, August 24–27, 2014, New York, NY, USA.

http://dx.doi.org/10.1145/2623330.2623751 .

in the distributions of the two classes, and the two entities have identical distributions. The subtle differences in distribution can be understood only upon closer examination. In particular, the setwise entity belonging to the class marked 'x' has marginally greater concentrations at the peripheries of the data ranges, whereas the setwise entity belonging to the class marked 'o' has marginally greater concentration at the central regions. The average behaviors of the records in the two entities are also not very different. In such cases, it may not be meaningful to classify any *single* data point, because of the fact the differences in distributions are very subtle over different regions of the data. The example in Figure 1 is a very simple case, in which we have shown the relative behavior of only two such entities. In practice, there may be thousands of such entities with subtle variations in their data distributions and shapes. For example, another entity belonging to class 'x' may not necessarily be concentrated at the peripheries, but may have a slightly different shape which is characteristic of that class. Typically, there may be a small number of characteristic properties in the data distributions *for a particular class*, but different entities may use a different subset of these characteristic properties. When the entire data is viewed as a distribution of individual records across different classes, it may be virtually impossible to distinguish the instances at the lowest level. The challenge is to learn these subtle differences and similarities at the *entity-distribution level* efficiently in the stream scenario. Since the data points for a particular set entity are not received sequentially, this further increases the challenge from the perspective of stream processing [1, 6]. In this paper, we will design an efficient classification method which captures the subtle entity-specific characteristics in the form of classification signatures. These classification signatures essentially create a summarized model of the typical patterns in the underlying class behavior of different entities. We will show how to use this model for effective classification.

This paper is organized as follows. We will present related work in the remainder of this section. In section 2, we design efficient methods for classification of multi-set streams. The experimental results are presented in section 3. The conclusions and summary are present in section 4.

1.1 Related Work

The problem of classification has been widely studied in the machine learning and data mining literature [9, 12, 21, 23]. Surveys on data classification may be found in [7]. Recently, the problem has also been extended to the stream scenario. The earliest work in the area focussed on the extension of decision trees for stream classification [6, 11, 14, 15, 16, 22]. A popular ensemble classifier was proposed in [24], and the use of data selection for stream classification for explored in [13]. A method for on-demand classification of data streams was proposed in [2]. Recently, stream classification has also been adapted to the rare-class detection problem [8, 17, 18, 19]. A survey of stream classification may be found in [3]. All these methods are proposed for the model construction and classification of test instances.

A setwise method for the clustering problem has recently been proposed in [4]. Other methods have also been proposed in which test instances are classified on the basis of the a-priori knowledge that all *test* instances belong to the same class [20], or for labels to be attached to bags of training instances [10]. However, we note that these problems still attach labels to individual instances at a *fundamental* level both during training and testing. The specification of labels with bags of instances is simply a result of either unavailability of labels with individual training instances, or additional meta-information provided with test instances. Individual instances can be meaningfully classified to labels in these cases. In the case of [10], the attaching of labels to bags of training instances is simply an approximation because of unavailability of labels about individual training instances instances. In the case of [20], the additional knowledge that a set of *test* instances belong to the same class simply enhances the accuracy of classification of individual instances, which could otherwise be performed without this information. Our model is fundamentally different, because labels are attached to setwise entities both during training and testing, and it is not even meaningful to attach labels to individual instances of data records. Rather, the classification behavior of an entity can only be defined on the basis of the *distribution* of the records inside it. This is a much more challenging scenario for the classification process, and especially so in the stream scenario.

2. SETWISE STREAM CLASSIFICATION

We will first introduce the notations and definitions which are relevant to our work. We assume that the different setwise entities in the training stream are denoted by $\mathcal{D}_1 \ldots \mathcal{D}_N$. Each entity $\mathcal{D}_i$ is associated with the class label l_i. We assume that there are a total of k classes, and the class label is drawn from $\{1 \ldots k\}$. The dimensionality of each data set is d, and each data set has the same set of features. It is assumed that the ith data set $\mathcal{D}_i$ has n_i records. The jth record of the ith training entity is denoted by $\overline{X_j(i)}$. Since the dimensionality of the data is d, it is evident that the record $\overline{X_j(i)}$ is a vector containing d components. In addition, we have a set of n test entities, which are denoted by $\mathcal{T}_1 \ldots \mathcal{T}_n$. The jth record of the ith test entity is denoted by $\overline{Z_j(i)}$.

DEFINITION 1 (SETWISE CLASSIFICATION). *Given a set of entities $\mathcal{D}_1 \ldots \mathcal{D}_N$, with associated labels $l_1 \ldots l_N$, construct a training model $\mathcal{M}$, which allows us to classify the different set entities $\mathcal{T}_1 \ldots \mathcal{T}_n$.*

The aforementioned problem definition is actually a simplification from the stream scenario. In the stream scenario, the individual records of an entity may be received in any particular order. Therefore, the individual records are tagged with the identifier of their entity, and also the corresponding entity label.

We assume that the data is received in the form of a stream $< \overline{Y_1}, entityid_1, label_1 > \ldots < \overline{Y_r}, entityid_r, label_r >$ $\ldots$. The tuple $\overline{Y_r}$ represents a d-dimensional data point which could be *either* from the training or the test data, the notation $entityid_r$ represents the id of the entity, and $label_r$ represents the label of the underlying data. The value of $label_r$ is drawn from $\{1 \ldots k\}$, if the record $\overline{Y_r}$ is drawn from an entity belonging to the training data. Otherwise, the record $\overline{Y_r}$ is drawn from an entity belonging to the test data, and the value of $label_r$ is -1. Thus, the records are not only out of order, *but the records from the training and test stream may also be mixed with one another.* Furthermore, we note that the class label for a test entity can be predicted as soon as a sufficient number of records are received in order to be able to predict its underlying distribution. As more records are received, the predicted label for a test entity will change (and typically become more accurate), because its underlying data distribution can also be estimated more accurately. The entity identifier is an integer drawn from $[1, N]$, if the entity is drawn from the training data. Otherwise, the entity identifier is an integer drawn from $[1, n]$. Therefore, assuming that $\overline{Y_r}$ is the jth data point of its entity, the value of $\overline{Y_r}$ is the same as either $\overline{X_j(entityid_r)}$ or $\overline{Z_j(entityid_r)}$ depending upon whether the rth record is a training record or test record respectively.

2.1 Setwise Model Maintenance

In this section, we will describe the process of setwise model maintenance of the different entities. The core idea is to create a set of supervised entity profiles which concisely characterize the distribution of the different entities. One possibility is to use a density estimation approach [25], which can model the relationships between the different classes and the corresponding data distributions. However, such an approach is unlikely to computationally efficient in the stream scenario, because of the need to track the densities over many different portions of the space; the number of such portions typically grows exponentially with the dimensionality of the space. Therefore, we will design a method which computes supervised class fingerprints in order to construct an effective classification model.

In order to concisely represent the distribution behavior of the different entities, we will use the concept of *fingerprints* in order to concisely summarize them. The idea of a fingerprint is to maintain the distribution patterns of the different entities in the data stream. These distribution patterns can be further leveraged to create concise representations of the profiles of different classes in the underlying data in *online fashion*. Clearly, such a model needs to be updated continuously. As more data points arrive in the stream, existing entity distribution patterns may evolve because of concept drift, and other entities with entirely new distribution patterns are received.

We note that the data points in the underlying data stream may belong to either labeled or unlabeled entities, depending upon whether they need to be used for model *building* (training data) or model-based *prediction* (test data). Clearly, this can be the case in many real applications, in which the model construction and prediction needs to be performed simultaneously. A given data point is used for model building, only if a label is associated with it, which is drawn from $\{1 \dots k\}$. Otherwise, if the label value is -1, the entity is a test instance, and we update its current classification status with the new data record, which is added to the distribution of the test instance. This goal is achieved by modeling the entity distributions in relation to landmarks or anchor points that are generated from the underlying data. The entity-specific statistical information, which are also referred to as fingerprints, are used to dynamically maintain the sets of class profiles. These represent the common entity distributions which are relevant to the different classes. A given class may contain *multiple class profiles*, since there may be distributional differences in the profiles belonging to that class. For a given test entity, we determine its class label by using the relationship of the existing class labels to the *current distribution of* that test entity. If a given test entity is classified multiple times during stream progression, its reported class label may change, as more and more data points are received for that entity, and its underlying distribution changes. The changed distribution may sometimes more closely match the profile for another class. Such situations are quite natural, because the test entity can be known more accurately over time, as new data points arrive.

The supervised model maintenance process continuously maintains the entity-specific profiles, and the different class profiles which represent the key entity distribution characteristics. At the same time, we maintain the class-specific profiles of the different fingerprints. Both these statistics need to be maintained simultaneously in the stream scenario. Correspondingly, we also need two input parameters that correspond to the granularity of the fingerprint maintenance and that of class profile maintenance. The granularity of the fingerprints is regulated by the parameter q, which represents the number of anchor points used for fingerprint construction. An additional input to the algorithm is the parameter p, which represents the total number of class profiles tracked in the data. The value of p is typically much larger than k, which is the total number of classes in the data. This ensures that the variations in the distributions of the entities belonging to a particular class can be captured by one of these class profiles. We will denote the q different anchor points by $\overline{W_1} \dots \overline{W_q}$. The simultaneous maintenance of the class profiles together with the fingerprints can be significantly challenging, because the former depends upon the latter, and the latter can change significantly, as new data points arrive and the distributions of the different entities evolve over time. The concept of *fingerprints* [4] is formally defined as follows;

Definition 2 (Fingerprints). *Let the entity containing the data points $\overline{Y_1} \dots \overline{Y_r}$ be partitioned into the q clusters $\mathcal{C}_1 \dots \mathcal{C}_q$, with anchors $\overline{W_1} \dots \overline{W_q}$ respectively, where each data point is assigned to its closest anchor. The corresponding (relative) cluster frequencies are denoted by $f_1 \dots f_q$, where $\sum_{i=1}^{q} f_i = 1$. Then, the fingerprint of the set of data points $\overline{Y_1} \dots \overline{Y_r}$, defined with respect to these anchors is denoted by the q-dimensional tuple $[f_1 \dots f_q]$.*

We denote the fingerprint with respect to anchors $\overline{W_1} \dots \overline{W_q}$ and set of data points $\mathcal{D}$ by $\mathcal{F}(\overline{W_1} \dots \overline{W_q}, \mathcal{D})$. It is important to notice that the fingerprints provide a way to represent the distribution of the data points in a given entity. As we will see later, this turns out to be very useful from the perspective of classification.

In order to dynamically maintain the classification profiles, a total of q anchors $\overline{W_1} \dots \overline{W_q}$ are used during classification. These anchors are fixed throughout the algorithm execution, and are generated in an initial step with the use of a k-means approach. Let $\mathcal{E}_i(t)$ be the subset of the training entity $\mathcal{D}_i$, at the time of the arrival of the tth point in the data stream. The fingerprints for all the entities encountered so far, are actively maintained, and are denoted by $\mathcal{F}(\overline{W_1} \dots \overline{W_q}, \mathcal{E}_1(t)) \dots \mathcal{F}(\overline{W_1} \dots \overline{W_q}, \mathcal{E}_N(t))$. Depending upon the number of such entities which have been encountered so far, these fingerprints can either be maintained in main memory, or they can be maintained on disk. If the training and test entities are arriving simultaneously, then the fingerprints of the test entities are maintained dynamically. As the test entity becomes successively more refined with the arrival of new data points, it is successively reclassified with its new representation. Presumably, the new fingerprint is a more accurate representation of the class structure and behavior. Let $\mathcal{H}_i(t)$ be the subset of the test entity $\mathcal{T}_i$, at the time of arrival of the tth point in the data stream. We corresponding fingerprint is denoted by $\mathcal{F}(\overline{W_1} \ldots \overline{W_q}, \mathcal{H}_i(t))$.

These finger prints are used in order to maintain the different *class distribution profiles*. Multiple class distribution profiles may be associated with a single class. This reflects the fact that many entity distributions may be relevant to a particular class. A class distribution profile is constructed from a set of fingerprints, *all of which belong to the same class*. Therefore, we define a class distribution profile as follows:

DEFINITION 3 (CLASS DISTRIBUTION PROFILES). *The class profiles for a set $S = \{\mathcal{L}_1, \ldots \mathcal{L}_s\}$ of q-dimensional fingerprints, which* **belong to the same class label** l *is defined as the following $(q+2)$-tuple containing the following components:*

- *We maintain q values containing the sum of each fingerprint component and denote the vector by $\overline{AG(\mathcal{S})}$.*
- *We maintain the number of fingerprints in the cluster, which is denoted by $n(\mathcal{S}) = |\mathcal{S}| = s$.*
- *We maintain the class label l of each fingerprint.*

We will next describe the overall process of fingerprint and class profile maintenance. As mentioned earlier, the fingerprints are actively maintained by the algorithm. Since the fingerprints are generated with the use of anchor points, it is important to have an efficient method for generation of the these anchors in the initial phase of the algorithm. Ideally, the anchor points should be dense regions of the data, around which the pattern of data points can be analyzed. Therefore, we use a sample of the data points, denoted by $InitSample$, and we apply a k-means clustering algorithm on these data points in order to generate these initial anchors. The initial anchors are the centroids of the clusters determined on the initial sample of the data points. We denote these anchors by $\overline{W_1} \ldots \overline{W_q}$.

In the event that the tth incoming point $\overline{Y_t}$ is from a training entity set (and belongs to entity set $\mathcal{D}_j$), we denote the subset of entity set $\mathcal{D}_j$ to which the point belongs by $\mathcal{U}_j(t)$. In the event that the tth incoming point is from a test entity (and belongs to entity set $\mathcal{T}_j$), we denote the subset of entity set $\mathcal{T}_j$ to which the point belongs by $\mathcal{V}_j(t)$. This data point is then assigned to its closest anchor point in the data. In order to compute the closest anchor point, we compute the euclidian distance between the data point $\overline{Y_t}$ and the anchors $\overline{W_1} \ldots \overline{W_q}$. Once the assignment has been performed, the fingerprints are correspondingly updated. The update process of a fingerprint needs to account for the addition of the new data point. The index of the selected anchor is denoted by m. The fingerprints for the data subsets before and after modification are denoted by $[f_1 \ldots f_q]$ and $[f'_1 \ldots f'_q]$ respectively. Then, if the tth incoming data point is a training point, the new fingerprint after the addition of a data point is denoted as follows:

$$f'_i = \begin{cases} \frac{f_i \cdot |U_j(t)|}{|U_j(t)|+1} & i \neq m \\ \frac{f_i \cdot |U_j(t)|+1}{|U_j(t)|+1} & i = m \end{cases} \quad (1)$$

```
Algorithm Set-Classify(Stream: Y, Profiles: p,
                       Anchors: q);
begin
  Generate q anchors W_1 ... W_q on
          first InitSample points;
  Divide p class profiles into k different classes
    in proportion to initial class presence, and
       denote by p_1 ... p_k;
  Cluster class-specific segment i with parameter p_i;
  t = 1;
  for each < Y_s, j > ∈ Y do begin
    if j ≥ 0 (training data point) do begin
      Determine closest anchor W_r to data point Y_s;
      Update the fingerprint F(W_1 ... W_q, E_j(t)) with
        data point Y_s by adding to rth bucket;
      if fingerprint has < min_stat points
        then add to tentative set R;
      else begin
        Determine closest profile with same
          class to F(W_1 ... W_q, E_j(t));
        Re-assign entity to closest class-profile if necessary;
        Update class profile statistics;
      end;
    end;
    else begin { Data point from test entity }
      Determine closest anchor W_r to data point Y_s;
      Update the fingerprint F(W_1 ... W_q, H_j(t)) with
        data point Y_s by adding a data point
        to rth bucket and updating relative frequencies;
      Determine closest profile to
          fingerprint F(W_1 ... W_q, H_j(t));
      report label of closest class profile;
    end
    t = t + 1;
  end
end
```

Figure 2: Setwise stream classification

In the event that the tth incoming data point is a test point, the new fingerprint after addition of the test point is as follows:

$$f'_i = \begin{cases} \frac{f_i \cdot |V_j(t)|}{|V_j(t)|+1} & i \neq m \\ \frac{f_i \cdot |V_j(t)|+1}{|V_j(t)|+1} & i = m \end{cases} \quad (2)$$

The denominator always increases by one point since the denominator represents the number of data points in the entity. However, the numerator increases by one for the case of the mth centroid, since only the fingerprint bucket for that bin has been updated.

At the same time, we maintain the class profiles for the different data points. Each class profile consists of a set of closely related fingerprints, all of which belong to the same class. A single class may of course contain multiple profiles, since there may be different entity distributions belonging to the same class. Only the entities which belong to the training data are used to update the class profiles. We assume that the p different class profiles which are consistently maintained are denoted by $\mathcal{P}_1 \ldots \mathcal{P}_p$. Each class profile $\mathcal{P}_i$ contains a number of different features which are tracked with it, according to Definition 3. The entities that belong to the test data are not assigned to any of the profiles. Rather, the fingerprints of these entities are continuously constructed over the course of the data stream and are used in order to perform the successively more accurate classifications as it gradually becomes possible to characterize the entity more and more accurately over time with the use of its fingerprint.

The average fingerprint characterization of the entities in a class profile $\mathcal{P}_i$ can be obtained by dividing each of the bins in $\overline{AG(\mathcal{P}_i)}$ by $n(\mathcal{S}_i)$. This averaged profile can be very useful for computing the similarity between a fingerprint and an averaged class profile. For each incoming data point, we update its underlying entity fingerprint, and assign it to its closest class profile. The closeness of an entity fingerprint to the class profile is computed with the use of the cosine distance between the fingerprint and the averaged class profile. Because an entity may contain many points, the fingerprint will be repeatedly updated, after it has already been assigned to a particular class profile. Correspondingly, the class-profile assignment may also vary with the arrival of additional data points.

In order to meaningfully assign a fingerprint to a class profile, the fingerprint needs to have a sufficient number of data points, so that it can be characterized in a statistically robust way. Therefore, we maintain a *tentative set* of fingerprints $\mathcal{R}$, which correspond to those entities for which a sufficient number of data points have not been received so far. We impose the condition that any fingerprint needs to have a minimum of *min_stat* data points in order to meaningfully assigned to a class profile. Otherwise, it is assigned to the tentative set $\mathcal{R}$, where it "waits" for more individual data points to be included in it. Therefore, a fingerprint will always be assigned to a tentative set at the initial stage of the algorithm. The first time that a fingerprint contains more than *min_stat* data points, it will be assigned to one of the p class profiles denoted by $\mathcal{P}_1 \dots \mathcal{P}_p$.

The other main issue is that each of the p different class profiles belongs to a specific label from the k different classes. In order to define the number of representatives of each class among the class profiles, we use the initial sample of *InitSample* points. Let $r_1 \dots r_k$ be the fraction of entities which belong to the k different classes in this initial sample. Then, the p different class profiles are divided up among the k different classes in proportion to $r_1 \dots r_k$. Specifically, the j-th class is assigned $\lfloor p \cdot r_j + 0.5 \rfloor$ different profiles. Furthermore, each class is assigned at least one profile, in the event that $\lfloor p \cdot r_j + 0.5 \rfloor$ evaluates to 0. Note that the profile distribution among the different classes may not necessarily sum to p. In the event that the number of profiles (assigned to the different classes) is more than p, we remove one profile allocation from each of the classes with the largest number of assigned profiles in decreasing order, until the total number is p. In the event that the number of profiles is less than p, we add one profile allocation to each of the classes with the least number of assigned profiles in increasing order, until the total number is p. We assume that the number of profiles allocated to the class i is denoted by p_i. Therefore, we have $\sum_{i=1}^{k} p_i = p$.

As an initial step in the algorithm, we use the *InitSample* (training) points in the data stream in order to create an initial profile set of classes. This is achieved by applying a k-means clustering algorithm to the entities (with at least *min_stat* points) from the initial sample of points. For each class i, a different k-means clustering is applied with the use of p_i centroids. The set of entities in each cluster are used to create a different class profile. Thus, a total of p profiles are available, which are distributed among the different classes. The entities which do not contain at least *min_stat* points are assigned to the tentative set $\mathcal{R}$.

Subsequently, the online profile maintenance and classification processes are executed simultaneously. The training and test data points may be mixed with one another. The training data points are used for profile maintenance, whereas the test data points are used for online classification. For each incoming (training) data point, we first update its entity fingerprint by adding the data point to the appropriate anchor bin within the fingerprint. At this point, if the fingerprint does not contain at least *min_stat* points, we allow it to stay in the tentative set $\mathcal{R}$. Otherwise, we determine the closest class profile **with the same class** among the current set of profiles, and update that class profile with the modified fingerprint. This process of modification requires us to remove the fingerprint from the profile to which it was assigned earlier, and assign it to a new profile. This requires us to subtract out the fingerprint from the old profile and add it to the new profile. Because the information stored in a profile is additive in nature, it is relatively easy to subtract out the information in one profile and add it to another. In some cases, the addition of a point to an entity may cause it to exceed the threshold of *min_stat*. In such cases, the setwise entity is moved out of the tentative set and added to the closest entity. In this case, the profile only needs to be updated in terms of adding an entity to the profile, but it does not need to be subtracted from a profile.

The fingerprints for the test entities are also maintained simultaneously with the training entities. For each incoming (test) data point, the fingerprint of its test entity is updated. These test entities are maintained in a separate test profile set $\mathcal{Q}$. Each time a fingerprint in $\mathcal{Q}$ is updated, it is assumed that the fingerprint is now presumably more "accurate" because of the addition of more data points to it. Therefore, this refined fingerprint is classified with the use of the training profiles already stored. The classification process determines the closest training profile to the test fingerprint with the use of the cosine metric. The label of this training profile is reported as the relevant label at that instant. This approach essentially re-classifies a test entity every time new information arrives in the stream in order to characterize it more accurately. This seems like a logical way to perform the classification in a scenario in which the entire entity is never available at any given time. The basic algorithm for classification is illustrated in Figure 2.

One observation about the process is that the change to each training entity fingerprint of $\mathcal{U}(t)$ is relatively small when the absolute number of elements in these sets (denoted by $|\mathcal{U}(t)|$) is large. Therefore, it is not necessary to update the class profile for a fingerprint, each time it is updated. Rather, we only update the fingerprint of the entity, but do not use it to update the class profile at all in most iterations. In fact, other than updating the fingerprint of the entity, we do not make any operation (such as cosine distance computations) on the class profiles at all. In order to decide the periods at which fingerprints have changed "sufficiently" in order to allow updates, we maintain an additional quantity for each training entity $\mathcal{U}(t)$ denoted by $\#^{\mathcal{U}(t)}$ at any given instant t. This quantity denotes the number of updates to the entity $\mathcal{U}(t)$ since the last time it was used to update a class profile. The quantity is updated each time the fingerprint is updated, and is reset to 0 every time the fingerprint is used to update a class profile. As long as the entity $\mathcal{U}(t)$ has a significantly larger number of points than the number of updates to it, we know that the fingerprint has not changed significantly enough to worry about issues with training. When the value of $\#^{\mathcal{U}(t)}/|\mathcal{U}(t)|$ is less than a pre-defined fraction (say 1%), we do not perform the updates. The updates are performed, only when this threshold is reached. An immediate observation is that the frequency of class profile updates will reduce with progression of the data stream, as the number of points in the fingerprint become larger and larger. Since a specific *percentage* of points in the fingerprint need to be added in order for the class profiles to be updated, it is evident that the frequency of profile updates reduces, as the *absolute* number of points in each fingerprint increases over the progression of the stream. In reality, the updates to the class profiles tend to be relatively infrequent in steady state, and continuously reduces over time. This results in an increasing efficiency of the algorithm with stream progression.

3. EXPERIMENTAL RESULTS

In this section, we present results on two real and one synthetic data sets. For the real data sets, the class labels were either available with the data set, or could be derived from one of the features of the data sets. For the synthetic data sets, each class was generated from a mixture model gaussian distribution.

3.1 Data Sets

We used two real data sets and one synthetic data set in order to test our approach. The classes in these data sets were highly mixed with one another, and could not be distinguished from one another on the basis of individual data points. These data sets are referred to as *Hub64 Data Stream*, *E-Cover Data Streams*, and *Gauss50Mix10D1000 Data Stream*. We describe these data sets in detail below:

- **Hub64 Data Stream:** The data stream was generated from the *Hub64 data set* and contains the voice signal of 64 different public personalities such as Wolf Blitzer, Bill Clinton, Al Gore, Candy Crowley etc. As we will see later, the identity of the speakers will be useful in order to judge the effectiveness of the clustering process. We derived an 8-dimensional GPCC format from the compressed domain. Each record in this format contained a micro-second sample of the underlying speech with the use of different features such as pitch, amplitude etc. The samples from two different speakers could be very similar, when this sample corresponds to a moment of silence or other sounds which are not easily distinguishable across different speakers. In such cases, the speakers can only be identified from *multiple sets* of records rather than individual records which did not contain meaningful information. In order to create the multi-set entities, we segmented each speaker data into 10 different multi-set entities, each of which was given a different multi-set identifier. This created a total of 640 entities spread out over a stream of 397,041 data points. We randomly mixed the data points for the different speakers, and created a stream of data points that were tagged with the corresponding multi-set identifiers. A total of 80% of the entities were treated as training data, whereas the remaining was treated as test data. The test and training data were randomly mixed with one another, which made the problem much more challenging.

- **E-Cover Data Stream:** This was a derivative data stream from the *forest cover data set*, which was designed to make it more challenging for the multi-set clustering problem. The original version of the problem was labeled with cover-type. We used the first attribute (elevation), in order to create the different multi-set entities. This is because the elevation attribute is very noisily related to the different attributes, and the classification can only be inferred from the overall distribution of the multi-set entities with the same elevation. Let μ and σ be the mean and standard deviations of the different elevations. The elevations were divided into 10 different categories, based on 9 different discretization points corresponding to $\mu - 1.3 \cdot \sigma$, $\mu - 0.7 \cdot \sigma$, $\mu - 0.3 \cdot \sigma$, $\mu - 0.1 \cdot \sigma$, μ, $\mu + 0.1 \cdot \sigma$, $\mu + 0.3 \cdot \sigma$, $\mu + 0.7 \cdot \sigma$, and $\mu + 1.3 \cdot \sigma$ respectively. We divided each of the 10 different categories into 150 different multi-set entities, which resulted in 1500 entities being spread over a stream of 581,012 records. The order of the records was randomized in the data set in order to create the stream. Each multi-data entity was tagged with the corresponding multi-set identifier. We removed the elevation attribute from the data set for clustering purposes, though the discretized value was retained as meta-information for evaluation purposes. Each of the quantitative attributes was normalized by its standard deviation. As before, used 80% of the entities are training entities and 20% of the entities as test entities.

- **Gauss50Mix10D1000 Data Stream:** The third data stream was a 10-dimensional synthetic data stream which was generated with the use of gaussian mixture models. We generated 50 different classes, each of which was a mixture model of 10 different clusters. Furthermore, the clusters for different classes overlapped with one another. Since each class was a mixture model containing many clusters The center of each cluster was chosen from a uniform distribution in $[0.1, 0.9]$, and the radius of each cluster along each dimension was chosen from a uniform distribution in $[1, 1.5]$. Note that the radius of each cluster is greater than the range from which the centers are drawn. Furthermore, since each multi-set distribution is drawn from a mixture model of 10 different clusters with randomly generated centers, it follows that the data sets from the different distributions will be highly overlapping with one another in terms of clustering behavior. An example of a 2-dimensional cross-section of a sample of 4 of the distributions is illustrated in Figure 1. It is evident that the different distributions are highly mixed with one another and show little clustering in terms of individual data points. The number of points in each of the $50 * 10 = 500$ different constituent clusters of the mixture model was generated from the Zipf distribution $1/(i + 100)^{\theta}$. The parameter of the Zipf distribution was chosen to 0.1. A total of 10^6 data points were distributed across the different clusters. Each of the dimensions was normalized so as to equalize the standard deviation across all attributes. For each of the 50 mixture model distributions, we tagged the corresponding data points with one of 20 different multi-set entities. Thus, the 10^6 different data points were distributed across 1000 different multi-set entities. We set 80% of the entities as training entities and the remaining as test entities. As in previous cases, the data points from the different entities were randomly mixed with one another in the form of a data stream.

3.2 Baseline Approach

We created multi-variate density distributions in order to characterize the different entities, and used these density distributions in order to construct the training models. The density distributions are constructed as sampled grid points in the data space. The number of such grid points are exponentially related to the number of dimensions. For each dimension, we had 3 possible grid points at $\mu_i - \sigma_i$, μ_i, and $\mu_i + \sigma_i$, where μ_i and σ_i are the mean and standard deviation of dimension i. Therefore, for a d-dimensional data set, we have 3^d possible grid points. Since this number can be very large, it is necessary to sample grid-points in order to create the density profiles in a reasonably efficient way. We used these density profiles were used as a surrogate for the fingerprints in conjunction with the approach in Figure 2 as the baseline technique. In order to create a comparable computational efficiency with the multi-set clustering technique, we constructed density estimates on as many grid points as the number of anchors which were used by our multi-set clustering technique. We used kernel density estimation on the incoming stream in order to create the density profiles at the grid points.

3.3 Effectiveness Results

All results were tested on an Lenovo X201 Thinkpad running Microsoft Windows XP, with a 2.4GHz CPU and 2.9 GB of main memory. The code was implemented with Microsoft Visual C++. In all cases, unless otherwise mentioned, the default number of anchors (or grid-points) used was 50, the default number of classification profiles was 80, and default initial number of sample points was 10,000. We first tested the classification accuracy with increasing number of anchors. The results for the *Hub64 data stream*, *E-cover data stream* and the *Gauss50Mix10D1000* data stream are illustrated in Figures 3(a), (b), and (c) respectively. The number of anchors (or grid-points for the baseline scheme) is illustrated on the X-axis, whereas the classification accuracy is illustrated on the Y-axis. The number of classification profiles was set to its default value of 80. In most cases, an increase in the number of anchors increased the classification accuracy, though this was not always the case. This is because a certain amount of noise is associated with the anchor construction process, and a large number of anchors may not always imply a higher classification accuracy. In all cases, the accuracy of the *Set-Classify* scheme was *significantly* higher than the density-based baseline. For example, in the case of the *Hub64* data stream, the classification accuracy of the *Set-Classify* scheme was greater than 40% with the use of 75 anchors and 80 classification profiles, whereas the classification accuracy of the density-based baseline was about 25%. This difference was even larger for the other two data sets. For example, for the case of the *E-Cover* data set, the density-based scheme performed disastrously with a classification accuracy of only about 20% at these same parameter values. On the other hand, the *Set-Classify* scheme had an accuracy which was greater than 80%. The different between the two schemes was also very significant in the case of the synthetic data set.

We also tested the classification accuracy of the schemes with increasing number of classification profiles. The results for the *Hub64 data stream*, *E-cover data stream* and the *Gauss50Mix10D1000* data stream are illustrated in Figures 3(d), (e), and (f) respectively. The number of classification profiles are illustrated on the X-axis, whereas the classification accuracy is illustrated on the Y-axis. The number of anchors was set to the default value of 50. As in the previous case, the *Set-Classify* scheme was significantly more accurate than the baseline methods. The other observation was that the trend with increasing classification profiles was much less clear as compared to the trend with increasing number of anchors. This is because an increase in the number of profiles increased the representation granularity (which improves accuracy), but also reduced the number of points in each profile (which reduces its robustness and therefore the overall accuracy).

Finally, we also tested the classification accuracy with progression of the data stream. The results for the *Hub64 data stream*, *E-cover data stream* and the *Gauss50Mix10D1000* data stream are illustrated in Figures 3(g), (h), and (i) respectively. The progression of the data stream (in terms of the number of points) is illustrated on the X-axis, whereas the classification accuracy (on the last block of points) is illustrated on the Y-axis. The number of anchors and classification profiles was set to 50 and 80 respectively. We note that the progression of the stream on the X-axis is illustrated in terms of the number of *test data points*, which are mixed randomly with the training data points. It is clear that in each case, the classification accuracy increases rapidly with stream progression, but stabilizes over time, as the distribution of classification profiles reaches steady state. As in the previous cases, the classification accuracy of the *Set-Classify* method is significantly greater than the density-based baseline for all the three data sets.

3.4 Efficiency Results

We also tested the efficiency of the scheme in terms of the number of data points processed per second. The processing rates for training and testing wee tabulated separately by separating out the running times for the algorithm loops which correspond to the training and testing data. The initialization times were charged to the training rates. We tested the processing rates with increasing number of anchors. The results for the *Hub64 data stream*, *E-cover data stream* and the *Gauss50Mix10D1000* data stream are illustrated in Figures 4(a), (b), and (c) respectively. The number of anchors are illustrated on the X-axis, whereas the processing rate (in terms of the number of data points processed per second) are illustrated on the Y-axis. The number of classification profiles was set to its default value of 80. The processing rates for all schemes reduces with an increasing number of anchors. This is because an increase in the number of anchors increases the amount of time it requires to update each fingerprint. It is evident that both the training and testing rates for the *Set-Classify* scheme are significantly greater than that for the baseline scheme. This is because the fingerprint generation process is much more efficient than the process of density estimation. Furthermore, the training rates tend to be significantly higher than the

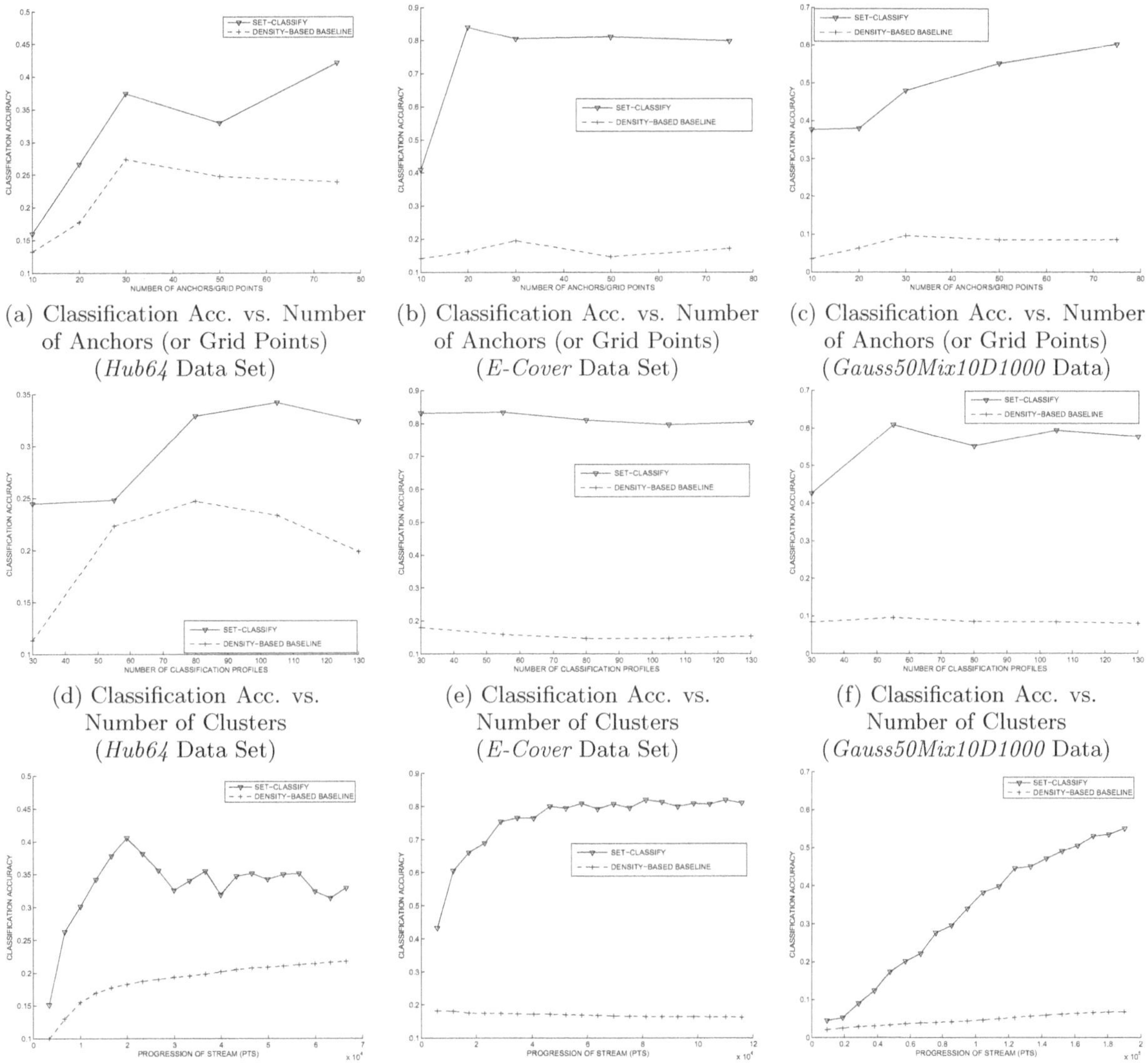

(a) Classification Acc. vs. Number of Anchors (or Grid Points) (*Hub64* Data Set)

(b) Classification Acc. vs. Number of Anchors (or Grid Points) (*E-Cover* Data Set)

(c) Classification Acc. vs. Number of Anchors (or Grid Points) (*Gauss50Mix10D1000* Data)

(d) Classification Acc. vs. Number of Clusters (*Hub64* Data Set)

(e) Classification Acc. vs. Number of Clusters (*E-Cover* Data Set)

(f) Classification Acc. vs. Number of Clusters (*Gauss50Mix10D1000* Data)

(g) Classification Accuracy with Stream Progression (*Hub64* Data Set)

(h) Classification Accuracy with Stream Progression (*E-Cover* Data Set)

(i) Classification Accuracy with Stream Progression (*Gauss50Mix10D1000* Data)

Figure 3: Effectiveness Results

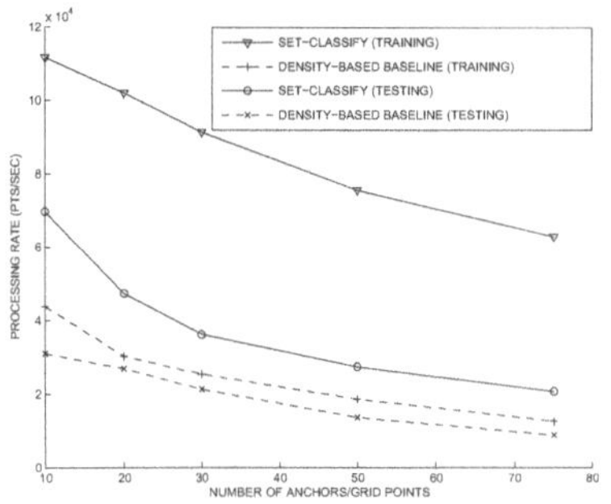

(a) Efficiency vs. Number of Anchors (or Grid Points) (*Hub64* Data Set)

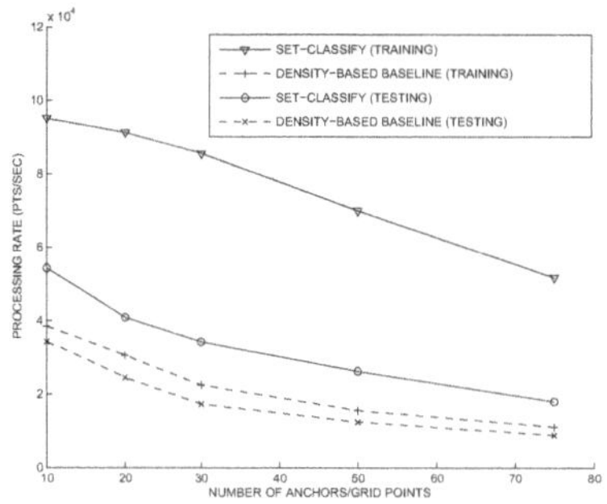

(b) Efficiency vs. Number of Anchors (or Grid Points) (*E-Cover* Data Set)

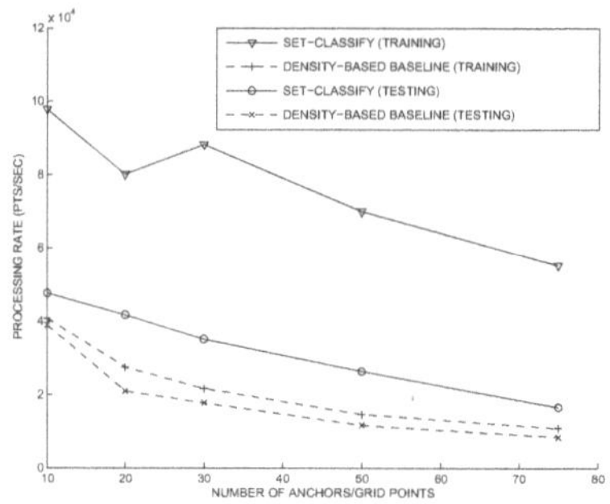

(c) Efficiency vs. Number of Anchors (or Grid Points) (*Gauss50Mix10D1000* Data)

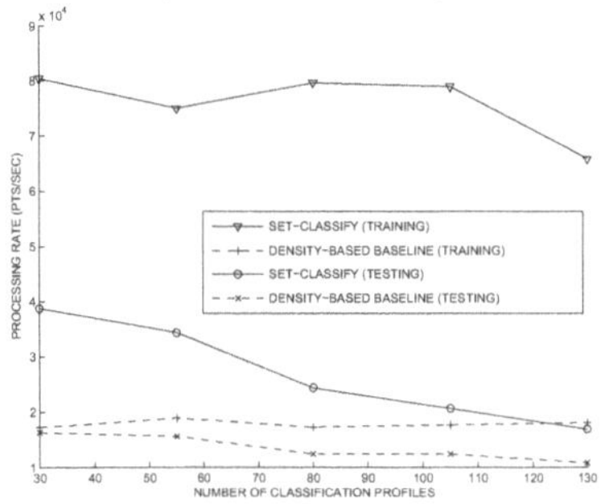

(d) Efficiency vs. Number of Clusters (*Hub64* Data Set)

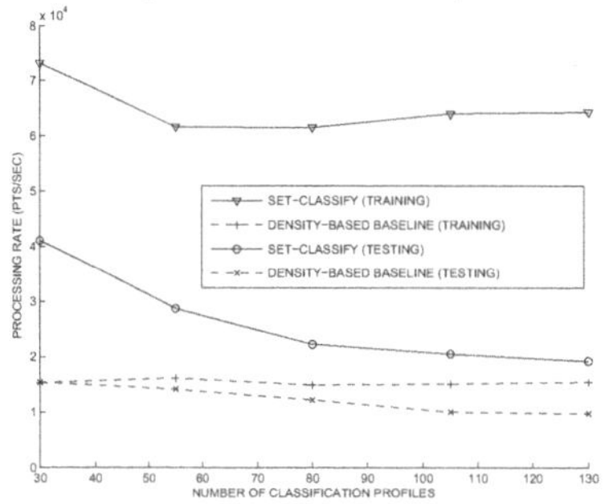

(e) Efficiency vs. Number of Clusters (*E-Cover* Data Set)

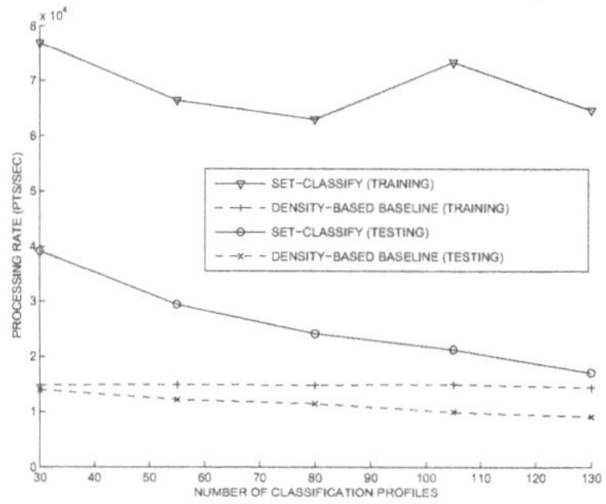

(f) Efficiency vs. Number of Clusters (*Gauss50Mix10D1000* Data)

Figure 4: Efficiency Results

testing rates. The reason for this was that the fingerprint of a training entity only needed to be compared with the class profiles which belonged *to the same class*, whereas the fingerprint of a testing entity need to be compared with the class profiles of *every class*. This ensured that the training rates were always much higher than the testing rates. Furthermore, the absolute training and testing rates were of the order of several thousand data points per second. This ensures that very large volumes of streams could be processed with the use of such an approach.

We also tested the processing rates with increasing number of classification profiles. The results for the *Hub64 data stream*, *E-cover data stream* and the *Gauss50Mix10D1000* data stream are illustrated in Figures 3(d), (e), and (f) respectively. The number of classification profiles are illustrated on the X-axis, whereas the processing rates is illustrated on the Y-axis. The number of anchors was set to the default value of 50. One observation was that while the processing rates reduces with increasing number of classification profiles, they were not quite as sensitive to this parameter, as they were to the number of anchors. The reason for this is that most of the time is spent in constructing the fingerprints, and this phase is essentially independent of the number of class profiles. Therefore, the processing rates are only mildly sensitive to the number of classification profiles. As in the previous case, the processing rates of the *Set-Classify* scheme are significantly greater than that of the density-based classification scheme. Furthermore, these processing rates are typically of the order of several thousands data points per second. This ensures that our approach is an effective and efficient method for setwise classification of data streams.

4. CONCLUSIONS AND SUMMARY

Setwise stream classification scenarios are increasingly common, where one needs to classify an entire set of data records, rather than an individual data point. An additional complicating factor is that the stream points from different multi-set entities may be mixed with one another. This can make the classification process much more challenging. This paper designs a technique for online generation of classification profiles, which are used for the purposes of classification. We presented experimental results illustrating its effectiveness and efficiency.

5. REFERENCES

[1] C. Aggarwal, J. Han, J. Wang, and P. Yu. A Framework for Clustering Evolving Data Streams, *VLDB Conference*, pp. 81–92, 2003.

[2] C. Aggarwal, J. Han, J. Wang, P. Yu. On Demand Classification of Data Streams, *ACM KDD Conference*, pp. 503–508, 2004.

[3] C. Aggarwal. A Survey of Stream Classification Algorithms, *Data Classification: Algorithms and Applications*, CRC Press, 2014.

[4] C. Aggarwal. The Multi-Set Stream Clustering Problem, *SIAM Conference on Data Mining*, pp. 59–69, 2012.

[5] C. Aggarwal. On Segment-based Stream Modeling and its Applications, *SIAM Conference on Data Mining*, pp. 721–732, 2009.

[6] C. Aggarwal. *Data Streams: Models and Algorithms*, Springer, New York, 2007.

[7] C. Aggarwal. *Data Classification: Algorithms and Applications*, CRC Press, Boca Raton, FL, 2014.

[8] T. Al-Khateeb, M. Masud, L. Khan, C. Aggarwal, J. Han, and B. Thuraisingham. Stream Classification with Recurring and Novel Class Detection Using Class-Based Ensemble. *IEEE ICDM Conference*, pp. 31–40, 2012.

[9] T. M. Cover, and P. E. Hart. Nearest Neighbor Pattern Classification. *IEEE Transactions on Information Theory*, 13(1), pp. 21–27, 1967.

[10] T. Dietterich, R. Lathrop, and T. Lozano-Perez. Solving the Multiple-Instance Problem with Axis-Parallel Rectangles. *Artificial Intelligence*, 89, pp. 31–71, 1997.

[11] P. Domingos, and G. Hulten. Mining High-Speed Data Streams. *ACM KDD Conference*, pp. 71–80, 2000.

[12] R. Duda, P. Hart, and D. Stork. *Pattern Classification*, Wiley-Interscience, 2000.

[13] W. Fan. Systematic Data Selection to Mine Concept Drifting Data Streams, *ACM KDD Conference*, pp. 128–137, 2004.

[14] J. Gama, R. Rocha, and P. Medas. Accurate Decision Trees for Mining High-Speed Data Streams, *ACM KDD Conference*, pp. 523–528, 2003.

[15] G. Hulten, L. Spencer, and P. Domingos. Mining Time Changing Data Streams. *ACM KDD Conference*, pp. 97–106, 2001.

[16] R. Jin, and G. Agrawal. Efficient Decision Tree Construction on Streaming Data, *ACM KDD Conference*, pp. 571–576, 2003.

[17] M. Masud, Q. Chen, L. Khan, C. Aggarwal, J. Gao, J. Han, and B. Thuraisingham. Addressing Concept-Evolution in Concept-Drifting Data Streams. *IEEE ICDM Conference*, pp. 929–934, 2010.

[18] M. Masud, T. Al-Khateeb, L. Khan, C. Aggarwal, J. Gao, J. Han, and B. Thuraisingham. Detecting Recurring and Novel Classes in Concept-Drifting Data Streams. *IEEE ICDM Conference*, pp. 1176–1181, 2011.

[19] M. Masud, Q. Chen, L. Khan, C. Aggarwal, J. Gao, J. Han, A. Srivastava, and N. Oza. Classification and Adaptive Novel Class Detection of Feature-Evolving Data Streams, *IEEE Transactions on Knowledge and Data Engineering*, 25(7), pp. 1484–1497, 2013.

[20] X. Ning, and G. Karypis. The Set Classification Problem and Solution Methods. *SIAM Conference on Data Mining*, pp. 847–858, 2009.

[21] J. R. Quinlan. C4.5: Programs for Machine Learning, *Morgan Kaufmann*, 1993.

[22] S. Ruping. Incremental Learning with Support Vector Machines. *IEEE ICDM Conference*, pp. 641–642, 2001.

[23] V. Vapnik. *The Nature of Statistical Learning Theory*, Springer, New York, 1995.

[24] H. Wang, W. Fan, P. Yu, J. Han. Mining Concept-Drifting Data Streams using Ensemble Classifiers. *ACM KDD Conference*, pp. 226–235, 2003.

[25] T. Zhang, R. Ramakrishnan, M. Livny. Fast Density Estimation Using CF-Kernel for Very Large Databases. *ACM KDD Conference*, pp. 312–316, 1999.

Streamed Approximate Counting of Distinct Elements

Beating Optimal Batch Methods

Daniel Ting
Facebook
1730 Minor Avenue
Seattle, WA
dting@fb.com

ABSTRACT

Counting the number of distinct elements in a large dataset is a common task in web applications and databases. This problem is difficult in limited memory settings where storing a large hash table table is intractable. This paper advances the state of the art in probabilistic methods for estimating the number of distinct elements in a streaming setting New streaming algorithms are given that provably beat the "optimal" errors for Min-count and HyperLogLog while using the same sketch.

This paper also contributes to the understanding and theory of probabilistic cardinality estimation introducing the concept of an area cutting process and the martingale estimator. These ideas lead to theoretical analyses of both old and new sketches and estimators and show the new estimators are optimal for several streaming settings while also providing accurate error bounds that match those obtained via simulation. Furthermore, the area cutting process provides a geometric intuition behind all methods for counting distinct elements which are not affected by duplicates. This intuition leads to a new sketch, Discrete Max-count, and the analysis of a class of sketches, self-similar area cutting decompositions that have attractive properties and unbiased estimators for both streaming and non-streaming settings.

Together, these contributions lead to multi-faceted advances in sketch construction, cardinality and error estimation, the theory, and intuition for the problem of approximate counting of distinct elements for both the streaming and non-streaming cases.

Categories and Subject Descriptors

G.3 [**Probability and Statistics**]: Probabilistic algorithms, Stochastic processes; H.2.8 [**Database Applications**]: Data mining

Keywords

distinct elements, martingale, cardinality estimation, randomized algorithms

KDD'14, August 24–27, 2014, New York, New York, USA.
ACM 978-1-4503-2956-9/14/08 ...$15.00.
http://dx.doi.org/10.1145/2623330.2623669.

1. INTRODUCTION

Approximating the number of distinct elements in a dataset while using a small amount of memory is an important problem with broad industrial applications. A web company may wish to count the number of distinct users accessing a service broken down by country of origin [12]. Other areas of application include counting network flows to detect denial of service attacks [6] and database warehousing [1].

A number of algorithms exist for approximately estimating these counts. Most tackle the problem by first constructing a summarization of the data or *sketch* and then estimating the number of distinct elements, the cardinality, from the sketch. In practice, Flajolet and Martin's HyperLogLog [8] and Chen et al's Self-learning bitmap [4] (S-bitmap) constitute the state of the art in the field when there is no prior estimate of the cardinality. Several theoretical results exist as well. Kane et al [11] give an algorithm with optimal space complexity but sub-optimal statistical efficiency while Giroire's Min-count algorithm [9] has optimal statistical efficiency but poor space requirements. Although these algorithms have been described as streaming algorithms, only the S-bitmap exploits the streaming property of data to achieve better accuracy.

This paper develops a general recipe for constructing streaming cardinality estimation algorithms by introducing the area cutting process and an estimator for the cardinality using martingale methods. The martingale methods extend the estimation methods used by the S-bitmap [4]. This recipe covers almost all sketching methods. Any sketch which is generated by hashing of each element in the data stream and is not affected by duplicates elements has a representation as an area cutting process. The associated martingale estimator is provably unbiased and provably optimal if queried immediately after a sketch update.

Streaming versions of HyperLogLog and Min-count are shown to have superior performance to their non-streaming counterparts. Regular HyperLogLog is shown to require approximately 1.5 times more bits than streaming HyperLogLog to achieve the same error, and Min-count requires twice the size of streaming Min-count. These streaming estimators are able to beat optimal estimators which use only the final sketch is because the streaming estimators are able to exploit the values of intermediate sketches as well. Furthermore, unlike the S-bitmap which can only be used in a streaming setting, these sketching methods have the advantage that they may also be used in distributed settings where results may be need to be aggregated over multiple servers or computed within a map-reduce framework.

A special class of decomposable self-similar area cutting processes is introduced and shown to have attractive properties. They are shown to have an unbiased estimator for non-streaming data as well as analytic formulas for the variance for both the streaming and non-streaming case. A new sketch construction, Discrete Max-count, yields a decomposable self-similar area cutting process which has good performance for small sketches. For a non-optimal encoding of the Discrete Max-count sketch, the space-complexity is derived and shown to have no term which jointly depends on both the error ϵ and cardinality n.

The empirical performance of each method is evaluated as well using both simulations and an anonymized Facebook test dataset. Unlike HyperLogLog which requires special corrections for small and medium sized cardinalities [10], the performance of the estimators is consistently good throughout the entire range of cardinalities tested.

Several ideas of note are introduced in this paper. To introduce these ideas the paper is structured as follows. In section 2, we formulate the cardinality estimation problem by describing the probabilistic data generating process for the sketches. This leads to the martingale estimator and its properties, including its optimality properties. Next, several existing sketches are described and shown to yield streaming estimates. The area cutting process and a geometric interpretation of the sketches are give in section 5. This paper then focuses on self-similar area cutting processes and their properties. Discrete Max-count is introduced as a special case and its space complexity is analyzed, and the optimal and near optimal estimators for the non-streaming versions of Min-count and HyperLogLog are shown to be non-optimal in streaming settings. The streaming methods are evaluated via simulation in section 7 and future research directions are discussed.

2. PROBABILITISTIC COUNTING

To fix the notation in this paper, let $\mathcal{X} = (X_1, X_2, ...)$ be a stream of elements and n denote the cardinality, the number of distinct elements, of $\mathcal{X}$. Cardinality estimation methods involve constructing a sequence of sketches S_i which are functions of the data seen up to some point, and then estimating the cardinality $\hat{N}(S_i)$ from the sketches. To ensure that only distinct elements are counted, the sketches should not be affected by duplicates. In other words, they should have the property $S_i = S_{i-1}$ if $X_i = X_j$ for some $j < i$. In most probabilistic methods, the sketches are based on a transformed stream of data which has been converted using a strong universal hash function h so that $(h(X_{i_1}), h(X_{i_2}), ...)$ forms a sequence of independent $Uniform(0,1)$ random variables where the subsequence (i_j) picks out the first occurrence of each distinct element. The hash function ensures that duplicates remain duplicates after transformation. The sketches S_i are then random elements from some distribution parameterized by n_i, the number of distinct elements encountered up to the ith element in the stream. Thus, the problem of estimating the cardinality is reduced to the statistical problem of estimating a parameter for a known family of distributions given the data S_i.

Our insight for exploiting the streaming nature of the data is that using just the last sketch S_{last} to estimate the cardinality throws away information contained in the entire sequence of sketches. We augment the sketch by including the current estimate into the sketch $\tilde{S}_i = (S_i, \hat{N}_i)$. This augmentation allows the construction of a provably unbiased martingale estimator with just an additional $O_p(\lg n)$ bits. Here, the notation $O_p(\lg n)$ is the probabilistic analog of $O(\lg n)$ where the bound holds for arbitrarily small probabilities.

Algorithm 1 Algorithm for updating an existing estimate $\hat{n}_{prev}$ and sketch with a new item.

```
function UpdateEstimate(n̂_prev, sketch, item_new)
    q ← P(sketch is modified)
    Add item_new to sketch
    if sketch is modified then
        return n̂_prev + 1/q
    else
        return n̂_prev
    end if
end function
```

2.1 Counting with Markov processes and Martingales

The key idea behind all streaming algorithms described in this paper is that a Markov chain is formed by the sequences of sketches generated from a data stream. This Markov chain is obtained by taking the original sequence of sketches $S_i^{(orig)}$ indexed by the number of items i encountered and considering only the subsequence S_t indexed by the number of *distinct* items t encountered.

THEOREM 1. *The sequence of sketches (S_t) forms a Markov chain when h is a strong universal hash.*

PROOF. The next sketch $S_{t+1} = f(S_t, h(X_t))$ is some function of the current sketch and the next hashed value. Since h is a strong universal hash, the $h(X_t)$ are independent and identically distributed, and the probability of transitioning to some value depends only on the previous value of the sketch S_t □

For ease of exposition, this paper will refer to the index t interchangeably as both time and the number of distinct elements encountered.

Define the *martingale estimator* to be the Markov chain

$$\hat{N}_{t+1} = \hat{N}_t + \frac{1}{q(S_t)} 1(S_{t+1} \neq S_t) \tag{1}$$

where $q(S_t)$ is the probability of modifying the current sketch and transitioning out of the current state. The initial state of the chain is $\hat{N}_0 = 0$. The idea behind this estimator is that with one time step the expected increase in the estimator is exactly 1. Note that although the underlying sequence (S_t) is not observed since the number of distinct items t is not known at an arbitrary location in the stream, the estimator depends only on observable events, namely on modifications to the sketch.

The resulting algorithm is simple and elegant and can be applied to any sketch which is unaffected by duplicates. Given a sketch, augment it with a counter c and add $1/q(S_{T_{t-1}})$ every time there is a change in the sketch. Note that the estimate is never updated when a duplicate item is encountered since duplicates do not modify the sketch. The algorithm is summarized in algorithm 1.

The name of the estimator comes from the fact that $\hat{N}_t - t$ is a martingale. A martingale M_t is a Markov process such that $\mathbb{E}(M_{t+1}|M_t) = M_t$. The martingale property aids in

Symbol	Description
n	True cardinality
m	Number of bins or samples
S_t	Sketch after t distinct items are encountered
T_i	Time of the ith modification of the sketch
$q(S_t)$	Probability that a new item modifies the sketch S_t
q_i	$q(S_{T_i})$
(Δ_t, Y_t)	offset and samples of an offset decomposition

Table 1: Table of symbols

deriving properties of the estimator. The most important property is given by the following theorem.

THEOREM 2. *The process $M_t = \hat{N}_t - t$ is a martingale. Hence, $\hat{N}_n$ is an unbiased estimate of the cardinality n.*

PROOF. The martingale property is trivial to check. $\mathbb{E}M_t = \mathbb{E}\mathbb{E}(M_t|M_{t-1}) = \mathbb{E}M_{t-1}$. By induction, $\mathbb{E}M_t = \mathbb{E}M_0 = 0$. In other words, $\mathbb{E}\hat{N}_n = n$, and $\hat{N}_n$ is unbiased. □

Another way to view the estimator comes from decomposing it in terms of holding times for the Markov chain. Let $T_1, T_2, \ldots$ be the jump times of the chain, so that T_i be the time of the ith modification to the sketch. The holding time $T_i - T_{i-1}$ is the time the chain remains in state $S_{T_{i-1}}$. Let T_K be the sketch's last modification time before time n.

$$n = \sum_{T_i \le n} (T_i - T_{i-1}) + (n - T_K) \tag{2}$$

$$\hat{N}_t = \sum_{T_i \le n} \mathbb{E}(T_i - T_{i-1}|S_{T_{i-1}}) = \sum_{T_i \le t} \frac{1}{q(S_{T_{i-1}})}. \tag{3}$$

Since the holding time $T_i - T_{i-1}$ of a discrete Markov chain has a *Geometric*$(q(S_{T_{i-1}}))$ distribution, the estimator is incremented by precisely the expected time it takes before the sketch is modified.

For convenience, we provide a table of commonly used symbols in table 1.

2.1.1 Bayesian approach

We also consider a Bayesian approach to estimation. This leads to subtlely different estimators which are biased but have slightly stronger optimality guarantees when the cardinality is drawn from a *Geometric*(α) prior. The Bayesian formulation is also of additional interest when estimating the error in section 2.2 since the posterior is tractable. The Bayesian estimate with lowest squared error given the sequence of observed sketches is the conditional expectation given the sketches

$$\hat{n}_{Bayes} = \mathbb{E}(N|S_{T_1}, \ldots, S_{T_K}, K) \tag{4}$$

$$= \sum_{t=1}^{K} \mathbb{E}(T_t - T_{t-1}|S_{T_{t-1}}) + \mathbb{E}(N - T_K|S_{T_K}, K). \tag{5}$$

Interestingly, this gives a slightly different decomposition than the one for the martingale estimator described by 3. The additional term $\mathbb{E}(N - T_K|S_{T_K}, K)$ means that the estimator is biased even under a uniform prior on N.

Under a *Geometric*(α) prior on the cardinality N, it is easy to derive

$$T_t - T_{t-1}|S_{T_{t-1}} \sim Geometric(1 - (1-\alpha)(1 - q_{t-1})) \tag{6}$$

$$N - T_K|S_{T_K}, K \sim Geometric(1 - (1-\alpha)(1 - q_{T_K})) \tag{7}$$

where $q_t = q(S_{T_t})$ and the holding times are conditionally independent given the sketches. Note that as $\alpha \to 0$ the prior approaches the improper uniform prior and the conditional distributions simplify to *Geometric*$(q(S_T))$ for appropriate T. In this case, the estimator is identical to the martingale estimator except that the Bayesian estimator has one additional term for the last holding time. The Bayesian conditional mean estimator is given by

$$\hat{N}_{Bayes} = \sum_{i=0}^{K} \frac{1}{q_i + \alpha(1 - q_i)}. \tag{8}$$

2.2 Error estimates

It is possible to maintain an estimate of the error in addition to keeping an estimate of the cardinality. We estimate the error using both a martingale approach and a Bayesian approach and describe the properties of each.

The martingale estimate of the variance gives an unbiased estimate of the variance, but only at jump times when the sketch is modified. The quadratic variation $\langle M_t \rangle$ of a process (M_t) is defined to the the sum of its squared increments:

$$\langle M_t \rangle = \sum_{i=0}^{t-1} (M_{i+1} - M_i)^2. \tag{9}$$

It follows from Doob's decomposition [5] that if M_t is a martingale then the quadratic variation process $\langle M_t \rangle$ is the unique predictable process such that $M_t^2 - \langle M_t \rangle$ is a martingale. In other words, since $\mathbb{E}M_t^2 = \text{Var}(M_t)$, the quadratic variation process is an unbiased streaming estimate of the variance.

For the martingale estimator, the quadratic variation conditional on the observed sketches yields an unbiased estimate of the martingale estimator's variance at jump times:

$$\widehat{\text{Var}}(\hat{N}_{T_k}) = \sum_{i=1}^{k} \text{Var}(T_i - T_{i-1}|q_{i-1}) = \sum_{i=1}^{k} \frac{1 - q_i}{q_i^2} \tag{10}$$

where the second line uses the fact that the increments are geometrically distributed and that the variance of a *Geometric*(q) random variable is $\frac{1-q}{q^2}$,

The reason this estimator is inadequate for estimating the variance at a fixed cardinality n, is that the increments after the last jump time involve the unobservable quantity $\sum_{t=T_K+1}^{n} 1^2 = (n - T_K)$. We may get around this by applying a Bayesian argument. Given a uniform prior on $n - T_k$, the posterior is given by $n - T_K \sim Geometric(q_K)$. This gives us a slightly modified estimate

$$\widehat{\text{Var}}(\hat{N}) = \sum_{i=1}^{k-1} \frac{1 - q_i}{q_i^2} + \frac{1}{q_k}. \tag{11}$$

A fully Bayesian approach is simple to analyze. Under a Bayesian model with a *Geometric*(α) prior, all of the holding times, including the last difference, are independent and geometrically distributed according to equations 6 and 7. The variance estimate for the Bayesian estimator at a fixed cardinality is

$$\widehat{\text{Var}}(\hat{N}_{Bayes}) = \sum_{i=0}^{K} \frac{1 - (q_i + \alpha(1 - q_i)}{(q_i + \alpha(1 - q_i))^2} \tag{12}$$

Note that if the estimate is at a stopping time, the Bayesian estimate for the variance also drops the last term in the sum. If $\alpha = 0$ and the estimate is at a jump time, the Bayesian estimate exactly matches the martingale estimator. However, if the estimate is at a fixed time n, the contribution of the last difference $N - T_K$ is $\frac{1-q_K}{q_K^2}$, the variance of a $Geometric(q_K)$ random variable, rather than $1/q_K$, the mean of a $Geometric(q_K)$ random variable and the contribution of the last term for the martingale estimator.

3. OPTIMALITY

3.1 Statistical efficiency versus space-complexity

The optimality results in this paper primarily address the notion of statistical efficiency. Given a sketch construction which yields a data generating distribution, what is the estimator with the lowest variance or risk? Much of the computer science theory literature focuses on optimal space-complexity. The primary differences between these two notions of optimality are three-fold. First, space-complexity is concerned with an asymptotic rate while statistical efficiency is concerned with the exact constant governing the rate. Second, statistical efficiency is always analyzed with respect to a given data generating distribution or the sketch construction in this case, while optimal space-complexity does not assume a particular construction. Third, space-complexity depends on both the estimation method from data and the encoding of the data while statistical efficiency only deals with estimation.

Although the method given by [11] has optimal space complexity, it has non-optimal statistical efficiency and a non-trivial probability of not returning any result whatsoever. Empirical results [13] show that HyperLogLog has lower error for the same sketch size. Because of these reasons, we do not consider finding an optimal algorithm for cardinality estimation to be a closed problem.

Given the current state-of-the-art in cardinality estimation, statistical efficiency has several advantages as a notion of optimality for practical algorithms. Since any decent statistical estimator for a parametric distribution has standard deviation on the order of $O(1/\sqrt{m})$ where m is the number of observations, the asymptotic rate of the standard deviation is typically meaningless. Statistical efficiency appropriately addresses the estimation problem while leaving the efficient encoding of the sketch as a separate issue. Furthermore, methods like HyperLogLog achieve a space-complexity of $O(\epsilon^{-2} \log\log n + \log n)$ compared to the optimal space-complexity $O(\epsilon^{-2} + \log n)$. The $\log\log n$ term is effectively constant as 6 bits allows estimation of cardinalities approaching 2^{64}. If the $\log\log n$ is ignored, the space-complexity matches the optimal one.

3.2 Optimality of the estimators

We establish that both the martingale estimator and its error estimate are optimal in the sense that they are minimum variance unbiased estimator at jump times. In other words, no other algorithm can also use the same sketch construction and have lower squared error if it gives an unbiased estimate. In Bayesian settings, the Bayesian cardinality estimators are optimal for both fixed cardinalities and at jump times when the cardinality is drawn from the prior distribution.

First, we consider the optimality of the martingale estimators at jump times for an infinite stream of data. Conditional on the sequence of sketches (S_i), the increments $T_{t+1} - T_t|(S_i)$ are independent random variables. This implies that the estimator $\hat{n}_T$ at a jump time T is the true conditional mean of the jump time given the sequence of sketches, and the martingale estimator of the variance is the true conditional variance. Hence, they are the optimal unbiased estimate under mean squared error. By the same reasoning, the variance estimate for the martingale estimator is also optimal at jump times. In the fixed n case, we are not able to prove that the estimator is a minimum variance unbiased estimator for fixed n.

In the Bayesian case, when the cardinality is a draw from the prior distribution, the Bayesian posterior mean is always optimal since it is the minimizer of squared error. However, it is biased, and an appropriate prior distribution is generally not known. For the same reason, the variance estimate for the Bayesian estimator is also optimal under these conditions.

4. EXISTING METHODS AND THEIR STREAMING COUNTERPARTS

The previous section presented universal estimators of the cardinality and error for any Markov chain of sketches. In this section, these estimators are applied to existing sketch constructions. HyperLogLog [8] and Min-count [9] are described and their streaming counterparts are derived using the martingale estimator. We also describe the S-bitmap streaming algorithm which already uses a martingale estimator and show that the martingale estimator for Linear Probabilistic Counting is nearly identical to the original non-streaming version. Furthermore, we show that the martingale estimator is optimal in non-streaming settings as well.

4.1 HyperLogLog

The HyperLogLog algorithm [8] estimates the cardinality based on the Flajolet-Martin (FM) sketch. The sketch is an integer valued m-vector $S_i = (S_{i1}, ..., S_{im})$. The sketch is highly compact since each vector entry may be represented in $O_p(\lg\lg(n/m))$ bits. For the FM-sketch, each element X_i is translated into a random pair

$$\begin{aligned} X_i &\to f(U_i) = (M_i, Y_i) \\ M_i &\sim Uniform([m]) \\ Y_i &\sim Geometric(1/2). \end{aligned}$$

The sketch updates bin M_i by taking the max of the current value in the bin and the new value Y_i

$$S_{i,j} = \begin{cases} \max\{S_{i-1,j}, Y_i\} & \text{if } j = M_i \\ S_{i-1,j} & \text{else} \end{cases}.$$

Sketch S_i is updated in one time step with probability

$$q(S_i) = \frac{1}{m}\sum_{j=1}^{m} P(Y_i > S_{ij}) = \frac{1}{m}\sum_{j=1}^{m} 2^{-S_{ij}}. \quad (13)$$

The HyperLogLog estimator is $\hat{N}_{hyperloglog} = \alpha/q(S_n)$ where S_n is the final sketch and α is an appropriate constant to correct for bias. Section 6.4 show that this modification yields a reduction in the variance by a factor of ≈ 1.56.

4.2 Min-count

Giroire's Min-count algorithm [9] maintains the mth-order statistics of the observed sample. In other words, it keeps the m smallest elements in the sample. Let $S^{(m)}$ denote the

m^{th} smallest element in S. Without loss of generality, assume the hashed values are distributed $Uniform(0, 1)$. The probability a sketch S_i is updated by a new element is

$$q(S_i) = S_i^{(m)}. \tag{14}$$

Like HyperLogLog, the non-streaming Min-count estimator of the cardinality is only a function of the final update probability $q(S_n)$ of the final sketch. The estimator is given by $\hat{N}_n^{(mincount)} = \frac{m-1}{q(S_n)}$. This estimator is provably optimal [3] when only the final sketch is observed. However, section 6.2 shows that the streaming estimator provably beats this optimal estimator.

4.3 Linear probabilistic counting

The Linear Probabilistic Counting algorithm (LPCA) [15] uses a simple bitmap as a sketch. Each item in the data stream is hashed to a bit, and that bit is set if it is not already. This algorithm is poor for large counts, as it requires space roughly linear in n. If B_t is the total number of bits set at time t, then the probability of transitioning out of the current state is $q(S_t) = 1 - B_t/m$. In this case, the martingale estimator has a simple analytic expression. This may be compared to the usual LPCA estimator.

$$\hat{N}_n^{(Harmonic)} = \sum_{i=1}^{B_n} \frac{m}{m-i} = m(H_m - H_{m-B_n}) \tag{15}$$

$$\hat{N}_n^{(LPCA)} = -m \log\left(1 - \frac{B_n}{m}\right) \tag{16}$$

where H_i denotes the ith harmonic number. Since $\log i \approx H_i$, the LPCA estimator is a very good approximation to the martingale estimator.

The martingale estimator is, in fact, provably optimal for both streaming and non-streaming cases. Since the estimator is a function of the number of bits set, B_n, in the final sketch and the sketch is not affected by the order in which elements are encountered, it is applicable in non-streaming settings. Furthermore, B_n uniquely determines the likelihood function, and hence, is a minimal sufficient statistic. Since the martingale estimator is an unbiased estimator and a function of a minimal sufficient statistic, the Rao-Blackwell theorem states that it is a minimum variance unbiased estimator [2].

4.4 S-bitmap

The S-bitmap algorithm also uses a simple bitmap as a sketch. The special property of the S-bitmap is that the relative error of the cardinality estimate defined to be $\sqrt{\text{Var}(\hat{N})/N}$ is constant over a chosen range. Like LPCA, the S-bitmap is highly efficient for smaller cardinalities. Table 2 in [4] shows that it often requires less space to achieve a desired error for cardinalities up to 10^7. One downside of the S-bitmap is that it is not applicable to distributed settings because the value of sketch S_i depends on the order in which the distinct elements are observed.

The derivation of the S-bitmap directly chooses transition probabilities $q(S_i)$ that yield a constant relative root mean squared error.

$$X_i \to (M_i, U_i)$$
$$M_i \sim Uniform([m])$$
$$U_i \sim Uniform(0, 1)$$

The sketch is updated by setting bit M_i if that bit is empty and $U_i > c(B_{i-1})$ for a carefully chosen cutoff function c that is monotonically increasing. The cutoff function is chosen in a manner that ensures that the relative error is constant up to the capacity of the sketch. This update process is further illustrated in section 5 and figure 2.

The S-bitmap estimator is identical to the martingale estimator. Like LPCA, the estimator is purely a function of the number of positive bits B_n in the final sketch, and B_n is a minimal sufficient statistic. Thus, the S-bitmap estimator is an optimal streaming estimate.

5. AREA CUTTING PROCESSES: A GEOMETRIC INTERPRETATION

So far, this paper has shown how the theory of Markov chains and martingales lead to cardinality estimators and their properties. We now give a geometric interpretation of sketch constructions via the *area cutting process*. This process is universally applicable as it can describe any sketch for counting distinct elements which is not affected by duplicates. It is useful as it can be used to create new sketches as well as to analyze existing ones.

Consider a Markov process that cuts out sections of a unit square. At each time step, a point is uniformly drawn from the unit square. Rather than hashing to a single random variable, hash each element to a pair of independent uniforms, $X_i \to (U_i, U_i')$. If that point falls on a portion of the square that has already been cut off, then do nothing. Otherwise, apply a deterministic procedure to cut off some section of the square that contains that point. It is easy to see that a duplicated point cannot induce more than one cut, so the sketch is not affected by duplicates and approximate for counting distinct items. The probability of an update at step i is equal to the remaining uncut area A_i.

THEOREM 3. *All sketches that are not affected by duplicates have a representation as an area cutting process whenever the universe from which elements are drawn is measureable.*

PROOF. The uncut area is simply the measure of the remaining elements which can affect the sketch. □

THEOREM 4. *The area process forms a sufficient statistic for the unknown cardinality n.*

PROOF. Write down the log-likelihood of the process. The only terms that depend on the holding times $T_i - T_j$ are functions of the area. □

Together with the likelihood and sufficiency principles [14], theorems 3 and 4 say that for any sketch construction, all information that is useful for estimating the cardinality is contained in the area process. More specifically, the Rao-Blackwell theorem [2] states that if $\hat{n}$ is an unbiased estimator and the sequence of areas (A_{T_i}) is a sufficient statistic, then $\mathbb{E}(\hat{n}|A_{T_1}, A_{T_2}, \ldots, A_n)$ has variance no worse than $\hat{n}$. Formally, this means that any estimator which is not a function of the area process can be improved by turning it into a function of the area process by taking the conditional mean.

5.1 Existing methods as area cutting processes

To illustrate the area cutting process, we describe several existing sketch constructions as area cutting processes.

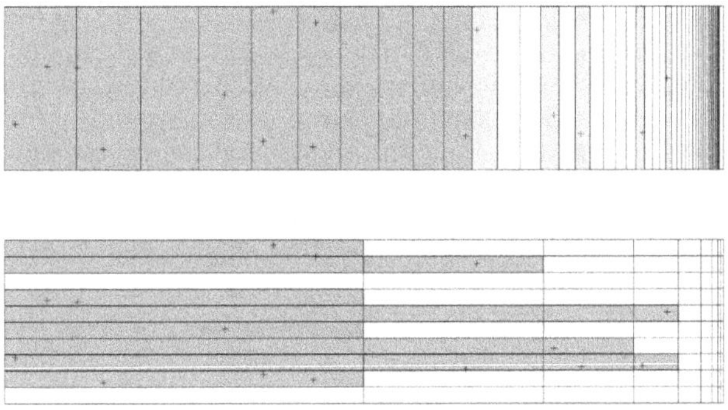

Figure 1: Pictoral representation of the Discretized Max-count (top) and FM (bottom) sketch. The + signs represent distinct items that are hashed uniformly to the rectangle. As each point is placed on the rectangle, shade an area covering the point if it is not already shaded. The shaded area represent the areas that are cut out of the sketch. New points that land in a shaded region do not affect the sketch. For the Discrete Max-count sketch, everything to the left of the cutoff is shaded regardless of whether or not a point falls in a particular box.

5.1.1 Hyperloglog

First, consider a continuous process corresponding to the FM-sketch used in HyperLogLog. Divide the unit square into m horizontal strips of equal size. The point (U_i, U_i') picks out a strip which contains the point and then cuts off everything to the left of U_i within that strip. At any given time, the remaining area in strip j is equal to the one minus the maximum of the U_i that fall into that strip.

A discretization of this continuous process leads to the FM-sketch. For each horizontal strip, divide it along the vertical axis into intervals $[2^v, 2^{v-1})$ indexed by the exponent v. Rather than store the exact location Z_j of the maximum element in the strip, store the exponent of the interval it belongs to. Equivalently, store $\lfloor -\lg Z_j \rfloor$. Since $\lfloor -\lg U_i \rfloor \sim Geometric(1/2)$ when $U_i \sim Uniform(0,1)$, this is equivalent to taking the maximum of $Geometric(1/2)$ random variables. Figure 1 illustrates this sketch as an area cutting process.

5.1.2 Min-count

The Min-count sketch is even simpler to visualize as an area cutting process. Instead of a unit square, the process cuts a unit interval. Everything greater than the mth sample is cut off. Note that each of the m samples that are stored also cut off the exact location of the unit interval on which it falls. That prevents duplicates from affecting the sketch. However, those locations form a set of measure 0 since two independent $Uniform(0,1)$ variables are equal with probability 0. This also highlights the primary weakness of the Min-count algorithm. In order to have enough precision to treat each sample as occupying an area of 0 measure, each sample requires many bits to store.

5.1.3 Linear probabilistic counting

Divide the unit square into m uniform vertical strips. Let each item in the stream hash to a uniformly distributed point on the square. Cutting out the vertical strip that an item falls into is equivalent to setting that bit. Figure 2 illustrates the difference between the S-bitmap and LPCA sketch.

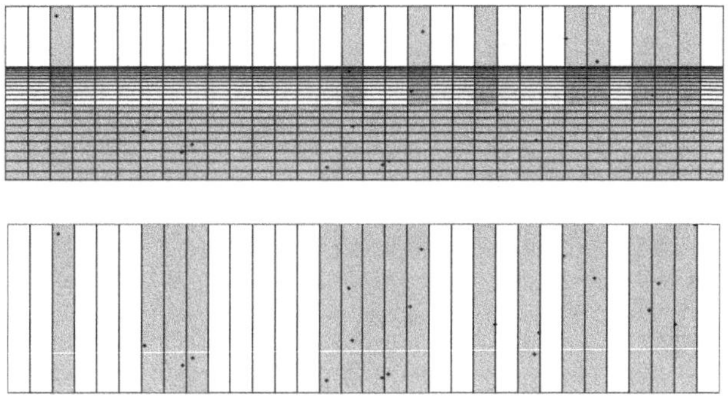

Figure 2: Pictoral representation of the (top) S-bitmap, (bottom) LPCA. Both share the same set of items that are hashed uniformly on the rectangle, but each cuts out a different area. Each vertical cut or equivalently, each bit that is set, results in a horizontal cut as well. Due to this, the S-bitmap sketch has fewer bits set and more remaining capacity.

5.1.4 S-bitmap

The area cutting process for the S-bitmap sketch is similar to the LPCA sketch. In addition to cutting a vertical strip out, every update to the square also cuts out an additional horizontal strip. Figure 2 illustrates this process. By cutting out a larger area with each bit, the capacity of the sketch is increased by extending the time until the next bit is set.

5.1.5 Virtual and Multiresolution bitmap

The virtual bitmap counting algorithm is the same as LPCA except that with probability $1 - \alpha$ an element is hashed to a null bucket and does not update the sketch. This is equivalent to starting with $1 - \alpha$ of the unit square already cut out and dividing the remaining area into m vertical strips like linear probabilistic counting. This allows the sketch to work for larger cardinalities at the cost of worse estimation for smaller cardinalities. The unbiased martingale estimator is simply $1/\alpha$ times the martingale LPCA estimator.

The multiresolution bitmap [6], covers a range of cardinalities effectively by using multiple virtual bitmaps. Similarly to all the other bitmap based sketches, it cuts out vertical strips corresponding to the bin each element hashes to. The difference between the multiresolution bitmap and virtual bitmap is that for the multiresolution the strips have varying widths.

5.1.6 Adaptive sampling

Adaptive sampling is a method similar to Min-count proposed by Wegman and analyzed by Flajolet [7]. Rather than always keeping a fixed number of samples m, adaptive sampling specifies a maximum number of samples. Whenever the maximum is exceeded, half of the remaining area is cut off, and the samples that fall below the cutoff are kept.

The adaptive sampling estimator is illustrative of the difference between traditional estimators and the martingale estimator. The usual estimator for adaptive sampling is k/p where p is the remaining area in the sketch. Each item stored in the sketch equally adds $1/p$ to the estimate. For the martingale estimator, the estimator is $\sum_x \frac{1}{p_x}$ where the sum is over all points that updated the sketch, including ones not stored in the final sketch, and p_x is the sampling probability or area at the time of adding x.

5.2 Creating new sketches: Discrete Max-count

In addition to better understanding of existing sketches, the area cutting process also leads to other sketches that may be used in approximate counting. The primary weakness of the Min-count algorithm is the number of bits required per sample stored, since each sample is a real number. We present the Discrete Max-count sketch which is a simple modification of the Min-count sketch that allows the sketch to be stored more efficiently. The Max-count sketch is obtained by hashing each distinct element to a discrete distribution F and taking the largest m values. The distribution F may be used as a tuning parameter which yields improves accuracy for targeted ranges of cardinalities. Note that when the distribution F is continuous, there is effectively no difference from the usual Min-count algorithm since F is monotonically increasing and $F(X) \sim Uniform(0,1)$ when $X \sim F$. Thus, the Min-count sketch is obtained by a simple variable transformation. We consider the case when the discrete distribution is $Geometric(1/m)$.

Under this distribution, Discrete Max-count has several interesting properties. First, it has infinite capacity since it can estimate arbitrarily large cardinalities. Second, the sketch may be decomposed into an offset which grows as $O(\log n)$ with the number of distinct elements encountered and a set of samples which does not grow with n. Third, the relative error of the algorithm is $O(1/\sqrt{m})$. Together this gives the sketch a space complexity of $O(\log n + \epsilon^{-2}g(\epsilon))$ where g is some function and ϵ is the relative error. If g is bounded by a constant, the sketch would have optimal space-complexity. Section 6.3 shows that $g(\epsilon)$ may be upper bounded by $\log \epsilon$ using a naive encoding of the samples. We also note that there is no interaction between the relative error ϵ and n in the space complexity bound. Kane et al [11] give an extensive list of space complexities for distinct counting algorithms. Only their theoretically optimal but empirically impractical [13] algorithm has this property.

We present the main tool to analyze this process, the notion of self-similarity, and give a dense set of proofs justifying these claims. An analysis of the method's running time is deferred to section 7.

6. SELF-SIMILAR AREA CUTTING

We introduce the notions of an offset decomposition and self-similarity for area cutting process. Consider a sequence of sketches S_t with areas $q(S_t)$ and jump times T_i. An area process is defined to be *self-similar* if $q(S_{T_i})/q(S_{T_{i+j}}) \stackrel{d}{=} q(S_0)/q(S_{T_j})$ for all $i > j$. In other words, it is self-similar when the proportion of the area cut out by j jumps remains the same in distribution over time. An area process is strongly self-similar if, in addition, the relative area cut off by a jump $q(S_T)/q(S_{T-1})$ is independent of $q(S_{T-1})$. If an area cutting process can be written as an offset Δ_t and a set of samples Y_t so that there is a bijection between S_t and (Δ_t, Y_t) and there exist functions q_0, q_1 such that for all t

$$q(S_t) = q_0(\Delta_t)q_1(Y_t)$$

$$Y_t \text{ is independent of } \Delta_t \text{ and } q_1(Y_t) \stackrel{d}{=} q_1(Y_1)$$

then (Δ_t, Y_t) is an offset decomposition of the area cutting process. An offset decomposition is (strongly) self-similar if the offset area $q_0(\Delta_t)$ is (strongly) self-similar and a process is a decomposable area cutting process if a non-trivial self-similar offset decomposition exists. When $0 \le q_0, q_1 \le 1$, the decomposition conditions state that the area may be obtained by first cutting off an area specified by the offset Δ_t and then independently cutting off part of the remaining area specified the samples Y_t. The condition also implies that the samples Y_t do not carry information about the cardinality since the distribution of Y_t does not depend on t. However, the samples do contain information that prevents double counting of duplicates.

The Min-count sketch is an example of a strongly self-similar area cutting process once at least m items have been encountered. The offset is equal to the mth smallest item $S_t^{(m)}$, and the samples are the remaining items in the sketch scaled by $S^{(m)}$. These rescaled samples are independent $Uniform(0,1)$ and independent of the offset. The proportion of area remaining after another cut is the maximum of these samples and a new independent $Uniform(0,1)$ variable. This maximum is always $Beta(m,1)$ distributed. Hence, the remaining proportion is independent of the offset, and its distribution does not change over time.

These self-similarity conditions lead to several attractive properties. Strong self-similarity ensures that a sketch has infinite capacity if the offset cannot cut off all the area, and it allows the variance of the martingale estimator to be computed exactly. An offset decomposition ensures that the size of the sketch is well-controlled. These properties are proved in the following theorems.

THEOREM 5. *The size required to store the samples Y_t of any offset decomposition does not depend on the cardinality n. Furthermore if the remaining area $q(\Delta_t, Y_t) > 0$ for all t almost surely, then the sketch can give unbiased estimates for arbitrarily large cardinalities almost surely.*

PROOF. The size required to store the samples Y_t is purely a function of the conditional distribution $Y_t|\Delta_t$ Since Y_t is independent of Δ_t and the marginal distribution of Y_t is the same for all t, the storage requirement for Y_t does not depend on n or Δ_t. If the remaining area is always greater than 0 then the martingale estimator will give an unbiased estimate for any cardinality. □

THEOREM 6. *For any area cutting process with an offset decomposition (Δ_t, Y_t), the variance of the martingale estimator is*

$$\mathrm{Var}(\hat{N}_n) = \sum_{t=1}^{n} \left(\mathbb{E}\left(\frac{1}{q_0(\Delta_{t-1})}\right) \mathbb{E}\left(\frac{1}{q_1(Y_1)}\right) - 1 \right) \quad (17)$$

PROOF. Consider the increments of the quadratic variation process for the martingale estimator. The expected squared increment for the tth distinct item is $\frac{1}{q(S_t)^2}q(S_t)(1 - q(S_t)) = 1/q(S_t) - 1$. The rest follows from the independence of Δ_t and Y_t and the product form for the area. □

THEOREM 7. *For any strongly self-similar offset decomposition, $1/q_0(\Delta_t) - ct$ is a martingale for some constant c. The variance of the martingale estimator has an analytic form given by*

$$\mathrm{Var}(\hat{N}_n) = n\left(\mathbb{E}\frac{1}{q_0(\Delta_0)} + c\frac{n-1}{2}\right)\mathbb{E}\frac{1}{q_1(Y_1)} - n \quad (18)$$

$$\approx \frac{n^2 r}{2}\mathbb{E}(q_1(Y_1))\mathbb{E}(q_1(Y_1)^{-1}) \quad (19)$$

where $r = \left(\mathbb{E}\frac{q_0(\Delta_{T-1})}{q_0(\Delta_T)} - 1\right)$.

PROOF. Note that $\frac{1}{q_0(\Delta_{t+1})} = \frac{1}{q_0(\Delta_t)}\frac{q_0(\Delta_t)}{q_0(\Delta_{t+1})}$ and that the two terms on the right hand side are independent conditional on $t+1$ being a jump time. Applying the law of total probability on $t+1$ being a jump time with probability $q_0(\Delta_t)q_1(Y_t)$, it is easy to show that $1/q_0(\Delta_t) - ct$ is a martingale with $c = r\mathbb{E}q_1(Y_1)$. The variance follows from equation 17. □

This theorem shows how the two components of an offset decomposition affects the variance of the estimate. The estimates are more accurate if the expected proportion r that is cut off is small and if the expected area cut off by the sample has low variance. This may be seen from applying the delta method to obtain $\mathbb{E}(1/q_1(Y_1)) \approx 1/\mathbb{E}q_1(Y_1) + \text{Var}(q_1(Y_1))/(\mathbb{E}q_1(Y_1))^2$. Furthermore, this gives a simple method to compute a closed form estimate of the error. Compute r,$\mathbb{E}(q_1(Y_1)^{-1})$, and $\mathbb{E}q_1(Y_1)$ analytically or via simulation and plug those values into equation 19.

6.1 Non-streaming estimators

Another consequence of theorem 7 is that a strongly self-similar decomposition leads to an unbiased estimator in non-streaming settings. Since $1/q_0(\Delta_t) - ct$ is a martingale,

$$\hat{N}_n^{(batch)} = \frac{1}{c}\left(\frac{1}{q_0(\Delta_n)} - \frac{1}{q_0(\Delta_0)}\right) \quad (20)$$

is an unbiased estimator that only depends on the final sketch S_n and a known initialization condition Δ_0. Note that the samples Y_n do not appear in the estimator. Since the distribution of Y_t does not depend on t and is independent of Δ_t, it is an ancillary statistic.

The variance of this estimator may be analyzed in the same manner as showing $1/q_0(\Delta_t) - ct$ is a martingale. Let $\kappa = \mathbb{E}\frac{q_0(\Delta_{T-1})^2}{q_0(\Delta_T)^2} - 1$ for a stopping time T.

$$\mathbb{E}\left(\frac{1}{q_0(\Delta_{t+1})^2}|q_0(\Delta_t)\right) = \frac{1}{q_0(\Delta_t)^2}\mathbb{E}\left(\frac{q_0(\Delta_t)^2}{q_0(\Delta_{t+1})^2}\right) \quad (21)$$

$$= \frac{1}{q_0(\Delta_t)^2} + \frac{\kappa\mathbb{E}q_1(Y_1)}{q_0(\Delta_t)} \quad (22)$$

Recursing and using the non-streaming estimator to compute $\mathbb{E}1/q_0(\Delta_t)$ yields that the variance of the non-streaming estimator is approximately

$$\text{Var}(\hat{N}_n^{(batch)}) \approx \left(\frac{\kappa}{2c} - 1\right)n^2. \quad (23)$$

6.2 Streaming versus Non-streaming Min-count

For Min-count, the optimal non-streaming estimator as well as its variance are known. Since it yields a strongly self-similar area cutting process, the variance of the martingale estimator is also known. The optimal non-streaming estimator [3] is $\frac{m-1}{\Delta_t}$. Since $\Delta_t \sim Beta(m, t-m+1)$, the estimator has variance $\frac{(t-m+1)t}{m-2} \approx t^2/(m-2)$. By equation 19, the martingale estimator has asymptotic variance $\frac{t^2}{2(m-1)}$. The streaming estimator easily beats the optimal non-streaming estimator and achieves the same error with half the number of samples. Furthermore, the non-streaming estimator in equation 20 is the same as the optimal non-streaming estimator, and the variance estimate converges to the true variance as $m \to \infty$.

6.3 Analysis of Discrete Max-count

THEOREM 8. *Discrete Max-count converges almost surely to an area cutting process with a strongly self-similar decomposition.*

PROOF. Let Δ_t be the mth largest element $S_t^{(m)}$ in the sketch and $Y_{ti} = S_t^{(i)} - S_t^{(m)}$. By the memoryless property of the geometric distribution, Δ_t and Y_t are independent, and this is an offset decomposition once the sketch contains at least m items. The proportion of area cut off by the offset $q(S_T)/q(S_{T-1})$ is the minimum of the samples Y_{T_i-1} and the newly observed value $h(X_T) - \Delta_{T-1}$ which is also independent of Δ_{T-1} by the memoryless property. Hence, the offset area process $q_0(\Delta_t)$ is strongly self-similar. □

The self-similarity property aids in upper bounding the variance and space-complexity of the algorithm. Since Discrete Max-count converges to a process with a strongly self-similar decomposition, the asymptotic variance is $O(r)$ where r is defined in theorem 7. The number of strips cut off by the offset at jump time T is obtained by taking the minimum of the samples Y_{T-1} along with the newly observed value $X_T - \Delta_{T-1}$. It may be upper bounded by taking the minimum of m independent $Geometric(1/m)$ variables rather than m unique $Geometric(1/m)$ variables. The probability that the minimum of m independent $Geometric(1/m)$ random variables is at most i is $1-(1-1/m)^{im}$. This is the distribution function of a $Geometric(1-(1-1/m)^m)$ variable. Using the moment generating function for the geometric distribution gives that $r < \frac{1}{m}\frac{1}{(1-(1-1/m)^m)(1-1/m)} \approx \frac{1}{m}\frac{1-e^{-1}}{\approx}1.58/m$. The term $\gamma = \mathbb{E}q_1(Y_1)\mathbb{E}(q_1(Y_1)^{-1})$ trivially satisfied the inequality $1 < \gamma < 1/(1-1/m)^{m+1} \approx e$. Empirically, we find that $\gamma \approx 1$ for a range of $m \in [100, 10000]$. This provides an both an approximate upper bound for the variance of $1.58n^2/m$ and proves that the relative error is order $O(1/\sqrt{m})$.

The space complexity of the sketch may be analyzed by considering the size required for the offset Δ_t and for the samples Y_t. In a naive encoding of the samples, each sample is encoded as a difference from the offset, and the number of bits required for each sample is on the order of $\log(m)/\log(1-1/m) \approx m\log m = O(\epsilon^{-2}\log\epsilon)$ where ϵ is the relative error. Naively encoding the offset as an integer requires $O(m\log n)$ space due to the fine granularity of the discretization. However, the non-streaming estimator in equation 20 demonstrates that the offset is close to a function of the current estimate. The offset may be encoded as a difference from this expectation. Equations 19 and 23 establish that $\frac{1}{c}\left(\frac{1}{q_0(\Delta_n)} - \frac{1}{q_0(\Delta_0)}\right)$ have mean n and variance $O(n^2m)$. Note that $q_0(\Delta_n) = (1-1/m)^{\Delta_n}$ is smooth. A simple Chebyshev bound and Taylor expansion yields that $\Delta_0 - m\log\hat{N}_n = O_p(n\sqrt{m})$. In other words, the offset may be stored in $O_p(\log n + \log\epsilon)$ bits. This gives the space complexity of Discrete Max-count to be $O(\log n + \epsilon^{-2}\log\epsilon)$.

6.4 Analysis of Streaming HyperLogLog

A trivial decomposition for any area cutting process always exists where the samples $Y_t = \{\}$. Theorem 6 gives that the variance that is approximately the sum of expected reciprocal areas. Since HyperLogLog estimates the cardinality in terms of the reciprocal area, $\hat{N}_{hll} = \alpha_m m/q(S_t)$ where

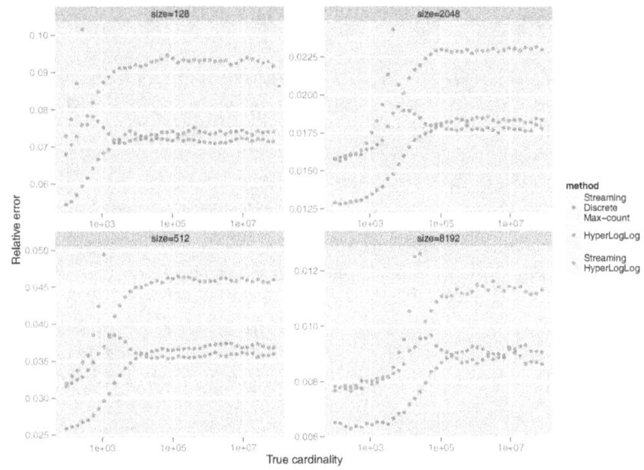

Figure 3: Relative error plot with *size* number of bins. Both streaming methods beat HyperLogLog over the entire range of cardinalities.

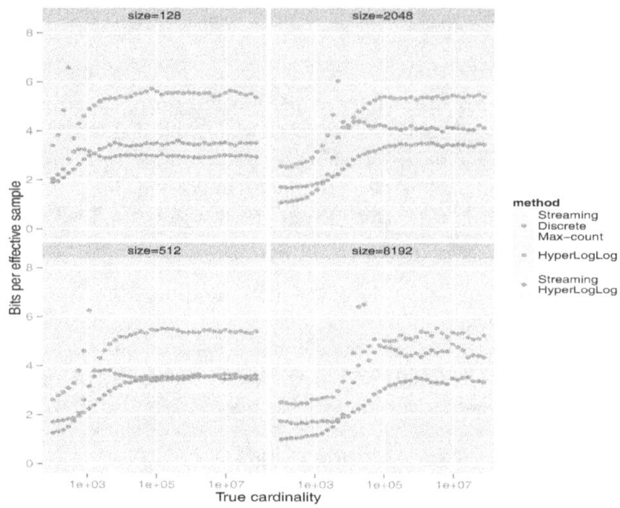

Figure 4: Effective bits per sample with *size* number of bins. For small sketches, Discrete Max-count outperforms both HyperLogLog based methods and requires half the size of HyperLogLog. For larger sketches, the encoding used by Discrete Max-count requires $O(\log m)$ bits per bin which results in worse performance for larger sketches.

$\alpha_m = 0.7213/(1 + 1.079/m)$ for $m \geq 128$, substituting n for $\hat{N}_{hll}$ gives the plug-in estimate

$$\text{Var}(\hat{N}_n^{(SHLL)}) \approx \frac{1}{\alpha_m m}\frac{n(n+1)}{2} - n \approx \frac{1}{1.4426\, m}n^2. \quad (24)$$

By comparison, the estimated variance for HyperLogLog is $\frac{1.04^2}{m}n^2$. In other words, HyperLogLog is predicted to use approximately $1.4426 \times 1.04^2 \approx 1.56$ times the space of Streaming HyperLogLog to achieve the same error. This matches extremely closely to our empirical evaluation where we found that Streaming HyperLogLog's variance bested HyperLogLog's by a factor of 1.57.

7. EXPERIMENTAL EVALUATION

The streaming cardinality and error estimates are empirically validated using both simulations and a real dataset. For all the simulations a 64 bit hash is used. A stream of 10^7 distinct elements is passed through each method and both cardinality and error estimates are obtained at regular intervals on a log scale. This is repeated 5×10^5 times for each method, and the results are averaged. The methods considered are HyperLogLog, Streaming HyperLogLog, and Streaming Discrete Max-count with a *Geometric*$(1/m)$ discretization.

To evaluate each method, we compare the relative error and effective bits per sample which are defined as

$$RelError(\hat{N}_n) = \frac{1}{n}\sqrt{\mathbb{E}(n - \hat{N}_n)^2}$$
$$m_{effective} = RelError(\hat{N}_n)^{-2}$$
$$BitPerSample(\hat{N}_n) = \frac{size_{sketch}}{m_{effective}}.$$

The definition of the effective sample size $m_{effective}$ is motivated by the fact that for many approximate counting methods including HyperLogLog, the relative error is approximately $1/\sqrt{m}$.

Note that the effective bits per sample is tied to the encoding of the sketch. For HyperLogLog, a typical implementation of the sketch which allocates five bits per bin is used. For Discrete Max-count, the sketch is encoded in three parts: the offset which is stored as an integer, a bitmap with $2m$ bits, and a sorted array of values above the offset plus $2m$. Each value in the array uses $\lceil \log_2 \max v - 2m \rceil$ bits where the max is taken over values in the array. We note this is not an optimal encoding of Discrete Max-Count, but it provides an upper bound on the optimal bits required per sample. In this case, the amortized running time of the method is $O_p(n \log m + m \log m \log n)$. Each distinct element requires $O(\log m)$ time to search through the sorted array, and each update requires $O(m \log m)$ time. There are $O_p(\log n / \log(1 - 1/m)) = O_p(m \log n)$ updates.

In addition to simulated data, the methods are evaluated on an anonymized Facebook test dataset. The sample contains 50 million rows containing approximately 1 million distinct users. To obtain accurate estimates of the relative error, each algorithm is run 4000 times with a randomly salted hash for each run. Figure 5 shows that the results on the dataset match the simulation.

8. DISCUSSION AND FUTURE WORK

There remain several questions of interest in this paper. In particular, questions about the space-complexity of these methods and the encoding used for each sketch remain. The ideas behind the self-similar area cutting processes and the decomposition into an offset Δ_t and set of samples Y_t leads to the Discrete Max-count sketch and space-complexities that only depend on the cardinality n through a counter. However, the encoding of the samples Y_t used in this paper has a space-complexity of $O(\epsilon^{-2} \log 1/\epsilon)$ rather than a rate of $O(\epsilon^{-2})$ to obtain the optimal space-complexity. Likewise, the FM-sketch yields a self-similar area cutting process. However, in the formulation of the process in section 6.4 the offset requires storage that grows at a rate greater than the optimal rate. We also conjecture that there are alternate decomposition of the FM-sketch into an offset and samples along with an encoding that yields optimal space-complexity. One possible offset is to take the median value of the bins.

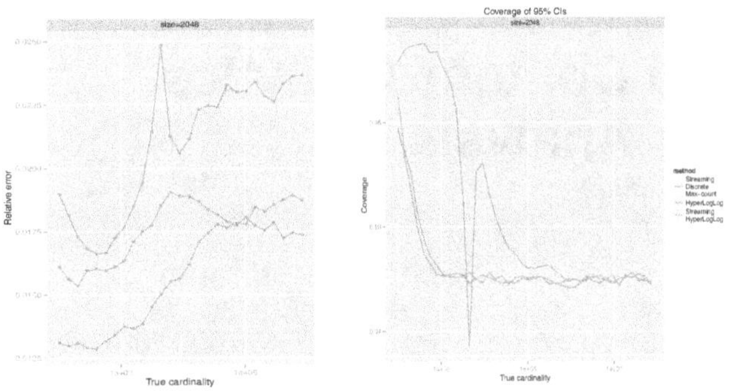

Figure 5: The left figure shows results on real data match the simulations. The right figure shows that the error estimates yield confidence intervals with the correct asymptotic coverage. HyperLogLog has worse coverage in an intermediate region due to bias. Bias corrected HyperLogLog [10] may improve on the observed coverage; however, the bias corrected method does include any improved estimates of the variance.

Another problem that remains is how to exploit the information in individual sketches that are merged. This may occur because the sketches are computed in a distributed fashion or because the cardinality of interest is the union of several sets with precomputed sketches. Although both HyperLogLog and Discrete Max-count have sketches that can be merged. Their estimators either only use the information contained in the final merged sketch or require access to the complete stream and cannot use precomputed sketches.

Another unexplored area is the effect of discretization on the underlying continuous area cutting process. HyperLogLog uses the $Geometric(1/2)$ distribution for discretization while Discrete Max-count uses the $Geometric(1-1/m)$ distribution. The discretizations lead can lead to different operating ranges as well as a different numbers of bits required per stored sample. The tradeoff between sketch size and accuracy due to discretization is not well-understood.

9. CONCLUSION

This paper presents a recipe for constructing practical algorithms that probabilistically estimate the number of distinct elements in a stream of data as well as the error of the estimate. These streaming algorithms provably outperform optimal non-streaming methods and yield substantial improvements in the storage requirements to obtain a desired relative error. This is born out in both theoretical and empirical results which show that HyperLogLog requires 50 percent more space than Streaming HyperLogLog to achieve the same error and Min-count requires twice as much space as Streaming Min-count.

We also provide a geometric interpretation to all sketches for distinct counting via the area-cutting process. Existing methods such as HyperLogLog, LPCA, and the S-bitmap are described via this process. This interpretation provides a link between different discretizations yielding different sketches and a common continuous area cutting process. Furthermore, we introduce the notion of decomposable self-similar area cutting process. Such processes have notable properties including infinite capacity and an encoding in which the sketch may be separated into two components, an offset which depends on the cardinality n and a set of samples whose the size depends only on the accuracy ϵ. This has interesting implications for the space-complexity of methods.

The proposed algorithms are analyzed under both frequentist and Bayesian settings. The cardinality estimators are proven to be optimal in various settings. In particular, the proposed martingale estimator is proven to be unbiased and optimal when queried immediately after a sketch is modified by an element in the stream. As a simple consequence of the analysis, we also give a provably optimal, unbiased estimator for the LPCA sketch which applies in both streaming and non-streaming settings.

These contributions lead to multi-faceted advances in sketch construction, cardinality and error estimation, theory, and intuition for the problem of approximate counting of distinct elements for both the streaming and non-streaming cases.

10. REFERENCES

[1] K. Aouiche and D. Lemire. A comparison of five probabilistic view-size estimation techniques in olap. In *DOLAP*, 2007.

[2] G. Casella and R. L. Berger. *Statistical inference.* Duxbury Press Belmont, CA, 2001.

[3] P. Chassaing and L. Gerin. Efficient estimation of the cardinality of large data sets. *DMTCS Proceedings*, pages 419–422, 2006.

[4] A. Chen, J. Cao, L. Shepp, and T. Nguyen. Distinct counting with a self-learning bitmap. *Journal of the American Statistical Association*, 106(495):879–890, 2011.

[5] R. Durrett. *Probability: theory and examples*, volume 3. Cambridge university press, 2010.

[6] C. Estan, G. Varghese, and M. Fisk. Bitmap algorithms for counting active flows on high speed links. In *Internet Measurement Conference*, 2003.

[7] P. Flajolet. On adaptive sampling. *Computing*, 43(4):391–400, 1990.

[8] P. Flajolet, É. Fusy, O. Gandouet, F. Meunier, et al. Hyperloglog: the analysis of a near-optimal cardinality estimation algorithm. In *AofA*, 2007.

[9] F. Giroire. Order statistics and estimating cardinalities of massive data sets. *Discrete Applied Mathematics*, 157(2):406–427, 2009.

[10] S. Heule, M. Nunkesser, and A. Hall. Hyperloglog in practice: Algorithmic engineering of a state of the art cardinality estimation algorithm. In *EDBT*, 2013.

[11] D. M. Kane, J. Nelson, and D. P. Woodruff. An optimal algorithm for the distinct elements problem. In *PODS*, 2010.

[12] A. Metwally, D. Agrawal, and A. E. Abbadi. Why go logarithmic if we can go linear?: Towards effective distinct counting of search traffic. In *EDBT*, 2008.

[13] J. Rae. Data stream cardinality: An empirical study of theoretically optimal algorithms. Master's thesis, University of Bristol, 2012.

[14] C. Robert. *The Bayesian Choice: From Decision-Theoretic Foundations to Computational Implementation.* Springer Texts in Statistics. Springer, 2001.

[15] K.-Y. Whang, B. T. Vander-Zanden, and H. M. Taylor. A linear-time probabilistic counting algorithm for database applications. *TODS*, 1990.

Time-Varying Learning and Content Analytics via Sparse Factor Analysis

Andrew S. Lan
Rice University
Houston, TX 77005
mr.lan@sparfa.com

Christoph Studer
Cornell University
Ithaca, NY 14853
studer@sparfa.com

Richard G. Baraniuk
Rice University
Houston, TX 77005
richb@sparfa.com

ABSTRACT

We propose SPARFA-Trace, a new machine learning-based framework for time-varying *learning* and *content analytics* for educational applications. We develop a novel message passing-based, blind, approximate Kalman filter for sparse factor analysis (SPARFA) that jointly traces learner concept knowledge over time, analyzes learner concept knowledge state transitions (induced by interacting with learning resources, such as textbook sections, lecture videos, etc., or the forgetting effect), and estimates the content organization and difficulty of the questions in assessments. These quantities are estimated solely from binary-valued (correct/incorrect) graded learner response data and the specific actions each learner performs (e.g., answering a question or studying a learning resource) at each time instant. Experimental results on two online course datasets demonstrate that SPARFA-Trace is capable of tracing each learner's concept knowledge evolution over time, analyzing the quality and content organization of learning resources, and estimating the question–concept associations and the question difficulties. Moreover, we show that SPARFA-Trace achieves comparable or better performance in predicting unobserved learner responses compared to existing collaborative filtering and knowledge tracing methods.

Keywords

Expectation maximization, Kalman filter, learning analytics, personalized learning, sparse factor analysis

1. INTRODUCTION

The traditional "one-size-fits-all" approach to education is a major bottleneck to improving learning outcomes worldwide. Fortunately, significant progress has been made over the past few decades on new technologies that provide timely feedback to learners as they follow personalized learning pathways through nonlinearly interconnected learning contents. Increasingly, these technologies are based on *machine learning algorithms* that automatically mine data from a potentially large number of learners interacting with learning contents (see [14, 15] for examples).

In our view, a *personalized learning system* (PLS) consists of two key components: (i) *learning analytics* (LA), which estimate each learner's knowledge state and dynamically trace its changes over time, as they either *learn* by interacting with various *learning resources* (e.g., textbook sections, lecture videos, labs) and *questions* (e.g., in quizzes, homework assignments, exams, and other assessments), or *forget* (see [30]), and (ii) *content analytics* (CA), which provide insight on the quality, difficulty, and organization of the learning resources and questions.

1.1 SPARse Factor Analysis (SPARFA)

The recently developed sparse factor analysis (SPARFA) framework [18] proposes a set of statistical model and algorithms for machine learning-based LA and CA. SPARFA models $Y_{i,j}$, the binary-valued graded response of learner j to question i, as a Bernoulli random variable (with 1 representing a correct response and 0 an incorrect one):

$$Y_{i,j} \sim Ber(\Phi(Z_{i,j})) \quad \text{with} \quad Z_{i,j} = \mathbf{w}_i^T \mathbf{c}_j - \mu_i.$$

Here, $\Phi(\cdot)$ is the inverse logit/probit link function, and the slack variable $Z_{i,j}$ depends on three factors: (i) the *question–concept association vector* $\mathbf{w}_i$ which characterizes how question i relates to each abstract concept, (ii) the *learner concept knowledge vector* $\mathbf{c}_j$ of learner j, and (iii) the *intrinsic difficulty* μ_i of question i. Given a dataset of graded learner response data $\mathbf{Y}$, SPARFA jointly estimates $\mathbf{c}_j, \forall j$ to effect LA and $\mathbf{w}_i$ and μ_i, $\forall i$ to effect CA.

While powerful, the SPARFA framework has two key limitations. First, it assumes that the learners' concept knowledge states remain *constant* over time; this reduces it's efficacy when applied to scenarios, where learners learn (and forget) concepts over time (weeks, months, years, decades) [4]. Second, SPARFA models only the learners' interactions with questions, which measure concept knowledge states, and not other kinds of learning opportunities, such as reading a textbook, viewing a lecture video, or conducting a laboratory or Gedankenexperiment; this complicates its application in automatically recommending new resources to individual learners for remedial or enrichment studies.

1.2 SPARFA-Trace: Time-varying Learning and Content Analytics

In this paper, we extend the SPARFA framework to address these limitations. We develop *SPARFA-Trace*, an on-

KDD'14, August 24–27, 2014, New York, NY, USA.
Copyright 2014 ACM 978-1-4503-2956-9/14/08 ...$15.00.
http://dx.doi.org/10.1145/2623330.2623631.

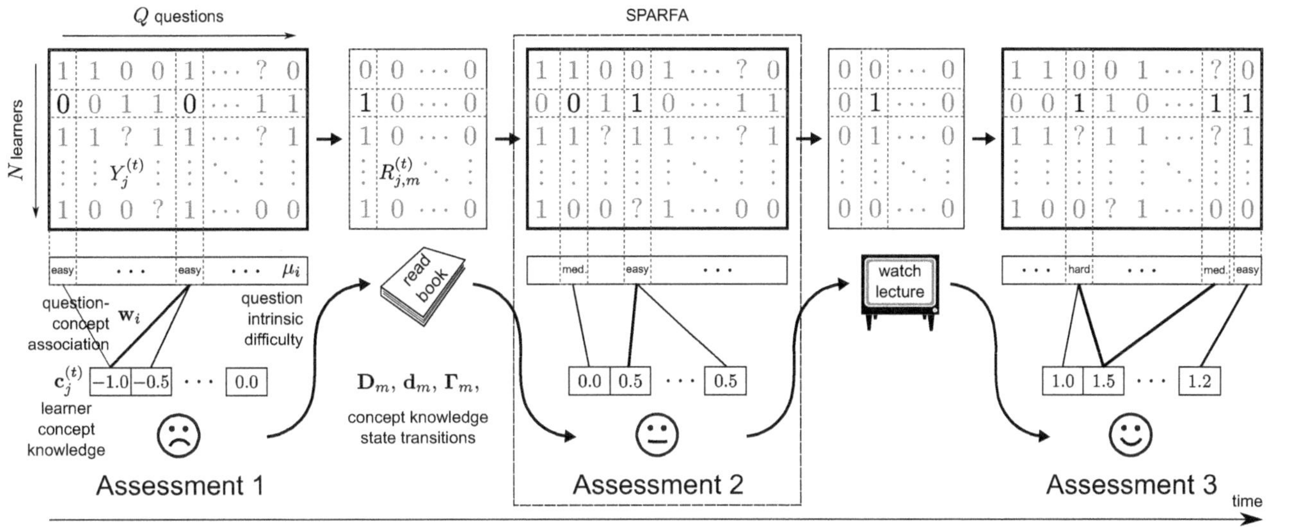

Figure 1: The SPARFA-Trace framework processes the graded learner response matrix $\mathbf{Y}$ (binary-valued, with '1' denoting a correct response, '0' an incorrect one, and '?' indicates an unobserved one) and the learner activity matrices $\{\mathbf{R}^{(t)}\}$ (binary-valued, with '1' denoting that a learner studied a particular learning resource, and '0' otherwise). Upon analyzing this data, SPARFA-Trace jointly traces the learner concept knowledge states $\mathbf{c}_j^{(t)}$ (a happy face represents high concept knowledge, and a sad face represents low concept knowledge) over time, and estimates the learning resource content organization and quality parameters $\mathbf{D}_m$, $\mathbf{d}_m$ and $\mathbf{\Gamma}_m$, together with question–concept association parameters $\mathbf{w}_i$ and question difficulty parameters μ_i.

line estimation algorithm that jointly performs *time-varying* LA and CA. The core machinery is based on blind approximate Kalman filtering. The working principles of SPARFA-Trace are illustrated in Figure 1. Time-varying LA is performed by tracing the evolution of each learner's concept knowledge state vector $\mathbf{c}_j^{(t)}$ over time t, based on observed binary-valued (correct/incorrect) graded learner responses to questions matrix $\mathbf{Y}$ and on the learner activity matrices $\mathbf{R}^{(t)}$. CA is performed by estimating the learner concept knowledge state transition parameters $\mathbf{D}_m$, $\mathbf{d}_m$, and $\mathbf{\Gamma}_m$, the question–concept associations and the question intrinsic difficulties $\mathbf{w}_i$ and μ_i, based on the estimated learner concept knowledge states at all time instances.

Tracing the learners' concept knowledge states over time is non-trivial due to the fact that the observations are noisy, binary-valued graded learner responses to questions. To perform this on-line estimation process, we develop a novel message passing-based algorithm in Section 3 that employs an approximate Kalman filter [12]. Furthermore, the underlying state-transition and observation parameters are, in general, unknown in real educational scenarios. Therefore, in Section 4, we introduce a set of novel convex optimization-based algorithms to estimate these parameters directly (and solely) from learner response data.

To test and validate the effectiveness of SPARFA-Trace, we conduct a series of validation experiments in Section 5 using real-world educational datasets collected with OpenStax Tutor [3, 21]. We show that SPARFA-Trace can effectively trace learner concept knowledge, estimate learner concept knowledge state transition parameters, and estimate the question-dependent parameters. Furthermore, we show that it achieves comparable or better performance than existing approaches on predicting unobserved learner responses.

1.3 Related work in knowledge tracing

The closest related work to SPARFA-Trace is *knowledge tracing* (KT), a popular technique for tracing learner knowledge evolution over time and for predicting future learner performance (see, e.g., [5, 22]). Powerful as it is, KT suffers from three drawbacks. First, KT uses binary learner knowledge state representations, characterizing learners as to whether they have mastered a certain concept or not, which provides limited explanatory power. Second, KT assumes that each question is associated with exactly one concept. This restriction limits KT to very narrow educational domains and prevents it from generalizing to typical courses/assessments involving multiple concepts. Third, KT uses a single "probability of learning" parameter to characterize learner knowledge state transitions. This limits KT's ability to analyze the quality and organization of different learning resources that would lead to different learner knowledge state transitions.

2. SPARFA-TRACE STATISTICAL MODEL

We start by extending SPARFA [18] to model learner concept knowledge evolution over time. Then, in Section 2.2, we characterize the transitions of a learner's concept knowledge states between consecutive time instances as an affine model.

2.1 Model for graded learner responses

The SPARFA-Trace statistical model characterizes the probability that a learner answers a question correctly at a particular time instance in terms of (i) the learner's knowledge on every concept at this particular time instance, (ii) how the question relates to each concept, and (iii) the intrinsic difficulty of the question. To this end, let N denote the number of learners, K the number of latent concepts in the course/assessment, and T the total number of time instances throughout the course/assessment. We define the K-dimensional vector $\mathbf{c}_j^{(t)} \in \mathbb{R}^K, t \in \{1, \ldots, T\}, j \in \{1, \ldots, N\}$, to represent the latent concept knowledge state of the jth learner at time instance t. Let Q be the total number of questions. We further define the mapping $i(t,j) : \{1,\ldots,T\} \times \{1,\ldots,N\} \mapsto \{1,\ldots,Q\}$, which maps learner and time instance indices to question indices; this information can be extracted from the learner activity log. We will use the shorthand notation $i_j^{(t)} = i(t,j)$ to denote the index of the question that the jth learner answers at time instance t as $i_j^{(t)}$. Under this notation, we define the K-dimensional vector $\mathbf{w}_{i_j^{(t)}} \in \mathbb{R}^K, i \in \{1,\ldots,Q\}$, as the question–concept association vector of this question. Finally, we define the scalar $\mu_{i_j^{(t)}} \in \mathbb{R}$ to be the intrinsic difficulty of question $i_j^{(t)}$, with positive values of $\mu_{i_j^{(t)}}$ representing difficult questions, and negative $\mu_{i_j^{(t)}}$ representing easy ones.

Given these quantities, we characterize the binary-valued graded response (where 1 denotes a correct response and 0 an incorrect one), of learner j to question $i_j^{(t)}$ at time instance t as a Bernoulli random variable:

$$Y_j^{(t)} \sim Ber(\Phi(Z_j^{(t)})), \qquad (t,j) \in \Omega_{\text{obs}},$$
$$Z_j^{(t)} = \mathbf{w}_{i_j^{(t)}}^T \mathbf{c}_j^{(t)} - \mu_{i_j^{(t)}}, \quad \forall t,j. \tag{1}$$

Here, the set $\Omega_{\text{obs}} \subseteq \{1,\ldots,T\} \times \{1,\ldots,N\}$ contains the indices associated with the observed graded learner response data, since some responses might not be observed in practice. $\Phi(z)$ denotes the *inverse probit link* function $\Phi_{\text{pro}}(z) = \int_{-\infty}^{z} \mathcal{N}(t)\,dt$, where $\mathcal{N}(t) = \frac{1}{\sqrt{2\pi}} \exp(-t^2/2)$ is the standard normal distribution. (The inverse logit link function could also be used; the inverse probit link function is preferred because it simplifies the calculations in Section 3.2.) The likelihood of an observation $Y_j^{(t)}$ can, alternatively, be written as

$$p(Y_j^{(t)} \,|\, \mathbf{c}_j^{(t)}) = \Phi\big((2Y_j^{(t)} - 1)(\mathbf{w}_{i_j^{(t)}}^T \mathbf{c}_j^{(t)} - \mu_{i_j^{(t)}})\big),$$

a shorthand expression we will use in what follows.

Following the original SPARFA framework [18], we impose the following model assumptions:

(A1) *The number of concepts is much smaller than the number of questions and the number of learners, $K \ll Q, N$*: This assumption imposes a low-dimensional model on the learners' responses to questions.

(A2) *The vector $\mathbf{w}_i$ is sparse*: This assumption is based on the observation that each question should only be associated with a few concepts out of all concepts in the domain of a course/assessment.

(A3) *The vector $\mathbf{w}_i$ has non-negative entries*: This assumption enables one to interpret the entries in $\mathbf{c}_j$ to be the latent concept knowledge of each learner, with positive values representing high concept knowledge, and negative values representing low concept knowledge.

These assumptions are reasonable in most real-world educational scenarios and alleviate the common *identifiability* issue inherent to factor analysis (if $Z_{i,j} = \mathbf{w}_i^T \mathbf{c}_j$, then we have $Z_{i,j} = \mathbf{w}_i^T \mathbf{Q}^T \mathbf{Q} \mathbf{c}_j = \widetilde{\mathbf{w}}_i^T \widetilde{\mathbf{c}}_j$ for any orthonormal matrix $\mathbf{Q}$. Hence, the estimation of $\mathbf{w}_i$ and $\mathbf{c}_j$ is non-unique up to a unitary transformation). The assumptions also improve the *interpretability* of the variables $\mathbf{w}_i$, $\mathbf{c}_j$, and μ_i.

2.2 Model for state transitions

In this section, we propose a latent state transition model that characterizes the learner concept knowledge evolution between two consecutive time instances. We assume here that the concept knowledge state evolves for two primary reasons: (i) A learner may interact with learning resources (e.g., read a section of an assigned textbook, watch a lecture video, conduct a lab experiment, run a computer simulation, etc.), all of which are likely to result in an increase of their concept knowledge. (ii) A learner may simply forget a learned concept, resulting in a decrease of their concept knowledge. For the sake of simplicity of exposition, we will treat the forgetting effect [30] as a special learning resource that reduces learners' concept knowledge over time.

We assume that there are a total of M distinct learning resources. We define the mapping $m(t,j) : \{1,\ldots,T\} \times \{1,\ldots,N\} \mapsto \{1,\ldots,M\}$ from time and learner indices to learning resource indices; this information can be extracted from the learner activity log. We will use the shorthand notation $m_j^{(t-1)} = m(t-1,j)$ to denote the index of the learning resource that learner j studies between time instance $t-1$ and time instance t. Armed with this notation, the learner activity summary matrices $\mathbf{R}^{(t)}$ illustrated in Figure 1 are defined by $R^{(t)}_{j,m_j^{(t)}} = 1, \forall (t,j)$, meaning that learner j interacted with learning resource $m_j^{(t)}$ between time instances t and $t+1$, and 0 otherwise. We are now ready to model the transition of learner j's latent concept knowledge state from time instance $t-1$ to t as

$$p(\mathbf{c}_j^{(t)} \,|\, \mathbf{c}_j^{(t-1)}) =$$
$$\mathcal{N}\Big(\mathbf{c}_j^{(t)} \,|\, (\mathbf{I}_K + \mathbf{D}_{m_j^{(t-1)}})\mathbf{c}_j^{(t-1)} + \mathbf{d}_{m_j^{(t-1)}}, \boldsymbol{\Gamma}_{m_j^{(t-1)}}\Big), \tag{2}$$

where $\mathcal{N}(\mathbf{x}|\boldsymbol{\mu}, \boldsymbol{\Sigma})$ represents a multivariate Gaussian distribution with mean vector $\boldsymbol{\mu}$ and covariance matrix $\boldsymbol{\Sigma}$. $\mathbf{I}_K$ is the $K \times K$ identity matrix; $\mathbf{D}_{m_j^{(t-1)}}$, $\mathbf{d}_{m_j^{(t-1)}}$, and $\boldsymbol{\Gamma}_{m_j^{(t-1)}}$ are latent learner concept knowledge state transition parameters, which define an affine model on the transition of the jth learner's concept knowledge state by interacting with learning resource $m_j^{(t-1)}$ between time instances $t-1$ and t. $\mathbf{D}_{m_j^{(t-1)}}$ is a $K \times K$ matrix, and $\mathbf{d}_{m_j^{(t-1)}}$ is a $K \times 1$ vector. The covariance matrix $\boldsymbol{\Gamma}_{m_j^{(t-1)}}$ characterizes the uncertainty induced in the learner concept knowledge state transition by interacting with learning resource $m_j^{(t-1)}$.

In order to reduce the number of parameters and to improve identifiability of the parameters $\mathbf{D}_{m_j^{(t-1)}}$, $\mathbf{d}_{m_j^{(t-1)}}$ and $\boldsymbol{\Gamma}_{m_j^{(t-1)}}$, we impose three additional assumptions on the learner knowledge state transition matrix $\mathbf{D}_{m_j^{(t-1)}}$:

(A4) $\mathbf{D}_{m_j^{(t-1)}}$ *is lower triangular*: This assumption means that, the kth entry in the learner concept knowledge vector $\mathbf{c}_j^{(t)}$ is only influenced by the the $1^{\text{st}}, \ldots, (k-1)^{\text{th}}$ entry in $\mathbf{c}_j^{(t-1)}$. As a result, the upper entries in $\mathbf{c}_j^{(t-1)}$ represent pre-requisite concepts covered early in the course, while lower entries represent advanced concepts covered towards the end of the course.

(A5) $\mathbf{D}_{m_j^{(t-1)}}$ *has non-negative entries*: This assumption ensures, for example, that having low concept knowledge at time instance $t-1$ (negative entries in $\mathbf{c}_j^{(t-1)}$) does not result in high concept knowledge at time instance t (positive entries in $\mathbf{c}_j^{(t)}$).

(A6) $\mathbf{D}_{m_j^{(t-1)}}$ *is sparse*: This assumption amounts for the observation that learning resources typically only cover a small subset of concepts among all concepts covered in a course.

In contrast to the learner concept knowledge transition matrix $\mathbf{D}_{m_j^{(t-1)}}$, we do not impose sparsity or non-negativity properties on the intrinsic learner concept knowledge state transition vector $\mathbf{d}_{m_j^{(t-1)}}$ in (2); this enables our framework to model cases of poorly designed, misleading, or off-topic learning resources that distract or confuse learners. Note that the *forgetting effect* can be modeled as a learning resource with negative entries in $\mathbf{d}_{m_j^{(t-1)}}$. To further reduce the number of parameters, we assume that the covariance matrix $\mathbf{\Gamma}_{m_j^{(t-1)}}$ is diagonal.

3. TIME-VARYING LEARNING ANALYTICS

Time-varying LA requires an on-line algorithm [13] that traces the evolution of learner concept knowledge over time. Designing such an algorithm is complicated by the fact that the binary-valued graded learner responses correspond to a non-linear and non-Gaussian observation model. The particle filter [6] is an on-line state estimation algorithm in non-linear and non-Gaussian systems, which uses a set of Monte-Carlo particles to approximate the latent state distribution. However, its excessive computational complexity prevents it from being applied to personalized learning at large scale (especially if immediate feedback is required). On the contrary, the Kalman filter [12] is an efficient on-line state estimation algorithm for linear dynamical systems (LDSs) with Gaussian observations, but it cannot be directly applied to time-varying LA because of the non-linear, non-Gaussian observation model (1).

In order to recast the time-varying LA problem as an approximate Kalman filter, we next introduce a set of approximations that build upon ideas in expectation propagation [20, 23]. We begin in Section 3.1 by reviewing the key elements of the Kalman filtering and smoothing approach, and then detail our approximate Kalman filter in Section 3.2. For notational simplicity, we will omit the learner index j in this section, i.e., the quantities $\mathbf{D}_{m_j^{(t-1)}}$ and $\mathbf{d}_{m_j^{(t-1)}}$ are replaced by $\mathbf{D}_{m^{(t-1)}}$ and $\mathbf{d}_{m^{(t-1)}}$. Moreover, we use the shorthand notation $\overline{\mathbf{D}}_{m^{(t-1)}}$ for the quantity $\mathbf{I}_K + \mathbf{D}_{m^{(t-1)}}$.

3.1 Kalman filtering and smoothing

The Kalman filter [9, 12] solves the problem of state estimation in LDSs, where the system consist of a series of continuous latent state variables that are separated by linear state transitions; the state observations are corrupted by Gaussian noise. We briefly summarize the main findings from [19]. Let the LDS consists of a series of T latent state variables $\mathbf{c}^{(t)}, t = 1, \ldots, T$, and observations $\mathbf{y}^{(t)}, t = 1, \ldots, T$. The factor graph [17, 28] associated to this LDS is visualized in Figure 2. The latent states (denoted by dashed circles) form a Markov chain, meaning that the next state only depends on the current state

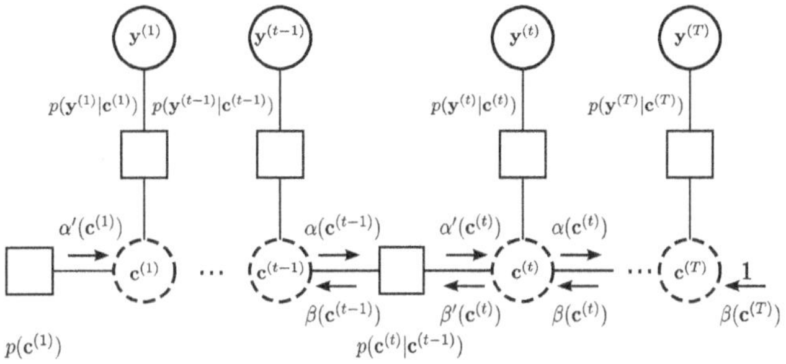

Figure 2: Factor graph message passing algorithm for the estimation of a set of T latent state variables with Markovian transition properties from (possibly noisy) observations.

but not on previous ones. The Kalman filter estimation procedure of the variables $\mathbf{c}^{(t)}, \forall t$ based on the observations $\mathbf{y}^{(t)}, \forall t$ (denoted by solid circles) can be formulated as a message-passing algorithm that consists of two phases. First, a forward message passing phase (i.e., the Kalman filtering phase) is performed. Then, using the estimates obtained during the Kalman filtering phase, a backward message passing phase—often referred to as Kalman smoothing or Rauch-Tung-Streibel (RTS) smoothing—is performed.

In the forward message passing phase (see Figure 2), the goal is to estimate latent state variables $\mathbf{c}^{(t)}$ based on the previous observations $\mathbf{y}^{(1)}, \ldots, \mathbf{y}^{(t)}$. In other words, the value of interest is $p(\mathbf{c}^{(t)} \mid \mathbf{y}^{(1)}, \ldots, \mathbf{y}^{(t)}), \forall t$. This quantity can be obtained via a left-right message passing algorithm outlined in Figure 2.

In Figure 2, the outgoing message $\alpha(\mathbf{c}^{(t)})$ from variable node $\mathbf{c}^{(t)}$ is given by [19]

$$\alpha(\mathbf{c}^{(t)}) = \alpha'(\mathbf{c}^{(t)})\, p(\mathbf{y}^{(t)} \mid \mathbf{c}^{(t)}) \\ = \left(\textstyle\prod_{\tau=1}^{t} b^{(\tau)}\right) p(\mathbf{c}^{(t)} \mid \mathbf{y}^{(1)}, \ldots, \mathbf{y}^{(t)}),$$

where $b^{(t)} = p(\mathbf{y}^{(t)} \mid \mathbf{y}^{(1)}, \ldots, \mathbf{y}^{(t-1)})$ is a scaling factor. We can see that a scaled version of $\alpha(\mathbf{c}^{(t)})$, $\widehat{\alpha}(\mathbf{c}^{(t)}) = \frac{\alpha(\mathbf{c}^{(t)})}{\prod_{\tau=1}^{t} b^{(\tau)}} = p(\mathbf{c}^{(t)} \mid \mathbf{y}^{(1)}, \ldots, \mathbf{y}^{(t)})$, is exactly the value of interest, which can be obtained in recursive fashion via

$$b^{(t)}\, \widehat{\alpha}(\mathbf{c}^{(t)}) = p(\mathbf{y}^{(t)} \mid \mathbf{c}^{(t)}) \int p(\mathbf{c}^{(t)} \mid \mathbf{c}^{(t-1)})\, \widehat{\alpha}(\mathbf{c}^{(t-1)}) d\mathbf{c}^{(t-1)}. \tag{3}$$

The key to obtaining a tractable and efficient estimator for $p(\mathbf{c}^{(t)} \mid \mathbf{y}^{(1)}, \ldots, \mathbf{y}^{(t)})$ is that the transition probability $p(\mathbf{c}^{(t)} \mid \mathbf{c}^{(t-1)})$ and the observation likelihood $p(\mathbf{y}^{(t)} \mid \mathbf{c}^{(t)})$ satisfy certain properties such that the messages $\widehat{\alpha}(\mathbf{c}^{(t)})$ and $\widehat{\alpha}(\mathbf{c}^{(t-1)})$ take on the same functional form, just with different parameters. A LDS satisfies this requirement, in which the transition probability and the observation likelihood are (multivariate) Gaussians of the following form:

$$p(\mathbf{c}^{(t)} \mid \mathbf{c}^{(t-1)}) = \mathcal{N}(\mathbf{c}^{(t)} \mid \overline{\mathbf{D}}_{m^{(t-1)}} \mathbf{c}^{(t-1)} + \mathbf{d}_{m^{(t-1)}}, \mathbf{\Gamma}_{m^{(t-1)}}),$$
$$p(\mathbf{y}^{(t)} \mid \mathbf{c}^{(t)}) = \mathcal{N}(\mathbf{y}^{(t)} \mid \mathbf{W}_{i^{(t)}} \mathbf{c}^{(t)}, \mathbf{\Sigma}_{i^{(t)}}).$$

Here, $\mathbf{\Gamma}_{m^{(t-1)}}$ is the covariance matrix for state transition, $\mathbf{W}_{i^{(t)}}$ is the measurement matrix, and $\mathbf{\Sigma}_{i^{(t)}}$ is the covariance matrix for the multivariate observation of the system. The functional form of the messages is also Gaussian, i.e., $\widehat{\alpha}(\mathbf{c}^{(t)}) \sim \mathcal{N}(\mathbf{c}^{(t)} \mid \mathbf{m}^{(t)}, \mathbf{V}^{(t)})$. Under these conditions, the forward message passing recursion (3) is given by

$$b^{(t)}\,\widehat{\alpha}(\mathbf{c}^{(t)}) = \mathcal{N}\Big(\mathbf{c}^{(t)}\,|\,\mathbf{m}^{(t)},\mathbf{V}^{(t)}\Big), \tag{4}$$

with the parameters $b^{(t)}$, $\mathbf{m}^{(t)}$ and $\mathbf{V}^{(t)}$ given by

$$\begin{aligned}
\mathbf{m}^{(t)} &= \overline{\mathbf{D}}_{m^{(t-1)}}\mathbf{m}^{(t-1)} + \mathbf{d}_{m^{(t-1)}} \\
&\quad + \mathbf{K}^{(t)}\Big(\mathbf{y}^{(t)} - \mathbf{W}_{i^{(t)}}(\overline{\mathbf{D}}_{m^{(t-1)}}\mathbf{m}^{(t-1)} + \mathbf{d}_{m^{(t-1)}})\Big), \\
\mathbf{V}^{(t)} &= (\mathbf{I} - \mathbf{K}^{(t)}\mathbf{W}_{i^{(t)}})\mathbf{P}^{(t-1)}, \\
b^{(t)} &= \mathcal{N}\Big(\mathbf{y}^{(t)}\,|\,\mathbf{W}_{i^{(t)}}(\overline{\mathbf{D}}_{m^{(t-1)}}\mathbf{m}^{(t-1)} + \mathbf{d}_{m^{(t-1)}}), \\
&\qquad \mathbf{W}_{i^{(t)}}\mathbf{P}^{(t-1)}\mathbf{W}^T_{i^{(t)}} + \mathbf{\Sigma}_{i^{(t)}}\Big),
\end{aligned}$$

in which the matrices $\mathbf{K}^{(t)}$ and $\mathbf{P}^{(t-1)}$ are

$$\begin{aligned}
\mathbf{K}^{(t)} &= \mathbf{P}^{(t-1)}\mathbf{W}^T_{i^{(t)}}(\mathbf{W}_{i^{(t)}}\mathbf{P}^{(t-1)}\mathbf{W}^T_{i^{(t)}} + \mathbf{\Sigma}_{i^{(t)}})^{-1}, \\
\mathbf{P}^{(t-1)} &= \overline{\mathbf{D}}_{m^{(t-1)}}\mathbf{V}^{(t-1)}\overline{\mathbf{D}}^T_{m^{(t-1)}} + \mathbf{\Gamma}_{m^{(t-1)}}.
\end{aligned}$$

The recursion starts with $p(\mathbf{c}^{(1)}) = \mathcal{N}(\mathbf{c}^{(1)} \mid \mathbf{m}^{(0)},\mathbf{V}^{(0)})$, where we assume $\mathbf{c}^{(1)}$ to be $\mathbf{m}^{(0)} = \mathbf{0}_K$ and $\mathbf{V}^{(0)} = \sigma_0^2\mathbf{I}_K$.

Kalman smoothing uses future observations $\mathbf{y}^{(\tau)}, \tau > t$ to obtain a better estimate of the latent state at time instance t. In other words, the value of interest is now $p(\mathbf{c}^{(t)} \mid \mathbf{y}^{(1)},\ldots,\mathbf{y}^{(T)})$. In order to estimate this value, a set of backward recursions similar to the set of forward recursions (3) can be used:

$$\begin{aligned}
&\widehat{\alpha}(\mathbf{c}^{(t-1)})\widehat{\beta}(\mathbf{c}^{(t-1)}) = \widehat{\alpha}(\mathbf{c}^{(t-1)}) \\
&\int_{\mathbf{c}^{(t)}} p(\mathbf{c}^{(t)}\,|\,\mathbf{c}^{(t-1)})p(\mathbf{y}^{(t)}\,|\,\mathbf{c}^{(t)})\frac{\widehat{\alpha}(\mathbf{c}^{(t)})\widehat{\beta}(\mathbf{c}^{(t)})}{b^{(t)}\,\widehat{\alpha}(\mathbf{c}^{(t)})}d\mathbf{c}^{(t)},
\end{aligned} \tag{5}$$

where $\widehat{\beta}(\mathbf{c}^{(t)}) = \frac{p(\mathbf{y}^{(t+1)},\ldots,\mathbf{y}^{(T)}|\mathbf{c}^{(t)})}{\prod_{\tau=t+1}^{T} b^{(\tau)}}$. The quantity of interest $p(\mathbf{c}^{(t)}\,|\,\mathbf{y}^{(1)},\ldots,\mathbf{y}^{(T)}) = \widehat{\alpha}(\mathbf{c}^{(t)})\widehat{\beta}(\mathbf{c}^{(t)})$ can be computed recursively as a backward message passing process, given the estimates (4) following the completion of the forward message passing process detailed above.

Specifically, in an LDS, the recursions take the form:

$$\widehat{\alpha}(\mathbf{c}^{(t-1)})\widehat{\beta}(\mathbf{c}^{(t-1)}) = \mathcal{N}(\mathbf{c}^{(t-1)}\,|\,\widehat{\mathbf{m}}^{(t-1)},\widehat{\mathbf{V}}^{(t-1)}), \tag{6}$$

with the parameters $\widehat{\mathbf{m}}^{(t-1)}$ and $\widehat{\mathbf{V}}^{(t-1)}$ given by

$$\begin{aligned}
\widehat{\mathbf{m}}^{(t-1)} &= \mathbf{m}^{(t-1)} + \mathbf{J}^{(t-1)}\Big(\widehat{\mathbf{m}}^{(t)} - \overline{\mathbf{D}}_{m^{(t-1)}}\mathbf{m}^{(t-1)} - \mathbf{d}_{m^{(t-1)}}\Big), \\
\widehat{\mathbf{V}}^{(t-1)} &= \mathbf{V}^{(t-1)} + \mathbf{J}^{(t-1)}\left(\widehat{\mathbf{V}}^{(t)} - \mathbf{P}^{(t-1)}\right)(\mathbf{J}^{(t-1)})^T, \\
\mathbf{J}^{(t-1)} &= \mathbf{V}^{(t-1)}(\overline{\mathbf{D}}_{m^{(t-1)}})^T(\mathbf{P}^{(t-1)})^{-1},
\end{aligned}$$

with $\widehat{\mathbf{m}}^{(T)} = \mathbf{m}^{(T)}$ and $\widehat{\mathbf{V}}^{(T)} = \mathbf{V}^{(T)}$.

3.2 Approximate Kalman filtering for Learning Analytics

The basic Kalman filtering and smoothing, i.e., (4) and (6) are only suitable for applications with a Gaussian latent state transition model and a Gaussian observation model, while the forward and backward recursions (3) and (5) hold for arbitrary state transition and observation models. When attempting to trace latent learner concept knowledge states under the SPARFA model, it is not possible to make Gaussian observations of these states. Concretely, we have only binary-valued graded learner responses as our observations. We will now detail approximations that enable the estimation of latent learner concept knowledge states for our model.

As introduced in Section 2, the observation model at time t is given by (1) and the state transition model is given by (2). Therefore, the recursion formula for the forward message passing process (3) becomes

$$\begin{aligned}
b^{(t)}\widehat{\alpha}(\mathbf{c}^{(t)}) &= p(Y^{(t)}\,|\,\mathbf{c}^{(t)})\int p(\mathbf{c}^{(t)}\,|\,\mathbf{c}^{(t-1)})\,\widehat{\alpha}(\mathbf{c}^{(t-1)})d\mathbf{c}^{(t)} \\
&= \Phi\Big(\big(2Y^{(t)}-1\big)\big(\mathbf{w}^T_{i^{(t)}}\mathbf{c}^{(t)} - \mu_{i^{(t)}}\big)\Big)\mathcal{N}\Big(\mathbf{c}^{(t)}|\,\widetilde{\mathbf{m}}^{(t)},\widetilde{\mathbf{V}}^{(t)}\Big),
\end{aligned} \tag{7}$$

where $\widetilde{\mathbf{m}}^{(t)} = \overline{\mathbf{D}}_{m^{(t-1)}}\mathbf{m}^{(t-1)} + \mathbf{d}_{m^{(t-1)}}$ and $\widetilde{\mathbf{V}}^{(t)} = \overline{\mathbf{D}}_{m^{(t-1)}}\mathbf{V}^{(t-1)}\overline{\mathbf{D}}^T_{m^{(t-1)}} + \mathbf{\Gamma}_{m^{(t-1)}}$.

Equation 7 shows that, $\widehat{\alpha}(\mathbf{c}^{(t)})$ is no longer Gaussian even if $\widehat{\alpha}(\mathbf{c}^{(t-1)})$ is Gaussian, under the probit binary observation model. Thus, the closed-form updates in (4) and (6) can no longer be applied. Therefore, we have to perform an approximate message passing approach within the Kalman filtering framework to arrive at a tractable estimator of $\mathbf{c}^{(t)}$.

A number of approaches has been proposed to approximate $\widehat{\alpha}(\mathbf{c}^{(t)})$ by a Gaussian distribution $\mathcal{N}\Big(\mathbf{c}^{(t)}\,|\,\overline{\mathbf{m}}^{(t)},\overline{\mathbf{V}}^{(t)}\Big)$; here, the *bar* on the variables denote the means and covariances of the *approximated* Gaussian messages. These approaches include the extended Kalman filter (EKF) [7, 10], which uses a linear approximation of the likelihood term around the point $\widetilde{\mathbf{m}}^{(t)}$, and thus reduce the non-Gaussian observation model to a Gaussian one; the unscented Kalman filter (UKF) [11, 27], which uses the unscented transform (UT) to create a set of "sigma vectors" from $p(\mathbf{c}^{(t-1)})$ and uses them to approximate the mean and covariance of $\widehat{\alpha}(\mathbf{c}^{(t)})$ after the non-Gaussian observation; and Laplace approximation [23, 31], which use an iterative algorithm to find the mode of $\widehat{\alpha}(\mathbf{c}^{(t)})$ and the Hessian at the mode to approximate the mean and covariance of the approximated Gaussian messages. We will employ an approximation approach first introduced in the expectation propagation (EP) literature [20].

It is known that the specific values for $\overline{\mathbf{m}}^{(t)}$ and $\overline{\mathbf{V}}^{(t)}$ that minimize the Kullback-Leibler (KL) divergence between $\mathcal{N}\Big(\mathbf{c}^{(t)}|\overline{\mathbf{m}}^{(t)},\overline{\mathbf{V}}^{(t)}\Big)$ and a target distribution $q(\mathbf{c})$ are the first and second moments of $q(\mathbf{c})$ [23]. Fortuneately, for the probit observation model $p(Y^{(t)}\mid\mathbf{c}^{(t)}) = \Phi\Big(\big(2Y^{(t)}-1\big)\big(\mathbf{w}^T_{i^{(t)}}\mathbf{c}^{(t)} - \mu_{i^{(t)}}\big)\Big)$, $\overline{\mathbf{m}}^{(t)}$, $\overline{\mathbf{V}}^{(t)}$ and $b^{(t)}$ have closed-form expressions (details omitted for simplicity):

$$\begin{aligned}
\overline{\mathbf{m}}^{(t)} &= \widetilde{\mathbf{m}}^{(t)} + \big(2Y^{(t)}-1\big)\frac{\widetilde{\mathbf{V}}^{(t)}\mathbf{w}_{i^{(t)}}}{\sqrt{1+\mathbf{w}^T_{i^{(t)}}\widetilde{\mathbf{V}}^{(t)}\mathbf{w}_{i^{(t)}}}}\frac{\mathcal{N}(z)}{\Phi(z)}, \\
\overline{\mathbf{V}}^{(t)} &= \widetilde{\mathbf{V}}^{(t)} - \frac{\widetilde{\mathbf{V}}^{(t)}\mathbf{w}_{i^{(t)}}\mathbf{w}^T_{i^{(t)}}\widetilde{\mathbf{V}}^{(t)}}{1+\mathbf{w}^T_{i^{(t)}}\widetilde{\mathbf{V}}^{(t)}\mathbf{w}_{i^{(t)}}}\left(z + \frac{\mathcal{N}(z)}{\Phi(z)}\right)\frac{\mathcal{N}(z)}{\Phi(z)}, \\
b^{(t)} &= \Phi(z),
\end{aligned} \tag{8}$$

with

$$z = \big(2Y^{(t)}-1\big)\frac{\mathbf{w}^T_{i^{(t)}}\widetilde{\mathbf{m}}^{(t)} - \mu_{i^{(t)}}}{\sqrt{1+\mathbf{w}^T_{i^{(t)}}\widetilde{\mathbf{V}}^{(t)}\mathbf{w}_{i^{(t)}}}},$$

and $\widetilde{\mathbf{m}}^{(t)}$, $\widetilde{\mathbf{V}}^{(t)}$ as given by (7).

The inverse probit link function is preferred over the inverse logit link function, due to the existence of the closed-form first and second moments described above. Therefore, we will focus on the inverse probit link function in the sequel.

Armed with the efficient approximation (8), the forward Kalman filtering and backward Kalman smoothing message passing scheme described in Section 3.1 can be applied to the problem at hand. Using these recursions, estimates of the desired quantities $p(\mathbf{c}^{(t)} \mid \mathbf{y}^{(1)}, \ldots, \mathbf{y}^{(T)})$ can be computed efficiently, providing a way for learner concept knowledge tracing under the model (1).

4. TIME-VARYING CONTENT ANALYTICS

So far, we have described an approximate Kalman filtering and smoothing approach for learner concept knowledge tracing, i.e., to estimate $p(\mathbf{c}_j^{(t)} \mid \mathbf{y}_j^{(1)}, \ldots, \mathbf{y}_j^{(T)}),\ \forall t, j$. The method proposed in Section 3 is only able to provide these estimates if all learner initial knowledge parameters $\mathbf{m}_j^{(0)}, \mathbf{V}_j^{(0)},\ \forall j$, all learner concept knowledge state transition parameters $\mathbf{D}_m$, $\mathbf{d}_m$, and $\mathbf{\Gamma}_m$, $\forall m$, and all question parameters, $\mathbf{w}_i$ and μ_i, $\forall i$, are given a priori.

However, in a typical PLS, these parameters are unknown and need to be estimated from the observed data. We now detail a set of convex optimization-based techniques to estimate the parameters $\mathbf{D}_m$, $\mathbf{d}_m$, and $\mathbf{\Gamma}_m$, $\forall m$, and $\mathbf{w}_i$, μ_i, $\forall i$,[1] given the estimates of the latent learner concept knowledge states $\mathbf{c}_j^{(t)}$ obtained from the approximate Kalman filtering approach described in Section 3. The techniques we detail in this chapter allows SPARFA-Trace to jointly trace learner concept knowledge and estimate learner, learning resource, and question-dependent parameters, using an expectation-maximization (EM) approach.

4.1 SPARFA-Trace as an EM algorithm

EM has been widely used in the Kalman filtering framework to estimate the parameters of interest in the system (see [2, Chap. 13] and [9] for more details) due to numerous practical advantages [24]. SPARFA-Trace performs parameter estimation in an iterative fashion in the EM framework. All parameters are initialized by random values, and then each iteration of the algorithm consist of two phases: (i) the current parameter estimates are used to estimate the latent state distributions $p(\mathbf{c}_j^{(t)} \mid \mathbf{y}_j^{(1)}, \ldots, \mathbf{y}_j^{(T)}),\ \forall t, j$, and (ii) these latent state estimates are then used to maximize the expected joint log-likelihood of all the observed and latent state variables, i.e.,

$$\underset{\mathbf{D}_m,\mathbf{d}_m,\mathbf{\Gamma}_m,\forall m,\mathbf{w}_i,\mu_i,\forall i}{\text{maximize}} \sum_{t=2}^{T}\sum_{j=1}^{N}\mathbb{E}_{\mathbf{c}_j^{(t-1)},\mathbf{c}_j^{(t)}}\Big[\log p(\mathbf{c}_j^{(t)}|\mathbf{c}_j^{(t-1)},\mathbf{D}_{m_j^{(t-1)}},$$
$$\mathbf{d}_{m_j^{(t-1)}},\mathbf{\Gamma}_{m_j^{(t-1)}})\Big] + \sum_{(t,j)\in\Omega_{\text{obs}}}\mathbb{E}_{\mathbf{c}_j^{(t)}}\big[\log p(Y_j^{(t)}|\mathbf{c}_j^{(t)},\mathbf{w}_{i_j^{(t)}},\mu_{i_j^{(t)}})\big], \quad (9)$$

in order to obtain new parameter estimates. SPARFA-Trace alternates between these two phases until convergence, i.e., a maximum number of iterations is reached or the change in the estimated parameters between two consecutive iterations falls below a given threshold.

[1]The estimation of the learner initial knowledge parameters $\mathbf{m}_j^{(0)}, \mathbf{V}_j^{(0)},\ \forall j$ is trivial and can be found in [2].

4.2 Estimating the state transition parameters

We start by estimating the latent learner concept knowledge state transition (i.e., learning resource) parameters $\mathbf{D}_m$, $\mathbf{d}_m$, and $\mathbf{\Gamma}_m$, $\forall m$. To this end, define $\mathcal{M}^m$ as the set containing time and learner indices (t, j) indicating that learner j studies the mth learning resource between time instances $t-1$ and t. With this definition, we aim to maximize the expected log-likelihood (9) with respect to $\mathbf{D}_m$ and $\mathbf{d}_m$, subject to the assumptions (A4)–(A6). We start by estimating $\mathbf{D}_m$ and $\mathbf{d}_m$ given $\mathbf{\Gamma}_m$. In order to induce sparsity on $\mathbf{D}_m$ to take (A6) into account, we impose an ℓ_1-norm penalty on $\mathbf{D}_m$, which is defined as the sum of the absolute values of all entries of $\mathbf{D}_m$ [8]. Taking only the terms containing $\mathbf{D}_m$ and $\mathbf{d}_m$, we can formulate the following augmented optimization problem:

$$(\text{P}_\text{d}) \quad \underset{\mathbf{D}_m\in\mathcal{L}^+,\mathbf{d}_m}{\text{minimize}} \sum_{t,j:(t,j)\in\mathcal{M}^m} \mathbb{E}_{\mathbf{c}_j^{(t-1)},\mathbf{c}_j^{(t)}}\Big[(\widetilde{\mathbf{D}}_m\widetilde{\mathbf{c}}_j^{(t-1)})^T\mathbf{\Gamma}_m^{-1}$$
$$(\widetilde{\mathbf{D}}_m\widetilde{\mathbf{c}}_j^{(t-1)}) - (\mathbf{c}_j^{(t)} - \mathbf{c}_j^{(t-1)})^T\mathbf{\Gamma}_m^{-1}(\mathbf{c}_j^{(t)} - \mathbf{c}_j^{(t-1)})\Big] + \gamma\|\mathbf{D}_m\|_1,$$

where $\mathcal{L}^+$ denotes the set of lower-triangular matrices with non-negative entries. For notational simplicity, we have written $[\mathbf{D}_m\ \mathbf{d}_m]$ as $\widetilde{\mathbf{D}}_m$. We also write the augmented latent state vectors $[(\mathbf{c}_j^{(t-1)})^T\ 1]^T$ as $\widetilde{\mathbf{c}}_j^{(t-1)}$, when multiplied by $\widetilde{\mathbf{D}}_m$, correspondingly. Note that the ℓ_1-norm penalty only applies to the matrix $\mathbf{D}_m$ in this notation.

The problem (P_d) is convex in $\widetilde{\mathbf{D}}_m$, and hence, can be solved efficiently. In particular, we use the iterative fast iterative shrinkage and thresholding algorithm (FISTA) framework [1]. In each iteration $\ell = 1, 2, \ldots, L_{\max}$, the algorithm performs two steps. First, a gradient step that aims to lower the objective function performs

$$\widehat{\mathbf{D}}_m^{\ell+1} \leftarrow \widetilde{\mathbf{D}}_m^{\ell} - \eta_\ell \nabla f(\widetilde{\mathbf{D}}_m), \quad (10)$$

where $f(\widetilde{\mathbf{D}}_m)$ corresponds to the differentiable part of the objective function (excluding the ℓ_1-norm penalty) in (P_d). The quantity η_ℓ is a step size parameter for iteration ℓ. Details on how to choose η_ℓ can be found in [1]. The gradient $\nabla f(\widetilde{\mathbf{D}}_m)$ in (10) is given by

$$\nabla f(\widetilde{\mathbf{D}}_m) = -\mathbf{\Gamma}_m^{-1} \sum_{t,j:(t,j)\in\mathcal{M}^m}\Bigg([\mathbf{J}_j^{(t-1)}\widehat{\mathbf{V}}_j^{(t)} + \widehat{\mathbf{m}}_j^{(t)}(\widehat{\mathbf{m}}_j^{(t-1)})^T$$
$$-\widehat{\mathbf{V}}_j^{(t-1)} - \widehat{\mathbf{m}}_j^{(t-1)}(\widehat{\mathbf{m}}_j^{(t-1)})^T \quad \widehat{\mathbf{m}}_j^{(t)} - \widehat{\mathbf{m}}_j^{(t-1)}]$$
$$-\mathbf{D}_m^{\ell}\begin{bmatrix}\widehat{\mathbf{V}}_j^{(t-1)} + \widehat{\mathbf{m}}_j^{(t-1)}(\widehat{\mathbf{m}}_j^{(t-1)})^T & \widehat{\mathbf{m}}_j^{(t-1)} \\ (\widehat{\mathbf{m}}_j^{(t-1)})^T & 1\end{bmatrix}\Bigg),$$

where the parameters $\mathbf{J}_j^{(t-1)}$, $\widehat{\mathbf{m}}_j^{(t-1)}$, $\widehat{\mathbf{m}}_j^{(t)}$, $\widehat{\mathbf{V}}_j^{(t-1)}$, and $\widehat{\mathbf{V}}_j^{(t)}$ are obtained from the backward recursions in (6). Next, the FISTA algorithm performs a projection step, which takes into account the sparsifying regularizer $\gamma\|\mathbf{D}_m\|_1$, and the assumptions (A4) and (A5):

$$\widetilde{\mathbf{D}}_m^{\ell+1} \leftarrow P_{\mathcal{L}^+}(\max\{\widehat{\mathbf{D}}_m^{\ell+1} - \gamma\eta_\ell, 0\}), \quad (11)$$

where $P_{\mathcal{L}^+}(\cdot)$ corresponds to the projection onto the set of lower-triangular matrices by setting all entries in the upper triangular part of $\mathbf{D}_m^{\ell+1}$ to zero. The maximum operator acts element-wise on $\mathbf{D}_m^{\ell+1}$. The updates (10) and (11) are repeated until convergence, eventually providing a new estimate $\widetilde{\mathbf{D}}_m^{\text{new}}$ for $[\mathbf{D}_m\ \mathbf{d}_m]$.

Using these new estimates, the update for $\boldsymbol{\Gamma}_m$ can be computed in closed form, which will be omitted for simplicity.

4.3 Estimating the question parameters

We next show how to estimate the question-dependent parameters $\mathbf{w}_i$, μ_i, $\forall i$. To this end, we define $\mathcal{Q}^i$ as the collection set of time and learner indices (t, j) that learner j answered the ith question at time instance t. We then minimize the expected negative log-likelihood of all the observed binary-valued graded learner responses (1) for the ith question, subject to (A2) and (A3). In order to impose sparsity on $\mathbf{w}_i$, we add an ℓ_1-norm penalty to the cost function, which leads to the following optimization problem:

$$(\mathrm{P_w}) \qquad \underset{\mathbf{w}_i : w_{i,k} \geq 0, \forall k}{\text{minimize}} \sum_{(t,j) \in \mathcal{Q}^i} \mathbb{E}_{\mathbf{c}_j^{(t)}}$$

$$\left[-\log\Phi((2Y_j^{(t)} - 1)(\mathbf{w}_i^T \mathbf{c}_j^{(t)} - \mu_i)) \right] + \lambda \|\mathbf{w}_i\|_1 .$$

The problem $(\mathrm{P_w})$ is convex in $\mathbf{w}_i$, thanks to the fact that the negative log-likelihood of the observation likelihood is convex and the linearity of the expectation operator (see [18] for details). However, the inverse probit link function prohibits us from obtaining a simple form of this expectation. In order to develop a tractable algorithm to approximately solve this problem, we utilize the unscented transform (UT) [27] to approximate the cost function of $(\mathrm{P_w})$.

Following the paradigms of the UT, we generate a set of sigma vectors $\{(\widetilde{\mathbf{c}}_j^{(t)})_n\}$ and a corresponding set of weights $\{u_n\}$, $n \in \{1, \ldots, 2K+1\}$, for each latent state vector $\mathbf{c}_j^{(t)}$, given the mean $\widehat{\mathbf{m}}_j^{(t)}$ and covariance $\widehat{\mathbf{V}}_j^{(t)}$. The cost function in the optimization problem $(\mathrm{P_w})$ can now be approximated by a weighted average of the cost function evaluated at $\{(\widetilde{\mathbf{c}}_j^{(t)})_n\}$. Once again, $(\mathrm{P_w})$ can be solved efficiently by using the FISTA framework [1]. The gradient step is given by

$$\widehat{\mathbf{w}}_i^{\ell+1} \leftarrow \mathbf{w}_i^{\ell} - \eta_\ell \nabla f(\mathbf{w}_i). \tag{12}$$

The gradient $\nabla f(\mathbf{w}_i)$ is given by $\nabla f(\mathbf{w}_i) = -\widetilde{\mathbf{C}}_i \widetilde{\mathbf{r}}_i$, where $\widetilde{\mathbf{r}}_i$ is a $(2K+1)|\mathcal{Q}^i| \times 1$ vector $\mathbf{r}_i = [\mathbf{a}_i^1 \ldots, \mathbf{a}_i^{|\mathcal{Q}^i|}]^T$. The vector $\mathbf{a}_i^q$ is defined by $\mathbf{a}_i^q = [(g_i^q)_1, \ldots, (g_i^q)_{2K+1}]$, where

$$(g_i^q)_n = u_n 2(Y_{j_q}^{(t_q)} - 1) \frac{\mathcal{N}\left(2(Y_{j_q}^{(t_q)} - 1)\mathbf{w}_i^T (\widetilde{\mathbf{c}}_{j_q}^{(t_q)})_n\right)}{\Phi\left(2(Y_{j_q}^{(t_q)} - 1)\mathbf{w}_i^T (\widetilde{\mathbf{c}}_{j_q}^{(t_q)})_n\right)},$$

in which (t_q, j_q) represents the qth time–learner index pair in $\mathcal{Q}^i$. The $K \times (2K+1)|\mathcal{Q}^i|$ matrix $\widetilde{\mathbf{C}}_i$ is defined as $\widetilde{\mathbf{C}}_i = [(\mathbf{G}_i)_1, \ldots, (\mathbf{G}_i)_{|\mathcal{Q}^i|}]$, where the $K \times (2K+1)$ matrix $(\mathbf{G}_i)_q$ is given by

$$(\mathbf{G}_i)_q = \left[(\widetilde{\mathbf{c}}_{j_q}^{(t_q)})_1, \ \ldots, \ (\widetilde{\mathbf{c}}_{j_q}^{(t_q)})_{2K+1}\right].$$

The projection step is given by

$$\mathbf{w}_i^{\ell+1} \leftarrow \max\{\widehat{\mathbf{w}}_i^{\ell+1} - \lambda\eta_\ell, 0\}. \tag{13}$$

For simplicity of exposition, the question intrinsic difficulties μ_i are omitted in the derivations above, as they can be included as an additional entry in $\mathbf{w}_i$ as $[\mathbf{w}_i^T \ \mu_i]^T$; the corresponding latent learner concept knowledge state vectors $\mathbf{c}_j^{(t)}$ are augmented accordingly as $[(\mathbf{c}_j^{(t)})^T \ -1]^T$.

Table 1: Comparisons of SPARFA-Trace against knowledge tracing (KT) on predicting responses for new learners using using Dataset 1. SPARFA-Trace slightly outperforms KT on all three metrics.

Performance metric	KT	SPARFA-Trace
Prediction accuracy	$86.42 \pm 0.16\%$	$\mathbf{87.49 \pm 0.12\%}$
Prediction likelihood	0.7718 ± 0.0011	$\mathbf{0.8128 \pm 0.0044}$
Area under the ROC curve	0.5989 ± 0.0056	$\mathbf{0.8157 \pm 0.0028}$

5. EXPERIMENTAL RESULTS

We now demonstrate the efficacy of SPARFA-Trace using real-world educational datasets. We begin by comparing SPARFA-Trace against two established methods on predicting unobserved binary-valued learner response data, namely knowledge tracing (KT) [5, 22] and SPARFA [18]. Then, we show how SPARFA-Trace is able to visualize learners' concept knowledge state evolution over time, and the learning resource and question quality and their content organization. The regularization parameters λ and γ are chosen via cross-validation [8], and all experiments are repeated for 25 independent Monte–Carlo trials.

5.1 Predicting responses for new learners

We now compare SPARFA-Trace against the KT method described in [22] for predicting responses for new learners that do not have previous recorded response history.

The dataset we use for this experiment is from an undergraduate computer engineering course collected using OpenStax Tutor (OST) [21]. We will refer to this dataset as "Dataset 1" in the following experiments. This dataset consists of the binary-valued graded response from 92 learners answering 203 questions, with 99.5% of the responses observed. The course is organized as three independent sections: The first section is on digital logic, the second on data structures, and the third on basic programming concepts. The full course consist of 11 assessments, including 8 homework assignments and an exam at the end of each section; we assume that the learners' concept knowledge state transitions can only happen between two consecutive assignments/exams, due to their interaction with all the lectures/readings/exercises.

Since KT is only capable of handling educational datasets that involve a single concept, we partition Dataset 1 into three parts, with each part corresponding to one of the three independent sections. We run KT independently on the three parts, and aggregate the prediction results. We initialize the four parameters of KT (learner prior, learning probability, guessing probability, slipping probability) with the best initial value we find over 5 different initializations. For SPARFA-Trace, we use $K = 3$, with each concept corresponding to one section of the dataset.

For cross-validation, we randomly partition Dataset 1 into 5 folds, with each fold consisting of 1/5 of the learners answering all questions. Four folds of the data are used as the training set and the other fold is used as the test set. We train both KT and SPARFA-Trace on the training set and obtain estimates on all learner, learning resource and question-dependent parameters, and test their prediction performances on the test set. For previously unobserved new learners in the test set, both algorithms make future predictions of $Y_j^{(t)}$ based on these estimates and observations $Y_j^{(1)}, \ldots, Y_j^{(t-1)}$, for $t = 1, \ldots, T$.

Table 2: Comparisons of SPARFA-Trace against SPARFA-M on predicting unobserved learner responses for Dataset 1.

	SPARFA-M		SPARFA-Trace	
	Dataset 1	Dataset 2	Dataset 1	Dataset 2
Accuracy	87.10 ± 0.04%	**86.64 ± 0.14%**	**87.31 ± 0.05%**	86.29 ± 0.25%
Likelihood	0.727 ± 0.001	0.704 ± 0.002	**0.730 ± 0.001**	**0.707 ± 0.003**

We compare both algorithms on three metrics: prediction accuracy, prediction likelihood, and area under the receiver operation characteristic (ROC) curve. The prediction accuracy corresponds to the percentage of correctly predicted responses; the prediction likelihood corresponds to the average the predicted likelihood of the unobserved responses, i.e., $\frac{1}{|\Omega^c_{\text{obs}}|}\sum_{t,j:(t,j)\in\Omega^c_{\text{obs}}} p(Y_j^{(t)}|\mathbf{w}_{i_j^{(t)}}, \mathbf{c}_j^{(t)}, \mu_{i_j^{(t)}})$ where Ω^c_{obs} is the set of unobserved learner responses in the test set; the area under the ROC curve is a commonly-used performance metric for binary classifiers (see [22] for details).

The means and standard deviations of all three metrics covering multiple cross-validation trials are shown in Table 1. We can see that SPARFA-Trace slightly outperforms KT on all performance metrics for Dataset 1. We also emphasize that SPARFA-Trace is capable of achieving superior prediction performance while simultaneously estimating the quality and content organization parameters of all learning resources and questions.

5.2 Predicting unobserved learner responses

We now compare SPARFA-Trace against the original SPARFA framework [18], which offers state-of-the-art collaborative filtering performance on predicting unobserved binary-valued graded learner responses.

We will use two datasets in this experiment. The first dataset is the full Dataset 1 with 92 learners answering 203 questions, explained in Section 5.1. The second dataset we use is from a signals and systems undergraduate course on OST, consisting of 41 learners answering 143 questions, with 97.1% of the responses observed. We will refer to this dataset as "Dataset 2" in the following experiments. All the questions were manually labeled with a number of $K = 4$ concepts, with the concepts being listed in Figure 5(b). The full course consist of 14 assessments, including 12 assignments and 2 exams.

We randomly partition the 143×43 (or 203×92) matrix $\mathbf{Y}$ of observed graded learner responses into 5 folds for cross-validation. Four folds of the data are used as the training set and the other fold is used as the test set. We train both the probit variant of SPARFA-M and SPARFA-Trace on the training set to obtain estimates of all model parameters and then use these estimates to predict unobserved held-out responses in the test set.

The means and standard deviations of the prediction accuracy and prediction likelihood metrics covering multiple cross-validation trials are shown in Tables 1 and 2. We see that SPARFA-Trace achieves comparable or better performance than the static SPARFA-M on both datasets.

5.3 Visualizing time-varying Learning and Content Analytics

In this section, we showcase another advantage of SPARFA-Trace over existing KT and collaborative filtering methods, i.e., the visualization of both learner knowledge state evolution over time and the estimated learning resource and question quality and content organization parameters.

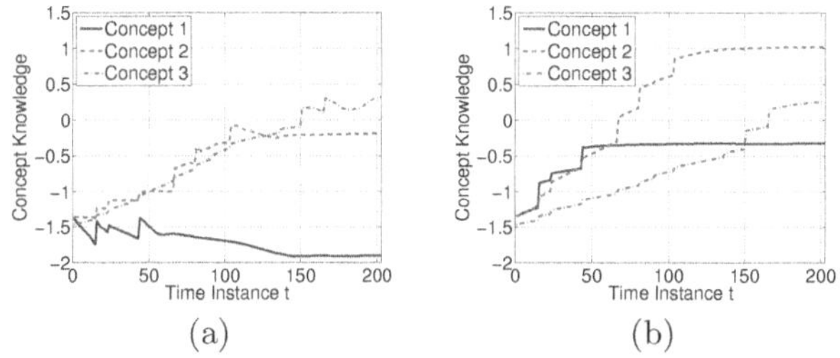

Figure 3: Estimated latent learner concept knowledge states for all time instances, for Dataset 1. (a) Learner 1's latent concept knowledge state evolution; (b) Average learner latent concept knowledge states evolution.

Figure 3(a) shows the estimated latent learner concept knowledge states at all time instances for Learner 1 in Dataset 1. We can see that their knowledge on Concepts 2 and 3 gradually improve over time, while their knowledge on Concept 1 does not. Therefore, recommending Learner 1 remedial material on Concept 1 seems necessary, which is verified by the fact that Learner 1 often responds incorrectly on questions covering Concept 1 towards the end of the course. Hence, SPARFA-Trace can enable a PLS to provide timely feedback to individual learners on the their concept knowledge at all times, which reveals the learning progress of the learners. Figure 3(b) shows the average learner concept knowledge states over the entire class at all time instances for Dataset 1. Using this information, SPARFA-Trace can also inform instructors on the trend of the concept knowledge state evolution of the entire class, in order to help them make timely adjustments to their course plans.

Figure 4(a) and Figure 4(b) show the quality and content organization of learning resources 3 and 9 for Dataset 2. These figures visualize the leaners' concept knowledge state transitions induced by interacting with Learning Resources 3 and 9. Circular nodes represent concepts; the leftmost set of dashed nodes represent the concept knowledge state vector $\mathbf{c}^{(t-1)}$, which are the learners' concept knowledge states before interacting with these learning resources, and the rightmost set of solid nodes represent the concept knowledge state vector $\mathbf{c}^{(t)}$, which are the learners' concept knowledge states after interacting with these learning resources. Arrows represent the the learner concept knowledge state transition matrix $\mathbf{D}_m$, the intrinsic quality vector of the learning resource $\mathbf{d}_m$, and their transformation effects on learners' concept knowledge states. Dotted arrows represent unchanged learner concept knowledge states; these arrows correspond to zero entries in $\mathbf{D}_m$ and $\mathbf{d}_m$. Solid arrows represent the intrinsic knowledge gain of some concepts, characterized by large, positive entries in $\mathbf{d}_m$. Dashed arrows represent the change in knowledge of advanced concepts due to their prerequisite concepts, characterized by non-zero entries in $\mathbf{D}_m$: High knowledge level on pre-requisite concepts can result in improved understanding and an increase on knowledge of advanced concepts, while low knowledge level on these prerequisite concepts can result in confusion and a decrease on knowledge of advanced concepts.

As shown in Figure 4(a), Learning Resource 3 is used in early stage of the course, and we can see that this learn-

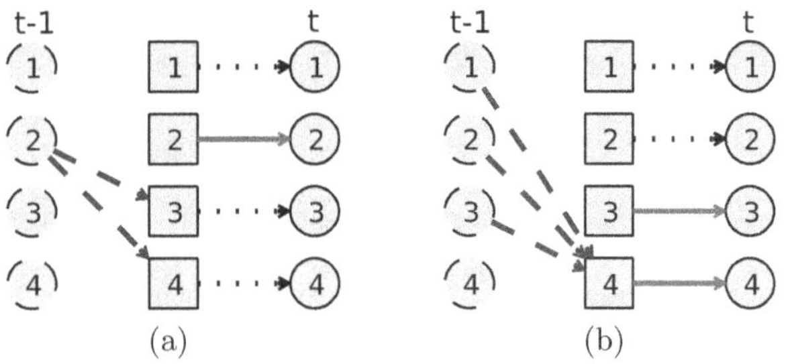

Figure 4: Visualized learner knowledge state transition effect of two distinct learning resources for Dataset 2. (a) Learner knowledge state transition effect for Learning Resource 3; (b) Learner knowledge state transition effect for Learning resource 9.

ing resource gives the learners a positive knowledge gain of Concept 2, while also helping on the more advanced Concepts 3 and 4. As shown in Figure 4(b), Learning resource 9 is used in later stage of the course, and we can see that it uses the learners' knowledge on all previous concepts to improve their knowledge on Concept 4, while also providing a positive knowledge gain on Concepts 3 and 4.

By analyzing the content organization of learning resources and their effects on learner concept knowledge state transitions, SPARFA-Trace enables a PLS to automatically recommend corresponding learning resources to learners based on their strengths and weaknesses. The estimated learning resource quality information also helps course instructors to distinguish between effective learning resources, and poorly-designed, off-topic, or misleading learning resources, thus helping them to manage these learning resources more easily.

Figure 5 shows the question–concept association graph obtained from Dataset 2. Circle nodes represent concept nodes, while square, box nodes represent question nodes. Each question box is labeled with the time instance at which it is assigned and its estimated intrinsic difficulty. From the graph we can see time-evolving effects, as questions assigned in the early stages of the course cover basic concepts (Concepts 1 and 2), while questions assigned in later stages cover more advanced concepts (Concepts 3 and 4). Some questions are associated with multiple concepts, and they mostly correspond to the final exam questions (boxes with dashed boundaries) where the entire course is covered.

Thus, by estimating the intrinsic difficulty and content organization of each question, SPARFA-Trace allows a PLS to generate feedback to instructors on the underlying knowledge structure of questions, which enables them to identify ill-posed or off-topic questions (such as questions that are not associated to any concepts in Figure 5(a)).

6. CONCLUSIONS

We have proposed SPARFA-Trace, a novel blind approximate Kalman filtering approach for time-varying learning and content analytics. The proposed method jointly traces latent learner concept knowledge evolution over time and simultaneously estimates the quality and content organization of the corresponding learning resources (such as textbook sections or lecture videos) and the questions in assessment sets. Being able to trace learners' concept knowledge evolution over time will enable a PLS to make timely feedback

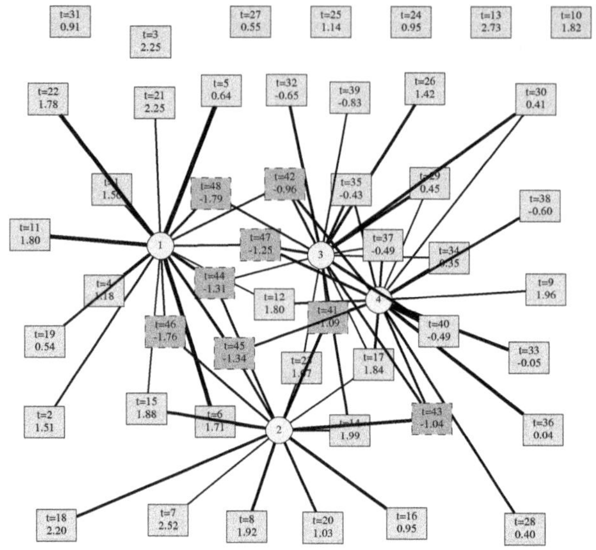

(a)

Concept 1	**Concept 2**
Laplace transform and filters	Sampling and reconstruction
Concept 3	**Concept 4**
Fourier series and Fourier transform	Signals and systems basics

(b)

Figure 5: (a) Question–concept association graph and concept labels for Dataset 2. (a) Question–concept association graph. Note that for the visualization to be compact, we show only 1/3 of all questions in the dataset; (b) Label of each concept.

to learners on their strengths and weaknesses. Furthermore, the estimated content-dependent parameters provide rich information on the knowledge structure and quality of learning resources. Together with the question parameters estimated, a PLS would be able to operate in an *autonomous* manner, requiring only minimal human input and intervention; this paves the way of applying SPARFA-Trace to MOOC-scale education scenarios, where the massive amount of data precludes manual intervention.

We note that SPARFA-Trace has potential to be applied to a wide range of other datasets, including (but not necessarily limited to) the analysis of temporal evolution in legislative voting data [29], and the study of temporal effects in general collaborative filtering settings [16, 25, 26, 32].

Acknowledgments

Thanks to Kim Davenport and JP Slavinsky for providing the OpenStax Tutor (OST) data and Andrew Waters and Ryan Ning for helpful discussions. This work was supported by the National Science Foundation under Cyberlearning grant IIS-1124535, the Air Force Office of Scientific Research under grant FA9550-09-1-0432, and the Google Faculty Research Award program. Visit the website `www.sparfa.com`, where you can learn more about the SPARFA project and purchase t-shirts and other merchandise.

References

[1] A. Beck and M. Teboulle. A fast iterative shrinkage-thresholding algorithm for linear inverse problems. *SIAM J. on Imaging Science*, 2(1):183–202, Mar. 2009.

[2] C. M. Bishop and N. M. Nasrabadi. *Pattern Recognition and Machine Learning*. Springer New York, 2006.

[3] A. C. Butler, E. J. Marsh, J. P. Slavinsky, and R. G. Baraniuk. Integrating cognitive science and technology improve learning in a STEM classroom. *Educational Psychology Review*, 26(1), Feb. 2014.

[4] M. Carrier and H. Pashler. The influence of retrieval on retention. *Memory & Cognition*, 20(6):633–642, Nov. 1992.

[5] A. T. Corbett and J. R. Anderson. Knowledge tracing: Modeling the acquisition of procedural knowledge. *User Modeling and User-adapted Interaction*, 4(4):253–278, Dec. 1994.

[6] A. Doucet, N. De Freitas, K. Murphy, and S. Russell. Rao-Blackwellised particle filtering for dynamic Bayesian networks. In *Proc.16th Conf. on Uncertainty in Artificial Intelligence*, pages 176–183, June 2000.

[7] G. A. Einicke and L. B. White. Robust extended Kalman filtering. *IEEE Trans. on Signal Processing*, 47(9):2596–2599, Sep. 1999.

[8] T. Hastie, R. Tibshirani, and J. Friedman. *The Elements of Statistical Learning*. Springer, 2010.

[9] S. S. Haykin. *Kalman Filtering and Neural Networks*. Wiley Online Library, 2001.

[10] A. H. Jazwinski. *Stochastic Processes and Filtering Theory*. Academic Press, New York, 1970.

[11] S. J. Julier and J. K. Uhlmann. New extension of the Kalman filter to nonlinear systems. In *Proc. 11th Intl. Symposium on Aerospace/Defense Sensing, Simulation and Controls*, pages 182–193, Apr. 1997.

[12] R. E. Kalman. A new approach to linear filtering and prediction problems. *ASME J. of Basic Engineering*, 82(1):35–45, 1960.

[13] S. P. Kasiviswanathan, H. Wang, A. Banerjee, and P. Melville. Online ℓ_1-dictionary learning with application to novel document detection. *Advances in Neural Information Processing Systems*, pages 2267–2275, Dec. 2012.

[14] G. Kennedy, I. Ioannou, Y. Zhou, J. Bailey, and S. O'Leary. Mining interactions in immersive learning environments for real-time student feedback. *Australasian J. of Educational Technology*, 29(2), 2013.

[15] Knewton. Knewton adaptive learning: Building the world's most powerful recommendation engine for education. *online*, June 2012.

[16] Y. Koren and J. Sill. OrdRec: an ordinal model for predicting personalized item rating distributions. In *Proc. of the 5th ACM Conf. on Recommender Systems*, pages 117–124, Oct. 2011.

[17] F. R. Kschischang, B. J. Frey, and H.-A. Loeliger. Factor graphs and the sum-product algorithm. *IEEE Trans. on Information Theory*, 47(2):498–519, Feb. 2001.

[18] A. S. Lan, A. E. Waters, C. Studer, and R. G. Baraniuk. Sparse factor analysis for learning and content analytics. *J. of Machine Learning Research, to appear*, 2014.

[19] T. P. Minka. From hidden Markov models to linear dynamical systems. Technical report, MIT, 1999.

[20] T. P. Minka. Expectation propagation for approximate Bayesian inference. In *Proc. 17th Conf. on Uncertainty in Artificial Intelligence*, pages 362–369, Aug. 2001.

[21] OpenStaxTutor. https://openstaxtutor.org/, 2013.

[22] Z. A. Pardos and N. T. Heffernan. Modeling individualization in a Bayesian networks implementation of knowledge tracing. In *Proc. 18th Intl. Conf. on User Modeling, Adaptation, and Personalization*, pages 255–266, June 2010.

[23] C. E. Rasmussen and C. K. I. Williams. *Gaussian Process for Machine Learning*. MIT Press, 2006.

[24] S. Roweis and Z. Ghahramani. Learning nonlinear dynamical systems using the expectation–maximization algorithm. *Kalman Filtering and Neural Networks*, 6:175–220, 2001.

[25] J. Silva and L. Carin. Active learning for online Bayesian matrix factorization. In *Proc. 18th Intl. Conf. on Knowledge Discovery and Data Mining*, pages 325–333, Aug. 2012.

[26] N. Thai-Nghe, T. Horvath, and L. Schmidt-Thieme. Factorization models for forecasting student performance. In *Proc. 4th Intl. Conf. on Educational Data Mining*, pages 11–20, July 2011.

[27] E. A. Wan and R. Van Der Merwe. The unscented Kalman filter for nonlinear estimation. In *Adaptive Systems for Signal Processing, Communications, and Control Symposium*, pages 153–158, Oct. 2000.

[28] C. Wang, J. Tang, J. Sun, and J. Han. Dynamic social influence analysis through time-dependent factor graphs. In *Intl. Conf. on Advances in Social Networks Analysis and Mining*, pages 239–246, July 2011.

[29] E. Wang, E. Salazar, D. Dunson, and L. Carin. Spatio-temporal modeling of legislation and votes. *Bayesian Analysis*, 8(1):233–268, Mar. 2013.

[30] B. Weiner and H. Reed. Effects of the instructional sets to remember and to forget on short-term retention: Studies of rehearsal control and retrieval inhibition (repression). *J. of Experimental Psychology*, 79(2):226, Feb. 1969.

[31] R. Wolfinger. Laplace's approximation for nonlinear mixed models. *Biometrika*, 80(4):791–795, Dec. 1993.

[32] H. Yu et al. Feature engineering and classifier ensemble for KDD cup 2010. *JMLR Workshop and Conference Proceedings*, 2010.

Active-Transductive Learning with Label-Adapted Kernels

Dan Kushnir*
Alcatel-Lucent Bell Laboratories
Murray Hill, NJ 07974
dan.kushnir@alcatel-lucent.com

ABSTRACT

This paper presents an efficient active-transductive approach for classification. A common approach of active learning algorithms is to focus on querying points near the class boundary in order to refine it. However, for certain data distributions, this approach has been shown to lead to uninformative samples. More recent approaches consider combining data exploration with traditional refinement techniques. These techniques typically require tuning sampling of unexplored regions with refinement of detected class boundaries. They also involve significant computational costs for the exploration of informative query candidates. We present a novel iterative active learning algorithm designed to overcome these shortcomings by using a linear running-time active-transductive learning approach that *naturally* switches from exploration to refinement. The passive classifier employed in our algorithm builds a random-walk on the data graph based on a modified graph geometry that combines the data distribution with current label hypothesis; while the query component uses the uncertainty of the evolving hypothesis. Our supporting theory draws the link between the spectral properties of our iteration matrix and a solution to the minimal-cut problem for a fused hypothesis-data graph. Experiments demonstrate computational complexity that is orders of magnitude lower than state-of-the-art, and competitive results on benchmark data and real churn prediction data.

Categories and Subject Descriptors

H.2.8 [**Database Management**]: Database Applications—*Data mining*

Keywords

classification; transductive learning; graph; active learning; uncertainty sampling

*Dan Kushnir is a member of technical staff at Bell Laboratories research arm

KDD'14, August 24–27, 2014, New York, NY, USA.

http://dx.doi.org/10.1145/2623330.2623673.

1. INTRODUCTION

Active learning is concerned with the design of algorithms that efficiently select a set of labeled training samples. The goal is to query those labels from a teacher which potentially optimize the prediction accuracy for the remaining unlabeled set. An active learner chooses at each trial a point (or possibly a batch) to be labeled by the teacher, and then learns a classification model. This process repeats itself until a label budget is used up. It has been shown that in some cases actively querying training samples expedites the learning process over traditional semi-supervised learning (e.g. [3, 15]), and is valuable especially when labels are scarce, expensive to obtain, or when unlabeled samples are abundant.

Past work on active learning can be roughly divided into two main approaches: First, an approach that focuses on refinement of the version space by actively probing the class decision boundary (e.g. [28]). This approach, typically an inductive one, often fails as it misses class boundaries that were not sampled, simply by focusing on refinement of boundaries already discovered and avoiding 'outlier' portions of the data. A second approach is a combined one, which employs both refinement of the version space and general exploration of the feature space (e.g. [3, 4, 6, 23]). These methods typically use graph-based techniques, where the exploration step samples pockets of data that the learner misclassifies and refines their class boundaries. However, the detection of such pockets is computationally challenging.

In this paper we focus on transductive learning and in particular on the second approach which combines exploration with boundary refinement since it captures both common types of classification failures. Our contribution is an active-transductive approach that yields competitive results while its implementation and computational effort are significantly simpler and lower than state-of-the-art algorithms. These advantages render it useful for real large data sets. In addition, unlike the combined approach that alternates between boundary refinement and exploration by use of pre-calculated parameters (e.g. [3, 23]), our method demonstrates early preference for exploration and naturally switches to refinement without the need for such parameters.

Our query strategy adapts the 'uncertainty sampling' criterion [20] to the graph setting, and shows that it can be used to *both* probe unexplored data pockets and refine decision boundaries in linear running time. It builds upon a probabilistic framework that combines the density and geometry of data with the current label hypothesis that emerges in the active learning process. Our framework uses *label-adapted kernels* which also improve the accuracy of the querying process when class distribution is *not smooth* over the data. This advantage is emphasized since many other (passive and) active-transductive approaches assume such limiting smoothness for their success (e.g. [8, 15, 32, 35]). In this paper we introduce theoretical justification for the use of label-adapted kernels as well as a convergence analysis, demonstrating its advantages in active-transductive learning. Our supporting theory relies on a careful spectral analysis of the iterative technique of Jacobi [13] for a particular system of equations and its connection with spectral graph theory [10].

Aside from the observed improved accuracy, the presented classifier and the query components both have asymptotic running time that is linear in the size of the data set. In particular, and unlike other active classifiers (e.g. [3,23,35]), our algorithm does not require a separate run of several classifiers for each query, and does not employ computationally demanding clustering algorithms, such as [4, 22]. It exhibits orders of magnitude speedup in empirical experiments, confirming its asymptotic complexity, while achieving superior accuracy.

The structure of the paper is as follows: in section 2 we review related work, and in section 3 we briefly introduce the problem of active learning. In section 4 we describe our approach and give a detailed description of our algorithm components and their running time. Section 5 consists of running time and accuracy experiments with benchmark and real data. We conclude in section 6.

2. RELATED WORK

The literature on semi-supervised learning is extensive (see [8] for an overview). Semi-supervised learning algorithms use unlabeled data during training to improve learning performance. In the transductive setting the unlabeled set is transduced with label information from other points. Graph-based algorithms have been developed to accurately transduce labels from a few training points to the unlabeled set of points by relying on graph structure (e.g. [5, 8, 11, 19, 32–34]). A basic assumption behind these methods is that class structure is smooth over the graph, or in other words, that classes separate well with respect to the data density patterns. This assumption allows to construct Markov processes whose transition probabilities rely on proximity in the data feature space (e.g. [8, 11, 27, 34]) in order to propagate label information. Alternatively, others use the smooth eigenvectors of the graph Laplacian (similar to the eigenvectors of the Markov matrix) as a basis to extend the labeling function from training samples to the unlabeled set (e.g. [26], [5]).

Much of the research in active learning focuses on the tradeoff between refinement and exploration (e.g. [3, 6, 23]), which is central in motivating our approach. As an example for algorithms that conduct merely refinement, we consider 'SIMPLE' [28]. 'SIMPLE' queries points closest to the center of the largest hypersphere that fits in the version space. Yet, 'SIMPLE' assumes a fairly symmetric version space and centrality of the hypersphere, which in many cases is not true. The geometry of the version space may be complex and requires exploration first, as naturally incorporated in our approach. Moreover, 'SIMPLE' has a high running time, which scales between $O(N^2) - O(N^3)$, as the number of support vectors is multiplied by the time to compute the kernel for each query. Other algorithms such as 'COMB' [3] incorporate exploration to overcome the shortcomings of 'refiner'-type algorithms. 'COMB' employs three active learners: the inductive 'SIMPLE' [28], a risk minimization active learner [24], and KFF (Kernel Farthest First) [3] which is an 'explorer'-type active learner. At each stage of 'COMB' a learner is chosen based on the reward utility assigned by each learner. While this approach, in fact, introduces a tradeoff between three different querying approaches, its implementation and choice of algorithm selection parameter are complex. Its computational complexity is also far from being negligible, as it uses 'SIMPLE'. A second example is the exploration method suggested in [23]. This algorithm combines 'SIMPLE' with KFF. The authors use an adaptable probabilistic parameter to choose the learner. However, the implementation is still demanding in terms of running time. As a third example we consider the algorithm +EXPLORE of [4]. The authors use spectral clustering [21] to expose uncovered clusters that the learner missed while querying samples. Otherwise they use uncertainty sampling [20]. +EXPLORE is augmented to graph-based active-transductive algorithms such as [5, 19, 32, 35] and introduces a remarkable improvement to these algorithms. Yet, +EXPLORE involves a significant computational effort in order to discover data clusters at each learning step. +EXPLORE is very close to our approach as its graph construction also relies on the currently available hypothesis to change the graph similarities. Even so, it also deviates from our approach in two fundamental ways: first, it uses the computationally consuming spectral clustering [21] (which has to be used after each query), whereas we use a iterative linear time diffusion kernel approach. And second, +EXPLORE uses a 'hard' decision criterion to connect same label nodes by an edge, while we use a 'soft' local one.

The algorithms [34] and [32] are two iterative graph transductive learning algorithms that inspired active learning extensions such as [34], [29], and [17]. These approaches rely on the limiting smoothness assumption, whereas we introduce a new label-adapted iteration to overcome this limitation. We note [26] and [11] that use variations of function-adapted kernels in the context of passive learning. However, these ideas were not used before or extended into the active learning setting.

In a recent work by [31], which focuses on active learning for unsupervised spectral clustering, the authors use the eigenvalue decomposition of the data graph Laplacian to probe query points that preserve matrix structure. Our supporting theory also relies on the spectral properties of the data graph. Yet, for our carefully designed iteration matrix the query component uses a linear combination of the dominant first and second eigenfunctions which are shown to minimize a combined cost function that captures *simultaneously* the labeling-function graph-cut and the data graph-cut. Finally, we consider recent work on batch-mode learning (e.g. [9, 18, 30]). Batch-mode active learning reduces the number of classifier calls per query, yet, it involves optimization procedures that are computationally demanding (polynomial or exponential in number of points). The tradeoff in running time should be carefully investigated with big data sets. For small data sets such as UCI's SEGMENTATION (as reported in [9]) the accuracy of our linear running time algorithm is favorable (see Sec. 5). Also, [9] reports running time results on data sets of a few hundred points and the reported ones (e.g. WAVEFORM) have higher running time than those reported for our algorithm in single-query mode. [18,30] do not report running times. Our experiments on big data sets include a simplistic uncertainty-based batch selection approach, and we mark more advanced batch-mode learning as future work.

3. PROBLEM SETTING

We address the problem of actively learning a classifier. Without loss of generality, consider the binary case with a set $S_{l+u} = \{x_i, y_i\}_{i=1}^{l+u} \subseteq \mathbb{R}^D \times \{+1, -1\}$ of $l + u$ points in $\mathbb{R}^D$ and their binary labels $h \in \{+1, -1\}$. In transductive learning the learner receives $X_{l+u} = \{x_i\}_{i=1}^{l+u}$ and a random training set $S_l = \{x_i, y_i\}_{i=1}^{l}$. The learner generates a soft prediction $\hat{\chi} = (\hat{\chi}_1, .., \hat{\chi}_{l+u})$, where $\hat{\chi}_i \in [+1, -1]$, and outputs $\hat{h} = \mathtt{sign}(\hat{\chi}_i)$. In our active-transductive setting the l training samples are *actively* chosen from X_u by the learner with the goal to minimize some loss-function on the remaining unlabeled points in X_u. We also consider in our experiments an active learning problem in which $X_u = \{X_{u1}, X_{u2}\}$ such that the learner is allowed to query points only from X_{u1}, and predicts for X_{u2}.

4. THE ALGORITHM AND ITS IMPLEMENTATION

We describe below our approach, supporting theory, and the detailed implementation of our algorithm, including its extension to the multi-class problem and its running-time complexity analysis.

4.1 Notation and Preliminary Setting.

We start by defining a finite weighted graph $G = (V, E)$ consisting of a set of *vertices* V, a set of *edges* $E \subset V \times V$, and a nonnegative *weighting* function $W : E \rightarrow \mathbb{R}^+$. We interpret the weight $W(v, \tilde{v})$ as a measure of similarity between the vertices v and $\tilde{v}$, when $(v, \tilde{v}) \in E$. The graph kernel is defined by

$$K = D^{-1}W, \tag{1}$$

where D is diagonal with $D_{ii} = d_i = \sum_j W(v_i, v_j)$. Thus Kf is a weighted averaging operator of some arbitrary function f to be studied: $f_i = (d_i)^{-1} \sum_{i\ j} w_{ij} f_j$, with the weights measured by the similarities W_{ij}; it has the 'averaging effect' of *smoothing* the function f over the graph.

In the data context, a graph G can be constructed in which the vertices of G correspond to the data points in X. W represents similarity between data points:

$$W(x_i, x_j) = m_1\left(\frac{\rho(x_i, x_j)^2}{\sigma_1(i, j)}\right), \tag{2}$$

where $\sigma_1(i, j)$ is a local scaling parameter, and typically $m_1(a) = exp(-a)$ with ρ as the Euclidean distance. The actual similarities used are the local ones in order to preserve local geometry and reduce computation time by using sparse matrices. These local similarities are realized by computing the k-nearest neighbors for each point x, denoted by $N_k(x)$. Throughout our experiments we select $\sigma_1(i, j)$ to be the median distance among the k nearest neighbors of x_i and x_j:

$$\sigma_1(i, j) = \text{median}\{\rho(x_i, x_l)_{l \in N_k(x_i)}, \rho(x_j, x_q)_{q \in N_k(x_j)}\}. \tag{3}$$

To facilitate notation $\sigma_1(i, j)$ will be typically denoted by σ_1. $K(x_i, x_j)$ follows immediately from (1):

$$K(x_i, x_j) = d_i^{-1} W(x_i, x_j). \tag{4}$$

4.2 Classification via Diffusion Kernels.

At the center of our algorithmic ideas lies a Markov process that is used to propagate labels from S_l to X_u. We start with the row-stochastic kernel defined by (1), which is viewed as the transition probabilities of a Markov random walk on the data neighborhood graph. The weights for each row i correspond exactly to the transition probabilities of a random walk starting at x_i. Specifically, the one step transition probability between states x_i and x_k is given by

$$p_{ik} = K(x_i, x_k) = \frac{W_{ik}}{\sum_j W_{ij}}, \tag{5}$$

where we denote $W(x_i, x_j)$ by W_{ij} to facilitate notation. We consider a random walk as means to assign a label to $x_i \in X_u$. The predicted label of x_i is associated with the probability of arriving to a labeled point of class 1 after performing a random walk starting at x_i [34] (we consider the binary case w.l.g.). Marking this probability as $p(y_{end} = 1|i)$, we consider the relation

$$p(y_{end} = 1|i) = \sum_j p(y_{end} = 1|j)p_{ij}, \tag{6}$$

and associate $p(y_{end} = 1|i)$ with the probability $p(y_i = 1|x_i)$. For labeled points $p(y_{end} = 1|i) = 1$, or 0 otherwise. Denoting $2p(y_{end} = 1|i) - 1$ by χ we see that $\chi \in [-1, 1]$ and its sign can be used to generate $\hat{h}$. χ can be partitioned as $\chi = [\chi_l, \chi_u]$. Similarly, D and W are partitioned into blocks

$$D = \begin{pmatrix} D_{ll} & 0 \\ 0 & D_{uu} \end{pmatrix} \text{ and } W = \begin{pmatrix} W_{ll} & W_{lu} \\ W_{ul} & W_{uu} \end{pmatrix}.$$

Eq. (6) can be transformed and re-written for the unlabeled points X_u and χ in matrix form as

$$\chi_u = (D_{uu}^{-1} W_{ul} \ \ D_{uu}^{-1} W_{uu}) \begin{pmatrix} \chi_l \\ \chi_u \end{pmatrix}, \tag{7}$$

resulting in the system

$$L_{uu}\chi_u = W_{ul}\chi_l \tag{8}$$

for the unlabeled samples, where $L = D - W$ is the graph Laplacian, and the sign of each χ_i gives the label of x_i. A similar system, motivated by quadratic energy minimization, is obtained by minimizing

$$C(\chi) = \frac{1}{2} \sum_{i,j=1}^{l+u} W_{ij}(\chi_i - \chi_j)^2 = \chi^T L \chi \tag{9}$$

while forcing equality on the labeled set $\chi_l = Y_l$ [8]. Specifically, minimizing (9) with respect to χ_u leads to

$$L_{ul}Y_l + L_{uu}\chi_u = 0 \Leftrightarrow L_{uu}\chi_u = -L_{ul}Y_l, \tag{10}$$

which is the same as (8), since $L_{ul} = -W_{ul}$.

The system (10) can be solved via the well-known Jacobi method [8,25]. The iterative Jacobi method solves the system $Mx = b$ by approximating the solution at the step $(t+1)$ by

$$x_i^{(t+1)} = \frac{1}{M_{ii}} \left(b_i - \sum_{j \neq i} M_{ij} x_j^{(t)}\right). \tag{11}$$

The Jacobi iteration matrix is defined to be $B_J = D^{-1}(R+L)$, where D is the diagonal matrix with M_{ii} on its i-th diagonal element, and R and L are the upper and lower triangular matrices of M. Hence, in matrix notation the iterative scheme is

$$x^{(t+1)} = D^{-1}(b - (R+L)x^{(t)}) \Leftrightarrow x^{(t+1)} = B_J x^{(t)} + D^{-1}b. \tag{12}$$

For faster convergence one may consider the damped iteration involving a parameter $\omega \in [0,1]$, where the iteration matrix is defined as $B_\omega = (1-\omega)I + \omega B_J$, so that

$$x^{(t+1)} = B_\omega x^{(t)} + \omega D^{-1}b. \tag{13}$$

For the system (10) we have $M = L_{uu}$, $x = \chi_u$, and $b = L_{ul}Y_l$, which then yields the iteration

$$\chi_i^{(t+1)} = \frac{1}{L_{uu}(x_i,x_i)}\left(-(L_{ul}Y_l)_i - \sum_{j\neq i} L_{uu}(x_i,x_j)\chi_j^{(t)}\right) \tag{14}$$

It is clear that (14) is a label diffusion process: transducing a label to x_i as a weighted average of the labels of its neighbors. In a slightly different view, it is equivalent to the iterative application of the kernel (1) on the characteristic vector χ, while restarting χ_l to Y_l after each iteration. Its probabilistic justification is in the random walk framework (6), which leads to classification. The summary of the label diffusion algorithm *DiffuseLabels* is given in Fig. 1.

We note that this formulation is related to various label propagation algorithms suggested in [11, 32, 33] except for the normalization steps there. Also, when $t \to \infty$ *DiffuseLabels* is related to the harmonic classifier of [34]. Yet, the equivalence we have just drawn between our label propagation and the Jacobi iteration plays an important role in deriving convergence and solution properties for the following iterative process that we propose for classification and active learning. We prove bellow that our label diffusion process converges, and provide a *multi-class extension* to our approach.

COROLLARY 1. ***The iteration in DiffuseLabels (14)***

$$\chi_i^{(t+1)} = \frac{1}{L_{uu}(x_i,x_i)}\left(-(L_{ul}Y_l)_i - \sum_{j\neq i} L_{uu}(x_i,x_j)\chi_j^{(t)}\right)$$

converges as $t \to \infty$.

PROOF. *The proof relies on the convergence proof of the Jacobi method [25]: if M (11) is strictly diagonally dominant then the iteration converges. Since for L_{uu} we have $L_{uu}(x_i,x_i) = \sum_{j=1}^{l+u} L(x_i,x_j)$, we have that $\forall i$ $L_{uu}(x_i,x_i) > \sum_j L_{uu}(x_i,x_j)$, therefore $M = L_{uu}$ is strictly diagonally dominant. This implies that the row sums $\{s_1,...,s_n\}$ of the iteration matrix B_J are smaller than 1. Since $\|L_{uu}\|_\infty = \max\{s_1,...,s_n\} < 1$, we obtain that the spectral radius of B_J is bounded by 1: $\max_i|\lambda_i| \leq \|L_{uu}\|_\infty < 1$, therefore B_J is a convergent matrix and the Jacobi iteration (14) converges.* □

The multi-class case. In the multi-class setting we consider $C = \{c_1,...,c_m\}$ classes, and $\Xi = \{\chi(c_1),...,\chi(c_m)\}$ characteristic assignment vectors instead of a single one as in the binary case. Each $\chi(c_j), 1 \leq j \leq m$, is a 'one vs. all' vector: $\chi_i(c_j) = 1$ if $x_i \in X_u$ belongs to c_j, or $\chi_i(c_j) = -1$, if $x_i \in X_u$ belongs to c_k, $k \neq j$, otherwise $\chi_i(c_j) = 0$. The label diffusion is applied to each vector and the classification is computed for a data point x_i as $\arg\max_j\{\bar{\chi}_i(c_j)\}$.

```
DiffuseLabels(X_{l+u}, S_l, t, K, χ)
Input: X_{l+u}: data, S_l: training set, K: kernel,
χ: current labeling approx. t: number of iterations.
Output: χ̄
if K and χ are empty:
  K = ConGeometKernel(X_{l+u})
  Initialize χ with labeling of S_l and 0 elsewhere.
for i = 1 to t, do:
  χ̄ = Kχ ;  χ̄_l = Y_l ;  χ = χ̄ ;
end for
Return χ̄.
```

Figure 1: The algorithm *DiffuseLabels*.

4.3 Classification via Label-Adapted Kernels.

The diffusion of labels (*DiffuseLabels*) depends only on information from data feature space encoded into the weights W_{ij}. In particular, the minimization of the quadratic energy (9) relies on the assumption that data points that belong to different classes will have a low similarity weight. It is this assumption on the smoothness and separability of the class label function which guarantees that the diffusion process will capture the class structure. This smoothness assumption, which is used in semi-supervised classification tasks, is often both local and global, i.e. h does not change much between nearest neighbors and on clusters of data points. However, in many real data sets this might not be the situation, as h may not be smooth with respect to W. To this end, we propose to modify the geometry captured by W so that the geometry of $\bar{\chi}$ - a smoothed version of χ that captures the current labeling hypothesis, is taken into account. To achieve this goal we consider the following label-adapted weight matrix in a second diffusion process:

Definition 1. **The label-adapted weight matrix is defined as**

$$W^{\bar{\chi}}(x_i,x_j) = m_1\left(\frac{\rho_1(x_i,x_j)^2}{\sigma_1}\right) m_2\left(\frac{\rho_2(\bar{\chi}(x_i),\bar{\chi}(x_j))^2}{\sigma_2}\right), \tag{15}$$

and its associated kernel is $K^{\bar{\chi}}$. m_1 and m_2 are decaying exponentials, ρ_1 and ρ_2 are distance metrics in $\mathbb{R}^D$ and $\mathbb{R}^k$ (typically $k=1$), σ_1 is a data scaling parameter that is chosen as in (3), σ_2 is a scaling parameter in the label feature space (its selection is discussed below), and $\bar{\chi}$ is a smoothed soft label estimate for h obtained via *DiffuseLabels* with the kernel K.

The construction in (15) assigns stronger affinity between points that are believed to belong to the same class, and weaker affinities between points of different classes. In particular, when $\sigma_2 << \sigma_1$, the associated averaging kernel K will average locally, but much more along the (estimated) contours of h than across them. Thus the selection of σ_2 depends on the importance of the estimation of h by $\bar{\chi}$. A median approach (3) can be used, which captures the level of uncertainty in $\bar{\chi}$. Or $\sigma_2 = 1$, which captures the average distance between the two labels {-1,1}.

We therefore consider a second label diffusion process involving the kernel (15), which follows a diffusion process with the kernel (4). This second diffusion process yields a new labeling estimation denoted by $\hat{\chi}$, as described in the pseudo-code *LAClassifier* in Fig. 2. The label diffusion process involving $K^{\bar{\chi}}$ will manifest fast label diffusion along the (suspected) same-class samples and slow diffusion along class boundaries. This property is advantageous to accelerate and improve classification, in particular when classes do not separate over the data, or in other words, the smoothness assumption does not hold. In this case our resulting iterant $\hat{\chi}$ will provide an approximation to h and not only to the data density distribution. In order to establish these claims, we first introduce Theorem 1 which shows that the Jacobi iteration with the label-adapted kernel (15) converges to an approximation of the class decision boundary *independently* of the smoothness assumption. Second, we show in Theorem 2 that in the modified graph geometry the energy function (9) is further minimized by $\hat{\chi}$.

THEOREM 1. ***Let $\hat{x}$ be the resulting iterant from the Jacobi iteration with the kernel (15) in LAClassifier. Then $\hat{x}$ approximates a minimal graph-cut in a graph constructed from the unknown true binary label function h and the data. In particular, $\hat{x}$ approximates h.***

PROOF. See appendix. □

THEOREM 2. ***Let $\bar{\chi}$ and $\hat{\chi}$ be the corresponding minima of the quadratic energy function (9) with W and $W^{\bar{\chi}}$. Then the label-adapted weight matrix and $\hat{\chi}$ further minimize (9). In particular,***

$$\sum_{i\in u, j\in l+u} W_{ij}^{\bar{\chi}}(\hat{\chi}_i - \hat{\chi}_j)^2 \leq \sum_{i\in u, j\in l+u} W_{ij}(\bar{\chi}_i - \bar{\chi}_j)^2$$

PROOF. See appendix. □

Theorem 1 and its proof reveal the structure of $\hat{\chi}$: it is dominated by the first eigenvectors of the kernel $W^{\bar{\chi}}$. The combination of the 1st and 2nd eigenvectors provides a real smooth approximation of a graph-cut of the points of the binary set h. As such it is simply an approximation of h. Most important, we show below how $\hat{\chi}$ is used within active learning: its transition from negative to positive values indicates the class decision boundary, and precise zero values indicate unexplored data portions. Another strength of Theorem 1 is in its independence from the smoothness assumption and class separation in data space: Popular data-constructed kernels (4) as, for example, in [5,11,32–34] result in a good estimate for h *only* if the smoothness assumption holds.

Theorem 2 establishes that the new solution $\hat{\chi}$ is smoother in the modified geometry as it minimizes the classification error (9) with $W^{\bar{\chi}}$. Using $W^{\bar{\chi}}$ in the quadratic energy function (9) is more meaningful than using W, because it contains a penalty that does not depend only on the data but also depends on the labels approximation $\bar{\chi}$. Connecting this with Theorem 1 and its proof, the resulting iterant $\bar{\chi}$ that minimizes the classification error contains the smooth components which better approximate h. As a result, the query component which relies on the absolute values of $\bar{\chi}$ attains better accuracy, as shown in the following section.

To this end the label-adapted diffusion suggests two key advantages: First, it computes the soft label approximation $\hat{\chi}$ in linear running time, while other methods, relying on black-box clustering algorithms, run with higher complexity (e.g. [4, 22, 23]) (see Sec. 4.5). Second, it suggests a classifier that is highly accurate and can be applied to classification problems where there is no class separation over the

LAClassifier(X_{l+u}, S_l, t)
Input: X_{l+u}: all data measurements,
S_l: the training set, t: number of iterations.
Output: $\hat{\chi}$
$K = ConGeometKernel(X_{l+u})$
Initialize χ with labeling of S_l and 0 elsewhere.
$\bar{\chi} = DiffuseLabels(t, K, \chi)$
$K^{\bar{\chi}} = ConstructLAKernel(W, \bar{\chi})$ (Eq. (15))
$\hat{\chi} = DiffuseLabels(t, K^{\bar{\chi}}, \chi)$
Return $\hat{\chi}$

Figure 2: Label propagation with label-adapted kernels *LAClassifier*.

data density. Our supporting theory links $\hat{\chi}$ directly with h, which is key in constructing an efficient active learning algorithm, referred to as **Label Adapted Active Learning (LAAL)**.

4.4 Active Learning with Label-Adapted Kernels.

Theorem 1 and its proof establish that the output of *LA-Classifier* - $\hat{\chi}$, is an approximation to the true binary labeling function h. As such, low $\hat{\chi}$ absolute values indicate either a class decision boundary or a yet unexplored region where a decision boundary could exist. With this observation we choose to adapt an uncertainty sampling criterion to perform active learning in our transductive setting. In general, representative points whose approximated soft labels $\{\hat{\chi}_i\}_{i=l+1}^{(l+u)}$ have a low absolute value: $q = \arg\min_i(|\hat{\chi}_i|)$ are queried. Such points indicate that the labeling function has not been sampled sufficiently or that a decision boundary exists. We distinguish between the two cases:

1. **Exploration**: Our fundamental observation is that after the iterative label-adapted diffusion process completes, regions of X_u that have not been explored will be identified as X_u points with label weights that are *essentially zero*: $\hat{\chi}_i = 0$. Zero-label points indicate clusters or even disconnected graph components that are unreachable by the labeling propagation process. Representative points of such data portions are potential candidates to reduce the hypotheses space, and should be explored. These representative points are identified by a high value of d_i which approximates the probability density function $p(x_i)$. This exploration is fast since the propagation algorithm has linear running time (see section 4.5), and the choice of the next query is based on merely sorting $\hat{\chi}$.

2. **Refinement:** Our second observation is that once exploration is mature, the label-adapted diffusion from S_l to X_u will essentially cover the whole graph. At that stage $\hat{\chi}$ will be non-zero everywhere. This situation naturally redirects LAAL's query selection process to query points along decision boundaries, since their soft labels are close to zero but numerically are *not* zero. The decision boundary points are captured by low $\hat{\chi}$ weights, as suggested by Theorem 1, which shows that $\hat{\chi}$ is a soft approximation of h.

Our query strategy is justified by the following probabilistic argument in Lemma 1:

```
LAAL(X_{l+u}, l)
  Input: X_{l+u}, l: number of points to query,
  Output: h = sign(χ̂)
  S_0 = ∅.
  for i = 1 to l
    χ̂ = LAClassifier(X_{l+u}, S_{i-1}).
    (x_q, y_q) = Query(χ̂, X_u);
    S_i = S_{i-1} ∪ (x_q, y_q);
    X_u = X_u \ x_q;
  end for
  χ̂ = LAClassifier(X_{l+u}, S_l).
  Return sign(χ̂)
```

Figure 3: Pseudo-code for *LAAL*.

LEMMA 1. ***Choosing $q = \arg\min_i\{|\hat{\chi}_i|\}$ minimizes the expected error criterion $E[(\hat{y}_i - y_i)^2|x_i]p(x_i)$, where $p(x)$ is the density of X.***

PROOF. *We expand the error expectation term:*

$$\begin{aligned} &E[(\hat{y}_i - y_i)^2|x_i] \\ &= p(y_i = 1|x_i)(\hat{y}_i - 1)^2 + p(y_i = -1|x_i)(\hat{y}_i + 1)^2 \\ &= (\hat{y}_i^2 + 1) - 2\hat{y}_i(p(y_i = 1|x_i) - p(y_i = -1|x_i)). \end{aligned}$$

Following Theorem 1, the difference $p(y_i = 1|x_i) - p(y_i = -1|x_i)$ can be well approximated by $|\hat{\chi}_i| : E[(\hat{y}_i - y_i)^2|x_i] \approx (\hat{y}_i^2 + 1) - 2|\hat{\chi}_i|$. Therefore, when $\hat{\chi}_i$ is minimal, and $p(x_i)$ (approximated by d_i) is maximal the expected error is maximal, which suggests querying such points. □

REMARK 1. ***If $|\hat{\chi}_q| \neq 0$ we do not use the representative criterion $\arg\max_i\{d_i : i = \arg\min_i |\hat{\chi}_i|\}$ since class decision boundary may not correspond to data density, and therefore choosing according to density may cause contamination.***

Description of the algorithm. We are now ready to describe the label-adapted active learning algorithm (LAAL) in Fig. 3. LAAL is a meta-algorithm that employs the label-adapted diffusion classifier *LAClassifier* (Fig. 2) to produce the current labeling hypothesis, and a query selection component *Query*. LAAL iterates the two procedures and outputs the final hypothesis once the required number of labels l had been queried. The query selection algorithm - *Query* uses the current soft hypothesis to select the point x_i^q that satisfies the criterion of a minimal absolute value: $q = \arg\min_i\{|\hat{\chi}_i|\}$, in accordance with Lemma 1. If $\hat{\chi}_i = 0$ *Query* selects x_i^q to be a representative of an unexplored data portion or cluster by choosing the candidate with the maximal sum of weights - d_i. Alternatively, when all $\bar{\chi}_i$'s are nonzero (i.e. exploration is saturated), *Query* will enforce the minimum criterion only.

A toy example. Fig. 4 illustrates the active learning process of LAAL on a simple XOR-type binary classification problem (A), where class separation does not correspond to the data density. In this example, points are queried using LAAL, a hypothesis is generated for the rest of the points X_u, and accuracy is reported. In sub-figures B-D black circles correspond to queried points, and the data points circle-filling colors correspond to the soft hypothesis generated by LAAL. Sub-figure B demonstrates the exploration stage: data portions for which the soft hypothesis is essentially zero are queried. In C all X_u points found to be assigned with a non-zero soft label - indicative of a saturated exploration phase. As seen, a rough sketch of the correct classes is well captured by the current hypothesis. Finally, in sub-figure D the query process is naturally redirected to the refinement of class boundaries. The advantages of using the label-adapted process are further discussed in our experimental results in Fig. 5-right for the same XOR problem, where we show that active learning with label adaptation attains significantly better error rates (10%) than without label-adaptation.

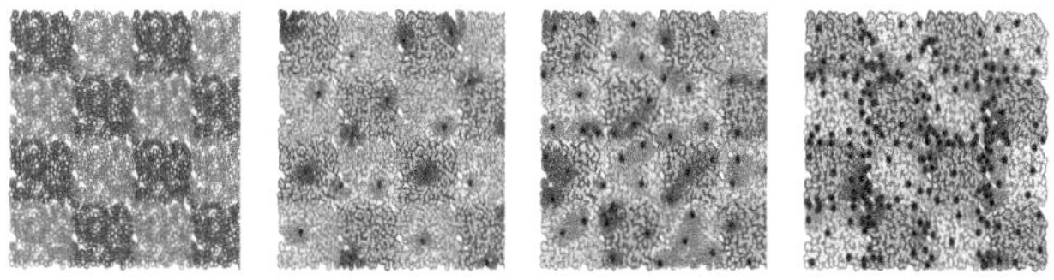

A B: 71% C: 84% D: 98%

Figure 4: Demonstration of LAAL with accuracy rates. A: the XOR data set. B: Exploration stage (20 queries). C: Maturity of exploration: most of X_u are assigned with soft labels (50 queries). D: Refinement stage: additional 190 queries concentrate mostly on class boundary refinement.

4.5 Running time of the algorithm.

In the following we show that the running time of LAAL is linear in the size of the data set and its dimension. We underline two key observations: First, the diffusion of labels in *DiffuseLabels* is an iteration of a product of a sparse matrix of size $N \times N$ ($N = l + u$) with a vector. Given that the kernel is $k-$sparse, the total complexity of *DiffuseLabels* is $O(t \cdot N \cdot k)$. In practice, t is small and was found to give optimal results in our experiments when $t = 2, 3$. Careful analysis shows that optimally $t \approx \frac{\log(N/l)}{\log(k)} \approx \log(N)$. Secondly, the first query selection process (*Query*) performs $O(|X_l|k^t \cdot log(|X_l| \cdot k^t))$ operations to sort and find the lowest values of $\hat{\chi}$. This running time can be further reduced on subsequent iterations by using simple book keeping on the last iteration sorting results and a heap: there are at most k^t elements in $|X_u|$ that are influenced by the last query which need to be updated. Therefore the query running time is $O(k^t log(|X_l| \cdot k^t))$. In practice of LAAL's running time is mostly dominated by the graph construction procedure, which involves finding nearest neighbors for all data points in X_{l+u}. Naive exact nearest neighbor algorithms have running time that is $O(N^2D)$, whereas space partitioning algorithms exhibit exponential complexity in high dimensions. We therefore resort to an approximate search (e.g. [1]) that suggests a tradeoff of an almost linear time complexity with a prescribed error constant ε.

For comparison, we discuss the running time of a few relevant active learners: Both [4] and [22] employ full clustering schemes for each query. '+ EXPLORE' [4] involves a spectral algorithm whose computational effort in general is cubic in N. As the authors report they had to half the size of standard benchmark UCI data sets in order to reduce a running time of over a month with 20 CPUs. [22] uses K-medoids clustering with complexity that scales as $O(i \cdot K \cdot (N - k)^2)$ with i as the number of iterations. Algorithms such as [35], also involve a computationally demanding procedure for es-

Table 1: Data sets used for experiments.

Data set / Info	size	D	type	m	source
XOR	6400	2	Real	2	[3, 23]
XOR-REDUCED	1000	2	Real	2	[3, 23]
XOR-HUGE	560000	2	Real	2	[3, 23]
MUSH	8124	139	Cat,Int	2	UCI
MUSK	476	166	Int	2	UCI
MAGIC	19020	11	Real	2	UCI
MAGIC-REDUCED	7762	10	Real	2	UCI
WAVEFORM	5000	21	Real	3	UCI
IONOSPHERE	351	34	Real,Int	2	UCI
CHURN	50000	171	Real,Int, Cat	2	[14]
COVERTYPE	581012	54	Real,Int	7	UCI
SUSY	1027000	18	Real	2	UCI
SEGMENTATION	2310	19	Real	7	UCI

timating the risk for each query candidate. In [23] and [3], support vector machines are used, and therefore for each query the running time is $O(|X_u| \cdot |V_h| \cdot T_k)$, where V_h is the number of support vectors and T_k is the time to compute the kernel. To this end LAAL's linear time complexity and observed accuracy suggest a significant improvement over current active algorithms, rendering it as practical for large data sets.

5. EXPERIMENTS

Active learning has already gained a significant body of algorithmic approaches. In our experiments we compare LAAL's performance with several carefully chosen representative baseline methods. First, the spectral-clustering based +EXPLORE of [4] with representative sampling which is closely related to our iterative approach mostly since it uses label adaptation via a 'hard' criterion, namely, by deleting graph edges of differently labeled points and establishing edges between similar label nodes. As shown in our accuracy experiments +EXPLORE indeed shows the closest performance to LAAL's; however, in our running time experiments it is significantly slower.

In addition, we compare LAAL with baseline uncertainty sampling approaches [20] where a variety of recent approaches have been proposed [12], [24]: We use a parametric version with a Bayes classifier [24], a non-parametric version referred to as 'Non-Adaptation' which amounts to using $\bar{\chi}$ for uncertainty sampling. We also compare with 'Large Margin' inductive approaches with Support Vector Machines [7], and with the ensemble approach of [23] and the algorithms of [3] and [28]. As control experiments we demonstrate LAAL's performance against a random query sampling approach and with and without label-adaptation. We use the 'XOR' data as a specific experiment to compare our performance on non-smooth data sets. We note that both [23] and [4] provide performance comparison with additional algorithms [3,5,19,28,32], therefore our comparison with [4] provides an even broader view of LAAL's performance. Other approaches focusing on batch learning [9,18,18,30], are fundamentally different and discussed in Sec. 2.

We start with an accuracy comparison that demonstrates LAAL's competitive accuracy, and then continue to a running time comparison on data sets of size up to 1 million which demonstrates LAAL's outstanding efficiency. The data sets used are summarized in table 1.

Parameters choice. $t = \log(N)$, σ_1 according to (3), and $\sigma_2 = 1$ (see 4.3).

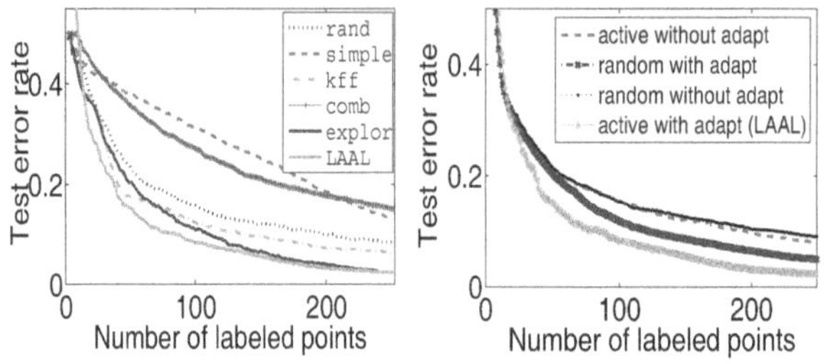

Figure 5: XOR-REDUCED data set. Left: results of [28] (SIMPLE), [3] (KFF and COMB), [23] (explor), random queries (random), and LAAL. Right: Comparison of LAAL with/without label-adapted kernels, and with random queries.

5.1 Accuracy experiments.

Non-smooth class function. We start with the binary 'XOR-REDUCED' classification problem which involves a synthetic data set from [3, 23], similar to Fig. 4. In 'XOR' the labeling function is not separable on the data, and therefore serves here as an example to compare LAAL's performance with various other methods some of which assume separability. The data is a generalization of the exclusive OR: a d-dimensional, $n \times n \times ... \times n$ "checkerboard" in which every square contains 250 points collected to a data set X ($\|X\| = 250n^d$). We repeated the following experiment 50 times: 100 points were randomly selected from X to serve as the test set X_{u2} and the remaining points were placed in X_{u1}. Classification error rates of LAAL as a function of the size of the training set X_l are shown in Fig. 5 [1] for $d = 2$, $n = 4$. Each curve is the average of 50 runs. The left sub-figure demonstrates a fast learning curve that LAAL exhibits over the other methods [3,23,28]. The result after 250 queried points is comparable to the best algorithm suggested in [23], with a faster convergence rate for LAAL. The right sub-figure depicts a performance comparison of LAAL with kernel methods that do not use the label-adapted kernel, but only the kernel that entails the geometric proximity of the data points, as in [32,33]. This figure also provides a comparison in which active learning is disabled, so that the data points are selected randomly. In this case LAAL performs with significant accuracy improvement when compared with the other diffusion-based methods: the label-adapted kernel improves classification, and, most important, it enhances accuracy when our active query process is used.

The following accuracy experiments involved UCI data sets MUSK, MUSH, MAGIC-REDUCED, IONOSPHERE, and IMAGE SEGMENTATION [2]. We used our codes for LAAL, '+EXPLORE' [4], uncertainty sampling [20] in 3 differen versions: 1. with the parametric Bayes classifier [24] (coded 'US'), 2. with non-parametric *DiffuseLabels* (without label-adapted kernel - using only $\bar{\chi}$) (coded 'NAdapt'), and 3. inductive SVM-based large margin approach [7, 28] (coded 'ISVM'). As a control experiment we also used a random query selection (coded 'Rand') with LAAL. In these experiments X_l was minimal and the test set includes the rest of the data X_u. We run each algorithm to query 50 data points and checked the accuracy at each step. To fairly com-

[1] left figure contains results of [23], courtesy of Kun Deng

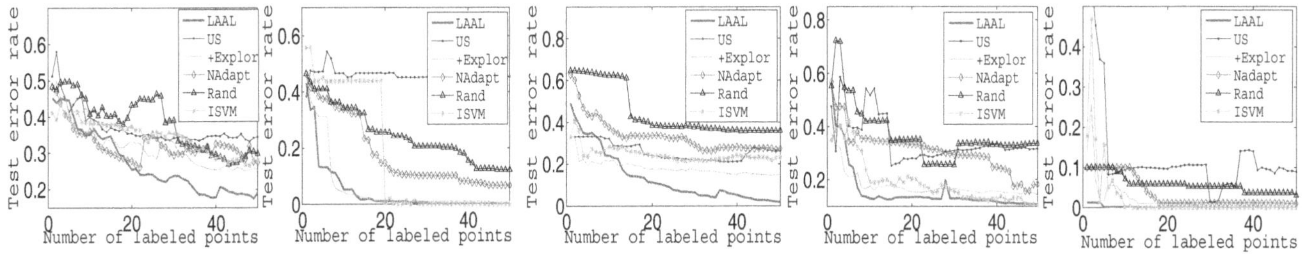

Figure 6: Error rate vs. number of labeled samples. Left to right: MUSK, MUSH, MAGIC, IONOSPHERE, and SEGMENTATION data sets.

pare LAAL and NAdapt with other methods we decided that points that have zero labels (typically because of being far away from labeled ones) will have a random label sampled which depends on the current proportion of positively classified labels. Results are reported in Fig. 6. LAAL demonstrates accuracy that is significantly better than the other algorithms over the full active learning period. '+EXPLORE' has a closer performance to LAAL and in early learning has short segments of better error performance; however, in all cases its overall behavior is less accurate than LAAL's, and we note again its higher running time. The Bayes classifier with uncertainty sampling shows to be less accurate, and diffusion without label-adapted kernels (using only $\bar{\chi}$) performs worse than LAAL, as it relies on the smoothness assumption. The inductive ISVM sometimes shows high accuracy at latent stage of learning - when enough points have been labeled. Lastly, we demonstrate the application of LAAL on a noisy large churn prediction tournament [14] data set, obtained from the telecommunication industry. The binary classification problem for predicting churn involves a noisy labeling function of a human decision process, and typically a rare class. We chose 10 random initial training sets and corresponding pool sets X_{u1} of size 5K. To simulate a realistic distribution of the churn class we selected a test set that contains 3% churn samples, and a training set with 50% churn class. We started with a preliminary experiment involving the Stochastic Gradient Boosting (SGB) classifier with decision trees [16]. We then introduced feature selection based on the output of SGB for the top 25 features. The selected features were used in a following experiment with LAAL and SGB. Results are reported in table 2 for the lift value of the top decile, showing an average improvement of 15% over SGB.

Table 2: Lift values for LAAL and SGB over 10 churn prediction data sets.

Alg./dataset	D1	D2	D3	D4	D5	D6	D7	D8	D9	D10	mean
LAAL	2.2	2.6	1.8	2.3	2.3	1.4	2.3	2.2	2.4	1.9	2.1
SGB	1.9	1.8	1.9	1.9	1.8	1.9	2.0	1.9	1.9	1.9	1.9

5.2 Running time experiments.

To demonstrate the efficiency of LAAL we performed running time comparisons with three representative algorithms: First, a baseline linear-running time parametric uncertainty sampling algorithm [20] with a Bayes classifier which in terms of speed should be the fastest algorithm to be examined (marked as 'US'). Second, the closely related clustering-based '+EXPLORE' [4] which uses the passive transductive classifier of [32] and spectral clustering [21] (marked as '+EXPLOR'). And third, an inductive active learning with SVM [7] (marked as 'ISVM'). We set an accuracy goal of 0.8 and run each algorithm until this accuracy is obtained, or until the query pool is exhausted. The experiment shows the tradeoff between accuracy and running time. CPU running time (log scale) vs. data size is reported in Fig. 7. The superiority of LAAL is clear: demonstrating 2-4 orders of magnitude speedup relative to 'US' and '+EXPLOR'. When data has a clear class-cluster structure (e.g. MUSH data set) '+EXPLORE' attains better running time than 'US'. However, LAAL, which also detects clusters, does so more efficiently. The results involving 'ISVM' demonstrate that once a single clear boundary exists, 'ISVM' is very accurate in refining it. However, its computational complexity is shown to be prohibitive. In many cases ISVM simply exhausted the query pool without reaching the desired accuracy: for example, in the 'XOR' data set where ISVM concentrated only on a single decision boundary.

Big data sets. To further demonstrate LAAL's efficiency we experimented with data sets that are 1-2 orders of magnitude bigger, including over 1,000,000 data points. There (as well as on previous experiments shown in Fig. 7) running time could not be measured for all algorithms as they mostly caused the system to crash, or simply run indefinitely beyond 10^5 seconds. In particular, in '+EXPLORE' the spectral clustering is a major computational bottleneck. We took a different approach with the other algorithms in order to provide the reader with an informative comparison: the algorithms were transformed to use batch learning with an uncertainty sampling criterion. Specifically, the query batch of size $b = 20$ was chosen as the sorted set $Q = \{q_{i_1}, ..., q_{i_b}\}$ of minimal $|\hat{\chi}_i|$ values. Batch learning has indeed accelerated the convergence of the algorithms to the desired accuracy. However, at $N \approx 10^4$ both US and ISVM exhausted the pool, run indefinitely, or crashed. We provide three experiments with big data sets: UCI COVERTYPE, UCI SUSY, and XOR-HUGE. Because of space limitations we plot running times for two of them in the bottom of Fig. 7. When applied to XOR-HUGE, ISVM exhausts the pool and crashes at $N \approx 10^4$. LAAL was running at $\sim 10^2$ seconds. For the COVERTYPE data set ISVM crashed at $N \approx 3 \times 10^4$, and shows a very steep slope. LAAL continues from $N \approx 10^4$ to $N = 5.8 \times 10^5$ with $10^2 - 10^3$ seconds. The experiments with the SUSY data set starting at $N = 4.8 \times 10^5$ show a similar trend towards and beyond 1M points.

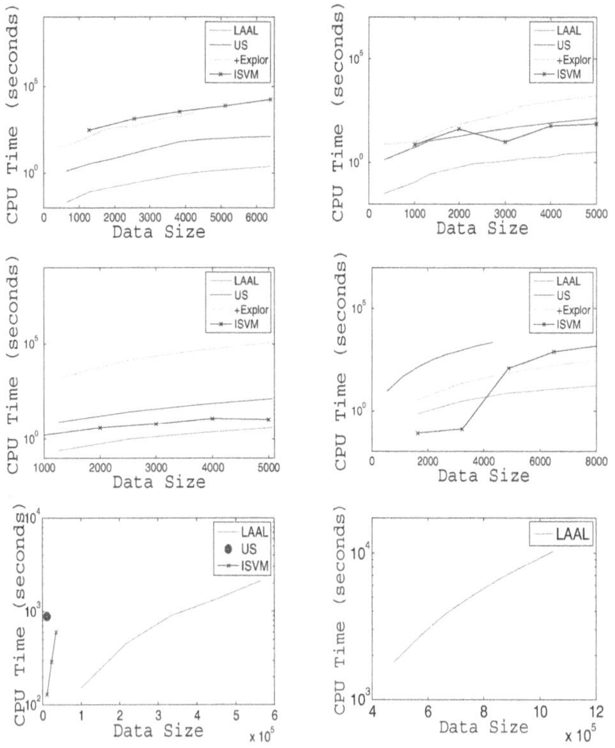

Figure 7: Running time (log-scale) vs. data size. Left to right: XOR and UCI data sets: WAVEFORM, MAGIC, MUSH, COVERTYPE, and SUSY.

6. CONCLUSIONS AND FUTURE WORK

We presented an efficient label diffusion method for active-transductive classification. LAAL demonstrates improved classification results over state-of-the-art active learning algorithms, and a significant reduction of running time. Our approach relies on the combination of classical geometric kernels with label-adapted kernels and on uncertainty sampling for query selection. These properties allow LAAL to efficiently overcome certain challenging situations in active learning such as non-smoothness of the class labeling function over the data distribution. Future work aims at accelerating the iteration process via low rank matrix approximation, an adaptive selection of the σ parameters to adapt to the distance from the nearest class decision boundary, imbalanced class distribution, and batch-mode learning.

7. ACKNOWLEDGMENTS

We thank Dr. Ron Begleiter and Prof. Ran El-Yaniv for the code of '+EXPLORE', and Kun Deng for his contribution of results from [23]. We also thank our anonymous reviewers for their useful comments.

8. REFERENCES

[1] A. Andoni, M. Datar, N. Immorlica, and V. Mirrokni. *Locality-sensitive hashing using stable distributions.* MIT Press, Cambridge, MA, 2006.

[2] K. Bache and M. Lichman. UCI machine learning repository, 2013.

[3] Y. Baram, R. El-Yaniv, and K. Luz. Online choice of active learning algorithms. *JMLR*, 5:255–291, December 2004.

[4] R. Begleiter, R. El-Yaniv, and D. Pechyony. Repairing self-confident active-transductive learners using systematic exploration. *Pattern Recogn. Lett.*, 29(9):1245–1251, July 2008.

[5] M. Belkin, I. Matveeva, and P. Niyogi. Regularization and semi-supervised learning on large graphs. In *COLT*, pages 624–638, 2004.

[6] A. Bondu, V. Lemaire, and B. M. Exploration vs. exploitation in active learning : A bayesian approach. In *IJCNN*, pages 1–7, 2010.

[7] C. Campbell, N. Cristianini, and A. J. Smola. Query learning with large margin classifiers. In *ICML*, pages 111–118, 2000.

[8] O. Chapelle, B. Schlkopf, and A. Zien. *Semi-Supervised Learning.* The MIT Press, 2006.

[9] R. Chattopadhyay, Z. Wang, W. Fan, I. Davidson, S. Panchanathan, and J. Ye. Batch mode active sampling based on marginal probability distribution matching. In *ACM SIGKDD*, pages 741–749, 2012.

[10] F. R. K. Chung. *Spectral Graph Theory.* CBMS Regional Conference Series in Mathematics 92, 1996.

[11] R. R. Coifman, S. Lafon, A. B. Lee, M. Maggioni, B. Nadler, F. Warner, and S. Zucker. Geometric diffusions as a tool for harmonic analysis and structure definition of data: Diffusion maps. *PNAS*, 102(21):7426–7431, June 2005.

[12] I. Dagan and S. P. Engelson. Committee-based sampling for training probabilistic classifiers. In *ICML*, pages 150–157, 1995.

[13] G. Dahlquist and A. Björck. *Numerical Methods.* Courier Dover, 2003.

[14] *Churn prediction tournament*, 2003. http://www.fuqua.duke.edu/centers/ccrm/index.html.

[15] E. J. Friedman. Active learning for smooth problems. In *COLT*, 2009.

[16] J. H. Friedman. Stochastic gradient boosting. *Comput. Stat. Data Anal.*, 38(4):367–378, February 2002.

[17] Q. Gu, C. Aggarwal, J. Liu, and J. Han. Selective sampling on graphs for classification. In *ACM SIGKDD*, pages 131–139, 2013.

[18] Y. Hu, D. Zhang, Z. Jin, D. Cai, and X. He. Active learning via neighborhood reconstruction. In *IJCAI*, pages 1415–1421, 2013.

[19] T. Joachims. Transductive learning via spectral graph partitioning. In *ICML*, pages 290–297, 2003.

[20] D. D. Lewis and W. A. Gale. A sequential algorithm for training text classifiers. In *ACM SIGIR*, pages 3–12, 1994.

[21] A. Y. Ng, M. I. Jordan, and Y. Weiss. On spectral clustering: Analysis and an algorithm. In *NIPS*, pages 849–856, 2001.

[22] H. T. Nguyen and A. Smeulders. Active learning using pre-clustering. In *PICML*, pages 623–630, 2004.

[23] T. Osugi, D. Kun, and S. Scott. Balancing exploration and exploitation: A new algorithm for active machine learning. In *ICDM*, pages 330–337, 2005.

[24] N. Roy and A. McCallum. Toward optimal active learning through sampling estimation of error reduction. In *ICML*, pages 441–448, 2001.

[25] Y. Saad. *Iterative Methods for Sparse Linear Systems.* Addison-Wesley Publishing, Boston, MA, 1996.

[26] A. D. Szlam, M. Maggioni, and R. R. Coifman. Regularization on graphs with function-adapted diffusion processes. *JMLR*, 9:1711–1739, June 2008.

[27] M. Szummer and T. Jaakkola. Partially labeled classification with markov random walks. In *NIPS*, pages 945–952, 2002.

[28] S. Tong and D. Koller. Support vector machine active learning with applications to text classification. *JMLR*, 2:999–1006, November 2001.

[29] X. Wang, R. Garnett, and J. Schneider. Active search on graphs. In *ACM SIGKDD*, pages 731–738, 2013.

[30] Z. Wang and J. Ye. Querying discriminative and representative samples for batch mode active learning. In *ACM SIGKDD*, pages 158–166, 2013.

[31] F. L. Wauthier, N. Jojic, and M. I. Jordan. Active spectral clustering via iterative uncertainty reduction. In *ACM SIGKDD*, pages 1339–1347, 2012.

[32] D. Zhou, O. Bousquet, T. N. Lal, J. Weston, and B. Schölkopf. Learning with local and global consistency. In *NIPS*, pages 321–328, 2003.

[33] X. Zhu and Z. Ghahramani. Learning from labeled and unlabeled data with label propagation. Technical report, Carnegie Melon, 2002.

[34] X. Zhu, Z. Ghahramani, and J. Lafferty. Semi-supervised learning using gaussian fields and harmonic functions. In *ICML*, pages 912–919, 2003.

[35] X. Zhu, J. Lafferty, and Z. Ghahramani. Combining active learning and semi-supervised learning using gaussian fields and harmonic functions. In *ICML 2003 workshop*, pages 58–65, 2003.

APPENDIX

Proof of Theorem 1

PROOF. We start with showing that a Jacobi iteration using an iteration matrix that is built from the *true* bi-class labels (using m_2 in (15)) results in an approximation to the class decision function:

Definition 2. ***The class weight matrix is defined as*** $W^h(x_i, x_j) = \exp\left(\frac{\rho_2(h(x_i),h(x_j))^2}{\sigma_2}\right)$**,** $K^h = (D^h)^{-1}W^h$ ***and*** B^h_J ***are the corresponding kernel and iteration matrix. Finally, the class graph Laplacian is defined as*** $L^h = D^h - W^h$**.**

L^h (and K^h) has similar eigenvectors to those of B^h_J. Let $v_1, ..., v_n$ and $\lambda_1, ..., \lambda_n$ be the set of eigenvectors of B^h_J ordered in the decreasing order of its eigenvalues. We have that a general solution is given by

$$\chi^{(t+1)} = (B^h_J)^t\chi^{(0)} = c_1\lambda_1^t v_1 + ... + c_n\lambda_n^t v_n, \tag{16}$$

where $c_1, ..., c_n$ are coefficients that are prescribed by the initial condition $\chi^{(0)}$: $\chi^{(0)} = c_1v_1 + ... + c_nv_n$. For a large enough t, and since $\forall i\ |\lambda_i| < 1$, we have that the dominant components in $\chi^{(t+1)}$ are the highest eigenvectors v_1 and v_2. v_1 has a constant sign, and the structure of h: it is piecewise constant on the indices belonging to the same class in h. A second component that may be dominant (for sufficiently small t and since c_2 is large because of negative and positive training samples), is v_2. v_2 obeys $v_2 \perp v_1$, and thus approximates a minimal cut in h [10]:

$$MinCut = \min_{h'} \sum_{i,j} W^h_{ij}|h'_i - h'_j|^2. \tag{17}$$

Therefore v_2 is an approximation for the binary function h, and its transition from negative to positive entries is corresponds to the decision boundary. λ_2 corresponds to how well h can be partitioned (the algebraic connectivity of the graph) [10], in particular, if h has a clear partition then λ_2 is close to λ_1. The combination of v_1 and v_2 in (16) forms an approximation to h, since $h' = h$ itself provides the minimum of (17). Clearly, h is partially known and we use instead $\bar{\chi}$ to build up a kernel and the Jacobi iteration process. Since $\bar{\chi}$ is approximates h from training samples and the propagated labels, the same spectral analysis applies for an iteration using $\bar{\chi}$ instead of h.

Now, consider the label-adapted kernel (15) in its matrix representation

$$K^{\bar{\chi}} = (D^{\bar{\chi}})^{-1}(W \cdot W^{\bar{\chi}}), \tag{18}$$

where $W^{\bar{\chi}}$ corresponds to m_2 in (15). The associated energy function is then

$$C(\chi) = \sum_{i,j} W_{ij} \cdot W^{\bar{\chi}}_{ij}|\chi_i - \chi_j|^2. \tag{19}$$

In this case the solution obtained by iterating with $B^{\bar{\chi}}_J$ will have components corresponding to the eigenvectors of $K^{\bar{\chi}}$: a constant sign component $v_1^{\bar{\chi}}$, and a second component $v_2^{\bar{\chi}}$ that reflects a cut in a fused graph constructed from a weight-by-weight multiplication of $W^{\bar{\chi}}_{ij}$ with W_{ij} - the weight of the graph constructed from X. In particular, it will capture a cut that minimizes (19). The cut reflects the data density and geometry as in (4), and, as shown above for W^h the currently approximated hypothesis $h \approx \bar{\chi}$. □

Proof of Theorem 2

PROOF. *Note that i does not include labeled points indices because those are always restarted in our algorithm to Y_l. We need to show that*

$$\exp\left(-\frac{\|x_i - x_j\|^2}{\sigma_1}\right)\exp\left(-\frac{|\hat{\chi}_i - \hat{\chi}_j|^2}{\sigma_2}\right)|\hat{\chi}_i - \hat{\chi}_j|^2$$
$$\leq \exp\left(-\frac{\|x_i - x_j\|^2}{\sigma_1}\right)|\bar{\chi}_i - \bar{\chi}_j|^2.$$

We distinguish between two cases 1. $|\bar{\chi}_i - \bar{\chi}_j| \leq |\hat{\chi}_i - \hat{\chi}_j|$, and 2. $|\hat{\chi}_i - \hat{\chi}_j| \leq |\bar{\chi}_i - \bar{\chi}_j|$.

1. *Since* $0 < |\bar{\chi}_i - \bar{\chi}_j| \leq |\hat{\chi}_i - \hat{\chi}_j| \leq 2$ *we can choose* σ_2 *so that*
$$\exp\left(-\frac{|\hat{\chi}_i - \hat{\chi}_j|^2}{\sigma_2}\right)|\hat{\chi}_i - \hat{\chi}_j|^2 \leq |\bar{\chi}_i - \bar{\chi}_j|^2.$$
Or alternatively we can choose a less tight σ_2 *s.t.*
$$\sum_{j\in l+u} \exp\left(-\frac{|\hat{\chi}_i - \hat{\chi}_j|^2}{\sigma_2}\right)|\hat{\chi}_i - \hat{\chi}_j|^2 \leq \sum_{j\in l+u} |\bar{\chi}_i - \bar{\chi}_j|^2.$$
2. *Since* $\exp\left(-\frac{|\bar{\chi}_i - \bar{\chi}_j|^2}{\sigma_2}\right) \leq 1$ *the result is immediate.*

□

Active Learning for Sparse Bayesian Multilabel Classification

Deepak Vasisht
MIT
deepakv@mit.edu

Andreas Damianou
University of Sheffield, UK
andreas.damianou@sheffield.ac.uk

Manik Varma
Microsoft Research
manik@microsoft.com

Ashish Kapoor
Microsoft Research
akapoor@microsoft.com

ABSTRACT

We study the problem of active learning for multilabel classification. We focus on the real-world scenario where the average number of positive (relevant) labels per data point is small leading to positive label sparsity. Carrying out mutual information based near-optimal active learning in this setting is a challenging task since the computational complexity involved is exponential in the total number of labels. We propose a novel inference algorithm for the sparse Bayesian multilabel model of [17]. The benefit of this alternate inference scheme is that it enables a natural approximation of the mutual information objective. We prove that the approximation leads to an identical solution to the exact optimization problem but at a fraction of the optimization cost. This allows us to carry out efficient, non-myopic, and near-optimal active learning for sparse multilabel classification. Extensive experiments reveal the effectiveness of the method.

Categories and Subject Descriptors

I.2.6 [**Artificial Intelligence**]: Learning

General Terms

Algorithms, Performance, Machine Learning, Optimization

Keywords

Multi-label Learning; Active Learning; Mutual Information

1. INTRODUCTION

The goal in multilabel classification is to learn a classifier which can automatically tag a data point with the most relevant *set* of labels. This is in contrast to multi-class classification where only a single label needs to be predicted per data point. Our objective, in this paper, is to develop an efficient, non-myopic and near-optimal active learning algorithm for multilabel classification employing a mutual information based data point selection criterion.

KDD'14, August 24–27, 2014, New York, NY, USA.

ACM 978-1-4503-2956-9/14/08 ...$15.00.
http://dx.doi.org/10.1145/2623330.2623759 .

There has been much recent interest in sparse multilabel learning [2, 15, 17]. In this scenario, each data point exhibits positive label sparsity in that only a small fraction of any point's labels are ever marked as positive or relevant. Note that this is a typical setting in most real world applications – the average number of positive labels per data point ranges from less than 5% on most UCI data sets to less than 0.001% on Wikipedia and other web data sets [2]. Sparse multilabel learning therefore presents an important, real-world and novel challenge to active learning techniques.

Traditional active learning techniques for multilabel learning do not take positive label sparsity into account [11, 13, 20,21,31]. Furthermore, these techniques are myopic and actively select only a single data point at a time for annotation. As a result, there is no provable guarantee that the final set of annotated points is optimal or even near-optimal. While mutual information based data sampling can provide near-optimal guarantees in certain regression settings [18,19], it is non-trivial to extend those to the active multilabel setting.

In this paper, we first develop an alternate inference technique for the sparse Bayesian multi-label graphical model of [17] which allows us to carry out efficient mutual information based active learning. We develop an approximation to the mutual information which is tightly coupled to our inference algorithm and which can be optimized much more efficiently than the exact mutual information. This approximation allows us to develop an active learning strategy that has the following desirable properties:

- The set of annotated points selected by our algorithm is provably near optimal.
- The selection of annotated points can be done in time independent of the size of the label space if all labels of the point are to be annotated, as opposed to the existing methods which scale linearly (at best) with the number of labels.
- The train and test times are considerably reduced due to the reduction of the label vector to a low dimensional space using a compressed sensing matrix.
- The method can be easily adapted to be integrated with different compressed sensing approaches in literature [3, 5, 8, 10, 12, 15–17, 28, 29, 32, 33].
- The method takes into account label sparsity which has been proven to be a desirable characteristic in past work on multilabel classification [2, 15, 17].

- The method allows us to generalize to other active learning scenarios like active diagnosis (selecting which labels to annotate for a point) and generalized active learning (selecting both the points and the labels to annotate).

Our main technical contribution is Theorem 1 where we prove that, at any given data point selection step, our approximation leads to an *identical* solution as would have been obtained using exact mutual information in the limiting case, but at a fraction of the optimization cost. Furthermore, by performing inference in a sparse Gaussian Process regression model, we can leverage the mutual information guarantees to provably show that the entire subset of data points selected for annotation by our proposed algorithm is near-optimal. This enables us to carry out active sparse multilabel learning in an efficient, non-myopic and theoretically principled fashion. Finally, as a natural extension of our method, the matrix inversions necessary for traditional active learning can be carried out in time that is independent of the size of the label vector for a point.

Extensive experiments reveal that our proposed active learning strategy consistently outperforms the state-of-the-art approaches based on variance sampling, SVM based active learning proposed in [20] and random sampling baselines. Furthermore, we demonstrate that our inference procedure leads to a better estimate of the variance needed for Bayesian active learning as compared to existing techniques. We also show that our method has significant gains (20 times gain over the `delicious` dataset with 983 labels) in time consumption over the state-of-the-art [20] as the number of labels increases. Finally, we demonstrate that our proposed approach can also be used to sample both labels as well as data points, thereby allowing learning at an even lower annotation cost as compared to existing techniques which have so far focussed on all the labels being annotated for a selected data point.

Our main contributions are as follows: (a) a novel inference procedure for the Bayesian sparse multilabel graphical model of [17]; (b) an approximation to the mutual information which follows naturally from our proposed inference procedure; (c) a proof that our proposed approximation selects the same data point as would have been chosen by optimizing mutual information (in the limiting case); and (d) an extensive evaluation of the proposed scheme on a diverse range of real world datasets to prove the gains obtained by our algorithm. These contributions allow us to carry out efficient mutual information based active sparse multilabel learning for the first time (to the best of our knowledge).

2. RELATED WORK

Past work in active learning has primarily focused on single label classification tasks [24]. However, multilabel classification has received wide interest in recent times [2,3,5,8, 10,12,15–17,28–30,32,33]. Active learning is more advantageous in this setting as label acquisition costs are higher for multilabel scenario. However, research in active learning for multilabel classification is still in its preliminary stage. Current multilabel active learning strategies train a binary SVM classifier for each label and combine the SVM margins using different heuristics to select the training set from a pool of available data for annotation [11, 21, 27]. [27] takes the average of the SVM uncertainties obtained by Platt scaling [23] and uses it as a selection criterion for greedily selecting the set of points to be annotated. [21] uses Mean Max Loss(MML) and Max Loss(ML) as two separate selection criteria for annotation of points. [31] uses logistic regression to predict the number of positive labels for each point and uses another SVM based heuristic to minimize expected loss for point selection. The state-of-the-art method [20] uses a combination of deviation from mean label cardinality and an SVM-based loss function for active learning. To the best of our knowledge, all these works are myopic and do not provide any theoretical guarantees on the optimality of the selected set.

On the other hand, mutual information has proved to be a very useful criterion for active learning with Gaussian Processes [18,19,26], both empirically and theoretically. In these schemes, each point is selected from a pool of available unlabeled data, so as to maximize the information gain over the remaining unlabeled data. The approximate submodularity of mutual information ensures that a set of points selected greedily based on this criterion will be near-optimal [19]. However, extending mutual information to multilabel classification is non-trivial as a straightforward computation of mutual information over the label space is exponential in the number of labels.

The Bayesian compressed sensing model proposed in [17] is closest to our work, in the sense that it models the multilabel classification task as a Gaussian Process. However, the approximations made in [17], for the inference procedure to be tractable, do not preserve the covariance matrix across labels and hence, render mutual information based active learning infeasible. The inference procedure proposed in section 4, however, preserves this covariance matrix and allows for efficient mutual information based active learning.

3. BACKGROUND

Our work builds upon a recently proposed Bayesian architecture for multilabel classification [17]. We briefly summarize this framework here. Given a set of N data points $\mathbf{X} = \{\mathbf{x}_i\}$ and the corresponding sparse l-dimensional binary label vectors $\mathbf{Y} = \{\mathbf{y}_i\}$, the key idea was to first reduce the classification task to a lower multidimensional regression task via a random projection matrix $\mathbf{\Phi}$, and then during test time, infer the labels for an unseen point via approximate Bayesian inference.

Specifically, a factor graph corresponding to the model consists of three potential functions: (1) the first potential term $f_{\mathbf{x}_i}(\mathbf{W}, \mathbf{z}_i) = \exp[-\frac{||\mathbf{W}^T\mathbf{x}_i - \mathbf{z}_i||^2}{2\sigma^2}]$ defines a regression function from each input point $\mathbf{x}_i$ to the k-dimensional latent variable $\mathbf{z}_i$ via $\mathbf{W}$. (2) The second potential term $g_{\mathbf{\Phi}}(\mathbf{y}_i, \mathbf{z}_i) = \exp[-\frac{||\mathbf{\Phi}\mathbf{y}_i - \mathbf{z}_i||^2}{2\chi^2}]$ corresponds to the transformation of l-dimensional labels $\mathbf{y}_i$ to the real-valued compressed space $\mathbf{z}_i$ via a $k \times l$, where $k \ll l$, random projection matrix $\mathbf{\Phi}$. (3) Finally, the third potential $h_{\boldsymbol{\alpha}_i}(\mathbf{y}_i) = \prod_{j=1}^{l} N(y_i^j; 0, \frac{1}{\alpha_i^j})$ enforces label sparsity by introducing a zero mean-Gaussian prior on each of the labels with precision α_i^j, which in turn are Gamma distributed. Formally, the joint probability distribution takes the following form:

$$p(\mathbf{Y}, \mathbf{Z}, \mathbf{W}, [\boldsymbol{\alpha}_i]_{i=1}^N | \mathbf{X}, \mathbf{\Phi})$$
$$= \frac{1}{Z} p(\mathbf{W}) \prod_{i=1}^{N} f_{\mathbf{x}_i}(\mathbf{w}, \mathbf{z}_i) g_{\mathbf{\Phi}}(\mathbf{y}_i, \mathbf{z}_i) h_{\boldsymbol{\alpha}_i}(\mathbf{y}_i) p(\boldsymbol{\alpha}_i). \quad (1)$$

Here, Z is the partition function (normalization term), $p(\mathbf{W}) = \prod_{i=1}^{K} N(\mathbf{w}_i, 0, I)$ is the spherical Gaussian prior on the linear regression functions, and $p(\boldsymbol{\alpha}_i) = \prod_{j=1}^{L} \Gamma(\alpha_i^j; a_0, b_0)$ is the product of Gamma priors on each individual label. Intuitively, the function $f_{\mathbf{x}_i}$ aligns the latent variable $\mathbf{z}_i$ with the output of the linear regression functions, and the function $g_{\boldsymbol{\Phi}}$ favors compatibility with the compressed label vector corresponding to $\mathbf{y}_i$. Finally, $h_{\boldsymbol{\alpha}_i}$ enforces sparsity over the labels.

Using $\mathbf{Y}_{\mathcal{L}}$ to denote labeled instances, inferring the exact posterior $P(\mathbf{Y}_{\mathcal{U}} \mid \mathbf{Y}_{\mathcal{L}}, \mathbf{X}, \boldsymbol{\Phi})$ over labels $\mathbf{Y}_{\mathcal{U}}$ for test points $\mathbf{X}_{\mathcal{U}}$ is prohibitive due to the product of Gaussian and non-Gaussian terms in the joint distribution. The approach in [17] resorts to variational inference by approximating the posterior over $\mathbf{Y}_{\mathcal{U}}$ as a Gaussian distribution. While this showed good performance in terms of classification accuracy, there is a significant disadvantage of using the same inference procedure for active learning tasks. The derived variational inference equations lead to loss in information about the variances between updates across the different layers of the graphical model. Specifically, the procedure approximates the posterior over $\mathbf{y}_i$ as a Gaussian, but the variance of the random variable $\mathbf{y}_i$ is completely independent of the variance of the random variable $\mathbf{z}_i$. Similarly, the variance of $\mathbf{z}_i$ is in turn independent of the variance of the random variable $\mathbf{W}$. The variance related to the Gaussian random variables is central to the use of mutual information in selective sampling tasks; hence, with the given inference procedure, mutual information cannot be optimally used as an active learning strategy.

4. OUR APPROACH

There are two key ingredients to our framework: first is an alternate approximate inference scheme that preserves variances due to the regression part of the graphical model. Given this inference scheme, the second part focuses on deriving an efficient near-optimal selective sampling strategy.

4.1 An Alternate Inference Procedure

Our goal here is to derive an inference scheme that would preserve the variances of the latent random variables and propagate correct uncertainties to $\mathbf{Y}$, thereby enabling an effective active learning strategy. The key observation here is the fact that such variances can in fact be preserved if instead of directly applying variational approximation, we first analytically integrate out the latent variables $\mathbf{Z}$ and $\mathbf{W}$ from the joint distribution (Eq. 1). Such analytic integration is feasible due to the form of potential functions $f_{\mathbf{x}_i}, g_{\boldsymbol{\Phi}}$ and the Gaussian Process prior $p(\mathbf{W})$. This results in a joint distribution over $\mathbf{Y}$ and $\boldsymbol{\alpha}$ that is a product of a Gaussian and a Gamma distribution. Formally,

$$p(\mathbf{Y}, [\boldsymbol{\alpha}_i]_{i=1}^N|\mathbf{X}, \boldsymbol{\Phi}) = \int_{\mathbf{Z},\mathbf{W}} p(\mathbf{Y}, \mathbf{Z}, \mathbf{W}, [\boldsymbol{\alpha}_i]_{i=1}^N|\mathbf{X}, \boldsymbol{\Phi})$$
$$= \frac{1}{Z} e^{\frac{\mathbf{Y}^T \boldsymbol{\Sigma}_{\mathbf{Y}}^{-1} \mathbf{Y}}{2}} \prod_{i=1}^{N} h_{\boldsymbol{\alpha}_i}(\mathbf{y}_i) p(\boldsymbol{\alpha}_i).$$

Here the label vector $\mathbf{Y}$ is an Nl-dimensional vector obtained by appending all l-dimensional $\mathbf{y}_i's$ one after the other. Similarly, $\mathbf{Z}$ is an Nk-dimensional vector resulting from stacking all k-dimensional $\mathbf{z}_i's$. Further, the term $\boldsymbol{\Sigma}_{\mathbf{Y}}$ takes the following form:

$$\boldsymbol{\Sigma}_{\mathbf{Y}}{}^{-1} = \tilde{\boldsymbol{\Phi}}^T (\boldsymbol{\Sigma}_{\mathbf{Z}} + \chi^2 \mathbf{I})^{-1} \tilde{\boldsymbol{\Phi}} \quad (2)$$

$$\text{where } \boldsymbol{\Sigma}_{\mathbf{Z}} = \begin{pmatrix} K_{11}\mathbf{I}_k & K_{12}\mathbf{I}_k & . & K_{1N}\mathbf{I}_k \\ K_{21}\mathbf{I}_k & K_{22}\mathbf{I}_k & . & K_{2N}\mathbf{I}_k \\ . & . & . & . \\ K_{N1}\mathbf{I}_k & K_{N2}\mathbf{I}_k & . & K_{NN}\mathbf{I}_k \end{pmatrix} \quad (3)$$

Here, the $Nk \times Nk$-dimensional matrix $\boldsymbol{\Sigma}_{\mathbf{Z}}$ is a special block matrix, where K_{ij} is the ith row and j^{th} column entry of $\mathbf{K} = (\mathbf{X}^T\mathbf{X} + \sigma^2\mathbf{I})^1$ and $\mathbf{I}_k$ is the $k \times k$ identity matrix. Finally, $\tilde{\boldsymbol{\Phi}}$ is another $Nk \times Nl$ block diagonal matrix with all the N diagonal entries set to $\boldsymbol{\Phi}$. Further, we'd like to explicitly point out that the matrix $\boldsymbol{\Sigma}_{\mathbf{Y}}{}^{-1}$ is a precision matrix and is not full-rank. Note that such non-invertible precision matrices are in-line with use of improper un-normalizable Gaussian distributions in Bayesian inference [9, 34] and do not pose any theoretical or practical problems.

The above mentioned marginalization preserves all the information about uncertainty due to the Gaussian Process regression part of the graphical model and is succinctly represented in the term $\boldsymbol{\Sigma}_{\mathbf{Y}}$. We propose to use variational inference and obtain an approximate posterior distribution over the label matrix $\mathbf{Y}$ that is a product of Gaussian terms and the corresponding Gamma terms over $\boldsymbol{\alpha}$. If we denote the approximation at the tth iteration as $q^t(\mathbf{Y}) = N(\boldsymbol{\mu}_{\mathbf{Y}}^t, \boldsymbol{\Sigma}_{\mathbf{Y}}^t)$ and $q^t([\boldsymbol{\alpha}]) = \prod_i \Gamma(a_i^t, b_i^t)$, the resulting update rules are as following:

$$\text{Update for } q^{t+1}(\mathbf{Y}): \ \boldsymbol{\Sigma}_{\mathbf{Y}}^{t+1} = [\text{diag}(\mathbb{E}(\boldsymbol{\alpha}^t)) + \boldsymbol{\Sigma}_{\mathbf{Y}}^{-1}]^{-1}$$
$$\text{Update for } q^{t+1}(\alpha^i): \ a_i^{t+1} = a_i^0 + 0.5,$$
$$b_i^{t+1} = b_i^0 + 0.5[\boldsymbol{\Sigma}^{t+1}(i,i)]$$

Given observed labels and $q(\mathbf{Y})$, the posterior distribution $q(\mathbf{Y}_{\mathcal{U}})$ over unobserved labels is simply the conditional Gaussian distribution obtained by using standard Gaussian identities. We'd like to point out that unlike the previous approach [17], the cross co-variances across all the labels for all the points are preserved in $\boldsymbol{\Sigma}_{\mathbf{Y}}^{-1}$. Further note that this algorithm results in the final variance over the label vectors in terms of the kernel function over the input features $\mathbf{X}$. This is a direct consequence of the fact that uncertainty from the regression part of the network has already been propagated to $\mathbf{Y}$ and sets a basis for an active learning scheme that is effective.

Selecting Hyperparameters a_0 and b_o: The choice of the hyperparameters a_0 and b_0 is critical to induce sparsity, as arbitrary assignments can lead to non-sparse solutions. To see this, consider the joint distribution $p(\mathbf{Y}, [\boldsymbol{\alpha}_i]_{i=1}^N|\mathbf{X}, \boldsymbol{\Phi})$ and analytically marginalize over $[\boldsymbol{\alpha}_i]_{i=1}^N$. This results in a distribution of the following form:

$$\int_{[\boldsymbol{\alpha}_i]_{i=1}^N} p(\mathbf{Y}, [\boldsymbol{\alpha}_i]_{i=1}^N|\mathbf{X}, \boldsymbol{\Phi})$$
$$= e^{-\frac{\mathbf{Y}^T \boldsymbol{\Sigma}_{\mathbf{Y}}^{-1} \mathbf{Y}}{2}} \prod_{i=1}^{N} \prod_{j=1}^{l} (1 + \frac{y_{ij}^2}{2b_0})^{-a_0}. \quad (4)$$

The above marginalization leads to a very intuitive interpretation where the term $\boldsymbol{\Sigma}_{\mathbf{Y}}{}^{-1}$ arises due to the regression part

[1]Extension to non-linear kernel is straightforward by replacing $\mathbf{X}^T\mathbf{X}$ with an appropriate kernel function.

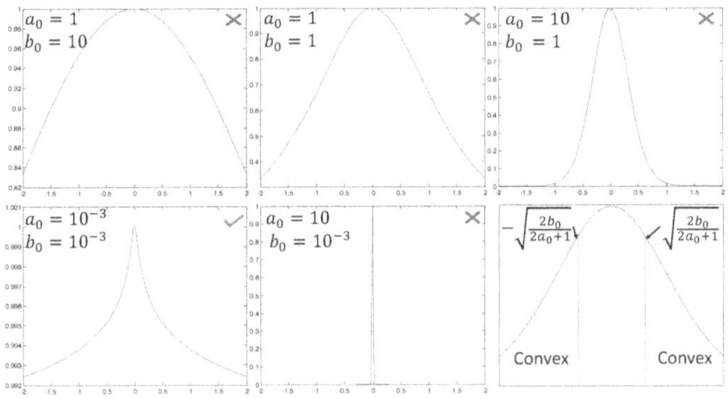

Figure 1: Plot of the sparsity inducing prior term $(1+\frac{y^2}{2b_0})^{-a_0}$ for different values of a_0 and b_0. The desirable shape of the prior term is shown in bottom-left corner (indicated by a green ✓) and occurs when a_0 and b_0 are set to 10^{-3} . The bottom-right figure characterizes the shape as a function of a_0 and b_0 and highlights that the shape is undesirably concave when $-\sqrt{\frac{2b_0}{2a_0+1}} < y < \sqrt{\frac{2b_0}{2a_0+1}}$.

of the framework and the terms $(1+\frac{y_{ij}^2}{2b_0})^{-a_0}$ induce the sparsity in the solution. Note that in the sparsity term, higher values of y_{ij} lead to a lower value of the potential, thereby penalizing non-zero instantiations. However, the shape of the penalty term critically depends upon the values of a_0 and b_0. Figure 1 plots these penalty prior functions for different values of a_0 and b_0. Figure 1 shows several shapes corresponding to different hyperparameter settings. Most of the shapes shown in the figure are undesirable for inducing sparsity due to their non-convexity localized around a large range near zero (highlighted by a red ×). The bottom-right panel on the other hand shows what a desirable penalty function should look like ($a_0 = b_0 = 10^{-3}$) (denoted by a green ✓).

The bottom-right subpanel in figure 1 characterizes the shape of the function in terms of the hyperparameters. In particular, the function can decomposed into three regions: (1) $y < -\sqrt{\frac{2b_0}{2a_0+1}}$, (2) $y > \sqrt{\frac{2b_0}{2a_0+1}}$, and (3) $-\sqrt{\frac{2b_0}{2a_0+1}} < y < \sqrt{\frac{2b_0}{2a_0+1}}$. It is straightforward to show that the second derivative of the function will always be greater than zero for region (1) and (2), thereby implying a nice locally convex behavior leading to a desirable shape of the penalty function. The region (3) on the other hand has the second derivative less than zero, thus leading to a shape with a flatter penalty structure. Consequently, in order to induce an appropriate sparsity inducing prior it is desirable to minimize the range where region (3) occurs. This is achieved when either a_0 takes a very high value or when b_0 tends to zero. However, setting a_0 to a high value will result in a very peaky penalty function (see figure 1 bottom-middle panel). A peaky penalty function is undesirable as it will override the potential arising due to the regression term in the overall mutilabel framework. Thus, a desirable prior can only be achieved when we select a very small value for both a_0 and b_0. It is no surprise that in prior research on Bayesian compressed sensing [6, 17, 25], a_0 and b_0 were set to very small values. Our analysis above validates such choices in order to incorporate a reasonable sparsity inducing prior. This observation about requiring a_0 and b_0 to be close to zero will be critical in the next section where we discuss non-myopic active learning.

4.2 Non-Myopic Selective Sampling

The goal of active learning is to select a set of points $\mathcal{A}$ to label from the available pool of unlabeled data $\mathcal{U}$ under budget constraints, $|\mathcal{A}| = n$, such that the resulting classifier is most accurate. Intuitively, we want to sample the n most informative points with respect to the classification task. Two potential criteria for the task are entropy and mutual information. Selecting points with maximum entropy boils down to choosing a set of points that jointly have the maximum uncertainty on their labels. The mutual information criterion [7], on the other hand, chooses $\mathcal{A}$ so that the uncertainty over the labels of remaining points is maximally reduced after the labels of $\mathcal{A}$ are incorporated in the predictive model.

The mutual information based criterion is the best of the two heuristics as the entropy criterion tends to select points that are far apart from each other in the feature space and hence ends up selecting points on the boundary. Since a point usually provides information about points in its nearby region, selecting points on the boundary wastes information gathering effort. In this paper, we present results in the context of mutual information as a criterion. Formally, if $H(\cdot)$ denotes the entropy, then we write the non-myopic subset selection problem as:

$$\mathcal{A}^* = \underset{\mathcal{A}\subseteq\mathcal{U},|\mathcal{A}|=n}{\arg\max}\ H(\mathbf{Y}_{\mathcal{U}\setminus\mathcal{A}}) - H(\mathbf{Y}_{\mathcal{U}\setminus\mathcal{A}}|\mathbf{Y}_{\mathcal{A}}). \quad (5)$$

We call this problem non-myopic due to the fact that the goal is to reason about the entire set $\mathcal{A}$ at once. This is different from the other schemes for active classification where a single point is chosen for querying a label, the model updated after observing the label and the process repeated for a total of n rounds. This non-myopic subset selection problem is NP-complete as shown below:

PROPOSITION 1. *The subset selection problem defined in equation 5 is NP-complete for the density* $p(\mathbf{Y}, [\boldsymbol{\alpha}_i]_{i=1}^N|\mathbf{X}, \boldsymbol{\Phi})$.

This proposition can easily be established by observing that, when the random variables $\boldsymbol{\alpha}$ are completely observed, the distribution reduces to the form of a multivariate Gaussian density. The proof simply follows from the fact that the subset selection problem for mutual information criterion has been previously shown to be NP-complete [19]. □

Given the hardness of this problem, we resort to a greedy approximation algorithm following recent ideas in submodular optimization. Specifically, if we can show that the objective (eq. 5) being optimized is submodular and non-decreasing, then we can derive a greedy strategy that sequentially selects data points based on marginal improvement of the objective. Note that the mutual information criterion is not submodular in general, but under some weak conditions, both submodularity and its non-decreasing property can be established. Formally, [18] have proved the following proposition for random variables $\mathcal{S}$ and $\mathcal{U}$ in a graphical model:

PROPOSITION 2. **[18]** *Let $\mathcal{S}$, $\mathcal{U}$ be disjoint subsets of random variables such that the variables in $\mathcal{S}$ are independent given $\mathcal{U}$. Let information gain be* $F(\mathcal{A}) = H(\mathcal{U}) -$

$H(\mathcal{U}\backslash\mathcal{A}|\mathcal{A})$, *where* $\mathcal{A} \subseteq \mathcal{U}$. *Then* F *is submodular and non-decreasing on* $\mathcal{U}$, *and* $F(\emptyset) = 0$.

The following observation identifies the graphical model corresponding to the joint distribution $p(\mathbf{Y}, [\boldsymbol{\alpha}_i]_{i=1}^N|\mathbf{X}, \boldsymbol{\Phi})$ as a special case of the above, thus establishing the submodularity and non-decreasing characteristic of our objective function.

COROLLARY 1. *Let* $\mathcal{S} = [\boldsymbol{\alpha}]_{i=1}^n$ *and* $\mathcal{U} = \mathbf{Y}_\mathcal{U}$, *then due to the form of* $h_{\boldsymbol{\alpha}_i}$ *and* $p(\boldsymbol{\alpha}_i)$, *we have* $[\boldsymbol{\alpha}_i]_{i=1}^N$ *independent given* $\mathbf{Y}_\mathcal{U}$. *Consequently, the objective in equation 5 is submodular and non-decreasing.* □

Given this observation, we can now propose a greedy algorithm that repeatedly picks the points with the highest increase in mutual information and adds them to the subset $\mathcal{A}$. The point $x^* \in \mathcal{U}$ selected to be added to the subset $\mathcal{A}$ is such that $x^* = \arg\max_x(MI(\mathcal{A} \cup x) - MI(\mathcal{A}))$. Here, $MI(\mathcal{A}) = H(\mathbf{Y}_{\mathcal{U}\backslash\mathcal{A}}) - H(\mathbf{Y}_{\mathcal{U}\backslash\mathcal{A}}|\mathbf{Y}_\mathcal{A})$ and it has been proved earlier that this algorithm selects the subset $\mathcal{A}^*$ such that the value of the objective function will at least be $(1 - \frac{1}{e})$ times the optimal solution [19, 22].

While the above mentioned corollary shows the existence of a greedy algorithm that has a good approximation guarantee, it is still non-trivial to compute the mutual information $MI(\mathcal{A})$ for the multilabel classification model. Specifically, in order to compute mutual information, we need to solve exact inference, which itself is non-trivial in our model. Here also, in order to derive an implementable solution, we need to establish a similar approximation $\hat{MI}$ to mutual information such that that the set of selected points $\mathcal{A}^*$ does not change when the approximated mutual information is used instead of the exact one. Formally, we prove the following theorem which in turn will imply that such an approximation is feasible:

Theorem 1. *Let* $\hat{MI}$ *denote the mutual information of any set* $\mathcal{A}$ *computed over the probability distribution,* $p(\mathbf{Y}) \propto \exp[\mathbf{Y}^T\boldsymbol{\Sigma}_\mathbf{Y}^{-1}\mathbf{Y}/2]$, *where* $\boldsymbol{\Sigma}_\mathbf{Y}^{-1}$ *is as defined in eq. 3, then for any* $x \in \mathcal{U}$:

$$\lim_{\substack{a_0\to 0\\ b_0\to 0}} MI(\mathcal{A}\cup x) - MI(\mathcal{A}) = \hat{MI}(\mathcal{A}\cup x) - \hat{MI}(\mathcal{A}).$$

Proof Sketch: To prove this theorem, we first use the fact that $MI(\mathcal{A} \cup x) - MI(\mathcal{A})$ can be written as $H(x|\mathcal{A}) - H(x|\mathcal{U}\backslash x)$ [19]. Next, we consider the joint distribution over $\mathbf{Y}$ given in eq. (4) that arises after analytically marginalizing over $[\boldsymbol{\alpha}_i]_{i=1}^N$. It is easy to show that given $\mathcal{A}$, the conditional predictive distribution of x takes a similar form:

$$p(x|\mathcal{A}) \propto \exp[-\frac{(x - m_\mathcal{A})^2}{2\sigma_\mathcal{A}^2}](1 + \frac{x^2}{2b_0})^{-a_0}$$

$$\text{where: } m_\mathcal{A} = \boldsymbol{\Sigma}_{x,\mathcal{A}}\boldsymbol{\Sigma}_{\mathcal{A},\mathcal{A}}^{-1}\mathbf{Y}_\mathcal{A}$$

$$\sigma_\mathcal{A}^2 = \boldsymbol{\Sigma}_{x,x} - \boldsymbol{\Sigma}_{x,\mathcal{A}}\boldsymbol{\Sigma}_{\mathcal{A},\mathcal{A}}^{-1}\boldsymbol{\Sigma}_{\mathcal{A},x}$$

The above reduction follows from simple algebraic manipulation where the terms corresponding to the set $\mathcal{A}$ are collected by using matrix inversion lemma. A similar form also can be derived for the conditional predictive distribution of x given $\mathcal{U}\backslash x$. Let us denote the conditional entropy of x given $\mathcal{A}$ computed via the Gaussian distribution as $\hat{H}(x|\mathcal{A})$. The proof then follows from the fact that $\lim_{\substack{a_0\to 0\\ b_0\to 0}} H(x|\mathcal{A}) = \hat{H}(x|\mathcal{A})$ (similarly for $H(x|\mathcal{U}\backslash x)$). Proof for the above statement is provided in appendix A. □

The implication of the above theorem is that the greedy selection strategy described above will yield nearly the same subset when $\hat{MI}$ is used instead of the true mutual information, as a_0 and b_0 are set to very small values in our algorithm. This is due to the fact that the greedy procedure seeks to include x such that $(MI(\mathcal{A} \cup x) - MI(\mathcal{A}))$ is maximized at each step and the above theorem guarantees that the order of selecting the points will not change when MI is replaced by $\hat{MI}$. This result enables us to derive an algorithm based on the approximate inference procedure described earlier in the paper. Note that the $\hat{MI}$ is defined over a Gaussian Process; thus, prior work [19] on near-optimal selective sampling can be directly applied here. Also, note that the discussion above only focuses where the Gaussian term has a zero mean for clarity purposes. It is fairly straightforward to extend the analysis to non-zero mean cases.

One of the surprising by-products of our result is the fact that, similar to Gaussian Process regression models, the observed labels do not affect the order in which the points should be selected, which in turn allows us to do non-myopic selection of points. Intuitively this is feasible by realizing that the mapping of the discrete label vectors to the continuous space via the matrix $\boldsymbol{\Phi}$ is almost 1-to-1 [15]. So, any subset selection via Gaussian Process regression on the continuous space, which is independent of observations, automatically transfers to the discrete labeled space. We wish to point out explicitly that $\boldsymbol{\Sigma}_\mathbf{Y}^{-1}$ is not full-rank; however, the computation over Gaussian mutual information is still feasible in such cases [14].

The proposed compressed sensing framework compresses the information about the labels, $\mathbf{Y}$ into the compressed space, $\mathbf{Z}$ and then couples the $\mathbf{Z}$ in a single covariance matrix, hence allowing us to do mutual information based active learning in time that is independent of the number of labels. The compressed sensing formulation also enables us to train lesser number of classifiers for the training process and reduce the training time significantly. Finally, note that the mutual information computation need not be done from scratch after each iteration of the active learner. We use lazy evaluations proposed in [19] to drastically reduce the computational cost for selection of subsequent points to be annotated.

5. ACTIVE LEARNING

It is interesting to note that selective sampling via $\hat{MI}$ can accommodate many different scenarios of selective sampling. The most popular setting in literature considers revealing all the labels for selected data points. Alternatively, in active diagnosis, different labels can be probed for one particular test case only. Finally, in the most general case, individual labels from different input points can be selected (generalized active learning).

5.1 Traditional Active Learning

In traditional active learning, we select a subset of points from the available data points for which all labels are revealed. Ideally, the goal is to choose a subset of size n that leads to maximum decrease in entropy over the remaining unlabeled points as described in equation 5. However, proposition 2 and corollary 1 allow us to greedily select points to be annotated so as to maximize the mutual information at each step. Algorithm 1 shows the outline of the method that allows efficient sampling of points based

Algorithm 1 Mutual information based active learning over the compressed space

Input: Input features $\mathcal{X}$ and budget n
Output: $\mathcal{A}$: The set of points to be labeled
  Compute $\mathbf{C} = \mathbf{\Sigma_Z} + \chi^2\mathbf{I}$ using $\mathbf{\Sigma_Z}$ defined in eq. 3
  $\mathcal{A} \leftarrow \phi$
  for $i \leftarrow 1$ to n **do**
    for $x \in \mathcal{X}\backslash\mathcal{A}$ **do**
      $\delta_x \leftarrow \frac{|\mathbf{C}(x,x)-\mathbf{C}(x,\mathcal{A})\mathbf{C}(\mathcal{A},\mathcal{A})^{-1}\mathbf{C}(\mathcal{A},x)|}{|\mathbf{C}(x,x)-\mathbf{C}(x,\mathcal{A})\mathbf{C}(\mathcal{A},\mathcal{A})^{-1}\mathbf{C}(\mathcal{A},x)|}$
    end
    $x_* \leftarrow \arg\max_x \delta_x$
    $\mathcal{A} \leftarrow \mathcal{A} \cup x^*$
  end

on mutual information. Note that, for this case, when all the labels are revealed per data point, we can be far more efficient in computation by directly using the Kernel matrix defined over the points alone.

5.2 Active Diagnosis

Such an active learning scenario is more specific to multilabel active learning, where obtaining each label for a point has significant cost associated with it. For example, in industrial or medical settings, where each label may be obtained as a result of an expensive test, it is wiser to select the labels which you want to be annotated for a selected point to decrease the overall cost, as opposed to annotating all the labels. If we denote the label vector as $\mathbf{y} = \{y_1, y_2, y_3, ...y_l\}$, then the active diagnosis problem is to select a subset of labels, $l' \subset \{1, 2, ...l\}$, which need to be annotated. This scenario can be easily handled by our model as we obtain the complete covariance matrix over the labels and the mutual information criterion $\hat{MI}$ treats each label independently. We can follow a greedy algorithm similar to the one followed in algorithm 1 to sample labels, wherein at each step, we select the label with index, $i = \arg\max_{i \in \mathcal{U}} \hat{MI}(\mathbf{y}_{\mathcal{L} \cup i}) - \hat{MI}(\mathbf{y}_{\mathcal{L}})$ to be labeled, where $\mathcal{U}$ and $\mathcal{L}$ denote the unlabeled and labeled indices respectively, as before. We present evaluation of our scheme for active diagnosis in the results section.

5.3 Generalized Active Learning

A combination of the above active learning scenarios leads to a general active learning problem, wherein the goal is to select both the points and the labels to be annotated within a given active learning budget. Given the budget to obtain n annotations, we select n document-label pairs from the set of pairs $\{(1,1), (1,2), ..., (N,l)\}$, where N is the number of documents with l labels each. To achieve this objective, we consider the information gain computed using $\hat{MI}$ obtained over the complete label matrix $\mathbf{Y}$. Once again, we use the greedy strategy to pick each pair. However, computing this metric over the entire space of document-label pairs is expensive and we resort to a two-way approach, wherein we first select the document to be annotated based on algorithm 1 and then select, the label to be revealed similar to active diagnosis. Note that, both active diagnosis and generalized active learning are novel active learning scenarios which are specific to the multilabel classification problem and can't be handled by SVM based state-of-the-art methods.

6. RESULTS

In this section, we present empirical results to demonstrate a) how the proposed approximate inference procedure compares to the prior work [17](denoted as BML-CS) in terms of accuracy as well as the capability to estimate variances, b) the comparison of mutual information based sampling with the state-of-the-art SVM based active learning method proposed in [20], uncertainity sampling and random sampling baselines, and c) performance of the method on novel active learning scenarios like active diagnosis and generalized active learning which are specific to multilabel classification.

6.1 Setup

Datasets: We used the datasets listed in Table 1 to evaluate our algorithm. As can be seen from the table, the datasets exhibit a wide range in type, feature vector size and label vector size. For each of the datasets, 4000 randomly sampled points were used as the active learning pool from which points had to be selected for training based on the different active learning strategies compared. Another set of 2000 points was used as the test data. For datasets with fewer than 6000 points (`enron`, `medical`, `MSRC` and `yeast`), the entire set was selected as the active learning pool and testing was done on the points not selected for training. All the results are reported after averaging over 5 such splits. For all the methods, an initial seed of 500 randomly sampled points was provided to the algorithms to start with (50 points, in case of `MSRC`, and 200, in case of `enron`, `medical` and `yeast`), as has been done in standard active learning literature. For all our experiments, we used features downloaded from the Mulan multilabel datasets [1]. For `MSRC`, we used 1024 bit features generated using the Picodes scheme [4].

Table 1: Datasets Used for Experiments

Dataset	Type	Instances	Features	Labels
Yeast	Biology	2417	103	14
MSRC	Image	591	1024	23
Medical	Text	978	1449	45
Enron	Text	1702	1001	53
Mediamill	Video	43907	120	101
RCV1	Text	6000	47236	101
Bookmarks	Text	87856	2150	208
Delicious	Text	16105	500	983

Baselines We compare the following methods for the evaluation of the proposed active learning strategy:

- **MIML**: Mutual Information for Multilabel classification as proposed in this paper
- **Uncert**: Uncertainty sampling on the model proposed in this paper. This method picks the point with the highest entropy after each iteration.
- **Rand**: Random sampling baseline wherein each point is randomly sampled.
- **Li-Adaptive:** SVM based adaptive active learning method proposed in [20], which is the state-of-the-art in multilabel active learning.

Parameters: For MIML and Uncert, the dimension of the compressed label space k was set to half of the number

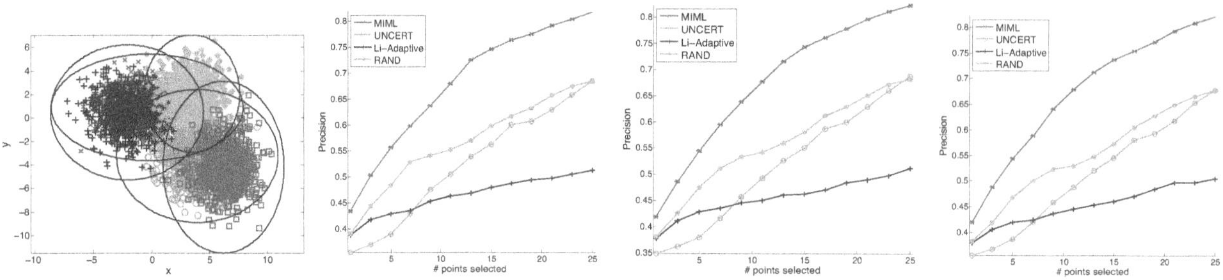

(a) Sample toy data, $L = 5$ (b) Precision at 1 (c) Precision at 2 (d) Precision at 3

Figure 2: Active Learning on Toy dataset:a)A sample toy dataset generated with 5 Gaussians. Points are generated from $L = 5$ Gaussians for this figure and are assigned labels based on the Euclidean distance from the Gaussian means. In our experiments, we use $L = 35$ Gaussians.b,c,d) The precision at 1,2 and 3 on the toy dataset obtained after averaging over 50 different runs. This clearly shows how mutual information quickly picks informative points to be annotated and hence, shows considerable increase in performance.

of labels for all datasets. The hyperparameters σ^2 and χ^2 in MIML and Uncert were selected via evidence maximization and a_0 and b_0 were set to 10^{-6}, which lead to fairly uninformative priors. The Li-Adaptive mechanism proposed in [20] has a hyperparameter β, which was selected from a prefixed set of values $0.1, 0.2, ..., 0.9, 1$ as suggested in [20]. Cross validation was done for all other parameters.

Performance Metric: Typically, the goal in multilabel classification is to predict the top k labels for each point. So, we use precision at 1, 2 and 3 to quantify the performance of different active learning schemes, which is in line with previous work. Precision at k is defined as the fraction of true positives over the top k predicted labels for each point. For novel active learning scenarios like generalized active learning and active diagnosis, the ultimate goal is to recover the whole label set of each single test point. So, we quantify our results using the F-1 measure which depends on all labels, rather than on the few top ones: F - measure $= 2 \frac{\text{precision} * \text{recall}}{\text{precision}+\text{recall}}$.

6.2 Toy Dataset

We first consider a toy dataset before assessing the performance of the different schemes on real-world datasets in 6.4. The toy dataset is created as follows: We create $L = 35$ two-dimensional Gaussians and assign a unique identifier to each of them. Their mean and standard deviation is randomly selected from a fixed interval such that the contours of the Gaussians, drawn for C standard deviation away from the mean, overlap with each other. Points are generated from each of the L Gaussians. The feature vector is just the 2-dimensional coordinate of the point and the labels are the Gaussians whose mean is no more than C standard deviations away from the point. For the experiments, C was selected such that each point belongs to 7 classes on average. To visualise the dataset, we plot the dataset generated by setting $L = 5$, i.e. a dataset generated with 5 Gaussians in Figure 2(a). For our experiments, we use $L = 35$ and start with a randomly sampled set of 20 points. We, then, select 25 more points based on different schemes from a pool of 1000 data points. The performance is averaged over 50 different runs and compared across all methods mentioned in section 6.1.

The precision at 1, precision at 2 and precision at 3 is shown in figure 2. As can be seen in the figure, the mutual information criterion quickly fills the training set with points that are helpful to the model. Uncertainty sampling on our model outperforms Li-Adaptive as points are added. In fact, Li-adaptive baseline performs worse than the random sampling baseline in this case. Intuitively, MIML starts by picking points across different Gaussians in order to maximize mutual information and hence leads to better prediction. On the other hand, the uncertainty sampling criterion picks points closer to the boundaries, hence missing out on information.

6.3 Exploration of the Alternate Inference Procedure:

In order to explore the properties of inference procedures (BML-CS [17] and proposed method(ML-OSS)), we compare the performance of both algorithms on the `MSRC` dataset, which has 23 labels. We used 1024-bit Picodes [4] image descriptors as features.

The results of the experiments are shown in Figure 4(a) and 4(b). Figure 4(a) plots the means of the labels inferred by both the methods for five randomly sampled test points and highlights that the means inferred by both the methods are highly correlated indicating that they are equally capable of modeling the means of the posterior distribution. However, similar correlation is not observed for variance estimates. Figure 4(b) plots the variances for the first label of all the test images inferred by the proposed method vs BML-CS on a negative log scale. Variances inferred by our inference method have a much wider spread indicating that BML-CS underestimates variances due to its limitation in propagating variances across the graphical model.

6.4 Evaluation of Active Learning Strategy

We compared the performance of the proposed mutual information (MIML) strategy with the strategy proposed in [20], uncertainty sampling (UNCERT) and random sampling (Rand). In these experiments, at every active learning round, all the labels corresponding to an input data point were revealed. Figure 3 shows the average of precision at 1,2 and 3 achieved on different datasets. Note that this is a significant metric as all our datasets except `delicious` have less than 3 positive labels per document on average.

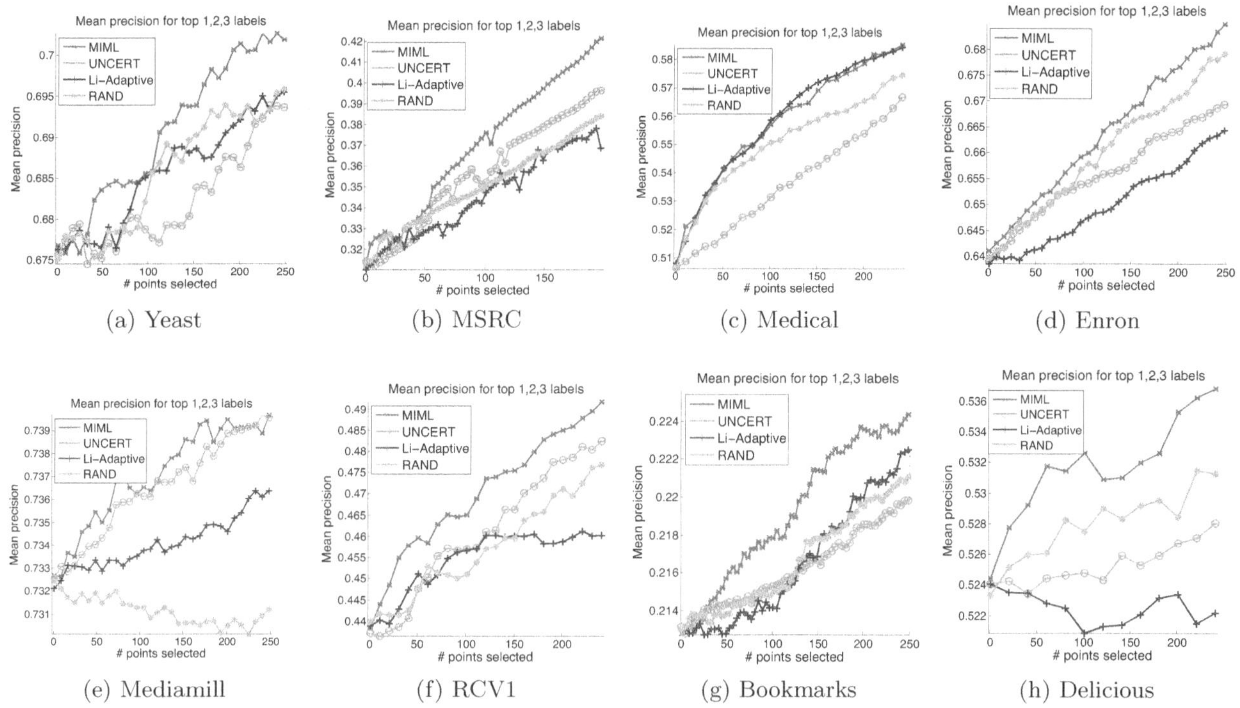

(a) Yeast (b) MSRC (c) Medical (d) Enron

(e) Mediamill (f) RCV1 (g) Bookmarks (h) Delicious

Figure 3: Active Learning with Mutual Information (IG): The averages of precision at 1, 2 and 3 on different datasets as points get added to the training set. Our method, MIML, comprehensively outperforms uncertainty sampling(UNCERT) and the random sampling baseline(Rand) as well as the state-of-the-art SVM based active learning approach, Li-Adaptive [20]. None of the other methods shows such consistent performance across the diverse range of datasets. Every other method is outperformed by the random sampling baseline in one or the other dataset.

Dataset	Labels	MIML	Li-Adaptive
Yeast	14	3m 25s	1m 54s
Mediamill	101	41m 29s	54m 35s
RCV1	101	30m 45s	37m 35s
Bookmarks	208	48m 58s	3h 57m
Delicious	983	1h 11m	20h 15m

Table 2: Time complexity analysis: Time taken to select 250 points from a pool of 4000 points for different datasets for our method (MIML) and the state-of-the-art SVM based approach [20]. For Yeast, the pool is 2000 points and other smaller datasets have been excluded. MIML scales much better than Li-Adaptive with the number of labels and achieves nearly 20x gain for Delicious.

We observe that the MIML criterion proposed in this paper outperforms all the compared methods consistently, on all the datasets. No other method beats the other methods across all datasets. For instance, Li-adaptive performs worse than random sampling on almost half of the datasets.

Evaluation of time complexity: Table 2 shows the time taken by the proposed method (MIML) and Li-adaptive, to select 250 points to be annotated from a pool of 4000 points. We do not include smaller datasets in this analysis. For `Yeast`, the pool is 2000 points as the dataset has only 2417 points. All these experiments were performed on a standard desktop PC with a 4 core, hyper-threaded Intel Core-i7 3.4GHz processor and 16GB RAM. As can be seen, the SVM based approach scales badly (even though training of binary classifiers per label was parallelized) with the number of labels and takes approximately 20 times the time taken by MIML on `delicious`. The only overhead in MIML with increasing number of labels is because of the time taken to learn the Gaussian process over the labels with an initial set of points. All other updates can be performed incrementally and hence, MIML is extremely time-efficient.

Active Diagnosis and Generalized Active Learning: Next, we demonstrate two active learning strategies specific to multilabel classification and show the benefits of our mutual information based strategy in these scenarios. As described before, in active diagnosis, one label per round is revealed for the test set based on the selection criteria. This scenario cannot be straightforwardly tackled by the method of [20], whereas it naturally fits in our model, as the employed joint distribution correlates both points and labels. Thus, we compare our results against the UNCERT and random sampling baselines. Since the ultimate goal is to recover the whole label set of each single test point, we quantify our results using the F-1 measure which depends on all labels, rather than on the few top ones: F - measure $= 2\,\frac{\text{precision} * \text{recall}}{\text{precision}+\text{recall}}$. We report the results of this experiment on the `RCV1` dataset; we randomly selected $n_* = 30$ points collected in a test set $\mathbf{Y}_*$ for which we did active diagnosis by selectively sampling their labels. Each test point has an unknown label vector of size $l = 101$ and the active diagnosis procedure was given a budget of

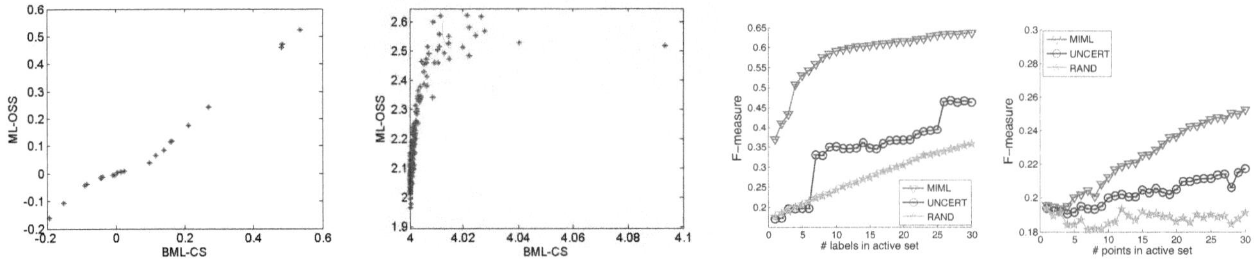

(a) Comparing means (b) Comparing Variances (c) Active Diagnosis (d) Generalized AL

Figure 4: (a, b) Comparison of the inference procedure with BML-CS: Figure (a) is a plot of means propagated by the proposed method (ML-OSS) vs means propagated by BML-CS for 5 randomly sampled test points. Mean values propagated by both the methods follow similar trends. Figure (b) plots variances inferred over the test points by our method vs variances propagated by BML-CS. Both the axis have been converted to negative log scale. Variances propagated by our approach have a wider spread and are higher. (c) Active Diagnosis: Plot of mean F-score against the number of active diagnosis rounds. Mutual information (MIML) outperforms uncertainity sampling (UNCERT) and random sampling (Rand). (d) Generalized Active Learning: Plot of mean F-score against the number of revealed points. Mutual information proves advantageous over the other methods.

$m = 30$ labels to select per point. An initial fully observed training set of 100 points kick started the experiment.

Fig. 4(c) summarizes the results in a plot averaged over 35 runs. We observe that the proposed criterion selects much more useful labels to reveal right from the start. The difference in the performance compared to the baselines is even larger than for the traditional active learning task. This is due to the fact that output labels within a data point are far more correlated than across data instances. For example, a test data corresponding to an article tagged as "investment" is very likely to also fall into the category "banking".

Generalized Active Learning is the scenario when both the input point and the label to be queried are selected based on the selection criteria. Since the goal here is to learn as much information as possible for the whole test set, we use the following criterion to evaluate the performance: after selecting $m = 30$ labels for each of the chosen data points, we compute the F-measure of the *whole* test set given the partially revealed label vectors of the current and all other data points already in the active set. We ran this experiment 35 times and present the averaged results for F-measure with number of points in the active set in figure 4(d). Note that, both active diagnosis and generalized active learning are enabled by the fact that our multilabel classification model can train on partially labelled datasets.

7. CONCLUSION

We presented a novel mutual information based active learning framework for multilabel classification, that enables a theoretically principled and non-myopic approach. We extensively evaluated our algorithm across various datasets in traditional active learning settings as well as active diagnosis and generalized active learning (which are specific to multilabel classification) and showed that it consistently outperforms the state-of-the-art, both in terms of time-efficiency and precision. Possible future work includes integration of the framework with other multilabel classification techniques.

8. REFERENCES

[1] Mulan Multilabel Datasets. http://mulan.sourceforge.net/datasets.html.

[2] R. Agrawal, A. Gupta, Y. Prabhu, and M. Varma. Multi-label learning with millions of labels: Recommending advertiser bid phrases for web pages. In *WWW*, 2013.

[3] K. Balasubramanian and G. Lebanon. The Landmark Selection Method for Multiple Output Prediction. In *ICML*, 2012.

[4] A. Bergamo, L. Torresani, and A. W. Fitzgibbon. PiCoDes: Learning a Compact Code for Novel-Category Recognition. In *NIPS*, 2011.

[5] W. Bi and J. T.-Y. Kwok. Efficient Multi-label Classification with Many Labels. In *ICML*, pages 405–413, 2013.

[6] C. M. Bishop and M. E. Tipping. Variational Relevance Vector Machines. In *UAI*, 2000.

[7] W. Caselton and J. Zidek. Optimal monitoring network designs . *Statistics and Probability Letters*, 1984.

[8] Y.-N. Chen and H.-T. Lin. Feature-aware Label Space Dimension Reduction for Multi-label Classification. In *NIPS*, pages 1538–1546, 2012.

[9] W. Chu, V. Sindhwani, Z. Ghahramani, and S. Keerthi. Relational Learning with Gaussian Processes. In *NIPS*, 2006.

[10] M. Cissé, N. Usunier, T. Artières, and P. Gallinari. Robust Bloom Filters for Large MultiLabel Classification Tasks. In *NIPS*, pages 1851–1859, 2013.

[11] A. Esuli and F. Sebastiani. Active Learning Strategies for Multi-Label Text Classification. In *ECIR*, 2009.

[12] C.-S. Feng and H.-T. Lin. Multi-label Classification with Error-Correcting Codes. *JMLR*, pages 289–295, 2011.

[13] A. Goldberg, X. Zhu, A. Furger, and J. Xu. OASIS: Online Active Semi-Supervised Learning. In *AAAI*, 2011.

[14] A. Gretton, R. Herbrich, and A. Hyvärinen. Kernel methods for measuring independence. *JMLR*, 2005.

[15] D. Hsu, S. Kakade, J. Langford, and T. Zhang. Multi-Label Prediction via Compressed Sensing. In *NIPS*, 2009.

[16] S. Ji, L. Tang, S. Yu, and J. Ye. Extracting Shared Subspace for Multi-label Classification. In *KDD*, pages 381–389, 2008.

[17] A. Kapoor, R. Viswanathan, and P. Jain. Multilabel Classification using Bayesian Compressed Sensing. In *NIPS*, 2012.

[18] A. Krause and C. Guestrin. Near-optimal Nonmyopic Value of Information in Graphical Models. In *UAI*, 2005.

[19] A. Krause, A. Singh, and C. Guestrin. Near-Optimal Sensor Placements in Gaussian Processes: Theory, Efficient Algorithms and Empirical Studies. *JMLR*, 2008.

[20] X. Li and Y. Guo. Active Learning with Multi-label SVM Classification. In *IJCAI*, 2013.

[21] X. Li, L. Wang, and E. Sung. Multi-label SVM Active Learning for Image Classification. In *ICIP*, 2004.

[22] G. Nemhauser, L. Wolsey, and M. Fisher. An analysis of approximations for maximizing submodular set functions. *Mathematical Programming*, 1978.

[23] J. C. Platt. Probabilistic Outputs for Support Vector Machines and Comparisons to Regularized Likelihood Methods. In *Advances In Large Margin Classifiers*. MIT Press, 1999.

[24] B. Settles. Active learning literature survey. Technical report, 2010.

[25] Shihao, Y. Xue, and L. Carin. Bayesian Compressive Sensing , 2007.

[26] A. Singh, A. Krause, C. Guestrin, and W. J. Kaiser. Efficient Informative Sensing using Multiple Robots.

[27] M. Singh, E. Curran, and P. Cunningham. Active learning for multi-label image annotation. Technical report, University College Dublin, 2009.

[28] F. Tai and H.-T. Lin. Multi-label Classification with Principal Label Space Transformation. In *Workshop proceedings of learning from multi-label data*, 2010.

[29] J. Weston, S. Bengio, and N. Usunier. Wsabie: Scaling Up To Large Vocabulary Image Annotation. In *IJCAI*, 2011.

[30] J. Weston, A. Makadia, and H. Yee. Label Partitioning for Sublinear Ranking. In *ICML*, 2013.

[31] B. Yang, J. Sun, T. Wang, and Z. Chen. Effective multi-label active learning for text classification. In *KDD*, 2009.

[32] H.-F. Yu, P. Jain, and I. S. Dhillon. Large-scale Multi-label Learning with Missing Labels. *ICML*, 2014.

[33] Y. Zhang and J. G. Schneider. Multi-Label Output Codes using Canonical Correlation Analysis. In *AISTATS*, pages 873–882, 2011.

[34] X. Zhu, J. Lafferty, and Z. Ghahramani. Semi-Supervised Learning: From Gaussian Fields to Gaussian Processes. Technical report, School of CS, CMU, 2003.

APPENDIX

Appendix A: Proof $\lim_{\substack{a_0\to 0\\ b_0\to 0}} H(x|\mathcal{A}) = \hat{H}(x|\mathcal{A})$

By definition $H(x|\mathcal{A}) = E_{\mathbf{Y}_\mathcal{A}}[H(x|\mathbf{Y}_\mathcal{A})]$ (also for $\hat{H}$). Here $E_{\mathbf{Y}_\mathcal{A}}[\cdot]$ is the expectation over the labels $\mathbf{Y}_\mathcal{A}$ at the active sites $\mathcal{A}$ under the distribution in eq. 4. Now,

$$\hat{H}(x|\mathbf{Y}_\mathcal{A}) - H(x|\mathbf{Y}_\mathcal{A}) = \frac{1}{\hat{Z}}\int_x e^{\frac{-(x-m_\mathcal{A})^2}{2\sigma_\mathcal{A}^2}} \frac{(x-m_\mathcal{A})^2}{2\sigma_\mathcal{A}^2}$$

$$-\frac{1}{Z}\int_x \frac{e^{\frac{-(x-m_\mathcal{A})^2}{2\sigma_\mathcal{A}^2}}}{[1+\frac{x^2}{2b_0}]^{a_0}}\left[\frac{(x-m_\mathcal{A})^2}{2\sigma_\mathcal{A}^2} + a_0\log(1+\frac{x^2}{2b_0})\right] + \log\frac{\hat{Z}}{Z}$$

Here, Z and $\hat{Z}$ are the corresponding normalizing constants. Now as $a_0 \to 0$, the term $a_0\log(1+\frac{x^2}{2b_0})$ vanishes. Further, using the binomial expansion $[1+\frac{x^2}{2b_0}]^{-a_0} = 1 - a_0 \cdot t + \frac{a_0(a_0-1)}{2!}\cdot t^2 + ..$, where $t = \frac{x^2}{2b_0+x^2}$, it is straightforward to show:

$$\lim_{\substack{a_0\to 0\\ b_0\to 0}} \hat{H}(x|\mathbf{Y}_\mathcal{A}) - H(x|\mathbf{Y}_\mathcal{A}) = \hat{H}(x|\mathbf{Y}_\mathcal{A})[1-\frac{\hat{Z}}{Z}] + \log\frac{\hat{Z}}{Z}$$

The required proof follows directly by using the binomial expansion and seeing that as $a_0 \to 0$, the expression $\frac{\hat{Z}}{Z} \to 1$ and the above quantity evaluates to zero.

Large-Scale Adaptive Semi-Supervised Learning via Unified Inductive and Transductive Model

[Extended Abstract]

De Wang *
University of Texas at Arlington
Department of Computer Science and Engineering,
500 UTA Boulevard
Arlington, Texas,76019-0015
wangdelp@gmail.com

Feiping Nie *
University of Texas at Arlington
Department of Computer Science and Engineering,
500 UTA Boulevard
Arlington, Texas,76019-0015
feipingnie@gmail.com

Heng Huang †
University of Texas at Arlington
Department of Computer Science and Engineering,
500 UTA Boulevard
Arlington, Texas,76019-0015
heng@uta.edu

ABSTRACT

Most semi-supervised learning models propagate the labels over the Laplacian graph, where the graph should be built beforehand. However, the computational cost of constructing the Laplacian graph matrix is very high. On the other hand, when we do classification, data points lying around the decision boundary (boundary points) are noisy for learning the correct classifier and deteriorate the classification performance. To address these two challenges, in this paper, we propose an adaptive semi-supervised learning model. Different from previous semi-supervised learning approaches, our new model needn't construct the graph Laplacian matrix. Thus, our method avoids the huge computational cost required by previous methods, and achieves a computational complexity linear to the number of data points. Therefore, our method is scalable to large-scale data. Moreover, the proposed model adaptively suppresses the weights of boundary points, such that our new model is robust to the boundary points. An efficient algorithm is derived to alternatively optimize the model parameter and class probability distribution of the unlabeled data, such that the induction of classifier and the transduction of labels are adaptively unified into one framework. Extensive experimental results on six real-world data sets show that the proposed semi-supervised learning model outperforms other related methods in most cases.

Categories and Subject Descriptors

H.2.8 [**Database Management**]: Database Applications-Data Mining

General Terms

Algorithms

* Authors contributed equally to this paper. † Corresponding author.

KDD'14, August 24–27, 2014, New York, NY, USA.

http://dx.doi.org/10.1145/2623330.2623731 .

Keywords

Semi-supervised learning; Large-scale semi-supervised learning; Unified inductive and transductive model

1. INTRODUCTION

In most data mining applications, the data are generally abundant, however, labeled data is often scarce. Labeling data is a tedious work, and costs huge amount of time and money. In this situation, how to fully utilize the abundant unlabeled data becomes very important.

Semi-supervised learning is a learning paradigm that suits for this situation, where both the labeled data and unlabeled data are used to learn the prediction model. There are two types of semi-supervised learning models: transductive learning models and inductive learning models. Transductive semi-supervised learning methods learn the labels of unlabeled data by propagating the label from labeled data to unlabeled data. The drawback of this kind of methods is that they can not be used for out-of-sample testing (*i.e.*, new testing data from not included in the unlabeled data). So when a new testing data arrives, such methods need to merge those new testing data into the previous data we have, and then reconstruct the whole model based on the merged data. Obviously, such a way is very inefficient for the testing of new out-of-sample data.

Inductive semi-supervised learning methods learn a classifier using both labeled data and unlabeled data. Then the learned classifier can be used for the classification of both unlabeled data using for training and also new out-of-sample testing data. In view of the convenience of out-of-sample testing, inductive semi-supervised learning methods are more attractive in practice.

Many graph based learning approaches have been proposed in recent years [1, 3, 5, 6, 13, 14, 15, 20]. Some of the most representative graph based semi-supervised learning models are: local and global consistency (LGC) [18], random walk (RW) [19], and gaussian field harmonic function (GFHF) [21], Laplacian regression [12], and semi-supervised discriminant analysis [2]. All of these models utilize the Laplacian graph and propagate the labels over the graph. Therefore, in order to use these models, an $n \times n$ graph Laplacian matrix has to be built beforehand.

However, the computational cost of building the $n \times n$ graph Laplacian matrix is at least $O(n^2)$. Such computational cost is daunting in the circumstance of large-scale data, where the number of data can easily reach billion level. So such graph based algorithms are not scalable to large-scale data.

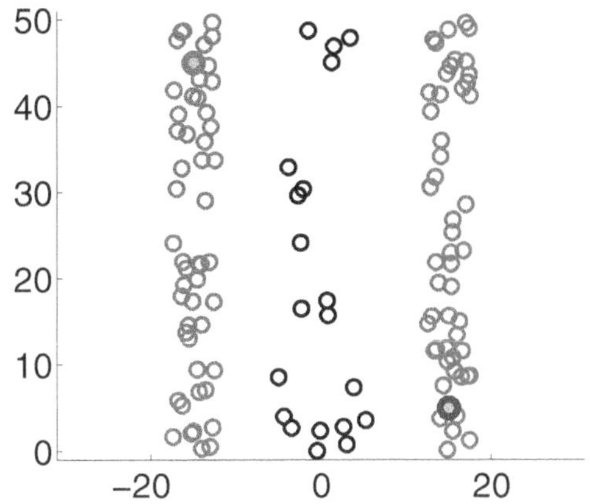

Figure 1: Data samples with boundary points (the black circles). The red circle point and the blue circle point are the labeled data points. All the rest data are unlabeled.

On the other hand, when we do classification, there are many data points lie around the decision boundary, which we call boundary points in the paper. These data points are very noisy for learning the correct classifier, and thus will deteriorate the classification performance of the learned classifier.

To address the above two challenges, a large-scale adaptive semi-supervised learning model is proposed in this paper. The proposed semi-supervised learning model has many good characteristics which will be discussed in detail after we introduce the model.

2. NEW LARGE-SCALE SEMI-SUPERVISED LEARNING MODEL

2.1 Motivation

Most semi-supervised learning methods are based on graph Laplacian matrix, like in the following works: local and global consistency (LGC) [18], random walk (RW) [19], and gaussian field harmonic function (GFHF) [21], Laplacian regression [12], and flexible manifold embedding (FME) [8].

One major drawback of such kind of methods is that the computational cost of constructing the $n \times n$ graph Laplacian matrix is very high, which is at least $O(n^2)$. What's more, if we use the gaussian kernel to construct the graph, the bandwidth parameter σ should be tuned carefully in order to achieve good performance. This makes the Laplacian graph based semi-supervised learning methods impractical to solve large-scale applications in which the number of samples n is often more than billion. If we can develop semi-supervised learning methods without constructing the graph Laplacian matrix, most of the computational cost can be avoided, such that the method can be applied to large-scale data.

On the other hand, when we do classification, there exist many *bad* data points that lie around the decision boundary. Consider the situation demonstrated in Figure 1. The red circle point and the blue circle point are the labeled data points. Considering the distribution of the data, the ideal decision boundary to classify these data points into two classes should be close to the vertical line $x = 0$. However, there are many data points lie around the decision boundary (the black circles in the figure). We call these points boundary points in the following. These boundary points will blur the clear distribution of the whole data, and are very noisy for learning the correct classifier. If these boundary points dominated the loss function, the learned classifier maybe distorted far way from the ground truth. In the example of Figure 1, if we consider too much of these boundary points, the learned classifier may become a horizontal line close to $y = 25$. If we do not consider these boundary points, and consider only the remaining clearly classified points, the correct vertical decision boundary can be easily discovered. Therefore, in order to learn the correct classifier, boundary points should be considered less. In fact, boundary points widely existed in all data sets. Especially when the class number of the data is large, boundary points existed around every decision boundary of each two classes. Therefore, it is very important to develop algorithms that is adaptive to boundary points. By adaptive, we mean that the algorithm can automatically distinguish the boundary points and clearly classified points, and pay less attention to boundary points while learning the classifier.

To address the above two important challenges, in this paper, we propose a new semi-supervised learning model.

2.2 Adaptive Semi-Supervised Learning

In [7], the label is obtained by the label propagation procedure and then used in a regression model. Inspired by [7], in this paper, we propose a new adaptive semi-supervised learning model where the label matrix Y is used as weights and optimized simultaneously with W. Our new model aims to solve the following objective function:

$$\min_{W,b,Y} \|X_l^T W + \mathbf{1}_{nl} b^T - Y_l\|_F^2 + \sum_{i=1}^{n} \sum_{k=1}^{c} y_{ik}^r \|x_i^T W + b^T - t_k^T\|_F^2$$
$$s.t. \;\; \forall i, y_{ik} \in [0,1], \sum_{k=1}^{c} y_{ik} = 1 \qquad (1)$$

where $X_l \in \Re^{d \times nl}$ is the labeled data set, nl is the number of labeled data, d is the number of feature, $\mathbf{1}_{nl}$ is a column vector of size nl whose elements are all one, $W \in \Re^{d \times c}$ is the model parameter matrix that need to be learned, c is the number of classes, $b \in \Re^{c \times 1}$ is the regression bias, $Y_l \in \Re^{nl \times c}$ is the label of labeled data; y_{ik} is the probability of the i-th unlabeled data belongs to the k-th class, which should be in a value between [0,1], $Y \in \Re^{n \times c}$ is the matrix formed by y_{ik}, which should also be learned along with W, n is the number of unlabeled data, $x_i \in \Re^{d \times 1}$ is the i-th unlabeled data, $t_k \in \Re^{c \times 1}$ is a class indicator vector for k-th class, where the k-th element of t_j: $t_{jk} = 1$, and the rest elements are zeros. r is an adaptive parameter that need to be tuned, and $r \geq 1$.

The first term in the objective function is the total loss of labeled data, the second term is the loss of unlabeled data, weighted by the probability distribution matrix Y. There is only one parameter, *i.e.* r, in our proposed ASL model. In our further analysis in the experiment section, we will show that the range of r can be fixed, and a reasonable interval is suggested.

It is interesting to note that the parameter actually serves for multiple purposes: **from the macro level, r balance the two terms in the objective function, decides how much unsupervised information is used; from the micro level, after r is fixed, the weights of boundary points will be suppressed to make the model robust to boundary points.** Following are some more detailed analysis for the conclusion.

From a macro point of view, r serves as a tradeoff between the first term (supervised part with label information available) and the second term (unsupervised part without label information). Note that we do not need another tradeoff parameter before the second term because r is able to balance the two terms. When r becomes large, y_{ik}^r will become small since it is a probability which is definitely less than 1, thus the weight of the second term become small.

In the extreme case, when r approaches infinity, the second term vanishes to zero, so only the first term counts, which means the objective function reduces to supervised learning.

From a micro point of view, r automatically adjust the importance (weight: y_{ik}^r in the objective function Eq. (1)) of each data instance. Consider the i-th data instance: if it is clearly classified, y_{ik} ($k = 1, ..., c$, the probability for x_i belongs to different class) will show obvious magnitude difference. For boundary points, however, y_{ik} ($k = 1, ..., c$) will be more likely equal to one another. Without loss of generality, assuming a binary classification problem, and $r = 2$. For clearly classified points, y_{i1} and y_{i2} would be one large and one small, say $y_{i1} = 0.9$ and $y_{i2} = 0.1$, then $y_{i1}^r = 0.9^2 = 0.81$, $y_{i2}^r = 0.1^2 = 0.01$. Thus, those clear classified points still have large weights in total and contribute a lot to the second term in the objective function. For boundary points, however, y_{i1} and y_{i2} would be more likely equal. Assuming $y_{i1} = y_{i2} = 0.5$, then $y_{i1}^r = y_{i2}^r = 0.5^2 = 0.25$. Thus, those boundary points will have small weights and contribute much less to the second term in the objective function. The above analysis is based on binary classification. Actually, in multi-class problems, for boundary points, y_{ik} ($k = 1, ..., c$) may tend to be $\frac{1}{c}$. Therefore, when c becomes larger, y_{ik} becomes smaller, and y_{ik}^r will be much smaller than the case in binary classification.

From the above analysis, we can see that: when r increases, y_{ik}^r will decrease for both clearly classified points and boundary points. However, the weights of boundary points are suppressed much more faster than clearly classified points. In this way, our model will relatively pay more attention to the clearly classified points and pay less attention to the boundary points. This makes our model adaptive and robust to boundary points, therefore, a better classifier can be learned.

It is innovative to use the class probability matrix of unlabeled data to do inductive learning. In our model, the induction of the classifier W is dependent on the class probability matrix Y of unlabeled data, and the transduction of labels to unlabeled data is dependent on the classifier W. The two steps are unified together by simultaneously optimize W and Y. This adaptive procedure is expected to benefit both the induction of classifier and also the transduction of labels to unlabeled data. However, in previous inductive semi-supervised learning methods, only the feature matrix X of unlabeled data is utilized to learn the classifier. And in those previous methods, an additional step is needed after the model is learned in order to predict the label of unlabeled data.

We summarize the characteristics of our model as following:

(1) **Computational efficient**: different from common graph-based semi-supervised learning methods, our model avoids the computational expensive step of constructing the graph Laplacian matrix.

(2) **Adaptive and robust to boundary points**: our model can adaptively adjust the weights of each data point. Boundary points will get much smaller weights than other points. This makes our model pay less attention to boundary points, and thus robust to boundary points.

(3) **Adaptive optimization procedure**: we simultaneously optimize the model parameter W and the class probability matrix Y of unlabeled data. This adaptive procedure is expected to benefit both the induction of classifier and also the transduction of labels to unlabeled data.

(4) **Only one parameter**: there is only one parameter to be tuned in our model, and the single parameter serves for multiple purposes. A reasonable range of the parameter can be given to facilitate the tuning procedure.

In the following section, an efficient iterative algorithm will be derived to solve the proposed objective function.

3. OPTIMIZATION ALGORITHM

In this section, we derive an efficient iterative algorithm that alternatively optimize over the model parameter W, b and the class probability matrix Y.

(1) When the model parameters W and b are fixed, we solve the class probability matrix Y. Since the first term becomes a constant, the objective function is reduced to:

$$\min_{Y} \sum_{i=1}^{n} \sum_{k=1}^{c} y_{ik}^r \left\| x_i^T W + b^T - t_k^T \right\|_2^2$$
$$s.t. \quad \forall i, y_{ik} \in [0,1], \sum_{k=1}^{c} y_{ik} = 1 \tag{2}$$

Denote $p_{ik} = \left\| x_i^T W + b^T - t_k^T \right\|_2^2$, Eq. (2) can be written as:

$$\min_{Y} \sum_{i=1}^{n} \sum_{k=1}^{c} y_{ik}^r p_{ik}$$
$$s.t. \quad \forall i, y_{ik} \in [0,1], \sum_{k=1}^{c} y_{ik} = 1 \tag{3}$$

Obviously, Eq. (3) can be decoupled between samples. So it is equivalent to solving:

$$\min_{y_{i\cdot}} \sum_{k=1}^{c} y_{ik}^r p_{ik}$$
$$s.t. \quad \forall i, y_{ik} \in [0,1], \sum_{k=1}^{c} y_{ik} = 1 \tag{4}$$

where $y_{i\cdot}$ represents the i-th row of Y.

When $r = 1$, obviously, the optimal solution of Eq. (4) is:

$$y_{ik} = 1, \text{if } k = k^*;$$
$$y_{ik} = 0, \text{if } k \neq k^*; \tag{5}$$

where $k^* = \arg\min_k p_{ik}$.

When $r > 1$, we solve Eq. (4) in the following way. The Lagrangian function of Eq. (4) is:

$$\sum_{k=1}^{c} y_{ik}^r p_{ik} - \beta\left(\sum_{k=1}^{c} y_{ik} - 1\right) \tag{6}$$

where β is the Lagrangian multiplier. In order to get the optimal solution of the subproblem, we set the derivative of Eq. (6) with respect to y_{ik} to zero. Thus, we get:

$$y_{ik} = \left(\frac{\beta}{r p_{ik}}\right)^{\frac{1}{r-1}}. \tag{7}$$

Substituting Eq. (7) into the constraint $\sum_{k=1}^{c} y_{ik} = 1$, we get the closed form solution of Y as following:

$$y_{ik} = \left(\frac{1}{p_{ik}}\right)^{\frac{1}{r-1}} / \sum_{k=1}^{c} \left(\frac{1}{p_{ik}}\right)^{\frac{1}{r-1}} \tag{8}$$

(2) When the class probability matrix Y is fixed, we solve the model parameter W and b. Note that the second term in the objective function in Eq. (1) sums over the number of unlabeled points n and the number of classes c. If we directly taking the derivative of the second term with respect to W, the resulting algorithm would need to iterate over n and c, which would be slow.

It is interesting to note that we can write the objective function in Eq. (1) into compact matrix representation in the following way:

$$\min_{W,b} \left\| X_l^T W + \mathbf{1}_{nl} b^T - Y_l \right\|_F^2 - 2Tr(F(W^T X + b\mathbf{1}_n^T))$$
$$+ Tr(W^T X + b\mathbf{1}_n^T) S (W^T X + b\mathbf{1}_n^T)^T \tag{9}$$

where $F = Y^r \in \Re^{n \times c}$ (here Y^r denotes to perform power operation on each element in Y), $S \in \Re^{n \times n}$ is a diagonal matrix with the i-th diagonal element equal to $s_{ii} = \sum_{k=1}^{c} F_{ik}$.

Setting the derivative of Eq. (9) with respect to b to zero, we get:

$$b = q[(Y_l^T - W^T X_l)\mathbf{1}_{nl} + (F^T - W^T XS)\mathbf{1}_n] \quad (10)$$

where q is a scalar, $q = \frac{1}{nl + \mathbf{1}_n^T S \mathbf{1}_n}$.

Setting the derivative of Eq. (9) with respect to W to zero, and plug in Eq. (10), we get:

$$[X_l(I_{nl} - Q_1)X_l^T + X(I_n - Q_2)SX^T - X_l Q_3 X^T - XQ_4 X_l^T]W \\ = X_l(I_{nl} - Q_1)Y + X(I_n - Q_2)F - X_l Q_3 F - XQ_4 Y \quad (11)$$

where $Q_1 = q\mathbf{1}_{nl}\mathbf{1}_{nl}^T$, $Q_2 = qS\mathbf{1}_n\mathbf{1}_n^T$, $Q_3 = q\mathbf{1}_{nl}\mathbf{1}_n^T$, $Q_4 = q\mathbf{1}_n\mathbf{1}_{nl}^T$.

Denote $C = X_l(I_{nl} - Q_1)X_l^T + X(I_n - Q_2)SX^T - X_l Q_3 X^T - XQ_4 X_l^T$, and $A = X_l(I_{nl} - Q_1)Y + X(I_n - Q_2)F - X_l Q_3 F - XQ_4 Y$, then the optimal solution of W is:

$$W = C^{-1}A \quad (12)$$

The optimization procedure is summarized in Algorithm 1. The two step optimization procedure alternatively optimize the model parameter W and the class probability matrix Y of unlabeled data. The induction of the classifier W is dependent on the class probability matrix Y of unlabeled data, and the transduction of labels to unlabeled data is dependent on the classifier W. This adaptive procedure is expected to benefit both the induction of classifier and also the transduction of labels to unlabeled data. It is novel to use the class probability matrix of unlabeled data to do inductive learning.

Because the algorithm get the minimum in each updates of W, b and Y, so the objective value decreases in each updates. What's more, the objective function is lower bounded by zero. Therefore, it is obvious that our algorithm will converge. We will show in the experiment section that the algorithm actually converges quite fast on all data sets.

Algorithm 1 Algorithm to solve the problem (1).

Initialize W.
repeat
  Update Y: using Eq. (5) if $r = 1$; using Eq. (8) if $r \neq 1$.
  Update W and b by Eq. (12) and Eq. (10), respectively.
until Converges

3.1 Complexity Analysis and Scalability

The major computational cost lies in our algorithm lies in the updating of $W = C^{-1}A$, where c is a $d \times d$ matrix. The computational cost of matrix inverting is $O(d^3)$. In fact, the computation of matrix inverse can be avoided. Note that we are aiming to compute $C^{-1}A$, which is the solution of the following problem:

$$\min_W W^T CW - 2W^T A \quad (13)$$

The solution of this minimization problem can be get iteratively using gradient descent method using the updating formula: $W_{t+1} = W_t - \alpha(CW_t - A)$, with a computational cost of $O(Td^2c)$, where T is the number of iterations, c is the number of columns in A.

In addition, getting the $d \times d$ matrix C cost $O(nd^2)$, getting the $d \times c$ matrix A cost $O(ndc)$. Therefore, the total computational cost of our algorithm is upper bounded by $O(nd^2) + O(ndc) + O(Td^2c)$. Consider in real situation c is always smaller in magnitude compared to d and n, the total computational cost can also be written as $O(nd^2) + O(Td^2)$. **This shows that the computational cost of our algorithm is linear with respect to the number of data samples n. Therefore our algorithm is able to scale to large-scale data.**

However, for those graph based semi-supervised learning methods, without taking into consideration of the huge computation cost for tuning the gaussian kernel bandwidth parameter and the running time of the algorithms themselves, constructing the Laplacian graph matrix already takes at least $O(n^2)$. In the big data applications, the number of data n can easily reach billion level. So such graph based algorithms are not scalable to large-scale data.

4. EXPERIMENTAL RESULTS

4.1 Data Sets Descriptions

In order to show the effectiveness of the proposed adaptive semi-supervised learning method, experiments are conducted on six real world data sets: AR [4], YALE-B [17], MSRC-V1 [16], PIE [11], FERET [10] and ORL [9]. These six data sets are all comprising of human faces, represented using gray scale pixel values. Figure 2 demonstrate some sample images from each data set. Important statistics are summarized in Table 1.

Table 1: Data Sets Descriptions

	# sample	# feature	# class
AR	840	768	120
YALE-B	2414	1024	38
MSRC-V1	1799	1024	12
CMU-PIE	3329	1024	68
FERET	1400	1296	200
ORL	400	644	40

4.2 Experimental Settings

In order to evaluate the effectiveness of the proposed Adaptive Semi-supervised Learning (ASL) method, we compare it with some most representative state-of-the-art semi-supervised learning methods. Since our method is a unified model which can simultaneously perform transduction and induction, we compare our methods with both transductive semi-supervised learning methods and inductive semi-supervised learning methods.

In this paper, we compare our method with three representative transductive semi-supervised learning methods: local and global consistency (LGC) [18], random walk (RW) [19], and gaussian field harmonic function (GFHF) [21].

Inductive semi-supervised learning methods learn a classifier using both labeled data and unlabeled data. Then the learned classifier can be used for the classification of both unlabeled data using for training and also new out-of-sample testing data. Compared with our method which can directly learn the labels of unlabeled data, common inductive semi-supervised learning methods need an additional step to get the labels for unlabeled data used in training.

Two representative inductive semi-supervised learning methods are compared with our method: flexible manifold embedding (FME) [8], and Laplacian regression (LapReg) [12]. LapReg aims to solve the manifold regularized problem, which has the following objective function:

$$\min_W ||Y_l - X_l^T W||_F^2 + \gamma_1 Tr(W^T XLX^T W) + \gamma_2 ||W||_F^2 \quad (14)$$

where Y_l,X_l are the labels and feature matrix of labeled data, respectively, X is formed by both labeled data and unlabeled data, L

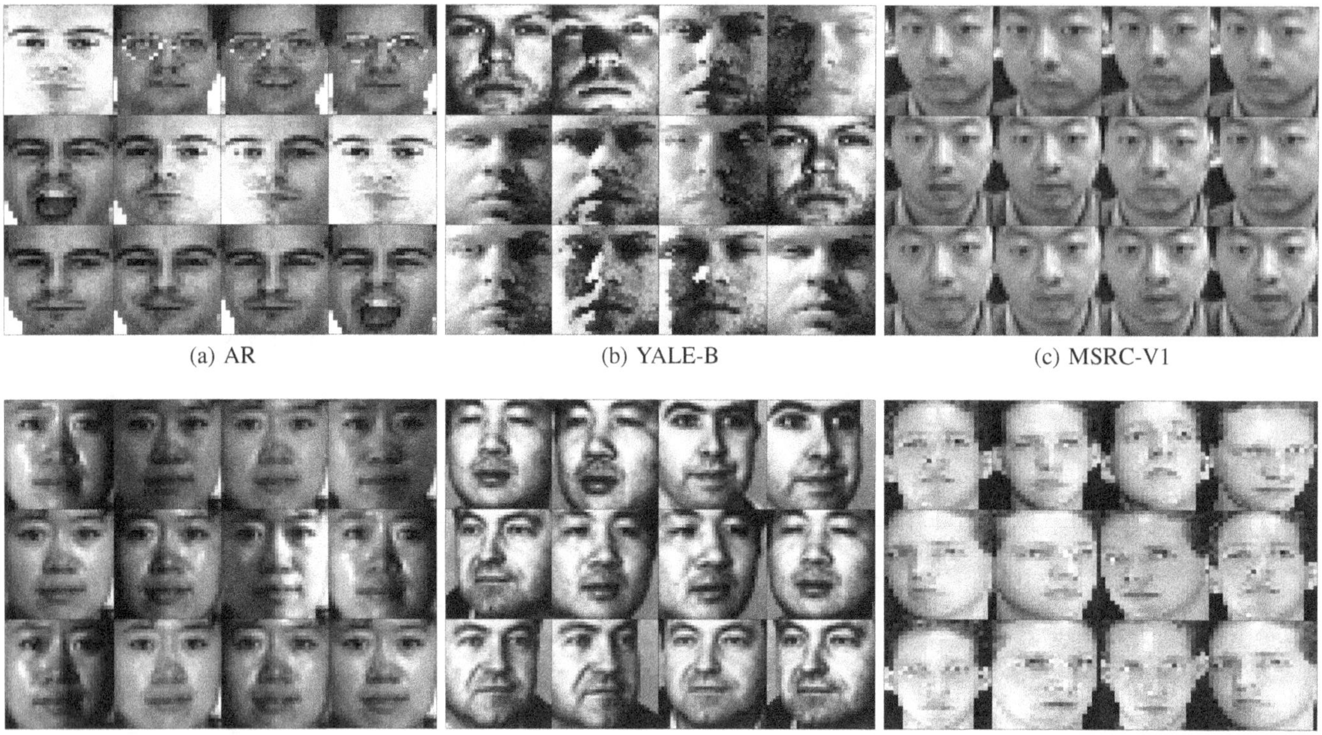

(a) AR (b) YALE-B (c) MSRC-V1

(d) CMU-PIE (e) FERET (f) ORL

Figure 2: Sample face images from each data set.

is the graph Laplacian matrix constructed using X, γ_1 and γ_2 are regularization parameters to balance the three terms.

Semi-supervised discriminant analysis (SDA) [2] is also a commonly used semi-supervised learning method. It aims to learn a projection matrix to map the data in high dimension to a lower dimension subspace. Since our method aims to learn a classifier rather than projection matrix for dimension reduction, we do not compare with SDA in this paper.

In our experiment, we repeat every methods 20 times to compute the average classification accuracy and standard deviation. Each data are first preprocessed using PCA such that 95% of the energy are retained. Different number of labeled points are used for training to study the sensitivity of those methods to the number of labeled data. We randomly choose 1,3,5 labeled points from each class as labeled data, and the remaining as unlabeled data. For transductive methods, since they can not perform out-sample testing, only the accuracy for unlabeled data is computed. For inductive methods, 33% of data are leaved out for out-of-sample testing, then the remaining training data is splited into labeled data and unlabeled data. The accuracy for both unlabeled data and out-of-sample testing are computed.

For our method, the parameter r is tuned from 1 to 2 with a step-size of 0.1. For LGC and RW, the tradeoff parameter α is tuned in [0.1:0.1:0.9,0.99] (*i.e.* from 0 to 0.99 with a step-size of 0.1, 0.99 is also included). GFHF is parameter-free. For LapReg and FME, both of them have two regularization parameters, and are tuned in $\{10^{-5}, 10^{-4}, ..., 10^4, 10^5\}$. The classification results of using the best tuned parameter are recorded.

4.3 Demonstration on Synthetic Data

In this section, we show the working mechanism of the proposed adaptive semi-supervised learning model on a synthetic data. The synthetic data (demonstrated in Figure 3(a)) is generated as following: 50 data points (corresponding to the samples in the left part of the figure) are sampled from a gaussian distribution with a mean of -15, and a standard deviation of 5 ; Another 50 data points (corresponding to the samples in the right part of the figure) are sampled from a gaussian distribution with a mean of 15, and also a standard deviation of 5. Then 20 boundary points are generated around the ideal decision boundary (*i.e.* the vertical line $x = 0$) with a mean of 0 and a standard deviation of 12. All the above data points are unlabeled data. After that, we add only one labeled point to each part (*i.e.*, red circle box in the left, blue circle box in the right). Note that we intentionally place the labeled point in the upper left corner and lower right corner. Compared to randomly label one point from each part, this labeling strategy will make it harder for a model to recover the correct decision boundary.

Figure 3 (c) shows the weights/importance of each unlabeled data point learned by our model . The weights of the i-th data point is $\sum_{k=1}^{c} y_{ik}^r$. If the weight of a data point is large, it will contribute more to the learning of the classifier. The last 20 samples are boundary points (points in the middle part of Figure 3 (a)). We can see that the weights of those boundary points are very small compared to other point. Therefore, our model can adaptively adjust the weights of each point, and thus robust to boundary points.

Figure 3 (b) shows the data after classification using our adaptive semi-supervised learning model. The size of each point is proportional to their weights. Boundary points in the middle part get smaller weights. The correct vertical decision boundary (the green line in the figure) is perfectly recovered, even with only one selected labeled point from each class, and the one labeled point is intentionally set to make it harder to recover the correct decision

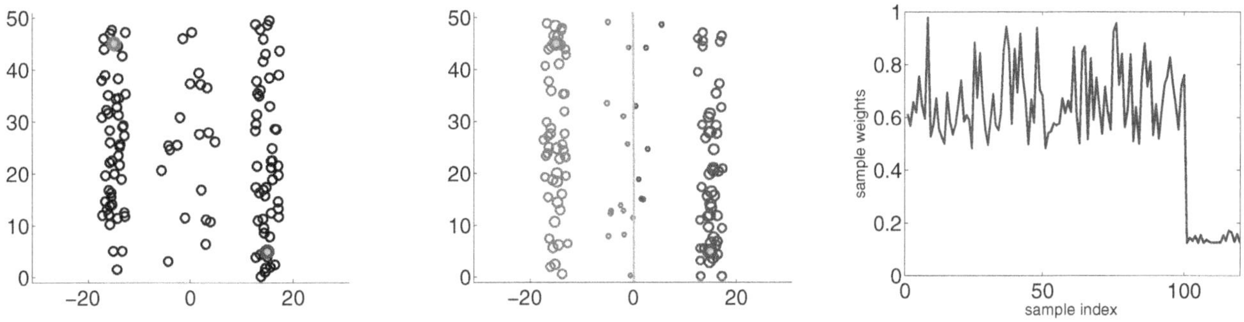

(a) Original toy data

(b) Toy data after classification using our model

(c) Sample weights

Figure 3: Demonstration on Synthetic Data: Figure (a) shows the original data distribution, the red circle box and the blue circle box are the labeled points, all other points are unlabeled; Figure (b) shows the data after classification by our model, the vertical green line is the recovered decision boundary. The size of each point is proportional to their weights. Boundary points in the middle part get smaller weights; Figure (c) shows the weights/importance of each sample learned by our model. The last 20 samples are the boundary points in Figure (a)

boundary. This shows that our model is able to learn the correct classifier with the presence of boundary points.

4.4 Parameter Discussions

There is only one parameter, *i.e.* r, in our proposed ASL model. As discussed before, the parameter actually serves for multiple purposes. In order to achieve the best performance, a proper r should be used to balance the supervised part and unsupervised part in the objective function, and in the meantime, make our model robust to boundary points.

If r is too large, the y_{ik}^r will tend to be zero, and the unsupervised information is lost. So r can not be too large. That's why r is suggested to vary in [1,2] (Consider the class number is often larger than 10, $r = 2$ is large enough to suppress; when the class number is small, the range of r can be extended correspondingly. Generally, [1,4] is totally sufficient for all small class number problems.)

In the following, we will show how the change of parameter r influence the weights of data points , and the influence on classification performance.

4.4.1 *r and Number of Important Points*

When r varies, the contribution of each data instance to the model also changes. We define a data point as an important point if the sum of weights over all classes exceeds an threshold value, *i.e.* it satisfies the following condition:

$$\sum_k^c y_{ik}^r > t \tag{15}$$

where t is a pre-specified threshold. In our experiment, t is set as 0.25 since it is reasonable to assume that an important point should belong to one certain class with a probability larger than 0.5, so $\sum_k^c y_{ik}^r > 0.5^2 = 0.25$ when $r < 2$.

Figure 4 shows the number of important points using different r values. From the figure we can see that:

(1)When $r = 1$, all points are regarded as important points because $\sum_k^c y_{ik}^1 = 1$. In this case, all samples contributes equally to the loss function since their sum of weights over all class are the same.

(2)When r increases, the number of important points will decrease. In this process, boundary points will become unimportant (contribute less to the objective function) with a small r value. This makes our model robust to boundary points. Some non boundary points may become unimportant with a relatively large r value. In the early stage of the increasing of r (say $r < 1.4$), the decreasing of important points is mainly because boundary points become unimportant. In the later stage of the increasing of r (say $r > 1.4$), the decrease of number of important points may also be due to that some non boundary points also become unimportant. Note that the number of important points on some data sets become zero in the later stage, but this does not mean unlabeled data points are not used in our model. Remember that the threshold we are using is 0.25, so the unlabeled data information is still utilized in the model with a relatively small weight. In the extreme case, when r approaches to infinity, all points will become totally unimportant with weight 0. In this case, unlabeled data points are not used in the model, which reduces to supervised learning.

Therefore, in order for the model to utilize the unlabeled data to the best degree, a proper r value should be chosen. The proper r value should: in the macro level, balance the supervised term and unsupervised term in the objective function; in the micro level, automatically adjust the weights of data points, so that the model become robust to boundary points, and thus learn a better classifier.

(3) On some data sets with large number of classes (FERET with 200 classes, AR with 120 classes), the number of important points will decrease drastically to zero. In the contrary, on some data sets with small number of classes (MSRC-V1 with 12 classes), the number of important points will decrease much slower, and still has many important points when $r = 2$. This is because when the class number is small, there tend to be less boundary points, and the probability y_{ik} will be relatively larger, so even with a large r value, there are still many important points. However, when the class number is large, there tend to be much more boundary points whose y_{ik} are small (tend to be $\frac{1}{c}$ in the worst case). So even with small r value, those boundary points become unimportant. In this case, the benefits of our proposed model, which suppresses the weights of boundary points, will be more obvious.

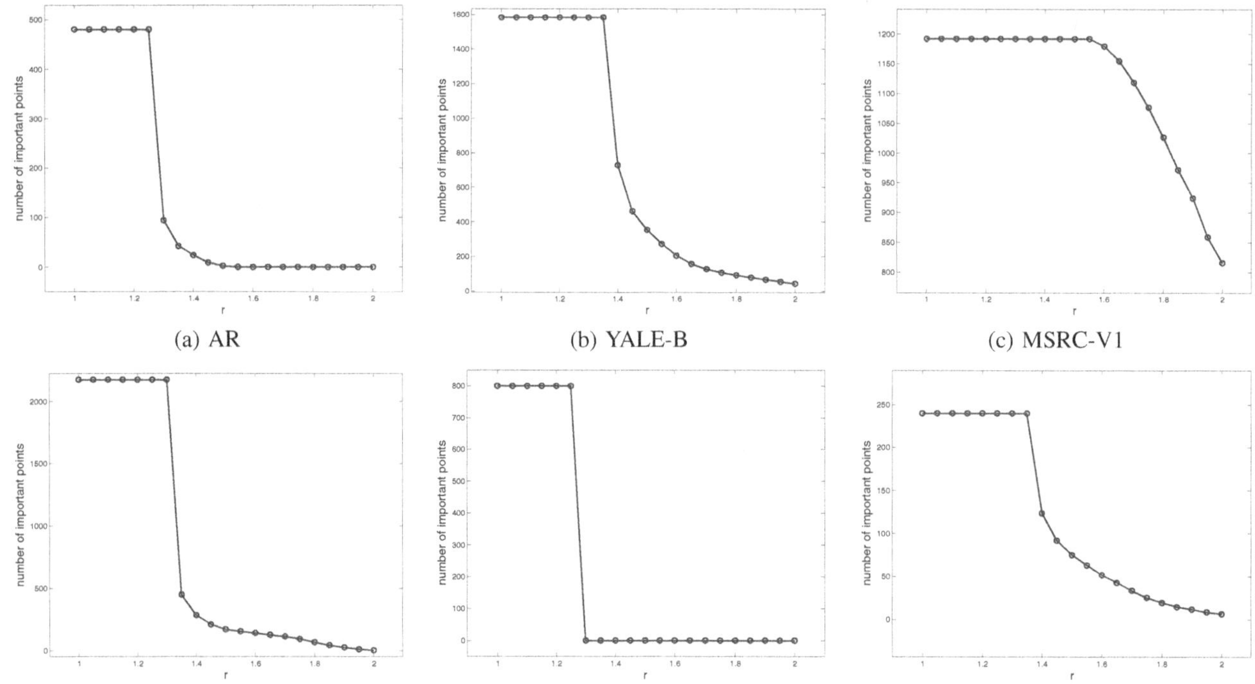

(a) AR (b) YALE-B (c) MSRC-V1

(d) CMU-PIE (e) FERET (f) ORL

Figure 4: The number of important points using different r values on six data sets. One labeled data point is used from each class.

4.4.2 *r and Classification Accuracy*

After the above analysis, we know that r will influence the learned model from both macro level (the weight of unsupervised term in the objective function) and micro level (suppress the weights of boundary points). Different model will lead to different classification results. In this section, we show how the r value will influence the classification performance.

Figure 5 shows the classification accuracy using different r value on the six data sets. From the figure we can see that: the classification accuracy changes with the parameter r, and the best classification results is achieved by different r value on different data sets.

On all the data sets, the best classfication accuracy is not achieved when $r = 1$, which is the common practice in many papers. This is because: by setting y_{ik}^r as data weights, our model is more robust to boundary points by suppressing the weights of boundary points. Therefore, by setting the weights of data as y_{ik}^r rather than the commonly used y_{ik} is more meaningful.

4.5 Classification Performance Comparison

In this section, we present extensive empirical study of the classification performance on six real world data sets. The classification accuracy and standard deviation for running different semi-supervised learning methods are reported in Table 2 to Table 7. From these tables, we can conclude that:

(1) The ASL method outperforms other comparing inductive semi-supervised learning methods (LapReg and FME) in most cases, and is significantly better than other transductive methods (LGC, RW, and GFHF) on all the six data sets. This justifies the effectiveness of the proposed ASL method. Because the ASL method is able to automatically balance the supervised part and unsupervised part in macro level. What's more, in the micro level, the ASL method can suppress the weights of boundary points, which makes the model robust to boundary points, and thus, learn a better classifier.

(2) In general, the inductive semi-supervised learning methods perform better than transductive methods.

(3) The performance of the three transductive methods are comparable to each other. The performance of these transductive methods is pretty good on the MSRC-V1 and ORL data sets. The reason maybe that the number of classes is small on these two data sets compared to other data sets. It seems that those transductive methods can not perform well when the data has large number of classes.

(4) The performance of LapReg and FME are comparable to each other. On the AR data set, the performance of FME is slightly better than the ASL method. This shows the effectiveness of using the manifold regularization to utilize the unlabeled data information. However, the drawback of LapReg and FME is that both of them have two regularization parameters, and the parameters' range is pretty large and not fixed (vary in $[10^{-5}, 10^{5}]$ or even larger). This makes it hard to tune the parameter.

(5) When the number of labeled data points from each class(*i.e.* kl) increases, the performance also become better on all data sets. Especially when number of labeled data points increase from 1 to 3, the classification accuracy improved significantly. Therefore, when the labeled information is scarce, to acquire more labeled data can be very helpful in semi-supervised learning.

4.6 Convergence Speed

In this section, we show the converge speed of the proposed algorithm empirically. Figure 6 shows the objective function value versus number of iterations. We can see that the proposed iterative algorithm converges in less than 20 iterations on all data sets.

In our experiment, running our algorithm 20 iterations only takes about 1 second on a laptop with 2.70GHz double core Intel Core i7 cpu, 16GB memory. Since the major computational cost in our al-

Table 2: Classification accuracy and standard deviation for running different semi-supervised learning methods 20 times on AR Data Set. "kl" represents the number of labeled points from each class used. The column "Unlabeled" record the classification accuracy of unlabeled data using transductive methods or inductive methods. The column "Testing" record the classification accuracy of out of sample testing data using inductive methods. "NA" represents the value is not available.

AR	kl=1		kl=3		kl=5	
	Unlabeled	Testing	Unlabeled	Testing	Unlabeled	Testing
LGC	22.42±1.57	NA	34.69±1.99	NA	41.92±3.53	NA
RW	20.40±1.60	NA	33.09±1.63	NA	40.40±2.65	NA
GFHF	20.89±1.43	NA	32.67±1.79	NA	40.96±2.41	NA
LapReg	75.56±1.64	73.65±1.94	92.63±1.72	92.92±1.81	94.67±1.89	94.77±1.09
FME	67.02±2.63	67.79±2.55	92.58±1.43	93.29±1.76	95.67±2.65	**95.83±1.23**
ASL	**77.36±2.23**	**76.08±2.81**	**93.15±1.60**	**93.46±1.67**	**96.83±1.96**	95.08±1.33

Table 3: Classification accuracy and standard deviation for running different semi-supervised learning methods 20 times on YALE-B Data Set.

YALE-B	kl=1		kl=3		kl=5	
	Unlabeled	Testing	Unlabeled	Testing	Unlabeled	Testing
LGC	42.47±2.11	NA	60.42±2.42	NA	68.16±1.48	NA
RW	43.98±2.43	NA	61.37±2.38	NA	68.69±1.42	NA
GFHF	43.75±1.96	NA	63.05±1.71	NA	70.32±2.12	NA
LapReg	51.36±2.88	50.88±3.11	86.09±1.73	86.51±1.92	94.90±0.82	95.02±1.07
FME	51.24±2.01	50.90±3.17	85.70±2.55	85.54±2.92	94.61±2.03	94.83±2.11
ASL	**59.35±2.91**	**58.98±8.08**	**96.06±1.86**	**96.13±1.92**	**99.14±0.54**	**99.00±0.85**

Table 4: Classification accuracy and standard deviation for running different semi-supervised learning methods 20 times on MSRC-V1 Data Set.

MSRC-V1	kl=1		kl=3		kl=5	
	Unlabeled	Testing	Unlabeled	Testing	Unlabeled	Testing
LGC	62.38±3.46	NA	88.34±5.38	NA	95.19±3.58	NA
RW	60.05±3.78	NA	88.98±5.29	NA	96.88±2.94	NA
GFHF	55.73±6.01	NA	89.73±4.39	NA	97.07±2.72	NA
LapReg	81.91±4.44	81.83±4.65	97.54±2.08	97.55±1.90	98.69±1.69	98.61±1.61
FME	80.72±4.34	80.45±4.50	97.17±2.64	97.28±2.57	99.29±0.88	99.22±0.98
ASL	**82.55±3.64**	**82.29±3.74**	**98.39±1.92**	**98.45±1.82**	**99.36±1.25**	**99.42±1.15**

Table 5: Classification accuracy and standard deviation for running different semi-supervised learning methods 20 times on CMU-PIE Data Set.

CMU-PIE	kl=1		kl=3		kl=5	
	Unlabeled	Testing	Unlabeled	Testing	Unlabeled	Testing
LGC	26.36±1.60	NA	44.76±0.85	NA	54.67±1.36	NA
RW	26.71±1.40	NA	44.03±1.15	NA	54.28±1.36	NA
GFHF	26.34±1.62	NA	45.33±1.72	NA	55.58±1.17	NA
LapReg	62.18±2.11	61.89±1.83	86.08±1.56	86.26±1.23	91.44±0.81	91.45±0.96
FME	60.31±1.53	60.68±1.73	86.68±1.78	85.36±1.66	91.35±1.05	91.31±1.42
ASL	**63.12±2.20**	**62.80±2.76**	**90.64±1.73**	**90.70±1.64**	**93.53±0.84**	**93.38±0.90**

Table 6: Classification accuracy and standard deviation for running different semi-supervised learning methods 20 times on FERET Data Set.

FERET	kl=1		kl=3		kl=5	
	Unlabeled	Testing	Unlabeled	Testing	Unlabeled	Testing
LGC	14.65±0.60	NA	26.74±1.13	NA	31.74±1.52	NA
RW	13.98±0.49	NA	25.02±1.14	NA	30.39±1.65	NA
GFHF	12.07±0.56	NA	21.57±1.38	NA	29.52±2.16	NA
LapReg	27.51±1.20	27.39±1.74	58.29±2.62	57.45±1.66	71.55±1.98	70.21±2.01
FME	26.14±1.42	26.64±1.95	57.61±2.63	56.58±2.51	70.50±2.61	71.10±2.27
ASL	**31.79±1.50**	**31.06±1.95**	**59.75±2.36**	**58.54±2.55**	**73.70±1.95**	**71.97±1.46**

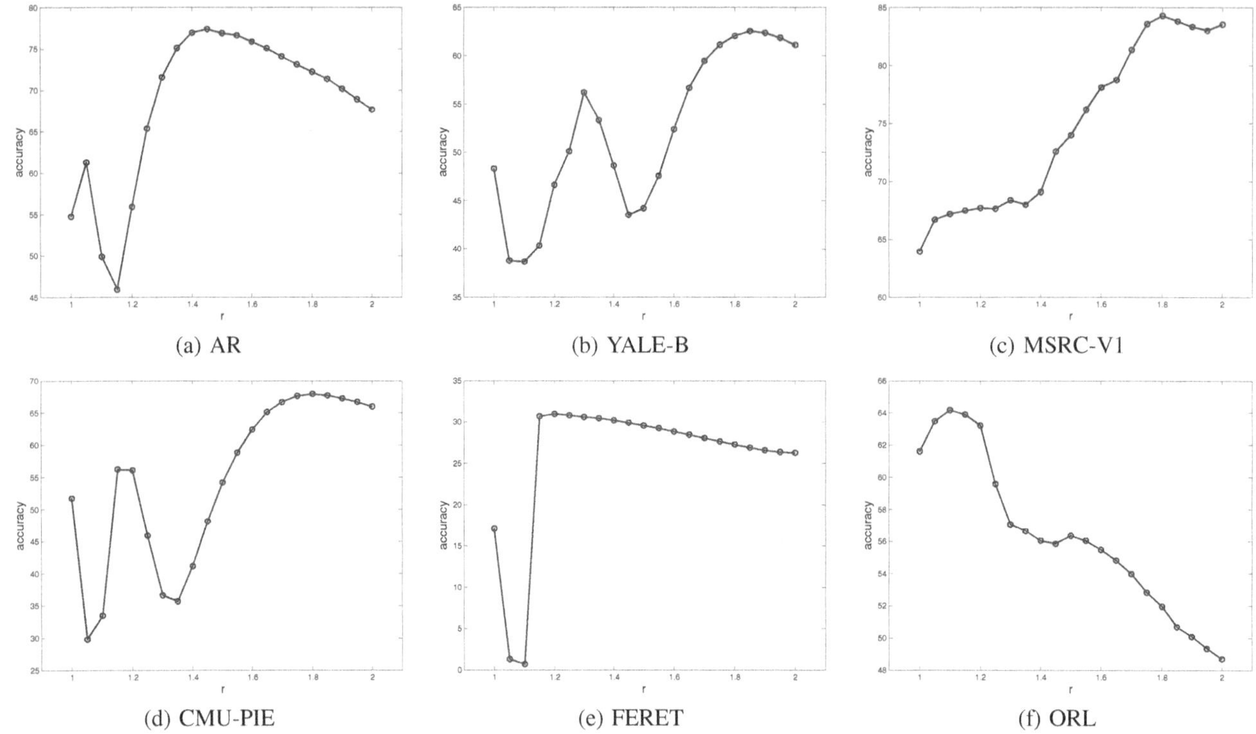

(a) AR (b) YALE-B (c) MSRC-V1 (d) CMU-PIE (e) FERET (f) ORL

Figure 5: The classification accuracy using different r values on the six data sets. One labeled data point is used from each class.

Table 7: Classification accuracy and standard deviation for running different semi-supervised learning methods 20 times on ORL Data Set.

ORL	kl=1		kl=3		kl=5	
	Unlabeled	Testing	Unlabeled	Testing	Unlabeled	Testing
LGC	75.95±2.48	NA	**88.84±2.78**	NA	90.20±2.54	NA
RW	75.86±1.46	NA	86.55±2.49	NA	90.65±1.70	NA
GFHF	74.99±1.73	NA	86.54±2.66	NA	89.85±2.27	NA
LapReg	72.38±2.44	68.58±3.95	87.16±2.54	84.50±2.98	92.94±2.41	90.29±3.03
FME	73.65±2.86	69.08±4.29	87.72±2.54	85.21±3.00	93.00±2.88	90.08±2.43
ASL	**76.42±2.02**	**72.17±3.01**	87.16±3.16	**86.08±3.33**	**93.75±2.91**	**90.47±2.54**

gorithm lies in the inverse of a d by d matrix, when the algorithm is used on data with high dimensionality, the computational cost can be reduced by using PCA for dimensionality reduction beforehand.

5. CONCLUSION

In this paper, we propose an adaptive semi-supervised learning model. Different from previous semi-supervised learning, our proposed model needn't construct the graph Laplacian matrix. Thus, our method avoids the huge computational cost required by previous methods, and achieves a computational complexity linear to the number of data points. Therefore, our method is scalable to large-scale data. Moreover, the proposed model adaptively suppresses the weights of boundary points. This makes our model robust to boundary points. An efficient algorithm is derived to alternatively optimize the model parameter and class probability distribution of unlabeled data, such that the induction of classifier and the transduction of labels are adaptively unified in one framework. Our model only has one parameter need to be tuned, and a fixed range is also suggested. Extensive experimental results show that the proposed semi-supervised learning model outperforms other state-of-the-art methods in most cases.

6. ACKNOWLEDGMENTS

This research was partially supported by NSF-IIS 1117965, NSF-IIS 1302675, NSF-IIS 1344152, NSF-DBI 1356628.

References

[1] M. Belkin, P. Niyogi, and V. Sindhwani. Manifold regularization: A geometric framework for learning from labeled and unlabeled examples. *The Journal of Machine Learning Research*, 7:2399–2434, 2006.

[2] D. Cai, X. He, and J. Han. Semi-supervised discriminant analysis. In *Computer Vision, 2007. ICCV 2007. IEEE 11th International Conference on*, pages 1–7. IEEE, 2007.

[3] X. Chang, F. Nie, Y. Yang, and H. Huang. A convex formulation for semi-supervised multi-label feature selection. In *The Twenty-Eighth AAAI Conference on Artificial Intelligence*, 2014.

[4] A. M. Martinez. The ar face database. *CVC Technical Report*, 24, 1998.

[5] F. Nie, S. Xiang, Y. Jia, and C. Zhang. Semi-supervised orthogonal discriminant analysis via label propagation. *Pattern Recognition*, 42(11):2615–2627, 2009.

[6] F. Nie, S. Xiang, Y. Liu, and C. Zhang. A general graph-based semi-supervised learning with novel class discovery. *Neural Computing and Applications*, 19(4):549–555, 2010.

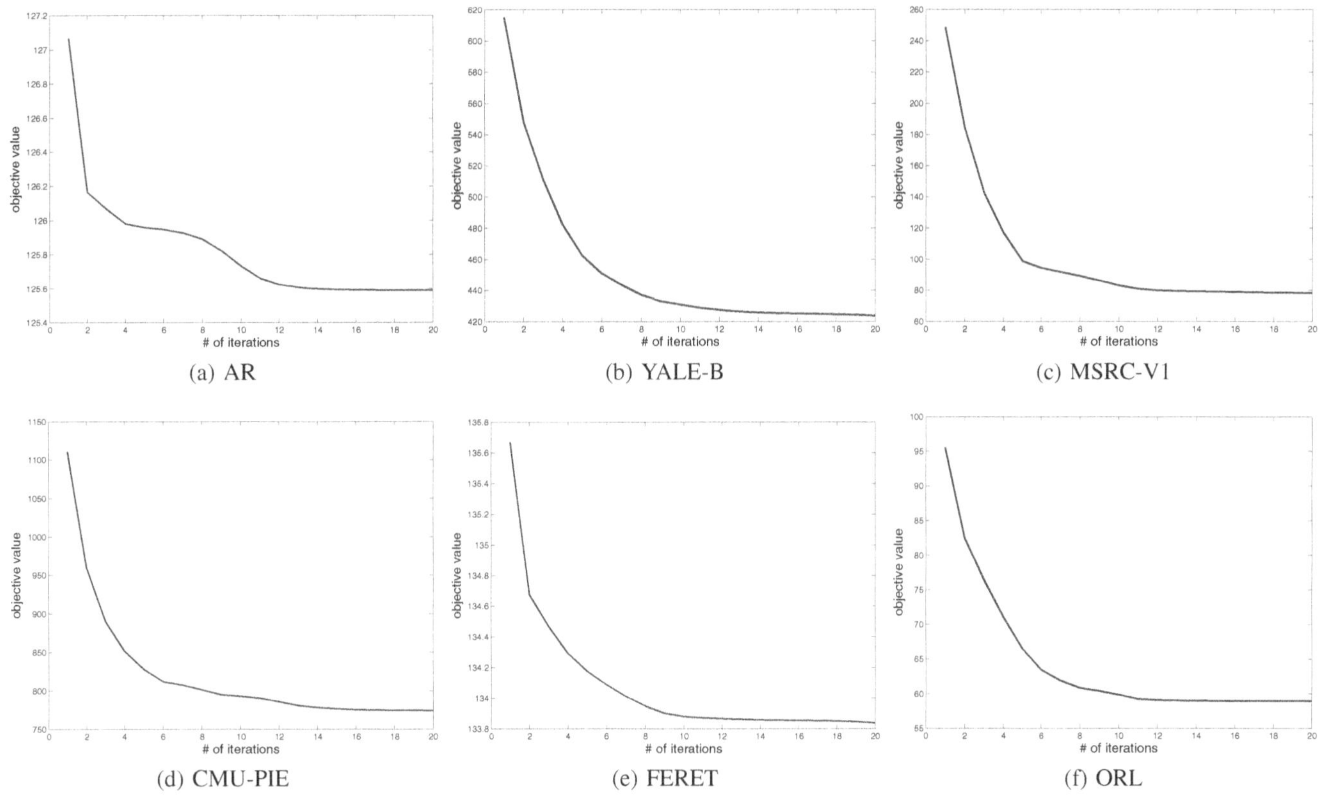

(a) AR (b) YALE-B (c) MSRC-V1

(d) CMU-PIE (e) FERET (f) ORL

Figure 6: Objective value versus the number of iterations.

[7] F. Nie, D. Xu, X. Li, and S. Xiang. Semisupervised dimensionality reduction and classification through virtual label regression. *Systems, Man, and Cybernetics, Part B: Cybernetics, IEEE Transactions on*, 41(3):675–685, 2011.

[8] F. Nie, D. Xu, I. W.-H. Tsang, and C. Zhang. Flexible manifold embedding: A framework for semi-supervised and unsupervised dimension reduction. *Image Processing, IEEE Transactions on*, 19(7):1921–1932, 2010.

[9] ORL Face Database, 2007. `http://www.cam-orl.co.uk/facedatabase.html`.

[10] P. J. Phillips, H. Moon, S. A. Rizvi, and P. J. Rauss. The feret evaluation methodology for face-recognition algorithms. *Pattern Analysis and Machine Intelligence, IEEE Transactions on*, 22(10):1090–1104, 2000.

[11] T. Sim, S. Baker, and M. Bsat. The cmu pose, illumination, and expression database. *IEEE Transactions on Pattern Analysis and Machine Intelligence*, 25(12):1615–1618, 2003.

[12] V. Sindhwani, P. Niyogi, M. Belkin, and S. Keerthi. Linear manifold regularization for large scale semi-supervised learning. In *Proc. of the 22nd ICML Workshop on Learning with Partially Classified Training Data*, volume 28, 2005.

[13] D. Wang, Y. Wang, F. Nie, J. Yan, W. Cai, A. Saykin, L. Shen, and H. Huang. Human connectome module pattern detection using a new multi-graph minmax cut model. In *Med Image Comput Comput Assist Interv*, 2014.

[14] H. Wang, C. Ding, and H. Huang. Directed Graph Learning via High-Order Co-linkage Analysis. In *Proceedings of the ECML PKDD*, pages 451–466, 2010.

[15] H. Wang, H. Huang, and C. Ding. Image annotation using multi-label correlated green's function. *IEEE Conference on Computer Vision*, pages 1–6, 2009.

[16] J. Winn and N. Jojic. Locus: Learning object classes with unsupervised segmentation. In *Computer Vision, 2005. ICCV 2005. Tenth IEEE International Conference on*, volume 1, pages 756–763. IEEE, 2005.

[17] Yale Univ. Face Database, 2002. `http://cvc.yale.edu/projects/yalefaces/yalefaces.html`.

[18] D. Zhou, O. Bousquet, T. Lal, J. Weston, and B. Schölkopf. Learning with local and global consistency. *Proc. Neural Info. Processing Systems*, 2003.

[19] D. Zhou and B. Schölkopf. Learning from labeled and unlabeled data using random walks. In *Pattern Recognition*, pages 237–244. Springer, 2004.

[20] X. Zhu. Semi-supervised learning literature survey. *Computer Science, University of Wisconsin-Madison*, 2:3, 2006.

[21] X. Zhu, Z. Ghahramani, and J. Lafferty. Semi-supervised learning using gaussian fields and harmonic functions. *Proc. Int'l Conf. Machine Learning*, 2003.

Active Semi-Supervised Learning Using Sampling Theory for Graph Signals

Akshay Gadde, Aamir Anis and Antonio Ortega
Department of Electrical Engineering
University of Southern California, Los Angeles
agadde@usc.edu, aanis@usc.edu, ortega@sipi.usc.edu

ABSTRACT

We consider the problem of offline, pool-based active semi-supervised learning on graphs. This problem is important when the labeled data is scarce and expensive whereas unlabeled data is easily available. The data points are represented by the vertices of an undirected graph with the similarity between them captured by the edge weights. Given a target number of nodes to label, the goal is to choose those nodes that are most informative and then predict the unknown labels. We propose a novel framework for this problem based on our recent results on sampling theory for graph signals. A graph signal is a real-valued function defined on each node of the graph. A notion of frequency for such signals can be defined using the spectrum of the graph Laplacian matrix. The sampling theory for graph signals aims to extend the traditional Nyquist-Shannon sampling theory by allowing us to identify the class of graph signals that can be reconstructed from their values on a subset of vertices. This approach allows us to define a criterion for active learning based on sampling set selection which aims at maximizing the frequency of the signals that can be reconstructed from their samples on the set. Experiments show the effectiveness of our method.

Categories and Subject Descriptors

I.5.2 [**Pattern Recognition**]: Design Methodology—*Classifier design and evaluation*; I.5.3 [**Pattern Recognition**]: Clustering—*Algorithms*

Keywords

Active semi-supervised learning; Graph signal processing; Sampling theory; Graph signal filtering

KDD'14, August 24–27, 2014, New York, NY, USA.

ACM 978-1-4503-2956-9/14/08 ...$15.00.
http://dx.doi.org/10.1145/2623330.2623760.

1. INTRODUCTION

In many real-life machine learning tasks, labeled data is scarce whereas unlabeled data is easily available. Active semi-supervised learning is an effective approach for such scenarios. A semi-supervised learning technique must not only learn from the labeled data but also from the inherent clustering present in the unlabeled data [29]. Further, when the labeling is expensive, it is better to let the learner choose the data points to be labeled so that it can pick the most informative and representative labels. Thus, in an active learning scenario, the goal is to achieve the maximum gain in terms of learning ability for a given, and small, number of label queries. In this paper, we propose a novel approach to active semi-supervised learning based on recent advances in sampling theory for graph signals.

Active learning has been studied in different problem scenarios such as online stream-based sampling, adaptive sampling etc. (see [23] for a review). We focus on the problem of pool-based batch-mode active semi-supervised learning, where there is a large static collection of unlabeled data from which a very small percentage of data points have to be selected in order to be labeled. Batch operation (i.e., selecting a *set* of data points to be labeled) is more realistic in scenarios such as crowdsourcing where it would not be practical to submit for labeling one data point at a time. Further, in this paper we focus on the problem of optimizing batches of any size without using any label information, which would be the case when selecting the first batch of data points to be labeled. We leave for future work the problem of incorporating labeled data, which would allow labels obtained for the first batch to be used to optimize data point selection for the second batch, and so on.

Applying a graph perspective to semi-supervised learning is not new. In a graph-based formulation, the data points are represented by nodes of a graph and the edges capture the similarity between the nodes they connect. For example, the weight on an edge might be a function of the distance between the two points in the feature space chosen for the classification task. The membership function of a given class can be thought of as a "graph signal", which has a scalar value at each of the nodes (e.g., 1 or 0 depending on whether or not the data point belongs to the class). Since features have been chosen to be meaningful for the classification task, it is reasonable to expect that nodes that are close together in the feature space will be likely to have the same label. Conversely, nodes that are far away in the feature space are less likely to have the same label. Thus, we expect the membership function to be *smooth* on the graph, i.e., moving from a node to its neighbors in the graph is unlikely to lead to changes in the membership. Thus, the semi-supervised learning problem can be viewed as a problem of interpolating a smooth graph signal. This view has led to many effective techniques such as MinCut [4], Gaussian random fields and harmonic functions [30], local and global consistency [28], manifold regularization [3] and spectral graph kernels [25].

Active learning has also benefited from this graph based-view. Many active learning approaches use the graph to quantify the quality of sampling sets [7, 9, 10]. One methodology is to try and pick a subset of nodes which captures the underlying low-dimensional manifold represented by the graph. Another is to pick the nodes to be labeled in such a way that unlabeled nodes are strongly connected to them. Some methods pick those samples which lead to minimization of generalization error bound. We discuss some of these methods in Section 4.

Many of the semi-supervised methods mentioned above are *global*, in the sense that they require inversion or eigen-decomposition of large matrices associated with the underlying graph. This poses a problem in scalable and distributed implementation of these algorithms. Most graph-based active learning methods suffer from the same problem. Another issue with these methods is that they do not give conditions under which the graph signal can be uniquely and perfectly interpolated from its samples on the chosen subset.

In recent years, there has been a significant amount of work devoted to the study of graph signal processing. The focus of this work has been to extend to the context of graph signals, theoretical results and tools that are well established in the context of conventional signal processing [24]. In particular, there have been contributions to the design of graph wavelets [11], graph filterbanks [17], etc. A key challenge in graph signal processing is to design *localized* algorithms that scale well with graph sizes, i.e., the output at each vertex should only depend on its local neighborhood.

In this paper we leverage our recent work on graph signal sampling and interpolation [18, 1]. We show that the newly developed theoretical results provide a rigorous and unified framework to select points to be labeled and subsequently perform semi-supervised learning. Our framework provides conditions under which a graph signal can be uniquely recovered from its values on a subset of vertices. These conditions lead to a powerful greedy algorithm for choosing the best nodes for labeling. The proposed algorithm is well motivated through a compelling graph theoretic interpretation. We give a numerically efficient way to implement the proposed algorithm which makes it scalable. We also give an effective and efficient semi-supervised learning method that is closely tied to the label selection algorithm and is theoretically well-justified. Both our algorithms are well-suited for a large-scale distributed implementation. We show that our method outperforms several state of the art methods by testing on multiple real datasets.

The rest of the paper is organized as follows. Section 2 reviews our recent work on sampling theory for graph signals. In Section 3 we apply the framework of sampling theory to derive the proposed active semi-supervised learning approach. Section 4 summarizes the related prior work. Experiments are presented in Section 5. Finally, we provide some concluding remarks in Section 6.

2. SAMPLING THEORY FOR GRAPH SIGNALS

We begin by briefly describing the theory of sampling for graph signals formulated in our previous work [18, 1].

2.1 Notation

Throughout this paper, we consider simple, connected, undirected, and weighted graphs $G = (\mathcal{V}, E)$ with nodes numbered from the set $\mathcal{V} = \{1, 2, \dots, N\}$, and edges $E = \{(i, j, w_{ij})\}, i, j \in \mathcal{V}$, where (i, j, w_{ij}) denotes an edge of weight w_{ij} between nodes i and j, with $w_{ii} = 0$. In the present context, the weights denote similarity between the respective nodes. The degree d_i of a node i is defined as the sum of the weights of edges connected to node i, and the degree matrix of the graph is a diagonal matrix defined as $\mathbf{D} = \text{diag}\{d_1, d_2, \dots, d_N\}$. The adjacency matrix $\mathbf{W}$ of the graph is an $N \times N$ matrix with $\mathbf{W}_{ij} = w_{ij}$ and the combinatorial Laplacian matrix is defined as $\mathbf{L} = \mathbf{D} - \mathbf{W}$. We shall use the symmetric normalized form of the adjacency and the Laplacian matrices defined as $\boldsymbol{\mathcal{W}} = \mathbf{D}^{-1/2}\mathbf{W}\mathbf{D}^{-1/2}$ and $\boldsymbol{\mathcal{L}} = \mathbf{D}^{-1/2}\mathbf{L}\mathbf{D}^{-1/2}$ respectively. $\boldsymbol{\mathcal{L}}$ is a symmetric positive semi-definite matrix and has a set of real eigenvalues $0 = \lambda_1 \leq \lambda_2 \leq \dots \leq \lambda_N \leq 2$ and a corresponding orthogonal set of eigenvectors denoted as $\mathbf{U} = \{\mathbf{u}_1, \mathbf{u}_2, \dots, \mathbf{u}_N\}$. A subset of nodes of the graph is denoted as a collection of indices $\mathcal{S} \subset \mathcal{V}$, with $\mathcal{S}^c = \mathcal{V} \setminus \mathcal{S}$ denoting its complement set. A restriction of a matrix $\mathbf{A}$ to rows in set $\mathcal{S}_1$ and columns in set $\mathcal{S}_2$ is denoted by the submatrix $\mathbf{A}_{\mathcal{S}_1,\mathcal{S}_2}$ and for the sake of brevity $\mathbf{A}_{\mathcal{S},\mathcal{S}} = \mathbf{A}_{\mathcal{S}}$. Also, $\mathbf{0}$ and $\mathbf{1}$ denote all-zeroes and all-ones vectors of appropriate sizes.

A graph signal is defined as a scalar-valued discrete mapping $f : V \rightarrow \mathbb{R}$, such that $f(i)$ is the value of the signal on node i. For ease of notation, it can also be represented as a vector $\mathbf{f} \in \mathbb{R}^N$ with indices corresponding to the node indices in the graph. In this paper, the signals of interest will be the membership functions associated with the various labels of interest in the classification problem. *Sampling* a graph signal $\mathbf{f}$ onto a subset of nodes $\mathcal{S}$, known as the *sampling set*, is realized by retaining the signal's values on the nodes in $\mathcal{S}$. The sampled signal is denoted by $\mathbf{f}(\mathcal{S})$, which is a vector of reduced length $|\mathcal{S}|$. In our context, a sampled graph signal will include the membership information for the data points that have been labeled.

2.2 Preliminaries

The classical Nyquist-Shannon sampling theorem establishes an upper limit on the bandwidth of signals that can be uniquely reconstructed when sampled at a given sampling rate. To have an analogous result in the realm of graphs, one needs a notion of frequency for graph signals. Such a spectral interpretation is provided by the eigenvalues and eigenvectors of the Laplacian matrix $\boldsymbol{\mathcal{L}}$, similar to the Fourier transform in traditional signal processing. The eigenvalues can be thought of as frequencies and indicate the variation in the eigenvectors: a high eigenvalue implies higher variation in the corresponding eigenvector [24]. Since the eigenvectors are orthogonal, they form a basis in $\mathbb{R}^N$. Thus, the *Graph Fourier Transform* (GFT) of a signal $\mathbf{f}$ is defined as its projection onto the eigenvectors of the graph Laplacian, i.e. $\tilde{\mathbf{f}}(\lambda_i) = \langle \mathbf{f}, \mathbf{u}_i \rangle$, or more compactly, $\tilde{\mathbf{f}} = \mathbf{U}^T\mathbf{f}$.

In this context, a smooth or low-pass graph signal can be obtained by forcing high frequency GFT coefficients to vanish. More formally, an *ω-bandlimited signal* on a graph is defined to have zero GFT coefficients for frequencies above its bandwidth ω, i.e. its spectral support is restricted to the set of frequencies $[0, \omega]$. The space of all ω-bandlimited signals is known as the *Paley-Wiener* space and is denoted by $PW_\omega(G)$ [20]. Note that $PW_\omega(G)$ is a subspace of $\mathbb{R}^N$.

With the notion of frequency introduced via the GFT, one can frame an adequate *sampling theory* for graph signals using the following ingredients:

P1: *Cutoff frequency* - For a given subset of nodes $\mathcal{S}$, find the cut-off frequency ω, such that any $\mathbf{f} \in PW_\omega(G)$ can be exactly recovered from its samples $\mathbf{f}(\mathcal{S})$.

P2: *Optimal sampling set* - For a given cut-off frequency ω, find the the smallest subset of nodes $\mathcal{S}_{\text{opt}}$ (i.e. with minimum $|\mathcal{S}_{\text{opt}}|$) such that all signals $\mathbf{f} \in PW_\omega(G)$ can be uniquely recovered from their samples $\mathbf{f}(\mathcal{S}_{\text{opt}})$ on $\mathcal{S}_{\text{opt}}$.

P3: *Reconstruction algorithm* - Given samples $\mathbf{f}(\mathcal{S})$ of a graph signal $\mathbf{f}$ on a subset of nodes $\mathcal{S}$, find the reconstructed signal values $\mathbf{f}(\mathcal{S}^c)$ on the complementary subset $\mathcal{S}^c$.

Note that for regular sampling in the traditional signal processing, problems **P1** and **P2** are reciprocal, i.e., knowing one automatically leads to the solution of the other. However, this does not hold for irregular sampling, as in the case of graph signals. Next, we briefly describe the solution to each of the problems above, and refer to [18, 1] for the details.

2.3 P1: Cut-off frequency

Let $L_2(\mathcal{S}^c)$ denote the space of all graph signals that are zero everywhere except possibly on the nodes in $\mathcal{S}^c$, i.e., $\forall \phi \in L_2(\mathcal{S}^c), \phi(\mathcal{S}) = 0$. Also, let $\omega(\phi)$ denote the bandwidth of a graph signal ϕ, i.e., the value of the maximum non-zero frequency of that signal. Then the following theorem can be proved [1]:

THEOREM 1 (SAMPLING THEOREM). *For a graph G, with normalized Laplacian $\boldsymbol{\mathcal{L}}$, any signal $\mathbf{f} \in PW_\omega(G)$ can be perfectly recovered from its values on a subset of nodes $\mathcal{S} \subset \mathcal{V}$ if and only if*

$$\omega < \omega_c(\mathcal{S}) \triangleq \inf_{\phi \in L_2(\mathcal{S}^c)} \omega(\phi) \tag{1}$$

where $\omega_c(\mathcal{S})$ is the cut-off frequency.

The theorem leads to a cut-off frequency that is *lower* than the minimum bandwidth of any signal in $L_2(\mathcal{S}^c)$. Intuitively, a signal $\phi \in L_2(\mathcal{S}^c)$ can be added to any input signal $\mathbf{f}$ without affecting its sampled version (since ϕ is identically zero for all vertices that are sampled, i.e., those in $\mathcal{S}$). Thus, if there existed a $\phi \in L_2(\mathcal{S}^c)$ such that $\phi \in PW_\omega(G)$ we would have that both $\mathbf{f}$ and $\phi + \mathbf{f}$ belong to $PW_\omega(G)$ *and* lead to the same set of samples on $\mathcal{S}$. So clearly it would not be possible to recover them both, and thus sampling of such signals in $PW_\omega(G)$ would not be possible. The condition in Theorem 1 ensures that $PW_\omega(G) \cap L_2(\mathcal{S}^c) = \{0\}$ and thus no such ϕ exists.

From Theorem 1, finding the maximum cut-off frequency for a set $\mathcal{S}$ requires finding the bandwidth $\omega(\phi^*)$ of the smoothest possible signal $\phi^* \in L_2(\mathcal{S}^c)$. A brute-force approach to this would entail computing the GFT of all signals in $L_2(\mathcal{S})$ and exhaustively searching for ϕ^*. We instead devise a computationally efficient way to approximate the bandwidth of any signal ϕ for a given integer parameter $k > 0$ as follows:

$$\omega_k(\phi) = \left(\frac{\phi^t \boldsymbol{\mathcal{L}}^k \phi}{\phi^t \phi} \right)^{1/k} \tag{2}$$

We then replace $\omega(\phi)$ in Theorem 1 by $\omega_k(\phi)$ in the objective function to obtain our estimated bandwidth:

$$\Omega_k(\mathcal{S}) = \inf_{\phi \in L_2(\mathcal{S}^c)} \omega_k(\phi) = \inf_{\phi \in L_2(\mathcal{S}^c)} \left(\frac{\phi^t \boldsymbol{\mathcal{L}}^k \phi}{\phi^t \phi} \right)^{1/k}. \tag{3}$$

Then, the smoothest possible signal ϕ^* in $L_2(\mathcal{S}^c)$ can be approximated by the minimizer ϕ_k^* in (3). Numerically, $\Omega_k(\mathcal{S})$ and ϕ_k^* can be determined from the smallest eigen-pair $(\sigma_{1,k}, \psi_{1,k})$ of the reduced matrix $(\boldsymbol{\mathcal{L}}^k)_{\mathcal{S}^c}$:

$$\Omega_k(\mathcal{S}) = \sigma_{1,k}, \tag{4}$$

$$\phi_k^*(\mathcal{S}^c) = \psi_{1,k},\ \phi_k^*(\mathcal{S}) = \mathbf{0}. \tag{5}$$

This approach does not require complete eigen-decomposition of $\boldsymbol{\mathcal{L}}$ and is computationally tractable. One can show that k controls the accuracy of the cut-off estimate (refer to [1] for details). As we increase the value of k, $\Omega_k(\mathcal{S})$ tends to give a better estimate of the cut-off frequency. Thus, there is a trade-off between accuracy of the estimate on the one hand, and complexity and numerical stability on the other that arise due to the power k in $\boldsymbol{\mathcal{L}}^k$. Moreover, $\Omega_k(\mathcal{S})$ can be proven to be always less than the actual cut-off $\omega_c(\mathcal{S})$, i.e. the Sampling Theorem still holds for the subset $\mathcal{S}$ except that the class of recoverable signals is determined to be narrower as a penalty for the cut-off approximation.

2.4 P2: Sampling set

We now describe the framework for the converse question: given a cut-off frequency ω_c for $PW_\omega(G)$, what is the smallest sampling set $\mathcal{S}_{\text{opt}}$ so that a signal $\mathbf{f} \in PW_\omega(G)$ is uniquely represented by $\mathbf{f}(\mathcal{S}_{\text{opt}})$. If K_c represents the number of eigenvalues of $\boldsymbol{\mathcal{L}}$ below ω_c, then by dimensionality considerations $|\mathcal{S}_{\text{opt}}| \geq K_c$. Also, note that $\mathcal{S}_{\text{opt}}$ may not be unique. Formally, one can use Theorem 1 and relax the true cut-off $\omega_c(\mathcal{S})$ by $\Omega_k(\mathcal{S})$, then $\mathcal{S}_{\text{opt}}$ can be found from the following optimization problem:

$$\underset{\mathcal{S}}{\text{Minimize}}\ |\mathcal{S}| \quad \text{subject to} \quad \Omega_k(\mathcal{S}) \geq \omega_c \tag{6}$$

This is a combinatorial problem because we need to compute $\Omega_k(\mathcal{S})$ for every possible subset $\mathcal{S}$.

However, this problem can be solved using a greedy heuristic to get an estimate $\mathcal{S}_{\text{est}}$ of the optimal sampling set. Starting with an empty sampling set $\mathcal{S}$ (with corresponding $\Omega_k(\mathcal{S}) = 0$) we keep adding nodes to $\mathcal{S}$ (from $\mathcal{S}^c$) one-by-one while trying to ensure maximum increase in $\Omega_k(\mathcal{S})$ at each step. The hope is that $\Omega_k(\mathcal{S})$ reaches the target cut-off ω_c with minimum number of node additions to $\mathcal{S}$. To understand which nodes should be included in $\mathcal{S}$, we introduce a binary relaxation of our cut-off formulation by defining the following matrix

$$\mathbf{M}_k^\alpha(\mathbf{t}) \triangleq \boldsymbol{\mathcal{L}}^k + \alpha\, \boldsymbol{\mathcal{D}}(\mathbf{t}), \quad k \in \mathbb{Z}^+, \alpha > 0, \mathbf{t} \in \mathbb{R}^N \tag{7}$$

where $\boldsymbol{\mathcal{D}}(\mathbf{t})$ is a diagonal matrix with $\mathbf{t}$ on its diagonal. Let $(\lambda_k^\alpha(\mathbf{t}), \mathbf{x}_k^\alpha(\mathbf{t}))$ denote the smallest eigen-pair of $\mathbf{M}_k^\alpha(\mathbf{t})$. Then, if $\mathbf{1}_{\mathcal{S}} : \mathcal{V} \to \{0, 1\}$ denotes the indicator function for the subset $\mathcal{S}$ (i.e. $\mathbf{1}(\mathcal{S}) = \mathbf{1}$ and $\mathbf{1}(\mathcal{S}^c) = \mathbf{0}$), one has

$$\lambda_k^\alpha(\mathbf{1}_\mathcal{S}) = \inf_{\mathbf{x}} \left(\frac{\mathbf{x}^t \boldsymbol{\mathcal{L}}^k \mathbf{x}}{\mathbf{x}^t \mathbf{x}} + \alpha \frac{\mathbf{x}(\mathcal{S})^t \mathbf{x}(\mathcal{S})}{\mathbf{x}^t \mathbf{x}} \right) \tag{8}$$

Note that the right hand side of the equation above is simply an *unconstrained regularization* of the constrained optimization problem in (3). When $\alpha \gg 1$, the components $\mathbf{x}(\mathcal{S})$ are highly penalized during minimization. Thus, if $\mathbf{x}_k^\alpha(\mathbf{1}_\mathcal{S})$ is the minimizer in (8), then $[\mathbf{x}_\alpha^k(\mathbf{1}_\mathcal{S})](\mathcal{S}) \to \mathbf{0}$, i.e. the values on nodes $\mathcal{S}$ tend to be very small. Therefore, for $\alpha \gg 1$, we have

$$\phi_k^* \approx \mathbf{x}_k^\alpha(\mathbf{1}_\mathcal{S}), \quad (\Omega_k(\mathcal{S}))^k \approx \lambda_k^\alpha(\mathbf{1}_\mathcal{S}) \tag{9}$$

From the above equation, we observe that the problem of greedily maximizing $\Omega_k(\mathcal{S})$ is equivalent to maximizing $\lambda_k^\alpha(\mathbf{1}_\mathcal{S})$, and thus, we simply need to study the variation of $\lambda_k^\alpha(\mathbf{t})$ with $\mathbf{t}$, a real-valued vector in $\mathbb{R}^N$, at $\mathbf{t} = \mathbf{1}_\mathcal{S}$. This relaxation circumvents the combinatorial nature of our problem and has been used earlier to study graph partitioning based on Dirichlet eigenvalues [19]. The gradient of $\lambda_k^\alpha(\mathbf{t})$ with respect to $\mathbf{t}(i)$ is given by

$$\left.\frac{d\lambda_\alpha^k(\mathbf{t})}{d\mathbf{t}(i)}\right|_{\mathbf{t}=\mathbf{1}_\mathcal{S}} = \alpha \left([\mathbf{x}_\alpha^k(\mathbf{1}_\mathcal{S})](i) \right)^2 \approx \alpha(\boldsymbol{\phi}_k^*(i))^2. \tag{10}$$

This equation forms the basis of our greedy heuristic: starting with an empty $\mathcal{S}$ (i.e., $\mathbf{1}_\mathcal{S} = \mathbf{0}$), if at each step, we include the node on which the smoothest signal $\phi_k^* \in L_2(\mathcal{S}^c)$ has maximum energy (i.e., $\mathbf{1}_\mathcal{S}(i) \leftarrow 1, i = \arg\max_j \left[(\boldsymbol{\phi}_k^*(j))^2\right]$), then the cut-off estimate $\Omega_k(\mathcal{S})$ tends to increase maximally.

While the algorithm in [1] has a goal of finding an $\mathcal{S}$ of smallest possible size that satisfies a target cut-off frequency, we can easily adapt it for our cut-off frequency maximization-based active learning algorithm. This will be discussed in detail in Section 3.1.

2.5 P3: Reconstruction

A graph signal $\mathbf{f} \in PW_\omega(G)$ can be written as a linear combination eigenvectors of $\boldsymbol{\mathcal{L}}$ with eigenvalues less than ω, i.e., $\mathbf{f} = \mathbf{U}_{\mathcal{V},\mathcal{K}}\boldsymbol{\alpha}$ where $\mathcal{K}$ is the index set of those eigenvectors and $\boldsymbol{\alpha}$ is a vector containing the corresponding GFT coefficients. When the unique recovery conditions of Theorem 1 are satisfied, $\boldsymbol{\alpha}$ and the signal $\mathbf{f}$, can be recovered from its subsampled version $\mathbf{f}(\mathcal{S})$ by solving the following least squares problem:

$$\mathbf{f}(\mathcal{S}) = \mathbf{U}_{\mathcal{S},\mathcal{K}}\boldsymbol{\alpha} \tag{11}$$

$$\Rightarrow \boldsymbol{\alpha} = \mathbf{U}_{\mathcal{S},\mathcal{K}}^{+}\mathbf{f}(\mathcal{S}). \tag{12}$$

Note that if the original signal $\mathbf{f}$ is not bandlimited, i.e., $\mathbf{f} \notin PW_\omega(G)$, then the least squares solution corresponds to an approximation of $\mathbf{f}$ in $PW_\omega(G)$ (in l_2 sense).

The least squares solution requires eigen-decomposition of $\boldsymbol{\mathcal{L}}$ which is computationally expensive and may not be practical for large graphs. We now describe the iterative, distributed algorithm developed in [18] based on projection onto convex sets (POCS). The proposed method is similar to the Papoulis-Gerchberg algorithm [22] in classical signal processing which is used to reconstruct a bandlimited signal from irregular samples. The convex sets of interest in this case are

$$C_1 = \{\mathbf{x} : \boldsymbol{\mathcal{D}}_\mathcal{S}\mathbf{x} = \boldsymbol{\mathcal{D}}_\mathcal{S}\mathbf{f}\} \tag{13}$$

$$C_2 = PW_\omega(G), \tag{14}$$

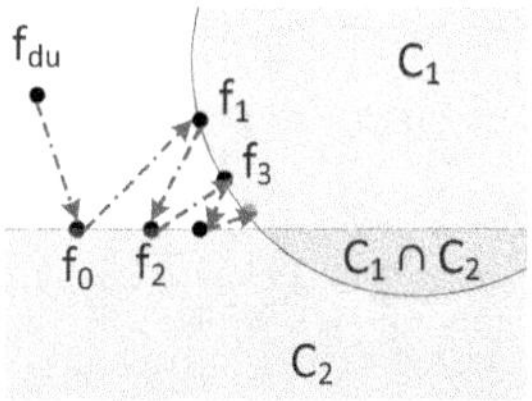

Figure 1: Iterative reconstruction using POCS

where $\boldsymbol{\mathcal{D}}_\mathcal{S}$ is the downsampling operator such that $\boldsymbol{\mathcal{D}}_\mathcal{S}\mathbf{f} = \mathbf{f}(\mathcal{S})$. The unique solution $\mathbf{f}$ to the least squares problem satisfies the following two constraints: (1) the signal equals the known values on the sampling set (i.e., $\mathbf{f} \in C_1$), (2) the signal is ω-bandlimited, where ω is computed using (4) (i.e., $\mathbf{f} \in C_2$). The projector for C_2 is $\boldsymbol{\mathcal{P}}_\omega : \mathbb{R}^N \to PW_\omega(G)$ which is a low-pass graph filter such that

$$\boldsymbol{\mathcal{P}}_\omega \mathbf{x} \in PW_\omega(G) \quad \forall\, \mathbf{x} \in \mathbb{R}^N \tag{15}$$

$\boldsymbol{\mathcal{P}}_\omega$ can be written in graph spectral domain as $\boldsymbol{\mathcal{P}}_\omega = \mathbf{H}(\boldsymbol{\mathcal{L}}) = \sum_{i=1}^N h(\lambda_i)\mathbf{u}_i\mathbf{u}_i^t$ where

$$h(\lambda) = \begin{cases} 1, & \text{if } \lambda < \omega \\ 0, & \text{if } \lambda \geq \omega \end{cases} \tag{16}$$

We define the projection operator for C_1 as $\boldsymbol{\mathcal{P}}_\mathcal{S} : \mathbb{R}^N \to C_1$ which replaces the samples on $\mathcal{S}$ by the known values.

$$\boldsymbol{\mathcal{P}}_\mathcal{S}\mathbf{x} = \mathbf{x} + \boldsymbol{\mathcal{D}}_\mathcal{S}^t(\mathbf{f}(\mathcal{S}) - \boldsymbol{\mathcal{D}}_\mathcal{S}\mathbf{x}). \tag{17}$$

With this notation the proposed iterative algorithm can be written as:

$$\begin{aligned} \mathbf{f}_0 &= \boldsymbol{\mathcal{P}}_\omega(\boldsymbol{\mathcal{D}}_\mathcal{S}^t\mathbf{f}(\mathcal{S})) \\ \mathbf{f}_{i+1} &= \boldsymbol{\mathcal{P}}_\omega\boldsymbol{\mathcal{P}}_\mathcal{S}\mathbf{f}_i \end{aligned} \tag{18}$$

At each iteration the algorithm resets the signal samples on $\mathcal{S}$ to the actual given samples and then projects the signal onto the low-pass space $PW_\omega(G)$. Figure 1 depicts this procedure graphically. It can be shown that $\boldsymbol{\mathcal{T}} = \boldsymbol{\mathcal{P}}_\omega\boldsymbol{\mathcal{P}}_\mathcal{S}$ is a non-expansive and asymptotically regular operator. Hence, the iterations in (18) converge to the unique point $\mathbf{f} \in C_1 \cap C_2$ which is the desired solution.

The low pass filter $\boldsymbol{\mathcal{P}}_\omega$ above is a spectral graph filter with an ideal brick-wall type spectral response. Thus, the exact computation of $\boldsymbol{\mathcal{P}}_\omega$ would require knowledge of the GFT, which we would like to avoid due to high computational complexity for large graphs. However, it is possible to approximate the ideal filtering operation as a matrix polynomial in terms of $\boldsymbol{\mathcal{L}}$, that can be implemented efficiently using only matrix vector products. Thus we replace $\boldsymbol{\mathcal{P}}_\omega$ in (18) with an approximate low pass filter $\boldsymbol{\mathcal{P}}_\omega^{\text{poly}}$ given by:

$$\boldsymbol{\mathcal{P}}_\omega^{\text{poly}} = \sum_{i=1}^N \left(\sum_{j=0}^p a_j \lambda_i^j \right) \mathbf{u}_i\mathbf{u}_i^t = \sum_{j=0}^p a_j \boldsymbol{\mathcal{L}}^j \tag{19}$$

We specifically use the truncated Chebychev polynomial expansion of any spectral kernel $h(\lambda)$, as proposed in [11], in our experiments. It is easy to show that an operator which is a p-degree polynomial in $\boldsymbol{\mathcal{L}}$ is p-hop localized on the graph and can be implemented in a distributed fashion. In order to ensure that the Chebyshev polynomial approximation is good, we first approximate the ideal spectral kernel by a

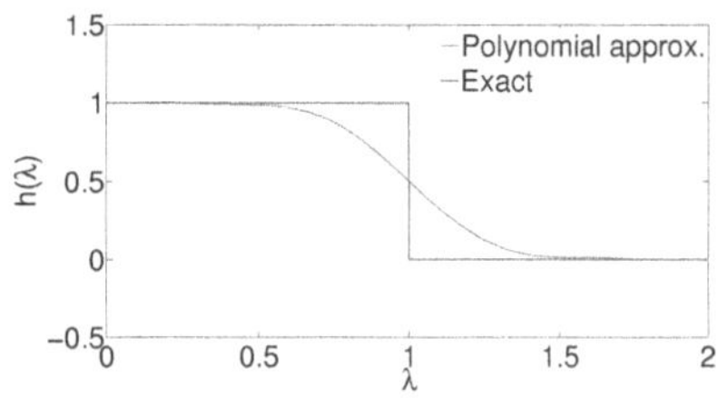

Figure 2: Spectral response of an approximate polynomial filter of degree 10. $\omega = 1, \alpha = 8$.

smooth, continuous sigmoid-like function (see Figure 2)

$$h'(\lambda) = \frac{1}{(1 + \exp(\alpha(\lambda - \omega)))} \tag{20}$$

Due to these approximations in the filter, the reconstructed signal obtained via POCS is different from the true bandlimited signal. However, in semi-supervised learning applications we do not expect the signals (i.e., class membership functions) to be exactly bandlimited anyway. So using a filter with slowly decaying spectral response ends up improving the classification accuracy slightly.

3. GRAPH SAMPLING BASED ACTIVE SEMI-SUPERVISED LEARNING

We now relate the sampling theory developed for graph signals to active semi-supervised learning and propose our solution to the problem. As noted earlier, if the edges of the graph represent similarity between the nodes, then a graph signal defined using the membership functions of a particular class tends to be smooth. This is illustrated experimentally in Figure 3. In Section 2.3 we showed how to estimate the sampling cut-off frequency for a set of vertices. In practice, class membership signals are not strictly bandlimited (see Figure 3). Thus we will be approximating a non-bandlimited signal with one that is bandlimited to the cut-off frequency of the chosen vertex set. The key observation in our work is that, even though we cannot recover the "true" membership signal exactly from its samples, an active learning approach *should aim at selecting the sampling set with maximum cut-off frequency.* This is obviously true since $PW_\omega(G) \subset PW_{\omega'}(G)$ if $\omega \leq \omega'$ and thus, for any signal, its best approximation with a signal from $PW_{\omega'}(G)$ can be no worse (in terms of l_2 error) than its best approximation with a signal from $PW_\omega(G)$.

In this setting, predicting the labels of the unknown datapoints using the labeled data amounts to reconstructing a bandlimited graph signal from its values on the sampling set. Thus, based on the above reasoning the active learning strategy, given a target number of datapoints to be labeled, should be to find a set $\mathcal{S}$, with that size, so that the cut-off frequency of $\mathcal{S}$ is maximized.

3.1 Proposed method

Now, we present the details of our method. We target a multi-class active semi-supervised learning problem with C classes. The true membership function for class j is denoted as $\mathbf{f}_j : \mathcal{V} \mapsto \{0, 1\}$, where $\mathbf{f}_j(i) = 1$ indicates that node i belongs to class j. These membership functions are taken to be the graph signals for our setting. The predicted membership functions for each class take real values and are denoted as $\hat{\mathbf{f}}_j : \mathcal{V} \mapsto \mathbb{R}$. The predicted label of node i is given by $\arg\max_j \hat{\mathbf{f}}_j(i)$. We denote the labeled set as $\mathcal{S}_L$ and the unlabeled set as $\mathcal{S}_U = \mathcal{V} \setminus \mathcal{S}_L$. Then, our solution to the active semi-supervised learning task can be formally summarized as follows:

1. Given a size m and parameter k, we first find the optimal labeled set $\mathcal{S}_L^*$ and corresponding cut-off frequency $\Omega_k(\mathcal{S}_L^*)$ as follows:

$$\mathcal{S}_L^* = \underset{\mathcal{S}:|\mathcal{S}|=m}{\arg\max}\ \Omega_k(\mathcal{S}) \tag{21}$$

   We solve this problem in a greedy fashion by adding nodes to $\mathcal{S}$ that maximize the increase in $\Omega_k(\mathcal{S})$ at each step (cf. Section 2.4). This procedure is summarized with Algorithm 1
2. Next, we query the labels of nodes in $\mathcal{S}_L^*$.
3. Finally, we determine the predicted membership functions $\hat{\mathbf{f}}_j$ for each class from $\mathbf{f}_j(\mathcal{S}_L^*), j = 1, \ldots, C$ using the POCS iterative method described in Section 2.5, where $\mathcal{S} = \mathcal{S}_L^*$ and $\omega = \Omega_k(\mathcal{S}_L^*)$ are used in (13) and (14) to construct the convex sets.

Algorithm 1 Greedy heuristic for finding $\mathcal{S}_L^*$

Input: $G = \{\mathcal{V}, E\}$, $\boldsymbol{\mathcal{L}}$, target size m, parameter $k \in \mathbb{Z}^+$.
Initialize: $\mathcal{S} = \{\emptyset\}$.
while $|\mathcal{S}| \leq m$ **do**
  For $\mathcal{S}$, compute the smoothest signal $\phi_k^* \in L_2(\mathcal{S}^c)$ using (4) and (5).
  $v \leftarrow \arg\max_i \left[(\phi_k^*(i))^2\right]$.
  $\mathcal{S} \leftarrow \mathcal{S} \cup v$.
end while
$\mathcal{S}_L^* \leftarrow \mathcal{S}$.

3.2 Graph Theoretic Interpretation

In this section, we will provide an intuitive interpretation for our node selection algorithm in terms of connected-ness among the nodes. To simplify the exposition, we consider the maximization problem (21) for $k = 1$:

$$\Omega_1(\mathcal{S}) = \inf_{\substack{\mathbf{x}(\mathcal{S})=\mathbf{0} \\ ||\mathbf{x}||=1}} \mathbf{x}^t \boldsymbol{\mathcal{L}} \mathbf{x} \tag{22}$$

This expression appears more commonly as part of discrete Dirichlet eigenvalue problems on graphs. Specifically, it is equal to the Dirichlet energy of the subset $\mathcal{S}^c$ [6, 19]. The sampling set selection problem seeks to identify the subset $\mathcal{S}$ that maximizes this objective function. To give an intuitive interpretation of our goal, we expand the objective function for any $\mathbf{x}$ with constraint $\mathbf{x}(\mathcal{S}) = \mathbf{0}$ as follows:

$$\begin{aligned}\mathbf{x}^t \boldsymbol{\mathcal{L}} \mathbf{x} &= \sum_{i \sim j} w_{ij} \left(\frac{x_i}{\sqrt{d_i}} - \frac{x_j}{\sqrt{d_j}} \right)^2 \\ &= \sum_{\substack{i \sim j \\ i \in \mathcal{S}, j \in \mathcal{S}^c}} w_{ij} \left(\frac{x_j^2}{d_j} \right) + \sum_{\substack{i \sim j \\ i, j \in \mathcal{S}^c}} w_{ij} \left(\frac{x_i}{\sqrt{d_i}} - \frac{x_j}{\sqrt{d_j}} \right)^2 .\end{aligned} \tag{23}$$

The minimizer in the equation above is the first Dirichlet eigenvector which is guaranteed to have strictly positive values on $\mathcal{S}^c$ [19]. Therefore, the contribution of the second

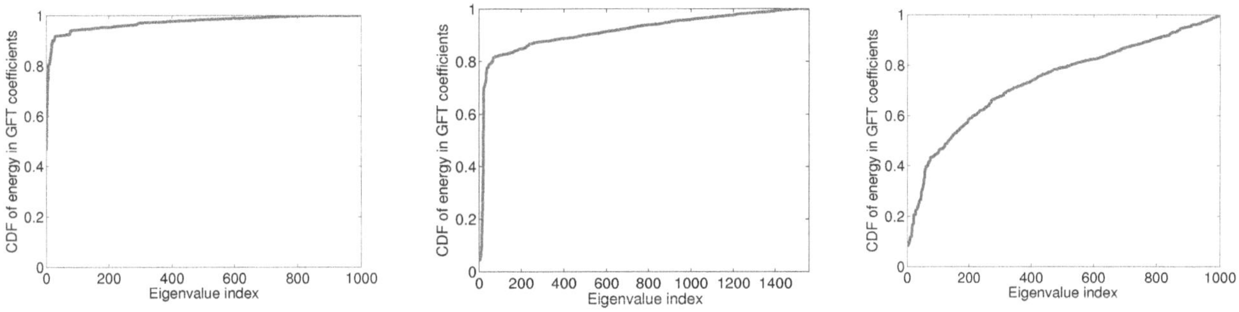

(a) USPS (b) Isolet (c) 20 newsgroups

Figure 3: Cumulative distribution of energy in the GFT coefficients of one of the class membership functions pertaining to the three real-world dataset experiments considered in Section 5. Note that most of the energy is concentrated in the low-pass region.

term is expected to be negligible as compared to the first one due to differencing, and we get

$$\mathbf{x}^t \boldsymbol{\mathcal{L}} \mathbf{x} \approx \sum_{j \in \mathcal{S}^c} \left(\frac{p_j}{d_j} \right) x_j^2, \tag{24}$$

where, $p_j = \sum_{i \in \mathcal{S}} w_{ij}$ is defined as the "partial out-degree" of node $j \in \mathcal{S}^c$, i.e., it is the sum of weights of edges crossing over to the set $\mathcal{S}$. Therefore, given a current selected $\mathcal{S}$, the greedy algorithm selects the next node, to be added to $\mathcal{S}$, that maximizes the increase in

$$\Omega_1(\mathcal{S}) \approx \inf_{||\mathbf{x}||=1} \sum_{j \in \mathcal{S}^c} \left(\frac{p_j}{d_j} \right) x_j^2. \tag{25}$$

Due to the constraint $||\mathbf{x}|| = 1$, the expression being minimized is essentially an infimum over a convex combination of the fractional out-degrees and its value is largely determined by nodes $j \in \mathcal{S}^c$ for which p_j/d_j is small. In other words, we must worry about those nodes that have a low ratio of partial degree to the actual degree. Thus, in the simplest case, our selection algorithm tries to remove those nodes from the unlabeled set that are weakly connected to nodes in the labeled set. This makes intuitive sense as, in the end, most prediction algorithms involve propagation of labels from the labeled to the unlabeled nodes. If an unlabeled node is strongly connected to various numerous points, its label can be assigned with greater confidence.

Note that using a higher power k in the cost function, i.e., finding $\Omega_k(\mathcal{S})$ for $k > 1$ involves $\mathbf{x}\boldsymbol{\mathcal{L}}^k\mathbf{x}$ which, loosely speaking, takes into account higher order interactions between the nodes while choosing the nodes to label. In a sense, we expect it to capture the connectivities in a more *global* sense, beyond local interactions, taking into account the underlying manifold structure of the data.

3.3 Complexity

We now comment on the time and space complexity of our algorithm. The most complex step in the greedy procedure for maximizing $\Omega_k(\mathcal{S})$ is computing the smallest eigen-pair of $(\boldsymbol{\mathcal{L}}^k)_{\mathcal{S}^c}$. This can be accomplished using an iterative Rayleigh-quotient minimization based algorithm. Specifically, the locally-optimal pre-conditioned conjugate gradient (LOPCG) method [14] is suitable for this approach. Note that $(\boldsymbol{\mathcal{L}}^k)_{\mathcal{S}^c}$ can be written as $\mathbf{I}_{\mathcal{S}^c,\mathcal{V}}.\boldsymbol{\mathcal{L}}.\boldsymbol{\mathcal{L}} \ldots \boldsymbol{\mathcal{L}}.\mathbf{I}_{\mathcal{V},\mathcal{S}^c}$, hence the eigenvalue computation can be broken into atomic matrix-vector products: $\boldsymbol{\mathcal{L}}.\mathbf{x}$. Typically, the graphs encountered in learning applications are sparse, leading to efficient implementations of $\boldsymbol{\mathcal{L}}.\mathbf{x}$. If $|\boldsymbol{\mathcal{L}}|$ denotes the number of non-zero elements in $\boldsymbol{\mathcal{L}}$, then the complexity of the matrix-vector product is $O(|\boldsymbol{\mathcal{L}}|)$. The complexity of each eigen-pair computation for $(\boldsymbol{\mathcal{L}}^k)_{\mathcal{S}^c}$ is then $O(k|\boldsymbol{\mathcal{L}}|r)$, where r is a constant equal to the average number of iterations required for the LOPCG algorithm (r depends on the spectral properties of $\boldsymbol{\mathcal{L}}$ and is independent of its size $|\mathcal{V}|$). The complexity of the label selection algorithm then becomes $O(k|\boldsymbol{\mathcal{L}}|mr)$, where m is the number of labels requested.

In the iterative reconstruction algorithm, since we use polynomial graph filters (Section 2.5), once again the atomic step is the matrix-vector product $\boldsymbol{\mathcal{L}}.\mathbf{x}$. The complexity of this algorithm can be given as $O(|\boldsymbol{\mathcal{L}}|pq)$, where p is the order of the polynomial used to design the filter and q is the average number of iterations required for convergence. Again, both these parameters are independent of $|\mathcal{V}|$. Thus, the overall complexity of our algorithm is $O(|\boldsymbol{\mathcal{L}}|(kmr + pq))$. In addition, our algorithm has major advantages in terms of space complexity: Since, the atomic operation at each step is the matrix-vector product $\boldsymbol{\mathcal{L}}.\mathbf{x}$, we only need to store $\boldsymbol{\mathcal{L}}$ and a constant number of vectors. Moreover, the structure of the Laplacian matrix allows one to perform the aforementioned operations in a distributed fashion. This makes it well-suited for large-scale implementations using software packages such as GraphLab [16].

3.4 Prediction Error and Number of Labels

As discussed in Section 2.5, given the samples $\mathbf{f}_{\mathcal{S}}$ of the true graph signal on a subset of nodes $\mathcal{S} \subset \mathcal{V}$, its estimate on $\mathcal{S}^c$ is obtained by solving the following problem:

$$\hat{\mathbf{f}}(\mathcal{S}^c) = \mathbf{U}_{\mathcal{S}^c,\mathcal{K}}\boldsymbol{\alpha}^* \text{ where, } \boldsymbol{\alpha}^* = \arg\min_{\boldsymbol{\alpha}} ||\mathbf{U}_{\mathcal{S},\mathcal{K}}\boldsymbol{\alpha} - \mathbf{f}(\mathcal{S})|| \tag{26}$$

Here, $\mathcal{K}$ is the index set of eigenvectors with eigenvalues less than the cut-off $\omega_c(\mathcal{S})$. If the true signal $\mathbf{f} \in PW_{\omega_c(\mathcal{S})}(G)$, then the prediction is perfect. However, this is not the case in most problems. The prediction error $\|\mathbf{f} - \hat{\mathbf{f}}\|$ roughly equals the portion of energy of the true signal in $[\omega_c(\mathcal{S}), \lambda_N]$ frequency band. By choosing the sampling set $\mathcal{S}$ that maximizes $\omega_c(\mathcal{S})$, we try to capture most of the signal energy and thus, reduce the prediction error.

An important question in the context of active learning is determining the minimum number of labels required so that the prediction error $\|\mathbf{f} - \hat{\mathbf{f}}\|$ is less that some given tolerance δ. To find this we first characterize the smoothness $\gamma(\mathbf{f})$ of a signal $\mathbf{f}$ as

$$\gamma(\mathbf{f}) = \min \theta \text{ s.t. } \|\mathbf{f} - \boldsymbol{\mathcal{P}}_\theta \mathbf{f}\| \leq \delta$$

The following theorem gives a lower bound on the minimum of number of labels required in terms of $\gamma(\mathbf{f})$.

THEOREM 2. *If $\hat{\mathbf{f}}$ is obtained by solving (26), then the minimum number of labels l required to satisfy $\|\mathbf{f} - \hat{\mathbf{f}}\| \leq \delta$ is greater than p, where p is the number of eigenvalues of $\boldsymbol{\mathcal{L}}$ less than $\gamma(\mathbf{f})$.*

PROOF. In order for (26) to have a unique solution, $\mathbf{U}_{\mathcal{S},\mathcal{K}}$ needs to have full column rank, which implies that $l = |\mathcal{S}| \geq |\mathcal{K}|$. Now, for $\|\mathbf{f} - \hat{\mathbf{f}}\| \leq \delta$ to hold the bandwidth of $\hat{\mathbf{f}}$ has to be at least $\gamma(\mathbf{f})$, or in other words, $|\mathcal{K}| \geq p$. This gives us the desired result as $l \geq |\mathcal{K}| \geq p$. □

4. RELATED WORK

Different frameworks have been proposed for pool-based batch-mode active semi-supervised learning including optimal experiment design [27, 26], generalization error bound minimization [7, 8] and submodular optimization [9, 10, 12]. We now point out connections between some of the graph based approaches in the above categories and our graph signal sampling theory based framework.

The notion of frequency given by GFT is closely related to Laplacian eigenmaps which is a well known dimensionality reduction technique [2]. GFT can be viewed as a way of measuring the signal variation on the manifold represented by Laplacian eigenmaps. By selecting nodes that maximize the bandwidth of the space of recoverable signals, we are trying to capture as many dimensions of the manifold structure of the data with as few samples as possible. A related active learning method proposed by Zhang et al. [27] uses optimal experiment design while considering local structure of the data in a way which is similar to local linear embedding (LLE) for approximating the underlying low-dimensional manifold [21]. This approach tries to choose the most representative data points from which one can recover the whole data set by local linear reconstruction. It is interesting to note that under certain conditions LLE and Laplacian eigenmaps are equivalent [15].

Gu and Han [7] propose a method based on minimizing the generalization error bound for learning with local and global consistency (LLGC) [28]. Their formulation boils down to choosing subset S that minimizes $\mathrm{Tr}\left((\mu \mathbf{L}_S + \mathbf{I})^{-2}\right)$. To relate this formulation to our proposed method, note that

$$\mathrm{Tr}\left((\mu \mathbf{L}_S + \mathbf{I})^{-2}\right) = \sum_i \frac{1}{(\zeta_i + 1)^2} \leq \frac{|S|}{(\zeta_1 + 1)^2}$$

where, $\zeta_1 \leq \ldots \leq \zeta_{|S|}$ denote the eigenvalues of $\mathbf{L}_S$. Loosely speaking, minimizing the above objective function is equivalent to maximizing the smallest eigenvalue ζ_1 of $\mathbf{L}_S$. So, this method essentially tries to ensure that the labeled set is well-connected to the unlabeled set whereas our method ensures that the unlabeled set is well-connected to the labeled set (cf. Section 3.2).

Submodular functions have been used for active semi-supervised learning on graphs by Guillory and Bilmes [10, 9]. In this work, the subset of nodes $S \subset \mathcal{V}$ is chosen to maximize

$$\Psi(S) = \min_{T \subseteq \mathcal{V} \setminus S : T \neq \emptyset} \frac{\Gamma(T)}{|T|}, \tag{27}$$

where $\Gamma(T)$ denotes the cut function $\sum_{i \in T, j \notin T} w_{ij}$. Intuitively, maximizing $\Psi(S)$ ensures that no subset of unlabeled nodes is weakly connected to the labeled set S. This agrees with the graph theoretic interpretation of our method given in Section 3.2. They also provide a bound on the prediction error in terms $\Psi(S)$ and a smoothness function $\Phi(\mathbf{f}) = \sum_{i,j} w_{ij}|f_i - f_j|$. This bound gives a theoretical justification for semi-supervised learning using min-cuts [4]. It also motivates a graph partitioning-based active learning heuristic [9] which says that to select l nodes to label, the graph should be partitioned into l clusters and one node should be picked at random from each cluster.

5. EXPERIMENTS

We compare our method against three active semi-supervised learning approaches mentioned in the previous section, namely, LLR [27], LLGC error bound minimization [7], METIS graph partitioning based heuristic [9] and Ψ-max [10]. The details of implementation of each method are as follows:

1. The LLR approach [27] allows any prediction method once the samples to be queried are chosen. We use the Laplacian regularized least squares (LapRLS) [3] method for prediction (used in [27]).

2. In our implementation of the LLGC bound method [7], we fix the parameter μ to 0.01. Since this approach is based on minimizing the generalization error bound for LLGC, we use the same method for prediction with the queried samples. [1]

3. The normalized cut based active learning heuristic of Guillory and Bilmes [9] is implemented using the METIS graph partitioning package [13]. This algorithm chooses a random node to label from each partition, so we average the error rates over a 100 trials.

In the implementation of our proposed method, we use approximate polynomial filters of degree 10 with $\alpha = 8$. The parameter k in our method is fixed as 8 for these experiments. Its effect on classification accuracy is studied in Section 5.4. In addition to the above methods, we also compare with the random sampling strategy. We use LapRLS to predict the unknown labels from the randomly queried samples and report the average error rates over 30 trials.

To intuitively demonstrate the effectiveness of our method, we first test it on a two circles toy data as shown in Figure 4. The data is comprised of 200 nodes from which we would like to select 8 nodes to query. We construct a weighted sparse graph by connecting each node to its 10 nearest neighbors while ensuring that the connections are symmetric. The edge weights are computed with the Gaussian kernel $\exp\left(-\frac{\|\mathbf{x}_i - \mathbf{x}_j\|^2}{2\sigma^2}\right)$ (except in the case of Ψ-max where the graph is unweighted). It can be seen from Figure 4 that all the methods choose 4 points from each of the two circles. Additionally, the proposed approach selects evenly

[1] In our experiments, we observed that the greedy algorithm given in [7] did not converge to a good solution. So we use Monte-Carlo simulations to minimize the objective function.

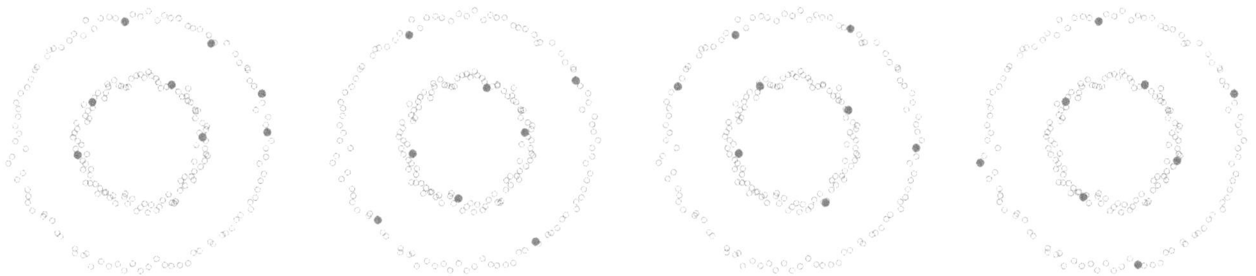

(a) Ψ-max (b) LLR (c) LLGC Bound (d) Proposed

Figure 4: Toy example comparing the nodes selected using different active learning methods

spaced data points within one circle, while at the same time maximizing the spacing between the selected data points in different circles. This is in accordance with the requirement of choosing points which are most representative of the data.

We tested our method in three application scenarios: Handwritten digit recognition, text classification and spoken letters recognition. In these experiments, we do not compare with Ψ-max since the method has computational complexity of $O(N^6)$ and, to the best of our knowledge, is not scalable. Next, we provide the details of each experiment. Both the datasets and the graph construction procedures used are typical of what has been used in the literature.

5.1 Handwritten digits classification

In this experiment, we used our proposed active semi-supervised learning algorithm to perform a classification task on the USPS handwritten digits dataset[2]. This dataset consists of 1100 16 × 16 pixel images for each of the digits 0 to 9. We used 100 randomly selected samples for each digit class to create one instance of our dataset. Thus each instance consists of 1000 feature vectors (100 samples/class × 10 digit classes) of dimension 256.

The graph is constructed using Gaussian kernel weights $w_{ij} = \exp\left(-\frac{||\mathbf{x}_i - \mathbf{x}_j||^2}{2\sigma^2}\right)$, where $\mathbf{x}_i$ is the 256-dimensional feature vector composed of pixel intensity values for each image. The parameter σ is chosen to be 1/3-rd of the average distance to the K-th nearest neighbor for all datapoints. This heuristic has been suggested in [5]. We fix $K = 10$. Additionally, the graph is sparsified approximately by restricting the connectivity of each datapoint to its K nearest neighbors, i.e., an edge between nodes i and j is removed unless node i is among the K-nearest neighbors of node j or vice-versa. This results in a symmetric adjacency matrix for the graph. Using the graph constructed, we select the points to label and report prediction error after reconstruction using our semi-supervised learning algorithm. We repeat the classification over 10 such instances of the dataset and report the average classification error. The results are illustrated in Figure (5a). We observe that our proposed method outperforms the others. A notable feature of our method is that we show very good classification results even for very few labeled samples. This is due to our inherent criterion for active learning that tries to select those points that maximize the recoverable dimensions of the underlying data manifold.

[2]`http://www.cs.nyu.edu/~roweis/data.html`

5.2 Text classification

For our text classification example, we use the 20 newsgroups dataset[3]. It contains around 20,000 documents, partitioned in 20 different newsgroups. For our experiment, we consider 10 groups of documents, namely, {comp.graphics, comp.os.ms-windows.misc, comp.sys.ibm.pc.hardware, comp.sys.mac.hardware, rec.autos, rec.motorcycles, sci.crypt, sci.electronics, sci.med, sci.space}, and randomly choose 100 datapoints from each group. We generate 10 such instances of 1000 data points each and report the average errors. We clean the dataset by removing the words that appear in fewer than 20 documents and then select only the 3000 most frequent ones from the remaining words. To form the feature vectors representing the documents, we use the tf-idf statistic of these words. The tf-idf statistic captures the relative importance of a word in a document in a corpus:

$$\text{tf-idf} = (1 + \log(\text{tf})) \times \log\left(\frac{N}{\text{idf}}\right) \tag{28}$$

where, tf is the frequency of a word in a document, idf is the number of documents in which the word appears and N is the total number of documents. Thus, we get 1000 feature vectors in 3000 dimensional space. To form the graph of documents, we compute the pairwise cosine similarity between their feature vectors. Each node is connected to the 10 nodes that are most similar to it and the resultant graph is then symmetrized. The classification results in Figure (5b) show that our method performs very well compared to others. However, the absolute error rates are not very good. This is due to the high similarity between different newsgroups which makes the problem inherently difficult.

5.3 Spoken letters classification

For the spoken letters classification example, we considered the Isolet dataset[4]. It consists of letters of the English alphabet spoken in isolation twice by 150 different subjects. The speakers are grouped into 5 sets of 30 speakers each, with the groups referred to as isolet1 through isolet5. Each alphabet utterance has been pre-processed beforehand to create a 617-dimensional feature vector.

For this experiment, we considered the task of active semi-supervised classification of utterances into the 26 alphabet categories. To form an instance of the dataset, 60 utterances are randomly selected out of 300 for each alphabet. Thus, each instance consists of 60 × 26 = 1560 datapoints

[3]`http://qwone.com/~jason/20Newsgroups/`

[4]`http://archive.ics.uci.edu/ml/datasets/ISOLET`

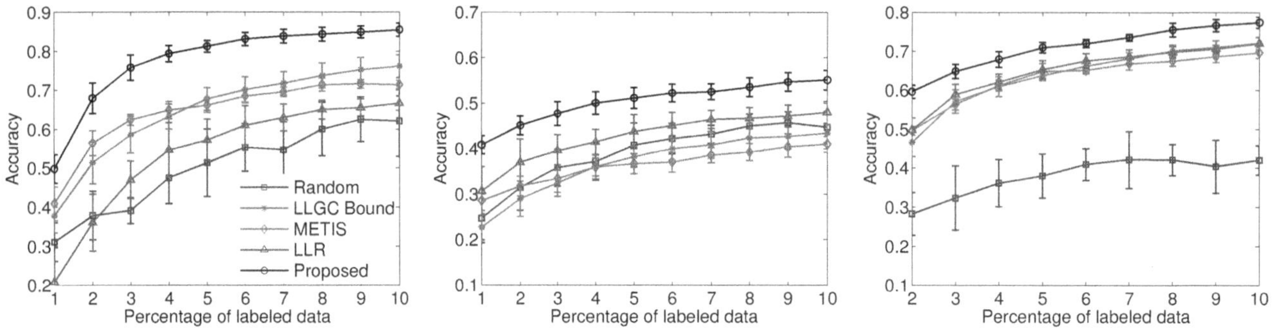

(a) USPS (b) 20 newsgroups (c) Isolet

Figure 5: Comparison of active semi-supervised learning methods on real datasets. Plots show the average classification accuracies for different percentages of labeled data.

of dimension 617. As in the hand-written digits classification problem, the graph is constructed using Gaussian kernel weights between nodes, with σ taken as 1/3-rd of the average distance to the K-th nearest neighbor for each datapoint. We select $K = 10$ for our experiment. Sparsification of the graph is carried out approximately using K-nearest neighbor criterion. With the constructed graph, we perform active semi-supervised learning using all the methods. The experiment is repeated over 10 instances of the dataset and average prediction error is reported in Figure (5c). Note that we start with 2% labeled points to ensure that each method gets a fair chance of selecting at least one point to label from each of the 26 classes. We observe that our method outperforms the others.

5.4 Effect of parameter k

To study the effect of parameter k in the proposed method on classification accuracy we repeat the above experiments for different values of k. Figure 6 shows the results. For the USPS and Isolet datasets, the classification accuracies remain largely unchanged for different values of k. For the 20 Newsgroups dataset, a slight improvement in classification accuracies is observed for higher values of k. This result agrees with the distribution of GFT coefficients of the class membership functions in each dataset shown in Figure 3. In USPS and Isolet datasets, most of the energy of the graph signal (i.e., the class membership functions) is contained in the first few frequencies. Thus, increasing the value of k, so that a better estimate of cut-off frequency is maximized during the choice of sampling set, is not necessary. In other words, maximizing a loose estimate of the cut-off frequency is sufficient. However, the membership functions in the 20 Newsgroups dataset have a significant fraction of their energy spread over high frequencies as shown in Figure 3. Due to this, maximizing a tighter estimate of the the cut-off allows the sampling set selection algorithm to pick nodes that capture more signal energy, resulting in higher accuracies.

6. CONCLUSION

In this paper, we introduce a novel framework for batch mode active semi-supervised learning based on sampling theory for graph signals. The proposed active learning framework aims to select the subset nodes which maximizes the dimension of the space of uniquely recoverable signals. In the context of sampling theory, this translates to selecting the subset with the maximum cut-off frequency. This interpretation leads to a very efficient greedy algorithm. We provide intuition about how the method tries to choose the nodes which are most representative of the data. We also present an efficient semi-supervised learning method based on bandlimited interpolation. We show, through experiments on real data, that our two algorithms, in conjunction, perform very well compared to state of the art methods.

In the future, we would like to provide bounds on the prediction error of the proposed method (when the true signal is not exactly bandlimited) in terms of signal smoothness and the cut-off frequency. We also hope to have tighter bounds on the number of labels required for desired prediction accuracy. It would be useful to consider an extension of the proposed framework to a partially batch setting so that we can incorporate the label information from previous batches to improve the choice of sampling sets.

7. REFERENCES

[1] A. Anis, A. Gadde, and A. Ortega. Towards a sampling theorem for signals on arbitrary graphs. *IEEE International Conference on Acoustics, Speech and Signal Processing (ICASSP), 2014.*

[2] M. Belkin and P. Niyogi. Semi-supervised learning on riemannian manifolds. *Machine learning*, 56(1-3):209–239, 2004.

[3] M. Belkin, P. Niyogi, and V. Sindhwani. Manifold regularization: A geometric framework for learning from labeled and unlabeled examples. *The Journal of Machine Learning Research*, 7:2399–2434, 2006.

[4] A. Blum and S. Chawla. Learning from labeled and unlabeled data using graph mincuts. In *Proceedings of the 18th International Conference on Machine Learning*, pages 19–26, 2001.

[5] O. Chapelle, B. Schölkopf, A. Zien, et al. *Semi-supervised learning*. MIT Press, Cambridge, 2006.

[6] F. R. K. Chung. *Spectral graph theory*, volume 92. CBMS Regional Conference Series in Mathematics, AMS, 1997.

[7] Q. Gu and J. Han. Towards active learning on graphs: An error bound minimization approach. In *Proceedings of 12th IEEE International Conference on Data Mining*, pages 882–887, 2012.

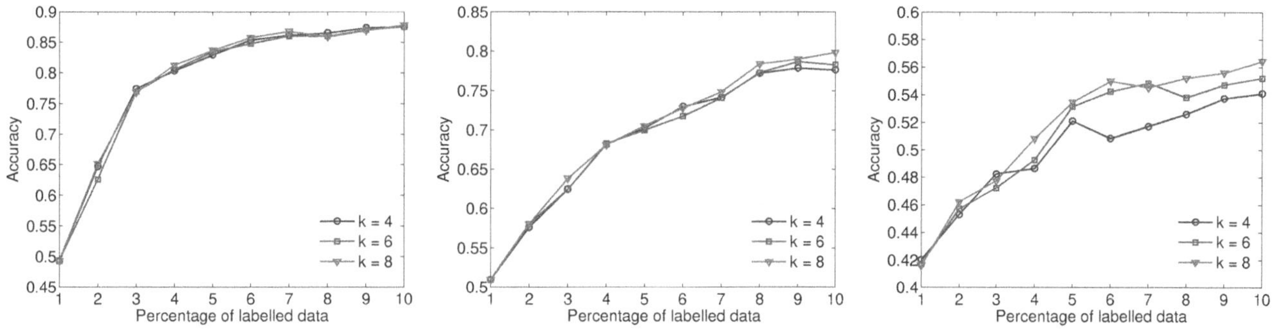

(a) USPS (b) Isolet (c) 20 newsgroups

Figure 6: Effect of k on classification accuracy of the proposed method. Plots show the average classification accuracy for different percentages of labelled data.

[8] Q. Gu, T. Zhang, C. Ding, and J. Han. Selective labeling via error bound minimization. In *Advances in Neural Information Processing Systems 25*, pages 332–340. 2012.

[9] A. Guillory and J. Bilmes. Label selection on graphs. In *Advances in Neural Information Processing Systems 22*, pages 691–699. 2009.

[10] A. Guillory and J. Bilmes. Active semi-supervised learning using submodular functions. In *Proceedings of 27th Conference on Uncertainty in Artificial Intelligence*, pages 274–282, 2011.

[11] D. Hammond, P. Vandergheynst, and R. Gribonval. Wavelets on graphs via spectral graph theory. *Applied and Computational Harmonic Analysis*, 30(2):129 – 150, 2011.

[12] S. C. Hoi, R. Jin, J. Zhu, and M. R. Lyu. Batch mode active learning and its application to medical image classification. In *Proceedings of the 23rd International conference on Machine learning*, pages 417–424, 2006.

[13] G. Karypis and V. Kumar. A fast and high quality multilevel scheme for partitioning irregular graphs. *SIAM Journal on Scientific Computing*, 20(1), 1998.

[14] A. V. Knyazev. Toward the optimal preconditioned eigensolver: Locally optimal block preconditioned conjugate gradient method. *SIAM journal on scientific computing*, 23(2):517–541, 2001.

[15] D. Kong, C. H. Ding, H. Huang, and F. Nie. An iterative locally linear embedding algorithm. In *Proceedings of the 29th International Conference on Machine Learning*, 2012.

[16] Y. Low, D. Bickson, J. Gonzalez, C. Guestrin, A. Kyrola, and J. M. Hellerstein. Distributed graphlab: A framework for machine learning and data mining in the cloud. *Proc. VLDB Endow.*, 5(8):716–727, Apr. 2012.

[17] S. Narang and A. Ortega. Perfect reconstruction two-channel wavelet filter banks for graph structured data. *IEEE Transactions on Signal Processing*, 60(6):2786–2799, June 2012.

[18] S. K. Narang, A. Gadde, E. Sanou, and A. Ortega. Localized iterative methods for interpolation in graph structured data. In *Signal and Information Processing (GlobalSIP), 2013 IEEE Global Conference on*, 2013.

[19] B. Osting, C. D. White, and E. Oudet. Minimal Dirichlet energy partitions for graphs. Aug. 2013. arXiv:1308.4915 [math.OC].

[20] I. Pesenson. Sampling in Paley-Wiener spaces on combinatorial graphs. *Transactions of the American Mathematical Society*, 360(10):5603–5627, 2008.

[21] S. T. Roweis and L. K. Saul. Nonlinear dimensionality reduction by locally linear embedding. *Science*, 290(5500):2323–2326, 2000.

[22] K. Sauer and J. Allebach. Iterative reconstruction of bandlimited images from nonuniformly spaced samples. *Circuits and Systems, IEEE Transactions on*, 34(12):1497–1506, 1987.

[23] B. Settles. Active learning literature survey. Computer Sciences Technical Report 1648, University of Wisconsin–Madison, 2010.

[24] D. I. Shuman, S. K. Narang, P. Frossard, A. Ortega, and P. Vandergheynst. Signal processing on graphs: Extending high-dimensional data analysis to networks and other irregular data domains. *Signal Processing Magazine, arXiv:1211.0053*, May. 2013.

[25] A. J. Smola and R. Kondor. Kernels and regularization on graphs. In *Learning theory and kernel machines*, pages 144–158. Springer, 2003.

[26] K. Yu, J. Bi, and V. Tresp. Active learning via transductive experimental design. In *Proceedings of the 23rd International conference on Machine learning*, pages 1081–1088, 2006.

[27] L. Zhang, C. Chen, J. Bu, D. Cai, X. He, and T. S. Huang. Active learning based on locally linear reconstruction. *Pattern Analysis and Machine Intelligence, IEEE Transactions on*, 33(10):2026–2038, 2011.

[28] D. Zhou, O. Bousquet, T. N. Lal, J. Weston, and B. Schölkopf. Learning with local and global consistency. In *Advances in Neural Information Processing Systems 16*. 2004.

[29] X. Zhu. Semi-supervised learning literature survey. Technical Report 1530, Computer Sciences, University of Wisconsin-Madison, 2008.

[30] X. Zhu, Z. Ghahramani, and J. Lafferty. Semi-supervised learning using gaussian fields and harmonic functions. In *ICML*, volume 3, pages 912–919, 2003.

Active Collaborative Permutation Learning

Jialei Wang
Dept. of Computer Science
University of Chicago
jialei@uchicago.edu

Nathan Srebro
Toyota Technological Institute
at Chicago
nati@ttic.edu

James A. Evans
Dept. of Sociology
University of Chicago
jevans@uchicago.edu

ABSTRACT

We consider the problem of Collaborative Permutation Recovery, i.e. recovering multiple permutations over objects (e.g. preference rankings over different options) from limited pairwise comparisons. We tackle both the problem of how to recover multiple related permutations from limited observations, and the active learning problem of which pairwise comparison queries to ask so as to allow better recovery. There has been much work on recovering single permutations from pairwise comparisons, but we show that considering several related permutations jointly we can leverage their relatedness so as to reduce the number of comparisons needed compared to reconstructing each permutation separately. To do so, we take a collaborative filtering / matrix completion approach and use a trace-norm or max-norm regularized matrix learning model. Our approach can also be seen as a collaborative learning version of Jamieson and Nowak's recent work on constrained permutation recovery, where instead of basing the recovery on known features, we learn the best features de novo.

Categories and Subject Descriptors

H.3.3 [**Information Storage and Retrieval**]: Information Filtering; I.2.6 [**Artificial Intelligence**]: Learning

General Terms

Theory, Algorithms, and Experimentation

Keywords

Collaborative Ranking; Active Learning; Matrix Factorization

1. INTRODUCTION

Recovering permutations or rankings from pairwise comparisons is an extensively studied problem with wide applications in information retrieval, knowledge discovery and machine learning. The standard setup is that of recovering a *single* permutation π over m objects based on information of the sort "A appears before B in the permutation". It is well known that if comparisons are indeed consistent with some underlying permutation (i.e. there are no discrepancies or errors) then $\Theta(m^2)$ random queries or $\Theta(m \log m)$ adaptively chosen queries are sufficient for recovering the permutation (this is essentially a sorting problem). Also when dealing with noisy comparisons, or when the comparisons are not transitive and consistent with some underlying permutation, methods are available for reconstructing the best consensus permutation from both random and adaptively chosen queries [2, 21].

But in many scenarios, we would like to recover multiple related permutations. Consider for example many people, each with their own tastes or preferences. We could try to recover a single permutation that best tries to explain the consensus among the people, treating comparisons made by different people as not-entirely-consistent noisy comparisons. This approach, seems absurd in the context of survey research, because it would fail to capture individual preferences and miss out entirely on the diversity of preferences in the population.

Alternatively, we could independently learn a separate permutation for each person. While this corresponds to the most common approach to imputing missing survey data, it breaks down in the context of sparse or much missing data. If we can only obtain a limited number of comparisons from each user, perhaps even less than the number of items m, this might not be enough to recover the permutations when each users' ranking is considered separately. By contrast, in this paper, we investigate the problem of *collaborative permutation learning*. That is, of jointly recovering multiple related, but not identical, permutations based on pairwise comparisons from different permutations. We will show through theoretical and empirical demonstrations that the solution of these problems could widen the application of learning with permutations to the design of novel, intelligent surveys that only require respondents to rank a few items in order to approximately recover their entire preference ranking. This would allow social and information science researchers to rapidly identify individually preferred products, services, opinions, policies and solutions, without wasting questions on answers that are likely predictable.

This type of collaborative ranking survey has become common for organizations that seek to identify preferred solutions to problems. Consider the survey platform "All our ideas" [1] in which individuals and organizations can field surveys or "idea marketplaces" of precisely the type we describe here. Individual respondents are posed with a question and an associated pair of possible responses. Respondents can either add a new response, or compare the presented pair. For example, in 2011, New York City Mayor Michael Bloomberg's office fielded such a survey that posed the question "Which do you think is better for creating a greener, greater New York City?" with possible responses including "open schoolyards across the city as public playgrounds", "increase targeted tree plantings in neighborhoods with high asthma rates", and "keep

KDD '14, August 24-27, 2014, New York City, USA.
Copyright 2014 ACM 978-1-4503-2956-9/14/08 ...$15.00.
http://dx.doi.org/10.1145/2623330.2623730.

[1] http://allourideas.org

NYC's drinking water clean by banning fracking in NYC's watershed" [25]. Collaborative ranking has been used in other academic projects to "crowdsource" common knowledge and impressions about the world. Consider the 2013 article, "the Collaborative Image of the City"[24], which employed a collaborative ranking survey through which thousands of respondents ranked pairs of urban street images from the United States and Europe to determine urban areas of more and less perceived safety and prosperity. In all of this research, however, comparison pairs are chosen randomly and are densely annotated by many respondents. Our research could dramatically improve the efficiency of these efforts.

More formally, we consider the following setup: we have n people and would like to learn for each person i a permutation π_i over m items. The information we obtain is through pairwise comparisons of the form "user i prefers item a over item b", i.e. that a appears before b in π_i ($\pi_i(a) > \pi_i(b)$). However, these pairwise comparisons might be noisy, or only partially consistent with some underlying permutation. Furthermore, we assume the permutations π_i are all related in some way, and modeling this relationship is part of our contribution here. In any case, based on such, possibly noisy and non-transitive, pairwise comparisons, our goal is to recover $\pi_1, \dots, \pi_n$. We also consider the "active" or "adaptive" setup where we can actively choose which queries to make, i.e. at each step we can choose a person i and a pair of items (a, b), and query user i as to whether the person prefers a over b (i.e. ask whether $\pi_i(a) < \pi_i(b)$ or $\pi_i(b) < \pi_i(a)$). The two questions we thus ask, and suggests answers for, are: (1) how can we recover the permutations for every person based on these pairwise preferences, and, (2) how should we adaptively choose queries so as to make our predictions more accurate and reduce the overall number of queries required.

In order to tackle the problem of collaborative permutation learning, we formulate the problem as a matrix completion problem with pairwise constraints, and use standard matrix-factorization regularizers, such as the trace-norm or max-norm, to reconstruct the matrix based on limited pairwise constraints. In Section 4 we discuss this matrix factorization approach, its underlying assumption about the relatedness of the permutation, and its relationship to the constrained single-permutation learning approach of [12]. We then leverage the existing understanding of methodology on matrix factorization regularizers to suggest efficient optimization methods for fitting our suggested models (Section 5) and to analyze the number of queries required for recovery—in Section 7 we show that under our model, $O(n+m)$ random queries are sufficient for approximate recovery, significantly less than the $O(nm)$ required for approximate recovery if learning each permutation independently. In order to further reduce this query complexity we turn to active learning and suggest an adaptive query heuristic based on biasing the queries towards more ambiguous pairs (Section 6).

Notation Let $[n] = \{1, 2, ..., n\}$. For a matrix $\mathbf{X} \in \mathbb{R}^{n\times m}$, let $\mathbf{X}_{i,j}$ be the (i, j)-th element; $\mathbf{X}_{i,\cdot}$ be the i-th row of $\mathbf{X}$, $\|\mathbf{X}\|_F = \sqrt{\sum_{i\in[n]}\sum_{j\in[m]}\mathbf{X}^2_{i,j}}$ be the Frobenius norm, $A \circ B = \mathrm{tr}(A^T B)$ be the matrix inner product of A and B, and denote $A \succeq 0$ to mean A is positive-semi-definite.

2. RELATED WORK

Rank aggregation from pairwise comparisons.

There has been much work on constructing a permutation based on pairwise comparisons. If the comparisons are transitive, that is consistent with some global permutation, then outputting this global permutation given enough pairwise comparisons is easy. Once the comparisons are noisy, or are not fully consistent, the task becomes trickier and one must both decide on a criteria for measuring the quality of a permutation (i.e. its degree of agreement with the comparisons) and devise an algorithm for finding the optimal permutation under this criteria. Some criteria and algorithms suggested for the problem include Borda Count [7], Rank Centrality [17], HodgeRank [13], Balanced Rank Estimation [31], and others. There are, however, two major differences between rank aggregation and the problem we pose here. For rank aggregation, it is typically assumed that: 1) there is only one globally optimal ranking, while here we assume each user holds a personal ranking; and 2) there are dense observations, i.e., with all, or at least many, pairwise comparisons being observed, while in our setting the observations are usually sparse, with only a very small fraction of pairwise preferences revealed. In particular, there is no hope of obtaining a meaningful global permutations with less than $m - 1$ comparisons, as even for perfectly consistent data, this does not enable linking relationships among all m items (more typically, in rank aggregation one has $O(m^2)$ comparisons).

Active learning for ranking.

Beyond the problem of rank aggregation given dense static data, there has also been interest in adaptive query strategies for learning the optimal distribution. Again, if all comparisons are guaranteed to be transitive and so consistent with some permutation, the problem is easy and boils down to sorting by comparisons, and can the permutation can be recovered using $O(m \log m)$ comparisons, e.g. using merge-sort. When the comparisons are not necessarily consistent, one might wish to obtain the most agreeing (optimal) permutation for all $\binom{m}{2}$ possible comparisons, but without actually making all these comparisons. I.e. the assumption is a user holds a system of pairwise preferences that is not necessarily consistent with a permutation, and we would like to uncover the most consistent permutation by making the least amount of pairwise queries. Recently, [1] showed that this problem too can be solved using only $O(m\text{poly}\log m)$ adaptively chosen queries. Furthermore, if we are willing to tolerate discrepancies in ϵ fraction of comparisons, relative to the optimal permutation, we need only $O(m\text{poly}\log 1/\epsilon)$ queries. This is in contrast to the $O(m/\epsilon^2)$ random queries required for solving the same task. This demonstrates the power of active learning in ranking, but is still limited to learning a single independent permutation.

(Active) Collaborative filtering.

The problem of collaborative ranking, as we consider it here, is related to widely studied problem of *collaborative filtering* as formalized through *matrix completion*, where we observe some ratings of items by users and would like to use these to predict the ratings of users on items they have not yet rated. Matrix factorization approaches have long been used collaborative filtering problems [11, 23], including using the trace-norm and max-norm [27] as well as other related matrix factorization regularizers. Active queries have also been investigated in this context, with heuristics suggested based on the *expected value of information*(EVIQ) [5] or the prediction margin [22], as well as using a Bayesian approach [14].

The main difference between standard collaborative filtering and the problem studied here, is that in the standard setting single-item ratings are observed, providing absolute information about a single entry in the unknown matrix. In contrast, we consider learning from pairwise comparisons, where we can only obtain relative information comparing two items. Our goal is also different, in that instead of seeking accuracy of specific ratings, we seek to capture a permutation for each user. Recent research [3, 32, 30] has also studied the problem of ranking in a collaborative filtering setup, but the objective of this work has been to optimize global ranking measures, such as NDCG or MAP. Moreover, their inputs are still rating scores, rather than pairwise information.

3. BACKGROUND: CONSTRAINED PERMUTATION LEARNING

In order to reduce the query complexity of ranking from pairwise comparisons, and allow learning permutations with less than m comparisons, we must use some external information and make assumptions on the permutation to be learned. [12] suggest associating with each item a a feature vector $v_a \in \mathbb{R}^d$ which encodes our prior information about a. Thinking of the feature vectors v_a as points in $\mathbb{R}^d$, a permutation is then specified as a direction in $\mathbb{R}^d$, where the rank order of items is given by their order when projected to this direction. Representing the direction in space as a vector $u \in \mathbb{R}^d$, the permutation π_u associated with u is defined by $\pi_u(a) < \pi_u(b)$ iff $\langle u, v_a \rangle < \langle u, v_b \rangle$ (we assume that u is in general position relative to the vectors v, i.e. that for no two items a, b, $\langle u, v_a \rangle = \langle u, v_b \rangle$). Alternatively, one can think of u as specifying a point in $\mathbb{R}^d$ and order items according to their distances from u: $\pi_u(a) < \pi_u(b)$ iff $\|u - v_a\| < \|u - v_b\|$. Ordering by the norm or by the projection are equivalent if u and all vectors v are normalized (i.e. on the unit sphere), and otherwise the difference between them amounts to adding one additional dimension. Although [12] focused mostly on ordering by distance, here it will be more convenient for us to order by projection.

In either case, for a given feature map, only a subset of permutations can be represented this way, allowing a significant reduction in the query complexity if we focus only on such permutations— [12] showed how $O(d \log m)$ adaptive queries are enough for learning the optimal permutation (among permutations of this form).

One can think of the feature map as specifying an embedding of items into a possible "preference space", with different axes specifying different attributes one might prefer or not prefer, and a direction u in this space specifying the preferences over these attributes, which in turn defines the preferences over items. The query complexity is then proportional to the dimensionality, or number of "attributes", d, instead of to the number of items m.

But the approach of [12] is still limited to a learning a single permutation at a time. Furthermore, the reduced query complexity relies on external information in the form of the feature embedding v_a. [12] did consider scenarios with individualized permutations, where each of many users has a different permutation over items (e.g. beer preferences in their application). But their proposed approach was to first obtain good features for each item using some external information source (in their case, the text of product reviews and descriptions) and then learn the permutation π_i for each user i separately, using only pairwise comparisons by this user i, based on the fixed feature maps. Here, we would like to avoid using a pre-determined feature map based on external information, and instead learn this map de novo by considering all users jointly, and leveraging information gleaned from one user's comparisons to improve the ranking of other users.

4. MATRIX COMPLETION BASED CPL

As in the model discussed above, we associate with each item a a vector $v_a \in \mathbb{R}^d$ and with each user a vector $u_i \in \mathbb{R}^d$, such that the permutation for user i is specified by $\pi_i(a) < \pi_i(b)$ iff $\langle u_i, v_a \rangle < \langle u_i, v_b \rangle$. However, instead of basing the model on pre-specified feature vectors v_a, we do not assume any prior knowledge on the items. Rather, following a collaborative approach, we jointly learn both the user vectors u_i *and* and item vectors v_a. Since the item vectors v_a are learned, the permutation for any single user is *not* constrained, unlike [12]. However, having observations on multiple users constrains the possible setting of the item vectors v_a and thus constraints the *relationship* between the multiple permutations. In other words, based on the observed comparisons from multiple users, we are learning the population space of possible permutations, which in turn allows us to learn individual permutations with significantly fewer observations.

$\pi_i(a) < \pi_i(b)$ iff $\mathbf{X}_{i,a} < \mathbf{X}_{i,b}$. Requiring that X decomposes as $X = UV^T$ of the appropriate dimensions is equivalent to requiring that it has rank at most d. We can thus consider performing collaborative permutation learning as searching for a low-rank matrix $\mathbf{X}$ such that $\text{sgn}(\mathbf{X}_{i,a} < \mathbf{X}_{i,b})$ matches our observed pairwise comparisons, or at least matches as many as possible to our observed pairwise comparisons.

However, as was suggested by [9, 27], we instead consider an infinite-dimensional model, where the dimensionality d is unbounded (one can think of $U_{a,\cdot}$ and $V_{b,\cdot}$ as vectors in an infinite-dimensional Hilbert space, or simply allow them to be vectors in an arbitrarily high dimensional space), where we instead constrain the *norms* $\|U_{a,\cdot}\|_2, \|V_{b,\cdot}\|_2$. Constraining the average squared-norm of these vectors corresponds to constraining the *trace-norm* (aka nuclear norm) of X, which is defined as[2]:

$$\|X\|_\Sigma = \min_{X=UV^T} \frac{1}{2}\left(\sum_{a=1}^{n} \|U_{a,\cdot}\|_2^2 + \sum_{b=1}^{m} \|V_{b,\cdot}\|_2^2\right). \quad (1)$$

Similarly, constraining the norm of all vectors (i.e. constraining the maximal norm) corresponds to constraining the *max-norm* of X, defined as:

$$\|X\|_{\max} = \min_{X=UV^T} \max\left(\max_a \|U_{a,\cdot}\|_2^2, \max_b \|V_{b,\cdot}\|_2^2\right). \quad (2)$$

Both the max-norm and the trace-norm can be thought of either as convex relaxations to the rank [10], or as more refined models, allowing an infinite-dimensional embedding, regularized through norm-regularization rather than a parametric constraint as in, e.g., Support Vector Machines [27]. Either way, in order for the norm-regularization to be meaningful, we must require not only that $X_{i,a} > X_{i,b}$ whenever we observe $\pi_i(a) > \pi_i(b)$, but that the inequality holds with a *margin*. And in order to allow for noisy or inconsistent observations, instead imposing a hard margin constraint, we seek to minimize an empirical *hinge loss*, defined below, which penalizes the extent of margin violations.

Let $\mathcal{S} : (i_1, a_1, b_1), (i_2, a_2, b_2), ..., (i_{|\mathcal{S}|}, a_{|\mathcal{S}|}, b_{|\mathcal{S}|})$ be the set of observed pairwise preferences, where (i, a, b) represents the comparison of user i prefers item a over b. $|\mathcal{S}|$ is the total set of observed pairwise comparisons. The empirical hinge loss of X is then defined as:

$$\hat{L}_{\text{hinge}}(\mathbf{X}) = \frac{\sum_{(i,a,b)\in\mathcal{S}} \max(1 - (\mathbf{X}_{i,a} - \mathbf{X}_{i,b}), 0)}{|\mathcal{S}|}$$

And our training objectives, with the trace-norm and max-norm respectively are:

$$\min_{\mathbf{X}} \|\mathbf{X}\|_\Sigma + \lambda \hat{L}_{\text{hinge}}(\mathbf{X}) \quad \text{and} \quad \min_{\mathbf{X}} \|\mathbf{X}\|_{\max} + \lambda \hat{L}_{\text{hinge}}(\mathbf{X}) \quad (3)$$

where λ is a regularization tradeoff parameter.

Both the trace-norm and max-norm are semi-definite-representable [9, 27] and thus both problems above can be rewritten and solved as semi-definite programs (SDP). This allows us to use standard SDP

[2]The trace-norm of X is also equal to the sum of the singular values of X, but we prefer thinking in terms of the matrix-factorization characterization of the trace-norm

solvers. However, in order to handle large-scale problem, special-purpose first-order optimization methods are required. Fortunately, in the past few years, there has been much progress in developing such methods for both trace-norm and max-norm regularized problems, and in the next Section we describe the methods we use here.

5. LARGE SCALE OPTIMIZATION

In this Section, we describe the accelerated first order methods we use to solve the optimization problems (3) and fit our models. For both the trace-norm and the max-norm we adapt recently proposed accelerated proximal methods.

5.1 Accelerated proximal gradient methods for trace-norm regularized CPL

For trace-norm regularized collaborative permutation learning, we use an accelerated version of Singular Value Thresholding (SVT): SVT optimization [6] consists of iterative updates corresponding to the optimization of a partial linearization of the objective function, where loss is linearized but the regularizer is not:

$$\begin{aligned} \mathbf{X}_k &= \arg\min_{\mathbf{X}} \hat{L}_{\text{hinge}}(\mathbf{X}_{k-1}) + (\mathbf{X} - \mathbf{X}_{k-1}) \circ \nabla \hat{L}_{\text{hinge}}(\mathbf{X}_{k-1}) \\ &+ \frac{1}{2\eta_k}\|\mathbf{X} - \mathbf{X}_{k-1}\|_F^2 + \frac{1}{\lambda}\|\mathbf{X}\|_\Sigma \end{aligned}$$

Such an update can be performed by soft-thresholding the singular-values of $\mathbf{X}_{k-1} - \eta_k \nabla \hat{L}_{\text{hinge}}(\mathbf{X}_{k-1})$, requiring a singular value decomposition at each iteration [6]. For a smooth loss function, such updates can be *accelerated* by combining two sequences of iterates $\mathbf{X}_k$ and $\mathbf{Z}_k$, as in [18, 20]. Although our objective function is not smooth, empirically we found that accelerated gradient methods can usually obtain better convergence than simple gradient descent for our problem. In particular, each iteration consists of the following updates:

$$\begin{aligned} \mathbf{X}_k &= \text{SVT}_{\frac{1}{2\lambda}}(\mathbf{Z}_k - \eta_k \nabla \hat{L}_{\text{hinge}}(\mathbf{Z}_k)) \\ \mathbf{Z}_{k+1} &= \mathbf{X}_k + (\frac{\alpha_k - 1}{\alpha_{k+1}})(\mathbf{X}_k - \mathbf{X}_{k-1}) \end{aligned}$$

where the SVT operator is defined as: $\text{SVT}_\lambda(\mathbf{X}) = U\Sigma_\lambda V^T$, where $\mathbf{X} = U\Sigma V^T$ is the singular value decomposition of $\mathbf{X}$, and $(\Sigma_\lambda)_{i,i} = \max\{0, \Sigma_{i,i} - \lambda\}$, and α_k is the parameter recursively defined as $\alpha_{k+1} = \frac{1+\sqrt{1+4\alpha_k^2}}{2}$ with $\alpha_1 = 1$.

5.2 Proximal iterative smoothing algorithm for max-norm regularized CPL

For the max-norm, we cannot take this approach, because the minimum of a quadratic function plus a max-norm regularizer is *not* given analytically in terms of the SVD. Instead, we take the proximal iterative smoothing (PRISMA) technique proposed by [19], where the goal is to solve a convex optimization which decomposes into three parts: a smooth part, a simple Lipschitz part, and a non-Lipschitz part. Although the pairwise hinge loss functions in max-norm regularized CPL problems are not smooth, we can also apply PRISMA to our problem because our objective function is

$$\min_{\mathbf{X}} \|\mathbf{X}\|_{\max} + \lambda \hat{L}_{\text{hinge}}(\mathbf{X})$$

. This problem can be rewritten as:

$$\min_{\mathbf{X},A,B} \frac{1}{\lambda} \max\text{diag}\begin{bmatrix} A & \mathbf{X} \\ \mathbf{X}^T & B \end{bmatrix} + \hat{L}_{\text{hinge}}(\mathbf{X}) + \delta_{\mathbb{S}_+^{m+n}}\begin{bmatrix} A & \mathbf{X} \\ \mathbf{X}^T & B \end{bmatrix}$$

where $\delta_{\mathbb{S}_+^{m+n}}$ is the indicator function of set of $(m+n) \times (m+n)$ positive semi-definite matrices (zeros inside $\mathbb{S}_+^{m+n}$ and infinite outside).

To apply PRISMA for this problem, we learn $A, B, \mathbf{X}$ simultaneously as a $(m+n) \times (m+n)$ matrix (we denote it as $\mathbf{Z}$): at each step, we first perform a gradient descent step on the function $\hat{L}_{\text{hinge}}(\mathbf{X})$, then add the proximal operator solution of the function $\frac{1}{\lambda}\max\text{diag}(\mathbf{Z})$, and then perform a proximal operator of the function $\delta_{\mathbb{S}_+^{m+n}}\mathbf{Z}$. Note that the proximal operator of $\max\text{diag}(\mathbf{Z})$ is equivalent to the proximal operator of the $\|\cdot\|_\infty$ on the diagonal vector of the matrix $\mathbf{Z}$, which has closed-form solution [8], and the proximal operator of $\delta_{\mathbb{S}_+^{m+n}}\mathbf{Z}$ can be solved by setting all negative eigenvalues of $\mathbf{Z}$ to zero. Thus the core updating steps are:

$$\begin{aligned} \mathbf{Y}_k &= \text{EVT}((1 - \frac{1}{\lambda\beta_k})\mathbf{Z}_k - \eta_k \nabla \hat{L}_{\text{hinge}}(\mathbf{Z}_k) + \frac{1}{\lambda\beta_k}\text{DVT}_{\beta_k}(\mathbf{Z}_k)) \\ \mathbf{Z}_{k+1} &= \mathbf{Y}_k + (\frac{\alpha_k - 1}{\alpha_{k+1}})(\mathbf{Y}_k - \mathbf{Y}_{k-1}) \end{aligned}$$

where DVT is the diagonal value thresholding operator: $\text{DVT}_{\beta_k}(\mathbf{X})_{i,i} = \text{sgn}(\mathbf{X}_{i,i})\min(\mathbf{X}_{i,i}, \beta_k)$ and $\text{DVT}_{\beta_k}(\mathbf{X})_{i,j} = \mathbf{X}_{i,j}$ for all $i \neq j$; and EVT is the Eigenvalue thresholding operator obtained by setting all negative eigenvalues to zero.

6. ACTIVE LEARNING STRATEGIES

In this section we discuss some active learning strategies for collaborative permutation learning. Although our goal is to create a system that actively makes queries to all possible pairs, for presentation clarity we consider the setting of pool-based batch mode active learning [26]. Suppose at learning stage t, we already have our learned model $\mathbf{X}^t$, as well as a candidate pool $\mathcal{P}_t = \{(i,a,b)\}$. We then need to ask users to reveal their comparison labels for a small batch of instances $\mathcal{Q}_{t+1} \subseteq \mathcal{P}_t$, and add these new training data to our current training set $\mathcal{S}_t$. Then we re-train the model using the combined training set $\mathcal{S}_{t+1} = \mathcal{S}_t \cup \mathcal{Q}_{t+1}$ to obtain improvement.

The baseline solution is uniform sampling where we randomly sample instances in $\mathcal{P}_t$ uniformly. We can also adopt some active ranking methods for single permutation learning in our setting: as inspired by [12], which actively query only the "ambiguous" pairs for labeling. "Ambiguous" is defined as the pair that can not be imputed from known pairwise comparisons based on the consistency assumption. (Suppose we know "a" is preferred to "b", "b" is preferred to "c"; pair "a" and "c" is not an "ambiguous" pair because we can transitively impute that "a" is preferred than "c"). We can use this approach in our setting: we uniformly sample "ambiguous" pairs for all users independently.

For our proposed approaches, the margin provides important information about the uncertainty of our learned model on the data. [29] proposed to actively query the instances with smallest margin for Support Vector Machines (SVMs), and [22] adopted this strategy and showed it's effectiveness for maximum-margin matrix factorization [27]. Likewise, we can use similar ideas to select pairs with the smallest difference in their estimated scores: $f_t(i,a,b) = |\mathbf{X}_{i,a}^t - \mathbf{X}_{i,b}^t|$.

Since our goal is to interactively estimate the model from data, when the model is inaccurate, the margin information could be misleading. As a result, we propose a stochastic sampling alternative. Given a temperature parameter T_t, we randomly sample query instances with probability proportional to $p_{(i,a,b)} = e^{-\frac{|\mathbf{X}_{i,a}^t - \mathbf{X}_{i,b}^t|}{T_t}}$. Thus we favor instances with smaller margin. At the beginning, we set the temperature high, which means we select instances tending to uniform randomness, and then we decrease the temperature during the learning process. In this way, we are more confident about our model and bias toward more of the instances with small margin. 1 described the detailed process of our proposed "CPL-Margin Sampling" algorithm.

Algorithm 1 CPL-Margin Sampling — Algorithm of active collaborative permutation learning from pairwise comparisons

Input: $\mathcal{P}_0 \in \mathbb{N}^{|\mathcal{P}| \times 3}$: the set of candidate pairwise preferences.
Initialization: The initialized model X^0 at time 0.
for $t = 1, 2, \ldots$ **do**
  Computing the margin score achieved by current model.
  Sampling k triplets from $\mathcal{P}_{t-1}$ with probability proportional to $e^{-\frac{|\mathbf{X}^{t-1}_{i,a} - \mathbf{X}^{t-1}_{i,b}|}{\tau_{t-1}}}$ to form the query set $\mathcal{Q}_t$, update the training set $\mathcal{S}_t = \mathcal{S}_{t-1} \cup \mathcal{Q}_t$.
  Learn the new $\mathbf{X}^t$ by solving the problem (3).
end for

7. THEORETICAL ANALYSIS

In this section we provide some theoretical analysis of the proposed algorithms. Suppose the true permutations are generated by the underlying matrix $\mathbf{X}^*$, we can define the expected loss for any matrix $\mathbf{X}$:

$$L(\mathbf{X}) = \frac{2\sum_{i=1}^{n}\sum_{a=1}^{m}\sum_{b\neq a}^{b\in[m]} \mathbb{I}_{\text{sgn}(\mathbf{X}^*_{i,a} - \mathbf{X}^*_{i,b}) \neq \text{sgn}(\mathbf{X}_{i,a} - \mathbf{X}_{i,b})}}{nm(m-1)}$$

and the empirical loss for matrix $\mathbf{X}$:

$$\hat{L}(\mathbf{X}) = \frac{1}{|\mathcal{S}|}\sum_{(i,a,b)\in\mathcal{S}} \mathbb{I}_{\mathbf{X}_{i,a} < \mathbf{X}_{i,b}}$$

and the expected hinge loss for matrix $\mathbf{X}$:

$$L_{\text{hinge}}(\mathbf{X}) = \frac{2\sum_{i=1}^{n}\sum_{a=1}^{m}\sum_{b\neq j}^{b\in[m]} l_{\text{hinge}}(i,a,b)}{nm(m-1)}$$

where $l_{\text{hinge}}(i,a,b) \max(1 - (\mathbf{X}_{i,a} - \mathbf{X}_{i,b}), 0)$ and the empirical hinge loss for matrix $\mathbf{X}$:

$$\hat{L}_{\text{hinge}}(\mathbf{X}) = \frac{1}{|\mathcal{S}|}\sum_{(i,a,b)\in\mathcal{S}} \max(1 - (\mathbf{X}_{i,a} - \mathbf{X}_{i,b}), 0)$$

7.1 Generalization bounds of CPL

The following theorems give generalization guarantees for the proposed collaborative permutation learning models.

THEOREM 1. *Let $\mathcal{X}^{\max}[A]$ be the set of matrices that with bounded max-norm A. Then for any $\delta > 0$, with probability at least $1-\delta$ over the choice of a sample $\mathcal{S}$, for every $\mathbf{X} \in \mathcal{X}^{\max}[A]$, the following holds:*

$$L(\mathbf{X}) \leq \hat{L}_{hinge}(\mathbf{X}) + 48\sqrt{\frac{A^2(n+m)}{|\mathcal{S}|}} + 3\sqrt{\frac{\ln\frac{2}{\delta}}{2|\mathcal{S}|}}$$

Proof Sketch. We treat the matrix $\mathbf{X}$ as a function $[n] \times [m] \to \mathbb{R}$, and use existing bounds on the Rademacher complexity [4] of matrices with bounded trace-norm or max-norm [28, 10]. The main difference here is that the instances, and hence the loss, depend on *two*, rather than only *one* evaluation of $\mathbf{X}$. Nevertheless, this only results in an increase by a factor of two in the Rademacher complexity of the loss class, and we can use standard arguments for obtaining uniform concentration and generalization guarantees as a function of the Rademacher complexity.

And we get the following generalization bound for trace-norm based methods:

THEOREM 2. *Let $\mathcal{X}^{\Sigma}[A]$ be the set of matrices with bounded trace-norm A. Then there exists a constant K, for any $\delta > 0$, with probability at least $1-\delta$ over the choice of a sample $\mathcal{S}$, for every $\mathbf{X} \in \mathcal{X}^{\Sigma}[A]$, the following holds:*

$$L(\mathbf{X}) \leq \hat{L}_{hinge}(\mathbf{X}) + 4K\sqrt{\frac{\frac{A^2}{nm}(n+m)\ln n}{|\mathcal{S}|}} + \sqrt{\frac{\ln\frac{1}{\delta}}{2|\mathcal{S}|}}$$

7.2 Sample complexity for approximate recovery

COROLLARY 3. *Suppose $\mathbf{X}^*$ is rank-r with bounded entries, let $\mathbf{X}_{\max}(\mathcal{S})$ be the max-norm regularized empirical loss minimizer: $\mathbf{X}_{\max}(\mathcal{S}) = \arg\min_{\mathbf{X}\in\mathcal{X}^{\max}[\sqrt{r}]} \hat{L}_{hinge}(\mathbf{X})$, with the sample size $|\mathcal{S}| \geq \frac{4608r(n+m)+18\ln\frac{2}{\delta}}{\epsilon^2}$, with probability at least $1-\delta$, we have*

$$L(\mathbf{X}_{\max}(\mathcal{S})) \leq \hat{L}_{hinge}(\mathbf{X}^*) + \epsilon$$

Proof Sketch. By error decomposition $L(\mathbf{X}_{\max}(\mathcal{S})) = L(\mathbf{X}_{\max}(\mathcal{S})) - \hat{L}_{\text{hinge}}(\mathbf{X}_{\max}(\mathcal{S})) + (\hat{L}_{\text{hinge}}(\mathbf{X}_{\max}(\mathcal{S})) - \hat{L}_{\text{hinge}}(\mathbf{X}^*)) + \hat{L}_{\text{hinge}}(\mathbf{X}^*)$, combining the fact of empirical loss minimizer, as well as basic mean inequalities.

Remark. If we further assume that the true scoring matrix suffers 0 hinge loss, i.e., that the following realizable condition holds: $\hat{L}_{\text{hinge}}(\mathbf{X}^*) = 0$, we get $L(\mathbf{X}_{\max}(\mathcal{S})) \leq \epsilon$, which means we obtain approximate recovery of all the permutations with ϵ-error.

Similarly, for the trace-norm regularized solution, we obtain the following result:

COROLLARY 4. *Suppose $\mathbf{X}^*$ is rank-r with bounded entries, let $\mathbf{X}_{\Sigma}(\mathcal{S})$ be the trace-norm regularized empirical loss minimizer: $\mathbf{X}_{\Sigma}(\mathcal{S}) = \arg\min_{\|\mathbf{X}\|_{\Sigma}\leq\sqrt{rnm}} \hat{L}_{hinge}(\mathbf{X})$. Then there exists a constant K, with the sample size $|\mathcal{S}| \geq \frac{32K^2r(n+m)\ln n + \ln\frac{1}{\delta}}{\epsilon^2}$, with probability at least $1-\delta$, we have*

$$L(\mathbf{X}_{\Sigma}(\mathcal{S})) \leq \hat{L}_{hinge}(\mathbf{X}^*) + \epsilon$$

Remark. By comparing the sample complexity of regularized CPL with trace-norm versus max-norm, we can see that max-norm is slightly superior by avoiding a $\log n$ factor, which is consistent with the analysis of classical collaborative filtering problems [28].

8. EMPIRICAL STUDIES

In this section, we conduct a set of experiments to demonstrate the effectiveness of our proposed approaches.

8.1 Experimental setting

Table 1: Statistics of data sets used in our experiments

Data	#Users	#Items	Size	Sparsity
Sushi	5,000	10	225,000	1
Vote200	16	67	6,459	0.182
Vote-wbc	339	369	10,658	0.0004
ML100K-500	500	500	1,659,704	0.027
ML100K-50	50	50	1,185	0.019
HetRec-600	600	600	1,042,049	0.010
HetRec-70	70	70	1,234	0.007

We test the performance of various algorithms for the CPL task on both real-world and synthetic data sets including actual pairwise comparison surveys, including the following:

- **Sushi** [15]: which is a data set contains 5,000 users' order lists over 10 kinds of sushi [3].
- **Vote-200**: a pairwise comparison survey associated with Washington Post's idea marketplace [25] implemented through the online platform [4]. In this survey, people were asked to propose who had the worst year in Washington in 2010, and then vote their comparisons between various people, agencies, organizations or classes according to the following form: "Entity A had a worse year than Entity B". Entities included "Representative Charlie Rangel", "The American Homeowner", "Senator Blanche Lincoln", "D.C. schoolchildren", and "The Political Center". Because the voting was anonymous, we have information on voting sessions, but not individual users. While it is very unlikely that multiple users compared items within a single "session," it is possible that the same person came back to the site and voted in multiple sessions, although we expect this behavior, if it occurred, was rare. As such, we treat each session as a singer user following the traditional collaborative filtering approach. There are 67 entities (items) in total, and voting results are very sparse. Thus we select a subset that each session contains at least 200 preferences.
- **Vote-wbc**: a pairwise comparison survey regarding the relative appeal of different Wikipedia advertisement banners [5] using the same platform as in the Vote-200 data. Here Wikipedia users propose and then compare pairs of possible banners for Wikipedia fundraising. Banner possibilities include "Knowledge is power. Keep the access to it free"; "A small donation for a world of information"; "A penny a thought? How many times has Wikipedia helped you?"; and "Open. Honest. Free."
- **Movielens data** [6]: a widely used collaborative filtering data set. We choose two subsets of 'Movielens 100K': 'ML100K-50' is a subset that contains 50 users on 50 items; 'ML100K-ML500' is a subset that contains 500 users on 500 movies. We generated all pairwise preferences in the subsets according to user ratings.
- **HetRec 2011 Movie data** [7]: another popular movie rating data set. We choose two subsets: 'HetRec-600' is the subset that contains 600 users on 600 movies, 'HetRec-70' is the subset that contains 70 users on 70 movies. We generated all pairwise preferences in the subsets according to user ratings.

Table 1 summarizes the statistics associated with these data sets, and shows that our data contains pairwise comparisons ranging up to several million. We measure the performance of algorithms using mean Kendell-Tau distance (MKTD), a generalization of Kendell-Tau distance to our multiple permutations setting. Kendll-Tau distance is widely used in single permutation learning evaluation [12] as it measure the fraction of pairwise preferences from the true permutation π recovered by the learned permutation $\hat{\pi}$: $d(\pi, \hat{\pi}) = \frac{\sum_{(a,b):\pi(a)<\pi(b)} \mathbb{I}\{\hat{\pi}(a)>\hat{\pi}(b)\}}{\binom{m}{2}}$. Suppose our model learns n ranking lists: $\pi_1, ...\pi_n$, given a ground truth set of test pairwise preferences $\mathcal{S}$, the MKTD is defined as:

$$\text{MKTD} = \frac{1}{|\mathcal{S}|} \sum_{(i,a,b)\in\mathcal{S}} \mathbb{I}_{(\pi_i(b)-\pi_i(a))>0}.$$

[3]http://www.kamishima.net/sushi/

[4]http://allourideas.org

[5]http://blog.allourideas.org/post/16175975017/

[6]http://movielens.umn.edu

[7]http://grouplens.org/datasets/hetrec-2011/

We test the performance of our model on the entire data set, and evaluate performance with a learning curve.

8.2 Compare CPL with rank aggregation

This set of experiments is designed to demonstrate how collaborative information is useful for our task. We compared the proposed CPL with a set of single permutation learning methods, including the following two that represent rank aggregation approaches: **Borda Count** [7] and **Balanced Rank Estimation** [31]. Because there are no natural active learning strategies for these approaches, we compare all algorithms to a uniform sampling of queries for fair comparison. We tune the λ parameter in our algorithms from $\{2^{-10}, 2^{-9}, ...2^{10}\}$ for all data sets. Note that we can use rank aggregation methods to learn multiple rankings: each user has one, and we can follow the traditional rank aggregation setting which learns a global ranking list. We add "Single" to denote the latter in the figures [8].

Figure 1 show the learning curves associated with our algorithms on various data sets. When comparing with Borda Count and Balanced Rank Estimation, we found that they perform reasonably well, and Balanced Rank Estimation usually performs slightly worse than Borda Count; When comparing the ranking aggregation method which learns multiple and single rankings, we find that the multiple rankings approach usually performs better, although single permutation methods might perform better in circumstances where we do not have enough observed data; when comparing the previous method with our collaborative approach, we can see that our algorithms performs significantly better. Finally, our method can improve rank aggregation approaches more on the voting data when we have more observations (Vote200 case), which illustrates the intrinsic difficulty of collaborative ranking on highly sparse and noisy data sets.

8.3 Comparison of active learning strategies

Knowing that CPL methods are superior, this set of experiments compares various active learning strategies. We compare the following methods: i) **Uniform Sampling**; ii) **Active Ranking**: as proposed in [12] for single permutation learning, note in our setting there are no given features for items, thus we perform a reduced SVD of our learned score matrix $X = U_r\Sigma_r V_r^T$, and use V_r as features for the items; iii) **SRRA**: the Smooth Relative Regret Approximation method proposed in [2], which suggests uniform sampling of the pairs for which rank position differences are within a certain range, as suggested by [2]. At first we narrow the range by 2 (which means we query the pairs with rank position differences of at most 2), then we double this range at each query stage; iv) **Simple Margin**: deterministic selection of pairs with the smallest margin; v) **Margin Sampling**: For simplicity, we begin with the following temperature attenuation scheme as $T_t = \frac{1}{t}$, where t is the learning stage. Since Active Ranking [12] needs to solve two linear programming problems in order to decide whether a pair is "Ambiguous", when the query pool is large (as in data sets with millions of pairs), the time cost becomes very high. Thus, we omit comparisons with Active Ranking on some large data sets. Figure 2 graphs the learning curves for various learning strategies. We can draw the following conclusions: i) Both Simple Margin and Margin Sampling perform significantly better than Uniform Sampling, which demonstrate the advantages that come from exploring a range of active learning strategies. While Active Ranking did not perform much better than Random Sampling, this is likely due

[8]We also tried to compare against Rank Centrality [17] and HodgeRank [13], but they failed in our setting due to the sparseness of the observations

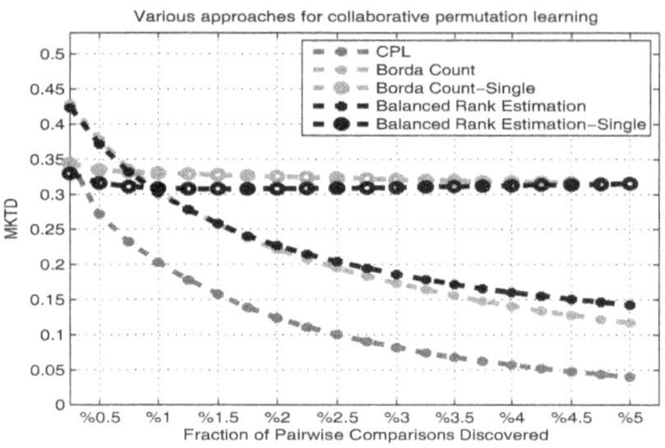

(a) *ML100K-500*

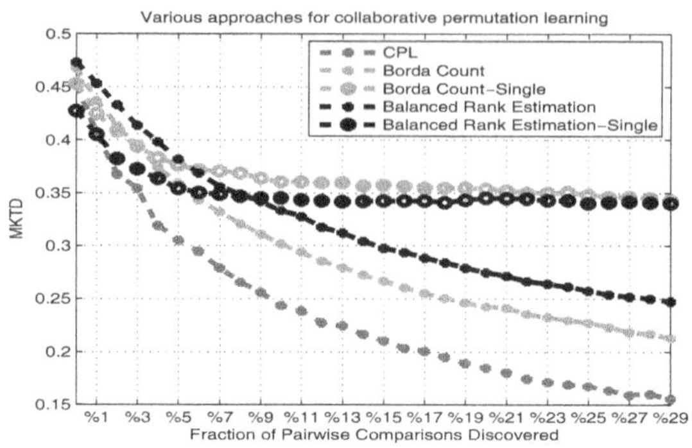

(b) *Vote200*

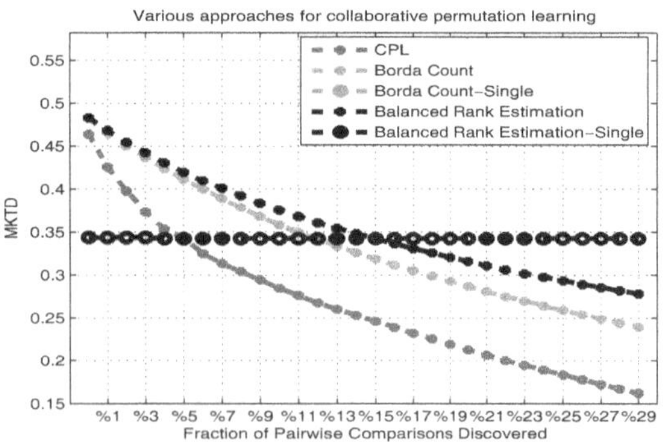

(c) *Sushi*

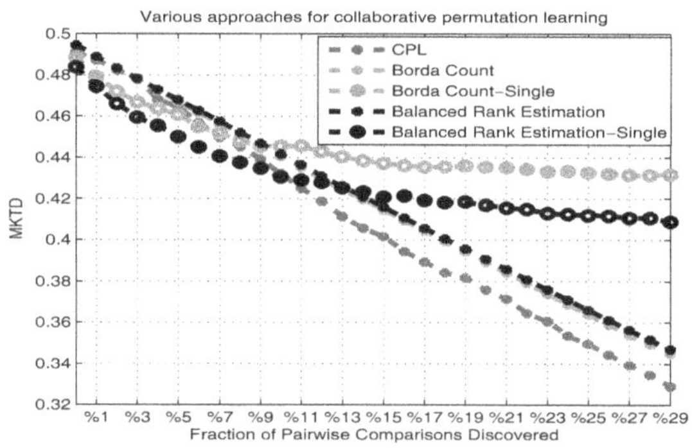

(d) *Vote-wbc*

Figure 1: Comparison of various learning methods for CPL

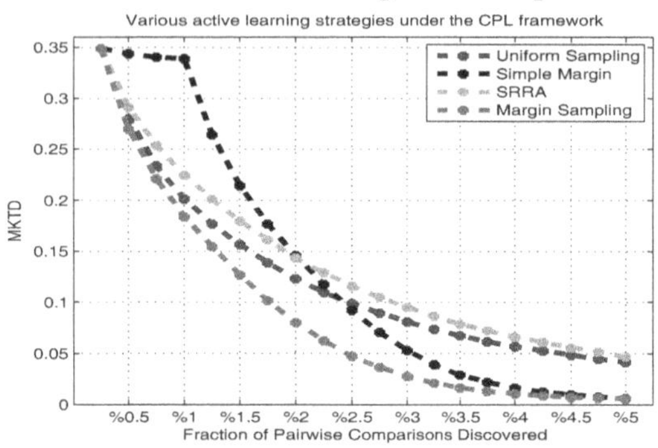

(a) *ML100K-500*

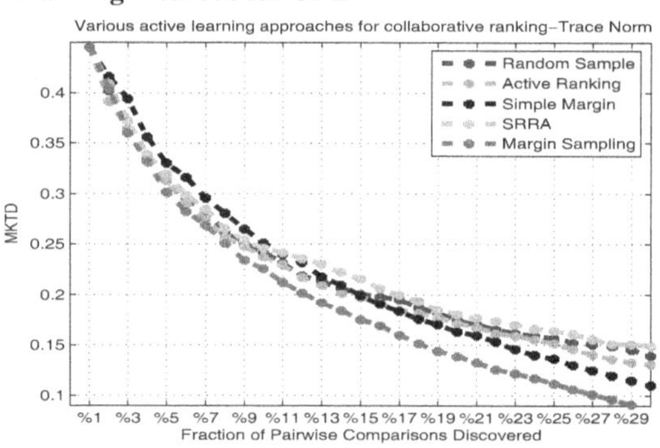

(b) *Vote200*

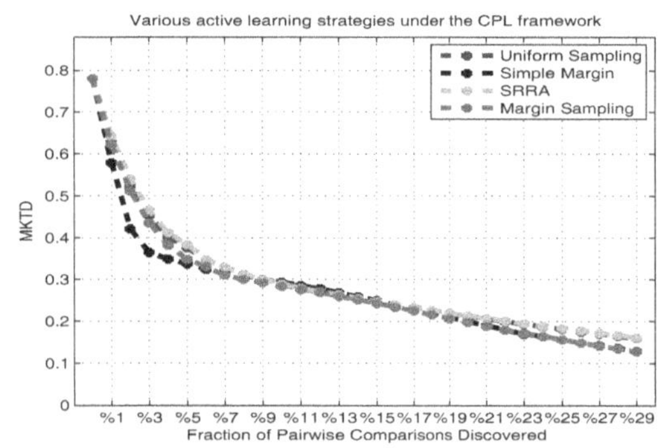

(c) *Sushi*

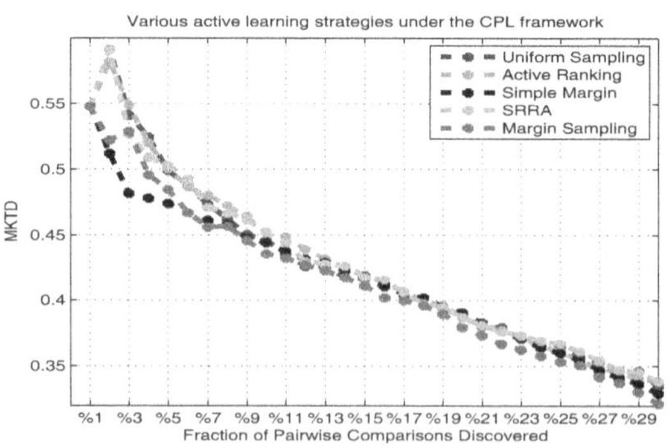

(d) *Vote-wbc*

Figure 2: Comparison of various active learning strategies for CPL

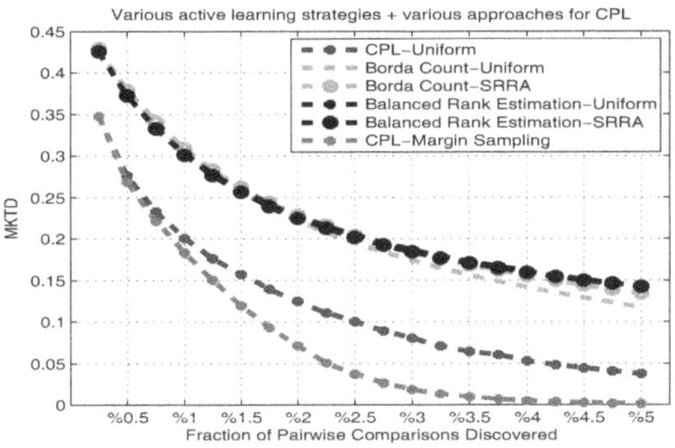

(a) *ML100K-500*

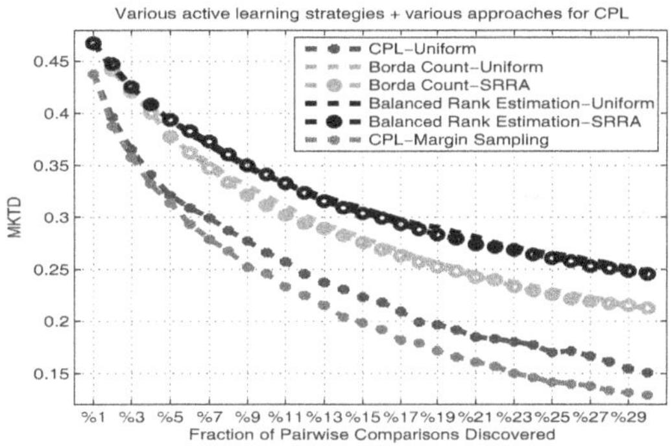

(b) *Vote200*

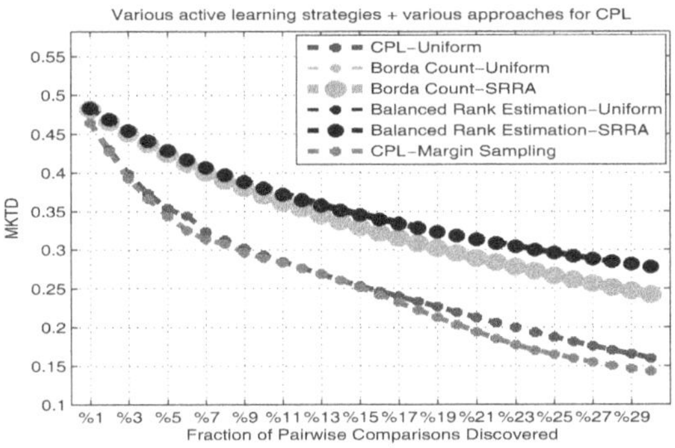

(c) *Sushi*

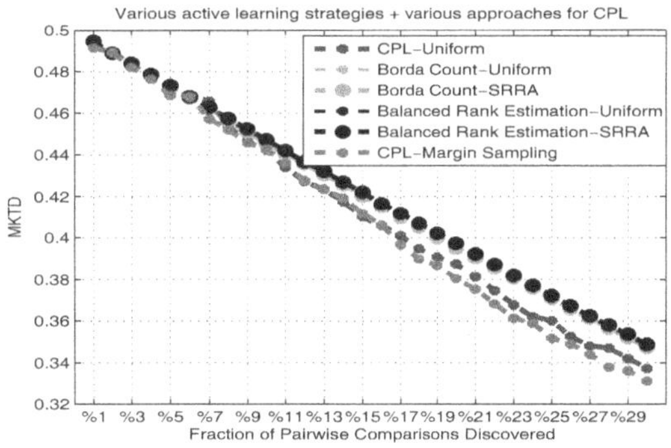

(d) *Vote-wbc*

Figure 3: Comparison of our system with single permutation based active learning + rank aggregation approaches

to 1) The active ranking approach, which is designed for the single ranking problem and so did not utilize collaborative information; 2) The "embedding" and "consistency" assumptions are not adequate for these real world data sets, especially when the features are not given; but most critically 3) the data are sparse and we can only test our algorithms on questions that were actually posed to and answered by users. Moreover, the SRRA method does not work in our setting, which may source from the reasons why Active Ranking performed poorly. ii) When comparing Simple Margin and Margin Sampling, we found that Margin Sampling performs significantly better, especially at the beginning of the learning process. This is likely because at the beginning, the model learned is not accurate as the margin information is somewhat misleading and thus we prefer more randomness. As the model becomes more accurate, we can put more trust in the margin information.

8.4 Comparison of the whole system

In this section we compare our proposed active collaborative permutation learning system(CPL+Margin Sampling) with some traditional rank aggregation methods, equipped with single permutation based active learning approaches. Figure 3 summarizes our results. We can see a significant advantage of our system over traditional approaches. SRRA based active methods cannot do better than uniform sampling in our collaborative setting, which further validates the emerging requirements of our collaborative permutation learning techniques on multiple permutation learning problems.

8.5 Simulations of sample complexity

The following experiment uses simulation on the sample complexity to evaluate our proposed methods. As shown in our theoretical analysis, under realizable condition, we only need $\mathcal{O}(\frac{r(n+m)}{\epsilon^2})$ pairwise observations to recover the multiple rankings list to ϵ error. We aim to validate the linear growth rates in our proven sample complexity bound. For simplicity, we set #users = #items = n, generalize two $n \times 5$ matrices U, V, where every elements of the two matrices are i.i.d. generated by a uniform distribution over $[0, 1]$, then we multiply these two matrices to form an $n \times n$ "rating" matrix, which is rank-5, and generate all pairwise comparisons according to the rating. Then, we test the MKTD on pair with margin at least 0.2(since we require realizable conditions for our analysis). We test the samples required to approximately recover $\%97$ of the whole pairwise preferences, test the CPL method using both uniform sampling and margin sampling strategies, and also compare with the single permutation learning methods. Figure 4 shows the sample complexity when n grows from 100 to 300. In the left figures, we see that the sample complexities of our methods look linear as n grows, and CPL requires significantly less samples than traditional methods. When comparing the sample complexities of uniform sampling and margin sampling, we found that margin sampling can usually reduce the samples needed, and it seems that sample complexity of margin sampling also grows linearly with n. We also compare the sample size needed for uniform sampling vs. margin sampling to achieve various ϵ-approximate recoveries when fixing $n = 200$, as left figure of 4 shows, the curves further validate the point that margin sampling does significantly better when we seek a very accurate solution.

8.6 CPL with Trace Norm vs Max Norm

In this section we compare the CPL with trace norm versus max norm. Figure 5 shows the curves learned by both trace-norm and max-norm regularized CPL algorithms. The basic observation is that trace-norm based methods and max-norm based algorithms usually perform similarly, and max-norm methods often performing slightly better.

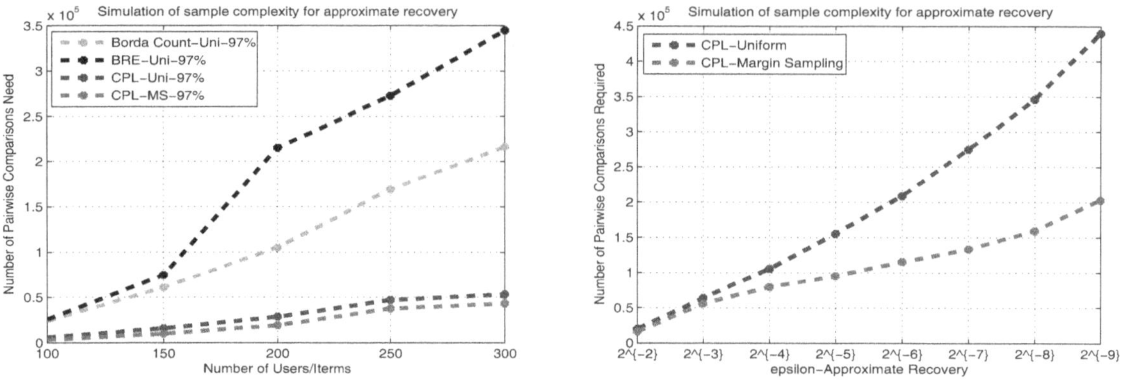

Figure 4: Simulation of Sample Complexity for Approximate Recovery, left: comparison of sample complexity as number of users/items increase; right: comparison of sample complexity for various ϵ-approximate recovery.

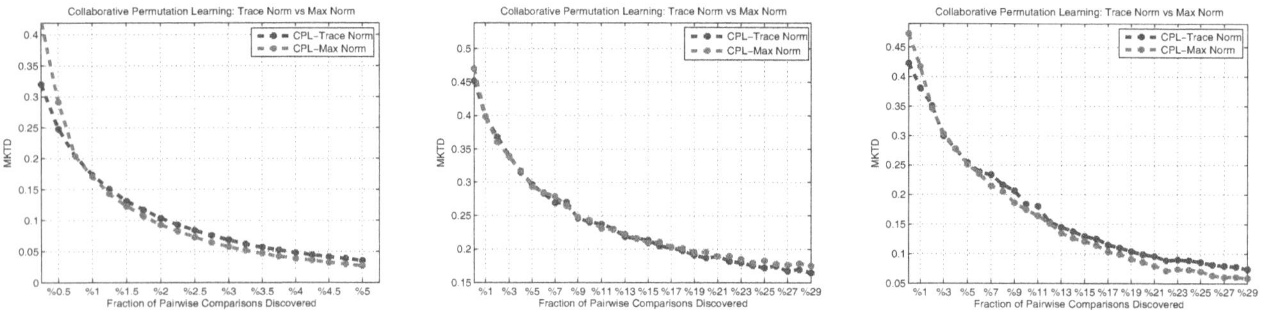

Figure 5: Evaluation on Trace Norm vs Max Norm for CPL: data sets from left to right: ML100K-500, Vote200, Hetrec 70.

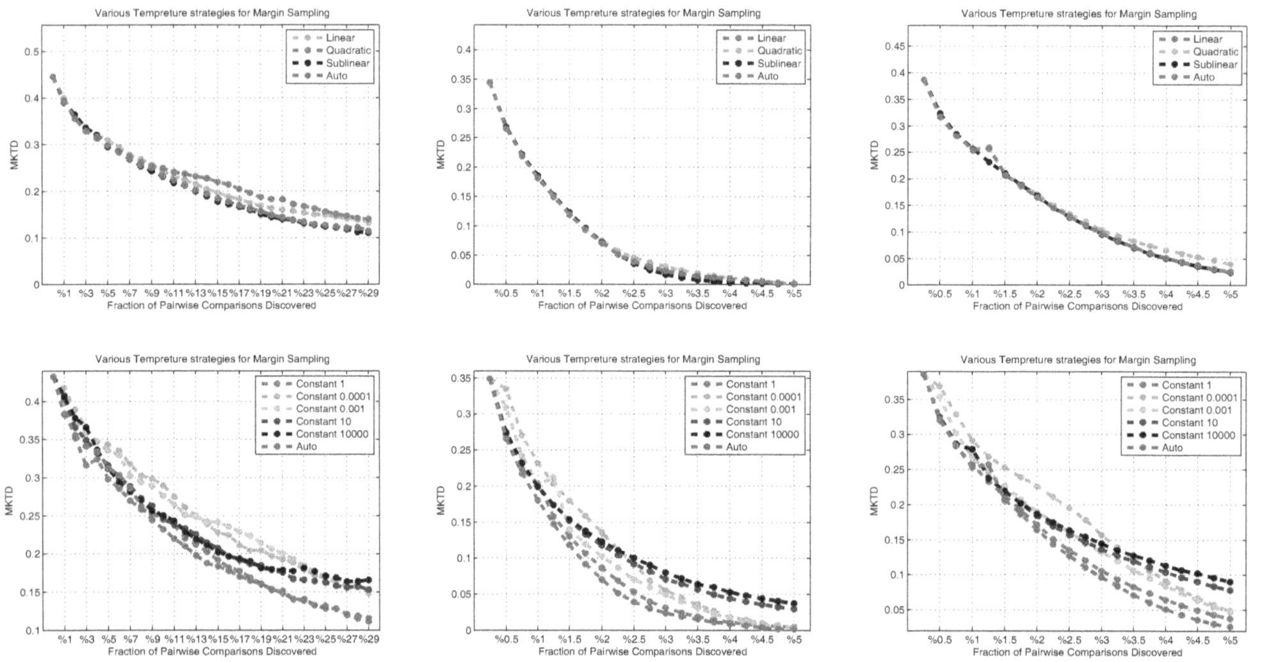

Figure 6: Evaluation of temperature decreasing schemes, top: evaluation of decreasing with different rates; bottom: evaluation of various constant temperatures. Data sets from left to right: Vote200, ML100K-50, Hetrec-600.

8.7 Temperature Decreasing Scheme

This experiment aims to study various temperature decreasing schemes for margin sampling. We consider the following general temperature model: $T_t = \frac{1}{c \cdot t^p}$, compared to the strategy we used in previous experiments where $c = 1, p = 1$, here we also test several schemes by varying c and p: first we fix $c = 1$, and vary $p = 0.5, 1, 2$, which represents sub-linear, linear, and quadratic temperature decreasing schemes, respectively. Moreover, we also adopt a "performance-driven" strategy by setting the temperature according to the MKTD we achieve: $T_t = \text{MKTD}_t$(We denote this method "auto" in the figures). Figure 6 summarizes the results. We can see that our margin sampling strategy is robust: it performs similar and quite well with different decreasing rates, when comparing different constant temperatures, we found that very low temperature tends to behave like simple margin(bad at the beginning), very high temperature tends to behave like uniform(bad at the end), adequate constant can performs reasonably well, although not so good as decreasing scheme. In addition, the proposed "performance-driven" temperature scheme appears promising. Thus, our margin sampling algorithms could be easily used in practical applications.

9. CONCLUSION

This paper studies the problem of collaborative permutation learning from pairwise comparisons, both passively and actively. We demonstrated that collaborative information is important, and propose to utilize collaborative information by matrix completion based algorithms. We then analyzed the generalization ability and sample complexity needed for approximate recovery of our proposed algorithms, and empirically demonstrated that our methods perform much better than traditional approaches. To reduce the number of comparisons required from users, we proposed various active learning strategies, and showed that active querying is very useful in reducing label costs. These approaches provide immediate application to a range of information retrieval and survey tasks. In particular, we highlight their power for creating efficient, just-in-time comparison surveys that can predict user preferences from small samples of comparisons.

We also identify several promising directions for further research, including: i) More scalable algorithms: we aim to apply our proposed methods on very large scale problems, where even the SVD is computationally prohibitive. Some existing large-scale trace-norm (and max-norm) optimization methods might be able to be adopted, e.g. [16]; ii) More theoretical analysis: currently we only explore generalization ability and approximate recovery analysis, but interesting theoretical questions remain, including: 1) the sample complexity required for exact recovery of the permutations (which might require additional assumptions); 2) the gap between active learning label complexity and uniform sample complexity.

References

[1] N. Ailon. An active learning algorithm for ranking from pairwise preferences with an almost optimal query complexity. *Journal of Machine Learning Research*, 13:137–164, 2012.

[2] N. Ailon, R. Begleiter, and E. Ezra. Active learning using smooth relative regret approximations with applications. *COLT*, 23:19.1–19.20, 2012.

[3] S. Balakrishnan and S. Chopra. Collaborative ranking. In *WSDM*, pages 143–152, 2012.

[4] P. L. Bartlett and S. Mendelson. Rademacher and gaussian complexities: Risk bounds and structural results. *Journal of Machine Learning Research*, 3:463–482, 2002.

[5] C. Boutilier, R. S. Zemel, and B. M. Marlin. Active collaborative filtering. In *UAI*, pages 98–106, 2003.

[6] J.-F. Cai, E. J. Candès, and Z. Shen. A singular value thresholding algorithm for matrix completion. *SIAM Journal on Optimization*, 20(4):1956–1982, 2010.

[7] J. C. de Borda. Mémoire sur les élections au scrutin. *Histoire de l'Académie Royale des Sciences*, 1784.

[8] J. C. Duchi and Y. Singer. Efficient online and batch learning using forward backward splitting. *Journal of Machine Learning Research*, 10:2899–2934, 2009.

[9] M. Fazel, H. Hindi, and S. P. Boyd. A rank minimization heuristic with application to minimum order system approximation. In *In Proceedings of the 2001 American Control Conference*, pages 4734–4739, 2001.

[10] R. Foygel and N. Srebro. Concentration-based guarantees for low-rank matrix reconstruction. In *COLT*, pages 315–340, 2011.

[11] T. Hofmann. Latent semantic models for collaborative filtering. *ACM Transactions on Information Systems (TOIS)*, 22(1):89–115, 2004.

[12] K. G. Jamieson and R. D. Nowak. Active ranking using pairwise comparisons. In *NIPS*, pages 2240–2248, 2011.

[13] X. Jiang, L.-H. Lim, Y. Yao, and Y. Ye. Statistical ranking and combinatorial hodge theory. *Math. Program.*, 127(1):203–244, 2011.

[14] R. Jin and L. Si. A bayesian approach toward active learning for collaborative filtering. In *UAI*, pages 278–285, 2004.

[15] T. Kamishima. Nantonac collaborative filtering: recommendation based on order responses. In *KDD*, pages 583–588, 2003.

[16] J. D. Lee, B. Recht, R. Salakhutdinov, N. Srebro, and J. A. Tropp. Practical large-scale optimization for max-norm regularization. In *NIPS*, pages 1297–1305, 2010.

[17] S. Negahban, S. Oh, and D. Shah. Iterative ranking from pair-wise comparisons. In *NIPS*, pages 2483–2491, 2012.

[18] Y. Nesterov. A method for solving a convex programming problem with convergence rate $o(\frac{1}{k^2})$. 1983.

[19] F. Orabona, A. Argyriou, and N. Srebro. Prisma: Proximal iterative smoothing algorithm. *CoRR*, abs/1206.2372, 2012.

[20] T. K. Pong, P. Tseng, S. Ji, and J. Ye. Trace norm regularization: Reformulations, algorithms, and multi-task learning. *SIAM Journal on Optimization*, 20(6):3465–3489, 2010.

[21] A. Rajkumar and S. Agarwal. A statistical convergence perspective of algorithms for rank aggregation from pairwise data. In *ICML*, 2014.

[22] I. Rish and G. Tesauro. Active collaborative prediction with maximum margin matrix factorization. In *ISAIM*, 2008.

[23] R. Salakhutdinov and A. Mnih. Probabilistic matrix factorization. In *NIPS*, 2007.

[24] P. Salesses, K. Schechtner, and C. A. Hidalgo. The collaborative image of the city: Mapping the inequality of urban perception. 8(7):e68400, 2013.

[25] M. J. Salganik and K. E. C. Levy. Wiki surveys: Open and quantifiable social data collection. *arXiv:1202.0500*, 2012.

[26] B. Settles. *Active Learning*. Synthesis Lectures on Artificial Intelligence and Machine Learning. Morgan & Claypool Publishers, 2012.

[27] N. Srebro, J. D. M. Rennie, and T. Jaakkola. Maximum-margin matrix factorization. In *NIPS*, 2004.

[28] N. Srebro and A. Shraibman. Rank, trace-norm and max-norm. In *COLT*, pages 545–560, 2005.

[29] S. Tong and D. Koller. Support vector machine active learning with applications to text classification. *Journal of Machine Learning Research*, 2:45–66, 2001.

[30] M. Volkovs and R. S. Zemel. Collaborative ranking with 17 parameters. In *NIPS*, pages 2303–2311, 2012.

[31] F. L. Wauthier, M. I. Jordan, and N. Jojic. Efficient ranking from pairwise comparisons. In *ICML (3)*, pages 109–117, 2013.

[32] M. Weimer, A. Karatzoglou, Q. V. Le, and A. J. Smola. Cofi rank - maximum margin matrix factorization for collaborative ranking. In *NIPS*, 2007.

Effective Global Approaches for Mutual Information Based Feature Selection

Nguyen Xuan Vinh Jeffrey Chan Simone Romano James Bailey
Department of Computing and Information Systems, The University of Melbourne, Australia
{ vinh.nguyen | jeffrey.chan | simone.romano | baileyj }@unimelb.edu.au

ABSTRACT

Most current mutual information (MI) based feature selection techniques are greedy in nature thus are prone to sub-optimal decisions. Potential performance improvements could be gained by systematically posing MI-based feature selection as a global optimization problem. A rare attempt at providing a global solution for the MI-based feature selection is the recently proposed Quadratic Programming Feature Selection (QPFS) approach. We point out that the QPFS formulation faces several non-trivial issues, in particular, how to properly treat feature 'self-redundancy' while ensuring the convexity of the objective function. In this paper, we take a systematic approach to the problem of global MI-based feature selection. We show how the resulting NP-hard global optimization problem could be efficiently approximately solved via spectral relaxation and semi-definite programming techniques. We experimentally demonstrate the efficiency and effectiveness of these novel feature selection frameworks.

Categories and Subject Descriptors

I.5.2 [**Pattern Recognition**]: Feature evaluation and selection

Keywords

Feature selection; mutual information; spectral relaxation; semi-definite programming; global optimization.

1. INTRODUCTION

Mutual information (MI) based approaches are an important feature selection paradigm in data mining. Over the years, these methods have gained increasing popularity, thanks especially to their ease of use, effectiveness and strong theoretical foundation rooted in information theory. Seventeen MI based feature selection approaches are listed in a recent comprehensive survey [3], summarizing nearly two decades of research in this area. The commonality of these methods lies in the fact that they all employ a greedy scheme to incrementally build the selected feature set, one at a time.

To gain some concreteness to our discussion, let us revisit a very popular mutual information-based feature selection family that is centred around the concepts of *redundancy* and *relevancy*. A particularly successful and well known instance of this family is the Minimum Redundancy Maximum Relevance (MRMR) framework [20]. Given a set of n features (which are often referred interchangeably to as variables, or attributes) $\mathbb{X} = \{X_1, \ldots, X_n\}$ and a target class variable C, the relevancy of X_i is measured by its mutual information (MI) with the class variable, i.e.,

$$Rel(X_i) \triangleq I(X_i; C) \triangleq \sum_{X_i, C} P(X_i, C) \log \frac{P(X_i, C)}{P(X_i)P(C)}$$

while its redundancy with respect to an already selected feature subset $\mathbb{S}$ is defined as

$$Red(X_i|\mathbb{S}) \triangleq \frac{1}{|\mathbb{S}|} \sum_{X_j \in \mathbb{S}} I(X_i; X_j)$$

Given these definitions of feature relevancy and redundancy, the MRMR framework [20] is a greedy scheme to select features one at a time, such that the i-th feature is selected maximizing the MRMR-objective:

$$\max_{X_i \in \mathbb{X} \setminus \mathbb{S}} \{Rel(X_i) - Red(X_i|\mathbb{S})\}$$

The generalized MRMR family is parameterized as

$$\mathcal{MRMR}: \max_{X_i \in \mathbb{X} \setminus \mathbb{S}} \left\{ I(X_i; C) - \alpha \sum_{X_j \in \mathbb{S}} I(X_i; X_j) \right\} \quad (1)$$

where α is a weighting factor that balances relevancy and redundancy, which is chosen to be $1/|\mathbb{S}|$ in the case of MRMR. The first member of this family, known as MIFS (Mutual Information Feature Selection) [2] with $\alpha = 1$, has been in fact introduced much earlier in the feature selection literature.

1.1 Global MI-based feature selection

Most current MI-based feature selection approaches are of an incremental nature, similar to the $\mathcal{MRMR}$ formulation. As such, these methods are prone to suboptimal decisions, as selected features cannot be deselected at a later stage. Potential performance improvement could be gained by systematically posing MI-based feature selection as a global optimization problem, and making a global decision considering the interaction between all features concurrently. The first attempt in this direction is the recently proposed

KDD'14, August 24–27, 2014, New York, NY, USA.
Copyright 2014 ACM 978-1-4503-2956-9/14/08 ...$15.00.
http://dx.doi.org/10.1145/2623330.2623611 .

Quadratic Programming Feature Selection (QPFS) approach [21]. QPFS reformulates the MRMR feature selection problem as the following quadratic program:

$$\mathcal{QPFS}: \min_{\mathbf{x}} \left\{ \alpha \mathbf{x}^T \mathbf{H} \mathbf{x} - \mathbf{x}^T \mathbf{f} \right\} \text{ s.t. } \sum_{i=1}^{n} x_i = 1, x_i \geq 0 \quad (2)$$

where $\mathbf{f}_{n\times 1} = [I(X_1; C), \ldots, I(X_n; C)]^T$ is the vector of feature relevancy, $\mathbf{H}_{n\times n} = [I(X_i; X_j)]_{i,j=1\ldots n}$ is the matrix of feature pairwise redundancy, and $\mathbf{x}_{n\times 1}$ represents relative feature weights. Note that $\mathbf{H}_{ii}$ *is set to feature self-redundancy,* i.e. entropy, $\mathbf{H}_{ii} = I(X_i; X_i) = H(X_i)$. The most attractive characteristic of the QPFS formulation in (2) is that if $\mathbf{H}$ is positive (semi)definite, then $\mathcal{QPFS}$ is a convex quadratic program which can be solved efficiently in polynomial time for the globally optimal solution. The output $\mathbf{x}$ of this program is used for global feature ranking.

1.2 Theoretical issues with the QPFS framework

The reformulation of the incremental $\mathcal{MRMR}$ as a global quadratic program $\mathcal{QPFS}$ as proposed in [21], although being very attractive, poses several non-trivial intriguing questions that we shall elaborate below.

• **Positive definiteness of H**: A pre-requisite for $\mathcal{QPFS}$ to be a convex quadratic program, thus admitting an efficient polynomial-time procedure to find the global minimum, is that the Hessian matrix $\mathbf{H}$ of pairwise feature mutual information be positive (semi)definite. In other words, the mutual information function on the space of features must be a proper kernel function. Our investigation into this problem shows that there is currently little understanding on whether the MI is a proper kernel. While we have not been able to theoretically prove nor disprove the positive definiteness of $\mathbf{H}$, our practical evaluation of QPFS using Matlab quadratic program solver sometimes numerically encounters indefinite $\mathbf{H}$ (for instance, the largest negative eigenvalue could be as large as -50 on a dataset of 2000 features), where Matlab solver declares the problem to be non-convex and aborts the operation.

In the original paper [21], this theoretical issue has been mostly neglected. For problems of a very large number of features, the authors proposed to approximate $\mathbf{H}$ using only its largest eigenvalues, so $\mathcal{QPFS}$ becomes convex. However, as there exist many small and medium size problems where an approximation might not be needed, establishing the positive definiteness of $\mathbf{H}$ is still required to ensure the theoretical soundness of the approach.

• **How to treat self-redundancy?** In $\mathcal{QPFS}$, note that the cost matrix $\mathbf{H}$ penalizes features for their redundancy with respect to other features. The 'self-redundancy' terms $\mathbf{H}_{ii} = I(X_i; X_i) = H(X_i)$, as designated in the original paper [21], in fact penalize features for their intrinsic entropy. The question of how to treat self-redundancy presents us with the following dilemmas:

– Arguably, features should not be penalized for self redundancy. Unfortunately, if we put $\mathbf{H}_{ii} = 0$, then the Hessian matrix $\mathbf{H}$ becomes indefinite, violating the pre-requisite for the $\mathcal{QPFS}$ formulation to be convex.

– If we put $\mathbf{H}_{ii} = H(X_i)$ as proposed in [21], then there will be selection bias in favor of features with low entropy. In general, discrete features may have higher entropy because of more uniform distribution across its categories, or having more categories. As we will theoretically and empirically show next in this paper, penalizing features for self-redundancy leads to undesired behaviors.

Example 1: We use a simple example here to show the counter-intuitive behavior of QPFS that penalizing features differently based on their entropy can lead to suboptimal decisions. Let us consider the following scenario, where a quaternary variable S (Smoking) takes 4 possible values ((1) none smoker; (2) 1 to 5 cigarettes per day; (3) 5 to 15 cigarettes per day; (4) more than 15 cigarettes per day). S causes the binary class variable C (0–none, 1–lung cancer) with joint probability distribution $P(S, C)$. C then in turn causes a binary characteristic feature G (Coughing, 0–occasionally, 1–frequently) with joint probability $P(C, G)$. The scenario is denoted by the Bayesian network and joint probability tables in Figure 1. The joint probability $P(S, G)$ can also be calculated as in Fig. 1. In this example, S can be used to perfectly classify C (using the rule $C = 0$ if $S \in \{1, 2\}$ and $C = 1$ otherwise), while if G were used the minimal error rate achievable, i.e. Bayes error rate, will be 5%. Thus S–smoking should be clearly preferred over G–coughing as a predictive feature for C–lung cancer, albeit having a higher entropy, i.e. 2 bits vs. 1 bit. We can compute the following quantities:

$$\begin{aligned} I(G; C) &= 0.7136 \text{ bit} \\ I(S; C) &= 1 \text{ bit} \\ I(S; G) &= 0.7136 \text{ bit} \end{aligned}$$

The optimal solution to the $\mathcal{QPFS}$ formulation

$$\min_{x_i > 0, \sum x_i = 1} \left\{ \mathbf{x}^T \begin{bmatrix} 2 & 0.7136 \\ 0.7136 & 1 \end{bmatrix} \mathbf{x} - \mathbf{x}^T \begin{bmatrix} 1 \\ 0.7136 \end{bmatrix} \right\} \quad (3)$$

is $\mathbf{x}^* = [0.42, 0.58]^T$, that is, the coughing G (weight 0.58) is ranked higher than smoking S (weight 0.42), which is incorrect.

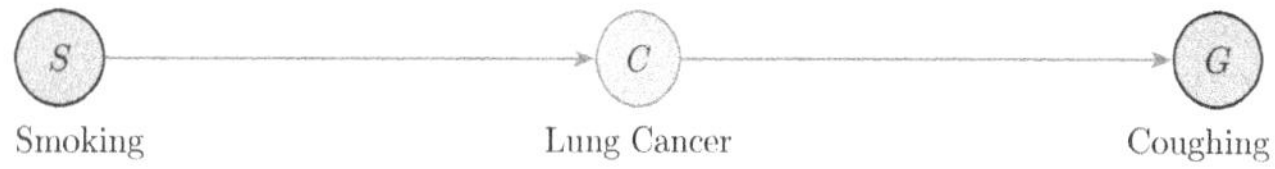

P(S,C)	C=0	C=1
S=1	0.25	0
S=2	0.25	0
S=3	0	0.25
S=4	0	0.25

P(C,G)	C=0	C=1
G=0	0.475	0.025
G=1	0.025	0.475

P(S,G)	G=0	G=1
S=1	0.2375	0.0125
S=2	0.2375	0.0125
S=3	0.0125	0.2375
S=4	0.0125	0.2375

Figure 1: The three-variable example: QPFS gives preference to the feature with smaller entropy G, while S is a better explanatory variable for C albeit having a higher entropy.

1.3 Contribution

Motivated by the initial success as well as the theoretical gap within the QPFS framework, we set out to systematically investigate the problem of global MI-based feature selection. Our first contribution in this paper is to reconsider the QPFS formulation and resolve the theoretical issues associated with its current form, as discussed above. Our second, and principal contribution, is to propose a novel formulation for global MI-based feature selection that can be solved effectively via spectral relaxation and semi-definite programming techniques. Via extensive experiments on a wide range of data sets, we establish the effectiveness and efficiency of our approach against other successful MI based feature selection techniques. We further show that for large data, low rank approximation can be applied to gain computational advantage to our global algorithm over its greedy counterpart.

2. PRELIMINARIES

It is worth noting that, in the original paper [21], the authors propose the quadratic formulation (2) without much explanatory detail. While that formulation is intuitively reasonable, let us take a more systematic, step-by-step derivation process implied behind QPFS, through which the inconsistency within QPFS itself will also be exposed. From a global optimization perspective, the incremental $\mathcal{MRMR}$ feature selection problem (1) can be reconsidered as a global *subset-selection* problem as follows:

$$\mathcal{SS}: \max_{\substack{\mathbb{S}\subset\mathbb{X}\\|\mathbb{S}|=k}} \left\{ \sum_{X_i\in\mathbb{S}} I(X_i;C) - \alpha \sum_{\substack{X_i,X_j\in\mathbb{S}\\i\neq j}} I(X_i;X_j) \right\} \quad (4)$$

which can in turn be equivalently formulated as a quadratic integer programming problem as

$$\mathcal{QIP}: \max_{\mathbf{x}} \left\{ \mathbf{x}^T\mathbf{f} - \alpha\mathbf{x}^T\mathbf{H}\mathbf{x} \right\} \text{ s.t. } \mathbf{x}\in\{0,1\}^n, \sum_{i=1}^{n} x_i = k \quad (5)$$

Here, k is the desired size for the final feature set, $\mathbf{f}_{n\times 1} = [I(X_1;C),\ldots,I(X_n;C)]^T$ is still the vector of feature relevancy, and $\mathbf{H}_{n\times n} = [I(X_i;X_j)]_{i,j=1\ldots n}$ is still the matrix of feature pairwise redundancy, except $\mathbf{H}_{ii} = 0$, i.e. zero-valued 'self-redundancy' terms. Note that this is also the critical difference between our global formulation and $\mathcal{QPFS}$: clearly and naturally, there should be no penalty for feature self-redundancy, as evidenced in the $\mathcal{MRMR}$ and $\mathcal{SS}$ formulations.

Unfortunately, there is no known efficient solution for both $\mathcal{SS}$ and $\mathcal{QIP}$. $\mathcal{SS}$ is a hard combinatorial problem for which an exhaustive search will cost $O(n^k)$, i.e. exponential in the target set size, while similarly $\mathcal{QIP}$ is known to be an NP-hard problem [5]. Noting that relaxing the problem to the continuous domain might lead to a more computationally tractable problem, we drop the integral 0–1 constraint, resulting in

$$\max_{\mathbf{x}} \left\{ \mathbf{x}^T\mathbf{f} - \alpha\mathbf{x}^T\mathbf{H}\mathbf{x} \right\} \text{ s.t. } \sum_{i=1}^{n} x_i = k,\ x_i \geq 0 \quad (6)$$

With a change of variable $y_i = x_i/k$, we arrive at:

$$\min_{\mathbf{y}} \left\{ k\alpha\mathbf{y}^T\mathbf{H}\mathbf{y} - \mathbf{y}^T\mathbf{f} \right\} \text{ s.t. } \sum_{i=1}^{n} y_i = 1,\ y_i \geq 0 \quad (7)$$

Herein, $k\alpha$ plays the role of a dynamic balancing factor. The $\mathcal{QPFS}$ formulation (2) is essentially a simplified variant of (7), where one disregards k and fixes the balancing factor to the same constant, i.e. α.

2.1 The extended MRMR family

Before providing a systematic analysis on how convexity could be ensured and 'self-redundancy' should be treated in the QPFS framework, let us gain further insight into both MRMR and QPFS by considering an extended MRMR family that incorporates second-order dependancy. The material discussed in this section will also serve as building blocks for our new approach, presented in Section 3. We start by elaborating the theoretical underpinnings behind MRMR and other similar heuristics. The ultimate goal of mutual information (MI) based feature selection is to select a subset of features $\mathbb{S}$ that shares the highest MI with C, i.e. $\max_{\mathbb{S}\subset\mathbb{X}} I(\mathbb{S};C)$. As this is a hard combinatorial problem, a practical approach is to build the feature subset incrementally, so that the i-th feature is selected as:

$$\arg\max_{X_i\in\mathbb{X}\setminus\mathbb{S}} I(\mathbb{S}\cup X_i;C) \equiv \arg\max_{X_i\in\mathbb{X}\setminus\mathbb{S}} I(X_i;C|\mathbb{S}) \quad (8)$$

As the high-dimensional MI term $I(X_i;C|\mathbb{S})$ is still hard to estimate from limited samples, MRMR and many other MI-based heuristics approximate (8) using low-order MI terms as:

$$I(X_i;C|\mathbb{S}) \simeq I(X_i;C) - \frac{1}{|\mathbb{S}|}\sum_{X_j\in\mathbb{S}} I(X_i;X_j) \quad (9)$$

However, the following natural decomposition of $I(X_i;C|\mathbb{S})$

$$I(X_i;C|\mathbb{S}) = I(X_i;C) - [I(X_i;\mathbb{S}) - I(X_i;\mathbb{S}|C)] \quad (10)$$

suggests that redundancy is in fact composed of two parts: an unconditional redundancy term $I(X_i;\mathbb{S})$ and a class conditional part $I(X_i;\mathbb{S}|C)$ [6]. This insight gives rise to the following extended minimal redundancy maximal relevance (EMRMR) objective:

$$\mathcal{EMRMR}: \max_{X_i} \left\{ I(X_i;C) - \alpha\sum_{X_j\in\mathbb{S}} [I(X_i;X_j) - I(X_i;X_j|C)] \right\} \quad (11)$$

This variant of MRMR has been introduced in the literature and observed to be more effective [3, 13, 14]. Similar to MRMR, EMRMR can be cast as an extended quadratic programming feature selection (EQPFS) problem as:

$$\mathcal{EQPFS} \ : \ \min_{\mathbf{x}} \left\{ \alpha\mathbf{x}^T[\mathbf{H}_1 - \mathbf{H}_2]\mathbf{x} - \mathbf{x}^T\mathbf{f} \right\}$$
$$\text{s.t.} \quad \sum_{i=1}^{n} x_i = 1, x_i \geq 0 \quad (12)$$

Here, $\mathbf{H}_1 = [I(X_i;X_j)]_{n\times n}$ and $\mathbf{H}_2 = [I(X_i;X_j|C)]_{n\times n}$ together make up the 'total-redundancy' matrix $\mathbf{H} = \mathbf{H}_1 - \mathbf{H}_2$. Similar to the QPFS formulation, we are presented with different choices about how to treat the total-self-redundancy terms, i.e. the diagonal elements of $\mathbf{H}_1$ and $\mathbf{H}_2$.

- If we set $\mathbf{H}_{1ii} = \mathbf{H}_{2ii} = 0$, i.e. no penalty for self-total-redundancy, then $\mathbf{H}$ is indefinite, hence $\mathcal{EQPFS}$ is non-convex and a global solution cannot be efficiently located.

- If we set $\mathbf{H}_{1ii} = I(X_i;X_i) = H(X_i)$ as in the original QPFS formulation [21], then analogously, $\mathbf{H}_{2ii}$ should be set to $I(X_i;X_i|C) = H(X_i|C)$. Thus $\mathbf{H}_{ii} = \mathbf{H}_{1ii} - \mathbf{H}_{2ii} = H(X_i) - H(X_i|C) = I(X;C)$, i.e. features which share more information with C are penalized more, which is clearly counter-intuitive and undesirable. In the next section, we provide a systematic analysis on how self-redundancy in the QPFS and EQPFS frameworks should be treated.

2.2 How to properly treat self-redundancy?

We argue that the most proper approach for treating self redundancy is that, *there should be no penalty for self redundancy*, i.e. $\mathbf{H}_{ii} = 0$, as clearly evident in the original

$\mathcal{MRMR}$ formulation. This choice however leads us to a non-convex quadratic program. We shall point out here that assigning $\mathbf{H}_{ii} = H(X_i)$ as in [21] in fact provides a convex approximation to the originally non-convex quadratic program. However, setting $\mathbf{H}_{ii} = H(X_i)$ leads to some counter-intuitive observation about $\mathcal{QPFS}$ (higher penalty for features with higher entropy) and $\mathcal{EQPFS}$ (higher penalty for features which share higher MI with C) as we have pointed out.

We propose that $\mathcal{QPFS}$ and $\mathcal{EQPFS}$ could be convexified by setting the diagonal elements of $\mathbf{H}$ to the same value $\lambda > 0$ sufficiently large to ensure the positive (semi)definiteness of the Hessian matrix. Formally, the general convexified $\mathcal{EQPFS}$ is as follows:

$$\min_{\mathbf{x},\sum_{i=1}^{n} x_i=1, x_i\geq 0} \left\{\alpha\mathbf{x}^T[\mathbf{H}_1 - \beta\mathbf{H}_2 + \lambda\mathbf{I}]\mathbf{x} - \mathbf{x}^T\mathbf{f}\right\} \quad (13)$$

where $\mathbf{I}$ is the identity matrix, both α and β play the role of balancing factors, and λ is a convexification parameter. β is employed to balance the unconditional redundancy (in $\mathbf{H}_1$) and the class conditional redundancy (in $\mathbf{H}_2$), as proposed in [14]. At $\beta = 0$, $\mathcal{EQPFS}$ reduces to the original $\mathcal{QPFS}$. With this approach, all features receive the same penalty for 'self-redundancy' λ, although the real purpose of λ is to convexify the problem, not to impose a penalty on self-redundancy. It is noted that different choices of $\{\alpha, \beta, \lambda\}$ can lead to different solutions corresponding to different feature rankings.

3. A NOVEL GLOBAL MI-BASED FEATURE SELECTION PARADIGM

In this section, we set out to design a novel, systematic global approach for MI-based feature selection. Our desiderata for such an ideal global framework is two-fold: (i) ability to handle second-order feature dependancy as in $\mathcal{EMRMR}$, (ii) strong theoretical foundation, with few or no ad-hoc parameters, such as the balancing parameters and convexification parameter as in the 'remedied' QPFS framework (13).

Our first ingredient for such new framework is the following nice theoretical result, which states that the relevancy, unconditional redundancy and class-conditional redundancy, can all be combined neatly into a single quantity, namely the conditional mutual information (CMI).

THEOREM 1. *We have:*

$$\sum_{X_j\in\mathbb{S}} I(X_i;C|X_j) = |\mathbb{S}|I(X_i;C) - \sum_{X_j\in\mathbb{S}} [I(X_i;X_j) - I(X_i;X_j|C)] \quad (14)$$

PROOF. The proof is straightforward using the following decomposition of the conditional MI:

$$I(X_i;C|X_j) = I(X_i;C) - I(X_i;X_j) + I(X_i;X_j|C) \quad (15)$$

□

In fact, now we can see a chain of relationship between the high-dimensional conditional relevancy term in (8), the CMI and the extended MRMR criteria:

$$I(X_i;C|\mathbb{S}) \simeq \textstyle\sum_{X_j\in\mathbb{S}} I(X_i;C|X_j) \quad (16)$$
$$\equiv |\mathbb{S}|I(X_i;C) - \textstyle\sum_{X_j\in\mathbb{S}}[I(X_i;X_j) + I(X_i;X_j|C)]$$

In light of these connections, we propose a global subset selection problem based on the CMI as follows:

$$\mathcal{SS}_{\mathcal{CMI}} : \max_{\substack{\mathbb{S}\subset\mathbb{X}\\ |\mathbb{S}|=k}} \left\{ \sum_{X_i\in\mathbb{S}} I(X_i;C) + \sum_{X_i,X_j\in\mathbb{S}} I(X_i;C|X_j) \right\} \quad (17)$$

which can be equivalently reformulated in the form of a quadratic integer programming problem:

$$\mathcal{QIP}_{\mathcal{CMI}} : \max_{\mathbf{x}} \left\{\mathbf{x}^T\mathbf{Q}\mathbf{x}\right\} \text{ s.t. } \mathbf{x}\in\{0,1\}^n, \|\mathbf{x}\| = \sqrt{k} \quad (18)$$

where $\mathbf{Q}_{ii} = I(X_i;C)$ and $\mathbf{Q}_{ij} = I(X_i;C|X_j), i\neq j$. Note that for $\mathbf{x}\in\{0,1\}^n$, we have $\sum_{i=1}^{n} x_i = k \Leftrightarrow \|\mathbf{x}\| = \sqrt{k}$. Here we use the norm constraint for set cardinality, as it results in more computationally tractable relaxations, as will be seen in the next sections. It is noted that $\mathbf{Q}$ is, in general, asymmetric. However, it could be replaced by the symmetric form $(\mathbf{Q}+\mathbf{Q}^T)/2$ without changing the objective value. Thus hereafter, $\mathbf{Q}$ refers to the matrix with $\mathbf{Q}_{ij} = \frac{1}{2}\{I(X_i;C|X_j) + I(X_j;C|X_i)\}, i\neq j$ and $\mathbf{Q}_{ii} = I(X_i;C)$. It can be seen that our Hessian matrix $\mathbf{Q}$ embodies both the notions of relevancy and total redundancy. With this novel formulation, we have resolved several issues associated with the self-redundancy terms, as well as eliminating the need of introducing (and thus, tuning) the balancing factors α, β and the convexification parameter λ, as in the general $\mathcal{EQPFS}$ formulation.

We now present an interesting geometrical interpretation for the CMI criterion as follows. Besides relevancy, the global subset selection formulations $\mathcal{SS}_{\mathcal{CMI}}$ and $\mathcal{QIP}_{\mathcal{CMI}}$ favor features having large total pairwise conditional relevance. It is interesting to note that the quantity $d_C(X_i, X_j) = I(X_i;C|X_j) + I(X_j;C|X_i)$ could be regarded as a *distance measure* in the feature space. Sotoca and Pla [22] further claimed that this distance measure, named the conditional mutual information distance, is a proper metric, that is, it satisfies the triangle inequality[1]. The interpretation of $d_C(X_i, X_j)$ as a distance measure brings about an interesting insight on $\mathcal{SS}_{\mathcal{CMI}}$, which can be rewritten as $\max_{\substack{\mathbb{S}\subset\mathbb{X}\\ |\mathbb{S}|=k}} \left\{\sum_{X_i\in\mathbb{S}} I(X_i;C) + \frac{1}{2}\sum_{X_i,X_j\in\mathbb{S}} d_C(X_i,X_j)\right\}$. This criterion selects k features such that their total relevance and total pairwise distance is maximized. In other words, the criterion aims to choose a set of highly relevant representative features that also provide good coverage over the feature space, i.e. far apart from each-other in CMI distance.

As $\mathcal{QIP}_{\mathcal{CMI}}$ is NP-hard, in the next sections we investigate efficient approximation techniques for solving this problem.

3.1 Global MI-based feature selection via spectral relaxation

We propose an efficient yet simple spectral relaxation technique for solving $\mathcal{QIP}_{\mathcal{CMI}}$. We shall relax $\mathcal{QIP}_{\mathcal{CMI}}$ to the continuous domain, by dropping the integral 0–1 constraints which in fact cause NP-hardness, while keeping only the

[1]We recently pointed out that Sotoca and Pla's proof is flawed, and that the triangle inequality holds true under the Naïve Bayes assumption, i.e. all the features are independent given the class variable [24]. Whether the CMI distance is a proper metric in general is still an open problem.

norm constraint, resulting in

$$\max_{\mathbf{x}} \left\{\mathbf{x}^T\mathbf{Q}\mathbf{x}\right\} \text{ s.t. } \|\mathbf{x}\| = \sqrt{k}, x_i \geq 0$$

$$\doteq \mathcal{SPEC}_{\mathcal{CMI}} \ : \ \max_{\mathbf{x}} \left\{\mathbf{x}^T\mathbf{Q}\mathbf{x}\right\} \text{ s.t. } \|\mathbf{x}\| = 1, x_i \geq 0 \quad (19)$$

where $\doteq$ denotes equivalence in feature *ordering*, noting that replacing $\|\mathbf{x}\| = \sqrt{k}$ with $\|\mathbf{x}\| = 1$ only scales the solution by a multiplicative constant $1/\sqrt{k}$. The non-negativity constraints $x_i \geq 0$ ensure that the relaxed solution can be reasonably interpreted as feature 'weights'.

Without the non-negativity constraints $x_i \geq 0$, albeit being a non-convex problem in general, $\mathcal{SPEC}_{\mathcal{CMI}}$ admits a simple global solution which coincides with that maximizing the well-known Rayleigh quotient of the form $\frac{\mathbf{x}^T\mathbf{Q}\mathbf{x}}{\mathbf{x}^T\mathbf{x}}$. The solution to this problem is *any unit-norm eigenvector corresponding to the dominant eigenvalue of* $\mathbf{Q}$ [10]. At optimality, the dominant eigenvalue of $\mathbf{Q}$ is also the maximum objective value. When the entries in $\mathbf{Q}$ are all non-negative, as $I(X_i; C|X_j) \geq 0$, then we can prove the following result:

THEOREM 2. *If $\mathbf{Q}_{ij} \geq 0 \ \forall i,j$ then:*
(i) the optimal solution $\mathbf{x}^*$ for $\max_{\|\mathbf{x}\|=1} \left\{\mathbf{x}^T\mathbf{Q}\mathbf{x}\right\}$ must be sign-consistent, i.e. having all x_i^*'s of the same sign.
(ii) any dominant eigenvector of $\mathbf{Q}$ must be sign-consistent.
(iii) if there exists a dominant eigenvector $\mathbf{x}^*$ having $x_i^* > 0, \forall i$, i.e. strictly positive, then its eigenvalue must be the unique dominant eigenvalue of $\mathbf{Q}$.

PROOF. (i) Assume that $\mathbf{x}^*$ has mixed-sign components, as $\mathbf{Q}_{ij} \geq 0 \ \forall i,j$ the value of the quadratic form $\mathbf{x}^{*T}\mathbf{Q}\mathbf{x}^* = \sum_{i,j} x_i^* x_j^* \mathbf{Q}_{ij}$ can always be increased by assigning the same sign to all x_i^*'s (still satisfying $\|\mathbf{x}^*\| = 1$), contradicting the assumption that $\mathbf{x}^*$ is the globally optimal solution.

(ii) We shall note that the critical points and critical values of $\max_{\|\mathbf{x}\|=1} \left\{\mathbf{x}^T\mathbf{Q}\mathbf{x}\right\}$ are respectively all the unit-norm eigenvectors of $\mathbf{Q}$ and their eigenvectors. In case $\mathbf{Q}$ has duplicate dominant eigenvalues, all their associated eigenvectors are globally optimal solution for $\max_{\|\mathbf{x}\|=1} \left\{\mathbf{x}^T\mathbf{Q}\mathbf{x}\right\}$, and therefore must be sign-consistent, as per (i).

(iii) As $x_i^* > 0$, there cannot exist any other sign-consistent (dominant) eigenvector that is orthogonal to $\mathbf{x}^*$, thus its eigenvalue must be the unique dominant eigenvalue of $\mathbf{Q}$. □

In view of this result, we can use any unit-norm dominant eigenvector of $\mathbf{Q}$ with all non-negative entries as the solution to $\mathcal{SPEC}_{\mathcal{CMI}}$. As for the feature ranking purpose, features with higher weights x_i will appear higher in the ranking, i.e. more important features. It is noted that in the $\mathcal{SPEC}_{\mathcal{CMI}}$ formulation, the Hessian $\mathbf{Q}$ is not required to be positive semidefinite as in the $\mathcal{QPFS}$ formulation.

Example 1 revisited: we have

$$I(G, C|S) = I(G; C) - I(G; S) + I(G, S|C) = 0 \text{ bit}$$
$$I(S, C|G) = I(S; C) - I(G; S) + I(G, S|C) = 0.2864 \text{ bit}$$

The solution to the $\mathcal{SPEC}_{\mathcal{CMI}}$ formulation

$$\max_{\|\mathbf{x}\|=1, x_i \geq 0} \left\{\mathbf{x}^T \begin{bmatrix} 1 & 0.2864/2 \\ 0.2864/2 & 0.7136 \end{bmatrix} \mathbf{x}\right\} \quad (20)$$

is $\mathbf{x}^* = [0.92, 0.38]^T$, that is, smoking S (weight 0.92) is ranked higher than coughing G (weight 0.38).

3.2 Global MI-based feature selection via semi-definite programming

In this section, we investigate another strategy for solving the integer quadratic programming problem $\mathcal{QIP}_{\mathcal{CMI}}$, via semi-definite programming. Semi-definite relaxation has recently gained increasing interest as an effective approximation tool for solving hard combinatorial problems. This significant interest was sparked by the seminal work of Goemans and Williamson [11] in approximating the NP-hard max-cut problem in graph theory,

$$\mathcal{MAXCUT} : \max_{\mathbf{x}} \{\mathbf{x}^T\mathbf{L}\mathbf{x}\} \quad \text{s.t. } \mathbf{x} \in \{-1, +1\}^n \qquad (21)$$

where $\mathbf{L}$ is the graph Laplacian matrix. As semidefinite programming (SDP) is known to generate tighter approximation for $\mathcal{MAXCUT}$ over spectral relaxation, here we are interested in seeing whether for the $\mathcal{QIP}_{\mathcal{CMI}}$ problem, SDP can significantly improve over spectral relaxation as presented above. In order to employ the semidefinite relaxation technique in [11], we first transform the binary 0–1 problem $\mathcal{QIP}_{\mathcal{CMI}}$ into a bipolar $-1/+1$ problem similar to $\mathcal{MAXCUT}$, via the transformation $x_i = \frac{y_i+1}{2}$, resulting in

$$\begin{aligned} \max_{\mathbf{y}} \quad & \left\{\frac{1}{4}(\mathbf{y}+\mathbf{1})^T\mathbf{Q}(\mathbf{y}+\mathbf{1})\right\} \qquad (22) \\ \text{s.t.} \quad & \mathbf{y} \in \{-1, 1\}^n, (\mathbf{y}+\mathbf{1})^T\mathbf{I}(\mathbf{y}+\mathbf{1}) = 4k \end{aligned}$$

where $\mathbf{1}_{n\times 1}$ is the vector of all 1's. Note that we could rewrite the norm constraint $\|\mathbf{x}\| = \sqrt{k}$ as $\mathbf{x}^T\mathbf{I}\mathbf{x} = k$ where $\mathbf{I}_{n\times n}$ is the identity matrix, hence $(\mathbf{y}+\mathbf{1})^T\mathbf{I}(\mathbf{y}+\mathbf{1}) = 4k$. Since the problem (22) is not in a homogeneous quadratic form, we shall transform it back to an equivalent homogeneous form via simply introducing an additional dummy variable $y_0 = 1$ (the variable expansion trick [27]), i.e. $\mathbf{y} = \{y_0 \equiv 1, y_1, \ldots, y_n\}$, resulting in

$$\begin{aligned} \max_{\mathbf{y}} \quad & \mathbf{y}^T\widehat{\mathbf{Q}}\mathbf{y} \qquad (23) \\ \text{s.t.} \quad & y_0 = 1, \mathbf{y} \in \{-1, 1\}^{n+1}, \mathbf{y}^T\widehat{\mathbf{I}}\mathbf{y} = 4k \end{aligned}$$

where $\widehat{\mathbf{Q}}_{(n+1)\times(n+1)} = \begin{bmatrix} \mathbf{1}^T\mathbf{Q}\mathbf{1} & \mathbf{1}^T\mathbf{Q} \\ \mathbf{Q}\mathbf{1} & \mathbf{Q} \end{bmatrix}$ and $\widehat{\mathbf{I}}_{(n+1)\times(n+1)} = \begin{bmatrix} \mathbf{1}^T\mathbf{I}\mathbf{1} & \mathbf{1}^T\mathbf{I} \\ \mathbf{I}\mathbf{1} & \mathbf{I} \end{bmatrix}$. We further note that the constraint $y_0 = 1$ could also be relaxed to $y_0 \in \{-1, 1\}$. This is because homogeneous quadratic problems are symmetric in $\mathbf{y}$ and $-\mathbf{y}$, therefore if $\mathbf{y}^*$ is optimal, then $-\mathbf{y}^*$ will also be optimal, and we simply need to pick the solution with $y_0^* = 1$ as the final solution. Now, note that the quadratic form $\mathbf{y}^T\widehat{\mathbf{Q}}\mathbf{y}$ can also be rewritten as $\widehat{\mathbf{Q}} \bullet \mathbf{y}\mathbf{y}^T$, where $\mathbf{U} \bullet \mathbf{V} = \sum_{i,j} U_{ij}V_{ij}$, we arrive at:

$$\begin{aligned} \max_{\mathbf{y}} \quad & \widehat{\mathbf{Q}} \bullet \mathbf{y}\mathbf{y}^T \qquad (24) \\ \text{s.t.} \quad & \mathbf{y} \in \{-1, 1\}^{n+1}, \widehat{\mathbf{I}} \bullet \mathbf{y}\mathbf{y}^T = 4k \end{aligned}$$

We next substitute $\mathbf{Y} = \mathbf{y}\mathbf{y}^T$, noting that an arbitrary matrix could only be factorized as such iff $\mathbf{Y} \succeq 0$, i.e. $\mathbf{Y}$ is positive semidefinite, and $\text{rank}(\mathbf{Y}) = 1$. Also note that for $y_i \in \{-1, 1\}$ we have $y_i.y_i = 1 \Leftrightarrow \text{diag}(\mathbf{Y}) = \mathbf{1}$, we arrive at

$$\begin{aligned} \max_{\mathbf{Y}} \quad & \widehat{\mathbf{Q}} \bullet \mathbf{Y} \qquad (25) \\ \text{s.t.} \quad & \widehat{\mathbf{I}} \bullet \mathbf{Y} = 4k, \text{diag}(\mathbf{Y}) = \mathbf{1}, \mathbf{Y} \succeq 0, \text{rank}(\mathbf{Y}) = 1 \end{aligned}$$

Until now we have not yet gained any computational advantage, as the problem (25) is still exactly equivalent to the NP-hard $\mathcal{QIP}_{\mathcal{CMI}}$ problem. The specific constraint that causes NP-hardness in this case is the rank-1 constraint, since without it, the following problem can be solved to optimality in polynomial time via semidefinite programming [18]:

$$\mathcal{SDP}_{\mathcal{CMI}} : \max_{\mathbf{Y}} \quad \widehat{\mathbf{Q}} \bullet \mathbf{Y} \qquad (26)$$
$$\text{s.t.} \quad \widehat{\mathbf{I}} \bullet \mathbf{Y} = 4k, \text{diag}(\mathbf{Y}) = \mathbf{1}, \mathbf{Y} \succeq 0$$

After solving $\mathcal{SDP}_{\mathcal{CMI}}$ we need to recover the discrete $\{-1, +1\}$ solution to (23), a process known as rounding. Herein, we simply adapt the random projection rounding technique proposed in [11], with 100 random projections. In each projection, the top k features are selected as the ones with corresponding rows $\mathbf{Y}_{i\cdot}$ having largest cosine similarity to a randomly picked vector uniformly distributed on the unit hypersphere in $\mathbb{R}^{n+1}$. Finally, the random projection that results in largest value for the original $\mathcal{QIP}_{\mathcal{CMI}}$ problem is selected. Interested readers are referred to [11] for these details.

3.3 Complexity analysis

For all methods, generally there will be time needed for computing the similarity matrix and the time needed for ranking the features. The time for computing MI quantities, such as $I(X_i; X_j)$ and $I(X_i; C|X_j)$ comprises mainly $O(d)$ time for computing the joint probability table. Thus, the time for computing the similarity matrix is $O(n^2 d)$. The ranking time complexity for MRMR, $\mathcal{SPEC}_{\mathcal{CMI}}$ and $\mathcal{SDP}_{\mathcal{CMI}}$ is provided in Table 1. The dominant time component for MRMR and $\mathcal{SPEC}_{\mathcal{CMI}}$ is in fact, for computing the similarity matrix, rather than ranking. In terms of ranking time, $\mathcal{SPEC}_{\mathcal{CMI}}$ is significantly less expensive than $\mathcal{QPFS}$, while $\mathcal{SDP}_{\mathcal{CMI}}$ is the most expensive.

Table 1: Ranking complexity in the number of features n.

Method	MRMR	$\mathcal{SPEC}_{\mathcal{CMI}}$	$\mathcal{QPFS}$	$\mathcal{SDP}_{\mathcal{CMI}}$
Complexity	$O(n^2)$	$O(n^2)$	$O(n^3)$	$O(n^{4.5})$

It is noted that greedy algorithms, such as MRMR, fill the similarity matrix gradually and could be stopped at any point to produce a partial ranking. In data mining and knowledge discovery, it is also often desirable to produce a complete ranking of all features. Indeed, while the top ranking features are important for building accurate classifiers, features with low ranks are important for understanding the data generating process. Such knowledge could be used, for example, to improve the data collecting process, where the least important features could be omitted from data collection. Also, a domain expert may be interested in studying how a feature of interest is ranked compared to others, in such case a complete ranking of all features is required.

3.4 Global feature selection for large data

For large data, computing the kernel-like matrix $\mathbf{Q}$ itself becomes expensive. Herein, we investigate a strategy to reduce this cost via low-rank approximation for $\mathbf{Q}$, in particular via the Nyström method. Nyström based methods for large-scale data analysis have been successfully applied on numerous problems in the pattern recognition and machine learning literature [9,15]. Without loss of generality, we can assume $\mathbf{Q}$ in the $\mathcal{SPEC}_{\mathcal{CMI}}$ formulation (19) to be positive semi-definite. Indeed

$$\mathcal{SPEC}_{\mathcal{CMI}} : \arg\max_{\|\mathbf{x}\|=1, x_i \geq 0} \left\{\mathbf{x}^T \mathbf{Q} \mathbf{x}\right\} \equiv \arg\max_{\|\mathbf{x}\|=1, x_i \geq 0} \left\{\mathbf{x}^T (\mathbf{Q} + \lambda \mathbf{I}) \mathbf{x}\right\}$$

where λ can be chosen as a sufficiently large positive constant without affecting the ranking. Nyström method approximates the positive semi-definite $\mathbf{Q}$ as

$$\widetilde{\mathbf{Q}} = \begin{bmatrix} \mathbf{A} & \mathbf{B} \\ \mathbf{B}^T & \mathbf{B}^T \mathbf{A}^{-1} \mathbf{B} \end{bmatrix}$$

using only a subset of $p = \gamma n$ rows of $\mathbf{Q}$, namely those comprising $[\mathbf{A}_{p\times p} \; \mathbf{B}_{p\times(n-p)}]$, where the rows are usually randomly sampled without replacement and $0 < \gamma < 1$ is the Nyström sampling rate. A useful characteristic of the Nyström approximation is that the approximated solution to the $\mathcal{SPEC}_{\mathcal{CMI}}$ formulation, namely the dominant eigenvector of $\widetilde{\mathbf{Q}}$, could be computed exactly from submatrices of much smaller size, without explicitly evaluating the block $\mathbf{B}^T \mathbf{A}^{-1} \mathbf{B}$ and fill in $\widetilde{\mathbf{Q}}$. This could be very useful for situations where the number of features is large, such that merely storing $\widetilde{\mathbf{Q}}_{n\times n}$ could already be a problem. Let $\mathbf{A}^{\frac{1}{2}}$ denote the symmetric positive definite square root of $\mathbf{A}$, define $\widehat{\mathbf{A}}_{p\times p} = \mathbf{A} + \mathbf{A}^{-\frac{1}{2}} \mathbf{B} \mathbf{B}^T \mathbf{A}^{-\frac{1}{2}}$ then the dominant eigenvector of $\widetilde{\mathbf{Q}}$ is simply

$$\sigma^{-\frac{1}{2}} \begin{bmatrix} \mathbf{A} \\ \mathbf{B}^T \end{bmatrix} \mathbf{A}^{-\frac{1}{2}} \mathbf{u}$$

where σ and $\mathbf{u}$ are the dominant eigenvalue and its associated eigenvector of $\widehat{\mathbf{A}}$ [9]. The complexity of the Nyström approximated solution is $O(\gamma n^2 d)$ for computing the similarity matrix and $O(\gamma n^2 + \gamma^2 n^2)$ for ranking. One remaining detail left is that although $\mathbf{Q}$ is entry-wise positive, it is not guaranteed that this property carries over to its approximation $\widetilde{\mathbf{Q}}$. Thus, $\widetilde{\mathbf{Q}}$ can have negative elements and as a results, its dominant eigenvector can have negative entries. In such cases, we induce a global ranking as follows. First, the problem is converted from a binary 0–1 problem to an equivalent bi-polar +1/-1 problem as in (22). Then a dummy variable $x_0 \equiv 1$, which is supposed to be always chosen, is included as in (23). The dominant eigenvector of $\begin{bmatrix} \mathbf{1}^T \widetilde{\mathbf{Q}} \mathbf{1} & \mathbf{1}^T \widetilde{\mathbf{Q}} \\ \widetilde{\mathbf{Q}} \mathbf{1} & \widetilde{\mathbf{Q}} \end{bmatrix}$ with the first entry (corresponding to x_0) being positive is chosen for feature ranking where the weights are sorted in descending order.

In [21] Nyström approximation was also applied for approximating the $\mathcal{QPFS}$ formulation (2). For $\mathcal{QPFS}$, a second level of approximation was further proposed, where the quadratic programming problem is approximated with one at a lower dimension, using only the largest eigenvalues of (the Nyström approximated) $\mathbf{H}$. As opposed to $\mathcal{QPFS}$, for the proposed $\mathcal{SPEC}_{\mathcal{CMI}}$ formulation, only one level of approximation, i.e. approximating $\mathbf{Q}$, is necessary. In general, Nyström approximation quality improves with increasing p. With a fixed sampling rate, approximation is better when there exists more redundancy in $\mathbf{Q}$, i.e. there are similar features.

4. EXPERIMENTAL EVALUATION

We perform a series of experiments to evaluate the efficiency and effectiveness of the two novel MI-based feature selection frameworks, namely $\mathcal{SPEC}_{\mathcal{CMI}}$ and $\mathcal{SDP}_{\mathcal{CMI}}$. First,

Table 2: Average time (in seconds) required for solving $\mathcal{SDP}_{\mathcal{CMI}}$ and $\mathcal{SPEC}_{\mathcal{CMI}}$ at different problem sizes (given pre-computed similarity matrices Q and H).

Dataset	#Features n	$\mathcal{SDP}_{\mathcal{CMI}}$	$\mathcal{SPEC}_{\mathcal{CMI}}$
Waveform	21	0.78 ± 0.07	0.005 ± 0.001
Promoter	57	1.18 ± 0.44	0.005 ± 0.001
Optdigits	64	1.59 ± 1.27	0.005 ± 0.001
Musk	166	3.38 ± 0.15	0.005 ± 0.000
Arrhythmia	257	9.46 ± 0.20	0.006 ± 0.001
Lung cancer	325	16.92 ± 0.73	0.007 ± 0.005
	$n > 700$	N/A	See Sec. 4.2

we compare $\mathcal{SPEC}_{\mathcal{CMI}}$ and $\mathcal{SDP}_{\mathcal{CMI}}$ in terms of their capability to approximate $\mathcal{QIP}_{\mathcal{CMI}}$, and draw the conclusion that $\mathcal{SPEC}_{\mathcal{CMI}}$ is the preferred approach. Second, we test $\mathcal{SPEC}_{\mathcal{CMI}}$ against $\mathcal{QPFS}$ in terms of scalability, and draw the conclusion that $\mathcal{SPEC}_{\mathcal{CMI}}$ is much more computationally scalable. Lastly, we compare $\mathcal{SPEC}_{\mathcal{CMI}}$ with other MI-based feature selection techniques on an extensive set of 15 small and medium sized real life data sets and 4 large datasets. The experiments were carried out on an Intel Core-i7 2.9Ghz PC with 16Gb of main memory.

4.1 $\mathcal{SPEC}_{\mathcal{CMI}}$ vs. $\mathcal{SDP}_{\mathcal{CMI}}$: a test of approximation tightness and scalability

We select several small size data sets in Table 4, namely Waveform ($n = 21$), Promoter ($n = 57$), Optdigits ($n = 64$), Musk ($n = 166$), Arrythmia ($n = 257$) and Lung cancer ($n = 325$) for this experiment. To solve the $\mathcal{SDP}_{\mathcal{CMI}}$ formulation, we employ the CVX toolbox for convex optimization [12], with the underlying solver being SDPT3 [23]. We set the number of features to be selected k to the range $[1, \min(n, 100)]$, thus in total there are 442 test cases. The average runtime comparison for $\mathcal{SDP}_{\mathcal{CMI}}$ and $\mathcal{SPEC}_{\mathcal{CMI}}$ (for the ranking phase) is reported in Table 2. For these small problems, the time required for $\mathcal{SPEC}_{\mathcal{CMI}}$ is negligible, while $\mathcal{SDP}_{\mathcal{CMI}}$ is orders of magnitude slower, but still acceptable. While $\mathcal{SDP}_{\mathcal{CMI}}$ running time does not seem a problem, it exhibits a large memory footprint. In fact, for problems with $n \sim 700$, CVX returns an out-of-memory error[2] on our PC. Note that the number of variables in the relaxed space for semidefinite programming is $O(\frac{1}{2}n^2)$. For example, with $n = 500$, CVX reports problem size of 125,751 variables and employs additionally $\sim$ 8Gb of memory.

We next compare $\mathcal{SDP}_{\mathcal{CMI}}$ and $\mathcal{SPEC}_{\mathcal{CMI}}$ in terms of the objective value of the original 0–1 problem $\mathcal{QIP}_{\mathcal{CMI}}$ in (18). Of all the 442 test cases, $\mathcal{SDP}_{\mathcal{CMI}}$ and $\mathcal{SPEC}_{\mathcal{CMI}}$ return different results in only 63 cases ($\sim$ 14%), within which $\mathcal{SDP}_{\mathcal{CMI}}$ 'wins' over in 46 cases ($\sim$ 73%). Thus it can be seen that $\mathcal{SDP}_{\mathcal{CMI}}$ tends to outperforms $\mathcal{SPEC}_{\mathcal{CMI}}$. This observation conforms well with previous studies, that semidefinite relaxation provides tighter approximation than spectral relaxation, as in other hard combinatorial problems such as graph max-cut. Nevertheless, the difference herein observed, if any, is often minor. More specifically, we have 58/63 cases in which the absolute relative difference, computed as $|obj_{SDP} - obj_{SPEC}|/obj_{SPEC}$ (where obj_{SDP} and obj_{SPEC} are the objective values of the $\mathcal{SDP}_{\mathcal{CMI}}$ and $\mathcal{SPEC}_{\mathcal{CMI}}$ approximated solution respectively), is $< 0.5\%$. Furthermore, a closer inspection reveals that in all cases, the feature sets differ in at most 2 features. For the rest 379/442 cases (86%), $\mathcal{SDP}_{\mathcal{CMI}}$ and $\mathcal{SPEC}_{\mathcal{CMI}}$ return identical objective value and identical feature sets. For the smallest Waveform data set, we also compute the optimal objective value found by exhaustive enumeration. In this case, the maximum relative difference between the optimal objective and that of $\mathcal{SPEC}_{\mathcal{CMI}}$ is only 0.07%, confirming the effectiveness of the two approximation schemes. For the other larger data sets, exhaustive enumeration is unacceptably slow, even with $k = 5$, ruling out this brute-force approach as a practical solution.

From this set of experiment, we draw the conclusion that, while semidefinite programming tends to generate tighter approximation, the difference is negligible. More importantly, the two techniques most often generate identical feature sets. In view of the fact that $\mathcal{SPEC}_{\mathcal{CMI}}$ is significantly simpler and more computationally efficient, we therefore promote $\mathcal{SPEC}_{\mathcal{CMI}}$ as the method of choice. In the next sections, we establish the efficiency and effectiveness of $\mathcal{SPEC}_{\mathcal{CMI}}$ against other popular MI-based feature selection approaches.

4.2 $\mathcal{SPEC}_{\mathcal{CMI}}$ vs. $\mathcal{QPFS}$: a test of scalability

To fix a concrete idea about how scalable and speedy dominant eigenvalue computation is, compared to quadratic convex optimization, we generate 10 random positive definite $\mathbf{Q}$ matrices for each size ranging from 1,000 to 30,000 (and also random relevancy vectors $\mathbf{f}$), and solve the $\mathcal{QPFS}$ and $\mathcal{SPEC}_{\mathcal{CMI}}$ problems using popular off-the-shelf solvers, specifically those provided by Matlab with default options. The average wall-clock time to solve these problems is provided in Table 3. Note that at $n > 16,000$, Matlab solver (`quadprog`) returned an out-of-memory error for $\mathcal{QPFS}$. On average, we observe that $\mathcal{QPFS}$ running time is two or more orders of magnitude slower than $\mathcal{SPEC}_{\mathcal{CMI}}$. For comparison, the ranking time for the incremental MRMR approach on the same similarity matrices is also reported in Table 3. With a carefully tuned implementation[3], MRMR outpaces $\mathcal{SPEC}_{\mathcal{CMI}}$ in running time, but practically this difference should not be a major concern.

In terms of practical implementation, the solution to $\mathcal{SPEC}_{\mathcal{CMI}}$ amounts to finding the dominant eigenvector of the Hessian matrix $\mathbf{Q}$. Algorithmically, this can be done as simply as repeatedly applying $\mathbf{Q}$ to any nondegenerate initial solution (the power method). In practice, dominant eigenvalue finding is a basic and efficient operation, which is built-in at the core of most, if not all, numerical packages. On the other hand, $\mathcal{QPFS}$ requires the solution to a quadratic convex optimization problem with linear constraints, which is arguably not always readily available as eigenvector computation. A further advantage of the $\mathcal{SPEC}_{\mathcal{CMI}}$ formulation over $\mathcal{QPFS}$ is that its solution via eigenvector decomposition is much more amenable to parallel computation, and can be implemented straightforwardly, readily exploiting the benefit of currently popular multi-core PC systems. Parallel implementation for quadratic and semi-definite programming on the other hand is an advanced research topic [26].

[2]Technically, we could employ more virtual memory using hard disk to circumvent memory shortage. But this results in a huge running time due to the high latency of hard disks.

[3]Implementation details can have considerable effects on the actual run time of the algorithms. Here, we employ our own optimized C++ implementation for MRMR to ensure its competitiveness, given that the same code implemented in Matlab could be 40-100 times slower.

Table 3: **Average time (in seconds) required for ranking the features at different problem sizes (given pre-computed similarity matrices Q and H).**

#Features	$\mathcal{QPFS}$	$\mathcal{SPEC}_{\mathcal{CMI}}$	MRMR
1,000	0.81 ± 0.11	0.03 ± 0.01	0.01 ± 0.00
5,000	55.94 ± 5.14	0.81 ± 0.03	0.17 ± 0.02
10,000	417.22 ± 25.23	2.91 ± 0.26	0.68 ± 0.04
13,000	1026.73 ± 85.99	5.12 ± 0.45	1.17 ± 0.06
16,000	2012.63 ± 157.15	7.66 ± 0.89	1.97 ± 0.41
20,000	N/A	10.64 ± 0.30	2.63 ± 0.11
30,000	N/A	25.03 ± 1.42	6.05 ± 0.25

Table 4: Dataset summary. n: #features, d: #samples, #C: #classes, Error: average cross validation error rate (%) using all features.

Data	n	d	#C	Error	Source
NCI60	9996	60	10	43.3	[21] [20]
SRBCT	2308	84	4	1.2	[21]
Lung	325	73	7	12.3	[20] [7]
Colon	2000	62	2	17.7	[7]
Leukemia	7129	73	2	1.4	[7]
Lymphoma	4026	96	9	3.1	[7]
Promoter	57	106	2	16.0	[1]
Spambase	57	4601	2	9.5	[1]
Musk2	166	6598	2	4.9	[1]
Arrhythmia	257	430	2	21.6	[1]
Multi-features	649	2000	10	1.6	[1]
Waveform	21	5000	3	13.0	[1]
Optdigits	64	3823	10	1.8	[1]
Gisette	5000	6000	2	50.0	[1]
Madelon	500	2000	2	34.7	[1]

4.3 Small and medium data sets

We compare the proposed $\mathcal{SPEC}_{\mathcal{CMI}}$ method with state of the art MI-based feature selection approaches on an extensive set of 15 well-known public datasets used in previous research [3, 14, 20, 21], covering a wide range of number of features, samples and classes. Feature selection methods are compared in terms of the average cross validation (CV) classification error rate on the range of 10 to 100 features in step of 1 (or 10 to n if $n < 100$). We employ 10-fold CV for datasets with number of samples $d \geq 100$ and leave-one-out CV otherwise. Following [14,21], the based classifier for most data sets is chosen as linear SVM (with the regularization parameter set to 1), except for the Gisette and Madelon datasets, where a 3-NN classifier was used following [3]. Details of the datasets used are given in Table 4. Continuous features were discretized using Fayyad and Irani's minimum description length (MDL) method [8]. Feature selection was done on discretized data, while classification was performed on the original feature space.

Apart from the feature selection approaches mentioned herein, namely MRMR, EMRMR, $\mathcal{QPFS}$ and $\mathcal{SPEC}_{\mathcal{CMI}}$, we also compare our approach with other well-known MI based methods, namely maximum relevance (maxRel), mutual information quotient (MIQ) [7] and conditional infomax feature extraction (CIFE) [16]. The connections between these methods are presented in great details in [3]. We note that [3] recommends the so-called joint mutual information (JMI), $\max_{X_i} \sum_{X_j \in \mathbb{S}} I(X_i, X_j; C)$, as the criterion of choice, for providing 'the best tradeoff in terms of accuracy, stability and flexibility with small samples'. We note that the JMI criterion is in fact exactly equivalent to the EMRMR criterion presented herein, and also the 'average-CMIM' criterion in [14]. For $\mathcal{QPFS}$ the balancing factor α was set as recommended in [21]. $\mathcal{SPEC}_{\mathcal{CMI}}$ requires no parameter tuning. We implemented and optimized the codes for all the above methods in Malab/C++, which are made publicly available via our website.

The experimental results for all methods are presented in Table 5. In order to summarize the statistical significance of the findings, as in [14], we employ the one sided paired t-test at 5% significance level to test the hypothesis that $\mathcal{SPEC}_{\mathcal{CMI}}$ or a compared method performs significantly better than the other. Overall, we found the proposed $\mathcal{SPEC}_{\mathcal{CMI}}$ framework to perform strongly against other popular MI-based criteria for feature selection. In particular, $\mathcal{SPEC}_{\mathcal{CMI}}$ consistently outperforms the alternative global formulation $\mathcal{QPFS}$. Of the incremental methods, $\mathcal{SPEC}_{\mathcal{CMI}}$ strongly outperforms maxRel, MIQ and CIFE. On the other hand, MRMR and EMRMR are two leading local algorithms, being only narrowly behind $\mathcal{SPEC}_{\mathcal{CMI}}$. The bold entries in Table 5 indicate the best performing algorithms (in terms of the average error rate and its standard deviation)—although the difference compared with other methods might not necessarily be statistically significant. The distribution of the 'bold entries' seems to suggest that no algorithm is universally dominant—a reminiscence of the no free lunch theorem for machine learning [25]. Nevertheless, from a practical viewpoint, for the supervised feature selection problem, one can, and should, try multiple feature selection strategies and use, e.g. the cross validation error rate as a guidance to choose the final set of features. From this perspective, we propose that $\mathcal{SPEC}_{\mathcal{CMI}}$ is a valuable addition to the current literature on feature selection.

4.4 Large data

We employ four datasets from the handwritten Chinese character database [17] as detailed in Table 6. These data are characterized by a large number of training samples, and especially a very large number of classes, making classification a challenging task. Indeed, the SVM implementation we employed, namely LibSVM [4], does not scale very well with this application where it has to train a large number ($\sim$ 3700) of one-versus-all classifiers. We therefore resort to a much simpler and more computationally efficient nearest class mean (NCM) classifier [19]. We select the top two performing greedy algorithms, namely MRMR and EMRMR, from section 4.3 together with $\mathcal{QPFS}$ and $\mathcal{SPEC}_{\mathcal{CMI}}$ for this test. In addition, we test the effectiveness of Nyström approximation with both $\mathcal{SPEC}_{\mathcal{CMI}}$ and $\mathcal{QPFS}$. We train the classifier on the train data and test accuracy is estimated on the separate test data. Since the number of samples is large, we expect this performance indicator to be representative. On these data, the MDL algorithm [8] binarizes most features, i.e. discretizing to only 2 states. Observing that the very large number of samples can support a finer discretization, we therefore also discretize the data to 5 and 10 equal-frequency bins. While finding the optimal discretization strategy is beyond the scope of this paper, we summarize our finding as follows: at lower number of bins, i.e. 2 and 5, methods that are based on the MI such as MRMR and $\mathcal{QPFS}$ outperform methods based on conditional MI, such that $\mathcal{SPEC}_{\mathcal{CMI}}$ and EMRMR. On the other hand,

Table 5: **Cross validation error rate comparison of $\mathcal{SPEC}_{\mathcal{CMI}}$ against other methods. W: win (+), T: tie (=), L: loss (−) for $\mathcal{SPEC}_{\mathcal{CMI}}$ against the compared method according to the 1-sided paired t-test.**

Data	maxRel	MIQ	CIFE	MRMR	EMRMR*	$\mathcal{QPFS}$	$\mathcal{SPEC}_{\mathcal{CMI}}$
Lung	14.2 ± 5.7 (+)	12.0±2.7 (+)	16.0±2.2 (+)	9.8±3.4 (+)	9.7±3.4 (+)	10.4±2.8 (+)	**9.4±2.5**
NCI60	35.1 ± 8.6 (+)	40.1±14.1 (+)	64.9±3.6 (+)	30.5±10.7 (=)	30.2±8.7 (−)	**28.1±9.4** (−)	31.3±8.4
Colon	12.8 ± 1.5 (=)	12.8±1.6 (=)	14.4±2.7 (+)	12.8±1.4 (=)	**12.0±1.0** (−)	13.2±1.4 (+)	12.7±1.2
Leukemia	3.1 ± 1.0 (+)	**1.0±1.6** (−)	5.0±1.0 (+)	2.4±0.8 (−)	2.5±0.6 (−)	3.0±1.0 (=)	2.9±1.0
Lymphoma	4.3 ± 2.5 (=)	6.0±5.0 (+)	16.6±2.9 (+)	4.1±2.1 (=)	**4.0±2.4** (=)	5.5±3.7 (+)	4.3±3.9
SRBCT	0.8 ± 1.1 (−)	2.1±3.5 (+)	11.8±3.7 (+)	0.6±1.2 (−)	0.9±1.2 (=)	**0.1±0.3** (−)	0.9±1.3
Promoter	8.7 ± 2.9 (=)	8.9±3.4 (=)	12.6±2.4 (+)	9.4±3.4 (+)	8.3±3.2 (=)	8.7±3.3 (=)	**8.3±3.1**
Spambase	11.5 ± 1.4 (+)	12.3±3.2 (+)	17.9±4.1 (+)	**11.3±1.5** (=)	11.4±1.5 (+)	12.0±1.9 (+)	**11.3±1.5**
Musk2	7.8 ± 1.8 (+)	**7.1±1.6** (−)	7.4±1.1 (=)	7.4±1.6 (=)	7.4±1.0 (=)	7.4±1.9 (=)	7.4±0.9
Arryth.	22.2 ± 1.0 (+)	24.0±3.5 (+)	24.6±1.8 (+)	22.3±1.5 (+)	22.2±0.8 (+)	22.8±2.0 (+)	**21.7±0.7**
Multifeat.	2.0 ± 0.9 (+)	3.2±2.8 (+)	2.8±0.7 (+)	**1.8±0.4** (=)	1.8±0.6 (=)	2.4±1.3 (+)	1.9±0.6
Optdigits	3.3 ± 2.5 (+)	3.3±2.6 (+)	3.4±2.5 (+)	**3.0±2.0** (=)	3.0±2.2 (=)	4.1±4.0 (+)	3.1±2.2
Waveform	13.9 ± 1.5 (=)	14.2±1.3 (+)	16.3±2.1 (+)	**13.7±1.0** (=)	13.7±1.1 (=)	**13.7±1.0** (=)	**13.7±1.0**
Gisette	7.8 ± 2.7 (+)	9.2±4.2 (+)	6.7±1.8 (+)	**6.0±2.5** (=)	6.4±2.4 (+)	8.0±2.3 (+)	6.1±2.2
Madelon	18.7 ± 3.2 (+)	37.4±3.7 (+)	17.5±3.4 (+)	28.2±2.2 (+)	16.0±3.1 (=)	23.3±3.5 (+)	**15.9±3.2**
#W/T/L:	10/4/1	11/2/2	14/1/0	4/9/2	4/8/3	9/4/2	

*Also equivalent to the JMI and ave-CMIM criteria, see [3, 14]

Table 6: **Large dataset summary. n: #features, d: #samples, #C: #classes, Error: test error rate (%) using all features with NCM classifier.**

Data	n	d (train)	d (test)	#C	Error
HWDB1.0	512	1,246,991	309,684	3,740	21.93
HWDB1.1	512	897,758	223,991	3,755	26.42
OLHWDB1.0	512	1,256,009	314,042	3,740	15.99
OLHWDB1.1	512	898,573	224,559	3,755	17.18

at higher number of bins, EMRMR and $\mathcal{SPEC}_{\mathcal{CMI}}$ performs slightly better than $\mathcal{QPFS}$ and MRMR. Our hypothesis is that a larger number of bins can leverage the large number of samples such that higher-dimensional mutual information quantities, such as the conditional MI, could be estimated at greater resolution. The test error rate on sets of up to 200 features on the 10-bin discretized data are reported in Figure 2(a-d). It is noted that $\mathcal{SPEC}_{\mathcal{CMI}}$+Nyström at a sampling rate of $\gamma = 0.2$ perform remarkably well on the HWDB1.0 and HWDB1.1 datasets, in fact better than $\mathcal{SPEC}_{\mathcal{CMI}}$—a somewhat intriguing observation, while being slightly better than $\mathcal{QPFS}$ on the OLHWDB1.0 and OLHWDB1.1 data. The effect of different sampling rate for $\mathcal{SPEC}_{\mathcal{CMI}}$+Nyström on the OLHWDB1.1 is presented in Fig. 2(e). The wall clock execution time of all algorithms on each data set is presented in Fig. 2(f). It is observed that methods that make use of the conditional MI such as $\mathcal{SPEC}_{\mathcal{CMI}}$ and EMRMR are more expensive than methods that make use of the MI such as $\mathcal{QPFS}$ and MRMR, mainly due to the fact that computing conditional MI is more time consuming. $\mathcal{SPEC}_{\mathcal{CMI}}$ and EMRMR admit similar execution time, while $\mathcal{QPFS}$ and MRMR admit similar execution time. Nyström approximation significantly reduces the execution time for both $\mathcal{SPEC}_{\mathcal{CMI}}$ and $\mathcal{QPFS}$.

5. CONCLUSION

In this paper, we have introduced a novel global optimization framework for the mutual information based feature selection problem. Our criterion for optimization is formulated based on the conditional mutual information, an information theoretic quantity which neatly captures feature relevancy, redundancy as well as class-conditional redundancy, leading to a neat homogeneous quadratic optimization criterion. We have demonstrated that this global formulation can be efficiently solved via spectral relaxation, admitting a very simple numerical solution. We also compared the spectral relaxation approach with the more sophisticated semidefinite relaxation, and establish that spectral relaxation returns mostly identical solution at a much cheaper computational cost. Compared to the local formulations MRMR and EMRMR, the global formulations can overcome the issue of local minima faced by local greedy schemes. Compared to the alternative global $\mathcal{QPFS}$ formulation, our new $\mathcal{SPEC}_{\mathcal{CMI}}$ framework naturally resolves several theoretical issues associated with the previous global $\mathcal{QPFS}$ formulation. Moreover, $\mathcal{SPEC}_{\mathcal{CMI}}$ admits a significantly simpler and much more efficient global solution, yet without any strict condition, such as positive definiteness, on the Hessian matrix.

Acknowledgments: This work is supported by the Australian Research Council via grant number FT110100112.

6. REFERENCES

[1] K. Bache and M. Lichman. UCI machine learning repository, 2013.

[2] R. Battiti. Using mutual information for selecting features in supervised neural net learning. *Neural Networks, IEEE Transactions on*, 5(4):537–550, 1994.

[3] G. Brown, A. Pocock, M.-J. Zhao, and M. Luján. Conditional likelihood maximisation: A unifying framework for information theoretic feature selection. *J. Mach. Learn. Res.*, 13:27–66, Mar. 2012.

[4] C.-C. Chang and C.-J. Lin. LIBSVM: A library for support vector machines. *ACM Transactions on Intelligent Systems and Technology*, 2:27:1–27:27, 2011. Software available at `http://www.csie.ntu.edu.tw/~cjlin/libsvm`.

[5] A. W. Chaovalitwongse, I. P. Androulakis, and P. M. Pardalos. Quadratic integer programming: complexity and equivalent forms quadratic integer programming: Complexity and equivalent forms. In C. A. Floudas and P. M. Pardalos, editors, *Encyclopedia of Optimization*, pages 3153–3159. 2009.

[6] H. Cheng, Z. Qin, W. Qian, and W. Liu. Conditional mutual information based feature selection. In *Knowledge Acquisition and Modeling*, pages 103–107, 2008.

[7] C. Ding and H. Peng. Minimum redundancy feature selection from microarray gene expression data. In *Bioinformatics Conference, 2003*, pages 523–528, 2003.

[8] U. M. Fayyad and K. B. Irani. Multi-interval discretization of continuous-valued attributes for classification learning. In *IJCAI*, pages 1022–1029, 1993.

[9] C. Fowlkes, S. Belongie, and J. Malik. Efficient spatiotemporal grouping using the nystrom method. In *CVPR 2001*, volume 1, pages I–231–I–238 vol.1, 2001.

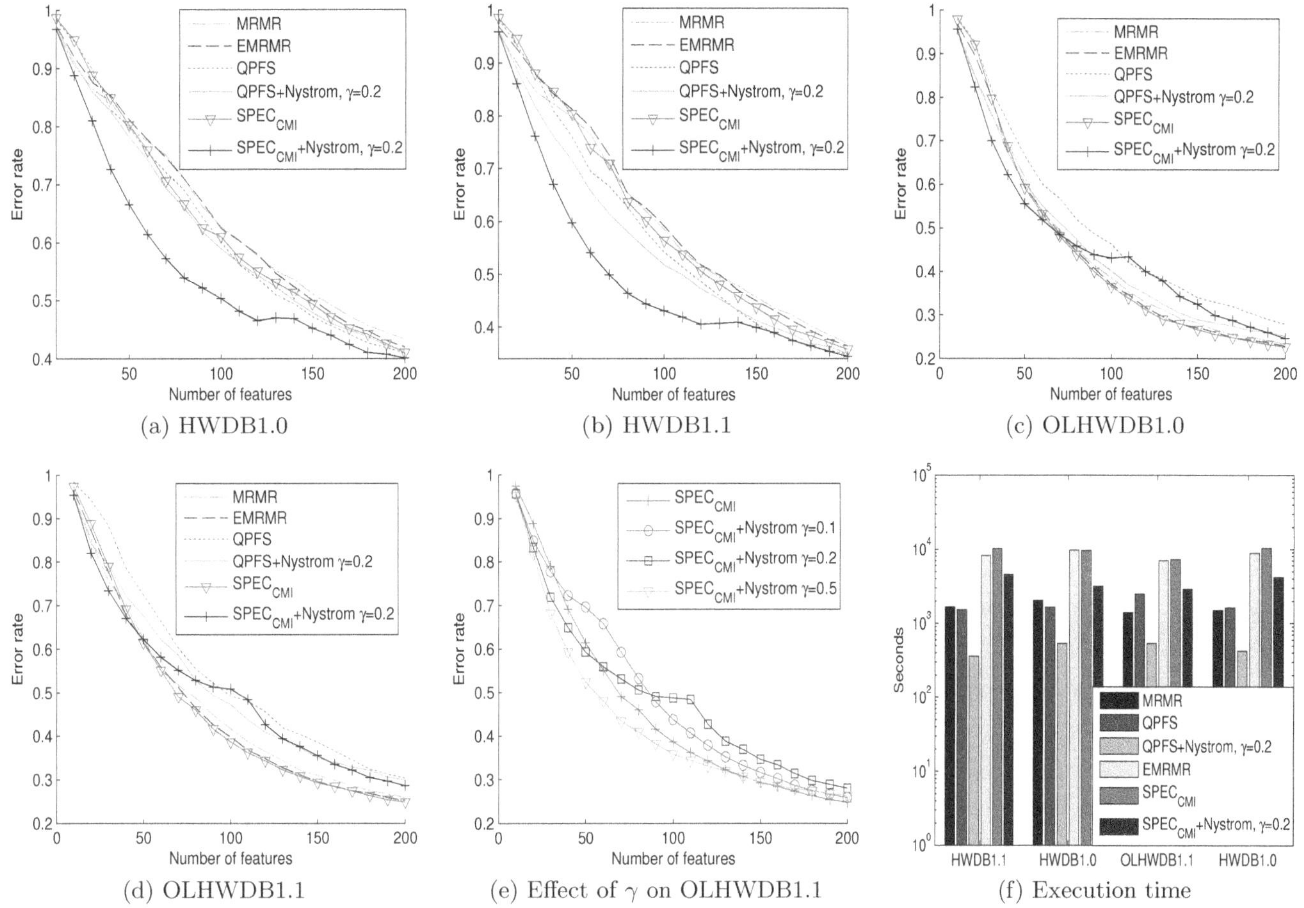

Figure 2: Test accuracy and execution time on the handwritten Chinese character database.

[10] J. Gallier. *Geometric Methods and Applications: For Computer Science and Engineering*. Texts in Applied Mathematics. Springer-Verlag GmbH, 2001.

[11] M. X. Goemans and D. P. Williamson. Improved approximation algorithms for maximum cut and satisfiability problems using semidefinite programming. *J. ACM*, 42(6):1115–1145, Nov. 1995.

[12] M. Grant and S. Boyd. CVX: Matlab software for disciplined convex programming, version 2.0 beta. http://cvxr.com/cvx, Sept. 2013.

[13] B. Guo and M. Nixon. Gait feature subset selection by mutual information. *IEEE Trans. Syst., Man, Cybern. A, Syst., Humans*, 39(1):36–46, 2009.

[14] G. Herman, B. Zhang, Y. Wang, G. Ye, and F. Chen. Mutual information-based method for selecting informative feature sets. *Pattern Recognition*, 46(12):3315 – 3327, 2013.

[15] M. Li, J. T. Kwok, and B.-L. Lu. Making large-scale nyström approximation possible. In J. Fürnkranz and T. Joachims, editors, *ICML*, pages 631–638. Omnipress, 2010.

[16] D. Lin and X. Tang. Conditional infomax learning: an integrated framework for feature extraction and fusion. In *ECCV'06*.

[17] C.-L. Liu, F. Yin, D.-H. Wang, and Q.-F. Wang. Casia online and offline chinese handwriting databases. In *Document Analysis and Recognition (ICDAR), 2011 International Conference on*, pages 37–41, Sept 2011.

[18] Z.-Q. Luo, W.-K. Ma, A.-C. So, Y. Ye, and S. Zhang. Semidefinite relaxation of quadratic optimization problems. *Signal Processing Magazine, IEEE*, 27(3):20–34, 2010.

[19] T. Mensink, J. Verbeek, F. Perronnin, and G. Csurka. Distance-based image classification: Generalizing to new classes at near-zero cost. *IEEE TPAMI*, 35(11):2624–2637, Nov 2013.

[20] H. Peng, F. Long, and C. Ding. Feature selection based on mutual information criteria of max-dependency, max-relevance, and min-redundancy. *IEEE Trans. Pattern Anal. Mach. Intell.*, 27(8):1226–1238, 2005.

[21] I. Rodriguez-Lujan, R. Huerta, C. Elkan, and C. S. Cruz. Quadratic programming feature selection. *J. Mach. Learn. Res.*, 11:1491–1516, 2010.

[22] J. M. Sotoca and F. Pla. Supervised feature selection by clustering using conditional mutual information-based distances. *Pattern Recognition*, 43(6):2068–2081, June 2010.

[23] K. C. Toh, M. Todd, and R. H. Tütüncü. Sdpt3 – a matlab software package for semidefinite programming. *Optimization methods and software*, 11:545–581, 1999.

[24] N. Vinh and J. Bailey. Comments on supervised feature selection by clustering using conditional mutual information-based distances. *Pattern Recognition*, 46(4):1220 – 1225, 2013.

[25] D. H. Wolpert. The lack of a priori distinctions between learning algorithms. *Neural computation*, 8(7):1341–1390, 1996.

[26] M. Yamashita, K. Fujisawa, M. Fukuda, K. Nakata, and M. Nakata. Algorithm 925: Parallel solver for semidefinite programming problem having sparse schur complement matrix. *ACM Trans. Math. Softw.*, 39(1):6:1–6:22, Nov. 2012.

[27] Y. Zhang, S. Burer, and W. N. Street. Ensemble pruning via semi-definite programming. *J. Mach. Learn. Res.*, 7:1315–1338, Dec. 2006.

Gradient Boosted Feature Selection

Zhixiang (Eddie) Xu *
Washington University in St. Louis
One Brookings Dr.
St. Louis, USA
xuzx@cse.wustl.edu

Gao Huang
Tsinghua University
30 Shuangqing Rd.
Beijing, China
huang-g09@mails.tsinghua.edu.cn

Kilian Q. Weinberger
Washington University in St. Louis
One Brookings Dr.
St. Louis, USA
kilian@wustl.edu

Alice X. Zheng *
GraphLab
936 N. 34th St. Ste 208
Seattle, USA
alicez@graphlab.com

ABSTRACT

A feature selection algorithm should ideally satisfy four conditions: reliably extract relevant features; be able to identify non-linear feature interactions; scale linearly with the number of features and dimensions; allow the incorporation of known sparsity structure. In this work we propose a novel feature selection algorithm, Gradient Boosted Feature Selection (GBFS), which satisfies all four of these requirements. The algorithm is flexible, scalable, and surprisingly straight-forward to implement as it is based on a modification of Gradient Boosted Trees. We evaluate GBFS on several real world data sets and show that it matches or outperforms other state of the art feature selection algorithms. Yet it scales to larger data set sizes and naturally allows for domain-specific side information.

Categories and Subject Descriptors

H.3 [**Information Storage and Retrieval**]: Miscellaneous; I.5.2 [**Pattern Recognition**]: Design Methodology—*Feature evaluation and selection*

General Terms

Learning

Keywords

Feature selection; Large-scale; Gradient boosting

*Work done while at Microsoft Research

KDD'14, August 24–27, 2014, New York, NY, USA.

ACM 978-1-4503-2956-9/14/08 ...$15.00.
http://dx.doi.org/10.1145/2623330.2623635 .

1. INTRODUCTION

Feature selection (FS) [8] is an important problems in machine learning. In many applications, *e.g.*, bio-informatics [21] or neuroscience [12], researchers hope to gain insight by analyzing *how* a classifier can predict a label and what features it uses. Moreover, effective feature selection leads to parsimonious classifiers that require less memory [25] and are faster to train and test [5]. It can also reduce feature extraction costs [29, 30] and lead to better generalization [9].

Linear feature selection algorithms such as LARS [7] are highly effective at discovering linear dependencies between features and labels. However, they fail when features interact in nonlinear ways. Nonlinear feature selection algorithms, such as Random Forest [9] or recently introduced kernel methods [32, 23], can cope with nonlinear interactions. But their computational and memory complexity typically grow super-linearly with the training set size. As data sets grow in size, this is increasingly problematic. Balancing the twin goals of *scalability* and *nonlinear* feature selection is still an open problem.

In this paper, we focus on the scenario where data sets contain a large number of samples. Specifically, we aim to perform efficient feature selection when the number of data points is much larger than the number of features ($n \gg d$). We start with the (NP-Hard) feature selection problem that also motivated LARS [7] and LASSO [26]. But instead of using a linear classifier and approximating the feature selection cost with an l_1-norm, we follow [31] and use gradient boosted regression trees [7] for which greedy approximations exist [2].

The resulting algorithm is surprisingly simple yet very effective. We refer to it as Gradient Boosted Feature Selection (GBFS). Following the gradient boosting framework, trees are built with the greedy CART algorithm [2]. Features are selected sparsely following an important change in the impurity function: splitting on new features is penalized by a cost $\lambda > 0$, whereas re-use of previously selected features incurs no additional penalty.

GBFS has several compelling properties. 1. As it learns an ensemble of regression trees, it can naturally discover nonlinear interactions between features. 2. In contrast to, *e.g.*, FS with Random Forests, it unifies feature selection and classification into a single optimization. 3. In contrast to existing nonlinear FS algorithms, its time and memory complexity scales as $O(dn)$, where d denotes the number of features dimensionality and n the number of data points[1], and is very fast in practice. 4. GBFS can naturally incorporate pre-specified feature cost structures or side-information, *e.g.*, select bags of features or focus on regions of interest, similar to generalized lasso in linear FS [19].

We evaluate this algorithm on several real-world data sets of varying difficulty and size, and we demonstrate that GBFS tends to match or outperform the accuracy and feature selection trade-off of Random Forest Feature Selection, the current state-of-the-art in nonlinear feature selection.

We showcase the ability of GBFS to naturally incorporate side-information about inter-feature dependencies on a real world biological classification task [1]. Here, features are grouped into nine pre-specified bags with biological meaning. GBFS can easily adapt to this setting and select entire feature bags. The resulting classifier matches the best accuracy of competing methods (trained on many features) with only *a single* bag of features.

2. RELATED WORK

One of the most widely used feature selection algorithms is Lasso [26]. It minimizes the squared loss with l_1 regularization on the coefficient vector, which encourages sparse solutions. Although scalable to very large data sets, Lasso models only linear correlations between features and labels and cannot discover non-linear feature dependencies.

[17] propose the Minimum Redundancy Maximum Relevance (mRMR) algorithm, which selects a subset of the most responsive features that have high mutual information with labels. Their objective function also penalizes selecting redundant features. Though elegant, computing mutual information when the number of instance is large is intractable, and thus the algorithm does not scale. HSIC Lasso [32], on the other hand, introduces non-linearity by combining multiple kernel functions that each uses a single feature. The resulting convex optimization problem aligns this kernel with a "perfect" label kernel. The algorithm requires constructing kernel matrices for all features, thus its time and memory complexity scale quadratically with input data set size. Moreover, both algorithms separate feature selection and classification, and require additional time and computation for training classifiers using the selected features.

Several other works avoid expensive kernel computation while maintaining non-linearity. Grafting [18] combines l_1 and l_0 regularization with a non-linear classifier based on a non-convex variant of the multi-layer perceptron. Feature Selection for Ranking using Boosted Trees [15] selects the top features with the highest relative importance scores. [27] and [9] use Random Forest. Finally, while not a feature selection method, [31] employ Gradient Boosted Trees to learn cascades of classifiers to reduce test-time cost by incorporating feature extraction budgets into the classifier optimization.

3. BACKGROUND

Throughout this paper we type vectors in bold ($\mathbf{x}_i$), scalars in regular math type (k or C), sets in cursive ($\mathcal{S}$) and matrices in capital bold ($\mathbf{F}$) font. Specific entries in vectors or matrices are scalars and follow the corresponding convention.

The data set consists of input vectors $\{\mathbf{x}_1, \ldots, \mathbf{x}_n\} \in \mathcal{R}^d$ with corresponding labels $\{y_1, \ldots, y_n\} \in \mathcal{Y}$ drawn from an unknown distribution. The labels can be binary, categorical (multi-class) or real-valued (regression). For the sake of clarity, we focus on binary classification $\mathcal{Y} \in \{-1, +1\}$, although the algorithm can be extended to multi-class and regression as well.

3.1 Feature selection with the l_1 norm

Lasso [26] combines linear classification and l_1 regularization

$$\min_{\mathbf{w}} \sum_{(\mathbf{x}_i, y_i)} \ell(\mathbf{x}_i, y_i, \mathbf{w}) + \lambda|\mathbf{w}|_1. \tag{1}$$

In its original formulation, $\ell(\cdot)$ is defined to be the squared loss, $\ell(\mathbf{x}_i, y_i, \mathbf{w}) = (\mathbf{w}^\top \mathbf{x}_i - y_i)^2$. However, for the sake of feature selection, other loss functions are possible. In the binary classification setting, where $y_i \in \{-1, +1\}$, we use the better suited log-loss, $\ell(\mathbf{x}_i, y_i, \mathbf{w}) = \log(1+\exp(y_i \mathbf{w}^\top x_i))$ [11].

3.2 The capped l_1 norm

l_1 regularization serves two purposes: It regularizes the classifier against overfitting, and it induces sparsity for feature selection. Unfortunately, these two effects of the l_1-norm are inherently tied and there is no way to regulate the impact of either one.

[33] introduce the *capped* l_1 norm, defined by the element-wise operation

$$q_\epsilon(w_i) = \min(w_i, \epsilon). \tag{2}$$

Its advantage over the standard l_1 norm is that once a feature is extracted, its use is not penalized further — *i.e.*, it penalizes using many features does not reward small weights. This is a much better approximation of the l_0 norm, which only penalizes feature use without interfering with the magnitude of the weights. When ϵ is small enough, *i.e.*, $\epsilon \leq \min_i |w_i|$, we can compute the exact number of features extracted with $q_\epsilon(\mathbf{w})/\epsilon$. In other words, penalizing $q_\epsilon(\mathbf{w})$ is a close proxy for penalizing the number of extracted features. However, the capped l_1 norm is not convex and therefore not easy to optimize.

The capped l_1 norm can be combined with a regular l_1 (or l_2) norm, where one can control the trade-off between feature extraction and regularization by adjusting the corresponding regularization parameters, $\mu, \lambda \geq 0$:

$$\min_{\mathbf{w}} \sum_{(\mathbf{x}_i, y_i)} \ell(\mathbf{x}_i, y_i, \mathbf{w}) + \lambda|\mathbf{w}|_1 + \mu q_\epsilon(\mathbf{w}). \tag{3}$$

Here $q_\epsilon(\mathbf{w})$ denotes $[q_\epsilon(\mathbf{w}_1), \ldots, q_\epsilon(\mathbf{w}_d)]$.

4. GRADIENT BOOSTED FEATURE SELECTION

The classifier in Eq. (3) is better suited for feature selection than plain l_1 regularization. However, it is still *linear*, which limits the flexibility of the classifer. Standard approaches for incorporating non-linearity include the kernel learning [22] and boosting [3]. HSIC Lasso [32] uses kernel learning to discover non-linear feature interactions at a price of quadratic memory and time complexity. Our method uses boosting, which is much more scalable.

[1] In fact, if the storage of the input data is not counted, the memory complexity of GBFS scales as $O(n)$.

Boosting assumes that one can pre-process the data with limited-depth regression trees. Let $\mathcal{H}$ be the set of all possible regression trees. Taking into account limited precision and counting trees that obtain identical values on the entire training set as one and the same tree, one can assume $|\mathcal{H}|$ to be finite (albeit possibly large). Assuming that inputs are mapped into $\mathcal{R}^{|\mathcal{H}|}$ through $\phi(\mathbf{x}) = [h_1(\mathbf{x}), \ldots, h_{|\mathcal{H}|}(\mathbf{x})]^\top$, we propose to learn a linear classifier in this transformed space. Eq. (3) becomes

$$\min_{\boldsymbol{\beta}} \sum_{(\phi(\mathbf{x}_i), y_i)} \ell(\phi(\mathbf{x}_i), y_i, \boldsymbol{\beta}) + \lambda|\boldsymbol{\beta}|_1 + \mu q_\epsilon(\boldsymbol{\beta}). \quad (4)$$

Here, $\boldsymbol{\beta}$ is a sparse linear vector that selects trees. Although it is extremely high dimensional, the optimization in Eq. (4) is tractable because $\boldsymbol{\beta}$ is extremely sparse. Assuming, without loss of generalization, that the trees in $\mathcal{H}$ are sorted so that the first T entries of $\boldsymbol{\beta}$ are non-zero, we obtain a final classifier

$$H(\mathbf{x}) = \sum_{t=1}^{T} \beta_t h_t(\mathbf{x}). \quad (5)$$

Feature selection.
Eq. (4) has two penalty terms: plain l_1 norm and capped l_1 norm. The first penalty term reduces overfitting while the second selects features. However, in its current form, the capped l_1 norm selects *trees* rather than features. We therefore have to modify our setup to explicitly penalize the extraction of features.

To model the total number of features extracted by an ensemble of trees, we define a binary matrix $\mathbf{F} \in \{0,1\}^{d \times T}$, where an entry $F_{ft} = 1$ if and only if the tree h_t uses feature f. With this notation, we can express the total weight assigned to trees that extract feature f as

$$\sum_{t=1}^{T} |F_{ft}\beta_t|. \quad (6)$$

We modify $q_\epsilon(\boldsymbol{\beta})$ to instead penalize the actual weight assigned to *features*. The final optimization becomes

$$\min_{\boldsymbol{\beta}} \ell(\boldsymbol{\beta}) + \lambda|\boldsymbol{\beta}|_1 + \mu \sum_{f=1}^{d} q_\epsilon\left(\sum_{t=1}^{T} |F_{ft}\beta_t|\right). \quad (7)$$

As before, if ϵ is sufficiently small ($\epsilon \leq \min_f |\sum_{t=1}^{T} F_{ft}\beta_t|$), we can set $\mu = 1/\epsilon$ and the feature selection penalty coincides exactly with the number of features used.

4.1 Optimization

The optimization problem in Eq. (7) is non-convex and non-differentiable. Nevertheless, we can minimize it effectively (up to a local fixed point) with gradient boosting [7]. Let $\mathcal{L}(\boldsymbol{\beta})$ denote the loss function to be minimized and $\nabla\mathcal{L}(\beta)_t$ the gradient w.r.t β_t. Gradient boosting can be viewed as coordinate descent where we update the dimension with the steepest gradient at every step. We can assume that the set of all regression trees $\mathcal{H}$ is negation closed, *i.e.*, for each $h \in \mathcal{H}$, we also have $-h \in \mathcal{H}$. This allows us to only follow negative gradients and always *increase* $\boldsymbol{\beta}$. Thus there is always a non-negative optimal β. The search for the dimensions t^* with the steepest negative gradient can be formalized as

$$t^* = \operatorname*{argmin}_t \nabla\mathcal{L}(\beta)_t. \quad (8)$$

In the remainder of this section we discuss approximate minimization strategies that does not require iterating over all possible trees.

l_1-regularization.
Since each step of the optimization increases a single dimension of $\boldsymbol{\beta}$ with a fixed step-size $\alpha > 0$, the l_1 norm of $\boldsymbol{\beta}$ can be written in closed form as $|\boldsymbol{\beta}|_1 = \alpha T$ after T iterations. This means that penalizing the l_1 norm of $\boldsymbol{\beta}$ is equivalent to early stopping after T iterations [7]. We therefore drop the $\lambda|\boldsymbol{\beta}|_1$ term and instead introduce T as an equivalent hyper-parameter.

Gradient Decomposition.
To find the steepest descent direction at iteration $T'+1$, we decompose the (sub-)gradient into two parts, one for the loss function $\ell()$, and one for the capped l_1 norm penalty

$$\nabla\mathcal{L}(\boldsymbol{\beta})_t = \frac{\partial \ell}{\partial \beta_t} + \mu \sum_{f=1}^{d} \nabla q_\epsilon\left(\sum_{t=1}^{T'} F_{ft}\beta_t\right). \quad (9)$$

(Hereafter we drop the absolute value around $F_{ft}\beta_t$, since both F_{ft} and β_t are non-negative.) The gradient of $q_\epsilon(\sum_t F_{ft}\beta_t)$ is not well-defined at the cusp when $\sum_t F_{ft}\beta_t = \epsilon$. But we can take the right-hand limit, since β_t never decreases,

$$\nabla q_\epsilon\left(\sum_{t=1}^{T'} F_{ft}\beta_t\right) = \begin{cases} F_{ft}, & \text{if } \sum_t F_{ft}\beta_t < \epsilon \\ 0, & \text{if } \sum_t F_{ft}\beta_t \geq \epsilon. \end{cases} \quad (10)$$

If we set $\epsilon = \alpha$, where $\alpha > 0$ is the step size, then $\sum_t F_{ft}\beta_t \geq \epsilon$ if and only if feature f has already been used in a tree from a previous iteration. Let $\phi_f = 1$ indicate that feature f is still *unused*, and $\phi_f = 0$ otherwise. With this notation we can combine the gradients from the two cases and replace $\nabla q_\epsilon\left(\sum_{t=1}^{T'} F_{ft}\beta_t\right)$ with $\phi_f F_{ft}$. We obtain

$$\nabla\mathcal{L}(\boldsymbol{\beta})_t = \frac{\partial \ell}{\partial \beta_t} + \mu \sum_{f=1}^{d} \phi_f F_{ft}. \quad (11)$$

Note that $\phi_f F_{ft} = 1$ if and only if feature f is extracted for the first time in tree t. In other words, the second term effectively penalizes trees that use many new (previously not selected) features.

Greedy Tree construction.
With Eq. (11) we can compute the gradient with respect to any tree. But finding the optimal t^* would still require searching all trees. In the remainder of this section, we transform the search for t^* from a search over all possible dimensions t to a search for the best tree h_t to minimize a pre-specified loss function. The new search can be approximated with the CART algorithm [2].

To this end, we apply the chain rule and decompose $\frac{\partial \ell}{\partial \beta_t}$ into the derivative of the loss ℓ w.r.t. the current prediction evaluated at each input $H(\mathbf{x}_i)$ and the partial derivative

Algorithm 1 GBFS in pseudo-code.

Input: data $\{\mathbf{x}_i, y_i\}$, learning rate ϵ, iterations T.
Initialize predictions $H = 0$ and selected feature set $\Omega = \emptyset$.
for $t = 1$ **to** T **do**
  Learn h_t using greedy CART to minimize the impurity function in Eq. (14).
  Update $H = H + \epsilon h_t$.
  For each feature f used in h_t, set $\phi_f = 0$ and $\Omega = \Omega \cup f$.
end for
Return H and Ω.

$\frac{\partial H(\mathbf{x}_i)}{\partial \beta_t}$,

$$\nabla \mathcal{L}(\beta)_t = \sum_{i=1}^{n} \frac{\partial \ell}{\partial H(\mathbf{x}_i)} \frac{\partial H(\mathbf{x}_i)}{\partial \beta_t} + \mu \sum_{f=1}^{d} \phi_f F_{ft}. \quad (12)$$

Note that $H(\mathbf{x}_i) = \boldsymbol{\beta}^\top \mathbf{h}(\mathbf{x}_i)$ is just a linear sum of all $h_t(\mathbf{x}_i)$, the predictions over training data. Thus $\frac{\partial H(\mathbf{x}_i)}{\partial \beta_t} = h_t(\mathbf{x}_i)$. If we let g_i denote the negative gradient $g_i = -\frac{\partial \ell}{\partial H(\mathbf{x}_i)}$, we can reformulate Eq. (12) as

$$h_t = \operatorname*{argmin}_{h_t \in \mathcal{H}} \sum_{i=1}^{n} -g_i h_t(\mathbf{x}_i) + \mu \sum_{f=1}^{d} \phi_f F_{ft}. \quad (13)$$

Similar to [3], we restrict $\mathcal{H}$ to only normalized trees (i.e. $\sum_i h_t^2(\mathbf{x}_i) = 1$). We can then add two constant terms $\frac{1}{2}\sum_i h_t^2(\mathbf{x}_i)$ and $\frac{1}{2}\sum_i g_i^2$ to eq. (13), and complete the binomial equation.

$$h_t = \operatorname*{argmin}_{h_t \in \mathcal{H}} \frac{1}{2} \sum_{i=1}^{n} \left(g_i - h_t(\mathbf{x}_i)\right)^2 + \mu \sum_{f=1}^{d} \phi_f F_{ft}. \quad (14)$$

This is now a penalized squared loss—an *impurity function*—and a good solutions can be found efficiently via the greedy CART algorithm for learning regression trees [7]. The first term in Eq. (14) encourages feature splits to best match the negative gradient of the loss function, and the second term rewards splitting on features which have already been used in previous iterations. Algorithm 1 summarizes the overall algorithm in pseudo-code.

4.2 Structured Feature Selection

In many feature selection applications, one may have additional qualitative knowledge about acceptable sparsity patterns. Sometimes features can be grouped into bags and the goal is to select as few bags as possible. Prior work on handling structured sparsity include group lasso [10, 20] and generalized lasso [19]. Our framework can easily handle structured sparsity via the feature cost identity function ϕ_f. For example, we can define $\phi_f = 1$ if and only if *no* feature from the same bag as f has been used in the past, and $\phi_f = 0$ otherwise. The moment a feature from a particular bag is used in a tree, all other features in the same bag become "free" and the classifier is encouraged to use features from this bag exclusively until it starts to see diminishing returns.

In the most general setting, we can define $\phi_f : \Omega \to \mathcal{R}_0^+$ as a function that maps from the set of previously extracted features to a cost. For example, one could imagine settings where feature extraction appears in stages. Extracting feature f makes feature g cheaper, but not free. One such application might be that of classifying medical images (e.g., MRI scans) where the features are raw pixels and feature groups are local regions of interest. In this case, $\phi_f(\Omega)$ may reduce the "price" of pixels surrounding those in Ω to encourage feature selection with local focus.

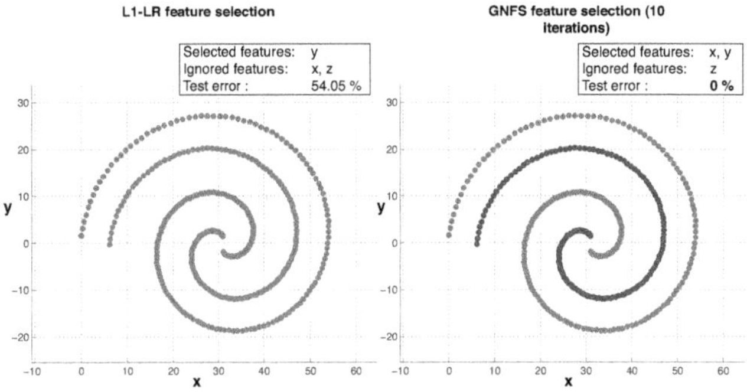

Figure 1: Feature selection and classification performance on a simulated data set. GBFS clearly out-performs the l_1 regularized logistic regression as it successfully captures the nonlinear relations between labels and features.

5. RESULTS

In this section, we evaluate GBFS against other state-of-the-art feature selection methods on synthetic as well as real-world benchmark data sets. We also examine at its capacity for dealing with known sparsity patterns in a bioinformatics application. All experiments were conducted on a desktop with dual 6-core Intel i7 cpus with 2.66GHz, 96 GB RAM, and Linux version 2.6.32.x86_64.

5.1 Synthetic data

Figure 1 illustrates a synthetic binary classification data set with three features. The data is not linearly separable in either two dimensions or three dimensions. However, a good nonlinear classifier can easily separate the data using x and y. The z feature is simply a linear combination of x and y and thus redundant. We randomly select 90% of the instances for training and the rest for testing.

Figure 1 (left panel) illustrates results from *l_1-regularized logistic regression* (L1-LR) [11, 16]. The regularization parameter is tuned on a hold-out set. Although L1-LR successfully detects and ignores the redundant feature z, it also assigns zero weight to x and only selects a single feature y. Consequently, it has poor classification error rate on the test set (54.05%). In contrast, GBFS (Figure 1, right panel) not only identifies the redundant feature z, but also detects that the labels are related to a nonlinear combination of x, y. It selects both x and y and successfully separates the data, achieving 0% classification error.

5.2 Structured feature selection

In many applications there may be prior constraints on the sparsity patterns. Since GBFS can naturally incorporate pre-specified feature structures, we use it to perform

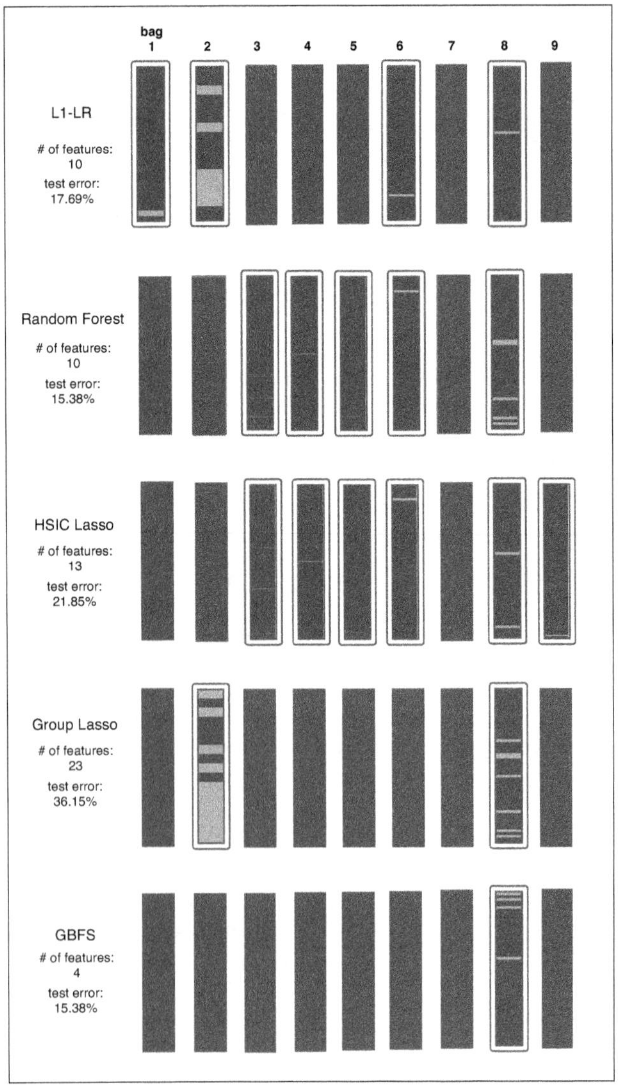

Figure 2: Feature selection on structured feature data set. Selected features are colored in green, and unselected are in blue. The bag is highlighted with a red/white box if at least one of its features is selected by the classifier. (Some bags may require zooming in to make the selected features visible.)

structured feature selection on the Colon data set[2]. In this dataset, 40 tumor and 22 normal colon tissues for 6500 human genes are measured using affymetrix gene chips. [1] select 2000 genes that have the highest minimal intensity across the samples. [13] further analyze these genes and cluster them into 9 clusters/bags by their biological meaning. The task is to classify whether a tissue is normal or tumor. We random split the 62 tissues into 80/20 training and testing datasets, repeated over 10 random splits. We use the feature-bag cost function ϕ_f mentioned in section 4.2 to incorporate this side-information (setting the cost of all features in a bag to *zero* once the first feature is extracted). Feature selection without considering these bag information not only performs and generalizes poorly, but are also difficult to interpret and justify.

Figure 2 shows the selected features from one random split and classification results averaged over 10 splits. Selected features are colored in green, and unselected ones are in blue. A bag is highlighted with a red/white box if at least one of its features is selected by the classifier. We compare against l_1-regularized logistic regression (L1-LR) [11, 16], Random Forest feature selection (RF-FS) [9], HSIC Lasso [32] and Group Lasso [14].

As shown in Figure 2, because GBFS can incorporate the bag structures, it focusses on selecting features in one specific bag. Throughout training, it only selects features from bag 8 (highlighted with a red/white box). This conveniently reveals the association between diseases and gene clusters/bags. Similar to GBFS, Group Lasso with logistic regression can also deal with structured features. However, its l_2 regularization has side effects on feature weights, and thus results in much higher classification error rate 36.15%. In contrast, l_1-regularized logistic regression, Random Forest and HSIC Lasso do not take bag information into consideration. They select scattered features from different bags, making results difficult to interpret. In terms of classification accuracy, GBFS and Random Forest has the lowest test set error rate (15.38%), whereas l_1-regularized logistic regression (L1-LR) and HSIC Lasso achieve error rates of 17.69% and 21.85%, respectively.

There are two reason why GBFS can be accurate with features from only a single bag. First, it is indeed the case that the genes in bag 8 are very predictive for the task of whether the tissue is malignant or benign (a result that may be of high biological value). Second, GBFS does not penalize further feature extraction inside bag 8 while other methods do; since bag 8 features are the most predictive, penalizing against them leads to a worse classifier.

5.3 Benchmark data sets

Data sets.

We evaluate GBFS on real-world benchmark data sets of varying sizes, domains and levels of difficulty. Table 1 lists data set statistics ordered by increasing numbers of training instances. We focus on data sets with a large number of training examples ($n \gg d$). All tasks are binary classification, though GBFS naturally extends to the regression setting, so long as the loss function is differentiable and continuous. Multi-class classification problems can be reduced to binary ones, either by selecting the two classes that are most easily confused or (if those are not known) by grouping labels into two sets.

Baselines.

The first baseline is *l_1-regularized logistic regression (L1-LR)* [11, 16]. We vary the regularization parameter to select different numbers of features and examine the test error rates under each setting.

We also compare against *Random Forest feature selection (RF-FS)* [9], a non-linear classification and feature selection algorithm. The learner builds many full decision trees by bagging training instances over random subsets of features. Features selection is done by ranking features based on their impurity improvement score, aggregated over all trees and all splits. Features with larger impurity improvements are

[2]Available through the Princeton University gene expression project (http://microarray.princeton.edu/oncology/)

data set	pcmac	uspst	spam	isolet	mnist3vs8	adult	kddcup99
#training	1555	1606	3681	6238	11982	32562	4898431
#testing	388	401	920	1559	1984	16282	311029
#features	3289	256	57	617	784	123	122

Table 1: Data sets statistics. Data sets are ordered by the number of training instances.

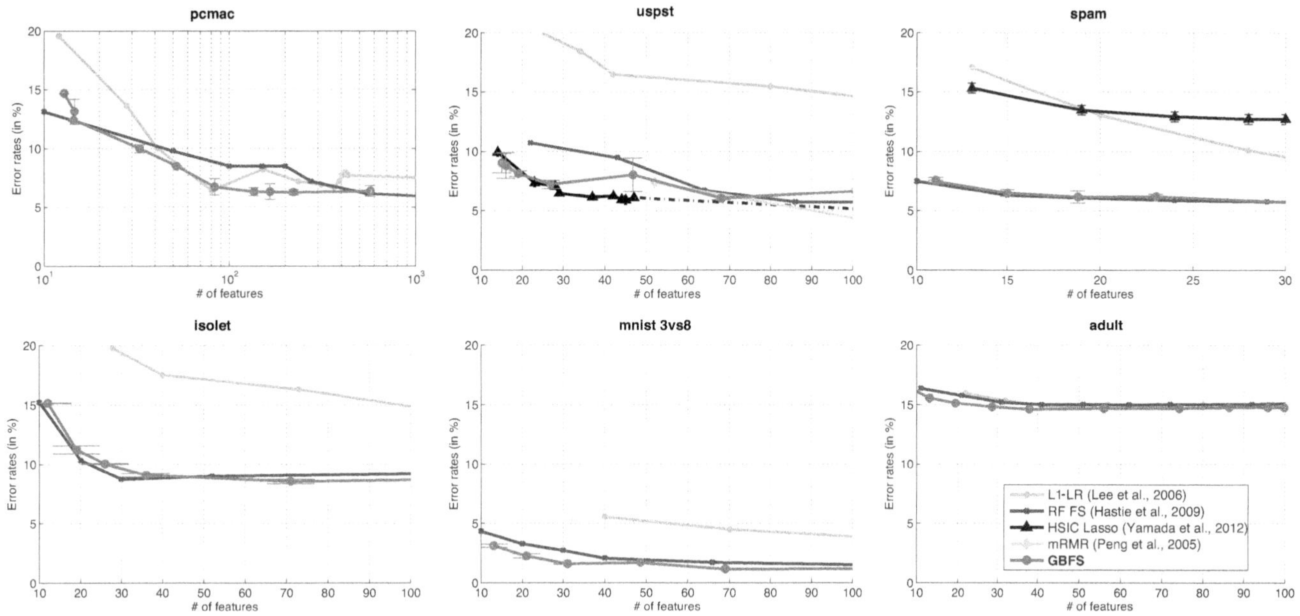

Figure 3: Classification error rates (in %) vs. feature selection performance for different algorithms on small to medium sized data sets.

considered more important. For each data set, we train a Random Forest with 2000 trees and a maximum number of 20 elements per leaf node. After training all 2000 trees, we rank all features. Starting from top of the list, we re-train a random forest with only the top-k features and evaluate its accuracy on the test set. We increase the number of selected features until all features are included.

The next state-of-the-art baseline is *Minimum Redundancy Maximum Relevance (mRMR)* [17], a non-linear feature selection algorithm that ranks features based on their mutual information with the labels. Again, we increase the selected feature set starting from the top of the list. At each stopping point, we train an RBF kernel SVM using only the features selected so far. The hyper-parameters are tuned on on 5 different random 80/20 splits of the training data. The final reported test error rates are based on the SVM trained on the full training set with the best hyper-parameter setting.

Finally, we compare against HSIC Lasso [32], a convex extension to Greedy HSIC [23]. HSIC Lasso builds a kernel matrix for each feature and combines them to best match an ideal kernel generated from the labels. It encourages feature sparsity via an l_1 penalty on the linear combination coefficients. Similar to l_1-regularized logistic regression, we evaluate a wide range of l_1 regularization parameters to sweep out the entire feature selection curve. Since HSIC Lasso is a two steps algorithm, we train a kernel SVM with the selected features to perform classification. Similar to the mRMR experiment, we use cross-validation to select hyper-parameters and average over 5 runs.

To evaluate GBFS, we perform 5 random 80/20 training/validation splits. We use the validation set to choose the depth of the regression trees and the number of iterations (maximum iterations is set to 2000). The learning rate is set to $\epsilon = 0.1$ for all data sets. In order to show the whole error rates curve, we evaluate the algorithm at 10 values for the feature selection trade-off parameter μ in Eq. (7) (i.e., $\mu = \{2^{-3}, 2^{-2}, 2^{-1}, 2^0, 2^1, 2^2, 2^3, 2^5, 2^7, 2^9\}$).

Error rates.

Figure 3 shows the feature selection and classification performance of different algorithms on small and medium sized data sets. We select up to 100 features except for *spam* ($d = 57$) and *pcmac* ($d = 3289$). In general, l_1-regularized logistic regression (L1-LR), Random Forest (RF-FS) and GBFS easily scale to all data sets. RF-FS and GBFS both clearly out perform L1-LR in accuracy on all data sets due to their ability to capture nonlinear feature-label relationships. HSIC Lasso is very sensitive to the data size (both the number of training instance and the number of features), and only scales to two small data sets (*uspst,spam*). mRMR is even more restrictive (more sensitive to the number of training instance) and thus only works for *uspst.* Both of them run out of memory on *pcmac*, which has the largest number of features. In terms of accuracy, GBFS clearly out-

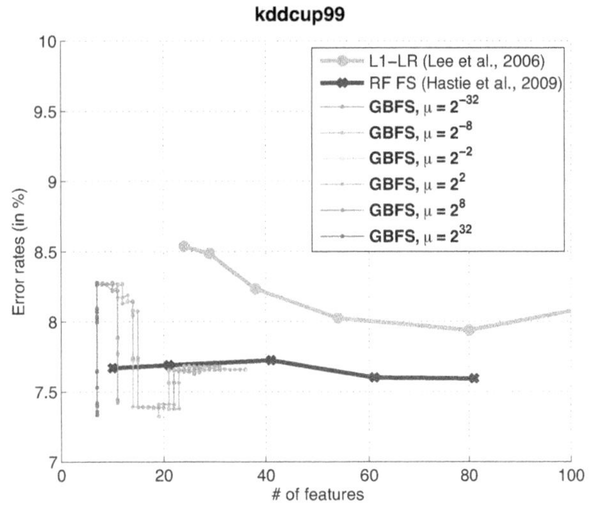

Figure 4: Feature selection and classification error rates (in %) for different algorithms on the large *kddcup99* data set.

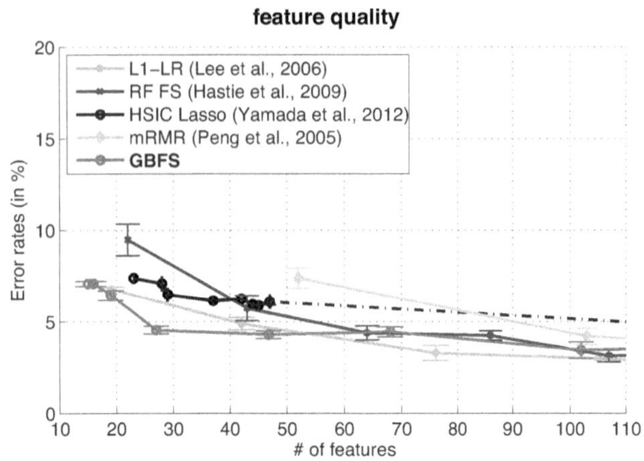

Figure 5: Error rates (in %) of SVM-RBF trained on various feature subset obtained with different features selection algorithms.

performs HSIC Lasso on *spam* but performs slightly worse on *uspst*. On all small and medium datasets, GBFS either outperforms RF-FS or matches its classification performance. However, very different from RF-FS, GBFS is a one step approach that selects features and learns a classifier at the same time, whereas RF-FS requires re-training a classifier after feature selection. This means that GBFS is much faster to train than RF-FS.

Large data set.

The last dataset in Table 1 (*kddcup99*) contains close to 5 million training instances. Training on such large data sets can be very time-consuming. We limit GBFS to $T = 500$ trees with the default hyper-parameters of tree depth $= 4$ and learning rate $= 0.1$. Training Random Forest with default hyper-parameters would take more than a week. Therefore, we limit the number of trees to 100 and the maximum number of instances per leaf node to 500. Feature selection and classification results are shown in Figure 4. For GBFS, instead of plotting the best performing results for each μ, we plot the whole feature selection iteration curve for multiple values of μ. GBFS obtains lower error rates than Random Forest (RF-FS) and l_1 regularized logistic regression (L1-LR) when few features are selected. (Note that due to the extremely large data set size, even improvements of $< 1\%$ are considered significant.)

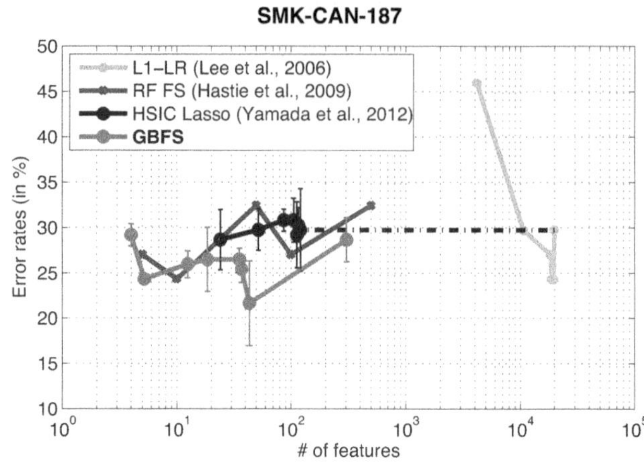

Figure 6: Classification error rates (in %) vs. feature selection performance for different algorithms on a high dimensional ($d \gg n$) data set.

Quality.

To evaluate the quality of the selected features, we separate the contribution of the feature selection from the effect of using different classifiers. We apply all algorithms on the smallest data set (*uspst*) to select a subset of the features and then train a SVM with RBF kernel on the respective feature subset. Figure 5 shows the error rates as a function of the number of selected features. GBFS obtains the lowest error rates in the (most interesting) regions of only few selected features. As more features are selected eventually all FS algorithms converge to similar values. It is worth noting that the linear classifier (L1-LR) slightly outperforms most nonlinear methods when given enough features, which suggests that the uspst digits data requires a nonlinear classifier for prediction but not for feature discovery.

$d \gg n$ scenario.

While GBFS focusses on the scenario where the number of training data points is much larger than the number of features ($n \gg d$), we also evaluate GBFS on a traditional feature selection benchmark data set SMK-CAN-187 [24], which is publicly available from [34]. This binary classification data set contains 187 data points and 19,993 features. We average results over 5 random 80/20 train-test splits. Figure 6 compares the results. GBFS out-performs l_1-regularized logistic regression (L1-LR), HSIC-Lasso and Random Forest feature selection (RF-FS), though by a small margin in some regions.

Computation time and complexity.

Not surprisingly, the linear method (L1-LR) is the fastest by far. Both mRMR and HSIC Lasso take significantly more time than Random Forest and GBFS because they involve either mutual information or kernel matrix computation, which scales as $O(d^2)$ or $O(n^2)$. Random Forest builds full trees, requiring a time complexity of $O(\sqrt{d}n \log n)$ per tree. The dependency on $\sqrt{d}$ is slightly misleading, as the number of trees required for Random Forests is also dependent on the number of features and scales as $O(\sqrt{d})$ itself. In contrast, GBFS only builds limited depth (depth $= 4, 5$) trees, and the computation time complexity is $O(dn)$. The number of iterations T is independent of the number of input features d; it is only a function of how the number of desired features. Empirically, we observe that the two algorithms are comparable in speed but GBFS is significantly faster on data sets with many instances (large n). The training time ranged from several seconds to minutes on the small data sets to about one hour on the large data set *kddcup99* (when Random Forest is trained with only 500 trees and large leaf sizes). Admittedly, the empirical comparison of training time is slightly problematic because our Random Forest implementation is based on highly optimized C++ code, whereas GBFS is implemented in Matlab^{TM}. We expect that GBFS could be made significantly faster if implemented in faster programming languages (*e.g.* C++) with the incorporation of known parallelization techniques for limited depth trees [28].

6. DISCUSSION

This paper introduces GBFS, a novel algorithm for non-linear feature selection. The algorithm quickly train very accurate classifiers while selecting high quality features. In contrast to most prior work, GBFS is based on a variation of gradient boosting of limited depth trees [7]. This approach has several advantages. It scales naturally to large data sets and it combines learning a powerful classifier and performing feature selection into a single step. It can easily incorporate known feature dependencies, a common setting in biomedical applications [1], medical imaging [6] and computer vision [4]. This has the potential to unlock interesting new discoveries in a variety of application domains. From a practitioners perspective, it is now worth investigating if a data set has inter-feature dependencies that could be provided as additional side-information to the algorithm.

One bottleneck of GBFS is that it explores features using the CART algorithm, which has a complexity of $O(dn)$. This may become a problem in cases with millions of features. Although this paper primarily focusses on the $n \gg d$ scenario, as future work we plan to consider improving the scalability with respect to d. One promising approach is to restrict the search to a random subsets of new features, akin to Random Forest. However, in contrast to Random Forest, the iterative nature of GBFS allows us to bias the sampling probability of a feature by its splitting value from previous iterations—thus avoiding unnecessary selection of unimportant features.

We are excited by the promising results of GBFS and believe that the use of gradient boosted trees for feature selection will lead to many interesting follow-up results. This will hopefully spark new algorithmic developments and improved feature discovery across application domains.

7. ACKNOWLEDGMENTS

KQW was supported by NSF grants 1149882 and 1137211. KQW and ZEX were supported by NSF IIS-1149882 and IIS- 1137211. Part of this work was done while ZEX was an intern at Microsoft Research, Redmond.

8. REFERENCES

[1] U. Alon, N. Barkai, D. A. Notterman, K. Gish, S. Ybarra, D. Mack, and A. J. Levine. Broad patterns of gene expression revealed by clustering analysis of tumor and normal colon tissues probed by oligonucleotide arrays. *Proceedings of the National Academy of Sciences*, 96(12):6745–6750, 1999.

[2] L. Breiman. *Classification and regression trees.* Chapman & Hall/CRC, 1984.

[3] O. Chapelle, P. Shivaswamy, S. Vadrevu, K. Weinberger, Y. Zhang, and B. Tseng. Boosted multi-task learning. *Machine learning*, 85(1):149–173, 2011.

[4] N. Dalal and B. Triggs. Histograms of oriented gradients for human detection. In *Computer Vision and Pattern Recognition, 2005. CVPR 2005. IEEE Computer Society Conference on*, volume 1, pages 886–893. IEEE, 2005.

[5] J. Duchi, S. Shalev-Shwartz, Y. Singer, and T. Chandra. Efficient projections onto the $l1$-ball for learning in high dimensions. In *Proceedings of the 25th international conference on Machine learning*, pages 272–279. ACM, 2008.

[6] J. A. Etzel, V. Gazzola, and C. Keysers. An introduction to anatomical ROI-based fMRI classification analysis. *Brain Research*, 1282:114–125, 2009.

[7] J. Friedman. Greedy function approximation: A gradient boosting machine. *The Annals of Statistics*, pages 1189–1232, 2001.

[8] I. Guyon and A. Elisseeff. An introduction to variable and feature selection. *The Journal of Machine Learning Research*, 3:1157–1182, 2003.

[9] T. Hastie, R. Tibshirani, and J. H. Friedman. *The elements of statistical learning.* Springer, 2009.

[10] J. Huang, T. Zhang, and D. Metaxas. Learning with structured sparsity. *The Journal of Machine Learning Research*, 12:3371–3412, 2011.

[11] S. Lee, H. Lee, P. Abbeel, and A. Y. Ng. Efficient l1 regularized logistic regression. In *Proceedings of the National Conference on Artificial Intelligence*, volume 21, page 401. Menlo Park, CA; Cambridge, MA; London; AAAI Press; MIT Press; 1999, 2006.

[12] Y. Liu, M. Sharma, C. Gaona, J. Breshears, J. Roland, Z. Freudenburg, E. Leuthardt, and K. Q. Weinberger. Decoding ipsilateral finger movements from ecog signals in humans. In *Advances in Neural Information Processing Systems*, pages 1468–1476, 2010.

[13] S. Ma, X. Song, and J. Huang. Supervised group lasso with applications to microarray data analysis. *BMC bioinformatics*, 8(1):60, 2007.

[14] L. Meier, S. Van De Geer, and P. Bühlmann. The group lasso for logistic regression. *Journal of the Royal Statistical Society: Series B (Statistical Methodology)*, 70(1):53–71, 2008.

[15] F. Pan, T. Converse, D. Ahn, F. Salvetti, and G. Donato. Feature selection for ranking using boosted trees. In *Proceedings of the 18th ACM conference on Information and knowledge management*, pages 2025–2028. ACM, 2009.

[16] M. Y. Park and T. Hastie. L1-regularization path algorithm for generalized linear models. *Journal of the Royal Statistical Society: Series B (Statistical Methodology)*, 69(4):659–677, 2007.

[17] H. Peng, F. Long, and C. Ding. Feature selection based on mutual information criteria of max-dependency, max-relevance, and min-redundancy. *Pattern Analysis and Machine Intelligence, IEEE Transactions on*, 27(8):1226–1238, 2005.

[18] S. Perkins, K. Lacker, and J. Theiler. Grafting: Fast, incremental feature selection by gradient descent in function space. *The Journal of Machine Learning Research*, 3:1333–1356, 2003.

[19] V. Roth. The generalized lasso. *Neural Networks, IEEE Transactions on*, 15(1):16–28, 2004.

[20] V. Roth and B. Fischer. The group-lasso for generalized linear models: Uniqueness of solutions and efficient algorithms. In *Proceedings of the 25th international conference on Machine learning*, pages 848–855. ACM, 2008.

[21] Y. Saeys, I. Inza, and P. Larrañaga. A review of feature selection techniques in bioinformatics. *bioinformatics*, 23(19):2507–2517, 2007.

[22] B. Schölkopf and A. Smola. *Learning with kernels: Support vector machines, regularization, optimization, and beyond*. MIT press, 2001.

[23] L. Song, A. Smola, A. Gretton, J. Bedo, and K. Borgwardt. Feature selection via dependence maximization. *The Journal of Machine Learning Research*, 98888:1393–1434, 2012.

[24] A. Spira, J. E. Beane, V. Shah, K. Steiling, G. Liu, F. Schembri, S. Gilman, Y.-M. Dumas, P. Calner, P. Sebastiani, et al. Airway epithelial gene expression in the diagnostic evaluation of smokers with suspect lung cancer. *Nature medicine*, 13(3):361–366, 2007.

[25] S. Sra. Fast projections onto $l1$, q-norm balls for grouped feature selection. In *Machine Learning and Knowledge Discovery in Databases*, pages 305–317. Springer, 2011.

[26] R. Tibshirani. Regression shrinkage and selection via the lasso. *Journal of the Royal Statistical Society. Series B (Methodological)*, pages 267–288, 1996.

[27] E. Tuv, A. Borisov, G. Runger, and K. Torkkola. Feature selection with ensembles, artificial variables, and redundancy elimination. *The Journal of Machine Learning Research*, 10:1341–1366, 2009.

[28] S. Tyree, K. Weinberger, K. Agrawal, and J. Paykin. Parallel boosted regression trees for web search ranking. In *WWW*, pages 387–396. ACM, 2011.

[29] Z. Xu, M. K., M. Chen, and K. Q. Weinberger. Cost-sensitive tree of classifiers. In S. Dasgupta and D. Mcallester, editors, *Proceedings of the 30th International Conference on Machine Learning (ICML-13)*, volume 28, pages 133–141. JMLR Workshop and Conference Proceedings, 2013.

[30] Z. Xu, M. Kusner, G. Huang, and K. Q. Weinberger. Anytime representation learning. In *Proceedings of the 30th International Conference on Machine Learning (ICML-13)*, pages 1076–1084, 2013.

[31] Z. Xu, K. Weinberger, and O. Chapelle. The greedy miser: Learning under test-time budgets. In *ICML*, pages 1175–1182, 2012.

[32] M. Yamada, W. Jitkrittum, L. Sigal, E. P. Xing, and M. Sugiyama. High-dimensional feature selection by feature-wise non-linear lasso. *arXiv preprint arXiv:1202.0515*, 2012.

[33] T. Zhang. Multi-stage convex relaxation for learning with sparse regularization. In D. Koller, D. Schuurmans, Y. Bengio, and L. Bottou, editors, *Advances in Neural Information Processing Systems 21*, pages 1929–1936. 2008.

[34] Z. Zhao, F. Morstatter, S. Sharma, S. Alelyani, A. Anand, and H. Liu. Advancing feature selection research. *ASU Feature Selection Repository*, 2010.

APPENDIX

A. SUPPLEMENTARY RESULTS

We further extend our experimental results by incorporating more one-vs-one pairs from MNIST data set. We randomly pick 6 one-vs-one pairs from MNIST and evaluate GBFS and other feature selection algorithms. The first baseline is l_1-regularized logistic regression (L1-LR). We vary the regularization parameter to select different number of features and examine the error rates under these different settings. We also compare against *Random Forest feature selection* [9]. Same to the procedure described in section 5, we run Random Forest with 2000 trees and a maximum number of 20 elements per leaf node. After training all 2000 trees, we rank all features. Starting from the most important feature, we re-train a random forest with only selected features and evaluate it on testing set. We gradually include less important features until we include all features. The other two baselines (include mRMR, HSIC-Lasso) do not scale on the MNIST data set.

Figure 7 indicates that GBFS consistently matches Random Forest FS, and clearly out-performs l_1-regularized logistic regression.

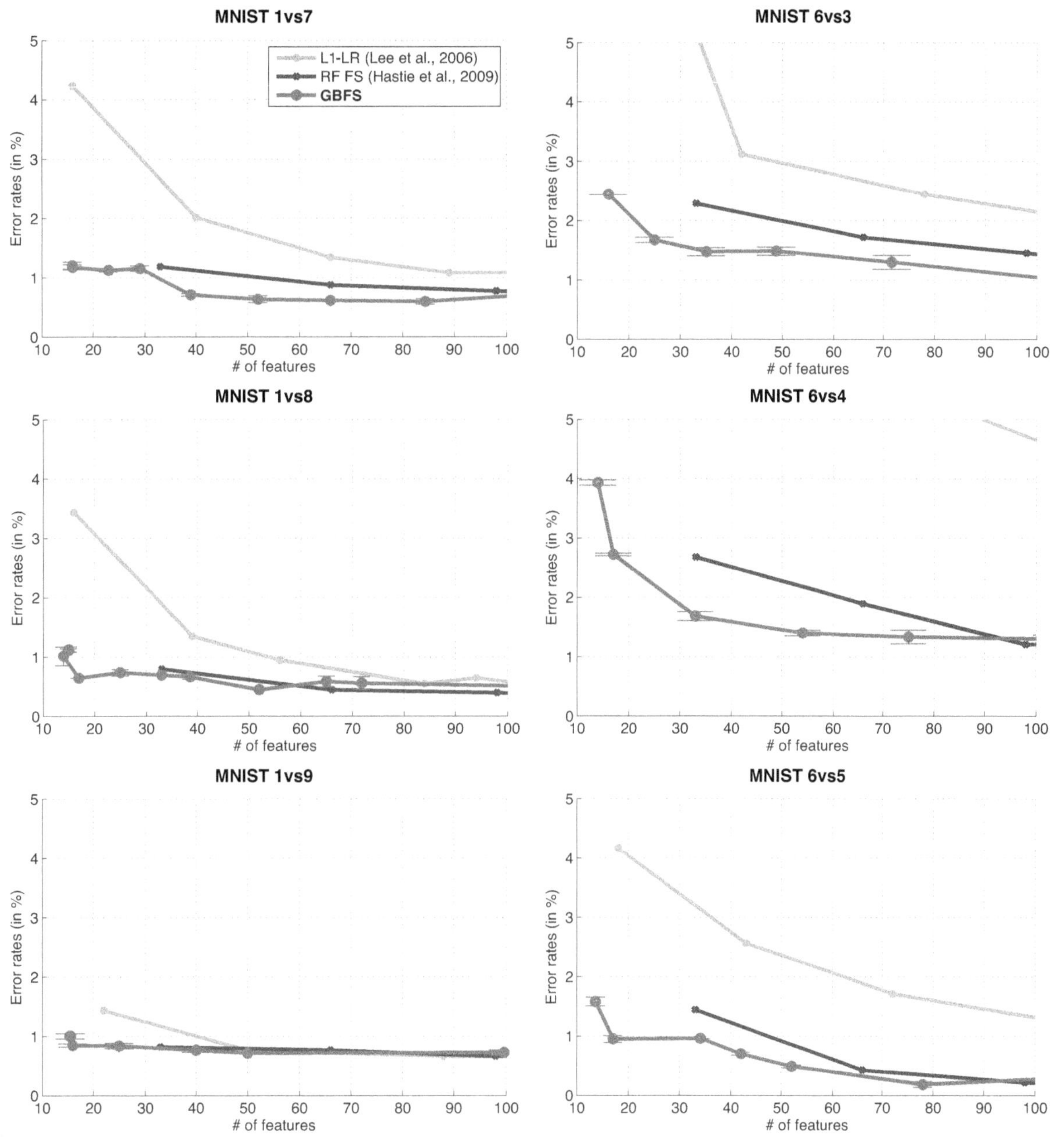

Figure 7: Classification error rates vs. feature selection performance for different algorithms on 6 random chosen pairs of binary classification tasks from MNIST data set.

Simultaneous Feature and Feature Group Selection through Hard Thresholding

Shuo Xiang
Arizona State University
Tempe, AZ 85287, USA
shuo.xiang@asu.edu

Tao Yang
Arizona State University
Tempe, AZ 85287, USA
t.yang@asu.edu

Jieping Ye
Arizona State University
Tempe, AZ 85287, USA
jieping.ye@asu.edu

ABSTRACT

Selecting an informative subset of features has important applications in many data mining tasks especially for high-dimensional data. Recently, simultaneous selection of features and feature groups (a.k.a bi-level selection) becomes increasingly popular since it not only reduces the number of features but also unveils the underlying grouping effect in the data, which is a valuable functionality in many applications such as bioinformatics and web data mining. One major challenge of bi-level selection (or even feature selection only) is that computing a globally optimal solution requires a prohibitive computational cost. To overcome such a challenge, current research mainly falls into two categories. The first one focuses on finding suitable continuous computational surrogates for the discrete functions and this leads to various convex and nonconvex optimization models. Although efficient, convex models usually deliver sub-optimal performance while nonconvex models on the other hand require significantly more computational effort. Another direction is to use greedy algorithms to solve the discrete optimization directly. However, existing algorithms are proposed to handle single-level selection only and it remains challenging to extend these methods to handle bi-level selection. In this paper, we fulfill this gap by introducing an efficient sparse group hard thresholding algorithm. Our main contributions are: (1) we propose a novel bi-level selection model and show that the key combinatorial problem admits a globally optimal solution using dynamic programming; (2) we provide an error bound between our solution and the globally optimal under the RIP (Restricted Isometry Property) theoretical framework. Our experiments on synthetic and real data demonstrate that the proposed algorithm produces encouraging performance while keeping comparable computational efficiency to convex relaxation models.

Categories and Subject Descriptors

H.2.8 [**Database Management**]: Database Applications-Data Mining

KDD'14, August 24–27, 2014, New York, NY, USA.

http://dx.doi.org/10.1145/2623330.2623662.

General Terms

Algorithms

Keywords

Feature selection, supervised learning, bi-level learning, combinatorics, optimization, dynamic programming

1. INTRODUCTION

Feature selection plays a critical role in many data mining applications that handle high-dimensional data and has been one of the most active research topics in machine learning. Over the past decades, with the development of compressive sensing techniques [24, 9, 11], joint modeling of prediction and feature selection gains its popularity and draws extensive studies [34, 19, 1, 33, 31, 30]. In the meantime, it is also believed that when the data possesses certain grouping structures, selecting feature groups together with individual features can be beneficial [32, 26, 7, 17, 28]. In the literature, simultaneous selection of features and feature groups is also referred to as bi-level selection [17, 29] and we will use these two terms interchangeably throughout the paper.

Formally, we consider the following linear model in this paper: the observations $\boldsymbol{y}$ can be generated via $\boldsymbol{y} = \boldsymbol{A}\bar{\boldsymbol{x}} + \boldsymbol{\epsilon}$, where each row of $\boldsymbol{A} \in \mathbb{R}^{n\times p}$ contains a sample and $\boldsymbol{\epsilon}$ represents the noise. $\bar{\boldsymbol{x}} \in \mathbb{R}^p$ is the parameter in this linear regression setting. In addition, the elements of $\bar{\boldsymbol{x}}$ are divided into $|G|$ mutually exclusive feature groups with G_i denoting the indices that belong to the ith group. The target is to find an accurate estimator $\boldsymbol{x}$ for $\bar{\boldsymbol{x}}$ based on our observations of $\boldsymbol{A}$ and $\boldsymbol{y}$. In the meantime, we expect the solution to yield sparsity in both feature level and group level, i.e., only a small number of features and feature groups are selected and thus a large potion of the elements/groups of $\boldsymbol{x}$ admits the value of zero. Mathematically, we formulate our problem in Eq. (1) below, where we attempt to find the best solution (in the sense of least squares) among all candidates containing no more than s_1 nonzero values and taking up to at most s_2 feature groups:

$$\begin{aligned} \underset{\boldsymbol{x}}{\text{minimize}} \quad & \frac{1}{2}\|\boldsymbol{A}\boldsymbol{x} - \boldsymbol{y}\|_2^2 \\ \text{subject to} \quad & \sum_{j=1}^{p} I(|x_j| \neq 0) \leq s_1 \\ & \sum_{j=1}^{|G|} I(\|\boldsymbol{x}_{G_j}\|_2 \neq 0) \leq s_2. \end{aligned} \tag{1}$$

Unfortunately, computing an optimal solution of the above problem requires enumerating all elements in the feasible set and thus incurs a prohibitive cost. A natural and popular approach is to replace the discrete constraints in Eq. (1) by their continuous computational surrogates. Sparse group lasso [14] applies the classical ℓ_1-relaxation on both feature-level and group-level and the resulting convex optimization problem can be efficiently solved. To enhance the quality of approximation, nonconvex relaxations using DC programming [28] and nonconvex penalties such as group MCP [7] and group bridge [16] are introduced, with extra computation effort. The connections between various convex and nonconvex bi-level learning models are investigated in the literature [29]. On the other hand, instead of finding suitable continuous surrogates, computing a local solution of the discrete optimization problem directly also receives plenty of attention. The iterative hard thresholding (IHT) [5, 6], orthogonal matching pursuit [25] and group orthogonal matching pursuit [20] all fall into this category. Although the optimization is by nature nonconvex, the efficiency of these algorithms is usually comparable (if not better) to that of convex relaxation models. However, to the best of our knowledge, these algorithms are proposed for feature selection only or group selection only. Whether they can be extended to handle bi-level selection properly and efficiently has not been much explored.

In this paper, we fulfill such a gap by introducing a hard thresholding model that is capable of bi-level selection. Our main contributions are: (1) we propose a novel bi-level selection model and show that the key combinatorial problem admits a globally optimal solution using dynamic programming; (2) we provide an error bound between our solution and the globally optimal under the RIP (Restricted Isometry Property) theoretical framework [9, 8]. We have evaluated the proposed algorithm on synthetic and real data. Results show that the proposed algorithm demonstrates encouraging performance while keeping comparable computational efficiency as convex relaxation models.

The remaining of the paper is organized as follows: We present our algorithm for Problem (1) and discuss different variants in Section 2. In Section 3, we investigate a key subproblem in our method and propose a dynamic programming algorithm that finds an optimal solution. The convergence property of the overall optimization framework is discussed in Section 4 and we present extensive empirical evaluation in Section 5. Section 6 concludes the paper and lists our plan of future work. For notations, we mainly follow the symbols introduced in Eq. (1), i.e., $\boldsymbol{A}$ stands for the design (sample) matrix, $\boldsymbol{y}$ is the response, $\boldsymbol{x}_{G_i}$ represents the regression model restricted on the ith group and f denotes the objective function.

2. OPTIMIZATION ALGORITHMS

Motivated by the iterative hard thresholding algorithm for ℓ_0-regularized problems [6] and the recent advances on nonconvex iterative shrinkage algorithm [15], we adopt the Iterative Shrinkage and Thresholding Algorithm (ISTA) framework and propose the following algorithm for solving Problem (1):

Algorithm 1 ISTA with Sparse Group Hard Thresholding

Input: $\boldsymbol{A}$, $\boldsymbol{y}$, s_1, s_2, $\eta > 1$
Output: solution $\boldsymbol{x}$ to Problem (1)
1: Initialize $\boldsymbol{x}^0$.
2: **for** $m \leftarrow 1, 2, \cdots$ **do**
3: Initialize L
4: **repeat**
5: $\boldsymbol{x}^m \leftarrow \text{SGHT}(\boldsymbol{x}^{m-1} - \frac{1}{L}\nabla f(\boldsymbol{x}^{m-1}))$
6: $L \leftarrow \eta L$
7: **until** line search criterion is satisfied
8: **if** the objective stops decreasing **then**
9: **return** $\boldsymbol{x}^m$
10: **end if**
11: **end for**

In the proposed algorithm above, f denotes the objective function and the "SGHT" in Algorithm 1 stands for the following **Sparse Group Hard Thresholding (SGHT)** problem with $\boldsymbol{v}$ as the input:

$$\begin{aligned} \underset{\boldsymbol{x}}{\text{minimize}} \quad & \frac{1}{2}\|\boldsymbol{x} - \boldsymbol{v}\|_2^2 \\ \text{subject to} \quad & \sum_{j=1}^{p} I(|x_j| \neq 0) \leq s_1 \\ & \sum_{j=1}^{|G|} I(\|\boldsymbol{x}_{G_j}\|_2 \neq 0) \leq s_2. \end{aligned} \tag{2}$$

Like most ISTA-based optimization algorithms, it is of critical importance that we can compute the projection step accurately and efficiently. In our case, the key part is exactly the SGHT problem. Although there are well established results on hard thresholding algorithms for ℓ_0-regularization, adding one more constraint on group cardinality greatly complicates the problem and requires deeper analysis. We will present detailed discussion on how to compute an optimal solution to this problem efficiently in the next section. Before that, we first introduce several possible variants of the proposed method. Notice that the target of Algorithm 1 is a nonconvex optimization problem. Different strategies for initialization and step-size may not only provide different convergence behavior, but also lead to a completely different solution. We consider three aspects in this paper: step-size initialization, line search criterion and acceleration option.

2.1 Step-size Initialization

To provide an initial value of the step-size (Line 6. in Algorithm 1), we consider two strategies: a constant value and the Barzilai-Borwein (BB) method [2]. The BB method essentially finds the best multiple of identity matrix to approximate the Hessian matrix such that the least squares error of the secant equation is minimized, i.e., L^k is initialized to

$$\begin{aligned} \alpha^k &= \arg\min_{\alpha} \|\alpha(x^k - x^{k-1}) - (\nabla f(x^k) - \nabla f(x^{k-1}))\| \\ &= \frac{(\Delta g)^T(\Delta x)}{\|\Delta x\|^2} \end{aligned}$$

with a safeguard bound, where $\Delta g = \nabla f(x^k) - \nabla f(x^{k-1})$ and $\Delta x = x^k - x^{k-1}$. In this paper, we set $L^k = \max(1, \alpha^k)$.

2.2 Line Search Criterion

We consider two line search termination criteria in this paper, which we name as Lipschiz criterion and sufficient decrease criterion. Specifically the Lipschiz criterion finds the smallest L that the following inequality is satisfied:

$$f(x^k) \leq f(x^{k-1}) + \langle \nabla f(x^{k-1}), x^k - x^{k-1} \rangle + \frac{L}{2} \|x^k - x^{k-1}\|_2^2. \quad (3)$$

On the other hand, the sufficient decrease criterion aims to find the smallest L such that:

$$f(x^k) \leq f(x^{k-1}) - \frac{L\delta}{2} \|x^k - x^{k-1}\|_2^2. \quad (4)$$

Inequality (3) is the standard way for ℓ_1-regularized optimization [3] and is applied extensively in structured sparse learning [19]. Inequality (4) and its variants are favored by most of the recent investigations on nonconvex regularized problems [4, 27, 15].

2.3 Acceleration Option

The ISTA framework has been shown to possess a convergence rate of $O(1/k)$ for a class of ℓ_1-regularized/constrained optimization problems and can be further improved to $O(1/k^2)$ via adding a carefully designed search point [21, 3]. However, whether the same strategy still works or makes the optimization diverge in the regime of nonconvex optimization remains unknown. In this paper we consider both of them and retain the notation of FISTA [3] to denote the ISTA with the acceleration trick. See Algorithm 2 for more detail about our FISTA.

Algorithm 2 FISTA with Sparse Group Hard Thresholding

Input: $\boldsymbol{A}$, $\boldsymbol{y}$, s_1, s_2, $\eta > 1$
Output: solution $\boldsymbol{x}$ to Problem (1)

Initialize $\boldsymbol{x}^{-1}$, $\boldsymbol{x}^0$, $\alpha^{-1} \leftarrow 0$, $\alpha^0 \leftarrow 1$
for $m \leftarrow 1, 2, \cdots$ **do**
  $\beta^m \leftarrow \frac{\alpha^{m-2}-1}{\alpha^{m-1}}$
  $\boldsymbol{u}^m \leftarrow \boldsymbol{x}^{m-1} + \beta^m(\boldsymbol{x}^{m-1} - \boldsymbol{x}^{m-2})$
  Initialize L
  repeat
    $\boldsymbol{x}^m \leftarrow \text{SGHT}(\boldsymbol{u}^m - \frac{1}{L}\nabla f(\boldsymbol{u}^m))$
    $L \leftarrow \eta L$
  until line search criterion is satisfied
  if the objective stops decreasing **then**
    return $\boldsymbol{x}^m$
  end if
end for

Table 1: Specific settings for each variant considered in the paper. The last two columns denote the Lipschiz and sufficient decrease line search criterion respectively.

VARIANTS	ISTA	ISTA	BB	CONST	LI S	DEC
ISTA		✓	✓			✓
ISTA-L		✓	✓		✓	
ISTA	✓		✓		✓	
ISTA-C	✓			✓	✓	

Table 1 summaries different variants we consider in this paper. All these variants will be examined in our experiments. We conclude this section by presenting several additional features of the proposed algorithm.

Remark 1. One significant advantage of adhering to the discrete model is that incorporating prior knowledge about the grouping structure is quite straight-forward. Remember that the two parameters in our model are just the upper-bound of features and feature groups respectively. In addition, model selection procedures such as cross-validation can be greatly facilitated since we only need to consider integer values, which are often quite small in real-world applications. On the contrary, the regularizers in most of the existing works are real-valued and may not provide much insights for parameter-tuning.

Remark 2. Although we consider our bi-level learning model in a linear regression setting, the technique can be readily extended to more general problems by choosing appropriate loss functions. Particularly, in order to extend our model to classification tasks, the widely-used logistic loss function can be applied instead of the least squares function in Eq. (1) and the proposed Algorithm 1 can be applied by changing the procedure that computes the gradient. In general, the proposed model can be extended to any convex loss functions with a simple gradient computation.

3. OPTIMAL SOLUTION OF SGHT

In this section, we show how to solve the SGHT problem in Eq. (2) efficiently using dynamic programming. Before presenting our algorithm, we first explore some key properties of Problem (2). As highlighted previously, the major challenge comes from the two coupled constraints. Therefore, we first consider the special case where only one of the two constraints is present. Some straight-forward analysis leads to the following results:

LEMMA 1. *If only the cardinality constraint is present, the optimal solution of Problem (2) can be obtained by setting the $p - s_1$ smallest (in absolute value) elements of $\boldsymbol{v}$ to zero. Similarly for group cardinality constraint, it suffices to find the $|G| - s_2$ smallest groups (in ℓ_2-norm) and set them to zero.*

Based on Lemma 1, it is also easy to verify that for any optimal solution $\boldsymbol{x}^*$ of Problem (2), each element x_i^* is either equal to v_i or zero, where the subscript i denotes the ith element of the vector. Therefore we have the following proposition providing an equivalent but discrete characterization of the original SGHT problem:

PRO OSITION 1. *Finding the optimal solution of problem* (2) *is e uivalent to the following* ***Sparse Group Subset Selection (SGSS)*** *problem:*

Given a set S on which a nonnegative value function f is defined. $C = \{C_1, C_2, \cdots, C_{|G|}\}$ is a collection of disjoint subsets of S such that $S = \bigcup_{i=1}^{|G|} C_i$. Find a subset $S' \subset S$ with the maximum value such that the cardinality of S is no more than s_1 and S' has nonempty intersections with at most s_2 elements from C. The value of a subset is defined as the summation of all the values of its elements.

We claim that the SGHT has an optimal solution if and only if we can find an optimal solution for the SGSS problem. We provide a one-way reduction (the "if" part) here. The other way is almost identical. The original SGHT problem can be reduced to SGSS by simply setting $S = \{1, 2, \cdots, p\}$ with the value function defined as $f(i) = v_i^2$ for all $1 \leq i \leq p$ and $C_i = G_i$ for all $1 \leq i \leq |G|$. Suppose S' is the optimal solution of SGSS. Then the optimal solution of SGHT can be readily obtained via:

$$x^* = \begin{cases} v_i & \text{if } i \in S' \\ 0 & \text{otherwise.} \end{cases} \quad (5)$$

In the sequel, we will focus on the SGSS problem and provide an efficient algorithm to compute its globally optimal solution. The term cardinality and group cardinality are used to characterize the size of S' and the number of elements from C with which S' has a nonempty intersection, respectively.

Let $T(i,j,k)$ denote the maximum value we can obtain by choosing a subset S', whose cardinality is no more than k and group cardinality is at most j. In addition, S' is only allowed to have nonempty intersection with $C_1, C_2, \cdots, C_i$. Therefore T is in essence a three-dimensional table of size $(|G|+1)\times(s_2+1)\times(s_1+1)$ (the table is zero-indexed). It is easy to verify that, if we are able to compute all the values in table T correctly, the maximum value one can get in the SGSS problem is given by $T(|G|, s_2, s_1)$.

Next we propose a dynamic programming algorithm to compute the table T. The motivation behind our method is the existence of optimal substructure and overlapping subproblems [18], two major ingredients for an efficient dynamic programming algorithm. More specifically, when we try to compute $T(i,j,k)$, the optimal solution must fall into one of the two situations: whether the C_i is selected or not. If not, we can simply conclude that $T(i,j,k) = T(i-1,j,k)$. On the other hand, if C_i is selected, we need to determine how many elements from C_i are included in the optimal solution. Suppose the optimal solution takes t elements from C_i, then we must have $T(i,j,k) = T(i-1,j-1,k-t) + CH(i,t)$, where $CH(i,t)$ denotes the maximum value one can get from choosing t elements out of C_i. The optimal t can be computed via enumeration. To sum up, the computation of $T(i,j,k)$ can be written in the following recursive form:

$$T(i,j,k) = \max \begin{cases} T(i-1,j,k) \\ \max\limits_{1\le t\le \min(k,|G_i|)} T(i-1,j-1,k-t) + CH(i,t). \end{cases}$$

It is clear from above that $T(i,j,k)$ can be computed using only the values in the table T with smaller indices. Therefore we can compute each element of the table T in increasing order for each index; see Figure 1 for more detail. In addition, to further reduce the complexity, function $CH(i,t)$ can be precomputed before the dynamic programming process. We present the detailed description of the proposed method in Algorithm 3. From table T, we are able to calculate the minimum objective value of the SGHT problem, which is exactly $\frac{1}{2}(\|\boldsymbol{v}\|_2^2 - T(|G|, s_2, s_1))$. In order to calculate the optimal solution $\boldsymbol{x}^*$, all we need to know is the indices of selected elements in S and the optimal solution can be constructed through Eq. (5). We compute such information by adding one table P (stands for path) in the proposed algorithm. Specifically, $P(i,j,k) = 0$ means the C_i is not selected in the computation of $T(i,j,k)$. Otherwise we set

$$P(i,j,k) = \arg \max_{1\le t\le \min(k,|G_i|)} T(i-1,j-1,k-t) + CH(i,t),$$

which is just the number of selected features in the ith group (C_i) in the optimal solution. To recover the indices of all the selected elements, we will start from $P(|G|, s_2, s_1)$ with a backtracking procedure and record the number of selected elements in each group. Algorithm 4 provides a formal description of this process. It accepts the table P as input and returns the *cnt* table which contains the number of selected elements in each group. Finally computing the optimal $\boldsymbol{x}^*$ only amounts to keeping the top selected elements for each group and setting the remains to zero.

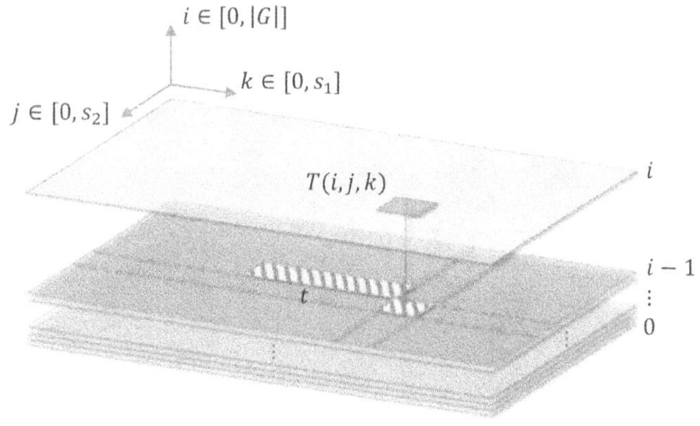

Figure 1: Illustration of the order of computation for each element in T. While computing $T(i,j,k)$, we only need values in those red squares, which are located in the previous rectangle (in terms of i-axis) and of equal or smaller coordinates on axes j and k. Therefore the computation can be naturally carried out in three nested loops, one for each axis respectively.

We analyze the time complexity of our proposed algorithm as follows. Notice that the time needed to precompute the table CH is give by:

$$O(\sum_{i=1}^{|G|} |G_i|\log(|G_i|)) = O(p\log p),$$

the dynamic programming part for computing both T and P takes

$$O(\sum_{i=1}^{|G|} s_2 s_1 |G_i|) = O(s_1 s_2 \sum_{i=1}^{|G|} |G_i|) = O(p s_1 s_2),$$

and the backtracking needs clearly $O(|G|)$ operations. Therefore the overall time complexity is

$$O(p(s_1 s_2 + \log p) + |G|) = O(s_1 s_2 p + p\log p).$$

When the number of features and feature groups selected is small, the SGHT problem can be solved efficiently.

4. CONVERGENCE ANALYSIS

In this section, knowing that the key SGHT sub-problem can be efficiently computed, we assess the quality of the solution produced by the overall optimization procedure (Algorithm 1). Specifically, since the constraints of Eq. (1) are nonconvex and only a local minimum can be found through our proposed method, we are interested in studying how close (in terms of Euclidean distance) the obtained solution to the optimal solution of the optimization problem (1). Although we are not aware of the optimal solution, the bound

Algorithm 3 Dynamic programming algorithm for SGSS

```
Input: S, C = ∪_{i=1}^{|G|} C_i, s_1, s_2
Output: T, P
T ← 0, CH ← 0, P ← 0
for i = 1 to |G| do
  sort C_i in decreasing order of magnitude
  for t = 1 to |G_i| do
    CH(i,t) ← CH(i,t − 1) + C_i(t)
  end for
end for
for i = 1 to |G| do
  for j = 1 to s_2 do
    for k = 1 to s_1 do
      T(i,j,k) ← T(i − 1,j,k)
      for t = 1 to G_i do
        w ← T(i − 1,j − 1,k − t) + CH(i,t)
        if w > T(i,j,k) then
          T(i,j,k) = w
          P(i,j,k) = t
        end if
      end for
    end for
  end for
end for
```

Algorithm 4 Linear backtracking algorithm for finding the number of selected elements in each group

```
Input: P , s_1, s_2
Output: cnt
j ← s_2, k ← s_1
for i = |G| downto 1 do
  cnt(i) ← P(i,j,k)
  if cnt(i) > 0 then
    j ← j − 1
    k ← k − cnt(i)
  end if
end for
```

between our solution and the optimal one can be analyzed under the theoretical framework of restricted isometry property (RIP) [9]. A matrix $\boldsymbol{A} \in \mathbb{R}^{n\times p}$ is said to satisfy the RIP property with constant δ_s if the following property holds for any s-sparse vector $\boldsymbol{x}$, i.e., $\|\boldsymbol{x}\|_0 \leq s$:

$$(1-\delta_s)\|\boldsymbol{x}\|_2^2 \leq \|\boldsymbol{A}\boldsymbol{x}\|_2^2 \leq (1+\delta_s)\|\boldsymbol{x}\|_2^2.$$

The RIP constant essentially assesses the extent to which the given matrix resembles an orthogonal matrix and theoretical analyses often require certain upperbound on the RIP constant. It is easy to see that δ_s is non-decreasing w.r.t s and a smaller value of δ_s indicates more rigid conditions we require from $\boldsymbol{A}$. In order to apply the RIP based analysis for our method, a group-RIP constant is introduced to incorporate the group structure. Matrix $\boldsymbol{A}$ has a group-RIP constant δ^g if for any vector $\boldsymbol{x}$ that spans no more than g groups, i.e., $\sum_{j=1}^{|G|} I(\|\boldsymbol{x}_{G_j}\|_2 \neq 0) \leq g$, the following relation are satisfied:

$$(1-\delta^g)\|\boldsymbol{x}\|_2^2 \leq \|\boldsymbol{A}\boldsymbol{x}\|_2^2 \leq (1+\delta^g)\|\boldsymbol{x}\|_2^2.$$

Our next result provides an error bound between an optimal solution of Problem (1) and the solution produced by our proposed Algorithm 1 with L fixed to 1.

THEOREM 1. *Let $\boldsymbol{x}^*$ be a globally optimal solution of Problem (1) and $\boldsymbol{x}^k$ be the solution we obtain after the kth iteration in Algorithm 1 with $L = 1$. If $c_1 < \frac{1}{2}$, the following result holds:*

$$\|\boldsymbol{x}^k - \boldsymbol{x}^*\|_2 \leq (2c_1)^k\|\boldsymbol{x}^0 - \boldsymbol{x}^*\|_2 + \frac{2\sqrt{1+c_2}}{1-2c_1}\|\boldsymbol{e}^*\|_2,$$

where $\boldsymbol{e}^* = \boldsymbol{y} - \boldsymbol{A}\boldsymbol{x}^*$, $c_1 = \min\{\delta_{3s_1}, \delta^{3s_2}\}$, $c_2 = \min\{\delta_{2s_1}, \delta^{2s_2}\}$. In addition, if $c_2 < \frac{1}{4}$, it is also true that:

$$\|\boldsymbol{x}^k - \boldsymbol{x}^*\|_2 \leq (4c_2)^k\|\boldsymbol{x}^0 - \boldsymbol{x}^*\|_2 + \frac{2\sqrt{1+c_2}}{1-4c_2}\|\boldsymbol{e}^*\|_2.$$

Theorem 1 clearly shows that the parameter estimation error of the proposed algorithm decreases linearly (with coefficient of $2c_1$ or $4c_2$) till a fixed error term is met. In addition, such an error term is proportional to the prediction error of the optimal solution of Problem (1). The proof of Theorem 1 mainly utilizes the technique in [12] and the details are left in the Appendix. We provide an illustrative example of the convergence procedure in Figure 2: if the assumptions on the (group) RIP constant hold, the sequence generated by running our algorithm is guaranteed to converge into a region centered at $\boldsymbol{x}^*$ with radius at most $c\|\boldsymbol{e}^*\|_2$, where c is a constant. As we can observe from Figure 2 and Theorem 1, the difference between the unknown globally optimal solution of Problem (1) and ours is upper-bounded by a multiple of the underlying error term $\|\boldsymbol{e}^*\|_2$. In addition, such a difference cannot be canceled unless we have $\boldsymbol{e}^* = 0$, in which case Theorem 1 essentially states that our method admits a linear convergence rate [22].

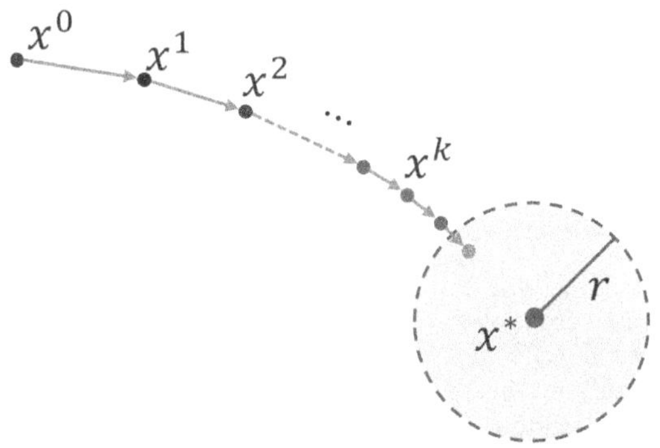

Figure 2: Illustration of the convergence behavior of the proposed algorithm. The parameter estimation error decreases linearly before entering into a region centered at x^* with radius proportional to the prediction error of x^*.

5. EXPERIMENTS

5.1 Evaluation of SGHT

Recall that solving SGHT (Problem (2)) accurately and efficiently is the key to our optimization procedure (Algorithm 1). We have theoretically analyzed the correctness and time complexity of our method in Section 3. In this part, we present empirical studies on the efficiency of our proposed Algorithm 3. As we have analyzed previously, three factors including the number of candidate features, the number of selected groups and the number of selected features determine the time complexity. We conduct the evaluation in four different scenarios, each of which demonstrates the relationship between the running time and some particular factors while keeping other factors unchanged. Specific settings are listed in Table 2.

Table 2: Experiment setup for evaluation of SGHT

IXED VARIA LE	# GRO	# EAT RE	s_1	s_2
SCENARIO 1	✓			
SCENARIO		✓		
SCENARIO		✓	✓	✓
SCENARIO 4	✓	✓		

- **Scenario 1. Varying number of features p with incremental candidate set.** We vary the number of features p from $1,000$ to $5,000,000$. The number of groups is fixed to 100 in this case, i.e., $|G| = 100$. s_2 is set to 20%, 40% and 60% of the total number of groups respectively and the value of s_1 is set to $5s_2$, i.e., we want to approximately select 5 features per group.
- **Scenario 2. Varying number of groups $|G|$ with incremental candidate set.** p is fixed to $1,000,000$ and G is chosen from the set of $\{10, 50, 100, 150, 200\}$. The value of s_1 and s_2 is set according to the same strategy in Scenario 1.
- **Scenario 3. Varying number of groups $|G|$ with fixed candidate set.** We conduct this evaluation in order to verify our theoretical result that the number of groups $|G|$ is not a dominating factor of time complexity. Specifically we fix the value of p to $1,000,000$ and choose $|G|$ from $\{50, 100, 500, 1000, 5000, 10000\}$. s_1 and s_2 are fixed as 50 and 5 respectively.
- **Scenario 4. Incremental candidate set with fixed number of groups and features.** In this case, $1,000,000$ variables are partitioned into 100 groups of equal size. We attempt to select $10\% \sim 60\%$ of all the groups and approximately 20 features per group.

Figure 3 demonstrates the running time (in seconds) of our SGHT algorithm of all four scenarios. Specifically, the nearly flat curve in our third experiment corroborates with the theoretical result that the number of groups is not a major factor of the time complexity. In other cases, our algorithm exhibits its capability of handling large-scale applications. Particularly, when only a small number of features and feature groups are wanted, as is the common situation in high-dimensional variable selection, our algorithm is capable of computing a globally optimial solution for SGHT with a performance competitive to its convex computational surrogate such as the soft-thresholding [10].

5.2 Evaluation of Convergence

We study the convergence behavior of different implementations of our discrete optimization approach proposed in Section 1. The evaluation is carried out on a collection of randomly generated data sets $(\boldsymbol{A}, \boldsymbol{y})$. Specifically, we generate $\boldsymbol{A} \in \mathbb{R}^{n \times p}, \boldsymbol{y} \in \mathbb{R}^n$, where the values of n and p are chosen from the following set:

$$\{(100, 2000), (100, 5000), (1000, 20000), (1000, 50000)\}.$$

All of the p features are partitioned into groups of size 100. The value of s_2 is selected from $\{0.1|G|, 0.2|G|\}$, i.e., we select 10% and 20% groups. s_1 is set to $5s_2$, which leads to the effect of within-group sparsity.

For all of the variants, we terminate the programs when either the relative change of objective value in two consecutive iterations or the gradient of the objective is less than a given threshold. The objective values of up to the first 100 iterations as well as the running time for each variant are reported in Figure 4. The results demonstrate the effect of BB to initialize the step-size. Both ISTA with lipschiz line search criterion (blue in Figure 4) and FISTA (black in Figure 4) deliver superior performance, particularly for large data sets and large number of selected groups/features.

5.3 Simulation Results

We examine the proposed bi-level method on synthetic data which consist of both group selection and bi-level variable selection. The data generation follows the procedures recommended in the literature [32, 29]: the data set is generated via the linear model $\boldsymbol{y} = \boldsymbol{A}\bar{\boldsymbol{x}} + \boldsymbol{\epsilon}$, where both of the design matrix $\boldsymbol{A} \in \mathbb{R}^{100 \times 200}$ and the noise term $\boldsymbol{\epsilon}$ follow a normal distribution. The ground truth $\bar{\boldsymbol{x}}$ is partitioned into 20 groups of equal size. In addition, two kinds of grouping structure are considered in this experiment; see Figure 5 for more detail. The goal is to obtain an accurate (in terms of least squares) estimator of $\bar{\boldsymbol{x}}$ that also preserves the grouping structure, given only $\boldsymbol{A}$ and $\boldsymbol{y}$.

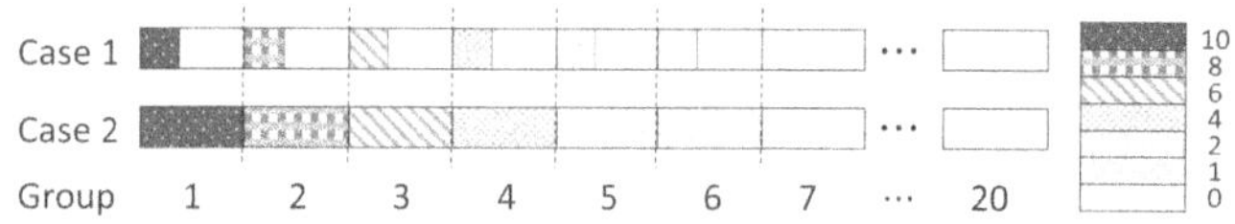

Figure 5: Illustraion of the grouping effect in the ground truth model $\bar{x}$. Both cases include redundant groups (group 7 to group 20). In addition, the first case contains a bi-level sparsity. The values within each group are identical, as shown in the color map.

State-of-the-art bi-level feature learning algorithms, including the convex sparse group lasso, two fractional models [29] (frac(1, 2) for bi-level variable selection and frac(2, 1) for group selection) and DC approximation approach [28], are included for comparison. It is worth mentioning that the DC approach deals with exactly the same formulation as ours but resort to using continuous computational surrogate. In addition, we also include orthogonal matching pursuit (OMP) and group orthogonal matching pursuit (gOMP) in the experiments as they provide baseline results for discrete optimization approach. For both fractional models, we choose 5 regularizers from the interval $[10^{-8}, 10^2]$. For DC approach and our method, s_2 is selected from $\{2, 4, 6, 8, 10\}$ and s_1 is chosen from the set of $\{2s_2, 4s_2, 6s_2, 8s_2, 10s_2\}$. Since the parameters of OMP and gOMP are just the number of selected features and feature groups respectively, we set $\{6, 12, 18, \cdots, 60\}$ as the candidate parameter set for OMP and similarly $\{2, 4, 6, \cdots, 10\}$ for gOMP. Five-fold cross-validation is carried out to choose the best parameter for each method. The tuned models are then tested on an i.i.d testing set. Following the setups in previous work [7, 28], the

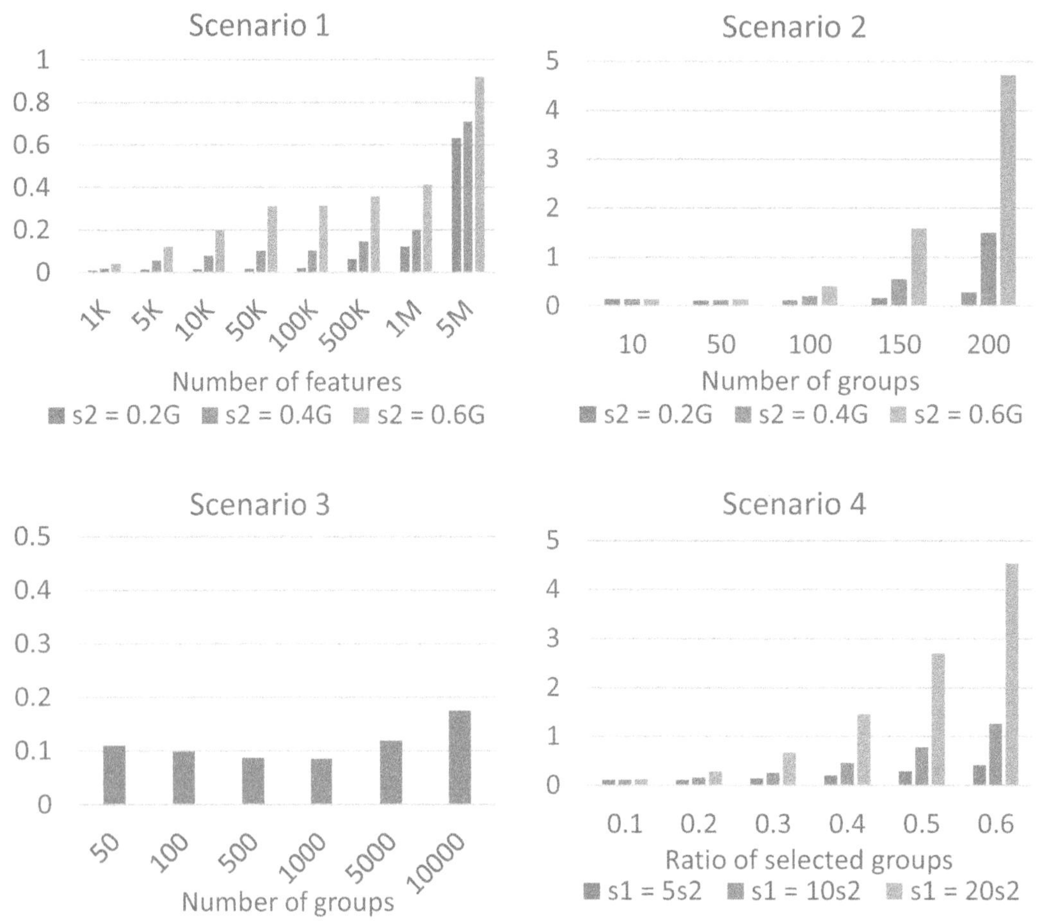

Figure 3: Running time (in seconds) of Algorithm 3 in different scenarios.

number of selected groups/features, the number of false positive selections and false negative selections and the running time (in seconds) are reported in Table 3. We can observe that the approaches with discrete parameters (OMP, gOMP, DC approach and our method) deliver more accurate estimation on the number of groups and features, compared to regularization-based approaches. Particularly, our method demonstrates the best performance in the bi-level selection tasks and is second only to gOMP in the scenario of group selection. The low false positive rate means that redundant groups are effectively screened. However, this could lead to a relatively high but still reasonable false negative rate. Such a phenomenon is also observed in existing work [7]. As of efficiency, it is expected that OMP and gOMP are the most efficient methods due to their cheap and small number of iterations. Among others, our method requires the least amount of running-time. In addition, the DC approach, which needs to refine the continous surrogate within each iteration, requires the most computational effort (nearly twice of the time of our method).

5.4 Real-world Applications

We conclude the experiment section with a study on the Boston Housing data set [13]. The original data set is used as a regression task which contains 506 samples with 13 features. Furthermore, to take into account the non-linear relationship between variables and response, up to third-degree polynomial expansion is applied on each feature, as suggested in previous works [23]. Specifically, for each variable x, we record x, x^2 and x^3 in the transformed data and gather them into one group. We randomly take 50% of the data as the training set and leave the rest for testing. The parameter settings for each method follow the same spirit in our last experiment and are properly scaled to fit this data set. We fit a linear regression model on the training data and report the number of selected features, feature groups as well as the mean squared error (MSE) on the testing set in Table 4. Five-fold cross validation is adopted for parameter tuning and all the results are averaged over 10 replications. We can observe from the table that our method shows the best prediction results with the least amount of features and feature groups.

6. CONCLUSIONS

In this paper, we study the problem of simultaneous feature and feature group selection. Unlike existing methods which are based on continuous computational surrogate for the discrete selection problem, we focus on the discrete model directly. Systematic investigations are carried out on optimization algorithms, convergence property as well as empirical evaluations. The proposed model delivers superior performance in both group selection and bi-level vari-

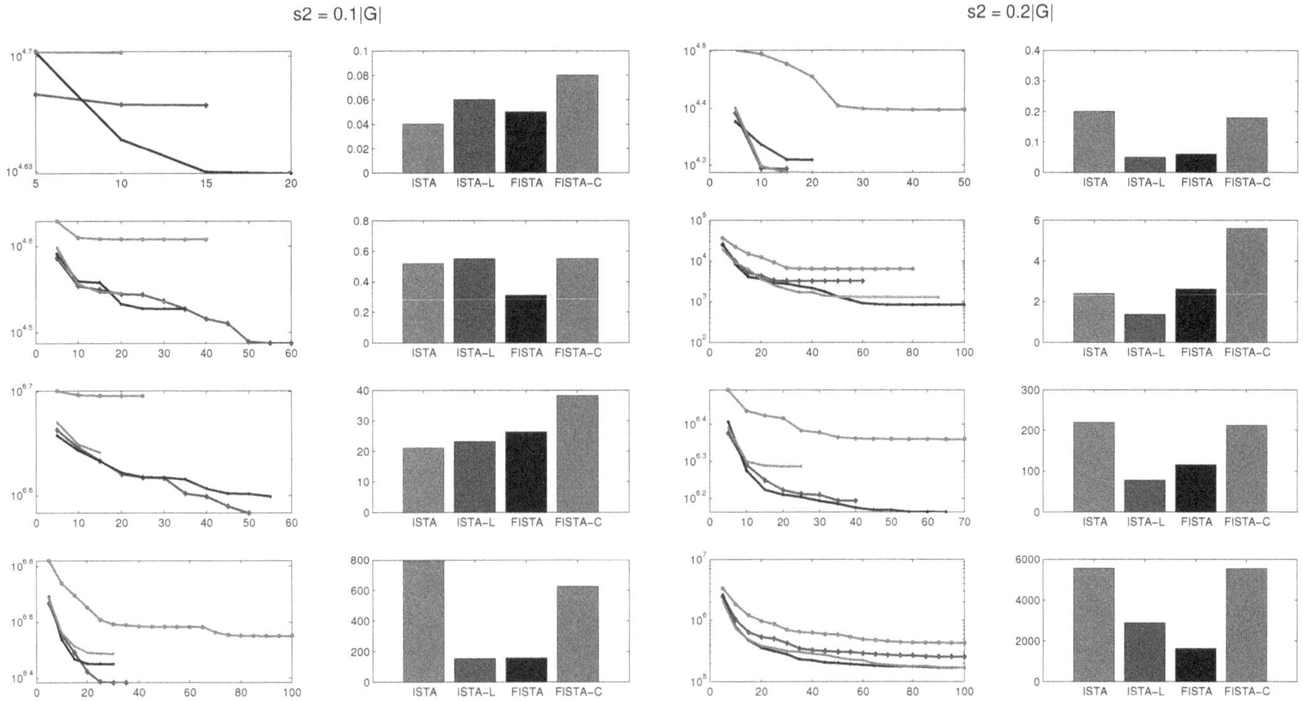

Figure 4: Convergence results of different variants of the proposed discrete optimization approach on synthetic data, where ISTA-L and FISTA-C stand for ISTA with Lipschiz line search criterion and FISTA with const step-size initialization. All the algorithms are evaluated on four data sets, from top to bottom, of which the size of A is $(100, 2000)$, $(100, 5000)$, $(1000, 20000)$ and $(1000, 50000)$ respectively. The number of selected group (s_2) is chosen from $0.1|G|$ and $0.2|G|$ and the corresponding results are listed from left to right. For each parameter setting, we report the objective values up to 100 iterations (the lines) as well as the running time in second (the histograms).

Table 4: Comparison of performance on the Boston Housing data set. All the results are averaged over 10 replications.

Methods	# Gro	# eat re	MSE
s Lasso	7.10	0. 0	60 .50
frac(1, 2)	9. 0	16.10	8485.1
frac(2, 1)	9.60	8.80	85 0.00
OMP	4. 0	6.00	8089.91
OMP	4. 0	1 .00	89 4.55
DC	.70	5. 0	8 .14
s ht	.10	.00	545. 7

able selection settings and possesses significant advantage on efficiency, particularly when only a small number of features and feature groups are demanded. In addition, due to the discrete parameters, model selection procedures such as parameter tuning can be greatly facilitated. We plan to extend our method to more challenging biomedical applications, particularly those with block-wise missing data.

7. ACKNOWLEDGMENTS

This work was supported in part by NIH (R01 LM010730) and NSF (IIS-0953662, MCB-1026710, and CCF-1025177).

8. REFERENCES

[1] F. Bach, R. Jenatton, J. Mairal, and G. Obozinski. *Convex Optimization with Sparsity-Inducing Norms.* 2010.

[2] J. Barzilai and J. M. Borwein. Two-point step size gradient methods. *IMA Journal of Numerical Analysis*, 8(1):141–148, 1988.

[3] A. Beck and M. Teboulle. A fast iterative shrinkage-thresholding algorithm for linear inverse problems. *SIAM Journal on Imaging Sciences*, 2(1):183–202, 2009.

[4] E. G. Birgin, J. M. Martínez, and M. Raydan. Nonmonotone spectral projected gradient methods on convex sets. *SIAM Journal on Optimization*, 10(4):1196–1211, 2000.

[5] T. Blumensath and M. E. Davies. Iterative thresholding for sparse approximations. *Journal of Fourier Analysis and Applications*, 14(5-6):629–654, 2008.

[6] T. Blumensath and M. E. Davies. Iterative hard thresholding for compressed sensing. *Applied and Computational Harmonic Analysis*, 27(3):265–274, 2009.

[7] P. Breheny and J. Huang. Penalized methods for bi-level variable selection. *Statistics and its interface*, 2(3):369–380, 2009.

Table 3: **Comparison of performance on synthetic data. NO, FP and FN denote number, false positive number and false negative number respectively. All the results are averaged over 10 replications.**

Methods	Bi-level Selection (case 1)							Gro Selection (case)						
	Gro s			eat res			Time	Gro s			eat res			Time
	NO.	P	N	NO.	P	N		NO.	P	N	NO.	P	N	
s Lasso	19.10	1 .10	0.00	9 . 0	75. 0	0.00	10.4	16.70	10.80	0.10	167.00	108.00	1.00	1 .
frac(1, 2)	8.90	.90	0.00	59.70	41.70	0.00	15.7	8. 0	. 0	0.90	59.00	19.90	0.90	9.9
frac(2, 1)	8.60	.80	0. 0	86.00	68.60	0.60	5.9	7.50	1.70	0. 0	75.00	17.00	.00	19.8
OMP	8.40	.00	0.60	1.00	5.90	.90	1.6	4.80	1.80	.00	7. 0	1.90	54.70	1.6
OMP	.80	0.00	. 0	8.00	6.60	6.60	0.85	4. 0	0.00	1.80	4 .00	0.00	18.00	0.85
DC	7.70	.00	0. 0	. 0	16. 0	1.00	4.	5.60	.00	.40	.90	7.00	.10	5.6
s HT	5. 0	0.00	0.80	19.60	4. 0	.60	17.4	5.60	1.50	1.90	51.60	1 .50	0.90	16.

[8] E. J. Candes. The restricted isometry property and its implications for compressed sensing. *Comptes Rendus Mathemati ue*, 346(9):589–592, 2008.

[9] E. J. Candes and T. Tao. Decoding by linear programming. *Information Theory, IEEE Transactions on*, 51(12):4203–4215, 2005.

[10] D. Donoho. De-noising by soft-thresholding. *Information Theory, IEEE Transactions on*, 41(3):613–627, 2002.

[11] D. L. Donoho. Compressed sensing. *Information Theory, IEEE Transactions on*, 52(4):1289–1306, 2006.

[12] S. Foucart. Sparse recovery algorithms: sufficient conditions in terms of restricted isometry constants. In *Approximation Theory XIII: San Antonio 2010*, pages 65–77. Springer, 2012.

[13] A. Frank and A. Asuncion. UCI machine learning repository, 2010.

[14] J. Friedman, T. Hastie, and R. Tibshirani. A note on the group lasso and a sparse group lasso. *Arxiv preprint arXiv:1001.0736*, 2010.

[15] P. Gong, C. Zhang, Z. Lu, J. Huang, and J. Ye. A general iterative shrinkage and thresholding algorithm for non-convex regularized optimization problems. In *The 30th International Conference on Machine Learning (ICML)*, pages 37–45, 2013.

[16] J. Huang, S. Ma, H. Xie, and C. Zhang. A group bridge approach for variable selection. *Biometrika*, 96(2):339–355, 2009.

[17] J. Huang, T. Zhang, et al. The benefit of group sparsity. *The Annals of Statistics*, 38(4):1978–2004, 2010.

[18] C. E. Leiserson, R. L. Rivest, C. Stein, and T. H. Cormen. *Introduction to algorithms.* The MIT press, 2001.

[19] J. Liu, S. Ji, and J. Ye. *SLEP: Sparse Learning with Efficient Projections.* Arizona State University, 2009.

[20] A. C. Lozano, G. Swirszcz, and N. Abe. Group orthogonal matching pursuit for variable selection and prediction. In *NIPS'09-23 th Annual Conference on Neural Information Processing Systems*, 2009.

[21] Y. Nesterov et al. Gradient methods for minimizing composite objective function, 2007.

[22] J. Nocedal and S. J. Wright. *Numerical Optimization.* Springer, 2000.

[23] G. Swirszcz, N. Abe, and A. C. Lozano. Grouped orthogonal matching pursuit for variable selection and prediction. In *Advances in Neural Information Processing Systems*, pages 1150–1158, 2009.

[24] R. Tibshirani. Regression shrinkage and selection via the lasso. *Journal of the Royal Statistical Society. Series B (Statistical Methodology)*, pages 267–288, 1996.

[25] J. A. Tropp and A. C. Gilbert. Signal recovery from random measurements via orthogonal matching pursuit. *Information Theory, IEEE Transactions on*, 53(12):4655–4666, 2007.

[26] L. Wang, G. Chen, and H. Li. Group scad regression analysis for microarray time course gene expression data. *Bioinformatics*, 23(12):1486–1494, 2007.

[27] S. J. Wright, R. D. Nowak, and M. A. Figueiredo. Sparse reconstruction by separable approximation. *Signal Processing, IEEE Transactions on*, 57(7):2479–2493, 2009.

[28] S. Xiang, X. Shen, and J. Ye. Efficient Sparse Group Feature Selection via Nonconvex Optimization. In *The 30th International Conference on Machine Learning (ICML)*, pages 284–292, 2013.

[29] S. Xiang, L. Yuan, W. Fan, Y. Wang, P. M. Thompson, and J. Ye. Multi-source learning with block-wise missing data for alzheimer's disease prediction. In *Proceedings of the 19th ACM SIGKDD international conference on Knowledge discovery and data mining*, pages 185–193. ACM, 2013.

[30] Y. Xu and D. Rockmore. Feature selection for link prediction. In *Proceedings of the 5th Ph. D. workshop on Information and knowledge*, pages 25–32. ACM, 2012.

[31] J. Ye and J. Liu. Sparse methods for biomedical data. *ACM SIGKDD Explorations Newsletter*, 14(1):4–15, 2012.

[32] M. Yuan and Y. Lin. Model selection and estimation in regression with grouped variables. *Journal of the Royal Statistical Society: Series B (Statistical Methodology)*, 68(1):49–67, 2006.

[33] T. Zhang. Multi-stage convex relaxation for feature selection. *Bernoulli*, 19(5B):2277–2293, 2011.

[34] H. Zou and R. Li. One-step sparse estimates in nonconcave penalized likelihood models. *Annals of statistics*, 36(4):1509, 2008.

APPENDIX

A. PROOF OF THEOREM 1

PROOF. Let $\boldsymbol{w}^k$ denote $\boldsymbol{x}^k - \nabla f(\boldsymbol{x}^k)$. It is clear that

$$\begin{aligned}&\|\boldsymbol{x}^{k+1} - \boldsymbol{w}^k\|_2^2\\ =&\|\boldsymbol{x}^{k+1} - \boldsymbol{x}^*\|_2^2 + \|\boldsymbol{x}^* - \boldsymbol{w}^k\|_2^2 + 2\langle \boldsymbol{x}^{k+1} - \boldsymbol{x}^*, \boldsymbol{x}^* - \boldsymbol{w}^k\rangle\\ \le&\|\boldsymbol{x}^* - \boldsymbol{w}^k\|_2^2,\end{aligned}$$

where the last inequality comes from the optimality of $\boldsymbol{x}^{k+1}$. After eliminating $\|\boldsymbol{x}^* - \boldsymbol{w}^k\|_2^2$ from both sides we can obtain:

$$\begin{aligned}&\|\boldsymbol{x}^{k+1} - \boldsymbol{x}^*\|_2\\ \le&2\langle \boldsymbol{x}^{k+1} - \boldsymbol{x}^*, \frac{\boldsymbol{w}^k - \boldsymbol{x}^*}{\|\boldsymbol{x}^{k+1} - \boldsymbol{x}^*\|_2}\rangle\\ =&2\langle \boldsymbol{x}^k - \boldsymbol{A}^T(\boldsymbol{A}\boldsymbol{x}^k - \boldsymbol{y}) - \boldsymbol{x}^*, \frac{\boldsymbol{x}^{k+1} - \boldsymbol{x}^*}{\|\boldsymbol{x}^{k+1} - \boldsymbol{x}^*\|_2}\rangle\\ =&2\langle \boldsymbol{x}^k - \boldsymbol{A}^T(\boldsymbol{A}\boldsymbol{x}^k - (\boldsymbol{A}\boldsymbol{x}^* + \boldsymbol{e}^*)) - \boldsymbol{x}^*, \frac{\boldsymbol{x}^{k+1} - \boldsymbol{x}^*}{\|\boldsymbol{x}^{k+1} - \boldsymbol{x}^*\|_2}\rangle\\ =&2\langle (\boldsymbol{I} - \boldsymbol{A}^T\boldsymbol{A})(\boldsymbol{x}^k - \boldsymbol{x}^*) - \boldsymbol{A}^T\boldsymbol{e}^*, \frac{\boldsymbol{x}^{k+1} - \boldsymbol{x}^*}{\|\boldsymbol{x}^{k+1} - \boldsymbol{x}^*\|_2}\rangle\\ =&2\langle (\boldsymbol{I} - \boldsymbol{A}_U^T\boldsymbol{A}_U)(\boldsymbol{x}^k - \boldsymbol{x}^*) - \boldsymbol{A}^T\boldsymbol{e}^*, \frac{\boldsymbol{x}^{k+1} - \boldsymbol{x}^*}{\|\boldsymbol{x}^{k+1} - \boldsymbol{x}^*\|_2}\rangle\\ \le&2(\|\boldsymbol{I} - \boldsymbol{A}_U^T\boldsymbol{A}_U\|_2\|\boldsymbol{x}^k - \boldsymbol{x}^*\|_2 + \|\boldsymbol{A}\frac{\boldsymbol{x}^{k+1} - \boldsymbol{x}^*}{\|\boldsymbol{x}^{k+1} - \boldsymbol{x}^*\|_2}\|_2\|\boldsymbol{e}^*\|_2)\\ \le&2(c_1\|\boldsymbol{x}^k - \boldsymbol{x}^*\|_2 + \sqrt{1+c_2}\|\boldsymbol{e}^*\|_2),\end{aligned}$$

where the set U is the union of support of $\boldsymbol{x}^*$, $\boldsymbol{x}^k$ and $\boldsymbol{x}^{k+1}$ and the last inequality is from the fact that the spectral norm of $I - A_U^T A_U$ is upperbounded by $\delta_{|U|}$ [6]. The first conclusion then follows from expanding the last term and compute the power series.

To prove the second result, a finer treatment of the set U above is needed. Specifically, we consider the following four sets:

$$\begin{aligned}I_1 &= \mathrm{supp}(\boldsymbol{x}^k), \quad I_2 = \mathrm{supp}(\boldsymbol{x}^{k+1})\\ I_3 &= \mathrm{supp}(\boldsymbol{x}^*) - \mathrm{supp}(\boldsymbol{x}^k)\\ I_4 &= \mathrm{supp}(\boldsymbol{x}^*) - \mathrm{supp}(\boldsymbol{x}^{k+1}),\end{aligned}$$

and it is easy to veryfy that:

$$\begin{aligned}&\mathrm{supp}(\boldsymbol{x}^k - \boldsymbol{x}^*) \subset I_{13}\\ &\mathrm{supp}(\boldsymbol{x}^{k+1} - \boldsymbol{x}^*) \subset I_{24}\\ &|I_{ij}| = |I_i \cup I_j| \le 2s_1, \quad \forall (i,j) \in \{1,2,3,4\}.\end{aligned}$$

Therefore we can conclude that:

$$\begin{aligned}&(\|\boldsymbol{x}^{k+1} - \boldsymbol{x}^*\|_2 - 2\sqrt{1+c_2}\|\boldsymbol{e}^*\|_2)\|\boldsymbol{x}^{k+1} - \boldsymbol{x}^*\|_2\\ \le&2\langle (\boldsymbol{I} - \boldsymbol{A}^T\boldsymbol{A})(\boldsymbol{x}^k - \boldsymbol{x}^*), \boldsymbol{x}^{k+1} - \boldsymbol{x}^*\rangle\\ =&2\langle (\boldsymbol{I} - \boldsymbol{A}^T\boldsymbol{A})\left((\boldsymbol{x}^k - \boldsymbol{x}^*)_{I_1} + (\boldsymbol{x}^k - \boldsymbol{x}^*)_{I_3}\right),\\ &(\boldsymbol{x}^{k+1} - \boldsymbol{x}^*)_{I_2} + (\boldsymbol{x}^{k+1} - \boldsymbol{x}^*)_{I_4}\rangle\\ \le&2\langle (\boldsymbol{I} - \boldsymbol{A}_{I_{12}}^T\boldsymbol{A}_{I_{12}})(\boldsymbol{x}^k - \boldsymbol{x}^*)_{I_1}, (\boldsymbol{x}^{k+1} - \boldsymbol{x}^*)_{I_2}\rangle\\ &+ 2\langle (\boldsymbol{I} - \boldsymbol{A}_{I_{14}}^T\boldsymbol{A}_{I_{14}})(\boldsymbol{x}^k - \boldsymbol{x}^*)_{I_1}, (\boldsymbol{x}^{k+1} - \boldsymbol{x}^*)_{I_4}\rangle\\ &+ 2\langle (\boldsymbol{I} - \boldsymbol{A}_{I_{32}}^T\boldsymbol{A}_{I_{32}})(\boldsymbol{x}^k - \boldsymbol{x}^*)_{I_3}, (\boldsymbol{x}^{k+1} - \boldsymbol{x}^*)_{I_2}\rangle\\ &+ 2\langle (\boldsymbol{I} - \boldsymbol{A}_{I_{34}}^T\boldsymbol{A}_{I_{34}})(\boldsymbol{x}^k - \boldsymbol{x}^*)_{I_3}, (\boldsymbol{x}^{k+1} - \boldsymbol{x}^*)_{I_4}\rangle\\ \le&2c_2(\|(\boldsymbol{x}^k - \boldsymbol{x}^*)_{I_1}\|_2\|(\boldsymbol{x}^{k+1} - \boldsymbol{x}^*)_{I_2}\|_2\\ &+ \|(\boldsymbol{x}^k - \boldsymbol{x}^*)_{I_1}\|_2\|(\boldsymbol{x}^{k+1} - \boldsymbol{x}^*)_{I_4}\|_2\\ &+ \|(\boldsymbol{x}^k - \boldsymbol{x}^*)_{I_3}\|_2\|(\boldsymbol{x}^{k+1} - \boldsymbol{x}^*)_{I_2}\|_2\\ &+ \|(\boldsymbol{x}^k - \boldsymbol{x}^*)_{I_3}\|_2\|(\boldsymbol{x}^{k+1} - \boldsymbol{x}^*)_{I_4}\|_2)\\ \le&2c_2\sqrt{2\|(\boldsymbol{x}^k - \boldsymbol{x}^*)_{I_1}\|_2^2 + 2\|(\boldsymbol{x}^k - \boldsymbol{x}^*)_{I_3}\|_2^2}\\ &\sqrt{2\|(\boldsymbol{x}^{k+1} - \boldsymbol{x}^*)_{I_2}\|_2^2 + 2\|(\boldsymbol{x}^{k+1} - \boldsymbol{x}^*)_{I_4}\|_2^2}\\ =&4c_2\|\boldsymbol{x}^k - \boldsymbol{x}^*\|_2\|\boldsymbol{x}^{k+1} - \boldsymbol{x}^*\|_2,\end{aligned}$$

where the first inequality is from our proof of the first result and we apply the Cauchy inequality to obtain the last inequality. The proof is completed by expanding the last term and computing the resulting power series. □

Safe and Efficient Screening For Sparse Support Vector Machine

Zheng Zhao, Jun Liu, James Cox
SAS Institute Inc. 600 Research Drive, Cary, NC 27513
{zheng.zhao, jun.liu, james.cox}@sas.com

ABSTRACT

Sparse support vector machine (SVM) is a robust predictive model that can effectively remove noise and preserve signals. Like Lasso, it can efficiently learn a solution path based on a set of predefined parameters and therefore provides strong support for model selection. Sparse SVM has been successfully applied in a variety of data mining applications including text mining, bioinformatics, and image processing. The emergence of big-data analysis poses new challenges for model selection with large-scale data that consist of tens of millions samples and features. In this paper, a novel screening technique is proposed to accelerate model selection for ℓ_1-regularized ℓ_2-SVM and effectively improve its scalability. This technique can precisely identify inactive features in the optimal solution of a ℓ_1-regularized ℓ_2-SVM model and remove them before training. The technique makes use of the variational inequality and provides a closed-form solution for screening inactive features in different situations. Every feature that is removed by the screening technique is guaranteed to be inactive in the optimal solution. Therefore, when ℓ_1-regularized ℓ_2-SVM uses the features selected by the technique, it achieves exactly the same result as when it uses the full feature set. Because the technique can remove a large number of inactive features, it can greatly increase the efficiency of model selection for ℓ_1-regularized ℓ_2-SVM. Experimental results on five high-dimensional benchmark data sets demonstrate the power of the proposed technique.

Categories and Subject Descriptors

H.2.8 [**Database Management**]: Database Applications—*data mining*; I.5.2 [**Pattern Recognition**]: Design Methodology—*feature evaluation and selection*

Keywords

Screening, sparse support vector machine, feature selection

KDD'14, August 24–27, 2014, New York, NY, USA.
Copyright 2014 ACM 978-1-4503-2956-9/14/08 ...$15.00.
http://dx.doi.org/10.1145/2623330.2623686.

1. INTRODUCTION

Sparse predictive modeling algorithms provide powerful tools to analyze high-dimensional data and generate results that have high-degree of interpretability and robustness [5, 11]. In general, an ℓ_1-regularized sparse predictive modeling algorithm can be formulated as $\min_{\boldsymbol{w}} \text{loss}(\boldsymbol{w}) + \lambda\|\boldsymbol{w}\|_1$. Here $\boldsymbol{w} \in \mathbb{R}^m$ contains the model coefficients, $\text{loss}(\boldsymbol{w})$ is a loss function, and $\lambda \geq 0$ is the regularization parameter that balances between the loss function and the regularizer. When the hinge loss or its square form is used as the loss function, the resulting sparse model is the ℓ_1-regularized support vector machine (SVM) [4, 18, 2, 6, 16]. An ℓ_1-regularized SVM model can simultaneously perform model fitting by margin maximization and remove noisy features by soft-thresholding. It has been successfully applied in a variety of data mining applications that include text mining, bioinformatics, and image processing. Compared to other variances of sparse SVM model [15, 8, 1], ℓ_1-regularized SVM enjoys two major advantages. First, it defines a convex problem; therefore, an optimal solution can always be achieved without any relaxation of the original problem. Second, its optimization is simple, and a well implemented ℓ_1-regularized SVM solver can readily handle large-scale problems with tens of millions samples and features [6].

The value of the regularization parameter λ is crucial to the performance of an ℓ_1-regularized SVM. To achieve good performance, model selection is often used to help choose an appropriate λ value. For example, given a series of regularization parameters, $\lambda_1 > \lambda_2 > \ldots > \lambda_k$, the corresponding solutions, $\boldsymbol{w}_1^*, \boldsymbol{w}_2^*, \ldots, \boldsymbol{w}_k^*$, can be obtained and the best solution can be chosen by using a prespecified criterion, such as the accuracy or the area under the curve (AUC) that is achieved by the resulting models on holdout samples.

Big-data analysis requires a higher standard of efficiency for predictive modeling. When data are huge, the computational cost of model selection can be prohibitive. An intuitive question is to ask whether the solution obtained in the kth step of model selection can be used in the $(k+1)$th step to speed up computation. For Lasso [11], the answer leads to the state-of-the-art screening techniques to accelerate model selection [17, 7, 14, 12, 10]. The key idea is that, given a solution $\boldsymbol{w}_1^*$ for $\lambda = \lambda_1$, one can identify many features that are guaranteed to have zero coefficients in $\boldsymbol{w}_2^*$ when $\lambda = \lambda_2$. By removing a large number of these inactive features, the cost for computing $\boldsymbol{w}_2^*$ can be greatly reduced.

Although screening algorithms have been designed for Lasso, very little research has been done for screening for ℓ_1-regularized SVMs except in [7], which proposes a safe screening technique for ℓ_1-regularized ℓ_1-SVM. This paper presents a novel screening technique that is designed to speed up model selection for ℓ_1-regularized ℓ_2-SVM. The technique makes use of the variational inequality [9] for constructing a tight convex set, which can be used to compute bounds for screening features. Features that are removed by this technique are guaranteed to be inactive in the optimal solution. Therefore, the screening is "safe." Experimental results on five high-dimensional benchmark data sets demonstrate that the proposed screening technique can dramatically speed up model selection for ℓ_1-regularized ℓ_2-SVM by efficiently removing a large number of inactive features.

2. ℓ_1-REGULARIZED ℓ_2-SVM

Assume that $\mathbf{X} \in \mathbb{R}^{m\times n}$ is a data set that contains n samples, $\mathbf{X} = (\mathbf{x}_1, \ldots, \mathbf{x}_n)$, and m features, $\mathbf{X} = \left(\mathbf{f}_1^\top, \ldots, \mathbf{f}_m^\top\right)^\top$. Assume also that $\mathbf{y} = (y_1, \ldots, y_n)$ contains n class labels, $y_i \in \{-1, +1\}$, $i = 1, \ldots, n$. Let $\mathbf{w} \in \mathbb{R}^m$ be the m-dimensional weight vector, let $\xi_i \geq 0, i = 1, \ldots, n$ be the n slack variables, and let $b \in \mathbb{R}$ and $\lambda \in \mathbb{R}^+$ be the bias and the regularization parameter, respectively. The primal form of the ℓ_1-regularized ℓ_2-SVM is defined as:

$$\min_{\boldsymbol{\xi},\mathbf{w}} \frac{1}{2}\sum_{i=1}^{n}\xi_i^2 + \lambda||\mathbf{w}||_1, \tag{1}$$
$$s.t.\ \ y_i\left(\mathbf{w}^\top\mathbf{x}_i + b\right) \geq 1 - \xi_i, \ \ \xi_i \geq 0.$$

Eq. (1) specifies a convex problem that has a non-smooth ℓ_1 regularizer, which enforces that the solution is sparse. Let $\boldsymbol{w}^\star(\lambda)$ be the optimal solution of Eq. (1) for a given λ. All the features that have nonzero values in $\boldsymbol{w}^\star(\lambda)$ are called active features, and the other features are called inactive. Let $\boldsymbol{\alpha} \in \mathbb{R}^n$ be the n-dimensional dual variable. By applying the Lagrangian multiplier [3], the dual of the problem defined in Eq. (1) can be obtained as:

$$\min_{\boldsymbol{\alpha}} ||\boldsymbol{\alpha} - \mathbf{1}||_2^2, \tag{2}$$
$$s.t.\ \ ||\hat{\mathbf{f}}_j^\top\boldsymbol{\alpha}|| \leq \lambda, \ \ j = 1, \ldots, m,$$
$$\sum_{i=1}^{n}\alpha_i y_i = 0, \ \ \boldsymbol{\alpha} \succcurlyeq \mathbf{0}.$$

Here, $\hat{\mathbf{f}} = \mathbf{Y}\mathbf{f}$, and $\mathbf{Y} = diag(\mathbf{y})$ is a diagonal matrix. By defining $\boldsymbol{\alpha} = \lambda\boldsymbol{\theta}$, Eq. (2) can be reformulated as:

$$\min_{\boldsymbol{\theta}} ||\boldsymbol{\theta} - \frac{\mathbf{1}}{\lambda}||_2^2, \tag{3}$$
$$s.t.\ \ ||\hat{\mathbf{f}}_j^\top\boldsymbol{\theta}|| \leq 1, \ \ j = 1, \ldots, m,$$
$$\sum_{i=1}^{n}\theta_i y_i = 0, \ \ \boldsymbol{\theta} \succcurlyeq \mathbf{0}.$$

In the primal formulation for the ℓ_1-regularized ℓ_2-SVM, the primal variables are b, $\mathbf{w}$, and $\boldsymbol{\xi}$. And in the dual formulation, the dual variables are $\boldsymbol{\alpha}$ or $\boldsymbol{\theta}$. When b and $\mathbf{w}$ are known, $\boldsymbol{\xi}$, $\boldsymbol{\alpha}$, and $\boldsymbol{\theta}$ can be obtained as:

$$\xi_i = \alpha_i = \lambda\theta_i = \max\left(0, 1 - y_i\left(\mathbf{w}^\top\mathbf{x}_i + b\right)\right). \tag{4}$$

The relation between $\boldsymbol{\alpha}$ and $\mathbf{w}$ can be expressed as:

$$\boldsymbol{\alpha}^\top\hat{\mathbf{f}}_j = \begin{cases} \operatorname{sign}(w_j)\,\lambda, & \text{if } w_j \neq 0 \\ [-\lambda, +\lambda], & \text{if } w_j = 0 \end{cases}, \quad j = 1, \ldots, m. \tag{5}$$

The relation between $\boldsymbol{\theta}$ and $\mathbf{w}$ can be expressed as:

$$\boldsymbol{\theta}^\top\hat{\mathbf{f}}_j = \begin{cases} \operatorname{sign}(w_j), & \text{if } w_j \neq 0 \\ [-1, +1], & \text{if } w_j = 0 \end{cases}, \quad j = 1, \ldots, m. \tag{6}$$

$\lambda_{\max}$ is defined as the smallest λ value that leads to $\mathbf{w} = \mathbf{0}$ when it is used in Eq. (1). Given an input data set $(\mathbf{X}, \mathbf{y})$, $\lambda_{\max}$ can be obtained in a closed form as:

$$\lambda_{\max} = \left\|\sum_{i=1}^{n}\left(y_i - \frac{n_+ - n_-}{n}\right)\mathbf{x}_i\right\|_\infty, \tag{7}$$

where n_+ and n_- denote the number of positive and negative samples, respectively. And when $\lambda \geq \lambda_{max}$, the optimal solution of the problem defined in Eq. (1) can be written as:

$$\mathbf{w}^\star = \mathbf{0}, \ \ b^\star = \frac{(n_+ - n_-)}{n}. \tag{8}$$

Denote $\mathbf{m} = \sum_{i=1}^{n}\left(y_i - \frac{n_+ - n_-}{n}\right)\mathbf{x}_i$. The first feature to enter the model is the one that corresponds to the element that has the largest magnitude in $\mathbf{m}$.

3. EFFICIENT AND SAFE SCREENING FOR ℓ_1-REGULARIZED ℓ_2-SVM

Eq. (6) shows that the necessary condition for a feature $\mathbf{f}$ to be active in an optimal solution is $|\boldsymbol{\theta}^\top\hat{\mathbf{f}}| = 1$. On the other hand, for any feature $\mathbf{f}$, if $|\boldsymbol{\theta}^\top\hat{\mathbf{f}}| < 1$, it must be inactive in the optimal solution. Given a λ value, this condition can be used to develop a screening rule for removing inactive features to speed up training for the ℓ_1-regularized ℓ_2-SVM. The key is to compute the upper bound of $|\boldsymbol{\theta}^\top\hat{\mathbf{f}}|$ for features. A feature can be safely removed if its upper bound value is less than 1. The cost of computing the upper bounds can be much lower than training ℓ_1-regularized ℓ_2-SVM. Therefore, screening can greatly lower the computational cost by removing many inactive features before training. To bound the value of $|\boldsymbol{\theta}^\top\hat{\mathbf{f}}|$, it is necessary to construct a closed convex set $\mathbf{K}$ that contains $\boldsymbol{\theta}$. The upper bound value can be then computed by maximizing $|\boldsymbol{\theta}^\top\hat{\mathbf{f}}|$ over $\mathbf{K}$.

3.1 Constructing the Convex Set K

In the following, Eq. (3) and the variational inequality [9] are used to construct a closed convex set $\mathbf{K}$ to bound $|\boldsymbol{\theta}^\top\hat{\mathbf{f}}|$. Proposition 3.1 introduces the variational inequality for a convex optimization problem.

PROPOSITION 3.1. *Let $\boldsymbol{\theta}^\star$ be an optimal solution of the following convex optimization problem:*

$$\min g(\boldsymbol{\theta}), \ \ s.t.\ \ \boldsymbol{\theta} \in \mathbf{K},$$

where g is continuously differentiable and $\mathbf{K}$ is closed and convex. Then the following variational inequality holds:

$$\nabla g\left(\boldsymbol{\theta}^\star\right)^\top\left(\boldsymbol{\theta} - \boldsymbol{\theta}^\star\right) \geq 0, \quad \forall\boldsymbol{\theta} \in \mathbf{K}.$$

The proof of this proposition can be found in [9].

Given $\lambda_2 < \lambda_{max}$, assume that there is a λ_1, such that $\lambda_{max} \geq \lambda_1 > \lambda_2$ and its corresponding solution $\boldsymbol{\theta}_1$ is known[1]. The reason to introduce λ_1 is that when λ_1 is close to λ_2 and $\boldsymbol{\theta}_1$ is known, $\boldsymbol{\theta}_1$ can be used to construct a tighter convex set that contains $\boldsymbol{\theta}_2$ to bound the value of $|\boldsymbol{\theta}_2^\top\hat{\mathbf{f}}|$.

[1]When $\lambda_1 = \lambda_{max}$, $\boldsymbol{\theta}_1$ is given in Eq. (4).

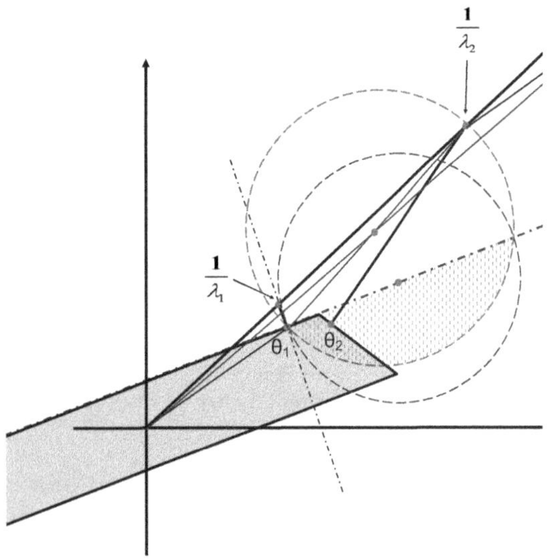

Figure 1: The K in a two-dimensional (2D) space when different t values are used. The red circle corresponds to $t = 0$, and the blue circle corresponds to $t = 1 + \left(\frac{1}{\lambda_2} - \frac{1}{\lambda_1}\right)\frac{\mathbf{a}^\top \mathbf{1}}{\left\|\frac{\mathbf{1}}{\lambda_1} - \boldsymbol{\theta}_1\right\|_2}$.

Let $\boldsymbol{\theta}_1$ and $\boldsymbol{\theta}_2$ be the optimal solutions of the problem defined in Eq. (3) for λ_1 and λ_2, respectively. Assume that $\lambda_1 > \lambda_2$ and that $\boldsymbol{\theta}_1$ is known. The following results can be obtained by applying Proposition 3.1 to the convex problem defined in Eq. (3) for $\boldsymbol{\theta}_1$ and $\boldsymbol{\theta}_2$, respectively:

$$\left(\boldsymbol{\theta}_1 - \frac{\mathbf{1}}{\lambda_1}\right)^\top (\boldsymbol{\theta} - \boldsymbol{\theta}_1) \geq 0, \tag{9}$$

$$\left(\boldsymbol{\theta}_2 - \frac{\mathbf{1}}{\lambda_2}\right)^\top (\boldsymbol{\theta} - \boldsymbol{\theta}_2) \geq 0. \tag{10}$$

By substituting $\boldsymbol{\theta} = \boldsymbol{\theta}_2$ into Eq. (9), and $\boldsymbol{\theta} = \boldsymbol{\theta}_1$ into Eq. (10), the following equations can be obtained:

$$\left(\boldsymbol{\theta}_1 - \frac{\mathbf{1}}{\lambda_1}\right)^\top (\boldsymbol{\theta}_2 - \boldsymbol{\theta}_1) \geq 0, \tag{11}$$

$$\left(\boldsymbol{\theta}_2 - \frac{\mathbf{1}}{\lambda_2}\right)^\top (\boldsymbol{\theta}_2 - \boldsymbol{\theta}_1) \leq 0. \tag{12}$$

In the preceding equations, $\boldsymbol{\theta}_1$, λ_1, and λ_2 are known. Therefore, Eq. (11) defines an n-dimensional halfspace and Eq. (12) defines an n-dimensional hyperball. Because $\boldsymbol{\theta}_2$ needs to satisfy both equations, it must reside in the intersection of the halfspace and the hyperball. Obviously, this region is a closed convex set, and it can be used as $\mathbf{K}$ to bound $|\boldsymbol{\theta}_2^\top \hat{\mathbf{f}}|$. Fig. 1 shows an example of the $\mathbf{K}$ in a two-dimensional space. In the figure, Eq. (11) defines the area below the blue line, Eq. (12) defines the area in the red circle, and $\mathbf{K}$ is indicated by the shaded area.

Besides the n-dimensional hyperball defined in Eq. (12), it is possible to derive a series of hyperballs by combining Eq. (11) and Eq. (12). Assume that $\boldsymbol{\theta}^\star$ is the optimal solution of Eq. (3) and $t \geq 0$. It is easy to verify that $\boldsymbol{\theta}^\star$ is also the optimal solution of the following problem:

$$\min_{\boldsymbol{\theta}} \left\|\boldsymbol{\theta} - \left(t\frac{\mathbf{1}}{\lambda} + (1-t)\,\boldsymbol{\theta}^\star\right)\right\|_2^2, \tag{13}$$
$$s.t. \ \|\hat{\mathbf{f}}_j^\top \boldsymbol{\theta}\| \leq 1, \ j = 1, \ldots, m,$$
$$\sum_{i=1}^n \theta_i y_i = 0, \ \boldsymbol{\theta} \succcurlyeq \mathbf{0}.$$

By applying Proposition 3.1 to the problem defined in Eq. (13) for $\boldsymbol{\theta}_1$, and $\boldsymbol{\theta}_2$, the following results can be obtained:

$$\left(\boldsymbol{\theta}_1 - \left(t_1\frac{\mathbf{1}}{\lambda_1} + (1-t_1)\,\boldsymbol{\theta}_1\right)\right)^\top (\boldsymbol{\theta} - \boldsymbol{\theta}_1) \geq 0, \tag{14}$$

$$\left(\boldsymbol{\theta}_2 - \left(t_2\frac{\mathbf{1}}{\lambda_2} + (1-t_2)\,\boldsymbol{\theta}_2\right)\right)^\top (\boldsymbol{\theta} - \boldsymbol{\theta}_2) \geq 0. \tag{15}$$

Let $t = \frac{t_1}{t_2} \geq 0$. By substituting $\boldsymbol{\theta} = \boldsymbol{\theta}_2$ and $\boldsymbol{\theta} = \boldsymbol{\theta}_1$ into Eq. (14) and Eq. (15), respectively, and then combining the two inequalities, the following equations can be obtained:

$$\mathbf{B}_t = \left\{\boldsymbol{\theta}_2 : (\boldsymbol{\theta}_2 - \mathbf{c})^\top (\boldsymbol{\theta}_2 - \mathbf{c}) \leq l^2\right\}, \tag{16}$$

$$\mathbf{c} = \frac{1}{2}\left(t\boldsymbol{\theta}_1 - t\frac{\mathbf{1}}{\lambda_1} + \frac{\mathbf{1}}{\lambda_2} + \boldsymbol{\theta}_1\right), l = \frac{1}{2}\left\|t\boldsymbol{\theta}_1 - t\frac{\mathbf{1}}{\lambda_1} + \frac{\mathbf{1}}{\lambda_2} - \boldsymbol{\theta}_1\right\|_2.$$

As the value of t changes from 0 to ∞, Eq. (16) generates a series of hyperballs. When $t = 0$, $\mathbf{c} = \frac{1}{2}(\frac{\mathbf{1}}{\lambda_2} + \boldsymbol{\theta}_1)$ and $l = \frac{1}{2}\|\frac{\mathbf{1}}{\lambda_2} - \boldsymbol{\theta}_1\|_2$. This corresponds to the hyperball defined by Eq. (12). The following theorems provide some insights about the properties of the hyperballs generated by Eq. (16):

THEOREM 3.2. *Let* $\mathbf{a} = \frac{\frac{\mathbf{1}}{\lambda_1} - \boldsymbol{\theta}_1}{\left\|\frac{\mathbf{1}}{\lambda_1} - \boldsymbol{\theta}_1\right\|_2}$. *The radius of the hyperball generated by Eq. (16) reaches it minimum when*

$$t = 1 + \left(\frac{1}{\lambda_2} - \frac{1}{\lambda_1}\right)\frac{\mathbf{a}^\top \mathbf{1}}{\left\|\frac{\mathbf{1}}{\lambda_1} - \boldsymbol{\theta}_1\right\|_2}.$$

Let $\hat{\mathbf{c}}$ *be the center of the ball and* l *be the radius. When the minimum is reached, they can be computed as:*

$$\hat{\mathbf{c}} = \frac{1}{2}\left(\frac{1}{\lambda_2} - \frac{1}{\lambda_1}\right)P_{\mathbf{a}}(\mathbf{1}) + \boldsymbol{\theta}_1, \ l = \frac{1}{2}\left(\frac{1}{\lambda_2} - \frac{1}{\lambda_1}\right)\|P_{\mathbf{a}}(\mathbf{1})\|.$$

Here, $P_{\mathbf{u}}(\mathbf{v}) = \mathbf{v} - \frac{\mathbf{v}^\top \mathbf{u}}{\|\mathbf{u}\|_2^2}\mathbf{u}$ *is an operator that projects* $\mathbf{v}$ *to the null-space of* $\mathbf{u}$. *Since* $\|\mathbf{a}\|_2 = 1$, $P_{\mathbf{a}}(\mathbf{1}) = \mathbf{1} - (\mathbf{a}^\top \mathbf{1})\,\mathbf{a}$.

PROOF. The theorem can be proved by minimizing the r defined in Eq. (16). □

THEOREM 3.3. *Let the intersection of the hyperplane* $\left(\boldsymbol{\theta}_1 - \frac{\mathbf{1}}{\lambda_1}\right)^\top (\boldsymbol{\theta}_2 - \boldsymbol{\theta}_1) = 0$ *and the hyperball defined by Eq. (16) be* $\mathbf{P}_t$. *The following equation holds:*

$$\mathbf{P}_{t_1} = \mathbf{P}_{t_2}, \ for \ \forall t_1, t_2 \geq 0, t_1 \neq t_2.$$

PROOF. The theorem can be proved by showing that $\mathbf{P}_t$ is independent of t. □

This theorem shows that the intersection between the hyperball $\mathbf{B}_t$ and the hyperplane $(\boldsymbol{\theta}_1 - \frac{\mathbf{1}}{\lambda_1})^\top (\boldsymbol{\theta}_2 - \boldsymbol{\theta}_1) = 0$ is the same for different t values.

THEOREM 3.4. *Let the intersection of the halfspace* $(\boldsymbol{\theta}_1 - \frac{\mathbf{1}}{\lambda_1})^\top (\boldsymbol{\theta}_2 - \boldsymbol{\theta}_1) \geq 0$ *and the hyperball defined by Eq. (16) be* $\mathbf{Q}_t$. *The following inequality holds:*

$$\mathbf{Q}_{t_1} \subseteq \mathbf{Q}_{t_2}, \ \textit{for} \ \forall t_1, t_2 \geq 0, t_1 \leq t_2.$$

PROOF. The theorem can be proved by showing that $\forall t_1, t_2 \geq 0$ and $t_1 \leq t_2$, if $\boldsymbol{\theta}_2 \in \mathbf{Q}_{t_1}$, then $\boldsymbol{\theta}_2 \in \mathbf{Q}_{t_2}$ also holds. □

This theorem shows that the volume of $\mathbf{Q}_t$ becomes larger when t becomes larger. And $\mathbf{Q}_{t_1} \subseteq \mathbf{Q}_{t_2}$ if $t_1 \leq t_2$.

Fig. 1 shows two circles in a 2D space. The red circle corresponds to the one obtained by setting $t_1 = 0$ in Eq. (16). The blue circle corresponds to the one obtained by setting

$$t_2 = 1 + \left(\frac{1}{\lambda_2} - \frac{1}{\lambda_1}\right) \frac{\mathbf{a}^\top \mathbf{1}}{\left\| \frac{\mathbf{1}}{\lambda_1} - \boldsymbol{\theta}_1 \right\|_2}$$

in Eq. (16). It can be observed that the intersections of the two circles pass the line $(\boldsymbol{\theta}_1 - \frac{\mathbf{1}}{\lambda_1})^\top (\boldsymbol{\theta}_2 - \boldsymbol{\theta}_1) = 0$. This is consistent with Theorem 3.3. Also since $t_1 \leq t_2$, $\mathbf{Q}_{t_1} \subseteq \mathbf{Q}_{t_2}$, which is consistent with Theorem 3.4.

Thereom 3.4 suggests that $\mathbf{Q}_{t=0}$ should be used to construct $\mathbf{K}$, because when $t = 0$, the volume of $\mathbf{Q}_t$ is minimized. The equality $\boldsymbol{\theta}^\top \mathbf{y} = 0$ in Eq. (3) of the dual formulation can also be used to further reduce the volume of $\mathbf{K}$.

$$\mathbf{K} = \left\{ \boldsymbol{\theta}_2 : (\boldsymbol{\theta}_2 - \mathbf{c})^\top (\boldsymbol{\theta}_2 - \mathbf{c}) \leq l^2, \right.$$
$$\left. \left(\boldsymbol{\theta}_1 - \frac{\mathbf{1}}{\lambda_1}\right)^\top (\boldsymbol{\theta}_2 - \boldsymbol{\theta}_1) \geq 0, \ \boldsymbol{\theta}_2^\top \mathbf{y} = 0 \right\}.$$

Here $\mathbf{c} = \frac{1}{2}\left(\frac{\mathbf{1}}{\lambda_2} + \boldsymbol{\theta}_1\right)$ and $l = \frac{1}{2}\left\|\frac{\mathbf{1}}{\lambda_2} - \boldsymbol{\theta}_1\right\|_2$. Let $\boldsymbol{\theta}_2 = \mathbf{c} + \mathbf{r}$, $\mathbf{a} = \frac{\frac{\mathbf{1}}{\lambda_1} - \boldsymbol{\theta}_1}{\left\|\frac{\mathbf{1}}{\lambda_1} - \boldsymbol{\theta}_1\right\|_2}$, and $\mathbf{b} = \frac{1}{2}\left(\frac{\mathbf{1}}{\lambda_2} - \boldsymbol{\theta}_1\right)$. $\mathbf{K}$ can be written as:

$$\mathbf{K} = \left\{ \boldsymbol{\theta}_2 : \boldsymbol{\theta}_2 = \mathbf{c} + \mathbf{r}, \ \|\mathbf{r}\|^2 \leq \|\mathbf{b}\|^2, \right.$$
$$\left. \mathbf{a}^\top (\mathbf{b} + \mathbf{r}) \leq 0, \ (\mathbf{c} + \mathbf{r})^\top \mathbf{y} = 0 \right\}. \quad (17)$$

Theorem 3.3 shows that when t varies, the intersection of the hyperball $\mathbf{B}_t$ and the hyperplane $(\boldsymbol{\theta}_1 - \frac{\mathbf{1}}{\lambda_1})^\top (\boldsymbol{\theta}_2 - \boldsymbol{\theta}_1) = 0$ remains unchanged. This suggests that if the maximum value of $|\boldsymbol{\theta}^\top \hat{\mathbf{f}}|$ is achieved with a $\boldsymbol{\theta}$ that is in this area, no matter which $\mathbf{B}_t$ is used, the maximum value will be the same. This property can be used to simplify the computation. Section 3.2.4 will show that when the maximum value of $|\boldsymbol{\theta}^\top \hat{\mathbf{f}}|$ is achieved with a $\boldsymbol{\theta}$ on the intersection of the hyperball $\mathbf{B}_{t=0}$ and the hyperplane $(\boldsymbol{\theta}_1 - \frac{\mathbf{1}}{\lambda_1})^\top (\boldsymbol{\theta}_2 - \boldsymbol{\theta}_1) = 0$, the computation of the maximum value can be simplified by switching to $\mathbf{B}_t$ with $t = 1 + \left(\frac{1}{\lambda_2} - \frac{1}{\lambda_1}\right) \frac{\mathbf{a}^\top \mathbf{1}}{\left\|\frac{\mathbf{1}}{\lambda_1} - \boldsymbol{\theta}_1\right\|_2}$.

3.2 Computing the Upper Bound

Given the convex set $\mathbf{K}$ defined in Eq. (17), the maximum value of $\left|\boldsymbol{\theta}_2^\top \hat{\mathbf{f}}\right|$ can be computed by solving the problem:

$$\max \left| (\mathbf{c} + \mathbf{r})^\top \hat{\mathbf{f}} \right| \quad (18)$$
$$s.t. \ \ \mathbf{a}^\top (\mathbf{b} + \mathbf{r}) \leq 0 \ , \|\mathbf{r}\|^2 - \|\mathbf{b}\|^2 \leq 0, \ \ (\mathbf{c} + \mathbf{r})^\top \mathbf{y} = 0.$$

In Eq. (18), $\boldsymbol{\theta}_2 = \mathbf{c} + \mathbf{r}$. Also, $\mathbf{r}$ is unknown, and $\hat{\mathbf{f}}$, $\mathbf{a}$, $\mathbf{b}$, $\mathbf{c}$, and $\mathbf{y}$ are known. Since the following equation holds:

$$\max |x| = \max \{-\min(x), \max(x)\}$$
$$= \max \{-\min(x), -\min(-x)\},$$

$\max \left|(\mathbf{c} + \mathbf{r})^\top \hat{\mathbf{f}}\right|$ can be decomposed to two subproblems:

$$m_1 = -\min \boldsymbol{\theta}_2^\top \hat{\mathbf{f}} = -\min \mathbf{r}^\top \hat{\mathbf{f}} - \mathbf{c}^\top \hat{\mathbf{f}} \quad (19)$$
$$s.t. \ \ \mathbf{a}^\top (\mathbf{b} + \mathbf{r}) \leq 0 \ , \|\mathbf{r}\|^2 - \|\mathbf{b}\|^2 \leq 0, \ \ (\mathbf{c} + \mathbf{r})^\top \mathbf{y} = 0,$$

$$m_2 = \max \boldsymbol{\theta}_2^\top \hat{\mathbf{f}} = -\min \mathbf{r}^\top \left(-\hat{\mathbf{f}}\right) + \mathbf{c}^\top \hat{\mathbf{f}} \quad (20)$$
$$s.t. \ \ \mathbf{a}^\top (\mathbf{b} + \mathbf{r}) \leq 0 \ , \|\mathbf{r}\|^2 - \|\mathbf{b}\|^2 \leq 0, \ \ (\mathbf{c} + \mathbf{r})^\top \mathbf{y} = 0,$$

and

$$\max \left|\boldsymbol{\theta}_2^\top \hat{\mathbf{f}}\right| = \max \left|(\mathbf{c} + \mathbf{r})^\top \hat{\mathbf{f}}\right| = \max (m_1, m_2).$$

Eq. (19) and Eq. (20) suggest that the key to bound $\left|\boldsymbol{\theta}_2^\top \hat{\mathbf{f}}\right|$ is to solve the following problem:

$$\min \mathbf{r}^\top \hat{\mathbf{f}} \quad (21)$$
$$s.t. \ \ \mathbf{a}^\top (\mathbf{b} + \mathbf{r}) \leq 0, \|\mathbf{r}\|^2 - \|\mathbf{b}\|^2 \leq 0, (\mathbf{c} + \mathbf{r})^\top \mathbf{y} = 0.$$

Its Lagrangian $L(\mathbf{r}, \alpha, \beta, \rho)$ can be written as:

$$\mathbf{r}^\top \hat{\mathbf{f}} + \alpha \mathbf{a}^\top (\mathbf{b} + \mathbf{r}) + \frac{1}{2}\beta \left(\|\mathbf{r}\|_2^2 - \|\mathbf{b}\|_2^2\right) + \rho (\mathbf{c} + \mathbf{r})^\top \mathbf{y}. \quad (22)$$

And the Karush-Kuhn-Tucker (KKT) conditions are:

$$\begin{aligned}
&\text{(dual feasibility)} & \alpha \geq 0, \beta \geq 0, \quad &(23)\\
&\text{(primal feasibility)} & \|\mathbf{r}\|_2^2 - \|\mathbf{b}\|_2^2 \leq 0, \quad &(24)\\
& & \mathbf{a}^\top (\mathbf{b} + \mathbf{r}) \leq 0, \quad &(25)\\
& & (\mathbf{c} + \mathbf{r})^\top \mathbf{y} = 0, \quad &(26)\\
&\text{(complementary slackness)} & \alpha \mathbf{a}^\top (\mathbf{b} + \mathbf{r}) = 0, \quad &(27)\\
& & \beta \left(\|\mathbf{r}\|_2^2 - \|\mathbf{b}\|_2^2\right) = 0, \quad &(28)\\
&\text{(stationarity)} & \nabla_{\mathbf{r}} L(\mathbf{r}, \alpha, \beta, \rho) = 0. \quad &(29)
\end{aligned}$$

Since $\|\mathbf{r}\|_2^2 \leq \|\mathbf{b}\|_2^2$, the problem specified in Eq. (21) is bounded from below by $-\|\mathbf{b}\|_2 \|\mathbf{f}\|_2$. Thus, $\min_{\mathbf{r}} L(\mathbf{r}, \alpha, \beta, \rho)$ is also bounded from below.

According to whether the inequality constraints are active, the problem can have different minimum values. This requires a discussion of the following four different cases: **(1)**, $\beta = 0$, $\hat{\mathbf{f}} + \alpha \mathbf{a} + \rho \mathbf{y} \neq 0$; **(2)**, $\beta = 0$, $\hat{\mathbf{f}} + \alpha \mathbf{a} + \rho \mathbf{y} = 0$; **(3)**, $\beta > 0$, $\alpha = 0$; **(4)**, $\beta > 0$, $\alpha > 0$. The following sections study these cases in detail.

3.2.1 *The Case* $\beta = 0$, $\hat{\mathbf{f}} + \alpha \mathbf{a} + \rho \mathbf{y} \neq \mathbf{0}$

In this case, set $\mathbf{r} = t(\mathbf{f} + \alpha \mathbf{a} + \rho \mathbf{y})$, and let $t \to -\infty$. Then $L(\mathbf{r}, \alpha, 0, \rho) \to -\infty$. This contradicts the observation that $\min_{\mathbf{r}} L(\mathbf{r}, \alpha, \beta, \rho)$ must be bounded from below. So when $\hat{\mathbf{f}} + \alpha \mathbf{a} + \rho \mathbf{y} \neq \mathbf{0}$, β must be positive.

3.2.2 *The Case* $\beta = 0$, $\hat{\mathbf{f}} + \alpha \mathbf{a} + \rho \mathbf{y} = \mathbf{0}$

Let $P_{\mathbf{u}}(\mathbf{v}) = \mathbf{v} - \frac{\mathbf{v}^\top \mathbf{u}}{\|\mathbf{u}\|_2^2} \mathbf{u}$ be the projection of $\mathbf{v}$ onto the null-space of $\mathbf{u}$. Given $\hat{\mathbf{f}} + \alpha \mathbf{a} + \rho \mathbf{y} = \mathbf{0}$, it is easy to verify that $\alpha P_{\mathbf{y}}(\mathbf{a}) = -P_{\mathbf{y}}(\hat{\mathbf{f}})$. This suggests that $\alpha P_{\mathbf{y}}(\mathbf{a})$ and $P_{\mathbf{y}}\left(\hat{\mathbf{f}}\right)$ are colinear. Also since $\alpha \geq 0$, the following must hold:

$$\frac{P_{\mathbf{y}}(\mathbf{a})^\top P_{\mathbf{y}}\left(\hat{\mathbf{f}}\right)}{\|P_{\mathbf{y}}(\mathbf{a})\|\|P_{\mathbf{y}}\left(\hat{\mathbf{f}}\right)\|} = -1.$$

Given $\alpha P_{\mathbf{y}}(\mathbf{a}) = -P_{\mathbf{y}}\left(\hat{\mathbf{f}}\right)$, α can be computed by:

$$\alpha = -\frac{P_{\mathbf{y}}(\mathbf{a})^\top P_{\mathbf{y}}\left(\hat{\mathbf{f}}\right)}{\|P_{\mathbf{y}}(\mathbf{a})\|_2^2} = \frac{\|P_{\mathbf{y}}\left(\hat{\mathbf{f}}\right)\|_2}{\|P_{\mathbf{y}}(\mathbf{a})\|_2}.$$

Similarly, the value of ρ can be computed by:

$$\rho = -\frac{\hat{\mathbf{f}}^\top \mathbf{y}}{\|\mathbf{y}\|_2^2} - \alpha\frac{\mathbf{a}^\top \mathbf{y}}{\|\mathbf{y}\|_2^2} = -\frac{\hat{\mathbf{f}}^\top \mathbf{y}}{\|\mathbf{y}\|_2^2} - \frac{\|P_{\mathbf{y}}\left(\hat{\mathbf{f}}\right)\|_2}{\|P_{\mathbf{y}}(\mathbf{a})\|_2}\frac{\mathbf{a}^\top \mathbf{y}}{\|\mathbf{y}\|_2^2}$$

By plugging $\beta = 0$ and the obtained value of α and ρ into Eq. (22), $L(\mathbf{r}, \alpha, 0, \rho)$ can be written as:

$$L(\mathbf{r}, \alpha, 0, \rho) = -\frac{\|P_{\mathbf{y}}\left(\hat{\mathbf{f}}\right)\|_2}{\|P_{\mathbf{y}}(\mathbf{a})\|_2}\mathbf{a}^\top \boldsymbol{\theta}_1 - \mathbf{c}^\top \hat{\mathbf{f}} \tag{30}$$

It can be verified that in this case, all KKT conditions specified in Eq. (23)–Eq. (29) are satisfied. Since the problem defined in Eq. (19) is convex and its domain is also convex, Eq. (30) defines the minimum value of the problem. The following theorem summarizes the result when $\beta = 0$.

THEOREM 3.5. *When* $\frac{P_{\mathbf{y}}(\mathbf{a})^\top P_{\mathbf{y}}(\hat{\mathbf{f}})}{\|P_{\mathbf{y}}(\mathbf{a})\|\|P_{\mathbf{y}}(\hat{\mathbf{f}})\|} = -1$, $\mathbf{r}^\top \hat{\mathbf{f}}$ *achieves its minimum value at* $\beta = 0$, *which can be computed as:*

$$\min_{\mathbf{r}} \mathbf{r}^\top \hat{\mathbf{f}} = -\frac{\|P_{\mathbf{y}}\left(\hat{\mathbf{f}}\right)\|_2}{\|P_{\mathbf{y}}(\mathbf{a})\|_2}\mathbf{a}^\top \boldsymbol{\theta}_1 - \mathbf{c}^\top \hat{\mathbf{f}}.$$

And in this case, the value of the dual variables are:

$$\alpha = \frac{\|P_{\mathbf{y}}\left(\hat{\mathbf{f}}\right)\|_2}{\|P_{\mathbf{y}}(\mathbf{a})\|_2},\ \beta = 0,\ \rho = -\frac{\hat{\mathbf{f}}^\top \mathbf{y}}{\|\mathbf{y}\|_2^2} - \frac{\|P_{\mathbf{y}}\left(\hat{\mathbf{f}}\right)\|_2}{\|P_{\mathbf{y}}(\mathbf{a})\|_2}\frac{\mathbf{a}^\top \mathbf{y}}{\|\mathbf{y}\|_2^2}.$$

Since $\alpha = \frac{\|P_{\mathbf{y}}(\hat{\mathbf{f}})\|_2}{\|P_{\mathbf{y}}(\mathbf{a})\|_2} > 0$, the minimum value is achieved on the hyperplane defined by $\mathbf{a}^\top(\mathbf{b} + \mathbf{r}) = 0$.

COROLLARY 3.6. *When* $\frac{|P_{\mathbf{y}}(\mathbf{a})^\top P_{\mathbf{y}}(\hat{\mathbf{f}})|}{\|P_{\mathbf{y}}(\mathbf{a})\|\|P_{\mathbf{y}}(\hat{\mathbf{f}})\|} = 1$, $\mathbf{r}^\top \hat{\mathbf{f}}$ *achieves its maximum value at* $\beta = 0$. *In this case* $-\min \boldsymbol{\theta}^\top \hat{\mathbf{f}}$ *can be computed as:*

$$-\min \boldsymbol{\theta}_2^\top \hat{\mathbf{f}} = -\min \mathbf{r}^\top \hat{\mathbf{f}} - \mathbf{c}^\top \hat{\mathbf{f}} = \frac{\|P_{\mathbf{y}}\left(\hat{\mathbf{f}}\right)\|_2}{\|P_{\mathbf{y}}(\mathbf{a})\|_2}\mathbf{a}^\top \boldsymbol{\theta}_1. \tag{31}$$

$\max \boldsymbol{\theta}_2^\top \hat{\mathbf{f}}$ can be computed by replacing $\hat{\mathbf{f}}$ with $-\hat{\mathbf{f}}$ in Eq. (31).

In the computation, $\|\mathbf{P}_{\mathbf{y}}\left(\hat{\mathbf{f}}\right)\|_2$ are independent to λ_1, λ_2, and $\boldsymbol{\theta}_1$. Therefore, it can be precomputed. $\|\mathbf{P}_{\mathbf{y}}(\mathbf{a})\|_2$ and $\mathbf{a}^\top \boldsymbol{\theta}_1$ are shared by all features. These properties can be used to accelerate the computation.

3.2.3 The Case: $\beta > 0$, $\alpha = 0$

In this case, since $\beta > 0$ and $\alpha = 0$, the minimum value of $\mathbf{r}^\top \hat{\mathbf{f}}$ is achieved on the boundary of the hyperball. In Figure 1, this corresponds to the arc of the red circle under the blue line. Plugging $\alpha = 0$ in Eq. (22) results in:

$$L(\mathbf{r}, 0, \beta, \rho) = \mathbf{r}^\top \hat{\mathbf{f}} + \frac{1}{2}\beta\left(\|\mathbf{r}\|_2^2 - \|\mathbf{b}\|_2^2\right) + \rho(\mathbf{c} + \mathbf{r})^\top \mathbf{y} \tag{32}$$

The dual function $g(0, \beta, \rho)$ can be obtained by setting

$$\nabla_{\mathbf{r}} L(\mathbf{r}, 0, \beta, \rho) = \hat{\mathbf{f}} + \beta\mathbf{r} + \rho\mathbf{y} = 0 \Rightarrow \mathbf{r} = -\frac{1}{\beta}\left(\hat{\mathbf{f}} + \rho\mathbf{y}\right).$$

Since $\beta > 0$, $\|\mathbf{b}\|_2 = \|\mathbf{r}\|_2$. Therefore β can be written as:

$$\beta = \frac{\|\hat{\mathbf{f}} + \rho\mathbf{y}\|_2}{\|\mathbf{b}\|_2}$$

Plugging the obtained $\mathbf{r}$ and β into $L(\mathbf{r}, 0, \beta, \rho)$ leads to:

$$g(\rho) = \min_{\mathbf{r}} L(\mathbf{r}, 0, \beta, \rho) = -\|\mathbf{b}\|_2\|\hat{\mathbf{f}} + \rho\mathbf{y}\|_2 + \rho\mathbf{c}^\top \mathbf{y}. \tag{33}$$

The dual function can be maximized by setting $\frac{\partial g(\rho)}{\partial \rho} = 0$. Also since $\mathbf{b}^\top \mathbf{y} = \mathbf{c}^\top \mathbf{y}$, the following equation holds:

$$-\|\mathbf{b}\|_2\frac{\rho\mathbf{y}^\top \mathbf{y} + \hat{\mathbf{f}}^\top \mathbf{y}}{\|\hat{\mathbf{f}} + \rho\mathbf{y}\|_2} + \mathbf{b}^\top \mathbf{y} = 0. \tag{34}$$

Squaring both sides of the equation and solving the obtained equation leads to the result:

$$\rho = -\frac{\hat{\mathbf{f}}^\top \mathbf{y}}{\mathbf{y}^\top \mathbf{y}} \pm \frac{\|P_{\mathbf{y}}\left(\hat{\mathbf{f}}\right)\|_2}{\|P_{\mathbf{y}}(\mathbf{b})\|_2}\frac{\mathbf{b}^\top \mathbf{y}}{\mathbf{y}^\top \mathbf{y}}.$$

To obtain this equation, the following facts are used:

$$\mathbf{b}^\top \mathbf{b} - \frac{\left(\mathbf{b}^\top \mathbf{y}\right)^2}{\mathbf{y}^\top \mathbf{y}} = \left\|\mathbf{b} - \frac{\mathbf{b}^\top \mathbf{y}}{\mathbf{y}^\top \mathbf{y}}\mathbf{y}\right\|_2^2 = \|P_{\mathbf{y}}(\mathbf{b})\|_2^2,$$

$$\hat{\mathbf{f}}^\top \hat{\mathbf{f}} - \frac{\left(\hat{\mathbf{f}}^\top \mathbf{y}\right)^2}{\mathbf{y}^\top \mathbf{y}} = \left\|\hat{\mathbf{f}} - \frac{\hat{\mathbf{f}}^\top \mathbf{y}}{\mathbf{y}^\top \mathbf{y}}\mathbf{y}\right\|_2^2 = \left\|P_{\mathbf{y}}\left(\hat{\mathbf{f}}\right)\right\|_2^2.$$

Since $(\mathbf{c} + \mathbf{r})^\top \mathbf{y} = 0$ and $\mathbf{r} = -\frac{1}{\beta}\left(\hat{\mathbf{f}} + \rho\mathbf{y}\right)$, it can be verified that $\beta = \frac{\hat{\mathbf{f}}^\top \mathbf{y} + \rho\mathbf{y}^\top \mathbf{y}}{\mathbf{c}^\top \mathbf{y}}$. To ensure that β is positive, the following equation must hold:

$$\rho = -\frac{\hat{\mathbf{f}}^\top \mathbf{y}}{\mathbf{y}^\top \mathbf{y}} + \frac{\|P_{\mathbf{y}}\left(\hat{\mathbf{f}}\right)\|_2}{\|P_{\mathbf{y}}(\mathbf{b})\|_2}\frac{\mathbf{b}^\top \mathbf{y}}{\mathbf{y}^\top \mathbf{y}}. \tag{35}$$

And in this case, β can be written in the form:

$$\beta = \frac{\|\hat{\mathbf{f}} + \rho\mathbf{y}\|_2}{\|\mathbf{b}\|_2} = \frac{\|P_{\mathbf{y}}\left(\hat{\mathbf{f}}\right)\|_2}{\|P_{\mathbf{y}}(\mathbf{b})\|_2} \tag{36}$$

To compute $\max_{\rho} g(\rho)$, first, Eq. (34) can be rewritten as:

$$\|\mathbf{b}\|_2\|\hat{\mathbf{f}} + \rho\mathbf{y}\|_2 = \|\mathbf{b}\|_2^2\frac{\rho\mathbf{y}^\top \mathbf{y} + \hat{\mathbf{f}}^\top \mathbf{y}}{\mathbf{b}^\top \mathbf{y}}. \tag{37}$$

Plugging Eq. (35) and Eq. (37) into Eq. (33) leads to:

$$\begin{aligned}\max_{\rho} g(\rho) &= -\|\mathbf{b}\|_2^2\frac{\rho\mathbf{y}^\top \mathbf{y} + \hat{\mathbf{f}}^\top \mathbf{y}}{\mathbf{b}^\top \mathbf{y}} + \rho\mathbf{b}^\top \mathbf{y} \\ &= -\|P_{\mathbf{y}}(\mathbf{b})\|_2\left\|P_{\mathbf{y}}\left(\hat{\mathbf{f}}\right)\right\|_2 - \frac{\hat{\mathbf{f}}^\top \mathbf{y}\mathbf{b}^\top \mathbf{y}}{\mathbf{y}^\top \mathbf{y}}\end{aligned}$$

Since $\frac{\hat{\mathbf{f}}^\top \mathbf{y}\mathbf{b}^\top \mathbf{y}}{\mathbf{y}^\top \mathbf{y}} = \hat{\mathbf{f}}^\top \mathbf{b} - P_{\mathbf{y}}^\top(\mathbf{b})P_{\mathbf{y}}\left(\hat{\mathbf{f}}\right)$, $\max_{\rho} g(\rho)$ can also be written in the following form:

$$\max_{\rho} g(\rho) = -\|P_{\mathbf{y}}(\mathbf{b})\|_2\left\|P_{\mathbf{y}}\left(\hat{\mathbf{f}}\right)\right\|_2 + P_{\mathbf{y}}(\mathbf{b})^\top P_{\mathbf{y}}\left(\hat{\mathbf{f}}\right) - \hat{\mathbf{f}}^\top \mathbf{b}.$$

It can be verified that in this case, all the KKT conditions specified in Eq. (23)–Eq. (24) and Eq. (26)–Eq.(29) are satisfied. The additional condition for Eq. (25) to be satisfied can be derived as follows. First setting the derivative of Eq. (22) to be zero leads to the following equation:

$$\mathbf{r} = -\frac{1}{\beta}\left(\hat{\mathbf{f}} + \alpha\mathbf{a} + \rho\mathbf{y}\right)$$

Plugging this equation to $\mathbf{a}^\top(\mathbf{b}+\mathbf{r}) \le 0$ results in:

$$\alpha \ge \beta\mathbf{a}^\top\mathbf{b} - \mathbf{a}^\top\mathbf{f} - \rho\mathbf{a}^\top\mathbf{y}.$$

If $\beta\mathbf{a}^\top\mathbf{b} - \mathbf{a}^\top\mathbf{f} - \rho\mathbf{a}^\top\mathbf{y} > 0$, $\alpha > 0$ must hold. According to the complementary slackness condition, $\mathbf{a}^\top(\mathbf{b}+\mathbf{r}) = 0$. Therefore, $\alpha = \beta\mathbf{a}^\top\mathbf{b} - \mathbf{a}^\top\mathbf{f} - \rho\mathbf{a}^\top\mathbf{y} > 0$. However, this contradicts the requirement that $\alpha = 0$. On the other hand, if $\beta\mathbf{a}^\top\mathbf{b} - \mathbf{a}^\top\mathbf{f} - \rho\mathbf{a}^\top\mathbf{y} \le 0$, $\alpha = 0$ must hold. Otherwise, $\alpha > 0$ and $\alpha = \beta\mathbf{a}^\top\mathbf{b} - \mathbf{a}^\top\mathbf{f} - \rho\mathbf{a}^\top\mathbf{y} \le 0$ form a contradiction. Therefore, to satisfy Eq. (25), the condition $\beta\mathbf{a}^\top\mathbf{b} - \mathbf{a}^\top\mathbf{f} - \rho\mathbf{a}^\top\mathbf{y} \le 0$ must be true. Plugging Eq. (35) and Eq. (36) in $\beta\mathbf{a}^\top\mathbf{b} - \mathbf{a}^\top\mathbf{f} - \rho\mathbf{a}^\top\mathbf{y} \le 0$ leads to:

$$\left\|P_{\mathbf{y}}\left(\hat{\mathbf{f}}\right)\right\|_2 P_{\mathbf{y}}(\mathbf{a})^\top \left(\frac{P_{\mathbf{y}}(\mathbf{b})}{\|P_{\mathbf{y}}(\mathbf{b})\|_2} - \frac{P_{\mathbf{y}}\left(\hat{\mathbf{f}}\right)}{\left\|P_{\mathbf{y}}\left(\hat{\mathbf{f}}\right)\right\|_2}\right) \le 0$$

Under this condition, the KKT condition $\mathbf{a}^\top(\mathbf{b}+\mathbf{r}) \ge 0$ must be satisfied. The following theorem summarizes the result for the case $\beta > 0$ and $\alpha = 0$.

THEOREM 3.7. *When* $P_{\mathbf{y}}(\mathbf{a})^\top \left(\frac{P_{\mathbf{y}}(\mathbf{b})}{\|P_{\mathbf{y}}(\mathbf{b})\|_2} - \frac{P_{\mathbf{y}}(\hat{\mathbf{f}})}{\|P_{\mathbf{y}}(\hat{\mathbf{f}})\|_2}\right) \le 0$, $\mathbf{r}^\top\hat{\mathbf{f}}$ *achieves its minimum value at* $\beta > 0$ *and* $\alpha = 0$:

$$\min_{\mathbf{r}} \mathbf{r}^\top\hat{\mathbf{f}} = -\|P_{\mathbf{y}}(\mathbf{b})\|_2 \left\|P_{\mathbf{y}}\left(\hat{\mathbf{f}}\right)\right\|_2 + P_{\mathbf{y}}(\mathbf{b})^\top P_{\mathbf{y}}\left(\hat{\mathbf{f}}\right) - \hat{\mathbf{f}}^\top\mathbf{b} \tag{38}$$

In this case, the values of the dual variables are:

$$\alpha = 0, \beta = \frac{\|P_{\mathbf{y}}\left(\hat{\mathbf{f}}\right)\|_2}{\|P_{\mathbf{y}}(\mathbf{b})\|_2}, \rho = -\frac{\hat{\mathbf{f}}^\top\mathbf{y}}{\mathbf{y}^\top\mathbf{y}} - \frac{\|P_{\mathbf{y}}\left(\hat{\mathbf{f}}\right)\|_2}{\|P_{\mathbf{y}}(\mathbf{b})\|_2}\frac{\mathbf{b}^\top\mathbf{y}}{\mathbf{y}^\top\mathbf{y}}. \tag{39}$$

COROLLARY 3.8. *When* $P_{\mathbf{y}}(\mathbf{a})^\top \left(\frac{P_{\mathbf{y}}(\mathbf{b})}{\|P_{\mathbf{y}}(\mathbf{b})\|_2} - \frac{P_{\mathbf{y}}(\hat{\mathbf{f}})}{\|P_{\mathbf{y}}(\hat{\mathbf{f}})\|_2}\right) \le 0$, $\mathbf{r}^\top\hat{\mathbf{f}}$ *achieves its minimum value at* $\beta > 0$ *and* $\alpha = 0$. *And in this case,* $-\min\boldsymbol{\theta}^\top\hat{\mathbf{f}}$ *can be computed as:*

$$\begin{aligned} -\min\boldsymbol{\theta}_2^\top\hat{\mathbf{f}} &= -\min\mathbf{r}^\top\hat{\mathbf{f}} - \mathbf{c}^\top\hat{\mathbf{f}} \\ &= \|P_{\mathbf{y}}(\mathbf{b})\|_2 \left\|P_{\mathbf{y}}\left(\hat{\mathbf{f}}\right)\right\|_2 - P_{\mathbf{y}}(\mathbf{b})^\top P_{\mathbf{y}}\left(\hat{\mathbf{f}}\right) - \hat{\mathbf{f}}^\top\boldsymbol{\theta}_1 \end{aligned} \tag{40}$$

$\max\boldsymbol{\theta}_2^\top\hat{\mathbf{f}}$ can be computed by replacing $\hat{\mathbf{f}}$ with $-\hat{\mathbf{f}}$ in Eq. (40).

In the computation, $\left\|P_{\mathbf{y}}\left(\hat{\mathbf{f}}\right)\right\|_2$ does not rely on λ_1, λ_2 and $\boldsymbol{\theta}_1$. Therefore, it can be precomputed. $P_{\mathbf{y}}(\mathbf{a})^\top P_{\mathbf{y}}(\mathbf{b})$ and $\|P_{\mathbf{y}}(\mathbf{b})\|_2$, although rely on λ_1, λ_2 or $\boldsymbol{\theta}_1$, are shared by all features and only need to be computed once. These properties can be used to accelerate computation.

3.2.4 The Case: $\beta > 0$, $\alpha > 0$

In this case, the minimum value of $\mathbf{r}^\top\hat{\mathbf{f}}$ is achieved on the intersection of the boundary of the hyperball and the hyperplane. In Figure 1, this corresponds to the two points on the intersection of the red circle and the blue line. It turns out that when $\beta > 0$ and $\alpha > 0$, deriving a closed form solution for the problem specified in Eq. (19) is difficult. Theorem 3.3 suggests that when the minimum value is achieved on the intersection of the hyperball and the hyperplane, one could switch the hyperball used in Eq. (19) to simplify the computation. It turns out that a closed form solution can be obtained by using the hyperball $\mathbf{B}_t$ with $t = 1 + \left(\frac{1}{\lambda_2} - \frac{1}{\lambda_1}\right)\frac{\mathbf{a}^\top\mathbf{1}}{\left\|\frac{\mathbf{1}}{\lambda_1} - \boldsymbol{\theta}_1\right\|_2}$. This corresponds to the hyperball defined in Theorem 3.2. As proved in Theorem 3.3, the intersections of different $\mathbf{B}_t$ and $(\frac{\mathbf{1}}{\lambda_1} - \boldsymbol{\theta}_1)^\top(\boldsymbol{\theta}_2 - \boldsymbol{\theta}_1) = 0$ are identical. Therefore, switching the hyperball $\mathbf{B}_t$ does not change the maximum value of $|\boldsymbol{\theta}^\top\hat{\mathbf{f}}|$.

When $\mathbf{B}_t$ with $t = 1 + \left(\frac{1}{\lambda_2} - \frac{1}{\lambda_1}\right)\frac{\mathbf{a}^\top\mathbf{1}}{\left\|\frac{\mathbf{1}}{\lambda_1} - \boldsymbol{\theta}_1\right\|_2}$ is used and assuming that the minimum is achieved on the intersection of the hyperball and the hyperplane, the problem specified in Eq. (19) can be rewritten as:

$$\begin{aligned} &\arg_{\mathbf{r}} \min \mathbf{r}^\top\hat{\mathbf{f}} \\ s.t.\quad &\mathbf{a}^\top\mathbf{r} = 0,\ \|\mathbf{r}\|_2^2 - l^2 \le 0,\ (\hat{\mathbf{c}} + \mathbf{r})^\top\mathbf{y} = 0. \end{aligned} \tag{41}$$

And its Lagrangian can be written as:

$$L(\mathbf{r}, \alpha, \beta, \rho) = \mathbf{r}^\top\hat{\mathbf{f}} + \alpha\mathbf{a}^\top\mathbf{r} + \frac{1}{2}\beta\left(\|\mathbf{r}\|_2^2 - l^2\right) + \rho(\hat{\mathbf{c}} + \mathbf{r})^\top\mathbf{y}.$$

In the preceding equation, $\mathbf{c}$ is the center of the hyperfall, and l is the radius of the hyperfall. They are defined as:

$$\hat{\mathbf{c}} = \frac{1}{2}\left(\frac{1}{\lambda_2} - \frac{1}{\lambda_1}\right)P_{\mathbf{a}}(\mathbf{1}) + \boldsymbol{\theta}_1,\ l = \frac{1}{2}\left(\frac{1}{\lambda_2} - \frac{1}{\lambda_1}\right)\|P_{\mathbf{a}}(\mathbf{1})\|.$$

The dual function $g(\alpha, \beta, \rho) = \min_{\mathbf{r}} L(\mathbf{r}, \alpha, \beta, \rho)$ can be obtained by setting $\nabla_{\mathbf{r}} L(\mathbf{r}, \alpha, \beta, \rho) = 0$, which leads to:

$$\mathbf{r} = -\frac{1}{\beta}\left(\hat{\mathbf{f}} + \alpha\mathbf{a} + \rho\mathbf{y}\right).$$

Since $\beta \ne 0$, $\|\mathbf{r}\|_2 = l$. Therefore, β can be written as:

$$\beta = \frac{\|\hat{\mathbf{f}} + \alpha\mathbf{a} + \rho\mathbf{y}\|_2}{l}$$

Since $\alpha \ne 0$, $\mathbf{a}^\top\mathbf{r} = 0$. Therefore, α can be written as:

$$\alpha = -\mathbf{a}^\top\left(\hat{\mathbf{f}} + \rho\mathbf{y}\right)$$

Plugging the obtained $\mathbf{r}$, α, and β into $L(\mathbf{r}, \alpha, \beta, \rho)$ leads to:

$$\begin{aligned} g(\rho) &= \min_{\mathbf{r}} L(\mathbf{r}, \alpha, \beta, \rho) \\ &= -l\|\hat{\mathbf{f}} + \alpha\mathbf{a} + \rho\mathbf{y}\|_2 + \rho\hat{\mathbf{c}}^\top\mathbf{y} \\ &= -l\|\hat{\mathbf{f}} - \mathbf{a}^\top\hat{\mathbf{f}}\mathbf{a} + \rho\mathbf{y} - \mathbf{a}^\top\mathbf{y}\mathbf{a}\|_2 + \rho\hat{\mathbf{c}}^\top\mathbf{y} \\ &= -l\|P_{\mathbf{a}}\left(\hat{\mathbf{f}}\right) + \rho P_{\mathbf{a}}(\mathbf{y})\|_2 + \rho\hat{\mathbf{c}}^\top\mathbf{y}. \end{aligned} \tag{42}$$

$g(\rho)$ can be maximized by setting $\frac{\partial g(\rho)}{\partial\rho} = 0$, which leads to:

$$l\frac{\rho P_{\mathbf{a}}(\mathbf{y})^\top P_{\mathbf{a}}(\mathbf{y}) + P_{\mathbf{a}}\left(\hat{\mathbf{f}}\right)^\top P_{\mathbf{a}}(\mathbf{y})}{\|P_{\mathbf{a}}\left(\hat{\mathbf{f}}\right) + \rho P_{\mathbf{a}}(\mathbf{y})\|_2} = \hat{\mathbf{c}}^\top\mathbf{y}. \tag{43}$$

Squaring both sides of the equation and solving the resulting problem yields a closed-form solution for ρ:

$$\rho = -\frac{P_{\mathbf{a}}\left(\hat{\mathbf{f}}\right)^\top P_{\mathbf{a}}(\mathbf{y})}{P_{\mathbf{a}}(\mathbf{y})^\top P_{\mathbf{a}}(\mathbf{y})} \pm \frac{\|P_{P_{\mathbf{a}}(\mathbf{y})}\left(P_{\mathbf{a}}\left(\hat{\mathbf{f}}\right)\right)\|_2}{\|P_{P_{\mathbf{a}}(\mathbf{y})}(P_{\mathbf{a}}(\mathbf{1}))\|_2}\frac{P_{\mathbf{a}}(\mathbf{1})^\top P_{\mathbf{a}}(\mathbf{y})}{P_{\mathbf{a}}(\mathbf{y})^\top P_{\mathbf{a}}(\mathbf{y})}.$$

To obtain this equation, the following facts are used:

$$\begin{aligned} \hat{\mathbf{c}}^\top\mathbf{y} &= \frac{1}{2}\left(\frac{1}{\lambda_2} - \frac{1}{\lambda_1}\right)P_{\mathbf{a}}(\mathbf{y})^\top P_{\mathbf{a}}(\mathbf{1}), \\ l^2 &= \frac{1}{4}\left(\frac{1}{\lambda_2} - \frac{1}{\lambda_1}\right)^2 P_{\mathbf{a}}(\mathbf{1})^\top P_{\mathbf{a}}(\mathbf{1}). \end{aligned}$$

Since $(\hat{\mathbf{c}}+\mathbf{r})^\top \mathbf{y}=0$, $\left(P_{\mathbf{a}}(\hat{\mathbf{c}})+P_{\mathbf{a}}(\mathbf{r})\right)^\top P_{\mathbf{a}}(\mathbf{y})=0$. It can be verified that $P_{\mathbf{a}}(\mathbf{r})=-\frac{1}{\beta}\left(P_{\mathbf{a}}\left(\hat{\mathbf{f}}\right)+\rho P_{\mathbf{a}}(\mathbf{y})\right)$. Therefore, $\beta=\frac{P_{\mathbf{a}}(\hat{\mathbf{f}})^\top P_{\mathbf{a}}(\mathbf{y})+\rho P_{\mathbf{a}}(\mathbf{y})^\top P_{\mathbf{a}}(\mathbf{y})}{P_{\mathbf{a}}(\hat{\mathbf{c}})^\top P_{\mathbf{a}}(\mathbf{y})}$. To ensure that β is positive, the following equation holds:

$$\rho=-\frac{P_{\mathbf{a}}\left(\hat{\mathbf{f}}\right)^\top P_{\mathbf{a}}(\mathbf{y})}{P_{\mathbf{a}}(\mathbf{y})^\top P_{\mathbf{a}}(\mathbf{y})}-\frac{\|P_{P_{\mathbf{a}}(\mathbf{y})}\left(P_{\mathbf{a}}\left(\hat{\mathbf{f}}\right)\right)\|_2}{\|P_{P_{\mathbf{a}}(\mathbf{y})}\left(P_{\mathbf{a}}(\mathbf{1})\right)\|_2}\frac{P_{\mathbf{a}}(\mathbf{1})^\top P_{\mathbf{a}}(\mathbf{y})}{P_{\mathbf{a}}(\mathbf{y})^\top P_{\mathbf{a}}(\mathbf{y})}$$

In this case, β can be written in the form:

$$\beta=2\left(\frac{1}{\lambda_2}-\frac{1}{\lambda_1}\right)^{-1}\frac{\|P_{P_{\mathbf{a}}(\mathbf{y})}\left(P_{\mathbf{a}}\left(\hat{\mathbf{f}}\right)\right)\|_2}{\|P_{P_{\mathbf{a}}(\mathbf{y})}\left(P_{\mathbf{a}}(\mathbf{1})\right)\|_2}$$

To compute $\max_\rho g(\rho)$, first, Eq. (43) can be rewritten as:

$$l\|P_{\mathbf{a}}\left(\hat{\mathbf{f}}\right)+\rho P_{\mathbf{a}}(\mathbf{y})\|_2=l^2\frac{\rho P_{\mathbf{a}}(\mathbf{y})^\top P_{\mathbf{a}}(\mathbf{y})+P_{\mathbf{a}}\left(\hat{\mathbf{f}}\right)^\top P_{\mathbf{a}}(\mathbf{y})}{\hat{\mathbf{c}}^\top\mathbf{y}}.$$

By plugging this equation and ρ into Eq. (42), $\max_\rho g(\rho)$ can be written in the following form:

$$\frac{1}{2}\left(\frac{1}{\lambda_2}-\frac{1}{\lambda_1}\right)\left(-\left\|P_{P_{\mathbf{a}}(\mathbf{y})}\left(P_{\mathbf{a}}\left(\hat{\mathbf{f}}\right)\right)\right\|_2\left\|P_{P_{\mathbf{a}}(\mathbf{y})}\left(P_{\mathbf{a}}(\mathbf{1})\right)\right\|_2 -\frac{P_{\mathbf{a}}^\top\left(\hat{\mathbf{f}}\right)^\top P_{\mathbf{a}}(\mathbf{y})P_{\mathbf{a}}(\mathbf{1})^\top P_{\mathbf{a}}(\mathbf{y})}{P_{\mathbf{a}}(\mathbf{y})^\top P_{\mathbf{a}}(\mathbf{y})}\right).$$

Since $P_{\mathbf{a}}(\mathbf{1})^\top P_{\mathbf{a}}(\mathbf{f})-\frac{P_{\mathbf{a}}\left(\hat{\mathbf{f}}\right)^\top P_{\mathbf{a}}(\mathbf{y})P_{\mathbf{a}}(\mathbf{1})^\top P_{\mathbf{a}}(\mathbf{y})}{P_{\mathbf{a}}(\mathbf{y})^\top P_{\mathbf{a}}(\mathbf{y})}$
$$=P_{P_{\mathbf{a}}(\mathbf{y})}\left(P_{\mathbf{a}}(\mathbf{1})\right)^\top P_{P_{\mathbf{a}}(\mathbf{y})}\left(P_{\mathbf{a}}\left(\hat{\mathbf{f}}\right)\right).$$

$\max_\rho g(\rho)$ can also be written in the form:

$$\frac{1}{2}\left(\frac{1}{\lambda_2}-\frac{1}{\lambda_1}\right)\left(-\left\|P_{P_{\mathbf{a}}(\mathbf{y})}\left(P_{\mathbf{a}}\left(\hat{\mathbf{f}}\right)\right)\right\|_2\left\|P_{P_{\mathbf{a}}(\mathbf{y})}\left(P_{\mathbf{a}}(\mathbf{1})\right)\right\|_2 +P_{P_{\mathbf{a}}(\mathbf{y})}\left(P_{\mathbf{a}}(\mathbf{1})\right)^\top P_{P_{\mathbf{a}}(\mathbf{y})}\left(P_{\mathbf{a}}\left(\hat{\mathbf{f}}\right)\right)-P_{\mathbf{a}}(\mathbf{1})^\top P_{\mathbf{a}}(\mathbf{f})\right).$$

Theorem 3.9 summarizes the result when $\beta>0$ and $\alpha>0$.

THEOREM 3.9. *When $\mathbf{r}^\top\hat{\mathbf{f}}$ achieves its minimum value at $\beta>0$ and $\alpha>0$, it can be computed as:*

$$\min_{\mathbf{r}}\mathbf{r}^\top\hat{\mathbf{f}}=$$
$$\frac{1}{2}\left(\frac{1}{\lambda_2}-\frac{1}{\lambda_1}\right)\left(-\left\|P_{P_{\mathbf{a}}(\mathbf{y})}\left(P_{\mathbf{a}}\left(\hat{\mathbf{f}}\right)\right)\right\|_2\left\|P_{P_{\mathbf{a}}(\mathbf{y})}\left(P_{\mathbf{a}}(\mathbf{1})\right)\right\|_2 +P_{P_{\mathbf{a}}(\mathbf{y})}\left(P_{\mathbf{a}}(\mathbf{1})\right)^\top P_{P_{\mathbf{a}}(\mathbf{y})}\left(P_{\mathbf{a}}\left(\hat{\mathbf{f}}\right)\right)-P_{\mathbf{a}}^\top(\mathbf{1})P_{\mathbf{a}}(\mathbf{f})\right).$$

COROLLARY 3.10. *When $\boldsymbol{\theta}^\top\hat{\mathbf{f}}$ achieves its minimum value at $\beta>0$ and $\alpha>0$, it can be computed as:*

$$-\min\boldsymbol{\theta}_2^\top\hat{\mathbf{f}}=-\min\mathbf{r}^\top\hat{\mathbf{f}}-\hat{\mathbf{c}}^\top\hat{\mathbf{f}}= \tag{44}$$
$$\frac{1}{2}\left(\frac{1}{\lambda_2}-\frac{1}{\lambda_1}\right)\left(\left\|P_{P_{\mathbf{a}}(\mathbf{y})}\left(P_{\mathbf{a}}\left(\hat{\mathbf{f}}\right)\right)\right\|_2\left\|P_{P_{\mathbf{a}}(\mathbf{y})}\left(P_{\mathbf{a}}(\mathbf{1})\right)\right\|_2 -P_{P_{\mathbf{a}}(\mathbf{y})}\left(P_{\mathbf{a}}(\mathbf{1})\right)^\top P_{P_{\mathbf{a}}(\mathbf{y})}\left(P_{\mathbf{a}}\left(\hat{\mathbf{f}}\right)\right)\right)-\hat{\mathbf{f}}^\top\boldsymbol{\theta}_1.$$

$\max\boldsymbol{\theta}_2^\top\hat{\mathbf{f}}$ can be computed by replacing $\hat{\mathbf{f}}$ with $-\hat{\mathbf{f}}$ in Eq. (44).

In the computation, $\left\|P_{P_{\mathbf{a}}(\mathbf{y})}\left(P_{\mathbf{a}}(\mathbf{1})\right)\right\|_2$ is shared by all features and needs to be computed only once. This property can be used to accelerate computation.

3.3 The Screening Algorithm

Algorithm 1 shows the procedure of screening features for ℓ_1-regularized ℓ_2-SVM. Given λ_1, λ_2, and $\boldsymbol{\theta}_1$, the algorithm returns a list $\mathbb{L}$, which contains the indices of the features that are potentially active in the optimal solution that corresponds to λ_2. The algorithm first weights all features using $\mathbf{Y}$ in Line 3. It then computes $\max|\hat{\mathbf{f}}^\top\boldsymbol{\theta}|$ for features in Line 4 and Line 5. If the value is larger than 1, it adds the index of the feature to $\mathbb{L}$ in Line 7. The function neg_min($\hat{\mathbf{f}}$) computes $-\min\boldsymbol{\theta}_2^\top\hat{\mathbf{f}}$. Since $P_{\mathbf{u}}(-\mathbf{v})=-P_{\mathbf{u}}(\mathbf{v})$, the intermediate results computed for neg_min($\hat{\mathbf{f}}$) can be used by neg_min($-\hat{\mathbf{f}}$) to accelerate its computation.

The algorithm needs to be implemented carefully to ensure efficiency. First, each step of the computation needs to be decomposed to many small substeps, so that the intermediate results obtained in the preceding substeps can be used by the following substeps to accelerate computation. Second, the substeps need to be organized and ordered properly so that no redundant computation is performed. It turns out the procedure listed in Algorithm 1 is surprisingly fast. First, $\mathbf{y}^\top\mathbf{1}$, $\mathbf{f}^\top\mathbf{1}$, $\mathbf{f}^\top\mathbf{y}$, and $\mathbf{f}^\top\mathbf{f}$ are independent of $\boldsymbol{\theta}_1$, λ_1, and λ_2. Therefore, they can been precomputed before training, and the cost is $O(mn)$. $\boldsymbol{\theta}_1^\top\mathbf{y}$, $\boldsymbol{\theta}_1^\top\mathbf{1}$, and $\boldsymbol{\theta}_1^\top\boldsymbol{\theta}_1$ are shared by all the features. So they can be computed at the begining of screening, and the cost is $O(n)$. Given these intermediate results, most substeps for computing $\max|\hat{\mathbf{f}}^\top\boldsymbol{\theta}|$ can be obtained in $O(1)$. The only expensive substep is to compute $\boldsymbol{\theta}_1^\top\mathbf{f}$, and its cost is $O(mn)$ for m features. However, when a solver fits a ℓ_1-regularized ℓ_2-SVM model, it might have already computed $\hat{\mathbf{f}}^\top\boldsymbol{\theta}_1$ as an intermediate result for all the features. In this case, $\hat{\mathbf{f}}^\top\boldsymbol{\theta}_1$ can be obtained from the solver for screening features at no cost.

In summary, in the worst case of the proposed procedure, the total computational cost for screening a data set that has m features and n samples is $O(mn)$. And if $\hat{\mathbf{f}}^\top\boldsymbol{\theta}_1$, $\mathbf{f}^\top\mathbf{1}$, $\mathbf{f}^\top\mathbf{y}$, and $\mathbf{f}^\top\mathbf{f}$ can be obtained from the intermediate results generated by the ℓ_1-regularized ℓ_2-SVM solver, the total cost can decrease to just $O(m)$.

4. EMPIRICAL STUDY

The proposed screening method was implemented in the C language and compiled as a library that can be conveniently accessed in a high-level programming language, such as the Python or SAS®. This section evaluates its power for accelerating model selection for ℓ_1-regularized ℓ_2-SVM. Experiments are performed on a Windows Server 2008 R2 with two Intel Xeon® L5530 CPUs and 72GB memory.

Input: $\mathbf{X} \in \mathbb{R}^{n \times m}$, $\mathbf{y} \in \mathbb{R}^n$, λ_1, λ_2, $\boldsymbol{\theta}_1 \in \mathbb{R}^n$.
Output: $\mathbb{L}$, the retained feature list.

$\mathbb{L} = \emptyset$, $i = 1$, $\mathbf{Y} = diag(\mathbf{y})$;
for $i \le m$ **do**
  $\hat{\mathbf{f}} = \mathbf{Y}\mathbf{f}_i$;
  m_1=neg_min($\hat{\mathbf{f}}$), m_2=neg_min($-\hat{\mathbf{f}}$);
  $m = \max\{m_1, m_2\}$;
  if $m \ge 1$ **then**
    $\mathbb{L} = \mathbb{L} \cup \{i\}$;
  end
  $i = i + 1$;
end
return $\mathbb{L}$;

Function neg_min($\hat{\mathbf{f}}$)
  if $\frac{P_{\mathbf{y}}(\mathbf{a})^\top P_{\mathbf{y}}(\hat{\mathbf{f}})}{\|P_{\mathbf{y}}(\mathbf{a})\| \|P_{\mathbf{y}}(\hat{\mathbf{f}})\|} = -1$ **then**
    compute m using Eq. (31);
    return m;
  end
  if $P_{\mathbf{y}}(\mathbf{a})^\top \left(\frac{P_{\mathbf{y}}(\mathbf{b})}{\|P_{\mathbf{y}}(\mathbf{b})\|_2} - \frac{P_{\mathbf{y}}(\hat{\mathbf{f}})}{\|P_{\mathbf{y}}(\hat{\mathbf{f}})\|_2} \right) \le 0$ **then**
    compute m using Eq. (40);
    return m;
  end
  compute m using Eq. (44);
  return m;
end

Algorithm 1: Screening for ℓ_1-regularized ℓ_2-SVM.

4.1 Experiment Setup

Five benchmark data sets are used in the experiment. One is a microarray data set: gli_85. Three are text data sets: rcv1.binary(rcv1b), real-sim, and news20.binary (news20b). And one is a educational data mining data set: kdd2010 bridge-to-algebra (kddb). The gli_85 data set is downloaded from Gene Expression Omnibus,[2] and the other four data sets are downloaded from the LIBSVM data repository.[3] According to the feature-to-sample ratio (m/n), the five data sets fall into three groups: (1) the $m \gg n$ group, including the gli_85 and news20b data sets; (2) the $m \approx n$ group, including the rcv1b and kddb data sets; and (3) the $m \ll n$ group, including the real-sim data set. Table 1 shows detailed information about the five benchmark data sets.

Table 1: Summary of the benchmark data sets

Data Set	sample (n)	feature (m)	m/n
gli_85	85	22283	262.15
rcv1b	20242	47236	2.33
real-sim	72309	20958	0.29
news20b	19996	1355191	67.77
kddb	19264097	29890095	1.55

A solver based on the coordinate gradient descent (cgd) algorithm [13] is implemented in the C language for training the ℓ_1-regularized ℓ_2-SVM model. This solver improves the one that is implemented in the liblinear package [6]. In liblinear, the bias term b is also penalized by the ℓ_1 regularizer and is inactive in most cases. In contrast, the improved one solves the problem specified in Eq. (1) exactly. Therefore, the bias term is not penalized and is alway active. Since $-\hat{\mathbf{f}}^\top \boldsymbol{\theta}_1$ is the gradient on a coordinate, $\hat{\mathbf{f}}^\top \boldsymbol{\theta}_1$ is computed in the solver as an intermediate result. Therefore, in screening, $\hat{\mathbf{f}}^\top \boldsymbol{\theta}_1$ values can be obtained from the solver at no cost.

For each given benchmark data set, the cgd solver is used to fit the ℓ_1-regularized ℓ_2-SVM model along a sequence of 20 λ values: $\{\lambda_k = \frac{1}{k}\lambda_{max} - \epsilon, k = 1, \ldots, 20, \epsilon = 10^{-8}\}$. When $\lambda = \lambda_{max} - \epsilon$, only one feature is active. Denote n_+ and n_- as the number of positive and negative samples, respectively. And let $\mathbf{m} = \sum_{i=1}^n \left(y_i - \frac{n_+ - n_-}{n} \right) \mathbf{x}_i$. This feature corresponds to the largest element in $\mathbf{m}$.

For each given benchmark data set, the cgd solver runs in seven different configurations: (1) In **org**, the solver runs without any accelerating technique. (2) In **warm**, the solver runs with warm-start. In the kth iteration, the $\mathbf{w}_{k-1}$ obtained in the $(k-1)$th iteration is used as the initial $\mathbf{w}_k$ for fitting the model. When λ_k and λ_{k-1} are close, warm-start can effectively speed up training by reducing the number of iterations for the solver to converge. (3) In **shr**, the solver runs with the shrinking strategy. During each iteration of the cgd solver run, if a feature's current weight is 0 and its gradient is very small, the feature is set to be inactive [6]. (4) In **warm_shr**, the solver runs with both warm-start and the shrinking strategy. (5) In **scr**, the solver runs with the screening technique. (6) In **warm_scr**, the solver runs with both warm-start and the screening technique. (7) In **scr_shr**, the solver runs with both the shrinking strategy and the screening technique.

Warm-start and screening are designed to speed up model selection, and shrinking is designed to speed up training. These techniques can be combined for further performance improvement. The main purpose of running the ℓ_1-regularized ℓ_2-SVM solver with different configurations is not only to compare different accelerating techniques, but also to provide a sensitivity study for exploring how these techniques can be combined to achieve the best performance.

Both screening and shrinking reduce computational cost by removing inactive features. Their major differences include the following: (1) Shrinking is performed in each iteration of training to reduce the search space of the solver, whereas screening is performed only once before training. (2) Shrinking is a heuristic method for removing inactive features. Sometimes it might also remove active features; when this happens, recovering the true result leads to extra cost. In contrast, the proposed screening technique is safe, because all the removed features are guaranteed to be inactive the optimal solution. (3) The introduced shrinking technique works only for the cgd solver. In contrast, the proposed screening technique can be applied with any ℓ_1-regularized ℓ_2-SVM solver to speed up model selection. Therefore, the proposed screening technique is more general.

[2] www.ncbi.nlm.nih.gov/geo/query/acc.cgi?acc=GSE4412
[3] www.csie.ntu.edu.tw/ cjlin/libsvmtools/datasets/

Table 2: Total run time of the ℓ_1-regularized ℓ_2-SVM solver when different combinations of accelerating techniques are used to speed up model selection.

Tech.	gli_85	rcv1b	real-sim	news20b	kddb
org	328.7	17.92	20.81	943.67	9209.06
warm	376.6	10.30	13.48	682.08	7752.80
shr	2.78	4.49	7.25	62.44	3374.53
warm_shr	3.10	2.31	4.32	32.62	2395.45
scr	0.78	3.35	6.67	25.53	1126.05
warm_scr	**0.74**	**1.78**	**4.30**	**17.84**	**831.87**
scr_shr	1.45	4.00	7.14	48.29	2603.94

Table 3: Total number of iterations for the ℓ_1-regularized ℓ_2-SVM solver to converge when different combinations of accelerating techniques are used.

Tech.	gli_85	rcv1b	real-sim	news20b	kddb
org	15535	1062	568	2579	755
warm	14610	615	**373**	**1898**	628
shr	16046	1737	815	4995	2008
warm_shr	14888	713	431	2157	1046
scr	15376	1059	596	2862	843
warm_scr	**14599**	**590**	390	1999	**569**
scr_shr	16150	1695	942	4908	1901

4.2 Results

Table 2 and Table 3 show the results of the total run time and the total number of iterations for the ℓ_1-regularized ℓ_2-SVM solver to converge when different combinations of accelerating techniques are used. The total run time and total number of iterations are obtained by aggregating the time and number of iterations used by the ℓ_1-regularized ℓ_2-SVM solver when it fits models using different regularization parameters. In terms of total running time, screening with warm-start (**warm_scr**) provides the best performance. Compared to **org**, for the $m \gg n$ group, the speed-up ratio is about 445 for the gli_85 data and 53 for the news20b data. For the $m \approx n$ group, the speed-up ratio is about 10 for the rcv1b data and 11 for the kddb data. And for the $m \ll n$ group, the speed-up ratio is about 5 for the real-sim data. The result shows that **warm_scr** is more effective when the number of features is larger than the number of samples. A similar trend is observed on **scr** and **scr_shr**. In terms of the total iteration number, the best performance is achieved by **warm** and **warm_scr**. This suggests that warm-start can effectively speed up convergence by providing a good start point for optimization. A similar trend is observed when **shr** is compared to **warm_shr**.

When **org** is compared to **scr**, the result suggests that the proposed screening technique can significantly improve the performance of the ℓ_1-regularized ℓ_2-SVM solver. This justifies that screening can effectively reduce the computational cost of training by removing most inactive features. When **shr** is compared to **scr**, the result suggests that screening performs faster. This is because shrinking is a heuristic method for removing inactive features. Sometimes, it might remove active features during training. When this happens, violations can be detected by using the KKT conditions for the optimal solution. However, recovering the optimal solution leads to extra cost. This is supported by the observation that with **shr** the solver usually takes more iterations to converge than with **org** and **src**. When **warm** is compared to **scr** and **shr**, the results suggest that removing inactive features for training is more effective than providing a good starting point for optimization.

The results presented in Table 2 and Table 3 suggest that the performance of screening and shrinking can be further improved by combining them with warm-start. This is because warm-start can effectively speed up convergence by providing a good starting point for optimization. However, combining screening with shrinking does not improve the performance of screening because that screening has already removed many inactive features before training is performed. When shrinking is used in training, its benefit for removing inactive features becomes insubstantial and is overwhelmed by the cost of recovering the optimal solution when it accidentally removes active features.

Figure 2 shows detailed information about how different combinations of accelerating techniques perform on the news20b data set when λ decreases from λ_{max} to $\frac{1}{20}\lambda_{max}$. The result shows that screening with warm-start is effective for accelerating and its performance is stable. It also shows that when λ decreases, the proposed screening technique can stably select a small set of features for reducing computational cost. Let k be the number of active features. On the news20b data set, when λ decreases from λ_{max} to $\frac{1}{20}\lambda_{max}$, the proposed screening technique retains about $k+430$ features for training the ℓ_1-regularized ℓ_2-SVM model. This number is much smaller than the dimensionality of the news20b data set, which is about 1.3 million. Similar trends are also observed on other data sets and are not presented in the paper because of the space limit.

Table 4: Comparison of screening to training time

Tech.	gli_85	rcv1b	real-sim	news20b	kddb
			scr		
scr	0.03	0.06	0.04	1.91	41.65
tr	0.75	3.29	6.63	23.63	1084.40
ratio	0.04	0.02	0.01	0.08	0.04
			warm_scr		
scr	0.03	0.07	0.04	1.91	41.71
tr	0.70	1.72	4.26	15.93	790.15
ratio	0.05	0.04	0.01	0.12	0.05

Table 4 compares the time used by screening to the time used by training. Notice that for training, the solver uses only the features that are selected by screening. Compared to training, the time used by screening is marginal.

The results presented in this section indicate that the proposed screening technqiue is effective for removing inactive features to improve training efficiency. And with warm-start they form the most powerful combination for accelerating model selection for the ℓ_1-regularized ℓ_2-SVM.

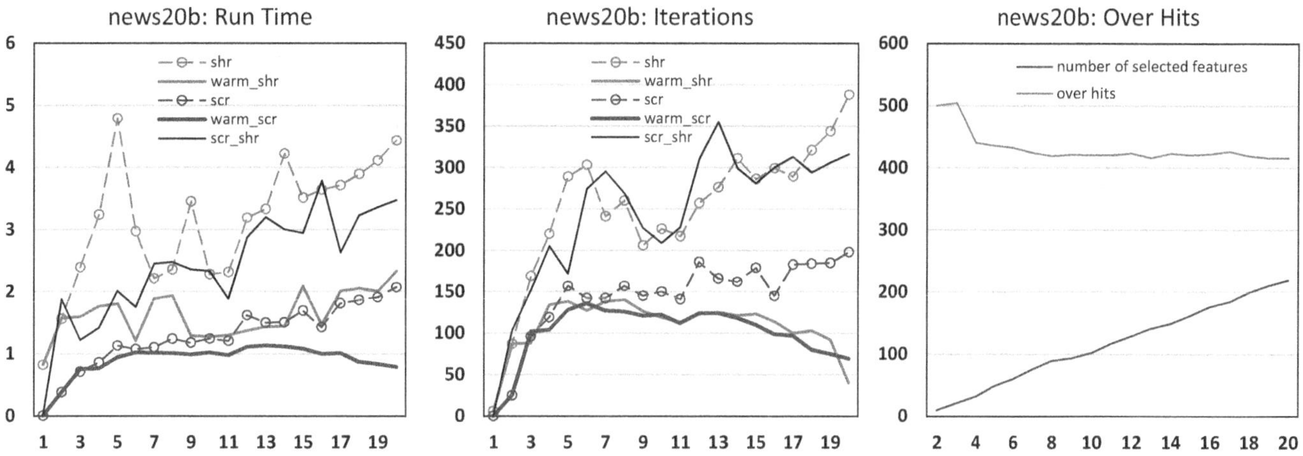

Figure 2: Detailed information about how different combinations of accelerating techniques perform when λ decreases from λ_{max} to $\frac{1}{20}\lambda_{max}$. Results are reported for the news20b data set. "Run time" is the time that is used for training. For scr, warm_scr, and scr_shr, run time includes screening time. "Iterations" is the number of iterations for the solver to converge. "Over hits" is the number of inactive features that are not removed by screening. The results show that the proposed screening technique improves efficiency significantly. And when λ decreases, the number of leftover inactive features is small and stable.

5. CONCLUSION

Screening is an effective technique for improving model selection efficiency by eliminating inactive features. This paper proposes a novel technique to screen features for ℓ_1-regularized ℓ_2-SVM. The key contribution of this paper is the usage of the variational inequality for deriving closed-form criteria to screen features for the ℓ_1-regularized ℓ_2-SVM model in different situations. Empirical study shows that the proposed technique can greatly improve model selection efficiency by stably eliminating a large number of inactive. Our ongoing work will extend the technique to screen features for the ℓ_1-regularized ℓ_1-SVM model.

6. ACKNOWLEDGMENTS

The authors would like to thank Anne Baxter, Russell Albright, and the anonymous reviewers for their valuable suggestions to improve this paper.

7. REFERENCES

[1] M. T. abd Li Wang and I. W. Tsang. Learning sparse svm for feature selection on very high dimensional datasets. In *ICML*, 2010.

[2] J. Bi, M. Embrechts, C. M. Breneman, and M. Song. Dimensionality reduction via sparse support vector machines. *JMLR*, 3:1229–1243, 2003.

[3] S. Boyd and L. Vandenberghe. *Convex Optimization*. Cambridge University Press, 2004.

[4] P. S. Bradley and L. O. Mangasarian. Feature selection via concave minimization and support vector machines. In *ICML*, 1998.

[5] E. Candes and M. Wakin. An introduction to compressive sampling. *IEEE Signal Processing Magazine*, 25:21–30, 2008.

[6] R.-E. Fan, K.-W. Chang, C.-J. Hsieh, X.-R. Wang, and C.-J. Lin. Liblinear: A library for large linear classification. *JMLR*, 9:1871–1874, 2008.

[7] L. Ghaoui, V. Viallon, and T. Rabbani. Safe feature elimination in sparse supervised learning. *Pacific Journal of Optimization*, 8:667–698, 2012.

[8] I. Guyon, J. Weston, S. Barnhill, and V. Vapnik. Gene selection for cancer classification using support vector machines. *Machine Learning*, 46:389–422, 2002.

[9] J. L. Lions and G. Stampacchia. Variational inequalities. *Communications on Pure and Applied Mathematics*, 20, (3):493–519, 1967.

[10] J. Liu, Z. Zhao, J. Wang, and J. Ye. Safe screening with variational inequalities and its application to lasso. In *ICML*, 2014.

[11] R. Tibshirani. Regression shrinkage and selection via the lasso. *Journal of the Royal Statistical Society, Series B*, 58:267–288, 1996.

[12] R. Tibshirani, J. Bien, J. H. Friedman, T. Hastie, N. Simon, J. Taylor, and R. J. Tibshirani. Strong rules for discarding predictors in lasso-type problems. *Journal of the Royal Statistical Society: Series B*, 74:245–266, 2012.

[13] P. Tseng and S. Yun. A coordinate gradient descent method for nonsmooth separable minimization. *Mathematical Programming*, 117:387–423, 2009.

[14] J. Wang and *et al.* Lasso screening rules via dual polytope projection. In *NIPS*, 2013.

[15] J. Weston, A. Elisseff, B. Schoelkopf, and M. Tipping. Use of the zero norm with linear models and kernel methods. *JMLR*, 3:1439–1461, 2003.

[16] G.-X. Yuan and K.-L. Ma. Scalable training of sparse linear svms. In *ICDM*, 2012.

[17] J. X. Zhen, X. Hao, and J. R. Peter. Learning sparse representations of high dimensional data on large scale dictionaries. In *NIPS*, 2011.

[18] J. Zhu, S. Rosset, T. Hastie, and R. Tibshirani. 1-norm support vector machines. In *NIPS*, 2003.

Factorized Sparse Learning Models with Interpretable High Order Feature Interactions

Sanjay Purushotham*
University of Southern California
Los Angeles, CA, USA
spurusho@usc.edu

Martin Renqiang Min†
NEC Labs America
Princeton, NJ, USA
renqiang@nec-labs.com

C.-C. Jay Kuo
University of Southern California
Los Angeles, CA, USA
cckuo@sipi.usc.edu

Rachel Ostroff‡
SomaLogic, Inc.
Boulder, CO, USA
rostroff@somalogic.com

ABSTRACT

Identifying interpretable discriminative high-order feature interactions given limited training data in high dimensions is challenging in both machine learning and data mining. In this paper, we propose a factorization based sparse learning framework termed FHIM for identifying high-order feature interactions in linear and logistic regression models, and study several optimization methods for solving them. Unlike previous sparse learning methods, our model FHIM recovers both the main effects and the interaction terms accurately without imposing tree-structured hierarchical constraints. Furthermore, we show that FHIM has oracle properties when extended to generalized linear regression models with pairwise interactions. Experiments on simulated data show that FHIM outperforms the state-of-the-art sparse learning techniques. Further experiments on our experimentally generated data from patient blood samples using a novel SOMAmer (Slow Off-rate Modified Aptamer) technology show that, FHIM performs blood-based cancer diagnosis and bio-marker discovery for Renal Cell Carcinoma much better than other competing methods, and it identifies interpretable block-wise high-order gene interactions predictive of cancer stages of samples. A literature survey shows that the interactions identified by FHIM play important roles in cancer development.

Categories and Subject Descriptors

J.3 [**Computer Applications**]: Life and Medical Sciences; I.2.6 [**Computing Methodologies**]: Artificial Intelligence—*sparse learning, feature selection*

Keywords

Sparse Learning; High-order interactions; Biomaker Discovery; Blood-based Cancer Diagnosis

*Co-first author

†Co-first author, corresponding author

‡To whom data request should be sent

KDD'14, August 24–27, 2014, New York, NY, USA.

http://dx.doi.org/10.1145/2623330.2623747.

1. INTRODUCTION

Identifying interpretable high-order feature interactions is an important problem in machine learning, data mining, and biomedical informatics, because feature interactions often help reveal some hidden domain knowledge and the structures of problems under consideration. For example, genes and proteins seldom perform their functions independently, so many human diseases are often manifested as the dysfunction of some pathways or functional gene modules, and the disrupted patterns due to diseases are often more obvious at a pathway or module level. Identifying these disrupted gene interactions for different diseases such as cancer will help us understand the underlying mechanisms of the diseases and develop effective drugs to cure them. However, identifying reliable discriminative high-order gene/protein or SNP interactions for accurate disease diagnosis such as early cancer diagnosis directly based on patient blood samples is still a challenging problem, because we often have very limited patient samples but a huge number of complex feature interactions to consider.

In this paper, we propose a sparse learning framework based on weight matrix factorizations and ℓ_1 regularizations for identifying discriminative high-order feature interactions in linear and logistic regression models, and we study several optimization methods for solving them. Experimental results on synthetic and real-world datasets show that our method outperforms the state-of-the-art sparse learning techniques, and it provides 'interpretable' blockwise high-order interactions for disease status prediction. Our proposed sparse learning framework is general, and can be used to identify any discriminative complex system input interactions that are predictive of system outputs given limited high-dimensional training data.

Our contributions are as follows: (1) We propose a method capable of simultaneously identifying both informative single discriminative features and discriminative block-wise high-order interactions in a sparse learning framework, which can be easily extended to handle arbitrarily high-order feature interactions; (2) Our method works on high-dimensional input feature spaces and ill-posed problems with much more features than data points, which is typical for biomedical applications such as biomarker discovery and cancer diagnosis; (3) Our method has interesting theoretical properties for generalized linear regression models; (4) The interactions identified by our method lead to biomedical insight into understanding blood-based cancer diagnosis.

2. RELATED WORK

Variable selection has been a well studied topic in statistics, machine learning, and data mining literature. Generally, variable selection approaches focus on identifying discriminative features using regularization techniques. Most recent methods focus on identifying discriminative features or groups of discriminative features based on Lasso penalty [18], Group Lasso [21], Trace-norm [6], Dirty model [8] and Support Vector Machines (SVMs) [16]. A recent approach [20] heuristically adds some possible high-order interactions into the input feature set in a greedy way based on lasso penalized logistic regression. Some recent approaches [2],[3] enforce strong and/or weak heredity constraints to recover the pairwise interactions in linear regression models. In strong heredity, an interaction term can be included in the model only if the corresponding main terms are also included in the model, while in weak heredity, an interaction term is included when either of the main terms are included in the model. However, recent studies in bioinformatics has shown that feature interactions need not follow heredity constraints for manifestation of the diseases, and thus the above approaches [2],[3] have limited chance of recovering relevant interactions. Kernel methods such as Gaussian Process [4] and Multiple Kernel Learning [10] can be used to model high-order feature interactions, but they can only tell which orders are important. Thus, all these previous approaches either failed to identify specific high-order interactions for prediction or identified sporadic pairwise interactions in a greedy way, which is very unlikely to recover the 'interpretable' blockwise high-order interactions among features in different sub-components (for example: pathways or gene functional modules) of systems. Recently, [14] proposed an efficient way to identify combinatorial interactions among interactive genes in complex diseases by using overlapping group lasso and screening. However, they use prior information such as gene ontology in their approach, which is generally not available or difficult to collect for some machine learning problems. Thus, there is a need to develop new efficient techniques to automatically capture the important 'blockwise' high-order feature interactions in regression models, which is the focus of this paper.

The remainder of the paper is organized as follows: in section 3 we discuss our problem formulation and relevant notations used in the paper. In section 4, we discuss the main idea of our approach, and in section 5 we give a overview of theoretical properties associated with our method. In section 6, we present the optimization methods which we use to solve our optimization problem. In section 7, we discuss our experimental setup and present our results on synthetic and real datasets. Finally, in section 8 we conclude the paper with discussions and future research directions.

3. PROBLEM FORMULATION

Consider a regression setup with a training set of n samples and p features, $\{(\mathbf{X}^{(i)}, y^{(i)})\}$, where $\mathbf{X}^{(i)} \in \mathbb{R}^p$ is the ith instance (column) of the design matrix $\mathbf{X}$ $(p \times n)$, $y^{(i)} \in \mathbb{R}$ is the ith instance of response variable $\mathbf{y}$ $(n \times 1)$, and $i = 1, \dots, n$. To model the response in terms of the predictors, we can set up a linear regression model

$$y^{(i)} = \boldsymbol{\beta}^T \mathbf{X}^{(i)} + \epsilon^{(i)}, \tag{1}$$

or a logistic regression model

$$p(y^{(i)} = 1 | \mathbf{X}^{(i)}) = \frac{1}{1 + \exp(-\boldsymbol{\beta}^T \mathbf{X}^{(i)} - \beta_0)}, \tag{2}$$

where $\boldsymbol{\beta} \in \mathbb{R}^p$ is the weight vector associated with single features (also called main effects), $\boldsymbol{\epsilon} \in \mathbb{R}^n$ is a noise vector, and $\beta_0 \in \mathbb{R}$ is the bias term. In many practical fields such as bioinformatics and medical informatics, the main terms (the terms only involving single features) are not enough to capture complex relationship between the response and the predictors, and thus high-order interactions are necessary. In this paper, we consider regression models with both main effects and high-order interaction terms. Equation 3 shows a linear regression model with pairwise interaction terms.

$$y^{(i)} = \boldsymbol{\beta}^T \mathbf{X}^{(i)} + \mathbf{X}^{(i)T} \mathbf{W} \mathbf{X}^{(i)} + \epsilon^{(i)}, \tag{3}$$

where $\mathbf{W}(p \times p)$ is the weight matrix associated with the pairwise feature interactions. The corresponding loss function (the sum of squared errors) is as follows (we center the data to avoid an additional bias term),

$$L_{sqerr}(\boldsymbol{\beta}, \mathbf{W}) = \frac{1}{2} \sum_{i=1}^{n} ||y^{(i)} - \boldsymbol{\beta}^T \mathbf{X}^{(i)} - \mathbf{X}^{T(i)} \mathbf{W} \mathbf{X}^{(i)}||_2^2. \tag{4}$$

We can similarly write the logistic regression model with pairwise interactions as follows,

$$p(y^{(i)} | \mathbf{X}^{(i)}) = \frac{1}{1 + \exp(-y^{(i)}(\boldsymbol{\beta}^T \mathbf{X}^{(i)} + \mathbf{X}^{(i)T} \mathbf{W} \mathbf{X}^{(i)} + \beta_0))} \tag{5}$$

and the corresponding loss function (the sum of the negative log-likelihood of the training data) is,

$$\begin{aligned} L_{logistic}(\boldsymbol{\beta}, \mathbf{W}, \beta_0) &= \sum_{i=1}^{n} \log(1 + \exp(-y^{(i)}(\boldsymbol{\beta}^T \mathbf{X}^{(i)} \\ &\quad + \mathbf{X}^{(i)T} \mathbf{W} \mathbf{X}^{(i)} + \beta_0)). \end{aligned} \tag{6}$$

4. OUR APPROACH

In this section, we propose an optimization-driven sparse learning framework to identify discriminative single features and groups of high-order interactions among input features for output prediction in the setting of limited training data. When the number of input features is huge (e.g. biomedical applications), it is practically impossible to explicitly consider quadratic or even higher-order interactions among all the input features based on simple lasso penalized linear regression or logistic regression. To solve this problem, we propose to factorize the weight matrix $\mathbf{W}$ associated with high-order interactions between input features to be a sum of K rank-one matrices for pairwise interactions or a sum of low-rank high-order tensors for higher-order interactions.

Each rank-one matrix for pairwise feature interactions is represented by an outer product of two identical vectors, and each m-order ($m > 2$) tensor is represented by the outer product of m identical vectors. Besides minimizing the loss function of linear regression or logistic regression, we penalize the ℓ_1 norm of both the weights associated with single input features and the weights associated with high-order feature interactions. Mathematically, we solve the optimization problem to identify the discriminative single and pairwise interaction features as follows,

$$\begin{aligned}\{\hat{\boldsymbol{\beta}}, \hat{\boldsymbol{a}}_k\} &= \arg\min_{\boldsymbol{a}_k, \boldsymbol{\beta}} L_{sqerr}(\boldsymbol{\beta}, \mathbf{W}) \\ &+ \lambda_\beta \|\boldsymbol{\beta}\|_1 + \sum_{k=1}^{K} \lambda_{a_k} \|\boldsymbol{a}_k\|_1\end{aligned} \tag{7}$$

where $\mathbf{W} = \sum_{k=1}^{K} \boldsymbol{a}_k \odot \boldsymbol{a}_k$, $\odot$ represents the tensor product/outer product, and $\hat{\boldsymbol{\beta}}, \hat{\boldsymbol{a}}_k$ represent the estimated parameters of our model and let Q represent objective function of (7) . For logistic regression, we replace $L_{sqerr}(\boldsymbol{\beta}, \mathbf{W})$ in (7) by $L_{logistic}(\boldsymbol{\beta}, \mathbf{W}, \beta_0)$. We call our model Factorization-based High-order Interaction Model (FHIM).

PROPOSITION 4.1. *The optimization problem in Equation 7 is convex in $\boldsymbol{\beta}$ and non-convex in $\boldsymbol{a}_k$.*

Because of the non-convexity property of our optimization problem, it is difficult to propose optimization algorithms which guarantee convergence to global optima. Here, we adopt a greedy alternating optimization methods to find the local optima for our problem. In the case of pairwise interactions, fixing other weights, we solve each rank-one weight matrix each time. Please note that our symmetric positive definite factorization of $\mathbf{W}$ makes this sub-optimization problem very easy. Moreover, for a particular rank-one weight matrix $\boldsymbol{a}_k \odot \boldsymbol{a}_k$, the nonzero entries of the corresponding vector $\boldsymbol{a}_k$ can be interpreted as the block-wise interaction feature indices of a densely interacting feature group. In the case of higher-order interactions, the optimization procedure is similar to the one for the pairwise interactions except that we have more rounds of alternating optimization. The parameter K of $\mathbf{W}$ is generally unknown in real datasets, thus, we greedily estimate K during the alternating optimization algorithm. In fact, the combination of our factorization formulation and the greedy algorithm is effective for estimating the interaction weight matrix $\mathbf{W}$. $\boldsymbol{\beta}$ is re-estimated when K is greedily added during the alternating optimization as shown in algorithm 1.

Algorithm 1 Greedy Alternating Optimization

Initialize $\boldsymbol{\beta}$ to $\mathbf{0}$, $K = 1$ and $\boldsymbol{a}_K = \mathbf{1}$
While (K==1) || ($\boldsymbol{a}_{K-1} \neq \mathbf{0}$ for $K > 1$)
  Repeat until convergence
    $\beta_j^t = \arg\min_j Q(\beta_1^t, ..., \beta_{j-1}^t, \beta_{j+1}^{t-1}, \beta_p^{t-1}), \boldsymbol{a_k}^{t-1})$
    $a_{k,j}^t = \arg\min_j Q((a_{k,1}^t, ..., a_{k,j-1}^t, a_{k,j+1}^{t-1}, a_{k,p}^{t-1}), \boldsymbol{\beta}^t)$
  End Repeat
  K = K + 1; $\boldsymbol{a}_K = \mathbf{1}$
End While
Remove $\boldsymbol{a}_K$ and $\boldsymbol{a}_{K-1}$ from $\boldsymbol{a}$.

5. THEORETICAL PROPERTIES

In this section, we study the asymptotic behavior of FHIM for the likelihood-based generalized linear regression models. The lemmas and theorems proved here are similar to the ones shown in the paper [3]. However, in their paper the authors make an assumption on the strong heredity (i.e. interaction term coefficients are dependent on the main effects), which is not assumed in our model since we are interested in identifying all high-order interactions irrespective of heredity constraints. Here, we discuss the asymptotic properties w.r.t to the main effects and factorized co-efficients.

Problem Setup: Assume that the data $\mathbf{V}_i = (\mathbf{X}_i, y_i), i = 1, ...n$ are collected independently and Y_i has a density of $f(g(\mathbf{X}_i), y_i)$ conditioned on $\mathbf{X}_i$, where g is a known regression function with main effects and all possible pairwise interactions. Let β_j^* and $a_{k,j}^*$ denote the underlying true parameters satisfying block-wise properties implied by our factorization. Let $Q_n(\boldsymbol{\theta})$ denote the objective with negative log-likelihood and $\boldsymbol{\theta}^* = (\boldsymbol{\beta}^{*T}, \boldsymbol{\alpha}^{*T})^T$, where $\boldsymbol{\alpha}^* = (\boldsymbol{a}_k^*), k = 1, ..., K$. We consider the estimates for FHIM as $\hat{\boldsymbol{\theta}}_n$:

$$\begin{aligned}\hat{\boldsymbol{\theta}}_n &= \arg\min_{\theta} Q_n(\boldsymbol{\theta}) \\ &= \arg\min_{\theta} -\frac{1}{n}\sum_{i=1}^{n}(L(g(\mathbf{X}_i), y_i) + \lambda_\beta|\boldsymbol{\beta}| + \sum_{k} \lambda_{\alpha_k}|\boldsymbol{\alpha_k}|\end{aligned} \tag{8}$$

where $L(g(\mathbf{X}_i), y_i)$ is the loss function of generalized linear regression models with pairwise interactions. In the case of linear regression, $g(\cdot)$ takes the form of Equation (3) without the noise term ϵ and $L(\cdot)$ takes the form of Equation (4). Now, let us define

$$\begin{aligned}\mathcal{A}_1 &= \{j : \beta_j^* \neq 0\} \\ \mathcal{A}_2 &= \{(k, l) : \alpha_{k,l}^* \neq 0\}, \\ \mathcal{A} &= \mathcal{A}_1 \cup \mathcal{A}_2\end{aligned} \tag{9}$$

where $\mathcal{A}_1$ contains the indices of the main terms which correspond to the nonzero true coefficients, and similarly $\mathcal{A}_2$ contains the indices of the factorized interaction terms whose true co-efficients are non-zero. Let us define

$$\begin{aligned}a_n &= \max\{\lambda_j^\beta, \lambda_l^{\alpha_k} : j \in \mathcal{A}_1, (k, l) \in \mathcal{A}_2\} \\ b_n &= \min\{\lambda_j^\beta, \lambda_l^{\alpha_k} : j \in \mathcal{A}_1^c, (k, l) \in \mathcal{A}_2^c\}\end{aligned} \tag{10}$$

Now, we show that our model possesses the oracle properties for (i) $n \to \infty$ with fixed p and (ii) $p_n \to \infty$ as $n \to \infty$ under some regularity conditions. Please refer to Appendix for proofs of the lemmas & theorems of sections 5.1 and 5.2.

5.1 Asymptotic Oracle Properties when $n \to \infty$

The asymptotic properties when sample size increases and the number of predictors is fixed are described in the following lemmas and theorems. FHIM possesses oracle properties [3] under certain regularity conditions (C1)-(C3) shown below. Let Ω denote the parameter space for $\boldsymbol{\theta}$.

(C1) The observations $\mathbf{V}_i : i = 1, ..., n$ are independent and identically distributed with a probability density $f(\mathbf{V}, \boldsymbol{\theta})$, which has a common support. We assume the density f satisfies the following equations:

$$E_{\boldsymbol{\theta}}\Big[\frac{\partial \log f(\mathbf{V}, \boldsymbol{\theta})}{\partial \theta_j}\Big] = 0 \qquad \text{for } j = 1, ..., p(K+1),$$

and

$$\begin{aligned}\mathbf{I}_{jk}(\boldsymbol{\theta}) =& E_{\boldsymbol{\theta}}\Big[\frac{\partial \log f(\mathbf{V}, \boldsymbol{\theta})}{\partial \theta_j}\frac{\partial \log f(\mathbf{V}, \boldsymbol{\theta})}{\partial \theta_k}\Big] \\ =& E_{\boldsymbol{\theta}}\Big[-\frac{\partial^2 \log f(\mathbf{V}, \boldsymbol{\theta})}{\partial \theta_j \partial \theta_k}\Big]\end{aligned}$$

(C2) The Fisher Information Matrix

$$\mathbf{I}(\boldsymbol{\theta}) = E\Big[\Big(\frac{\partial \log f(\mathbf{V},\boldsymbol{\theta})}{\partial \boldsymbol{\theta}}\Big)\Big(\frac{\partial \log f(\mathbf{V},\boldsymbol{\theta})}{\partial \boldsymbol{\theta}}\Big)^T\Big]$$

is finite and positive definite at $\boldsymbol{\theta} = \boldsymbol{\theta}^*$.

(C3) There exists an open set ω of Ω that contains the true parameter point $\boldsymbol{\theta}^*$ such that for almost all $\mathbf{V}$ the density $f(\mathbf{V},\boldsymbol{\theta})$ admits all third derivatives $(\partial^3 f(\mathbf{V},\boldsymbol{\theta}))/(\partial\theta_j \partial\theta_k\partial\theta_l)$ for all $\boldsymbol{\theta} \in \omega$ and any $j,k,l = 1,...,p(K+1)$. Furthermore, there exist functions M_{jkl} such that

$$\left|\frac{\partial^3}{\partial\theta_j\partial\theta_k\partial\theta_l}\log f(\mathbf{V},\boldsymbol{\theta})\right| \le M_{jkl}(\mathbf{V}) \qquad \text{for all } \boldsymbol{\theta} \in \omega$$

where $m_{jkl} = E_{\boldsymbol{\theta}^*}[M_{jkl}(\mathbf{V})] < \infty$. These regularity conditions are the existence of common support and first, second derivatives for $f(\mathbf{V},\boldsymbol{\theta})$; Fisher Information matrix being finite and positive definite; and existence of bounded third derivative for $f(\mathbf{V},\boldsymbol{\theta})$. These regularity conditions guarantee asymptotic normality of the ordinary maximum likelihood estimates [11].

LEMMA 5.1. *Assume $a_n = o(1)$ as $n \to \infty$. Then under regularity conditions (C1)-(C3), there exists a local minimizer $\hat{\boldsymbol{\theta}}_{\boldsymbol{n}}$ of $Q_n(\boldsymbol{\theta})$ such that $||\hat{\boldsymbol{\theta}}_{\boldsymbol{n}} - \boldsymbol{\theta}^*|| = O_P(n^{-1/2} + a_n)$*

THEOREM 5.2. *Assume $\sqrt{n}b_n \to \infty$ and the minimizer $\hat{\boldsymbol{\theta}}_{\boldsymbol{n}}$ given in lemma 5.1 satisfies $||\hat{\boldsymbol{\theta}}_{\boldsymbol{n}} - \boldsymbol{\theta}^*|| = O_P(n^{-1/2})$. Then under regularity conditions (C1)-(C3), we have*

$$P(\hat{\boldsymbol{\beta}}_{\mathcal{A}_1^C} = 0) \to 1, \qquad P(\hat{\boldsymbol{\alpha}}_{\mathcal{A}_2^C} = 0) \to 1$$

Lemma 5.1 implies that when the tuning parameters associated with the non-zero coefficients of main effects and pairwise interactions tend to 0 at a rate faster than $n^{-1/2}$, then there exists a local minimizer of $Q_n(\boldsymbol{\theta})$, which is $\sqrt{n}$–consistent (the sampling error is $O_p(n^{-1/2})$). Theorem 5.2 shows that our model removes noise consistently with high probability ($\to 1$). If $\sqrt{n}a_n \to 0$ and $\sqrt{n}b_n \to \infty$, then lemma 5.1 and theorem 5.2 imply that the $\sqrt{n}$–consistent estimator $\hat{\boldsymbol{\theta}}_n$ satisfies $P(\hat{\boldsymbol{\theta}}_{\mathcal{A}^c} = 0) \to 1$.

THEOREM 5.3. *Assume $\sqrt{n}a_n \to 0$ and $\sqrt{n}b_n \to \infty$. Then under the regularity conditions (C1)-(C3), the component $\hat{\boldsymbol{\theta}}_{\boldsymbol{\mathcal{A}}}$ of the local minimizer $\hat{\boldsymbol{\theta}}_{\boldsymbol{n}}$ (given in lemma 5.1) satisfies*

$$\sqrt{n}(\hat{\boldsymbol{\theta}}_{\mathcal{A}} - \boldsymbol{\theta}^*_{\mathcal{A}}) \to_d N(0, \mathbf{I}^{-1}(\boldsymbol{\theta}^*_{\mathcal{A}})),$$

where $\mathbf{I}(\boldsymbol{\theta}^*_{\mathcal{A}})$ is the Fisher information matrix of $\boldsymbol{\theta}_{\mathcal{A}}$ at $\boldsymbol{\theta}_{\mathcal{A}} = \boldsymbol{\theta}^*_{\mathcal{A}}$ assuming that $\boldsymbol{\theta}^*_{\mathcal{A}^c} = 0$ is known in advance.

Theorem 5.3 shows that our model estimates the non-zero coefficients of the true model with the same asymptotic distribution as if the zero coefficients were known in advance. Based on theorems 5.2 and 5.3, we can say that our model has the oracle property [3], [5], when the tuning parameters satisfy the conditions $\sqrt{n}a_n \to 0$ and $\sqrt{n}b_n \to \infty$. To satisfy these conditions, we have to consider adaptive weights $w_j^\beta, w_l^{\alpha_k}$ [23] for our tuning parameters $\lambda_\beta, \lambda_{\alpha_k}$ (see appendix for more details). Thus, our tuning parameters are:

$$\lambda_j^\beta = \frac{\log n}{n}\lambda_\beta w_j^\beta, \qquad \lambda_l^{\alpha_k} = \frac{\log n}{n}\lambda_{\alpha_k} w_l^{\alpha_k}$$

5.2 Asymptotic Oracle Properties When $p_n \to \infty$ as $n \to \infty$

In this section, we consider the asymptotic behavior of our model when the number of predictors p_n grows to infinity along with the sample size n. If certain regularity conditions (C4)-(C6) (shown below) hold, then we can show that our model possesses the oracle property.

We denote the total number of predictors by p_n. We denote all the quantities that change with sample size by adding n as their subscript. $\mathcal{A}_1, \mathcal{A}_2, \mathcal{A}$ are defined as in section 5 and let $s_n = |\mathcal{A}_n|$. The asymptotic properties of our model when the number of predictors increases along with the sample size are described in the following lemma and theorem. The regularity conditions (C4)-(C6) are given below: Let Ω_n denote the parameter space for $\boldsymbol{\theta}_n$.

(C4) The observations $\mathbf{V}_{ni} : i = 1,...,n$ are independent and identically distributed with a probability density $f_n(\mathbf{V}_n, \boldsymbol{\theta}_n)$, which has a common support. We assume the density f_n satisfies the following equations:

$$E_{\boldsymbol{\theta}_n}\Big[\frac{\partial \log f_n(\mathbf{V}_n,\boldsymbol{\theta}_n)}{\partial\theta_{nj}}\Big] = 0 \qquad \text{for } j = 1,...,p_n,$$

and

$$\begin{aligned}\mathbf{I}_{jk}(\boldsymbol{\theta}_n) =& E_{\boldsymbol{\theta}_n}\Big[\frac{\partial \log f_n(\mathbf{V}_n,\boldsymbol{\theta}_n)}{\partial\theta_{nj}}\frac{\partial \log f_n(\mathbf{V}_n,\boldsymbol{\theta}_n)}{\partial\theta_{nk}}\Big]\\ =& E_{\boldsymbol{\theta}_n}\Big[-\frac{\partial^2 \log f_n(\mathbf{V}_n,\boldsymbol{\theta}_n)}{\partial\theta_{nj}\partial\theta_{nk}}\Big]\end{aligned}$$

(C5) $I_n(\boldsymbol{\theta}_n) = E[(\frac{\partial \log f_n(\mathbf{V}_{n1},\boldsymbol{\theta}_n)}{\partial\boldsymbol{\theta}_n})(\frac{\partial \log f_n(\mathbf{V}_{n1},\boldsymbol{\theta}_n)}{\partial\boldsymbol{\theta}_n})^T]$ satisfies
$0 < C_1 < \lambda_{\min} I_n(\boldsymbol{\theta}_n) \le \lambda_{\max} I_n(\boldsymbol{\theta}_n) < C_2 < \infty$ for all n, where $\lambda_{\min}(.)$ and $\lambda_{\max}(.)$ represent the smallest and largest eigenvalues of a matrix respectively. Moreover, for any $j,k = 1,...,p_n$,

$$E_{\boldsymbol{\theta}_n}\left\{\frac{\partial \log f_n(\mathbf{V}_{n1},\boldsymbol{\theta}_n)}{\partial\theta_{nj}}\frac{\partial \log f_n(\mathbf{V}_{n1},\boldsymbol{\theta}_{n1})}{\partial\theta_{nk}}\right\}^2 < C_3 < \infty,$$

and

$$E_{\boldsymbol{\theta}_n}\left\{\frac{\partial^2 \log f_n(\mathbf{V}_{n1},\boldsymbol{\theta}_n)}{\partial\theta_{nj}\partial\theta_{nk}}\right\} < C_4 < \infty$$

(C6) There exists a large open set $\omega_n \subset \Omega_n \in \mathbb{R}^{p_n}$ which contains the true parameters $\boldsymbol{\theta}_n^*$ such that for almost all $\mathbf{V}_{ni}$ the density admits all third derivatives $\partial^3 f_n(\mathbf{V}_{ni},\boldsymbol{\theta}_n)/\partial\theta_{nj}\partial\theta_{nk}\partial\theta_{nl}$ for all $\boldsymbol{\theta}_n \in \omega_n$. Furthermore, there are functions M_{njkl} such that

$$\left|\frac{\partial^3 f_n(\mathbf{V}_{ni},\boldsymbol{\theta}_n)}{\partial\theta_{nj}\partial\theta_{nk}\partial\theta_{nl}}\right| \le M_{njkl}(\mathbf{V}_{ni})$$

for all $\boldsymbol{\theta}_n \in \omega_n$ and

$$E_{\boldsymbol{\theta}_n} M^2_{njkl}(\mathbf{V}_{ni}) < C_5 < \infty$$

for all p_n, n, and j,k,l.

LEMMA 5.4. *Assume that the density $f_n(\boldsymbol{V_n}, \boldsymbol{\theta}^*_{\boldsymbol{n}})$ satisfies some regularity conditions (C4)-(C6). If $\sqrt{n}a_n \to 0$ and $p_n^5/n \to 0$ as $n \to \infty$, then there exists a local minimizer $\hat{\boldsymbol{\theta}}_{\boldsymbol{n}}$ of $Q_n(\boldsymbol{\theta})$ such that $||\hat{\boldsymbol{\theta}}_{\boldsymbol{n}} - \boldsymbol{\theta}^*_{\boldsymbol{n}}|| = O_P(\sqrt{p_n}(n^{-1/2} + a_n))$*

THEOREM 5.5. *Suppose that the density $f_n(\boldsymbol{V_n}, \boldsymbol{\theta_n^*})$ satisfies some regularity conditions (C4)-(C6). If $\sqrt{np_n}a_n \to 0$, $\sqrt{n/p_n}b_n \to \infty$ and $p_n^5/n \to 0$ as $n \to \infty$, then with probability tending to 1, the $\sqrt{n/p_n}$-consistent local minimizer $\hat{\boldsymbol{\theta}}_{\boldsymbol{n}}$ in Lemma 5.4 satisfies the following:*

- *Sparsity:* $\hat{\boldsymbol{\theta}}_{n\mathcal{A}_n^c} = \boldsymbol{0}$
- *Asymptotic normality:*
$$\sqrt{n}\boldsymbol{A}_n\boldsymbol{I}_n^{\frac{1}{2}}(\hat{\boldsymbol{\theta}}_{n\mathcal{A}_n} - \boldsymbol{\theta}^*_{n\mathcal{A}_n}) \to_d N(\boldsymbol{0}, \boldsymbol{G})$$

where $\boldsymbol{A}_n$ is an arbitrary $m \times s_n$ matrix with finite m such that $\boldsymbol{A}_n\boldsymbol{A}_n^T \to \mathbf{G}$ and $\mathbf{G}$ is a $m \times m$ nonnegative symmetric matrix and $\mathbf{I}_n(\boldsymbol{\theta}^*_{n\mathcal{A}_n})$ is the Fisher information matrix of $\boldsymbol{\theta}_{n\mathcal{A}_n}$ at $\boldsymbol{\theta}_{n\mathcal{A}_n} = \boldsymbol{\theta}^*_{n\mathcal{A}_n}$. Since the dimension of $\hat{\boldsymbol{\theta}}_{n\mathcal{A}_n} \to \infty$ as sample size $n \to \infty$, we could consider arbitrary linear combination $\mathbf{A}_n\hat{\boldsymbol{\theta}}_{n\mathcal{A}_n}$ for the asymptotic normality of our model's estimates. Similar to section 5.1, to satisfy oracle property, we have to consider an adaptive weights $w_{nj}^{\beta}, w_{nl}^{\alpha_k}$ [23] for our tuning parameters $\lambda_\beta, \lambda_{\alpha_k}$ as:

$$\lambda_{nj}^{\beta} = \frac{\log(n)p_n}{n}\lambda_\beta w_{nj}^{\beta}, \qquad \lambda_{n,l}^{\alpha_k} = \frac{\log(n)p_n}{n}\lambda_{\alpha_k} w_{nl}^{\alpha_k}$$

6. OPTIMIZATION

In this section, we outline three optimization methods that we employ to solve our objective function (7), which corresponds to Line 4 and 5 in Algorithm 1. [15] provides a good survey on several optimization approaches for solving ℓ_1-regularized regression problems. In this paper, we use the sub-gradient and co-ordinate wise soft-thresholding based optimization methods since they work well and are easy to implement. We compare these methods in the experimental results in section 7.

6.1 Sub-Gradient Methods

Sub-gradient based strategies treat the non-differentiable objective as a non-smooth optimization problem and use sub-gradients of the objective function at the non-differentiable points. For our model, the optimality conditions w.r.t parameter vectors $\boldsymbol{\beta}$ and $\boldsymbol{a}_k$ can be written out separately based on the objective function (7). Optimality conditions w.r.t $\boldsymbol{a}_k$ is:

$$\begin{cases} \nabla_j \mathcal{L}(\boldsymbol{a}_k) + \lambda_{a_k} sgn(a_{kj}) = 0 & |a_{kj}| > 0 \\ |\nabla_j \mathcal{L}(\boldsymbol{a}_k)| \le \lambda_{a_k} & a_{kj} = 0 \end{cases}$$

where $\mathcal{L}(\boldsymbol{a}_k)$ is the loss function of our linear regression model or logistic regression model in Equation (7) w.r.t $\boldsymbol{a}_k$. Similarly, optimality conditions can be written for $\boldsymbol{\beta}$. The sub-gradient $\nabla_j^s f(\boldsymbol{a}_k)$ for each a_{kj} is given by

$$\nabla_j^s f(\boldsymbol{a}_k) = \begin{cases} \nabla_j \mathcal{L}(\boldsymbol{a}_k) + \lambda_{a_k} sgn(a_{kj}), & |a_{kj}| > 0 \\ \nabla_j \mathcal{L}(\boldsymbol{a}_k) + \lambda_{a_k}, & a_{kj} = 0, \nabla_j \mathcal{L}(\boldsymbol{a}_k) < -\lambda_{a_k} \\ \nabla_j \mathcal{L}(\boldsymbol{a}_k) - \lambda_{a_k}, & a_{kj} = 0, \nabla_j \mathcal{L}(\boldsymbol{a}_k) > \lambda_{a_k} \\ 0, & -\lambda_{a_k} \le \nabla_j \mathcal{L}(\boldsymbol{a}_k) \le \lambda_{a_k} \end{cases}$$

where

$$\nabla_j \mathcal{L}(\boldsymbol{a}_k) = \frac{1}{2}\sum_i(-2\mathbf{X}_j^{(i)}\mathbf{X}^{T(i)}\boldsymbol{a}_k)[y^{(i)} - \boldsymbol{\beta}^T\mathbf{X}^{(i)} - \mathbf{X}^{T(i)}\mathbf{W}\mathbf{X}^{(i)}].$$

for our linear regression model. The negation of the sub-gradient represents the steepest descent direction. Similarly the sub-gradients for $\boldsymbol{\beta}$ ($\nabla_j^s f(\boldsymbol{\beta})$) can be calculated. Differential of the loss function of the linear regression in Equation (7) w.r.t $\boldsymbol{\beta}$ is given by

$$\nabla_j \mathcal{L}(\boldsymbol{\beta}) = \frac{1}{2}\sum_i(-2\mathbf{X}_j^{(i)})[y^{(i)} - \boldsymbol{\beta}^T\mathbf{X}^{(i)} - \mathbf{X}^{T(i)}\mathbf{W}\mathbf{X}^{(i)}]$$

6.1.1 Orthant-Wise Descent (OWD)

Andrew and Gao [1] proposed an effective strategy for solving large-scale ℓ_1-regularized regression problems based on choosing an appropriate steepest descent direction for the objective function and taking a step like a Newton iteration in this direction (with an L-BFGS Hessian approximation [12]). The orthant-wise learning descent method for our model takes the following form

$$\boldsymbol{\beta} \leftarrow \mathcal{P}_{\mathcal{O}}[\boldsymbol{\beta} - \gamma_{\boldsymbol{\beta}}\mathcal{P}_{\mathcal{S}}[H_{\boldsymbol{\beta}}^{-1}\nabla^s f(\boldsymbol{\beta})]]$$
$$\boldsymbol{a_k} \leftarrow \mathcal{P}_{\mathcal{O}}[\boldsymbol{a_k} - \gamma_{a_k}\mathcal{P}_{\mathcal{S}}[H_{a_k}^{-1}\nabla^s f(\boldsymbol{a_k})]]$$

where $\mathcal{P}_{\mathcal{O}}$ and $\mathcal{P}_{\mathcal{S}}$ are two projection operators and $H_{\boldsymbol{\beta}}$ is the positive definite approximation of Hessian of quadratic approximation of objective function $f(\boldsymbol{\beta})$, and $\gamma_{\boldsymbol{\beta}}$ and $\gamma_{\boldsymbol{a}_k}$ are step sizes. $\mathcal{P}_{\mathcal{S}}$ projects the Newton-like direction to guarantee that it is in the descent direction. $\mathcal{P}_{\mathcal{O}}$ projects the step onto the orthant containing $\boldsymbol{\beta}$ or $\boldsymbol{a}_k$ and ensures that line search does not cross points of non-differentiability.

6.1.2 Projected Scaled Sub-Gradient (PSS)

Schmidt [15] proposed optimization methods called Projected Scaled Sub-Gradient methods where the iterations can be written as the projection of a scaling of a sub-gradient of the objective. Please refer to [1] and [15] for more details on OWD and PSS methods.

6.2 Soft-thresholding

Soft-thresholding based co-ordinate descent optimization method can be used to find $\boldsymbol{\beta}, \boldsymbol{a}_k$ updates in the alternating optimization algorithm for our FHIM model. The $\boldsymbol{\beta}$ updates are $\tilde{\beta}_j$ and are given by

$$\tilde{\beta}_j(\lambda_\beta) \leftarrow S\Big(\tilde{\beta}_j(\lambda_\beta) + \sum_{i=1}^{n} X_{ij}(y_i - \sum_{k\neq j} X_{jk}\tilde{\beta}_k - \sum_k X_{ik}\mathbf{W}X_{ki}), \lambda_\beta\Big)$$

where $\mathbf{W} = \sum_k \boldsymbol{a_k} \odot \boldsymbol{a_k}$, and S is the soft-thresholding operator [7]. Similarly, the updates for $\boldsymbol{a_k}$ are $\tilde{a}_{kj}$ and given by

$$\tilde{a}_{kj}(\lambda_{a_k}) \leftarrow S\Big(\tilde{a}_{kj}(\lambda_{a_k}) + \sum_{i=1}^{n} X_{ij}(\sum_k\sum_{r=1}^{p} a_{kr}X_{ir})[y_i - \sum_{k\neq j} X_{jk}\tilde{\beta}_k - \sum_k X_{ik}\mathbf{W}_{\sim j}X_{ki}], \lambda_{a_k}\Big)$$

where $\mathbf{W}_{\sim j}$ is $\mathbf{W}$ with j^{th} column and j^{th} row elements are all zero.

7. EXPERIMENTS

In this section, we use synthetic and real datasets to demonstrate the efficacy of our model (FHIM), and compare its performance with LASSO [18], All-Pairs Lasso [2], Hierarchical LASSO [2], Group Lasso [21], Trace-norm [9], Dirty model [8] and QUIRE [14]. For all these models, we perform 5 runs of 5-fold cross-validation on training dataset (80 %)

to find the optimal parameters and evaluate prediction error on a test dataset (20 %). We search tuning parameters for all methods using grid search and for our model the parameters λ_β and λ_{a_k} are searched in the range of $[0.01, 10]$. We also discuss the support recovery of $\boldsymbol{\beta}$ and $\mathbf{W}$ for our model.

7.1 Datasets

We use synthetic datasets and a real dataset for classification and support recovery experiments. We give detailed description of these datasets below.

7.1.1 *Synthetic Dataset*

We generate the predictors of the design matrix $\mathbf{X}$ using a normal distribution with mean zero and variance one. The weight matrix $\mathbf{W}$ was generated as a sum of K rank one matrices i.e. $\mathbf{W} = \sum_{k=1}^{K} \boldsymbol{a}_k \boldsymbol{a}_k^T$. $\boldsymbol{\beta}, \boldsymbol{a_k}$ were generated as a sparse vector from a normal distribution with mean 0 and variance 1, while noise vector $\boldsymbol{\epsilon}$ is generated from a normal distribution with mean 0 and variance 0.1. Finally, the response vectors $\mathbf{y}$ of the linear and logistic regression models with pairwise interactions were generated using Equations (3) and (5) respectively. We generated several synthetic datasets by varying number of instances (n), number of variables/predictors (p), rank of $\mathbf{W}$ i.e. K and sparsity level of $\boldsymbol{\beta}$, $\boldsymbol{a}_k$. We denote the combined total predictors (that is main effects predictors + predictors for interaction terms) by q, here $q = p(p+1)/2$. Sparsity level (non-zeros) was chosen as $2 \sim 4\%$ for large $p(> 100)$, and $5 \sim 10\%$ for small $p(< 100)$ for both $\boldsymbol{\beta}, \boldsymbol{a}_k$. In this paper, we show results for synthetic data in these settings: Case (1) $n > p$ and $q > n$ (high-dimensional setting w.r.t combined predictors) and, Case (2) $p > n$ (high-dimensional w.r.t original predictors).

7.1.2 *Real Dataset*

To predict cancer progression status directly from blood samples, we generated our own dataset. All samples and clinical information were collected under Health Insurance Portability and Accountability Act compliance from study participants after obtaining written informed consent under clinical research protocols approved by the institutional review boards for each site. Blood was processed within 2 hours of collection according to established standard operating procedures. To predict RCC status, serum samples were collected at a single study site from patients diagnosed with RCC or benign renal mass prior to treatment. Definitive pathology diagnosis of RCC and cancer stage was made after resection. Outcome data was obtained through follow-up from 3 months to 5 years after initial treatment. Our RCC dataset contains 212 RCC samples from benign and 4 different stages of tumor. Expression levels of 1092 proteins based on a high-throughput SOMAmer protein quantification technology are collected. The number of Benign, Stage 1, Stage 2, Stage 3 and Stage 4 tumor samples are 40; 101; 17; 24 and 31 respectively.

7.1.3 *Experimental Design*

We use linear regression models (Equation 3) for all the following experiments and we only use logistic regression models (Equation 5) for synthetic data experiments shown in table 2. We evaluate the performance of our method (FHIM) by the following experiments:

1. Prediction error and support recovery experiments on synthetic datasets
2. Classification experiments using RCC samples: We perform three stage-wise binary classification experiments using RCC samples:
   (a) Case 1: Classification of Benign samples from Stage $1-4$ samples.
   (b) Case 2: Classification of Benign and Stage 1 samples from Stage $2-4$ samples.
   (c) Case 3: Classification of Benign, Stage $1, 2$ samples from Stage $3, 4$ samples.

7.1.4 *Performance on Synthetic dataset*

We evaluate the performance of our model (FHIM) on synthetic dataset by the following experiments: (i) Comparison of optimization methods presented in section 6, (ii) Prediction error on the test data for $q > n$ and $p > n$ (high-dimensional settings), (iii) Support recovery accuracy of $\boldsymbol{\beta}$, $\mathbf{W}$ and (iv) Prediction of rank of $\mathbf{W}$ using greedy approach.

Table 3 shows the prediction error on test data when different optimization methods (discussed in section 6) are used for our model (FHIM). From table 3, we see that both OWD and PSS methods perform nearly similar (OWD is marginally better), and are better than the soft-thresholding method. This is because, in soft-thresholding, co-ordinate updates of variables might not be accurate in high dimensional settings (i.e. the solution is affected by the path taken during updates). We observed that soft-thresholding in general is slower than OWD and PSS methods. For all the other experiments discussed in this paper, we choose OWD as the optimization method for FHIM. Table 1 and Table 2 shows

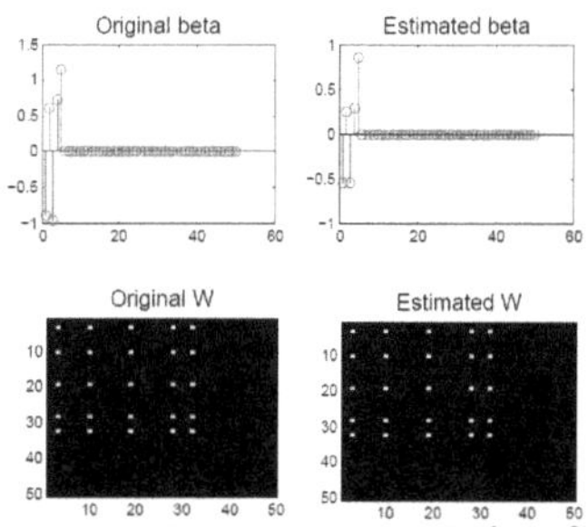

Figure 1: Support Recovery of $\boldsymbol{\beta}$ (90 % sparse) and W (99 % sparse) for synthetic data Case 1: $n > p$ and $q > n$ where $n = 1000, p = 50, q = 1275$.

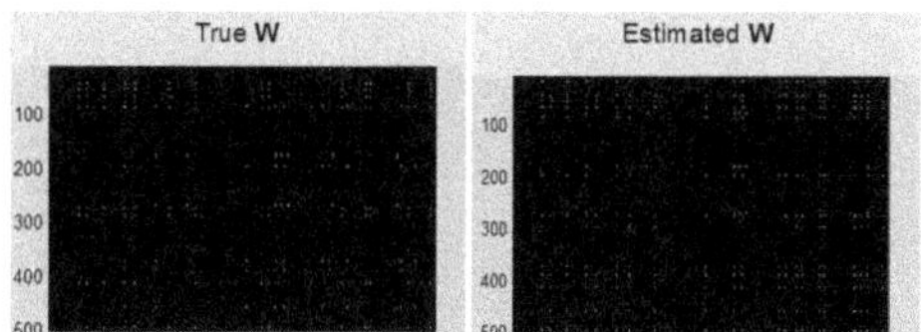

Figure 2: Support Recovery of W (99.5 % sparse) for synthetic data Case 2: $p > n$ where p = 500, n = 100. Online supplementary materials contain high-quality images for this figure.

the performance comparison (in terms of prediction error on test dataset) of FHIM for linear and logistic regression models with respect to the state-of-the-art approaches such as Lasso, Fused Lasso, Trace-Norm and Hierarchical Lasso (HLasso is a general version of SHIM [3]). From tables 1 and 2, we see that FHIM generally outperforms all the state-of-the-art approaches for both linear and logistic pairwise regression models. For $q > n$, we see that test data prediction

	n, p, K	FHIM	Fused Lasso	Lasso	HLasso	Trace norm	Dirty Model
$q > n$	1000, 50, 1	**338.4(14.5)**	425.9(20.7)	474.7(15.3)	354.32 (24.82)	464.4(36.3)	613.5(0.76)
	1000, 50, 5	**343.7(12.9)**	1888.3(121.1)	1922.9(143.9)	889.1 (112.5)	1822.6(99.8)	2453.8(0.76)
	10000, 500, 1	**1093.1(19.5)**	2739.57(155.1)	3896.3(129.5)	-	3887.9(101.1)	4674.7(0.8)
	10000, 500, 5	**1090.76(12.21)**	22720(597.8)	23279.6(231.3)	-	22916.5(321.4)	29214(0.8)
$p > n$	100, 500, 1	**230.49 (50.3)**	1157.2(355.0)	1335.0(159.2)	-	1160.3(299.7)	1651.9(62.6)
	100, 1000, 1	**340.1 (40.02)**	770.9(127.6)	879.1(180.3)	-	699.9(208.7)	808.1(5.1)
	100, 2000, 1	**907.8 (100.1)**	1022.3(406.2)	919.2(132.1)	-	880.42(471.6)	1916.7(63.4)

Table 1: Performance comparison for synthetic data on linear regression model with high-order interactions. Prediction Error (MSE) and Std. deviation of MSE (shown inside brackets) on test data is used to measure the model's performance. For $p >= 500$, Hierarchical Lasso (HLasso) has heavy computational complexity, hence we don't show it's results here.

	n, p, K	FHIM	Fused Lasso	Lasso	HLasso	Trace norm
$q > n$	1000, 50, 1	**0.127 (0.009)**	0.128 (0.017)	0.156 (0.017)	0.136 (0.02)	0.128 (0.016)
	1000, 50, 5	**0.189 (0.03)**	0.227 (0.024)	0.292 (0.042)	0.257 (0.022)	0.503 (0.027)
	10000, 500, 1	**0.135 (0.002)**	0.265 (0.007)	0.161 (0.012)	-	0.225 (0.077)
	10000, 500, 5	**0.390 (0.05)**	0.514 (0.006)	0.507(0.108)	-	0.514 (0.006)
$p > n$	100, 500, 1	**0.325 (0.04)**	0.352 (0.086)	0.4323(0.054)	-	0.40(0.079)
	100, 1000, 1	**0.390 (0.056)**	0.409(0.086)	0.458(0.083)	-	0.438(0.011)

Table 2: Performance comparison for synthetic dataset on logistic regression model with high-order interactions. Misclassification Error on test data is used to measure the model's performance

error for FHIM is consistently lower compared to all other approaches. For $p > n$, FHIM performs slightly better than other approaches, however, the prediction error for all the approaches is high since it's hard to accurately recover the coefficients of main effects and pairwise interactions in very high-dimensional settings.

From figure 1 and table 4, we see that our model performs very well ($F1$ score close to 1) in the support recovery of $\boldsymbol{\beta}$ and $\mathbf{W}$ for the $q > n$ setting. From figure 2 and table 5, we see that our model performs fairly well in the support recovery of $\mathbf{W}$ for $p > n$ setting. We observe that when the tuning parameters are correctly chosen, support recovery of $\mathbf{W}$ works very well when $\mathbf{W}$ is low-rank (see table 4 and 5), and the $F1$ score for the support recovery of $\mathbf{W}$ decreases with increase in rank of $\mathbf{W}$. Table 5 shows that for $q > n$ the greedy strategy of FHIM accurately recovers the rank K of $\mathbf{W}$, while for $p > n$, the greedy strategy might not correctly recover K. This is because the tensor factorization is not unique and slightly correlated variables can enter our model during optimization.

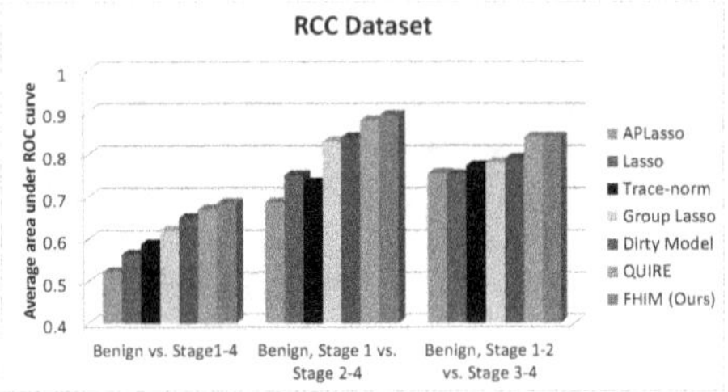

Figure 3: Comparison of the classification performances of different feature selection approaches with our model in identifying the different stages of RCC. We perform five fold cross validation five times and average AUC score is reported.

7.1.5 Classification Performance on RCC

In this section, we report systematic experimental results on classification of samples from different stages of RCC. The predictive performance of the markers and pairwise interactions selected by our model (FHIM) is compared against the markers selected by Lasso, All-Pairs Lasso [2], Group Lasso, Dirty model [8] and QUIRE. We use SLEP [13], MALSAR [22] and QUIRE packages for the implementation of these models. The overall performance of the algorithms are shown in Figure 3. In this figure, we report average AUC score for five runs of 5-fold cross validation experiments for cancer stage prediction in RCC. In 5-fold cross validation experiments, we train our model on the four folds to identify the main effects and pairwise interactions and we use the remaining one fold for testing prediction. The average AUC achieved by features selected with our model are 0.68, 0.89 and 0.84 respectively for the three cases discussed in section 7.1.3. We performed pairwise t-tests for the comparisons of our method vs. the other methods, and all p-values are below 0.0075. From figure 3, it is clear that our model outperforms all the other algorithms that do not use prior feature group information for all the three classification cases of RCC prediction. In addition, our model has similar performance to the state-of-the-art technique - QUIRE [14], which uses Gene Ontology based functional annotation for grouping and clustering of genes to identify high order interactions.

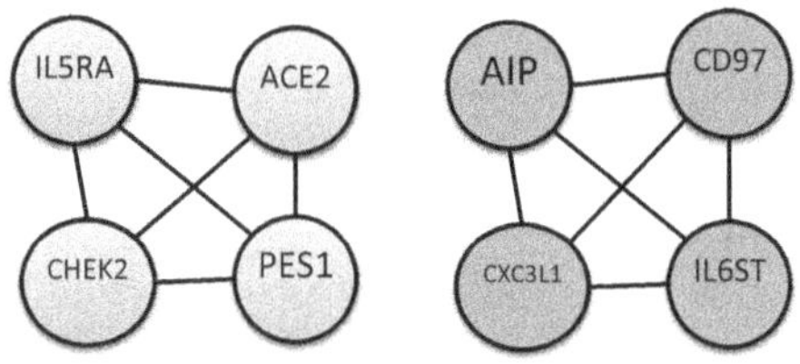

Figure 4: Examples of functional modules for RCC Case 3, induced by markers and interactions discovered by our model and enriched in pathways and functions associated with RCC

7.1.6 Informative interactions discovered by FHIM

An investigation of the pairwise interactions identified by our model on RCC dataset reveals that many of these interactions are indeed relevant to the prediction of cancer. Figure 4 shows some of the interactions associated with higher weighted pairwise co-efficients for Case 3 of RCC classification experiment. The interactions include *CX3CL1- CD97*, *CHEK2-IL5RA* which are known to be related to proteins in blood. *CX3CL1* was recently found to promote breast cancer [17], while *CD97* was found to promote colorectal cancer [19]. We believe these protein interactions might lead to renal cell cancer. Further investigations of the interactions identified by our model might reveal novel protein interactions associated with renal cell cancer and thus leading to testable hypothesis.

7.1.7 Time Complexity

FHIM has $O(np)$ time complexity for algorithm 1. In general, FHIM takes more time than the Lasso approach since we do alternating optimization of $\boldsymbol{\beta}, \boldsymbol{a_k}$. For $q \sim n$ setting with $n = 1000$, $q = 1275$, our OWD learning optimization method on Matlab takes around ~ 1 minute for 5-fold cross-validation, while for $p > n$ with $p = 2000$, $n = 100$, our FHIM model took around 2 hours for 5-fold cross-validation. Our experiments were run on intel i3 dual-core 2.9 GHz CPU with 8 GB RAM.

n, p	OWD	Soft-thres -holding	PSS
100, 500	**230.5**	276.2	239.5
100, 1000	**340.1**	710.5	358.7
100, 2000	**907.8**	1174.1	927.4

Table 3: Comparison of optimization methods for our FHIM model based on test data prediction error

n, p	Sparsity $\boldsymbol{\beta}, \boldsymbol{a}_k$	K	Support recovery $\boldsymbol{\beta}, \boldsymbol{W}$(F1 score)
1000, 50	5, 5	1	1.0, 1.0
1000, 50	5, 5	3	1.0, 0.95
1000, 50	5, 5	5	1.0, 0.82
10000, 500	10, 20	1	0.95, 0.72
10000, 500	10, 20	3	0.80, 0.64
10000, 500	10, 20	5	0.72, 0.55

Table 4: Support recovery of $\boldsymbol{\beta}, \mathbf{W}$

n, p	true K	estimated K	W support recovery F1 score
1000, 50	1	1	1.0
1000, 50	3	3	1.0
1000, 50	5	5	0.8
100, 100	1	2	0.75
100, 500	3	2	0.6
100, 1000	5	4	0.5

Table 5: Recovering K using greedy strategy

8. CONCLUSIONS

In this paper, we proposed a factorization based sparse learning framework called FHIM for identifying high-order feature interactions in linear and logistic regression models, and studied several optimization methods for our model. Empirical experiments on synthetic and real datasets showed that our model outperforms several well-known techniques such as Lasso, Trace-norm, GroupLasso and achieves comparable performance to the current state-of-the-art method - QUIRE, while not assuming any prior knowledge about the data. Our model gives 'interpretable' results for high-order feature interactions on RCC dataset which can be used for biomarker discovery for disease diagnosis.

In the future, we will consider the following directions: (i) We will consider factorization of the weight matrix $\mathbf{W}$ as $\mathbf{W} = \sum_k \boldsymbol{a}_k \boldsymbol{b}_k^T$ and higher-order feature interactions, which is more general, but the optimization problem is non-convex; (ii) We will extend our optimization methods from Single-Task Learning to Multi-Task Learning; (iii) We will consider groupings of features for both Single Task Learning and Multi-Task Learning.

References

[1] G. Andrew and J. Gao. Scalable training of l1-regularized log-linear models. In *Proceedings of the 24th international conference on Machine learning*, pages 33–40. ACM, 2007.

[2] J. Bien, J. Taylor, and R. Tibshirani. A lasso for hierarchical interactions. *The Annals of Statistics*, 41(3):1111–1141, 2013.

[3] N. H. Choi, W. Li, and J. Zhu. Variable selection with the strong heredity constraint and its oracle property. *Journal of the American Statistical Association*, 105(489):354–364, 2010.

[4] D. K. Duvenaud, H. Nickisch, and C. E. Rasmussen. Additive gaussian processes. In *NIPS*, pages 226–234, 2011.

[5] J. Fan and R. Li. Variable selection via nonconcave penalized likelihood and its oracle properties. *Journal of the American Statistical Association*, 96(456):1348–1360, 2001.

[6] R. Foygel, N. Srebro, and R. Salakhutdinov. Matrix reconstruction with the local max norm. *arXiv preprint arXiv:1210.5196*, 2012.

[7] J. Friedman, T. Hastie, H. Höfling, and R. Tibshirani. Pathwise coordinate optimization. *The Annals of Applied Statistics*, 1(2):302–332, 2007.

[8] A. Jalali, P. Ravikumar, and S. Sanghavi. A dirty model for multiple sparse regression. *arXiv preprint arXiv:1106.5826*, 2011.

[9] S. Ji and J. Ye. An accelerated gradient method for trace norm minimization. In *Proceedings of the 26th Annual International Conference on Machine Learning*, pages 457–464. ACM, 2009.

[10] G. R. G. Lanckriet, N. Cristianini, P. Bartlett, L. E. Ghaoui, and M. I. Jordan. Learning the kernel matrix with semidefinite programming. *J. Mach. Learn. Res.*, 5:27–72, Dec. 2004.

[11] E. L. Lehmann and G. Casella. *Theory of point estimation*, volume 31. Springer, 1998.

[12] D. C. Liu and J. Nocedal. On the limited memory bfgs method for large scale optimization. *Mathematical programming*, 45(1-3):503–528, 1989.

[13] J. Liu, S. Ji, and J. Ye. *SLEP: Sparse Learning with Efficient Projections*. Arizona State University, 2009.

[14] R. Min, S. Chowdhury, Y. Qi, A. Stewart, and R. Ostroff. An integrated approach to blood-based cancer diagnosis and biomarker discovery. In *Proceedings of the Pacific Symposium on Biocomputing*, 2014.

[15] M. Schmidt. *Graphical model structure learning with l1-regularization.* PhD thesis, UNIVERSITY OF BRITISH COLUMBIA, 2010.

[16] J. A. Suykens and J. Vandewalle. Least squares support vector machine classifiers. *Neural processing letters*, 9(3):293–300, 1999.

[17] M. Tardaguila, E. Mira, M. A. García-Cabezas, A. M. Feijoo, M. Quintela-Fandino, I. Azcoitia, S. A. Lira, and S. Manes. Cx3cl1 promotes breast cancer via transactivation of the egf pathway. *Cancer research*, 2013.

[18] R. Tibshirani. Regression shrinkage and selection via the lasso. *Journal of the Royal Statistical Society. Series B (Methodological)*, pages 267–288, 1996.

[19] M. Wobus, O. Huber, J. Hamann, and G. Aust. Cd97 overexpression in tumor cells at the invasion front in colorectal cancer (cc) is independently regulated of the canonical wnt pathway. *Molecular carcinogenesis*, 45(11):881–886, 2006.

[20] T. T. Wu, Y. F. Chen, T. Hastie, E. Sobel, and K. Lange. Genome-wide association analysis by lasso penalized logistic regression. *Bioinformatics*, 25(6):714–721, 2009.

[21] M. Yuan and Y. Lin. Model selection and estimation in regression with grouped variables. *Journal of the Royal Statistical Society: Series B (Statistical Methodology)*, 68(1):49–67, 2006.

[22] J. Zhou, J. Chen, and J. Ye. *MALSAR: Multi-tAsk Learning via StructurAl Regularization.* Arizona State University, 2011.

[23] H. Zou. The adaptive lasso and its oracle properties. *Journal of the American statistical association*, 101(476):1418–1429, 2006.

APPENDIX

A. PROOFS FOR SECTION 5.1

PROOF OF LEMMA 5.1:. Let $\eta_n = n^{-1/2} + a_n$ and $\{\boldsymbol{\theta}^* + \eta_n\boldsymbol{\delta} : ||\boldsymbol{\delta}|| \leq d\}$ be the ball around $\boldsymbol{\theta}^*$, where $\boldsymbol{\delta} = (u_1, ..., u_p, v_{11}, ...v_{Kp})^T = (\mathbf{u}^T, \mathbf{v}^T)^T$. Define

$$D_n(\boldsymbol{\delta}) \equiv Q_n(\boldsymbol{\theta}^* + \eta_n\boldsymbol{\delta}) - Q_n(\boldsymbol{\theta}^*)$$

Where $Q_n(\boldsymbol{\theta}^*)$ is defined in equation (8). For $\boldsymbol{\delta}$ that satisfies $||\boldsymbol{\delta}|| = d$, we have

$$\begin{aligned}
D_n(\boldsymbol{\delta}) =& - L_n(\boldsymbol{\theta}^* + \eta_n\boldsymbol{\delta}) + L_n(\boldsymbol{\theta}^*)\\
&+ n\sum_j \lambda_j^\beta(|\beta_j^* + \eta_n u_j| - |\beta_j^*|)\\
&+ n\sum_{k,l} \lambda_l^{\alpha_k}(|\alpha_{k,l}^* + \eta_n v_{kl})| - |\alpha_{k,l}^*|\\
\geq& - L_n(\boldsymbol{\theta}^* + \eta_n\boldsymbol{\delta}) + L_n(\boldsymbol{\theta}^*)\\
&+ n\sum_{j\in\mathcal{A}_1} \lambda_j^\beta(|\beta_j^* + \eta_n u_j| - |\beta_j^*|)\\
&+ n\sum_{(k,l)\in\mathcal{A}_2} \lambda_l^{\alpha_k}(|\alpha_{k,l}^* + \eta_n v_{kl})| - |\alpha_{k,l}^*|\\
\geq& - L_n(\boldsymbol{\theta}^* + \eta_n\boldsymbol{\delta}) + L_n(\boldsymbol{\theta}^*)\\
&- n\eta_n\sum_{j\in\mathcal{A}_1} \lambda_j^\beta|u_j| - n\eta_n\sum_{(k,l)\in\mathcal{A}_2} \lambda_l^{\alpha_k}|v_{kl}|\\
\geq& - L_n(\boldsymbol{\theta}^* + \eta_n\boldsymbol{\delta}) + L_n(\boldsymbol{\theta}^*)\\
&- n\eta_n^2(\sum_{j\in\mathcal{A}_1}|u_j| + \sum_{(k,l)\in\mathcal{A}_2}|v_{kl}|)\\
\geq& - L_n(\boldsymbol{\theta}^* + \eta_n\boldsymbol{\delta}) + L_n(\boldsymbol{\theta}^*) - n\eta_n^2(|\mathcal{A}_1| + |\mathcal{A}_2|)d\\
=& - [\nabla L_n(\boldsymbol{\theta}^*)]^T(\eta_n\boldsymbol{\delta}) - \frac{1}{2}(\eta_n\boldsymbol{\delta})^T[\nabla^2 L_n(\boldsymbol{\theta}^*)]\\
&(\eta_n\boldsymbol{\delta})(1 + o_p(1)) - n\eta_n^2(|\mathcal{A}_1| + |\mathcal{A}_2|)d
\end{aligned}$$

We used Taylor's expansion in above step. We split the above into three parts and we get:

$$\begin{aligned}
K_1 =& - \eta_n[\nabla L_n(\boldsymbol{\theta}^*)]^T\boldsymbol{\delta}\\
=& - \sqrt{n}\eta_n(\frac{1}{\sqrt{n}}\nabla L_n(\boldsymbol{\theta}^*))^T\boldsymbol{\delta}\\
=& - O_p(n\eta_n^2)\boldsymbol{\delta}\\
K_2 =& \frac{1}{2}n\eta_n^2\{\boldsymbol{\delta}^T[-\frac{1}{n}\nabla^2 L_n(\boldsymbol{\theta}^*)\boldsymbol{\delta}](1 + o_p(1))\}\\
=& \frac{1}{2}n\eta_n^2\{\boldsymbol{\delta}^T[I(\boldsymbol{\theta}^*)\boldsymbol{\delta}](1 + o_p(1))\}\\
K_3 =& - n\eta_n^2(|\mathcal{A}_1| + |\mathcal{A}_2|)d
\end{aligned}$$

Thus,

$$\begin{aligned}
D_n(\boldsymbol{\delta}) \geq& K_1 + K_2 + K_3\\
=& - O_p(n\eta_n^2)\boldsymbol{\delta} + \frac{1}{2}n\eta_n^2\{\boldsymbol{\delta}^T[I(\boldsymbol{\theta}^*)\boldsymbol{\delta}](1 + o_p(1))\}\\
&- n\eta_n^2(|\mathcal{A}_1| + |\mathcal{A}_2|)d
\end{aligned}$$

We see that K_2 dominates the rest of the terms and is positive since $I(\boldsymbol{\theta})$ is positive definite at $\boldsymbol{\theta} = \boldsymbol{\theta}^*$ from regularity condition (C2). Therefore, for any given $\epsilon > 0$ there exists a large enough constant d such that

$$P\{\inf_{||\delta||=d} Q_n(\boldsymbol{\theta}^* + \eta_n\boldsymbol{\delta}) > Q_n(\boldsymbol{\theta}^*)\} \geq 1 - \epsilon$$

This implies that with probability at-least $1-\epsilon$, there exists a local minimizer in the ball $\{\boldsymbol{\theta}^* + \eta_n\boldsymbol{\delta} : ||\boldsymbol{\delta}|| \leq d\}$. Thus, there exists a local minimizer of $Q_n(\boldsymbol{\theta})$ such that $||\hat{\boldsymbol{\theta}}_n - \boldsymbol{\theta}^*|| = O_p(\eta_n)$. □

PROOF OF THEOREM 5.2:. Let us first consider $P(\hat{\alpha}_{\mathcal{A}_2^c} = 0) \to 1$. It is sufficient to show that for any $(k, l) \in \mathcal{A}_2^c$

$$\frac{\partial Q_n(\hat{\boldsymbol{\theta}}_n)}{\partial \alpha_{k,l}} < 0 \text{ for } -\epsilon_n < \hat{\alpha}_{k,l} < 0 \tag{11}$$

$$\frac{\partial Q_n(\hat{\boldsymbol{\theta}}_n)}{\partial \alpha_{k,l}} > 0 \text{ for } \epsilon_n > \hat{\alpha}_{k,l} > 0 \tag{12}$$

with probability tending to 1, where $\epsilon_n = Cn^{-1/2}$ and $C > 0$ is any constant. To show (12), notice

$$\begin{aligned}
\frac{\partial Q_n(\hat{\boldsymbol{\theta}}_n)}{\partial \alpha_{k,l}} =& - \frac{L_n(\hat{\boldsymbol{\theta}}_n)}{\partial \alpha_{k,l}} + n\lambda_l^{\alpha_k} sgn(\hat{\alpha}_{k,l})\\
=& - \frac{L_n(\boldsymbol{\theta}^*)}{\partial \alpha_{k,l}} - \sum_{j=1}^{p(K+1)} \frac{\partial^2 L_n(\boldsymbol{\theta}^*)}{\partial \alpha_{k,l}\partial \theta_j}(\hat{\theta}_j - \theta_j^*)
\end{aligned}$$

$$-\sum_{j=1}^{p(K+1)}\sum_{m=1}^{p(K+1)}\frac{\partial^3 L_n(\tilde{\boldsymbol{\theta}})}{\partial\alpha_{k,l}\partial\theta_j\partial\theta_m}(\hat{\theta}_j-\theta_j^*)(\hat{\theta}_m-\theta_m^*)$$
$$+n\lambda_l^{\alpha_k}sgn(\hat{\alpha}_{k,l})$$

where $\tilde{\boldsymbol{\theta}}$ lies between $\hat{\boldsymbol{\theta}}_{\boldsymbol{n}}$ and $\boldsymbol{\theta}^*$. By regularity conditions (C1)-(C3) and the Lemma 5.1, we have

$$\frac{\partial Q_n(\hat{\boldsymbol{\theta}}_n)}{\partial\alpha_{k,l}}=\sqrt{n}\{O_p(1)+\sqrt{n}\lambda_l^{\alpha_k}sgn(\hat{\alpha}_{k,l})\}$$

As $\sqrt{n}\lambda_l^{\alpha_k}\to\infty$ for $(k,l)\in\mathcal{A}_2^c$ from the assumption, the sign of $\frac{\partial Q_n(\hat{\boldsymbol{\theta}}_n)}{\partial\alpha_{k,l}}$ is dominated by $sgn(\hat{\alpha}_{k,j})$. Thus,

$$P\left(\frac{\partial Q_n(\hat{\boldsymbol{\theta}}_n)}{\partial\alpha_{k,l}}>0 \text{ for } 0<\hat{\alpha}_{k,l}<\epsilon_n\right)\to 1 \text{ as } n\to\infty$$

(11) has identical proof as above. Also, $P(\hat{\boldsymbol{\beta}}_{\mathcal{A}_1^c}=0)\to 1$ can be proved similarly since in our model $\boldsymbol{\beta}$ and $\boldsymbol{\alpha}$ are independent of each other. □

PROOF OF THEOREM 5.3. Let $Q_n(\boldsymbol{\theta}_{\mathcal{A}})$ denote the objective function Q_n only on the $\mathcal{A}-$component of $\boldsymbol{\theta}$, that is $Q_n(\boldsymbol{\theta})$ with $\boldsymbol{\theta}_{\mathcal{A}^c}$. Based on Lemma 5.1 and Theorem 5.2, we have $P(\hat{\boldsymbol{\theta}_{\mathcal{A}^c}}=0)\to 1$. Thus,

$$P\Big(\arg\min_{\boldsymbol{\theta}_{\mathcal{A}}}Q_n(\boldsymbol{\theta}_{\mathcal{A}})=(\mathcal{A}-\text{component of}$$
$$\arg\min_{\boldsymbol{\theta}}Q_n(\boldsymbol{\theta}))\Big)\to 1$$

Thus, $\hat{\boldsymbol{\theta}}_{\mathcal{A}}$ should satisfy

$$\frac{\partial Q_n(\boldsymbol{\theta}_{\mathcal{A}})}{\partial\theta_j}\Big|_{\boldsymbol{\theta}_{\mathcal{A}}=\hat{\boldsymbol{\theta}}_{\mathcal{A}}}=0 \qquad \forall j\in\mathcal{A} \tag{13}$$

with probability tending to 1. Let $L_n(\boldsymbol{\theta}_{\mathcal{A}})$ and $P_\lambda(\boldsymbol{\theta}_{\mathcal{A}})$ denote the log-likelihood function of $\boldsymbol{\theta}_{\mathcal{A}}$ and the penalty function of $\boldsymbol{\theta}_{\mathcal{A}}$ respectively so that we have

$$Q_n(\boldsymbol{\theta}_{\mathcal{A}})=-L_n(\boldsymbol{\theta}_{\mathcal{A}})+nP_\lambda(\boldsymbol{\theta}_{\mathcal{A}})$$

From (13), we have

$$\nabla_{\mathcal{A}}Q_n(\hat{\boldsymbol{\theta}}_{\mathcal{A}})=-\nabla_{\mathcal{A}}L_n(\hat{\boldsymbol{\theta}}_{\mathcal{A}})+n\nabla_{\mathcal{A}}P_\lambda(\hat{\boldsymbol{\theta}}_{\mathcal{A}})=0, \tag{14}$$

with probability tending to 1.
Now, consider by Taylor expansion of first term and second terms at $\boldsymbol{\theta}_{\mathcal{A}}=\boldsymbol{\theta}_{\mathcal{A}}^*$, we get the following:

$$\begin{aligned}-\nabla_{\mathcal{A}}L_n(\hat{\boldsymbol{\theta}}_{\mathcal{A}})=&-\nabla_{\mathcal{A}}L_n(\boldsymbol{\theta}_{\mathcal{A}}^*)-[\nabla_{\mathcal{A}}^2L_n(\boldsymbol{\theta}_{\mathcal{A}}^*)+o_p(1)]\\&(\hat{\boldsymbol{\theta}}_{\mathcal{A}}-\boldsymbol{\theta}_{\mathcal{A}}^*)\\=&\sqrt{n}\Bigg[-\frac{1}{\sqrt{n}}\nabla_{\mathcal{A}}L_n(\boldsymbol{\theta}_{\mathcal{A}}^*)+\\&\mathbf{I}(\boldsymbol{\theta}_{\mathcal{A}}^*)\sqrt{n}(\hat{\boldsymbol{\theta}}_{\mathcal{A}}-\boldsymbol{\theta}_{\mathcal{A}}^*)+o_p(1)\Bigg]\end{aligned}$$

$$\begin{aligned}n\nabla_{\mathcal{A}}P_\lambda(\hat{\boldsymbol{\theta}}_{\mathcal{A}})=&n\Bigg\{\begin{bmatrix}\lambda_j^\beta sgn(\beta_j)\\\lambda_l^{\alpha_k}sgn(\alpha_{k,l})\end{bmatrix}_{j\in\mathcal{A}_1,(k,l)\in\mathcal{A}_2}\\&+o_p(1)(\hat{\boldsymbol{\theta}}_{\mathcal{A}}-\boldsymbol{\theta}_{\mathcal{A}}^*)\Bigg\}\\=&\sqrt{n}o_p(1)\end{aligned}$$

since $\sqrt{n}a_n=o(1)$ and $||\hat{\boldsymbol{\theta}}_{\mathcal{A}}-\boldsymbol{\theta}_{\mathcal{A}}^*||=O_p(n^{-1/2})$

Thus, we get,

$$\begin{aligned}0=&\sqrt{n}\Bigg[-\frac{1}{\sqrt{n}}\nabla_{\mathcal{A}}L_n(\boldsymbol{\theta}_{\mathcal{A}}^*)\\&+\mathbf{I}(\boldsymbol{\theta}_{\mathcal{A}}^*)\sqrt{n}(\hat{\boldsymbol{\theta}}_{\mathcal{A}}-\boldsymbol{\theta}_{\mathcal{A}}^*)+o_p(1)\Bigg]\end{aligned}$$

Therefore, from central limit theorem,

$$\sqrt{n}(\hat{\boldsymbol{\theta}}_{\mathcal{A}}-\boldsymbol{\theta}_{\mathcal{A}}^*)\to_d N(\mathbf{0},\mathbf{I}^{-1}(\boldsymbol{\theta}_{\mathcal{A}}^*))$$

□

The proofs for lemma and theorem of section 5.2 are along the same lines as above. Please refer to Appendix section C for more details.

B. COMPUTING ADAPTIVE WEIGHTS

Here, we explain how the adaptive weights $w_j^\beta, w_l^{\alpha_k}$ can be calculated for tuning parameters $\lambda_\beta, \lambda_{\alpha_k}$ in Theoretical properties (Theorems 5.3 & 5.5) of Section 5. Let q be the total number of predictors, let n be total number of instances. When $n>q$, we can compute the adaptive weights $w_j^\beta, w_l^{\alpha_k}$ for tuning parameters $\lambda_j^\beta, \lambda_l^{\alpha_k}$ using ordinary least squares (OLS) estimates of the training observations.

$$\lambda_j^\beta=\frac{\log n}{n}\lambda_\beta w_j^\beta, \qquad \lambda_l^{\alpha_k}=\frac{\log n}{n}\lambda_{\alpha_k}w_l^{\alpha_k}$$

where

$$w_j^\beta=|\frac{1}{\hat{\beta}_j^{OLS}}|, \qquad w_l^{\alpha_k}=|\frac{1}{\hat{\alpha_k}_l^{OLS}}|,$$

When $q>n$, the OLS estimates are not available and so we compute the weights using the ridge regression estimates, that is, replacing all the above OLS estimates with the ridge regression estimates. The tuning parameter for ridge regression can be selected using cross-validation. Note, we find $\hat{\alpha_k}_j^{OLS}$ by taking least squares w.r.t to each α_k where $k\in[0,K]$ for some $K\geq trueK$. Without loss of generality we can assume $K=trueK$ for proving the Theoretical properties in section 5. Even if $K\geq trueK$, it does not affect the Theoretical properties since the cardinality of $\mathcal{A}_2(|\mathcal{A}_2|)$ does not affect the root-n consistency (see, proof of lemma 5.1). In practice, K is greedily chosen by algo. 1 in our paper.

C. SUPPLEMENTARY MATERIALS

For interested readers, we provide online supplementary materials at `http://www.cs.toronto.edu/~cuty/FHIM_Supp.pdf` with detailed proofs for Lemma 5.4 and Theorem 5.5. These proofs do not affect the understanding of this paper. We also provide high quality images for figure 1 in the supplementary materials. We provide more details about the experimental settings for state-of-the-art techniques used in this paper.

Parallel Gibbs Sampling for Hierarchical Dirichlet Processes via Gamma Processes Equivalence

Dehua Cheng
University of Southern California
Los Angeles, CA 90089
dehua.cheng@usc.edu

Yan Liu
University of Southern California
Los Angeles, CA 90089
yanliu.cs@usc.edu

ABSTRACT

The hierarchical Dirichlet process (HDP) is an intuitive and elegant technique to model data with latent groups. However, it has not been widely used for practical applications due to the high computational costs associated with inference. In this paper, we propose an effective parallel Gibbs sampling algorithm for HDP by exploring its connections with the gamma-gamma-Poisson process. Specifically, we develop a novel framework that combines bootstrap and Reversible Jump MCMC algorithm to enable parallel variable updates. We also provide theoretical convergence analysis based on Gibbs sampling with asynchronous variable updates. Experiment results on both synthetic datasets and two large-scale text collections show that our algorithm can achieve considerable speedup as well as better inference accuracy for HDP compared with existing parallel sampling algorithms.

Categories and Subject Descriptors

G.3 [**Mathematics of Computing**]: Probability and Statistics

Keywords

Parallel Inference; Hierarchical Dirichlet Process; Topic Model

1. INTRODUCTION

Modeling large, complex, real-world domains often demands powerful models which can handle rich relational structures. Mixture models, such as those to model groups of data with shared characteristics by enforcing a shared set of mixture components, are one of the most intuitive and also effective solutions. For instance, the latent Dirichlet allocation (LDA) model has been proven successful in modeling a collection of documents [4] and the nonparametric extensions with hierarchical Dirichlet processes (HDP) inherit the advantage of LDA and allow the flexibility to learn the number of mixture components automatically from the data [14].

The HDP has achieved success in modeling many different types of data. However, the biggest challenge towards applications is their inability to scale to large datasets. Recently, some excellent work has been conducted to address this challenging problem, which can be summarized into two directions. One is the general-purpose implementation of parallel inference algorithms [7, 8, 9]. These algorithms are general enough to be applied to any type of graphical models, but it is difficult for them to achieve the desired speedup in specific models. The other direction is the approximation or vanilla parallelism of specific models, such as [10, 2, 16] for parallel inference of LDA models. Furthermore, [17] proposes an exact parallel sampling algorithm for HDP, which is the first nontrivial distributed sampling algorithm for HDP that converges to the true distribution provably. However, there is still room for improvement since the algorithm suffers from unbalanced workload and increasing rejection rate of the Metropolis Hasting step with increasing number of processors.

In this paper, we propose a parallel Gibbs sampling algorithm for HDP by exploring its connection with the gamma-gamma-Poisson process, which has a rich potential for developing various parallel inference algorithms. We propose a parallel sampling algorithm based on the augmented gamma-gamma-Poisson process model and reconstruct the dataset using a bootstrap technique which brings the independence across different mixture components. Therefore we can perform independent variable update for each mixture component. We also provide theoretical convergence analysis for the parallel Gibbs sampling algorithm with asynchronous variable updates, i.e., each variable updates without explicit coordination, which is common in a distributed system. We demonstrate the accuracy of our proposed algorithm on the synthetic datasets and faster convergence rate on large-scale real world datasets.

The rest of the paper is organized as follows: we first review the basic ideas in Section 2. In Section 3, we describe our parallel sampling algorithm based on gamma-gamma-Poisson process and discuss theoretical convergence analysis. Finally, we show the experiment results in Section 4.

2. BACKGROUND AND NOTATIONS

A *Dirichlet process mixture model* (DPMM) is a mixture model with an infinite number of mixture components, where the *Dirichlet process* (DP), with the base distribution H and concentration parameter α, serves as the non-

KDD'14, August 24–27, 2014, New York, NY, USA.
Copyright 2014 ACM 978-1-4503-2956-9/14/08 ...$15.00.
http://dx.doi.org/10.1145/2623330.2623708 .

parametric prior of the mixing measure over all components. Given a dataset $\{x_i\}_{i=1}^N$ of size N, DPMM assumes that the ith data point $x^{(i)}$ is generated from the mixture component $\eta^{(i)}$ as follows:

$$\begin{aligned} G|\{\alpha, H\} &\sim \mathrm{DP}(\alpha, H), \\ \eta^{(i)}|G &\sim G, \\ x^{(i)}|\eta^{(i)} &\sim p(x^{(i)}|\eta^{(i)}), \qquad i \in \{1, \ldots, N\}. \end{aligned}$$

As proved by Ferguson in [5], $G = \sum_{k=1}^{\infty} \pi_k \delta_{\theta_k}$ with the discrete support $\{\theta_k\}_{k=1}^{\infty} \subset H$ where H is the space of all mixture components, δ_{θ_k} is Dirac-delta function of component θ_k and π_k is the associated mixture weight. Each $\theta_k \in H$ represents a mixture component, and each mixture component has its distribution over the data space $p(x|\theta_k)$.

In some applications, we may be interested in modeling groups of data with shared mixture components and prior over mixing measures. Therefore the *hierarchical Dirichlet process* (HDP) mixture model is proposed as a hierarchical structural extension of DPMM [14]. That is, given a dataset with groups $X_d = \{x_d^{(i)}\}_{i=1}^{N_d}$, with $d \in \{1, \ldots, D\}$ as the group index, and N_d as the size of dth group, HDP assumes that they are generated as follows:

$$\begin{aligned} G_0|\{\alpha, H\} &\sim \mathrm{DP}(\alpha, H), \\ G_d|\{\gamma, G_0\} &\sim \mathrm{DP}(\gamma, G_0), \\ \eta_d^{(i)}|G_d &\sim G_d, \\ X_d^{(i)}|\eta_d^{(i)} &\sim p(x_d^{(i)}|\eta_d^{(i)}), \qquad i \in \{1, \ldots, N_d\}. \end{aligned}$$

The upper level DP generates G_0 from the mixture component space H as the common base measure to ensure that each group shares mixture components with a positive probability. Then each group is generated from DPMM based on the mixture component space G_0, with independent concentration parameter γ. Topic model is one nice example for HDP, where each latent topic corresponds to the mixture component, the collection of documents is the groups of data, and each data point is a word in the document.

The HDP has achieved success in modeling observations with latent groups in hierarchical structures [14, 13, 12]. However, the computational cost of inference over HDP makes it infeasible for practical applications. Various inference techniques have been investigated to solve this problem, such as variational inference, sampling techniques and so on. Among them, sampling algorithms have become popular due to their simplicity and high inference quality [14]. However, they are also known to suffer from the slow convergence rate. Therefore several parallel sampling algorithms have been proposed to speed up the convergence via parallel computing paradigm.

Slice sampler [15] is one example of parallel sampling algorithm for DPMM. It reduces the infinite mixture component space to a finite subset at each step, where the mixture component assignment for each data point is conditionally independent of the rest and thus can be updated simultaneously. Parallelizing slice sampler is simple but requires multiple times of synchronization within each update, which could lead to significant communication overhead and makes it impractical for the distributed learning scenario.

In [2], an approximation of the HDP is introduced and a parallel sampling algorithm is developed for the approximate model. It divides the data into subsets and each processor synchronously updates the variable through a Gibbs sampler based on the current state of its local dataset and the previous state of the global dataset. The processors communicate with each other asynchronously to ensure the global convergence. This algorithm is well suited for the parallel environment with distributed storage but the inference results may not be as accurate as the original HDP.

The first real-sense parallel sampling algorithm for HDP has been proposed in [17]. It is based on examining an equivalent generative model of HDP with auxiliary variables. Conditioned on the auxiliary variables, each processor can update its local variables independently. Data points are assigned to processors based on the status of auxiliary variables, and each processor learns the mixture component independently. That is, the algorithm implicitly separates the mixture components space to each processor. One major issue with the algorithm is the potential imbalanced workload across processors. In addition, the rejection rate of the Metropolis Hasting step for updating auxiliary variables could be high and thus resulting in slower convergence rate.

As we can see, most existing work on parallel sampling for HDP has limitations either in inference accuracy or convergence rate. Given the large demand in practical applications, seeking an effective parallel sampling algorithm remains an important and challenging task.

3. PARALLEL GIBBS SAMPLING FOR HDP

In this section, we describe in detail our approach: we first review the gamma-gamma-Poisson process and its equivalence to HDP, and then introduce the parallel Gibbs sampling algorithms on the equivalent model.

3.1 Gamma-Gamma-Poisson Process

Introduction.

A *gamma-Poisson process* is a two-level hierarchy of completely random process defined on base measurable space H[19].It is known that a random process Π' drawn from gamma-Poisson process with parameter $\{m, H\}$ is defined as follows:

$$\begin{aligned} G' &\sim \mathrm{GaP}(H), \\ \Pi' &\sim \mathrm{PoisP}(mG'), \end{aligned}$$

where PoisP refers to Poisson process and GaP refers to Gamma process. If H is discrete and $H = \sum_{k=1}^{\infty} \alpha_k \delta_{\theta_k}$, where α_k is the associated atom weight (which becomes the mixture weight in the equivalent mixture model of HDP defined later), the generation process of Π' can also be described as:

$$G' = \sum_{k=1}^{\infty} \pi'_k \delta_{\theta_k}, \quad \pi'_k \sim \mathrm{Gamma}(\alpha_k, 1), \tag{1}$$

and

$$\Pi' = \sum_{k=1}^{\infty} n_k \delta_{\theta_k}, \quad n_k|G' \sim \mathrm{Pois}(m\pi'_k). \tag{2}$$

The *gamma-gamma-Poisson process* is defined by replacing the based measure H in *gamma-Poisson process* with another random measure G' drawn from a gamma process $\mathrm{GaP}(\alpha H)$. The equivalence between HDP and gamma-gamma-Poisson process is well-studied in [19] section 3.1. The generative process of both HDP and gamma-gamma-Poisson process are summarized in Table 1. Note that unlike G_i,

Table 1: Summary of the generative process of HDP and gamma-gamma-Poisson processes

HDP	Gamma-gamma-Poisson Process
$G_0 \mid \{\alpha, H\} \sim \mathrm{DP}(\alpha, H)$	$G_0' \mid \{\alpha, H\} \sim \mathrm{GaP}(\alpha H)$
$G_d \mid \{\gamma, G_0\} \sim \mathrm{DP}(\gamma, G_0)$	$G_d' \mid \{G_0'\} \sim \mathrm{GaP}(G_0')$
$\eta_d^{(i)} \mid G_d \sim G_d$	$\Pi_d' \mid \{m, G_d'\} \sim \mathrm{PoisP}(mG_d')$
$X_d^{(i)} \mid \eta_d^{(i)} \sim p(x_d^{(i)} \mid \eta_d^{(i)})$	$X_d \mid \Pi_d' \sim p(X \mid \Pi_d')$

the sum of the weight of G_i' is no longer 1, so it does not represent a distribution. But since G_i' is proportional to G_i, we can obtain G_i easily by normalization. Furthermore, instead of normalizing the weights explicitly, we can resort to the property of Poisson process that given the sum of several independent Poisson random variables, the Poisson random variables are conditionally distributed as multinomial distributions with the normalized weights. Thus the normalization is achieved implicitly.

An Example of Topic Models.

We take topic models as an example to illustrate the generative process of gamma-gamma-Poisson process. The upper level DP which generates the global topic space G_0 in HDP is replaced by the gamma process with same parameters $G_0' = \sum_{k=1}^{\infty} \alpha_k \delta_{\theta_k} \sim \mathrm{GaP}(\alpha H)$, where α_k represents the weight for the kth topic. For each document, we first draw the topic mixing parameter $G_d' \mid \{G_0'\} \sim \mathrm{GaP}(G_0')$. Similar to eq(1), we can also have $G_d' = \sum_{k=1}^{\infty} \pi_{dk}' \delta_{\theta_k}$, where π_{dk}' is the weight for the kth topic in the dth document. According to G_d', we use the Poisson process to generate the count measure $\Pi_d' \mid \{m, G_d'\} \sim \mathrm{PoisP}(mG_d')$, which can be represented as $\Pi_d' = \sum_{k=1}^{\infty} n_{dk} \delta_{\theta_k}$. Each n_{dk} has its definitive meaning: the number of words that belongs to topic k in document d. Finally, we generate the words for each document according to n_{dk} and the conditional word distribution given the topic. Notice that [19] provides similar derivations except that the last two steps are combined to directly generate n_{dkx}, i.e., the number of word x that belongs to topic k in document d.

3.2 Parallel Gibbs Sampling Algorithm

Motivation.

Even though we establish the equivalence between HDP and gamma-gamma-Poisson process, these two models, however, behave differently. For simplicity, we use the topic models to illustrate the difference. The advantage of gamma-gamma-Poisson process is that for each different topic, the generative process is completely independent with each other in the entire process, which is the merit of composing completely random processes. Note that when we mention the kth topic, we are referring to all variables α_k, θ_k, π_{dk}' and n_{dk} with the same topic index k. This key property lays the foundation of the parallel Gibbs sampling algorithm.

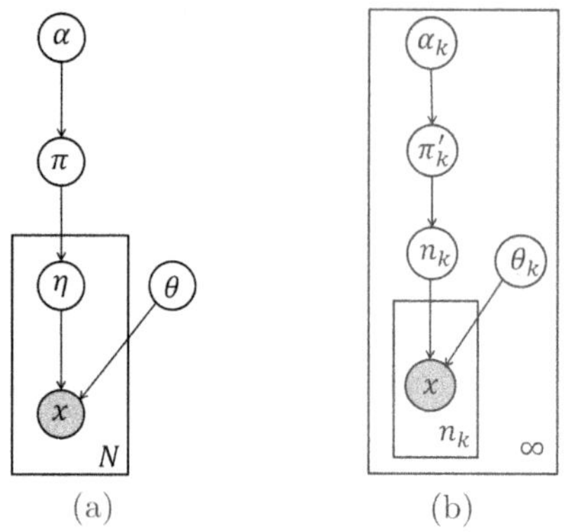

Figure 1: Graphical model representation of topic models by (a) HDP and (b) gamma-gamma-Poisson process for one document.

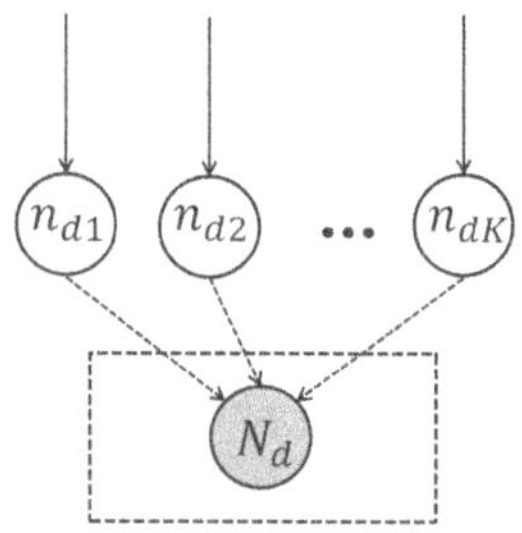

Figure 2: Dependency between n_{dk} and N_d. With N_d observed, $\{n_{dk}\}_{k=1}^{K}$ will form a clique. Otherwise, they are independent with each other.

Another major difference is how we treat the variables n_{dk} and N_d (see in Figure 1). In HDP, n_{dk} does not directly appear in the model, but N_d is given. This agrees better with the real world setting, where the size of the dataset is usually observed. In gamma-gamma-Poisson process, N_d is implicitly determined after we generate n_{dk}, and it cannot be acquired beforehand. This raises one major challenge to parallel inference algorithms because any explicit assumption on N_d will breakdown the cross-topic independence. Therefore we develop a technique that combines bootstrap and Reversible Jump MCMC algorithm to address this particular challenge.

Algorithm.

The inference task of HDP is defined as follows: given the hyperparameters of the model and the observation, how can we infer the parameter θ_k which characterizes the conditional word distribution given the topic as well as the associated topic distribution π_{0k} and $\pi_{dk}, d \in \{1, \ldots, D\}$ for each topic k? The input is a collection of documents. We represent the dth document by X_d and its length by N_d.

Applying the finite approximation on the number of topic K as in [19], we have a much simpler model representation as follows:

$$\alpha_k \mid \alpha \sim \mathrm{Gamma}(\frac{\alpha}{K}, 1),$$

$$\pi_{dk}' \mid \{\alpha_k\} \sim \mathrm{Gamma}(\alpha_k, 1),$$

$$\theta_k \sim H_\theta,$$

$$n_{dk}|\{m, \pi'_{dk}\} \sim \text{Pois}(m\pi'_{dk}),$$

$$X_{dk}|\{\theta_k, n_{dk}\} \sim p(X|\theta_k, n_{dk}),$$

$$k \in 1, 2, \ldots, K, \qquad d \in 1, 2, \ldots, D.$$

where H_θ represents the generative model for θ_k, e.g., the Dirichlet distribution.

The joint distribution can be computed as

$$p(n_{dk}, \pi'_{dk}, X_{dk}, \alpha_k, \theta_k) = \prod_{k=1}^{K} \frac{\alpha_k^{\frac{\alpha}{K}-1}}{\Gamma(\frac{\alpha}{K})} e^{-\alpha_k} \tag{3}$$

$$\times \prod_{k=1}^{K} \prod_{d=1}^{D} \frac{\pi_{dk}'^{\alpha_k - 1}}{\Gamma(\alpha_k)} e^{-\pi'_{dk}} \frac{(m\pi'_{dk})^{n_{dk}}}{n_{dk}!} e^{-m\pi'_{dk}}$$

$$\times \prod_{k=1}^{K} H_\theta(\theta_k) \times \prod_{k=1}^{K} \prod_{d=1}^{D} \prod_{i=1}^{n_{dk}} p(x_{dk}^{(i)}|\theta_k).$$

Our goal is to design a parallel sampling algorithm which can update each topic and its associated variables asynchronously in parallel. Thus, it is important to analyze variable dependence across topics. From the graphical model in Figure 1(b), we can see that different topics are only connected by their common child nodes x. All θ_k are dependent with each other through x_{dk}, which is necessary for learning topics jointly. But they are independent given the topic assignment for each word, so we can achieve independent update by grouping the word by topic. All n_{dk} for any given d are connected by N_d, as shown in Figure 2. This dependence among n_{dk} is the "side effect" of the new model, which is undesirable and impedes us from developing efficient parallel sampling algorithms. Our solution is to "unobserve" the variable N_d, by constructing a document with flexible length. Details are provided in the sampling step for updating n_{dk}.

We propose the updating rules for α_k, θ_k, π'_{dk} and n_{dk} as follows: (See Algorithm 1 for pseudocode.)

Updating n_{dk}. We update n_{dk} by the Metropolis-Hasting step based on Reversible Jump MCMC with two equally weighted proposed jumps: "$n_{dk} \to n_{dk}+1$" (n_{dk}^{++}) or "$n_{dk} \to n_{dk}-1$" (n_{dk}^{--}). In the likelihood function, the factors regarding n_{dk} (given d and k) are

$$\frac{(m\pi'_{dk})^{n_{dk}}}{n_{dk}!} \prod_{i=1}^{n_{dk}} p(x_{dk}^{(i)}|\theta_k). \tag{4}$$

In addition, with the dataset X_d given, the likelihood function becomes

$$\frac{(m\pi'_{dk})^{n_{dk}}}{n_{dk}!} \prod_{i=1}^{n_{dk}} p_{x_{dk}^{(i)}}(k), \tag{5}$$

where $p_x(k) \propto p(x|\theta_k)$ is the normalized likelihood of topic assignment. Such normalization is equivalent as conditioning on observation X, which is necessary for deriving correct acceptance rate since the length of document is different before and after the jump.

As we can see, the change of n_{dk} also leads to the change of topic assignment in the dth document, which changes n_{d*} in other topics. Given X_d, this operation cannot be conducted within the kth topic. Therefore, as discussed above, we need to construct a new document X'_d of flexible length X'_d based on the original X_d. In this way, we can increase or decrease n_{dk} without affecting other topics directly.

Algorithm 1 Parallel Sampling Algorithm for Gamma-Gamma-Poisson Process

```
Inputs: Group of dataset X_d, parameter α, m. Number
  of iteration to update n_dk in each iteration maxNIter
Outputs: Mixture component θ_k and corresponding
  normalized weight π_0k, π_dk
Construct stacks S_d for each dataset d
Construct empty collection X'_dk and empty buffer B_dk
  for all dataset d and mixture component k, and initialize
  n_dk to 0
Initialize α_k, θ_k, π'_dk randomly
for each mixture component k asynchronously in parallel do
  repeat
    for each dataset d do
      for nIter from 1 to maxNIter do
        Draw u ~ Uniform(0, 1)
        if u < 0.5 then
          Pop x* from S_d and add it to X'_dk with acceptance
          rate A_{n_dk^++}. If failed, add x* to B_dk
        else
          Pop x* from X'_dk randomly and add it to B_dk
          with acceptance rate A_{n_dk^--}. If failed, add x*
          back to X'_dk
        end if
      end for
      Push all element from B_dk to S_d if B_dk exceeds
      certain size.
      Update π'_dk by equation 8
    end for
    Update α_k by equation 9
    Update θ_k by equation 10, and update partition
    function Z.
  until convergence
end for
Normalize {α_k} → {π_0k} and {π'_dk} → {π_dk}
Return mixture component θ_k and corresponding
  weight π_dk
```

First, we build a stack S_d to store X'_d. Each element $x^* \in S_d$ is randomly drawn from X_d with replacement. This ensures that, for all n, the empirical distribution of the first n elements in S_d is an approximation to the empirical distribution of X_d. We also pre-group the elements in X'_d as X'_{dk} by the topic assignment.

When we propose an increase on n_{dk}, we pop a new word x^* from S_d and accept the increase with acceptance rate $A_{n_{dk}^{++}}$ as:

$$A_{n_{dk}^{++}} = min(1, \frac{m\pi'_{dk}}{n_{dk}+1} p_{x^*}(k)). \tag{6}$$

If the proposal is accepted, we will add x^* to X'_{dk} and assign it to the kth topic. Otherwise it returns to S_d.

When we propose a decrease on n_{dk}, we randomly choose one word x^* from X'_{dk}. The acceptance rate $A_{n_{dk}^{--}}$ is

$$A_{n_{dk}^{--}} = min(1, \frac{n_{dk}}{m\pi'_{dk}} \frac{1}{p_{x^*}(k)}). \tag{7}$$

If the proposal is accepted, we will delete x^* from X'_{dk} and return it to the stack S_d.

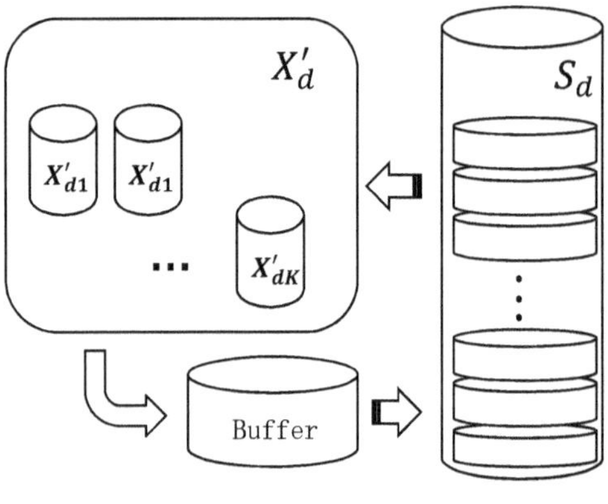

Figure 3: The structure of reconstructed dataset and data flow.

In our implementation, we also add a buffer B_{dk} between X'_{dk} and S_d. The word returning to S_d will be first stored at B_{dk}, and returned to S_d shortly after. This is helpful to avoid consecutive rejections on outliers. m can be empirically set proportional to $1/K$, which increases the acceptance rate. Note that a larger value of m will impede convergence at the initial stage, when n_{dk} is small. The overall flow is illustrated in Figure 3. X'_d serves as an approximation to the original dataset X_d. There might be bias in X'_d due to unassigned but visited elements in stack S_d. The accuracy of this approximation is tested with synthetic datasets in Section 4.1.

This approach appears to be similar to online algorithms, but they are fundamental different: in online settings, we only have one pass of the observations. In our algorithm, although we feed X'_{dk} with the data in stream, the rejected data will return to the stack eventually and similarly for the deleted data from X'_{dk}. This is crucial because it helps to maintain that the empirical distribution of X'_d is close to X_d, otherwise X'_d could be strongly affected by the selection bias during the *add-and-delete* process.

Updating π'_{dk}. In the likelihood function, the factors regarding π'_{dk} are

$$\pi'^{\alpha_k+n_{dk}-1}_{dk} e^{-(m+1)\pi'_{dk}},$$

which means that π'_{dk} follows a gamma distribution with $n_{dk}+\alpha_k$ and $m+1$ as its scale and shape parameter respectively. Therefore, we update π'_{dk} based on n_{dk} and α_k as follows

$$\pi'_{dk} \sim \text{Gamma}(n_{dk}+\alpha_k, m+1). \tag{8}$$

Updating α_k. In the likelihood function, the factors regarding α_k are

$$\frac{\alpha_k^{\frac{\alpha}{K}-1}}{(\Gamma(\alpha_k))^D} e^{\alpha_k \sum_{d=1}^{D} log(\pi'_{dk})-1}.$$

Because α_k is usually quite small, the first order Laurent expansion provides a simple and accurate approximation, which is $\Gamma(z) \approx 1/z$ when $|z| < 1$. α_k is approximately distributed as

$$\alpha_k \sim \text{Gamma}(\frac{\alpha}{K} + D, \sum_{d=1}^{D} -log(\pi'_{dk})). \tag{9}$$

Table 2: Rules of update for all variables

Variable	Rule of update
n_{dk}	n^{++}_{dk} with $A_{n^{++}_{dk}}$; n^{--}_{dk} with $A_{n^{--}_{dk}}$
π'_{dk}	$\text{Gamma}(n_{dk}+\alpha_k, m+1)$
θ_k	$H_\theta(\theta_k)\prod_{d=1}^{D} p(X_{dk}\|\theta_k)$
α_k	$\text{Gamma}(\frac{\alpha}{K}+D, \sum_{d=1}^{D} -log(\pi'_{dk}))$

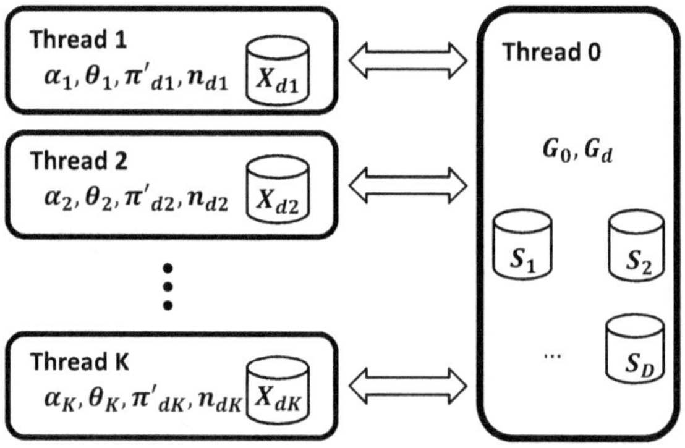

Figure 4: The thread architecture for the proposed parallel sampling algorithm

We can either use this approximation, or treat it as the proposed distribution in a Metropolis-Hasting step.

Updating θ_k. We update θ_k based on its posterior distribution.

$$\theta_k \propto H(\theta_k) \prod_{i=1}^{n_i} p(x_k^{(i)}|\theta_k). \tag{10}$$

The updating rules for all variables are summarized in Table 2.

3.3 Parallel Structure

As mentioned before, our algorithm updates each topic and its associated variables asynchronously in parallel. Each topic is assigned to a thread. The architecture is showed is Figure 4. Moreover, to minimize the possible conflicts when the same document is accessed by different topics at the same time, we separate the documents to several disjoint subsets at step 8 in Algorithm 1. In each iteration, we update the topic only based on a subset of documents and rotate through all subsets, so the conflict can be avoided completely. Similar techniques have been used by [18] in a parallel GPU sampling algorithm for LDA to reduce parameter storage redundancy and avoid access conflicts.

The only connection across topics is through computing term $p_{x^*}(k)$ when updating n_{dk}. We store the partition function $Z(x^*) = \sum_{k=1}^{K} p(x^*|\theta_k)$ locally, so we can obtain $p_{x^*}(k) = p(x^*|\theta_k)/Z(x^*)$. We update Z periodically to ensure the accuracy.

Because the updates are made asynchronously for each topic, we store each topic update with its time stamp. So we can sort the updates according to its time stamp and reconstruct the parameters for the whole model.

3.4 Convergence Analysis

For Gibbs sampling based parallel sampling algorithm, the variables are updated asynchronously in parallel, which is different from that in sequential Gibbs sampling algorithm, where the order of updates is fixed. The proof of convergence for Gibbs sampler does not generalize to all parallel Gibbs sampling algorithms. Fortunately, for some of them, the order of updates has been proven to be irrelevant to a certain extent. For instance, in chromatic Gibbs sampler [6], all possible orders of updates within the same color are indeed equivalent. In this section, we study the convergence for general parallel sampling algorithm based on Gibbs sampling. There are two differences:

- In a global iteration, some variables have been updated more than once.
- The order of updates can be different in each global iteration.

The term "global iteration" is not well defined in asynchronous settings. Here we use it loosely: we separate the clock time to disjoint intervals. If in each time interval, every random variable has been updated at least once, we call such interval as a global iteration. We also define the order of update as follows:

Definition 3.1 (Order of update). *An order of update is a sequence of index from the index set of random variables, where each index must occur at least once.*

For example, $(1,2,1,3)$ and $(3,2,1)$ are legitimate orders of update for the index set $\{1,2,3\}$, while $(1,2,1)$ is not. We model the order of update by a random distribution $P_{\mathcal{O}}$, which depends on various factors including the algorithm itself, the computation hardware, the probabilistic model (i.e. the graph structure of the graphical model), and current state of the sample. We prove in the following theorem that if the distribution $P_{\mathcal{O}}$ is independent with the current state of the sample, the convergence is guaranteed.

Theorem 3.1. *If a probabilistic model $P(\cdot)$ has positive support and the distribution $P_{\mathcal{O}}$ on order of update is independent with the current state of the sample, the convergence of Gibbs sampler is guaranteed, and it converges to the true distribution $P(\cdot)$.*

Proof. First, we exam the stationary measure of the Markov chain defined by Gibbs sampler with an arbitrary order of updates $\mathcal{O}$, we first prove that, if the probabilistic model $P(\cdot)$ has positive support, the stationary measure is the true distribution $P(\cdot)$. The proof is very similar to that for Gibbs sampler. Assume that we have $x = (x_1, x_2, \dots, x_n) \sim P(\cdot)$, we update the variables according to the order of updates $\mathcal{O} = (i_1, i_2, \dots, i_{n_{\mathcal{O}}})$. For the first step, we have

$$\sum_{x_{i_1}} p(x_1, x_2, \dots, x_n) p(x^*_{i_1} | x_{-i_1}) = p(x_1, \dots, x^*_{i_1}, \dots, x_n),$$

where x_{-i} represents the set $\{x_1, \dots, x_{i-1}, x_{i+1}, \dots, x_n\}$. So we have that $x^{(1)} = (x_1, \dots, x^*_{i_1}, \dots, x_n) \sim P(\cdot)$. Similarly, after second step, the result $x^{(2)}$ also has the distribution $P(\cdot)$. By simple induction, we prove that after updating $x_{n_{\mathcal{O}}}$, we have $x^* = (x^*_1, x^*_2, \dots, x^*_n) \sim P(\cdot)$, which proves the statement. Note that it indicates that the stationary measure is invariant to different order of updates, and it is indeed the true distribution $P(\cdot)$.

With this statement, we then prove our main theorem with help of the main result in [11], which indicates that for an inhomogeneous Markov chain, when there exists a probability measure $P(\cdot)$ such that each of the different steps corresponds to a nice ergodic Markov kernel with stationary measure $P(\cdot)$, it will converge to $P(\cdot)$. We have already proved that $P(\cdot)$ is the stationary measure of any order of updates, so the Markov kernel at each step has the same stationary measure $P(\cdot)$, which proves the theorem. □

The assumption of the independence with the current state of the sample is essential to the conclusion, and similar issue has been discussed in [1] for *adaptive MCMC*. The validity of such assumption relies on the algorithm and its implementation. For example, in LDA, the speed of updating the word distribution for a topic depends on the current number of words assigned to the topic. However, such dependence is not strong enough to affect the convergence of our algorithm, which is confirmed by later experimental results.

4. EXPERIMENTAL RESULTS

In this section, we first study the accuracy of our parallel sampling algorithm (G2PP) on the synthetic dataset, then we test the interpretability of the G2PP on the *Bitcoin Blog* dataset, and finally we compare with with other baseline algorithms on large real world dataset in terms of convergence rate.

We implement the *synchronous Gibbs sampler* (Synch) [2] based on the posterior sampling with auxiliary variable algorithm described in [14], the *AVparallel* algorithm (AVP) based on the *Chinese restaurant franchise* (CRF) with global update scheme proposed in [17] and the *slice sampler* based on [15]. All algorithms are implemented in C++. We test all algorithms under the same hyperparameter setting. Note that the iteration for G2PP and other algorithms are not equivalent, so it is unreasonable to compare the performance based on number of iteration. Therefore, we present our results based on actual runtime.

In our experiments, the convergence rate of AVP is significantly slower than the rest of candidates. The reported convergence time for CRF of a java implementation in the original paper is around 4000 minutes on the same NIPS dataset, which is far longer than the convergence time of other algorithms. The slice sampler also suffers from slow convergence in the preliminary experiments. Note that AVP and slice sampler are theoretically accurate. In contrast, G2PP and Synch are approximate sampling algorithms. Therefore, we only present the results of G2PP, Synch and Gibbs, which is Synch with one processor.

4.1 Inference Accuracy

In order to demonstrate the inference accuracy of G2PP, we design two experiments on the synthetic datasets. The algorithm performance is measured by the prediction accuracy and model perplexity.

Table 3: F1 Scores on mixture of Gaussian dataset by G2PP and Synch

ALGORITHM	F1 SCORE
G2PP	0.94
GIBBS	0.91

Table 4: F1 Scores on LDA dataset by G2PP and Synch

ALGORITHM	F1 SCORE
G2PP	0.65
GIBBS	0.60
SYNCH-2	0.57
SYNCH-4	0.54
SYNCH-8	0.48

4.1.1 *Mixture of Gaussians*

We first generate a synthetic dataset with mixture of Gaussian, which consists of 50 bivariate Gaussian distributions, each with mean distributed according to Norm(0, 10) and variance of 0.01. The dataset contains one million data points in total.

We evaluate the results according to the F1 score between clusters obtained by each algorithm and the ground truth. We adopt the definition of F1 score in [17], which is defined on the pairwise observations. We define the *precision* and *recall* as $|P^{(g)} \cap P^{(p)}|/|P^{(p)}|$ and $|P^{(g)} \cap P^{(p)}|/|P^{(g)}|$ respectively, where $P^{(g)}$ is the set of pairs of data point of the same cluster under the ground truth, and $P^{(p)}$ is all pairs of data points of the same cluster under the prediction. The result is shown in Table 3. The F1 scores shown in the table represent the average prediction results on the Markov chain, excluding the burn-in period. We can see that G2PP yields comparable and even better performance in terms of prediction accuracy than Gibbs sampler.

4.1.2 *Latent Dirichlet Allocation*

We also test our algorithm on a second synthetic dataset generated by latent Dirichlet allocation (LDA). The synthetic corpus contains 1000 documents and 10 latent topics. Each document is of the same length of 1000. The vocabulary size is set to 1000. The concentration parameters of all Dirichlet distributions are set to 1. We compare the performance of G2PP with Gibbs sampler and synchronous Gibbs sampler (Synch) [2] on F1 score and model perplexity.

The F1 scores for each method are listed in Table 4 and the perplexity curves over time is shown in Figure 5. As we can see, G2PP performs better in both F1 score and perplexity. In addition, Synch shows decreasing accuracy when the number of processors increases, because each processor owns smaller subset of data.

In summary, we empirically show that our parallel sampling algorithm not only does not compromise on accuracy, but also may achieve slight improvement in part due to the bias induced by X'_d (which makes it more robust on outliers).

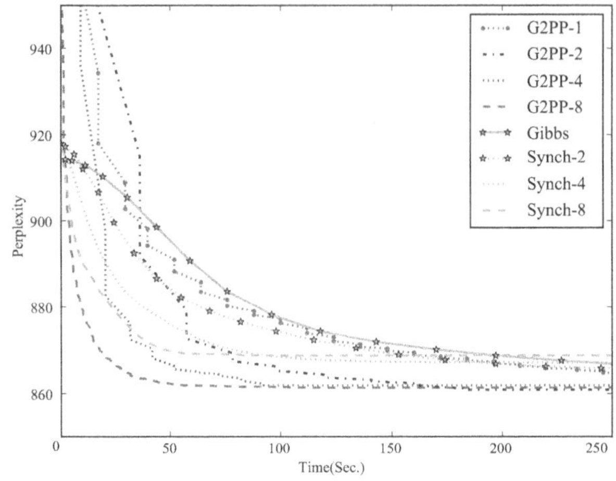

Figure 5: The convergence plot for G2PP and Synch with 1, 2, 4, 8 processors on LDA dataset.

Table 5: Latent topics Inferred by G2PP on Bitcoin dataset

TOPIC 1	TOPIC 2	TOPIC 3	TOPIC 4	TOPIC 5
BITCOIN	LIKE	BITCOIN	GOLD	SECURITY
CURRENCY	PEOPLE	CURRENCY	MARKET	MALWARE
ONLINE	BITCOIN	CHINA	PRICE	DATA
PAYMENT	ONE	BANK	FED	NSA
SAID	SEE	VIRTUAL	YEAR	COMPUTER
DIGITAL	WOULD	CENTRAL	ECONOMY	USERS
FIRST	WAY	EXCHANGE	US	ATTACKS
COMPANY	COULD	PRICE	INVESTORS	INTERNET
TRANSACTIONS	EVEN	CHINESE	BUBBLE	INFORMATION
ONE	RE	SYSTEM	RATE	WASHINGTON

4.2 Interpretability on Real World Dataset

We test our G2PP algorithm on a real world dataset for topic modeling. We collected the online blogs related to the *Bitcoin* posted between Nov. 19th, 2013 and Dec. 20th, 2013 based on Google News search results. *Bitcoin* is a peer-to-peer payment system and digital cryptocurrency introduced as open source software in 2009 by pseudonymous developer Satoshi Nakamoto, which becomes extremely popular in the last few months of 2013.

We preprocessed the dataset in a standard manner. We only consider the blog posts in English, which leads to a collection of 1899 documents with averaged length of 292 and 7379 unique words. The top 5 latent topics and the top 10 words associated with each topic by G2PP is listed in Table 5. We also present the results of Gibbs sampler in Table 6. Both results are intuitive and reasonable. For example, in Table 5, Topic 1 is the introduction of *Bitcoin*, Topic 3 is the events related to China, which is the main cause for both soar and drop in *Bitcoin* price. Moreover, the resemblance between the results from Gibbs and G2PP is remarkable, which indicates that the results of G2PP are as reliable as the Gibbs sampler. Moderate differences in the word and topic ranking are due to the randomness in the inference process.

Table 6: Latent topics inferred by Gibbs on the Bitcoin dataset

Topic 1	Topic 2	Topic 3	Topic 4	Topic 5
BITCOIN	ONE	CHINA	YEAR	DATA
CURRENCY	PEOPLE	BITCOIN	MARKET	NSA
EXCHANGE	LIKE	CHINESE	FED	COMPANY
DIGITAL	WOULD	CURRENCY	ECONOMY	INTERNET
VALUE	TIME	BTC	US	SECURITY
VIRTUAL	EVEN	BANK	LAST	GOVERNMENT
SAID	COULD	SAID	GROWTH	SNOWDEN
MONEY	RE	TRADING	MONTH	PRIVACY
ONE	GET	YUAN	WEEK	SOCIAL
WAY	TRANSACTIONS	CENTRAL	INVESTORS	ONLINE

Table 7: Statistics of NIPS and NYT datasets

Dataset	# Documents	Vocabulary Size
NIPS1-17	2484	14036
NYTimes news	300000	102660

With the results on the synthetic datasets and this real-world application dataset, we can safely confirm that the inference results by G2PP is accurate in terms of both statistical criteria and topic interpretation. Next, we investigate the performance of convergence rate.

4.3 Convergence Rate

We choose two benchmark datasets, i.e., NIPS1-17 (NIPS) dataset[1] and NYTimes news (NYT) dataset[2] for convergence analysis. The statistics of the two datasets are listed in Table 7.

4.3.1 NIPS 1-17 Dataset

We split the dataset into a training set with 2284 documents and a test set with 200 documents. We evaluate the algorithm by the perplexity on the test set. The convergence time and final perplexity are listed in Table 8. The typical convergence curves are shown in Figure 6. The result shows that G2PP performs well in terms of convergence speed, accuracy and scalability with respect to the number of processors.

Note that as the number of processors increases, the perplexity value by Synch increases, which means that the accuracy decreases. Moreover, Synch becomes more likely to be trapped in local optimal. By "local optimal", we refer to the phenomenon that the perplexity stably stays at a higher level than the known optimal value before reaching it. For Synch on 16 processors, it is possible that all runs are trapped in local optimal.

4.3.2 NYTimes news Dataset

NYTimes news dataset is a large dataset contains over 100 million words. The inference of HDP on such a dataset is extreme time-consuming and impractical. Efficient inference algorithm on such scale will significantly widen the range of application for the powerful HDP.

We selected a test set of 3000 articles from the dataset and used the rest as the training set. We evaluate the algorithm by the perplexity on the test set. The convergence curves are illustrated in Figure 7. All the results are obtained on 16 processors.

On NYTimes dataset, G2PP can converge in a short time. While there is no good way (except for running the experiment for infinite time) to tell whether Synch finally converged or trapped in "local optimal", it is safe to conclude that G2PP can provide better parameter estimation than Synch within a reasonable time limit.

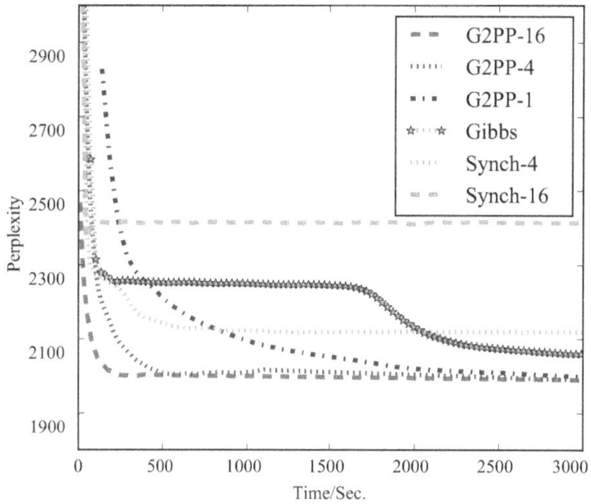

Figure 6: The convergence plot for G2PP and Synch with 1, 4, 16 processors on NIPS dataset.

Table 8: The experiment results of different sampling algorithms on NIPS dataset. Note that the results marked by ∗ represent those didn't converge within limited time.

Algorithm	# Proc.	Conv. time(sec.)	Perp.
G2PP	1	$1467 \pm 345(1164)$	2020
G2PP	4	$481 \pm 101(306)$	2016
G2PP	16	$102 \pm 45(63)$	2004
Gibbs	1	$1920 \pm 880(701)$	2060
Synch	2	$922 \pm 419(368)*$	2080
Synch	4	$519 \pm 331(188)*$	2117
Synch	16	$85.5 \pm 42(49)*$	2413

4.4 Comparison with Subsampling

In section 4.3, the G2PP algorithm performs consistently better than other baselines. But the underlying reason is unclear at this point. The major question is that because the G2PP performs bootstrap on the original dataset, is the speedup merely an outcome of subsampling on the original dataset? As the computation complexity is approximately proportional to the total length of documents, inference on the subsampled dataset should yield competitive speedup at the expenses of inference accuracy. Subsampling on the original dataset also places an unknown effect on the "local

[1] `http://ai.stanford.edu/~gal/data.html`

[2] `http://archive.ics.uci.edu/ml/datasets/Bag+of+Words`[3]

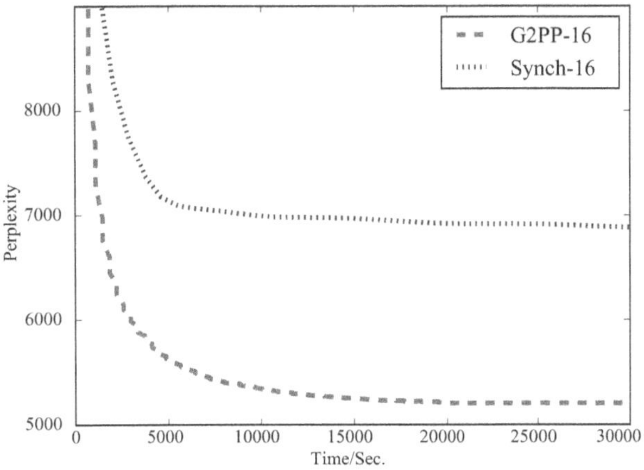

Figure 7: The convergence plot on NYT dataset for G2PP and Synch with 16 processors.

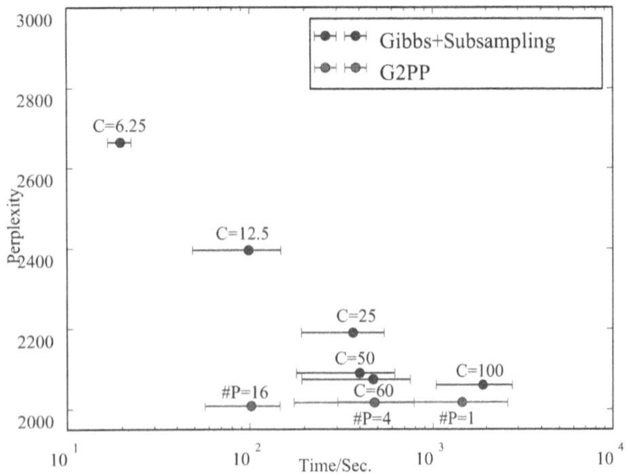

Figure 8: The convergence plot for Gibbs with subsampling on NIPS. $\#P$ denotes the number of processors, and C is the percentage of subsampling.

optimal" phenomenon. We design a series of experiments to answer this question.

In one experiment, we test the speedup and the accuracy of Gibbs algorithm with dataset subsampling. For each run, we first subsample the training set of NIPS dataset to the $C\%$ of its original length, then we conduct the inference only based on the subsampled dataset. The perplexity is tested on same test set as in section 4.3.1. We choose C from $\{6.75, 12.5, 50, 60\}$. The results are illustrated in Figure 8. The results by G2PP on the original dataset are also included for comparison.

As shown in Figure 8, subsampling provides a flexible tradeoff between speed and accuracy. Note that the speedup is not proportional to $1/C$, because subsampling affects both the computational complexity of each iteration and the overall convergence rate. By varying the subsampling rate, we can achieve comparable speedup similar to parallel algorithms with 4 processors on the NIPS dataset. But the accuracy decreases quickly when we further lower the subsampling rate. More importantly, we observe that the G2PP algorithm provides better trade off between accuracy and convergence rate comparing to Gibbs sampling with subsampling. This demonstrates that unique factors other than bootstrapping contribute to the gain in performance by G2PP.

5. CONCLUSION AND FUTURE WORK

In this paper, we proposed a parallel Gibbs sampling algorithm for HDP based on gamma-gamma-Poisson process. By actively bootstrapping the dataset, we constructed a *new* dataset with flexible size. Together with Reversible Jump MCMC, we proposed a parallel Gibbs sampling algorithm where each mixture component can update in parallel. The proposed algorithm is also suitable for distributed system. We showed its accuracy on synthetic datasets and remarkable speedup comparing with other HDP sampling algorithms on large scale real world dataset. We also examined convergence for parallel Gibbs sampling algorithm with asynchronous variable updates, and we provided the necessary condition to ensure convergence.

For future work, we will further improve the proposed algorithm from the following perspectives: First, we will study the systematic approach for setting parameter m; Second, we will investigate how to choose a dynamic upper bound on the number of mixture components; Lastly, we will examine the generality of the gamma-gamma-Poisson process for parallel inference over other nonparametric mixture models.

6. ACKNOWLEDGMENT

We thank Shang-Hua Teng, Eric Xing, Jun Zhu for discussions, and Xinran He for proof-reading. The research was sponsored by the NSF research grants IIS-1134990, NSF research grants IIS-1254206, and Okawa Foundation Research Award. The views and conclusions are those of the authors and should not be interpreted as representing the official policies of the funding agency, or the U.S. Government.

References

[1] C. Andrieu, N. De Freitas, A. Doucet, and M. I. Jordan. An introduction to mcmc for machine learning. *Machine learning*, 50(1-2):5–43, 2003.

[2] A. Asuncion, P. Smyth, and M. Welling. Asynchronous distributed learning of topic models. *Advances in Neural Information Processing Systems*, 21(81-88):17, 2008.

[3] K. Bache and M. Lichman. UCI machine learning repository, 2013.

[4] D. M. Blei, A. Y. Ng, and M. I. Jordan. Latent dirichlet allocation. *the Journal of Machine Learning Research*, 3:993–1022, 2003.

[5] T. S. Ferguson. A bayesian analysis of some nonparametric problems. *The Annals of Statistics*, pages 209–230, 1973.

[6] J. Gonzalez, Y. Low, A. Gretton, C. Guestrin, and U. Gatsby Unit. Parallel gibbs sampling: From colored fields to thin junction trees. *Journal of Machine Learning Research*, 2011.

[7] J. Gonzalez, Y. Low, and C. Guestrin. Residual splash for optimally parallelizing belief propagation. In *In Artificial Intelligence and Statistics*, Clearwater Beach, Florida, April 2009.

[8] J. Gonzalez, Y. Low, C. Guestrin, and D. O'Hallaron. Distributed parallel inference on large factor graphs.

In *Conference on Uncertainty in Artificial Intelligence*, Montreal, Canada, July 2009.

[9] Y. Low, J. Gonzalez, A. Kyrola, D. Bickson, C. Guestrin, and J. M. Hellerstein. Graphlab: A new parallel framework for machine learning. In *Conference on Uncertainty in Artificial Intelligence*, Catalina Island, California, July 2010.

[10] D. Newman, A. Asuncion, P. Smyth, and M. Welling. Distributed inference for latent dirichlet allocation. *Advances in Neural Information Processing Systems*, 20(1081-1088):17–24, 2007.

[11] L. Saloff-Coste and J. Zúñiga. Convergence of some time inhomogeneous markov chains via spectral techniques. *Stochastic processes and their applications*, 117(8):961–979, 2007.

[12] K.-A. Sohn and E. P. Xing. A hierarchical dirichlet process mixture model for haplotype reconstruction from multi-population data. *The Annals of Applied Statistics*, pages 791–821, 2009.

[13] E. Sudderth, A. Torralba, W. Freeman, and A. Willsky. Describing visual scenes using transformed dirichlet processes. *Advances in Neural Information Processing Systems*, 18:1297, 2006.

[14] Y. W. Teh, M. I. Jordan, M. J. Beal, and D. M. Blei. Hierarchical dirichlet processes. *Journal of the American Statistical Association*, 101(476), 2006.

[15] S. G. Walker. Sampling the dirichlet mixture model with slices. *Communications in Statistics-Simulation and Computation*, 36(1):45–54, 2007.

[16] Y. Wang, H. Bai, M. Stanton, W.-Y. Chen, and E. Y. Chang. Plda: Parallel latent dirichlet allocation for large-scale applications. In *Algorithmic Aspects in Information and Management*, pages 301–314. Springer, 2009.

[17] S. Williamson, A. Dubey, and E. P. Xing. Parallel markov chain monte carlo for nonparametric mixture models. In *Proceedings of the 30th International Conference on Machine Learning*, pages 98–106, 2013.

[18] F. Yan, N. Xu, and Y. Qi. Parallel inference for latent dirichlet allocation on graphics processing units. In *Advances in Neural Information Processing Systems*, pages 2134–2142, 2009.

[19] M. Zhou and L. Carin. Augment-and-conquer negative binomial processes. In *Advances in Neural Information Processing Systems*, pages 2555–2563, 2012.

Empirical Glitch Explanations

Tamraparni Dasu
AT&T Labs - Research
tamr@research.att.com

Ji Meng Loh
New Jersey Institute of Technology
ji.m.loh@njit.edu

Divesh Srivastava
AT&T Labs - Research
divesh@research.att.com

ABSTRACT

Data glitches are unusual observations that do not conform to data quality expectations, be they logical, semantic or statistical. By applying data integrity constraints, potentially large sections of data could be flagged as being noncompliant. Ignoring or repairing significant sections of the data could fundamentally bias the results and conclusions drawn from analyses. In the context of Big Data where large numbers and volumes of feeds from disparate sources are integrated, it is likely that significant portions of seemingly noncompliant data are actually legitimate usable data.

In this paper, we introduce the notion of *Empirical Glitch Explanations* – concise, multi-dimensional descriptions of subsets of potentially dirty data – and propose a scalable method for empirically generating such explanatory characterizations. The explanations could serve two valuable functions: (1) Provide a way of identifying legitimate data and releasing it back into the pool of clean data. In doing so, we reduce cleaning-related *statistical distortion* of the data; (2) Used to refine existing data quality constraints and *generate and formalize domain knowledge*.

We conduct experiments using real and simulated data to demonstrate the scalability of our method and the robustness of explanations. In addition, we use two real world examples to demonstrate the utility of the explanations where we reclaim over 99% of the suspicious data, keeping data repair related statistical distortion close to 0.

1. INTRODUCTION

While much attention has been paid to identifying data quality constraint violations and developing cleaning strategies, there has not been much focus on whether all data that is noncompliant should be subject to repair, and if all data that violate a given constraint should be treated as a homogeneous set. By unnecessarily or incorrectly remediating noncompliant data, there is a danger of changing the data to such an extent that it is unrecognizable and suffers a high *statistical distortion* as defined in [6]. Conclusions and inferences drawn from over-treated and distorted data could likely be misleading.

KDD'14, August 24–27, 2014, New York, NY, USA.

http://dx.doi.org/10.1145/2623330.2623716.

Empl.	Status	Phone	Dept.	Room	Super.
ID_1	Active	1AAA3600000	D4000	———	ID_4
ID_2	———	1AAA3600000	———	———	———
ID_3	Retired	1AAA3600000	D2200	E260	ID_6
ID_5	Active	1AAA3608776	D2300	A115	ID_9
ID_7	New Hire	1AAA3608776	D2300	D284	ID_5
ID_8	New Hire	1AAA3608776	D2300	B106	ID_5
ID_10	Active	1AAA3605519	D8000	A132	ID_13
ID_11	Active	1AAA3605519	D8000	A132	ID_13
ID_12	Active	1AAA3605519	D8000	A132	ID_13

Table 1: *Sample data from a Human Resources database: Employee ID, Employee Status, Phone number, Department ID, Room Number, Supervisor ID. Three sets of duplicates corresponding to three different phone numbers violate the data quality constraint "Any given phone number must have only one record associated with it."*

Given that data quality constraints tend to be fairly broad and flag significantly large tracts of data as suspect, it is critical to study this data for additional, potentially explanatory relationships in the data that could reduce the cost and distortion associated with cleaning, as well as add to our domain knowledge of the data. Data quality is so highly context and domain dependent that any empirical method that facilitates the gathering of domain knowledge, particularly in Big Data scenarios, is valuable in itself.

In this paper, we provide evidence that significant portions of data that seem to violate constraints have valid explanations and can be released back into the clean pool of data without being altered. Identifying empirical explanations for seemingly suspicious data based on attribute patterns is a valuable contribution to the data quality process that preserves the original characteristics of the data, and to the best of our knowledge, has not been addressed before. Formalizing and generating domain knowledge, or suggesting repair strategies are outside the current scope of the paper and will be addressed in future research.

1.1 An Illustrative Example

For illustrative purposes, we focus on a small instance from the Human Resources (HR) database of a big corporation. We will explore the example in detail in Section 5.

In Table 1, we present nine records, each with six attributes – Employee ID, Employee Status, Phone Number, Department ID, Room Number, Supervisor ID. In principle, a phone number is supposed to be unique and hence the attribute should follow the constraint: "Any given phone number must have only one record associated with it." However, we found several duplicates. We discuss three instances here, where each of the three phone numbers occurs three times. We have changed the actual values for proprietary reasons while preserving the attribute relationships.

In the first set of 3 duplicates corresponding to phone number `1AAA3600000`, there are five missing values. In the second set corresponding to phone number `1AAA3608776`, the employees are from the same department. Furthermore, employee with `ID_5` is the supervisor of the other two employees, both new hires. Finally, in the third set corresponding to phone number `1AAA3605519`, the three employees are again from the same department. In addition, they are all in the same room `A132` and report to the same supervisor `ID_13`.

Note that even though each of the examples violates the same constraint, namely "a given phone number must have only one record associated with it", it is possible that the explanation could be different. The first set could represent genuinely bad data or even a default value, since the set contains other bad data (missing values). The second set could reflect the legitimate use of the supervisor's phone number for new hires. Finally the third set could reflect employees sitting in the same room `A132` and hence sharing a physical phone. If these explanations are consistent with real world experience, we can return the second and third sets (6 records = 67% of bad data) to the "clean" data pool and modify the "no duplicates for a given phone number" rule to include the two exceptions – namely, if the employees are new hires and have the same phone number as their supervisor, or if they sit in the same physical room.

Our goal in this paper is to empirically discover such multi-attribute explanations for data quality violations. In doing so, we enable data consumers to sift through data glitches and identify positives that can be returned to the clean data pool, at the same time refining data quality constraints to better reflect the changing nature of the data. This is particularly important in the context of Big Data analytics where not just the data, but also the rules that govern them are in a state of flux, and where automation and speed are of essence.

1.2 Related Work

Data quality is an active area of research with extensive literature that covers a vast spectrum of topics. We briefly mention a small subset here, and refer the reader to literature that takes a broader overview of data quality such as the introductory [5] which focuses on an exploratory and analytical approach, or the more recent [8] which provides an overview of recent advances in the theory and application of data quality, including data inconsistencies, data deduplication, characterizing incomplete data, and data currency models; and applications in automatically discovering data quality rules, detecting errors in real-life data, and for correcting errors with performance guarantees.

There has also been considerable interest in refining data quality constraints. In [9], the authors focus on identifying subsets of data that do not conform to consistency constraints that are specified as functional dependencies. They propose a method for automatically generating "tableaux" that either violate or satisfy a given constraint.

In [3], the authors propose a new data-driven tool that focuses on the discovery of context-dependent rules and conditional functional dependencies (CFDs) that almost hold. The tool returns the rules together with the noncompliant records. In subsequent work [4], the authors propose that in contemporary scenarios, the constraints evolve constantly as the underlying data processes change. They describe a framework where the data and the constraints are modified in conjunction to minimize the cost of repair.

Other work has focused on glitch patterns and correlations [1] and introduced the idea of multi-type and multidimensional glitches. The authors use glitch dependencies and patterns for identifying data-driven cleaning strategies. In [2], the authors propose a *masking index* to estimate the impact of glitches hidden by masking (e.g. missing data mask duplicates). The idea of *statistical distortion*, the distortion in data caused by well-intentioned data repair efforts was introduced as a critical criterion for measuring the utility of data cleaning strategies in [6].

Our work is fundamentally different and novel and goes beyond validating or modifying constraints. We aim to *empirically explain* the violations in order to reduce the amount of data to be be cleaned and modified. In fact, as we demonstrated in our illustrative example, the same constraint ("duplicate phone numbers") could generate different explanations. Using the same repair for all data that violate this constraint could introduce new data glitches where none existed. This is an important contribution because existing literature makes no further distinction once the set of data that violates a constraint has been identified. We do not merely verify, validate or modify existing constraints, we explain the constraint violations to redeem good data, and lay the groundwork for the refinement of existing constraints and automatic generation of new constraints.

1.3 Our Contributions

In this paper, we turn our attention to the fundamental task of explaining seemingly anomalous data by empirically discovering patterns, and characterizing subsets that can be returned to the clean data pool, thus reducing the statistical distortion induced by unnecessary repairs. We:

(1) Introduce the novel and important notion of *explainable glitches* which are seeming violations that can be collectively described by a succinct empirical description. Such descriptions have the potential to explain the glitches, either by consulting subject matter experts ("supervisor's phone number used initially for new hires") or other heuristics ("shared physical device in a shared room"). The explanations could serve two valuable functions:

- (a) Provide a way to identify legitimate data and release it back into the pool of clean data. In doing so, we reduce *statistical distortion* of the data due to misguided data repair;
- (b) Used to refine existing data quality constraints and *generate and formalize domain knowledge.*

(2) Propose a *robust and scalable* method for empirically generating the explanations by developing the new notion of *crossover subsampling* to create subsets that are similar to the noncompliant set. In doing so we reduce the redundancy of the resampling procedure caused by the disparity in sizes between dataset D and the suspicious subset A and ensure that our results are statistically significant. In addition, we define *two objective metrics, size and merit,* for evaluating and ranking the explanations. The metrics make

the method flexible and customizable depending on the application. Such flexibility is key to a highly domain dependent task like data cleaning.
(3) We evaluate the methodology within a comprehensive experimental framework using real and synthetic data sets, and explore the robustness and scalability of explanations. In one real data instance, we are able to reclaim 99% of the data flagged as suspicious, reducing the potential statistical distortion considerably.

In this paper we focus on the notion that data that violate constraints can be explained and reclaimed for normal use without any alteration, thus preserving the authenticity of the original data. Generating and formalizing domain knowledge is outside the current scope and will be addressed in future work.

1.4 Paper Organization

The rest of the paper is organized as follows. In Section 2, we introduce the problem and in Section 3, present our approach to solving it. We discuss our empirical framework in Section 4. We present two real world case studies in Section 5 and Section 6. Finally, we summarize our results and identify future research in Section 7.

2. PROBLEM DESCRIPTION

Suppose that we are given a data set D with N rows (records) and d columns (attributes), and a constraint C. Constraints are rules (logical, semantic, statistical) that are imposed on data, typically to ensure conformity to expectations about the data e.g. "social security numbers must have 9 digits". Let the set A consist of all "suspicious" records in D that violate C. In our illustrative example, D would be the HR data, C would be the constraint "any given phone number must have only one record associated with it" and A would be the set of nine records in Table 1. In the absence of explanations, the problematic set Q that needs to be cleaned is given by

$$Q = A.$$

Our objective is to reduce the size of set Q by identifying portions of the set A that can be explained as "clean" using characteristics derived from other attributes and data values. By doing so, we cut the cost of cleaning *and* reduce distorting the statistical properties of the original data. A cleaning process typically makes an educated guess about the correct values. By adopting a frugal cleaning approach, we preserve more of the original data and stay faithful to the original statistical properties of the data.

Briefly, we achieve our objective by generating empirical explanations $\mathcal{E}$, each of which describes a set of records $P \subseteq A$. Explanations are typically of the form $\{s_j\}$, where s_j describes a condition on a value v_j in the suspicious set A.

For example, from the illustrative example in Section 1.1, for the suspicious sets corresponding to the phone numbers in parentheses, the following explanations were generated (we drop the attribute name when there is no ambiguity):
A (`1AAA3600000`) : $\mathcal{E}_1$ = {"blank" is frequent and occurs in multiple attributes}
A (`1AAA3608776`) : $\mathcal{E}_2$ = { `ID_5 in attributes 1 and 6, New Hire, D2300` }
A (`1AAA3608519`) : $\mathcal{E}_3$ = { `ID_13, A132, D8000` }
The empirical descriptions were then presented to an expert, who provided a real world description:
$\mathcal{E}_1$ = {"blank" is frequent and occurs in multiple attributes } → "Bad data, needs remediation."
$\mathcal{E}_2$ = { `ID_5 in attributes 1 and 6, New Hire, D2300` } → "Clean data : New hires assigned supervisor's phone #."
$\mathcal{E}_3$ = { `ID_13, A132, D8000` } → "Clean data : Members of same department working for the same supervisor, sharing a physical room, and a phone."
Therefore, in our example, of the three suspicious sets, only the one associated with `1AAA3600000` was truly problematic.

3. OUR APPROACH

We take a nonparametric approach to the problem. By doing so, we ensure a general applicability that is agnostic to any underlying data distributions. The main steps are:
(1) Identify the set A by applying the constraints C to the data set D as shown in Figure 1. In the absence of further explanation, the entire set A is deemed *suspicious*. We avoid the word anomalous since our objective is to establish that not all of A is anomalous.
(2) For each value $v \in A$, generate a *propensity signature, s*. The signature is probabilistic and captures the propensity of occurrence of a value v across all records and attributes of A, as shown in Figure 1.
(3) Rank the signatures based on their *suspiciousness*, using statistical criteria. The significant signatures together constitute an explanation

$$\mathcal{E} = \{s_j\}.$$

The signatures can be used collectively in a conjunctive (conditioned upon multiple attributes), disjunctive (conditioned upon multiple values of same attribute), or in some other manner to define the explanation.
(4) Apply the explanation $\mathcal{E}$ to A, to isolate the corresponding set of records P of A.
(5) Quantify the *effectiveness* of an explanation using its *size* and *merit* in reducing the statistical distortion of impacted records.

3.1 Suspicious Set

Given a data quality constraint C, we apply the constraint to the entire data set D and identify A, the suspicious subset of data violations. Identifying A is relatively easy for obvious glitches like null missing values or exact duplicates. However, it is non-trivial in more complex cases such as disguised missing values [12] and where the glitches are masked or hidden [2]. In addition, if the glitch detection is dependent on thresholds, for example in outliers, then determining A is even more task dependent. However, methods for formulating C and determining A are outside the scope of this paper. We assume that the data quality constraint C and the resultant set of violations A are both clearly specified.

DEFINITION 3.1. *The set of records $A \subseteq D$ that violate the data quality constraint C constitute the suspicious set.*

Usually $|A| << |D|$, but as we will see in the case studies, there could be exceptions. Let the "good" or non-suspicious data be given by

$$A' = D - A,$$

the complement of A with respect to the entire data set D. Our objective is to identify values $v \in A$ that exhibit different statistical behavior in A and A'.

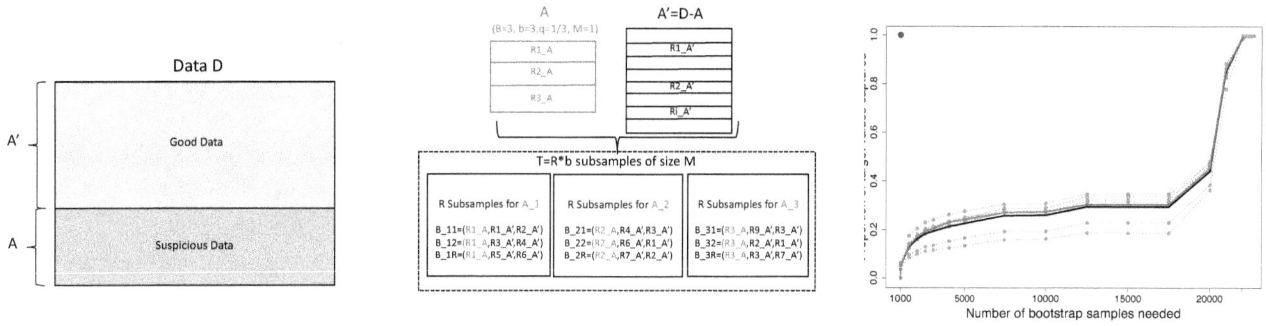

Figure 1: (a) Given a data set D, and a subset A of potentially suspicious data, we can compute *propensity signatures* for every value v in A by estimating its propensity of occurrence across the attributes $\{C_k\}$. (b) Crossover Subsampling: The suspicious set A of size $B = 3$ is divided into $b = 3$ parts of crossover proportion $q = 1/3$. Each part A_i is equivalent to a record R_i_A by construction. For each part R_i_A of size $M = B/b = 1$, the remaining $B - M = 2$ records R_j_D are drawn randomly from $D - A_i$ and a subsample of size $B = 3$ is created. This is repeated $R = 3$ times for each A_i, yielding $R * b = 3 * 3 = 9$ crossover subsamples in all. (c) Crossover sampling (blue dot), due to its design, captures all the values in a "suspicious set" in a specified number of samples (1000) while simple random sampling will require more than 20,000 samples to capture half the suspicious set, as shown by 10 iterations (grey dots), and mean (red) and median (black) over the 10 iterations.

3.2 Propensity Signatures

In order to capture the behavior of a value v in a set, we propose propensity signatures. Let v be a value in A, the suspicious set. Further, let the total number of attributes in A be d, and let p_k be the probability of v occurring in attribute C_k of A, where $k = 1, \ldots, d$. Then,

DEFINITION 3.2. *The propensity signature of a value v in set A is a d-dimensional vector given by*

$$s_A(v) = (p_1, \ldots, p_k, \ldots, p_d), k = 1, \ldots, d,$$

and captures the propensity of occurrence of v in A.

Analogously, the signature of v in A' is given by:

$$s_{A'}(v) = (P_1, \ldots, P_k, \ldots, P_d), k = 1, \ldots, d,$$

where P_k is the probability of occurrence of v across A'.

Note that propensity signatures differ from the traditional joint density functions which focus on the joint occurrence of different values in a record, while propensity signatures focus on the occurrence of a value across all records and attributes in a sample.

Since we do not know the distributions of v *a priori*, we will use the empirical estimates of propensity signatures $\widehat{s(v)}$ to identify the set of *suspicious* values $\mathbf{V} = \{v\}$ that have statistically different signatures in the suspicious data set A compared to the "good" data A'.

For example, given the suspicious set A of duplicate phone numbers corresponding to `1AAA3608776` discussed in Section 1.1, the *estimated propensity signatures* are:

$$s_A\widehat{(ID_5)} = (1/3, 0, 0, 0, 0, 2/3)$$

and

$$s_A(\widehat{NewHire}) = (0, 2/3, 0, 0, 0, 0).$$

We describe the empirical estimates in detail in Section 4.2. We wish to demonstrate that not all suspicious values are necessarily "dirty", and can be reclaimed without cleaning or altering in any way.

3.3 Statistical Significance

How do we determine whether the propensity signature of a value is statistically significant? One approach would be to compute the distances of propensity signatures of all values in A from the corresponding value signatures in the good set A', and rank the values based on the signature distances. The values with the greatest signature distances (say top 10%) could be considered statistically different. However, the problem with this approach is that the signatures of different values are not comparable, nor the distances between them. The signature of a common numeric value like 0 that spans multiple attributes and serves both as a real value as well as a default, is bound to be different from that of a specific character string like "Florida", for example. The relative ranking of signatures and distances of different values might be distorted by inherent differences in the way the values are used.

3.3.1 Crossover Subsampling

An alternate approach is to use resampling, where we draw samples repeatedly, compute propensity signatures of a given value in each sample, and construct a *sampling distribution* of the propensity signatures. From the sampling distribution, we can infer the expected signature of the value, as well as the expected variability in its signature. Resampling is an established technique for capturing the variability of statistical and empirical estimates, see [7, 11]. Since all the signatures in the sampling distribution pertain to the *same* value, the question of comparability does not arise.

In addition to the comparability of propensity signatures, we need to ensure that the signatures are computed from like sized data sets. The size of the set influences the variability of statistical estimates, and when we compare the propensity signature of a value from the suspicious set A, it is important to draw sample sets of similar size. This is achieved through *subsampling*, i.e. choosing a sample of a smaller size from a bigger sample, and in our case, choosing one the same size as A from the good set $A' = D - A$.

However, A is significantly smaller than D, and therefore A', because we expect the suspicious set of data quality violations to be fairly small. This makes random subsampling unsuitable for our purposes where it is likely that many of the subsamples drawn from A' will not capture the values in the records of A, and therefore make no contribution to the sampling distribution estimation. We would like to construct specialized subsamples that share some characteristics of A, in addition to being like-sized.

We accomplish this by proposing a novel subsampling technique called *crossover subsampling*. Note that crossover subsampling described below is different from stratified subsampling, where the subsample is drawn randomly and proportionally from each of the classes of interest, for example, A and $D - A$. However, with crossover subsampling, we are guaranteed that *every* record in A is represented in a specified proportion of the subsamples. Figure 1(c) empirically shows that over 10 iterations, given a target "suspicious set", crossover sampling (blue dot), due to its design, captures all the target values in a specified number of samples (e.g. 1000), while simple random sampling will require more than 20,000 samples to capture half the target values in any of the 10 iterations (grey dots), or the mean (red) and median (black) computed over the 10 iterations.

DEFINITION 3.3. *A q-crossover subsample of size B drawn from two sets D and $A \subset D$ where the size of set A is $|A| = B$, is defined to be a set that contains q proportion of samples from A, and the rest from $D - A$, and every record in A occurs in exactly q proportion of the subsamples.*

A q-crossover subsample is constructed as follows. In the absence of any prior knowledge, we partition A (size B) into $b = 1/q$ chunks of size $M = B/b$, denoted by $A = A_1 + A_2 + \ldots + A_b$, and cross each piece A_i with a random piece of size $B - M$ drawn from $D - A_i$ to create a like-sized sample of size B. We replicate this process R times, holding A_i fixed but drawing randomly without replacement from $D - A_i$. This yields R samples of size B corresponding to A_i. We then compute the sampling distribution of propensity signatures of each value v in A_i from these R replications corresponding to chunk A_i, denoted by $\widehat{\mathcal{F}_{A_i}(v)}$.

We test the estimated signature $\widehat{s_A(v)}$ against $\widehat{\mathcal{F}_{A_i}(v)}$, and establish whether that particular value has a statistically different pattern of occurrence in A_i using the method described in Section 3.3.2. Each chunk A_i then gets to vote on the suspiciousness of the value v.

DEFINITION 3.4. *A value v in set A is voted to be suspicious with respect to the empirical sampling distribution $\widehat{\mathcal{F}_{A_i(v)}}$ corresponding to chunk A_i of A if it is statistically significant with respect to that distribution. The vote is denoted by the indicator function $I_{A_i}(v)$ which takes the value 1 if significant, 0 otherwise.*

We repeat this step with each of the b pieces of A. Each chunk yields a vote $I_{A_i}(v)$ for each value v. The more votes a value has, the more confident we are about its significance and the more informative it is in an explanation.

DEFINITION 3.5. *The informativeness of a value v is measured by the proportion of votes*

$$K = \sum_i I_{A_i}(v)/b.$$

In summary, the crossover sampling process results in a total of $T = R * b$ samples of size B, and a collection of *empirical sampling distributions* $\{\widehat{\mathcal{F}_{A_i}(v)}\}_{i=1}^{b}$ corresponding to the b chunks $\{A_1, \ldots, A_b\}$, each of which gets one vote for each value v.

We demonstrate the process in Figure 1(b), where:
B (subsample size, same as size of suspicious set A) = 3,
b (number of chunks) = 3,
M (chunk size) = $B/b = 1$,
q (crossover proportion) = $1/b = 1/3$,
R (the number of replications) = 3, and
T (the total number of subsamples) = $R * b = 9$.

In the process described above, all the R replications correspond to a given partition of $A = A_1 + A_2 + \ldots + A_b$ into b chunks. We could make the process more general by spreading the number of replications R over a small number of randomized partitions of A. For example, we could run $R/5$ replications for a given partition $A = A_1 + A_2 + \ldots + A_b$, another $R/5$ replications for $A = B_1 + B_2 + \ldots + B_b$ and so on until a final $R/5$ replications for the fifth partition $A = E_1 + E_2 + \ldots + E_b$. This would make it possible to combine the votes from each chunk with greater generality.

3.3.2 Testing for Statistical Significance

We flag a value v as significant if its propensity signature lies outside the chosen error bounds of its corresponding sampling distribution $\widehat{\mathcal{F}_A(v)}$. These bounds are computed component-wise for each attribute. We compare each element of the signature with the corresponding bootstrap distribution and if any element lies above or below the chosen bounds, (mean $\pm$ 2 standard deviations; 97.5 and 2.5 percentiles), we declare the signature to be significant. For example, consider the propensity signature

$$\widehat{s_A(ID_5)} = (1/3, 0, 0, 0, 0, 2/3)$$

from our illustrative example. The following error bounds are based on the mean $\pm$ 2 standard deviations (hence the negative and fractional values of the bounds) of the bootstrap sampling distribution corresponding to ID_5 :

```
Lower (2.5%) Bound:  (-0.18, 0, 0, 0, 0, 0.44)
Upper (97.5%) Bound:  (0.2, 0, 0, 0, 0, 0, 1.80).
```

Now, given that $\widehat{s_A(ID_5)}$'s first component corresponding to component (attribute 1), 1/3=0.33 is above the upper bound 0.2 for the corresponding component, we declare the value ID_5 to be significant even though for component (attribute) 6, 2/3=0.67 lies within the interval [0.44,1.8].

We use statistically significant propensity signatures that have been identified in this way to construct *explanations*.

3.4 Glitch Explanations

Let the collection of values v in A with statistically significant signatures be $\mathbf{V} = \{v_1, v_2, \ldots, v_L\}$.

DEFINITION 3.6. *A glitch explanation $\mathcal{E} \subseteq \mathbf{V}$ is a collection of values in A that have statistically significant propensity signatures.*

For example, for the suspicious set A of duplicate phone numbers corresponding to phone number `1AAA3608776` discussed in Section 1.1, the estimated signatures of ID_5 and $NewHire$ are significant and lead to the explanation: $\mathcal{E} = ID_5, NewHire$.

Note that explanations need to be human interpretable (vetted by domain experts), and therefore the more succinct they are, the easier to understand and explain. To capture this aspect, we introduce the notion of the size of an explanation.

DEFINITION 3.7. *The size of an explanation is the smallest number of informative, non-redundant values in the explanation.*

We can use a threshold on the informativeness (Definition 3.5) i.e. $K > \alpha$ for including a value v in an explanation, providing a measure of customizability to the data consumer.

In addition, the set of values with statistically significant propensity signatures could exhibit redundancy. For instance, if two values have a one-to-one relationship and always occur together in every record of the suspicious set A (e.g., unique organizational code such as "DEPT007" and a unique name like "Department of Shaken, Not Stirred"). Finally, values such as blanks are usually not informative and do not contribute towards a general explanation. Note that many redundancies can be automatically generated using algorithms for discovering functional dependencies and conditional dependencies e.g. in [9].

3.5 Evaluating an Explanation

We measure the efficacy of an explanation by the *statistical distortion* of the data prevented by reclaiming the data corresponding to the explanation. Statistical distortion can be measured in many ways, from simple measures like difference in aggregates such as means and medians, to more complex measures such as the histogram distance between two data sets D and D'. Different ways of measuring statistical distortion, including the Earth Mover Distance, are described in [6].

For the purpose of this paper, we use the general notion of the proportion of records that are touched by data repair. This is because any other metric, such as histogram distance, would need a knowledge of the actual repairs and changes made to the data. Since our focus is on explaining glitches and not statistical distortion *per se*, this general notion is enough for the purpose of illustration.

Any records that are reclaimed by glitch explanations and left untouched, result in a *reduction* in the statistical distortion caused by cleaning. Let S be the reclaimed set with size $|S|$. Then, the *reduction* τ in the statistical distortion is given by:

$$\tau = \frac{|S|}{|A|}.$$

DEFINITION 3.8. *The merit τ of an explanation $\mathcal{E}$ is the reduction in statistical distortion caused by reclaiming the records explained by $\mathcal{E}$.*

For instance, we can reclaim 6 of the 9 suspicious records in the example of Section 1.1, resulting in a merit of

$$\tau = 6/9 = 0.667.$$

3.6 Automation and Scale

In general, we expect the suspicious set A to be small, and therefore the number of values for which to compute signatures to be relatively small as well. If not, the target values for which to compute propensity signatures can be selected on a prioritized basis e.g. top 5% of frequently occurring values.

In addition, the choice of parameters such as crossover proportion, q, and informativeness, K, while customizable, are rooted in statistical theory. We have found that $q \in [0.1, 0.25]$ and $K > 0.8$ are good default values.

Finally, while explanations are often validated by human experts, it is possible to refine and cross-validate them automatically by empirical repetition and replication.

4. EMPIRICAL FRAMEWORK

From the preceding discussion, it is is clear that our approach for generating signatures and explanations is data-driven and necessarily requires a rigorous experimental basis to ensure the validity of the empirical results. We describe the experimental framework.

4.1 Identifying the Suspicious Set

For the purpose of this paper, we assume that identifying the suspicious set A of data quality violations is simply a matter of testing well-defined constraints. However, it is likely that identifying A might involve uncertainty, in which case we might need an empirical approach, as in the case of disguised missing values [10].

4.2 Constructing Propensity Signatures

Each of the sets A and $D - A$ contain a collection of distinct values. We construct the empirical estimates of the propensity signatures described in Section 3.2 in a single pass over the data, for each distinct value in A and $D - A$. Let A have N_A rows (records). Suppose that v occurs n_k times in column (attribute) C_k in the suspicious set A. Let

$$\widehat{p_k} = n_k/N_A,$$

be an empirical estimate of the probability p_k. For example, in Figure 1, an estimate of the propensity signature of v is given by:

$$\widehat{s_A(v)} = (0, 2/3, 2/3, 1/3, 3/3, 0).$$

Similarly, the estimated propensity signature of v in $A' = D - A$ is given by

$$\widehat{s_{A'}(v)} = (\widehat{P_1}, \ldots, \widehat{P_k}, \ldots, \widehat{P_d}), k = 1, \ldots, d,$$

where $\widehat{P_k} = m_k/N_{A'}$, m_k is the number of occurrences of v in attribute C_k of A' , $N_{A'}$ is the number of rows (records) in A'. Note that $\widehat{p_k} = n_k/N_A$ is the maximum likelihood estimate (MLE) [13] of the true probability p_k that v will occur in the kth column (attribute) of A, and similarly $\widehat{P_k} = m_k/N_{A'}$ is the MLE with respect to P_k, the probability that v will occur in the kth column (attribute) of A'.

4.3 Resampling and Subsampling

Once we have identified A and $A' = D - A$, we need to isolate values $v \in A$ that help us to statistically differentiate A from A', in order to explain the suspiciousness. We accomplish this using crossover subsampling discussed in Section 3.3.1.

In our experiments in this paper, we used a thousand bootstrap replications ($R = 1000$) to generate 1000 signatures for each value $v \in A$. Note that the actual signature contributed by the suspicious set A is included in the 1000. We flag value v to be significant if any element in its signature lies outside the error bounds computed from the sampling distribution based on the 1000 bootstrap signatures. For the rest of this paper we use quantile based error bounds at the 0.005 level of significance. The results in the case studies in Sections 5 and 6 are based on a crossover proportion of $q = 0.1$, except in one set of experiments where we vary the crossover proportion. The computation was performed in 10 parallel R language batch jobs on a cluster of Intel multi-core Xeon processors (2.53GHz) running Scientific Linux 5.5 operating system.

5. ORGANIZATIONAL DATA

Our first real world data consisted of the Human Resources database of a large company. It contained 50,084 records, each record with 17 attributes. Our data quality constraint was "Given any telephone number, there should be only one record". Note that validating this constraint involves multiple records. When we applied the constraint, we found that 14,872 (29%) records were in violation, generated by 530 distinct phone numbers, each of which gave rise to a suspicious set of duplicates. The sets came in 54 distinct sizes. Only a handful of suspicious sets had significant sizes, most had fewer than 100 records, considerably fewer than the overall set size of 50K records. The distribution of the size of the suspicious sets is shown in Figure 2(a), where the X-axis is the size of the suspicious set and the Y-axis the number of suspicious sets with that size. The axes are staggered with variable scales for better readability. Only two sets have more than 1000 records, and most have fewer than 50 records, with suspicious sets with just 2 records accounting for more than 100 such sets. We list the 5 most duplicated phone numbers below. While we have anonymized the actual values for proprietary reasons, the explanations are real.

```
+1 (BBB) 999-9999 (8011 duplicates);
+ CCC9999999      (2209 duplicates);
+1 (DDD) 392-2600 (619 duplicates);
                  (538 duplicates);
+1 (EEE) 000-0000 (475 duplicates).
```

It is interesting that at first glance, the worst offenders (with the exception of `+1 (DDD) 392-2600`) seem to be bogus phone numbers used as defaults.

Let us first consider the explanation corresponding to the non-trivial duplicate phone number `1 (DDD) 392-2600` which is duplicated 619 times. It is given by:

$\mathcal{E}$ `(1 (DDD) 392-2600)`={ MeanBoss, USA, HER MAJESTY'S CUSTOMER SERVICE, MIRAMAR, FL, C, Contractor, Bogus Co., =33027, LAKESIDE DR STE 620 }

The signature provides an interesting explanation. The phone number corresponds to `Contractors` that work for the company `Bogus` under supervisor `MeanBoss`; and are located at `LAKESIDE DR STE 620, MIRAMAR, FL, 33027, USA`; shared the phone number `1 (DDD) 392-2600`; and were dedicated to working on `HER MAJESTY'S CUSTOMER SERVICE`. It is a centralized office number, and is therefore acceptable as a duplicate.

Similarly, consider the explanation for the phone number `1 (EEE) 000-0000` duplicated 475 times:

$\mathcal{E}$ `(1 (EEE) 000-0000)` = { USA , C, SuperBoss, WESTLAKE VILLAGE , Q's SOLUTIONS, TX , Shady Marketing, MI, Fishy Co. , CA , =91361, =76054, TOWNSGATE RD, NORWOOD DR }

The phone numbers corresponds to employees that work for supervisor `SuperBoss`, and were contracted from the companies Fishy Co. or Shady Marketing, to work on Q's SOLUTIONS and given the default phone number of `1 (EEE) 000-0000`.

The explanation for the worst offender `+1 (BBB) 999-9999`, after removing redundancies like blanks and other values like states and cities, consisted of 18 zip codes, corresponding to locations of contractors working across the USA. The zip codes appeared only in this suspicious set and not in any of the other suspicious sets, making them distinctive.

These examples show that while the phone numbers were "dirty" and violated a constraint, the other attributes provide enough of an explanation for us to trust that data and reclaim it for regular use. With just the five suspicious sets described above, we were able to reclaim 11,852 of the 14,872 duplicate records.

5.1 Reclaiming data with Explanations

In general, explanations consisting of between 3 to 20 values are ideal. Very small explanations might not be specific enough (e.g. "USA"), and those with too many values might be hard to interpret. Sometimes, by relaxing the threshold K from 1 to 0.8, we found more useful explanations.

On other occasions, despite our best efforts, the explanations were not useful. Consider the one associated with a small suspicious set of 29 duplicates.

$\mathcal{E}$ `(1 0)` = { C }

Clearly, even the phone number `1 0` is mangled. And the significant value in the explanation, "C", does not provide any useful information other than the fact that it is a code associated with contractors. The locations were spread across multiple cities in multiple countries, across multiple services and supervisors. There was no discernible pattern. Therefore we could not salvage these records.

In total, using our method we could explain all but around 70 records corresponding to suspicious sets of size 29, 16, 6, and 2 (multiple sets) which did not garner enough votes to pass confidence guarantees. Therefore, in this real world case study, our explanations reclaimed around 14,800 records and caused a total reduction in statistical distortion of

$$\sum \tau = (14800)/14872 = 0.9951.$$

Therefore the collective merit of our explanations for the Organizational data is 0.9951. Next, we ran experiments to test various sampling parameters.

5.2 Experiment 1: Robustness of Explanations

To test whether the explanations for close variants of a phone number are similar, we took a suspicious set and created two syntactically different variants. One set corresponding to `FFF7474014` with $|A|$=298, and second set corresponding to `FFF 747 4014` with $|A|$=30. We were gratified that our method generated the same explanation for both, namely:

$\mathcal{E}$ = { "M", IIND, II, GURGAON, GRGNIIAF, DLF ATRIA PHASE II GURGAON HARYANA, Desi Company, Contractor, BOND CUSTOMER EXPERIENCE, C, =122 002 }

From this we could infer that both sets of duplicate phone numbers corresponded to contractors from an Indian company assigned to supervisor `"M"`, and that the two phone numbers were *near-duplicates*, but our method was robust

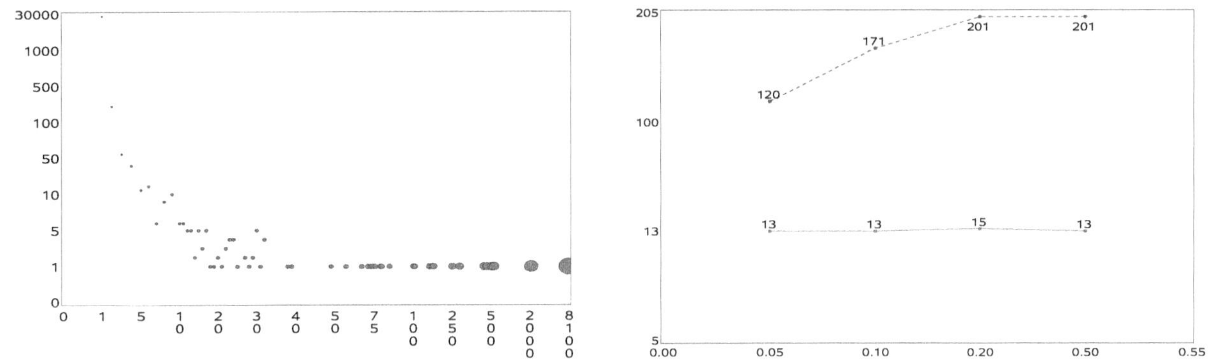

Figure 2: (a) For the case study in Section 5, the distribution of the size of suspicious sets; (b) The change in the size of explanations with crossover proportion q. For the suspicious set of `+1 (BBB) 999-9999` (shown as blue dashed curve), the size of the explanations increases with the crossover proportion. For the suspicious set of `FFF7474014` (shown as solid red curve), the size of the explanation is very steady, implying a well-defined succinct set.

enough to generate the same set of values in the explanation, despite the difference in sizes of the suspicious sets.

5.3 Experiment 2: Crossover Proportion

For our second experiment, we chose two suspicious sets corresponding to two different phone numbers in the HR data. The first suspicious set consisted of duplicates of `+1 (BBB) 999-9999` and had 8011 records with 33,063 unique values. The second suspicious set consisted of duplicates of `FFF7474014` and had 298 records with 1,364 unique values. We varied $q = (0.05, 0.1, 0.2, 0.5)$ and measured three quantities for each of the two suspicious sets: (1) the number of significant values that got at least one vote from the $b = 1/q$ chunks, (2) the size of the explanation defined as the number of values within each proportion q that got a unanimous vote, i.e. $K = 1$ from Definition 3.5, and (3) the number of "clean" values in the explanation that got a perfect vote of $K = 1$ for all four values of the crossover proportion q.

Figure 2 (b) shows the size of the explanations with each crossover proportion. The X-axis shows the crossover proportion q, the Y-axis shows the size of the explanation. In this particular discussion, the size is based solely on votes, and not on redundancy. We chose to keep the redundant values in order to maintain comparability since they will be consistently included in all signatures. In Figure 2(b), the suspicious set of `+1 (BBB) 999-9999` (shown as blue dashed curve) had 283 significant values of which 100 were unanimous in all the proportions. The size of the explanations increases with the crossover proportion, almost doubling. This indicates that there is no succinct explanation, it just expands as the bootstraps include more and more of the suspicious set. (Most of these were redundant values like geographical states and "USA". As noted above, we reduced these to 18 non-redundant values of zip codes.) The suspicious set of `FFF7474014` (shown as solid red curve) had 36 significant values of which 13 were unanimous in all four proportions. The size of the explanation is very steady, implying a well-defined succinct set.

6. MOBILE TELEPHONY DATA

Our second example consists of mobile telephony data, collected over a period of two weeks. We anonymized the data by preserving the NPA (area code) of each phone number and hashing the 7 digit phone number in a consistent fashion. Next, we aggregated the data by zip codes and into 15 minute bins. Each zip code was associated with a Metro area. The variables of interest include number of calls made, number of texts sent, number of calls dropped during set up, and number of calls dropped while the call was in progress. The aggregated data set had 27,291,446 records. A sample:

```
ZIP|UNIX-TIME|CALLS|BAD-1|BAD-2|TEXTS|METRO AREA
10001|1360231200|208|0|0|463|Manhattan
10001|1360232100|227|0|2|410|Manhattan
```

We suspect that some of the data might be erroneous for reasons that are probably data quality related, rather than anything to do with the actual network performance. A rationale is outside the scope of this paper, but the data quality constraint was specified by experts as:

$$C_T \leq 0.25,$$

where C_T is the ratio of the sum of `BAD-1` and `BAD-2` calls to the total number of calls handled. Any records that violated this constraint i.e. $C_T > 0.25$ were considered suspicious and put in the set A. In reality, there were only 78,464 records across more than 27 Million records. Note that this instance is (1) a valid case where $|A| << |D|$, and (2) an example of a single-record constraint where each record can be assessed for constraint violation independently of other records.

Even though the suspicious records were scattered, we wanted to study if we could (1) recover patterns if they existed in such large data of millions of records and (2) study the impact of scale on our method. The mobility data used in the following two studies study was synthetic data created from the real mobility data described above, by injecting suspicious data from the set A in a controlled manner.

Suspicious Zip Codes: We took 174,326 records corresponding to the zip codes from metro areas labelled New York, Other NYC Boroughs, Chicago, Chicago Loop and San Francisco and created a test data set D_T. This particular data set had no bad records at all. We simulated bad data by injecting bad records from the suspicious set A into the test data set D_T. We selected the worst 6 zip codes from

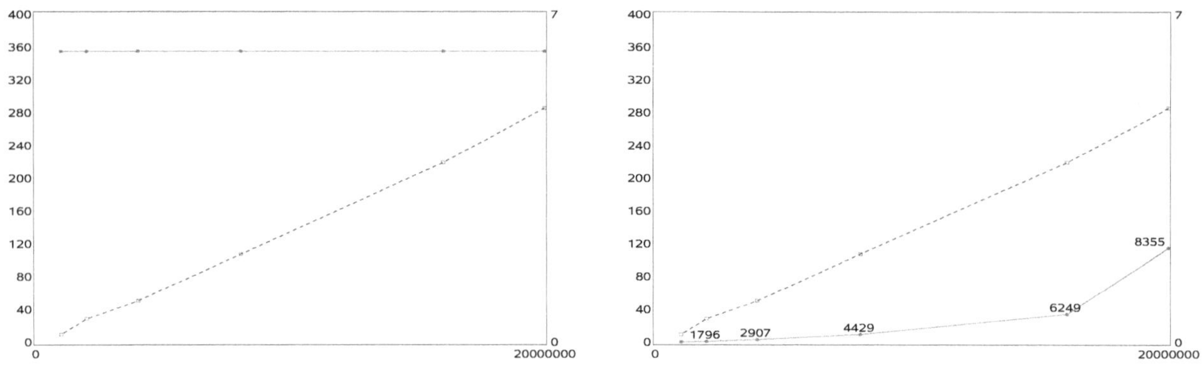

Figure 3: Plots (a) and (b) show the run times of (1) creating the crossover samples (blue dashed line) and (2) computing the signatures and the bootstrap sampling distribution (solid red curve) as the sizes of the good and bad data set vary. In (a) the bad data set is fixed at 78000 while the good data set varies as shown on the X-axis. In (b) the sizes of both the data sets vary. The two curves are measured on different scales (Y-axes), the red curve against the Y-axis on the left side, the blue curve on the Y-axis on the right side of the plots. The numbers on the curve represent the number of unique values in the bad data set.

A listed under the column "Worst Zip" of Table 2. These 6 zip codes contributed 1,517 bad records, and a total of 7,146 records. We then chose 6 zip codes in D_T that had a similar distribution of records as the 6 worst zips. We removed all these records, and replaced them with all the records corresponding to the 6 worst zips. Finally, we mapped the actual zip codes of the worst 6 zips to the zip codes of the records that we removed from the data set D_T. The mapping is shown in Table 2. While mapping the zips is not necessary, we do it for reasons of consistency to keep the zip codes within the metro areas for interpretation purposes. Note that the simulated bad zip codes correspond to the three metro areas Chicago Loop, San Francisco and Manhattan.

The resulting data set D_{ZIP} now has 174,391 total records with 1,517 bad records concentrated in 6 zips listed under the column "Mapped To Zip" of Table 2. That is, if the bad records occur in these zip codes, then they are not suspicious since we put them there. Our method correctly generated the zip codes `94143, 94119, 60603, 60602, 10041, 10020` as significant values, each with 10 votes from each of the randomizations. In addition, the following explanation for the Metro areas were generated. The number of votes are shown in parentheses: `Chicago Loop(10), San Francisco(10)` for the upper tail (much higher). Chicago Loop and San Francisco are as expected due to the zip code mapping, and are redundant to the zip codes. However, the metro area Manhattan did not show up. This is because the proportion of Manhattan was the same in the bad data as it was in the good data. But this has no impact on our explanations since Metro areas are redundant to the zip codes.

Worst Zip	MappedTo Zip	MappedTo Metro	Total Records	Suspicous Records
88434	60602	Chicago	1329	395
80744	94119	San Fran	1303	252
55925	10041	Manhattan	900	229
93225	60603	Chicago	1344	220
03278	10020	Manhattan	1249	212
67481	94143	San Fran	1021	209

Table 2: Zip mapping

Therefore our minimal explanation is that bad records in the following zip codes will not be considered "dirty" since we expect them to be there.
$\mathcal{E} = \{$ zip codes: 94143, 94119, 60603, 60602, 10041, 10020 $\}$.
As a consequence, we are able to reclaim all the suspicious records, resulting in a statistical distortion of 0. The merit τ of our explanation is 1.

Had we not used the explanations, the statistical distortion associated with the dirty data would have been $\mathit{StatisticalDistortion} = 1517/174391 = 0.0087$.

Suspicious Time Periods: We simulated badly behaved time periods in a manner similar to the zip codes. We took the worst 6 15-minute time slots, namely `2.45 AM, 3.00 AM, 3.15 AM, 3.30 AM, 3.45 AM, 4.00 AM`, from the master file of 27 Million records. These contributed 7908 records. We replaced the data corresponding to these time slots in the test dataset D_T with the bad data. Table 3 shows the number of injected records corresponding to the time slot, and the corresponding suspicious records contained in them.

Time Slot	Suspicious Records	Total Records
02:45 AM	1266	1338
03:00 AM	1247	1326
03:15 AM	1271	1322
03:30 AM	1212	1276
03:45 AM	1301	1356
04:00 AM	1229	1290

Table 3: Simulated time slots

We derived the time and day of the week from the Unix time stamp and generated the following explanations.
$\mathcal{E} = \{$ Tue, Wed, Thurs, Sat, Sun; 2.45 AM, 3.00 AM, 3.15 AM, 3.30 AM, 3.45 AM, 4.00 AM $\}$
The explanation of the bad time periods holds for 5 days of the week, but doesn't seem to include Mondays and Fridays. The bad records corresponding to these two days that fall

in the 6 identified time slots, 1,090 and 1,148 respectively, cannot be explained. Therefore the merit of our explanation is:

$$\tau = (7908 - (1090 + 1148))/7908 = 0.717.$$

6.1 Experiment 3: Size of Data Sets

Finally, we wanted to test the scalability of our method, in terms of computation as well as robustness of explanations, by varying the sizes of both the suspicious set A and the good set $A' = D - A$. We resampled from the mobility data described at the beginning of this section to create the following synthetic data. The experiments are summarized in Figure 3 which features two Y-axes, on the left and right side of the plotting frames, one for each of the two curves that are measured on different scales. The X-axis denotes the number of records in the good data set.

First, we kept the bad data set at the fixed size of 78,464 records (10,111 unique values) and varied the size of the good data set from 1Million records to 2, 4, 8, 16 and 20 Million records. We split the task into two steps (1) create the bootstrap crossover subsamples (dashed blue curve in Figure 3 measured against the Y-axis on the right side of the plotting frame) and (2) compute the signatures and the corresponding sampling distribution from the bootstrap samples (solid red curve in Figure 3 measured against the Y-axis on the left side of the plotting frame). We found, as expected, that creating the crossover subsamples from the good data set to form the 1000 bootstrap samples took longer with the increase in the size of the good data. In Figure 3(a), the dashed blue curve increases with the size of the good data, measured against the second Y-axis on the right side of the frame. The computation of the bootstrap signatures and the sampling distribution depends only on the size of the samples (fixed at 78000) and the number of bootstraps (fixed at 1000). This is reflected in the solid straight line at the top of the plot measured against the first Y-axis on the left side of the frame. We also found that the set of suspicious values, and hence the resulting explanations, were the same in all cases.

Next, we changed the sizes of both the good and bad data. The good data was varied just as above, but in addition we varied the size of the bad data over 1250, 2500, 5000, 10000, 20000 and 40000 records. Number of unique values in the bad set are denoted on the red curve. As expected, the computing times increased with both the data set sizes, for both the sample creation (dashed blue) and the signature and sampling distribution computation (solid red). However, fewer suspicious values were deemed significant in the instances with smaller bad data sets. This phenomenon was mainly due to the smaller number of unique values in the bad data records. For example, the smallest bad data set of 1250 records is about 1.5% of the original bad data set of 78,464 records. In addition, there is more uncertainty (variance) in the distribution of the bootstrap signatures for the smaller bad data sets. Many of the values, even when significant, fail the strict criterion of $K = 1$, i.e. all 10 blocks generated by the $q = 0.1$ crossover proportion must vote for the signatures.

7. CONCLUSION

In this paper, we introduced the notion of *empirical glitch explanations*, which are data-driven, multi-attribute descriptions of subsets of potentially dirty data. The explanations are used by domain experts to decide whether the data is genuinely dirty, or is acceptable based on the explanations. The explanations reduce the amount of data subjected to unnecessary repair, and reduce the statistical distortion induced by cleaning. We evaluate explanations based on their *size*, which is related to usefulness and interpretability, and *merit*, the amount of statistical distortion prevented by the explanations.

We described an empirical framework for generating glitch explanations by proposing a novel subsampling technique called *crossover subsampling*. We demonstrated the utility of our approach based on real world data sets where we could reclaim up to 99% of the data, and ran experiments to demonstrate the scalability and robustness of our method.

A major thrust of our future work, which could have critical applications in Big Data, involves generating and formalizing the domain knowledge we learn from the glitch explanations, in order to: (1) Reason with it and answer questions e.g. "what is the most common explanation for glitches in one organization vs another?" and (2) Analyze explanations over time as new data gets added to understand the temporal nature and frequency of glitch patterns.

8. REFERENCES

[1] L. Berti-Equille, T. Dasu, and D. Srivastava. Discovery of complex glitch patterns: A novel approach to quantitative data cleaning. In *ICDE*, 2011.

[2] L. Berti-Equille, J. M. Loh, and T. Dasu. A masking index for quantifying hidden glitches. In *ICDM*, 2013.

[3] F. Chiang and R. J. Miller. Discovering data quality rules. *PVLDB*, 1(1):1166–1177, 2008.

[4] F. Chiang and R. J. Miller. A unified model for data and constraint repair. *ICDE*, 2011.

[5] T. Dasu and T. Johnson. *Exploratory Data Mining and Data Cleaning*. John Wiley, New York, 2003.

[6] T. Dasu and J. M. Loh. Statistical distortion: Consequences of data cleaning. *PVLDB*, 5(11):1674–1683, 2012.

[7] B. Efron and R. J. Tibshirani. *An Introduction to the Bootstrap*. Chapman and Hall, 1993.

[8] W. Fan. Data quality: Theory and practice. In H. Gao, L. Lim, W. Wang, C. Li, and L. Chen, editors, *Web-Age Information Management*, volume 7418 of *Lecture Notes in Computer Science*, pages 1–16. Springer Berlin Heidelberg, 2012.

[9] L. Golab, H. J. Karloff, F. Korn, D. Srivastava, and B. Yu. On generating near-optimal tableaux for conditional functional dependencies. *PVLDB*, 1(1):376–390, 2008.

[10] M. Hua and J. Pei. Cleaning disguised missing data: A heuristic approach. *KDD*, 2007.

[11] R. Kohavi. A study of cross-validation and bootstrap for accuracy estimation and model selection. *IJCAI*, 1995.

[12] R. K. Pearson. The problem of disguised missing data. *SIGKDD Explor. Newsl.*, 8(1):83–92, June 2006.

[13] C. R. Rao. *Linear Statistical Inference and Its Applications*. Wiley, New York, 1973.

Learning with Dual Heterogeneity: A Nonparametric Bayes Model

Hongxia Yang
IBM Watson Research Center
1101 Kitchawan Rd
Yorktown Heights, NY, 10598
yangho@us.ibm.com

Jingrui He
School of Computing, Informatics, Decision Systems Engineering
Arizona State University
699 S Mill Ave, Tempe, AZ 85281
jingrui.he@gmail.com

ABSTRACT

Traditional data mining techniques are designed to model a single type of heterogeneity, such as multi-task learning for modeling task heterogeneity, multi-view learning for modeling view heterogeneity, etc. Recently, a variety of real applications emerged, which exhibit dual heterogeneity, namely both task heterogeneity and view heterogeneity. Examples include insider threat detection across multiple organizations, web image classification in different domains, etc. Existing methods for addressing such problems typically assume that multiple tasks are equally related and multiple views are equally consistent, which limits their application in complex settings with varying task relatedness and view consistency. In this paper, we advance state-of-the-art techniques by adaptively modeling task relatedness and view consistency via a nonparametric Bayes model: we model task relatedness using normal penalty with sparse covariances, and view consistency using matrix Dirichlet process. Based on this model, we propose the *NOBLE* algorithm using an efficient Gibbs sampler. Experimental results on multiple real data sets demonstrate the effectiveness of the proposed algorithm.

Categories and Subject Descriptors

G.3 [**Probability and Statistics**]: [nonparametric statistics]; I.5.1 [**Pattern Recognition**]: Models—*statistical*

Keywords

Nonparametric Bayes modeling; multi-task multi-view; Gibbs sampler.

1. INTRODUCTION

Nowadays, we are facing large amount of data in a variety of areas, such as social media, manufacturing, traffic analytics, etc. A common challenge in these areas is how to handle multiple types of data heterogeneity. For example, in social media, we may have micro-blogs coming from heterogeneous sources, such as Facebook and Twitter, and each micro-blog may be characterized by heterogeneous features, such as key words, hashtags, number of re-tweets, number of Facebook likes, etc; in manufacturing, we may have products from heterogeneous manufacturing lines, and each product may be characterized by heterogeneous environmental variables, such as temperature, pressure, etc; in traffic analytics, we can collect traffic information from heterogeneous geographic locations (e.g., different states), and for each location, we may have heterogeneous traffic indicators, such as volume, GPS positions, etc.

Recent years have seen growing interest in addressing problems with multiple types of data heterogeneity [22, 19, 14, 43, 20, 21, 42]. In particular, for problems with dual heterogeneity, i.e., both task and view heterogeneity, researchers have proposed multi-task multi-view learning, or M^2TV learning, to jointly learn in multiple related tasks with overlapping, partially overlapping or completely different feature spaces [22, 43, 21, 42]. Compared with traditional multi-task learning [12, 46, 11, 38, 30], where the feature space is *homogeneous* across different tasks, i.e., a single view, M^2TV learning is able to handle *heterogeneous* feature spaces; compared with traditional multi-view learning [13, 24, 16, 28, 8], where the examples come from a *homogeneous* task, i.e., a single task, M^2TV learning is able to leverage *heterogeneous* (related) tasks to improve the learning performance in each task.

A key question in M^2TV learning is how to model the relatedness among multiple tasks/views. Existing methods for M^2TV learning [22, 43, 21, 42] usually assume that all the tasks are equally related, and all the views are equally consistent. Therefore, they mainly focus on exploring various types of task relatedness and view consistency. In this paper, we go one step further, and study: (1) if all the tasks are equally related and all the views are equally consistent; (2) to what extent the multiple tasks are related and the multiple views are consistent. This is motivated by the fact that in many real applications, it is often not known a priori the degree of relatedness among multiple tasks and consistency among multiple views. In the adversarial cases where some tasks are *negatively* related to the others and some views are contaminated by noise, simply applying the existing methods for M^2TV learning may even hurt the performance. Although in traditional multi-task learning, there has already been some work accommodating various task

KDD'14, August 24–27, 2014, New York, NY, USA.

http://dx.doi.org/10.1145/2623330.2623727.

relatedness [45, 46, 12, 11], to the best of our knowledge, our work is the first to study this problem in the context of M^2TV learning.

To this end, motivated by the successful application of Bayesian hierarchical modeling in multi-task learning and multi-view learning [19, 3, 5], we propose a nonparametric Bayes method for M^2TV learning. In this method, task relatedness is modeled via a normal penalty that decomposes the full covariance matrix into the Kronecker product, and view consistency is modeled via a matrix Dirichlet process. Furthermore, we design the *NOBLE* algorithm, which stands for ***NO***nparametric ***B***ayes ***LE***arning with dual heterogeneity. It is based on an efficient Gibbs sampler scalable to relatively high dimensions. The main contributions of this paper can be summarized as follows.

1. For the first time, in the context of M^2TV learning, we study problems where multiple tasks may exhibit different degree of relatedness, and multiple views may exhibit different degree of consistency;

2. We propose a nonparametric Bayes method for M^2TV learning which adaptively learns various task relatedness and view consistency;

3. We design the *NOBLE* algorithm based on an efficient Gibbs sampler scalable to relatively high dimensions;

4. We compare the performance of our proposed *NOBLE* algorithm with state-of-the-art techniques on various real data sets.

The rest of the paper is organized as follows. In Section 2, we briefly review the related work. The nonparametric Bayes method for M^2TV learning is proposed in Section 3, followed by the algorithm description of *NOBLE* in Section 4. Section 5 compares *NOBLE* with state-of-the-art methods on real data sets. Finally, we conclude in Section 6.

2. RELATED WORK

In this section, we briefly review the related work in heterogeneous learning and Dirichlet process mixture models.

2.1 Heterogeneous Learning

The goal of heterogeneous learning is to leverage multiple types of heterogeneities (e.g., task heterogeneity, view heterogeneity, instance heterogeneity, label heterogeneity, etc) to improve the performance of predictive modeling. For example, in [22, 23, 33, 43, 19, 21, 42], the authors jointly modeled the task and view heterogeneities; in [41] the authors jointly modeled the view and instance heterogeneities; in [26], the authors jointly modeled the instance and label heterogeneities.

For problems with both task and view heterogeneity, the authors of [22] focused on multiple tasks with completely different feature spaces, and proposed to construct a single prediction model in the shared induced space; the authors of [23] proposed to learn shared predictive structures on common views from multiple related tasks, and used the consistency among different views to improve the performance; the authors of [43] used co-regularization in each task to obtain a linear mapping, and used additional regularization functions across different tasks to impose task relatedness; the authors of [19] proposed a latent probit model to jointly learn the domain transforms, and a probit classifier shared in the common domain; the authors of [42] proposed a large margin framework to address transfer learning problems[1] with the same set of views in the source and target domains; the authors of [21] proposed a graph-based framework to model the relationship among multiple tasks/views, and designed an iterative algorithm $IteM^2$ to find the classification function. The major difference between our work and the existing work is the following. Existing methods assume that all the tasks are equally related and all the views are equally consistent. Therefore, they mainly focus on exploring various kinds of task relatedness and view consistency. In our work, we go one step further, and study: (1) if all the tasks are equally related and all the views are equally consistent; and (2) to what extent the multiple tasks are related and the multiple views are consistent.

The problem of varying task relatedness has been studied in traditional multi-task learning. For example, in [37], the authors proposed to use bipartite graphs to represent multi-task learning, and made use of Gaussian process to model varying task relatedness; in [12], the authors proposed a robust multi-task learning (RMTL) algorithm that learns multiple tasks simultaneously as well identifies the irrelevant tasks; in [46], the authors showed the equivalent relationship between alternating structure optimization and clustered multi-task learning; etc. However, the above methods and analysis only apply in the multi-task setting, and it is not straightforward to extend them to M^2TV learning.

In particular, Bayesian modeling has been widely used in multi-task learning and multi-view learning over the last decade. Research work dedicated to Bayesian hierarchical modeling has demonstrated effectiveness and improvement in performance [19, 3, 5]. The proposed methods have been successfully applied to different areas, such as information retrieval [7] and computer vision [30]. Typical approaches to transfer information among multiple tasks/views include: sharing hidden nodes in neural networks, placing a common prior in hierarchical models, sharing a common structure on the predictor space, and structured regularization in kernel methods, among others [19, 38, 9, 40, 39].

2.2 Dirichlet Process Mixture Models

In this paper, we propose to use Dirichlet process (DP) prior to encourage view clustering in the context of M^2TV learning. Before presenting our model, we briefly review DP mixture models. In a Bayesian mixture model, we assume that the true density of the response $\boldsymbol{Y}$ can be written as a mixture of parametric densities, conditioned on a hidden parameter θ. For example, in a Gaussian mixture, θ corresponds to the mean μ and variance σ^2. The marginal probability of an observation is given by a continuous mixture, $f(y) = \int_{\mathcal{T}} f(y|\theta)P(d\theta)$, where $\mathcal{T}$ is the set of all possible parameters and the prior P is a measure on that space. DP models uncertainty about the prior density P [17, 2]. If P is drawn from a Dirichlet process then it can be analytically integrated out of the conditional distribution of θ_T given $\theta_{1:(T-1)}$, where θ_T denotes the Tth parameter for observation y_T. Specifically, the random variable θ_T has a Polya

[1]Transfer learning is very similar to multi-task learning except that in transfer learning, we only care about the learning performance in the target domain.

urn distribution [6]:

$$\theta_T|\theta_{1:(T-1)} \sim \frac{1}{\alpha+T-1}\sum_{t=1}^{T-1}\delta_{\theta_t} + \frac{\alpha}{\alpha+T-1}G_0.$$

The above equation reveals the clustering property of the joint distribution of $\theta_{1:T}$, where there is a positive probability that each θ_t will take on the value of another $\theta_{t'}$, leading some of the parameters to share values. This equation also makes clear the roles of α and G_0. The unique values of $\theta_{1:(T-1)}$ are drawn independently from G_0; the parameter α controls how likely θ_T is to be a newly drawn value from G_0 rather than to take one of values from $\theta_{1:(T-1)}$. G_0 controls the distribution of a new component.

In a DP mixture, θ is a latent parameter to an observed data point y [2]: $P \sim \mathrm{DP}(\alpha G_0)$, $\theta_t \sim P$, $y_t|\theta_t \sim f(\cdot|\theta_t)$. Examining the posterior distribution of $\theta_{1:T}$ given $y_{1:T}$ brings out its interpretation as an "infinite clustering" model. Because of the clustering property, observations are grouped by their shared parameters. Unlike finite clustering models, however, the number of groups is random and unknown. Moreover, a new data point can be assigned to a new cluster that was not previously seen in the data.

However, the DP prior does not allow local clustering of tasks/views with respect to a subset of the feature vector without making independence assumptions. Considering sample s ($s = 1,\ldots,n_t$) from task (or view) t ($t = 1,\ldots,T$), suppose that the response variable is y_{ts} and related feature vector is $\boldsymbol{x}_{ts}$ with dimension n_p by 1. A common strategy for such problem is to use a hierarchical model of the form $y_{ts} \sim p(\boldsymbol{x}_{ts}, \boldsymbol{f}_t, \boldsymbol{\phi})$, where $p(\boldsymbol{x}, \boldsymbol{f}, \boldsymbol{\phi})$ is the conditional distribution of y given feature vector $\boldsymbol{x}$, parameters $\boldsymbol{f}$ and $\boldsymbol{\phi}$. $\boldsymbol{\phi}$ are global parameters and $\boldsymbol{f} = (\boldsymbol{f}_1,\ldots,\boldsymbol{f}_T)$ is a vector of task-specific (or view-specific) coefficients. We could specify independent DP priors for the coefficients [35, 14]: $f_{tp} \overset{\text{iid}}{\sim} G_t, G_t \sim DP(\alpha_j, G_{0j})$ for $p = 1,\ldots,n_p$. This approach allows differential clustering of the coefficients for different feature components, however, independence is assumed across the feature components. This is unappealing, because $f_{tp} = f_{t'p}$ provides information that tasks t and t' are similar, which should intuitively increase the probability that $f_{tp} = f_{t'p'}$, for $p \neq p'$. Motivated by this desire to borrow information across related feature components and tasks simultaneously, [35] propose a matrix stick-breaking process (MSBP) by assuming

$$f_{tp} \overset{\text{ind}}{\sim} G_{tp}, \quad \mathcal{G} \sim \mathcal{P},$$

where $\mathcal{G} = \{G_{tp}, p = 1,\ldots,n_p, t = 1,\ldots,T\}$ is a matrix of random probability measures, and $\mathcal{P}$ is a probability measure on $(\Omega, \mathcal{G})$, with Ω the space of $T \times n_p$ matrices with the (t,p)th element a probability measure on $(\mathcal{X}_t, \mathcal{B}_t)$. Here, $\mathcal{G}$ is a σ-algebra of subsets of Ω and $\mathcal{B}_t$ is a Borel σ-algebra of subsets of $\mathcal{X}_t$, $f_{tp} \in \mathcal{X}_t$. The proposed MSBP allows separate clustering and borrowing of information for the different feature components through

$$G_{tp} = \sum_{h=1}^{H}\{V_{tph}\prod_{l<h}V_{tpl}\}\delta_{\Theta_{ph}}, \quad \Theta_{ph} \overset{\text{ind}}{\sim} G_{0p},$$

$$V_{tph} = U_{th}W_{ph}, \quad U_{th} \overset{\text{iid}}{\sim} \mathrm{Beta}(1,\alpha), \quad W_{ph} \overset{\text{iid}}{\sim} \mathrm{Beta}(1,\beta).$$

To provide an intuitive explanation for the above formulation, we first consider the sticks W_{ph}. If W_{ph} is large for a particular index h^*, then the corresponding parameters Θ_{ph^*} is likely to be shared among multiple tasks. We also note that this sharing among tasks is encouraged by large U_{th^*}. Since U_{th^*} may be large for multiple different tasks t, this implies that if parameter sharing occurs for one predictor among the multiple tasks, then it is also likely that there will be sharing for other predictors. We can therefore generalize the following key properties of MSBP: (i) if a given parameter for predictor p, Θ_{ph^*}, is shared among some of the tasks, it is more likely to be shared among other tasks; (ii) if sharing occurs between multiple predictors for a subset of tasks, then it is more encouraged that sharing will occur between other predictors within these tasks.

3. NONPARAMETRIC BAYES LEARNING WITH DUAL HETEROGENEITY

3.1 Notation

Suppose that we have T tasks and V views in total. For the vth view, there are d_v features. For the tth task ($t = 1,\ldots,T$), there are n_t examples and each example can be represented as $\boldsymbol{x}_{ts} = [(\boldsymbol{x}_{ts1})',\ldots,(\boldsymbol{x}_{tsV})']'$ with label $\hat{y}_{ts}$ ($s = 1,\ldots,n_t$), where $()'$ denotes vector transpose. $\boldsymbol{x}_{tsv} \in \mathbb{R}^{d_v}$ denotes the features from the vth view ($v = 1,\ldots,V$) of the sth example in the tth task, and $\hat{y}_{ts}$ is either discrete for classification problems, or real-valued for regression problems. Notice that if a certain view is missing, the associated features will all be 0. Therefore, our problem setting is essentially the same as in [21] where some views are shared by multiple tasks, and some views are task specific. Without loss of generality, suppose that we know the output $\hat{y}_{t1},\ldots,\hat{y}_{tm_t}$ of the first m_t examples, where m_t is usually much smaller than n_t. Our goal is to leverage both the label information from all the related tasks, as well as the consistency among different views of a single task to predict the output of the remaining $n_t - m_t$ examples.

3.2 Model Formulation

In our proposed model, we first decompose each task into multiple single-view models. Each of them generates a predictor based on the features in the single view, which can be used to make predictions on future unseen examples. Here we relax the common assumption in multi-view learning [8, 29, 34] that different views are conditionally independent given the class label. To be specific, for the tth task ($t = 1,\ldots,T$), we use a mixture linear regression model for the estimated output $\hat{y}_{ts}$ ($s = 1,\ldots,n_t$) by averaging the prediction results from all single-view models as follows:

$$\hat{y}_{ts} = \sum_{v=1}^{V}(\boldsymbol{x}_{tsv})'\boldsymbol{f}_{tv} + \epsilon_{ts},$$

where $\boldsymbol{f}_{tv} \in \mathbb{R}^{d_v}$ is the coefficient vector, and $\epsilon_{tsv} \in \mathbb{R}$ is the observational error. Based on the above model, we estimate the task relatedness and the view consistency as follows.

1. **Task Relatedness**: Here we use a Gaussian process defined on ϵ_{ts} to model the task relatedness. To be specific, we assume that $\boldsymbol{\epsilon}_s = \{\epsilon_{ts}\}_{t=1,\ldots,T} \sim \mathrm{N}(0, K)$, where $K \in \mathbb{R}^{T\times T}$ is the kernel matrix of the Gaussian process, and it is the key to determining the various task relatedness. Different from [37], where only a single information source is used to obtain the kernel function,

in this paper, we fully leverage the multi-view property to estimate K in a more reliable way. To be specific, in order to estimate K, we define a task graph as follows: the graph consists of T nodes with each node representing a single task; let $B \in \mathbb{R}^{T\times T}$ denote the adjacency matrix of the graph, whose element in the tth row and t'^{th} column is $B_{tt'} = \frac{1}{n_t n_{t'}} \sum_{s=1}^{n_t} \sum_{s'=1}^{n_{t'}} < \boldsymbol{x}_{ts}, \boldsymbol{x}_{t's'} >$, where $t, t' = 1, \ldots, T$, and $< \cdot, \cdot >$ denotes vector inner product. For this graph, we can compute the Laplacian $\Delta = D - B$, where $D \in \mathbb{R}^{T\times T}$ is a diagonal matrix with each diagonal element equal to the row sum of B. Using Δ, we obtain K as follows:

$$K = \left[\beta(\Delta + \frac{1}{\sigma^2}\mathbf{I})\right]^{-1},$$

where both β and σ^2 are positive parameters. In particular, β controls the overall sharpness of the distribution: large values of β mean that the distribution is more peaked around its mean. For more flexibility, we let $\beta \sim \text{Ga}(a, b)$, which stands for Gamma distribution with shape parameter a and scale parameter b. It will be adapted to the data through adjusting the distribution related parameters a and b. σ^2 controls the amount of regularization. For this parameter, we could use the following prior $\sigma^2 \sim \text{IG}(c, d)$, which stands for Inverse-Gamma distribution with shape parameter c and scale parameter d.

We would like to point out several important aspects of the proposed Gaussian process. First, the kernel matrix K, whose elements indicate the similarity among various tasks, depends on the inverse of the regularized graph Laplacian Δ. Therefore, the relatedness between two tasks is global in the sense that it depends on all the tasks. Second, if we also have unlabeled data in addition to the labeled training data, all the unlabeled data can be used to define the adjacency matrix B (since it does not require label information), thus making it more robust to noise. Finally, the adjacency matrix B depends on the features from all the views through $\boldsymbol{x}_{ts}$. It tends to be more reliable if certain views have been contaminated by noise.

2. **View Consistency**: To estimate the various view consistency, we jointly model the coefficient vectors $\boldsymbol{f}_{tv}$ ($v = 1, \ldots, V$) through:

$$\begin{pmatrix} \boldsymbol{f}_{t1} \\ \vdots \\ \boldsymbol{f}_{tV} \end{pmatrix} \sim \text{N}\left(\mathbf{0}, \begin{bmatrix} \Psi_{11} & \Psi_{12} & \cdots & \Psi_{1V} \\ \vdots & \vdots & \ddots & \vdots \\ \Psi_{V1} & \Psi_{V2} & \cdots & \Psi_{VV} \end{bmatrix} \right)$$

where $\Psi_{vv'} \in \mathbb{R}_+^{d_v \times d_{v'}}$ denotes the covariance matrix between the vth and the v'^{th} views. $\Psi_{vv'} = \Psi_{v'v}$.

Furthermore, a Dirichlet Process (DP) prior can be used here to encourage view cluster. However, without the conditional independence assumption, the DP prior does not allow local clustering of views with respect to a subset of the feature vectors. To address this problem, we extend the matrix DP prior [15] to define the covariance matrix $\Psi_{vv'}$, which encourages cross-view sharing of data. To be specific, we borrow information by incorporating dependency in the prior distributions for the matrices $\{\Psi_{vv'}\}$.

We start by assuming for $v \geq v' \geq 1$,

$$\Psi_{vv'} \overset{\text{ind}}{\sim} F_{vv'}, \quad \mathcal{F} \sim \mathcal{P},$$

Here $\mathcal{F} = \{F_{vv'}, V \geq v \geq v' \geq 1\}$ is a matrix of random probability measures. Let Ω be the space of symmetric $V \times V$ matrices and $\mathcal{F}$ will be a σ-algebra of subsets of Ω. $\mathcal{P}$ is a probability measure on $(\Omega, \mathcal{F})$.

Next, our focus is on the specification of $\mathcal{P}$. Assuming each element in $\mathcal{F}$ has a stick-breaking representation, i.e.,

$$F_{vv'} = \sum_{h=1}^{\infty} \{W_{vv',h} \prod_{l<h} (1 - W_{vv',l})\} \delta_{\Theta_h}, \Theta_h \overset{\text{ind}}{\sim} G, \quad (1)$$

where $\boldsymbol{W}_{vv'} = \{W_{vv',h}, h = 1, \ldots, \infty\}$, for $V \geq v \geq v' \geq 1$, is an array of random stick-breaking weights. $\Theta_h \in \mathbb{R}_+^{d_v \times d_v}$ stands for the latent covariance matrix[2] that is drawn from the base measure G, which usually takes the Inverse-Wishart (IW) distribution. Notice that similar to the usual Dirichlet Process, $\Psi_{vv'}$ equals to Θ_h with probability proportional to $W_{vv',h} \prod_{l<h} (1 - W_{vv',l})$.

Dependency within dimensions of $\mathcal{F}$ will be incorporated through dependent stick-breaking weights and the common parametric prior G. For the stick-breaking weights, we decompose them as follows

$$W_{vv',h} = \gamma_{vh}\gamma_{v'h}, \gamma_{vh} \sim \text{Beta}(1, \alpha), \alpha \overset{\text{ind}}{\sim} \text{Ga}(1, \alpha_0),$$

where both γ_{vh} and $\gamma_{v'h}$ are random variables with the same Beta distribution, $\alpha > 0$ is a parameter in the Beta distribution, and $\alpha_0 > 0$ is the scale parameter in the Gamma distribution. In this way, we guarantee the symmetric property: $W_{vv',h} = W_{v'v,h}$. Furthermore, according to [15], the definition of γ_{vh} ensures that

$$\sum_{h=1}^{\infty} \{W_{vv',h} \prod_{l<h} (1 - W_{vv',l}) = 1\}$$

Therefore, Equation (1) is a valid probability measure.

We use the following example to show the intuition of the above formulation. Let $V = 4$, and $V_1, \ldots, V_4$ stand for the four different views. Then the probability that two covariance matrices $\Psi_{V_1V_2}$ and $\Psi_{V_1V_3}$ are same can be computed as follows.

$$\Pr(\Psi_{V_1V_2} = \Psi_{V_1V_3}) = \frac{1}{(\alpha+1)(\alpha+2) - 1}$$

Furthermore, the conditional probability of these two matrices being the same given that $\Psi_{V_4V_2} = \Psi_{V_4V_3}$ can be computed as follows.

$$\lim_{\alpha \to 0} \Pr(\Psi_{V_1V_2} = \Psi_{V_1V_3} | \Psi_{V_4V_2} = \Psi_{V_4V_3}) = \frac{1}{\alpha+1}$$

From the above equations, we can see that the probability of $\Psi_{V_1V_2}$ and $\Psi_{V_1V_3}$ being the same ranges between 0 and 1, depending on the value of the parameter α. Both converge to 1 in the limit as $\alpha \to 0$ and to 0 as $\alpha \to \infty$. We can verify that $\Pr(\Theta_{V_1V_2} = \Theta_{V_1V_3}) \leq \Pr(\Theta_{V_1V_2} = \Theta_{V_1V_3} | \Theta_{V_4V_2} = \Theta_{V_4V_3})$. It means given that view 2, 4 and

[2]For the sake of explanation, we assume that d_v is a constant for $v = 1, \ldots, V$; otherwise we fill in 0 values to make the dimensionality of each view equal.

view 3, 4 are equally correlated in terms of the covariance matrices, then there will be an increased probability that view 1, 2 and view 1, 3 are equally correlated.

Finally, for the base measure G of the view covariance matrix, we consider the following degenerate distribution:

$$G = \pi \mathrm{I}_0 + (1-\pi)G_0, G_0 \sim \mathrm{IW}(\nu, \Psi_0)$$

where $0 \leq \pi \leq 1$, ν is the degrees of freedom of the Inverse-Wishart distribution, $\Psi_0 \in \mathbb{R}_+^{d_v \times d_v}$ is the scale matrix. When $\Psi_{vv'}$ falls into the I_0 cluster, the corresponding covariance matrix will be a zero matrix, and the nonsignificant $\boldsymbol{f}_{tv}$ will be set to 0.

Figure 1 shows the graphical representation of the proposed model. To generalize, for each example s in the task t (y_{st}), task relatedness is characterized through K where β controls the overall sharpness of the distribution and σ^2 controls the amount of regularization. On the other hand, there is a view-specific feature $\boldsymbol{x}_{tsv}$ for the s example in the tth task and we use $\boldsymbol{f}_{tv}$ to characterize v^{th} view effect in the tth task. We extend the DP to characterize the covariance matrix $\Psi_{vv'}$ in order to cluster the coefficients $\boldsymbol{f}_{tv}$. $\mathbf{W}$ and α characterize the stick weights; G characterizes the base measure for DP, which is a degenerate distribution with probability π to be the null matrix and with probability $1-\pi$ to be an Inverse-Wishart distribution G_0 with degrees of freedom ν and scale matrix Ψ_0.

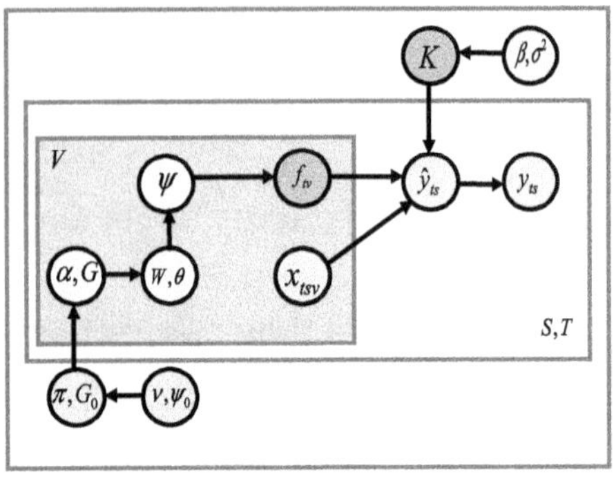

Figure 1: Graphical representation for the proposed model.

4. THE PROPOSED ALGORITHM

In this section, we present the *NOBLE* algorithm, which stands for ***NO***nparametric ***B***ayes ***LE***arning with dual heterogeneity. It is based on an efficient Gibbs algorithm that is scalable to relatively high dimensions. For simplicity, we assume that $n_t = S$ in the following. In particular, each iteration of the Gibbs sampler draws samples through the following sequence. The joint likelihood of the samples is as follows:

$$p(\boldsymbol{y}|\boldsymbol{X}, \boldsymbol{f}, K) = (2\pi)^{-\frac{TS}{2}} |\mathrm{I}_S \otimes K|^{-\frac{1}{2}} \cdot \exp\Big\{ -\frac{1}{2}(\boldsymbol{y} - \boldsymbol{X}\boldsymbol{f})'(\mathrm{I}_S \otimes K)^{-1}(\boldsymbol{y} - \boldsymbol{X}\boldsymbol{f})\Big\} \quad (2)$$

where

$$\boldsymbol{y} = \begin{pmatrix} y_{11} \\ \vdots \\ y_{1S} \\ \vdots \\ y_{21} \\ \vdots \\ y_{2S} \\ \vdots \\ y_{TS} \end{pmatrix}, \quad \boldsymbol{X} = \begin{pmatrix} \boldsymbol{x}_{11} & & \\ \vdots & & \\ \boldsymbol{x}_{1S} & & \\ & \boldsymbol{x}_{21} & \\ & \vdots & \\ & \boldsymbol{x}_{2S} & \\ & & \boldsymbol{x}_{T1} \\ & & \vdots \\ & & \boldsymbol{x}_{TS} \end{pmatrix},$$

with $\boldsymbol{x}_{ts} = \begin{pmatrix} \boldsymbol{x}_{ts1} \\ \vdots \\ \boldsymbol{x}_{tsV} \end{pmatrix}$, and $\boldsymbol{f} = \begin{pmatrix} \boldsymbol{f}_1 \\ \vdots \\ \boldsymbol{f}_T \end{pmatrix}$, $\boldsymbol{f}_t = \begin{pmatrix} \boldsymbol{f}_{t1} \\ \vdots \\ \boldsymbol{f}_{tV} \end{pmatrix}$.

The posterior distribution of $\boldsymbol{f}_{tv}$ is proportional to combining the joint likelihood and the prior in Equation (1). Therefore we can update $\boldsymbol{f}_{tv}$ jointly from the following conjugate mulvariate normal distribution:

$$p(\boldsymbol{f}|\cdots) \sim \mathrm{MN}\Big((\boldsymbol{X}(K^{-1} \otimes \mathrm{I}_S)\boldsymbol{X} + \mathrm{I}_T \otimes \Psi)^{-1} \boldsymbol{X}'(K^{-1} \otimes \mathrm{I}_S \hat{\boldsymbol{y}}), (\boldsymbol{X}(K^{-1} \otimes \mathrm{I}_S)\boldsymbol{X} + \mathrm{I}_T \otimes \Psi)^{-1}\Big), \quad (3)$$

Similarly, by combining the joint likelihood as in Equation (2) and the prior $\mathrm{Ga}(a, b)$, β is updated directly through the following Gamma distribution $p(\beta|\cdots)$:

$$\mathrm{Ga}\Big(a + \frac{1}{2}TV, b + \frac{1}{2}(\hat{\boldsymbol{y}} - \boldsymbol{X}\boldsymbol{f})'((\Delta + \frac{1}{\sigma^2}\mathrm{I}_T) \otimes \mathrm{I}_S)(\hat{\boldsymbol{y}} - \boldsymbol{X}\boldsymbol{f})\Big). \quad (4)$$

In each iteration, given the prior $\mathrm{IG}(c, d)$, σ^2 is drawn through:

$$p(\sigma^2|\cdots) \sim \mathrm{IG}\Big(c + \frac{1}{2}TV, d + \frac{1}{2}\beta(\hat{\boldsymbol{y}} - \boldsymbol{X}\boldsymbol{f})'(\hat{\boldsymbol{y}} - \boldsymbol{X}\boldsymbol{f})\Big). \quad (5)$$

Since the DP prior implies that D is almost surely discrete, the prior will automatically group the m coefficient-specific hyperparameters $\Psi_{vv'}$ into L clusters Ψ_l^*, where $L \leq \frac{1}{2}V(V-1)$. One of these clusters will most likely correspond to $\Psi_l^* = I_{d_v \times d_v}$, and the other clusters will not be 0. We denote $J_{vv'} = l$ if the (v, v')th covariance matrix is clustered in the lth latent cluster. Our proposed prior can be seen more clearly through the equivalent stick breaking form $J_{vv'} \sum_{l=1}^{\infty} W_l \delta_l$ with

$$\Psi_l^* \sim \begin{cases} \pi\delta_0, & \text{for } l = 1 \\ (1-\pi)\mathrm{IW}(\nu, \Psi_0), & \text{for } l > 1. \end{cases}$$

Extending the exact block Gibbs sampler of [36], the joint prior distributions of $J_{vv'}$ and a latent variable $\zeta_{vv'}$ can be written as

$$f(J_{vv'}, \zeta_{vv'}|\boldsymbol{W}) = \sum_{l:W_l > \zeta_{vv'}} \delta_l(\cdot) = \sum_{l=1}^{\infty} 1(\zeta_{vv'} < W_l)\delta_l(\cdot).$$

We implement the following exact block Gibbs sampler steps:

(1). Sample $\zeta_{vv'} \sim \mathrm{uniform}(0, W_{J_{vv'}})$, for $v \geq v' \geq 1$ with $W_l = \gamma_l \prod_{h<l}(1-\gamma_h)$.

Sample the stick-breaking random variables γ_l from $\gamma_l \sim \text{beta}\left(1 + m_l, \alpha + \sum_{s=l+1}^{L} m_s\right)$, for $l = 1, \ldots, L$ with L the minimum value satisfying $W_1 + \ldots + W_L > 1 - \min\{\zeta_{vv'}\}$. m_l is the number of components clustered into the lth cluster.

Sample Ψ_l^* for $l = 1, \ldots, L$ by
(1) For $l = 1, \Psi_1^* = 0$.
(2) For $2 \leq l \leq L$, since $(\boldsymbol{f}_{tv} | \boldsymbol{f}_{t(-v)}) \propto \exp\left\{-\frac{1}{2}\boldsymbol{f}_{tv}{}'\Psi_{vv'}\boldsymbol{f}_{tv} - \boldsymbol{f}_{tv}\sum_{v\sim v'}\Psi_{vv'}\boldsymbol{f}_{tv'}\right\}$, Ψ_l^* can be drawn directly from:

$$\Psi_l^* \sim \text{IW}\left(m_l + \nu + 1, \Psi_0 + \textstyle\sum_t \sum_{J_{vv'}=l} \boldsymbol{f}_{tv}\boldsymbol{f}_{tv'}\right).$$

(2). Sample $J_{vv'}$ for $v \geq v' \geq 1$ from the multinomial conditional with

$$\Pr(J_{vv'} = l|\cdot) \propto 1(\zeta_{vv'} < \pi_l) \prod_t \exp\{-\boldsymbol{f}_{tv}\Psi_l^*\boldsymbol{f}_{tv'}\}.$$

After updating γ_h, with the relationship $\gamma_{vh} \sim \text{beta}(1, \alpha), \alpha \overset{\text{ind}}{\sim} \text{Ga}(1, \alpha_0)$, we sample α through

$$p(\alpha|\cdots) \sim \mathcal{E}\left(\alpha_0 - \sum_{v,h}\log(1 - \gamma_{vh})\right). \tag{6}$$

where $\mathcal{E}(x; \lambda) = \lambda\exp(-\lambda x)$ is the exponential density.

Based on the above discussion, the proposed *NOBLE* algorithm is summarized in Algorithm 1.

Algorithm 1 *NOBLE* Algorithm

Require: y_{ts}, $\boldsymbol{x}_{tsv}$, IN_{tsv}, K $t = 1, \ldots, T$, $s = 1, \ldots, S$, $v = 1, \ldots, V$
Ensure: the initial value for $\boldsymbol{f}_{tv}$, β, σ^2, $\Psi_{vv'}$ and α

```
for i = 1 to Total number of iterations do
  for t = 1 to T do
    for v, v' = 1 to V do
      Update f through the multivariate normal distribution in Equation (3);
      Update β through the Gamma distribution as in Equation (4);
      Draw σ^2 directly from Inverse Gamma distribution in Equation (5);
      Update DP related parameters using exact block Gibbs sampler as described in the above Step 4;
      Update α using truncated exponential distribution as in equation (6).
    end for
  end for
end for
```

---

5. EXPERIMENTS

In this section, we present some experimental results showing the effectiveness of the proposed *NOBLE* algorithm and compare against the following algorithms[3]:

1. regMVMT [44]: an inductive multi-view learning algorithm for multiple related tasks through a co-regularized framework.
2. SMTL [27]: a Bayesian semi-supervised learning framework for problems with multiple tasks using unlabeled data based on Markov random walk.
3. CASO [10]: a multi-task learning algorithm improving the ASO algorithm [1] through a novel regularizer.

For all 4 algorithms, we repeat the experiments 10 times and report the average classification error[4]. For regMVMT, the parameters are optimized using cross-validation. For SMTL and CASO, the parameters are set according to [27] and [10] respectively. For the proposed *NOBLE* algorithm, we simply set non-informative hyperparameters as $\alpha_0 = 1$, $\pi = 1/2$, $\nu = 2n_p + 1$ and $\Psi_0 = \mathbf{I}_{n_p}$ without prior knowledge about the correlation among the tasks and the relative importance of each view in the predictive model of each task. We also performed convergence diagnostics, such as trace plots and Geweke's convergence diagnostic for randomly selected parameters. No signs of adverse mixing have been found. All results are based on 3,000 Gibbs sampling iterations after a burn-in period of 2,000.

In our experiments, to generate multiple views from the original feature space, we adopt a similar strategy as in [25], and apply different linear/nonlinear dimensionality reduction methods, including ICA with different functions (pow[3] or order 3 polynomial kernel, Tanh, Gaussian, skew) [18], PCA based (PCA, Prob PCA [31], and kernel PCA), MDS, diffusion maps, Laplacian, and Laplacian Eigenmaps [32], resulting in 11 views total.

20 newsgroups data set. We first consider the 20 newsgroups data set [4]. This data set consists of articles from 20 different newsgroups forming a hierarchical structure. Here we focus on the "comp" and "rec" categories (similar experimental results are observed for the other categories and thus omitted for brevity), and create 4 tasks from them. To be specific, for each task, we pick one subcategory from "comp" and "rec" respectively and randomly sample 100 articles from each subcategory to form 2 classes, each described by 53975 features.

To test the capability of our proposed algorithm to recover data sets with different sparsity, we experiment on data sets with various numbers of labeled examples: varying from randomly selecting 20 to 180 observed samples and use the remaining as test set.

Figure 2 shows the comparison results of the 4 algorithms with varying training set size. Each subfigure shows the average classification error for a single task. From these figures, we can see that the performance of *NOBLE* dominates the other methods, and the margin becomes more significant as the number of labeled examples increases. This is because *NOBLE* is able to learn from data: (1) if all the tasks/views are related, and (2) how much they are related to each other.

Figure 3 shows that by using the DP prior, we are able to partition the 11 views into 2 groups roughly: one consists of 7 views generated using ICA and PCA based dimensionality reduction methods, and the other consists of 4 views generated using MDS, diffusion maps, Laplacian, and Laplacian Eigenmaps. In each iteration of the algorithm, there is a positive probability that $\Psi_{V_iV_j} = \Psi_{V_iV_{j'}}$ for every $j \neq j'$. Two views $j \neq j'$ are said to be clustered in terms of sharing covariance matrices if and only if $\Psi_{V_iV_j} = \Psi_{V_iV_{j'}}$ and Figure 3 is the average over the iterations. The clustering

[3]We did not compare with $IteM^2$ [21] since in our experiments, the features are not guaranteed to be non-negative. As shown in [43], the performance of $IteM^2$ is not satisfactory in this case.

[4]For the sake of clarity, we did not display the error bars.

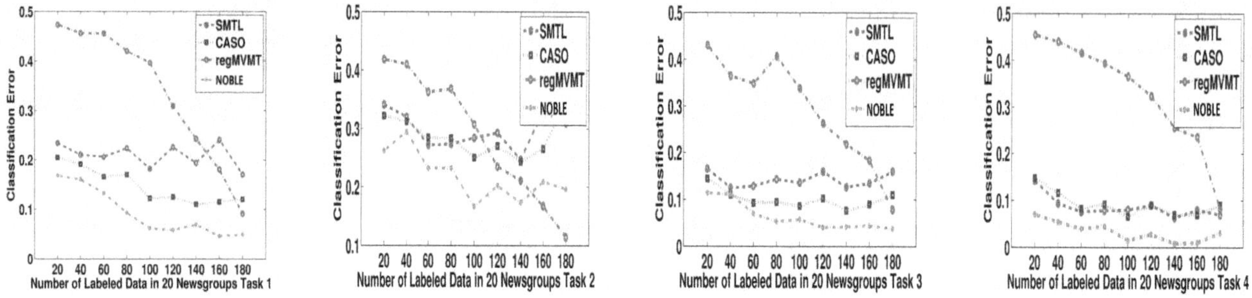

Figure 2: Comparison results on the 20 Newsgroups data.

of the views encoded by the ties among the covariance matrices will simply be referred to as the "clustering of the views", although it should be understood that it is the data themselves that are clustered. The fact that our model induces ties among the views is the means by which it borrows strength across objects for estimation.

WebKB data set. Next we test the performance of *NOBLE* on WebKB data set, where the goal is to classify whether a web page is course related or not [8]. We also create 4 tasks from this data set, each including 200 web pages collected from the same university.

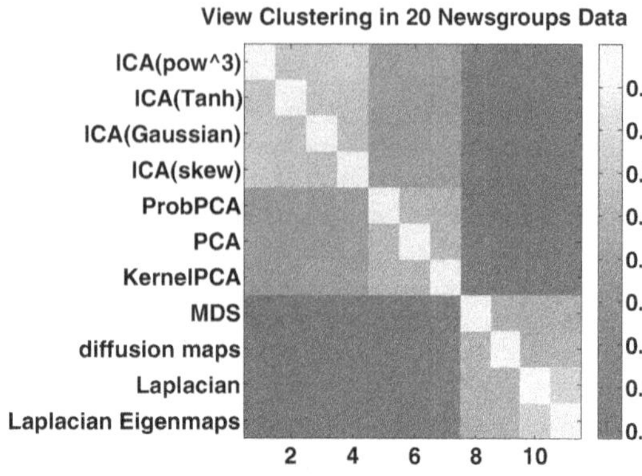

Figure 3: *NOBLE* clustering probability for 11 views of the 20 newsgroups data.

Figure 4 shows the comparison results with varying training set size. Similarly as before, we can see that the performance of *NOBLE* is better than the other 3 competitors in each of the 4 tasks.

Email spam data set. Finally, we compare on the email spam data set from ECML 2006 discovery challenge.[5] The goal is to classify if each email is spam or ham. In problem A, There are 3 users with 2,500 emails each, which are considered as 3 related tasks.

Comparison results are shown in Figure 5. On this data set, we also see improved performance of *NOBLE* over the competitors except for Task 1: when the training set size is small, *NOBLE* and CASO are pretty close to each other; when the training set size is large, the performance of *NOBLE* is consistently improved whereas the performance of CASO fluctuates. We notice that throughout the extensive experiments, regMVMT cannot perform well when the training sample size is small.

We also test the computation time per iteration in *NOBLE* as we vary the training set size, which is shown in Figure 6. From this figure, we can see that *NOBLE* scales linearly with respect to the total number of labeled examples, thus it is scalable to relatively large data sets.

6. CONCLUSION

In this paper, we propose a nonparametric Bayes model for addressing problems with dual-heterogeneity, i.e., task heterogeneity (multiple related tasks) and view heterogeneity (multiple views). Compared with state-of-the-art techniques which assume that the tasks are equally related and the views are equally consistent, we aim at answering the following two questions: (1) Are all the tasks equally related and all the views equally consistent? (2) To what extent are the tasks related to each other, and the views consistent with each other? To this end, we make use of the normal penalty with sparse inverse covariances and the matrix DP prior to adaptively learn the task relatedness and the view consistency. Furthermore, we propose the *NOBLE* algorithm based on an efficient Gibbs sampler, which constructs predictors for all the tasks leveraging both the multi-task and multi-view nature. Experimental results on several real data sets show that *NOBLE* outperforms existing methods in M^2TV learning.

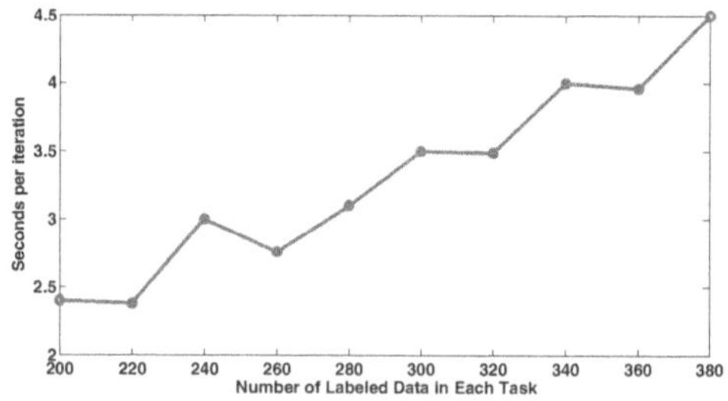

Figure 6: Computation time per iteration of *NOBLE*.

References

[1] R. Ando and T. Zhang. A framework for learning predictive structures from multiple tasks and unlabeled data. *Journal of Machine Learning Research*, 6:1817–1853, 2005.

[5] `http://www.ecmlpkdd2006.org/challenge.html`.

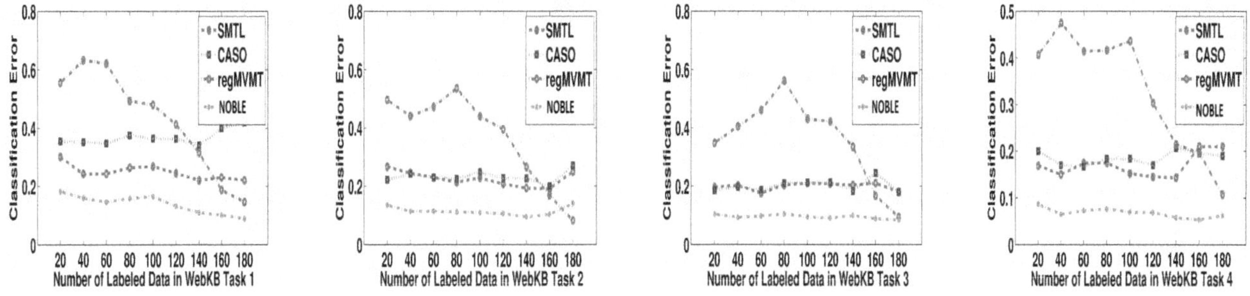

Figure 4: Comparison results on the WebKB data.

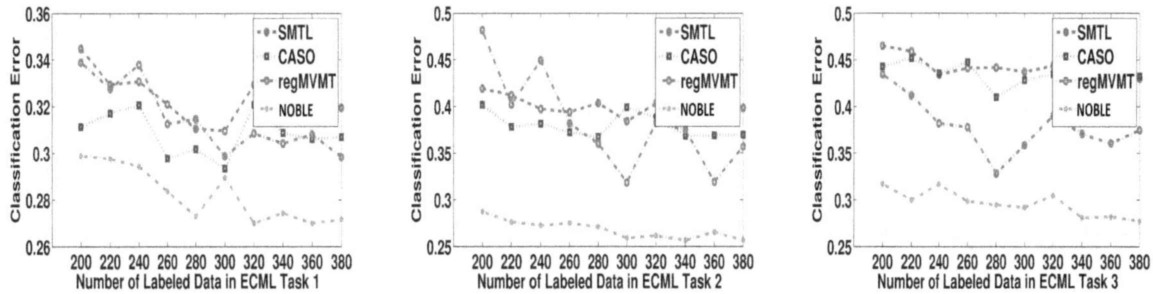

Figure 5: Comparison results on the email spam data.

[2] C. Antoniak. Mixtures of dirichlet processes with applications to bayeisan nonparametric problems. *The Annals of Statistics*, 2:1152–1174, 1974.

[3] C. Archambeau, S. Guo, and O. Zoeter. Sparse bayesian multi-task learning. *NIPS*, 2011.

[4] A. Asuncion and D. Newman. UCI machine learning repository, 2007.

[5] B. Bakker and T. Hesks. Task clustering and gating for bayesian multitask learning. *JMLR*, 4:83–99, 2003.

[6] D. Blackwell and J. MacQueen. Ferguson distributions via polya urn schemes. *The Annals of Statistics*, 1:353–355, 1973.

[7] D. M. Blei, T. L. Griffiths, M. I. Jordan, and J. B. Tenenbaum. Hierarchical topic models and the nested chinese restaurant process. In *NIPS*, 2003.

[8] A. Blum and T. M. Mitchell. Combining labeled and unlabeled sata with co-training. In *COLT*, 1998.

[9] D. Burr and H. Doss. A bayesian semiparametric model for random-effects meta-analysis. *Journal of the American Statistical Association*, 100(469):242–251, 2005.

[10] J. Chen, T. Lei, J. Liu, and J. Ye. A convex formulation for learning shared structures from multiple tasks. *ICML*, 2009.

[11] J. Chen, J. Liu, and J. Ye. Learning incoherent sparse and low-rank patterns from multiple tasks. In *KDD*, pages 1179–1188, 2010.

[12] J. Chen, J. Zhou, and J. Ye. Integrating low-rank and group-sparse structures for robust multi-task learning. In *KDD*, pages 42–50, 2011.

[13] C. Christoudias, R. Urtasun, and T. Darrell. Multi-view learning in the presence of view disagreement. In *UAI*, pages 88–96, 2008.

[14] L. Ding, A. Yilmaz, and R. Yan. Interactive image segmentation using dirichlet process multiple-view learning. *IEEE Transactions on Image Processing*, 21(4):2119–2129, 2012.

[15] D. Dunson, Y. Xue, and L. Carin. The matrix stick-breaking process: flexible bayes meta analysis. *Journal of the American Statistical Association*, 103:317–327, 2008.

[16] J. Farquhar, D. Hardoon, H. Meng, J. Shawe-Taylor, and S. Szedmak. Two view learning: Svm-2k, theory and practice. *NIPS*, 2005.

[17] T. Ferguson. A bayesian analysis of some nonparametric problems. *The Annals of Statistics*, 1:209–230, 1973.

[18] H. Gavert, J. Hurri, J. Sarela, and A. Hyvarinen. The fastica package for matlab. `http://research.ics.aalto.fi/ica/fastica/`, 2005.

[19] S. Han, X. Liao, and L. Carin. Cross-domain multitask learning with latent probit models. *NIPS*, 2012.

[20] M. Harel and S. Mannor. Learning from multiple outlooks. In *ICML*, pages 401–408, 2011.

[21] J. He and R. Lawrence. A graphbased framework for multi-task multi-view learning. In *ICML*, pages 25–32, 2011.

[22] J. He, Y. Liu, and Q. Yang. Linking heterogeneous input spaces with pivots for multi-task learning. In *SDM*, 2014.

[23] X. Jin, F. Zhuang, S. Wang, Q. He, and Z. Shi. Shared structure learning for multiple tasks with multiple views. In *ECML/PKDD (2)*, pages 353–368, 2013.

[24] S. M. Kakade and D. P. Foster. Multi-view regression via canonical correlation analysis. In *COLT*, pages 82–96, 2007.

[25] A. Kumar, P. Rai, and H. D. III. Co-regularized multi-view spectral clustering. In *NIPS*, pages 1413–1421, 2011.

[26] Y.-X. Li, S. Ji, S. Kumar, J. Ye, and Z.-H. Zhou. Drosophila gene expression pattern annotation through multi-instance multi-label learning. *IEEE/ACM Trans. Comput. Biology Bioinform.*, 9(1):98–112, 2012.

[27] Q. Liu, X. Liao, and L. Carin. Semi-supervised multi-task leraning. *NIPS*, 2007.

[28] I. Muslea, S. Minton, and C. A. Knoblock. Active + semi-supervised learning = robust multi-view learning. In *ICML*, pages 435–442, 2002.

[29] K. Nigam and R. Ghani. Analyzing the effectiveness and applicability of co-training. In *CIKM*, pages 86–93, 2000.

[30] J. O'Sullivan and S. Thrun. Discovering structure in multiple learning tasks: The tc algorithm. *ICML*, pages 489–497, 1996.

[31] M. Tipping and C. Bishop. Probabilistic principal component analysis. *Journal of the Royal Statistical Society, Series B*, 61:611–622, 1999.

[32] L. van der Maaten, E. Postma, and H. van den Herik. Dimensionality reduction: A comparative review. *Tilburg University Technical Report, TiCC-TR 2009-005*, 2009.

[33] H. Wang, F. Nie, H. Huang, S. L. Risacher, A. J. Saykin, and L. Shen. Identifying disease sensitive and quantitative trait-relevant biomarkers from multidimensional heterogeneous imaging genetics data via sparse multimodal multitask learning. *Bioinformatics*, 28(12):127–136, 2012.

[34] W. Wang and Z.-H. Zhou. A new analysis of co-training. In *ICML*, pages 1135–1142, 2010.

[35] Y. Xue, X. Liao, L. Carin, and B. Krishnapuram. Multi-task learning for classification with dirichlet process priors. *Journal of Machine Learning Research*, 8:35–63, 2007.

[36] C. Yau, O. Papaspiliopoulos, G. Roberts, and C. Holmes. Nonparametric hidden markov models with application to the analysis of copy-number-variation in mammalian genomes. *Journal of Royal Statistical Society: Series B*, 73(1):37–57, 2010.

[37] K. Yu and W. Chu. Gaussian process models for link analysis and transfer learning. In *NIPS*, 2007.

[38] K. Yu, A. Schwaighofer, and V. Tresp. Learning gaussian processes from multiple tasks. *ICML*, 2005.

[39] K. Yu, A. Schwaighofer, V. Tresp, W. Ma, and H. Zhang. Collaborative ensemble learning: Combining collaborative and content-based information filtering via hierarchical bayes. *UAI*, 2003.

[40] K. Yu, V. Tresp, and S. Yu. A nonparametric hierarchical bayesian framework for information filtering. *Proceedings of the 27th Annual International ACM SIGIR Conference on Research and Development in Information Retrieval*, 2004.

[41] D. Zhang, J. He, and R. D. Lawrence. Mi2ls: multi-instance learning from multiple informationsources. In *KDD*, pages 149–157, 2013.

[42] D. Zhang, J. He, Y. Liu, L. Si, and R. D. Lawrence. Multi-view transfer learning with a large margin approach. In *KDD*, pages 1208–1216, 2011.

[43] J. Zhang and J. Huan. Inductive multi-task learning with multiple view data. In *KDD*, pages 543–551, 2012.

[44] J. Zhang and J. Huan. Inductive multi-task learning with multiple view data. In *KDD*, pages 543–551, 2012.

[45] Y. Zhang and D.-Y. Yeung. A convex formulation for learning task relationships in multi-task learning. *CoRR*, abs/1203.3536, 2012.

[46] J. Zhou, J. Chen, and J. Ye. Clustered multi-task learning via alternating structure optimization. In *NIPS*, pages 702–710, 2011.

Online Chinese Restaurant Process

Chien-Liang Liu
Industrial Technology Research Institute
Computational Intelligence Technology Center
Rm. 709, Bldg. 51, 195, Sec. 4. Chung Hsing Rd., Chutung. Hsinchu, Taiwan 310, ROC
jackyliu@itri.org.tw

Tsung-Hsun Tsai
National Chiao Tung University
Department of Computer Science
1001 University Road, Hsinchu, Taiwan 300, ROC
artsuu@gmail.com

Chia-Hoang Lee
National Chiao Tung University
Department of Computer Science
1001 University Road, Hsinchu, Taiwan 300, ROC
chl@cs.nctu.edu.tw

ABSTRACT

Processing large volumes of streaming data in near-real-time is becoming increasingly important as the Internet, sensor networks and network traffic grow. Online machine learning is a typical means of dealing with streaming data, since it allows the classification model to learn one instance of data at a time. Although many online learning methods have been developed since the development of the Perceptron algorithm, existing online methods assume that the number of classes is available in advance of classification process. However, this assumption is unrealistic for large scale or streaming data sets. This work proposes an online Chinese restaurant process (CRP) algorithm, which is an online and nonparametric algorithm, to tackle this problem. This work proposes a relaxing function as part of the prior and updates the parameters with the likelihood function in terms of the consistency between the true label information and predicted result. This work presents two Gibbs sampling algorithms to perform posterior inference. In the experiments, the online CRP is applied to three massive data sets, and compared with several online learning and batch learning algorithms. One of the data sets is obtained from Wikipedia, which comprises approximately two million documents. The experimental results reveal that the proposed online CRP performs well and efficiently on massive data sets. Finally, this work proposes two methods to update the hyperparameter α of the online CRP. The first method is based on the posterior distribution of α, and the second exploits the property of online learning, namely adapting to change, to adjust α dynamically.

Categories and Subject Descriptors

I.2.6 [**Artificial Intelligence**]: Learning—*Parameter Learning*; F.1.2 [**Theory of Computation**]: Modes of Computation—*Online computation*

KDD'14, August 24–27, 2014, New York, NY, USA.

http://dx.doi.org/10.1145/2623330.2623636.

General Terms

Algorithms, Experimentation, Theory

Keywords

Adaptive Learning; Chinese Restaurant Process; Nonparametric; Online Learning

1. INTRODUCTION

Online learning has attracted a significant amount of interest in the field of machine learning, and an important family of efficient and scalable machine learning algorithms exist for large-scale applications. Like massive data sets, streaming data sources are commonly important, particularly when data sets are generated in real time, as are many log files, sensor data, and network data. The distributions that underlie the streaming data typically change over time, so the predictive model should be adapted accordingly. One important property of online learning is that the true label of the instance is available after the prediction is made. The true label information can then be used to refine the predictive model, so that subsequent predictions will be closer to the true labels.

Although many online learning algorithms have been developed over the past few decades, most online learning algorithms require the number of classes of the clasification model to be determined in advance of information processing. However, this requirement is unreasonable in real world applications, since the number of classes is usually unknown for massive data sets. Additionally, many application settings require models to be able to deal with a *nonexhaustive* training data set, from which some classes may be missing and therefore absent from the training data set. Detecting new classes from streaming or massive data sets is an important issue in the era of big data, motivating the development herein of a new algorithm to solve this problem. For example, the biosensing problem requires rapid identification of new, emerging classes of microorganisms, which are not represented in the initial training library. Detecting the sudden presence of a new class is an important element of an automated outbreak-identification strategy [11]. E-mail classification is another typical example of online learning. An e-mail system that can identify new classes that are not present in the existing class set and suggest possible labels could constitute an extension of an existing e-mail classification system.

Bayesian nonparametric (BNP) models provide an alternative means of solving this problem; their complexity increases with the number of observed data instances. BNP models can incorporate prior knowledge into the model by placing a prior on an unbounded number of parameters. The Dirichlet process (DP), introduced by Ferguson [14], is a stochastic process that is frequently used as a prior in Bayesian nonparametric statistics. The idea of using a Dirichlet process as the prior of the mixing proportions of a simple distribution was first introduced by Antoniak [2]. The DP is an elegant alternative to parametric model selection using the Dirichlet process mixture model, which comprises a countably infinite number of components [2, 31, 28]. The Chinese restaurant process (CRP) [1] mixture model is one of the representations of the DP mixture model. The CRP induces an exchangeable distribution over partitions, so that the joint distribution is invariant to the order in which observations are assigned to clusters, and each observation can be treated as the last in a sequence of observations. This property yields a very useful representation in the inferences of DP mixture models [36, 28].

This work develops a nonparametric online learning algorithm that is called the online Chinese restaurant process. The proposed algorithm retains the ability of nonparametric models to automatically infer an adequate model complexity from data without determining the number of classes in advance. The online CRP is also an online learning algorithm, indicating that the online CRP is adapted as more data instances are observed. This work proposes a relaxing function to represent part of the prior and updates the parameters according to the likelihood function in terms of the consistency between the true label information and the predicted result. The online CRP is influenced by the true label information, which is used to adjust the parameters of the model, so the online CRP relaxes the assumption of exchangeability used by CRP. Unlike existing online learning algorithms, the online CRP is a nonparametric method, so its model complexity is determined by data. Additionally, the proposed algorithm allows the creation of new classes, and so is more practical and flexible model when applied to massive data sets. In the experiments, three massive data sets are used to assess the online CRP and compare it with several online learning and batch learning algorithms. One of the data sets is obtained from Wikipedia, and includes approximately two million articles. The experimental results demonstrate that the online CRP works well and efficiently on the massive data sets.

The main contribution of this paper is to develop a nonparametric online learning algorithm. To the best of our knowledge, this is the first work that combines Bayesian nonparametric learning with online learning, allowing the classification model to grow with the data rather than requiring that the number of classes be determined in advance of the classification process. This work presents two Gibbs sampling algorithms for making posterior inferences. One of these algorithms is a collapsed Gibbs sampling algorithm, which is more efficient than the other and is used in the experiments. This work proposes two methods for updating hyperparameter α of the online CRP; the first one is based on the posterior distribution of α, while the second exploits the property of online learning, namely adapting to change, to adjust α dynamically.

The rest of this paper is organized as follows. Section 2 then reviews the Chinese restaurant process, and introduces online Chinese restaurant process algorithms. Next, Section 3 summarizes the results of several experiments. Section 4 discusses the experimental results and analyzes the online Chinese restaurant process. Section 5 draws conclusions.

2. ONLINE CHINESE RESTAURANT PROCESS

The goal of clustering is to identify latent information in data, such that objects in the same cluster are more similar to each other than objects from different clusters. The finite mixture model (FMM) is commonly used in clustering applications. The FMM assumes the existence of finite models, each of which is associated with a parameter. Each data point is generated by one of the mixture models. Inferring the parameters associated with the models and identifying which model generated each data point yields the clustering of the data points. However, the FMM must determine the number of models in advance of the clustering. The usual trade off in model order selection problems arises: with too many components, the mixed models may overfit the data, while a mixture with too few components may not be sufficiently flexible to approximate the true underlying model [15]. The Bayesian nonparametric mixture model, which is called a Chinese restaurant process mixture or a Dirichlet process mixture, infers the number of clusters from the data and allows the number of clusters to grow as new data instances are observed [17].

2.1 Notation

This section presents the notation that will be used throughout this study. The notation is based on the metaphor of the CRP, which involves customers, tables and dishes. Customer $\mathbf{x}_i$ corresponds to a data point, while the table is the cluster in the CRP or a class in the online CRP. Accordingly, the customers who sit at the same table correspond to data points in the same class. Meanwhile, the dish at table j is the parameter of the class j, denoted as θ_j, and the number of customers who sit at table j is m_j. The preference of customer $\mathbf{x}_i$ for the dish served at table j is $H(\mathbf{x}_i, \theta_j)$, which is the likelihood that $\mathbf{x}_i$ belongs to class j. Unlike the CRP, the online CRP allows each customer to move to another table after he has first been assigned to a table. The assigned table and the final table at which customer $\mathbf{x}_i$ sits are z_i and y_i, respectively.

The online CRP is a nonparametric method: the number of possible tables is infinite. In this work, the number of occupied tables is denoted as k. The base distribution and the concentration parameter are G_o and α, respectively. Finally, this work proposes a relaxing function $g(\gamma_1, \gamma_2, e_j, f_j)$ to adjust the prior in the online CRP, in which γ_1 and γ_2 are regret rates, and f_j and e_j are used to track the misassignment of the previous $i-1$ customers on table j. Finally, $\mathbf{x}_{-i}$ is introduced to represent all of the customers except for customer i, and $\mathbf{x}_{-i,c}$ represents all of the customers in class c except for customer i. The terms y_{-i} and z_{-i} have similar meanings.

2.2 Chinese Restaurant Process

The Chinese restaurant process (CRP) [1], a discrete-time stochastic process, defines a distribution over partitions that embodies the assumed prior distribution over cluster structures [30]. The CRP receives the name from the following metaphor. Imagine a Chinese restaurant with an infinite number of tables each with infinite capacity, and a sequence of n customers who enter the restaurant and sit down. The first customer enters the restaurant and sits at the first table. The ith subsequent customer sits at an occupied table, or at the next unoccupied table as follows.

$$P(z_i = j | z_{-i}, \alpha) \quad \propto \quad \begin{cases} \frac{m_j}{i-1+\alpha} & \text{if } j \leq k \\ \frac{\alpha}{i-1+\alpha} & \text{if } j = k+1 \end{cases} \tag{1}$$

The CRP induces an exchangeable distribution over partitions, so that the joint distribution is invariant in the order in which observations are assigned to clusters. Hence, each customer's table assignment z_i can be made by pretending that $\mathbf{x}_i$ is the last person to sit down. As given by Equation (1), the ith customer sits at an occupied table j with a probability that is proportional to the number of already seated customers m_j, or sits at a new table with a probability that is proportional to α. The tables are analogous to clusters, and customers to observations or data points. A larger m_j is more likely to grow. Therefore, the CRP exhibits a clustering property due to a rich-gets-richer phenomenon. Additionally, as a prior on the number of tables, the CRP is a nonparametric model, meaning that the number of occupied tables grows as more customers enter the restaurant.

The exact computation of posterior expectations for a DP mixture model is infeasible when the data include just a few observations. Markov chain methods enable the systematic computation of the posterior distribution of the parameters [12, 36, 26, 13, 28, 20]. Several Markov chain methods for sampling from distribution of a DP mixture model have been presented [28]. Markov chain Monte Carlo (MCMC) sampling methods can be slow to converge and their convergence can be difficult to diagnose. Variational inference is an alternative, giving deterministic approach to approximate likelihoods and posteriors [6, 35].

The CRP offers great flexibility for clustering applications, and has motivated many extensions. For example, the nested Chinese restaurant process (nCrp) [5, 4] extends the CRP to a hierarchy of partitions, allowing arbitrarily large branching factors. While exchangeability is commonly considered to be an advantageous property, much of the data in text, image and audio domains are not exchangeable. The distance-dependent Chinese restaurant process (dd-CRP) [3] relaxes the assumption of exchangeability, and provides a better fit to sequential data and network data. Socher et al. [33] further uses spectral clustering [32, 29] to reduce dimensionality and cluster data using the dd-CRP on spectral space.

2.3 Relaxing Function

The metaphor of the online CRP is an extension of that of the CRP. The first customer sits at the first table, as in the CRP. When a subsequent customer enters the restaurant, the table is assigned differently from that in the CRP. In the online CRP, a waiter tracks the dishes at all the tables, and assigns the customer to a appropriate table based on the waiter's prior knowledge of the dishes and the customer's preference for dishes. However, the customer may be dissatisfied with the table assignment, and move to another table. The restaurant will be in chaos, if the customers move too frequently. To reduce the probability of misassignment, the waiter tracks the movements of customers to adjust the probabilities associated with the assignment of the next new customer to the various tables, and adjusts table dish information to avoid the misassignment. It is noted that table assignments for ith customer comprise two results, one is assigned by waiter, denoted as z_i, and the other one is the final sitting table, represented as y_i. For table j and customer i, f_j and e_j track the misassignment of the previous $i-1$ customers as shown in Equation (2), where $\mathbb{I}$ is an indicator function.

$$\begin{aligned} f_j &= \sum_{a=1}^{i-1} \mathbb{I}\{y_a = j \wedge z_a \neq j\} \\ e_j &= \sum_{a=1}^{i-1} \mathbb{I}\{z_a = j \wedge y_a \neq j\} \end{aligned} \tag{2}$$

$$g(\gamma_1, \gamma_2, e_j, f_j) \quad = \quad (1+\gamma_1)^{f_j}(1-\gamma_2)^{e_j} \tag{3}$$

For table j, $f_j > 0$ indicates that the assignment to table j should be increased, since customers tend to move to table j. Conversely, the assignment to table j should be reduced if $e_j > 0$, since the assignments to table j may cause the customers to move to other tables. Inspired by regret theory [25], this work proposes a relaxing function, Equation (3), where γ_1 and γ_2 are regret rates, and the information about misassignment that is carried by f_j and e_j are viewed as prior knowledge in determining the distribution of table assignment probabilities.

$$\begin{aligned} &P(z_i = j | z_{-i}, \mathbf{x}_i, y_i, \theta, G_0, \alpha) \\ &\propto \begin{cases} g(\gamma_1, \gamma_2, e_j, f_j)\frac{m_j}{i-1+\alpha} H(\mathbf{x}_i, \theta_j) & \text{if } j \leq k \\ \frac{\alpha}{i-1+\alpha} \int H(\mathbf{x}_i, \theta_j) \mathrm{d}G_0(\theta_j) & \text{if } j = k+1 \end{cases} \end{aligned} \tag{4}$$

Equation (4) presents the posterior distribution estimation of online CRP, in which the prior comprises the relaxing function and the prior of the CRP, and $H(\mathbf{x}_i, \theta_j)$ denotes the likelihood that datum $\mathbf{x}_i$ is a member of class j. Notably, the online CRP reduces to the CRP when $f_j = 0$ and $e_j = 0$ for all j. Although the metaphor of the online CRP is similar to that of the CRP, several differences exist between the two processes. First, the CRP is an unsupervised learning method, and it is usually used in clustering applications. Conversely, the online CRP is an online algorithm, in which the label information y_i is available after the prediction of $\mathbf{x}_i$ is made. Second, the prior of the online CRP differs from that of the CRP. Third, the movement of the datum $\mathbf{x}_i$ between classes simultaneously alters the parameters of the classes that are indexed as z_i and y_i in the online CRP.

2.4 Inference and Learning

Figure 1 shows the graphical model of the online CRP, in which the observed random variables include the datum $\mathbf{x}_i$ and its corresponding label y_i. The sampling process is as follows:

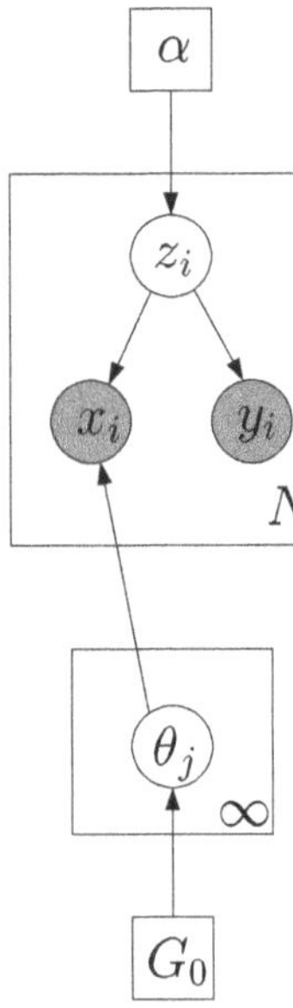

Figure 1: Graphical Model of Online Chinese Restaurant Process

$$
\begin{aligned}
z_i|\alpha &\sim \text{Mult(Online CRP}(\alpha))\\
\theta_{z_i}|G_0 &\sim G_0\\
\mathbf{x}_i|\theta, z_i &\sim F(\theta_{z_i})
\end{aligned}
\tag{5}
$$

Equation (5) specifies that z_i is a class indicator variable, referring to the predicted class of datum $\mathbf{x}_i$. For each datum $\mathbf{x}_i$, the predicted label z_i can be sampled using the online CRP. The class parameter θ_{z_i} is drawn from the base distribution, G_0, and each data point $\mathbf{x}_\text{l}$ is generated by a distribution F associated with parameter θ_{z_i}. The proposed algorithm is an online algorithm, so the correct label information y_i becomes available after the prediction is made. The model uses z_i and y_i to update class parameters.

Unlike most online learning algorithms, such as Perceptron and Winnow [24], the online CRP is not a mistake-driven model, but updates parameters whenever correct or incorrect predictions have been made. If the prediction is incorrect, $z_i \neq y_i$, then the likelihood that datum $\mathbf{x}_i$ belongs to class z_i is overestimated. To adjust the estimate, a pseudo data point $\mathbf{x}'_i = -b \times \mathbf{x}_i$ is assumed to join class z_i, where $b > 0$ is a constant that specifies the weighting of the pseudo data point. Then, the model samples a new class parameter θ_{z_i} with the posterior probability of θ_{z_i} that is conditional on $\mathbf{x}'_i$, $\mathbf{x}_{-i,z_i}$, α, G_0 and all of the pseudo data points that are associate with table z_i. Conversely, the likelihood that datum $\mathbf{x}_i$ belongs to class y_i is underestimated, so a pseudo data point $\mathbf{x}''_i = b \times \mathbf{x}_i$ rather than $\mathbf{x}_i$ is assumed to join class y_i. Similarly, the model samples a new class parameter θ_{y_i} with the posterior probability of θ_{y_i} that is conditional on $\mathbf{x}''_i$, $\mathbf{x}_{-i,y_i}$, α ,G_0 and all of the pseudo data points that are associate with table y_i. Conversely, if the prediction is correct ($z_i = y_i$), then the model samples a new class parameter θ_{z_i} using the posterior probability of θ_{z_i} that is conditional on $\mathbf{x}_i$, $\mathbf{x}_{-i,z_i}$, α, G_0 and all of the pseudo data points that are associated with table z_i.

The graphical model that is presented in Figure 1 reveals that random variables z and θ are latent variables. In this work, Gibbs sampling is conducted to carry out posterior inference. The Gibbs sampling involves iterations that alternatively draw samples from one of the variables while the others are kept fixed. Accordingly, the conditional posterior distributions of these variables must be derived. The conditional posterior distribution of θ_j is given above. The sampling of z_i is based on the following equation, in which $P(z_i = j|z_{-i}, y_i, \alpha)$ is the prior, and $P(\mathbf{x}_i|\theta_j)$ is the likelihood that θ_j generates datum $\mathbf{x}_i$:

$$P(z_i = j|z_{-i}, y_{-i}, \mathbf{x}_i, \theta_j, \alpha, G_0) \propto P(z_i = j|z_{-i}, y_{-i}, \alpha)P(\mathbf{x}_i|\theta_j) \tag{6}$$

This study uses the prior of online CRP to represent $P(z_i = j|z_{-i}, y_{-i}, \alpha)$, and uses $H(\mathbf{x}_i, \theta_j)$ to represent likelihood, $P(\mathbf{x}_i|\theta_j)$. Hence, Equation (6) becomes Equation (4) in the online CRP. Algorithm 1 is the online CRP algorithm. Notably, the true label information is used to adjust model parameters, so the online CRP is not exchangeable.

Algorithm 1: Online Chinese Restaurant Process

Input: The dispersion parameter α and base distribution G_0, and regret rates γ_1 and γ_2

Initialize m_s, f_s, and e_s as 0 for all $s \in \mathbb{N}$
$k \leftarrow 0$
$b \leftarrow 1$
for $i \leftarrow 1$ **to** ∞ **do**
    Get a data $\mathbf{x}_i$
    if $k = 0$ **then**
        $z_i \leftarrow 1$
    else
        Sample z_i from $P(z_i = j|z_{-i}, \mathbf{x}_i, \theta, G_0, \alpha) \propto$
$$\begin{cases} (1+\gamma_1)^{f_j}(1-\gamma_2)^{e_j}\frac{m_j}{i-1+\alpha}H(x_i,\theta_j) & \text{if } j \le k \\ \frac{\alpha}{i-1+\alpha}\int H(\mathbf{x}_i,\theta_j)\mathrm{d}G_0(\theta_j) & \text{if } j = k+1 \end{cases}$$
        Get label information y_i
        if $z_i = y_i$ **then**
            Sample a new θ_{z_i} from the posterior of θ_{z_i} conditional on G_0 and all the real and pseudo data points associated with the table z_i
            $m_{z_i} \leftarrow m_{z_i} + 1$
        else
            Sample a new θ_{z_i} from the posterior of θ_{z_i} conditional on G_0 and all the real and pseudo data points associated with the table z_i
            Sample a new θ_{y_i} from the posterior of θ_{y_i} conditional on G_0 and all the real and pseudo data points associated with the table y_i
            $m_{y_i} \leftarrow m_{y_i} + 1$
            $e_{z_i} \leftarrow e_{z_i} + 1$
            $f_{y_i} \leftarrow f_{y_i} + 1$
        end
    end
end

2.5 Collapsed Sampling

The marginalization of some variables from a joint distribution always reduces the variance, consistent with the Rao-Blackwell Theorem [21]. In a conjugate context, we can integrate analytically over θ_j, eliminating θ_j from the algorithm to simplify the sampling process. Then, for each data point $\mathbf{x}_i$, only z_i has to be sampled using Equation (7), in which $F(\theta_j)_{-i}$ is the posterior probability of θ_j conditional on $\mathbf{x}_{-i,j}$, the pseudo data points in table j and G_0.

$$P(z_i = j | z_{-i}, \mathbf{x}_i, y_{-i}, \theta, G_0, \alpha) \propto \begin{cases} g(\gamma_1, \gamma_2, e_j, f_j) \frac{m_j}{i-1+\alpha} \int H(\mathbf{x}_i, \theta_j) \mathrm{d}F(\theta_j)_{-i} & \text{if } j \leq k \\ \frac{\alpha}{i-1+\alpha} \int H(\mathbf{x}_i, \theta_j) \mathrm{d}G_0(\theta_j) & \text{if } j = k+1 \end{cases} \quad (7)$$

Algorithm 2: Collapsed Online Chinese Restaurant Process

```
Input: The dispersion parameter α and base
       distribution G0, and regret rates γ1 and γ2
1  Initialize m_s, f_s, and e_s as 0 for all s ∈ ℕ
2  k ← 0
3  b ← 1
4  for i ← 1 to ∞ do
5      Get a data x_i
6      if k = 0 then
7          z_i ← 1
8      else
9          Sample z_i from the distribution as listed in
           Equation (7)
10         Get label information y_i
11         if z_i = y_i then
12             Update the sufficient statistics of table z_i on
               joining x_i to table z_i
13             m_{z_i} ← m_{z_i} + 1
14         else
15             Update the sufficient statistics of table z_i on
               joining −b × x_i to table z_i
16             Update the sufficient statistics of table y_i on
               joining b × x_i to table y_i
17             m_{y_i} ← m_{y_i} + 1
18             e_{z_i} ← e_{z_i} + 1
19             f_{y_i} ← f_{y_i} + 1
20         end
21     end
22 end
```

Algorithm 2 shows the collapsed sampling for the online CRP, and Algorithm 2 is used in the experiments herein. The proposed algorithm is an online algorithm, so the algorithm processes datum $\mathbf{x}_i$ sequentially, as in Line 5. The first datum is assigned to the first class, as in Line 7. For subsequent data, z_i are sampled using Equation (7), as in Line 9. Since the number of classes is k, the sampling process must be conducted k times to estimate the posterior probabilities for all the k classes. The model should consider the probability of assigning $\mathbf{x}_i$ to a new class, labeled as $k+1$ in the algorithm. The model selects the most likely class from the $k+1$ classes, which is given by z_i in the algorithm. When the predicted class is available, the model receives the true label information y_i. The model compares z_i with y_i and updates parameters based on the results of the comparison. As in Line 12, the model updates the sufficient statistics of class z_i with the added $\mathbf{x}_i$ and increases the number of data within class z_i by one when $z_i = y_i$. However, classes z_i and y_i update the sufficient statistics of classes z_i and y_i with the addition of a pseudo data point when $z_i \neq y_i$. Besides sufficient statistics, the algorithm updates the information about the number of data and misassignment. The above processes are found in Lines 15-19. Additionally, this work develops two methods for updating hyperparameter α of the online CRP. The first is based on the posterior distribution of α, while the second exploits the property of online learning, namely adapting to change, to adjust α dynamically. They are described in the Appendix. In the experiments herein, the second method is used to adjust α dynamically with an initial value of one.

3. EXPERIMENTS

The implementation of the proposed online CRP assumes that the text of a document follows a multinomial distribution, and that the parameters of the multinomial follow a Dirichlet distribution, such that the conjugate prior can be used to perform collapsed sampling as in Algorithm 2. In this work, three data sets are used to assess system performance and several methods are compared with the proposed algorithm.

3.1 Data Corpora

The 20 Newsgroups, RCV1, and Wikipedia are all popular data sets that are commonly used in text analysis experiments.

- The 20 Newsgroups data set is a collection of approximately 20,000 newsgroup documents, partitioned (nearly) evenly across 20 different newsgroups. The 20 Newsgroups data set has become popular for experiments involving text applications of machine learning techniques, such as text classification and text clustering.
- Reuters Corpus Volume I (RCV1) [22] is an archive of over 800,000 manually categorized newswire stories that has recently been made available by Reuters, Ltd. for research purposes. RCV1 documents are categorized with respect to three controlled vocabularies - topics, industries, and regions. We follow the category tree and use the second layers as the labels of documents. In the experiments, the documents that appear only in the first layers and those documents that belong to more than one category are removed. The remaining number of categories is 53, and the total number of documents is 534,135.
- The Wikipedia data set is obtained from the Wikimedia database dump, which comprises approximately three million documents. Terms with frequency ranking lower than 50,000 are used as features and the documents without any of those features are removed. The number of remaining documents is approximately two million. The class label information is the category information that is presented in a Wikipedia document. The Wikipedia data set comprises 24 categories.

In the preprocessing stage, the stop words are removed from the data sets, since they fail to provide sufficient information to be useful in the clustering task. Punctuation marks are removed and all English letters are converted to lower case. Finally, stemming is applied to the words.

3.2 Evaluation Measurements

Classification F_1 metric is commonly used to assess the performance of text classification applications. However, the use of classification F_1 assumes that the number of classes is fixed. The proposed algorithm is a nonparametric method in which the number of classes is unbounded. Therefore, the classification F_1 metric could not be used in the experiments herein. The generated classes are compared using the clustering F_1 metric [27]. The clustering F_1 metric considers both precision and recall, which are computed over pairs of documents whose label assignments either agree or disagree. Similarly, one can obtain true positives (TP), false positives (FP), true negatives (TN) and false negatives (FN) in terms of the clustering conditions of the pairs. Then, precision, recall and clustering F_1 metric can be obtained from the confusion matrix. Not only clustering F_1 metric, but also error rates are used as evaluation measures. The execution time is also recorded.

3.3 Online Learning Experiments

The experiments herein involve massive data sets, so classification takes a relatively long time. Different approaches are used in the experiments on the 20 Newsgroups data set and the other two data sets. The 20 Newsgroups data set comprises approximately 20,000 documents, and five-fold cross-validation is used on this data set. Experimental results are presented as average and standard deviation, and the mean plus or minus two standard deviations is presented in the tables. The RCV1 and Wikipedia data sets contain numerous documents, so uniform random sampling is used to select training data and testing data from these. The experiments on the two data sets are only conducted once, since each experiment takes a long time. All the methods are implemented using Matlab. The online CRP involves a parameter b that specifies the weighting of the pseudo data point, and its value is one in the experiments.

Hoi et al. [18] developed a library for online learning algorithms that is called LIBOL, which comprises a large family of recently developed state-of-the-art online learning algorithms for large-scale online classification tasks. The LIBOL provides binary and multi-class classification algorithms. The experiments involve multi-class data sets, so multi-class classification algorithms are considered in the comparison of methods. Among these multi-class algorithms, the first-order algorithms include the online gradient descent (OGD) [38] algorithm, passive aggressive (PA) [8] algorithms, and the relaxed online maximum margin algorithm (ROMMA) [23]. The second-order algorithms include adaptive regularization of weight vectors (AROW) [10] algorithm, multi-class confidence weighted (CW) algorithms [9], and soft confidence-weighted learning (SCW) [19] algorithms. The LIBOL further includes variants of some of these algorithms, all of which are used in the experiments. Crammer et al. [8] developed three variants of the passive-aggressive algorithms - PA, PA-I and PA-II. The LIBOL includes the multi-class aggressive ROMMA algorithm called aROMMA. Finally, the LIBOL includes two variants of SCW called SCW-I and SCW-II, respectively.

Besides LIBOL, this work uses additional methods in the experiments, including several variants of Perceptron and online logistic regression [37]. Perceptron is a typical online learning algorithm, and Freund and Schapire [16] proposed several variants of online Perceptron algorithms, including voted Perceptron, average Perceptron, last Perceptron and random Perceptron. This work uses the first three variants in the experiments. The Perceptron algorithm is well known to be able to be employed in a nonlinear way by means of the kernel trick, which depends on only the dot products between the vectors in feature space, and selects the mapping such that these high-dimensional dot products can be computed in the original space by means of a kernel function. The kernelized algorithms of the variants of Perceptron are applied to the data sets. Although these variants of Perceptron belong to batch learning algorithms, they can process data sequentially in the training phase, explaining why they are used in the experiments.

The algorithms that are implemented in LIBOL belong to online learning, while the variants of Perceptron belong to batch learning. Therefore, the experiments herein are conducted using online learning and batch learning settings. The online learning setting concerns the algorithms in the LIBOL, since these do not have a training phase, and they evaluate system performances from when they receive the first data point until they receive the last data point. They are online learning algorithms, so the models that are used in the algorithms can be continually adapted. In contrast, the algorithms of the variants of Perceptron comprise a training phase and a prediction phase, so the batch learning setting uses supervised learning approach to evaluate system performances, in which the algorithms adapt their models during the training phase, and use the trained model to predict testing data without any further change to the model. The proposed online CRP can use online learning and batch learning settings, and we compare online CRP with the comparison algorithms with the two settings.

The first data set to be used in the experiments is the 20 Newsgroups data set, which includes 20 categories and approximately 20,000 documents. Table 1 presents the experimental results obtained using the online learning setting, and Table 2 lists the experimental results obtained using the batch learning setting. All of the algorithms complete classification of the 20 Newsgroups data set. The second data set to be used is RCV1, which is massive. In a practical application setting, classification performance and execution time must both be considered. The methods in the LIBOL fail to complete the task owing to insufficient memory problem, so they are absent from the experimental results, and the batch learning setting is used in the experiments to compare the proposed online CRP with variants of Perceptron algorithms. As indicated in Table 2, the online CRP, the variants of Perceptron and their kernelized extensions can complete the classification in reasonable time. However, the kernelized extensions require the computation of the kernel matrix, which encounters the memory problem with RCV1 and Wikipedia data sets. Additionally, the execution time of the variants of Perceptron are all much longer than the proposed algorithm on the RCV1 and Wikipedia data sets. Therefore, the remaining experiments were performed using the online CRP and last Perceptron. Table 3 and Table 4 present the experimental results obtained using the RCV1 and Wikipedia data sets, respectively. Table 4 presents only the error rate, since clustering F_1 metric depends on pairwise comparisons between all of the classification results. The number of documents in Wikipedia is approximately two millions, yielding a large number of pairwise combinations.

Table 1: Experimental Results on 20 Newsgroups with Online Learning Setting

	Error Rate	Cluster F_1	Execution Time (sec)
Online CRP	0.2471 ± 0.0057	0.6056 ± 0.0045	277 ± 7
ROMMA	0.9451 ± 0.0123	0.0950 ± 0.0003	92 ± 0
aROMMA	0.9449 ± 0.0128	0.0950 ± 0.0003	84 ± 1
OGD	0.3931 ± 0.0396	0.4056 ± 0.0432	85 ± 1
PA	0.9432 ± 0.0170	0.0950 ± 0.0003	84 ± 0
PA-I	0.2762 ± 0.0042	0.5507 ± 0.0058	82 ± 2
PA-II	0.2693 ± 0.0036	0.5605 ± 0.0046	82 ± 2
CW	0.2362 ± 0.0027	0.6076 ± 0.0040	$48,382 \pm 1,167$
AROW	0.4423 ± 0.0197	0.3322 ± 0.0232	$46,865 \pm 675$
SCW-I	0.2358 ± 0.0036	0.6083 ± 0.0047	$46,276 \pm 432$
SCW-II	0.2345 ± 0.0034	0.6102 ± 0.0054	$46,360 \pm 455$

Table 2: Experimental Results on 20 Newsgroups with Batch Learning Setting

	Error Rate	Cluster F_1	Execution Time (sec)
Online CRP	0.2010 ± 0.0100	0.6790 ± 0.0224	313 ± 9
Last Perceptron	0.3904 ± 0.0313	0.4005 ± 0.0302	256 ± 27
Voted Perceptron	0.3206 ± 0.0127	0.4938 ± 0.0187	267 ± 11
Average Perceptron	0.3928 ± 0.0391	0.4100 ± 0.0460	269 ± 9
Kernel Last Perceptron	0.3903 ± 0.0304	0.4060 ± 0.0395	63 ± 3
Kernel Voted Perceptron	0.3100 ± 0.0287	0.5085 ± 0.0399	407 ± 19
Kernel Average Perceptron	0.3936 ± 0.0209	0.3972 ± 0.0360	404 ± 5
Online Logistic Regression	0.3177 ± 0.0162	0.5010 ± 0.0196	$113,527 \pm 2,755$

Table 3: Experimental Results on RCV1 Data Set

	Error Rate	Cluster F_1	Execution Time
Online CRP	0.1477	0.8517	54,958
Last Perceptron	0.1176	0.8905	259,512

Table 4: Experimental Results on Wikipedia Data Set

	Error Rate	Execution Time
Online CRP	0.3602	112,030
Last Perceptron	0.3888	2,249,000

4. DISCUSSION AND ANALYSIS

Table 1 reveals that the online CRP performs similar to some of the second-order algorithms in the LIBOL. In the LIBOL, the second-order online learning methods such as CW, SCW-I and SCW-II perform well on the 20 Newsgroups data set, but their execution times greatly exceed those of first-order methods. For the high-dimensional data sets, the calculation of covariance matrix is highly complex and therefore difficult. Table 2 and Table 4 show that the online CRP outperforms the variants of Perceptron on 20 Newsgroups and Wikipedia data sets.

Last Perceptron outperforms the proposed method on the RCV1 data set as shown in Table 3, but its execution time is much longer. In the experiments on the compared methods that involve binary classifiers, such as Perceptron variants, the one-against-all technique is used to extend these methods to multi-class scenarios. Therefore, the number of classes should be available when a k-class problem is decomposed into a series of two-class problems. In contrast, the proposed online CRP grows to accommodate the complexity of the data without requiring the number of classes in advance, providing flexibility in processing massive or streaming data sets. To evaluate the proposed algorithm when used on a streaming data set, the proposed algorithm is applied to a sorted 20 Newsgroups data set, in which the documents are sorted by timestamps. The experimental results are almost the same as those presented in Table 2.

The experiments involve balanced and imbalanced data sets, and the experimental results demonstrate that the proposed method can perform well on the two kinds of data sets. The experimental results also indicate that the proposed method can complete classification within reasonable time, even though the Wikipedia data set comprises two million documents. The proposed method is analyzed, compared with supervised learning methods, and the performance is assessed with different numbers of training documents. Finally, the settings of the parameters are discussed.

4.1 Analysis of Online CRP Algorithm

The proposed online CRP is an online learning algorithm. The prediction depends on the posterior probabilities of all the existing classes and a new class, so the model need retain sufficient statistics only for these classes. When the prediction of a data point is completed, the model updates the required sufficient statistics rather than undergoing retraining. Thus, the online CRP can process the streaming data in almost real-time. Additionally, the model is memory-efficient, since only the model and a single data point have to be retained in memory.

The sampling process that is listed in Line 9 of Algorithm 2 shows that the computational cost of each sampling update is proportional to the number of classes, k. The value of k approaches $\alpha \log(n)$ asymptotically as n approaches infinity [2, 34]. Meanwhile, the worst case for the model to update parameters is $z_i \neq y_i$, since the model should update the parameters of class z_i and y_i. The time complexity for updating model parameters is a constant, since the update involves only the sufficient statistics. Therefore, the total time complexity for processing n data points is $O(k \times n) = O(\alpha n \log(n))$. In most cases, the time complexity approaches $O(n)$ since $n \gg k$. The experimental results are consistent with the analysis.

4.2 Comparison with Supervised Learning

The proposed method is compared with supervised learning methods on the three data sets using SVM, logistic regression, and Naive Bayes methods. Table 5 presents the experimental results on the 20 Newsgroups. Experiments on SVM are conducted using libsvm [7] with linear kernel. The above supervised learning methods require that model parameters to be determined in classifying documents, so a subset of the data is used as a validation set to determine appropriate values of parameters. Table 6 and Table 7 present the experimental results concerning RCV1 and Wikipedia data sets, respectively.

The experimental results reveal that SVM generally outperforms other methods, but it fails to classify the Wikipedia data set, owing to the computation of the kernel matrix. The proposed online CRP outperforms Naive Bayes, and is comparable to logistic regression. The above three supervised learning methods require that the number of classes is known in advance of classification process. Although many differences exist between the proposed online CRP and the CRP, the proposed online CRP and the CRP share an important property: both are nonparametric methods. The number of classes in the online CRP is determined by the data, and provides a practical and flexible model for dealing with massive data sets.

4.3 Assessment of Performance with Different Numbers of Training Documents

Experiments were conducted herein to determine whether the online CRP benefits from more training examples. Although the proposed method is an online learning algorithm, the online CRP can be very easily converted into a supervised learning algorithm. We can use the online CRP to process available labeled examples sequentially, yielding a classification model. The classification model can then be used to classify the testing examples sequentially, and the classification performance can be evaluated.

In the experiments, 15,000 documents were randomly selected from the RCV1 data set as testing documents. To analyze further the impact of the number of training documents on classification performance, various numbers of labeled examples are used to train the classification model. Figure 2 presents the experimental results, in which the testing error rates for various numbers of training documents are recorded. The experimental results indicate that the testing error generally declines as the number of training documents increases.

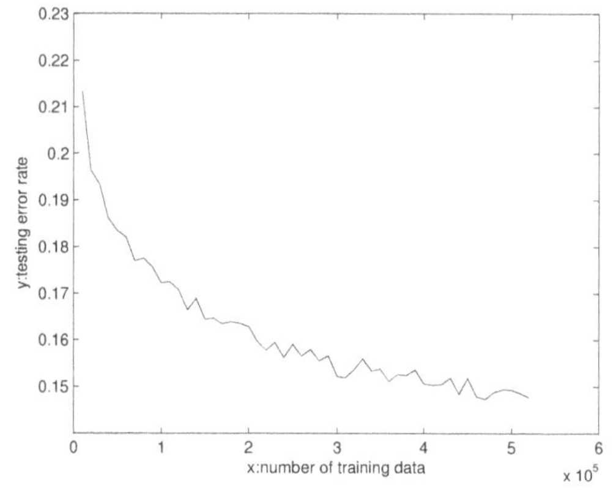

Figure 2: Testing Error on RCV1 Data Set

4.4 Parameter Setting

This section conducts experiments on 20 Newsgroups and evaluates performance with various settings of the parameters γ_1, γ_2, b, and α. First experiments with various values of γ_1 and γ_2 are conducted and the performance is evaluated. The settings are simplified by setting γ_1 equal to γ_2. When their values are less than 0.5, clustering F_1 metric is around 0.66. In contrast, increasing γ_1 and γ_2 significantly degrades performance. A small value of regret rate was preferred in the experiments. Second, experiments were performed using various values of b, which specifies the weighting of the pseudo data point. The experimental results indicate that when b is ten, the best F_1 value, 0.6949, is obtained. If b is larger than 100 or less than 0.1, the performance will be poor. The above evaluation suggests the setting of parameter b. Finally, the technique that is mentioned in the Appendix is used to enable the model to automatically determine α from the data. Experiments with two initial values, 1 and 1000, are conducted. The above experimental settings can evaluate whether the proposed scheme can automatically adjust α to maintain performance. The experimental results indicate that their performance is almost the same as that in Table 2. Therefore, even if the initial value of α is unreasonable, the proposed dynamic setting scheme can adjust α according to the data.

5. CONCLUSION

This work develops a nonparametric online learning algorithm that adjusts the parameters and complexity of the model as more data instances are observed. The online CRP is more flexible in dealing with massive and streaming data sets than are traditional online learning algorithms. This work proposes a new prior and model parameter updating mechanism that are based on the property of online learning. The experimental results indicate that the online CRP performs well and efficiently on massive data sets. A simple mechanism for converting the online CRP into a supervised learning algorithm is also proposed, and experiments are

Table 5: Compared with Supervised Learning on 20 Newsgroups

	Error Rate	Cluster F_1	Execution Time
Online CRP	0.2010 ± 0.0100	0.6790 ± 0.0224	312.8182 ± 8.9205
SVM	0.2030 ± 0.0092	0.6516 ± 0.0104	$5,931.9255 \pm 56.2376$
Logistic Regression	0.1793 ± 0.0195	0.6929 ± 0.0285	$8,576.3864 \pm 315.3372$
Naive Bayes	0.2276 ± 0.0120	0.6139 ± 0.0217	$2,909.1719 \pm 30.3903$

Table 6: Compared with Supervised Learning on RCV1 Data Set

	Error Rate	Cluster F_1	Execution Time
Online CRP	0.1477	0.8517	54, 958
SVM	0.0748	0.9318	346, 112
Logistic Regression	0.1409	0.8394	12, 367
Naive Bayes	0.1800	0.7850	143, 831

Table 7: Compared with Supervised Learning on Wikipedia Data Set

	Error Rate	Execution Time
Online CRP	0.3602	112, 030
Logistic Regression	0.3488	40, 952
Naive Bayes	0.3887	389, 209

performed with various numbers of training examples. The experimental results indicate that the online CRP benefits from more training examples, but the performance gain is small when the number of training examples exceeds a specific threshold. This finding gives a direction for the future work: the online CRP with the stochastic gradient descent (SGD) trick can be used to deal with massive data sets when training time is an important issue. Central to the proposed method is nonparametric online learning approach, which we argue provides a more flexible and realistic means of dealing with streaming data sets. The nonparametric models make weaker assumptions and let the data "speak for themselves", and online learning allows the model to adapt to observed data.

6. ACKNOWLEDGMENTS

This work was sponsored by Ministry of Economic Affairs, Taiwan, R.O.C. through project No. D352B23100 conducted by Industrial Technology Research Institute (ITRI).

7. REFERENCES

[1] D. Aldous. Exchangeability and related topics. In *École d'Été St Flour 1983*, pages 1–198. Springer-Verlag, 1985. Lecture Notes in Math. 1117.

[2] C. E. Antoniak. Mixtures of dirichlet processes with applications to bayesian nonparametric problems. *Annals of Statistics*, 2(6), November 1974.

[3] D. M. Blei and P. I. Frazier. Distance dependent chinese restaurant processes. *J. Mach. Learn. Res.*, 12:2461–2488, Nov. 2011.

[4] D. M. Blei, T. L. Griffiths, and M. I. Jordan. The nested chinese restaurant process and bayesian nonparametric inference of topic hierarchies. *J. ACM*, 57(2):7:1–7:30, Feb. 2010.

[5] D. M. Blei, T. L. Griffiths, M. I. Jordan, and J. B. Tenenbaum. Hierarchical topic models and the nested chinese restaurant process. In *NIPS*, 2003.

[6] D. M. Blei and M. I. Jordan. Variational inference for dirichlet process mixtures. *Bayesian Analysis*, 1(1):121–144, 2006.

[7] C.-C. Chang and C.-J. Lin. LIBSVM: A library for support vector machines. *ACM Transactions on Intelligent Systems and Technology*, 2:27:1–27:27, 2011. Software available at http://www.csie.ntu.edu.tw/ cjlin/libsvm.

[8] K. Crammer, O. Dekel, J. Keshet, S. Shalev-Shwartz, and Y. Singer. Online passive-aggressive algorithms. *J. Mach. Learn. Res.*, 7:551–585, Dec. 2006.

[9] K. Crammer, M. Dredze, and A. Kulesza. Multi-class confidence weighted algorithms. In *Proceedings of the 2009 Conference on Empirical Methods in Natural Language Processing: Volume 2 - Volume 2*, EMNLP '09, pages 496–504, Stroudsburg, PA, USA, 2009. Association for Computational Linguistics.

[10] K. Crammer, A. Kulesza, and M. Dredze. Adaptive regularization of weight vectors. *Machine Learning*, 91(2):155–187, 2013.

[11] M. Dundar, F. Akova, A. Qi, and B. Rajwa. Bayesian nonexhaustive learning for online discovery and modeling of emerging classes. In *ICML*, 2012.

[12] M. D. Escobar. Estimating normal means with a dirichlet process prior. *Journal of the American Statistical Association*, 89(425):268âĂŞ277, 1994.

[13] M. D. Escobar and M. West. Bayesian density estimation and inference using mixtures. *Journal of the american statistical association*, 90(430):577âĂŞ588, 1995.

[14] T. S. Ferguson. A bayesian analysis of some nonparametric problems. *The annals of statistics*, page 209âĂŞ230, 1973.

[15] M. A. T. Figueiredo and A. K. Jain. Unsupervised learning of finite mixture models. *IEEE Trans. Pattern Anal. Mach. Intell.*, 24(3):381–396, Mar. 2002.

[16] Y. Freund and R. E. Schapire. Large margin classification using the perceptron algorithm. *Mach. Learn.*, 37(3):277–296, Dec. 1999.

[17] S. J. Gershman and D. M. Blei. A tutorial on Bayesian nonparametric models. *Journal of Mathematical Psychology*, 56(1):1–12, Feb. 2012.

[18] S. C. Hoi, J. Wang, and P. Zhao. *LIBOL: A Library for Online Learning Algorithms*. Nanyang Technological University, 2012.

[19] S. C. H. Hoi, J. Wang, and P. Zhao. Exact soft confidence-weighted learning. In *ICML*. icml.cc / Omnipress, 2012.

[20] H. Ishwaran and L. F. James. Gibbs sampling methods for stick-breaking priors. *Journal of the American Statistical Association*, 96(453):161–173, 2001.

[21] S. M. Kay. *Fundamentals of statistical signal processing: estimation theory*. Prentice-Hall, Inc., Upper Saddle River, NJ, USA, 1993.

[22] D. D. Lewis, Y. Yang, T. G. Rose, and F. Li. Rcv1: A new benchmark collection for text categorization research. *J. Mach. Learn. Res.*, 5:361–397, Dec. 2004.

[23] Y. Li and P. M. Long. The Relaxed Online Maximum Margin Algorithm. *Mach. Learn.*, 46(1-3):361–387, Jan. 2002.

[24] N. Littlestone. Learning quickly when irrelevant attributes abound: A new linear-threshold algorithm. *Mach. Learn.*, 2(4):285–318, Apr. 1988.

[25] G. Loomes and R. Sugden. Regret theory: An alternative theory of rational choice under uncertainty. *Economic Journal*, 92(368):805–24, 1982.

[26] S. N. MacEachern. Estimating normal means with a conjugate style Dirichlet process prior. *Communications in Statistics - Simulation and Computation*, 23(3):727–741, 1994.

[27] C. D. Manning, P. Raghavan, and H. Schtze. *Introduction to Information Retrieval*. Cambridge University Press, New York, NY, USA, 2008.

[28] R. M. Neal. Markov chain sampling methods for dirichlet process mixture models. *Journal of computational and graphical statistics*, pages 249–265, 2000.

[29] A. Y. Ng, M. I. Jordan, and Y. Weiss. On Spectral Clustering: Analysis and an algorithm. In *Advances in Neural Information Processing Systems 14*, pages 849–856. MIT Press, 2001.

[30] J. Pitman. Combinatorial stochastic processes. Technical Report 621, Dept. Statistics, U.C. Berkeley, 2002. Lecture notes for St. Flour course, July 2002.

[31] C. E. Rasmussen. The infinite gaussian mixture model. In *NIPS*, pages 554–560, 1999.

[32] J. Shi and J. Malik. Normalized Cuts and Image Segmentation. *IEEE Trans. Pattern Anal. Mach. Intell.*, 22(8):888–905, 2000.

[33] R. Socher, A. L. Maas, and C. D. Manning. Spectral chinese restaurant processes: Nonparametric clustering based on similarities. *Journal of Machine Learning Research - Proceedings Track*, 15:698–706, 2011.

[34] E. B. Sudderth. *Graphical models for visual object recognition and tracking*. PhD thesis, Cambridge, MA, USA, 2006. AAI0809973.

[35] M. J. Wainwright and M. I. Jordan. Graphical models, exponential families, and variational inference. *Found. Trends Mach. Learn.*, 1(1-2):1–305, Jan. 2008.

[36] M. West, P. Müller, and M. D. Escobar. Hierarchical priors and mixture models, with applications in regression and density estimation. *Aspects of Uncertainty: A Tribute to D. V. Lindley*, pages 363–386, 1994.

[37] F. Zhdanov and V. Vovk. Competitive online generalized linear regression under square loss. In *Proceedings of the 2010 European conference on Machine learning and knowledge discovery in databases: Part III*, ECML PKDD'10, pages 531–546, Berlin, Heidelberg, 2010. Springer-Verlag.

[38] M. Zinkevich. Online convex programming and generalized infinitesimal gradient ascent. In *ICML*, pages 928–936, 2003.

APPENDIX

A. SAMPLE α WITH POSTERIOR PROBABILITY

As in the CRP mixture, the concentration parameter α can be sampled from the posterior probability conditional on $\mathbf{z}$ as indicated in Equation (8). Equation (9) gives the likelihood that α generates $\mathbf{z}$, where n is the number of data points, $g(\gamma_1, \gamma_2, e_{z_i}, f_{z_i})$ denotes the relaxing function for $\mathbf{x}_i$ joining to table z_i, m_{z_i} represents the number of people who sit at the table z_i when $\mathbf{x}_i$ joins it. If the prior distribution of α is available, we can sample α using Equation (8) and the observed data points.

$$P(\alpha|\mathbf{z}) \propto P(\mathbf{z}|\alpha)P(\alpha) \tag{8}$$

$$P(\mathbf{z}|\alpha) = \prod_{i=1}^{n} \frac{\mathbb{1}\{m_{z_i} = 0\}\alpha + \mathbb{1}\{m_{z_i} \neq 0\}g(\gamma_1, \gamma_2, e_{z_i}, f_{z_i})m_{z_i}}{\alpha + \sum_{j=1}^{k} g(\gamma_1, \gamma_2, e_j, f_j)m_j} \tag{9}$$

B. DYNAMIC α

This work proposes to use a dynamic approach that is adapting to change to determine the value of α. The value of α specifies the probability of creating a new class. If the class prediction of $\mathbf{x}_i$ is a new class, but the true class of $\mathbf{x}_i$ is in one of the existing ones, the value of α should be reduced. In contrast, the value of α should be increased if the predicted class is in one of the existing classes, but the true class label is new. This approach is used in the experiments to adjust α dynamically.

Knowledge Vault: A Web-Scale Approach to Probabilistic Knowledge Fusion

Xin Luna Dong*, Evgeniy Gabrilovich, Geremy Heitz, Wilko Horn, Ni Lao,
Kevin Murphy†, Thomas Strohmann, Shaohua Sun, Wei Zhang
Google, 1600 Amphitheatre Parkway, Mountain View, CA 94043
{lunadong|gabr|geremy|wilko|nlao|kpmurphy|tstrohmann|sunsh|weizh}@google.com

ABSTRACT

Recent years have witnessed a proliferation of large-scale knowledge bases, including Wikipedia, Freebase, YAGO, Microsoft's Satori, and Google's Knowledge Graph. To increase the scale even further, we need to explore automatic methods for constructing knowledge bases. Previous approaches have primarily focused on text-based extraction, which can be very noisy. Here we introduce Knowledge Vault, a Web-scale probabilistic knowledge base that combines extractions from Web content (obtained via analysis of text, tabular data, page structure, and human annotations) with prior knowledge derived from existing knowledge repositories. We employ supervised machine learning methods for fusing these distinct information sources. The Knowledge Vault is substantially bigger than any previously published structured knowledge repository, and features a probabilistic inference system that computes calibrated probabilities of fact correctness. We report the results of multiple studies that explore the relative utility of the different information sources and extraction methods.

Keywords

Knowledge bases; information extraction; probabilistic models; machine learning

1. INTRODUCTION

> *"The acquisition of knowledge is always of use to the intellect, because it may thus drive out useless things and retain the good. For nothing can be loved or hated unless it is first known."*
>
> – Leonardo da Vinci.

In recent years, several large-scale knowledge bases (KBs) have been constructed, including academic projects such as YAGO [39], NELL [8], DBpedia [3], and Elementary/ DeepDive [32], as well as commercial projects, such as those by Microsoft[1], Google[2], Facebook[3], Walmart [9], and others. (See Section 7 for a detailed discussion of related work.) These knowledge repositories store millions of facts about the world, such as information about people, places and things (generically referred to as entities).

Despite their seemingly large size, these repositories are still far from complete. For example, consider Freebase, the largest open-source knowledge base [4]. 71% of people in Freebase have no known place of birth, and 75% have no known nationality[4]. Furthermore, coverage for less common relations/predicates can be even lower.

Previous approaches for building knowledge bases primarily relied on direct contributions from human volunteers as well as integration of existing repositories of structured knowledge (e.g., Wikipedia infoboxes). However, these methods are more likely to yield head content, namely, frequently mentioned properties of frequently mentioned entities. Suh et al. [41] also observed that Wikipedia growth has essentially plateaued, hence unsolicited contributions from human volunteers may yield a limited amount of knowledge going forward. Therefore, we believe a new approach is necessary to further scale up knowledge base construction. Such an approach should automatically extract facts from the whole Web, to augment the knowledge we collect from human input and structured data sources. Unfortunately, standard methods for this task (cf. [44]) often produce very noisy, unreliable facts. To alleviate the amount of noise in the automatically extracted data, the new approach should automatically leverage already-cataloged knowledge to build prior models of fact correctness.

In this paper, we propose a new way of automatically constructing a Web-scale probabilistic knowledge base, which we call the *Knowledge Vault*, or KV for short. Like many other knowledge bases, KV stores information in the form

*Authors are listed alphabetically
†Corresponding author

KDD'14, August 24–27, 2014, New York, NY, USA.

ACM 978-1-4503-2956-9/14/08 ...$15.00.
http://dx.doi.org/10.1145/2623330.2623623.

[1] `http://www.bing.com/blogs/site_blogs/b/search/archive/2013/03/21/satorii.aspx`
[2] `http://www.google.com/insidesearch/features/search/knowledge.html`
[3] `http://www.insidefacebook.com/2013/01/14/facebook-builds-knowledge-graph-with-info-modules-on-community-pages/`
[4] Numbers current as of October 2013, cf. [28]. Freebase data is publicly available at `https://developers.google.com/freebase/data`.

of RDF triples (subject, predicate, object).An example is </m/02mjmr, /people/person/place_of_birth /m/02hrh0_>, where /m/02mjmr is the Freebase id for Barack Obama, and /m/02hrh0_ is the id for Honolulu. Associated with each such triple is a confidence score, representing the probability that KV "believes" the triple is correct.

Entity types and predicates come from a fixed ontology, which is similar to that used in other systems, such as YAGO [39], NELL [8], DeepDive [32], and various systems participating in the TAC-KBP slot-filling competition [22]. Knowledge bases that use a fixed ontology should be contrasted with open information extraction (Open IE) approaches, such as Reverb [12], which work at the lexical level. Open IE systems usually have multiple redundant facts that are worded differently, such as <Barack Obama, was born in, Honolulu> and <Obama, place of birth, Honolulu>. In contrast, KV separates facts about the world from their lexical representation. This makes KV a structured repository of knowledge that is language independent.

The contributions of this paper are threefold. First, the Knowledge Vault is different from previous works on automatic knowledge base construction as it combines noisy extractions from the Web together with prior knowledge, which is derived from existing knowledge bases (in this paper, we use Freebase as our source of prior data). This approach is analogous to techniques used in speech recognition, which combine noisy acoustic signals with priors derived from a language model. KV's prior model can help overcome errors due to the extraction process, as well as errors in the sources themselves. For example, suppose an extractor returns a fact claiming that Barack Obama was born in Kenya, and suppose (for illustration purposes) that the true place of birth of Obama was not already known in Freebase. Our prior model can use related facts about Obama (such as his profession being US President) to infer that this new fact is unlikely to be true. The error could be due to mistaking Barack Obama for his father (entity resolution or co-reference resolution error), or it could be due to an erroneous statement on a spammy Web site (source error).

Second, KV is much bigger than other comparable KBs (see Table 1). In particular, KV has 1.6B triples, of which 324M have a confidence of 0.7 or higher, and 271M have a confidence of 0.9 or higher. This is about 38 times more than the largest previous comparable system (DeepDive [32]), which has 7M confident facts (Ce Zhang, personal communication). To create a knowledge base of such size, we extract facts from a large variety of sources of Web data, including free text, HTML DOM trees, HTML Web tables, and human annotations of Web pages. (Note that about 1/3 of the 271M confident triples were not previously in Freebase, so we are extracting new knowledge not contained in the prior.)

Third, we perform a detailed comparison of the quality and coverage of different extraction methods, as well as different prior methods. We also demonstrate the benefits of using multiple extraction sources and systems. Finally, we evaluate the validity of the closed world assumption, which is often used to automatically evaluate newly extracted facts given an existing knowledge base (see Section 6).

In the following sections, we describe the components of KV in more detail. We then study the performance of each part of the system in isolation and in combination, and show that fusion of multiple complementary systems and data sources considerably improves precision at a given recall level

2. OVERVIEW

KV contains three major components:

- **Extractors**: these systems extract triples from a huge number of Web sources. Each extractor assigns a confidence score to an extracted triple, representing uncertainty about the identity of the relation and its corresponding arguments.
- **Graph-based priors**: these systems learn the prior probability of each possible triple, based on triples stored in an existing KB.
- **Knowledge fusion**: this system computes the probability of a triple being true, based on agreement between different extractors and priors.

Abstractly, we can view the KV problem as follows: we are trying to construct a weighted labeled graph, which we can view as a very sparse $E \times P \times E$ 3d matrix G, where E is the number of entities, P is the number of predicates, and $G(s,p,o) = 1$ if there is a link of type p from s to o, and $G(s,p,o) = 0$ otherwise. We want to compute $\Pr(G(s,p,o) = 1|\cdot)$ for candidate (s,p,o) triples, where the probability is conditional on different sources of information. When using extractions, we condition on text features about the triple. When using graph-based priors, we condition on known edges in the Freebase graph (obviously we exclude the edge we are trying to predict!). Finally, in knowledge fusion, we condition on both text extractions and prior edges.

We describe each of three components in more detail in the following sections. Before that, we discuss our training and test procedure, which is common to all three approaches.

2.1 Evaluation protocol

Using the methods to be described in Section 3, we extract about 1.6B candidate triples, covering 4469 different types of relations and 1100 different types of entities. About 271M of these facts have an estimated probability of being true above 90%; we call these "confident facts". The resulting KB is much larger than other automatically constructed KBs, as summarized in Table 1.

To evaluate the quality of our methods, we randomly split this data into a training set (80% of the data) and a test set (20% of the data); we infer labels for these triples using the method described below. To ensure that certain common predicates (e.g., relating to geographical containment) did not dominate the performance measures, we took at most 10k instances of each predicate when creating the test set. We then pooled the samples from each predicate to get a more balanced test set.

If the test set contains the triple (s,p,o), then the training set is guaranteed not to contain the same triple. However, it may contain (s,p,o') or (s,p',o) or (s',p,o). For example, suppose s is Barack Obama, p is father-of, and o is Sasha Obama. Then the training set may contain the fact that Barack is the father of Malia Obama, or that Barack lives in the same place as Sasha Obama, etc. In graph terminology, we are leaving out edges at random from the training set, and asking how well we can predict their presence or absence.

Name	# Entity types	# Entity instances	# Relation types	# Confident facts (relation instances)
Knowledge Vault (KV)	1100	45M	4469	271M
DeepDive [32]	4	2.7M	34	7M[a]
NELL [8]	271	5.19M	306	0.435M[b]
PROSPERA [30]	11	N/A	14	0.1M
YAGO2 [19]	350,000	9.8M	100	4M[c]
Freebase [4]	1,500	40M	35,000	637M[d]
Knowledge Graph (KG)	1,500	570M	35,000	18,000M[e]

Table 1: Comparison of knowledge bases. KV, DeepDive, NELL, and PROSPERA rely solely on extraction, Freebase and KG rely on human curation and structured sources, and YAGO2 uses both strategies. Confident facts means with a probability of being true at or above 0.9.

[a] Ce Zhang (U Wisconsin), private communication

[b] Bryan Kiesel (CMU), private communication

[c] Core facts, `http://www.mpi-inf.mpg.de/yago-naga/yago/downloads.html`

[d] This is the number of non-redundant base triples, excluding reverse predicates and "lazy" triples derived from flattening CVTs (complex value types).

[e] `http://insidesearch.blogspot.com/2012/12/get-smarter-answers-from-knowledge_4.html`

An alternative approach to constructing the test set would have been to leave out all edges emanating from a particular node. However, in such a case, the graph-based models would have no signal to leverage. For example, suppose we omitted all facts about Barack Obama, and asked the system to predict where he lives, and who his children are. This would be possible given text extractions, but impossible given just a prior graph of facts. A compromise would be to omit all edges of a given type; for example, we could omit connections to all his children, but leave in other relations. However, we think the random sampling scenario more accurately reflects our actual use-case, which consists of growing an existing KB, where arbitrary facts may be missing.

2.2 Local closed world assumption (LCWA)

All the components of our system use supervised machine learning methods to fit probabilistic binary classifiers, which can compute the probability of a triple being true. We give the details on how these classifiers are constructed in the following sections. Here, we describe how we determine the labels (we use the same procedure for the training and test set).

For (s, p, o) triples that are in Freebase, we assume the label is true. For triples that do not occur in Freebase, we could assume the label is false (corresponding to a closed world assumption), but this would be rather dangerous, since we know that Freebase is very incomplete. So instead, we make use a somewhat more refined heuristic that we call the *local closed world assumption.*

To explain this heuristic, let us define $O(s, p)$ as the set of existing object values for a given s and p. This set will be a singleton for functional (single-valued) predicates such as place of birth, but can have multiple values for general relations, such as children; of course, the set can also be empty. Now, given a candidate triple (s, p, o), we assign its label as follows: if $(s, p, o) \in O(s, p)$, we say the triple is correct; if $(s, p, o) \notin O(s, p)$, but $|O(s, p)| > 0$, we say the triple is incorrect (because we assume the KB is *locally complete* for this subject-predicate pair); if $O(s, p)$ is empty, we do not label the triple, and we throw it out of our training / test set.

This heuristic is also used in previous works such as [15]. We empirically evaluate its adequacy in Section 6, by comparing to human-labeled data. There are more sophisticated methods for training models that don't make this assumption (such as [28, 36]), but we leave the integration of such methods into KV to future work.

3. FACT EXTRACTION FROM THE WEB

In this section, we summarize the extractors that we use to build KV, and then we evaluate their relative performance.

3.1 Extraction methods

3.1.1 Text documents (TXT)

We use relatively standard methods for relation extraction from text (see [16] for a recent overview), but we do so at a much larger scale than previous systems.

We first run a suite of standard NLP tools over each document. These perform named entity recognition, part of speech tagging, dependency parsing, co-reference resolution (within each document), and entity linkage (which maps mentions of proper nouns and their co-references to the corresponding entities in the KB). The in-house named entity linkage system we use is similar to the methods described in [18].

Next, we train relation extractors using distant supervision [29]. Specifically, for each predicate of interest, we extract a seed set of entity pairs that have this predicate, from an existing KB. For example, if the predicate is `married_to`, the pairs could be `(BarackObama, MichelleObama)` and `(BillClinton, HillaryClinton)`. We then find examples of sentences in which this pair is mentioned, and extract features/ patterns (either from the surface text or the dependency parse) from all of these sentences. The features that we use are similar to those described in [29].

In a bootstrapping phase, we look for more examples of sentences with these patterns occurring between pairs of entities of the correct type. We use the local closed world assumption to derive labels for the resulting set of extractions. Once we have a labeled training set, we fit a binary classifier (we use logistic regression) for each predicate independently in parallel, using a MapReduce framework. We have trained extractors for 4469 predicates, which is much more than previous machine reading systems.

3.1.2 HTML trees (DOM)

A somewhat different way to extract information from Web pages is to parse their DOM trees. These can either come from text pages, or from "deep web" sources, where data are stored in underlying databases and queried by filling HTML forms; these sources together generate more than 1B pages of data in DOM tree format [7]. To extract triples from DOM trees, we train classifiers as in the text case, except that we derive features connecting two entities from the DOM trees instead of from the text. Specifically, we use the lexicalized path (along the tree) between the two entities as a feature vector. The score of the extracted triples is the output of the classifier.

3.1.3 HTML tables (TBL)

There are over 570M tables on the Web that contain relational information (as opposed to just being used for visual formatting) [6]. Unfortunately, fact extraction techniques developed for text and trees do not work very well for tables, because the relation between two entities is usually contained in the column header, rather than being close by in the text/ tree. Instead, we use the following heuristic technique. First, we perform named entity linkage, as in the text case. Then we attempt to identify the relation that is expressed in each column of the table by looking at the entities in each column, and reasoning about which predicate each column could correspond to, by matching to Freebase, as in standard schema matching methods [42]. Ambiguous columns are discarded. The score of the extracted triple reflects the confidence returned by the named entity linkage system.

3.1.4 Human Annotated pages (ANO)

There are a large number of webpages where the webmaster has added manual annotations following ontologies from *schema.org*, *microformats.org*, *openGraphProtocol.org*, etc. In this paper, we use *schema.org* annotations. Many of these annotations are related to events or products, etc. Such information is not currently stored in the knowledge vault. So instead, in this paper we focus on a small subset of 14 different predicates, mostly related to people. We define a manual mapping from *schema.org* to the Freebase schema for these different predicates. The score of the extracted triple reflects the confidence returned by the named entity linkage system (the same one we use for TXT triples).

3.2 Fusing the extractors

We have described 4 different fact extraction methods. A simple way to combine these signals is to construct a feature vector $\vec{f}(t)$ for each extracted triple $t = (s, p, o)$, and then to apply a binary classifier to compute $\Pr(t = 1|\vec{f}(t))$. For simplicity and speed, we fit a separate classifier for each predicate.

The feature vector is composed of two numbers for each extractor: the square root[5] of the number of sources that the extractor extracted this triple from, and the mean score of the extractions from this extractor, averaging over sources (or 0 if the system did not produce this triple).

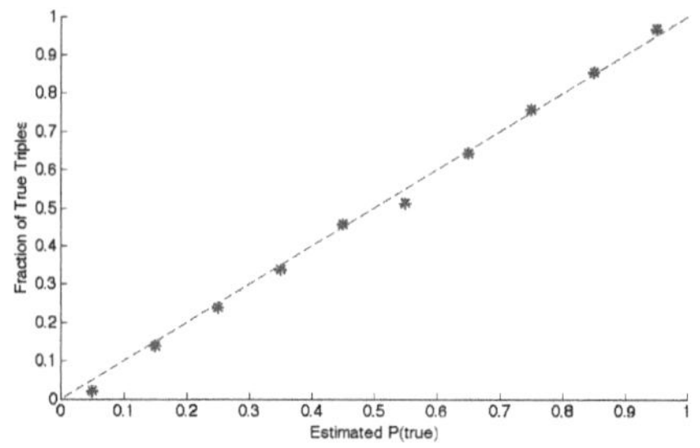

Figure 1: True probability vs estimated probability for each triple in KV.

The classifier learns a different weight for each component of this feature vector, and hence can learn the relative reliabilities of each system. In addition, since we fit a separate classifier per predicate, we can model their different reliabilities, too.

The labels for training the fusion system come from applying the local closed world assumption to the training set. Since this is a very low-dimensional classification problem, we initially used a linear logistic regression model. However, we observed considerably better performance by using boosted decision stumps [35]. This kind of classifier can learn to quantize the features into bins, and thus learn a non-linear decision boundary.

3.3 Calibration of the probability estimates

The confidence scores from each extractor (and/or the fused system) are not necessarily on the same scale, and cannot necessarily be interpreted as probabilities. To alleviate this problem, we adopt the standard technique known as Platt Scaling (named after [33]), which consists of fitting a logistic regression model to the scores, using a separate validation set. Figure 1 shows that our (fused) probability estimates are well-calibrated, in the following sense: if we collect all the triples that have a predicted probability of 0.9, then we find that about 90% of them are indeed true. Each individual extractor is also calibrated (results not shown).

3.4 Comparison of the methods

Using the four extractors described earlier applied to a very large web corpus, we extract about 1.6B triples. Table 2 shows the number of triples from each system. We see that the DOM system extracts the largest number of triples overall (about 1.2B), of which about 94M (or 8%) are high confidence (with a probability of being true at or above 0.9; see the penultimate column of Table 2). The TBL system extracts the least number of triples overall (about 9.4M). One reason for this is that very few columns in webtables (only 18% according to [17]) map to a corresponding Freebase predicate. The ANO and TXT systems both produce hundreds of millions of triples.

In addition to measuring the number of triples at different confidence levels, it is interesting to consider the area under the ROC curve (AUC score). This score is equal to the probability that a classifier will rank a randomly chosen positive

[5]The motivation for using $\sqrt{n}$, where n is the number of sources, is to reduce the effect of very commonly expressed facts (such as the birth place of Barack Obama). Results are similar if we use $\log(1 + n)$. Note that we perform de-duplication of sources before running the extraction pipelines.

System	#	# > 0.7	# > 0.9	Frac. >0.9	AUC
TBL	9.4M	3.8M	0.59M	0.06	0.856
ANO	140M	2.4M	0.25M	0.002	0.920
TXT	330M	20M	7.1M	0.02	0.867
DOM	1200M	150M	94M	0.08	0.928
FUSED-EX.	1600M	160M	100M	0.06	0.927

Table 2: Performance of different extraction systems.

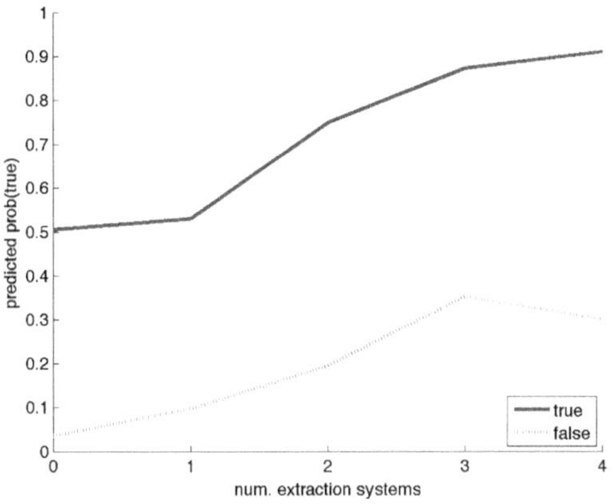

Figure 2: Predicted probability of each triple vs. the number of systems that predicted it. Solid blue line: correct (true) triples. Dotted red line: incorrect (false) triples.

instance higher than a randomly chosen negative one. We computed the AUC scores for the different extraction methods on different test sets, namely, only using the extractions produced by each system (obviously, the test sets were distinct from the training sets). The test set for computing the AUC score for the fused extractors was the union of all the test sets of the individual systems.

We see that the DOM system has the highest AUC score, so although it produces a large number of low confidence triples, the system "knows" that these are likely to be false. The table also illustrates the benefits of fusing multiple extractors: we get about 7% more high confidence triples, while maintaining a high AUC score (see the last row of the table). Not surprisingly, however, the performance of the fusion system is dominated by that of the DOM system. In Section 5, we shall show much greater gains from fusion, when we combine graph priors with extractors.

3.5 The beneficial effects of adding more evidence

Figure 2 shows how the overall predicted probability of each triple changes as more systems extract it. When no systems extract a given triple, we rely on our prior model (described in Section 4); averaging over all the triples, we see that the prior probability for the true triples is about 0.5, whereas the prior probability for the false triples is close to 0. As we accumulate more evidence in favor of the triple, our belief in its correctness increases to near 1.0 for the true triples; for the false triples, our belief also increases, although it stays well below 0.5.

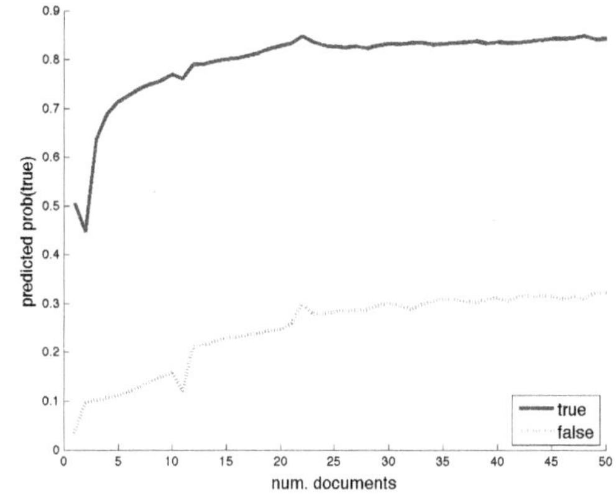

Figure 3: Predicted probability of each triple vs. the number of unique web sources that contain this triple (axis truncated at 50 for clarity).

Figure 3 shows how the probability of a triple increases with the number of sources where the triple is seen. Again, our final belief in true triples is much higher than in false triples. To prevent over-counting of evidence, we only count each triple once per domain, as opposed to once per URL; for example, if we extract a triple asserting that Barack Obama was born in Kenya from `myblogger.com/page1` and `myblogger.com/page2`, we only count this once.

4. GRAPH-BASED PRIORS

As mentioned in the introduction, facts extracted from the Web can be unreliable. A good way to combat this is to use prior knowledge, derived from other kinds of data. In this paper, we exploit existing triples in Freebase to fit prior models, which can assign a probability to any possible triple, even if there is no corresponding evidence for this fact on the Web (cf. [2]). This can be thought of as link prediction in a graph. That is, we observe a set of existing edges (representing predicates that connect different entities), and we want to predict which other edges are likely to exist. We have tried two different approaches to solving this problem, which we describe below.

4.1 Path ranking algorithm (PRA)

One way to perform link prediction is to use the path ranking algorithm of [24]. Similar to distant supervision, we start with a set of pairs of entities that are connected by some predicate p. PRA then performs a random walk on the graph, starting at all the subject (source) nodes. Paths that reach the object (target) nodes are considered successful. For example, the algorithm learns that pairs (X, Y) which are connected by a marriedTo edge often also have a path of the form $X \xrightarrow{\text{parentOf}} Z \xleftarrow{\text{parentOf}} Y$, since if two people share a common child, they are likely to be married. The quality of these paths can be measured in terms of their support and precision, as in association rule mining (cf., [15]).

The paths that PRA learns can be interpreted as rules. For example, consider the task of predicting where someone went to college. The algorithm discovers several useful rules, shown in Table 3. In English, the first rule says: a person X is likely to have attended school S if X was drafted from

F1	P	R	W	Path
0.03	1	0.01	2.62	/sports/drafted-athlete/drafted,/sports/sports-league-draft-pick/school
0.05	0.55	0.02	1.88	/people/person/sibling-s, /people/sibling-relationship/sibling, /people/person/education, /education/education/institution
0.06	0.41	0.02	1.87	/people/person/spouse-s, /people/marriage/spouse, /people/person/education, /education/education/institution
0.04	0.29	0.02	1.37	/people/person/parents, /people/person/education, /education/education/institution
0.05	0.21	0.02	1.85	/people/person/children, /people/person/education, /education/education/institution
0.13	0.1	0.38	6.4	/people/person/place-of-birth, /location/location/people-born-here, /people/person/education, /education/education/institution
0.05	0.04	0.34	1.74	/type/object/type, /type/type/instance, /people/person/education, /education/education/institution
0.04	0.03	0.33	2.19	/people/person/profession, /people/profession/people-with-this-profession, /people/person/education, /education/education/institution

Table 3: Some of the paths learned by PRA for predicting where someone went to college. Rules are sorted by decreasing precision. Column headers: F1 is the harmonic mean of precision and recall, P is the precision, R is the recall, W is the weight given to this feature by logistic regression.

sports team T, and T is from school S. The second rule says: a person is likely to attend the same school as their sibling.

Since multiple rules or paths might apply for any given pair of entities, we can combine them by fitting a binary classifier (we use logistic regression). In PRA, the features are the probabilities of reaching O from S following different types of paths, and the labels are derived using the local closed world assumption. We can fit a classifier for each predicate independently in parallel. We have trained prior predictors for 4469 predicates using Freebase as training data. At test time, given a new (s, p, o) triple, we look up all the paths for predicate p chosen by the learned model, and perform a walk (on the training graph) from s to o via each such path; this gives us a feature value that can be plugged in to the classifier.

The overall AUC is 0.884, which is less than that of the fused extractor system (0.927), but is still surprisingly high.

4.2 Neural network model (MLP)

An alternative approach to building the prior model is to view the link prediction problem as matrix (or rather, tensor) completion. In particular, the original KB can be viewed as a very sparse $E \times P \times E$ 3d matrix G, where E is the number of entities, P is the number of predicates, and $G(s,p,o) = 1$ if there is a link of type p from s to o, and $G(s,p,o) = 0$ otherwise. We can perform a low-rank decomposition of this tensor by associating a latent low dimensional vector to each entity and predicate, and then computing the elementwise inner product:

$$\Pr(G(s,p,o) = 1) = \sigma\left(\sum_{k=1}^{K} u_{sk} w_{pk} v_{ok}\right) \tag{1}$$

where $\sigma(x) = 1/(1+e^{-x})$ is the sigmoid or logistic function, and $K \sim 60$ is the number of hidden dimensions. Here $\vec{u}_s$, $\vec{w}_p$ and $\vec{v}_o$ are K-dimensional vectors, which embed the discrete tokens into a low dimensional "semantic" space. If we ignore the sigmoid transform (needed to produce binary responses), this is equivalent to the PARAFAC method of tensor decomposition [14, 5, 11].

A more powerful model was recently proposed in [37]; this associates a different *tensor* with each relation, and hence has the form

$$\Pr(G(s,p,o) = 1) = \sigma\left(\vec{\beta}_p^T f\left[\vec{u}_s^T \vec{W}_p^{1:M} \vec{v}_o\right]\right) \tag{2}$$

where $f()$ is a nonlinear function such as tanh, $\vec{\beta}_p$ is a $K \times 1$ vector, and $\vec{W}_p^m$ is a $K \times K$ matrix. Unfortunately, this model requires $O(KE + K^2MP)$ parameters, where M is the number of "layers" in the tensor W.

In this paper, we considered a simpler approach where we associate one *vector* per predicate, as in Equation 1, but then use a standard multi layer perceptron (MLP) to capture interaction terms. More precisely, our model has the form

$$\Pr(G(s,p,o) = 1) = \sigma\left(\vec{\beta}^T f\left[\vec{A}\left[\vec{u}_s, \vec{w}_p, \vec{v}_o\right]\right]\right) \tag{3}$$

where $\vec{A}$ is a $L \times (3K)$ matrix (where the $3K$ term arises from the K-dimensional $\vec{u}_s$ and $\vec{w}_p$ and $\vec{v}_o$) representing the first layer weights (after the embeddings), and $\vec{\beta}$ is a $L \times 1$ vector representing the second layer weights. (We set $L = K = 60$.) This has only $O(L+LK+KE+KP)$ parameters, but achieves essentially the same performance as the one in Equation 2 on their dataset.[6]

Having established that our MLP model is comparable to the state of the art, we applied it to the KV data set. Surprisingly, we find that the neural model has about the same performance as PRA when evaluated using ROC curves (the AUC for the MLP model is 0.882, and for PRA is 0.884).

To illustrate that the neural network model learns a meaningful "semantic" representation of the entities and predicates, we can compute the nearest neighbors of various items in the a K-dimensional space. It is known from previous work (e.g., [27]) that related entities cluster together in the space, so here we focus on predicates. The results are shown in Table 4. We see that the model learns to put semantically related (but not necessarily similar) predicates near each other. For example, we see that the closest predicates (in the $\vec{w}$ embedding space) to the 'children' predicate are 'parents', 'spouse' and 'birth-place'.

4.3 Fusing the priors

We can combine the different priors together using the fusion method described in Section 3.2. The only difference is the features that we use, since we no longer have any extractions. Insead, the feature vector contains the vector of confidence values from each prior system, plus indicator values specifying if the prior was able to predict or not. (This lets us distinguish a missing prediction from a prediction score of 0.0.) We train a boosted classifier using these signals, and calibrate it with Platt Scaling, as before. Fusing

[6]More precisely, [37] reported an 88.9% accuracy on the subset of Freebase data they have worked with (75,043 entities, 13 relations) when they replaced entities such as `Barack-Obama` by their constituting words `Barack` and `Obama`. Applying the same technique of replacing entities with consituting words, our simpler model got an accuracy of 89.1%.

Predicate	Neighbor 1	Neighbor 2	Neighbor 3
children	0.4 parents	0.5 spouse	0.8 birth-place
birth-date	1.24 children	1.25 gender	1.29 parents
edu-end	1.41 job-start	1.61 edu-end	1.74 job-end

Table 4: Nearest neighbors for some predicates in the 60d embedding space learned by the neural network. Numbers represent squared Euclidean distance. Edu-start and edu-end represent the start and end dates of someone attending a school or college. Similarly, job-start and job-end represent the start and end dates of someone holding a particular job.

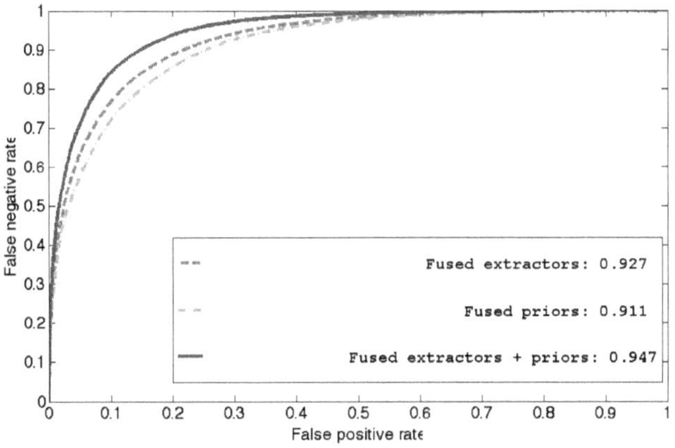

Figure 4: ROC curves for the fused extractor, fused prior, and fused prior + extractor. The numbers in the legend are the AUC scores.

the two prior methods helps performance, since they have complementary strengths and weaknesses (different inductive biases): the AUC of the fused system is 0.911.

5. FUSING EXTRACTORS AND PRIORS

We have described several different fact extraction methods, and several different priors. We can combine all these systems together using the fusion method described in Section 3.2. Figure 4 shows the benefits of fusion quantitatively. We see that combining prior and extractor together results in a significant boost in performance.

To more clearly illustrate the effect of adding the prior, Figure 5 plots the number of triples in each confidence bin for the (fused) extractor, the (fused) prior, and the overall system. We see that compared with considering only extractions, combining priors and extractors increases the number of high confidence facts (those with a probability greater than 0.9) from about 100M to about 271M. Of these, about 33% are new facts that were not yet in Freebase.

Figure 5 illustrates another interesting effect: when we combine prior and extractor, the number of triples about which we are uncertain (*i.e.*, the predicted probability falling in the range of [.3, .7]) has gone down; some of these triples we now believe to be true (as we discussed previously), but many we now believe to be false. This is a visual illustration that the prior can reduce the false positive rate.

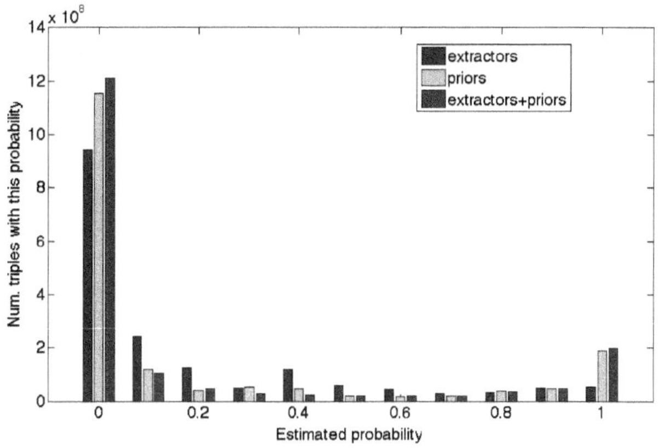

Figure 5: Number of triples in KV in each confidence bin.

We now give a qualitative example of the benefits of combining the prior with the extractor. The extraction pipeline extracted the following triple:[7]

```
<Barry Richter (/m/02ql38b),
/people/person/edu./edu/edu/institution,
Universty of Wisconsin-Madison (/m/01yx1b)>
```

The (fused) extraction confidence for this triple was just 0.14, since it was based on the following two rather indirect statements:[8]

```
In the fall of 1989, Richter accepted a scholarship
to the University of Wisconsin, where he played for
four years and earned numerous individual accolades...
```

```
The Polar Caps' cause has been helped by the impact of
knowledgable coaches such as Andringa, Byce and former
UW teammates Chris Tancill and Barry Richter.
```

However, we know from Freebase that Barry Richter was born and raised in Madison, WI. This increases our prior belief that he went to school there, resulting in a final fused belief of 0.61.

6. EVALUATING LCWA

So far, we have been relying on the local closed world assumption (LCWA) to train and test our system. However, we know that this is just an approximation to the truth. For example, Freebase often lists the top 5 or so actors for any given movie, but it is unreasonable to assume that this list is complete (since most movies have a cast of 10–20 actors); this can result in false negatives (if our system predicts the

[7] Here the predicate is a conjunction of two primitive predicates, `/people/person/education` and `/education/education/institution`, obtained by passing through a complex value type (CVT) node, aka an anonymous or "blank" node, representing the temporal event that Barry attended Madison.

[8] Sources: `http://www.legendsofhockey.net/LegendsOfHockey/jsp/SearchPlayer.jsp?player=11377` and `http://host.madison.com/sports/high-school/hockey/numbers-dwindling-for-once-mighty-madison\-high-school\-hockey-programs/article_95843e00-ec34-11df-9da9-001cc4c002e0.html`

Labels	Prior	Extractor	Prior+ex
LCWA	0.943	0.872	0.959
Human	0.843	0.852	0.869

Table 5: AUC scores for the fused prior, extractor and prior+extractor using different labels on the 10k test set.

name of an actor that is not on the list). Conversely (but less frequently), Freebase can contain errors, which can result in false positives.

To assess the severity of this problem, we manually labeled a subset of our balanced test set, using an in-house team of raters. This subset consisted of 1000 triples for 10 different predicates. We asked each rater to evaluate each such triple, and to determine (based on their own research, which can include web searches, looking at wikipedia, etc) whether each triple is true or false or unknown; we discarded the 305 triples with unknown labels.

We then computed the performance of our systems on this test set, using both LCWA labels and the human labels. In both cases, the system was trained on our full training set (i.e., 80% of 1.6B) using LCWA labels. The results are shown in Table 5. We see that the performance on the human labeled data is lower, although not by that much, indirectly justifying our use of the LCWA.

7. RELATED WORK

There is a growing body of work on automatic knowledge base construction [44, 1]. This literature can be clustered into 4 main groups: (1) approaches such as YAGO [39], YAGO2 [19], DBpedia [3], and Freebase [4], which are built on Wikipedia infoboxes and other structured data sources; (2) approaches such as Reverb [12], OLLIE [26], and PRISMATIC [13], which use open information (schema-less) extraction techniques applied to the entire web; (3) approaches such as NELL/ ReadTheWeb [8], PROSPERA [30], and DeepDive/ Elementary [32], which extract information from the entire web, but use a fixed ontology/ schema; and (4) approaches such as Probase [47], which construct taxonomies (is-a hierarchies), as opposed to general KBs with multiple types of predicates.

The knowledge vault is most similar to methods of the third kind, which extract facts, in the form of disambiguated triples, from the entire web. The main difference from this prior work is that we fuse together facts extracted from text with prior knowledge derived from the Freebase graph.

There is also a large body of work on link prediction in graphs. This can be thought as creating a joint probability model over a large set of binary random variables, where $G(s,p,o) = 1$ if and only if there is a link of type p from s to o. The literature can be clustered into three main kinds of methods: (1) methods that directly model the correlation between the variables, using discrete Markov random fields (e.g., [23]) or continuous relaxations thereof (e.g., [34]); (2) methods that use latent variables to model the correlations indirectly, using either discrete factors (e.g., [48]) or continuous factors (e.g., [31, 11, 20, 37]); and (3) methods that approximate the correlation using algorithmic approaches, such as random walks [24].

In the knowledge vault, we currently employ graph priors of the second and third kind. In particular, our neural tensor model is a continuous latent variable model, which is similar to, but slightly different from, [37] (see Section 4.2 for a discussion). Our PRA model is similar to the method described in [24], except it is trained on Freebase instead of on NELL. In addition, it uses a more scalable implementation.

Another related literature is on the topic of probabilistic databases (see e.g., [40, 43]). KV is a probabilistic database, and it can support simple queries, such as `BarackObama BornIn ?`, which returns a distribution over places where KV thinks Obama was born. However, we do not yet support sophisticated queries, such as JOIN or SELECT.

Finally, there is a small set of papers on representing uncertainty in information extraction systems (see e.g., [45, 25]). KV also represents uncertainty in the facts it has extracted. Indeed, we show that its uncertainty estimates are well-calibrated. We also show how they change as a function of the amount of evidence (see Figure 2).

8. DISCUSSION

Although Knowledge Vault is a large repository of useful knowledge, there are still many ways in which it can be improved. We discuss some of these issues below.

Modeling mutual exclusion between facts. Currently (for reasons of scalability) we treat each fact as an independent binary random variable, that is either true or false. However, in reality, many triples are correlated. For example, for a functional relation such as born-in, we know there can only be one true value, so the (s, p, o_i) triples representing different values o_i for the same subject s and predicate p become correlated due to the mutual exclusion constraint. A simple way to handle this is to collect together all candidate values, and to force the distribution over them to sum to 1 (possibly allowing for some "extra" probability mass to account for the fact that the true value might not be amongst the extracted set of candidates). This is similar to the notion of an X-tuple in probabilistic databases [40]. Preliminary experiments of this kind did not work very well, since the different o_i often represent the same entity at different levels of granularity. For example, we might have a fact that Obama was born in Honolulu, and another one stating he was born in Hawaii. These are not mutually exclusive, so the naive approach does not work. We are currently investigating more sophisticated methods.

Modeling soft correlation between facts. For some kinds of relations, there will be soft constraints on their values. For example, we know that people usually have between 0 and 5 children; there is of course a long tail to this distribution, but it would still be surprising (and indicative of a potential error) if we extracted 100 different children for one person. Similarly, we expect the date of birth of a person to be about 15 to 50 years earlier than the date of birth of their child. Preliminary experiments using joint Gaussian models to represent correlations amongst numerical values show some promise, but we still need to fully integrate this kind of joint prior into KV.

Values can be represented at multiple levels of abstraction. We can represent the world at different levels of granularity. For example, we can say that Obama is born in Honolulu, or in Hawaii, or in the USA. When matching extracted facts with those stored in Freebase, we use prior geographical knowledge to reason about compatibility. For example, if we extract that Obama was born in Hawaii, and we already know he was born in Honolulu, we consider this a correct extraction. In the future, we would like to generalize this approach to other kinds of values. For example, if we extract that Obama's profession is politician, and we already know his profession is president, we should regard the extracted fact as true, since it is implied by what we already know.

Dealing with correlated sources. In Figure 3, we showed how our belief in a triple increased as we saw it extracted from more sources. This is of course problematic if we have duplicated or correlated sources. Currently we have a very simple solution to this, based on counting each domain only once. In the future, we plan to deploy more sophisticated copy detection mechanisms, such as those in [10].

Some facts are only temporarily true. In some cases, the "truth" about a fact can change. For example, Google's current CEO is Larry Page, but from 2001 to 2011 it was Eric Schmidt. Both facts are correct, but only during the specified time interval. For this reason, Freebase allows some facts to be annotated with beginning and end dates, by use of the CVT (compound value type) construct, which represents n-ary relations via auxiliary nodes. (An alternative approach is to reify the pairwise relations, and add extra assertions to them, as in the YAGO2 system [19].) In the future, we plan to extend KV to model such temporal facts. However, this is non-trivial, since the duration of a fact is not necessarily related to the timestamp of the corresponding source (cf. [21]).

Adding new entities and relations. In addition to missing facts, there are many entities that are mentioned on the Web but are not in Freebase, and hence not in KV either. In order to represent such information, we need to automatically create new entities (cf. [46]); this is work in progress. Furthermore, there are many relations that are mentioned on the Web but cannot be represented in the Freebase schema. To capture such facts, we need to extend the schema, but we need to do so in a controlled way, to avoid the problems faced by open IE systems, which have many redundant and synonymous relations. See [17] for one possible approach to this problem.

Knowledge representation issues. The RDF triple format seems adequate for representing factual assertions (assuming a suitably rich schema), but it might be less appropriate for other kinds of knowledge (e.g., representing the difference between running and jogging, or between jazz music and blues). There will always be a long tail of concepts that are difficult to capture in any fixed ontology. Our neural network is one possible way to provide semantically plausible generalizations, but extending it to represent richer forms of knowledge is left to future work.

Inherent upper bounds on the potential amount of knowledge that we can extract. The goal of KV is to become a large-scale repository of all of human knowledge. However, even if we had a perfect machine reading system, not all of human knowledge is available on the Web. In particular, common sense knowledge may be hard to acquire from text sources. However, we may be able to acquire such knowledge using crowdsourcing techniques (c.f., [38]).

9. CONCLUSIONS

In this paper we described how we built a Web-scale probabilistic knowledge base, which we call Knowledge Vault. In contrast to previous work, we fuse together multiple extraction sources with prior knowledge derived from an existing KB. The resulting knowledge base is about 38 times bigger than existing automatically constructed KBs. The facts in KV have associated probabilities, which we show are well-calibrated, so that we can distinguish what we know with high confidence from what we are uncertain about. In the future, we hope to continue to scale KV, to store more knowledge about the world, and to use this resource to help various downstream applications, such as question answering, entity-based search, etc.

Acknowledgments

We thank John Giannandrea, Fernando Pereira, and Amar Subramanya for constructive suggestions that helped us improve this paper, and Kevin Lerman, Abhijit Mahabal, and Oksana Yakhnenko for developing most of the extraction pipeline. We also thank Eric Altendorf and Alex Smola, who were instrumental in the early phases of the project.

10. REFERENCES

[1] AKBC-WEKEX. The Knowledge Extraction Workshop at NAACL-HLT, 2012.

[2] G. Angeli and C. Manning. Philosophers are mortal: Inferring the truth of unseen facts. In *CoNLL*, 2013.

[3] S. Auer, C. Bizer, G. Kobilarov, J. Lehmann, R. Cyganiak, and Z. Ives. DBpedia: A nucleus for a web of open data. In *The semantic web*, pages 722–735, 2007.

[4] K. Bollacker, C. Evans, P. Paritosh, T. Sturge, and J. Taylor. Freebase: a collaboratively created graph database for structuring human knowledge. In *SIGMOD*, pages 1247–1250. ACM, 2008.

[5] A. Bordes, X. Glorot, J. Weston, and Y. Bengio. Joint learning of words and meaning representations for open-text semantic parsing. In *AI/Statistics*, 2012.

[6] M. Cafarella, A. Halevy, Z. D. Wang, E. Wu, and Y. Zhang. WebTables: Exploring the Power of Tables on the Web. *VLDB*, 1(1):538–549, 2008.

[7] M. J. Cafarella, A. Y. Halevy, and J. Madhavan. Structured data on the web. *Commun. ACM*, 54(2):72–79, 2011.

[8] A. Carlson, J. Betteridge, B. Kisiel, B. Settles, E. H. Jr., and T. Mitchell. Toward an architecture for never-ending language learning. In *AAAI*, 2010.

[9] O. Deshpande, D. Lambda, M. Tourn, S. Das, S. Subramaniam, A. Rajaraman, V. Harinarayan, and A. Doan. Building, maintaing and using knowledge bases: A report from the trenches. In *SIGMOD*, 2013.

[10] X. L. Dong, L. Berti-Equille, and D. Srivastatva. Integrating conflicting data: the role of source dependence. In *VLDB*, 2009.

[11] L. Drumond, S. Rendle, and L. Schmidt-Thieme. Predicting RDF Triples in Incomplete Knowledge Bases with Tensor Factorization. In *10th ACM Intl. Symp. on Applied Computing*, 2012.

[12] A. Fader, S. Soderland, and O. Etzioni. Identifying relations for open information extraction. In *EMNLP*, 2011.

[13] J. Fan, D. Ferrucci, D. Gondek, and A. Kalyanpur. Prismatic: Inducing knowledge from a large scale

lexicalized relation resource. In *First Intl. Workshop on Formalisms and Methodology for Learning by Reading*, pages 122–127. Association for Computational Linguistics, 2010.

[14] T. Franz, A. Schultz, S. Sizov, and S. Staab. TripleRank: Ranking Semantic Web Data by Tensor Decomposition. In *ISWC*, 2009.

[15] L. A. Galárraga, C. Teflioudi, K. Hose, and F. Suchanek. Amie: association rule mining under incomplete evidence in ontological knowledge bases. In *WWW*, pages 413–422, 2013.

[16] R. Grishman. Information extraction: Capabilities and challenges. Technical report, NYU Dept. CS, 2012.

[17] R. Gupta, A. Halevy, X. Wang, S. Whang, and F. Wu. Biperpedia: An Ontology for Search Applications. In *VLDB*, 2014.

[18] B. Hachey, W. Radford, J. Nothman, M. Honnibal, and J. Curran. Evaluating entity linking with wikipedia. *Artificial Intelligence*, 194:130–150, 2013.

[19] J. Hoffart, F. M. Suchanek, K. Berberich, and G. Weikum. YAGO2: A Spatially and Temporally Enhanced Knowledge Base from Wikipedia. *Artificial Intelligence Journal*, 2012.

[20] R. Jenatton, N. L. Roux, A. Bordes, and G. Obozinski. A latent factor model for highly multi-relational data. In *NIPS*, 2012.

[21] H. Ji, T. Cassidy, Q. Li, and S. Tamang. Tackling Representation, Annotation and Classification Challenges for Temporal Knowledge Base Population. *Knowledge and Information Systems*, pages 1–36, August 2013.

[22] H. Ji and R. Grishman. Knowledge base population: successful approaches and challenges. In *Proc. ACL*, 2011.

[23] S. Jiang, D. Lowd, and D. Dou. Learning to refine an automatically extracted knowledge base using markov logic. In *Intl. Conf. on Data Mining*, 2012.

[24] N. Lao, T. Mitchell, and W. Cohen. Random walk inference and learning in a large scale knowledge base. In *EMNLP*, 2011.

[25] X. Li and R. Grishman. Confidence estimation for knowledge base population. In *Recent Advances in NLP*, 2013.

[26] Mausam, M. Schmitz, R. Bart, S. Soderland, and O. Etzioni. Open language learning for information extraction. In *EMNLP*, 2012.

[27] T. Mikolov, K. Chen, G. Corrado, and J. Dean. Efficient estimation of word representations in vector space. In *ICLR*, 2013.

[28] B. Min, R. Grishman, L. Wan, C. Wang, and D. Gondek. Distant supervision for relation extraction with an incomplete knowledge base. In *NAACL*, 2013.

[29] M. Mintz, S. Bills, R. Snow, and D. Jurafksy. Distant supervision for relation extraction without labeled data. In *Prof. Conf. Recent Advances in NLP*, 2009.

[30] N. Nakashole, M. Theobald, and G. Weikum. Scalable knowledge harvesting with high precision and high recall. In *WSDM*, pages 227–236, 2011.

[31] M. Nickel, V. Tresp, and H.-P. Kriegel. Factorizing YAGO: scalable machine learning for linked data. In *WWW*, 2012.

[32] F. Niu, C. Zhang, and C. Re. Elementary: Large-scale Knowledge-base Construction via Machine Learning and Statistical Inference. *Intl. J. On Semantic Web and Information Systems*, 2012.

[33] J. Platt. Probabilities for SV machines. In A. Smola, P. Bartlett, B. Schoelkopf, and D. Schuurmans, editors, *Advances in Large Margin Classifiers*. MIT Press, 2000.

[34] J. Pujara, H. Miao, L. Getoor, and W. Cohen. Knowledge graph identification. In *International Semantic Web Conference (ISWC)*, 2013.

[35] L. Reyzin and R. Schapire. How boosting the margin can also boost classifier complexity. In *Intl. Conf. on Machine Learning*, 2006.

[36] A. Ritter, L. Zettlemoyer, Mausam, and O. Etzioni. Modeling missing data in distant supervision for information extraction. *Trans. Assoc. Comp. Linguistics*, 1, 2013.

[37] R. Socher, D. Chen, C. Manning, and A. Ng. Reasoning with Neural Tensor Networks for Knowledge Base Completion. In *NIPS*, 2013.

[38] R. Speer and C. Havasi. Representing general relational knowledge in conceptnet 5. In *Proc. of LREC Conference*, 2012.

[39] F. Suchanek, G. Kasneci, and G. Weikum. YAGO - A Core of Semantic Knowledge. In *WWW*, 2007.

[40] D. Suciu, D. Olteanu, C. Re, and C. Koch. *Probabilistic Databases*. Morgan & Claypool, 2011.

[41] B. Suh, G. Convertino, E. H. Chi, and P. Pirolli. The singularity is not near: slowing growth of wikipedia. In *Proceedings of the 5th International Symposium on Wikis and Open Collaboration*, WikiSym '09, pages 8:1–8:10, 2009.

[42] P. Venetis, A. Halevy, J. Madhavan, M. Pasca, W. Shen, F. Wu, G. Miao, and C. Wi. Recovering semantics of tables on the web. In *Proc. of the VLDB Endowment*, 2012.

[43] D. Z. Wang, E. Michelakis, M. Garofalakis, and J. Hellerstein. BayesStore: Managing Large, Uncertain Data Repositories with Probabilistic Graphical Models. In *VLDB*, 2008.

[44] G. Weikum and M. Theobald. From information to knowledge: harvesting entities and relationships from web sources. In *Proceedings of the twenty-ninth ACM SIGMOD-SIGACT-SIGART symposium on Principles of database systems*, pages 65–76. ACM, 2010.

[45] M. Wick, S. Singh, A. Kobren, and A. McCallum. Assessing confidence of knowledge base content with an experimental study in entity resolution. In *AKBC workshop*, 2013.

[46] M. Wick, S. Singh, H. Pandya, and A. McCallum. A Joint Model for Discovering and Linking Entities. In *AKBC Workshop*, 2013.

[47] W. Wu, H. Li, H. Wang, and K. Q. Zhu. Probase: A probabilistic taxonomy for text understanding. In *SIGMOD*, pages 481–492. ACM, 2012.

[48] Z. Xu, V. Tresp, K. Yu, and H.-P. Kriegel. Infinite hidden relational models. In *UAI*, 2006.

Improving the Modified Nyström Method Using Spectral Shifting

Shusen Wang
College of Computer Science and Technology
Zhejiang University
wss@zju.edu.cn

Chao Zhang
College of Computer Science and Technology
Zhejiang University
zczju@zju.edu.cn

Hui Qian
College of Computer Science and Technology
Zhejiang University
qianhui@zju.edu.cn

Zhihua Zhang
*Department of Computer Science and Engineering
Shanghai Jiao Tong University
zhihua@sjtu.edu.cn

ABSTRACT

The Nyström method is an efficient approach to enabling large-scale kernel methods. The Nyström method generates a fast approximation to any large-scale symmetric positive semidefinete (SPSD) matrix using only a few columns of the SPSD matrix. However, since the Nyström approximation is low-rank, when the spectrum of the SPSD matrix decays slowly, the Nyström approximation is of low accuracy. In this paper, we propose a variant of the Nyström method called the modified Nyström by spectral shifting (SS-Nyström). The SS-Nyström method works well no matter whether the spectrum of SPSD matrix decays fast or slow. We prove that our SS-Nyström has a much stronger error bound than the standard and modified Nyström methods, and that SS-Nyström can be even more accurate than the truncated SVD of the same scale in some cases. We also devise an algorithm such that the SS-Nyström approximation can be computed nearly as efficient as the modified Nyström approximation. Finally, our SS-Nyström method demonstrates significant improvements over the standard and modified Nyström methods on several real-world datasets.

Categories and Subject Descriptors

G.1.0 [**Numerical Analysis**]: General—*Numerical algorithms*; G.1.3 [**Numerical Analysis**]: Numerical Linear Algebra—*Sparse, structured, and very large systems*

Keywords

Kernel approximation; the Nyström method; large-scale machine learning

*Corresponding Author

KDD'14, August 24–27, 2014, New York, NY, USA.

http://dx.doi.org/10.1145/2623330.2623614 .

1. INTRODUCTION

With the advent of the big-data era, how to efficiently learn from big-data has become a major concern and a hot topic of machine learning research. When data are large, many expensive matrix operations, e.g., matrix inverse and eigenvalue decomposition, which cost $\mathcal{O}(m^3)$ time and $\mathcal{O}(m^2)$ space for an $m \times m$ matrix, become computational prohibitive. Such expensive matrix operations are indispensable for many classical machine learning methods like kernel methods [22, 23], so these machine learning methods are infeasible when facing big-data problems. One possible approach to making matrix computation and kernel methods scalable is to use randomized matrix approximations to reduce the time and space costs [18], among which the most famous one is perhaps the Nyström method [5, 10, 14, 15, 20, 26, 30, 31].

The Nyström method approximates an arbitrary symmetric positive semidefinite (SPSD) kernel matrix using a small subset of its columns, and the method reduces the time complexity of many matrix operations from $\mathcal{O}(m^3)$ or $\mathcal{O}(m^2k)$ to $\mathcal{O}(mc^2)$ and space complexity from $\mathcal{O}(m^2)$ to $\mathcal{O}(mc)$, where k is the target rank, c is the number of selected columns, and it holds in general that $k < c \ll m$. In this way, time and space costs are only linearly in m, so many kernel methods can be efficiently solved even when m is large.

Williams & Seeger [30] used the Nyström method to speedup matrix inverse such that the inference of large-scale Gaussian process regression can be efficiently performed. Later on, the Nyström method has been applied to spectral clustering [7, 17], kernel SVMs [33], kernel PCA and manifold learning [26, 32, 33], kernel ridge regression [3], determinantal point processes [1], etc.

However, although the Nyström method is usually effective and efficient, its approximation quality can be very low in some cases. Wang & Zhang [28] showed that the relative-error (with respect to the best rank-k approximation) of the Nyström approximation grows with the matrix size m at least linearly. Thus the approximation can be rather rough when m is large, unless a large number of columns are selected to construct the Nyström approximation, which will violate the intention of using matrix approximations. To improve the approximation quality without sampling a large amount of columns, some other fast matrix approximation models have been proposed. Particularly, Wang & Zhang [28] developed the *modified Nyström method* to generate a low-rank approximation in a similar way to the standard Nyström method. The modified

Nyström method is much more accurate than the standard Nyström method in that it only samples an acceptable amount of columns and its relative error does not grow with matrix size m. In addition, the modified Nyström method only requires the original matrix to be symmetric, which is milder than SPSD required by the standard Nyström method.

The standard/modified Nyström methods generate low-rank approximations to kernel matrices, and their approximation errors cannot be better than the rank c truncated SVD, where c is the number of columns selected by the Nyström methods. When the spectrum of a kernel matrix decays slowly (that is, the $c+1$ to m largest eigenvalues are not small enough), the low-rank approximations constructed by either the truncated SVD or the standard/modified Nyström methods are far from the original kernel matrix. Cortes *et al.* [3] showed that the accuracy of kernel approximations affects the accuracy of learning algorithms. Therefore, when the spectrum of the kernel matrix decays slowly, the standard/modified Nyström methods cannot generate effective approximations to be used in learning algorithms.

To make the approximation still effective even when the spectrum of the original kernel matrix decays slowly, we propose in this paper a new method called *the modified Nyström by spectral shifting (SS-Nyström)*. Unlike the standard/modified Nyström methods which approximate the kernel matrix $\mathbf{K} \in \mathbb{R}^{m\times m}$ by a low-rank factorization $\mathbf{K} \approx \mathbf{C}\mathbf{U}\mathbf{C}^T$, our SS-Nyström approximates $\mathbf{K}$ by $\mathbf{K} \approx \bar{\mathbf{C}}\bar{\mathbf{U}}\bar{\mathbf{C}}^T + \delta\mathbf{I}_m$, where $\mathbf{C}, \bar{\mathbf{C}} \in \mathbb{R}^{m\times c}$, $\mathbf{U}, \bar{\mathbf{U}} \in \mathbb{R}^{c\times c}$, and $\delta \geq 0$. When the spectrum of $\mathbf{K}$ decays slowly, the term $\delta\mathbf{I}_m$ significantly improves the approximation accuracy. We show that SS-Nyström method has a provably tighter bound than the standard/modified Nyström methods. In sum, this paper offers the following contributions:

- We propose a kernel approximation method called the modified Nyström by Spectral Shifting (SS-Nyström), which is provably superior over the standard/modified Nyström methods (see Theorem 3). SS-Nyström can be even tighter than the truncated SVD in some conditions (See Example 1).
- We devise an efficient algorithm such that the SS-Nyström approximation can be computed nearly as efficient as the modified Nyström approximation. The proposed algorithm is also pass-efficient in that it goes only four passes through the kernel matrix, thus SS-Nyström is still efficient even when data do not fit in RAM.

The kernel approximation models proposed in the very recent work [15, 24] are also variants of the Nyström method and reported to achieve higher approximation accuracy. It is also straightforward to improve the ensemble Nyström method [15] and the memory efficient kernel approximation method [24] using the spectral shifting method proposed in this paper.

The remainder of this paper is organized as follows. In Section 2 we define the notation that will be used in this paper. In Section 3 we formally introduce the standard Nyström method and the modified Nyström method. In Section 4 we formulate our SS-Nyström method and show that our SS-Nyström can speedup several kernel methods in the same way as the standard Nyström method does. In Section 5 we theoretically show the superiority of SS-Nyström over the standard/modified Nyström methods. In Section 6 we devise an efficient algorithm for computing SS-Nyström. In Section 7 we empirically evaluate the SS-Nyström method and the proposed efficient algorithm. The proof of the theorems are deferred to the appendix.

2. NOTATION

For a matrix $\mathbf{A} = [a_{ij}]$, we let $\mathbf{a}_j$ be its j-th column, and $\|\mathbf{A}\|_F = (\sum_{i,j} a_{ij}^2)^{1/2}$ be its Frobenius norm. For a squared matrix, the matrix trace $\mathrm{tr}(\cdot)$ is the sum of the diagonal entries. We also let $\mathbf{I}_m$ be the $m \times m$ identity matrix and let $\mathbf{1}_m$ be the size-m all-one vector.

Letting $\rho = \mathrm{rank}(\mathbf{A})$, we write the condensed singular value decomposition (SVD) of $\mathbf{A}$ as $\mathbf{A} = \mathbf{U}_\mathbf{A}\mathbf{\Sigma}_\mathbf{A}\mathbf{V}_\mathbf{A}^T$, where the (i,i)-th entry of $\mathbf{\Sigma}_\mathbf{A} \in \mathbb{R}^{\rho\times\rho}$ is the i-th largest singular value of $\mathbf{A}$, denoted $\sigma_i(\mathbf{A})$. We also let $\mathbf{U}_{\mathbf{A},k}$ and $\mathbf{V}_{\mathbf{A},k}$ be the first k ($< \rho$) columns of $\mathbf{U}_\mathbf{A}$ and $\mathbf{V}_\mathbf{A}$, respectively, and $\mathbf{\Sigma}_{\mathbf{A},k}$ be the $k \times k$ top left block of $\mathbf{\Sigma}_\mathbf{A}$. Then the matrix $\mathbf{A}_k = \mathbf{U}_{\mathbf{A},k}\mathbf{\Sigma}_{\mathbf{A},k}\mathbf{V}_{\mathbf{A},k}^T$ is the "closest" rank-k approximation to $\mathbf{A}$. If $\mathbf{A}$ is a squared matrix, we let $\lambda_i(\mathbf{A})$ be the i-th largest eigenvalue. If $\mathbf{A}$ is SPSD, then the eigenvalue decomposition and SVD are equivalent.

For an $m\times n$ matrix, the full SVD costs time $\mathcal{O}(\min\{m^2n, mn^2\})$, and the rank k truncated SVD costs time $\mathcal{O}(mnk)$. Although multiplying an $m\times n$ matrix by an $n\times p$ matrix runs in $\mathcal{O}(mnp)$ flops, the constant in the big-$\mathcal{O}$ notation is tremendously smaller than that of SVD, and matrix multiplication can be highly efficiently performed in parallel computing facilities. So we instead denote the time complexity of matrix multiplication by $T_{\text{multiply}}(mnp)$, which is far less than $\mathcal{O}(mnp)$ in practice [12, 28].

3. RELATED WORK

Given an $m \times m$ SPSD matrix $\mathbf{K}$, we let $\mathcal{J}$ ($\mathcal{J} \subset [m] \triangleq \{1, 2, \ldots, m\}$ and $|\mathcal{J}| = c$) be an index set computed by some column selection algorithm. Then we let $\mathbf{C} \in \mathbb{R}^{m\times c}$ be the columns of $\mathbf{K}$ indexed by $\mathcal{J}$, and let $\mathbf{W} \in \mathbb{R}^{c\times c}$ be the rows of $\mathbf{C}$ indexed by $\mathcal{J}$. The *standard Nyström method* [30] approximates $\mathbf{K}$ by

$$\tilde{\mathbf{K}}_c^{\text{nys}} = \mathbf{C}\mathbf{U}^{\text{nys}}\mathbf{C}^T = \mathbf{C}\mathbf{W}^\dagger\mathbf{C}^T,$$

where $\mathbf{W}^\dagger$ is the Moore-Penrose inverse of $\mathbf{W}$. The *modified Nyström method* [28, 29] is defined by

$$\tilde{\mathbf{K}}_c^{\text{mod}} = \mathbf{C}\mathbf{U}^{\text{mod}}\mathbf{C}^T = \mathbf{C}(\mathbf{C}^\dagger\mathbf{K}(\mathbf{C}^\dagger)^T)\mathbf{C}^T.$$

The only difference between the standard and the modified Nyström methods is their intersection matrices: $\mathbf{U}^{\text{nys}} = \mathbf{W}^\dagger$ for the standard Nyström method and $\mathbf{U}^{\text{mod}} = \mathbf{C}^\dagger\mathbf{K}(\mathbf{C}^\dagger)^T$ for the modified Nyström method.

When $\mathrm{rank}(\mathbf{K}) = \mathrm{rank}(\mathbf{U}^{\text{nys}}) = \mathrm{rank}(\mathbf{U}^{\text{mod}})$, that is, when $\mathbf{K}$ is low-rank, both of the standard/modified Nyström approximations are exact [29]. The modified Nyström method is in general more accurate than the standard Nyström method due to $\|\mathbf{K} - \tilde{\mathbf{K}}_c^{\text{mod}}\|_F \leq \|\mathbf{K} - \tilde{\mathbf{K}}_c^{\text{nys}}\|_F$. With the selected columns at hand, it costs time $\mathcal{O}(c^3)$ to compute the standard Nyström approximation and $\mathcal{O}(mc^2) + T_{\text{multiply}}(m^2c)$ to compute the modified Nyström approximation.

The quality of the Nyström approximations is largely determined by whether the selected columns are informative, so a better column selection algorithm makes the Nyström approximations more accurate. In the previous work much attention has been paid to the relative-error column selection algorithms [2, 4, 6, 10, 11], among which the uniform sampling [10] and adaptive sampling [4] are the most widely used ones. The following lemma is the strongest theoretical result for the Nyström methods [28].

LEMMA 1. *Given an $m \times m$ symmetric matrix $\mathbf{K}$ and a target rank k, by selecting $c = \mathcal{O}(k\epsilon^{-2})$ columns of $\mathbf{K}$ to form $\mathbf{C} \in \mathbb{R}^{m\times c}$ using the adaptive sampling based algorithm of [28], the following inequality holds:*

$$\mathbb{E}\big\|\mathbf{K} - \tilde{\mathbf{K}}_c^{mod}\big\|_F \leq (1+\epsilon)\big\|\mathbf{K} - \mathbf{K}_k\big\|_F,$$

where $\mathbf{K}_k$ denotes the top k truncated SVD approximation of K. The algorithm takes time $\mathcal{O}(mc^2 + mk^3\epsilon^{-2/3}) + T_{multiply}(m^2c)$ and space $\mathcal{O}(mc)$ in computing $\mathbf{C}$ and $\mathbf{U}$ of the modified Nyström approximation.

Lemma 1 indicates that by selecting $c = \mathcal{O}(k\epsilon^{-2})$ columns of $\mathbf{K}$, the modified Nyström approximation achieves comparable accuracy as the rank k truncated SVD. When the spectrum of $\mathbf{K}$ decays fast, the approximation generated by the truncated SVD is highly accurate, and so is the modified Nyström approximation. Otherwise, if the bottom $m - k$ singular values (i.e. eigenvalues) of $\mathbf{K}$ are large, then $\|\mathbf{K} - \mathbf{K}_k\|_F$ is large, and so is $\|\mathbf{K} - \tilde{\mathbf{K}}_c^{\mathrm{mod}}\|_F$.

This work is closely related to the matrix ridge approximation (MRA) [34], which improves approximation accuracy by preserving the eigenvalues both large and small. When the bottom eigenvalues of $\mathbf{K}$ are large, MRA is much more accurate than the truncated SVD and the Nyström method [27, 34]. However, MRA is solved by iterative algorithms and is thus not pass-efficient and memory-efficient, it is thus limited to medium-scale data problems. Inspired by MRA, we propose a kernel approximation model which inherits the efficiency of the Nyström method and is effective when the bottom eigenvalues are large.

4. THE SS-NYSTRÖM APPROXIMATION

In the first subsection we formulate and justify our SS-Nyström method. In the second subsection we discuss how to apply SS-Nyström to speedup Gaussian process regression, kernel SVM, and kernel ridge regression problems.

4.1 Problem Formulation

Given a target rank k ($\leq c \ll m$), the SS-Nyström approximation of $\mathbf{K}$ is defined as

$$\tilde{\mathbf{K}}_c^{\mathrm{ss}} \;=\; \bar{\mathbf{C}}\bar{\mathbf{U}}\bar{\mathbf{C}}^T + \delta\mathbf{I}_m. \tag{1}$$

Here $\delta \geq 0$ is called the spectral shifting term and $\bar{\mathbf{C}}\bar{\mathbf{U}}\bar{\mathbf{C}}^T$ is the rank c modified Nyström approximation of $\bar{\mathbf{K}} = \mathbf{K} - \delta\mathbf{I}_m$. Notice that since $\bar{\mathbf{K}}$ is symmetric but possibly not SPSD, the $c \times c$ intersection matrix $\bar{\mathbf{U}}$ is also in general indefinite. Later we will see that the term $\delta\mathbf{I}_m$ has a direct effect on the spectrum of $\mathbf{K}$, that is why we call our method the modified Nyström by *spectrum shifting*.

Now we consider how to choose δ. It follows from the definition directly that the approximation error is $\mathbf{K} - \tilde{\mathbf{K}}_c^{\mathrm{ss}} = \bar{\mathbf{K}} - \bar{\mathbf{C}}\bar{\mathbf{U}}\bar{\mathbf{C}}^T$; Lemma 1 indicates that by selecting sufficiently many columns of $\bar{\mathbf{K}}$ to construct $\bar{\mathbf{C}}$ and $\bar{\mathbf{U}}$, it holds in expectation that

$$\mathbb{E}\big\|\mathbf{K} - \tilde{\mathbf{K}}_c^{\mathrm{ss}}\big\| \;=\; \mathbb{E}\big\|\bar{\mathbf{K}} - \bar{\mathbf{C}}\bar{\mathbf{U}}\bar{\mathbf{C}}^T\big\| \;\leq\; (1+\epsilon)\big\|\bar{\mathbf{K}} - \bar{\mathbf{K}}_k\big\|_F.$$

Apparently, for fixed k, the smaller the error $\|\bar{\mathbf{K}} - \bar{\mathbf{K}}_k\|_F$ is, the tighter error bound the SS-Nyström has; if $\|\bar{\mathbf{K}} - \bar{\mathbf{K}}_k\|_F \leq \|\mathbf{K} - \mathbf{K}_k\|_F$, then SS-Nyström has a better error bound than the modified Nyström. Therefore, to make the error bound as strong as possible, we formulate the following optimization problem to compute δ:

$$\min_{\delta \geq 0} \;\big\|\bar{\mathbf{K}} - \bar{\mathbf{K}}_k\big\|_F^2; \qquad \text{s.t. } \bar{\mathbf{K}} = \mathbf{K} - \delta\mathbf{I}_m.$$

However, since $\bar{\mathbf{K}}$ is in general indefinite, it needs all of the eigenvalues of $\mathbf{K}$ to solve the problem exactly. Since computing the full eigenvalue decomposition is expensive, we attempt to relax the problem. Considering that

$$\begin{aligned} \big\|\bar{\mathbf{K}} - \bar{\mathbf{K}}_k\big\|_F^2 \;&=\; \min_{|\mathcal{J}|=m-k} \sum_{j\in\mathcal{J}} \big(\sigma_j(\mathbf{K}) - \delta\big)^2 \\ &\leq\; \sum_{j=k+1}^{m} \big(\sigma_j(\mathbf{K}) - \delta\big)^2, \end{aligned} \tag{2}$$

we seek to minimize the upper bound of $\|\bar{\mathbf{K}} - \bar{\mathbf{K}}_k\|_F^2$ to compute δ, leading to the solution

$$\delta^{\mathrm{opt}} = \frac{1}{m-k}\sum_{j=k+1}^{m}\sigma_j(\mathbf{K}) = \frac{1}{m-k}\Big(\mathrm{tr}(\mathbf{K}) - \sum_{j=1}^{k}\sigma_j(\mathbf{K})\Big). \tag{3}$$

If we choose $\delta = 0$, then SS-Nyström degenerates to the modified Nyström method. The following theorem indicates that the SS-Nyström with any $\delta \in (0, \delta^{\mathrm{opt}}]$ has a stronger relative-error bound than the modified Nyström method.

THEOREM 2. *Give an $m \times m$ SPSD matrix $\mathbf{K}$, we let $\bar{\mathbf{K}} = \mathbf{K} - \delta\mathbf{I}_m$ and δ^{opt} be defined in (3). Then for any $\delta \in (0, \delta^{opt}]$, the following inequality holds:*

$$\big\|\bar{\mathbf{K}} - \bar{\mathbf{K}}_k\big\|_F^2 \;\leq\; \big\|\mathbf{K} - \mathbf{K}_k\big\|_F^2.$$

We give an example in Figure 1 to illustrate why SS-Nyström is useful. From the plot of the eigenvalues we can see that the "tail" of the eigenvalues becomes thinner after the spectral shifting. Specifically, $\|\mathbf{K} - \mathbf{K}_k\|_F^2 = 0.52$ and $\|\bar{\mathbf{K}} - \bar{\mathbf{K}}_k\|_F^2 \leq 0.24$. When the same number of columns are selected to construct the SS-Nyström or the modified Nyström approximations, SS-Nyström has much tighter error bound because $\|\bar{\mathbf{K}} - \bar{\mathbf{K}}_k\|_F^2$ is much smaller than $\|\mathbf{K} - \mathbf{K}_k\|_F^2$.

4.2 Applications to Kernel Methods

We discuss in this section how to speed up matrix inverse and eigenvalue decomposition using the Nyström methods.Many kernel methods will become scalable if the matrix inverse and eigenvalue decomposition can be efficiently solved.

- Gaussian process regression [30], least squares SVM [25], and kernel ridge regression [21] all require computing this kind of linear system:

  $$(\mathbf{K} + \alpha\mathbf{I}_m)\mathbf{b} = \mathbf{y}, \tag{4}$$

  which amounts to the matrix inverse problem $\mathbf{b} = (\mathbf{K} + \alpha\mathbf{I}_m)^{-1}\mathbf{y}$. Here α is a constant.

- Spectral clustering [7, 17], kernel PCA [32], and many manifold learning [33, 26] need to perform the truncated eigenvalue decomposition; the sampling algorithm of determinantal point processes [13, 1] performs the full eigenvalue decomposition.

Let $\mathbf{K} \in \mathbb{R}^{m\times m}$ be the kernel matrix, and let the SS-Nyström approximation of $\mathbf{K}$ be defined by

$$\tilde{\mathbf{K}}_c^{\mathrm{ss}} \;=\; \bar{\mathbf{C}}\bar{\mathbf{U}}\bar{\mathbf{C}}^T + \delta\mathbf{I}_m.$$

We show that when $\mathbf{K}$ is replaced by $\tilde{\mathbf{K}}_c^{\mathrm{ss}}$, the aforementioned linear system and eigenvalue decomposition can be efficiently solved. When using $\tilde{\mathbf{K}}_c^{\mathrm{nys}}$ or $\tilde{\mathbf{K}}_c^{\mathrm{mod}}$ to replace $\mathbf{K}$, one can still use the results by setting $\delta = 0$.

We first show how to approximately compute $\mathbf{b} = (\mathbf{K} + \alpha\mathbf{I}_m)^{-1}\mathbf{y}$. Let $\bar{\mathbf{U}} = \mathbf{Z}\mathbf{\Lambda}\mathbf{Z}^T$ be the condensed eigenvalue decomposition of the intersection matrix of SS-Nyström, where $\mathbf{Z} \in \mathbb{R}^{c\times\rho}$, $\mathbf{\Lambda} \in \mathbb{R}^{\rho\times\rho}$, and $\rho = \mathrm{rank}(\bar{\mathbf{U}}) \leq c$. We expand

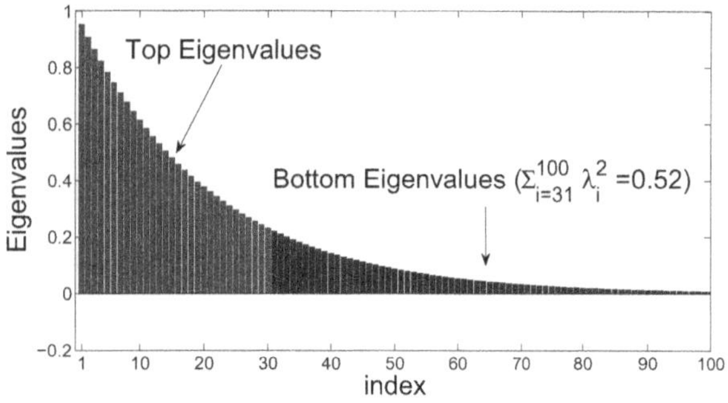

(a) Before spectral shifting.

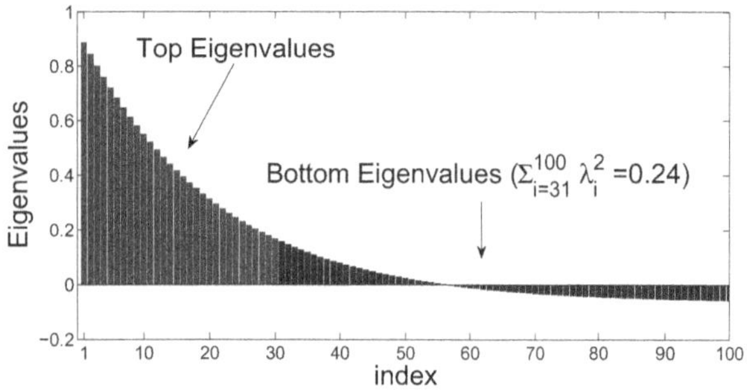

(b) After spectral shifting.

Figure 1: Toy data: 100×100 SPSD matrix whose the t-th eigenvalue is 1.05^{-t}. We set $m = 100$, $k = 30$, and thus $\delta^{\text{opt}} = 0.064$. We plot the eigenvalues of K in Figure 1(a) and $\bar{\mathbf{K}} = \mathbf{K} - \delta^{\text{opt}} \mathbf{I}_{100}$ in Figure 1(b).

$(\tilde{\mathbf{K}}_c^{\text{ss}} + \alpha \mathbf{I}_m)^{-1}$ by the Sherman-Morrison-Woodbury formula and obtain

$$
\begin{aligned}
(\tilde{\mathbf{K}}_c^{\text{ss}} + \alpha \mathbf{I}_m)^{-1} &= (\bar{\mathbf{C}} \mathbf{Z} \mathbf{\Lambda} \mathbf{Z}^T \bar{\mathbf{C}}^T + \tau \mathbf{I}_m)^{-1} \\
&= \tau^{-1} \mathbf{I}_m - \tau^{-1} \bar{\mathbf{C}} \mathbf{Z} (\tau \mathbf{\Lambda}^{-1} + \mathbf{Z}^T \bar{\mathbf{C}}^T \bar{\mathbf{C}} \mathbf{Z})^{-1} \mathbf{Z}^T \bar{\mathbf{C}}^T,
\end{aligned}
$$

where $\tau = \delta + \alpha$. In this way the linear system (4) can be computed in only $\mathcal{O}(mc^2)$ time and $\mathcal{O}(mc)$ space.

Now we show how to approximately compute the eigenvalue decomposition of $\mathbf{K}$. We let $\bar{\mathbf{C}} = \mathbf{U}_{\bar{\mathbf{C}}} \mathbf{\Sigma}_{\bar{\mathbf{C}}} \mathbf{V}_{\bar{\mathbf{C}}}$ be the condensed SVD of $\bar{\mathbf{C}}$. Suppose $\rho = \text{rank}(\bar{\mathbf{C}})$, we let

$$
\mathbf{S} \;=\; \mathbf{\Sigma}_{\bar{\mathbf{C}}} \mathbf{V}_{\bar{\mathbf{C}}} \bar{\mathbf{U}} \mathbf{V}_{\bar{\mathbf{C}}}^T \mathbf{\Sigma}_{\bar{\mathbf{C}}}^T \;\in\; \mathbb{R}^{\rho \times \rho},
$$

and we write the eigenvalue decomposition of $\mathbf{S}$ as $\mathbf{S} = \mathbf{U}_\mathbf{S} \mathbf{\Lambda}_\mathbf{S} \mathbf{U}_\mathbf{S}^T$. Now we can write the eigenvalue decomposition of $\tilde{\mathbf{K}}_c^{\text{ss}}$ as

$$
\begin{aligned}
\tilde{\mathbf{K}}_c^{\text{ss}} &= (\mathbf{U}_\mathbf{C} \mathbf{U}_\mathbf{S}) \mathbf{\Lambda}_\mathbf{S} (\mathbf{U}_\mathbf{C} \mathbf{U}_\mathbf{S})^T + \delta \mathbf{I}_m \\
&= (\mathbf{U}_\mathbf{C} \mathbf{U}_\mathbf{S})(\mathbf{\Lambda}_\mathbf{S} + \delta \mathbf{I}_\rho)(\mathbf{U}_\mathbf{C} \mathbf{U}_\mathbf{S})^T + \mathbf{U}_\perp (\delta \mathbf{I}_m) \mathbf{U}_\perp^T.
\end{aligned}
$$

Here $\mathbf{U}_\perp \in \mathbb{R}^{m \times (m-\rho)}$ is a column orthogonal matrix orthogonal to $(\mathbf{U}_\mathbf{C} \mathbf{U}_\mathbf{S})$.

5. THEORETICAL ANALYSIS

We provide theoretical analysis for the SS-Nyström method in Theorem 3, which shows that SS-Nyström has a much tighter error bound than the modified Nyström method. We also demonstrate in Example 1 that in some cases the SS-Nyström method can be better than any other low-rank matrix approximation methods.

THEOREM 3. *Suppose there is a column selection algorithm $\mathcal{A}_{col}$ such that for any $m \times m$ symmetric matrix $\mathbf{S}$ and target rank k ($\ll m$), by selecting $c \geq C(m, k, \epsilon)$ columns of $\mathbf{S}$ using algorithm $\mathcal{A}_{col}$, the modified Nyström method attains the error bound*

$$
\big\| \mathbf{S} - \tilde{\mathbf{S}}_c^{mod} \big\|_F^2 \;\leq\; (1+\epsilon) \, \big\| \mathbf{S} - \mathbf{S}_k \big\|_F^2 .
$$

Then for any $m \times m$ SPSD matrix $\mathbf{K}$, we compute δ^{opt} according to (3) and compute $\bar{\mathbf{K}} = \mathbf{K} - \delta^{opt} \mathbf{I}_m$. By using $\mathcal{A}_{col}$ to select $c \geq C(m, k, \epsilon)$ columns of $\bar{\mathbf{K}}$, the SS-Nyström defined in (1) attains the error bound

$$
\big\| \mathbf{K} - \tilde{\mathbf{K}}_c^{ss} \big\|_F^2 \;\leq\; (1+\epsilon) \bigg(\big\| \mathbf{K} - \mathbf{K}_k \big\|_F^2 - \frac{\big[\sum_{i=k+1}^m \lambda_i(\mathbf{K}) \big]^2}{m-k} \bigg).
$$

If the columns of $\bar{\mathbf{K}}$ are selected by the adaptive sampling based algorithm of [28], which satisfies the assumption in Theorem 3 and is the best practical algorithm for the modified Nyström method, then the error bound incurred by SS-Nyström is given in the following corollary.

COROLLARY 4. *Suppose we are given an SPSD matrix $\mathbf{K}$. By sampling $c = \mathcal{O}(k\epsilon^{-2})$ columns of $\bar{\mathbf{K}}$ using the adaptive sampling based algorithm of [28], SS-Nyström attains the following error bound:*

$$
\mathbb{E} \big\| \mathbf{K} - \tilde{\mathbf{K}}_c^{ss} \big\|_F^2 \leq (1+\epsilon) \bigg(\big\| \mathbf{K} - \mathbf{K}_k \big\|_F^2 - \frac{\big[\sum_{i=k+1}^m \lambda_i(\mathbf{K}) \big]^2}{m-k} \bigg).
$$

Recall from Lemma 1 that the best known error bound of the modified Nyström method is

$$
\mathbb{E} \big\| \mathbf{K} - \tilde{\mathbf{K}}_c^{\text{mod}} \big\|_F^2 \;\leq\; (1+\epsilon) \, \big\| \mathbf{K} - \mathbf{K}_k \big\|_F^2 ,
$$

where $c = \mathcal{O}(k\epsilon^{-2})$ columns are selected from $\mathbf{K}$. When the bottom eigenvalues $\lambda_{k+1}(\mathbf{K}), \cdots, \lambda_m(\mathbf{K})$ are large, we can see from Lemma 1 and Corollary 4 that the error bound of SS-Nyström is much better than that of the modified Nyström method. Here we give an example to demonstrate the superiority of SS-Nyström over the the standard/modified Nyström methods and even the truncated SVD of the same scale.

EXAMPLE 1. *Let $\mathbf{K}$ be an $m \times m$ SPSD matrix such that $\lambda_1(\mathbf{K}) \geq \cdots \geq \lambda_k(\mathbf{K}) > \theta = \lambda_{k+1}(\mathbf{K}) = \cdots = \lambda_m(\mathbf{K}) > 0$. By sampling $c = \mathcal{O}(k)$ columns by the adaptive sampling based algorithm of [28], we have that*

$$
\big\| \mathbf{K} - \tilde{\mathbf{K}}_c^{ss} \big\|_F^2 \;=\; 0,
$$

and that

$$
\begin{aligned}
(m-c)\theta^2 \;&=\; \big\| \mathbf{K} - \mathbf{K}_c \big\|_F^2 \\
&\leq\; \big\| \mathbf{K} - \tilde{\mathbf{K}}_c^{mod} \big\|_F^2 \;\leq\; \big\| \mathbf{K} - \tilde{\mathbf{K}}_c^{nys} \big\|_F^2 .
\end{aligned}
$$

In this example SS-Nyström is far better than the other approximation methods if we set θ a large constant.

6. EFFICIENT ALGORITHM

Notice that computing the spectral shifting term δ in (1) according to (3) requires the truncated SVD which costs time $\mathcal{O}(m^2 k)$ and space $\mathcal{O}(m^2)$. This can be accelerated by computing the top-k singular values approximately using random projection techniques [2, 12]. We depict the whole algorithm for computing SS-Nyström using random projections in Algorithm 1. The performance of the approximation is analyzed in the following theorem.

Algorithm 1 The Modified Nyström by Spectral Shifting.

1: **Input:** an $m \times m$ SPSD matrix $\mathbf{K}$, a target rank k, the oversampling parameter l.
2: *// compute δ^{opt} approximately*
3: $\mathbf{\Omega} \longleftarrow m \times l$ standard Gaussian matrix;
4: $\mathbf{Q} \longleftarrow$ the l orthonormal basis of $\mathbf{Y} = \mathbf{K\Omega} \in \mathbb{R}^{m \times l}$;
5: $s \longleftarrow$ sum of the top k singular values of $\mathbf{A} = \mathbf{Q}^T\mathbf{K} \in \mathbb{R}^{l \times m}$;
6: $\tilde{\delta} = \frac{1}{m-k}\big(\mathrm{tr}(\mathbf{K}) - s\big) \approx \delta^{\mathrm{opt}}$;
7: *// spectral shifting*
8: $\bar{\mathbf{K}} \leftarrow \mathbf{K} - \tilde{\delta}\mathbf{I}_m \in \mathbb{R}^{m \times m}$;
9: *// compute the modified Nyström approximation for $\bar{\mathbf{K}}$*
10: $\bar{\mathbf{C}} \longleftarrow c$ columns of $\bar{\mathbf{K}}$ selected by some column sampling algorithm;
11: $\bar{\mathbf{U}} \longleftarrow \bar{\mathbf{C}}^\dagger \bar{\mathbf{K}} (\bar{\mathbf{C}}^\dagger)^T \in \mathbb{R}^{c \times c}$;
12: **return** the SS-Nyström approximation $\tilde{\mathbf{K}}_c^{\mathrm{ss}} = \bar{\mathbf{C}}\bar{\mathbf{U}}\bar{\mathbf{C}}^T + \tilde{\delta}\mathbf{I}_m$.

THEOREM 5. *Let δ^{opt} be defined in (3) and $\tilde{\delta}$, k, l, m be defined in Algorithm 1. The following inequality holds in expectation:*

$$\mathbb{E}\big[|\delta^{opt} - \tilde{\delta}| \,/\, \delta^{opt}\big] \;\leq\; k/\sqrt{l},$$

where the expectation is taken w.r.t. the Gaussian random matrix $\mathbf{\Omega}$ in Algorithm 1. Lines 2–6 in Algorithm 1 compute $\tilde{\delta}$ in time $\mathcal{O}(ml^2) + T_{multiply}(m^2 l)$ and space $\mathcal{O}(ml)$.

By using Algorithm 1 to compute δ^{opt} approximately, it costs only $\mathcal{O}(ml^2) + T_{\mathrm{multiply}}(m^2 l)$ more time to compute the SS-Nyström approximation than the modified Nyström approximation. Our experiments show that a small l (say, $l = 4k$) is sufficient for obtaining a highly accurate approximation to δ^{opt}, no matter whether the spectrum of $\mathbf{K}$ decays fast or slow. Since it costs $\mathcal{O}(mc^2) + T_{\mathrm{multiply}}(m^2 c)$ time to compute the modified Nyström and c can be set as $\mathcal{O}(k\epsilon^{-2})$, if we set $l = 4k$, then the time complexity for computing SS-Nyström is the same as computing the modified Nyström.

7. EXPERIMENTS

We conduct experiments on several real-world datasets to evaluate the method and algorithm proposed in this paper. In Section 7.1 we describe the setup of the experiments. In Section 7.2 we evaluate the fast approximation of δ^{opt} proposed in Section 6. In Section 7.3 we compare SS-Nyström with the standard/modified Nyström methods on several middle-size datasets. In Section 7.4 we compare the methods on a large-scale dataset where the kernel matrix does not fit in RAM.

7.1 The Setup

We perform experiments on several datasets released by UCI [8] and Statlog [19]. We obtain the data collected on the LIBSVM website[1] where the data are scaled to [0,1]. We summarize the datasets in Table 1.

For each dataset, we generate a radial basis function (RBF) kernel $\mathbf{K}^\alpha$ defined by

$$k_{ij}^{\alpha} = \exp\Big(-\frac{1}{2\alpha}\|\mathbf{x}_i - \mathbf{x}_j\|_2^2\Big)$$

and a sparse RBF kernel $\mathbf{K}^{\alpha,\nu,C}$ [9] defined by

$$k_{ij}^{\alpha,\nu,C} = \bigg[\Big(1 - \frac{\|\mathbf{x}_i - \mathbf{x}_j\|_2}{C}\Big)^{\nu}\bigg]_+ \cdot \exp\Big(-\frac{\|\mathbf{x}_i - \mathbf{x}_j\|_2^2}{2\alpha}\Big).$$

[1]http://www.csie.ntu.edu.tw/~cjlin/libsvmtools/datasets/

Here $\mathbf{x}_1, \cdots, \mathbf{x}_m$ are the data instances, $\alpha > 0$ is the scaling parameter, $C > 0$ is the cutting-off point, d is the number of attributes, $\nu > (d+1)/2$, and $[z]_+ \triangleq \max\{z, 0\}$. The larger the scaling parameter α is, the faster the spectrum of the kernel decays. For the sparse RBF kernel, following [10], we fix $\nu = \lceil (d+1)/2 \rceil$ and $C = 3\alpha$.

We implement all the algorithms in MATLAB and run the algorithms on a workstation with Intel Xeon 2.40GHz CPUs, 24GB RAM, and 64bit Windows Server 2008 system. To compare the running time, we set MATLAB in single thread mode by the command "maxNumCompThreads(1)".

7.2 Performance of the Approximation to δ^{opt}

We evaluate the accuracy of the approximation to δ^{opt} (Lines 2–6 in Algorithm 1) proposed in Theorem 5. We generate RBF kernel matrices of the listed datasets, where we set the scaling parameter $\alpha = 0.1$ or $\alpha = 1$. We use the error ratio $|\delta^{\mathrm{opt}} - \tilde{\delta}|/\delta^{\mathrm{opt}}$ to evaluate the approximation performance. We repeat the experiments 20 times and plot the average error ratio versus l/k in Figure 2. Here $\tilde{\delta}$, l, and k are defined in Theorem 5. We can see from Figure 2 that the approximation to δ^{opt} is of very high quality: when $l = 4k$, the error ratios are less than 0.03 in all cases. So we set $l = 4k$ in all of the subsequent kernel approximation experiments in order to obtain a low over-sampling rate with a high accuracy at the same time.

7.3 Performance of Kernel Approximation

We evaluate the kernel approximation accuracy of SS-Nyström mainly in comparison with the standard/modified Nyström methods. In this paper our attention is mainly focused on kernel matrices whose spectrum decay slowly, so we set the scaling parameter α a small value. Otherwise if α is large, the bottom eigenvalues will be very small, and consequently the spectral shifting parameter δ^{opt} will be so small that there is no significant difference between SS-Nyström and the modified Nyström. Specifically, we set $k = 50$ and $\alpha = 0.2$ for the dense RBF kernels and $\alpha = 2$ for the sparse RBF kernels. We use Algorithm 1 to compute the SS-Nyström approximation, in which we set $l = 4k$. For each of the standard/modified/SS Nyström methods, we use two algorithms to select columns: the uniform sampling algorithm [10] and the adaptive sampling algorithm [28].

We report the approximation accuracy and running time of each algorithm for each method. The approximation accuracy is evaluated by

$$\text{Approximation Error} \;=\; \|\mathbf{K} - \tilde{\mathbf{K}}\|_F / \|\mathbf{K}\|_F,$$

where $\tilde{\mathbf{K}}$ is the approximation generated by each method. Every time when we do column sampling, we run each sampling algorithm 10 times and report the minimal approximation error of the 10 repeats since the error bound of each method is actually guaranteed with expectations and we can get a quite accurate approximation within 10 repeats according to [28]. We report the average elapsed time of the 10 repeat rather than the total elapsed time because the 10 repeats can be done in parallel on 10 machines. We depict the approximation errors and the average elapsed time of the dense RBF kernels in Figures 3 and Figure 4 and those of the sparse RBF kernels are in Figure 5 and Figure 6. In the figures, we use $\frac{c}{m}$ as the X-axis because the compared methods have the same RAM cost when c and m are fixed.

The results clearly show that our SS-Nyström works significantly better than the standard/modified Nyström methods when the spectrum of the kernel matrix decays slowly. As for the running

Table 1: A summary of the datasets for the Nyström approximation.

Dataset	MNIST	Letters	Wine Quality	Satimage	Segment	DNA	German	Splice	Breast Cancer
#Instance	60,000	15,000	4,898	4,435	2,310	2,000	1,000	1,000	683
#Attribute	780	16	12	36	19	180	24	60	10

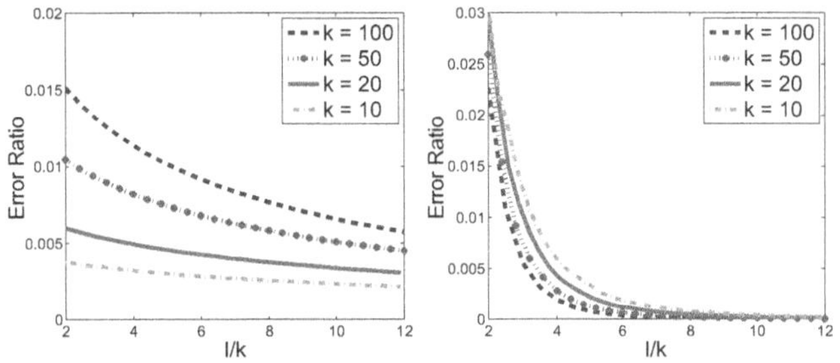

(a) Letters.

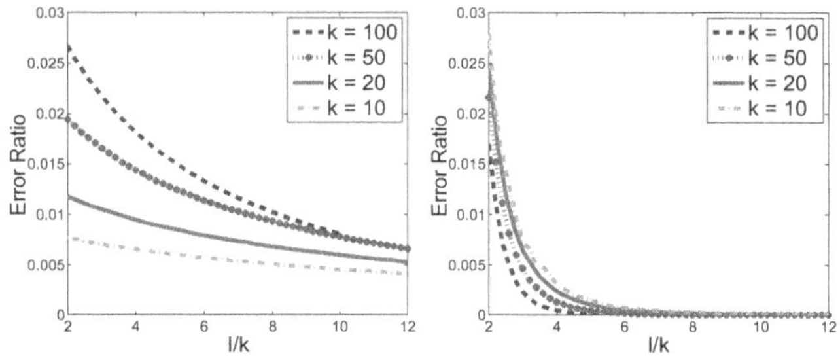

(b) Wine Quality.

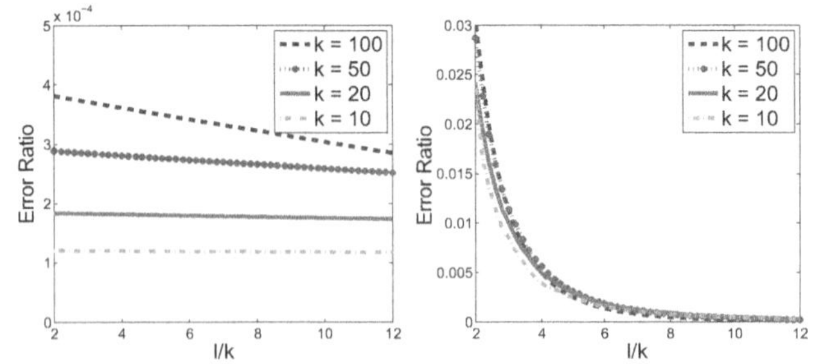

(c) Satimage.

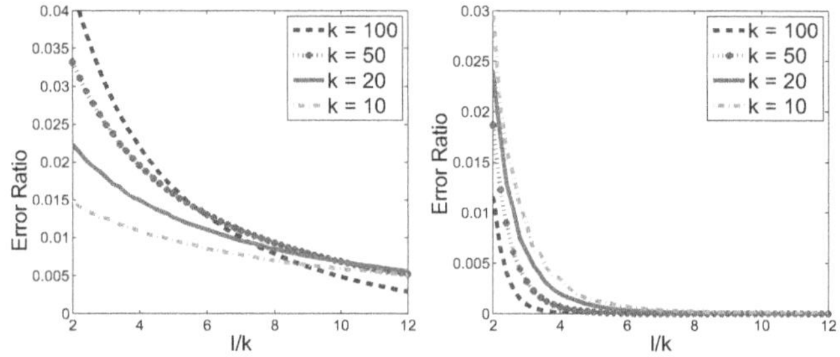

(d) Segment.

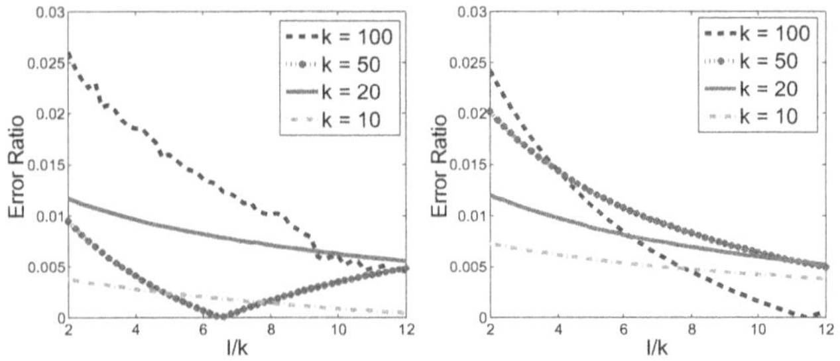

(e) DNA.

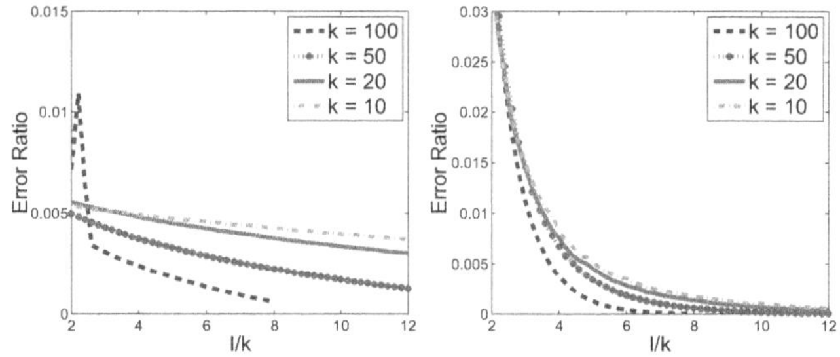

(f) German.

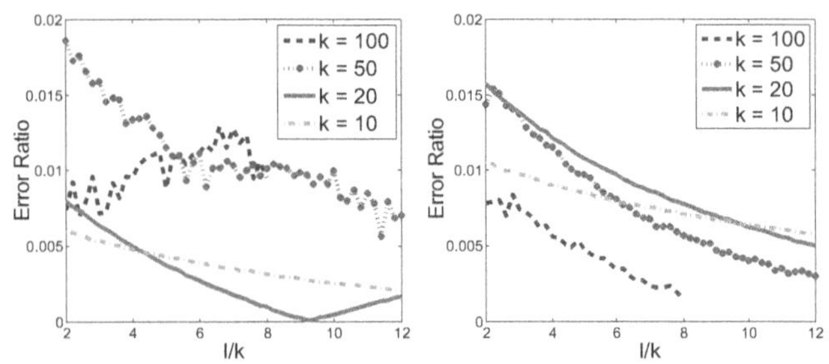

(g) Splice.

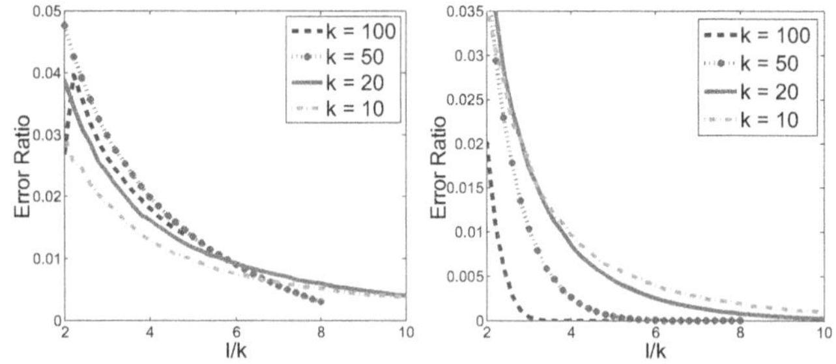

(h) Breast Cancer.

Figure 2: The error ratio $|\delta^{\text{opt}} - \tilde{\delta}|/\delta^{\text{opt}}$ versus l/k. In each subfigure, the left corresponds to the RBF kernel matrix with scaling parameter $\alpha = 0.1$, and the right corresponds to $\alpha = 1$.

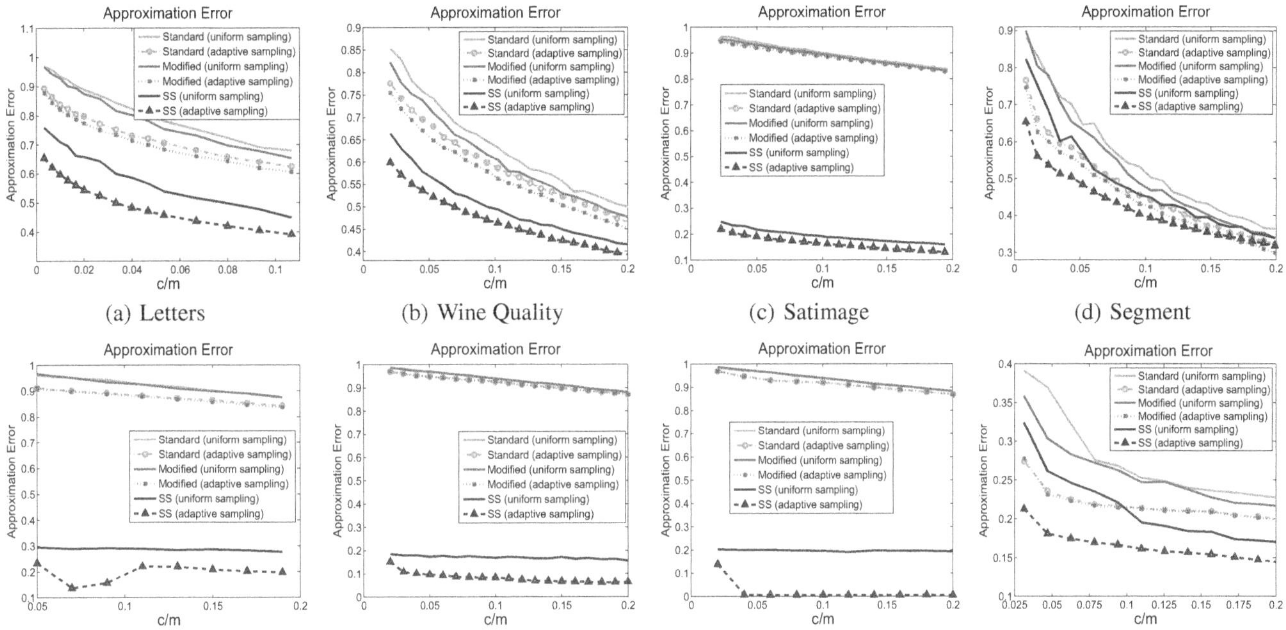

(a) Letters (b) Wine Quality (c) Satimage (d) Segment

(e) DNA (f) German (g) Splice (h) Breast Cancer

Figure 3: The kernel approximation error incurred by the standard Nyström, modified Nyström, and SS-Nyström on the dense RBF kernels.

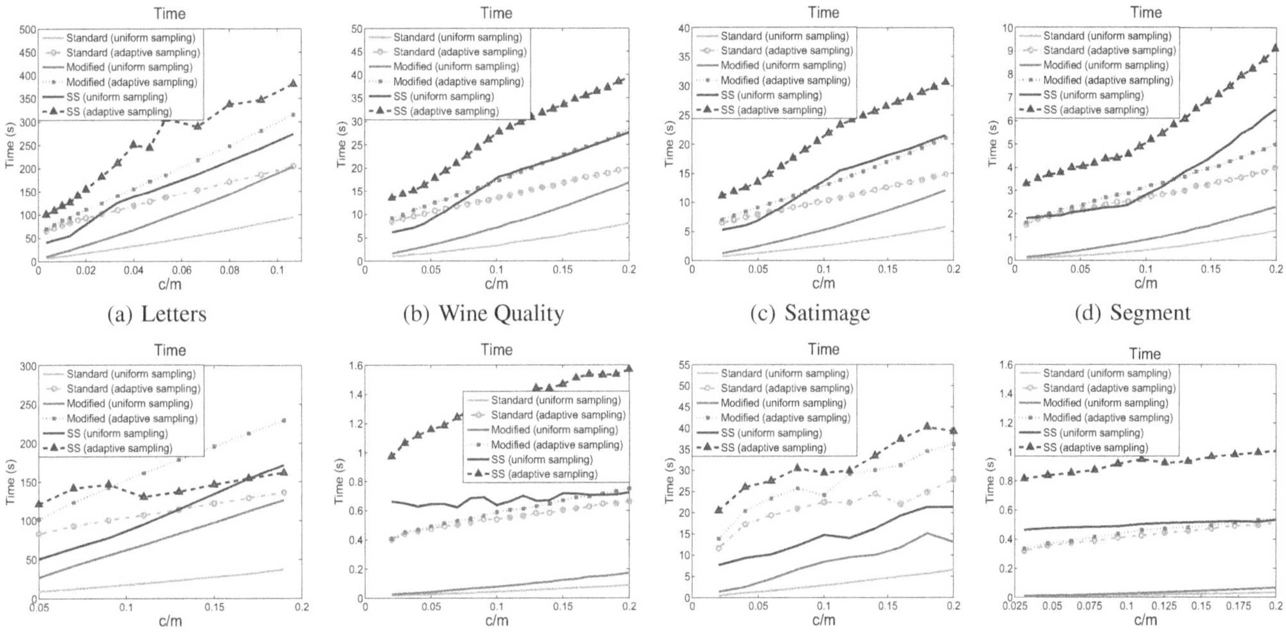

(a) Letters (b) Wine Quality (c) Satimage (d) Segment

(e) DNA (f) German (g) Splice (h) Breast Cancer

Figure 4: The elapsed time of the standard Nyström, modified Nyström, and SS-Nyström on the dense RBF kernels.

time, our SS-Nyström is a little slower than the modified Nyström because SS-Nyström needs to compute δ^{opt} approximately by randomized SVD, which costs time $\mathcal{O}(mk^2) + T_{\text{multiply}}(m^2k)$ (as we set $l = 4k$). Since it costs time $\mathcal{O}(mc^2) + T_{\text{multiply}}(m^2c)$ to compute the modified Nyström approximation, so our SS-Nyström should be only constant times slower than the modified Nyström; this is verified by experiments.

7.4 Large-Scale Experiment

Finally, we compare SS-Nyström with the standard/modified Nyström methods on a large-scale dataset. We use the MNIST

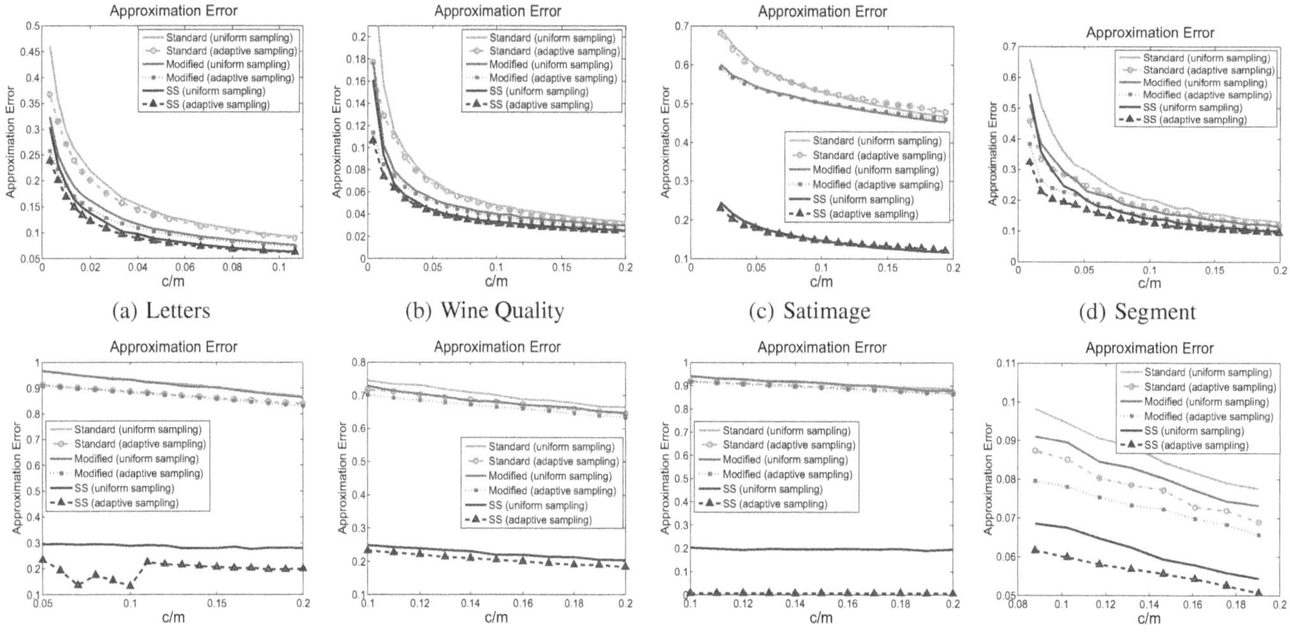

(a) Letters (b) Wine Quality (c) Satimage (d) Segment

(e) DNA (f) German (g) Splice (h) Breast Cancer

Figure 5: The kernel approximation error incurred by the standard Nyström, modified Nyström, and SS-Nyström on the sparse RBF kernels.

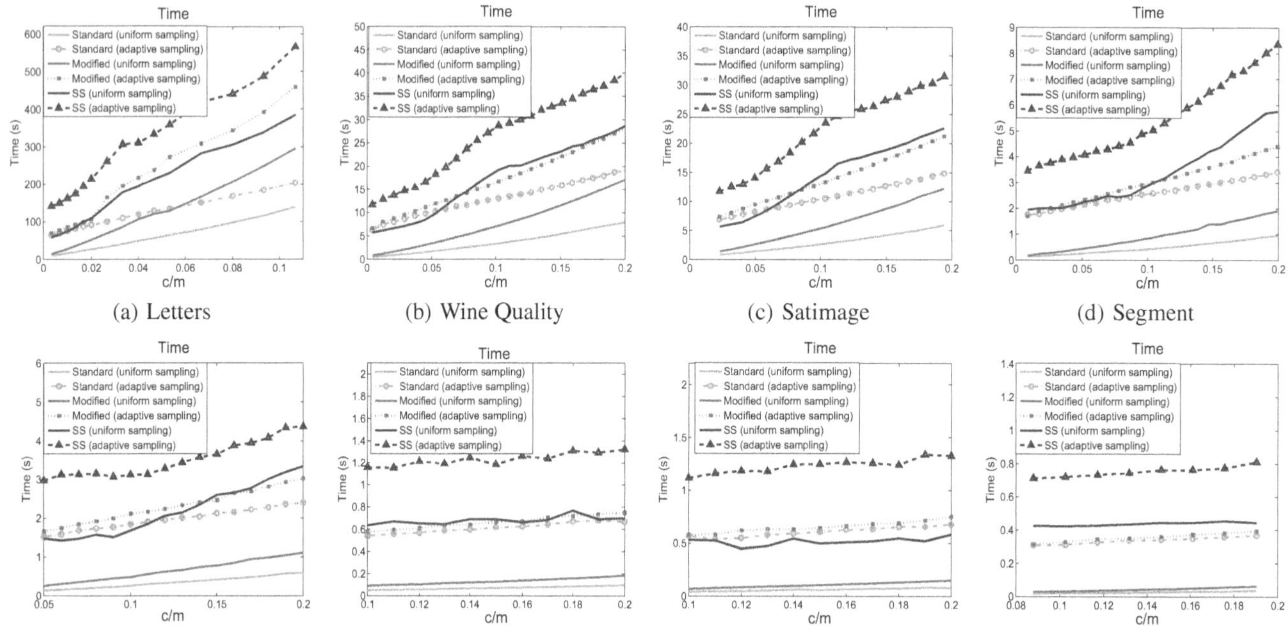

(a) Letters (b) Wine Quality (c) Satimage (d) Segment

(e) DNA (f) German (g) Splice (h) Breast Cancer

Figure 6: The elapsed time of the standard Nyström, modified Nyström, and SS-Nyström on the sparse RBF kernels.

[16] dataset which has $60,000$ instance. We generate an RBF kernel with the scaling parameter $\alpha = 5$. The kernel matrix of MNIST has size of $60,000 \times 60,000$ which exceed the RAM of our workstation. We partition the kernel matrix to 30 blocks of size $60,000 \times 2,000$ and store them in the disk; at each time at most one block is loaded into the RAM. We only use uniform sampling to construct the approximations because other sampling methods are much more expensive, and we set $k = c/3$ for SS-Nyström. The standard Nyström method goes one pass through the data, the modified Nyström method goes two passes, and SS-Nyström (Algorithm 1) goes four passes. We report the approximation error (the minimum of 10 repeats) in Figure 7. We can see that the error

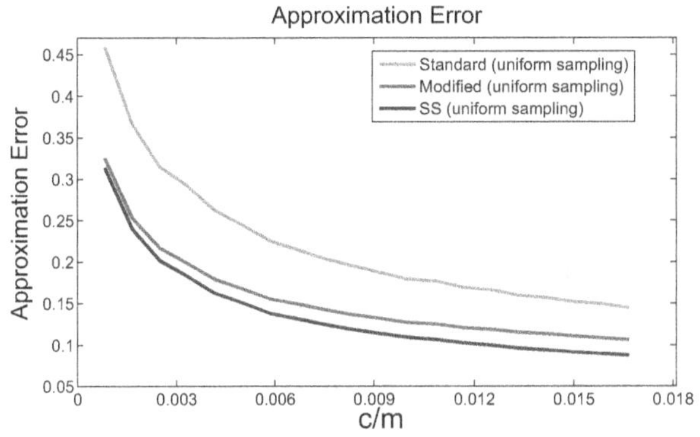

Figure 7: The kernel approximation error incurred by the standard Nyström, modified Nyström, and SS-Nyström on the MNIST dataset.

incurred by SS-Nyström is lower than that of the standard/modified Nyström methods. This set of experiments demonstrates that our proposed SS-Nyström method is still feasible for large-scale data that do not fit in RAM.

8. CONCLUSIONS

The Nyström method is an important kernel approximation method for enabling large-scale machine learning algorithms. In this paper we have proposed the SS-Nyström method which is a variant of the Nyström method and can speedup many kernel methods in the same way as the standard/modified Nyström methods. We have shown that SS-Nyström has a much stronger error bound than the standard/modified Nyström methods. Especially, when the bottom eigenvalues of a kernel matrix are not sufficiently small, the approximation accuracy of the standard/modified Nyström method or even the truncated SVD is unsatisfactory, while our SS-Nyström can still generate approximations of high accuracy. We have also devised an algorithm for computing SS-Nyström efficiently. Finally, the experiments have further demonstrated the effectiveness and efficiency of our SS-Nyström method.

9. ACKNOWLEDGEMENT

Shusen Wang is supported by Microsoft Research Asia Fellowship 2013 and the Scholarship Award for Excellent Doctoral Student granted by Chinese Ministry of Education. Hui Qian is supported by the National Natural Science Foundation of China (No. 61272303) and the National Program on Key Basic Research Project of China (973 Program, No. 2010CB327903). Zhihua Zhang is supported by the National Natural Science Foundation of China (No. 61070239).

APPENDIX

A. PROOF OF THEOREMS

We prove the three theorems of this paper respectively in the following subsections.

A.1 Proof of Theorem 2

PROOF. Since (2) is in convex and δ^{opt} is the minimizer of (2), then for any $\delta \in (0, \delta^{\text{opt}}]$, it holds that

$$\sum_{j=k+1}^{m} \big(\sigma_j(\mathbf{K}) - \delta\big)^2 \leq \sum_{j=k+1}^{m} \big(\sigma_j(\mathbf{K}) - 0\big)^2 = \big\|\mathbf{K} - \mathbf{K}_k\big\|_F^2.$$

Then the theorem follows by the inequality (2) that any δ in the given interval can result in a smaller error. □

A.2 Proof of Theorem 3

PROOF. The error incurred by SS-Nyström is

$$\begin{aligned}\big\|\mathbf{K} - \tilde{\mathbf{K}}_c^{\text{ss}}\big\|_F^2 &= \big\|\big(\bar{\mathbf{K}} + \delta^{\text{opt}}\mathbf{I}_m\big) - \big(\bar{\mathbf{C}}\bar{\mathbf{U}}\bar{\mathbf{C}}^T + \delta^{\text{opt}}\mathbf{I}_m\big)\big\|_F^2 \\ &= \big\|\bar{\mathbf{K}} - \bar{\mathbf{C}}\bar{\mathbf{U}}\bar{\mathbf{C}}^T\big\|_F^2 \leq (1+\epsilon)\big\|\bar{\mathbf{K}} - \bar{\mathbf{K}}_k\big\|_F^2 \\ &= (1+\epsilon)\sum_{i=k+1}^{m} \sigma_i^2(\bar{\mathbf{K}}) = (1+\epsilon)\sum_{i=k+1}^{m} \lambda_i(\bar{\mathbf{K}}^2).\end{aligned}$$

Here the inequality follows from the property of the column selection algorithm $\mathcal{A}_{\text{col}}$. The i-th largest eigenvalue of $\bar{\mathbf{K}}$ is $\lambda_i(\mathbf{K}) - \delta^{\text{opt}}$, so the m eigenvalues of $\bar{\mathbf{K}}^2$ are all in the set $\{(\lambda_i(\mathbf{K}) - \delta^{\text{opt}})^2\}_{i=1}^m$. The sum of the least $m-k$ of the m eigenvalues of $\bar{\mathbf{K}}^2$ must be less than or equal to the sum of any $m-k$ of the eigenvalues, thus we have

$$\begin{aligned}\sum_{i=k+1}^{m} \lambda_i(\bar{\mathbf{K}}^2) &\leq \sum_{i=k+1}^{m} \Big(\lambda_i(\mathbf{K}) - \delta^{\text{opt}}\Big)^2 \\ &= \sum_{i=k+1}^{m} \lambda_i^2(\mathbf{K}) - 2\sum_{i=k+1}^{m} \delta^{\text{opt}}\lambda_i(\mathbf{K}) + (m-k)(\delta^{\text{opt}})^2 \\ &= \|\mathbf{K} - \mathbf{K}_k\|_F^2 - \frac{1}{m-k}\Big[\sum_{i=k+1}^{m} \lambda_i(\mathbf{K})\Big]^2,\end{aligned}$$

by which the theorem follows. □

A.3 Proof of Theorem 5

PROOF. Let $\tilde{\mathbf{K}} = \mathbf{Q}(\mathbf{Q}^T\mathbf{K})_k$, where $\mathbf{Q}$ is defined in Line 4 in Algorithm 1. It was shown in [2] that

$$\mathbb{E}\|\mathbf{K} - \tilde{\mathbf{K}}\|_F^2 \leq (1 + k/l)\,\|\mathbf{K} - \mathbf{K}_k\|_F^2, \tag{5}$$

where the expectation is taken w.r.t. the random Gaussian matrix $\mathbf{\Omega}$.

It follows from Lemma 6 that

$$\|\boldsymbol{\sigma}_{\mathbf{K}} - \boldsymbol{\sigma}_{\tilde{\mathbf{K}}}\|_2^2 \leq \|\mathbf{K} - \tilde{\mathbf{K}}\|_F^2,$$

where $\boldsymbol{\sigma}_{\mathbf{K}}$ and $\boldsymbol{\sigma}_{\tilde{\mathbf{K}}}$ contain the singular values in a descending order. Since $\tilde{\mathbf{K}}$ has a rank at most k, the $k+1$ to n entries of $\boldsymbol{\sigma}_{\tilde{\mathbf{K}}}$ are zero. We split $\boldsymbol{\sigma}_{\mathbf{K}}$ and $\boldsymbol{\sigma}_{\tilde{\mathbf{K}}}$ into vectors of length k and $m-k$:

$$\boldsymbol{\sigma}_{\mathbf{K}} = \begin{bmatrix} \boldsymbol{\sigma}_{\mathbf{K},k} \\ \boldsymbol{\sigma}_{\mathbf{K},-k} \end{bmatrix} \quad \text{and} \quad \boldsymbol{\sigma}_{\tilde{\mathbf{K}}} = \begin{bmatrix} \boldsymbol{\sigma}_{\tilde{\mathbf{K}},k} \\ \mathbf{0} \end{bmatrix}$$

and thus

$$\|\boldsymbol{\sigma}_{\mathbf{K},k} - \boldsymbol{\sigma}_{\tilde{\mathbf{K}},k}\|_2^2 + \|\boldsymbol{\sigma}_{\mathbf{K},-k}\|_2^2 \leq \|\mathbf{K} - \tilde{\mathbf{K}}\|_F^2. \tag{6}$$

Since $\|\boldsymbol{\sigma}_{\mathbf{K},-k}\|_2^2 = \|\mathbf{K} - \mathbf{K}_k\|_F^2$, it follows from (5) and (6) that

$$\mathbb{E}\|\boldsymbol{\sigma}_{\mathbf{K},k} - \boldsymbol{\sigma}_{\tilde{\mathbf{K}},k}\|_2^2 \leq \frac{k}{l}\|\boldsymbol{\sigma}_{\mathbf{K},-k}\|_2^2.$$

Since $\|\mathbf{x}\|_2 \leq \|\mathbf{x}\|_1 \leq \sqrt{k}\|\mathbf{x}\|_2$ for any $\mathbf{x} \in \mathbb{R}^k$, we have that

$$\mathbb{E}\big\|\boldsymbol{\sigma}_{\mathbf{K},k} - \boldsymbol{\sigma}_{\tilde{\mathbf{K}},k}\big\|_1 \leq \frac{k}{\sqrt{l}}\big\|\boldsymbol{\sigma}_{\mathbf{K},-k}\big\|_1.$$

Then it follows from (3) and Line 6 in Algorithm 1 that

$$\begin{aligned}\mathbb{E}\big|\delta^{\text{opt}} - \tilde{\delta}\big| &= \mathbb{E}\left[\frac{1}{m-k}\left|\sum_{i=1}^{k}\sigma_i(\mathbf{K}) - \sum_{i=1}^{k}\sigma_i(\tilde{\mathbf{K}})\right|\right] \\ &\leq \frac{1}{m-k}\mathbb{E}\big\|\boldsymbol{\sigma}_{\mathbf{K},k} - \boldsymbol{\sigma}_{\tilde{\mathbf{K}},k}\big\|_1 \\ &\leq \frac{k}{\sqrt{l}}\frac{1}{m-k}\big\|\boldsymbol{\sigma}_{\mathbf{K},-k}\big\|_1 = \frac{k}{\sqrt{l}}\delta^{\text{opt}}.\end{aligned} \tag{7}$$

□

The following lemma is used to prove the theorem. The lemma is easy to prove, so here we do not show the detailed proof.

LEMMA 6. *Let* $\mathbf{A}$ *and* $\mathbf{B}$ *be square matrices and* $\boldsymbol{\sigma}_{\mathbf{A}}$ *and* $\boldsymbol{\sigma}_{\mathbf{B}}$ *contain the singular values in a descending order. Then we have that*

$$\|\boldsymbol{\sigma}_{\mathbf{A}} - \boldsymbol{\sigma}_{\mathbf{B}}\|_2^2 \leq \|\mathbf{A} - \mathbf{B}\|_F^2.$$

References

[1] R. H. Affandi, A. Kulesza, E. B. Fox, and B. Taskar. Nyström approximation for large-scale determinantal processes. In *International Conference on Artificial Intelligence and Statistics (AISTATS)*, 2013.

[2] C. Boutsidis, P. Drineas, and M. Magdon-Ismail. Near optimal column-based matrix reconstruction. In *Annual Symposium on Foundations of Computer Science (FOCS)*, 2011.

[3] C. Cortes, M. Mohri, and A. Talwalkar. On the impact of kernel approximation on learning accuracy. In *Conference on Artificial Intelligence and Statistics (AISTATS)*, 2010.

[4] A. Deshpande, L. Rademacher, S. Vempala, and G. Wang. Matrix approximation and projective clustering via volume sampling. *Theory of Computing*, 2(2006):225–247, 2006.

[5] P. Drineas and M. W. Mahoney. On the Nyström method for approximating a gram matrix for improved kernel-based learning. *Journal of Machine Learning Research*, 6:2153–2175, 2005.

[6] P. Drineas, M. W. Mahoney, and S. Muthukrishnan. Relative-error CUR matrix decompositions. *SIAM Journal on Matrix Analysis and Applications*, 30(2):844–881, Sept. 2008.

[7] C. Fowlkes, S. Belongie, F. Chung, and J. Malik. Spectral grouping using the Nyström method. *IEEE Transactions on Pattern Analysis and Machine Intelligence*, 26(2):214–225, 2004.

[8] A. Frank and A. Asuncion. UCI machine learning repository, 2010.

[9] M. G. Genton. Classes of kernels for machine learning: A statistics perspective. *Journal of Machine Learning Research*, 2:299–312, 2001.

[10] A. Gittens and M. W. Mahoney. Revisiting the nyström method for improved large-scale machine learning. In *International Conference on Machine Learning (ICML)*, 2013.

[11] V. Guruswami and A. K. Sinop. Optimal column-based low-rank matrix reconstruction. In *Proceedings of the 23rd Annual ACM-SIAM Symposium on Discrete Algorithms (SODA)*, pages 1207–1214. SIAM, 2012.

[12] N. Halko, P.-G. Martinsson, and J. A. Tropp. Finding structure with randomness: Probabilistic algorithms for constructing approximate matrix decompositions. *SIAM Review*, 53(2):217–288, 2011.

[13] J. B. Hough, M. Krishnapur, Y. Peres, B. Virág, et al. Determinantal processes and independence. *Probability Surveys*, 3:206–229, 2006.

[14] R. Jin, T. Yang, M. Mahdavi, Y. Li, and Z. Zhou. Improved bounds for the nystrom method with application to kernel classification. *IEEE Transactions on Information Theory*, 59(10):6939–6949, 2013.

[15] S. Kumar, M. Mohri, and A. Talwalkar. Sampling methods for the Nyström method. *Journal of Machine Learning Research*, 13:981–1006, 2012.

[16] Y. LeCun, L. Bottou, Y. Bengio, and P. Haffner. Gradient-based learning applied to document recognition. *Proceedings of the IEEE*, 86(11):2278–2324, 1998.

[17] M. Li, X.-C. Lian, J. T. Kwok, and B.-L. Lu. Time and space efficient spectral clustering via column sampling. In *IEEE Conference on Computer Vision and Pattern Recognition (CVPR)*, 2011.

[18] M. W. Mahoney. Randomized algorithms for matrices and data. *Foundations and Trends in Machine Learning*, 3(2):123–224, 2011.

[19] D. Michie, D. J. Spiegelhalter, and C. C. Taylor. *Machine Learning, Neural and Statistical Classification*. Prentice Hall, 1994.

[20] E. J. Nyström. Über die praktische auflösung von integralgleichungen mit anwendungen auf randwertaufgaben. *Acta Mathematica*, 54(1):185–204, 1930.

[21] C. Saunders, A. Gammerman, and V. Vovk. Ridge regression learning algorithm in dual variables. In *International Conference on Machine Learning (ICML)*, 1998.

[22] B. Schölkopf and A. J. Smola. *Learning with Kernels: Support Vector Machines, Regularization, Optimization, and Beyond.* MIT Press, 2002.

[23] J. Shawe-Taylor and N. Cristianini. *Kernel Methods for Pattern Analysis*. Cambridge University Press, 2004.

[24] S. Si, C.-J. Hsieh, and I. Dhillon. Memory efficient kernel approximation. In *International Conference on Machine Learning (ICML)*, pages 701–709, 2014.

[25] J. A. Suykens and J. Vandewalle. Least squares support vector machine classifiers. *Neural processing letters*, 9(3):293–300, 1999.

[26] A. Talwalkar, S. Kumar, M. Mohri, and H. Rowley. Large-scale svd and manifold learning. *Journal of Machine Learning Research*, 14:3129–3152, 2013.

[27] S. Wang, C. Zhang, H. Qian, and Z. Zhang. Using the matrix ridge approximation to speedup determinantal point processes sampling algorithms. In *The 28th AAAI Conference on Artificial Intelligence (AAAI)*, 2014.

[28] S. Wang and Z. Zhang. Improving CUR matrix decomposition and the Nyström approximation via adaptive sampling. *Journal of Machine Learning Research*, 14:2729–2769, 2013.

[29] S. Wang and Z. Zhang. Efficient algorithms and error analysis for the modified Nyström method. In *International Conference on Artificial Intelligence and Statistics (AISTATS)*, 2014.

[30] C. Williams and M. Seeger. Using the Nyström method to speed up kernel machines. In *Advances in Neural Information Processing Systems (NIPS)*, 2001.

[31] T. Yang, Y.-F. Li, M. Mahdavi, R. Jin, and Z.-H. Zhou. Nyström method vs random fourier features: A theoretical and empirical comparison. In *Advances in Neural Information Processing Systems (NIPS)*, 2012.

[32] K. Zhang and J. T. Kwok. Clustered Nyström method for large scale manifold learning and dimension reduction. *IEEE Transactions on Neural Networks*, 21(10):1576–1587, 2010.

[33] K. Zhang, I. W. Tsang, and J. T. Kwok. Improved Nyström low-rank approximation and error analysis. In *International Conference on Machine Learning (ICML)*, 2008.

[34] Z. Zhang. The matrix ridge approximation: algorithms and applications. *Machine Learning*, pages 1–32, 2014.

Fast Flux Discriminant for Large-Scale Sparse Nonlinear Classification

Wenlin Chen
Department of Computer Science and Engineering
Washington University in St. Louis, USA
wenlinchen@wustl.edu

Yixin Chen
Department of Computer Science and Engineering
Washington University in St. Louis, USA
chen@cse.wustl.edu

Kilian Q. Weinberger
Department of Computer Science and Engineering
Washington University in St. Louis, USA
kilian@wustl.edu

ABSTRACT

In this paper, we propose a novel supervised learning method, Fast Flux Discriminant (FFD), for large-scale nonlinear classification. Compared with other existing methods, FFD has unmatched advantages, as it attains the efficiency and interpretability of linear models as well as the accuracy of nonlinear models. It is also sparse and naturally handles mixed data types. It works by decomposing the kernel density estimation in the entire feature space into selected low-dimensional subspaces. Since there are many possible subspaces, we propose a submodular optimization framework for subspace selection. The selected subspace predictions are then transformed to new features on which a linear model can be learned. Besides, since the transformed features naturally expect non-negative weights, we only require smooth optimization even with the ℓ_1 regularization. Unlike other nonlinear models such as kernel methods, the FFD model is interpretable as it gives importance weights on the original features. Its training and testing are also much faster than traditional kernel models. We carry out extensive empirical studies on real-world datasets and show that the proposed model achieves state-of-the-art classification results with sparsity, interpretability, and exceptional scalability. Our model can be learned in minutes on datasets with millions of samples, for which most existing nonlinear methods will be prohibitively expensive in space and time.

Categories and Subject Descriptors

H.2.8 [**Database Management**]: Database Applications-Data Mining; J.3 [**Computer Applications**]: Life and Medical Sciences

Keywords

classification; interpretability; sparsity; submodularity

KDD'14, August 24–27, 2014, New York, NY, USA.
Copyright 2014 ACM 978-1-4503-2956-9/14/08 ...$15.00.
http://dx.doi.org/10.1145/2623330.2623627.

1. INTRODUCTION

In supervised classification, there are several potentially competing needs. For example in biomedical applications, classifiers often need to be *feature-sparse*, in order to identify leading risk factors for prevention and intervention of critical medical conditions. In addition, the training sets can be very large, thus requiring good *scalability*, but the classifier should also be expressive enough to model *nonlinear* feature interaction. Finally, and possibly most importantly, the classifier must also achieve *high accuracy*. These requirements are by no means specific to biomedical applications. In fact, they are representative for many machine learning application domains. Although several methods excel at various aspects, to date none manages to capture all of them.

Linear classifiers [33] cover many of these needs: they can be highly scalable [8], learn weights that are naturally interpretable and, if paired with ℓ_1 regularization, can also be feature-sparse [7, 29]. Because of these strengths, they are a common choice for machine learning practitioners. However, linear classifiers fall short on at least two of the desired requirements: they cannot learn nonlinear decision boundaries, which inherently limits their accuracy on difficult or lower-dimensional datasets. Further, they cannot discover the relevance of features that are beneficial only through nonlinear interactions with each other.

Nonlinear classifiers can model such feature interactions and are not limited by linear decision boundaries, but they typically suffer from different limitations. For example, deep neural nets [12] are highly nonlinear and scalable, but do not naturally incorporate feature sparsity and the decisions are hard to interpret. Similarly, tree ensembles, such as Random Forests [4], share the same weaknesses. The kernel trick [26] is a popular method to extend linear classifiers to learn nonlinear decision boundaries, but it also removes their natural interpretability and scalability.

To get the best out of both nonlinear methods (nonlinear separability) and linear methods (high efficiency), a recent trend in data mining and machine learning is to replace heavy nonlinear machineries with simpler linear ones, and to achieve high accuracy by introducing certain nonlinearity in **feature mapping**. That is, they map the original input data $\mathbf{x} \in \mathcal{R}^D$ to a feature vector $\phi(\mathbf{x}) \in \mathcal{R}^M$ and then learn a linear hyperplane $\mathbf{w}^T\phi(x)$, $\mathbf{w} \in \mathcal{R}^M$ [17, 22, 24, 30]. A linear classifier, trained on $\phi(\mathbf{x}) \in \mathcal{R}^M$ instead of the "raw" features $\mathbf{x} \in \mathcal{R}^D$, can learn nonlinear decision boundaries in the original input space while maintaining its high scalability. Unfortunately, however, this approach does not also maintain its interpretability and feature-sparseness. The classifier weights can no longer be interpreted, which drastically limits the usefulness of this approach for many applications tied to the discovery of feature importance.

As our first contribution, we propose a novel algorithm, which we refer to as Fast Flux Discriminant (FFD). FFD is designed to combine *all* the strengths of linear and nonlinear supervised learning. It maintains the scalability, feature-sparsity and interpretability of linear classifiers, yet can learn non-linear decision boundaries, discover pairwise feature interactions and it matches the high accuracy of state-of-the-art nonlinear models.

At its core, FFD is based on kernel density estimation (KDE) [3]. The ultimate goal of (discriminative) supervised learning is to estimate the conditional label distribution $p(y|\mathbf{x})$, for a label y of an input $\mathbf{x} \in \mathcal{R}^D$. If unlimited labeled data were available, this distribution could be estimated directly with KDE. In practice, however, such a naïve approach does often not work. The curse of dimensionality [3] makes the data requirements of KDE grow *exponentially* with the data dimensionality, thus quickly exceeding any realistic limitations, if the data is sufficiently high dimensional. However, if the dimensionality is low, KDE is very effective.

Chen *et al.* [6] make use of KDE as a feature transformation. They point out that if features do not interact with each other, the conditional label distribution can be decomposed as $\log \frac{p(y=1|\mathbf{x})}{p(y=-1|\mathbf{x})} = w_0 + \sum_{d=1}^{D} w_d \log \frac{p(y=1|[\mathbf{x}]_d)}{p(y=-1|[\mathbf{x}]_d)}$, where $[\mathbf{x}]_d$ denotes the dth dimension of $\mathbf{x}$ and the weights w_d are estimated from the data.[1] Similar to Rahimi and Recht [24], this approach learns an explicit feature transformation that enables linear classifiers to learn non-linear decision boundaries. Unfortunately, it cannot discover non-linear feature interactions.

In this paper we follow this insight but *relax* the restriction that features cannot interact with each others. Instead, we assume that features *can* interact, but their interactions are limited to $r \ll D$ features. Let A denote a set or "bag" of features, with $|A| \leq r$, and let $[\mathbf{x}]_A$ denote the *shortened* input vector $\mathbf{x}$ with only those features in A. We assume that r is small enough, so that $p(y|[\mathbf{x}]_A)$ can still be computed fast and accurately via KDE. FFD learns a new representation $\mathbf{x} \rightarrow \Phi(\mathbf{x})$, where each dimension of $\Phi(\mathbf{x})$ corresponds to the conditional label distribution $p(y|[\mathbf{x}]_A)$ for some feature bag A. A *linear* classifier learned on the data $\Phi(\mathbf{x})$ can learn nonlinear decision boundaries and its weights indicate which feature "bags" are most important. If in addition the classifier is regularized to be sparse, we can identify which feature bags are in fact *sufficient* to make accurate predictions. Because KDE is highly non-linear and approximates the true conditional distribution, FFD reliably learns the within-bag feature interactions.

One immediate challenge with this setup is the exponentially growing number, $\binom{D}{r}$, of possible sets A. How can we identify which such sets of features to include in our representation? Our second contribution is to formulate this as a tractable optimization problem. We propose a novel optimization framework which maximizes the similarity coverage and minimizes redundancy of the selected feature set. Moreover, the optimization formulation contains cardinality penalty for sparsity and interpretability. We formulate this selection problem as a combinatorial optimization with a submodular objective. Previous work [9] proves that for this category of problems, there exists a 1/3-approximation bound in the worst case.

To further promote feature sparsity of the FFD model, we also employ ℓ_1 regularization. A disadvantage of typical ℓ_1 regularization is that it is not differentiable everywhere and requires non-smooth optimization techniques such as sub-gradient descent. However, since the KDE features in FFD model conditional label distribution, their weights are naturally expected to be non-negative. Based on this key insight, we add non-negativity constraints to the training objective and make it a *smooth* optimization problem even with ℓ_1 regularization. This enables us to employ fast smooth optimization algorithms.

Finally, we carry out extensive experiments on real-world datasets and show that the proposed FFD model achieves state-of-the-art classification results with exceptional scalability. FFD can be learned in minutes on datasets with millions of samples, for which other nonlinear methods will be prohibitively expensive in space and time. FFD also demonstrates interpretability and results in very sparse models.

This paper is organized as follows. In Section 2, we present the notations and preliminaries. We describe the proposed FFD model in Section 3. We discuss related work in Section 4 and present experimental results in Section 5. Section 6 gives conclusions.

2. PRELIMINARIES

In this section, we introduce the notations and review the density-based logistic regression (DLR) model [6], which is highly related to the proposed model.

Assume we are given a dataset $\mathcal{D} = \{\mathbf{x}_i, y_i\}$, $i = 1, \cdots, N$, $\mathbf{x}_i \in \mathcal{R}^D$ where D is the number of attributes[2], and the label $y_i \in \{-1, 1\}$. Let the input vector be $\mathbf{x}_i = ([\mathbf{x}_i]_1, \cdots, [\mathbf{x}_i]_D)$.

$\mathcal{D}$ can be further partitioned into two datasets $\mathcal{D}_1$ and $\mathcal{D}_{-1}$, which include all the data points whose labels are $y = 1$ and $y = -1$, respectively.

In the training phase, the DLR model first maps each training sample to a new feature space in a dimension-wise manner, i.e. $\mathbf{x} \rightarrow \mathbf{\Phi}(\mathbf{x})$ where

$$\mathbf{\Phi}(\mathbf{x}) = (\phi_1(\mathbf{x}), \phi_2(\mathbf{x}), \cdots, \phi_D(\mathbf{x})).$$

Similar to logistic regression, DLR models the conditional probability of y given a sample $\mathbf{x}$ by a sigmoid function on the transformed features.

$$p(y = 1|\mathbf{x}) = \frac{1}{1 + \exp(-(\mathbf{w}\mathbf{\Phi}(\mathbf{x})))} \tag{1}$$

where the parameter $\mathbf{w}$ can be learned via maximum likelihood estimation or equivalently the empirical risk minimization with logistic loss:

$$\underset{\mathbf{w}}{\text{minimize}} \ \frac{1}{N}\sum_{i=1}^{N}\left(1 + e^{-y_i(\mathbf{w}\Phi(\mathbf{x}_i))}\right) + \lambda\|\mathbf{w}\|_2 \tag{2}$$

[1]This approximation is exact for $w_d = 1$ if the features are label conditionally independent, which is also often referred to as the Naïve Bayes assumption [3].

[2]For simplicity, here we only discuss datasets with numerical features. The proposed method also applies to datasets with categorical and mixed features.

If we use the original attributes without feature mapping, i.e. $\phi_d(\mathbf{x}) = [\mathbf{x}]_d$ for $d = 1, \cdots, D$, Eq. (1) is the original LR.

Unlike LR, DLR introduces a nonlinear feature mapping based on the following rationale. First, Eq. (1) can be rewritten as:

$$\mathbf{w\Phi}(\mathbf{x}) = \ln \frac{p(y=1|\mathbf{x})}{p(y=-1|\mathbf{x})} \quad (3)$$

Assuming conditional independence of the attributes given the class label y, it can be shown that [6]

$$\ln \frac{p(y=1|\mathbf{x})}{p(y=-1|\mathbf{x})} = w_0 + \sum_{d=1}^{D} \left(\ln \frac{p(y=1|[\mathbf{x}]_d)}{p(y=-1|[\mathbf{x}]_d)} \right) \quad (4)$$

where $w_0 = (D-1)\ln \frac{p(y=1)}{p(y=-1)}$. Comparing (3) with (4) and setting $\mathbf{w} = 1$, we can naturally derive the following feature transformation used by DLR. For each dimension d, the DLR feature mapping is:

$$\phi_d(\mathbf{x}) = \ln \frac{p(y=1|[\mathbf{x}]_d)}{p(y=-1|[\mathbf{x}]_d)}, \quad (5)$$

which is a logit transformation on the conditional probability of y given a single feature $[\mathbf{x}]_d$.

In order to compute the features $\phi_d(\mathbf{x})$ in (5), DLR estimates $p(y|[\mathbf{x}]_d)$ by treating categorial and numerical attributes in different ways.

- If $[\mathbf{x}]_d$ is a categorical attribute, $p(y=1|[\mathbf{x}]_d)$ is estimated by counting the proportion of samples with label $y = 1$ among all the samples whose d^{th} attribute is $[\mathbf{x}]_d$. Let $\mathcal{D}_{[\mathbf{x}]_d}$ be the set of of samples in $\mathcal{D}$ whose d^{th} attribute equals to $[\mathbf{x}]_d$. The DLR estimate is

$$\phi_d(\mathbf{x}) = \ln \frac{|\mathcal{D}_1 \bigcap \mathcal{D}_{[\mathbf{x}]_d}|}{|\mathcal{D}_{-1} \bigcap \mathcal{D}_{[\mathbf{x}]_d}|}. \quad (6)$$

- If $[\mathbf{x}]_d$ is a numerical attribute, then DLR calculates $\phi_d(\mathbf{x})$ by kernel density estimation (KDE) [3]. The DLR estimate is

$$\phi_d(\mathbf{x}) = \ln \frac{\sum_{i\in\mathcal{D}_1} \exp(-\frac{([\mathbf{x}]_d-[\mathbf{x}_i]_d)^2}{h_d^2})}{\sum_{i\in\mathcal{D}_{-1}} \exp(-\frac{([\mathbf{x}]_d-[\mathbf{x}_i]_d)^2}{h_d^2})}, \quad (7)$$

  where h_d is a parameter called the kernel bandwidth.

In the training phase, DLR first computes the feature mapping and then calls a standard LR package to learn $\mathbf{w}$. In the testing phase, given a testing sample $\mathbf{x}$, the DLR model first transforms it to $\mathbf{\Phi}(\mathbf{x})$ via KDE or counting depending on the feature type. The conditional probability of y given $\mathbf{x}$ is then calculated by Eq. (1).

Though DLR offers good interpretability as it assigns a weight to each original dimension, it has some serious drawbacks. 1) DLR has high training and testing complexity. Although DLR is more efficient in its training time, its feature computation is still expensive. For a dataset with N samples and D dimensions, DLR requires $O(DN^2)$ time for training and $O(DN)$ time for testing one single sample. Such a testing cost is the same as kernel SVM, making it too expensive for applications where extensive testings are required. 2) DLR generates dense vectors and does not offer sparsity. 3) DLR assumes conditional independence of each dimension give the class label, which is often violated in practice and may suffer from high correlation between dimensions.

3. FAST FLUX DISCRIMINANT (FFD)

In this section, we propose our FFD model. Like DLR, FFD also performs a feature mapping based on density estimation and then learns a linear machine after the feature mapping. However, FFD is significantly different from DLR and offers a few salient advantages. It does not assume conditional independence and is able to capture the correlation between features. Also, it preserves the interpretability and explicitly promotes sparsity of the model. Moreover, the learning process of FFD is far more efficient than DLR, leveraging on the fast computing of low-dimensional density estimation via histogram estimation.

In summary, the main steps of FFD include the following.

1. Subspace feature mapping, which generates features based on non-parametric kernel density estimation.
2. Submodular subspace selection, which selects subspace features based on submodular optimization.
3. Model training, which learns a sparse and interpretable linear machine with smooth ℓ_1 regularization.

All the above steps are designed to be highly efficient and capable of scaling to large data. Below, we discuss the main components of FFD before putting them together.

3.1 Subspace feature mapping

This step generates features that can effectively model the conditional probability $p(y|\mathbf{x})$, which enables the nonlinear separability of the model. It is based on non-parametric density estimation which does not make any parametric assumption of the data distribution and is particular suitable for large data since it can make full use of all the data samples. Here, we first describe the histogram-based density estimation in general for the full feature space, which is unrealistic due to the curse of dimensionality. But the same idea can be applied to and is very efficient for low-dimensional subspaces. We then combine the predictions from all subspaces via a linear model and generate nonlinear classification decision boundary.

First, each dimension is divided into equal-length bins. Let b_d be the number of bins for the dth dimension. If $[\mathbf{x}]_d$ is categorical, b_d is always the number of categories for this feature. If $[\mathbf{x}]_d$ is numerical, b_d is a parameter we need to set.

In the training phase, given the training dataset $\mathcal{D} = \{\mathbf{x}_i, y_i\}$, $i = 1, \cdots, N$, we assign each training sample to the corresponding bin. If $[\mathbf{x}_i]_d$ is a categorical feature, $B([\mathbf{x}_i]_d)$, the bin index for dimension d is the category index of $[\mathbf{x}_i]_d$. For a numerical feature, suppose the bins of the dth dimension start at

$$start_d = \min_{k=1..N} \{[\mathbf{x}_k]_d\}$$

and end at

$$end_d = \max_{k=1..N} \{[\mathbf{x}_k]_d\}.$$

The bin length l_d is given by:

$$l_d = \frac{end_d - start_d}{b_d} \quad (8)$$

Let $B([\mathbf{x}_i]_d)$ be the bin index for $[\mathbf{x}_i]_d$. We have that

$$B([\mathbf{x}_i]_d) = \frac{[\mathbf{x}_i]_d - start_d}{l_d} \quad (9)$$

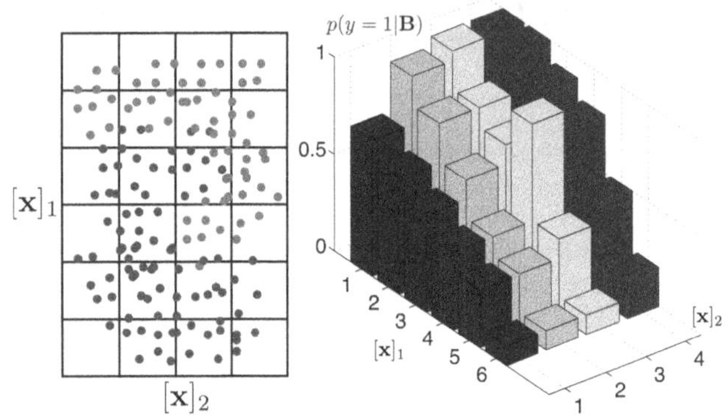

Figure 1: Histogram estimation for a 2-D subspace. Left: a snapshot of a 2-D grid. Right: The proportion of $y = 1$ in each grid cell based on counting.

Each data sample $\mathbf{x}_i$ corresponds to a grid cell[3] (a vector of bin indices):

$$B(\mathbf{x}_i) = (B([\mathbf{x}_i]_1), \cdots, B([\mathbf{x}_i]_D)).$$

After assigning each training sample to the corresponding grid cell, a naive histogram-based density method would estimate the the probability of $p(y|\mathbf{x})$ by counting the proportion of samples with different labels in grid cell $B(\mathbf{x})$. This naive histogram-based density estimation is efficient and does not make any assumption on the distribution of the underlying data. However, if the number of training samples is not enough, this estimation would suffer from huge bias and variance. In addition, the number of grid cells grows exponentially with the number of dimensions, leading to the curse of dimensionality. As a result, this simple histogram method is not practical.

To overcome this problem, instead of directly modeling $p(y|\mathbf{x})$ by density estimation for the whole space, FFD expresses $p(y|\mathbf{x})$ by a number of density estimation for low dimensional subspaces. Each subspace contains a small number (less than r) of features. In essence, we assume that features can interact with each other, but their interactions are limited to $r \ll D$ features. We assume that r is small enough, so that the density estimation for r-dimensional subspaces can still be computed fast. For example, Figure 1 shows the histogram-based density estimation for a 2-dimensional subspace. This subspace is discretized into a grid as shown on the left subfigure. The proportion of training samples with $y = 1$, i.e. $p(y = 1|\mathbf{B})$, is then computed for each grid cell by simple counting as shown on the right subfigure.

To combine the density estimations from all subspaces, we convert the result from each subspace to a new feature and then apply a linear model on these new features. Specifically, FFD learns a new representation $\mathbf{x} \to \Phi(\mathbf{x})$, where

$$\Phi(\mathbf{x}) = (\phi_1(\mathbf{x}), \cdots, \phi_M(\mathbf{x}))$$

is a vector of M subspace features. For each $m = 1, \cdots, M$, FFD uses the following feature

$$\phi_m(\mathbf{x}) = \ln \frac{p(y = 1|[\mathbf{x}]_{A_m})}{p(y = -1|[\mathbf{x}]_{A_m})}, \tag{10}$$

[3]In this paper, the meanings of "bin" and "grid cell" are interchangeable. We often refer to "bin" in the context of a single dimension and "grid cell" otherwise

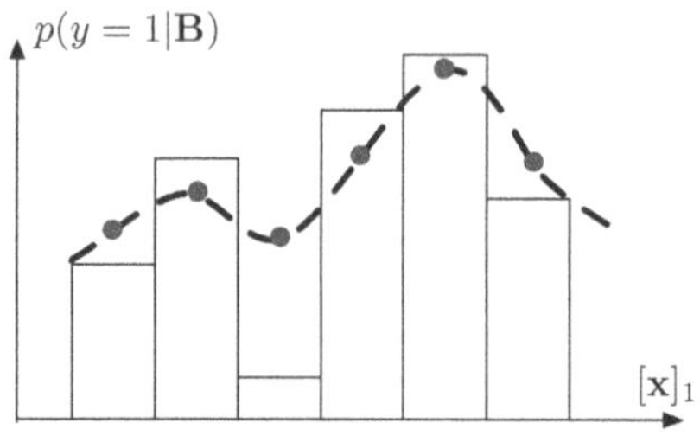

Figure 2: Kernel smoothing for a 1-D histogram. The height of each bin is the proportion of $y = 1$ in each bin based on counting. The purple dots are the new $p(y = 1|\mathbf{B})$ for each bin after kernel smoothing.

where $A_m \subset \{1, \cdots, D\}$, $|A_m| \le r$, is a subset of feature dimensions and $[\mathbf{x}]_{A_m} = ([\mathbf{x}]_{d \in A_m})$ are $\mathbf{x}$'s values in the dimensions included in A_m.

Following the design of logistic regression, FFD models the following probability:

$$p(y = 1|\mathbf{x}) = \frac{1}{1 + \exp\left(-\sum_{m=1}^{M} w_m \phi_m(\mathbf{x})\right)}. \tag{11}$$

3.2 Kernel smoothing for histogram

FFD estimates $p(y = 1|[\mathbf{x}]_{A_m})$ via histogram-based density estimation. Since the cardinality $|A_m| \le r$ where $r \ll D$, it avoids the curse of dimensionality.

For relatively small datasets, the histogram estimation for the subspace specified by A_m is still unstable. First, if the length of bins is too small, there would be few data samples in each bin, resulting in inaccurate estimation. Second, the histogram estimation could be non-smooth for neighboring bins.

To address these issues, we propose to use a *bin kernel smoothing* technique, which allows the bins to affect each other according to their mutual kernel. Suppose $\mathbf{B} = (B_1, \cdots, B_{|A_m|})$ is a grid cell in the subspace specified by the dimensions in A_m and denote G_{A_m} as the set of all the grid cells in this subspace. We have the following smoothed estimate for grid cell $\mathbf{B}$

$$p(y|\mathbf{B}) = \frac{\sum_{\mathbf{B}' \in G_{A_m}} n_{\mathbf{B}'}(y) K^{bin}(\mathbf{B}, \mathbf{B}')}{\sum_{\mathbf{B}' \in G_{A_m}} N_{\mathbf{B}'} K^{bin}(\mathbf{B}, \mathbf{B}')} \tag{12}$$

where $n_{\mathbf{B}'}(y)$ is the the number of training samples with label y in $\mathbf{B}'$, and $N_{\mathbf{B}'}$ is the total number of training samples in $\mathbf{B}'$. The kernel between two grid cells $\mathbf{B}$ and $\mathbf{B}'$ is a Guassian kernel given by

$$K^{bin}(\mathbf{B}, \mathbf{B}') = \exp\left(-\sum_{d \in A_m} \frac{(B_d - B'_d)^2 l_d^2}{2h_d^2}\right) \tag{13}$$

where $h_d > 0$ is a parameter called the *bandwidth* of the kernel density function. A popular rule of thumb [27] for deciding the value of h_d is as follow:

$$h_d^* = 1.06\sigma_d N^{-1/5}, \tag{14}$$

where σ_d is the standard deviation of the training samples on d^{th} dimension. Figure 2 illustrates the kernel smoothing for a 1-dimensional histogram. As we can observe, $p(y = 1|\mathbf{B})$ in the third bin is originally very low due to the lack of data.

However, after kernel smoothing, this value gets higher and the overall histogram becomes smoother.

In essence, the proposed bin kernel smoothing is an approximation of KDE by discretizing each dimension into bins and treating all samples in the bin as located at the center of the bin. Not surprisingly, we can show that the approximation error approaches zero as the discretization is fine enough.

PROPOSITION 1. *As $b_d \to \infty$, the conditional probability estimated by (12) approaches the result by the Nadaraya-Watson estimator [3]*

$$\hat{p}(y=1|[\boldsymbol{x}]_{A_m}) = \frac{\sum_{i\in\mathcal{D}_1} K_{A_m}(\boldsymbol{x},\boldsymbol{x}_i)}{\sum_{i=1}^{N} K_{A_m}(\boldsymbol{x},\boldsymbol{x}_i)} \tag{15}$$

where $\mathcal{D}_1$ is the set of training samples with label $y=1$ and $K_{A_m}(\boldsymbol{x}_1,\boldsymbol{x}_2)$ is a Guassian kernel function on variables specified by A_m, namely,

$$K_{A_m}(\boldsymbol{x}_1,\boldsymbol{x}_2) = \exp\left(-\sum_{d\in A_m}\frac{([\boldsymbol{x}_1]_d-[\boldsymbol{x}_2]_d)^2}{2h_d^2}\right). \tag{16}$$

The size of memory required to store all histogram information is $O\left(\sum_{m=1}^{M} b_{A_m}\right)$ where $b_{A_m}=\prod_{d\in A_m} b_d$ is the total number of grid cells required for the subspace specified by A_m. Since $|A_m|$ is always very small (e.g. less than 3), the memory cost will not be large. One advantage of FFD is that the size of the model does not increase as the training dataset gets larger. This is different from other popular non-parametric models such as RBF-SVM and KNN. For example, in RBF-SVM all the support vectors should be stored. As the training set gets larger, the number of support vectors will also increase.

In addition, in the testing phase, the kernel matrix between support vectors and testing samples needs to be computed, resulting in $O(N_tN_s)$ running time where N_t is the size of the testing data and N_s is the number of support vectors. In contrast, FFD has a linear test time $O(N_t)$, since for a given testing sample FFD only needs to retrieve the value stored in the histogram in order to compute ϕ_m.

3.3 Submodular subspace selection

Let U be the ground set containing all subspace candidates, i.e. all $A_m \subset \{1,\cdots,D\}$ such that $|A_m|\le r$. The cardinality of U is $\sum_{k=1}^{r}\binom{D}{k}$. With so many candidates, one key challenge is to determine which subspaces in U to choose from. Here we propose a combinatorial optimization framework to address this problem. Suppose $S\subseteq U$ is the set of subspaces we select, we propose to find S such that

$$\underset{S}{\text{maximize}} \sum_{i\in S}\sum_{j\in U-S} c_{i,j} - \alpha\sum_{i,j\in S,i\neq j} c_{i,j} + \beta\sum_{i\in S} a_i - \mu|S|^2 \tag{17}$$

where $c_{i,j}$ is the Pearson correlation between ϕ_i and ϕ_j based on A_i and A_j, respectively. a_i is the training accuracy of the subspace estimation for G_{A_i}, which can be computed efficiently by simply checking the number of mislabeled samples in all grid cells of G_{A_i}. (α,β,μ) are all non-negative hyper-parameters.

The four components in (17) correspond to four different goals, respectively. 1) The first term, which is a cut function [10], maximizes the similarity coverage of the set U so that set S is a good representative of U. 2) The second term minimizes the pair-wise correlations within S to reduce the redundancy and relieve the problem of highly correlated features and co-linearity. 3) The third term maximizes the overall accuracy of histogram estimation of the selected subspaces. 4) The fourth term minimizes the cardinality of S for sparsity.

The maximization of (17) is a NP-hard problem. However, we show that (17) is a submodular maximization problem and good approximation bound can be achieved. We first introduce the concept of submodular set functions.

Definition 1. [10] Suppose U is the ground set, a set function $f: 2^U \to \mathcal{R}$ is submodular if it satisfies the property of diminishing return: for every $A,B\in U$, $A\subseteq B$, and every $e\in U-B$, we have that

$$f(A\cup e)-f(A) \ge f(B\cup e)-f(B). \tag{18}$$

If equality always holds in (18), f is modular.

It has been shown that maximizing a submodular function without any constraints can achieve a 1/3-approximation bound using a deterministic local search (DLS) algorithm [9, 13]. That is,

$$f_{obj}(S_g) \ge \frac{1}{3} f_{obj}(S^*),$$

where f_{obj} is the objective function in (17), S_g is the solution by the DLS algorithm, and S^* is the optimal solution. Note that this lower bound only occurs in the worst case. In practice, the performance is typically much better.

Now we prove the submodularity of (17).

THEOREM 1. *The objective function in (17) is submodular if $c_{i,j}\ge 0, \forall i,j\in U$.*

PROOF. Let

$$f_c(S) = \sum_{i\in S}\sum_{j\in U-S} c_{i,j} - \alpha\sum_{i,j\in S,i\neq j} c_{i,j}. \tag{19}$$

It has been shown that $f_c(S)$ is submodular if $c_{i,j}\ge 0, \forall i,j\in U$ [20]. Moreover, it is easy to verify that $\beta\sum_{i\in S} a_i$ is a modular function and that $-\mu|S|^2$ is submodular function according to Definition 1. Since submodularity is preserved under non-negative linear combination of submodular functions [10], we see that the the objective function in (17) is submodular. □

In practice, we find that most $c_{i,j}$ are non-negative, since each ϕ_m is an indicator of the label y and they are not likely to have negative correlation. For completeness, we have the following lemma to help guarantee the submodularity of (17).

LEMMA 1. *Let $\gamma = -\min\{\min_{i,j}\{c_{i,j}\},0\}$, then $f_c(S)-\gamma(1+\alpha)|S|^2$ is submodular where $f_c(S)$ is defined in (19).*

PROOF. Let e_S be the $|U|\times 1$ indicator vector of set S where U is the ground set, and $e_S(i)=1$ if $A_i\in S$ and 0 otherwise [4] (so e_U is a vector whose elements are all 1). Let C be the correlation matrix of all elements in U where its element (i,j) is $c_{i,j}$. We rewrite the function in matrix form as follows

$$\begin{aligned} f_c(S) &= e_S^\top C(e_U-e_S) - \alpha e_S^\top (C-I)e_S \\ &= e_S^\top Ce_U + \alpha e_S^\top Ie_S - (\alpha+1)e_S^\top Ce_S \\ &= e_S^\top Ce_U + \alpha|S| - (\alpha+1)e_S^\top Ce_S \end{aligned} \tag{20}$$

[4] $e_S(i)$ is the ith element in e_S

Suppose E is a $|U| \times |U|$ matrix with all elements being 1. It is easy to show that $|S|^2 = e_S^\top E e_S$. Thus, we have that

$$\begin{aligned} & f_c(S) - \gamma(1+\alpha)|S|^2 \\ =& e_S^\top C e_U + \alpha|S| - (\alpha+1)(e_S^\top C e_S + \gamma e_S^\top E e_S) \\ =& e_S^\top C e_U + \alpha|S| - (\alpha+1)e_S^\top (C+\gamma E) e_S \end{aligned} \quad (21)$$

Now we define

$$C^+ = C + \gamma E. \quad (22)$$

According to the definition of γ, we have that $\gamma \geq 0$ and elements in C^+ are all non-negative. Thus, $-(\alpha+1)e_S^\top(C + \gamma E)e_S$ is submodular due to the submodularity of negative quadratic function [2]. In addition, we can see that $e_S^\top C e_U + \alpha|S|$ is modular. Thus, $f_c(S) - \gamma(1+\alpha)|S|^2$ is submodular. $\square$

THEOREM 2. *When $\mu \geq \gamma$, the objective function in (17) is submodular and the DLS algorithm has a 1/3-approximation bound in the worst case.*

PROOF. According to Lemma 1, (17) can be rewritten as

$$\sum_{i\in S}\sum_{j\in U-S} c_{i,j}^+ - \alpha \sum_{i,j\in S, i\neq j} c_{i,j}^+ + \beta\sum_{i\in S} a_i - (\mu-\gamma)|S|^2, \quad (23)$$

where c^+i,j are elements in C^+ defined in (22). Since $c_{i,j}^+ \geq 0$, we see that (23) has the same form as defined in Theorem 1 if $\mu - \gamma \geq 0$. Thus, it is submodular and has a 1/3-approximation bound [9]. $\square$

In practice, we can first compute all the $c_{i,j}$ and γ, and then choose a μ value such that $\mu \geq \gamma$. Therefore, we can always guarantee the submodularity and optimization bound.

3.4 Sparse learning algorithm

Since the dimensionality of subspaces should be relatively small to avoid the curse of dimensionality, in this paper we have a restriction that $|A_m| \leq 2$. So there are $M = O(D(D+1)/2)$ potential $\phi_m(\mathbf{x})$ including 1-dimensional and 2-dimensional subspaces. After all those $\phi_m(\mathbf{x})$ are computed by smoothed histogram estimation and filtered by submodular subspace selection, we need to learn the weight vector $\mathbf{w} = (w_1, \cdots, w_M)$[5] in (11). We require strong sparsity on $\mathbf{w}$, which is not satisfied by the learning framework in (2).

One simple alternative is to replace the ℓ_2 regularization with ℓ_1 regularization [11] which promotes sparsity. However, the FFD model has a nice structure and can offer an even better solution. Let us rewrite (10) as

$$\phi_m(\mathbf{x}) = \ln\frac{p(y=1|[\mathbf{x}]_{A_m})}{1-p(y=1|[\mathbf{x}]_{A_m})} = g\left(p(y=1|[\mathbf{x}]_{A_m})\right) \quad (24)$$

where $g(z) = \ln\frac{z}{1-z}$ is a logit function. We can observe that $\phi_m(\mathbf{x})$ is an increasing function of $p(y=1|[\mathbf{x}]_{A_m})$. In addition, $\phi_m(\mathbf{x}) \geq 0$ if $p(y=1|[\mathbf{x}]_{A_m}) \geq 0.5$ and less than 0 otherwise. Given the monotonic relation between $p(y=1|\mathbf{x})$ and $\phi_m(\mathbf{x})$ in (11), the weight w_m on $\phi_m(\mathbf{x})$ is supposed to be non-negative under the assumption that $p(y=1|[\mathbf{x}]_{A_m})$ estimated by histogram is a weak learner. Given that $\mathbf{w}$ is non-negative, we have that $\|\mathbf{w}\|_1 = \sum_{m=1}^{M} w_m$. The learning formulation with ℓ_1 regularization becomes:

$$\begin{aligned} \underset{\mathbf{w}}{\text{minimize}} \quad & \frac{1}{N}\sum_{i=1}^{N}\left(1+e^{-y_i(\mathbf{w}\Phi(\mathbf{x}_i))}\right) + \lambda\sum_{m=1}^{M} w_m \\ \text{subject to} \quad & \mathbf{w} \geq 0 \end{aligned} \quad (25)$$

Compared with other ℓ_1 norm method, the ℓ_1 norm in our framework is differentiable for all feasible $\mathbf{w}$. Such a smooth optimization problem with simple bound constraints can be efficiently solved by gradient-descent solvers.

Using (25), FFD also enforces more sparsity than traditional ℓ_1 regularization. To see that, assume that the gradient of a positive w_m is negative. When doing gradient descent on it, w_m will tend to decrease its value. But due to the non-negative constraint, it cannot go below 0 and will thus end up at 0, which leads to even more sparse solution than ℓ_1 regularization.

The overall learning algorithm for FFD is shown in Algorithm 1.

[5]Now M is the number of ϕ_m after submodular subspace selection.

Algorithm 1 The learning algorithm for FFD

for $m = 1$ *to* M **do** ▷ Histogram estimation
    Build grid G_{A_m}.
    for $i = 1$ *to* N **do**
        Assign $\mathbf{x}_i$ to the grid cell indexed by (9)
    end for
    for $\mathbf{B} \in G_{A_m}$ **do**
        Compute $p(y|\mathbf{B})$ by (12)
    end for
end for
for $i = 1$ *to* N **do** ▷ Computing $\phi_m(\mathbf{x}_i)$
    for $m = 1$ *to* M **do**
        Compute $\phi_m(\mathbf{x}_i)$ by (10)
    end for
end for
Select subspaces by solving (17) using the DLS algorithm
Learn $\mathbf{w}$ by solving (25)

3.5 Discussions

We make a few further comments about FFD.

Cross validation. Before executing the complete algorithm of FFD as stated in Algorithm 1, all the hyperparameters should be pre-specified including λ in (25) and (α, β, μ) in (17). Experts can set these hyper-parameters by good intuition. For non-experts, a typical way to tune them is utilizing a k-fold cross-validation where grid search is performed on all hyper parameters to minimize the validation error. However, this brute-force algorithm has a high computational cost. In addition, it does not make use of the validation errors during the grid search.

As a better solution,we use a recent Bayesian optimization technique [28] to tune the hyper-parameters in order to globally minimize the validation error. Specifically, the validation error is modeled as a sample from a Gaussian Process (GP). Each time, we sample the hyper-parameters $(\lambda,\alpha, \beta, \mu)$ which minimize the expectation of its validation error under the assumption of GP. Then, Algorithm 1 is run on this hyper-parameter sample to evaluate its actual cross-validation error. This sample with its validation error are then incorporated in the previous GP and forms a new GP. This process keeps running until a maximum iteration limit is reached. The best hyper-parameters are the one that have the minimum cross-validation error among all the samples. It has been shown that this Bayesian optimization method for cross validation largely outperforms normal grid search [28].

Usefulness of submodular subspace selection. Though ℓ_1 regularization encourages sparsity, the performance of linear methods with ℓ_1 regularization (including logistic regression) suffers if the input variables are highly correlated or even co-linear [11,14]. Thus, before training FFD by solving (25), it is necessary and important to do subset selection on all ϕ_m in order to reduce their correlation.

Interpretability. Similar to LR, FFD can provide probability of its prediction in addition to the predicted label. However, in LR model the weights on different features may not be directly comparable. For example, the measurement of blood pressure has a vastly different scale than that of height, and their weights are not comparable. In contrast, the weights $\mathbf{w}$ in FFD do not suffer from this problem because all ϕ_m are on the same scale as they model conditional probabilities. In addition, each $\phi_m(\mathbf{x})$ is an indicator of $p(y = 1|[\mathbf{x}]_{A_m})$ because they have a monotonic relationship as shown in (10). With the sparsity of FFD, we can also identify which feature bags A_m are in fact *sufficient* to make accurate predictions based on the weights. Since kernel density estimation for the subspaces is highly nonlinear and approximates the true conditional distribution, FFD reliably learns the feature interactions.

4. RELATED WORK

Our FFD model is related to density-based logistic regression (DLR) [6] which transforms the original raw features to a new feature representation by KDE and then trains a logistic regression model on the new feature vectors. However, it does not promote sparsity and is not capable of handling feature interaction. In addition, compared to DLR, the feature transformation in FFD allows much faster computation, reducing the training time from $O(DN^2)$ to $O(DN)$ and the testing time from $O(DN)$ to $O(D)$.

In general, FFD is related to recent works on learning linear models with explicit nonlinear feature transformations. For example, random kitchen sinks (RKS) [24] transforms each data $\mathbf{x}$ into a finite-dimensional vector $\phi(\mathbf{x}) \in \mathcal{R}^M$ to approximate the RBF-kernel function for any two inputs $\mathbf{x}$ and $\mathbf{y}$ in such way that $\phi(\mathbf{x})^T\phi(\mathbf{y}) \approx K(x, y)$, where $K(\mathbf{x}, \mathbf{y})$ is the RBF kernel function. This allows highly scalable *linear* classifiers in the transformed space to learn approximately the same decision boundaries as SVM with a RBF kernel in the original input space. The recent fastfood algorithm [17] further speeds up RKS using matrix approximation techniques and reduces the time and space complexities. Other feature mapping techniques include those based on random projection [1,15,18,23], polynomial approximation [21], and hashing [19,32]

Existing feature mapping techniques, when combined with linear classifiers, can achieve both nonlinear separability and higher scalability of linear classifiers. However, they cannot take advantage of the interpretability of linear classifiers. The feature mapping techniques such as Fourier transformation, random projection, and hashing are all defined in a different space than that of the original features. As a result, these models do not provide a weight for each original feature dimension and cannot offer a clear notion of interpretability. Moreover, all these works except for [18] do not explicitly support sparsity.

Table 1: Comparison of the characteristics of different classifiers.

	LR	SVM-rbf	DLR	RKS	FFD
Interpretable	Yes	No	Yes	No	Yes
Efficient	Yes	No	No	Yes	Yes
Nonlinear	No	Yes	Yes	Yes	Yes
Sparse	Yes	No	No	No	Yes

5. EXPERIMENTAL RESULTS

In this section, we conduct extensive experiments to evaluate the proposed FFD model. We evaluate three versions of FFD.

- FFD-1: FFD with only 1-dimensional subspaces, i.e. $|A_m| \leq 1$, and without submodular subspace selection.
- FFD-2: FFD with 1-dimensional and 2-dimensional subspaces, i.e. $|A_m| \leq 2$, and without submodular subspace selection.
- FFD-sfo: FFD-2 with submodular optimization for subspace selection.

In FFD-2 and FFD-sfo, for ϕ_m involving two dimensions, we picks the top $3D$ out of $D(D-1)/2$ such ϕ_m's according to their accuracies for histogram estimation, where D is the dimensionality of the training samples. For all the three methods, we set the number of bins for numerical features to 50, i.e. $b_d = 50$. For submodular maximization in (17), we use the *sfo* toolbox developed by Andreas Krause [16]. To solve the sparse learning problem in (25), we use the minConf_TMP function[6]. This function is superior at optimizing smooth objective functions subject to bound constraints, which is exactly our case.

Baseline methods. We also consider four other methods for comparison. 1) Logistic regression with ℓ_1 regularization (LR) [11], implemented by Mark Schmidt [25]. 2) Support vector machines with the RBF kernel (SVM-rbf). We use the LibSVM library [5]. 3) Density-based Logistic Regression (DLR) [6], a linear classifier with nonlinear feature mapping based on the naive Bayes assumption. 4) Random Kitchen Sink (RKS) [24], a linear classifier with nonlinear feature mapping that approximates the RBF kernel.

A comparison of the characteristics of these models is given in Table 1. We can see that FFD is the only model that can support *all* of the desirable properties including interpretability, nonlinearity, efficiency, and sparsity.

Cross validation. The hyper-parameters in all methods are tuned via cross validation. The cross validations are performed by Bayesian optimization which has been proved to be far more efficient and accurate than a simple grid search [28]. For the RKS model, we also cross validate all

[6]Available at
`http://www.di.ens.fr/~mschmidt/Software/minConf`

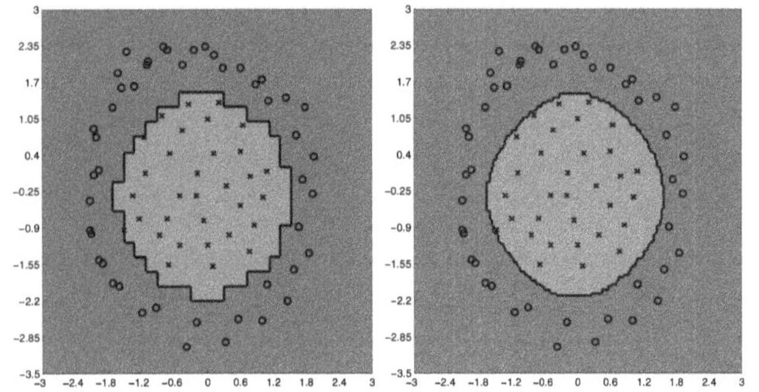

Figure 3: The decision boundary of FFD-1 on a toy example. Left: FFD-1 with 20 bins for each dimension. Right: FFD-1 with 100 bins for each dimension.

types of features including random Fourier features and random binning features.

Visualization of a toy example. We create a nonlinearly separable dataset to visualize the classification ability of FFD method and the effect of using different number of bins, as shown in Figure 3. We can observe that the FFD-1 can perfectly separate the two classes while other linear methods cannot. We also see that, as the number of bins increases, the decision boundary gets smoother.

Comprehensive evaluation. Table 2 shows a comprehensive comparison of all methods on various datasets. All these datasets are publicly available at the UCI repository[7] or the LibSVM website[8]. The datasets are sorted by the number of samples in the datasets. The experiments are run on an off-the-shelve desktop with two 8-core Intel(R) Xeon(R) processors of 2.67 GHz and 128*GB* of RAM. The implementations of all methods are in or through the interface of MATLAB^{TM}. In order for SVM-rbf to run as fast as possible, we set the cache size of LibSVM to 10*GB* which is sufficiently large for all the tested datasets.

From Table 2, we can observe the following facts.

In terms of accuracy, the performance of FFD methods is fairly strong in general. Datasets including checkboard, banana, mnist38 and cod-rna are well-known for its high non-linearity, which can be told by the poor performance of LR on these datasets. However, both FFD-2 and FFD-sfo perform almost as good as SVM-rbf and RKS, which demonstrates their superior nonlinear classification ability. And for datasets including splice and Adult, FFD methods largely outperforms all the other methods.

In terms of running time, we can see that FFD models are very efficient in general, which is fairly comparable with and sometimes even better than the linear machines LR and RKS. For example, the Adult dataset has 14 features, among which 8 are categorical. Models such as LR, SVM-rbf and RKS should first convert the categorical features to numerical features before training. The most popular method, as recommended in [31], is using k binary numerical features to represent an k-category feature. For example, (red,blue,green) can be represented by (1,0,0), (0,1,0) and (0,0,1). We observe that the original 14 features increase to 104 features at the end, which adds to the burden of training. In contrast, our FFD models naturally handle categorical features since each category is a bin in its dimension and no kernel smoothing is needed, leading to superior time efficiency.

We also see that FFD models are much more efficient than nonlinear models such as SVM-rbf and DLR. For the cod-rna dataset with 0.27 million samples, it takes FFD models less than 1 second while SVM-rbf spends over 10 minutes and DLR cannot finish. The improvement is even more salient on the kddcup99 dataset which contains almost 5 million samples. We make kddcup99 a binary classified dataset by setting class 6 to a positive class and other classes to a negative class, since class 6 contains 57% of the samples. It takes FFD models less than one minute while it is prohibitively large for both SVM-rbf and DLR.

However, though FFD-sfo generally has good accuracy and efficiency, we also point out that the cost of submodular optimization is sensitive to the dimensionality of the datasets, and using submodular subspace selection may not be the most sensible for image datasets such as mnist38. However, even for the mnist38 dataset, FFD-sfo is much faster than SVM-rbf and DLR, while FFD-1 and FFD-2 are extremely fast.

In terms of practical usability, FFD models give interpretability and sparsity, while other nonlinear models including SVM-rbf and RKS do not. In summary, FFD is a clear winner considering all the aspects.

Cases of highly correlated features. As stated in Section 3, linear methods including models with ℓ_1 regularization become more unstable and less accurate when highly correlated features or co-linearity exist. Although FFD methods are capable of classifying nonlinear datasets, they are linear models on ϕ_m and thus may also suffer from this issue. In this case, FFD-sfo is better than FFD-2 since it rules out highly correlated ϕ_m by maximizing the submodular objective function in (17). This effect has been partially reflected in Table 2.

To demonstrate the advantage of FFD-sfo over FFD-2 in a more observable way, we conduct another experiment in the feature selection context. First, we make a new splice data set by duplicating each feature, which makes them co-linear. Then, we run FFD-2 and FFD-sfo on both the original and new datasets. For reference, we also run the LR and Lasso [11] models which are state-of-the-art feature selection methods. For FFD methods, one feature is considered selected if it is used by any ϕ_m whose $w_m \neq 0$. Figure 4 shows the curves about accuracy versus number of selected features. First, we observe that FFD methods is much better than LR and Lasso since FFD offers nonlinear separability. Second, although FFD-2 and FFD-sfo have comparable performance on the original dataset, FFD-sfo is way better than FFD-2 on the new dataset, demonstrating the ability of FFD-sfo in addressing the issue of highly correlated or co-linear features.

Real-world clinical prediction. In addition to evaluation on public benchmark datasets, we also test FFD models on a real-world clinical application. This is a collaboration with Barnes-Jewish Hospital, one of the largest hospitals in the US. The task is to predict potential ICU transfers for hospitalized patients based on 34 vital signs. The data col-

[7]`https://archive.ics.uci.edu/ml/datasets.html`
[8]`http://www.csie.ntu.edu.tw/~cjlin/libsvmtools/datasets/binary.html`

Table 2: Performance of various methods on various datasets. Note that the FFD models have the additional advantages of interpretability and sparsity, which are not found in SVM-rbf and RKS. "N/A" means unfinished in 2 hours or memory overflow.

Dataset	N	D	Performance	LR	SVM-rbf	DLR	RKS	FFD-1	FFD-2	FFD-sfo
breast	683	9	accuracy(%)	96.63	96.05	97.36	97.07	96.34	97.51	97.07
			time(sec)	0.0164	0.0165	0.0574	0.0573	0.0278	0.4242	0.5779
splice	1000	60	accuracy(%)	80.70	87.20	92.00	90.10	91.60	94.60	94.50
			time(sec)	0.0144	0.2468	0.4069	0.0679	0.0835	1.235	2.2159
checkboard	2000	2	accuracy(%)	49.70	93.95	51.00	92.50	51.25	92.20	92.30
			time(sec)	0.0143	0.1454	0.0589	0.8763	0.0188	0.0434	0.07
banana	5300	2	accuracy(%)	56.70	90.45	71.89	89.57	71.74	89.72	89.91
			time(sec)	0.0126	0.6449	0.2354	0.5021	0.0326	0.0516	0.0298
musk	6598	166	accuracy(%)	94.33	90.69	95.21	96.42	96.88	95.06	94.71
			time(sec)	1.2882	58.6402	23.1885	0.7666	1.0141	4.1618	25.139
mnist38	11982	784	accuracy(%)	96.77	99.11	97.09	97.28	96.32	98.69	98.98
			time(sec)	0.9187	230.1897	1621	0.4323	2.0696	1.0952	122.419
magic04	14226	10	accuracy(%)	79.50	86.38	82.59	84.57	81.40	82.21	84.98
			time(sec)	0.2639	20.145	21.6976	1.6225	0.3211	0.188	0.4033
Adult	30162	14	accuracy(%)	84.71	80.43	85.41	83.96	85.40	85.31	85.42
			time(sec)	6.8223	492.7818	81.8001	3.8515	0.4057	3.1718	1.1399
cod-rna	271617	8	accuracy(%)	75.08	91.75	N/A	92.29	77.34	89.53	89.73
			time(sec)	0.785	629.759	N/A	5.7484	0.6583	1.0074	0.7651
kddcup99	4898431	41	accuracy	99.99	N/A	N/A	99.92	99.99	99.99	99.99
			runtime(sec)	179.2541	N/A	N/A	41.3827	46.2968	50.0306	54.0227

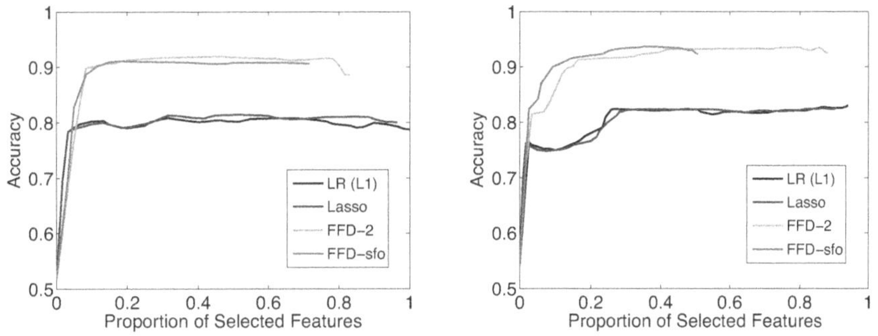

Figure 4: Accuracy vs. proportion of selected features. Left: The original splice dataset; Right: The new splice dataset with co-linear features.

lection process can be found in [6]. On this dataset, FFD-sfo and FFD-2 have 95.37% and 94.59% accuracy, respectively. The results outperform the DLR model with a 93.26% accuracy which is found to be better than LR and SVM [6]. Moreover, FFD is the only model that can offer sparsity and interpretability. This is vitally important in clinical practice since healthcare personnel can be informed of the most important risk factors and take proper actions for prevention and intervention.

6. CONCLUSIONS

Many applications in the big data era find existing classifiers inadequate. They often require not only high accuracy but also high efficiency, sparsity, and interpretability. To date no classifier, linear or nonlinear, excel at all these aspects. We have presented a novel Fast Flux Discriminant (FFD) model which delivers all these desirable properties. FFD learns a linear discriminant on top of a non-parametric feature mapping which captures nonlinear feature interactions. FFD addresses the curse of dimensionality by decomposing the kernel density estimation in the original feature space into low-dimensional subspaces. We have also proposed a submodular optimization framework to select subspaces and to address the problem of highly correlated features and collinearity. Moreover, FFD attains feature sparsity using ℓ_1 regularization. A nice feature of FFD is that its density-based features naturally have non-negative weights and hence allows for smooth optimization, which is not previously possible for ℓ_1 regularization. Empirical results have shown that FFD delivers similar accuracy as state-of-the-art nonlinear classifiers, but with sparsity, interpretability, and much better scalability. To the best of our knowledge, this is the first classifier that possesses all these merits. Given its unprecedented combination of advantages, we believe FFD will become a popular general-purpose classification model for a large scope of real-world applications such as biomedical prediction.

7. ACKNOWLEDGMENTS

WC and YC are supported in part by the CNS-1017701, CCF-1215302, and IIS-1343896 grants from the National Science Foundation of the United States, a Microsoft Research New Faculty Fellowship, a Washington University URSA grant, and a Barnes-Jewish Hospital Foundation grant. KQW is supported by NSF grants 1149882, 1137211.

8. REFERENCES

[1] D. Achlioptas. Database-friendly random projections: Johnson-Lindenstrauss with binary coins. *Journal of Computer and System Science*, 66:671–687, 2003.

[2] F. Bach. Learning with submodular functions: A convex optimization perspective. *Foundations and Trends in Machine Learning*, 2013.

[3] C. M. Bishop. *Pattern Recognition and Machine Learning*. Springer-Verlag New York, Inc., Secaucus, NJ, USA, 2006.

[4] L. Breiman. Random forests. *Machine Learning*, 45(1):5–32, 2001.

[5] C.-C. Chang and C.-J. Lin. LIBSVM: A library for support vector machines. *ACM Transactions on Intelligent Systems and Technology*, 2:27:1–27:27, 2011.

[6] W. Chen, Y. Chen, Y. Mao, and B. Guo. Density-based logistic regression. In *Proceedings of the 19th ACM SIGKDD*, KDD '13, pages 140–148, New York, NY, USA, 2013. ACM.

[7] B. Efron, T. Hastie, I. Johnstone, and R. Tibshirani. Least angle regression. *The Annals of statistics*, 32(2):407–499, 2004.

[8] R.-E. Fan, K.-W. Chang, C.-J. Hsieh, X.-R. Wang, and C.-J. Lin. Liblinear: A library for large linear classification. *The Journal of Machine Learning Research*, 9:1871–1874, 2008.

[9] U. Feige and V. S. Mirrokni. Maximizing non-monotone submodular functions. In *In Proceedings of 48th Annual IEEE Symposium on Foundations of Computer Science (FOCS*, page 2007, 2007.

[10] S. Fujishige. *Submodular Functions and Optimization: Second Edition*. Annals of Discrete Mathematics. Elsevier Science, 2005.

[11] T. Hastie, R. Tibshirani, and J. H. Friedman. *The Elements of Statistical Learning*. Springer, 2009.

[12] G. E. Hinton, S. Osindero, and Y.-W. Teh. A fast learning algorithm for deep belief nets. *Neural computation*, 18(7):1527–1554, 2006.

[13] R. Iyer, S. Jegelka, and J. A. Bilmes. Fast semidifferential-based submodular function optimization. In *International Conference on Machine Learning (ICML)*, Atlanta, Georgia, 2013.

[14] G. James, T. Hastie, D. Witten, and R. Tibshirani. *An Introduction to Statistical Learning: With Applications in R*. Springer, 2013.

[15] P. Kar and H. Karnick. Random feature maps for dot product kernels. In *Proc. AISTATS*, 2012.

[16] A. Krause. Sfo: A toolbox for submodular function optimization. *The Journal of Machine Learning Research*, 11:1141–1144, 2010.

[17] Q. Le, T. Sarlos, and A. Smola. Fastfood - computing hilbert space expansions in loglinear time. In *Proceedings of the 30th International Conference on Machine Learning*, volume 28, pages 244–252, May 2013.

[18] P. Li, T. J. Hastie, and K. W. Church. Very sparse random preojections. In *Proc. SIGKDD*, pages 287–296, 2006.

[19] P. Li and A. Konig. b-bit minwise hasing. In *Proc. WWW*, 2010.

[20] H. Lin and J. Bilmes. Multi-document summarization via budgeted maximization of submodular functions. ACL-HLT '10, pages 912–920, Stroudsburg, PA, USA, 2010. Association for Computational Linguistics.

[21] K. Lin and M. Chen. Efficient kernel approximation for large-scale support vector machine classification. In *Proc. SIGKDD*, 2011.

[22] O. Pele, B. Taskar, A. Globerson, and M. Werman. The pairwise piecewise-linear embedding for efficient non-linear classification. In *Proceedings of The 30th International Conference on Machine Learning*, pages 205–213, 2013.

[23] N. Pham and R. Pagh. Fast and scalable polynomial kernels via explicit feature maps. In *Proc. SIGKDD*, 2013.

[24] A. Rahimi and B. Recht. Random features for large-scale kernel machines. In J. Platt, D. Koller, Y. Singer, and S. Roweis, editors, *Advances in Neural Information Processing Systems 20*. MIT Press, Cambridge, MA, 2008.

[25] M. Schmidt, G. Fung, and R. Rosales. Fast optimization methods for l1 regularization: A comparative study and two new approaches. In *ECML*, volume 4701, pages 286–297. 2007.

[26] B. Schölkopf and A. J. Smola. *Learning with kernels*. The MIT Press, 2002.

[27] B. W. Silverman and P. J. Green. *Density Estimation for Statistics and Data Analysis*. Chapman and Hall, 1986.

[28] J. Snoek, H. Larochelle, and R. Adams. Practical bayesian optimization of machine learning algorithms. In *Advances in Neural Information Processing Systems 25*, pages 2960–2968. 2012.

[29] R. Tibshirani. Regression shrinkage and selection via the lasso. *Journal of the Royal Statistical Society. Series B (Methodological)*, pages 267–288, 1996.

[30] A. Vedaldi and A. Zisserman. Efficient additive kernels via explicit feature maps. *Pattern Analysis and Machine Intelligence, IEEE Transactions on*, 34(3):480–492, 2012.

[31] C. wei Hsu, C. chung Chang, and C. jen Lin. A practical guide to support vector classification, 2010.

[32] K. Weinberger, A. Dasgupta, J. Langford, A. Smola, and J. Attenberg. Feature hashing for large scale multitask learning. In *Proc. ICML*, 2009.

[33] G. Yuan, C. Ho, and C. Lin. Recent advances of large-scale linear classification. *Proceedings of the IEEE*, 100:2584–2603, 2012.

Scalable Histograms on Large Probabilistic Data

Mingwang Tang and Feifei Li
School of Computing, University of Utah, Salt Lake City, USA
{tang, lifeifei}@cs.utah.edu

ABSTRACT

Histogram construction is a fundamental problem in data management, and a good histogram supports numerous mining operations. Recent work has extended histograms to probabilistic data [5–7]. However, constructing histograms for probabilistic data can be extremely expensive, and existing studies suffer from limited scalability [5–7]. This work designs novel approximation methods to construct scalable histograms on probabilistic data. We show that our methods provide constant approximations compared to the optimal histograms produced by the state-of-the-art in the worst case. We also extend our methods to parallel and distributed settings so that they can run gracefully in a cluster of commodity machines. We introduced novel synopses to reduce communication cost when running our methods in such settings. Extensive experiments on large real data sets have demonstrated the superb scalability and efficiency achieved by our methods, when compared to the state-of-the-art methods. They also achieved excellent approximation quality in practice.

Categories and Subject Descriptors

H.2.4 [**Information Systems**]: Database Management—*Systems*

Keywords

histogram; scalable method; probabilistic database

1. INTRODUCTION

In many applications, uncertainty naturally exists in the data due to a variety of reasons. For instance, data integration and data cleaning systems produce fuzzy matches [10, 21]; sensor/RFID readings are inherently noisy [4, 9]. Numerous research efforts were devoted to represent and manage data with uncertainty in a probabilistic database management system [18, 21]. Many interesting mining problems have recently surfaced in the context of uncertain data e.g., mining frequent pattern and frequent itemset [1, 3, 24]. In the era of big data, along with massive amounts of data from different application and science domains, uncertainty in the data is only expected to grow with larger scale.

Histograms are important tools to represent the distribution of feature(s) of interest (e.g., income values) [15, 19]. Not surprisingly, using the possible worlds semantics [8, 21], histograms are also useful tools in summarizing and working with probabilistic data [5–7]. Given that answering queries with respect to all possible worlds is in #P-complete complexity [8], obtaining a compact synopsis or summary of a probabilistic database is of essence for understanding and working with large probabilistic data [5–7]. For example, they will be very useful for mining frequent patterns and itemsets from big uncertain data [1, 3, 24].

Cormode and Garofalakis were the first to extend the well-known V-optimal histogram (a form of bucketization over a set of one dimension values) [15], and wavelet histogram [16] to probabilistic data [6, 7], followed by the work by Cormode and Deligiannakis [5]. Note that histogram construction can be an expensive operation, even for certain data, e.g., the exact algorithm for building a V-optimal histogram is based on a dynamic programming formulation, which runs in $O(Bn^2)$ for constructing B buckets over a domain size of n [15]. Not surprisingly, building histograms on probabilistic data is even more challenging. Thus, existing methods [5–7] do not scale up to large probabilistic data, as evident from our analysis and experiments in this work.

Thus, this work investigates the problem of scaling up histogram constructions in large probabilistic data. Our goal is to explore quality-efficiency tradeoff, when such tradeoff can be analyzed and bounded in a principal way. Another objective is to design methods that can run efficiently in parallel and distributed fashion, to further mitigate the scalability bottleneck using a cluster of commodity machines.

Overview. A probabilistic database characterizes a probability distribution of an exponential number of possible worlds, and each possible world is a realization (deterministic instance) of the probabilistic database. Meanwhile, the query result on a probabilistic database essentially determines a distribution of possible query answers across all possible worlds. Given the possible worlds semantics, especially for large probabilistic data, approximate query answering based on compact synopsis (e.g., histogram) is more desirable in many cases, e.g., cost estimations in optimizers and approximate frequent items [3, 5–7, 21, 24, 26].

Conventionally, histograms on a deterministic database seek to find a set of constant bucket representatives for the

KDD'14, August 24–27, 2014, New York, NY, USA.
Copyright 2014 ACM 978-1-4503-2956-9/14/08 ...$15.00.
http://dx.doi.org/10.1145/2623330.2623640 .

data distribution subject to a given space budget of buckets and an error metric. Building histograms on deterministic databases has been widely explored and understood in the literature. In probabilistic databases, building the corresponding histograms need to address the following problems: (I) how to combine the histograms on each possible world; (II) how to compute the histogram efficiently without explicitly instantiating all possible worlds.

One meaningful attempt is building histograms that seek to minimize the expected error of a histogram's approximation of item frequencies across all possible worlds, using an error metric, which was first proposed in [6, 7]. One concrete application example might be estimating the expected result size of joining two probabilistic relations based on the corresponding histograms, or evaluating queries asking for an expected value approximately.

It is *important to note that for many error metrics, this histogram is not* the same as simply building a histogram for expected values of item frequencies; and the latter always provides (much) worse quality in representing the probabilistic database with respect to a number of commonly used error metrics, as shown in [6, 7]

Based on this definition, a unified dynamic programming (DP) framework of computing optimal histograms on the probabilistic data was proposed in [6, 7] with respect to various kinds of error metrics. Specifically, for the widely used sum of square error (SSE), it costs $O(Bn^2)$ time where B is the number of buckets and n is the domain size of the data. Immediately, we see that the optimal histogram construction suffers from quadratic complexity with respect to the domain size n. For a domain of merely 100,000 values, this algorithm could take almost a day to finish and render it unsuitable for many data sets in practice.

Summary of contributions. Inspired by these observations, we propose constant-factor approximations for histograms on large probabilistic data. By allowing approximations, we show that it is possible to allow users to adjust the efficiency-quality tradeoff in a principal manner.

We propose a novel "partition-merge" method to achieve this objective. We introduce "recursive merging" to improve the efficiency, while the histogram quality achieved will not significantly deviate from the optimal version. We also devise novel synopsis techniques to enable distributed and parallel executions in a cluster of commodity machines, to further mitigate the scalability bottleneck. To that end,

- We review the problem of histogram constructions on probabilistic data in Section 2, and highlight the limitations in the state-of-the-art.
- We design PMERGE in Section 3, which gives constant-factor approximations and scales up the histogram construction on large probabilistic data. PMERGE uses a "partition-merge" approach to realize efficiency-quality tradeoff. It also admits "recursive-merging" to allow further efficiency-quality tradeoff.
- We extend our investigation to distributed and parallel settings in Section 4, and introduce novel synopsis methods to support computation- and communication-efficient execution of our methods in distributed and parallel fashion in Section 5.
- We conduct extensive experiments on large data sets in Section 6. The results suggest that our approximation methods have achieved significant (orders of magnitude) run-time improvement compared to the state-of-the-art approach with high-quality approximation.

In addition, we survey other related works in Section 7 and conclude the paper in Section 8. *Unless otherwise specified*, proofs of theorems and lemmas were omitted due the space constraint and for brevity; they are available in Appendix B of our online technical report [25].

2. BACKGROUND AND STATE OF THE ART

Uncertain data models. Sarma *et al.* [20] describes various models of uncertainty, varying from the simplest *basic model* to the (very expensive) *complete model* that can describe any probability distribution of data instances.

Basic model is a over-simplification with no correlations. Existing work on histograms on uncertain data [5–7] adopted two popular models that extend the basic model, i.e., the *tuple model* and the *value model*, and compared their properties and descriptive abilities. The *tuple* and *value* models are two common extensions of the basic model in terms of the tuple- and attribute-level uncertainty [20], that were extensively used in the literature (see discussion in [5–7]).

Without loss of generality, we consider that a probabilistic database $\mathcal{D}$ contains one relation (table). We also concentrate on the one dimension case or one attribute of interest.

Definition 1 *The tuple model* was originally proposed in TRIO [2]. An uncertain database $\mathcal{D}$ has a set of tuples $\tau = \{t_j\}$. Each tuple t_j has a discrete probability distribution function (pdf) of the form $\langle(t_{j1}, p_{j1}), \ldots, (t_{j\ell_j}, p_{j\ell_j})\rangle$, specifying a set of mutually exclusive *(item, probability)* pairs. Any t_{jk}, for $k \in [1, \ell_j]$, is *an item drawn from a fixed domain* and p_{jk} is the probability that t_j takes the value t_{jk} in the jth row of a relation.

When instantiating this uncertain relation to a possible world W, each tuple t_j either draws a value t_{jk} with probability p_{jk} or generates no item with probability of $1 - \sum_{k=1}^{\ell_j} p_{jk}$. The probability of a possible world W is simply the multiplication of the relevant probabilities.

Definition 2 *The value model* is a sequence τ of independent tuples. Each tuple gives the *frequency distribution of a distinct item* of the form $\langle\, j : f_j = ((f_{j1}, p_{j1}), \ldots, (f_{j\ell_j}, p_{j\ell_j}))\,\rangle$. Here, j is an item drawn from a fixed domain (e.g., source IP) and its associated pdf f_j describes the distribution of j's possible frequency values.

In particular, $\Pr[f_j = f_{jk}] = p_{jk}$ where f_{jk} is a frequency value from a frequency value domain $\mathcal{V}$; f_j is subject to the constraint that $\sum_{jk} p_{jk} \leq 1$ for $k \in [1, \ell_j]$. When it is less than 1, the remaining probability corresponds that *the item's frequency is zero.* When instantiating this uncertain relation to a possible world W, for an item j, its frequency f_j either takes a frequency value f_{jk} with probability p_{jk} or takes zero as its frequency value with probability $1 - \sum_{k=1}^{\ell_j} p_{jk}$. So the probability of a possible world W is computed as the multiplication of the possibilities of f_j's taking the corresponding frequency in each tuple.

2.1 Histograms on probabilistic data

Without loss of generality, in both models, we consider the items are drawn from the integer domain $[n] = \{1, ..., n\}$ and use $\mathcal{W}$ to represent the set of all possible worlds. Let N be the size of a probabilistic database, i.e., $N = |\tau|$.

For an item $i \in [n]$, g_i *is a random variable for the distribution of i's frequency over all possible worlds*, i.e,

$$g_i = \{(g_i(W), \Pr(W)) | W \in \mathcal{W}\}, \quad (1)$$

where $g_i(W)$ is item i's frequency in a possible world W and $\Pr(W)$ is the possibility of W.

Example 1 Consider an ordered domain $[n]$ with three items $\{1, 2, 3\}$ for both models, i.e., $n = 3$.

The input $\tau = \{\langle(1, \frac{1}{2}), (3, \frac{1}{3})\rangle, \langle(2, \frac{1}{4}), (3, \frac{1}{2})\rangle\}$ *in the tuple model* defines eight possible worlds:

W	$\emptyset$	1	2	3	1, 2	1, 3	2, 3	3, 3
$\Pr(W)$	$\frac{1}{24}$	$\frac{1}{8}$	$\frac{1}{24}$	$\frac{1}{6}$	$\frac{1}{8}$	$\frac{1}{4}$	$\frac{1}{12}$	$\frac{1}{6}$

The input $\tau = \{\langle 1 : (1, \frac{1}{2})\rangle, \langle 2 : (1, \frac{1}{3})\rangle, \langle 3 : ((1, \frac{1}{2}), (2, \frac{1}{2}))\rangle\}$ *in the value model* defines eight possible worlds:

W	3	1, 3	2, 3	3, 3	1, 2, 3	1, 3, 3	2, 3, 3	1, 2, 3, 3
$\Pr(W)$	$\frac{1}{6}$	$\frac{1}{6}$	$\frac{1}{12}$	$\frac{1}{6}$	$\frac{1}{12}$	$\frac{1}{6}$	$\frac{1}{12}$	$\frac{1}{12}$

Consider the *tuple model* example from above and denote the eight possible worlds (from left to right) as $W_1, \ldots, W_8$. It's easy to see that $g_3(W) = 1$ for $W \in \{W_4, W_6, W_7\}$, $g_3(W) = 2$ for $W \in \{W_8\}$ and $g_3(W) = 0$ on the rest. Thus, the frequency random variable g_3 of item 3 is $g_3 = \{(0, \frac{1}{3}), (1, \frac{1}{2}), (2, \frac{1}{6})\}$ with respect to $\mathcal{W}$ in this example. Meanwhile, it's also easy to see $g_3 = \{(1, \frac{1}{2}), (2, \frac{1}{2})\}$ over $\mathcal{W}$ in the value model example from above.

Definition 3 A *B-bucket representation* partitions domain $[n]$ into B non-overlapping consecutive buckets (s_k, e_k) for $k \in [1, B]$, where $s_1 = 1$, $e_B = n$ and $s_{k+1} = e_k + 1$. Frequencies within each bucket b_k are approximated by a single representative $\widehat{b}_k$ and we represent it as $b_k = (s_k, e_k, \widehat{b}_k)$.

The B-bucket histogram achieving the minimal SSE error for approximating a deterministic data distribution is known as the V-optimal histogram [14]. It can be found using a dynamic programming formulation in $O(Bn^2)$ time [15], where n is the domain size of the underlying data distribution. We denote this method from [15] as the OptVHist method.

To extend histogram definitions to probabilistic data, we first consider a single possible world $W \in \mathcal{W}$ for a probabilistic data set $\mathcal{D}$, where W is *a deterministic data set*. Hence, the frequency vector of W is given by $G(W) = \{g_1(W), ..., g_n(W)\}$ (recall that $g_i(W)$ is item i's frequency in W). Given a B-bucket representation for approximating $G(W)$, the SSE of a bucket b_k in the world W is given as: $SSE(b_k, W) = \sum_{j=s_k}^{e_k} (g_j(W) - \widehat{b}_k)^2$. The SSE of the B-bucket representation in W is simply $\sum_{k=1}^{B} SSE(b_k, W)$.

Cormode and Garofalakis have extended B-bucket histogram to probabilistic data [6,7] by asking for the minimal expected SSE. Formally,

Definition 4 Given the (uncertain) frequency sequence of random variables $\{g_1, \ldots, g_n\}$ as defined in (1), the problem seeks to construct a B-bucket representation (typically $B \ll n$) such that the expected SSE over all possible worlds is minimized, i.e., the histogram with the value given by:

$$\mathcal{H}(n, B) = \min\{\mathrm{E}_{\mathcal{W}} \left[\sum_{k=1}^{B} \sum_{j=s_k}^{e_k} (g_j - \widehat{b}_k)^2 \right] \} \quad (2)$$

In (2), the expectation of the sum of bucket errors is equal to the sum of expectations of bucket errors [6,7], i.e.,

$$\mathrm{E}_{\mathcal{W}} \left[\sum_{k=1}^{B} \sum_{j=s_k}^{e_k} (g_j - \widehat{b}_k)^2 \right] = \sum_{k=1}^{B} \mathrm{E}_{\mathcal{W}} \left[\sum_{j=s_k}^{e_k} (g_j - \widehat{b}_k)^2 \right]. \quad (3)$$

Consequently, the optimal histogram could be derived by a dynamic programming formulation as follows:

$$\mathcal{H}(i, j) = \min_{1 \le \ell < i} \mathcal{H}(\ell, j-1) + \min_{\widehat{b}}(\ell + 1, i, \widehat{b}), \quad (4)$$

where $\mathcal{H}(i, j)$ represents the minimal error from the optimal j-buckets histogram on interval $[1, i]$; $\min_{\widehat{b}}(\ell + 1, i, \widehat{b})$ is the minimal bucket error for the bucket spanning the interval $[\ell + 1, i]$ using a single representative value $\widehat{b}$.

Previous work [6,7] showed that the cost of the optimal histogram is $O(Bn^2)$ and $\min_{\widehat{b}}(\ell+1, i, \widehat{b})$ could be computed in constant time using several precomputed prefix-sum arrays which we will describe in the following subsection. We dub this state-of-art method from [7] *the* OptHist *method.*

2.2 Efficient computation of bucket error

Cormode and Garofalakis [7] show that, for SSE, the minimal error of a bucket $b = (s, e, \widehat{b})$ is achieved by setting the representative $\widehat{b} = \frac{1}{e-s+1} \mathrm{E}_{\mathcal{W}} \left[\sum_{i=s}^{e} g_i \right]$. The corresponding bucket error is given by:

$$SSE(s, e, \widehat{b}) = \sum_{i=s}^{e} \mathrm{E}_{\mathcal{W}}[g_i^2] - \frac{1}{e - s + 1} \mathrm{E}_{\mathcal{W}}[\sum_{i=s}^{e} g_i]^2. \quad (5)$$

In order to answer the $\min_{\widehat{b}}(s, e, \widehat{b})$ query in (4) for any (s, e) values in constant time, prefix-sum arrays of $\mathrm{E}_{\mathcal{W}}[g_i^2]$ and $\mathrm{E}_{\mathcal{W}}[g_i]$ in equation (5) are precomputed as follows (details can be found in [7]):

$$A[e] = \sum_{i=1}^{e} \mathrm{E}_{\mathcal{W}}[g_i^2] = \sum_{i=1}^{e} (\mathrm{Var}_{\mathcal{W}}[g_i] + \mathrm{E}_{\mathcal{W}}[g_i]^2) \quad B[e] = \sum_{i=1}^{e} \mathrm{E}_{\mathcal{W}}[g_i] \quad (6)$$

tuple model: $\mathrm{E}_{\mathcal{W}}[g_i] = \sum_{t_j \in \tau} \Pr[t_j = i]$ and $\mathrm{Var}_{\mathcal{W}}[g_i] = \sum_{t_j \in \tau} \Pr[t_j = i](1 - \Pr[t_j = i])$.

value model: $\mathrm{E}_{\mathcal{W}}[g_i] = \sum_{v_j \in \mathcal{V}} v_j \Pr[g_i = v_j]$ and $\mathrm{Var}_{\mathcal{W}}[g_i] = \sum_{v_j \in \mathcal{V}} (v_j - \mathrm{E}_{\mathcal{W}}[g_i])^2 \Pr[g_i = v_j]$

Set $A[0] = B[0] = 0$, then the minimal SSE $\min_{\widehat{b}}(s, e, \widehat{b})$ for both models is computed as:

$$A[e] - A[s-1] - \frac{(B[e] - B[s-1])^2}{e - s + 1}.$$

In both models, in addition to the $O(Bn^2)$ cost as shown in last subsection, it also takes $O(N)$ cost to compute the A, B arrays ($N = |\tau|$, number of probabilistic tuples).

3. APPROXIMATE HISTOGRAMS

The state-of-the-art OptHist method from [7] is clearly not scalable, when given larger domain size.

A baseline method. A natural choice is to consider computing a B-bucket histogram for the *expected frequencies of all items.* Note that this histogram is not the same as the desired histogram as defined in equation (2) and (3) since in general $\mathrm{E}[f(X)]$ does not equal $f(\mathrm{E}[X])$ for arbitrary function f and random variable X.

However, we can show in our histogram, the SSE error of a bucket $[s, e]$ using $\widehat{b}$ as its representative is:

$$SSE(s, e, \widehat{b}) = \mathrm{E}_{\mathcal{W}}[\sum_{i=s}^{e} (g_i - \widehat{b})^2] = \sum_{i=s}^{e} (\mathrm{E}_{\mathcal{W}}[g_i^2] - 2\mathrm{E}_{\mathcal{W}}[g_i]\widehat{b} + \widehat{b}^2).$$

On the other hand, if we build a B-bucket histogram over the expected frequencies of all items, the error of a bucket $[s, e]$ using $\bar{b}$ as its representative is:

$$SSE(s,e,\bar{b}) = \sum_{i=s}^{e}(\mathrm{E}_{\mathcal{W}}[g_i]-\bar{b})^2 = \sum_{i=s}^{e}((\mathrm{E}_{\mathcal{W}}[g_i])^2-2\mathrm{E}_{\mathcal{W}}[g_i]\bar{b}+\bar{b}^2).$$

When using the same bucket configurations (i.e., the same boundaries and $\widehat{b} = \bar{b}$ for every bucket), the two histograms above differ by $\sum_{j=s}^{e}(\mathrm{E}_{\mathcal{W}}[g_i^2] - (\mathrm{E}_{\mathcal{W}}[g_i])^2) = \sum_{j=s}^{e} \mathrm{Var}_{\mathcal{W}}[g_i]$ on a bucket $[s, e]$. Hence, the overall errors of the two histograms differ by $\sum_{i\in[n]} \mathrm{Var}_{\mathcal{W}}[g_i]$ which is a constant. Given this and computing the expected frequencies of all items can be done in $O(N)$ time, computing the optimal B-bucket histogram for them (now a deterministic frequency vector) still requires the OptVHist method from [15], taking $O(Bn^2)$ for a domain of size n, which still suffers the same scalability issue.

A natural choice is then to use an approximation for the B-bucket histogram on expected frequencies (essentially a V-optimal histogram), as an approximation for our histogram. The best approximation for a V-optimal histogram is an $(1+\varepsilon)$-approximation [23] (in fact, to the best of our knowledge, it is the only method with theoretical bound on approximation quality). But when using approximations, one cannot guarantee that the same bucket configurations will yield the same approximation bound with respect to both histograms. So its theoretical guarantee is no longer valid with respect to our histogram. Nevertheless, it is worth comparing to this approach as a baseline method, which is denoted as the *EF-Histogram* method.

3.1 The PMerge method

Hence, we search for novel approximations that can provide error guarantees on the approximation quality and also offer quality-efficiency tradeoff, for the histograms from [6,7] as defined in (2). To that end, we propose a constant approximation scheme, PMerge, by leveraging a "partition-merge" principle. It has a *partition phase* and a *merge phase*.

Partition. The *partition phase* partitions the domain $[n]$ into m equally-sized sub-domains, $[s_1, e_1], \ldots, [s_m, e_m]$ where $s_1 = 1, e_m = n$ and $s_{k+1} = e_k + 1$. For the kth sub-domain $[s_k, e_k]$, we compute the A, B arrays on this domain as A_k, B_k for $k \in [1, m]$. A_k and B_k are computed using $[s_k, e_k]$ as an input domain and equation (6) for the value and the tuple models respectively,

Next, for each sub-domain $[s_k, e_k]$ ($k \in [1, m]$), we apply the OptHist method from [7] (as reviewed in Section 2.1) over the A_k, B_k arrays to find the *local optimal B-buckets histogram* for the kth sub-domain. The partition phase produces m local optimal B-bucket histograms, which lead to mB buckets in total.

Merge. The goal of the merge phase is to merge the mB buckets from the partition phase into optimal B buckets in terms of the SSE error using one merging step. To solve this problem, naively, we can view an input bucket $b = (s, e, \widehat{b})$ as having $(e - s + 1)$ items with identical frequency value $\widehat{b}$. Then, our problem reduces to precisely constructing an V-optimal histogram instance [15]. But the cost will be $O(B(\sum_{i=1}^{mB}(e_i - s_i + 1))^2)$ using the OptVHist method, which is simply $O(Bn^2)$.

A critical observation is that a bucket $b = (s, e, \widehat{b})$ can also be viewed as a *single weighted frequency* $\widehat{b}$ with a weight of $(e - s + 1)$, such that we can effectively reduce the domain size while maintaining the same semantics. Formally, let $Y = mB$. A weighted frequency vector $\{f_1, f_2, \ldots, f_Y\}$

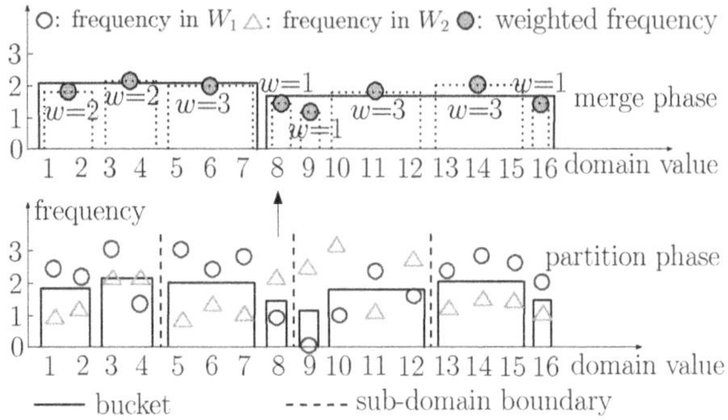

Figure 1: An example of PMerge: $n = 16, m = 4, B = 2$.

on an ordered domain $[Y]$ has a weight w_i for each f_i. It implies w_i items with a frequency f_i at i. The weighted version of the V-optimal histogram seeks to construct a B-bucket histogram such that the SSE between these buckets and the input weighted frequency vector is minimized. This problem is the same as finding:

$$\mathcal{H}_w(Y, B) = \min\{\sum_{k=1}^{B}\sum_{j=s_k}^{e_k} w_j(f_j - \widehat{b}_k)^2\},$$

where $s_1 = 1$ and $e_B = Y$. The optimal B buckets can be derived by a similar dynamic programming formulation as that shown in equation (4). The main challenge is to compute the optimal one-bucket $\min_{\widehat{b}}(s, e, \widehat{b})$ for any interval $[s, e]$ now in the weighted case. We show in Appendix A how to do this efficiently using several prefix sum arrays.

Thus the weighted optimal B-bucket histogram can be derived by filling a $Y \times B$ matrix, and each cell (i, j) takes $O(Y)$ time. Thus, the weighted B-bucket histogram is computed in $O(BY^2) = O(m^2B^3)$ time, which is much less than $O(Bn^2)$ since both B and m are much smaller than n.

An example. An example of PMerge is given in Figure 1, where $n = 16$, $B = 2$, and $m = 4$. To ensure clarity, we show only two possible worlds W_1 (blue circle) and W_2 (green triangle) from the set of possible worlds $\mathcal{W}$ of this database. In the partition phase, each sub-domain of size 4 is approximated by 2 local optimal buckets. In total, the partition phase has produced 8 buckets in Figure 1. In the merge phase, each input bucket maps to a weighted frequency as discussed above. For example, the first bucket covering frequencies in $[1, 2]$ represents a weighted frequency of 1.8 with weight 2. These 8 buckets were merged into two buckets as the final output.

Complexity analysis. In the partition phase, it takes linear time to compute the corresponding A_k, B_k arrays within each sub-domain $[s_k, e_k]$ for $k \in [1, m]$, following the results from [7]. The size of sub-domain $[s_k, e_k]$ is roughly n/m for $k \in [1, m]$. It takes $O(Bn^2/m^2)$ to run the OptHist method on A_k, B_k to find the kth local optimal B-bucket histogram. Next, the merge phase takes only $O(B^3m^2)$ time as analyzed above. Hence,

Lemma 1 PMerge *takes* $O(N + Bn^2/m + B^3m^2)$.

3.2 Approximation quality

In order to evaluate the absolute value of the histogram approximation error, we adopt the ℓ_2 distance (square root of SSE error) between the data distribution and the histogram synopsis. Next, we show the approximation quality of PMerge compared to the *optimal* B-bucket histogram found by OptHist in terms of the ℓ_2 distance.

Theorem 1 *Let $\|\mathcal{H}(n,B)\|_2$ and $\|\mathcal{H}_{\text{PMERGE}}(n,B)\|_2$ be the ℓ_2 norm of the SSE error of B-bucket histogram produced by* OPTHIST *and* PMERGE *respectively on domain $[n]$. Then, $\|\mathcal{H}_{\text{PMERGE}}(n,B)\|_2 < 3.17 \cdot \|\mathcal{H}(n,B)\|_2$.*

3.3 Recursive PMERGE

Note that the problem size of mB in the merge phase of PMERGE may still be too large to be handled efficiently by a DP method. Fortunately, we can further improve the efficiency by doing "recursive merging" as follows.

First of all, the partition phase will partition the input domain into m^ℓ equal-sized sub-domains, instead of only m sub-domains, for some integer ℓ (user specified).

The merge phase now *recursively* merges the $m^\ell B$ buckets from the partition phase into B buckets using ℓ iterations. Each iteration reduce the number of input buckets by a factor of m by applying a sequence of *merging steps*. Specifically, each merging step merges mB consecutive buckets (from left to right) from the current iteration into B buckets in the next iteration, which is done using the same merging step from the standard PMERGE method (i.e., using the weighted B-bucket histogram idea). We dub the recursive PMERGE methods RPMERGE.

Extending the analysis from Lemma 1 and Theorem 1 gives the following result, w.r.t the ℓ_2 norm of the SSE:

Theorem 2 *Using $O(N + B\frac{n^2}{m^\ell} + B^3\sum_{i=1}^{\ell} m^{(i+1)})$ time, the* RPMERGE *method gives a 3.17^ℓ approximation of the optimal B-bucket histogram found by* OPTHIST.

It is important to note that the approximation bounds in both Theorems 1 and 2 reflect the *worst-case analysis*. The extreme cases leading to the worst-case bounds are almost impossible in real data sets. In practice, PMERGE and its recursive version RPMERGE always provide *(very) close to optimal approximation quality* (much better than what these worst-case bounds indicate), as shown in our experiments.

4. DISTRIBUTED AND PARALLEL PMERGE

PMERGE allows efficient execution in a distributed and parallel framework. In the partition phase, each sub-domain can be handled independently in parallel.

The recursive PMERGE offers even more venues for parallelism. In this case, *its merge phase* can also run in a distributed and parallel fashion, since each merging step from every iteration can be processed independently.

Next, we'll address the challenge on computing the local A_k, B_k arrays efficiently for each sub-domain $[s_k, e_k]$ in a distributed and parallel setting . For both models, we assume that the underlying probabilistic database has been split into β chunks $\{\tau_1, \ldots, \tau_\beta\}$ and stored in a distributed file system (DFS). It is important to note that the input data is not necessarily sorted by the values of the items when stored into chunks in a DFS.

4.1 The partition phase in the value model

Recall that in the value model, f_i is a pdf describing item i's possible frequency values and their associated probabilities. We first show that:

Lemma 2 *In the value model, $\Pr[g_i = v] = \Pr[f_i = v]$ for any frequency value $v \in \mathcal{V}$ ($\mathcal{V}$ is the domain of all possible frequency values).*

Lemma 2 and equation (6) imply that:

Lemma 3 *The A, B arrays for the value model also equal: $A[j] = \sum_{i=1}^{j} \mathrm{E}[f_i^2]$, $B[j] = \sum_{i=1}^{j} \mathrm{E}[f_i]$.*

Without loss of generality, we assume β "data nodes (aka processes)" to consume the input data chunks, and also m "aggregate nodes/processes" to produce the local optimal B-bucket histograms. Each data chunk is processed by one data node in parallel. Each data node produces m partitions, each of which corresponds to a sub-domain of size (roughly) n/m, using a partition function $h : [n] \to [m]$, $h(i) = (\lceil i/\lceil n/m \rceil \rceil)$.

The ℓth data node processing chunk τ_ℓ reads in tuples in τ_ℓ in a streaming fashion. For each incoming tuple (i, f_i) found in τ_ℓ, it computes two values $(\mathrm{E}[f_i], \mathrm{E}[f_i^2])$. It then writes a key-value pair $(i, (\mathrm{E}[f_i], \mathrm{E}[f_i^2]))$ to the $h(i)$th partition. The $h(i)$th aggregate node will collect the $h(i)$th partitions from all β data nodes, the union of which forms the $h(i)$th sub-domain of the entire data.

Thus, the kth ($k \in [1, m]$) aggregate node will have all the key-value pairs $(i, (\mathrm{E}[f_i], \mathrm{E}[f_i^2]))$ for all $i \in [s_k, e_k]$ in the kth sub-domain, if item i exists in the database; otherwise it simply produces a $(i, (0, 0))$ pair for such $i \in [s_k, e_k]$.

That said, the kth aggregate node can easily compute the A_k, B_k arrays for the kth sub-domain using Lemma 3. It then uses the OPTHIST method on A_k, B_k to produce the kth local optimal B-bucket histogram. Clearly, all m aggregate nodes can run independently in parallel.

4.2 The partition phase in the tuple model

In the tuple model, the tuples needed to compute $\mathrm{Var}_\mathcal{W}[g_i]$ and $\mathrm{E}_\mathcal{W}[g_i]$ for each item i are distributed over β tuple chunks. Hence, we rewrite equation (6) for computing A, B arrays in the tuple model as follows:

Lemma 4 *The A, B arrays in the tuple model can also be computed as:*

$$A[j] = \sum_{i=1}^{j}\left(\sum_{\ell=1}^{\beta} \mathrm{Var}_{\mathcal{W},\ell}[g_i] + \left(\sum_{\ell=1}^{\beta} \mathrm{E}_{\mathcal{W},\ell}[g_i]\right)^2\right) \quad B[j] = \sum_{i=1}^{j}\sum_{\ell=1}^{\beta} \mathrm{E}_{\mathcal{W},\ell}[g_i],$$

where $\mathrm{Var}_{\mathcal{W},\ell}[g_i] = \sum_{t \in \tau_\ell} \Pr[t = i](1 - \Pr[t = i])$ and $\mathrm{E}_{\mathcal{W},\ell}[g_i] = \sum_{t \in \tau_\ell} \Pr[t = i]$.

A similar procedure as that described for the value model could then be applied. The difference is that the ℓth data node processing chunk τ_ℓ emits a key-value pair $(i, (\mathrm{E}_{\mathcal{W},\ell}[g_i], \mathrm{Var}_{\mathcal{W},\ell}[g_i]))$ instead, for *each distinct item i from the union of all possible choices of all tuples in τ_ℓ*. Thus, the kth aggregate node will reconstruct A_k, B_k arrays according to Lemma (4) and then use the OPTHIST method on A_k, B_k arrays to produce the local optimal B-bucket histogram for the kth sub-domain in the partition phase.

4.3 Recursive PMERGE and other remarks

For RPMERGE, we carry out the partition phase for each model using the method from Section 4.1 and Section 4.2 respectively. In the merge phase, we can easily invoke multiple independent nodes/processes to run all merging steps in one iteration in parallel. In the following, we denote the distributed and parallel PMERGE and RPMERGE methods as parallel-PMERGE and parallel-RPMERGE respectively.

5. PARALLEL-PMERGE WITH SYNOPSIS

A paramount concern in distributed computation is the communication cost. The parallel-PMERGE method may incur high communication cost for large domain size.

This cost is $O(n)$ in the value model. Given a set τ of tuples in a value model database with size $N = |\tau|$; τ is stored in β distributed chunks in a DFS. Each tuple will produce a key-value pair to be emitted by one of the data nodes. In the worst case $N = n$ (one tuple for each item of the domain), thus $O(n)$ cost. On the other hand, this cost is $O(\beta n)$ in the tuple mode. The worst case is when possible choices from all tuples in every distributed tuple chunk have covered all distinct items from the domain $[n]$.

There are only $O(Bm)$ bytes communicated in the merge phase of parallel-PMERGE for both models, where every aggregate node sends B buckets to a single node for merging. Thus, the communication cost of parallel-PMERGE is dominated by the partition phase.

We present novel synopsis to address this issue. The key idea is to approximate the A_k, B_k arrays at the kth aggregate node ($k \in [1, m]$) with unbiased estimators $\widehat{A}_k, \widehat{B}_k$ constructed by *either samples or sketches* sent from the data nodes. Since parallel-PMERGE and parallel-RPMERGE share the same partition phase, hence, the analysis above and the synopsis methods below *apply to both methods.*

5.1 Sampling methods for the value model

The VS method. One way of interpreting $\mathrm{E}[f_i^2]$ and $\mathrm{E}[f_i]$ is treating each of them as *an count of item* i in the arrays A_k and B_k respectively. Then $A_k[j]$ and $B_k[j]$ in Lemma 3 can be interpreted as *the rank* of j, i.e. the number of appearance of items from $[s_k, e_k]$ that are less than or equal to j in array A_k, B_k respectively. Using this view, we show how to construct an estimator $\widehat{B}_k[j]$ with the value model sampling method VS. The construction and results of $\widehat{A}_k[j]$ are similar.

Considering the ℓth data node that processes the ℓth tuple chunk τ_ℓ, we first define $T1(i,\ell) = \mathrm{E}[f_i^2]$ and $T2(i,\ell) = E[f_i]$ respectively if $(i, f_i) \in \tau_\ell$; otherwise we assign them as 0. We then define $A_{k,\ell}, B_{k,\ell}$ as follows, for every $k \in [1, m]$:

$$A_{k,\ell}[j] = \sum_{i=s_k}^{j} T1(i,\ell), B_{k,\ell}[j] = \sum_{i=s_k}^{j} T2(i,\ell), \text{ for any } j \in [s_k, e_k].$$

Using τ_ℓ, the ℓth data node can easily compute $A_{k,\ell}, B_{k,\ell}$ locally for all k and j values. It's easy to get the following results at *the kth aggregate node* for any $j \in [s_k, e_k]$:

$$A_k[j] = \sum_{\ell=1}^{\beta} A_{k,\ell}[j], B_k[j] = \sum_{\ell=1}^{\beta} B_{k,\ell}[j], \text{ for any } k \in [1, m]. \quad (7)$$

We view $B_{k,\ell}[j]$ as the *local rank* of j from τ_ℓ at the ℓth data node. By (7), $B_k[j]$ is simply *the global rank of* j that equals the sum of all local ranks from β nodes. We also let $M_k = \sum_{j=s_k}^{e_k} \mathrm{E}[f_j]$.

For every tuple (i, f_i) from τ_ℓ, data node ℓ unfolds (conceptually) $\mathrm{E}[f_i]$ copies of i, and samples each i independently with probability $p = \min\{\Theta(\sqrt{\beta}/\varepsilon M_k), \Theta(1/\varepsilon^2 M_k)\}$. If a copy of i is sampled, it is added to a sample set $S_{k,\ell}$ where $k = h(i)$, using the hash function in Section 4.1. If c_i copies of i are sampled, we add $(i,1), \ldots, (i, c_i)$ into $S_{k,\ell}$. The pairs of values in $S_{k,\ell}$ are sorted by the item values from the first term, and ties are broken by the second term. Data node ℓ sends $S_{k,\ell}$ to the kth aggregate node for $k \in [1, m]$.

We define the *rank* of a pair (i, x) in $S_{k,\ell}$ as the number of pairs ahead of it in $S_{k,\ell}$, denoted as $r((i, x))$. For any $j \in [s_k, e_k]$ and $\ell \in [1, \beta]$, aggregate node k computes an estimator $\widehat{B}_{k,\ell}[j]$ for the local rank $B_{k,\ell}[j]$ as: $\widehat{B}_{k,\ell}[j] = r((j, c_j))/p + 1/p$, if item j is present in $S_{k,\ell}$.

If an item $j \in [s_k, e_k]$ is not in $S_{k,\ell}$, let y be the predecessor of j in $S_{k,\ell}$ in terms of *item values*, then $\widehat{B}_{k,\ell}[j] = \widehat{B}_{k,\ell}[y] + 1/p$. If no predecessor exists, then $\widehat{B}_{k,\ell}[j] = 0$.

It then estimates the global rank $B_k[j]$ for $j \in [s_k, e_k]$ as:

$$\widehat{B}_k[j] = \sum_{\ell=1}^{\beta} \widehat{B}_{k,\ell}[j]. \quad (8)$$

Lemma 5 *$\widehat{B}_k[j]$ in (8) is an unbiased estimator of $B_k[j]$ and* $\mathrm{Var}[\widehat{B}_k[e]]$ *is* $O((\varepsilon M_k)^2)$.

The communication cost is $\sum_{\ell,j} p = O(\min\{\sqrt{\beta}/\varepsilon, 1/\varepsilon^2\})$ for $\ell \in [1, \beta]$ and $j \in [s_k, e_k]$ for aggregate node k in the worst case. Hence, the total communication cost in the partition phase of PMERGE with VS is $O(\min\{m\sqrt{\beta}/\varepsilon, m/\varepsilon^2\})$. Note that $\{M_1, \ldots, M_m\}$ can be easily precomputed in $O(m\beta)$ communication cost.

5.2 Sketching methods for the tuple model

The TS (tuple model sketching) method. Observe that we can rewrite equations in Lemma 4 to get:

$$A_k[j] = \sum_{\ell=1}^{\beta} \sum_{i=s_k}^{j} \mathrm{Var}_{\mathcal{W},\ell}[g_i] + \sum_{i=s_k}^{j} (\sum_{\ell=1}^{\beta} \mathrm{E}_{\mathcal{W},\ell}[g_i])^2$$

$$B_k[j] = \sum_{\ell=1}^{\beta} \sum_{i=s_k}^{j} \mathrm{E}_{\mathcal{W},\ell}[g_i]. \quad (9)$$

We can view $\sum_{i=s_k}^{j} \mathrm{Var}_{\mathcal{W},\ell}[g_i]$ and $\sum_{i=s_k}^{j} \mathrm{E}_{\mathcal{W},\ell}[g_i]$ as a local rank of j in a separate local array computed from τ_ℓ. Similarly, estimation of the global rank, i.e., the first term of $A_k[j]$ and $B_k[j]$ in (9), can be addressed by the VS method.

The challenge is to approximate $\sum_{i=s_k}^{j} (\mathrm{E}_{\mathcal{W}}[g_i])^2$, the second term of $A_k[j]$ in (9). It is the second frequency moment (F_2) of $\{\mathrm{E}_{\mathcal{W}}[g_{s_k}], \ldots, \mathrm{E}_{\mathcal{W}}[g_j]\}$. Given that each $\mathrm{E}_{\mathcal{W}}[g_i]$ is a distributed sum and j varies over $[s_k, e_k]$, we actually need a *distributed method* to answer a *dynamic F_2 (energy) range query* approximately on a sub-domain $[s_k, e_k]$.

The key idea is to build AMS sketches [17] for a set of *intervals from a carefully constructed binary decomposition* on each sub-domain locally at every data node.

For a sub-domain $[s_k, e_k]$ at the kth aggregate node, let $M_k'' = \sum_{i=s_k}^{e_k} (\mathrm{E}_{\mathcal{W}}[g_i])^2$. The leaf-level of the binary decomposition partitions $[s_k, e_k]$ into $1/\varepsilon$ intervals, where each interval's F_2 equals $\varepsilon M_k''$. An index-level (recursively) concatenates every two consecutive intervals from the level below to form a new interval (thus, the height of this binary decomposition is $O(\log\lceil \frac{1}{\varepsilon} \rceil)$). Figure 2(a) illustrates this idea.

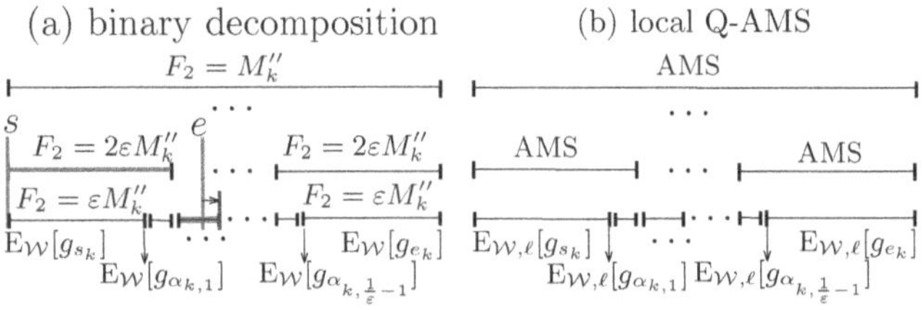

Figure 2: Binary decomposition and local Q-AMS.

Once the $(\frac{1}{\varepsilon} - 1)$ partition boundaries $\{\alpha_{k,1}, \ldots, \alpha_{k,\frac{1}{\varepsilon}-1}\}$ at the leaf-level were found, aggregate node k sends them to all β data nodes. Each data node builds a set of AMS sketches, one for each interval from the binary decomposition (of all levels), over its local data. We denote it as the local *Q-AMS sketch* (Queryable-AMS).

In other words, data node ℓ builds these AMS sketches using $\{E_{\mathcal{W},\ell}[g_{s_k}], \ldots, E_{\mathcal{W},\ell}[g_{e_k}]\}$ as shown in Figure 2(b). Then data node ℓ sends its Q-AMS sketch for $[s_k, e_k]$ to the kth aggregate node, which combines β local Q-AMS sketches into a *global Q-AMS* sketch for the kth sub-domain $[s_k, e_k]$, leveraging on the linearly-mergeable property of each individual AMS sketch [12, 17]. The global Q-AMS sketch is equivalent to a Q-AMS sketch that is built from $\{E_{\mathcal{W}}[g_{s_k}], \ldots, E_{\mathcal{W}}[g_{e_k}]\}$ directly; recall that $E_{\mathcal{W}}[g_i] = \sum_{\ell=1}^{\beta} E_{\mathcal{W},\ell}[g_i]$.

For a query range (s, e), $s_k \leq s < e \leq e_k$, we find the intervals that form the canonical cover of (s, e) in the global Q-AMS sketch, and approximate $(E_{\mathcal{W}}[g_s])^2 + \cdots + (E_{\mathcal{W}}[g_e])^2$ by the summation of the F_2 approximations (from the AMS sketches) of these intervals. If (s, e) is not properly aligned with an interval at the leaf-level of an Q-AMS sketch, we snap s and/or e to the nearest interval end point.

The error from the snapping operation in the leaf-level is at most $O(\varepsilon M''_k)$. By the property of the AMS sketch [17], the approximation error of any AMS sketch in the global Q-AMS sketch is at most $O(\varepsilon F_2(I))$, with at least probability $(1 - \delta)$, for an interval I covered by that AMS sketch. Also $F_2(I) \leq M''_k$ for any I in the global Q-AMS sketch. Furthermore, there are at most $O(\log \frac{1}{\varepsilon})$ intervals in a canonical cover since the height of the tree in Q-AMS is $\log\lceil \frac{1}{\varepsilon} \rceil$. Hence, the approximation error for any range F_2 query in the global Q-AMS sketch is $O(\varepsilon M''_k \log \frac{1}{\varepsilon})$ with probability at least $(1 - \delta)$, for $\varepsilon, \delta \in (0, 1)$ used in the construction of the Q-AMS sketch. Finally, the size of an AMS sketch is $O(\frac{1}{\varepsilon^2} \log \frac{1}{\delta})$ [12, 17]. Thus, we can show that:

Lemma 6 *Given the partition boundaries* $\{\alpha_{k,1}, \ldots, \alpha_{k,\frac{1}{\varepsilon}-1}\}$ *for a sub-domain* $[s_k, e_k]$*, for any* s, e *such that* $s_k \leq s < e \leq e_k$*, Q-AMS can approximate* $(E_{\mathcal{W}}[g_s])^2 + (E_{\mathcal{W}}[g_{s+1}])^2 + \cdots + (E_{\mathcal{W}}[g_e])^2$ *within an additive error of* $O(\varepsilon M''_k \log \frac{1}{\varepsilon})$ *with probability* $\geq (1 - \delta)$ *using space of* $O(\frac{1}{\varepsilon^3} \log \frac{1}{\delta})$.

Communication cost and partition boundaries. Each aggregate node needs to send $(\frac{1}{\varepsilon} - 1)$ values per sub-domain to all β data nodes, and there are m sub-domains in total. So the communication cost of this step is $O(m\beta/\varepsilon)$. Then, each data node needs to send out m local Q-AMS sketches, one for each sub-domain. The communication cost of this step is $O(\frac{m\beta}{\varepsilon^3} \log \frac{1}{\delta})$. Hence, the total communication is $O(\frac{m\beta}{\varepsilon^3} \log \frac{1}{\delta})$, which caters for the worst-case analysis.

But the above method and analysis depend on the calculation of the partition boundaries $\{\alpha_{k,1}, \ldots, \alpha_{k,\frac{1}{\varepsilon}-1}\}$ for any sub-domain $[s_k, e_k]$, for $k \in [1, m]$. To calculate this exactly we need $\{E_{\mathcal{W}}[g_{s_k}], \ldots, E_{\mathcal{W}}[g_{e_k}]\}$ at the kth aggregate node, which obviously are not available (unless using $O(n\beta)$ total communication for β data nodes for all sub-domains, which defeats our purpose). Fortunately, given that VS can estimate each $B_k[j]$ with an ε error efficiently, each $E_{\mathcal{W}}[g_i]$ can be estimated as $(\widehat{B}_k[i] - \widehat{B}_k[i-1])$ By (9).

6. EXPERIMENTS

We implemented all methods in Java. We test OPTHIST, EF-Histogram, PMERGE and RPMERGE methods in centralized environment without parallelism, and parallel-PMERGE and parallel-RPMERGE methods (with and without synopsis) in distributed and parallel settings. The centralized experiments were executed over a Linux machine running a single Intel i7 3.2GHz cpu, with 6GB of memory and 1TB disk space. We then used MapReduce as the distributed and parallel programming framework and tested all methods in a Hadoop cluster with 17 machines (of the above configuration) running Hadoop 1.0.3. The default HDFS (Hadoop distributed file system) chunk size is 64MB.

Datasets. We executed our experiments using the WorldCup data set and the SAMOS data set. The WorldCup data set is the access logs of 92 days from the 1998 World Cup servers, composed of 1.35 billion records. Each record consists of client id, file type and time of access etc. We choose the client id as the item domain, which has a maximum possible domain size of 2,769,184. We vary the domain size of client ids from 10,000 up to 1,000,000. Records in the entire access log are divided into continuous but disjoint groups, in terms of access time. We generate a discrete frequency distribution pdf for items within each grouping interval and assign the pdf to a tuple in the *tuple model*. For the *value model*, we derive a discrete pdf for each client id based on its frequency distribution in the whole log with respect to 13 distinct requested file types and assign the pdf to the tuple with that client id in the value model. The SAMOS data set is composed of 11.8 million records of various atmospheric measurements from a research vessel and we care about the temperature field, which has a domain size of about 10,000 (by counting two digits after the decimal point of a fraction reading). In a similar way, we form the tuple model and value model data on the SAMOS data.

Setup. The default data set is WorldCup. To accommodate the limited scalability of OPTHIST, we initially vary the value of n from 10,000 up to 200,000 and test the effects of different parameters. The default values of parameters are $B = 400$ and $n = 100,000$. For RPMERGE, the recursion depth is $\ell = 2$. We set $m = 16$ and $m = 6$ as the default values for PMERGE and RPMERGE respectively. We then explore the scalability of our methods, up to a domain size of $n = 1,000,000$. The running time of all methods are only linearly dependent on N, number of tuples in a database. Hence, we did not show the effect of N; all reported running time are already *start-to-end wall-clock* time.

In each experiment, unless otherwise specified, we vary the value of one parameter, while using the default values of other parameters. The approximation ratios of our approximate methods were calculated with respect to the optimal B-buckets histogram produced by OPTHIST [6, 7].

6.1 Centralized environment

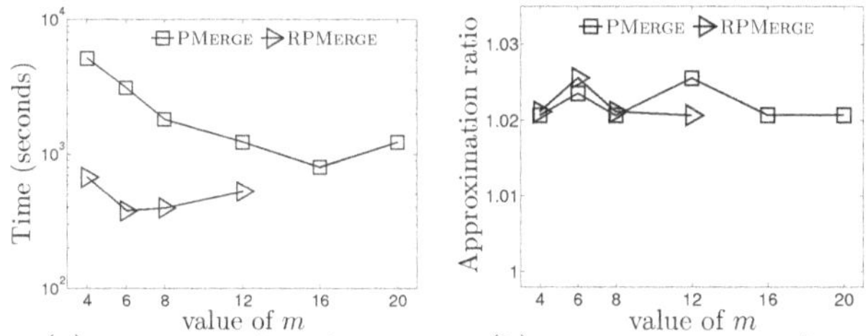

(a) m vs running time. (b) m vs approx. ratio.

Figure 4: Vary m on the tuple model.

Effect of m. Figure 4 shows the running time and approximation ratio when we vary m from 4 to 20 on the tuple model data sets. Recall that PMERGE will produce m sub-domains, while RPMERGE will produce m^{ℓ} sub-domains, in the partition phase. Hence, RPMERGE gives the same number of sub-domains using a (much) smaller m value. For both methods, a larger m value will reduce the size of each

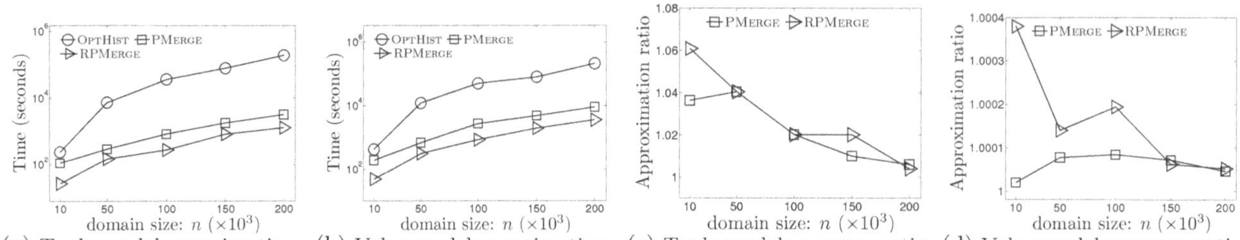

(a) Tuple model: running time. (b) Value model: running time. (c) Tuple model: approx. ratio. (d) Value model: approx. ratio.

Figure 5: Approximation ratio and running time: vary n.

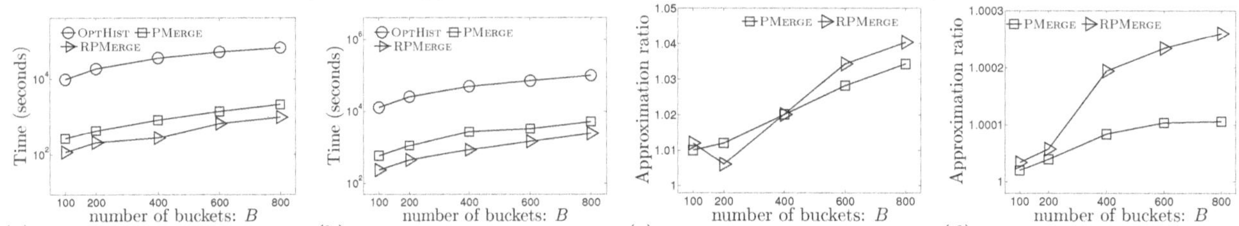

(a) Tuple model: running time. (b) Value model: running time. (c) Tuple model: approx. ratio. (d) Value model: approx. ratio.

Figure 6: Approximation ratio and running time: vary B.

sub-domain, hence, reducing the runtime of the OPTHIST method on each sub-domain and the overall cost of the partition phase. But a larger m value increases the cost of the merge phase. As a result, we expect to see a sweet point of the overall running time across all m values. Figure 4(a) reflects exactly this trend and the same trend holds on the value model data set as well. They consistently show that $m = 16$ and $m = 6$ provide the best running time for PMERGE and RPMERGE respectively. Note that this sweet point can be analytically analyzed, by taking derivative of the cost function (partition phase + merge phase) with respect to m.

Figure 4(b) shows their approximation ratios on the tuple model data set. The approximation quality of both methods fluctuates slightly with respect to m; but they both produce B-buckets histograms of extremely high quality with approximation ratio very close to 1. The quality is much better than their worst-case theoretical bounds, as indicated by Theorems 1 and 2 respectively.

The results of varying m from the value model are very similarly, and have been omitted for brevity. Also, we have investigated the results of varying the recursive depth ℓ from 1 to 3. They consistently show that $\ell = 2$ achieves a nice balance between running time and approximation quality. For brevity, we ommited the detailed results.

Effect of n. Figure 5 shows the results with respect to n on both value and tuple models. In both models, the running time of OPTHIST increases quadratically with respect to n. In contrast, both PMERGE and RPMERGE are much more scalable, and have outperformed OPTHIST by at least one to two orders of magnitude in all cases. For example, in Figure 5(b), when $n = 100,000$, OPTHIST took nearly 14 hours while RPMERGE took only 861 seconds. RPMERGE further improves the running time of PMERGE by about 2-3 times and is the most efficient method.

Meanwhile, both PMERGE and RPMERGE achieve close to 1 approximation ratios across all n values in Figures 5(c) and Figure 5(d). The approximation quality gets better (approaching optimal) as n increases on both models.

Effect of B. We vary the number of buckets from 100 to 800 in Figure 6. Clearly, RPMERGE outperforms OPTHIST by two orders of magnitude in running time in both models, as see in Figures 6(a) and 6(b). Figures 6(c) and 6(d) show the approximation ratios in each model respectively. The approximation ratio of both PMERGE and RPMERGE slightly increases when B increases on both models. Nevertheless, the quality of both methods are still excellent, remaining very close to the optimal results in all cases.

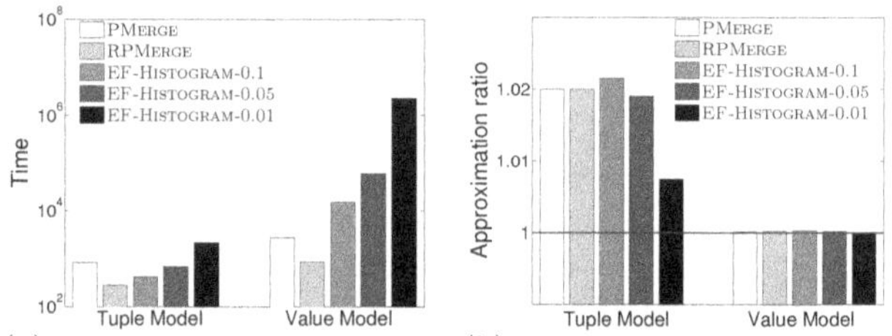

(a) Running time: WorldCup. (b) Approx. ratio: WorldCup.

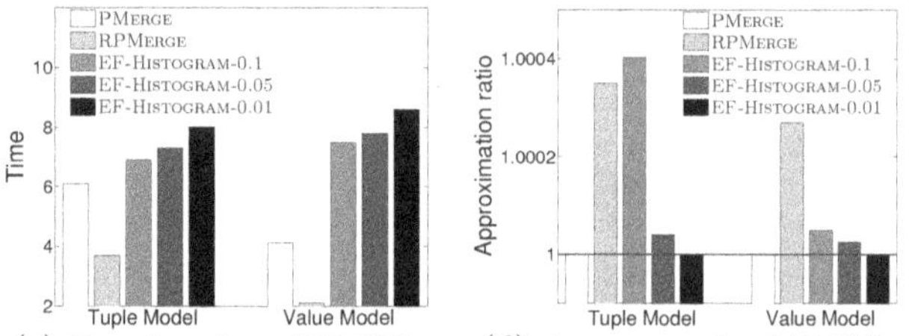

(c) Running time: SAMOS. (d) Approx. ratio: SAMOS.

Figure 7: Comparison against the baseline method.

Comparison with the baseline. Lastly, we compare the running time and approximation ratios of our methods against the baseline EF-Histogram method (with $\varepsilon = 0.1, \varepsilon = 0.05$ and $\varepsilon = 0.01$ respectively) on two data sets. Our methods used their default parameter values on the WorldCup data set. For the SAMOS data set, we set $n = 10,000$ and $B = 100$. Clearly, small ε values does help improve the approximation quality of EF-Histogram as shown in Figure 7(b) and Figure 7(d). But our methods have provided almost the same approximation quality on both data sets, while offering worst-case bounds in theory as well. Note that EF-Histogram only provides the $(1+\varepsilon)$ approximation bound with respect to the B-buckets histogram on expected frequencies, but not on the probabilistic histograms.

Meanwhile, the running time of EF-Histogram increases significantly (it is actually quadratic to the inverse of ε value,

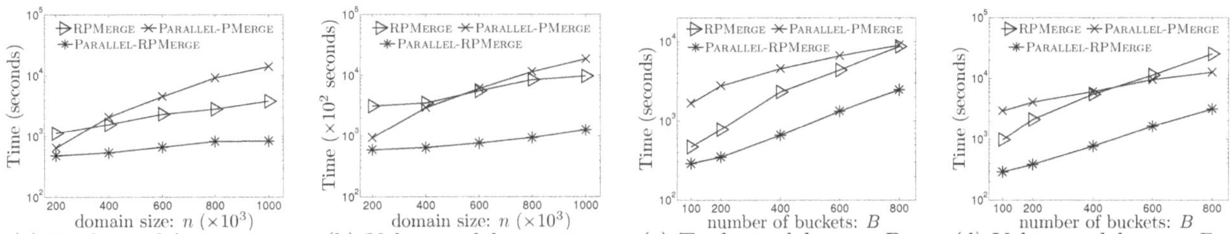

(a) Tuple model: vary n. (b) Value model: vary n. (c) Tuple model: vary B. (d) Value model: vary B.

Figure 8: Scalability of the parallel approximate methods.

i.e., $1/\varepsilon^2$), especially on the much larger WorldCup data set. In all cases our best centralized method, RPMERGE, has significantly outperformed the EF-Histogram as shown in Figure 7(a) and Figure 7(c). Furthermore, the distributed and parallel fashion of PMERGE and RPMERGE further improves the efficiency of these methods, as shown next.

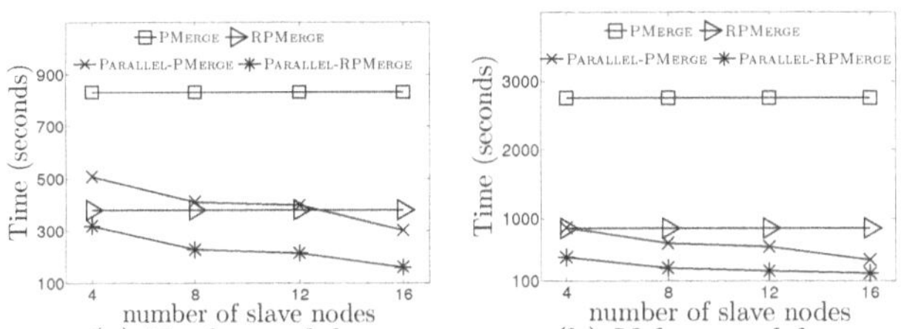

(a) Tuple model. (b) Value model.

Figure 9: Time: vary number of slave nodes.

6.2 Distributed and parallel setting

Effect of size of the cluster. Figure 9 shows the running time of different methods when we vary the number of slave nodes in the cluster from 4 to 16. For reference, we have included the running time of centralized PMERGE and RPMERGE. We can see a (nearly) linear dependency between the running time and the number of slave nodes for both parallel-PMERGE and parallel-RPMERGE methods. The speed up for both methods is not as much as the increasing factor of the number of slave nodes used. The reason is that Hadoop always includes some extra overhead such as job launching and tasks shuffling and IO cost of intermediate HDFS files, which reduces the overall gain from parallelism.

Scalability. Next, we investigate the scalability of RPMERGE (the best centralized method), parallel-PMERGE and parallel-RPMERGE on very large probabilistic data sets. We used all 16 slave nodes in the cluster, and varied either the values of n from 200,000 to 1000,000 when $B = 400$, or the values of B from 100 to 800 when $n = 600,000$. We omit OPTHIST and PMERGE methods in this study, since they are too expensive compared to these methods.

Figures 8(a) and 8(b) show that with recursive merging RPMERGE can even outperform parallel-PMERGE as n increases. But clearly parallel-RPMERGE is the best method and improves the running time of RPMERGE by 8 times on the value model and 4 times on the tuple model when $n = 1000,000$. It becomes an order of magnitude faster than parallel-PMERGE in both models when n increases.

Figures 8(c) and 8(d) show the running time when we vary B and fix $n = 600,000$. Running time of all methods increase with larger B values. This is because large B values increase the computation cost of the merging step, especially for recursive PMERGE. Nevertheless, parallel-RPMERGE significantly outperforms both parallel-PMERGE and RPMERGE in all cases on both models.

6.3 Distributed and parallel synopsis

Lastly, we study the communication saving and approximation quality of parallel-PMERGE and parallel-RPMERGE with synopsis. The default values are $n = 600,000$, $B = 400$ and $\varepsilon = 0.002$ for VS and $\varepsilon = 0.1$ for TS. We have omitted the results for the running time of Parallel-PMERGE and Parallel-RPMERGE with synopsis, since they are very close to that of Parallel-PMERGE and Parallel-RPMERGE respectively (since the running time of all these methods are dominated by solving the DP instances in the partition and merging phases).

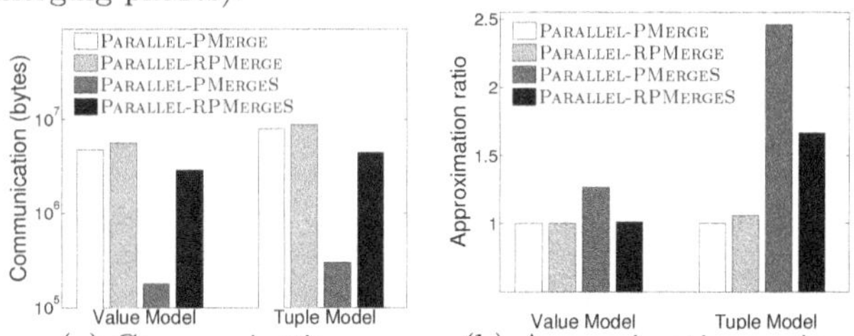

(a) Communication. (b) Approximation ratio.

Figure 10: Effects of using synopsis.

Comparing effects of synopsis in both models. Here we use parallel-PMERGES (parallel-RPMERGES) to denote a parallel-PMERGE (parallel-RPMERGE) method with a synopsis in either model. In value model, the synopsis is VS; and in tuple model, the synopsis is TS.

Figure 10(a) shows that parallel-PMERGES outperforms parallel-PMERGE and parallel-RPMERGE by more than an order of magnitude in communication cost for both models. Parallel-RPMERGES has much higher communication cost than parallel-PMERGES since the sampling cost in the partition phase has increased by an order of m using m^2 subdomains (when $\ell = 2$). Nevertheless, it still saves about 2-3 times of communication cost compared to that of parallel-PMERGE and parallel-RPMERGE for both models.

Figure 10(b) shows that parallel-PMERGES and parallel-RPMERGES have excellent approximation quality on the value model (very close to optimal histograms). They give less optimal approximations in the tuple model, since Q-AMS in the TS method has higher variances in its estimated A, B arrays in the tuple model, compared to the estimations on A, B arrays given by VS in the value model.

Remarks. The communication cost of all of our synopsis methods are independent of n, whereas the communication cost of both parallel-PMERGE and parallel-RPMERGE are linearly dependent on n, as shown from our analysis in Section 5. This means the synopsis methods introduce even more savings when domain size increases.

7. RELATED WORK

We have reviewed the most relevant related work in Section 2. That said, extensive efforts were devoted to constructing histograms in deterministic data, motivated by the early work in [14–16,19]. An extensive survey for histograms on deterministic data is in [13]. There are also numerous efforts on modeling, querying, and mining uncertain data; see [1, 3, 21, 24]. A good histogram for large probabilistic data is very useful for many such operations, e.g, finding frequent items, patterns, and itemsets [1,3,24,26].

However, little is known about histograms over probabilistic data till three recent studies [5–7]. Cormode and Garofalakis have extended the bucket-based histogram and the wavelet histogram to probabilistic data by seeking to minimize the expectation of bucket errors over all possible worlds [6,7]. The details of which can be found in Section 2. Cormode and Deligiannakis then extend the probabilistic histogram definition to allowing bucket with a pdf representation rather than a single constant value [5]. A main limitation of these studies is the lack of scalability, when the domain size of the probabilistic data increases.

Allowing some approximations in histogram construction is also an important subject on deterministic data, e.g., [11, 22, 23] and many others. One possible choice is to run these methods on expected frequencies of all items, and simply use the output as an approximation to our histogram. But the theoretical approximation bound with respect to the deterministic data (in our case, the expected frequencies of all items) does not carry over to probabilistic histogram definition with respect to n random variables (frequency distributions of every item i). To the best of our knowledge, the $(1+\varepsilon)$ approximation from [23] is the best method with theoretical guarantees for histograms over deterministic data (in fact, to the best of our knowledge, other methods are mostly heuristic-based approaches). We did explore this approach as a baseline method in our study.

8. CONCLUSION

This paper designed novel approximation methods for constructing optimal histograms on large probabilistic data. Our approximations run much faster and have much better scalability than the state-of-the-art. The quality of the approximate histograms are almost as good as the optimal histograms in practice. We also introduced novel techniques to extend our methods to distributed and parallel settings, which further improve the scalability. Interesting future work include but not limited to how to extend our study to probabilistic histograms with pdf bucket representatives [5] and how to handle histograms of other error metrics.

9. ACKNOWLEDGMENT

Mingwang Tang and Feifei Li were supported in part by NSF Grants IIS-1251019 and IIS-1200792.

10. REFERENCES

[1] C. C. Aggarwal, Y. Li, J. Wang, and J. Wang. Frequent pattern mining with uncertain data. In *SIGKDD*, 2009.

[2] P. Agrawal, O. Benjelloun, A. D. Sarma, C. Hayworth, S. Nabar, T. Sugihara, and J. Widom. Trio: A system for data, uncertainty, and lineage. In *VLDB*, 2006.

[3] T. Bernecker, H.-P. Kriegel, M. Renz, F. Verhein, and A. Zuefle. Probabilistic frequent itemset mining in uncertain databases. In *SIGKDD*, 2009.

[4] R. Cheng, D. Kalashnikov, and S. Prabhakar. Evaluating probabilistic queries over imprecise data. In *SIGMOD*, 2003.

[5] G. Cormode and A. Deligiannakis. Probabilistic histograms for probabilistic data. In *VLDB*, 2009.

[6] G. Cormode and M. Garofalakis. Histograms and wavelets on probabilistic data. In *ICDE*, 2009.

[7] G. Cormode and M. Garofalakis. Histograms and wavelets on probabilistic data. *IEEE TKDE*, 22(8):1142–1157, 2010.

[8] N. Dalvi and D. Suciu. Efficient query evaluation on probabilistic databases. In *VLDB*, 2004.

[9] A. Deshpande, C. Guestrin, S. Madden, J. Hellerstein, and W. Hong. Model-driven data acquisition in sensor networks. In *VLDB*, 2004.

[10] X. Dong, A. Y. Halevy, and C. Yu. Data integration with uncertainty. In *VLDB*, 2007.

[11] P. B. Gibbons, Y. Matias, and V. Poosala. Fast incremental maintenance of approximate histograms. In *VLDB*, 1997.

[12] M. G. Graham Cormode and D. Sacharidis. Fast approximate wavelet tracking on streams. In *EDBT*, 2006.

[13] Y. E. Ioannidis. The history of histograms. In *VLDB*, 2003.

[14] Y. E. Ioannidis and V. Poosala. Balancing histogram optimality and practicality for query result size estimation. In *SIGMOD*, 1995.

[15] H. V. Jagadish, N. Koudas, S. Muthukrishnan, V. Poosala, K. Sevcik, and T. Suel. Optimal histograms with quality guarantees. In *VLDB*, 1998.

[16] Y. Matias, J. S. Vitter, and M. Wang. Wavelet-based histograms for selectivity estimation. In *SIGMOD*, 1998.

[17] Y. M. Noga Alon and M. Szegedy. The space complexity of approximating the frequency moments. In *STOC*, 1996.

[18] J. Pei, M. Hua, Y. Tao, and X. Lin. Query answering techniques on uncertain and probabilistic data: tutorial summary. In *SIGMOD*, 2008.

[19] V. Poosala, Y. E. Ioannidis, P. J. Haas, and E. J. Shekita. Improved histograms for selectivity estimation of range predicates. In *SIGMOD*, 1996.

[20] A. D. Sarma, O. Benjelloun, A. Y. Halevy, S. U. Nabar, and J. Widom. Representing uncertain data: models, properties, and algorithms. *VLDBJ*, 18(5):989–1019, 2009.

[21] D. Suciu, D. Olteanu, C. Ré, and C. Koch. *Probabilistic Databases*. Synthesis Lectures on Data Management. 2011.

[22] K. S. Sudipto Guha and J. Woo. Rehist: Relative error histogram construction algorithms. In *VLDB*, 2004.

[23] N. K. Sudipto Guha and K. Shim. Approximation and streaming algorithms for histogram construction problems. *TODS*, 31(1):396–438, 2006.

[24] L. Sun, R. Cheng, D. W. Cheung, and J. Cheng. Mining uncertain data with probabilistic guarantees. In *SIGKDD*, 2010.

[25] M. Tang and F. Li. Scalable histograms on large probabilistic data. In *Technical report, http://www.cs.utah.edu/~lifeifei/papers/ph.pdf*, 2014.

[26] Q. Zhang, F. Li, and K. Yi. Finding frequent items in probabilistic data. In *SIGMOD*, 2008.

Appendix A: The Weighted Histogram

Fast computation of bucket Error. We can show that in the weighted case the $\min_{\widehat{b}}(s,e,\widehat{b})$ is achieved by setting $\widehat{b} = \frac{\sum_{k=s}^{e} w_k f_k}{\sum_{k=s}^{e} w_k}$ and the corresponding bucket error for the bucket b is as follows: $SSE(b,\widehat{b}) = \sum_{j=s}^{e} w_j(f_j^2 - \widehat{b}^2)$. The prefix sum arrays need to be precomputed are:

$$P[e] = \sum_{i=1}^{e} w_j f_j, \quad PP[e] = \sum_{i=1}^{e} w_j f_j^2, \quad W[e] = \sum_{i=1}^{e} w_j.$$

Given these arrays, $\min_{\widehat{b}}(s,e,\widehat{b})$ is computed as:

$$PP[e] - PP[s] - \frac{(P[e]-P[s])^2}{W[e]-W[s]}.$$

Correlation Clustering in MapReduce

Flavio Chierichetti*
Sapienza University
Rome, Italy
flavio@di.uniroma1.it

Nilesh Dalvi†
Trooly, Inc.
Mountain View, CA
nileshdalvi@gmail.com

Ravi Kumar
Google, Inc.
Mountain View, CA
ravi.k53@gmail.com

ABSTRACT

Correlation clustering is a basic primitive in data miner's toolkit with applications ranging from entity matching to social network analysis. The goal in correlation clustering is, given a graph with signed edges, partition the nodes into clusters to minimize the number of disagreements. In this paper we obtain a new algorithm for correlation clustering. Our algorithm is easily implementable in computational models such as MapReduce and streaming, and runs in a small number of rounds. In addition, we show that our algorithm obtains an almost 3-approximation to the optimal correlation clustering. Experiments on huge graphs demonstrate the scalability of our algorithm and its applicability to data mining problems.

Categories and Subject Descriptors: H.2.8 [Database Management]: Database Applications - *Data Mining*

Keywords: Scalable clustering; Signed networks.

1. INTRODUCTION

Correlation clustering is a basic primitive underlying several data management and data mining tasks such as deduplication [5,19,24], identifying communities [15] and network link prediction [12].

The correlation clustering problem is the following: given an undirected signed graph where each edge is labeled either positive or negative, partition the nodes into clusters so that the total number of disagreements is minimized. Here, a disagreement is said to happen if a positive edge becomes an inter-cluster edge or a negative edge becomes an intra-cluster edge. Note that the problem definition does not contain the number of clusters; this is one of the main attractions of correlation clustering, since in many applications it is not possible to specify the number of clusters a priori. Correlation clustering was first introduced by Bansal, Blum, and Chawla [9]. They showed the problem is NP-hard in general and presented a constant-factor approximation for complete graphs. The factor was later improved to three by Ailon, Charikar, and Newman [3]; Gionis, Mannila, and Tsaparas [22] obtained a deterministic three-approximation algorithm for weighted graphs obeying the triangle inequality.

Even though correlation clustering is defined for signed graphs, such graphs arise in a variety of contexts, some obvious and some less obvious. A sign (positive or negative) on an edge in graph can connote different semantics depending on the underlying setting. In case of social networks and trust/opinion networks, a positive sign denotes endorsement whereas a negative sign denotes disapproval; signed networks in social media have been extensively studied recently [29,30]. If the nodes of the graph are items that are possibly duplicated, a positive edge can signify that the items might be the same and negative edges could mean they are not the same. If the nodes of the graph are vectors, the sign could correspond to the angle between the vectors, denoting how aligned or different they are to each other.

Correlation clustering has been used in a wide range of data mining applications. We outline a few here; see Section 2 for more.

(i) In the entity deduplication problem, the goal is to remove entities that are duplicates of one another. Such duplicates can arise if the entities were obtained through independent sources/feeds. A positive edge between two entities indicates that the entities could be the same and a negative edge indicates that they could be different. Correlation clustering has been used in this setting to cluster this graph and produce entities that are duplicates [5,19,24].

(ii) In signed social networks, where positive edge denote friendship and negative edges denote enmity, correlation clustering is a natural way to identify communities [15]. It has also been used as a tool for the link classification problem, i.e., to predict the sign of a missing edge [12], with formal interpretations to the prediction complexity of link classification in a supervised transductive learning framework.

(iii) In machine learning and data mining, the problem of aggregating multiple clusterings and the problem of consensus clustering can be viewed as special cases of the correlation clustering problem [22]; here, the edge weights correspond to the fraction of clusters separating the two nodes.

In many of these applications, the signed graphs exhibit the following two key properties: the positive degree of each node is typically *bounded* and the graph is *complete*, with the understanding that the missing edges are to be interpreted as negative. The randomized algorithm of Ailon et al. [3], which obtains a three-approximation for such graphs, will be the starting point of our work. Their algorithm is tantalizingly simple: pick a *pivot* node uniformly at random, remove it and all its positive neighbors as a cluster, repeat. Despite its simplicity, it is clearly inefficient on massive graphs since it is inherently sequential, possibly removing only a few nodes in each round of processing the graph.

*Part of this work was done while the author was visiting Google. ~~This work was partially supported~~ by a Google Focused Research Award, and by a Google Faculty Award.

†This work was done while the author was at Facebook.

KDD'14, August 24–27, 2014, New York, NY, USA.

http://dx.doi.org/10.1145/2623330.2623743.

Our results. In this work we obtain an efficient scalable algorithm for the correlation clustering problem. In particular, we show how to make the approximation algorithm of [3] round-efficient by picking multiple pivots in *parallel* and repeating. While this idea is natural, we show that one has to be careful in how the pivots must be picked in parallel; a less judicious choice can lead to poor quality solutions. We show two key features of our parallel pivot algorithm. (i) It runs in a logarithmic number of rounds for graphs with a constant number of positive neighbors; for arbitrary graphs, the number of rounds gets further multiplied by the logarithm of the maximum positive degree. (ii) For complete graphs, it outputs a solution that is a close to three-approximation to the optimal correlation clustering solution. Our algorithm is extremely easy to implement in MapReduce, streaming, and message-passing models.

Our proof for the running time is a delicate charging argument that tracks the node with large positive degrees and shows that each of them either disappears or has its degree halved after a certain number of rounds. Our proof for the approximation guarantee proceeds by getting a lower bound on the optimal by considering the dual of a linear program. In contrast, for general graphs, we show that the bounded positive degree (or, for that matter, a bounded degree) assumption does not buy much algorithmic benefit: the problem is as hard as the unbounded degree case.

We then implement our algorithm in a real MapReduce system. We run our algorithm on a graph corresponding to an entity deduplication instance; this graph consists of around 30M nodes and close to a billion edges. The ability to run our algorithm on such a large instance shows its scalability and applicability. We also show that our algorithm achieves performance very close to that of [3], despite being much efficient in terms of its round complexity. We also implement our algorithm in the streaming model and demonstrate its ability to handle graphs with more than 2.5B edges, but only using a very limited amount of main memory.

2. RELATED WORK

The related work falls into three categories: the extensive theoretical work on correlation clustering, the applications of correlation clustering to web mining and machine learning problems, and the theme of efficient, scalable algorithms for web-scale mining.

As discussed earlier, there has been a lot of work on obtaining good approximation algorithms for correlation clustering on complete graphs [3, 9, 22]. The algorithm of Ailon et al. (known as Pivot) will be the starting point for our work. For general graphs, Demaine et al. [18] presented an $O(\log n)$-approximation algorithm; they also showed a logarithmic integrality gap for a natural linear program for the problem. There have been some work on considering natural extensions of the vanilla correlation clustering problem; for example, bipartite correlation clustering was studied by Ailon et al. [2], overlapping correlation clustering was studied by Bonchi, Gionis, and Ukkonen [11], chromatic correlation clustering was studied by Bonchi et al. [10], and subspace correlation clustering was studied by Günnemann et al. [23]. To the best of our knowledge, there has been no result on scalable algorithms with provable bounds for correlation clustering.

Correlation clustering is such a basic primitive that it finds a multitude of applications in web mining applications; in many of these situations, the freedom to not specify the number of clusters to a clustering algorithm is often desirable. Correlation clustering has been extensively used in the general problem of deduplication. For example, a modification of correlation clustering (by including hard constraints) was considered [5] to perform large-scale deduplication of entity references; for an extensive survey on this topic, see [19, 24]. Further applications include disambiguation in people search [25], co-reference resolution [34], and many NLP applications (see the references in [20]). In web search context, correlation clustering has been used to cluster query refinements in web search [36], automatically label query-URL pairs with human-like judgments [1], and segment Web pages [13]. In social network setting, it has been used for link classification in signed networks such as trust and opinion networks [12] and for clustering sparse graphs that arise in social networks [15]. Correlation clustering has also been applied in learning settings such as support vector machines [21] and cluster aggregation [11]. See the surveys [27, 38].

MapReduce algorithms have been developed for basic graph problems such as minimum spanning trees [26], triangle counting [37], and matching [28, 35]. In the combinatorial optimization setting, MapReduce algorithms for the problems of maximum coverage [16], densest subgraph [7], and k-means clustering [8] were obtained recently. All these algorithms have the flavor that they show how to parallelize an *inherently* sequential algorithm, but still almost preserving the original guarantees. Our work is yet another instance of this theme, though the actual techniques we use are vastly different from that of the above. The scalability of correlation clustering algorithms has been addressed before [5, 6, 20] but none of these proposes provably scalable and provably good algorithms.

3. BACKGROUND

In this section we set up the basic notation and problem definitions. Let $G = (V, E)$ be an undirected graph, with $|V| = n$. Each edge $e \in E$ is labeled either *positive* or *negative*; let E^+ be the set of all positive edges and let $E^- = E \setminus E^+$ be the set of all negative edges. Let $\Gamma(v) = \{w \mid \{v, w\} \in E\}$ be the *neighbors* of $v \in V$, let $\deg(v) = |\Gamma(v)|$ be its *degree*, and let $\Delta = \max_{v \in V} \deg(v)$ be the maximum degree in G. Similar concepts are defined with respect to the labels: for example, let $\Gamma^+(v) = \{w \mid \{v, w\} \in E^+\}$, $\deg^+(v) = |\Gamma^+(v)|$, and $\Delta^+ = \max_{v \in V} \deg^+(v)$. If G is *weighted*, let $w^+ : E \to [0, 1]$ and $w^- : E \to [0, 1]$ be the edge weight functions; here by weighted we mean that each edge has a positive weight and a negative weight and they sum to 1.

DEFINITION 3.1 (CORRELATION CLUSTERING). *Given a labeled graph $G = (V, E)$, find a partition of V that minimizes the sum of positive edges across two clusters and the sum of negative edges inside the clusters.*

In other words, the goal of correlation clustering is to minimize the total number of disagreements. Note that the number of clusters is not specified as part of the objective; this is one of the major attractions of correlation clustering. Also, the above definition naturally extends to weighted graphs, where the weight of an edge is used in charging for the disagreements. As we mentioned in Section 1, we will be stating our results in terms of Δ^+ (i.e, the number of positive edges incident on every node); we will be interested in very efficient algorithms when Δ^+ is bounded.

Correlation clustering is an NP-hard problem [9] and hence there has been work on developing approximation algorithms for it (see Section 2). A clustering is said to be an *α-approximation* if its cost is at most α times the cost of the optimal correlation clustering. (Note that the number of clusters produced by an approximation algorithm need not be the same as the number of optimal clusters.) We focus on an elegant algorithm of Ailon, Charikar, and Newman [3], henceforth referred to as the Pivot algorithm.

The basic idea in Pivot is simple: pick a node uniformly at random; designate all the nodes connected to it by positive edges as a cluster; remove this cluster; and repeat. For future convenience, we state this algorithm in the following manner. The subroutine

Algorithm 1 CreateCluster(V, E^+, v)

```
C ← {v} ∪ Γ⁺(v)                         // positive neighbors
V ← V \ C
E⁺ ← E⁺ ∩ (V choose 2)
output C as a cluster
return (V, E⁺)
```

CreateCluster implements the task of creating a cluster and updating the graph, once a pivot is chosen. Given this, the Pivot algorithm follows easily. An analysis of this algorithm shows that it obtains a three-approximation when G is a complete graph [3].

Algorithm 2 Pivot$(G = (V, E^+))$

```
while V ≠ ∅ do
    v ← uniform at random node in V
    (V, E⁺) ← CreateCluster(V, E⁺, v)
```

Given the simplicity of Pivot, it is somewhat tempting to use it in large-scale applications. A careful scrutiny however indicates that the algorithm makes expensive multiple passes over the input, i.e., every time a new cluster is output. In fact, this behavior can be pathological: for example, if the graph has only negative edges or if the graph is a line, then Pivot makes a linear number of passes. This clearly limits its applicability on massive real-world graphs.

4. ALGORITHMS

In this section we present a fast, scalable algorithm for correlation clustering. This algorithm guarantees a constant-factor approximation when the graph is complete and runs in polylogarithmically many rounds. For general graphs, we show that the problem is as hard to approximate even in the bounded-degree case.

A natural way to obtain a scalable parallel algorithm for correlation clustering would be to parallelize Pivot by picking many pivots in parallel and grow clusters around them (using CreateCluster) and hope that the graph shrinks significantly in each round. To proceed in this direction, we need to stipulate the distribution with which multiple pivots should be picked. One has to be careful in choosing a distribution: we illustrate two plausible approaches and indicate their pitfalls on complete graphs.

Suppose multiple pivots are chosen with probability proportional to their degrees (this is desirable since it will also shrink the graph faster). One can show that with high probablity this algorithm produces a non-constant approximation on a graph composed of $\ln n$ stars of positive edges having $n/\ln n$ nodes each, and such that each star center pair is joined by a negative edge.

On the other hand, suppose multiple pivots are chosen inversely proportional to their degrees (this approach was used by Luby [32] to obtain a parallel algorithm for the maximal independent set problem). In our setting, however, one can verify the following: for a positive-edge clique of $n/2$ nodes, where each node in the clique is connected with a positive edge to a new node and where the rest of the edges are negative, this algorithm would produce a non-constant approximation with high probability. In general, even if a particular way of choosing multiple pivots looks appealing, it is unclear how to preserve the approximation properties of Pivot.

4.1 A parallel pivot algorithm

We present our algorithm called ParallelPivot (see Algorithm 3). As stated before, the idea behind the algorithm is to choose pivots in parallel and grow clusters around them. The pivots are chosen in a delicate manner in a two-step process: in the first step, each node is sampled with probability inversely proportional to the current maximum positive degree; this results in a set of *active* nodes. In the second step, active nodes that are adjacent to each other (line 6) are deactivated; the remaining active nodes are the *pivots* (line 7). If a non-pivot node is adjacent to more than one pivot, then it is assigned to the smallest of them (lines 10–11) according to a uniform random permutation of the nodes (π in the algorithm). Then, as in Pivot, each pivot grows its own cluster (in parallel) using its positive neighbors (line 13). In the next section, we show two properties of this algorithm: (i) unlike Pivot, it runs in logarithmically many rounds and (ii) like Pivot, it still outputs a constant-factor approximation for complete graphs.

Algorithm 3 ParallelPivot$(G = (V, E^+), \epsilon)$

```
1:  π ← a random permutation of V
2:  while E⁺ ≠ ∅ do
3:      Δ⁺ ← max_{v∈V} deg⁺(v)                  // current max +ve degree
4:      for v ∈ V do
5:          A ← A ∪ {v} with prob. p = ε/Δ⁺     // active node
6:      A' ← A ∩ ⋃_{v∈A} Γ⁺(v)                  // adjacent active nodes
7:      P ← A \ A'                               // pivots
8:      B ← {v | v ∈ V \ P ∧ |Γ⁺(v) ∩ P| ≥ 2}
                                 // non-pivots with multiple adjacent pivots
9:      for v ∈ B do
10:         w ← arg min_{w'∈Γ⁺(v)∩P} π(w')       // pick one using π
11:         E⁺ ← E⁺ \ {{v, w'} | w' ∈ Γ⁺(v) ∩ (P \ {w})}
                                 // remove positive edges to others
12:     for p ∈ P do
13:         (V, E⁺) ← CreateCluster(V, E⁺, p)
14: for v ∈ V do
15:     output {v} as a cluster
```

4.2 Analysis

Number of rounds. We first prove a crucial point about the progress made by the algorithm in each round. A natural approach to track the progress of the algorithm is by lower bounding the number of nodes or edges removed in each round. Unfortunately, such a lower bound would be too weak to show that ParallelPivot finishes in a small number of rounds; we therefore resort to a subtler argument. We track the maximum positive degree of the graph, and show that after logarithmically many rounds of the algorithm, nodes with large positive degree either disappear, or their positive degree shrinks by a constant factor.

LEMMA 1. *Suppose that $\epsilon < \frac{1}{2}$. Fix a constant $c > 0$ and let $\Delta^+ \geq 1$ be the maximum positive degree before beginning a round of the loop at line 2. Then, for any node v, after $\lceil \frac{8c}{\epsilon} \ln n \rceil$ rounds, with probability at least $1 - n^{-c}$, either v will have been removed from the graph or it will have degree at most $\Delta^+/2$.*

PROOF. Consider the graph at the beginning of an arbitrary round of the algorithm and let $\Delta^+, \deg^+(\cdot), \Gamma^+(\cdot)$ be defined with respect to this graph. The probability that a node is activated in this round is $p = \epsilon/\Delta^+$. Let v be an arbitrary node and consider the event ξ_v = "in this round of the loop exactly one neighbor w of v gets activated and no neighbor of this neighbor w gets activated."

Then,

$$\Pr[\xi_v] = \sum_{w\in\Gamma(v)} \left(p\cdot(1-p)^{\left|\Gamma^+(w)\cup\Gamma^+(v)\setminus\{w\}\right|}\right)$$

$$\geq \sum_{w\in\Gamma(v)} \left(p\cdot(1-p)^{\deg^+(v)}\cdot(1-p)^{\deg^+(w)}\right).$$

Now, observe that since $\Delta^+ \geq \max\left(\deg^+(v),\deg^+(w)\right)$, we have $p\cdot\max\left(\deg^+(v),\deg^+(w)\right)\leq\epsilon$. Thus,

$$\deg^+(v)+\deg^+(w)\leq\frac{2\epsilon}{p},$$

and

$$\Pr[\xi_v]\geq\sum_{w\in\Gamma(v)}\left(p\cdot(1-p)^{\frac{2\epsilon}{p}}\right).$$

By calculus, it holds that $(1-x)^{\frac{1}{x}}\geq\frac{1}{4}$, for each $x\in\left(0,\frac{1}{2}\right]$. Since $\epsilon\leq\frac{1}{2}$, we have $p\leq\frac{1}{2}$ and therefore

$$\left((1-p)^{\frac{1}{p}}\right)^{2\epsilon}\geq\left(\frac{1}{4}\right)^{2\epsilon}\geq\frac{1}{4}.$$

We thus obtain,

$$\Pr[\xi_v]\geq\frac{p\cdot\deg^+(v)}{4}.$$

If $\deg^+(v)>\frac{\Delta^+}{2}$, then we have

$$p\cdot\deg^+(v)>\frac{\epsilon}{2},$$

and hence $\Pr[\xi_v]>\epsilon/8$.

Now consider round i and let Δ_i^+ be the maximum positive degree before this round. Consider any node v that had positive degree at least $\Delta_i^+/2$ in round i, and consider any subsequent round $j>i$. If the positive degree of v in round j is at most $\Delta_i^+/2$, then v will have shrunk its positive degree (with respect to round i) by a factor of at least 2. Otherwise, since the maximum positive degree is non-increasing during the execution of the algorithm, we will have that $\Pr[\xi_v]>\epsilon/8$ even at round j. Therefore, after $\left\lceil\frac{8c}{\epsilon}\ln n\right\rceil$ rounds, either v's positive degree shrinks by a factor of at least 2 or the probability that v will end up in a cluster is at least

$$1-\left(1-\frac{\epsilon}{8}\right)^{\frac{8c}{\epsilon}\ln n}\geq 1-n^{-c}.\quad\square$$

From this, we can bound the number of passes the algorithm makes on the input graph.

COROLLARY 2. *Algorithm 3 terminates after at most*

$$O\left(\frac{1}{\epsilon}\log n\cdot\log\Delta^+\right)$$

rounds of its loop, with probability at least $1-1/n^c$, *for any constant* $c>0$.

Approximation factor. We now proceed to prove the approximation guarantee when G is a complete graph. We start by recalling a definition from [3]. Consider the original graph $G=(V,E)$, and call a set $T\subseteq V$ of three nodes a *bad triangle* if it induces two edges in E^+ and one edge in E^-. Let $\mathcal{T}\subseteq\binom{V}{3}$ be the set of bad triangles in the original graph $G=(V,E)$. Let $S_{v,v'}=\bigcup_{\{v,v'\}\subset T\in\mathcal{T}}T$ be the union of the sets of nodes of the bad triangles that contain both v and v'. We now show that the distribution with which nodes as picked as pivots by ParallelPivot is close to the distribution induced by Pivot.

LEMMA 3. *Suppose that* $\epsilon<\frac{1}{7}$. *Let* $v',v''\in V$ *be two nodes in the instance that are contained in at least one bad triangle and let* P *be the set of pivots chosen in a round of Algorithm 3 at the beginning of which no node in* $S_{v',v''}$ *was part of a cluster. Then,*

$$\Pr\left[\{v',v''\}\cap P\neq\emptyset\mid S_{v',v''}\cap P\neq\emptyset\right]\leq\frac{2}{|S_{v',v''}|\cdot(1-7\epsilon)}.$$

PROOF. For simplicity, let $S=S_{v',v''}$. Clearly, $|S|\geq 3$. Note that before a pivot is chosen in S, the maximum of the degree of v' and the degree of v'' in the graph induced by S will be at least $\frac{|S|-2}{2}$. Therefore, before a pivot is chosen in S, we have $\Delta^+\geq\frac{|S|-2}{2}\geq\frac{|S|}{6}\implies|S|\leq 6\Delta^+$.

We compute the probability that an arbitrary node $v\in S$ becomes a pivot, given that $S\cap P\neq\emptyset$. By Bayes' rule,

$$\Pr[v\in P\mid S\cap P\neq\emptyset]=\frac{\Pr[v\in P\wedge S\cap P\neq\emptyset]}{\Pr[S\cap P\neq\emptyset]}.$$

Observe that since $v\in S$, the event "$v\in P\wedge S\cap P\neq\emptyset$" is equal to the event "$v\in P$". Moreover, the event "$v\in P$" is a subset of the event "v has been activated"; the latter event has probability p. Therefore,

$$\Pr[v\in P\mid S\cap P\neq\emptyset]\leq\frac{p}{\Pr[S\cap P\neq\emptyset]}.$$

Now, consider the probability of the event "$S\cap P\neq\emptyset$"; it is not smaller than the probability that exactly one node $v\in S$ gets activated and that none of its neighbors outside of S gets activated. Since Δ^+ is an upper bound on the maximum positive degree,

$$\begin{aligned}\Pr[S\cap P\neq\emptyset] &\geq |S|\cdot p\cdot(1-p)^{|S|+\Delta^+}\\ &\geq |S|\cdot p\cdot(1-p)^{7\Delta^+}.\end{aligned}$$

Recall that $(1-x)^y\geq 1-xy$ for each $0<x<1, y\geq 1$. Hence,

$$\Pr[S\cap P\neq\emptyset]\geq|S|\cdot p\cdot\left(1-7\Delta^+p\right)=(1-7\epsilon)\cdot|S|\cdot p.$$

Therefore for any node $v\in S$, we have

$$\Pr[v\in P\mid S\cap P\neq\emptyset]\leq\frac{1}{|S|\cdot(1-7\epsilon)}.$$

The main claim can be then proved by a union bound on the two events given by $v=v'$ and $v=v''$. $\square$

We now prove our main algorithmic result. Our proof follows the one in [3], adapting its single-pivot choice charging argument to our parallel multiple-pivot process.

THEOREM 4. *Suppose that* $\epsilon<\frac{1}{7}$. *Then, Algorithm 3 returns a* $\left(1+\frac{2}{1-7\epsilon}\right)$*-approximate correlation clustering.*

PROOF. Observe that the total cost of the clustering $\mathcal{C}$ produced by Algorithm 3 can be upper bounded by the number of bad triangles that will be removed from the graph because of the selection of one of their nodes as a pivot. For $T\in\mathcal{T}$, let p_T be the probability that at least one of its nodes is chosen as a pivot while T is a completely part of the graph. Then, the expected cost incurred by the algorithm can be upper bounded by

$$E[\mathcal{C}]\leq\sum_{T\in\mathcal{T}}p_T. \tag{1}$$

For lower bounding the cost of the optimum, we consider the following linear program (LP) relaxation of correlation clustering.

$$\begin{cases}\text{minimize}\sum_{\{v,v'\}\in\binom{V}{2}}x_{v,v'}\\ \text{subject to}\\ x_{v,v'}+x_{v,v''}+x_{v',v''}\geq 1 & \forall\{v,v',v''\}\in\mathcal{T},\\ 0\leq x_{v,v'} & \forall\{v,v'\}\in\binom{V}{2}.\end{cases}$$

Note that in the integral solution, $x_{v,v'} = 1$ if the edge between v and v' is not satisfied, and 0 otherwise. The dual of the above program can be written as follows.

$$\begin{cases} \text{maximize} \sum_{T \in \mathcal{T}} y_T \\ \text{subject to} \\ \sum_{T \in \mathcal{T} \wedge T \supset \{v,v'\}} y_T \leq 1 \quad \forall \{v,v'\} \in \binom{V}{2}, \\ 0 \leq y_T \qquad\qquad\qquad \forall T \in \mathcal{T}. \end{cases}$$

The value of any feasible solution of this dual is a lower bound on the optimal value of the LP, which in turn is a lower bound on the value of the optimal correlation clustering. We will show that

$$y_T = \frac{p_T}{1 + \frac{2}{1-7\epsilon}}, \tag{2}$$

is a feasible solution to the dual. Then, (1) and (2) will prove that the algorithm returns a $1 + \frac{2}{1-7\epsilon}$-approximation in expectation.

To show (2), consider any edge $\{v, v'\} \in E$ and for simplicity, let $S = S_{v,v'}$. Recall that a bad triangle will increment the total cost of the algorithm's solution if and only if at least one of its nodes is chosen as a pivot before the triangle disappears. The expected total cost of the $|S| - 2$ bad triangles containing $\{v, v'\}$ can then be upper bounded in the following manner. If any node $v'' \in S \setminus \{v, v'\}$ is chosen before any of $\{v, v'\}$, then a cost of 1 (i.e., the cost of the bad triangle $\{v, v', v''\}$) is incurred and all the bad triangles containing $\{v, v'\}$ will be eliminated; the probability of this event is at most 1. If, on the other hand, at least one of v and v' is chosen as a pivot before any other node in S, then the cost will be $|S| - 2$ (i.e., a cost 1 for each of the $|S| - 2$ triangles). By Lemma 3, the probability of this event is at most $\frac{2}{|S|(1-7\epsilon)}$. Thus, the expected total cost of the $|S| - 2$ bad triangles containing $\{v, v'\}$ is at most

$$\sum_{T \supset \{v,v'\}} p_T \leq 1 \cdot 1 + (|S| - 2) \cdot \frac{2}{|S|(1 - 7\epsilon)} \leq 1 + \frac{2}{1 - 7\epsilon},$$

since the expected cost of a bad triangle is p_T. Therefore, if $y_T = p_T/(1 + \frac{2}{1-7\epsilon})$, then all the dual constraints will be satisfied. □

Suppose that we fix an upper bound of $\tau < \frac{1}{7}$ on ϵ. Then, the approximation ratio of our algorithm, as long as $\epsilon \leq \tau$, can be upper bounded by $3 + \frac{14\epsilon}{1-7\tau}$. As ϵ approaches 0, this ratio approaches $3 + 14\epsilon + O(\epsilon^2) = 3 + O(\epsilon)$. Concretely, if $\epsilon \leq \tau = \frac{1}{14}$, then we have that the approximation ratio is at most $3 + 28\epsilon$.

We observe that the total number of bits communicated in a round is at most $O(n \log n)$, which is also the size of the output and is therefore, in a sense, inevitable. We also observe that the analysis can be extended to weighted graphs that satisfy the so-called *probability constraints*, as in [3] (the algorithm still remains the same); we omit the analysis details in this version of the paper.

Tightness of the running time. We show that our running time analysis is near-tight. To this end, we construct the following complete instance $G = (V, E)$ by only specifying the positive edges; the rest of the edges will be negative. Choose some integer $1 \leq k < (1 - \epsilon) \lceil \log_2 n \rceil$, and for each $i = 1, \ldots, k$, create $\lceil n/2^k \rceil$ disjoint stars with 2^i leaves each and add them to G. It is easy to see that $|V| = \Theta(n)$ and $\Delta^+ = 2^k$, and that the number of executions of the algorithm's loop on this instance is $\Theta(\log n \cdot \log \Delta^+)$.

4.3 Realizations in scalable models

MapReduce. Recall that in the MapReduce model of computation [17], the input is partitioned across a set of machines and the computation is split into a map phase and a reduce phase. In the map phase, each machine consumes its portion of the input and outputs a set of key-value tuples. In the reduce phase, all the tuples with the same key are processed by a single machine and output, if any, is emitted. These two phases can be repeated, yielding a multi-round algorithm. Since each phase is expensive from both computational and data access points of view, it is desirable to have MapReduce algorithms with a small number of rounds.

We now illustrate how ParallelPivot can be implemented in a small number of rounds in MapReduce. Clearly, the maximum positive degree of a graph can be computed in one round of MapReduce. Likewise, the task of (randomly) selecting active nodes and computing pivots by removing adjacent active nodes (lines 5–7) can also be computed in one round. Once the pivots are computed, assigning each non-pivot node to a unique pivot neighbor (lines 10–11) can be done with an additional round. Finally, it is easy to observe that CreateCluster itself, with the graph update, can be implemented in yet another round. In Section 5.1 we show the performance of a MapReduce realization of our algorithm.

Streaming. In the streaming model of computation [4], the input is read sequentially by a machine with a limited amount of main memory (typically, sublinear in the size of the input). The goal is design an algorithm that makes a few passes over the input in order to compute the function. In the graph case, input is assumed to be available as a stream of edges. It is easy to check that each of the steps of ParallelPivot can be implemented in the streaming model, where the only amount of memory is to store the pivots and their neighbors in each pass; in Section 5.3 we show the performance of a realization of our algorithm in the streaming model.

Pregel. Pregel is a large-scale graph computing framework that is based on the bulk synchronous message-passing model [33]. In this model, each node of the graph is a computational unit, the computation proceeds in supersteps, and within each superstep, messages can be asynchronously exchanged between the nodes. It is easy to check that the two communication-intensive steps in our algorithm, namely, finding the current maximum degree and computing the pivot nodes from the active nodes can themselves be implemented in a constant number of Pregel supersteps.

4.4 General graphs

In this section we consider the correlation clustering problem on general (i.e., not necessarily complete) graphs. For general graphs, the best known is an $O(\log n)$-approximation algorithm. This algorithm, however, is based on rounding a linear program [18]. Given this, we turn our attention to the case when Δ is bounded (which is stronger than assuming Δ^+ is bounded). Unfortunately, we show that correlation clustering on bounded-degree graphs is as hard as solving correlation clustering on arbitrary graphs, thereby dashing any hopes for an improved centralized algorithm.

THEOREM 5. *There exists a constant c such that if there is a polynomial time α-approximation algorithm for correlation clustering on graphs with $\Delta \leq c$, then there is a polynomial time α-approximation algorithm for correlation clustering on every graph.*

PROOF. We show a reduction from an arbitrary graph G to a bounded-degree graph G'. Let $G = (V, E^+, E^-)$, where $|V| = n$ is sufficiently large. From G, we will construct (in polynomial time) G' with the following properties: there exists a canonical form of the (correlation clustering) solutions of G' such that every solution of G' can be transformed in polynomial time into a canonical solution having equal or smaller cost and there is a polynomial-time computable bijective mapping between canonical solutions of G' and solutions of G that leaves the cost of the solutions unchanged. These properties will complete the proof.

The key gadget we use in our proof is a constant-degree regular expander graph $H = (W, F)$ with the following properties: (i) $|W| = 2n$, (ii) $\forall v \in W, \deg(v) = 2|F|/|W| = O(1)$, and (iii) for each set $S \subseteq W$ such that $|S| \leq |W|/2$, it holds that the cut $(S, W \setminus S)$ has at least $2|S|$ edges. Such graphs exist and can be constructed in polynomial time [31]. The idea then is to "tensor" each node in G with H so that the resulting graph will have constant degree and if the tensoring is done carefully, then the correlation clustering solutions will be preserved as well.

The target graph $G' = (V', E'^{+}, E'^{-})$ will be made up of n copies of H, one for each node in V. Each edge in each of these copies will be labeled positive. These copies will be connected with each other through what we call *instance* edges. Fix $v_i \in V$ and consider v_i's copy of H denoted $H_i = (W_i, F_i)$. Since $|W_i| = 2n$, it is possible to find an injective function from $\Gamma^{+}(v_i) \cup \Gamma^{-}(v_i)$ to W_i; we use $w_{i,j}$ to denote the node in W_i corresponding to the (v_i's side of) the edge $\{v_i, v_j\}$ in $E^{+} \cup E^{-}$. If $\{v_i, v_j\}$ is a positive (resp., negative) edge, then we add a positive (resp., negative) instance edge between $w_{i,j}$ and $w_{j,i}$. This completes the description of the instance G'. Note that no node in V' will be hit by more than one instance edge and therefore Δ' will still be a constant.

Next, we show correctness. We say that a clustering of G' is *canonical* if no W_i gets partitioned among two or more clusters. Observe that a canonical clustering of G' will have cost equal to the number of instance edges that are incorrectly clustered. More precisely, if $\{v_i, v_j\} \in E^{+}$, then a canonical clustering of G' will pay 1 for that edge if it places W_i and W_j in two different clusters. Analogously, if $\{v_i, v_j\} \in E^{-}$, then a canonical clustering of G' will pay 1 for that edge if it places W_i and W_j in the same cluster. Therefore, if we produce a clustering of G from a canonical clustering of G' by putting v_i and v_j together if and only if W_i and W_j are together in the canonical clustering, then the cost of the clustering of G will equal the cost of the canonical clustering of G'. Conversely, to go from a clustering of G to a canonical clustering of G' with the same cost, it suffices to cluster the sets W_i and W_j together in G' if and only if v_i and v_j are clustered together in G.

Therefore, we only need to show that at least one optimal clustering of G' is canonical. We show this by methodically transforming a non-canonical solution to a canonical solution of smaller or equal cost in polynomial time. Indeed, suppose in the current non-canonical solution, W_i is partitioned between $k \geq 2$ clusters into mutually disjoint parts $P_1, \ldots, P_k$, with $|P_1| \leq \cdots \leq |P_k|$ and $|P_1| + \cdots + |P_k| = |W_i|$. Necessarily, we have $|P_{k-1}| \leq n/2$ and therefore the number of non-instance (positive) edges that are cut by the original clustering is at least $2 \cdot |W_i \setminus P_k|/2$; this follows from the expansion property (iii) of H_i. If t_k was the number of instance edges hitting P_k that were misplaced by the original clustering, we then have that the contribution[1] of W_i to the cost function is at least $2 \cdot |W_i \setminus P_k|/2 + t_k/2$. On the other hand if for each $i = 1, \ldots, k-1$, we disconnect the nodes in P_i from their current cluster and we put them in P_k's cluster, then we will have that all the non-instance edges of W_i will be correctly clustered. Therefore, the cost of the set $W_i \setminus P_k$ will be at most the cost of its instance edges, i.e., at most $|W_i \setminus P_k|$. The cost of P_k will also be limited to the cost of its instance edges, i.e., $t_k/2$. Therefore, the total cost will be at most $|W_i \setminus P_k| + t_k/2$. Therefore, merging all the P_i's together will not increase the cost of the clustering. By repeating this merging operation, we will end up with a canonical clustering of cost not larger than that of the original clustering. □

[1]The contribution of a set of nodes to the cost function is defined as follows: a misplaced edge fully contained in the set has cost 1, whereas a misplaced edge half-contained in the set has cost $\frac{1}{2}$.

In light of this negative result, to obtain a scalable algorithm in the general case, one has to resort to heuristics. A few possibilities are:

(i) One could run Algorithm 3 on general graphs, hoping that it will produce a reasonably good solution. Note however that the algorithm is still efficient, i.e., runs in $O(\log n \cdot \log \Delta^{+})$ rounds.

(ii) Instead of minimizing the number of disagreements in the correlation clustering objective (Definition 3.1), one could instead maximize the number of agreements. One way to do that would be to find a maximal matching M of (V, E^{+}) and take each matched edge in M as a cluster and the remaining nodes as singletons. Note that this heuristic can be implemented scalable using the methods in [28]. The heuristic does produce an $O(\Delta)$ approximation for the maximization version[2]. Indeed, since no negative edges are clustered, no mistakes are made on the edges in E^{-}. Since $M \subseteq E^{+}$ is a maximal matching, $|M| \geq \frac{|E^{+}|}{2\Delta - 1}$ for otherwise there must exist an edge in E^{+} whose endpoints are not covered by M. Thus, the proposed clustering correctly joins at least an $\Omega\left(\frac{1}{\Delta}\right)$ fraction of the edges in E^{+}.

(iii) One could try to adapt the LP rounding algorithm of [18]. To do so, though, one would need to (1) solve the linear program, and (2) round its fractional solution to an integral one. It is unclear whether these two steps can be carried out efficiently in a MapReduce-like framework.

5. EXPERIMENTS

We implemented our techniques in MapReduce and streaming, and evaluated it on the following datasets. The goal our experiments will be to show that (i) the solution quality of ParallelPivot is very close to that of Pivot and (ii) ParallelPivot runs in a very small number of rounds.

Datasets. For our first dataset, we use the structured dataset embedded in HTML pages that was extracted by the Web Data Commons project (`webdatacommons.org/`). The project extracts all Microformat, Microdata, and RDFa data from the Common Crawl web corpus (`commoncrawl.org/`), the largest and most up-to-data web corpus that is currently available to the public, and provide the extracted data for download in the form of RDF-quads. From this dataset, we constructed all entities that correspond to *places*, where a place is defined as any entity that has a `name`, either a street address or geo co-ordinates, and optionally `phone` and `website`. Appendix 6 describes the mapping that we used from the RDF types to our schema, which can be used to reproduce our dataset. We extracted around 35M places from Web Data Commons. Our goal is to resolve duplicates in this dataset. Given a pair of entities, we use the *TF-IDF* similarity between their fields to determine if they are duplicates. Since we cannot compute the similarity between all pairs, we use an n-gram index [14] on the fields to generate candidate pairs, and run our similarity condition on all candidates to generate duplicate edges. The resulting dataset has around 900M edges. We call this dataset WDC.

The second dataset that we use is the Cora dataset (`people.cs.umass.edu/~mccallum/data.html`). The Cora dataset consists of 1,878 citations to real papers. This dataset has been hand-clustered into groups referring to the same paper. While this is a much smaller dataset, the availability of ground truth enables us to study the accuracy of our algorithm, as well as compare it with Pivot. On this dataset, we trained a similarity classifier, and ran it on all pairs of node. The classifier resulted in 68,882 positive edges. We denote this dataset by CORA.

[2]We recall that there exists a trivial 2-approximation for the maximization version: return the best of the all-in-one-cluster, and the each-in-its-own-cluster, partitions.

The third dataset that we use is an undirected version of a Twitter follower graph (`an.kaist.ac.kr/traces/WWW2010.html`). This graph consists of more than 41M nodes and 2.5B edges, with the maximum degree of 2.9M. In addition to being larger, this dataset has a higher average degree, a very high maximum degree, and a skewed degree distribution. We denote this dataset by TWITTER. As before, we treat the follower edges as positive and the missing edges as negative.

5.1 Results on WDC

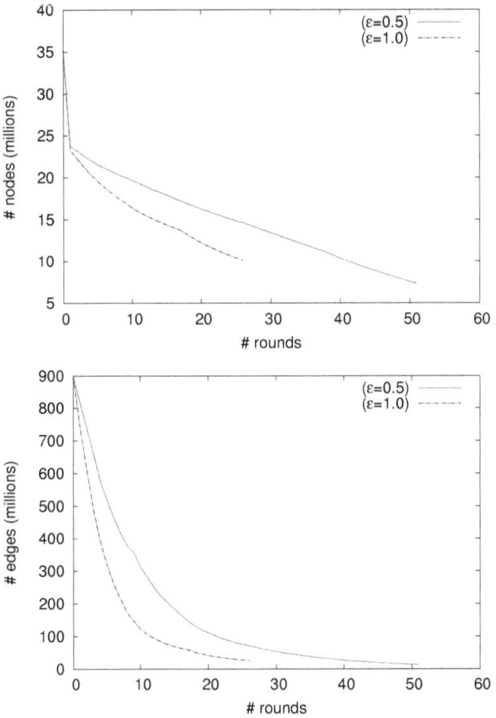

Figure 1: Number of nodes and edges remaining after each round on the WDC dataset ($\epsilon = 0.5, 1$).

We ran 50 rounds of ParallelPivot on the WDC dataset with a setting of $\epsilon = 0.5$, and 25 rounds with a setting of $\epsilon = 1$. After each round, we plotted the number of remaining nodes, the number of remaining edges, the maximum and the average degree, the number of active nodes and the number of pivots.

Figure 1 shows the plots of number of remaining nodes and edges respectively. We see that the nodes decay almost linearly with the number of rounds. The large drop in the first round is due to the fact that a large number of nodes had degree 0 (they did not generate any candidate), and hence got removed in the first round. The number of edges show a more dramatic decay. The edge roughly halve in size after every 6 rounds for $\epsilon = 0.5$ and 3 rounds for $\epsilon = 1$. For $\epsilon = 0.5$, after around 30-40 rounds, the graph is small enough to fit in the memory of singe machines, at which point we can simply use the Pivot algorithm to cluster the remaining graph. For $\epsilon = 1$, we need around 15-20 rounds.

Figure 2 plots Δ^+ (the maximum positive degree) of the graph after each round. The initial graph has $\Delta^+ = 1,400$, but it falls rapidly with each round. It also plots the average degree of the graph, which itself falls rapidly. This indicates that the graph becomes progressively sparser.

The number of active nodes chosen at each round is directly proportional to the number of total remaining nodes and inversely proportional to Δ^+, both of which decrease over time. But Δ^+ decays faster, resulting is more active nodes chosen at each round. Figure 3 shows this plot. It also plots the number of pivots (number of active nodes not adjacent to any other active node). We see that most active nodes end up being pivots. As Figure 3 shows, this ratio remains flat at around 98% throughout the entire run for $\epsilon = 0.5$. A ratio of 100% would mean that all the pivots are truly random, and the algorithm would be equivalent in accuracy to the Pivot algorithm. Thus, a high ratio of 98% indicates that we are close to Pivot accuracy. For $\epsilon = 1$, the ratio is still very high, between 95% and 98%. Note that the theoretical guarantee of ParallelPivot is a $3 + O(\epsilon)$, which could be quite larger (for constant ϵ) than the 3-approximation returned by Pivot. Still, Figure 3 shows that, in practice, the two algorithms seem to be on par. Since Pivot cannot be run on such a large dataset, we cannot provide a direct comparison of accuracy on this dataset.

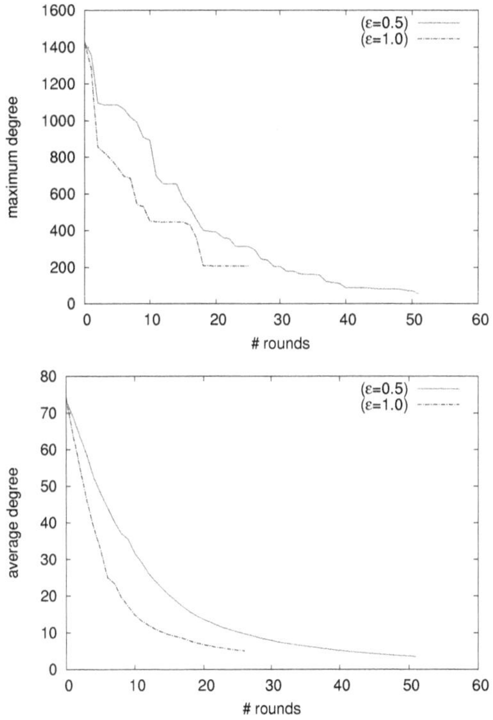

Figure 2: Maximum and average degree after each round on the WDC dataset ($\epsilon = 0.5, 1$).

5.2 Results on CORA

We use CORA to evaluate the accuracy of our techniques. Even for this small dataset, running the optimal clustering is infeasible. Thus, we cannot directly evaluate the accuracy of ParallelPivot with respect to the optimum. Instead, we evaluate its accuracy with respect to the golden truth, and compare it with Pivot. For each of the two algorithms, we define two notions of accuracy. The first is the number of disagreements with respect to the golden truth, which is the sum of the false positives and false negatives. The second is the F-measure of each algorithm, which is the harmonic mean of the precision and the recall with respect to the golden truth.

Figures 4 plot the two measures of accuracy for ParallelPivot, for ϵ ranging from 0.1 to 0.9, and compare it with Pivot. For each ϵ, we ran ParallelPivot 100 times and took the average. The shaded regions in each plot represent the error bars consisting of one stan-

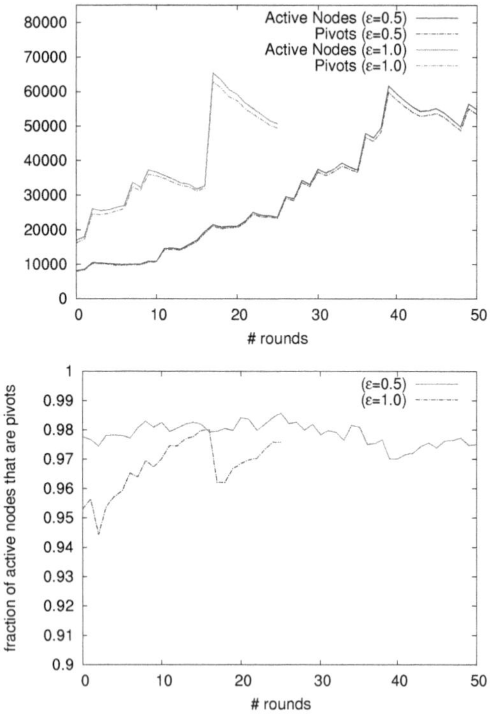

Figure 3: Number and fraction of active nodes chosen as pivots at each round on the WDC dataset ($\epsilon = 0.5, 1$).

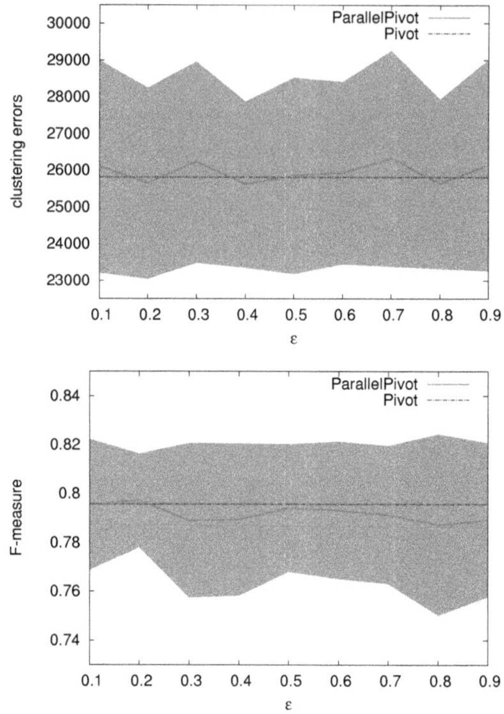

Figure 4: The number of clustering disagreements and the F-measure as a function of ϵ on CORA.

dard deviation. We see that for the entire range of ϵ, both the disagreements and F-measure of ParallelPivot are on par with Pivot.

Figure 5 shows the number of rounds that ParallelPivot takes, as a function of ϵ. Note that the ground truth has 190 clusters, so Pivot, that processes one cluster as a time, will require 190 rounds. ParallelPivot starts with 140 rounds for $\epsilon = 0.1$, but only requires around 25 rounds when ϵ is close to 1. Note that our algorithm is not defined for $\epsilon > 1$, since the probability ϵ/Δ^+ of choosing active nodes can become greater than 1. While our guarantee of $(3 + \epsilon)$ approximation for ParallelPivot only holds for $\epsilon < \frac{1}{7} \simeq 0.14$, Figures 4 and 5 together show that ParallelPivot is at par with Pivot over the entire range of ϵ, and the number of rounds significantly go down when ϵ is close to 1.

5.3 Results on TWITTER

We use TWITTER to demonstrate ParallelPivot in the streaming model. Since the number of edges in this dataset is more than 2.5B, which makes it hard to store the graph entirely on a machine with a small amount of main memory. The algorithm ran for 140 rounds.

Figure 6 shows the number of nodes and edges after each round of ParallelPivot. Perhaps because of the skewed nature of the degree distribution, the behaviors are different: the number of nodes decrease slowly in the beginning and rapidly towards the end, whereas the number of edges has the opposite behavior. Figure 7 shows the average and maximum degrees in each round. The behavior is similar to the number of edges, though the maximum degree drops rapidly; this enables more pivots to be chosen in subsequent rounds of ParallelPivot, which in turn contributes to an increased drop in the number of nodes as seen in Figure 6.

Figure 8 shows the number and fraction of active nodes chosen as pivots in each round of the algorithm. The number of active nodes (and pivots) is unimodal in nature, peaking at around the 100th round. Note that this fully determines the memory required by the streaming algorithm. Using the average degree from Figure 7, we see that the the memory used by the algorithm is upper bounded by the space require to store a graph of around 200K nodes of average degree around 2, which is insignificant (especially, when compared to the size of the original graph).

6. CONCLUSIONS

In this paper we considered the problem of how to efficiently perform correlation clustering on massive graphs. We obtained a simple algorithm that runs in a provably small number of rounds and obtains a constant-factor approximation to correlation clustering. Since correlation clustering is a basic web mining problem, our algorithm opens up the possibility of it being applied to very large instance. We illustrate this by running our algorithm on a real MapReduce and streaming systems on huge real-world instance;

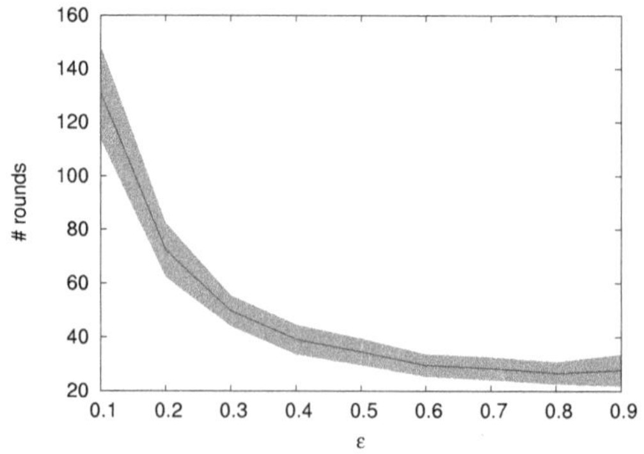

Figure 5: The number of rounds as a function of ϵ on CORA.

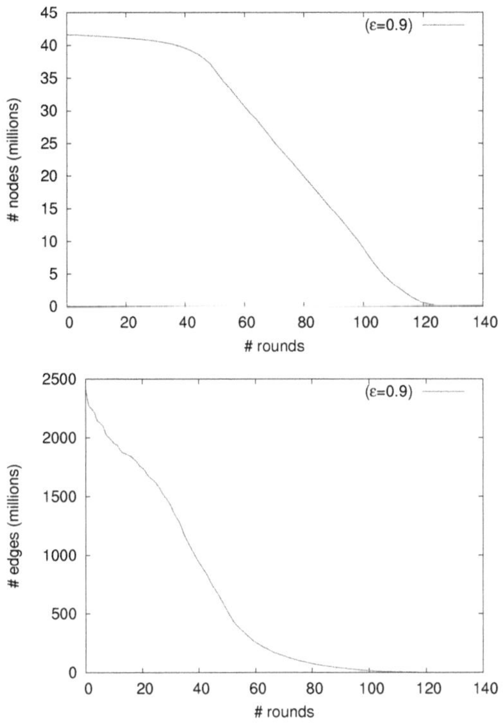

Figure 6: Number of nodes and edges remaining after each round on the TWITTER dataset.

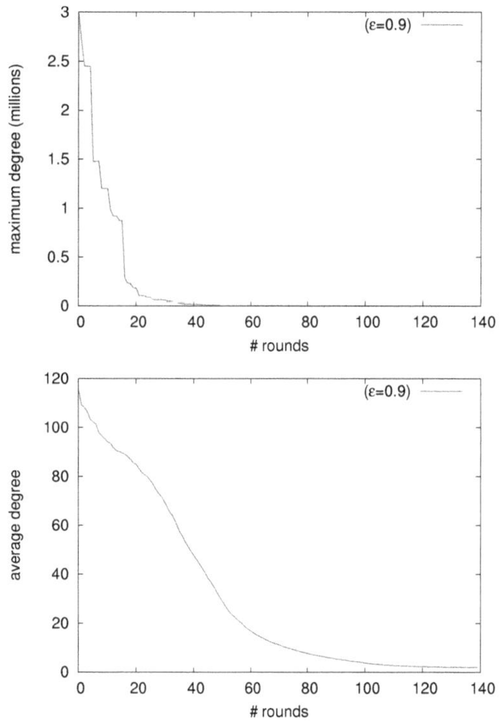

Figure 7: Maximum and average degree after each round on the TWITTER dataset.

this is one of the largest instances where a correlation clustering algorithm has been run. It will be interesting to consider variants of correlation clustering have been used in data mining applications to see if such variants also admit an efficient parallel algorithm.

7. REFERENCES

[1] R. Agrawal, A. Halverson, K. Kenthapadi, N. Mishra, and P. Tsaparas. Generating labels from clicks. In *WSDM*, pages 172–181, 2009.

[2] N. Ailon, N. Avigdor-Elgrabli, E. Liberty, and A. van Zuylen. Improved approximation algorithms for bipartite correlation clustering. *SICOMP*, 41(5):1110–1121, 2012.

[3] N. Ailon, M. Charikar, and A. Newman. Aggregating inconsistent information: Ranking and clustering. *JACM*, 55(5), 2008.

[4] N. Alon, Y. Matias, and M. Szegedy. The space complexity of approximating the frequency moments. *JCSS*, 58(1):137–147, 1999.

[5] A. Arasu, C. Ré, and D. Suciu. Large-scale deduplication with constraints using dedupalog. In *ICDE*, pages 952–963, 2009.

[6] S. Bagon and M. Galun. Large scale correlation clustering optimization. *CoRR*, abs/1112.2903, 2011.

[7] B. Bahmani, R. Kumar, and S. Vassilvitskii. Densest subgraph in streaming and MapReduce. In *VLDB*, pages 454–465, 2012.

[8] B. Bahmani, B. Moseley, A. Vattani, R. Kumar, and S. Vassilvitskii. Scalable k-means++. *PVLDB*, 5(7):622–633, 2012.

[9] N. Bansal, A. Blum, and S. Chawla. Correlation clustering. *Machine Learning*, 56(1-3):89–113, 2004.

[10] F. Bonchi, A. Gionis, F. Gullo, and A. Ukkonen. Chromatic correlation clustering. In *KDD*, pages 1321–1329, 2012.

[11] F. Bonchi, A. Gionis, and A. Ukkonen. Overlapping correlation clustering. *Knowl. Inf. Syst.*, 35(1):1–32, 2013.

[12] N. Cesa-Bianchi, C. Gentile, F. Vitale, and G. Zappella. A correlation clustering approach to link classification in signed networks. *JMLR*, 23:34.1–34.20, 2012.

[13] D. Chakrabarti, R. Kumar, and K. Punera. A graph-theoretic approach to webpage segmentation. In *WWW*, pages 377–386, 2008.

[14] S. Chaudhuri, V. Ganti, and R. Kaushik. A primitive operator for similarity joins in data cleaning. In *ICDE*, 2006.

[15] Y. Chen, S. Sanghavi, and H. Xu. Clustering sparse graphs. In *NIPS*, pages 2213–2221, 2012.

[16] F. Chierichetti, R. Kumar, and A. Tomkins. Max-cover in Map-Reduce. In *WWW*, pages 231–240, 2010.

[17] J. Dean and S. Ghemawat. MapReduce: Simplified data processing on large clusters. *C. ACM*, 51(1):107–113, 2008.

[18] E. D. Demaine, D. Emanuel, A. Fiat, and N. Immorlica. Correlation clustering in general weighted graphs. *TCS*, 361(2-3):172–187, 2006.

[19] A. K. Elmagarmid, P. G. Ipeirotis, and V. S. Verykios. Duplicate record detection: A survey. *TKDE*, 19(1):1–16, 2007.

[20] M. Elsner and W. Schudy. Bounding and comparing methods for correlation clustering beyond ILP. In *NAACL-HLT Workshop on ILP-NLP*, 2009.

[21] T. Finley and T. Joachims. Supervised clustering with support vector machines. In *ICML*, pages 217–224, 2005.

[22] A. Gionis, H. Mannila, and P. Tsaparas. Clustering aggregation. *TKDD*, 1(1), 2007.

[23] S. Günnemann, I. Färber, K. Virochsiri, and T. Seidl. Subspace correlation clustering: Finding locally correlated dimensions in subspace projections of the data. In *KDD*, pages 352–360, 2012.

[24] O. Hassanzadeh, F. Chiang, H. C. Lee, and R. J. Miller. Framework for evaluating clustering algorithms in duplicate detection. *VLDB*, 2(1):1282–1293, 2009.

[25] D. V. Kalashnikov, Z. Chen, S. Mehrotra, and R. Nuray-Turan. Web people search via connection analysis. *TKDE*, 20(11):1550–1565, 2008.

[26] H. Karloff, S. Suri, and S. Vassilvitskii. A model of computation for MapReduce. In *SODA*, pages 938–948, 2010.

[27] H.-P. Kriegel, P. Kröger, and A. Zimek. Clustering high-dimensional data: A survey on subspace clustering, pattern-based clustering, and correlation clustering. *TKDD*, 3(1):1–58, 2009.

[28] S. Lattanzi, B. Moseley, S. Suri, and S. Vassilvitskii. Filtering: A method for solving graph problems in MapReduce. In *SPAA*, pages 85–94, 2011.

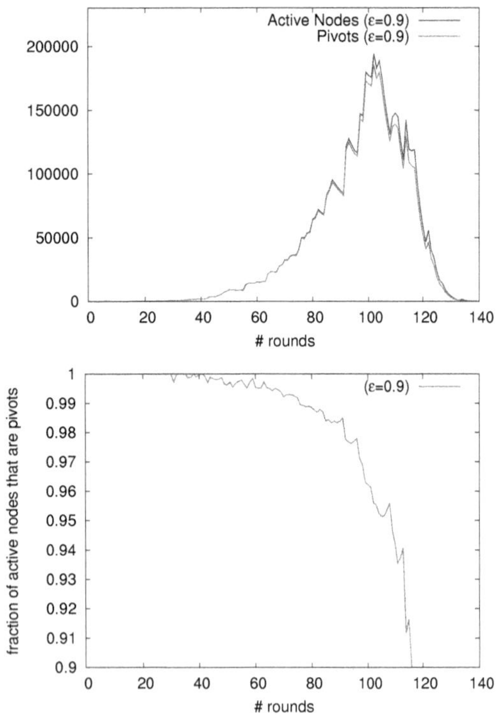

Figure 8: Number and fraction of active nodes chosen as pivots in each round on the TWITTER dataset.

[29] J. Leskovec, D. P. Huttenlocher, and J. M. Kleinberg. Predicting positive and negative links in online social networks. In *WWW*, pages 641–650, 2010.

[30] J. Leskovec, D. P. Huttenlocher, and J. M. Kleinberg. Signed networks in social media. In *CHI*, pages 1361–1370, 2010.

[31] A. Lubotzky, R. Phillips, and P. Sarnak. Ramanujan graphs. *Combinatorica*, 8(3):261–277, 1988.

[32] M. Luby. A simple parallel algorithm for the maximal independent set problem. In *STOC*, pages 1–10, 1985.

[33] G. Malewicz, M. H. Austern, A. J. Bik, J. C. Dehnert, I. Horn, N. Leiser, and G. Czajkowski. Pregel: A system for large-scale graph processing. In *SIGMOD*, pages 135–146, 2010.

[34] A. McCallum and B. Wellner. Toward conditional models of identity uncertainty with application to proper noun coreference. In *IIWeb*, pages 79–84, 2003.

[35] G. D. F. Morales, A. Gionis, and M. Sozio. Social content matching in MapReduce. In *PVLDB*, pages 460–469, 2011.

[36] E. Sadikov, J. Madhavan, L. Wang, and A. Y. Halevy. Clustering query refinements by user intent. In *WWW*, pages 841–850, 2010.

[37] S. Suri and S. Vassilvitskii. Counting triangles and the curse of the last reducer. In *WWW*, pages 607–614, 2011.

[38] A. Zimek. Correlation clustering. *SIGKDD Explor. Newsl.*, pages 53–54, 2009.

APPENDIX

Web Commons Data

The schema for our places data consists of `name`, `address`, `street`, `locality`, `region`, `country`, `zip`, `category`, `description`, `phone`, `geo`, and `url`. The following table shows all the RDF types in Web Data Commons that we mapped to each of our attribute. Not all attributes are present in all entities.

name
http://rdf.data-vocabulary.org/#name
http://rdf.data-vocabulary.org/name
http://schema.org/LocalBusiness/name
http://data-vocabulary.org/Organization/title
http://www.data-vocabulary.org/Organization/name
http://www.w3.org/2006/vcard/ns#given-name
http://data-vocabulary.org/Organization/name
http://www.w3.org/2006/vcard/ns#n
http://rdf.data-vocabulary.org/#nickname
http://www.w3.org/2006/vcard/ns#additional-name
http://www.w3.org/2006/vcard/ns#nickname
http://rdf.data-vocabulary.org/#title
http://rdf.data-vocabulary.org/title
address
http://data-vocabulary.org/Organization/address
http://rdf.data-vocabulary.org/#addr
http://rdf.data-vocabulary.org/#address
http://rdf.data-vocabulary.org/address
http://schema.org/LocalBusiness/address
http://www.data-vocabulary.org/Organization/address
http://www.w3.org/2006/vcard/ns#adr
street
http://data-vocabulary.org/Organization/street-address
http://rdf.data-vocabulary.org/#street-address
http://rdf.data-vocabulary.org/#street
http://rdf.data-vocabulary.org/street-address
http://rdf.data-vocabulary.org/streetAddress
http://schema.org/LocalBusiness/streetAddress
http://www.w3.org/2006/vcard/ns#street-address
region
http://data-vocabulary.org/Organization/region
http://rdf.data-vocabulary.org/#region
http://rdf.data-vocabulary.org/addressRegion
http://rdf.data-vocabulary.org/region
http://www.w3.org/2006/vcard/ns#region
zip
http://data-vocabulary.org/Organization/postal-code
http://rdf.data-vocabulary.org/#postal-code
http://rdf.data-vocabulary.org/postal-code
http://rdf.data-vocabulary.org/postalCode
http://schema.org/LocalBusiness/postalCode
http://www.w3.org/2006/vcard/ns#postal-code
country
http://data-vocabulary.org/Organization/country-name
http://rdf.data-vocabulary.org/#country-name
http://www.w3.org/2006/vcard/ns#country-name
category
http://rdf.data-vocabulary.org/#category
http://www.w3.org/2006/vcard/ns#category
phone
http://data-vocabulary.org/Organization/tel
http://rdf.data-vocabulary.org/#tel
http://rdf.data-vocabulary.org/tel
http://schema.org/LocalBusiness/telephone
http://www.data-vocabulary.org/Organization/tel
http://www.w3.org/2006/vcard/ns#tel
http://www.w3.org/2006/vcard/ns#workTel
http://schema.org/LocalBusiness/faxNumber
http://www.w3.org/2006/vcard/ns#fax
geo
http://data-vocabulary.org/Organization/geo
http://rdf.data-vocabulary.org/#geo
http://rdf.data-vocabulary.org/geo
http://schema.org/LocalBusiness/geo
http://www.w3.org/2006/vcard/ns#geo
http://rdf.data-vocabulary.org/#latitude
http://www.data-vocabulary.org/Organization/longitude
http://www.w3.org/2006/vcard/ns#longitude
http://rdf.data-vocabulary.org/#longitude
http://www.data-vocabulary.org/Organization/latitude
http://www.w3.org/2006/vcard/ns#latitude
url
http://rdf.data-vocabulary.org/url
http://data-vocabulary.org/Organization/url
http://rdf.data-vocabulary.org/#url
http://rdf.data-vocabulary.org/url
http://schema.org/LocalBusiness/url
http://www.data-vocabulary.org/Organization/url
http://www.w3.org/2006/vcard/ns#url
http://rdf.data-vocabulary.org/acquireURL

Scaling Out Big Data Missing Value Imputations

(Pythia vs. Godzilla)

Christos Anagnostopoulos
School of Computing Science
University of Glasgow, G12 8QQ, Glasgow, UK
christos.anagnostopoulos@glasgow.ac.uk

Peter Triantafillou
School of Computing Science
University of Glasgow, G12 8QQ, Glasgow, UK
peter.triantafillou@glasgow.ac.uk

ABSTRACT

Solving the missing-value (MV) problem with small estimation errors in big data environments is a notoriously resource-demanding task. As datasets and their user community continuously grow, the problem can only be exacerbated. Assume that it is possible to have a single machine ('Godzilla'), which can store the massive dataset and support an ever-growing community submitting *MV imputation* requests. Is it possible to replace Godzilla by employing a large number of cohort machines so that imputations can be performed much faster, engaging cohorts in parallel, each of which accesses much smaller partitions of the original dataset? If so, it would be preferable for obvious performance reasons to access only a subset of all cohorts per imputation. In this case, can we decide swiftly which is the desired subset of cohorts to engage per imputation? But efficiency and scalability is just one key concern! Is it possible to do the above while ensuring comparable or even better than Godzilla's imputation estimation errors? In this paper we derive answers to these fundamentals questions and develop principled methods and a framework which offer large performance speedups and better, or comparable, errors to that of Godzilla, independently of which missing-value imputation algorithm is used. Our contributions involve Pythia, a framework and algorithms for providing the answers to the above questions and for engaging the appropriate subset of cohorts per MV imputation request. Pythia functionality rests on two pillars: (i) dataset (partition) signatures, one per cohort, and (ii) similarity notions and algorithms, which can identify the appropriate subset of cohorts to engage. Comprehensive experimentation with real and synthetic datasets showcase our efficiency, scalability, and accuracy claims.

Categories and Subject Descriptors: H. Information Systems; I.5.3 Clustering.

Keywords: Big data; Missing value; Clustering.

1. INTRODUCTION

Data quality is a major concern in big data processing and knowledge management systems. One relevant problem in data quality is the presence of missing values (MVs). The MV problem should be carefully addressed, otherwise bias might be introduced into the induced knowledge. Common solutions to the MV problem either fill-in the MVs (*imputation*) or ignore / exclude them. Imputation entails a *MV substitution algorithm* (MVA) that replaces MVs in a dataset with some plausible values. Imputed data can be treated as reliable as the observed data, but they are as good estimations as the assumptions used to create them.

On the one hand, most computational intelligence and machine learning (ML) techniques (such as neural networks and support vector machines) fail if one or more inputs contains MVs and thus cannot be used for decision-making purposes [1]. Furthermore, the choice of different MVAs affects the performance of ML techniques that are subsequently used with imputed data [2]. On the other hand, the MV problem abounds: it can be found, for instance, in results from medical experimentation and chemical analysis, in datasets from domains such as meteorology and microarray gene monitoring technology [4], and in survey databases [5]. MVs can occur e.g., due to wireless sensor faults, not reacting experiments, or participants skipping survey questions. Industrial and research databases include MVs [6], e.g., maintenance databases have up to 50% of their entries missing [7]. Patient records in medical databases lack some values; interestingly, a database of patients with cystic fibrosis missing more than 60% of its entries was analyzed in [8]. Moreover, gene expression microarray data sets contain MVs, making the need for robust MVAs apparent, since algorithms for gene expression analysis require complete gene array data [9].

Motivations. Given the significance of MVAs, three notes are in order: Firstly, MVAs which can ensure low estimation errors are computationally expensive and typically their performance is largely dependent on dataset sizes. Secondly, nowadays, datasets can be massive. Even worse, existing datasets grow significantly with time; it is not surprising that most MVAs in the literature are typically tested over small-to medium sized datasets. Lastly, as if the scalability limitations imposed by dataset sizes were not enough, in many applications the user community (e.g., in shared scientific datasets in data centers accessed by scientists from all over the world) can be very large and thus the MV imputation input arrival rates can become high as well. These facts pose a scalability nightmare.

The scalability gospel (as established by the seminal work from Google researchers producing the Map-Reduce (MR) [10] data-access paradigm and systems such as the Google

KDD'14, August 24–27, 2014, New York, NY, USA.

http://dx.doi.org/10.1145/2623330.2623615.

File System [11]) rests on the notion of *scaling out*: that is, (i) employ a large number of commodity (off-the-shelf and thus inexpensive) machines, each storing a much smaller partition of the original dataset, and (ii) access them in parallel.

However, MR is not a panacea, for two reasons. First, not all complex problems are 'embarrassingly parallelizable' and amenable to MR techniques. In particular, there exist sophisticated MVAs ensuring small errors, which are not MR-able [12]. Second, in the context of MVAs, even if they were 'embarrassingly parallelizable', not all partitions may be relevant. It may very well be the case that a number of the machines hold data that cannot help (or even hurt) in the MV imputation process. And, obviously, engaging only a fraction of all machines will introduce large benefits: First with respect to performance. MV imputation will be shorter, as these times typically depend on the worst performing machine and with increasing machine numbers the probability of a mall-performing machine increases. Further, overall MV imputation throughput will be higher, as each imputation will be taxing fewer overall system resources (processors, communication bandwidth and disks). Second, with respect to MV estimation errors. In fact, as we shall formally show later, engaging all machines and their dataset partitions may actually introduce large additional MV estimation errors.

Goals. In this work, we will consider a stream of MV inputs (or inputs), i.e., multi-dimensional vectors with some MVs in certain dimensions, arriving at a data system. Typically, the system is presented with a batch of data items with MVs, which must be added to the system after MVs have been estimated. There are two system alternatives. The first is based on employing a single machine which stores the whole of the dataset. We affectionately call this machine *Godzilla*. Godzilla can employ any MVA to perform the MV imputations. As motivated earlier, this approach suffers from several disadvantages. The second alternative employs a (potentially large) number of machines, referred to as *cohorts*, each storing a partition of Godzilla's dataset. Imputation execution engages cohorts in parallel, whereby each cohort runs an MVA on a much smaller local dataset. This can introduce dramatic performance improvements. As an illustration, assuming, say, 50 cohorts and an MVA operating on a dataset of size n with asymptotic complexity $O(n^2)$ (or $O(n^3)$; [3], [4]) a scale-out execution is expected to speedup input processing by a factor of $50^2 = 2,500$ (or $50^3 = 125,000$) as such MVA runs in parallel on a dataset of size $\frac{1}{50}n$. Moreover, this alternative affords the possibility of accessing only a subset of all cohorts for a given input. We will not make any restricting assumptions as to specific characteristics of this system or the method for partitioning the dataset.

The formidable challenges here entail: (i) for data accuracy (estimation-error) reasons, we should ensure that the subset of cohorts contacted achieve similar, if not smaller estimation errors, compared to the errors that Godzilla would yield; (ii) *swiftly* determine the subset of cohorts to engage per imputation, achieving large efficiency/scalability gains.

Contributions. To our knowledge, this is the first study on scaling out MV imputations. We shall derive fundamental knowledge regarding meeting the estimation error and performance goals outlined above. Armed with this knowledge, we shall propose a novel, principally derived framework, *Pythia*, which offers large performance speed-ups and better, or comparable, errors to that of Godzilla given a stream of MV inputs. Pythia's salient contribution is that, given an input (of imputation requests), Pythia is able to predict and engage the appropriate subset of cohorts to employ per imputation. Pythia's prediction process relies on (i) the concept of per cohort-dataset *signature*, which derives from the (local) dataset of a cohort and (ii) novel similarity notions and algorithms which, based on each imputation request and cohort signatures, can determine the best subset of cohorts to engage. Finally, we will provide comprehensive experimental evidence substantiating and showcasing Pythia's accuracy and performance, using a variety of metrics and real and synthetic datasets.

The paper is structured as follows: Section 2 reports on background and discusses related work, while Section 3 introduces the problem fundamentals of scaling out the MV imputations. In Section 4 and Section 5 we introduce the Pythia framework and propose two schemes. In Section 6 we evaluate our framework and Section 7 concludes the paper.

2. BACKGROUND & RELATED WORK

2.1 Missing data

Assume a data set $\mathcal{X}$ of d-dimensional data points with some MVs on a certain dimension X_i. Data on X_i are said to be *missing completely at random* (MCAR) if the probability of MV on X_i, q, is unrelated to the value of X_i itself or to the values of any other dimensions. If data are MCAR, a reduced sample of $\mathcal{X}$ will be a random sub-sample of $\mathcal{X}$; MCAR assumes that the distributions of MVs and complete data are the same. Data on X_i are said to be *missing at random* (MAR) if q depends on the observed data, but does not depend on the MV itself. In MAR, the dimension associated with MVs has a relation to other dimensions, i.e., MVs can be estimated by using the complete data of other dimensions. It is impossible to test whether the MAR condition is satisfied for $\mathcal{X}$ because, since the (actual) values of missing data are not known, we cannot compare the values of those with and without missing data to see if they differ systematically on that X_i. Data on X_i are *missing not at random* (MNAR) if q depends on the MVs and, thus, missing data cannot be estimated by using the existing dimensions; MNAR is rarely applicable in practice.

2.2 Related work

Missing data hinder the application of many statistical analysis and ML techniques available in off-the-shelf software. To analyze $\mathcal{X}$ with MVs, certain MVAs have been proposed [13]. The simplest method is discarding the data points with MVs or removing the corresponding dimensions. Both removals of such points and dimensions result in decreasing the information content of $\mathcal{X}$ and are applicable only when (i) $\mathcal{X}$ contains a small amount of MVs, and (ii) the analysis of the remaining complete points will not be biased by the removal. There are many MVAs varying from naïve methods, e.g., mean imputation, to some more robust methods based on relationships among dimensions. In the *dummy variable adjustment*, MVs are set to some arbitrary value. The *mean / mode imputation* replaces MVs of a dimension by the sample mean / mode of all observed values of that dimension. In *hot deck* MVA [14], a MV is filled in with a value from an estimated distribution w.r.t. $\mathcal{X}$. In the K-nearest neighbors MVA [15], the MVs of a point are imputed considering the K most similar (observed) points from $\mathcal{X}$. The regression- and likelihood-based MVAs are introduced in [16]. In *regression-based imputation* [17], the MVs of a point are estimated by regression of the dimensions corresponding to MVs on the dimensions associated to the observed values of that point. This approach argues that dimensions have relationships among themselves; if no relationships exist among dimensions in $\mathcal{X}$ and the dimensions corresponding to MVs, such MVA will not be precise for imputation. *Likelihood-based imputation* [16] is based on parameter estimation in the presence of MVs, i.e., $\mathcal{X}$'s parameters are estimated by maximum likelihood or maximum a posteriori procedures relying on variants of the Expectation-Maximization algorithm. The *multiple imputation* MVA [18], instead of filling in a single value for each MV, replaces each MV with a set of plausible values that represent the uncertainty about the actual value to impute. These multiply-imputed datasets are then analyzed by using standard procedures for complete data and combining the results from these analyses. In case of MVs in time series, the models in [19] (using dynamic Bayesian networks), [20] (using matrix completion), and [21] (using Gaussian mixtures clustering) recover MVs in motion capture sequences, vital signs, and micro-array gene expression streams, respectively. Furthermore, ML-based MVAs, e.g., decision-trees and rule-based methods, generate a model from $\mathcal{X}$ that contain MVs, which is used to perform classification that imputes the MVs (see [2] and the references therein). Finally, the imputation framework [6] applies most existing MVAs (base methods) to improve their accuracy of imputation while preserving the asymptotic computational complexity of the base methods. The interested reader could also refer to [6], [9] and [22] (and the references therein) for a comprehensive survey of the most recent MVAs.

3. PROBLEM ANALYSIS & FUNDAMENTALS

3.1 Definitions & Notations

Definition 1. Given a set $\mathcal{X}$ of d-dimensional data points, $\mathcal{X} = \{\mathbf{x}_1, \ldots, \mathbf{x}_{|\mathcal{X}|}\}$, for each $\mathbf{x}_i$ we define $\mathbf{w}_i = [w_{ik}]^\top$ with $w_{ik} = 0$ whenever $\mathbf{x}_i$'s k-th dimensional value is missing; otherwise $w_{ik} = 1$. We express $\mathbf{x}_i$ as $(\mathbf{z}_i, \mathbf{z}_i^{\mathbf{m}})$, where $\mathbf{z}_i \in \mathbb{R}^n$ denotes observed values and $\mathbf{z}_i^{\mathbf{m}} \in \mathbb{R}^{(d-n)}$ denotes MVs, with $n = \sum_{k=1}^{d} w_{ik}$.

Definition 2. Given a finite integer $m > 0$, $\mathcal{X}_i$ is a partition of $\mathcal{X}$ such that $\mathcal{X} \equiv \cup_{i=1}^{m} \mathcal{X}_i$ and $\mathcal{X}_i \neq \mathcal{X}_j, i \neq j$. S_i denotes the machine (*cohort*), which maintains $\mathcal{X}_i$, performs a MVA over $\mathcal{X}_i$, and is indexed by i, $i = 1, \ldots, m$. $\mathcal{S} = \{S_i\}_{i=1}^{m}$ is the set of all cohorts. The (imaginary) *Godzilla* S_0 assembles all $\mathcal{X}_i$ and is capable of performing a MVA over $\mathcal{X}$.

Definition 3. A single MV input on MVA is $\mathbf{i} = (\mathbf{x}, \mathbf{w})$ and output is $\hat{\mathbf{x}}$ expressed by $(\mathbf{z}, \hat{\mathbf{z}}^{\mathbf{m}})$. $\hat{\mathbf{x}} \in \mathbb{R}^d$ is referred to as *estimate* containing $\hat{\mathbf{z}}^{\mathbf{m}} \in \mathbb{R}^{(d-n)}$ of imputed MVs by MVA. If $\mathbf{x}_a$ is the actual vector, the absolute reconstruction error is $e = \| \hat{\mathbf{x}} - \mathbf{x}_a \|$; $\| \mathbf{x} \|$ denotes the Euclidean norm.

3.2 MVAs in our framework

As our contributions are independent of any particular MVA, we overview two popular and representative MVAs as would be used in our framework. To exemplify our framework and methods, we employ the weighted K-nearest neighbors (KNN) [15] and sequential multivariate regression imputation method (REG) [17]. These MVAs are widely used for multivariate imputation in many scientific areas.

3.2.1 Weighted K-nearest neighbors imputation

KNN is widely used [22] since it has many attractive characteristics: it is a non-parametric method, which does not require the creation of a predictive model for each dimension with MV and takes into account the correlation structure of the data. KNN is based on the assumption that points close in distance are potentially similar. For given input $(\mathbf{x}_i, \mathbf{w}_i)$ with $\mathbf{x}_i = (\mathbf{z}_i, \mathbf{z}_i^{\mathbf{m}})$, KNN calculates a weighted Euclidean distance D_{ij} between $\mathbf{x}_i$ and $\mathbf{x}_j \in \mathcal{X}$ such that

$$D_{ij} = \left(\frac{\sum_{k=1}^{d} w_{ik} w_{jk} (x_{ik} - x_{jk})^2}{\sum_{k=1}^{d} w_{ik} w_{jk}} \right)^{1/2}.$$

The MV of the k-th dimension of $\mathbf{x}_i$ (i.e., $z_{ik}^{\mathbf{m}}$ of $\mathbf{z}_i^{\mathbf{m}}$) is estimated by the weighted average of non-MVs of the K most similar $\mathbf{x}_j$ to $\mathbf{x}_i$, i.e., $\hat{z}_{ik}^{\mathbf{m}} = \sum_{j=1}^{K} \frac{D_{ij}^{-1}}{\sum_{v=1}^{K} D_{iv}^{-1}} x_{jk}$. KNN is typically used with K=10,15,20; theses values have been favored in previous studies [22], [23]. (In our experiments we will use K=10).

3.2.2 Sequential multivariate regression imputation

REG estimates the MVs by fitting a sequence of regression models and drawing values from the corresponding predictive distributions. Let $Y_1, \ldots, Y_{d-n}$ denote $d-n$ (dependent) variables with MVs, sorted in ascending order to the number of MVs and $\mathbf{X} = [X_1, \ldots, X_n]^\top$ denote n (predictor) variables with no MVs. REG consists of c rounds. In round 1, step 1, we regress the variable with the fewest number of MVs, Y_1, on $\mathbf{X}$ imputing the MVs under the appropriate regression model; e.g., if Y_1 is continuous, categorical, or binary then ordinary least squares, generalized logit, or logistic linear regression is applied, respectively. In step 2, after estimating the regression coefficients β of the model from step 1, we use the estimated $\hat{\beta}$ to impute the MVs of Y_1. In step 3, we update $\mathbf{X}$ by appending Y_1 and continue to variable, say Y_2, with the next fewest MVs and repeat the process using updated $\mathbf{X}$ as predictors until all the variables have been imputed. That is, Y_1 is regressed on $\mathbf{U} = \mathbf{X}$; Y_2 is regressed on $\mathbf{U} = (\mathbf{X}, Y_1)$, where Y_1 has imputed MVs; Y_3 is regressed on $\mathbf{U} = (\mathbf{X}, Y_1, Y_2)$, where Y_1 and Y_2 have imputed MVs, and so on. Steps 1 to 3 are then repeated in rounds 2 through c, modifying the predictors set to include all Ys except the one used as the dependent variable. Hence, regress Y_1 on $\mathbf{X}$ and $Y_2, \ldots, Y_{d-n}$; regress Y_2 on $\mathbf{X}$ and $Y_1, Y_3, \ldots, Y_{d-n}$, and so on. Repeated cycles continue for c rounds, or until stable imputed MVs occur.

3.3 On Cohort vs. Godzilla errors

We consider a discrete time domain $t \in \mathbb{T}$ and at instance $t = 1, 2, \ldots$, we are given input $\mathbf{i}[t]$. Assume that Godzilla S_0 exists and is capable of invoking a certain MVA for $\mathbf{i}[t]$. At first thought, one could claim that, since Godzilla has global knowledge (i.e., the union of all $\mathcal{X}_i$), the corresponding estimate $\hat{\mathbf{x}}_G[t]$ would be *better* (in terms of reconstruction error $e_G[t]$) than $\hat{\mathbf{x}}_i[t]$ of each S_i (with error $e_i[t]$). However, this does not always hold true. It depends on the probability density function (pdf) of $\{\mathcal{X}_i\}$ and the (possibly unknown) pdf of $\mathbf{z}[t]$, $\mathbf{z}^{\mathbf{m}}[t]$, and $\mathbf{w}[t]$.

THEOREM 1. *Let e_G and e_i denote the estimate error of Godzilla S_0 and cohort S_i. It is not always true that $e_G < e_i, \forall S_i \in \mathcal{S}$.*

PROOF. To prove Theorem 1, suppose its converse were true. Then it suffices to show counterexamples. Consider the mean imputation (MEAN) and the KNN. Consider that points in $\mathcal{X}_i$ are normally distributed, $\mathcal{N}(\mu_i, \sigma_i^2)$, with mean μ_i and variance σ_i^2 and $|\mu_i - \mu_j| >> 0, i \neq j$. Evidently, S_0's data set $\mathcal{X} = \cup_{i=1}^m \mathcal{X}_i$ follows the mixture $\mathcal{N}(\mu, \sigma^2)$ with $\mu = \sum_{i=1}^m a_i \mu_i$, $\sigma^2 = \sum_{i=1}^m a_i((\mu_i - \mu)^2 + \sigma_i^2)$; $a_i > 0, \sum_{i=1}^m a_i = 1$. If we were told that all (both observed $\mathbf{z}$ and unobserved $\mathbf{z^m}$) inputs followed $\mathcal{N}(\mu_j, \sigma_j^2)$ for some $j, 1 \leq j \leq m$ then we should have engaged only S_j thus yielding $e_j < e_G$ in case of MEAN, and $e_j = e_G$ in case of KNN (for $K << |\mathcal{X}_j|$) and avoiding engaging all S_i. □

Furthermore, consider that all $\mathcal{X}_i$ follow exactly the same distribution; consequently, S_0's $\mathcal{X}$ follows the same distribution. Then, regardless of any knowledge on the pdfs of inputs, we could randomly select one cohort from $\mathcal{S}$, thus, yielding $e_i = e_G, \forall S_i \in \mathcal{S}$, and avoiding engaging all cohorts.

Example 1: Consider $m = 3$ cohorts S_1, S_2, S_3 with 2D datasets $\mathcal{X}_i$, corresponding joint pdfs f_1, f_2, f_3 and a Godzilla S_0 with $\mathcal{X} = \cup_{i=1}^3 \mathcal{X}_i$ whose joint pdf f_G is shown in Fig. 1(a). Assume REG, KNN, and MEAN MVAs. We are given a stream of 10^4 inputs $\mathbf{i}[1], \ldots, \mathbf{i}[t]$ and assume that we *know* the pdf of each $\mathbf{i}[t]$, i.e., its observed and MVs are known to be produced either by f_1, f_2, or f_3. For each $\mathbf{i}[t]$, we invoke a MVA (a) on S_0 and obtain $e_G[t]$, (b) only on the cohort S_j with the same pdf f_j as that of the input and obtain $e_j[t]$, and (c) on all cohorts, aggregate their estimates by taking their average and obtain $e_{all}[t]$. Fig. 1(b) shows the root-mean-square error (RMSE) e_G, e_j, and e_{all} for all MVAs. We observe that the knowledge of the pdf of each input results to a significantly lower error e_j, because we engage only the cohort S_j corresponding to the same pdf as that of the input. Godzilla produces a relatively high e_G (for all MVAs) with high computational cost due to processing high volumes of data. Moreover, the parallel execution of MVAs over all cohorts for each input produces a high e_{all}. Unfortunately, the pdf of an incoming input is not known, especially, the pdf of the MVs is unknown since they are never observed. Moreover, we can achieve high parallelism with concurrently engaging all cohorts but, we also obtain high error, because there might be a subset of cohorts that *adversely* contribute to the aggregated estimate, e.g., due to the fact that the corresponding pdfs of their data sets are different from those of the inputs (see Example 2). Note, however, that in the case of MEAN, $e_G = e_{all}$.

3.4 On computing good cohort subsets

Here we show: (i) that computing the best cohorts subset is computationally hard, (ii) that even if an efficient heuristic can be found, it would not be desirable for our purpose since it would require communication with all cohorts, hence, another approach is needed, like our signature-based prediction approach and (iii) that as exemplified using our reference popular MVAs, it is highly beneficial to engage only a good cohort subset per imputation. The above showcases thus the traits and benefits of our approach.

In our framework, we utilize a node called Pythia that attempts to predict the best cohorts subset per input. Pythia receives input $\mathbf{i}[t] = (\mathbf{x}[t], \mathbf{w}[t])$ with $0 < n[t] = \sum_{k=1}^d w_k[t] < d$. In the remainder, the time index t is omitted for the sake of readability. Of course, Pythia can, trivially, engage all cohorts in parallel. Each cohort S_i locally produces an estimate $\hat{\mathbf{x}}_i$ (through MVA invocation) and provides it to Pythia. Then, Pythia takes their average value $\hat{\mathbf{x}} = \frac{1}{m}\sum_{i=1}^m \hat{\mathbf{x}}_i$. Let us denote such method as the *All Cohorts Method*, notated by ACM, so to differentiate it from Pythia's sophisticated methods. ACM implies that all cohorts are equal candidates and available for providing an estimate. It would have been preferable if Pythia could engage a subset $\mathcal{S}' \subset \mathcal{S}$ of cohorts whose average estimate $\hat{\mathbf{x}}' = \frac{1}{|\mathcal{S}'|}\sum_{S_i \in \mathcal{S}'} \hat{\mathbf{x}}_i$ would be equal to $\hat{\mathbf{x}}$, or more interestingly, if Pythia could engage the minimum subset of cohorts whose average estimate is close to $\hat{\mathbf{x}}$ for each input.

Determining the minimum cohorts subset whose aggregate estimate is close to $\hat{\mathbf{x}}$ calls to mind the Subset Sum Problem (SSP) [24]: Consider a pair $(\mathcal{I}, s)$, where $\mathcal{I}$ is a set of $m > 0$ positive integers and s is a positive integer. SSP asks for a subset of $\mathcal{I}$ whose sum is closest to, but not greater than, s. SSP is NP-hard [24]. Consider now the following problem, referred to as Minimum Subset Average Problem (MSAP).

Problem 1. (MSAP) Given $(\mathcal{I}, s)$, find the minimum subset $\mathcal{I}'$ with average s' subject to $\lfloor s' \rfloor = s$ or $\lceil s' \rceil = s$ (C1).

THEOREM 2. *MSAP is NP-hard.*

PROOF. If there is a polynomial-time algorithm for MSAP, then a polynomial-time algorithm can be developed for SSP. Assume there exists a polynomial algorithm $A(\mathcal{I}, s)$ that solves MSAP, i.e., $A(\mathcal{I}, s)$ finds in polynomial time the minimum subset $\mathcal{I}'$ subject to constraint C1 in Problem 1. Then, $A(\mathcal{I}, s)$ can be used to solve SSP with $(\mathcal{I}, ms)$, $m = |\mathcal{I}|$. In general, any solution $B(\mathcal{I}, s)$ of SSP with $(\mathcal{I}, s)$ can be formulated as Algorithm 1. If the complexity of $A(\mathcal{I}, s)$ is a polynomial $\mathcal{Q}(m)$ then the complexity of $B(\mathcal{I}, s)$ is $O(m\mathcal{Q}(m))$. But, this implies that there is a polynomial-time algorithm for SSP. Hence, no polynomial-time algorithm exists for MSAP. □

ALGORITHM 1: $B(\mathcal{I}, s)$

```
Input: I, s
Output: I'
for 1 ≤ k ≤ |I| do
    call A(I, s/k);
    If a subset I' of I with k elements is found, whose
    elements have an average k' such that ⌊k'⌋ = s/k or
    ⌈k'⌉ = s/k Then return I'
end
```

THEOREM 3. *Given input $\mathbf{i}$, the problem of finding the minimum subset $\mathcal{S}' \subset \mathcal{S}$ of cohorts, whose average estimate $\hat{\mathbf{x}}'$ gives the same reconstruction error as $\hat{\mathbf{x}}$ is NP-hard.*

PROOF. Let $e = \| \hat{\mathbf{x}} - \mathbf{x}_a \|$ and $e' = \| \hat{\mathbf{x}}' - \mathbf{x}_a \|$. In order to show that the problem of finding the minimum subset $\mathcal{S}'$ with $e' = e$ is NP-hard, it suffices to show that finding the minimum subset $\mathcal{S}' \subset \mathcal{S}$ of cohorts such that $\| \hat{\mathbf{x}}' \| = \| \hat{\mathbf{x}} \|$ subject to C1 is NP-hard. Consider the set $\mathcal{I}^0 = \{\lfloor \| \hat{\mathbf{x}}_i \| \rfloor\}_{i=1}^m$, and $\mathcal{I}^1 = \{\lceil \| \hat{\mathbf{x}}_i \| \rceil\}_{i=1}^m$, $\| \hat{\mathbf{x}}_i \| > 0, \forall i$. Since MSAP, which deals with integers is NP-hard from Theorem 2, MSAP with $(\mathcal{I}^0, \lfloor \| \hat{\mathbf{x}} \| \rfloor)$ and $(\mathcal{I}^1, \lceil \| \hat{\mathbf{x}} \| \rceil)$ is also NP-hard. □

SSP and MSAP are NP-hard, however, one is often satisfied with an approximate, sub-optimal solution, i.e., in polynomial time; see [25] for SSP. Nevertheless, even if Pythia

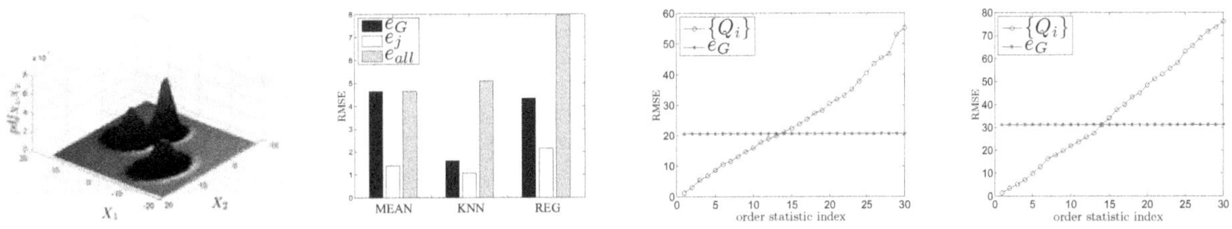

(a) Joint pdf $f_G(X_1, X_2)$ (b) RMSE using MEAN, KNN, REG (c) RMSE using KNN (d) RMSE using REG

Figure 1: (a) Joint pdf; (b) RMSE e_G, e_j, e_{all} using MEAN, KNN and REG for $m = 3$ in Example 1; (c-d) RMSE of Godzilla and order statistics Q_i of ACM using KNN and REG for $m = 30$ in Example 2.

were able to use such heuristic to find the minimum set $\mathcal{S}'$ for given input (let m be small) then this would still not be preferable given our goals. That is because, in order to obtain $\mathcal{S}'$ for a given input, Pythia would *firstly* have to engage all cohorts and consequently, based on their estimates, produce $\mathcal{S}'$. What we want is for Pythia to guess/predict the most appropriate $\mathcal{S}'$, which gives the same or, hopefully, smaller reconstruction error than that of $\mathcal{S}$ *without having to access all cohorts*! For instance, this guess can be interpreted as follows: cohort $S_i \in \mathcal{S}$ might consider $\mathbf{z}$ (of input $\mathbf{i}$) as an observation which is deemed *unlikely* w.r.t. $\mathcal{X}_i$. Based on the fact that a MVA highly depends on $\mathcal{X}_i$, S_i will probably provide a bad estimate for $\mathbf{i}$ (w.r.t. e_i). Were Pythia capable of predicting the *unsuitability* of S_i providing a good estimate *before* engaging S_i then Pythia could have excluded S_i from $\mathcal{S}'$.

The task of predicting $\mathcal{S}'$ per input involves the following issues: (a) the joint pdf of the MVs is evidently unknown since the actual values of $\mathbf{z}^\mathbf{m}$ are not observed; (b) it is not feasible to identify the joint pdf that generates $\mathbf{z}$, since we have only one sample from this at a time; (c) it is not suitable to assume that $\mathbf{z}$ is produced by a certain pdf at time t, which remains also the same for subsequent $\mathbf{z}[\tau], \tau > t$. This is getting more difficult when dealing with non-stationary distributions of $\mathbf{z}$ and $\mathbf{w}$, which is not a rare situation.

Example 2: Consider $m = 30$ cohorts. We are given a stream of 10^4 inputs where the joint pdf of each input is unknown. For each input, we invoke a MVA (KNN and REG) on Godzilla and on all cohorts in parallel, and aggregate their estimates (ACM). For each input, we obtain the order statistics $Q_1 = \min_i\{e_i\}, \ldots, Q_{30} = \max_i\{e_i\}$ of the corresponding errors of all cohorts and plot their average values in Fig. 1(c-d); the e_G is shown for comparison. We can observe that more than 40% of cohorts provide lower error to that of Godzilla for KNN and REG. This indicates that it is of high importance to predict such subset of cohorts for each input while knowing neither the pdfs of the cohorts' sets nor the pdf of each input. Note that ACM in this case produces a higher average error than even Godzilla. Furthermore, we observe that for each input there is an *ideal* cohort that gives the minimum error; note that $\bar{Q}_1$ is 93% / 95% smaller than e_G for KNN / REG. An *ideal* Pythia has to predict $\mathcal{S}'$ hopefully including the ideal cohort and/or those S_i with $e_i < e_G$ for each input. We now formulate our problems.

Problem 2. Determine what *information* each $S_i \in \mathcal{S}$ a-priori must convey to Pythia in order to predict whether S_i is suitable for providing a (local) good estimate $\hat{\mathbf{x}}_i$ given an input, i.e., whether S_i should be a member of $\mathcal{S}'$. This information is referred to as the *signature* P_i of $\mathcal{X}_i$.

Problem 3. Determine how signatures $\{P_i\}_{i=1}^m$ are updated for each input.

4. THE PYTHIA FRAMEWORK

Pythia aims to solve the above problems. Predicting $\mathcal{S}'$ for each input, based on per-cohort signatures, avoids the fundamental problems of NP-hardness of exact solutions and of the need to on-the-fly engage all cohorts for approximate heuristic solutions.

Each cohort S_i constructs a signature P_i from $\mathcal{X}_i$. P_i reflects the current structure of data points in $\mathcal{X}_i$. The idea behind a signature is that S_i is engaged for a given $\mathbf{i}$ once $\mathbf{x}$ can be 'explained' through P_i. S_i provides its (locally) created P_i to Pythia, which stores all signatures forming $\mathcal{P} = \{P_i\}_{i=1}^m$. Figure 2(a) pictorially depicts the framework's operation. The operation of the framework is as follows: Given $\mathbf{i}$,

1. Pythia predicts $\mathcal{S}' \subseteq \mathcal{S}$ w.r.t. $\mathcal{P}$
2. Pythia then engages only the cohorts from S' sending $\mathbf{i}$ to them.
3. Each $S_i \in \mathcal{S}'$
   (a) invokes a MVA and
   (b) provides its estimate $\hat{\mathbf{x}}_i$ to Pythia.
4. Pythia constructs the aggregate estimate $\hat{\mathbf{x}}$ that is sent to cohorts from $\mathcal{S}'$.
5. Each $S_i \in \mathcal{S}'$ can exploit $\hat{\mathbf{x}}$ for updating its P_i.
6. Pythia uses $\hat{\mathbf{x}}$ for updating $\mathcal{P}$.

4.1 Signatures

In this work, P_i refers to a clustering structure over $\mathcal{X}_i$ providing a set of representative points (clusters) $\mathcal{C}_i$. Each cohort $S_i \in \mathcal{S}$ employs the Adaptive Resonance Theory (ART) [26], an unsupervised learning model from the competitive learning paradigm, in order to locally construct P_i over $\mathcal{X}_i$. In ART, whose algorithm is shown as Algorithm 2, each $\mathbf{x}_k \in \mathcal{X}_i$ is processed by finding the nearest cluster $\mathbf{c}^* \in \mathbb{R}^d$ to $\mathbf{x}_k$, i.e., $\mathbf{c}^* = \arg\min_{\mathbf{c}\in\mathcal{C}_i} \parallel \mathbf{c} - \mathbf{x}_k \parallel$, where $\mathcal{C}_i$ is the set of clusters. Then, it is allowed $\mathbf{x}_k$ to modify/update $\mathbf{c}^*$ only if $\mathbf{c}^*$ is sufficiently close to $\mathbf{x}_k$ ($\mathbf{c}^*$ is said to 'resonate' with $\mathbf{x}_k$) i.e., if $\parallel \mathbf{c}^* - \mathbf{x}_k \parallel \leq \rho_i$ for some *vigilance* $\rho_i > 0$. In this case, $\mathbf{c}^*$ is updated through the rule $\mathbf{c}^* \leftarrow \mathbf{c}^* + \eta_i(\mathbf{x}_k - \mathbf{c}^*)$, where $\eta_i \in (0, 1)$ is a learning rate, which gradually decreases. Otherwise, i.e., $\parallel \mathbf{c}^* - \mathbf{x}_k \parallel > \rho_i$, a new cluster $\mathbf{c}$ is formed handling $\mathbf{x}_k$ such that $\mathbf{c} = \mathbf{x}_k$ and $\mathcal{C}_i \leftarrow \mathcal{C}_i \cup \{\mathbf{c}\}$.

Definition 4. Cohort S_i's signature P_i over $\mathcal{X}_i$ is the triple

$$P_i = \langle \mathcal{C}_i, \rho_i, \eta_i \rangle. \tag{1}$$

ALGORITHM 2: ART algorithm at cohort S_i

Input: $\mathcal{X}_i, \eta_i, \rho_i$
Output: $\mathcal{C}_i$
$\mathcal{C}_i = \{\mathbf{x}_1\}$;
for $1 < k \leq |\mathcal{X}_i|$ **do**
  $b^* = \| \mathbf{c}^* - \mathbf{x}_k \| = \min_{\mathbf{c} \in \mathcal{C}_i} \| \mathbf{c} - \mathbf{x}_k \|$;
  if $b^* > \rho_i$ **then**
    $\mathcal{C}_i \leftarrow \mathcal{C}_i \cup \{\mathbf{x}_k\}$;
  else
    $\mathbf{c}^* \leftarrow \mathbf{c}^* + \eta_i(\mathbf{x}_k - \mathbf{c}^*)$;
  end
end

Definition 5. We say that $\mathbf{x}$ is a *member* of P_i, notated $\mathbf{x} \in P_i$, iff $\min_{\mathbf{c} \in \mathcal{C}_i} \| \mathbf{c} - \mathbf{x} \| \leq \rho_i$; otherwise, $\mathbf{x} \notin P_i$.

The statement '$\mathbf{x} \in P_i$' denotes that there is at least one $\mathbf{c} \in \mathcal{C}_i$ such that $\mathbf{x}$ is placed close to $\mathbf{c}$ with distance less than ρ_i, for instance, the closest cluster $\mathbf{c}^*$ to $\mathbf{x}$. The more clusters $\mathbf{c} \in \mathcal{C}_i$ satisfy the criterion $\| \mathbf{c} - \mathbf{x} \| \leq \rho_i$, the more appropriate $\mathcal{C}_i$ is for $\mathbf{x}$. In this sense, if $\mathbf{x} \in P_i$ then $\mathbf{x}$ can be represented by at least one cluster from $\mathcal{X}_i$. Based on this intuition, if $\mathbf{x} \in P_i$, cohort S_i provides a rather good estimate for some missing parts of $\mathbf{x}$ compared to a cohort S_j associated with a P_j for which it holds true that $\mathbf{x} \notin P_j$. The latter case indicates that no cluster from $\mathcal{C}_j$ can be a representative point for $\mathbf{x}$.

Since ρ_i represents a threshold of similarity between points and clusters, thus, guiding ART in determining when a new cluster should be formed, it should depend on $\mathcal{X}_i$. In order to give a physical meaning to ρ_i, it is expressed through a set of percentages $\alpha_k \in (0, 1)$ of the ranges between the lowest $x_k^{\min}$ and highest $x_k^{\max}$ values of each dimension k of points in $\mathcal{X}_i$, $k = 1, \ldots, d$. Let $\mathbf{r}_i = [(x_1^{\max} - x_1^{\min}), \ldots, (x_d^{\max} - x_d^{\min})]^\top$ and the diagonal $d \times d$ matrix $\mathbf{A}$ with $\mathbf{A}[k, k] = \alpha_k$. Then $\rho_i = \| \mathbf{A}\mathbf{r}_i \|$. High α_k values result to a low number of clusters and vice versa. Each S_i determines a ρ_i over $\mathcal{X}_i$, creates P_i through Algorithm 2, and sends P_i to Pythia.

Note: when dealing with mixed-type data points, e.g., consisting of categorical, binary, and continuous attributes, we can adopt appropriate distance metrics [27] for the distance between $\mathbf{x}_k$ and $\mathbf{x}_l$ instead of using the Euclidean distance $\| \mathbf{x}_k - \mathbf{x}_l \|$; this does not spoil the generality of signature creation.

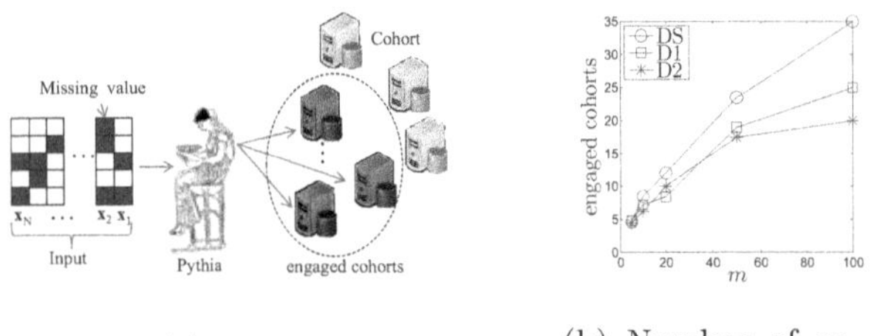

(a) Pythia (b) Number of engaged cohorts

Figure 2: (a) Inputs with MVs, Pythia and engaged cohorts; (b) Engaged cohorts against m (COE).

4.2 Cohort prediction schemes

Up to this point, we have shown how to use signatures as a guiding light to select appropriate cohorts for MV imputations. Now, our concern is twofold: MV imputations must be (i) low cost and (ii) high accuracy. Low cost (once signature processing is performed) refers to the communication cost between Pythia and cohorts and to the cost of running MVAs at cohorts. High accuracy refers to low RMSE. Therefore, we present algorithms with these in mind.

4.2.1 Cost-aware algorithm: Top-$\mathcal{K}$ Cohort scheme

For simplicity we present the top-1 (Best) Cohort (BC) scheme, i.e., $\mathcal{K} = 1$. Pythia is not involved in producing the (final) estimate $\hat{\mathbf{x}}$, instead, only one cohort (best cohort) is engaged for doing this locally. Pythia communicates only with the best cohort, which runs the MVA, thus, this optimizes our cost metric. Given $\mathbf{i}$, Pythia determines the best cohort $S^* \in \mathcal{S}$ with $P^* = \langle \mathcal{C}^*, \rho^*, \eta^* \rangle$ such that **(A1)** $\mathbf{c}^* = \arg\min_{\mathbf{c} \in \cup_{i=1}^m \mathcal{C}_i} \| \mathbf{c} - \mathbf{z} \|$ and $\mathbf{c}^* = \arg\min_{\mathbf{c} \in \mathcal{C}^*} \| \mathbf{c} - \mathbf{z} \|$, i.e., $\mathbf{c}^* \in \mathcal{C}^*$ is the closest cluster to $\mathbf{z}$ among all clusters from all signatures, and **(A2)** $\mathbf{z} \in P^*$. Note that $\mathbf{z} \in \mathbb{R}^n$ with $0 < n = \sum_{k=1}^d w_k < d$ provided that $\mathbf{x}$ contains $d - n$ MVs. In order to evaluate '$\mathbf{z} \in P^*$' Pythia calculates $\rho^{*(n)} \leq \rho^*$ associated with the n dimensions of $\mathbf{r}^*$ corresponding to the n non-MVs. Then, it checks if $\| \mathbf{c}^* - \mathbf{z} \| \leq \rho^{*(n)}$ dealing only with the n dimensions of $\mathbf{c}^*$. Pythia engages only S^*, which produces the final $\hat{\mathbf{x}}$. If there is no cohort that satisfies criteria A1 and A2, BC engages the cohort that satisfies only criterion A1. If $\mathcal{K} > 1$ one can repeat the above criteria for the top $\mathcal{K}$ cohorts ranked with the distance between the corresponding $\mathbf{c}_j^*$ and $\mathbf{z}$, $1 \leq j \leq \mathcal{K} < m$. In this case the final $\hat{\mathbf{x}}$ is produced by aggregating all $\hat{\mathbf{x}}_j$.

4.2.2 Accuracy-aware algorithm: Cohorts Outlier Elimination scheme

Cohorts Outlier Elimination (COE) trades off additional cost for improving our other metric, accuracy. Given $\mathbf{i}$, Pythia checks whether $\mathbf{z} \in P_i$. This is achieved once Pythia, for each cohort S_i, calculates $\rho_i^{(n)} \leq \rho_i$ associated with the n dimensions of $\mathbf{r}_i$ corresponding to the n non-MVs. If $\| \mathbf{c}_i^* - \mathbf{z} \| \leq \rho_i^{(n)}$ (dealing only with the n dimensions of $\mathbf{c}^*$) with $\mathbf{c}_i^* = \arg\min_{\mathbf{c} \in \mathcal{C}_i} \| \mathbf{c} - \mathbf{z} \|$ then $\mathcal{S}' \leftarrow \mathcal{S}' \cup \{S_i\}$. Once $\mathcal{S}'$ is determined with $\ell = |\mathcal{S}'| \leq |\mathcal{S}| = m$, Pythia engages only cohorts from $\mathcal{S}'$ and obtains their corresponding estimates $\hat{\mathbf{x}}_i, i = 1, \ldots, \ell$. The aggregate estimate $\hat{\mathbf{x}}$ determined by Pythia is

$$\hat{\mathbf{x}} = \sum_{S_i \in \mathcal{S}''} \hat{\mathbf{x}}_i b_i \ , \ b_i = \frac{\| \mathbf{z} - \mathbf{c}_i^* \|^{-1}}{\sum_{S_j \in \mathcal{S}''} \| \mathbf{z} - \mathbf{c}_j^* \|^{-1}}, \tag{2}$$

where b_i is the weight for estimate $\hat{\mathbf{x}}_i$ normalized by the sum of inverse distance from the closest cluster $\mathbf{c}_i^*$ to $\mathbf{z}$ from cohort $S_i \in \mathcal{S}''$. The set $\mathcal{S}'' \subseteq \mathcal{S}'$ contains cohorts $S_i \in \mathcal{S}'$ whose estimates are not considered *outliers* in $\mathcal{E} = \{\| \hat{\mathbf{x}}_1 \|, \ldots, \| \hat{\mathbf{x}}_\ell \|\}$. This is achieved by computing the statistic

$$u_{i,\mathcal{E}} = \frac{| \| \hat{\mathbf{x}}_i \| - median(\mathcal{E})|}{mad(\mathcal{E})} \tag{3}$$

for each $\| \hat{\mathbf{x}}_i \| \in \mathcal{E}$ and then considering $\hat{\mathbf{x}}_i$ as outlier if $u_{i,\mathcal{E}}$ exceeds a certain cutoff, usually 2.5 or 3.0 [28]. The $median(\mathcal{E})$ and $mad(\mathcal{E})$ is the sample median and median absolute deviation about the median of $\mathcal{E}$, respectively. Pythia provides $\hat{\mathbf{x}}$ to each $S_i \in \mathcal{S}''$ for updating their signatures; see Section 5.1. If $\mathcal{S}' = \emptyset$, Pythia engages all cohorts; if $\mathcal{S}'' = \emptyset$, Pythia engages all cohorts from $\mathcal{S}'$.

4.3 Pythia asymptotic complexity

In COE, given $\mathbf{i}$ Pythia evaluates '$\mathbf{z} \in P_i$', $\forall P_i \in \mathcal{P}$, i.e., it performs one nearest neighbor (1NN) search for each P_i over $\mathcal{C}_i$. We adopt a d-dimensional tree structure [31] for each P_i over the clusters of $\mathcal{C}_i$. Let $\xi = \frac{1}{m}\sum_{i=1}^{m}|\mathcal{C}_i|$ be the average number of clusters in signature P_i. The corresponding time complexity per input $\mathbf{i}$ in COE is $O(md\log(\xi))$. In BC, we also adopt a d-dimensional tree structure over all clusters from all signatures in $\mathcal{P}$. Given $\mathbf{i}$, Pythia performs a 1NN search with $O(d\log(m\xi))$ time since it searches over all clusters from all signatures $\cup_{i=1}^{m}\mathcal{C}_i$. COE and BC require $O(md\xi)$ space. Pythia requires $O(\ell)$ and $O(1)$ communication with cohorts from $\mathcal{S}'$ and the best cohort in COE and BC schemes, respectively.

5. PYTHIA SIGNATURE UPDATE

5.1 COE signature update

Once Pythia has produced $\hat{\mathbf{x}}$ given an input, it updates $\mathcal{P}$. Only $P_i \in \mathcal{P}$, which correspond to cohorts $S_i \in \mathcal{S}''$, need to be updated. The update of P_i is based on the rule $\mathbf{c}_i^* \leftarrow \mathbf{c}_i^* + \eta_i(\mathbf{z} - \mathbf{c}_i^*)$ where $\mathbf{c}_i^* = \arg\min_{\mathbf{c}\in\mathcal{C}_i} \parallel \mathbf{z} - \mathbf{c} \parallel$, i.e., only the dimensions of $\mathbf{c}_i^*$ are modified, which correspond to the n dimensions of the non-MVs of $\mathbf{x}$. This denotes that no new clusters at P_i are formed after the update w.r.t. $\hat{\mathbf{x}}$, since $\mathbf{z} \in P_i$. The exact update can be locally reflected by $S_i \in \mathcal{S}''$ to its signature in order to be secured against a Pythia break-down situation. The magnitude of change in P_i w.r.t. $\hat{\mathbf{x}}$ is $\delta_i = \eta_i \parallel \mathbf{z} - \mathbf{c}_i^* \parallel$.

Let the sum involving the y moments of the reciprocals of binomial coefficients $F_x^{(y)} = \sum_{k=0}^{x} k^y \binom{x}{k}^{-1}$ for non-negative integers x, y. From [29] we obtain that $F_x^{(0)} = \frac{x+1}{2^{x+1}}\sum_{k=1}^{x+1}\frac{2^k}{k}$ and $F_x^{(1)} = \frac{x}{2}F_x^{(0)}$.

THEOREM 4. *The expected magnitude of change in P_i, $E[\delta_i|S_i \in \mathcal{S}'']$, in COE is bounded above by $\delta_i^{\max} = \eta_i\rho_i(F_d^{(0)} - 2)$ and $\delta_i^{\max} \sim (\frac{2}{d-1} - \frac{1}{2^{d-1}})\eta_i\rho_i$ for very large d.*

PROOF. Consider input $\mathbf{i}$ with $1 \le n \le d-1$ non-MVs and $S_i \in \mathcal{S}''$. The probability of choosing a subset of n out of d dimensions corresponding to non-MVs is $\binom{d}{n}^{-1}$. The expected magnitude of change of P_i is $E[\delta_i] = \sum_{n=1}^{d-1}\binom{d}{n}^{-1}\eta_i \parallel \mathbf{z} - \mathbf{c}_i^* \parallel \le \sum_{n=1}^{d-1}\binom{d}{n}^{-1}\eta_i\rho_i^{(n)} \le \sum_{n=1}^{d-1}\binom{d}{n}^{-1}\eta_i\rho_i = (F_d^{(0)} - 2)\eta_i\rho_i$. The asymptotic expansion of $F_d^{(0)} \sim 2 + \frac{2}{d-1} - \frac{1}{2^{d-1}}$ as $d \to \infty$ (proved in [30]). Hence, $\delta_i^{\max} \sim (\frac{2}{d-1} - \frac{1}{2^{d-1}})\eta_i\rho_i$. □

THEOREM 5. *The expected magnitude of change in $\mathcal{P}$, $E[\delta]$, in COE is bounded above by $\delta^{\max} = \eta^{\max}\rho^{\max}(F_m^{(1)} - 1)(F_d^{(0)} - 2)$ and $\delta^{\max} \sim (m-1)(\frac{2}{d-1} - \frac{1}{2^{d-1}})\eta^{\max}\rho^{\max}$ for very large m and d, where $\eta^{\max} = \max\{\eta_i\}_{i=1}^{m}$, $\rho^{\max} = \{\rho_i\}_{i=1}^{m}$.*

PROOF. The probability that a subset $\mathcal{S}''$ of ℓ cohorts is determined by Pythia is $\binom{m}{\ell}^{-1}$. Hence (from Theorem 4),

$$\begin{aligned} E[\delta] &\le \sum_{\ell=1}^{m}\binom{m}{\ell}^{-1}\sum_{i=1}^{\ell}\sum_{n=1}^{d-1}\binom{d}{n}^{-1}\eta_i\rho_i \\ &\le \eta^{\max}\rho^{\max}\sum_{\ell=1}^{m}\ell\binom{m}{\ell}^{-1}(F_d^{(0)} - 2) \\ &= \eta^{\max}\rho^{\max}(F_m^{(1)} - 1)(F_d^{(0)} - 2) \end{aligned}$$

Since $\lim_{m\to\infty}\frac{F_m^{(1)}}{m} \to 1$ (Theorem 11; [29]) and from Theorem 4, we obtain $\delta^{\max} \sim (m-1)(\frac{2}{d-1} - \frac{1}{2^{d-1}})\eta^{\max}\rho^{\max}$. □

5.2 BC signature update

The best cohort S^* updates its signature w.r.t. $\hat{\mathbf{x}}$ as described in Section 5.1, with magnitude of change bounded by $\delta^{*\max}$ (Theorem 4). Note that the change in S^*'s signature is not reflected at Pythia's $\mathcal{P}$ and specifically at the corresponding $P^* \in \mathcal{P}$.

THEOREM 6. *The expected magnitude of change in $\mathcal{P}$, $E[\delta]$, in BC is bounded above by $(F_d^{(0)} - 2)\eta^{\max}\rho^{\max}$.*

PROOF. Each $S_i \in \mathcal{S}$ is equally probable to be selected by Pythia as the best cohort given an input. Hence, from Theorem 5 we obtain $E[\delta] \le \sum_{i=1}^{m}\frac{1}{m}(F_d^{(0)} - 2)\eta_i\rho_i \le (F_d^{(0)} - 2)\eta^{\max}\rho^{\max}$. □

Pythia determines a frequency $\propto (F_d^{(0)} - 1)\eta^{\max}\rho^{\max}$ for a batch update of $\mathcal{P}$ by asking from all (previously engaged as best) cohorts to send their updated signatures changes (referring only to modified clusters), provided that they have not changed from the previous batch update. However, a batch update can be avoided once the best cohort sends the final estimate to Pythia for updating $\mathcal{P}$.

6. PERFORMANCE EVALUATION

6.1 Experiments

Setup. We conducted an extensive series of experiments to assess the performance of Godzilla, ACM and Pythia's schemes COE and BC on two real datasets (D1 and D2) and a synthetic dataset (DS). Real datasets are adopted from the UCI Machine Learning Repository [32]. D1 contains $|\mathcal{X}| = 5 \cdot 10^5$ real valued vectors of $d = 90$ corresponding to audio features. D2 contains $|\mathcal{X}| = 5 \cdot 10^4$ real valued vectors of $d = 384$ corresponding to features extracted from Computed Tomography images. Each vector of DS is a 20-dimensional point with the first fifteen dimensions randomly sampled from a Gaussian mixture of five component Gaussian pdfs with equal mixture weights and mean values of each component randomly selected from the uniform distribution $U(0, 15)$. The other five dimensions are drawn, independently, from the univariate Gaussian distribution $\mathcal{N}(0, 1)$. The first fifteen dimensions are informative dimensions, while the rest dimensions are random noises artificially added to test Pythia's capability of predicting $\mathcal{S}'$. For each dataset, we synthetically produce MVs from each $\mathbf{x}_t$ for $t = 1, \ldots, T$ as follows: each dimension $k = 1, \ldots, d$ from $\mathbf{x}_t$ is randomly and independently marked as missing with MV probability q. In this case, we expect $|\mathcal{X}|\sum_{k=1}^{d-1}\binom{d}{k}q^k(1-q)^{d-k}$ points with MVs; we exclude the cases of missing all dimensions or none. We set $q = 0.3$, which is a relatively high probability of MVs per dimension, thus, being able to test Pythia's robustness in terms of accuracy. On average, a signature P_i contains 0.32% of points of cohort's set $\mathcal{X}_i$ (this amount refers to the number of clusters stored in Pythia) using ART with initial learning rate $\eta = 0.2$, which gradually decreases. Moreover, we set the range percentage $\alpha_k = \alpha = 0.1$ for all dimensions in order to construct ρ. We run all experiments 100 times and took their average values for all performance metrics, with a stream of $T = 1000$ inputs. Pythia's schemes and MVAs

(Section 3.2) were written in Matlab. Table 1 summarizes the parameter values used in our experiments.

Parameter	Notation	Value/Range
d	dimensions	{20,90,384}
α	vigilance range pct.	0.1
η	init. learning rate	0.2
q	MV probability	0.3
m	number of cohorts	$\{5, 10, 20, 50, 100\}$
T	number of inputs	1000

Table 1: Experiment parameters.

Performance metrics. Our metrics include *efficiency metrics* and *accuracy metrics*. A scale-out system consisting of m cohorts affords two types of parallelism: *intra-imputation* and *inter-imputation* parallelism. The former refers to the capability of processing any single imputation using a number of cohorts in parallel, each accessing a dataset partition. The latter refers to the systems' capability of running in parallel a number of imputations, each of which engages a subset of cohorts. It is crucial to note that Godzilla affords neither of these parallelism types and that ACM affords only intra-imputation parallelism. This latter scenario is particularly important as typically a system is presented with a (large) batch of (vector-) inputs, each with missing values and the goal is to impute all input vectors in the batch as quickly/scalably as possible. Given this, our efficiency metrics embody various efficiency aspects impacting scalability. First, we report on *imputation latency*, defined as the time (in seconds) a system (i.e., Godzilla, ACM, Pythia-COE, or Pythia-BC) requires to impute a single input (vector) using a MVA. The rate of latency increase as dataset sizes grow is a strong aspect of scalability. In ACM, latency refers to the time a single cohort requires to impute a single input on its local dataset partition, assuming m cohorts run in parallel. In Pythia, latency refers to the time for COE / BC to predict best cohort(s) $\mathcal{S}''/\mathcal{S}^*$, plus the latency to run MVA in parallel at cohort(s). *Imputation speedup* is defined as the ratio of Godzilla latency over ACM / COE / BC latency; it indicates how much a system is faster than Godzilla for a single imputation. *Imputation throughput* is defined as the rate of imputations delivered by a system (number of imputations per second) given a finite stream (batch) of T inputs: with this we capture the inter-imputation parallelism, *in addition to* the intra-imputation parallelism.

We measure *imputation accuracy* using the RMSE metric (root-mean squared difference) between $\mathbf{x}_a$ and $\hat{\mathbf{x}}$:

$$RMSE = \left(\frac{1}{T} \sum_{t=1}^{T} \frac{\sum_{k=1}^{d} w_{tk}(x_{(a)tk} - \hat{x}_{tk})^2}{\sum_{k=1}^{d} w_{tk}} \right)^{1/2}. \quad (4)$$

6.2 Performance results

6.2.1 Imputation efficiency

Fig. 3(a-b) shows the imputation speedup against m for all systems using KNN and REG over D2. Similar results are obtained for D1 which are omitted due to space limitations. Overall ACM, COE and BC achieve an almost linear speedup using both REG and KNN. The speedup of COE and BC drops slightly as m increases since higher m implies more signatures to be processed at Pyhtia.

Fig. 3(c-d) shows the latency of Godzilla and Pythia-COE (Pythia-BC curves are very close to Pythia-COE) using REG when $m = \{10, 50, 100\}$ and the size of D1 and D2 varies from 5000 to 300,000 points; (similar results exist for KNN, but are omitted for space reasons). Godzilla struggles with increasing dataset sizes: with over 200,000 and 100,000 points, a high latency over 20s and 35s per input for D1 and D2, respectively, is observed. Pythia scales nicely with its latency per input increasing linearly. Moreover, when the number of cohorts increases, we obtain a sublinear increase in latency. Pythia can easily handle large datasets if more cohorts are available to scale to big data missing values.

Fig. 4(a-b) shows the throughput of each system indicating the capability of handling a stream of T inputs. COE engages S' for an input (or S^* in case of BC) thus the other cohorts ($\in S \setminus S'$) are available to be potentially engaged for other inputs in the stream. Now, recall Fig. 2(b) which shows the average number of cohorts engaged by COE per input for all data sets. For $m = 100$, about 26% of cohorts (average for all data sets) are engaged per input. Obviously, the distribution of the engaged cohorts plays an important role. That is, for a stream of inputs heading for imputation, we achieve very high throughput when (i) $|S'|$ is relatively small (in case of COE) and (ii) different imputations engage different subsets of cohorts. On the other hand, in ACM, all cohorts are concurrently occupied by the same input. The impact of the cohort engagement policy of Pythia's schemes on the throughput is illustrated in Fig. 4(a-b) using REG, where the y-axis is plotted in logarithmic scale for readability. (Similar results exist with KNN). Pythia can handle up to tens of thousands of inputs per second, compared to ACM and Godzilla, which deal with tens of inputs and a few inputs, respectively. As expected, Pythia achieves higher throughput as m increases, as the possibilities for intra-imputation parallelism increase. However, note that in Fig. 4(a) as m increases, we do not achieve further significant increase in throughput, because Pythia's processing over signatures becomes significant. The latter is higher for higher dimensions. In Fig. 4(b), as m increases, Pythia achieves high throughput. We can observe the impact of the number of dimensions d on throughput. D2 contains points with 326% more dimensions than those in D1. Pythia achieves a throughput over 10^4 (inputs/sec) with $m = 20$ in D1, while it achieves the same throughput with $m = 100$ in D2 (five times more cohorts).

Our results up to now clearly make a strong case for the scale-out advantages of the Pythia framework.

6.2.2 Imputation accuracy

Fig. 4(c-d) shows the RMSE against m using KNN and REG on synthetic data. COE and BC, as anticipated based on discussions of Example 1 and 2, obtain significant lower RMSE than Godzilla and ACM. However, this occurs with decreasing benefits as the number of cohorts increases; for $m > 50$ no further decrease in RMSE is achieved. Specifically, COE predicts a subset of cohorts, out of m cohorts, which achieves quite similar RMSE as that obtained by a subset of cohorts out of m' with $m' > m > 50$. In addition, BC engages the best cohort whose estimate is very close to the aggregate estimate of the subset of cohorts engaged by COE. Please note that ACM may yield a higher RMSE depending on the MVA used, even compared to Godzilla. For instance, using KNN, Godzilla would provide the *global* best

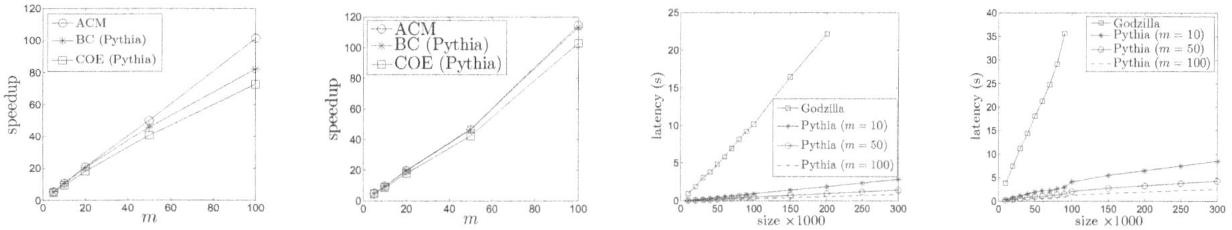

(a) Speedup; (KNN) (b) Speedup; (REG) (c) Latency; (REG) (d) Latency; (REG)

Figure 3: (a-b) Imputation speedup against m of ACM, COE and BC in dataset D2 using KNN and REG; (c-d) Imputation scalability against m of Godzilla and Pythia (COE) in datasets D1 & D2 using REG.

K points, whereas in ACM each cohort, even when storing irrelevant data, will be contributing its best K points. The latter necessarily implies that ACM's imputation involves points which adversely affect imputation errors.

Fig. 5 shows the RMSE against m using KNN and REG on real datasets. Pythia's schemes achieve comparable RMSE with Godzilla, with COE assuming relatively the lowest RMSE for both MVAs and datasets. In addition, the RMSE of COE remains at its lowest value from a certain m value (e.g., $m = 50$ in D2) thus there is no need to involve more cohorts. BC performs slightly better than Godzilla for both MVAs and datasets. Moreover, BC assumes higher RMSE than COE. This denotes the robustness of COE compared to BC in terms of accuracy due to the aggregate estimate from multiple engaged cohorts. ACM has higher RMSE than Godzilla in both datasets since it aggregates the estimates of all cohorts possibly incorporating estimates that spoil the final result.

6.3 Discussion

The central conclusions of our study are the following:

- Godzilla suffers from obvious severe scalability / efficiency limitations. Furthermore, it can have a poor performance even in terms of imputation accuracy.
- ACM offers efficiency performance comparable to what Map-Reduce solutions to scalability would offer, in that it requires all cohorts to be engaged for MV imputation. As such, it can only improve per-imputation efficiency. Our results show that ACM performs poorly in terms of both MV imputation throughput (compared to Pythia) and accuracy (compared to Pythia *and even* Godzilla).
- Pythia is a great all-around performer, significantly outperforming both ACM and Godzilla in terms of both overall efficiency and accuracy. Note that, even though ACM enjoys a smaller per-imputation latency than Pythia, this is achieved at a significant cost for overall imputation throughput and accuracy.
- Finally, the two Pythia schemes BC and COE, as expected can trade-off efficiency for accuracy with BC offering higher throughput but at lower accuracy.

7. CONCLUSIONS

We have tackled the problem of scaling out MV imputations, a common problem in many big data applications. We studied and developed some of the fundamentals of the problem, based on which we developed Pythia, a framework and algorithms designed for this aim. The Pythia framework is drastically different, as it on the one hand avoids the need to access all cohorts (and all associated costs for communication and for running MVAs at all cohorts), while on the other can achieve better or comparable MV imputation accuracy, compared to centralized solutions. Specifically, our comprehensive experiments showed that it can provide drastically better efficiency/scalability and accuracy compared to a centralized approach (Godzilla) and a massively parallel, a la Map-Reduce, solution (ACM). Future work plans entail the study of additional cohort prediction schemes, straddling the line between efficiency and accuracy.

8. ACKNOWLEDGEMENTS

This research has been co-financed by the European Union (European Social Fund - ESF) and Greek national funds through the Operational Program 'Education and Lifelong Learning' of the National Strategic Reference Framework (NSRF) - Research Funding Program: Thales. Investing in knowledge society through the European Social Fund.

9. REFERENCES

[1] X. Su, *et al*, 'Using Classifier-Based Nominal Imputation to Improve Machine Learning', *Proc. 15th PAKDD*, Part I, LNAI 6634, pp. 124–135, 2011.

[2] A. Farhangfar, *et al*, 'Impact of imputation of missing values on classification error for discrete data', *Pattern Recognition*, 41(12): 3692–3705, Dec 2008.

[3] M.T. Asif, *et al*, 'Low-Dimensional Models for Missing Data Imputation in Road Networks', *Proc. 38th IEEE ICASSP*, pp.3527–3531, 2013.

[4] E.C. Chi, *et al*, 'Genotype imputation via matrix completion', *Genome Research*, 23(3):509–18, Mar 2013.

[5] I.B. Aydilek, *et al*, 'A novel hybrid appoach to estimating missing values in databases using k-nearest neighbors and neural networks', *Innovative Computing, Information and Control*, 8(7A): 1349–4198, Jul 2012.

[6] A. Farhangfar, *et al*, 'A Novel Framework for Imputation of Missing Values in Databases', *IEEE Trans. Sys. Man Cyber. (A)*, 37(5): 692–709, Sep 2007.

[7] K. Lakshminarayan, *et al*, 'Imputation of missing data in industrial databases', *Appl. Intell.*, 11(3): 259–275, Nov / Dec 1999.

[8] L. A. Kurgan, *et al*, 'Mining the cystic fibrosis data', J. Zurada & M. Kantardzic (Eds.), *Next Generation of Data-Mining Applications*, IEEE Press, 415–444, 2005.

[9] A.W. Liew, *et al*, 'Missing value imputation for gene expression data: computational techniques to recover missing data from available information', *Brief. Bioinform.*, 12(5): 498–513, Sep 2011.

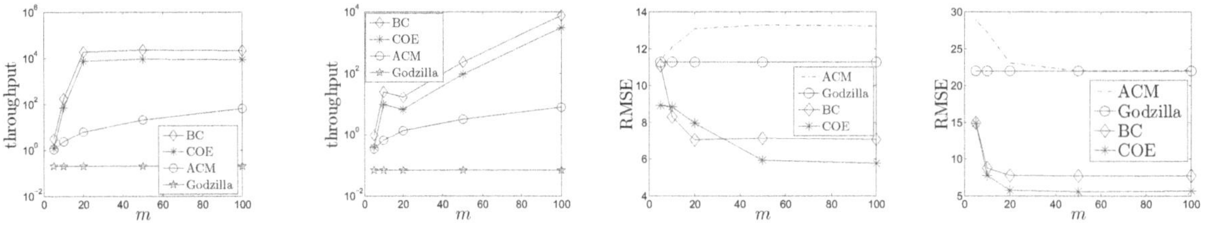

(a) Throughput; REG (b) Throughput; REG (c) RMSE; KNN (d) RMSE; REG

Figure 4: (a-b) System throughput against m of Godzilla, ACM, COE and BC in dataset D1 & D2 using REG; (c-d) RMSE against m of Godzilla, ACM, COE and BC in dataset DS using KNN and REG.

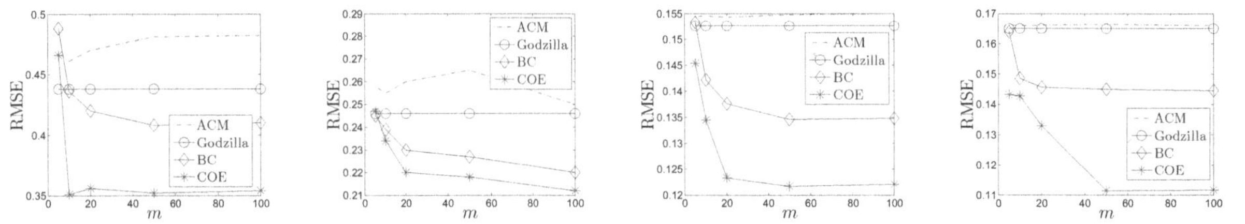

(a) RMSE; D1 (KNN) (b) RMSE; D1 (REG) (c) RMSE; D2 (KNN) (d) RMSE; D2 (REG)

Figure 5: RMSE against m of Godzilla, ACM, COE and BC in dataset D1 (a-b) and D2 (c-d) using KNN and REG.

[10] J. Dean, *et al*, 'MapReduce: Simplified Data Processing on Large Clusters', *Proc. USENIX OSDI*, 2004.

[11] S. Ghemawat, *et al*, 'The Google File System', *Proc. ACM SOSP*, 2003.

[12] C-T. Chu, *et al*, 'Map-Reduce for Machine Learning on Multicore', *NIPS 19*, MIT press, 281–288, 2006.

[13] C. K. Enders, 'Applied Missing Data Analysis', *Guilford Press*, NY, 2010.

[14] D. W. Joenssen, *et al*, 'Hot Deck Methods for Imputing Missing Data', *Proc. 8th MLDM* , LNCS 7376, pp.63–75, 2012.

[15] O. Troyanskaya, *et al*, 'Missing value estimation methods for DNA microarrays', *Bioinformatics*, 17(6):520–525, 2001.

[16] R.J. Little, *et al*, 'Statistical Analysis with Missing Data', *Wiley*, NY, 1987.

[17] T.E. Raghunathan, *et al*, 'A multivariate technique for multiply imputing missing values using a sequence of regression models', *Survey Methodology*, 27(1):85–95, 2001.

[18] D.B. Rubin, 'Multiple Imputation After 18+ Years', *J. of the American Statistical Association*, 91(434):473–489, 1996.

[19] L. Li, *et al*, 'DynaMMo: mining and summarization of coevolving sequences with missing values', *Proc. 15th KDD*, 527–534, 2009.

[20] S. Yang, *et al*, 'Online recovery of missing values in vital signs data streams using low–rank matrix completion', *Proc. 11th IEEE ICMLA*, 281–287, 2012.

[21] M. Ouyang, *et al*, 'Gaussian mixture clustering and imputation of microarray data', *Bioinformatics*, 20(6): 917–923, Apr 2004.

[22] T. Aittokallio, *et al*, 'Dealing with missing values in large-scale studies: microarray data imputation and beyond' *Brief. Bioinform.* 11(2):253–264, 2010.

[23] D-W. Kim, *et al*, 'Iterative Clustering Analysis for Grouping Missing Data in Gene Expression Profiles', *Proc. PAKDD 2006*, LNAI 3918, pp.129–138, 2006.

[24] M.R. Garey, *et al*, 'Computers and Intractability; A Guide to the Theory of NP–Completeness', *W. H. Freeman & Co.*, NY, 1990.

[25] B. Przydatek, 'A fast approximation algorithm for the subset–sum problem', *Intl. Trans. in Op. Res.*, 9(4): 437–459, Jul 2002.

[26] G. A. Carpenter, *et al*, 'The ART of adaptive pattern recognition by a self–organizing neural network', *IEEE Computer*, 21(3): 77–88, Mar 1988.

[27] A. Ahmad, *et al*, 'A k–mean clustering algorithm for mixed numeric and categorical data' *Data & Knowledge Engineering*, 63(2):503–527, 2007.

[28] P. J. Rousseeuw, *et al*, 'Alternatives to the median absolute deviation', *J. American Statistical Association*, 88(424): 1273–1283, Dec 1993.

[29] H. Belbachir, *et al*, 'Sums involving moments of reciprocals of binomial coefficients', *J. Integer Sequences*, 14(6), Article 11.6.6, 16p, 2011.

[30] J-H. Yang, *et al*, 'The asymptotic expansions of certain sums involving inverse of binomial coefficient', *Intl. Mathematical Forum*, 5(16): 761–768, 2010.

[31] J.L. Bentley, 'Multidimensional binary search trees used for associative searching', *Communications of the ACM*, 18(9):509–517, 1975.

[32] K. Bache, *et al*, UCI Machine Learning Repository [http://archive.ics.uci.edu/ml] Irvine, Uni. of California, School of Inform. and Comp. Sci., 2013.

Efficient Mini-batch Training for Stochastic Optimization

Mu Li[1,2], Tong Zhang[2,3], Yuqiang Chen[2], Alexander J. Smola[1,4]
[1]Carnegie Mellon University [2]Baidu, Inc. [3]Rutgers University [4]Google, Inc.
muli@cs.cmu.edu, tzhang@stat.rutgers.edu, chenyuqiang@baidu.com, alex@smola.com

ABSTRACT

Stochastic gradient descent (SGD) is a popular technique for large-scale optimization problems in machine learning. In order to parallelize SGD, minibatch training needs to be employed to reduce the communication cost. However, an increase in minibatch size typically decreases the rate of convergence. This paper introduces a technique based on approximate optimization of a conservatively regularized objective function within each minibatch. We prove that the convergence rate does not decrease with increasing minibatch size. Experiments demonstrate that with suitable implementations of approximate optimization, the resulting algorithm can outperform standard SGD in many scenarios.

1. INTRODUCTION

The recent years have witnessed a rapid growth of data in variety and volume. The sheer amount of data has led to increasing interest in scalable optimization. Stochastic gradient descent (SGD) is one of the most popular methods. It has been successfully applied to large scale natural language processing [11], deep learning [7], matrix factorization [10], image classification [17], and latent variable models [22].

Traditional SGD processes one example per iteration. This sequential nature makes SGD challenging for distributed inference. A common practical solution is to employ minibatch training, which aggregates multiple examples at each iteration. However, the synchronization cost of mini-batch training is potentially still too large for large scale applications. For instance, in a distributed implementation, machines may need to communicate with each other for every mini-batch in order to synchronize the shared variables, such as gradients or parameters [8]. Given that both bandwidth and latency of networks are often 100x worse than physical memory, this overhead cannot be ignored.

Although large mini-batches are preferable to reduce the communication cost, they may slow down convergence rate in practice [4]. That is, if SGD converges by T iterations, the mini-batch training with batch size b may need more than T/b iterations. The increase in computation diminishes the benefits of the reduced communication cost due to large b. In addition, the I/O costs increases if the data is too large to fit into memory so that one need to fetch the minibatch from disk or network [25].

KDD'14, August 24–27, 2014, New York, NY, USA.

http://dx.doi.org/10.1145/2623330.2623612 .

This paper considers the problem that we want to use *large mini-batches* to reduce *communication cost* but at the same time retain *good convergence properties*. It is known that for general convex objective functions, the convergence of SGD is $\mathcal{O}(1/\sqrt{T})$; for mini-batch SGD with minibatch size b, the convergence is $\mathcal{O}(1/\sqrt{bT} + 1/T)$ [8]. Since the total number of examples examined is bT while there is only a $\sqrt{b}$ times improvement, the convergence speed degrades with increasing minibatch size.

To address this issue we propose an alternative mini-batch update strategy that does not slow down in convergence as the mini-batch size increases. The key observation is that, when a mini-batch is large, it is desirable to solve a more complex optimization problem, rather than simply update the solution by the gradients. Specifically, in each iteration, we *solve* a conservative risk minimization subproblem. It consists of two components: the original objective function on the mini-batch and a conservative penalty. Accordingly we are able to gain more from a mini-batch before moving to the next. The conservative penalty reduces variance and prevents divergence from the previous consensus. For our goal we need two ingredients: a more sophisticated update strategy and secondly, an efficient means of solving the conservative subproblem such that the increase of computation does not overwhelm the reduced synchronization cost.

Many previous works aimed at improving mini-batch SGD optimization. [11] proposed to use asynchronous communication. [23] studied the accelerated version. At a more fundamental level, [20, 27] consider the problem of solving subproblems in parallel, followed by averaging. They can be viewed as the extreme case where the mini-batch size is the entire partition. These strategies, however, are wasteful since no communication occurs during the compute phase.

Our approach differs from previous work by the addition of a conservative penalty and the use of each data partition in a nontrivial manner beyond simple gradient computation:

- We propose a new and general way of performing mini-batch updates beyond simple parameter averaging.

- We show that the proposed algorithm has an optimal $\mathcal{O}(1/\sqrt{bT})$ convergence rate, which improves [8] when the batch size b is large. Furthermore, we show it can be improved to $\mathcal{O}(\log T/(\lambda bT) + \lambda/(\sqrt{b}T))$ for a λ-strongly convex objective function.

- We propose two strategies to solve the conservative subproblem and demonstrate how to extend them in a communication efficient distributed implementation.
- We demonstrate the efficacy of the algorithm on a large scale dataset.

2. ALGORITHM

For concreteness of our exposition we need to introduce the inference problem formally. Our goal is to solve

$$w_* = \operatorname*{argmin}_{w\in\Omega} \phi(w) \text{ where } \phi(w) = \frac{1}{n}\sum_{i=1}^{n} \phi_i(w). \quad (1)$$

Here $\phi_i : \Omega \to \mathbb{R}$ is a convex loss function and w is a shared parameter. This general form addresses a large group of machine learning problems. We give two examples:

Risk Minimization [12]**:** Here the objective is to minimize a loss function $\ell(x, y, w)$, such as the regression or classification error that depends on data x and label y. Moreover, one commonly adds a regularizer $c(w)$. Assume there are n example pairs $(x_1, y_1), \ldots, (x_n, y_n)$, then we obtain the objective function by setting

$$\phi_i(w) = \ell(x_i, y_i, w) + \lambda c(w) \quad (2)$$

where λ is the regularization coefficient.

Graphical Model Inference [15, 14]**:** In undirected graphical models (and factor graphs) the relationship between random variables can be encoded by clique potentials $\psi_C(w)$, as given by the Hammersley-Clifford theorem [1]. Assume the clique set $\mathcal{C} = \{C_1, \ldots, C_n\}$, then pseudolikelihood can be decomposed into terms

$$\phi_i(w) = \log \psi_{C_i}(w). \quad (3)$$

Note that this only applies to fully observed models. For partial observations we need to interleave this with an expectation step (or any other method for addressing nonconvex inference problems).

A much larger family of problems has been characterized by the ADMM algorithms of [2]. They can all be viewed as special cases of the above setting where different $\phi_i(w)$ only act on a subset of variables.

2.1 Mini-Batch Stochastic Gradient Descent

We begin with a brief review of a naive variant of mini-batch SGD. During training it processes a group of examples per iteration. For notational simplicity, assume that n is divisible by the number of mini-batches m. Then we partition the examples into m mini-batches, each of size $b = n/m$. Note that this assumption is not required neither for the proof nor for the implementation. Likewise, the pre-partitioning step is also not necessary in practice, however, it simplifies the exposition of what follows.

Given a random minibatch $I \subset \{1, \ldots, n\}$ of size b, we can define the objective function on I as

$$\phi_I(w) = \frac{1}{|I|}\sum_{i\in I} \phi_i(w) \text{ we have } \phi(w) = \mathbf{E}_I\left[\phi_I(w)\right]. \quad (4)$$

In the simple case that $\Omega = \mathbb{R}^d$ the mini-batch SGD employs the following stochastic update rule: at each iteration t, we pick mini-batch $I_t \subset \{1, \ldots, n\}$ of size b at random and let

$$w_t = w_{t-1} - \eta_t \nabla \phi_{I_t}(w). \quad (5)$$

Whenever Ω has a nontrivial shape we would need to add a projection step, which finds the nearest neighbor of w_t in the feasible set Ω [26].

For convex ϕ_i, this method converges to the minimum objective value at a rate of $\mathcal{O}(1/\sqrt{bT} + 1/T)$, where T is the number of iterations [8]. Although b times more examples are processed in an iteration, the mini-batch training can converge much slower than that of standard SGD with the same number of processed examples. In practice, the convergence rate slows down dramatically in terms of the number of examples processed, when we use a large mini-batch size.

2.2 Efficient Mini-Batch Training

The above empirical finding was a key motivation for our approach. To gain some intuition note that for general domains Ω the update (5) can be rewritten as an optimization problem on a mini-batch:

$$w_t = \operatorname*{argmin}_{w\in\Omega}\Big[\phi_{I_t}(w_{t-1}) + \langle \nabla\phi_{I_t}(w_{t-1}), w - w_{t-1}\rangle + \frac{1}{2\eta_t}\left\|w - w_{t-1}\right\|_2^2\Big]$$

Note that this can be regarded as an approximation of $\phi_{I_t}(w)$, the loss on the minibatch plus a conservative penalty relative to w_{t-1}. While the above optimization problem is easy to solve, the first order Taylor approximation of $\phi_{I_t}(w)$ might be too coarse to achieve sufficient progress towards the optimal solution. Such an aggressive trade-off of fast convergence in favor of computational efficiency is highly undesirable for mini-batches of large sizes: often there is high overhead of switching to the next mini-batch, e.g. due to process synchronization, data reads from disk and network communication.

Note that SGD often uses a small step size due to the variance of the randomly chosen mini-batch. However, when the size of a mini-batch increases, its variance decreases. More sophisticated methods may be used towards faster convergence rate. In this paper, we propose to update the parameter by solving the following subproblem at iteration t:

$$w_t = \operatorname*{argmin}_{w\in\Omega}\left[\phi_{I_t}(w) + \frac{\gamma_t}{2}\left\|w - w_{t-1}\right\|_2^2\right]. \quad (6)$$

It consists of two components: the first part minimizes the objective function on mini-batch I_t, aiming to achieve full utilization of this mini-batch. The second component is a conservative constraint which limits dramatic changes of the parameter to avoid overutilization.

Algorithm 4 shows the proposed algorithm. Compared to the SGD rule, we need to solve the more complex conservative subproblem for each mini-batch. For the sake of simplicity in the theoretical analysis, we assume that the optimization is performed exactly; in practice, an approximate solution will be sufficient, particularly in the early stages of inference. If the computational cost for this approximate optimization is not too expensive compared to SGD, then this method has similar overall complexity per step relative to SGD, while at the same time drastically reducing the amount of network communication required between steps.

Algorithm 1 Single node template

Input: Initial w_0, conservative coefficients $\gamma_1, \ldots, \gamma_T$

for $t = 1, \ldots, T$ **do**

randomly choose mini-batch $I_t \subset \{1, \ldots, n\}$ of size b

solve the conservative subproblem:

$$w_t = \operatorname*{argmin}_{w \in \Omega} \left[\phi_{I_t}(w) + \frac{\gamma_t}{2} \|w - w_{t-1}\|_2^2 \right].$$

end for

2.3 Theoretical Analysis

The advantage of solving the conservative subproblem (6) is that the convergence does not slow down dramatically when the mini-batch size increases. This is reflected in our main result. Before stating the theorem, we need to introduce the notion of a Bregman divergence for convex functions f as follows:

$$D_f(w; w') := f(w) - f(w') - \nabla f(w')^\top (w - w') \quad (7)$$

This is the difference between $f(w)$ and the value of the first-order Taylor expansion of f at w', when evaluated at w. The properties of Bregman divergence include:

Non-negativity: $D_f(w; w') \geq 0$

Convexity: $D_f(w; w')$ is convex with respect to w

Linearity: $D_f(w; w')$ is linear with respect to f, namely

$$D_{f+cf'}(w; w') = D_f(w; w') + c D_{f'}(w; w').$$

We need the following assumption for our theorem:

ASSUMPTION 1. *We assume that for all t:*

$$\mathbf{E}_{I_t}\left[D_\phi(w_t; w_{t-1})\right] \leq \mathbf{E}_{I_t}\left[D_{\phi_{I_t}}(w_t; w_{t-1}) + \frac{\gamma_t}{2}\|w_t - w_{t-1}\|_2^2\right]$$

Note that $D_\phi(w; w_{t-1}) = \mathbf{E}_{I_t}\left[D_{\phi_{I_t}}(w; w_{t-1})\right]$ holds for general w that does not depend on I_t. However, since w_t depends on I_t we require some $\gamma_t > 0$ to satisfy the condition. Essentially, Assumption 1 bounds the amount of 'surprise' we can expect when replacing the full Bregman Divergence by one on the subset plus a conservative penalty.

Note that the assumption holds as long as we pick γ_t greater than or equal to the smoothness parameter of ϕ:

$$\phi(w) - \phi(w') - \nabla \phi(w')^\top (w - w') \leq \frac{\gamma_t}{2}\|w - w'\|_2^2.$$

In other words, the counterpart of strong convexity, namely that there exists a quadratic *upper* bound on the amount of change, suffices to guarantee this condition. In practice, however, one may be more aggressive and allow a much smaller γ_t when the mini-batch size is large. In fact, one may show that a choice of $\gamma_t = O(1/b)$ is sufficient. We have the following theorem:

THEOREM 1. *Consider the stochastic update rule (6). Assume that ϕ_i is λ-strongly convex for all i:*

$$\phi_i(w) - \phi_i(w') - \nabla \phi_i(w')^\top (w - w') \geq \frac{\lambda}{2}\|w - w'\|_2^2.$$

Under Assumption 1 and when choosing the update parameter $\gamma_t = \gamma + \lambda(t-1)$, we have for all $w_* \in \Omega$:

$$\sum_{t=1}^T \mathbf{E}[\phi(w_t) - \phi(w_*)] \leq \frac{\gamma}{2}\|w_* - w_0\|_2^2 + \frac{A^2}{b}\sum_{t=1}^T \frac{1}{\gamma_t}$$

$$\text{where } A^2 = \sup_{w \in \Omega} n^{-1} \sum_{i=1}^n \|\nabla \phi_i(w) - \nabla \phi(w)\|_2^2.$$

For convex functions, the modulus of strong convexity $\lambda = 0$ vanishes. This amounts to a constant update rate γ. In this case, choosing

$$\gamma = \sqrt{\frac{2T}{b}} \frac{A}{\|w_* - w_0\|_2}$$

minimizes the right hand side of the bound. Note that there is no a-priori guarantee that a correspondingly small γ is feasible. However, since the variance decreases with $\mathcal{O}(1/b)$ for increasing minibatch size, the scaling of $\gamma = \mathcal{O}(1/\sqrt{b})$ is appropriate. This yields the following aggregate regret bound

$$\frac{1}{T}\sum_{t=1}^T \mathbf{E}[\phi(w_t) - \phi(w_*)] \leq \frac{\sqrt{2}A}{\sqrt{Tb}}\|w_* - w_0\|_2.$$

This means that if mini-batch size is b, after T steps, we have a convergence bound of $1/\sqrt{bT}$. Therefore increasing mini-batch size does not affect convergence in terms of the number of training examples processed by the algorithm. For strongly convex $\lambda > 0$, we can achieve a regret bound of $\mathcal{O}(\log T/(\lambda b T) + \lambda/(\sqrt{b}T))$ with optimal choice of γ.

2.4 Proof of Theorem 1

For convenience, we define the regularized mini-batch loss

$$h_t(w) = \phi_{I_t}(w) + \frac{\gamma_t}{2}\|w\|_2^2.$$

Our proof relies on three lemmas. First, we upper bound $\|w_t - \bar{w}_t\|_2$, where $\bar{w}_t$ is similar to w_t except for optimizing over all examples. That is, the gradients differ via $\|\nabla \phi(\bar{w}_t) - \nabla \phi_{I_t}(\bar{w}_t)\|_2$. Next we show that the expectation of the latter, namely the variance of gradient over a mini-batch, is bounded from above by A^2/b. Finally we characterize the progress from time $t-1$ to t. The proofs of these auxiliary lemmas are presented in the Appendix.

LEMMA 1. *Let*

$$\bar{w}_t = \operatorname*{argmin}_{w \in \Omega} \left[\phi(w) + \frac{\gamma_t}{2}\|w - w_{t-1}\|_2^2\right], \quad (8)$$

be the minimizer of the conservative version of the risk. Then the difference between the full solution $\bar{w}_t$ and the minibatch solution w_t is bounded by

$$\|w_t - \bar{w}_t\|_2 \leq \frac{1}{\gamma_t}\|\nabla \phi(\bar{w}_t) - \nabla \phi_{I_t}(\bar{w}_t)\|_2.$$

LEMMA 2. *Assume that $w \in \Omega$ and assume that we randomly choose a mini-batch I of size b independent of w. Then the expected deviation between gradients is bounded by*

$$\mathbf{E}_I\left[\|\nabla \phi_I(w) - \nabla \phi(w)\|_2^2\right] = \frac{n-b}{n-1}\frac{B^2}{b} \leq \frac{A^2}{b}.$$

where $B^2 = \frac{1}{n}\sum_{i=1}^n \|\nabla \phi_i(w) - \nabla \phi(w)\|_2^2.$

LEMMA 3. *Given any $w_* \in \Omega$, the expected improvement in terms of Bregman Divergence is bounded via*

$$\begin{aligned} &\mathbf{E}\left[D_{h_t}(w_*, w_t)\right] - \mathbf{E}\left[D_{h_t}(w_*, w_{t-1})\right] \\ \leq &\phi(w_*) - \mathbf{E}\left[\phi(w_t)\right] - \mathbf{E}\left[D_\phi(w_*; w_{t-1})\right] + \frac{1}{\gamma_t}\frac{A^2}{b}. \end{aligned} \tag{9}$$

PROOF OF THEOREM 1. Under the assumption that ϕ_i is λ-strongly convex, it follows by construction that h_t is strongly convex with modulus $\gamma_t + \lambda$. Consequently the Bregman divergence is bounded by

$$D_{h_t}(w_*, w_t) \geq \frac{\gamma_t + \lambda}{2}\left\|w_* - w_t\right\|_2^2.$$

Together with Lemma 3, we have

$$\begin{aligned} &\mathbf{E}\left[\phi(w_t) - \phi(w_*) + \frac{\gamma_{t+1}}{2}\left\|w_* - w_t\right\|_2^2\right] \\ = &\mathbf{E}\left[\phi(w_t) - \phi(w_*) + \frac{\gamma_t + \lambda}{2}\left\|w_* - w_t\right\|_2^2\right] \\ \leq &\mathbf{E}\left[\phi(w_t)\right] - \phi(w_*) + \mathbf{E}\left[D_{h_t}(w_*, w_t)\right] \\ \leq &\mathbf{E}\left[D_{h_t}(w_*, w_{t-1}) - D_\phi(w_*; w_{t-1})\right] + \frac{A^2}{b\gamma_t} \\ = &\mathbf{E}\left[D_{\phi_{I_t}}(w_*, w_{t-1}) - D_\phi(w_*; w_{t-1})\right] \\ &+ \frac{\gamma_t}{2}\mathbf{E}\left[\left\|w_* - w_{t-1}\right\|_2^2\right] + \frac{A^2}{b\gamma_t} \\ = &\frac{\gamma_t}{2}\mathbf{E}\left[\left\|w_* - w_{t-1}\right\|_2^2\right] + \frac{A^2}{b\gamma_t} \end{aligned}$$

Here the first equality follows from the definition of γ_t; the second equality follows from the definition of h_t and simple algebra; the third equality uses the fact that we are drawing I_t independently. Hence we have

$$\mathbf{E}_{I_t|w_{t-1}} D_{\phi_{I_t}}(w_*, w_{t-1}) = D_\phi(w_*; w_{t-1}).$$

Summing over $t = 1, \ldots, T$, we obtain the desired bound. □

3. PRACTICAL CONSIDERATIONS

Our analysis assumes that we solve the conservative subproblem (6) exactly; in practice, we only need to perform this optimization approximately. In this section, we propose two approximate approaches and their distributed implementation.

3.1 Approximation by Early Stopping

Optimization algorithms solving the original problem (1) can often be applied to the conservative subproblem (6): the latter consists of a part of the former with a simple quadratic term with respect to the parameter. While the most suitable optimization methods vary for different objective functions, a natural idea is to reuse the one to solve (6) but to stop it earlier. It is understood that real applications are complex; here we propose two simple but general methods that allow us to solve (6).

The first one is a direct extension of SGD. Note that, if we set $\gamma = 0$, then SGD equals to performing gradient descent with a single pass of the mini-batch with w_{t-1} as the start point. We relax the single pass constraint such that we could obtain a more accurate solution of the conservative subproblem. The algorithm, named EMSO-GD, is shown in Algorithm 2. It solves (6) by gradient descent. Standard stopping criteria can be used to achieve early stopping. For instance, we may stop when the relative objective improvement is less than a thresholds. In practice we found it most convenient to use the simplest strategy: limit the maximal iteration number L. That is, the for loop will stop if we pass the mini-batch L times. A major benefit of this strategy is to simplify the synchronization of the distributed implementation we will introduce in the next section.

Algorithm 2 EMSO-GD: solve (6) by gradient descent

Input: previous parameter w_{t-1}, mini-batch I_t
conservative coefficient γ_t, learning rate η_t
Output: new parameter w_t
$w_t \leftarrow w_{t-1}$
for $\ell = 0, \ldots, L$ **do**
  update
$$w_t \leftarrow w_t - \eta_t\left(\nabla\phi_{I_t}(w_t) + \gamma_t(w_t - w_{t-1})\right) \tag{10}$$
end for

The second method is motivated by [25], where coordinate descent is applied to solve the dual form of the linear SVM in a mini-batch. Unlike [25], we directly solve the subproblem by coordinate descent in the *primal* form. Algorithm 3 shows the proposed algorithm, which is named EMSO-CD. In each time, EMSO-CD chooses a random coordinate $j \in [1, p]$, where p is the total number of coordinates, and then solves the one dimension problem

$$\underset{w_j}{\operatorname{argmin}}\left\{\phi_{I_k}(w) + \frac{\gamma_t}{2}\left\|w - w_{t-1}\right\|_2\right\}.$$

This minimization problem may have a closed form solution. But generally it could be solved by the Newton method. Similar to EMSO-GD, we use the maximal iteration number as the early stop criteria.

Algorithm 3 EMSO-CD: solve (6) by coordinate descent

Input: previous parameter w_{t-1}, mini-batch I_t
conservative coefficient γ_t
Output: new parameter w_t
$w_t \leftarrow w_{t-1}$
for $\ell = 0, \ldots, Lp$ **do**
  randomly choose coordinate $j \in [0, p]$
  update
$$w_{t,j} \leftarrow w_{t,j} - \eta_t\frac{\nabla_j\phi_{I_t}(w_t) + \gamma_t(w_{t,j} - w_{t-1,j})}{\nabla_{jj}^2\phi_{I_t}(w_t) + \gamma_t} \tag{11}$$
end for

3.2 Distributed Model Averaging

In distributed computing, we assume there are d machines, which are connected by network. Then the conservative subproblem could be solved by all these machine together. Specifically, we first divide a mini-batch into d partitions, next assign one partition to each of the machines, and then obtain the solution via communication. One possible approach is that all machines communicate in each iteration when solving the subproblem. However, this may introduce a large amount of communication.

Instead, we propose to use a more communication friendly approach where each machine solves the conservative subproblem independently, and then all machines average their

name	KDD04	URL	CTR
# examples	146 K	2.4 M	142 M
# features	74	3.2 M	28 M
# entries	11 M	277 M	8.4 G
# features per example	73±0.8	116±17	59±26
label ratio $+1 : -1$	1:111	1:2	1:15

Table 1: A collection of real datasets.

name	update	iteration	distributed
L-BFGS	[18]	batch	yes
LIBLINEAR	[9]	batch	no
Mini-Batch SGD	(5)	mini-batch	yes
EMSO-GD	(10)	mini-batch	yes
EMSO-CD	(11)	mini-batch	yes

Table 2: Evaluated Algorithms.

results. The algorithm is shown in Algorithm 4. Note that there is no restriction in terms of the choice of methods for solving the subproblems locally. In particular, the algorithms introduced in the previous section apply.

Algorithm 4 EMSO: Efficient Mini-Batch for Stochastic Optimization

Input: initialization w_0, conservative coefficients $\{\gamma_t\}_{t=1}^T$ learning rate $\{\eta_t\}_{t=1}^T$, number of machines k

partition examples into m mini-batches $I_1, \ldots, I_m$
for $t = 1, \ldots, T$ **do**
  randomly choose mini-batch I_t
  partition I_t into $I_{t,1}, \ldots, I_{t,d}$
  for $i = 1, \ldots, d$ **do** {in parallel}
    machine i get partition $I_{t,i}$
    solve the conservative subproblem on $I_{t,i}$ by Algorithm 2 or 3 to obtain $w_t^{(i)}$
  end for
  average $w_t = \frac{1}{d}\sum_{i=1}^d w_t^{(i)}$ via communication
end for

4. EXPERIMENTS

4.1 Dataset

To evaluate the proposed algorithms, we used three binary classification datasets of varying scales, which are listed on Table 1. KDD04 comes from the particle physics task at KDD Cup 2004[1], whose goal is to classify two types of particles generated in high energy collider experiments. The URL dataset aims to detect malicious URLs[2]. CTR is a private dataset containing displayed advertisements which are randomly sampled within a period of three months. The goal is to predict whether or not an advertisement will be clicked. KDD04 is a dense dataset, while the other two are extremely sparse. The largest dataset CTR has more than 100 million examples and the raw text file size is approximately 300 GB.

4.2 Setup

For the sake of simplicity we study the case of classification via logistic regression. There the objective function can be written in the form of (1) by letting

$$\phi_i(w) = \log(1 + \exp(-y_i\langle x_i, w\rangle)).$$

Here we let (y_i, x_i) to be the i-th sample pair.

We evaluated five algorithms, as summarized in Table 2. With the exception of LibLinear all algorithms were implemented in C++ using MPI for communication. The linear algebra operations are mainly performed by eigen3[3], which is a highly efficient C++ template library.

L-BFGS This is a parallelized version of the classical memory-limited BFGS method, as described in [18]. That is, the root machine obtains subgradients from each of the client machines to aggregate into a global subgradient. Subsequently the parameters are updated and we broadcast its new value. By construction the method is a batch optimization solver.

LibLinear This is the single-machine implementation as obtained from Chih-Jen Lin's site[4]. We include it to provide a reference point to existing and well-known solvers. This is a sophisticated batch solver for convex problems.

Mini-Batch SGD This effectively computes subgradients for a small minibatch on each machine. These subgradients are then aggregated to obtain a full mini-batch supgradient. After that, we take an update on the server using (5) and rebroadcast the parameters.

We used an $\mathcal{O}(1/\sqrt{t})$ decay learning rate for the mini-batch algorithms. Specifically, we set

$$\eta_t = \eta\sqrt{\frac{\alpha}{t+\alpha}}$$

for iteration t, where constants η and α specify the initial scale and decaying speed, respectively. We performed grid search to choose the best values by examining the convergence progress. We search the range of $\eta \in \{10^0, \ldots, 10^{-5}\}$ and $\alpha \in \{10^0, \ldots, 10^4\}$.

EMSO-GD This uses the parameter-averaging approach introduced in Algorithm 4 while performing parameter updates per client via (10). It differs from the previous methods by taking the higher order information of the loss function into account when processing a minibatch.

EMSO-CD The key difference to EMSO-GD is that it uses coordinate descent to update parameters within a minibatch. Other than that, the structure is essentially identical. For both EMSO variants we set $\lambda = 0$, the number of inner iterations to be 5 and 2, respectively, and search γ from $\{10^0, \ldots, 10^5\}$.

All experiments were carried on a cluster, where each machine is equipped with four AMD Opteron Interlagos 16 core 6272 CPUs, 128GB memory and 10Gbit Ethernet.

[1] http://osmot.cs.cornell.edu/kddcup/datasets.html
[2] http://sysnet.ucsd.edu/projects/url/
[3] http://eigen.tuxfamily.org/
[4] http://www.csie.ntu.edu.tw/~cjlin/liblinear/

4.3 Minibatch Size and Convergence

A first sanity check is to ascertain that the convergence results regarding mini-batch methods on a single node hold. For this purpose we increase the batch size from 10^3 to 10^5. The objective values after processing 10^7 examples are shown on Figure 1. As expected, when the mini-batch size increases, there is an increment of objective value for mini-batch SGD due to the rather crude approximation of the dataset by a first order Taylor expansion. That is, the convergence in terms of examples processed slows down. This degeneration is worst on the dataset KDD04, which is dense and extremely unbalanced in terms of its labels. This problem is alleviated by EMSO-GD. It performs 5 iterations of gradient descent in a mini-batch and therefore potentially gains more information about the higher order structure than SGD.

However, the convergence is much more stable when solving the conservative subproblem by coordinate descent. As can be seen from Figure 1, the objective value of EMSO-CD does not increase. It even slightly decreases, with the increasing mini-batch sizes. A possible explanation is that, even though each mini-batch is passed only twice, the coordinate descent with the previous parameter as a warm start gives satisfactory solutions to the conservative subproblem. So it provides sufficient progress to compensate for the loss due to increasing the mini-batch size.

In summary, solving conservative optimization problems on a minibatch is beneficial when compared to a naive gradient computation.

4.4 Comparison to other algorithms

In a next step we compare the algorithms listed in Table 2 by objective value versus run time. We use the same setting as Section 4.3 for the mini-batch algorithms, but only report the result with the best batch size, namely 10^5 for EMSO-CD and 10^3 for the other two algorithms. Figure 2 shows the results. It can be seen that the convergence the two batch algorithms, L-BFGS and LibLinear is similar: slow at the beginning but fast at the end. This is not too unsurprising given LibLinear's heritage.

For the mini-batch algorithms, EMSO-GD is comparable to SGD: While EMSO-GD converges faster in terms of number of minibatch iterations, it consumes 5 times more computational time than SGD. Note that, even with a larger mini-batch size, EMSO-CD is 10 times faster than the other two, and furthermore, it is faster than the batch algorithm at the end.

4.5 Minibatch Size and Synchronization Cost

Recall that a major benefit of large mini-batch sizes is the potential reduction in synchronization cost. Figure 3 shows the contribution of synchronization cost to the overall runtime of the algorithm when using 12 machines. Even with such a small number of computers the proportion is considerable. As expected, this cost decreases with increasing mini-batch size. It is due to the increase in the amount of computation between synchronization passes. Furthermore, because both EMSO-GD and EMSO-CD solve a more complex optimization problem in each mini-batch than SGD, their synchronization cost is correspondingly smaller than that of SGD. In addition, although coordinate descent passes a mini-batch twice in our experiment, it requires significant more exponentiation operations than the gradient descent (a

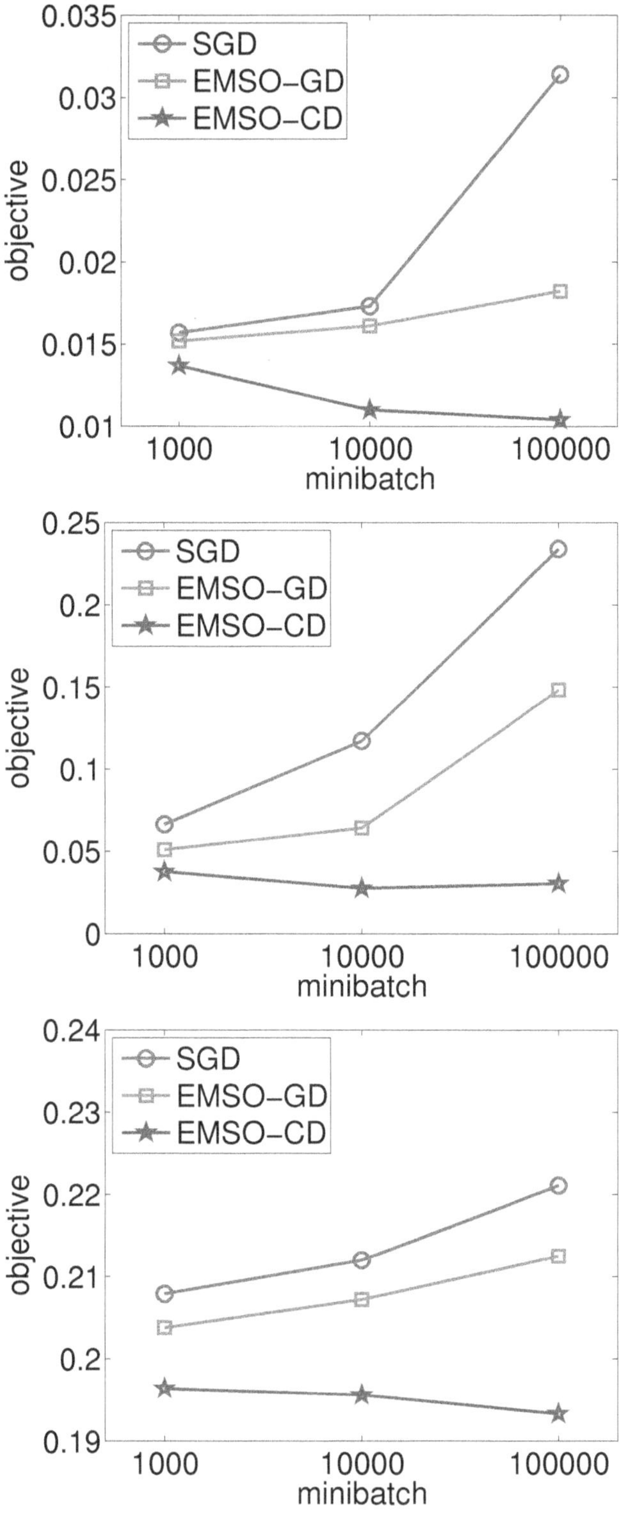

Figure 1: Objective value versus mini-batch size after in total 10^7 examples are processed in a single node. From top to bottom, datasets are KDD04, URL, and CTR, respectively, where CTR is downsampled to 4 millions examples due to the limited capacity of a single node.

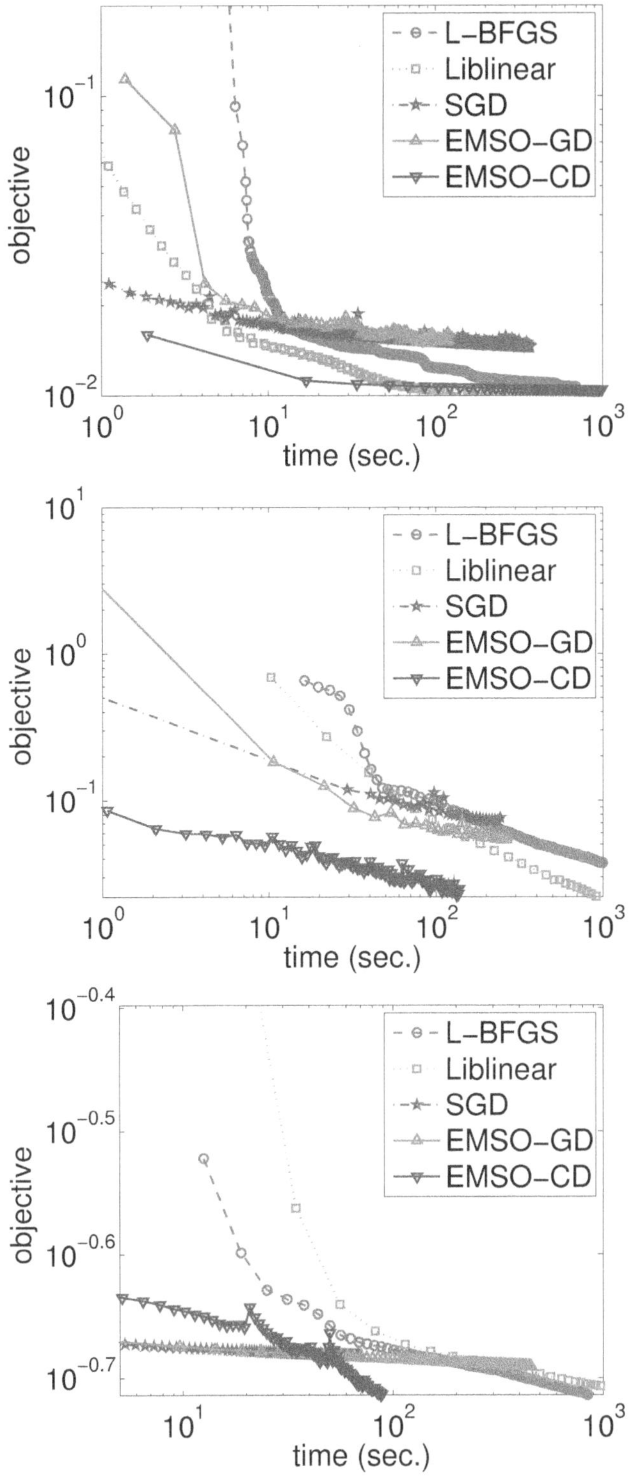

Figure 2: Objective value versus run time by a single node. Datasets are the same as Figure 1, which are KDD04, URL, and CTR from top to bottom.

fast special functions library would probably address this issue). As a result, it consumes more CPU time than gradient descent, even though the latter processes a min-batch five

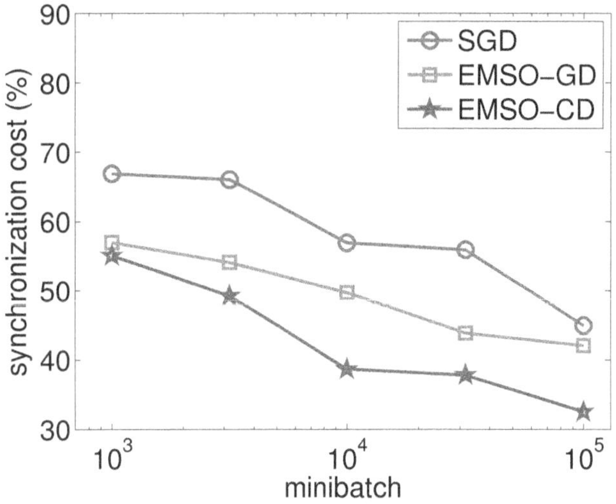

Figure 3: The fraction of synchronization cost as a function of minibatch size when communicating between 12 and 12 nodes.

	objective = 0.2		objective = .1972	
#nodes	time	speedup	time	speedup
5	879s	1.00x	2439s	1.00x
10	499s	1.76x	1367s	1.78x
20	363s	2.42x	962s	2.54x

Table 3: Run time and speedup for EMSO-CD to reach the same objective value when running on 5, 10 and 20 nodes.

times, and therefore has a further decreased synchronization cost.

The convergence results under various mini-batch sizes are shown in Figure 4. We first fix the total number of examples processed to be 5×10^6. As can be seen from the top figure, the results are similar to the single node results of Figure 1. That is, EMSO-GD slightly improves SGD while EMSO-CD is resilient to increase the mini-batch size. The bottom of Figure 4 shows the results by fixing the run time to be 1,000 seconds. The trend then is total different. Because the portion of synchronization cost decrease, more time can be allocated to process the examples, therefore a large mini-batch size is faster. Furthermore, although SGD is comparable to EMSO-GD in the single node experiment, as shown in Figure 2, the latter outperforms the former here, due to the communication cost in distributed environment. In addition, there are clear advantages for EMSO-CD to use large batch size, as it converges faster when the mini-batch size increases.

4.6 Scalability

We conclude our experimental evaluation by assessing runtime results for varying numbers of nodes. We primarily compare the following two algorithms: EMSO-CD and L-BFGS. Figure 5 shows the convergence results. As can be seen, both algorithms benefits from an increase in the number of nodes. But L-BFGS gains more than EMSO-CD, because the former passes the whole training data in each iteration so the portion of synchronization cost is small—15% comparing 30% of EMSO-CD. However, EMSO-CD is

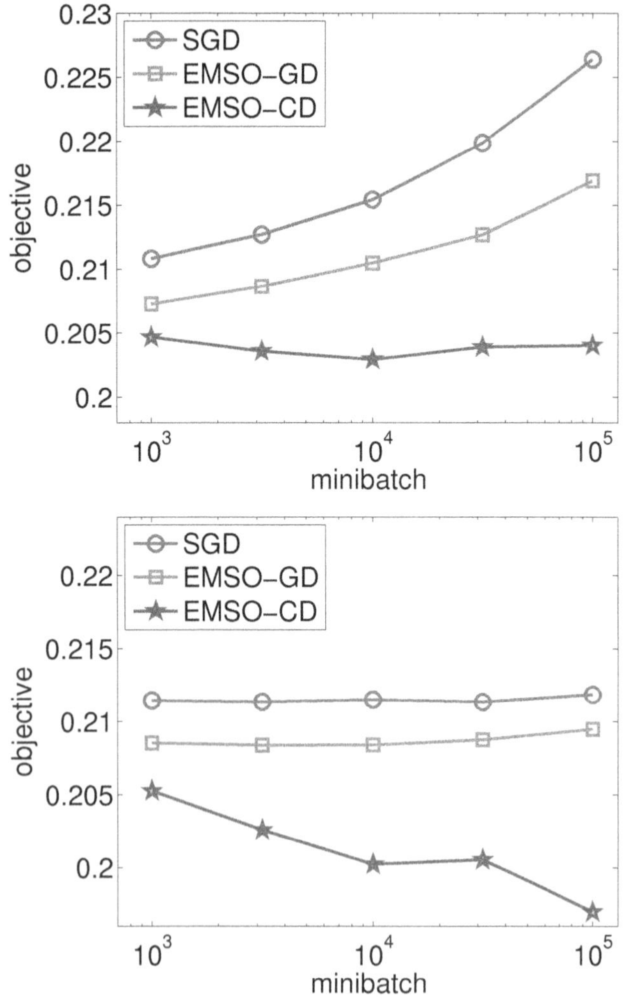

Figure 4: Objective values when varying the mini-batch size using 12 nodes. Top: for a fixed total number of examples set to 5×10^6. Bottom: for fixed runtime set to 1000 seconds.

still 10 times faster than L-BFGS, due to the faster convergence rate.

Table 3 shows the quantitative speedup for EMSO-CD to reach specific objective values. When the number of nodes doubled from 5 to 10, there is an average 1.75x speedup for both objective values, and if the nodes number is increased by 4 times, the speedup increases to 2.5x.

5. RELATED WORK AND DISCUSSION

The idea of using mini-batch in stochastic optimization has been studied by a number of researchers. For example, it was shown in [8] that distributed mini-batch gradient can achieve a convergence rate of $\mathcal{O}(1/\sqrt{Tb}+1/T)$, which is comparable to that of serial SGD when the minibatch size is small. Additional studies include [6, 24, 23].

There is also a large volume of works to improve the standard mini-batch approach. For example, [16] proposed to solve $\min_w \phi_{I_t}(w)$ directly, while [3] presented a L-BFGS style updating. In addition, [19, 13] argued to reduce the stochastic variance via gradients computed on the whole dataset.

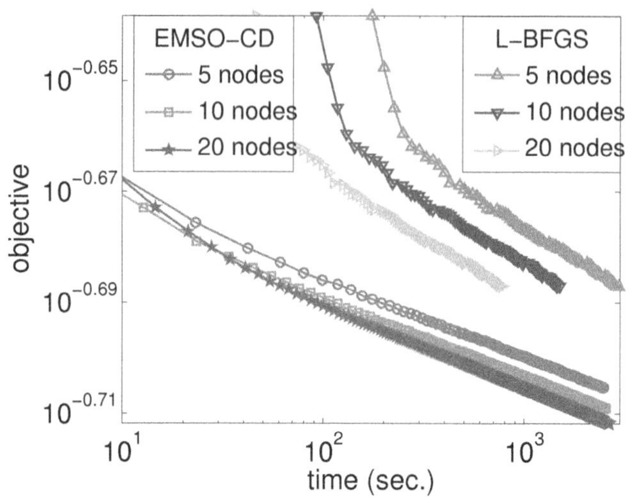

Figure 5: Objective function value versus run time for both EMSO-CD and L-BFGS using varying numbers of nodes.

Another line of research focuses on the practical performance, especially when data cannot fit into memory. For example, [25] studied solving linear SVM in the dual form by processing a block of data at each time. [21] showed that having both I/O and computational threads working together can further improve the performance. [5] studied how to select the data block.

Our work is different from previous ones in several aspects. First, we propose a novel mini-batch algorithm that solves a regularized optimization problem in primal form at each step. We show that the method can also achieve the optimal convergence rates theoretically, and presented practical implementations of the approach. The practical performance of the resulting methods outperform minibatch SGD under various scenarios.

Conclusion.

In this paper we proposed a variant of mini-batch SGD whose convergence rate does not degrade when the batch size increases. It solves a conservative subproblem in each iteration to maximize the utilization of the mini-batch while at the same time controlling the variance via a conservative constraint. We showed that it enjoys an optimal convergence rate and proposed practical distributed implementations. Furthermore, we demonstrated its efficiency on serial and distributed experiments on large scale datasets.

6. REFERENCES

[1] J. Besag. Spatial interaction and the statistical analysis of lattice systems (with discussion). *Journal of the Royal Statistical Society. Series B*, 36(2):192–236, 1974.

[2] S. Boyd, N. Parikh, E. Chu, B. Peleato, and J. Eckstein. Distributed optimization and statistical learning via the alternating direction method of multipliers. *Foundations and Trends in Machine Learning*, 3(1):1–123, 2010.

[3] R. Byrd, S. Hansen, J. Nocedal, and Y. Singer. A stochastic quasi-newton method for large-scale optimization. *arXiv preprint arXiv:1401.7020*, 2014.

[4] R. H. Byrd, G. M. Chin, J. Nocedal, and Y. Wu. Sample size selection in optimization methods for machine learning. *Mathematical programming*, 134(1):127–155, 2012.

[5] K.-W. Chang and D. Roth. Selective block minimization for faster convergence of limited memory large-scale linear models. In *Conference on Knowledge Discovery and Data Mining*, pages 699–707, 2011.

[6] A. Cotter, O. Shamir, N. Srebro, and K. Sridharan. Better mini-batch algorithms via accelerated gradient methods. In *NIPS*, volume 24, pages 1647–1655, 2011.

[7] J. Dean, G. Corrado, R. Monga, K. Chen, M. Devin, Q. Le, M. Mao, M. Ranzato, A. Senior, P. Tucker, K. Yang, and A. Ng. Large scale distributed deep networks. In *Neural Information Processing Systems*, 2012.

[8] O. Dekel, R. Gilad-Bachrach, O. Shamir, and L. Xiao. Optimal distributed online prediction using mini-batches. Technical report, `http://arxiv.org/abs/1012.1367`, 2010.

[9] R.-E. Fan, J.-W. Chang, C.-J. Hsieh, X.-R. Wang, and C.-J. Lin. LIBLINEAR: A library for large linear classification. *Journal of Machine Learning Research*, 9:1871–1874, Aug. 2008.

[10] R. Gemulla, E. Nijkamp, P. J. Haas, and Y. Sismanis. Large-scale matrix factorization with distributed stochastic gradient descent. In *Proceedings of the 17th ACM SIGKDD international conference on Knowledge discovery and data mining*, pages 69–77. ACM, 2011.

[11] K. Gimpel, D. Das, and N. A. Smith. Distributed asynchronous online learning for natural language processing. In *Proceedings of the Fourteenth Conference on Computational Natural Language Learning*, pages 213–222. Association for Computational Linguistics, 2010.

[12] T. Hastie, R. Tibshirani, and J. Friedman. *The Elements of Statistical Learning*. Springer, New York, 2 edition, 2009.

[13] R. Johnson and T. Zhang. Accelerating stochastic gradient descent using predictive variance reduction. In *Advances in Neural Information Processing Systems*, pages 315–323, 2013.

[14] M. I. Jordan. *An Introduction to Probabilistic Graphical Models*. MIT Press, 2008. To Appear.

[15] F. Kschischang, B. J. Frey, and H. Loeliger. Factor graphs and the sum-product algorithm. *IEEE Transactions on Information Theory*, 47(2):498–519, 2001.

[16] B. Kulis and P. L. Bartlett. Implicit online learning. In *Proc. Intl. Conf. Machine Learning*, 2010.

[17] Y. Lin, F. Lv, S. Zhu, M. Yang, T. Cour, K. Yu, L. Cao, and T. Huang. Large-scale image classification: fast feature extraction and svm training. In *Computer Vision and Pattern Recognition (CVPR), 2011 IEEE Conference on*, pages 1689–1696. IEEE, 2011.

[18] D. C. Liu and J. Nocedal. On the limited memory BFGS method for large scale optimization. *Mathematical Programming*, 45(3):503–528, 1989.

[19] D. Mahajan, S. S. Keerthi, S. Sundararajan, and L. Bottou. A parallel sgd method with strong convergence. *arXiv preprint arXiv:1311.0636*, 2013.

[20] G. Mann, R. McDonald, M. Mohri, N. Silberman, and D. Walker. Efficient large-scale distributed training of conditional maximum entropy models. In Y. Bengio, D. Schuurmans, J. Lafferty, C. K. I. Williams, and A. Culotta, editors, *Advances in Neural Information Processing Systems 22*, pages 1231–1239, 2009.

[21] S. Matsushima, S. Vishwanathan, and A. Smola. Linear support vector machines via dual cached loops. In Q. Yang, D. Agarwal, and J. Pei, editors, *The 18th ACM SIGKDD International Conference on Knowledge Discovery and Data Mining, KDD*, pages 177–185. ACM, 2012.

[22] D. Mimno, M. Hoffman, and D. Blei. Sparse stochastic inference for latent dirichlet allocation. In *International Conference on Machine Learning*, 2012.

[23] S. Shalev-Shwartz and T. Zhang. Accelerated mini-batch stochastic dual coordinate ascent. In *Advances in Neural Information Processing Systems*, pages 378–385, 2013.

[24] M. Takáč, A. Bijral, P. Richtárik, and N. Srebro. Mini-batch primal and dual methods for svms. *arXiv preprint arXiv:1303.2314*, 2013.

[25] H.-F. Yu, C.-J. Hsieh, K.-W. Chang, and C.-J. Lin. Large linear classification when data cannot fit in memory. In B. Rao, B. Krishnapuram, A. Tomkins, and Q. Yang, editors, *Knowledge Discovery and Data Mining*, pages 833–842. ACM, 2010.

[26] M. Zinkevich. Online convex programming and generalised infinitesimal gradient ascent. In *Proceedings of the International Conference on Machine Learning*, pages 928–936, 2003.

[27] M. Zinkevich, A. J. Smola, M. Weimer, and L. Li. Parallelized stochastic gradient descent. In nips23e, editor, *nips23*, pages 2595–2603, 2010.

APPENDIX

PROOF OF LEMMA 1. Since $w_t = \operatorname{argmin}_{w \in \Omega} h_t(w)$, we have from the first order KKT condition at w_t:

$$\nabla h_t(w_t)^\top (w_t - \bar{w}_t) \leq 0$$

In addition, the first order KKT condition of (8) at $\bar{w}_t$ combined with the fact that $h_t(w) = \phi_{I_t}(w) + \frac{\gamma_t}{2} \|w - w_{t-1}\|_2^2$ implies that

$$(\nabla h_t(\bar{w}_t) + \nabla \phi(\bar{w}_t) - \nabla \phi_{I_t}(\bar{w}_t))^\top (w_t - \bar{w}_t) \geq 0.$$

By substracting the first inequality from the second inequality, and rearranging terms, we obtain:

$$\begin{aligned} &(\nabla h_t(w_t) - \nabla h_t(\bar{w}_t))^\top (w_t - \bar{w}_t) \\ &\leq (\nabla \phi(\bar{w}_t) - \nabla \phi_{I_t}(\bar{w}_t))^\top (w_t - \bar{w}_t). \end{aligned} \tag{12}$$

By additivity of Bregman divergences we have

$$D_{h_t}(\bar{w}_t; w_t) = D_{\phi_{I_t}}(\bar{w}_t; w_t) + \frac{\gamma_t}{2} \|\bar{w}_t - w_t\|_2^2.$$

hence $D_{h_t}(\bar{w}_t; w_t) \geq \frac{\gamma_t}{2} \|\bar{w}_t - w_t\|_2^2$.

Similarly $D_{h_t}(w_t; \bar{w}_t) \geq \frac{\gamma_t}{2} \|\bar{w}_t - w_t\|_2^2$. It follows that

$$\begin{aligned}
\gamma_t \|w_t - \bar{w}_t\|_2^2 &\leq D_{h_t}(\bar{w}_t; w_t) + D_{h_t}(w_t; \bar{w}_t) \\
&= (\nabla h_t(w_t) - \nabla h_t(\bar{w}_t)^\top (w_t - \bar{w}_t) \\
&\leq (\nabla \phi(\bar{w}_t) - \nabla \phi_{I_t}(\bar{w}_t))^\top (w_t - \bar{w}_t) \\
&\leq \|\nabla \phi(\bar{w}_t) - \nabla \phi_{I_t}(\bar{w}_t)\|_2 \|w_t - \bar{w}_t\|_2,
\end{aligned}$$

where the second inequality is due to (12). The third inequality is Cauchy-Schwarz inequality. □

PROOF OF LEMMA 2. This bound is essentially a conversion of variances from a minibatch I to the full set when using sampling without replacement. To simplify notation we use the abbreviation of $\psi_i := \nabla \phi_i(w) - \nabla \phi(w)$ and $\psi_I = \nabla \phi_I(w) - \nabla \phi(w)$. Note that by construction

$$\mathbf{E}_i [\psi_i] = \mathbf{E}_I [\psi_I(w)] = \psi \tag{13}$$

and therefore $B^2 = \mathbf{E}_i [\|\psi_i\|^2]$ and $B^2 \leq A^2$. The latter inequality follows since A^2 is a uniform upper bound on the variance over all $w \in \Omega$. This yields

$$\begin{aligned}
\mathbf{E}_I [\|\psi_I\|_2^2] &= \mathbf{E}_I \left[\left\| \frac{1}{b} \sum_{i \in I} \psi_i \right\|_2^2 \right] = \frac{1}{b^2} \mathbf{E}_I \left[\sum_{i,j \in I} {\psi_i}^\top \psi_j \right] \\
&= \frac{1}{b^2} \mathbf{E}_I \left[\sum_{i \neq j \in I} {\psi_i}^\top \psi_j \right] + \frac{B^2}{b} \\
&= \frac{b-1}{bn(n-1)} \sum_{i \neq j} {\psi_i}^\top \psi_j + \frac{B^2}{b} \\
&= \frac{b-1}{bn(n-1)} \sum_{i,j} \psi_i^\top \psi_j + \frac{B^2}{b} - \frac{B^2}{b} \frac{b-1}{n-1} \\
&= 0 + \frac{B^2}{b} \frac{n-b}{n-1} < \frac{A^2}{b}
\end{aligned}$$

The last equality used the fact that ψ_i has zero-mean. □

PROOF OF LEMMA 3. We have

$$\begin{aligned}
&D_{h_t}(w_*, w_t) - D_{h_t}(w_*, w_{t-1}) \\
&= D_{h_t}(w_{t-1}, w_t) + (\nabla h_t(w_{t-1}) - \nabla h_t(w_t))^\top (w_* - w_t) \\
&\quad + (\nabla h_t(w_{t-1}) - \nabla h_t(w_t))^\top (w_t - w_{t-1}) \\
&\leq D_{h_t}(w_{t-1}, w_t) + \nabla \phi_{I_t}(w_{t-1})^\top (w_* - w_t) \\
&\quad + (\nabla h_t(w_{t-1}) - \nabla h_t(w_t))^\top (w_t - w_{t-1}) \\
&= \phi(w_*) - \phi(w_t) - D_\phi(w_*; w_{t-1}) \\
&\quad - (\nabla \phi(w_{t-1}) - \nabla \phi_{I_t}(w_{t-1}))^\top (w_* - w_t) \\
&\quad + (D_\phi(w_t; w_{t-1}) - D_{h_t}(w_t; w_{t-1})),
\end{aligned}$$

where the equalities follow from algebraic manipulations and the definition of Bregman divergence; in the inequality, we used the first order KKT condition of (6) at w_t, implying that

$$\begin{aligned}
&(\nabla \phi_{I_t}(w_{t-1}) + \nabla h_t(w_t) - \nabla h_t(w_{t-1}))^\top (w_* - w_t) \\
&= \nabla h_t(w_t)^\top (w_* - w_t) \geq 0.
\end{aligned}$$

Taking expectation, we have

$$\begin{aligned}
&\mathbf{E} D_{h_t}(w_*, w_t) - \mathbf{E} D_{h_t}(w_*, w_{t-1}) \\
&\leq \phi(w_*) - \mathbf{E}\phi(w_t) - \mathbf{E} D_\phi(w_*; w_{t-1}) \\
&\quad - \mathbf{E}(\nabla \phi(w_{t-1}) - \nabla \phi_{I_t}(w_{t-1}))^\top (w_* - w_t) \\
&\quad + \mathbf{E}(D_\phi(w_t; w_{t-1}) - D_{h_t}(w_t; w_{t-1})) \\
&\leq \phi(w_*) - \mathbf{E}\phi(w_t) - \mathbf{E} D_\phi(w_*; w_{t-1}) \\
&\quad - \mathbf{E}(\nabla \phi(w_{t-1}) - \nabla \phi_{I_t}(w_{t-1}))^\top (w_* - w_t) \\
&= \phi(w_*) - \mathbf{E}\phi(w_t) - \mathbf{E} D_\phi(w_*; w_{t-1}) \\
&\quad - \mathbf{E}(\nabla \phi(w_{t-1}) - \nabla \phi_{I_t}(w_{t-1}))^\top (\bar{w}_t - w_t),
\end{aligned} \tag{14}$$

where the second inequality follows from $\mathbf{E}(D_\phi(w_t; w_{t-1}) - D_{h_t}(w_t; w_{t-1})) \leq 0$, which is a consequence of Assumption 1. The equality holds because

$$\begin{aligned}
&\mathbf{E}(\nabla \phi(w_{t-1}) - \nabla \phi_{I_t}(w_{t-1}))^\top w_* \\
&= \mathbf{E}(\nabla \phi(w_{t-1}) - \nabla \mathbf{E}_{I_t | w_{t-1}} \phi_{I_t}(w_{t-1}))^\top w_* \\
&= 0 = \mathbf{E}(\nabla \phi(w_{t-1}) - \nabla \phi_{I_t}(w_{t-1}))^\top \bar{w}_t.
\end{aligned}$$

Note further that

$$\begin{aligned}
&- \mathbf{E}(\nabla \phi(w_{t-1}) - \nabla \phi_{I_t}(w_{t-1}))^\top (\bar{w}_t - w_t) \\
&\leq \sqrt{\mathbf{E}\|\nabla \phi(w_{t-1}) - \nabla \phi_{I_t}(w_{t-1}))\|_2^2 \, \mathbf{E}\|\bar{w}_t - w_t\|_2^2} \\
&\leq \sqrt{\mathbf{E}\|\nabla \phi(w_{t-1}) - \nabla \phi_{I_t}(w_{t-1}))\|_2^2 \, \mathbf{E}\|\nabla \phi(\bar{w}_t) - \nabla \phi_{I_t}(\bar{w}_t)\|_2^2 / \gamma_t} \\
&\leq A^2 / (\gamma_t b),
\end{aligned}$$

where the first inequality follows from Cauchy-Schwarz inequality, the second inequality is due to Lemma 1, and the third inequality is due to Lemma 2. Plugging the above estimate into (14), we obtain the desired bound. □

Streaming Submodular Maximization: Massive Data Summarization on the Fly

Ashwinkumar Badanidiyuru
Cornell Unversity
ashwinkumarbv@gmail.com

Baharan Mirzasoleiman
ETH Zurich
baharanm@inf.ethz.ch

Amin Karbasi
ETH Zurich
Yale University
amin.karbasi@gmail.com

Andreas Krause
ETH Zurich
krausea@ethz.ch

ABSTRACT

How can one summarize a massive data set "on the fly", i.e., without even having seen it in its entirety? In this paper, we address the problem of extracting representative elements from a large stream of data. I.e., we would like to select a subset of say k data points from the stream that are most representative according to some objective function. Many natural notions of "representativeness" satisfy submodularity, an intuitive notion of diminishing returns. Thus, such problems can be reduced to maximizing a submodular set function subject to a cardinality constraint. Classical approaches to submodular maximization require full access to the data set. We develop the first efficient streaming algorithm with constant factor $1/2 - \varepsilon$ approximation guarantee to the optimum solution, requiring only a single pass through the data, and memory independent of data size. In our experiments, we extensively evaluate the effectiveness of our approach on several applications, including training large-scale kernel methods and exemplar-based clustering, on millions of data points. We observe that our streaming method, while achieving practically the same utility value, runs about 100 times faster than previous work.

Categories and Subject Descriptors

H.2.8 [**Database Management**]: Database applications—*Data mining*

Keywords

Submodular functions; Streaming algorithms

1. INTRODUCTION

The unprecedented growth in modern datasets – coming from different sources and modalities such as images, videos, sensor data, social networks, etc. – demands novel techniques that extract useful information from massive data, while still remaining computationally tractable. One compelling approach that has gained a lot of interest in recent years is *data summarization*: selecting representative subsets of manageable size out of large data sets. Applications range from exemplar-based clustering [8], to document [23, 7] and corpus summarization [33], to recommender systems [10, 9], just to name a few. A systematic way for data summarization, used in all the aforementioned applications, is to turn the problem into selecting a subset of data elements optimizing a utility function that quantifies "representativeness" of the selected set. Often-times, these objective functions satisfy *submodularity*, an intuitive notion of diminishing returns (c.f., [27]), stating that selecting any given element earlier helps more than selecting it later. Thus, many problems in data summarization require maximizing submodular set functions subject to cardinality constraints [14, 18], and big data means we have to solve this problem at scale.

Submodularity is a property of set functions with deep theoretical and practical consequences. The seminal result of Nemhauser et al. [27], that has been of great importance in data mining, is that a simple greedy algorithm produces solutions competitive with the optimal (intractable) solution. This greedy algorithm starts with the empty set, and iteratively locates the element with maximal marginal benefit (increasing the utility the most over the elements picked so far). This greedy algorithm (and other standard algorithms for submodular optimization), however, unfortunately requires *random access* to the data. Hence, while it can easily be applied if the data fits in main memory, it is impractical for data residing on disk, or arriving over time at a fast pace.

In many domains, data volumes are increasing faster than the ability of individual computers to store them in main memory. In some cases, data may be produced so rapidly that it cannot even be stored. Thus, it becomes of crucial importance to process the data in a *streaming* fashion where at any point of time the algorithm has access only to a small fraction of data stored in primary memory. This approach not only avoids the need for vast amounts of random-access memory but also provides predictions in a timely manner based on the data seen so far, facilitating real-time analytics.

In this paper, we provide a simple streaming protocol, called SIEVE-STREAMING, for monotone submodular function maximization, subject to the constraint that at most k points are selected. It requires only a *single pass* over the data, in *arbitrary* order, and provides a *constant factor* $1/2 - \varepsilon$ approximation to the optimum solution, for any $\varepsilon > 0$. At the same time, it only requires $O((k \log k)/\varepsilon)$

KDD'14, August 24–27, 2014, New York, NY, USA.

ACM 978-1-4503-2956-9/14/08 ...$15.00.
http://dx.doi.org/10.1145/2623330.2623637.

memory (i.e., independent of the data set size), and processes data points with $O((\log k)/\varepsilon)$ update time. To the best of our knowledge, it is the first streaming protocol that provides such strong theoretical guarantees if nothing but monotone submodularity is assumed. Our experimental results demonstrate the effectiveness of our approach on several submodular maximization problems. We show that for problems such as exemplar-based clustering and active set selection in nonparametric learning, our approach leads to streaming solutions that provide competitive utility when compared with those obtained via classical methods, at a dramatically reduced fraction of the computational cost (about 1% in both the exemplar based clustering and active set selection applications).

2. BACKGROUND AND RELATED WORK

Over the recent years, submodular optimization has been identified as a powerful tool for numerous data mining and machine learning applications including viral marketing [17], network monitoring [22], news article recommendation [10], nonparametric learning [14, 29], document and corpus summarization [23, 7, 33], network inference [30], and Determinantal Point Processes [13]. A problem of key importance in all these applications is to maximize a monotone submodular function subject to a cardinality constraint (i.e., a bound on the number k of elements that can be selected). See [18] for a survey on submodular maximization.

Classical approaches for cardinality-constrained submodular optimization, such as the celebrated greedy algorithm of Nemhauser et al. [27], or its accelerated variants [24, 22, 3] require random access to the data. Once the size of the dataset increases beyond the memory capacity (typical in many modern datasets) or the data is arriving incrementally over time, neither the greedy algorithm, nor its accelerated versions can be used.

Scaling up: distributed algorithms.

One possible approach to scale up submodular optimization is to distribute data to several machines, and seek parallel computation methods. In particular, Mirzasoleiman et al. [25] in parallel to Kumar et al. [20] devised distributed algorithms for maximizing submodular functions, under some additional assumptions on the objective function: Lipschitz continuity [25] or bounded spread of the non-zero marginal gains [20]. Prior to [25] and [20], specific instances of distributed submodular maximization, that often arise in large-scale graph mining problems, have been studied. In particular, Chierichetti et al. [6] and later Blelloch et al. [5] addressed the MAX-COVER problem and provided a constant approximation to the centralized algorithm. Lattanzi et al. [21] addressed more general graph problems by introducing the idea of *filtering*: reduce the size of the input in a distributed fashion so that the resulting, much smaller, problem instance can be solved on a single machine. Our streaming method SIEVE-STREAMING employs a similar filtering idea.

Streaming algorithms for submodular maximization.

Another natural approach to scale up submodular optimization, explored in this paper, is to use streaming algorithms. In fact, in applications where data arrives at a pace that does not allow even storing it, this is the only viable option. The first approach, STREAM-GREEDY, for submodular maximization on data streams is presented by [14]. However, their approach makes strong assumptions about the way the data stream is generated, and unless their assumptions are met, it is fairly easy to construct examples (and we demonstrate one in this paper) where the performance of their algorithm degrades quickly when compared to the optimum solution. Furthermore, the update time (computational cost to process one data point) of their approach is $\Omega(k)$, which is prohibitive for large k. We compare against their approach in this paper.

The work of [20] claims a multi-pass and a single-pass streaming algorithm. The claimed guarantees for the single pass algorithm depend on the maximum increase in the objective any element can offer (Thm. 27, [20]), while the multi-pass algorithm has a memory requirement depending on the data size n (Thm. 28, [20]). Our algorithm SIEVE-STREAMING lazily tracks the maximum valued element, enabling a single pass streaming algorithm which *does not depend* on the maximum increase in the objective any element can offer. We cannot empirically compare against [20] as the details of both algorithms are omitted.

There is further related work on the *submodular secretary problem* [15, 4]. While also processing elements in a stream, these approaches are different in two important ways: (i) they work in the stronger model where they must either commit to or permanently discard newly arriving elements; (ii) they require *random* arrival of elements, and have a worse approximation ratio (≤ 0.1 vs. $1/2-\epsilon$). If elements arrive in arbitrary order, performance can degrade arbitrarily. Some approaches also require large (i.e., $O(n)$) memory [15].

In this paper, we provide the first streaming algorithm for cardinality-constrained submodular maximization with 1) constant factor approximation guarantees, that 2) makes no assumptions on the data stream, 3) requires only a single pass, 4) only $O(k \log k)$ memory and 5) only $O(\log k)$ update time, assuming 6) nothing but monotone submodularity.

3. STREAMING SUBMODULAR MAX

We consider the problem of selecting subsets out of a large data set of size n, indexed by V (called ground set). Our goal is to maximize a non-negative set function $f : 2^V \rightarrow \mathbb{R}_+$, where, for $S \subseteq V$, $f(S)$ quantifies the utility of set S, capturing, e.g., how well S represents V according to some objective. We will discuss concrete instances of functions f in Section 4. A set function f is naturally associated with a *discrete derivative*, also called the *marginal gain*,

$$\triangle_f(e|S) \doteq f(S \cup \{e\}) - f(S), \tag{1}$$

where $S \subseteq V$ and $e \in V$, which quantifies the increase in utility obtained when adding e to set S. f is called *monotone* iff for all e and S it holds that $\triangle_f(e|S) \geq 0$. Further, f is *submodular* iff for all $A \subseteq B \subseteq V$ and $e \in V \setminus B$ the following diminishing returns condition holds:

$$\triangle_f(e|A) \geq \triangle_f(e|B). \tag{2}$$

That means, adding an element e in context of a set A helps at least as much as adding e in context of a superset B of A. Throughout this paper, we focus on such monotone submodular functions. For now, we adopt the common assumption that f is given in terms of a value oracle (a black box) that computes $f(S)$ for any $S \subseteq V$. In Section 6, we will discuss the setting where $f(S)$ itself depends on the entire data set V, and not just the selected subset S. Submodular functions contain a large class of functions that naturally arise in data mining and machine learning applications (c.f., [17, 22, 10, 14, 9, 23, 7, 33, 30, 18]).

Cardinality-constrained submodular maximization.

The focus of this paper is on maximizing a monotone submodular function subject to a cardinality constraint, i.e.,

$$\max_{S \subseteq V} f(S) \quad \text{s.t.} \quad |S| \leq k. \tag{3}$$

We will denote by S^* the subset of size at most k that achieves the above maximization, i.e., the optimal solution, with value $\texttt{OPT} = f(S^*)$. Unfortunately, problem (3) is NP-hard, for many classes of submodular functions [11]. However, a seminal result by Nemhauser et al. [27] shows that a simple greedy algorithm is highly effective. It starts with the empty set $S_0 = \emptyset$, and at each iteration i over the whole dataset, it chooses an element $e \in V$ maximizing (1), i.e.,

$$S_i = S_{i-1} \cup \{\arg\max_{e \in V} \triangle_f(e|S_{i-1})\}. \tag{4}$$

Let S^g denote this greedy solution of size at most k. Nemhauser et al. prove that $f(S^g) \geq (1 - 1/e)\texttt{OPT}$, i.e., the greedy algorithm obtains a $(1-1/e) \approx 0.63$ approximation. For several classes of monotone submodular functions, it is known that $(1 - 1/e)$ is the best approximation guarantee that one can hope for [26, 11, 19]. Moreover, the greedy algorithm can be accelerated using lazy evaluations [24, 22].

Submodular optimization over data streams.

In many today's data mining and machine learning applications, running the standard greedy algorithm or its variants [24, 22] is computationally prohibitive: either the data set does not fit in main memory on a single computer, precluding random access, or the data itself arrives in a stream (e.g., activity logs, video streams), possibly in a pace that precludes storage. Hence, in such applications, we seek methods that can process quickly arriving data in a timely manner. *Streaming algorithms* with a limited memory available to them (much less than the ground set) and limited processing time per item [12] are practical solutions in such scenarios. They access only a small fraction of data at any point in time and provide approximate solutions.

More formally, in context of streaming submodular maximization, we assume that the ground set $V = \{e_1, \dots, e_n\}$ is ordered (in some arbitrary manner, w.l.o.g., the natural order $1, 2, \dots, n$), and any streaming algorithm must process V in the given order. At each iteration t, the algorithm may maintain a memory $M_t \subset V$ of points, and must be ready to output a candidate feasible solution $S_t \subset M_t$ of size at most $|S_t| \leq k$. Whenever a new point arrives from the stream, the algorithm may elect to remember it (i.e., insert it into its memory). However, if the memory exceeds a specified capacity bound, it must discard elements before accepting new ones. The performance of a streaming algorithm is measured by four basic parameters:

- the *number of passes* the algorithm needs to make over the data stream,
- the *memory* required by the algorithm (i.e., $\max_t |M_t|$),
- the *running time* of the algorithm, in particular the number of oracle queries (evaluations of f) made,
- the *approximation ratio*, i.e., $f(S_T)/\texttt{OPT}$ where S_T is the final solution produced by the algorithm[1].

[1]Note that T can be bigger than n, if the algorithm makes multiple passes over the data.

Towards Streaming Submodular Maximization.

The standard greedy algorithm (4) requires access to all elements of the ground set and hence cannot be directly applied in the streaming setting. A naive way to implement it in a streaming fashion, when the data is static and does not increase over time, is to pass k times over the ground set and at each iteration select an element with the maximum marginal gain. This naive approach will provide a $(1 - 1/e)$ approximation at the price of passing many (i.e, k) times over the data, using $O(k)$ memory, $O(nk)$ function evaluations. Note that, if the data size increases over time (e.g., new elements are added to a log, video is being recorded, etc.) we can no longer implement this naive approach. Moreover, the accelerated versions of the greedy algorithm do not provide any benefit in the streaming setting as the full ground set is not available for random access.

An alternative approach is to keep a memory of the best elements seen so far. For instance, we can start from the empty set $S_0 = \emptyset$. As long as no more than k elements $e_1, e_2, \dots, e_t$ have arrived (or no more than k elements are read from the ground set), we keep all of them, i.e., $S_t = S_{t-1} \cup \{e_t\}$, for $t \leq k$. Then for each new data point e_t, where $t > k$, we check whether switching it with an element in S_{t-1} will increase the value of the utility function f. If so, we switch it with the one that maximizes the utility. Formally, if there exists an $e \in S_{t-1}$ such that $f(S_{t-1} \cup \{e_t\} \setminus \{e\}) > f(S_{t-1})$, then we swap e and e_t, setting $S_t = S_{t-1} \cup \{e_t\} \setminus \{e\}$. This greedy approach is the essence of Stream-Greedy of [14]. However, unless strong conditions are met, the performance of Stream-Greedy degrades arbitrarily with k (see Appendix).

Very recently, the existence of another streaming algorithm – Greedy-Scaling – was claimed in [20]. As neither the algorithm nor its proof were described in the paper, we were unable to identify its running time in theory and its performance in practice. Based on their claim, if nothing but monotone submodularity is assumed, Greedy-Scaling has to pass over the dataset $O(1/\delta)$ times in order to provide a solution with $\delta/2$ approximation guarantee. Moreover, the required memory also increases with data as $O(kn^\delta \log n)$. With a stronger assumption, namely that all (non-zero) marginals are bounded between 1 and Δ, the existence of a one-pass streaming algorithm with approximation guarantee $1/2-\epsilon$, and memory $k/\epsilon \log(n\Delta)$ is claimed. Note that the above requirement on the bounded spread of the nonzero marginal gains is rather strong and does not hold in certain applications, such as the objective in (6) (here, Δ may increase exponentially in k).

In this paper, we devise an algorithm– Sieve-Streaming – that, for any $\varepsilon > 0$, within only one pass over the data stream, using only $O(k \log(k)/\varepsilon)$ memory, running time of at most $O(n \log(k)/\varepsilon)$ produces a $1/2 - \varepsilon$ approximate solution to (3). So, while the approximation guarantee is slightly worse compared to the classical greedy algorithm, a single pass suffices, and the running time is dramatically improved. Moreover, ε serves as a tuning parameter for trading accuracy and cost.

4. APPLICATIONS

We now discuss two concrete applications, with their submodular objective functions f, where the size of the datasets or the nature of the problem often requires a streaming solution. We report experimental results in Section 7. Note that

	# passes	approx. guarantee	memory	update time
Standard Greedy [27]	$O(k)$	$(1-1/e)$	$O(k)$	$O(k)$
GREEDY-SCALING [20]	$O(1/\delta)$	$\delta/2$	$kn^\delta \log n$	?
STREAM-GREEDY [14]	multiple	$(1/2-\varepsilon)$	$O(k)$	$O(k)$
SIEVE-STREAMING	1	$(1/2-\varepsilon)$	$O(k\log(k)/\varepsilon)$	$O(\log(k)/\varepsilon)$

Table 1: Comparisons between the existing streaming methods in terms of number of passes over the data, required memory, update time per new element and approximation guarantee. For GREEDY-SCALING we report here the performance guarantees claimed in [20]. However, as the details of the streaming algorithm are not presented in [20] we were unable to identify the update time and compare with them in our experiments. For STREAM-GREEDY no upper bound on the number of rounds is provided in [14]. The memory and update times are not explicitly tied to ε.

many more data mining applications have been identified to rely on submodular optimization (e.g., [17, 22, 10, 9, 23, 33, 30]), which can potentially benefit from our work. Providing a comprehensive survey is beyond the scope of this article.

4.1 Exemplar Based Clustering

We start with a classical data mining application. Suppose we wish to select a set of exemplars, that best represent a massive data set. One approach for finding such exemplars is solving the k-medoid problem [16], which aims to minimize the sum of pairwise dissimilarities between exemplars and elements of the dataset. More precisely, let us assume that for the data set V we are given a distance function $d: V\times V \to \mathbb{R}$ such that $d(\cdot,\cdot)$ encodes dissimilarity between elements of the underlying set V. Then, the k-medoid loss function can be defined as follows:

$$L(S) = \frac{1}{|V|}\sum_{e\in V}\min_{v\in S} d(e,v).$$

By introducing an auxiliary element e_0 (e.g., $=\mathbf{0}$, the all zero vector) we can turn L into a monotone submodular function [14]:

$$f(S) = L(\{e_0\}) - L(S\cup\{e_0\}). \tag{5}$$

In words, f measures the decrease in the loss associated with the set S versus the loss associated with just the auxiliary element. It is easy to see that for suitable choice of e_0, maximizing f is equivalent to minimizing L. Hence, the standard greedy algorithm provides a very good solution. But the problem becomes computationally challenging when we have a large data set and we wish to extract a small subset S of exemplars. Our streaming solution SIEVE-STREAMING addresses this challenge.

Note that in contrast to classical clustering algorithms (such as k-means), the submodularity-based approach is very general: It does not require *any* properties of the distance function d, except nonnegativity (i.e., $d(\cdot,\cdot)\geq 0$). In particular, d is not necessarily assumed to be symmetric, nor obey the triangle inequality.

4.2 Large-scale Nonparametric Learning

Besides extracting representative elements for sake of explorative data analysis, data summarization is a powerful technique for speeding up learning algorithms.

As a concrete example, consider kernel machines [31] (such as kernelized SVMs/logistic regression, Gaussian processes, etc.), which are powerful non-parametric learning techniques. The key idea in these approaches is to reduce non-linear problems such as classification, regression, clustering etc. to linear problems – for which good algorithms are available – in a, typically high-dimensional, transformed space. Crucially, the data set $V=\{e_1,\dots,e_n\}$ is represented in this transformed space only implicitly via a kernel matrix

$$K_{V,V} = \begin{pmatrix} \mathcal{K}_{e_1,e_1} & \dots & \mathcal{K}_{e_1,e_n} \\ \vdots & & \vdots \\ \mathcal{K}_{e_n,e_1} & \dots & \mathcal{K}_{e_n,e_n} \end{pmatrix}.$$

Hereby $\mathcal{K}_{e_i,e_j}$ is the similarity of item i and j measured via a symmetric positive definite kernel function. For example, a commonly used kernel function in practice where elements of the ground set V are embedded in a Euclidean space is the squared exponential kernel

$$\mathcal{K}_{e_i,e_j} = \exp(-|e_i - e_j|_2^2/h^2).$$

Many different kernel functions are available for modeling various types of data beyond Euclidean vectors, such as sequences, sets, graphs etc. Unfortunately, when scaling to large data sets, even representing the kernel matrix $K_{V,V}$ requires space quadratic in n. Moreover, solving the learning problems (such as kernelized SVMs, Gaussian processes, etc.) typically has cost $\Omega(n^2)$ (e.g., $O(n^3)$ for Gaussian process regression).

Thus, a common approach to scale kernel methods to large data sets is to perform *active set selection* (c.f., [28, 32]), i.e., select a small, representative subset $S\subseteq V$, and only work with the kernel matrix $K_{S,S}$ restricted to this subset. The key challenge is to select such a representative set S.

One prominent procedure that is often used in practice is the Informative Vector Machine (IVM) [32], which aims to select a set S maximizing the following objective function

$$f(S) = \frac{1}{2}\log\det(\mathbf{I}+\sigma^{-2}\Sigma_{S,S}), \tag{6}$$

where σ is a regularization parameter. Thus, sets maximizing $f(S)$ maximize the log-determinant $\mathbf{I}+\sigma^{-2}\Sigma_{S,S}$, and therefore capture diversity of the selected elements S. It can be shown that f is monotone submodular [32]. Note that similar objective functions arise when performing MAP inference in Determinantal Point Processes, powerful probabilistic models for data summarization [13].

When the size of the ground set is small, standard greedy algorithms (akin to (4)) provide good solutions. Note that the objective function f only depends on the selected elements (i.e., the cost of evaluating f does not depend on the size of V). For massive data sets, however, classical greedy algorithms do not scale, and we must resort to streaming.

In Section 7, we will show how SIEVE-STREAMING can choose near-optimal subsets out of a data set of 45 million vectors (user visits from Yahoo! Front Page) by only accessing a small portion of the dataset. Note that in many nonparametric learning applications, data naturally arrives over time. For instance, the Yahoo! Front Page is visited by thousands of people every hour. It is then advantageous, or sometimes the only way, to make predictions with kernel methods by choosing the active set on the fly.

5. THE SIEVE-STREAMING ALGORITHM

We now present our main contribution, the SIEVE-STREAMING algorithm for streaming submodular maximization. Our approach builds on three key ideas: 1) a way of simulating the (intractable) optimum algorithm via thresholding, 2) guessing the threshold based on the maximum singleton element, and 3) lazily running the algorithm for different thresholds when the maximum singleton element is updated. As our final algorithm is a careful mixture of these ideas, we showcase each of them by making certain assumptions and then removing each assumption to get the final algorithm.

5.1 Knowing OPT helps

The key reason why the classical greedy algorithm for submodular maximization works, is that at every iteration, an element is identified that reduces the "gap" to the optimal solution by a significant amount. More formally, it can be seen that, if S_i is the set of the first i elements picked by the greedy algorithm (4), then the marginal value $\triangle_f(e_{i+1}|S_i)$ of the next element e_{i+1} added is at least $(\texttt{OPT} - f(S_i))/k$. Thus, our main strategy for developing our streaming algorithm is identify elements with similarly high marginal value. The challenge in the streaming setting is that, when we receive the next element from the stream, we must immediately decide whether it has "sufficient" marginal value. This will require us to compare it to OPT in some way which gives the intuition that knowing OPT should help.

With the above intuition, we could try to pick the first element with marginal value $\texttt{OPT}/k$. This specific attempt does not work for instances that contain a single element with marginal value just above $\texttt{OPT}/k$ towards the end of the stream, and where the rest of elements with marginal value just below $\texttt{OPT}/k$ appear towards the beginning of the stream. Our algorithm would have then rejected these elements with marginal value just below $\texttt{OPT}/k$ and can never get their value. But we can immediately observe that if we had instead lowered our threshold from $\texttt{OPT}/k$ to some $\beta\texttt{OPT}/k$, we could have still gotten these lower valued elements while still making sure that we get the high valued elements when β is reasonably large. Below, we use $\beta = 1/2$.

Our algorithm will be based on the above intuition. Suppose we know OPT up to a constant factor α, i.e., we have a value v such that $\texttt{OPT} \geq v \geq \alpha \cdot \texttt{OPT}$ for some $0 \leq \alpha \leq 1$. The algorithm starts with setting $S = \emptyset$ and then, after observing each element, it adds it to S if the marginal value is at least $(v/2 - f(S))/(k - |S|)$ and we are still below the cardinality constraint. Thus, it "sieves" out elements with large marginal value. The pseudocode is given in algorithm 1

PROPOSITION 5.1. *Assuming input v to algorithm 1 satisfies $\texttt{OPT} \geq v \geq \alpha$ OPT, the algorithm satisfies the following properties*

- *It outputs a set S such that $|S| \leq k$ and $f(S) \geq \frac{\alpha}{2}$ OPT*
- *It does 1 pass over the data set, stores at most k elements and has $O(1)$ update time per element.*

Algorithm 1 SIEVE-STREAMING-KNOW-OPT-VAL

```
Input: v such that OPT ≥ v ≥ α OPT
S = ∅
for i = 1 to n do
    if △_f(e_i | S) ≥ (v/2 − f(S))/(k − |S|) and |S_v| < k then
        S := S ∪ {e_i}
return S
```

5.2 Knowing $\max_{e\in V} f(\{e\})$ is enough

Algorithm 1 requires that we know (a good approximation) to the value of the optimal solution OPT. However, obtaining this value is a kind of chicken and egg problem where we have to estimate OPT to get the solution and use the solution to estimate OPT. The crucial insight is that, in order to get a very crude estimate on OPT, it is enough to know the maximum value of any singleton element $m = \max_{e\in V} f(\{e\})$. From submodularity, we have that

$$m \leq \texttt{OPT} \leq k \cdot m.$$

This estimate is not too useful yet; if we apply Proposition 5.1 directly with $v = km$ and $\alpha = 1/k$, we only obtain the guarantee that the solution will obtain a value of $\texttt{OPT}/2k$.

Fortunately, once we get this crude upper bound $k \cdot m$ on OPT, we can immediately refine it. In fact, consider the following set

$$O = \{(1+\epsilon)^i | i \in \mathbb{Z}, m \leq (1+\epsilon)^i \leq k \cdot m\}.$$

At least one of the thresholds $v \in O$ should be a pretty good estimate of OPT, i.e there should exist at least some $v \in O$ such that $(1-\epsilon)\texttt{OPT} \leq v \leq \texttt{OPT}$. That means, we could run Algorithm 1 once for each value $v \in O$, requiring multiple passes over the data. In fact, instead of using multiple passes, a single pass is enough: We simply run several copies of Algorithm 1 in parallel, producing one candidate solution for each threshold $v \in O$. As final output, we return the best solution obtained.

More formally, the algorithm proceeds as follows. It assumes that the value $m = \max_{e\in V} f(\{e\})$ is given at the beginning of the algorithm. The algorithm discretizes the range $[m, k \cdot m]$ to get the set O. Since the algorithm does not know which value among O is a good estimate for OPT, it simulates Algorithm 1 for each of these values v: Formally it starts with a set S_v for each $v \in O$ and after observing each element, it adds to every S_v for which it has a marginal value of at least $(v/2 - f(S_v))/(k - |S_v|)$ and S_v is below the cardinality constraint. Note that $|O| = \mathcal{O}((\log k)/\epsilon)$, i.e., we only need to keep track of $\mathcal{O}((\log k)/\epsilon)$ many sets S_v of size at most k each, bounding the size of the memory $M = \cup_{v\in O} S_v$ by $\mathcal{O}((k \log k)/\epsilon)$. Moreover, the update time is $\mathcal{O}((\log k)/\epsilon)$ per element. The pseudocode is given in Algorithm 2.

PROPOSITION 5.2. *Assuming input m to Algorithm 2 satisfies $m = \max_{e\in V} f(\{e\})$, the algorithm satisfies the following properties*

- *It outputs a set S such that $|S| \leq k$ and $f(S) \geq \left(\frac{1}{2} - \epsilon\right)$ OPT*
- *It does 1 pass over the data set, stores at most $O\left(\frac{k \log k}{\epsilon}\right)$ elements and has $O\left(\frac{\log k}{\epsilon}\right)$ update time per element.*

Algorithm 2 SIEVE-STREAMING-KNOW-MAX-VAL

Input: $m = \max_{e \in V} f(\{e\})$
$O = \{(1+\epsilon)^i | i \in \mathbb{Z}, m \leq (1+\epsilon)^i \leq k \cdot m\}$
For each $v \in O, S_v := \emptyset$
for $i = 1$ to n **do**
  for $v \in O$ **do**
    if $\triangle_f(e_i \mid S_v) \geq \frac{v/2 - f(S_v)}{k - |S_v|}$ and $|S_v| < k$ **then**
      $S_v := S_v \cup \{e_i\}$
return $\text{argmax}_{v \in O_n} f(S_v)$

5.3 Lazy updates: The final algorithm

While Algorithm 2 successfully removed the unrealistic requirement of knowing OPT, obtaining the maximum value m of all singletons still requires one pass over the full data set, resulting in a two-pass algorithm.

It turns out that it is in fact possible to estimate m on the fly, within a *single* pass over the data. We will need two ideas to achieve this. The first natural idea is to maintain an auxiliary variable m which holds the current maximum singleton element after observing each element e_i and lazily instantiate the thresholds $v = (1+\epsilon)^i, m \leq (1+\epsilon)^i \leq k \cdot m$. Unfortunately, this idea alone does not yet work: This is because when we instantiate a threshold v we could potentially have already seen elements with marginal value $v/(2k)$ that we should have taken for the solution corresponding to S_v.

The second idea is to instead instantiate thresholds for an *increased range* $v = (1+\epsilon)^i, m \leq (1+\epsilon)^i \leq 2 \cdot k \cdot m$. It can be seen that when a threshold v is instantiated from this expanded set O, every element with marginal value $v/(2k)$ to S_v will appear on or after v is instantiated.

We now state the algorithm formally. It maintains an auxiliary variable m that holds the current maximum singleton element after observing each element e_i. Whenever m gets updated, the algorithm lazily instantiates the set O_i and deletes all thresholds outside O_i. Then it includes the element e_i into every S_v for $v \in O_i$ if e_i has the marginal value $(v/2 - f(S_v))/(k - |S_v|)$ to S_v. Finally, it outputs the best solution among S_v. We call the resulting algorithm SIEVE-STREAMING, and present its pseudocode in Algorithm 3, as well as an illustration in Figure 1.

Algorithm 3 SIEVE-STREAMING

$O = \{(1+\epsilon)^i | i \in \mathbb{Z}\}$
For each $v \in O, S_v := \emptyset$ (maintain the sets only for the necessary v's lazily)
$m := 0$
for $i = 1$ to n **do**
  $m := \max(m, f(\{e_i\}))$
  $O_i = \{(1+\epsilon)^i | m \leq (1+\epsilon)^i \leq 2 \cdot k \cdot m\}$
  Delete all S_v such that $v \notin O_i$.
  for $v \in O_i$ **do**
    if $\triangle_f(e_i \mid S_v) \geq \frac{v/2 - f(S_v)}{k - |S_v|}$ and $|S_v| < k$ **then**
      $S_v := S_v \cup \{e_i\}$
return $\text{argmax}_{v \in O_n} f(S_v)$

THEOREM 5.3. SIEVE-STREAMING *(Algorithm 3) satisfies the following properties*

- *It outputs a set S such that $|S| \leq k$ and $f(S) \geq \left(\frac{1}{2} - \epsilon\right)$ OPT*
- *It does 1 pass over the data set, stores at most $O\left(\frac{k \log k}{\epsilon}\right)$ elements and has $O\left(\frac{\log k}{\epsilon}\right)$ update time per element.*

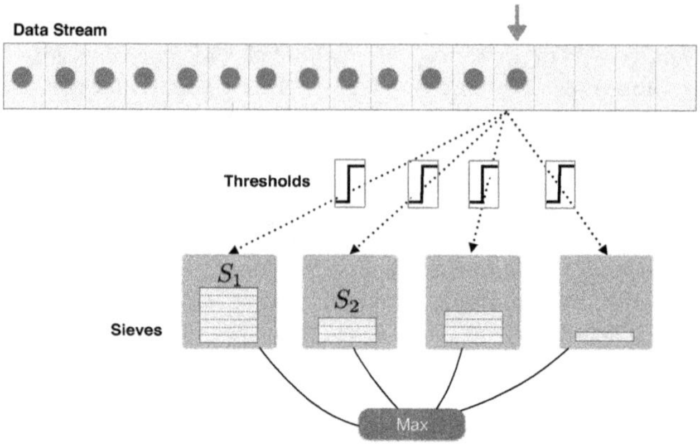

Figure 1: Illustration of SIEVE-STREAMING. Data arrives in any order. The marginal gain of any new data point is computed with respect to all of the sieves. If it exceeds the specific threshold of any sieve that does not yet meet the cardinality constraint, the point will be added. Otherwise it will be discarded. SIEVE-STREAMING ensures that the number of sieves is bounded. Moreover, it can provide statistics about the data accumulated at any time by returning the elements of the sieve with maximum utility.

Note that the total computation cost of SIEVE-STREAMING is $O(\frac{n \log k}{\epsilon})$. This is in contrast to the cost of $O(nk)$ for the classical greedy algorithm. Thus, not only does SIEVE-STREAMING require only a single pass through the data, it also offers an accuracy–performance tradeoff by providing the tuning parameter ϵ. We empirically evaluate this tradeoff in our experiments in Section 7. Further note that when executing SIEVE-STREAMING, some sets S_v do not "fill up" (i.e., meet the cardinality constraint). The empirical performance can be improved – without sacrificing any guarantees – by maintaining a reservoir (cf., Sec. 6) of $O(k \log k)$ random elements, and augment the non-full sets S_v upon termination by greedily adding elements from this reservoir.

6. BEYOND THE BLACK-BOX

In the previous sections, we have effectively assumed a so called *black-box* model for the function evaluations: given any set S, our algorithm SIEVE-STREAMING can evaluate $f(S)$ independently of the ground set V. I.e., the black-box implementing f only needs access to the selected elements S, but not the full data stream V. In several practical settings, however, this assumption is violated, meaning that the utility function f depends on the entire dataset. For instance, in order to evaluate (5) we need to know the loss function over the entire data set. Fortunately, many such functions (including (5)) share an important characteristic; they are *additively decomposable* [25] over the ground set V. That means, they can be written as

$$f(S) = \frac{1}{|V|} \sum_{e \in V} f_e(S), \tag{7}$$

where $f_e(S)$ is a non-negative submodular function. Decomposability requires that there is a separate monotone submodular function associated with every data point $e \in V$

and the value of $f(S)$ is nothing but the average of $f_e(S)$. For the remaining of this section, we assume that the functions $f_e(\cdot)$ can all be evaluated without accessing the full ground set. We define the evaluation of the utility function f restricted to a subset $W \subseteq V$ as follows:

$$f_W(S) = \frac{1}{|W|} \sum_{e \in W} f_e(S).$$

Hence $f_W(S)$ is the empirical average of f w.r.t. to set W. Note that as long as W is large enough and its elements are randomly chosen, the value of the empirical mean $f_W(S)$ will be a very good approximation of the true mean $f(S)$.

PROPOSITION 6.1. *Assume that all of $f_e(S)$ are bounded and w.l.o.g. $|f_e(S)| \leq 1$. Moreover, let W be uniformly sampled from V. Then by Hoeffding's inequality we have*

$$\Pr(|f_W(S) - f(S)| > \xi) \leq 2 \exp\left(\frac{-|W|\xi^2}{2}\right).$$

There are at most $|V|^k$ sets of size at most k. Hence, in order to have the RHS $\leq \delta$ for *any* set S of size at most k we simply (using the union bound) need to ensure

$$|W| \geq \frac{2\log(2/\delta) + 2k\log(|V|)}{\xi^2}. \tag{8}$$

As long as we know how to sample uniformly at random from a data stream, we can ensure that for decomposable functions defined earlier, our estimate is close (within the error margin of ξ) to the correct value. To sample randomly, we can use a *reservoir sampling* technique [35]. It creates a reservoir array of size $|W|$ and populates it with the first $|W|$ items of V. It then iterates through the remaining elements of the ground set until it is exhausted. At the i-th element where $i > |W|$, the algorithm generates a random number j between 1 and i. If j is at most $|W|$, the j-th element of the reservoir array is replaced with the ith element of V. It can be shown that upon finishing the data stream, each item in V has equal probability of being chosen for the reservoir.

Now we can devise a two round streaming algorithm, which in the first round applies reservoir sampling to sample an evaluation set W uniformly at random. In the second round, it simply runs SIEVE-STREAMING and evaluates the utility function f only with respect to the reservoir W.

Algorithm 4 SIEVE-STREAMING + Reservoir Sampling

1: Go through the data and find a reservoir W of size (8)
2: Run SIEVE-STREAMING by only evaluating $f_W(\cdot)$

THEOREM 6.2. *Suppose* SIEVE-STREAMING *uses a validation set W of size $|W| \geq \frac{2\log(2/\delta)k^2+2k^3\log(|V|)}{\varepsilon^2}$. Then with probability $1-\delta$, the output of Alg 4 will be a set S of size at most k such that*

$$f(S) \geq (\frac{1}{2} - \varepsilon)(OPT - \varepsilon).$$

This result shows how SIEVE-STREAMING can be applied to decomposable submodular functions if we can afford enough memory to store a sufficiently large evaluation set. Note that the above approach naturally suggests a heuristic one-pass algorithm for decomposable functions: Take the first $\frac{2\log(2/\delta)k^2+2k^3\log(|V|)}{\varepsilon^2}$ samples as validation set and run the greedy algorithm on it to produce a candidate solution. Then process the remaining stream, updating the validation set via reservoir sampling, and applying SIEVE-STREAMING, using the current validation set in order to approximately evaluate f. We report our experimental results for the exemplar-based clustering application using an evaluation set W.

7. EXPERIMENTS

In this section, we address the following questions:

- How good is the solution provided by SIEVE-STREAMING compared to the existing streaming algorithms?
- What computational benefits do we gain when using SIEVE-STREAMING on large datasets?
- How good is the performance of SIEVE-STREAMING on decomposable utility functions?

To this end, we run SIEVE-STREAMING on the two data mining applications we described in Section 4: exemplar-based clustering and active set selection for nonparametric learning. For both applications we report experiments on large datasets with millions of data points. Throughout this section we consider the following benchmarks:

- *random selection*: the output is k randomly selected data points from V.
- *standard greedy*: the output is the k data points selected by algorithm (4). This algorithm is not applicable in the streaming setting.
- *lazy greedy*: the output produced by the accelerated greedy method [24]. This algorithm is not applicable in the streaming setting.
- STREAM-GREEDY: The output is the k data points provided by STREAM-GREEDY as described in Section 3

In all of our experiments, we stop the streaming algorithms if the utility function does not improve significantly (relative improvement of at least γ for some small value $\gamma > 0$). In all of our experiment, we chose $\gamma = 10^{-5}$. This way, we can compare the performance of different algorithms in terms of computational efforts in a fair way. Throughout this section, we measure the computational cost in terms of the number of function evaluations used (more precisely, number of oracle queries). The advantage of this measure is that it is independent of the concrete implementation and platform. However, to demonstrate that the results remain almost identical, we also report the actual wall clock time for the exemplar-based clustering application. The random selection policy has the lowest computational cost among the streaming algorithms we consider in this paper. In fact, in terms of function evaluations its cost is one; at the end of the sampling process the selected set is evaluated once. To implement the random selection policy we can employ the reservoir sampling technique discussed earlier. On the other end of the spectrum, we have the standard greedy algorithm which makes k passes over the ground set, providing typically the best solution in terms of utility. Since it is computationally prohibitive we cannot run it for the large-scale datasets. However, we also report results on a smaller data set, where we compare against this algorithm.

7.1 Active Set Selection

For the active set selection objective described in Section 4.2, we chose a Gaussian kernel with $h = 0.75$ and

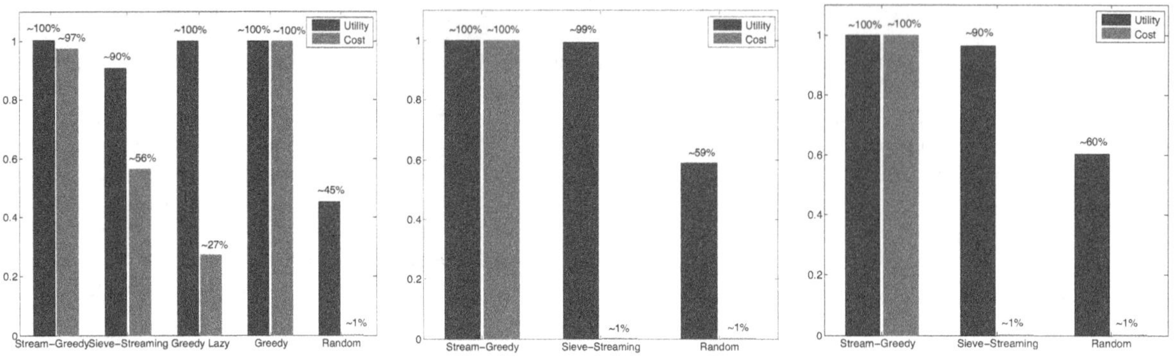

(a) Parkinsons (b) Census (c) Y! front page

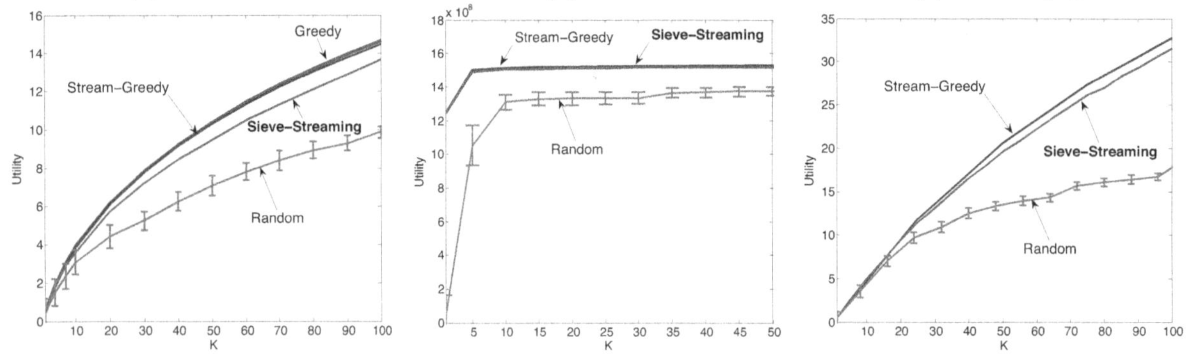

(d) Parkinsons (e) Census (f) Y! front page

Figure 2: Performance comparison. a), b) and c) show the utility obtained, along with the computational cost, by the algorithms on 3 different datasets. SIEVE-STREAMING achieves the major fraction of the utility with orders of magnitude less computation time. d), e) f) demonstrate the performance of all the algorithms for different values of k on the same datasets. In all of them SIEVE-STREAMING performs close to the (much more computationally expensive) STREAM-GREEDY benchmark.

$\sigma = 1$. For the small-scale experiments, we used the *Parkinsons Telemonitoring* dataset [34] consisting of 5,875 bio-medical voice measurements with 22 attributes from people with early-stage Parkinson's disease. We normalized the vectors to zero mean and unit variance. Fig. 2a compares the performance of SIEVE-STREAMING to the benchmarks for a fixed active set size $k = 20$. The computational costs of all algorithms, as well as their acquired utilities, are normalized to those of the standard greedy. As we can see, SIEVE-STREAMING provides a solution close to that of the standard greedy algorithm with a much reduced computational cost. For different values of k, Fig. 2d shows the performance of all the benchmarks. Again, SIEVE-STREAMING operates close to STREAM-GREEDY and (lazy) greedy.

For our large-scale scale experiment, we used the *Yahoo! Webscope* data set consisting of 45,811,883 user visits from the Featured Tab of the Today Module on the Yahoo! Front Page [2]. For each visit, the user is associated with a feature vector of dimension six. Fig. 2c compares the performance of SIEVE-STREAMING to the benchmarks for a fixed active set size $k = 100$. Since the size of the data set is large, we cannot run the standard (or lazy) greedy algorithm. As a consequence, computational costs and utilities are normalized to those of the STREAM-GREEDY benchmark. For such a large dataset, the benefit of using SIEVE-STREAMING is much more pronounced. As we see, SIEVE-STREAMING provides a solution close to that of STREAM-GREEDY while having several orders of magnitude lower computational cost. The performance of all algorithms (expect the standard and lazy greedy) for different values of k is shown in Fig. 2f.

7.2 Exemplar-Based Clustering

Our exemplar-based clustering experiment involves SIEVE-STREAMING applied to the clustering utility function (described in Section 4.1) with the squared Euclidean distance, namely, $d(x, x') = \|x - x'\|^2$. We run the streaming algorithms on the *Census1990* dataset [1]. It consists of 2,458,285 data points with 68 attributes. We compare the performance of SIEVE-STREAMING to the benchmarks as well as the classical online k-means algorithm (where we snap each mean to the nearest exemplar in a second pass to obtain a subset $S \subseteq V$). Again, the size of the dataset is too large to run the standard greedy algorithm. As discussed in Section 6, the clustering utility function depends on the whole data set. However, it is decomposable, thus an evaluation set W can be employed to estimate the utility of any set S based on the data seen so far. For our experiments, we used reservoir sampling with $|W| = 1/10|V|$.

Fig 2b shows the performance of SIEVE-STREAMING compared to the benchmarks for a fixed active set size $k = 5$. The computational costs of all algorithms, as well as their acquired utilities, are normalized to those of STREAM-GREEDY. We did not add the performance of online k-means to this figure as online k-means is not based on submodular function maximization. Hence, it does not query the clustering utility function. As we observe again, SIEVE-STREAMING provides a solution close to that of STREAM-GREEDY with substantially lower computational cost. For different values of k, Fig. 2e shows the performance of all the benchmarks. To compare the computational cost of online k-means with the benchmarks that utilize the clustering utility function, we measure the wall clock times of all the methods. This is reported in Table 2. We see again that the utility of Sieve-Streaming is comparable to Stream-Greedy and online k-means with much lower wall clock time.

8. CONCLUSIONS

We have developed the first efficient streaming algorithm–Sieve-Streaming–for cardinality-constrained submodular maximization. Sieve-Streaming provides a constant factor $1/2 - \varepsilon$ approximation guarantee to the optimum solution and requires only a single pass through the data and memory independent of the data size. In contrast to previous work, which makes strong assumptions on the data stream V or on the utility function (e.g., bounded spread of marginal gains, or Lipschitz continuity), we assumed nothing but monotonicity and submodularity. We have also demonstrated the effectiveness of our approach through extensive large scale experiments. As shown in Section 7, Sieve-Streaming reaches the major fraction of the utility function with much (often several orders of magnitude) less computational cost. This property of Sieve-Streaming makes it an appealing and sometimes the only viable method for solving very large scale or streaming applications. Given the importance of submodular optimization to numerous data mining and machine learning applications, we believe our results provide an important step towards addressing such problems at scale.

Acknowledgments. This research was supported in part by NSF AF-0910940, SNF 200021-137971, DARPA MSEE FA8650-11-1-7156, ERC StG 307036, a Microsoft Faculty Fellowship and an ETH Fellowship.

9. REFERENCES

[1] Census1990, UCI machine learning repository, 2010.
[2] Yahoo! academic relations. r6a, yahoo! front page today module user click log dataset, version 1.0, 2012.
[3] A. Badanidiyuru and J. Vondrák. Fast algorithms for maximizing submodular functions. In *SODA*, 2014.
[4] M. Bateni, M. Hajiaghayi, and M. Zadimoghaddam. Submodular secretary problem and extensions. In *APPROX-RANDOM*, pages 39–52, 2010.
[5] G. E. Blelloch, R. Peng, and K. Tangwongsan. Linear-work greedy parallel approximate set cover and variants. In *SPAA*, 2011.
[6] F. Chierichetti, R. Kumar, and A. Tomkins. Max-cover in map-reduce. In *WWW*, 2010.
[7] A. Dasgupta, R. Kumar, and S. Ravi. Summarization through submodularity and dispersion. In *ACL*, 2013.
[8] D. Dueck and B. J. Frey. Non-metric affinity propagation for unsupervised image categorization. In *ICCV*, 2007.
[9] K. El-Arini and C. Guestrin. Beyond keyword search: Discovering relevant scientific literature. In *KDD*, 2011.
[10] K. El-Arini, G. Veda, D. Shahaf, and C. Guestrin. Turning down the noise in the blogosphere. In *KDD*, 2009.
[11] U. Feige. A threshold of ln n for approximating set cover. *Journal of the ACM*, 1998.
[12] M. M. Gaber, A. Zaslavsky, and S. Krishnaswamy. Mining data streams: a review. *SIGMOD Record*, 34(2):18–26, 2005.
[13] J. Gillenwater, A. Kulesza, and B. Taskar. Near-optimal map inference for determinantal point processes. In *NIPS*, pages 2744–2752, 2012.
[14] R. Gomes and A. Krause. Budgeted nonparametric learning from data streams. In *ICML*, 2010.
[15] A. Gupta, A. Roth, G. Schoenebeck, and K. Talwar. Constrained non-monotone submodular maximization: Offline and secretary algorithms. In *WINE*, 2010.
[16] L. Kaufman and P. J. Rousseeuw. *Finding groups in data: an introduction to cluster analysis*, volume 344. Wiley-Interscience, 2009.
[17] D. Kempe, J. Kleinberg, and E. Tardos. Maximizing the spread of influence through a social network. In *Proceedings of the ninth ACM SIGKDD*, 2003.
[18] A. Krause and D. Golovin. Submodular function maximization. In *Tractability: Practical Approaches to Hard Problems*. Cambridge University Press, 2013.
[19] A. Krause and C. Guestrin. Near-optimal nonmyopic value of information in graphical models. In *UAI*, 2005.
[20] R. Kumar, B. Moseley, S. Vassilvitskii, and A. Vattani. Fast greedy algorithms in mapreduce and streaming. In *SPAA*, 2013.
[21] S. Lattanzi, B. Moseley, S. Suri, and S. Vassilvitskii. Filtering: a method for solving graph problems in mapreduce. In *SPAA*, 2011.
[22] J. Leskovec, A. Krause, C. Guestrin, C. Faloutsos, J. VanBriesen, and N. Glance. Cost-effective outbreak detection in networks. In *KDD*, 2007.
[23] H. Lin and J. Bilmes. A class of submodular functions for document summarization. In *NAACL/HLT*, 2011.
[24] M. Minoux. Accelerated greedy algorithms for maximizing submodular set functions. *Optimization Techniques, LNCS*, pages 234–243, 1978.
[25] B. Mirzasoleiman, A. Karbasi, R. Sarkar, and A. Krause. Distributed submodular maximization: Identifying representative elements in massive data. In *Neural Information Processing Systems (NIPS)*, 2013.
[26] G. L. Nemhauser and L. A. Wolsey. Best algorithms for approximating the maximum of a submodular set function. *Math. Oper. Research*, 1978.
[27] G. L. Nemhauser, L. A. Wolsey, and M. L. Fisher. An analysis of approximations for maximizing submodular set functions - I. *Mathematical Programming*, 1978.
[28] C. E. Rasmussen and C. K. I. Williams. *Gaussian Processes for Machine Learning (Adaptive Computation and Machine Learning)*. 2006.
[29] C. Reed and Z. Ghahramini. Scaling the indian buffet process via submodular maximization. In *ICML*, 2013.
[30] M. G. Rodriguez, J. Leskovec, and A. Krause. Inferring networks of diffusion and influence. *ACM Transactions on Knowledge Discovery from Data*, 5(4):21:1–21:37, 2012.
[31] B. Schölkopf and A. Smola. *Learning with Kernels: Support Vector Machines, Regularization, Optimization, and Beyond*. MIT Press, Cambridge, MA, USA, 2001.
[32] M. Seeger. Greedy forward selection in the informative vector machine. Technical report, University of California, Berkeley, 2004.

	SIEVE-STREAMING	online k-means	STREAM-GREEDY
wall clock time	4376 s	11905 s	77160 s
utility	$152 \cdot 10^6$	$152 \cdot 10^6$	$153 \cdot 10^6$

Table 2: Performance of SIEVE-STREAMING with respect to STREAM-GREEDY and online k-means. To compare the computational cost, we report the wall clock time in second. In this experiment we used $k = 100$.

[33] R. Sipos, A. Swaminathan, P. Shivaswamy, and T. Joachims. Temporal corpus summarization using submodular word coverage. In *CIKM*, 2012.

[34] A. Tsanas, M. A. Little, P. E. McSharry, and L. O. Ramig. Enhanced classical dysphonia measures and sparse regression for telemonitoring of parkinson's disease progression. In *ICASSP*, 2010.

[35] J. Vitter. Random sampling with a reservoir. *ACM Trans. Mathematical Software*, 11(1):37–57, 1985.

APPENDIX

PROOF OF PROPOSITION 5.1. We will first prove by induction that after adding $|S|$ elements to S the solution will satisfy the following inequality

$$f(S) \geq \frac{v|S|}{2k} \tag{9}$$

The proof is by induction. The base case $f(\emptyset) \geq 0$ is easy to see. Assume by induction that equation 9 holds for set S and we add element e. Then we know by the condition of the algorithm that $f(S \cup \{e\}) - f(S) \geq \frac{v/2 - f(S)}{k-|S|}$. Simplifying we get $f(S \cup \{e\}) \geq f(S)(1 - \frac{1}{k-|S|}) + \frac{v}{2(k-|S|)}$. Substituting equation 9 into this equation and simplifying we get the desired result $f(S \cup \{e\}) \geq \frac{v(|S|+1)}{2k}$.

The rest of the proof is quite simple. There are two cases.

- Case 1: At the end of the algorithm S has k elements. Then from equation 9 we get $f(S) \geq \frac{v}{2k} \cdot k = \frac{v}{2} \geq \frac{\alpha}{2}$ OPT.
- Case 2: At the end of the algorithm $|S| < k$. Then let A^* be the optimal solution with $A^* - S = \{a_1, a_2, \ldots, a_l\}$ and $A^* \cap S = \{a_{l+1}, a_{l+2}, \ldots, a_k\}$. Let for each element $a_j \in A^* - S$, it be rejected from including into S when the current solution was $S_j \subseteq S$. Then we have the two inequalities that $f_{S_j}(a_j) \leq \frac{v/2 - f(S_j)}{k - |S_j|}$ and that $f(S_j) \geq \frac{v|S_j|}{2k}$. Combining the two we get $f_{S_j}(a_j) \leq \frac{v}{2k}$ which implies that $f_S(a_j) \leq \frac{v}{2k}$. Let A_j denote $\{a_1, a_2, \ldots, a_j\}$.

$$\begin{aligned} f(S \cup A^*) - f(S) &= \sum_{j=1}^{l} f(S \cup A_j) - f(S \cup A_{j-1}) \\ &\leq \sum_{j=1}^{l} f(S_j \cup \{a_j\}) - f(S_j) \\ &\leq \sum_{j=1}^{l} \frac{v}{2k} \leq \frac{v}{2} \leq \frac{\texttt{OPT}}{2} \\ \Rightarrow \texttt{OPT} - f(S) \leq \frac{\texttt{OPT}}{2} &\Rightarrow f(S) \geq \frac{1}{2}\texttt{OPT} \end{aligned}$$

Here the first inequality is due to submodularity, second is by definition of $A^* - S$.

□

PROOF OF PROPOSITION 5.2. The proof directly follows from Theorem 5.1 and the fact that there exists a $v \in O$ such that $(1-\epsilon)\texttt{OPT} \leq v \leq \texttt{OPT}$. □

PROOF OF THEOREM 5.3. First observe that when a threshold v is instantiated any element with marginal value at least $v/(2k)$ to S_v appears on or after v is instantiated. This is because if such an element e_i appeared before v was instantiated then $v \in O_i$ and would have been instantiated when e_i appeared. Then the proof directly follows from Theorem 5.2 and the fact that Algorithm 3 is the same as Algorithm 2 with a lazy implementation. □

PROOF OF THEOREM 6.2. The proof closely follows the proof of the algorithm when we evaluate the submodular function exactly from Proposition 5.1, 5.2 and Theorem 5.3. From Proposition 6.1 we get that for any set S, $|f_W(S) - f(S)| \leq \frac{\epsilon}{k}$. Hence, as we are taking k elements, the error for the solution after taking each element adds up and we get $f(S) \geq (1/2 - \epsilon)\texttt{OPT} - \frac{\epsilon}{k} \cdot k$ which is the desired result. □

Bad example for STREAM-GREEDY

We show that there exists a family of problem instances of streaming submodular maximization under a k cardinality constraint, where it holds for the solution S produced by STREAM-GREEDY after one pass through the data, that $f(S)/\texttt{OPT} \leq 1/k$. For this claim, take the weighted coverage of a collection of sets: Fix a set X and a collection V of subsets of X. Then for a subcollection $S \subseteq V$, the monotone submodular function f is defined as

$$f_{\text{cov}}(S) = \sum_{x \in \cup_{v \in S} v} w(x).$$

Here, $w(\cdot)$ is the weight function that assigns positive weights to any element from X. Now, let us assume that X is the set of natural numbers and elements arrive as follows:

$$\begin{aligned} &\{1\}, \{2\}, \ldots, \{k\}, \{1, 2, \ldots, k\} \\ &\{k+1\}, \{k+2\}, \ldots, \{2k\}, \{k+1, k+2, \ldots, 2k\} \ldots \\ &\{k^2+1\}, \{k^2+2\}, \ldots, \{k^2+k\}, \{k^2+1, k^2+2, \ldots, k^2+k\} \end{aligned}$$

Let $\epsilon << 1$. We define the weights as

$$\begin{aligned} w(1) = w(2) = \cdots = w(k) &= 1 \\ w(k+1) = w(k+2) = \cdots = w(2k) &= 1+\epsilon \\ &\vdots \\ w(k^2+1) = w(k^2+2) = \cdots = w(k^2+k) &= 1+k\epsilon \end{aligned}$$

Then it is clear that STREAM-GREEDY skips the non-singleton sets as they do not provide any benefit. In contrast, the optimum solution only consists of those sets. Now, after observing $O(k^2)$ elements from the above data stream, the ratio between the solution provided by STREAM-GREEDY and the optimum algorithm decays as $O(1/k)$.

Distance Queries from Sampled Data: Accurate and Efficient

Edith Cohen
Microsoft Research
Mountain View, CA, USA
editco@microsoft.com

ABSTRACT

Distance queries are a basic tool in data analysis. They are used for detection and localization of change for the purpose of anomaly detection, monitoring, or planning. Distance queries are particularly useful when data sets such as measurements, snapshots of a system, content, traffic matrices, and activity logs are collected repeatedly.

Random sampling, which can be efficiently performed over streamed or distributed data, is an important tool for scalable data analysis. The sample constitutes an extremely flexible summary, which naturally supports domain queries and scalable estimation of statistics, which can be specified after the sample is generated. The effectiveness of a sample as a summary, however, hinges on the estimators we have.

We derive novel estimators for estimating L_p distance from sampled data. Our estimators apply with the most common weighted sampling schemes: Poisson Probability Proportional to Size (PPS) and its fixed sample size variants. They also apply when the samples of different data sets are independent or coordinated. Our estimators are admissible (Pareto optimal in terms of variance) and have compelling properties.

We study the performance of our Manhattan and Euclidean distance ($p = 1, 2$) estimators on diverse datasets, demonstrating scalability and accuracy even when a small fraction of the data is sampled. Our work, for the first time, facilitates effective distance estimation over sampled data.

1. INTRODUCTION

Data is commonly generated or collected repeatedly, where each *instance* has the form of a value assignment to a set of *keys*: Daily summaries of the number of queries containing certain keywords, activity in a social network, transmitted bytes for IP flow keys, performance parameters (delay, throughput, or loss) for IP source destination pairs, environmental measurements for sensor locations, and requests for resources. In these examples, each set of values (instance) corresponds to a particular time or location. The universe of possible key values is fixed across instances but the values of a key are different.

One of the most basic operations in data analysis are *Distance queries*, which are used to detect, measure, and localize change [7, 26]. Their applications include anomaly detection, monitoring, and planning. Formally, a difference query between instances is specified by a meta-data based selection predicate that is applied to the keys. The result is the distance between the vectors projected on the selected keys. The simple example in Figure 1 shows two instances on 7 keys, and some queries specified on this data using Euclidean and Manhattan distances.

data set

key h:	a	b	c	d	e	f
$v_1(h)$	5	0	4	5	8	7
$v_2(h)$	7	10	3	0	6	7

L_p**-distance** for $H \subset \{a, b, c, d, e, f\}$: $L_p(H) = (L_p^p(H))^{\frac{1}{p}}$
where $L_p^p(H) = \sum_{h \in H} |v_1(h) - v_2(h)|^p$

Example Queries:

$L_1(\{a, \ldots, f\}) = 20 \quad L_2(\{a, \ldots, f\}) = \sqrt{134} \approx 11.6$
$L_1(\{d, e, f\}) = 7 \quad L_2^2(\{a, e\}) = 4$

Figure 1: Distances between two instances, Table shows a data set with two instances $i \in \{1, 2\}$ and 7 keys $\{a, \ldots, f\}$ and the values $v_i(h)$ of key h in instance i. The figure also provides example distance queries, specified for a selected set H of keys.

The collection and warehousing of massive data is subject to limitations on storage, throughput, and bandwidth. Even when the data is stored in full, exact processing of queries may be slow and resource consuming. Random sampling of datasets is widely used as a means to obtain a flexible summary over which we can query the data while meeting these limitations [27, 36, 6, 5, 8, 20, 21, 3, 17, 3, 22, 12, 19, 10, 13].

The sampling scheme is applied to our data, and a set of random bits, and returns a small subset of the entries. Our sample includes these entries and their values and has a fraction of the size of the original dataset. The sample only includes nonzero entries, this is particularly important when the data is sparse, meaning that the vast majority of keys have associated value 0. When the values distribution is skewed, we often apply *weighted* sampling, meaning that the probability a key is sampled depends on its value – Favoring heavier keys allow for more accurate estimates of sums and other statistics.

Perhaps the most basic sampling scheme is Poisson sampling, where keys are sampled independently. Weighting is often done using Probability Proportional to Size (PPS) sampling [23], where the inclusion probability is proportional to the value. Other common sampling schemes are bottom-k (order) samples, which have the advantage over independent sampling of yielding a sample size of exactly k. Bottom-k sampling generalizes reservoir sampling and includes Priority (Sequential Poisson) sampling and weighted sampling without replacement [33, 32, 30, 11, 19, 12, 13]. These sampling schemes are very efficient to apply also when the data is streamed or distributed.

Once we have the sample, we can quickly process approximate queries posed over the original data. This is done by applying an

KDD'14, August 24–27, 2014, New York, NY, USA.

ACM 978-1-4503-2956-9/14/08 ...$15.00.
http://dx.doi.org/10.1145/2623330.2623680.

estimator to the sample. We seek estimators that provide good results when a small fraction of the data is sampled. In particular, we would like them to be *admissible*, that is, optimally use the information we have in the sample, and be efficient to compute. When estimating nonnegative quantities, such as distances, we are interested in nonnegative estimators.

Consider the basic problem of estimating, for a given selection predicate, the sum of values of keys selected by the predicate. This problem is solved well by the classic Horvitz-Thompson (HT) [24] estimator. The estimate is the sum, over sampled keys i satisfying the predicate, of the ratio v_i/p_i, where v_i is the value and p_i is the inclusion probability of i. This *inverse-probability* estimate is clearly unbiased (if $v_i > 0 \implies p_i > 0$): if the key is not sampled, the estimate is 0 and otherwise it is v_i/p_i, giving expectation v_i. The estimate is also nonnegative when values are. Moreover, the inverse-probability estimator is a UMVUE (uniform minimum variance unbiased estimator), meaning that among all unbiased and nonnegative estimators, it minimizes variance point wise. To apply this estimator, we need the inclusion probability p_i to be available to it when v_i is. This is the case with both Poisson and bottom-k sampling, when implemented correctly.

The HT estimate is a sum estimator: conceptually, we apply an estimator to each key in the universe. Keys that are not sampled have an estimate of 0. Keys that are sampled have a positive estimate. We then sum the estimators of different keys. This makes it highly suitable for domain (selection) queries, which aggregate over a subset of keys that can be specified by a predicate.

We now turn to our problem of estimating the distance between instances from their samples. We seek an estimator with similar properties to the HT estimator: a sum estimator, unbiased and nonnegative, and with optimal use of the information in the sample.

This problem turns out to be significantly more challenging. One can attempt to apply again the HT estimator: When the outcome reveals the value of the estimated quantity, the estimate is equal to the value divided by the probability of such an outcome. The estimate is 0 otherwise. Inverse probability estimates, however, are inapplicable to distance estimation over weighted samples, since they require that there is a positive probability for an outcome which reveals the exact value of the estimated quantity: the absolute difference between the values of the key in two instances. With multiple instances and weighted sampling, keys that have zero value in one instance and positive value in another have positive contribution to the distance but because zero values are never sampled, there is zero probability for determining the value from the outcome: In the Example in Figure 1, key c has value 5 in the first instance and value 0 in the second, and thus has a contribution of 5 to the L_1 distance. The key however will never be included in a weighted sample of instance 2.

When considering multiple instances, we also need to specify how their samples relate to each other. The sampling schemes we mentioned, Poisson and bottom-k, specify the distribution for a single instance. Our first requirement, since data of different instances can be distributed or collected in different times, is that the sample of one instance can not depend on values assumed in another [16, 14]. The random bits, however, can be reused (using random hash functions), to make sampling probabilities dependent. The two extremes of the joint distribution of samples of different instances are *independent sampling* (independent sets of random bits for each instance) and *coordinated sampling* (identical sets of random bits). With coordinated sampling, which is a form of locality sensitive hashing, similar instances have similar samples whereas independent samples of identical instances can be completely disjoint. Each of these two relations has unique advantages and therefore in our work here we address both: Coordination [4, 34, 31, 33, 6, 5, 8, 20, 21, 3, 12, 22, 13, 16] allows for tighter estimates of many basic queries including distinct counts (set union) [8, 20, 21, 13], quantile sums [16], Jaccard similarity [6, 5], and more recently L_1 distance [16]. The drawbacks of coordination are that it results in unbalanced "burden" where same keys tend to be sampled across instances – an issue when, for example, being sampled translates to overhead which would like to balance across keys. Moreover, while beneficial for some queries, the variance on other queries – notably sum queries that span values from multiple instances ("total number of search queries by Californians on Monday-Wednesday", from daily summaries) – is larger than with independent sampling – an issue if our samples are primarily used for such queries.

Contributions:

We derive unbiased nonnegative estimators for L_p^p distance queries over weighted samples. These include the two important cases of Manhattan distances L_1 and Euclidean distances L_2 (which is the square root of L_2^2). Our estimators apply with either Poisson or bottom-k sampling. We also address the two important cases where the samples of different instances are independent or coordinated. Our work facilitates, for the first time, the use of weighted samples as summaries that support distance queries.

Our estimators have several compelling properties. Similarly to the HT estimator, our estimators are *sum* estimators: We estimate L_p^p as a sum, over *the selected keys*, of nonnegative unbiased estimates of $\text{RG}_p = |v_1 - v_2|^p$ of the values assumed by the key (see Figure1). Our estimators are unbiased, nonnegative, and admissible (Pareto optimal), meaning that another (nonnegative and unbiased) estimator with strictly lower variance on some data must have strictly higher variance on another data. The estimate $\hat{\text{RG}}_p$ obtained for a particular key has high variance, since most likely, the key is not sampled in any instance (in which case the estimate is 0), but unbiasedness allows for diminishing relative error when more keys are selected. The distance L_p can be estimated by the pth root of our L_p^p estimate.

Our estimates $\hat{\text{RG}}_p$ can be positive also when the samples do not reveal the respective value RG_p but only partial information on it. This property turns out to be critical for obtaining admissible estimators, what is not possible, as we mentioned above, with the inverse-probability estimate. It also means, however, that the estimators we derive have to be carefully tailored to the power p.

For independently-sampled instances, we present an estimator for RG_p of two values ($p > 0$). This derivation uses a technique we presented in [14]. Our estimator, which we call the L^* estimator, is the unique symmetric and *monotone* admissible estimator, where monotonicity means that the estimate is non-decreasing with the information we can glean from the outcome.

For coordinated samples of instances, we apply our framework of monotone sampling [9]. We derive the L* and U* estimators for the RG_p functions, which are admissible, unbiased, and nonnegative. The L* estimator is monotone and has lower variance for data with small difference (range) whereas the U* estimator performs better when the range is large. This choice is important, because it allows us to customize estimation to properties of the data set. Network traffic data, for example, is likely to have larger differences and thus the U* estimator may perform better whereas the L* estimator would be preferable when differences are smaller. The L* estimator also exhibits a compelling theoretical property of being "variance competitive" [15], meaning that for all data vectors, its variance is not too far off the minimum possible variance for the vector by a nonnegative unbiased estimator. This property makes the L* estimator a good default choice.

For $p = 1, 2$, which are the important special cases of the Manhattan and the Euclidean distances, we compute closed form expressions of estimators and their variance and also obtain tighter bounds on the "competitiveness" of the L* estimator. We evaluate and compare the performance of our L_1 and L_2^2 distance estimators on queries over diverse data sets. The queries vary in the support size (number of keys in the data set satisfying the selection predicate) and in the relative difference (difference normalized by norm). We show that in all cases, we achieve good results when a small fraction of the data is sampled. Over coordinated samples, we examine the behavior of the L* and U* estimators and also consider the *optimally competitive* estimator, which minimizes the worst-case ratio, and we compute by a program. Finally, we provide guidelines to choosing between these estimators based on properties of the data.

Roadmap: Section 2 contains necessary background and definitions. We present difference estimators for independent samples in Section 3 and for coordinated samples in Section 4. Section 7 contains an experimental evaluation.

2. PRELIMINARIES

We denote by $v_{ih} \in \mathbb{R}_{\geq 0}$ the value of key $h \in K$ in instance $i \in [r]$ and by the vector $\boldsymbol{v}(h)$, the values of key h in all instances (the column vector v_{ih}). The *exponentiated range* of a vector $\boldsymbol{v}$ is:

$$\text{RG}_p(\boldsymbol{v}) = (\max(\boldsymbol{v}) - \min(\boldsymbol{v}))^p \quad (p > 0) \tag{1}$$

where $\max(\boldsymbol{v}) \equiv \max_i v_i$ and $\min(\boldsymbol{v}) = \min_i v_i$ are the maximum and minimum entry values of the vector $\boldsymbol{v}$. We omit the subscript when $p = 1$.

We are interested in queries which specify a selected subset $H \subset K$ of keys, through a predicate on K, and return

$$L_p^p(H) = \sum_{h \in H} \text{RG}_p(\boldsymbol{v}(h)) . \tag{2}$$

The L_p-distance of two instances ($r = 2$) is $L_p(H) \equiv (L_p^p(H))^{1/p}$.

When data is sampled, we estimate L_p^p, by summing estimates $\hat{\text{RG}}_p$ for the respective single-key primitive $\text{RG}_p(\boldsymbol{v}(h))$ over keys $h \in H$. We use nonnegative unbiased estimators for the primitives, which result, from linearity of expectation, in unbiased estimates for the sums. We measure error by the coefficient of variation (CV), which is the ratio of the square root of the variance to the mean. Our estimates for each key have high variance, but when inclusions of different keys are pairwise independent, variance is additive and the CV decreases with $|H|$, allowing for accurate estimates of the sum. Finally, we can estimate $L_p(H)$ by taking the pth root of the estimate for $L_p^p(H)$. This estimate is biased, but the error is small when the CV of our $L_p^p(H)$ estimate is small.

A basic component in applying sum estimators is obtaining from basic sampling schemes of instances the respective estimation problems for a *single key*. We cast the basic sampling schemes discussed in the introduction in the following form, which facilitates separate treatment of each key.

The sampling of the entry v_{ih} is specified by a threshold value $\tau_{ih} \geq 0$, and random *seed* values $u_{ih} \sim U[0, 1]$ chosen uniformly at random.

$$h \text{ is sampled in instance } i \iff v_{ih} \geq \tau_{ih} u_{ih} . \tag{3}$$

The estimation problem for a single key h is then as follows. We know $\boldsymbol{\tau} = (\tau_{1h}, \ldots, \tau_{rh})$, the seeds $\boldsymbol{u} = (u_{1h}, \ldots, u_{rh})$, and the results of the sampling for h (the value v_{ih} in all instances i where h was sampled). We apply an estimator $\hat{\text{RG}}_p$ to this information, which we refer to as the *outcome* S, to estimate $\text{RG}_p(\boldsymbol{v})$. The availability of the seeds u_{ih} to the estimator turns out to be critical for estimation quality [14, 9]. We facilitate it by generating the seeds using random hash functions (pairwise independence between keys suffices for variance bounds). When we treat a single key h, we omit the reference to h from the notation.

Sampling scheme of instances. We now briefly return to sampling schemes of instances, and show how we obtain the single-key formulation (3) from them.

With Poisson PPS (Probability Proportional to Size) sampling of instance i, each key h is sampled with probability proportional to v_{ih}. An equivalent formulation is to use a global threshold value T_i, such that a key h is sampled if and only if $v_{ih} \geq u_{ih} T_i$. The expected sample size $\mathsf{E}[|S|] = \sum_{h \in K} \min\{1, v_{ih}/T_i\}$ is determined by T_i. The sampling can be easily implemented with respect to either a desired sample size or a fixed threshold value. The respective estimation problem (3) for key h has $\tau_{ih} \equiv T_i$. As an example, we can obtain a PPS Poisson sample of expected size $\mathsf{E}[|S|] = 3$ for the instances in Figure 1 using $T_1 = 29/3$ (instance 1) and $T_2 = 33/3 = 11$ (instance 2).

Priority (sequential Poisson) sampling [30, 19, 35] is performed by assigning each key a *priority* $r_{ih} = v_{ih}/u_{ih}$. The sample of instance i includes the k keys with largest priorities, the $(k + 1)^{\text{th}}$ largest priority T_i, and the kth largest priority T_i'.

To obtain the single-key formulation (3) for key h, we consider the sampling *conditioned* on fixing the seeds u_{ij} (and thus the priorities r_{ij}) for all $j \neq h$ [12, 19]. The *effective* threshold τ_{ih} is the kth largest priority in $K \setminus \{h\}$: Key h is then sampled if and only if $v_{ih}/u_{ih} > \tau_{ih}$. When $h \in S$, $\tau_{ih} = T_i$ and when $h \notin S$, $\tau_{ih} = T_i'$.

When sampling several instances, we can make the samples *independent* when we use independent u_{ih} for all i. The samples are *coordinated* (shared-seed) if the same seed is used for the same key in all instances, that is, $\forall h \in K, \forall i \in [r], u_{ih} = u_{1h} \equiv u_h$.

Figure 2 shows Poisson PPS and priority samples, independent and coordinated, obtained for the two instances in Figure 1 from a random seed assignment u_{ih}. The figure also shows the threshold values τ_{ih}, which are available to the estimators $\hat{\text{RG}}_p(S)$. As an example, the outcome for key 4, (the outcome is the input to the estimator), is as follows. When instances are independently Poisson sampled the outcome includes: $v_1 = 5$ (key 4 is sampled only in instance 1 so we know v_{14} exactly), $u_1 = 0.15$, $u_2 = 0.36$ (seeds available by applying hash functions to the key), and $\tau_1 = 29/3$, $\tau_2 = 11$ (with Poisson PPS sampling, the same threshold applies to all keys in each instance). With coordinated priority sampling of instances the outcome includes $v_1 = 5$, $u = 0.15$, $\tau_1 = 13.8$ (since key 4 is sampled in instance 1) and $\tau_2 = 30.4$ (since key 4 is not sampled in instance 2).

From here onward, we focus on estimating $\text{RG}_p(\boldsymbol{v})$ for a single key from the respective outcome S. We return to sum aggregates only for the experiments in Section 7.

Estimators: For an outcome S, we denote by

$$\begin{aligned} S^* &= \{\boldsymbol{v} \mid S = S(\boldsymbol{u}, \boldsymbol{v})\} \\ &= \{\boldsymbol{z} \mid i \in S \implies z_i = v_i\, ,\, i \notin S \implies z_i < \tau_i u_i\} \end{aligned} \tag{4}$$

the set of all data vectors consistent with S. We can equivalently define the outcome as the set S^* since it captures all the information available to the estimator on $\boldsymbol{v}$ and hence on $\text{RG}_p(\boldsymbol{v})$. For our example in Figure 2, considering independent Poisson sampling and key 4, the set S^* includes all vectors $(5, x)$ such that $x < u_2\tau_2 = 0.36 \cdot 11 = 3.96$. The actual data vector for key 4 is $(5, 0)$, but the outcome only partially reveals it.

	1	2	3	4	5	6
Instance 1	5	0	4	5	8	7
Instance 2	7	10	3	0	6	7

Independent sampling, PPS

seeds u_1	0.23	0.29	0.84	0.15	0.58	0.19
seeds u_2	0.81	0.17	0.48	0.36	0.15	0.49
v_1/u_1	21.7	0	4.8	33.3	13.8	36.8
v_2/u_2	8.6	58.8	6.25	0	41.7	14.3

Coordinated sampling, PPS

seeds u	0.23	0.29	0.84	0.15	0.58	0.19
v_1/u	21.7	0	4.8	33.3	13.8	36.8
v_2/u	30.4	34.5	3.6	0	10.3	36.8

Poisson samples $E[|S|] = 3$:

	τ_i	S
independent		
1	29/3	$\{1, 4, 5, 6\}$
2	11	$\{2, 5, 6\}$
coordinated $u \equiv u_1$		
1	29/3	$\{1, 4, 5, 6\}$
2	11	$\{1, 2, 5, 6\}$

priority samples $|S| = 3$:

	τ_{ih}: $h \in S, h \notin S$	S
independent		
1	13.8, 21.7	$\{4, 5, 6\}$
2	8.6, 14.3	$\{2, 5, 6\}$
coordinated $u \equiv u_1$		
1	13.8, 21.7	$\{4, 5, 6\}$
2	10.3, 30.4	$\{1, 2, 6\}$

Figure 2: Independent and coordinated samples of two instances. Poisson PPS samples of expected size 3 and priority samples of size 3 ($k = 3$).

We denote by $\mathcal{S}$ the set of all possible outcomes, that is, any outcome consistent with any data vector $\boldsymbol{v}$ in our domain. For data $\boldsymbol{v}$, we denote by $\mathcal{S}_{\boldsymbol{v}}$ the probability distribution over outcomes consistent with $\boldsymbol{v}$. As mentioned, we are seeking *nonnegative* estimators $\hat{\text{RG}}_p(S) \geq 0$ for all $S \in \mathcal{S}$, since RG_p are nonnegative. Since we sum many estimates, we would like each estimate to be *unbiased* $\mathsf{E}_{S\sim\mathcal{S}_{\boldsymbol{v}}}[\hat{\text{RG}}_p(S)] = \text{RG}_p(\boldsymbol{v})$. We also seek *bounded variance* on all data $\boldsymbol{v}$, $\mathsf{E}_{S\sim\mathcal{S}_{\boldsymbol{v}}}[\hat{\text{RG}}_p(S)^2] < \infty$, and *admissibility* (Pareto variance optimality): there is no nonnegative unbiased estimator with same or lower variance on all data and strictly lower on some data. An intuitive property that is sometimes desirable is *monotonicity*: the estimate value is non decreasing with the information on the data that we can glean from the outcome $S^* \subset S'^* \implies \hat{\text{RG}}_p(S) \geq \hat{\text{RG}}_p(S')$.

When S^* includes vectors $\boldsymbol{v}$ such that $\text{RG}_p(\boldsymbol{v}) = 0$, any unbiased and nonnegative estimator must have $\hat{\text{RG}}_p(S) = 0$ (with probability 1). We therefore limit our attention to estimators satisfying this property.

We can also see that when the key h is not sampled in any instance, then S^* is consistent with $\text{RG}_p(\boldsymbol{v}) = 0$, which means that $\hat{\text{RG}}_p(S) = 0$ and we therefore do not need to explicitly compute the contribution of the vast majority of keys that are not sampled in at least one instance.

Finally, we will use the following definition of order optimality of estimators in our constructions. Given a partial order $\prec$ on the data domain an estimator $\hat{f}$ is $\prec$-optimal (respectively, $\prec^+$-optimal) if it is unbiased (resp., and nonnegative) for all data $\boldsymbol{v}$, and minimizes variance for $\boldsymbol{v}$ conditioned on the variance being minimized for all preceding vectors. Formally, if there is no other unbiased (resp., nonnegative) estimator that has strictly lower variance on some data $\boldsymbol{v}$ and at most the variance of $\hat{f}$ on all vectors that precede $\boldsymbol{v}$. An order optimal estimator is admissible.

3. INDEPENDENT PPS SAMPLING

We derive estimators for $\text{RG}_p(\boldsymbol{v})$, where $\boldsymbol{v} = (v_1, v_2)$ (two instances $r = 2$). The estimation scheme is specified by $\boldsymbol{\tau} = (\tau_1, \tau_2)$. The outcome $S(\boldsymbol{u}, \boldsymbol{v})$ is determined by the data vector $\boldsymbol{v} = (v_1, v_2)$ and $\boldsymbol{u} = (u_1, u_2)$, where $u_i \sim U[0, 1]$ are independent. The set S^* of vectors consistent with S is (4).

We derive the L* estimator, $\hat{\text{RG}}_p^{(L)}$, which is the unique symmetric, monotone, and admissible estimator. The construction adapts a framework from [14], which was used to estimate $\max\{v_1, v_2\}$: We specify an order $\prec$ on the data domain. We then formulate a set of sufficient constraints for an unbiased symmetric and order-optimal estimator $\hat{f}^{(\prec)}$ of $\text{RG}_p(\boldsymbol{v})$. The constraints, however, do not incorporate nonnegativity, as this results in much more complex dependencies. But if we find a nonnegative solution $\hat{f}^{(\prec)}$, then we find an estimator with all the desired properties. We therefore hope for a good "guess" of $\prec$.

We work with $\prec$ that prioritizes smaller distances, that is, $\boldsymbol{v} \prec \boldsymbol{z}$ if and only if $\text{RG}(\boldsymbol{v}) < \text{RG}(\boldsymbol{z})$. With each outcome $S \in \mathcal{S}$, we associate its *determining vector* $\phi(S)$, which we define as the $\prec$-minimal vector in (the closure of) S^*. The closure is the set obtained when using a non-strict inequality in (4). The determining vector is unique for all outcomes S that are not consistent with $\text{RG}_p(\boldsymbol{v}) = 0$, that is, $\text{RG}_p(\boldsymbol{v}) > 0$ for all $\boldsymbol{v} \in S^*$. As we mentioned earlier, we only need to specify the estimator on these outcomes, since we only consider estimators that are 0 on outcomes consistent with $\text{RG}_p(\boldsymbol{v}) = 0$. The mapping of outcomes S to the determining vector $\phi(S)$ is shown in Table 1 (Bottom).

We now formulate sufficient constraints for $\prec$-optimality. Conditioned on fixing the estimator on outcomes S such that $\phi(S) \prec \boldsymbol{v}$, the "best" we can do, in terms of minimizing variance, is to set it to a fixed value on all outcomes such that $\phi(S) = \boldsymbol{v}$. This fixed value is determined by the unbiasedness requirement. Since $\hat{f}^{(\prec)}$ is the same for all outcomes with same determining vector, we specify it as a function of the determining vector $\hat{f}^{(\prec)}(S) \equiv \hat{f}^{(\prec)}(\phi(S))$.

We use the notation $\mathcal{S}_0(\boldsymbol{v})$ for the set of outcomes S that are consistent with $\boldsymbol{v}$ but also consistent with a vector that precedes $\boldsymbol{v}$:

$$\mathcal{S}_0(\boldsymbol{v}) = \{S | \boldsymbol{v} \in S^* \wedge \phi(S) \prec \boldsymbol{v}\}$$

The contribution of the outcomes $\mathcal{S}_0(\boldsymbol{v})$ to the expectation of $\hat{f}^{(\prec)}$ when data is $\boldsymbol{v}$ is

$$f_0(\boldsymbol{v}) = \mathsf{E}_{S\sim\mathcal{S}_{\boldsymbol{v}}}[I_{S\in\mathcal{S}_0(\boldsymbol{v})}\hat{f}^{(\prec)}(S)] ,$$

where I is the indicator function. We obtain the following sufficient constraints for a $\prec$-optimal unbiased estimator, that may not be nonnegative, but is forced to be 0 on all outcomes consistent with $\text{RG}_p(\boldsymbol{v}) = 0$. For all $\boldsymbol{v}$,

$$\text{PR}_{S\sim\mathcal{S}_{\boldsymbol{v}}}[\phi(S) = \boldsymbol{v}] = 0 \implies f_0(\boldsymbol{v}) \equiv f(\boldsymbol{v}) \quad (5)$$

$$\text{PR}_{S\sim\mathcal{S}_{\boldsymbol{v}}}[\phi(S) = \boldsymbol{v}] > 0 \implies \hat{f}^{(\prec)}(\boldsymbol{v}) = \frac{f(\boldsymbol{v}) - f_0(\boldsymbol{v})}{\text{PR}_{S\sim\mathcal{S}_{\boldsymbol{v}}}[\phi(S) = \boldsymbol{v}]} \quad (6)$$

We derive $\hat{\text{RG}}_p^{(L)}$ by solving the right hand side of (6) for all $\boldsymbol{v}$ such that $\text{PR}_{S\sim\mathcal{S}_{\boldsymbol{v}}}[\phi(S) = \boldsymbol{v}] > 0$. The solution $\hat{\text{RG}}_p^{(L)}(\boldsymbol{\phi})$ ($p > 0$) is provided in Table 1 through a mapping of determining vectors to estimate values. The estimator is specified for $\phi_1 \geq \phi_2$, as the other case is symmetric. We can verify that for all $p > 0$, the estimator $\hat{\text{RG}}_p^{(L)}$ is nonnegative, monotone (for all y, $\hat{\text{RG}}_p^{(L)}(y, x)$ is non-increasing for $x \in (0, y]$) and has finite variances (follow from $\int_0^y \hat{\text{RG}}_p^{(L)}(y, x)^2 dx < \infty$). We can also verify that condition (5) holds. Vectors $\boldsymbol{v}$ with $\text{PR}_{S\sim\mathcal{S}_{\boldsymbol{v}}}[\phi(S) = \boldsymbol{v}] = 0$ are exactly those with one positive and one zero entry. We can verify that (5)

$\boldsymbol{\phi} = (\phi_1, \phi_2)$	$\widehat{\text{RG}}_p^{(L)}(\boldsymbol{\phi})$
$\boldsymbol{\phi} = (0, 0)$	0
$\phi_1 \geq \phi_2 > \tau_2$	$\frac{\tau_1}{\min\{\tau_1, \phi_1\}}(\phi_1 - \phi_2)^p$
$\phi_1 \geq \phi_2 \leq \tau_2$	$\frac{p\tau_1\tau_2}{\min\{\phi_1, \tau_1\}} \int_{\max\{0, \phi_1 - \tau_2\}}^{\phi_1 - \phi_2} \frac{y^{p-1}}{\phi_1 - y} dy + \frac{\tau_1 \max\{0, \phi_1 - \tau_2\}^p}{\min\{\phi_1, \tau_1\}}$

outcome S		$\phi(S)_1$	$\phi(S)_2$
$S = \emptyset$	:	0	0
$S = \{1\}$	:	v_1	$\min\{u_2\tau_2, v_1\}$
$S = \{2\}$	:	$\min\{u_1\tau_1, v_2\}$	v_2
$S = \{1, 2\}$	:	v_1	v_2

Table 1: Top: Estimator $\widehat{\text{RG}}_p^{(L)}$ for $p > 0$ over independent samples, stated as a function of the determining vector $\boldsymbol{\phi} = (\phi_1, \phi_2)$ when $\phi_1 \geq \phi_2$ (case $\phi_2 > \phi_1$ is symmetric). Bottom: mapping of outcomes to determining vectors.

is satisfied, that is, $\mathsf{E}_{S \sim \mathcal{S}_{\boldsymbol{v}}} \widehat{\text{RG}}_p^{(L)}(S) = \text{RG}_p(\boldsymbol{v})$ on these vectors. Table 2 shows explicit expressions of $\widehat{\text{RG}}^{(L)}$ and $\widehat{\text{RG}}_2^{(L)}$.

$\boldsymbol{\phi} = (\phi_1, \phi_2)$	$\widehat{\text{RG}}^{(L)}(\boldsymbol{\phi})$
$\boldsymbol{\phi} = (0, 0)$	0
$\phi_1 \geq \phi_2 > \tau_2$	$\frac{\tau_1}{\min\{\tau_1, \phi_1\}}(\phi_1 - \phi_2)$
$\phi_1 \geq \phi_2 \leq \tau_2$	$\frac{\tau_1\tau_2}{\min\{\tau_1, \phi_1\}} \ln\left(\frac{\min\{\phi_1, \tau_2\}}{\phi_2}\right) + \frac{\tau_1 \max\{0, \phi_1 - \tau_2\}}{\min\{\phi_1, \tau_1\}}$

$\boldsymbol{\phi} = (\phi_1, \phi_2)$	$\widehat{\text{RG}}_2^{(L)}(\boldsymbol{\phi})$
$\boldsymbol{\phi} = (0, 0)$	0
$\phi_1 \geq \phi_2 > \tau_2$	$\frac{\tau_1}{\min\{\tau_1, \phi_1\}}(\phi_1 - \phi_2)^2$
$\phi_1 \geq \phi_2 \leq \tau_2$	$\frac{2\tau_1\tau_2}{\min\{\tau_1, \phi_1\}}\left(\phi_2 - \min\{\phi_1, \tau_2\} + \phi_1 \ln \frac{\min\{\phi_1, \tau_2\}}{\phi_2}\right) + \frac{\tau_1 \max\{0, \phi_1 - \tau_2\}^2}{\min\{\phi_1, \tau_1\}}$

Table 2: Explicit form of estimators $\widehat{\text{RG}}^{(L)}$ and $\widehat{\text{RG}}_2^{(L)}$ for $r = 2$ over independent samples. Estimator is stated as a function of the determining vector (ϕ_1, ϕ_2) when $\phi_1 \geq \phi_2$ (case $\phi_2 \geq \phi_1$ is symmetric).

We now provide the derivation. We consider vectors $\boldsymbol{v}$ in increasing $\prec$ order and solve (6) for $f^{(\prec)}$ on outcomes with determining vector $\boldsymbol{v} = (v, v - \Delta)$, where $v \geq \Delta \geq 0$.

• **Case:** $v - \Delta \geq \tau_2$. The outcomes always reveals the second entry. The determining vector is $\boldsymbol{v}$ when $u_1\tau_1 \leq v$, which happens with probability $\min\{1, v/\tau_1\}$. Otherwise, the outcome is consistent with $(v - \Delta, v - \Delta)$ and the estimate is 0. We solve the equality $\Delta^p = \min\{1, v/\tau_1\}\widehat{\text{RG}}_p^{(L)}$, obtaining

$$\widehat{\text{RG}}_p^{(L)}(v, v - \Delta) = \frac{\tau_1}{\min\{v, \tau_1\}}\Delta^p . \quad (7)$$

• **Case:** $v - \Delta < \tau_2$. The determining vector is $(v, v - \Delta)$ with probability $\frac{\min\{v, \tau_1\}}{\tau_1}\frac{v - \Delta}{\tau_2}$. Otherwise, it is $(v, v - y)$ for some $y < \Delta$. We use (6) to obtain an integral equation:

$$\begin{aligned}\Delta^p &= \frac{\min\{v, \tau_1\}}{\tau_1}\frac{v - \Delta}{\tau_2}\widehat{\text{RG}}_p^{(L)}(v, v - \Delta) + \\ &+ \frac{\min\{v, \tau_1\}}{\tau_1\tau_2}\int_{\max\{0, v - \tau_2\}}^{\Delta} \widehat{\text{RG}}_p^{(L)}(v, v - y) dy\end{aligned}$$

Taking a partial derivative with respect to Δ, we obtain

$$\frac{\partial \widehat{\text{RG}}_p^{(L)}(v, v - \Delta)}{\partial \Delta} = \frac{p\tau_1\tau_2}{\min\{v, \tau_1\}}\frac{\Delta^{p-1}}{v - \Delta}$$

We use the boundary value for $\Delta = \max\{0, v - \tau_2\}$:

$$\widehat{\text{RG}}_p^{(L)}(v, \min\{v, \tau_2\}) = \frac{\tau_1}{\min\{v, \tau_1\}} \max\{0, v - \tau_2\}^p ,$$

and obtain the solution

$$\widehat{\text{RG}}_p^{(L)}(v, v - \Delta) = \quad (8)$$
$$\frac{p\tau_1\tau_2}{\min\{v, \tau_1\}} \int_{\max\{0, v - \tau_2\}}^{\Delta} \frac{y^{p-1}}{v - y} dy + \frac{\tau_1 \max\{0, v - \tau_2\}^p}{\min\{v, \tau_1\}}$$

The special case $\tau_1 = \tau_2 = \tau$: The estimators $\widehat{\text{RG}}^{(L)}$ and $\widehat{\text{RG}}_2^{(L)}$ as a function of the determining vector and their variance are provided in Tables 3 and 4.

Determining vector $\phi_1 \geq \phi_2$	$\widehat{\text{RG}}^{(L)}(\boldsymbol{\phi})$
$\phi_1 \geq \phi_2 \geq \tau$	$\phi_1 - \phi_2$
$\phi_1 \geq \tau \geq \phi_2$	$\tau \ln \frac{\tau}{\phi_2} + \phi_1 - \tau$
$\phi_2 \leq \phi_1 \leq \tau$	$\frac{(\tau)^2}{\phi_1} \ln \frac{\phi_1}{\phi_2}$

Data $v_1 \geq v_2$	$\text{VAR}_{\mathcal{S}_{\boldsymbol{v}}}[\widehat{\text{RG}}^{(L)}]$
$v_1 \geq v_2 \geq \tau$	0
$v_1 \geq \tau \geq v_2$	$-2\tau v_2 \ln(\frac{\tau}{v_2}) - v_2^2 + \tau^2$
$v_2 \leq v_1 \leq \tau$	$2\tau^2(1 - \frac{v_2}{v_1}\ln\frac{v_1}{v_2} - \frac{v_2}{v_1}) - (v_1 - v_2)^2$

Table 3: $\widehat{\text{RG}}^{(L)}$ and its variance for independent samples.

4. SHARED-SEED SAMPLING

We derive estimators for $\text{RG}_p(\boldsymbol{v})(p > 0)$, where $\boldsymbol{v} = (v_1, \ldots, v_r)$ for $r \geq 2$. The sampling uses the same random seed u for all entries. The outcome $S(u, \boldsymbol{v})$ is determined by the data $\boldsymbol{v}$ and a *scalar* seed value $u \in (0, 1]$, drawn uniformly at random: Entry i is included in S if and only if $v_i \geq \tau_i u$.

We apply our work on estimators for monotone sampling [9] to derive two unbiased nonnegative admissible estimators: The L* estimator $\widehat{\text{RG}}_p^{(L)}$ and the U* estimator $\widehat{\text{RG}}_p^{(U)}$. We present closed form expressions of estimators and variances when $\boldsymbol{\tau}$ has all entries equal (to the scalar τ). The derivations easily extend to non-uniform $\boldsymbol{\tau}$.

The set of data vectors consistent with outcome $S(u, \boldsymbol{v})$ is

$$S^* = \{\boldsymbol{z} | \forall i \in [r], i \in S \implies z_i = v_i \, , \, i \notin S \implies z_i < \tau_i u\} .$$

Observe that the sets $S^*(u, \boldsymbol{z})$ are the same for all consistent data vectors $\boldsymbol{z} \in S^*(u, \boldsymbol{v})$. Fixing the data $\boldsymbol{v}$, the set $S^*(u, \boldsymbol{v})$ is non-decreasing with u, which means that the information on the data that we can glean from the outcome can only increase when u decreases. This makes the sampling scheme *monotone* in the randomization, which allows us to apply the estimator derivations in [9].

The lower bound function. The derivations use the *lower bound function* $\underline{\text{RG}}_p$, which maps an outcome S to the infimum of RG_p

condition	$\widehat{\text{RG}}_2^{(L)}(\boldsymbol{\phi})$
$\phi_1 \geq \phi_2 \geq \tau$	$(\phi_1 - \phi_2)^2$
$\phi_1 \geq \tau \geq \phi_2$	$\phi_1^2 - (\tau)^2 - 2\tau(\phi_1 - \phi_2) + 2\tau\phi_1 \ln \frac{\tau}{\phi_2}$
$\phi_2 < \phi_1 \leq \tau$	$2(\tau)^2(\ln \frac{\phi_1}{\phi_2} - \frac{\phi_1 - \phi_2}{\phi_1})$

Data $v_1 \geq v_2$	$\text{VAR}_{\mathcal{S}_{\boldsymbol{v}}}[\widehat{\text{RG}}_2^{(L)}]$
$v_1 \geq v_2 \geq \tau$	0
$v_1 \geq \tau \geq v_2$	$-4v_1v_2\tau(2v_1 - v_2)\ln\frac{\tau}{v_2}$ $+4v_1v_2(\tau)^2 + \frac{(\tau)^4}{3} + \frac{8v_2^3\tau}{3}$ $-6v_1v_2^2\tau - 4v_1^2v_2^2$ $-v_2^4 + 4v_1v_2^3 + 4v_1^2(\tau)^2 - 2v_1(\tau)^3$
$v_2 \leq v_1 \leq \tau$	$\frac{2(\tau)^2}{3v_1}\left(4v_2^3 + 5v_1^3 - 9v_1v_2^2\right) - (v_1 - v_2)^4$ $-4(\tau)^2(2v_1 - v_2)v_2\ln(\frac{v_1}{v_2})$

Table 4: $\widehat{\text{RG}}_2^{(L)}$ and its variance for independent samples.

values on vectors that are consistent with the outcome:

$$\underline{\text{RG}}_p(S) = \inf_{\boldsymbol{v}\in S^*} \text{RG}_p(\boldsymbol{v}) \; .$$

For RG, the lower bound is the difference between a lower bound on the maximum entry and an upper bound on the minimum entry.

$$\underline{\text{RG}}(S) \quad = \quad \max_{i\in S} v_i - \min\{\min_{i\in S} v_i, \min_{i\notin S} \tau_i u\} \; .$$

The lower bound on RG_p is the pth power of the respective bound on RG, that is, $\underline{\text{RG}}_p(S) = \underline{\text{RG}}(S)^p$. For $S(u,\boldsymbol{v})$, we use the notation $\underline{\text{RG}}_p(S(u,\boldsymbol{v})) \equiv \underline{\text{RG}}_p(u,\boldsymbol{v})$. For all-entries-equal $\boldsymbol{\tau}$:

condition	$\lvert S\rvert$	$\underline{\text{RG}}(S)$
$u > \frac{\max(\boldsymbol{v})}{\tau}$	0	0
$\frac{\max(\boldsymbol{v})}{\tau} \geq u \geq \frac{\min(\boldsymbol{v})}{\tau}$	$1 \ldots r-1$	$\max(\boldsymbol{v}) - u\tau$
$u < \frac{\min(\boldsymbol{v})}{\tau}$	r	$\text{RG}(\boldsymbol{v})$

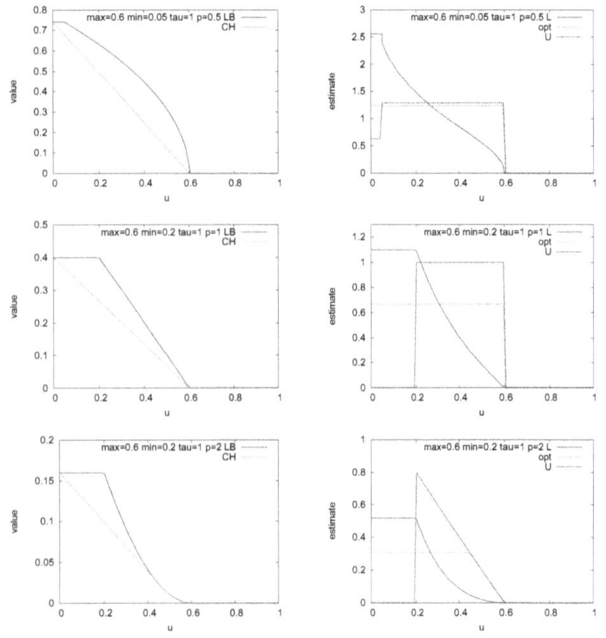

Figure 3: Left: The lower bound function and corresponding lower hull for example vectors and $p \in \{0.5, 1, 2\}$. Right: the corresponding optimal, L*, and U* estimates on outcomes consistent with the vector.

The L* estimator. The L* estimator [9] is defined for any monotone estimation problem for which an unbiased and nonnegative estimator exists. This estimator is specified as a function of the corresponding lower bound function. For RG_p we have

$$\forall S(\zeta,\boldsymbol{v}),\ \hat{\text{RG}}_p^{(L)}(S) = \frac{\underline{\text{RG}}_p(\zeta,\boldsymbol{v})}{\zeta} - \int_{\zeta}^{1} \frac{\underline{\text{RG}}_p(u,\boldsymbol{v})}{u^2} du \; . \tag{9}$$

From [9], we know that $\hat{\text{RG}}_p^{(L)}$ has the following properties:

- It is nonnegative and unbiased.
- It is the unique (up to equivalence) admissible unbiased nonnegative monotone estimator, meaning that the estimate is nondecreasing with u.
- It is $\prec^+$-optimal with respect to the partial order $\prec$

$$\boldsymbol{v} \prec \boldsymbol{z} \iff \text{RG}_p(\boldsymbol{v}) < \text{RG}_p(\boldsymbol{z}) \; .$$

$\prec^+$-optimality with respect to this particular order means that any estimator with a strictly lower variance for a data vector must have strictly higher variance on some vector with a smaller range – this means that the L* estimator "prioritizes" data where the range (or difference when aggregated) is small.

The L* estimator has finite variances when the monotone estimation problem admits a nonnegative estimator with finite variances. It is also 4-*competitive* in terms of variance [15], meaning that for any data vector, the ratio of the expectation of the square to the minimum one possible for the data via an unbiased nonnegative estimator is at most 4

$$\forall \boldsymbol{v}, \mathsf{E}_{S\sim\mathcal{S}_{\boldsymbol{v}}}[\hat{\text{RG}}_p^{(L)}(S)^2] \leq 4\mathsf{E}_{S\sim\mathcal{S}_{\boldsymbol{v}}}[\hat{\text{RG}}_p^{(\boldsymbol{v})}(S)^2] \; ,$$

where $\hat{\text{RG}}_p^{(\boldsymbol{v})}(S)$ is a nonnegative unbiased estimator which minimizes the variance for $\boldsymbol{v}$ (We will present a construction of this estimator). Competitiveness, is a strong property that means that for *all* data vectors, the variance under the L* estimator is not too far off the minimum possible variance for that vector by a nonnegative unbiased estimator.

For our sampling scheme with all entries equal τ, we define $\max(\boldsymbol{v}) \equiv \max_i v_i$ (which is available from S whenever $|S| > 0$) and $v_{\min} = \min(\boldsymbol{v})$ if $|S| = r$ and $v_{\min} = u\tau$ otherwise, which is also always available from S, the estimator is

$$\hat{\text{RG}}_p^{(L)}(S) = \begin{cases} |S| = 0: & 0 \\ |S| \geq 1: & (\max(\boldsymbol{v}) - v_{\min})^p \max\{1, \frac{\tau}{v_{\min}}\} - \\ & \int_{\min\{1, \frac{v_{\min}}{\tau}\}}^{\min\{1, \frac{\max(\boldsymbol{v})}{\tau}\}} \frac{(\max(\boldsymbol{v}) - x\tau)^p}{x^2} dx \end{cases} \tag{10}$$

Estimators and variance for RG and RG_2 are provided in Tables 6 and 7. We also compute a tight ratio on variance competitiveness for $p = 1, 2$:

LEMMA 4.1.

$$\forall \boldsymbol{v},\ E_{S\sim\mathcal{S}_{\boldsymbol{v}}}[\hat{\text{RG}}^{(L)}(S)^2] \;\leq\; 2E_{S\sim\mathcal{S}_{\boldsymbol{v}}}[\hat{\text{RG}}^{(\boldsymbol{v})}(S)^2] \tag{11}$$

$$\forall \boldsymbol{v},\ E_{S\sim\mathcal{S}_{\boldsymbol{v}}}[\hat{\text{RG}}_2^{(L)}(S)^2] \;\leq\; 2.5E_{S\sim\mathcal{S}_{\boldsymbol{v}}}[\hat{\text{RG}}_2^{(\boldsymbol{v})}(S)^2] \tag{12}$$

The U* estimator. The U* estimator [9] is the solution of the integral equation

$$\forall S(\zeta,\boldsymbol{v}),\ \hat{\text{RG}}_p(\zeta,\boldsymbol{v}) = \sup_{\boldsymbol{z}\in S^*} \inf_{0\leq\eta<\zeta} \frac{\underline{\text{RG}}_p(\eta,\boldsymbol{z}) - \int_\zeta^1 \hat{\text{RG}}_p(u,\boldsymbol{v})du}{\zeta - \eta}$$

From [9], we know that $\hat{\text{RG}}_p^{(U)}$ has the following properties:

- It is nonnegative and unbiased.
- It is $\prec^+$-optimal with respect to the partial order $\prec$

$$\boldsymbol{v} \prec \boldsymbol{z} \iff \text{RG}_p(\boldsymbol{v}) > \text{RG}_p(\boldsymbol{z}) \; .$$

This means that the U* estimator "prioritizes" data where the range (or difference when aggregated) is large. In particular, it is the nonnegative unbiased estimator with minimum variance on data with $\min(\boldsymbol{v}) = 0$.

The solution for all-entries equal τ is provided as Algorithm 1 (details are omitted due to space limitations). The estimator is admissible and has finite variances for all data vectors.

Expressions for the variance of $\hat{\text{RG}}_p^{(U)}$ for $p = 1, 2$ are omitted due to space limitations.

***v*-optimality.** We say that an estimator is $\boldsymbol{v}$-*optimal* (for data $\boldsymbol{v}$), if amongst all estimators that are nonnegative and unbiased for all data, it has the minimum possible variance when the data is $\boldsymbol{v}$.

In order to measure the competitiveness of our estimators, as in Lemma 4.1, we derive an expression for the *$\boldsymbol{v}$-optimal estimate values* $\hat{\text{RG}_p}^{(\boldsymbol{v})}$. It turns out that the values assumed by a $\boldsymbol{v}$-optimal estimator on outcomes consistent with $\boldsymbol{v}$ are unique (almost everywhere on $\mathcal{S}_{\boldsymbol{v}}$ [15]. Note that there is no single estimator that is $\boldsymbol{v}$-optimal for all $\boldsymbol{v}$, that is, there is no uniform minimum variance unbiased nonnegative estimator for RG_p. Therefore, the $\boldsymbol{v}$-optimal estimates for all possible values of $\boldsymbol{v}$ can not be combined into a single estimator.

We now obtain an explicit representation of $\hat{\text{RG}}_p^{(\boldsymbol{v})}$. We use the notation $H^{(\boldsymbol{v})}_{\text{RG}_p}(u)$ for the lower boundary of the convex hull (lower hull) of $\underline{\text{RG}}_p(u,\boldsymbol{v})$ and the point $(1,0)$. This function is monotone non-increasing in u and therefore differentiable almost everywhere. We apply the following

THEOREM 4.1. *[15] A nonnegative unbiased estimator* $\hat{\text{RG}}_p$ *minimizes* $\text{VAR}_{S\sim\mathcal{S}_{\boldsymbol{v}}}[\hat{\text{RG}}_p] \iff$ almost everywhere *on* $\mathcal{S}_{\boldsymbol{v}}$

$$\hat{\text{RG}}_p^{(\boldsymbol{v})}(u) = -\frac{dH^{(\boldsymbol{v})}_{\text{RG}_p}(u)}{du}\ . \tag{13}$$

The estimates (13) are monotone non-increasing in u.

We can now specify $\hat{\text{RG}}_p^{(\boldsymbol{v})}$ for PPS sampling with all-entries-equal τ. The function $\underline{\text{RG}}_p(u,\boldsymbol{v})$ is $\max\{0,\max(\boldsymbol{v})-\tau\}$ for $u \geq \frac{\max(\boldsymbol{v})}{\tau}$ and equal to $\text{RG}_p(\boldsymbol{v})$ for $u \leq \frac{\min(\boldsymbol{v})}{\tau}$. Therefore for $u \geq \frac{\max(\boldsymbol{v})}{\tau}$, the lower hull is $H^{(\boldsymbol{v})}_{\text{RG}_p}(u) = 0$ and $\hat{\text{RG}}_p^{(\boldsymbol{v})}(u) = 0$.

For $p \leq 1$, the function is concave for $u \in [\frac{\min(\boldsymbol{v})}{\tau}, \frac{\max(\boldsymbol{v})}{\tau}]$. The lower hull is therefore a linear function for $u \leq \frac{\max(\boldsymbol{v})}{\tau}$: when $\max(\boldsymbol{v}) \leq \tau$, $H^{(\boldsymbol{v})}_{\text{RG}_p}(u) = \text{RG}_p(\boldsymbol{v})(1-u\frac{\tau}{\max(\boldsymbol{v})})$ and when $\max(\boldsymbol{v}) \geq \tau$, $H^{(\boldsymbol{v})}_{\text{RG}_p}(u) = \text{RG}_p(\boldsymbol{v}) - u(\text{RG}_p(\boldsymbol{v}) - (\max(\boldsymbol{v})-\tau)^p)$. The $\boldsymbol{v}$-optimal estimates are therefore constant for $u \leq \min\{1, \frac{\max(\boldsymbol{v})}{\tau}\}$: $\hat{\text{RG}}_p^{(\boldsymbol{v})}(u) = \text{RG}(\boldsymbol{v})\frac{\tau}{\max(\boldsymbol{v})}$ when $\max(\boldsymbol{v}) \leq \tau$, and $\hat{\text{RG}}_p^{(\boldsymbol{v})}(u) = \text{RG}_p(\boldsymbol{v}) - (\max(\boldsymbol{v})-\tau)^p$ when $\max(\boldsymbol{v}) \geq \tau$.

For $p > 1$, $\underline{\text{RG}}_p(u,\boldsymbol{v})$ is convex for $u \in [\frac{\min(\boldsymbol{v})}{\tau}, \frac{\max(\boldsymbol{v})}{\tau}]$. Geometrically, the lower hull follows the lower bound function for $u > \alpha$, where α is the point where the slope of the lower bound function is equal to the slope of a line segment connecting the current point to the point $(0, \text{RG}_p(\boldsymbol{v}))$. For $u \leq \alpha$, the lower hull follows this line segment and is linear. Formally, the point α is the solution of

$$\text{RG}_p(\boldsymbol{v}) = (\max(\boldsymbol{v}) - x\tau)^{p-1}(p\tau + \max(\boldsymbol{v}) - x\tau)\ .$$

If there is no solution $\alpha \in [\frac{\min(\boldsymbol{v})}{\tau}, \min\{1, \frac{\max(\boldsymbol{v})}{\tau}\}]$, we use $\alpha = \min\{1, \frac{\max(\boldsymbol{v})}{\tau}\}$. The estimates for $u \in [\alpha, \min\{1, \frac{\max(\boldsymbol{v})}{\tau}\}]$ are $\hat{\text{RG}}_p(u,\boldsymbol{v}) = -\frac{d\underline{\text{RG}}_p(u,\boldsymbol{v})}{du} = p\tau(\max(\boldsymbol{v}) - u\tau)^{p-1}$ and for $u \leq \alpha$, $\hat{\text{RG}}_p^{(\boldsymbol{v})}(u) = \frac{\text{RG}_p(\boldsymbol{v}) - (\max(\boldsymbol{v})-\alpha\tau)^p}{\alpha}$.

Figure 3 (top) illustrates $\underline{\text{RG}}_p(u,\boldsymbol{v})$ and the corresponding lower hull $H^{(\boldsymbol{v})}_{\text{RG}_p}$ as a function of u for example vectors with $p \in \{0.5, 1, 2\}$.

Now that we expressed $\hat{\text{RG}}_p^{(\boldsymbol{v})}(S)$ on all outcomes consistent with $\boldsymbol{v}$, we can compute (for any vector $\boldsymbol{v}$), the minimum possible variance attainable for it by an unbiased nonnegative estimator:

$$\text{VAR}_{\mathcal{S}_{\boldsymbol{v}}}[\hat{\text{RG}}_p^{(\boldsymbol{v})}] = \int_0^1 \hat{\text{RG}}_p^{(\boldsymbol{v})}(u)^2 du - \text{RG}_p(\boldsymbol{v})^2\ . \tag{14}$$

We use the expectation of the square to measure the "variance competitiveness" of estimators (Since the second summand in (14) is the same for all estimators). The ratio for a particular $\boldsymbol{v}$ is the expectation of the square for $\boldsymbol{v}$ divided by the optimal one which is $\mathsf{E}_{S\sim\mathcal{S}_{\boldsymbol{v}}}[\hat{\text{RG}}_p^{(\boldsymbol{v})}(S)^2] = \int_0^1 \hat{\text{RG}}_p^{(\boldsymbol{v})}(u)^2 du$. The competitive ratio is the maximum ratio over all $\boldsymbol{v}$.

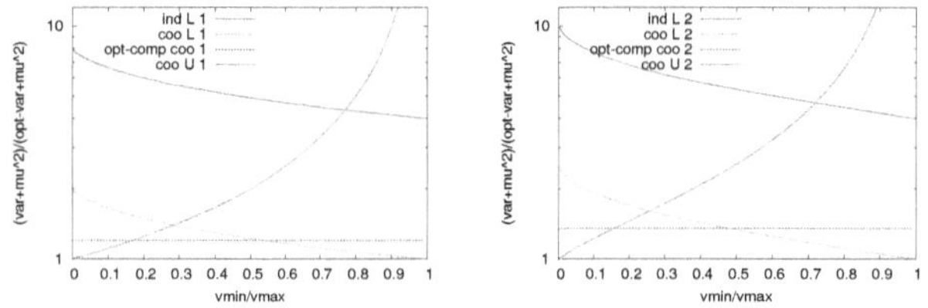

$p = 1, \frac{\max(\boldsymbol{v})}{\tau} = 0.25$ $\qquad$ $p = 2, \frac{\max(\boldsymbol{v})}{\tau} = 0.25$

Figure 4: Ratio of the expectation of the square to the minimum possible expectation of the square for the data point (over shared-seed samples), as a function of the ratio $\min(\boldsymbol{v})/\max(\boldsymbol{v})$. Estimator $\hat{\text{RG}}_p^{(L)}$ over independent samples, and $\hat{\text{RG}}_p^{(L)}$, $\hat{\text{RG}}_p^{(U)}$, and the optimally competitive estimator over shared-seed samples. Sampling with all-entries equal τ.

The optimally competitive (OC) estimator. We used a program to compute the estimator with minimum competitive ratio. The estimator was computed for an outcome that revealed $\max(\boldsymbol{v})$ and provided an upper bound $x < \max(\boldsymbol{v})$ on $\min(\boldsymbol{v})$. The domain was discretized and the estimates were computed iteratively for decreasing x so that the estimates satisfy a certain ratio c. We then performed a search to find the minimum c for which the computation is successful.

Choosing between the L*, U*, and OC estimators. Figure 3 shows the $\boldsymbol{v}$-optimal estimates and the L* and U* estimators for example vectors, illustrating the monotonicity of L* and how the estimators relate to each other. The estimators and their variances depend only on $\boldsymbol{\tau}$ and the maximum and minimum entry values $\max(\boldsymbol{v})$ and $\min(\boldsymbol{v})$. We study the variance for all-entries-equal $\boldsymbol{\tau}$ and $\max(\boldsymbol{v}) \leq \tau$.

Figure 4 shows the expectation of the square of the L* estimator over independent samples and of the L*, U*, and OC estimators over shared-seed samples. This is as a function of the ratio of the minimum to the maximum value in the data vector. The expectation of the square plotted is the ratio to the minimum possible expectation of the square over coordinated samples (the $\boldsymbol{v}$-optimum). Recall that the $\boldsymbol{v}$-optimum is not simultaneously attainable for all vectors and is used only as a reference for variance competitiveness. We can see that the L* estimator is nearly optimal when the ratio is large and that the U* estimator is nearly optimal when the ratio is small. The OC estimator outperforms both in the mid range. For the L* estimator, the ratio is always at most 2 (for $p = 1$) and 2.5 (for $p = 2$) from the optimum whereas the U* estimator can have large ratios. The OC estimator has optimal worst-case ratios of 1.204 (for $p = 1$) and 1.35 (for $p = 2$), but the ratio is the same across the range for all data vectors with $\min(\boldsymbol{v}) < \max(\boldsymbol{v}) \leq \tau$.

We study the variance as a function of $\frac{\min(\boldsymbol{v})}{\max(\boldsymbol{v})}$. The variance is 0 when $\text{RG}(\boldsymbol{v}) = 0$ (ratio is 1). Otherwise, it is lower for $\hat{\text{RG}}_p^{(U)}$ when the ratio is sufficiently small. The threshold point is ϕ_p which satisfies

$$\text{VAR}_{\mathcal{S}_{\boldsymbol{v}}}[\hat{\text{RG}}_p^{(U)}] < \text{VAR}_{\mathcal{S}_{\boldsymbol{v}}}[\hat{\text{RG}}_p^{(L)}] \iff \frac{\min(\boldsymbol{v})}{\max(\boldsymbol{v})} < \phi_p\ .$$

For $p = 1$, $\phi_1 \approx 0.285$ (is the solution of the equality $(1-x)/(2x) = \ln(1/x)$). For $p = 2$, $\phi_2 \approx 0.258$.

This suggests selecting an estimator according to expected characteristics of the data. If typically $\text{RG}(\mathbf{v}) > (1-\phi_p)\max(\mathbf{v})$, we choose $\hat{\text{RG}}_p^{(U)}$. If typically $\text{RG}(\mathbf{v}) < (1-\phi_p)\max(\mathbf{v})$ we choose $\hat{\text{RG}}_p^{(L)}$, and otherwise, we choose the OC estimator.

5. EXTENSIONS

The *one-sided distance*, which isolates the growth or decline components, is defined as $L_{p+}^p(H) = \sum_{h\in H} \text{RG}_{p+}(\boldsymbol{v}(h))$, where $\text{RG}_{p+}(\boldsymbol{v}) = \max\{0, v_1 - v_2\}^p$. We can use any of our RG_p estimators $\hat{\text{RG}}_p(S)$ to estimate RG_{p+} as follows: If S^* includes $\boldsymbol{v}$ such that $v_1 \leq v_2$ then $\hat{\text{RG}}_{p+}(S) = 0$. Otherwise, $\hat{\text{RG}}_{p+}(S) = \hat{\text{RG}}_p(S)$. We can symetrically define L_{p-}^p and RG_{p-} and $\hat{\text{RG}}_{p-}$.

Our derivations can be extended to other sampling schemes. One such extension is to weighted sampling without replacement (PPSWR), which is bottom-k sampling with priorities $r_{ih} = -\frac{\ln(1-u_{ih})}{v_{ih}}$ [33, 32, 11, 12].

6. RELATED WORK

Prior to our work, the only distance estimator we are aware of which obtained good estimate with small fraction of data sampled is for L_1 over coordinated samples. This estimator uses the relation $|v_1 - v_2| = \max\{v_1, v_2\} - \min\{v_1, v_2\}$ to obtain an indirect estimate as the difference of two inverse probability estimates for the maximum and minimum [16]. Our U* estimator for $p = 1$ is a strengthening of this L_1 estimator.

Distance estimation over *unweighted* coordinated [28] or independent [14] sampling is a much simpler problem. With unweighted sampling, the inclusion probability of positive entries is independent of their weight. When carefully implemented, we can use inverse-probability estimates, which as discussed in the introduction, do not work with weighted sampling. An unweighted sample, however, is much less informative for its size when the data is skewed, as "heavy hitters" can be easily missed out. The estimators we develop here are applicable with, and take advantage, of weighted sampling.

Distance estimation of vectors (each instance in our terminology is presented as a vector of key values) was extensively studied using *linear sketches*, which are random linear projections, e.g. [25, 2, 1, 18]. Random projections have the property that the difference vector of sketches is the sketch of the difference of the two vectors. This means they are tailored for distance-like queries which aggregate over functions of the coordinate-wise differences. In particular, with linear sketches we can accurately estimate distances that are very small relative to the input vectors norms, whereas even with weighted sampling, accuracy depends on the relation of the distance to the vectors norms. A significant disadvantage of linear sketches, however, is lack of flexibility: Unlike samples, they do not support domain (selection) queries that are specified after the summary structure is computed and can only estimate distance between the full vectors. Moreover, each sketch is tailored for a specific metric, such as L_2^2. Lastly, linear sketches are not suitable for estimating one-sided distances. Moreover, linear sketches have size which often depends (poly) logarithmically on the number of keys. To summarize, the two techniques, sampling and linear sketches, have different advantages. Sampling provides much greater flexibility in terms of supported queries and often admits a smaller summary structure.

7. EXPERIMENTAL EVALUATION

We selected several datasets that have the form of values assigned to a set of keys, on two instances, and natural selection predicates. We consider the L_1 and L_2^2 distances on keys satisfying these predicates. Properties of the data sets with selections are summarized below and in Table 5.

- **destIP** (IP packet traces): keys: (anonymized) IP destination addresses. value: the number of IP flows to this destination IP. Instances: two consecutive time periods. Selection: all IP destination addresses in a certain subnetwork.

- **Server** (WWW activity logs): Keys: (anonymized) source IP address and Web site pairs. value: the number of HTTP requests issued to the Web site from this address. Instances: two consecutive time periods. Selection: A particular Web site.

- **Surnames and OSPD8:** keys: all words (terms). value: the number of occurrences of the term in English books digitized by Google and published within the time period [29]. Instances: the years 2007 and 2008. Surnames selection: the 18.5×10^3 most common surnames in the US. OSPD8 selection: the 7.5×10^4 8 letter words that appear in the Official Scrabble Players Dictionary (OSPD).

Each of the two instances were Poisson PPS [23] sampled (see Section 2) with different sampling threshold T, to obtain a range of sample sizes. We used both coordinated (shared-seed) and independent sampling of the two instances.

We study the quality of the L_p^p estimates obtained from our RG_p estimators. We estimate $L_p^p = \sum_{h\in H} \text{RG}_p(\boldsymbol{v}(h))$ as the sum over selected keys H of RG_p estimates: $\hat{L}_p^p = \sum_{h\in H} \hat{\text{RG}}_p(\boldsymbol{v}(h))$. We consider the estimator $\hat{\text{RG}}_p^{(L)}$ for independent samples (Section 3) and the estimators $\hat{\text{RG}}_p^{(L)}$ and $\hat{\text{RG}}_p^{(U)}$ for coordinated samples (Section 4). To apply the estimators, we apply the selection predicate to sampled keys to identify all the ones satisfying the predicate. The estimators are then computed for keys that are sampled in at least one instance (the estimate is 0 for keys that are not sampled in any instance and do not need to be explicitly computed).

Since all our RG_p estimators are unbiased and nonnegative, so is the corresponding sum estimate $\hat{L}_p^p$. The variance is additive and is $\sum_{h\in H} \text{VAR}_{\mathcal{S}_{\boldsymbol{v}(h)}}[\hat{\text{RG}}_p]$. We measure the performance of the estimators using the variance normalized by the square of the expectation, which is the squared coefficient of variation $\text{CV}^2(\hat{L}_p^p) = \frac{\sum_{h\in H} \text{VAR}_{\mathcal{S}_{\boldsymbol{v}(h)}}[\hat{\text{RG}}_p]}{(\sum_{h\in H} \text{RG}_p(\boldsymbol{v}(h)))^2}$.

Figure 5 shows the CV^2 of our L_p^p estimators ($p = 1, 2$) as a function of the sampled fraction of the dataset. We can see qualitatively, that all estimators, even over independent samples, are satisfactory, in that the CV is small for a sample that is a small fraction of the full data set. The estimator $\hat{\text{RG}}_p^{(L)}$ over coordinated shared-seed samples outperforms, by orders of magnitude, the estimator $\hat{\text{RG}}_p^{(L)}$ over independent samples. The gap widens for more aggressive sampling (higher T).

On the IP flows and WWW logs data, there are significant differences on the values of keys between instances: the L_1 distance is a large fraction of the total sum of values $\sum_{h\in H}\sum_{i\in[2]} v_i(h)$. Therefore, for the destIP and Server selections, $\hat{\text{RG}}_p^{(U)}$ outperforms $\hat{\text{RG}}_p^{(L)}$ on shared-seed samples. On the term count data there is typically a small difference between instances. We can see that for the Surnames and OSPD8 selections, $\hat{\text{RG}}_p^{(L)}$ outperforms $\hat{\text{RG}}_p^{(U)}$ on shared seed samples. These trends are more pronounced for the Euclidean distance ($p = 2$). In this case, on Surnames and OSPD8, $\hat{\text{RG}}_p^{(L)}$ over independent samples outperform $\hat{\text{RG}}_p^{(U)}$ over shared-seed samples. We can see that we can significantly improve accuracy by tailoring the selection of the estimator to properties of the data. The performance of the U* estimator, however, can significantly diverge for very similar instances whereas the competitive L* estimator is guaranteed not to be too far off. Therefore, when

data	# keys	p1%	p2%	$\sum_{ih} v_{ih}$	p1%	p2%	$L_1 / \sum_{ih} v_{ih}$	$L_{1+} / \sum_{ih} v_{ih}$	$L_{1-} / \sum_{ih} v_{ih}$
destIP	3.8×10^4	65%	65%	1.1×10^6	49%	51%	0.36	0.19	0.18
Server	2.7×10^5	53%	56%	2.9×10^6	50%	50%	0.75	0.38	0.37
Surnames	1.9×10^4	100%	100%	8.9×10^7	48.6%	51.4%	0.094	0.0617	0.0327
OSPD8	7.5×10^5	99%	99%	1.57×10^{10}	46.8%	53.2%	0.0826	0.0727	0.0099

Table 5: Datasets with subset selections. Table shows total number of distinct keys H satisfying selection predicate that had a positive value in at least one of the two instances, corresponding percentage in each instance, total sum of values $\sum_{ih} v_{ih}$, and fraction (shown as percentage), sum in each instance $i = 1, 2$: $\frac{\sum_h v_{ih}}{\sum_{jh} v_{jh}}$, and normalized L_1, L_{1+} and L_{1-} distances.

there is no prior knowledge on the difference, we suggest using the L* estimator.

The datasets also differ in the symmetry of change. The change is more symmetric in the IP flows and WWW logs data $L_{p+} \approx L_{p-}$ whereas there is a general growth trend $L_{p+} \gg L_{p-}$ in the term count data. Estimator performance on one-sided distances (not shown) is similar to the corresponding distance estimators.

8. CONCLUSION

Distance queries are essential for monitoring, planning, and anomaly and change detection. Random sampling is an important tool for retaining the ability to query data under resource limitations. We provide the first satisfactory solution for estimating L_p distance from sampled data sets. Our solution is comprehensive, covering common sampling schemes. It is supported by rigorous analysis and novel techniques. Our estimators scale well with data size and we demonstrated that accurate estimates are obtained for queries with small support size.

Acknowledgement. The author is grateful to Haim Kaplan for many comments, helpful feedback, and suggesting the use of the ngrams data.

	$\hat{\text{RG}}^{(L)}$
$\lvert S\rvert = 0$	0
$\lvert S\rvert \geq 1$	$\max\{\max(\boldsymbol{v}) - \tau, 0\} - \max\{\min(\boldsymbol{v}) - \tau, 0\} + \tau \ln \frac{\min\{\max(\boldsymbol{v}), \tau\}}{\min\{v_{\min}, \tau\}}$

Condition	$\text{VAR}_{S_{\boldsymbol{v}}}[\hat{\text{RG}}^{(L)}]$
$\min(\boldsymbol{v}) \geq \tau$	0
$\max(\boldsymbol{v}) \leq \tau,\ \min(\boldsymbol{v}) = 0$	$2\text{RG}(\boldsymbol{v})\tau - \text{RG}(\boldsymbol{v})^2$
$\max(\boldsymbol{v}) \leq \tau,\ \min(\boldsymbol{v}) > 0$	$2\text{RG}(\boldsymbol{v})\tau - \text{RG}(\boldsymbol{v})^2 - 2\tau \min(\boldsymbol{v}) \ln(\frac{\max(\boldsymbol{v})}{\min(\boldsymbol{v})})$
$0 < \min(\boldsymbol{v}) \leq \tau \leq \max(\boldsymbol{v})$	$(\tau)^2 - \min(\boldsymbol{v})^2 - 2\tau \min(\boldsymbol{v}) \ln(\frac{\tau}{\min(\boldsymbol{v})})$
$0 = \min(\boldsymbol{v}),\ \tau \leq \max(\boldsymbol{v})$	$(\tau)^2 - \min(\boldsymbol{v})^2$

Table 6: $\hat{\text{RG}}^{(L)}$ **and variance for shared-seed sampling.**

Algorithm 1 $\hat{\text{RG}}_p^{(U)}(S)$

if $|S| = 0$ **then return** 0 ▷ from hereafter $|S| > 0$
$m \leftarrow \max_{i \in S} v_i$ ▷ $m = \max(\boldsymbol{v})$
if $|S| < r$ **then** $n \leftarrow 0$
else $n \leftarrow \min_{i \in S} v_i$ ▷ $n = \underline{\min}(S)$
if $n \geq \tau$ **then return** $(m - n)^p$ ▷ case: $\min(\boldsymbol{v}) \geq \tau$
if $p \leq 1$ **then** ▷ case: $\min(\boldsymbol{v}) \leq \tau$ and $p \leq 1$
  if n=0 **then return** $m^p \frac{\tau}{\min\{m, \tau\}}$
  else **return** $\frac{\tau}{n}\left((m - n)^p - \frac{\min\{m,\tau\} - n}{\min\{m,\tau\}} m^p\right)$
if $m \leq \tau$ **then** ▷ case: $\max(\boldsymbol{v}) \leq \tau, p > 1$
  if $\zeta\tau > n$ **then return** $p\tau(m - \zeta\tau)^{p-1}$
  else **return** 0
▷ case: $n < \tau < \max(\boldsymbol{v})$ and $p > 1$
$\eta_0 \leftarrow \frac{p\tau - m}{(p-1)\tau}$
if $\eta_0 \in (0, 1)$ **then** ▷ subcase: $\eta_0 \in (0, 1)$
  if $\zeta \geq \max\{\eta_0, n/\tau\}$ **then return** $\frac{(m - \eta_0\tau)^p}{1 - \eta_0}$
  if $n/\tau < \zeta < \eta_0$ **then return** $p\tau(m - \zeta\tau)^{p-1}$
  if $\zeta \leq n/\tau \leq \eta_0$ **then return** 0
  if $\zeta \leq n/\tau \geq \eta_0$ **then**
    return $\frac{\tau(m-n)^p}{n} - \frac{(\tau - n)(m - \eta_0\tau)^p}{n(1 - \eta_0)}$
else ▷ subcase: $\eta_0 \notin (0, 1)$
  if $\zeta\tau > n$ **then return** m^p
  else **return** $\frac{\tau}{n}(m - n)^p - m^p\left(\frac{\tau}{n} - 1\right)$

9. REFERENCES

[1] N. Alon, Y. Matias, and M. Szegedy. The space complexity of approximating the frequency moments. *J. Comput. System Sci.*, 58:137–147, 1999.

[2] B. Bahmani, A. Goel, and R. Shinde. efficient distributed locality sensitive hashing. In *CIKM*. ACM, 2012.

[3] K. S. Beyer, P. J. Haas, B. Reinwald, Y. Sismanis, and R. Gemulla. On synopses for distinct-value estimation under multiset operations. In *SIGMOD*, pages 199–210. ACM, 2007.

[4] K. R. W. Brewer, L. J. Early, and S. F. Joyce. Selecting several samples from a single population. *Australian Journal of Statistics*, 14(3):231–239, 1972.

[5] A. Z. Broder. On the resemblance and containment of documents. In *Proceedings of the Compression and Complexity of Sequences*, pages 21–29. IEEE, 1997.

[6] A. Z. Broder. Identifying and filtering near-duplicate documents. In *Proc.of the 11th Annual Symposium on Combinatorial Pattern Matching*, volume 1848 of *LNCS*, pages 1–10. Springer, 2000.

[7] S. S. Chawathe, A. Rajaraman, H. Garcia-Molina, and J. Widom. Change detection in hierarchically structured information. In *Proceedings of the 1996 ACM SIGMOD international conference on Management of data*, 1996.

[8] E. Cohen. Size-estimation framework with applications to transitive closure and reachability. *J. Comput. System Sci.*, 55:441–453, 1997.

[9] E. Cohen. Estimation for monotone sampling: Competitiveness and customization. In *PODC*. ACM, 2014. full version `http://arxiv.org/abs/1212.0243`.

[10] E. Cohen, N. Duffield, C. Lund, M. Thorup, and H. Kaplan. Efficient stream sampling for variance-optimal estimation of subset sums. *SIAM J. Comput.*, 40(5), 2011.

[11] E. Cohen and H. Kaplan. Summarizing data using bottom-k sketches. In *ACM PODC*, 2007.

[12] E. Cohen and H. Kaplan. Tighter estimation using bottom-k sketches. In *Proceedings of the 34th VLDB Conference*, 2008.

[13] E. Cohen and H. Kaplan. Leveraging discarded samples for tighter estimation of multiple-set aggregates. In *ACM SIGMETRICS*, 2009.

[14] E. Cohen and H. Kaplan. Get the most out of your sample: Optimal unbiased estimators using partial information. In *Proc. of the 2011*

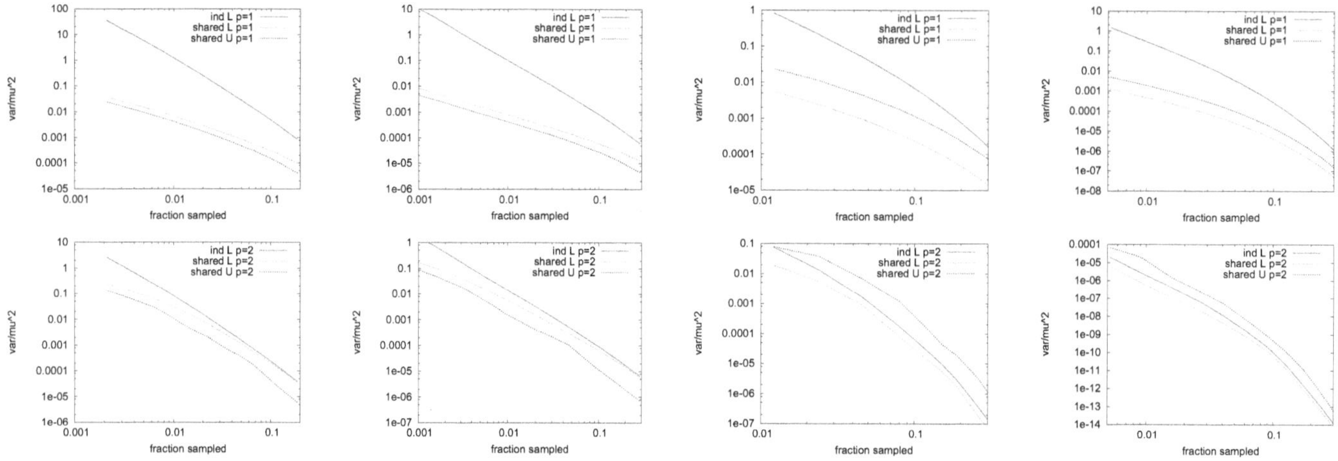

Figure 5: Queries (left to right): destIP, Server, Surnames, OSPD8. Plot shows CV^2 of L_p^p estimate for fraction of sampled items from the query support. Top shows $p = 1$ (L_1) bottom shows $p = 2$ (L_2^2).

	$\hat{\mathrm{RG}}_2^{(L)}$
$\lvert S\rvert = 0$	0
$\lvert S\rvert \geq 1$	$\max\{\max(\boldsymbol{v}), \tau\}^2 - \max\{\min(\boldsymbol{v}), \tau\}^2$ $-2\max\{\min(\boldsymbol{v}), \tau\}(\max(\boldsymbol{v}) - v_{\min})$ $+2\tau \max(\boldsymbol{v}) \ln \frac{\min\{\max(\boldsymbol{v}),\tau\}}{\min\{v_{\min},\tau\}}$

Condition	$\mathrm{VAR}_{\mathcal{S}_{\boldsymbol{v}}}[\hat{\mathrm{RG}}_2^{(L)}]$
$\min(\boldsymbol{v}) \geq \tau$	0
$\max(\boldsymbol{v}) \leq \tau$	$-4\tau \max(\boldsymbol{v}) \min(\boldsymbol{v}) \ln(\frac{\max(\boldsymbol{v})}{\min(\boldsymbol{v})})(2\max(\boldsymbol{v}) - \min(\boldsymbol{v}))$ $-(\max(\boldsymbol{v}) - \min(\boldsymbol{v}))^4$ $+\frac{2\tau}{3}(5\max(\boldsymbol{v})^3 + 4\min(\boldsymbol{v})^3 - 9\max(\boldsymbol{v})\min(\boldsymbol{v})^2)$
$\min(\boldsymbol{v}) \leq \tau$ $\wedge$ $\max(\boldsymbol{v}) \geq \tau$	$4\max(\boldsymbol{v})\min(\boldsymbol{v})\tau(\min(\boldsymbol{v}) - 2\max(\boldsymbol{v})) \ln \frac{\tau}{\min(\boldsymbol{v})}$ $+4\max(\boldsymbol{v})\min(\boldsymbol{v})(\tau)^2 + \frac{(\tau)^4}{3} + \frac{8\min(\boldsymbol{v})^3\tau}{3}$ $-6\max(\boldsymbol{v})\min(\boldsymbol{v})^2\tau - 4\max(\boldsymbol{v})^2\min(\boldsymbol{v})^2$ $-\min(\boldsymbol{v})^4 + 4\max(\boldsymbol{v})\min(\boldsymbol{v})^3 + 4\max(\boldsymbol{v})^2(\tau)^2$ $-2\max(\boldsymbol{v})(\tau)^3$

Table 7: $\hat{\mathrm{RG}}_2^{(L)}$ and variance for shared-seed sampling

ACM Symp. on Principles of Database Systems (PODS 2011). ACM, 2011. full version: http://arxiv.org/abs/1203.4903.

[15] E. Cohen and H. Kaplan. What you can do with coordinated samples. In *The 17th. International Workshop on Randomization and Computation (RANDOM)*, 2013. full version: http://arxiv.org/abs/1206.5637.

[16] E. Cohen, H. Kaplan, and S. Sen. Coordinated weighted sampling for estimating aggregates over multiple weight assignments. *Proceedings of the VLDB Endowment*, 2(1–2), 2009. full version: http://arxiv.org/abs/0906.4560.

[17] T. Dasu, T. Johnson, S. Muthukrishnan, and V. Shkapenyuk. Mining database structure; or, how to build a data quality browser. In *Proc. SIGMOD Conference*, pages 240–251, 2002.

[18] W. Dong, M. Charikar, and K. Li. Asymmetric distance estimation with sketches for similarity search in high-dimensional spaces. In *SIGIR*, 2008.

[19] N. Duffield, M. Thorup, and C. Lund. Priority sampling for estimating arbitrary subset sums. *J. Assoc. Comput. Mach.*, 54(6), 2007.

[20] P. Gibbons and S. Tirthapura. Estimating simple functions on the union of data streams. In *Proceedings of the 13th Annual ACM Symposium on Parallel Algorithms and Architectures*. ACM, 2001.

[21] P. B. Gibbons. Distinct sampling for highly-accurate answers to distinct values queries and event reports. In *International Conference on Very Large Databases (VLDB)*, pages 541–550, 2001.

[22] M. Hadjieleftheriou, X. Yu, N. Koudas, and D. Srivastava. Hashed samples: Selectivity estimators for set similarity selection queries. In *Proceedings of the 34th VLDB Conference*, 2008.

[23] J. Hájek. *Sampling from a finite population*. Marcel Dekker, New York, 1981.

[24] D. G. Horvitz and D. J. Thompson. A generalization of sampling without replacement from a finite universe. *Journal of the American Statistical Association*, 47(260):663–685, 1952.

[25] P. Indyk and R. Motwani. Approximate nearest neighbors: Towards removing the curse of dimensionality. In *Proc. 30th Annual ACM Symposium on Theory of Computing*, pages 604–613. ACM, 1998.

[26] D. Kifer, S. Ben-David, and J. Gehrke. Detecting change in data streams. In *VLDB*, 2004.

[27] D.E. Knuth. *The Art of Computer Programming, Vol. 2: Seminumerical Algorithms*. Addison-Wesley, 1969.

[28] P. Li, , K. W. Church, and T. Hastie. Conditional random sampling: A sketch-based sampling technique for sparse data. In *NIPS*, 2006.

[29] J. B. Michel, Y. K. Shen, A. Presser Aiden, A. Veres, M. K. Gray, W. Brockman, The Google Books Team, J. P. Pickett, D. Hoiberg, D. Clancy, P. Norvig, J. Orwant, S. Pinker, M. A. Nowak, and E. L. Aiden. Quantitative analysis of culture using millions of digitized books. *Science*, 331(6014):176–182, 2011. http://www.sciencemag.org/content/331/6014/176.

[30] E. Ohlsson. Sequential poisson sampling. *J. Official Statistics*, 14(2):149–162, 1998.

[31] E. Ohlsson. Coordination of pps samples over time. In *The 2nd International Conference on Establishment Surveys*, pages 255–264. American Statistical Association, 2000.

[32] B. Rosén. Asymptotic theory for successive sampling with varying probabilities without replacement, I. *The Annals of Mathematical Statistics*, 43(2):373–397, 1972.

[33] B. Rosén. Asymptotic theory for order sampling. *J. Statistical Planning and Inference*, 62(2):135–158, 1997.

[34] P. J. Saavedra. Fixed sample size pps approximations with a permanent random number. In *Proc. of the Section on Survey Research Methods, Alexandria VA*, pages 697–700. American Statistical Association, 1995.

[35] M. Szegedy. The DLT priority sampling is essentially optimal. In *Proc. 38th Annual ACM Symposium on Theory of Computing*. ACM, 2006.

[36] J.S. Vitter. Random sampling with a reservoir. *ACM Trans. Math. Softw.*, 11(1):37–57, 1985.

Improved Testing of Low Rank Matrices

Yi Li
Max-Planck Institute for Informatics
yli@mpi-inf.mpg.de

Zhengyu Wang
Institute for Interdisciplinary Informatics Science (IIIS)
Tsinghua University
wangsincos@163.com

David P. Woodruff
IBM Research, Almaden
dpwoodru@us.ibm.com

ABSTRACT

We study the problem of determining if an input matrix $A \in \mathbb{R}^{m\times n}$ can be well-approximated by a low rank matrix. Specifically, we study the problem of quickly estimating the rank or stable rank of A, the latter often providing a more robust measure of the rank. Since we seek significantly sublinear time algorithms, we cast these problems in the property testing framework. In this framework, A either has low rank or stable rank, or is far from having this property. The algorithm should read only a small number of entries or rows of A and decide which case A is in with high probability. If neither case occurs, the output is allowed to be arbitrary. We consider two notions of being far: (1) A requires changing at least an ϵ-fraction of its entries, or (2) A requires changing at least an ϵ-fraction of its rows. We call the former the "entry model" and the latter the "row model". We show:

- For testing if a matrix has rank at most d in the entry model, we improve the previous number of entries of A that need to be read from $O(d^2/\epsilon^2)$ (Krauthgamer and Sasson, SODA 2003) to $O(d^2/\epsilon)$. Our algorithm is the first to *adaptively* query the entries of A, which for constant d we show is necessary to achieve $O(1/\epsilon)$ queries. For the important case of $d = 1$ we also give a new non-adaptive algorithm, improving the previous $O(1/\epsilon^2)$ queries to $O(\log^2(1/\epsilon)/\epsilon)$.
- For testing if a matrix has rank at most d in the row model, we prove an $\Omega(d/\epsilon)$ lower bound on the number of rows that need to be read, even for adaptive algorithms. Our lower bound matches a non-adaptive upper bound of Krauthgamer and Sasson.
- For testing if a matrix has stable rank at most d in the row model or requires changing an ϵ/d-fraction of its rows in order to have stable rank at most d, we prove that reading $\tilde{\Theta}(d/\epsilon^2)$ rows is necessary and sufficient.

We also give an empirical evaluation of our rank and stable rank algorithms on real and synthetic datasets.

KDD'14, August 24–27, 2014, New York, NY, USA.

ACM 978-1-4503-2956-9/14/08 ...$15.00.
http://dx.doi.org/10.1145/2623330.2623736.

Categories and Subject Descriptors

F.2.1 [**Analysis of Algorithms and Problem Complexity**]: Numerical Algorithms and Problems—*Computation on matrices*; G.2.3 [**Discrete Mathematics**]: Applications

General Terms

Algorithms, Theory

Keywords

dimensionality reduction, principal component analysis, property testing, robustness, stable rank

1. INTRODUCTION

Low rank approximation is a popular tool in computer science with applications to computer vision, information retrieval, and machine learning. In many of these applications, such as image, video, multimedia processing, web data, and bioinformatics the dimensionality of the data is very large. This makes designing algorithms for processing such data more challenging, requiring very low memory and extremely fast processing time.

A saving grace of large-scale data is that it is often of low intrinsic dimension. For example, in Principal Component Analysis (PCA) [6, 7, 13] the data points are column vectors of a matrix A with the assumption that A can be expressed as $L+N$ for L a matrix of low rank and N a matrix of small Frobenius norm, which could typically model noise that has been added to A. Replacing A with the matrix L provides a good low rank approximation to A. PCA has a wide range of applications, including non-negative matrix factorization [9], latent dirichlet allocation [1], clustering [3], and geometric shape fitting problems [4]. There is a large body of work on randomized algorithms for low rank approximation; we refer the reader to Section 5 of the survey by Mahoney [11].

Recently, a new form of PCA called robust PCA was introduced [2]. In this problem, the data points are again column vectors of a matrix $A = L+N$, where L is a low rank matrix, but now N is only guaranteed to be a sparse matrix. Unlike classical PCA, the entries of N can be arbitrarily large provided there are a small number of non-zero entries (the locations of the non-zero entries of N are unknown). This makes robust PCA less sensitive to outlier contamination. We refer the reader to [2] in which applications of robust PCA to video surveillance, face recognition, latent semantic indexing, ranking and collaborative filtering are given. In typical applications, such as recommender systems [15], L is a matrix of a small constant rank. Surprisingly, under certain assumptions there are efficient algorithms for recovering L and N. One assumption is that the number of non-zero entries of N is at most a sufficiently small constant fraction of the total number of entries.

Independently of the work above, the property testing community has also studied whether a matrix can be expressed as a small perturbation of a low rank matrix [8, 12]. In the property testing model there is an unknown, typically very large object, such as a graph, a matrix, or a vector. This object is queried in certain positions in order to determine if it satisfies a property $\mathcal{P}$ or is far from satisfying $\mathcal{P}$. For an introduction to property testing, we refer the reader to a survey by Goldreich [5]. The relevant results in the property testing literature for robust PCA are those for what we refer to as the Rank property. In this problem, the input matrix A is either of rank at most d, or requires changing an ϵ-fraction of its entries in order to become a matrix of rank at most d. Note that this is a decision version of the robust PCA problem: either $A = L$ in the notation above, or if $A = L + N$ for a matrix L of rank at most d, then necessarily more than an ϵ-fraction of entries of N are non-zero. Distinguishing these two cases allows one to decide whether the assumptions required for a robust PCA algorithm to succeed hold. If the input A is in neither case, then it is allowed for the algorithm to output an arbitrary answer, which is acceptable for the robust PCA application since robust PCA is guaranteed to work if N has at most an ϵ-fraction of non-zero entries.

The Rank problem was studied by Krauthgamer and Sasson [8], who showed there exists a randomized algorithm succeeding with 99% probability on every input matrix A and reading only $O(d^2/\epsilon^2)$ entries of A. This bound is independent of the dimensions of the matrix A. This provides a quick, provably correct method for determining whether robust PCA procedures will work on A, without having to run them in case A is not well-approximated by a low rank matrix. Other methods such as clustering and recommendation systems can also benefit by first running an algorithm for Rank to determine if A is close to a low rank matrix.

Despite this progress, there are several natural questions that remain:

1. In machine learning problems a quadratic dependence on ϵ is often prohibitive. Can one improve the $O(d^2/\epsilon^2)$ algorithm of [8] to have a linear dependence on $1/\epsilon$?
2. In differential equation applications, one often has a sparse matrix stored in Compressed Sparse Row (CSR) or Compressed Sparse Columns (CSC) representation, which allows the retrieval of an entire row or column almost as quickly as a single entry. What is the complexity of the Rank problem in this model? To distinguish this model from the previous model, we refer to this as the "row model", while the model in which individual entries are changed is the "entry model".
3. It is often more common for a matrix to have low *stable rank* than low rank, where the stable rank is defined as $\|A\|_F^2/\|A\|^2$. Here $\|A\|_F$ is the Frobenius norm and $\|A\|$ the operator norm. The stable rank is a continuous, robust relaxation of the rank, with applications to finding well-conditioned submatrices [16]. Can we design algorithms for the StableRank problem, of determining if A has stable rank at most d, or requires changing an ϵ/d-fraction of rows to have stable rank at most d? For this question to make sense, we assume as is often done when working with the stable rank [16], that the rows of A have Euclidean norm at most 1, as otherwise one can increase the norm of a single row of A until its stable rank is arbitrarily close to 1. It also makes sense to parameterize the problem in terms of changing an ϵ/d-fraction of rows rather than an ϵ-fraction of rows, since by replacing a $1/d$ fraction of rows with the vector v for an arbitrary unit vector v, one can always reduce the stable rank to at most d.

Our Contributions: In this paper we thoroughly study both the Rank and StableRank problems. We answer the questions above, providing new theoretical and empirical guarantees for these problems.

Results for the Rank Problem:

1. In the entry model, by allowing queries (i, j) to be adaptively chosen based on the values $A_{i',j'}$ of previously queried entries (i', j'), we are able to improve the algorithm of [8] to give an algorithm which makes only $O(d^2/\epsilon)$ rather than $O(d^2/\epsilon^2)$ queries. Our algorithm, like that of [8] has one-sided error, meaning that if A is of rank at most d the algorithm will be correct with probability 1, while if A is ϵ-far from this property, the algorithm succeeds with probability .99.
2. We show that, for constant d, adaptivity is necessary for achieving this improved algorithm. That is, we show that any algorithm which makes only non-adaptive queries, meaning it chooses its query set before reading any of the entries of A, requires reading $\Omega((\log 1/\epsilon)/\epsilon)$ entries of A. As our upper bound for constant d is $O(1/\epsilon)$ queries, this demonstrates a separation in the power of adaptivity.
3. We further study the problem when $d = 1$, which has important applications to parsing images of building facades [17]. In this case we design a non-adaptive algorithm which achieves $O((1/\epsilon)\log^2(1/\epsilon))$ queries in the entry model, improving the $O(1/\epsilon^2)$ non-adaptive algorithm of [8].
4. In the row model, we show that any, possibly adaptive, algorithm requires reading $\Omega(d/\epsilon)$ rows of A. This matches a non-adaptive $O(d/\epsilon)$ algorithm of [8].

Results for the StableRank Problem:

1. We show in the row model that reading a total of $O(d \log n \log(d \log n)/\epsilon^2)$ non-adaptively chosen rows suffices to solve the problem.
2. We also show an $\Omega(d/\epsilon^2)$ lower bound in the row model. Our lower bound holds even for adaptive algorithms, and is optimal up to an $O(\log n \log(d \log n))$ factor.

We experimentally validate our algorithms for Rank and StableRank on several natural input distributions on A and sparsity patterns N.

For the StableRank problem, we use real datasets from the University of Florida Sparse Matrix Collection. We show that for a large fraction of the matrices in this dataset, our algorithms only need to sample a very small fraction of rows to solve the StableRank problem. We parameterize the number of rows that need to be read as a function of the stable rank parameter d for these datasets.

For the Rank problem, we use synthetic datasets. Our experiments show particularly noticeable improvements for adaptive query algorithms over non-adaptive query algorithms for small ϵ. For example, for $\epsilon = 0.01$ and $d = 1$, for one of our input distributions the number of adaptive queries is 7% of the number of non-adaptive queries required.

Paper Outline: We give our adaptive algorithm for the Rank problem in the entry model in Section 2, and show that adaptivity is essential by proving a lower bound for non-adaptive algorithms in Section 3. In Section 4, we give a new non-adaptive algorithm for the important case of $d = 1$, which comes close to the lower bound we prove for non-adaptive algorithms in Section 3. In Section 5 we consider the row model, and prove a lower bound on the number of rows read for the RANK problem. In Section 6 we give an algorithm for the StableRank problem and show a nearly matching lower bound, both in the row model. Finally, we present our experimental results in Section 7.

2. ALGORITHM FOR RANK PROBLEM

In this section we study the Rank problem with adaptive queries. We assume that $\min(m, n) = \omega(d/\epsilon)$, that is, that $\min(m, n)$ is larger than cd/ϵ for any fixed constant $c > 0$. This is consistent with our goal of testing if A has small rank.

We first review the algorithm for Rank in [8]. Suppose that the input matrix A has rank greater than d. That algorithm tries to find a submatrix with rank greater than d. The algorithm starts with an empty submatrix and iteratively grows the submatrix by appending one random row and one random column. Let B_t be the submatrix maintained at step t and $X_t = \text{rank}(B_t)$. It was shown in [8] that $\Pr\{X_{t+1} > X_t | X_t \leq d\} \geq \epsilon/3$ and thus by a Chernoff bound, $t = O(d/\epsilon)$ suffices to reach $X_t > d$ with constant probability.

Algorithm 1 Our Algorithm for the Rank problem

$I \leftarrow \emptyset, J \leftarrow \emptyset$
for $t = 1$ to $O(d^2/\epsilon)$ **do**
  Pick (i, j) uniformly random from $I^c \times J^c$
  Query $A_{I,j}$, $A_{i,J}$ and $A_{i,j}$
  if $\text{rank}(A_{I\cup\{i\},J\cup\{j\}}) > \text{rank}(A_{I,J})$ **then**
    $I \leftarrow I \cup \{i\}, J \leftarrow J \cup \{j\}$
  end if
  $B_t \leftarrow A_{I,J}$
  if $\text{rank}(B_t) > d$ **then**
    return "A is ϵ-far from rank d"
  end if
end for
return "A is of rank d"

In our adaptive algorithm, we also augment B_t in each step until $\text{rank}(B_t) > d$. We formally write our algorithm in Algorithm 1. Suppose at step t, $\text{rank}(B_t) < d$ and I and J are the index sets of the rows and columns of B_t, respectively. Consider the index pairs $I^c \times J^c$, where $I^c = [m] \setminus I$ and $J^c = [n] \setminus J$, where for an integer ℓ, $[\ell] = \{1, 2, \ldots, \ell\}$. We claim that at least an $\Omega(\epsilon)$ fraction of the index pairs in $I^c \times J^c$ would increase $\text{rank}(B_t)$. Assume that this is true for the moment. Then in expectation, $O(1/\epsilon)$ random samples in $I^c \times J^c$ suffice for there to exist a sample index pair that would increase the rank B_t after augmenting with respect to that index pair. We can find one such pair by checking each chosen possible augmentation of B_t. Call the pair found B_{t+1}. By linearity of expectation and a Chernoff bound, $t = O(d)$ steps suffice to give $\text{rank}(B_t) > d$. The number of entries read is, in expectation, bounded by

$$\sum_{t=0}^{O(d)} O\left(\frac{2t+1}{\epsilon}\right) = O\left(\frac{d^2}{\epsilon}\right).$$

Now we prove our claim above to complete the proof. We can assume, without loss of generality, that B_t consists of an upper left submatrix of A. Since we assume that $\min(m, n) = \omega(d/\epsilon)$, and B_t has at most d rows and columns, we can change all the entries of A in the first t columns and first t rows so that the rows restricted to the first t columns are in the row span of B_t, and the columns restricted to the first t rows are in the column span of B_t. This only changes at most an $\epsilon/2$-fraction of the total number of entries of A. Next, for each entry (i, j) not among the first t columns or rows, we can change the value of $A_{i,j}$ so that augmenting B_t by the pair (i, j) does not increase the rank of B_t. Since we must change at least an ϵ-fraction of overall entries of A to reduce the rank to at most d, and B_t has rank at most d, the number of index pairs in $I^c \times J^c$ that would increase $\text{rank}(B_t)$ must be at least $\epsilon mn/2$.

Our algorithm is optimal for constant d, because it requires $\Omega(1/\epsilon)$ queries just to distinguish a zero matrix from a matrix with ϵmn randomly placed non-zero entries.

3. LOWER BOUND FOR RANK PROBLEM FOR NON-ADAPTIVE ALGORITHMS

In this section, we start with a simple example to demonstrate that it is generally hard to improve the non-adaptive upper bound of $O(1/\epsilon^2)$ for Rank even for $d = 1$, for a class of natural non-adaptive algorithms which query submatrices and make their decision based on the maximum rank of them. Next, we give a proof that any randomized non-adaptive algorithm requires $\Omega((\log 1/\epsilon)/\epsilon)$ queries for $d \geq 1$.

3.1 A Hard Input for a Class of Natural Non-adaptive Algorithms

To design non-adaptive algorithms, a natural way is to select some submatrices of A to query, namely $A_1, \cdots, A_t$, and then make a decision based on whether $\max_{i\in[t]} \text{rank}(A_i) > d$. However, there is an example of A such that the number of queries required is at least $\Omega(1/\epsilon^2)$ for such algorithms, even when $d = 1$. In the following we fix $d = 1$. One can easily extend the result to any d.

Denote

$$M = \begin{pmatrix} 0_{\epsilon n\times\epsilon n} & 1_{\epsilon n\times(1-\epsilon)n} \\ 1_{(1-\epsilon)n\times\epsilon n} & 0_{(1-\epsilon)n\times(1-\epsilon)n} \end{pmatrix},$$

where $1_{r,c}$ is an r-by-c matrix whose entries are all 1s. Let A be the matrix obtained from uniformly randomly permuting the rows and columns of M.

In order to find a fully queried submatrix whose rank is more than 1, one must query an entry in A corresponding to an entry of the top-left submatrix in M (we call such an entry critical), whose size is just $\epsilon n \times \epsilon n$. Therefore, if the total query size is $o(1/\epsilon^2)$, the probability is $o(1)$ that one has queried a critical entry in order to find that $\text{rank}(A) = 2$ instead of 1. Hence, a lower bound of $\Omega(1/\epsilon^2)$ holds for non-adaptive algorithms which query a set of submatrices and decide on whether the maximum rank of those submatrices is more than d.

In fact, for more complicated algorithms, it is possible to reduce the non-adaptive query size when $d = 1$. We shall study it in Section 4.

The example here also illustrates the superiority of adaptive queries over non-adaptive ones. An adaptive algorithm needs $O(1/\epsilon)$ queries (in expectation) to find an entry of value 1, and based on the position of that entry, the algorithm can then extend it to a matrix of rank 2 with $O(1/\epsilon)$ more queries; while a non-adaptive algorithm does not know which rank-1 matrix to extend.

3.2 An $\Omega(\frac{1}{\epsilon}\log\frac{1}{\epsilon})$ Non-adaptive Lower Bound for Constant d

In this subsection, we prove the following theorem, which can be automatically extended to arbitrary d.

THEOREM 1. *Any randomized non-adaptive algorithm for the* Rank *problem with $d = 1$ requires $\Omega((1/\epsilon)\log(1/\epsilon))$ queries.*

To give a lower bound for non-adaptive queries for any randomized algorithm, we apply Yao's Lemma, and (1) define two distributions D_0, D_1, such that D_0 is a distribution of matrices of rank at most d (or $\Pr_{M\sim D_0}\{\text{rank}(M) \le d\} = 1$, the same below), while D_1 is a distribution of matrices which are ϵ-far from rank d; (2) prove that with high probability, any deterministic non-adaptive set of $(c/\epsilon)\log(1/\epsilon)$ entries cannot distinguish D_0 from D_1, where $c > 0$ is a constant.

Algorithm 2 Hard Distribution

1: Let i be uniformly sampled in $[k]$.
2: Let $r = n/2^{i-1}$, $c = \epsilon n \cdot 2^i$, and x_1, x_2, y_1, y_2 be i.i.d. $N(0, I_n)$ vectors.
3: Let $M_0, M_1 \in \mathbb{R}^{n\times n}$ be

$$M_0 = \begin{pmatrix} x_1 y^T & 0_{r,n-c} \\ 0_{n-r,c} & 0_{n-r,n-c} \end{pmatrix}$$

and

$$M_1 = \begin{pmatrix} x_1 y_1^T + x_2 y_2^T & 0_{r,n-c} \\ 0_{n-r,c} & 0_{n-r,n-c} \end{pmatrix},$$

where $y_i = \sqrt{(y_1)_i^2 + (y_2)_i^2}$.
4: Let $P_r, P_c \in \mathbb{R}^{n\times n}$ be two uniformly random permutation matrices.
5: Let $\mathcal{D}_0$ be the distribution of $P_r M_0 P_c$ and D_1 the distribution of $P_r M_1 P_c$.

We define the distributions $\mathcal{D}_0$ and $\mathcal{D}_1$ on $\mathbb{R}^{n\times n}$ in Algorithm 2. Notice that $\mathcal{D}_0$ is a distribution of matrices of rank 1 with probability 1 while $\mathcal{D}_1$ is a distribution such that a random sample is ϵ-far from a rank-1 matrix with probability 1.

Now consider a deterministic algorithm for testing the matrix A sampled from either of the two distributions with equal probability. The queries of the algorithm can be written as a deterministic subset $S \subseteq [n] \times [n]$. The following lemma is straightforward by the construction of the distributions, together with the property of normal distributions that $N(\mu_1, \sigma_1^2) + N(\mu_2, \sigma_2^2) \sim N(\mu_1 + \mu_2, \sigma_1^2 + \sigma_2^2)$.

LEMMA 1. *If for each row and column of A the number of observed non-zero entries is at most 1, then the algorithm cannot determine whether A is "of rank 1" or "ϵ-far from any rank-1 matrix" better than a random guess. Formally,*

$$\begin{aligned}&(\forall j \in [n], |\{(i,j) \in S \,|\, A_{i,j} \ne 0\}| \le 1)\\ &\wedge (\forall i \in [n], |\{(i,j) \in S \,|\, A_{i,j} \ne 0\}| \le 1)\ .\\ &\Rightarrow \Pr\{\text{rank}(A) \le 1 \,|\, A_S\} = \tfrac{1}{2}\end{aligned}$$

To upper-bound the probability that two or more non-zero observations are in a query row or column, we need the following lemma. It follows from a union bound argument and simple inequalities.

LEMMA 2. *Suppose that there are n bins, m of which contain a ball each. Then choosing b bins uniformly at random collects at least 2 balls with probability at most $(bm/n)^2$.*

PROOF. We pick b bins one by one. The probability that two particular bins both contain balls is at most $(m/n)^2$. Also notice that if at least 2 balls are picked, it must be the case that there exist two attempts both of which have balls. Applying a union bound, we obtain the probability that we collect at least 2 balls is at most $\binom{b}{2}\cdot\left(\frac{m}{n}\right)^2 \le \left(\frac{bm}{n}\right)^2$. □

The next is the most important lemma, which is a bit technical. It says that if the number of non-adaptive queries is small, then the probability will be small that there exists one column such that the number of non-zero observations on that column is larger than 1.

LEMMA 3. *If $|S| \le \frac{1}{192\epsilon}\log\frac{1}{\epsilon}$, then*

$$\Pr\{\exists j \in [n], |\{(i,j) \in S \,|\, A_{i,j} \ne 0\}| \ge 2\} \le 1/8.$$

PROOF. We start with some definitions. For every $i \in [k-1]$, let x_i be the number of columns in $[n]$ such that the number of entries observed on that column is larger than 2^{i-1} but no more than 2^i. Let x_k be the number of columns in $[n]$ such that the number of entries observed on that column is larger than 2^{k-1}. More formally, for $i \in [k-1]$, let

$$x_i = \left|\left\{j \,\middle|\, 2^{i-1} < |(\cdot,j) \cap S| \le 2^i\right\}\right|,$$

and for $i = k$,

$$x_i = \left|\left\{j \,\middle|\, 2^{i-1} < |(\cdot,j) \cap S|\right\}\right|.$$

We know that

$$2|S| \ge \sum\nolimits_{i\in[k]} 2^i \cdot x_i.$$

For $i \in [k]$, let P_i bet the probability that there exists one column containing 2 or more observed non-zero entries, conditioned on the event that A has an $(n/2^{i-1}) \times (\epsilon n 2^i)$ submatrix of non-zero entries (i.e., i is chosen when it is generated in Algorithm 2). By Lemma 2, we obtain that for all $j \in [k]$,

$$P_j \le \epsilon \cdot 2^j \cdot \left(\sum_{i=1}^{j-1} x_i \cdot 4^{1+i-j} + \sum_{i=j}^{k} x_i\right).$$

Notice that the factor $\epsilon 2^j$ comes from the fact that there are only $\epsilon 2^j n$ columns that are non-zero in A. If we visit

2^i entries on a column of $n/2^{j-1}$ non-zero entries, the probability that we hit at least 2 non-zero entries is at most $\left(\frac{2^i \cdot n/2^{j-1}}{n}\right)^2 = 4^{1+i-j}$. If it is more than 1, we bound it by 1 since it is a probability. Therefore,

$$P_j \le \epsilon \cdot \left(\sum_{i=1}^{j-1} x_i \cdot 2^{2+2i-j} + \sum_{i=j}^{k} 2^j \cdot x_i\right).$$

Summing over all $j \in [k]$ yields that

$$\sum_{j\in[k]} P_j \le 12\epsilon \cdot \sum_{j\in[k]} 2^j \cdot x_j \le 24\epsilon\,|S|\,.$$

Therefore, if $|S| \le \frac{1}{192\epsilon}\log\frac{1}{\epsilon}$, then

$$\frac{1}{k}\sum_{j\in[k]} P_j \le 1/8,$$

i.e.,

$$\Pr\left\{\exists j \in [n]\,, |\{(i,j) \in S\,|A_{i,j} \ne 0\}| \ge 2\right\} \le 1/8.$$

□

Extending Lemma 3 to rows and combining with Lemma 1, we can prove Theorem 1, i.e., any non-adaptive algorithm that solves our problem takes $\Omega\left(\frac{1}{\epsilon}\log\frac{1}{\epsilon}\right)$ queries.

4. NON-ADAPTIVE RANK ONE ALGORITHM

In this section, we give a non-adaptive algorithm for the Rank problem with $O(\frac{1}{\epsilon}\log^2\frac{1}{\epsilon})$ queries when $d = 1$ and $\epsilon \le 1/e$. Let η be such that $\eta\log(1/\eta) = \epsilon$ and $\eta < 1/2$. Also let $k = \log 1/\eta$. The proposed algorithm is as follows. We describe it for an $n \times n$ matrix A, though it immediately extends to rectangular matrices as well.

Choose $R_1, \cdots, R_k$ and $C_1, \cdots, C_k$ from $[n]$ uniformly at random such that

$$R_1 \subseteq \cdots \subseteq R_k, \quad C_1 \supseteq \cdots \supseteq C_k,$$

and

$$|R_i| = c_0 2^i d, \quad |C_i| = c_0 d/2^i\eta,$$

where c_0 is a sufficiently large constant to be determined later. Denote $Q = \bigcup_{i=1}^{k}(R_i \times C_i)$, the overall set of entries the algorithm will query. Then, the algorithm computes

$$\min_{A_{(R_k,C_1)\setminus Q}} \operatorname{rank}(A_{R_k,C_1}),$$

the minimum possible rank of the matrix, and decides that "A is ϵ-far from being rank-d" iff the minimum possible rank is more than d.

Notice that the total number of entries the algorithm queries is $O(d^2\log(1/\eta)/\eta) = O((d^2/\epsilon)\log^2(1/\epsilon))$. Now we justify the correctness of the proposed algorithm for $d = 1$.

For fixed $A \in \mathbb{R}^{n\times n}$ which is ϵ-far from being rank -d, call (r,c) an augment for $R \times C \subseteq [n]\times[n]$ if $r \in [n]\setminus R$, $c \in [n]\setminus C$ and $\operatorname{rank}(A_{R\cup\{r\},C\cup\{c\}}) > \operatorname{rank}(A_{R,C})$. Let $aug(R,C)$ be the set of all the augments, that is,

$$aug(R,C) = \{(r,c) \in ([n]\setminus R)\times([n]\setminus C) : \operatorname{rank}(M_{R\cup\{r\},C\cup\{c\}}) > \operatorname{rank}(M_{R,C})\}.$$

For fixed R, C and A, define $count_r$ ($r \in [n]\setminus R$) to be the number of c's such that $(r,c) \in aug(R,C)$. Let $count^*_{i\in[n-|R|]}$ be the non-increasing reordering of the sequence $(count_r)_{r\in[n]\setminus R}$. For simplicity of notation, let $count^*_i = 0$ if $i > n-|R|$. The following lemma follows from the fact that the number of augments is at least ϵn^2 if A is ϵ-far from being rank-d and $\operatorname{rank}(A_{R,C}) \le d$, as argued in Section 2.

LEMMA 4. *If A is ϵ-far from being rank-d and $rank(A_{R,C}) \le d$, then*

$$|aug(R,C)| = \sum_{r\in[n]\setminus R} count_r = \sum_i count^*_i \ge \epsilon n^2.$$

We define the concept of an augment pattern below.

Definition 1. For M, R, C and $i \in [\log(1/\eta)]$, we say that (R,C) has augment pattern i on A iff $count^*_{n/2^i} \ge 2^{i-1}\eta n$.

Following the definition, we show the existence of at least one augment pattern for (R,C) when A is ϵ-far from being rank-d and $\operatorname{rank}(M_{R,C}) \le d$.

LEMMA 5. *If A is ϵ-far from being rank-d and $\operatorname{rank}(A_{R,C}) \le d$, then there exists i such that (R,C) has augment pattern i.*

PROOF. We prove the lemma by contradiction. Suppose that (R,C) does not have augment pattern i for all $i \in [\log(1/\eta)]$, i.e.,

$$count^*_{n/2^i} < 2^{i-1}\eta n, \quad i = 1,2,\ldots,\log(1/\eta).$$

It follows that

$$\begin{aligned}\sum_i count^*_i &= \sum_{i=\frac{n}{2}+1}^{n} count^*_i + \sum_{i=\frac{n}{4}+1}^{\frac{n}{2}} count^*_i + \cdots \\ &+ \sum_{i=\frac{n}{2^{\log(1/\eta)}}+1}^{\frac{n}{2^{\log(1/\eta)-1}}} count^*_i + \sum_{i=1}^{\eta n} count^*_i \\ &< \frac{\eta n^2}{2}\cdot(\log(1/\eta)+1) \\ &< \eta\log(1/\eta)\,n^2 \quad (\text{since } \eta < 1/2) \\ &= \epsilon n^2,\end{aligned}$$

which contradicts Lemma 4. □

Note that if (R,C) has augment pattern i on A, a uniformly random rectangle sample of dimension $c2^i \times c/2^i\eta$ will hit at least one augment with high probability, which is at least

$$\left(1-\left(1-2^{-i}\right)^{c2^i}\right)\left(1-\left(1-2^{i-1}\eta\right)^{c/2^i\eta}\right) \ge 1 - \frac{2}{e^{c/2}}.$$

We conclude this fact as

LEMMA 6. *Suppose that (R,C) has augment pattern i on A and $j \in \{i-1, i\}$. Let $R', C' \subseteq [n]$ be uniformly random such that $|R'| = c2^j$, $|C'| = c/2^j\eta$. Then the probability that (R',C') contains at least one augment of (R,C) on A is at least $1 - 2e^{-c/2}$.*

Now we are ready to show the correctness for the proposed algorithm.

THEOREM 2. *Suppose that $\epsilon \le 1/e$. For any matrix A (either of rank at most $d = 1$, or at least ϵ-far from it), the probability that the proposed algorithm is erroneous is at most $1/3$, provided that $c_0 \ge 12$.*

PROOF. If A is of rank at most 1, the algorithm will never be wrong. Now we analyze the case that A is ϵ-far from being rank-1. We discuss the two cases based on the number of augment patterns for $(\emptyset, \emptyset)$ on A.

Case (i) $(\emptyset, \emptyset)$ has only one single augment pattern.

Let i denote the only augment pattern that $(\emptyset, \emptyset)$ has. We divide R_i uniformly at random into two even parts, $R_i^{(1)}$ and $R_i^{(2)}$. Do the same with C_i, obtaining $C_i^{(1)}$ and $C_i^{(2)}$. By Lemma 6, the probability that $A_{R_i^{(1)}, C_i^{(1)}}$ contains at least one non-zero entry is at least $1 - 2e^{-c_0/4}$. Let us condition on this event.

Let $(r, c) \in (R_i^{(1)}, C_i^{(1)})$ be such that $A_{r,c} \neq 0$. Then $(\{r\}, \{c\})$ has augment pattern i by Lemma 5, while on the other hand it is impossible that $(\{r\}, \{c\})$ has augment pattern other than i, since $(\emptyset, \emptyset)$ does not have the augment pattern. Now consider the probability that $(R \backslash \{r\}, C \backslash \{c\})$ contains an augment for $(\{r\}, \{c\})$. We claim that this probability is also at least $1 - 2e^{-c_0/4}$. Since $R_i^{(2)}$ and $C_i^{(2)}$ are uniformly random given $R_i^{(1)}$ and $C_i^{(1)}$, we can use a coupling argument to show that the probability that $(R_i \backslash \{r\}, C_i \backslash \{c\})$ contains at least one augment for $(\{r\}, \{c\})$ is greater than a uniformly random sample of dimension $c_0 2^i/2 \times c_0/2^{i+1}\eta$ in $([n] \setminus \{r\}) \times ([n] \setminus \{c\})$ does.

Therefore, the probability to augment one empty matrix to a 2×2 full rank matrix is at least $1 - 4e^{-c_0/4} > 2/3$, and the algorithm answers correctly in this case.

Case (ii) $(\emptyset, \emptyset)$ has multiple augment patterns.

In this case, suppose that $(\emptyset, \emptyset)$ has augment patterns i and j $(i < j)$. Divide R_i uniformly at random into two even parts $R_i^{(1)}$ and $R_i^{(2)}$, and C_j into $C_j^{(1)}$ and $C_j^{(2)}$. Also divide $R_j \backslash R_i$ evenly into $R^{(1)}$ and $R^{(2)}$, $C_i \backslash C_j$ into $C^{(1)}$ and $C^{(2)}$. According to Lemma 6, the probability that both $(R_i^{(1)}, C_j^{(1)} \cup C^{(1)})$ and $(R_i^{(1)} \cup R^{(1)}, C_j^{(1)})$ intersect with $aug(\emptyset, \emptyset)$ is at least $1 - 4^{-c_0/4}$. Conditioned on this, we discuss two cases based on whether $(R_i^{(1)}, C_j^{(1)})$ intersects with $aug(\emptyset, \emptyset)$.

Case (ii.1): $(R_i^{(1)}, C_j^{(1)}) \cap aug(\emptyset, \emptyset) = \emptyset$. Let $(r_i, c_i) \in (R_i^{(1)}, C^{(1)})$ be such that $A_{r_i,c_i} \neq 0$ and $(r_j, c_j) \in (R^{(1)}, C_j^{(1)})$ be such that $A_{r_j,c_j} \neq 0$. Since $A_{r_i,c_j} = 0$, we know that $\mathrm{rank}(A_{(\{r_i,r_j\},\{c_i,c_j\})}) = 2$ so the algorithm answers correctly.

Case (ii.2): $(R_i^{(1)}, C_j^{(1)}) \cap aug(\emptyset, \emptyset) \neq \emptyset$. Let $(r, c) \in (R_i^{(1)}, C_j^{(1)}) \cap aug(\emptyset, \emptyset)$. Following a similar argument of case (ii.1), we can prove that the probability is at least $1 - 2e^{-c_0/4}$ that (r, c) could be augmented with augment pattern i by $(R_i \backslash \{r\}, C_i \backslash \{c\})$ (or with augment pattern j by $(R_j \backslash \{r\}, C_j \backslash \{c\})$. So the overall probability is at least $1 - 6e^{-c_0/4} > 2/3$ that the algorithm answers correctly in this case by finding a submatrix of rank 2. □

5. LOWER BOUND FOR RANK IN THE ROW MODEL

In this section, we discuss the Rank problem in the row model. Recall that we say A is ϵ-far from having property P if at least ϵn rows of A have to be changed for A to have property P. The Rank problem in this model is to test whether the matrix has rank at most d or is ϵ-far from having rank at most d.

In this model, the algorithm of [8] gives an upper bound of $O(d/\epsilon)$ rows. Next we show a matching lower bound when the entries of A come from any field $\mathbb{F}$, e.g., the real numbers. Assume that $n \geq 2d/\epsilon$ throughout this section.

First assume $\mathbb{F}$ is a finite field. Let $\mathcal{D}_1$ be a distribution over $n \times n$ matrices defined as follows. Choose a random d-dimensional subspace W in $\mathbb{F}^n$ and then choose $2\epsilon n$ uniformly random vectors from W. Place these $2\epsilon n$ vectors on $2\epsilon n$ uniformly random rows of an $n \times n$ matrix. The resulting distribution is $\mathcal{D}_1$. We define $\mathcal{D}_2$ similarly, except that W is a uniformly random $(d + \epsilon n)$-dimensional subspace in $\mathbb{F}^n$. Clearly $\mathrm{rank}(A) \leq d$ when $A \sim \mathcal{D}_1$. When $B \sim \mathcal{D}_2$, with probability $1 - o(1)$, one needs to change at least ϵn rows of B to reduce its rank to d.

By construction, adaptively choosing rows does not help in distinguishing $\mathcal{D}_1$ from $\mathcal{D}_2$, and so we may assume the query algorithm is non-adaptive. Fix $Q \subseteq \{1, \ldots, n\}$ with $|Q| = q$. Let $A_Q = (A_{ij})_{i \in Q, 1 \leq j \leq n}$ and define B_Q similarly. Each defines a distribution on $q \times n$ matrices, denoted by $\mathcal{L}(A_Q)$ and $\mathcal{L}(B_Q)$, respectively.

LEMMA 7. *Suppose that $\mathbb{F}$ is a finite field. When $q \leq \alpha d/(8\epsilon)$, it holds that $d_{TV}(\mathcal{L}(A_Q), \mathcal{L}(B_Q)) \leq \alpha + |\mathbb{F}|^{-d/4} + o(1)$, where d_{TV} denotes total variation distance.*

PROOF. When $q \leq \alpha d/(8\epsilon)$, by a Markov bound, with probability $\geq 1 - \alpha$ at most $d/4$ vectors of the chosen $2\epsilon n$ ones are read. For distribution $\mathcal{D}_1$, with probability $\geq 1 - |\mathbb{F}|^{-d/4}$, the vectors are linearly independent. For distribution $\mathcal{D}_2$, with probability $\geq 1 - o(1)$, the vectors are linearly independent. The conclusion follows immediately from the observation that conditioned on the vectors being linearly independent, they are distributed as a set of uniformly chosen $d/4$ linearly independent vectors in $\mathbb{F}^n$. □

For $\mathbb{F} = \mathbb{R}$, we define $\mathcal{D}_1$ and $\mathcal{D}_2$ similarly, except that the $2\epsilon n$ random vectors are chosen subject to the multidimensional Gaussian measure on W. Similarly to the lemma above, we have,

LEMMA 8. *Suppose that $\mathbb{F} = \mathbb{R}$ and $\alpha > 0$. When $q \leq \alpha d/(8\epsilon)$, it holds that $d_{TV}(\mathcal{L}(A_Q), \mathcal{L}(B_Q)) \leq \alpha + o(1)$.*

PROOF. When $q \leq \alpha d/(8\epsilon)$, by a Markov bound, with probability $\geq 1 - \alpha$ at most $d/4$ vectors of the chosen $2\epsilon n$ ones are read. For both distributions, the randomly chosen vectors are linearly independent almost surely. The conclusion follows immediately from the observation that conditioned on the vectors being linearly independent, they are distributed as a set of uniformly chosen $d/4$ linearly independent vectors in $\mathbb{R}^n$. □

The lower bound follows immediately as a corollary.

COROLLARY 1. *In the row model, any algorithm for the Rank problem needs to sample $\Omega(d/\epsilon)$ rows.*

6. STABLE RANK IN THE ROW MODEL

6.1 Upper Bound

Definition 2. (stable rank) Let $A \in \mathbb{R}^{n \times n}$ be a non-zero matrix. The *stable rank* of A is $\mathrm{srank}(A) = \|A\|_F^2 / \|A\|^2$.

We will design an algorithm for the StableRank problem for $n \times n$ matrices. We denote the i-th row of A by $A_{i,\cdot}$.

Algorithm 3 Algorithm for the StableRank problem

```
    // c = (1/8)(1 - 1/d)^2
1:  q ← Θ( d/((1 - 1/d)^6 ε^2) log n + d log n log(d log n) )
2:  Sample q rows of A, forming Ã
3:  X ← (n/q) ||Ã||_F^2
4:  if X ≤ (9/10)(1 - 1/d)εn then
5:      output 'stable rank ≤ d'
6:  else
7:      if (n/q)||Ã||^2 ≥ X/((1 + cd/(d-1))d) then
8:          output 'stable rank ≤ d'
9:      else
10:         output 'εn/d-far from having stable rank ≤ d'
11:     end if
12: end if
```

LEMMA 9. *Suppose that $d/\epsilon \geq 2$. If A is (ϵ/d)-far from having stable rank $\leq d$, then*

$$\|A\|_F^2 \geq (\frac{\epsilon n}{d} - 1)(d-1) \tag{1}$$

$$\|A\|^2 \leq (1 + \frac{\epsilon}{d}(1 - \frac{1}{d}))\frac{\|A\|_F^2}{d} - (1 - \frac{1}{d})(\frac{\epsilon n}{d} - 1). \tag{2}$$

PROOF. Suppose that $x \in S^{n-1}$ satisfies $\|A\| = \|Ax\|_2$. Without loss of generality, assume that $\langle A_{1,\cdot}, x\rangle^2 \leq \langle A_{2,\cdot}, x\rangle^2 \leq \cdots \leq \langle A_{n,\cdot}, x\rangle^2$. Let $m = \lceil \epsilon n/d \rceil - 1$, so that $n > 2m$. Changing each $A_{i,\cdot}$ $(1 \leq i \leq m)$ to x forms a new matrix B, and it must hold that $\operatorname{srank}(B) > d$.

It is clear that $\|B\|^2 \geq m$ and $\|B\|_F^2 \leq \|A\|_F^2 + m$, so

$$d < \operatorname{srank}(B) \leq \frac{\|A\|_F^2 + m}{m},$$

whence (1) follows.

Next we prove the second conclusion. It is clear that

$$S_m := \sum_{i=1}^m \langle A_{i,\cdot}, x\rangle^2 \leq \frac{m}{n}\sum_{i=1}^n \langle A_{i,\cdot}, x\rangle^2 = \frac{m}{n}\|A\|^2 \leq \frac{m}{n}\cdot\frac{\|A\|_F^2}{d}.$$

Observe that

$$\|B\|_F^2 \leq \|A\|_F^2 - \sum_{i=1}^m \|A_{i,\cdot}\|_2^2 + m \leq \|A\|_F^2 - S_m + m$$

and

$$\|B\|^2 \geq \|A\|^2 - S_m + m.$$

It follows that

$$d < \operatorname{srank}(B) \leq \frac{\|A\|_F^2 - S_m + m}{\|A\|^2 - S_m + m}$$

whence (2) follows. □

LEMMA 10. *In Algorithm 3, it holds that $|X - \|A\|_F^2| \leq \frac{1}{8}(1 - \frac{1}{d})^2 \epsilon n$ with probability $\geq 9/10$.*

PROOF. Let $\tau = \frac{1}{8}(1 - \frac{1}{d})^2$. By a Chernoff bound, sampling q rows uniformly gives failure probability $2e^{-2q(\tau\epsilon)^2} < 0.1$, that is, $q = \Omega(1/(\tau\epsilon)^2)$. □

LEMMA 11 ([10]). *Let $\tilde{A}$ be a matrix formed by r independent row samples of A according to probability $p_t \geq \beta\|A_{t,\cdot}\|_2^2/\|A\|_F^2$. If $r \geq \frac{4\operatorname{srank}(A)}{\beta\eta^2}\ln\frac{2n}{\delta}$ then with probability at least $1 - \delta$, it holds that $(1-\eta)\|A\|^2 \leq \frac{n}{r}\|\tilde{A}\|^2 \leq (1+\eta)\|A\|^2$.*

LEMMA 12. *Let $X \sim \operatorname{Unif}(S^{n-1})$ then $\|x\|_\infty \leq \sqrt{\frac{2\log n}{n}}$ with probability $\geq 1 - n^{-2}$.*

THEOREM 3. *Suppose that $\|A\|_{\text{row}} = 1$, then Algorithm 3 is a correct algorithm for the* **StableRank** *problem with success probability ≥ 0.6 in the row model. It reads $O(\frac{d\log n}{(1-\frac{1}{d})^6\epsilon^2} + d\log n\log(d\log n))$ rows.*

PROOF. By Lemma 1, if A is far from having stable rank at most d, it must hold that $\|A\|_F^2 \geq (1 - 1/d)\epsilon n$. Conditioned on the event that X is a good estimator to $\|A\|_F^2$, that is, X satisfies the conclusion of Lemma 10, it holds that $X \geq \frac{9}{10}(1 - \frac{1}{d})\epsilon n$. Hence the algorithm is correct on Line 5. Now we assume that $\|A\|_F^2 \geq (1 - 1/d)\epsilon n$. Let $\eta = \frac{c\epsilon n}{\|A\|_F^2} \leq \frac{cd}{d-1} =: \eta'$ then $(1 - \frac{\tau\eta'}{c})\|A\|_F^2 \leq X \leq (1 + \frac{\tau\eta'}{c})\|A\|_F^2$.

Now suppose that $\operatorname{srank}(A) > c_1 d$. Let U be a uniformly random $n \times n$ orthogonal matrix. Since we only care about norms of $\tilde{A}$ we can replace $\tilde{A}$ with $\tilde{A}U$, which is a random sample of q rows of AU. Observe that $(AU)_{i,\cdot}$ is a random vector uniform on $\|A_{i,\cdot}\|_2 S^{n-1}$, it follows from Lemma 12 and a union bound that $\|A_{i,\cdot}\|_\infty \leq 2\|A_{i,\cdot}\|_2^2(\log n)/n$ for all i with probability $\geq 1 - 1/n$. Conditioned on this event, $\|A\|_{\text{col}}^2 \leq 2\|A\|_F^2(\log n)/n \leq 2\log n$. Invoking [14, Theorem 1.8],

$$\begin{aligned}\mathbb{E}\|\tilde{A}'\| &\leq C_1\sqrt{\frac{q}{n}}\|A\| + C_2\sqrt{\log q}\cdot\sqrt{\frac{2\log n}{n}}\|A\|_F \\ &\leq C_1\sqrt{\frac{q}{c_1 d}}\cdot\frac{\|A\|_F}{\sqrt{n}} + 2C_2\sqrt{\log q\log n}\cdot\frac{\|A\|_F}{\sqrt{n}}\end{aligned}$$

and thus with probability ≥ 0.9,

$$\begin{aligned}\|\tilde{A}'\| &\leq 10C_1\sqrt{\frac{q}{c_1 d}}\cdot\frac{\|A\|_F}{\sqrt{n}} + 20C_2\sqrt{\log q\log n}\cdot\frac{\|A\|_F}{\sqrt{n}} \\ &\leq \frac{1}{\sqrt{1 - \frac{\tau\eta'}{c}}}\left(10C_1\sqrt{\frac{q}{c_1 d}} + 20C_2\sqrt{\log q\log n}\right)\sqrt{\frac{X}{n}}\end{aligned}$$

On the other hand, when $\operatorname{srank}(A) \leq d$, it holds with probability ≥ 0.9 that

$$\|\tilde{A}'\| \geq \frac{1}{2}\sqrt{\frac{q}{n}}\|A\| \geq \frac{1}{2}\sqrt{\frac{q}{n}}\frac{\|A\|_F}{\sqrt{d}} \geq \frac{1}{2}\sqrt{\frac{q}{n}}\sqrt{1 - \frac{\tau\eta'}{c}}\sqrt{\frac{X}{d}}$$

By our choice of parameters,

$$\begin{aligned}&\frac{1}{2}\sqrt{\frac{q}{n}}\sqrt{1 - \frac{\tau\eta'}{c}}\sqrt{\frac{X}{d}} \\ &\geq \frac{1}{\sqrt{1 - \frac{\tau\eta'}{c}}}\left(10C_1\sqrt{\frac{q}{c_1 d}} + 20C_2\sqrt{\log q\log n}\right)\sqrt{\frac{X}{n}},\end{aligned}$$

provided that c_1 is less than a constant times $1/(1 - \frac{1}{d})^2$ and $c = \tau$. Hence we can distinguish the two cases.

Now we assume that $\operatorname{srank}(A) \leq c_1 d$. Let $\beta = \|A\|_F^2/n$, so $\beta\|A_{i,\cdot}\|_2^2/\|A\|_F^2 \leq 1/n$ for all i, that is, uniform sampling satisfies the assumption of Lemma 11. It then follows from Lemma 11 that with probability at least 0.9, it holds that

$$(1-\eta)\|A\|^2 \leq \frac{n}{q}\|\tilde{A}\|^2 \leq (1+\eta)\|A\|^2.$$

Conditioned on this event; in the first case, $\|A\|^2 \geq \|A\|_F^2/d$; in the second case, by Lemma 9, $\|A\|^2 \leq (1 + \frac{\epsilon}{d}(1 - \frac{1}{d}))\frac{\|A\|_F^2}{d} -$

$(1-\frac{1}{d})(\frac{\epsilon n}{d}-1)$ and thus

$$\frac{n}{q}\|\tilde{A}\|^2 \le (1+\eta)\left(\frac{1+\frac{\epsilon}{d}(1-\frac{1}{d})}{1-\tau\eta/c}\frac{X}{d} - (1-\frac{1}{d})(\frac{\epsilon n}{d}-1)\right).$$

It is not difficult to establish that

$$(1+\eta)\left(\frac{1+\frac{\epsilon}{d}(1-\frac{1}{d})}{1-\tau\eta/c}\frac{X}{d} - (1-\frac{1}{d})(\frac{\epsilon n}{d}-1)\right) < \frac{1-\eta}{1+\tau\eta/c}\cdot\frac{X}{d}$$

when $c = \tau = \frac{1}{8}(1-\frac{1}{d})^2$. Therefore we can distinguish the two cases. Combining with the discussion above for the case where $\mathrm{srank}(A) > c_1 d$, we see that Line 8 and Line 10 are correct. □

6.2 Lower bound

Let $\mathcal{D}_1$ be a distribution over $n\times n$ matrices defined as follows. Choose a random $x_0 \in S^{n-1}$ and place x_0 in n/d randomly chosen rows of an $n\times n$ matrix A. Place the first $n-n/d$ rows of a random orthogonal matrix in the remaining $n-n/d$ rows of A. Let $\mathcal{D}_1$ be the distribution of A.

We define $\mathcal{D}_2$ similarly as follows. Choose random $x_0 \in S^{n-1}$ and place x_0 in $(1-2\epsilon)n/d$ randomly chosen rows of an $n\times n$ matrix B. Place the first $n-(1-2\epsilon)n/d$ rows of a random orthogonal matrix in the remaining $n-(1-\epsilon)n/d$ rows of B. Let $\mathcal{D}_2$ be the distribution of B.

Suppose that $A\sim\mathcal{D}_1$ and $B\sim\mathcal{D}_2$. It is clear $\|A\|_F^2 = n$ and $\|A\|^2 \ge n/d$, and so $\mathrm{srank}(A)\le d$. Now we upper bound $\|B\|^2$. With probability 1, we know that x_0 does not lie in the span of the orthogonal rows, and so $\|Bx\|^2 < 1+(1-3\epsilon)n/d$, that is, $\|B\|^2 < 1+(1-3\epsilon)n/d \le (1-2\epsilon)n/d$. Changing $\delta n/d$ rows of B forms a new matrix B' with $\mathrm{srank}(B')\le d$. We know that $\|B'\|_F^2 \ge \|B\|_F^2 - \delta n/d = (1-\delta/d)n$ and $\|B'\|^2 \le \|B\|^2 + \delta n/d$. It follows from $\|B'\|_F^2/d \le \|B'\|^2$ that $1-\delta/d \le 1-2\epsilon+\delta$, thus $\delta \ge 2\epsilon(1+1/d) > \epsilon$, and we conclude that with probability 1, the matrix B is (ϵ/d)-far from having stable rank $\le d$.

Fix $Q\subseteq\{1,\dots,n\}$ with $|Q|=q$. Let $A_Q = (A_{ij})_{i\in Q,1\le j\le n}$ and define B_Q similarly. Each defines a distribution on $q\times n$ matrices, denoted by $\mathcal{L}(A_Q)$ and $\mathcal{L}(B_Q)$, respectively. Also denote by $B(n,p)$ the binomial distribution of n trials and success probability p.

LEMMA 13. *The Hellinger distance between two binomial distributions is given by*

$$d_H(B(n,p),B(n,q)) = \sqrt{1-(\sqrt{pq}+\sqrt{(1-p)(1-q)})^n}.$$

LEMMA 14. *Suppose that $d\ge 2$. When $q\le \alpha^2 d/(18\epsilon^2)$, it holds that $d_{TV}(\mathcal{L}(A_Q),\mathcal{L}(B_Q)) \le \alpha + o(1)$.*

PROOF. Observe that A_Q and B_Q contain the same number of rows of x_0 then the conditional distributions are the same. Note that the distance between $\mathcal{L}(A_Q)$ and $B(q,1/d)$ is $o(1)$ and a similar result holds for $\mathcal{L}(B_Q)$ and $B(q,\frac{1-3\epsilon}{d})$. Therefore using that $\sqrt{2}$ times the Hellinger distance is at least as large as the variation distance, we have,

$$\begin{aligned} &d_{TV}(\mathcal{L}(A_Q),\mathcal{L}(B_Q)) \\ &= d_{TV}(B(q,\frac{1}{d}),B(q,\frac{1-3\epsilon}{d})) + o(1) \\ &\le \sqrt{2}d_H(B(q,\frac{1}{d}),B(q,\frac{1-3\epsilon}{d})) + o(1) \\ &\le 2\left(1-\left(\sqrt{\frac{1-3\epsilon}{d^2}}+\sqrt{\left(1-\frac{1}{d}\right)\left(1-\frac{1}{d}+\frac{3\epsilon}{d}\right)}\right)^q\right) + o(1) \end{aligned}$$

It is not difficult to verify that

$$\sqrt{\frac{1-3\epsilon}{d^2}}+\sqrt{\left(1-\frac{1}{d}\right)\left(1-\frac{1}{d}+\frac{3\epsilon}{d}\right)} \ge 1-\frac{9\epsilon^2}{d}$$

whenever $d\ge 2$ and $0<\epsilon<\frac{1}{3}$. Therefore, it holds that

$$d_{TV}(\mathcal{L}(A_Q),\mathcal{L}(B_Q)) \le \sqrt{2\cdot\frac{9q\epsilon^2}{d}} + o(1) \le \alpha + o(1).$$

whenever $q \le \frac{\alpha^2}{18}\cdot\frac{d}{\epsilon^2}$. □

The lower bound follows immediately as a corollary.

COROLLARY 2. *Suppose that $d\ge 2$. Under the row sampling model, any algorithm that is correct on the* STABLERANK *problem needs to sample $\Omega(d/\epsilon^2)$ rows.*

7. EMPIRICAL RESULTS

All programs are written in MATLAB and the source code can be found at `http://www.mpi-inf.mpg.de/~yli/codes.pdf`.

7.1 Stable Rank Testing

Algorithm 3 takes $\tilde{O}(\frac{d}{\epsilon^2}\log n)$ row samples with a theoretical guarantee, however, a literal interpretation of the bound makes it less useful in practice, since for $d=2$, $\epsilon=0.1$, it holds that $d\log n/\epsilon^2 > n$ for $n\le 1500$. Indeed, the theoretical upper bound is too pessimistic, i.e., very often we do not need so many samples for real data sets. We justify our thoughts in the following experiment.

We test our algorithm with the University of Florida Sparse Matrix Collection[1]. There are 628 square real matrices with dimension between 100 and 1000 (inclusive). Among them, there are 220 matrices at least 0.1-far from having stable rank 2. There are also 35 square matrices with stable rank ≤ 2. For each matrix A of the 255 matrices, we determine the minimum q such that our algorithm, when sampling q rows at random, succeeds with probability ≥ 0.9 in distinguishing whether its stable rank is at most 2, or it is at least 0.1-far from having stable rank 2. The probability is determined by 100 independent trials. The cumulative distribution of q/n (where n is the dimension of A) is plotted in Figure 2. We can see that our algorithm needs to sample only at most 15% of the rows for 90% of the matrices. The remaining 10% have relatively small stable rank and it is natural to expect that more rows are needed.

We conducted similar experiments for $d=3$ and $d=5$, too. The results are also plotted in Figure 2. Regarding $d=3$, there are 174 matrices at least 0.1-far from having stable rank 3 and 67 matrices with stable rank ≤ 3. We ran our algorithm on each of the 81 matrices and plotted the cumulative distribution of q/n. We can see that our algorithm needs to sample only at most 15% of the rows for 90% of the 241 matrices. Regarding $d=5$, there are 105 matrices at least 0.1-far from having stable rank 5 and 161 matrices with stable rank ≤ 5. We can see that our algorithm needs to sample only at most 10% of the rows for 90%, and 15% of the rows for 95%, of the 266 matrices.

7.2 Rank Testing

We have seen there is a gap of a $1/\epsilon$ factor in the theoretical results between $O(d^2/\epsilon^2)$ samples for the non-adaptive

[1] `http://www.cise.ufl.edu/research/sparse/matrices/`

algorithm and $O(d^2/\epsilon)$ samples for the adaptive one. As above, both bounds could be too pessimistic as well. Thus we design the following experiments to show that the adaptive tester has a real advantage over the non-adaptive algorithm even when both algorithms read much fewer samples than the respective theoretical upper bound.

We conducted three sets of experiments on different matrix distributions as follows.

- strip distribution:

$$A = P\begin{pmatrix}\sum_{j=1}^{d+1} x_j y_j^T & 0 \\ 0 & 0\end{pmatrix} Q,$$

where $x_1, \ldots, x_{d+1}$ are i.i.d. $N(0, I_{\epsilon n})$ vectors, $y_1, \ldots, y_{d+1}$ are i.i.d. $N(0, I_n)$ vectors, P and Q are independent random $n \times n$ permutation matrices.

- rectangular distribution:

$$A = P\begin{pmatrix}\sum_{j=1}^{d+1} x_j y_j^T & 0 \\ 0 & 0\end{pmatrix} Q,$$

where $x_1, \ldots, x_{d+1}$ are i.i.d. $N(0, I_{n/2^i-1})$ vectors and $y_1, \ldots, y_{d+1}$ are i.i.d. $N(0, I_{\epsilon n 2^i})$ vectors, i is chosen uniformly at random from $\{1, \ldots, \lfloor\log(1/\epsilon)\rfloor\}$, P and Q are independent random $n\times n$ permutation matrices.

- square distribution:

$$A = P\begin{pmatrix}\sum_{j=1}^{d+1} x_j x_j^T & 0 \\ 0 & 0\end{pmatrix} Q,$$

where $x_1, \ldots, x_{d+1}$ are i.i.d. $N(0, I_{\lfloor\sqrt{\epsilon} n\rfloor})$ vectors, P and Q are independent random $n\times n$ permutation matrices.

In each case it holds that $\text{rank}(A) = d + 1$ with probability 1. We consider three cases of d: $d = 1, 2, 5$. For both the strip and the square distribution, we set $n = 1000$ and $\epsilon = 0.01$, 0.03, 0.05, 0.07, 0.09, 0.11, 0.15, 0.20, 0.25, 0.30, 0.35, 0.40, 0.45, 0.5; for the rectangular distribution we set $n = 1024$ and $\epsilon = 1/128$, 1/64, 1/32, 1/16, 1/8, 1/4, 1/2. For each configuration of d and ϵ and each matrix distribution, we ran both the non-adaptive query algorithm [8] and the adaptive query algorithm (Algorithm 1) for 1000 times independently to obtain the number of queries needed to conclude $\text{rank}(A) > d$ with a success probability of at least 0.9. The results are shown in Figure 1 in logarithmic scale.

In all settings above, adaptive queries outperform non-adaptive ones, and particularly heavily for small ϵ. It is also notable that the strip distribution is especially adversarial for the non-adaptive tester, which needs to makes at least $1/\epsilon^2$ queries. When $\epsilon = 0.01$, the number of adaptive queries is only 7.1%, 9.4%, 12.4% of that of non-adaptive queries for $d = 1$, 2, 5, respectively. Even when $\epsilon = 0.5$, the number of adaptive queries is less than 1/3 of that of non-adaptive queries. The difference between non-adaptive and adaptive queries is less pronounced under the other two distributions, still the number of adaptive queries is at most a half of that of non-adaptive ones.

8. ACKNOWLEDGEMENTS

David Woodruff would like to acknowledge the support from the XDATA program of the Defense Advanced Research Projects Agency (DARPA), administered through Air Force Research Laboratory contract FA8750-12-C0323.

9. REFERENCES

[1] D. M. Blei, A. Y. Ng, and M. I. Jordan. Latent dirichlet allocation. *the Journal of machine Learning research*, 2003.

[2] E. J. Candès, X. Li, Y. Ma, and J. Wright. Robust principal component analysis? *J. ACM*, 58(3):11, 2011.

[3] C. H. Q. Ding and X. He. *K*-means clustering via principal component analysis. In *ICML*, 2004.

[4] D. Feldman, M. Schmidt, and C. Sohler. Turning big data into tiny data: Constant-size coresets for k-means, pca and projective clustering. In *Proceedings of the Annual ACM-SIAM Symposium on Discrete Algorithms*, 2013.

[5] O. Goldreich. A brief introduction to property testing. In *Studies in Complexity and Cryptography*, pages 465–469. 2011.

[6] H. Hotelling. Analysis of a complex of statistical variables into principal components. *Journal of educational psychology*, 24(6):417, 1933.

[7] I. T. Jolliffe. *Graphical Representation of Data Using Principal Components*. Springer, 2002.

[8] R. Krauthgamer and O. Sasson. Property testing of data dimensionality. In *SODA*, pages 18–27, 2003.

[9] D. D. Lee and H. S. Seung. Algorithms for non-negative matrix factorization. *Advances in Neural Information Processing Systems*, 2001.

[10] M. Magdon-Ismail. Row sampling for matrix algorithms via a non-commutative bernstein bound. arXiv:1008.0587, 2010.

[11] M. W. Mahoney. Randomized algorithms for matrices and data. *Foundations and Trends in Machine Learning*, 3(2):123–224, 2011.

[12] M. Parnas and D. Ron. Testing metric properties. In *STOC*, pages 276–285, 2001.

[13] K. Pearson. On lines and planes of closest fit to systems of points in space. *Philosophical Magazine*, 2(6):559–572, 1901.

[14] M. Rudelson and R. Vershynin. Sampling from large matrices: An approach through geometric functional analysis. *J. ACM*, 54(4), July 2007.

[15] B. M. Sarwar, G. Karypis, J. A. Konstan, and J. Riedl. Application of dimensionality reduction in recommender systems ï£¡ a case study. In *Proceedings of the ACM WebKDD Workshop*, 2000.

[16] J. A. Tropp. Column subset selection, matrix factorization, and eigenvalue optimization. In *SODA*, pages 978–986, 2009.

[17] C. Yang, T. Han, L. Quan, and C.-L. Tai. Parsing façade with rank-one approximation. In *CVPR*, pages 1720–1727, 2012.

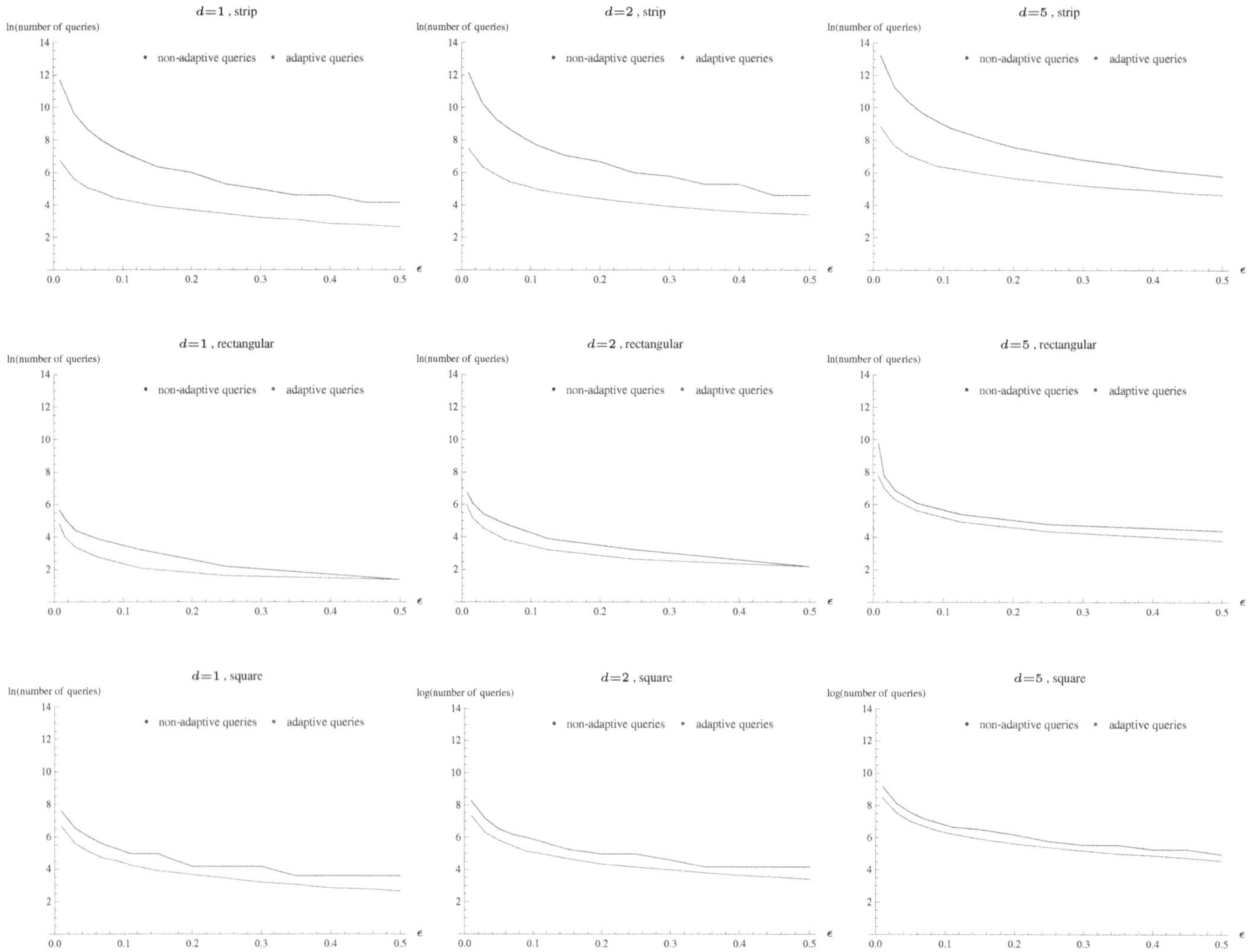

Figure 1: Experiment results for rank. The first row corresponds to the case where A is subject to the strip distribution, the second row the rectangular distribution and the third row the square distribution.

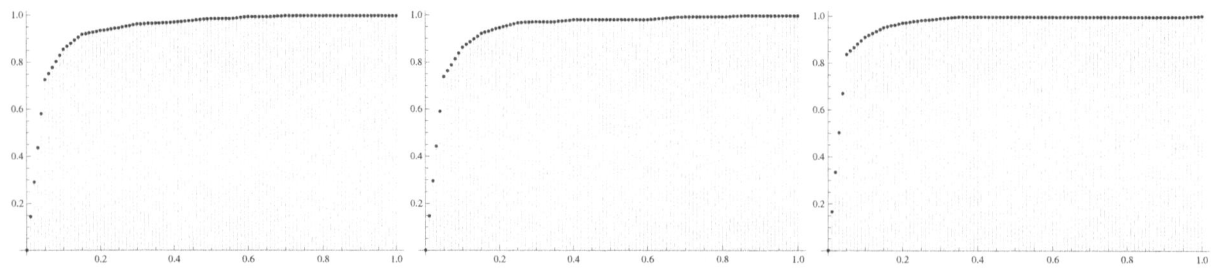

Figure 2: Experiment results for stable rank under row access model. The horizontal axis represents q/n, the percentage of rows sampled. The vertical axis is percentage of the tested matrices for which the algorithm succeeds with probability ≥ 0.9 at the corresponding sampling rate. The three plots correspond to $d = 2, 3, 5$, respectively, from left to right.

DeepWalk: Online Learning of Social Representations

Bryan Perozzi
Stony Brook University
Department of Computer Science

Rami Al-Rfou
Stony Brook University
Department of Computer Science

Steven Skiena
Stony Brook University
Department of Computer Science

{bperozzi, ralrfou, skiena}@cs.stonybrook.edu

ABSTRACT

We present DEEPWALK, a novel approach for learning latent representations of vertices in a network. These latent representations encode social relations in a continuous vector space, which is easily exploited by statistical models. DEEPWALK generalizes recent advancements in language modeling and unsupervised feature learning (or *deep learning*) from sequences of words to graphs.

DEEPWALK uses local information obtained from truncated random walks to *learn* latent representations by treating walks as the equivalent of sentences. We demonstrate DEEPWALK's latent representations on several multi-label network classification tasks for social networks such as BlogCatalog, Flickr, and YouTube. Our results show that DEEPWALK outperforms challenging baselines which are allowed a global view of the network, especially in the presence of missing information. DEEPWALK's representations can provide F_1 scores up to 10% higher than competing methods when labeled data is sparse. In some experiments, DEEPWALK's representations are able to outperform all baseline methods while using 60% less training data.

DEEPWALK is also scalable. It is an online learning algorithm which builds useful incremental results, and is trivially parallelizable. These qualities make it suitable for a broad class of real world applications such as network classification, and anomaly detection.

Categories and Subject Descriptors

H.2.8 [**Database Management**]: Database Applications - Data Mining; I.2.6 [**Artificial Intelligence**]: Learning; I.5.1 [**Pattern Recognition**]: Model - Statistical

Keywords

social networks; deep learning; latent representations; learning with partial labels; network classification; online learning

KDD'14, August 24–27, 2014, New York, NY, USA.

ACM 978-1-4503-2956-9/14/08 ...$15.00.
http://dx.doi.org/10.1145/2623330.2623732

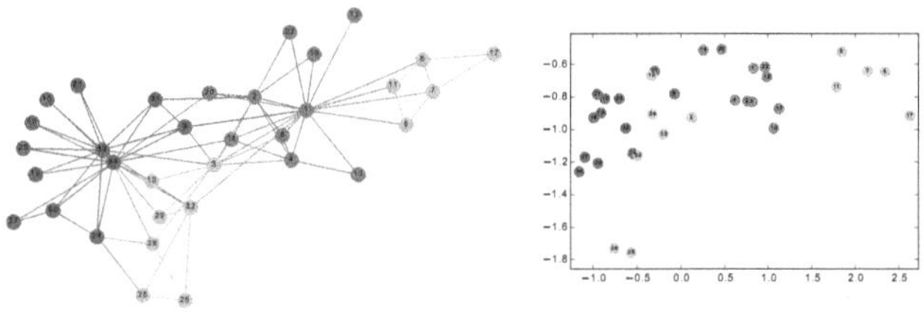

(a) Input: Karate Graph (b) Output: Representation

Figure 1: Our proposed method *learns* a latent space representation of social interactions in $\mathbb{R}^d$. The learned representation encodes community structure so it can be easily exploited by standard classification methods. Here, our method is used on Zachary's Karate network [44] to generate a latent representation in $\mathbb{R}^2$. Note the correspondence between community structure in the input graph and the embedding. Vertex colors represent a modularity-based clustering of the input graph.

1. INTRODUCTION

The sparsity of a network representation is both a strength and a weakness. Sparsity enables the design of efficient discrete algorithms, but can make it harder to generalize in statistical learning. Machine learning applications in networks (such as network classification [16, 37], content recommendation [12], anomaly detection [6], and missing link prediction [23]) must be able to deal with this sparsity in order to survive.

In this paper we introduce *deep learning* (unsupervised feature learning) [3] techniques, which have proven successful in natural language processing, into network analysis for the first time. We develop an algorithm (DEEPWALK) that learns *social representations* of a graph's vertices, by modeling a stream of short random walks. Social representations are latent features of the vertices that capture neighborhood similarity and community membership. These latent representations encode social relations in a continuous vector space with a relatively small number of dimensions. DEEPWALK generalizes neural language models to process a special language composed of a set of randomly-generated walks. These neural language models have been used to capture the semantic and syntactic structure of human language [7], and even logical analogies [29].

DEEPWALK takes a graph as input and produces a latent representation as an output. The result of applying our method to the well-studied Karate network is shown in Figure 1. The graph, as typically presented by force-directed layouts, is shown in Figure 1a. Figure 1b shows the output of our method with 2 latent dimensions. Beyond the striking similarity, we note that linearly separable portions of (1b) correspond to clusters found through modularity maximization in the input graph (1a) (shown as vertex colors).

To demonstrate DeepWalk's potential in real world scenarios, we evaluate its performance on challenging multi-label network classification problems in large heterogeneous graphs. In the relational classification problem, the links between feature vectors violate the traditional *i.i.d.* assumption. Techniques to address this problem typically use approximate inference techniques [32] to leverage the dependency information to improve classification results. We distance ourselves from these approaches by learning label-independent representations of the graph. Our representation quality is not influenced by the choice of labeled vertices, so they can be shared among tasks.

DeepWalk outperforms other latent representation methods for creating *social dimensions* [39, 41], especially when labeled nodes are scarce. Strong performance with our representations is possible with very simple linear classifiers (e.g. logistic regression). Our representations are general, and can be combined with any classification method (including iterative inference methods). DeepWalk achieves all of that while being an online algorithm that is trivially parallelizable.

Our contributions are as follows:

- We introduce deep learning as a tool to analyze graphs, to build robust representations that are suitable for statistical modeling. DeepWalk learns structural regularities present within short random walks.
- We extensively evaluate our representations on multi-label classification tasks on several social networks. We show significantly increased classification performance in the presence of label sparsity, getting improvements 5%-10% of Micro F_1, on the sparsest problems we consider. In some cases, DeepWalk's representations can outperform its competitors even when given 60% less training data.
- We demonstrate the scalability of our algorithm by building representations of web-scale graphs, (such as YouTube) using a parallel implementation. Moreover, we describe the minimal changes necessary to build a streaming version of our approach.

The rest of the paper is arranged as follows. In Sections 2 and 3, we discuss the problem formulation of classification in data networks, and how it relates to our work. In Section 4 we present DeepWalk, our approach for Social Representation Learning. We outline ours experiments in Section 5, and present their results in Section 6. We close with a discussion of related work in Section 7, and our conclusions.

2. PROBLEM DEFINITION

We consider the problem of classifying members of a social network into one or more categories. Let $G = (V, E)$, where V represent the members of the network, E are their connections, $E \subseteq (V \times V)$, and $G_L = (V, E, X, Y)$ is a partially labeled social network, with attributes $X \in \mathbb{R}^{|V| \times S}$ where S is the size of the feature space for each attribute vector, and $Y \in \mathbb{R}^{|V| \times |\mathcal{Y}|}$, $\mathcal{Y}$ is the set of labels.

In a traditional machine learning classification setting, we aim to learn a hypothesis H that maps elements of X to the labels set $\mathcal{Y}$. In our case, we can utilize the significant information about the dependence of the examples embedded in the structure of G to achieve superior performance.

In the literature, this is known as the relational classification (or the *collective classification* problem [37]). Traditional approaches to relational classification pose the problem as an inference in an undirected Markov network, and then use iterative approximate inference algorithms (such as the iterative classification algorithm [32], Gibbs Sampling [15], or label relaxation [19]) to compute the posterior distribution of labels given the network structure.

We propose a different approach to capture the network topology information. Instead of mixing the label space as part of the feature space, we propose an unsupervised method which learns features that capture the graph structure *independent* of the labels' distribution.

This separation between the structural representation and the labeling task avoids cascading errors, which can occur in iterative methods [34]. Moreover, the same representation can be used for multiple classification problems concerning that network.

Our goal is to learn $X_E \in \mathbb{R}^{|V| \times d}$, where d is small number of latent dimensions. These low-dimensional representations are distributed; meaning each social phenomena is expressed by a subset of the dimensions and each dimension contributes to a subset of the social concepts expressed by the space.

Using these structural features, we will augment the attributes space to help the classification decision. These features are general, and can be used with any classification algorithm (including iterative methods). However, we believe that the greatest utility of these features is their easy integration with simple machine learning algorithms. They scale appropriately in real-world networks, as we will show in Section 6.

3. LEARNING SOCIAL REPRESENTATIONS

We seek to learn social representations with the following characteristics:

- **Adaptability** - Real social networks are constantly evolving; new social relations should not require repeating the learning process all over again.
- **Community aware** - The distance between latent dimensions should represent a metric for evaluating social similarity between the corresponding members of the network. This allows generalization in networks with homophily.
- **Low dimensional** - When labeled data is scarce low-dimensional models generalize better, and speed up convergence and inference.
- **Continuous** - We require latent representations to model partial community membership in continuous space. In addition to providing a nuanced view of community membership, a continuous representation has smooth decision boundaries between communities which allows more robust classification.

Our method satisfies these requirements by learning representation for vertices from a stream of short random walks, using optimization techniques originally designed for language modeling. Here, we review the basics of both random walks and language modeling, and describe how their combination satisfies our requirements.

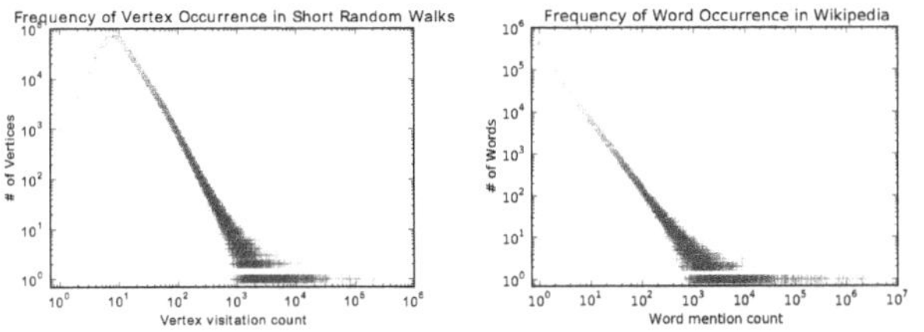

(a) YouTube Social Graph (b) Wikipedia Article Text

Figure 2: The distribution of vertices appearing in short random walks (2a) follows a power-law, much like the distribution of words in natural language (2b).

3.1 Random Walks

We denote a random walk rooted at vertex v_i as $\mathcal{W}_{v_i}$. It is a stochastic process with random variables $\mathcal{W}^1_{v_i}, \mathcal{W}^2_{v_i}, \dots, \mathcal{W}^k_{v_i}$ such that $\mathcal{W}^{k+1}_{v_i}$ is a vertex chosen at random from the neighbors of vertex v_k. Random walks have been used as a similarity measure for a variety of problems in content recommendation [12] and community detection [2]. They are also the foundation of a class of *output sensitive* algorithms which use them to compute local community structure information in time sublinear to the size of the input graph [38].

It is this connection to local structure that motivates us to use a *stream* of short random walks as our basic tool for extracting information from a network. In addition to capturing community information, using random walks as the basis for our algorithm gives us two other desirable properties. First, local exploration is easy to parallelize. Several random walkers (in different threads, processes, or machines) can simultaneously explore different parts of the same graph. Secondly, relying on information obtained from short random walks make it possible to accommodate small changes in the graph structure without the need for global recomputation. We can iteratively update the learned model with new random walks from the changed region in time sub-linear to the entire graph.

3.2 Connection: Power laws

Having chosen online random walks as our primitive for capturing graph structure, we now need a suitable method to capture this information. If the degree distribution of a connected graph follows a power law (i.e. *scale-free*), we observe that the frequency which vertices appear in the short random walks will also follow a power-law distribution.

Word frequency in natural language follows a similar distribution, and techniques from language modeling account for this distributional behavior. To emphasize this similarity we show two different power-law distributions in Figure 2. The first comes from a series of short random walks on a scale-free graph, and the second comes from the text of 100,000 articles from the English Wikipedia.

A core contribution of our work is the idea that techniques which have been used to model natural language (where the symbol frequency follows a power law distribution (or *Zipf's law*)) can be re-purposed to model community structure in networks. We spend the rest of this section reviewing the growing work in language modeling, and transforming it to learn representations of vertices which satisfy our criteria.

3.3 Language Modeling

The goal of language modeling is to estimate the likelihood of a specific sequence of words appearing in a corpus. More formally, given a sequence of words $W_1^n = (w_0, w_1, \cdots, w_n)$, where $w_i \in \mathcal{V}$ ($\mathcal{V}$ is the vocabulary), we would like to maximize the $\Pr(w_n | w_0, w_1, \cdots, w_{n-1})$ over all the training corpus. Recent work in representation learning has focused on using probabilistic neural networks to build general representations of words which extend the scope of language modeling beyond its original goals.

In this work, we present a generalization of language modeling to explore the graph through a stream of short random walks. These walks can be thought of as short sentences and phrases in a special language; the direct analog is to estimate the likelihood of observing vertex v_i given all the previous vertices visited so far in the random walk, i.e.

$$\Pr\left(v_i \mid (v_1, v_2, \cdots, v_{i-1})\right) \tag{1}$$

Our goal is to learn a latent representation, not only a probability distribution of node co-occurrences, and so we introduce a mapping function $\Phi\colon v \in V \mapsto \mathbb{R}^{|V| \times d}$. This mapping Φ represents the latent social representation associated with each vertex v in the graph. (In practice, we represent Φ by a $|V| \times d$ matrix of free parameters, which will serve later on as our X_E). The problem then, is to estimate the likelihood:

$$\Pr\Big(v_i \mid \left(\Phi(v_1), \Phi(v_2), \cdots, \Phi(v_{i-1})\right)\Big) \tag{2}$$

However, as the walk length grows, computing this conditional probability becomes unfeasible.

A recent relaxation in language modeling [27, 28] turns the prediction problem on its head. First, instead of using the context to predict a missing word, it uses one word to predict the context. Secondly, the context is composed of the words appearing to both the right and left of the given word. Finally, it removes the ordering constraint on the problem, instead, requiring the model to maximize the probability of any word appearing in the context without the knowledge of its offset from the given word. In terms of vertex representation modeling, this yields the optimization problem:

$$\underset{\Phi}{\text{minimize}} \quad -\log \Pr\left(\{v_{i-w}, \cdots, v_{i+w}\} \setminus v_i \mid \Phi(v_i)\right) \tag{3}$$

We find these relaxations are particularly desirable for social representation learning. First, the order independence assumption better captures a sense of 'nearness' that is provided by random walks. Moreover, this relaxation is quite useful for speeding up the training time by building small models as one vertex is given at a time.

Solving the optimization problem from Eq. 3 builds representations that capture the shared similarities in local graph structure between vertices. Vertices which have similar neighborhoods will acquire similar representations (encoding co-citation similarity), allowing generalization on machine learning tasks.

By combining both truncated random walks and language models we formulate a method which satisfies all of our desired properties. This method generates representations of social networks that are low-dimensional, and exist in a continuous vector space. Its representations encode latent forms of community membership, and because the method

Algorithm 1 DEEPWALK(G, w, d, γ, t)

Input: graph $G(V, E)$
window size w
embedding size d
walks per vertex γ
walk length t
Output: matrix of vertex representations $\Phi \in \mathbb{R}^{|V| \times d}$
1: Initialization: Sample Φ from $\mathcal{U}^{|V| \times d}$
2: Build a binary Tree T from V
3: **for** $i = 0$ to γ **do**
4: $\quad \mathcal{O} = \text{Shuffle}(V)$
5: $\quad$ **for each** $v_i \in \mathcal{O}$ **do**
6: $\quad\quad \mathcal{W}_{v_i} = RandomWalk(G, v_i, t)$
7: $\quad\quad$ SkipGram(Φ, $\mathcal{W}_{v_i}$, w)
8: $\quad$ **end for**
9: **end for**

outputs useful intermediate representations, it can adapt to changing network topology.

4. METHOD

In this section we discuss the main components of our algorithm. We also present several variants of our approach and discuss their merits.

4.1 Overview

As in any language modeling algorithm, the only required input is a corpus and a vocabulary $\mathcal{V}$. DEEPWALK considers a set of short truncated random walks its own corpus, and the graph vertices as its own vocabulary ($\mathcal{V} = V$). While it is beneficial to know V and the frequency distribution of vertices in the random walks ahead of the training, it is not necessary for the algorithm to work as we will show in 4.2.2.

4.2 Algorithm: DEEPWALK

The algorithm consists of two main components; first a random walk generator, and second, an update procedure. The random walk generator takes a graph G and samples uniformly a random vertex v_i as the root of the random walk $\mathcal{W}_{v_i}$. A walk samples uniformly from the neighbors of the last vertex visited until the maximum length (t) is reached. While we set the length of our random walks in the experiments to be fixed, there is no restriction for the random walks to be of the same length. These walks could have restarts (i.e. a teleport probability of returning back to their root), but our preliminary results did not show any advantage of using restarts. In practice, our implementation specifies a number of random walks γ of length t to start at each vertex.

Lines 3-9 in Algorithm 1 shows the core of our approach. The outer loop specifies the number of times, γ, which we should start random walks at each vertex. We think of each iteration as making a 'pass' over the data and sample one walk per node during this pass. At the start of each pass we generate a random ordering to traverse the vertices. This is not strictly required, but is well-known to speed up the convergence of stochastic gradient descent.

In the inner loop, we iterate over all the vertices of the graph. For each vertex v_i we generate a random walk $|\mathcal{W}_{v_i}| = t$, and then use it to update our representations (Line 7). We use the SkipGram algorithm [27] to update

Algorithm 2 SkipGram(Φ, $\mathcal{W}_{v_i}$, w)

1: **for each** $v_j \in \mathcal{W}_{v_i}$ **do**
2: $\quad$ **for each** $u_k \in \mathcal{W}_{v_i}[j - w : j + w]$ **do**
3: $\quad\quad J(\Phi) = -\log \Pr(u_k \mid \Phi(v_j))$
4: $\quad\quad \Phi = \Phi - \alpha * \frac{\partial J}{\partial \Phi}$
5: $\quad$ **end for**
6: **end for**

these representations in accordance with our objective function in Eq. 3.

4.2.1 SkipGram

SkipGram is a language model that maximizes the co-occurrence probability among the words that appear within a window, w, in a sentence. It approximates the conditional probability in Equation 3 using an independence assumption as the following

$$\Pr\left(\{v_{i-w}, \cdots, v_{i+w}\} \setminus v_i \mid \Phi(v_i)\right) = \prod_{\substack{j=i-w \\ j \neq i}}^{i+w} \Pr(v_j | \Phi(v_i)) \tag{4}$$

Algorithm 2 iterates over all possible collocations in random walk that appear within the window w (lines 1-2). For each, we map each vertex v_j to its current representation vector $\Phi(v_j) \in \mathbb{R}^d$ (See Figure 3b). Given the representation of v_j, we would like to maximize the probability of its neighbors in the walk (line 3). We can learn such a posterior distribution using several choices of classifiers. For example, modeling the previous problem using logistic regression would result in a huge number of labels (that is equal to $|V|$) which could be in millions or billions. Such models require vast computational resources which could span a whole cluster of computers [4]. To avoid this necessity and speed up the training time, we instead use the Hierarchical Softmax [30, 31] to approximate the probability distribution.

4.2.2 Hierarchical Softmax

Given that $u_k \in V$, calculating $\Pr(u_k \mid \Phi(v_j))$ in line 3 is not feasible. Computing the partition function (normalization factor) is expensive, so instead we will factorize the conditional probability using Hierarchical softmax. We assign the vertices to the leaves of a binary tree, turning the prediction problem into maximizing the probability of a specific path in the hierarchy (See Figure 3c). If the path to vertex u_k is identified by a sequence of tree nodes $(b_0, b_1, \ldots, b_{\lceil \log |V| \rceil})$, $(b_0 = \text{root}, b_{\lceil \log |V| \rceil} = u_k)$ then

$$\Pr(u_k \mid \Phi(v_j)) = \prod_{l=1}^{\lceil \log |V| \rceil} \Pr(b_l \mid \Phi(v_j)) \tag{5}$$

Now, $\Pr(b_l \mid \Phi(v_j))$ could be modeled by a binary classifier that is assigned to the parent of the node b_l as Equation 6 shows,

$$\Pr(b_l \mid \Phi(v_j) = 1/(1 + e^{-\Phi(v_j) \cdot \Psi(b_l)}) \tag{6}$$

where $\Psi(b_l) \in \mathbb{R}^d$ is the representation assigned to tree node b_l's parent. This reduces the computational complexity of calculating $\Pr(u_k \mid \Phi(v_j))$ from $O(|V|)$ to $O(\log |V|)$.

We can speed up the training process further, by assigning shorter paths to the frequent vertices in the random walks. Huffman coding is used to reduce the access time of frequent elements in the tree.

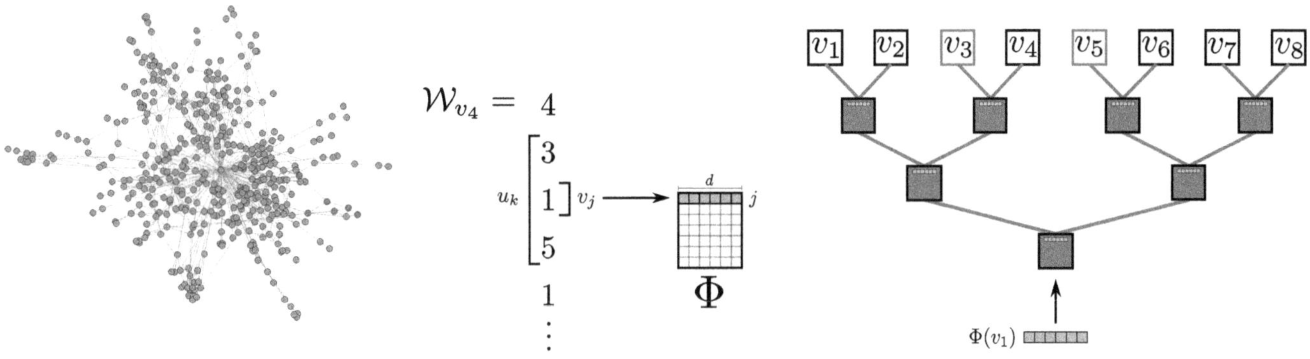

(a) Random walk generation. (b) Representation mapping. (c) Hierarchical Softmax.

Figure 3: Overview of DeepWalk. We slide a window of length $2w + 1$ over the random walk $\mathcal{W}_{v_4}$, mapping the central vertex v_1 to its representation $\Phi(v_1)$. Hierarchical Softmax factors out $\Pr(v_3 \mid \Phi(v_1))$ and $\Pr(v_5 \mid \Phi(v_1))$ over sequences of probability distributions corresponding to the paths starting at the root and ending at v_3 and v_5. The representation Φ is updated to maximize the probability of v_1 co-occurring with its context $\{v_3, v_5\}$.

4.2.3 Optimization

The model parameter set is $\theta = \{\Phi, \Psi\}$ where the size of each is $O(d|V|)$. Stochastic gradient descent (SGD) [5] is used to optimize these parameters (Line 4, Algorithm 2). The derivatives are estimated using the back-propagation algorithm. The learning rate α for SGD is initially set to 2.5% at the beginning of the training and then decreased linearly with the number of vertices that are seen so far.

4.3 Parallelizability

As shown in Figure 2 the frequency distribution of vertices in random walks of social network and words in a language both follow a power law. This results in a long tail of infrequent vertices, therefore, the updates that affect Φ will be sparse in nature. This allows us to use asynchronous version of stochastic gradient descent (ASGD), in the multi-worker case. Given that our updates are sparse and we do not acquire a lock to access the model shared parameters, ASGD will achieve an optimal rate of convergence [36]. While we run experiments on one machine using multiple threads, it has been demonstrated that this technique is highly scalable, and can be used in very large scale machine learning [9]. Figure 4 presents the effects of parallelizing DeepWalk. It shows the speed up in processing BlogCatalog and Flickr networks is consistent as we increase the number of workers to 8 (Figure 4a). It also shows that there is no loss of predictive performance relative to the running DeepWalk serially (Figure 4b).

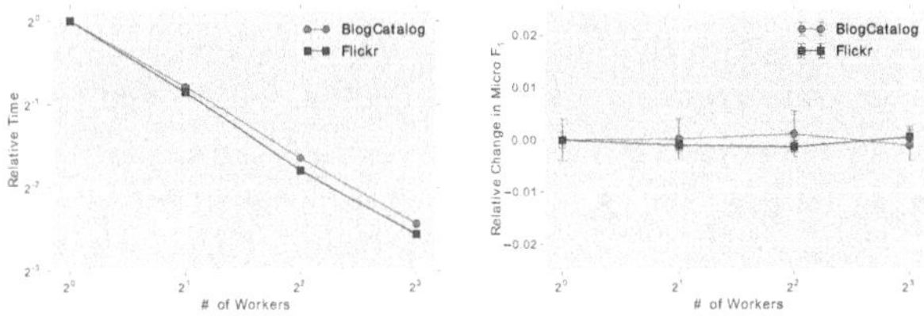

(a) Running Time (b) Performance

Figure 4: Effects of parallelizing DeepWalk

4.4 Algorithm Variants

Here we discuss some variants of our proposed method, which we believe may be of interest.

4.4.1 Streaming

One interesting variant of this method is a *streaming* approach, which could be implemented without knowledge of the entire graph. In this variant small walks from the graph are passed directly to the representation learning code, and the model is updated directly. Some modifications to the learning process will also be necessary. First, using a decaying learning rate may no longer be desirable as it assumes the knowledge of the total corpus size. Instead, we can initialize the learning rate α to a small constant value. This will take longer to learn, but may be worth it in some applications. Second, we cannot necessarily build a tree of parameters any more. If the cardinality of V is known (or can be bounded), we can build the Hierarchical Softmax tree for that maximum value. Vertices can be assigned to one of the remaining leaves when they are first seen. If we have the ability to estimate the vertex frequency a priori, we can also still use Huffman coding to decrease frequent element access times.

4.4.2 Non-random walks

Some graphs are created as a by-product of agents interacting with a sequence of elements (e.g. users' navigation of pages on a website). When a graph is created by such a stream of *non-random* walks, we can use this process to feed the modeling phase directly. Graphs sampled in this way will not only capture information related to network structure, but also to the frequency at which paths are traversed.

In our view, this variant also encompasses language modeling. Sentences can be viewed as purposed walks through an appropriately designed language network, and language models like SkipGram are designed to capture this behavior.

This approach can be combined with the streaming variant (Section 4.4.1) to train features on a continually evolving network without ever explicitly constructing the entire graph. Maintaining representations with this technique could enable web-scale classification without the hassles of dealing with a web-scale graph.

Name	BlogCatalog	Flickr	YouTube
$\|V\|$	10,312	80,513	1,138,499
$\|E\|$	333,983	5,899,882	2,990,443
$\|\mathcal{Y}\|$	39	195	47
Labels	Interests	Groups	Groups

Table 1: Graphs used in our experiments.

5. EXPERIMENTAL DESIGN

In this section we provide an overview of the datasets and methods which we will use in our experiments. Code and data to reproduce our results will be available at the first author's website.[1]

5.1 Datasets

An overview of the graphs we consider in our experiments is given in Figure 1.

- BlogCatalog [39] is a network of social relationships provided by blogger authors. The labels represent the topic categories provided by the authors.
- Flickr [39] is a network of the contacts between users of the photo sharing website. The labels represent the interest groups of the users such as *'black and white photos'*.
- YouTube [40] is a social network between users of the popular video sharing website. The labels here represent groups of viewers that enjoy common video genres (e.g. *anime* and *wrestling*).

5.2 Baseline Methods

To validate the performance of our approach we compare it against a number of baselines:

- SpectralClustering [41]: This method generates a representation in $\mathbb{R}^d$ from the d-smallest eigenvectors of $\widetilde{\mathcal{L}}$, the normalized graph Laplacian of G. Utilizing the eigenvectors of $\widetilde{\mathcal{L}}$ implicitly assumes that graph cuts will be useful for classification.
- Modularity [39]: This method generates a representation in $\mathbb{R}^d$ from the top-d eigenvectors of B, the Modularity matrix of G. The eigenvectors of B encode information about modular graph partitions of G [35]. Using them as features assumes that modular graph partitions will be useful for classification.
- EdgeCluster [40]: This method uses k-means clustering to cluster the adjacency matrix of G. Its has been shown to perform comparably to the Modularity method, with the added advantage of scaling to graphs which are too large for spectral decomposition.
- wvRN [25]: The weighted-vote Relational Neighbor is a relational classifier. Given the neighborhood $\mathcal{N}_i$ of vertex v_i, wvRN estimates $\Pr(y_i|\mathcal{N}_i)$ with the (appropriately normalized) weighted mean of its neighbors (i.e $\Pr(y_i|\mathcal{N}_i) = \frac{1}{Z}\sum_{v_j\in\mathcal{N}_i} w_{ij}\Pr(y_j \mid \mathcal{N}_j))$. It has shown surprisingly good performance in real networks, and has been advocated as a sensible relational classification baseline [26].
- Majority: This naïve method simply chooses the most frequent labels in the training set.

[1] `http://bit.ly/deepwalk`

6. EXPERIMENTS

In this section we present an experimental analysis of our method. We thoroughly evaluate it on a number of multi-label classification tasks, and analyze its sensitivity across several parameters.

6.1 Multi-Label Classification

To facilitate the comparison between our method and the relevant baselines, we use the exact same datasets and experimental procedure as in [39, 40]. Specifically, we randomly sample a portion (T_R) of the labeled nodes, and use them as training data. The rest of the nodes are used as test. We repeat this process 10 times, and report the average performance in terms of both Macro-F_1 and Micro-F_1. When possible we report the original results [39, 40] here directly.

For all models we use a one-vs-rest logistic regression implemented by LibLinear [11] extended to return the most probable labels as in [39]. We present results for DeepWalk with ($\gamma = 80$, $w = 10$, $d = 128$). The results for (SpectralClustering, Modularity, EdgeCluster) use Tang and Liu's preferred dimensionality, $d = 500$.

6.1.1 BlogCatalog

In this experiment we increase the training ratio (T_R) on the BlogCatalog network from 10% to 90%. Our results are presented in Table 2. Numbers in bold represent the highest performance in each column.

DeepWalk performs consistently better than EdgeCluster, Modularity, and wvRN. In fact, when trained with only 20% of the nodes labeled, DeepWalk performs better than these approaches when they are given 90% of the data. The performance of SpectralClustering proves much more competitive, but DeepWalk still outperforms when labeled data is sparse on both Macro-F_1 ($T_R \leq 20\%$) and Micro-F_1 ($T_R \leq 60\%$).

This strong performance when only small fractions of the graph are labeled is a core strength of our approach. In the following experiments, we investigate the performance of our representations on even more sparsely labeled graphs.

6.1.2 Flickr

In this experiment we vary the training ratio (T_R) on the Flickr network from 1% to 10%. This corresponds to having approximately 800 to 8,000 nodes labeled for classification in the entire network. Table 3 presents our results, which are consistent with the previous experiment. DeepWalk outperforms all baselines by at least 3% with respect to Micro-F_1. Additionally, its Micro-F_1 performance when only 3% of the graph is labeled beats all other methods even when they have been given 10% of the data. In other words, DeepWalk can outperform the baselines with 60% less training data. It also performs quite well in Macro-F_1, initially performing close to SpectralClustering, but distancing itself to a 1% improvement.

6.1.3 YouTube

The YouTube network is considerably larger than the previous ones we have experimented on, and its size prevents two of our baseline methods (SpectralClustering and Modularity) from running on it. It is much closer to a real world graph than those we have previously considered.

The results of varying the training ratio (T_R) from 1% to 10% are presented in Table 4. They show that DeepWalk significantly outperforms the scalable baseline for creating

	% Labeled Nodes	10%	20%	30%	40%	50%	60%	70%	80%	90%
	DeepWalk	**36.00**	**38.20**	**39.60**	**40.30**	**41.00**	**41.30**	41.50	41.50	42.00
	SpectralClustering	31.06	34.95	37.27	38.93	39.97	40.99	**41.66**	**42.42**	**42.62**
	EdgeCluster	27.94	30.76	31.85	32.99	34.12	35.00	34.63	35.99	36.29
Micro-F1(%)	Modularity	27.35	30.74	31.77	32.97	34.09	36.13	36.08	37.23	38.18
	wvRN	19.51	24.34	25.62	28.82	30.37	31.81	32.19	33.33	34.28
	Majority	16.51	16.66	16.61	16.70	16.91	16.99	16.92	16.49	17.26
	DeepWalk	**21.30**	**23.80**	25.30	26.30	27.30	27.60	27.90	28.20	28.90
	SpectralClustering	19.14	23.57	**25.97**	**27.46**	**28.31**	**29.46**	**30.13**	**31.38**	**31.78**
	EdgeCluster	16.16	19.16	20.48	22.00	23.00	23.64	23.82	24.61	24.92
Macro-F1(%)	Modularity	17.36	20.00	20.80	21.85	22.65	23.41	23.89	24.20	24.97
	wvRN	6.25	10.13	11.64	14.24	15.86	17.18	17.98	18.86	19.57
	Majority	2.52	2.55	2.52	2.58	2.58	2.63	2.61	2.48	2.62

Table 2: Multi-label classification results in BlogCatalog

	% Labeled Nodes	1%	2%	3%	4%	5%	6%	7%	8%	9%	10%
	DeepWalk	**32.4**	**34.6**	**35.9**	**36.7**	**37.2**	**37.7**	**38.1**	**38.3**	**38.5**	**38.7**
	SpectralClustering	27.43	30.11	31.63	32.69	33.31	33.95	34.46	34.81	35.14	35.41
Micro-F1(%)	EdgeCluster	25.75	28.53	29.14	30.31	30.85	31.53	31.75	31.76	32.19	32.84
	Modularity	22.75	25.29	27.3	27.6	28.05	29.33	29.43	28.89	29.17	29.2
	wvRN	17.7	14.43	15.72	20.97	19.83	19.42	19.22	21.25	22.51	22.73
	Majority	16.34	16.31	16.34	16.46	16.65	16.44	16.38	16.62	16.67	16.71
	DeepWalk	**14.0**	17.3	**19.6**	**21.1**	**22.1**	**22.9**	**23.6**	**24.1**	**24.6**	**25.0**
	SpectralClustering	13.84	**17.49**	19.44	20.75	21.60	22.36	23.01	23.36	23.82	24.05
Macro-F1(%)	EdgeCluster	10.52	14.10	15.91	16.72	18.01	18.54	19.54	20.18	20.78	20.85
	Modularity	10.21	13.37	15.24	15.11	16.14	16.64	17.02	17.1	17.14	17.12
	wvRN	1.53	2.46	2.91	3.47	4.95	5.56	5.82	6.59	8.00	7.26
	Majority	0.45	0.44	0.45	0.46	0.47	0.44	0.45	0.47	0.47	0.47

Table 3: Multi-label classification results in Flickr

	% Labeled Nodes	1%	2%	3%	4%	5%	6%	7%	8%	9%	10%
	DeepWalk	**37.95**	**39.28**	**40.08**	**40.78**	**41.32**	**41.72**	**42.12**	**42.48**	**42.78**	**43.05**
	SpectralClustering	—	—	—	—	—	—	—	—	—	—
Micro-F1(%)	EdgeCluster	23.90	31.68	35.53	36.76	37.81	38.63	38.94	39.46	39.92	40.07
	Modularity	—	—	—	—	—	—	—	—	—	—
	wvRN	26.79	29.18	33.1	32.88	35.76	37.38	38.21	37.75	38.68	39.42
	Majority	24.90	24.84	25.25	25.23	25.22	25.33	25.31	25.34	25.38	25.38
	DeepWalk	**29.22**	**31.83**	**33.06**	**33.90**	**34.35**	**34.66**	**34.96**	**35.22**	**35.42**	**35.67**
	SpectralClustering	—	—	—	—	—	—	—	—	—	—
Macro-F1(%)	EdgeCluster	19.48	25.01	28.15	29.17	29.82	30.65	30.75	31.23	31.45	31.54
	Modularity	—	—	—	—	—	—	—	—	—	—
	wvRN	13.15	15.78	19.66	20.9	23.31	25.43	27.08	26.48	28.33	28.89
	Majority	6.12	5.86	6.21	6.1	6.07	6.19	6.17	6.16	6.18	6.19

Table 4: Multi-label classification results in YouTube

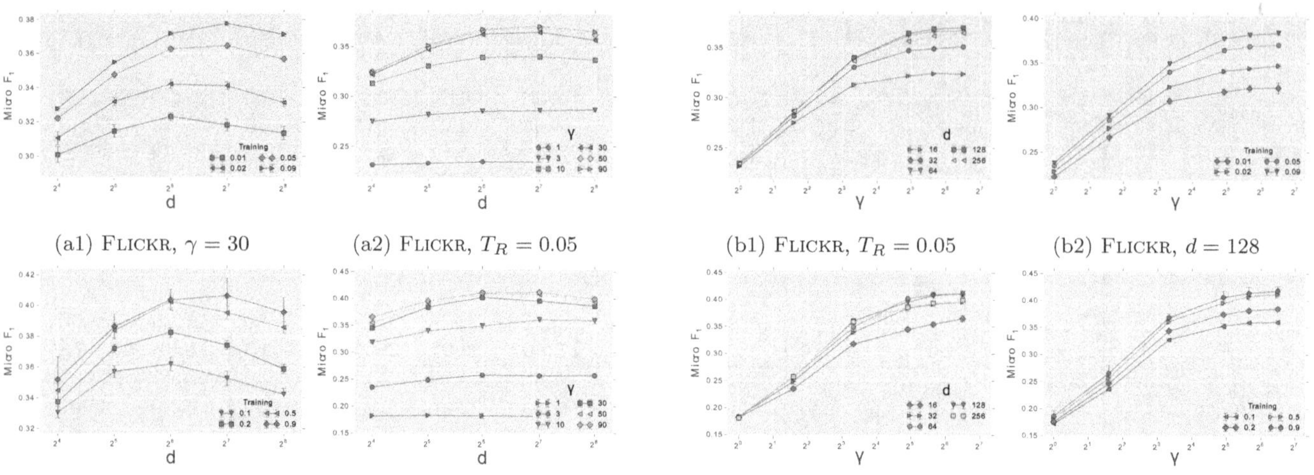

(a1) FLICKR, $\gamma = 30$ (a2) FLICKR, $T_R = 0.05$ (b1) FLICKR, $T_R = 0.05$ (b2) FLICKR, $d = 128$

(a3) BLOGCATALOG, $\gamma = 30$ (a4) BLOGCATALOG, $T_R = 0.5$ (b3) BLOGCATALOG, $T_R = 0.5$ (b4) BLOGCATALOG, $d = 128$

(a) Stability over dimensions, d (b) Stability over number of walks, γ

Figure 5: Parameter Sensitivity Study

graph representations, EdgeCluster. When 1% of the labeled nodes are used for test, the Micro-F_1 improves by 14%. The Macro-F_1 shows a corresponding 10% increase. This lead narrows as the training data increases, but DEEPWALK ends with a 3% lead in Micro-F_1, and an impressive 5% improvement in Macro-F_1.

This experiment showcases the performance benefits that can occur from using social representation learning for multi-label classification. DEEPWALK, can scale to large graphs, and performs exceedingly well in such a sparsely labeled environment.

6.2 Parameter Sensitivity

In order to evaluate how changes to the parameterization of DEEPWALK effect its performance on classification tasks, we conducted experiments on two multi-label classifications tasks (FLICKR, and BLOGCATALOG). In the interest of brevity, we have fixed the window size and the walk length to emphasize local structure ($w = 10$, $t = 40$). We then vary the number of latent dimensions (d), the number of walks started per vertex (γ), and the amount of training data available (T_R) to determine their impact on the network classification performance.

6.2.1 *Effect of Dimensionality*

Figure 5a shows the effects of increasing the number of latent dimensions available to our model.

Figures 5a1 and 5a3 examine the effects of varying the dimensionality and training ratio. The performance is quite consistent between both FLICKR and BLOGCATALOG and show that the optimal dimensionality for a model is dependent on the number of training examples. (Note that 1% of FLICKR has approximately as many labeled examples as 10% of BLOGCATALOG).

Figures 5a2 and 5a4 examine the effects of varying the dimensionality and number of walks per vertex. The relative performance between dimensions is relatively stable across different values of γ. These charts have two interesting observations. The first is that there is most of the benefit is accomplished by starting $\gamma = 30$ walks per node in both graphs. The second is that the relative difference between different values of γ is quite consistent between the two graphs. FLICKR has an order of magnitude more edges than BLOGCATALOG, and we find this behavior interesting.

These experiments show that our method can make useful models of various sizes. They also show that the performance of the model depends on the number of random walks it has seen, and the appropriate dimensionality of the model depends on the training examples available.

6.2.2 *Effect of sampling frequency*

Figure 5b shows the effects of increasing γ, the number of random walks that we start from each vertex.

The results are very consistent for different dimensions (Fig. 5b1, Fig. 5b3) and the amount of training data (Fig. 5b2, Fig. 5b4). Initially, increasing γ has a big effect in the results, but this effect quickly slows ($\gamma > 10$). These results demonstrate that we are able to learn meaningful latent representations for vertices after only a small number of random walks.

7. RELATED WORK

The main differences between our proposed method and previous work can be summarized as follows:

1. We *learn* our latent social representations, instead of computing statistics related to centrality [13] or partitioning [41].
2. We do not attempt to extend the classification procedure itself (through collective inference [37] or graph kernels [21]).
3. We propose a scalable online method which uses only local information. Most methods require global information and are offline [17,39–41].
4. We apply unsupervised representation learning to graphs.

In this section we discuss related work in network classification and unsupervised feature learning.

7.1 Relational Learning

Relational classification (or *collective classification*) methods [15, 25, 32] use links between data items as part of the classification process. Exact inference in the collective classification problem is NP-hard, and solutions have focused on the use of approximate inference algorithm which may not be guaranteed to converge [37].

The most relevant relational classification algorithms to our work incorporate community information by learning clusters [33], by adding edges between nearby nodes [14], by using PageRank [24], or by extending relational classification to take additional features into account [43]. Our work takes a substantially different approach. Instead of a new approximation inference algorithm, we propose a procedure which learns representations of network structure which can then be used by existing inference procedure (including iterative ones).

A number of techniques for generating features from graphs have also been proposed [13, 17, 39–41]. In contrast to these methods, we frame the feature creation procedure as a representation learning problem.

Graph Kernels [42] have been proposed as a way to use relational data as part of the classification process, but are quite slow unless approximated [20]. Our approach is complementary; instead of encoding the structure as part of a kernel function, we learn a representation which allows them to be used directly as features for any classification method.

7.2 Unsupervised Feature Learning

Distributed representations have been proposed to model structural relationship between concepts [18]. These representations are trained by the back-propagation and gradient descent. Computational costs and numerical instability led to these techniques to be abandoned for almost a decade. Recently, distributed computing allowed for larger models to be trained [4], and the growth of data for unsupervised learning algorithms to emerge [10]. Distributed representations usually are trained through neural networks, these networks have made advancements in diverse fields such as computer vision [22], speech recognition [8], and natural language processing [1, 7].

8. CONCLUSIONS

We propose DeepWalk, a novel approach for learning latent social representations of vertices. Using local information from truncated random walks as input, our method learns a representation which encodes structural regularities. Experiments on a variety of different graphs illustrate the effectiveness of our approach on challenging multi-label classification tasks.

As an online algorithm, DeepWalk is also scalable. Our results show that we can create meaningful representations for graphs which are too large for standard spectral methods. On such large graphs, our method significantly outperforms other methods designed to operate for sparsity. We also show that our approach is parallelizable, allowing workers to update different parts of the model concurrently.

In addition to being effective and scalable, our approach is also an appealing generalization of language modeling. This connection is mutually beneficial. Advances in language modeling may continue to generate improved latent representations for networks. In our view, language modeling is actually sampling from an unobservable language graph. We believe that insights obtained from modeling observable graphs may in turn yield improvements to modeling unobservable ones.

Our future work in the area will focus on investigating this duality further, using our results to improve language modeling, and strengthening the theoretical justifications of the method.

Acknowledgements

The authors thank the reviewers for their helpful comments. This research was partially supported by NSF Grants DBI-1060572 and IIS-1017181, and a Google Faculty Research Award.

9. REFERENCES

[1] R. Al-Rfou, B. Perozzi, and S. Skiena. Polyglot: Distributed word representations for multilingual nlp. In *Proceedings of the Seventeenth Conference on Computational Natural Language Learning*, pages 183–192, Sofia, Bulgaria, August 2013. ACL.

[2] R. Andersen, F. Chung, and K. Lang. Local graph partitioning using pagerank vectors. In *Foundations of Computer Science, 2006. FOCS'06. 47th Annual IEEE Symposium on*, pages 475–486. IEEE, 2006.

[3] Y. Bengio, A. Courville, and P. Vincent. Representation learning: A review and new perspectives. 2013.

[4] Y. Bengio, R. Ducharme, and P. Vincent. A neural probabilistic language model. *Journal of Machine Learning Research*, 3:1137–1155, 2003.

[5] L. Bottou. Stochastic gradient learning in neural networks. In *Proceedings of Neuro-Nîmes 91*, Nimes, France, 1991. EC2.

[6] V. Chandola, A. Banerjee, and V. Kumar. Anomaly detection: A survey. *ACM Computing Surveys (CSUR)*, 41(3):15, 2009.

[7] R. Collobert and J. Weston. A unified architecture for natural language processing: Deep neural networks with multitask learning. In *Proceedings of the 25th ICML*, ICML '08, pages 160–167. ACM, 2008.

[8] G. E. Dahl, D. Yu, L. Deng, and A. Acero. Context-dependent pre-trained deep neural networks for large-vocabulary speech recognition. *Audio, Speech, and Language Processing, IEEE Transactions on*, 20(1):30–42, 2012.

[9] J. Dean, G. Corrado, R. Monga, K. Chen, M. Devin, Q. Le, M. Mao, M. Ranzato, A. Senior, P. Tucker, K. Yang, and A. Ng. Large scale distributed deep networks. In P. Bartlett, F. Pereira, C. Burges, L. Bottou, and K. Weinberger, editors, *Advances in Neural Information Processing Systems 25*, pages 1232–1240. 2012.

[10] D. Erhan, Y. Bengio, A. Courville, P.-A. Manzagol, P. Vincent, and S. Bengio. Why does unsupervised pre-training help deep learning? *The Journal of Machine Learning Research*, 11:625–660, 2010.

[11] R.-E. Fan, K.-W. Chang, C.-J. Hsieh, X.-R. Wang, and C.-J. Lin. LIBLINEAR: A library for large linear classification. *Journal of Machine Learning Research*, 9:1871–1874, 2008.

[12] F. Fouss, A. Pirotte, J.-M. Renders, and M. Saerens. Random-walk computation of similarities between nodes of a graph with application to collaborative recommendation. *Knowledge and Data Engineering, IEEE Transactions on*, 19(3):355–369, 2007.

[13] B. Gallagher and T. Eliassi-Rad. Leveraging label-independent features for classification in sparsely

labeled networks: An empirical study. In *Advances in Social Network Mining and Analysis*, pages 1–19. Springer, 2010.

[14] B. Gallagher, H. Tong, T. Eliassi-Rad, and C. Faloutsos. Using ghost edges for classification in sparsely labeled networks. In *Proceedings of the 14th ACM SIGKDD*, KDD '08, pages 256–264, New York, NY, USA, 2008. ACM.

[15] S. Geman and D. Geman. Stochastic relaxation, gibbs distributions, and the bayesian restoration of images. *Pattern Analysis and Machine Intelligence, IEEE Transactions on*, (6):721–741, 1984.

[16] L. Getoor and B. Taskar. *Introduction to statistical relational learning*. MIT press, 2007.

[17] K. Henderson, B. Gallagher, L. Li, L. Akoglu, T. Eliassi-Rad, H. Tong, and C. Faloutsos. It's who you know: Graph mining using recursive structural features. In *Proceedings of the 17th ACM SIGKDD*, KDD '11, pages 663–671, New York, NY, USA, 2011. ACM.

[18] G. E. Hinton. Learning distributed representations of concepts. In *Proceedings of the eighth annual conference of the cognitive science society*, pages 1–12. Amherst, MA, 1986.

[19] R. A. Hummel and S. W. Zucker. On the foundations of relaxation labeling processes. *Pattern Analysis and Machine Intelligence, IEEE Transactions on*, (3):267–287, 1983.

[20] U. Kang, H. Tong, and J. Sun. Fast random walk graph kernel. In *SDM*, pages 828–838, 2012.

[21] R. I. Kondor and J. Lafferty. Diffusion kernels on graphs and other discrete input spaces. In *ICML*, volume 2, pages 315–322, 2002.

[22] A. Krizhevsky, I. Sutskever, and G. E. Hinton. Imagenet classification with deep convolutional neural networks. In *NIPS*, volume 1, page 4, 2012.

[23] D. Liben-Nowell and J. Kleinberg. The link-prediction problem for social networks. *Journal of the American society for information science and technology*, 58(7):1019–1031, 2007.

[24] F. Lin and W. Cohen. Semi-supervised classification of network data using very few labels. In *Advances in Social Networks Analysis and Mining (ASONAM), 2010 International Conference on*, pages 192–199, Aug 2010.

[25] S. A. Macskassy and F. Provost. A simple relational classifier. In *Proceedings of the Second Workshop on Multi-Relational Data Mining (MRDM-2003) at KDD-2003*, pages 64–76, 2003.

[26] S. A. Macskassy and F. Provost. Classification in networked data: A toolkit and a univariate case study. *The Journal of Machine Learning Research*, 8:935–983, 2007.

[27] T. Mikolov, K. Chen, G. Corrado, and J. Dean. Efficient estimation of word representations in vector space. *CoRR*, abs/1301.3781, 2013.

[28] T. Mikolov, I. Sutskever, K. Chen, G. S. Corrado, and J. Dean. Distributed representations of words and phrases and their compositionality. In *Advances in Neural Information Processing Systems 26*, pages 3111–3119. 2013.

[29] T. Mikolov, W.-t. Yih, and G. Zweig. Linguistic regularities in continuous space word representations. In *Proceedings of NAACL-HLT*, pages 746–751, 2013.

[30] A. Mnih and G. E. Hinton. A scalable hierarchical distributed language model. *Advances in neural information processing systems*, 21:1081–1088, 2009.

[31] F. Morin and Y. Bengio. Hierarchical probabilistic neural network language model. In *Proceedings of the international workshop on artificial intelligence and statistics*, pages 246–252, 2005.

[32] J. Neville and D. Jensen. Iterative classification in relational data. In *Proc. AAAI-2000 Workshop on Learning Statistical Models from Relational Data*, pages 13–20, 2000.

[33] J. Neville and D. Jensen. Leveraging relational autocorrelation with latent group models. In *Proceedings of the 4th International Workshop on Multi-relational Mining*, MRDM '05, pages 49–55, New York, NY, USA, 2005. ACM.

[34] J. Neville and D. Jensen. A bias/variance decomposition for models using collective inference. *Machine Learning*, 73(1):87–106, 2008.

[35] M. E. Newman. Modularity and community structure in networks. *Proceedings of the National Academy of Sciences*, 103(23):8577–8582, 2006.

[36] B. Recht, C. Re, S. Wright, and F. Niu. Hogwild: A lock-free approach to parallelizing stochastic gradient descent. In *Advances in Neural Information Processing Systems 24*, pages 693–701. 2011.

[37] P. Sen, G. Namata, M. Bilgic, L. Getoor, B. Galligher, and T. Eliassi-Rad. Collective classification in network data. *AI magazine*, 29(3):93, 2008.

[38] D. A. Spielman and S.-H. Teng. Nearly-linear time algorithms for graph partitioning, graph sparsification, and solving linear systems. In *Proceedings of the thirty-sixth annual ACM symposium on Theory of computing*, pages 81–90. ACM, 2004.

[39] L. Tang and H. Liu. Relational learning via latent social dimensions. In *Proceedings of the 15th ACM SIGKDD*, KDD '09, pages 817–826, New York, NY, USA, 2009. ACM.

[40] L. Tang and H. Liu. Scalable learning of collective behavior based on sparse social dimensions. In *Proceedings of the 18th ACM conference on Information and knowledge management*, pages 1107–1116. ACM, 2009.

[41] L. Tang and H. Liu. Leveraging social media networks for classification. *Data Mining and Knowledge Discovery*, 23(3):447–478, 2011.

[42] S. Vishwanathan, N. N. Schraudolph, R. Kondor, and K. M. Borgwardt. Graph kernels. *The Journal of Machine Learning Research*, 99:1201–1242, 2010.

[43] X. Wang and G. Sukthankar. Multi-label relational neighbor classification using social context features. In *Proceedings of the 19th ACM SIGKDD*, pages 464–472. ACM, 2013.

[44] W. Zachary. An information flow model for conflict and fission in small groups1. *Journal of anthropological research*, 33(4):452–473, 1977.

Open-domain Quanity Queries on Web Tables: Annotation, Response and Consensus Models

Sunita Sarawagi
IIT Bombay

Soumen Chakrabarti
IIT Bombay

ABSTRACT

Over 40% of columns in hundreds of millions of Web tables contain numeric quantities. Tables are a richer source of structured knowledge than free text. We harness Web tables to answer queries whose target is a quantity with natural variation, such as **net worth of zuckerburg**, **battery life of ipad**, **half life of plutonium**, and **calories in pizza**. Our goal is to respond to such queries with a ranked list of quantity distributions, suitably represented. Apart from the challenges of informal schema and noisy extractions, which have been known since tables were used for non-quantity information extraction, we face additional problems of noisy number formats, as well as unit specifications that are often contextual and ambiguous.

Early "hardening" of extraction decisions at a table level leads to poor accuracy. Instead, we use a probabilistic context free grammar (PCFG) based unit extractor on the tables, and retain several top-scoring extractions of quantity types and numerals. Then we inject these into a new collective inference framework that makes global decisions about the relevance of candidate table snippets, the interpretation of the query's target quantity type, the value distributions to be ranked and presented, and the degree of consensus that can be built to support the proposed quantity distributions. Experiments with over 25 million Web tables and 350 diverse queries show robust, large benefits from our quantity catalog, unit extractor, and collective inference.

1. INTRODUCTION

Web search engines enhance "organic" search results with data from structured knowledge bases (KBs), curated from diverse sources using information extraction [13] and entity annotation [5] techniques. With very few exceptions [10, 19, 3, 1], a vast majority of work on extracting typed text segments, entities, attributes and relations involve discrete symbols and not *measurable quantities*[1]. And yet, the Web is as rich a source of quantities as it is of symbolic knowledge. There are hundreds of millions of information-rich HTML tables on the Web. In our sample, a full 40% of their columns exclusively contain quantities. On the other hand, *quantity-seeking* Web queries are well-served only in verticals like shopping, food and travel where structured databases contain columns that are matched against the query, aggregated, and presented as quantities throughout. With one mild exception [20], the emerging Web tables literature [17, 4, 7, 11] does not regard quantity extractions as any different from discrete symbolic value extractions.

[1]"When you can measure what you are speaking about, and express it in numbers, you know something about it." — Lord Kelvin.

KDD'14, August 24–27, 2014, New York, NY, USA.

http://dx.doi.org/10.1145/2623330.2623749.

1.1 Our goal

Our goal is to bridge the gap between the noisy presentation of quantities in Web tables and open-domain, one-off quantity-seeking queries. Asking for an attribute of an entity is a common case, e.g., **average revenue of microsoft**, **half-life of plutonium** and **mass of pluto**. Note that we are primarily interested in seeking quantities with *uncertainty* and *imprecision*, unlike "cosmic truths" like the number of primes under 1000, or the value of π. For this reason, our queries cannot be answered from Wikipedia Infoboxes, which mostly offer point answers, and without directly accumulating evidence from the Web. To this end, we present a new, robust, open-domain, quantity search system QEWT.

QEWT is a large system with very many details. Here we distill three major contributions: a quantity catalog and a new table column unit annotator based on a probabilistic context free grammar (PCFG), a query response model based on ranked value distributions, and a new algorithm for collective consensus inference. Our unit catalog, query workloads, labeled data, and code are publicly available at `http://www.cse.iitb.ac.in/~sunita/wwt`.

1.2 Our contributions

Table column unit annotator. Quantity columns in web tables are notoriously challenging to extract. Unit expressions may be ambiguous ("m.") or even missing, syntactic clues though present might be noisy, and units may not follow clear-cut representations in table headers. We compiled a quantity catalog QuTree, and designed a new unit annotator for table columns based on probabilistic context free grammars (PCFGs). The PCFG technique exploits a diverse set of clues, including co-occurrence statistics between quantity types, units and phrases mined from an *unlabeled* corpus of table headers.

Quantity response model. In IR, the response is a list of URLs or documents. In expert or entity search [2], it is a list of entities. Queries that seek uncertain quantities require a very different treatment. In particular, extracted quantities can be distinct from each other for extraneous reasons, or there may be systematic variations (which isotope of Plutonium, or Microsoft revenue in which year). A more intuitive uniform output representation is a *distribution over quantities*. We describe techniques to represent, score and rank such distributions h, given the query.

Earlier work [3, "QCQ"] is a restrictive special case of our framework. Each response in QCQ is a single *interval*, and a model was trained to score these using labeled data. Here we can create distributions and intervals in a query-driven manner without labeled data. Since our target is open-domain query answering, we ensure that our response model can handle data at arbitrary scales and from arbitrary distributions via a data-driven distance metric.

Collective extraction framework. The centerpiece of our approach is a collective model for extracting quantities from raw Web tables. Instead of "hardening" extraction decisions on quantity columns eagerly, we keep around multiple uncertain values and units, which are finally collectively resolved over multiple tables at query time. We depend on a consensus model that defines a joint distribution h over all candidate extractions to assign collectively resolved probabilities on the relevance of each snippet and the extracted unit and value. Another valuable input is from a classifier that provides a distribution over the target quantity type. We train the classifier via a novel method of tapping our huge unlabeled table corpus.

Experimental evaluation. We report on experiments with 350 queries spanning three query benchmarks compiled from QCQ [3], InfoGather [20] and World Bank data [18]. The base corpus tables is accessed through the Google API at research.google.com/tables and our corpus of 25 million tables extracted [11] from a commercial Web crawl of 500 million pages. Our experimental results can be summarized as:

- Our PCFG-based column annotator is considerably more accurate than rule-based (82% vs 40%) or simpler baselines (74%). However, it is not nearly perfect.
- As a consequence, choosing locally best extractions from each table independently gives poor accuracy. Collective judgment of snippet relevance and extractions improves answer precision from 28% to 42%.
- Smooth notions of consensus between contributing quantities is important; accumulating counts for point estimates (collapsing distribution h to a histogram over discrete values) causes a 6% drop in precision.
- The quantity type classifier trained from the unlabeled table corpus provides a 8% boost in precision.

2. SYSTEM OVERVIEW AND ROADMAP

We present an overview of our system QEWT in Figure 1. The user submits a quantity query q which has two parts. The first part a_q is a sequence of word/s that are a verbal description of the response quantity type (e.g., distance from sun, speed, annual revenue). The second part e_q is a free-form sequence of words that indicate an entity for which a quantity attribute is being sought (e.g. Pluto, Concorde, Microsoft). The query words are submitted to indices over Web table corpora and a set of tables retrieved. Figure 3 shows sample tables for the query `co2 emissions of china` with $e_q =$ `china` and $a_q =$ `co2 emissions`. A snippet generator module processes the retrieved tables for potential answer snippets and attaches a relevance score to each. Next, a number/unit extractor parses the noisy snippets to output an uncertain list of values and units based on a unit ontology. The uncertain extractions from all tables are collectively resolved to get a distribution over the target quantity. Finally the response as a continuous distribution or ranked quantity intervals is output to the user. We next present an overview of the main components.

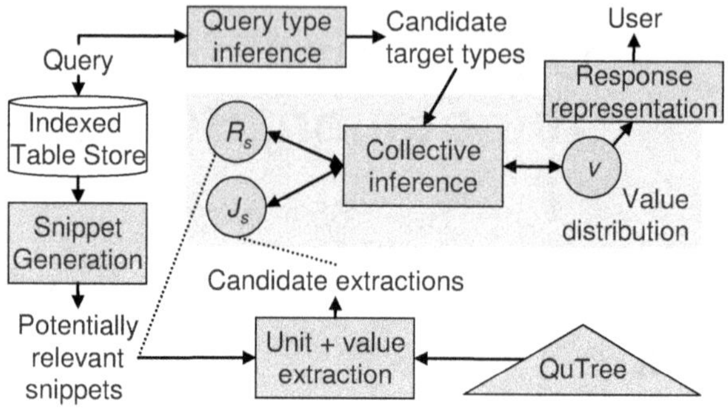

Figure 1: System sketch of QEWT.

Table corpus. We use two sources of tables: a commercial crawl of 500 million Web pages, from which we extracted and indexed 25 million non-decorative HTML tables, and tables collected per-query via the API provided by research.google.com/tables. We extract from each table zero or more top rows as the header for each of its columns, and selected text from the page embedding the table as the context as described in [11]. A type interpreter labels table columns as numeric or textual; in our corpus of 25 million tables we recognized 40% of the table columns as numeric.

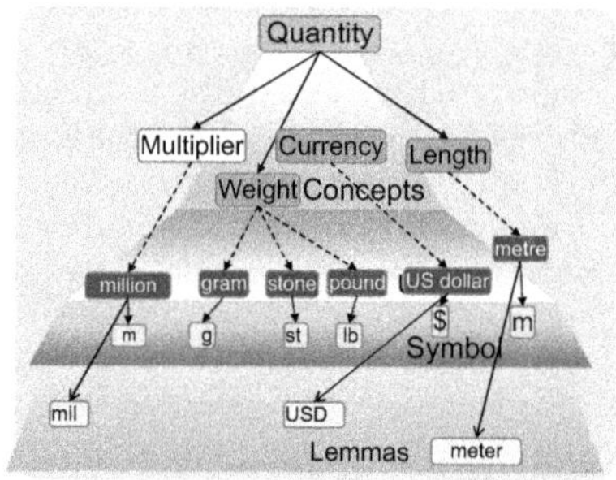

Figure 2: Fragment of QuTree.

Unit catalog QuTree. Starting from Category:Units_of_-measurement in Wikipedia, we created a unit catalog we call QuTree. It has 44 quantity types such as *Length*, *Area*, *Speed*, and 750 units. Each quantity type has a *canonical* unit, and other units come with conversion factors to/from the canonical unit. A fragment of QuTree is shown in Figure 2. Each catalog unit is associated with one or more full names (e.g., kilometre per hour), one or more symbols (e.g., kmph, km/h) and an optional list of lemmas to account for the common variant names of a unit, (e.g., meter-metre, kmph-kilometre per hour). QuTree also includes the concept of a "multiplier" to denote dimensionless quantities, with unit instances like thousand, million and billion, which capture scales of measurements. QuTree can be downloaded from goo.gl/542L2Y. It is to quantities what YAGO [14] is to discrete entities.

Query target type. In the user query, a_q is a textual hint at a quantity type t from the quantity catalog. We must build an estimate of the distribution $\Pr(t|q) = \Pr(t|a_q)$. For example, for attribute `co2 emissions` $\Pr(t|a_q)$ is expected to assign high probability to the quantity type *mass*. In Section 3.1 we show how to train $\Pr(t|a_q)$ via an innovative use of the table corpus, and without requiring tedious manual labeling. We will see in Section 6.4 that this signal is very useful to the collective extractor in finding relevant answers.

Country	Total Emissions (1000's tons carbon)
UNITED STATES OF AMERICA	92,739,807
RUSSIAN FEDERATION*	37,562,270
CHINA (MAINLAND)	29,575,206
GERMANY	22,283,279
UNITED KINGDOM	19,895,515
JAPAN	13,857,045
FRANCE (INCLUDING MONACO)	9,175,102

	Energy-saving scenario[b] (billion metric tons of CO_2)	Current trends scenario[c] (billion metric tons of CO_2)
Countries	**1990**	**2000**
OECD	10.4	11.3
North America	5.6	6.2
Europe	3.4	3.5
Pacific OECD	1.4	1.6
FSU and CEE[d]	4.4	3.2
Rest of world	5.9	8.8
China	2.4	3.4

Country	CO2 Emissions 2000 thousands of metric tons of carbon	Per Capita CO2 Emissions 2000 metric tons of carbon
United States of America	1,535,910.00	5.31
China	771,057.00	0.60
Russian Federation	391,664.00	2.69
Japan	323,281.00	2.54
India	292,265.00	0.29

List of countries sorted by CO2 Emission

Rank	Country Name	CO2 emissions (kt)
1	China	6.533.018
2	United States	5.832.194
3	South Asia	1.828.941
4	India	1.611.042
5	Russia	1.536.099
6	Japan	1.253.517

Figure 3: Sample tables responding to query $e_q =$ `china` and $a_q =$ `co2 emissions`.

Snippet relevance. The index search returns a set of candidate tables that match the query keywords q in the header, context, or body. On each candidate table, we use a snippet generation module to match e_q to a row header, a_q to a column header, and identify candidate cells for quantity extraction. Observe from Figures 3 and 4 the challenges of identifying potentially relevant rows, e.g., "China" vs. "China (mainland)", and relevant columns, e.g. multiple columns might be relevant and column headers may not match a_q at all as shown in Figure 4. Therefore, relevance of a snippet is uncertain. We use a random variable R_s to denote the uncertainty in the relevance of a snippet s and associate a score $r_s \in [0, 1]$ to denote $\Pr(R_s = 1)$. We will describe snippet generation and relevance score assignment further in Section 3.2.

Number and unit extraction. From each snippet s, we extract a float value from the table cell, and annotate it with a unit from QuTree based on signals in the column header and the table cell. Note that a unit node in QuTree belongs to exactly one quantity type, so a unit annotation also gives its quantity type. Both these tasks are highly challenging because of the extreme diversity of writing down quantities on the web: multipliers expressed separately in the column header, locale-dependent use of commas, periods, and spaces, scientific notation, etc. can confound any simplistic local extractor. Unit extraction from headers has its own challenges of dealing with drastic formatting differences in both column headers and cell quantities E.g., one column header may say "Total Emissions (1000's tons carbon)" whereas another may say "(billion metric tons of CO_2)" — these are different, whereas yet another table saying "CO2 emissions (kt)" is comparable to the second case. In Section 5 we present our design of a parser based on a context free grammar and a rich feature set. The output of this step is a weighted list of possible extractions of values and units from each snippet.

Collective inference. The candidate extractions are inputs to the centerpiece of QEWT: a novel collective inference procedure that simultaneously estimates the relevance of each snippet and each of its possible extractions, and the target quantity type basing its judgement on a global estimate of the distribution of values around the quantity. We describe this in Section 3.5.

Answer representation. As challenging as robustness to input variation is the issue of answer representation. The vast body of work on search has to rank discrete items such as URLs (pages) [8] or entities [2]. Here our true response is an uncertain quantity, but how best is this shown to the user? Rather than take an inflexible stand, QEWT supports three different types of answer formats each of which is suited for a different kind of quantitative queries. QEWT's internal response representation is a quantity distribution, but QEWT can provide simplified digests in the form of ranked value intervals [3], or degenerated to ranked point values (in case the query has little or no uncertainty, such as physical constants, or are categorical queries in disguise, such as the number of USB ports in a laptop).

3. COLLECTIVE CONSENSUS INFERENCE

As shown in Figure 1, the collective inference module, which we describe in this section, mediates between the type distribution, snippet relevance uncertainty, and the uncertainty of snippet unit and value extractions. Section 3.1 is about estimating the target type of the query. Section 3.2 discusses scoring snippets wrt the query. Section 3.3 describes how a single snippet can lead to many possible extractions of a unit and value, and how to score these extractions. Section 3.4 deals with the design of distributions for consensus inference. Finally, Section 3.5 describes the consensus inference algorithm itself.

3.1 Query target quantity type $\Pr(t|q)$

Given query $q = (a_q, e_q)$, its target quantity type, which is uncertain, is modeled as a distribution $\Pr(t|a_q)$. A good estimate of $\Pr(t|a_q)$ is vital for generating relevant responses.

3.1.1 Dictionary match

A baseline method may look for matches of the attribute words with type and unit names/lemmas in our quantity catalog. It may correctly find the target type of queries like `length of nile` or `year of crash`. But many queries like `usa co2 emissions`, `walton net worth`, `miami rainfall`, and `ebay revenue` have no match in the catalog, leading to loss of recall. Surprisingly, there is also precision loss. E.g., query `fan speed` which matches well the type *speed* in QuTree but misses the correct target type *frequency*.

3.1.2 Data-driven approach

Ideally, we would like to recognize that query word `revenue` targets type *money amount* and that `distance`, `length`, `height` and `width` all target the type *length* (dimension).

This form of association between (potential query) words and quantity types is evident in a fraction (but still a large absolute number) of tables, with column headers like "Width in inches", "co2 emissions in kiloton", "Average rainfall in inches", "Fan speed (rpm)", and "Annual revenue ($ million)". To take advantage of these headers, they must be mapped to types, which is, in general, a highly nontrivial job (see Section 5). However, starting from over 25 million tables, we could find 1.1 million headers which could be mapped with high precision (99%) to types, using simple rules discussed in Section 5.1, and restricting to headers with an exact and unique match with a unit in QuTree.

We thus get (automatically) labeled instances with observed features consisting of the words $\mathbf{x}_k$ in the header not included in the unit, and a quantity type t_k derived by generalizing its extracted unit. E.g., from the header text "Annual revenue ($ million)" we extract an instance with bag of words $\mathbf{x} = \{annual, revenue\}$ and type *money amount*. These labeled instances are used to train a logistic regression classifier for $\Pr(t|q)$. 3-fold cross validation gave 94% accuracy, higher than using PMI models [16]. If the posterior entropy was large (e.g., for a query on `refractive index`), we prefered the "dimensionless" type in favor of other types.

3.2 Snippet match with query

Each table retrieved from the index generates one or more snippets. We represent the uncertainty of relevance of a snippet s to q by $R_{s,q}$, or R_s if q is fixed. The uncertainty of relevance is reflected in a score r_{sq} or $r_s \in [0, 1]$. Based on query q, the local evidence in favor of relevance ($R_s = 1$) is r_s, and the local evidence in favor of irrelevance ($R_s = 0$) is $1 - r_{qs}$.

Given query $q = (a_q, e_q)$ and a candidate table T, we describe how we match these two parts of the query to generate one or more snippets from T. We view web tables as vertical stores of entity and their attributes[2]. Accordingly, a candidate snippet is generated by matching e_q to a row r in a column c_e and matching a_q to a different column c_a and generating the snippet from cell (r, c_a). For most queries, we find a single snippet per table but sometimes the entity e_q could match multiple rows of a table, or a_q could match multiple columns of T. For example, in Figure 3 the first three web tables generate a single snippet for query `co2 emissions of china`. In contrast, for the query `refractive index of flint glass`, in Figure 4, the second table matches the entity "flint glass" in the last two rows whereas the first web table provides the attribute "Refractive index" in three different forms over columns 2, 3, and 4. We next elaborate on our method for generating such snippets.

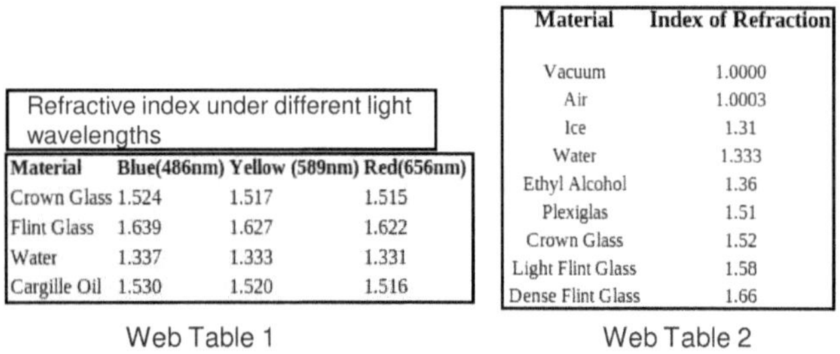

Figure 4: Snippet match with query.

The candidate tables are required to match all high-IDF terms in the query in either the body, header, or context. This ensures that our candidate snippets are minimally relevant. Thereafter, we separately measure the similarity score $\text{sim}(e_q, r, c_e, T)$ of entity e_q to cell (r, c_e) and similarity score $\text{sim}(a_q, c_a, T)$ of attribute string a_q to column c_a's header. These match scores are custom designed to depend on matches beyond the immediate cells to include T's context, title, and other parts of its body. In [11] we presented the design of a segmented similarity function that shows how to measure the relevance of a table's column to a query keyword while combining column-specific match with matches from the rest of the table. We use this segmented similarity function as the match function: $\text{sim}(e_q, r, c_e, T)$ and $\text{sim}(a_q, c_a, T)$.

The snippets from a table are generated as follows. We first find the (r, c) with the best value of $\text{sim}(e_q, r, c, T)$. Call it (r^*, c_e^*). Fix c_e^* as the entity column. We then find the column c that is numeric and has maximum similarity $\text{sim}(a_q, c, T)$. Call it c_a^*. Next, as snippets we select those cells r_s, c_s for which:

$$\begin{aligned}\text{sim}(e_q, r_s, c_e^*, T) &\geq \max(\text{sim}(e_q, r^*, c_e^*, T) - \epsilon, \sigma)\\ \text{sim}(a_q, c_s, T) &\geq \max(\text{sim}(a_q, c_a^*, T) - \epsilon, 0)\}\end{aligned}$$

This criteria makes sure that we select all snippets $s = (r_s, c_s)$ whose match is close enough (within ϵ) of the best possible match from T, provided the entity match is at least σ. In our experiments we used 0.2 for both ϵ and σ. The reason we have a minimum match threshold for entities and not for attributes is because the number of numeric columns in a table is typically much smaller than the number of rows. We depend on the global consensus model to prefer the columns that are correct. We use the entity and attribute match scores to assign the relevance score of a snippet as $r_s = (\text{sim}(a_q, c_s, T) + \text{sim}(e_q, r_s, c_e^*, T))/2$.

3.3 Possible extractions from snippet

We model each snippet s as extracting exactly one value and one unit (therefore, type). However, given the noise in extraction, we model the extracted value and type as uncertain, but drawn from a finite, usually small set of alternative extractions. This set of possible extractions is indexed by j. For example, consider the web table in Figure 1 obtained in response to query `height of washington monument`.

Height (m)	Year	Building
168,7	1884	Washington Monument
95,8	1899	Old Post Office
91,5	1990	Washington National Cathedral
87,6	1892	United States Capitol
39,2	1943	Jefferson Memorial

Table 1: An example web table for query `height of washington monument`.

We get one snippet from this table at the cell (1,1), but we have uncertainty over its value: does 168,7 equal 168.7, or a list of two numbers 168 and 7. This gives rise to two possible values: 168.7 and 168? Also, from the header Height (m), the unit parser extracts three possible units: meter, million, and mile. So, we consider all six combinations of unit and value as possibilities for j. Each j is attached with a score g_{sj} that we generate as follows: First, parse the value in the cell based on different locale specific parsers and get the set of successful parses of the value $v_{s1}, \ldots, v_{sn}$. Second, use the CFG unit parser described in Section 5 to get a list of units along with their scores: $(u_{s1}, w_1), \ldots, (u_{sm}, w_{sm})$. The set j consists of the mn possible cross product of value,unit combination where each j is associated with: a value v_{sj}, a unit u_{sj} and therefore its type t_{sj}, and a confidence score

[2]We omit a discussion of horizontal tables for simplicity [6].

$g_{sj} = \frac{w_{sj}}{n} \geq 0$. (Note that a specific extraction j has an extracted unit, and each unit maps to a unique quantity type. For convenience, we can convert a specific extraction to some canonical unit that we associate with the quantity type.) Summarizing, for each snippet s, there are two hidden random variables:

- $R_s \in \{0,1\}$, the snippet relevance bit.
- J_s, an extraction index. If $R_s = 0$, then $J_s = \perp$ is undefined. Otherwise, J_s tells us what value and unit/type s contributes to the global consensus.

3.4 Value distribution h

In abstract terms, a quantity query should be answered with a type (unit) and a value distribution h. For each potential response type τ, we will build a distribution $h_\tau(v)$, with the usual constraint $\int_\bullet h_\tau(\bullet)d\bullet = 1$.

h_τ will be estimated from a set of values $\{v_i\}$, but, based on the previous sections, each value v_i is associated with a probability π_i that the value should actually contribute to h_τ. This is expressed with the notation $h_\tau(\bullet|\{(v_i, \pi_i)\})$.

Simple parametric distributions are not a good choice for h, given that we have to deal with numbers of arbitrary scale, coming from arbitrary domains, with a high level of extraction noise. Therefore, we focus on non-parametric distributions. We briefly mention two standard forms of h_τ for the sake of completeness.

3.4.1 Kernel density

A natural option is a kernel density estimate:

$$h_\tau(\bullet; \{v_i, \pi_i\}) = \frac{1}{Z}\sum_i \frac{\pi_i}{\sqrt{2\pi}\sigma_i} e^{(\bullet - v_i)^2/2\sigma_i^2}, \quad (1)$$

where σ_i is a kernel width parameter that may be the same for all i as a special case, and $Z = \sum_i \pi_i$. A problem that we faced with a fixed width is that they do not adapt well to numbers of arbitrary scales. Consider the query that seeks to find the half-life of Plutonium. Plutonium has many isotopes with extremely diverse half-lives: 14, 88, 6560, 24100, and 376000 years. Naturally these are stated approximately, with errors that are commensurate with the magnitude of the quantity being expressed. We associated a different width σ_i around each data point that increases with the scale of the point v_i as max(10% of v_i, minimum non-zero gap between numbers).

3.4.2 Wavelet

Another popular non-parametric density estimator is based on Wavelets. Wavelets are believed to outperform kernel density estimators at representing discontinuities and local variations, features rampant in our data. We use the Haar wavelet as our basis function. Due to lack of space, we refer the reader to standard textbooks on the topic and omit further details.

3.5 Consensus inference algorithm

3.5.1 Intuition

Now we are in a position to verbally express how collective consensus is formed, given a query. We will state that various scores "should be large", with the understanding that, in a collective scheme, we want some sort of aggregate (say their product) to be large. We will then translate this description into a formal model.

- If τ is a top-scoring response quantity type, then $\Pr(\tau|q)$ should be large.
- Suppose we choose specific values for all snippet relevance variables R_s. Then the score of that configuration is
$$\prod_{s:R_s=1} r_s \prod_{s:R_s=0} (1 - r_s), \quad (2)$$
and this should be large.
- If a snippet is irrelevant, no specific extraction needs to be chosen for that snippet. If snippet s is relevant, we need to pick one extraction $J_s = j$, for which $t_{sj} = \tau$ (i.e., the extracted type matches the query target type), and g_{sj} is large.
- Consider now all relevant snippets s and their chosen extractions J_s. These induce a multiset of values $\{v\}$. If we are to propose value distribution h to the user, we want the density at $\{v\}$ to be large. Assuming iid extraction events[3], this can be written as $\prod_{s:R_s=1} h(v_{s,J_s})$.
- If h were an arbitrary distribution of unlimited complexity, it could support an arbitrary set of extracted values, no matter how disparate from each other. Therefore h needs to be *regularized*, and there needs to be consensus among the values claimed to be contributing to h.

In the rest of this section, we fill in the details of the above framework.

Inputs: $\Pr(t|q)$; for all snippets s, r_s and t_{sj}, v_{sj}, g_{sj} for all candidate extractions j.
Evolving variables: $\check{r}_s, \check{g}_{sj}$
initialize hidden variables $\check{g}_{sj} \leftarrow g_{sj}\, r_s \Pr(t_{sj}|q)$
for iterations $i = 1, 2, \ldots$ **do**
  for each snippet s **do**
    let $h_\tau^{\setminus s}(\bullet)$ be a value distribution estimated from all snippets except s, using weights $\check{g}_{sj}$
    for each candidate extraction j **do**
      $\phi_{sj} \leftarrow g_{sj}\, r_s \Pr(t_{sj}|q)\, h_{t_{sj}}^{\setminus s}(v_{sj})$ {consensus}
    end for
    $\phi_{s\perp} \leftarrow 1 - r_s$
    $D \leftarrow \phi_{s\perp} + \sum_j \phi_{sj}$
    $\check{r}_s \leftarrow (1/D)\sum_j \phi_{sj}$
    for each j **do**
      $\check{g}_{sj} \leftarrow \phi_{sj}/D$
    end for
  end for
end for

Figure 5: Collective inference pseudocode.

3.5.2 Iterative update algorithm

Each snippet s that potentially contributes information to the response of a query has the associated hidden variables R_s and J_s. The collective inference algorithm will build estimates of the posterior distributions over R_s, J_s through the procedure shown in Figure 5. Specifically, let $\check{r}_s \in [0,1]$ be the posterior probability of relevance of snippet s. If the snippet is relevant, then the probability of extraction j being valid is $\check{g}_{sj}$, with $\sum_j \check{g}_{sj} = 1$ for each s. We also maintain, for all possible response types τ, the value distributions denoted $h_\tau(\bullet)$.

The consensus update $\phi_{sj} \leftarrow g_{sj}\, r_s \Pr(t_{sj}|q)\, h_{t_{sj}}^{\setminus s}(v_{sj})$ can also be interpreted as a "leave-one-out" validation of v_{sj} in

[3]Multiple extractions from a table are not iid. QEWT handles them, but we skip discussing them for simplicity.

the backdrop of other contributing values, as explained below. (Think of index i here as $\langle s,j\rangle$.) If v_i is dropped while making the estimate h_τ, we will write it as $h_\tau^{\setminus i}(\bullet|\{(v_i,\pi_i)\})$. A natural notion of consensus among $\{(v_i,\pi_i)\}$ can be obtained by dropping each (v_i,π_i) in turn, forming the estimate $h_\tau^{\setminus i}(\bullet|\{(v_i,\pi_i)\})$, and evaluating $h^{\setminus i}(v_i,\{(v_i,\pi_i)\})$. It tells us how strongly v_i itself is supported by the rest of the observed values.

The lines after the consensus are to update $\breve{r}_s$ and $\breve{g}_{sj}$ to normalized posterior probabilities. After (sufficient) convergence, we are left with these posterior probabilities, from which we construct h_τ on all values (with their posterior probabilities). The resulting h_τ and/or values with their posterior probabilities are then sent to the answer interval representation module, described next.

4. INTERVAL REPRESENTATION

Expressive densities described in the previous section give us a great deal of power to fit the extracted values. However, the user may wish to view something simpler than such a general density. Following QCQ [3], we propose approaches to present ranked *intervals* as the query response. We associate each interval I with a lower limit ℓ_I and upper limit u_I and a p_I that denotes the probability that the answer lies within $[\ell_I,u_I]$. The final answer is a set $\mathcal{I}$ of non-overlapping intervals $I_1,\ldots,I_k$ such that $\sum_{I\in\mathcal{I}} p_I=1$. A baseline approach would be to cluster the relevant values, but the relevance of a value is not known for sure, and the number of clusters is also unknown. Therefore, we need more sophisticated methods.

For this part snippet boundaries are not relevant, so we denote our input as a set of (v_i,π_i) pairs where a i corresponds to some sj and $\pi_i=\breve{g}_{sj}$.

4.1 Uniform density mixture

$\mathcal{I}$ can also be thought of as a mixture of uniform distribution with density

$$h_{\mathcal{I}}(v)=\int_v\sum_{I\in\mathcal{I}}\frac{p_I}{u_I-\ell_I}\delta(v\in[\ell_I,u_I])dv \tag{3}$$

Thus, one method of obtaining $\mathcal{I}$ is to approximate a more expressive density (Section 3.4) to a mixture of uniform distributions. Let $h(\bullet|\{(v_i,\pi_i)\})$ be a density (such as a Kernel density). We find our desired intervals $I_1,\ldots,I_k$ such that within each $I=[\ell_I,u_I]$, the error of approximating density h by a constant is within a tolerance ϵ while minimizing the number of such intervals. We measure error in terms of KL divergence between h and $h_{\mathcal{I}}$; this makes the error per interval as $\int_{v=\ell_I}^{u_I}h(v)\log h(v)\,dv-p_I\log\frac{p_I}{u_I-\ell_I}$ where $p_I=\int_{v=\ell_I}^{u_I}h(v)\,dv$. We allow intervals to be single points $\ell_I=u_I$, and assign an error of 0 for such intervals.

Since we restrict the interval boundaries to values in V, we can easily find the optimal set of intervals in $O(|V|)^2$ time using a simple range segmentation algorithm.

4.2 MDL-intervals

One problem with the above method is the difficulty of finding one tolerance ϵ to fit all query types. We next present a method based on the minimum description length (MDL) principle [12] that is more adaptive to per-query variations in value distributions.

Assume we have a set S_q of values sampled from all rows of the snippet columns for query q. For example, in Figure 3 the set S_q will be sampled from all distinct co2 emission values over all countries. Our goal is to find intervals $\mathcal{I}=I_1,\ldots,I_k$ to represent the point answers $V=\{(v_i,\pi_i)\}$. Note that each $v_i\in S_q$. Using MDL, we interpret this as a compression problem from a hypothetical sender of V to a receiver, with the intervals serving as a compression model for V. We assume S_q is known to both parties. The cost of sending V has two parts: the cost of the model, which in our case is the set of intervals, and the cost of sending the data V given model.

The cost of sending the data V given intervals $\mathcal{I}=I_1,\ldots I_k$ is the sum of the cost of data in each interval. Let S_I denote the set of numbers from S_q that lie in interval $I=[\ell_I,u_I],p_I$. As per $\mathcal{I}$, all values within $[\ell_I,u_I]$ have probability $r_I=\frac{p_I}{|S_I|}$ of being relevant. Each entry v_i in V is relevant with probability π_i, thus the expected number of bits for sending v_i is: $-\pi_i\log r_I-(1-\pi_i)\log(1-r_I)$. Other values in S_I are irrelevant and require $-\log(1-r_I)$ bits each. Summing up, data cost over all intervals is $-\sum_{I\in I_1,\ldots I_k}\sum_{v_i\in I}-\pi_i\log r_I+\pi_i\log(1-r_I)-|S_I|\log(1-r_I)$.

The model cost is the cost of sending the parameters r_I and the boundary $[\ell_I,u_I]$. Following MDL, we encode r_I by finding a good fit distribution $p(r_I)$, and setting the cost as $-\log p(r_I)$. Since r_I is between 0 and 1, a natural choice is the Beta distribution whose density is $\Pr(p;m,n)=\frac{1}{B(m,n)}p^{m-1}(1-p)^{n-1}$ where $B(m,n)$ is the Beta function and m,n are parameters. We need to choose m,n so as to minimize the cost of sending r_Is over all intervals and all queries. Since S_q is typically larger than V, we choose the prior parameters as $m=1,n=2$ so that smaller values of r_I get lower cost. The set of intervals that minimize the sum of data and model cost can be found in $O(|V|^2)$ time using the same segmentation algorithm as in Section 4.1.

5. UNIT EXTRACTOR

So far we have abstracted the role of the extractor that finds likely units from table columns. Given the noise in tables bearing quantities, the module that annotates table columns with units needs to be fairly sophisticated.

Problem statement. Given a numeric table column with a textual header $\mathbf{x}$ our goal is to extract the units (if any) from $\mathbf{x}$ that associate with the numbers in the column. Figure 6

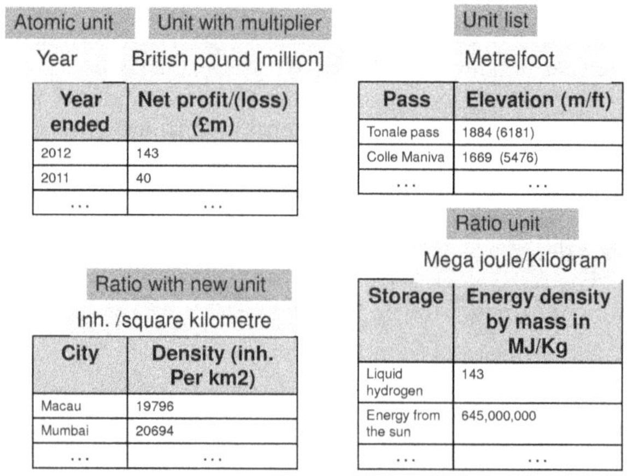

Figure 6: Example unit annotations (in yellow) on table columns.

shows some example unit annotations to table columns. As shown, we handle four types of unit occurrences:

- atomic units like year and meter that have exact match with a unit node in our quantity ontology QuTree,
- units with multipliers (e.g. million pounds),
- compound units formed by taking a ratio or product of two units (e.g. mega joule/kilogram), and
- a list of units (e.g. metre|foot).

5.1 An initial rule-based extractor

We initially attempted to extract based on a set of intuitive rules capturing various lexical clues and matches with the unit catalog, since all previous work on quantities have relied on rule-based unit extractors [3, 20].

Let the term MATCH refer to the longest sequence of tokens in a header $\mathbf{x}$ that matches a unit name, symbol, or lemma in QuTree. Annotating a unit based purely on a MATCH leads to many false positives because there are several words like "in", "at", "last", "s", "stone", "point" that are unit names/symbols but are commonly used as non-unit words. Therefore, we defined rules that require additional evidences for a MATCH in $\mathbf{x}$ to be tagged a unit:

1. AFTER-IN: A MATCH after IN is a unit e.g. "Price in \$", "Distance in km", "Wind velocity in miles per hour".
2. BRACKETED: A MATCH within brackets is a unit e.g "Net profit (\$)", "CO2 emissions (kiloton)"
3. TYPE-NAME: A MATCH tied to a unit U whose parent type name appears in the header is unit U. E.g. "Length of race, m" is annotated U=`Metre` and "Cruise Speed, mph." is annotated `Miles per hour`

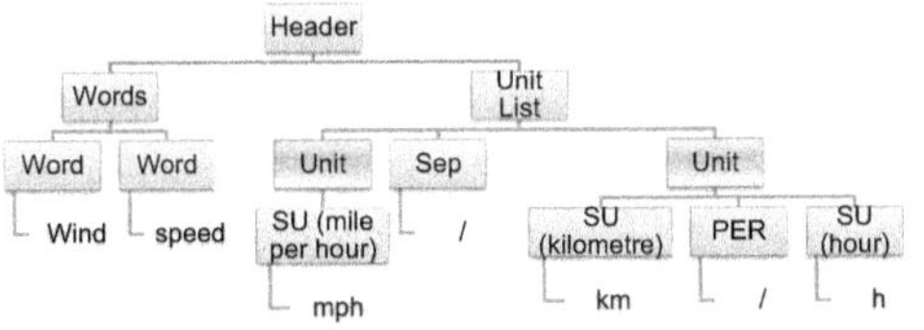

Figure 7: An example parse for the column header `Wind␣speed␣(mph␣/␣km/h)`. SimpleUnit is abbreviated to SU, and unary nodes like CUnit and AtomUnit have been deleted for compactness.

Header	::=	Words? Unit-List Words?
Unit	::=	CUnit | Multiplier Msep CUnit | CUnit Msep Multiplier | Msep Multiplier
Msep	::=	Empty | OF | IN
CUnit	::=	SimpleUnit | SimpleUnit UnitOp SimpleUnit
UnitOp	::=	Empty | PER | '/' | ×
SimpleUnit	::=	AtomUnit | Multiplier AtomUnit
AtomUnit	::=	Unit_in_QuTree | New_word
Multiplier	::=	Multiplier_Unit_in_QuTree | Number

Figure 8: Grammar used by the CFG

On deploying these rules on our table corpus we were surprised by their large number of errors. For example, the rule AFTER-IN wrongly labels the header "Scores in last match" as unit `Last` (a unit of Volume), and cannot disambiguate between units `Carat, Knot,` and `Kiloton` in header "Capacity in kt" since "kt" is a symbol for each of these three units. The rule BRACKETED wrongly labels word "dec" in header "Population (Dec 2006)" as unit Decade. Also, it cannot differentiate between units in headers "duration(s)" and "year(s)" where the unit annotation of the first should be `Seconds` but the second should have no unit. The rule TYPE-NAME wrongly annotates header "Length of song(m:s)" as `Meter` whereas the correct annotation for "m" is `Minute`. The rule is particularly bad for compound units, for example in "Energy density by volume (MJ/L)", volume helps annotate L as `Liter`. Rules for compound units are not easy because they require simultaneous labeling of many different parts of the headers. Finally, these set of rules have poor recall, for example, the header "CO2 Emissions 2000 thousands of metric tons of carbon" from the third table in Figure 3 is not covered by any of the three rules.

We therefore explored alternative models that combine multiple soft evidence from additional resources and are more expressive in their modeling of compound units and other unit patterns like multipliers. The rampant ambiguity of a mention with language words and a unit and with other units, implied that just depending on clues derived from the header string may not be adequate. Further, since the system of derived units is based on a well-defined grammar, it seemed natural to use a grammar to drive the extraction. Feature-based context free grammars seemed perfect for the task. Regular grammars cannot capture patterns that encourage alternative units to be of the same type, as in "Meters per second (m/s)".

5.2 Feature-based context free grammar

In this approach we use a discriminative Context Free Grammar (CFG) with scores attached to each possible production in the grammar [15]. In Table 8 we show the CFG (without scores) for unit extraction from table headers. The grammar supports all four different types of compound units illustrated in Figure 6. In Figure 7 we present an example parse tree for the header: "Wind speed (mph / km/h)" that this grammar supports.

In general, the grammar allows many possible parses of a header $\mathbf{x}$. Each parse-tree has a score that is additive over each of the productions in the tree. A production P of the form: $R ::= R_1 R_2$ is scored as:

$$\text{score}(P) = \mathbf{w}.\mathbf{f}(P, \mathbf{x}, i, j, k) \tag{4}$$

where (i, j) and $(j + 1, k)$ are the text spans in $\mathbf{x}$ that R_1 and R_2 cover, respectively. When R_2 is empty ($j = k$), we have a unary production. The feature vector $\mathbf{f}$ can be used to capture various clues that help identify units. We list the set of features we used in sections 5.2.1,... 5.2.5. The weight vector $\mathbf{w}$ corresponding to the features could be trained using the discriminative framework of [15], but since the number of features in our case was small (seven) and easily interpretable, we fixed their values manually.

The task of annotating units in an input $\mathbf{x}$ reduces to the task of finding the tree of production with the highest sum of scores, and outputing the list of units under the "Unit" nodes in the tree. Since we have scores, as against hard rules, we can output multiple extractions each weighted with a score. The well-known Inside-outside algorithm [13, 9] for inference in PCFGs can be easily extended to output the top-K highest scoring extractions in polynomial time.

We next list the features used in $\mathbf{f}(P, \mathbf{x}, i, j, k)$. We first list the features for leaf-level productions where R is a unit name U which could be either a Multiplier or an AtomicUnit, and finally in Section 5.2.5 present features for other internal nodes of the parse tree. We will use the short form $\mathbf{x}_{ij}$ to denote the token subsequence $x_i \ldots, x_j$ of $\mathbf{x}$.

5.2.1 Matches with the Unit Catalog

The TF-IDF similarity of $\mathbf{x}_{ij}$ to various parts of unit $U's$ entry in QuTree, including U's name, lemmas, and symbol is an important feature for productions that tag $\mathbf{x}_{ij}$ as a unit name. Another feature analogous to the TYPE-NAME rule, is the TF-IDF similarity of the words in the parent quantity type of U and tokens in $\mathbf{x}$ *excluding* $\mathbf{x}_{ij}$. For example, in the header "Length (m)", this feature will apply for production `Meter :=` $\mathbf{x}_{22}$ since the word "Length" matches the parent type of unit Meter. However, it does not fire for production `million :=` $\mathbf{x}_{22}$.

5.2.2 Lexical clues

When each of the AFTER-IN and BRACKETED rules apply on a $\mathbf{x}_{ij}$ we fire a feature when R is the unit state "Unit". To allow for occasional extraneous tokens, (e.g. length in approx meter), we also fire these tokens with a tolerance of one token.

5.2.3 Relative frequency

We exploit ontologies such as WordNet that provide relative frequency of word usage to get disambiguation clues between units and non-units and between different symbols of the same unit. WordNet provides relative frequency of various senses of nouns in its ontology. Each noun sense s is associated with a list of word-forms and a frequency $f(s)$. Let $S = \{s_1, \ldots, s_m\}$ be the set of senses whose word-forms match $\mathbf{x}_{ij}$. If one of these senses, say s, is a descendant of the Quantity type in Wordnet and matches the base name of the unit U in QuTree, we fire a feature with value $1 - \frac{f(s)}{\sum_{t \in S} f(t)}$. For example, with $\mathbf{x}_{ij}$="last", we found eight matching senses in Wordnet, with more than 99% frequency on the non-unit meaning of last as "finish" or "end". This provided strong evidence to not tag "last" as a unit.

5.2.4 Co-occurrence statistics from table corpus

Another strong clue for correctly assigning a unit U to $\mathbf{x}$ is obtained from the presence of strongly co-occurring words in $\mathbf{x}$ outside unit words $\mathbf{x}_{ij}$. For example, for $\mathbf{x}$ = "width in m", and unit U = `metre` for token x_{22}, we can exploit the fact that "width" often co-occurs with `Length` units. We use the unlabeled corpus of table headers to train a query type classifier as described in Section 3.1.2. Using this, we assign a feature with value $\Pr(t_U|\mathbf{x})$ where t_U is the parent type of unit U.

5.2.5 Compound, Multiple, Multiplier units

We next add a set of features to handle compound units. For each compound unit type: unit-multiplier pair (e.g. dollar [million]), and ratio/product of two units (MJ/L) we add bias terms so that atomic units are preferentially related via these operations instead of being treated as a list of unrelated units. Finally, when two units belong to the same type, we add a bias term so that they are treated as alternatives (e.g. metre|feet).

6. EXPERIMENTS

After describing our testbed in Section 6.1, we perform controlled studies on collective extraction (§6.2), choice of value distribution h (§6.3), query type inference (§6.4), response interval generation approaches (§6.5), and the effect of various unit extractors (§6.6).

6.1 Testbed

Table corpora. Our corpus of tables was collected from two sources: a commercial Web crawl with 500M pages similar to ClueWeb09[4] from which we extracted 25 million tables [11], and tables returned by research.google.com/tables in response to queries.

Queries and ground truth. We used three sources of queries:

QCQ: 28 diverse queries used in [3].

WorldBank: 172 queries on four quantity attributes of countries: forest area, co2 emissions, land area, and population. Ground truth is from World Bank documents [18].

InfoGather: 146 queries used in InfoGather [20], on three different types of quantities: population of 50 large cities of the world and revenue and profit of 34 large corporations. Land area of countries was also part of this workload, but since we had already included in WorldBank, we dropped it from this set.

Queries with ground truth are at goo.gl/542L2Y.

Measurements. As in QCQ [3], we need to design how the performance of QEWT is measured. Most commonly, ground truth G is available as a set of values, or one or a few ranges. Similar to QCQ, we assume that the query specifies a multiplicative confidence band ϵ. I.e., if a true point value is v, the user would be satisfied with a value in $[(1-\epsilon)v, (1+\epsilon)v]$ (Our results are with $\epsilon = 0.02$). Meanwhile, QEWT presents a distribution h. The *probabilistic precision* of h is

$$\int_v h(v)\delta\Big([(1-\epsilon)v, (1+\epsilon)v] \in G\Big) dv, \qquad (5)$$

which is the total area matching a ground truth value band. Recall is defined as the fraction of G supported by h[5]. The probabilistic F1 score is the harmonic mean of probabilistic precision and recall. Given the total area under h is always 1, any attempt to recall all ground values by "smearing out" h will result in large swathes of h never being touched by a ground truth band. Since the form of h shown to the user is a set probability weighted set intervals, we use $h_{\mathcal{I}}$ (Equation 3) for h.

6.2 Benefits of collective answer extraction

QEWT potentially improves upon two simpler baselines. In **CollectiveHard**, for each snippet s, we greedily and locally choose the extraction with the best scoring unit and value. I.e., J_s is pinned. The only uncertainty is in relevance R_s, for which h is used. For $\Pr(t|q)$ we use the hard scores from Section 3.1.1 which is 1 when a_q matches the catalog, and uniform otherwise. In **Independent**, h is missing but the rest of the setting is exactly the same as in **Collective**. The default representation for h is variable width kernel density. Figure 9 shows that the full power of QEWT's collective extraction is vital. In workload InfoGather, **CollectiveHard** suffers particularly severely because of the hard method of query type assignment on the `corporate tax rate` queries.

6.3 Effect of choices of h

With the value of h established, in Figure 10 we compare choices for h: variable and fixed width kernel density, wavelets, and a degenerate distribution with impulse probabilities only at point values seen in the snippets, essentially treating quantities as discrete symbolic extractions. Whereas there is no clear winner among the continuous distributions, they are all better than point histograms, which

[4]lemurproject.org/clueweb09

[5]Note, an alternative definition of probabilistic recall is precision times the fraction of G supported by h. But that causes precision to be counted twice in F1 and is redundant.

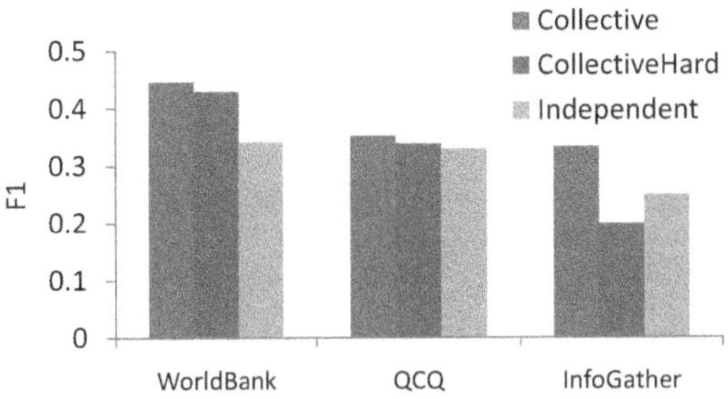

Figure 9: Comparing collective extraction models.

are bad for queries like net worth of a celebrity, or revenue of a company that are often stated approximately; it gets no benefit of consensus from values that are close by (e.g. \$ 111.5 billion versus \$ 111.05 billion).

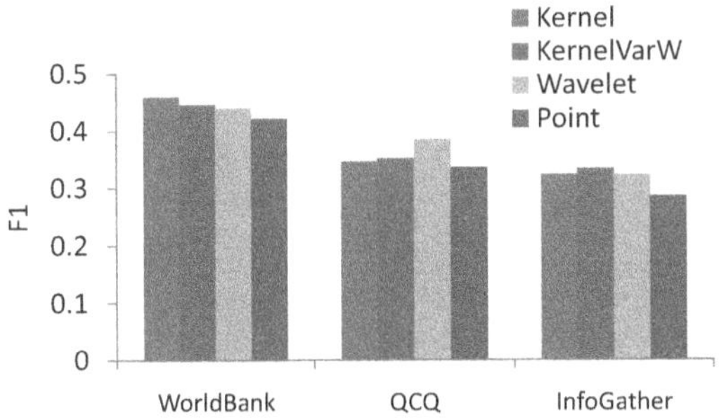

Figure 10: Comparing different models for h(.)

6.4 Effect of query type prediction $\Pr(t|q)$

We compare the dictionary match approach (§3.1.1) with the data-driven approach (§3.1.2). Out of the 35 distinct attribute names spanning the three workloads, dictionary match correctly identified only ten of the query types. In contrast, our data-driven approach correctly classified 34 of them with confidence at least 0.66. Some example attributes and their type and score from this method appear in Figure 11. When the data-driven unit extractor is plugged into the collective answer extractor, the result is a significant boost to end-to-end accuracy, as shown in Figure 12.

6.5 Interval generation methods compared

Figure 13 compares MDL-intervals (§4.2) vs. uniform mixture approximations (§4.1). The x-axis is proportional to the (assigned) marginal cost of an additional segment (one uniform distribution). The y-axis shows F1. At low segment cost, responses are over-fragmented, losing recall. At high segment cost, precision is lost.

Part of the reason for MDL's superiority is the guidance from the reference value distribution. Figure 14 shows an example, for the query "corporate tax rate of united states". There are 12 distinct correct answers in the tight interval [39.05, 39.34] (%), shown as green crosses. The candidate extracted values $V = \{(v_i, p_i)\}$ are shown as red squares (some wide off the mark). About 100 reference values forming S_q, sampled from tables on corporate tax rates of several countries are between 20% and 40%, shown as blue diamonds. Because of the large reference density in [35, 45], the intervals (with probabilities) created by MDL are **[39.2,39.4]: 0.61**, [35,35]: 0.1, [40,40]: 0.09, and [39.0,39.1]: 0.09. The most likely one is shown as a green box, containing most true values. In contrast, the top response from UniformMix is the low-precision interval [35.0,45]: 0.91, because it

Attribute	Type	$\Pr(\tau \vert a_q)$
annual rainfall	Length	0.92
revenue	Currency	0.71
weight	Mass	0.96
CO2 emissions	Mass	0.87
depth	Length	0.97
distance to sun	Length	0.97
net worth	Currency	0.83
population	Multiples	0.73
half life	Time	0.67

Figure 11: Query attributes a_q, labeled type τ and $\Pr(\tau|a_q)$ via logistic classifier.

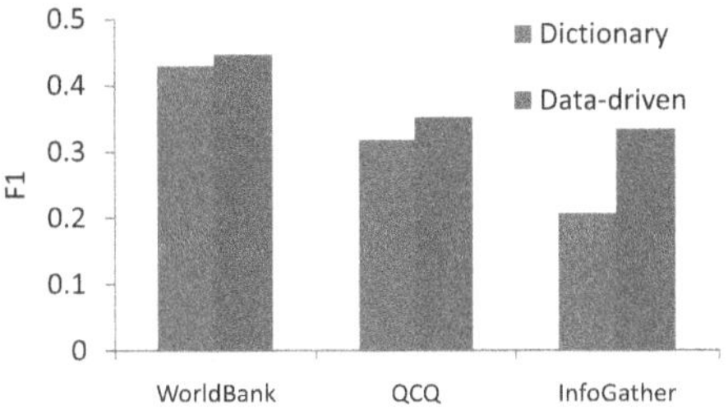

Figure 12: Query F1 accuracy under different query-type classification models.

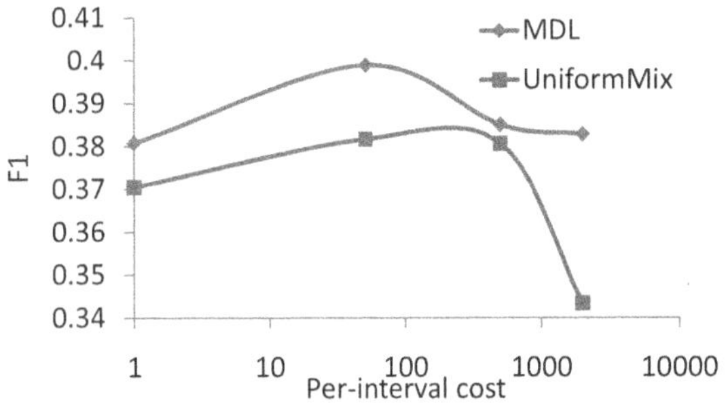

Figure 13: Comparing the MDL and UniformMix models for generating final intervals in the answer for increasing Segment cost.

has no query-specific method of measuring relative distances between points.

6.6 Benefits of PCFG-based unit extractor

Here we evaluate different parsers for extracting units discussed in Section 5 and also study their impact on end-to-end query processing.

In order to estimate the extraction accuracy of unit parsers, we created a dataset of 617 table headers from our corpus that have been manually labeled with the correct units. In Figure 15 we plot the extraction accuracy of different parsers under varying settings. **Rule** is a rule-based parser that includes among others the rules of Section 5.1 refined to label only unambiguous matches. This has an accuracy of only

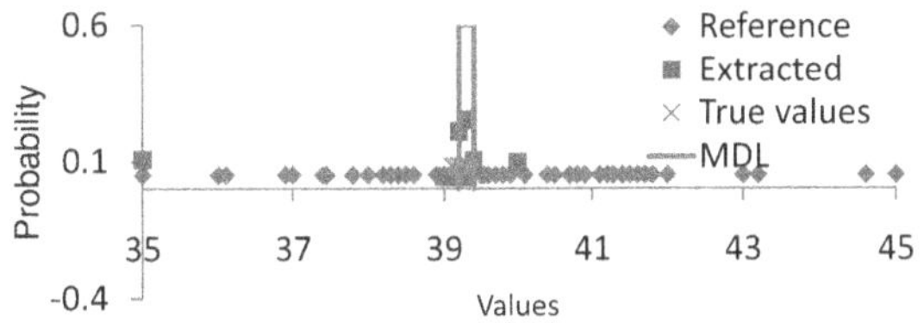

Figure 14: An example showing how a reference set of numbers helps the MDL approach select the correct intervals.

40%, and almost all of this error is due to poor recall — the precision of the rule-based parser is 99%. In contrast, our proposed CFG-based parser that we call **QuantCFG** achieves an accuracy of 82%. We created another parser called **Sequence** that uses all the features of **QuantCFG** but not its grammar, and chooses the unit with highest score **w**.**f** among all word sequences that match QuTree. The drop in accuracy to 74% establishes the importance of the grammar. The next three bars establish the importance of features in Sections 5.2.2, 5.2.3, 5.2.4 by reporting accuracy of **QuantCFG** without various subsets of them.

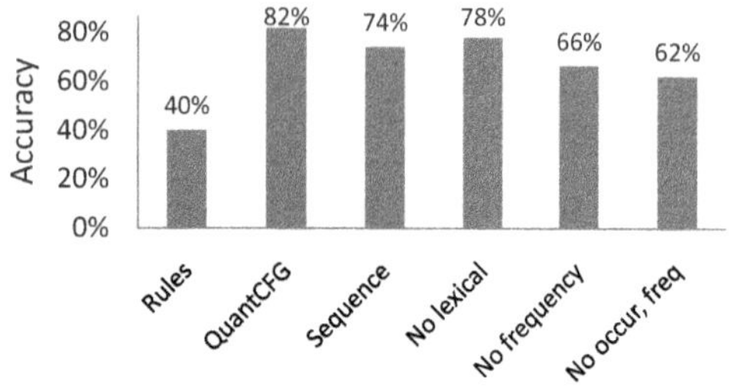

Figure 15: Comparing different parsers.

We next assess the impact of the unit extraction accuracy on the final answer quality in the end-to-end system. In Figure 16, we compare F1 scores of the answer on the three workloads on three different parsers described above: the rule-based parser, the feature-based sequence parser, and our QuantCFG parser. We observe that it is necessary to use parsers both with high precision and high recall for getting quality answers.

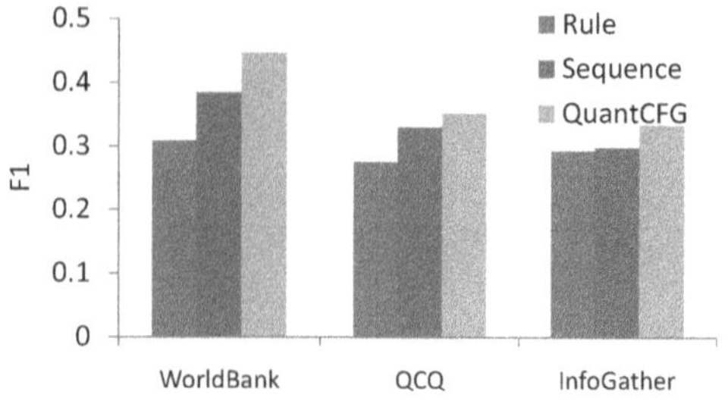

Figure 16: Comparing different parsers on their impact on the answer quality in the end to end system.

7. RELATED WORK

Moriceau [10] was among the earliest to formalize quantity search, and provide some initial notions of temporal trends and aggregation of values. A more extensive system was built by Wu and Marian [19, "W&M"]. Banerjee *et al.* [3, "QCQ"] proposed the quantity interval ranking problem. None of these exploited source HTML tables, none delayed per-snippet extraction decisions, and none proposed an inference procedure that collectively estimated snippet relevance, snippet extractions, and the value distribution. SCAD [1] collected quantities while satisfying domain-guided numeric constraints between them (e.g., a laptop screen is wider than it is tall). But SCAD did not use a unit extractor or consensus inference as in QEWT. Zhang *et al.* [20, "InfoGather"] also extract units and values from Web tables. They focus on identifying correspondences among tables based on column types. They do not model uncertain value distributions. Their aggregation/consensus is based on exact match of values, which we demonstrate as weaker than QEWT's value distribution model. InfoGather extracts column units using rules, which cannot handle compound units and noisy headers, unlike our PCFG unit extractor. Their "query" resembles a table completion task, with ~100 entities, units, and scales explicitly provided. In contrast, QEWT is a robust, open-domain system for ad-hoc, single-entity queries.

Acknowledgments. This work was partly supported by research grants from the Indo-German Max Planck Centre for Computer Science (IMPECS) and from Yahoo! Research.

8. REFERENCES

[1] A. Bakalov, A. Fuxman, P. P. Talukdar, and S. Chakrabarti. SCAD: collective discovery of attribute values. In *WWW Conference*, pages 447–456, 2011.

[2] K. Balog, L. Azzopardi, and M. de Rijke. A language modeling framework for expert finding. *Information Processing and Management*, 45(1):1–19, 2009.

[3] S. Banerjee, S. Chakrabarti, and G. Ramakrishnan. Learning to rank for quantity consensus queries. In *SIGIR Conference*, 2009.

[4] M. J. Cafarella, A. Y. Halevy, and N. Khoussainova. Data integration for the relational web. *PVLDB*, 2(1), 2009.

[5] M. Cornolti, P. Ferragina, and M. Ciaramita. A framework for benchmarking entity-annotation systems. In *WWW Conference*, pages 249–260, Rio de Janeiro, Brazil, 2013.

[6] E. Crestan and P. Pantel. Web-scale table census and classification. In *Proceedings of the fourth ACM international conference on Web search and data mining*, WSDM '11, 2011.

[7] G. Limaye, S. Sarawagi, and S. Chakrabarti. Annotating and searching web tables using entities, types and relationships. In *VLDB*, 2010.

[8] T.-Y. Liu. Learning to rank for information retrieval. In *Foundations and Trends in Information Retrieval*, volume 3, pages 225–331. Now Publishers, 2009.

[9] C. D. Manning and H. Schütze. *Foundations of Statistical Natural Language Processing*. The MIT Press, Cambridge, Massachusetts, 1999.

[10] V. Moriceau. Numerical data integration for cooperative question-answering. In *EACL Workshop on Knowledge and Reasoning for Language Processing*, pages 42–49, 2006.

[11] R. Pimplikar and S. Sarawagi. Answering table queries on the web using column keywords. In *Proc. of the 38th Int'l Conference on Very Large Databases (VLDB)*, 2012.

[12] J. Rissanen. Stochastic complexity in statistical inquiry. In *World Scientific Series in Computer Science*, volume 15. World Scientific, Singapore, 1989.

[13] S. Sarawagi. Information extraction. *FnT Databases*, 1(3), 2008.

[14] F. M. Suchanek, G. Kasneci, and G. Weikum. YAGO: A core of semantic knowledge unifying WordNet and Wikipedia. In *WWW Conference*, pages 697–706. ACM Press, 2007.

[15] B. Taskar, D. Klein, M. Collins, D. Koller, and C. Manning. Max-margin parsing. In *EMNLP*, July 2004.

[16] P. D. Turney. Mining the Web for synonyms: PMI-IR versus LSA on TOEFL. In *ECML*, 2001.

[17] P. Venetis, A. Y. Halevy, J. Madhavan, M. Pasca, W. Shen, F. Wu, G. Miao, and C. Wu. Recovering semantics of tables on the web. *PVLDB*, 4(9), 2011.

[18] Worldbank. http://data.worldbank.org/, 2014.

[19] M. Wu and A. Marian. Corroborating answers from multiple web sources. In *WebDB: Tenth International Workshop on the Web and Databases*, 2007.

[20] M. Zhang and K. Chakrabarti. Infogather+: semantic matching and annotation of numeric and time-varying attributes in web tables. In *SIGMOD Conference*, 2013.

Crowdsourced Time-sync Video Tagging using Temporal and Personalized Topic Modeling

Bin Wu[1], Erheng Zhong[1], Ben Tan[1], Andrew Horner[1], Qiang Yang[1,2]
[1]Department of Computer Science and Engineering,
Hong Kong University of Science and Technology, Hong Kong
[2]Noah's Ark Lab, Huawei, Hong Kong
{bwuaa,ezhong,btan,horner,qyang}@cse.ust.hk

ABSTRACT

Time-sync video tagging aims to automatically generate tags for each video shot. It can improve the user's experience in previewing a video's timeline structure compared to traditional schemes that tag an entire video clip. In this paper, we propose a new application which extracts time-sync video tags by automatically exploiting crowdsourced comments from video websites such as Nico Nico Douga, where videos are commented on by online crowd users in a time-sync manner. The challenge of the proposed application is that users with bias interact with one another frequently and bring noise into the data, while the comments are too sparse to compensate for the noise. Previous techniques are unable to handle this task well as they consider video semantics independently, which may overfit the sparse comments in each shot and thus fail to provide accurate modeling. To resolve these issues, we propose a novel temporal and personalized topic model that jointly considers temporal dependencies between video semantics, users' interaction in commenting, and users' preferences as prior knowledge. Our proposed model shares knowledge across video shots via users to enrich the *short* comments, and peels off user interaction and user bias to solve the *noisy*-comment problem. Log-likelihood analyses and user studies on large datasets show that the proposed model outperforms several state-of-the-art baselines in video tagging quality. Case studies also demonstrate our model's capability of extracting tags from the crowdsourced *short* and *noisy* comments.

Categories and Subject Descriptors

H.2.8 [**Database Management**]: Data Mining

Keywords

Video tagging; crowdsourcing; topic modeling; temporal and personalized model

1. INTRODUCTION

Online videos have become indispensable to peoples' daily lives. Everyday, millions of people watch online videos for entertainment, news, and education. Traffic created by online video websites such as Youtube, Hulu, and Netflix occupied 56.6% of the total global consumer internet traffic in 2012 [1]. At the same time, the volume of online videos is extremely large. On YouTube, over 6 billion hours of video are watched each month and 100 hours of video are uploaded to YouTube every minute [2]. The huge traffic and volume of online videos have made data management and indexing, the key parts of video searching, very challenging.

Figure 1: Videos with time-sync descriptions improve the user's experience in previewing and locating video content. We magnified the thumbnails and time-sync description for illustration.

To solve the aforementioned problems, automatic video tagging techniques have been proposed to generate keywords to represent a video for fast and accurate video indexing [20, 17]. However, these techniques can only provide video-level tags, that is, keywords corresponding to entire video clips. The problem is that even if the generated tags can perfectly summarize the video content, users have no idea how these tags are associated with the video playback time, which results in a long wait for video buffering, and having to either slide through the entire video or randomly approximate the informativeness of the video content.

To this end, time-sync video tagging has been proposed as a new paradigm. Time-sync video tags are synchronized to a video's playback time, and are therefore well structured in a timeline manner. Users will be able to better preview and search videos. For example, Youku.com, one of the biggest online video websites in China, has started to provide such a feature on some videos. As shown in Figure 1[1], users can preview video content in both thumbnails and text/tags by indicating the playback time. Also, this textual information can enrich search results with playback time positions.

[1]http://goo.gl/Fol6t, accessed 9 July.

KDD'14, August 24–27, 2014, New York, NY, USA.

http://dx.doi.org/10.1145/2623330.2623625.

In addition to improving user experience and indexing precision, time-sync tags and the corresponding video shots also act as an accurate labeled set for extrinsic tasks such as video classification. All in all, time-sync video tagging offers several advantages compared to traditional video tagging schemes which only tag for the entire video.

However, generating time-sync video tags automatically usually requires image to text transformation [19] and subtitles/annotations, both of which are either too difficult to realize or too expensive to obtain. Fortunately, video sharing websites such as Nico Nico Douga[2] and acfuntv[3], where users can comment on playback timestamps, provide opportunities to solve this problem. In such video websites, comments are overlaid directly over the video, synchronized to a specific playback time. This allows comments to respond directly to the corresponding video semantics, in sync with users - creating a sense of shared watching experience. For simplicity, we call this type of online video as time-sync commented (TSC) videos. In this paper, our objective is to extract time-sync video tags for TSC videos using comments only, which is a new application.

Given the well-structured comments of TSC videos, the learning problem of time-sync video tagging can be regarded as topic extraction for each video shot. Nevertheless, extracting tags from TSC videos is not only a new application but also brings up a new crowdsourcing problem. The challenge in TSC videos is that crowd users with different preferences interact with one another frequently and bring noise into the data, while the comments are too sparse to compensate for the noise, i.e., the text content in each video shot is very *short* and *noisy*. More specifically, there are only ten comments for each video shot on average, and each comment normally contains less than five words. This is because in TSC videos, each comment is only allowed to stay on the screen for a few seconds, which restricts users to *short* comments. Comments are also *noisy* because they usually contain information from multiple sources. As in traditional crowdsourcing problems [22, 23], users may have their own preferences on topics, which are not necessarily related to the current video semantics, and therefore introduce user bias in their comments. Moreover, the shared video watching experience allows users to interact with one another. In many cases, users write irrelevant comments such as replying to a previous comment, which may bury the most valuable information.

Previous methods cannot be applied to solve the *short* and *noisy* issues. Some researchers have taken advantage of the huge number of real-time comments for big events generated by crowds on social media applications such as Twitter, which are similar to TSC videos due to their *short* and *noisy* properties. For instance, Chakrabarti *et al.* proposed to summarize key tweets for live football video events [5]. However, the videos they explored were typically live videos such as big sports games which are important enough for large number of related tweets in real-time. Extending these schemes to online video tagging is more difficult because of the lack of viewers and comments. More importantly, since these approaches did not consider knowledge enrichment and user modeling in mining crowdsourced content, the *short* and *noisy* (e.g., user bias and interaction) issues cannot be solved.

Some unsupervised methods have been proposed to consider knowledge sharing across instances in crowdsourced data and collecting high quality labels by integrating noisy-labels. They achieved this goal by modeling information such as labeling ability [22, 23], by assuming that users' labeling follows an Independent Identical Distribution (*i.i.d.*). Nevertheless, in a TSC video, users can see previous comments before commenting, which means labeling is not independent (commenting can be regarded as labeling on video semantics). In fact, the dependencies between users' labels might have strong effects on modeling users' preferences. Intuitively, a user might have a preference on a specific topic if s/he often comments about it, while users who follow this topic may be simply responding to the previous comments, not necessarily indicating the same preference. Ignoring the interactions in comments may lead to inaccurate modeling of users' preferences, and fail to remove user bias in topic extraction. Therefore, the typical *i.i.d.* assumption does not hold for users' labeling, and thus previous methods may not be suitable in TSC videos.

To solve these problems, we propose an unsupervised method to automatically generate time-sync video tags using crowdsourced comment data only. More specifically, the technical contribution of this paper is that we build a novel temporal and personalized topic model which integrates users' preferences, users' interaction, and the temporal semantics of videos. On one hand, it encodes the temporal semantics correlation between successive video shots, which can enrich the *short* comments of the current video shot. On the other hand, to recover topics of the current video semantics accurately, our proposed model removes user interaction and user bias to address the *noisy* problem. This is achieved by encoding semantics dependencies between comments within the same shot, and utilizing an adaptive variable of each user to denote their latent preferences that decide their global commenting preferences.

The main contributions of our paper are as follows:

1. We propose a novel time-sync video tagging application for time-sync commented videos. To the best of our knowledge, this is the first work on automatic time-sync video tagging using video comments only.
2. We propose a novel temporal and personalized topic model for automatic video tagging, which addresses *short* and *noisy* (i.e., user bias and interaction) problems of time-sync comments.
3. We evaluate our proposed model with real-world large datasets, user studies, and a case study. The results show that our proposed model outperforms baselines in terms of tagging quality with similar computational complexity.

2. PROBLEM DEFINITION

In this section, we first present an example video to illustrate what is a TSC video. Then, we define our problem formally. After the definition, we show statistics on TSC videos to give some insights on the data.

2.1 Illustration of Time-sync Commented Videos

Two snapshots (with a one-minute gap) of an example video[4] are shown in Figure 2. Users can write comments with respect to the current video semantics (e.g., 'bento', 'shrimps'). Moreover, users' views can be affected by previous comments. For example, in the first snapshot, user B's comment "...SHIMPS..." may help other users (e.g., user A) recognize the unobvious shrimps. Then, the comment "Eating the shrimps" provided by user D is probably generated under the co-effect of both previous comments ("shimps") and the current semantics ("eating"). Note that users' IDs can be retrieved by parsing the website. In this paper, we refer to such videos as time-sync commented (TSC) videos.

[2]http://www.nicovideo.jp/. Nico Nico Douga is the most popular video sharing website in Japan, with 25 million users (19.6% of Japnese population) according to the statistics in May, 2012.

[3]http://www.acfun.tv

[4]http://live.nicovideo.jp/watch/lv139636921

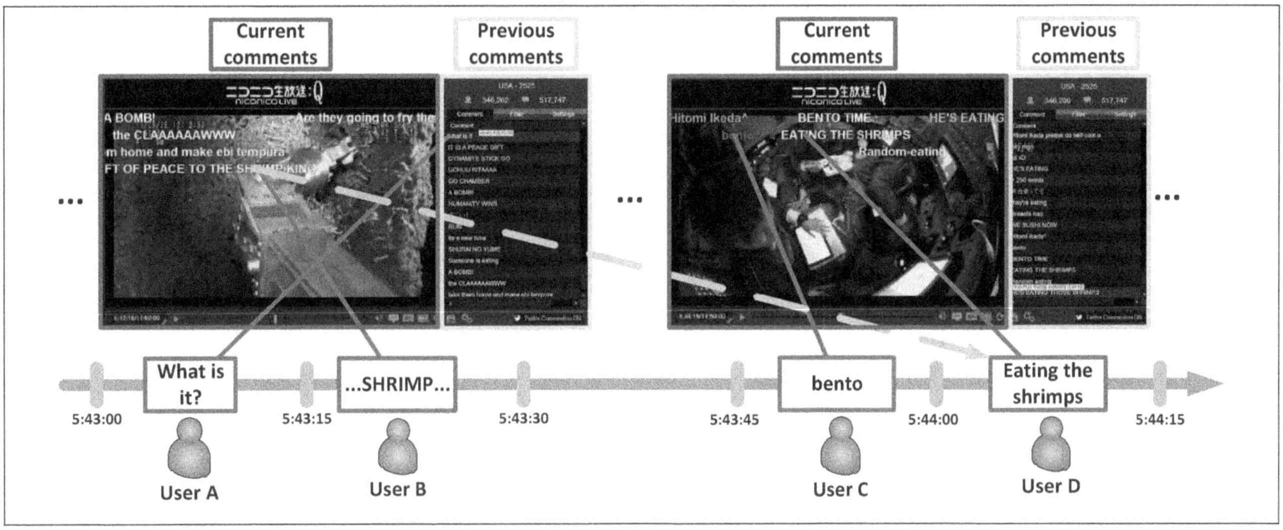

Figure 2: Snapshot of an example Time-Sync Commented (TSC) video. Users share their watching experience by providing time-sync comments that appear on the screen.

Table 1: Notation List

Notation	Definition
V	Set of videos, containing $\|V\|$ videos
U	Set of users, containing $\|U\|$ users
v	A video, containing $\|v\|$ shots
s	A shot, containing $\|s\|$ comments
v_s	Video which contains s
c	A comment, containing $\|c\|$ words
w	A word
W	Vocabulary set
u_c	User who commented comment c
s_c	Shot which contains comment c
pre_s	Preceding shots of s in v_s
pre_c	Preceding comments of c in s_c
T	Number of tags to be generated for each shot
m_{pre_s}	Semantics prior distribution of s, generated by pre_s
m_{pre_c}	Semantics prior distribution of c, generated by pre_c
K	Number of hidden topics
N	Number of comments
M	Size of vocabulary
$\boldsymbol{x_u}$	u's preference vector.
$\boldsymbol{\lambda_s}$	s's topic prior distribution vector.
$\boldsymbol{\alpha_c}$	Dirichlet prior distribution vector for c's topic distribution.
β	Dirichlet prior for word-topic distribution.
$\boldsymbol{\varphi_t}$	Word distribution of topic t
$\boldsymbol{\pi_c}$	c's topic prior distribution base vector
$\boldsymbol{\theta_c}$	c's topic distribution

2.2 Formal Problem Definition

In this section, we present the problem definition formally. We have a set of videos $V = \{v_1, v_2, \dots, v_{|V|}\}$ of size $|V|$, and users $U = \{u_1, u_2, \dots, u_{|U|}\}$ of size $|U|$ who have written comments on these videos V. Each video $v \in V$ has a number of shots which have been segmented previously, $v = \{s_{(v)1}, s_{(v)2}, \dots, s_{(v)|v|}\}$ where $|v|$ denotes the number of shots in video v. Shots in a video are organized according to playback time. For example, $s_{(v)i}$ means the i-th shot appears in video v and $s_{(v)i+1}$ is the $(i+1)$-th shot. We denote a set of shots s as $pre_s = \{s'|s, s' \in v, s'$ appears before $s\}$. Each shot has a number of comments $s = \{c_{(s)1}, c_{(s)2}, \dots, c_{(s)|s|}\}$, where $|s|$ is the number of comments in shot s. Note that each comment corresponds to a specific timestamp in a video, and all comments are organized according to playback time. Users may write their comments after seeing the preceding comments, and the set of preceding comments is denoted as $pre_c = \{c'|c, c' \in s, c'$ appears before $c\}$. Each comment c consists of a set of words $c = \{w_{(c)1}, w_{(c)2}, \dots, w_{(c)|c|}\}$, where $w_{(c)i}$ is the i-th obseved word in c and $|c|$ denotes the number of words in comment c. Usually, both $|s|$ and $|c|$ are small. For each comment c, the user is known and denoted as u_c. Similarly, we denote the shot containing comment c as s_c. We also denote the total number of comments as N and the size of the vocabulary as M for simplicity.

Given that comments in each video shot are *short* and *noisy* (i.e., $|s|$ is small and each c is affected by pre_c), our task is to extract tags $W_s = \{w_1, w_2, \dots, w_T\}$ from each shot s so that the tags well describe the shot, that is to find:

$$W_s = \max_{W'_s \subset W} P(W'_s|s, u_c, Pre_c, Pre_s), \forall c \in s. \tag{1}$$

where W is the vocabulary set, and W'_s is a candidate of W_s. For reference, the above notations have been listed in Table 1.

2.3 Inspection of Time-Sync Commented Videos

For better insight into the time-sync comments, we have conducted data inspection of the video comments from acfuntv[5], a typical time-sync commented video website. Statistics of pairwise Jaccard similarity [14] and the number of Chinese characters in the comments have been investigated, as shown in Figure 3 and Table 2.

Table 2: Jaccard Similarity for the Average Comment

Statistics	Average Comments Jaccard Similarity
Overall Comments	0.008
Intra-user	0.036
Overall Shots	0.038
Intra-shot	0.065
Comment with Preceding Comments	0.080
Shot with Preceding Shots	0.099

The number of Chinese characters is usually small in most comments, i.e., about 15 characters on average (see Figure 3(a)). The average similarity between a comment and its preceding comments is much higher than the intra-shot similarity (the average pairwise

[5]http://www.acfun.tv

similarity between comments within the same shot), which indicates the tight correlation between a comment and its preceding comments. Moreover, a large number of comments are very similar, e.g., with an average similarity higher than 0.8 compared to their preceding comments (see Figure 3(f)). These two observations numerically describe the *short* comment property and user-interactions for time-sync comments.

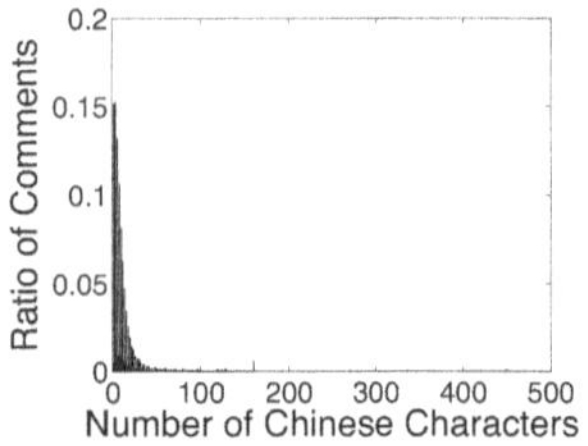

(a) Number of characters in each comment.

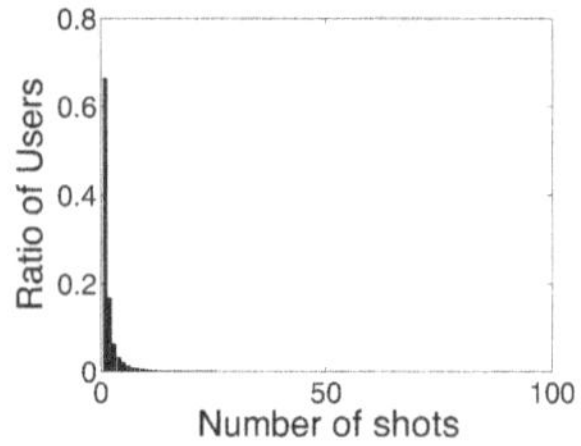

(b) Number of shots for each user.

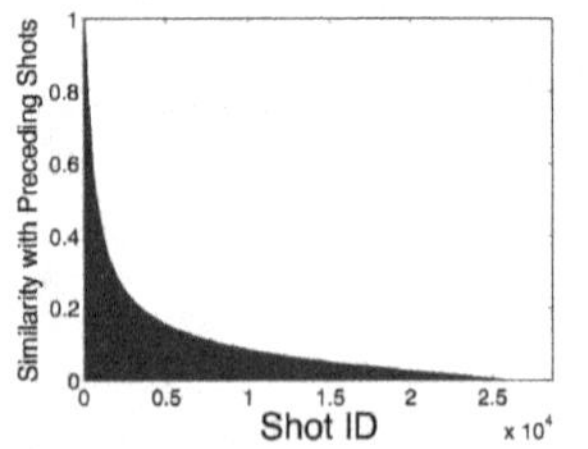

(c) Similarity between a shot and its preceding shot(s).

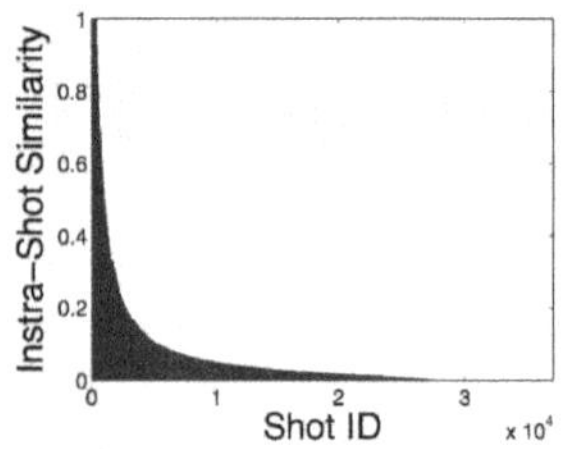

(d) Similarity between comments for each shot.

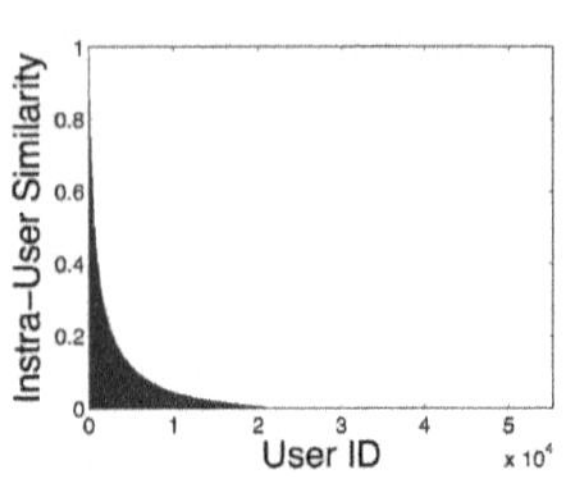

(e) Similarity between comments for each user.

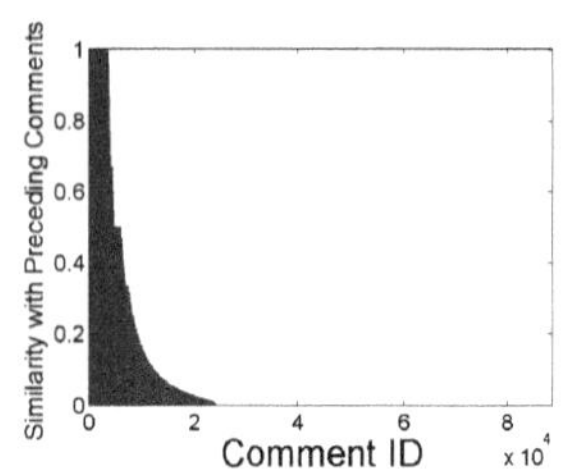

(f) Similarity between a comment and its preceding comment(s).

Figure 3: Data Inspection of Time-Sync Comments.

On the other hand, as shown in Table 2, the average intra-user (i.e., comments by the same user) similarity (0.036) and average inter-shot similarity (0.099) are much higher than the overall similarity (0.008). This observation indicates users' preferences in comments and the temporal dependency of video semantics.

3. EXTRACTING TAGS FROM TIME-SYNC COMMENTED VIDEOS

We propose to exploit knowledge from the preceding video shots to solve the *short* and *noisy* comment problems. On one hand, we enrich the knowledge in the current video shot by considering its temporal dependencies. On the other hand, we model user preferences and interactions to remove content-irrelevant data from each comment. Specifically, we consider the generative process of a comment as a probabilistic model, where the words in comments are observed and the underlying video semantic topics are hidden. To better infer the hidden topics, we incorporate the above factors as prior knowledge in generating topics, such that knowledge can be shared across videos and shots accurately through users.

Topic modeling, which aims to extract semantically valid topics from document collections, is a natural choice for solving the problem. Before describing our proposed model, we first briefly introduce Latent Dirichlet Allocation [4], the most well-known topic model which has been successfully applied in text analysis tasks such as tag recommendation [13].

3.1 Latent Dirichlet Allocation

Latent Dirichlet Allocation (LDA) assumes words in a document/comment (for simplification, hereafter referred to as comment) are generated by some hidden topics. For example, a comment containing "soccer", "NBA", "Kobe Bryant" is probably about sports while "predicting" and "LDA" are probably about machine learning. LDA aims to infer hidden topics of a given comment. For instance, what topic or mixture of topics would "soccer" and "predicting" be about? Are they about sports, machine learning, or both? More specifically, LDA represents the mixture of topics as a probability distribution over topics. Note that LDA is an unsupervised method, and the topics are latent variables.

3.2 Temporal and Personalized Topic Model

In this section, we introduce our proposed temporal and personalized topic model (TPTM). Consider when user u writes comment c on video shot s. On the one hand, both user u's preference and video shot s's semantics determine the prior knowledge of comment c's topics, making the process personal. On the other hand, since user u can see the preceding comments in s_c when generating comment c, c is also affected by its preceding comments. Moreover, preceding shots are semantically similar to current shots with high probability. The temporal dependencies between comments and the similarity between shots' semantics make the process temporal.

Formally, we denote $\mathcal{MN}()$ as a sampling process with respect to Multinomial distribution, $\mathcal{D}(\alpha)$ and $\mathcal{D}(\beta)$ as sampling processes with respect to a Dirichlet distribution with parameter α for per-comment topic distributions and β for per-topic word distributions. The generative process of TPTM is as follows, and the corresponding graphical model is shown in Figure 4:

1. For each user u
   (a) Generate u's **preference vector**
   $\boldsymbol{x_u} \sim \mathcal{N}(\boldsymbol{0}, \sigma_u \boldsymbol{I_K}), \boldsymbol{x_u} \in \mathbb{R}^K$
2. For each video v
   (a) For each shot $s \in v$
      i. Generate s's **topic prior distribution vector**
      $\boldsymbol{\lambda_s} \sim \mathcal{N}(\boldsymbol{m_{pre_s}}, \sigma_s \boldsymbol{I_K}), \boldsymbol{\lambda_s} \in \mathbb{R}^K$
3. For each topic t
   (a) Generate the word distribution for topic t
   $\boldsymbol{\varphi_t} \sim \mathcal{D}(\beta)$
4. For each comment $c \in s$, where c is commented by u_c
   (a) Let c's **topic prior distribution base vector** be
   $\boldsymbol{\pi_c} = \boldsymbol{\lambda_{s_c}} \odot \boldsymbol{x_{u_c}} + \boldsymbol{m_{pre_c}}$
   (b) Let c's **topic prior distribution vector** be
   $\boldsymbol{\alpha_c} = lgt(\boldsymbol{\pi_c})$
   (c) Generate c's topic distribution
   $\boldsymbol{\theta_c} \sim \mathcal{D}(\boldsymbol{\alpha_c})$
   (d) For each observed token $w_j \in c$
      i. Generate $z_{cj} \sim \mathcal{MN}(\boldsymbol{\theta_c})$

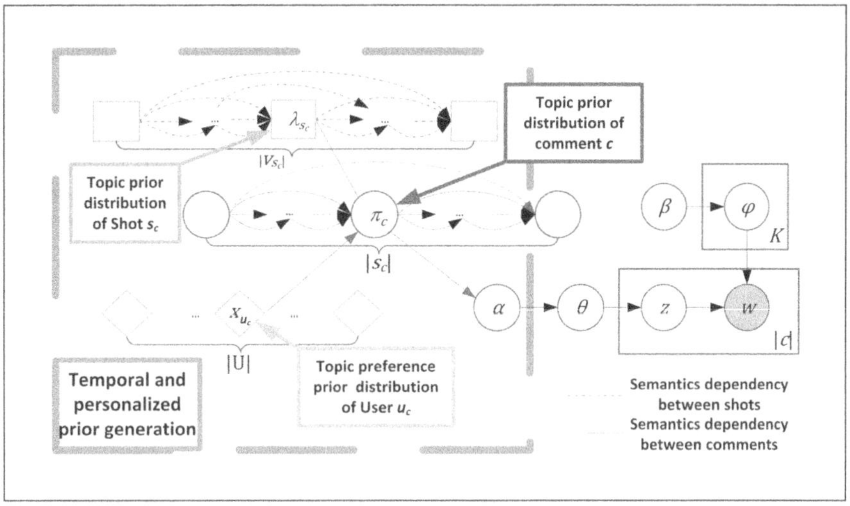

Figure 4: The graphical model of our temporal and personalized topic model (TPTM). For simplification, we only show a simple example where a user u_c writes a comment c on a shot s_c. In the exact model, a shot can contain multiple comments while a user can write multiple comments on multiple shots and videos.

ii. Generate $w_j \sim \mathcal{MN}(\boldsymbol{\varphi}_{\boldsymbol{z}_{cj}})$

where $\odot$ denotes element-wise multiplication, and $lgt(y) = log[1 + e^y]$. $\boldsymbol{m}_{\boldsymbol{pre_s}}$ is defined as the average temporal semantics of pre_s, the preceding shots of shot s, acting as prior distribution of s's semantics. As shots that are closer in sequential order tend to be more similar in semantics, we assume a semantic similarity between shot s and shots in pre_s subject to an exponential decay, which is formally defined as:

$$\boldsymbol{m}_{\boldsymbol{pre_s}} = \frac{\sum_{s' \in pre_s} \exp^{-\gamma_s \Delta(s,s')} \boldsymbol{\lambda}_{\boldsymbol{s'}}}{\sum_{s' \in pre_s} \exp^{-\gamma_s \Delta(s,s')}} \tag{2}$$

where $\Delta(s, s')$ is the absolute difference in appearance order between s and one of its preceding shots s', γ_s is the decay rate. Similarly, $\boldsymbol{m}_{\boldsymbol{pre_c}}$ is defined as:

$$\boldsymbol{m}_{\boldsymbol{pre_c}} = \frac{\sum_{c' \in pre_c} \exp^{-\gamma_c \Delta(c,c')} \boldsymbol{\pi}_{\boldsymbol{c'}}}{\sum_{c' \in pre_c} \exp^{-\gamma_c \Delta(c,c')}} \tag{3}$$

We observed that both $\boldsymbol{m}_{\boldsymbol{pre_s}}$ and $\boldsymbol{m}_{\boldsymbol{pre_c}}$ are essential for dealing with the *short* and *noisy* comment challenges. $\boldsymbol{m}_{\boldsymbol{pre_c}}$ explicitly models the user interaction by encoding semantic dependencies between comments within the same shot, which peels off co-user interference and makes the extracted video topics less *noisy*. Also, on the one hand, videos are connected via the common users, where knowledge can be implicitly propagated via modeling users' latent preference x_u adaptively; on the other hand, modeling temporal dependency between shots (i.e., $\boldsymbol{m}_{\boldsymbol{pre_s}}$) encodes semantics gained from preceding shots. Such knowledge propagation enriches the current shot semantics and therefore addresses the *short* comment problem.

3.3 Inference

The inference of TPTM has two steps: 1) infer the topic distribution for each comment; 2) extract the most probable words for each shot. The first step can be achieved by maximizing the joint distribution $P(z, \lambda, x, \theta, \varphi)$. In the second step, to extract the most probable words of a shot s, we generate topics from the topic distribution $\mathcal{T}_s$ of s obtained by averaging each comment c's topic distribution θ_c, where $c \in s$. Then, tags of shot s are extracted by picking the most probable words.

Observe that for each comment c, if α_c is fixed (i.e., π_c is fixed), the model is equivalent to multiple independent LDAs, where each comment has a different prior distribution for each topic. Therefore, we can perform a collapsed Gibbs sampling by integrating out θ and φ, and sampling z. After integrating out θ and φ, the complete likelihood $P(z, \lambda, x)$ is given by:

$$\begin{aligned} P(z,\lambda,x) =& P(z|\lambda,x)P(\lambda)P(x) \\ =& \prod_{c:c\in s_c, s_c\in v, v\in V} \Bigg\{ \frac{\Gamma\big(\sum_t lgt(x_{u_c t}\lambda_{s_c t} + m_{pre_{ct}})\big)}{\Gamma\big(\sum_t lgt(x_{u_c t}\lambda_{s_c t} + m_{pre_{ct}}) + n_c\big)} \\ & \prod_t \frac{\Gamma\big(lgt(x_{u_c t}\lambda_{s_c t} + m_{pre_{ct}}) + n_{t|c}\big)}{\Gamma\big(lgt(x_{u_c t}\lambda_{s_c t} + m_{pre_{ct}})\big)} \\ & \prod_t \frac{1}{\sqrt{2\pi}\sigma_s} \exp\left(- \frac{(\lambda_{s_c t} + m_{pre_{s_c t}})^2}{2\sigma_s^2} \right) \\ & \prod_t \frac{1}{\sqrt{2\pi}\sigma_u} \exp\left(- \frac{x_{u_c t}^2}{2\sigma_u^2} \right) \Bigg\} \end{aligned} \tag{4}$$

Here we maximize $P(z, \lambda, x)$ with respect to z, λ, and x respectively. A Gibbs sampler as described in [11] is used to sample z, and λ and x are updated using gradient descent. As for λ, the derivative of the log of equation Equation (4) with respect to λ_{st} given shot s and topic t is:

$$\begin{aligned} \frac{\partial P(z,\lambda,x)}{\partial \lambda_{st}} =& - \frac{\lambda_{st} + m_{pre_{st}}}{\sigma_s^2} \\ & + \sum_{c:s_c=s} \Bigg\{ x_{u_c t} dlgt(x_{u_c t}\lambda_{st} + m_{pre_{ct}}) \\ & \times \Big[\Psi\big(\sum_t lgt(x_{u_c t}\lambda_{st} + m_{pre_{ct}})\big) \\ & - \Psi\big(\sum_t lgt(x_{u_c t}\lambda_{st} + m_{pre_{ct}}) + n_c\big) \\ & + \Psi\big(lgt(x_{u_c t}\lambda_{st} + m_{pre_{ct}}) + n_{t|c}\big) \\ & - \Psi\big(lgt(x_{u_c t}\lambda_{st} + m_{pre_{ct}})\big)\Big] \Bigg\} \end{aligned} \tag{5}$$

where $dlgt(y) := \partial lgt(y)$. Similarly, the derivative with respect to x_{ut} given user u and topic t is:

$$
\begin{aligned}
\frac{\partial P(z,\lambda,x)}{\partial x_{ut}} = &-\frac{x_{ut}}{\sigma_u^2} + \sum_{c:u_c=u} \Bigg\{ \lambda_{s_c t} dlgt(x_{ut}\lambda_{s_c t} + m_{pre_c t}) \\
&\times \Big[\Psi\big(\sum_t lgt(x_{ut}\lambda_{s_c t} + m_{pre_c t})\big) \\
&- \Psi\big(\sum_t lgt(x_{ut}\lambda_{s_c t} + m_{pre_c t}) + n_c\big) \\
&+ \Psi\big(lgt(x_{ut}\lambda_{s_c t} + m_{pre_c t}) + n_{t|c}\big) \\
&- \Psi\big(lgt(x_{ut}\lambda_{s_c t} + m_{pre_c t})\big)\Big]\Bigg\}
\end{aligned} \tag{6}
$$

where $m_{pre_c t}$ can be regarded as a constant given user u_c since pre_c does not contain comments written by u_c (according to our definition). Finally, the updating equations for λ_{st} and x_{ut} are:

$$
\lambda_{st} \leftarrow \lambda_{st} - \eta \frac{\partial P(z,\lambda,x)}{\partial \lambda_{st}} \tag{7}
$$

$$
x_{ut} \leftarrow x_{ut} - \eta \frac{\partial P(z,\lambda,x)}{\partial x_{ut}} \tag{8}
$$

where η is the learning rate. The inference procedure, inspired by [15], is as follows: fixing λ and x, the model is equivalent to multiple independent LDAs where the standard LDA Gibbs sampler is used to sample z and φ. After several iterations of sampling, we alternatively update λ and x using Eq (7) and Eq (8). The implementation details is described in Section 4.2.

After inference, we can obtain the topic distribution $\mathcal{T}_{st}$ of each shot s given a topic t:

$$
\mathcal{T}_{st} = \frac{\sum_{c \in s} \theta_{ct}}{|s|} \tag{9}
$$

Then, the T most probable words can be extracted from shot s. The probability of choosing a word is defined as:

$$
P(w|s) = \sum_t \mathcal{T}_{st} * \varphi_{tw} \tag{10}
$$

Framework. The complete algorithm of our proposed temporal and personalized model is shown in Algorithm 1. Overall, it is an iterative process. In each iteration, Gibbs sampling is used to infer lower level variables such as the topic distribution θ, word distribution for topic φ, and topic z, which is identical to LDA. For every 200 iterations, higher level variables such as user preference x and video shot semantics prior distribution λ are updated in turn with respect to the joint distribution $P(z,\lambda,x)$ using Eq. (7) and Eq. (8). Then the temporal semantics prior distributions m_{pre_s} and m_{pre_c} are updated.

Time complexity. The time complexity of Gibbs sampling for lower level variables is $\mathcal{O}(NMK)$ for each iteration. The complexity of updating λ and x for each iteration are both equal to $\mathcal{O}(NK)$. For updating m_{pre_s} and m_{pre_c}, the upper bounds are $\mathcal{O}(N^2K)$ and $\mathcal{O}(\sum_{v \in V} |v|^2 K)$, respectively. Actually, these bounds can be much tighter in our problem setting. Since the average number of comments $|s|$ for each shot s and the average number of shots $|v|$ for each video v is about 10 (see Table 3), and both m_{pre_c} and m_{pre_s} are close to 0 when $\Delta \approx 10$ (according to Eq. (2) and Eq. (3)), the complexity of updating m_{pre_c} and m_{pre_s} can be further bounded as $\mathcal{O}(10NK) < \mathcal{O}(NMK)$. Therefore, the complexity of TPTM is $\mathcal{O}(NMK)$.

4. EXPERIMENTS

We empirically answer the following questions in this section: 1) Does the proposed temporal and personalized model generate better tags for video shots? 2) How do the model parameters (e.g., the number of topics K and the decay rate γ) affect the model performance? To answer these questions, we first introduce the data we used. We then compare the performance of our method to some

Algorithm 1 Temporal and Personalized Topic Model

```
Input Videos V; each video v ∈ V contains shots; each
  shot s ∈ v contains comments; each comment c corresponds
  to a specific playback timestamp, with observed words and a
  known user u_c ∈ U. Number of topics K.
Output Time-sync tags of each shot s.
Given a topic t, initialize the topic prior distribution of shot
  λ_st ~ N(0, σ_s^2), initialize the user preference vector x_ut ~
  N(0, σ_u^2).
for i = 1 to #sampling iterations do
    if i is the odd multiples of 200 then
        Update λ_st using Eq. (7).
    else if i is the even multiples of 200 then
        Update x_ut using Eq. (8).
    end if
    if i is the integer multiples of 200 then
        Update m_pre_s and m_pre_c using Eq. (2) and Eq. (3).
    end if
    Sample topic of each given observed token in c.
end for
for each shot s do
    Extract time-sync tags using Eq. (10).
end for
```

state-of-the-art methods. We use log-likelihood as the evaluation metric for both 1) and 2), which is described in detail in Section 4.3. Moreover, we conduct human evaluation and a case study to show the quality of the tags generated by our method.

4.1 Data Description

Our data was retrieved from a Chinese TSC video website[6]. We use two datasets for experimental studies: comments for videos uploaded in the music section[7] and the fun section[8] snapshot on Oct 2012, with 9,992 videos and 10,187 videos, respectively. Tokenizing and stemming of the raw comments were done by a Chinese natural language processing toolbox, ICTCLAS[9]. However, since comments in TSC videos contain a large amount of internet slang, the resulting tokens missed many meaningful words, and had a large number of single Chinese characters due to incorrect tokenization. Although some single characters have their own merits, most had negative impact according to our experiments. Therefore, to best recover the internet slang, we applied a bigram concatenation of the previous results and obtained a new vocabulary. All single characters were then deleted and about 300,000 words remained. Next, we segmented each video according to the number of comments over playback time. We used a peakfinder[10] to find the peaks and troughs of the comments density, and then segment the videos into shots. Each shot contained at least eight comments, and each video contained at least one shot. Videos not satisfying these requirements were filtered out[11]. Finally, there were 6922 videos, 46,078 shots, 420,125 comments, and 150,838 users for music videos; 9492 videos, 68,069 shots, 683,759 comments, and

[6] http://www.acfun.tv/

[7] http://www.acfun.tv/v/list58/index.htm

[8] http://www.acfun.tv/v/list60/index.htm

[9] http://www.ictclas.org/index.html

[10] http://www.mathworks.com/matlabcentral/fileexchange/25500-peakfinder

[11] For videos without comments where our approach (text-based) is not applicable, content-based approaches such as [9] can be adopted.

Table 3: Summary of data.

Type	Number	Average Number
Data: Music Videos		
Videos	6922	-
Users	150,838	-
Shots	46,078	6.7 per video
Comments	420,125	9.11 per shot
Data: Fun Videos		
Videos	9492	-
Users	231,914	-
Shots	68,069	7.3 per video
Comments	683,759	10.04 per shot

231,914 users for fun videos[12]. 14% of the users published more than 3 comments, and these users occupied 60% of all comments. This means that there are many long-tail users, which makes the problem even more challenging. The data is summarized in Table 3.

4.2 Experimental Setup

For comparison purposes, we introduce two baselines: LDA and Sembler [23]. Sembler has been proposed to integrate crowd-sourced labels for tasks with temporal content such as name entity recognition (NER) and part of speech tagging (POS). For implementation, we mimic Sembler by modifying TPTM to ignore the dependencies between users. Note that Algorithm 2 described in [23] was not adopted because the labeling space in our problem setting is exponential to the vocabulary size, which makes it computationally intractable to generate valid sequential labelings. Also, we did not introduce Dynamic Topic Models (DTM) as baselines due to two reasons: 1). DTM models the dynamics of the prior β, which is not applicable for our problem setting as each video shot can be commented at different time stamps; 2). DTM is also a simplified version of Sembler in modeling α by ignoring the user preference $\boldsymbol{x_u}$.

The model parameters of each baseline are described as follows: In LDA, each comment was treated as an independent document, and the prior parameter α was fixed at 0.5. In Sembler, videos are considered temporal while users' labelings are assumed to follow an independent identical distribution (*i.i.d.*). That is, comments are assumed to be independent of preceding comments. More specifically, we set $m_{pre_{ct}} = 0$ for each comment c and topic t. In TPTM, dependencies between shots and between users' comments are modeled. We implemented these three models based on a Gibbs Sampler, with the number of sampling iterations set to 1000, α_c for each comment initialized to 0.5, and β to 0.1. In TPTM, we alternatively optimized λ and x using Eq. (7) and Eq. (8) (see Algorithm 1). In Sembler, only λ is optimized five times. The learning rate in both TPTM and Sembler is defined as $\eta = \frac{0.1}{2^{i\%10}}$, where i is the current iteration number. γ_s and γ_c were both set to 1.

We observe that the computational time increases linearly with larger data size for all three methods. For TPTM on full music video data, every 200 iterations of Gibbs sampling and one iteration of optimizing λ or x take about 1.5 hours in our computer, which has 16G of memory and a 3.2 Gz CPU, while LDA takes about 1 hour. All three methods converge within 600 Gibbs sampling iterations.

Table 4 shows the top words for four music video topics[13]. The first topic is about the background music of videos; the second describes the video structure[14]; the third topic refers to comments on music videos concepts; the fourth is about the well-known song 'Gangnam Style'.

4.3 Performance Analyses

We examined the held-out log-likelihood $P(\mathbf{c}'|\alpha, \varphi)$ of the three methods, where $\mathbf{c}'$ is the held-out comment set, and α and φ are obtained in the training process. The higher the held-out log-likelihood, the better the model predicts the topic distribution of the held-out data [21]. We used the first half videos for the training set and the second half for the held-out set. More specifically, if a video was commented on only by new users (i.e., users who did not write comments in the training set), no prior knowledge of personal information was available for these new users. Therefore, we only considered the 108,364 users who provided comments in both the training and held-out sets. The results are a ten run average.

As shown in Figure 5(a), both TPTM and Sembler achieved higher held-out log-likelihood as compared to LDA, which shows the benefits of modeling user preferences and the temporal dependencies between video shots. Moreover, on average, the initial log-likelihoods of TPTM and Sembler are already notably better than or close to the converged log-likelihood of LDA, which indicates the accurate estimation of α by the first two methods. Furthermore, TPTM, exploiting temporal dependencies and user interactions, shows superior performance compared to Sembler.

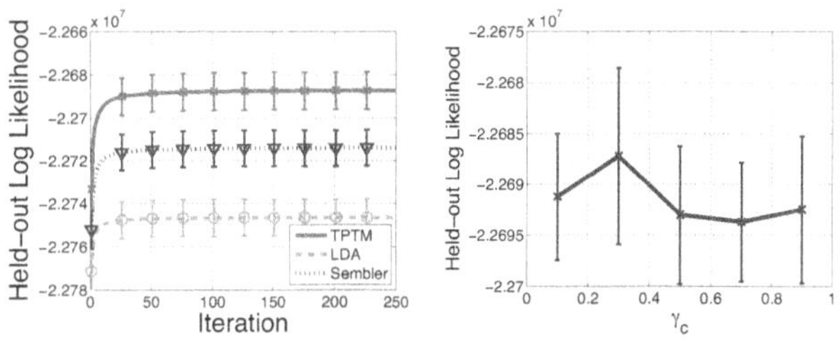

(a) Held-out log-likelihood of three methods.

(b) Held-out log-likelihood with different γ_c.

Figure 5: Held-out log-likelihood analyses

Log-likelihood with respect to the number of topics K is shown in Table 5. We trained TPTM by 25, 50, 75, 100 topics respectively with the best at 25. TPTM outperforms both Sembler and LDA consistently and significantly, which shows the power of modeling temporal and personalized factors in TPTM. We also observe that in both datasets, log-likelihood decreases when the number of topics increases. This may be due to the data we used. For example, music video users mainly appreciated hot songs and therefore topics were limited. For fun videos, although the semantics of different videos vary, the main topics may be limited to only a few such as daily life and pets. In practice, K can be optimized using cross-validation or non-parametric methods.

We also studied γ_c which decides how much a comment is affected by its preceding comments. We tested γ_c from 0.1 to 0.9, and the result is shown in Figure 5(b). When γ_c was set to 0.3, TPTM performed the best. Referring to Equation 3, when $\gamma_c = 0.3$, the temporal effect of the current comment semantics decays by 25% after one comment, and 78% after five comments.

4.4 User Study

We have also conducted a set of user studies (Figure 6) to evaluate the quality of tags generated by TPTM compared to Sembler

[12]We have made the data publicly available at http://www.cse.ust.hk/~bwuaa/TSC/TSC.zip.

[13]These words were manually translated to English by the authors.

[14]For example, 'high energy' is a Chinese internet slang often used to forecast the coming eye-catching video event.

Table 4: Top words for four selected topics for each model ($K = 100$).

Method	Topic 1	Topic 2	Topic 3	Topic 4
TPTM	'BGM[15]', 'Tacata', 'download'	'high energy', 'high energy ahead', 'low energy'	'divine tune', 'good', 'jazz'	'style', 'oba', 'gangnam'
Sembler	'music', 'miku', 'dating'	'high energy', 'high energy ahead', 'low energy'	'divine tune', 'hungry', 'awesome'	'style', 'oba', 'pickled vegetables'
LDA	'BGM', 'train', 'translation'	'ice', 'high energy', 'low energy'	'divine tune', 'little hero', 'monster'	'oba', 'I cry', 'gangnam'

Table 5: Held-out log-likelihood performance ($\times 10e7$) with different number of topics K.

Method \ K	25	50	75	100
Data: Music Videos				
TPTM	**-2.269 $\pm$ 9e-5**	**-2.2816 $\pm$ 5e-5**	**-2.2884 $\pm$ 3e-5**	**-2.2939 $\pm$ 5e-5**
Sembler	-2.2714 $\pm$ 8e-5	-2.2826 $\pm$ 8e-5	-2.2892 $\pm$ 2e-5	-2.2948 $\pm$ 6e-5
LDA	-2.2746 $\pm$ 9e-5	-2.2859 $\pm$ 6e-5	-2.2925 $\pm$ 3e-5	-2.2974 $\pm$ 5e-5
Data: Fun Videos				
TPTM	**-3.8995 $\pm$ 3e-5**	**-3.9227 $\pm$ 4e-5**	**-3.9359 $\pm$ 4e-5**	**-3.9448 $\pm$ 4e-5**
Sembler	-3.9021 $\pm$ 4e-5	-3.9242 $\pm$ 4e-5	-3.9370 $\pm$ 4e-5	-3.9460 $\pm$ 4e-5
LDA	-3.9084 $\pm$ 3e-5	-3.9302 $\pm$ 3e-5	-3.9424 $\pm$ 3e-5	-3.9511 $\pm$ 4e-5

and LDA. Three labelers evaluated the randomly selected 673 shots from the music videos.

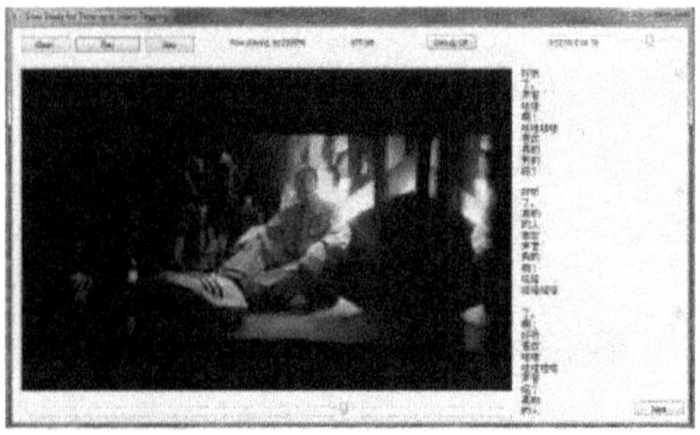

Figure 6: User study interface.

As illustrated in Figure 6, shots were played one by one and the corresponding tags generated by the three methods were displayed on the right-hand-side. Specifically, the order of the three sets of tags were random for each shot. The number of tags in each set was at most ten and the tag order represents its ranking and relevance. Labelers were asked to choose the best set of tags by clicking on one of the three radio buttons in the right-hand-side. One of the methods then received a single vote for each shot. The results listed in Table 6 show that TPTM received 28% more votes than the other methods. Fleiss' Kappa [10], a measure of inter-rater reliability, was then evaluated. The Fleiss' Kappa of the votings was 0.20 with a p-value at 10^{-4}, which can be interpreted as fair but statistically significant agreement among the labelers.

Table 6: Results of user study.

Method	A	B	C	Overall
TPTM	267	275	240	782
LDA	207	192	209	608
Sembler	179	186	204	569

4.5 Case Study

We randomly picked a video[16] and examined its time-sync tags. As listed in Table 7, we extracted six shots of the tags from the video and listed the corresponding snapshots in the first row. Words below the snapshots are generated by the three methods. Note that words are in descending order of relevance, and words in bold are manually labeled as meaningful tags. In general, all three methods generated some meaningful words from the *short* and *noisy* comments. TPTM provided a more reasonable rankings for these tags. Moreover, TPTM captured more valuable words given the *short* and *noisy* content, such as 'good looking' in shot 2, 'princess' in shot 4 and 'American' in shot 6. More specifically, the mean average precision at ten tags (MAP@10), a standard evaluation metric of ranking, was calculated. TPTM achieved 0.187, which is 30% higher than Sembler and LDA (0.146 and 0.144 respectively).

[16]http://www.acfun.tv/v/ac268521

5. RELATED WORK

Traditional video tagging techniques generate tags for an entire video clip [17, 20]. Some content-based methods for time-sync tagging have been proposed (e.g., Feng *et al.* designed a model to generate time-sync tags by predicting tags for extracted keyframes [9]). However, content-based methods rely on a large amount of human-labeled data, which is difficult to acquire in real-world applications because the types of videos vary widely and human labor is expensive. Some researchers have turned to the cheap or free data acquired from the internet. For example, Xu *et al.* and Chiu *et al.* used web-casting text to detect events in broadcast videos [24, 6]. Chakrabarti *et al.* [5] summarized live sports videos events using user-generated information in social networks, the output of which, however, are multiple key tweets instead of a few tags. Also, the above methods mainly focused on big events such as sports games, which cannot be extended to daily online videos. Davis *et al.* designed a system to study time-sync tagging by social network users [8]. However, their data was acquired from an experimental system, which is not scalable. To the best of our knowledge, no previous work has been done on text based time-sync video tagging, and none has solved the *short* and *noisy* comment problem of crowdsourced content.

Crowdsourcing is a process that involves outsourcing tasks to a distributed group of people, which is normally much cheaper than hiring experts. Machine learning and data mining researchers have been using crowdsourcing services (e.g., Amazon Mechanical Turk) to solve the lack of labeled-data problem for applications such as sentiment classification [18] and Name Entity Recognition [23]. However, crowdsourced labels need to be cleaned before utilization because labels from the crowd are usually contaminated by

Table 7: Example of time-sync video tagging. Description of the six segments: 1) At the beginning of the video, Taylor Swift showed up as an office lady. 2) Taylor Swift is working in an office. 3) A man is playing card games in the computer. 4) Taylor Swift is taking the elevator. 5) Taylor Swift is recalling the moments with her boyfriends using a Sony tablet. 6) Taylor Swift picks up her soldier boyfriend at the airport.

	31.3”-45.9”	105.8”-116.0”	149.8”-153.4”	161.0”-172.0”	178.4”-190.8”	235.7”-241.6”	
Shots							MAP@10
TPTM	‘subtitles’ ‘+1’ **‘like’** ‘„’ ‘mine’ **‘love her’** ‘you’ ‘really’ **‘big love’** **‘my love’**	‘......’ **‘divine tune’** **‘like’** ‘ah..’ ‘holy cow’ ‘the’ **‘MV’** **‘sister’** ‘pressure’ **‘good looking’**	‘have to’ **‘game’** ‘to’ ‘have to be’ ‘just now’ **‘memory’** **‘computer’** **‘on the screen’** ‘what’ ‘and’	‘mine’ ‘you’ **‘sister’** ‘have to’ ‘ah,’ ‘it’s me’ ‘again’ ‘a little’ **‘singer’** **‘princess’**	‘you’ ‘the’ **‘I love’** ‘in fact’ ‘yours’ ‘my’ **‘love you’** ‘truth’ **‘ads’** **‘expression’**	‘feeling’ **‘girl’** ‘have to’ **‘bastard’** ‘all are’ **‘ads’** **‘beautiful’** ‘is?’ **‘man’** **‘American’**	0.187
Sembler	‘subtitles’ ‘+1’ **‘like’** ‘„’ ‘mine’ ‘no’ ‘really’ ‘think’ ‘OK’ ‘you’	‘......’ ‘holy cow’ **‘divine tune’** **‘like’** ‘the’ **‘MV’** **‘sister’** **‘I like’** ‘pressure’ ‘ah..’	‘have to’ **‘game’** ‘to’ ‘just now’ ‘have to be’ **‘computer’** **‘memory’** **‘on the screen’** ‘what’ ‘and’	‘mine’ ‘again’ ‘you’ **‘sister’** ‘ah,’ ‘it’s me’ ‘have to’ ‘a little’ ‘people’ **‘singer’**	‘you’ **‘I love’** ‘the’ ‘yours’ ‘in fact’ ‘truth’ **‘love you’** ‘my’ **‘expression’** **‘ads’**	‘feeling’ **‘girl’** ‘all are’ ‘have to’ ‘is?’ **‘man’** ‘is,’ **‘ads’** **‘bastard’** **‘beautiful’**	0.146
LDA	‘+1’ ‘subtitles’ **‘like’** ‘„’ ‘mine’ ‘really’ ‘you’ ‘I will’ **‘I love’** **‘love her’**	‘......’ **‘divine tune’** **‘like’** ‘holy cow’ **‘sister’** ‘the’ ‘pressure’ ‘ah..’ **‘MV’** ‘great’	‘have to’ **‘game’** ‘to’ ‘just now’ ‘have to be’ **‘memory’** **‘computer’** **‘on the screen’** ‘what’ ‘and’	‘mine’ ‘have to’ ‘you’ **‘sister’** ‘again’ ‘ah,’ ‘a little’ ‘it’s me’ ‘people’ **‘singer’**	‘you’ ‘the’ **‘I love’** ‘yours’ ‘truth’ ‘in fact’ ‘my’ **‘love you’** **‘expression’** **‘ads’**	‘feeling’ **‘girl’** ‘all are’ ‘have to’ **‘man’** ‘is?’ **‘ads’** **‘bastard’** **‘beautiful’** ‘is’	0.144

errors and bias. Several approaches have been proposed recently for label by emphasizing labels provided by high quality labelers cleaning[3, 22, 23]. For example, Welinder *et al.* [22] designed a probabilistic graphical model to evaluate skill and knowledge for each image annotator, as well as quality for each image. Sembler [23] was proposed to improve the quality of the collected labels in a sequential labeling problem by modeling users' abilities and sequential dependencies of instances. In summary, most traditional methods infer the true label for a given instance by modeling both user ability and the question difficulty, assuming that users answer questions independently. However, user labeling does not follow the *i.i.d.* assumption in TSC videos due to users' interaction in the shared watching experience. Therefore, traditional methods may fail to accurately remove users' bias. Although Das *et al.* addressed the user interaction problem in a crowdsourcing setting [7], only single-real-value label space and explicit social network were considered. These are not applicable to a video tagging/topic extraction problem. Ritter *et al.* modeled twitter dialogues, another type of interacting short message, by assuming fixed topics, and homogeneous users [16]. Their model, however, is essentially a similar, simpler version of Sembler and TPTM for a different purpose (discovering dialogue acts).

Time-sync commented videos have been exploited by Yoshii *et al.*. The authors developed an automatic music commentator using TSC videos [25]. Their method, however, failed to work in our problem setting because once their model is trained, the most probable words for each hidden state are fixed. This limits the vocabulary of generated comments or tags, which can be observed from their online demo[17]. Moreover, they did not address the *short* and *noisy* comment problems.

6. CONCLUSIONS AND FUTURE WORK

In this paper, we have exploited crowdsourced texual data from time-sync commented video websites for automatic time-sync video tagging, which is a new application. Based on the challenge that time-sync comments in each video shot are *short* and *noisy*, we proposed a novel temporal and personalized topic model which enriches knowledge of *short* comments across videos and shots by collectively exploiting multiple users' preferences. It also peels off user interactions in time-sync comments to address the *noisy* comment problem. Held-out log-likelihood analyses and user studies show that our proposed model outperforms state-of-the-art baselines. Case studies have also been conducted to demonstrate our proposed model's capability in mining *short* and *noisy* comments.

Discussion. According to Section 3.3, to train the model (i.e., to infer variables such as user preference x and the topic distribution of a shot $\mathcal{T}$), we need to scan through all the data. This can be a problem in tagging online videos where video collections are large scale and growing, which makes the training process very slow. Our model can be easily modified into an online and paral-

[17]http://staff.aist.go.jp/k.yoshii/commentator/index.html

lel scheme to handle large scale data. For updating the lower level variables (e.g., θ and φ), parallel and online LDA have been proposed for efficient topic inference [12]. And for updating higher level variables (e.g., λ and x), the user preference x is the only factor learned from the old data that relates to topics of the new videos. Therefore, we only need to load user preference x learned in the old data to absorb new data, which makes online updating trivial. Again, since variables such as λ, m_{pre_s}, and m_{pre_c} only depend on the corresponding video, the updating process can be easily partitioned with respect to each video, that is to update multiple videos in parallel. The online and parallel scheme is essential for handling large scale data (though the details are not elaborated here due to page limits). In addition, although our proposed model is specifically designed for time-sync tagging of online videos, it can also serve as a basic technique for other applications such as time-sync tagging of news video and movies with the help of subtitles or speech-to-text transcription. Moreover, our proposed pure text-based model can also be applied to many tasks other than video tagging such as event summarization based on social networks.

Future Work. In the future, we can extend our work as follows:

1) By building internet slang collections to improve tokenization. According to Table 7 and our observations, the quality of the generated tags heavily depends on pre-processing such as tokenization. However, to the best of our knowledge, no large internet slang collections are available. Although we have not analyzed TSC from a linguistic point of view due to the limits of time and our knowledge, we consider it the most important area for future work.

2) By designing a unified model incorporating video segmentation. Video segmentation is essential to the user-experience of time-sync tagging. However, to simplify the problem, video segmentation has been conducted by a simple segmentation scheme as a part of data pre-processing in this paper, which is not satisfactory in terms of quality. In the future, we can incorporate video segmentation as a latent factor, and infer better segmentation simultaneously considering the semantics of the comments .

3) By improving tagging quality by knowledge transfer among multiple data sources. In this paper, connection between different TSC video sources was not considered. In fact, videos in different sections can be very different in terms of both video semantics and users' comments. For example, videos in the music section usually consists of multiple short clips, while videos in the movie section are likely much longer in terms of per-video duration. The underlying topics are probably different as well. It would be interesting to investigate how users comment in different sections.

4) By extending our results to extrinsic tasks such as video scene classification and object recognition. The automatic time-sync tagging approach proposed in this paper is actually a crowdsourced label collection and integration process. Therefore, a natural extension is to use the generated tags and the corresponding video shots as labeled pairs for extrinsic tasks. On the other hand, the quality of the generated tags can also be evaluated by existing ground-truth measures of extrinsic tasks.

7. ACKNOWLEDGMENTS

This work was undertaken thanks to the support of China National 973 project 2014CB340304 and Hong Kong RGC Projects 621013, 620812, and 621211.

8. REFERENCES

[1] Cisco visual networking index: Global mobile data traffic forecast update, 2012-2017. white paper. Online: http://goo.gl/wt9Dy (9 July 2013).

[2] Youtube statistics. Online: http://goo.gl/jLcaFP (9 July 2013).

[3] Y. Bachrach, T. Graepel, T. Minka, and J. Guiver. How to grade a test without knowing the answers - a bayesian graphical model for adaptive crowdsourcing and aptitude testing. In *ICML*, 2012.

[4] D. Blei, A. Ng, and M. Jordan. Latent dirichlet allocation. *the Journal of machine Learning research*, 3:993–1022, 2003.

[5] D. Chakrabarti and K. Punera. Event summarization using tweets. In *ICWSM*, pages 66–73, 2011.

[6] C. Chiu, P. Lin, S. Li, T. Tsai, and Y. Tsai. Tagging webcast text in baseball videos by video segmentation and text alignment. *Circuits and Systems for Video Technology, IEEE Transactions on*, 22(7):999–1013, 2012.

[7] A. Das, S. Gollapudi, R. Panigrahy, and M. Salek. Debiasing social wisdom. In *Proceedings of the 19th ACM SIGKDD international conference on Knowledge discovery and data mining*, pages 500–508. ACM, 2013.

[8] S. Davis, I. Burnett, and C. Ritz. Using social networking and collections to enable video semantics acquisition. *IEEE MultimediaS*, 16(4):52–60, 2009.

[9] S. Feng, R. Manmatha, and V. Lavrenko. Multiple bernoulli relevance models for image and video annotation. In *CVPR*, pages 1002–1009, 2004.

[10] J. L. Fleiss, B. Levin, and M. C. Paik. The measurement of interrater agreement. *Statistical Methods for Rates and Proportions*, 2:212–236, 1981.

[11] T. Griffiths and M. Steyvers. Finding scientific topics. *Proceedings of the National Academy of Sciences of the United States of America*, 101(Suppl 1):5228–5235, 2004.

[12] D. K. JinYeong Bak and A. Oh. Distributed online learning for latent dirichlet allocation. In *NIPS Workshop on Big Learning, 2012*, pages 1–8, 2012.

[13] R. Krestel, P. Fankhauser, and W. Nejdl. Latent dirichlet allocation for tag recommendation. In *RecSys*, pages 61–68. ACM, 2009.

[14] C. D. Manning and H. Schütze. *Foundations of Statistical Natural Language Processing*, volume 999. MIT Press, 1999.

[15] D. M. Mimno and A. McCallum. Topic models conditioned on arbitrary features with dirichlet-multinomial regression. In *UAI*, pages 411–418, 2008.

[16] A. Ritter, C. Cherry, and B. Dolan. Unsupervised modeling of twitter conversations. In *Human Language Technologies: The 2010 Annual Conference of the North American Chapter of the Association for Computational Linguistics*, pages 172–180, 2010.

[17] S. Siersdorfer, J. San Pedro, and M. Sanderson. Automatic video tagging using content redundancy. In *SIGIR*, pages 395–402, 2009.

[18] R. Snow, B. O'Connor, D. Jurafsky, and A. Ng. Cheap and fast—but is it good?: evaluating non-expert annotations for natural language tasks. In *EMNLP*, pages 254–263, 2008.

[19] S. Tan, H. Tan, and C. Ngo. Topical summarization of web videos by visual-text time-dependent alignment. In *MM*, pages 1095–1098. ACM, 2010.

[20] A. Ulges, C. Schulze, M. Koch, and T. Breuel. Learning automatic concept detectors from online video. *Computer Vision and Image Understanding*, 114(4):429–438, 2010.

[21] H. M. Wallach, I. Murray, R. Salakhutdinov, and D. Mimno. Evaluation methods for topic models. In *Proceedings of the 26th ICML*, pages 1105–1112. ACM, 2009.

[22] P. Welinder, S. Branson, S. Belongie, and P. Perona. The multidimensional wisdom of crowds. In *NIPS*, pages 2424–2432, 2010.

[23] X. Wu, W. Fan, and Y. Yu. Sembler: Ensembling crowd sequential labeling for improved quality. In *AAAI*, pages 1713–1719, 2012.

[24] C. Xu, J. Wang, K. Wan, Y. Li, and L. Duan. Live sports event detection based on broadcast video and web-casting text. In *Proceedings of the 14th ACM MM*, pages 221–230. ACM, 2006.

[25] K. Yoshii and M. Goto. Musiccommentator: Generating comments synchronized with musical audio signals by a joint probabilistic model of acoustic and textual features. *Entertainment Computing–ICEC 2009*, pages 85–97, 2009.

Identifying and Labeling Search Tasks via Query-based Hawkes Processes

Liangda Li[†], Hongbo Deng[‡], Anlei Dong[‡], Yi Chang[‡], and Hongyuan Zha[¶†]

[†]College of Computing
Georgia Institute of Technology
Atlanta, GA 30032

[‡]Yahoo Labs
701 First Avenue
Sunnyvale, CA 94089

[¶]Software Engineering Institute
East China Normal University
Shanghai, China 200062

ldli@cc.gatech.edu, {hbdeng, anlei, yichang}@yahoo-inc.com, zha@cc.gatech.edu

ABSTRACT

We consider a search task as a set of queries that serve the same user information need. Analyzing search tasks from user query streams plays an important role in building a set of modern tools to improve search engine performance. In this paper, we propose a probabilistic method for identifying and labeling search tasks based on the following intuitive observations: queries that are issued temporally close by users in many sequences of queries are likely to belong to the same search task, meanwhile, different users having the same information needs tend to submit topically coherent search queries. To capture the above intuitions, we directly model query temporal patterns using a special class of point processes called Hawkes processes, and combine topic models with Hawkes processes for simultaneously identifying and labeling search tasks. Essentially, Hawkes processes utilize their self-exciting properties to identify search tasks if influence exists among a sequence of queries for individual users, while the topic model exploits query co-occurrence across different users to discover the latent information needed for labeling search tasks. More importantly, there is mutual reinforcement between Hawkes processes and the topic model in the unified model that enhances the performance of both. We evaluate our method based on both synthetic data and real-world query log data. In addition, we also apply our model to query clustering and search task identification. By comparing with state-of-the-art methods, the results demonstrate that the improvement in our proposed approach is consistent and promising.

Categories and Subject Descriptors:
H.3.3 [**Information Storage and Retrieval**]: Information Search and Retrieval; I.2.6 [**Artificial Intelligence**]: Learning; J.4 [**Computer Applications**]: Social and Behavioral Sciences

Keywords: Hawkes process, latent Dirichlet allocation, variational Inference, search task

1. INTRODUCTION

Nowadays, search engines have become the most important and indispensable Web portal, whereby people pursue a wide range of searches in order to satisfy a variety of *information needs*. To better understand users' information needs and search behaviors, one important research direction is to detect and split users' temporal sequences of queries into disjoint *query sessions*, which are often defined as a sequence of queries issued within a fixed period of time, ranging from 5 to 120 minutes. However, a user's single session may contain queries with multiple intents, or consist of seeking information on single or multiple topics [28]. Going beyond a search session, a *search task* [23, 17, 30], which is defined as a set of queries serving for the same *information need*, has been recognized as a more suitable atomic unit than a single query or session, not only for better modeling user search intent but also for improving other downstream search engines' applications, such as query suggestion [9, 17] and personalized search [33]. Additionally, analyzing the formation of search tasks also deepens our understanding of the simultaneous temporal diffusion of multiple memes, i.e., intents or ideas, in social networks [34]. Therefore, how to effectively identify and label search tasks becomes an interesting and challenging problem.

Recently, there have been attempts to extract in-session tasks [28, 23, 17], and cross-session tasks [18, 19, 1, 30] from sequences of queries. They build clustering or classification methods to identify tasks based on time splitting, lexicon similarity, and query reformulation patterns. Even though the temporal submission patterns in query sequences carry valuable information for mining search tasks, those existing methods only use them for either simply splitting sequences of queries into temporally-demarcated sessions [18, 19, 23], or transforming them as features among queries [19, 17, 30]. We believe that by directly modeling temporal information as part of extracting search tasks in a richer way, we can substantially improve search task mining. Another key drawback of those existing methods is that most of them focus only on the query sequences of individual users instead of considering the whole query log. Only very recently, there has been an attempt which tries to take advantage of the collective intelligence of many users for discovering tasks [24]. It is obvious that different users may have the same information need, and share the same search task, thus modeling query sequences across different users will be very valuable for capturing semantically similar search tasks in a global context.

Generally, two consecutive queries issued by a user are more likely to belong to the same search task than two non-contiguous queries, but that is not necessary always the case. For example, as shown in Figure 1, the consecutive queries "autotrader" and "Yahoo autos" issued by user u_a belong to the same search task, while the consecutive queries "Yahoo autos" and "wells fargo" belong to two separate search tasks. Another complicated case is that two non-contiguous queries may belong to the same or different tasks

KDD'14, August 24–27, 2014, New York, NY, USA.

http://dx.doi.org/10.1145/2623330.2623679.

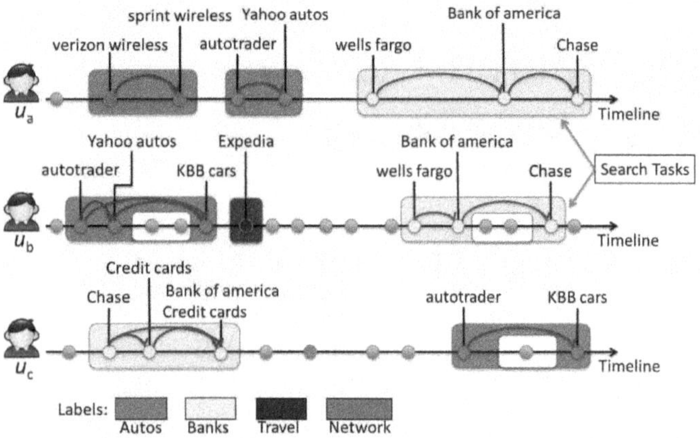

Figure 1: An Illustration of Relationship between Consecutive Queries and Search Tasks. Every circle represents a query issued by a user at time t_n. The blue arrow line indicates an influence exists between queries. A set of queries linked by blue lines denotes a search task, and some topically coherent search tasks across three users are labeled by different colors.

as well, e.g., "verizon wireless" and "autotrader" issued by user u_a belong to two different search tasks, but "Yahoo autos" and "KBB cars" issued by users u_b belong to the same search task. These examples show that in reality we cannot simply rely on the time splitting or an individual user behavior for identifying search tasks. It makes more sense to take into account the explicit temporal information of query sequences exhibited by many different users in the whole query logs. *The basic intuition is that if two consecutive or temporally-close queries are issued many times by the same user or many others users, it is more likely these two queries are semantically related to each other, i.e., belong to the same search task.* As we can see, the consecutive queries "wells fargo" and "Bank of america" are issued by both u_a and u_b (and possible many other users), while the consecutive queries "Yahoo autos" and "wells fargo" are only issued by user u_a. Therefore, according to the above intuition, "wells fargo" and "bank of america" are more likely to belong to the same search task compared with "Yahoo auto" and "wells fargo". Similarly, for non-contiguous queries, "autotrader" and "KBB cars" are issued temporally very close by both u_b and u_c, which indicates they have higher chance of belonging to the same search task. Moreover, different users may engage in different search patterns, e.g., user u_b searches more frequently than user u_a, which indicates how likely the search tasks may change within a certain time period for different users, and then they should be treated differently based on their search activities. All in all, we choose to identify search tasks by leveraging the temporally weighted query co-occurrence — this not only guarantees sound performance by making full use of both textual and temporal information of the entire query sequences, but also enables the labeling of the identified search tasks since semantically related queries are clustered together through query links determined by co-occurrence.

To model temporally close query co-occurrences, we turn to Latent Dirichlet Allocation (LDA) [7], one powerful graphical model that exploits co-occurrence patterns of queries in query sequences. Existing temporal LDA models [16, 32] learned distinguished topic distributions from temporal fragments of data, while ignored query co-occurrence across different fragments, thus failed to make full use of the temporal information. Recently, some spatial-LDA models [31] encouraged queries that are very close in space to share similar topic distributions, i.e., weighing the reliability of query co-occurrence based on spatial closeness. However, there exists no uniform standards for measuring such closeness across different instances, especially in temporal data. Our research, on the other hand, considers making full use of temporal information by weighing the reliability of each co-occurrence of a pair of queries based on how likely an *influence* exists between this pair of queries. Here we define query *influence* as:

- The occurrence of one query raises the probability that the other query will be issued in the near future.

Influence, rather than closeness, enables us to distinguish temporally close query co-occurrence from temporally regular query co-occurrence for each user based on his own propensity of query submission. For instance, in Figure 1, the absolute temporal distance between "KBB cars" and "Expedia" is smaller than that between "verizon wireless" and "sprint wireless", however, *influence* exists between the latter pair of queries rather than the former one, since user u_b's query submission propensity is much larger than that of user u_a. To model such personal propensity and *influence*, in this paper, we utilize Hawkes processes [14], a special class of point processes, whose intensity functions characterize how likely an event will happen at each timestamp. The intensity function of Hawkes includes a base intensity, along with a positive influence of the past events on the current one. Such a positive influence is originated from the *self-exciting* property that the occurrence of one event in the past increases the probability of events happening in the future. We find that Hawkes's *self-exciting* property coincides with the concept of *influence* in our situation, and its base intensity captures the personal propensity. Thus we employ Hawkes processes to fully utilize temporal information in query sequences for identifying the existence of query *influence*.

From the perspective of Hawkes processes, *influence* generally exists between temporally-close queries. However, for an observed query sequence, not all temporally-close query-pairs have the actual *influence* in between, since in some cases the occurrence of the later queries may result from the base intensity rather than *self-exciting* property. Furthermore, existing Hawkes models [20, 35] find it intractable to obtain an optimal solution of *influence* existence based on temporal information only. Last but the most important, it is unable to directly identify search tasks by either generating topics based on query co-occurrence using LDA, or estimating all *influence* candidates by Hawkes. To address the above issues, we concentrate on the *influence* existence between semantically related queries, whose estimation can be simplified by the joint efforts of LDA and Hawkes and enable a direct identification of search tasks.

According to the above intuition, a search task can be viewed as a sequence of semantically related queries linked by *influence*. A query that does not satisfy user's *information need* will *self-excite* the submission of another semantically related query in the near future. On the other hand, a query rarely excites the submission of another semantically unrelated query even if their timestamps are very close. Thus we believe that those semantic *influence* are the *influence* that actually take effect, and our paper solves search task identification directly by identifying those *influence*. To limit the solution space of such *influence*, we cast both *influence* existence and query-topic membership into latent variables, and identify the existence probability of pairwise *influence* with the similarity of the memberships of associated two queries. This identification works as a bridge between LDA and Hawkes processes, as LDA assigns high *influence*-qualified co-occurred queries to the same topic, while query co-occurrence frequency narrows the solution space of *influence*. In this way, LDA and Hawkes mutually benefit each other in identifying search tasks using both temporal and textual information. To this end, we propose a probabilistic model that incorporates this equalization to combine the LDA model with Hawkes processes, and develop a mean-field variational inference algorithm to estimate the *influence* by optimizing the data likelihood. We evaluate our method on synthetic data, and also apply it to mine search tasks in both AOL and Yahoo query log data. Experimental results show that the proposed method can achieve significantly better performance than existing state-of-the-art methods.

In a nutshell, our major contributions include: (1) We cast search task identification into the problem of identify semantic *influence* in observed query sequences, and propose a probabilistic model by combining LDA model with Hawkes processes to address the problem. Most importantly, there is mutual reinforcement between Hawkes processes and the topic model in the unified model that enhances the performance of both. (2) We employ Hawkes processes to directly model temporal information as part of search task identification, which has never been explicitly exploited in the existing works.

The rest of the paper is organized as follows. We first introduce Hawkes processes, and the proposed model by combining LDA with Hawkes processes in Section 2. In Section 3, we develop a fast mean-field variational inference algorithm for the resulting optimization problem. We then describe and report the experimental results in Section 4. Finally, we introduce the related work in Section 5, and present our conclusions and future work in Section 6.

2. PROBLEM DEFINITION

Let us consider a typical scenario where M users issue M corresponding query sequences, and we mark the query sequence of user m as $T_m = \{t_{m,n}, n = 1, \dots, N_m\}$, where $t_{m,n}$ is the time-stamp of the n-th query. We denote the word set of the n-th query of user m as $W_{m,n} = \{w_{m,n,1}, \dots, w_{m,n,c_{m,n}}\}$. Existing works generally identify search task by sequentially solve two subproblems: 1) using queries' textual information to cluster queries in observed query sequences, and 2) using obtained clusters together with temporal information to partition query sequences into search tasks. In this section, we show how these two subproblems can be simultaneously addressed by combining Hawkes processes with the LDA model, and how temporal and textual information can be combined to address the above two subproblems in a mutually-beneficial way. We also show how our model can be used to automatically label search tasks along with search task identification.

2.1 Query Co-occurrence and LDA

We address the query clustering problem using graphical models like LDA [7], which has been proven to be effective in topic discovery by clustering words that co-occur in the same document into topics. Let us first introduce how to use LDA to cluster queries based on their textual information only. One straightforward idea is to treat each user's query sequence as a document, and cluster queries that co-occur in the same query sequence into topics, since queries issued by the same user are generally more likely to share the same *information need* than queries issued by different users. Since we focus on query co-occurrence instead of word co-occurrence, we enforce that words in one query belong to the same topic. Our LDA model assumes K topics lie in the given query sequences, and each user m is associated with a randomly drawn vector π_m, where $\pi_{m,k}$ denotes the probability that a query issued by user m belongs to topic k. For the n-th query in the query sequence of user m, a K-dimensional binary vector $Y_{m,n} = [y_{m,n,1}, \dots, y_{m,n,K}]^T$ is used to denote the query's topic membership. One challenge we encounter in the inference of topic membership Y is that, without temporal information of queries, it is difficult to judge whether two non-contiguous co-occurred queries should belong to the same topic or not. The reason is that the reliability of the co-occurrence of queries heavily depends on their temporal distances. A pair of queries that co-occurs many times may be completely unrelated if the temporal gap between them is always large.

Since the co-occurrence of queries with large temporal gap can be harmful, we make use of temporal information to decide which query co-occurrence should be taken into account by LDA, i.e., how a document in LDA model should be constructed. One simple way of utilizing temporal information is to define a document as consecutive queries in a fixed time window (or time session), which enables us to focus on temporally close query co-occurrence. Temporally close queries that issued many times by the same user or many other users are more likely to be semantically related to each other, i.e., belong to the same search task. However, a time window based LDA model may suffer from the following drawbacks: 1) Usually no optimal solution exists for cutting the entire query sequence into different time-sessions. If we allow different time-sessions to overlap, redundant query co-occurrence will be taken into account; otherwise, pairs of queries with very small temporal gap can be partitioned into different tasks, which may cause information loss. 2) Using time windows will ignore or misunderstand users' own temporal patterns in searching.

To address the above drawbacks, we can weigh each query co-occurrence based on how likely an *influence* exists between this pair of queries, i.e., the degree to which the occurrence of one query raises the probability that the other query will be issued in the near future. That is to say, one document is a subsequence of queries linked through *influence*. This *influence*, rather than time window, enables us to distinguish temporally close query co-occurrence from temporally regular query co-occurrence for each user based on his/her own propensity of query submission. To model such personal propensity and *influence*, we will utilize Hawkes processes to capture the temporal information in different query sequences.

2.2 Hawkes Process

One powerful tool in statistics for modeling event (query) sequence data is temporal point processes, which are widely used to describe data that are localized at a finite set of time points $\{t_1, \dots, t_N\}$ [27]. In a temporal point process, $N(t)$ counts the number of events that has occurred up to and including time t, and the conditional intensity function $\lambda(t|\mathcal{H}_t)$ denotes the expected infinitesimal rate at which events occur at timestamp t depending on $\mathcal{H}_t$, the history of events preceding t. For clarity, hereafter we use $*$ to imply the dependence on $\mathcal{H}_t$, i.e., $\lambda(t|\mathcal{H}_t)$ will be denoted $\lambda^*(t)$.

The Hawkes process is a class of self- or mutually-exciting point process models [14]. A univariate Hawkes process $\{N(t)\}$ is defined by its intensity function

$$\lambda^*(t) = \mu(t) + \int_{-\infty}^{t} \kappa(t-s)dN(s),$$

where $\mu > 0$ is a base intensity, κ is a kernel function capturing the positive influence of past events on the current value of the intensity process, which is the process's *self-exciting* property that the occurrence of one event in the past will trigger events happening in the future. Such *self-exciting* property can either exists between every pair of events as assumed in a normal univariate Hawkes process, or only exists between limited pair of events. For instance, any query but the last one in a search task can imply an increased probability of future queries issued in the same search task, since the user's *information need* in this search task hasn't been satisfied. Meanwhile, queries from different search tasks may rarely affect each other.

Since our definition of *influence* coincides with the *self-exciting* property of Hawkes process, we propose to identify the *influence* among queries by building one separate Hawkes process on each user's query sequence. In the query sequence of user m, we use $R_{m,n,n'}$ to denote whether *influence* exists between the n-th and n'-th query. If *influence* exists, we believe that the occurrence of n-th query has a time-decay effect on increasing the intensity at the timestamp of the occurrence of the n'-th query. Thus based on *influence* R_m, we model the query sequence issued by user m with a univariate Hawkes process, whose intensity can be written as:

$$\lambda_m(t) = \mu_m + \sum_{t_{m,l}<t} R_{m,l,n}\beta_m\kappa(t - t_{m,l}). \quad (1)$$

Here the baseline intensity μ_m captures how often user m issues a query spontaneously[1] (i.e., not triggered by any other queries), while β_m models the degree of *influence* between sequential queries issued by user m, and $\kappa(t - t_{m,l})$[2] captures the time-decay effect only.

Influence R can be estimated together with μ and β by maximizing the likelihood of the proposed Hawkes model on observed query sequence $\{T_m = \{t_{m,n}\}\}$. The estimation of R is actually to identify query-pairs in which the occurrence of the later query most likely violates the normal query-submission propensity, and gets triggered by the earlier one. In other words, if *influence* exists between two queries, the corresponding temporal gap can be significantly less than the average temporal gap of pairs of queries in the same query sequence (issued by the same user). Since the definition of *influence* suggests that queries linked by significant *influence* naturally form search tasks, a thresholding of $R_{m,l,n}\beta_m\kappa(t-t_{m,l})$ with a small constant automatically results in search task partition. The estimation of R consequently partitions observed query sequences into search tasks.

2.3 LDA-Hawkes

Estimated by Hawkes processes, *influence* R captures the unique temporal pattern of each user's query sequence. We use R to weight the query co-occurrence, which bridges the LDA model and Hawkes process through:

$$R_{m,n,n'} = Y_{m,n}^T * Y_{m,n'}, \quad (2)$$

that is to say, *influence* exists between these two queries if and only if the two queries share the same topic. Since queries in the same search task are linked by *influence*, all queries in the same search task share the same topic, which labels this search task as well.

Through our defined bridge between *influence* R and query-topic membership Y, the Hawkes process and the LDA model mutually benefit each other in identifying and labeling search tasks. On the one hand, provided *influence* among queries, we obtain 0-1 weighted query co-occurrence of each candidate query-pair in observed query sequences, and generate topics accordingly. For instance, in Figure 2, although 8 pairs of queries (9 possible combinations with 8 unique query-pairs) co-occur in query sequences, only the co-occurrences of query-pairs "bank of america"–"wells fargo" and "Expedia"–"american airline" have positive weights. These weighted query co-occurrences contain personal temporal information, thus are expected to lead to improved topics compared with existing LDA-based methods [16, 32, 31] that used no weight scheme or only unifom standard weight scheme.

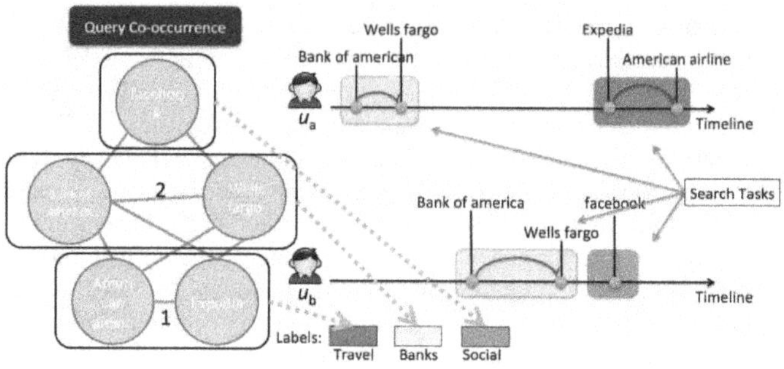

Figure 2: A Toy Example of our LDA-Hawkes model. Blue line denotes the influence among queries. Green dash line shows the label each query belongs to.

On the other hand, the estimation of *influence* R only based on temporal data $\{T_m\}$ can be intractable, since the exploration of the whole space of R is known to very costly ($2^{\sum_m N_m}$ possible solutions). LDA-Hawkes further makes use of textual data to limit the output space of R to the most probable subspace, since topics learned by the LDA part in turn justify the *influence* existence between each pair of queries. Two queries rarely co-occur can be clustered into different topics by the LDA part, based on such query-topic membership no *influence* exists between these two queries. For example, in the query sequence of user u_b shown in Figure 2, the temporal gap between query-pair "bank of america"–"wells fargo" is larger than the temporal gap between query-pair "wells fargo"–"facebook". However, the pair of queries "bank of america"–"wells fargo" also co-occurs in the query sequence of user u_a, while "wells fargo"–"facebook" does not, which in turn emphasizes that *influence* should exist between "bank of america" and "wells fargo" rather than between "wells fargo" and "facebook". To sum up, combined through *influence*, Hawkes process and LDA reciprocally contribute to the search task identification and labeling.

Finally, we present our generative model that combines Hawkes process and LDA as follows:

- For each topic k, draw a V dimensional membership vector $\sigma_k \sim \text{Dirichlet}(\alpha')$.
- For each user m, draw a K dimensional membership vector $\pi_m \sim \text{Dirichlet}(\alpha)$.
- For the content of the n-th query issued by user m,
  - $Y_{m,n} \sim \text{Multinomial}(\pi_m)$;
  - For the i-th word in the n-th query issued by user m,
    - $w_{m,n,i} \sim \text{Multinomial}(Y_{m,n}, \sigma)$;
- For the timestamp of the sequence of queries issued by user m,
  - draw personal base intensity μ_m and degree of *influence* β_m;
  - derive R_m from $\{Y_{m,n}\}$ through Eqn (2);
  - $N_m(\cdot) \sim \text{HawkesProcess}(\lambda_m(\cdot))$, where the intensity λ_m is defined as in Eqn (1).

[1]For simplicity, we assume this cascade-birth process is a homogeneous Possion process with $\mu_m(t) = \mu_m$.

[2]Our paper uses the exponential kernel in experiments, i.e., $\kappa(\Delta t) = \omega e^{-\omega\Delta t}$ if $\Delta t \geq 0$ or 0 otherwise. However, the model development and inference is independent of kernel choice and extensions to other kernels such as power-law, Rayleigh, nonparametric kernels are straightforward.

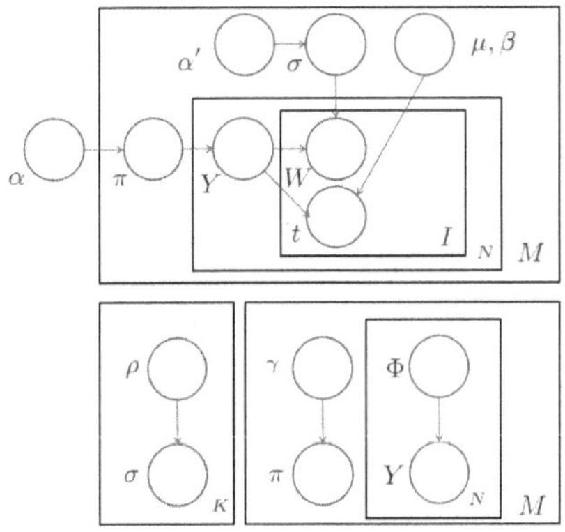

Figure 3: Graphical model representation of LDA-Hawkes and the variational distribution that approximates the likelihood. The upper figure shows the graphical model representation of LDA-Hawkes, while the lower figure shows the variational distribution that approximates the likelihood.

Here V is the size of vocabulary. Note that in our LDA-Hawkes model, queries issued by one user share the same topic distribution, while words in one query belong to the same topic. The topic membership of the n-th query of user m, $Y_{m,n}$, determines not only the words the query owns, but also the timestamp of its occurrence through Hawkes process $\lambda_m(\cdot)$.

Under our LDA-Hawkes model, the joint probability of data $T = \{N_m(\cdot)\} = \{\{t_{m,n}\}_{n=1}^{N_m}\}$, $W = \{\{W_{m,n}\}_{n=1}^{N_m}\}$ and latent variables $\{\pi_{1:M}, Y\}$ can be written as follows:

$$
\begin{aligned}
& p(T, W, \pi_{1:M}, Y, \sigma|\alpha,\alpha', \mu, \beta) \\
&= \prod_m P(\{t_{m,n}\}_{n=1}^{N_m}|Y_{m,1:N_m}, \mu_m, \beta_m) \prod_m \prod_n \prod_i P(w_{m,n,i}|Y_{m,n}, \sigma) \\
& \prod_m \prod_n P(Y_{m,n}|\pi_m) \prod_m P(\pi_m|\alpha) \prod_k P(\sigma_k|\alpha').
\end{aligned}
$$

3. INFERENCE

Despite that a tremendous amount of work on inference of topic models have been published, none of them are designed to address topic model combined with point processes. In this section, we derive a mean-field variational Bayesian inference algorithm for our proposed LDA-Hawkes model.

3.1 Variational Inference

Under LDA-Hawkes model, given observations of both temporal information $T = \{N_m(\cdot)\} = \{\{t_{m,n}\}_{n=1}^{N_m}\}$ and textual information $W = \{\{W_{m,n}\}_{n=1}^{N_m}\}$ of query sequences, the log-likelihood for the complete data is given by $\log P(T, W|\mu, \beta, \alpha,\alpha')$. Since this true posterior is hard to infer directly, we turn to variational methods [6], whose main idea is to posit a distribution over the latent variables with variational parameters, and find the settings of the parameters so as to make the distribution close to the true posterior in Kullback-Leibler (KL) divergence. In Figure 3, the lower part shows the variational distribution that approximates the data likelihood. Our paper chooses to introduce a distribution of latent variables q specified as the mean-field fully factorized family as follows:

$$
\begin{aligned}
& q(\pi_{1:M}, Y, \sigma_{1:K}|\gamma_{1:M}, \Phi, \rho_{1:K}) \\
&= \prod_m q_1(\pi_m|\gamma_m) \prod_m \prod_n q_2(y_{m,n}|\phi_{m,n}) \prod_k q_1(\sigma_k|\rho_k)
\end{aligned}
$$

where q_1 is a Dirichlet, q_2 is a multinomial, and $\{\gamma_{1:M}, \Phi, \rho_{1:K}\}$ are the set of variational parameters. We optimize those free parameters to tight the following lower bound $\mathcal{L}'$ for our likelihood:

$$
\begin{aligned}
\log p(T, W|\mu, \beta, \alpha,\alpha') \geq & E_q[\log p(T, W, \pi_{1:M}, Y, \sigma|\alpha,\alpha', \mu, \beta)] \\
& - E_q[\log q(\pi_{1:M}, Y, \sigma_{1:K})]. \qquad (3)
\end{aligned}
$$

Isolating terms containing λ in Eqn (3), we have

$$
\mathcal{L}_h = \sum_{m=1}^{M} \sum_n E_q(\log \lambda(t_{m,n})) - \sum_{m=1}^{M} \int_0^T E_q(\lambda(s))ds, \quad (4)
$$

as the partial likelihood on temporal data assuming query-topic distribution is known. On one hand, we have $\sum_{m=1}^{M} \int_0^T E_q(\lambda(s))ds = \sum_{m=1}^{M} b_m + T \sum_{m=1}^{M} \mu_m$. Here

$$
b_m = \sum_{n=1}^{N_m} \sum_{l=1}^{n-1} r(\phi_{m,l}, \phi_{m,n})(K(t_{m,n} - t_{m,l}) - K(t_{m,n-1} - t_{m,l})),
$$

where $K(t) = \int_0^t \kappa(s)ds$, and we define function $r(\phi_{m,l}, \phi_{m,n}) = \sum_k \phi_{m,l,k}\phi_{m,n,k}$, which can be viewed as the latent variable that approximates *influence* R. On the other hand, in order to update each Hawkes hyper-parameter μ and β independently, we adopt the strategy in [34], and break down the log sum $E_q(\log \lambda(t_{m,n}))$ based on Jensen's inequality as:

$$
\begin{aligned}
\mathbb{E}_q(\log(\lambda(t_{m,n}))) \geq & \eta_{m,nn} \log(\mu_m) + \sum_{l=1}^{n-1} \eta_{m,ln} \log(\beta_m \kappa(t_{m,n} - t_{m,l})) \\
& - \eta_{m,nn} \log(\eta_{m,nn}) - \sum_{l=1}^{n-1} r(\phi_{m,l}, \phi_{m,n}) \eta_{m,ln} \log(\eta_{m,ln}),
\end{aligned}
$$

where $\{\eta\}$ is a set of branching variables constrained by:

$$
\eta_{m,ln} \geq 0, \; \eta_{m,nn} + \sum_{l=1}^{n-1} r(\phi_{m,l}, \phi_{m,n}) \eta_{m,ln} = 1.
$$

Under a coordinate descent framework, we optimize the lower bound as in Eqn (3) against each variational latent variable[3] and the model hyper-parameter, including both LDA hyper-parameters and Hawkes hyper-parameters. For variational latent variables, we have the following process

- update rules for ϕ's as:

$$
\begin{aligned}
\phi_{m,n,k} \propto \exp(& \sum_m (\Psi(\gamma_{m,k}) - \Psi(\sum_k \gamma_{m,k})) \\
& + \sum_i \sum_v w_{m,n,i,v} [\Psi(\rho_{k,v}) - \Psi(\sum_v \rho_{k,v})] \\
& + \sum_{l=1}^{n-1} f_{l,n} + \sum_{l'=n+1}^{N_m} f_{n,l'}),
\end{aligned}
$$

  where we define $f_{l,n} = \phi_{m,l,k}(\eta_{m,ln} \log(\frac{\beta_m \kappa(t_{m,n} - t_{m,l})}{\eta_{m,ln}}) - \beta_m(K(t_{m,n} - t_{m,l}) - K(t_{m,n-1} - t_{m,l})))$;

- update rules for γ's as:

$$
\gamma_{m,k} = \alpha_k + \sum_n \phi_{m,n,k};
$$

- update rules for ρ's as:

$$
\rho_{k,v} \propto \alpha'_v + \sum_m \sum_n \sum_i \phi_{m,n,k} w_{n,i,v};
$$

[3]Here we categorize branching variables η as variational latent variables.

- and update rules for η as:

$$\eta_{m,nn} = \frac{\mu_m}{\mu_m + \sum_{l=1}^{n-1} r(\phi_{m,l}, \phi_{m,n})\beta_m \kappa(t_{m,n} - t_{m,l})},$$

$$\eta_{m,ln} = \frac{\beta_m \kappa(t_{m,n} - t_{m,l})}{\mu_m + \sum_{l=1}^{n-1} r(\phi_{m,l}, \phi_{m,n})\beta_m \kappa(t_{m,n} - t_{m,l})}.$$

3.2 Learning

We use a variational expectation-maximization (EM) algorithm [11] to compute the empirical Bayes estimates of the LDA hyper-parameters α and α' in our LDA-Hawkes model. This variational EM algorithm optimizes the lower bound as in Eqn (3) instead of the real likelihood, it iteratively approximates the posterior by fitting the variational distribution q and optimizes the corresponding bound against the parameters.

In updating α, we use a Newton-Raphson method, since the approximate maximum likelihood estimate of α doesn't have a closed form solution. The Newton-Raphson method is conducted with a gradient and Hessian as follows:

$$\frac{\partial \mathcal{L}'}{\partial \alpha_k} = N(\Psi(\sum_k \alpha_k) - \Psi(\alpha_k)) + \sum_m (\Psi(\gamma_{m,k}) - \Psi(\sum_k \gamma_{m,k})),$$

$$\frac{\partial \mathcal{L}'}{\partial \alpha_{k_1} \alpha_{k_2}} = N(\mathbb{I}_{(k_1=k_2)} \Psi'(\alpha_{k_1}) - \Psi'(\sum_k \alpha_k)).$$

Similar update rules can be derived for α'.

On the other hand, to obtain the approximate maximimum likelihood estimation of Hawkes hyper-parameters, we optimize the lower bound as in Eqn (3) against each Hawkes hyper-parameter, and update μ and β independently with closed-form solutions as follows:

$$\beta_m = \frac{1}{b_m} \sum_{n=1}^{N_m} \sum_{l=1}^{n-1} r(\phi_{m,l}, \phi_{m,n}) \eta_{m,ln}, \quad \mu_m = \frac{1}{T} \sum_{n=1}^{N_m} \eta_{m,nn}.$$

Our variation inference algorithm, named LDA-Hawkes, can be interpreted intuitively in the following way. The label/topic distribution γ in each user's query sequence is determined by both the topic prior and the topic assignment of each query. The word distribution ρ in each topic is determined by both the word prior and the topic assignment of each word. The probability of a query n issued by user m belonging to topic k is jointly determined by: (a) Users' label/topic distributions; (b) how queries are semantically clustered; (c) the influence from labels of queries in the past to the label of the current query; and (d) the influence from the label of the current query to labels of queries in the future.

In our mean-field variation inference algorithm, the computational cost of inferring variational variables is $O((\sum_m N_m)K\bar{C})$, where $\bar{C}$ is the average number of words in a query. The computational cost of the estimation of LDA hyper-parameters is $O(K+V)$. The computational cost of the estimation of Hawkes hyper-parameters is $O(\sum_m N_m^2)$, which can be reduced to $O(\sum_m N_m)$ by controlling the number of *influence* candidate for each query. Most queries have only limited number of *influence* associated, since for each query, most of the rest queries are far from it, and there exist many other queries in between. Thus the total computational cost of our algorithm is $O((\sum_m N_m)K\bar{C} + V)$.

4. EXPERIMENTS

We evaluated our LDA-Hawkes model on both synthetic and real-world data sets, and compared the performance with the following baselines:

- two alternative LDA-based probabilistic models:

  Time-Window(TW): This model assumes queries belong to the same search task only if they lie in a fixed or flexible time window, and uses LDA to cluster queries into topics based on the query co-occurrences within the same time window. We tested time windows of various sizes.

  Word-Related: This model assumes queries belongs to the same search task only if they share at least one word, and uses LDA to cluster queries into topics based on the co-occurrences of queries that sharing at least one word.

- two state-of-the-art query clustering approaches:

  Session-Similarity[36]: This method evaluated query similarity based on both query sessions and query content, and used those similarity scores for query clustering.

  GATE[2]: This is a Greedy Agglomerative Topic Extraction algorithm. It extracted topics based on a pre-defined topic similarity function, which considered both semantic similarity and mission similarity. Here mission similarity refers to the likelihood that two queries appear in the same mission, while missions are sequences of queries extracted from users' query logs through a mission detector.

- and three state-of-the-art search task identification approaches:
  Bestlink-SVM [30]: This method identified search tasks using a semi-supervised clustering model based on the latent structural SVM framework. A set of effective automatic annotation rules were proposed as weak supervision to release the burden of manual annotation.

  QC-HTC/QC-WCC [23]: This series of methods viewed search task identification as the problem of best approximating the manually annotated tasks, and proposed both clustering and heuristic algorithms to solve it. QC-WCC conducted clustering by dropping query-pairs with low weights, while QC-HTC considered the similarity between the first and last queries of two clusters in agglomerative clustering.

  Reg-Classifier[18]: This method designed a diverse set of syntactic, temporal, query log and web search features, and used them in a logistic regression model to detect search tasks.

4.1 Synthetic data

Data Generation. Given parameters $(M, N, K, \alpha, \alpha', \mu, \beta)$, the synthetic data is sampled according to the proposed generative model. We record the sampled values of Y, and calculate the ground-truth *influence* R for evaluating the accuracy of our prediction of *influence* among queries. Notice μ and β are both vectors of size M, where the elements μ_m and β_m are randomly generated in $[0.5\hat{\mu}, 1.5\hat{\mu}]$ and $[0.5\hat{\beta}, 1.5\hat{\beta}]$ respectively before the simulation. Vectors α and α' are of size K and V respectively, where the element α_k and α'_v are generated in $[0.5\hat{\alpha}, 1.5\hat{\alpha}]$ and $[0.5\hat{\alpha'}, 1.5\hat{\alpha'}]$ respectively before the simulation.

Our synthetic data are simulated with two different settings:

- `Small`: $M = 100$, $N = 120$, $K = 10$, $\hat{\mu} = 0.01$, $\hat{\beta} = 0.5$, $\hat{\alpha} = 0.1$, $\hat{\alpha'} = 0.1$. Simulations were run 1,000 times using the pre-generated parameters μ, β;
- `Large`: $M = 10{,}000$, $N = 10{,}000$, $K = 50$, $\hat{\mu} = 0.01$, $\hat{\beta} = 0.5$, $\hat{\alpha} = 0.1$, $\hat{\alpha'} = 0.1$. Simulations were run 10 times.

To test the robustness of our method, we add two types of noise to the original synthetic data:

`Event Noisy`: We generate additional 10% of total number of queries randomly in the time window of each already sampled query sequence, and add them to the sequence;

`Intensity Noisy`: Instead of using $\lambda(t)$ to simulate the query occurrence at time t, we use a noisy value $\lambda'(t)$, which is obtained by adding Guassian noise on $\lambda(t)$:

$$\lambda'(t) = \max(0.1e + 1, 0)\lambda(t), \; e \sim \mathcal{N}(0, \sigma). \quad (5)$$

The default value of σ is set to be 1.

Inference and Estimation. Table 1 evaluates both training likelihood, and the accuracy of our proposed variational inference algorithm in parameter estimation and latent variable inference on the synthetic data. We can find that, on the small synthetic data, LDA-Hawkes can recover the Hawkes parameters μ and β very well, which represent users' personal temporal patterns of query submission. Meanwhile, based on the inferred query-topic membership $\hat{Y}$, we predict the *influence* $\hat{R}$ among queries, and compare with the ground-truth *influence* R to evaluate the accuracy of our *influence* prediction through:

$$\text{Proc}_R = \sum_m \frac{1}{N_m(N_m-1)/2} \sum_{n=1}^{N_m} \sum_{n'=n+1}^{N_m} I(R_{n,n'} = \hat{R}_{n,n'}).$$

Results in Table 1 show that LDA-Hawkes can accurately predict *influence*. We also find an interesting phenomenon that the accuracy of our estimated Hawkes parameters and the accuracy of our predicted *influence* are highly correlated, since given different predicted *influence* $\hat{R}$, the optimal parameters μ and β that maximize the likelihood of Hawkes processes on a query sequence can be very different. On the large synthetic data, LDA-Hawkes's performance on parameter estimation becomes worse, while the accuracy of *influence* prediction also decreases. Due to the shapely increased data size, the combination of textual and temporal information becomes more complicated, which makes *influence* prediction more difficult, and further affects the learning of users' personal temporal patterns. On both noisy data sets, LDA-Hawkes's performances in both inference and estimation become worse.

4.2 Real-world Data

We also conducted extensive experiments on two real-world data sets. The first data set is adapted from the query log of `AOL` search engine [4]. The entire collection consists of 19.4 million search queries from about 650,000 users over a 3-month period. We cleaned the data by removing the duplicated queries which were submitted consecutively within 1 minute. We randomly selected a subset of users who submitted over 1,000 queries during this period, and collected their corresponding search activities, including the anonymized user ID, query string, timestamp, the clicked URL. As a result, we collected 1,786 users with 2.2 million queries, and their activities span from 18 days to 3 months. The second data set is collected from Yahoo search engine, from Jan 2013 to September 2013. Similarly, we cleaned the data and randomly selected a subset of users who submitted over 3,000 queries during this period. As a result, we collected 1,475 users with 1.9 million queries, and their activities span from 54 days to 9 months.

Model Fitness. Table 2 shows the log predictive likelihood on events falling in the final 10% of the total time of query data. To avoid overfitting issues, we adopt a k-fold cross validation strategy, and select the optimal number of topics K. According to Table 2, LDA-Hawkes fits both synthetic and real-world data better than TW and Word-Related. This illustrates that a Hawkes process can better utilize the temporal information in benefiting LDA's learning of textual data than simply considering the co-occurrence of queries within a time session or queries sharing at least one same word. The larger a time-window TW uses, the worse its performance will be. Time-window based LDA models generally perform better than

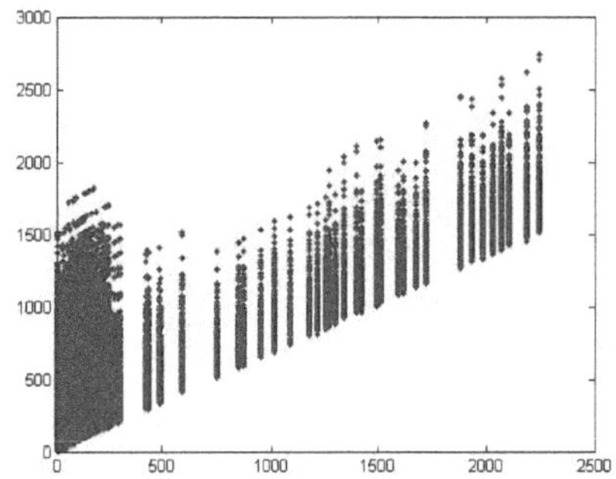

Figure 4: Q-Q plot of the predictive query sequence simulated with inferred Hawkes parameters versus the real query sequence.

Word-Related. Word-Related performs the worst, which illustrates that using lexicon-similarity only is far from enough for grouping semantically related queries. On both noisy data sets, the performances of all models become worse. However, the decrease of the performance of LDA-Hawkes is smaller than that of TW and Word-Related, which demonstrates the robustness of our proposed model.

In addition, another experiment is conducted to study how well the proposed model can fit the temporal data of query logs. Figure 4 shows the Q-Q plot of the predictive query sequences based on Hawkes parameters inferred from `AOL` versus the real query sequences in `AOL`. If the distribution of the timestamps of the predictive query sequences and that of the real query sequences are similar, the points in the Q-Q plot will approximately lie around the diagonal. If these two distributions are linearly related, the points in the Q-Q plot will approximately lie on a line, but not necessarily on the diagonal. From Figure 4, we can find that LDA-Hawkes fits the temporal data of real-world query logs very well.

Query clustering. Along with search task identification, the proposed model simultaneously clusters queries into topics, and automatically labels identified search tasks. According to our definition of search tasks, the performance of their identification depends heavily on the accuracy of per-query topic prediction. Moreover, whether our identified search tasks are labeled appropriately depends on how well our inferred topics match real-world semantic concepts. Thus the performance of identifying and labeling search tasks mainly depends on how we cluster query words into different topics. In this series of experiments, we evaluate the quality of obtained query clusters/topics, which depends on their purity, or semantic coherence. Since no ground truth about the correct composition of a topic is available, we assess purity by the average similarity of each pair of queries within the same topic as:

$$\text{Purity} = \frac{1}{K} \sum_k \frac{\sum_{q_i, q_j \in t_k} \text{Sim}(q_i, q_j)}{N_k(N_k-1)/2} \times 100\%,$$

where N_k is the number of queries in topic k.

We evaluate the query similarity based on their categorical labels from the Open Directory Project (ODP)[4], which has been widely used to measure the semantic relations between queries [5, 12]. The ODP , also known as DMOZ, is a human-edited directory of more than 4 million URLs. These URLs belong to over 590,000 categories organized in a tree-structured taxonomy where more general topics are located at higher levels. Users can issue queries in ODP and use the returned categories to categorize those queries. For instance, the URL {tech.groups.yahoo.com/group/amrc-l/} belongs

[4]http://www.dmoz.org/

Table 1: Inference and Estimation of LDA-Hawkes on Synthetic data

Data set	$\frac{1}{M}\sum_m \lvert\frac{\bar{\mu}_m-\mu_m}{\mu_m}\rvert$	$\frac{1}{M}\sum_m \lvert\frac{\bar{\beta}_m-\beta_m}{\beta_m}\rvert$	Prec_R	log likelihood
Small Synthetic	0.058	0.204	0.9175	-92.38
Small Event Noisy	0.083	0.317	0.8847	-95.02
Small Intensity Noisy	0.101	0.362	0.8675	-96.80
Large Synthetic	0.174	0.381	0.8573	-115.29
Large Event Noisy	0.202	0.413	0.8291	-119.38
Large Intensity Noisy	0.219	0.436	0.8107	-122.25

Table 2: Log Predictive Likelihood on Both Synthetic and Real-world Data

Model/Data set	LDA-Hawkes	TW(5 min)	TW(1 hour)	TW(1 day)	TW(1 week)	Word-Related
Small Synthetic	-110.32	-121.87	-124.08	-137.21	-168.40	-504.83
Small Event Noisy	-122.83	-135.23	-139.37	-152.15	-184.50	-536.21
Small Intensity Noisy	-127.36	-139.21	-146.59	-159.42	-192.23	-543.19
Large Synthetic	-163.84	-177.48	-182.43	-198.20	-239.04	-846.14
Large Event Noisy	-179.34	-193.05	-200.13	-221.49	-263.91	-880.04
Large Intensity Noisy	-184.27	-198.30	-207.23	-228.91	-270.92	-889.36
AOL	-153.12	-165.03	-169.83	-184.27	-221.32	-815.42
Yahoo	-192.36	-217.32	-222.95	-236.03	-275.74	-896.17

to Top/Arts/Animation/Anime/Clubs_and_Organizations, while the URL {http://valleyofazure.tripod.com/} belongs to another directory Top/Arts/Animation/Anime/Characters. Hence, to measure how related these two queries are, we can use a notion of similarity between the corresponding categories provided by ODP. In particular, we measure the similarity between category C_i of query q_i and category C_j of query q_j as the length of their longest common prefix $P(C_i, C_j)$ divided by the length of the longest path between C_i and C_j. More precisely, we define this similarity as:

ODP Similarity

$$\text{Sim}(q_i, q_j) = |P(C_i, C_j)| / \max(|C_i|, |C_j|),$$

where $|C|$ denotes the length of a path. For instance, the similarity between the two queries above is 3/5 since they share the path "Top/Arts/Animation" and the longest one is made of five directories. We evaluate the similarity between two queries by measuring the similarity between the most similar categories of the two queries, among the top 5 answers provided by ODP.

Figure 5 compares the purity of topics detected by LDA-Hawkes, alternative probabilistic models, and state-of-the-art query clustering approaches on AOL and Yahoo data sets. We can find that LDA-Hawkes outperforms all compared approaches. It improves over the second best method by up to 10%. `Gate` and TW(5 min) take the second place, both of them are slightly better than `Session-Similarity` and TW(1 hr), which again demonstrates that a small time window better benefits the LDA model in detecting semantically related queries. Word-Related performs significantly worse than other methods, which shows that considering only the co-occurrence of queries sharing words is very limited. Meanwhile, we find that compared with TW, LDA-Hawkes, `Session-Similarity`, and `Gate` perform relatively better on Yahoo data set, which implies that LDA-Hawkes works for various real-world query logs. Notice that the absolute value of topic purity is not very high, since the ODP categories are fine-grained, the categories of queries from the same search task are very likely to be different, but share paths, i.e., have common prefix.

Search Task Identification. To justify the effectiveness of the proposed model in identifying search tasks in query logs, we employ a public AOL data subset[5] with 554 annotated search tasks. This subset contains 13 users with around 110 queries per user. We also recruit eight editors to annotate 1150 search tasks in a randomly chosen subset from the Yahoo data, which contains 100 users with around 50 queries per user. We measure the performance by a widely used evaluation metric,

F_1 score

$$F_1 = \frac{2 * p_{pair} * r_{pair}}{p_{pair} + r_{pair}},$$

where p_{pair} denotes the percentage of query-pairs in our predicted search tasks that also appear in the same ground-truth task, while r_{pair} denotes the percentage of query-pairs in the ground-truth tasks that also appear in the same predicted task.

[5]http://miles.isti.cnr.it/ tolomei/?page_id=36.

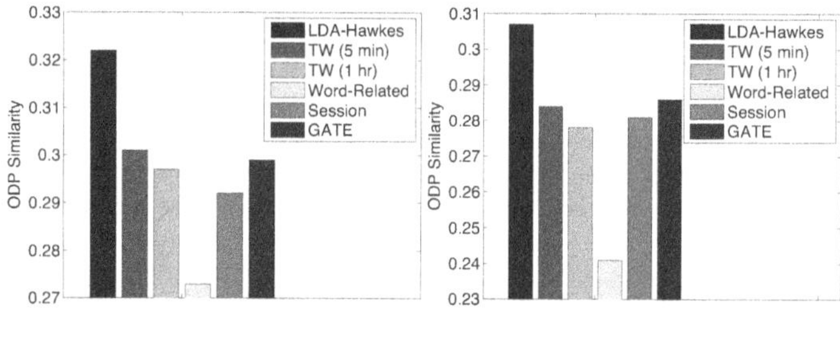

(a) AOL (b) Yahoo

Figure 5: Query Clustering measured by Topic Purity. This metric relies on ODP Similarity to evaluate the pairwise similarity between queries.

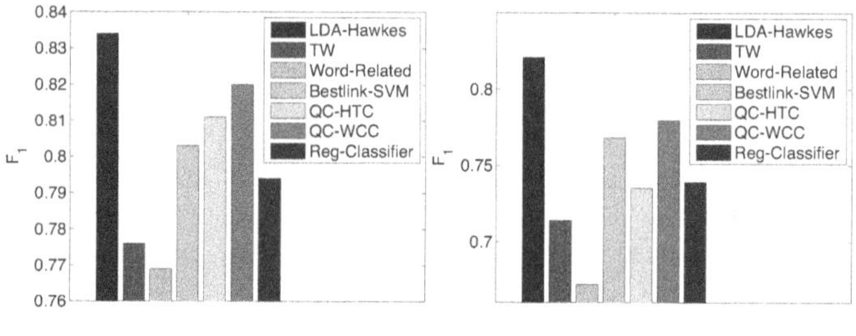

(a) AOL (b) Yahoo

Figure 6: Performance Comparison of Search Task Identification measured by F_1 Score.

Figure 6 compares the proposed model with alternative probabilistic models and state-of-the-art search task identification approaches by F_1 score. Here among TW models with various time-window sizes, we only include the "5 min" sized Time-Window in comparison, since it performs the best in both model fitness and query clustering. From Figure 6, we find that LDA-Hawkes performs the best among all compared approaches, and outperforms the second best approach by over 5%. Furthermore, LDA-Hawkes outperforms baselines in terms of both accuracy and recall. TW and Word-Related perform the worst since their assumptions on query-relationship within the same search task are too strong. Moreover, LDA-Hawkes's advantage over Bestlink-SVM and Reg-Classifier illustrates that employing self-exciting point processes like Hawkes to utilize the temporal information in query logs can be a better choice than incorporating temporal information in features. The advantage over QC-HTC and QC-WCC demonstrates that appropriate usage of temporal information in query logs can even better reflect the semantic relationship between queries, rather than exploiting it in some collaborative knowledge. The advantage of the performance of LDA-Hawkes over other baselines on Yahoo query log is greater than that on AOL. One possible reason is that the average length of search tasks in Yahoo is larger than that in AOL, which results in more influence occurrences, and enables LDA-Hawkes to better learn the temporal patterns of users.

Case Study of Identified Search Tasks. In this part, we try to show a few examples that LDA-Hawkes identify and label search tasks in Yahoo query log, so as to illustrate the validity of our identified search tasks and their labeling. From Figure 7, we can find that both the word co-occurrence and temporal gap play a important role in predicting *influence* among sequential queries. Although chances are very small that queries "aircract carrier" and "aircraft carrier" will co-occur, we predict an *influence* between them, since they are temporally close. On the other hand, query-pair "tibet" and "ryukyu islands", and query-pair "aircraft carrier" and "battleships us" are not consecutive, however, we predict that *influence* exist between those pairs of queries, as they co-occur in quite a few number of users' query sequences. Thus we may conclude that the existence of *influence* demands both temporal and sematic closeness. Queries linked by *influence* belong to the same search task since the user's *information need* is not satisfied by the former query, which makes the user additionally issue the later semantically related query, whose occurrence violates that user's regular query submission propensity. The figure also shows that LDA-Hawkes is able to assign the same label to different search tasks which are semantically related, despite that the temporal gap between them are very long.

5. RELATED WORK

Search query logs have been extensively studied to improve the search relevance and provide better user experience. There has been a large body of work focused on the problem of identifying search tasks or sessions from sequences of queries. Many of these methods use the idea of a "timeout" cutoff between queries, where two consecutive queries are considered as two different sessions or tasks if the time interval between them exceeds a certain threshold. Often a 30-minute timeout is used to segment sessions [9, 22, 30]. In addition, other timeout thresholds have been proposed, from 1 to 120 minutes [15, 18, 23]. However, the experimental results of these methods indicate that the timeouts, whatever their lengths, are of limited utility in predicting whether two queries belong to the same task, and unsuitable for identifying session boundaries. Beyond that, Wang et al. [30] and Hua et al. [17] treated the time intervals between queries as pairwise features in their models. But

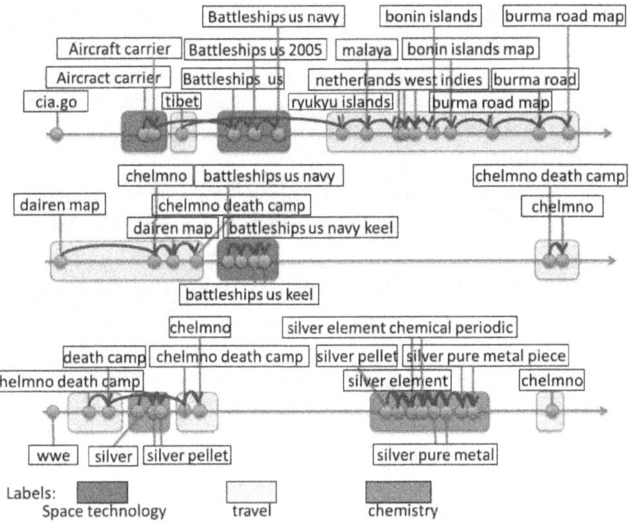

Figure 7: Case Study: Purple arrow line denotes the *influence* identified by the proposed model, rounded rectangle denotes the identified search tasks, rectangle denotes the labels our model assigns to search tasks.

no previous work has explicitly exploited the temporal information directly in their models. In our work, we directly integrate the temporal information into our model, rather than highly relying on different timeouts, for identifying search tasks.

There have been attempts to extract in-session tasks [28, 18, 23], and cross-session tasks [18, 19, 1, 30] from query sequences based on classification and clustering methods. Jones and Klinkner [18] proposed to learn a binary classifier to detect whether two queries belong to the same task or not, which organized and segmented query sequences into hierarchical units. Moreover, Kotov et al. [19] and Agichtein et al. [1] studied the problem of cross-session task extraction via binary same-task classification, and found different types of tasks demonstrate different life spans. Another suitable mechanism for identifying sessions or tasks may rely on *unsupervised learning* approaches, i.e., query clustering algorithms, especially when no labeled training set is available. The intuition for using query clustering is based on the assumption that if two queries belong to the same cluster, then they are topically related. Cao et al. [9] proposed a clustering algorithm for summarizing queries into concepts throughout a click-through bipartite graph built from a search log. Lucchese et al. [23, 24] and Hua et al. [17] exploited the knowledge base for detecting semantically related query pairs that are not similar from a lexical content point of view. In addition, Wang et al. [30] proposed a semi-supervised clustering method for identifying cross-session tasks. Different from these existing methods, our paper assumes that queries belonging to the same search task are linked by influence. Moreover, instead of focusing on the query sequence of each single user, we take into account the query sequences issued by different users simultaneously in a unified framework, such that our model can identify and label coherent search tasks across users.

Our proposed model is closely related to point processes, which have been used to model social networks [8] and natural events [37]. People find self-exciting point processes naturally suitable to model continuous-time events where the occurrence of one event can affect the likelihood of subsequent events in the future. One important self-exciting process is Hawkes process, which is first used to analyze earthquakes [25, 37], and then widely applied to many different areas, such as market modeling [13, 3], crime modeling [29], terrorist [26], conflict [35, 21], and viral videos on the Web [10]. A novel Hawkes model was also proposed to model both temporal and textual information in viral [34]. To solve such models, an EM algorithm is generally adopted to estimate the maximum likelihood of Hawkes process [20].

6. CONCLUSION AND FUTURE WORK

In this paper, we have presented a probabilistic model to integrate the LDA model with Hawkes processes for identifying and labeling search tasks. Basically, Hawkes processes utilize their self-exciting properties to identify search tasks if influence exists among a sequence of queries for individual users, while the LDA model exploits query co-occurrence across different users to discover the latent information needed for labeling search tasks. By leveraging the temporally weighted query co-occurrence, our model not only guarantees sound performance by making full use of both textual and temporal information of the entire query sequences, but also enables the labeling of the identified search tasks since semantically related queries are clustered together through query links determined by co-occurrence. We have applied the proposed LDA-Hawkes model to analyze search tasks on both AOL and Yahoo query logs, and compare with several alternative approaches. Experimental results show that the improvements of our proposed model are consistent, and our LDA-Hawkes model achieves the best performance. In future work, it would be interesting to consider other information, e.g., click-through data, into this framework, and investigate the performance of LDA-Hawkes in other domains.

7. ACKNOWLEDGMENT.

This work is supported in part by NSF grant IIS-1116886, NIH grant R01 GM108341 and NSFC grant NSFC-61129001/F010403.

8. REFERENCES

[1] E. Agichtein, R. W. White, S. T. Dumais, and P. N. Bennett. Search, interrupted: understanding and predicting search task continuation. In *SIGIR*, pages 315–324, 2012.

[2] L. M. Aiello, D. Donato, U. Ozertem, and F. Menczer. Behavior-driven clustering of queries into topics. In *CIKM*, pages 1373–1382, New York, NY, USA, 2011. ACM.

[3] Y. Ait-Sahalia, J. Cacho-Diaz, and R. Laeven. Modeling financial contagion using mutually exciting jump processes. *Tech. rep.*, 2010.

[4] AOL. http://gregsadetsky.com/aol-data/.

[5] R. Baeza-Yates and A. Tiberi. Extracting semantic relations from query logs. KDD, pages 76–85, New York, NY, USA, 2007. ACM.

[6] D. Blei and M. Jordan. Variational inference for dirichlet process mixtures. In *Bayesian Analysis*, volume 1, pages 121–144, 2005.

[7] D. M. Blei, A. Y. Ng, and M. I. Jordan. Latent dirichlet allocation. *J. Mach. Learn. Res.*, 3:993–1022, March 2003.

[8] C. Blundell, K. A. Heller, and J. M. Beck. Modelling reciprocating relationships with hawkes processes. *NIPS*, 2012.

[9] H. Cao, D. Jiang, J. Pei, Q. He, Z. Liao, E. Chen, and H. Li. Context-aware query suggestion by mining click-through and session data. In *KDD*, pages 875–883, 2008.

[10] R. Crane and D. Sornette. Robust dynamic classes revealed by measuring the response function of a social system. *Proceedings of the National Academy of Sciences of the United States of America*, 105(41):15649–15653, 2008.

[11] A. P. Dempster, N. M. Laird, and D. B. Rubin. Maximum likelihood from incomplete data via the EM algorithm. *Journal of the Royal Statistical Society. Series B (Methodological)*, pages 1–38, 1977.

[12] H. Deng, I. King, and M. R. Lyu. Entropy-biased models for query representation on the click graph. SIGIR, pages 339–346, New York, NY, USA, 2009. ACM.

[13] E. Errais, K. Giesecke, and L. R. Goldberg. Affine point processes and portfolio credit risk. *SIAM J. Fin. Math.*, 1(1):642–665, Sep 2010.

[14] A. G. Hawkes. Spectra of some self-exciting and mutually exciting point processes. *Biometrika*, 58:83–90, 1971.

[15] D. He, A. Göker, and D. J. Harper. Combining evidence for automatic web session identification. *Inf. Process. Manage.*, 38(5):727–742, 2002.

[16] M. D. Hoffman, D. M. Blei, and F. Bach. Online learning for latent dirichlet allocation. In *NIPS*, 2010.

[17] W. Hua, Y. Song, H. Wang, and X. Zhou. Identifying users' topical tasks in web search. In *WSDM*, pages 93–102, 2013.

[18] R. Jones and K. L. Klinkner. Beyond the session timeout: automatic hierarchical segmentation of search topics in query logs. In *CIKM*, pages 699–708, 2008.

[19] A. Kotov, P. N. Bennett, R. W. White, S. T. Dumais, and J. Teevan. Modeling and analysis of cross-session search tasks. In *SIGIR*, pages 5–14, 2011.

[20] E. Lewisa and G. Mohlerb. A nonparametric em algorithm for multiscale hawkes processes. *Journal of Nonpara-metric Statistics*, 1, 2011.

[21] L. Li and H. Zha. Dyadic event attribution in social networks with mixtures of hawkes processes. CIKM, pages 1667–1672, New York, NY, USA, 2013. ACM.

[22] Z. Liao, Y. Song, L.-w. He, and Y. Huang. Evaluating the effectiveness of search task trails. In *Proceedings of the 21st international conference on World Wide Web*, pages 489–498. ACM, 2012.

[23] C. Lucchese, S. Orlando, R. Perego, F. Silvestri, and G. Tolomei. Identifying task-based sessions in search engine query logs. In *WSDM*, pages 277–286, 2011.

[24] C. Lucchese, S. Orlando, R. Perego, F. Silvestri, and G. Tolomei. Discovering tasks from search engine query logs. *ACM Trans. Inf. Syst.*, 31(3):14, 2013.

[25] Y. Ogata. Statistical models for earthquake occurrences and residual analysis for point processes. *Journal of the American Statistical Association.*, 83(401):9–27, 1988.

[26] M. D. Porter and G. White. Self-exciting hurdle models for terrorist activity. *The Annals of Applied Statistics*, 6(1):106–124, 2011.

[27] F. Schoenberg. Introduction to point processes. *Wiley Encyclopedia of Operations Research and Management Science*, pages 616–617, 2010.

[28] A. Spink, S. Koshman, M. Park, C. Field, and B. J. Jansen. Multitasking web search on vivisimo.com. In *ITCC (2)*, pages 486–490, 2005.

[29] A. Stomakhin, M. B. Short, and A. L. Bertozzi. Reconstruction of missing data in social networks based on temporal patterns of interactions. *Inverse Problems.*, 27(11), Nov 2011.

[30] H. Wang, Y. Song, M.-W. Chang, X. He, R. W. White, and W. Chu. Learning to extract cross-session search tasks. In *WWW*, pages 1353–1364, 2013.

[31] X. Wang and E. Grimson. Spatial latent dirichlet allocation. NIPS, pages 1577–1584, 2007.

[32] Y. Wang, E. Agichtein, and M. Benzi. Tm-lda: efficient online modeling of latent topic transitions in social media. In *KDD*, pages 123–131, New York, NY, USA, 2012. ACM.

[33] R. W. White, W. Chu, A. Hassan, X. He, Y. Song, and H. Wang. Enhancing personalized search by mining and modeling task behavior. In *WWW*, pages 1411–1420, 2013.

[34] S. Yang and H. Zha. Mixture of mutually exciting processes for viral diffusion. In *ICML*, volume 28, pages 1–9, 2013.

[35] A. Z.-Mangion, M. Dewarc, V. Kadirkamanathand, and G. Sanguinetti. Point process modelling of the afghan war diary. *PNAS*, 109(31):12414–12419, July 2012.

[36] Z. Zhang and O. Nasraoui. Mining search engine query logs for query recommendation. In *WWW*, pages 1039–1040, New York, NY, USA, 2006. ACM.

[37] J. Zhuang, Y. Ogata, and D. V. Jones. Stochastic declustering of space-time earthquake occurrences. *Journal of the American Statistical Association.*, 97(458):369–380, 2002.

LaSEWeb: Automating Search Strategies over Semi-structured Web Data

Oleksandr Polozov*
University of Washington
polozov@cs.washington.edu

Sumit Gulwani
Microsoft Research
sumitg@microsoft.com

ABSTRACT

We show how to programmatically model processes that humans use when extracting answers to queries (e.g., "Who invented typewriter?", "List of Washington national parks") from semi-structured Web pages returned by a search engine. This modeling enables various applications including automating repetitive search tasks, and helping search engine developers design micro-segments of factoid questions.

We describe the design and implementation of a domain-specific language that enables extracting data from a webpage based on its structure, visual layout, and linguistic patterns. We also describe an algorithm to rank multiple answers extracted from multiple webpages.

On 100,000+ queries (across 7 micro-segments) obtained from Bing logs, our system LaSEWeb answered queries with an average recall of 71%. Also, the desired answer(s) were present in top-3 suggestions for 95%+ cases.

Categories and Subject Descriptors

H.2.3 [**Database Management**]: Languages—*query languages*; H.3.3 [**Information Storage and Retrieval**]: Information Search and Retrieval—*clustering, search process, information filtering*

Keywords

Semi-structured data; domain-specific languages; structure extraction; Web programming; question answering.

1. INTRODUCTION

The creation of search engines changed the way people locate information on the Web. 91% of online adults currently use search engines to find information on the Web, 59% of them daily [21]. 84% of research undertaken by college students begins with a search engine query [3], and the same trend is observed for faculty and professional researchers [11]. Search engines dictate our habits of knowledge discovery on the Web.

Even though many of the queries submitted to search engines represent one-off tasks, a significant percent of them are repetitive. First, end-users often have to *process batch data* that requires making a series of similar queries to a search engine. A typical example is finding a similar piece of information about every item in a given list, e.g. acquiring contact information about a list of people, getting BibTeX entries for a list of articles, etc.

Second, so called *factoid questions* ("Who invented radio?", "What is the population of Germany?", etc.) still constitute a significant portion of all user queries in search engine logs [23]. Search engines have recognized the importance of factoid questions, and introduced a notion of a *micro-segment* of queries – a specific category of questions, for which the search engine shows the instant answer underneath the search bar, along with the list of search results. The source of data for answering micro-segment questions is typically a structured knowledge database, such as FreeBase. This implies that (a) the information presented in an answer is limited to the content of the database; (b) answer extraction code is hard-coded for every micro-segment; (c) time-sensitive information is not tracked consistently. In constrast, any desired knowledge is usually present in the free-text Web data, but it is usually unstructured or semi-structured (i.e., partially labeled to be accessible and recognizable by humans, but not by data collection algorithms).

Even when a search engine provides instant response, it may not be exactly what the end-user wants. According to [24], people prefer to locate their target in iterations, by observing the context of an answer and refining the query as necessary. They mostly look at multiple pages related to their desired answer, although seldom at more than ten [13]. Moreover, there may be multiple possible "answers" to a user's query, and the user is often interested in exploring the context related to each of them. For this, end-users like to explore the list of search results manually, since the task of *extracting and ranking multiple answer candidates along with their context* lies beyond the capabilities of current micro-segment search. This is the problem addressed in this paper.

All mentioned repeatable search tasks share the same generic features. A repeatable search task is a parameterized Web query that takes a tuple of string *arguments*, and returns a set of string *answers*. Essentially, a parameterized Web query is a *function* over the Web data, which is defined once, and later executed multiple times for various specific

*Work done during an internship at Microsoft Research.

KDD'14, August 24–27, 2014, New York, NY, USA.

ACM 978-1-4503-2956-9/14/08...$15.00.
http://dx.doi.org/10.1145/2623330.2623761 .

arguments. Currently, the only automated component in the execution of such a function is a search engine. The rest of the execution is defined by end-users' search strategies over the search engine results, and is entirely manual.

We observe that for any repeatable search task people follow similar strategies in extracting knowledge from the Web. They compose a search query aimed to bring a list of results with high recall, but not necessarily high precision (i.e. the desired knowledge is present among the suggested links, but it may not be ranked high enough by the search engine). People then navigate to the suggested links, and explore the content of webpages to build a list of answer candidates and associated context. In order to locate an answer candidate on a webpage, they use a set of patterns that form a basis of their *search strategy*. These patterns include:

- Linguistic patterns: sentence structure, semantic information, textual content of the webpage.
- Structural patterns: any relational or otherwise semi-structured information on the webpage, tables, lists.
- Visual patterns: layout and styling of the webpage, presentational attributes of its elements, emphasis.

These patterns serve as a way to create structure and add semantics on top of the semi-structured content of the Web.

In this paper, we present LASEWEB[1] – a system for automating repetitive search tasks from end-users' descriptions of their search strategies involving the above-mentioned patterns. LASEWEB consists of a novel domain-specific language (DSL) for programming search strategies, and an interpreter for it, built on top of the search engine Bing. A LASEWEB program takes a tuple of user query arguments, and returns a set of answer strings from the Web, ranked by their confidence scores, along with their corresponding source URLs. It does so by (a) exploring the list of search results returned by Bing for our *seed query*, (b) executing a LASEWEB *query* on each webpage in the list to extract multiple answer string representations from it, and (c) clustering these representations using an application-specific *similarity function*. The language of LASEWEB queries includes textual, structural, and visual search patterns that we collected from our observations of typical search strategies. The interpreter for this language makes use of semi-structured content of a webpage and CSS attributes of HTML nodes along with state-of-the-art natural language processing (NLP) algorithms and programming by example (PBE) algorithms. We intend LASEWEB to be used by both end-users and micro-segment developers.

We evaluated LASEWEB on two different applications of Web programming: (a) 7 factoid micro-segments, represented by 100,000+ user queries from Bing logs, and (b) 5 repeatable academic search tasks, related to PLDI-2014 committee. The system achieved 95%+ precision in all micro-segments, and 73% precision in repeatable search, with an average recall of 71%.

This paper makes the following contributions:

- We define and motivate the problem of Web programming with two different applications (§2).
- We introduce LASEWEB, our DSL for writing Web programs that incorporate humans' search strategies in a declarative format (§3).
- We provide an efficient interpreter for our DSL (§4). Besides other things, it makes use of novel *logical table parsing* techniques that utilize textual, structural, and visual features of a webpage to extract structural information from semi-structured data (§4.1.2).
- We evaluate LASEWEB on two applications of Web programming: 7 factoid micro-segments and 5 batch search tasks (§5).

2. MOTIVATION

2.1 Examples

We begin with two scenarios that illustrate the problem of Web programming. These scenarios are: factoid micro-segments in search engines, and repetitive Web searches.

Scenario 1. Alice is a software developer in a search engine department. She is responsible for a "micro-segment" search: providing instant answers to simple factoid questions underneath the search bar, along with a list of usual search results. She wants to implement a new micro-segment that can answer questions about inventors/creators of various products or discoveries. A fraction of this information exists in FreeBase and similar databases, but they lack data about (a) less fundamental inventions, like "paper clip", and (b) ambiguous attributions, like "radio" (N. Tesla vs. G. Marconi vs. A. Popov, etc.) Such information is available on the Web, in the list of provided search results. However, in order to discover any contextual information, a user has to navigate to every webpage in the list manually.

Instead of hard-coding FreeBase information, Alice might want to implement the following pseudocode, which represents her own search strategy in locating inventor infomation on the Web. This pseudocode describes a set of linguistic patterns that match sentences about inventors on webpages, returned by a search engine.

$w \leftarrow$ product name
$q \leftarrow w \circ$ "inventor"
$U \leftarrow$ search results for q
for all urls $u_j \in U$ **do**
  $\mathcal{Q}_1 \leftarrow$ pattern "Entity(Person) ␣ ∗ ␣ Syn(invented) ␣ ∗ ␣ w"
  $S \leftarrow$ {strings s within the content of u_j | s is an Entity(Person) component in a match of $\mathcal{Q}_1$ }
  $\mathcal{Q}_2 \leftarrow$ pattern "Entity(Person) ␣ ∗ ␣ Syn(creator) ␣ POS(Prep) ␣ w"
  $S \leftarrow S \cup$ {strings s within the content of u_j | s is a Entity(Person) component in a match of $\mathcal{Q}_2$ }
  ...
  Assume more confidence in the more frequent results in S
return all collected results with confidence scores and URLs

In this pseudocode Syn(s) matches any word that is synonymic to s, $*$ matches any number of words, POS(Prep) matches a preposition, Entity(Person) matches several words that constitute a person name (such as "John Atanasoff"). $\circ$ denotes string concatenation.

When executed against a user query w = "computer", this program produces a set of results, similar to the following:

Answer	Confidence	Sources
John Atanasoff	14.5%	http://www.computerhope.com http://www.ehow.com http://inventors.about.com
Charles Babbage	10.2%	http://www.buzzle.com http://www.ask.com
...	...	...

We note that with this approach, *every* micro-segment turns into a "repetitive search": a parameterized search task that is defined once by a search engine developer, and executed multiple times with different arguments by end-users. The input of this search task are micro-segment arguments –

[1] **La**nguage for **S**tructure **E**xtraction.

Figure 1: Screenshot of the personal webpage of Dr. Shaz Qadeer[2] (retrieved in October 2013).

for example, for "inventor" micro-segment this is the product name. The output of the task are answers to the factoid question of the micro-segment, ranked by confidence scores, along with their source URLs for additional context.

Scenario 2. Sofus has a table of KDD 2014 committee member names, which he wants to fill in with their corresponding phone numbers. Phone numbers can be extracted from their personal webpages automatically via regular expressions, but there are two challenges: (a) these webpages have to be identified first; (b) regular expressions may have false positives. Consider a webpage in Fig. 1. A simple regular expression for phone numbers will match both "Phone" and "Fax" lines on the page. Moreover, on different webpages it might also match a secretary's phone number, lab numbers, university numbers, etc. Also, retrieval of all personal webpages is still manual and tedious.

Without any automation, a human typically looks for a phone number on a personal webpage using visual and linguistic cues: proximity to header, words like "Phone" or "Fax", string pattern (regular expressions), table-like structure "⟨field name⟩ : ⟨value⟩". The following pseudocode describes this manual search strategy:

$w_i \leftarrow i^{\text{th}}$ committee member's name
$q_i \leftarrow w_i \circ$ "`phone number`"
$U \leftarrow$ search results for q_i
for all urls $u_j \in U$ **do**
  $S \leftarrow$ {strings s within the content of $u_j \mid s$ appears close to w_i or a picture $\wedge$ w_i is emphasized (bold/colored) $\wedge s$ is a value in a table-like structure where key is similar to "Phone"/"Voice" $\wedge$ s matches a phone number }
  Assume more confidence in the more frequent results in S
return all collected results with confidence scores and URLs

We note that the information on a webpage could be presented in an entirely different format: as a series of lines with a separator other than a colon, as an HTML table, with different layout, etc. However, people interpret any of these formats as a generic "table-like" structure, and locate information in them in a similar manner.

In this scenario, the repetitive search task lies in collecting similar knowledge for each item in the list. The input is a person's name, and the output is the set of found phone numbers. There may be multiple "correct" answers (e.g., home/cell phone number).

2.2 Observations

Examples in §2.1 show two different applications of parameterized Web queries, and expose several features that most people share in their search strategies. We summarize the list of our observations about these features below. They form the foundation for the definition of the problem of Web programming (which we tackle in this paper), and the LASEWEB system (which is our approach to solving it).

2.2.1 Problem definition

Repetitive search tasks are parameterized. People often need to use the same strategy for a series of similar Web search tasks with different parameters. Scenario 2 showed a case of an end-user dealing with a single problem of finding a phone number, applied to multiple people. In Scenario 1 the task is defined by a micro-segment developer, and later used multiple times by different end-users.

Search tasks have multiple answers. Depending on the nature of the search task, there may be multiple pieces of information that should be extracted from the Web as possible "answers". A user is often interested in (a) exploring different answers ranked by some measure of their respective confidence/relevance, and (b) exploring some context related to the various answers.

These observations motivate our problem definition:

Definition 1. A *Web program* is a process that takes a tuple of user *query arguments*, and returns a set of *answer strings*, ranked by their confidence, along with corresponding *source URLs* for every answer string.

A Web program is essentially defined as a *function* from strings to sets of strings. The *execution* of such a function happens over data on the Web. The *definition* of such a function consists of various typical patterns that constitute humans' *search strategy*. Both definition and execution of Web programs are currently entirely manual, with the search engine being the only automatic bridge between the user's goal and the Web data; our LASEWEB system automates the execution of such Web programs.

2.2.2 Our approach

We propose LASEWEB, our approach to Web programming. It implements a Web program by automating a typical human's search strategy for it. The automation is based on our observations about common features of such search strategies, summarized below.

Exploring multiple webpages. When there are multiple "correct" answers to the question, people explore multiple webpages in order to adjust their confidence in some of these answers. In order to retrieve a list of relevant webpages to explore, an end-user typically starts with a query to a search engine. This initial query is expected to yield a set of results with high recall but possibly low precision. A simple combination of arguments does not necessarily constitute a good initial query for a search engine: based on the application, the user might want to use additional keywords or some features of a search engine front-end in the query.

In our approach, every LASEWEB program contains a *seed query builder* – a function that composes the initial query to a search engine (§3.1).

Answers have multiple representations. A single answer can be found on the Web in multiple string representations. For example, a person's name can be written with or without middle initial, with given name or family name first, with or without proper capitalization, etc. The nature of such multiple representations depends on the application.

[2]`http://research.microsoft.com/en-us/people/qadeer/`

We *cluster* multiple representations of the same answer together using a *similarity function* that defines an application-specific logic of answer similarity (§3.1). We then rank the resulting clusters by our measure of answer confidence, and choose a *representative answer* for every cluster (§4.2).

People look for patterns. When looking for an answer on a particular webpage, people use a set of patterns that locate relevant information within the content of the webpage. These patterns can be categorized as follows:

1. **Linguistic patterns**, as in Scenario 1, use syntax and semantic characteristics of text to find appropriate matches within the content of a webpage. The required answer of a LASEWEB query typically exists at this lowest level surrounded by text that we can fuzzily describe using linguistic patterns. End-users usually do not build such patterns consciously, but domain experts can easily extrapolate their search strategy into simple linguistic patterns, as was shown in Scenario 1.
2. **Structural patterns**, as in Scenario 2, use structured or semi-structured content of the webpage to extract required information according to the implicit schema. The majority of text content on the Web is not structured, but rather semi-structured: tables are not normalized, and often not even marked as a table. However, people identify any of the following as a "table":
   - HTML `<table>`, `<ul>`, or `<ol>`.
   - plain text with separators (e.g. colon).
   - block elements, spatially aligned in a table-like structure.
3. **Visual patterns**, as in Scenario 2, use spatial layout of the webpage, colors, proximity and other stylistic features to locate relevant information. The exact instantiation of these patterns (i.e., specific colors or layout) differs among webpages, but human brain is capable of checking them in a generic manner.

We present an appropriate query language that includes linguistic, structural, and visual patterns of search strategies (§3.2). This language is the main component of LASEWEB.

3. LASEWEB LANGUAGE

In this section, we present the language of LASEWEB. §3.1 introduces LASEWEB *programs* – our representation of parameterized queries, described and motivated before in §2. We describe the syntax and semantics of LASEWEB *queries*, the main component of LASEWEB programs, in §3.2. The implementation of our interpreter for LASEWEB programs is discussed in §4.

3.1 LaSEWeb programs

Every LASEWEB *program* $\mathcal{P}$ represents a single parameterized query that takes a tuple of user query arguments $\vec{v}$ and returns a set of answer strings, annotated with their confidence scores along with their source URLs. The execution of a LASEWEB program $\mathcal{P}$ on a tuple of user query arguments $\vec{v}$ is defined as $\mathcal{P}\colon \vec{v} \mapsto \{\langle a_i, \beta_i, U_i \rangle\}$, where a_i is the ith *answer string*, β_i is its *confidence score*, and U_i is the set of its *source URLs*. Higher confidence scores correspond to more relevant answers.

The syntax and semantics of LASEWEB programs is based on our observations, summarized in §2.2. A LASEWEB program $\mathcal{P}$ first constructs a *seed query* for Bing, executes a LASEWEB *query* on each of the returned search results, extracts the desired *answer strings* from the matches of the LASEWEB query, and clusters these answer strings together, according to the *similarity function*.

Definition 2. A LASEWEB program $\mathcal{P}$ is parameterized by $\vec{v}$ that is replaced by a tuple of user-provided arguments at runtime for every specific search invocation. It is defined as a tuple $\langle q, \sigma, \mathcal{Q}, \ell_a \rangle$, where:

- q is a *seed query builder* function, which builds an initial query for Bing from $\vec{v}$. This query should be likely to produce a set of relevant links with high recall.
- σ is a *similarity function*, which compares two answer strings from the Web, and determines whether they describe the same "answer" in the application logic.
- $\mathcal{Q}$ is a LASEWEB *query*, which describes a set of patterns that humans use to find this kind of information on the Web. As a result of its execution, $\mathcal{Q}$ matches none or many answer strings on a single webpage.
- ℓ_a is a label in $\mathcal{Q}$ that specifies what subexpression of the match is extracted as an "answer" (this is similar to named capturing groups in regular expressions).

EXAMPLE 1. *In Scenario 1 the "inventor" micro-segment is described with* LASEWEB *program* $\mathcal{P} = \langle q, \sigma, \mathcal{Q}, \ell_a \rangle$*, where:*

- $q(w) = w \circ$ "`inventor`"
- $\sigma(w_1, w_2) = \mathsf{true}$ *iff* w_1 *and* w_2 *describe the same person name (e.g., "Charles Babbage" and "C. Babbage").*
- $\mathcal{Q}$ *is the* LASEWEB *query equivalent to* $\mathcal{Q}_1 \vee \mathcal{Q}_2$ *in Scenario 1. We show this query in Example 4.*
- ℓ_a *is a label of the subexpression* Entity(Person) *in* $\mathcal{Q}$.

Specific search invocations of $\mathcal{P}$ *apply it on specific user parameters, such as* $\vec{v} =$ ("`computer`"), *or* $\vec{v} =$ ("`paper clip`").

The rest of this section focuses on the syntax and semantics of the main component of a LASEWEB program – a LASEWEB query $\mathcal{Q}$. Our interpreter for LASEWEB programs, which makes use of the other components as well (q, σ, and ℓ_a), is described in §4.

3.2 LaSEWeb queries

A LASEWEB query $\mathcal{Q}$ is executed against a webpage. A *webpage* is a tree of HTML nodes $\mathcal{N}$. For each HTML node $\mathcal{N}$ we define two auxiliary functions $\mathsf{BBox}(\mathcal{N})$ and $\mathsf{Text}(\mathcal{N})$, which are used by LASEWEB to determine the result of the execution. $\mathsf{BBox}(\mathcal{N})$ returns a rectangle b that is the smallest bounding box of node $\mathcal{N}$ on the page, when rendered by a browser (assuming a fixed resolution). $\mathsf{Text}(\mathcal{N})$ is a string that is a displayed textual content of $\mathcal{N}$, with all HTML tags stripped off. The result of executing a LASEWEB query $\mathcal{Q}$ against such a webpage is a multi-set of possible *answer strings*, each labeled with some label ℓ – the subexpression of $\mathcal{Q}$ that matched this answer string. A subset of this multi-set that is labeled with the "answer label" ℓ_a in the definition of $\mathcal{P}$, is selected for the final answer set.

Fig. 2 shows the syntax of LASEWEB. A LASEWEB query $\mathcal{Q}$ unites three types of expressions: *visual expressions* $\mathcal{B}$, *structural expressions* $\mathcal{S}$, and *linguistic expressions* $\mathcal{L}$. They are aligned in a *hierarchical structure* of three layers that match separate webpage elements:

- The topmost layer of visual expressions describes webpage elements with particular stylistic propeties. They make use of presentational attributes of an HTML node, its CSS, position, and bounding box. A visual expression $\mathcal{B}$ is executed against a *bounding box* b.

(a)

Linguistic expression $\mathcal{L}$	$:= \mathsf{Ling}(\mathcal{E}, \Phi) \mid \mathcal{L}_1 \vee \mathcal{L}_2$
Linguistic pattern $\mathcal{E}$	$:= \mathcal{E}^+ \mid \mathcal{E}^* \mid \mathcal{E}? \mid \mathcal{E}_1\ \mathcal{E}_2 \mid \ell\colon \mathcal{E} \mid \mathsf{Word}$
	$\mid \mathsf{ConstWord}(s) \mid \mathsf{ConstPhrase}(s_1, \ldots, s_k)$
	$\mid \mathsf{Syn}(s) \mid \mathsf{POS}(p) \mid \mathsf{Entity}(e) \mid \mathsf{NP} \mid \ldots$
Linguistic constraint Φ	$:= \mathsf{SameSentence}(\ell_1, \ell_2) \mid \mathsf{Regex}(\ell, s) \mid \ldots$
	$\mid \Phi_1 \wedge \Phi_2 \mid \Phi_1 \vee \Phi_2 \mid \neg\Phi \mid \mathsf{true} \mid \mathsf{false}$
String s	$:= w \mid v_k$
ID labels ℓ, η	$:= w$
Part of speech p	$\in \{\mathsf{Noun}, \mathsf{Verb}, \mathsf{Prep} \ldots\}$
Entity type e	$\in \{\mathsf{Person}, \mathsf{Org}, \mathsf{Place} \ldots\}$

LASEWEB query $\mathcal{Q}$	$:= \mathsf{FW}(\mathcal{B}, \Psi) \mid \mathcal{Q}_1 \vee \mathcal{Q}_2$
Visual expression $\mathcal{B}$	$:= \mathcal{S} \mid \mathsf{Union}(\mathcal{B}_1, \mathcal{B}_2) \mid \eta\colon \mathcal{B}$
Visual constraint Ψ	$:= \mathsf{Nearby}(\eta_1, \eta_2) \mid \mathsf{Emphasized}(\eta) \mid \mathsf{Layout}(\eta_1, \eta_2, d) \mid \ldots$
	$\mid \Psi_1 \wedge \Psi_2 \mid \Psi_1 \vee \Psi_2 \mid \neg\Psi \mid \mathsf{true} \mid \mathsf{false}$
Structural expression $\mathcal{S}$	$:= \mathsf{Leaf}(\mathcal{L}) \mid \mathsf{VLOOKUP}(\mathcal{L}_1, \mathcal{L}_2, \mathcal{L}_3) \mid \mathsf{AttrLookup}(\mathcal{L}_1, \mathcal{L}_2)$
Direction d	$\in \{\mathsf{Up}, \mathsf{Down}, \mathsf{Left}, \mathsf{Right}\}$

(b)

$\mathsf{Ling}(\mathcal{E}, \mathsf{true}) \equiv \mathcal{E}$ $\quad \mathsf{FW}(\mathcal{B}, \mathsf{true}) \equiv \mathcal{B}$ $\quad \ell\colon \mathsf{Word} \equiv \ell$ $\quad \mathsf{Word}^* \equiv *$

$\mathsf{ConstWord}(s) \equiv \text{“}s\text{”}$ $\quad \mathsf{ConstPhrase}(s_1, \ldots, s_k) \equiv \text{“}s_1 \sqcup \cdots \sqcup s_k\text{”}$

Figure 2: (a) LASEWEB query language syntax. v_k denotes the kth argument in a tuple of user query arguments $\vec{v}$, k denotes an integer constant, and w denotes a string constant. (b) Common shorthands in LASEWEB, used for brevity.

- The middle layer of structural expressions describes a structural pattern of information within any *logical tables* in a webpage. A structural expresion $\mathcal{S}$ is executed against an HTML node. $\mathcal{S}$ is the simplest form of a visual expression: it matches a bounding box b if $\mathcal{S}$ matches a node $\mathcal{N}$, encompassed by b.
- The bottom layer of linguistic expressions $\mathcal{L}$ describes a string pattern using syntactic and semantic matching constructors. $\mathcal{L}$ is the simplest form of a structural expresion. It is executed against an input string t, which is the content $\mathsf{Text}(\mathcal{N})$ of some HTML node $\mathcal{N}$.

Together these three expression types cover the entire range of typical patterns of search strategies, defined in §2.2.

A LASEWEB query $\mathcal{Q}$ is parameterized with a tuple of parameters $\vec{v}$, which are replaced by user-provided query arguments v_k (before its execution on a webpage). Thus, in Fig. 2 every string (which is not a label name) can be either a constant string literal w, or a user query argument v_k.

We begin with an explanation of linguistic expressions in §3.2.1, and proceed with structural expression in §3.2.2, and visual expressions in §3.2.3. Examples 4 and 5 give examples of full LASEWEB queries on applications from §2.

3.2.1 Linguistic expressions

A *linguistic expression* $\mathcal{L}$ consists of a *linguistic pattern* $\mathcal{E}$ and a *linguistic constraint* Φ. Here linguistic patterns, when executed against an input string t, collect multiple matches M, and linguistic constraints filter out matches with undesired properties.

A linguistic pattern $\mathcal{E}$ is executed against an input string t. In our system, we consider strings as lists of *tokens*. A token is a natural language primitive (word, punctuation, etc.).

The result of the execution of $\mathcal{E}$ on t is a set W of *linguistic matches* M. Every linguistic match M is a mapping from ID labels ℓ of $\mathcal{E}$'s subexpressions to *matched substrings* of t. Intuitively, $\mathcal{E}$ acts similarly to a regular expression: when $\mathcal{E}$ finds a succesful match within t, every subexpression of $\mathcal{E}$ corresponds to some substring t' of t. Some of these subexpressions $\ell\colon \mathcal{E}$ are explicitly marked with labels ℓ; this is similar to named capturing groups in regular expressions.

Linguistic patterns are similar to regular expressions in a sense of their composition methods. They are divided into three kinds as described below.

Primitive. A linguistic pattern Word matches any single token. We usually denote $\ell\colon$ Word simply as ℓ, since label ℓ is essentially a variable that captures a word match in the mapping M. Linguistic patterns $\mathsf{ConstWord}(s)$ and $\mathsf{ConstPhrase}(s_1, \ldots, s_k)$ match a fixed token s or a fixed sequence of tokens “$s_1 \sqcup \cdots \sqcup s_k$”, respectively, in t.

Composite. Operators $+$, ?, and $*$ (Kleene star) borrow their semantics from regular expressions. Each of them has a single linguistic pattern as a subexpression, and their resulting mappings M are composed from the matches found in subexpressions. For $+$ and $*$, whose subexpression matches multiple times in the substring, we put all the found mappings in the final linguistic match M. Thus, the same label ℓ may occur multiple times in the linguistic match M.

Linguistic predicates. Most of the forms of linguistic patterns are *predicates*, which match a token or a sequence of tokens only if it satisfies some linguistic property. We show several representatives of linguistic predicates in Fig. 2; more can be implemented, assuming the existence of corresponding NLP algorithms. In this paper we use the following representative predicates:

- $\mathsf{POS}(p)$: matches a token if its part of speech is p.
- $\mathsf{Entity}(e)$: matches a sequence of tokens, classified as a *named entity* of type e (person name, place, etc.).
- NP: matches a sequence of tokens if it constitutes a *noun phrase* in the parse tree of the sentence.
- $\mathsf{Syn}(s)$: matches a single token if it is synonymic to s.

We assume the existence of corresponding functions $\mathsf{IsNP}(s)$, $\mathsf{PosValue}(s)$, $\mathsf{AreSynonyms}(s_1, s_2)$, $\mathsf{EntityValue}(s)$, which implement required NLP algorithms on strings. §4 discusses our implementation of these functions.

Linguistic constraints. Every match M, returned by a linguistic pattern $\mathcal{E}$, is filtered through a linguistic constraint Φ. The final set of matches W, returned by a linguistic expression $\mathcal{L}$, consists only of those matches M that haven't been filtered out by Φ.

We present two representatives of linguistic constraints:

- $\mathsf{SameSentence}(\ell_1, \ell_2)$ returns true iff matches captured by ℓ_1 and ℓ_2 belong to the same sentence within t.
- $\mathsf{Regex}(\ell, s)$ returns true iff the match captured by ℓ satisfies the regular expression s.

EXAMPLE 2. *The “inventor” micro-segment in Scenario 1 can be described with the following linguistic expression:*

$\mathcal{L} = \mathsf{Ling}(\mathcal{E}_1, \Phi) \vee \mathsf{Ling}(\mathcal{E}_2, \Phi)$ *where:*

$\mathcal{E}_1 = (\ell_{ans}\colon \mathsf{Entity}(\mathsf{Person})) \sqcup * \sqcup \mathsf{Syn}(\text{“}\texttt{invent}\text{”}) \sqcup * \sqcup (\ell_q\colon v_1)$

$\mathcal{E}_2 = (\ell_q\colon v_1) \sqcup \mathsf{Syn}(\text{“}\texttt{created}\text{”}) \sqcup \mathsf{POS}(\mathsf{Prep}) \sqcup * \sqcup (\ell_{ans}\colon \mathsf{Entity}(\mathsf{Person}))$

$\Phi = \mathsf{SameSentence}(\ell_{ans}, \ell_q)$

Suppose the specific search invocation looks for the inventor of typewriters. We set $\vec{v} = (\text{“}\texttt{typewriter}\text{”})$ *and apply the resulting query to strings found on the pages returned by Bing. One of these strings is* $t =$ “**In 1714, a patent to something like a typewriter was granted to a man named Henry Mill in England, but no example of Mills' invention survives. Finally, in 1867, a Milwaukee, Wisconsin printer-publisher-**

politician named Christopher Latham Sholes, with assistance from Carlos Glidden and Samuel Soule, patented what was to be the first useful typewriter."[3]

$\mathcal{E}_2$ will capture no matches. $\mathcal{E}_1$, however, will capture 4 matches. In each of them ℓ_q will capture the word "`typewriter`*", and ℓ_{ans} will capture named entities "`Henry Mill`", "`Christopher Latham Sholes`", "`Carlos Glidden`", "`Samuel Soule`", respectively. All of them are possible matches of $\mathcal{E}_1$, because there is a word "`patented`", the synonym of "`invent`", between them and the last occurence of "`typewriter`" in t. However, the first match will be eliminated by Φ, because captures of ℓ_{ans} and ℓ_q occur in different sentences. The final result of $\mathcal{L}$ is a multi-set W of three matches. Out of them, all three can be considered "inventors" of the typewriter, although one (Christopher Latham Sholes) is arguably more relevant than two others.*

We note several features of LASEWEB in this example:

- The optimal structure of $\mathcal{E}$ can be easily deduced from a single look at an example of a desired answer on the Web, and refined later in 1-2 iterations, based on the execution results.
- Most of the features of the desired answer strings can be generally described with just 2-3 linguistic predicates in LASEWEB.
- Multiple ways to extract an intended answer can be expressed as a disjunction of linguistic patterns.
- Linguistic constraints Φ and linguistic predicates within $\mathcal{E}$ filter out false positives. Without them, more erroneous matches would be found by $\mathcal{L}$ on the webpage.
- Not all strings in the resulting answer set are equally likely to serve as "the answer" to the question. Therefore, our interpreter for LASEWEB programs, described in §4, assigns confidence scores to answer strings based on their relative frequency on the Web.

3.2.2 Structural expressions

A structural expression $\mathcal{S}$ is executed against an HTML node $\mathcal{N}$ and returns an answer set W. Two representative constructors of structural expressions, $\mathsf{AttrLookup}(\mathcal{L}_1, \mathcal{L}_2)$ and $\mathsf{VLOOKUP}(\mathcal{L}_1, \mathcal{L}_2, \mathcal{L}_3)$, describe two structural patterns that arise in the real-word webpages. A structural pattern is a particular alignment of structured information on a webpage, such as a relational table or a list of attributes. For such structured forms we can use any relational techniques (of which VLOOKUP and AttrLookup are two examples) to select the required information from the structure.

In real-world webpages, the information is seldom present in a clean tabular format. However, the information is often *semi-structured*: it follows a recognizable pattern, from which the implicit tabular structure can be recovered. For example, consider a list of "$\langle$attribute$\rangle$: $\langle$value$\rangle$" lines, each presenting an attribute and its value, separated by a colon. Such a list can be interpreted as a 2-column table of attributes along with their corresponding values. We call such implicit tables *logical tables* and assume the existence of a $\mathsf{Tables}(\mathcal{N})$ function that returns a set of logical tables present in the HTML node $\mathcal{N}$. Each table T is indexed from 1 through the number of rows/columns. Each cell $T[j,k]$ is the textual content of the corresponding logical cell (e.g. the content of a `<td>` node, or a substring of an "$\langle$attribute$\rangle$: $\langle$value$\rangle$" line in a paragraph, etc.). We discuss our implementation of $\mathsf{Tables}(\mathcal{N})$ in §4.

[3] `http://ideafinder.com/history/inventions/typrwriter.htm`

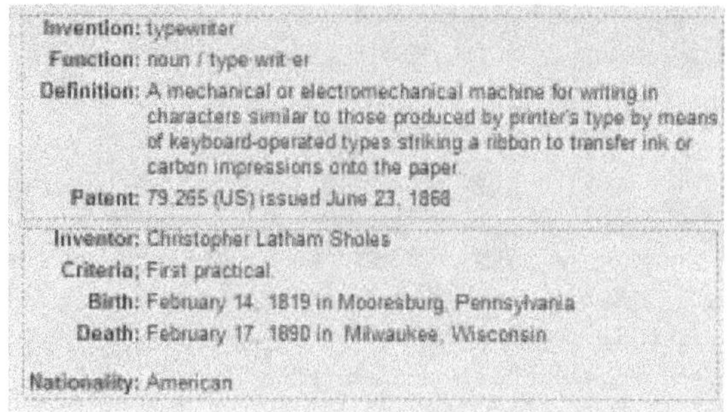

Figure 3: Textual attribute table about the typewriter inventor. Two separate HTML `<table>`s are highlighted.

Constructor $\mathsf{VLOOKUP}(\mathcal{L}_1, \mathcal{L}_2, \mathcal{L}_3)$ represents a Microsoft Excel `VLOOKUP` operation. Its arguments are the *key expression* $\mathcal{L}_1$, the *header expression* $\mathcal{L}_2$, and the *content expression* $\mathcal{L}_3$. Given a logical table T, if $\mathcal{L}_1$ matches a cell $T[j,k']$ in j^{th} row, and $\mathcal{L}_2$ matches a header cell $T[1,k]$ in k^{th} column of the first row, LASEWEB executes the content expression $\mathcal{L}_3$ on the intersection cell $T[j,k]$, and returns the result.

Constructor $\mathsf{AttrLookup}(\mathcal{L}_1, \mathcal{L}_2)$ represents a *two-column attribute lookup* operation. Its arguments are the *attribute expression* $\mathcal{L}_1$ and the *content expression* $\mathcal{L}_2$. Given a logical table T of ≥ 2 columns where $\mathcal{L}_1$ matches any cell $T[j,1]$ in the jth row of the first column (attribute name), LASEWEB executes the content expression $\mathcal{L}_2$ on the neighboring cell $T[j,2]$, and returns the result.

EXAMPLE 3. *Fig. 3 shows an example of a logical table about the inventor of a typewriter, taken from the Web. This table is not a 2-column* `<table>` *tag, as it might appear to the viewer. Instead, it is represented as two* `<table>` *tags (highlighted in green), with pieces of plain text information within. Nevertheless, if $\mathcal{N}$ is a* `<div>` *containing both* `<table>`*s, our function* $\mathsf{Tables}(\mathcal{N})$ *extracts a single 2-column attribute table from it.*

The following structural expression is used to extract information from such logical table:

$$\mathcal{S} = \mathsf{AttrLookup}(\mathsf{Syn}(\text{"}\mathtt{inventor}\text{"}),\ \mathsf{Entity}(\mathsf{Person}))$$

*This expression is not parameterized with any user arguments, it extracts the attribute value for **any** "inventor" row. In order to bind $\mathcal{S}$ to the particular invention ("`typewriter`"), we introduce additional constraints on it in Example 4.*

3.2.3 Visual expressions

A visual expression $\mathcal{B}$ is executed against a *bounding box* b. We use bounding boxes instead of HTML nodes here, because not every visually distinguishable webpage element is represented by a single HTML node. We made LASEWEB accessible to end-users, according to our observations of their search strategies. As §2.2 shows, they often make use of the stylistic properties of the webpage, *as seen by end-users*.

The result of the execution of $\mathcal{B}$ is a tuple of a linguistic answer set W, matched by the lower subexpressions, and a *visual match* V. A visual match is a mapping of ID labels of visual expressions η to bounding boxes b.

Constructor $\mathsf{Union}(\mathcal{B}_1, \mathcal{B}_2)$ matches a union of two bounding boxes $\mathsf{unite}(b_1, b_2)$ if its subexpressions $\mathcal{B}_1$ and $\mathcal{B}_2$ match b_1 and b_2, respectively. The union of two bounding boxes is the smallest rectangle that contains both b_1 and b_2.

Visual constraints. The top-level LASEWEB query $\mathcal{Q}$ consists of a visual expression $\mathcal{B}$ with a *visual constraint* Ψ. Similarly to linguistic constraints, visual constraints filter out false positive matches V, returned by the execution of $\mathcal{B}$. We present three representatives of visual constraints here:

- Constraint $\mathsf{Nearby}(\eta_1, \eta_2)$ checks the bounding boxes $V[\eta_1]$ and $V[\eta_2]$ for proximity. It compares the distance between them with a predefined relative *proximity threshold* δ.
- Constraint $\mathsf{Layout}(\eta_1, \eta_2, d)$ checks whether bounding boxes $b_1 = V[\eta_1]$ and $b_2 = V[\eta_2]$ are aligned according to the layout d. In other words, b_1 should lie within a sector defined by the center of b_2 and the two corners of b_2 in the direction d.
- Constraint $\mathsf{Emphasized}(\eta)$ checks whether the content of the bounding box $V[\eta]$ is emphasized with respect to its surrounding elements. This includes colors, fonts, font sizes, headers (`<h1>` through `<h6>`), etc.

EXAMPLE 4. *The complete* LASEWEB *query for the "inventor" micro-segment is shown below:*

$\mathcal{Q} = \mathsf{FW}(\mathsf{Union}(\eta_v : \mathsf{Leaf}(\mathsf{Syn}(v_1)),\ \eta_t : \mathcal{S}),\ \mathsf{Nearby}(\eta_v,\ \eta_t)) \vee \mathsf{Leaf}(\mathcal{L})$

where $\mathcal{L}$ *is the linguistic expression from Example 2*

$\mathcal{S}$ *is the structural expression from Example 3*

EXAMPLE 5. *Scenario 2 shows a repetitive task of collecting phone numbers from multiple personal contact pages of researchers, similar to the one shown in Fig. 1. The following* LASEWEB *query collects the desired phone number(s) from such a webpage:*

$\mathcal{Q} = \mathsf{FW}(\mathsf{Union}(\eta_t : \mathsf{Leaf}(v_1),\ \eta_b : \mathcal{S}_b),\ \Psi)$

$\Psi = \mathsf{Layout}(\eta_t, \eta_b, \mathsf{Down}) \wedge \mathsf{Nearby}(\eta_t, \eta_b) \wedge \mathsf{Emphasized}(\eta_t)$

$\mathcal{S}_b = \mathsf{AttrLookup}(\mathsf{Syn}(\texttt{"phone"}),\ \mathcal{L}_a)$

$\mathcal{L}_a = \mathsf{Ling}(\ell,\ \mathsf{Regex}(\ell,\ \texttt{"\textbackslash(?\textbackslash d+\textbackslash)?\textbackslash W\textbackslash d+\textbackslash W\textbackslash d+"}))$

When $\mathcal{Q}$ *is executed with the arguments* $\vec{v} = (\texttt{"Shaz Qadeer"})$, *it matches any phone number in a logical attribute table such that "Shaz Qadeer" can be found above the table within the proximity threshold, and is somehow emphasized.*

4. IMPLEMENTATION

In this section, we discuss our implementation of the interpreter for LASEWEB programs. It consists of two important components: the interpreter for LASEWEB queries $\mathcal{Q}$, and the execution engine for the entire LASEWEB program $\mathcal{P}$. We discuss important aspects of the LASEWEB query interpreter implementation in §4.1, and present our LASEWEB program execution algorithm in §4.2.

4.1 Query interpreter

4.1.1 Linguistic expressions

The key ideas in our interpretation of linguistic expressions are: (a) usage of state-of-the-art NLP algorithms, and (b) our refinement of the semantics of $\mathcal{E}$ for better performance on large webpages, called *anchoring*.

NLP algorithms. To support interpretation of linguistic predicates, our implementation requires algorithms for the functions $\mathsf{IsNP}(s)$, $\mathsf{PosValue}(s)$, $\mathsf{EntityValue}(s)$. They are implemented using state-of-the-art algorithms in NLP: Stanford CoreNLP [7, 15, 26] and MSR SPLAT [22] for named entity recognition, syntactic parsing, and part-of-speech tagging. To implement the $\mathsf{AreSynonyms}(s_1, s_2)$ function, we used S. W.-t. Yih's PILSA word synonymy library [27].

Anchoring. A naïve implementation of matching a linguistic expression $\mathcal{E}$ against a string t would try to find a linguistic match for every possible starting token in t. This is extremely inefficient, especially when dealing with Kleene star operator $*$. Instead, we *anchor* our matching procedure, identifying a set of constant strings (*anchors*), if any, that *must* match as particular subexpressions of $\mathcal{E}$. If anchors are given, we start the matching with a linear search for anchor occurences in text, and proceed with matching other subexpressions of $\mathcal{E}$ around every occurence. If no anchors are given, the algorithm resorts to naïve matching.

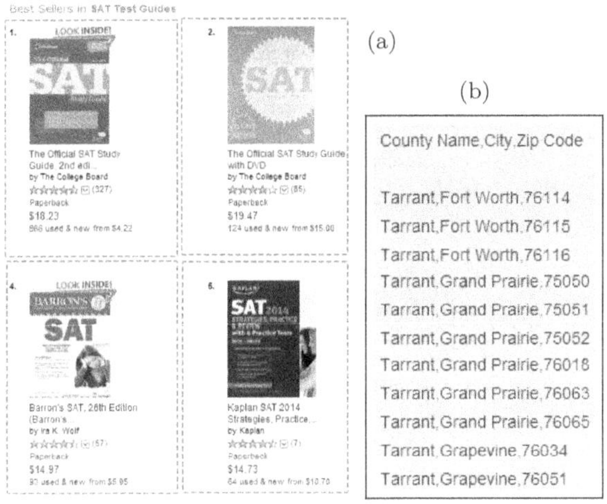

Figure 4: (a) A logical table on the Amazon website, built with a grid of `<div>` elements (shown in green). (b) A logical table, built in plain text with commas as column separators.

4.1.2 Structural expressions

The key idea in our interpretation of structural expressions is the $\mathsf{Tables}(\mathcal{N})$ function, which implements *logical table detection*. Its goal is to extract any information from the HTML node $\mathcal{N}$ that is likely to be *perceived* as a table by an end-user. We implement three basic strategies for detecting logical tables within an HTML node:

HTML tables. A `<table>` tag defines a logical table unless it is used for webpage layout (i.e. has multiple non-primitive pieces of content within it, possibly nested tables).

Visual tables. Any grid of `<div>`s or similar block elements constitutes a logical table if its bounding boxes are precisely aligned in a grid structure. Fig. 4a shows an example of a logical table built with `<div>` elements. We detect such tables by collecting a tree of bounding boxes of all HTML nodes within $\mathcal{N}$, and then building grids of those bounding boxes that are aligned next to each other.

Plain text tables. Often the information is presented as a table by marking it with punctuation signs and separators in plain text, instead of HTML tags. Fig. 1 and Fig. 3 show examples of such plain text tables, with colon being a separator between two columns. Fig. 4b shows another example, where the intended table is relational, and the separator between the columns is comma.

The simplest approach for detecting plain text tables would be to maintain a set of common separators (i.e. a colon, a comma, a space, etc.), and attempt to split entire paragraphs of text by them, picking the one that gives most results. However, even if the separator is "correct" (i.e., it actually splits the logical columns in the paragraph), it can also be present within some of the logical cells. For example, if Fig. 4b used whitespace instead of comma for column

function SEARCH($\mathcal{P} = \langle q, \sigma, \mathcal{Q}, \ell_a \rangle,\ \vec{v}$)
1: $U \leftarrow$ the results of Bing on $q(\vec{v})$
2: Substitute v_k in $\mathcal{Q}$ with values from $\vec{v}$
3: $\mathcal{C} \leftarrow \emptyset$ // *set of clusters,* $C_i = \{\langle s_k, \{u_j\}_{j=1}^{n_{ik}} \rangle\}_{k=1}^{m_i}$
4: **for all** URLs $u_j \in U$ **do**
5: $\mathcal{N} \leftarrow$ the `<body>` node of u_j
6: $S_j \leftarrow \{M[\ell_a] \mid M$ is the result of executing $\mathcal{Q}$ on $\mathcal{N}\}$
7: **for all** answer strings $s_k \in S_j$ **do**
8: $C_j \leftarrow \{\langle s_k, \{u_j\} \rangle\}$
9: **for all** $C \in \mathcal{C}$ such that $\exists s' \in C \colon \sigma(s_k, s')$ **do**
10: Merge C_j with C
11: $\mathcal{C} \leftarrow \mathcal{C} \cup \{C_j\}$
12: **for all** final clusters $C_i \in \mathcal{C}$ **do**
13: $a_i \leftarrow$ the most frequent string representation $s_k \in C_i$
14: $\beta_i \leftarrow \frac{1}{|U|} \sum_{j=1}^{|U|} \sum_{s \in C_i} \frac{c(s, u_j)}{|S_j|}$ where:
$c(s, u_j) = \#$ of times s was found at URL u_j
15: $U_i \leftarrow$ union of all source URLs for all $s_k \in C_i$
16: **yield return** $\langle a_i, \beta_i, U_i \rangle$

Figure 5: LASEWEB program execution algorithm. It takes a LASEWEB program $\mathcal{P}$ and tuple of user query arguments $\vec{v}$, and returns a set of triples $\langle a_i, \beta_i, U_i \rangle$ where a_i is an answer, β_i is its confidence score, U_i is a set of its source URLs.

separation, this naïve algorithm would detect four columns instead of three for "Fort Worth" and "Grand Prairie" rows.

However, there exists an approach to figure out correct splits automatically. Fix a candidate separator from the common list. For this separator and a fixed HTML node $\mathcal{N}$, we first build a list of lines in $\mathsf{Text}(\mathcal{N})$ that have consistent splitting with respect to this separator (i.e. the same number of columns > 1). The rest of the lines are passed to the PBE system FlashFill [9], which automatically figures out likely syntactic string transformations from few examples by using sophisticated ranking schemes. We use their publicly available implementation from the Microsoft Excel spreadsheet system. The list of consistent lines is used as a list of positive examples for FlashFill. The output of FlashFill is the list of correct outputs (splits) for the rest of the lines, or a failure signal. Our LASEWEB program interpreter automatically checks the correctness of this output later, by comparing it with other answer candidates during clustering.

4.1.3 Visual expressions

The key idea in interpretation of visual expressions is usage of runtime presentational attributes of HTML nodes $\mathcal{N}$. Specifically, we ask a browser to render each webpage in memory, on a virtual canvas of 1920×1080 pixels. After rendering, we collect the information about the bounding box of each HTML node $\mathcal{N}$, and use it as a value of $\mathsf{BBox}(\mathcal{N})$. Similarly, we collect the run-time values of CSS attributes, and use them for evaluating visual constraints Ψ.

4.2 Program execution

Fig. 5 shows the algorithm of LASEWEB program execution. It takes a LASEWEB *program* $\mathcal{P}$ and a tuple of user query arguments $\vec{v}$, and returns a set of *answer strings*, augmented with their *confidence scores* and *source URLs*.

The execution algorithm is shown as SEARCH($\mathcal{P}, \vec{v}$) function. It starts with querying the search engine for URLs with a seed query (line 1) and filling in user arguments in the LASEWEB query $\mathcal{Q}$ (line 2). After that it proceeds with matching the query $\mathcal{Q}$ with every URL in the obtained list of search results U.

During matching, the algorithm maintains a set of clusters $\mathcal{C}$. Every cluster $C_i \in \mathcal{C}$ represents a single logical answer. A cluster is a multi-set of string representations s_k, augmented with sets of their source URLs. A cluster can contain multiple occurences of the same answer string s_k, and the same answer string may occur multiple times on a single webpage (URL). Every time the algorithm finds a new answer string s_k on some webpage u_j, it constructs a new singleton cluster $\{\langle s_k, \{u_j\} \rangle\}$ and merges it with all existing clusters in $\mathcal{C}$ that contain strings similar to s_k, according to the similarity function σ (lines 7-11).

After matching, the algorithm extracts logical answers and their confidence scores from the collected set of clusters $\mathcal{C}$ (lines 12-16). For each cluster $C_i \in \mathcal{C}$, it considers the most frequent answer string in it as a *representative answer* of this cluster. Its confidence score is calculated with Bayes Law:

$$\beta_i = \frac{1}{|U|} \sum_{j=1}^{|U|} p(C_i \mid u_j) \qquad p(C_i \mid u_j) = \sum_{s \in C_i} \frac{c(s, u_j)}{|S_j|}$$

where $|S_j|$ is the number of answer strings extracted from u_j, and $c(s, u_j)$ is the number of times s was found in u_j.

5. EVALUATION

We implemented LASEWEB in C# programming language in approximately 5000 lines of code. In this section, we present the results of its evaluation over two applications of parametrized Web programming, shown in §2. It aims to verify the following usability requirements of LASEWEB:

1. Low number of iterations (refinements) during LASEWEB program development.
2. High total number of correctly answered real-life queries.

For the first goal, we observed that in all experiments, the number of iterations required to compose and evaluate every program on our own search strategies was at most 5. We present the detailed results of evaluating the second goal below for every application.

Micro-segments. We extracted 100,000+ user queries across 7 micro-segments from the logs of a popular search engine over the 12 month period. These micro-segments were chosen by our Bing partners as possible targets because of a substantial query traffic. Since LASEWEB does not have an NLP front-end, we used regular expressions to extract user queries that belonged to certain factoid micro-segments.

Fig. 6a reports the results of micro-segment evaluation. For each micro-segment we show the recall (fraction of answered user queries), and comparison with the existing Bing question answering module. Given the absence of ground truth data for real-life user queries, we evaluated LASEWEB precision by manually sampling 30-50 queries for each micro-segment at random. On average, the top 3 results contained "correct" answers to the query in 95% of cases.

As Fig. 6a shows, LASEWEB handles a much greater fraction of user queries than Bing question answering module. Bing module gives definite answers from structured databases, thus achieving 100% precision, but low recall. Additionally, LASEWEB found alternative answer options for many questions, providing additional context, whereas Bing provided only a single answer from the database. Low recall of "ASCII" and "Lyrics" micro-segments can be improved by additional refinement of our LASEWEB programs.

We refrained from comparison of LASEWEB with state-of-the-art Web question answering engines for two reasons. First, question answering engines mostly operate on a lin-

(a)

Micro-segment	# queries	Recall	Bing recall
ASCII code of a symbol	1,551	32.88%	0%
Calories in a food	9,207	71.80%	0%
Inventor of a product	8,994	75.91%	16.01%
Lyrics of a song	48,995	24.36%	0%
Phone number of a company	6,881	95.49%	0%
Population of a place	18,151	92.53%	57.58%
Release date of a product	12,339	97.24%	12.60%

(b)

Search task	Recall	Precision
Phone #	29/37	21/29
Affiliation	34/37	22/34
PhD institution	21/37	13/21
General chair	21/28	17/21
Invited talks	13/28	11/13
Average	**71%**	**73%**

Figure 6: (a) Evaluation results of factoid micro-segments. For each micro-segment: number of queries, fraction of queries answered by LASEWEB (recall), fraction of queries, answered by Bing. LASEWEB examined 50 top Bing results. (b) Evaluation results of repeatable search tasks. For each task: fraction of answered (recall), and correctly answered queries (precision). Precision was evaluated manually. LASEWEB examined 30 top Bing results. In both applications, the running time is linearly proportional to the number of examined webpages, and a single webpage took from 0.1 to 20 sec to process.

guistic level, taking a query in natural language, and converting it into a logical representation. LASEWEB solves an orthogonal problem: it takes a query in a logical representation, and searches for answers on the Web. Second, prior question answering approaches were evaluated on a *narrow* set of *unique* factoid questions (e.g. TREC corpus). In contrast, LASEWEB focuses on *large micro-segments* of *similar* questions. Both of these aspects make direct comparison of approaches infeasible: LASEWEB does not focus on user query analysis, and spending time on writing LASEWEB programs for 500 different TREC questions was not meaningful. We note that any state-of-the-art user query analysis module can be used as a LASEWEB front-end that converts a query into a logical representation, as discussed in §6.

The running time of LASEWEB on a single webpage ranges from 0.1 to 20 seconds, and the time to interpret a single query is linearly proportional to the number of webpage examined. Since this performance is not sufficient for answering user queries in real-time, our engine can be used to generate answers to logged queries offline, and the results can be stored in a database to answer future queries in real-time.

Repeatable search tasks. We chose 5 categories of repeatable academic search tasks, and used them for LASEWEB evaluation. The test data for 3 people-related tasks is a list of PLDI 2014 committee members (37 people), and the data for 2 conference-related tasks is a list of 21st century POPL and PLDI conferences (28 items). We evaluated precision and recall of all results manually.

Fig. 6b shows the results of the evaluation. Most of the desired information was easily extracted from the Web. The average precision is 73%, which is lower than that of a micro-segment search due to (a) inconsistensies in named entity recognition for organizations, and (b) name collisions for some of committee members. The recall in influenced by the recall of Bing results (for this application it is much lower that that of a factoid questions). In some of the cases we couldn't find the correct answers ourselves (e.g., for some invited talks). Also, LASEWEB currently does not handle non-HTML formats: for example, a researcher's PhD institution is often listed in the CV, in PDF format, and Bing couldn't find any alternative sources of information.

6. RELATED WORK

Question answering. The problem of answering factoid questions in natural language has been studied for several decades. The most notable examples include Watson [12], KNOWITALL [6], START [14], AskMSR [4], etc.

Most of these systems focus on understanding user intent, expressed as a question in natural language, and assume the existence of structured knowledge databases. In contrast, LASEWEB extracts data from semi-structured sources on the Web, by restructuring this data according to the guidance, provided by an end-user in a form of a program in our language. These two efforts are orthogonal and can be integrated to provide a natural language front-end for extracting arguments for programs in our query language.

Some of the question answering systems [4, 6] use an automatic approach to extract answers from the Web. LASEWEB is semi-automatic: it does not generalize the patterns automatically, mostly because it allows for specifying structural/visual patterns in addition to linguistic patterns, used by question answering systems. This allows for higher recall of LASEWEB, but requires an end-user to construct a program manually, by exploring several examples. The integration of NLP technologies for user intent understanding will eliminate the need for manual program construction.

Repeatable search. A concept similar to our definition of repeatable search tasks are Web mashups, which are websites that combine information from public APIs into a single visualization. Ennals and Gay [5] proposed MashMaker, a GUI and a language for creating mashup websites. However, mashups use only structured information from public APIs as their data sources. In contrast, LASEWEB allows to automate arbitrary repeatable search task over semi-structured Web data. Unlike MashMaker, LASEWEB doesn't provide a GUI for constructing programs in our language, but we intend to explore automated synthesis of such programs from examples or natural language [10]. A similar work has been done on mashups: Vegemite [19] generates mashup expressions using programming by demonstration.

CoScripter [18] is a system that automates repetition of Web-based tasks using demonstration. It records scripts of actions on a webpages into a central public repository, from which they are later available for execution. CoScripter focuses on multiple Web-based tasks, not necessarily search-related. However, it is limited in a way in which scripts can process information on a webpage. LASEWEB includes a wide range of webpage features, generalized from our observations of typical search strategies, which allow for a more precise capturing of the end-user's search intent.

SXPath. SXPath [20] is the language that extends popular XML query language XPath [2] towards queries upon visual layout of XML elements. It is built on the system of *visual axes* and *bouding boxes* in addition to XPath concepts.

LASEWEB includes visual expressions as part of its query language, because they often appear in patterns that end-users use to extract information from the Web. In contrast to SXPath, LASEWEB also includes linguistic and structural expressions, which allow for querying a HTML document on the levels, semantically different from XML.

Table detection. An important portion of LaSEWeb is its logical table detection algorithm, that lies in the core of structural expression matching. Table detection has been studied in the past. Tengli et al. [25] develop an algorithm that extracts information from semi-structured HTML and plaintext tables using examples – marked row/column labels. Krüpl et al. [16] and, similarly, Gatterbauer et al. [8] propose techniques for using visual cues (bounding boxes) for automatic table extraction. Cafarella et al. [1] perform table extraction from linguistic cues.

LaSEWeb integrates *all* table extraction approaches (textual, visual and structural) in a *single automatic* function. Our implementation also uses a state-of-the-art PBE system [9] in a novel manner for parsing plain text tables with inconsistent separators. However, any off-the-shelf table extraction technique (e.g., [1, 16, 17, 25]) can be used to complement the logical table extraction module for LaSEWeb.

7. CONCLUSION

This paper investigated the problem of Web programming – a novel programming model, where functions are defined as repeatable search procedures, operating over semi-structured content of webpages returned by a search engine. These functions can be used multiple times with different user query arguments. We explored two of the many possible applications of Web programming, namely factoid micro-segments in search engines, and repeatable batch queries.

We present a DSL that allows end-users and software developers to express semantic patterns of their search strategies, eliminating the need for manual exploration of search engine results. Our implementation of the DSL leverages cross-disciplinary technologies: browser rendering APIs, state-of-the-art NLP tools, and programming by example technologies. Our system LaSEWeb achieves good precision and recall in practice, and is an important step towards automation of knowledge discovery on the Web.

LaSEWeb can be seen as bridging the gap between PL technologies for processing structured data formats, and numerous semi-structured data on the Web. Our programming model is a natural evolution of the prior effort on integrating structured Web queries into programming environments.

8. ACKNOWLEDGMENTS

We thank Saurabh Tiwary and the Bing team for providing us access to the valuable user search query data.

References

[1] M. J. Cafarella, C. Re, D. Suciu, O. Etzioni, and M. Banko. Structured querying of Web text. *CIDR'07*.

[2] J. Clark, S. DeRose, et al. XML path language (XPath), 1999.

[3] C. De Rosa, B. Gauder, D. Cellentani, T. Dalrymple, and L. J. Olszewski. *Perceptions of Libraries, 2010: Context and Community: a Report to the OCLC Membership*. OCLC, 2011.

[4] S. Dumais, M. Banko, E. Brill, J. Lin, and A. Ng. Web question answering: Is more always better? *SIGIR'02*.

[5] R. Ennals and D. Gay. User-friendly functional programming for web mashups. In *ICFP*, 2007.

[6] O. Etzioni, M. Cafarella, D. Downey, S. Kok, A.-M. Popescu, T. Shaked, S. Soderland, D. S. Weld, and A. Yates. Web-scale information extraction in KnowItAll. In *WWW*, 2004.

[7] J. R. Finkel, T. Grenager, and C. Manning. Incorporating non-local information into information extraction systems by Gibbs sampling. In *ACL*, 2005.

[8] W. Gatterbauer and P. Bohunsky. Table extraction using spatial reasoning on the CSS2 visual box model. In *AAAI*, 2006.

[9] S. Gulwani. Automating string processing in spreadsheets using input-output examples. *POPL'11*.

[10] S. Gulwani. Synthesis from examples: Interaction models and algorithms. In *SYNASC*, 2012.

[11] R. Housewright, R. C. Schonfeld, and K. Wulfson. Ithaka S+ R US Faculty Survey 2012. *April*, 8, 2013.

[12] A. Ittycheriah, M. Franz, W.-J. Zhu, A. Ratnaparkhi, and R. J. Mammone. IBM's statistical question answering system. In *TREC*, 2000.

[13] B. J. Jansen and A. Spink. How are we searching the World Wide Web? A comparison of nine search engine transaction logs. *IPM*, 42(1), 2006.

[14] B. Katz, G. Marton, G. C. Borchardt, A. Brownell, S. Felshin, D. Loreto, J. Louis-Rosenberg, B. Lu, F. Mora, S. Stiller, et al. External knowledge sources for question answering. In *TREC*, 2005.

[15] D. Klein and C. D. Manning. Accurate unlexicalized parsing. In *ACL*, 2003.

[16] B. Krüpl, M. Herzog, and W. Gatterbauer. Using visual cues for extraction of tabular data from arbitrary HTML documents. In *WWW*, 2005.

[17] V. Le and S. Gulwani. FlashExtract: a framework for data extraction by examples. In *PLDI*, 2014.

[18] G. Leshed, E. M. Haber, T. Matthews, and T. Lau. Coscripter: automating & sharing how-to knowledge in the enterprise. In *CHI*, 2008.

[19] J. Lin, J. Wong, J. Nichols, A. Cypher, and T. A. Lau. End-user programming of mashups with vegemite. In *IUI*, 2009.

[20] E. Oro, M. Ruffolo, and S. Staab. SXPath: extending XPath towards spatial querying on web documents. *VLDB*, 4(2), 2010.

[21] K. Purcell, J. Brenner, and L. Rainie. *Search engine use 2012*. Pew Internet & American Life Project, 2012.

[22] C. Quirk, P. Choudhury, J. Gao, H. Suzuki, K. Toutanova, M. Gamon, W.-t. Yih, L. Vanderwende, and C. Cherry. MSR SPLAT, a language analysis toolkit. In *ACL*, 2012.

[23] A. Spink, H. C. Ozmutlu, E. Aversa, and C. Manley. What do people ask for on the web and how do they ask it: Ask Jeeves query analysis. 2001.

[24] J. Teevan, C. Alvarado, M. S. Ackerman, and D. R. Karger. The perfect search engine is not enough: a study of orienteering behavior in directed search. In *CHI*, 2004.

[25] A. Tengli, Y. Yang, and N. L. Ma. Learning table extraction from examples. In *ACL*, 2004.

[26] K. Toutanova, D. Klein, C. D. Manning, and Y. Singer. Feature-rich part-of-speech tagging with a cyclic dependency network. In *HLT-NAACL*, 2003.

[27] W.-t. Yih, G. Zweig, and J. C. Platt. Polarity inducing latent semantic analysis. In *ACL*, 2012.

Personalized Search Result Diversification via Structured Learning

Shangsong Liang
s.liang@uva.nl

Zhaochun Ren
z.ren@uva.nl

Maarten de Rijke
derijke@uva.nl

University of Amsterdam, Amsterdam, The Netherlands

ABSTRACT

This paper is concerned with the problem of personalized diversification of search results, with the goal of enhancing the performance of both plain diversification and plain personalization algorithms. In previous work, the problem has mainly been tackled by means of unsupervised learning. To further enhance the performance, we propose a supervised learning strategy. Specifically, we set up a structured learning framework for conducting supervised personalized diversification, in which we add features extracted directly from the tokens of documents and those utilized by unsupervised personalized diversification algorithms, and, importantly, those generated from our proposed user-interest latent Dirichlet topic model. Based on our proposed topic model whether a document can cater to a user's interest can be estimated in our learning strategy. We also define two constraints in our structured learning framework to ensure that search results are both diversified and consistent with a user's interest. We conduct experiments on an open personalized diversification dataset and find that our supervised learning strategy outperforms unsupervised personalized diversification methods as well as other plain personalization and plain diversification methods.

Categories and Subject Descriptors

H.3.3 [**Information Storage and Retrieval**]: Information Search and Retrieval

Keywords

Personalization; diversity; structured SVMs; ad hoc retrieval

1. INTRODUCTION

Search result diversification has recently gained attention as a method to tackle query ambiguity. In search result diversification one typically considers the relevance of a document in light of the other retrieved documents. The goal is to identify the probable "aspects" of the ambiguous query, retrieve documents for each of these aspects and make the search results more diverse [13]. By doing so, in the absence of any knowledge of users' context or preferences, the chance that any user issuing an ambiguous query will find at least one of these results to be relevant to the underlying information need is maximized [10].

KDD '14, August 24–27, 2014, New York, NY, USA.

ACM 978-1-4503-2956-9/14/08 ... $15.00.
http://dx.doi.org/10.1145/2623330.2623650 .

In both search result diversification and personalized web search, an issued query is often viewed as an incomplete expression of a user's underlying need [22]. Unlike search result diversification, where the system accepts and adapts its behavior to a situation of uncertainty, personalized web search strives to change this situation by enhancing the system's knowledge about users' information needs. Rather than aiming to satisfy as many users as possible, personalization aims to build a sense of who the user is, and maximize the satisfaction of a specific user [26].

Although different, diversification and personalization are not incompatible and do not have mutually exclusive goals [23]. Search results generated by diversification techniques should be more diverse when a user's preferences are unrelated to the query. Likewise, personalization can improve the effectiveness of aspect weighting in diversification, by favoring query interpretations which are predicted to be more related to each specific user [26].

In this paper we study the problem of *personalized diversification of search results*, with the goal of enhancing both diversification and personalization performances. The problem has previously been investigated by Radlinski and Dumais [19] and Vallet and Castells [26]. They have presented a number of effective *unsupervised learning* approaches that combine both personalization and diversification components to tackle the problem. To further improve the performance we propose a *supervised learning* approach.

There are a couple of advantages to considering a supervised learning approach. Such approaches can leverage useful information underlying labeled training data, apply existing optimization techniques to the problem and are easier to adaptation. Of course, they also have disadvantages, one of which is that it is expensive to create training data for supervised learning methods. This is, however, a shortcoming for any supervised learning strategy and we leave it as future work.

Accordingly, we formulate the task of personalized search result diversification as a problem of predicting a diverse set of documents given a specific user and a query. Specifically, we formulate a discriminant based on maximizing search result diversification, and perform training using the well-known structured support vector machines (SSVMs) framework [25]. The main idea is first to propose a user-interest LDA-style [5, Latent Dirichlet Allocation] topic model, from which we can infer a per-document multinomial distribution over topics and determine whether a document can cater for a specific user. Then, during training we use features extracted directly from the tokens' statistical information in the documents and those utilized by unsupervised personalized diversification algorithms, and, more importantly, those generated from our proposed topic model. Additionally, two types of constraint in SSVMs are explicitly defined to enforce the search results to be both diverse and relevant to a user's personal interest.

We evaluate our proposed approach on a publicly available personalized diversification dataset and compare it to unsupervised approaches, that focus on either personalization or diversification alone, to combined approaches like those in [19] and [26], and to two standard structured learning approaches [32, 33]. The three main contributions of our work are:(1) We tackle the problem of personalized diversification of search results differently, using a supervised learning method. (2) We propose a user-interest latent topic model to capture a user's interest and infer per-document multinomial distributions over topics. (3) We explicitly enforce diversity and personalization through two types of constraints in structured learning for personalized diversification.

2. RELATED WORK

Three major types of research relate to our work: personalized diversification, structured learning, and topic modeling.

2.1 Personalized search result diversification

Two main components, viz., personalized web search and search result diversification, play important roles in tackling the problem of personalized search result diversification. The task of personalized web search aims at identifying the most relevant search results for an individual by leveraging their information. Many personalized web search methods have been proposed, such as the one based on social tagging profiles [27], ranking model adaption for personalized search [29], search personalization by modeling the impact of users' behavior [4], and personalized search using interaction behaviors in search sessions [17]. In contrast, diversification aims to make the search results diversified given an ambiguous query so that users can find at least one of these results to be relevant to their underlying information need [2]. Well-known diversification methods include the maximal marginal relevance model [8], probabilistic model [9], subtopic retrieval model [35], xQuAD [21], RxQuAD [28], IA-select [2], PM-2 [12], and more recently, matroid constraints [1], DSPApprox [13], text-based measures [3], term-level [13], and fusion-based [16]. All of the above methods focus on either personalization or diversification only.

To the best of our knowledge, only Radlinski and Dumais [19] and Vallet and Castells [26] have studied the problem of combining both personalization and diversification. Radlinski and Dumais [19] analyze a large sample of individual users' query logs from a web search engine such that individual users' query reformulations can be obtained. Then they personalize web search by reranking some top results using query reformulations to introduce diversity into those results. Their evaluation suggests that using diversification is a promising method to improve personalized reranking of search results. Vallet and Castells [26] present a number of approaches that combine personalization and diversification components. They investigate the introduction of the user as an explicit variable in state-of-the-art diversification models. Their personalized search result diversification algorithms achieve competitive performance and improve over plain personalization and plain diversification baselines.

All of the previous personalized diversification models are unsupervised. However, we argue that to enhance the performance, it is better to employ a supervised learning approach, and our experiments show that supervised learning can indeed improve the performance of unsupervised approaches. To the best of our knowledge, this is the first attempt to tackle the problem of personalized diversification using supervised learning methods.

2.2 Structured learning

Structured learning has provided principled techniques for learning structured-output models, with the structured support vector machines (SSVMs) being one of the most important ones [25]. In structured learning, a set of training pairs, $\{(\mathbf{x},\mathbf{y})|\mathbf{x}\in\mathcal{X},\mathbf{y}\in\mathcal{Y}\}$, is assumed to be available to the learning algorithm, and the goal is to learning a mapping $f : \mathcal{X} \rightarrow \mathcal{Y}$ from the input space $\mathcal{X}$ to the output space $\mathcal{Y}$, such that a regularized task-dependent loss function $\Delta : \mathcal{Y}\times\mathcal{Y}\rightarrow\mathbb{R}^+$ can be minimized, where $\Delta(\mathbf{y},\bar{\mathbf{y}})$ denotes the cost of predicting output $\bar{\mathbf{y}}$ when the correct prediction is $\mathbf{y}$. In the past few years, Structured SVMs (SSVMs) have been studied and applied in many areas, such as speech recognition [36], optimizing average precision of a ranking [33], and diversification [32]. For us, the most interesting prior application of SSVMs is the one for predicting diverse subsets [32]. However, our personalized search result diversification method differs from that proposed in [32]: we work on personalized diversification where we propose a user-interest LDA-style model to capture a user's interest distribution over topics, whereas they directly apply existing SSVMs algorithm to tackle the problem of search result diversification but not personalized diversification; our model explicitly makes results diverse and consistent to the user's interest by enforcing both diversity and interest constraints, whereas their model only implicitly diversifies the results by adopting standard SSVMs. Prior work on diversification [12, 21, 28], however, has shown that explicit approaches outperform implicit ones in most cases. To the best of our knowledge, this is the first attempt to explicitly enforce diversity and personalization through additional constraints in SSVMs.

2.3 Topic modeling

Topic modeling provides a suite of algorithms to discover hidden thematic structure in a collection of documents. A topic model takes a collection of documents as input, and discovers a set of "latent topics"—recurring themes that are discussed in the collection—and the degree to which each document exhibits those topics [5]. *Latent dirichlet allocation* (LDA) [5] is one of the simplest topic models, and it decomposes a collection of documents into topics—biased probability distributions over terms—and represents each document with a subset of these topics. Many LDA-style models have been proposed, such as the syntactic topic model [6], multilingual topic model [7], topic over time model [30], and more recently, the max-margin model [37], spatio-temporal model [31], fusion-based model [16] and multi-contextual model [24]. We propose a user-interest LDA-style model to capture a multinomial distribution of topics specific to a user. From our model, we infer a per-document multinomial distribution over the topics so that we can easily identify whether a document caters to a user's interest. Our experimental results demonstrate that the model can help to enhance the performance of personalized search result diversification. To the best of our knowledge, this is the first time that a topic model is utilized to enhance the performance of personalized diversification.

3. THE LEARNING PROBLEM

Let $\mathbf{u} = \{d_1,\ldots,d_{|\mathbf{u}|}\} \in \mathcal{U}$ be a set of documents of size $|\mathbf{u}|$ which a user u is interested in. For each query q, we assume that we are given $\mathbf{u}$ and a set of candidate documents $\mathbf{x} = \{x_1,\ldots,x_{|\mathbf{x}|}\} \in \mathcal{X}$, where $\mathcal{X}$ denotes the set of all possible document sets. Our task is to select a subset $\mathbf{y}\in\mathcal{Y}$ of K documents from $\mathbf{x}$ that maximizes the performance of personalized search result diversification given q and $\mathbf{u}$, where we let $\mathcal{Y}$ denote the space of predicted subsets $\mathbf{y}$. Following the standard machine learning setup, we formulate our task as learning a hypothesis function $h : \mathcal{X} \times \mathcal{U} \to \mathcal{Y}$ to predict a $\mathbf{y}$ given $\mathbf{x}$ and $\mathbf{u}$. To this end, we assume that a set of labeled training data is available:

$$\{(\mathbf{x}^{(i)}, \mathbf{u}^{(i)}, \mathbf{y}^{(i)}) \in \mathcal{X} \times \mathcal{U} \times \mathcal{Y} : i = 1, \ldots, N\},$$

where $\mathbf{y}^{(i)}$ is the ground-truth subset of K documents from $\mathbf{x}^{(i)}$, and $\mathbf{u}^{(i)}$ is the set of documents that user u_i is interested in, and N is the size of the training data. We aim to find a function h such that the empirical risk $R_S^{\Delta}(h) = \frac{1}{N}\sum_{i=1}^{N} \Delta(\mathbf{y}^{(i)}, h(\mathbf{x}^{(i)}, \mathbf{u}^{(i)}))$ can be minimized, where we quantify the quality of a prediction by considering a loss function $\Delta : \mathcal{Y} \times \mathcal{Y} \to \mathbb{R}^+$ that measures the penalty of choosing $\bar{\mathbf{y}} = h(\mathbf{x}^{(i)}, \mathbf{u}^{(i)})$. Here, given the ground-truth $\mathbf{y}$, viz., the ground truth ranking of relevant documents, and the predicting $\bar{\mathbf{y}}$, viz., the ranking of predicted documents, we define the loss function based on a diversity metric, α-nDCG [10] (other diversity metrics are possible but we obtain the best performance when adopting this metric), as:

$$\Delta(\mathbf{y}, \bar{\mathbf{y}}) = 1 - \alpha\text{-nDCG}(\mathbf{y}, \bar{\mathbf{y}}). \tag{1}$$

We focus on hypothesis functions which are parameterized by a weight vector $\mathbf{w}$, and thus wish to find $\mathbf{w}$ to minimize the risk, $R_S^{\Delta}(\mathbf{w}) \equiv R_S^{\Delta}(h(\cdot;\mathbf{w}))$. We let a discriminant $\mathcal{F} : \mathcal{X} \times \mathcal{U} \times \mathcal{Y} \to \mathbb{R}^+$ compute how well the predicting $\bar{\mathbf{y}}$ fits for $\mathbf{x}$ and $\mathbf{u}$. Then the hypothesis predicts the $\bar{\mathbf{y}}$ that maximizes $\mathcal{F}$:

$$\bar{\mathbf{y}} = h(\mathbf{x}, \mathbf{u}; \mathbf{w}) = \arg\max_{\mathbf{y}\in\mathcal{Y}} \mathcal{F}(\mathbf{x}, \mathbf{u}, \mathbf{y}). \tag{2}$$

We describe each $(\mathbf{x}, \mathbf{u}, \mathbf{y})$ through a feature vector $\Psi(\mathbf{x}, \mathbf{u}, \mathbf{y})$; the extraction will be discussed later. The discriminant function $\mathcal{F}(\mathbf{x}, \mathbf{u}, \mathbf{y})$ is assumed to be linear in the feature vector $\Psi(\mathbf{x}, \mathbf{u}, \mathbf{y})$ such that:

$$\mathcal{F}(\mathbf{x}, \mathbf{u}, \mathbf{y}) = \mathbf{w}^T \Psi(\mathbf{x}, \mathbf{u}, \mathbf{y}), \tag{3}$$

where $\mathbf{w}$ is a weight vector to be learned from training data.

4. STRUCTURED LEARNING FOR PERSONALIZED DIVERSIFICATION

In this section, we introduce the standard SSVMs learning problem, propose constraints for personalized diversification and describe our optimization problem and the way we make predictions.

4.1 Standard structured SVMs

Our personalized diversification model builds on an existing standard structured learning framework. In our setting, the standard structured learning framework can be described as: given a training set $\{(\mathbf{x}^{(i)}, \mathbf{u}^{(i)}, \mathbf{y}^{(i)}) \in \mathcal{X}\times\mathcal{U}\times\mathcal{Y} : i = 1, \ldots, N\}$, structured SVMs are employed to learn a weight vector $\mathbf{w}$ for the discriminant function $\mathcal{F}(\mathbf{x}, \mathbf{u}, \mathbf{y})$ through the following quadratic programing problem:

Optimization Problem 1. (Standard structured SVMs)

$$\min_{\mathbf{w},\xi\geq 0} \frac{1}{2}||\mathbf{w}||^2 + \frac{C}{N}\sum_{i=1}^{N} \xi_i \tag{4}$$

subject to $\forall i, \forall \mathbf{y} \in \mathcal{Y}\backslash\mathbf{y}^{(i)}, \xi_i \geq 0,$

$$\mathbf{w}^T\Psi(\mathbf{x}^{(i)}, \mathbf{u}^{(i)}, \mathbf{y}^{(i)}) \geq \mathbf{w}^T\Psi(\mathbf{x}^{(i)}, \mathbf{u}^{(i)}, \mathbf{y}) + \Delta(\mathbf{y}^{(i)}, \mathbf{y}) - \xi_i.$$

In the objective function (4), the parameter C is a tradeoff between model complexity, $||\mathbf{w}||^2$, and a hinge loss relaxation of the training loss for each training example, $\sum \xi_i$. The constraints enforce the requirement that the ground-truth personalized diversity document set $\mathbf{y}^{(i)}$ should have a greater function value than other alternative $\mathbf{y} \in \mathcal{Y}$, and $\mathbf{y} \neq \mathbf{y}^{(i)}$.

4.2 Additional constraints

As discussed above, we aim at training a personalized diversification model that can enforce both diversity and consistency with the user's interest. This can be achieved by introducing additional constraints to the structured SVM optimization problem defined in (4). To start, diversity requires a set of retrieved documents that should not discuss the same aspects of an ambiguous query. In other words, aspects of documents returned by a diversification model should have little overlap with one another. Formally, we enforce diversity with the following constraint.

Constraint for diversity:

$$\mathbf{w}^T\Psi(\mathbf{x}^{(i)}, \mathbf{u}^{(i)}, \mathbf{y}^{(i)}) \geq \sum_{y\in\mathbf{y}^{(i)}} \mathbf{w}^T\Psi(\mathbf{x}^{(i)}, \mathbf{u}^{(i)}, y) - \xi_i. \tag{5}$$

In (5), the sum of each document's score, $\sum \mathbf{w}^T\ \Psi(\mathbf{x}^{(i)}, \mathbf{u}^{(i)}, y)$, should not be greater than the overall score when they are considered as an ideal ranking of the document sets. As a result, commonly shared features will be associated with relatively low weights, and a document set with less redundancy will be predicted.

Additionally, personalization requires a set of returned documents to match the user's personal interest. Formally, we enforce personalization with the following constraint.

Constraint for consistency with user's interest:

$$\begin{aligned}\mathbf{w}^T\Psi(\mathbf{x}^{(i)}, \mathbf{u}^{(i)}, \mathbf{y}^{(i)}) \ \geq\ & \mathbf{w}^T\Psi(\mathbf{x}^{(i)}, \mathbf{u}^{(i)}, \mathbf{y}) + \\ & (1 - \text{sim}(\mathbf{y}, \mathbf{u}^{(i)})) - \mu - \xi_i,\end{aligned} \tag{6}$$

where $\text{sim}(\mathbf{y}, \mathbf{u}^{(i)}) \in [0, 1]$ is a function (see (14)) that measures subtopic distribution similarity between a set of documents $\mathbf{y}$ and the documents user u_i is interested in, i.e., $\mathbf{u}^{(i)}$, μ is a slack variable that tends to give slightly better performance, which can be defined as $\mu = \frac{1}{N}\sum_{i=1}^{N}(1 - \text{sim}(\mathbf{y}^{(i)}, \mathbf{u}^{(i)}))$.

In (6), $(1 - \text{sim}(\mathbf{y}, \mathbf{u}^{(i)}))$ quantifies how well a set of documents matches a user's interest. If the topics discussed in a set of documents $\mathbf{y}$ are not consistent with a user's personal interest, $\mathbf{w}^T\Psi(\mathbf{x}, \mathbf{u}, \mathbf{y})$ will result in a relatively low score. During prediction, documents consistent with a user's interest will be preferred.

4.3 Our optimization problem

A set of documents produced in response to an ambiguous query should be diverse and consistent to the user's personal interest. To this end we integrate the proposed additional constraints with standard structured SVMs. We propose to train a personalized diversification model by tackling the following optimization problem:

Optimization Problem 2. (Structured SVMs for personalized diversification)

$$\min_{\mathbf{w},\xi\geq 0} \frac{1}{2}||\mathbf{w}||^2 + \frac{C}{N}\sum_{i=1}^{N} \xi_i \tag{7}$$

subject to $\forall i, \forall \mathbf{y} \in \mathcal{Y}\backslash\mathbf{y}^{(i)}, \xi_i \geq 0,$

$$\begin{aligned}
\text{i.}\ \ \mathbf{w}^T\Psi(\mathbf{x}^{(i)}, \mathbf{u}^{(i)}, \mathbf{y}^{(i)}) \ &\geq \mathbf{w}^T\Psi(\mathbf{x}^{(i)}, \mathbf{u}^{(i)}, \mathbf{y}) + \\
&\quad \Delta(\mathbf{y}^{(i)}, \mathbf{y}) - \xi_i, \\
\text{ii.}\ \ \mathbf{w}^T\Psi(\mathbf{x}^{(i)}, \mathbf{u}^{(i)}, \mathbf{y}^{(i)}) \ &\geq \sum_{y\in\mathbf{y}^{(i)}} \mathbf{w}^T\Psi(\mathbf{x}^{(i)}, \mathbf{u}^{(i)}, y) - \xi_i, \\
\text{iii.}\ \ \mathbf{w}^T\Psi(\mathbf{x}^{(i)}, \mathbf{u}^{(i)}, \mathbf{y}^{(i)}) \ &\geq \mathbf{w}^T\Psi(\mathbf{x}^{(i)}, \mathbf{u}^{(i)}, \mathbf{y}) + \\
&\quad ((1 - \text{sim}(\mathbf{y}, \mathbf{u}^{(i)})) - \mu) - \xi_i.
\end{aligned}$$

Algorithm 1: Cutting plane algorithm

Input : $(\mathbf{x}^{(1)}, \mathbf{u}^{(1)}, \mathbf{y}^{(1)}), \ldots, (\mathbf{x}^{(N)}, \mathbf{u}^{(N)}, \mathbf{y}^{(N)}), C, \epsilon$

$\mathcal{W}_i \leftarrow \emptyset, \mathcal{W}_i' \leftarrow \emptyset, \mathcal{W}_i'' \leftarrow \emptyset$ for all $i = 1, \ldots, N$

$\mu = \frac{1}{N}\sum_{i=1}^{N}(1 - \mathrm{sim}(\mathbf{y}^{(i)}, \mathbf{u}^{(i)}))$

repeat

  for $i = 1, \ldots, N$ **do**

    $H(\mathbf{y}; \mathbf{w}) \equiv \Delta(\mathbf{y}^{(i)}, \mathbf{y}) + \mathbf{w}^T\Psi(\mathbf{x}^{(i)}, \mathbf{u}^{(i)}, \mathbf{y}) - \mathbf{w}^T\Psi(\mathbf{x}^{(i)}, \mathbf{u}^{(i)}, \mathbf{y}^{(i)})$

    $H'(\mathbf{y}; \mathbf{w}) \equiv \sum_{y \in \mathbf{y}^{(i)}} \mathbf{w}^T\Psi(\mathbf{x}^{(i)}, \mathbf{u}^{(i)}, y) - \mathbf{w}^T\Psi(\mathbf{x}^{(i)}, \mathbf{u}^{(i)}, \mathbf{y}^{(i)})$

    $H''(\mathbf{y}; \mathbf{w}) \equiv \mathbf{w}^T\Psi(\mathbf{x}^{(i)}, \mathbf{u}^{(i)}, \mathbf{y}) + ((1 - \mathrm{sim}(\mathbf{y}, \mathbf{u}^{(i)})) - \mu) - \mathbf{w}^T\Psi(\mathbf{x}^{(i)}, \mathbf{u}^{(i)}, \mathbf{y}^{(i)})$

    compute $\bar{\mathbf{y}} = \mathrm{argmax}_{\mathbf{y}} H(\mathbf{y}; \mathbf{w})$, $\bar{\mathbf{y}}' = \mathrm{argmax}_{\mathbf{y}} H'(\mathbf{y}; \mathbf{w})$ and $\bar{\mathbf{y}}'' = \mathrm{argmax}_{\mathbf{y}} H''(\mathbf{y}; \mathbf{w})$

    compute $\xi_i = \max\{0, \max_{\mathbf{y} \in \mathcal{W}_i} H(\mathbf{y}; \mathbf{w}), \max_{\mathbf{y} \in \mathcal{W}_i'} H'(\mathbf{y}; \mathbf{w}), \max_{\mathbf{y} \in \mathcal{W}_i''} H''(\mathbf{y}; \mathbf{w})\}$

    if $H(\bar{\mathbf{y}}; \mathbf{w}) > \xi_i + \epsilon$ **or** $H'(\bar{\mathbf{y}}'; \mathbf{w}) > \xi_i + \epsilon$ **or** $H''(\bar{\mathbf{y}}''; \mathbf{w}) > \xi_i + \epsilon$ **then**

      Add constraint to working set $\mathcal{W}_i \leftarrow \mathcal{W}_i \cup \{\bar{\mathbf{y}}\}$, $\mathcal{W}_i' \leftarrow \mathcal{W}_i' \cup \{\bar{\mathbf{y}}'\}$, $\mathcal{W}_i'' \leftarrow \mathcal{W}_i'' \cup \{\bar{\mathbf{y}}''\}$

      $\mathbf{w} \leftarrow$ optimize (7) over $\bigcup_i \{\mathcal{W}_i, \mathcal{W}_i', \mathcal{W}_i''\}$

until *no* $\mathcal{W}_i$, $\mathcal{W}_i'$ *and* $\mathcal{W}_i''$ *have changed during iteration*

Algorithm 2: Greedy subset selection for prediction

Input : $\mathbf{w}, \mathbf{x}, \mathbf{u}$

$\bar{\mathbf{y}} \leftarrow \emptyset$

for $k = 1, \ldots, K$ **do**

  $\bar{x} = \arg\max_{x: x \in \mathbf{x}, x \notin \bar{\mathbf{y}}} \mathbf{w}^T\Psi(\mathbf{x}, \mathbf{u}, \bar{\mathbf{y}} \cup \{x\})$

  $\bar{\mathbf{y}} \leftarrow \bar{\mathbf{y}} \cup \{\bar{x}\}$

return $\bar{\mathbf{y}}$

4.4 The learning algorithm

We can solve the optimization problem defined in (7) by employing the cutting plane algorithm [25]. The learning algorithm is shown in Algorithm 1. The algorithm iteratively adds constraints until we have solved the original problem within a desired tolerance ϵ. It starts with empty working sets $\mathcal{W}_i$, $\mathcal{W}_i'$ and $\mathcal{W}_i''$, for $i = 1, \ldots, N$. Then it iteratively finds the most violated constraints $\bar{\mathbf{y}}$, $\bar{\mathbf{y}}'$ and $\mathbf{y}''$ for each $(\mathbf{x}^{(i)}, \mathbf{u}^{(i)}, \mathbf{y}^{(i)})$ in terms of the three constraints (i), (ii) and (iii) in (7), respectively. If they are violated by more than ϵ, we add them into the corresponding working sets. We iteratively update $\mathbf{w}$ by optimizing (7) over the updated working sets. The outer loop in Algorithm 1 can halt within a polynomial number of iterations for any desired precision ϵ; see [25].

4.5 Prediction

After $\mathbf{w}$ has been learned, given an ambiguous query, a set of candidate documents $\mathbf{x}$, and a set of documents $\mathbf{u}$ the user u is interested in, we try to predict a set of documents $\bar{\mathbf{y}}$ by tackling the following prediction problem:

$$\bar{\mathbf{y}} = \arg\max_{\mathbf{y} \in \mathcal{Y}} \mathcal{F}(\mathbf{x}, \mathbf{u}, \mathbf{y}) = \mathbf{w}^T\Psi(\mathbf{x}, \mathbf{u}, \mathbf{y}). \tag{8}$$

This is a special case of the Budgeted Max Coverage problem [15], and can be efficiently solved by Algorithm 2.

5. USER-INTEREST TOPIC MODEL AND FEATURE SPACE

In this section, we first review the notation and terminology used in our user-interest topic model, and then describe the model and the features used in our structured learning framework.

Table 1: Main notation used in user-interest topic model.

Notation	Gloss	Notation	Gloss
q	query	d	document
u	user	z	topic
T	number of topics	U	number of users
D	number of documents	V	number of tokens
N_d	number of tokens in d		
$\widetilde{\mathbf{u}}$	a set of users	$\widetilde{\mathbf{w}}$	a set of tokens
b_z	Beta distribution parameter for z		
α	the parameter of user Dirichlet prior		
β	the parameter of token Dirichlet prior		
θ_d	multinomial distribution of topics specific to d		
ϕ_z	multinomial distribution of tokens specific to z		
ϑ_u	multinomial distribution of topics specific to u		
z_{di}	topic associated with the i-th token in d		
w_{di}	the i-th token in d		
r_{di}	relevance of the i-th token in d		

5.1 Notation and terminology

We summarize the main notation used in our user-interest topic model (UIT) in Table 1. We distinguish between queries, aspects and topics. A *query* is a user's expression of an information need. An *aspect* (sometimes called *subtopic* at the TREC Web tracks [11]) is an interpretation of an information need. We use *topic* to refer to latent topics as identified by a topic modeling method (LDA).

5.2 User-interest topic model

To capture per-user and per-document multinomial distributions over topics such that we can measure whether a document can cater for the user's interest, we propose a user-interest latent topic model (UIT). Topic discovery in UIT is influenced not only by token co-occurrences, but also by the relevance scores of documents evaluated by users. In our UIT model, we use a Beta distribution over a (normalized) document relevance span covering all the data, and thus various skewed shapes of rising and falling topic prominence can be flexibly represented.

The latent topic model used in UIT is a generative model of relevance and tokens in the documents. The generative process used in Gibbs sampling [18] for its parameter estimation, is as follows:

i. Draw T multinomials ϕ_z from a Dirichlet prior β, one for each topic z;

ii. For each user u, draw a multinomial ϑ_u from a Dirichlet prior α; then for each token w_{di} in document $d \in \mathbf{u}$:

  (a) Draw a topic z_{di} from multinomial ϑ_u;

  (b) Draw a token w_{di} from multinomial $\phi_{z_{di}}$;

  (c) Draw a relevance score r_{di} for w_{di} from Beta $(b_{z_{di}1}, b_{z_{di}2})$.

Fig. 1 shows a graphical representation of our model. In the generative process, the relevance scores of tokens observed in the same document are the same and evaluated by a user, although a relevance score is generated for each token from the Beta distribution. In our experiments, there is a fixed number of latent topics, T, although a non-parametric Bayes version of UIT that automatically integrates over the number of topics would certainly be possible. The posterior distribution of topics depends on the information from two modalities: tokens and the documents' relevance scores.

Inference is intractable in this model. Following [6, 7, 14, 18, 30], we employ Gibbs sampling to perform approximate inference. We adopt a conjugate prior (Dirichlet) for the multinomial distributions, and thus we can easily integrate out ϑ and ϕ, analytically capturing the uncertainty associated with them. In this way we

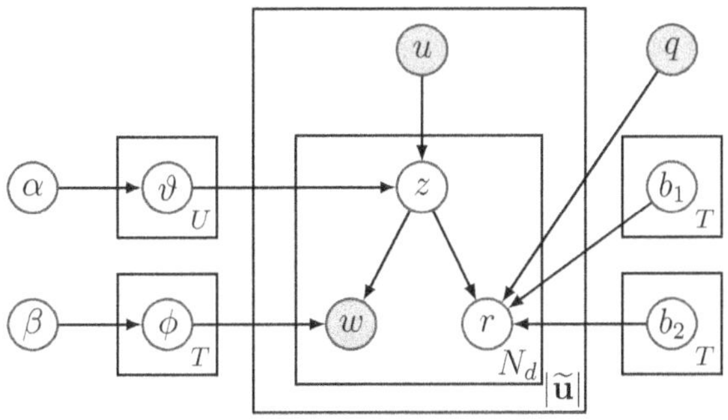

Figure 1: Graphical representation of user-interest topic model.

facilitate the sampling, i.e., we need not sample ϑ and ϕ at all. Because we use the continuous Beta distribution rather than discretizing document relevance scores, sparsity is not a big concern in fitting the model. For simplicity and speed we estimate these Beta distributions (b_{z1}, b_{z2}) by the method of moments, once per iteration of Gibbs sampling. We find that the sensitivity of the hyperparameters α and β is not very strong. Thus, for simplicity, we use fixed symmetric Dirichlet distributions ($\alpha = 50/T$ and $\beta = 0.1$) in all our experiments.

In the Gibbs sampling procedure above, we need to calculate the conditional distribution $P(z_{di}|\widetilde{\mathbf{w}}, \mathbf{r}, \mathbf{z}_{-di}, \widetilde{\mathbf{u}}, \alpha, \beta, \mathbf{b}, q)$, where $\mathbf{z}_{-di}$ represents the topic assignments for all tokens except w_{di}. We begin with the joint probability of a dataset, and using the chain rule, we can obtain the conditional probability conveniently as:

$$P(z_{di}|\widetilde{\mathbf{w}}, \mathbf{r}, \mathbf{z}_{-di}, \widetilde{\mathbf{u}}, \alpha, \beta, \mathbf{b}, q) \propto \frac{n_{z_{di}w_{di}} + \beta_{w_{di}} - 1}{\sum_{v=1}^{V}(n_{z_{di}v} + \beta_v) - 1} \frac{n_{u_{di}z_{di}} + \alpha_{z_{di}} - 1}{\sum_{z=1}^{T}(n_{u_{di}z} + \alpha_z) - 1} \times \frac{(1-r_{di})^{b_{z_{di}1}-1} r_{di}^{b_{z_{di}2}-1}}{B(b_{z_{di}1}, b_{z_{di}2})},$$

where n_{zv} is the total number of tokens v that are assigned to topic z, n_{uz} represents the number of topics z that are assigned to user u.

After the Gibbs sampling procedure, we can easily infer a user's interest, i.e., multinomial distributions over topics for user u as:

$$\vartheta_{uz} = p(z|u) = \frac{n_{uz} + \alpha_z}{\sum_{z=1}^{T}(n_{uz} + \alpha_z)}, \tag{9}$$

and easily infer multinomial distributions over tokens for topic z:

$$\phi_{zv} = p(v|z) = \frac{n_{zv} + \beta_v}{\sum_{v=1}^{V}(n_{zv} + \beta_v)}, \tag{10}$$

where n_{zv} is the number of tokens of word v that are assigned to topic z. To obtain the multinomial distribution over topics for document d, i.e., θ_{dz}, we first apply the Bayes' rule:

$$\theta_{dz} = p(z|d) = \frac{p(d|z)p(z)}{p(d)}, \tag{11}$$

where $p(d|z)$ is the probability of d belonging to topic z, and $p(z)$ is the probability of topic z. According to (10), $p(d|z)$ can be obtained as $p(d|z) = \prod_{v\in d} p(v|z) = \prod_{v\in d} \phi_{zv}$. According to (9), $p(z)$ can be obtained as $p(z) = \sum_{u=1}^{U} p(z|u)p(u)$, where U is the total number of users. Therefore, 11 can be represented as:

$$\theta_{dz} = \frac{\prod_{v\in d} \phi_{zv} \sum_{u=1}^{U} p(z|u)p(u)}{p(d)}. \tag{12}$$

As any d has the same chance to be considered to be returned in response to q, we can assume that $p(d)$ is a constant, and likewise we also assume that $p(u)$ is a constant, such that (12) becomes:

$$\theta_{dz} = \tfrac{1}{E} \prod_{v\in d} \phi_{zv} \sum_{u=1}^{U} \vartheta_{uz}, \tag{13}$$

where $E = \sum_{z=1}^{T} \prod_{v\in d} \phi_{zv} \sum_{u=1}^{U} \vartheta_{uz}$ is a normalization constant. Then, the topic distribution similarity $\text{sim}(\mathbf{y}, \mathbf{u})$ between a set of documents $\mathbf{y}$ and the documents $\mathbf{u}$ a user u is interested in can be measured as:

$$\text{sim}(\mathbf{y}, \mathbf{u}) = \tfrac{1}{|\mathbf{y}|} \sum_{d\in\mathbf{y}} \cos(\theta_d, \vartheta_u), \tag{14}$$

where vectors $\theta_d = (\theta_{d1}, \cdots, \theta_{dT})$ and $\vartheta_u = (\vartheta_{d1}, \cdots, \vartheta_{dT})$ are the multinomial distribution of topics specific to document d and user u, respectively. We use the cos function in (14); other distance functions such as one based on Euclidean distance can be employed but we found that the results were not significantly different.

5.3 Feature space

The feature representation Ψ must enable meaningful discrimination between high quality and low quality predictions [32]. To predict a set of documents in the personalized diversification task, we propose to consider three main types of feature space.

Tokens. Following [32], we define L token sets $V_1(\mathbf{y}), \ldots, V_L(\mathbf{y})$. Each token set $V_l(\mathbf{y})$ contains the set of tokens that appear at least l times in some document in $\mathbf{y}$. Then we use thresholds on the ratio $|D_l(v)|/|\mathbf{u}|$ (or $|D_l(v)|/|\mathbf{x}|$) to define feature values of $\psi_l(v, \mathbf{u})$ (or $\psi_l(v, \mathbf{x})$) that describe word v at l-th importance level. Here, $D_l(v)$ is the set of documents that have at least l copies of v in the whole set of documents $\mathbf{u}$ (or $\mathbf{x}$). We let $L = 20$ in our experiments, as quite a few tokens can appear more than 20 times in a document. Besides, we propose to directly utilize the tokens' statistics to capture similarity between a document $x \in \mathbf{y}$ and a set of documents $\mathbf{u}$ that a user u is interested in as features. We consider cosine, Euclidean and Kullback-Leibler (KL) divergence similarity metrics. For each of these three metrics, we compute the minimal, maximal, and average similarity scores of the document $x \in \mathbf{y}$ and the standard deviations to a set of documents $\mathbf{u}$ based on the content of the documents and the standard LDA model [5]. In total, we have 49 features that fall in this feature category.

Interest. In addition, based on our UIT topic model, we also compute the cosine, Euclidean and KL similarity between a document $x \in \mathbf{y}$ and a set of documents $\mathbf{u}$ based on a multinomial distribution over topics and the user's multinomial distribution over topics generated by UIT. Again, for each of these three similarity metrics, we compute the minimal, maximal, and average similarity scores and the standard deviation scores. In total, we have $S = 36$ features $\omega_s(x, \mathbf{u})$ that fall in this feature category.

Probability. The main probabilities used in state-of-the-art unsupervised personalized diversification methods are utilized in our learning model as features, i.e., $\gamma_m(x, \mathbf{x}, \mathbf{u})$. These probabilities include $p(d|q)$, the probability of d relevant to q, $p(c|d)$, the probability of d belonging to a category c, $p(c|q, u)$, the personalized query aspect distribution, $p(c|d, u)$, the personalized aspect distribution over d, and $p(d|c, u)$, the personalized aspect-dependent document distribution, where c is a category that d belongs to in the Textwise Open Directory Project category service.[1] For $p(d|q)$, we obtain 3 versions of this feature value produced by BM25 [20], Jelinek-Mercer and Dirichlet language models [34]. To get the feature value of $p(c|d)$, we make use of the Textwise service which returns up to 3 possible categories for d, ranked by a score in $[0, 1]$, and we use the normalized scores as features. We adopt 5 ways of

[1] `http://textwise.com`

computing $p(c|q,u)$ as feature values [26]; for details on how to compute $p(c|q,u)$, $p(c|d,u)$ and $p(d|c,u)$ we refer to [26].

Then, we define $\Psi(\mathbf{x},\mathbf{u},\mathbf{y})$ as follows:

$$\Psi(\mathbf{x},\mathbf{u},\mathbf{y}) = \begin{bmatrix} \frac{1}{|\mathbf{y}|}\sum_{v\in V_1(\mathbf{y})}\psi_1(v,\mathbf{u}) \\ \frac{1}{|\mathbf{y}|}\sum_{v\in V_1(\mathbf{y})}\psi_1(v,\mathbf{x}) \\ \vdots \\ \frac{1}{|\mathbf{y}|}\sum_{v\in V_L(\mathbf{y})}\psi_L(v,\mathbf{u}) \\ \frac{1}{|\mathbf{y}|}\sum_{v\in V_L(\mathbf{y})}\psi_L(v,\mathbf{x}) \\ \frac{1}{|\mathbf{y}|}\sum_{x\in\mathbf{y}}\omega_1(x,\mathbf{u}) \\ \vdots \\ \frac{1}{|\mathbf{y}|}\sum_{x\in\mathbf{y}}\omega_S(x,\mathbf{u}) \\ \frac{1}{|\mathbf{y}|}\sum_{x\in\mathbf{y}}\gamma_1(x,\mathbf{x},\mathbf{u}) \\ \vdots \\ \frac{1}{|\mathbf{y}|}\sum_{x\in\mathbf{y}}\gamma_M(x,\mathbf{x},\mathbf{u}) \end{bmatrix}.$$

6. EXPERIMENTAL SETUP

In this section, we describe our experimental setup; §6.1 lists our research questions; §6.2 describes our dataset; §6.3 and §6.4 lists the baselines and metrics for evaluation, respectively; §6.5 details the settings of the experiments.

6.1 Research questions

The research questions guiding the remainder of the paper are: (RQ1) Can supervised personalized diversification methods outperform state-of-the-art unsupervised methods? Can our method beat state-of-the-art supervised methods? See §7.1. (RQ2) What is the contribution of the user-interest topic model in our proposed method? See §7.2. (RQ3) What is the effect of the constraints for diversity and consistence with user's interest in our method? See §7.3. (RQ4) Does our method outperform the best supervised baseline method on each query? See §7.4. (RQ5) Can our method retrieve a competitive number of subtopics per query? See §7.5. (RQ6) What is the performance of our supervised methods when the C parameter is varied? See §7.6.

6.2 Dataset

In order to answer our research questions we work with a publicly available personalized diversification dataset.[2] This dataset contains private evaluation information from 35 users on 180 search queries. The queries are quite ambiguous, as the length of each query is no more that two keywords. In total, there are 751 subtopics for the queries, with most of the queries having more than 2 subtopics. Over 3800 relevance judgements are available, for at least the top 5 results for each query. Each relevance judgement includes 3 main assessments: a 4-grade scale assessment on how relevant the result is to the user's interests (resulting in the *user relevance* ground truth and the set of users' interesting documents being created); a 4-grade scale assessment on how relevant the result is to the evaluated query (resulting in the *topic relevance* ground truth being created); and a 2-grade assessment whether a specific subtopic is related to the evaluated query (resulting in the subjective subtopics related to the search query being created). Details of this dataset can be found in [26]. For pre-processing, we apply Porter stemming, tokenization, and stopword removal (using the INQUERY list) to the documents using the Lemur toolkit.[3]

[2] http://ir.ii.uam.es/~david/persdivers/

[3] http://www.lemurproject.org

Two well-known corpora, ClueWeb09 and ClueWeb12,[4] have been proposed for search result diversification tasks in the TREC 2009–2013 Web tracks [11]. However, they do not contain any user information or relevance judgments provided by specific users, and thus do not fit our experiments.

6.3 Baselines

Let PSVM$_{div}$ denote our personalized diversification via structured learning method. We compare PSVM$_{div}$ to 11 baselines: a traditional web search algorithm, BM25 [20]; 2 well-known plain (in the sense of "not personalized") search result diversification approaches, IA-Select [2] and xQuAD [21]; a plain (in the sense of "not diversified") personalized search approach based on BM25 [27], Pers$_{BM25}$; a two-stage diversification and personalization approach, xQuAD$_{BM25}$, as suggested by [19], that first applies the xQuAD algorithm and then Pers$_{BM25}$; 4 state-of-the-art unsupervised personalized diversification methods [26], PIA-Select, PIA-Select$_{BM25}$, PxQuAD, and PxQuAD$_{BM25}$. As PSVM$_{div}$ builds on standard structured learning framework, we also consider 2 structured learning algorithms: SVM$_{div}$ [32] that directly tries to retrieve relevant documents covering as many subtopics as possible, and a standard structured learning method, denoted as SVM$_{rank}$ [33] that directly ranks documents by optimizing a relevance-biased evaluation metric (we use α-nDCG and nDCG to define the loss functions for SVM$_{div}$ and SVM$_{rank}$, respectively).[5]

For the supervised methods, PSVM$_{div}$, SVM$_{div}$ and SVM$_{rank}$, we use a 130/40/10 split for our training, validation and test sets, respectively. We train PSVM$_{div}$, SVM$_{div}$ and SVM$_{rank}$ using values of C (see (7)) that vary from 1e-4 to 1.0. The best C value is then chosen on the validation set, and evaluated on the test queries. The train/validation/test splits are permuted until all 180 queries were chosen once for the test set. We repeat the experiments 10 times and report the average evaluation results.

6.4 Evaluation

We use the following diversity metrics for evaluation, most of which are official evaluation metrics in the TREC Web tracks [11] and are widely used in the literature on result diversification:

α-nDCG@k. A version of normalized discounted cumulative gain at k in which the role of the parameter α is emphasized in computing the novelty of the top k documents. α-nDCG@k scores a ranking by rewarding newly-found subtopics and penalizing redundant subtopics geometrically, discounting all rewards with a log-harmonic discount function of rank. See [10] for details on how α-nDCG@k is computed.

S-Recall@k. Subtopic recall at k [35] is computed at retrieval depth k using the following procedure. Assume there are Q ambiguous queries. Let z be an aspect of query q and N_q the number of aspects (subtopics) associated with q. Then, the subtopic recall at rank k [35] is defined as the percentage of subtopics covered by one of the top k documents:

$$\text{S-Recall@}k = \frac{1}{Q}\sum_{q=1}^{Q}\frac{|\bigcup_{i=1}^{k}\text{subtopics}(d_i|q)|}{N_q},$$

where subtopics$(d_i|q)$ is the number of aspects covered by d_i in response to q.

ERR-IA@k. Intent-aware expected reciprocal rank at retrieval depth k, similarly, is computed as

$$\text{ERR-IA@}k = \frac{1}{Q}\sum_{q=1}^{Q}\frac{1}{N_q}\sum_{z=1}^{N_q}\text{ERR}(k|z,q),$$

[4] http://boston.lti.cs.cmu.edu/clueweb12/

[5] The source code for SVM$_{rank}$ [33] and SVM$_{div}$ [32] is available at http://www.cs.cornell.edu/People/tj/.

where ERR$(k|z,q)$ is the expected reciprocal rank score at k in terms of aspect z of query q.

Prec-IA@k. Intent-aware precision at k [2] is defined as

$$\text{Prec-IA@}k = \frac{1}{Q}\sum_{q=1}^{Q}\frac{1}{N_q}\sum_{z=1}^{N_q}\text{Prec}(k|z,q),$$

where Prec$(k|z,q)$ is the precision at k in terms of the aspects z of q, and can be computed as $\frac{1}{k}\sum_{j=1}^{k} j_q(z,j)$. Here, $j_q(z,j)=1$ if the document returned for q at depth j is judged relevant to aspect z of q; otherwise, $j_q(z,j)=0$.

MAP-IA@k. Intent-aware MAP at k [2] is computed as

$$\text{MAP-IA@}k = \frac{1}{Q}\sum_{q=1}^{Q}\frac{1}{N_q}\sum_{z=1}^{N_q}\text{MAP}(k|z,q),$$

where MAP$(k|z,q)$ is the MAP score for top k returned documents in terms of aspect z of q.

For evaluating accuracy, we use nDCG [10], ERR, Prec@k and MAP. Since users mainly evaluated the top 5 returned results [26], we compute the scores at depth 5 for all metrics. Statistical significance of observed differences between the performance of two runs is tested using a two-tailed paired t-test and is denoted using ▲ (or ▼) for significant differences for $\alpha = .01$, or △ (and ▽) for $\alpha = .05$.

6.5 Experiments

We report on 6 main experiments aimed at answering the research questions listed in §6.1. Our first experiment aims at understanding whether supervised personalized diversification methods outperform unsupervised ones and whether PSVM$_{div}$ beats the supervised algorithms that apply structured learning technique directly. We compare PSVM$_{div}$ to 2 supervised baselines, SVM$_{div}$ and SVM$_{rank}$, and the 9 unsupervised baselines with both topic relevance and user relevance ground truths, respectively.

To understand the contribution of the user-interest topic model, we conduct our second experiment where we perform comparisons between PSVM$_{div}$ using all features ("token", "interest" and "probability," see §5.3) including those extracted from the topic model and PSVM$_{div}$ using basic features ("token" and "probability" only, see §5.3). In our third experiment, aimed at understanding the effect of our new constraints in PSVM$_{div}$, a series of experiments is conducted by employing different sets of constraints while training.

In order to understand how PSVM$_{div}$ compares to the best baseline, our fourth and fifth experiment provide a query- and subtopic-level analysis, respectively. Finally, to understand the influence of the key parameter in our structured learning framework, C, we train PSVM$_{div}$, SVM$_{div}$ and SVM$_{rank}$ by varying C from 1e-4 to 1.0 and report the performance.

7. RESULTS AND ANALYSIS

The following subsections report, analyze and discuss our experimental results.

7.1 Supervised vs. unsupervised

Table 2 lists the diversity scores of the unsupervised baseline methods. For all metrics in terms of either user relevance or topic relevance, none of the plain methods, viz., BM25, IA-Select, Pers$_{BM25}$, xQuAD and xQuAD$_{BM25}$, beats the best unsupervised personalized diversification methods, viz., PIA-Select, PIA-Select$_{BM25}$, PxQuAD or PxQuAD$_{BM25}$. Moreover, in some cases the performance differences between the best plain method and the best unsupervised personalized diversification method are significant. This indicates that diversity and personalization are complementary and can enhance each other. The same observation can be found in Table 5 where performance is evaluated by relevance-oriented metrics.

Table 2: Performance of unsupervised methods on diversification metrics. The best performance per metric is in boldface. The best plain retrieval method (BM25, IA-Select, Pers$_{BM25}$, xQuAD and xQuAD$_{BM25}$) is underlined. Statistically significant differences between the best performance per metric and the best plain retrieval method are marked in the upper left hand corner of the best performance score.

	α-nDCG	S-Recall	ERR-IA	Prec-IA	MAP-IA
User relevance					
BM25	.6443	.4557	.2267	.1659	.1245
IA-Select	.6099	.4282	.2241	.1624	.1177
Pers$_{BM25}$	.6427	.4541	.2318	.1639	.1206
xQuAD	.6421	.4635	.2299	.1675	.1267
xQuAD$_{BM25}$	.6270	.4558	.2249	.1646	.1123
PIA-Select	.5766	.4407	.2006	.1480	.1085
PIA-Select$_{BM25}$	.6457	▲**.4752**	.2364	.1581	.1180
PxQuAD	.6409	.4588	.2313	.1629	.1296
PxQuAD$_{BM25}$	**.6497**	.4713	△**.2367**	**.1676**	**.1296**
Topic relevance					
BM25	.7599	.4456	.2315	.1717	.1241
IA-Select	.7685	.4425	.2365	.1767	.1212
Pers$_{BM25}$	.7746	.4555	.2330	.1794	.1219
xQuAD	.7711	.4600	.2348	.1747	.1245
xQuAD$_{BM25}$	.7763	.4741	.2336	.1773	.1225
PIA-Select	.7410	.4641	.2227	.1650	.1206
PIA-Select$_{BM25}$	△**.7854**	**.4798**	△**.2415**	.1740	▲**.1300**
PxQuAD	.7744	.4543	.2350	.1747	.1278
PxQuAD$_{BM25}$	.7827	.4718	.2396	**.1797**	.1245

Table 3 shows the diversity-oriented evaluation results of 3 supervised methods using basic features ("token", and "probability" features, see §5.3) in terms of both ground truths. In terms of diversity-oriented evaluation metrics all of the supervised methods significantly outperform the best unsupervised methods when making comparisons between the scores and the scores of unsupervised methods in Table 2 in most cases. We make further comparisons in Tables 5 and 6 in terms of relevance-oriented metrics, and find that supervised methods can statistically significantly outperform unsupervised ones. These two findings attest to the merits of taking supervised personalized diversification methods for the task of personalized search result diversification.

Next, we compare supervised strategies to each other. Tables 3 and 4 show the diversity-oriented evaluation resutls in terms of both grounth truths. It is clear from both tables that our supervised method PSVM$_{div}$ statistically significantly beats plain supervised methods, SVM$_{rank}$ and SVM$_{div}$. This is because PSVM$_{div}$ considers both personalization and diversity factors, whereas the other two do not take both two factors into account. SVM$_{rank}$ only tries to return more relevant documents, and SVM$_{div}$ directly utilizes standard structured learning for diversification.

As shown in Table 6, in terms of the relevance-oriented metrics, PSVM$_{div}$ does not significantly outperform SVM$_{rank}$ and SVM$_{div}$. This is because PSVM$_{div}$ returns the same number of relevant documents that do, however, cover more subtopics than the other supervised methods. Hence, PSVM$_{div}$ mainly outperforms the other two in terms of diversity-oriented metrics. We provide further analyses in §7.4 (query-level) and §7.5 (subtopic-level).

7.2 Effect of the proposed UIT model

Next, to understand the contribution of our UIT topic model, we compare the performance of the supervised methods using basic

Table 3: Performance of supervised methods utilizing basic features on diversification metrics. The best performance per metric is in boldface. Statistically significant differences between supervised and the best unsupervised method (in Table 2) per metric, between PSVM$_{div}$ and SVM$_{div}$, are marked in the upper left hand corner of the supervised method' score, in the right hand corner of the PSVM$_{div}$ score, respectively.

	User relevance				
	α-nDCG	S-Recall	ERR-IA	Prec-IA	MAP-IA
SVM$_{rank}$	▲.6667	△.4837	.2396	.1683	▲.1856
SVM$_{div}$	▲.6750	△.4887	.2412	△.1698	▲.1974
PSVM$_{div}$	▲**.7234**▲	▲**.5756**▲	▲**.2514**▲	▲**.1702**△	▲**.2037**△
	Topic relevance				
SVM$_{rank}$	.7889	.4805	.2437	△.1812	▲.1848
SVM$_{div}$	▲.8003	△.4893	△.2479	△.1833	▲.2045
PSVM$_{div}$	▲**.8533**▲	▲**.5834**▲	▲**.2649**▲	▲**.1846**△	▲**.2113**▲

Table 4: Performance of supervised methods utilizing all features on diversification metrics. The best performance per metric is in boldface. All the scores here are statistically significant compared to those in Table 2. Statistically significant differences between the method here and the method in Table 3, between PSVM$_{div}$ and SVM$_{div}$, are marked in the upper left hand corner of the corresponding score, in the right hand corner of the PSVM$_{div}$ score, respectively.

	User relevance				
	α-nDCG	S-Recall	ERR-IA	Prec-IA	MAP-IA
SVM$_{rank}$	△.6782	△.4973	.2416	△.1710	▲.2887
SVM$_{div}$	△.6867	△.4973	.2456	△.1729	▲.2911
PSVM$_{div}$	▲**.7513**▲	▲**.6140**▲	△**.2628**▲	△**.1742**△	▲**.2979**△
	Topic relevance				
SVM$_{rank}$	▲.8422	▲.5068	▲.2554	△.1903	▲.3001
SVM$_{div}$	△.8569	▲.5068	▲.2628	▲.1907	▲.3036
PSVM$_{div}$	▲**.9549**▲	▲**.6730**▲	▲**.2849**▲	△**.1917**△	▲**.3096**△

Table 5: Performance of unsupervised methods on relevance metrics. Notational conventions are the same as in Table 2.

	User relevance				Topic relevance			
	nDCG	ERR	Prec	MAP	nDCG	ERR	Prec	MAP
BM25	.5697	.9364	.7113	.2038	.7775	.9440	.9146	.2239
IA-Select	.5126	.9389	.6796	.1813	.7340	.9452	.9250	.2299
Pers$_{BM25}$	.5713	.9276	.7183	.2076	.7741	.9374	.9298	.2316
xQuAD	.5526	.9352	.6858	.1915	.7518	.9367	.9125	.2231
xQuAD$_{BM25}$	.5540	.9133	.6921	.1841	.7605	.9278	.9312	.2281
PIA-Select	.4783	.9034	.6417	.1774	.6709	.9062	.8667	.2043
PIA-Select$_{BM25}$	.5482	.9271	.6687	.1803	.7264	.9418	.9042	.2223
PxQuAD	.5631	.9246	.7050	.2073	.7679	.9435	.9229	.2306
PxQuAD$_{BM25}$	**.5764**	**.9374**△	**.7258**△	**.2145**	**.7793**	**.9466**	**.9396**	**.2355**

features, i.e., all other features but not the features generated from the UIT model, with those using all the features.

We turn to Tables 3 and 4, that list the results of the supervised methods in terms of diversity-oriented metrics when using the basic features and all features, respectively. For all supervised methods, the performance of using all features is better than that of only using the basic features. That is, our proposed UIT model can capture users' interest distributions and this kind of information can be applied to improve performance. Due to space limitations, we do not report the results in terms of relevance-oriented metrics; the findings there are qualitatively similar.

Table 6: Performance of supervised methods utilizing basic features on relevance metrics. The best performance per metric is in boldface. Statistically significant differences between supervised and the best unsupervised method (in Table 5) per metric, between PSVM$_{div}$ and SVM$_{div}$, are marked in the upper left hand corner of the supervised method' score, in the right hand corner of the PSVM$_{div}$ score, respectively.

	User relevance				Topic relevance			
	nDCG	ERR	Prec	MAP	nDCG	ERR	Prec	MAP
SVM$_{rank}$	△.5805	△.9456	△.7345	△.2238	△.7864	.9478	▲.9763	△.2446
SVM$_{div}$	△.5813	△.9467	△.7396	△.2240	△.7858	.9493	▲.9806	△.2482
PSVM$_{div}$	△**.5833**	△**.9485**	△**.7412**	△**.2281**	△**.7922**△	△**.9521**	▲**.9834**	△**.2496**

Table 7: Performance of PSVM$_{div}$ involving different constraints using basic features on diversification metrics with user relevance ground truth. The best performance per metric is in boldface. Statistically significant differences against PSVM$_{div}$-C$_i$ are marked in the upper right hand corner of the corresponding scores.

	User relevance				
	α-nDCG	S-Recall	ERR-IA	Prec-IA	MAP-IA
PSVM$_{div}$-C$_i$	.6713	.4842	.2403	.1673	.1969
PSVM$_{div}$-C$_{i,ii}$	.6973▲	.5262▲	.2437	.1681	.1977
PSVM$_{div}$-C$_{i,iii}$	.6994▲	.5275▲	.2478△	.1687△	.1983
PSVM$_{div}$-All	**.7234**▲	**.5756**▲	**.2514**▲	**.1702**▲	**.2037**△

Table 8: Performance of PSVM$_{div}$ involving different constraints using all features on diversification metrics with user relevance ground truth. Statistically significant differeneces between the score here and that in Table 7 are marked in the upper left hand corner of the scores. Other notational conventions are the same as in Table 7.

	User relevance				
	α-nDCG	S-Recall	ERR-IA	Prec-IA	MAP-IA
PSVM$_{div}$-C$_i$	▲.6843	▲.4965	△.2434	△.1714	▲.2906
PSVM$_{div}$-C$_{i,ii}$	▲.7156▲	▲.5334▲	△.2494△	△.1720△	▲.2932
PSVM$_{div}$-C$_{i,iii}$	▲.7194▲	▲.5388▲	△.2501△	△.1723△	▲.2937△
PSVM$_{div}$-All	▲**.7513**▲	▲**.6140**▲	△**.2628**▲	△**.1742**▲	▲**.2979**△

7.3 Effect of the proposed constraints

Next, to understand the effect of the newly proposed constraints, we conduct experiments by employing different sets of constraints while training. The comparisons are again divided into those using all features and those using basic features. We write PSVM$_{div}$-C$_i$, PSVM$_{div}$-C$_{i,ii}$, PSVM$_{div}$-C$_{i,iii}$, and PSVM$_{div}$-All to denote the methods trained with the standard constraint (constraint i in (7)), standard and diversity-biased constraints (constraints i and ii in (7)), standard and interest-biased (constraints i and iii in (7)), and all constraints involved (constraints i, ii and iii in (7)), respectively. Again, we only report results on diversity-oriented metrics.

According to Tables 7 and 8, when employing one more constraint, either diversity-biased or interest-biased, the performance is statistically significantly better than that of only employing the standard constraint. In terms of all metrics, the performance of PSVM$_{div}$ employing all constraints statistically significantly outperforms the performance of using at most two constraints. The positive effect of the proposed constraints again demonstrates that combining diversification (the diversity-biased constraint) and personalization (the interest-biased constraint) boosts the performance.

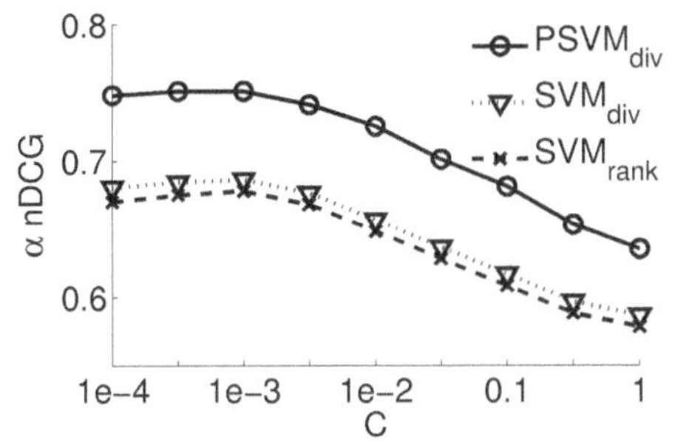

Figure 4: Performance of the supervised methods using all features when varying the value of parameter C.

7.4 Query-level analysis

In order to figure out why PSVM$_{div}$ enhances other supervised baselines, we take a closer look at per test query improvements of PSVM$_{div}$ over the best supervised baseline method, viz., SVM$_{div}$, which outperforms SVM$_{rank}$ in most cases. Fig. 2 shows the per query performance differences in terms of the diversify-oriented metrics of PSVM$_{div}$ against SVM$_{div}$ when they use all the features. PSVM$_{div}$ achieves performance improvements for many queries, especially in terms of α-nDCG, S-Recall, ERR-IA.

In a very small number of cases, PSVM$_{div}$ performs poorer than SVM$_{div}$. This appears to be due to the fact that PSVM$_{div}$ promotes some non-relevant documents when it tries to cover as many subtopics as possible for a given query.

7.5 Subtopic-level analysis

Next, we zoom in on the number of different subtopics that are returned by PSVM$_{div}$ and SVM$_{div}$, respectively, to further analyze why PSVM$_{div}$ beats SVM$_{div}$. Here, again, we use SVM$_{div}$ as a representative. Specifically, we report changes in the number of subtopics for PSVM$_{div}$ against SVM$_{div}$ in Fig. 3 when they use all features. Red bars indicate the number of subtopics that appear in the run of PSVM$_{div}$ but not in the run of SVM$_{div}$, white bars indicate the number of subtopics in both runs, whereas blue bars indicate the number of subtopics that are not in PSVM$_{div}$ but in SVM$_{div}$; queries are ordered first by the size of the red bar, then the size of the white bar, and finally the size of the blue bar.

Clearly, the differences between PSVM$_{div}$ and SVM$_{div}$ in the top 2 and 3 are more limited than the differences in the top 4 and 5, but in all cases PSVM$_{div}$ outperforms SVM$_{div}$. E.g., in total there are 68 more subtopics in the top 5 of the run produced by PSVM$_{div}$ than those in the SVM$_{div}$ run (in terms of all the 180 test queries, 68 subtopics in PSVM$_{div}$ but not in SVM$_{div}$, 7 subtopics in SVM$_{div}$ but not in PSVM$_{div}$).

7.6 Performance of parameter tuning

To understand the performance of the tradeoff parameter C used in (4) and (7), which balances between weights and slacks, we show the performance of PSVM$_{div}$ as well as the 2 supervised baselines using all features. To save space, we only report the performance on α-nDCG. Fig. 4 plots the results and it illustrates that PSVM$_{div}$ performs best when C is small. This indicates the merit of our new constraints (as well as the standard constraint used in the baselines) focusing on weight modification rather than on low training loss.

8. CONCLUSION

Most previous work on personalized diversification of search results produce a ranking using unsupervised methods, either implicitly or explicitly. In this paper, we have adopted a different perspective on the problem, based on structured learning. We propose to boost the diversity and match to users' personal interests of search results by introducing two additional constraints into the standard structured learning framework. We also propose a user-interest topic model to capture users' multinomial distribution of interest over topics and infer per-document multinomial distributions over topics. Based on this a number of user interest features are extracted and the similarity between a user and a document can be effectively measured for our learning method.

Our evaluation shows that supervised personalized diversification approaches outperforms state-of-the-art unsupervised personalization diversification, plain personalization and plain diversification algorithms. The two proposed constraints are shown to play a significant role in the supervised method. We also find that the user-interest topic model helps to improve performance. Our proposed learning method is able to return more subtopics.

As to future work, we aim to study other types of learning strategies for personalized diversification of search results. Our method employed the α-nDCG metric in the loss function; we plan to use other alternative metrics. Finally, our experimental results were only evaluated on a single dataset. In future work we plan to invite users to label the existing datasets, e.g., ClueWeb09, such that they can also be used for personalized diversification algorithms.

Acknowledgments. This research was partially supported by the China Scholarship Council, the European Community's Seventh Framework Programme (FP7/2007-2013) under grant agreements nr 288024 (LiMoSINe) and nr 312827 (VOX-Pol), the Netherlands Organisation for Scientific Research (NWO) under project nrs 727.011.005, 612.001.116, HOR-11-10, 640.006.013, the Center for Creation, Content and Technology (CCCT), the QuaMerdes project funded by the CLARIN-nl program, the TROVe project funded by the CLARIAH program, the Dutch national program COMMIT, the ESF Research Network Program ELIAS, the Elite Network Shifts project funded by the Royal Dutch Academy of Sciences (KNAW), the Netherlands eScience Center under project number 027.012.105, the Yahoo! Faculty Research and Engagement Program, the Microsoft Research PhD program, and the HPC Fund.

9. REFERENCES

[1] Z. Abbassi, V. S. Mirrokni, and M. Thakur. Diversity maximization under matroid constraints. In *KDD*, pages 32–40, 2013.

[2] R. Agrawal, S. Gollapudi, A. Halverson, and S. Ieong. Diversifying search results. In *WSDM*, pages 5–14, 2009.

[3] K. Bache, D. Newman, and P. Smyth. Text-based measures of document diversity. In *KDD*, pages 23–31, 2013.

[4] P. N. Bennett, R. W. White, W. Chu, S. T. Dumais, P. Bailey, F. Borisyuk, and X. Cui. Modeling the impact of short- and long-term behavior on search personalization. In *SIGIR*, pages 185–194, 2012.

[5] D. M. Blei, A. Y. Ng, and M. I. Jordan. Latent dirichlet allocation. *J. Mach. Learn. Res.*, 3:993–1022, 2003.

[6] J. Boyd-Graber and D. M. Blei. Syntactic topic models. In *NIPS*, 2008.

[7] J. Boyd-Graber and D. M. Blei. Multilingual topic models for unaligned text. In *UAI*, pages 75–82, 2009.

[8] J. Carbonell and J. Goldstein. The use of MMR, diversity-based reranking for reordering documents and producing summaries. In *SIGIR*, pages 335–336, 1998.

[9] H. Chen and D. R. Karger. Less is more: probabilistic models for retrieving fewer relevant documents. In *SIGIR*, pages 429–436, 2006.

[10] C. L. A. Clarke, M. Kolla, G. V. Cormack, O. Vechtomova, A. Ashkan, S. Büttcher, and I. MacKinnon. Novelty and

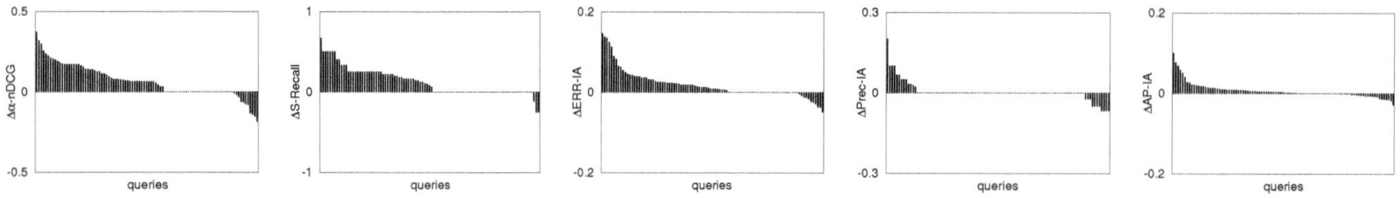

Figure 2: Per query performance differences of PSVM$_{div}$ against SVM$_{div}$. The figures shown are for α-nDCG, S-Recall, ERR-IA, Prec-IA and MAP-IA, respectively. A bar extending above the center of a plot indicates that PSVM$_{div}$ outperforms SVM$_{div}$, and vice versa for bars extending below the center. Note that figures are not in the same scale.

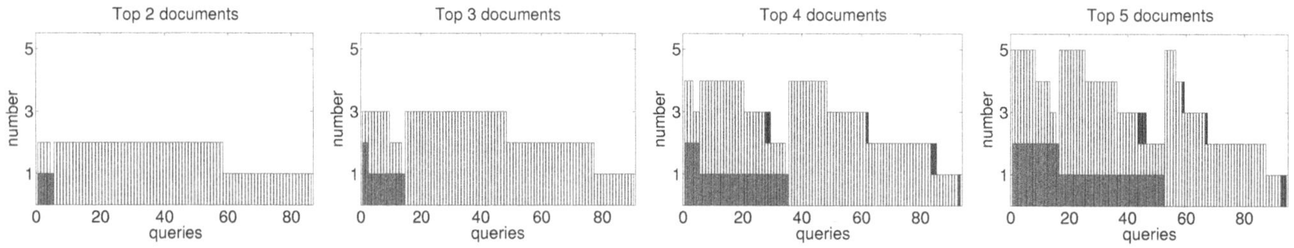

Figure 3: How runs produced by PSVM$_{div}$ and SVM$_{div}$ differ. Red, white, blue bars indicate the number of different subtopics that appear in PSVM$_{div}$ but not in SVM$_{div}$, in both runs and not in PSVM$_{div}$ but in SVM$_{div}$, respectively, at corresponding depth k (for k=2, 3, 4, 5). Figures should be viewed in color.

diversity in information retrieval evaluation. In *SIGIR*, pages 659–666, 2008.

[11] C. L. A. Clarke, N. Craswell, and E. M. Voorhees. Overview of the TREC 2012 web track. In *TREC*, pages 1–8, 2012.

[12] V. Dang and W. B. Croft. Diversity by proportionality: An election-based approach to search result diversification. In *SIGIR*, pages 65–74, 2012.

[13] V. Dang and W. B. Croft. Term level search result diversification. In *SIGIR*, pages 603–612, 2013.

[14] S. Jameel and W. Lam. An unsupervised topic segmentation model incorporating word order. In *SIGIR*, pages 203–212, 2013.

[15] S. Khuller, A. Moss, and J. S. Naor. The budgeted maximum coverage problem. *Inf. Proc. Lett.*, 70(1):39–45, 1999.

[16] S. Liang, Z. Ren, and M. de Rijke. Fusion helps diversification. In *SIGIR*, 2014.

[17] C. Liu, N. J. Belkin, and M. J. Cole. Personalization of search results using interaction behaviors in search sessions. In *SIGIR*, 2012.

[18] J. S. Liu. The collapsed Gibbs sampler in Bayesian computations with applications to a gene regulation problem. *J. Am. Stat. Assoc.*, 89(427):958–966, 1994.

[19] F. Radlinski and S. Dumais. Improving personalized web search using result diversification. In *SIGIR*, pages 691–692. ACM, 2006.

[20] S. E. Robertson and D. A. Hull. The TREC-9 filtering track final report. In *TREC*, pages 25–40, 2000.

[21] R. L. Santos, C. Macdonald, and I. Ounis. Exploiting query reformulations for web search result diversification. In *WWW*, pages 881–890, 2010.

[22] X. Shen, B. Tan, and C. Zhai. Implicit user modeling for personalized search. In *CIKM*, pages 824–831. ACM, 2005.

[23] Y. Shi, X. Zhao, J. Wang, M. Larson, and A. Hanjalic. Adaptive diversification of recommendation results via latent factor portfolio. In *SIGIR*, pages 175–184. ACM, 2012.

[24] J. Tang, M. Zhang, and Q. Mei. One theme in all views: Modeling consensus topics in multiple contexts. In *KDD*, pages 5–13, 2013.

[25] I. Tsochantaridis, T. Joachims, T. Hofmann, and Y. Altun. Large margin methods for structured and interdependent output variables. *J. Mach. Learn. Res.*, 6:1453–1484, 2005.

[26] D. Vallet and P. Castells. Personalized diversification of search results. In *SIGIR'12*, 2012.

[27] D. Vallet, I. Cantador, and J. M. Jose. Personalizing web search with folksonomy-based user and document profiles. In *ECIR*, pages 420–431. Springer, 2010.

[28] S. Vargas, P. Castells, and D. Vallet. Explicit relevance models in intent-oriented information retrieval diversification. In *SIGIR*, pages 75–84, 2012.

[29] H. Wang, X. He, M.-W. Chang, Y. Song, R. W. White, and W. Chu. Personalized ranking model adaptation for web search. In *SIGIR*, pages 323–332, 2013.

[30] X. Wang and A. McCallum. Topics over time: A non-markov continuous-time model of topical trends. In *KDD*, pages 424–433, 2006.

[31] Q. Yuan, G. Cong, Z. Ma, A. Sun, and N. M. Thalmann. Who, where, when and what: Discover spatio-temporal topics for twitter users. In *KDD*, pages 605–613, 2013.

[32] Y. Yue and T. Joachims. Predicting diverse subsets using structural svms. In *ICML*, pages 1224–1231. ACM, 2008.

[33] Y. Yue, T. Finley, F. Radlinski, and T. Joachims. A support vector method for optimizing average precision. In *SIGIR*, pages 271–278. ACM, 2007.

[34] C. Zhai and J. Lafferty. A study of smoothing methods for language models applied to ad hoc information retrieval. In *SIGIR*, pages 334–342, 2001.

[35] C. Zhai, W. W. Cohen, and J. Lafferty. Beyond independent relevance: methods and evaluation metrics for subtopic retrieval. In *SIGIR*, pages 10–17, 2003.

[36] S.-X. Zhang and M. Gales. Structured SVMs for automatic speech recognition. *IEEE Trans. on Audio, Speech, and Lang. Proc.*, 21(3):544–555, 2013.

[37] J. Zhu, X. Zheng, L. Zhou, and B. Zhang. Scalable inference in max-margin topic models. In *KDD*, pages 964–972, 2013.

Efficient Multi-Task Feature Learning with Calibration

Pinghua Gong[1,2], Jiayu Zhou[1,2], Wei Fan[3], Jieping Ye[1,2]
[1]Center for Evolutionary Medicine and Informatics, The Biodesign Institute, ASU, Tempe, AZ 85287
[2]Department of Computer Science and Engineering, ASU, Tempe, AZ 85287
[3]Huawei Noah's Ark Lab, Hong Kong, China
[1,2]{pinghua.gong, jiayu.zhou, jieping.ye}@asu.edu, [3]david.fanwei@huawei.com

ABSTRACT

Multi-task feature learning has been proposed to improve the generalization performance by learning the shared features among multiple related tasks and it has been successfully applied to many real-world problems in machine learning, data mining, computer vision and bioinformatics. Most existing multi-task feature learning models simply assume a common noise level for all tasks, which may not be the case in real applications. Recently, a Calibrated Multivariate Regression (CMR) model has been proposed, which calibrates different tasks with respect to their noise levels and achieves superior prediction performance over the non-calibrated one. A major challenge is how to solve the CMR model efficiently as it is formulated as a composite optimization problem consisting of two non-smooth terms. In this paper, we propose a variant of the calibrated multi-task feature learning formulation by including a squared norm regularizer. We show that the dual problem of the proposed formulation is a smooth optimization problem with a piecewise sphere constraint. The simplicity of the dual problem enables us to develop fast dual optimization algorithms with low per-iteration cost. We also provide a detailed convergence analysis for the proposed dual optimization algorithm. Empirical studies demonstrate that, the dual optimization algorithm quickly converges and it is much more efficient than the primal optimization algorithm. Moreover, the calibrated multi-task feature learning algorithms with and without the squared norm regularizer achieve similar prediction performance and both outperform the non-calibrated ones. Thus, the proposed variant not only enables us to develop fast optimization algorithms, but also keeps the superior prediction performance of the calibrated multi-task feature learning over the non-calibrated one.

Categories and Subject Descriptors

H.2.8 [**Database Management**]: Database Applications—*Data Mining*

KDD'14, August 24–27, 2014, New York, NY, USA.

ACM 978-1-4503-2956-9/14/08 ...$15.00.
http://dx.doi.org/10.1145/2623330.2623641.

Keywords

Multi-task learning; feature selection; calibration; dual problem; accelerated gradient descent

1. INTRODUCTION

Multi-task feature learning aims to improve the generalization performance by learning multiple related tasks together and exploring the shared features among tasks. It has received a lot of interests and has been successfully applied to a wide range of applications including gene data analysis [18], breast cancer classification [34], neural semantic basis discovery [21] and disease progression prediction [36, 37]. Most existing multi-task feature learning models can be formulated as a regularized optimization problem and they usually focus on how to design a good regularizer to capture the underlying shared features among tasks; examples include group lasso multi-task feature learning [1, 19, 23, 25, 29, 33, 34], tree-guided group lasso multi-task feature learning [18], composite regularized multi-task feature learning [14, 16] and non-convex regularized multi-task feature learning [13, 15].

However, most existing multi-task feature learning models simply assume a common noise level for all tasks, which may not hold in real applications. Moreover, theoretical analysis in Lounici et al. [26] shows that, to achieve the optimal parameter estimation error bounds, the regularized parameter should be chosen in proportion to the maximum standard deviations of the noise for all tasks. In practice, the standard deviations of the noise are unknown or very difficult to estimate, which makes the parameter tuning quite challenging. To this end, Liu et al. [22] propose a Calibrated Multivariate Regression (CMR) model which calibrates each task by employing different noise levels for all tasks and achieve superior prediction performance over the non-calibrated one. Moreover, their theoretical analysis shows that the CMR model can achieve the optimal parameter estimation error bounds by properly tuning the regularized parameter which does not depend on the standard deviations of the noise for all tasks. This makes the parameter tuning of the CMR model much more insensitive to the noise levels. However, one major challenge in the practical use of the CMR model is that it is formulated as a composite optimization problem consisting of two non-smooth terms, which makes the optimization problem challenging to solve.

In this paper, inspired by the great success of the elastic net [38], we propose a variant of the calibrated multi-task feature learning formulation by including a squared norm regularizer. The major contributions of this paper include:

(1) We show that the dual problem of the proposed formulation is a smooth optimization problem with a piecewise sphere constraint. (2) The simplicity of the dual problem enables us to develop fast dual optimization algorithms with low per-iteration cost. (3) We provide a detailed convergence analysis for the proposed algorithm. (4) Experimental results demonstrate that, the dual optimization algorithm quickly converges and it is much more efficient than the primal optimization algorithm. Moreover, the calibrated multi-task feature learning algorithms with and without the squared norm regularizer achieve similar prediction performance and both outperform the non-calibrated ones. These results demonstrate that the proposed variant not only enables us to develop fast optimization algorithms, but also keeps the superior prediction performance of the calibrated multi-task feature learning over the non-calibrated one.

The rest of the paper is organized as follows: We introduce preliminaries in Section 2. We propose a variant of the multi-task feature formulation and develop fast optimization algorithms in Section 3. We report experimental results in Section 4 and we conclude in Section 5.

2. PRELIMINARIES

Assume that we are given m learning tasks associated with the data $\{(X_1, \mathbf{y}_1), \cdots, (X_m, \mathbf{y}_m)\}$ and a linear model:

$$\mathbf{y}_i = X_i \mathbf{w}_i^\star + \boldsymbol{\epsilon}_i, \; i \in \{1, \cdots, m\},$$

where $X_i \in \mathbb{R}^{n_i \times d}$ is the data matrix and $\mathbf{y}_i \in \mathbb{R}^{n_i}$ is the response vector for the i-th task, respectively; $\mathbf{w}_i^\star \in \mathbb{R}^d$ is the underlying true weight and $\boldsymbol{\epsilon}_i \in \mathbb{R}^{n_i}$ is the noise vector for the i-th task, respectively; each entry of $\boldsymbol{\epsilon}_i$ is sampled from the normal distribution with mean zero and standard deviation σ_i. The ordinary (non-calibrated) multi-task feature learning model is formulated as the following problem:

$$\min_{W \in \mathbb{R}^{d\times m}} \left\{ \sum_{i=1}^m \|X_i \mathbf{w}_i - \mathbf{y}_i\|^2 + \lambda r(W) \right\}, \tag{1}$$

where $\|\cdot\|$ is the Euclidean norm; $W = [\mathbf{w}_1, \cdots, \mathbf{w}_m] \in \mathbb{R}^{d\times m}$ is the weight matrix with the i-th column $\mathbf{w}_i \in \mathbb{R}^d$ being the weight vector for the i-th task; $\lambda > 0$ is a regularized parameter; $r(W)$ is a model-specific regularizer (such as group lasso, tree-guided group lasso, a composite regularizer and a non-convex regularizer). To calibrate each task by considering the different noise levels of all tasks, Liu et al. [22] propose to use the square-root function [6, 11] instead of the least squares function, resulting in the following Calibrated Multivariate Regression (CMR) model:

$$\min_{W \in \mathbb{R}^{d\times m}} \left\{ \sum_{i=1}^m \|X_i \mathbf{w}_i - \mathbf{y}_i\| + \lambda r(W) \right\}. \tag{2}$$

Liu et al. [22] interpret the CMR model in Eq. (2) as the following weighted regularized least squares problem:

$$\min_{W \in \mathbb{R}^{d\times m}} \left\{ \sum_{i=1}^m \frac{1}{\sigma_i \sqrt{n_i}} \|X_i \mathbf{w}_i - \mathbf{y}_i\|^2 + \lambda r(W) \right\}, \tag{3}$$

where $\frac{1}{\sigma_i \sqrt{n_i}}$ is the weight for calibrating the i-th task. When we do not have any prior knowledge on σ_i's, σ_i is chosen as

$$\sigma_i = \frac{1}{\sqrt{n_i}} \|X_i \mathbf{w}_i - \mathbf{y}_i\|, \; i \in \{1, \cdots, m\}. \tag{4}$$

Thus, using the weight defined in Eq. (4), the CMR model in Eq. (2) calibrates different tasks via solving the weighted regularized least squares model in Eq. (3). Although the Robust Feature Selection (RFS) algorithm in [28] also uses a similar square-root loss, it is quite different from the CMR model in Eq. (2) that RFS "calibrates" different samples but not different tasks via the square-root loss. Notice that the regularizer and the loss function in Eq. (2) are usually both non-smooth, which makes the optimization problem challenging to solve.

3. FORMULATION AND EFFICIENT OPTIMIZATION ALGORITHMS

Inspired by the great success of the elastic net [38], we propose a variant of the calibrated multi-task feature learning model by adding a squared norm regularizer as follows:

$$\min_{W \in \mathbb{R}^{d\times m}} \left\{ \sum_{i=1}^m \|X_i \mathbf{w}_i - \mathbf{y}_i\| + \lambda_1 \|W\|_{1,2} + \frac{\lambda_2}{2}\|W\|_F^2 \right\}, \tag{5}$$

where $\|W\|_{1,2} = \sum_{j=1}^d \|\mathbf{w}^j\|$ with $\mathbf{w}^j$ being the j-th row of W; $\|W\|_F^2 = \sum_{i=1}^m \sum_{j=1}^d w_{ij}^2$ with w_{ij} being the (i,j)-th entry of W; $\lambda_1, \lambda_2 > 0$ are regularized parameters. The major benefit of the proposed formulation is that we can derive a smooth dual optimization problem with a piecewise sphere constraint. The simplicity of the dual problem enables us to develop fast optimization algorithms with low per-iteration cost. Moreover, the proposed variant keeps the superior prediction performance of the calibrated multi-task feature learning over the non-calibrated one.

3.1 The Dual Ascent Optimization Algorithm

We first derive the dual problem of the optimization problem in Eq. (5) and then present key properties of the dual problem. Finally, we propose fast algorithms to solve the dual problem and provide detailed convergence analysis accordingly. Let $\mathbf{z}_i = X_i \mathbf{w}_i - \mathbf{y}_i$. Then Eq. (5) is equivalent to the following constrained optimization problem:

$$\min_{W,\mathbf{z}} \left\{ \sum_{i=1}^m \|\mathbf{z}_i\| + \lambda_1 \|W\|_{1,2} + \frac{\lambda_2}{2}\|W\|_F^2 \right\},$$
$$s.t. \; \mathbf{z}_i = X_i \mathbf{w}_i - \mathbf{y}_i, \; i \in \{1, \cdots, m\}, \tag{6}$$

where $\mathbf{z} = [\mathbf{z}_1^T, \cdots, \mathbf{z}_m^T]^T \in \mathbb{R}^{\sum_{i=1}^m n_i}$. It is easy to verify that the strong duality [9] holds for the optimization problem in Eq. (6). We can write down the Lagrange function of the above problem as follows:

$$\mathcal{L}(W, \mathbf{z}, \boldsymbol{\theta}) = \sum_{i=1}^m \|\mathbf{z}_i\| + \lambda_1 \|W\|_{1,2} + \frac{\lambda_2}{2}\|W\|_F^2 + \sum_{i=1}^m \boldsymbol{\theta}_i^T (X_i \mathbf{w}_i - \mathbf{y}_i - \mathbf{z}_i), \tag{7}$$

where $\boldsymbol{\theta} = [\boldsymbol{\theta}_1^T, \cdots, \boldsymbol{\theta}_m^T]^T \in \mathbb{R}^{\sum_{i=1}^m n_i}$ with $\boldsymbol{\theta}_i \in \mathbb{R}^{n_i}$ being the Lagrange multiplier corresponding to the constraint $\mathbf{z}_i = X_i \mathbf{w}_i - \mathbf{y}_i$. Minimizing $\mathcal{L}(W, \mathbf{z}, \boldsymbol{\theta})$ with respect to W and $\mathbf{z}$, we obtain the objective function of the dual problem of

Eq. (6) as follows:

$$\tilde{\mathcal{D}}(\boldsymbol{\theta}) = \min_W \left\{ \lambda_1 \|W\|_{1,2} + \frac{\lambda_2}{2}\|W\|_F^2 + \sum_{i=1}^m \boldsymbol{\theta}_i^T (X_i \mathbf{w}_i - \mathbf{y}_i) \right\} + \sum_{i=1}^m \min_{\mathbf{z}_i} \left\{ \|\mathbf{z}_i\| - \boldsymbol{\theta}_i^T \mathbf{z}_i \right\}, \quad (8)$$

where

$$\min_{\mathbf{z}_i} \left\{ \|\mathbf{z}_i\| - \boldsymbol{\theta}_i^T \mathbf{z}_i \right\} = \begin{cases} 0, & \text{if } \|\boldsymbol{\theta}_i\| \le 1, \\ -\infty, & \text{otherwise.} \end{cases} \quad (9)$$

Thus, we obtain the dual problem of Eq. (6) as follows:

$$\max_{\boldsymbol{\theta}} \mathcal{D}(\boldsymbol{\theta}), \quad s.t. \ \|\boldsymbol{\theta}_i\| \le 1, \ i \in \{1, \cdots, m\}, \quad (10)$$

where the objective function is

$$\mathcal{D}(\boldsymbol{\theta}) = \min_W \left\{ \lambda_1 \|W\|_{1,2} + \frac{\lambda_2}{2}\|W\|_F^2 + \sum_{i=1}^m \boldsymbol{\theta}_i^T (X_i \mathbf{w}_i - \mathbf{y}_i) \right\}. \quad (11)$$

We show that the optimization problem in Eq. (11) has nice properties which enable us to develop fast algorithms for solving the dual problem in Eq. (10).

THEOREM 1. *The optimization problem in Eq. (11) has a unique solution $W(\boldsymbol{\theta})$. Moreover, $\mathcal{D}(\boldsymbol{\theta})$ is continuously differentiable and L-Lipschitz continuous gradient. Specifically, the gradient of $\mathcal{D}(\boldsymbol{\theta})$ is*

$$\nabla \mathcal{D}(\boldsymbol{\theta}) = [(X_1 \mathbf{w}_1(\boldsymbol{\theta}) - \mathbf{y}_1)^T, \cdots, (X_m \mathbf{w}_m(\boldsymbol{\theta}) - \mathbf{y}_m)^T]^T, \quad (12)$$

where $\mathbf{w}_i(\boldsymbol{\theta})$ is the i-th column of $W(\boldsymbol{\theta})$. The Lipschitz constant of $\nabla \mathcal{D}(\boldsymbol{\theta})$ is

$$L = \frac{\max_{i \in \{1, \cdots, m\}} \sigma_{\max}^2(X_i)}{\lambda_2}, \quad (13)$$

where $\sigma_{\max}(X_i)$ is the largest singular value of X_i.

PROOF. Denote the objective function of the optimization problem in Eq. (11) as

$$f(W, \boldsymbol{\theta}) = \lambda_1 \|W\|_{1,2} + \frac{\lambda_2}{2}\|W\|_F^2 + \sum_{i=1}^m \boldsymbol{\theta}_i^T (X_i \mathbf{w}_i - \mathbf{y}_i). \quad (14)$$

Obviously, $f(W, \boldsymbol{\theta})$ is strongly convex and coercive with respect to W. Hence, the optimization problem in Eq. (11) has a unique solution $W(\boldsymbol{\theta})$.

To prove the remaining part of Theorem 1, we rewrite $f(W, \boldsymbol{\theta})$ in the following compact form:

$$f(W, \boldsymbol{\theta}) = \lambda_1 \|W\|_{1,2} + \frac{\lambda_2}{2}\|W\|_F^2 + \mathrm{Tr}(W^T U(\boldsymbol{\theta})) - \boldsymbol{\theta}^T \mathbf{y},$$

where $\mathrm{Tr}(\cdot)$ denotes the trace norm and

$$U(\boldsymbol{\theta}) = [X_1^T \boldsymbol{\theta}_1, \cdots, X_m^T \boldsymbol{\theta}_m] \in \mathbb{R}^{d \times m},$$
$$\boldsymbol{\theta} = [\boldsymbol{\theta}_1^T, \cdots, \boldsymbol{\theta}_m^T]^T \in \mathbb{R}^{\sum_{i=1}^m n_i},$$
$$\mathbf{y} = [\mathbf{y}_1^T, \cdots, \mathbf{y}_m^T]^T \in \mathbb{R}^{\sum_{i=1}^m n_i}.$$

Denote

$$g(W) = \lambda_1 \|W\|_{1,2} + \frac{\lambda_2}{2}\|W\|_F^2. \quad (15)$$

Then we have

$$\begin{aligned} \mathcal{D}(\boldsymbol{\theta}) &= \min_W \left\{ f(W, \boldsymbol{\theta}) = g(W) + \mathrm{Tr}(W^T U(\boldsymbol{\theta})) - \boldsymbol{\theta}^T \mathbf{y} \right\} \\ &= -\max_W \left\{ \mathrm{Tr}(-W^T U(\boldsymbol{\theta})) - g(W) \right\} - \boldsymbol{\theta}^T \mathbf{y} \\ &= -g^\star(-U(\boldsymbol{\theta})) - \boldsymbol{\theta}^T \mathbf{y}, \end{aligned} \quad (16)$$

where $g^\star(\cdot)$ is the conjugate function of $g(\cdot)$. Recalling the definition of $g(\cdot)$ in Eq. (15), we know that $g(\cdot)$ is a proper, lower semi-continuous and convex function. Thus, we have $g^{\star\star}(\cdot) = g(\cdot)$ and $g^\star(\cdot)$ is also a proper, lower semi-continuous and convex function. Moreover, $g(\cdot)$ is strongly convex with the parameter λ_2. Thus, by Proposition 12.60 in [31], we obtain that $g^\star(\cdot)$ is continuously differentiable and $\nabla g^\star(\cdot)$ is Lipschitz continuous with constant $1/\lambda_2$. Hence, $\mathcal{D}(\boldsymbol{\theta})$ is continuously differentiable. Noting that $W(\boldsymbol{\theta})$ is the minimizer of the optimization problem in Eq. (11), we have

$$W(\boldsymbol{\theta}) = \arg\max_W \left\{ \mathrm{Tr}(-W^T U(\boldsymbol{\theta})) - g(W) \right\},$$

and hence

$$-U(\boldsymbol{\theta}) \in \partial g(W(\boldsymbol{\theta})).$$

According to Corollary 23.5.1 in [30], we have $-U(\boldsymbol{\theta}) \in \partial g(W(\boldsymbol{\theta}))$ if and only if $W(\boldsymbol{\theta}) = \nabla g^\star(-U(\boldsymbol{\theta}))$, which together with Eq. (16) and the definition of $U(\boldsymbol{\theta})$ implies that

$$\begin{aligned} \nabla \mathcal{D}(\boldsymbol{\theta}) &= X \mathbf{s}(\boldsymbol{\theta}) - \mathbf{y} \\ &= [(X_1 \mathbf{w}_1(\boldsymbol{\theta}))^T, \cdots, (X_m \mathbf{w}_m(\boldsymbol{\theta}))^T]^T - \mathbf{y}, \end{aligned} \quad (17)$$

where

$$X = \begin{bmatrix} X_1 & & \\ & \ddots & \\ & & X_m \end{bmatrix}, \mathbf{s}(\boldsymbol{\theta}) = \begin{bmatrix} \nabla_1 g^\star(-U(\boldsymbol{\theta})) \\ \vdots \\ \nabla_m g^\star(-U(\boldsymbol{\theta})) \end{bmatrix}$$

with $\nabla_i g^\star(-U(\boldsymbol{\theta}))$ being the partial derivative of $g^\star(-U(\boldsymbol{\theta}))$ with respect to the i-th column of $-U(\boldsymbol{\theta})$. Thus, Eq. (12) immediately follows from Eq. (17). Moreover, for any $\boldsymbol{\theta}, \boldsymbol{\gamma} \in \mathbb{R}^{\sum_{i=1}^m n_i}$, we have

$$\|\nabla \mathcal{D}(\boldsymbol{\theta}) - \nabla \mathcal{D}(\boldsymbol{\gamma})\| = \|X(\mathbf{s}(\boldsymbol{\theta}) - \mathbf{s}(\boldsymbol{\gamma}))\|,$$

Recalling that $\nabla g^\star(\cdot)$ is Lipschitz continuous with constant $1/\lambda_2$, we have

$$\begin{aligned} &\|\nabla \mathcal{D}(\boldsymbol{\theta}) - \nabla \mathcal{D}(\boldsymbol{\gamma})\| \le \sigma_{\max}(X)\|\mathbf{s}(\boldsymbol{\theta}) - \mathbf{s}(\boldsymbol{\gamma})\| \\ &\le \frac{\sigma_{\max}(X)}{\lambda_2}\|U(\boldsymbol{\theta}) - U(\boldsymbol{\gamma})\|_F = \frac{\sigma_{\max}(X)}{\lambda_2}\|X^T(\boldsymbol{\theta} - \boldsymbol{\gamma})\| \\ &\le \frac{\sigma_{\max}^2(X)}{\lambda_2}\|\boldsymbol{\theta} - \boldsymbol{\gamma}\|, \end{aligned}$$

where $\sigma_{\max}(X)$ is the largest singular value of X. By noticing that X is a block diagonal matrix, we have

$$\|\nabla \mathcal{D}(\boldsymbol{\theta}) - \nabla \mathcal{D}(\boldsymbol{\gamma})\| \le \frac{\max_{i \in \{1, \cdots, m\}} \sigma_{\max}^2(X_i)}{\lambda_2}\|\boldsymbol{\theta} - \boldsymbol{\gamma}\|.$$

That is, $\nabla \mathcal{D}(\boldsymbol{\theta})$ is Lipschitz continuous with constant L defined in Eq. (13). □

REMARK 1. *The squared norm regularizer $\frac{\lambda_2}{2}\|W\|_F^2$ in Eq. (5) is critical for the establishment of Theorem 1 and hence is crucial to develop fast optimization algorithms on solving the dual problem in Eq. (10).*

Based on Theorem 1, we know that the objective function of the dual problem in Eq. (10) is smooth (Lipschitz continuous gradient) and the constraint is a piecewise sphere. Thus, we can use the framework of FISTA [4, 24, 12, 2] to solve the dual problem in Eq. (10). We present the pseudo codes in Algorithm 1. Notice that the dual problem in Eq. (10) is a *maximization* problem. Therefore, the gradient projection step in Eq. (20) and the line search criterion in Eq. (21) are modified accordingly.

In Algorithm 1, there are two critical steps. In the following, we show that both steps have closed-form solutions with low cost. The first critical step is how to efficiently compute the dual objective function value $\mathcal{D}(\boldsymbol{\theta})$ and the gradient $\nabla\mathcal{D}(\boldsymbol{\theta})$, which depends on how to efficiently obtain the optimal solution $W(\boldsymbol{\theta})$ for the problem in Eq. (11). Next, we show how to efficiently solve the optimization problem in Eq. (11). By exploring the special structure of Eq. (11), we have for all $j \in \{1, \cdots, d\}$:

$$\mathbf{w}^j(\boldsymbol{\theta}) = \arg\min_{\mathbf{w}^j} \left\{ \frac{\lambda_2}{2}\|\mathbf{w}^j\|^2 + \mathbf{u}^j(\boldsymbol{\theta})(\mathbf{w}^j)^T + \lambda_1\|\mathbf{w}^j\| \right\}, \tag{18}$$

where $\mathbf{w}^j(\boldsymbol{\theta}), \mathbf{w}^j$ and $\mathbf{u}^j(\boldsymbol{\theta})$ are the j-th row of $W(\boldsymbol{\theta}), W$ and $U(\boldsymbol{\theta}) = [X_1^T\boldsymbol{\theta}_1, \cdots, X_m^T\boldsymbol{\theta}_m]$, respectively. Eq. (18) has the following closed-form solution [14, 23]:

$$\begin{aligned}\mathbf{w}^j(\boldsymbol{\theta}) &= \arg\min_{\mathbf{w}^j} \left\{ \frac{\lambda_2}{2}\left\|\mathbf{w}^j + \frac{\mathbf{u}^j(\boldsymbol{\theta})}{\lambda_2}\right\|^2 + \lambda_1\|\mathbf{w}^j\| \right\} \\ &= \arg\min_{\mathbf{w}^j} \left\{ \frac{1}{2}\left\|\mathbf{w}^j + \frac{\mathbf{u}^j(\boldsymbol{\theta})}{\lambda_2}\right\|^2 + \frac{\lambda_1}{\lambda_2}\|\mathbf{w}^j\| \right\} \\ &= -\frac{1}{\lambda_2}\max\left(0, 1 - \frac{\lambda_1}{\|\mathbf{u}^j(\boldsymbol{\theta})\|}\right)\mathbf{u}^j(\boldsymbol{\theta}). \end{aligned} \tag{19}$$

The second critical step is how to efficiently solve the gradient projection subproblem. Due to the simplicity of the piecewise sphere constraint, the gradient projection subproblem has a closed-form solution in Eq. (20).

By Theorem 4.4 in [4], we have the following result.

THEOREM 2. *(Theorem 4.4 [4]) Let $\{\boldsymbol{\theta}^k\}$ be the sequence generated by Algorithm 1 and $\boldsymbol{\theta}^\star$ be an optimal solution for the problem in Eq. (10). Then for all $k \geq 1$, we have*

$$\mathcal{D}(\boldsymbol{\theta}^\star) - \mathcal{D}(\boldsymbol{\theta}^k) \leq \frac{2\beta L\|\boldsymbol{\theta}^0 - \boldsymbol{\theta}^\star\|^2}{(k+1)^2},$$

where $\boldsymbol{\theta}^0$ is the initial point; $\beta > 1$ is the factor used in the line search (β is defined in Algorithm 1); L is the Lipschitz constant defined in Eq. (13).

Based on Theorem 2, we establish a convergence rate for the sequence $\{W^k\}$ generated by Algorithm 1 in the following theorem:

THEOREM 3. *Let $\{W^k\}$ and $\{\boldsymbol{\theta}^k\}$ be the sequences generated by Algorithm 1, and let $W^\star$ and $\boldsymbol{\theta}^\star$ be any optimal solutions for the problems in Eq. (5) and Eq. (10), respectively. Then for all $k \geq 1$, we have*

$$\|W^k - W^\star\|_F \leq 2\sqrt{\frac{\beta L}{\lambda_2}}\frac{\|\boldsymbol{\theta}^0 - \boldsymbol{\theta}^\star\|}{k+1}.$$

Algorithm 1: Accelerated Dual Ascent Algorithm

Input : $\boldsymbol{\theta}^0 \in \mathbb{R}^{\sum_{i=1}^m n_i}$, $\eta_0 > 0$, $\beta > 1$

Initialize $\boldsymbol{\theta}^1 \leftarrow \boldsymbol{\theta}^0$; $t_0 \leftarrow 1$; $t_1 \leftarrow 1$;

for $k = 1, 2, \cdots$ **do**

  $\alpha_k \leftarrow \frac{t_{k-1}-1}{t_k}$;

  $\boldsymbol{\nu}^k \leftarrow \boldsymbol{\theta}^k + \alpha_k(\boldsymbol{\theta}^k - \boldsymbol{\theta}^{k-1})$;

  for $j = 0, 1, 2, \cdots$ **do**

    $\eta_k \leftarrow \beta^j \eta_{k-1}$;

    Compute $\boldsymbol{\theta}^k$ via gradient projection:

$$\boldsymbol{\theta}^k = \left[\frac{(\tilde{\boldsymbol{\nu}}_1^k)^T}{\max(1, \|\tilde{\boldsymbol{\nu}}_1^k\|)}, \cdots, \frac{(\tilde{\boldsymbol{\nu}}_m^k)^T}{\max(1, \|\tilde{\boldsymbol{\nu}}_m^k\|)}\right]^T \text{ with}$$
$$\left[(\tilde{\boldsymbol{\nu}}_1^k)^T, \cdots, (\tilde{\boldsymbol{\nu}}_m^k)^T\right]^T = \tilde{\boldsymbol{\nu}}^k = \boldsymbol{\nu}^k + \frac{1}{\eta_k}\nabla\mathcal{D}(\boldsymbol{\nu}^k). \tag{20}$$

    if *the following line search criterion*

$$\mathcal{D}(\boldsymbol{\theta}^k) \geq \mathcal{D}(\boldsymbol{\nu}^k) + \nabla\mathcal{D}(\boldsymbol{\nu}^k)^T(\boldsymbol{\theta}^k - \boldsymbol{\nu}^k) - \frac{\eta_k}{2}\|\boldsymbol{\theta}^k - \boldsymbol{\nu}^k\|^2 \tag{21}$$

    is satisfied **then**

      break;

    end

  end

  Compute $W^k \leftarrow W(\boldsymbol{\theta}^k)$ via Eq. (19);

  if *some convergence criterion is satisfied* **then**

    Let $\boldsymbol{\theta}^\star \leftarrow \boldsymbol{\theta}^k$ and $W^\star \leftarrow W^k$;

    break;

  end

  $t_{k+1} \leftarrow \frac{1+\sqrt{1+4t_k^2}}{2}$;

end

Output: $\boldsymbol{\theta}^\star$, $W^\star$

PROOF. We follow the proof of Theorem 4.1 in [5]. Denote

$$h(\mathbf{z}, \boldsymbol{\theta}) = \sum_{i=1}^m \left\{\|\mathbf{z}_i\| - \boldsymbol{\theta}_i^T\mathbf{z}_i\right\}, \tag{22}$$

$$\mathbf{z}^k \in \arg\min_{\mathbf{z}} h(\mathbf{z}, \boldsymbol{\theta}^k), \tag{23}$$

where $\{\boldsymbol{\theta}^k\}$ is the sequence generated by Algorithm 1. Considering Eqs. (7), (14), (22) together, we have

$$\mathcal{L}(W, \mathbf{z}, \boldsymbol{\theta}^k) = f(W, \boldsymbol{\theta}^k) + h(\mathbf{z}, \boldsymbol{\theta}^k). \tag{24}$$

From Algorithm 1, we have

$$W^k = W(\boldsymbol{\theta}^k) = \arg\min_W f(W, \boldsymbol{\theta}^k). \tag{25}$$

By the optimality condition of Eq. (25), we have

$$O \in \partial_{W^k} f(W^k, \boldsymbol{\theta}^k), \tag{26}$$

where O denotes the zero matrix and $\partial_{W^k} f(W^k, \boldsymbol{\theta}^k)$ denotes the sub-differential of $f(W, \boldsymbol{\theta}^k)$ with respect to W at the point $W = W^k$. Recalling that $f(W, \boldsymbol{\theta}^k)$ is strongly convex with respect to W with the parameter λ_2, which together with Eq. (26) implies that for all $W \in \mathbb{R}^{d\times m}$

$$f(W, \boldsymbol{\theta}^k) - f(W^k, \boldsymbol{\theta}^k) \geq \frac{\lambda_2}{2}\|W - W^k\|_F^2. \tag{27}$$

By Eq. (23), we have for all $\mathbf{z} \in \mathbb{R}^{\sum_{i=1}^m n_i}$

$$h(\mathbf{z}, \boldsymbol{\theta}^k) - h(\mathbf{z}^k, \boldsymbol{\theta}^k) \geq 0. \quad (28)$$

Adding Eqs. (27), (28) together and considering Eq. (24), we have for all $W \in \mathbb{R}^{d\times m}$ and $\mathbf{z} \in \mathbb{R}^{\sum_{i=1}^m n_i}$:

$$\mathcal{L}(W, \mathbf{z}, \boldsymbol{\theta}^k) - \mathcal{L}(W^k, \mathbf{z}^k, \boldsymbol{\theta}^k) \geq \frac{\lambda_2}{2}\|W - W^k\|_F^2. \quad (29)$$

From Eqs. (11), (25), we know that

$$\mathcal{D}(\boldsymbol{\theta}^k) = f(W^k, \boldsymbol{\theta}^k). \quad (30)$$

Recalling that the sequence $\{\boldsymbol{\theta}^k\} = \{[(\boldsymbol{\theta}_1^k)^T, \cdots, (\boldsymbol{\theta}_m^k)^T]^T\}$ satisfies the constraint in Eq. (10) and considering Eqs. (9), (23), we have for all $k \geq 1$:

$$h(\mathbf{z}^k, \boldsymbol{\theta}^k) = 0,$$

which together with Eqs. (24), (30) implies that

$$\mathcal{D}(\boldsymbol{\theta}^k) = \mathcal{L}(W^k, \mathbf{z}^k, \boldsymbol{\theta}^k). \quad (31)$$

Denote by $(W^\star, \mathbf{z}^\star)$ as an optimal solution for the optimization problem in Eq. (6). Then by the equality constraint in Eq. (6), we have for all $i \in \{1, \cdots, m\}$

$$\mathbf{z}^\star = X_i\mathbf{w}_i^\star - \mathbf{y}_i,$$

which together with Eq. (7) implies that

$$\mathcal{L}(W^\star, \mathbf{z}^\star, \boldsymbol{\theta}^k) = \sum_{i=1}^m \|\mathbf{z}_i^\star\| + \lambda_1\|W^\star\|_{1,2} + \frac{\lambda_2}{2}\|W^\star\|_F^2. \quad (32)$$

Noticing that Eq. (32) attains the minimum objective function value in Eq. (6) and strong duality holds for the optimization problem in Eq. (6), we have

$$\mathcal{D}(\boldsymbol{\theta}^\star) = \mathcal{L}(W^\star, \mathbf{z}^\star, \boldsymbol{\theta}^k), \quad (33)$$

where $\boldsymbol{\theta}^\star$ is an optimal solution of the dual problem in Eq. (10). Substituting $W = W^\star, \mathbf{z} = \mathbf{z}^\star$ into Eq. (29) and considering Eqs. (31), (33), we obtain

$$\mathcal{D}(\boldsymbol{\theta}^\star) - \mathcal{D}(\boldsymbol{\theta}^k) \geq \frac{\lambda_2}{2}\|W^\star - W^k\|_F^2,$$

which together with Theorem 2 immediately implies that the inequality in Theorem 3 holds. □

REMARK 2. *In additional to FISTA [4], we can use many other optimization algorithms to solve the dual problem in Eq. (10). For example, the SpaRSA framework [32] can be adopted to efficiently solve the dual problem. The theoretical convergence rate of SpaRSA is no better than that of FISTA. However, due to the utilization of the Barzilai-Borwein (BB) rule [3, 32], the empirical convergence performance of SpaRSA is much better than that of FISTA for solving the dual problem in Eq. (10) [see Section 4.2].*

3.2 Discussion

Notice that the objective function in Eq. (5) consists of a differentiable term $\frac{\lambda_2}{2}\|W\|_F^2$ and a non-differentiable term $\sum_{i=1}^m \|X_i\mathbf{w}_i - \mathbf{y}_i\| + \lambda_1\|W\|_{1,2}$. Theoretically, we can use the framework of FISTA [4] to directly solve the optimization problem in Eq. (5), achieving a convergence rate of $O(1/k^2)$. If we additionally consider the strong convexity of the objective function in Eq. (5), the proximal gradient method (PGM) can achieve a geometrically linear convergence rate. However, both FISTA and PGM are not practical for directly solving the optimization problem in Eq. (5). Specifically, *at each iteration* of both FISTA and PGM, we need to solve the following proximal operator problem:

$$\min_W \left\{\frac{1}{2}\|W - B\|_F^2 + \rho\left(\sum_{i=1}^m \|X_i\mathbf{w}_i - \mathbf{y}_i\| + \lambda_1\|W\|_{1,2}\right)\right\},$$

where $B \in \mathbb{R}^{d\times m}$ and $\rho > 0$ are both constant with respect to W. Obviously, solving the above proximal operator problem is as difficult as solving the original optimization problem in Eq. (5).

We can also use a similar primal smoothed optimization algorithm (more details are provided in the Appendix A) proposed in [22] to solve the primal problem in Eq. (5) directly. One problem is that the smoothing parameter is quite challenging to tune while this parameter is crucial to the convergence performance of the SPG algorithm.

Another approach which can solve the optimization problem in Eq. (5) is the Alternating Direction Method of Multipliers (ADMM) method [8] (more details are provided in the Appendix B). One problem is that, at each step, we need to solve a Lasso problem which does *not* admit a closed-form solution. Moreover, the penalty parameter is very hard to tune while this parameter is critical for the efficiency of the ADMM method.

A very straightforward approach to solve the optimization problem in Eq. (5) is the sub-gradient method [10]. In the non-smooth case, the objective function value sequence $\{l(W^k)\}$ generated by the sub-gradient method converges to the optimal value $l^\star$ at a rate of $O(1/\sqrt{k})$ under certain conditions [10], where $l(W)$ denotes the objective function in Eq. (5). However, this convergence rate is established without exploiting the strong convexity of the objective function $l(W)$. By considering the strong convexity of $l(W)$, Beck and Teboulle [5] show that the convergence rate of the objective function value has been improved from $O(1/\sqrt{k})$ to $O(\ln(k)/k)$ using the sub-gradient method. However, the sub-gradient method still converges slowly because the sub-gradient method is a very general method for solving non-smooth optimization problems without exploring the special structure of Eq. (5) and the step size at each step is shrinking to zero (or the step size is a very small constant).

The cutting plane method [7] and the level set method [20] are another two approaches which can solve the optimization problem in Eq. (5). They can be viewed as improved methods of the sub-gradient method. Similar to the sub-gradient method, the cutting plane and the level set methods are general methods for solving non-smooth optimization problems and do not exploit the the special structure of Eq. (5).

4. EXPERIMENTS

In this section, we first evaluate the prediction performance of the calibrated multi-task feature algorithms with and without the squared norm regularizer. Then, we present computational efficiency studies for our proposed algorithms. Matlab codes are included at MALSAR package [35].

4.1 Prediction Performance

We include the following algorithms for comparison: (1) **Calibration**: the calibrated multi-task feature learning formulation in Eq. (5) by setting $\lambda_2 = 0$; (2) **Calibration-**

Table 1: **The averaged MSE (standard deviation) over 10 random splittings of training and test samples. Training ratio refers to the ratio of training samples to the total samples.**

data sets	training ratio	Calibration	Calibration-L2	LeastSquares	LeastSquares-L2
Synthetic	60%	*11.73(0.37)*	11.80(0.42)	12.03(0.29)	12.03(0.29)
	70%	9.19(0.43)	*9.18(0.40)*	10.09(0.49)	10.09(0.49)
	80%	*7.24(0.42)*	7.25(0.42)	8.28(0.65)	8.28(0.65)
ADNI ADAS-Cog	60%	*37.27(2.31)*	37.45(2.24)	38.92(2.75)	39.02(2.81)
	70%	*32.95(1.88)*	33.57(2.21)	34.19(1.99)	34.15(1.98)
	80%	27.11(2.12)	*26.73(1.72)*	27.38(1.82)	27.35(1.75)
ADNI MMSE	60%	21.93(0.87)	*21.80(0.97)*	23.63(0.71)	23.69(0.71)
	70%	18.75(0.24)	*18.52(0.39)*	20.26(0.86)	20.30(0.87)
	80%	15.20(1.00)	*15.08(1.12)*	16.53(0.76)	16.54(0.78)

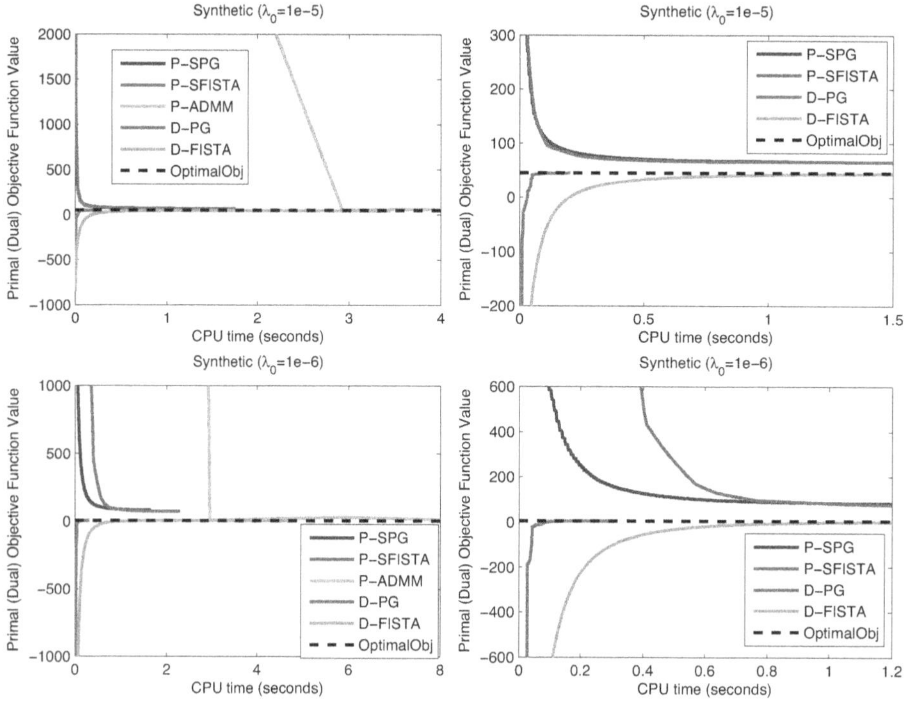

Figure 1: The primal objective function value (P-SPG, P-SFISTA and P-ADMM) and the dual objective function value (D-PG and D-FISTA) vs. CPU time (seconds) plots on the Synthetic data set. The right figures are magnified views of the left figures. The legend "PrimalObj" denotes the optimal primal objective function value in Eq. (5) and regularized parameters are set as $\lambda_1 = \lambda_2 = \lambda_0 \sum_{i=1}^{m} n_i$, where n_i is the number of samples from the i-th task.

L2: the calibrated multi-task feature learning formulation in Eq. (5) by setting $\lambda_2 \neq 0$; (3) **LeastSquares**: the non-calibrated multi-task feature learning formulation in Eq. (1) by setting $r(W) = \|W\|_{1,2}$; (4) **LeastSquares-L2**: the non-calibrated multi-task feature learning formulation in Eq. (1) by setting $r(W) = \|W\|_{1,2}$ and adding a squared norm regularizer $\frac{\lambda_2}{2}\|W\|_F^2$. We conduct experiments on both synthetic and real-world data sets which are described as follows:

Synthetic Data: We adopt the similar procedure in [22] to generate the synthetic data as follows: we set the number of tasks as $m = 10$ and each task has $n_i = 100$ samples which have $d = 200$ features (i.e., the dimensionality is $d = 200$); each row of the data matrix $X_i \in \mathbb{R}^{n_i \times d}$ of the i-th task is independently sampled from the multivariate normal distribution $N(\mathbf{0}, \Sigma)$ with $\sigma_{jj} = 1$ and $\sigma_{jk} = 0.5$ for all $j \neq k$, and it is normalized such that the length of each column of X_i is 1; each entry of the underlying ground truth matrix $W \in \mathbb{R}^{d \times m}$ is independently sampled from the uniform distribution $U(-10, 10)$ and then we randomly set 95% rows of W as zero vectors; each entry of the noise vector $\boldsymbol{\delta}_i \in \mathbb{R}^{n_i}$ is independently sampled from the normal distribution $N(0, \sigma_i^2)$, where $\sigma_i = 2^{-(i-1)/4}$ for $i = 1, \cdots, m$; the response vector $\mathbf{y}_i \in \mathbb{R}^{n_i}$ of the i-th task is computed by $\mathbf{y}_i = X_i\mathbf{w}_i + \sigma_{\max}\boldsymbol{\delta}_i$, where $\sigma_{\max} = 2\sqrt{2}$.

Real-World Data: We conduct experiments on two real-world data sets which are summarized as follows: (I) The Alzheimer's Disease Neuroimaging Initiative (ADNI)[1] is a longitudinal study aiming at identifying important neuroimaging biomarkers that are predictive of the progression of the Alzheimer's disease and building predictive models for prognosis of the disease. In our experiments, we use 310 MRI features from 648 patients to predict the MMSE value, which is a cognitive score that indicates the cognitive functionality of the patients. According to the medical diagnosis, there

[1] `www.loni.ucla.edu/ADNI/`

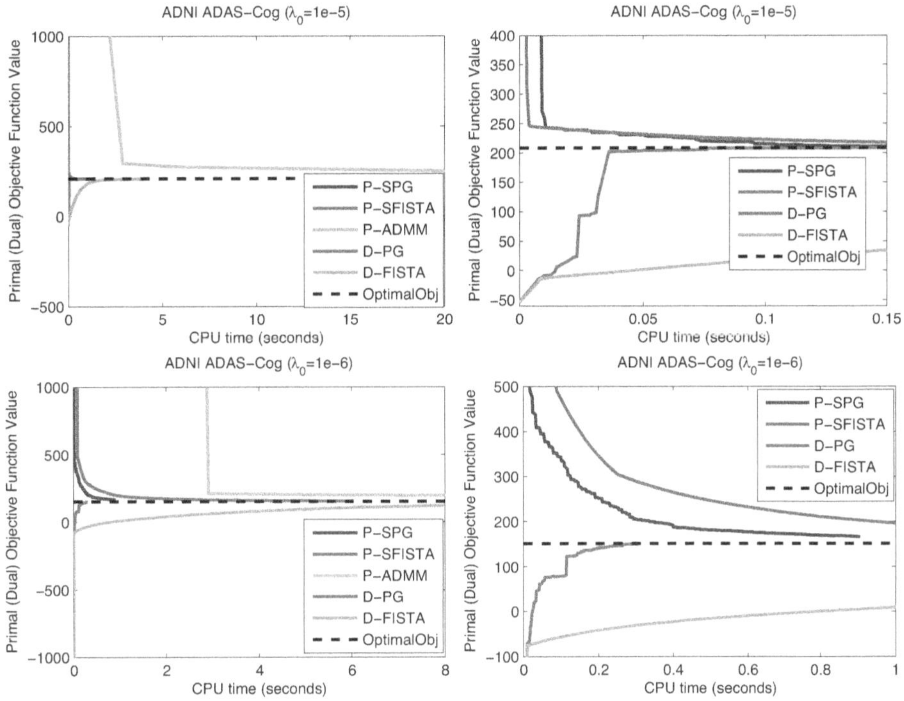

Figure 2: The primal objective function value (P-SPG, P-SFISTA and P-ADMM) and the dual objective function value (D-PG and D-FISTA) vs. CPU time (seconds) plots on the ADNI ADAS-Cog data set. The right figures are magnified views of the left figures. The legend "PrimalObj" denotes the optimal primal objective function value in Eq. (5) and regularized parameters are set as $\lambda_1 = \lambda_2 = \lambda_0 \sum_{i=1}^{m} n_i$, where n_i is the number of samples from the i-th task.

are 191 normal control (NC), 319 mild cognitive impairment (MCI), and 138 patients with probably Alzheimer's disease (AD) [please refer to [36, 37] for more details about the data]. We thus construct three tasks, and in each medical group we build one regression model to predict the corresponding MMSE scores. (II) We also use the ADNI data set and build multi-task regression models for predicting the ADAS-Cog score, which is another important cognitive score. We construct the task in the same way as in (I).

In the prediction performance experiments, we terminate the comparative algorithms when the relative change of the two consecutive objective function values is less than 10^{-6} or the number of iterations exceeds 10000. We randomly split the samples from each task into training and test samples with different training ratios (60%, 70% and 80%). All parameters of the comparative algorithms are tuned via 5-fold cross validation. For each training ratio, we report the averaged mean squared error (MSE) and the standard deviation over 10 random splittings of training and test samples as shown in Table 1. From these results, we have the following observations: (a) The calibrated multi-task feature learning algorithms (Calibration and Calibration-L2) outperform the non-calibrated ones (LeastSquares and LeastSquares-L2), which shows the superior prediction performance of the calibrated algorithms over the non-calibrated ones. (b) Calibration and Calibration-L2 achieve very similar prediction performance, which demonstrates that the proposed variant keeps the superior prediction performance of the calibrated multi-task feature learning over the non-calibrated one. In the next subsection, we will show that solving the smooth dual problem using a proper optimization algorithm is much more efficient than solving the primal problem directly.

4.2 Computational Efficiency Studies

We study the computational efficiency of solving the optimization problem in Eq. (5) by comparing the following algorithms: (1) **D-PG**: solve the primal optimization problem in Eq. (5) via using SpaRSA [32] to solve the dual optimization problem in Eq. (10); (2) **D-FISTA**: solve the primal optimization problem in Eq. (5) via using FISTA [4] to solve the dual optimization problem in Eq. (10); (3) **P-SPG**: solve the primal optimization problem in Eq. (5) via using SpaRSA [32] to solve the smoothed optimization problem in Eq. (37); (4) **P-SFISTA**: solve the primal optimization problem in Eq. (5) via using FISTA [4] to solve the smoothed optimization problem in Eq. (37); (5) **P-ADMM**: solve the primal optimization problem in Eq. (5) by using ADMM [8]. We conduct the experiments on the same data sets (both synthetic and real-world) described in the last subsection. We initialize D-PG and D-FISTA with $\boldsymbol{\theta}^0$ whose entries are independently sampled from the standard normal distribution, and initialize P-SPG, P-FISTA and P-ADMM with W^0 which is computed by Eq. (19) using $\boldsymbol{\theta}^0$. We terminate the comparative algorithms when the relative change of the two consecutive objective function values[2] is less than 10^{-6} or the number of iterations exceeds 10000. All algorithms are implemented in Matlab and executed on an Intel Core i7-3770 CPU (@3.4GHz) with 32GB memory.

[2]The objective function value indicates the dual objective function value in Eq. (10) and the primal objective function value in Eq. (5) for dual optimization algorithms (D-PG and D-FISTA) and for primal optimization algorithms (P-SPG, P-FISTA and P-ADMM), respectively.

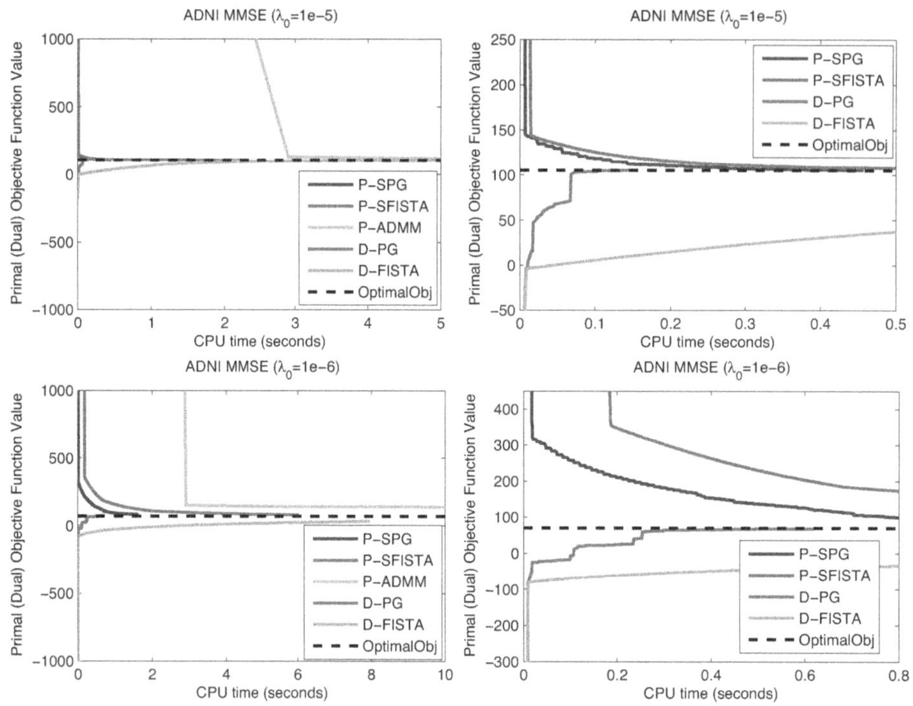

Figure 3: The primal objective function value (P-SPG, P-SFISTA and P-ADMM) and the dual objective function value (D-PG and D-FISTA) vs. CPU time (seconds) plots on the ADNI MMSE data set. The right figures are magnified views of the left figures. The legend "PrimalObj" denotes the optimal primal objective function value in Eq. (5) and regularized parameters are set as $\lambda_1 = \lambda_2 = \lambda_0 \sum_{i=1}^{m} n_i$, where n_i is the number of samples from the i-th task.

To show detailed convergence behaviors of the comparative algorithms and compare their computational efficiency, we report the primal objective function value (for P-SPG, P-FISTA and P-ADMM) and the dual objective function value (for D-PG and D-FISTA) vs. CPU time plots as shown in Figure 1, Figure 2 and Figure 3. To better compare the efficiency of dual and primal optimization algorithms, in each figure, we also draw a horizontal line indicating the optimal primal objective function value in Eq. (5). From these results, we have the following observations: (a) D-PG and D-FISTA increase the dual objective function value which finally converges to the optimal primal objective function value. This validates the fact that the strong duality holds for the optimization problem in Eq. (5). (b) D-PG is the most efficient among all algorithms on all data sets. Specifically, D-PG always quickly increases the dual objective function and rapidly terminates by approaching the optimal primal objective function value. (c) D-PG converges faster than D-FISTA and D-SPG converges faster than P-SFISTA, which demonstrates that SpaRSA indeed has very good empirical convergence performance. Although there is no rigorous proof that D-PG is the most efficient, empirical studies demonstrate that using SpaRSA to solve the dual problem is much more efficient than that by solving the primal problem directly. This may be due to the nice properties of the dual problem and the empirically fast convergence of SpaRSA.

5. CONCLUSIONS

In this paper, we study a variant of the calibrated multi-task feature learning by adding a squared norm regularizer. We derive a smooth dual optimization problem with a piecewise sphere constraint, which enables us to develop fast dual optimization algorithms. We also provide a detailed convergence analysis for the proposed dual optimization algorithm. Empirical studies demonstrate that, the dual optimization algorithm quickly converges and it is much more efficient than the primal optimization algorithm. Moreover, the calibrated multi-task feature learning algorithms with and without the squared norm regularizer achieve similar prediction performance and both outperform the non-calibrated ones. In our future work, we will analyze statistical properties of the proposed formulation and apply it to other applications such as Drosophila image annotation [17].

Acknowledgements

This work is supported in part by China 973 Fundamental R&D Program (No.2014CB340304), NIH (R01 LM010730), and NSF (IIS-0953662, CCF-1025177).

6. REFERENCES

[1] A. Argyriou, T. Evgeniou, and M. Pontil. Convex multi-task feature learning. *Machine Learning*, 73(3):243–272, 2008.

[2] F. Bach, R. Jenatton, J. Mairal, and G. Obozinski. Optimization with sparsity-inducing penalties. *Foundations and Trends® in Machine Learning*, 4(1):1–106, 2011.

[3] J. Barzilai and J. Borwein. Two-point step size gradient methods. *IMA Journal of Numerical Analysis*, 8(1):141–148, 1988.

[4] A. Beck and M. Teboulle. A fast iterative shrinkage-thresholding algorithm for linear inverse problems. *SIAM Journal on Imaging Sciences*, 2(1):183–202, 2009.

[5] A. Beck and M. Teboulle. A fast dual proximal gradient algorithm for convex minimization and applications. *Operations Research Letters*, 42(1):1–6, 2014.

[6] A. Belloni, V. Chernozhukov, and L. Wang. Square-root lasso: pivotal recovery of sparse signals via conic programming. *Biometrika*, 98(4):791–806, 2011.

[7] D. Bertsekas. *Nonlinear Programming*. Athena Scientific, 1999.

[8] S. Boyd, N. Parikh, E. Chu, B. Peleato, and J. Eckstein. Distributed optimization and statistical learning via the alternating direction method of multipliers. *Foundations and Trends® in Machine Learning*, 3(1):1–122, 2011.

[9] S. Boyd and L. Vandenberghe. *Convex optimization*. Cambridge university press, 2004.

[10] S. Boyd, L. Xiao, and A. Mutapcic. Subgradient methods. *Lecture notes of EE392o, Stanford University*, 2003.

[11] F. Bunea, J. Lederer, and Y. She. The group square-root lasso: Theoretical properties and fast algorithms. *arXiv preprint arXiv:1302.0261*, 2013.

[12] P. Gong, K. Gai, and C. Zhang. Efficient euclidean projections via piecewise root finding and its application in gradient projection. *Neurocomputing*, 74(17):2754–2766, 2011.

[13] P. Gong, J. Ye, and C. Zhang. Multi-stage multi-task feature learning. In *NIPS*, pages 1997–2005, 2012.

[14] P. Gong, J. Ye, and C. Zhang. Robust multi-task feature learning. In *SIGKDD*, pages 895–903, 2012.

[15] P. Gong, J. Ye, and C. Zhang. Multi-stage multi-task feature learning. *Journal of Machine Learning Research*, 14(1):2979–3010, 2013.

[16] A. Jalali, P. Ravikumar, S. Sanghavi, and C. Ruan. A dirty model for multi-task learning. *NIPS*, 2010.

[17] S. Ji, L. Sun, R. Jin, S. Kumar, and J. Ye. Automated annotation of drosophila gene expression patterns using a controlled vocabulary. *Bioinformatics*, 24(17):1881–1888, 2008.

[18] S. Kim and E. Xing. Tree-guided group lasso for multi-task regression with structured sparsity. In *ICML*, 2009.

[19] M. Kolar, J. Lafferty, and L. Wasserman. Union support recovery in multi-task learning. *Journal of Machine Learning Research*, 12:2415–2435, 2011.

[20] C. Lemaréchal, A. Nemirovskii, and Y. Nesterov. New variants of bundle methods. *Mathematical Programming*, 69(1):111–147, 1995.

[21] H. Liu, M. Palatucci, and J. Zhang. Blockwise coordinate descent procedures for the multi-task lasso with applications to neural semantic basis discovery. In *ICML*, pages 649–656, 2009.

[22] H. Liu, L. Wang, and T. Zhao. Multivariate regression with calibration. *arXiv preprint arXiv:1305.2238*, 2013.

[23] J. Liu, S. Ji, and J. Ye. Multi-task feature learning via efficient $\ell_{2,1}$-norm minimization. In *UAI*, 2009.

[24] J. Liu, S. Ji, and J. Ye. Slep: Sparse learning with efficient projections. *Arizona State University*, 2009.

[25] K. Lounici, M. Pontil, A. Tsybakov, and S. Van De Geer. Taking advantage of sparsity in multi-task learning. In *COLT*, 2009.

[26] K. Lounici, M. Pontil, S. Van De Geer, and A. Tsybakov. Oracle inequalities and optimal inference under group sparsity. *The Annals of Statistics*, 39(4):2164–2204, 2011.

[27] Y. Nesterov. Smooth minimization of non-smooth functions. *Mathematical Programming*, 103(1):127–152, 2005.

[28] F. Nie, H. Huang, X. Cai, and C. Ding. Efficient and robust feature selection via joint $\ell_{2,1}$-norms minimization. In *NIPS*, pages 1813–1821, 2010.

[29] G. Obozinski, B. Taskar, and M. Jordan. Multi-task feature selection. *Statistics Department, UC Berkeley, Tech. Rep*, 2006.

[30] R. T. Rockafellar. *Convex Analysis*. Princeton University Press, 1997.

[31] R. T. Rockafellar and R. Wets. *Variational Analysis*. Springer, 1998.

[32] S. Wright, R. Nowak, and M. Figueiredo. Sparse reconstruction by separable approximation. *IEEE Transactions on Signal Processing*, 57(7):2479–2493, 2009.

[33] X. Yang, S. Kim, and E. Xing. Heterogeneous multitask learning with joint sparsity constraints. In *NIPS*, 2009.

[34] Y. Zhang, D. Yeung, and Q. Xu. Probabilistic multi-task feature selection. In *NIPS*, 2010.

[35] J. Zhou, J. Chen, and J. Ye. *MALSAR: Multi-tAsk Learning via StructurAl Regularization*. Arizona State University, 2011.

[36] J. Zhou, J. Liu, V. Narayan, and J. Ye. Modeling disease progression via fused sparse group lasso. In *SIGKDD*, pages 1095–1103, 2012.

[37] J. Zhou, L. Yuan, J. Liu, and J. Ye. A multi-task learning formulation for predicting disease progression. In *SIGKDD*, pages 814–822, 2011.

[38] H. Zou and T. Hastie. Regularization and variable selection via the elastic net. *Journal of the Royal Statistical Society: Series B (Statistical Methodology)*, 67(2):301–320, 2005.

APPENDIX

A. Primal Smoothed Optimization Algorithm

We use the smoothing technique [27] to derive a primal smoothed optimization algorithm to solve Eq. (5). Based on the definition of the dual norm, we have

$$\sum_{i=1}^{m} \|X_i\mathbf{w}_i - \mathbf{y}_i\| = \sum_{i=1}^{m} \max_{\|\mathbf{v}_i\|\leq 1} \mathbf{v}_i^T(X_i\mathbf{w}_i - \mathbf{y}_i). \tag{34}$$

Define a function as

$$\sum_{i=1}^{m} \|X_i\mathbf{w}_i - \mathbf{y}_i\|_\mu = \sum_{i=1}^{m} \max_{\|\mathbf{v}_i\|\leq 1} \left\{\mathbf{v}_i^T(X_i\mathbf{w}_i - \mathbf{y}_i) - \frac{\mu}{2}\|\mathbf{v}_i\|^2\right\}, \tag{35}$$

where $\mu > 0$ is a smoothing parameter. We show in the following proposition that $\sum_{i=1}^{m} \|X_i\mathbf{w}_i - \mathbf{y}_i\|_\mu$ is smooth.

THEOREM 4. *The optimization problem in Eq. (35) has a unique solution in the following closed-form:*

$$\mathbf{v}_i(\mathbf{w}_i) = \frac{X_i\mathbf{w}_i - \mathbf{y}_i}{\max(\mu, \|X_i\mathbf{w}_i - \mathbf{y}_i\|)}.$$

Moreover, $\sum_{i=1}^{m} \|X_i\mathbf{w}_i - \mathbf{y}_i\|_\mu$ is continuously differentiable and Lipschitz continuous gradient with respect to W. Specifically, the gradient $G^\mu(W)$ of $\sum_{i=1}^{m} \|X_i\mathbf{w}_i - \mathbf{y}_i\|_\mu$ is

$$G^\mu(W) = [X_1^T\mathbf{v}_1(\mathbf{w}_1), \cdots, X_m^T\mathbf{v}_m(\mathbf{w}_m)],$$

and the Lipschitz constant of $G^\mu(W)$ is

$$\tilde{L} = \frac{\max_{i\in\{1,\cdots,m\}} \sigma_{\max}^2(X_i)}{\mu}. \tag{36}$$

Based on Theorem 4 (the proof of Theorem 4 is very similar to that of Theorem 1 and is thus omitted here), we know that $\sum_{i=1}^{m} \|X_i\mathbf{w}_i - \mathbf{y}_i\|_\mu$ is a smoothed surrogate of the non-smooth term $\sum_{i=1}^{m} \|X_i\mathbf{w}_i - \mathbf{y}_i\|$. Thus, we consider solving the following smoothed version of the optimization problem in Eq. (5):

$$\widehat{W} = \arg\min_{W\in\mathbb{R}^{d\times m}} \left\{\sum_{i=1}^{m} \|X_i\mathbf{w}_i - \mathbf{y}_i\|_\mu + \frac{\lambda_2}{2}\|W\|_F^2 + \lambda_1\|W\|_{1,2}\right\}. \tag{37}$$

The primal smoothed algorithm in fact solves the optimization problem in Eq. (5) via solving the smoothed optimization problem in Eq. (37). To be more specific, we present a primal smoothed optimization algorithm called accelerated primal smoothed algorithm given in Algorithm 2, in which FISTA [4] is used to solve the smoothed optimization problem in Eq. (37) and some notations are defined as follows:

$$l(W)_\mu = \sum_{i=1}^{m} \|X_i\mathbf{w}_i - \mathbf{y}_i\|_\mu + \frac{\lambda_2}{2}\|W\|_F^2 + \lambda_1\|W\|_{1,2},$$

$$s(W)_\mu = \sum_{i=1}^{m} \|X_i\mathbf{w}_i - \mathbf{y}_i\|_\mu + \frac{\lambda_2}{2}\|W\|_F^2.$$

The convergence analysis of Algorithm 2 is similar to Theorem 2.2 in [22] and is thus omitted here.

Algorithm 2: Accelerated Primal Smoothed Algorithm

Input : $W^0 \in \mathbb{R}^{d\times m}$, $\eta_0 > 0$, $\beta > 1$;

Initialize $W^1 \leftarrow W^0$; $t_0 \leftarrow 1$; $t_1 \leftarrow 1$;
for $k = 1, 2, \cdots$ **do**
 $\alpha_k \leftarrow \frac{t_{k-1}-1}{t_k}$;
 $V^k = W^k + \alpha_k(W^k - W^{k-1})$;
 for $j = 0, 1, 2, \cdots$ **do**
  $\eta_k \leftarrow \beta^j \eta_{k-1}$; $\widetilde{V}^k \leftarrow V^k - \frac{1}{\eta_k}\nabla s(V^k)_\mu$;
  Compute W^k via proximal gradient:

$$W^k = \arg\min_W \left\{\frac{\eta_k}{2}\|W - \widetilde{V}^k\|_F^2 + \lambda_1\|W\|_{1,2}\right\};$$

  if *the following line search criterion*

$$l(W^k)_\mu \le l(W^k)_\mu + tr(\nabla l(V^k)_\mu^T(W^k - V^k)) + \frac{\eta_k}{2}\|W^k - V^k\|_F^2$$

  is satisfied **then**
   break;
  end
 end
 if *some convergence criterion is satisfied* **then**
  Let $W^\star \leftarrow W^k$;
  break;
 end
 $t_{k+1} \leftarrow \frac{1+\sqrt{1+4t_k^2}}{2}$;
end

Output: $W^\star$

REMARK 3. *Similar to the dual optimization algorithm, we can also use SpaRSA [32] to solve the smoothed optimization problem in Eq. (37). Due to the use of the Barzilai-Borwein (BB) rule [3, 32], SpaRSA achieves very good empirical convergence performance.*

B. Alternating Direction Method of Multipliers (ADMM)

We know that the optimization problem in Eq. (5) is equivalent to the constrained optimization problem in Eq. (6) and we can write down the augmented Lagrange function of Eq. (6) as follows:

$$\mathcal{L}_\mathcal{A}(W, \mathbf{z}, \boldsymbol{\theta}, \rho) = \sum_{i=1}^{m}\|\mathbf{z}_i\| + \lambda_1\|W\|_{1,2} + \frac{\lambda_2}{2}\|W\|_F^2, + \sum_{i=1}^{m}\left\{\boldsymbol{\theta}_i^T(\mathbf{y}_i - \mathbf{z}_i - X_i\mathbf{w}_i) + \frac{\rho}{2}\|\mathbf{y}_i - \mathbf{z}_i - X_i\mathbf{w}_i\|^2\right\},$$

where $\mathbf{z} = [\mathbf{z}_1^T, \cdots, \mathbf{z}_m^T]^T \in \mathbb{R}^{\sum_{i=1}^m n_i}$; $\boldsymbol{\theta} = [\boldsymbol{\theta}_1^T, \cdots, \boldsymbol{\theta}_m^T]^T \in \mathbb{R}^{\sum_{i=1}^m n_i}$ with $\boldsymbol{\theta}_i \in \mathbb{R}^{n_i}$ being the Lagrange multiplier corresponding to the constraint $\mathbf{z}_i = \mathbf{y}_i - X_i\mathbf{w}_i$; $\rho > 0$ is a penalty parameter.

The ADMM solves the optimization problem in Eq. (5) by alternatively updating the variables as follows:
(1) Update W:

$$\begin{aligned} W^k &= \arg\min_W \Big\{\lambda_1\|W\|_{1,2} + \frac{\lambda_2}{2}\|W\|_F^2 \\ &\quad + \sum_{i=1}^{m}\Big[(\boldsymbol{\theta}_i^{k-1})^T(\mathbf{y}_i - \mathbf{z}_i^{k-1} - X_i\mathbf{w}_i) \\ &\quad + \frac{\rho}{2}\|\mathbf{y}_i - \mathbf{z}_i^{k-1} - X_i\mathbf{w}_i\|^2\Big]\Big\} \\ &= \arg\min_W \Big\{\lambda_1\|W\|_{1,2} + \frac{\lambda_2}{2}\|W\|_F^2 \\ &\quad + \frac{\rho}{2}\sum_{i=1}^{m}\left\|\frac{\boldsymbol{\theta}_i^{k-1}}{\rho} - \mathbf{z}_i^{k-1} + \mathbf{y}_i - X_i\mathbf{w}_i\right\|^2\Big\} \end{aligned}$$

We can use FISTA [4] or SpaSRA [32] to efficiently solve the above problem, where the gradient of the smooth part of the objective function is given by:

$$\nabla_W f_s(W) = \lambda_2 W + [\mathbf{t}_1 \ldots \mathbf{t}_m] \text{ with}$$
$$\mathbf{t}_i = -\rho X_i^T\left(\frac{\boldsymbol{\theta}_i^{k-1}}{\rho} - \mathbf{z}_i^{k-1} + \mathbf{y}_i - X_i\mathbf{w}_i\right).$$

(2) Update $\mathbf{z}$:

$$\begin{aligned} \mathbf{z}^k &= \arg\min_{\mathbf{z}} \Big\{\sum_{i=1}^{m}\|\mathbf{z}_i\| + \sum_{i=1}^{m}\Big[(\boldsymbol{\theta}_i^{k-1})^T(\mathbf{y}_i - \mathbf{z}_i - X_i\mathbf{w}_i^k) \\ &\quad + \frac{\rho}{2}\|\mathbf{y}_i - \mathbf{z}_i - X_i\mathbf{w}_i^k\|^2\Big]\Big\} \\ &= \arg\min_{\mathbf{z}} \sum_{i=1}^{m}\left\{\|\mathbf{z}_i\| + \frac{\rho}{2}\left\|\frac{\boldsymbol{\theta}_i^{k-1}}{\rho} + \mathbf{y}_i - \mathbf{z}_i - X_i\mathbf{w}_i^k\right\|^2\right\}. \end{aligned}$$

For the above problem, the optimal solution is given by the following closed-form:

$$\begin{aligned} \mathbf{z}_i^k &= \arg\min_{\mathbf{z}_i}\left\{\frac{1}{\rho}\|\mathbf{z}_i\| + \frac{1}{2}\left\|\mathbf{z}_i - \left(\frac{\boldsymbol{\theta}_i^{k-1}}{\rho} + \mathbf{y}_i - X_i\mathbf{w}_i^k\right)\right\|^2\right\} \\ &= \max\left(0, 1 - \frac{1}{\rho\|\mathbf{v}_i\|}\right)\mathbf{v}_i, \end{aligned}$$

where $\mathbf{v}_i = \dfrac{\boldsymbol{\theta}_i^{k-1}}{\rho} + \mathbf{y}_i - X_i\mathbf{w}_i^k$.

(3) Update $\boldsymbol{\theta}$:

$$\boldsymbol{\theta}_i^k = \boldsymbol{\theta}_i^{k-1} + \rho\left(\mathbf{y}_i - \mathbf{z}_i^k - X_i\mathbf{w}_i^k\right).$$

Multi-task Copula by Sparse Graph Regression

Tianyi Zhou
[1] Centre for Quantum Comp. & Intelligent Sys.
University of Technology, Sydney, Australia
[2] Computer Science & Engineering,
University of Washington, Seattle, WA, USA
tianyi.david.zhou@gmail.com

Dacheng Tao
Centre for Quantum Comp. & Intelligent Sys.
Faculty of Engineering & IT,
University of Technology, Sydney
235 Jones Street, Ultimo, NSW 2007, Australia
dacheng.tao@uts.edu.au

ABSTRACT

This paper proposes multi-task copula (MTC) that can handle a much wider class of tasks than mean regression with Gaussian noise in most former multi-task learning (MTL). While former MTL emphasizes shared structure among models, MTC aims at joint prediction to exploit inter-output correlation. Given input, the outputs of MTC are allowed to follow arbitrary joint continuous distribution. MTC captures the joint likelihood of multi-output by learning the marginal of each output firstly and then a sparse and smooth output dependency graph function. While the former can be achieved by classical MTL, learning graphs dynamically varying with input is quite a challenge. We address this issue by developing sparse graph regression (SpaGraphR), a non-parametric estimator incorporating kernel smoothing, maximum likelihood, and sparse graph structure to gain fast learning algorithm. It starts from a few seed graphs on a few input points, and then updates the graphs on other input points by a fast operator via coarse-to-fine propagation. Due to the power of copula in modeling semi-parametric distributions, SpaGraphR can model a rich class of dynamic non-Gaussian correlations. We show that MTC can address more flexible and difficult tasks that do not fit the assumptions of former MTL nicely, and can fully exploit their relatedness. Experiments on robotic control and stock price prediction justify its appealing performance in challenging MTL problems.

Categories and Subject Descriptors

K.4.1.4 [**Computing Methodologies**]: Machine Learning—*Learning Paradigms, Multi-task Learning*; K.4.3.5.3 [**Computing Methodologies**]: Machine Learning Approaches—*Learning in Probabilistic Graphical Models*

General Terms

Machine Learning, Statistics

Keywords

Multi-task learning; Copula; Semi-parametric model; Sparse Structured learning; Covariance Regression

KDD'14, August 24–27, 2014, New York, NY, USA.
Copyright 2014 ACM 978-1-4503-2956-9/14/08 ...$15.00.
http://dx.doi.org/10.1145/2623330.2623697.

1. INTRODUCTION

Effectiveness of multi-task learning (MTL) has been broadly proved in massive real applications such as gene expression analysis [41][24], brain activity prediction [22], collaborative filtering [38], information retrieval [25] and economic forecasting [13]. MTL studies how to exploit the underlying task relatedness in learning multiple tasks' models so that tasks can benefit from each other. Precisely, let $x \in \mathcal{X}$ be input features in domain $\mathcal{X} \subseteq \mathbb{R}^p$ and $y = \{y_i\}_{i=1}^k \in \mathcal{Y}$ be outputs of k tasks in domain $\mathcal{Y} = \prod_{i=1}^k \mathcal{Y}_i \subseteq \mathbb{R}^k$. Given associated k training sets $\{X_i, Y_i\}_{i=1}^k$ with $X_i \in \mathbb{R}^{n_i \times p}$ and $Y_i \in \mathbb{R}^{n_i \times 1}$, in machine learning it is of general interest to learn a joint conditional probability model $p(y|x)$, which contains all predictive information of outputs y given x. Classical MTL methods study the case when $p(y|x)$ is a product distribution $\prod p(y_i|x)$ with each component a mean regression model $f_i(x) : \mathcal{X} \to \mathcal{Y}_i$ plus an i.i.d. Gaussian noise $\epsilon_i \sim \mathcal{N}(0, \sigma_i^2)$

$$p(y|x) = \prod_{i=1}^{k} p(y_i|x), y_i|x \sim \mathcal{N}\left(f_i(x), \sigma_i^2\right), \qquad (1)$$

where $y_i = f_i(x) + \epsilon_i$. Note the above model reduces the model complexity of $p(y|x)$ on the expense of ignoring the dependency among outputs. Two families of MTL methods have been developed based on (1) and exploit task relatedness in different ways.

1.1 Classical Multi-task Learning

We first consider the case when $f_i(x)$ is a parametric function $f_i(x; w_i)$ with parameter w_i. While maximizing the likelihood $p(y|x; W)$ with $W = \{w_i\}_{i=1}^k$ leads to k independent M-estimators of $\hat{w}_i = \arg\max p(y_i|x; w_i)$, which introduce trivial single-task learning regardless of task-relatedness; maximizing the posterior of W with a joint prior $p(W)$ has motivated a line of MTL methods, which relate different tasks by endowing shared structures across $\{w_i\}_{i=1}^k$. MAP estimator $\hat{W} = \arg\max_W \log[p(W) \prod_{i=1}^k p(y_i|x; w_i)]$ yields a regularization based learning framework d

$$\hat{W} = \arg\min_{W} \sum_{i=1}^{k} \|f_i(X_i; w_i) - Y_i\|_F^2 + \lambda \mathcal{R}(W), \qquad (2)$$

where $f_i(X_i; w_i)$ extends $f_i(x; w_i)$ by applying f_i to each sample in X_i, and $\mathcal{R}(W)$ is a regularization term resulting from $p(W)$ and encoding the shared structure. In previous MTL methods, a linear function $f_i(x; w_i) = xw_i$ is usually adopted, whereas their used regularizers $\mathcal{R}(W)$ are of different types. For instance, an ℓ_1/ℓ_q $(q > 1)$ norm regularizer $\mathcal{R}(W) = \sum_{i=1}^k \|w_i\|_q$ results in shared nonzero patterns among different w_i and thus yields joint feature selection across tasks [2, 23, 29]; a trace norm regularizer $\mathcal{R}(W) = \|W\|_*$ restricts vectors $\{w_i\}_{i=1}^k$ lying in a low-dimensional space that indicates each w_i is generated from a few shared basis vectors [16, 30]; the vector fields [3] of predictor functions span a low-dimensional subspace, a graph regularizer $\mathcal{R}(W) = \text{tr}(WLW^T)$ can equip $\{w_i\}_{i=1}^k$ with clustered [39], tree [17], manifold or graph weighted fusion structure [6]. Moreover, sum mixture of two regularizers for $W = P+Q$ is proposed, where P encodes shared structure and Q captures task-specific structure [1, 5, 15, 14], which includes alternating structure optimization (ASO), incoherent sparse low-rank (ISLR) formulation, robust multi-task feature learning (rMTFL), robust multi-task learning (rMTL), and so forth. In these methods, the task relatedness refers to shared model structures that lead to smaller hypothesis parameter space. When the prior $p(W)$ agrees with the true models, a better generalization performance is provably achieved.

The model (1) also gives rise to a non-parametric MTL scheme named "multi-task Gaussian process (GP) regression (MTGP)" [4], which admits more flexible form of $f_i(x)$ and assumes identical input $X \equiv X_{i\in[k]}$ in training set (so $n \equiv n_{i\in[k]}$). However, rather than imposing a GP prior to each single $f_i(x)$, a task-related GP prior is placed over all latent functions $\{f_i(x)\}_{i=1}^k$. This GP covariance is the Kronecker product of a covariance function $k^x(x, x')$ over input x and a "free form" positive semi-definite task similarity matrix $K^f \in \mathbb{R}^{k\times k}$. The key assumption added to (1) here is $\langle f_i(x), f_j(x')\rangle = K_{ij}^f k^x(x, x')$, which defines correlation between different predictive function values on different input data points. Learning hyper-parameters θ_x in k^x and K^f is conducted by likelihood maximization rather than MAP. In MTGP, it is the stationary hyperparameter K^f rather than the structure shared by task-wise parameters $\{w_i\}_{i=1}^k$ encodes the task relatedness. Instead of reducing the hypothesis parameter space to gain a better generalization performance, it abridges the output space.

So the inference of one task output on a new data point requires weighted averaging of kn outputs from the whole training set. Inverse of an $kn \times kn$ (assume identical input $X \equiv X_{i\in[k]}$ so $n \equiv n_{i\in[k]}$) covariance matrix is needed in weight computing and might cause computational burden. Learning hyperparameters θ_x of k^x and K^f is conducted by likelihood maximization rather than MAP,

$$\left\{\hat{\theta_x}, \hat{K^f}\right\} = \arg\max_{\theta_x, K^f} \log \prod_{i=1}^{k} p\left(y_i \,\middle|\, x, \theta_x, \left\{K_{ij}^f\right\}_{j=1}^k\right), \quad (3)$$

which can be solved by EM algorithm that requires $kn \times kn$ matrix inverse per iterate.

1.2 Motivation and Main Contributions

Although the model in (1) has long been favored and thoroughly studied in former MTL research, its effectiveness is only limited to tasks that are mean regressions with independent Gaussian noise.

Firstly, in a wider range of MTL problems, the k tasks may vary in diverse types and in different combinations. This implies the conditional marginal $p(y_i|x)$ may be non-Gaussian, or the marginals for different outputs y_i are from different classes of distributions. In the following, we discuss some non-Gaussian examples of $p(y_i|x)$. Comparing to mean regression with Gaussian noise, median regression with symmetric heavy-tailed noise such as Cauchy or Laplace is more robust to outliers in practice; quantile regression with asymmetric heavy-tailed noise is commonly used in ecology and econometrics to discover input-output relationship when input has weak ties with output mean; Poisson distribution is naturally used in count data regression; Gamma distribution is the best model for studying the emission mechanism of gamma-ray burst data; mixture model is better to fit a multi-mode distribution that can capture $p(y_i|x)$ where y_i is the prediction from multi-model or multi-expert [27], which could be multiple user groups in recommendation system [19], multiple mechanisms resulting in brain activities, or multiple systems for economics forecasting. Thus a flexible and expressive multi-task learning model should allow the combination of such different choices of $p(y_i|x)$. However, most previous MTL models cannot provide such rich possible options of $p(y_i|x)$.

Secondly, correlations among output variables $\{y_i\}_{i=1}^k$ are ignored in (1) to obtain a decomposable model in learning. However, they are natural task-relatedness that are possible to be directly estimated from data and improve prediction. Instead of employing a joint likelihood to capture such relatedness, exploration of task-relatedness in previous MTL relies on the joint prior of parameters or prediction functions for multiple models. In this case, it is required either to know them (e.g., joint prior $p(W)$ or K^f) in advance, or to learn them indirectly from data in a complicated fashion, like EM algorithm. Both are difficult.

In contrast, if we consider about learning the joint likelihood as a multivariate Gaussian $p(y|x)$, a direct idea embedding output correlations in $p(y|x) = p(\epsilon = y - f(x))$ is to posit dependent noises $\{\epsilon_i\}_{i=1}^k$. We also face difficulty because this demands learning a covariance function $\Sigma(x) : \mathcal{X} \to \mathbb{R}^{k\times k}$, which is a difficult open problem in former studies [10, 20]. It becomes even harder when marginals $\{p(y_i|x)\}_{i=1}^k$ are allowed to be arbitrary continuous densities to express more general tasks, because in this case the joint density $p(y|x)$ falls into a broad category of general distributions, in which the output correlations are usually hard to be even parametrized.

In this paper, we propose multi-task copula (MTC) that can choose arbitrary continuous marginal distributions $p(y_i|x)$ for different tasks to build a joint predictive distribution $p(y|x)$, which also encodes the output correlations as a decomposable parametric part $c(\cdot|x)$ in its density function. Thanks to the flexibility of copula model, MTC overcomes the aforementioned two main drawbacks of previous MTL methods, and can handle more general task types as well as fully exploit their relatedness via output correlations. A two-stage learning scheme for MTC will be advocated, in which we first learn the marginal $p(y_i|x)$ for each task independently, and then learn the copula density $c(\cdot|x)$ encoding outputs dependency. One merit of this scheme is that previous MTL methods can be seamlessly incorporated into the first stage, so the task relatedness can be encoded and fully exploited by both joint prior from previous MTL and joint likelihood in MTC. Another merit is that, in the special case of Gaussian copula, learning the non-Gaussian correlations among outputs encoded in $c(\cdot|x)$ can be reduced to estimating a Gaussian covariance on each given x.

In order to provide a reliable estimation of the Gaussian covariance function of x that defines the Gaussian copula, we develop an efficient non-parametric estimator "sparse graph regression" (SpaGraphR) to predict input-dependent Gaussian covariance, whose inverse (i.e., precision matrix) is sparse and encodes a structured dependency graph. The zero entries correspond to the conditional independence between outputs on the graph. In MTC, rather than estimating a stationary dependency graph by "covariance selection" [7], SpaGraphR enables the graph of y to dynamically vary with input x and thus provides a more expressive and flexible model for describing output correlations. Such local covariance has been broadly observed in various real problems, and verified to be a helpful information for prediction. For example, the correlations of different factors describing climate or market behaviors are always changing with time and locations. The prediction of these factors essentially relies on these changes in their correlations.

Similar problem of learning covariance function has rarely been studied before. SpaGraphR updates graphs on all given input data points in a hierarchical order and is a result of kernel smoothing in conjunction with ℓ_1 regularized likelihood maximization. In learning algorithm, it starts with sparse precision matrices on a small set of representative points, and then updates the precision matrices on other points for several rounds by a fast proximal operator. In each round, a few new points joined in the set of points with updating graphs, and thus the graph estimator is refined in a coarse-to-fine multi-resolution style. Each update merely requires small matrix multiplications and entry-wise soft-thresholding. Hence, SpaGraphR has promising efficiency on big data. Experiments on challenging real problems, i.e., robotic control and stock prediction, rigidly demonstrate the effectiveness of MTC and SpaGraphR in MTL problems.

2. MULTI-TASK COPULA

Table 1: Comparison between MTL and MTC models.

	Marginals $p(y_i\|x)$	Joint Prior $p(W)$	Outputs Dependency $c(\{F_i(y_i)\}_{i=1}^k\|x)$
MTL	Gaussian/Logistic	Allow	-
MTC	Any continuous dist.	Allow	Allow

We propose MTC that tailors the copula model [35] to the MTL problem as

$$p(y|x) = c\left(F_1(y_1), F_2(y_2), \cdots, F_k(y_k)|\, x\right) \prod_{i=1}^{k} p(y_i|x), \quad (4)$$

where $F_i(y_i)$ is the cumulative distribution function (CDF) of output y_i associated with density $g_i(y_i) = p(y_i|x)$ so that $F_i(y_i) \equiv \Pr(z \leq y_i|x) \equiv \int_{-\infty}^{y_i} g_i(z)\mathrm{d}z$. The copula density function $c(\cdot|x)$ takes all marginal CDFs $\{F_i(y_i)\}_{i=1}^k$ as its augments, and maintains the output correlations in a parametric form conditioned on x. As a semi-parametric model for joint prediction, MTC is easier to learn and less prone to over-fitting than a fully non-parametric model, while more expressive and flexible than a fully parameterized model. In theory, let $F(y)$ be the joint CDF, (1) can be derived from the kth order partial derivative of a copula function $C(\cdot)$.

DEFINITION 1. *Let $Y_1, \ldots, Y_k$ be real random variables marginally uniformly distributed on $[0,1]$. A copula function $C : [0,1]^k \rightarrow [0,1]$ is a joint (cumulative) distribution*

$$C\left(y_1, \ldots, y_k\right) = F(y) \equiv \Pr\left(\bigwedge_{i=1}^{k} Y_i \leq u_i\right). \quad (5)$$

By Sklar's seminal theorem [35], any joint CDF $F(y)$ can be represented as a copula function $C(\cdot)$ of its univariate marginals $\{F_i(y_i)\}_{i=1}^k$. Moreover, $C(\cdot)$ is unique in the case of continuous marginals. Furthermore, the converse is also true, i.e., any copula function defined on a combination of any marginal functions gives a valid joint distribution with the same marginals.

This property is critical to MTC. Firstly, it provides a theoretical guarantee that MTC is able to model the multi-task learning model $p(y|x)$ by arbitrary joint joint distribution with continuous marginals. So it overcomes the two limitations of previous MTL models mentioned in the beginning of Section 1.2. Secondly, it indicates that the model is decomposable, so we can separately learn the marginal prediction model $p(y_i|x)$ for each task and the then learn the outputs dependency conditional on x encoded in $C(\cdot)$. In addition, we do not need to estimate the partition function for normalization in MTC. The copula model $p(y|x)$ (4) automatically turns into a legal joint prediction model taking output correlations into account.

Theoretically, we can construct any legal copula $C(\cdot)$ by a copula trick derived from inverting Sklar's theorem. For example, Gaussian copula [9, 21]

$$C\left(\{F_i(y_i)\}_{i=1}^k\right) = \Phi_\Sigma\left(\{\Phi^{-1}\left(F_i(y_i)\right)\}_{i=1}^k\right), \quad (6)$$

where Φ is the standard normal distribution and Φ_Σ is the zero mean multivariate Gaussian with covariance matrix Σ, and Archimedean copula [26]

$$C\left(\{F_i(y_i)\}_{i=1}^k\right) = \psi\left(\sum_{i=1}^{k} \psi^{-1}\left(F_i(y_i)\right)\right), \quad (7)$$

where ψ is the so called generator function with a single parameter are two families of copulas widely applied in practice. Both have the strength to model dependency in high dimensions (i.e., with large k). While Archimedean copula is easier to estimate due to its single parameter, Gaussian copula is more powerful for expressing the sophisticated dependency graph structure.

When the structure of a graphical model $G = (V, E)$ (where V is the vertex set and E is the edge set) is known in advance, we can decompose the joint density into the product of several components based on local copulas. Two recent examples are tree-structured copula [18] with density

$$g(y) = \left[\prod_{i=1}^{k} f_i(y_i)\right] \prod_{(i,j)\in E} c_{ij}\left(F_i(y_i), F_j(y_j)\right), \quad (8)$$

where c_{ij} is a bivariate copula density associated with y_i and y_j, and copula Bayesian network (CBN) [8] with density

$$g(y) = \prod_{i=1}^{k} R_{c_i}\left(F_i(y_i), F_{i1}(\mathrm{pa}_{i1}), \ldots, F_{i1}(\mathrm{pa}_{ik_i})\right) f_i(y_i), \quad (9)$$

where $\{\mathrm{pa}_{ij}\}_{j=1}^{k_i}$ is the parents of node i and R_{c_i} is the so called "copula ratio" computed from a local copula associated with y_i and its parents.

It is not hard to verify that the density functions of all the above copula models can be written in the same form as $p(y|x)$ in MTC (4), i.e., a parametric component [1] encoding the conditional dependency of y multiplied by the product of all marginals $\{p(y_i|x)\}_{i=1}^k$. In addition, since all of them are capable of handling an arbitrary number of outputs, after they have been learned from training data, they can be freely plugged into MTC (4) and results in a joint prediction model.

In Table 1, we provide a comparison between classical MTL (1) and MTC (4) from the perspective of model. In addition, an illustration of MTC is also given in Figure 2.

3. TWO-STAGE LEARNING FOR MULTI-TASK COPULA

Note the parameters in both $c(\cdot|x)$ and the marginals $\{p(y_i|x)\}_{i=1}^k$ of copula models introduced before are assumed to depend on x in MTC. Therefore, before producing a valid prediction model, these

[1] In CBN it is not always a legal copula density $c(\cdot|x)$, but can still be treated as a parametric component conditioned on x in MTC, and thus causes no difference in learning and inference.

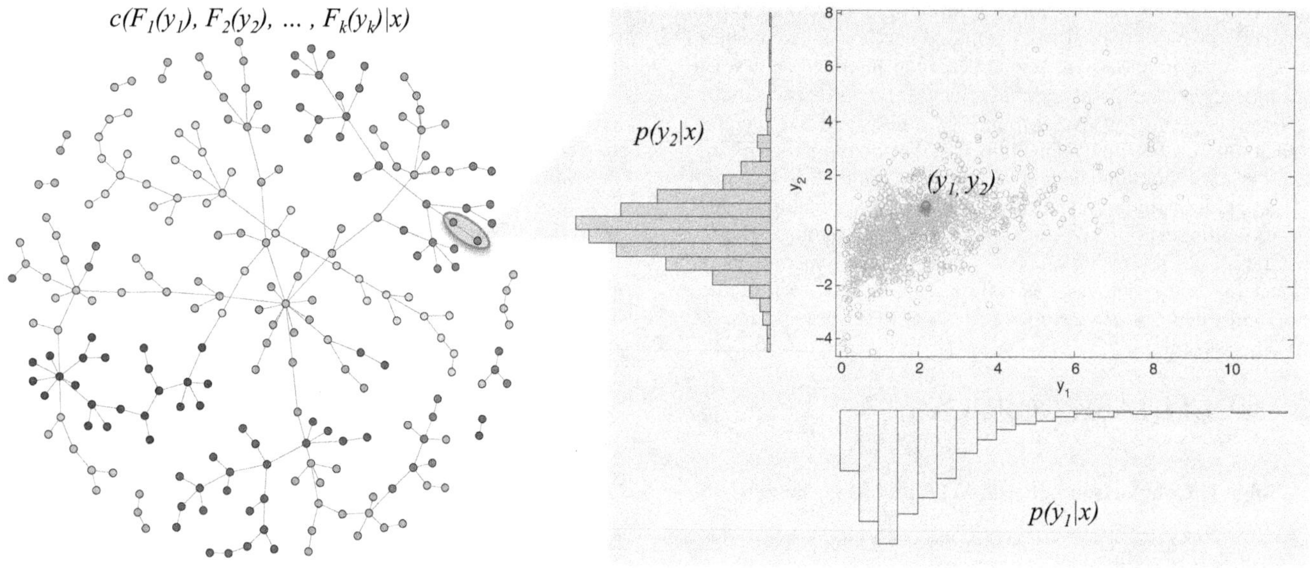

Figure 1: Illustration of multi-task copula (4) in generating outputs y given inputs x. Left: the copula density $c\left(F_1(y_1), F_2(y_2), \cdots, F_k(y_k) \middle| x\right)$ as a function of x and defined by an outputs dependency graph. Right: the marginal conditional density for y_1 and y_2 can be any continuous density functions, and MTC defines the dependent joint distribution of y, from which we draw a sample (y_1, y_2). MTC fully captures the outputs correlations varying with inputs, and fits the conditional marginals by arbitrary continuous density functions. Thus it provides an expressive joint likelihood model with small complexity.

parameters have to be learned as parametric or non-parametric functions of x from training data. According to the "distribution generation" mechanism of copula suggested by Sklar's theorem, we adopt a two-stage learning scheme that estimates the marginal distributions $\{p(y_i|x)\}_{i=1}^k$ at first and then the parameters in $c(\cdot|x)$ as functions of x to build the joint prediction model.

A primary advantage of this scheme is that its first stage is exactly equal to likelihood or posterior maximization ignoring outputs dependency, and thus can be accomplished by off-the-shelf classical MTL methods in Section 1.1 or their trivial variants. For example, in the case of robust regression, we consider a general task with output $y_i = f_i(x) + \epsilon_i$, where noise ϵ_i is a random variable obeying symmetric (for mean regression) or asymmetric (for quantile regression) distribution, and function $f_i(x)$ is a constant computed from x. When $f_i(x)$ is assumed to have a parametric form $f_i(x; w_i)$ like linear or log-linear functions, the parameters $\{w_i\}_{i=1}^k$ sharing structures can be immediately learned by the regularization based MTL (2). When a more flexible non-parametric function $f_i(x)$ is preferred, the multi-task GP regression can be applied to achieve k predictive functions with related GP priors.

In addition, in the case of multi-model or multi-expert, we can consider a more general task whose output y_i obeys a conditional 1-D Gaussian mixture model such that

$$p(y_i|x) = \sum_{j=1}^{m} \frac{w_j}{\sigma\sqrt{2\pi}} \exp\left\{\frac{(y_i - f_{ij}(x))^2}{2\sigma^2}\right\}. \quad (10)$$

When $f_{ij}(x) = xw_{ij}$, each task is exactly the "Gaussian mixture regression" (GMR) [12], and an MAP estimator of W with any joint prior $p(W)$ mentioned in Section 1.1 can result in an EM algorithm, whose M-step invokes the regularized MTL (2). When $f_{ij}(x)$ is selected as a non-parametric function, each task collapses to the "mixture of Gaussian processes" (MGP) model [33]. The GPs associated with different tasks can be related by the same trick used in multi-task GP regression via positing a task-similarity matrix K^f. An EM algorithm is also required in learning K^f and kernel parameters. Since the above EM algorithms can be directly derived by standard procedures, we will not go into their details in this paper and leave them to a longer version.

Therefore, the first stage allows lots of flexible choices of tasks and their corresponding marginal prediction models. Moreover, the first stage enables MTC to take the advantage of the task relatedness exploited by joint prior in classical MTL methods, whose merits thus can be fully inherited in MTC. Together with the task relatedness complied in the output dependency graph, which will be learned in the second stage, MTC can achieve a considerable performance boost. This is because the output dependency encoded by $c(\cdot|x)$ and the task-relatedness encoded by joint prior in classical MTL play independent roles in MTC model, and thus cannot be transferred to each other. To see this, we investigate the two terms on the right hand side of (4). While the outputs dependency is encoded by the first term $c(\cdot|x)$, the coherent latent structures exploited by classical MTL are embedded in the second term, i.e., the product of marginals. It is worthy noting that the marginals can also be trained independently as single tasks, and the MTC can still give promising prediction. The benefit of doing this is we can enjoy faster speed from divide-and-conquer or distributed computation naturally in this stage.

After the first stage, we obtain the estimates of all the marginal densities, as well as those of their associated cumulative functions $\{\hat{F}_i(y_i)\}_{i=1}^k$. In the second stage, we estimate copula density $c(\cdot|x)$ in the form of $c\left(\{F_i(y_i)\}_{i=1}^k \middle| \Theta(x)\right)$ from the training set

$$\left\{Z \equiv \{\hat{F}_i(Y_i)\}_{i=1}^k, X\right\}, \quad (11)$$

where the copula parameter $\Theta(x)$ is a function of x. For an Archimedean copula with only one parameter, and copula models built from local copulas defined on a given graphical model, the regular maximum likelihood estimate is able to achieve an accurate estimate $\hat{\Theta}(x)$.

In this paper, an primary challenge is to learn a locally smooth or piece-wise linear covariance function $\Sigma(x)$ in accompany with sparse precision $S(x) = (\Sigma(x))^{-1}$ for Gaussian copula (6) applied to MTC. The main reason for choosing Gaussian copula here is its capability of modeling high dimensional distributions. Learning Gaussian copula in MTC requires a simultaneous learning of the graph structure and the corresponding edge weights, both varying with x. This problem is extremely challenging because: 1) a parametric $\Sigma(x)$ easily suffers from over-fitting in large k and p case, for example, k^2p parameters are required to be estimated even when each entry of $\Sigma(x)$ is a linear function of x; 2) a non-parametric $\Sigma(x)$ by kernel smoothing of local covariance matrices is unlikely to also be sparse; 3) point-wise covariance selection based on only one sample of y on each point x is seriously ill-posed and computationally intractable.

4. SPARSE GRAPH REGRESSION

In this section, we propose an efficient algorithm called "sparse graph regression" (SpaGraphR), which learns a non-parametric covariance function $\Sigma(x)$ that has sparse inverse $S(x)$ on any x in the dataset and are locally smooth. SpaGraphR leverages the local smoothness to avoid a great amount of costly computations, and achieves sparse . From the perspective of non-parametric regression, we need to estimate a sparse precision $S(x)$ for multivariate Gaussian variable $z = \{\Phi^{-1}(\hat{F}_i(y_i))\}_{i=1}^k$ from its i.i.d. samples on each point x. However, we usually have only one output sample $y^i \in \mathbb{R}^k$ on the ith input sample x^i in training set $X = \{x^i\}_{i=1}^n$, which indicates only one sample z^i is available for estimating $S(x^i)$. This brings difficulty in estimation. We will firstly discuss two possible classes of covariance estimator that have been investigated recently.

Covariance selection (CS), first proposed in [7] and drawing tremendous interests recently [11, 34], aims to estimate a sparse precision matrix from insufficient samples in a high-dimensional space. In this case, maximum likelihood estimate $\hat{S} = \hat{\Sigma}^{-1}$ cannot offer a legal $\hat{S}$, because the sample covariance matrix $\hat{\Sigma}$ is singular and thus does not have an inverse. Additional ℓ_1 regularization is applied to S in CS for two purposes: 1) to obtain a valid S, and 2) to make the entries of S sparse, where the zeros indicate conditional independence and suggest a structured Gaussian Markov random field. CS is formulated as

$$\hat{S}_{\hat{\Sigma},\lambda} = \arg\min_{S\succ 0} -\log\det(S) + \mathrm{tr}(\hat{\Sigma}\mathrm{S}) + \lambda \left\|\mathrm{vec}(S)\right\|_1. \quad (12)$$

The estimate $\hat{S}_{\hat{\Sigma},\lambda}$ has been proved to converge to the true S at different rates in different norms by recent papers. These convergence rates differs in the order of dimension p yet share the same order $\mathcal{O}(1/\sqrt{n})$ of sample number n. However, in our case $n = 1$ for each x^i, the variance of CS estimate (12) with $\hat{\Sigma} = z^i z^{iT}$ (z^i is z corresponding to x^i) is unbearable. In addition, applying expensive CS algorithm to each data point is impractical on computation.

Different from CS, another strategy that is able to achieve a $\hat{\Sigma}$ with lower variance is to take the local smoothness of $\Sigma(x)$ into account, which results in Nadaraya-Watson (NW) estimator [28, 36] based on kernel smoothing (with kernel function $K(x,\cdot)$) of covariance, i.e.,

$$\Sigma_K(x) = \frac{\sum_{i=1}^n K(x,x^i) z^i z^{iT}}{\sum_{i=1}^n K(x,x^i)}. \quad (13)$$

NW estimator involves the neighbors of x^i in the covariance estimation on x^i, and thus could provide a more precise estimator $\Sigma_K(x^i)$ than $z^i z^{iT}$ under the assumption that $\Sigma(x)$ is a smooth function of x. However, in practice, the resulting $\hat{S}(x) = (\Sigma_K(x))^{-1}$ does not hold a guarantee of sparsity, so we usually cannot gain a structured graph from directly taking the inverse. A straightforward approach to obtain a sparse graph regression in this case is to plug a NW estimator into CS by replacing $\hat{\Sigma}$ in (12) with $\Sigma_K(x)$, i.e., $\hat{S}(x) := \hat{S}_{\Sigma_K(x),\lambda}$. However, its computational cost is prohibitive when applied to a great number of data points, because we have to apply CS algorithm to each point.

According to the density function of multivariate Gaussian, it is the entries in precision matrix S that encode the weights of all edges on the dependency graph. Therefore, it is more preferable to seek a smooth precision function $S(x)$ rather than a smooth covariance function $\Sigma(x)$, when the generated sparse graphs are expected to exhibit structures and edge weights smoothly varying with x. In contrast to (13), we define an NW estimator for $S(x)$ as

$$S_K(x,X) = \frac{\sum_{i\in B_\epsilon(x,X)} K(x,x^i) S(x^i)}{\sum_{i\in B_\epsilon(x,X)} K(x,x^i)}. \quad (14)$$

Note $S_K(x,X)$ is defined as the kernel smoothing of the precision matrices on training data points within the ϵ-ball $B_\epsilon(x,X) \equiv \{i : \|x - x^i\|_2 \le \epsilon, x^i \in X\}$ of x. If the neighboring precision matrices $\{S(x^i)\}_{i\in B_\epsilon(x,X)}$ are sparse, $S_K(x,X)$ is also sparse on the union of their support sets. In addition, due to the non-negative kernel weights, $S_K(x,X)$ is a symmetric positive definite (PSD) matrix if all the involved $S(x^i)_{i:i\in B_\epsilon(x)} \succ 0$ is PSD. Thus $S_K(x,X)$ is a legal precision matrix estimator encoding underlying graph structure, and will be used for outputs dependency graph prediction in SpaGraphR.

Unfortunately, $\{S(x^i)\}_{i\in B_\epsilon(x,X)}$ in (14) are unknown and need to be estimated in advance. We cannot obtain them by applying $S_K(x,X)$ again because it turns out to be the "chicken or the egg" dilemma. We also cannot apply the aforementioned CS estimate $\hat{S}_{\Sigma_K(x),\lambda}$ because the training set could be huge and thus causes heavy computational burden. Nevertheless, it is possible to start from a few graphs by applying $\hat{S}_{\Sigma_K(x),\lambda}$ to a small subset of training points $\Omega \subseteq X$, and then develop an efficient operator to update graphs on the other points from the known ones in an incremental or propagation manner. By incorporating the likelihood maximization on point x, ℓ_1 regularization in (12), and local smoothness of $S_K(x,X)$, we develop an operator $S_+(x,\Omega)$ for updating $S(x)$ in SpaGraphR

$$\begin{aligned} S_+(x,\Omega) := {} & \eta_\lambda \left\{ \left[(1-\gamma) z z^T + \gamma \left(S_K(x,\Omega)\right)^{-1} \right]^{-1} \right\} \\ = {} & \eta_\lambda \left\{ \frac{1}{\gamma} \left[S_K(x,\Omega) - \frac{1-\gamma}{\gamma + (1-\gamma) z^T [S_K(x,\Omega) z]} \right.\right. \\ & \left.\left. [S_K(x,\Omega) z] \left[S_K(x,\Omega) z\right]^T \right] \right\}, \end{aligned} \quad (15)$$

where $\eta_\lambda(\cdot)$ is an matrix element-wise soft-thresholding operator $[\eta_\lambda(X)]_{i,j} = \mathrm{sgn}\left(X_{i,j}\right) \max\left(|X_{i,j}| - \lambda, 0\right)$ that results in sparse update $S_+(x,\Omega)$, and γ is a parameter adjusting the trade-off between likelihood maximization and local smoothness. Kailath variant of Woodbury identity is used to obtain the equality between the two representations in (15). As an important consequence, the second representation merely requires simple matrix-vector multiplication and entry-wise substraction, and thus makes $S_+(x,\Omega)$ considerably efficient to compute.

Let's look at some motivations behind (15). Equivalently, it can be derived by applying a proximal operator [31] to PSD matrix $S_V(x,\Omega) = \left[(1-\gamma) z z^T + \gamma \left(S_K(x,\Omega)\right)^{-1}\right]^{-1}$ with ℓ_1 regularization, i.e.,

$$\begin{aligned}&\text{prox}_{\lambda\|\text{vec}(S)\|_1}\left(S_V(x,\Omega)\right)=\\&\arg\min_S\left\{\|\text{vec(S)}\|_1+\tfrac{1}{2\lambda}\|S-S_V(x,\Omega)\|_F^2\right\}.\end{aligned}\tag{16}$$

According to the property of proximal operator, $S_+(x,\Omega)$ finds a sparse precision matrix (whose sparsity is controlled by λ) close to $S_V(x,\Omega)$, whose inverse is a "pseudo sample covariance" $(1-\gamma)zz^T+\gamma\left(S_K(x,\Omega)\right)^{-1}$ comprised of a rank-1 sample covariance zz^T and a covariance matrix estimated by inverting the NW estimator $S_K(x,\Omega)$. The weight $\gamma\in[0,1]$ adjusts the contributions of the two terms in building the pseudo sample covariance. When the neighboring graphs used in $S_K(x,\Omega)$ are precise with preferred sparsity, a large γ is applied so that zz^T is a minor maximum likelihood correction term to $(S_K(x,\Omega))^{-1}$. Hence the resulting $S_+(x,\Omega)$ has sparse graph structure and edge weights close to those of $S_K(x,\Omega)$ and fitting training data z well. This can be verified more clearly in the second row of (15), in which $S_V(x,\Omega)$ is comprised of the NW estimator $S_K(x,\Omega)$ and a rank-1 correction term caused by z. With a large γ, the resulting $S_+(x,\Omega)$ encodes a similar dependency graph as $S_K(x,\Omega)$, while the likelihood on the unique sample z is properly maximized and the sparsity is maintained by soft-thresholding. Hence, the proximal operator (15) allows us to update sparse precision matrices on arbitrary points given those on a small subset Ω.

In SpaGraphR, we start from a small subset Ω_0 storing the most representative points whose $S(x)$ have been estimated by CS $\hat{S}_{\Sigma_K(x),\lambda}$ as "seeds", and a sequence of disjoint subsets $\{\Omega_i\}_{i=1}^M\subseteq X$ that are ordered by their capability to represent the whole training set X. When the representative capability of a subset is measured by the squared error, the subset sequence can be built by top-down hierarchical k-means clustering. In this case, cluster centers of the second layer constitute Ω_0, and $\Omega_{t\in[M]}$ is comprised of the training points closest to the cluster centers at the $(t+2)^{th}$ layer. In iterations, $S(x)$ on points of each subset is updated given $S(x)$ estimated on all the prior subsets by (15). For example, $S(x)$ on points in subset Ω_t is updated as $\left\{S(x^j):=S_+(x^j,\cup_{l=1}^{t-1}\Omega_l)\right\}_{j\in\Omega_t}$.

In SpaGraphR, graph regression $S(x)$ on a smaller Ω places a warm start for the regression on a larger Ω, and thus the dependency graphs encoded by $S(x)$ in $\mathcal{X}$ are updated in a coarse to fine multi-resolution manner by incrementing Ω of $S_K(x,\Omega)$ in $S_+(x,\Omega)$. In addition, SpaGraphR is equal to applying a special proximal Newton-like method [31] to a CS problem (12) with $\hat{\Sigma}=S_V(x,X)$ for each involved x. Since we do not know $\hat{\Sigma}=S_V(x,X)$, in the tth iterate, a quadratic approximation of CS object function (12) on $S=S_V(x,\cup_{l=1}^{t-1}\Omega_l)$ and with $\hat{\Sigma}=S_V(x,\cup_{l=1}^{t-1}\Omega_l)$ is minimized. We summarize SpaGraphR in Algorithm 4.

Algorithm 1 Sparse Graph Regression (SpaGraphR)

Input: $\left\{X,\{Y_i\}_{i=1}^k\right\}$, $\{\hat{F}_i(y_i)\}_{i=1}^k$, λ, γ, M
Output: precision matrices $S(x)$ on all points
Compute $\{Z_i\}_{i=1}^k$ by applying $z_i=\Phi^{-1}\left(\hat{F}_i(y_i)\right)$ to each sample in $\{Y_i\}_{i=1}^k$;
Generate subset sequence $\{\Omega_i\}_{i=0}^M$ by $(M+2)$-layer top-down hierarchical k-means on X;
Estimate $S(x)$ on $x\in\Omega_0$ by $\hat{S}(x)=\hat{S}_{\Sigma_K(x),\lambda}$, where any CS algorithm can be applied;
for $t=1\to M$ **do**
  Update $\{S(x)\}_{x\in\Omega_t}$:$\left\{S(x^j):=S_+(x^j,\cup_{l=1}^{t-1}\Omega_l)\right\}_{j\in\Omega_t}$;
end for

---

5. JOINT PREDICTION BY MAP INFERENCE

Given a new instance x, the predictive distribution of y can be obtained by plugging x into the learned MTC model (4). Specifically, the precision matrix S in Gaussian copula density is estimated by $S_K(x,X)$, while the marginals are achieved by plugging x into the classical MTL model learned in the first stage. If the goal is to achieve a distribution of y or its clustering structure, the above procedure directly provides the results. However, when exact values for outputs y are required for prediction, an additional MAP inference needs to be conducted to $p(y|x)$ in (4)

$$\hat{y}=\arg\min_y\left\{-\log c\left(\{F_i(y_i)\}_{i=1}^k\middle|x\right)-\sum_{i=1}^k\log p(y_i|x)\right\}.\tag{17}$$

Without loss of generality, we study the case of Gaussian copula, the above optimization is equal to

$$\hat{y}=\arg\min_{y:\{F_i(y_i)=\Phi(z_i)\}_{i=1}^k}\left\{\frac{1}{2}z^TSz-\sum_{i=1}^k\log p(y_i|x)\right\},\tag{18}$$

which can be solved by alternating direction method of multipliers (ADMM) [31]

$$\begin{cases}z^{t+1}:=&\arg\min_z\sum_{i=1}^k\left[\frac{p}{2}\left\|F_i(y_i^t)-\Phi(z_i)\right\|_2^2+\right.\\&\left.q_i^k\left(F_i(y_i^t)-\Phi(z_i)\right)\right]+\frac{1}{2}z^TSz,\\\{y_i^{t+1}:=&\arg\min_{y_i}\frac{p}{2}\left\|F_i(y_i)-\Phi(z_i^{t+1})\right\|_2^2+\\&q_i^k\left(F_i(y_i)-\Phi(z_i^{t+1})\right)-\log p(y_i|x)\}_{i=1}^k,\\q^{t+1}:=&q^t+p\cdot\left\{F_i(y_i^{t+1})-\Phi(z_i^{t+1})\right\}_{i=1}^k,\end{cases}\tag{19}$$

where the subscript $\cdot^t$ denotes the tth iterate, $p/2$ is the weight of quadratic penalty in augmented Lagrangian, $q\in\mathbb{R}^k$ is the Lagrangian multiplier, and the diagonal of S is set to zero. In the above inference algorithm, the k outputs in y are updated independently as in classical MTL except an additional regularizer linking y_i with z_i. The k elements in z are jointly updated according to their dependency graph encoded in S and relationship to y. Dual variable q is updated by gradient ascent. In practice, we usually initialize y by classical MTL such that

$$\{y_i^0=\arg\min_{y_i}-\log p(y_i|x)\}_{i=1}^k.\tag{20}$$

So only a few subsequent iterates are required to gain an appealing joint prediction. Moreover, linear approximation could be applied to $F_i(y_i)-\Phi(z_i)$ in the updates of y and z for obtaining analytical solutions to the minimizations. Hence, the joint prediction conducted by (19) is efficient.

Another optimization algorithm for solving (18) can be derived by computing the finite difference approximation of Jacobi matrix in computing the first order gradient. In particular, if we substitute $z(y)=\{\Phi^{-1}(\hat{F}_i(y_i))\}_{i=1}^k$ into (18), the problem is reduced to an unconstrained optimization, which can be efficiently solved by gradient descent method or accelerated first order optimization like Nesterov's method. By using chain rule, the gradient of the objective function $G(y)$ in (18) can be approximated by

$$\frac{\partial G(y)}{\partial y}\approx\left[\frac{2}{h}\right]\left[z\left(y+h\right)-z\left(y-h\right)\right]^TSz-\frac{\partial\sum_{i=1}^k\log p(y_i|x)}{\partial y},\tag{21}$$

where h is a difference vector for y.

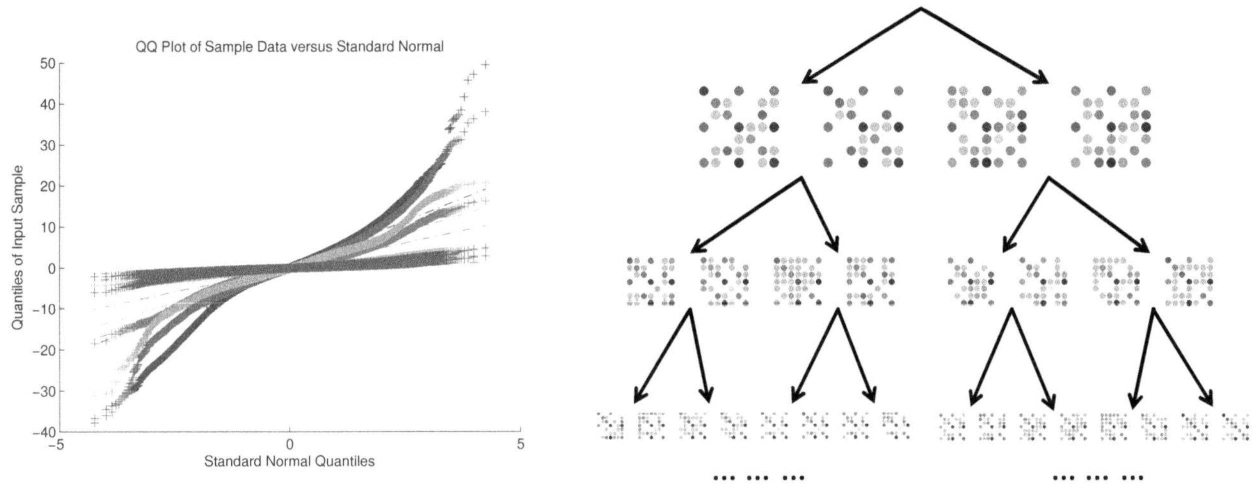

Figure 2: LEFT: Q-Q plot showing non-Gaussian noises obtained by classical MTL. RIGHT: sparse precision matrices by SpaGraphR on representative points selected by hierarchical k-means.

6. NUMERICAL RESULTS

6.1 Robotic Control

In the first experiment, we apply MTC and MTL algorithms to inverse dynamics dataset Sarcos [2] collected from a 7 degrees-of-freedom robot arm. It contains 48933 samples, each has 21 input features including 7 joint positions, 7 joint velocities plus 7 joint accelerations, and 7 joint torques as task outputs. In experiments, 400 samples are randomly selected for training and the rest are for test, in which averaged normalized MSE (nMSE) is measured for evaluation. We firstly apply single-task regression and regularization based MTL methods embedded in [40], and obtain 7 mean regression models. However, the Q-Q plot of the model noises $\{\epsilon_i = y_i - xw_i\}_{i=1}^7$ in Figure 2(a) shows that 3 outputs tend to have non-Gaussian noises, and thus implies the contradiction to assumed model in (1). This may cause sensitiveness to outliers and weaken the prediction performance.

We then apply MTC with Gaussian copula for achieving a joint conditional model $p(y|x)$ that can fit data better. In particular, we change the predictive models for the 3 outputs to a median regression with symmetric Laplacian noise and two quantile regression with asymmetric Laplacian noise, while keep the mean regression models for the rest outputs. In learning, these marginal models are estimated at first and then SpaGraphR is invoked to obtain a sparse precision function of x depicting the correlations among the Gaussian and non-Gaussian marginals. In Figure 2(b), we show the resultant sparse precision matrices on representative points identified by hierarchical k-means (2 points per cluster and 2^t clusters on t^{th} layer). It could be seem that both the graph sparse structure and the edge weights vary smoothly in local area of $\mathcal{X}$. Hence SpaGraphR provides a flexible model for outputs conditional correlations without losing robustness. In prediction, MTC has competitive performance comparing ro most classical MTL methods. The nMSE of different methods are listed in Table 2. In this case when the number of tasks is closed to the number of features, MTC exploiting outputs dependency is more effective in reducing model complexity.

[2] `http://gaussianprocess.org/gpml/data/`

6.2 Stock Price Prediction

In this experiment, we establish an MTC model for stock price prediction by learning from historical quote data collected from Yahoo! Finance [3]. Then we test and compare the prediction performance of MTC and other MTL methods for recently stock prices. In particular, we collect the weekly closing price of 35 famous companies' stocks from their historical quotes on NASDAQ between 01/01/2000 and 09/23/2013, which are 35 time series of stock prices in 716 weeks. For each stock, given historical prices in the pasting v weeks $\{q_{t-i}\}_{i=1}^v$, the price q_t in t^{th} week can be predicted by linear autoregression (AR) model $\hat{q}_t = \sum_{i=1}^v w_i q_{t-i} + w_0$. Hence, we sample 600 weeks with equal time intervals, and let the stock prices in these 600 weeks as responses. For each week out of the 600, we let the stock prices in the pasting 10 weeks as its input features. Therefore, for s^{th} stock, we have a dataset with outputs $Y_s \in \mathbb{R}^{600}$ and inputs $X_s \in \mathbb{R}^{600\times 10}$.

Table 2: Comparison of single-task regression (STR), dirty model for MTL [15], clustered MTL (CMTL) [39] and MTC on Sarcos dataset (nMSE).

	STR	Dirty	CMTL	MTC
nMSE	0.1828	0.1651	0.2733	0.1204

However, when predicting multiple stocks, we expect the historical prices of other stocks can also help the prediction. Therefore, we expand the input features and the AR model predicting the sth stock's price in the tth week turns to

$$\hat{q}_{s,t} = \sum_{i=1}^{k}\sum_{j=1}^{v} w_{i,j} q_{i,t-j} + w_{s,0}, \tag{22}$$

where $s \in [35]$ indexes the $k = 35$ stocks and $t \in [600]$ indexes the 600 weeks, and $v = 10$. The inputs of the dataset for each stock changes to the same matrix $[X_1, \ldots, X_{35}] \in \mathbb{R}^{600\times 350}$. In the experiment, we split the dataset by choosing the prices in the

[3] http://finance.yahoo.com/

first 400 weeks out of the 600 weeks as training set, and the prices in the rest 200 weeks for test. Note this setting is more challenging than random split and is closer to real problem, in which we expect to gain a reliable model for future prices only from historical prices.

Our goal here is to build a joint prediction model for all 35 stocks by not only using all of their historical prices' information captured by the AR model (22), but also by leveraging the dynamically varying correlations among different stocks. When modeling the conditional marginal $p(q_{s,t}|\{q_{i,t-j}\}_{i\in[35],j\in[10]})$ in (4) by AR model (22), an interesting and broadly verified phenomenon is that $\hat{q}_{s,t}$ in (22) performs more robust and reliable when assigned to the τth quantile (e.g., median, 25%, 75%) of the conditional marginal rather than the mean. This indicates that the conditional marginals are non-Gaussian, possibly asymmetric and heave tailed, and the conditional correlations among outputs are also non-Gaussian. The former fact leads to the failure of most MTL methods based on mean regression with Gaussian noise, while the latter fact leads to the failure of most covariance regression/selection methods based on Gaussian covariance assumption.

Fortunately, MTC is able to precisely model the non-Gaussian conditional marginals and correlations by learning the marginal model and copula density model separately. In particular, we adopt a τth quantile regression with skewed Laplace noise for each marginal model, i.e.,

$$p(y_i|x,w) = b\tau(1-\tau)\cdot \begin{cases} \exp(-b(1-\tau)(xw-y_i)), & y_i < xw; \\ \exp(-b\tau(y_i-xw)), & y_i \geq xw; \end{cases} \quad (23)$$

In the first learning stage, we impose additional ℓ_1 regularization to the coefficients w as a sparse prior. This is essentially helpful to our problem because 1) the current price of one stock is usually related to the prices of a few other stocks at a few historical time intervals rather than all stocks over all intervals; and 2) the number of training samples 400 is very close to the feature dimensions 350 and thus may introduce large variance. Given w, b can be easily obtained via MLE. The quantile τ (reported in Table 3) and the weight of ℓ_1 regularization (either 0.2 or 0.3) for each stock are achieved by hypothesis testing and cross-validation, respectively.

In the second learning stage, we compute 400 Gaussian samples Z from Y and the CDF of marginal models obtained in the first stage as training set for SpaGraphR, which learns the sparse and smooth graph function describing the dynamic graph over stocks. The sparse prior of the graph function also plays an important role here, because one stock currently is only related to a subset of other stocks in the same or related areas, and the influence of one area to another varies over time, which makes the edges in the graph changing over time.

We report both the ℓ_1 relative error $|\hat{q}-q|/|q|$ averaged over all 200 testing weeks for each stock in Table 3. The performance of marginal models before joint inference (STR) is also reported in order to make the improvement solely brought by the sparse graph function more clear. For comparison, we also apply existing MTL methods to this problem and report their performance in the same ways. Different from modeling $\hat{q}_{s,t}$ in (22) by quantile regression, all of them model it by least square regression yet with different joint priors/regularization over all w.

The results in Table 3 show that MTC successfully and precisely predict most of the stock prices over time, while the other classic MTL fail on most of them (their training errors are between $[0.5, 2]$ but the test errors are much worse, indicating their joint likelihood is very far from the truth, which can be accurately modeled by MTC). This is because the mean regression with Gaussian noise has large variance on stock data, and classical MTL cannot correctly capture and leverage the conditional non-Gaussian correlations by joint prior. Comparing to the prediction by single quantile regression models, the additional improvement of MTC prediction proves the essential role of SpaGraphR in relating multiple tasks to help prediction.

7. CONCLUSION

Multi-task learning (MTL) covers a rich class of machine learning and statistical problems expecting to let different tasks benefit each other by exploring their relatedness [32][37]. However, in order to reduce MTL to a easier regularization problem, most previous MTL methods limit the types of tasks, ignore the conditional dependency among outputs and merely rely on the pre-defined joint prior distribution of models to capture the relatedness. So they can hardly handle more complex tasks in practice, and usually achieve limited improvement over single task learning.

In this paper, we adapt copula model from semi-parametric statistics to the joint likelihood function $p(y|x)$ in MTL. The capability of copula in generating arbitrary continuous joint distribution results in an expressive model that allows combination of different types of marginal models $p(y_i|x)$ for different tasks, and an unified parametric description of outputs dependency. This structure enables us to develop a two-stage learning scheme for the proposed "multi-task copula (MTC)". While the first stage learns the marginals by using single task learning or any previous MTL method, the second stage aims at learning a conditional covariance function $\Sigma(x)$ (or precision function $\Sigma^{-1}(x)$ encoding a sparse dependency graph of y varying with inputs x.

Although this covariance regression is an open challenging problem in recent machine learning community, we proposes an efficient nonparametric estimator for $\Sigma(x)$ called "sparse graph regression (SpaGraphR)" that incorporates local likelihood maximization, kernel smoothing, and sparse structure of graph. SpaGraphR enables both the edge weighs and the sparse graph structure smoothly changing with varying x, which can be rarely achieved by previous methods. In addition, SpaGraphR starts from a few seed graphs on a small number of representative x and updates the graphs on other points from the known graphs by cheap matrix multiplication and entry-wise soft-thresholding. So it can refine the estimation accuracy of $\Sigma^{-1}(x)$ in a coarse-to-fine grained space of x efficiently for big data.

Different from previous MTL methods relying on given joint prior applied to task models, MTC automatically learns the conditional dependency of task outputs which directly serves the joint prediction. The joint prediction can be obtained by solving an easy optimization problem.

We applied MTC to robotic control and stock price prediction problems, in which there exist strong correlations between task outputs that cannot be correctly captured by previous MTL methods due to the non-Gaussian and asymmetric properties of their data distribution. In experimental comparison, we verify that the capability of both integrating different types of marginal distributions and capturing their conditional dependency lends MTC the power to outperform other MTL methods.

It is worth noting that the models presented in this paper and used in experiments are merely special instances of MTC. MTC allows rich combination of marginal models from different distribution classes or even non-parametric distributions, and arbitrary copula density functions that describe the output dependency. Similar to copula which is a "distribution generator", MTC plays a role of "model generator" for multi-task learning that can fit each task with the suitable marginal model and simultaneously fully leverage the task-relatedness encoded by both output dependency and joint

Table 3: **Comparison of Dirty, CMTL, MTL with trace norm penalty, STR, MTC on stock price data (test relative ℓ_1 error).**

Stock	τ	Dirty	CMTL	Trace	STR	MTC
ATT	0.1	3.9653	4.8156	2.2068	0.1239	0.0937
BOA	0.1	6.0347	4.4945	5.7678	0.0920	0.0679
Boeing	0.9	8.0096	8.3798	8.142	0.2544	0.2102
CVS	0.2	6.2283	4.8732	3.7163	0.0879	0.0841
FeDex	0.1	2.7012	9.976	5.6893	0.2353	0.2193
Ford	0.5	9.7238	2.1568	6.481	0.1142	0.1048
GE	0.4	3.9807	4.7537	2.388	0.0733	0.0707
HP	0.2	3.8119	8.3573	17.4959	0.1000	0.0910
IBM	0.1	1.9552	3.8116	4.0757	0.0997	0.0948
JPMorgan	0.2	3.2578	5.5316	2.4995	0.1555	0.1262
Macy	0.1	5.8561	5.8208	3.2293	0.1128	0.1115
Adobe	0.1	5.2789	5.1415	4.3769	0.1317	0.0814
Amazon	0.2	6.5161	0.6358	31.5366	0.3619	0.3204
Apple	0.1	8.7289	1.8109	21.0517	0.7708	0.5172
Autodesk	0.1	5.5317	8.3711	5.12	0.1936	0.1458
Chevron	0.1	2.8925	3.8882	2.8397	0.0366	0.0366
Cisco	0.2	5.2039	5.5257	5.1972	0.1619	0.1071
Costco	0.4	8.1616	5.6682	5.6519	0.4100	0.3601
Dell	0.1	7.0798	5.3801	8.6039	0.1481	0.1339
Ebay	0.9	4.6712	3.1633	3.374	0.1150	0.1050
Intel	0.1	7.1312	3.7495	7.6896	0.1004	0.0947
Maxim	0.2	4.7308	3.4045	2.473	0.1706	0.1145
Microsoft	0.9	6.7137	3.1567	4.2504	0.0485	0.0492
Oracle	0.2	16.283	4.0686	3.7193	0.0886	0.0820
Priceline	0.2	44.4155	148.1859	151.665	1.3897	1.0205
Qualcomm	0.1	2.5908	3.8174	2.5528	0.1125	0.0944
Sandisk	0.2	9.0629	5.6423	12.1588	0.1947	0.1748
SouthwestAir	0.1	12.7343	4.438	6.107	0.0878	0.0704
Target	0.9	8.8795	6.8072	5.1398	0.2976	0.2432
TI	0.1	6.3444	4.4869	4.503	0.1427	0.1085
Vodafone	0.1	14.3038	5.5485	3.5616	0.0818	0.0721
Walmart	0.2	4.6541	4.4191	3.9601	0.0551	0.0550
Wholefood	0.1	3.3218	6.0992	7.2131	0.1108	0.0857
Xilinx	0.1	6.1487	3.1605	1.6395	0.1889	0.1555
Yahoo	0.1	7.4028	6.0218	6.2141	0.2003	0.1862

prior of marginal models. Therefore, we believe lots of possible future contributions can be made to improve either MTC model for specified MTL problems or the efficiency of its learning/inference algorithms.

Acknowledgement

We would like to thank Prof. Carlos Guestrin, Prof. Ben Taskar and Prof. Emily Fox for their important suggestions in improving this draft. This work is supported by Australian Research Council Projects FT-130101457 and DP-140102164.

References

[1] R. Ando and T. Zhang. A framework for learning predictive structures from multiple tasks and unlabeled data. *Journal of Machine Learning Research*, 6:1817–1853, 2005.

[2] A. Argyriou, T. Evgeniou, and M. Pontil. Multi-task feature learning. In *Advances in Neural Information Processing Systems (NIPS)*, 2007.

[3] C. Z. J. Y. B. Lin, S. Yang and X. He. Multi-task vector field learning. In *Advances in Neural Information Processing Systems (NIPS)*, 2013.

[4] E. Bonilla, K. Chai, and C. Williams. Multi-task gaussian process prediction. In *Advances in Neural Information Processing Systems (NIPS)*, 2007.

[5] J. Chen, J. Liu, and J. Ye. Learning incoherent sparse and low-rank patterns from multiple tasks. In *Proceedings of the 16th ACM SIGKDD International Conference on Knowledge Discovery and Data Mining (KDD)*, 2010.

[6] X. Chen, Q. Lin, S. Kim, J. Carbonell, and E. Xing. Smoothing proximal gradient method for general structured sparse learning. In *The Conference on Uncertainty in Artificial Intelligence (UAI)*, 2011.

[7] A. Dempster. Covariance selection. *Biometrics*, 28:157–175, 1972.

[8] G. Elidan. Copula bayesian networks. In *Advances in Neural Information Processing Systems (NIPS)*, 2010.

[9] P. Embrechts, F. Lindskog, and A. McNeil. *Modeling dependence with copulas and applications to risk management.* Handbook of Heavy Tailed Distributions in Finance. 2003.

[10] E. Fox and D. Dunson. Bayesian nonparametric covariance regression. *arXiv:1101.2017*, 2011.

[11] J. Friedman, T. Hastie, and R. Tibshirani. Sparse inverse covariance estimation with the graphical lasso. *Biostatistics*, 9(3):432–441, 2008.

[12] Z. Ghahramani and M. Jordan. Supervised learning from incomplete data via an em approach. In *Advances in Neural Information Processing Systems (NIPS)*, 1994.

[13] J. Ghosn and Y. Bengio. Multi-task learning for stock selection. In *Advances in Neural Information Processing Systems (NIPS)*, 1997.

[14] P. Gong, J. Ye, and C. Zhang. Robust multi-task feature learning. In *Proceedings of the 18th ACM SIGKDD International Conference on Knowledge Discovery and Data Mining (KDD)*, 2012.

[15] A. Jalali, P. Ravikumar, S. Sanghavi, and C. Ruan. A dirty model for multi-task learnin. In *Advances in Neural Information Processing Systems (NIPS)*, 2010.

[16] S. Ji and J. Ye. An accelerated gradient method for trace norm minimization. In *International Conference on Machine Learning (ICML)*, 2009.

[17] S. Kim and E. Xing. Tree-guided group lasso for multi-task regression with structured sparsity. In *International Conference on Machine Learning (ICML)*, 2010.

[18] S. Kirshner. Learning with tree-averaged densities and distributions. In *Advances in Neural Information Processing Systems (NIPS)*, 2007.

[19] B. Liu, Y. Fu, Z. Yao, and H. Xiong. Learning geographical preferences for point-of-interest recommendation. In *Proceedings of the 19th ACM SIGKDD International Conference on Knowledge Discovery and Data Mining (KDD)*, pages 1043–1051, 2013.

[20] H. Liu, X. Chen, J. Lafferty, and L. Wasserman. Graph-valued regression. In *Advances in Neural Information Processing Systems (NIPS)*, 2010.

[21] H. Liu, J. Lafferty, and L. Wasserman. The nonparanormal: Semiparametric estimation of high dimensional undirected graphs. *Journal of Machine Learning Research*, 10:2295–2328, 2009.

[22] H. Liu, M. Palatucci, and J. Zhang. Blockwise coordinate descent procedures for the multi-task lasso, with applications to neural semantic basis discovery. In *International Conference on Machine Learning (ICML)*, 2009.

[23] J. Liu, S. Ji, and J. Ye. Multi-task feature learning via efficient l2,1-norm minimization. In *The Conference on Uncertainty in Artificial Intelligence (UAI)*, 2009.

[24] Q. Liu, Q. Xu, V. W. Zheng, H. Xue, Z. Cao, and Q. Yang. Multi-task learning for cross-platform sirna efficacy prediction: an in-silico study. *BMC Bioinformatics*, 11:181, 2010.

[25] X. Mao, B. Lin, D. Cai, X. He, and J. Pei. Parallel field alignment for cross media retrieval. In *Proceedings of the 21st ACM International Conference on Multimedia*, MM '13, pages 897–906, 2013.

[26] A. McNeil and J. Nešlehová. Multivariate archimedean copulas, d-monotone functions and ℓ_1-norm symmetric distributions. *Annals of Statistics*, 37(5b).

[27] K. Mo, E. Zhong, and Q. Yang. Cross-task crowdsourcing. In *Proceedings of the 19th ACM SIGKDD International Conference on Knowledge Discovery and Data Mining (KDD)*, pages 677–685, 2013.

[28] E. Nadaraya. On estimating regression. *Theory of Probability and its Applications*, 9(1):141–200.

[29] G. Obozinski, B. Taskar, and M. Jordan. High-dimensional union support recovery in multivariate regression. In *Advances in Neural Information Processing Systems (NIPS)*, 2009.

[30] G. Obozinski, B. Taskar, and M. Jordan. Joint covariate selection and joint subspace selection for multiple classi?cation problems. *Statistics and Computing*, 20:231–252, 2010.

[31] N. Parikh and S. Boyd. Proximal algorithms. *Foundations and Trends in Optimization*, 2013.

[32] N. Quadrianto, A. J. Smola, T. S. Caetano, S. V. N. Vishwanathan, and J. Petterson. Multitask learning without label correspondences. In *Advances in Neural Information Processing Systems (NIPS)*, pages 1957–1965, 2010.

[33] C. Rasmussen and Z. Ghahramani. Infinite mixtures of gaussian process experts. In *Advances in Neural Information Processing Systems (NIPS)*, 2001.

[34] B. Rolfs, B. Rajaratnam, D. Guillot, I. Wong, and A. Maleki. Iterative thresholding algorithm for sparse inverse covariance estimation. In *Advances in Neural Information Processing Systems (NIPS)*, 2012.

[35] A. Sklar. Fonctions de repartition a n dimensions et leurs marges. *Publications de l'Institut de Statistique de L'Universite de Paris*, 8:229–231.

[36] G. Watson. Smooth regression analysis. *Sankhya: The Indian Journal of Statistics, Series A*, 26(4):359–372.

[37] S. Yang, Y. Jiang, and Z.-H. Zhou. Multi-instance multi-label learning with weak label. In *International Joint Conference on Artificial Intelligence (IJCAI)*, 2013.

[38] S. Yu, K. Yu, V. Tresp, and H. Kriegel. Collaborative ordinal regression. In *International Conference on Machine Learning (ICML)*, 2006.

[39] J. Zhou, J. Chen, and J. Ye. Clustered multi-task learning via alternating structure optimization. In *Advances in Neural Information Processing Systems (NIPS)*, 2011.

[40] J. Zhou, J. Chen, and J. Ye. *MALSAR: Multi-tAsk Learning via StructurAl Regularization.* Arizona State University, 2011.

[41] J. Zhu, B. Zhang, E. Smith, B. Drees, R. Brem, L. Kruglyak, R. Bumgarner, , and E. Schadt. Integrating large-scale functional genomic data to dissect the complexity of yeast regulatory networks. *Nature Genetics*, 40:854–861, 2008.

Unifying Learning to Rank and Domain Adaptation: Enabling Cross-Task Document Scoring *

Mianwei Zhou, Kevin Chen-Chuan Chang
Department of Computer Science, University of Illinois at Urbana-Champaign, Urbana, IL, USA
zhou18@illinois.edu, kcchang@illinois.edu

ABSTRACT

For document scoring, although *learning to rank* and *domain adaptation* are treated as two different problems in previous works, we discover that they actually share the same challenge of adapting keyword contribution across different queries or domains. In this paper, we propose to study the *cross-task document scoring* problem, where a task refers to a query to rank or a domain to adapt to, as the first attempt to unify these two problems. Existing solutions for learning to rank and domain adaptation either leave the heavy burden of adapting keyword contribution to feature designers, or are difficult to be generalized. To resolve such limitations, we abstract the *keyword scoring principle*, pointing out that the contribution of a keyword essentially depends on, first, its importance to a task and, second, its importance to the document. For determining these two aspects of keyword importance, we further propose the concept of *feature decoupling*, suggesting using two types of easy-to-design features: *meta-features* and *intra-features*. Towards learning a scorer based on the decoupled features, we require that our framework fulfill *inferred sparsity* to eliminate the interference of noisy keywords, and employ *distant supervision* to tackle the lack of keyword labels. We propose the *Tree-structured Boltzmann Machine* (T-RBM), a novel two-stage Markov Network, as our solution. Experiments on three different applications confirm the effectiveness of T-RBM, which achieves significant improvement compared with four state-of-the-art baseline methods.

Categories and Subject Descriptors

H.3.3 [**Information Search and Retrieval**]: Retrieval models; I.2.7 [**Natural Language Processing**]: Text analysis

Keywords

Learning to Rank; Domain Adaptation; Feature Decoupling; Tree-Structured Restricted Boltzmann Machine

*This material is based upon work partially supported by NSF Grant IIS 1018723, the Advanced Digital Science Center of UIUC and the Multimodal Information Access and Synthesis Center at UIUC. Any opinions, findings, and conclusions or recommendations expressed in this publication are those of the author(s) and do not necessarily reject the views of the funding agencies.

KDD'14, August 24–27, 2014, New York, NY, USA.

ACM 978-1-4503-2956-9/14/08 ...$15.00.
http://dx.doi.org/10.1145/2623330.2623739.

1. INTRODUCTION

With much information in the world represented by unstructured text, many applications study how to develop document *scorers*, which can analyze the content of a document and determine its relevance for some information need, *e.g.*, text categorization [8], document retrieval [5]. Since manually crafting scorers is difficult, people are interested in how to automatically *learn* such scorers from labeled documents.

Scorer learning techniques have been actively studied for years – unlike early applications which usually deal with only one topic (*e.g.*, judging if a document is about "finance" [8]), with the prevalence of the Web serving the whole world of users and connecting numerous sources of data, most applications nowadays must handle various user needs, *i.e.*, *queries*, and diverse sources, *i.e.*, *domains*.

First, in terms of *queries*, many applications aim at ranking documents for queries that represent users' information needs, *i.e.*, realizing *learning to rank*. Unlike traditional IR which deals with short queries, learning to rank applications nowadays have to handle more sophisticated queries:

Application 1: *Verbose-Query-based Retrieval* [11, 2], which addresses verbose queries that consist of one or more long sentences. It is more challenging than traditional IR, because long queries usually contain extraneous terms which might hinder retrieval of relevant documents.

Application 2: *Entity-Centric Document Filtering* [22], which studies, given an entity (*e.g.*, a person) characterized by an identification page (*e.g.*, her Wikipedia page) as a query, how to identify documents relevant to the entity. Since an identification page is usually long and noisy, the solution has to identify keywords that represent the characteristics of the entity (*e.g.*, "microsoft" for entity "Bill Gates") for better retrieval accuracy.

Second, in terms of *domains*, traditional scorer learning techniques work well only when the training and testing documents use similar distributions of keywords, *i.e.*, documents are from the same domain. Due to the expensive cost of labeling, we expect to learn a document scorer that could be adapted across different domains, *i.e.*, realizing *domain adaptation*, for example:

Application 3: *Cross-Domain Sentiment Analysis* [4], which studies how to adapt a sentiment scorer across different domains of reviews. It is challenging because people tend to use different sentiment keywords in different domains, *e.g.*, "boring" in book reviews, and "leaking" in kitchen appliance reviews instead.

We observe that, although learning to rank and domain adaptation seem distinct from each other, both of them have to handle the varying importance of each *keyword* in different queries/domains (in this paper, we do not consider other properties which are orthogonal to the keyword content, *e.g.*, pagerank, although they can be easily incorporated as well). For example, in entity-centric document filtering, keyword "Microsoft" is important for query "Bill Gates," but not for "Michael Jordan;" in sentiment analysis, as mentioned earlier, different domains would use different keywords to represent the same sentiment. Therefore, as the common challenge for these two types of applications, both of them have to consider how to bridge keywords across different queries or domains.

Problem – Cross-Task Document Scoring. As the *first contribution* of this paper, observing such a common challenge, we propose to study a general *cross-task document scoring* problem, which, as far as we know, is the first attempt to unify learning to rank and domain adaptation. Formally, cross-task document scoring aims at learning a scorer $\mathcal{F}(d, t)$ to predict the relevance of document d for task t, where the notion of "*task*" represents the scoring of documents for one query in one domain. In the training phase, we are given some documents labeled for some tasks t (*e.g.*, some queries) to learn $\mathcal{F}(d, t)$; in the testing phase, as highlighted by "cross-task," $\mathcal{F}(d, t)$ should be capable of handling new tasks t' (*e.g.*, new queries) which do not appear in the labeled data.

Challenge – Learning to Adapt Keyword Contribution. As our *second contribution*, we identify the core challenge of cross-task document scoring as learning to adapt keyword contribution across tasks. Formally, if we use $Contrib(w, d, t)$ to denote the contribution of keyword w for document d with respect to task t, the relevance of document d is essentially the accumulation of its keywords' contribution $Contrib(w, d, t)$. Therefore, the challenge of learning $\mathcal{F}(d, t)$ lies in how to determine keyword contribution $Contrib(w, d, t)$ for tasks that do not appear in the training data, *i.e.*, *learning to adapt keyword contribution*.

Learning to adapt keyword contribution is critical for enabling cross-task scoring; however, traditional learning to rank frameworks (*e.g.*, RankSVM [10]) simply circumvent the problem. To learn a scorer, such frameworks adopt an ensembling idea to combine a set of manually crafted sub-scorers $f_k(d, t)$ as features, *e.g.*, in document retrieval [5, 14], $f_k(d, t)$ could be BM25, language model. These learning to rank frameworks are feasible for traditional document retrieval, as there exist many readily studied scorers that could be used as features; however, for newly proposed applications, such scorers are seldom available, and we need laborious feature engineering in order to adopt these frameworks.

Insight – Keyword Scoring Principle. As our *third contribution*, towards learning to adapt keyword contribution, we propose our key insight:

Keyword Scoring Principle – the importance of keyword w for document d with respect to task t, i.e., $Contrib(w, d, t)$, depends on: 1. the importance of keyword w for task t; 2. the importance of keyword w for document d.

Although such a principle is not abstracted before, it is intuitive and implicitly followed in the previous design of manually crafted scorers. Take BM25 as example: in terms of the first aspect, BM25 assumes that keywords with high inverse document frequency (*i.e.*, high *IDF*) are more important for the query; in terms of the second aspect, BM25 assumes that keywords mentioned a lot in the document (*i.e.*, high *TF*) should have higher contribution.

Abstract – Feature Decoupling. As our *fourth contribution*, to fulfill our goal of learning $Contrib(w, d, t)$ based on the principle, we propose the idea of *feature decoupling*, which suggests "decoupling" the original scorer-as-feature design in traditional learning to rank frameworks into two types of more elementary features:

To determine "the importance of keyword w for task t," we design *meta-features*, denoted by $f_k^{(M)}(w, t)$, to represent task-related keyword properties. In learning to rank, some recent works [1, 11, 3, 22] adopt such an idea, *e.g.*, using meta-features such as keyword position to identify important keywords from queries. In domain adaptation, Blitzer *et al.* [4] propose a model to use keyword correlation to bridge keywords from different domains. We can use meta-features to realize the same insight, which will be discussed in details in Section 3.4.

To determine "the importance of keyword w for document d," we propose the concept of *intra-features*, denoted by $f_k^{(I)}(w, d)$, to characterize how keyword w occurs in document d. The motivation is that, besides simply counting keywords as most applications do, we can characterize the keyword occurrence more generally and systematically for higher prediction accuracy. For example, keywords that appear in the title, anchor text or URL usually have larger contribution to the relevance.

Given such a decoupled feature design, we have to appropriately "re-couple" $f_k^{(M)}(w, t)$ and $f_k^{(I)}(w, d)$ to determine $Contrib(w, d, t)$, and $\mathcal{F}(d, t)$ finally takes the following abstraction:

$$\mathcal{F}(d, t) : \langle f_1^{(M)}(w, t), ...; f_1^{(I)}(w, d), ... \rangle \rightarrow \mathbb{R} \qquad (1)$$

To the best of our knowledge, such a learning framework, which aims at learning a scorer upon two types of elementary features, has not been studied before (previous works [1, 11, 3, 22] which have the concept of meta-features do not model intra-features).

Towards learning keyword contribution based on decoupled features, our framework has to fulfill two requirements:

<u>*Requirement 1: Inferred Sparsity.*</u> Unlike traditional learning to rank frameworks [5, 14] which do not model the concept of keywords, our scorer should be aware of the potential interference from noisy keywords. For example, both verbose-query-based retrieval and entity-centric document filtering focus on long queries, in which many keywords are unrelated to user intent or target entities; in sentiment analysis, a review usually contains many keywords that are irrelevant to sentiment. Even if we assign such keywords with small contribution, their values, once accumulated, will still severely affect the document score.

Therefore, in order to filter noisy keywords, we require that the keyword contribution function $Contrib(w, d, t)$ be *sparse*, which only outputs non-zero values for important keywords. Different from traditional sparse learning [20] which aims at learning sparse feature weightings to enforce feature sparsity, our goal is to *sparsify the inferred value of a function, i.e.*, achieving *inferred sparsity* (their difference will be further discussed in Section 4.1).

<u>*Requirement 2: Distant Supervision.*</u> Toward realizing learning to score keywords, another challenge arises from the lack of the keyword labels. In most applications, we are only provided with document labels, and it is impractical to request manual keyword labels for learning $Contrib(w, d, t)$. Therefore, we require that the scorer should fulfill *distant supervision*, by only using document labels to "distantly" guide the adaptation of keyword contribution.

Solution – Tree-Structured Restricted Boltzmann Machine. As our *fifth contribution*, to fulfill these two requirements, we propose a novel *Tree-structured Restricted Boltzmann Machine* (T-RBM) model for the cross-task document scoring problem.

First, to achieve *inferred sparsity*, the model needs a scoring scheme which can eliminate the contribution of noisy keywords. We develop a *two-stage* procedure: in the first stage, we learn a classifier to discretize the importance of keywords into different levels based on their meta-features, and *regularize* the classifier to enforce the elimination of noisy keywords; in the second stage, we determine the contribution of important keywords by their intra-features and set the contribution of unimportant ones to be zero.

Second, to achieve *distant supervision*, we propose to *join* the two stages in one model. Specifically, we take advantage of Markov Network to connect keyword importance and document relevance, such that we can use document labels to directly supervise the learning of the keyword classifier.

Based on these ideas, we design T-RBM, which, as a variant of Restricted Boltzmann Machine [19] (one type of bipartite Markov Network), models each document as a tree graph with the root node representing a document and the leaf nodes representing its keywords. Free of loop structures, T-RBM could be efficiently trained by exact belief propagation [17].

In the experiments, we performed our evaluation on verbose-query-based retrieval, entity-centric document filtering and cross-domain sentiment analysis in three different datasets. By comparing T-RBM with four state-of-the-art baselines, we observed that our framework not only provides a conceptually unified modeling but also significantly improves the results on different applications.

2. RELATED WORK

In terms of *abstraction*, learning to rank and domain adaptation are separately abstracted and studied in previous works, *e.g.*, document retrieval [5, 1, 11, 3], entity-centric document filtering [22], cross-domain sentiment analysis [4]. Inspired by their works, we identify their common challenge and propose a novel framework to unify these two problems for achieving a more general solution.

In terms of *challenge*, cross-task document scoring boils down to learning to adapt keyword contribution across different tasks.

1. For *learning to rank*, most previous works [5, 14] simply circumvent the challenge, leaving the burden of determining keyword contribution to feature designers. Some of the recent works [1, 11, 3, 22] start to confront the challenge by modeling keyword-level features, *i.e.*, meta-features, to learn keyword contribution; however, none of them explicitly model intra-features, failing to capture different kinds of keyword occurrences in the document.
2. For *domain adaptation*, Blitzer *et al.* [4] propose structural correspondence learning (SCL) to bridge keywords from different domains. The intuition is that, given two domain-specific keywords (*e.g.*, "boring" from book reviews and "leaking" from kitchen appliance reviews), if both of them co-occur a lot with some pivot keywords (*i.e.*, keywords like "bad," "worst" which are commonly used in all domains), these two keywords should share similar sentiment (*e.g.*, both "boring" and "leaking" represent negative sentiment). To realize such an insight, SCL learns a set of pivot predictors, each of which predicts the occurrence of one pivot keyword based on other domains-specific keywords, to relate different domains. Li *et al.* [13] and Pan *et al.* [16] follow the same intuition but use different approaches such as feature alignment [16] and matrix decomposition [13]. Different from these approaches which "hardcode" the logic of keyword adaptation in the model design, our feature decoupling idea allows designers to conveniently incorporate different ways of keyword adaptation by meta-features.

In terms of *technique*, we propose T-RBM, a novel two-stage Markov Network taking the decoupled features as input and fulfilling the requirements of inferred sparsity and distant supervision.

1. With respect to *inferred sparsity*, unlike sparse learning [20] which learns sparse parameters as feature weightings, we aim at sparsifying the inferred value of the keyword contribution function. Existing meta-feature-based solutions have different limitations in fulfilling this requirement. The solutions proposed by Lease *et al.* [11], Bendersky *et al.* [3] and Zhou *et al.* [22] do not fulfill the requirement, making the prediction result vulnerable to noisy keywords. Zhou *et al.* [22] propose another BoostMapping model, which achieves inferred sparsity by clustering keywords based on their meta-features and eliminating noisy clusters; as the limitations, BoostMapping is difficult to solve when we have to model multiple intra-features, and might overfit the training data. We will compare T-RBM with these models in details in Section 4.1.
2. With respect to the requirement of *distant supervision*, similar to T-RBM, Bendersky *et al.* [1] propose to learn a keyword classifier to discover important concepts for retrieval; however, their solution relies on the existence of keyword labels, which is impractical for most applications. Different from their work, taking the advantage of Markov Network, T-RBM manages to train the keyword classifier based on only document labels.
3. With respect to the *model structure*, the most related work to ours is the Markov Random Field model proposed by Lease *et al.* [11]. As the key difference, their solution is a generative model characterizing $P(q, d)$ – the joint probability of observing query q and document d, while our T-RBM model directly models the conditional probability $P(d|q)$. It has been repeatedly confirmed that a discriminative model usually yields better generalization performance compared with a generative model [21]; furthermore, as mentioned earlier, their solution does not fulfill the inferred sparsity requirement.
4. Restricted Boltzmann Machine (RBM), as one type of bipartite Markov Network, is adopted in many applications such as topic modeling [18], deep learning [6], *etc.*With distinct settings and objectives, our proposed T-RBM is different from traditional RBM models in two aspects: first, T-RBM takes a tree structure which can be trained efficiently; second, T-RBM adopts a novel hidden variable regularization technique, which allows the model to control the inferred sparsity of keyword contribution.

3. CROSS-TASK DOCUMENT SCORING

In this section, we formally define the *cross-task document scoring* problem. To tackle the challenge of *learning to adapt keyword contribution*, we propose the insight of *keyword scoring principle* and the concept of *feature decoupling*.

3.1 Problem: Cross-Task Document Scoring

In document scoring, we aim at predicting the relevance of a document d for a particular task t. Formally, task t could be represented as a function $t : d \to \mathbb{R}$, which takes a document d as input, and outputs a score denoting the relevance of d. We define that two tasks t_1 and t_2 are different, if there exists one document d satisfying $t_1(d) \neq t_2(d)$. Therefore, identifying relevant documents for different queries belongs to two different tasks, as one document usually has different relevance for two queries; similarly, the sentiment judgement of a book review is also different from that of a kitchen appliance review.

In contrast with *single-task document scoring* which tackles only one task (*e.g.*, text categorization [8] learns a scorer to predict if a document is about a fixed topic such as "finance"), in a *cross-task document scoring* problem, we are interested in a set of different but related tasks $\mathcal{T}$. For example, in verbose-query-based retrieval and entity-centric document filtering, each $t \in \mathcal{T}$ represents a task of predicting document relevance for one verbose query or one entity; in cross-domain sentiment analysis, each task t is to judge the sentiment of reviews form one particular domain.

Formally, in *cross-task document scoring*, our goal is to automatically learn a document scorer $\mathcal{F}(d, t)$, which could output the relevance of document d for task $t \in \mathcal{T}$.

In *the training phrase*, we are given a set of training documents $\mathbf{d} = \{d_1, d_2, ..., d_N\}$ and a list of document labels $\hat{\mathbf{y}} = \{\hat{y}_1, ..., \hat{y}_N\}$, where each d_i is labeled by $\hat{y}_i$ denoting the relevance of d_i for task $t_i \in \mathcal{T}$ (t_i and t_j could refer to the same task, indicating d_i and d_j are labeled for the same query or in the same domain). Here, $\hat{y}_i$ could be either binary (*e.g.*, 0–negative, 1–positive) or ordinal (*e.g.*, 0–irrelevant, 1–relevant or 2–perfectly relevant).

Based on the training documents, we aim at learning $\mathcal{F}$, which, in *the testing phase*, could predict the relevance of a new document d' for task $t' \in \mathcal{T}$. Specifically, as highlighted by "cross-task," we require that t' should differ from all the training tasks, *i.e.*, $t' \neq t_i$ for all i. That is because, in most applications, the target task set $\mathcal{T}$ could not be covered by finite training examples (*e.g.*, there are infinite possible queries in document retrieval) and thus, $\mathcal{F}$ should be adaptable to unseen queries or domains, *i.e.*, new tasks.

3.2 Challenge: Learning to Adapt Keyword Contribution

To score a document d for a task t, the scorer has to assess the content of document d. Formally, we use $\mathcal{V}(t)$ to represent the vocabulary of keywords that are considered in task t, where each keyword $w \in \mathcal{V}(t)$ could be 1-gram, 2-gram, noun phrases, *etc.* Following previous works [3, 22, 4], in verbose-query-based retrieval and entity-centric document filtering, $\mathcal{V}(t)$ covers keywords that are mentioned in the query or the entity identification page, while in cross-domain sentiment analysis, $\mathcal{V}(t)$ includes all the keywords. We then define $\mathcal{W}(d,t) \subseteq \mathcal{V}(t)$ as the content of document d that is related with task t.

Based on the document content $\mathcal{W}(d,t)$, the relevance of document d could be viewed as the accumulation of its containing keywords' contribution. Formally, if we use *Conrib*(w,d,t) to denote the contribution of keyword w to document d with respect to task t, $\mathcal{F}(d,t)$ takes the form of

$$\mathcal{F}(d,t) \propto \sum_{w \in \mathcal{W}(d,t)} \mathit{Conrib}(w,d,t) \tag{2}$$

As Eq. 2 shows, the challenge of cross-task document scoring becomes how to learn *Conrib*(w,d,t) to determine the keyword contribution for new tasks t' which do not appear in the training data, *i.e.*, *learning to adapt keyword contribution*.

3.3 Insight: Keyword Scoring Principle

Due to the requirement of "cross-task," the learning of *Conrib*(w,d,t) is non-trivial. If our target is a single-task document scoring problem (*i.e.*, tackling the same task in both training and testing phases), as a common solution [8], we can define *Conrib*$(w,d,t) = \alpha_w * \mathit{TF}_w(d)$, where each feature function $\mathit{TF}_w(d)$ represents how many times document d contains a specific keyword w, and α_w, as its weighting, characterizes the importance of keyword w (*e.g.*, in text categorization , if the target topic is about finance, keyword "stock" should have value of α_w). The scorer is then defined by

$$\mathcal{F}(d,t) = \sum_{w \in \mathcal{W}(d,t)} \alpha_w * \mathit{TF}_w(d) \tag{3}$$

where α_w could be learned by standard learners. However, such a design could not be applied in cross-task document scoring, because, as we mentioned in Section 1, one keyword usually has very different importance for different tasks, and thus, α_w learned from training data could not be adapted to new tasks.

Traditional learning to rank frameworks (*e.g.*, RankSVM [10]) manage to tackle different tasks (*i.e.*, queries); however, they circumvent the problem of learning *Conrib*(w,d,t), which define the scorer by

$$\mathcal{F}(d,t) = \sum_{k=1}^{N} \beta_k f_k(d,t) \tag{4}$$

where $f_{k \in \{1...N\}}(d,t)$ is a set of handcrafted sub-scorer features and β_k is learned to represent the confidence of $f_k(d,t)$, *e.g.*, in document retrieval [5], $f_k(d,t)$ could be vector space model, BM25 and language model. As we discussed in Section 1, such frameworks require designers to manually determine the keyword contribution in the feature design, laying heavy burden on designers.

In order to automatically learn the contribution of keywords, as our key insight, we propose the keyword scoring principle:

Definition 1 (Keyword Scoring Principle). If we use $\mathcal{R}_t(w,t)$ to denote the importance of keyword w for task t, and $\mathcal{R}_d(w,d)$ to denote the importance of keyword w for document d, the keyword contribution *Contrib*(w,d,t) should take the following form:

$$\mathit{Contrib}(w,d,t) : \mathcal{R}_t(w,t), \mathcal{R}_d(w,d) \rightarrow \mathbb{R} \tag{5}$$

3.4 Abstract: Feature Decoupling

As we introduced in Section 1, towards automatically learning the keyword contribution *Contrib*(w,d,t) based on the principle, we propose the concept of *feature decoupling*, which suggest "decoupling" the original scorer-as-feature design (*i.e.*, $f_k(d,t)$ used in Eq. 4) into two types of more elementary features:

Definition 2 (Feature Decoupling). To learn *Contrib*(w,d,t), we propose to design, first, *meta-features* $f_k^{(M)}(w,t)$, which characterize task-t-related properties of keyword w, for determining the importance of keyword w for task t, *i.e.*, defining $\mathcal{R}_t(w,t)$ by

$$\mathcal{R}_t(w,t) : \langle f_1^{(M)}(w,t), f_2^{(M)}(w,t), ...\rangle \rightarrow \mathbb{R} \tag{6}$$

and, second, *intra-features* $f_k^{(I)}(w,d)$, which describe how document d contains keyword w, for determining the importance of keyword w for document d, *i.e.*, defining $\mathcal{R}_d(w,d)$ by

$$\mathcal{R}_d(w,d) : \langle f_1^{(I)}(w,d), f_2^{(I)}(w,d), ...\rangle \rightarrow \mathbb{R}. \tag{7}$$

Figure 1 lists all the features we use for verbose-query-based retrieval, entity-centric document filtering, and cross-domain sentiment analysis.

First, for *meta-features*, the designs vary a lot across applications:
a) In verbose-query-based retrieval, meta-features are designed to identify important keywords in the query. For example, *QueryPos* is used, as keywords mentioned earlier in the query tend to be more important. Following previous works [3], we model not only unigram, but also adjacent bigrams in the query. To discriminate their importance, we design separate features for them, *e.g.*, *QueryPos*[unigram] and *QueryPos*[bigram].
b) In entity-centric document filtering, we only model unigrams, because the query is already very long, and we find that considering bigrams does not help improve the performance. In additional to the features used in verbose-query-based retrieval, we also design meta-features like *TFInTitle*, *TFInInfoBox*, to leverage the structure of Wikipedia pages for identifying importance keywords.
c) In cross-domain sentiment analysis, the design of meta-features is very different from the other applications. In order to realize the insight proposed by Blitzer *et al.* [4] (introduced in Section 2), given a domain-specific keyword w, we propose to calculate a list of meta-features *Corr*$[w_p]$, each of which measures the Pearson correlation between w and one particular pivot keyword w_p – the correlation is positive if two keywords are positively correlated, negative if negatively correlated and zero if independent.

Second, *intra-features* characterize how a document contains a keyword. As discussed in Section 1, our designed intra-features describe how a keyword appears in different positions of a document (*e.g.*, title, anchor text) by different representations of term frequency (*e.g.*, term frequency normalized by document length). In verbose-query-based retrieval, as suggested by Bendersky *et al.* [3], we also design *WindowTF* specifically for bigrams, which counts the number of times that two keywords appear within a fixed size of window.

Name	Description
Meta-Feature $f_k^{(M)}(w,t)$	
QueryTF	Term Frequency of w is in the query (or the Wiki page).
IDF	The inverse term frequency of w
IsNoun (Vb/ Adj/ Adv/Num)	If w is a noun/verb/adjective/adverb/number
QueryPos	The first position where w is mentioned.
TFInTitle (InfoBox/OpenPara /AnchorEntity)	Term Frequency of w in the Wikipedia title/ the InfoBox/ the Wikipedia opening paragraph/ the anchor entities.
Corr[w_p]	Pearson Correlation between w and one pivot keyword w_p
Intra-Feature $f_k^{(I)}(w,d)$	
DocTF(Raw/Normalized/Log -Scaled)	Term frequency of w in d, which is represented by three features: raw frequency, frequency normalized by length, and logarithmically scaled frequency computed by log (f(w,d) + 1).
AnchorTF(Raw/...)	Term frequency of w in the anchor text of d
TitleTF(Raw/...)	Term frequency of w in the title of d
WindowsTF(Raw/...)	Only for Bigram. The number of times two keywords appear within a fixed size of window.
Doc-Feature $f_k^{(D)}(d)$	
DocLen	The document length of d
PivotTF[w_p]	Term Frequency of pivot keyword w_p in document d

Type	Feature List
Verbose-Query-based Retrieval	
Meta-Feature	[UniGram/Bigram] *QueryTF, IDF, QueryPos* [UniGram] *IsNoun(Vb/...)*
Intra-Feature	[UniGram/Bigram] *DocTF(Raw/...), AnchorTF(Raw/...), TitleTF(Raw/...)* [Bigram] WindowTF (Raw/...)
Doc-Feature	*DocLen*
Entity-centric document Filtering	
Meta-Feature	*QueryTF, IDF, IsNoun(Vb/ ...), QueryPos, TFInTitle(InfoBox/...)*
Intra-Feature	*DocTF(Raw/...), DocAnchorTF(Raw/...), DocTitleTF(Raw/...)*
Doc-Feature	*DocLen*
Cross-domain Sentiment Analysis	
Meta-Feature	*Corr[w_p]*
Intra-Feature	*DocTF(Raw/...)*
Doc-Feature	*DocLen, PivotTF[w_p]*

Figure 1: Feature design for three applications.

Training Phase:

Given: Training documents $\boldsymbol{d} = \{d_1, d_2, ..., d_N\}$, each d_i is labeled by y_i denoting the relevance of d_i with respect to task t_i, represented by its content $\mathcal{W}(d_i, t_i)$, and characterized by meta-features $f_k^{(M)}(w, t_i)$, intra-features $f_k^{(I)}(w, d_i)$ and doc-features $f_k^{(D)}(d_i)$

Output: A document scorer $\mathcal{F}(d, t)$ learned from training data.

Testing Phase:

Given: A new task t' ($t' \neq t_i$, for all i), document d' represented by $\mathcal{W}(d', t')$, features $f_k^{(M)}(w, t')$, $f_k^{(I)}(w, d')$ and $f_k^{(D)}(d')$

Output: The relevance of d' with respect to t', i.e., $\mathcal{F}(d', t')$

Figure 2: Cross-task document scoring.

Finally, we design doc-features $f_k^{(D)}(d)$, which characterize document features that have the same weightings across different tasks. For example, in cross-domain sentiment analysis, we design *PivotTF*$[w_p]$ for each pivot keyword w_p (*e.g.*, "good," "bad"), which represents the same sentiment in all domains. The design of doc-features is not the main focus of this paper, as they are the same with the features used in traditional learning models.

Given such a decoupled feature design, the cross-task document scoring problem is summarized in Figure 2.

4. TREE-STRUCTURED RESTRICTED BOLTZMANN MACHINE

Towards realizing learning to adapt keyword contribution, we require that our framework fulfill the requirements of *inferred sparsity* and *distant supervision*. As our solution, we propose *Tree-Structured Restricted Boltzmann Machine* (T-RBM) to learn a two-stage document scorer based on the decoupled features.

4.1 Requirement: Inferred Sparsity & Distant Supervision

As we motivated in Section 1, in many applications, the keyword vocabulary $\mathcal{V}(t)$ we model is very noisy. If such noisy keywords are not appropriately filtered, their inferred values of *Contrib*(w, d, t), once accumulated, will severely affect the prediction accuracy of $\mathcal{F}(d, t)$. Therefore, we require that our framework achieve *inferred sparsity*:

Requirement 1 (Inferred Sparsity for Keyword Contribution). *Contrib*(w, d, t) should equal to zero for unimportant keywords w.

This concept of inferred sparsity is closely related with feature sparsity, which traditional sparse learning works [20] aim to achieve. The goal of feature sparsity is to learn a sparse feature weighting vector, in which only a few features have non-zero weightings, for the purpose of reducing model complexity and increasing prediction accuracy. One common technique for achieving feature sparsity is l_1 regularization. For example, in single-task document scoring (which defines $\mathcal{F}(d, t)$ by Eq. 3), we can add an l_1 regularization term $|\alpha_w|_1$ to the objective function to learn sparse feature weightings α_w.

In contrast with feature sparsity which aims at learning sparse feature weightings, in inferred sparsity, we would like to "sparsify" the inferred value of a function, *i.e.*, *Contrib*(w, d, t). Traditional feature sparsity techniques simply do not work, because the value of *Contrib*(w, d, t) is jointly determined by a set of decoupled features – setting some of their weightings to be zero can not make the whole function become sparse.

Besides inferred sparsity, due to the lack of keyword labels, the learning framework should also achieve *distant supervision*:

Requirement 2 (Distant Supervision by Document Labels). The learning of keyword contribution *Contrib*(w, d, t) should be distantly guided by only document labels $\hat{\mathbf{y}}$.

As we introduced in Section 2, some existing works [3, 11, 22] on verbose-query-based retrieval and entity-centric document filtering also adopt the concept of meta-features. Although we can extend their works to support multiple intra-features, their models still have different limitations in fulfilling our requirements.

First, the concept weighting model proposed by Bendersky *et al.* [3], the Markov random field model proposed by Lease *et al.* [11] and the linear weighting model proposed by Zhou *et al.* [22] all belong to same the category, which define *Contrib*$(w, d, t) = [\sum_i \beta_i * f_i^{(M)}(w, t)] * DocTF(w, d)$ as a linear function over meta-features. Since *DocTF*(w, d) is just one type of intra-feature, we can easily extend it to support multiple intra-features, by defining *Contrib*$(w, d, t) = \sum_{i,j} \beta_{ij} * f_i^{(M)}(w, t) * f_j^{(I)}(w, d)$, and the scorer becomes

$$\mathcal{F}(d, t) = \sum_{i,j} \beta_{ij} \sum_{w \in \mathcal{W}(d,t)} f_i^{(M)}(w, t) * f_j^{(I)}(w, d) \quad (8)$$

where each $\sum_{w \in \mathcal{W}(d,t)} f_i^{(M)}(w, t) * f_j^{(I)}(w, d)$ could be treated as a generated feature, and β_{ij} could be learned by standard learners.

Such a linear design of *Contrib*(w, d, t) fails to fulfill the requirement of inferred sparsity. Actually, except the trivial solution which sets all β_{ij} to be 0, for other assignments of β_{ij}, we can only get a small number of keywords (no more than the number of β_{ij}) which have zero contribution. The drawback of failing to achieve inferred sparsity could be observed by checking the semantics of the generated features. Take meta-feature *QueryPos* and intra-feature *DocTF* as example. The generated feature denotes the *QueryPos* summation of keywords from a document, which fails to capture the intuition that keywords with low *QueryPos* are more important, and documents containing more low-*QueryPos* keywords are more relevant.

Second, realizing the limitations of linear models, Zhou *et al.* [22] propose BoostMapping, which first adopts a boosting framework to generate a set of clusters $c_1, c_2, ...$, with each cluster c_i containing keywords sharing similar meta-features, *e.g.*, "*IDF* > 10 and *QueryPos* < 5," and then assumes that keywords from the same cluster c_i share the same contribution $Contrib_i(w, d, t) = \gamma_i * DocTF(w, d)$. Similar to the linear weighting model, we can extend it to support multiple intra-features by defining $Contrib_i(w, d, t) = \sum_j \gamma_{ij} * f_j^{(I)}(w, d)$, and the scorer becomes

$$\mathcal{F}(d, t) = \sum_{i,j} \gamma_{ij} \sum_{w \in \mathcal{W}(d,t) \cap c_i} f_j^{(I)}(w, d). \quad (9)$$

BoostMapping manages to achieve inferred sparsity, as the learner will assign $\gamma_{ij} = 0$ for unimportant clusters. However, it is difficult to extend the learning algorithm of BoostMapping (specifically, for generating clusters c_i) to support multiple intra-features. Furthermore, as reported in the paper [22] and confirmed in our experiment, BoostMapping might overfit to training tasks in some specific settings, which would lead to poor generalization capability.

4.2 Proposal: Two-Stage Scoring Model

To fulfill these two requirements, we develop a *two-stage* scoring procedure. Specifically, to achieve inferred sparsity, we *discretize* the importance of a keyword into different levels, and explicitly define $Contrib(w, d, t) = 0$ for unimportant keywords; to realize distant supervision, we unify the two stages in one single model, and learn the feature weightings by only document labels. The model is described in the following:

- In the first stage, we build a keyword classifier $\mathcal{C}(w, t) \in \{0, 1, ..., L\}$ based on meta-features $f_k^{(M)}(w, t)$ to discretize the importance of keywords, where $\mathcal{C}(w, t) = 0$ indicates that w is a noisy keyword for task t, and $\mathcal{C}(w, t) \in \{1, ..., L\}$ represents keywords of different importance levels.
- In the second stage, we determine contribution of each keyword w based on its importance level $\mathcal{C}(w, t)$. For important keywords with $\mathcal{C}(w, t) = l \neq 0$, the value of $Contrib(w, d, t)$ should depend on intra-features $f_k^{(I)}(w, d)$, while for unimportant ones (*i.e.*, $\mathcal{C}(w, t) = 0$), we set $Contrib(w, d, t) = 0$ to fulfill the requirement of inferred sparsity.

Formally, such a two-stage model defines $Contrib(w, d, t)$ as,

$$Contrib(w, d, t) = \begin{cases} \mathcal{U}_l(w, d) & \text{if } \mathcal{C}(w, t) = l \neq 0; \\ 0 & \text{if } \mathcal{C}(w, t) = 0. \end{cases} \quad (10)$$

where $\mathcal{U}_l(w, d)$ is a function defined over intra-features $f_k^{(I)}(w, d)$.

4.3 Solution: Tree-Structured Restricted Boltzmann Machine

In order to realize the design of $Contrib(w, d, t)$ in Eq. 10, the model should, first, characterize how keyword classifier $\mathcal{C}(w, t)$ depends on meta-features $f^{(M)}(w, t)$, second, determine how the contribution of important keywords, *i.e.*, $\mathcal{U}(w, d)$, is defined based on intra-features $f^{(I)}(w, d)$, and, third, be capable of learning $\mathcal{C}(w, t)$ in the absence of keyword labels. To achieve these three goals, we propose a novel *Tree-structured Restricted Boltzmann Machine* (T-RBM), in the framework of Markov Network, as our solution. Restricted Boltzmann Machine (RBM) [19] refers to one type of bipartite Markov network, which is widely used in many applications (*e.g.*, deep learning [6], topic modeling [18]). As a simplified

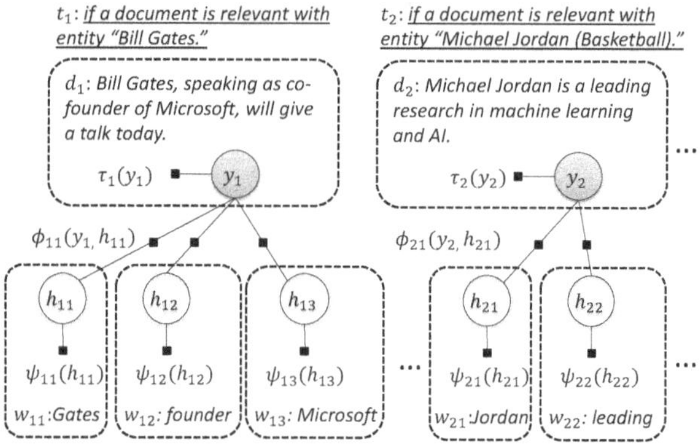

Figure 3: Tree-structured Restricted Boltzmann Machine.

RBM, our proposed T-RBM takes a tree structure to characterize the dependency between documents and keywords.

We highlight three important features of our proposed T-RBM model. First, to tackle the lack of keyword labels, T-RBM models the importance of keywords as *hidden variables*, and only uses document labels to guide the learning. Second, T-RBM adopts a novel *hidden variable regularization* idea, which allows the model to control the inferred sparsity of keyword contribution. Third, taking a tree structure, T-RBM could be *efficiently learned* by standard optimization techniques.

4.3.1 Model Overview

Figure 3 shows a T-RBM model designed for entity-centric document filtering. Generally, T-RBM is composed of N tree-structured Markov Networks, each of which corresponds to one document. There are no edges between trees, indicating that the documents are independent with each other. Each tree contains two types of nodes y_i and $\mathbf{h_i} = \{h_{i1}, ..., h_{i|\mathbf{h_i}|}\}$, with $y_i \in \{0, 1\}$ denoting the relevance of document d_i ($y_i = 1$ if d_i is relevant, and $y_i = 0$ otherwise) and $h_{ij} \in \{0, 1, ..., L\}$ is a hidden variable denoting the importance of w_{ij} for task t_i (for notational convenience, we use $\mathbf{w_i} = \{w_{i1}, w_{i2}, ...\}$ to represent document content $\mathcal{W}(d_i, t_i)$, where w_{ij} denotes the j-th keyword in document d_i). More specifically, $h_{ij} = 0$ indicates that w_{ij} is unimportant, and $h_{ij} \in \{1, ..., L\}$ corresponds to different importance levels of keywords, *e.g.*, in sentiment analysis, both "good" and "bad" are important keywords, but have different contribution to the document sentiment.

Three types of factors $\psi_{ij}(h_{ij})$, $\phi_{ij}(y_i, h_{ij})$ and $\tau_i(y_i)$ are defined in T-RBM. Specifically, $\psi_{ij}(h_{ij})$ characterizes whether keyword w_{ij} is important for task t_i, $\phi_{ij}(y_i, h_{ij})$ models how keyword w_{ij} contributes its importance to document d_i, and $\tau_i(y_i)$ models the effect of other document features $f_k^{(D)}(d_i)$. Based on the factors, the conditional probability $P(y_i, \mathbf{h_i}|d_i, \mathbf{w_i}, t_i)$ is defined to represent the probability of a specific assignment of y_i and $\mathbf{h_i}$, given in the following,

$$P(y_i, \mathbf{h_i}|d_i, \mathbf{w_i}, t_i) \propto \tau_i(y_i) \prod_{j=1}^{|\mathbf{w_i}|} \phi_{ij}(y_i, h_{ij}) \psi_{ij}(h_{ij}) \quad (11)$$

We are interested in document scorer $\mathcal{F}(d_i, t_i)$, which, in the language of probability, is formally described by $P(y_i = 1|d_i, \mathbf{w_i}, t_i)$. Based on Eq. 11, we can represent $P(y_i = 1|d_i, \mathbf{w_i}, t_i)$ in the form of graph factors, by marginalizing $P(y_i = 1, \mathbf{h_i}|d_i, \mathbf{w_i}, t_i)$ over all possible assignments of $\mathbf{h_i}$,

$$P(y_i = 1|d_i, \mathbf{w_i}, t_i) = \sum_{\mathbf{h_i}} P(y_i = 1, \mathbf{h_i}|d_i, \mathbf{w_i}, t_i) \quad (12)$$

To enforce inferred sparsity, we also want to control the percentage of noisy keywords in the model learning. In the language of probability, the inferred sparsity of keyword contribution could be represented by $P(\mathbf{h_i} = 0|d_i, \mathbf{w_i}, t_i)$, defined as follows,

$$P(\mathbf{h_i} = 0|d_i, \mathbf{w_i}, t_i) = \sum_{y=0}^{1} \prod_{j=1}^{|\mathbf{w_i}|} P(y_i = y, h_{ij} = 0|d_i, \mathbf{w_i}, t_i) \tag{13}$$

4.3.2 Factor Design

In T-RBM, we design factors $\psi_{ij}(h_{ij})$, $\phi_{ij}(y_i, h_{ij})$ and $\tau_i(y_i)$ to characterize the dependency required by Eq. 10.

First, $\psi_{ij}(h_{ij})$ characterizes how keyword classifier $\mathcal{C}(w_{ij}, t_i)$ judges if w_{ij} is an important keyword for task t_i, which should depend on meta-features $f_k^{(M)}(w_{ij}, t_i)$:

$$\psi_{ij}(h_{ij}) = \begin{cases} e^{\sum_k \theta_{kl}^{(M)} f_k^{(M)}(w_{ij}, t_i)} & \text{if } h_{ij} = l > 0; \\ 1 & \text{if } h_{ij} = 0. \end{cases} \tag{14}$$

Eq. 14 characterizes different levels of important keywords by defining L sets of feature weightings $\theta_{k,l}^{(M)}$. Note that we set $\tau_i(0) = 1$ since only relative value between $\tau_i(l)$ and $\tau_i(0)$ matters in the Markov Network.

Second, $\phi_{ij}(y_i, h_{ij})$ models how noisy keywords are filtered, and how the contribution of important keywords $\mathcal{U}_l(w, d)$ depends on intra-features $f_k^{(I)}(w_{ij}, d_i)$,

$$\phi_{ij}(y_i, h_{ij}) = \begin{cases} \exp[\sum_k \theta_{kl0}^{(I)} f_k^{(I)}(w_{ij}, d_i)] & \text{if } h_{ij} = l \ \& \ y_i = 0; \\ \exp[\sum_k \theta_{kl1}^{(I)} f_k^{(I)}(w_{ij}, d_i)] & \text{if } h_{ij} = l \ \& \ y_i = 1; \\ 1 & \text{if } h_{ij} = 0. \end{cases} \tag{15}$$

We set $\phi_{ij}(0, 0) = \phi_{ij}(1, 0) = 1$ to represent that if w_{ij} is an unimportant keyword, w_{ij} would not contribute any score to document d_i. When w_{ij} is important, *i.e.*, $h_{ij} = l > 0$, the value of $\phi_{ij}(y_i, h_{ij})$ depends on how w_{ij} appears in document d_i, *i.e.*, intra-features $f_k^{(I)}(w_{ij}, d_i)$. It should be noted that, even if we assume only one keyword importance level with $L = 1$, such a factor design can still discriminate keywords of different importance, because the contribution of keyword w_{ij} is the marginalization result of $P(y_i, h_{ij} = 1|d_i, \mathbf{w_i}, t_i)$ and $P(y_i, h_{ij} = 0|d_i, \mathbf{w_i}, t_i)$.

Finally, we define $\tau_i(d_i)$ to incorporate document features $f_k^{(D)}(d_i)$ that are generalizable across tasks:

$$\tau_i(y_i) = \begin{cases} \exp[\sum_k \theta_k^{(D)} f_k^{(D)}(d_i)] & \text{if } y_i = 1; \\ 1 & \text{if } y_i = 0. \end{cases} \tag{16}$$

We use $\boldsymbol{\theta} = \{\theta^{(M)}_{1..K^{(M)},1..L}, \theta^{(I)}_{1..K^{(I)},1..L,0..1}, \theta^{(D)}_{1..K^{(D)}}\}$ to denote the set of parameters that need to be determined in T-RBM, where $K^{(M)}$, $K^{(I)}$ and $K^{(D)}$ denote the number of designed meta-features, intra-features and doc-features respectively, and the total number of parameters is $K^{(M)} * L + K^{(I)} * L * 2 + K^{(D)}$.

4.3.3 Model Learning

Following the maximal likelihood principle, our objective is to learn $\boldsymbol{\theta}$ to maximize the likelihood $\mathcal{L}(\boldsymbol{\theta}; \hat{\mathbf{y}})$ of observing document labels $\hat{\mathbf{y}}$, regularized by $\mathcal{G}(\boldsymbol{\theta}) = \sum_{i=1}^{N} \log P(\mathbf{h_i} = \mathbf{0}|d_i, \mathbf{w_i}, t_i)$ to control the inferred sparsity of all the keywords. Formally the likelihood is defined by

$$\begin{aligned}
&\underset{\boldsymbol{\theta}}{\text{argmax}} \mathcal{L}(\boldsymbol{\theta}; \hat{\mathbf{y}}) + \lambda \mathcal{G}(\boldsymbol{\theta}) \\
&= \underset{\boldsymbol{\theta}}{\text{argmax}} \sum_{i=1}^{N} \log P(y_i = \hat{y}_i|d_i, \mathbf{w_i}, t_i) + \lambda \log P(\mathbf{h_i} = \mathbf{0}|d_i, \mathbf{w_i}, t_i) \\
&= \underset{\boldsymbol{\theta}}{\text{argmax}} \sum_{i=1}^{N} \log \sum_{\mathbf{h_i}} \tau_i(\hat{y}_i) \prod_{j=1}^{|\mathbf{w_i}|} \phi_{ij}(\hat{y}_i, h_{ij}) \psi_{ij}(h_{ij}) \\
&+ \lambda \log \sum_{y=0}^{1} \tau_i(y) \prod_{j=1}^{|\mathbf{w_i}|} \phi_{ij}(y, 0) \psi_{ij}(0) + (1 + \lambda) \log \sum_{y=0}^{1} \sum_{\mathbf{h_i}} \tau_i(y) \\
&\cdot \prod_{j=1}^{|\mathbf{w_i}|} \phi_{ij}(y, h_{ij}) \psi_{ij}(h_{ij})
\end{aligned} \tag{17}$$

where λ controls the inferred sparsity of keyword contribution. Specifically, when $\lambda > 0$, the model will favor more sparse keyword contribution, and vice versa. Here we first study document scoring as a classification problem by assuming that document labels are all binary (*i.e.*, $\hat{y}_i \in \{0, 1\}$), and will later extend our solution to document ranking problems which accept ordinal labels.

To optimize the objective function, we use the Limited-memory Broyden-Fletcher-Goldfarb-Shanno (L-BFGS) algorithm, which is a popular gradient-based method for solving unconstrained nonlinear problems – specifically, we adopt the LibLBFGS library [15], a c-implementation of L-BFGS. As the optimization routine, in each step, we compute the current gradient value of the objective function at $\boldsymbol{\theta}$, and LibLBFGS will update $\boldsymbol{\theta}$ according to the gradient value. The optimization routine stops until the objective function converges.

The gradient value of the objective function at $\boldsymbol{\theta}$, as required by LibLBFGS, is computed as follows,

$$\begin{aligned}
\frac{\partial \mathcal{L}(\boldsymbol{\theta}; \hat{\mathbf{y}})}{\partial \theta_{kl}^{(M)}} &= \sum_{i=1}^{N} \sum_{j=1}^{|\mathbf{w_i}|} [P(h_{ij} = l|y_i = \hat{y}_i, d_i, \mathbf{w_i}, t_i) \\
&-(1 + \lambda) P(h_{ij} = l|d_i, \mathbf{w_i}, t_i)] f_k^{(M)}(w_{ij}, t_i)
\end{aligned} \tag{18}$$

$$\begin{aligned}
\frac{\partial \mathcal{L}(\boldsymbol{\theta}; \hat{\mathbf{y}})}{\partial \theta_{kly}^{(I)}} &= \sum_{i=1}^{N} \sum_{j=1}^{|\mathbf{w_i}|} [P(h_{ij} = l, y_i = y|y_i = \hat{y}_i, d_i, \mathbf{w_i}, t_i) \\
&-(1 + \lambda) P(h_{ij} = l, y_i = y|d_i, \mathbf{w_i}, t_i)] f_k^{(I)}(w_{ij}, d_i)
\end{aligned} \tag{19}$$

$$\begin{aligned}
\frac{\partial \mathcal{L}(\boldsymbol{\theta}; \hat{\mathbf{y}})}{\partial \theta_{k}^{(D)}} &= \sum_{i=1}^{N} [P(y_i = 1|y_i = \hat{y}_i, d_i, \mathbf{w_i}, t_i) \\
&-(1 + \lambda) P(y_i = 1|d_i, \mathbf{w_i}, t_i)] f_k^{(D)}(d_i)
\end{aligned} \tag{20}$$

In Eq. 18, Eq. 19 and Eq. 20, all the probabilities could be computed by belief propagation [17]. As T-RBM is a tree-structured graph, belief propagation could efficiently compute the exact result.

In general, the time complexity of T-RBM is $O[T * (N_d * K^{(D)} + N_e * K^{(I)} + N_w * K^{(M)})]$, where T denotes the number of total iterations, N_d, N_e and N_w represent the number of documents, keyword-document pairs and keywords respectively. Such time complexity stems from the computation of factors $\psi_{ij}(h_{ij})$, $\phi_{ij}(y_i, h_{ij})$ and $\tau_i(y_i)$ given current model parameters $\boldsymbol{\theta}$. After computing the factors, the time complexity of belief propagation is $O(N_e)$, and updating parameter $\boldsymbol{\theta}$ takes $O(|\boldsymbol{\theta}|)$, which are much faster than the factor computation and could be ignored.

4.3.4 Extension to Ranking Problem

This section discusses how to extend T-RBM to ranking problems, where training labels are ordinal instead of binary, *e.g.*, $\hat{y}_i \in \{0, 1, 2\}$, denoting {"irrelevant", "relevant", "perfectly relevant"}.

As the solution, we apply the cumulative logits approach [12] to convert the ranking problem back to a binary classification problem. Assume that each $\hat{y}_i \in \{0, 1, ..., V\}$, we will construct V different binary document classifier separately. For the v-th document classifier, we partition the data into two groups: $\{y_i < v\}$ and $\{y_i \geq v\}$, and learn a document classifier $P(y_i \geq v|d_i, \mathbf{w}_i, t_i)$ based on the learning algorithm in Section 4.3.3. Given the results of the classifiers, we can compute the expected relevance as the ranking score of each document, given as follows,

$$\mathcal{F}(d_i, t_i) = \sum_{v=1}^{V} v * P(y_i = v|d_i, \mathbf{w}_i, t_i) \tag{21}$$

$$= \sum_{v=1}^{V} v * [P(y_i \geq v|d_i, \mathbf{w}_i, t_i) - P(y_i \geq v-1|d_i, \mathbf{w}_i, t_i)] \tag{22}$$

5. EXPERIMENT

In this section, we compare the overall performance of T-RBM with four state-of-the-art baselines, to demonstrate the effectiveness of applying T-RBM for cross-task document scoring problems.

5.1 Experiment Setting

To demonstrate the capacity of T-RBM on general cross-task document scoring problems, we study three different applications – verbose-query-based retrieval, entity-centric document filtering and cross-domain sentiment analysis – on different datasets with specification shown in Figure 4.

1. *Robust (Verbose-query-based Retrieval).* In order to construct a large dataset, we combined two newswire collections released by TREC 2004 and 2005 Robust tracks. Unlike most datasets that contain only short keyword queries, these two collections are the largest publicly available datasets that have detailed query descriptions, which could be used as verbose queries. Following previous verbose query works [3], we only used the $\langle desc \rangle$ portions of TREC queries, and ignored the $\langle title \rangle$ portions. Given one query, each document is labeled as 2–perfectly relevant, 1–relevant and 0–irrelevant.
2. *TREC-KBA (Entity-centric Document Filtering).* This dataset includes 29 Wikipedia entities covering living persons from different domains and a few organizations. For each entity, 100~3000 candidate documents are collected and labeled as garbage, neutral, relevant or central. Following the same procedure in the previous work [22], we got binary labels by viewing central and relevant documents as positive, and others negative.
3. *Review (Cross-domain Sentiment Analysis).* This dataset was constructed by Blitzer *et al.* [4] through selecting Amazon product reviews from four different domains: books, DVDs, electronics and kitchen appliances. Each domain contains 1000 positive, 1000 negative and 3000~5000 unlabeled reviews. We selected 60 pivot keywords by mutual information as suggested by Blitzer *et al.* [4], and learned pivot predictors (for SCL) and Pearson Correlation (for T-RBM) based on unlabeled reviews.

Among the three applications, verbose-query-based retrieval was studied as a ranking problem in previous works, while entity-centric document filtering and cross-domain sentiment analysis were treated as classification problems. Following such conventions, we used ranking-oriented metrics like NDCG@k and MAP (Mean Average Precision) for verbose-query-based retrieval, and classification-oriented metrics including precision, recall, F1-measure and accuracy for the other two tasks.

Dataset	Num of Tasks	Num of Docs	Num of Positive Docs	Classification / Ranking
Robust	249 Queries	349,093	Perfectly Relevant: 3,821 Relevant: 20,147	Ranking
TREC-KBA	29 Entities	52,238	24,704	Classification
Review	4 Domains	8,000	4000	Classification

Figure 4: Dataset specification.

To confirm the confidence of the comparison, for both verbose-query-based retrieval and entity-centric document filtering, we divided queries into 5 sets, and adopted 5-fold cross validation with standard t-test. For cross-domain sentiment analysis, we applied the evaluation method in [4], which trained one model for each domain, adapted the model to the other three domains and reported the average ranking performance over 12 sets of results.

To deal with unbalanced data, we reweighed the training instances to balance positive and negative data. All features were first standardized to reduce the impact of different feature scales. In those baselines which require classifier or ranker learning, we used SVM-Light [9] and RankSVM [10] to learn the feature weightings with default parameters. In T-RBM, we empirically set the number of keyword importance level L to be 2 and regularization factor λ to be 0.005, and will later investigate their impact.

5.2 Quantitative Evaluation

5.2.1 Overall Performance

We designed different baselines to incrementally validate the performance of our proposed T-RBM model. First, we experimented the StandardLearner baseline to demonstrate the necessity of realizing learning to score keywords. Second, we compared T-RBM with LinearMapping [22, 3, 11] and BoostMapping [22] to verify the effectiveness of T-RBM on learning to adapt keyword contribution. In cross-domain sentiment analysis, we also compared T-RBM with SCL [4] to demonstrate that T-RBM well realizes the domain adaptation insight proposed by Blizter *et al.* [4].

1. *Standard Learning Model* (StandardLearner). This baseline solves the problems by standard learning to rank/classify techniques, which defines the scorer by Eq. 4. In the feature design, for verbose-query-based retrieval, we followed the LETOR benchmark [14] to extract ranking features such as TFIDF, BM25 and Language model for each query-document pair; for entity-centric document filtering, as the input query is an entity document, we designed features to calculate the document similarity using different metrics introduced in [7], *e.g.*, Euclidean distance, cosine similarity; in cross-domain sentiment analysis, we used all keywords as features and disregarded domain differences.
2. *Linear Weighting Model* (LinearWeight). As discussed in Section 4.1, the models proposed by Bendersky *et al.* [3], Lease *et al.* [11], and Zhou *et al.* [22] all belong to the same category. This baseline extends such models to support multiple intra-features, which defines the scorer by Eq. 8.
3. *Boosting Mapping Model* (BoostMapping). This baseline adopts the boosting framework proposed by Zhou *et al.* [22], which defines the document scorer by Eq. 9. Since learning keyword clusters based on multiple intra-features is difficult, we first learned the keyword clusters c_i based on only $DocTF(w, d)$, and then applied the SVM or RankSVM again to re-learn the feature weightings γ_{ij}.
4. *Structural Correspondence Learning* (SCL) [4]. This baseline implements the SCL algorithm (introduced in Section 2) proposed by Blitzer *et al.* We used SVMLight to train pivot predictors and the final classifiers, and adopted the same parameter setting used in [4].

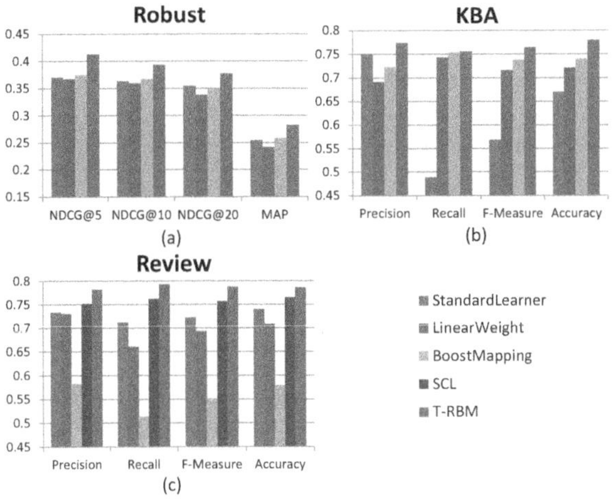

Figure 5: Performance comparison with baselines.

Figure 5 demonstrates T-RBM consistently outperforms other baselines in three applications. Specifically, we observe that T-RBM achieves encouraging improvement against runner-up BoostMapping in verbose-query-based retrieval (NDCG@5 +10.2%, NDCG@10 +7.3%, NDCG@20 +8.5% and MAP +9.4%) and entity-centric document filtering (F-Measure +3.5% and accuracy +5.4%) with p-value$<$ 0.05, while in cross-domain sentiment analysis, T-RBM outperforms runner-up SCL (F-Measure +4.4% and accuracy +2.7%). We analyze the performance differences between T-RBM and other baselines in the following.

First, for the StandardLearner baseline, its performance largely depends on the quality of the adopted features. The results in Figure 5 show that, intuitive feature designs fail to achieve satisfactory results for general cross-document scoring problems. Specifically, in verbose-query-based retrieval, using traditional document scorers as features does not perform well because of the existence of noisy keywords. In entity-centric document filtering, since there exist many relevant documents that are not similar to the identification page (*e.g.*, they might discuss only one or two aspects of the entity), StandardLearner based on document similarity fails as well. In cross-domain sentiment analysis, the result confirms the necessity of adapting keyword importance for different domains.

Second, LinearWeight does not perform well. As we discussed in Section 4.1, the linear definition of keyword contribution function makes it vulnerable to noisy keywords. From the result, we can observe that LinearWeight achieves relatively better performance in verbose-query-based retrieval, which is a task that involves less noisy keywords compared with the other two. The results confirm the importance of fulfilling the inferred sparsity requirement.

Third, BoostMapping fulfills the inferred sparsity requirement, by eliminating the contribution of keywords from noisy clusters; however, it might easily overfit the dataset in some specific settings. In the experiment, we can observe that BoostMapping outperforms LinearWeight over Robust and KBA datasets, but achieves very poor performance on the Review dataset. That is because, unlike the first two applications where the training dataset contains many different tasks (*i.e.*, queries or entities), in cross-domain sentiment analysis, the training data only contains one domain at a time. As the result, BoostMapping severely over-fits the training domain and fails to be generalized to the other domains.

Fourth, SCL outperforms other baselines, and the result is consistent with the performance reported in [4]. However, SCL relies on the idea of pivot predictors to realize domain adaptation, which could not be generalized to other cross-task document scoring problems that do not have the concept of pivot keywords. Moreover, in

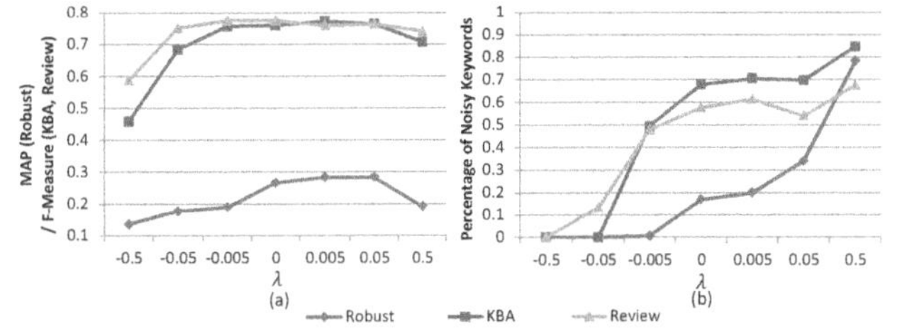

Figure 6: Effect of different parameters.

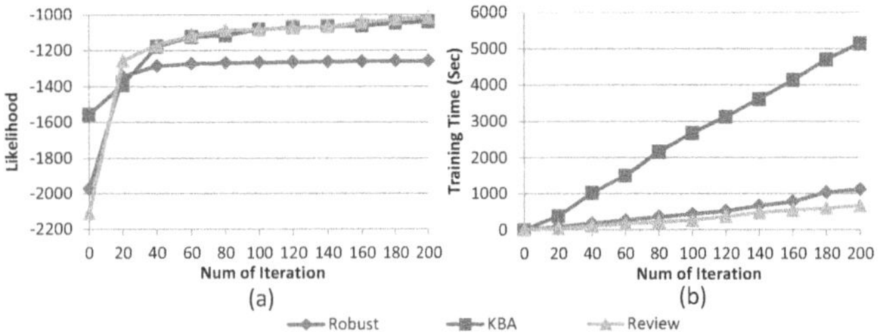

Figure 7: Learning efficiency.

the experiment, we discover that the performance of SCL is sensitive to the model used for training the pivot predictors – different pivot predictors (*e.g.*, trained by SVM and logistic regression) tend to result in very different prediction performance.

Finally, T-RBM outperforms all the four baselines on three different applications. Essentially, the insight of T-RBM is very similar to BoostMapping, which classifies keywords into groups based on their meta-features, and learns the importance of different groups. However, different from BoostMapping which adopts a greedy algorithm to generate clusters, T-RBM takes advantage of Markov Network to jointly learn the weightings for meta-features and intra-features, which greatly reduces the risk of over-fitting. The results demonstrate that T-RBM achieves satisfactory performance on both learning to rank and domain adaptation.

5.2.2 *Different Parameters*

In T-RBM, we have to manually determine two parameters: the number of keyword importance levels L and regularization parameter λ. We experimented different values of L ranging from 1 to 5, and discovered that the performance of T-RBM is not sensitive to L. That is because, as we discussed in Section 4.3.2, even if we set $L = 1$, T-RBM can still model different levels of keyword importance by the marginalization of hidden variables.

In this section, we only investigate the impact of λ. Figure 6 shows how different values of regularization parameter λ affect the performances of T-RBM (in Figure 6 (a)) and the number of keywords that are classified as noise (in Figure 6 (b)). In Figure 6 (a), we can discover that, when λ is negative, the performance of T-RBM decreases significantly for all three datasets. That is because, as Figure 6 (b) illustrates, a negative value of λ will tempt the model to judge more keywords as important, making the scorer vulnerable to noisy keywords. The result again confirms the importance of fulfilling the requirement of inferred sparsity. T-RBM usually achieves the best performance when λ is around 0.005 and 0.05. Continually increasing the value of λ will over-regularize the model and lower down the performance.

5.2.3 *Training Efficiency*

In this section, we are going to investigate the training efficiency of T-RBM. Figure 7(a) shows that the likelihood value converges very quickly within around 100 iterations in all three applications, which, as Figure 7(b) displays, takes 358 seconds for verbose-query-

Data set	*Task*	*Unimportant (L=0)*	*Important (L=1)*
Robust 2005	Query: Marine Vegetation	as, of, purpose	Drug purpose, marine vegetation, harvest
	Query: Abuse of E-Mail	by, in, through	prevent excess, many people, mail
KBA	Entity: Jim Steyer	2011, http, media	privacy, manager, expert, professor
	Entity: Douglas Carswell	http, UK, time	donate, foundation, enthusiast, localist
Review	Domain: DVD	was, you, just	amazing, great performance, great dvd
	Domain: electronics	what, get	inexpensive, works great, fit into, faster

(a) Examples of important/unimportant keywords.

Data set	*Meta-Feature ($\theta_{k1}{}^{(M)}$)*	*Intra-Feature ($\theta_{k11}{}^{(I)} - \theta_{k10}{}^{(I)}$)*
Robust 2005	IDF[Uni](1.118), IDF[Bi](0.535), QueryTF [Bi](0.301), IsVerb[Uni](0.209)	DocTF_Log[Uni](0.744), HeadTF_Log [Uni](0.178), WindowTF_Raw[Bi](0.103)
KBA	QueryPos (-0.829), IsNum(-0.353), IDF (0.169), TextTF (0.082), TFInInfoBox(0.075)	DocTF_Noramlized(0.082), TitleTF_Log (0.034) AnchorTF_Raw(-0.072)
Review	Cor[a_wonerful](14.662), Cor [easy_to](9.097), Cor[poorly] (-7.746), Cor[enjoable](7.694)	DocTF_Raw(0.0362), DocTF_Log(0.023) DocTF_Normalized(0.005)

(b) Features with highest absolute weightings.

Figure 8: Case study.

based retrieval, 2672 seconds for entity-centric document filtering, and 211 seconds for cross-sentiment analysis. In general, the training speed is very fast to get a stable solution.

5.3 Case Study

To give an intuitive illustration of how T-RBM identifies important/unimportant keywords for cross-task document scoring applications, in Figure 8 (a), we perform case studies by showing 2 example tasks per dataset, and listing some of their unimportant ($L = 0$) and important keywords ($L = 1$) based the value of $P(h_{ij})$ derived by T-RBM. To analyze the effect of our designed features, we list the meta-features and intra-features which have the maximal absolute weightings in Figure 8 (b).

As Figure 8 displays, in terms of meta-features, in verbose-query-based retrieval, it meets our expectation that *IDF*, for both unigrams and bigrams, has the highest weightings; the result also includes *QueryTF[Bigram]*, implying that bigrams (*e.g.*, "drug purpose," "prevent excess") usually have higher importance than unigrams. In entity-centric document filtering, *QueryPos* is the most important meta-feature, demonstrating the position of a keyword is a very useful signal for identifying important keywords from a long Wikipedia page; *TFInfoBox* also has high weighting, which verifies our intuition of using Wikipedia page structure to identify important keywords. In cross-domain sentiment analysis, the result shows that the correlation with keywords such as "a_wonderful" and "easy_to" is helpful for identifying the sentiment of a keyword, demonstrating that our framework successfully realizes the insight proposed by Blizter *et al.* [4]. In terms of intra-features, we can observe *DocTF* always has the highest weighting, whereas, different applications favor different term frequency representations. For example, in entity-centric document filtering, *DocTF_Normalized* has higher weighting because the TREC-KBA dataset contains a large number of short documents (*e.g.*, tweets), and without normalization, the scorer would severely bias towards long documents.

6. CONCLUSION

In this paper, we proposed to study the cross-task document scoring problem – given some labeled documents for some user queries or data domains, how to learn a scorer which could predict the relevance of a new document for a new query or domain. As the key insight, towards facilitating the feature design, we proposed the idea of feature decoupling. To design a document scorer based on the decoupled features, we proposed a novel T-RBM model as our solution. Experiments on three applications confirmed the effectiveness of T-RBM.

7. REFERENCES

[1] M. Bendersky and W. B. Croft. Discovering key concepts in verbose queries. In *Proc. of SIGIR '11*, page 491. ACM, 2008.

[2] M. Bendersky, D. Metzler, and W. B. Croft. Learning concept importance using a weighted dependence model. In *Proc. of WSDM '10*, pages 31–40. ACM, 2010.

[3] M. Bendersky, D. Metzler, and W. B. Croft. Parameterized concept weighting in verbose queries. In *Proc. SIGIR '11*, pages 605–614. ACM, 2011.

[4] J. Blitzer, M. Dredze, and F. Pereira. Biographies, bollywood, boom-boxes and blenders: Domain adaptation for sentiment classification. In *Proc. of ACL '07*, number 1, page 440, 2007.

[5] Y. Cao, J. Xu, T.-Y. Liu, H. Li, Y. Huang, and H.-W. Hon. Adapting ranking svm to document retrieval. In *Proc. SIGIR '06*, pages 186–193. ACM, 2006.

[6] G. E. Hinton, S. Osindero, and Y.-W. Teh. A fast learning algorithm for deep belief nets. *Neural computation*, 18(7):1527–1554, 2006.

[7] A. Huang. Similarity measures for text document clustering. In *Proc. of NZCSRSC '08*, pages 49–56, 2008.

[8] T. Joachims. Text categorization with support vector machines: Learning with many relevant features. In *LNCS*, volume 1398, pages 137–142, 1998.

[9] T. Joachims. Making large scale svm learning practical. 1999.

[10] T. Joachims. Optimizing search engines using clickthrough data. In *Proc. SIGKDD '02*, pages 133–142. ACM, 2002.

[11] M. Lease. An improved markov random field model for supporting verbose queries. In *Proc. of SIGIR '09*, pages 476–483. ACM, 2009.

[12] P. Li, Q. Wu, and C. J. Burges. Mcrank: Learning to rank using multiple classification and gradient boosting. In *Proc. of NIPS '07*, pages 897–904, 2007.

[13] T. Li, V. Sindhwani, C. Ding, and Y. Zhang. Knowledge transformation for cross-domain sentiment classification. In *Proceedings of the 32nd international ACM SIGIR conference on Research and development in information retrieval*, pages 716–717. ACM, 2009.

[14] T.-Y. Liu, J. Xu, T. Qin, W. Xiong, and H. Li. Letor: Benchmark dataset for research on learning to rank for information retrieval. In *Proc. of SIGIR '07 workshop*, pages 3–10, 2007.

[15] N. Okazaki. Liblbfgs: a library of limited-memory broyden-fletcher-goldfarb-shanno (l-bfgs). *URL http://www.chokkan. org/software/liblbfgs/index. html*, 2011.

[16] S. J. Pan, X. Ni, J.-T. Sun, Q. Yang, and Z. Chen. Cross-domain sentiment classification via spectral feature alignment. In *Proceedings of the 19th international conference on World wide web*, pages 751–760. ACM, 2010.

[17] J. Pearl. *Probabilistic reasoning in intelligent systems: networks of plausible inference*. Morgan Kaufmann, 1988.

[18] R. Salakhutdinov and G. E. Hinton. Replicated softmax: an undirected topic model. In *NIPS '09*, pages 1607–1614, 2009.

[19] P. Smolensky. Information processing in dynamical systems: Foundations of harmony theory. 1986.

[20] R. Tibshirani. Regression shrinkage and selection via the lasso. *Journal of the Royal Statistical Society. Series B (Methodological)*, pages 267–288, 1996.

[21] V. Vapnik. Statistical learning theory, 1998.

[22] M. Zhou and K. C.-C. Chang. Entity-centric document filtering: boosting feature mapping through meta-features. In *Proc. of CIKM '13*, pages 119–128. ACM, 2013.

Scalable Heterogeneous Translated Hashing

Ying Wei[§], Yangqiu Song[†], Yi Zhen[‡], Bo Liu[§], Qiang Yang[§,¶]
[§]Hong Kong University of Science and Technology, Hong Kong
[†]University of Illinois at Urbana-Champaign, Urbana, IL, USA
[‡]Duke University, Durham, NC, USA
[¶]Huawei Noah's Ark Lab, Hong Kong
[§]{yweiad,bliuab,qyang}@cse.ust.hk, [†]yqsong@illinois.edu, [‡]zhenyisx@gmail.com

ABSTRACT

Hashing has enjoyed a great success in large-scale similarity search. Recently, researchers have studied the multi-modal hashing to meet the need of similarity search across different types of media. However, most of the existing methods are applied to search across multi-views among which explicit bridge information is provided. Given a heterogeneous media search task, we observe that abundant multi-view data can be found on the Web which can serve as an auxiliary bridge. In this paper, we propose a *Heterogeneous Translated Hashing* (HTH) method with such auxiliary bridge incorporated not only to improve current multi-view search but also to enable similarity search across heterogeneous media which have no direct correspondence. HTH simultaneously learns hash functions embedding heterogeneous media into different Hamming spaces, and translators aligning these spaces. Unlike almost all existing methods that map heterogeneous data in a common Hamming space, mapping to different spaces provides more flexible and discriminative ability. We empirically verify the effectiveness and efficiency of our algorithm on two real world large datasets, one publicly available dataset of Flickr and the other MIRFLICKR-Yahoo Answers dataset.

Categories and Subject Descriptors: H.3 [Information Storage and Retrieval]: Information Search and Retrieval; H.4 [Information Systems Applications]: Miscellaneous.

Keywords: Hash Function Learning; Heterogeneous Translated Hashing; Scalability.

1. INTRODUCTION

With the explosive growth of data on and off the Web, heterogeneity arising from different data sources has become ubiquitous. There exist numerous interactions among a diverse range of heterogeneous media: summarizing a piece of video with textual keywords, displaying advertisements by understanding the content of a mobile game, and recommending products based on social activities including sending messages, checking in at places, adding friends, and posting pictures. Figure 1 shows a simple example of leveraging images to provide more accurate answers in Question-Answering systems. All these applications boil down to a fundamental problem: *similarity search across heterogeneous modalities*.

Figure 1: An example of using images to help better question-answering. With a specific poster of "Night of Champions", the answer to where to buy can be more precise.

The challenges of similarity search across heterogeneous modalities are two-fold: 1) how to efficiently perform the computation to meet the large amount of data available; and 2) how to effectively compare the similarity with the existence of heterogeneity. A brute force similarity comparison between the examples from different media is prohibitively expensive for large-scale datasets. Traditional space partitioning methods which accelerate similarity search, such as KD-trees [2] and Metric trees [24], have poor performance in high dimensional spaces [26]. Due to their constant or sub-linear query speed and low storage cost, hashing based methods initiated by locality sensitive hashing (LSH) [1, 7], have aroused more and more interest and become a main-stream technique for fast approximate nearest neighbour (ANN) search. The key principle of hashing is to learn compact binary codes that can preserve similarity. In other words, similar points in the original feature space are projected to similar hash codes in the Hammming space. However, these methods all work with homogeneous data points.

To apply hashing across heterogeneous media is a non-trivial task. First, data from different media sources have incommensurable representation structures. Second, besides preserving homogeneous media similarity in the way as traditional hashing does, heterogeneous media similarity should be preserved simultaneously. Heterogeneous media similarity is defined as semantic relatedness between a pair of entities in different modalities. For instance, a query image and a document in database are similar if they derive from the same topic, e.g., "sports". Such heterogeneous correspondence data that are labelled as similar or dissimilar are the "bridge" to search across heterogeneous media. However, in the task of illustrating questions with pictures as Figure 1 shows, questions as queries do not have any correspondence with the pre-defined database of images. Thus, the third challenge is that in most of practical applications, the explicit relationships between query en-

KDD'14, August 24–27, 2014, New York, NY, USA.
Copyright 2014 ACM 978-1-4503-2956-9/14/08 ...$15.00.
http://dx.doi.org/10.1145/2623330.2623688.

tities (in one domain) and the database entities (in another domain) probably do not apparently exist.

So far limited attempts have been made towards hashing across heterogeneous media. The existing works such as [4, 12, 32, 15] all focus on the situation where explicit relationships are given. For example, the method proposed in [12] assumes that the data is formatted in a multi-view fashion, i.e., each data instance in the database should have a representation in each view. Therefore, explicit relationship is clearly given for each data instance. Particularly, the method proposed in [15] even relies on the explicit relationships between queries and the database in the testing phase.

Moreover, most existing approaches embed multiple media data into a common Hamming space, thus generating hash codes with the same number of bits for all modalities. However, such an embedding is unreasonable because different media types usually have different dimensionality and distributions. In fact, researchers have argued that in uni-modal hashing using the same number of bits for all projected dimensions is unsound because dimensions of larger variances carry more information [8, 13]. Analogously, heterogeneous media data with incommensurable representations and distributions also carry different amounts of information so that they should not be collectively hashed into binary codes of the same length. Otherwise, the equal treatment of different modalities can deteriorate the hashing performance. To the best of our knowledge, the work of [15] is among the first to adopt different bits for different modalities and correlating these bits with mapping functions. However, as mentioned above, it re-learns hash codes for out-of-sample data highly reliant on the given relationships between queries and the database, which is neither practical nor efficient.

In this paper, we propose a novel learning method to enable translation-based hashing across heterogeneous media called *Heterogeneous Translated Hashing* (HTH) to address these limitations. Given a heterogeneous media search task, we observe that some multi-modal data are available on the Web which can serve as a bridge to preserve heterogeneous media similarity, while massive uncorrelated examples in each individual modality can be incorporated to enhance homogeneous media similarity preservation. Learning from such auxiliary heterogeneous correspondence data and homogeneous unlabelled data, HTH generates a set of hash functions for each modality that can project entities of each media type onto an individual Hamming space. All of the Hamming spaces are aligned with a learned translator. In practice, we formulate the above learning procedure as a joint optimization model. Despite the non-convex nature of the learning objective, we express it as a difference of two convex functions to enable the application of the concave-convex procedure (CCCP) [29] iteratively. Then we employ the stochastic sub-gradient strategy [20] to efficiently find the local optimum in each CCCP iteration. Finally, we conduct extensive experiments on two real-world large scale datasets and demonstrate our proposed method to be both effective and efficient.

The remainder of this paper is organized as follows. We review the related work in Section 2. In Section 3, we present the formulation and optimization details of the proposed method. Experimental results and analysis on two real-world datasets are shown in Section 4. Finally, Section 5 concludes the paper.

2. RELATED WORK

In this section, we briefly review the related work in two categories. We first introduce the recently developed learning to hash methods, which is the background of our approach. Then we review several current state-of-the-art hashing methods across heterogeneous modalities.

2.1 Learning to Hash

LSH [1, 7] and its variations [6, 10, 11, 17] , as the earliest exploration of hashing, generate hash functions from random projections or permutations. Nevertheless, these data-independent hash functions may not confirm to every application, and hence require very long hash codes, which increases costs of storage and online query, to achieve acceptable performances. Recently, data-dependent learning to hash methods attempt to alleviate the problem via learning hash functions from data. Unsupervised learning (spectral hashing (SH) [27], self-taught hashing (STH) [31], anchor graph hashing (AGH) [13]), supervised learning (Boosting [19], semantic hashing [18], LDAHash [23]) and semi-supervised learning (semi-supervised hashing [25]) have been explored since then. These approaches have significantly improved the hashing results for many specific tasks.

2.2 Hash acorss Heterogeneous Modalities

To the best of our knowledge, only a few research attempts towards multi-modal hashing have been made to speed up similarity search across different feature spaces or modalities.

Bronstein et al. [4] first explored the cross-modality similarity search problem and proposed cross-modal similarity sensitive hashing (CMSSH). It embeds multi-modal data into a common Hamming space. Later, several works [12, 28, 30, 32, 33, 34] were proposed. Both cross-view hashing (CVH) [12] and inter-media hashing (IMH) [22] extend spectral hashing to preserve intra-media and inter-media similarity simultaneously. Nevertheless, CVH enables cross-view similarity search given multi-view data whereas IMH adds a linear regression term to learn hash functions for efficient code generation of out-of-sample data. Zhen et al. [32] extended label-regularized max-margin partition (LAMP) [14] to the multi-modal case. Multimodal latent binary embedding (MLBE) [33] presents a probabilistic model to learn binary latent factors which are regarded as hash codes in the common Hamming space. Parametric local multimodal hashing (PLMH) [30] extends MLBE and learns a set of local hash functions for each modality. Recently, Zhu et al. [34] and Wu et al. [28] presented two new techniques for obtaining hash codes in multi-modal hashing. [34] obtains k-bit hash codes of a specific data point via thresholding its distances to k cluster centres while [28] thresholds the learned sparse coefficients for each modality as binary codes.

All these methods assume that the hashed data reside in a common Hamming space. However, this may be inappropriate especially when the modalities are quite different. Relational-aware heterogeneous hashing (RaHH) [15] addresses this problem by generating hash codes with different lengths (one for each modality) together with a mapping function. Unfortunately, RaHH has to adopt a fold-in scheme to generate hash codes for out-of-sample data, which is time-consuming, because it learns codes directly instead of explicit hash functions. In the next section, we elaborate our approach to eliminate these restrictions.

3. HETEROGENEOUS TRANSLATED HASHING

In this section, we present our approach in detail. We first introduce the general framework which consists of an offline training phase and an online querying phase. After introducing the notations and problem definitions, we show that HTH can be achieved by solving a novel optimization problem, and we develop an effective and efficient algorithm accordingly. The whole algorithm and the complexity analysis are given at the end of this section.

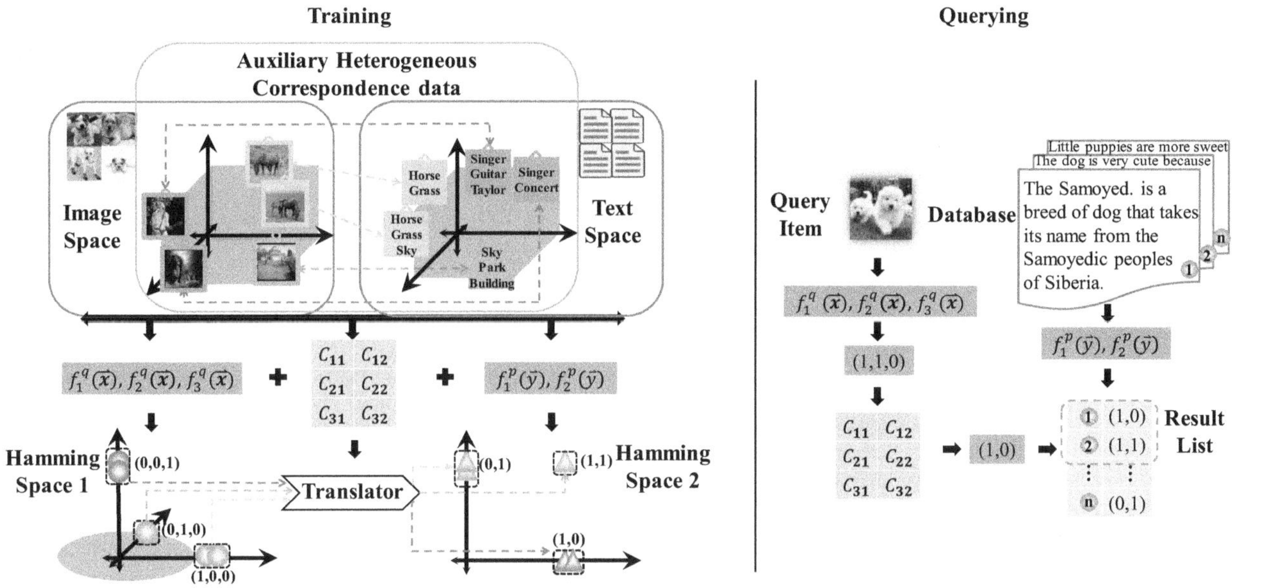

Figure 2: The flowchart of the proposed Heterogeneous Translated Hashing framework. The left corresponds to the offline training of hash functions and the translator, and the right summarizes the process of online querying.

3.1 Overview

We illustrate the HTH framework in Figure 2. HTH involves two phases: an offline training phase (left) and an online querying phase (right). For the simplicity of presentation, we focus on two heterogeneous media types, namely, images and text documents. Nevertheless, it is straightforward to extend HTH to more general cases with three or more types of media. During the offline training phase, HTH learns: 1) the hash functions for each media type to map the data to their individual Hamming space, which has dimensions of the number equalling the code length; and 2) a translator to align the two Hamming spaces. Since effective hash codes should simultaneously preserve homogeneous and heterogeneous media similarity, the correspondence between different domains is needed. In this work, we use auxiliary tagged images crawled from Flickr as the "bridge" shown in the central pink bounding box in Figure 2 which encloses images, documents and their relationships. Meanwhile, a proportion of queries, e.g., images, are incorporated to enhance intra-similarity preservation together with auxiliary images as the left blue bounding box which encloses all images shows. The same applies to text documents. With hash functions, similar homogeneous instances of each media type should be hashed into the same or close bucket in its Hamming space as displayed in Figure 2. Moreover, hash codes of one media type can be translated into the other Hamming space so that mutually correlated data points across different domains are expected to have small Hamming distances.

In the online querying phase, the database, e.g., a pile of text documents, is pre-encoded into a hash table via applying corresponding learned hash functions. When a new query instance comes, we first generate its hash codes using the domain specific hash functions. Subsequently, the hash codes are translated to the Hamming space of the database via the learned translator. Using existing hardware techniques such as bit operations, we can compute the Hamming distances between the query and all database instances, and retrieve its nearest neighbours efficiently.

3.2 Notations and Problem Definition

Suppose we are given a few query data instances $\tilde{\mathbf{X}}^q = \{\tilde{\mathbf{x}}_i\}_{i=1}^N$ and a large database $\tilde{\mathbf{Y}}^p = \{\tilde{\mathbf{y}}_j\}_{j=1}^M$, where $\tilde{\mathbf{x}}_i \in \mathbb{R}^{d_q}$ is a d_q dimensional feature vector in the query domain and $\tilde{\mathbf{y}}_j \in \mathbb{R}^{d_p}$ represents a d_p-dimensional vector in the feature space of the database. In addition, we are given a set of auxiliary data points from both modalities and their relationships which are expressed as a triple set $\mathcal{A}_{xy} = \cup_{i=1}^{N_1} \cup_{j=1}^{N_2} \{\mathbf{x}_i^*, \mathbf{y}_j^*, s_{ij}\}$, in which $s_{ij} = 1$ indicates that the instances $\mathbf{x}_i^*$ and $\mathbf{y}_j^*$ are correlated while $s_{ij} = 0$ otherwise. We construct the training set $\mathcal{T}_x = \{\mathbf{x}_i\}_{i=1}^{N_x}$ of the query domain as follows: randomly sample n instances from $\tilde{\mathbf{X}}^q$ and select all auxiliary data points corresponding to the query domain, i.e., $N_x = n + N_1$. Similarly, $\mathcal{T}_y = \{\mathbf{y}_j\}_{j=1}^{N_y}$ with $N_y = m + N_2$. Our goal is to learn two sets of hash functions and a translator from the training set $\mathcal{A}_{xy}$, $\mathcal{T}_x$ and $\mathcal{T}_y$. The two sets of hash functions, $\mathcal{F}^q(\mathbf{x}) = \{f_k^q(\mathbf{x})\}_{k=1}^{k_q}$ and $\mathcal{F}^p(\mathbf{y}) = \{f_l^p(\mathbf{y})\}_{l=1}^{k_p}$, project the query and database domain into a

Table 1: Definition of Notations

Notation	Description	Number	Set Notation
		Input	
$\tilde{\mathbf{x}}_i$	ith query instance	N	$\tilde{\mathbf{X}}^q = \{\tilde{\mathbf{x}}_i\}_{i=1}^N$
$\tilde{\mathbf{y}}_j$	jth database instance	M	$\tilde{\mathbf{Y}}^p = \{\tilde{\mathbf{y}}_j\}_{j=1}^M$
$\{\mathbf{x}_i^*, \mathbf{y}_j^*, s_{ij}\}$	a triple set of auxiliary pairs	$N_{xy} = N_1 \times N_2$	$\mathcal{A}_{xy} = \cup_{i=1}^{N_1} \cup_{j=1}^{N_2} \{\mathbf{x}_i^*, \mathbf{y}_j^*, s_{ij}\}$
$\mathbf{x}_i$	ith training instance in query domain	N_x	$\mathcal{T}_x = \{\mathbf{x}_i\}_{i=1}^{N_x}$
$\mathbf{y}_j$	jth training instance in database domain	N_y	$\mathcal{T}_y = \{\mathbf{y}_j\}_{j=1}^{N_y}$
		Output	
$f_k^q(\mathbf{x})$	kth hash function in query domain	k_q	$\mathcal{F}^q(\mathbf{x}) = \{f_k^q(\mathbf{x})\}_{k=1}^{k_q}$
$f_l^p(\mathbf{y})$	lth hash function in database domain	k_p	$\mathcal{F}^p(\mathbf{y}) = \{f_l^p(\mathbf{y})\}_{l=1}^{k_p}$
$\mathbf{C}^{k_q \times k_p}$	the $k_q \times k_p$ translator		
$\mathbf{h}_k^q$	kth hash code in query domain	k_q	$\mathbf{H}^q = \{\mathbf{h}_k^q\}_{k=1}^{k_q}$
$\mathbf{h}_l^p$	lth hash code in database domain	k_p	$\mathbf{H}^p = \{\mathbf{h}_l^p\}_{l=1}^{k_p}$

k_q dimensional and a k_p dimensional Hamming space respectively. The translator $\mathbf{C}^{k_q \times k_p}$ aligns the two Hamming spaces in a bitwise manner. Based on the hashing functions and the translator, we can generate hash codes $\mathbf{H}^q = \{\mathbf{h}_k^q\}_{k=1}^{k_q} \in \{-1,+1\}^{N \times k_q}$ in the query domain and $\mathbf{H}^p = \{\mathbf{h}_l^p\}_{l=1}^{k_p} \in \{-1,+1\}^{M \times k_p}$ in the database domain and perform accurate nearest neighbour retrieval across different media types. For brevity, we summarize these notations in Table 1.

3.3 Learning Hash Functions and Translators

In this section, we introduce the objective function of our proposed HTH integrating both the homogeneous similarity preservation term and the heterogeneous similarity preservation term.

3.3.1 *Homogeneous media similarity preservation*

A core criterion to preserve homogeneous media similarity is that similar data points in the original space should share similar hash codes within each single media type. To meet this criterion, in this work we first define the kth (lth) bit hash function of the query domain (the database domain) $f_k^q(\mathbf{x})$ ($f_l^p(\mathbf{y})$) as a linear projection which has been widely adopted in existing related works [22, 31, 32]:

$$f_k^q(\mathbf{x}) = sgn((\mathbf{w}_k^q)^T\mathbf{x}) \text{ and } f_l^p(\mathbf{y}) = sgn((\mathbf{w}_l^p)^T\mathbf{y}), \tag{1}$$

where $sgn(\cdot)$ is the sign function, and $\mathbf{w}_k^q$ and $\mathbf{w}_l^p$ denote projection vectors for the kth and lth bit hash codes in the query and database domain respectively.

In each domain, we can treat each hash function above as a binary classifier and each bit $h_k^{q(i)} \in \{-1,+1\}$ of the ith query data point as a binary class label. The goal is to learn binary classifiers $f_1^q, \cdots, f_{k_q}^q$ to predict k_q labels (bits) $h_1^q, \cdots, h_{k_q}^q$ for any query item $\mathbf{x}$. Moreover, we train binary classifiers for all the bits independently because different bits $h_1^q, \cdots, h_{k_q}^q$ should be uncorrelated. We propose to learn the hash function for the kth bit by solving the following optimization problem:

$$\mathcal{J}_{\mathbf{w}_k^q}^{ho} = \frac{1}{N_x}\sum_{i=1}^{N_x} \ell((\mathbf{w}_k^q)^T\mathbf{x}_i) + \gamma_q \Omega(\|\mathbf{w}_k^q\|_{\mathcal{H}}), \tag{2}$$

where $\ell(\cdot)$ denotes the loss function on one data point and Ω is a regularization term about functional norm $\|\mathbf{w}_k^q\|_{\mathcal{H}}$ in Hilbert spaces. Inspired by the large-margin criterion adopted by Support Vector Machine (SVM), we define ℓ using the hinge loss function $\ell((\mathbf{w}_k^q)^T\mathbf{x}_i) = [1 - h_k^{q(i)}(\mathbf{w}_k^q)^T\mathbf{x}_i]_+$, where $[a]_+$ returns a if $a >= 0$ and 0 otherwise. Ω is commonly defined as the L_2-norm $\frac{1}{2}\|\mathbf{w}_k^q\|^2$. Note that $h_k^{q(i)} = f_k^q(\mathbf{x}_i) = sgn((\mathbf{w}_k^q)^T\mathbf{x}_i)$, the optimization objective (2) can be rewritten as:

$$\mathcal{J}_{\mathbf{w}_k^q}^{ho} = \frac{1}{N_x}\sum_{i=1}^{N_x}[1 - |(\mathbf{w}_k^q)^T\mathbf{x}_i|]_+ + \frac{\gamma_q}{2}\|\mathbf{w}_k^q\|^2 + [\frac{1}{N_x}|\sum_{i=1}^{N_x}(\mathbf{w}_k^q)^T\mathbf{x}_i| - \delta]_+, \tag{3}$$

where γ_q is a balancing parameter controlling the impact of the regularization, and the last term is to avoid a trivially optimal solution which assigns all N_x data points to the same bit. Without the last constraint, the data points may be classified into the same side with large $|(\mathbf{w}_k^q)^T\mathbf{x}_i|$ value so that $[1 - |(\mathbf{w}_k^q)^T\mathbf{x}_i|]_+$ equals to 0 for all N_x data points which is meaningless in hashing. Thus we enforce $-\delta \le \frac{1}{N_x}|\sum_{i=1}^{N_x}(\mathbf{w}_k^q)^T\mathbf{x}_i| \le \delta$ with a pre-defined constant δ.

Similarly, we can learn the hash functions for the database domain by minimizing the following objective function:

$$\mathcal{J}_{\mathbf{w}_l^p}^{ho} = \frac{1}{N_y}\sum_{j=1}^{N_y}[1 - |(\mathbf{w}_l^p)^T\mathbf{y}_j|]_+ + \frac{\gamma_p}{2}\|\mathbf{w}_l^p\|^2 + [\frac{1}{N_y}|\sum_{j=1}^{N_y}(\mathbf{w}_l^p)^T\mathbf{y}_j| - \delta]_+, \tag{4}$$

where γ_p controls the impact of regularization. To learn hash functions from both query and database domains that preserve the homogeneous similarity, we combine (3) and (4) and derive the following objective function:

$$\begin{aligned}
&\mathcal{J}^{ho}(\mathbf{W}^q, \mathbf{W}^p) \\
&= \sum_{k=1}^{k_q}\left\{\frac{1}{N_x}\sum_{i=1}^{N_x}[1 - |(\mathbf{w}_k^q)^T\mathbf{x}_i|]_+ + [\frac{1}{N_x}|\sum_{i=1}^{N_x}(\mathbf{w}_k^q)^T\mathbf{x}_i| - \delta]_+\right\} \\
&+ \sum_{l=1}^{k_p}\left\{\frac{1}{N_y}\sum_{j=1}^{N_y}[1 - |(\mathbf{w}_l^p)^T\mathbf{y}_j|]_+ + [\frac{1}{N_y}|\sum_{j=1}^{N_y}(\mathbf{w}_l^p)^T\mathbf{y}_j| - \delta]_+\right\} \\
&+ \frac{\gamma_q}{2}\|\mathbf{W}^q\|_F^2 + \frac{\gamma_p}{2}\|\mathbf{W}^p\|_F^2,
\end{aligned} \tag{5}$$

where $\mathbf{W}^q = \{\mathbf{w}_1^q, \cdots, \mathbf{w}_{k_q}^q\}$, $\mathbf{W}^p = \{\mathbf{w}_1^p, \cdots, \mathbf{w}_{k_p}^p\}$ and $\|\cdot\|_F^2$ denotes the Frobenius norm.

3.3.2 *Heterogeneous media similarity preservation*

In the last subsection, we learn the hash codes that can preserve homogeneous media similarity for each media type. For the sake of flexibility and discrimination between two modalities, we adopt hash codes with different numbers of bits for different domains. To perform similarity search across different Hamming spaces, in this subsection, we introduce a translator $\mathbf{C}^{k_q \times k_p}$ to map the hash codes from a k_q-dimensional Hamming space to a k_p-dimensional Hamming space or vice versa. We also show that $\mathbf{C}$ can be learned from auxiliary heterogeneous pairs $\mathcal{A}_{xy} = \cup_{i=1}^{N_1}\cup_{j=1}^{N_2}\{\mathbf{x}_i^*, \mathbf{y}_j^*, s_{ij}\}$.

A good translator should have the following three properties: 1) semantically related points across different domains should have similar hash codes after translation; 2) semantically uncorrelated points across different domains should be far away from each other in the translated Hamming space; 3) it should have good generalization power. To obtain such a good translator, we propose to minimize the following heterogeneous loss function:

$$\mathcal{J}^{he} = \sum_{i,j}^{N_{xy}}[s_{ij}d_{ij}^2 + (1 - s_{ij})\tau(d_{ij})] + \frac{\gamma_C}{2}\|\mathbf{C}\|_F^2, \tag{6}$$

where $d_{ij} = \sum_{l=1}^{k_p}[\sum_{k=1}^{k_q} C_{kl}(\mathbf{w}_k^q)^T\mathbf{x}_i^* - (\mathbf{w}_l^p)^T\mathbf{y}_j^*]^2$ represents the distance in the Hamming space of the database between the ith translated hash code from the query domain and the jth code string from the database domain. $\tau(\cdot)$ is the SCISD [16] function specified by two parameters a and λ:

$$\tau(d_{ij}) = \begin{cases} -\frac{1}{2}d_{ij}^2 + \frac{a\lambda^2}{2} & \text{if } \; 0 \le |d_{ij}| \le \lambda \\ \frac{d_{ij}^2 - 2a\lambda|d_{ij}| + a^2\lambda^2}{2} & \text{if } \; \lambda < |d_{ij}| \le a\lambda \\ 0 & \text{if } \; |d_{ij}| > a\lambda \end{cases}. \tag{7}$$

Note that if two data points are semantically similar, that is, $s_{ij} = 1$, we require that they have small d_{ij}; if they are semantically dissimilar, we require that they have small SCISD value which implies that they are far apart in the Hamming space.

3.3.3 *Overall optimization problem*

Combining the objective functions introduced in the previous two subsections, the overall optimization problem of HTH can be written as follows:

$$\min_{\mathbf{W}^q, \mathbf{W}^p, \mathbf{C}} \; \mathcal{J}^{ho} + \beta\mathcal{J}^{he} \tag{8}$$

where β is a trade-off parameter between homogeneous and heterogeneous loss functions.

3.4 Optimization

Problem (8) is non-trivial to solve because it is discrete and non-convex *w.r.t.* $\mathbf{W}^q$, $\mathbf{W}^p$ and $\mathbf{C}$. In the following, we develop an alternating algorithm to solve this problem which converges to a local minimum very quickly.

We first describe how to learn the projection vector $\mathbf{w}_k^q$ for the kth bit while fixing other variables. Note that projection vectors for different bits can be learned independently using the same algorithm. The objective function *w.r.t.* $\mathbf{w}_k^q$ is:

$$\mathcal{J}_{\mathbf{w}_k^q} = \frac{1}{N_x}\sum_{i=1}^{N_x}[1-|(\mathbf{w}_k^q)^T\mathbf{x}_i|]_+ + [\frac{1}{N_x}|\sum_{i=1}^{N_x}(\mathbf{w}_k^q)^T\mathbf{x}_i|-\delta]_+ + \beta\sum_{i,j}^{N_{xy}}[s_{ij}d_{ij}^2+(1-s_{ij})\tau(d_{ij})]+\frac{\gamma_q}{2}\|\mathbf{w}_k^q\|^2. \tag{9}$$

Although (9) is not convex, it can be expressed as the differences of two convex functions, and hence can be minimized efficiently using *constrained concave-convex-procedure* (CCCP) [29].

We briefly introduce the idea of CCCP here. Given an optimization problem in the form of $\min_x f(x)-g(x)$ where f and g are real-valued convex functions, the key idea of CCCP is to iteratively evaluate an upper bound of the objective function by replacing g with its first-order Taylor expansion around the current solution, x_t, i.e., $\mathcal{R}(g(x_t)) = g(x_t)+\partial_x g(x_t)(x-x_t)$. Then the relaxed sub-problem $f(x)-\mathcal{R}(g(x_t))$ is in convex form and can be solved by off-the-shelf convex solvers. The solution sequence $\{x_t\}$ obtained by CCCP is guaranteed to reach a local optimum.

Specifically, the upper bound of (9) in the tth CCCP iteration is:

$$\mathcal{J}^{(t)}_{\mathbf{w}_k^q} = \tag{10}$$
$$\frac{1}{N_x}\sum_{i=1}^{N_x}[f_1(\mathbf{w}_k^q)-\mathcal{R}(g_1(\mathbf{w}_k^{q(t)}))] + [\frac{1}{N_x}|\sum_{i=1}^{N_x}(\mathbf{w}_k^q)^T\mathbf{x}_i|-\delta]_+ + \beta\sum_{i,j}^{N_{xy}}s_{ij}d_{ij}^2 + \beta\sum_{i,j}^{N_{xy}}(1-s_{ij})[\tau_1(d_{ij})-\mathcal{R}(\tau_2(d_{ij}^{(t)}))]+\frac{\gamma_q}{2}\|\mathbf{w}_k^q\|^2,$$

where $f_1(\mathbf{w}_k^q) = 1+[|(\mathbf{w}_k^q)^T\mathbf{x}_i|-1]_+$, $g_1(\mathbf{w}_k^{q(t)}) = |(\mathbf{w}_k^{q(t)})^T\mathbf{x}_i|$, $\tau_2(d_{ij}) = \frac{1}{2}d_{ij}^2-\frac{a\lambda^2}{2}$ and

$$\tau_1(d_{ij}) = \begin{cases} 0 & \text{if } \ 0 \le |d_{ij}| \le \lambda \\ \frac{ad_{ij}^2-2a\lambda|d_{ij}|+a\lambda^2}{2(a-1)} & \text{if } \ \lambda < |d_{ij}| \le a\lambda \\ \frac{1}{2}d_{ij}^2-\frac{a\lambda^2}{2} & \text{if } \ |d_{ij}| > a\lambda \end{cases}. \tag{11}$$

The Taylor expansion of $g_1(\cdot)$ and $\tau_2(\cdot)$ around the value of $\mathbf{w}_k^q$ in the tth iteration are $\mathcal{R}(g_1(\mathbf{w}_k^{q(t)})) = |(\mathbf{w}_k^{q(t)})^T\mathbf{x}_i| + sgn((\mathbf{w}_k^{q(t)})^T\mathbf{x}_i)\cdot\mathbf{x}_i(\mathbf{w}_k^q-\mathbf{w}_k^{q(t)})$ and $\mathcal{R}(\tau_2(d_{ij}^{(t)})) = \frac{1}{2}d_{ij}^{(t)2}-\frac{a\lambda^2}{2}+d_{ij}^{(t)}\frac{\partial d_{ij}^{(t)}}{\mathbf{w}_k^q}(\mathbf{w}_k^q-\mathbf{w}_k^{q(t)})$ respectively. Note that

$$d_{ij}^{(t)} = \sum_{l=1}^{k_p}[\sum_{k=1}^{k_q}C_{kl}(\mathbf{w}_k^{q(t)})^T\mathbf{x}_i^* - (\mathbf{w}_l^p)^T\mathbf{y}_j^*]^2. \tag{12}$$

However, minimizing (10) is time-consuming if the data dimensionality is high. As a result, we employ Pegasos [21] which is a sub-gradient based solver and reported to be one of the fastest gradient-based solvers, to solve the problem. In each Pegasos iteration, the key step is to evaluate the sub-gradient of $\mathcal{J}^{(t)}_{\mathbf{w}_k^q}$ *w.r.t.* $\mathbf{w}_k^q$ from l_1 random homogeneous data points and l_2 random heterogeneous pairs:

Algorithm 1 Heterogeneous Translated Hashing (HTH)

Input:

$\mathcal{T}_x = \{\mathbf{x}_i\}_{i=1}^{N_x}$ – query training set

$\mathcal{T}_y = \{\mathbf{y}_j\}_{j=1}^{N_y}$ – database training set

$\mathcal{A}_{xy} = \cup_{i=1}^{N_1}\cup_{j=1}^{N_2}\{\mathbf{x}_i^*, \mathbf{y}_j^*, s_{ij}\}$ – auxiliary heterogeneous data

$\beta, \gamma_q, \gamma_p, \gamma_C$ – regularization parameters

δ – partition balance parameter

a, λ – SCISD function parameter

k_q; k_p – length of hash codes

Output:

$\mathbf{W}^q, \mathbf{W}^p, \mathbf{C}$

Initialize $\mathbf{W}^q$, $\mathbf{W}^p$ with CVH and $\mathbf{C} = \mathbf{I}$;
while $\mathbf{W}^q$, $\mathbf{W}^p$ and $\mathbf{C}$ are not converged **do**
  Fix $\mathbf{W}^p$ and $\mathbf{C}$, optimize $\mathbf{W}^q$:
  for $k = 1\cdots k_q$ **do**
    for $t = 1\cdots t_{max}$ **do**
      $\mathbf{w}_k^{q(t+1)} = \arg\min \mathcal{J}^{(t)}_{\mathbf{w}_k^q}$;
    end for
  end for
  Fix $\mathbf{W}^q$ and $\mathbf{C}$, optimize $\mathbf{W}^p$
  for $k = 1\cdots k_p$ **do**
    for $t = 1\cdots t_{max}$ **do**
      $\mathbf{w}_l^{p(t+1)} = \arg\min \mathcal{J}^{(t)}_{\mathbf{w}_l^p}$;
    end for
  end for
  Fix $\mathbf{W}^q$ and $\mathbf{W}^p$, optimize $\mathbf{C}$:
  for $t = 1\cdots t_{max}$ **do**
    solve $\mathbf{C}^{(t+1)} = \arg\min \mathcal{J}^{(t)}_{\mathbf{C}}$;
  end for
end while

$$\frac{\partial\mathcal{J}^{(t)}_{\mathbf{w}_k^q}}{\mathbf{w}_k^q} = \frac{1}{N_x}\sum_{i=1}^{N_x}[\frac{\partial(f_1(\mathbf{w}_k^q))}{\mathbf{w}_k^q} - sgn((\mathbf{w}_k^{q(t)})^T\mathbf{x}_i)\mathbf{x}_i] + \eta_{\mathbf{w}_k^q} + \gamma_q\mathbf{w}_k^q + 2\beta\sum_{i,j}^{N_{xy}}s_{ij}d_{ij}\frac{\partial d_{ij}}{\mathbf{w}_k^q} + \beta\sum_{i,j}^{N_{xy}}(1-s_{ij})(\frac{\partial\tau_1(d_{ij})}{\mathbf{w}_k^q} - d_{ij}^{(t)}\frac{\partial d_{ij}^{(t)}}{\mathbf{w}_k^q}), \tag{13}$$

where

$$\frac{\partial(f_1(\mathbf{w}_k^q))}{\mathbf{w}_k^q} = \begin{cases} 0 & \text{if } \ |(\mathbf{w}_k^q)^T\mathbf{x}_i| \le 1 \\ sgn((\mathbf{w}_k^q)^T\mathbf{x}_i)\mathbf{x}_i & \text{otherwise,} \end{cases} \tag{14}$$

$$\eta_{\mathbf{w}_k^q} = \begin{cases} 0 & \text{if } \ \frac{1}{N_x}|(\sum_{i=1}^{N_x}\mathbf{w}_k^q)^T\mathbf{x}_i| \le \delta \\ sgn(\frac{1}{N_x}\sum_{i=1}^{N_x}(\mathbf{w}_k^q)^T\mathbf{x}_i - \delta)\cdot\frac{1}{N_x}\sum_{i=1}^{N_x}\mathbf{x}_i & \text{otherwise,} \end{cases} \tag{15}$$

$$\frac{\partial d_{ij}}{\mathbf{w}_k^q} = \sum_{l=1}^{k_p}\{2\cdot[\sum_{k=1}^{k_q}C_{kl}(\mathbf{w}_k^q)^T\mathbf{x}_i^* - (\mathbf{w}_l^p)^T\mathbf{y}_j^*]\cdot C_{kl}\mathbf{x}_i^*\}, \tag{16}$$

$$\frac{\partial d_{ij}^{(t)}}{\mathbf{w}_k^q} = \sum_{l=1}^{k_p}\{2\cdot[\sum_{k=1}^{k_q}C_{kl}(\mathbf{w}_k^{q(t)})^T\mathbf{x}_i^* - (\mathbf{w}_l^p)^T\mathbf{y}_j^*]\cdot C_{kl}\mathbf{x}_i^*\}, \tag{17}$$

$$\frac{\partial\tau_1(d_{ij})}{\mathbf{w}_k^q} = \frac{\partial d_{ij}}{\mathbf{w}_k^q}\cdot\begin{cases} 0 & \text{if } \ 0 \le |d_{ij}| \le \lambda \\ \frac{ad_{ij}-a\lambda sgn(d_{ij})}{a-1} & \text{if } \ \lambda < |d_{ij}| \le a\lambda \\ d_{ij} & \text{if } \ |d_{ij}| > a\lambda. \end{cases} \tag{18}$$

Similarly, the objective function and sub-gradient *w.r.t.* $\mathbf{w}_l^p$ at the tth CCCP iteration are :

$$\mathcal{J}_{\mathbf{w}_l^p}^{(t)} = \tag{19}$$

$$\frac{1}{N_y}\sum_{j=1}^{N_y}[f_1(\mathbf{w}_l^p) - \mathcal{R}(g_1(\mathbf{w}_l^{p(t)}))] + [\frac{1}{N_y}|\sum_{j=1}^{N_y}(\mathbf{w}_l^p)^T\mathbf{y}_j| - \delta]_+$$

$$+\beta\sum_{i,j}^{N_{xy}} s_{ij}d_{ij}^2 + \beta\sum_{i,j}^{N_{xy}}(1 - s_{ij})[\tau_1(d_{ij}) - \mathcal{R}(\tau_2(d_{ij}^{(t)}))] + \frac{\gamma_p}{2}\|\mathbf{w}_l^p\|^2,$$

and

$$\frac{\partial\mathcal{J}_{\mathbf{w}_l^p}^{(t)}}{\mathbf{w}_l^p} = \frac{1}{N_y}\sum_{j=1}^{N_y}[\frac{\partial(f_1(\mathbf{w}_l^p))}{\mathbf{w}_l^p} - sgn((\mathbf{w}_l^{p(t)})^T\mathbf{y}_j)\mathbf{y}_j]] + \eta_{\mathbf{w}_l^p} + \gamma_p\mathbf{w}_l^p$$

$$+ 2\beta\sum_{i,j}^{N_{xy}} s_{ij}d_{ij}\frac{\partial d_{ij}}{\mathbf{w}_l^p} + \beta\sum_{i,j}^{N_{xy}}(1 - s_{ij})(\frac{\partial\tau_1(d_{ij})}{\mathbf{w}_l^p} - d_{ij}^{(t)}\frac{\partial d_{ij}^{(t)}}{\mathbf{w}_l^p}), \tag{20}$$

where

$$\frac{\partial d_{ij}}{\mathbf{w}_l^p} = 2\cdot[\sum_{k=1}^{k_q} C_{kl}(\mathbf{w}_k^q)^T\mathbf{x}_i^* - (\mathbf{w}_l^p)^T\mathbf{y}_j^*]\cdot\mathbf{y}_j^*. \tag{21}$$

Note that both $\frac{\partial d_{ij}^{(t)}}{\mathbf{w}_l^p}$ and $\frac{\partial\tau_1(d_{ij})}{\mathbf{w}_l^p}$ can easily be derived and we omit them here due to space limitations.

To update the translator $\mathbf{C}$, we also use CCCP. The objective function and sub-gradient *w.r.t.* every element C_{kl} in the tth CCCP iteration:

$$\mathcal{J}_{C_{kl}}^{(t)} = \beta\sum_{i,j}^{N_{xy}} s_{ij}d_{ij}^2 + \beta\sum_{i,j}^{N_{xy}}(1 - s_{ij})[\tau_1(d_{ij}) - \mathcal{R}(\tau_2(d_{ij}^{(t)}))] + \frac{\gamma_C}{2}\|\mathbf{C}\|_F^2,$$

and

$$\frac{\partial\mathcal{J}_{C_{kl}}^{(t)}}{C_{kl}} = \beta\sum_{i,j}^{N_{xy}}(1-s_{ij})(\frac{\partial\tau_1(d_{ij})}{C_{kl}} - d_{ij}^{(t)}\frac{\partial d_{ij}^{(t)}}{C_{kl}}) + \gamma_C C_{kl} + 2\beta\sum_{i,j}^{N_{xy}} s_{ij}d_{ij}\frac{\partial d_{ij}}{C_{kl}},$$

where

$$\frac{\partial d_{ij}}{C_{kl}} = 2\cdot[\sum_{k=1}^{k_q} C_{kl}(\mathbf{w}_k^q)^T\mathbf{x}_i^* - (\mathbf{w}_l^p)^T\mathbf{y}_j^*]\cdot(\mathbf{w}_k^q)^T\mathbf{x}_i^*.$$

The overall procedure of the HTH method, alternating learning $\mathbf{W}^q$, $\mathbf{W}^p$ and the translator $\mathbf{C}$ with CCCP and Pegasos, is presented in Algorithm 1.

3.5 Complexity Analysis

The computational cost of the proposed algorithm comprises three parts: updating $\mathbf{W}^q$, $\mathbf{W}^p$ and $\mathbf{C}$. Hence, the total time complexity of training HTH is $O(k_qd_q(l_1+l_3)+k_pd_p(l_2+l_3)+l_3k_pk_q)$ where l_1 and l_2 are the numbers of stochastically selected training data points in the query domain and database domain by the Pegasos solver. l_3 is the number of randomly sampled auxiliary data pairs from N_{xy} auxiliary heterogeneous co-occurrence data pairs. Clearly, the time complexity for our algorithm scales linearly with the number of training data points and quadratic with the length of hash codes. In practice, the code length is short, otherwise, the technique of "hashing" will be meaningless. Hence our algorithm is very computationally efficient.

During the online query phase, given a query instance $\tilde{\mathbf{x}}_i \in \tilde{\mathbf{X}}^q$, we apply our learned hash functions for the query domain to it by performing two dot-product operations, $\mathbf{H}_i^q = \mathbf{x}_i\cdot\mathbf{W}^q$ and translation $\mathbf{H}_i^q\cdot\mathbf{C}$, which are quite efficient. The translated query hash codes are then compared with the hash codes of the database by quick XOR and bit count operations. These operations enjoy the sub-linear time-complexity *w.r.t.* the database size.

4. EXPERIMENTS

In this section, we evaluate the performance of HTH on two real world datasets and compare it with the state-of-the-art multi-modal hashing algorithms.

4.1 Experimental Settings

4.1.1 Datasets

In this work, we use two real world datasets, NUS-WIDE[1] and MIRFLICKR-Yahoo Answers.

NUS-WIDE is a Flickr dataset containing 269,648 tagged images [5]. The annotation for 81 semantic concepts is provided for evaluation. We prune this dataset via keeping the image-tag pairs that belong to the ten largest concepts. For image features, 500 dimensional SIFT vectors are used. On the other side, a group of tags for an image composes a single text document. For each text document, we use the probability distribution of 100 Latent Dirichlet Allocation (LDA) [3] topics as the feature vector. Therefore, NUS-WIDE is a multi-view dataset. Each data instance has an image view and a text view. When searching images using text query or searching text documents using image query, the groundtruth is derived by checking whether an image and a text document share at least one of the ten selected largest concepts.

MIRFLICKR-Yahoo Answers is a heterogeneous media dataset consisting of images from MIRFLICKR-25000 [9] and QAs from Yahoo Answers. MIRFLICKR-25000 is another Flickr collection consisting of 25,000 images. We utilize 5,018 tags provided by NUS-WIDE to filter irrelevant pictures in MIRFLICKR-25000 by cross-checking tags of each image with these 5,018 tags. The 500 dimensional sift feature vector is also applied. Yahoo Answers are crawled from a public API of Yahoo Query Language (YQL)[2]. The 5,018 tags are taken as keywords to search relevant QAs on Yahoo Answers. For each keyword, we extract top 100 results returned by YQL. Finally, we obtain a pool of about 300,000 QAs, each of which is regarded as a text document in the experiment. Each QA is represented in a 100 dimensional LDA based feature vector. For the task using image query to retrieve QAs in the database, those QAs which share at least two words with tags corresponding to the image query (images in MIRFLICKR-25000 are also tagged) are labelled as the groundtruth. The groundtruth for the task using QA as query to retrieve the image database is obtained similarly. More importantly, we randomly select a number of multi-view instances, e.g., 2,000, in the NUS-WIDE dataset as the "bridge". As a result, we obtain $2,000^2 = 4\times10^6$ auxiliary heterogeneous pairs.

4.1.2 Baselines

We compare our method with the following four baseline algorithms.

Cross-modality similarity-sensitive hashing (CMSSH) [4], to the best of our knowledge, is the first approach that tackles hashing across multimodal data. CMSSH uses Adaboost to construct a group of hash functions sequentially for each modality while only preserving inter-modality similarity.

Cross-view hashing (CVH) [12] extends spectral hashing to the multi-view case via a CCA (canonical correlation analysis) alike

[1]http://lms.comp.nus.edu.sg/research/NUS-WIDE.htm
[2]http://developer.yahoo.com/yql/

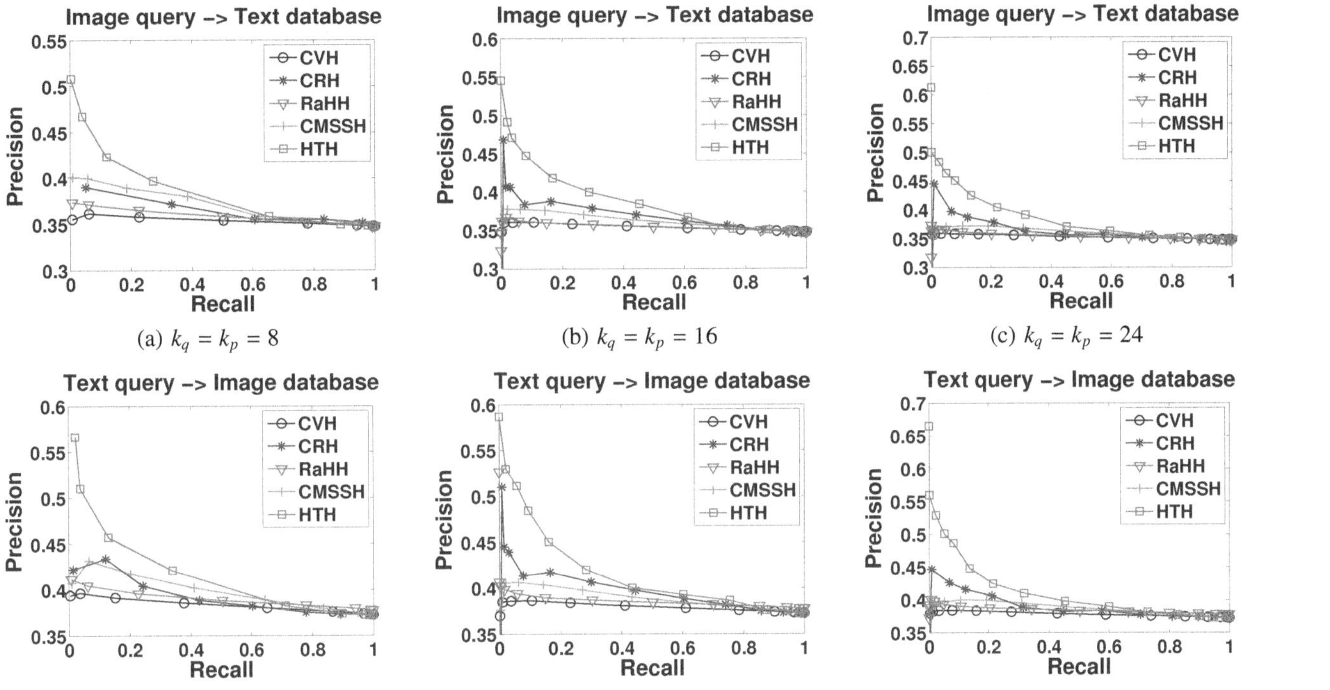

(a) $k_q = k_p = 8$ (b) $k_q = k_p = 16$ (c) $k_q = k_p = 24$

(d) $k_q = k_p = 8$ (e) $k_q = k_p = 16$ (f) $k_q = k_p = 24$

Figure 3: Precision-recall curves on NUS-WIDE dataset.

procedure. In our implementation, CVH learns two hash functions which can directly be applied to out-of-sample data.

Co-regularized hashing (CRH) [32] proposes a boosted co-regularization framework to learn two sets of hash functions for both the query and database domain.

Relation-aware heterogeneous hashing (RaHH) [15] adopts uneven bits for different modalities and a mapping function between them. During testing we add no heterogeneous relationship between queries and the database in our setting. In [15], however, they used the explicit relationship and attained higher accuracies.

4.1.3 Evaluation metric

In this paper, Mean Average Precision (MAP), precision and recall are adopted as our evaluation metrics of effectiveness.

MAP stands out among performance measures in virtue of its competitive stability and discrimination. To compute MAP, Average Precision (AP) of top R retrieved documents for a single query is first calculated. $AP = \frac{1}{L}\sum_{r=1}^{R} P(r)\delta(r)$ where L is the number of groundtruth in the R retrieved set, $P(r)$ indicates the precision of top-r retrieved documents and $\delta(r) = 1$ denotes whether the rth retrieved document is a true neighbour otherwise $\delta(r) = 0$. MAP is then averaged over all queries' APs. The larger the MAP score, the better the retrieval performance. In our experiments, we set R= 50. The precision and recall scores reported in this paper are averaged over all queries. The larger the area under the curves, the better the achieved performance.

4.2 Results on NUS-WIDE Dataset

We perform two kinds of tasks on the NUS-WIDE dataset: 1) retrieving text documents by using images as queries; 2) retrieving images by using text documents as queries. In either task, we randomly select $300^2 = 90,000$ image-tag pairs from the NUS-WIDE dataset to be our training pairs. For the task of retrieving texts by image queries (retrieving images by text queries), we select 2,000 images (text documents) as queries and 10,000 text documents (images) to be the database. We perform our experiment on four such randomly sampled datasets and the average MAP results for all the compared algorithms are reported in Table 2. To be comparable with CVH, CMSSH and CRH, HTH adopts the same code length for different domains. From Table 2, we have the following observation. HTH outperforms all state-of-the-art methods in almost all settings at most 30%.

Table 2: MAP comparison on NUS-WIDE.

Task	Algorithm	Code Length ($k_q = k_p$)			
		8	16	24	32
Image→Text	CVH	0.4210	0.4085	0.4066	0.4112
	CMSSH	0.4447	0.4209	0.4109	0.4123
	CRH	0.4645	0.5003	0.5255	0.3207
	RaHH	0.4120	0.4122	0.4098	0.4182
	HTH	**0.5013**	**0.5357**	**0.5362**	**0.5151**
Text→Image	CVH	0.4483	0.4323	0.4296	0.4361
	CMSSH	0.4779	0.4485	0.4378	0.4373
	CRH	0.4986	0.5327	**0.5774**	0.3378
	RaHH	0.4595	0.4396	0.4351	0.4315
	HTH	**0.5398**	**0.5688**	0.5508	**0.5525**

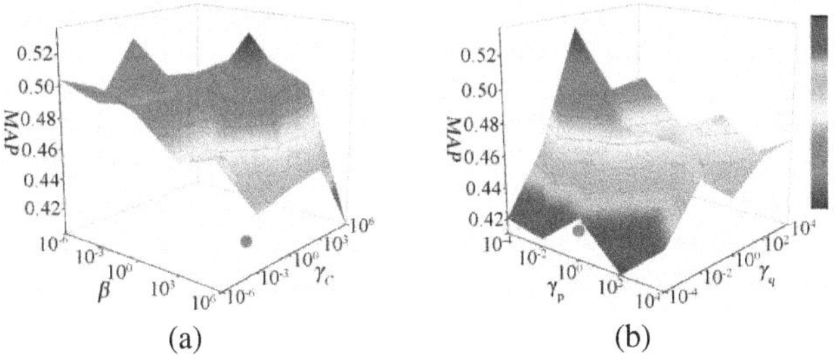

(a) (b)

Figure 4: Study of parameter sensitivity on NUS-WIDE dataset. Parameter settings in our experiments are labelled in red dots and correspond to the best performances.

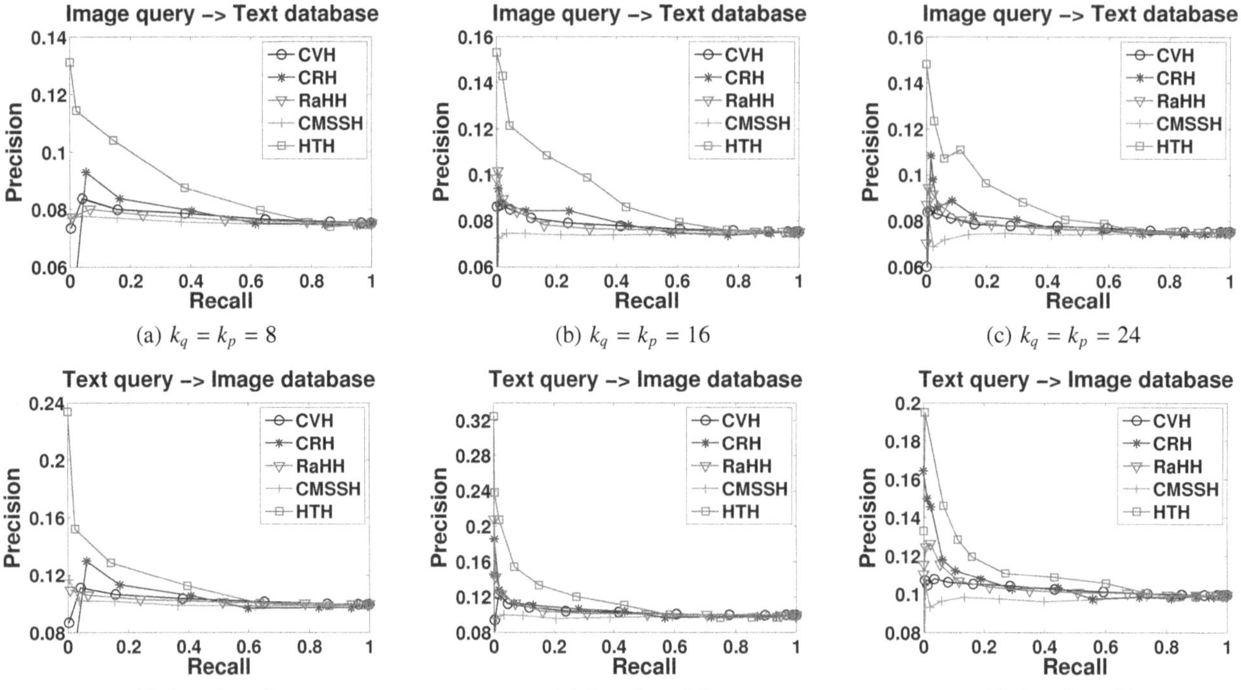

(a) $k_q = k_p = 8$ (b) $k_q = k_p = 16$ (c) $k_q = k_p = 24$

(d) $k_q = k_p = 8$ (e) $k_q = k_p = 16$ (f) $k_q = k_p = 24$

Figure 5: Precision-recall curves on MIRFLICKR-Yahoo Answer dataset.

The precision-recall curves for 8, 16 and 24 bits are plotted in Figure 3. The superior performance of HTH in precision-recall curves agrees with the results of MAP in Table 2.

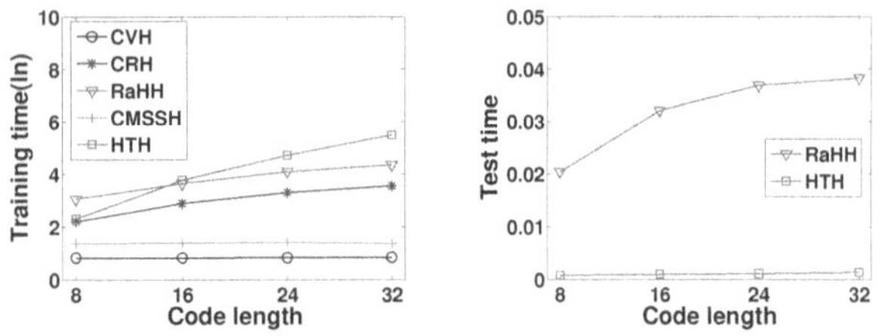

(a) Training time (b) Test time

Figure 6: Time cost of training and testing on NUS-WIDE dataset with different code lengths. The time is measured in seconds. Y-axis in (a) is the natural logarithm of training time.

We also study the effect of different parameter settings on the performance of HTH. We fix the code lengths of both modalities to be 16. There are four trade-off parameters, β, γ_q, γ_p and γ_C as shown in objective function (8). We perform grid search on β and γ_C in the range of $\{10^{-6}, 10^{-3}, 10^0, 10^3, 10^6\}$ by fixing γ_q and γ_p. HTH gains the best MAP at $\beta = 1,000$, $\gamma_C = 1$ as Figure 4(a) shows. When fixing the β and γ_C, grid search of γ_q and γ_p in the range of $\{10^{-4}, 10^{-2}, 10^0, 10^2, 10^4\}$ shows that $\gamma_q = \gamma_p = 0.01$ performs the best. We adopt $\gamma_C = 1, \beta = 1,000, \gamma_q = 0.01, \gamma_p = 0.01$ in our experiments.

The time costs of HTH and other baselines are shown in Figure 6 as the code length changes. Since the training complexity of HTH is quadratic with respect to the code length, it takes more training time when the codes are longer. However, hashing with less bits is expected, thereby HTH is practical. In online querying phase, since CVH, CMSSH and CRH have the same time complexity as HTH, we only compare HTH with RaHH. The average query search time of HTH is much less than RaHH because RaHH does not learn explicit hash functions and has to adopt the fold-in scheme for out-of-sample data.

4.3 Results on MIRFLICKR-Yahoo Answers Dataset

We also report the results of the two tasks (using images to search text documents and using text documents to search images) on the MIRFLICKR-Yahoo Answers dataset which contains a larger number of images and text documents.

In this experiment, $N_{xy} = 2,000^2 = 4\times10^6$ image-tags pairs from NUS-WIDE dataset, 500 randomly selected images from MIRFLIC -KR as well as 500 sampled QAs from Yahoo Answers are chosen for training. In this case, these image-tag pairs from NUS-WIDE serve as the auxiliary bridge while queries and the database have no direct correspondence since MIRFLICKR images and Yahoo Answers are obtained independently.

Table 3: MAP comparison on MIRFLICKR-Yahoo Answers.

Task	Algorithm	Code Length($k_q = k_p$)			
		8	16	24	32
Image→QA	CVH	0.1331	0.1443	0.1460	0.1506
	CMSSH	0.1373	0.1268	0.1210	0.1295
	CRH	0.0979	0.1419	0.1317	0.1216
	RaHH	0.1346	0.1437	0.1474	0.1275
	HTH	**0.1577**	**0.1738**	**0.1824**	**0.1617**
QA→Image	CVH	0.1515	0.1758	0.1694	0.1721
	CMSSH	0.1735	0.1483	0.1518	0.1544
	CRH	0.1048	0.2234	0.1793	0.1862
	RaHH	0.1669	0.1731	0.1686	0.1452
	HTH	**0.1785**	**0.2460**	**0.2055**	**0.2324**

To apply CVH, CMSSH, CRH to this dataset, we simply train hash functions for images and texts using the image-tag pairs from NUS-WIDE and generate hash codes of images from MIRFLICKR and QAs from Yahoo Answers by directly applying corresponding hash functions. For RaHH, in the training phase, the data is the same as those used in CVH, CMSSH and CRH. In the testing phase, we do not add any relationships between queries and database entities when applying the fold-in algorithm to generate hash codes for out-of-sample data. For HTH, we train the hash functions with the auxiliary heterogeneous pairs and unlabelled homogeneous data. In the testing phase, it is easy to apply the learned hash functions to out-of-sample data without any correspondence information.

Table 4: MAP of RaHH and HTH on MIRFLICKR-Yahoo Answer with different combinational code length.

k_q \ k_p	8		16		24		32	
	RaHH	HTH	RaHH	HTH	RaHH	HTH	RaHH	HTH
8	0.1346	0.1577	0.1315	0.1410	0.1442	0.1583	0.1366	0.1725
16	0.1346	0.1525	0.1437	0.1738	**0.1545**	**0.1894**	0.1274	0.1638
24	0.1346	0.1692	0.1437	0.1736	0.1474	0.1824	0.1378	0.1625
32	0.1346	0.1761	0.1437	0.1626	0.1474	0.1701	0.1275	0.1617

The MAP results are summarized in Table 3 with various code length settings. It shows that HTH outperforms all the other algorithms under all settings. This demonstrates that HTH shows more superiority in situations where queries and the database do not interrelate. Similarly, the precision-recall curves are plotted in Figure 5.

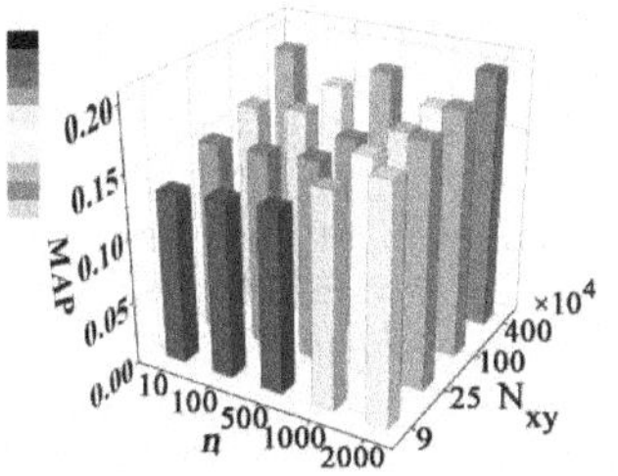

Figure 7: The influence of varying N_{xy}, the number of auxiliary heterogeneous pairs, and n, the number of added unlabelled images/QAs, on MAP performance.

More importantly, our proposed HTH method adopts uneven bits for different modalities so that it discriminates between the query and database domain flexibly. In Table 4, we compare HTH with RaHH, which also supports different code lengths. The row represents code length of images while the column is for that of QAs. HTH and RaHH both attain the best MAP results at $k_q = 16$ and $k_p = 24$. This code length combination is regarded as the best trade-off between effective translator learning and original information preservation. Moreover, images require less bits to achieve comparable performance compared to QAs because instances in text domain are more dispersed so that more bits are called for encoding all the instances.

The influence of N_{xy}, the number of auxiliary heterogeneous training pairs, and n, the number of added unlabelled images/QAs, on MAP performance is investigated in Figure 7. Reasonably, larger n and N_{xy} result in better MAP performance. In practice, we choose $N_{xy} = 4 \times 10^6$ and $n = 500$, which is competitive with $N_{xy} = 4 \times 10^6$ and $n = 2,000$, to be more efficient during training.

The time costs of HTH on MIRFLICKR-Yahoo Answers dataset is also reported in Figure 8. The results are similar to Figure 6 except that HTH is more efficient by contrast. This demonstrates that HTH is less sensitive to the size of the training data, which can be further proved in Figure 9. CVH and CMSSH rely on eigen-decomposition operations which are efficient especially when the dimensions of the dataset are comparatively low. However, they do not consider homogeneous similarity or the regularization of pa rameters, thus resulting in less accurate out-of-sample testing performance. Although HTH takes more training time than CRH and RaHH when the number of auxiliary heterogeneous pairs, N_{xy}, is small, it shows more efficiency compared with CRH and RaHH as N_{xy} increases. Therefore, HTH has good scalability and can be applied to large-scale datasets. Note that we do not report results of CMSSH when $N_{xy} = 2.5 \times 10^7, 10^8$ since the algorithm has "out-of-memory" at these scales.

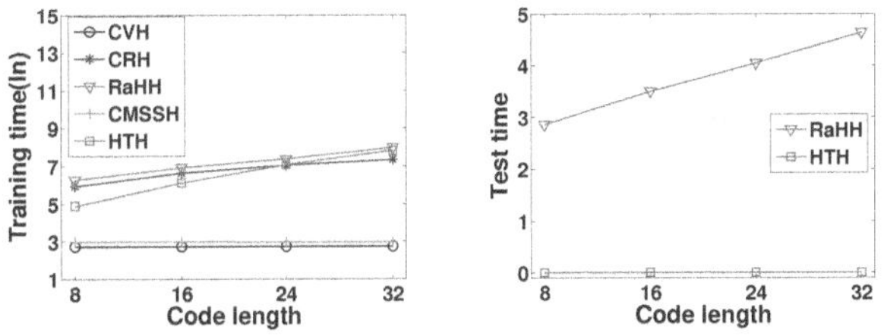

(a) Training time (b) Test time

Figure 8: Time cost of training and testing on MIRFLICKR-Yahoo Answers dataset with code lengths. The time is measured in seconds. Y-axis in (a) is the natural logarithm of training time.

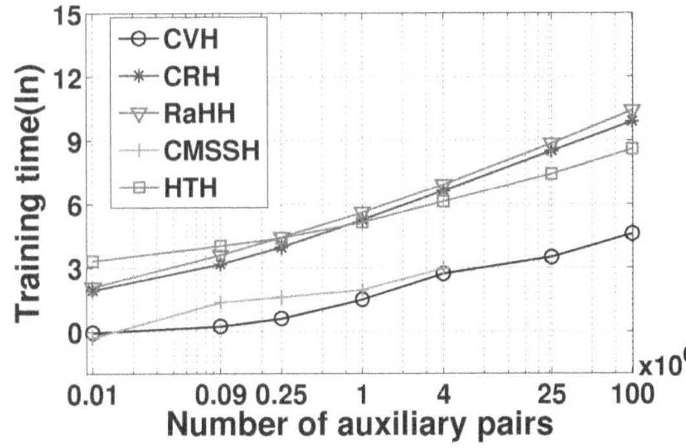

Figure 9: Scalability of training on MIRFLICKR-Yahoo Answers dataset as the number of auxiliary heterogeneous pairs, N_{xy}, increases. The time is measured in seconds. X-axis is in logarithmic scale. Y-axis is the natural logarithm of training time.

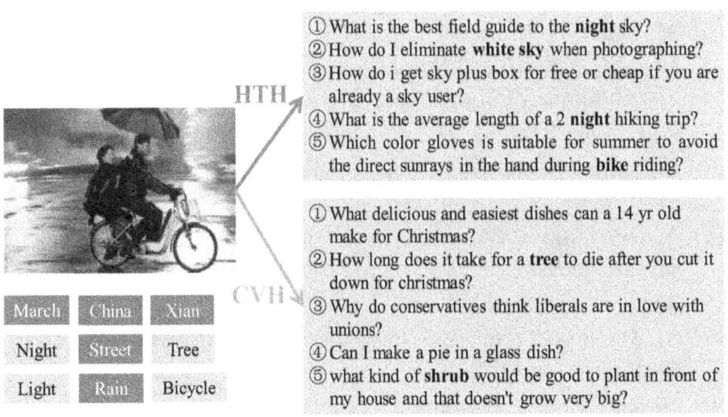

Figure 10: Given a picture in the MIRFLICKR dataset as query, we retrieve top-5 nearest questions from the Yahoo Answers dataset by HTH and CVH. Whether there exist corresponding keywords in a retrieved question to the labels of the picture indicates the relevance of this question to the picture.

We finally provide a similarity search example in Figure 10 to visually show the effectiveness of HTH. Given an image from MIRFLICKR, we compare the relevance of top-5 nearest questions to the image by HTH and CVH[3]. The retrieved questions via HTH are more relevant to this picture as shown in Figure 10.

[3]For space limitation, we only compare with CVH.

5. CONCLUSIONS

In this paper, we propose a novel heterogeneous translated hashing (HTH) model to perform similarity search across heterogeneous media. In particular, by leveraging auxiliary heterogeneous relationship on the web as well as massive unlabelled instances in each modality, HTH learns a set of hash functions to project instances of each modality to an individual Hamming space and a translator aligning these Hamming spaces. Extensive experimental results demonstrate the superiority of HTH over state-of-the-art multi-modal hashing methods. In the future, we plan to apply HTH to other modalities from social media and mobile computing, and to devise a more appropriate scheme to translate between different Hamming spaces, thereby further improving HTH.

6. ACKNOWLEDGEMENTS

We thank the reviewers for their valuable comments to improve this paper. The research has been supported in part by China National 973 project 2014CB340304 and Hong Kong RGC Projects 621013, 620812, and 621211.

7. REFERENCES

[1] A. Andoni and P. Indyk. Near-optimal hashing algorithms for approximate nearest neighbor in high dimensions. In *FOCS*, pages 459–468, 2006.

[2] J. L. Bentley. Multidimensional binary search trees used for associative searching. *Communications of the ACM*, 18(9):509–517, 1975.

[3] D. M. Blei, A. Y. Ng, and M. I. Jordan. Latent dirichlet allocation. *the Journal of machine Learning research*, 3:993–1022, 2003.

[4] M. Bronstein, A. Bronstein, F. Michel, and N. Paragios. Data fusion through cross-modality metric learning using similarity-sensitive hashing. In *CVPR*, pages 3594–3601, 2010.

[5] T.-S. Chua, J. Tang, R. Hong, H. Li, Z. Luo, and Y.-T. Zheng. Nus-wide: A real-world web image database from national university of singapore. In *VLDB*, pages 48:1–48:9, 2009.

[6] M. Datar, N. Immorlica, P. Indyk, and V. S. Mirrokni. Locality-sensitive hashing scheme based on p-stable distributions. In *SCG*, pages 253–262, 2004.

[7] A. Gionis, P. Indyk, and R. Motwani. Similarity search in high dimensions via hashing. In *VLDB*, pages 518–529, 1999.

[8] Y. Gong and S. Lazebnik. Iterative quantization: A procrustean approach to learning binary codes. In *CVPR*, pages 817–824, 2011.

[9] M. J. Huiskes and M. S. Lew. The mir flickr retrieval evaluation. In *MIR*, 2008.

[10] B. Kulis and K. Grauman. Kernelized locality-sensitive hashing for scalable image search. In *CVPR*, pages 2130–2137, 2009.

[11] B. Kulis, P. Jain, and K. Grauman. Fast similarity search for learned metrics. *Pattern Analysis and Machine Intelligence, IEEE Transactions on*, 31(12):2143–2157, 2009.

[12] S. Kumar and R. Udupa. Learning hash functions for cross-view similarity search. In *IJCAI*, pages 1360–1365, 2011.

[13] W. Liu, J. Wang, S. Kumar, and S.-F. Chang. Hashing with graphs. In *ICML*, pages 1–8, June 2011.

[14] Y. Mu, J. Shen, and S. Yan. Weakly-supervised hashing in kernel space. In *CVPR*, pages 3344–3351, 2010.

[15] M. Ou, P. Cui, F. Wang, J. Wang, W. Zhu, and S. Yang. Comparing apples to oranges: A scalable solution with heterogeneous hashing. In *KDD*, pages 230–238, 2013.

[16] N. Quadrianto and C. Lampert. Learning multi-view neighborhood preserving projections. In *ICML*, pages 425–432, 2011.

[17] M. Raginsky and S. Lazebnik. Locality-sensitive binary codes from shift-invariant kernels. In *NIPS*, pages 1509–1517. 2009.

[18] R. Salakhutdinov and G. Hinton. Semantic hashing. *International Journal of Approximate Reasoning*, 50(7):969 – 978, 2009.

[19] G. Shakhnarovich, P. Viola, and T. Darrell. Fast pose estimation with parameter-sensitive hashing. In *ICCV*, pages 750–757, 2003.

[20] S. Shalev-Shwartz, Y. Singer, and N. Srebro. Pegasos: Primal estimated sub-gradient solver for svm. In *ICML*, pages 807–814, 2007.

[21] S. Shalev-Shwartz, Y. Singer, N. Srebro, and A. Cotter. Pegasos: primal estimated sub-gradient solver for svm. *Mathematical Programming*, 127(1):3–30, 2011.

[22] J. Song, Y. Yang, Y. Yang, Z. Huang, and H. T. Shen. Inter-media hashing for large-scale retrieval from heterogeneous data sources. In *SIGMOD*, pages 785–796, 2013.

[23] C. Strecha, A. Bronstein, M. Bronstein, and P. Fua. Ldahash: Improved matching with smaller descriptors. *Pattern Analysis and Machine Intelligence, IEEE Transactions on*, 34(1):66–78, 2012.

[24] J. K. Uhlmann. Satisfying general proximity/similarity queries with metric trees. *Information processing letters*, 40(4):175–179, 1991.

[25] J. Wang, S. Kumar, and S.-F. Chang. Semi-supervised hashing for scalable image retrieval. In *CVPR*, pages 3424–3431, 2010.

[26] R. Weber, H.-J. Schek, and S. Blott. A quantitative analysis and performance study for similarity-search methods in high-dimensional spaces. In *VLDB*, pages 194–205, 1998.

[27] Y. Weiss, A. Torralba, and R. Fergus. Spectral hashing. In *NIPS*, pages 1753–1760, 2008.

[28] F. Wu, Z. Yu, Y. Yang, S. Tang, Y. Zhang, and Y. Zhuang. Sparse multi-modal hashing. *Multimedia, IEEE Transactions on*, 16(2):427–439, 2014.

[29] A. L. Yuille, A. Rangarajan, and A. Yuille. The concave-convex procedure (cccp). *Advances in neural information processing systems*, 2:1033–1040, 2002.

[30] D. Zhai, H. Chang, Y. Zhen, X. Liu, X. Chen, and W. Gao. Parametric local multimodal hashing for cross-view similarity search. In *IJCAI*, pages 2754–2760, 2013.

[31] D. Zhang, J. Wang, D. Cai, and J. Lu. Self-taught hashing for fast similarity search. In *SIGIR*, pages 18–25, 2010.

[32] Y. Zhen and D. Y. Yeung. Co-regularized hashing for multimodal data. In *NIPS*, pages 1385–1393. 2012.

[33] Y. Zhen and D. Y. Yeung. A probabilistic model for multimodal hash function learning. In *KDD*, pages 940–948, 2012.

[34] X. Zhu, Z. Huang, H. T. Shen, and X. Zhao. Linear cross-modal hashing for efficient multimedia search. In *MM*, pages 143–152, 2013.

Matching Users and Items Across Domains to Improve the Recommendation Quality

Chung-Yi Li
Department of Computer Science and Information Engineering,
National Taiwan University, Taiwan
r00922051@csie.ntu.edu.tw

Shou-De Lin
Department of Computer Science and Information Engineering,
National Taiwan University, Taiwan
sdlin@csie.ntu.edu.tw

ABSTRACT

Given two homogeneous rating matrices with some overlapped users/items whose mappings are unknown, this paper aims at answering two questions. First, can we identify the unknown mapping between the users and/or items? Second, can we further utilize the identified mappings to improve the quality of recommendation in either domain? Our solution integrates a latent space matching procedure and a refining process based on the optimization of prediction to identify the matching. Then, we further design a transfer-based method to improve the recommendation performance. Using both synthetic and real data, we have done extensive experiments given different real life scenarios to verify the effectiveness of our models. The code and other materials are available at http://www.csie.ntu.edu.tw/~r00922051/matching/

Categories and Subject Descriptors

I.2.6 [**ARTIFICIAL INTELLIGENCE**]: Learning—*Parameter learning*

Keywords

Collaborative Filtering; Transfer Learning; Matrix Factorization

1. INTRODUCTION

Nowadays, recommendation systems are widely deployed for not only e-business services but also brick and mortar stores. In general there are two possible strategies in designing a recommendation system: content-based [10] and collaborative filtering (CF) based [5] approaches. The former relies on the content and profile information of users and items to perform recommendation, while the latter relies mainly on the ratings of items given by users to identify similar users and items for recommendation. This paper mainly focuses on the analysis of CF-based models and assumes only rating data are available.

Collecting sufficient amount of rating data has been recognized as a critical factor in designing a successful CF-based recommendation system. As CF-based recommendation systems become increasingly popular, it is not hard to imagine more and more rating data would become available to models for different businesses. One might wonder what kind of useful knowledge one can extract from several different rating sets of completely independent services.

For example, a newly established online song requesting service, which possesses some internal ratings about its users' preferences to songs, can take advantage of the publicly available rating data from other similar services (e.g. Yahoo! music service). The reason is that we know there exists some overlapping between users and/or items in the two services, only the exact mappings are unknown. We call the newly established service "the target domain" and the other service "the source domain". One would then appreciate a model that, based only on the two sets of rating data, is able to identify not only the user mappings but the item mappings between the two domains. Such connection can then be used to enrich the understanding of the users and items in the target domain. One would be even happier if the model can exploit the likely "marginally correct" correspondence it found previously to boost the performance of a CF system built in the target domain. In our experiments, we provide 8 effective scenarios (e.g. whether user sets are completely overlapped, partially overlapped, or completely independent; or whether the ratings are disjoint across matrices or not) to verify the usefulness of such model.

Formally, we assume there are two homogeneous rating matrices: a target matrix $\mathbf{R}_1$ and an auxiliary data matrix $\mathbf{R}_2$. The rows and columns represent users and items, and each entry in the matrix represents the rating of an item given by a user. In these matrices, the two user sets and two item sets are overlapped to some extent, but we do not know how to associate the users and the items between the matrices. We want to answer the following two questions:

1. Given only $\mathbf{R}_1$ and $\mathbf{R}_2$, is it possible to find out the mapping of users and the mapping of items between them?
2. Given the noisy mapping we obtained, is it possible to transfer information from $\mathbf{R}_2$ to improve the rating prediction in $\mathbf{R}_1$?

The underlying assumption we made is that the rating behavior of both domains are similar; we call such rating data the "homogeneous". The problems sound hard because the user and item correspondences are both unknown, which prevents us from exploiting any supervised learning algorithm. If one side is already matched (e.g. if the items are matched), then one can use approaches like nearest neighbor to match the other side (e.g. users), as discussed in [13]. Unfortunately, such method cannot be applied when the columns and rows of the rating matrices both have gone through an unknown permutation process.

KDD'14, August 24–27, 2014, New York, NY, USA.
Copyright 2014 ACM 978-1-4503-2956-9/14/08 ...$15.00.
http://dx.doi.org/10.1145/2623330.2623657.

Fortunately, the matching problem is not impossible to solve. Recall the underlying assumption of collaborative filtering: similar users shall rate items similarly and similar items shall receive similar ratings from users. Viewing collaborative filtering as a matrix completion process, the above assumption actually suggests the rows/columns of the rating matrix are indeed dependent. That is, the matrix is of low-rank. The low-rank assumption has been validated by experiments. Owing to this assumption, researchers have proposed a family of strategies based on matrix factorization (MF), which has proven to be one of the most successful solutions for collaborative filtering [6, 1].

Extending from the concept of CF, our key hypothesis is that if two users rated some items similarly in one domain, they shall rate similar items similarly in the other domain. The low-rank assumption on both matrices plays a key role to the solution we propose in this paper. Our idea is to find a way to transform the incomplete matrices $\mathbf{R}_1$ and $\mathbf{R}_2$ into low-rank approximation, and match users/items in the latent space. One plausible solution is to perform matrix factorization on $\mathbf{R}_1$ and $\mathbf{R}_2$ then try to match users/items in the latent space. Figure 1 shows an illustrative example.

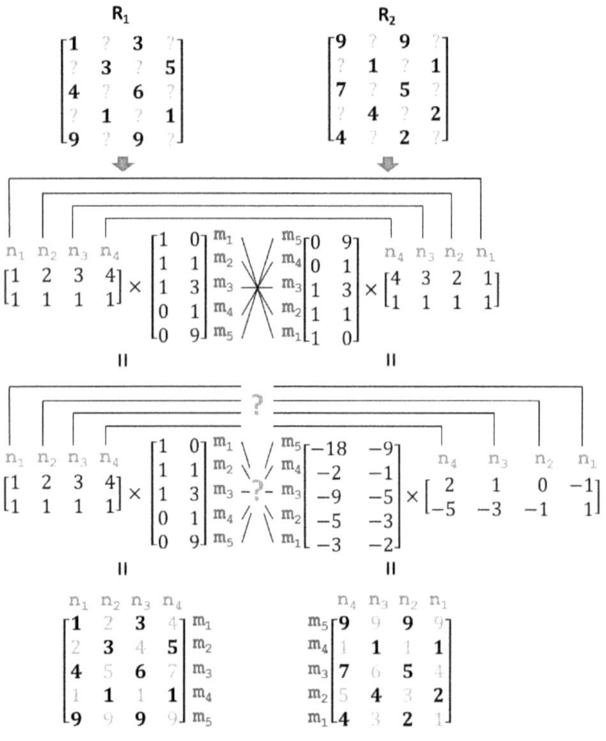

Figure 1: User and Item Matching on Low-Rank Matrices

At the first glance, it seems non-trivial to find the relationship between $\mathbf{R}_1$ and $\mathbf{R}_2$. Assuming that both matrices are of low-rank, they can be factorized into a user-latent matrix and item-latent matrix. Then it might be possible to match users based on the two user-latent matrices, as shown in the first decomposition in Figure 1. Unfortunately, matrix factorization is not unique, so $\mathbf{R}_1$ and $\mathbf{R}_2$ can be factorized using different latent space, prohibiting any further matching of users or items (see the second decomposition in Figure 1).

Another plausible idea is to exploit the idea of singular value decomposition (SVD) on the rating matrices $\mathbf{R}_1$ and $\mathbf{R}_2$, and then match users and items based on the singular vectors. This paper proposes a trick that allows us to obtain singular value decomposition on an incomplete matrix. However, the solution of SVD is still not unique, i.e. sign difference may exist, and the decomposition is unstable when noise occurs. We then propose a greedy-based algorithm that solves the sign problem and searches the nearest neighbors in the latent space. Then, we propose to adjust the matching results through a process that minimizes the prediction error on the existing ratings of $\mathbf{R}_1$ using $\mathbf{R}_2$, making the matching results more resistant to noise. Experiments show that our method can accurately find the correspondence given clean low-rank data, while achieving much higher matching accuracy than other competitors if given real, noisy data. Finally, based on the discovered matching outcome, we propose a transfer learning approach that transfers the rating information from $\mathbf{R}_2$ to $\mathbf{R}_1$ to boost the performance of the recommendation system in $\mathbf{R}_1$. We conduct extensive experiments including a variety of scenarios to verify the effectiveness of our model.

2. RELATED WORK

2.1 User Identification

User identification has been studied under different settings by different research communities. In natural language processing, author identification [2] is formulated as a text categorization problem, in which a supervised learning model is built based on features extracted from the authors' manuscripts. In social network analysis, Narayanan and Shmatikov [14] propose to link two social networks and de-anonymize users by first identifying some seed nodes and then iteratively propagating the mapping.

Some approaches have recently been proposed to link users from different social media sites. Zafarani and Liu propose MOBIUS for cross-media user identification [20]. Based on features extracted from user names, they learn a classification model to determine whether an account belongs to a certain person. Liu et al. [9] associates users with an unsupervised approach by calculating the rareness of the names. When a rare name (such as pennystar881) occurs on different websites, it is very likely that the two accounts are owned by the same person. Yuan et al. [19] propose another unsupervised approach to link users. They find that some users may explicitly display their other accounts on the profile page or disclose the account links when they share a post across websites. They design an algorithm to automatically capture all such information to link users.

Most of the studies differ from us because our model relies on rating data, and we do not assume there are any labeled pairs available for training. The closest work to us is [13], in which Narayanan and Shmatikov study how to de-anonymize users from rating data. In their setup the item mapping is known, which makes the task easier than the one we are trying to solve. Moreover, our model embeds itself a second objective: to improve the rating prediction in the target matrix.

2.2 Transfer Learning in Collaborative Filtering Given Correspondence

Many models have been proposed for transfer learning in collaborative filtering [17, 11, 18, 21, 15, 16, 4, 3]. The common goal is to transfer information across several data matrices. Most of the models assume that there is a one-to-one correspondence between users or between items across domains.

For example, in collective matrix factorization [17], there is a rating matrix (users by movies) and a label matrix (genres by movies) for transferring. The shared movie side then becomes the bridge for transferring, as they assume the latent factors of the movies are similar. Similar ideas can be applied on matrices of different time frames [18], on binary versus numerical matrices [15, 16], or on a rating matrix and a social relation matrix [11, 4].

To sum up, the above models transfer information across two or more heterogeneous data matrices based on restrictions that the latent factors of the shared user side or item side are similar. Our setting is quite the opposite: the data matrices are homogeneous while both the user and item correspondence are unknown.

2.3 Transfer Learning in Collaborative Filtering When Correspondence is Unknown

We only find two models that transfer information between rating matrices without exploiting user and item correspondences and will discuss them in details here.

Codebook transfer (CBT) [7] and rating-matrix generative model (RMGM) [8] transfer information between two rating matrices without assuming user correspondence or item correspondence. The basic assumption of the two models are of the form:

$$\mathbf{R}_1 \approx \mathbf{U}_1\mathbf{B}\mathbf{V}_1^T,$$
$$\mathbf{R}_2 \approx \mathbf{U}_2\mathbf{B}\mathbf{V}_2^T,$$

where $\mathbf{B}$ is a shared K by K matrix. The major difference between these models and our model is that these models do not assume user correspondence or item correspondence between $\mathbf{R}_1$ and $\mathbf{R}_2$. Instead, they assume that $\mathbf{R}_1$ and $\mathbf{R}_2$ have homogeneous rating pattern; they enforce constraints on $\mathbf{U}$'s and $\mathbf{V}$'s while assuming the homogeneous pattern matrix, $\mathbf{B}$, is shared across $\mathbf{R}_1$ and $\mathbf{R}_2$. However, the constraints make the optimization process complicated and limit the expressive power of the model.

In CBT, $\mathbf{U}$ and $\mathbf{V}$ are constrained to be 0-1 matrices, and there can only be one entry with value 1 in each row. After adding the constraints, $\mathbf{R} \approx \mathbf{U}\mathbf{B}\mathbf{V}^T$ can be viewed as a co-clustering process that simultaneously divide users and items into groups. Assume a user is in i-th user group and an item is in j-th item group, then the rating of such user and item (r_{ij} in $\mathbf{R}$) is predicted to be the value of corresponding group rating value in $\mathbf{B}$ (b_{ij}). Thus, the formulation of CBT is actually associating groups of users (items) in $\mathbf{R}_1$ with groups of users (items) in $\mathbf{R}_2$.

However, the hard clustering constraint greatly reduces the expressive power of CBT; many lower-rank matrices cannot be factored under such constraint. Furthermore, to solve CBT, the optimization process requires the auxiliary matrix $\mathbf{R}_2$ to be fully observed, or it has to fill in missing entries with data mean before factorization. Since there are much more missing entries than observed ones in a sparse rating matrix, filling in the missing values manually can seriously bias the model.

RMGM relaxes the constraints in CBT from hard clustering to soft clustering by using a probabilistic graphical model, and it does not require $\mathbf{R}_2$ to be fully observed. To be more specific, the joint probability defined in RMGM is

$$P(r, m^{(i)}, n^{(i)}, C_m, C_n) = P(m^{(i)}|C_m)P(n^{(i)}|C_n)P(r|C_m, C_n)P(C_m)P(C_n),$$

and the rating prediction is

$$\sum_r r \sum_{k_1,k_2} P(r|C_m = k_1, C_n = k_2)P(C_m = k_1|m^{(i)})P(C_n = k_2|n^{(i)}),$$

where $m^{(i)}$ and $n^{(i)}$ are user and item in i-th domain, and C_m and C_n are the cluster for the user and item, respectively. If we rewrite the rating prediction as

$$\sum_{k_1,k_2}\left(P(C_m = k_1|m^{(i)})P(C_n = k_2|n^{(i)})\sum_r rP(r|C_m = k_1, C_n = k_2)\right),$$

the term $\sum_r rP(r|C_m, C_n)$ is similar to $\mathbf{B}$ in CBT. $P(C_m|m^{(i)})$ and $P(C_n|n^{(i)})$ are similar to $\mathbf{U}_i$ and $\mathbf{V}_i$, respectively. When the rating prediction is perfect, $\mathbf{R} = \mathbf{U}_i\mathbf{B}\mathbf{V}_i^T$.

Even though RMGM relaxes the hard clustering constraints in CBT, constraints still exist: the elements in each row of $\mathbf{U}$ and $\mathbf{V}$ must be nonnegative and sum up to 1. This again limits the expressive power of the model and complicate the optimization task. Besides, the objective function of RMGM is the self-defined likelihood. It deviates from common evaluation measures such as root mean square error. Consider the following example:

$$\mathbf{R} = \begin{bmatrix}1 & 1\\3 & 3\\2 & 2\end{bmatrix}, \mathbf{U} = P(C_m|m^{(i)}) = \begin{bmatrix}1 & 0\\0 & 1\\0.5 & 0.5\end{bmatrix}, \mathbf{V}^T = P(C_n|n^{(i)})^T = \begin{bmatrix}1 & 1\\0 & 0\end{bmatrix},$$

$$\mathbf{B} = \textstyle\sum_r rP(r|C_m, C_n) = 1 \times \begin{bmatrix}1 & 1\\0 & 0\end{bmatrix} + 2 \times \begin{bmatrix}0 & 0\\0 & 0\end{bmatrix} + 3 \times \begin{bmatrix}0 & 0\\1 & 1\end{bmatrix} = \begin{bmatrix}1 & 1\\3 & 3\end{bmatrix}.$$

When we evaluate this model by root mean square error, the error is 0 because $\mathbf{R}$ is exactly the product of the three matrices. However, the data likelihood defined by RMGM is also 0 because the term $P(r = 2|C_m, C_n)$ is always 0. Thus, RMGM will try to find other parameters to fit the data, but they are not necessarily minimizing the prediction error. Nevertheless, RMGM is considered as the state-of-the-art and will be our main competitor in the evaluation.

In conclusion, past models do not try to solve correspondence and impose extra constraints in the factorization equation. Our model directly solves the correspondence problem and leverages such information to transfer across matrices.

3. METHODOLOGY

Given two partially observed rating matrices $\mathbf{R}_1$ and $\mathbf{R}_2$, we made the following assumptions:

1. There are some common users and common items across $\mathbf{R}_1$ and $\mathbf{R}_2$, but we do not know the correspondence.
2. The two matrices represent the same homogeneous domain. That is, if we can link the common users/items (rows/columns) between $\mathbf{R}_1$ and $\mathbf{R}_2$, we can merge them into one single matrix (Figure 2), and such matrix is likely to be low-rank which allows the collaborative filtering models to perform recommendation.

To find out the correspondence between $\mathbf{R}_1$ and $\mathbf{R}_2$, intuitively we want to solve

$$\mathbf{R}_1 \approx \mathbf{G}_{\text{user}}\mathbf{R}_2\mathbf{G}_{\text{item}}^T,$$

where $\mathbf{G}_{\text{user}}$ and $\mathbf{G}_{\text{item}}$ are 0-1 matrices that represent user and item correspondences. The symbol $\approx$ implies the corresponding entries in $\mathbf{R}_1$ and $\mathbf{G}_{\text{user}}\mathbf{R}_2\mathbf{G}_{\text{item}}^T$ shall be as similar as possible. The apparent challenge is that the rating matrices are partially observed, and very few entries are observed in both $\mathbf{R}_1$ and $\mathbf{R}_2$. Thus, we want to modify the above equation to deal with this problem.

We want to exploit the low-rank property of the rating matrices to solve the problem. To do so, we replace the original rating matrix by its fully filled low-rank approximation (i.e. no missing values). We propose the following two objective functions:

1. $\hat{\mathbf{R}}_1 \approx \mathbf{G}_{\text{user}}\hat{\mathbf{R}}_2\mathbf{G}_{\text{item}}^T$
2. $\mathbf{R}_1 \approx \mathbf{G}_{\text{user}}\hat{\mathbf{R}}_2\mathbf{G}_{\text{item}}^T$

We want to find $\mathbf{G}$'s that satisfies the above criteria. The symbol $\hat{\mathbf{R}}$ stands for the low-rank approximation of $\mathbf{R}$. In Equation 1, we hope to map the low-rank approximation $\mathbf{R}_2$ to the low-rank approximation of $\mathbf{R}_1$. In Equation 2, we hope the observed entries

$$\mathbf{R}_1 = \begin{bmatrix} \mathbf{1} & ? & ? & ? \\ ? & \mathbf{2} & \mathbf{3} & ? \\ \mathbf{1} & ? & ? & ? \\ ? & \mathbf{2} & \mathbf{3} & \mathbf{4} \end{bmatrix}, \quad \mathbf{R}_2 = \begin{bmatrix} \mathbf{1} & \mathbf{2} & ? & ? \\ \mathbf{1} & ? & ? & \mathbf{4} \\ ? & ? & \mathbf{3} & ? \\ ? & \mathbf{2} & ? & \mathbf{4} \end{bmatrix}$$

$$\mathbf{R} = \begin{bmatrix} \mathbf{1} & \mathbf{2} & ? & ? \\ \mathbf{1} & \mathbf{2} & \mathbf{3} & \mathbf{4} \\ \mathbf{1} & ? & \mathbf{3} & ? \\ ? & \mathbf{2} & \mathbf{3} & \mathbf{4} \end{bmatrix}$$

Figure 2: if the correspondence between $\mathbf{R}_1$ and $\mathbf{R}_2$ are known (e.g. the i-th column/row of $\mathbf{R}_1$ are mapped to the i-th column/row of $\mathbf{R}_2$), then $\mathbf{R}_1$ and $\mathbf{R}_2$ can be merged into one denser matrix.

in $\mathbf{R}_1$ can be matched by the corresponding entries of the low-rank approximation of $\mathbf{R}_2$. In theory we can swap $\mathbf{R}_1$ and $\mathbf{R}_2$ in Equation 2, but we chose to match the observation of $\mathbf{R}_1$ since it is the target matrix which we want to improve the rating prediction later on.

Optimizing the first objective function is easier but yields less accurate solutions, while the second objective function is more reliable but harder to solve. Therefore, our complete matching algorithm solves the two equations sequentially: the matching obtained from the first equation is used as initialization and to reduce the search space of second objective. We describe our solution to Equation 1 in Section 3.1. The main idea is to conduct singular value decomposition on the incomplete matrix $\hat{\mathbf{R}}$. We also design a greedy search on the latent factors for user matching and item matching. Section 3.2 solves Equation 2 in a way similar to two-block coordinate descent. At last, in Section 3.3, we describe our transfer learning model that exploits the matching result to boost the quality of rating prediction on the target domain.

In the following discussion, we do not constrain correspondence matrix $\mathbf{G}$ to be pure permutation matrix to simplify the optimization process. We only impose constraints on each row – such that one entry is 1 and the rest are all 0s – but not on columns. In other words, for each user/item in $\mathbf{R}_1$, we want to find its most similar neighbor in $\mathbf{R}_2$, rather than enforce the 1-to-1 mapping between users/items. This relaxation also makes our model more general as it can then handle situations with low or even no overlapping across domains.

3.1 Latent Space Matching

3.1.1 Singular Value Decomposition

The fundamental idea of our latent space matching approach is based on the uniqueness of singular value decomposition (SVD). Given a completely observed matrix $\mathbf{R}$, the singular value decomposition is $\mathbf{R} = \mathbf{UDV}^T$, where $\mathbf{D}$ is diagonal and $\mathbf{U}$ and $\mathbf{V}$ are unitary. We know that $\mathbf{D}$ is unique for every $\mathbf{R}$ when d_i's are sorted. Moreover, when all the singular values are distinct, the singular vectors ($\mathbf{U}$ and $\mathbf{V}$) are unique except sign differences. We can always multiply a column of U and the corresponding column of V by -1 and they become another valid solution for singular value decomposition.

The sign difference is indeed an important issue which we will address later. Assuming the sign problem is solved, it is possible to obtain a unique latent vector to represent any user or item. Then we can solve the user/item matching problem by conducting nearest neighbor search on the latent factors.

3.1.2 From Matrix Factorization to Singular Value Decomposition

Conventional singular value decomposition solvers cannot be applied to decompose the partially observed rating matrix. In collaborative filtering, matrix factorization (MF)[6, 12] – an unconstrained two-factor decomposition – is usually used. Here we provide a simple yet efficient process to transform unconstrained matrix factorization to a form of singular value decomposition.

Let $\mathbf{R}$ be a rating matrix and $\mathbf{W}$ an indicator matrix, where $\mathbf{W}_{ij} = 1$ means user i rated item j or 0 otherwise. Let M denote the number of users, N be the number of items, and K be the parameter that estimates the rank. We omit the regularization term for clarity. Then the objective of matrix factorization is to find $\mathbf{P}_{M\times K}$ and $\mathbf{Q}_{N\times K}$ such that

$$\min_{P,Q} \|\mathbf{W} \odot \left(\mathbf{R} - \mathbf{PQ}^T\right)\|^2_{\text{Fro}},$$

where $\odot$ is the Hadamard (entrywise) product and Fro stands for Frobenius norm. The $\mathbf{P}$ and $\mathbf{Q}$ are usually solved by stochastic gradient descent or alternating least square [6].

Singular value decomposition is composed of $\mathbf{U}_{M\times K}$, $\mathbf{D}_{K\times K}$ and $\mathbf{V}_{N\times K}$ such that

$$\min_{U,V,D} \quad \|\mathbf{W} \odot \left(\mathbf{R} - \mathbf{UDV}^T\right)\|^2_{\text{Fro}}$$
$$\text{subject to} \quad \mathbf{U}^T\mathbf{U} = \mathbf{I}, \mathbf{V}^T\mathbf{V} = \mathbf{I}, \mathbf{D} \text{ is diagonal}$$

Our trick starts from performing factorization on $\mathbf{R}$ to obtain $\mathbf{P}$ and $\mathbf{Q}$, and then transform $(\mathbf{P}, \mathbf{Q})$ to $(\mathbf{U}, \mathbf{D}, \mathbf{V})$ by applying conventional SVD on $\mathbf{P}$ and $\mathbf{Q}$. Note that $\mathbf{P}$ and $\mathbf{Q}$ are not partially observed so we can exploit conventional methods to obtain the decomposition. [1] The process is illustrated in Figure 3. Assume ($\mathbf{U}_P$, $\mathbf{D}_P$, $\mathbf{V}_P$) is the SVD of $\mathbf{P}$ and ($\mathbf{U}_Q$, $\mathbf{D}_Q$, $\mathbf{V}_Q$) is the SVD of $\mathbf{Q}$. Let ($\mathbf{U}_X$, $\mathbf{D}_X$, $\mathbf{V}_X$) be the SVD of $(\mathbf{D}_P\mathbf{V}_P^T\mathbf{V}_Q\mathbf{D}_Q^T)$. Then,

$$\mathbf{PQ}^T = \mathbf{U}_P\mathbf{D}_P\mathbf{V}_P^T\left(\mathbf{U}_Q\mathbf{D}_Q\mathbf{V}_Q^T\right)^T = \mathbf{U}_P\mathbf{U}_X\mathbf{D}_X\mathbf{V}_X^T\mathbf{U}_Q^T.$$

We have obtained the SVD for $\mathbf{PQ}^T$ as $\mathbf{UDV}^T$, where $\mathbf{U} = \mathbf{U}_P\mathbf{U}_X$, $\mathbf{V} = \mathbf{U}_Q\mathbf{V}_X$ and $\mathbf{D} = \mathbf{D}_X$.

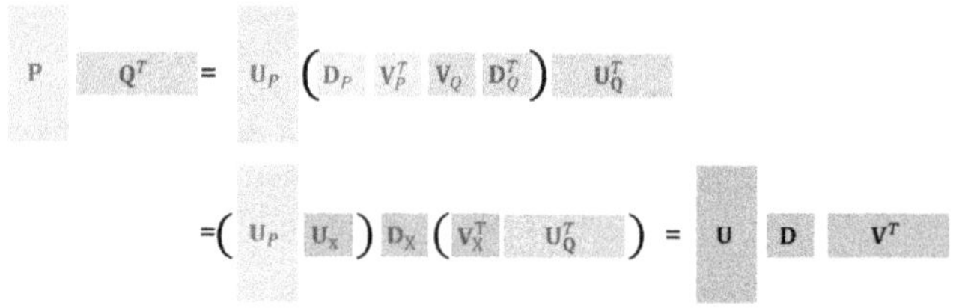

Figure 3: From MF to SVD

One practical issue to be aware of is that SVD normalizes the norm of each column of $\mathbf{U}$ and $\mathbf{V}$ to 1, so the values of $\mathbf{U}$ and $\mathbf{V}$ tend to be smaller for larger matrices. Since $\mathbf{R}_1$ and $\mathbf{R}_2$ may be of different sizes, it is necessary to scale the values in $\mathbf{U}$ and $\mathbf{V}$ to make sure later on when we want to compare $\mathbf{U}_1$ with $\mathbf{U}_2$ and $\mathbf{V}_1$ with $\mathbf{V}_2$, they are of the same scale. $\mathbf{U}$, $\mathbf{D}$ and $\mathbf{V}$ are re-scaled as

$$\mathbf{U} = \mathbf{U} \times \sqrt{M}, \mathbf{D} = \mathbf{D} \times \sqrt{M} \times \sqrt{N}, \mathbf{V} = \mathbf{V} \times \sqrt{N},$$

where M and N are scalars representing the number of users and items respectively.

[1] the matrix is highly asymmetric so thin SVD (economical SVD) is used and the decomposition only takes seconds.

3.1.3 Objective Function of Latent Space Matching

Remember our first goal is to find $\mathbf{G}_{\text{user}}$ and $\mathbf{G}_{\text{item}}$ such that

$$\hat{\mathbf{R}}_1 \approx \mathbf{G}_{\text{user}}\hat{\mathbf{R}}_2\mathbf{G}_{\text{item}}^T.$$

From the previous section, we have obtained the low-rank approximation of two matrices as $\hat{\mathbf{R}}_1 = \mathbf{U}_1\mathbf{D}_1\mathbf{V}_1^T$ and $\hat{\mathbf{R}}_2 = \mathbf{U}_2\mathbf{D}_2\mathbf{V}_2^T$. The above equation becomes

$$\mathbf{U}_1\mathbf{D}_1\mathbf{V}_1^T \approx \mathbf{G}_{\text{user}}\mathbf{U}_2\mathbf{D}_2\mathbf{V}_2^T\mathbf{G}_{\text{item}}^T.$$

Then, we can decouple the user/item matching problem because of the uniqueness of singular value decomposition. When the decomposition is unique, the latent factors of the same user in $\mathbf{R}_1$ and $\mathbf{R}_2$ should be similar, and the latent factors of the same item should be similar, too. Thus, we can decouple the above equation into two matching problems:

$$\min_{\mathbf{G}_{\text{user}},\mathbf{S}_{\text{user}}} \|\mathbf{U}_1\mathbf{D}_1^{0.5} - \mathbf{G}_{\text{user}}\mathbf{U}_2\mathbf{D}_2^{0.5}\mathbf{S}_{\text{user}}\|_{\text{Fro}}^2$$

$$\min_{\mathbf{G}_{\text{item}},\mathbf{S}_{\text{item}}} \|\mathbf{V}_1\mathbf{D}_1^{0.5} - \mathbf{G}_{\text{item}}\mathbf{V}_2\mathbf{D}_2^{0.5}\mathbf{S}_{\text{item}}\|_{\text{Fro}}^2$$

We have mentioned that singular value decomposition is unique except the sign of column vectors. Thus, in the equation we add a sign matrix $\mathbf{S}$, a small diagonal matrix (K by K) where each diagonal element is either 1 or -1. Since the formulations of user matching and item matching are identical, here we will discuss user side only.

When $\mathbf{S}$ is fixed, the previous equation becomes

$$\min_{\mathbf{G}_{\text{user}}} \|\mathbf{Z}_1 - \mathbf{G}_{\text{user}}\mathbf{Z}_2\|_{\text{Fro}}^2,$$

where

$$\mathbf{Z}_1 = \mathbf{U}_1\mathbf{D}_1^{0.5}, \mathbf{Z}_2 = \mathbf{U}_2\mathbf{D}_2^{0.5}\mathbf{S}.$$

Now all rows of $\mathbf{G}$ become independent because we only enforce constraints on rows but not columns. Thus, it becomes a simple nearest neighbor search problem. For each row in $\mathbf{Z}_1$, the goal is to select the most similar row in $\mathbf{Z}_2$ (illustrated in Figure 4). It takes $\Theta(M_1M_2K)$ time to solve $\mathbf{G}$, where M_1 and M_2 are the number of users in $\mathbf{R}_1$ and $\mathbf{R}_2$, respectively.

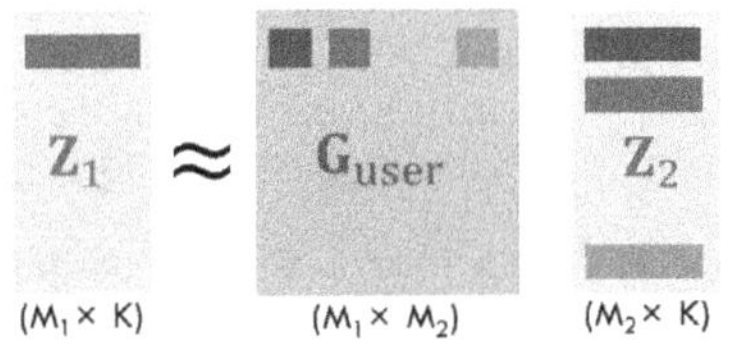

Figure 4: Subroutine when $\mathbf{S}$ is fixed – Nearest Neighbor Search. The purple entry in $\mathbf{G}$ becomes 1 when the purple row in $\mathbf{Z}_2$ is the nearest neigbor to the grey row in $\mathbf{Z}_1$.

Unfortunately, for the problem we are facing, the sign matrix is unknown and there are 2^K possible combinations. We therefore design a greedy approach to search for a plausible solution. Assume $d_1 \geq d_2 \geq \cdots \geq d_K$, where d_i is a singular value. In the k-th iteration, we try both $s_k = 1$ and $s_k = -1$ and solve $\mathbf{G}$ twice. We choose the s_k and $\mathbf{G}$ that results in a smaller objective value in nearest neighbor. After determining s_k, we move on to the next iteration and solve s_{k+1}. We illustrate how to solve $\mathbf{S}$ in Figure 5.

Ideally, we can simply use the $\mathbf{G}$ obtained in the last iteration as our matching result. However, smaller singular values and their singular vectors are more noisy, resulting in a noisy $\mathbf{G}$. That says, picking the matching function $\mathbf{G}$ in the final iteration might not be the best choice. Here we propose a simple strategy to perform such "dimension selection" to pick the most suitable $\mathbf{G}_{\text{user}}$ and $\mathbf{G}_{\text{item}}$. Our goal is to select one $\mathbf{G}$ from $\mathbf{G}_{(1:K)}$, where the $\mathbf{G}_{(1:K)}$ is the output in every iteration while solving $\mathbf{S}$. We collect all pairs of $\mathbf{G}_{\text{user}}$ and $\mathbf{G}_{\text{item}}$, and then select the pair that leads to the best rating prediction in $\mathbf{R}_1$. We choose the $\mathbf{G}_{\text{user}}$ and $\mathbf{G}_{\text{item}}$ that minimize

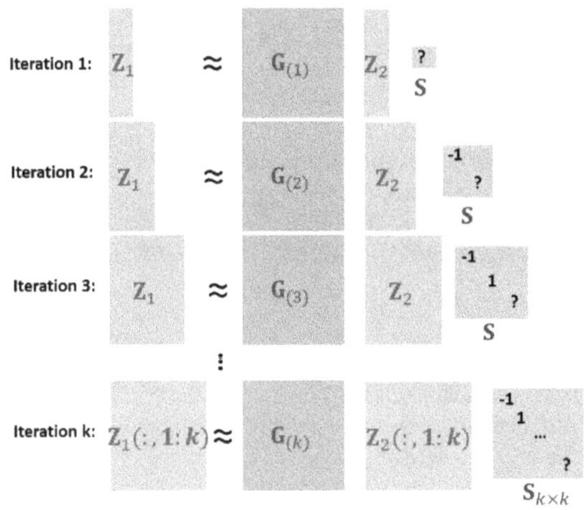

Figure 5: Sign Solving Process

$$\|\mathbf{W}_1 \odot \left(\mathbf{R}_1 - \mathbf{G}_{\text{user}}\mathbf{U}_2\mathbf{D}_2\mathbf{V}_2\mathbf{G}_{\text{item}}^T\right)\|_{\text{Fro}}^2.$$

The complete procedure for our latent space matching is described in Algorithm 1.

Finally, we enter the discussion about time complexity. In the MATCHING function of Algorithm 1, we actually maintain a distance table T that records all pair distance between $\mathbf{Z}_1$ and $\mathbf{Z}_2$ for fast look-up. After k iterations, T records the distance calculated using the latent dimension 1 to k, so in the next iteration we can quickly update the distance by considering the latent dimension $k+1$ only. Thus, the complete time complexity of the MATCHING function in Algorithm 1 is still $\Theta(M_1M_2K)$ for user matching and $\Theta(N_1N_2K)$ for item matching. The dimension selection part takes $\Theta(K \times L \times K) = \Theta(K^2L)$, where L is the number of ratings in $\mathbf{R}_1$.

3.1.4 Remarks on Latent Space Matching

The main advantage of the proposed latent space matching method is that it decouples user/item matching problem. In the ideal case where the matrix is low-rank, latent space matching is capable of producing perfect matching (our experiment will show this). However, there are some potential concerns when noise exists. First, latent space matching is based on matrix factorization, which is only an approximation of the original rating matrix. Second, when some singular values are close and the intensity of noise increases, the corresponding singular vectors are mixed together. In such degenerate cases, singular value decomposition is not unique.

It is known that singular value decomposition is equivalent to principle component analysis when the data mean is zero. We can illustrate the degenerate case in Figure 6(a) and Figure 6(b). Figure 6(a) is an example where the singular value decomposition is unique. The major axis of the ellipse represents the first singular vector and the minor axis represents the second singular vector. In contrast, Figure 6(b) shows a degenerate case. We cannot identify the major axis in the graph and the singular value decomposition of the data matrix is not unique.

Algorithm 1 Latent Space Matching

Require: $\mathbf{U}_1, \mathbf{D}_1, \mathbf{V}_1, \mathbf{U}_2, \mathbf{D}_2, \mathbf{V}_2$ and $\mathbf{R}_1$
Ensure: $\mathbf{G}^*_{\text{user}}$ and $\mathbf{G}^*_{\text{item}}$
function NN($\mathbf{Z}_1, \mathbf{Z}_2, T$)
 ▷ perform nearest neighbor search
 ▷ T is the distance cache for speed-up
 $\alpha = \min_{\mathbf{G}} \|\mathbf{Z}_1 - \mathbf{G}\mathbf{Z}_2\|^2_{\text{Fro}}$
 $\mathbf{G} = \operatorname{argmin}_{\mathbf{G}} \|\mathbf{Z}_1 - \mathbf{G}\mathbf{Z}_2\|^2_{\text{Fro}}$
 return (α, $\mathbf{G}$)
end function
function MATCHING($\mathbf{Z}_1, \mathbf{Z}_2$)
 ▷ T is a cache for speed-up
 initialize all elements of the distance table T to 0
 for k = 1 to K **do**
  let $s_k = +1$
  $(\alpha_+, \mathbf{G}_+) = \text{NN}(\mathbf{Z}_{1\,(:,1:k)}, \mathbf{Z}_{2\,(:,1:k)}\mathbf{S}_{(1:k,1:k)}, \text{T})$
  let $s_k = -1$
  $(\alpha_-, \mathbf{G}_-) = \text{NN}(\mathbf{Z}_{1\,(:,1:k)}, \mathbf{Z}_{2\,(:,1:k)}\mathbf{S}_{(1:k,1:k)}, \text{T})$
  if $\alpha_+ \le \alpha_-$ **then**
   $\mathbf{G}_{(k)} = \mathbf{G}_+$, $s_k = +1$
  else
   $\mathbf{G}_{(k)} = \mathbf{G}_-$, $s_k = -1$
  end if
  update T according to $\mathbf{G}_{(k)}$
 end for
 return $\mathbf{G}_{(1)}, \cdots, \mathbf{G}_{(K)}$
end function
$\mathbf{G}_{\text{user}\,(1:K)}$ = MATCHING($\mathbf{U}_1\mathbf{D}_1^{0.5}, \mathbf{U}_2\mathbf{D}_2^{0.5}$)
$\mathbf{G}_{\text{item}\,(1:K)}$ = MATCHING($\mathbf{V}_1\mathbf{D}_1^{0.5}, \mathbf{V}_2\mathbf{D}_2^{0.5}$)
for k = 1 to K **do** ▷ dimension selection
 $\text{error}_k = \|\mathbf{W}_1 \odot (\mathbf{R}_1 - \mathbf{G}_{\text{user}\,(k)}\mathbf{U}_2\mathbf{D}_2\mathbf{V}_2\mathbf{G}^T_{\text{item}\,(k)})\|^2_{\text{Fro}}$.
end for
$(\text{error}_{\min}, k_{\min}) = \min_k \text{error}_{1:K}$
$\mathbf{G}^*_{\text{user}} = \mathbf{G}_{\text{user}\,(k_{\min})}$
$\mathbf{G}^*_{\text{item}} = \mathbf{G}_{\text{item}\,(k_{\min})}$

Such deficiency can be observed in the experiment, which leads to our design of a refinement approach which we will describe in the next section.

3.2 Matching Refinement through Optimization

We talked about how the user and item correspondences, $\mathbf{G}_{\text{user}}$ and $\mathbf{G}_{\text{item}}$, can be obtained through latent space matching. Here we propose a method to further refine them using the previously learned $\mathbf{G}_{\text{user}}$ and $\mathbf{G}_{\text{item}}$. Since our ultimate goal is to transfer knowledge from $\mathbf{R}_2$ to help rating prediction of $\mathbf{R}_1$, a reasonable way to evaluate the quality of $\mathbf{G}_{\text{user}}$ and $\mathbf{G}_{\text{item}}$ is to check whether $\mathbf{G}_{\text{user}}\mathbf{P}_2\mathbf{Q}_2^T\mathbf{G}^T_{\text{item}}$ can reproduce the corresponding ratings in $\mathbf{R}_1$, where $\mathbf{P}_2\mathbf{Q}_2^T$ is the low-rank approximation of $\mathbf{R}_2$. Therefore, we want to adjust $\mathbf{G}_{\text{user}}$ and $\mathbf{G}_{\text{item}}$ to satisfy the following equation

$$\min_{\mathbf{G}_{\text{user}}, \mathbf{G}_{\text{item}}} \|\mathbf{W}_1 \odot \left(\mathbf{R}_1 - \mathbf{G}_{\text{user}}\mathbf{P}_2\mathbf{Q}_2^T\mathbf{G}^T_{\text{item}}\right)\|_{\text{Fro}}.$$

Note that in our previous latent space matching, for each user/item we identify its nearest neighbor. Here we propose to record the top nearest candidates for each user and item, and reevaluate their quality based on the above equation. Assume in latent space matching, we have recorded the top C neighboring users/items. Then the $\mathbf{G}_{\text{user}}$ and $\mathbf{G}_{\text{item}}$ we want to solve now become $M_1 \times C$ and $N_1 \times C$

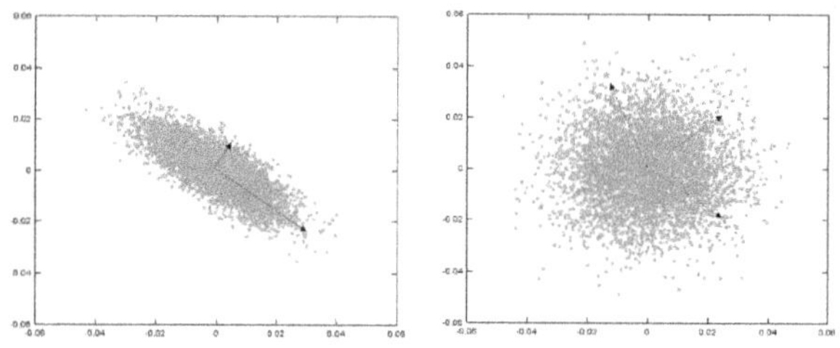

(a) Normal Data (b) A Degenerate Case

Figure 6: If the data distribution is like (a), the principal component is the major axis. In (b) we cannot identify the principal component.

matrices, respectively. M_1 and N_1 are the number of users and the number of items in $\mathbf{R}_1$.

We solve $\mathbf{G}$ in a similar manner as two-block coordinate descent, except here the variables in $\mathbf{G}$ are discrete. When $\mathbf{G}_{\text{item}}$ is fixed, each row in $\mathbf{G}_{\text{user}}$ becomes independent, and finding the best $\mathbf{G}_{\text{user}}$ becomes a straightforward search problem. For each user in $\mathbf{R}_1$, we are finding the candidate (the corresponding row in $\mathbf{P}_2$) that minimizes the rating prediction error in the row of $\mathbf{R}_1$. It takes $\Theta(LCK)$ time to solve $\mathbf{G}_{\text{user}}$, where L is the number of ratings in $\mathbf{R}_1$.

It can be easily seen that this process leads to a local optimal solution as every time when we update $\mathbf{G}$, the objective value is guaranteed to become smaller. Our algorithm solves $\mathbf{G}_{\text{user}}$ and $\mathbf{G}_{\text{item}}$ alternately until both $\mathbf{G}$'s become stable. There is only a finite number of possibilities, so the algorithm will converge. Since the procedure only reaches local optimum, a good initialization is very important to guarantee the quality of the output. Our latent space matching serves such purpose. We set the initial value of $\mathbf{G}$ here to the $\mathbf{G}$ outputted in the original latent space matching.

3.3 Transferring Imperfect Matching to Predict Ratings on the Target Domain

Here we emphasize on transferring the matching information to the target domain to improve rating prediction. We modify matrix factorization [6, 12] for rating prediction. In the original matrix factorization model, the goal is to find $\mathbf{P}$ and $\mathbf{Q}$ to minimize

$$\|\mathbf{W} \odot \left(\mathbf{R} - \mathbf{P}\mathbf{Q}^T\right)\|^2 + \lambda\left(\|\mathbf{P}\|^2 + \|\mathbf{Q}\|^2\right).$$

Once $\mathbf{P}$ and $\mathbf{Q}$ are identified, we can multiply them to obtain the full matrix as the prediction. The norms here are Frobenius norm.

When the user and item correspondences are both given, let g_m be the corresponding user in $\mathbf{R}_2$ of user m in $\mathbf{R}_1$ and g_n be the corresponding item in $\mathbf{R}_2$ of item n in $\mathbf{R}_1$. We modify the original formula of matrix factorization by adding a "matching-based" regularization term:

$$\begin{aligned}&\|\mathbf{W}_1 \odot \left(\mathbf{R}_1 - \mathbf{P}_1\mathbf{Q}_1^T\right)\|^2 + \|\mathbf{W}_2 \odot \left(\mathbf{R}_2 - \mathbf{P}_2\mathbf{Q}_2^T\right)\|^2 \\ &+\lambda\left(\|\mathbf{P}_1\|^2 + \|\mathbf{Q}_1\|^2 + \|\mathbf{P}_2\|^2 + \|\mathbf{Q}_2\|^2\right) \\ &+\beta\sum_m^{M_1} \arctan\left(\|\mathbf{P}_1(m,:) - \mathbf{P}_2(g_m,:)\|^2\right) \\ &+\beta\sum_n^{N_1} \arctan\left(\|\mathbf{Q}_1(n,:) - \mathbf{Q}_2(g_n,:)\|^2\right)\end{aligned}$$

The extra regularization terms associated with β restrict the latent factors of matched users/items to be the same. Therefore, if the matching is correct, since the corresponding users or items are forced to align in their latent space, the extra information from the other domain can then be exploited.

Acknowledging the fact that our matching is not perfect, special care needs to be taken to prevent incorrect matching from hampering the prediction performance. Thus, we add an arctan function to alleviate the influence of outliers. When the matching results become unreliable, our model degenerates into regular matrix factorization model as β would become 0 after parameter selection. The objective is still differentiable and can be solved via standard approaches such as gradient descent.

4. EXPERIMENTS

4.1 Experimental Setup

Table 1: Statistics of $\mathbf{R}$

Dataset	# of Users and Items	Rating Scale	Sparsity
Low Rank	(20000, 10000)	real, [-1,1]	5%
Yahoo! Music	(20000, 10000)	integer, 0-100	5.4%

Our goal is to link the users and items in two homogeneous rating matrices, $\mathbf{R}_1$ and $\mathbf{R}_2$, and then use the corresponding information in $\mathbf{R}_2$ to improve rating prediction in $\mathbf{R}_1$. However, we cannot find two independent datasets that provide the ground truth for user/item mappings to evaluate our model. Fortunately, we can use a real dataset and split it into two rating sets as $\mathbf{R}_1$ and $\mathbf{R}_2$. Another advantage of using such strategy for evaluation is that we can then test different scenarios (i.e. different splitting condition) to evaluate the usefulness of our model under a variety of different assumptions. The user and item ids of $\mathbf{R}_2$ are randomly permuted, while the permutation (unknown to our model) becomes the ground truth of the correspondence.

We conduct experiments on a synthetic dataset and a real dataset, Yahoo! music dataset. The synthetic dataset is a noise-free low-rank matrix for verifying the soundness of different models. It is a rank-50 matrix, generated by the following MATLAB command

randn(20000,50)*diag(1.1.^[1:50])*randn(50,10000).

We sample 5% of it as $\mathbf{R}$ and linearly scale the minimum and maximum values to -1 and 1. Yahoo! music dataset has been used as the benchmark data in KDD Cup 2011 [1]. For both datasets, we take out a subset $\mathbf{R}$ and split it into $\mathbf{R}_1$ and $\mathbf{R}_2$. The statistics of $\mathbf{R}$ are listed in Table 1.

With the capability to control the mapping condition, now we are ready to test the effectiveness of our model under different assumptions. Below lists the conditions (see Figure 7 for details):

1. **Disjoint Split.** We assume a user will not rate the same item twice, so the same rating will not appear in both $\mathbf{R}_1$ and $\mathbf{R}_2$. Real world scenario is in ratings for durable goods. For example, assume $\mathbf{R}_1$ and $\mathbf{R}_2$ are two nearby retailers that sells laptops, and thus have similar customers and products. When a user buys a laptop in $\mathbf{R}_1$, he or she is unlikely to buy the same laptop again in the other store.
2. **Overlap Split.** We assume ratings given in $\mathbf{R}_1$ may or may not appear in $\mathbf{R}_2$. This is a very common situation. For example, given two supermarkets in the same area, a customer can buy identical or different products in both stores.
3. **Contained Split.** We assume $\mathbf{R}_2$ is more frequently visited and all rating information in $\mathbf{R}_1$ is also available in $\mathbf{R}_2$. This is an extreme case of overlap split when the overlap ratio is maximized, and it is presumably the easiest situation for linking users and items between $\mathbf{R}_1$ and $\mathbf{R}_2$.

For the three splits, we vary the overlap ratio for ratings, but we assume that every user and item in $\mathbf{R}_1$ can be found in $\mathbf{R}_2$ and vice versa. This assumption may not be true in some cases so we created two additional scenarios.

4. **Subset Split.** We assume the users and items in $\mathbf{R}_1$ are subsets of that in $\mathbf{R}_2$. This is a common situation when $\mathbf{R}_1$ and $\mathbf{R}_2$ are two stores selling same type of goods in the same area, where $\mathbf{R}_2$ is a much larger and potentially cheaper store that has more products for sale.
5. **Partial Split.** We assume the user/item set in $\mathbf{R}_1$ are partially overlapped with that in $\mathbf{R}_2$. This is also a very common situation that two stores have overlapping but not identical customers and products for sell. We want to first discover the mapping between the overlapped users/items, and then use such information to improve the rating prediction.

For subset split and partial split, we simply assume that their overlap ratio for ratings is similar to that of the overlap split.

Because $\mathbf{R}_1$ is the target domain in which we want to evaluate whether rating prediction accuracy can be boosted by knowledge transfer, we divide its data into training, validation and testing sets. $\mathbf{R}_2$, on the other hand, belongs to the source domain, thus we only need to divide it into training and validation set. Validation sets are used for parameter tuning in factorization models. Each of the two validation sets takes up 2.5% of the original data $\mathbf{R}$, while the testing set takes up 5%. Each of the validation and testing sets does not overlap with any other set so as to ensure the sanity of our experiment. The training sets of $\mathbf{R}_1$ and $\mathbf{R}_2$ are sampled from $\mathbf{R}$ according to the scenarios described above (Figure 7).

4.2 Competing Models

The first experiment is to evaluate the matching quality. To our knowledge, there has not yet been solutions proposed to utilize only incomplete rating information to perform user/item alignment, so we compare our method with other baseline models.

We define the following three baseline models. Here we only describe the user-matching procedure as the item-matching procedure is identical.

1. **Matching based on Regular Matrix Factorization.** We conduct the regular matrix factorization and then perform nearest neighbor matching based on Euclidean distances between the obtained latent factors.
2. **Matching based on User Mean/Item Mean.** Find nearest users for matching based on the mean of their ratings. In other words, users with similar rating averages are matched.
3. **Matching based on Rating Lists.** We first sort the ratings of each user from large to small into a list. For any two users, we align the two rating lists and use the Euclidean distance of these two vectors as the matching criteria. In other words, two users are paired if their sorted rating lists are similar.

As mentioned in the introduction section, latent factor matching from simple matrix factorization does not work. The solution of matrix factorization is not unique since

$$\mathbf{P}\mathbf{Q}^T = \mathbf{P}\mathbf{A}\mathbf{A}^{-1}\mathbf{Q}^T,$$

Figure 7: Illustration of Splits

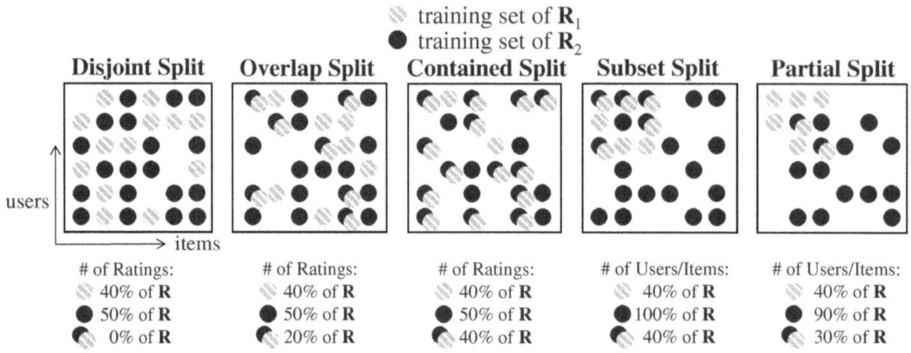

Even when $\mathbf{R}_1 = \mathbf{R}_2$, we can still obtain very different $\mathbf{P}_1$ and $\mathbf{P}_2$. In fact, experiment results show that the first two baselines perform no better than random guess, so we omit them from the result table to save space. We found the third baseline that works much better than the first two, and therefore its results are included in our table.

Second, we conduct an experiment to evaluate the quality boost of rating prediction in $\mathbf{R}_1$ after transferring information from $\mathbf{R}_2$. There has not yet been much work on information transfer without knowing the underlying correspondence. Hence, for rating prediction we use rating-matrix generative model (RMGM) as the state-of-the-art for comparison.

4.3 Implementation Details

For our factorization models, we use gradient descent and backtracking line search to solve the objective function. The dimension K is fixed to 50, and the parameters λ and β are automatically selected by observing the error rate of the validation set. After selection, λ is determined to be 0 for noise-free low-rank dataset and 5 for Yahoo! music dataset, and β ranges from 0 to 400. Besides, we employ the data scaling and early stopping procedure. We scale the ratings in the training set to zero mean and unit variance, and scale the values back in the prediction phase; the training process stops when validation error starts to increase.

We implement two versions of rating-matrix generative model (RMGM) [8] for comparison. They can be solved by standard expectation-maximization algorithm. [2] The original RMGM uses categorical distribution for $P(r|C_m, C_n)$. However, categorical distribution does not reflect the ordinal relation among the rating values. Therefore, we implement another version of RMGM that uses Gaussian distribution. For both models, the original and Gaussian RMGMs, we set the latent dimension K to 50 (we find that a larger K leads to similar performance), and we conduct the same early stopping procedure. For Gaussian RMGM, we find that the variance of Gaussian is better set to a constant parameter that can be tuned by observing the error rate of the validation set. We have also conducted the data scaling process for Gaussian RMGM.

4.4 Results of User and Item Matching

In the matching process, the matching can output either the most likely candidate or a ranked list of candidates for each user/item in $\mathbf{R}_1$. Therefore, we can use accuracy as well as mean average precision (MAP) as the evaluation criteria. However, in the partial split, some users and items in $\mathbf{R}_1$ do not appear in $\mathbf{R}_2$. Thus, when evaluating the matching result of such scenario, we remove these users and items from consideration.

[2]An example code is provided by the author of RMGM: https://sites.google.com/site/libin82cn/

Table 2: Matching Result on the Low-Rank Dataset

	Rating List	Latent Space	Refinement
Disjoint Split			
Accuracy(user)	0.000	1.000	1.000
MAP(user)	0.003	1.000	1.000
Accuracy(item)	0.001	1.000	1.000
MAP(item)	0.007	1.000	1.000
Overlap Split			
Accuracy(user)	0.025	1.000	1.000
MAP(user)	0.048	1.000	1.000
Accuracy(item)	0.051	1.000	1.000
MAP(item)	0.089	1.000	1.000
Contained Split			
Accuracy(user)	0.538	1.000	1.000
MAP(user)	0.612	1.000	1.000
Accuracy(item)	0.703	1.000	1.000
MAP(item)	0.765	1.000	1.000
Subset Split			
Accuracy(user)	0.013	1.000	1.000
MAP(user)	0.029	1.000	1.000
Accuracy(item)	0.029	1.000	1.000
MAP(item)	0.058	1.000	1.000
Partial Split			
Accuracy(user)	0.007	1.000	1.000
MAP(user)	0.019	1.000	1.000
Accuracy(item)	0.018	1.000	1.000
MAP(item)	0.042	1.000	1.000

The matching results are shown in Table 2 and Table 3. The results on the noise-free low-rank dataset demonstrate the soundness of our approach. When there is no noise in the rating matrix, our latent space matching can precisely match all users and items by comparing the singular vectors regardless of the splits. On the other hand, the performance of baseline model (rating list) improves when more ratings are shared between domains , but the results are still far from perfect.

On Yahoo! music dataset, we see a similar trend: when more ratings are shared, the results are generally better. We observe that the contained split is easier to match than overlap split, while both are easier to match than disjoint split. The matching accuracy for the subset split and partial split are slightly worse (though still comparable) than that of the overlap split. It is because although the

Table 3: Matching Result on Yahoo! Music

	Rating List	Latent Space	Refinement
Disjoint Split			
Accuracy(user)	0.074	0.310	0.633
MAP(user)	0.126	0.419	0.717
Accuracy(item)	0.019	0.204	0.325
MAP(item)	0.047	0.325	0.463
Overlap Split			
Accuracy(user)	0.150	0.547	0.960
MAP(user)	0.226	0.652	0.973
Accuracy(item)	0.056	0.442	0.786
MAP(item)	0.107	0.578	0.859
Contained Split			
Accuracy(user)	0.419	0.851	0.997
MAP(user)	0.526	0.905	0.998
Accuracy(item)	0.323	0.815	0.975
MAP(item)	0.423	0.886	0.986
Subset Split			
Accuracy(user)	0.122	0.392	0.918
MAP(user)	0.190	0.510	0.941
Accuracy(item)	0.047	0.297	0.686
MAP(item)	0.090	0.433	0.780
Partial Split			
Accuracy(user)	0.109	0.350	0.871
MAP(user)	0.175	0.470	0.906
Accuracy(item)	0.043	0.272	0.573
MAP(item)	0.081	0.402	0.684

ratio of shared ratings is similar among these splits, some users and items can never be aligned in the subset split and partial split.

For all cases, the latent space matching we proposed already enjoys a significant boost comparing to the best baseline model, while the matching refinement through optimization further leads to great improvement over latent space matching. It is reasonable because there are some drawbacks of latent space matching, which have been discussed in Section 3.1.4.

4.5 Results for Rating Prediction by Transferring

Table 4: Rating Prediction (RMSE) on Yahoo! Music

	RMGM	Gaussian RMGM	MF	Proposed Approach
Disjoint Split	27.47	26.59	24.24	**23.34** †
Overlap Split	27.54	26.48	24.23	**23.49** †
Contained Split	27.58	26.53	24.29	**23.92** †
Subset Split	27.65	26.56	24.13	**23.40** †
Partial Split	27.57	26.51	24.21	**23.77** †

Those significantly better then the second best results are marked with †

Next we want to evaluate whether our matching can indeed be used to improve the quality of a recommendation system in the target domain. We resort to the experiment on rating prediction and use root mean square error (RMSE) as the evaluation criterion. The hypothesis to be verified with this experiment is that despite the existence of user/item mis-matching, our model can still improve the prediction accuracy of the target domain after information transfer. Here we focus on the Yahoo! music dataset because in the noise-free low-rank dataset the RMSE before transferring is already close to 0.

The results are shown in Table 4. Gaussian RMGM outperforms the original RMGM, likely due to the fact that the actual rating itself does not follow categorical distribution. However, RMGM does not perform well in this experiment. One of the reason is that the likelihood function optimized by RMGM does not directly reflect the objective for evaluation (discussed in Section 2.3), while in our model minimizing the prediction error (i.e. RMSE in this experiment) is one of the direct objectives.

For all cases, our proposed approach leads to significant improvement over the original matrix factorization (MF) model, which is widely considered as one of the most effective single domain model. Interestingly, although the results in Table 3 show that the matching accuracy can be ranked as disjoint < overlap < contained split, results in Table 4 show that in terms of rating prediction, the improvement for the disjoint split is the best, while the improvement for the contained split is the worst. We believe this is because when there is less overlap of ratings, the amount of information $\mathbf{R}_2$ provides to $\mathbf{R}_1$ increases, and our solution is capable of leveraging the extra information to provide better prediction outcome.

4.6 When Users/Items Do Not Overlap

Figure 8: Illustration of Three New Splits

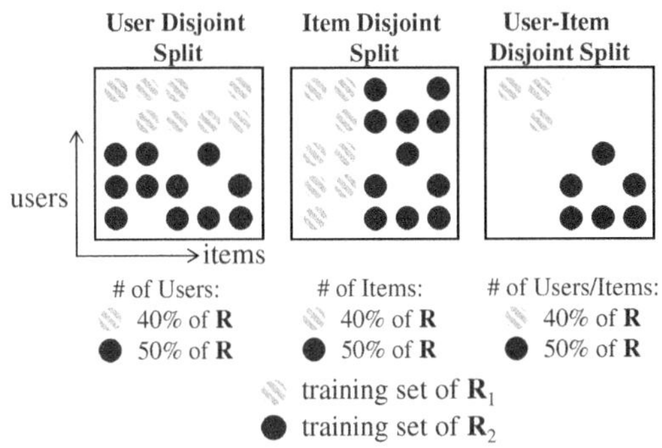

Finally, we want to test what happens when the original assumption of our model is violated: that is, what happens if the user sets or the item sets do not overlap at all. It implies the matching is always wrong and our matching algorithm can at best identify some "similar" users/items. Thus, we create three other splits and they are illustrated in Figure 8.

1. **User Disjoint Split.** The user sets of $\mathbf{R}_1$ and $\mathbf{R}_2$ are disjoint and the item sets are the same though the mapping is still unknown. It is also a common scenario in the real world. For example, there are two DVD-rental stores located in different states. Although they have similar items to be rented, the customer bases are completely disjoint.

2. **Item Disjoint Split.** The user sets are identical (without knowing the mapping), while the item sets are disjoint. For example, two near-by restaurants, one of which serves eastern food and the other serves western food, may share similar set of customers.

3. **User-Item Disjoint Split.** The user sets and item sets are both non-overlapped. It is conceivably the most challenging task of all.

The results are shown in Table 5 and Table 6. For the disjoint dimension, our algorithm can only identify the "similar" entities. (thus we do not report their matching accuracy.) Despite this, it is very promising to see that the rating prediction can still be improved, most likely due to the fact that on the other overlapped dimension the correspondence can be identified. If both sides are disjoint, our model cannot yield any boost, as β becomes 0 after parameter tuning and our model degenerates into regular matrix factorization model.

In short, when original assumption is violated, our model may still lead to some improvement and it is at least no worse than regular matrix factorization model. Such discovery delivers an encouraging and important message for practical usage because the aforementioned scenarios are all very common in the real world.

Table 5: Matching Result on Yahoo! Music

	Rating List	Latent Space	Refinement
User Disjoint Split			
Accuracy(item)	0.017	0.148	0.247
MAP(item)	0.044	0.257	0.370
Item Disjoint Split			
Accuracy(user)	0.070	0.159	0.579
MAP(user)	0.121	0.250	0.663

Table 6: Rating Prediction (RMSE) on Yahoo! Music

	MF	Proposed Approach
User Disjoint Split	23.24	**23.15** †
Item Disjoint Split	23.88	**23.35** †
User-Item Disjoint Split	24.21	24.21

Those significantly better then the second best results are marked with †

5. CONCLUSION

We present a novel yet intuitive two-step algorithm for a very challenging and seldom tackled task of identifying user/item correspondences between two homogeneous rating matrices. After the correspondences are identified, we introduce a transfer learning approach to boost the rating prediction accuracy in the target domain. Our two-stage matching algorithm not only aims at matching users/items in the latent space, but also refines the matching based on the objective to predict the observed values in the target domain. The refinement not only boosts the quality of matching but also facilitates further transferring process to enhance rating prediction. We test our model on 8 different scenarios, each corresponds to a real-world scenario of transferring. The results are very promising as our model can identify the matching between user/item sets from different domains to some extent. More importantly, except one extremely difficult scenario where the users/items are both completely disjoint, our model significantly boosts the rating prediction performance.

6. ACKNOWLEDGEMENTS

This work was sponsored by AOARD grant number No. FA2386-13-1-4045, Ministry of Science and Technology, National Taiwan University and Intel Corporation under grants NSC102-2911-I-002-001 and NTU103R7501, and grant 102-2923-E-002-007-MY2, 102-2221-E-002-170, 101-2628-E-002-028-MY2.

References

[1] G. Dror, N. Koenigstein, Y. Koren, and M. Weimer. The yahoo! music dataset and kdd-cup'11. *Journal of Machine Learning Research-Proceedings Track*, 2012.

[2] M. Gamon. Linguistic correlates of style: authorship classification with deep linguistic analysis features. In *Proc. COLING*, 2004.

[3] L. Hu, J. Cao, G. Xu, L. Cao, Z. Gu, and C. Zhu. Personalized recommendation via cross-domain triadic factorization. In *Proc. WWW*, 2013.

[4] M. Jamali and L. Lakshmanan. Heteromf: recommendation in heterogeneous information networks using context dependent factor models. In *Proc. WWW*, 2013.

[5] Y. Koren and R. Bell. Advances in collaborative filtering. In *Recommender Systems Handbook*, pages 145–186. Springer, 2011.

[6] Y. Koren, R. Bell, and C. Volinsky. Matrix factorization techniques for recommender systems. *Computer*, 2009.

[7] B. Li, Q. Yang, and X. Xue. Can movies and books collaborate? cross-domain collaborative filtering for sparsity reduction. In *Proc. IJCAI*, 2009.

[8] B. Li, Q. Yang, and X. Xue. Transfer learning for collaborative filtering via a rating-matrix generative model. In *Proc. ICML*, 2009.

[9] J. Liu, F. Zhang, X. Song, Y.-I. Song, C.-Y. Lin, and H.-W. Hon. What's in a name?: an unsupervised approach to link users across communities. In *Proc. WSDM*, 2013.

[10] P. Lops, M. de Gemmis, and G. Semeraro. Content-based recommender systems: State of the art and trends. In *Recommender Systems Handbook*, pages 73–105. Springer, 2011.

[11] H. Ma, H. Yang, M. R. Lyu, and I. King. Sorec: social recommendation using probabilistic matrix factorization. In *Proc. CIKM*, 2008.

[12] A. Mnih and R. Salakhutdinov. Probabilistic matrix factorization. In *Proc. NIPS*, 2008.

[13] A. Narayanan and V. Shmatikov. Robust de-anonymization of large sparse datasets. In *Security and Privacy, IEEE Symposium on*, 2008.

[14] A. Narayanan and V. Shmatikov. De-anonymizing social networks. In *Security and Privacy, IEEE Symposium on*, 2009.

[15] W. Pan, E. W. Xiang, N. N. Liu, and Q. Yang. Transfer learning in collaborative filtering for sparsity reduction. In *Proc. AAAI*, 2010.

[16] W. Pan and Q. Yang. Transfer learning in heterogeneous collaborative filtering domains. *Artificial Intelligence*, 2013.

[17] A. P. Singh and G. J. Gordon. Relational learning via collective matrix factorization. In *Proc. SIGKDD*, 2008.

[18] L. Xiong, X. Chen, T.-K. Huang, J. G. Schneider, and J. G. Carbonell. Temporal collaborative filtering with bayesian probabilistic tensor factorization. In *SDM*, 2010.

[19] N. J. Yuan, F. Zhang, D. Lian, K. Zheng, S. Yu, and X. Xie. We know how you live: exploring the spectrum of urban lifestyles. In *Proc. COSN*, 2013.

[20] R. Zafarani and H. Liu. Connecting users across social media sites: a behavioral-modeling approach. In *Proc. KDD*, 2013.

[21] Y. Zhang, B. Cao, and D.-Y. Yeung. Multi-domain collaborative filtering. In *Proc. UAI*, 2010.

Optimal Recommendations under Attraction, Aversion, and Social Influence

Wei Lu[†] Stratis Ioannidis[‡] Smriti Bhagat[‡] Laks V.S. Lakshmanan[†]

[†]University of British Columbia
Vancouver, B.C., Canada
{welu,laks}@cs.ubc.ca

[‡]Technicolor Los Altos Research Center
Los Altos, CA, USA
{stratis.ioannidis,smriti.bhagat}@technicolor.com

ABSTRACT

People's interests are dynamically evolving, often affected by external factors such as trends promoted by the media or adopted by their friends. In this work, we model interest evolution through dynamic interest cascades: we consider a scenario where a user's interests may be affected by (a) the interests of other users in her social circle, as well as (b) suggestions she receives from a recommender system. In the latter case, we model user reactions through either attraction or aversion towards past suggestions. We study this interest evolution process, and the utility accrued by recommendations, as a function of the system's recommendation strategy. We show that, in steady state, the optimal strategy can be computed as the solution of a semi-definite program (SDP). Using datasets of user ratings, we provide evidence for the existence of aversion and attraction in real-life data, and show that our optimal strategy can lead to significantly improved recommendations over systems that ignore aversion and attraction.

Categories and Subject Descriptors

H.2.8 [**Database Applications**]: Data Mining

Keywords

Recommender Systems; Interest Evolution; Attraction; Aversion

1. INTRODUCTION

Users' content consumption patterns evolve over time. For example, a user may be attracted towards content that is popular, content recommended to her by a service, or content being enjoyed by her friends. Alternatively, users may get tired of certain types of content, e.g., romantic comedy movies, and desire to consume something different and new. A key challenge for recommender systems is accurately modeling such user preferences as they evolve over time. Although traditional matrix factorization approaches can be extended to incorporate temporal dynamics of user behavior [19,20], such extensions do not identify or explicitly analyze the *factors* that influence the drift in interests.

KDD'14, August 24–27, 2014, New York, NY, USA.

http://dx.doi.org/10.1145/2623330.2623744.

A "classic" factor influencing user interests is *attraction*: users may be attracted to content they are exposed to repeatedly and often (such as, e.g., a song played often on the radio). This phenomenon, known in psychology as the "*mere-exposure effect*" [33], is natural and intuitive, and is the main premise behind advertising [10, 15]. Nonetheless, repetition and/or overexposure can also have the opposite effect, leading to *aversion*: recent research argues that users often desire serendipitous, novel, previously unseen content [1,3,23,27]. This notion is also quite natural and intuitive, but is usually not taken into account by recommender systems, yielding over-specialized, predictable recommendations [3,23].

A third factor affecting a user's interests is *social influence*: users may feel attracted to content consumed and liked by their friends. Trend adoption through "word-of-mouth" or "viral" marketing is also a well documented phenomenon [7,9], and has been extensively studied since the seminal paper by Kempe et al. [17]. Nonetheless, to the best of our knowledge, the effect of social influence on interests, and its implications for recommender systems, has received attention only recently [16,27].

Incorporating these influence factors in a recommender system raises several challenges. To begin with, under attraction and aversion, a recommender can no longer be treated as a passive entity: recommendations it makes may alter user interests, pushing them either towards or away from certain topics. Hence, traditional methods that merely profile a user and then cater to this specific profile may fall short of keeping up with these dynamics. Second, social influence implies that recommendation decisions to different users cannot be made in isolation anymore: as recommendations alter a user's interests through attraction and aversion, social influence can spread these changes, resulting in an *interest cascade*. Therefore, optimal recommendation decisions across users need to be computed *globally*, taking into account the joint effect they have over the user's social network.

In this work, we make the following contributions:

- We formulate a global recommendation problem in the pretense of attraction, aversion, and social influence. In particular, we propose a mathematical model that incorporates these phenomena, and study the steady state behavior of user interests as a function of the recommender's strategy in selecting which items to show to users. Under this model, we seek the optimal recommendation strategy, i.e., one that maximizes the users' social welfare in steady state (Section 3).
- We show that, for a large recommender item catalog, obtaining the optimal recommendation strategy amounts to solving a quadratically-constrained quadratic optimization problem (QCQP). Though this problem may not be convex, we present a semi-definite program (SDP) relaxation that can be solved in polynomial time. In many cases, this solution is also

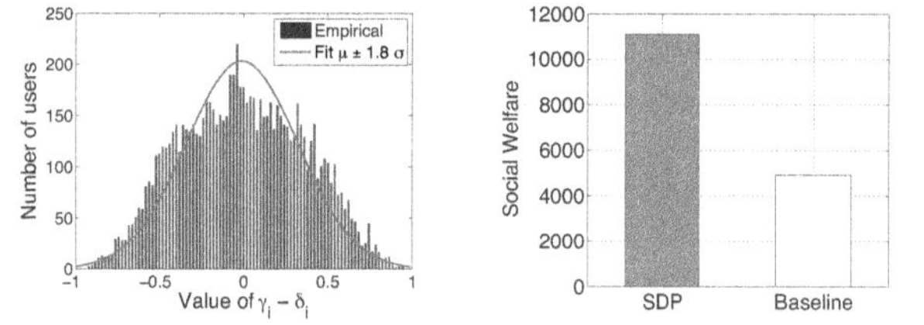

(a) Attraction-Aversion (b) Gains from SDP solution

Figure 1: Illustration of aversion and attraction in MovieLens, and gains from accounting for them in optimization.

guaranteed to be an optimal solution; when the solution is not optimal, we show how a solution with a provable approximation guarantee can be constructed through randomization. We discuss how to determine whether the solution is optimal, and identify special cases for which an optimal solution is always reached, and randomization is unnecessary (Section 4).

- We provide evidence for the existence of attraction and aversion in three real-life rating datasets. We do so by developing and applying a method for learning the weight (i.e., importance) of these factors from rating data (Section 5). Applied to three real life datasets, our method indicates that between 14.0% to 19.6% of users show strong aversive or attractive behavior (Section 6).
- We conduct extensive experiments on real world datasets, and show that our recommendation algorithm is 17.5% to 125% better than a baseline algorithm in terms of social welfare achieved (Section 6).

Our analysis indicates that (a) the above phenomena are present in real-life datasets and (b) accounting for them can lead to significant gains in the improvement of recommendations. Figure 1 provides a quick illustration of these two facts (see Section 6 for a detailed account on the derivation these two figures). Figure 1(a) presents the distribution of a score measuring aversion and attraction among different users in MovieLens (with -1 indicating users with the strongest aversive behavior, and $+1$ indicating users with the strongest attractive behavior). About 7.0% of users are strongly aversive (score ≤ -0.5) while 9.0% are strongly attractive (score ≥ 0.5). Accounting for such users can lead to a significant impact on recommendations: as shown in Figure 1(b), the user social welfare more than doubles when incorporating this knowledge in recommendation decisions. Though there are clearly many factors of user behavior that are not accounted for in our analysis, we believe that these two facts, along with the SDP relaxation yielding optimal recommendations, indicate that investigating and accommodating for such phenomena is both important and tractable.

2. RELATED WORK

There has been a significant interest in modeling the temporal dynamics of user interests for various settings close to ours [19, 26, 27, 30]. Early work on matrix factorization (MF) by Koren [19] incorporates time-variant user profiles, an approach that we also adopt. We depart from this line of work by modeling, and also including in the MF process (see Section 5), factors that impact these drifts, including attraction, aversion, and social influence.

Several studies have highlighted the need for serendipity and diversity in the context of recommender systems, both of which relate to the notion of aversion we describe here. The need for serendipity was first identified by McNee et al. [23]. To address this, Yu et al. [32] and Abbassi et al. [1] propose algorithms for recommending items that maximize a score that combines both relevance to a user as well as diversity. Ge et al. [12] focus on evaluating the lack of serendipity and diversity, and how it hurts the quality of recommendations. We depart from these works by modeling how recommendations themselves may instigate aversion or attraction among users, through a dynamic evolution of user interests.

Our approach to aversion is closer to Das Sarma et al. [27], who consider users that iteratively consume items in one out of several categories. They incorporate "boredom" and social influence in a manner similar to us: inherent item values decrease as a function of a weighted frequency of past consumption, and a user's utility is averaged among her friend's utilities. The authors provide bounds of the steady state performance of different consumption strategies under such dynamics. We depart by modelling user interests as multi-dimensional vectors, and using a factor-based model for user utilities, whose dynamics and steady state behavior cannot be captured by the (one-dimensional) model in [27].

The literature on social influence is vast, motivated by the viral marketing applications introduced by Domingos and Richardson [9] and further studied by Kempe et al. [17]. Our influence model is closer to *gossiping* [28], in that the interest/state of each user results from averaging the interests of her neighbors. Though we depart from classic gossiping protocols in that we incorporate additional dynamics (through attraction and aversion), similar techniques as in [28] could potentially be used to study our system in scenarios where interest evolution is asynchronous across users. In the context of matrix factorization, Jamali et al. [16] propose incorporating the distance of a user's profile to the average profile of users in their social circle as a regularization factor in MF. This is consistent with the social influence behavior we outline in Section 3.3. We depart from this work by modeling dynamic profiles, and studying the additional effect of recommendations on user profiles through attraction and aversion.

Semi-definite programming (SDP) relaxation for quadratically-constrained quadratic programs (QCQP) lies at the core of our algorithmic contribution. Building on the seminal work by Goemans and Williamson [13], several papers have demonstrated classes of QCQPs for which an SDP relaxation gives a constant approximation guarantee [24, 25, 31]. Moreover, exact solutions of rank 1 are known to be attainable for several classes of QCQP, including when the problem has one [6] or two quadratic constraints [5]. Of special interest is the case where the quadratic objective involves non-negative off-diagonal elements, and constraints involve only quadratic terms of one variable [34], as the attraction-dominant case of our problem falls into this class (see Section 4.3). We refer the interested reader to [29] for SDP in general, and to [22, 25] for applications to quadratic programming.

3. PROBLEM FORMULATION

In what follows, we present our mathematical model of users interacting with a recommender system. We use bold script (e.g., $\mathbf{x}, \mathbf{y}, \mathbf{u}, \mathbf{v}$) to denote vectors, and capital script (e.g., A, B, H) to denote matrices. For either matrices or vectors, we use $\geq$ to indicate element-wise inequalities. For symmetric matrices, we use $\succeq$ to indicate dominance in the positive semidefinite sense; in particular, $A \succeq 0$ implies that A is positive semidefinite. For square matrices A, we denote by $\mathrm{tr}(A), \mathrm{diag}(A), \mathrm{rank}(A)$ the trace, diagonal and rank of A, respectively. Finally, given an $n \times m$ matrix A, we denote by $\mathrm{col} : \mathbb{R}^{n \times m} \to \mathbb{R}^{nm}$ the column-major order representation of A: i.e., $\mathrm{col}(A)$ maps the elements of A to a vector, by stacking the m columns of A on top of each other.

3.1 Overview

Our model assumes that user interests are dynamic: they are affected both by recommendations users receive, as well as by how other users' interests evolve. In particular, our model of user behavior takes into account the following factors:

1. *Inherent interests.* Our model accounts for an inherent predisposition users may have, e.g., towards particular topics or genres. This is static and does not change through time.

2. *Attraction.* As per the mere-exposure effect, users may exhibit attractive behavior: if a type of content is shown very often by the recommendation service, this might reinforce the desire of a user to consume it.

3. *Aversion.* Users may also exhibit aversive behavior: a user can grow tired of a topic that she sees very often, and may want to see something new or rare.

4. *Social influence.* A user's behavior can be affected by what people in her social circle (e.g., her friends or family) are interested in.

Under the joint effect of the factors above, suggestions made by the recommender instigate an *interest cascade* over the users. Suggestions alter user interests through attraction or aversion; in turn, these changes affect neighboring users as well, on account of their social behavior. These effects propagate dynamically over the users' social network. Next, we formally describe how each of these factors is incorporated in our model.

3.2 Recommender System and User Utilities

We consider n users receiving recommendations from an entity we call the recommender. We denote by $[n] \equiv \{1, 2, \ldots, n\}$ the set of all users. At each time step $t \in \mathbb{N}$, the recommender suggests an item to each user in $[n]$, selected from a catalog C of available items. The user accrues a utility from the item recommended. As discussed below, the recommender's goal is to suggest items that maximize the aggregate user utility, i.e., the social welfare.

Following the standard convention in recommender systems, we assume factor-based user utilities. At each $t \in \mathbb{N}$, each user $i \in [n]$ has an *interest profile* represented by a d-dimensional vector $\mathbf{u}_i(t) \in \mathbb{R}^d$. Moreover, the item recommended to user i at time t is represented by a d-dimensional *feature profile* $\mathbf{v}_i(t) \in \mathbb{R}^d$. Then, the expected rating[1] a user i would give to the item suggested to her at time t is given by $F(\mathbf{u}_i(t), \mathbf{v}_i(t))$, where

$$F(\mathbf{u}, \mathbf{v}) = \langle \mathbf{u}, \mathbf{v} \rangle = \textstyle\sum_{k=1}^{d} \mathbf{u}_k \mathbf{v}_k, \qquad (1)$$

i.e., the inner product between the interest and feature profiles [18,20]. Intuitively, each coordinate of a feature profile can be perceived as an item-specific feature such as, e.g., a movie's genre or an article's topic. The corresponding coordinate in an interest profile captures the propensity of the user to react positively or negatively to this feature.

We call $F(\mathbf{u}_i(t), \mathbf{v}_i(t))$ the *utility* of user i from the suggested item at time t. Without loss of generality[2], we assume that the item profiles $\mathbf{v}_i \in \mathbb{R}^d$ are normalized, i.e.: $\|\mathbf{v}_i(t)\|_2 = 1$ for all $i \in [n]$, $t \in \mathbb{N}$. Under this assumption, given that a user's profile is $\mathbf{u}$, the best item to recommend to user i is the one that yields the highest expected rating; indeed, this is

$$\underset{\mathbf{v}\in\mathbb{R}^d : \|\mathbf{v}\|_2 = 1}{\arg\max} \quad F(\mathbf{u}, \mathbf{v}) = \mathbf{u}/\|\mathbf{u}\|_2,$$

i.e., the item that maximizes the utility of a user i. Note that identifying items that maximize the *aggregate* utility across users (i.e., the sum of expected ratings to suggested items), is a natural goal for the recommender.

[1] In practice, (1) best approximates *centered* ratings, i.e., ratings offset by a global average across users.

[2] Note that $F(\mathbf{u}, \mathbf{v}) = F(s\mathbf{u}, \frac{1}{s}\mathbf{v})$, for any scalar $s \in \mathbb{R}$, so we can assume that either user or feature profiles have a bounded norm.

3.3 Interest Evolution

The evolution of user interests captures the four factors outlined in Section 3.1. At each time step $t \in \mathbb{N}$, the interest profile of a user $i \in [n]$ is chosen alternately between either a *personalized* or a *social* behavior. If personalized, the behavior of a user is again selected among three possible outcomes, each corresponding to inherent interests, attraction, and aversion, respectively.

The selection of which of these four behaviors takes place at a given time step is random, and occurs independently of selections at other users as well as selections at previous time slots. We denote with $\beta \in [0, 1]$ the probability that the user selects a social behavior at time slot t. The probability of selecting a personalized behavior is thus $1-\beta$. Interests at these two distinct events are as follows:

Personalized Behavior. If a user's interest is selected through a personalized behavior, the user selects her profile through one of the three personalized factors outlined in Section 3.1. In particular, for every $i \in [n]$, there exist probabilities $\alpha_i, \gamma_i, \delta_i \in [0, 1]$ such that $\alpha_i + \gamma_i + \delta_i = 1$, and:

- **Inherent interests.** With probability α_i, user i follows her *inherent interests*. That is, $\mathbf{u}_i(t)$ is sampled from a probability distribution μ_i^0 over $\mathbb{R}^d$. This distribution does not vary with t and captures the user's inherent predisposition.

- **Attraction.** With probability γ_i, user i selects a profile that is *attracted* to the items suggested to her in the past. To capture this notion denote by $\mathcal{V}_i(t) = \{\mathbf{v}_i(\tau)\}_{\tau \le t}$ the *history* of (profiles of) items suggested to a user i. Then, the interest of a user under attraction is given by $g(\mathcal{V}_i(t-1))$, a weighted average of the items suggested to it in the past. That is:

$$\mathbf{u}_i(t) = g(\mathcal{V}_i(t-1)) = \frac{\sum_{\tau=0}^{t-1} w_{t-\tau}\mathbf{v}(\tau)}{\sum_{\tau=0}^{t-1} w_{t-\tau}}. \qquad (2)$$

- **Aversion.** With probability δ_i, user i selects a profile that is *repulsed* by the items suggested to her in the past; that is, her interest profile is given by

$$\mathbf{u}_i(t) = -g(\mathcal{V}_i(t-1)) = -\frac{\sum_{\tau=0}^{t-1} w_{t-\tau}\mathbf{v}(\tau)}{\sum_{\tau=0}^{t-1} w_{t-\tau}}. \qquad (3)$$

To gain some intuition on (2) and (3), recall that a user's utility at time t is given by (1). Therefore, a profile generated under (2) implies that the suggestion that *maximizes* her utility at time t would be one that aligns perfectly (i.e., points in the same direction as) the weighted average g up to time $t-1$. In contrast, under the aversive behavior (3), the same suggestion *minimizes* the user's utility.

Note that the weighted average g is fully determined by the sequence weights $\{w_\tau\}_{\tau\in\mathbb{N}}$. By selecting decaying weights, a higher importance can be placed on more recent suggestions.

Social Behavior. User i's profile is selected through social behavior with probability β. Conditioned on this event:

- **Social Influence.** A user aligns her interests with a user j selected from her social circle with probability P_{ij}. That is:

$$\mathbf{u}_i(t) = \mathbf{u}_j(t-1), \quad \text{with probability } P_{ij}, \tag{4}$$

where $\sum_j P_{ij} = 1$.

The probability $P_{ij} \in [0,1]$ captures the influence that user j has on user i. Note that users j for which $P_{ij} = 0$ (i.e., outside i's social circle) have no influence on i. Moreover, the set of pairs (i,j) s.t. $P_{ij} \neq 0$, defines the social network among users. We denote by $P \in [0,1]^{n\times n}$ the stochastic matrix with elements P_{ij}, $i,j \in [n]$; we assume that P is ergodic (i.e., irreducible and aperiodic) [11].

Under these dynamics, interests evolve in the form of a dynamic cascade: suggestions made by the recommender act as a forcing function, altering interests either through attraction or aversion. Such changes propagate across users through the social network.

3.4 Recommended Item Distribution

In practice, the recommender has access to a finite "catalog" of items. Recalling that feature profiles have norm 1, the recommender's catalog can be represented as a set $C \subseteq \mathbb{B}$, where $\mathbb{B} = \{\mathbf{v} \in \mathbb{R}^d : \|\mathbf{v}\|_2 = 1\}$ is the set of items of norm 1 (i.e., the d-dimensional unit ball).

We assume that the recommender selects the items $\mathbf{v}_j(t) \in \mathbb{B}$ suggested to user $i \in [n]$ by sampling them from a discrete distribution ν_i over $\mathbb{B}$, whose support is C. Note that the expected feature profile of a suggested item is a weighted average among the vectors in C. As such, it belongs to the *convex hull* of catalog C; formally:

$$\bar{\mathbf{v}}_i = \int_{\mathbf{v}\in\mathbb{B}} \mathbf{v} d\nu_i \in \text{conv}(C), \tag{5}$$

Note that conv(C) is a convex polytope included in $\mathbb{B}$.

As we will see later in our analysis (c.f. Theorem 1), the steady state user utilities depend only on the expectations $\bar{\mathbf{v}}_i$, $i \in [n]$, rather than the entire distributions ν_i. We will thus refer to $\{\bar{\mathbf{v}}_i\}_{i\in[n]}$ as the *recommender strategy*; it is worth keeping in mind that, given a $\bar{\mathbf{v}}_i \in \text{conv}(C)$, finding a ν_i such that (5) holds can be computed in polynomial time in $|C|$ (see also Section 4.4).

We further assume that the catalog C is large; in particular, for large catalog size $|C|$, we have:

$$\text{conv}(C) \simeq \mathbb{B}. \tag{6}$$

This would be true if, for example, each item in the catalog are generated in an i.i.d. fashion from a distribution that covers the entire ball $\mathbb{B}$; this distribution need not be uniform[3]. We revisit the issue of how to pick a distribution ν_i given $\bar{\mathbf{v}}_i$, as well as how to interpret our results in the case of a finite catalog, in Section 4.4.

3.5 Recommendation Objective

Observe that, under the above dynamics, the evolution of the system is a Markov chain, whose state comprises the interest and feature profiles. We define the objective of the recommender as maximizing the social welfare, i.e., the sum of expected user utilities, in *steady state*. Formally, we wish to determine a strategy $\{\bar{\mathbf{v}}_i\}_{i\in[n]}$ (and, hence, distributions ν_i) that maximizes:

$$\lim_{T\to\infty} \frac{1}{T}\sum_{t=0}^{T}\sum_{i\in[n]} \langle \mathbf{u}_i(t), \mathbf{v}_i(t)\rangle = \lim_{t\to\infty} \sum_{i\in[n]} \mathbb{E}[\langle \mathbf{u}_i(t), \mathbf{v}_i(t)\rangle],$$

[3]Formally, $\lim_{|C|\to\infty} \text{conv}(C) = \mathbb{B}$ w.p. 1 if, e.g., items in catalog C are sampled independently from a probability distribution absolutely continuous to the uniform distribution on $\mathbb{B}$.

where the equality above holds w.p. 1 by the renewal theorem [11]. It is important to note that, under the interest dynamics described in 3.3, optimal recommendations to a user i cannot be obtained independently of recommendations to other users: user i's profile depends on recommendations made not only directly to this user, but also to any user reachable through i's social network.

4. OPTIMAL RECOMMENDATIONS

In this section, we discuss how the recommender selects which items to present to users to maximize the system's social welfare. We begin by obtaining a closed-form formula for the social welfare in steady state, and then discuss algorithms for its optimization.

4.1 Steady State Social Welfare

Recall that μ_i^0 is the inherent profile distribution of user $i \in [n]$, and let μ_i be the steady state distribution of the profile of user i. We denote by $\bar{\mathbf{u}}_i = \int_{\mathbf{u}\in\mathbb{R}^d} \mathbf{u} d\mu_i$ and $\bar{\mathbf{u}}_i^0 = \int_{\mathbf{u}\in\mathbb{R}^d} \mathbf{u} d\mu_i^0$ the expected profile of $i \in [n]$ under the steady state and inherent profile distributions, respectively. Moreover, denote by $\bar{U}, \bar{U}^0, \bar{V} \in \mathbb{R}^{n\times d}$ the matrices of dimensions $n \times d$ whose rows comprise the expected profiles $\bar{\mathbf{u}}_i$, $\bar{\mathbf{u}}_i^0$, $\bar{\mathbf{v}}_i$, $i \in [n]$, respectively. Let also A, Γ, $\Delta \in \mathbb{R}^{n\times n}$ be the $n \times n$ diagonal matrices whose diagonal elements are the coefficients $(1-\beta)\alpha_i$, $(1-\beta)\gamma_i$, and $(1-\beta)\delta_i$, respectively.

Then, the steady state social welfare can be expressed in closed form according to the following theorem.

THEOREM 1. *The expected social welfare in steady state is:*

$$G(\bar{V}) \equiv \text{tr}\left[(I-\beta P)^{-1}\left(\text{A}\bar{U}^0\bar{V}^\mathsf{T} + (\Gamma-\Delta)\bar{V}\bar{V}^\mathsf{T}\right)\right], \tag{7}$$

where tr$(\cdot)$ *denotes the matrix trace.*

PROOF. Observe that at any time step $t \in [n]$ the profiles $\mathbf{u}_i(t)$ and $\mathbf{v}_i(t)$ are independent random variables. Hence,

$$\lim_{t\to\infty}\sum_{i\in[n]} \mathbb{E}[\langle \mathbf{u}_i(t), \mathbf{v}_i(t)\rangle] = \lim_{t\to\infty}\sum_{i\in[n]} \langle \mathbb{E}[\mathbf{u}_i(t)], \mathbb{E}[\mathbf{v}_i(t)]\rangle$$
$$= \sum_{i\in[n]} \langle \bar{\mathbf{u}}_i, \bar{\mathbf{v}}_i\rangle = \text{tr}(\bar{U}\bar{V}^\mathsf{T}). \tag{8}$$

Observe that by the linearity of expectation $\mathbb{E}[g(\mathcal{V}_i(t))] = \bar{\mathbf{v}}_i$ for all $t \in \mathbb{N}$ and $i \in [n]$. Thus, for $U(t) = [\mathbf{u}_i(t)]_{i\in[n]} \in \mathbb{R}^{n\times d}$ the matrix of user profiles at time t, we get that

$$\mathbb{E}[U(t)] = A\bar{U}^0 + \beta P\mathbb{E}[U(t-1)] + \Gamma\bar{V} - \Delta\bar{V}.$$

As βP is sub-stochastic and ergodic, the Perron-Frobenius theorem [11] implies that $\bar{U} = \lim_{t\to\infty}\mathbb{E}[U(t)]$ exists and

$$\bar{U} = A\bar{U}^0 + \beta P\bar{U} + (\Gamma-\Delta)\bar{V}.$$

Solving this linear system, and substituting the solution for $\bar{U}$ in (8), yields the theorem. □

An important consequence of Theorem 1 is that the steady state social welfare depends only on the expected profiles $\bar{V}$, rather than the entire distributions ν_i, $i \in [n]$. Hence, determining the optimal recommender strategy amounts to solving the following quadratically-constrained quadratic optimization problem (QCQP):

GLOBAL RECOMMENDATION

$$\begin{aligned} \text{Max.:} \quad & \text{tr}\left[(I-\beta P)^{-1}\left(\text{A}\bar{U}^0\bar{V}^\mathsf{T} + (\Gamma-\Delta)\bar{V}\bar{V}^\mathsf{T}\right)\right] \\ \text{subj. to:} \quad & \|\bar{\mathbf{v}}_i\|_2^2 \leq 1, \text{ for all } i \in [n]. \end{aligned} \tag{9}$$

where the norm constraint comes from (6). Note that this is indeed a global optimization: to solve it, recommendations across different users need to be taken into account jointly. This manifests in (9) through the quadratic term in the social welfare objective.

4.2 SDP Relaxation

The QCQP (9) is not necessarily convex. It is thus not a priori clear whether it can be solved in polynomial time. However, there is a way to reduce to a semi-definite program (SDP) relaxation, which can be solved in polynomial time. Interestingly, in many cases, the solution obtained for the SDP relaxation turns out to be an optimal solution to our original problem (9), and there is a simple and efficient test that can verify whether the obtained solution is optimal. Finally, when the solution is not optimal, it can be transformed to yield a constant-factor approximation. We are thus able to obtain a strong and elegant theoretical result for solving the GLOBALRECOMMENDATION problem.

It is important to note that the large-catalog assumption (6) is crucial to tractability: replacing the quadratic constraints with the linear constraints (5) does not lead to a problem that is amenable to an SDP relaxation. In fact, generic quadratic problems with linear constraints are known to be inapproximable, unless P = NP [25].

Deriving an SDP Relaxation. We begin by describing first how to express (9) as "almost" an SDP, except for a rank constraint:

THEOREM 2. *There exists a symmetric matrix* $H \in \mathbb{R}^{(nd+1)\times(nd+1)}$ *and a convex polyhedral set* $\mathcal{D} \in \mathbb{R}^{nd+1}$ *such that* GLOBAL RECOMMENDATION (9) *is equivalent to:*

$$\begin{aligned} \text{Max.:} \quad & \mathrm{tr}(HY) \\ \text{subj. to:} \quad & Y \succeq 0,\ \mathrm{diag}(Y) \in \mathcal{D},\ \mathrm{rank}(Y) = 1, \end{aligned} \tag{10}$$

where $Y \in \mathbb{R}^{(nd+1)\times(nd+1)}$.

PROOF. Let $\mathbf{x} = \mathrm{col}(\bar{V}) \in \mathbb{R}^{nd}$ be the column-major order vector representation of the recommender's strategy, and $\mathbf{b} = \mathrm{col}((I-\beta P)^{-1}\mathrm{A}\bar{U}^0) \in \mathbb{R}^{nd}$ the vector representation of the linear term in (7). Moreover, for $Q = (I-\beta P)^{-1}(\Gamma - \Delta) \in \mathbb{R}^{n\times n}$, consider the following block-diagonal symmetric matrix, where $\frac{Q+Q^\top}{2}$ is repeated d times:

$$H_0 = \begin{bmatrix} \frac{Q+Q^\top}{2} & \mathbf{0} & \cdots & \mathbf{0} \\ \mathbf{0} & \frac{Q+Q^\top}{2} & \cdots & \mathbf{0} \\ \cdots & \cdots & \cdots & \cdots \\ \mathbf{0} & \mathbf{0} & \cdots & \frac{Q+Q^\top}{2} \end{bmatrix} \in \mathbb{R}^{nd\times nd}.$$

Under this notation, (9) can be written as

$$\begin{aligned} \text{Max.} \quad & \mathbf{b}^\top\mathbf{x} + \mathbf{x}^\top H_0 \mathbf{x} \\ \text{subj. to} \quad & \mathbf{x}^2 \in \mathcal{D}_0, \end{aligned} \tag{11}$$

where $\mathbf{x}^2 = [\mathbf{x}_k^2]_{k\in[nd]} \in \mathbb{R}_+^{nd}$ results from squaring the elements of $\mathbf{x}$, and $\mathcal{D}_0$ the set implied by the norm constraints:

$$\mathcal{D}_0 = \{\mathbf{x}' \in \mathbb{R}^{nd} \mid \forall i \in [n], \textstyle\sum_{j=1}^{nd} \mathbb{1}_{j \bmod n = i \bmod n}\, \mathbf{x}'_j \le 1\}.$$

Note that $\mathcal{D}_0$ is a convex polyhedral set defined by linear equality constraints. Moreover, (11) can be homogenized to a quadratic program without linear terms using the following standard trick (see also [22, 25, 29]). Introducing an auxiliary variable t, the objective can be replaced by $t\mathbf{b}^\top\mathbf{x} + \mathbf{x}^\top H_0\mathbf{x}$, where t satisfies the constraint $t^2 \le 1$. Setting $\mathbf{y} = (\mathbf{x}, t) \in \mathbb{R}^{nd+1}$, this yields:

$$\begin{aligned} \text{Max.:} \quad & \mathbf{y}^\top H\mathbf{y} \\ \text{subj. to:} \quad & \mathbf{y}^2 \in \mathcal{D}, \end{aligned} \tag{12}$$

Algorithm 1: GLOBAL RECOMMENDATION ALGORITHM

Solve SDP RELAXATION (13); let Y be its solution;
if rank$(Y) = 1$ **then**
  Let $\lambda > 0$ be the unique positive eigenvalue of Y, and $\mathbf{e}$ the corresponding eigenvector;
  $(\mathbf{x}, t) \leftarrow \sqrt{\lambda}\cdot\mathbf{e}$;
else
  Construct a factorization $Y = Z^\top Z$, $Z \in \mathbb{R}^{(nd+1)\times(nd+1)}$;
  Sample a random $u \in \mathbb{R}^{nd+1}$ from $\mathcal{N}(0, I_{nd+1})$;
  $\sigma \leftarrow \mathrm{sgn}(Z^\top u)$;
  $D \leftarrow$ a diagonal matrix containing $\sqrt{\mathrm{diag}\, Y}$;
  $(\mathbf{x}, t) \leftarrow D\sigma$;
end if
Let $\bar{V} \in \mathbb{R}^{n\times d}$ be such that $\mathrm{col}(\bar{V}) = t\cdot\mathbf{x}$;
return $\bar{V}$;

where H is the following symmetric matrix:

$$H = \begin{bmatrix} H_0 & \mathbf{b}/2 \\ \mathbf{b}^\top/2 & 0 \end{bmatrix} \in \mathbb{R}^{(nd+1)\times(nd+1)},$$

and

$$\mathcal{D} = \{\mathbf{y}' = (\mathbf{x}', t') \in \mathbb{R}^{nd+1} \mid \mathbf{x}' \in \mathcal{D}_0, t' \le 1\}.$$

To see that (12) and (11) are equivalent, observe that an optimal solution $(\mathbf{x}, t)$ to (12) must be such that $t = -1$ or $t = +1$. If $t = +1$, then $\mathbf{x}$ is an optimal solution to (11); if $t = -1$, then $-\mathbf{x}$ is an optimal solution to (11). Finally, (12) is equivalent to (10), by setting $Y = \mathbf{y}\mathbf{y}^\top$ and using the fact that $\mathbf{y}^\top H\mathbf{y} = \mathrm{tr}(H\mathbf{y}\mathbf{y}^\top)$.

In particular, given an optimal solution Y to (10), an optimal solution to GLOBALRECOMMENDATION can be constructed as follows. Since $Y \succeq 0$ and rank$(Y) = 1$, there exists $\mathbf{y} \in \mathbb{R}^{nd+1}$ such that $Y = \mathbf{y}\mathbf{y}^\top$. More specifically, Y has a unique positive eigenvalue λ. If $\mathbf{e}$ is the corresponding eigenvector, $\mathbf{y} = (\mathbf{x}, t) = \sqrt{\lambda}\cdot\mathbf{e}$. An optimal solution to (9) is thus the matrix $\bar{V} \in \mathbb{R}^{n\times d}$ with column-major order representation $\mathrm{col}(\bar{V}) = t\cdot\mathbf{x}$. □

Problem (10) is still not convex, on account of the rank constraint on Y. However, in light of Theorem 2, a natural relaxation for GLOBAL RECOMMENDATION is the following semi-definite program, resulting from dropping this rank constraint:

SDP RELAXATION

$$\begin{aligned} \text{Max.:} \quad & \mathrm{tr}(HY) \\ \text{subj. to:} \quad & Y \succeq 0,\ \mathrm{diag}(Y) \in \mathcal{D}. \end{aligned} \tag{13}$$

This is a relaxation, in the sense that it increases the feasible set: any solution to (10) will also be a solution to (13). Crucially, (13) is a convex SDP problem, and can be solved in polynomial time. Moreover, if it happens that the optimal solution Y of (13) has rank 1, this solution is also guaranteed to be an optimal solution to (10), and can thus be used to construct an optimal solution to GLOBAL RECOMMENDATION, by Theorem 2. If, on the other hand, rank$(Y) > 1$, we are not guaranteed to retrieve an optimal solution to (10). However, a solution with a provable approximation guarantee can still be constructed through a randomization technique, originally proposed by Goemans and Williamson [13].

Approximation Algorithm. Algorithm 1 summarizes the steps in the approach outlined above to solving GLOBAL RECOMMENDATION. First, the algorithm obtains an optimal solution Y to the SDP (13). It then tests if rank$(Y) = 1$, i.e., if this solution happens to have rank 1. If it does, then it is also a solution to (10), and an optimal solution to (9) can be constructed as outlined in the proof of Theorem 2. In particular, Y can be written as $Y = \mathbf{y}\mathbf{y}^\top$, where

$\mathbf{y} = (\mathbf{x}, t) \in \mathbb{R}^{nd+1}$ can be computed from the unique positive eigenvalue of Y and its corresponding eigenvector. The optimal solution to (9) can subsequently be obtained as the matrix $\bar{V} \in \mathbb{R}^{n\times d}$ that has a column-major order representation $\text{col}(V) = t \cdot \mathbf{x}$.

If, on the other hand, $\text{rank}(Y) > 1$, the algorithm returns a vector $(\mathbf{x}, t)$ constructed in a randomized fashion. In particular, the algorithm returns the vector $\sqrt{\text{diag}(Y)}$, namely the square root of Y's diagonal elements, with each coordinate multiplied by a random sign ($+1$ or -1). The random sign vector $\sigma \in \{-1, +1\}^{nd+1}$ used in this multiplication is constructed as follows. Given that $Y \succeq 0$, there exists a matrix $Z \in \mathbb{R}^{n\times n}$ that factorizes Y, i.e., $Y = Z^\top Z$. Such a matrix can be obtained in polynomial time from the eigendecomposition of Y. Having Z, the algorithm proceeds by sampling a random vector $u \in \mathbb{R}^{nd+1}$ from a standard Gaussian distribution. Then, σ is the binary vector computed by applying the sign operator on the coordinates of vector $Z^\top u$.

The resulting random $\mathbf{y} = (\mathbf{x}, t) \in \mathbb{R}^{nd+1}$ is guaranteed to be a feasible solution to (10). Most importantly, the following approximation guarantee for the quality of the corresponding solution to GLOBAL RECOMMENDATION can be provided:

THEOREM 3 (YE [25]). *Let G^*, G_* be the maximal and minimal values of the social welfare G given by (7), evaluated over the feasible domain of (9). Let also $\bar{V}$ be the solution generated by Algorithm 1 when* $\text{rank}(Y) > 1$. *Then*

$$\frac{G^* - \mathbb{E}_u[\bar{V}]}{G^* - G_*} \leq \frac{\pi}{2} - 1 < \frac{4}{7},$$

where the expectation $\mathbb{E}_u[\cdot]$ is over the Gaussian vector u.

The existence of a simple test (namely, $\text{rank}(Y) = 1$) verifying that the solution produced by Algorithm (1) is optimal is important. In fact, in Section 6, we study an extensive set of instances, involving several social network topologies and combinations of aversive and attractive behavior. *In each and every instance studied, Algorithm 1 yielded an optimal solution.* Hence, although the quadratic program (9) is not known to be within the class of problems that can be solved exactly through an SDP relaxation, the experiments in Section 6 suggest that a stronger guarantee than the one provided by Theorem 3 is attained in practice.

4.3 Special Cases

Though for generic instances of (9) we cannot obtain a better theoretical guarantee than Theorem 3, there are specific instances of (9) for which optimality is always attained, and the approximation through randomization is not necessary. As these cases are also of practical interest, we briefly review them below.

Attraction Dominance. Consider a scenario where (a) $\gamma_i > \delta_i$ for all $i \in [n]$ and (b) $\bar{U}^0 \geq \mathbf{0}$. Intuitively, (a) implies that attraction to proposed content is more dominant than aversion to content, while (b) implies that user profile features take only positive values. Hence, the matrix H in Theorem 2 has nonnegative off-diagonal elements. Although the QCQP (9) in this case is not convex, it is known that in this specific case Algorithm 1 provides an optimal, rank-1 solution [34].

Uniform Aversion Dominance. Consider a scenario where (a) all parameters are uniform across users, i.e.,$\gamma_i = \gamma$ and $\delta_i = \delta$, for all $i \in [n]$, and (b) $\gamma < \delta$, i.e., aversion dominates user behavior. In this case, the QCQP (9) is convex and can thus be solved optimally by standard interior point methods in polynomial time [6].

No Personalization. Consider the scenario where *the same item is recommended to all users, i.e.,* $\mathbf{v}_i(t) = \mathbf{v}(t)$, $\forall i \in [n]$. In this case, GLOBAL RECOMMENDATION reduces to a quadratic objective with a single quadratic constraint, in which case even though the problem may not be convex, Algorithm 1 is guaranteed to find a rank-1, optimal solution [6].

No Social Network. In the case where $\beta = 0$, and there is no social component to the optimization, the social welfare (7) becomes separable in $\bar{\mathbf{v}}_i$, i.e., $G(\bar{V}) = \sum_{i\in[n]} G_i(\bar{\mathbf{v}}_i)$, where G_i is a quadratic function. Then, the optimization is separable, and a solution to (9) can be obtained by solving $\max_{\bar{\mathbf{v}}_i\in\mathbb{R}^d:\|\mathbf{v}\|\leq 1} G(\bar{\mathbf{v}}_i)$ for each $i \in [n]$; these are again quadratic problems with a single quadratic constraint, and can be solved exactly by Algorithm 1 [6].

4.4 Finite Catalog

Recall that our analysis assumes (6), which becomes applicable for a large catalog C covering the unit ball $\mathbb{B}$. We describe below how a computed profile $\bar{\mathbf{v}}_i$, $i \in [n]$ can be used to construct a distribution ν_i over catalog C.

If $\bar{\mathbf{v}}_i \in \text{conv}(C)$, the recommender can select probabilities $\nu_i(\mathbf{v})$, for $\mathbf{v} \in C$, that satisfy (5); this equality, along with the positivity constraints, and the constraint$\sum_{\mathbf{v}\in C} \nu_i(\mathbf{v}) = 1$ (as ν_i is a distribution), are linear, and define a feasible set. Thus, finding a probability distribution satisfying (5) (i.e., that lies in the feasible set) is a linear program, which can be solved in polynomial time.

If, on the other hand, $\bar{\mathbf{v}}_i \notin \text{conv}(C)$, the same procedure can be applied to the projection of $\bar{\mathbf{v}}_i$ to $\text{conv}(C)$. Given that $\text{conv}(C)$ is a convex polytope, this can again be computed in polynomial time. Moreover, under (6), if the catalog C is large this projection will be close to the optimal value $\bar{\mathbf{v}}_i$.

5. PARAMETER LEARNING FROM DATA

In this section, we provide an algorithm for validating the existence of attraction and aversion phenomena in real datasets. In short, our approach involves incorporating aversion and attraction parameters into Matrix Factorization (MF) [18, 20]; we treat parameters α_i, γ_i and δ_i as regularization terms, which are learned through cross validation.

Extending MF. We focus on datasets that comprise ratings generated by users, at known times (such as the datasets used in Section 6). More specifically, we assume access to a dataset represented by tuples of the form (i, j, r_{ij}, t) where $i \in [n] \equiv \{1, \ldots, n\}$ is the id of a user, $j \in [m] \equiv \{1, \ldots, m\}$ the id of an item, $r \in \mathbb{R}$ the feedback (rating) provided by user i to item j and $t \in [T]$ the time at which the rating took place. Denoting by $E \subset [n] \times [m]$ the pairs appearing in tuples in this dataset, recall that matrix factorization (MF) amounts to constructing profiles $\mathbf{u}_i \in \mathbb{R}^d$, $\mathbf{v}_j \in \mathbb{R}^d$ that are solutions to:

$$\min_{\substack{\mathbf{u}_i,\mathbf{v}_j,\\ i\in[n],j\in[m]}} \sum_{(i,j)\in E}(r_{ij} - \langle \mathbf{u}_i, \mathbf{v}_j\rangle)^2 + \lambda \sum_{i\in[n]} \|\mathbf{u}_i\|_2^2 + \mu \sum_{j\in[m]} \|\mathbf{v}_j\|_2^2 \quad (14)$$

where $\lambda, \mu > 0$ are regularization parameters to be learned through cross validation. Though this is not a convex problem, it is typically solved either through gradient descent or alternating least squares techniques, both of which perform well in practice [18, 20].

We incorporate attraction and aversion in this formulation as follows. First, at any time step $t \in [T]$, the profile of a user i is given by $\mathbf{u}_i(t) \in \mathbb{R}^d$. Let $E_i(t) \subseteq [m]$ be the set of items rated by user i at time t and

$$\mathcal{V}_i(t) = \{\mathbf{v}_j : j \in E_i(\tau), 1 \leq \tau \leq t\}$$

be the set of items the user has interacted with up to time t (inclusive). As in Section 3, we denote by $g(\mathcal{V}_i(t))$ the weighted average

Algorithm 2: Attraction-Aversion Learning Algorithm

Obtain $\mathbf{u}_i^0, \forall i \in [n]$, and $\mathbf{v}_j, \forall j \in [m]$ through standard MF (14);
Compute $g(\mathcal{V}_i(t)), \forall i \in [n], \forall t \in [T]$;
Split the dataset into k folds;
Initialize values in α,γ,δ uniformly at random from [0, 1] and project $(\alpha_i, \gamma_i, \delta_i)$ to the set $\{(x, y, z) \geq 0 : x + y + z = 1\}, \forall i \in [n]$;
repeat
  $(\alpha, \gamma, \delta, \kappa) \leftarrow (\alpha, \gamma, \delta, \kappa) - \rho \nabla \bar{\text{SE}}_{\texttt{test}}(\alpha, \gamma, \delta, \kappa)$;
  Project $(\alpha_i, \gamma_i, \delta_i)$ to $\{(x, y, z) \geq 0 : x + y + z = 1\}, \forall i \in [n]$;
until Change of $\bar{\text{SE}}_{\texttt{test}}$ in two consecutive iterations is small enough

Case	Flixster	FilmTipSet	MovieLens
# users	4.6K	443	8.9K
# items	25K	4.3K	3.8K
# ratings	1.8M	118K	1.3M
# SN edges	44K	N/A	N/A

Table 1: Datasets statistics

of items in $\mathcal{V}_i(t)$. Then, we propose obtaining $\mathbf{u}_i(t)$ as solutions to:

$$\min_{\substack{\mathbf{u}_i(t), i \in [n],\\ t \in [T]}} \sum_{\substack{t \in [T], i \in [n],\\ (i,j) \in E_i(t)}} (r_{ij} - \langle \mathbf{u}_i(t), \mathbf{v}_j \rangle)^2 + \sum_{i \in [n], t \in [T]} \left(\|\mathbf{u}_i(t) - \alpha_i \mathbf{u}_i^0 - (\gamma_i - \delta_i) g(\mathcal{V}_i(t))\|_2^2 + \kappa \|\mathbf{u}_i(t)\|_2^2 \right), \quad (15)$$

where $\mathbf{u}_i^0$, $\mathbf{v}_j$ are computed through standard MF (14), and α_i, $\gamma_i, \delta_i, i \in [n]$ and κ are also treated as regularization parameters, to be learned through cross validation. Note that, in contrast to (14), (15) is a simple linear regression problem, and the profiles $\mathbf{u}_i(t)$, where $i \in [n]$, $t \in [T]$, can be computed in closed form.

Learning Procedure. Based on this approach, our algorithm for learning the vectors α, γ, and δ is outlined in Algorithm 2. First, we learn the inherent profiles $\mathbf{u}_i^0$ and the item feature profiles $\mathbf{v}_j$ by solving (14), through stochastic gradient descent. Then, we use these profiles to learn $\alpha_i, \gamma_i, \delta_i$ through cross validation. In particular, we split the ratings dataset in k folds, and use $k-1$ folds as a training set, and one fold as a test set. In our evaluation, we set $k = 5$. We learn $\mathbf{u}_i(t)$ by solving (15) on this restricted dataset. Using these, we compute the square error on the test set as:

$$\text{SE}_{\texttt{test}} = \sum_{(i,j,t) \in \texttt{test}} (r_{ij} - \langle \mathbf{u}_i(t), \mathbf{v}_j \rangle)^2.$$

We repeat this process across k folds and obtain an average $\bar{\text{SE}}_{\texttt{test}}$.

We compute vectors α,γ,δ that minimize the average $\bar{\text{SE}}_{\texttt{test}}$. Note that this is a function of the regularization parameters of (15), i.e., $\bar{\text{SE}}_{\texttt{test}} = \bar{\text{SE}}_{\texttt{test}}(\alpha, \gamma, \delta, \kappa)$. As (15) admits a closed form solution, so does $\bar{\text{SE}}_{\texttt{test}}(\alpha, \gamma, \delta, \kappa)$. Using this, we find α,γ,δ through projected gradient descent, requiring that they sum to 1.

6. EXPERIMENTS

We perform experiments to evaluate our parameter learning and social welfare-maximizing algorithms on three real-world rating datasets: Flixster, FilmTipSet, and MovieLens, as well as several synthetically generated traces. The implementations are in Matlab and we use the CVX library [14] to solve the SDP in Algorithm 1. All experiments were run on a server with AMD Opteron 6272 CPUs (eight cores at 2.1GHz) and 128GB memory.

Dataset Preparations. We first describe the three real-world rating datasets. Their statistics are summarized in Table 1.

Flixster is a social movie rating site[4]. The original dataset, collected by Jamali et al. [16], comprises 1M users, 14M undirected friendship edges, and 8.2M timestamped ratings (ranging from 0.5 to 5 stars). We use Graclus[5] to extract a dense subgraph of the social network. Further, we filter out users and movies with less than 100 ratings so that there is enough data to learn temporal profile vectors. This gives a core of 4.6K users, 44K edges, and 25K movies.

FilmTipSet[6] is Swedish movie fans community. The data was originally published for a research competition in the CAMRa workshop[7]. It has 16K users, 67K movies, 2.8M timestamped ratings (on the scale of 1 to 5). We select users rating no less than 100 movies in both 2004 and 2005. This gives a core of 443 users, 4.3K movies, and 118K ratings.

The third dataset is MovieLens[8] (the 10M-user version). We focus on users that have rated at least 20 movies in the year of 2000. Note that there is no social network in MovieLens. FilmTipSet contains some social networking information, which we were unable to use in our analysis due to its extreme sparsity (85 edges for the 443 core users).

6.1 Evaluation of Parameter Learning

Learning on Synthetic Data. We first run Algorithm 2 on a synthetically generated dataset to examine its accuracy. We set $n = 100$, $T = 100$, and $d = 5$. Each user $i \in [n]$ consumes one random item at every time step $t \in [T]$. For all users i, we generate "ground-truth" α_i, γ_i, and δ_i uniformly at random from [0, 1] and normalize them so that $\alpha_i + \gamma_i + \delta_i = 1$. The expected inherent interest profiles and item profiles are generated uniformly at random from $[0, 1]^d$. Interest profiles evolve according to the dynamics in Section 3.3, with $\beta = 0$, and weighted average g with equal weights. At each step, users generate ratings computed by taking the inner product of appropriate profile vectors.

The learning rate ρ and regularization parameter κ in Algorithm 2 are both set to be 0.001 (determined by cross validation). The convergence condition of Algorithm 2 is set to be the change in $\bar{\text{SE}}_{\texttt{test}}$ being smaller than 10^{-6}. We repeat the process ten times with different random starting points and report the results obtained in the repetition that gives the smallest $\bar{\text{SE}}_{\texttt{test}}$.

Let α_i^ℓ, γ_i^ℓ, and δ_i^ℓ be the learned evolution probabilities. We use RMSE to define the learning error w.r.t. α_i's:

$$\text{RMSE}_\alpha = \sqrt{\frac{\sum_{i=1}^n |\alpha_i - \alpha_i^\ell|^2}{n}}.$$

RMSE_γ and RMSE_δ can thus be defined in the same way. Figure 2a shows the decrease of these RMSEs as the number of iterations goes up. At convergence, they are 0.08, 0.58 and 0.56 respectively. In addition, Figure 2a also shows that the test RMSE (computed as $\sqrt{\bar{\text{SE}}_{\texttt{test}}/|\texttt{test}|}$) drops steadily as the learning proceeds, which finally converges to 0.02 in a total of 5300 iterations.

In Figure 2b, we show a scatter plot of the ground-truth probabilities and the learned probabilities (at convergence). Each data point has one ground-truth probability value in x-coordinate and the corresponding learned value in y-coordinate. The $y = x$ line indicates points for which the learned and ground truth probabilities are equal. As can be seen, the algorithm recovers α_i's almost perfectly, while the results for γ_i's and δ_i's are also reasonably good.

[4]http://www.flixster.com/
[5]http://www.cs.utexas.edu/users/dml/Software/graclus.html
[6]http://www.filmtipset.se/
[7]http://www.dai-labor.de/camra2010/
[8]http://grouplens.org/datasets/movielens/

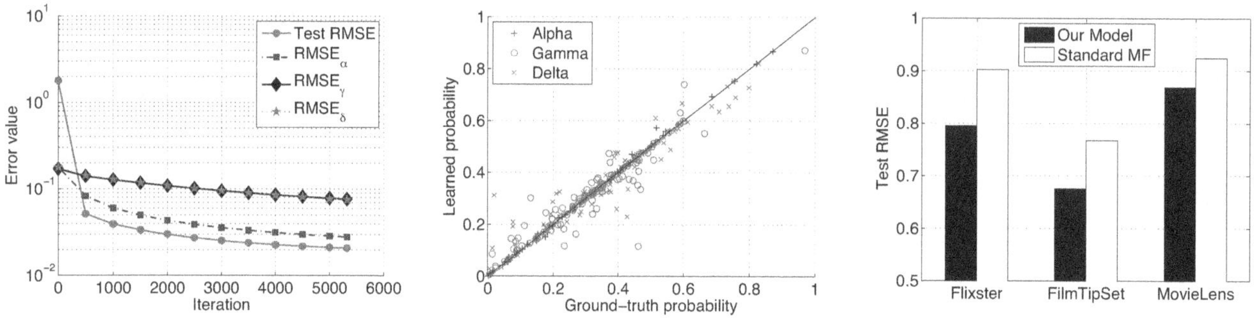

(a) Test RMSE, RMSE_α, RMSE_γ, and RMSE_δ over iterations (b) Interest evolution probabilities learned on synthetic data (c) Test RMSE comparisons

Figure 2: Evaluating parameter learning

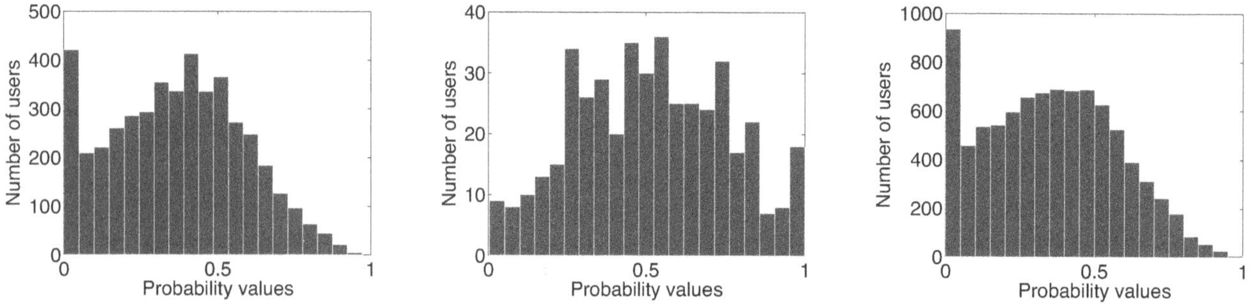

(a) Flixster (b) FilmTipSet (c) MovieLens

Figure 3: Learned values of α_i on three real-world datasets

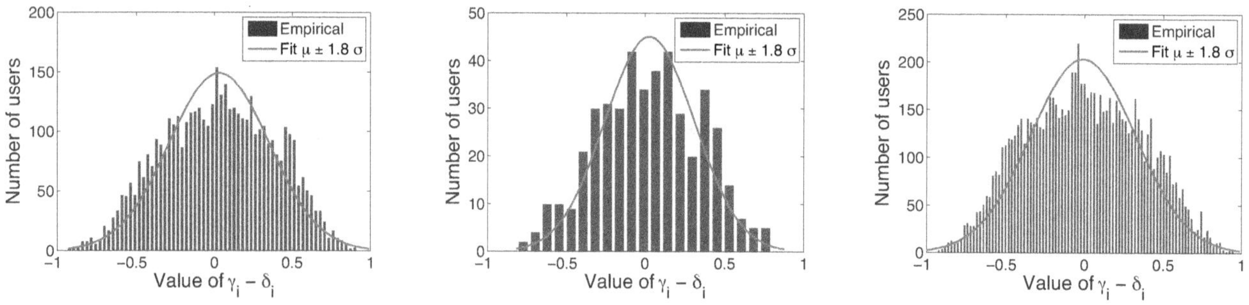

(a) Flixster (b) FilmTipSet (c) MovieLens

Figure 4: Values of $\gamma_i - \delta_i$ on three real-world datasets

This gives us confidence in deploying the algorithm on real-world rating data, in which ground-truth parameters are not known.

Learning on Real Data. For each dataset, we sort the ratings in chronological order and split them into $T = 10$ time steps. A single time step corresponds to 3, 1.2, and 2.5 calendar months in Flixster, MovieLens, and FilmTipSet, respectively. We then run Algorithm 2 with learning rate $\rho = 0.001$, regularization parameter $\kappa = 0.001$, and number of latent features $d = 10$. Figure 3 shows the distributions of values learned for α_i's. Furthermore, to compare the number of attraction-dominant users and the number of aversion dominant users, in Figure 4 we display the distribution of $\gamma_i - \delta_i$, along with a Gaussian distribution fitted by data within the interval $[\mu - 1.8\sigma, \mu + 1.8\sigma]$ (capturing 90% of a Gaussian distribution), where μ and σ^2 is the mean and variance of all $\gamma_i - \delta_i$'s. As can be seen, the empirical distribution has tails that are heavier than the Gaussian (at about -0.5 and 0.5), indicating the existence of strongly aversive and strongly attracted users.

For reference, we also compare the average test RMSE on five-fold cross-validation achieved by our model and by standard MF. For standard MF, we implement the stochastic gradient descent method as in [20] with $d = 10$, learning rate 0.002, and regularization parameters determined by cross validation. As shown in Figure 2c, profiles learned by Algorithm 2 outperform standard MF in rating prediction, lowering the test RMSE by 11.8%, 11.9%, 6.18% on Flixster, FilmTipSet, and MovieLens respectively.

6.2 Social Welfare Performance

Next, we evaluate Algorithm 1, hereafter referred to as *GRA*, and compare the social welfare it yields with a baseline that ignores interest evolution. This baseline recommends to each user

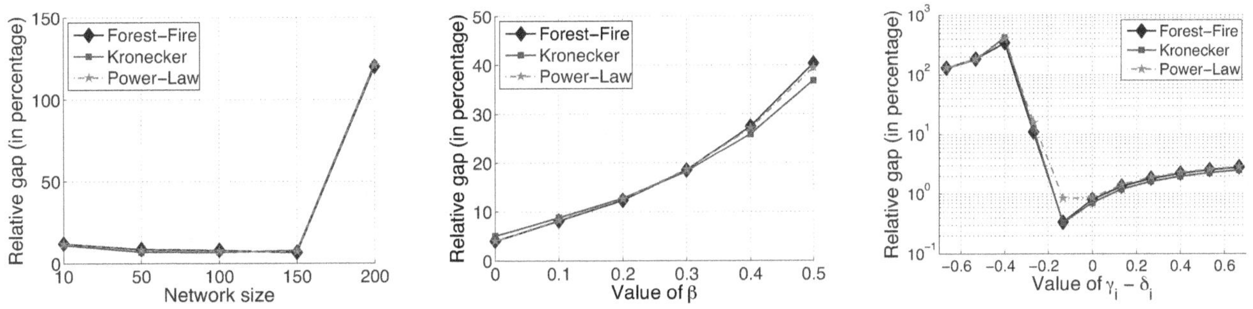

(a) Varying network size (n) (b) Varying β (c) Varying $\gamma_i - \delta_i$

Figure 5: Relative increase in social welfare by *GRA* over *MF-Local* on synthetic datasets.

the item profile maximizing the user's utility under the inherent profile computed by standard MF. For each user $i \in [n]$, this is $\mathbf{v}_i = \mathbf{u}_i^0/||\mathbf{u}_i^0||_2$, for all $i \in [n]$. It is thus easy to see that $||\mathbf{v}_i||_2 = 1$ and it is in fact co-linear w.r.t. $\mathbf{u}_i^0$. We hereafter refer to this baseline as *MF-Local*. In all experiments, following the literature of social influence propagation and maximization [8, 17], we set the influence probability of user j on user i to be $1/\deg^{\text{in}}(i)$, where $\deg^{\text{in}}(i)$ is the in-degree of node i in the network graph.

6.2.1 Experiments on Synthetic Networks

We start by evaluating the social welfare achieved by *GRA* and *MF-Local* on three different of random networks that mimic the structure of a social network: Forest-Fire [4], Kronecker [21], and Power-Law [2]. For each type, we consider the following settings: Forest-Fire with forward and backward burning probability being 0.38 and 0.32 respectively, Kronecker with initiator matrix being $[0.9, 0.5; 0.5, 0.3]$, and Power-Law with exponent 2.1.

We vary the size of network graphs (i.e., number of users, n), the value of β (i.e, users' tendency of getting influenced by friends), and the difference between γ_i and δ_i, to evaluate their effects on the performance of our *GRA* algorithm in comparison to *MF-Local*. Unless otherwise noted, α_i's, γ_i's, δ_i's, and inherent user profiles are sampled randomly and the process is repeated ten times, of which we take the average social welfare. Also, d is fixed to be 10. In all cases, we plot the *relative gap* in social welfare, i.e.,

$$(\text{Social Welfare}_{GRA} - \text{Social Welfare}_{\textit{MF-Local}})/|\text{Social Welfare}_{\textit{MF-Local}}|.$$

Effect of Network Size. We test five different values for n: $10, 50, 100, 150$, and 200 for Forest-Fire and Power-Law, and $16, 32, 64, 128$, and 256 for Kronecker (by definition a random Kronecker graph has 2^w nodes where $w \in \mathbb{N}_+$ is the number of iterations of Kronecker product taken in the generation process [21]). As can be seen from Figure 5a, the gap between *GRA* and *MF-Local* is close to 10% for small graphs, but increases on all three networks for larger values of n: *GRA* achieves twice as much social welfare as *MF-Local*, for $n = 200$.

Effect of β. In this test, we vary the value of β from 0 up to 0.5. Network size is fixed at 100 for Forest-Fire and Power-Law, and 128 for Kronecker. Figure 5b shows that *GRA* significantly outperforms *MF-Local*, and more interestingly, the relative gap increases as β increases. This intuitively suggests that when the influence among users is higher, ignoring the joint effect of recommendations becomes more detrimental to maximizing the social welfare.

Effects of $\gamma_i - \delta_i$. Next, we test different values of $\gamma_i - \delta_i$, representing cases from extreme aversion dominance to attraction dominance. Network size is $n = 100$ and $\beta = 0.25$, while $\alpha_i = \alpha$, $\gamma_i = \gamma$ and $\delta_i = \delta$ for all $i \in [n]$. We set α s.t. $\alpha(1-\beta) = 0.25$, and vary $\gamma - \delta$, where $\alpha + \gamma + \delta = 1$. Relative gaps are shown in Figure 5c. All in all, we see that gaps are far more pronounces in the strongly aversive regime, as targeting to the existing profiles of users leads to suboptimal recommendations. For values less than -0.3, the social welfare under *MF-Local* is actually negative; it goes up as $\gamma - \delta$ increases, i.e., users tend towards attractive behavior. In contrast, the social welfare of *GRA* is always positive, and always greater than the one under *MF-Local*. As a result, there is a large gap for values at less than -0.3; the relative gap becomes small (but still positive) near -0.1, and then steadily increases.

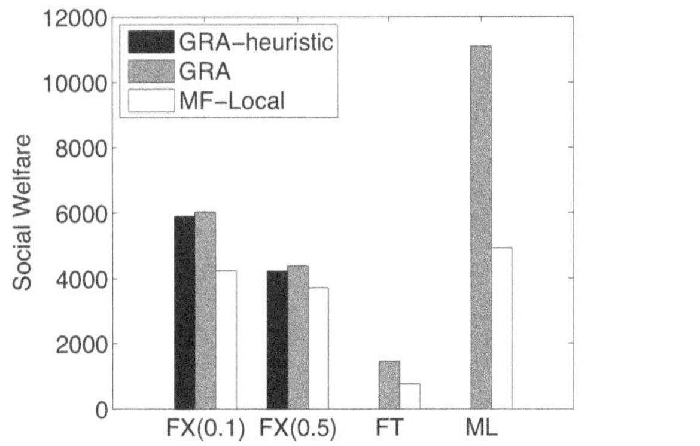

Figure 6: Social welfare achieved on: FX(0.1) and FX(0.5) – Flixster with $\beta = 0.1$ and 0.5; FT – FilmTipSet; ML – MovieLens.

It is important to note that in all evaluations of *GRA* over synthetic datasets, as well as the ones listed below on real datasets, *GRA returned an optimal solution.* That is, for all inputs tested, the matrix Y computed had rank 1. Hence, although the QCQP problem (9) is not known to be solvable in polynomial time, in practice, *GRA* outperforms the guarantee of Theorem 3.

6.2.2 Experiments on Real Data

We next compare the social welfare attained on Flixster, FilmTipSet, and MovieLens by *GRA* and *MF-Local*. For FilmTipSet and MovieLens where there is no social network considered, GLOBAL RECOMMENDATION is separable and can thus be *parallelized* (see Section 4.3): we can divide users into arbitrary subsets, run *GRA* on each of them, and then combine the total social welfare over all subsets as the final solution without any loss.

To improve the scalability of GPA over Flixster, and parallelize its execution, we adopt the following heuristic. First, we split the social graph into 50 subgraphs using Graclus. Then, we solve SDP on each subgraph separately. Note that, in effect, this optimization ignores the edges between subgraphs, and thus only yields an approximation to the social welfare.

Figure 6 illustrates the performance of *GRA* and *MF-Local* on those datasets, where the values of α_i, γ_i, and δ_i are all from the learning results in Section 6.1 and dimensionality d is set to 10. We can see that *GRA* is significantly superior to *MF-Local*: on FilmTipSet (1461 vs. 757) and MovieLens (11092 vs. 4926), it achieves approximately twice the social welfare. On Flixster, we test two cases for β: 0.1 and 0.5, representing weak and strong social behavior respectively. For *GRA*, we adopt the aforementioned clustering-based heuristic to compute $\bar{\mathbf{v}}_i$'s, and evaluate the welfare achieved by *GRA* in two ways: (i) simply calculating the welfare on the subgraph and taking the sum over all subgraphs (termed *GRA*-heuristic); (ii) taking the $\bar{\mathbf{v}}_i$'s to calculate the social welfare on the entire graph (termed *GRA*). The values computed by method (ii) are only slightly different from (i), indicating that our clustering heuristic closely follows the true social welfare, while enabling parallelization. The relative gain of *GRA*-heuristic over *MF-Local* is 39.0% when $\beta = 0.1$ and 13.4% when $\beta = 0.5$. The running time of *GRA* is reasonably good, e.g., on a subgraph of Flixster with 94 nodes and 276 edges, *GRA* finishes in 90 seconds.

In summary, through extensive empirical evaluation on both real and synthetic data, we have demonstrated that first, the phenomenon of interest evolution, especially attraction and aversion, can indeed by observed from real-world rating data, and second, both of our learning algorithm and global recommendation algorithm are highly effective in their respective tasks.

7. CONCLUSIONS

Our study of attraction, aversion, and social influence suggests that such phenomena can be incorporated in recommendation decisions, and that the SDP relaxation approach brings relevant optimizations within the realm of tractability. The heuristic we exploited in Section 6, namely, parallelizing execution over weakly connected partitions of the social graph, highlights an approach for scalable, parallelizable solutions to the SDP relaxation. Nevertheless, further opportunities for improving efficiency exist: the sparse, block structure of the matrices in our SDP was not exploited by the generic solvers we employed. Investigating solutions that exploit this structure for higher efficiency is an interesting future direction. Moreover, although the QCQP that expresses our problem is not known to be exactly solvable through an SDP relaxation, all solutions we obtained through our experiments were actually optimal. Understanding if optimality holds for a wider class than the ones presented in Section 4.3 is also an important open problem. Finally, there are many phenomena beyond attraction, aversion and social influence that may affect a user's interests. The quadratic nature of our problem arises from the standard factor-based model for utilities: understanding if other phenomena inducing drift on profiles can also be cast in this framework is also an open question.

8. REFERENCES

[1] Z. Abbassi et al. Getting recommender systems to think outside the box. In *Proceedings of the third ACM conference on Recommender systems*, pages 285–288. ACM, 2009.

[2] W. Aiello, F. R. K. Chung, and L. Lu. A random graph model for massive graphs. In *STOC*, pages 171–180, 2000.

[3] S. Amer-Yahia et al. Battling predictability and overconcentration in recommender systems. *IEEE Data Eng. Bull.*, 32(4):33–40, 2009.

[4] A.-L. Barabási and R. Albert. Emergence of scaling in random networks. *science*, 286(5439):509–512, 1999.

[5] A. Beck and Y. C. Eldar. Strong duality in nonconvex quadratic optimization with two quadratic constraints. *SIAM Journal on Optimization*, 17(3):844–860, 2006.

[6] S. Boyd and L. Vandenberghe. *Convex Optimization*. Cambridge University Press, 2004.

[7] J. J. Brown and P. H. Reingen. Social ties and word-of-mouth referral behavior. *Journal of Consumer research*, 1987.

[8] W. Chen, L. V. S. Lakshmanan, and C. Castillo. *Information and Influence Propagation in Social Networks*. Synthesis Lectures on Data Management. Morgan & Claypool Publishers, 2013.

[9] P. Domingos and M. Richardson. Mining the network value of customers. In KDD, pages 57–66. ACM, 2001.

[10] X. Fang, S. Singh, and R. Ahluwalia. An examination of different explanations for the mere exposure effect. *Journal of consumer research*, 34(1):97–103, 2007.

[11] R. G. Gallager. *Discrete stochastic processes*, volume 101. Kluwer Academic Publishers Boston, 1996.

[12] M. Ge et al. Beyond accuracy: Evaluating recommender systems by coverage and serendipity. RecSys '10.

[13] M. X. Goemans and D. P. Williamson. Improved approximation algorithms for maximum cut and satisfiability problems using semidefinite programming. *JACM*, 42(6):1115–1145, 1995.

[14] M. Grant and S. Boyd. CVX: Matlab software for disciplined convex programming, version 2.0 beta. `http://cvxr.com/cvx`, Sept. 2013.

[15] A. Grimes and P. J. Kitchen. Researching mere exposure effects to advertising-theoretical foundations and methodological implications. *International Journal of Market Research*, 49(2):191–219, 2007.

[16] M. Jamali and M. Ester. A matrix factorization technique with trust propagation for recommendation in social networks. In *RecSys*, 2010.

[17] D. Kempe, J. Kleinberg, and É. Tardos. Maximizing the spread of influence through a social network. In KDD, pages 137–146, 2003.

[18] Y. Koren. Factorization meets the neighborhood: a multifaceted collaborative filtering model. In *KDD*, 2008.

[19] Y. Koren. Collaborative filtering with temporal dynamics. *Commun. ACM*, 53(4), 2010.

[20] Y. Koren, R. Bell, and C. Volinsky. Matrix factorization techniques for recommender systems. *IEEE Computer*, 2009.

[21] J. Leskovec et al. Kronecker graphs: An approach to modeling networks. *J. of Machine Learning Research*, 11:985–1042, 2010.

[22] Z.-q. Luo et al. Semidefinite relaxation of quadratic optimization problems. *Signal Processing Magazine, IEEE*, 27(3):20–34, 2010.

[23] S. M. McNee et al. Being accurate is not enough: how accuracy metrics have hurt recommender systems. In *CHI EA*, pages 1097–1101, 2006.

[24] Y. Nesterov. Semidefinite relaxation and nonconvex quadratic optimization. *Optimization methods and software*, 9(1-3):141–160, 1998.

[25] Y. Nesterov, et al. Semidefinite programming relaxations of nonconvex quadratic optimization. In *Handbook of semidefinite programming*, pages 361–419. Springer, 2000.

[26] K. Radinsky, et al. Modeling and predicting behavioral dynamics on the web. In *WWW*, 2012.

[27] A. D. Sarma et al. Understanding cyclic trends in social choices. In *WSDM*, pages 593–602, 2012.

[28] D. Shah. *Gossip algorithms*. Now Publishers Inc, 2009.

[29] L. Vandenberghe and S. Boyd. Semidefinite programming. *SIAM review*, 38(1):49–95, 1996.

[30] J. Yang and J. Leskovec. Patterns of temporal variation in online media. In *WSDM*, 2011.

[31] Y. Ye. Approximating quadratic programming with bound and quadratic constraints. *Math. Prog.*, 84(2):219–226, 1999.

[32] C. Yu, L. Lakshmanan, and S. Amer-Yahia. It takes variety to make a world: Diversification in recommender systems. In *EDBT*, 2009.

[33] R. B. Zajonc. Attitudinal effects of mere exposure. *Journal of personality and social psychology*, 9:1–27, 1968.

[34] S. Zhang. Quadratic maximization and semidefinite relaxation. *Mathematical Programming*, 87(3):453–465, 2000.

ClusCite: Effective Citation Recommendation by Information Network-Based Clustering

Xiang Ren, Jialu Liu, Xiao Yu, Urvashi Khandelwal, Quanquan Gu, Lidan Wang, Jiawei Han
University of Illinois at Urbana-Champaign, Urbana, IL
{xren7, jliu64, xiaoyu1, khndlwl2, qgu3, lidan, hanj}@illinois.edu

ABSTRACT

Citation recommendation is an interesting but challenging research problem. Most existing studies assume that all papers adopt the same criterion and follow the same behavioral pattern in deciding relevance and authority of a paper. However, in reality, papers have distinct citation behavioral patterns when looking for different references, depending on paper content, authors and target venues. In this study, we investigate the problem in the context of heterogenous bibliographic networks and propose a novel cluster-based citation recommendation framework, called **ClusCite**, which explores the principle that citations tend to be *softly* clustered into *interest groups* based on multiple types of relationships in the network. Therefore, we predict *each* query's citations based on related interest groups, each having its own model for paper authority and relevance. Specifically, we learn group memberships for objects and the significance of relevance features for each interest group, while also propagating relative authority between objects, by solving a joint optimization problem. Experiments on both DBLP and PubMed datasets demonstrate the power of the proposed approach, with 17.68% improvement in Recall@50 and 9.57% growth in MRR over the best performing baseline.

Categories and Subject Descriptors

H.3.3 [**Information Storage and Retrieval**]: Information Search and Retrieval

Keywords

Citation Recommendation; Heterogeneous Information Network; Clustering; Citation Behavioral Pattern

1. INTRODUCTION

A research paper needs to cite relevant and important previous work to help readers understand its background, context and innovation. However, the already large, and rapidly growing body of scientific literature makes it hard for anyone to go through and digest all the papers. It is thus

KDD'14, August 24–27, 2014, New York, NY, USA.

http://dx.doi.org/10.1145/2623330.2623630.

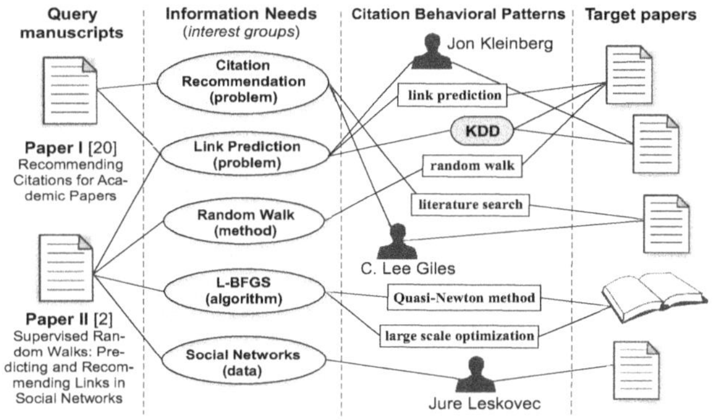

Figure 1: A toy example showing the diverse information needs of two query manuscripts and the corresponding citation behavioral patterns.

desirable to design a system that could automatically generate quality citation recommendations. Traditional literature search engines, such as Google Scholar, can retrieve a list of relevant papers using keyword-based queries. But casting one's rich information needs into a few keywords may not be feasible. Moreover, a user may be looking for papers that are not only relevant to their work, but also important and of high quality. To this end, citation recommendation aims to suggest a small number of publications that can be used as high quality references to satisfy such citation requirements.

There exist some interesting studies on citation recommendation. Context-aware recommendation [10, 12] analyzes each citation's local context to capture its specific information needs. However, local context can be ambiguous or too short a query, causing inaccurate predictions. Topical similarity-based methods [18, 24] find conceptually related papers by taking advantage of latent topic models. But solely relying on topic distributions to measure relevance is insufficient. A large number of papers may share the same topic, making topical similarity weak in indicating importance of a paper. Both methods primarily focus on recommending relevant papers based on content, but ignore critical information related to importance and quality.

Recent studies [16, 20] utilize citation links to derive structural similarity and authority, which serve as good complements to content-based relevance features. With paper text, authors and target venues as queries, one can further generate a rich set of structural features [5, 27] based on multiple types of relations between different entities. However, existing hybrid methods have difficulty in handling the diverse information needs since they impose the same citation behavioral pattern on every query manuscript. Fig. 1 il-

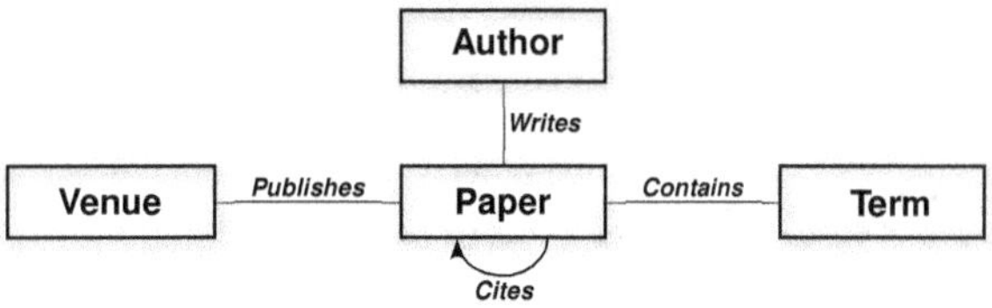

Figure 2: Schema for DBLP bibliographic network.

lustrates the diversity of these behavioral patterns using a toy example. Paper I is on "citation recommendation" and "link prediction", which are studied by a relatively compact group of researchers and venues, and one can find useful papers through related researchers, venues and key terms effectively. On the other hand, for "random walk", relations through authors and venues would be less informative on paper relevance since this method is widely studied by authors working on a variety of topics, and published at venues focusing on a variety of fields. Previous hybrid methods learn and apply the same recommendation model across all queries, ignoring the variations in citation behaviors when seeking quality references. Intuitively, paper citations should be organized into different groups and each group should have its own behavior pattern to identify information of interest.

In this paper, we propose a novel citation recommendation framework to capture citation behaviors for *each* query manuscript, based on both paper relevance and importance. By softly clustering citations into different interest groups, we aim to study the significance of different relevance features for each interest group, and derive paper relative authority within each group. In doing so, the challenge of satisfying diverse information needs behind a paper's citations can be properly tackled by making a paper-specific recommendation according to the query's interest group membership. Meanwhile, integration of paper importance can be accurately accomplished using relative authority. This idea, though interesting, leads to two critical problems: (1) how to discover hidden interest groups for effective citation recommendation, and (2) how to derive behavioral patterns on relevance and authority for each group.

To facilitate our study, a heterogenous bibliographic network, encoding the multiple types of relations between different objects, is constructed (Fig. 2). A rich set of structural features is derived from the network, representing various relation semantics (Table 1) between two papers. We then formulate a joint optimization problem to learn the proposed model such that prediction error along with graph regularization is minimized over known citations, based on the network. Specifically, the optimization problem conducts graph-regularized co-clustering to learn group membership for attribute objects and weights on relevance features for each group. It also propagates relative authority between different objects. An alternative minimization algorithm, called **ClusCite**, is further designed to iterate between co-clustering and authority propagation. Intuitively, feature weights and relative authority can be better learned with high quality interest groups, and in turn they assist in mining higher quality interest groups.

Our experiments on the DBLP and PubMed datasets demonstrate the power of the proposed model. ClusCite achieves 17.68% improvement in Recall@50 and 9.57% growth in MRR over the best baseline on the DBLP dataset. Our performance analysis shows that ClusCite can achieve even better results with richer attribute objects, and our case studies demonstrate the effectiveness of discovered interest groups and object relative authority for citation recommendation.

The rest of the paper is organized as follows. Sec. 2 gives background and the problem definition. Sec. 3 introduces our new model. The learning algorithm and its computational complexity analysis are in Sec. 4. We present and analyze our experimental results in Sec. 5, discuss the related work in Sec. 6, and conclude this study in Sec. 7.

Table 1: Meta paths with different semantics.

Meta path	Semantic meaning of the relation
$P-A-P$	p_i and p_j share same author(s)
$P-T-P$	p_i and p_j contain same term(s)
$P-V-P$	p_i and p_j are in the same venue
$P-T-P \to P$	p_i share term(s) with the paper(s) that cite p_j
$P-A-P \leftarrow P$	p_i share the same author(s) with the paper(s) cited by p_j

2. BACKGROUND

This section introduces concepts on heterogeneous bibliographic networks and presents the formal problem definition.

A **heterogeneous bibliographic network** [27, 23] is a directed graph G, that consists of multiple types of objects and relationships, derived from a bibliographic dataset.

Suppose there are n papers $\mathcal{P} = \{p_1, \ldots, p_n\}$, $|\mathcal{A}|$ authors $\mathcal{A} = \{a_1, \ldots, a_{|\mathcal{A}|}\}$, $|\mathcal{V}|$ venues (conferences or journals) $\mathcal{V} = \{v_1, \ldots, v_{|\mathcal{V}|}\}$, and $|\mathcal{T}|$ terms $\mathcal{T} = \{e_1, \ldots, e_{|\mathcal{T}|}\}$ in the network. Citations between papers form a directed subgraph denoted by an adjacency matrix $\mathbf{Y} \in \mathbb{R}^{n\times n}$ with $Y_{ij} = 1$ if paper p_i cites paper p_j and $Y_{ij} = 0$ otherwise. For relationships between papers and authors, we use an undirected bipartite graph, denoted by a biadjacency matrix $\mathbf{R}^{(\mathcal{A})} \in \mathbb{R}^{n\times|\mathcal{A}|}$, where $R^{(\mathcal{A})}_{ij} = 1$ if paper p_i has the author a_j and $R^{(\mathcal{A})}_{ij} = 0$ otherwise. Similarly, the relationships between papers and venues can also be represented by a biadjacency matrix $\mathbf{R}^{(\mathcal{V})} \in \mathbb{R}^{n\times|\mathcal{V}|}$, $R^{(\mathcal{V})}_{ij} = 1$ if paper p_i is published in the venue v_j and $R^{(\mathcal{V})}_{ij} = 0$ otherwise. We extract a set of term objects $\mathcal{T}$ from the paper's free-text and further construct an undirected bipartite subgraph between these terms and papers to represent paper content. We use the weight matrix $\mathbf{R}^{(\mathcal{T})} \in \mathbb{R}^{n\times|\mathcal{T}|}$ to denote the paper-term subgraph where $R^{(\mathcal{T})}_{ij}$ is the term frequency of term e_j in paper p_i.

We adopt the concept of **network schema** to describe the heterogeneous bibliographic network at the meta level [22, 23]. An example is shown in Fig. 2.

As shown in [22, 27], meta path-based features in heterogeneous information networks describe a rich set of relation semantics that can capture textual similarity, conceptual relevance and several kinds of social relatedness. A *meta path* is defined over network schema, where nodes are object types and edges are relation types. Table 1 shows some examples that use meta paths to measure paper relevance for the citation recommendation problem. Moreover, structural similarity measures can be defined on each meta path to generate relevance features, as shown in [22, 27].

In general, we represent the meta path-based relevance score between p_i and p_j as $\phi(p_i, p_j)$. Suppose we generate L different meta path-based relevance features by combining different meta paths with different structural similarity measures, we can define a relevance scores matrix $\mathbf{S}^{(i)} \in \mathbb{R}^{n\times L}$ for every paper $p_i \in \mathcal{P}$ where $S^{(i)}_{jl} = \phi^{(l)}(p_i, p_j)$ is the l-th meta path-based relevance score between p_i and p_j[1].

In this work, we cast the citation recommendation problem into the problem of learning a recommendation score function $s(q,p) : \mathcal{Q} \times \mathcal{P} \mapsto \mathbb{R}$ for a query manuscript $q \in \mathcal{Q}$ and a target paper $p \in \mathcal{P}$ based on the heterogeneous bibliographic network. The learned function is later used to

[1]Details of the meta path-based similarity computation in heterogeneous bibliographic network can be found in [22].

compute scores between query and target papers to make a recommendation. Formally, we define the **citation recommendation problem** as follows.

DEFINITION 1 (PROBLEM DEFINITION). *Given a heterogeneous bibliographic network G, and the terms, authors and target venues for a query manuscript $q \in \mathcal{Q}$, we aim to build a recommendation model specifically for q, and recommend a small subset of target papers $p \in \mathcal{P}$ as high quality references for q, by ranking the papers with the score function $s(q, p)$.*

3. THE PROPOSED FRAMEWORK

At a high level, the proposed cluster-based citation recommendation framework consists of two major steps:

1. Learning the model parameters based on known citations by solving a joint optimization problem (Sec. 4).
2. Making paper-specific recommendations for each query manuscript based on the learned ClusCite model, which is introduced in detail in this section.

3.1 Model Overview

We first provide an overview of the proposed model by defining the major components in the score function $s(q, p)$.

Given a query manuscript q, its citations will focus on several interest groups each having its own behavioral patterns in finding relevant and high authority work (Fig. 1). It is desirable to recommend papers that are highly ranked in multiple interest groups of the query, since they best capture diverse information needs. We propose a cluster-based score function to decide relative relevance and importance of target papers in the context of each interest group. It assigns a final recommendation score by integrating scores computed with respect to different interest groups.

Mathematically, suppose paper citations can be softly clustered into K interest groups, based on multiple types of relationships between objects in the heterogeneous bibliographic network, then we define the score function $s(q, p)$ as follows:

$$s(q,p) = \sum_{k=1}^{K} \theta_q^{(k)} \cdot \Big\{ r^{(k)}(q,p) + f_{\mathcal{P}}^{(k)}(p) \Big\}. \qquad (1)$$

Function $s(q, p)$ measures how likely a query manuscript $q \in \mathcal{Q}$ is to cite a target paper $p \in \mathcal{P}$. It is decomposed into a set of cluster-based functions: the cluster-based relevance function $r^{(k)}(q, p) : \mathcal{Q} \times \mathcal{P} \mapsto \mathbb{R}$ measures the relatedness between q and p according to the k-th interest group, and paper relative authority function $f_{\mathcal{P}}^{(k)}(p) : \mathcal{P} \mapsto \mathbb{R}$ computes the relative importance of p within the k-th interest group. The weighted combination of these functions defines the final recommendation score with respect to the group membership indicators of q, *i.e.*, $\{\theta_q^{(k)} : \theta_q^{(k)} > 0\}$, which represent how likely query q is to belong to the K different interest groups.

3.2 Feature Weights for Paper Relevance

As mentioned in Sec. 2, one can compute a rich set of meta path-based features to describe paper relevance under various relation semantics. Each meta path-based feature, could play a distinct role in identifying relevant work in different interest groups.

In Fig. 1, incorporating meta path $P - V - P$ along with textual similarity $P - T - P$ can effectively suggest related papers under the interest "link prediction (problem)" because only a compact set of venues (*e.g.*, KDD, ICML and ICDM) study this problem. However, if the interest switches to "L-BFGS (algorithm)", using $P - V - P$ probably will hurt the results since a much broarder set of venues involve studying this algorithm, and thus, sharing a venue with the query provides very weak evidence for paper relevance.

Table 2: Learned weights on seven different meta paths for four mined interest groups ($K = 40$).

Meta path	Group 1	Group 2	Group 3	Group 4
$P-V-P$	0.0024	0.0113	0.0158	0.3076*
$P-A-P$	0.0054	0.0006	0.0192	0.1243
$P-A-P \to P$	0.6133**	0.2159*	0.2254	0.0213
$P-T-P$	0.1227	0.0947	0.1579	0.1095
$P-T-P \to P$	0.0442	0.5448**	0.3250*	0.0231
$P-T-P \leftarrow P$	0.1938*	0.0870	0.3578**	0.2409**

In order to capture the biased significance of different relevance features for different interest groups, we assign feature weights for each interest group individually, leading to the definition of a cluster-based relevance function as follows:

$$r^{(k)}(q,p) = \sum_{l=1}^{L} w_k^{(l)} \cdot \phi^{(l)}(q,p). \qquad (2)$$

For each interest group k, we use a set of weights $\{w_k^{(l)} : w_k^{(l)} > 0\}$ to measure the significance of the L different meta path-based features $\{\phi^{(l)}(q, p)\}$ for the group.

These K feature weights are estimated through a joint optimization problem (Sec. 4). We demonstrate in Table 2 the learned feature patterns over 7 meta paths for 4 example interest groups (* and ** highlight first and second most significant values), using the random walk-based similarity measure on DBLP. All 4 groups show distinct weights on the 7 meta paths, justifying the claim that different interest groups hold different feature weights. In particular, we find meta paths which impose textual similarity (*e.g.*, $P-T-P \leftarrow P$) as well as references of co-author's papers ($P-A-P \to P$) play critical roles in finding relevant papers in these 4 groups, which matches human intuitions very well.

3.3 Object Relative Authority

A paper may have very different visibility or authority among different interest groups even if it has many citations. In the DBLP dataset [25], paper ObjectRank [3] (132 citations) got 47 citations from VLDB but only 12 from WWW, while RankSVM [14] (250 citations) obtained only 27 citations from VLDB but 109 from WWW, implying the bias of authority in different interest groups.

Instead of learning object's group membership and deriving relative authority separately, we propose to estimate them jointly using graph regularization, which preserves consistency over each subgraph. By doing so, paper relative authority serves as a feature for learning interest groups, and better estimated groups can in turn help derive relative authority more accurately (Fig. 3).

We adopt the semi-supervised learning framework [8] that leads to iteratively updating rules as authority propagation between different types of objects.

$$\begin{aligned} \mathbf{F}_{\mathcal{P}} &= G_{\mathcal{P}}(\mathbf{F}_{\mathcal{P}},\ \mathbf{F}_{\mathcal{A}},\ \mathbf{F}_{\mathcal{V}}; \lambda_{\mathcal{A}},\ \lambda_{\mathcal{V}}), \\ \mathbf{F}_{\mathcal{A}} &= G_{\mathcal{A}}(\mathbf{F}_{\mathcal{P}}) \ \text{ and } \ \mathbf{F}_{\mathcal{V}} = G_{\mathcal{V}}(\mathbf{F}_{\mathcal{P}}). \end{aligned} \qquad (3)$$

We denote relative authority score matrices for paper, author and venue objects by $\mathbf{F}_{\mathcal{P}} \in \mathbb{R}^{K \times n}$, $\mathbf{F}_{\mathcal{A}} \in R^{K \times |\mathcal{A}|}$ and $\mathbf{F}_{\mathcal{V}} \in R^{K \times |\mathcal{V}|}$. Generally, in an interest group, relative importance of one type of object could be a combination of the relative importance from different types of objects [23].

In our solution, the propagation function $G_{\mathcal{P}}$ updates paper relative authority scores for all groups, following the intuition: High quality papers from an interest group are often published in highly reputed venues, written by authoritative authors and related to other high quality papers, from this group. Trade-off parameters $\lambda_{\mathcal{A}}$ and $\lambda_{\mathcal{V}}$ control the relative importance of paper-author and paper-venue relations. On the other hand, propagation functions $G_{\mathcal{A}}$ and $G_{\mathcal{V}}$ capture the rules: highly regarded authors often write good quality papers, and highly reputed venues often publish good quality papers. We include detailed formulae for the three propagation functions in Sec. 4.

3.4 Paper-Specif c Citation Recommendation

In practice, to derive interest group memberships for newly emerged queries, one has to re-estimate the model using these queries and training data, which is highly inefficient. Moreover, as the number of papers grows rapidly, the size of the model parameter space will increase a lot, making the model learning even more unscalable.

To tackle these two challenges, we leverage group memberships of the query's related attribute objects, *i.e.*, authors, terms and target venues, to approximately represent group membership of the query manuscript.

Intuitively, terms of the query manuscript describe its information needs based on paper content, whereas its author(s) and venue complement the content with research interests and other conceptual information. Specifically, we represent the query's group membership $\theta_q^{(k)}$ by weighted integration of group memberships of its attribute objects.

$$\theta_q^{(k)} = \sum_{\mathcal{X}\in\{\mathcal{A},\mathcal{V},\mathcal{T}\}} \sum_{x\in N_{\mathcal{X}}(q)} \frac{\theta_x^{(k)}}{|N_{\mathcal{X}}(q)|}. \quad (4)$$

We use $N_{\mathcal{X}}(q)$ to denote type $\mathcal{X}$ neighbors for query q, *i.e.*, its attribute objects. How likely a type $\mathcal{X}$ object is to belong to the k-th interest group is represented by $\theta_x^{(k)}$.

Paper-specific citation recommendation can be efficiently conducted for each query manuscript q by applying Eq. (1) along with definitions in Eqs. (2), (3) and (4).

4. MODEL LEARNING

This section introduces the learning algorithm for the proposed citation recommendation model in Eq. (1).

There are three sets of parameters in our model: group memberships for attribute objects; feature weights for interest groups; and object relative authority within each interest group. A straightforward way is to first conduct hard-clustering of attribute objects based on the network and then derive feature weights and relative authority for each cluster. Such a solution encounters several problems: (1) one object may have multiple citation interests, (2) mined object clusters may not properly capture distinct citation interests as we want, and (3) model performance may not be best optimized by the mined clusters.

In our solution, we formulate a joint optimization problem to estimate all model parameters simultaneously, which minimizes prediction error as well as graph regularization. By doing so, we can softly cluster attribute objects in terms of their citation interests and guarantee the learned model can yield good performance on training data.

We explain the joint optimization problem in Sec. 4.1 and design an efficient algorithm to solve it in Sec. 4.2 along with its computational complexity analysis in Sec. 4.3.

4.1 The Joint Optimization Problem

To learn model parameters, we use a citation network as training data, where value 1 indicates observed citation relationships while value 0 represents a mixture of negatives (should not cite) or unobserved (unaware and may cite in the future) examples. Traditional learning methods adopt classification [27] or learning-to-rank [1] objective functions and usually treat all 0s in training data as negative examples, which does not fit the real cases.

Without loss of generality, we adopts weighted square error [11] on the citation matrix as the loss function to measure the prediction performance, which is defined as follows:

$$\begin{aligned}\mathcal{L} &= \sum_{i,j=1}^{n} M_{ij}\Big(Y_{ij} - \sum_{k=1}^{K}\sum_{l=1}^{L}\theta_{p_i}^{(k)} w_k^{(l)} S_{jl}^{(i)} - \sum_{k=1}^{K}\theta_{p_i}^{(k)} F_{\mathcal{P},kj}\Big)^2,\\ &= \sum_{i=1}^{n}\big\|\mathbf{M}_i\odot\Big(\mathbf{Y}_i - \mathbf{R}_i\mathbf{P}(\mathbf{W}\mathbf{S}^{(i)T} + \mathbf{F}_{\mathcal{P}})\Big)\big\|_2^2.\end{aligned} \quad (5)$$

We define the weight indicator matrix $\mathbf{M}\in\mathbb{R}^{n\times n}$ for the citation matrix, where M_{ij} takes value 1 if the citation relationship between p_i and p_j is observed and 0 in other cases. By doing so, the model can focus on positive examples and get rid of noise in the 0 values. One can also define other loss functions to optimize with respect to precision or recall.

For ease of optimization, the loss can be further rewritten in a matrix form, where matrix $\mathbf{P}\in\mathbb{R}^{(|\mathcal{T}|+|\mathcal{A}|+|\mathcal{V}|)\times K}$ is group membership indicator for all attribute objects while $\mathbf{R}_i\in\mathbb{R}^{n\times((|\mathcal{T}|+|\mathcal{A}|+|\mathcal{V}|))}$ is the corresponding neighbor indicator matrix such that $\mathbf{R}_i\mathbf{P} = \sum_{\mathcal{X}\in\{\mathcal{A},\mathcal{V},\mathcal{T}\}}\sum_{x\in N_{\mathcal{X}}(p_i)}\frac{\theta_x^{(k)}}{|N_{\mathcal{X}}(p_i)|}$. Feature weights for each interest group are represented by each row of the matrix $\mathbf{W}\in\mathbb{R}^{K\times L}$, *i.e.*, $W_{kl} = w_k^{(l)}$. Hadamard product $\odot$ is used for the matrix element-wise product.

As discussed in Sec. 3.3, to achieve authority learning jointly, we adopt graph regularization to preserve consistency over the paper-author and paper-venue subgraphs, which takes the following form:

$$\begin{aligned}\mathcal{R} = &\frac{\lambda_{\mathcal{A}}}{2}\sum_{i=1}^{n}\sum_{j=1}^{|\mathcal{A}|} R_{ij}^{(\mathcal{A})}\Big\|\frac{\mathbf{F}_{\mathcal{P},i}}{D_{ii}^{(\mathcal{PA})}} - \frac{\mathbf{F}_{\mathcal{A},j}}{D_{jj}^{(\mathcal{AP})}}\Big\|_2^2\\ &+ \frac{\lambda_{\mathcal{V}}}{2}\sum_{i=1}^{n}\sum_{j=1}^{|\mathcal{V}|} R_{ij}^{(\mathcal{V})}\Big\|\frac{\mathbf{F}_{\mathcal{P},i}}{D_{ii}^{(\mathcal{PV})}} - \frac{\mathbf{F}_{\mathcal{V},j}}{D_{jj}^{(\mathcal{VP})}}\Big\|_2^2.\end{aligned} \quad (6)$$

The intuition behind the above two terms is natural: Linked objects in the heterogeneous network are more likely to share similar relative authority scores [13]. To reduce impact of node popularity, we apply a normalization technique on authority vectors, which helps suppress popular objects to keep them from dominating the authority propagation. Each element in the diagonal matrix $\mathbf{D}^{(\mathcal{PA})}\in\mathbb{R}^{n\times n}$ is the degree of paper p_i in subgraph $R^{(\mathcal{A})}$ while each element in $\mathbf{D}^{(\mathcal{AP})}\in\mathbb{R}^{|\mathcal{A}|\times|\mathcal{A}|}$ is the degree of author a_j in subgraph $R^{(\mathcal{A})}$. Similarly, we can define the two diagonal matrices for subgraph $R^{(\mathcal{V})}$.

Integrating the loss in Eq. (5) with graph regularization in Eq. (6), we formulate a joint optimization problem following the semi-supervised learning framework [8]:

$$\begin{aligned}\min_{\mathbf{P},\mathbf{W},\mathbf{F}_{\mathcal{P}},\mathbf{F}_{\mathcal{A}},\mathbf{F}_{\mathcal{V}}}\ &\frac{1}{2}\mathcal{L} + \mathcal{R} + \frac{c_p}{2}\|\mathbf{P}\|_F^2 + \frac{c_w}{2}\|\mathbf{W}\|_F^2\\ &\text{s.t. } \mathbf{P}\geq 0;\ \ \mathbf{W}\geq 0.\end{aligned} \quad (7)$$

To ensure stability of the obtained solution, Tikhonov regularizers are imposed on variables $\mathbf{P}$ and $\mathbf{W}$ [4], and we use c_p, $c_w > 0$ to control the strength of regularization. In addition, we impose non-negativity constraints to make sure learned group membership indicators and feature weights can provide semantic meaning as we want.

4.2 The ClusCite Algorithm

Directly solving Eq (7) is not easy because the objective function is non-convex. We develop an alternative minimization algorithm, called **ClusCite**, which alternatively optimizes the problem with respect to each variable.

The learning algorithm essentially accomplishes two things simultaneously and iteratively: Co-clustering of attribute objects and relevance features with respect to interest groups, and authority propagation between different objects. During an iteration, different learning components will mutually enhance each other (Fig. 3): Feature weights and relative authority can be more accurately derived with high quality interest groups while in turn they serve a good feature for learning high quality interest groups.

First, to learn group membership for attribute objects, we take the derivative of the objective function in Eq. (7) with respect to $\mathbf{P}$ while fixing other variables, and apply the Karush-Kuhn-Tucker complementary condition to impose the non-negativity constraint [7]. With some simple algebraic operations, a multiplicative update formula for $\mathbf{P}$ can be derived as follows:

$$P_{jk} \leftarrow P_{jk} \frac{\left[\sum_{i=1}^{n} \mathbf{R}_i^T \tilde{\mathbf{Y}}_i \mathbf{S}^{(i)} \mathbf{W}^T + \mathbf{L}_{\mathbf{P}1}^{+} + \mathbf{L}_{\mathbf{P}2}^{-}\right]_{jk}}{\left[\mathbf{L}_{\mathbf{P}0} + \mathbf{L}_{\mathbf{P}1}^{-} + \mathbf{L}_{\mathbf{P}2}^{+} + c_p \mathbf{P}\right]_{jk}}, \quad (8)$$

where matrices $\mathbf{L}_{\mathbf{P}0}$, $\mathbf{L}_{\mathbf{P}1}$ and $\mathbf{L}_{\mathbf{P}2}$ are defined as follows:

$$\begin{aligned}
\mathbf{L}_{\mathbf{P}0} &= \sum_{i=1}^{n} \mathbf{R}_i^T \mathbf{R}_i \mathbf{P} \mathbf{W} \tilde{\mathbf{S}}^{(i)T} \tilde{\mathbf{S}}^{(i)} \mathbf{W}^T; \; \mathbf{L}_{\mathbf{P}1} = \sum_{i=1}^{n} \mathbf{R}_i^T \tilde{\mathbf{Y}}_i \mathbf{F}_{\mathcal{P}}^T; \\
\mathbf{L}_{\mathbf{P}2} &= \sum_{i=1}^{n} \mathbf{R}_i^T \mathbf{R}_i \mathbf{P} \tilde{\mathbf{F}}_{\mathcal{P}}^{(i)} \tilde{\mathbf{F}}_{\mathcal{P}}^{(i)T} + \sum_{i=1}^{n} \mathbf{R}_i^T \mathbf{R}_i \mathbf{P} \mathbf{W} \tilde{\mathbf{S}}^{(i)T} \mathbf{F}_{\mathcal{P}}^T \\
&\quad + \sum_{i=1}^{n} \mathbf{R}_i^T \mathbf{R}_i \mathbf{P} \mathbf{F}_{\mathcal{P}} \tilde{\mathbf{S}}^{(i)} \mathbf{W}^T.
\end{aligned}$$

In order to preserve non-negativity throughout the update, $\mathbf{L}_{\mathbf{P}1}$ is decomposed into $\mathbf{L}_{\mathbf{P}1}^{-}$ and $\mathbf{L}_{\mathbf{P}1}^{+}$ where $A_{ij}^{+} = (|A_{ij}| + A_{ij})/2$ and $A_{ij}^{-} = (|A_{ij}| - A_{ij})/2$. Similarly, we decompose $\mathbf{L}_{\mathbf{P}2}$ into $\mathbf{L}_{\mathbf{P}2}^{-}$ and $\mathbf{L}_{\mathbf{P}2}^{+}$, but note that the decomposition is applied to each of the three components of $\mathbf{L}_{\mathbf{P}2}$, respectively. We denote the masked $\mathbf{Y}_i$ as $\tilde{\mathbf{Y}}_i$, which is the Hadamard product of $\mathbf{M}_i$ and $\mathbf{Y}_i$. Similarly, $\tilde{\mathbf{S}}^{(i)}$ and $\tilde{\mathbf{F}}_{\mathcal{P}}^{(i)}$ denote row-wise masked $\mathbf{S}^{(i)}$ and $\mathbf{F}_{\mathcal{P}}$ by $\mathbf{M}_i$.

Second, to learn feature weights for interest groups, the multiplicative update formula for $\mathbf{W}$ can be derived following a similar derivation as that of $\mathbf{P}$, taking the form:

$$W_{kl} \leftarrow W_{kl} \frac{\left[\sum_{i=1}^{n} \mathbf{P}^T \mathbf{R}_i^T \tilde{\mathbf{Y}}_i \mathbf{S}^{(i)} + \mathbf{L}_{\mathbf{W}}^{-}\right]_{kl}}{\left[\sum_{i=1}^{n} \mathbf{P}^T \mathbf{R}_i^T \mathbf{R}_i \mathbf{P} \mathbf{W} \tilde{\mathbf{S}}^{(i)T} \tilde{\mathbf{S}}^{(i)} + \mathbf{L}_{\mathbf{W}}^{+} + c_w \mathbf{W}\right]_{kl}}, \quad (9)$$

where we have $\mathbf{L}_{\mathbf{W}} = \sum_{i=1}^{n} \mathbf{P}^T \mathbf{R}_i^T \mathbf{R}_i \mathbf{P} \mathbf{F}_{\mathcal{P}} \tilde{\mathbf{S}}^{(i)}$.

Similarly, to preserve non-negativity of $\mathbf{W}$, $\mathbf{L}_{\mathbf{W}}$ is decomposed into $\mathbf{L}_{\mathbf{W}}^{+}$ and $\mathbf{L}_{\mathbf{W}}^{-}$, which can be computed same before.

Finally, we derive the authority propagation functions in Eq. (3) by optimizing the objective function in Eq. (7) with respect to the authority score matrices of papers, authors

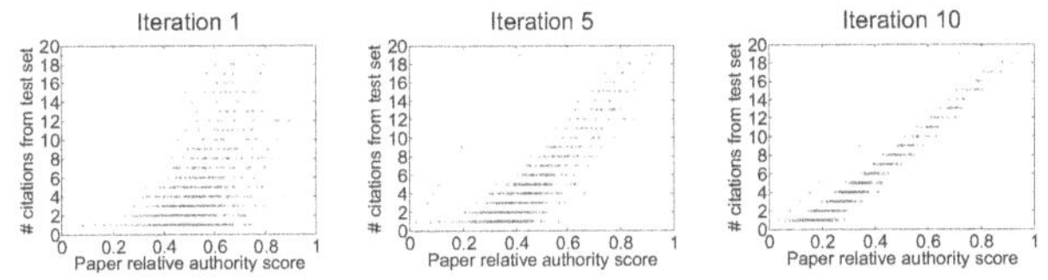

Figure 3: Correlation between paper relative authority and # ground truth citations, during different iterations.

and venues. Specifically, we take the derivative of the objective function with respect to $\mathbf{F}_{\mathcal{P}}$, $\mathbf{F}_{\mathcal{A}}$ and $\mathbf{F}_{\mathcal{V}}$, and follow traditional semi-supervised learning frameworks [8] to derive the update rules, which take the form:

$$\begin{aligned}
\mathbf{F}_{\mathcal{P}} &= G_{\mathcal{P}}(\mathbf{F}_{\mathcal{P}}, \mathbf{F}_{\mathcal{A}}, \mathbf{F}_{\mathcal{V}}; \lambda_{\mathcal{A}}, \lambda_{\mathcal{V}}) \\
&= \frac{1}{\lambda_{\mathcal{A}} + \lambda_{\mathcal{V}}} \left(\lambda_{\mathcal{A}} \mathbf{F}_{\mathcal{A}} \mathbf{S}_{\mathcal{A}}^T + \lambda_{\mathcal{V}} \mathbf{F}_{\mathcal{V}} \mathbf{S}_{\mathcal{V}}^T + \mathbf{L}_{\mathbf{F}_{\mathcal{P}}}\right) \quad (10) \\
\mathbf{F}_{\mathcal{A}} &= G_{\mathcal{A}}(\mathbf{F}_{\mathcal{P}}) = \mathbf{F}_{\mathcal{P}} \mathbf{S}_{\mathcal{A}}; \quad (11) \\
\mathbf{F}_{\mathcal{V}} &= G_{\mathcal{V}}(\mathbf{F}_{\mathcal{P}}) = \mathbf{F}_{\mathcal{P}} \mathbf{S}_{\mathcal{V}}. \quad (12)
\end{aligned}$$

where we have normalized adjacency matrices and the paper authority guidance terms defined as follows:

$$\begin{aligned}
\mathbf{S}_{\mathcal{A}} &= (\mathbf{D}^{(\mathcal{PA})})^{-1/2} \mathbf{R}^{(\mathcal{A})} (\mathbf{D}^{(\mathcal{AP})})^{-1/2} \\
\mathbf{S}_{\mathcal{V}} &= (\mathbf{D}^{(\mathcal{PV})})^{-1/2} \mathbf{R}^{(\mathcal{V})} (\mathbf{D}^{(\mathcal{VP})})^{-1/2} \\
\mathbf{L}_{\mathbf{F}_{\mathcal{P}}} &= \sum_{i=1}^{n} \mathbf{P}^T \mathbf{R}_i^T \left\{\tilde{\mathbf{Y}}_i - \mathbf{R}_i \mathbf{P} (\mathbf{W} \tilde{\mathbf{S}}^{(i)} + \tilde{\mathbf{F}}_{\mathcal{P}}^{(i)})\right\}
\end{aligned}$$

Using normalized adjacency matrices $\mathbf{S}_{\mathcal{A}}$ and $\mathbf{S}_{\mathcal{V}}$ to propagate relative authority can suppress popular objects in the network. In this way, they will not dominate the authority propagation. At each iteration, the guidance term $\mathbf{L}_{\mathbf{F}_{\mathcal{P}}}$ adjusts paper relative authority such that the model can fit known citations in a more accurate way.

Algorithm 1 summarizes the ClusCite algorithm. For convergence analysis, ClusCite essentially applies block coordinate descent on the optimization problem in Eq. (7). The proof procedure in [26] can be adopted to prove convergence for ClusCite (to the local minimum). For lack of space, we do not include it here.

Fig. 3 illustrates the quality change of estimated paper relative authority. Given an interest group, citations from test set to training papers serve as our ground truth for the relative authority of this group. We study the change of correlation between estimated relative authority and the ground truth, during different iterations. The initialization (global citation count) shows poor quality based on the correlation. As the algorithm iterates, we observe significant enhancement on the correlation, which justifies the effectiveness of the proposed authority propagation approach.

4.3 Computational Complexity Analysis

In this section, we analyze the computational complexity of the proposed ClusCite algorithm. Let d denote the total number of attribute objects and $|E|$ the total number of links in the heterogeneous network. First, it takes $O(K(n+d))$ time to initialize all the variables and $O(|E|L)$ time to pre-compute the constants in the update formula. In addition, we apply the fact that: $\sum_n \mathbf{A}_n \mathbf{X} \mathbf{B}_n = \mathbf{C}$ is equivalent to $(\sum_n \mathbf{B}_n^T \otimes \mathbf{A}_n) \operatorname{vec}(\mathbf{X}) = \operatorname{vec}(\mathbf{C})$, in our implementation so that we can avoid summations over all papers by pre-computing several matrix Kronecker products ($\otimes$). This step takes totally $O(L^2|E|^2/n + L|E|^3/n^2)$ time.

We then study the time complexity at each iteration of ClusCite with pre-computed matrices. Learning the group

Algorithm 1 Model Learning by ClusCite

Input: adjacency matrices $\{\mathbf{Y}, \mathbf{S}_{\mathcal{A}}, \mathbf{S}_{\mathcal{V}}\}$, neighbor indicator $\mathbf{R}$, mask matrix $\mathbf{M}$, meta path-based features $\{\mathbf{S}^{(i)}\}$, parameters $\{\lambda_{\mathcal{A}}, \lambda_{\mathcal{V}}, c_w, c_p\}$, number of interest groups K
Output: group membership $\mathbf{P}$, feature weights $\mathbf{W}$, relative authority $\{\mathbf{F}_{\mathcal{P}}, \mathbf{F}_{\mathcal{A}}, \mathbf{F}_{\mathcal{V}}\}$

```
Initialize P, W with positive values, and {F_P, F_A, F_V}
  with citation counts from training set
repeat
   Update group membership P by Eq. (8)
   Update feature weights W by Eq. (9)
   Compute paper relative authority F_P by Eq. (10)
   Compute author relative authority F_A by Eq. (11)
   Compute venue relative authority F_V by Eq. (12)
until objective in Eq. (7) converges
```

membership matrix $\mathbf{P}$ by Eq. (8) takes $O(L|E|^3/n^3+L^2|E|^2/n^2 + Kdn)$ time. Learning the feature weights $\mathbf{W}$ by Eq. (9) takes $O(L|E|^3/n^3 + L^2|E|^2/n^2 + Kdn)$ time. Updating all three relative authority matrices takes $O(L|E|^3/n^3 + |E| + Kdn)$ time. Let the number of iterations to compute ClusCite be T ($T \ll n$). The total time complexity is $O(L|E|^3/n^2 + L^2|E|^2/n + T|E| + TKdn)$. In our experiments, ClusCite usually converges within 50 iterations.

5. EXPERIMENTS

In this section, we evaluate the recommendation performance of the proposed method on real world data and conduct case studies to demonstrate its effectiveness.

5.1 Data Preparation

In the experiments, two different bibliographic datasets are used: the DBLP dataset[2] [25] and the PubMed dataset[3]. Statistics of the two constructed heterogeneous bibliographic networks are summarized in Table 3.

5.1.1 Heterogeneous Bibliographic Networks

Tang *et al.* [25] extracted citation information and built a DBLP citation dataset. We generated a subset of the aforementioned dataset by filtering out papers with incomplete meta information or less than 5 citations. Keywords and key phrases are extracted from paper titles and abstracts using the TF-IDF measure and the TextBlob noun phrase extractor[4]. The PubMed Central dataset is processed by the same method as described above to generate a subset[5]. We converted both datasets into heterogeneous bibliographic networks according to the network schema in Fig. 2.

5.1.2 Training and Evaluation Sets

We split the network to generate training, validation and testing subsets according to the paper publication year. We considered three time intervals T_0, T_1 and T_2. The subnetwork associated with papers in T_0 was used for model training. Papers in T_1 were then used as the validation set for parameter tuning and papers in T_2 were used as the test set for evaluations. Tables 4(a) and 4(b) summarize the statistics of the subsets. During evaluation, we consider citations from the evaluation sets (T_1 and T_2) to the training set (T_0) as the ground truth. Such an evaluation practice is more realistic because a citation recommendation system only knows the related attribute objects of a newly written manuscript. Also, it predicts future citations based on models which are learned from past citations.

Table 3: Statistics of two bibliographic networks.

Data sets	DBLP	PubMed
# papers	137,298	100,215
# authors	135,612	212,312
# venues	2,639	2,319
# terms	29,814	37,618
# relationships	~2.3M	~3.6M
Paper avg citations	5.16	17.55

Table 4: Training, validation and testing paper subsets from the DBLP and PubMed datasets

(a) The DBLP dataset

Subsets	Train	Validation	Test
Years	T_0=[1996, 2007]	T_1=[2008]	T_2=[2009, 2011]
# papers	62.23%	12.56%	25.21%

(b) The PubMed dataset

Subsets	Train	Validation	Test
Years	T_0=[1966, 2008]	T_1=[2009]	T_2=[2010, 2013]
# papers	64.50%	7.81%	27.69%

5.1.3 Feature Generation

In the experiments, without loss of generality, we selected 15 different meta-paths between paper objects including $(P-X-P)^y$, $P-X-P \to P$ and $P-X-P \leftarrow P$ where $X = \{A, V, T\}$ and $y = \{1, 2, 3\}$. Note that $(P-X-P)^2$ denotes $P-X-P-X-P$. We used two different structural similarity measures: PathSim [22] measure and the random-walk based measure [27]. We applied the random-walk based measure to all meta-paths and the PathSim measure to only symmetric meta-paths due to its requirement. This provides us with 24 meta-path based relevance features. Note that all the "cited" and "citing" relations in the meta-paths were only measured between papers in the training set.

5.2 Experimental Settings

We provide details on the experimental settings for conducting evaluations on all the methods.

5.2.1 Compared Methods

We compared the proposed method (ClusCite) with its variation which considered only relevance features (ClusCite-Rel). Several widely deployed or state-of-the-art citation recommendation approaches were also implemented, including content-based methods, link-based methods and hybrid methods. All compared methods were first tuned on validation set to pick the tuning parameters.

BM25: BM25 is a text-based method, which computes similarity scores using only text information.

PopRank [19]: PopRank is a link-based method which derives an object's importance based on authority propagation in the heterogeneous bibliographic network.

TopicSim: We measure similarity between papers with topic modeling technique (LDA) and return the papers with the most similar topic distribution compared with the query.

Link-PLSA-LDA [18]: Link-PLSA-LDA[6] is a hybrid method that leverages both document text and citation links

[2] `http://arnetminer.org/DBLP_Citation`
[3] `http://www.ncbi.nlm.nih.gov/pmc/`
[4] `http://textblob.readthedocs.org/en/latest/`
[5] `https://github.com/shanzhenren2/PubMed_subset`
[6] `https://sites.google.com/site/rameshnallapati/software`

Table 5: Recommendation performance comparisons on DBLP and PubMed datasets in terms of Precision, Recall and MRR. We set the number of interest groups to be 200 ($K = 200$) for ClusCite and ClusCite-Rel.

Method	DBLP					PubMed				
	P@10	P@20	R@20	R@50	MRR	P@10	P@20	R@20	R@50	MRR
BM25	0.1260	0.0902	0.1431	0.2146	0.4107	0.1847	0.1349	0.1754	0.2470	0.4971
PopRank	0.0112	0.0098	0.0155	0.0308	0.0451	0.0438	0.0314	0.0402	0.0814	0.2012
TopicSim	0.0328	0.0273	0.0432	0.0825	0.1161	0.0761	0.0685	0.0855	0.1516	0.3254
Link-PLSA-LDA	0.1023	0.0893	0.1295	0.1823	0.3748	0.1439	0.1002	0.1589	0.2015	0.4079
L2-LR	0.2274	0.1677	0.2471	0.3547	0.4866	0.2527	0.1959	0.2504	0.3981	0.5308
RankSVM	0.2372	0.1799	0.2733	0.3621	0.4989	0.2534	0.1954	0.2499	0.382	0.5187
MixFea	0.2261	0.1689	0.2473	0.3636	0.5002	0.2699	0.2025	0.2519	0.4021	0.5041
ClusCite-Rel	0.2402	0.1872	0.2856	0.4015	0.5156	0.2786	0.2221	0.2753	0.4305	0.5524
ClusCite	**0.2429**	**0.1958**	**0.2993**	**0.4279**	**0.5481**	**0.3019**	**0.2434**	**0.3129**	**0.4587**	**0.5787**

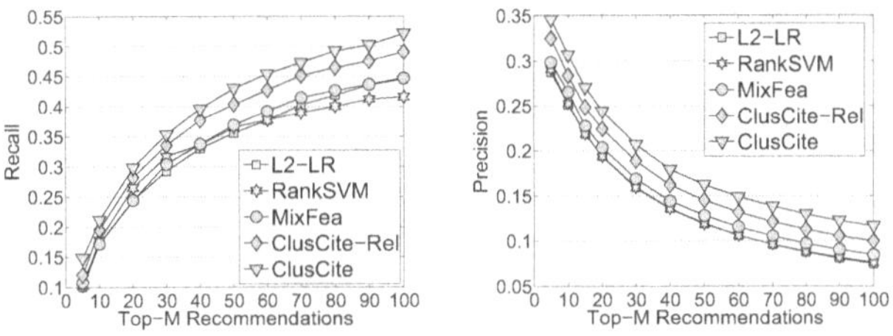

(a) Recall on DBLP (b) Precision on PubMed

Figure 4: Performance comparisons measured by Recall and Precision at different positions.

when modeling topics. The candidates were ranked in terms of the conditional probability of citations from the query manuscript to the candidate papers.

L2-LR [27]: This technique changes the problem into classification with a linearly weighted combination of meta path-based relevance features. Positive examples are observed citations and negative examples are randomly sampled paper pairs.

RankSVM [14]: RankSVM considers the preference between paper-paper relationships, instead of assuming all unobserved relationships are negative examples.

MixFea: the candidates were ranked by a linear combination of meta path-based relevance features, topic distributions and PopRank's features. We used RankSVM to estimate feature weights.

ClusCite: candidates were ranked based on the scores computed by Eq. (1). We set the number of interest groups $K = 200$, $c_p = 10^{-6}$, $c_w = 10^{-7}$, $\lambda_{\mathcal{A}} = \lambda_{\mathcal{V}} = 0.3$ after tuning them on validation sets (Fig. 5 and Sec. 5.6).

ClusCite-Rel: candidates were ranked based on the proposed model with only meta path-based relevance features, *i.e.*, by dropping $\mathbf{F}_{\mathcal{P}}$ in Eq. (1). It used the same settings on K, c_p and c_w as those of ClusCite.

5.2.2 Evaluation Metrics

We employed Precision and Recall at position M (P@M and R@M) as the evaluation metrics. Recall@M is defined as the percentage of original citing papers that appear in the top-M recommended list. A high recall with a lower M indicates a better citation recommendation system. Precision@M was also used to measure the effectiveness of the recommendation system by checking whether the original citing papers were ranked high for the query manuscript.

Furthermore, it is desirable that ground truth papers should appear earlier in the top-M recommended list. Therefore, Mean Reciprocal Rank (MRR) was also employed over the target papers, which is defined as $\mathrm{MRR} = \frac{1}{|\mathcal{Q}_T|}\sum_{q\in\mathcal{Q}_T}\frac{1}{\mathrm{rank}(q)}$, where $\mathcal{Q}_T$ is the testing set and rank(q) denotes the rank of its first ground truth paper (positive example).

5.3 Performance Comparison

We now compare the proposed recommendation model (ClusCite) with its variation (ClusCite-Rel) and other baselines in terms of the citation recommendation performance.

First, we compare the proposed methods with seven different baselines using Precision@10, 20, Recall@20, 50 and MRR. Table 5 summarizes the comparison results on both DBLP and PubMed datasets. Overall, the proposed ClusCite method and its variation ClusCite-Rel outperform other methods on all metrics. In particular, ClusCite obtains a 17.68% improvement in Recall@50 and 9.57% improvement in MRR compared to the best baseline on the DBLP dataset. On the PubMed dataset, it improves Recall@20 by 20.19% and MRR by 14.79% compared to MixFea. Even though MixFea has incorporated a rich set of features, ClusCite obtained superior performance because it not only explores citation behaviors by learning group-based feature weights over different relation semantics, but also integrates relative paper authority to augment the recommendation process.

The ClusCite-Rel method outperforms all other baselines and improves Recall@50 by 10.42% compared to the best baseline, MixFea, on the DBLP dataset. Comparing ClusCite-Rel with methods such as RankSVM and L2-LR, one can clearly notice the performance gain from distinguishing relevance feature weights for different interest groups. ClusCite always outperforms ClusCite-Rel, improving MRR by 12.21% and Recall@50 by 6.57% on the DBLP dataset. The enhancement mainly comes from utilizing paper relative authority with respect to different interest groups. Also, the derived relative authority can assist recommendation since it is jointly learned through the unified optimization.

MixFea is another method that incorporates paper authority information, but it does not distinguish paper authority in different interest groups. However, it still obtained better results than RankSVM and L2-LR did in most cases. This demonstrates the effectiveness of paper authority information in the citation recommendation process. Furthermore, poor performance of PopRank shows that using only global authority is not sufficient to conduct good citation recommendation. Different from the conclusions in [10], We found that Link-PLSA-LDA and TopicSim can only achieve 0.0893 and 0.0273 for Precision@20 (compared to 0.1677 with L2-LR), respectively. Also, BM25 outperformed both of the topic-based methods in all cases. This shows that topic-based features are not good enough for finding relevant papers, since the features may be of coarse granularity.

For more comprehensive comparisons, we computed the precision and recall at different positions (5 to 100) to study the trends in performance changes. Due to space limits, Fig. 4 only shows the comparison results of Recall on DBLP and comparison results of Precision on PubMed, respec-

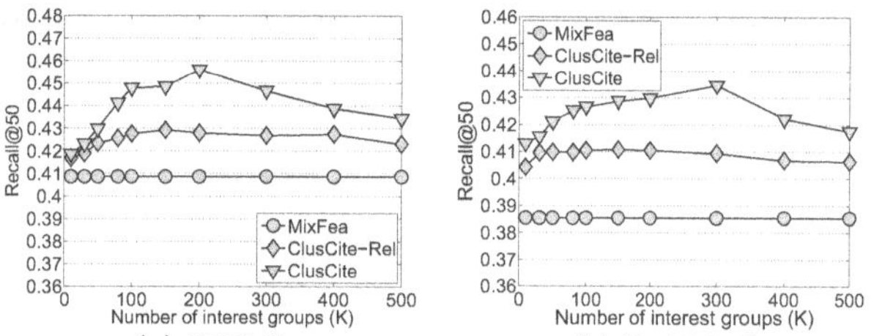

(a) DBLP (b) PubMed

Figure 5: Performance change (Recall@50) on validation sets, with respect to number of interest groups (K) (MixFea as baseline).

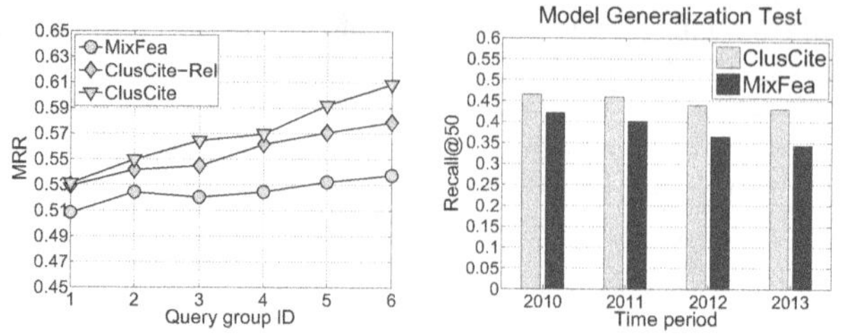

(a) # attribute objects (b) time periods of queries

Figure 6: Performance change with number of attribute objects and time periods of query papers.

tively. For both precision and recall, the performance gap between ClusCite and ClusCite-Rel gets slightly larger as more candidates are returned. This indicates that authority information played a critical role in identifying papers with moderate relevance to the query (people may cite relevant papers even though they are new and less reputed, but they prefer authoritative ones among the less relevant papers).

5.4 Performance Analysis

In this section, we analyze the performance of ClusCite, ClusCite-Rel and MixFea in different recommendation scenarios. We ran the following experiments on both datasets and observed similar performance changes in both. However, in the interest of brevity, we only present results from the PubMed dataset for some analyses.

First, we studied performance change with respect to the number of interest groups for ClusCite and ClusCite-Rel. As presented in Fig. 5(a) and 5(b), although not very sensitive to K, these two methods did perform differently when the number of groups were varied. Also, the performance changes were more notable at smaller K, *i.e.*$K < 100$. This indicates that the proposed methods cannot determine citation behavior well when the number of groups is small. On the other hand, a large K (*e.g.*$K > 300$) caused a performance drop due to the insufficiency of training data in deriving interest groups. We found that ClusCite achieved the best performance when the number of groups was $K = 200$ while ClusCite-Rel obtained the best performance with a large number $K = 300$. This shows that biomedical domain has more diverse citation behavior patterns.

In ClusCite and ClusCite-Rel, the paper-specific recommendation makes a prediction for a query based on its attribute objects. Therefore, we want to examine their performance change by studying the correlation between recommendations of the two proposed methods and the number of attribute objects in the query manuscript. We divided the test set into 6 groups with respect to the number of attribute objects. The resulting query groups had an average number of attribute objects ranging from 6.46 (group 1) to 18.98 (group 6). The results by MRR are summarized in Fig. 6(a). Overall, ClusCite outperformed ClusCite-Rel, and both outperformed MixFea. The proposed methods achieved a larger performance improvement when the number of attribute objects increased (*e.g.*from 0.02 in group 1 to 0.08 in group 6) while the performance of MixFea seemed less sensitive between different query groups. This demonstrates that with more attribute objects provided by the query manuscript, the proposed method can make better paper-specific recommendations because richer attribute objects provide better estimation on group membership of the query manuscript.

Finally, we tested the model generalization by evaluating performance on test papers from different time periods. We generated four test subsets using papers in T_2 of the PubMed dataset where each subset consists of papers from one specific year. By applying the methods on each subset, we want to study how the model, learned from papers in T_0, can predict citations for future papers. The study results are shown in Fig. 6(b). Overall, the performance of both methods dropped when recommending for newer papers but ClusCite always outperformed MixFea. Recall@50 of MixFea decreased by 16.42% from year 2010 to 2013 while Recall@50 of ClusCite dropped only about 7.72%, which indicates the better generalization of the proposed method.

5.5 Case Studies

To demonstrate the effectiveness of mining hidden interest groups, we conduct two sets of case studies on the DBLP dataset to show citation behavioral patterns (Fig. 7) and relative authority ranking of authors and venues, (Table 6) within an example of mined interest groups.

First, we show that the learned interest groups have distinct citation behavioral patterns and can satisfy different information needs. We apply K-means clustering on all objects' group membership indicators and derive their most likely groups (we set $K = 40$). Two representative groups were picked where group A contained 8,345 papers and 208 venues and group B contained 10,922 papers and 291 venues. We found that major venues in group A were database venues (*e.g.*, "SIGMOD" and "VLDB") and those in group B were computer vision venues (*e.g.*, "TPAMI" and "IJCV"). To study how the four venues were cited by papers in the two interest groups, we calculated the average number of citations from papers in group A and B to the four venues, respectively. The results are in Fig. 7(a). One can see that papers in group A prefer to cite database papers while those in group B cite computer vision papers more frequently.

Following a similar procedure, we selected two more representative groups and studied their papers' citations on four different authors: data mining researchers "Pillip S. Yu" and "Rakesh Agrawal" from group A and programming language researchers "Thomas W. Reps" and "Ken Kenndedy" from group B. The average number of citations for these four authors are summarized in Fig. 7(b). Similar behavioral patterns were observed that papers in group A cite data mining researchers more frequently while papers in group B prefer programming language researchers. The derived interest groups show two different behavioral patterns on citations, and justify that they can capture different citation interests.

Second, we study the effectiveness of the relative authority propagation process in the proposed ClusCite algorithm. By setting the number of interest groups as $K = 40$, we apply ClusCite on the training data and obtain relative authority scores for authors ($\mathbf{F}_\mathcal{A}$) and venues ($\mathbf{F}_\mathcal{V}$). We can list the top ranked objects based on their relative authority scores within different interest groups. Table 6 shows the ranked lists for two example interest groups. One can easily identify

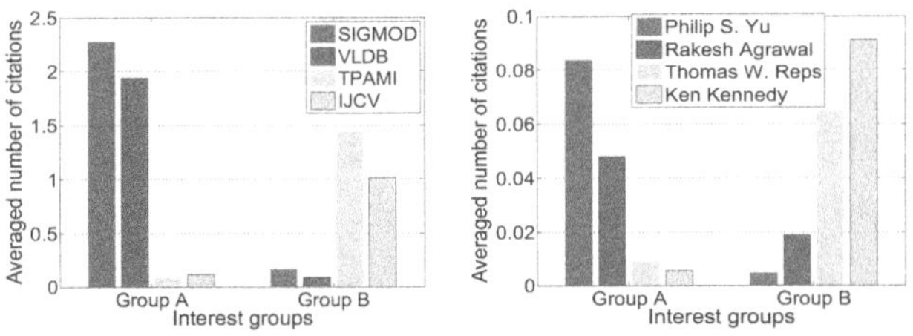

(a) Citations on venues (b) Citations on authors

Figure 7: Case studies on citation behavioral patterns among different interest groups. We show the averaged number of citations on four venues and four authors, for two groups of papers.

the research areas that these two interest groups belong to: Group I is on database and information system while Group II is on computer vision and multimedia. There is a high degree of consensus between the ranking list generated by ClusCite and the top venues and reputed authors in each research area. This demonstrates that the relative authority propagation can generate meaningful authority scores with respect to different interest groups.

Table 6: Top-5 authority venues and authors from two example interest groups derived by ClusCite.

Rank	Venue		Author	
	Group I (database and information system)			
1	VLDB	0.0763	Hector Garcia-Molina	0.0202
2	SIGMOD	0.0653	Christos Faloutsos	0.0187
3	TKDE	0.0651	Elisa Bertino	0.0180
4	CIKM	0.0590	Dan Suciu	0.0179
5	SIGKDD	0.0488	H. V. Jagadish	0.0178
	Group II (computer vision and multimedia)			
1	TPAMI	0.0733	Richard Szeliski	0.0139
2	ACM MM	0.0533	Jitendra Malik	0.0122
3	ICCV	0.0403	Luc Van Gool	0.0121
4	CVPR	0.0401	Andrew Blake	0.0117
5	ECCV	0.0393	Alex Pentland	0.0114

5.6 Parameter Study

In this section, we study the impact of four parameters: c_p and c_w in ClusCite and ClusCite-Rel, and $\lambda_{\mathcal{A}}$ and $\lambda_{\mathcal{V}}$ in ClusCite, on validation sets. The number of interest groups are set as $K = 200$. MixFea, the best baseline, is the only one used here. For conciseness, only DBLP dataset results are presented in Fig. 8, where the x-axes are in log scale.

In the joint optimization problem in Eq. (7), c_p and c_w control the strength of Tikhonov regularizers on group membership indicators and relevance feature weights. A larger value imposes a higher penalty on the magnitude of variable values. We vary one of these two parameters while fixing the other as zero. For ClusCite, we set $\lambda_{\mathcal{A}} = \lambda_{\mathcal{V}} = 0.1$. Both ClusCite and ClusCite-Rel show robust performance over a large range of c_w (Fig. 8(a)) and achieve significant improvement compared to MixFea. We observe a similar trend when varying c_w (Fig. 8(b)) but ClusCite performs slightly better when $c_w = 10^{-7}$. Such changes are because $\mathbf{W}$ plays a role in balancing relevance and authority scores for the ClusCite model while scaling of $\mathbf{P}$ will not affect the ranking results.

ClusCite has two more parameters $\lambda_{\mathcal{A}}$ and $\lambda_{\mathcal{V}}$, which control relative importance of authority information from authors and venues, respectively. By setting one to zero and varying the other, we aim to see a performance change when only one information source is utilized in the authority propagation process. Using ClusCite-Rel and MixFea as baselines, one can see that both information sources help improve the performance of ClusCite significantly. ClusCite achieves the best performance when $\lambda_{\mathcal{A}} = 0.3$ (Fig. 8(c)) and $\lambda_{\mathcal{V}} = 0.3$ (Fig. 8(d)). In particular, we found that applying venue information to authority propagation led to better results.

6. RELATED WORK

6.1 Citation Recommendation

Existing work leverages different kinds of information to recommend citations for a query manuscript, from paper content, known citations to authors and venues of a paper.

Traditional keyword-based approaches have difficulty in finding conceptually similar work due to the ambiguity of short-text queries [20, 5]. One can notice that the performance of BM25 in our experiments is much worse than those of the hybrid methods like L2-LR. Using citation local contexts, *i.e.*, text surrounding the citation positions, context-based methods can capture diverse information needs more precisely [24, 10, 12]. However, the local context might be irrelevant to the ideas of cited paper. Moreover, picking the size of each context window is non-trivial. Also, it will be interesting to study different intents and purposes behind the citation contexts to leverage them more accurately.

On the other hand, known citations can be used to measure paper structural similarity. Traditional link prediction techniques [16, 2] and collaborative filtering techniques [11] encounter cold-start issue since in practice little or no citations are provided for query manuscript. Heterogenous link prediction techniques [17, 6] tackle this issue by taking advantages of multiple types of relationships between papers, authors and venues. However, these link-based methods cannot achieve satisfactory results without considering content-based features. Therefore, recent studies start integrating both content and structure information to augment the performance [20]. Latent topic models are used to predict citations for new documents by modeling citation links jointly[18, 24]. However, topical similarity may be too coarse to serve as good evidence for citation prediction and experimental results on TopicSim and Link-PLSA-LDA show their limited performance. Yu *et al.* [27] derive a rich set of meta-path based features from heterogeneous bibliographic networks in modeling citation recommendation, which can capture text-based similarity, conceptual relevance as well as several types of social relatedness.

Aforementioned methods consider only paper relevance but ignore another critical information for citation recommendation, namely the importance and quality of target papers [20]. Bethard and Jurafsky [5] built a literature search system by learning a linearly weighted model over both relevance and authority features.

Our work considers diverse citation interests by imposing different feature patternsaccording to the interest groups of each query (see comparisons between ClusCite-Rel and L2-LR [27]). Yu *et al.* [28] study personalized entity recommendation, which shares the similar idea of building local retrieval model for each cluster specifically. Our work is also related to [5] in terms of incorporating paper authority, but we derive paper relative authority within each group specifically (see comparisons between ClusCite and MixFea).

6.2 Authority Ranking on Graphs

Ranking objects on graphs by their importance and popularity has been extensively studied [15, 19] and combined with keyword search system [3]. In particular, Sun and

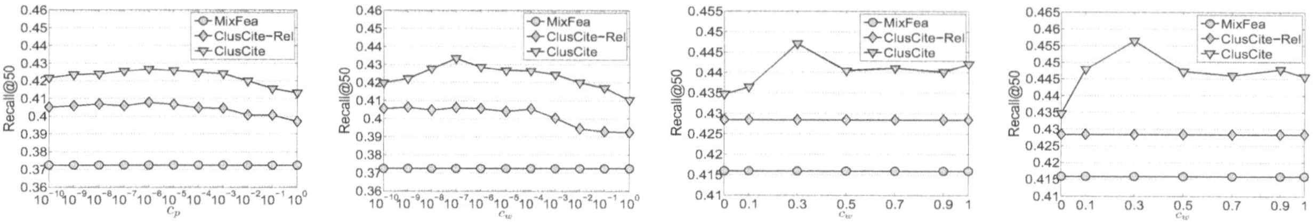

(a) Varying c_p (b) Varying c_w (c) Varing $\lambda_{\mathcal{A}}$ (d) Varing $\lambda_{\mathcal{V}}$

Figure 8: Performance change (Recall@50) of ClusCite-Rel and ClusCite on DBLP validation set when varying parameters c_p and c_w for both methods, and $\lambda_{\mathcal{A}}$ and $\lambda_{\mathcal{V}}$ for ClusCite. MixFea is used as a baseline.

Giles [21] consider both citation impacts as well as venue influence when propagating paper authority scores in bibliographic networks. With ranking supervision, graph-based semi-supervised ranking frameworks can be further applied[1, 8]. However, these methods do not capture the bias of authority when topics or interests of the query change. (see comparison between PopRank [19] and ClusCite)

Haveliwala [9] personalizes the PageRank algorithm by considering query topics to derive query-specific authority score. Similar ideas were explored when performing clustering [23] and classification [13] in heterogeneous information networks, where object relative authority served as features for representing classes. To our best knowledge, the proposed method is the first to learn object relative authority through optimizing the citation recommendation model, based on multiple types of relationships in heterogeneous bibliographic networks.

7. CONCLUSION AND FUTURE WORK

In this paper, we study citation recommendation in the context of heterogeneous bibliographic networks and propose a novel cluster-based citation recommendation framework to satisfy a user's diverse citation intents. By organizing paper citations into interest groups, the proposed method is able to determine the significance of different structural relevance features for each group, and derive paper's relative authority within each group. In this way, we can make paper-specific recommendations to capture each query's diverse information needs. We formulate a joint optimization problem to learn model parameters by taking advantage of multiple relationships in the network, and develop an efficient algorithm to solve it. Performance evaluation results show a significant improvement compared to state-of-the-art methods and the case studies demonstrate the effectiveness of the proposed method.

Interesting future work includes extending the proposed clustering-based recommendation framework for Web search tasks or entity recommendation so that one can capture local relevance and authority jointly. In addition, there is potential to adjust the network structure for each interest group so that relative authority can more accurately propagate within the corresponding sub-networks. Finally, one can integrate object authority information with each meta path instance to design novel features for citation recommendation.

8. ACKNOWLEDGEMENTS

The work was supported in part by the U.S. Army Research Laboratory under Cooperative Agreement No. W911NF-09-2-0053 (NS-CTA), the U.S. Army Research Office under Cooperative Agreement No. W911NF-13-1-0193, U.S. National Science Foundation grants CNS-0931975, IIS-1017362, IIS-1320617, IIS-1354329, NASA NRA-NNH10ZDA001N, DTRA, and MIAS, a DHS-IDS Center for Multimodal Information Access and Synthesis at UIUC.

9. REFERENCES

[1] A. Agarwal, S. Chakrabarti, and S. Aggarwal. Learning to rank networked entities. In *SIGKDD*, 2006.

[2] L. Backstrom and J. Leskovec. Supervised random walks: predicting and recommending links in social networks. In *WSDM*, 2011.

[3] A. Balmin, V. Hristidis, and Y. Papakonstantinou. ObjectRank: Authority-based keyword search in databases. In *VLDB*, 2004.

[4] M. Belkin, P. Niyogi, and V. Sindhwani. Manifold regularization: A geometric framework for learning from labeled and unlabeled examples. *JMLR*, 7:2399–2434, 2006.

[5] S. Bethard and D. Jurafsky. Who should I cite: learning literature search models from citation behavior. In *CIKM*, 2010.

[6] Y. Dong, J. Tang, S. Wu, J. Tian, N. V. Chawla, J. Rao, and H. Cao. Link prediction and recommendation across heterogeneous social networks. In *ICDM*, 2012.

[7] Q. Gu, J. Zhou, and C. Ding. Collaborative filtering: Weighted nonnegative matrix factorization incorporating user and item graphs. In *SDM*, 2010.

[8] Z. Guan, J. Bu, Q. Mei, C. Chen, and C. Wang. Personalized tag recommendation using graph-based ranking on multi-type interrelated objects. In *SIGIR*, 2009.

[9] T. H. Haveliwala. Topic-sensitive pagerank. In *WWW*, 2002.

[10] Q. He, J. Pei, D. Kifer, P. Mitra, and L. Giles. Context-aware citation recommendation. In *WWW*, 2010.

[11] Y. Hu, Y. Koren, and C. Volinsky. Collaborative filtering for implicit feedback datasets. In *ICDM*, 2008.

[12] W. Huang, S. Kataria, C. Caragea, P. Mitra, C. L. Giles, and L. Rokach. Recommending citations: translating papers into references. In *CIKM*, 2012.

[13] M. Ji, J. Han, and M. Danilevsky. Ranking-based classification of heterogeneous information networks. In *SIGKDD*, 2011.

[14] T. Joachims. Optimizing search engines using clickthrough data. In *SIGKDD*, 2002.

[15] J. M. Kleinberg. Authoritative sources in a hyperlinked environment. *Journal of the ACM*, 46(5):604–632, 1999.

[16] D. Liben-Nowell and J. Kleinberg. The link prediction problem for social networks. In *CIKM*, 2003.

[17] Z. Lu, B. Savas, W. Tang, and I. S. Dhillon. Supervised link prediction using multiple sources. In *ICDM*, 2010.

[18] R. M. Nallapati, A. Ahmed, E. P. Xing, and W. W. Cohen. Joint latent topic models for text and citations. In *SIGKDD*, 2008.

[19] Z. Nie, Y. Zhang, J.-R. Wen, and W.-Y. Ma. Object-level ranking: bringing order to web objects. In *WWW*, 2005.

[20] T. Strohman, W. B. Croft, and D. Jensen. Recommending citations for academic papers. In *SIGIR*, 2007.

[21] Y. Sun and C. L. Giles. Popularity weighted ranking for academic digital libraries. In *ECIR*. 2007.

[22] Y. Sun, J. Han, X. Yan, S. P. Yu, and T. Wu. PathSim: Meta Path-Based Top-K Similarity Search in Heterogeneous Information Networks. In *VLDB*, 2011.

[23] Y. Sun, Y. Yu, and J. Han. Ranking-based clustering of heterogeneous information networks with star network schema. In *SIGKDD*, 2009.

[24] J. Tang and J. Zhang. A discriminative approach to topic-based citation recommendation. In *PAKDD*. 2009.

[25] J. Tang, J. Zhang, L. Yao, J. Li, L. Zhang, and Z. Su. Arnetminer: extraction and mining of academic social networks. In *SIGKDD*, 2008.

[26] P. Tseng. Convergence of a block coordinate descent method for nondifferentiable minimization. *Journal of optimization theory and applications*, 109(3):475–494, 2001.

[27] X. Yu, Q. Gu, M. Zhou, and J. Han. Citation prediction in heterogeneous bibliographic networks. In *SDM*, 2012.

[28] X. Yu, X. Ren, Y. Sun, Q. Gu, B. Sturt, U. Khandelwal, B. Norick, and J. Han. Personalized entity recommendation: A heterogeneous information network approach. In *WSDM*, 2014.

GeoMF: Joint Geographical Modeling and Matrix Factorization for Point-of-Interest Recommendation

Defu Lian[†‡], Cong Zhao[†], Xing Xie[‡], Guangzhong Sun[†], Enhong Chen[†], Yong Rui[‡]
[†]University of Science and Technology of China
[‡]Microsoft Research, Beijing, China
[†]{liandefu,congzhao}@mail.ustc.edu.cn,
[‡]{xingx,yongrui}@microsoft.com, [†]{gzsun,cheneh}@ustc.edu.cn

ABSTRACT

Point-of-Interest (POI) recommendation has become an important means to help people discover attractive locations. However, extreme sparsity of user-POI matrices creates a severe challenge. To cope with this challenge, viewing mobility records on location-based social networks (LBSNs) as implicit feedback for POI recommendation, we first propose to exploit weighted matrix factorization for this task since it usually serves collaborative filtering with implicit feedback better. Besides, researchers have recently discovered a spatial clustering phenomenon in human mobility behavior on the LBSNs, i.e., individual visiting locations tend to cluster together, and also demonstrated its effectiveness in POI recommendation, thus we incorporate it into the factorization model. Particularly, we augment users' and POIs' latent factors in the factorization model with activity area vectors of users and influence area vectors of POIs, respectively. Based on such an augmented model, we not only capture the spatial clustering phenomenon in terms of two-dimensional kernel density estimation, but we also explain why the introduction of such a phenomenon into matrix factorization helps to deal with the challenge from matrix sparsity. We then evaluate the proposed algorithm on a large-scale LBSN dataset. The results indicate that weighted matrix factorization is superior to other forms of factorization models and that incorporating the spatial clustering phenomenon into matrix factorization improves recommendation performance.

Categories and Subject Descriptors

H.2.8 [**Database Management**]: Database Applications—*data mining*; H.3.3 [**Information Storage and Retrieval**]: Information Search and Retrieval—*clustering, information filtering*

Keywords

Weighted Matrix Factorization; Location Recommendation; Kernel Density Estimation; Location-based Social Network

KDD'14, August 24–27, 2014, New York, NY, USA.
Copyright 2014 ACM 978-1-4503-2956-9/14/08 ...$15.00.
http://dx.doi.org/10.1145/2623330.2623638 .

1. INTRODUCTION

With the popularity of smart mobile devices and the diversification of positioning technologies, it has become easier for people to acquire real-time information regarding their locations. This development has triggered the advent of location-based social networks (LBSNs), such as Foursquare, Jiepang, Facebook Place and so on. This emergence has not only led to location-based socializing becoming a new form of social interaction, but has also helped people speed up familiarization of the surroundings. To achieve the latter goal, Point-of-Interest (POI) recommendation has become one important means.

Recently, POI recommendation has become a popular research topic due to easy access of large-scale mobility records and inclusion of social network information. One of the most important problems in POI recommendation is how to deal with a severe challenge stemming from extreme sparsity of user-POI matrices. To this end, viewing mobility records on the LBSNs, i.e., check-ins, as implicit feedback for POI recommendation, we first propose to exploit weighted matrix factorization for this task because it usually serves collaborative filtering with implicit feedback better than the other approaches [8, 18]. In this algorithm, users and POIs are mapped onto a joint latent space by approximating a user-POI 0/1 rating matrix (each 0/1 in the matrix indicates whether a user has checked in at a POI) in a weighted way, such that a user's preference for a POI is modeled as inner product between them in that space. The reasons that check-ins can be considered as implicit feedback for POI recommendation lies in the following three aspects: first, check-in datasets just include the locations where users have been and therefore they likely prefer. In other words, they just provides *positive* examples. Second, the visit frequencies of a user to her visiting locations reflect her confidences of being fond of them. The visiting patterns of higher frequency indicate the preferences of higher confidence. Third, locations where a user has never visited are either really unattractive or undiscovered but potentially appealing. However, these two cases are usually difficult to differentiate from each other if no extra information is provided.

Fortunately, due to inclusion of geographical information of POIs, some researchers have recently discovered a spatial clustering phenomenon [21] in human mobility behavior on the LBSNs, i.e., individual visiting locations tend to cluster together, and leveraged it to assist POI recommendation. For example, Ye et al. [24] characterized it by a power law distribution on the distance between any pair of visited locations. Instead of making the power law distributed assumption, Zhang et al. [26] directly performed kernel density estimation to this distribution. To avoid the cost in computing the distance between paired locations, in [2, 12], the authors modeled the spatial clustering phenomenon in terms of geo-clustering and tried to estimate individual spatial distribution. Actually, by modeling the spatial clustering phenomenon, it becomes possible to partially distinguish unattractive locations from undiscovered but potentially appealing ones. In particular, it is much more likely that unvisited POIs near a frequently visited location are really unattractive and this likelihood depends on the visit frequency to that location. This is because if a user often visits a certain POI but has never patronized surrounding POIs, it is highly unlikely for her to visit them in the future. Therefore, weighted matrix factorization will benefit from the introduction of such a phenomenon.

For the sake of joint geographical modeling and matrix factorization, we augment users' and POIs' latent factors of the factorization model with non-negative activity area vectors of users and non-negative influence area vectors of POIs, as shown in Figure 1. These augmenting vectors consist of a set of grids with the same fixed size. Each entry in a user's activity area vector represents the possibility of this user showing up in the corresponding grid while each entry in a POI's influence vector indicates the degree of influence that this POI has on the corresponding grid. The reason for such an explicit augmentation with geographical information is that there is still no evidence showing that the latent space has included geographical information (It is easy for other information, e.g., POI categories, to be incorporated into this framework in a similar manner). In this way, a user's preference for a POI is modeled as inner product between them in the augmented space and thus includes both the interest of the user from the latent space and her preference for the location of the POI. If a user's preference for the location of a POI is non-zero, the activity areas of the user intersect with the influence areas of the POI so that this POI is reachable from the activity areas of the user. In other words, it is possible for the attractiveness of the POI to cross the gap arising from the distance.

More importantly, it is possible to exploit such a representation of users' preference to partially distinguish unattractive locations from undiscovered ones. Let's go back to the previous example, where a user often visited a POI i, but has never patronized POIs nearby. Using such a representation, the user has similar location preference for the POIs around i. However, since this user has never visited nearby POIs, from the perspective of approximation, such a representation requires inner product in the latent space to offset the location preference. Therefore, we have introduced more potentially unattractive locations (*negative* examples) into matrix factorization. Thus, it explains why the incorporation of spatial clustering phenomenon into the factorization model can help to deal with the challenge stemming from the user-POI matrix sparsity.

When only considering augmenting vectors in the proposed model and assuming that influence areas of POIs are fixed in advance, the proposed model is reduced to a non-negative weighted least square problem. Supposing that influence on a grid from a POI is determined by the density at the grid's center of the two-dimensional normal distribution centered at this POI, the reduced model encompasses two-dimensional kernel density estimation on individual visiting

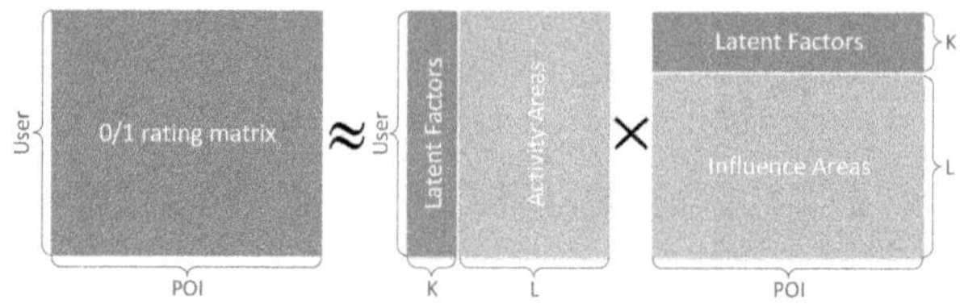

Figure 1: The augmented model for weighted matrix factorization, where the dimension of latent space is K and the number of grid areas is L.

locations. In particular, the estimated density at a location i with respect to a user equals to the averaging density at the location i of the normal distributions centered at each of her visiting locations, or inversely, it equals to the averaging density at each of her visiting locations of the normal distribution centered at the location i. When mapping POIs onto grids and constituting users' activity area vectors with grids and their visited frequency, the estimated density is in proportion to inner product between the augmenting vectors. Thus, two-dimensional kernel density estimation is a special case of the reduced model so that our model captures the spatial clustering phenomenon from the perspective of kernel density estimation (KDE). However, different from KDE, the advantage of the proposed model lies in its consistent objective goal with weighted matrix factorization. Therefore, the modeling of the spatial clustering phenomenon is seamlessly incorporated into matrix factorization.

To summarize, in this paper, we have made the following contributions to POI recommendation.

- According to the analysis to mobility records from a location-based social network for POI recommendation, these mobility records are considered as implicit feedback for recommendation systems. Therefore, we propose to leverage weighted matrix factorization to conduct POI recommendation.
- Due to the existence of accurate geographical locations of POIs, we propose augmenting users' and POIs' latent factors with activity area vectors of users and influence area vectors of POIs. Based on such an augmented model, we can not only capture the spatial clustering phenomenon from the aspect of two-dimensional kernel density estimation, but we are also able to explain why the modeling of the spatial clustering phenomenon can help to cope with the challenge of recommendation arising from the user-POI matrix sparsity. Moreover, since its objective goal is consistent with weighted matrix factorization, the modeling of the spatial clustering phenomenon is seamlessly incorporated into matrix factorization.
- We evaluate the proposed algorithm on a large-scale location-based social network dataset. The results not only show the superiority of weighted matrix factorization on POI recommendation to other forms for factorization models, but they also indicate that incorporating the spatial clustering phenomenon into matrix factorization improves recommendation performance.

2. PRELIMINARY

POI recommendation is commonly studied on a user-POI matrix $\mathbf{C} \in \mathbb{N}^{M \times N}$, where there are M users and N items.

Then each entry $c_{u,i}$ in the matrix $\mathbf{C}$ records the visit frequency of a user u to a POI i, where u and i is reserved indexing users and POIs respectively. Here, following common symbolic notation, upper case bold letters denote matrices, lower case bold letters denote column vectors without any specification, and non-bold letters represent scalars.

2.1 Matrix Factorization

Given this frequency matrix, one possible approach to POI recommendation is low rank matrix factorization with respect to it. This involves mapping users and POIs into a joint latent space with dimension $K \ll \min(M, N)$, such that a user's preference for a POI is modeled as inner product between them in that latent space. The mapping is achieved by approximating the frequency matrix by solving the following optimization problem,

$$\min_{\mathbf{P},\mathbf{Q}} \|\mathbf{C} - \mathbf{P}\mathbf{Q}^T\|_F^2 \tag{1}$$

where $\mathbf{P} \in \mathbb{R}^{M\times K}$ and $\mathbf{Q} \in \mathbb{R}^{N\times K}$ are users' latent vectors and POIs' latent vectors, respectively. $\|\cdot\|_F$ is the Frobenius norm of matrices, simply the square root of the sum of the squared values in matrices. And this optimization can be uniquely solved by singular value decomposition (SVD) by taking the first K pairs of singular vectors. However, due to the large number of users and POIs, it is more practical to alternate these two kinds of latent factors to solve the least square problem. For the sake of further scalability, it has become a popular solution to simply approximate the observed ratings (frequency), that is, minimizing the following weighted square errors,

$$\min_{\mathbf{P},\mathbf{Q}} \|\mathbf{W} \odot (\mathbf{C} - \mathbf{P}\mathbf{Q}^T)\|_F^2 \tag{2}$$

where $\odot$ is the Hadamard product operator, i.e., element-wise multiplication of matrices. $\mathbf{W}$ is a binary weighted matrix whose entry $w_{u,i}$ indicates whether a user u has visited a POI i, i.e., $w_{u,i} = \mathbb{I}(c_{u,i} > 0)$. In order to reduce the generalization error (performance on unseen data), regularization terms are usually added to this objective goal to shrinking the latent vectors toward zero, i.e.,

$$\min_{\mathbf{P},\mathbf{Q}} \left(\|\mathbf{W} \odot (\mathbf{C} - \mathbf{P}\mathbf{Q}^T)\|_F^2 + \gamma(\|\mathbf{P}\|_F^2 + \|\mathbf{Q}\|_F^2)\right) \tag{3}$$

2.2 Weighted Matrix Factorization for Implicit Feedback

The previously discussed matrix factorization is designed for rating predictions in a typical scenario of movie recommendation. In such cases, users not only reveal their favorite movies with high ratings, but also their least favoriate movies with low ratings. However, in POI recommendation, a user's visit to a location reflects her preference for it. The visit frequency to this location determines the confident level of her preference for it. In particular, a higher visit frequency corresponds to a larger confidence of preference for the location. Therefore, in the frequency matrix, there are only *positive* examples observed so that POI recommendation is considered as a well-known One Class Collaborative Filtering (OCCF) problem [18, 8].

One solution to such an OCCF problem is to randomly sample some negative examples for each user and to assign them smaller weights than positive ones since the confidence in their negative attitude is less than the positive attitude of the positive examples. It is also possible and effective to consider all the unvisited locations as negative examples when the weights to all negative examples are assigned the same value, i.e., 1. In particular, we set the weighting matrix as follows,

$$w_{u,i} = \begin{cases} \alpha(c_{u,i}) + 1 & \text{if } c_{u,i} > 0 \\ 1 & \text{otherwise} \end{cases} \tag{4}$$

where $\alpha(c_{u,i}) > 0$ is a monotonically increasing function with respect to $c_{u,i}$. Such a setting exactly encodes the observation that the frequency is a confidence of users' preferences. Based on this weighted matrix, the objective function for the implicit feedback is represented as follows:

$$\min_{\mathbf{P},\mathbf{Q}} \left(\|\mathbf{W} \odot (\mathbf{R} - \mathbf{P}\mathbf{Q}^T)\|_F^2 + \gamma(\|\mathbf{P}\|_F^2 + \|\mathbf{Q}\|_F^2)\right) \tag{5}$$

It is similar to Eq (3), except that the frequency matrix $\mathbf{C}$ is substituted with a 0/1 rating matrix $\mathbf{R}$, where each entry $r_{u,i} \in \{0, 1\}$ indicates whether a user u has visited a POI i. Therefore, this new form of objective actually approximates whether users have visited locations in a weighted way. However, due to the weight setting, the approximation error is summed over all entries in the user-POI matrix. Fortunately, the approximate error can be efficiently reduced via alternative least square and its time complexity for each iteration is in proportion to the total number of visited locations, i.e., the number of non-zero entries in the frequency matrix. We will provide detailed analysis in a later section.

3. JOINT GEOGRAPHICAL MODELING AND MATRIX FACTORIZATION

Weighted matrix factorization works well in most of implicit feedback datasets since it takes all unvisited locations as negative examples and assigns larger weights to positive examples than negative ones. However, in the case of POI recommendation, since POIs are naturally equipped with geographical information, there is still room for improvement in this algorithm. For example, if a user often visits a POI i but never patronizes POIs around i, it is more likely that these unvisited POIs surrounding i will become negative examples than unvisited but distant ones, and this likelihood depends on the visit frequency to the POI i. Although there are some recent studies that leverage this geographical information to assist POI recommendation [24, 2, 12, 26] by modeling the well-known spatial clustering phenomenon, these approaches are almost independent of the procedure for collaborative filtering, particularly, matrix factorization. The incorporation of geographical information into matrix factorization, in particular weighted matrix factorization for implicit feedback datasets, is important, because it may not only help to understand how to recommend POIs in the presence of geographical information, but may also help to explain why the modeling of the spatial clustering phenomenon can help to cope with the challenges of matrix sparsity. More importantly, it may boost the overall recommendation performance. To this end, we propose GeoMF for joint geographical modeling and matrix factorization.

3.1 Representation

Before presenting the GeoMF model, for the sake of convenience, we must first clarify two terms involved: user's activity areas and POI's influence areas. Roughly speaking, a user's activity areas consist of location regions where the

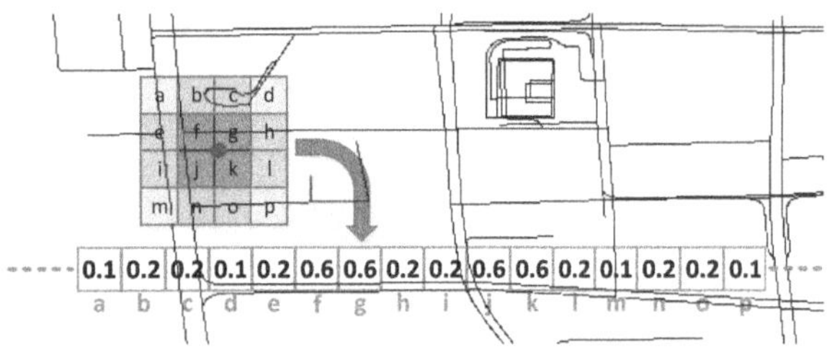

Figure 2: Generating an influence area vector for a POI (the red point).

user will show up and POI's influence areas are those regions to which the influence of this POI can be propagated. As for influence areas, we take Eiffel Tower as an example of a POI. Its influence areas may consist of all the areas in Paris since it is a famous symbol of Paris. More specifically and formally, when we assume the areas are obtained by splitting the whole world into L even grids, denoted as $\mathbb{L} = \{g_1, g_2, ..., g_L\}$, we have the following definitions:

DEFINITION 1 (USER'S ACTIVITY AREAS). *A user's activity areas are determined by a set of pairs of a grid area $l \in \mathbb{L}$ where the user may show up and a non-negative real value $v \in \mathbb{R}_+$ indicating the possibility of appearing.*

We can represent a user's activity areas as a non-negative vector $\mathbf{x} \in \mathbb{R}_+^L$. Each entry x_l in the vector $\mathbf{x}$ indicates the possibility that this user will appear in the grid $g_l \in \mathbb{L}$.

DEFINITION 2 (POI'S INFLUENCE AREAS). *Influence areas of a POI consist of a collection of pairs of a grid area $l \in \mathbb{L}$ to which the influence of this POI can be propagated and a non-negative real value $v \in \mathbb{R}_+$ indicating the quantity of influence from this POI.*

A POI's influence areas can also be similarly converted into a non-negative vector $\mathbf{y} \in \mathbb{R}_+^L$. Usually, influence areas are different from POI to POI. For simplicity, we assume the influence areas of a POI are fixed in advance and have a normal distribution centered at this POI. In particular, the influence y_l at a grid g_l from a POI i is $y_l = \frac{1}{\sigma}K(\frac{d(l,i)}{\sigma})$, where $K(\cdot)$ is standard normal distribution and σ is the standard deviation. Figure 2 shows an example of such a setting.

The advantage of setting the influence areas in this way is that inner product between $\mathbf{x}$ and $\mathbf{y}$ encompasses two-dimensional kernel density estimation on a user's visiting locations. Specifically, the estimated density of a user u at a POI i equals to $\frac{1}{|\mathbb{P}_u|\sigma}\sum_{j\in\mathbb{P}_u} K(\frac{d(i,j)}{\sigma})$, where $\mathbb{P}_u$ is a set of visited POIs by user u. If these POIs $\mathbb{P}_u$ are mapped into her visited areas of grids $\mathbb{L}_u \subseteq \mathbb{L}$, this estimation becomes $\frac{1}{|\mathbb{P}_u|}\sum_{l\in\mathbb{L}_u} \frac{n_l}{\sigma}K(\frac{d(i,l)}{\sigma})$, where n_l is her visiting frequency to the grid g_l, and thus is in proportion to $\mathbf{x}^T\mathbf{y}$ by setting $\mathbf{x}$ as the visit frequency to the corresponding grid areas. In this way, we actually model the spatial clustering phenomenon using two-dimensional kernel density estimation. However, different from kernel density estimation, a user's activity area vector $\mathbf{x}$ is a variable learned by the subsequent optimization.

We then leverage $\mathbf{x}$ and $\mathbf{y}$ to augment user's and POI's latent factors in the matrix factorization, respectively, as shown in Figure 1. We obtain the estimated preference matrix for our proposed GeoMF model as follows

$$\tilde{\mathbf{R}} = \mathbf{P}\mathbf{Q}^T + \mathbf{X}\mathbf{Y}^T \quad (6)$$

where we stack the activity area vector of each user by row to obtain a users' activity area matrix $\mathbf{X} \in \mathbb{R}^{*M\times L}$ and stack the influence area vector of each POI by row to obtain a POIs' influence area matrix $\mathbf{Y} \in \mathbb{R}^{*N\times L}$. One reason for such an explicit augmentation with geographical information is that there is still no evidence showing that the latent space has already included them (It is easy for other information, e.g., the POI categories, to be incorporated into this framework in a similar way). In this way, a user's preference for a POI is modeled as an inner product in this augmented space and thus includes both the interest of the user from the latent space and her preference for the locations of the POI. If her preference for the locations of a POI is non-zero, her activity areas intersect with the influence areas of the POI so that the POI is reachable from her activity areas.

Another reason for this kind of augmentation is that it explains why the modeling of the spatial clustering phenomenon can help to deal with the challenge of matrix sparsity. In particular, returning to the example in the first paragraph of this section, where a user has often visited a POI i, but never patronized POIs around i. Using such a representation, this user has similar *non-negative* location preference for the POIs around i. However, since this user has never visited these surrounding POIs, such a representation requires the inner product in the latent space to offset the location preference, from the perspective of approximation (Minimizing weighted square loss similar to weighted matrix factorization; discussed later). In this way, we introduce more potential unattractive locations (confidently *negative* examples) into matrix factorization.

3.2 Optimization

The learning of these three matrices is achieved by minimizing a similar objective function to weighted matrix factorization for implicit feedback, i.e.,

$$\min_{\mathbf{P},\mathbf{Q},\mathbf{X}} \|\mathbf{W}\odot(\mathbf{R}-\mathbf{P}\mathbf{Q}^T-\mathbf{X}\mathbf{Y}^T)\|_F^2+\gamma(\|\mathbf{P}\|_F^2+\|\mathbf{Q}\|_F^2)+\lambda\|\mathbf{X}\|_1$$

$$\text{subject to } \mathbf{X} \geq 0 \quad (7)$$

where $\|\mathbf{X}\|_1$ is ℓ_1 norm of matrix $\mathbf{X}$. One reason for imposing such a matrix norm is that users are usually constrained around several long-stay locations, such as, home or workplace, while ℓ_1 norm of the matrix is generally exploited to restrict the sparsity of matrices [16]. Another benefit of placing the sparse constraint is that it can also improve the effectiveness and the efficiency of recommendation (shown in experimental section).

This objective function is minimized with an alternative optimization, consisting of one procedure of learning latent factors when fixing $\mathbf{X}$ and another one of non-negative weighted sparse least square with respect to $\mathbf{X}$ when fixing latent factors. Since in each procedure, the objective function is not increasing, the iteration of such an alternative optimization can guarantee the non-increase of the objective function.

When fixing activity area matrix $\mathbf{X}$, the optimization of this objective function with respect to the users' and POIs' latent factors is similar to alternative least square in weighted matrix factorization discussed previously. More specifically, the latent factors of user u is updated based on

$$\mathbf{p}_u = (\mathbf{Q}^T\mathbf{W}^u\mathbf{Q} + \gamma\mathbf{I})^{-1}\mathbf{Q}^T\mathbf{W}^u(\mathbf{r}_u - \mathbf{Y}\mathbf{x}_u) \quad (8)$$

where $\mathbf{W^u}$ is an $N \times N$ diagonal matrix, subject to $W^u_{i,i} = w_{u,i}$ and $\mathbf{r}_u$ is a column rating vector of user u. Here, since we have set the same weight, i.e., 1 to the unvisited locations, there is a trick to speed up its calculation [8]. In particular, $\mathbf{Q}^T\mathbf{W}^u\mathbf{Q} = \mathbf{Q}^T(\mathbf{W}^u - \mathbf{I})\mathbf{Q} + \mathbf{Q}^T\mathbf{Q}$. In this case, the second part is independent of users so that it can be precomputed while the first part only requires $O(\|\mathbf{r}_u\|_0 K^2)$, where ℓ_0 norm of matrix (vector) is the number of non-zero entries in this matrix (here, it is also the number of visited locations of user u). For the inverse of a $K \times K$ matrix, we assume it requires $O(K^3)$ time even though more efficient algorithms exist but probably are less relevant for the typically small values of K. Applying the similar trick to calculate the remaining part $\mathbf{Q}^T\mathbf{W}^u\hat{\mathbf{r}}_u$, where $\hat{\mathbf{r}}_u = (\mathbf{r}_u - \mathbf{Y}\mathbf{x}_u)$, it costs $O(\|\hat{\mathbf{r}}_u\|_0 K)$ to get a $K \times \|\hat{\mathbf{r}}_u\|_0$ matrix. Completing the final matrix multiplication between the inversed matrix and the intermediate matrix requires $O(\|\hat{\mathbf{r}}_u\|_0 K^2)$ time. Therefore, it will cost $O(\|\hat{\mathbf{r}}_u\|_0 K^2 + K^3)$ to update latent factors for user u in total. If we update all users' latent factors in sequence (parallel updating is possible since there is no dependence between users), the total update time is $O(\|\hat{\mathbf{R}}\|_0 K^2 + MK^3)$, where $\hat{\mathbf{R}} = \mathbf{R} - \mathbf{X}\mathbf{Y}^T$.

Similarly, we can update the latent factor of a POI i as:

$$\mathbf{q}_i = (\mathbf{P}^T\mathbf{W}^i\mathbf{P} + \gamma\mathbf{I})^{-1}\mathbf{P}^T\mathbf{W}^i(\mathbf{r}_i - \mathbf{X}\mathbf{y}_i) \quad (9)$$

where $\mathbf{W}^i$ is an $M \times M$ diagonal matrix, subject to $W^i_{u,u} = w_{u,i}$ and $\mathbf{r}_i$ is a column rating vector of the POI i. Applying the similar optimization trick, we can complete the update of POIs' latent factors in $O(\|\hat{\mathbf{R}}\|_0 K^2 + NK^3)$ time.

Since $\|\hat{\mathbf{R}}\|_0 > (M + N) \times K$ is usually satisfied, the total complexity of updating latent factors in one iteration is $O(\|\hat{\mathbf{R}}\|_0 K^2)$. K is set as a small number ($50 \sim 200$) so that it can be considered as proportional to the number of non-zero entries in new matrix $\hat{\mathbf{R}}$, but larger than the original one $\mathbf{R}$. Therefore, the sparsity constraint of $\mathbf{X}$ is also important to the efficiency of updating these latent factors. Additionally, for the sake of higher efficiency, we assume that the two-dimensional normal distribution for generating influence areas of POIs is truncated so that the sparsity structure of $\mathbf{Y}$ can also be guaranteed. In other words, only those areas within a certain threshold of distance (i.e., d km) from a POI are considered as its influence areas. This is reasonable to some extent since the normal distribution usually decays quickly with the increase of the distance from its center.

According to previous analysis, the updating of latent factors corresponds to approximating the new matrix $\hat{\mathbf{R}} = \mathbf{R} - \mathbf{X}\mathbf{Y}^T$. Therefore, by introducing the geographical information, we have added many negative examples for the latent factor model. These negative examples in this new matrix $\hat{\mathbf{R}}$ have negative ratings due to the non-negativeness of $\mathbf{X}$ and $\mathbf{Y}$, and their absolute values are in proportion to a user's preference for the locations of POIs. Thus it is more likely that unvisited POIs near frequently visited POIs will become negative examples. This confirms the preceding explanation why incorporating the spatial clustering phenomenon into collaborative filtering can help to cope with the challenge of matrix sparsity.

Now let's turn to learning users' activity area matrix $\mathbf{X}$. When fixing the latent factors, the objective function with respect to $\mathbf{X}$ is similar to a non-negative weighted least square problem, which can be further generalized as a bounded-variable least square problem [10]. Such kinds of problems have been solved by several approaches, including active set method [10], sequential coordinate-wise algorithm [4], projected gradient descent method [11] and so on. Among these methods, projected gradient descent is highly efficient and has been extensively studied in non-negative matrix factorization, which can also be cast into two sub-problems related to non-negative least square [11]. The general idea of the projected gradient descent algorithm is to update parameters by gradient descent and then to project the updated ones into feasible regions defined by bound constraints. Nevertheless, the choice of learning rate in the gradient descent needs to guarantee that the projected parameters can sufficiently decrease the objective function. Thus we leverage the methods proposed in [11] to update users' activity area matrix. However, due to the existence of the weighting matrix and latent factors, the gradient of this objective function with respect to $\mathbf{X}$ is a full matrix. It is impractical to update all the parameters at one time. Thus, instead, we update the activity area vectors for each user independently.

Let's rewrite the objective function with respect to the activity area vector of a user u and discard the irrelevant terms.

$$\begin{gathered} L(\mathbf{x}_u) = \|\mathbf{W}^u(\mathbf{r}_u - \mathbf{Q}\mathbf{p}_u - \mathbf{Y}\mathbf{x}_u)\|_F^2 + \lambda\|\mathbf{x_u}\|_1 \\ \text{subject to } \mathbf{x}_u \geq 0 \end{gathered} \quad (10)$$

The gradient of $L(\mathbf{x}_u)$ with respect to $\mathbf{x}_u$ is

$$\nabla L(\mathbf{x}_u) = \mathbf{Y}^T\mathbf{W}^u(\mathbf{Y}\mathbf{x}_u - (\mathbf{r}_u - \mathbf{Q}\mathbf{p}_u)) + \lambda \quad (11)$$

Based on this gradient, we update $\mathbf{x}_u$ as follows

$$\mathbf{x}_u^{(t+1)} = P_+(\mathbf{x}_u^{(t)} - \alpha\nabla L(\mathbf{x}_u)) \quad (12)$$

where $P_+(\mathbf{x})$ is a function to project a vector $\mathbf{x} \in \mathbb{R}^L$ onto its non-negative orthant $\mathbb{R}^L_+$. In particular,

$$P_+(x_l) = \begin{cases} x_l & \text{if } x_l > 0 \\ 0 & \text{otherwise} \end{cases}, \quad l \in \{1, ..., L\} \quad (13)$$

The learning rate, α is chosen so as to ensure the sufficient decrease of the objective function, i.e.,

$$L(\mathbf{x}_u^{(t+1)}) - L(\mathbf{x}_u^{(t)}) \leq \varepsilon\nabla L(\mathbf{x}_u)^T(\mathbf{x}_u^{(t+1)} - \mathbf{x}_u^{(t)}) \quad (14)$$

where ε is a parameter of this condition and commonly set as 0.01. Since our objective is a quadratic function w.r.t $\mathbf{x}_u$, this condition can be quickly evaluated via the gradient and Hessian matrix ($\nabla^2 L(\mathbf{x}_u) = \mathbf{Y}^T\mathbf{W}^u\mathbf{Y}$), i.e.,

$$(1 - \varepsilon)\nabla L(\mathbf{x}_u)^T\Delta\mathbf{x}_u + \frac{1}{2}\Delta\mathbf{x}_u^T\nabla^2 L(\mathbf{x}_u)\Delta\mathbf{x}_u \leq 0 \quad (15)$$

where $\Delta\mathbf{x}_u = \mathbf{x}_u^{(t+1)} - \mathbf{x}_u^{(t)}$ is the change of $\mathbf{x}_u$. In this case, in each step, although the objective function has decreased sufficiently, it requires repeatedly searching the learning rate (based on some heuristic rules). And with the change in learning rate, the gradient increases by $\nabla^2 L(\mathbf{x}_u)\Delta\mathbf{x}_u$. Since there are approximately an equal number of influence areas (denoted as $n_{\bar{i}}$) for different POIs, the increase of the gradient along with evaluating the sufficient decrease condition costs at most $O(\|\mathbf{x}_u\|_0 n_{\bar{i}})$. The part that is irrelevant to $\mathbf{x}_u$ in the gradient can be computed in a way that is similar to updating the latent factors and its complexity is denominated by the calculation of the Hessian matrix, that is, $O(\|\mathbf{r}_u\|_0 n_{\bar{i}}^2)$. If we perform an updating operation for each user in sequence (it can be done in parallel), the overall complexity is $O(\#iter \times t \|\mathbf{X}\|_0 n_{\bar{i}} + \|\mathbf{R}\|_0 n_{\bar{i}}^2)$, where $\#iter$ is the number of iterations to be updated and t is the average number of trials for searching the learning rate. Here, we once again observe the importance of the sparse structure in the efficiency of optimization.

Someone may be curious about what a user's activity areas will be based on such an updating strategy. Thus we will try to conduct an analysis from this perspective. For simplicity, assume that the latent factors are not taken into account. The users' activity area matrix $\mathbf{X}$ is initialized to zero. After the first iteration, $\mathbf{x}_u = \alpha P_+(\mathbf{Y}^T \mathbf{W}^u \mathbf{r}_u - \lambda)$, thus including the regions that can be directly reached from a user's visiting POIs by means of $\mathbf{Y}$. The possibility of showing up in a grid area depends on the visiting frequency via the weighting matrix $\mathbf{W}^u$. Thus, the update in this first iteration is similar to kernel density estimation except that it is subject to the decrease of the objective function. In the subsequent iterations, a user's activity areas are expanded by $\mathbf{Y}^T \mathbf{W}^u \mathbf{Y}$, which encodes the personalized spatial correlation between POIs, under the condition of decreasing the objective function.

4. EXPERIMENT

4.1 Dataset and Experimental setup

We evaluate the proposed algorithm on a large-scale location-based social network dataset. This dataset was crawled from Jiepang, a Chinese location-based social network, similar to Foursquare and spanned almost two years from March. 2011 to March. 2013. Although check-ins of Jiepang users are not publicly available on Jiepang itself, they are synchronized to other social networks, i.e., Weibo, so that they can be obtained by the open APIs of these social networks. In this way, we crawled 36,143,085 Jiepang check-ins at 1,000,457 POIs from 454,375 users. If this data is represented as a user-POI matrix, its density is 7.95×10^{-5}. In this dataset, each user made 80 check-ins on average and these check-ins are dispersed at 47 POIs on average. If we distribute these check-ins by their date, we find that each user only make 1.5 check-ins each day on average. If we distribute these POIs into 3 km^2 regions, each region contains 13 POIs on average and up to 13,068 POIs in the maximal case. Then we select POIs that are visited by at least two users and users who have been to at least 10 distinct locations. Finally, 276,450 users and 574,095 POIs are then reserved and the density of these users on these POIs is 1.27×10^{-4}.

For each user, we randomly select 30% of her visiting locations as ground truth for testing. The remaining portions from each user constitute a training dataset for learning the parameters of the proposed model. The learned model scores each unvisited location for each user (i.e., not in her training portion) and then ranks them according to the scores. The learned model is then assessed by its capacity of finding the ground truth locations for each user among the ranked locations. Such a capacity is usually measured by two widely-used metrics, i.e., Recall@k and Precision@k, in the top k POI recommendation [24, 12, 5]. The former metric w.r.t each user indicates what percentage of her visiting locations can emerge in the top k recommended POIs while the latter metric w.r.t each user indicates what percentage of locations among the top k recommended POIs has been visited by her. Formally, if we define $\mathbb{S}_u(k)$ as the top k recommended POIs and $\mathbb{V}_u$ as the visited locations of user u,

$$\begin{aligned} Recall@k &= \frac{1}{M} \sum_{u=1}^{M} \frac{|\mathbb{S}_u(k) \cap \mathbb{V}_u|}{|\mathbb{V}_u|} \\ Precision@k &= \frac{1}{M} \sum_{u=1}^{M} \frac{|\mathbb{S}_u(k) \cap \mathbb{V}_u|}{k}. \end{aligned} \tag{16}$$

The above procedure corresponds to one trial. The final performance of the recommendation algorithms is obtained by averaging on the metrics of 5 times independent trials.

Next we set up the parameters controlling the complexity and being not learned via optimization. All these parameters are set by cross validation. The dimension of the latent space is set as 50 and the weighted matrix is set by $\alpha(c_{u,i}) = 1 + \log(1 + c_{u,i} \times 10^{\epsilon})$ where $\epsilon = 10$. However, the recommendation performance is not sensitive to the regularization coefficient γ for shrinking latent factors since all negative examples (unvisited locations) are taken into account and thus we set it as $\gamma = 0.01$. For the parameters related to modeling locations, including the ℓ_1 regularization coefficient λ for the sparsity constraint and the distance d for truncated normal distribution for setting the influence area matrix, we examine them in the result part.

In the following sections, we will evaluate the proposed algorithm according to three aspects. First, we compare the different approaches to using matrix factorization for POI recommendation. Then we study the modeling of spatial clustering phenomenon, denoted as *GeoWLS* (which just ignores the latent factors in GeoMF), under the different parameter settings and compare it with kernel density estimation. Finally, we compare the proposed model (*GeoMF*) with weighted matrix factorization (*WMF*) and *GeoWLS* in order to understand the benefit of geographical information.

4.2 Study of Matrix Factorization

For the sake of understanding the effectiveness of WMF for POI recommendation, we compare it with user-based collaborative filtering (*UCF*) [24] and the following factorization algorithms.

- ***UCF***. In this *UCF*, the similarity between users is related to the number of their common visited locations and the weight of a user w.r.t a location is 0/1 indicating whether the user has visited the location. In other words, *UCF* is built based on the user-POI 0/1 rating matrix $\mathbf{R}$.

- ***MF-01***. A non weighted version of WMF, performs factorization on user-POI 0/1 rating matrix $\mathbf{R}$, based on the following optimization $\min_{\mathbf{P},\mathbf{Q}} \|\mathbf{R} - \mathbf{P}\mathbf{Q}^T\|_F^2 + \gamma(\|\mathbf{P}\|_F^2 + \|\mathbf{Q}\|_F^2)$, where γ is set by cross validation.

- ***MF-Freq***. A factorization algorithm is directly conducted on user-POI frequency matrix $\mathbf{C}$, denoted as *MF-Freq*, based on a similar optimization procedure to *MF-01* except for substituting $\mathbf{R}$ with $\mathbf{C}$. Such a factorization algorithm has been exploited in [17, 5] for POI recommendation

- ***B-NMF***. B-NMF is a Bayesian non-negative matrix factorization algorithm that places Gamma prior on its latent factors. It tries to optimizes the following objective function [15],

$$\min_{\mathbf{P},\mathbf{Q}} D(\mathbf{C}\|\mathbf{P}\mathbf{Q}^T) - \sum_{u,k} \ln \Gamma(p_{u,k}|\alpha_k, \beta_k) - \sum_{i,k} \ln \Gamma(q_{u,k}|\alpha_k, \beta_k)$$

where $D(\mathbf{A}\|\mathbf{B}) = \sum_{i,j} A_{i,j} \log \frac{A_{i,j}}{B_{i,j}} - A_{i,j} + B_{i,j}$ is the divergence from matrix $\mathbf{A}$ to $\mathbf{B}$ [20] and $\Gamma(x|\alpha, \beta)$ is a Gamma distribution, parametrized by a share parameter α and a rate parameter β. It should be noted that we can not optimize it over all entries in the matrix for the sake of efficiency. Thus we randomly sample the same number of negative POIs as positive ones. This algorithm has been exploited in [2, 12] for POI recommendation.

- ***WMF-B***. This algorithm introduces the popularity of POIs into weighted matrix factorization for POI recommendation since it is common to retain items' biases in the factorization models [9]. This algorithm minimize $\|\mathbf{W} \odot (\mathbf{R} - \mathbf{P}\mathbf{Q}^T - \mathbf{1}\mathbf{b}^T)\|_F^2 + \gamma(\|\mathbf{P}\|_F^2 + \|\mathbf{Q}\|_F^2) + \eta\|\mathbf{b}\|_2^2$ with respect to users' and items' latent factors $\mathbf{P}$ and $\mathbf{Q}$ as well as the items' biases $\mathbf{b} \in \mathbb{R}^N$. Here, $\mathbf{1}$ is a column vector of length M with all entries one.

The result of the comparison is shown in Figures 3(a) and 3(d). The **first** observation is that factorization on frequency matrix (*MF-Freq*) based on square loss function performs worst among all the factorization models (even if we apply logarithm to the frequency). However, if we make use of divergence instead of square loss, the performance (i.e., *B-NMF*) improves compared to *MF-Freq* since it can model the skewness of visit frequency [2, 12]. This constitutes our **second** observation. Unfortunately, according to the **third** observation, it doesn't perform as well as the factorization on 0/1 rating matrix (*MF-01*) and user-based collaborative filtering (*UCF*). This indicates that approximating frequency, in spite in terms of Poisson likelihood in *B-NMF*, will attenuate the capacity of factorization models for recommendation. Additionally, in the **next** observation, *MF-01* is superior to both *B-NMF* and *UCF*. This may arise from the sparsity of individual visited locations because *B-NMF* only optimizes over a small subset of all the entries in the matrix for the sake of efficiency and *UCF* is modeled on the observed individual visited locations, while *MF-01* considers all unvisited locations as negative examples efficiently. The superiority of *MF-01* to *UCF* also confirms the advantage of matrix factorization models in recommendation systems compared to memory-based collaborative filtering [1]. When using the visiting frequency as the confidence of a user's preference for locations, we can further improve the recommendation performance, based on the **fifth** observation, that *WMF* outperforms *MF-01*. In summary, weighted matrix factorization works better for collaborative filtering on implicit feedback than the other forms of matrix factorization and user-based collaborative filtering. The **final** observation, which we make by comparing the results of *WMF* with *WMF-B*, is that we can't observe a significantly large improvement due to the introduction of the POIs' biases. One reason for this is that weighted matrix factorization may already imply such bias information. Also, the common reason to introduce the bias in the traditional matrix factorization algorithm is to center user-item rating matrix, but in weighted matrix factorization, the user-item rating matrix is filled with 0/1 entries, indicating that users has a certain action on items, so that there is no special requirement for centering. In other words, it is not essential to include the items' biases when applying weighted matrix factorization for collaborative filtering with implicit feedback.

4.3 Study of Modeling Spatial Clustering Phenomenon

By ignoring the latent factors in the GeoMF model, the reduced model (GeoWLS) tries to capture the spatial clustering phenomenon. In this model, the sparsity structure of the activity area matrix of users and the influence area matrix of POIs are important to the effectiveness and efficiency of GeoMF. These two parts are captured by two separated parameters, i.e., the regularization coefficient λ of ℓ_1 matrix norm and d km of truncated normal distribution for generating POIs' influence areas. Thus, in this section, we examine the effect of these two parameters and show the results in Figure 3(b) and 3(e). We can make the following observations:

First, we compare the recommendation performance under different distance thresholds for truncated normal distribution. In particular, we take grid regions within 0.5km and 1km of POIs to generate the influence area matrix of POIs while setting λ to zero, i.e., without any sparsity constraints, and then train two GeoWLS models based on such settings. According to the recommendation performance of these two models, we only observe a small improvement after taking more grid regions into account. One major reason lies in the high density of POIs. For such a sake, we analyze the density of POIs in our check-in dataset, which we measure via the number of POIs reached by expanding visited POIs to their nearby locations. In particular, if we expand visited POIs to nearby locations within d km distance, we would like to know how many unvisited locations can be added to the candidates for recommendation. Thus we draw a scatter plot between them, shown in Figure 4(a), where the x axis indicates the expanded distance while the y axis represents the number of candidate POIs (Since this value is different from person to person, we plot the (25%,50%,75%) quantile of its distribution over the population). We can see that when we expand visited POIs to nearby locations within 0.5 km, the number of candidate locations will be around 8,000 among half users and when expanded to 1 km, this number increases to 11,000. Therefore, expanding to 0.5 km may already include sufficient candidates for top-k recommendation ($k \ll 8,000$). Moreover, with the help of this analysis, we can see that it is really difficult to recommend POIs based only on location information. Therefore, the recommendation performance that only uses locations is lower than collaborative filtering approaches.

Second, by fixing the distance to 0.5 km but varying λ, we explore the effect of sparsity constraints of users' activity area matrix on recommendation performance. According to these two figures, increasing from 0 to 10, the performance of GeoWLS improves consistently. In other words, the sparsity structure of users' activity area matrix can help improve the recommendation performance because this constraint reduces some of the noisy activity areas. Moreover, the sparsity constraint reduces the number of non-zero entries in the matrix and increases the efficiency of our GeoMF model. However, when continuing to increase its value from 10 to 20, the performance only improves in the top positions

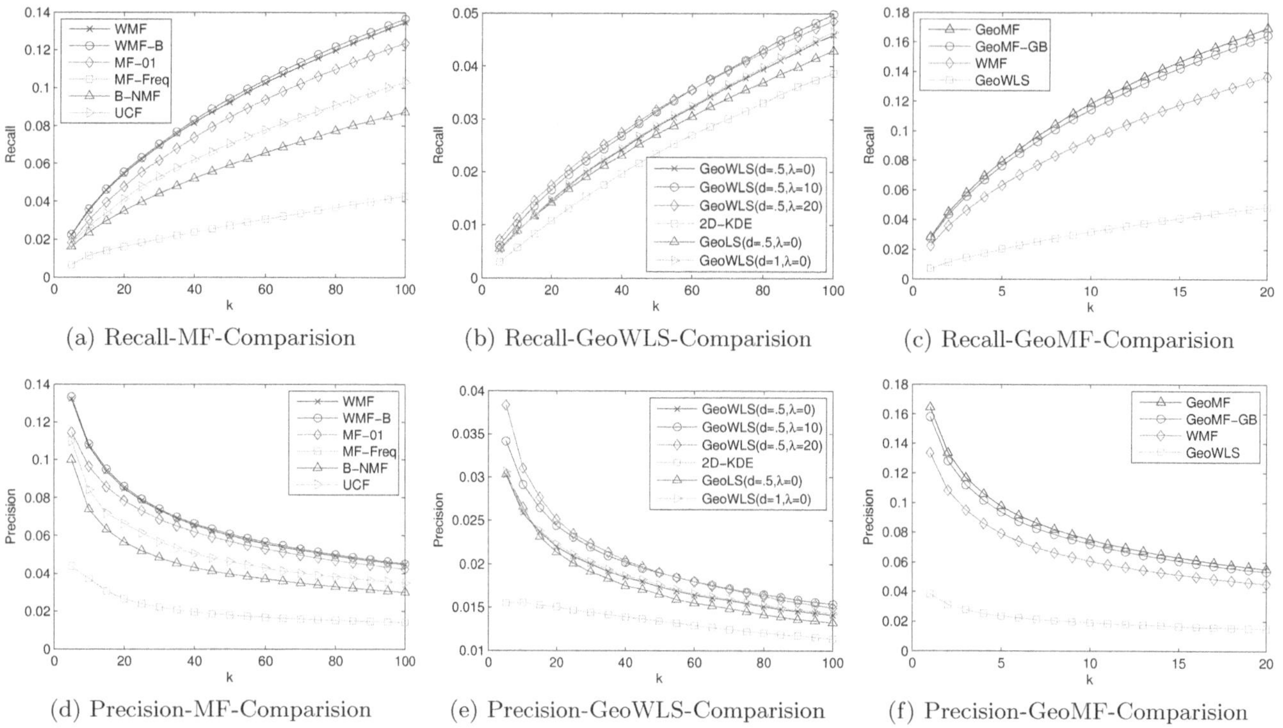

(a) Recall-MF-Comparision (b) Recall-GeoWLS-Comparision (c) Recall-GeoMF-Comparision

(d) Precision-MF-Comparision (e) Precision-GeoWLS-Comparision (f) Precision-GeoMF-Comparision

Figure 3: Figures (a) and (d) compare the performance of different kinds of matrix factorization for POI recommendation. Figures (b) and (e) compare the performances of GeoWLS with different settings of the coefficients of sparse constraints and with two-dimensional kernel density estimation. Figures (c) and (f) compare GeoMF with two components (WMF and GeoWLS).

while those at the bottom start to decrease. The underlying reason is that stronger sparsity constraints also remove some significant activity areas at the same time of reducing noise.

It is possible to suspend the necessity of weighted square loss instead of square loss, since this procedure may be independent of matrix factorization. To this end, we compare GeoWLS with a non-weighted version *GeoLS* under the same setting of parameters in the **third** step. From the results, we can see that GeoWLS outperforms GeoLS. Thus the goal of geographical modeling is consistent with weighted matrix factorization w.r.t POI recommendation so that geographical modeling is seamlessly incorporated into matrix factorization for recommending POIs.

Although GeoWLS encompasses two-dimensional kernel density estimation (*2D-KDE*), it is subject to the minimization of weighted square loss and is different from 2D-KDE. Hence, **finally**, we compare GeoWLS with 2D-KDE. Based on the results, we observe that GeoWLS is much better than 2D-KDE and that the formalization in terms of weighted non-negative least square is effective for POI recommendation. Moreover, we also study the reasonableness of GeoWLS by plotting the activity areas of a sample user in Figure 4(b). The results show that it is similar to 2D-KDE, that is, in the areas with larger number of visited locations, users have a higher possibility of showing up. However, the difference is that in GeoWLS there will be a larger possibility of showing up in less popular areas given two areas with the same visit frequency (these two regions are indistinguishable via 2D-KDE). This is reasonable, considering that a visit to less popular areas implies a larger preference for it compared to popular ones.

4.4 Comparison with Baselines

In this section, we will compare GeoMF with its two components, i.e., WMF and GeoWLS in order to determine the benefits of introducing geographical information into WMF. Additionally, we use Gradient Boosting [6] to integrate these two components, denoted as *GeoMF-GB*, since our GeoMF model can be considered an additive model of WMF and GeoWLS. It is similar to one round of GeoMF optimization (it alternates between GeoWLS and WMF three times in our experiments) starting with GeoWLS. However, we can set different weighting strategies for GeoWLS and WMF since these two models are independent of each other in the Gradient Boosting framework. We omit the implementation here due to space limitation. We simply show the results in Figure 3(c) and 3(f). We **first** observed that GeoMF greatly outperforms WMF, indicating that GeoMF benefits from the knowledge of geographical information. In other words, latent vectors in the WMF may not capture the geographical information so that its explicit modeling in GeoMF can remedy this weakness. **Second**, GeoMF is slightly better than GeoMF-GB. This, on the one hand, indicates GeoMF can benefit from multiple alternation between GeoWLS and WMF; on the other hand, it implies the information obtained by the negative examples from GeoWLS is limited with respect to WMF. One potential reason is that all the unvisited locations are already considered as negative examples in WMF. Another possible reason is that these two models are relatively independent of each other so that multiple alternation can not boost the recommendation performance a great deal.

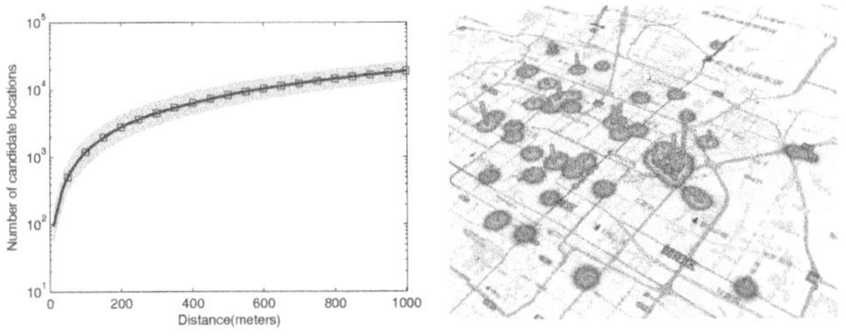

Figure 4: (a) Number of candidate locations vs. the expansion distance (b) The density plot of activity areas of one user

4.5 Discussion and Future Work

Our proposed GeoMF model is a general framework for using the content information of POIs in matrix factorization. POIs also include category attributes and these categories are organized by two-level hierarchy. The top level only contains several coarse categories while the bottom ones include finer categories. Therefore we also try to incorporate finer categories into the factorization models. However, our results show no significant improvement to the factorization models. One reason is that POIs' latent factors may already encode such information. Another one lies in the incompleteness of POIs' categories. According to a statistics to the categories of POIs, we find that over 40% of POIs don't have finer categories. Nevertheless, one interesting thing is that the visit time of users' to locations may help us to deduce the category information according to [23]. Thus, one future task is to exploit the time information in matrix factorization for POI recommendation.

Another assumption for the GeoMF model is that normal distribution would be truncated with the same influence distance of all POIs. However, in practice, different POIs may have different influence distances. In other words, some locations (i.e., restaurants) are only visited by nearby users while others (i.e., hotels, attractions) may be visited by many non-natives. Thus, it is interesting to learn the influence distance of POIs and to study the correlation between it and POIs' categories.

Besides, social network information is not taken into consideration in our model. This is because our model focuses on incorporating location into matrix factorization. However, our model can be easily extended with social interaction, e.g., by imposing a Graph Laplacian regularization. Due to space limitation, we will discuss it in the future work.

5. RELATED WORK

Location recommendation has been an important topic in location-based services. For example, some research has focused on recommending some specific types of locations. Park et al. [19] designed a system based on Bayesian learning with both users' preferences and location contexts to recommend restaurants. Similarly, Horozov et al. [7] developed a user-based collaborative filtering system to recommend restaurants to a user, by finding which restaurants similar users have visited before. Zheng et al. [28] designed a random walk style model to do tourism hot spot recommendation by taking into account both users' travel experiences and location attractiveness. In addition to single-type location recommendation mentioned above, there is also some other work considering multiple-activity-type location recommendation. For example, Zheng et al. considered location recommendation and activity recommendation together, so that they can provide location recommendation w.r.t. different types of activities [27]. The proposed model formulates a location-activity matrix for collaborative filtering and uses some additional information such as location features to help recommendation.

With the growing popularity of location-based social networks, location recommendation is drawing plenty of attention once again, since it is possible to obtain large-scale location visit records and several new challenges, including an extremely sparse user-location matrix and the presence of social networks, have arisen from this data. To address these challenges, several methods have been proposed. For example, Ye et al. [24] discovered the spatial clustering phenomenon of individual visited locations and characterized it by a power law distributed distance of any pair of visited locations [24]. In addition, they also exploited the similarity between users based on location history and social relationships on social networks for collaborative filtering. To better incorporate social relationships from social networks into collaborative filtering, Noulas et al. [17] conducted random walk with a restart on user-POI bipartite graph and social graph. With regard to modeling the spatial clustering phenomenon, instead of making the power law distribution assumption, Zhang et al. [26] suggested using kernel density estimation to estimate the distribution of distance between pairs of locations. Concentrating on modeling the distance distribution may ignore the multi-center characteristics of individual visiting locations according to [2]. Thus, the authors tried to apply clustering techniques on individual visited locations for encoding the spatial clustering phenomenon. They also exploited Bayesian non-negative matrix factorization for location recommendation, placing a Gamma prior on non-negative latent factors since this model can capture the skewness of the visit frequency to locations. These two models are then multiplied together since both of them are modeled in a probabilistic way. To improve the ad hoc integration between them, Liu et al. [12] proposed a geographical probabilistic factor analysis framework to takes geo-clustering and Bayesian non-negative matrix factorization into consideration by defining a user's preference for locations as a multiplication of her interest in the locations, the locations' popularity and the distance between her and POIs.

In addition to studying the effect of social network information and of spatial clustering phenomenon, there has also been research into studying the impact of context information, e.g., time, and the textual content of locations on POI recommendation. For example, in [13, 25, 22], they tried to leverage content information of locations via topic modeling to assist POI recommendation; In [5], Gao et al. proposed distinguishing a user's latent factors at different times and exploiting several strategies to aggregate a user's time-dependent latent factors; In [3, 14], the authors leveraged the information from previous POIs, including the POIs themselves, categories and so on, for next POI recommendation.

Comparing our work with these existing ones, there are many differences. First, we leverage weighted matrix factorization for POI recommendation since according to our experimental results it may be more appropriate than other methods for collaborative filtering from implicit feedback. Second, the modeling of the spatial clustering phenomenon is similar to two-dimensional kernel density estimation and thus doesn't make any assumption about the distribution of visited locations. Finally, geographical modeling is seamlessly incorporated into weighted matrix factorization and this incorporation explains why modeling the spatial clustering phenomenon helps to deal with the challenge of matrix sparsity. However, we don't take the content information into consideration in our proposed model since we don't have any other information except the categories of POIs in our dataset. This information can easily be incorporated into the current framework. Actually, we have tried to incorporate the categories of POIs, but haven't found much benefit from doing so. We have elaborated on the related issues in the discussion of Experimental section.

6. CONCLUSIONS

In this paper, we first studied POI recommendation from the viewpoint of weighted matrix factorization. We then augmented the latent space obtained from weighted matrix factorization with geographical information. Particularly, users' latent factors were augmented with users' activity areas while POIs' latent factors were augmented with POIs' influence areas. At the same time, sparse and non-negative constraints were imposed on both of them. Based on this augmented model, we did not only modeled the spatial clustering phenomenon from the novel perspective of two-dimensional kernel density estimation, but we also explained why the modeling of the spatial clustering phenomenon can help to deal with the challenge of matrix sparsity. Then we evaluated the proposed model on a large-scale check-in dataset. The experimental results showed that weighted matrix factorization is superior to other kinds of factorization models for POI recommendation and that incorporating the modeling of the spatial clustering phenomenon into matrix factorization improved the recommendation performance. Moreover, the imposed sparsity constraint also boosted the recommendation performance at the same time of promoting efficiency.

7. REFERENCES

[1] G. Adomavicius and A. Tuzhilin. Toward the next generation of recommender systems: A survey of the state-of-the-art and possible extensions. *IEEE Trans. Know. Data. Eng.*, 17(6):734–749, 2005.

[2] C. Cheng, H. Yang, I. King, and M. Lyu. Fused matrix factorization with geographical and social influence in location-based social networks. In *Proceedings of AAAI'12*, 2012.

[3] C. Cheng, H. Yang, M. R. Lyu, and I. King. Where you like to go next: successive point-of-interest recommendation. In *Proceedings of IJCAI'13*, pages 2605–2611. AAAI Press, 2013.

[4] V. Franc, V. Hlaváč, and M. Navara. Sequential coordinate-wise algorithm for the non-negative least squares problem. In *Computer Analysis of Images and Patterns*, pages 407–414. Springer, 2005.

[5] H. Gao, J. Tang, X. Hu, and H. Liu. Exploring temporal effects for location recommendation on location-based social networks. In *Proceedings of RecSys'13*, pages 93–100. ACM, 2013.

[6] T. Hastie, R. Tibshirani, and J. Friedman. The elements of statistical learning: data mining, inference, and prediction, 2001.

[7] T. Horozov, N. Narasimhan, and V. Vasudevan. Using location for personalized poi recommendations in mobile environments. In *Proceedings of SAINT'06*. IEEE Computer Society, 2006.

[8] Y. Hu, Y. Koren, and C. Volinsky. Collaborative filtering for implicit feedback datasets. In *Proceedings of ICDM'08*, pages 263–272. IEEE, 2008.

[9] Y. Koren, R. Bell, and C. Volinsky. Matrix factorization techniques for recommender systems. *Computer*, 42(8):30–37, 2009.

[10] C. L. Lawson and R. J. Hanson. *Solving Least Squares Problems*, volume 15. SIAM, 1995.

[11] C.-J. Lin. Projected gradient methods for nonnegative matrix factorization. *Neural computation*, 19(10):2756–2779, 2007.

[12] B. Liu, Y. Fu, Z. Yao, and H. Xiong. Learning geographical preferences for point-of-interest recommendation. In *Proceedings of KDD'13*, pages 1043–1051. ACM, 2013.

[13] B. Liu and H. Xiong. Point-of-interest recommendation in location based social networks with topic and location awareness. In *Proceedings of SDM'13*, pages 396–404. SIAM, 2013.

[14] X. Liu, Y. Liu, K. Aberer, and C. Miao. Personalized point-of-interest recommendation by mining users' preference transition. In *Proceedings of CIKM'13*, pages 733–738. ACM, 2013.

[15] H. Ma, C. Liu, I. King, and M. R. Lyu. Probabilistic factor models for web site recommendation. In *Proceedings of SIGIR'11*, pages 265–274. ACM, 2011.

[16] K. P. Murphy. *Machine learning: a probabilistic perspective.* The MIT Press, 2012.

[17] A. Noulas, S. Scellato, N. Lathia, and C. Mascolo. A random walk around the city: New venue recommendation in location-based social networks. In *Proceedings of SocialCom'12*, pages 144–153. IEEE, 2012.

[18] R. Pan, Y. Zhou, B. Cao, N. Liu, R. Lukose, M. Scholz, and Q. Yang. One-class collaborative filtering. In *Proceedings of ICDM'08*, pages 502–511. IEEE, 2008.

[19] M. Park, J. Hong, and S. Cho. Location-based recommendation system using bayesian user's preference model in mobile devices. *Ubiquitous Intelligence and Computing*, pages 1130–1139, 2007.

[20] D. Seung and L. Lee. Algorithms for non-negative matrix factorization. *Advances in neural information processing systems*, 13:556–562, 2001.

[21] W. Tobler. A computer movie simulating urban growth in the detroit region. *Economic geography*, 46:234–240, 1970.

[22] D. Yang, D. Zhang, Z. Yu, and Z. Wang. A sentiment-enhanced personalized location recommendation system. In *Proceedings of the 24th ACM Conference on Hypertext and Social Media(HT'13)*, pages 119–128. ACM, 2013.

[23] M. Ye, D. Shou, W. Lee, P. Yin, and K. Janowicz. On the semantic annotation of places in location-based social networks. In *Proceedings of KDD'11*, pages 520–528. ACM, 2011.

[24] M. Ye, P. Yin, W.-C. Lee, and D.-L. Lee. Exploiting geographical influence for collaborative point-of-interest recommendation. In *Proceedings of SIGIR'11*, pages 325–334. ACM, 2011.

[25] H. Yin, Y. Sun, B. Cui, Z. Hu, and L. Chen. Lcars: a location-content-aware recommender system. In *Proceedings of KDD'13*, pages 221–229. ACM, 2013.

[26] J.-D. Zhang and C.-Y. Chow. igslr: Personalized geo-social location recommendation-a kernel density estimation approach. In *Proceedings of GIS'13*.

[27] V. Zheng, Y. Zheng, X. Xie, and Q. Yang. Collaborative location and activity recommendations with gps history data. In *Proceedings of WWW'10*, pages 1029–1038. ACM, 2010.

[28] Y. Zheng, L. Zhang, Z. Ma, X. Xie, and W. Ma. Recommending friends and locations based on individual location history. *ACM Trans. Web*, 5(1):5, 2011.

Detecting Anomalies in Dynamic Rating Data: A Robust Probabilistic Model for Rating Evolution

Stephan Günnemann Nikou Günnemann Christos Faloutsos
Carnegie Mellon University, USA
{sguennem, nguennem, christos}@cs.cmu.edu

ABSTRACT

Rating data is ubiquitous on websites such as Amazon, TripAdvisor, or Yelp. Since ratings are not static but given at various points in time, a temporal analysis of rating data provides deeper insights into the evolution of a product's quality. In this work, we tackle the following question: Given the time stamped rating data for a product or service, how can we detect the general rating behavior of users as well as time intervals where the ratings behave anomalous?

We propose a Bayesian model that represents the rating data as sequence of categorical mixture models. In contrast to existing methods, our method does not require any aggregation of the input but it operates on the original time stamped data. To capture the dynamic effects of the ratings, the categorical mixtures are temporally constrained: Anomalies can occur in specific time intervals only and the general rating behavior should evolve smoothly over time. Our method automatically determines the intervals where anomalies occur, and it captures the temporal effects of the general behavior by using a state space model on the natural parameters of the categorical distributions. For learning our model, we propose an efficient algorithm combining principles from variational inference and dynamic programming. In our experimental study we show the effectiveness of our method and we present interesting discoveries on multiple real world datasets.

Categories and Subject Descriptors

H.2.8 [**Database Management**]: Database Applications —*Data mining*; I.2.6 [**Artificial Intelligence**]: Learning

Keywords

robust mining; anomaly detection; categorical mixtures

1. INTRODUCTION

Online rating data provides customers valuable information about products and services and supports their decision making process. Exploiting and presenting this data is a key feature of websites such as Amazon, Yelp, or Tripadvisor. Besides the usefulness of rating data for customers, also companies and manufactures can benefit from it by, e.g., using the data to detect functional weaknesses of their products or changes in the customers' satisfaction.

In this work, we propose a method for analyzing rating data that incorporates the data's temporal characteristics. Given the time stamped rating data for a product or service, we aim at detecting the general rating behavior of the users (called the base behavior) as well as time intervals in which these ratings deviate from the general population (anomalous behavior). The base behavior describes the general quality of a product or service accounting for temporal evolutions, e.g., resulting from decreasing quality due to technical progress of competing products. The anomalies, in contrast, deviate from the base behavior and might, e.g., occur due to spammers trying to push the success of a product or due to changes in the service quality.

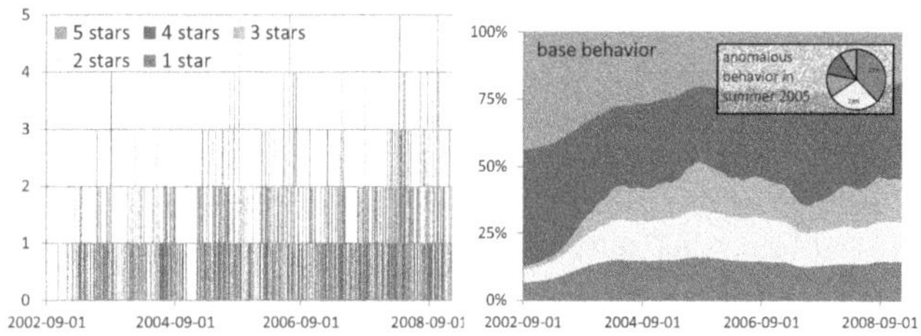

Fig. 1: Left: Time-stamped rating data analyzed by our method (here: a hotel from TripAdvisor). Right: Extracted base behavior. Upper corner: Anomalous behavior detected in summer 2005.

In Figure 1, we show a real world example for such an effect. The data we analyzed here is a hotel from the TripAdvisor database. On the left, we show a subset of the original time stamped data. The colors indicate the different star ratings, and the height of each bar the number of these ratings at the current time. Obviously, it is hard to analyze such data by hand. In particular, keep in mind that the ratings are not uniformly distributed over time.

On the right, we illustrate the detected *base behavior* of our method. As one can see, the base behavior nicely shows the general rating behavior of the users and evolves smoothly over time with primarily medium to high ratings. Additionally, our method has found anomalous behavior in the months of July and August 2005. As shown on the upper right, in these intervals, the fraction of low ratings (red and yellow) is highly increased compared to the base behavior (65% low ratings compared to around 30% in the base behavior). As we will show in Section 5, these anomalies occurred due to problems in the service of the hotel.

KDD'14, August 24–27, 2014, New York, NY, USA.
Copyright 2014 ACM 978-1-4503-2956-9/14/08 ...$15.00.
http://dx.doi.org/10.1145/2623330.2623721.

In general, our method detects time intervals in dynamic rating data which show anomalous behavior and – at the same time – it detects the base behavior if the data would *not* be polluted by anomalies. Besides using this principle to detect weaknesses in products and services, it can generally be used to filter out rating information which behave anomalous. Thereby, prospective customers might be provided with a cleaned history about the product; or, one might specifically highlight these time intervals to the users to provide the whole picture on a product (since otherwise these anomalous ratings are hidden in the larger set of normal behavior). As an additional benefit, we can exploit our method to predict the base behavior of future ratings. Accordingly, when new ratings arrive, we can estimate whether they match or deviate from the predicted behavior – thus, giving indication of new anomalies.

So far, there exists only a single method which analyzes temporal rating data under the presence of anomalies [7]. A potential drawback of [7], however, is the necessary aggregation/binning of the data. When using a coarse aggregation, the temporal effects of the data are not well captured (in the extreme, all data is a single bin). When using a fine aggregation, the analyzed distributions might degenerate (in the extreme, many bins are empty). In our model we avoid this problem by directly operating on the time stamped data which is modeled via a sequence of categorical mixture models. We explicitly keep into account that ratings might not uniformly arrive over time. Furthermore, the work [7] assumes that anomalies occur at individual points in time. Our work captures the effects of real data much better by accounting for multiple different types of anomalies appearing across several *time intervals*. Our contributions are:

- *Mining task:* We present a technique for the analysis of time stamped rating data. Our method detects the base behavior of users as well as time intervals where potential anomalies occurred. Additionally, our technique can be used to predict the rating behavior at future time points.
- *Theoretical soundness:* Our method is based on a sound Bayesian model that represents the rating data as a sequence of temporally constrained categorical mixture models. To capture the temporal effects of the base behavior we use a state space model on the natural parameters of the categorical distributions.
- *Algorithm design:* We propose an efficient algorithm for learning our model which combines principles from variational inference and dynamic programming.
- *Effectiveness:* We evaluate our method on different real world datasets and we show its effectiveness by presenting interesting findings.

2. BAYESIAN FRAMEWORK

In this section, we introduce our model for detecting the base rating behavior of users as well as time intervals in which anomalies have been occurred. Following convention, we do not distinguish between a random variable X and its realization $X = x$ if it is clear from the context. As an abbreviation, we denote sets of random variables with the index $*$, e.g. $z_*^{(t)}$ is the set $\{z_i^{(t)}\}$ with i in the corresponding domain, and z is an abbreviation for the set $z_*^{(*)}$. Vectors of (random) variables are written in bold font, e.g. $\boldsymbol{b}$, while the entries of the vectors are given in standard font, e.g. b_i. We write $t \in T$, as a shortcut for $t \in \{1, \ldots, T\}$.

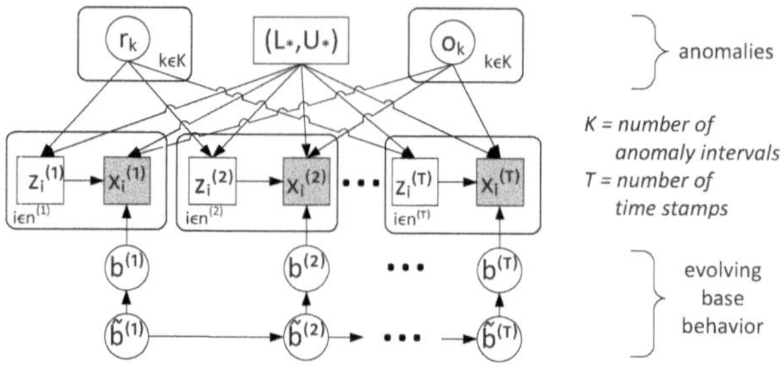

Fig. 2: Graphical model of our approach

Preliminaries. The data we consider is a time stamped collection of ratings. Let $x_i^{(t)}$ denote the i-th rating occurred at *time index* t, and $s^{(t)}$ the *time stamp* at time index t. At each time index we might observe multiple ratings (e.g. if time stamps are only measured/provided on a daily basis). We denote with $n^{(t)}$ the number of ratings at time index t. We assume the data to be ordered according to time, i.e. $s^{(t)}$ occurs after $s^{(t-1)}$. We denote with $\Delta^{(t_1,t_2)}$ the elapsed time between time stamp $s^{(t_1)}$ and $s^{(t_2)}$ and we set $\Delta^{(t)} := \Delta^{(t-1,t)}$. Note that for each t a different $\Delta^{(t)}$ might be observed since we do not require a fixed binning or aggregation of the rating data. We denote with T the number of time indices (i.e. the number of *distinct* time stamps) and we assume that users can choose ratings based on a rating scale with S different ratings (e.g. stars from 1 to S). As an abbreviation for later use, we define $n_s^{(t)} := |\{i \in \{1, \ldots, n^{(t)}\} \mid x_i^{(t)} = s\}|$ to be the number of ratings at time t which possess the evaluation $s \in S$.

Generative Process.

We model the rating data including potential anomalies via a probabilistic generative process. An overview of our generative process showing the used variables and their dependencies is illustrated by the graphical model in Figure 2. In the following we discuss the details of this process.

Given the observed rating data X, our aim is to extract the base behavior of the users and intervals in time where anomalies occur. Since the observed data might already be polluted by anomalies, we cannot directly use it to estimate the base behavior. Instead, we assume that the observed data is obtained by mixing the (unkown) base user behavior with the (unknown) anomaly behavior. Thus, both types of behavior are represented as *latent* variables which are not directly observed but inferred by our technique. Technically, at each point in time we have a categorical mixture model as illustrated in Figure 3. To incorporate the temporal properties of the data, we perform additional modeling:

Part 1: Mixing anomalies and base behavior. In contrast to the base behavior, which is present over the whole timespan, we assume that anomalies are rare events (otherwise, they would correspond to the majority of the data, making the term "anomaly" rather meaningless) and occur only in a specific time interval like, e.g., during a short attack of spam. Technically, instead of using an individual anomaly at each point in time, we restrict the number of anomalies to be small, i.e. smaller than a number K (we discuss later how to choose this parameter), and we temporally constrain the "influence" of each anomaly to a small time interval. For each anomaly, we define this interval by the random variables L_k and U_k, denoting the lower and upper bound of time indices at which the kth anomaly occurs.

In the following, we will use the function

$$k(t) = \begin{cases} k & \text{if } \exists x : x = k \wedge L_x \leq t \leq U_x \\ 0 & \text{else} \end{cases} \quad (1)$$

which maps the time index t to the corresponding anomaly (or to 0 if no anomaly exists at this point in time). Here, we require disjointness of the different intervals.

Note that the use of anomaly *intervals* is a huge advantage in contrast to [7], which models the anomalies at each time point individually. The potential of this extension is best shown for the case of very fine grained time stamps: In this case, we usually expect only a single rating per time stamp, i.e. $n^{(t)} = 1$. To capture anomalies at multiple consecutive points in time, the work of [7] has to use multiple anomalies, while in our work a single interval suffices.

At this point we want to mention the difference between outliers and anomalies [7]: While *outliers* are irregular behavior attributed to mostly random corruptions of the data (like, e.g., measurement errors), *anomalies* are irregular behavior that follow a specific pattern (like, e.g., time points with consistently low ratings due to a change in the product's quality). In our work, we consider anomalous behavior.

Giving the above information, the observed data at time t is modeled as a categorical mixture model defined by

$$x_i^{(t)} \sim \begin{cases} \text{Categorical}(\boldsymbol{\pi}^{(t)}) & \text{if } z_i^{(t)} = 0 \\ \text{Categorical}(\mathbf{o}_{k(t)}) & \text{if } z_i^{(t)} = 1 \end{cases} \quad (2)$$

$$z_i^{(t)} \sim \begin{cases} 0 & \text{if } k(t) = 0 \\ \text{Bernoulli}(r_{k(t)}) & \text{else} \end{cases} \quad (3)$$

Here, $z_i^{(t)}$ is the indicator variable showing which ratings are anomalies. $\boldsymbol{\pi}^{(t)} \in [0...1]^S$ is the vector describing the base behavior at time t, $\mathbf{o}_k \in [0...1]^S$ is the kth anomaly behavior, and r_k is the mixing proportion. The higher the value of r_k, the higher the proportion of anomalies within the corresponding interval. If no anomaly is present at time t, all variables $z_*^{(t)}$ are set to zero, corresponding of using only the base behavior at this point in time. Thus, the mixture model's components referring to the anomalies are constrained to specific intervals (cf. Figure 3).

For a Bayesian treatment, we equip the variables with corresponding prior distributions. We use

$$\mathbf{o}_k \sim Dir(\hat{\boldsymbol{\alpha}}) \qquad r_k \sim Beta(\hat{\alpha}, \hat{\beta})$$

due to the properties of conjugacy. The vector $\hat{\boldsymbol{\alpha}}$, for example, can be used to specify prior knowledge about potential anomalies (e.g. anomalies should represent primarily low ratings). In all of our experiments we use $\hat{\boldsymbol{\alpha}} = \mathbf{1}$ and $\hat{\alpha} = \hat{\beta} = 1$ corresponding to non-informative priors.

For the lower and upper bounds we exploit the idea that anomalies should appear primarily in short time intervals. That is, we assume that the probability to observe an anomaly over a very long time frame is lower than the probability to observe anomalies over only a few time points. We capture this effect by drawing the lower and upper bounds according to an exponential distribution controlled by the duration $\Delta^{(L_k,U_k)}$ of the anomaly interval. Formally

$$p(L_*, U_*) \propto \begin{cases} \prod_{k=1}^{K} e^{-\lambda \cdot \Delta^{(L_k,U_k)}} & \text{if disjoint intervals} \\ 0 & \text{else} \end{cases} \quad (4)$$

Please note that this is the joint distribution over all intervals since we require their disjointness. The larger λ, the larger the bias to small anomaly intervals. Per default, if no prior knowledge is given, one should select $\lambda = 0$. In this case, any combination of L_*, U_* is equally likely, corresponding to a non-informative prior. Note also that $\lambda = 0$ is a *valid* prior since the domain of L_*, U_* is finite.

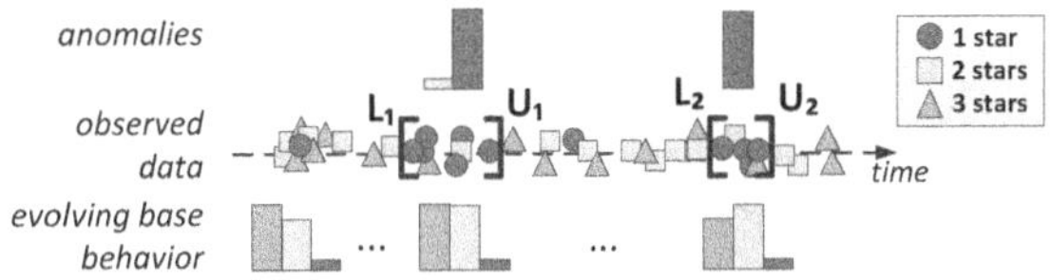

Fig. 3: Illustration of the generative process using temporally constrained categorical mixture models

Part 2: Smoothness of the base behavior. So far, we have not specified any distribution on the base behavior $\boldsymbol{\pi}^{(t)}$. The core idea is that the base behavior should evolve smoothly over time according to the general behavior of the users. That is, we want to incorporate the temporal properties of the data.

As pointed out in [6], the (mean) parameters of the categorical distribution and their corresponding Dirichlet hyperparameters are not amenable to sequential modeling. Therefore, we exploit a similar idea as proposed in [6, 17]: instead of operating on the (mean) parameters $\boldsymbol{\pi}^{(t)}$, we operate on the natural parameters (cf. exponential family [5]). For the categorical distribution, the natural parameters are simply given by the logs of the mean values, i.e. $b_s^{(t)} = log(\pi_s^{(t)}/\pi_S^{(t)})$. While the mean parameters are restricted to lie on the simplex, the natural parameters are unconstrained, leading to an elegant way of sequential modeling.

In the following, we only operate on the natural parameters $\mathbf{b}^{(t)}$. If the mean parameters are required (e.g. as in Equation 2), we can simply apply the transformation

$$\pi_s^{(t)} = \frac{exp(b_s^{(t)})}{\sum_{j \in S} exp(b_j^{(t)})} =: \pi(\mathbf{b}^{(t)})_s$$

Note that the term $b_S^{(t)}$ is always 0. Therefore, we can ignore it for the remainder of the discussion, thus, operating effectively on an $S-1$ dimensional space.

Given the natural parameters $\mathbf{b}^{(t)}$ at each time index $t \in T$, we model their smoothness by exploiting the idea of linear state space systems [5] in combination with Brownian motion [11, 17]. First, we assume an underlying state space $\widetilde{\mathbf{b}}^{(t)}$ which temporally evolves over time via

$$\widetilde{\mathbf{b}}^{(t)} \sim \mathcal{N}(\widetilde{\mathbf{b}}^{(t-1)}, \Delta^{(t)} \cdot \mathbf{Q}) \quad (5)$$

$$\widetilde{\mathbf{b}}^{(1)} \sim \mathcal{N}(\widetilde{\mathbf{b}}_0, \mathbf{Q}_0)$$

We call this space the "smoothed" base behavior. Intuitively, the state of the smoothed base behavior at time t corresponds to the old state plus a small deviation governement by the noise covariance matrix $\Delta^{(t)} \cdot \mathbf{Q}$. The larger the time difference between two observed ratings, the larger the corresponding covariance. That is, we effectively allow a higher change in the base behavior if the elapsed time between two ratings is high. If time points are very close to each other, we allow only small changes in the base behavior. In the limit, this discrete-time Gaussian random walk corresponds to Brownian motion [11, 17].

This process captures naturally the effects of rating data. In the case of movies, for example, one might see many ratings appearing in short time frames during the time the movie has been released to the theaters and again many ratings a few month later when the DVD has been released. Both time frames potentially describe different base behavior due to different audiences.

Given the smoothed base behavior, the actual base behavior is now obtained by the simple random process

$$\mathbf{b}^{(t)} \sim \mathcal{N}(\widetilde{\mathbf{b}}^{(t)}, \mathbf{R}) \tag{6}$$

which again allows a small deviation between the base behavior and its smoothed counterpart. Note that we do not directly impose the temporal evolution between the variables $\mathbf{b}^{(*)}$, but via the state space $\widetilde{\mathbf{b}}^{(*)}$. This additional layer is in particular beneficial if the number of ratings varies strongly between the time points. If we would not use $\widetilde{\mathbf{b}}^{(*)}$, a single time point with a huge amount of ratings could dominate most of the temporal behavior.

Finally, we add corresponding priors to the newly introduced parameters. By exploiting the fact of conjugacy it follows that $\mathbf{Q}$ is drawn from an Inverse-Wishart distribution, i.e. $\mathbf{Q} \sim \mathcal{W}^{-1}(\Psi_q^0, \nu_q^0)$. The parameters Ψ_q^0 and ν_q^0 can be used to control the smoothness of the base behavior by providing prior knowledge about the noise covariance. Similarly, $\mathbf{R}$ follows an Inverse-Wishart distribution and $(\widetilde{\mathbf{b}}_0, \mathbf{Q}_0)$ a Normal-Inverse-Wishart distribution.

Summary and Discussion.

Overall, our generative process captures the temporal properties of the data by modeling a smooth base behavior as well as accounting for anomalies which are constrained to occur at certain time intervals. We will show in Section 3 how we perform efficient (approximate) inference for this model.

Model Selection. So far, we assumed the number K of anomalies is given. If not apriori known, we can estimate it via model selection. We choose the Bayesian information criterion [5]. Any other criterion can be used as well.

As we will see in Sec. 3, we will integrate out all latent variables except of $\Theta = \{L_*, U_*, \boldsymbol{Q}, \boldsymbol{R}\}$. Thus, increasing the value of K by one, increases the number of free parameters in our model by about 2 (the lower and upper bound of the new anomaly interval). This is a slight overestimate since the intervals need to be disjoint and, thus, they are not completely independently free variables. Given this result, we can choose the K minimizing the BIC equation

$$BIC(K) = -2 \cdot \ln \mathcal{L}_K + (2 \cdot K + c) \cdot \ln(\sum_t n^{(t)})$$

Here, the constant c denotes the parameters of the model which do not increase when increasing K. Since the value of c does not affect the optimal choice for K, we can simply set it to 0. The term $\mathcal{L}_K$ denotes the likelihood of the data when using K anomaly intervals. We can approximate it with the technique shown in Section 3.

Prediction. Since the base behavior evolves via a linear state space system, we are able to predict the behavior at future points in time. Combining Eq. 5 and 6, it follows

$$\mathbf{b}^{(T+1)} \sim \mathcal{N}(\widetilde{\mathbf{b}}^{(T)}, \mathbf{R} + \Delta^{(T+1)} \cdot \mathbf{Q}) \tag{7}$$

Thus, given estimates for $\widetilde{\mathbf{b}}^{(T)}$, $\mathbf{R}$, and $\mathbf{Q}$ (cf. Section 3), comparing the observed ratings at time $T+1$ against the predicted base behavior can be used as an indicator whether new anomalies have been occurred.

3. ALGORITHM

While the previous section focused on the model's generative process, we now present our learning technique. That is, *given* a set of observations X we aim at inferring the values of the hidden variables which best describe the observed data. There are multiple ways to formulate this objective. In this work, we treat the variables $\Theta = \{L_*, U_*, \boldsymbol{Q}, \boldsymbol{R}\}$ as parameters and we are interested in finding their maximum a posteriori estimate Θ_{MAP} as well as the posterior distribution $p(V|X, \Theta_{MAP})$ of the latent variables $V = \{\mathbf{o}_*, r_*, z_*^{(*)}, \mathbf{b}^{(*)}, \widetilde{\mathbf{b}}^{(*)}\}$ (which can then, e.g., be used to pick specific realizations of the latent variables).

3.1 Variational EM

Since exact inference in our model is intractable, we compute an approximation using variational expectation-maximization [5]. The idea is to approximate $p(V|X, \Theta)$ by a tractable family of parametrized distributions $q(V|\Omega)$. The parameters Ω are the free variational parameters. These parameters are optimized such that the best approximation between q and p is obtained. This corresponds to the expectation step of the variational EM method. Technically, we minimize the Kullback-Leibler divergence between q and p by optimizing over Ω. Using Jensen's inequality, minimizing the KL divergence is equivalent to maximizing the following lower bound on the log marginal likelihood [5]:

$$\mathcal{L}(X; \Theta, \Omega) = \mathbb{E}_q[\ln p(X, V, \Theta)] + H(q) \tag{8}$$

where $\mathbb{E}_q[.]$ denotes the expectation w.r.t. the q distribution and H the entropy.

Given an approximation of $p(V|X, \Theta)$ via $q(V|\Omega)$, we then determine updated parameter values for Θ by again maximizing Equation 8. This corresponds to the maximization step of the EM method.[1]

In short, the general processing scheme of our method is to alternatingly maximize $\mathcal{L}(X; \Theta, \Omega)$ w.r.t. Ω and Θ. *As we will later see, we actually interweave both steps by simultaneously optimizing parts of Θ and Ω.*

3.1.1 Variational distribution

In contrast to the frequently used mean field approximation, which assumes a fully factorized distribution, we use

$$p(V \mid X, \Theta) \approx q(V|\Omega) := \prod_k q_1(\mathbf{o}_k) \cdot \prod_k q_2(r_k) \cdot \prod_t \prod_i q_3(z_i^{(t)}) \cdot \prod_t q_4(\mathbf{b}^{(t)}) \cdot q_5(\widetilde{\mathbf{b}}^{(1)}) \cdot \prod_{t>1} q_5(\widetilde{\mathbf{b}}^{(t)} \mid \widetilde{\mathbf{b}}^{(t-1)})$$

We retain the sequential structure of the smoothed base behavior in q_5. Indeed, as described later, we determine q_5 via a Kalman filter where it follows that $q_5(\widetilde{\mathbf{b}}^{(t)}|\widetilde{\mathbf{b}}^{(t-1)})$ is a Normal distribution given by $\mathcal{N}(\widetilde{\mathbf{b}}^{(t)} \mid \widetilde{\boldsymbol{\mu}}_{t|T}, \mathbf{P}_{t|T})$. For the remaining variational distributions we use

$$q_1(\mathbf{o}_k) = Dir(\mathbf{o}_k|\boldsymbol{\alpha}_k) \qquad q_3(z_i^{(t)}) = Bernoulli(z_i^{(t)}|\phi_{t,i})$$
$$q_2(r_k) = Beta(r_k|\alpha_k, \beta_k) \quad q_4(\mathbf{b}^{(t)}) = \mathcal{N}(\mathbf{b}^{(t)}|\boldsymbol{\mu}^{(t)}, v^{(t)} \cdot I)$$

where $\Omega = \{\boldsymbol{\alpha}_*, \alpha_*, \beta_*, \phi_{*,*}, \boldsymbol{\mu}^{(*)}, v^{(*)}\}$ are the variational parameters to be optimized.

[1]The only actual difference between these steps is that Θ represents a point estimate of the random variables, while Ω represents the hyperparameters of a full distribution.

Note that the distributions $q_3(z_i^{(t)})$ and $q_3(z_{i'}^{(t)})$ are identical when $x_i^{(t)} = x_{i'}^{(t)}$, i.e. when both ratings have the same value. Thus, in practice we do not need to keep track of $n^{(t)}$ many different distributions at time t but it is sufficient to record S many distributions; one for each possible evaluation. We denote with ϕ_t^s the variational parameter of the distribtion q_3 for all ratings showing evaluation s at time t.

3.1.2 *Optimization Procedures*

As described above, our goal is to update the values of Ω and Θ by maximizing (or more generally increasing) the value of Equation 8. One crucial requirement of our technique was to ensure the efficiency of our method. In the following, we want to highlight the most important results.

3.2 Optimizing the Lower/Upper Bounds

A first naive solution to update the lower/upper bounds of the anomaly intervals would be to test any possible combination. Obviously, this solution is not efficient and requires time $O(T^2)$ already for a single anomaly. We provide a principle which is *linear* in the number of time stamps.

We start with the case of a single anomaly and uniform gaps between all time stamps, i.e. it holds K=1 and $\Delta^{(t)}$=1 for all t.

3.2.1 *Simultaneous Optimization*

Equation 3 shows the dependency between L_1/U_1 and z. Intuitively, the bounds act as a switch on the distribution of z: if z is outside of the interval, it is the trivial 0 distribution; if it is inside, it is a Bernoulli. Accordingly, assuming the posterior distribution for z (or its approximation q_3) is *given*, an optimization of L_1/U_1 is rather meaningless since one trivially has to capture all time points where the distribution is not the constant 0. Therefore, we propose to *simultaneously* optimize L_1/U_1 and q_3 to maximize Equation 8.

Observation: If we know that a time point t fulfills $t \in [L_k, U_k]$, the optimal distribution of $q_3(z_i^{(t)})$ can be computed independent from all other points in time. The optimal distribution is obtained by setting its variational parameter $\phi_{t,i}/\phi_t^s$ to the value as derived in Sec. 3.3. In particular, this value is independent of the actual values of L_k and U_k (knowing that $t \in [L_k, U_k]$). Based on this result we can also compute the entropy

$$h_{t,s} := H(q_3(z_i^{(t)})) = -\phi_t^s \ln \phi_t^s - (1-\phi_t^s)\ln(1-\phi_t^s)$$

for all $z_i^{(t)}$ fulfilling $x_i^{(t)}$=s. If $t \notin [L_k, U_k]$, we have $q_3(z_i^{(t)} = 0) = 1$ and we define the entropy $H(q_3)$ to be zero.

Using these results and the derivations of the appendix, as well as removing all terms which are independent of L_1, U_1 and q_3, we can reformulate Equation 8 to:

$$\ln p(L_*, U_*) + \sum_{t \in T} \sum_{i \in n^{(t)}} \mathbb{E}_q[\ln p(z_i^{(t)}|\ldots) + \ln p(x_i^{(t)}|\ldots)] + H(q_3(z_i^{(t)}))$$

$$= -\lambda \cdot \Delta^{(L_1,U_1)} + \sum_{t \notin [L_1,U_1]} \sum_{s=1}^{S} n_s^{(t)} \cdot \mathbb{E}_q\left[\ln \pi(\mathbf{b}^{(t)})_s\right] + \sum_{t \in [L_1,U_1]} \Big($$

$$\sum_{s=1}^{S} [n_s^{(t)} \cdot h_{t,s} + n_s^{(t)} \cdot \phi_t^s \cdot (\mathbb{E}_q[\ln r_{k(t)}] + \mathbb{E}_q[\ln o_{k(t),s}])$$

$$+ n_s^{(t)} \cdot [1-\phi_t^s] \cdot (\mathbb{E}_q[\ln(1-r_{k(t)})] + \mathbb{E}_q[\ln \pi(\mathbf{b}^{(t)})_s])]\Big)$$

$$= \lambda + \sum_{t \in T} \sum_{s=1}^{S} n_s^{(t)} \cdot \mathbb{E}_q\left[\ln \pi(\mathbf{b}^{(t)})_s\right] + \sum_{t \in [L_1,U_1]} f_1(t) \quad (9)$$

where we used the fact $\Delta^{(L_k,U_k)} = U_k - L_k$ and we defined

$$f_k(t) := -\lambda + \sum_{s=1}^{S} n_s^{(t)} \cdot \phi_t^s \cdot [\mathbb{E}_q[\ln r_k] + \mathbb{E}_q[\ln o_{k,s}] - \mathbb{E}_q\left[\ln \pi(\mathbf{b}^{(t)})_s\right]]$$
$$+ n_s^{(t)} \cdot [1-\phi_t^s] \cdot \mathbb{E}_q[\ln(1-r_k)] + n_s^{(t)} \cdot h_{t,s}$$

Intuitively, the function $f_1(t)$ measures the "gain" in the log-likelihood when adding t to the anomaly interval.

The first two terms of Eq. 9 can be removed since they are constant w.r.t. the bounds and q_3 and thus do *not* affect the optimal solution. Accordingly, maximizing Eq. 8/9 w.r.t. L_1, U_1, and q_3 is equivalent to solving

$$(L_1^*, U_1^*) = \arg\max_{(L_1,U_1)} \sum_{t=L_1}^{U_1} f_1(t) \quad \text{with } 1 \le L_1 \le U_1 \le T$$

Since the function f_1 is independent of L_1/U_1, i.e. the terms $f_1(t)$ are constant within the current optimization step, we can record all values $f_1(t)$ in a finite array of length T. Thus, the above problem corresponds to the *Maximum Subarray Problem*. Using Kadane's algorithm [4], this problem can be solved in time $O(T)$.

3.2.2 *Non-uniform gaps between timestamps*

So far, we assumed $\Delta^{(t)} = 1$ for all $t \in T$. We now generalize the above result to handle varying values for $\Delta^{(t)}$.

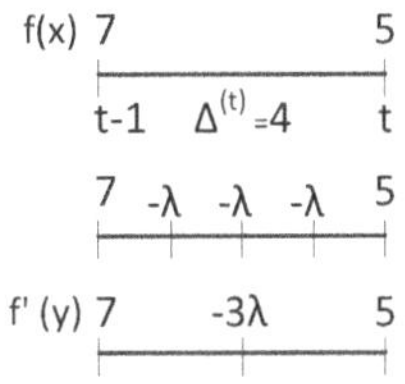

Fig. 4: Handling non-uniformity

W.l.o.g., due to finite precision in the measurement of time (e.g. UTC timestamps are usually measured in seconds), we can assume $\Delta^{(t)} \in \mathbb{N}^+$. Thus, a naive approach to handle the scenario of non-uniform gaps is to "blow up" the actual data by "artificial" time points where no ratings occur. After including the artificial time points, the Δ values are again equal to 1, and the previous technique can be applied. Figure 4 top and middle show this principle. Obviously, this principle is not suitable for huge time gaps and the new size of the array can be arbitrarily large.

Considering $f_1(t)$, it becomes apparent that its value evaluates to $-\lambda$ for each artificial time point. When searching for the subarray with maximal sum, these negative entries will never occur at the beginning/end of the anomaly interval [3]. If they would be at the beginning/end, one could easily shorten the interval to obtain a new one with higher sum. Thus, artificial time points are either completely contained in the interval or not included at all.

Using this result, we can safely "merge" all adjacent artificial time points to a single one with the function value $-\lambda \cdot u^{(t)}$, where $u^{(t)}$ is the number of artificial time points between time index t and $t-1$. Clearly, $u^{(t)} = \Delta^{(t)} - 1$ and the number of merged artificial time points is bounded by $T-1$. Overall, we can define a new array f' of size $2 \cdot T - 1$ where

$$f_k'(y) = \begin{cases} f_k(\frac{y+1}{2}) & \text{if } y \text{ is odd} \\ -\lambda \cdot (\Delta^{(\frac{y}{2}+1)} - 1) & \text{if } y \text{ is even} \end{cases}$$

for $y \in [1, 2 \cdot T - 1]$. And we now solve the problem

$$(a^*, b^*) = \arg\max_{(a,b)} \sum_{y=a}^{b} f_1'(y)$$

and set $(L_1^*, U_1^*) = (\frac{a^*+1}{2}, \frac{b^*+1}{2})$. Since the size of f' is bounded by $2 \cdot T - 1$ the runtime complexity is $O(T)$.

3.2.3 Extension to multiple intervals

We now extend our result to multiple different anomalies/intervals. Using multiple anomalies affects the choice of the optimal q_3 distribution (cf. paragraph 'Observation' in Section 3.2.1). It is no longer sufficient to know whether $t \in [L_k, U_k]$ but we also have to know *which* k we consider.[2] Accordingly, for each anomaly k we have to use its individual function f_k/f'_k to measure the gain of adding a time point to the anomaly interval k. Overall, maximizing Eq. 8 using multiple intervals corresponds to solving

$$\underset{(a_1,b_1),\ldots,(a_K,b_K)}{\arg\max} \sum_{k\in K}\sum_{y=a_k}^{b_k} f'_k(y) \text{ with } a_k \le b_k < a_{k+1} \quad (10)$$

We solve the above problem by a dynamic programming technique. The necessary recursions are given by

$$g(1,1) = f'_1(1) \qquad g(1,t) = \max\{g(1,t-1) + f'_1(t), f'_1(t)\}$$
$$g(k,k) = m(k-1,k-1) + f'_k(k)$$
$$g(k,t) = \max\{g(k,t-1) + f'_k(t), m(k-1,t-1) + f'_k(t)\}$$
$$m(k,k) = g(k,k) \qquad m(k,t) = \max\{g(k,t), m(k,t-1)\}$$

Here, $m(k,t)$ (for $t \ge k$) denotes the maximal value of Eq. 10 when using k intervals and data up to point t. In contrast, $g(k,t)$ denotes the maximal value of Eq. 10 when the kth interval is forced to end at the t-th point in time (using k intervals and data up to t). Obviously, $g(k,t) \le m(k,t)$ holds. The value of $m(K,T)$ is the optimal value of Eq. 10.

We only provide a brief idea of these recursions: Assume we know the optimal intervals when using $k-1$ anomalies and data up to time point $t-1$. Let these intervals be denoted $(L_1,U_1),\ldots,(L_{k-1},U_{k-1})$. Additionally, assume the optimal intervals for k anomalies and data up to time point $t-1$ are given, denoted with $(L'_1,U'_1),\ldots,(L'_k,U'_k)$. Finally, assume the optimal intervals are given when the last interval is forced to end at time $t-1$ (we call these the g-intervals). Denote these with $(\hat{L}'_1,\hat{U}'_1),\ldots,(\hat{L}'_k,\hat{U}'_k)$, here $\hat{U}'_k = t-1$.

How will the solution for k intervals and data up to t look like? We can distinguish the following cases: (1) The time point t will be included in the optimal intervals. Obviously, since we are at the last point in time, it can only be represented by the kth interval. We can distinguish two subcases: (1a) The time point t is the beginning of the kth interval. In this case, the optimal intervals are $(L_1,U_1),\ldots,(L_{k-1},U_{k-1}),(t,t)$ and $m(k,t) = m(k-1,t-1) + f'_k(t)$. Since the last interval already ends at t, we also have $g(k,t) = m(k-1,t-1) + f'_k(t)$. (1b) The time point t is *not* the beginning of the kth interval. Thus, the optimal solution needs to be $(\hat{L}'_1,\hat{U}'_1),\ldots,(\hat{L}'_k,t)$ and we obtain $m(k,t) = g(k,t) = g(k,t-1) + f'_k(t)$.

(2) The time point t will *not* be included in the optimal intervals. In this case, since we want to find k intervals, the optimal solution is $(L'_1,U'_1),\ldots,(L'_k,U'_k)$ and $m(k,t) = m(k,t-1)$. For the g-intervals we have to distinguish two cases: (2a) The time point t is the beginning of the kth g-interval. In this case, the new g-intervals are $(L_1,U_1),\ldots,(L_{k-1},U_{k-1}),(t,t)$ and $g(k,t) = m(k-1,t-1) + f'_k(t)$. (Note that we use the optimal intervals from $m(k-1,t-1)$, not the g-intervals!) (2b) The time point t is *not* the beginning of the kth g-interval. Thus, leading to the solution $(\hat{L}'_1,\hat{U}'_1),\ldots,(\hat{L}'_k,t)$ with $g(k,t) = g(k,t-1) + f'_k(t)$.

[2] Technically, we could write $\phi^s_{t,k}$ to denote the optimal hyperparameter of q_3 assuming $t \in [L_k, U_k]$. We omitted k for brevity.

Exploiting the fact $g(x,y) \le m(x,y)$ and that we want to maximize $m(x,y)$, leads to the recursion as defined above. It is easy to add data structures to the method which record the start/end positions of the optimal intervals. Solving the above recursions via dynamic programming, we obtain:

THEOREM 1. *The optimal values for L_*, U_* and the optimal distributions q^*_3 can be computed in time $O(K \cdot T)$.*

3.3 Optimization of q_1, q_2, q_3

Following the principle of [5], the optimal distribution for q_3 can be determined by

$$\ln q^*_3(z_i^{(t)}) = \mathbb{E}_{q\setminus z_i^{(t)}}[\ln p(X,V,\Theta)] + const$$

Here, the constant $const$ absorbs all terms which are independent of $z_i^{(t)}$ and, thus, do not affected the optimal distribution of q_3. The term $\mathbb{E}_{q\setminus z_i^{(t)}}[.]$ denotes the expectation with respect to the distribution q taken overall all variables except of $z_i^{(t)}$. Assuming $k(t) = k \neq 0$, and using the results from the appendix, it follows that

$$\ln q^*_3(z_i^{(t)} = 1) = \mathbb{E}_q[\ln r_k] + \mathbb{E}_q[\ln o_{k,s}] =: x$$
$$\ln q^*_3(z_i^{(t)} = 0) = \mathbb{E}_q[\ln(1-r_k)] + \mathbb{E}_q[\ln \pi(\mathbf{b}^{(t)})_s] =: y$$

where $s = x_i^t$. Therefore, the optimal value of the variational parameter is $\phi_{t,i} = \phi^s_t = \frac{e^x}{e^x + e^y}$.

The same principle can be applied for the distributions q_1 and q_2, leading to

$$\alpha_{k,s} = (\hat{\boldsymbol{\alpha}})_s + \sum_{t=L_k}^{U_k} n_s^{(t)} \cdot \phi^s_t$$

$$\alpha_k = \hat{\alpha} + \sum_{t=L_k}^{U_k}\sum_{s=1}^{S} n_s^{(t)} \cdot \phi^s_t \qquad \beta_k = \hat{\beta} + \sum_{t=L_k}^{U_k}\sum_{s=1}^{S} n_s^{(t)} \cdot (1-\phi^s_t)$$

3.4 Remaining Optimizations

Optimizing the base behavior. The base behavior can be updated for each $\mathbf{b}^{(t)}$ independently. Removing all terms from Equation 8 which are independent of $\mathbf{b}^{(t)}$ leads to

$$\mathbb{E}_q[\sum_i \ln p(x_i^{(t)}|\ldots)] + \mathbb{E}_q[\ln p(\mathbf{b}^{(t)}|\tilde{\mathbf{b}}^{(t-1)}, \mathbf{R})] + H(q_4(\mathbf{b}^{(t)})) \quad (11)$$

The first term is given in the appendix, and $H(q_4(\mathbf{b}^{(t)})) = \frac{S-1}{2}\ln(2\pi e v^{(t)})$. For the second term we derive:

$$\mathbb{E}_q\left[\ln p(\mathbf{b}^{(t)} \mid \ldots)\right] = -\frac{1}{2}\cdot\mathbb{E}_q\left[(\mathbf{b}^{(t)} - \tilde{\mathbf{b}}^{(t)})^T \cdot \mathbf{R}^{-1} \cdot (\mathbf{b}^{(t)} - \tilde{\mathbf{b}}^{(t)})\right] + c_1$$
$$= -\frac{1}{2}\mathbb{E}_q\left[\mathbf{b}^{(t)^T} \cdot \mathbf{R}^{-1} \cdot \mathbf{b}^{(t)}\right] + \mathbb{E}_q\left[\mathbf{b}^{(t)^T} \cdot \mathbf{R}^{-1} \cdot \tilde{\mathbf{b}}^{(t)}\right] + c_2$$
$$= -\frac{1}{2}\left[Tr(\mathbf{R}^{-1} \cdot v^{(t)}) + \boldsymbol{\mu}^{(t)^T} \cdot \mathbf{R}^{-1} \cdot \boldsymbol{\mu}^{(t)}\right] + \tilde{\boldsymbol{\mu}}^T_{t|T} \cdot \mathbf{R}^{-1}\boldsymbol{\mu}^{(t)} + c_3$$

We absorbed all terms which are independent of $\mathbf{b}^{(t)}$ into the constants c_i. Overall, Eq. 11 can be written as a function of $\boldsymbol{\mu}^{(t)}$ and $v^{(t)}$, which we optimize using gradient ascent.

Optimizing the smoothed base behavior. Since our model corresponds to a linear system, we can use a Kalman filter/smoother to determine the distribution of q_5. We use the Rauch-Tung-Striebel smoother. Thus, the distribution of q_5 can be computed efficiently by a forward and backward pass, leading to an update with runtime complexity $O(T)$.

Since the outputs $\mathbf{b}^{(t)}$ of the dynamic system are not observations but distributions, we slightly adapt the Kalman update/innovation equations. Following the standard calculus of Kalman filters, the predicted mean and covariance matrix for time t (given data up to time $t-1$) are given by $\widetilde{\boldsymbol{\mu}}_{t|t-1} = \widetilde{\boldsymbol{\mu}}_{t-1|t-1}$ and $\mathbf{P}_{t|t-1} = \mathbf{P}_{t-1|t-1} + \Delta^{(t)} \cdot \mathbf{Q}$. Given the measurement at time t, the measurement residual can be computed as $\mathbf{e}_t = \mathbb{E}_q[\mathbf{b}^{(t)}] - \widetilde{\boldsymbol{\mu}}_{t|t-1}$. Accordingly, the residual covariance is given by $\mathbf{S}_t = \mathbf{P}_{t|t-1} + \mathbf{R} + v^{(t)} \cdot I$. Note the increased variance due to the uncertainty of the base behavior. Letting the Kalman gain be defined by $\mathbf{K}_t = \mathbf{P}_{t|t-1} \cdot \mathbf{S}_t^{-1}$, we see that the Kalman gain is smaller for time points showing a high variance, i.e. high uncertainty, in the base behavior. These points affect the smoothed base behavior less strongly.

Continuing with the standard calculus, the updated mean and covariance are $\widetilde{\boldsymbol{\mu}}_{t|t} = \widetilde{\boldsymbol{\mu}}_{t|t-1} + \mathbf{K}_t \cdot \mathbf{e}_t$ and $\mathbf{P}_{t|t} = (I - \mathbf{K}_t) \cdot \mathbf{P}_{t|t-1} \cdot (I - \mathbf{K}_t)^T + \mathbf{K}_t \cdot \mathbf{R} \cdot \mathbf{K}_t^T$. Here, we used the Joseph form of the covariance update equation since it holds for any value of $\mathbf{K}_t$. For the backward pass, the RTS smoother leads to $\widetilde{\boldsymbol{\mu}}_{t|T} = \widetilde{\boldsymbol{\mu}}_{t|t} + C_t \cdot (\widetilde{\boldsymbol{\mu}}_{t+1|T} - \widetilde{\boldsymbol{\mu}}_{t+1|t})$ and $\mathbf{P}_{t|T} = \mathbf{P}_{t|t} + C_t \cdot (\mathbf{P}_{t+1|T} - \mathbf{P}_{t+1|t}) \cdot C_t^T$, with $C_t = \mathbf{P}_{t|t} \cdot \mathbf{P}_{t+1|t}^{-1}$. Due to space limitations, we kindly refer to the rich literature on Kalman filter/smoother, for details about the derivations.

Optimization of Q and R. Updating $\mathbf{Q}$ and $\mathbf{R}$ follows from the properties of the conjugate prior. Note that Eq. 5 can also be written in the form $\widetilde{\mathbf{b}}^{(t)} - \widetilde{\mathbf{b}}^{(t-1)} \sim \mathcal{N}(0, \Delta^{(t)} \cdot \mathbf{Q})$. Also, by the definition of the normal distribution it holds that $\mathcal{N}(\mathbf{x}|0, \Delta \cdot \Sigma) = \Delta^{-d/2} \cdot \mathcal{N}(\mathbf{x}/\sqrt{\Delta}|0, \Sigma)$, where d is the dimensionality of the distribution. Since the terms $\Delta^{-d/2}$ are constant when optimizing the log-likelihood, they can be ignored. Thus, $\mathbf{Q}$ can be seen as the covariance matrix of a Normal distribution with *known* mean of zero. Correspondingly, we can use the Inverse-Wishart distribution as its (conjugate) prior. Following the results of conjugacy, the posterior distribution of $\mathbf{Q}$ is an Inverse-Wishart distribution $\mathcal{W}^{-1}(\Psi_q, \nu_q)$ with $\nu_q = \nu_q^0 + T - 1$ and scale matrix

$$\Psi_q = \Psi_q^0 + \sum_{t=2}^{T} \mathbb{E}_q \left[\frac{1}{\Delta^{(t)}} \left(\widetilde{\mathbf{b}}^{(t)} - \widetilde{\mathbf{b}}^{(t-1)} \right)^T \cdot \left(\widetilde{\mathbf{b}}^{(t)} - \widetilde{\mathbf{b}}^{(t-1)} \right) \right]$$

which can easily be computed by plugging in the known expectations. Given this distribution, the MAP estimate for $\mathbf{Q}$ can efficiently determined by selecting the mode of the Inverse-Wishart distribution, i.e. $\mathbf{Q}^* = \frac{1}{(S-1)+1+\nu_q} \cdot \Psi_q$. The same principle can be applied for $\mathbf{R}$.

3.5 Overall Processing and Complexity

Using the above optimizations and update equations, our method iteratively recomputes the values for Θ and Ω. If the change in Equation 8 is less than 0.1% we assume convergence and terminate. Based on the previous results, and assuming that $K, S << T$, each iteration is linear in the number of time stamps, i.e. we have a complexity of $O(T)$.

4. RELATED WORK

Spotting anomalies in rating data: So far, only [7] considers the temporal analysis of rating data incorporating potentially anomalous behavior. The work models the rating data as distributions over time. As mentioned in the introduction, it requires an aggregation/binning of the data and it cannot handle intervals of anomalies. We compare our technique against [7] in the experimental analysis.

Modeling of temporal continuous data: Similar to the work [7], traditional time series modeling methods such as vector autoregression [14, 13] or Kalman filter/smoother [5], analyze continuous data. They are not directly suited for our scenario of categorical data (or require a problematic binning). Furthermore, traditional approaches for time series modeling are sensitive to outliers. Thus, these models fail to find good approximations of the data corrupted by anomalies. Therefore, robust techniques to handle outliers have been proposed [16]. These methods are designed to handle *outliers* which are attributed to mostly independent, random corruptions of the data, while our work is designed to handle *anomalies* following a specific pattern.

Since in our work the Kalman filter operates on the (clean) base behavior, i.e. the anomalies have been 'removed' by the other mixture model components, the problem of anomalies is circumvented. We compare our technique against a Kalman filter in the experimental analysis.

Modeling of temporal documents: One might represent the ratings at a certain point in time as a document with the words corresponding to the ratings' evaluations. Modeling temporal document collections is handled by dynamic topic mining [6, 17, 2]. Applying these methods on the 'documents' generated via the ratings is questionable since each document most likely would contain only a single 'word'. Ignoring this issue, further problems for our scenario are: First, [6, 2] require a binning of the documents in fixed time slots. Second, [6, 17] require that topics exist over the whole lifetime. In our work, however, anomalies exist only in specific time intervals. While [2] allows topics to appear and disappear, they prefer smooth evolutions. In our case, however, anomalies abruptly appear/disappear in time. Also, all of these techniques are (of course) designed to detect multiple topics. In our scenario, however, we want to find a single base behavior which captures the general temporal evolution, enriched by a few number of anomalies.

Related applications: Multiple techniques have been proposed in the area of *outlier detection* [1]. While the majority of techniques tackles the case of independently distributed data, time-series outlier detection and outlier detection for streaming data are also an active field of research [1]. Both areas differ from our work since they are designed for continuous data. Also, most existing techniques consider outlier in the sense of independent, random errors in the data. *Change detection* techniques detect points in time where the state of the underlying system has changed [15]. A change might not generally indicate anomalous behavior. Indeed, even the base behavior might change over time.

Studying product ratings has been done in multiple research areas, all following different goals and objectives. *Recommender Systems* incorporate ratings and their temporal information [9, 10] to improve the prediction performance. *Opinion mining* aims at extracting the sentiment of users regarding specific products or features of a product [18]. *Modeling* of social rating networks, e.g., to compactly describe the underlying mechanism driving the network or to generate synthetic data, has been studied, e.g, in [12].

None of the existing methods is designed to detect anomalies and the underlying evolving base behavior in rating data.

5. EXPERIMENTAL ANALYSIS

We applied our method (called SpotRate due to its potential to spot anomalies in rating data) on *over six million* product ratings representing varies categories: an extract of the Amazon website [8] evaluating multiple different products, another subset of the Amazon website evaluating

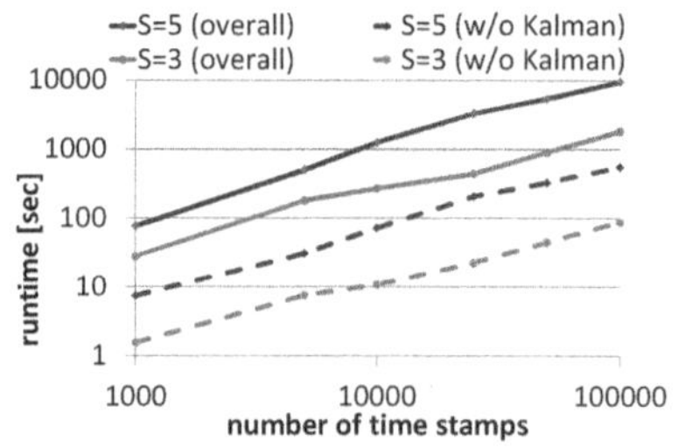

Fig. 5: Runtime vs. number of time stamps

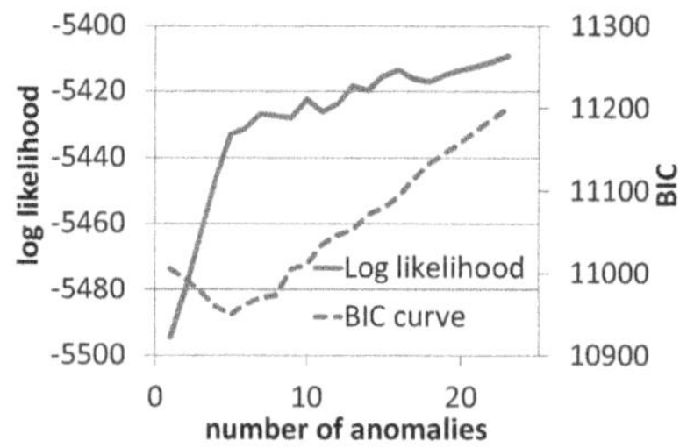

Fig. 6: Likelihood and BIC vs. K (synthetic data)

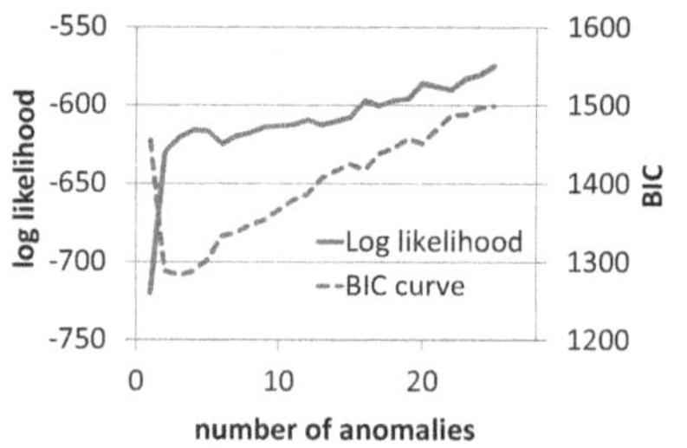

Fig. 7: Likelihood and BIC vs. K (real world data)

food products[3], ratings of restaurants in the area of Phoenix based on Yelp, and an extract of the TripAdvisor website[4] for hotel ratings. The data consists of tuples representing the ID of a product/service to be rated, the user who evaluated the product, the time stamp when the rating occurred, and a star rating in the range from 1 up to 5. Additionally, these datasets contain textual reviews, which we used to understand and describe the results of our method.

Besides these real world datasets we used synthetic data generated based on the presented process to analyze the scalability and robustness of our method.

5.1 Runtime Analysis

We briefly analyze the runtime of SpotRate. The runtime is primarily affected by the number of time stamps T and the rating scale S. The actual number of ratings does not affect the runtime (cf. Sec. 3.1.1). For the runtime analysis, we selected the product B00003TL7P from the Amazon dataset and we extended it to different length (from 1,000 to 100,000) by concatenation. Besides the original rating scale of $S = 5$, we used a rating scale of $S = 3$ by merging 1/2 and 4/5 ratings. All experiments were conducted on commodity hardware with 3 GHz CPU's and 4 GB main memory.

The results are shown in Fig. 5. Confirming our study of Sec. 3.5, the runtime increases linearly, showing the method's high scalability (note the slope of 1 in the log-log plot). The overall runtime for 100,000 time stamps (which would corresponds to 273 years when measured on a daily basis) is only about 158 minutes on commodity hardware. A brief study shows that the currently most rated products have around 20,000 (Amazon: Kindle Fire) or 8,000 (Yelp: Bottega Louie) ratings. Thus, even when considering the finest granularity, we highly exceed this number.

Additionally, we measured the runtime of our method when ignoring the time required for the Kalman smoother (dashed lines). As shown, the Kalman smoother contributs to around 90% of the absolute runtime. The remaining parts of our method are highly efficient.

We also studied the effect of the number of anomalies K on the runtime. According to Sec. 3.2.3, K linearly affects the runtime of the dynamic programming technique. Since the Kalman smoother (whose runtime is independent of K) accounts for most of the absolute runtime, we only observed a very small change of only a few seconds. Thus, overall, only T and S influence our method's practical applicability.

5.2 Effectiveness

In the following, we analyze the effectiveness of SpotRate considering different aspects. We start with the model selection principle. For this experiment, we generated synthetic data according to our model. We used 4000 ratings with 5 anomaly intervals. Figure 6 shows on the (first) y-axis the obtained log-likelihood of our method when varying the number K of potential anomalies. Obviously, the general trend shows that increasing K also increases the log-likelihood: more flexibility to describe the data is given. A very high increases is obtained until the value of 5, which corresponds to the true number of anomalies. After this point, the benefit of allowing further anomalies decreases.

This effect is well captured by the BIC score, which is shown on the second y-axis of the figure. The minimal BIC value is obtained for the value of 5. Thus, the model selection principle introduced before can be used as a good indicator how to select the number of anomalies.

The same behavior can be observed for real world data as, e.g., shown in Fig. 7. Here we plotted the log-likelihood and BIC score for a coconut-water sold on Amazon (cf. Sec. 5.4). Again, one sees a clear minimum of the BIC value, indicating that three anomaly intervals describe the data very well.

Next, we analyze our iterative optimization. In Fig. 8 we analyze how the log-likelihood increases when we increase the number of iterations until convergence. That is, on the x-axis we count how often the variables have been updated, while the y-axis shows the log-likelihood. We plotted the curves for different values of K, again for the product B00003TL7P. As expected, the first iterations lead to the highest improvement in the log-likelihood. Still, we see an improvement in the later iterations, showing the effectiveness of the optimization step. As also shown in the previous experiment, a higher value of K leads to a better likelihood. Additionally, for this product, we observed that a smaller number of intervals can lead to a lower number of required iterations. In general, however, the difference in the number of iterations was not as significant as shown for this product.

Finally, we analyze the effect of λ. Per default, a value of 0 can be selected to realize a non-informative prior. In Figure 9, we varied the value of λ between 1 and 0. We selected $K = 10$. As shown, for larger values of λ, shorter intervals are preferred. In particular, for $\lambda = 1$ the average interval length is close to the shortest possible length of 1. For $\lambda = 0$ larger intervals are captured. Note that $\lambda = 0$ does not mean that the whole set of time stamps is represented as an anomaly interval. Even in the case of $\lambda = 0$, we only report time intervals where the behavior is anomalous.

5.3 Comparison with related techniques

We compare SpotRate against the related technique RLA [7] and a Kalman smoother. Doing a fair comparison between these approaches is challenging since the data they analyze and goals they follow are different. In particular, the

[3] `http://snap.stanford.edu/data/`

[4] `http://sifaka.cs.uiuc.edu/~wang296/Data/`

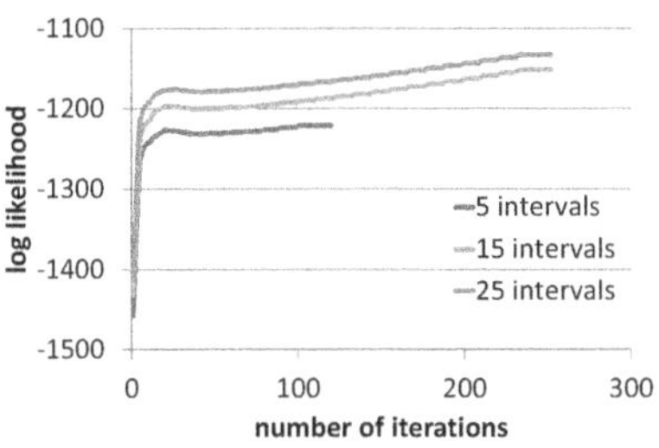

Fig. 8: Convergence analysis

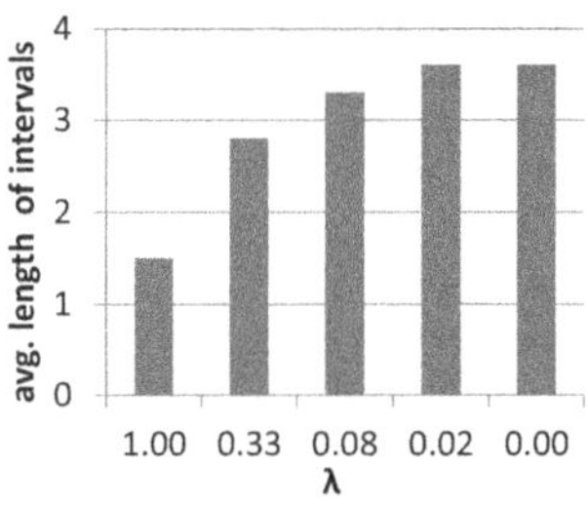

Fig. 9: Effect of λ

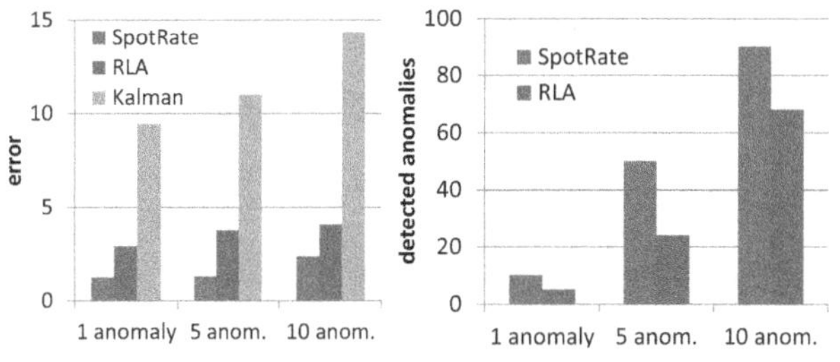

Fig. 10: Comparison with related methods

work [7] requires an aggregation of the data since it operates on the rating distributions. Thus, e.g., measuring the likelihood on the categorical data is questionable. Since RLA, however, is the only existing technique which also analyzes dynamic rating data, we try to study some effects.

For comparing the methods, we use two principles: In the first experiment, we compare the base behavior detected by the methods against the known base behavior for synthetically generated data. The base behavior is continuous in our model as well as in RLA, and for the Kalman smoother. Thus, it is fair to, e.g., measure the Frobenius norm between the ground truth base behavior and the detected ones. We generated data with 1000 time points and added a varying number of anomaly intervals to it, each covering 10 time points. We ensured that the anomaly intervals exactly match the aggregation required for RLA. Thus, this method gets a huge advantage since this assumption does not necessarily hold for real data. Fig. 10 (left) shows the results: Our method obtains the lowest error, it is able to detect the hidden base behavior. The Kalman smoother cannot handle anomalies and shows a high deviation to the ground truth.

In a second experiment, we evaluated whether the methods are able to detect the anomalous points in time (this is only possible for SpotRate and RLA). As shown in Figure 10 (right), our method almost perfectly detects all anomalous points in time. RLA in contrast is not able to spot all points, which also explains the previously observed higher error to the base behavior. Overall, our method outperforms the competing techniques in detecting the correct base behavior as well as spotting the anomalous points in time.

5.4 Discoveries

In the following, we will demonstrate the application of SpotRate by illustrating some of our interesting discoveries.

(1) We start with the example illustrated in Fig. 1. It represents a hotel in the Caribbean evaluated on TripAdvisor. While understanding the original time-stamped data is difficult, the extracted base behavior allows an easy understanding: clearly, the hotel is evaluated with mostly 4 and 5 stars. Our method found anomalous behavior in July and August 2005. In this time frame, the negative ratings highly increased. Analyzing the reviews at the detected time points, the reviewers criticized *"the restaurants with ridiculous reservation rules"* often showing overbooking and *"the nonfunctional air-conditions"*. These reviews indicate that in the given months the service of the hotel has dropped, potentially due to a highly increased number of guests. Our method was able to spot these anomalies, and it successfully smoothed out these points from the base behavior.

(2) Next, we show the result for a coconut-water sold on Amazon (http://www.amazon.com/dp/B000CNB4LE). Applying our method leads to the base behavior as shown in Figure 11. The three detected anomaly intervals appear at the end of 2010. As shown next to the figure, the detected anomalies are described by distributions $\mathbf{o}_k$ representing primarily low ratings. They clearly deviate to the base behavior. Inspecting the product's reviews during these times, most customers are not satisfied with the *"new plastic bottles"* the manufacturer has introduced, leading to a bad taste. Later time points do not show this anomalous behavior, indicating that the manufacturer has solved this problem (*"I can understand a lot of the initial bad reviews as I thought the new plastic bottle had a bad after taste. ... I can say that the taste is much improved ..."*).

(3) Next, we want to show the benefit of extracting an evolving base behavior. Figure 12 shows the base behavior of a baby bouncer (B00005QI1G) from the Amazon data. Looking at its evaluation, it is recognizable that the majority of reviewers evaluated this product with 5 stars. At the later time points, however, the number of low and medium ratings increases. Note that these intervals are not classified as anomalies but they represent the general evolution of the product. A closer look at the product's reviews at these time points explains that over time the customers were more and more unsatisfied by the product since it is *"nice to play but not long lasting"* and the *"battery simply does not last very long with the vibrating feature"*.

Discoveries via prediction. Finally, we want to show the potential of our method to detect anomalies via prediction. According to Eq. 7, we can predict the base behavior at future points in time. By comparing it against newly arriving ratings, anomalies can be spotted. We removed from all restaurants of the Yelp dataset the last 10 points in time. We applied our method on the remaining data. Figure 13 shows three restaurants whose predicted base behavior (left bar [a] of each diagram) highly deviates to the observed ratings (right bar [b]), thus, potentially indicating anomalies.

Inspecting the reviews of the first restaurant, we see comments like *"I've been eating at Stacy's for over a year so it pains me to kill them but the service [...] was pathetic. [...] I don't know if its a new employee or something going wrong but I'm probably not going back..."*. Thus, indicating that the service quality of the (previously very highly rated) restaurant has suddenly dropped.

For the second restaurant, we observed comments like *"All the prices have went up"* and *"The picture of the menu and prices is out dated"*, which again indicates a recent deviation to the previous behavior, potentially due to increased prices.

Finally, the reason for the abruptly appearing low ratings of the third restaurant seems to be caused by expanding/remodeling the old building. The old atmosphere of the restaurant seems not to be preserved and the larger capacity could not be handled by the service staff: *"the expanded building is nice [...] but something was lost. we didn't have*

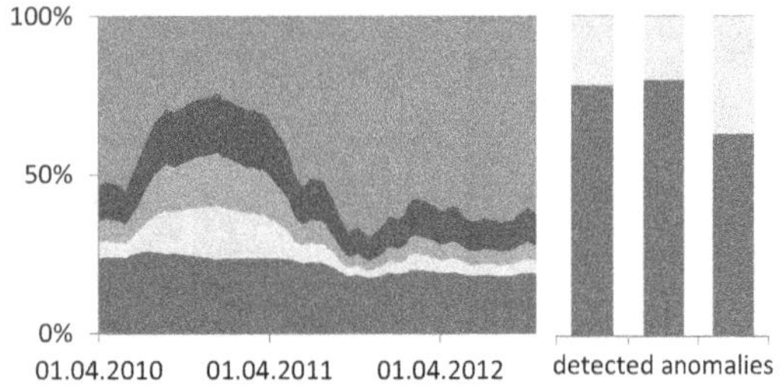

Fig. 11: Base behavior and anomalies (intervals spotted at the end of 2010).

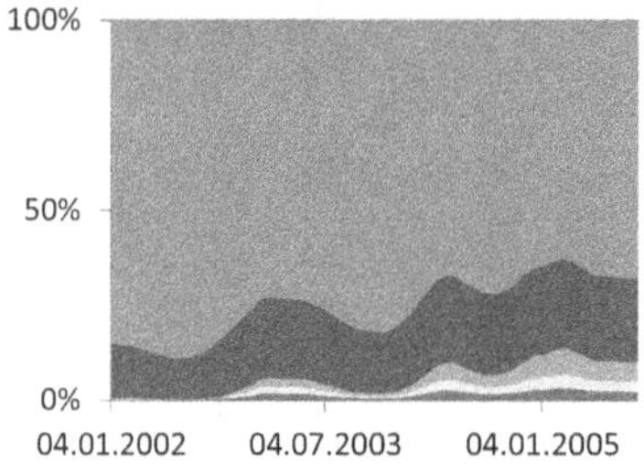

Fig. 12: Evolving base behavior (Amazon)

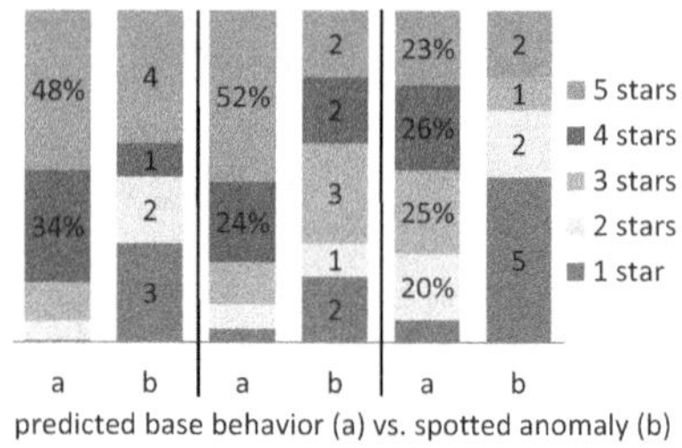

Fig. 13: Spotting anomalies via prediction (Yelp)

that hometown feel. we miss all the signatures and pictures." and *"I think its rad that you expanded, but if you cant handle the customer load then whats the point?"*.

Overall, by modeling the temporal evolution of the base behavior, our method is able to detect these newly occurring anomalies, which can then, e.g., be used to inform the corresponding companies.

6. CONCLUSION

We developed the method SpotRate for analyzing time stamped rating data. Our method detects the users' base behavior as well as time intervals representing anomalies. We proposed a sound Bayesian framework which represents the rating data via temporally constrained categorical mixture models. It accounts for the temporal evolution of the base behavior and enables us to predict the rating behavior for newly occurring ratings. We developed an efficient algorithm which exploits principles of variational inference and dynamic programming. Our experimental study has shown the potential of our method to spot anomalies and to use the base behavior for studying the evolution of a product.

Acknowledgments. Stephan Günnemann has been supported by a fellowship within the postdoc-program of the German Academic Exchange Service (DAAD). Research was also sponsored in part by the Army Research Laboratory and was accomplished under Cooperative Agreement Number W911NF-09-2-0053. Any opinions, findings, and conclusions or recommendations expressed in this material are those of the author(s) and do not necessarily reflect the views of the funding parties. The U.S. Government is authorized to reproduce and distribute reprints for Government purposes notwithstanding any copyright notation here on.

7. REFERENCES

[1] C. C. Aggarwal. *Outlier Analysis.* Springer, 2013.

[2] A. Ahmed and E. P. Xing. Timeline: A dynamic hierarchical dirichlet process model for recovering birth/death and evolution of topics in text stream. In *UAI*, pages 20–29, 2010.

[3] F. Bengtsson et al. Computing maximum-scoring segments in almost linear time. In *Computing and Combinatorics*, pages 255–264. Springer, 2006.

[4] J. Bentley. Programming pearls: algorithm design techniques. *Communications of the ACM*, 27(9):865–873, 1984.

[5] C. M. Bishop. *Pattern recognition and machine learning.* Springer, 2007.

[6] D. M. Blei and J. D. Lafferty. Dynamic topic models. In *ICML*, pages 113–120, 2006.

[7] N. Günnemann, S. Günnemann, and C. Faloutsos. Robust multivariate autoregression for anomaly detection in dynamic product ratings. In *WWW*, pages 361–372, 2014.

[8] N. Jindal and B. Liu. Opinion spam and analysis. In *WSDM*, pages 219–230, 2008.

[9] N. Koenigstein, G. Dror, and Y. Koren. Yahoo! music recommendations: modeling music ratings with temporal dynamics and item taxonomy. In *RecSys*, pages 165–172, 2011.

[10] Y. Koren. Collaborative filtering with temporal dynamics. In *KDD*, pages 447–456, 2009.

[11] G. F. Lawler. *Introduction to stochastic processes.* CRC Press, 2006.

[12] K. Lerman. Dynamics of a collaborative rating system. In *WebKDD/SNA-KDD*, pages 77–96, 2007.

[13] R. B. Litterman. Forecasting with bayesian vector autoregressions. *Journal of Business & Economic Statistics*, 4(1):25–38, 1986.

[14] H. Lütkepohl. *New introduction to multiple time series analysis.* Cambridge University Press, 2005.

[15] X. Song, M. Wu, C. M. Jermaine, and S. Ranka. Statistical change detection for multi-dimensional data. In *KDD*, pages 667–676, 2007.

[16] J.-A. Ting, E. Theodorou, and S. Schaal. Learning an outlier-robust kalman filter. In *ECML*, pages 748–756, 2007.

[17] C. Wang, D. M. Blei, and D. Heckerman. Continuous time dynamic topic models. In *UAI*, pages 579–586, 2008.

[18] H. Wang, Y. Lu, and C. Zhai. Latent aspect rating analysis on review text data: a rating regression approach. In *KDD*, pages 783–792, 2010.

APPENDIX

Let $[\![.]\!]$ denote the Iverson bracket, it holds: $\mathbb{E}_q[[\![z_i^{(t)}{=}1]\!]]{=}\phi_{t,i}$ $\mathbb{E}_q[[\![z_i^{(t)}{=}0]\!]]{=}1-\phi_{t,i}$ $\quad$ $\mathbb{E}_q[\ln \mathbf{o}_{k,s}]{=}\psi(\alpha_{k,s})-\psi(\sum_j \alpha_{k,j})$ $\mathbb{E}_q[\ln r_k]{=}\psi(\alpha_k){-}\psi(\alpha_k{+}\beta_k)$ $\mathbb{E}_q[\ln(1{-}r_k)]{=}\psi(\beta_k){-}\psi(\alpha_k{+}\beta_k)$

Given the definition of the distribution p, it follows:

- For $k(t) = k \neq 0$ it holds:
  $\mathbb{E}_q[\ln p(z_i^{(t)}|\ldots)] = \mathbb{E}_q[\ln r_k^{[\![z_i^{(t)}=1]\!]} \cdot (1-r_k)^{[\![z_i^{(t)}=1]\!]}]$
  $= \mathbb{E}_q[[\![z_i^{(t)}=1]\!]] \cdot \mathbb{E}_q[\ln r_k] + \mathbb{E}_q[[\![z_i^{(t)}=0]\!]] \cdot \mathbb{E}_q[\ln(1-r_k)]$
- $\mathbb{E}_q[\ln p(x_i^{(t)}|...)] = \mathbb{E}_q[[\![z_i^{(t)}=1]\!]] \cdot \mathbb{E}_q[\ln o_{k(t),s}] +$ $\mathbb{E}_q[[\![z_i^{(t)}=0]\!]] \cdot \mathbb{E}_q[\ln \pi(\mathbf{b}^{(t)})_s]$ for $x_i^{(t)} = s$
- $\mathbb{E}_q[\sum_i \ln p(x_i^{(t)}|...)] = \mathbb{E}_q\left[\sum_{s=1}^S n_s^{(t)} \cdot \ln p(x=s \mid \ldots)\right]$
  $= \sum_{s=1}^S n_s^{(t)} \cdot \phi_t^s \cdot \mathbb{E}_q[\ln o_{k(t),s}] + n_s^{(t)} \cdot [1-\phi_t^s] \cdot \mathbb{E}_q\left[\ln \pi(\mathbf{b}_t)_s\right]$
- $\mathbb{E}_q\left[\ln \pi(\mathbf{b}^{(t)})_s\right] = \mathbb{E}_q\left[\ln \frac{e^{b_s^{(t)}}}{1+\sum_{s=1}^{S-1} e^{b_s^{(t)}}}\right] = \mathbb{E}_q\left[\mathbf{b}_s^{(t)}\right] -$
  $\mathbb{E}_q\left[\ln(1+\sum_{s=1}^{S-1} e^{\mathbf{b}_i^{(t)}})\right] \geqslant \mu_s^{(t)} - \ln(\mathbb{E}_q\left[1+\sum_{s=1}^{S-1} e^{\mathbf{b}_s^{(t)}}\right])$
  $= \mu_s^{(t)} - \ln(1+\sum_{s=1}^{S-1} e^{\mu_s^{(t)}+\frac{v^{(t)}}{2}})$

Product Selection Problem: Improve Market Share by Learning Consumer Behavior

Silei Xu
slxu@cse.cuhk.edu.hk

John C.S. Lui
cslui@cse.cuhk.edu.hk

Department of Computer Science and Engineering
The Chinese University of Hong Kong
New Territories, Hong Kong

ABSTRACT

It is often crucial for manufacturers to decide what products to produce so that they can increase their market share in an increasingly fierce market. To decide which products to produce, manufacturers need to analyze the consumers' requirements and how consumers make their purchase decisions so that the new products will be competitive in the market. In this paper, we first present a general distance-based product adoption model to capture consumers' purchase behavior. Using this model, various distance metrics can be used to describe different real life purchase behavior. We then provide a learning algorithm to decide which set of distance metrics one should use when we are given some historical purchase data. Based on the product adoption model, we formalize the *k most marketable products (or k-MMP)* selection problem and formally prove that the problem is *NP-hard*. To tackle this problem, we propose an efficient greedy-based approximation algorithm with a provable solution guarantee. Using submodularity analysis, we prove that our approximation algorithm can achieve at least 63% of the optimal solution. We apply our algorithm on both synthetic datasets and real-world datasets (TripAdvisor.com), and show that our algorithm can easily achieve five or more orders of speedup over the exhaustive search and achieve about 96% of the optimal solution on average. Our experiments also show the significant impact of different distance metrics on the results, and how proper distance metrics can improve the accuracy of product selection.

Categories and Subject Descriptors

F2.2 [**Analysis of Algorithms and Problem Complexity**]: Nonnumerical Algorithms and Problems

Keywords

Product selection; consumer behavior; model learning; submodular set function; approximation algorithm

KDD'14, August 24–27, 2014, New York, NY, USA.
Copyright 2014 ACM 978-1-4503-2956-9/14/08 ...$15.00.
http://dx.doi.org/10.1145/2623330.2623692.

1. INTRODUCTION

Product competition in the current digital age is becoming increasingly fierce. Consumers can easily access the information about a given product via the Internet. Moreover, consumers can share their opinions on products in the form of ratings or reviews via various web services, e.g., Amazon. Therefore, instead of relying on the sales pitch by salesmen or traditional TV advertisements, consumers can now review many competing products before they make their final purchase decision. Manufacturers, on the other hand, can use the web information, such as ratings and reviews, to gain a better understanding of consumers' requirements on various products. This leads to a new challenge on how to discover consumers' preferences, and how these preferences may help manufacturer to select appropriate new products so to compete with other manufacturers in the market.

To introduce new products into a market, a manufacturer usually has a set of *candidate products* to consider. However, due to budget constraints, the manufacturer can only produce a small subset of these candidate products. The objective of a manufacturer is to select a subset of products which can maximize its profit or market share. In this study, we consider the following scenario: In a market consisting of a set of existing products from various manufacturers and a set of consumers, a manufacturer wants to select "*k most marketable products*" from a set of candidate products so as to maximize the market share of all products from this manufacturer (this includes the possibility that some existing products in the market are from the same manufacturer).

One of the major challenges of the "*k most marketable products*" problem is how to model various consumers' adoption behavior, i.e., how consumers make their purchase decisions. Different adoption behavior may lead to different product selection results. However, there is a lack of formal work of how to model these behaviors using available data. Furthermore, finding the optimal solution to the "*k most marketable products*" problem can be shown to be *NP-hard* in general.

In this paper, we first model the consumers' adoption behavior with a generalized distance-based model where different distance metrics can be used to describe many different consumers behaviors. We then propose a method to learn which set of distance metrics one should use when we are given some historical purchase data. We also present a computationally efficient approximation algorithm to solve the k most marketable products problem. To the best of our knowledge, this is the first paper that provides the formal consumers' adoption model and the analysis of product selection. The contributions of this paper are:

- We formulate the problem of finding the k most marketable products (k-*MMP*) for a manufacturer.
- We model the adoption behavior of consumers using a general *distance-based product adoption model* which can take on various different distance metrics.
- We provide a learning method to determine the appropriate set of distance metrics using the historical purchase data on market share of a subset of the existing products.
- We prove that the k-*MMP* problem is *NP-hard* and propose a computationally efficient approximation algorithm. By proving the monotonicity and submodularity properties of the objective function, we show that our approximation algorithm provides a $(1-1/e)$-approximation as compared with the optimal solution.
- We carry out experiments on synthetic and real-world datasets to demonstrate the computational efficiency of our algorithm and quality of its solutions. We also illustrate how one can select the appropriate distance metrics by learning from the historical purchase data so as to improve the market share.

The outline of the paper is as follows. In Section 2, we propose a general product adoption model which can accommodate different distance metrics to describe the consumers' adoption behavior, and we formulate the k-*MMP* problem. In Section 3, we present a learning method to select the appropriate set of distance metrics according to the historical market share of existing products. In Section 4, we propose an exact algorithm for the case of $k = 1$ and prove that finding the exact solution for $k > 1$ is *NP-hard*. To tackle the computational challenge, we present an approximation algorithm in Section 5. We show that this algorithm is computationally efficient and also provides a high quality solution guarantee. In Section 6, we perform experiments on both the synthetic data and the real-world data. Related work is shown in Section 7, and Section 8 concludes.

2. MATHEMATICAL MODELS AND PROBLEM FORMULATION

In this section, we first present a model of a market by considering both products and consumers. Then we present a *distance-based product adoption model* to describe various consumers' product adoption behaviors. Based on these models, we formulate the k-*MMP* problem.

2.1 Market Model

Let us consider a market which consists of a set of l consumers $\mathcal{C} = \{c_1, c_2, \ldots, c_l\}$ and a set of m existing products $\mathcal{P}_E = \{p_1, p_2, \ldots, p_m\}$. Let M represent a manufacturer in the market, and $\mathcal{P}_M$ denote the set of existing products produced by M, where $\mathcal{P}_M \subseteq \mathcal{P}_E$ and $|\mathcal{P}_M| = m_M$. The remaining products in $\mathcal{P}_E$ are from other manufacturers who are the competitors of M. These competing products are denoted by $\mathcal{P}_C$, where $\mathcal{P}_C \subseteq \mathcal{P}_E$ and $|\mathcal{P}_C| = m_C$. According to these definitions, we have $m = m_M + m_C$, $\mathcal{P}_E = \mathcal{P}_M \cup \mathcal{P}_C$, and $\mathcal{P}_M \cap \mathcal{P}_C = \emptyset$.

Suppose the manufacturer M wants to produce some new products to maximize its utility, i.e., the market share. M has a set of n *candidate new products* to choose from, which we denote by $\mathcal{P}_N = \{p_{m+1}, p_{m+2}, \ldots, p_{m+n}\}$. Note that all the products in $\mathcal{P}_N$ are *new* to the market, in other words, $\mathcal{P}_N \cap \mathcal{P}_E = \emptyset$. Due to the budget, technological and manufacturing constraints, the manufacturer M can only produce $k \leq n$ of these candidate products in $\mathcal{P}_N$.

Each product in $\mathcal{P}_E \cup \mathcal{P}_N$ is associated with d attributes denoted by $\mathcal{A} = \{a_1, a_2, \ldots, a_d\}$. Each attribute a_i is represented by a non-negative real number, and higher value implies higher quality. One can use a_i to represent various attributes of a given product, e.g., durability, ratings, inverse of price. Hence, the quality of a product can be described by a d-dimensional vector. Specially, the quality of product p_j is described by the vector $\boldsymbol{q}_j = (q_j[1], q_j[2], \ldots, q_j[d])$, where $q_j[t] \in [0, \infty)$, $\forall t \in \{1, 2, .., d\}$ indicates p_j's quality on attribute a_t. Similarly, each consumer in $\mathcal{C}$ is also associated with $\mathcal{A}$ to describe his requirements on different attributes. Let $\boldsymbol{r}_i = (r_i[1], r_i[2], \ldots, r_i[d])$ be the requirement vector of consumer c_i, where $r_i[t] \in [0, \infty)$, $\forall t \in \{1, 2, \ldots, d\}$ indicates c_i's *minimum* requirement on attribute a_t, i.e., c_i requires that the product's quality on attribute a_t is at least $r_i[t]$, or he will not adopt (or purchase) that product.

EXAMPLE 1. *To illustrate the notations, we present an example in Figure 1. Consider a market of smart phones where we have two existing products $\mathcal{P}_E = \{p_1, p_2\}$ and three consumers $\mathcal{C} = \{c_1, c_2, c_3\}$. Manufacturer M is considering two candidate products $\mathcal{P}_N = \{p_3, p_4\}$. Let say each product is described by two attributes: a_1 is the inverse of price (units per thousand dollars, UPM for short) and a_2 is durability (years), and they are represented in the horizontal and the vertical axis respectively. The quality vectors of products and the requirement vectors of consumers are shown in the figure (with $\mathcal{P}_E$:◇, $\mathcal{P}_N$:□, $\mathcal{C}$:○). For instance, the quality vector of p_1 is $(2,6)$, so we can purchase two units of p_1 with one thousand dollars (or the price of p_1 is \$500), and the durability of p_1 is six years. Similarly, the requirement vector of c_1 is $(1,5)$, so consumer c_1 wants a product which is at most \$1000 and can last for at least five years.*

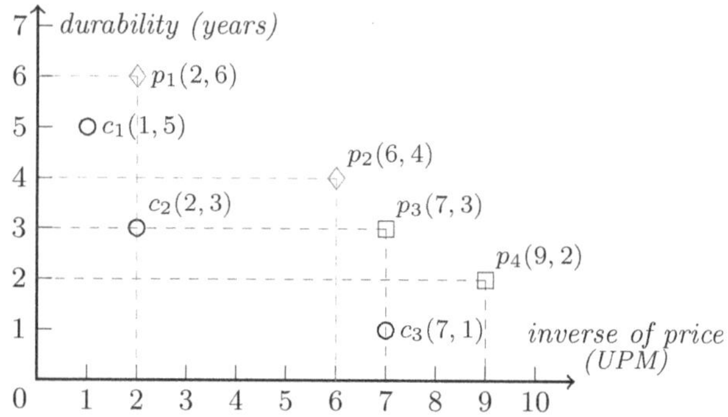

Figure 1: An illustration of the market model

2.2 Product Adoption Model

We assume that a consumer may adopt a product if the product satisfies his requirement. We say that a product satisfies a consumer's requirements if and only if the product meets the requirements of that consumer on *all* attributes. Formally, we define the product satisfiability condition.

DEFINITION 1. **(Product satisfiability)** *Consider a consumer c_i and a product p_j. We say the product p_j satisfies* *the consumer c_i if and only if $q_j[t] \geq r_i[t]$, $\forall t=1,\ldots,d$. We denote this relationship as $p_j \succsim c_i$, and p_j is said to be a satisfactory product of c_i, while c_i is a potential consumer of p_j in other words.*

For example, consider the products and consumers depicted in Figure 1. One can observe that the quality vector of p_1 is $(2,6)$ and the requirement vector of c_1 is $(1,5)$. Since $2>1$ and $6>5$, so p_1 satisfies c_1, or $p_1 \succsim c_1$. Similarly, we have $p_3 \succsim c_2$ and $p_3 \succsim c_3$.

We assume that if a consumer has some satisfactory products, then he will adopt one unit of product from any of these feasible products. When a consumer c_i has only one satisfactory product, say p_j, then c_i will adopt p_j for sure. However, it becomes complicated when there are multiple satisfactory products. All previous works [7, 12, 13, 16] assume that the consumer will *randomly* adopt one of the satisfactory products, but this is not realistic in many situations. In the following, we present the *distance-based adoption model* to describe some realistic and representative product adoption behavior when consumers make their purchase decisions. Our model is very general to model various product adoption behaviors in the real world scenarios.

In a real world market, products with higher quality usually attract more consumers. Therefore, we use a distance measure between a product's quality and a consumer's requirement to decide which product the consumer may adopt. Note that consumers will only consider their satisfactory products. Furthermore, larger distance implies better quality. Let $d_{i,j}$ be the distance between the consumer c_i's requirement vector ($\boldsymbol{r}_i$) and the product p_j's quality vector ($\boldsymbol{q}_j$). We assume that c_i will adopt the product p_j which has the largest distance among all his satisfactory products. If there are multiple satisfactory products which have the same largest distance measure with c_i, then c_i will randomly select one of these products. Mathematically, we define the *distance-based adoption model* as follows.

DEFINITION 2. **(Distance-based adoption model)** *Given a consumer c_i and a set $\mathcal{P}$ of products available in the market, let $\mathcal{FP}(c_i|\mathcal{P})$ be the set of products which have the largest distance between their quality vectors and c_i's requirement vector among all c_i's satisfactory products. The probability that c_i adopts a product $p_j \in \mathcal{P}$ is*

$$\Pr(i,j|\mathcal{P}) = \begin{cases} \frac{1}{|\mathcal{FP}(c_i|\mathcal{P})|} & \textit{if } p_j \in \mathcal{FP}(c_i|\mathcal{P}), \\ 0 & \textit{otherwise.} \end{cases} \quad (1)$$

Note that we can use many *distance metrics*, e.g., l_1, l_2, l_∞ norms. For instance, if l_1 norm (or the *Manhattan distance*) is used, then consumers will choose the satisfactory products which have the largest sum of all components' values in the quality vectors. To describe different adoption behaviors of different consumers in a real world market, we also take into account the weighted distance metrics. Let w_t be the weight of attribute a_t, $w_t \geq 0, \forall a_t \in \mathcal{A}$, then under the l_1 norm, the distance $d_{i,j}$ can be expressed as:

$$d_{i,j} = \sum_{a_t \in \mathcal{A}} w_t \cdot (q_j[t] - r_i[t]). \quad (2)$$

It is important to point out that the algorithms we present in this paper are general to all distance metrics. Readers can use other distance metrics when appropriate. In here, we present four representative distance metrics which we use as examples for illustrations and experiments.

- ***Discrete metric (DM).*** We define $d_{i,j}=1$ for consumers c_i and c_i's satisfactory product p_j in the discrete metric. This distance metric simplifies the adoption model that consumers will randomly select one from all his satisfactory products. Using this distance metric, our work subsumes the adoption models of previous works [7, 12, 13, 16].
- ***Norm metric (NM).*** In this distance metric, we set the weight $w_t = 1.0$, $\forall a_t \in \mathcal{A}$ based on the l_1 norm metric as defined in Equation (2). Note that in general, one can use other norm as distance metric and our algorithms still apply.
- ***Price metric (PM).*** In a real world market, one common situation is that if a consumer's requirements are satisfied, then he will select the cheapest product, i.e., the one with the highest quality on the attribute of "price". In this case, we can set the weight of all attributes to zero except the "price" based on the l_1 norm metric as defined in Equation (2).
- ***Richman metric (RM).*** Unlike the *price metric*, some consumers may be rich and they are insensitive to the price but only want the best product. In this case, we can set the weight of "price" attribute to zero while setting the weight of other attributes to one.

EXAMPLE 2. *To illustrate, let us consider the products and consumers depicted in Figure 1. Suppose that manufacturer M decides to produce p_3, then the set of available products in the market is $\mathcal{P}=\mathcal{P}_E \cup \{p_3\} = \{p_1,p_2,p_3\}$. Let us consider the probability c_2 will adopt p_3, i.e.,* $\Pr(2,3|\mathcal{P})$, *when c_2 uses the above four distance metrics. From Figure 1, one can observe that c_2 is satisfied by p_1, p_2, and p_3. If c_2 uses the* discrete metric, *then $d_{2,1}=d_{2,2}=d_{2,3}=1$, so* $\Pr(2,3|\mathcal{P})=1/3$. *If c_2 uses the* norm metric, *then we have $d_{2,1}=3$, $d_{2,2}=d_{2,3}=5$. Hence, c_2 will select p_2 and p_3 with probability* $\Pr(2,2|\mathcal{P})=Pr(2,3|\mathcal{P})=1/2$. *If c_2 uses the* price metric, *then we only need to consider the attribute* inverse of price. *We have $d_{2,1}=0$, $d_{2,2}=4$, $d_{2,3}=5$, so* $\Pr(2,3|\mathcal{P})=1$, *c_2 will adopt p_3. If c_2 uses the* richman metric, *we have $d_{2,1}=3$, $d_{2,2}=1$, $d_{2,3}=0$. Thus c_2 will adopt p_1 only, or* $\Pr(2,1|\mathcal{P})=1$ *and* $\Pr(2,3|\mathcal{P})=0$.

2.3 Problem Formulation

To find the k most marketable products, we first need to define the expected market share of a set of products under the distance-based adoption model. Given the market condition, i.e., the consumers $\mathcal{C}$ and the existing products $\mathcal{P}_E$, let P be the set of products we consider, then the expected market share of P is defined as

$$MS(P) = \frac{1}{l} \cdot \sum_{p_j \in P} \sum_{c_i \in \mathcal{PC}(p_j)} \Pr(i,j|\mathcal{P}_E \cup P), \quad (3)$$

where $l=|\mathcal{C}|$, $\mathcal{PC}(p_j)$ denotes the set of potential consumers of product p_j, and $\Pr(i,j|\mathcal{P}_E \cup P)$ is defined in Equation (1).

EXAMPLE 3. *Let us illustrate the expected market share of p_3, or $MS(\{p_3\})$, by considering the scenario depicted in Figure 1. There are two existing products ($P_E = \{p_1,p_2\}$) and three consumers ($\mathcal{C} = \{c_1,c_2,c_3\}$) in the market. By adding product p_3 into the market, p_3 satisfies consumers c_2 and c_3. Assume that c_2 uses the* norm metric, *then according to Example 2, we have* $\Pr(2,3|\mathcal{P})=1/2$. *Now consider consumer c_3. Since we have not added p_4 into the market,*

p_3 is c_3's only satisfactory product, so c_3 will adopt p_3 for sure. Therefore, in this scenario, c_2 and c_3 will adopt p_3 with probability 1/2 and 1, respectively. So the expected sales of p_3 is 1.5 units, It follows that the expected market share of p_3 is 1.5/3=50% since there are three consumers in total.

Based on the definition of market share in Equation (3), we formulate the k-**M**ost **M**arketable **P**roducts (k-*MMP*) problem as follows.

DEFINITION 3. (k-*MMP*) *Given a set of consumers $\mathcal{C}$, a set of existing products $\mathcal{P}_E = \mathcal{P}_C \cup \mathcal{P}_M$ in the market, and $\mathcal{P}_N$, a set of candidate products by the manufacturer M, select a set $P \subseteq \mathcal{P}_N$ where $|P| = k$ so to maximize $MS(P \cup \mathcal{P}_M)$ for manufacturer M.*

To solve the k-*MMP* problem, we need to tackle the following two issues: (1) Find the proper distance metrics for the market. (2) Design an efficient algorithm to find the solution to the k-*MMP* problem. Since there are various potential distance metrics and manufacturers usually do not know which distance metrics the consumers may adopt, we present a learning approach to discover the proper set of distance metrics for a given market from historical purchase data. This is presented in Section 3. After deciding on the proper distance metrics, we present the algorithmic design in solving the k-*MMP* problem. In Section 4, we present an efficient and exact algorithm for the 1-*MMP* problem and prove that the k-*MMP* problem is *NP-hard* when $k \geq 2$. In Section 5, we present an efficient approximation algorithm. By exploiting the monotonicity and submodularity properties of the market share function $MS(\cdot)$, we prove that our approximation algorithm can provide high performance guarantee on the quality of the solutions.

3. DISTANCE METRIC LEARNING

As discussed in Section 2, there are various distance metrics one can use and the product selection results can vary significantly depending on the distance metrics according to the results shown in Section 6. Hence, it is important to "*learn*" about the proper distance metrics (in other words, consumers' product adoption behavior) from the available data. In this work, we propose a learning method based on the market share of a set of products in the market so to discover the appropriate distance metrics.

Note that in real life, some manufacturers may not release full information about their market share. Therefore, we assume that we only know the market share of a *subset* of existing products. Formally, let $\mathcal{P}'_E$ be the n' products that we know the market share data, where $\mathcal{P}'_E \subseteq \mathcal{P}_E$. Let ms_j be the market share of $p_j \in \mathcal{P}'_E$.

Assume that we have a *model set* consisting of distance-based product adoption models using m' different potential distance metrics, which are numbered from 1 to m'. Let e_{ji} be the expected market share of product p_j under the product adoption model using the i-th potential distance metric. Let θ_i be the probability that consumers use the i-th distance metric, and $\Theta = (\theta_1, \theta_2, \ldots, \theta_{m'})^T$. Then we can forecast the market share for each product $p_j \in \mathcal{P}'_E$ as:

$$f_j(\Theta) = \Theta \cdot (e_{j1}, e_{j2}, \ldots, e_{jm'}) = \theta_1 e_{j1} + \theta_2 e_{j2} + \ldots + \theta_{m'} e_{jm'}, \tag{4}$$

where $f_j(\Theta)$ is the forecast market share of product p_j.

We can find the best fit for Θ by minimizing the squared difference between the forecast market share f_j and the real-world market share ms_j. Let Δ_j be the difference between f_j and ms_j, or mathematically, $\Delta_j(\Theta) = |f_j(\Theta) - ms_j|$. We can formalize the model selection problem as follows.

$$\begin{aligned} \text{Minimize} \quad & \sum_{p_j \in \mathcal{P}'_E} \Delta_j^2(\Theta), \\ \text{subject to} \quad & \Theta \geq \mathbf{0}, \quad \theta_1 + \theta_2 + \ldots + \theta_{m'} = 1, \end{aligned} \tag{5}$$

where $\Theta \geq 0$ means that $\theta_i \geq 0, \forall i \in \{1, \ldots, m'\}$. Thus, the problem is reduced to a linear regression problem with constrained least squares approach, which can be solved using the technique in [3]. Once we solve this linear regression problem, we can forecast the market share $f_j(\Theta)$ based on the probability vector Θ.

EXAMPLE 4. *Consider a* model set *consisting of adoption models using the norm metric (NM), the price metric (PM) and the richman metric (RM). Assume we obtain the real-world market share of three products p_1, p_2, and p_3 and we want to forecast the market share of p_4. The real-world market share and the expected market share under three different models of these products are shown in Table 4.*

	NM	*PM*	*RM*	*real-world*
p_1	20%	1%	50%	5%
p_2	30%	10%	10%	15%
p_3	5%	30%	0%	20%
p_4	10%	40%	5%	unknown

Table 1: An example of model selection

Let θ_1, θ_2, and θ_3 be the probability of consumers using the norm metric*, the* price metric*, and the* richman metric*, respectively. Then we can formalize the problem as follows.*

$$\begin{aligned} \textit{Minimize} \quad & \left\| \begin{matrix} 20\% \cdot \theta_1 & 1\% \cdot \theta_2 & 50\% \cdot \theta_3 & -5\% \\ 30\% \cdot \theta_1 & 10\% \cdot \theta_2 & 10\% \cdot \theta_3 & -15\% \\ 5\% \cdot \theta_1 & 30\% \cdot \theta_2 & 0\% \cdot \theta_3 & -20\% \end{matrix} \right\|_2^2 \\ \textit{subject to} \quad & \Theta \geq \mathbf{0}, \quad \theta_1 + \theta_2 + \theta_3 = 1. \end{aligned} \tag{6}$$

We obtain $\Theta = (0.3074, 0.6926, 0)^T$ by solving the above optimization problem. Thus, we can forecast that the real-world market share of p_4 as $(10\%, 40\%, 5\%) \cdot \Theta = 30.78\%$.

In Section 6, we will show that we can estimate the probability vector Θ with high accuracy if we know the model set and the market share of a small number of products, based on which, we can find products with higher market share.

4. EXACT ALGORITHM AND HARDNESS

Let us first present the exact algorithm for solving a special case of the k-*MMP* problem when $k = 1$. This will serve as the foundation of our approximation algorithm in Section 5. Then we prove the *NP-hardness* of the k-*MMP* problem when $k \geq 2$.

4.1 Exact Top-1 Algorithm

One way to find the exact solution of the 1-*MMP* problem is via exhaustive search: Calculate the expected market share for all candidate products in $\mathcal{P}_N$ and select the product with the largest market share. To calculate the expected market share of a product, we need to check the requirement vectors of all l consumers and the quality vectors of their satisfactory products with time complexity $O(mld)$, where m is the number of existing products and d is the dimension of the attribute vector $\mathcal{A}$. Assume that we consider a model set S consisting of m' potential product adoption models. Since there are n candidate products, the computational complexity of the exhaustive search is $O(m'mnld)$.

In the following, we present an enhanced algorithm for the 1-*MMP* problem based on precomputation. This enhanced algorithm has a lower computational complexity, or $O(m'(m+n)ld)$. The pseudo code of this algorithm is shown in Algorithm 1.

Algorithm 1: Exact top-1 algorithm

```
Input: P_E, P_M, P_N, C, S, Θ
Output: 1-MMP
for all model t in S do
    d_max_t[i] ← d_{i,j} where p_j ∈ FP(c_i|P_E);
    e_t[i] ← |FP(c_i|P_E)|;
    m_t[i] ← |FP(c_i|P_E) ∩ P_M|;
end
max_increase ← 0;
for all p_j ∈ P_N do
    for all c_i ∈ PC(p_j) under each model t in S do
        Δsales_t(p_j) ← 0;
        if d(i,j) > d_max_t[i] then
            Δsales_t(p_j) ← Δsales_t(p_j) + (1 − m_t[i]/e_t[i]);
        else if d(i,j) = d_max_t[i] then
            Δsales_t(p_j) ← Δsales_t(p_j) + ((m_t[i]+1)/(e_t[i]+1) − m_t[i]/e_t[i]);
    end
    ΔSales(p_j) ← θ_1 Δsales_1(p_j) + ... + θ_m' Δsales_m'(p_j)
    if ΔSales(p_j) > max_increase then
        res ← p_j;
        max_increase ← ΔSales(p_j);
    end
end
return res
```

LEMMA 1. *The computational complexity of Algorithm 1 is* $O(m'(m+n)ld)$*, where* $m' = |S|$*,* $m = |\mathcal{P}_E|$*,* $n = |\mathcal{P}_N|$*,* $l = |\mathcal{C}|$*,* $d = |\mathcal{A}|$*.*

PROOF. Firstly, it takes $O(d)$ time to calculate the distance for each pair of consumer and product under each adoption model, while there are l consumers, m existing products, and m' product adoption models, so it takes $O(m'mld)$ in total. Then, for each product $p_j \in \mathcal{P}_N$, we calculate the increase of sales caused by adding p_j, which takes $O(m'ld)$ time. Since there are n candidate new products, the complexity of these steps is $O(m'nld)$. Therefore, the total computational complexity of Algorithm 1 is $O(m'(m+n)ld)$. □

4.2 Top-*k* Exact Algorithm

Similarly, exhaustive search is a direct approach to find the exact solution of the k-*MMP* problem. By enumerating all possible subsets of size k from $\mathcal{P}_N$, and calculating the expected market share of each subset, one can find the set of product with size k which achieves the largest market share. However, the exhaustive approach is *not scalable* since there exist exponentially many possible subsets. In the following theorem, we formally show that finding the exact solution of the k-*MMP* problem is NP-hard.

THEOREM 1. *Finding the exact solution for the* k*-MMP selection problem is NP-hard when* $k \geq 2$ *and the number of attributes is* $d \geq 3$*.*

PROOF. Please refer to the appendix. □

5. APPROXIMATION ALGORITHM

In this section, we extend the top-1 algorithm for the k-*MMP* problem using a greedy-based approximation algorithm. The algorithm is not only computationally efficient, but also provide at least $(1-1/e)$-approximation by exploiting that the market share function is monotone and submodular. In the following, let us first present our approximation algorithm. Then we formally prove its performance guarantee, and finally prove that the market share function we consider is indeed monotone and submodular.

5.1 Greedy-based Approximation Algorithm

Our approximation algorithm is based on the exact top-1 algorithm to solve the top-k problem. The main idea is as follows. We select k products in k steps. In each step, we select the product which is the solution of the exact top-1 algorithm. Furthermore, instead of building the farthest product tables at each step, we only build them in the first step, and then update the tables in the remaining steps. The pseudo code of this algorithm is depicted in Algorithm 2.

Algorithm 2: Approximation top-*k* algorithm

```
Input: P_E, P_M, P_N, C, S, Θ, k
Output: k-MMP
P_res ← ∅;
while |P_res| < k do
    p_new ← solution of the exact top-1 algorithm;
    for c_i ∈ PC(p_new) under each model t in S do
        if d(i,new) > fd_t[i] then
            fd_t[i] ← d(i,new), e_t[i] ← 1, m_t[i] ← 1;
        else if d(i,new) = fd_t[i] then
            e_t[i] ← e_t[i] + 1, m_t[i] ← m_t[i] + 1;
    end
    P_res ← P_res ∩ {p_new};
    P_M ← P_M ∪ {p_new};
    P_N ← P_N \ {p_new};
end
return P_res
```

THEOREM 2. **(Computational complexity)** *The computational complexity of Algorithm 2 is* $O(m'(m+kn)ld)$*, where* $m' = |S|$*,* $m = |\mathcal{P}_E|$*,* $n = |\mathcal{P}_N|$*,* $l = |\mathcal{C}|$*,* $d = |\mathcal{A}|$*.*

PROOF. Based on Lemma 1, it takes $O(m'mld)$ time to build these farthest product tables and $O(m'nld)$ time to find the exact solution of 1-*MMP*. The complexity of updating tables is only $O(ld)$. Since we only build the tables once and find the 1-*MMP* k times in Algorithm 2, the computational complexity of Algorithm 2 is $(m'(m+kn)ld)$. □

5.2 Guarantee on Solution Quality

To prove the performance guarantee of our approximation algorithm, let us first introduce the notion of "*submodular set function*" [11].

Definition 4. **(Submodular set function)** *Given a finite ground set U, a function f that maps subsets of U to real numbers is called* submodular *if*

$$f(S\cup\{u\})-f(S)\geq f(T\cup\{u\})-f(T),\ \forall S\subseteq T\subseteq U, u\in U. \quad (7)$$

Next, we show one interesting property of submodular set functions [5], based on which we design our approximation algorithm with theoretical performance guarantee.

Theorem 3. *For a non-negative monotone submodular function $f: 2^U \rightarrow R$, let $S\subseteq U$ be the set of size k obtained by selecting elements from U one at a time, each time choosing the element that provides the largest marginal increase in the function value. Let $S^*\subseteq U$ be the set that maximizes the value of f over all k-element sets. Then we have $f(S) \geq (1-1/e)\cdot f(S^*)$. In other words, S provides a $(1-1/e)$-approximation, or guarantees a lower bound on the quality of solution as compared to the optimal solution.*

Applying to the *k-MMP* problem, the ground set is $\mathcal{P}_M\cup\mathcal{P}_N$, the market share function $MS(\cdot)$ defined in Section 2 maps subsets of $\mathcal{P}_M\cup\mathcal{P}_N$ to real numbers, i.e., the expected market share of products. According to Theorem 3, if we can prove that $MS(\cdot)$ is a non-negative monotone submodular set function, then our approximation Algorithm 2 can provide a $(1-1/e)$-approximation. We leaves the proof of these properties in the next subsection, and once we prove them, we have the following theorem.

Theorem 4. **(Performance guarantee)** *The approximation algorithm stated in Algorithm 2 provides at least $(1-1/e)$-approximate solutions compared with the optimal ones, where e is the base of the natural logarithm.*

Proof. According to Theorem 5, which will be proved in the following sub-section, the market share function $MS(\cdot)$ in Equation (3) is non-negative, monotone submodular. So, according to Theorem 3, Algorithm 2 provides $(1-1/e)$-approximate solutions. □

5.3 Submodular Market Share Function

Let us consider the market share function $MS(\cdot)$ defined in Section 2. According to the definition of $MS(\cdot)$, it is obviously non-negative, so we seek to prove the monotonicity and submodularity properties. For the ease of presentation, we define the following notations. For any set $S\subseteq\mathcal{P}_M\cup\mathcal{P}_N$ of products, let $\mathcal{P}_S=\mathcal{P}_E\cup S$ and $S_j=S\cup\{p_j\}$, let $pr_i(S)=\sum_{p_j\in S}\Pr(i,j|\mathcal{P}_S)$ denote the probability of the consumer c_i adopting products in S when a set $\mathcal{P}_S$ of products is available in the market. Furthermore, when a set $\mathcal{P}$ of products is available in the market, we define $\mathcal{FC}(p_j|\mathcal{P})$ as the set of consumers that p_j is their farthest product, and recall that $\mathcal{FP}(c_i|\mathcal{P})$ is the set of farthest products from c_i.

One key fact we use in our proof is that by adding a new product, say p_u, only those consumers in $\mathcal{FC}(p_u|\mathcal{P}_u)$ will change their product adoption decisions. Therefore, to calculate the change of market share caused by adding p_u, we only need to consider the consumers in $\mathcal{FC}(p_u|\mathcal{P}_u)$. Mathematically, we have the following proposition.

Proposition 1. *Let $\mathcal{P}_S$ be the set of products in the market, by adding a new product p_u into the market, $p_u\in\mathcal{P}_N\backslash\mathcal{P}_S$, the increase of the market share of products in S_u is*

$$MS(S_u)-MS(S)=\sum_{c_i\in\mathcal{FC}(p_u|S_u)}\frac{1}{l}\left[pr_i(S_u)-pr_i(S)\right]. \quad (8)$$

Based on Proposition 1, we now proceed to prove the monotonicity and submodularity of the market share function $MS(\cdot)$. First, we prove two lemmas (Lemma 2 and 3). Based on these two lemmas, we prove the monotonicity and submodularity properties in Theorem 5.

Lemma 2. *Let $S\subseteq\mathcal{P}_M\cup\mathcal{P}_N$ be a set of products, and p_u be another product in $\mathcal{P}_N$, $p_u\in\mathcal{P}_N\backslash S$. For a consumer $c_i\in\mathcal{C}$, if $c_i\in\mathcal{FC}(p_u|\mathcal{P}_{S_u})$, then we have*

$$pr_i(S_u)-pr_i(S)\geq 0. \quad (9)$$

Proof. Please refer to the appendix. □

Lemma 3. *Let S and T be two sets of products, $S\subseteq T\subseteq\mathcal{P}_M\cup\mathcal{P}_N$, and p_u be another product in $\mathcal{P}_N$, $p_u\in\mathcal{P}_N\backslash T$. For a consumer $c_i\in\mathcal{C}$, if $c_i\in\mathcal{FC}(p_u|\mathcal{P}_{T_u})$, then we have*

$$pr_i(S_u)-pr_i(S)\geq pr_i(T_u)-pr_i(T). \quad (10)$$

Proof. Please refer to the appendix. □

Theorem 5. *Suppose consumers adopt products following the distance-based adoption model, then the market share function $MS(\cdot)$ defined in Equation (3) is monotone submodular for the k-MMP problem.*

Proof. We prove the monotonicity property first. To prove the monotonicity property, we need to show

$$MS(S_u)-MS(S)\geq 0\quad \forall S\subseteq\mathcal{P}_N\cup\mathcal{P}_M, p_u\in\mathcal{P}_N \quad (11)$$

holds, which can be proved by combining the results of Proposition 1 and Lemma 2.

To prove the submodularity property, according to Definition 4, we need to show

$$MS(S_u)-MS(S)\geq MS(T_u)-MS(T) \quad (12)$$

holds $\forall S\subseteq T\subseteq\mathcal{P}_N\cup\mathcal{P}_M$ and $p_u\in\mathcal{P}_N$.

In the case of $p_u\in S$, Inequality (12) holds since both sides are equal to 0. In the case of $p_u\in T\backslash S$, the right side of the inequality equals 0, while according to the monotonicity, which has been proved, the left side is non-negative. Hence Inequality (12) also holds. In the case of $p_u\in\mathcal{P}_N\backslash T$, Inequality (12) can be easily proved by combining the results of Proposition 1 and Lemma 3. Thus, Inequality (12) holds $\forall S\subseteq T\subseteq\mathcal{P}_N\cup\mathcal{P}_M$ and $p_u\in\mathcal{P}_N$. □

6. EXPERIMENTS

We perform experiments on both synthetic datasets and real-world web datasets. We implement our approximation algorithm and the exhaustive search algorithm in C++ and perform experiments on a PC with a 16-core 2.4GHz CPU, 30 GB of main memory under the 64-bit Debian 6.0. First, we use synthetic datasets to evaluate the computational efficiency and accuracy of our approximation algorithm. Then we apply our algorithm on the real-world web datasets to show the impact of different distance metrics, and how to learn distance metrics from some historical sales data and to perform product selection.

6.1 Speedup and Accuracy

We generate the synthetic datasets using the generator provide by [1]. In a real-world market, products usually do not have high quality on *all* attributes. Instead, they have high quality on some subset of attributes only. For example, a smart phone with a large screen will have high quality on display but low quality on portability. Furthermore, if a product has high quality on most attributes, then the price of this product will be high in general, which indicates low quality on the price attribute. We generate the datasets of products with negative correlation on attributes: Products which have high quality in one attribute tends to have low quality on at least one other attribute. On the other hand, we generate the consumers' requirement of each attribute independently using a uniform distribution.

We compare the running time and the market share between our approximation algorithm (or *greedy*) and the exhaustive search algorithm (or *exh*). We examine the impact of various factors, including the size of datasets (n, m, l, d), the number of new products we need to select (k), and models using different distance metrics (four distance metrics as introduced in Section 2). The default settings of these parameters are: $m = 100$, $n = 20$, $l = 10,000$, $d = 10$, $k = 2$. The computational efficiency and accuracy our experiments are similar under all distance models, so we only show the results for the *norm distance metric*.

Note that both the running time of our approximation algorithm and the exhaustive algorithm increases linearly with m, l, and d, due to the page limit, we only show the results of varying k and n while keeping other parameters as default values. Table 2 shows the speedup of our approximation algorithm over the exhaustive algorithm. Figure 2 shows the running time of these two algorithms, where the horizontal axis depicts the variation on parameters n (number of candidate products we need to consider) and k (number of products we need to select), while the vertical axis depicts the log scale of the running time, in seconds.

From the table and the figure, one can observe that our approximation algorithm is significantly faster than the exhaustive algorithm: $O(n^k)$ times faster when selecting k products from n candidate products. The speedup is around 285,000 even for a small dataset (i.e., select $k = 5$ products from $n = 20$ candidates). In this case, the running time of exhaustive algorithm is around 40 hours. In the case of selecting five products from $n = 80$ candidates, our conservative estimate on the running time of the exhaustive algorithm is about 10 years. In contrast, the running time of our approximation algorithm for all cases remain in less than one second. We also test our approximation algorithm on a larger dataset where $m = 1,000$, $n = 100$, $l = 1,000,000$. We select $k = 8$ new products from the 100 candidates. Our approximation algorithm still only takes about 7 minutes.

Figure 3 depicts the expected market share of the two algorithms. One can observe that our approximation algorithm provides high accuracy: about 0.96 approximation on average as compared with the optimal solution obtained using the exhaustive algorithm. This shows that our algorithm generates results which is much better than the theoretical lower bound guarantee. In fact, the results of the two algorithms are exactly the same for over 80% of all experiments we performed and our approximation algorithm still provides a 0.82 approximation even under the worst case scenario among all experiments.

	$k = 2$	$k = 3$	$k = 4$	$k = 5$
$n = 20$	65.89	1160.37	18799.17	285804.08
$n = 40$	256.62	8111.76	287626.53	$\approx 1\times10^7$
$n = 60$	535.29	26511.67	$\approx 1\times10^6$	$\approx 5\times10^7$
$n = 80$	915.38	57812.33	$\approx 4\times10^6$	$\approx 2\times10^8$

Table 2: Speedup: varying k and n

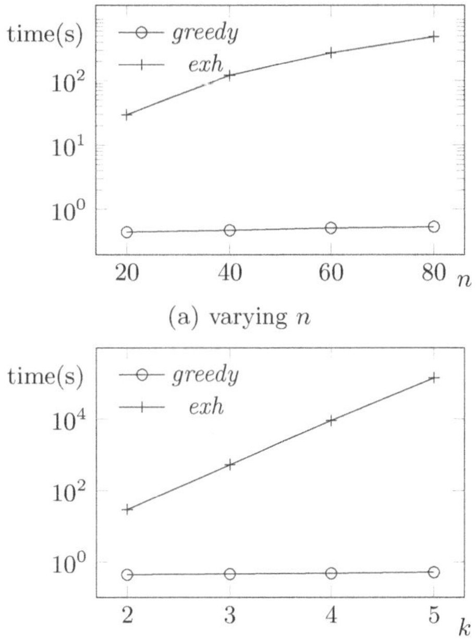

(a) varying n

(b) varying k

Figure 2: Running time: *greedy* vs. *exh*

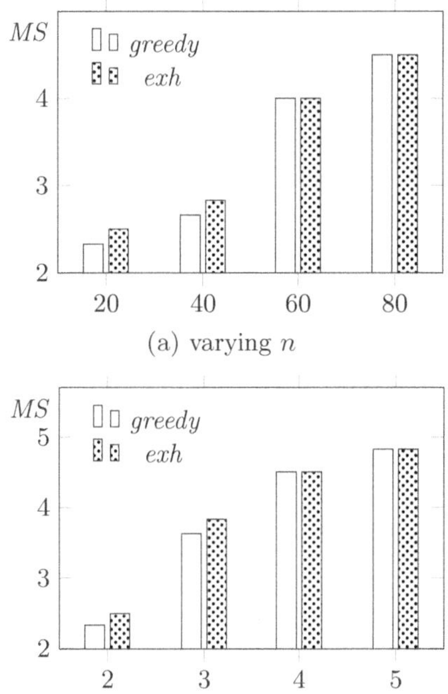

(a) varying n

(b) varying k

Figure 3: Market share (%): *greedy* vs. *exh*

6.2 Impact of Distance Metrics

In this subsection, we perform experiments on a real-world web dataset, and we aim to show the influence of using different distance metrics.

We extract the *TripAdvisor* dataset from [15]. Hotels and reviewers of these hotels are considered as products and consumers respectively in this dataset. The reviewers rated hotels on seven attributes: value, room, location, cleanliness, front desk, service, and business service. We use the average rating of an attribute as the quality of that attribute for each hotel. We also add the inverse of the average price of the hotel as the eighth attribute, which is normalized in the range of (1, 5). For each consumer, we extract requirement vector as follows. Let $\bar{r}$ be the average rating of a hotel's attribute and r_i be the rating from the consumer c_i. If r_i is lower than $\bar{r}$, it means that c_i has a higher requirement than average, and if r_i is higher than $\bar{r}$, c_i may have a lower requirement than the average. Thus, we set the requirement of c_i as $\bar{r}+(\bar{r}-r_i)$. For example, if $\bar{r}=3.5$ and $r_i=4$, then the requirement of c_i will be $3.5+(3.5-4)=3$. Table 3 shows the overall statistics of the dataset.

# of products	# of consumers	# of attributes
1,605	186,249	8

Table 3: Parameters of our web datasets

We select the first 605 hotels as the candidate products and set the remaining 1000 hotels as the existing products. We apply our approximation algorithm to solve the 2-*MMP* problem using the four distance metrics introduced in Section 2: *discrete metric (DM)*, *norm metric (NM)*, *price metric (PM)*, and *richman metric (RM)*. The results are shown in the first four rows of the second column in Table 4. One can observe that the results vary greatly when we use different distance metrics. This implies the importance of inferring and understanding consumers' adoption behavior.

distance metrics	*ID of selected products*	*market share of selected products*
DM	214, 566	32.33%
NM	284, 214	11.20%
PM	566, 350	35.43%
RM	284, 214	11.20%
$\hat{\Theta}$	566, 284	38.09%

Table 4: Results of the 2-*MMP* problem

6.3 Learning Distance Metrics

In the following, we evaluate the accuracy of our learning method using the same dataset in the last subsection. Since we do not have the information about products' real-world market share and consumers' adoption models, we manually set the probability $\hat{\Theta}$ that consumers use the above four distance metrics. Then we randomly set the distance metric for each consumer according to $\hat{\Theta}$ and estimate the "real-world market share" by enumerating each consumer's choice. We estimate the probability as Θ using the learning method in Section 3 and compare the *normalized root-mean-square error (NRMSE)* between Θ and $\hat{\Theta}$ to evaluate the accuracy of our learning method. Note that *NRMSE* ranges in $(0,1)$ and lower value implies higher accuracy.

We present the experimental results in the case that $\hat{\Theta}=(0.1,0.2,0.6,0.1)^T$ and the "real-world market share" of a set $\mathcal{P}'_E$ of five products are known. Firstly, we calculate the expected market share of these products under all the four potential models. The results are shown in Table 5 along with the "real-world market share".

ID	*DM*	*NM*	*PM*	*RM*	*real-world*
91	0.21	0.13	4.81	0.13	2.93
500	0.40	0.14	0.33	0.07	0.27
517	1.30	49.83	2.10	25.38	13.75
746	1.07	0.79	0.81	11.40	1.87
350	0.68	1.09	3.80	1.09	2.64

Table 5: Market share (%)

Then, by solving the following optimization problem, we can estimate $\Theta=(0.1084,0.1979,0.5953,0.0984)^T$. One can observe that Θ is very close to $\hat{\Theta}$ (*NRMSE*$\approx$0.0099), which indicates a high accuracy of the estimation.

$$\text{Minimize}\quad \left\| \begin{matrix} 0.21\%\theta_1 & 0.13\%\theta_2 & 4.81\%\theta_3 & 0.13\%\theta_4 & -2.93\% \\ 0.40\%\theta_1 & 0.14\%\theta_2 & 0.33\%\theta_3 & 0.07\%\theta_4 & -0.27\% \\ 1.30\%\theta_1 & 49.83\%\theta_2 & 2.10\%\theta_3 & 25.38\%\theta_4 & -13.75\% \\ 1.07\%\theta_1 & 0.79\%\theta_2 & 0.81\%\theta_3 & 11.40\%\theta_4 & -1.87\% \\ 0.70\%\theta_1 & 0.15\%\theta_2 & 1.68\%\theta_3 & 0.15\%\theta_4 & -2.64\% \end{matrix} \right\|_2^2$$

$$\text{subject to}\quad \Theta \geq \mathbf{0},\quad \theta_1+\theta_2+\theta_3+\theta_4=1.$$

Based on the derived probability Θ, one can forecast the market share of products and make a better product selection decision. The result of the 2-*MMP* problem in this scenario is shown in the last row of Table 4. For the selected products under each adoption model in Table 4, we estimate the "real-world market share" and list the result in the last column. One can observe that, the product selection result based on learning the proper weighting of distance metrics achieves a better market share than other distance metrics.

We also select different sets $\mathcal{P}'_E$ of products that we know the market share and examine the *NRMSE*. The results are shown in Figure 4, where the vertical axis is the *NRMSE* of the estimation, the horizontal axis of (a) is n' which is the size of $\mathcal{P}'_E$, and the horizontal axis of (b) is the average variance σ^2 of the expected market share of products in $\mathcal{P}'_E$ under different models when $n'=5$ and $n'=20$.

One can observe that our estimation maintains a high accuracy in general. The average accuracy is about 0.035 even in the case that we only know the market share of five products. Furthermore, the accuracy increases exponentially fast when the size of $\mathcal{P}'_E$ increases. On the other hand, product sets with larger σ^2 have higher accuracy, which is realistic since if the market share varies slightly under different models, it may be difficult to estimate.

Due to the page limit, we only present the above example. We like to note that our results and conclusions are consistent when we vary $\hat{\Theta}$, model set, or any other parameters.

7. RELATED WORK

Product selection: Let us provide some related work on product selection. In [6], authors formulated a number of microeconomic applications as optimization problems via data mining perspective. Inspired by [6], Li et al. [7] extended

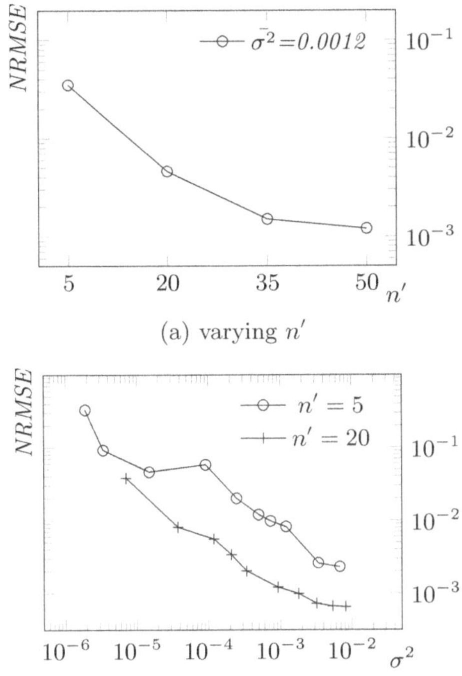

(a) varying n'

(b) varying σ^2

Figure 4: Accuracy of distance metric learning

the concept of dominance, which is used as skyline operators [1] to analyze various forms of relationships between products and consumers. A manufacturer can position popular products effectively while remaining profitable by analyzing the dominance relationships. The works in [16, 14, 13, 12] considered the situation that there exist multiple manufacturers. The authors of [16] derived the Nash Equilibrium when each manufacturer modifies its product in a round robin manner to maximize the market share. Wan et al. [14] aimed to find the most competitive products which are not dominated by any competitors without taking into account the consumers. They extended their work in [13, 12] by considering the consumers' preferences. However, the above papers all aimed to maximize the *number of potential consumers*, which is not equivalent to the *market share* derived in this paper. In fact, potential consumers may not lead to higher market share because different consumers have different probability to adopt new products. Authors in [8] aimed to find the products with the maximum expected number of total adopters, which is similar with the market share in our paper. But their algorithm could not provide any theoretical performance guarantee. Furthermore, none of the previous works consider the complicated product adoption behavior of consumers. Instead, they assumed that consumers will make randomly product adoption decisions, which corresponds to a special case of our product adoption model using the *discrete norm*.

Maximization of submodular functions: Submodular functions have properties which are very similar to the convex and concave functions. The authors of [2, 11] showed that a natural greedy hill-climbing strategy can achieve a provable performance guarantee for a problem of maximizing a non-negative monotone submodular function: at least 63% of optimal. Due to the generality of this performance guarantee, this results has found applications in a number of areas, e.g., discrete optimization [10], materialized view [4], and influence maximization [5].

8. CONCLUSIONS

In this work, we present the problem of finding the k most marketable products (k-*MMP*) under a distance-based adoption model. Our adoption model is general in that we can use different distance metrics to describe various consumers' adoption behaviors. Given some historical data sets on market share, we propose a learning method to select the appropriate distance metrics to describe consumers' production adoption behavior. We prove that the k-*MMP* problem is *NP-hard* when $k \geq 2$ and the number of products' attributes, d, is three or more. We propose a polynomial time approximation algorithm to solve the k-*MMP* problem. Using the submodularity analysis, we formally prove that our approximation algorithm can guarantee a $(1-1/e)$-approximation as compared to the optimal solution. We compared our approximation algorithm with the exhaustive search algorithm on the synthetic datasets. The results showed that our approximation algorithm can achieve $O(n^k)$ times speedup when selecting k products from n candidates. Furthermore, the solution quality of our algorithm is about 96% on average, which is much higher than the theoretical lower bound. We also perform experiments on the real-world web datasets to show the crucial impact of different distance metrics and how we can improve the accuracy of product selection using our distance metric selection method.

9. ACKNOWLEDGMENTS

The work of John C.S. Lui is supported in part by the GRF Grant 415112.

10. REFERENCES

[1] S. Borzsony, D. Kossmann, and K. Stocker. The skyline operator. In *ICDE*, pages 421–430, 2001.

[2] G. Cornuejols, M. L. Fisher, and G. L. Nemhauser. Location of bank accounts to optimize float. *Management science*, 23(8):789–810, 1977.

[3] P. E. Gill, W. Murray, and M. H. Wright. Practical optimization. 1981.

[4] V. Harinarayan, A. Rajaraman, and J. D. Ullman. Implementing data cubes efficiently. In *ACM SIGMOD Record*, volume 25, pages 205–216. ACM, 1996.

[5] D. Kempe, J. Kleinberg, and É. Tardos. Maximizing the spread of influence through a social network. In *KDD*, pages 137–146, 2003.

[6] J. Kleinberg, C. Papadimitriou, and P. Raghavan. A microeconomic view of data mining. *Data mining and knowledge discovery*, pages 311–324, 1998.

[7] C. Li, B. C. Ooi, A. K. Tung, and S. Wang. Dada: a data cube for dominant relationship analysis. In *SIGMOD*, pages 659–670, 2006.

[8] C.-Y. Lin, J.-L. Koh, and A. L. Chen. Determining k-most demanding products with maximum expected number of total customers. In *TKDE*, pages 1732–1747, 2012.

[9] X. Lin, Y. Yuan, Q. Zhang, and Y. Zhang. Selecting stars: the k most representative skyline operator. In *ICDE*, pages 86–95, 2007.

[10] G. L. Nemhauser and L. A. Wolsey. *Integer and combinatorial optimization*, volume 18. Wiley New York, 1988.

[11] G. L. Nemhauser, L. A. Wolsey, and M. L. Fisher. An analysis of approximations for maximizing submodular set functions - I. *Mathematical Programming*, pages 265–294, 1978.

[12] Y. Peng, R. C.-W. Wong, and Q. Wan. Finding top-k preferable products. In *TKDE*, pages 1774–1788, 2012.

[13] Q. Wan, R. Wong, and Y. Peng. Finding top-k profitable products. In *ICDE*, pages 1055–1066, 2011.

[14] Q. Wan, R. C.-W. Wong, I. F. Ilyas, M. T. Özsu, and Y. Peng. Creating competitive products. In *VLDB*, pages 898–909, 2009.

[15] H. Wang. `http://times.cs.uiuc.edu/~wang296/Data`.

[16] Z. Zhang, L. V. S. Lakshmanan, and A. K. H. Tung. On domination game analysis for microeconomic data mining. In *TKDD*, pages 18:1–18:27, 2009.

APPENDIX

• **Proof of Theorem 1:**

PROOF. The *NP-hardness* proof can be achieved by transforming an *NP-hard* problem, called the *top-k Representative Skyline Product* (top-k RSP) [9], to a special case of the k-*MMP* problem.

Let us state the top-k RSP [9]. Given a set U of points and a positive integer k, compute a set S of k skyline points such that the number of points dominated by these k points is maximized. A point $p = (p[1], p[2], \ldots, p[d])$ *dominates* another point $q = (q[1], q[2], \ldots, q[d])$ iff $p[i] \geq q[i]$ $\forall 1 \leq i \leq d$ and there exists at least one dimension k such that $p[k] > q[k]$, and we denote this as $p \succ q$. Consequently, the *skyline* point is defined as follows. Given a set U of points, the skyline points of U are the set of $S \subseteq U$ points which are not dominated by any points in U.

Given an instance of top-k RSP problem, we construct an instance of k-*MMP* problem, which can be carried out as follows. Set $\mathcal{P}_E = \emptyset$, i.e., $m = 0$. Let $\mathcal{P}_N$ be the set of skyline points in U, and $\mathcal{C}$ be the rest, i.e., $\mathcal{C} = U \backslash \mathcal{P}_N$. Note that in general, the concept of *dominance* is different from *product satisfiability* as stated in Definition 1. Formally, we have $p_j \succ c_i \Rightarrow p_j \succsim c_i$, but $p_j \succsim c_i \nRightarrow p_j \succ c_i$. However, if $p_j \succsim c_i$ but $p_j \nsucc c_i$, then the quality vector of p_j is exactly the same with the requirement vector of c_i, i.e., p_j and c_i have the same location in the d-dimensional space. But in our construction, the product points are skyline points while the consumer points are not, so there *does not exist* such kind of c_i and p_j pairing in our construct. Therefore, we can treat *dominance* and *product satisfiability* to be the same in this instance.

Let P be the set of k products we select from $\mathcal{P}_N$. In this case, since there is no existing product, so if a consumer has any satisfactory product in P, the consumer will adopt one unit of products in P, otherwise, 0. As a result, the expected number of adopters is equal to the number of consumers who have satisfactory products in P. In another word, $MS(P)$ is equal to the total number of points dominated by the skyline points in P divide by the total number of non-skyline points. Since the total number of non-skyline points is fixed, the result of the corresponding top-k RSP problem is also the result of this instance of the k-*MMP* problem.

Therefore, any instance of the top-k RSP problem can be transformed to an instance of the k-*MMP* problem. Since the top-k RSP problem has been proved to be an *NP-hard* problem, the k-*MMP* problem is also *NP-hard*. □

• **Proof of Lemma 2:**

PROOF. To simplify the proof, we define the following notations. Let $\sigma = |\mathcal{FP}(c_i|\mathcal{P}_{S_u})|$ and $s = |\mathcal{FP}(c_i|\mathcal{P}_{S_u})| \cap S_u|$, where $\sigma \geq s \geq 1$. Let $d = d_{i,j}$ where $p_j \in \mathcal{FC}(c_i|\mathcal{P}_S)$. Since $c_i \in \mathcal{FC}(p_u|\mathcal{P}_{S_u})$, we have $d_{i,u} \geq d$. If $d_{i,u} > d$, then c_i will adopt p_u with probability 1, i.e., $pr_i(S_u) = 1$. While $pr_i(S) \leq 1$, so Inequality (9) holds. If $d_{i,u} = d$, then $\mathcal{FP}(c_i|\mathcal{P}_{S_u}) = \mathcal{FP}(c_i|\mathcal{P}_S) \cup \{p_u\}$, so $|\mathcal{FP}(c_i|\mathcal{P}_S)| = \sigma - 1$. Similarly, we have $|\mathcal{FP}(c_i|\mathcal{P}_S) \cap S| = s - 1$. When $\sigma = 1$, $\mathcal{FP}(c_i|\mathcal{P}_S)$ is an empty set, which means p_u is c_i's only choice, the situation is the same with the case of $d_{i,u} = d$. So we only need to consider the case when $\sigma > 1$. Bring the notations into Inequality (9), we have

$$pr_i(S_u) - pr_i(S) = \frac{s}{\sigma} - \frac{s-1}{\sigma-1} = \frac{\sigma - s}{\sigma(\sigma-1)} \geq 0, \qquad (13)$$

which can be proved by observing that $\sigma \geq s$ and $\sigma > 1$. □

• **Proof of Lemma 3:**

PROOF. Because $S_u \subseteq T_u$, p_u has more competitors when a set T_u of products is available in the market. As a result, $\mathcal{FC}(p_u|T_u) \subseteq \mathcal{FC}(p_u|S_u)$. Since $c_i \in \mathcal{FC}(p_u|T_u)$, we have $c_i \in \mathcal{FC}(p_u|S_u)$. Follow the same notations in the proof of Lemma 2, let us consider the case of $\sigma = 1$ first. In this case, $pr_i(S_u) = 1$, $pr_i(S) = 0$, so the left side of Inequality (10) equals to 1. While the right side of the inequality is obviously no larger than 1, so the Inequality (10) holds. Now let us consider the case when $\sigma > 1$. According to the proof of Lemma 2, we have

$$pr_i(S_u) - pr_i(S) = \frac{s}{\sigma} - \frac{s-1}{\sigma-1}. \qquad (14)$$

Let d_T and d_S denote the distance between c_i and the products in $\mathcal{FP}(c_i|\mathcal{P}_T)$ and $\mathcal{FP}(c_i|\mathcal{P}_S)$, respectively, where $d_{i,u} \geq d_T \geq d_S$. In the case of $d_{i,u} > d_S$, then the left side of Inequality 10 equals to 1, so the inequality holds. Thus, the remaining thing is to prove the inequality holds when $d_{i,u} = d_T = d_S$. In this case, $\mathcal{FP}(c_i|\mathcal{P}_{S_u}) = \mathcal{FP}(c_i|\mathcal{P}_S) \cup \{p_u\}$, $\mathcal{FP}(c_i|\mathcal{P}_{T_u}) = \mathcal{FP}(c_i|\mathcal{P}_T) \cup \{p_u\}$, and $\mathcal{FP}(c_i|\mathcal{P}_S) \subseteq \mathcal{FP}(c_i|\mathcal{P}_T)$. Let $\delta = |\mathcal{FP}(c_i|\mathcal{P}_{T_u})| - |\mathcal{FP}(c_i|\mathcal{P}_{S_u})|$, then it follows that $\delta \geq 0$, $\sigma + \delta = |\mathcal{FP}(c_i|\mathcal{P}_{T_u})|$, $s + \delta = |\mathcal{FP}(c_i|\mathcal{P}_{T_u}) \cup T_u|$. Thus we have

$$pr_i(T_u) - pr_i(T) = \frac{s+\delta}{\sigma+\delta} - \frac{s+\delta+1}{\sigma+\delta+1}. \qquad (15)$$

According to Equation (14) and (15), we can derive Inequality (10) as follows.

$$\text{Inequality (10) holds}$$
$$\Leftrightarrow \frac{s}{\sigma} - \frac{s-1}{\sigma-1} \geq \frac{s+\delta}{\sigma+\delta} - \frac{s+\delta-1}{\sigma+\delta-1}$$
$$\Leftrightarrow \frac{\sigma - s}{\sigma(\sigma-1)} \geq \frac{\sigma - s}{(\sigma+\delta)(\sigma+\delta-1)} \qquad (16)$$

Hence, we only need to show that Inequality (16) holds, which can be proved by observing that $\sigma > 1$, $\delta \geq 0$ and $\sigma \geq s$. □

TCS: Efficient Topic Discovery over Crowd-oriented Service Data

Yongxin Tong Caleb Chen Cao Lei Chen
Hong Kong University of Science & Technology, Hong Kong, China
{yxtong, caochen, leichen}@cse.ust.hk

ABSTRACT

In recent years, with the widespread usage of Web 2.0 techniques, crowdsourcing plays an important role in offering human intelligence in various service websites, such as Yahoo! Answer and Quora. With the increasing amount of crowd-oriented service data, an important task is to analyze latest hot topics and track topic evolution over time. However, the existing techniques in text mining cannot effectively work due to the unique structure of crowd-oriented service data, *task-response pairs*, which consists of the task and its corresponding responses. In particular, existing approaches become ineffective with the ever-increasing crowd-oriented service data that accumulate along the time. In this paper, we first study the problem of discovering topics over crowd-oriented service data. Then we propose a new probabilistic topic model, the *Topic Crowd Service Model* (TCS model), to effectively discover latent topics from massive crowd-oriented service data. In particular, in order to train TCS efficiently, we design a novel parameter inference algorithm, the *Bucket Parameter Estimation* (BPE), which utilizes belief propagation and a new sketching technique, called *Pairwise Sketch* (pSketch). Finally, we conduct extensive experiments to verify the effectiveness and efficiency of the TCS model and the BPE algorithm.

Categories and Subject Descriptors

H.2.8 [**Database Applications**]: Data Mining

General Terms

Design, Experimentation, Performance

Keywords

Crowd-oriented Service, Probabilistic Topic Model, Crowdsourcing

KDD'14, August 24–27, 2014, New York, NY, USA.

http://dx.doi.org/10.1145/2623330.2623647.

1. INTRODUCTION

Crowdsourcing refers to outsourcing works traditionally performed by an employee to an "undefined, generally large group of people in the form of an open call"[13]. In general, crowdsourcing-based service has a common framework: each employer (a.k.a the task publisher) poses a task, and then this task is responded or finished by many different and unknown crowd employees. Thus, the "task-response pairs" is the unique structure of crowdsourcing data. In this paper, we call information services provided by crowdsourcing, which include massive task-response pairs, as *crowd-oriented services*. Examples of crowd-oriented services include Yahoo! Answers, Quora, and Baidu Recommender, etc.

Given a crowd-oriented service system, one of the most significant problems is the "assignment problem"[11], namely how the crowd-oriented service system assigns a task to a right employee or helps an employee to find a right task. In order to enhance the accuracy of assignments, an effective method is to match them in terms of the semantic topic distribution of tasks and historical responses of employees. Thus, the problem of discovering topic is a fundamental task for crowd-oriented service systems. For example, stackoverflow[1] is a crowd-oriented website regarding programming techniques. By means of discovering the topic distributions of tasks and responses in stackoverflow, we can know which programming technique is the most popular one in current communities of programmers and guide the crowdsourcing platform to find hidden speciality of crowd employee according to their responses.

Although topic discovery is a basic operator for crowd-oriented service data, it is not trivial to capture hidden topics over crowd oriented service data using existing techniques of text mining. Back to the example about stackoverflow, Table 1 includes several real tasks and responses downloaded from the stackoverflow. The crowd-oriented service data in Table 1 contains infinite entries that are chronologically ordered and each entry contains a task and its corresponding responses (if any). We can observe that the first and second task-response entries discuss the topic related with Android-based developing techniques, and the third one is about iPhone techniques. If we use existing text mining techniques, such as Latent Dirichlet allocation (LDA) model, to discover the hidden topic distribution, a straightforward solution is to consider each task and response as a document and applies LDA model. For the first two entries in Table 1, this method can capture the topic about Android-based technique in the tasks and their responses since "An-

[1] http://stackoverflow.com/

Table 1: Crowd-oriented Service Data from the stackoverflow

ID	Tasks	Responses
1	Android application database to save images ...	Android SQLite database with multiple tables can...
2	How to use simpleadapter with activity Android...	An Android ListView with adapter is shown as follows...
3	Find mobilephones on hotspot networks in iPhone?...	iOS 7 system of Apple devices provide an IP address of ...
...	......	......

droid" occur in both of them. However, for the third entry, LDA model might not return similar topic distribution because there is no common words appeared in both of the task and the response.

Thus, for crowd-oriented service data, it is the necessary to discover hidden topics by considering both the task-response pair correlation and the specific semantic feature of each task and response. Furthermore, a real-time crowd-oriented service should be viewed as an online updateable data of crowd-oriented task-response pairs, which is referred as a series of consecutively submitted crowd-oriented tasks (task for short) and corresponding responses from crowds. Therefore, for these online service data, the efficiency of training the model is another major concern. The latent topics need to be discovered from massive crowd-oriented service data in real time. To achieve these goals in discovering topics over crowd-oriented service data, we have to address the following two challenges.

- Challenge 1: How to design an effective model to capture the task-response correlation over dynamic evolving crowd-oriented service data?
- Challenge 2: Facing the high volume of crowd-oriented service data, how to guarantee the training efficiency? There are two critical issues need to be addressed. The first problem is how to efficiently store and process massive task-response pairs. The other one is how to design an efficient parameter estimation approach, which can help deriving the proper parameter settings for the proposed topic detection model over crowd-oriented service data.

The aforementioned challenges reflect the high demand of an advanced probabilistic model which is tailored to meet the crowd data form and large data size. In answering this demand, we design and present the *Topic Crowd Service Model* (TCS), which features the capability of discovering latent topics from massive crowd-oriented service data with high accuracy. One essential niche of TCS is that it captures the the structure of task-response pair by preserving the mutual correlation. The massive size of incoming data, which is continuously increasing everyday, is the nightmare for most conventional parameter estimation methods such as collapsed Gibbs Sampling(GS)[20] and Variational Bayes(VB)[1], due to the high computational cost while traversing the dataset. It is observed that such computational cost attributes to the iterative behaviour of scanning the entire corpus and visit the complete topic space. This procedure leads to a linearly increasing computational time cost of the size of the data, the number of topics and the number of training iterations. In answering such challenge, we propose the *Block Parameter Estimation*(BPE), which is a fast parameter estimation method. The BPE features the *Pair Sketch*(pSketch) technique, which is a storage space reduction approach that alleviates the pain of updating new data trunks. Moreover, in order to achieve the convergence of parameter inference process, BPE integrates belief propagation[18] into the stochastic gradient descent framework [3], in which a series of online gradient updates lead to the stationary point of the likelihood function of TCS. Such design of the BPE brings in significantly speedup for the parameter inference process by simplifying the updates of TCS during the iterations: in each iteration, only a small portion of the crowd-oriented service data are selected as well as a part of topic space for message updating and passing. In sum, we make following major contributions:

- We design and present a new probabilistic topic model, the *Topic Crowd Service Model* (TCS model), which features the capability of discovering latent topics from massive crowd-oriented service data with high accuracy.
- We propose a fast parameter estimation algorithm, the *Bucket Parameter Estimation* (BPE), which utilizes a new sketching technique, called *pSketch*, and belief propagation to enhance the efficiency of the training process significantly.
- We verify the effectiveness and efficiency of the proposed methods through extensive experiments on real datasets. The experimental evaluation shows that TCS model and BPE algorithm outperform several existing probabilistic topic models and parameter estimation methods.

The rest of the paper is organized as follows. Our problem formulation is introduced in Section 2. In Section 3, we discuss the assumptions and generative process of the *Topic Crowd Service Model* (TCS). In addition, to train *TCS* efficiently, we present a new pairwise data-based sketch (pSkech) to quickly select the significant words in crowd-oriented service data in Section 4. Based on the significant words, we propose an effective parameter estimation algorithm, called *Bucket Parameter Estimation* (BPE), to train TCS in a specific bucket and multiple consecutive buckets of crowd-oriented service data in Section 5. We present the experimental results, related work and conclude the paper in Sections 6, 7, and 8, respectively.

2. PROBLEM FORMULATION

In this section, we formally define the related concepts and the problem of discovering hot topics over crowd-oriented service data. Let us begin with defining a few basic concepts as follows.

DEFINITION 1 (TASK-RESPONSE PAIR). *Given a crowd-oriented task T_i, a set of corresponding responses $\{R_{i,1}, \cdots, R_{i,m}\}$, the arbitrary pair $(T_i, R_{i,j})$ for $j \in [1, m]$ is called a task-response pair.*

Table 2: Notation

Notation	Description
D	the set of all documents
W	the set of all words
W_T	the set of all words from tasks
W_R	the set of all words from responses
T	the set of distinct words from tasks
R	the set of distinct words from responses
K	the number of topics
d	document
s	sentence
z	topic
w	word
θ	multinomial distribution over topics
ϕ	multinomial distribution over words
α	Dirichlet prior vector for θ
β	Dirichlet prior vector for ϕ
$z^k_{d,s}$	the sentence s of document d is assigned to topic k
$z^k_{d,s,w}$	the word w in sentence s of document d is assigned to topic k
$n_{d,s,w}$	the number of w in sentence s of document d
λ_T	the significant threshold of words in tasks
λ_R	the significant threshold of words in responses
ρ_D	the proportion of documents for message passing
ρ_K	the proportion of topics for message passing
l_d	the related documents with the document d
ζ	the influence of related documents

DEFINITION 2 (CROWD-ORIENTED SERVICE DATA). *Let CS=$\{(T_1, R_{1,1}), \cdots, (T_n, R_{n,1}), \cdots, (T_n, R_{n,m})\}$ be a set of task-response pairs, where each task and response is a document. Each document d is represented by a subset of the collection of words W=$\{w_1, \cdots, w_{|W|}\}$. Given arbitrary task-response pair, a word-pair includes two words, one word is from the document of the task, the other word is from the document of the response.*

DEFINITION 3 (TOPIC). *A semantically coherent topic ϕ is a multinomial distribution of words $\{p(w|\phi)\}_{w\in W}$ with the constraint $\sum_{w\in W} p(w|\phi) = 1$.*

According to the definitions of related concepts, we can now formally define the major task in the problem of discovering topics over crowd-oriented service data as follows.

Discovering Topics over Crowd-oriented Service Data Problem: *Given the input of a crowd-oriented service data CS, we are required to infer the latent topics ϕ over in CS.*

Moreover, we list notations used in this paper in Table 2.

3. TOPIC CROWD SERVICE MODEL

In this section, we present a novel probabilistic model, *Topic Crowd Service Model* (TCS), for discovering topics over crowd-oriented service data. As shown in Table 1 and aforementioned definitions, each *document* is either a *task* or a *response from crowd employees*. Then, we illustrate the underlying logic of TCS. The generative process of TCS is shown in Algorithm 1.

Each document has a topic distribution. According to the pairs generated by pSketch, which will be introduced in Section 4, the topically coherency of each document is related. When composing the documents, the user first decides the topic that is aligned with his or her current task requirement and then selects some words according to the chosen topic. Notably, the topic distribution is determined by the document itself and the documents related by the corresponding task-response pairs. Furthermore, since each sentence is usually topically coherent, we impose the constraint that the words in each sentence should share the same topic, in order to capture semantic coherency.

Algorithm 1: Generative process of TCS

```
for each topic k ∈{1, ··· , K} do
    draw a word distribution φ_k ~ Dirichlet(β);
for each document d ∈{1, ··· , D} do
    draw topic distribution θ_d ~ Dirichlet(α);
    if d is a task then
        sample a response d' with regard to the number
        of sketch pairs between d and d';
    if d is a response then
        select the corresponding task d';
    generate new document topic distribution θ' by
    combining θ_d and θ_d';
    for each sentence s ∈ d do
        choose a topic z ~ Multinomial(θ');
        generate words w ~ Multinomial(φ_z);
```

Although existing parameter inference techniques, such as Gibbs sampling and variational Bayes, can be used to train the TCS model according to Algorithm 1, they have to spend higher computational cost. In order to enhance the efficiency of training process significantly, we will consider the problem of training the TCS model as a labelling problem. In other words, the training objective is equal to assign a set of topic labels to explain the observed data.

4. PAIRWISE SKETCH

As discussed in Section 3, the latent topic distribution is influenced by corresponding task-response pairs in the proposed TCS model. Thus, it is crucial for the training process to calculate frequencies of word pairs from task-response pairs. However, due to high-volume of online crowd-oriented service data, it is infeasible to count and store all word pairs due to the excessively high cost. Fortunately, word pairs with significant frequencies provide most information for discovering latent topics. So we propose to give priority to capture the contents of these pairs. Since finding significant word pairs is the foundation of our parameter estimation algorithm, we present a novel sketching structure, called *Pairwise Sketch* (*pSketch*), to efficiently select the significant word pairs from massive online task-response pairs. Before discussing the new data structure and algorithm, we first introduce several basic concepts and notations.

Given the set of all words of the given crowd-oriented service data W, it can be partitioned into two disjoint subsets, denoted by W_T and W_R, which consist of all words from tasks and responses, respectively. Moreover, the sets of distinct words in W_T and W_R are denoted by T and R, respectively. Then, a significant word pair is defined as follows.

DEFINITION 4 (SIGNIFICANT WORD PAIR). *Given a crowd-oriented service data CS, two significant thresholds λ_T and λ_R where $\lambda_T, \lambda_R \in (0, 1)$, a word pair (t,r) is a significant word pair if and only if $f(t,r) > \lceil \lambda_T f(t) \rceil$ and $f(t,r) > \lceil \lambda_R f(r) \rceil$, where $f(t,r)$ means the frequency of the word pair (t,r), $f(t)$ is the sum of frequencies of all word pairs with t as the word in tasks, and $f(r)$ is similar.*

Please note that duplicates of a task in CS is only counted as one task. In general, $|W_R| >> |W_T|$, hence we set two dif-

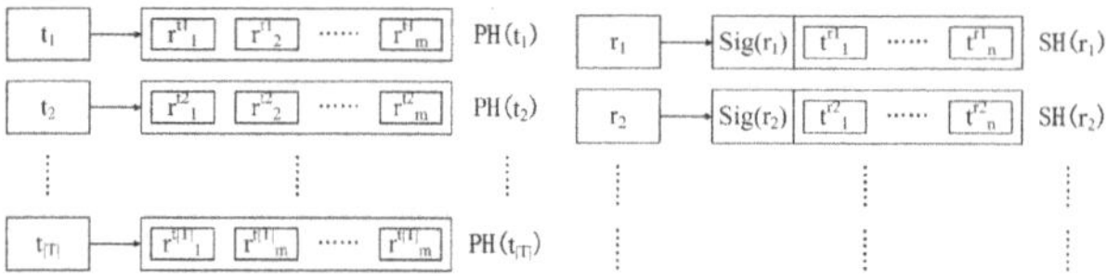

(a) Primary Hashing (PH) (b) Secondary Hashing (SH)

Figure 1: Pairwise Sketch (pSketch)

ferent significant thresholds for them. In order to discover all significant word pairs for online crowd-oriented service data efficiently, a straightforward idea is to utilize existing streaming algorithms of finding frequent items, such as the CM-Sketch algorithm[7], the lossy-counting algorithm[15], the space-saving algorithm[17], and etc. However, the existing researches only handle single item rather than correlated pairs. Hence, we have to design a novel solution to find all significant word pairs. Inspired by the space-saving algorithm[17], which is one of the fastest streaming algorithms, we propose a novel sketching structure, called the *PairwiseSketch* (*pSketch*) and algorithm to find all significant word pairs. The pSketch is defined as follows.

Pairwise Sketch: It consists of two hashing structure components: the *primary hashing structure* (denoted *PH*) and the *secondary hashing structure* (denoted *SH*).

Primary Hashing Structure (PH): It includes |T| *primary hashing units* since the crowd-oriented service data has |T| distinct words from tasks. Each primary hashing unit (denoted PH(t_i)) uses t_i as the hashing key and maps a space-saving structure, which is also called the Stream-Summary in [17], to maintain the information about which words from responses are approximate significant for t_i. In other words, r_j is approximate significant for t_i if $f(t_i, r_j) > \lceil(\lambda_T - \epsilon)f(t)\rceil$. ϵ is the error ratio for λ_T. Moreover, based on [17], the number of elements of each space-saving structure is equal to $\lceil\frac{1}{\epsilon}\rceil$, namely $m = \lceil\frac{1}{\epsilon}\rceil$. Figure 1(a) shows a primary hashing structure.

Secondary Hashing Structure (SH): Similar to the *Primary Hashing Structure*, it consists of the set of *secondary hashing units*. Similarly, the number of elements of each space-saving structure, $n = \lceil\frac{1}{\delta}\rceil$ where δ is the error ratio for λ_R. However, there are two differences between the two hashing structures. On the one hand, the number of *secondary hashing units* is scalable rather than |R|. As discussed above, we choose the set of words from tasks as the primary hashing set since $|W_R| >> |W_T|$. Thus, our basic idea is to construct secondary hashing units only for the words from responses in current significant word pairs. On the other hand, an additional element, called the significant counter (denoted Sig(r_j)), appears in each secondary hashing units SH(r_j) and is used to filter out redundant secondary hashing units , where $Sig(r_j)$ records the number of currently significant word pairs from tasks with r_j. Once Sig(r_j)=0, r_j can be safely deleted from *SH*. Finally, in practice, in order to discover potential significant words from responses, we relax the monitoring requirement to the concept of *ϵ-significant words from responses*. Namely, a word r_j is *ϵ-significant* for a word t_i if $f(t_i, r_j) > \epsilon f(t_i)$. Figure 1(b) shows a secondary hashing structure.

According to the aforementioned pSketch structure, we design the significant word pair sketching algorithm in Algorithm 2. For each word pair (t,r), the algorithm first checks whether t constructs its primary hashing unit $PH(t)$ in lines 1-2. Then, the algorithm calls the space-saving algorithm subroutine to maintain frequencies of the word pairs including t in line 4. If r becomes ϵ-significant for t and has $SH(r)$ in the current secondary hashing structure, the algorithm pluses one for Sig(r) in lines 5-7. Otherwise, $SH(r)$ is constructed in lines 8-9. When r is not ϵ-significant for t, Sig(r) is decreased by 1. In particular, the $SH(r)$ will be deleted from current secondary hashing structure if Sig(r) is equal to zero. In other words, the current r is never included by any significant word pairs. Finally, the algorithm also call the space-saving algorithm subroutine to maintain frequencies of the word pairs including r if $SH(r)$ is not deleted from SH. Hence, the pSketch structure not only maintains all significant word pairs but also returns them while traversing the sketch structure.

Algorithm 2: Significant Word Pairs Sketching

Input: a crowd-oriented service data CS, a error ratio ϵ for λ_T, a error ratio δ for λ_R,

```
1  for each word pair (t,r)∈CS do
2      if t does not construct its PH(t) in PH then
3          Construct PH(t);
4      Call Space-Saving(PH(t),r,ε);
5      if r becomes ε-significant for F(t) then
6          if SH(r) exists in SH then
7              Sig(r)← Sig(r)+1;
8      else
9          Construct SH(r) and Sig(r)← 1;
10     if r is not ε-significant for F(t) then
11         Sig(r)← Sig(r)-1;
12         if Sig(r)=0 then
13             Delete SH(r);
14     if SH(t)∈SH then
15         Call Space-Saving(SH(t),t,δ);
```

Computational Complexity Analysis: The time complexity and space complexity of Algorithm 2 are shown as follows. Since crowd-oriented service data is online in most cases, the number of word pairs may be currently unknown. Hence, we mainly analyze the time of processing each word pair in Algorithm 2. The processing time for each word pair in Algorithm 2 is an amortized constant time, which can be directly obtained because Algorithm 2 calls the space-saving subroutine in constant time, and the space-saving subroutine has the amortized constant processing time[17].

The space complexity of Algorithm 2 is $\mathcal{O}(\frac{1+\delta}{\epsilon\delta}|T|)$. In the following, the space usages of primary and secondary hash structures are analyzed, respectively. For primary hash structures, Algorithm 2 assigns a space-saving structure for each distinct word from task. Each space-saving structure spends $\mathcal{O}(\frac{1}{\epsilon})$ according to its definition[17]. Hence, the space usage of primary hash structures is totally $\mathcal{O}(\frac{|T|}{\epsilon})$. Furthermore, according to the definition of ϵ-significant word pairs, the maximum number of words that come from responses and satisfy $f(t, r) > \epsilon \cdot f(t)$ for any word t from tasks is $\frac{1}{\epsilon}$. Thus, the total space usage of secondary hash structures is $\frac{|T|}{\epsilon\delta}$. To sum up, the total space complexity of Algorithm 2 is $\mathcal{O}(\frac{|T|}{\epsilon} + \frac{|T|}{\epsilon\delta}) = \mathcal{O}(\frac{1+\delta}{\epsilon\delta}|T|)$.

5. PARAMETER ESTIMATION

In this section, we discuss the details of the *Bucket Parameter Estimation* (BPE). Section 5.1 first shows the procedure of utilizing BPE to train TCS with crowd-oriented service data in a specific bucket. Section 5.2 also extends the BPE approach to the scenario of multiple consecutive buckets.

5.1 Parameter Estimation in Single Bucket

Section 4 introduces a novel sketching structure to select the significant task-response pairs in crowd-oriented service data. According to these task-response pairs, we propose a new latent parameter estimation approach in a bucket in this subsection, a. Since each sentence is the basic unit for topic assignment, we first aim to infer the probability that a sentence s of the document d is assigned to the topic k, namely the following formula,

$$P(z^k_{d,s}|\mathbf{z}^k_{d,-s}, \mathbf{n}_{d,-s}, \mathbf{z}^k_{\cdot,-s,w}, \mathbf{n}_{\cdot,-s,w}, \mathbf{l}_d) \quad (1)$$

where l_d denotes the related documents which include a word occurring with the other word of the current document d in at least a significant word pair in pSketch, $-s$ means all sentences in the current document d without s, and $\mathbf{z}_{d,-s}$ and $\mathbf{z}_{\cdot,-s,w}$ are all possible topic assignments of neighbouring variables.

Therefore, we denote the belief message by $\mu^k_{d,s}$, indicating a sentence s of the document d is generated by the topic k. It is represented by the following formula:

$$\mu^k_{d,s} \propto \frac{(1-\zeta)\mu^k_{d,-s} + \zeta\mu^k_{l_d} + \alpha_k}{\sum_{k'}\Big((1-\zeta)\mu^{k'}_{d,-s} + \zeta\mu^{k'}_{l_d} + \alpha_{k'}\Big)}$$
$$\frac{\Gamma\Big(\sum_{r'}(n_{\cdot,-s,w'}\mu^k_{\cdot,-s,w'} + \beta_{w'})\Big)}{\Gamma\Big(\sum_{w'}(n_{\cdot,-s,w'}\mu^k_{\cdot,-s,w'} + \beta_{w'} + n_{d,s,w'})\Big)} \quad (2)$$
$$\prod_{w\in s}\Big(\frac{\Gamma(n_{\cdot,-s,w}\mu^k_{\cdot,-s,w} + \beta_w + n_{d,s,w})}{\Gamma(n_{\cdot,-s,w}\mu^k_{\cdot,-s,w} + \beta_w)}\Big)$$

where ζ denotes a ratio to influence the intensity between the current document d and the related documents l_d. In addition, belief message $\mu^k_{d,s,w}$ that a word w in the sentence s can be also updated by $\mu^k_{d,s,w} = \mu^k_{d,s}$..

According to Equation 2, we need to perform a series of iterations to update beliefs and infer parameters. In order to guarantee the efficiency and effectiveness of training the TCS model, there are two crucial challenges: 1) What is the best strategy for the training process? 2) when should the iteration process terminates?

For the first challenge, our main idea is to choose the largest belief residual, which is denoted by $r^k_{d,s} = \Big|\mu^k_{d,s}(t) - \mu^k_{d,s}(t-1)\Big|$, as the updating goal in the updating process from the $(t-1)^{th}$ iteration to the tth iteration. It is reasonable for the updating method in each iteration because the largest belief residuals speed up the convergence of iterations as much as possible. Based on the aforementioned updating strategy, we have to update all non-zero belief residuals, whose number is too huge. Hence, to further enhance the efficiency of the training process, we select only significant task-response pairs, topics, and documents in the training process according to the pSketch. Before introducing more details of our selection strategy, we first extend the concept of $r^k_{d,s}$ to the residuals of higher levels. We denote the residual of the document d on the topic k as $r^k_d = \sum_s r^k_{d,s}$. In other words, the residual of the document d on the topic k is equal to the sum of all residuals of sentences of the document d in the topic k. Similarly, we also denote the residual of the document d as $r_d = \sum_s r^k_d$. Then, we define two selected proportions, denoted by ρ_D and ρ_K, of documents and topics for message passing in each iteration.

Based on the above concepts, our selection updating strategy in each iteration is shown as follows.

- Step 1: We sort all r_d in a descending order and choosing $\rho_D \times D$ documents having the $\rho_D \times D$ largest r_d, where D is the number of documents.
- Step 2: For each selected document d, we sort all r^k_d in a descending order and choose $\rho_K \times K$ topics having the $\rho_K \times K$ largest r^k_d in d, where K is the number of topics.
- Step 3: We only update belief messages in the set of $\rho_D \times D$ documents and $\rho_K \times K$ topics.

According to the above selection updating strategy, we can obtain the normalized estimated messages as follows.

$$\hat{\mu}^k_{d,s}(t) = \frac{\mu^k_{d,s}(t)\sum_k \hat{\mu}^k_{d,s}(t-1)}{\sum_k \mu^k_{d,s}(t)} \quad (3)$$

$$\hat{\mu}^k_{d,s,w}(t) = \frac{\mu^k_{d,s,w}(t)\sum_k \hat{\mu}^k_{d,s,w}(t-1)}{\sum_k \mu^k_{d,s,w}(t)} \quad (4)$$

where $(t-1)$ and t are the previous iteration and the current iteration, respectively. Based on the aforementioned belief messages, we can infer the following parameters: the distribution of topics, θ, and the distribution of words, ϕ, respectively. Namely,

$$\theta^k_d = \frac{\mu^k_{d,\cdot} + \alpha_k}{\sum_{k'}\Big(\mu^{k'}_{d,\cdot} + \alpha_{k'}\Big)}. \quad (5)$$

$$\phi^k_w = \frac{\mu^k_{\cdot,\cdot,w} + \beta_w}{\sum_{w'}\Big(\mu^k_{\cdot,\cdot,w'} + \beta_{w'}\Big)}. \quad (6)$$

For the second challenge, the iteration process also plays a important role. We give two termination conditions for the iteration process. The first condition is a predefined number of iterations. The second condition is when the convergence of the iteration process occurs.

To sum up, based on the solutions to the above two challenges, Algorithm 3 presents the Bucket Parameter Estimation (BPE) algorithm. According to the pseudocode in Algorithm 3, BPE algorithm first initializes and normalizes $\mu^k_{d,s}(0)$ and $\mu^k_{d,s,w}(0)$ in line 2. The pSketch stores the frequencies of significant task-response pairs and assists the initialization of $\mu^k_{d,s,w}(0)$. Then, in each iteration, BPE algorithm sorts the documents according to corresponding r_d and selects $\rho_D \times D$ documents having the largest residuals in lines 3-10. For each selected documents, BPE algorithm also sorts topics and selects $\rho_K \times K$ topics having the largest residuals in lines 4-8. After the selection, this algorithm updates and normalizes $\mu^k_{d,s}(t)$ and $\mu^k_{d,s,w}(t)$ in line 5. In particular, please note that BPE algorithm has to sort and calculates all residuals of all documents and topics in the first iteration because there is no previous information. Finally, BPE algorithm terminates when one of two termination conditions, the maximum iteration number and the convergence of iteration, is satisfied.

5.2 Parameter Estimation in Multiple Consecutive Buckets.

Section 5.1 have introduced the Bucket Parameter Estimation algorithm within a bucket, we extend the BPE algorithm to the scenario of multiple consecutive buckets. In

Algorithm 3: Bucket Parameter Estimation (BPE)

```
for each task-response pair in each document d and each topic k do
    Random initialization and normalization μ^k_{d,s}(0) and μ^k_{d,s,w}(0) based on pSketch;
for each iteration do
    for each document do
        compute μ^k_{d,s}(t) and μ^k_{d,s,w}(t);
        compute r^k_{d,s}(t), r^k_d(t) and r_d(t);
        Sort r^k_d(t) in a descending order;
        Select the ρ_K × K documents having the largest residuals.
    Sort r_d(t) in a descending order;
    Select the ρ_D × D documents having the largest residuals.
```

fact, there are many real applications for the scenario of multiple consecutive buckets. For example, incremental crowd-oriented service data, updating crowd-oriented service data, crowd-oriented service data steams, and so on. For such data, we can partition the complete data into multiple buckets, then extend BPE algorithm to infer latent topics and capture the evaluation of topics.

First of all, we define several new input parameters for the scenario of multiple consecutive buckets. We denote m as the index of multiple buckets and D_m as the number of documents in the mth bucket. Please note that $m \in [1, \infty]$, $d \in [1, D_m]$, and $w \in [1, \infty]$. The indexes of multiple buckets and words reach infinity because infinity crowd-oriented service data are considered in the scenario of multiple consecutive buckets.

Then, we introduce how to extend BPE algorithm to the scenario of multiple consecutive buckets. Different from the updating strategy in the single bucket, the basic idea is that the updating parameters not only consider the information on the current bucket but also integrate the information on the previous buckets. Specifically, in the mth bucket, the extended BPE algorithm first randomly initializes and normalizes the belief messages, denoted by $\mu^k_{d,s}[m]$, then initializes the sufficient statistics, denoted by $\Omega^k_w[m-1] = n_{\cdot,\cdot,w}[m-1]\mu^k_{\cdot,\cdot,w}[m-1]$. Hence, the belief message that a sentence s of the document d on the topic k in Equation 2 should be extended as follows,

$$\mu^k_{d,s}[m] \propto \frac{(1-\zeta)\mu^k_{d,-s}[m] + \zeta\mu^k_{l_d}[m] + \alpha_k}{\sum_{k'}\Big((1-\zeta)\mu^{k'}_{d,-s}[m] + \zeta\mu^{k'}_{l_d}[m] + \alpha_{k'}\Big)}$$
$$\frac{\Gamma\Big(\sum_{w'}(n_{\cdot,-s,w'}[m]\mu^k_{\cdot,-s,w'}[m] + \Omega^k_{w'}[m-1] + \beta_{w'})\Big)}{\Gamma\Big(\sum_{w'}(n_{\cdot,-s,w'}[m]\mu^k_{\cdot,-s,w'}[m] + \Omega^k_{w'}[m-1] + \beta_{w'} + n_{d,s,w'})\Big)}$$
$$\prod_{w \in s}\Big(\frac{\Gamma(n_{\cdot,-s,w}[m]\mu^k_{\cdot,-s,w}[m] + +\Omega^k_w[m-1] + \beta_w + n_{d,s,w})}{\Gamma(n_{\cdot,-s,w}[m]\mu^k_{\cdot,-s,w}[m] + \Omega^k_w[m-1] + \beta_w)}\Big) \quad (7)$$

According to the aforementioned belief message updating strategy, the BPE algorithm (Algorithm 3) can be extended to perform until at least one of the two termination conditions is satisfied.

6. EXPERIMENTAL STUDY

In this section, we evaluate the performance of TCS and BPE with a large-scale crowd-oriented service data. Section 6.1 describes the experimental setup. Section 6.2 presents the experimental results of BPE in terms of the efficiency. Section 6.3 measures the memory cost of BPE. Section 6.4 evaluates the effectiveness of TCS model with several standard metrics. Section 6.5 illustrates some results of topics and analyzes topic evolution in multiple consecutive buckets.

6.1 Experimental Setup

A crowd oriented service data (a.k.a question-answer data) from Yahoo is used as our experimental data. The data contains 142,612 questions and corresponding answers. Similar to [20], we set the hyperparameters as $\alpha = 2/K$ and $\beta = 0.01$. Furthermore, for sampling based parameter inference methods, we report the topic modeling results after 300 iterations, which practically ensures convergence in terms of perplexity that is a standard measure for evaluating the generalization of a probabilistic model [21].

6.2 Efficiency

We first demonstrate the TCS performance concerning the efficiency aspect. Specifically, we compare BPE with a set of state-of-the-art practices including variational Bayes [1] (VB) and collapsed Gibbs sampling (GS) [10, 20]. We train all the models on the same dataset from pSketch in order to achieve a fair evaluation. Please refer to Figure 2 for the performance evaluation results. In Figure 2(a), the training time with the increase of the data size of a bucket is illustrated, where we set the topic amount $K = 300$. We summarize two findings via this experiment: 1) As shown in the figure, the training time of TCS(GS) slightly decreases with the data size of a bucket even it involves the additional cost of residual sorting, while that of TCS(VB) and TCS(BPE) increases. This is because the larger data size of a budget leads to a slightly faster convergence of the sampling based parameter inference methods. 2)TCS(BPE) shows less sensitivity to the change of the size of a bucket, which is a great character concerning online service with dynamic changes.

We then increase the topic amount K while fixing the data size of a bucket at 512MB, and we record the time cost of the three parameter inference methods. The results are shown in Figure 2(b), in which the running time of all three algorithms increase with K. However, since GS and VB require visiting all documents and the entire topic space, their time cost increase quickly when the data size grows larger. On the contrary, BPE only entails a subset of documents and a fraction of topic space, which qualifies itself as a fast topic modeling of massive crowd oriented service data.

We then answer the question that TCS(BPE) outperforms the other topic models in terms of training efficiency. We vary the data size of a bucket and the topic amount, and then we evaluate the time consumption of different models and present the result in Figure 2(c) and 2(d). Here all baseline methods are trained on full data while TCS(BPE) is trained selectively. In Figure2(c) we set the topic amount to be 300 and the result demonstrates the superiority of TCS(BPE) over other models: 1) TCS is a relatively light-weight topic model and does not involve much complicated calculation; 2) TCS(BPE) utilizes pSketch to reduce the crowd oriented service data that need to be digested by the downstream topic modeling process; and 3) TCS(BPE) reduces the amount of documents and the scope of the topic space that need to be

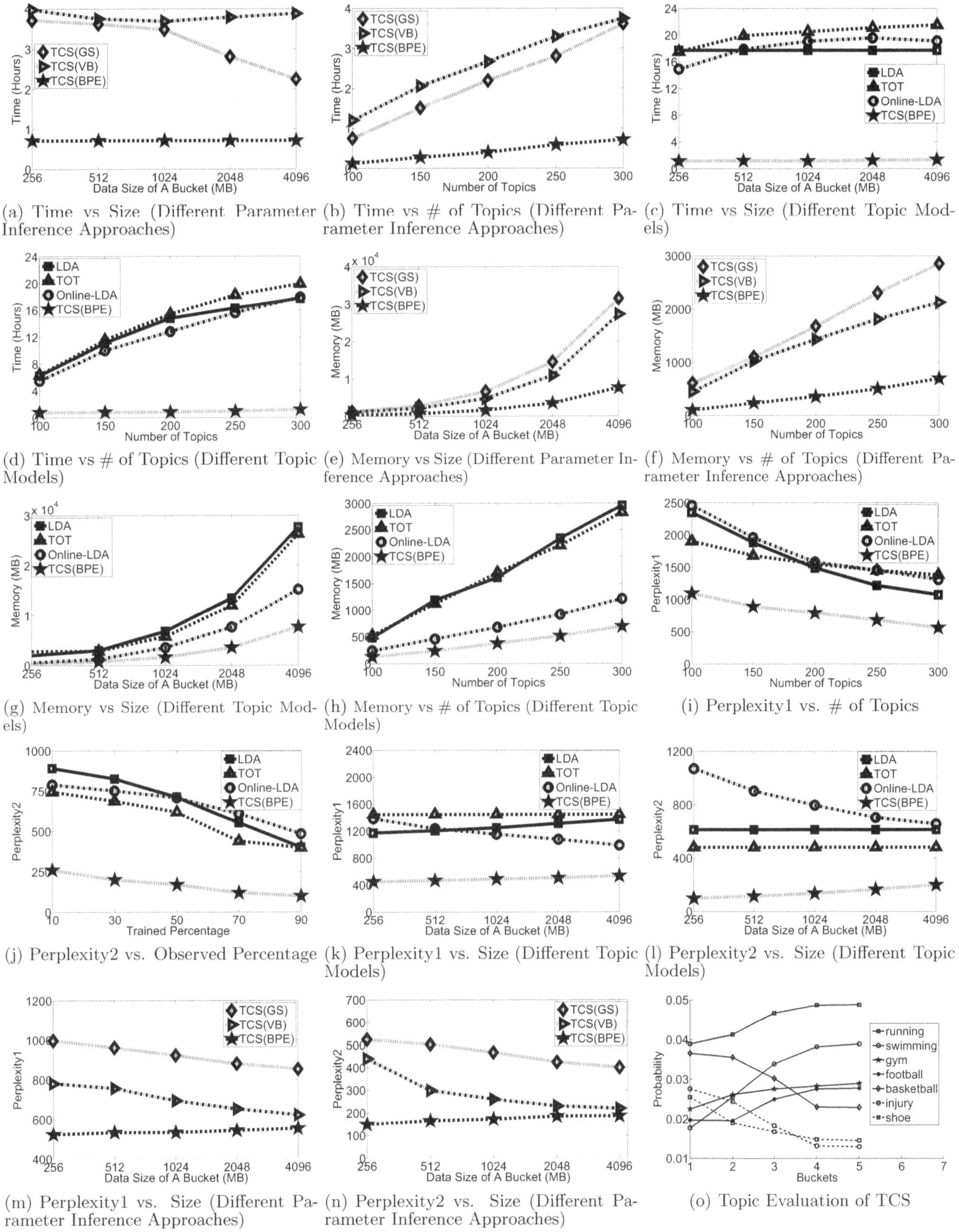

(a) Time vs Size (Different Parameter Inference Approaches)

(b) Time vs # of Topics (Different Parameter Inference Approaches)

(c) Time vs Size (Different Topic Models)

(d) Time vs # of Topics (Different Topic Models)

(e) Memory vs Size (Different Parameter Inference Approaches)

(f) Memory vs # of Topics (Different Parameter Inference Approaches)

(g) Memory vs Size (Different Topic Models)

(h) Memory vs # of Topics (Different Topic Models)

(i) Perplexity1 vs. # of Topics

(j) Perplexity2 vs. Observed Percentage

(k) Perplexity1 vs. Size (Different Topic Models)

(l) Perplexity2 vs. Size (Different Topic Models)

(m) Perplexity1 vs. Size (Different Parameter Inference Approaches)

(n) Perplexity2 vs. Size (Different Parameter Inference Approaches)

(o) Topic Evaluation of TCS

Figure 2: Performance Evaluation

scanned in each iteration. We then fix the data size of a bucket to be 512MB while varying the topic amount K increasingly and evaluate the time cost. The results are shown in Figure 2(d), where the TCS(BPE) exhibits significantly better scalability over other methods with a rather moderate linear increase.

6.3 Memory Cost

Memory cost is another significant concern when evaluating topic modeling techniques. In this subsection, Figure 2(e) and Figure 2(f) show the results of comparing the memory cost of different parameter inference methods for training TCS. The BPE approach always outperforms both GS and VB in terms of memory cost.

Moreover, we also evaluate the performance of different topic models by varying the data size of a bucket. Please refer to Figure 2(g) as the results, where TCS(BPE) consumes much less memory resource than LDA and TOT. The reason is two-fold, firstly, classical topic models need to process all data and inevitably occupy large memory resources; secondly, small data size of each bucket helps other three topic models exploit the memory more effectively. For example, when the bucket size is set to 512MB, the typical memory cost of TCS(BPE) is only 617MB, which is much less than those consumed by the representative topic models. And this value even outperforms the result of Online-LDA, which demonstrates the merit of pSketch in Section 4. Then we demonstrate the memory cost in terms of a varying amount of topics while the data size of a bucket is set to be 512MB. The results are depicted in Figure 2(h), where linear increasing behavior is observed for every topic models. However, Online-LDA and TCS(BPE) shows lowest memory usage when the amount grows larger, which indicates its potential as a scalable practice.

6.4 Effectiveness

In this subsection, we discuss the effectiveness of TCS model. Specifically, the evaluation are conducted based on the concept of perplexity measurement[21]. Before we elaborate the details of the experiment, we first generalize its definition as below:

$$Perplexity1(\theta,\phi) = (\prod_{d=1}^{D}\prod_{i=1}^{N_d} p(w_i|\theta,\phi))^{\frac{-1}{\sum_{d=1}^{D}(N_d)}}, \tag{8}$$

$$Perplexity2(\theta,\phi) = (\prod_{d=1}^{D}\prod_{i=P+1}^{N_d} p(w_i|\theta,\phi,w_{a:P}))^{\frac{-1}{\sum_{d=1}^{D}(N_d-P)}}. \tag{9}$$

The difference between $Perplexity1$ and $Perplexity2$ is that the former one is used to describe the $held-out$ perplexity on the learned model ϕ, and the latter one is used to evaluate the effectiveness of *prediction* of the TCS model.

The design of TCS aims to achieve better generalization performance, which can be associated to a lower value of perplexity. In order to facilitate the empirical study, we integrate about ten thousand questions and corresponding responses into a dataset. We then evaluate the TCS capability of predicting unknown task and response words on such dataset, and we notice that the perplexity has a monotonically decreasing relationship with the likelihood of the dataset. Moreover, we adopt LDA [20] and TOT [25](both classical topic models) and Online-LDA [12](dynamic topic model) as the baseline approaches while following their corresponding parameter estimation methods. We summarize the results in Figure 2(i), where the lowest line(TCS) shows lower perplexity and therefore better capability to predicting unseen data comparing with the baselines. Note that for the online models(Online-LDA and TCS(BPE)), we assume the crowd oriented service data of each hour as a bucket.

Moreover, we aim to measure how effective the proposed models is in terms of predicting the future task and response words based on a portion of available tasks and responses. Specifically, given the task words $t_{1:P}$ from a user's log of tasks and response, we try to find out which model provides a better predictive distribution $p(t|t_{1:P})$ of the remaining words. In particular, eighty percent of tasks and responses data are set as the training data and the remaining twenty percent as the test data. The calculation of the perplexity is shown in Equation (9) and we summarize the comparison results in Figure 2(j). As shown in the figure, TCS(BPE) shows good capability to predict the future released tasks and responses given the historical tasks and responses.

We then present Figures 2(k) and (l) to show the perplexity1 and perplexity2 measurements while increasing the data size of a bucket. In Figure 2(k) the topic amount is fixed to 300. We can observe that all topic models is not sensitive for changing the data size of a bucket since they show stable value of the perplexity1 in terms of increasing data size of a bucket. Then, Figure 2(l) shows the perplexity2 measurement with the increase of the data size of a bucket. Not surprisingly, all the topic models remains stable on the perplexity2 measurement, and TCS(BPE) shows obvious superiority over other methods in terms of perplexity.

We further demonstrate in Figure 2(m) the perplexity1 measurement with increasingly varying data size of a bucket, while the topic amount K is set to 300. TCS(VB) exhibits lower perplexity when the data size of a bucket increases, because larger data size of bucket ushers in more robust online gradient descents for higher accuracy. On the contrary, TCS(GS) and TCS(BPE) often perform worse when the data size of a bucket increases, because smaller data size of a bucket helps correct the global biases. In all cases, TCS(BPE) achieves the lowest predictive perplexity, indicating the highest topic modeling accuracy. Figure 2(n) shows the performance of the perplexity2 measurement with the same setting above. We report similar result to that in Figure 2(m), where TCS(BPE) achieves highest topic modeling accuracy.

These experimental results above verify that TCS is a robust and effective topic model for crowd oriented service data in terms of the topic modeling accuracy.

6.5 Analysis of Topic Results and Evolution

Based on the topic modeling results of TCS, it is observed that TCS is designed to discover semantically meaningful topics by different parameter inference methods. The top ten words of four topics extracted by VB, GS and BPE on the same dataset are summarized in Table 3. All three parameter inference methods exhibit effectiveness in grouping semantically coherent task words together as topics, where their results observe high level overlapping of task words except slightly different word ranking. For instance, task words "running", "swimming" "gym", "football" and "basketball" are all contained in the topic *Sport*. And the rankings of these task words also show great resemblance with each other. Therefore we conclude that the discovered topics are comparable among all the three parameter inference algorithms, which means that using BPE to train TCS can achieve paramount topic modeling accuracy while significantly better efficiency is observed.

The evolution of each topic is another informal but important measure of the success of topic models. We compare the topics that are discovered from consecutive different buckets and show the results in Figure 2(o),. Again we take the topic *Sport* as an example of topic evolution. In the first bucket, the task word "swimming"(solid line with circle marker) does not exist in the top five words. Then after receiving more data from the crowd oriented service data flow, the rank of "swimming" climbs from the sixth to the second in the following several buckets. The task words "gym" and "football" present similar trajectories where they gradually become more and more important in the topic of *Sport*. Word emergence and word perishment, in the meantime, is another important phenomenon in topic modeling results. For example, in the fourth bucket, the word "injury" appears in the topic for the first time and its rank reaches the 7th position in the fifth bucket. On the other hand, the word "shoe"(dotted lines) loses its importance to the topic as more and more crowd oriented service data are processed, and in the fourth bucket it eventually disappeared. All these results demonstrate the capability of TCS via BPE to detect the topic evolution.

7. RELATED WORK

In this section, we review the related work in two categories, crowd-oriented service computation and topic modeling problems.

7.1 Crowd-oriented Service Computation

Crowd-oriented service computation is a long-existing concept and has been practiced for centuries. With the emergence of Internet web service, especially the one that facilitates online question-and-answer websites like Yahoo! Answer and Baidu Recommender, crowd-oriented service starts to experience a new age where the source of human is broadened to a vast pool of crowds, instead of designated experts. This type of outsourcing to crowds, i.e. crowdsourcing, is now receiving countless success in many areas such as fund raising, logistics, monitoring and so on.

In crowd-oriented service applications, human cognitive abilities are mainly exploited in two types: voting among many options, and providing contents according to certain requirements. Most of basic queries in database [8] can be decomposed into simple voting as human tasks: such as filtering [5, 6, 19] into two-option voting (Yes or No), entity resolution [24], join [16], data cleaning[23], ranking [9], etc.

7.2 Topic Modeling

Since Blei et al. proposed the concept of topic modeling[2], topic modeling has attracted tremendous attention in both academic and industrial areas since its emergence. Especially along with the development of Web2.0 techniques, textual data plays a more and more important role in real-life application. Among these textual data, social network or social media like Facebook or Twitter exhibits great value due to their popularity and diversity in contents. Topic modeling is thus adopted to track emerging events in social communities [14] and to capture geographical topics [29].

Besides aforementioned wide applications, one of important issues is how to efficiently train the probabilistic models. The collapsed variational Bayesian inference for latent Dirichlet Allocation(LDA)[22] is proposed to beat its counterpart in terms of both computation cost and training accuracy. The work in [30, 31] then enables the classic loopy belief propagation for parameter estimation by considering the LDA as a factor graph. Topic distribution for new documents can also be inferred without retraining[28]. These parameter inference methods tackle the efficiency issue in training probabilistic topic models in different angles, but none of them are able to be easily adapted to meet the requirements from massive crowd oriented service data.

Moreover, another set of related researches with our work is the Community Question Answering (CQA). In this field, most previous work focused on bridging the lexical gap between the queried question and the historical questions [26]. Recently, a few work has studied how to utilize latent information to fill up the lexical gap [32, 4] and how to discover latent topics[27]. However, the biggest difference between researches of CQA and our work lies in the research objective. Our work focus on enhancing the efficiency of training process and save the space cost as much as possible through the proposed sketching techniques. However, the main goals of CQA are to bridge the lexical gap between the queried question and the historical questions and to recommend best answers to new questions.

To sum up, to the best of our knowledge, the TCS model together with the BPE algorithm and the pSketch structure is the first technique that systematically investigates the problem of topic discovery over massive crowd-oriented service data and provides solutions with solid performance.

8. CONCLUSIONS

In this paper, we study the problem of discovering latent topics over massive crowd-oriented service data efficiently. In order to guarantee the efficiency and effectiveness of the mining process, we design a novel probabilistic topic model, called *Topic Crowd Service Model*, which seamlessly incorporates a new data structure, called *Pairwise Sketch (pSketch)* and an efficient parameter estimation algorithm, called *Bucket Parameter Estimation (BPE)*. We conduct extensive experiments in real data to verify the effectiveness and efficiency of TCS and BPE. In particular, we verify that BPE algorithm not only significantly enhances the efficiency of topic modeling but also decrease the memory cost than that of existing approaches.

9. ACKNOWLEDGMENTS

The authors thank the anonymous reviewers for their insightful and constructive comments. This work is supported in part by the Hong Kong RGC Project N_HKUST637/13, National Grand Fundamental Research 973 Program of China under Grant 2012-CB316200, National Natural Science Foundation of China (NSFC) Grant No. 61232018, Microsoft Research Asia Gift Grant, Microsoft Research Asia Fellowship 2012 and Google Faculty Award 2013.

10. REFERENCES

[1] H. Attias. Inferring parameters and structure of latent variable models by variational bayes. In *UAI*, 1999.

[2] D. M. Blei, A. Y. Ng, and M. I. Jordan. Latent dirichlet allocation. *Journal of Machine Learning Research*, 3:993–1022, 2003.

[3] L. Bottou. Online learning and stochastic approximations. *Online learning in neural networks*, 1998.

[4] L. Cai, G. Zhou, K. Liu, and J. Zhao. Learning the latent topics for question retrieval in community qa. In *IJCNLP*, pages 273–281, 2011.

Table 3: Evaluation of the Topic Results

Topics	Bucket Parameter Estimation (BPE)		Gibbs Sampling (GS)		Varitional Bayes	
Computer Programming	language	0.049678	language	0.045369	language	0.041782
	software	0.040128	code	0.042315	code	0.039274
	Java	0.038941	C++	0.035129	Java	0.036855
	code	0.036762	Java	0.031524	software	0.033937
	C++	0.032754	python	0.030671	python	0.031726
Restaurant	menu	0.051437	menu	0.059744	menu	0.058472
	food	0.045139	food	0.050024	food	0.049647
	flavour	0.039116	drink	0.042367	drink	0.046438
	drink	0.035406	pizza	0.036694	flavour	0.041082
	pizza	0.032773	wine	0.030431	pizza	0.037568
Sport	running	0.048745	running	0.031074	running	0.058742
	swimming	0.038868	swimming	0.020345	swimming	0.051286
	gym	0.028912	football	0.019074	basketball	0.047921
	football	0.027712	basketball	0.016109	football	0.041235
	basketball	0.022902	gym	0.014321	gym	0.030039
Tourism	visitor	0.068868	visitor	0.060202	visitor	0.061964
	hotel	0.053937	hotel	0.052887	hotel	0.050129
	beach	0.048002	price	0.047609	price	0.042129
	price	0.038868	museum	0.041298	beach	0.036812
	shop	0.034149	beach	0.031011	museum	0.029432
Weather	hot	0.039623	hot	0.041102	hot	0.038729
	cold	0.036009	stormy	0.037210	cold	0.032808
	stormy	0.030854	cold	0.031852	rain	0.029458
	earth	0.028791	wind	0.026197	stormy	0.024912
	wind	0.026486	rain	0.023843	wind	0.019247

[5] C. C. Cao, J. She, Y. Tong, and L. Chen. Whom to ask? jury selection for decision making tasks on micro-blog services. *PVLDB*, 5(11):1495–1506, 2012.

[6] C. C. Cao, Y. Tong, L. Chen, and H. V. Jagadish. Wisemarket: a new paradigm for managing wisdom of online social users. In *KDD*, pages 455–463, 2013.

[7] G. Cormode and S. Muthukrishnan. An improved data stream summary: the count-min sketch and its applications. *J. Algorithms*, 55(1):58–75, 2005.

[8] M. J. Franklin, D. Kossmann, T. Kraska, S. Ramesh, and R. Xin. Crowddb: answering queries with crowdsourcing. In *SIGMOD*, pages 61–72, 2011.

[9] S. Guo, A. G. Parameswaran, and H. Garcia-Molina. So who won?: dynamic max discovery with the crowd. In *SIGMOD*, pages 385–396, 2012.

[10] G. Heinrich. Parameter estimation for text analysis. *Web: http://www. arbylon. net/publications/text-est. pdf*, 2005.

[11] C.-J. Ho, S. Jabbari, and J. W. Vaughan. Adaptive task assignment for crowdsourced classification. In *ICML (1)*, pages 534–542, 2013.

[12] M. Hoffman, F. R. Bach, and D. M. Blei. Online learning for latent dirichlet allocation. In *NIPS*, 2010.

[13] J. Howe. *Crowdsourcing: Why the Power of the Crowd Is Driving the Future of Business.* Crown Business, 2009.

[14] C. X. Lin, B. Zhao, Q. Mei, and J. Han. Pet: a statistical model for popular events tracking in social communities. In *KDD*, pages 929–938, 2010.

[15] G. S. Manku and R. Motwani. Approximate frequency counts over data streams. In *VLDB*, pages 346–357, 2002.

[16] A. Marcus, E. Wu, D. R. Karger, S. Madden, and R. C. Miller. Human-powered sorts and joins. *PVLDB*, 5(1):13–24, 2011.

[17] A. Metwally, D. Agrawal, and A. El Abbadi. An integrated efficient solution for computing frequent and top-k elements in data streams. *ACM Trans. Database Syst.*, 31(3):1095–1133, 2006.

[18] K. P. Murphy, Y. Weiss, and M. I. Jordan. Loopy belief propagation for approximate inference: An empirical study. In *UAI*, 1999.

[19] A. G. Parameswaran, H. Garcia-Molina, H. Park, N. Polyzotis, A. Ramesh, and J. Widom. Crowdscreen: algorithms for filtering data with humans. In *SIGMOD*, pages 361–372, 2012.

[20] I. Porteous, D. Newman, A. Ihler, A. Asuncion, P. Smyth, and M. Welling. Fast collapsed gibbs sampling for latent dirichlet allocation. In *SIGKDD*, 2008.

[21] M. Rosen-Zvi, T. Griffiths, M. Steyvers, and P. Smyth. The author-topic model for authors and documents. In *UAI*, 2004.

[22] Y. W. Teh, D. Newman, and M. Welling. A collapsed variational bayesian inference algorithm for latent dirichlet allocation. In *NIPS*, 2006.

[23] Y. Tong, C. C. Cao, C. J. Zhang, Y. Li, and L. Chen. Crowdcleaner: Data cleaning for multi-version data on the web via crowdsourcing. In *ICDE*, pages 1182–1185, 2014.

[24] J. Wang, T. Kraska, M. J. Franklin, and J. Feng. Crowder: Crowdsourcing entity resolution. *PVLDB*, 5(11):1483–1494, 2012.

[25] X. Wang and A. McCallum. Topics over time: a non-markov continuous-time model of topical trends. In *SIGKDD*, 2006.

[26] X. Xue, J. Jeon, and W. B. Croft. Retrieval models for question and answer archives. In *SIGIR*, pages 475–482, 2008.

[27] L. Yang, M. Qiu, S. Gottipati, F. Zhu, J. Jiang, H. Sun, and Z. Chen. Cqarank: jointly model topics and expertise in community question answering. In *CIKM*, pages 99–108, 2013.

[28] L. Yao, D. Mimno, and A. McCallum. Efficient methods for topic model inference on streaming document collections. In *SIGKDD*, 2009.

[29] Z. Yin, L. Cao, J. Han, C. Zhai, and T. S. Huang. Geographical topic discovery and comparison. In *WWW*, pages 247–256, 2011.

[30] J. Zeng, W. Cheung, and J. Liu. Learning topic models by belief propagation. *PAMI*, 2011.

[31] J. Zeng, Z.-Q. Liu, and X.-Q. Cao. Online belief propagation for topic modeling. *arXiv*, 2012.

[32] T. C. Zhou, C.-Y. Lin, I. King, M. R. Lyu, Y.-I. Song, and Y. Cao. Learning to suggest questions in online forums. In *AAAI*, 2011.

SigniTrend: Scalable Detection of Emerging Topics in Textual Streams by Hashed Significance Thresholds

Erich Schubert, Michael Weiler, Hans-Peter Kriegel
Ludwig-Maximilians Universität München
Oettingenstr. 67, 80538 München, Germany
http://www.dbs.ifi.lmu.de/
{schube,weiler,kriegel}@dbs.ifi.lmu.de

ABSTRACT

Social media such as Twitter or weblogs are a popular source for live textual data. Much of this popularity is due to the fast rate at which this data arrives, and there are a number of global events – such as the Arab Spring – where Twitter is reported to have had a major influence. However, existing methods for emerging topic detection are often only able to detect events of a global magnitude such as natural disasters or celebrity deaths, and can monitor user-selected keywords or operate on a curated set of hashtags only. Interesting emerging topics may, however, be of much smaller magnitude and may involve the combination of two or more words that themselves are not unusually hot at that time. Our contributions to the detection of emerging trends are threefold: first of all, we propose a significance measure that can be used to detect emerging topics early, long before they become "hot tags", by drawing upon experience from outlier detection. Secondly, by using hash tables in a heavy-hitters type algorithm for establishing a noise baseline, we show how to track even all keyword pairs using only a fixed amount of memory. Finally, we aggregate the detected co-trends into larger topics using clustering approaches, as often as a single event will cause multiple word combinations to trend at the same time.

Categories and Subject Descriptors

H.2.8 [**Database Management**]: Database Applications—*Data Mining*; I.5.m [**Pattern Recognition**]: Miscellaneous—*Emerging Topic Detection*

Keywords

Trend Detection; Hashing; Text-Mining; Outlier Detection

1. INTRODUCTION

Social networks and microblogging services like Facebook and Twitter are known for the large amount of data published every second by their users. But also news agencies like Reuters and Bloomberg publish thousands of articles daily covering a wide range of topics. The information explosion calls for new tools and approaches to process this amount of data, as a single user can no longer read all the information available. Instead, automatic filters are used everywhere: email servers reject two thirds of our email traffic deemed as spam; the Facebook news feed is also heavily filtered: Facebook reported that the average user would have 1500 potential stories each day, out of which around 300 are automatically prioritized and shown by Facebook; yet most users even only read about half of these on average. In addition, some hard coded filters are used to e.g. merge all birthday wishes into a single story to reduce clutter.

Traditional text mining techniques such as clustering and topic modeling cannot be used trivially when processing a live stream of data. They can provide meaningful insight to refine e.g. a search query or to analyze a static text corpus, but are not applicable to fast-flowing, ever changing data streams. To cope with this flow of data, emerging topic detection is a useful tool, yet itself an emerging area. The goal of emerging topic detection is to identify new trends early, to notify the user of the evolving story. Intuitively the goal is to have an automated "breaking news" detection. When the user is able to customize and prioritize the data sources, this will ultimately allow personalized breaking news and trend detection, and corporations could use the additional knowledge to quickly react to future market needs and thus increase their profit. But the detection of trends in such fast-flowing data remains challenging because most documents contain raw unstructured natural language text; often abbreviated such that the interpretation is hard for both humans and computers. Ambiguity, homonyms and synonyms further add to these challenges. Even if some semantic annotations like tags are available, these are not necessarily helpful for the problem at hand, as they may be ambiguous as well and not all of them have an actual meaning [24]. Due to these problems, the resulting analysis quality still does often not meet the expectations in practise.

Scalability of textual analysis continues to be a problem. Many approaches are based on simple preprocessing such as stopword removal and stemming, and then use distributed algorithms to simply count and track word occurrences over time; very few methods seem to be able to extract meaning from sentences, correlate words and model complex information in near real time on high volume data [13]. This may explain why text analytics seems to take off very slowly.[1] As

KDD'14, August 24–27, 2014, New York, NY, USA.

http://dx.doi.org/10.1145/2623330.2623740.

[1]`http://www.kdnuggets.com/2014/02/poll-results-te\ xt-analytics-use-shows-no-significant-change.html`

marketing professor Hausman recently noted (commerical) sentiment analysis software often is less accurate than a coin toss [20], it may be necessary to first reduce the amount of data, then analyze this part thoroughly but manually.

In this article, we propose a statistics-based score for evaluating trends as well as scalability improvements to allow tracking arbitrary word pairs. The detected trends are then aggregated into a cluster to be further analyzed by the user.

2. RELATED WORK

The field of emerging topics detection receives much attention, as the daily flood of information available in social media and news agencies is impossible to overlook – in fact, the media are reporting on the increasing volume of data every day. To know what topics are currently "hot" could be an enormous advantage both for private uses and businesses. To solve these demands, commercial systems like Dataminr, Sysomos, Brandwatch, MediaMiser, and Topsy have been established. There are also a number of non-commercial systems like the CMU system [37], the UMass system [4], Meme-Detection System [26] or Blogscope [8]. Most of the published research focusses on Twitter as primary source of information inter alia due to its public streaming API[2] for accessing random samples of all public statuses and the contained hashtags, which help to reduce the dimensionality of the incoming text and could provide some additional semantic information.

First Story Detection (FSD) is a closely related task to emerging topic detection, with the subtle difference that the focus is to identify the actual first report of an event, not necessarily a topic gaining substantially in popularity. The CMU system [37] attempts to cluster continuously arriving news streams into groups that share the same event. They present an on-line method to accumulate events for a retrospective event detection. The UMass system [4] represents documents in a vector space such as a term frequency vector. Incoming documents are first compared to the database of previous documents using a nearest-neighbor search, then added to the corpus. Documents that differ enough from the most similar earlier document are considered to be first stories. This approach however does not scale well to large data sets such as Twitter due to the need to maintain the database corpus [29]. To scale this nearest-neighbor approach to Twitter streams, the use of locality sensitive hashing (LSH [21]) was proposed [29]. To limit database size, buckets are limited in size and the oldest document is removed from the bucket when the bucket would overflow.

Kleinberg [23] uses an infinite state automaton to model frequency bursts of incoming documents such as emails. Different states of the automaton correspond to different message frequencies, and a hierarchy is extracted from the state transitions. In Blogosphere [30], Kleinberg's approach was applied to the titles of blog posts. To improve performance, they had to omit keywords cooccurring with other keywords in the same title. In a post-processing stage they enrich bursty keywords with semantically correlated terms by looking at the five nearest neighbours using an Euclidean-based distance metric on the automatons' state series. Kleinberg's burst modeling was also used in [33], where it was applied to topics estimated by a dynamic topic model (DTM).

Cataldi et al. [12] proposed a method that extracts terms from tweets to model a life cycle inspired by biological processes. They define a term as *emerging*, if it is now frequent but was rare in the past. To improve results, they also consider social relationships (like the followers count) to determine the user authority. Although they do a post-processing step to enrich detected trending terms with semantically related keywords, they cannot detect when two keywords that have already been frequent before now are frequently co-mentioned such as when *obama* and *merkel* meet.

TwitterMonitor [27] first identifies bursty keywords that have a higher absolute frequency than usual and uses them as a seed to explore them further. Keywords that cooccur in the same tweets (within a small history window) are grouped together. For each such keyword set a singular value decomposition (SVD, [16]) is applied on all tweets containing them. The extracted terms are used to build a better description for each bursty keyword set.

EDCoW [35] applies a wavelet analysis on words to model their frequencies. Trivial words are identified with their cross correlation value. In Hip and Trendy [28], the focus lies on building a taxonomy from trends for a specific geographic area and to categorise them, rather than finding cooccurence trends. Similarly CiteSpace II [14] has a strong focus on visualizing emerging trends.

Density estimation on data streams as performed in stream clustering approaches such as CluStream [3] is also related to our approach. However these algorithms assume you have a stream of coordinates, and want to estimate the resulting coordinate-based density. Such vector data arises for example in sensor networks, where the need of compressing historical information [17] can be satisfied using wavelets, discrete cosine or histograms. Temporal velocity profiles [2] are then applicable to such data, and can be used to predict the positions of dense regions of moving objects. In our approach, we will be estimating a density on the temporal domain only, as if we would split the input stream into separate streams for each word and process them separately. These techniques therefore do not apply here.

The problem of top-k monitoring [7] is related, but it does not take relative significance into account. These approaches, often aimed at detecting denial-of-service (DOS) attacks in network flows, are interested in the most frequently occurring patterns only. In the context of monitoring textual streams, these approaches would likely monitor popular terms such as *justin* and *bieber*.

Exponential histograms [15] have been proposed for probabilistic counting as well as for weakly additive functions. This was then extended to continuously monitor variance over data streams [6] similar to our approach. However, we use a simpler yet effective approach: their techniques are designed with the requirement to take exactly the previous N observations into account. Our approach uses exponential weighting, which will never fully forget data, but aggregates historical values into a single figure, in which old results will eventually have a weight of effectively zero.

A rather similar approach to our system is enBlogue [5]: Like our approach, they are also interested in the cooccurrence of words, instead of relying on single terms. The central measure of their approach is Jaccard similarity [22] of two words in relation to their overall popularity. Like most other approaches processing Twitter data, they first preprocess the data, in order to extract hashtags and named entities as tokens. In order to find cooccurrences, they start

[2]`https://dev.twitter.com/docs/streaming-apis`

with a reduced seed list of frequent tokens; then track all token combinations that contain at least one of these seeds. For each token pair, a short history of ρ recent occurrence counts and popularities is kept; token pairs not seen during the last ρ epochs are discarded. Similar to our method, exponential smoothing is applied to predict future values from history. The score is computed based on the relative deviation from the estimate, weighted by logarithmic popularity:

$$score(t) = \frac{(x(t) - E[x])/x(t)}{|\log(popularity(t))|}$$

A key limitation of enBlogue is the need for controlling the memory usage. A number of mechanisms are employed to reduce the data volume: only hashtags and named entities are used for the analysis. Then seed tags are chosen based on a minimum occurrence threshold as well as a top-k filter. However, the experiments indicate that the accurracy drops linearly with the seed tags parameter, so these thresholds do not appear to be beneficial. Last but not least, since enBlogue keeps a history of 2ρ historical values for any pair of tags tracked, it scales badly with respect to memory usage. In our experiments, we observed as much as 700 million word and word pairs (see Table 1). While not all of them will be kept in memory at the same time, this requires a substantial amount of memory and update cost.

The method we propose improves over enBlogue in multiple ways. Instead of keeping a history, we only need two floating point values per record. Secondly, by storing this data only approximately in a hash table, we are not as much affected by the large number of potential word pairs. As we cleverly exploit hash collissions, we only need the hash table to be large enough to store all frequent word pairs, which due to the long-tailedness of the distribution is a substantially smaller number (as seen from the quantiles in Table 2). Petrović et al. [29] proposed a method for first story detection based on locality sensitive hashing. While our approach borrows on ideas from LSH and MinHash, we do not use this for nearest neighbor search, and do not need to store the individual documents for similarity search.

3. SIGNIFICANT TREND DETECTION

In information retrieval and text mining, a popular similarity measure for text is cosine similarity on the term frequency (TF) vectors, weighted by the inverse document frequency (IDF). This model is commonly referred to as TF-IDF vector model. Depending on the definitions used, term frequency can either be the absolute counts of each term, or the relative frequency. In the context of trend detection, such similarity measures are difficult to use: they are designed to quantify the similarity of two documents, but trending topics may span many documents, and documents will often cover more than one topic. In particular, topics may have subtopics; and within a larger topic (such as pop music) a subtopic (such as a particular artist) may be trending, even when the larger topic is not.

A naïve approach to perform topic detection would be the use of cluster analysis. However, cluster analysis on streaming data is far from a solved problem. Often, these clustering algorithms are unable to recognize hierarchies of clusters, and may need parameter fine tuning. Because of these limitations, the algorithms are mainly useful to cluster the result set of an information retrieval task for user presentation. Another similarly naïve approach maintains a database of recent documents, and searches the nearest neighbor (i.e. the most similar earlier document) for each new document. While this works reasonably well in a controlled corpus, it will fail on many noisy real data sets: while a low nearest-neighbor distance is indicative that the document is a near duplicate, the contrary does not hold: not every document will be the start of an interesting emerging topic, but it may also be just noise. In fact, nearest-neighbor distances are a popular measure of outlierness [31].

When detecting emerging topics in data streams, we cannot assume that we already have a cluster for the topic. In fact, it is desired to detect the topic as soon as possible. Yet at the same time, we are only interested in topics that both have a minimum size, but also show an "unusual" growth rate. When looking for trending subtopics, this becomes even more challenging – here, we may not be interested in the main topic, but only in the restriction to a subdomain.

In the following subsections, we will discuss some important aspects for emerging trend detection. First of all, we discuss how to measure *significance* of trends, as opposed to just some deviation score. Secondly, we will elaborate briefly on the *relationship to outlier detection*. Then we will discuss the importance of *word cooccurrences* for detecting trends that may be masked otherwise and additional challenges for *early detection* when using the suggested statistics. Finally, we will discuss *hashing* approaches for *scalability* to monitoring all pairwise cooccurrences.

3.1 Emerging and Trending Topics

When users see "trending topics", they usually assume that these are simply the most popular terms. However, users do not only want popularity, but they also expect *novelty*. Therefore, we must not simply look at the most popular tags, but we must take this popularity into its historical context. Furthermore, the absolute popularity is subject to seasonal trends. Depending on the data source, working hours and weekdays result in "seasonal" patterns that need to be accounted for. Relative popularity – normalized by the total number of documents for the day – proved much more robust in our experiments.

To evaluate the significance of a trend, we suggest to make use of statistical best practice such as the z-score (formally, the z-score assumes a normal distribution; while this will likely not hold, it nevertheless can serve as a reasonable heuristic for our purposes):

$$z(x) := (x - \mu)/\sigma$$

To use this on data streams, we need a moving average and moving standard deviation such as the exponentially weighted average ($EWMA$) and the associated standard deviation or variance ($EWMVar$):

$$sig(x) := \frac{x - EWMA}{\sqrt{EWMVar}} \tag{1}$$

in order to increase stability (the variance could be 0) as well as to account for non-interesting fluctuations of rare terms, we will ensure a minimum average and minimum standard deviation of β, which we call the bias term:

$$sig_\beta(x) := \frac{x - \max\{EWMA, \beta\}}{\sqrt{EWMVar} + \beta} \tag{2}$$

This bias term β not only avoids a division by 0, but also serves as a noise filter. For low volume data $EWMA < \beta$

with a small value of β we cannot statistically argue about trends. Intuitively, we should set β to the expected background noise level, i.e. how often rare terms occur naturally in the data stream, without trending. This bias term also takes into account that our input data is discrete – there are no "half occurrences" of words.

In order to estimate the average $EWMA$ and the variance $EWMVar$ for a data stream and a learning rate α, we can rely on earlier work by Welford [34] and West [36] on incremental mean and variance. The update equations given by Finch [18] for the exponentially weighted variants allow these values to be efficiently maintained on a data stream:

$$\Delta \leftarrow x - EWMA$$

$$EWMA \leftarrow EWMA + \alpha \cdot \Delta \quad (3)$$

$$EWMVar \leftarrow (1-\alpha) \cdot (EWMVar + \alpha \cdot \Delta^2) \quad (4)$$

The learning rate α can be set using the half-life time $t_{1/2}$; a parameter a domain expert will be able to choose easily based on his experience and needs:

$$\alpha_{half\text{-}life} = 1 - \exp\left(\log\left(\tfrac{1}{2}\right)/t_{1/2}\right) \quad (5)$$

This update equation is best used with a fixed update cycle. While we could adjust the update cycle dynamically by adjusting α or $t_{1/2}$ accordingly, there are good reasons not to update too often: first of all, a fixed recomputation interval gives better performance guarantees, and secondly we have more control over the statistical validity of our estimates. We cannot use above equations to update the statistics on every arriving record, but we must perform some aggregation to estimate the popularity x reliably. When using a too high update rate, we will have more variance in our estimation of x, which will in turn harm the estimation of $EWMA$ and $EWMVar$. When using a data source with a natural cycle, such as a news ticker having a daily pattern, we can expect best results aligning our updates with this cycle.

Note that we avoid the popular equation $E(X^2) - E(X)^2$ for estimating the variance, because this equation is prone to numerical instability due to catastrophic cancellation with floating point arithmetic. This instability may be the reason why variance on data streams seems to be rarely used yet. Equation 4 is numerically stable [18], and thus preferable.

3.2 Emerging Topics are Outliers

Emerging topics, when defined as "a set of documents which grows faster than expected from comparable other document sets", essentially are a specific kind of outliers. Schubert et al. [32] discuss a generalized local outlier detection model, and demonstrate its applicability to video streams. A similar interpretation for outlier detection is possible for our approach: for each topic (approximated as word or word pair), we compute a reference model consisting of an average frequency and variance based on an exponentially weighted *temporal neighborhood* set. We then compare the current frequency to this reference, and measure the trend by the deviation from this model.

The relationship to outlier detection not only exists on a formal level, but we are also seeing many problems typical to this domain [38]: we do not know beforehand what data we are searching for, and we do not have labeled training data so popular machine learning approaches such as random forests cannot be trained for this problem. Instead, we have to fight the problems of masking and swamping [9, 19], where for example a continuously popular word such as *obama* may prevent the detection of related trends, or a single strong trend may mask other trends in the data set.

3.3 Trend Detection on Cooccurrences

Equation 3 and Equation 4 can be applied to any numerical variable X. In order to apply this approach to trend detection in textual data, we need to represent the incoming data stream appropriately. We will not only build one variable for each word, but also for each word coocurrence. The reason is that we may be unable to reliably detect or analyze some trends on single words only. In Figure 1 we visualize the Boston Marathon bombing on news data. In Figure 1a the raw word occurrences are presented. The word *boston* shows a comparable peak three days before the Marathon. Figure 1b visualizes the EWMA moving average. In this figure, it becomes evident that *boston* is (unsurprisingly) frequently mentioned, but even *explosion* (as e.g. "the explosion of mobile traffic", "stock explosion" and "Dreamliner battery explosion") is occurring quite often. The exact combination however of these three words first occurs on April 15. Using the proposed significance measure, as visualized in Figure 1d, shows a 48σ event for this combination. For other related words, this event of global media interest also shows a peak, but not quite as strong. On April 19, we observe a similar peak for the combination *boston*, *suspect*; on this day the suspects were identified and the manhunt began. This example demonstrates the benefits of tracking word cooccurrences instead of single words.

3.4 Early Detection of Trends

Equation 3 and Equation 4 are not designed for continuous updating of the $EWMA$ and $EWMVar$ estimates, but we first need to have a robust estimate of the value of x. While we can easily adjust $\alpha_{half\text{-}life}$ to dynamic time windows, the value of x will become noisy and exhibit a too high variance to be useful for trend detection. A simple but reliable approach estimating x is to use temporal slicing on natural cycles and volume of the data source (which may be a day for a news feed, or an hour for Twitter). Even when not updating $EWMA$ continuously, we can still perform an online detection of trends. In order to evaluate the significance of a trend, it is even desirable to compare the current estimate of x with estimations based on delayed data only, i.e. we want to compare the observed value x with the predicted value $EWMA$ based on the previous day, and not including the latest data in the prediction yet. By solving Equation 1 for x, we can obtain an alerting threshold τ if we fix a desired significance niveau s.

$$x > EWMA + s \cdot EWMVar =: \tau \quad (6)$$

Intuitively, when $x > \tau$, we are observing an $s \cdot \sigma$ significant increasing trend in the data. We do however need to acknowledge that this is not based on proper statistical hypothesis testing, so we cannot assume that 3σ events are rare: the $66 - 95 - 99.7\%$ rule (the three sigma rule) does not apply here, as we will be monitoring thousands of trends in parallel and have some margin of error; on the other hand we are interested in seeing multiple event every day, and not just the most significant events of the year. This approach can be seen as a variant of Bollinger Bands as used in stock

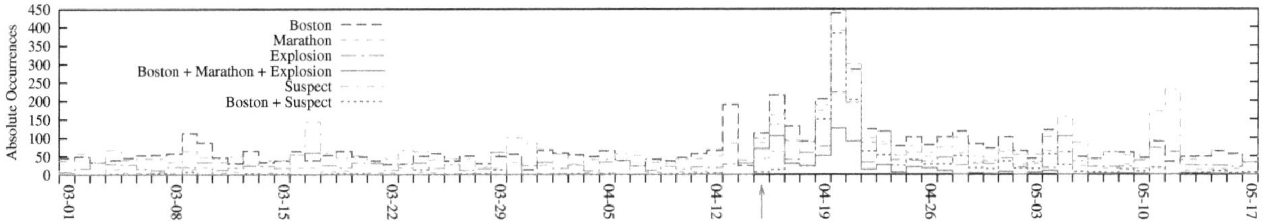

(a) Boston Marathon event – raw absolute occurences

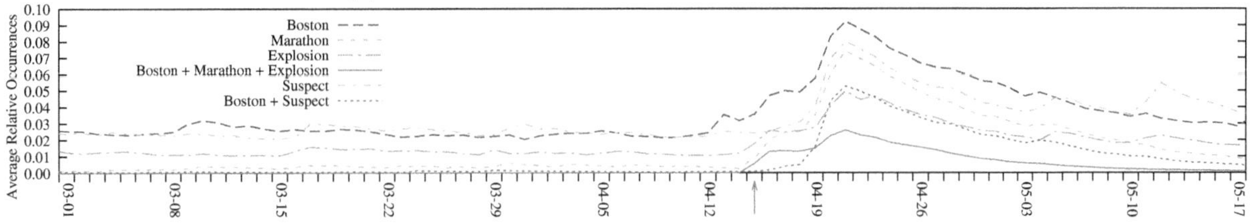

(b) Boston Marathon event – *EWMA* averages

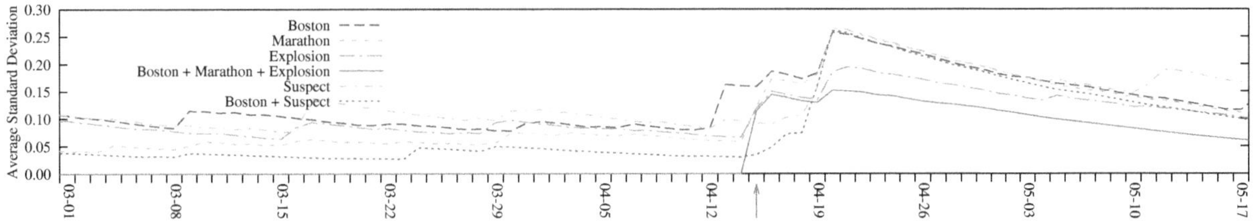

(c) Boston Marathon event – standard deviations ($\sqrt{EWMVar}$)

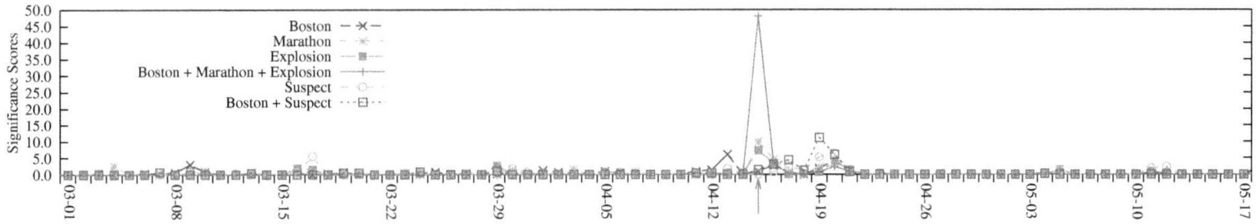

(d) Boston Marathon event – significance scores

Figure 1: Visualization of selected word occurrences for the Boston Marathon bombing on news data

market analysis, except that our data sources do not exhibit the fast negative feedback loop driving the stock market.[3]

The main difficulty with this approach is getting a robust estimate of x while the epoch is not yet complete. On the news data set, for example, it is common not to see any news posted before 6am in the morning. The first news item each day will naturally produce terms with a naïve document frequency of 1; yet they do not constitute a reliable trend so far. However, we also do not know how many news will be posted during the day in total. Therefore, in order to estimate x, we need to learn to predict the number of documents to be posted during the epoch; we can then compare the absolute number of occurrences, the number of documents seen so far, and the number of documents expected to obtain a better estimate of x.

3.5 Scalability by Hashing

Although Equation 3 and Equation 4 are efficient to compute, we would still need to perform this for any word pair. As seen in Table 1, this is not scalable. Instead of restricting the set of candidates to monitor beforehand, we propose to use a probabilistic approach based on hash tables. The popularity of words follows a long-tailed distribution: the majority of words has a low occurrence rate in the data. This property can be exploited using clever hashing techniques. Our approach is related to heavy-hitters algorithms such as Bloom filter [10] and MinHash [11]. Instead of probabilistic set membership testing, our hashing scheme is designed for providing an upper bound of the *EWMA* and *EWMVar* values. We use 2^ℓ buckets (each storing an *EWMA* and *EWMVar* value), and k hash functions, so that each word is mapped to at most k buckets. When updating the *EWMA* hash tables – when transitioning from one epoch to the next – we first hash each word (with a frequency larger than β) into its k buckets. For each bucket we track the *maximum* popularity x observed in the current epoch. Next, we update the *EWMA* and *EWMVar* values in the hash table with the *maximum* x observed for all words in this bucket only. When computing the alerting threshold τ for an observed word w, we again inspect the k buckets given by the hash functions. The threshold is then obtained by taking the *minimum* alerting threshold of all buckets (Equation 6). Assuming there exists at least one hash bucket where the candidate word w has the maximum popularity x_w of all words in this bucket, then the *EWMA* value stored in this bucket will not be overwritten by a different word w'; and at the same time none of the k buckets was last updated with a lower popularity

[3]It is therefore unlikely that the proposed method is beneficial for stock market analysis.

than x_w. Otherwise, i.e. if in each of the k buckets there was a hash collission with a more popular word w', we will overestimate the *EWMA* and *EWMVar* values, and we may miss an emerging trend. To avoid this, we need to choose ℓ large enough, such that the majority of bins are not filled with frequent keywords.

Using this hashing strategy, we can control the amount of memory and computation needed for maintaining the trend statistics very well. In fact, this allows us to scale our approach beyond tracking single word (or hashtag) occurrences to monitoring even word-pair occurrences in large data streams. Word-pair occurrences prove very effective in our experiments at detecting subtopics. For example when Edward Snowden traveled from Hong Kong to Moscow, all of the individual words {*edward, snowden, hong, kong, moscow*} themselves have not been trending (events surrounding Edward Snowden have continuously been in the media at that time), but various combinations of these words such as *snowden* and *moscow* exhibit a significant peak.

The use of hashing yields a number of benefits. First of all, updating the statistics becomes a vectorized bulk operation. Secondly, the memory usage is constant, and the data can easily be serialized either for transmission to a different system, but also for checkpointing and crash recovery. After loading the last checkpoint, either a replay of the latest data can be used to restore the exact state, or the system can even decide to only process new data, and rely on the statistics to recover (it may then be desirable to disable alerting for this epoch).

3.6 Trend Redundancy and Refinement

A secondary challenge is the redundancy of trends. Assuming that a word such as *snowden* is trending, then we will likely see other related words such as *edward* also trend at the same time. But we may also see uninteresting combinations such as {*snowden, the*} trend significantly compared to previous usage of this word combination. Probably the most important step here is to perform stopword removal: by not including known stopwords in the trend analysis, we both have to analyze much less pairs, but we will also remove a large share of uninteresting co-trends. In addition to a language-specific set of stopwords, it is also beneficial to include domain specific stopwords, such as *follow, tweet, retweet* (*rt*), *lol* and *twitter* for Twitter.

In the refinement phase, we can use an inverted index to both verify observed trends (as the hash table may have had a collission), but also compute the overlap between any two words involved in the detected trends. For this we employed the clustering toolkit ELKI [1], and used hierarchical clustering with Ward linkage. Similarity is measured by how significant the two words trend together. We cannot assume that related words form a clique: consider for example *fiscal, cliff, barack* and *obama*. The last two will usually not qualify as a trending topic, but the names are in fact one of the most mentioned words in news on any day; however all four together form a known topic.

Alternatives at this stage – which we plan to investigate in future work – include finding maximum-weight cliques (as used in [25]) and topic modeling techniques such as pLSI and LDA. However, topic modeling is not guaranteed to produce a more meaningful output either [13].

In Algorithm 1 we give a pseudocode for the overall detection process, but we have to omit some details for brevity.

Algorithm 1: Document Processing

```
Data: epoch Epoch identifier
Data: EWMA[c] Averages hash table
Data: EWMVar[c] Variance hash table
Data: h_i Hash functions
Input: s Threshold for refinement / alerting

open index[epoch] shard for writing
initialize frequency map
initialize stats map
/* Index a new document                                  */
foreach doc in current epoch do
    foreach unique word and word-pair in doc do
        add doc.id to index[epoch][word]
        increment frequency[word]
        /* Get word statistics from hash table           */
        if not stats[word] then
            (μ, σ) ← (∞, ∞)
            foreach hash function h_i do
                c ← h_i(word)
                if EWMA[c] < μ then
                    μ ← EWMA[c]
                    σ ← √EWMVar[c]
            stats[word] ← (μ, σ)
        (μ, σ) ← stats[word]
        /* Test for significance threshold              */
        x ← estimate frequency of word
        if (x − max(β, μ))/(σ + β) > s then
            send to refinement for early alerting

/* Perform end-of-day analysis                           */
initialize trending topics list
foreach unique word and word-pair in frequency do
    (μ, σ) ← stats[word]
    /* Test for significance threshold                  */
    x ← frequency[word]/|documents|
    if (x − max(β, μ))/(σ + β) > s then
        add word to trending topics
close index[epoch] shard for writing
Refine trending topics
Cluster trending topics
Produce end-of-day report

/* Update the statistics table for next epoch            */
/* Aggregate into maximum for each bucket                */
initialize update-table
foreach word and word-pair in frequency do
    frequency ← frequency of word
    foreach hash function h_i do
        c ← h_i(word)
        if frequency > update-table[c] then
            update-table[c] ← frequency
/* Update statistics table                               */
foreach hash code c do
    freq ← update-table[c]/number of documents
    Δ ← freq − EWMA[c]
    EWMA[c] ← EWMA[c] + α · Δ
    EWMVar[c] ← (1 − α) · (EWMVar[c] + α · Δ²)
/* End epoch                                             */
```

4. EXPERIMENTS

We demonstrate the scalability of our system as well as its ability to detect statistically significant trends in real data sets, without the need to reduce the candidate set as required in related work such as enBlogue [5]. For all data sets, we employed best practises for text mining such as language-specific stemming using the Xapian search engine library.[4] We also removed a standard set of English stopwords as well as domain specific stopwords (e.g. *retweet* for Twitter).

The implementation of the main analysis (not including the web spider and preprocessing) was done in Java using a single thread and Apache Lucene[5] as backing index. To save disk space and comply with copyright requirements, we did not store complete documents for the news data set, but only inverted lists, the URL and the headline.

4.1 Data Sets

For our experiments we focused on three data sets that exhibit very different charactersistics, as it can be seen from Table 1 and Table 2. The first data set, consisting of news articles, contains much fewer documents, but the documents obviously are much longer than those of the Twitter data set. The longer paragraphs of the news articles then yield even more word pairs than the Twitter data. But there is also a more subtle difference than the size. Where Twitter contained 25 million unique tokens, 99% of these occurred less than 14 times in the data set. In the news data, the vocabulary was much more evenly used, with the top 1% of words occurring 3476 times or more.

4.1.1 News Articles

We used a web spider to index news articles from popular news agencies such as Reuters and Bloomberg as our first data source. We limited the index process to the year 2013 plus a window of 10 days. As these news contents have restrictive copyright requirements, we must not store the full documents, but only use the data to perform trend detection and construct a search index for refinement; but the original article can be accessed on the publisher's website.

Nevertheless, the news article corpus is very interesting, because it is editorially managed, and of a different nature than Twitter: where Twitter users tend to re-share the exact same text to their followers, news agencies try to avoid duplication. For some trending topics, we do however see "update" documents in this data source. For the use case of a corporate user interested e.g. in financial trends, news agencies may be the more interesting data source than Twitter. Methods such as enBlogue [5] cannot be applied on this data set without modifications, as it relies on hashtags to seed its search process. Our method does not have such restrictions, but monitors all frequent word pairs.

4.1.2 Twitter

Because of the low latency and high volume, Twitter has become one of the most popular data sources for trend detection on the Internet. Events such as the Arab Spring led to a wide acceptance of Twitter as a medium capable of real-time monitoring. As such, this data source is an interesting complement to the news organization data sources we used for most of our experiments: Twitter data is even noisier and larger in volume, but it is also prone to bias due to its non-representative user base. We used Twitter's public streaming API at the "Spritzer" sampling rate (approximately 1% of tweets) to process about 279 million tweets over a period of 114 days. For analysis purposes we only used English language tweets, removed all retweets (about 10%) and used a simple near-duplicate detector to remove obvious spam and bulk (about 1.5%), which yields 94 million tweets to analyze. When including *#hashtags* and *@usermentions* as tokens, the results were dominated by teen idols, which are massively "spammed" by their fans. But as these tweets include few other words (except stopwords such as *ilysim*) they become essentially empty when skipping these tags. Without *#hashtags* and *@usermentions*, the analysis become more focused on the textual content, and thus the results became much more interesting (as seen in Table 4).

4.1.3 Stack Overflow

Stack Overflow is a Q&A website, which publishes its data under a creative commons license.[6] We analyzed the contents of the main website, years 2010 to 2013, totaling to 5.9 million questions. There were few significant trends in this data set, corresponding to important software releases (OS X Mavericks, OS X Mountain Lion, iOS6, iOS7, TypeScript), the `facebook.stackoverflow.com` launch and holidays (new years, christmas), so we omit details for brevity (included in the online demonstration).

4.2 Manual Analysis of Real World Trends

Table 3 examines the top 50 most significant trends in the news data set for the year 2013. For brevity, we omitted economic and sport news outside the top 10. Finance and sports dominate the results due to their extensive coverage in these data sources. In particular, "game days" of sports leagues trend every week due to some new word pair combinations. This may require future work to automatically classify the detected trends into categories such as sports. Nevertheless, a number of events also made it into the top 40, such as the Boston Marathon bombing discussed before, the algeria gas plant attack and Syrias use of chemical weapons.

In Table 4 we also discuss the top 40 trends in Twitter detected. All of these are easily verifiable with Internet search. Detected trends consist of single words, up to almost complete sentences by Twitter standards. Despite not using retweets, many topics such as the Oscar selfie (the most retweeted tweet so far) still surfaced, because a substantial amount of users add a reply text to their tweet.

4.3 Scalability

Due to the use of hash tables, we were able to run the experiments on a single i7-3770 CPU core without the need to use distributed computation or multiple threads. For the news data set, the preprocessed data volume was 1.1 GB (2.6 MB per day on average). Analyzing a year of data took 18 minutes, i.e. 2.5-3 seconds on average per day. The refinement index only stores the headlines, for which we need only 745 KB per day, and 305 MB total for a whole year.

The raw 1% Twitter input data was 228 GB compressed, after filtering retweets and non-English tweets, and preprocessing, 6.7 GB remained. Processing Twitter took 1.5 hours; 46 seconds on average per day. The actual analysis

[4]Open-Source, `http://xapian.org/`

[5]Open-Source, `https://lucene.apache.org/`

[6]`https://archive.org/details/stackexchange`

Table 1: Data set statistics (after stopword removal)

Data set	Documents	Paragraphs	Unique Words	Total Words	Unique Pairs	Total Pairs
News	424,704	5,867,457	300,141	56,661,782	71,289,359	660,430,059
Twitter	94,127,149	94,127,149	25,581,022	245,140,695	179,105,233	473,871,456
StackOverflow	5,932,320	30,423,831	2,040,932	138,205,636	91,460,397	545,570,530

Table 2: Vocabulary statistics (after stopword removal)

	Word Frequency			Pair Frequency		
Data set	Median	90% Quantile	99% Quantile	Median	90% Quantile	99% Quantile
News	3	81	3476	2	18	124
Twitter	1	at 92.9: 2	14	1	at 91.3: 4	29
StackOverflow	1	at 90.1: 7	185	1	at 90.9: 5	73

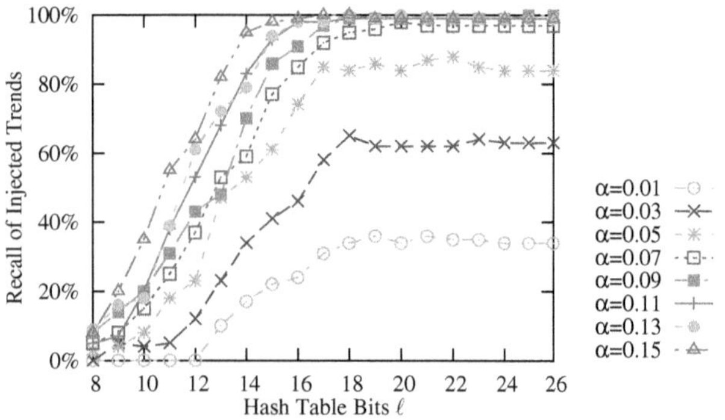

Figure 2: Performance with varying hash table size ℓ, $k = 4$

ran in 48 minutes; 25 seconds per day. The inverted index for Twitter occupied 18 GB of disk space, storing about 160 MB per day of Twitter data. Therefore, this approach should be scalable to the full Twitter "firehose" stream. In particular, there are a number of easy ways for distributing the load: for example, building the backing index, maintaining the hash tables, and refining the detected events can easily be distributed on separate systems. As the backing indexes are sharded already, the shards can also be distributed onto different machines trivially. In fact, we were able to process the news data sets on a Raspberry Pi (700 MHz ARM CPU, 512 MB RAM) at a processing speed of 104.1 seconds on average per day.

4.4 Hash Table Size

For the hash table sizes, we expect a saturation effect to happen. Too small hash tables will lead to masking and swamping [9, 19]; but once the hash table has become big enough to not have collissions, the *EWMA* estimates are expected to be good. To verify this, we used semi-synthetically data sets derived from the news data sets. Into these, we injected artificial words following a narrow Poisson distribution with $\lambda = 2 \dots 9$ weakened by a constant factor of α. After then random onset of the artificial trend, we modified each document with a probability of

$$\alpha \cdot pmf_{Poisson}(\lambda, k) = \alpha \frac{\lambda^k}{k!} e^{-\lambda}$$

Due to the randomization of λ, some trends will be easier to spot, others will be harder. Furthermore, both the existing natural trends in the data and injected trends may mask the injected trends. The maximum value of the probability mass function is 0.27, so for $\alpha = 0.15$ about 4% of documents were modified to include the artificial keyword. For $\alpha = 0.01$, the chance of trend injection drops to 0.27%. Figure 2 summarizes the results on the injected trends data using $k = 4$ hash functions. As you can see, at $\alpha > 0.05$ the artificial trends are detected reliably, and the hash tables show a typical saturation effect, where the performance no longer increases once we have reached a reasonable size. A hash table of 20 bits requires just 2^{25} bytes of memory (32 Megabytes).

4.5 Online Demonstration

The results of our trend detection system are available at `http://signi-trend.appspot.com/` for exploration.

5. CONCLUSIONS

In this article, we first discussed the use of exponentially weighted floating averages and variance to score a trending topic with respect to its recent occurrences in the data stream. The proposed statistic needs litte memory – two floating point values only – and can be efficiently updated using an incremental equation. The numerical properties of this equation are well understood, and it was shown to be more stable than the naïve equation of the variance involving a difference of squares. This improved scoring function is able to capture the background noise as well as general trends in the data, and by measuring variability it can produce a much more meaningful significance score than e.g. nearest-neighbor distances that were used in state-of-the-art prior work to measure emerging topics.

Secondly, we showed how to scale our statistical approach to monitoring every word and word pair of a data stream with limited memory, by using hashing techniques and exploiting that the majority of words and word pairs occurrs only rarely in the stream. By resolving hash collissions in favor of the more common word or word pair, we will usually have an exact statistic for these words and only occur information loss on rarely seen words – which then by definition are not trending yet. Scalability of this approach was demonstrated by analyzing state-of-the-art data sets faster than real time on a single CPU.

Third, we suggested and demonstrated the use of clustering techniques to aggregate the observed trends – which usually only affect a small subset of the vocabulary, for which the results can be refined from an inverted index – into larger trends. This has become more important than in previous work, as we monitor a much larger set of candidates; and in particular cooccurrences tend to overlap and form clusters.

To the best of our knowledge, this is the first system that can monitor all word pair cooccurrences on a large data stream without the need for parallelization, whereas previous work can only monitor a filtered set of terms or word pairs, based on a seed set. Such a restriction is no longer necessary with the memory reduction obtained via hashing.

Table 3: Excerpt of top 50 trends on news data set 2013 (dominated by economy, sports and politics)

Score	Date	Stemmed Keywords (excerpt, edited for readability)	Explanation
58	11-18	thomson text summary 3000xtra alert outperform eikon	Reuters artifact – 233 research alerts
13	10-09	janet yellen ben bernank vice barack obama nomin	Obama nominates Yellen as U.S. Fed Chief
10	02-14	heinz buffett gdp hj merger shrank berkshir hathaway warren	Berkshire Hathaway, 3G Capital buy Heinz
9.7	07-03	turmoil armi unrest egyptian lisbon egypt mursi portug bailout	Yen rises because of turmoil in Egypt, Portugal
9.4	04-19	boston search bomb suspect marathon manhunt	Boston Marathon suspect manhunt
9.3	04-15	boston explos marathon	Boston Marathon bombing
9.3	01-28	durabl caterpillar pend	Four-month high oil, strong durable goods
8.8	09-19	inning era	Baseball end of season reports
8.8	02-26	ben bernank testimoni defend deadlock stalem	Bernanke defends bond-buying, Italian stalemate
8.6	07-11	ben bernank minut accommod forese dovish	Bernanke reassures euro bonds markets
Economical, financial and sports news largely omitted outside the top 10 for brevity			
8.6	04-16	finish sharp metal boston marathon rebound terror bomb explos injur	Boston Marathon attack details
8.6	03-25	rescu cyprus bailout eurogroup guarante relief dutch jeroen dijsselbloem	EU cyprus bailout
8.5	01-17	hostag desert milit algeria algerian	Algerian gas plant attack
8.5	09-03	finnish wireless handset nokia smartphon microsoft	Microsoft buys Nokia's handset business
8.3	01-23	davo forum switzerland cameron referendum	Cameron promises referendum to leave EU
7.8	11-24	atom reactor iranian geneva enrich breakthrough lift uranium	Breakthrough on Iran nuclear activity
7.8	08-26	chemic weapon secretari holiday durabl	Kerry comments on Syria over chemical weapons
7.7	05-21	oklahoma moor tornado	Moore, Oklahoma hit by deadly tornados
7.6	09-23	merkel angela coalit victori william dudley shutdown	German elections succes for Angela Merkel
7.3	10-01	deadlock shutdown midnight began trillion unpaid barack obama	U.S. government partial shutdown
7.2	08-27	syrian chemic weapon strike assad tension kerri secretari	Escalations in Syria
6.9	04-20	dzhokhar tamerlan tsarnaev brother suspect captur dead watertown injur	Boston Marathon suspects captured
6.8	07-24	appl iphon smartphon markit flash beat faster	Surge in iPhone sales
6.8	12-06	nelson mandela die apartheid african africa	Nelson Mandela died
6.7	02-15	moscow communiqu	G20 finance ministers in Moscow
6.7	04-08	thatcher iron margaret	Margaret Thatcher died
6.6	07-12	airport dreamlin ethiopian heathrow boe	Boeing Dreamliner catches fire

6. REFERENCES

[1] E. Achtert, H.-P. Kriegel, E. Schubert, and A. Zimek. Interactive data mining with 3D-Parallel-Coordinate-Trees. In *Proc. SIGMOD*, pages 1009–1012, 2013.

[2] C. C. Aggarwal. A framework for diagnosing changes in evolving data streams. In *Proc. SIGMOD*, pages 575–586, 2003.

[3] C. C. Aggarwal, J. Han, J. Wang, and P. S. Yu. A framework for clustering evolving data streams. In *Proc. VLDB*, pages 81–92, 2003.

[4] J. Allan, V. Lavrenko, D. Malin, and R. Swan. Detections, bounds, and timelines: UMass and TDT-3. In *TDT-3*, pages 167–174, 2000.

[5] F. Alvanaki, S. Michel, K. Ramamritham, and G. Weikum. See what's enBlogue: real-time emergent topic identification in social media. In *Proc. EDBT*, pages 336–347, 2012.

[6] B. Babcock, M. Datar, R. Motwani, and L. O'Callaghan. Maintaining variance and k-medians over data stream windows. In *Proc. PODS*, pages 234–243, 2003.

[7] B. Babcock and C. Olston. Distributed top-k monitoring. In *Proc. SIGMOD*, pages 28–39, 2003.

[8] N. Bansal and N. Koudas. Blogscope: a system for online analysis of high volume text streams. In *Proc. VLDB*, pages 1410–1413, 2007.

[9] V. Barnett and T. Lewis. *Outliers in Statistical Data*. John Wiley&Sons, 3rd edition, 1994.

[10] B. H. Bloom. Space/time trade-offs in hash coding with allowable errors. *Commun. ACM*, 13(7):422–426, 1970.

[11] A. Z. Broder. On the resemblance and containment of documents. In *Proc. SEQUENCES*, pages 21–29, 1997.

[12] M. Cataldi, L. D. Caro, and C. Schifanella. Emerging topic detection on Twitter based on temporal and social terms evaluation. In *Proc. MDM/KDD*, page 4, 2010.

[13] J. Chang, J. L. Boyd-Graber, S. Gerrish, C. Wang, and D. M. Blei. Reading tea leaves: How humans interpret topic models. In *Proc. NIPS*, volume 22, pages 288–296, 2009.

[14] C. Chen. CiteSpace II: Detecting and visualizing emerging trends and transient patterns in scientific literature. *ASIS&T*, 57(3):359–377, 2006.

[15] M. Datar, A. Gionis, P. Indyk, and R. Motwani. Maintaining stream statistics over sliding windows. *SICOMP*, 31(6):1794–1813, 2002.

[16] S. C. Deerwester, S. T. Dumais, T. K. Landauer, G. W. Furnas, and R. A. Harshman. Indexing by latent semantic analysis. *ASIS*, 41(6):391–407, 1990.

[17] A. Deligiannakis, Y. Kotidis, and N. Roussopoulos. Compressing historical information in sensor networks. In *Proc. SIGMOD*, pages 527–538, 2004.

[18] T. Finch. Incremental calculation of weighted mean and variance. Technical report, University of Cambridge, 2009.

[19] A. S. Hadi, A. H. M. Rahmatullah Imon, and M. Werner. Detection of outliers. *WIREs Comp. Stat.*, 1(1):57–70, 2009.

[20] A. Hausman. The sad state of sentiment analysis. Online: `http://www.hausmanmarketingletter.com/sad-state-sentiment-analysis/`, 2013.

[21] P. Indyk and R. Motwani. Approximate nearest neighbors: towards removing the curse of dimensionality. In *Proc. STOC*, pages 604–613, 1998.

[22] P. Jaccard. Distribution de la florine alpine dans la Bassin de Dranses et dans quelques regiones voisines. *Bulletin de la Societe Vaudoise des Sciences Naturelles*, 37:241–272, 1901.

Table 4: Top 40 trends on Twitter data (dominated by celebrities and teen idols)

Score	Date	Keywords	Explanation
174	03-06	boosi releas jail	Rapper Lil Boosie released from jail early
154	05-28	rip author poet inspir angelou maya peac dr	Civil rights activist Dr. Maya Angelou died
127	05-12	elev jayz attack jay solang beyonc	Solange, Jay Z and Beyonce elevator incident
98	03-03	ellen degener host selfi pizza	Ellen's Oscar Selfie and Pizza
76	05-22	ewok	Band 5SOS changed its name on Twitter to "Ewok Village"
76	03-21	bracket mercer duke	Mercer surprise win over Duke in March Madness
73	05-24	ronaldo bale gareth	Champions league final
63	04-07	geldof dead rip peach	Peaches Geldof died of heroin
61	04-15	moon eclips lunar blood	Blood moon (lunar eclipse)
60	05-05	shovel	Snow in May + "shovel girl fight" viral video
51	05-24	ramo sergio	Champions league final
51	04-14	zac efron	Zac Efron shirtless at the MTV movie awards
50	03-17	punch pinch green	St. Patricks Day
50	05-06	mimi	Mimi Faust and Nikko announce private video
49	03-17	lizzi	Lizzie in the series The Walking Dead
48	02-19	angela	Talking Angela hoax
47	04-29	ban silver adam clipper donald sterl nba owner	Donald Sterling banned for life from NBA
46	05-15	sm exo kris	Rumor of Kris (of Exo-M) parting
43	05-10	austria	Austria wins the Eurovision song contest
43	03-03	arm bradley longer cooper	Oscar selfie: "If only Bradley's arm was longer. Best photo ever"
43	02-24	rip harold ghostbust rami	Actor Harold Ramis died
42	04-10	sibl nation	National siblings day
42	03-09	arsenal wigan	Arsenal vs. Wigan Athletic in FA cup
41	04-13	million matt	Matthew Espinosa follow spree (#mattTo1Mil)
41	03-17	earthquak	4.4 earthquake strongly felt in Los Angeles
41	05-09	billionair dre dr beat billion appl	Apple buys Dr. Dre
40	05-10	eurovis	Eurovision Song Contest
38	05-06	bambi	Love & Hip Hop Atlanta Premiere with Bambi
38	03-19	ezra dead	Ezra gets shot in series "Pretty little liars"
38	04-16	bale gareth goal	Winning goal in Copa del Rey final
38	03-03	actor oscar mcconaughey matthew leo leonardo dicaprio	No Oscar for Leonardo di Caprio, again
37	05-06	scrappi	Love & Hip Hop Atlanta Premiere with Scrappy
36	05-09	cleveland johnni manziel dalla footbal draft brown	Johnny Manziel draft in NFL
35	04-30	rip bob actor hoskin	Actor Bob Hoskins died
35	04-26	racist donald clipper sterl owner	Donald Sterlin accused of racism (see above!)
35	03-18	allison	Allison in TV series "teen wolf"
34	04-02	warn tsunami chile magnitud earthquak quak	Chile 8.2 magnitude earthquake
34	05-21	cav	Cleveland Cavaliers win NBA draft lottery again
34	05-06	joselin	Love & Hip Hop Atlanta Premiere with Joseline Hernandez
34	03-14	pie pi	π day (3.14)

[23] J. Kleinberg. Bursty and hierarchical structure in streams. *Data Min. Knowl. Disc.*, 7(4):373–397, 2003.

[24] D. Laniado and P. Mika. Making sense of Twitter. In *ISWC*, pages 470–485. Springer, 2010.

[25] T. Lappas, M. R. Vieira, D. Gunopulos, and V. J. Tsotras. On the spatiotemporal burstiness of terms. *PVLDB*, 5(9):836–847, 2012.

[26] J. Leskovec, L. Backstrom, and J. Kleinberg. Meme-tracking and the dynamics of the news cycle. In *Proc. KDD*, pages 497–506, 2009.

[27] M. Mathioudakis and N. Koudas. Twittermonitor: trend detection over the Twitter stream. In *Proc. SIGMOD*, pages 1155–1158, 2010.

[28] M. Naaman, H. Becker, and L. Gravano. Hip and trendy: Characterizing emerging trends on Twitter. *ASIS&T*, 62(5):902–918, 2011.

[29] S. Petrović, M. Osborne, and V. Lavrenko. Streaming first story detection with application to twitter. In *Human Language Technologies*, pages 181–189, 2010.

[30] M. Platakis, D. Kotsakos, and D. Gunopulos. Searching for events in the blogosphere. In *Proc. WWW*, pages 1225–1226, 2009.

[31] S. Ramaswamy, R. Rastogi, and K. Shim. Efficient algorithms for mining outliers from large data sets. In *Proc. SIGMOD*, pages 427–438, 2000.

[32] E. Schubert, A. Zimek, and H.-P. Kriegel. Local outlier detection reconsidered: a generalized view on locality with applications to spatial, video, and network outlier detection. *Data Min. Knowl. Disc.*, 28(1):190–237, 2014.

[33] Y. Takahashi, T. Utsuro, M. Yoshioka, N. Kando, T. Fukuhara, H. Nakagawa, and Y. Kiyota. Applying a burst model to detect bursty topics in a topic model. In *Adv. NLP*, pages 239–249, 2012.

[34] B. P. Welford. Note on a method for calculating corrected sums of squares and products. *Technometrics*, 4(3):419–420, 1962.

[35] J. Weng and B.-S. Lee. Event detection in Twitter. In *ICWSM*, 2011.

[36] D. H. D. West. Updating mean and variance estimates: an improved method. *Commun. ACM*, 22(9):532–535, 1979.

[37] Y. Yang, T. Pierce, and J. Carbonell. A study of retrospective and on-line event detection. In *Proc. SIGIR*, pages 28–36, 1998.

[38] A. Zimek, E. Schubert, and H.-P. Kriegel. A survey on unsupervised outlier detection in high-dimensional numerical data. *Stat. Anal. Data Min.*, 5(5):363–387, 2012.

Experiments with Non-parametric Topic Models

Wray Buntine*
Monash University
Clayton, VIC, Australia
wray.buntine@monash.edu

Swapnil Mishra
RSISE, The Australian National University
Canberra, ACT, Australia
swapnil.mishra@anu.edu.au

ABSTRACT

In topic modelling, various alternative priors have been developed, for instance asymmetric and symmetric priors for the document-topic and topic-word matrices respectively, the hierarchical Dirichlet process prior for the document-topic matrix and the hierarchical Pitman-Yor process prior for the topic-word matrix. For information retrieval, language models exhibiting word burstiness are important. Indeed, this burstiness effect has been show to help topic models as well, and this requires additional word probability vectors for each document. Here we show how to combine these ideas to develop high-performing non-parametric topic models exhibiting burstiness based on standard Gibbs sampling. Experiments are done to explore the behavior of the models under different conditions and to compare the algorithms with previously published. The full non-parametric topic models with burstiness are only a small factor slower than standard Gibbs sampling for LDA and require double the memory, making them very competitive. We look at the comparative behaviour of different models and present some experimental insights.

Categories and Subject Descriptors

I.7 [**Document and Text Processing**]: Miscellaneous; I.2.6 [**Artificial Intelligence**]: Learning

Keywords

topic modelling; experimental results; non-parametric prior; text

1. INTRODUCTION

Topic models are now a recognised genre in the suite of exploratory software available for text data mining and other semi-structured tasks. Moreover, it is also recognised that a broad class of variants can be developed based around extended graphical models that capture some additional domain requirements. Examples of these extensions include author-topic modelling [19], document segmentation [8] and word-sense disambiguation [1], however the list is extensive. Here we consider the task of improving the vanilla topic model, but in the back of our mind is the requirement that the techniques need to easily be transferred to the host of variants that make up a significant part of use in applications.

While the standard model is Latent Dirichlet Allocation (LDA), and many techniques exist to scale this up significantly, better quality topic models are available. Two clear and related innovations are available here. The first is the use of more sophisticated priors for the probability vectors rather than the simple symmetric Dirichlet [25], and the second is the use of non-parametric methods, best characterised by the HDP-LDA model [24], again to improve the priors, the standard being the hierarchical Dirichlet process. These have the goals of better estimating prior topic or word proportions, and also estimating the "right" number of topics. Note these are related in that a technique to estimate the proportions for different topics can also make some topics insignificant, thus effectively changing the number of topics.

Another innovation, not so well known, is to model *burstiness* [5], which is the idea that once we see a word, we can expect to see it again. Consider the following news snippet:

> Despite their separation, Charles and Diana stayed close to their *boys William* and Harry. Here, they accompany the *boys* for 13-year-old *William*'s first day school at Eton College on Sept. 6, 1995, with housemaster Dr. Andrew Gayley looking on.

We see here that two words, "boys" and "William" appear twice. In the information retrieval literature, a related phenomenen is the notion of *eliteness* [12] whereby words are said to have different "levels" of occurrence, and this influenced the development of the dominant relevance paradigm in information retrieval [18].

These innovations, non-parametric priors and burstiness, have so far been bogged down by computationally intensive techniques that prevent their wider use. The original implementation of DCMLDA for burstiness [5] was only able to be applied to small data sets of less than a 1000 documents. A theme of research in recent machine learning conferences have been a variety of alternative algorithms for inference with HDP-LDA [22, 27, 2]. One technique of note is the use of stochastic variational methods that allows application to streaming data [27, 13]. An excellent theoretical and em-

*Part of this author's contribution was done while at NICTA, Canberra.

KDD'14, August 24–27, 2014, New York, NY, USA.
ACM 978-1-4503-2956-9/14/08.
http://dx.doi.org/10.1145/2623330.2623691.

pirical comparison of a variety of sampling and variational methods can be found in [20].

These newer algorithms, however, are usually based on the standard stick-breaking formulation for Dirichlet processes and variational methods for these and the simpler Dirichlet distribution. Recently, an alternative sampling scheme for the more general Pitman-Yor process has been developed [4] called *table indicator sampling*. It uses prebuilt tables of second order generalised Stirling numbers, and the scheme has seen use on problems such as document segmentation [9] and topic models on structured text [7]. Its key advantages are that it requires no dynamic memory for implementation, and that the convergence is usually significantly faster and better quality (it is a collapsed Gibbs sampler) [6].

This table indicator sampling allows easy development of non-parametric topic models including HDP-LDA, its extension to the Pitman-Yor process (PYP) and power-law models [21] which place the PYP on the topic-word matrix. What is interesting, however, which is our first major contribution, is that we can easily extend this broader variety of non-parametric topic models by adding a burstiness component on the front end of the model. Moreover, an implementation trick lets this be done with little additional memory/time overhead. These models are available in our recently MLOSS-released open source multi-core software `hca`[1].

The resulting non-parametric LDA algorithms turn out to be fast. Generally, they are a factor or two (in memory and time) slower than standard Gibbs implementations of vanilla LDA and typically 5 times faster than comparable variational HDP-LDA implementations but with the same memory requirements. Although, we also show that Mallet's [16] asymmetric-symmetric LDA is a form of truncated HDP-LDA and it is an order of magnitude faster again. The experimental results show improvement over all the existing methods in perplexity, including Mallet. We also conduct a number of experiments to explore the nature of the new algorithms. The full experiments with burstiness are the first done at moderate scale with these sort of models and the experimental insights are our second major contribution. Our implementation runs bursty HDP-LDA with K=1000 topics on 800k news articles at 10 minutes per major Gibbs cycle using a standard 8-core CPU.

We first discuss, at a general level, how we use Pitman-Yor processes and the nature of the inference with them, in Section 2. Section 3 presents the different models used here. Because our inference schemes are standard block Gibbs samplers in the table indicator framework, we do not detail the algorithms here other than describing how we implement burstiness. Section 4 then presents our experimental setup, and a sequence of empirical investigations follow in Section 5.

2. THE HIERARCHICAL PITMAN-YOR PROCESS

Here we briefly review the methods used for inference on the hierarchical Pitman-Yor processes that one can see embedded in the model we use [3]. Those not needing to understand the fundamentals of the sampling methods can skip this section.

All our samplers use standard block table indicator Gibbs samplers for the network of Pitman-Yor processes [4, 9] and adaptive rejection sampling [10] for the many hyperparameters. Slice sampling is usually of similar performance but can suffer with the extremely peaked posteriors for the concentration parameter of a Pitman-Yor process.

We use the Pitman-Yor process as a distribution on a probability vector. The distribution has a mean (*i.e.*, another probability vector), a variance parameter represented as a concentration (usually given as b_X when on vector $\vec{X}$), and a third parameter called discount (usually given as a_X when on vector $\vec{X}$), so one has $\vec{p} \sim \text{PYP}\left(a_p, b_p, \vec{\theta}\right)$. The Pitman-Yor process, when used in this way, can be used hierarchically to form distributions on a network of probability vectors.

The inference on a network of probability vectors is based on a basic property of species sampling schemes [14] that is best understood using the framework of message passing over networks. Figure 1a shows the context of a probability vector $\vec{p}$ having a Pitman-Yor process with base distribution $\vec{\theta}$. Two multinomial style likelihood messages are passed up to $\vec{p}$ with counts $\vec{n}$ and $\vec{m}$. The standard message then passed on from $\vec{p}$ to $\vec{\theta}$ using the multinomial-Dirichlet distribution [3] is a complex set of gamma functions obtained using the normalising term for a Dirichlet distribution, represented in the figure as $l_p^{Dir}(\vec{\theta})$ (assuming a concentration at the node of b_p)

$$l_p^{Dir}(\vec{\theta}) \;=\; \frac{\Gamma(b_p)}{\Gamma(b_p+N+M)}\prod_k \frac{\Gamma\left(b_p\theta_k+n_k+m_k\right)}{\Gamma(b_p\theta_k)}\,, \quad (1)$$

where the total statistics are $N=\sum_k n_k$ and $M=\sum_k m_k$. This functional complexity on $\vec{\theta}$ prevents any further network inference.

Figure 1b shows the alternative after marginalising out the vector $\vec{p}$ using Pitman-Yor process theory [3]. One however must introduce a new latent count vector $\vec{t}$ that represents the fraction of the data $\overrightarrow{n+m}$ that passes up in a message to $\vec{\theta}$. These are called *table multiplicities* and they correspond to the number of tables in the corresponding Chinese restaurant process (CRP) [24]. The multiplicites have a bounding constraint $t_k \le n_k + m_k$ and moreover $t_k \equiv 0$ if and only if $n_k + m_k \equiv 0$. Thus at the expense of introducing a latent count vector $(\vec{t})$ one gets a simple multinomial likelihood passed up the hierarchy, albiet with a complex looking but O(1) normalising constant, in the form

$$l_p^{PYP}(\vec{\theta}) \;=\; \frac{(b_p|a_p)_T\Gamma(b_p)}{\Gamma(b_p+N+M)}\prod_k S^{n_k+m_k}_{t_k,a_p}\theta_k^{t_k}\,, \quad (2)$$

where the total $T=\sum_k t_k$ and $(x|y)_T$ denotes the Pochhammer symbol, $(x|y)_T = x(x+y)\ldots(x+(T-1)y)$. $S^c_{t,a}$ is a generalized second-order Stirling number [23]. Libraries[2] exist for efficiently dealing with this making it in most cases an $O(1)$ computation.

The counts of $\vec{t}$ then contribute to the data at the parent node $\vec{\theta}$ and thus its posterior probability. Thus network inference is feasible, and moreover no dynamic memory is required, unlike CRP methods, because $\vec{t}$ is the same dimension as $\overrightarrow{n+m}$. Sampling the $\vec{t}$ directly, however, leads

[1]See `http://mloss.org/software/view/527/`

[2]See `https://mloss.org/software/view/424/` and `https://mloss.org/software/view/528`

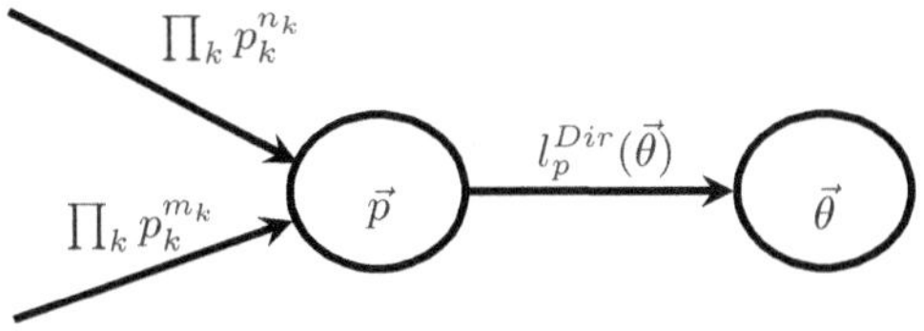

(a) Embedded probability vector with messages.

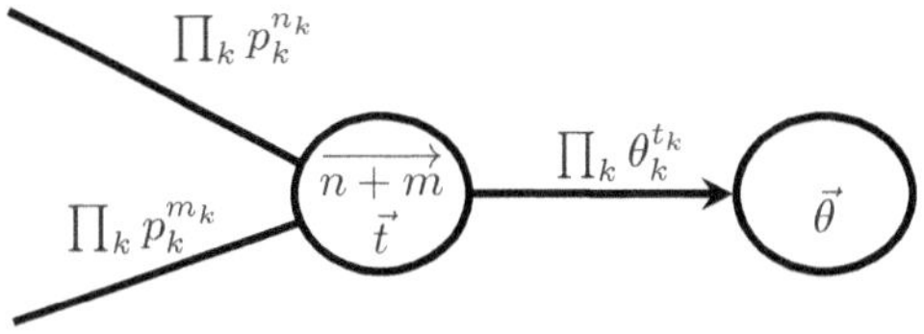

(b) Embedded count vectors after marginalising.

Figure 1: Computation with species sampling models.

to a poor algorithm because they may have a large range (above, $0 \leq t_k \leq n_k + m_k$) and the impact of data at the node $\vec{p}$ on the node $\vec{\theta}$ is buffered by $\vec{t}$, leading to poor mixing.

Table indicators are introduced by [4] to allow the sampling of the table multiplicity vectors $\vec{t}$ to be done incrementally and thus allow more rapid mixing and simpler sampling. Note the table indicators are Boolean values indicating if the current data item increments the table multiplicity at its node and thus the data item contributes to the message to the parent. The assignment of indicators to data can be done because of the above constraint $t_k \leq n_k + m_k$. So the data item contributes a +1 to $n_k + m_k$ and the matched table indicator contributes either 0 or +1 to t_k, which is the change in the message to the parent. If there is a grandparent node, then a corresponding table indicator in the parent node might also propagate a +1 up to the grandparent.

For inference on a network of such vectors, each probability vector node contributes a factor to the posterior probability. For the above example with table indicators this is given by Formula (3) [3]

$$\frac{(b_p|a_p)_T \Gamma(b_p)}{\Gamma(b_p + N + M)} \prod_k S^{n_k+m_k}_{t_k,a_p} \binom{n_k + m_k}{t_k}^{-1}, \quad (3)$$

where the addition of the $\binom{n_k+m_k}{t_k}$ term over Equation (2) simply divides by the number of choices there are for picking the t_k boolean table indicators to be on out of a possible $n_k + m_k$.

In sampling, a data point coming from the node source for $\vec{n}$ contributes a +1 to n_k (for some k), and either contributes a +1 or a 0 to t_k depending on the value of the table indicator. If $n_k = t_k = 0$ initially, then it must contribute a +1 to t_k, so there is no choice. The change in posterior probability of Formula (3) due to the new data point at this node is, given the Boolean indicator r_l

$$\begin{aligned}&\left((t_k+1)\,(b_p + T * a_p)\, S^{n_k+m_k+1}_{t_k+1,a_p}\right)^{r_l \equiv 1} \\ &\left((n_k + m_k - t_k + 1) S^{n_k+m_k+1}_{t_k,a_p}\right)^{r_l \equiv 0} \\ &\left((n_k + m_k + 1)\,(b_p + N + M)\, S^{n_k+m_k}_{t_k,a_p}\right)^{-1} \quad (4)\end{aligned}$$

depending on the value of the table indicator r_l for the data point. In a network, one has to jointly sample table indicators for all reachable ancestor nodes in the network, and standard discrete graphical model inference is done in closed form. Examples are given by [7, 8].

For estimation, one requires the expected probabilities $\mathbb{E}_{\vec{n},\vec{m},\vec{t},\vec{\theta}}[\vec{p}]$ at a node. In the table indicator framework this is harder to compute. Fortunately, with a trivial change of latent variables (drop the table indicators and reintroduce the table occupancies for the CRP) we get the usual estimation formula for the CRP [23] given by Equation (5)

$$\mathbb{E}_{\vec{n},\vec{m},\vec{t},\vec{\theta}}[\vec{p}] \;=\; \frac{b_p + T * a_p}{b_p + N + M}\vec{\theta} + \frac{\vec{n} + \vec{m} - a_p\vec{t}}{b_p + N + M}\,. \quad (5)$$

Since this does not involve knowing the table occupancies for the CRP, no additional sampling is needed to compute the formula, just the existing counts (*i.e.*, $\vec{n}, \vec{m}, \vec{t}$) are used. Moreover, we know the estimates normalise correctly.

3. MODELS

3.1 Basic Models

The basic non-parametric topic model we consider is given in Figure 2. Here, the document-topic proportions $\vec{\theta}_i$ (for i running over documents) have a PYP with mean $\vec{\alpha}$ and the topic-word proportions $\vec{\phi}_k$ (for k running over topics) have a PYP with mean $\vec{\beta}$. The mean vectors $\vec{\alpha}$ and $\vec{\beta}$ correspond to the asymmetric priors of [25].

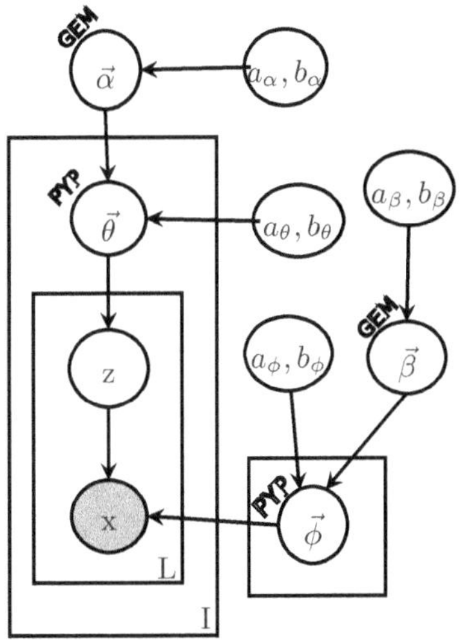

Figure 2: Non-parametric topic model.

While we show $\vec{\alpha}$ and $\vec{\beta}$ having a GEM prior [15, 24] in the figure, allowing different priors covers a range of LDA styles, as shown in Table 1. For instance, when $\vec{\alpha}$ is finite and the discount for the PYP on $\vec{\theta}$, a_θ, is zero, then $\vec{\theta} \sim \text{Dirichlet}(b_\theta\vec{\alpha})$. Thus the two PYPs in the figure can be configured to be Dirichlets, giving the standard LDA set-up for $\vec{\theta}$ and likewise for $\vec{\phi}_k$. The GEM is equivalent to the stick-breaking prior that is at the core of a DP or PYP, so

Table 1: Family of LDA Models. The "tr" abbreviates "truncated" and "symm" abbreviates "symmetric".

	$\vec{\alpha}$ prior	a_α	a_θ	$\vec{\beta}$ prior	a_ϕ
LDA	finite $\vec{u}$	0	0	finite $\vec{u}$	0
tr. HDP-LDA	tr. GEM	0	0	finite $\vec{u}$	0
tr. HDP-LDA	symm. Dir.	0	0	finite $\vec{u}$	0
tr. NP-LDA	tr. GEM	-	0	tr. GEM	-

using this with $\vec{\alpha}$ and a truncated K, and setting $\vec{\phi}_k$ up to be Dirichlet distributed as just shown, we have truncated HDP-LDA. Notice there are different ways of provided a truncated prior to ensure a fixed dimensional $\vec{\alpha}$. The truncated GEM is used in various versions of truncated HDP-LDA [22, 27], and the simpler truncation, just using a Dirichlet, is implicit in the asymmetric priors of [25]. That is, the asymmetric-symmetric (AS) variant of LDA [25] is equivalent to a truncated HDP-LDA. This means that `Mallet` [16] has implemented a truncated HDP-LDA (via AS-LDA) since 2008, and it is indeed both one of the fastest and the best performing.

Thus we reproduce several alternative variants of LDA [25], as well as truncated versions of HDP-LDA, HPYP-LDA and a fully non-parametric asymmetric version (with the truncated GEM prior on both $\vec{\alpha}$ and $\vec{\beta}$) we refer to as NP-LDA. Sampling algorithms for dealing with the HPYP-LDA case are from earlier work [4], and the other cases are similar.

3.2 Bursty Models

The extension with burstiness we consider [5] is given in Figure 3. Here, each topic $\vec{\phi}_k$ is specialised to a variant

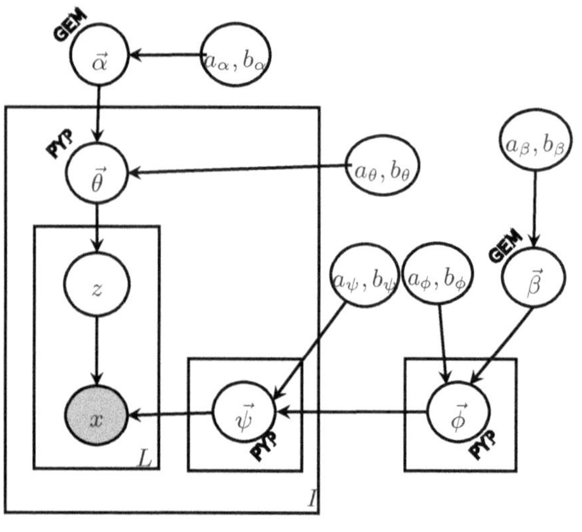

Figure 3: Model with topic burstiness.

specific to each document i, $\vec{\psi}_{k,i}$. Thus

$$\vec{\psi}_{k,i} \sim \text{PY}\left(a_\phi, b_{\phi,k}, \vec{\phi}_k\right) .$$

On the surface one would think introducing potentially $K * W$ (number of words by number of topics) new parameters *for each document*, for the $\vec{\psi}_k$, seems statistically impractical. In practice, the $\vec{\psi}_k$ are marginalised out during inference and book-keeping only requires a small number of additional latent variables. Note that each topic k has its own concentration parameter $b_{\phi,k}$. This feature will be illustrated in Subsection 5.5.

3.3 Inference with Burstiness

In LDA style topic modelling using our approach, we get a formula for sampling a new topic z for a word w in position l in a document d. Suppose all the other data and the rest of the document is $\mathcal{D}_{-(d,l)}$ and this is some model $\mathcal{M}$ (maybe NP-LDA or LDA, *etc.*) with hyperparameters. Then denote this Gibbs sampling formula as $p\left(z \,|\, w, \mathcal{D}_{-(d,l)}, \mathcal{M}\right)$. For LDA, this is just the standard collapsed Gibbs sampling formula [11]. It also forms the first step of the block Gibbs sampler we use for HDP-LDA [4]: first we sample the topic z, and then we sample the various table indicators give z in the model.

The burstiness model built on $\mathcal{M}$, denote it $\mathcal{M}$-$\mathcal{B}$, is sampled using $p\left(z \,|\, w, \mathcal{D}_{-(d,l)}, \mathcal{M}\text{-}\mathcal{B}\right)$ which is computed using $p\left(z \,|\, w, \mathcal{D}_{-(d,l)}, \mathcal{M}\right)$. Thus we say the burstiness model $\mathcal{M}$-$\mathcal{B}$ is a front end to the Gibbs sampler. At the position l in a document we have a word of type w and wish to resample its topic $z = k$. Let $n_{w,k}$ be the number of other existing words of the type w already in topic k for the current document, and let $s_{w,k}$ be the corresponding table multiplicities. They are statistics for the parameters $\vec{\psi}_k$ in the burstiness model. Note by keeping track of which words in a document are unique, one knows that $n_{w,k} = 0$ for those words, thus computation can be substantially simplified. Let $N_{\cdot,k}$ and $S_{\cdot k}$ be the corresponding totals for the topic k in the document (*i.e.*, summed over words). The matrices of counts $n_{w,k}$ and $s_{w,k}$ and vectors $N_{\cdot,k}$ and $S_{\cdot k}$ can be recomputed as each document in processed in time proportional to the length of the document.

The Gibbs sampling probability for choosing $z = k$ at position l for the burstiness model is obtained using Equation (4).

$$
\begin{aligned}
& p\left(z = k \,|\, w, \mathcal{D}_{-(d,l)}, \mathcal{M}\text{-}\mathcal{B}\right) \;\propto \qquad (6)\\
& p\left(z \,|\, w, \mathcal{D}_{-(d,l)}, \mathcal{M}\right) \frac{b_{\psi,k} + a_\psi S_{\cdot k}}{b_{\psi,k} + N_{\cdot,k}} \frac{s_{w,k}+1}{n_{w,k}+1} \frac{S^{n_{w,k}+1}_{s_{w,k}+1,a_\psi}}{S^{n_{w,k}}_{s_{w,k},a_\psi}} \\
& \quad + \frac{1}{b_{\psi,k} + N_{\cdot,k}} \frac{n_{w,k} - s_{w,k} + 1}{n_{w,k}+1} \frac{S^{n_{w,k}+1}_{s_{w,k},a_\psi}}{S^{n_{w,k}}_{s_{w,k},a_\psi}} .
\end{aligned}
$$

This has a special case when $s_{w,k} = n_{w,k} = 0$ of

$$p\left(z \,|\, w, \mathcal{D}_{-(d,l)}, \mathcal{M}\right) \frac{b_{\psi,k} + a_\psi S_{\cdot k}}{b_{\psi,k} + N_{\cdot,k}} . \qquad (7)$$

Once topic $z = k$ is sampled, the second term of Equation (6) is proportional to the probability that the table indicator for word w in the $\vec{\psi}_k$ PYP is zero, it does not contribute data to the parent node $\vec{\phi}_k$, *i.e.*, the original model $\mathcal{M}$ will ignore this data point. The first term of Equation (6) is proportional to the probability that the table indicator is one, so it does contribute data to the parent node $\vec{\phi}_k$, *i.e.*, back to the original model $\mathcal{M}$. This table indicator is sampled according to the two terms and the $n_{w,k}, s_{w,k}, N_{\cdot,k}, S_{\cdot k}$ are all updated. If the table indicator is one then the original model $\mathcal{M}$ processes the data point in the manner it usually would.

Thus Equation (6) is used to filter words, so we refer to it as the burstiness front-end. Only words with table indicators of one are allowed to pass through to the regular model $\mathcal{M}$ and contribute to its statistics for $\vec{\phi}_k$ and, for instance, any further PYP vectors in the model.

4. EXPERIMENTAL SETUP

4.1 Implementation

The publically available `hca` suite used in these experiments is coded in C using 16 and 32 bit integers where needed for saving space. All data preparation is done using the DCA-Bags[3] package, a set of scripts, and input data can be handled in a number of formats including the LdaC format. All algorithms are run on a desktop with an Intel(R) Core(TM) i7 8-core CPU (3.4Ghz) using a single core.

The algorithms have no dynamic memory, so we set the maximum number of topics K ahead of time. This is like the truncation level in variational implementations of HDP-LDA. Moreover, initialisation is done by setting the number of topics to this maximum and randomly assigning words to topics. Other authors [22] report initialising to the maximum number of topics, rather than 1, leads to substantially better results, an experimental finding with which we agree.

Note, inference and learning for burstiness requires the word by topic counts $n_{w,k}$ and word by topic multiplicities $s_{w,k}$ be maintained for each document, as well as their totals. There is an implementation trick used to achieve space efficiency here. First one computes, for each document, which words appear more than once in the document (*i.e.*, those for which $n_{w,k}$ can become greater than 1). These words require special handling, the full Equation (6), and lists of these are stored in preset variable length arrays. Words that occur only once in a document are easy to deal with since their sampling is governed by Equation (7) and no sampling of the table indicator is needed. Second, the count and multiplicity statistics (the $n_{w,k}$ and $s_{w,k}$ which are statistics for $\vec{\psi}_{i,k}$) are not stored but recomputed as each document is about to be processed. Moreover, this only needs to be done for words appearing more than once in the document (hence why lists of these are prestored). All one needs to recompute these statistics is the Boolean table indicators and the topic assignments. The statistics $n_{w,k}, s_{w,k}$ can be recomputed in time proportional to the length of the document.

4.2 Data

We have used several datasets for our experiments, the PN, MLT, RML, TNG, NIPS and LAT datasets. Not all data sets were used in all comparisons.

The PN dataset is taken from 805K News articles (Reuters RCV1) using the query "person", excluding stop words and words appearing <5 times. The MLT dataset is abstracts from the JMLR volumes 1-11, the ICML years 2007-2011, and IEEE Trans.of PAMI 2006-2011. Stop words were discarded along with words appearing <5 or >2900 times. The RML dataset is the Reuters-21578 collection, made up using standard ModLewis split. The TNG dataset is the 20-newsgroup dataset using the standard split. For both stop words were discarded along with words appearing <5 times. The LAT dataset is the LA Times articles from TREC disk 4. Stop words were discarded along with words appearing <10 times. Only words made up entirely of alphabetic characters or dashes were allowed. Roweis' NIPS dataset[4] was left as is.

[3] http://mloss.org/software/view/522/

Table 2: Characteristic Sizes of Datasets

	PN	MLT	RML	TNG	LAT	NIPS
W	26037	4662	16994	35287	78953	13649
D	8616	2691	19813	18846	131896	1740
T	1000	306	6188	7532	0	348
N	1.76M	224k	1.27M	1.87M	34.5M	23.0M

Characteristics of these six datasets are given in Table 2, where dictionary size is W, number of documents (including test) is D, number of test documents is T and total number of words in the collection is N.

4.3 Evaluation

The algorithms are evaluated on two different measures, test sample perplexity and point-wise mutual information (PMI). Perplexity is calculated over test data and is done using document completion [26], known to be unbiased and easy to implement for a broad class of models. The document completion estimate is averaged over 40 cycles per document done at the end of the training run and uses a 80-20% split, so every fifth word is used to evaluate perplexity and the remaining to estimate latent variables for the document. Topic comprehensibility can be measured in terms of PMI [17]. It is done by measuring average word association between all pairs of words in the top-10 topic words (using the English Wikipedia articles). Here the PMI reported is average across all topics. PMI files are prepared with the `DCA-Bags` package using `linkCoco` and projected onto the specific data-sets using `cooc2pmi.pl` in the `hca` suite.

We also compare results with two other systems, `online-hdp` [27] is a stochastic variational algorithm for HDP-LDA coded in Python from C. Wang[5], and `HDP` a Matlab+C combination doing Gibbs sampling from Y.W. Teh. To do the comparisons, at various timepoints we take a snapshot of the $\vec{\alpha}$ vector and the $\vec{\phi}_k$ vectors. This is already supported in `onlinehdp`, and C. Chen provided the support for this task with `HDP`. We then load these values along with the hyperparameter settings into `hca` and use its document completion and PMI evaluation options "-V -p -hdoc,5." In this way, all algorithms are compared using identical software.

5. EXPERIMENTS

5.1 Runtime Comparisons

To see how the algorithms work at scale, we consider the cycle times and memory requirements of the different versions running on the full LAT data set. These are given in Table 3. Cycle times in minutes are for a full pass through all documents and memory requirements are given in megabytes. LDA, HDP-LDA (where $a_\theta = 0$) and NP-LDA are as described in Section 3. The right half of the table gives performance for the burstiness model of Figure 3. Note only a portion of the computation is linear in K so, for instance NP-LDA with burstiness using $K = 2000$ topics on the same dataset takes roughly 90 minutes a cycle and 2.43GB memory. Moreover, given it is coded in Python using inefficient

[4] `http://www.cs.nyu.edu/~roweis/data.html`

[5] Some C++ versions also exist.

Table 3: Cycle times and memory requirements on the LA Times TREC 4 data using $K = 500$ topics. "Burst" is the burstiness version.

	w/out Burst		with Burst	
Alg.	mins.	Mb	mins.	Mb
LDA	11	630	20	690
HDP-LDA	20	760	30	850
NP-LDA	35	840	45	930
onlinehdp	236	1800		

allocation, `onlinehdp` has comparable memory requirements to `hca`. In subsequent experiments, we also saw `HDP` required 5-7 times more memory than `hca`.

Experiments show that the convergence rates (in cycle counts not time) are similar for the various Gibbs algorithms (LDA, Burst LDA, Burst NP-LDA, etc.). Gibbs for full non-parametric LDA with the burstiness front end gives substantial improvements over vanilla Gibbs LDA while requiring only 50% more memory and 3 times greater computation time. Note that the table indicator samplers have previously been reported to give 1-2% improvement in perplexity over Chinese restaurant samplers [4], which in turn retain a substantial improvement over earlier variational algorithms for HDP-LDA [22].

We find that sampling hyper-parameters (for instance, discounts and concentrations of Pitman-Yor processes) to be important for performance. A substantial part of the time for topic burstiness is hyper-parameter sampling, something that is usually less than 5% for the other models. This is because the model has a different concentration parameter for every topic, thus much more of the inefficient adaptive rejection sampling is done for the bursty models versus others.

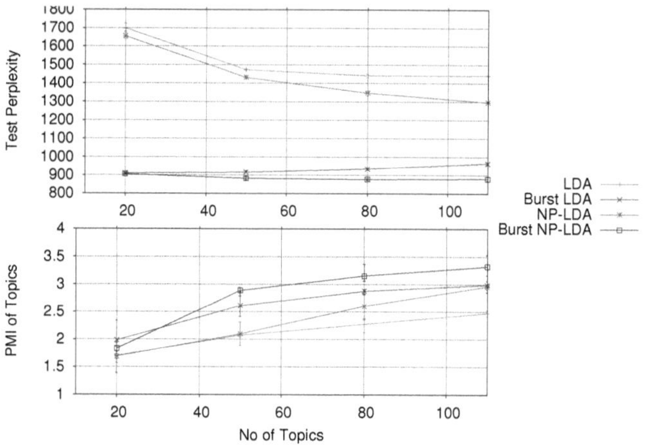

Figure 4: Perplexity and PMI on the RML data for LDA, Burst LDA and NP-LDA, Burst NP-LDA.

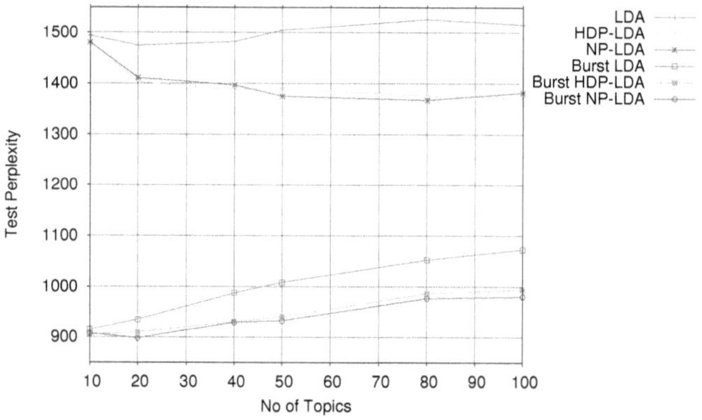

Figure 5: Perplexity as the number of topics (K) changes for different algorithms on the MLT data.

5.2 General Results

A subset of the results are presented in Table 4 and some informative plots given in Figure 4 and Figure 5. These represent the average values computed over 4 independent runs. Note that the differences between `hca`'s "Burst HDP" and "Burst NP-LDA" in the table are not significant at the 5% level, but are only mildy significant.

LDA reaches an earlier minimum for perplexity and then it usually increases, though PMI does increase as well. Models like HDP-LDA and NP-LDA usually keep on improving in PMI as the number of topics increases and hold-out perplexity often waivers about, gradually increasing after a later minimum. For instance, for the small MLT data set they reach a minimum perplexity at about K=20. All the while, PMI keeps improving. For data sets like Reuters-21578 a much larger number of topics can be supported, for instance $K > 500$ easily. The eventual increase in perplexity for larger K seems counter-intuitive given the non-parametric slogan of "estimating the right dimension of the model from the data". However, remember, we have initialization artifacts to deal with. Initializing with substantially too many topics leads to fragmentation/duplication of the topics not subsequently handled by simple Gibbs sampling. To deal with this sort of affect, we need something like split-merge operators in the sampler [2].

With the burstiness models, however, the change in performance is dramatic. Burstiness almost always improves PMI, sometimes substantially and the drop in perplexity is always dramatic. Burstiness makes perplexity peak much earlier w.r.t. the number of topics, but for the non-parametric models the subsequent rise in perplexity thereafter is mild. The non-parametric models cope better with the challenges of sampling behind the bursty front-end. However the best perplexity is reached for low number of topics on MLT where all the different models (LDA, HDP-LDA, NP-LDA) have similar perplexity. For the larger RML data set, LDA's perplexity again peaks earlier but NP-LDA's keeps improving for the number of topics considered.

5.3 Performance Comparisons

This section compares `hca` performance with previous algorithms.

5.3.1 *Comparison with* `onlinehdp` *and* `HDP`

In order to compare the different systems, `hca` versus `onlinehdp` and `HDP` we use the RML and TNG data. We used a fixed set of hyperparameters with no sampling so all discount parameters are set to 0 and the relevant concentration parameters set to 1 (b_α, b_θ) and a symmetric $\beta = (0.01)\vec{1}$ is used. For `onlinehdp` we did a large number of runs vary-

Table 4: Document completion perplexity and PMI for hca variants. Data is presented as "Perplexity/PMI". "HDP" is short for "HDP-LDA".

Data (K)	LDA	Burst LDA	HDP	Burst HDP	NP-LDA	Burst NP-LDA
MLT(10)	1493.62/2.33	915.46/2.47	1480.85/2.61	**904.29**/2.59	1480.20/2.38	907.74/**2.70**
MLT(50)	1504.63/2.94	1008.68/3.26	1389.29/3.70	940.69/3.63	1375/3.47	**932.88/3.93**
RML(50)	1472.87/2.07	915.65/2.61	1427.28/2.25	891.07/2.73	1431.29/2.10	**882.06/2.89**
RML(110)	1441.55/2.43	965.56/2.99	1308.83/3.05	889.42/3.31	1297.08/2.96	**880.22/3.32**
PN(160)	4232.08/3.69	2988.69/4.18	3801.42/4.50	2689.19/4.62	3785.05/4.39	**2657.78/4.70**
PN(240)	4306.63/4.07	3081.19/4.45	3726.05/4.75	**2720.98**/4.76	3676.35/4.72	2734.66/**4.78**

ing $\tau = 1, 4, 16, 64$. $\kappa = 0.5, 0.8$ and $K = 150, 300$ and $batchsize = 250, 1000$. Note $\tau = 64, \kappa = 0.8$ are recommend in [27]. Only the fastest and best converging result is given for onlinehdp. We did one run of both hca and HDP with these settings noting that the differences are way outside of the range of typical statistical variation between individual runs. Plots of the runs over time are given in Figures 6 and 7. The final PMI scores for the 3 algorithms are given

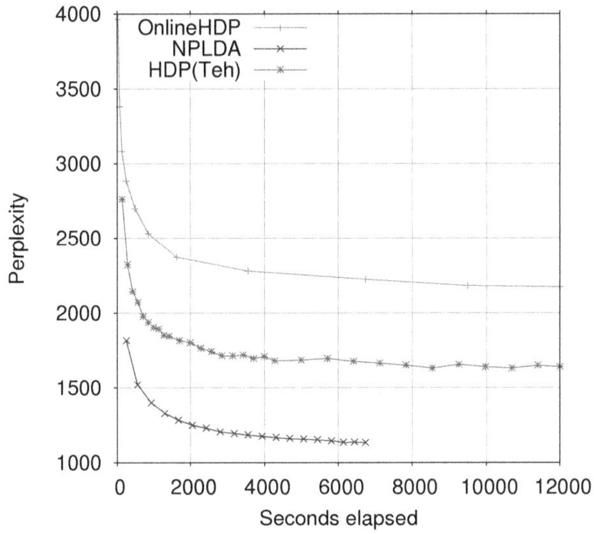

Figure 6: Comparative perplexity for one run on the RML data.

in Table 5.

Table 5: PMI scores for the comparative runs.

	onlinehdp	hca	HDP
RML	2.607	3.47	4.452
TNG	4.042	4.017	4.887

Table 6: Effective Number of Topics for the comparative runs.

	onlinehdp	hca	HDP
RML	37.0	155	149
TNG	7.1	92.7	89.6

The improvement in perplexity of hca over HDP is not that surprising because comparative experiments on even simple

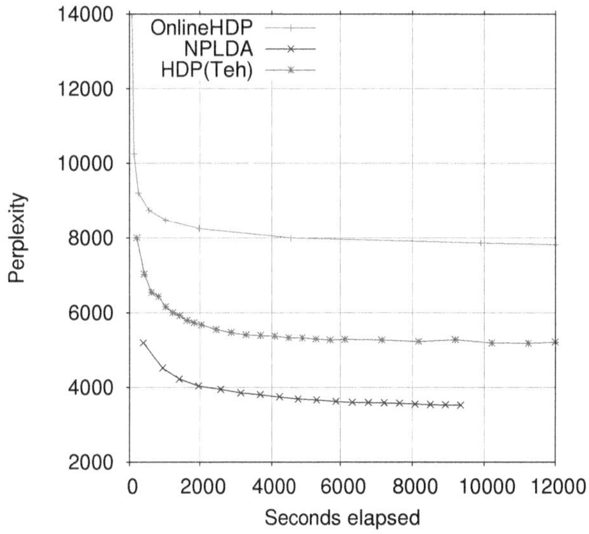

Figure 7: Comparative perplexity for one run on the TNG data.

models show the significant improvement of table indicator methods over CRP methods [6], and Sato et al. [20] also report substantial differences between different formulations for variational HDP-LDA. However, the poor performance of onlinehdp needs some explanation. On looking at the topics discovered by onlinehdp, we see there are many duplicates. Moreover, the topic proportions given by the $\vec{\alpha}$ vector show extreme bias towards earlier topics. It is known, for instance, that variational methods applied to the Dirichlet make the probability estimates more extreme. In this model one is working with a tree of Betas, so it seems the effect is confounded. A useful diagnostic here is the "Effective Number of Topics" which is given by exponentiating the entropy of the estimated $\vec{\alpha}$ vector, shown in Table 6. One can see hca and HDP are similar here but onlinehdp has a dramatically reduced number of topics. The non-duplicated topics in the onlinehdp result, however, look good in terms of comprehensability, so the online stochastic variational method is clearly a good way to get a smaller number of topics from a very large data set.

5.3.2 Comparison with Mallet

Mallet suppports asymmetric-symmetric LDA, which is a form of truncated HDP-LDA using finite symmetric Dirichlet to truncate a GEM. We compare the implementation of HDP-LDA in Mallet and hca. Results are reported for

Table 7: Comparative Results for Mallet.

Dataset(K)	Mallet	hca (HDP-LDA)	hca (NP-LDA)
RML(300)	1404 ± 8	1280 ± 2	1145 ± 2
TNG(300)	4081 ± 27	3999 ± 10	3586 ± 8
MLT(50)	1357 ± 14	1389 ± na	1375 ± na
PN(240)	3844 ± 24	3726 ± na	3676 ± na

Table 8: Comparative Results for PCVB0

K	PCVB0	hca (HDP-LDA)	hca (NP-LDA)
200	1285 ± 10	1267 ± 5	1193 ± 5
300	1275 ± 10	1223 ± 5	1151 ± 5

"RML" and "TNG" datasets with 300 topics as per previous, and also some from Table 4. As suggested in [16] we run `Mallet` for 2000 iterations, and optimise the hyperparameters every 10 major Gibbs cycles after an initial burn-in period of 50 cycles, to get the best results. Table 7 presents the comparative results. We can see that `hca` generally produces better results. Note that results produced by the full asymmetric version NP-LDA are even better, an option not implemented in `Mallet`.

5.3.3 Comparison with PCVB0

We also sought to compare `hca` with the variants of `PCVB0` reported in [20]. These are a family of simplified variational algorithms, though the different variants seem to perform similarly. Without details of the document pre-processing, it was difficult to reproduce comparable datasets. Thus only results for their "KOS blog corpus," available preprocessed from the UCI Machine Learning Repository, where used in producing the comparisons presented in Table 8. We note the smaller difference here in perplexity is such that better hyper-parameter estimation with PCVB0 could well make the algorithms more equal. Interestly, Sato et al. report little difference between the symmetric or asymmetric priors on the Dirichlet on $\vec{\phi}_k$. In contrast, our corresponding asymmetric version NP-LDA shows significant improvements.

5.3.4 Comparison on NIPS 1988-2000 Dataset

A split-merge variant of HDP-LDA has been developed [2] that was compared with online and batch variational algorithms. For the NIPS data they have made runs with $K = 300$ and they estimate all hyperparameters. They use a 80-20% split for document completion and we replicated the experiment with the same dataset, parameter settings and sampling. The results are show in Figure 8 and should be compared with [2, Figure 2(b)]. Their results show plots for 40 hours whereas we ran for 4.5 hours, so our algorithm is approximately 4 times faster per document. Our Gibbs implementation of HDP-LDA substantially beats all other non-split-merge algorithms. Not surprisingly, the sophisticated split-merge sampler eventually reaches the performance of ours. Note the NP-LDA model is superior to HDP-LDA on this data, and the bursty versions are clearly superior to all others.

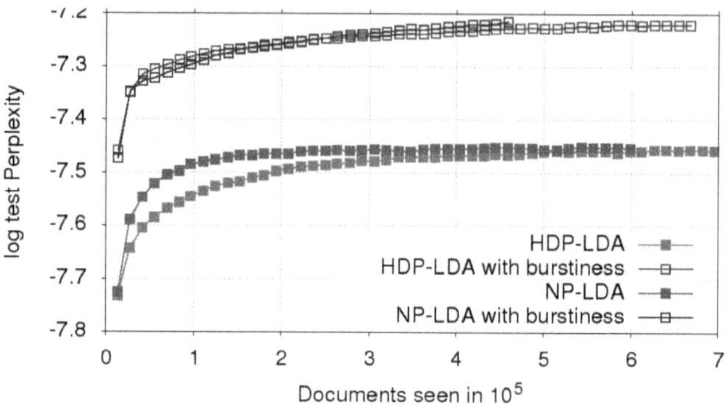

Figure 8: Convergence on Roweis' NIPS data for $K = 300$.

5.4 Effect of Hyperparameters on the Number of Topics

Standard reporting of experiments using HDP-LDA usually sets the β parameter which governs the symmetric prior for the $\vec{\phi}_k$. For instance, some authors [13] call this η and it is set to 0.01. Here we explore what happens when we vary this parameter for the RML data. Note we have done this experiment on most of the data sets and the results are comparable. We train HDP-LDA for 1000 Gibbs cycles and

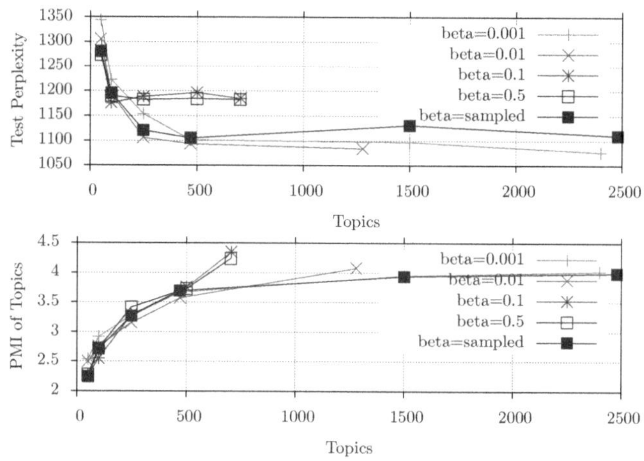

Figure 9: Perplexity and PMI for the RML data when varying β in the symmetric prior for HDP-LDA.

then record the evaluation measures. This takes 60 minutes on the desktop for each value of β. We also do a run where β is sampled. For each of the curves, the stopping point on the right gives the number of full topics used by the algorithms (ignoring trivially populated topics with 1-2 words). So the lowest perplexity is achieved by HDP-LDA with $\beta = 0.001$ where roughly $K = 2,400$ topics are used. Sampling β roughly tracks the lowest achieved for each number of topics.

The PMI results also indicate that for larger β one obtains more comprehensible topics, though less of them. Thus there is a trade-off: if you want less but more comprehensible topics, for instance a coarser summary of the content, then make β larger. If you want a better fit to the data, or more finely grained topics, then estimate β properly.

Table 9: Low proportion topics (proportion below 0.001) with lower variance factor for LAT data when $K = 500$.

PMI	topic words
0.31	Zsa gabor capos slapping avert anhalt enright rolls-Royce cop-slapping Hensley judgeship Leona
2.32	herald tribune examiner dailies gannet batten numeric press-telegram petersburg sentinel
4.02	Baker PT evangelist bakers Tammy Faye swagged evangelists televangelists defrocked

Thus we can see that the number of topics found by HDP-LDA is significantly affected by the hyper parameter β, and thus it is probably inadvisable to fix it without careful experimentation, consideration or sampling. Moreover, the number of topics on RML, with roughly 20,000 documents is up to 2,000. Inspection shows a good number of these are comprehensible. With larger collections we claim it would be impractical to attempt to "estimate" the right number of topics. For larger collections, one could be estimating tens of thousands of topics. Is this large number of topics even useful?

5.5 Topic Specific Concentrations

For the topic burstiness model of Figure 3 we had topic specific concentrations to the PYP, $b_{\phi,k}$. Now the concentration and discount together control the variance. So for document i and topic k, the variance of a word probability $\psi_{i,k,w}$ from its mean $\phi_{k,w}$ will be $\left(\frac{1-a_\phi}{1+b_{\phi,k}}\right)\phi_{k,w}$ [3]. We call the ratio the variance factor. If it is close to one then the word proportions $\vec{\psi}_{i,k}$ for the topic have little relationship to their mean $\vec{\phi}_k$. If close to zero they are similar. Figure 10 considers 500 topics from a model built on the LAT data with $K = 500$ using PYP-LDA and topic burstiness. About

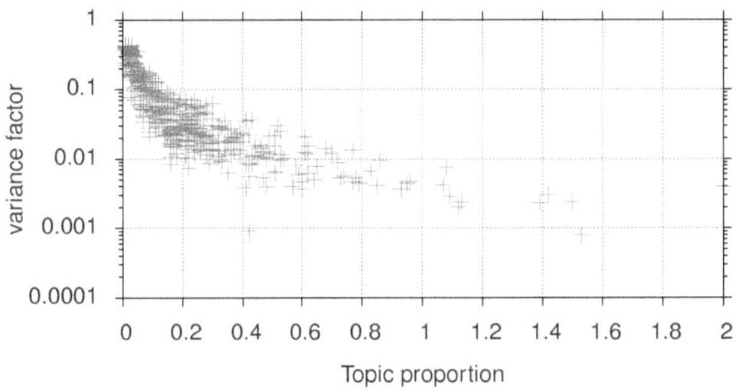

Figure 10: Topic proportions versus the variance factor for LAT data when $K = 500$.

15% of the topics have low values for concentration that make the topics effectively random, and thus not properly used. Examples of topics with low proportions but variance factor below 0.4, so the topics are still use able, are given in Table 9. The first topic is actually about two issues: the first is the Zsa Zsa Gabor slapping incident, and the second is about Orange County Dist. Atty.s Avert and Enright.

6. CONCLUSION

We have shown that an implementation of the HDP-LDA non-parametric topic model and related non-parametric extension NP-LDA using block table indicator Gibbs sampling methods [4] are significantly superior to recent variational methods in terms of perplexity of results. The NP-LDA is also significantly superior in perplexity to the `Mallet` implementation of truncated HDP-LDA (masquerading as asymmetric symmetric LDA). Taking account of the different implementation languages, the newer Gibbs samplers and variational methods also have the same memory footprint. `Mallet` is substantially faster, however, and performs well for HDP-LDA.

We note that these have two goals, (A) better estimating prior topic or word proportions, and (B) estimating the "right" number of topics. The non-parametric methods seem superior at the first goal (A) over the parametric equivalents. Given that the estimated number of topics grows substantially with the collection sizes, it is not clear how important goal (B) can be. Arguably, goal (A) is the more important one.

Moreover, we have developed a Gibbs theory of burstiness that:

- Is implemented as a front-end so can in principle readily be applied to most variants of a topic model that use a Gibbs sampler.
- It is a factor of 1.5-2 slower per major Gibbs cycle.

This will allow the wide variety of topic-model variants to easily take advantage of the burstiness model.

Through the experiments, we have illustrated some characterizations of the models, for instance:

- Our asymmetric-asymmetric NP-LDA model is about 75% slower than HDP-LDA but generally performs better than HDP-LDA, a different result to published results [25, 20] due to the different algorithms.
- The topic comprehensibility (as measured using PMI) is substantially improved by the burstiness version, as reported in the original work [5].
- The topic concentration parameter in the burstiness model goes very low when the topic is insignificant. We can use this to estimate which topics have become inactive in the model.
- The concentration parameter for the topic-word vectors significantly affects results, so care should be taken in experiments using these models.

7. ACKNOWLEDGEMENTS

Both authors were funded partly by NICTA. NICTA is funded by the Australian Government through the Department of Communications and the Australian Research Council through the ICT Centre of Excellence Program. Thanks to Changyou Chen and Kar Wai Lim for their feedback and Changyou for running the `HDP` experiments.

8. REFERENCES

[1] J. Boyd-Graber, D. Blei, and X. Zhu. A topic model for word sense disambiguation. In *EMNLP-CoNLL*, pages 1024–1033, 2007.

[2] M. Bryant and E. Sudderth. Truly nonparametric online variational inference for hierarchical Dirichlet processes. In P. Bartlett, F. Pereira, C. Burges,

L. Bottou, and K. Weinberger, editors, *Advances in Neural Information Processing Systems 25*, pages 2708–2716. 2012.

[3] W. Buntine and M. Hutter. A Bayesian view of the Poisson-Dirichlet process. Technical Report arXiv:1007.0296 [math.ST], arXiv, Feb. 2012.

[4] C. Chen, L. Du, and W. Buntine. Sampling table configurations for the hierarchical Poisson-Dirichlet process. In *Machine Learning and Knowledge Discovery in Databases: European Conference, ECML PKDD*, pages 296–311. Springer, 2011.

[5] G. Doyle and C. Elkan. Accounting for burstiness in topic models. In *Proc. of the 26th Annual Int. Conf. on Machine Learning*, ICML '09, pages 281–288, 2009.

[6] L. Du. *Non-parametric Bayesian Methods for Structured Topic Models A Mixture Distribution Approach.* PhD thesis, School of Computer Science, the Australian National University, Canberra, Australia, 2011.

[7] L. Du, W. Buntine, and H. Jin. Modelling sequential text with an adaptive topic model. In *Proc. of the 2012 Joint Conf. on EMNLP and CoNLL*, pages 535–545. ACM, 2012.

[8] L. Du, W. Buntine, and M. Johnson. Topic segmentation with a structured topic model. In *HLT-NAACL*, pages 190–200. The Association for Computational Linguistics, 2013.

[9] L. Du, W. Buntine, and M. Johnson. Topic segmentation with a structured topic model. In *Proceedings of NAACL-HLT*, pages 190–200, 2013.

[10] W. R. Gilks and P. Wild. Adaptive rejection sampling for Gibbs sampling. *Applied Statistics*, pages 337–348, 1992.

[11] T. Griffiths and M. Steyvers. Finding scientific topics. *PNAS Colloquium*, 2004.

[12] S. Harter. A probabilistic approach to automatic keyword indexing. Part II. An algorithm for probabilistic indexing. *Jnl. of the American Society for Information Science*, 26(5):280–289, 1975.

[13] M. Hoffman, D. Blei, C. Wang, and J. Paisley. Stochastic variational inference. *Journal of Machine Learning Research*, 14:1303–1347, 2013.

[14] H. Ishawaran and L. James. Generalized weighted Chinese restaurant processes for species sampling mixture models. *Statistica Sinica*, 13:1211–1235, 2003.

[15] H. Ishwaran and L. James. Gibbs sampling methods for stick-breaking priors. *Journal of ASA*, 96(453):161–173, 2001.

[16] A. K. McCallum. Mallet: A machine learning for language toolkit. http://mallet.cs.umass.edu, 2002.

[17] D. Newman, J. Lau, K. Grieser, and T. Baldwin. Automatic evaluation of topic coherence. In *Proc. of the 2010 Annual Conf. of the NAACL*, pages 100âĂŞ108, 2010.

[18] S. Robertson and H. Zaragoza. The probabilistic relevance framework: BM25 and beyond. *Found. Trends Inf. Retr.*, 3(4):333–389, Apr. 2009.

[19] M. Rosen-Zvi, T. Griffiths, M. Steyvers, and P. Smyth. The author-topic model for authors and documents. In *Proc. of the 20th Annual Conf. on Uncertainty in Artificial Intelligence (UAI-04)*, pages 487–49, 2004.

[20] I. Sato, K. Kurihara, and H. Nakagawa. Practical collapsed variational Bayes inference for hierarchical Dirichlet process. In *Proc. of the 18th ACM SIGKDD international conf. on Knowledge discovery and data mining*, pages 105–113. ACM, 2012.

[21] I. Sato and H. Nakagawa. Topic models with power-law using Pitman-Yor process. KDD '10, pages 673–682. ACM, 2010.

[22] Y. Teh, K. Kurihara, and M. Welling. Collapsed variational inference for HDP. In *NIPS '07*. 2007.

[23] Y. W. Teh. A Bayesian interpretation of interpolated Kneser-Ney. Technical Report TRA2/06, School of Computing, National University of Singapore, 2006.

[24] Y. W. Teh, M. I. Jordan, M. J. Beal, and D. M. Blei. Hierarchical Dirichlet processes. *Journal of the ASA*, 101(476):1566–1581, 2006.

[25] H. Wallach, D. Mimno, and A. McCallum. Rethinking LDA: Why priors matter. In *Advances in Neural Information Processing Systems 19*, 2009.

[26] H. Wallach, I. Murray, R. Salakhutdinov, and D. Mimno. Evaluation methods for topic models. In *ICML '09*, pages 672–679. 2009.

[27] C. Wang, J. Paisley, and D. Blei. Online variational inference for the hierarchical Dirichlet process. In *AISTATS '11*. 2011.

Reducing the Sampling Complexity of Topic Models

Aaron Q. Li
CMU Language Technologies
Pittsburgh, PA
aaronli@cmu.edu

Amr Ahmed
Google Strategic Technologies
Mountain View, CA
amra@google.com

Sujith Ravi
Google Strategic Technologies
Mountain View, CA
sravi@google.com

Alexander J. Smola
CMU MLD and Google ST
Pittsburgh PA
alex@smola.org

ABSTRACT

Inference in topic models typically involves a sampling step to associate latent variables with observations. Unfortunately the generative model loses sparsity as the amount of data increases, requiring $O(k)$ operations per word for k topics. In this paper we propose an algorithm which scales linearly with the number of actually instantiated topics k_d in the document. For large document collections and in structured hierarchical models $k_d \ll k$. This yields an order of magnitude speedup. Our method applies to a wide variety of statistical models such as PDP [16, 4] and HDP [19].

At its core is the idea that dense, slowly changing distributions can be approximated efficiently by the combination of a Metropolis-Hastings step, use of sparsity, and amortized constant time sampling via Walker's alias method.

Keywords

Sampling; Scalability; Topic Models; Alias Method

1. INTRODUCTION

Topic models are some of the most versatile tools for modeling statistical dependencies. Given a set of observations $x_i \in \mathcal{X}$, such as documents, logs of user activity, or communications patterns, we want to infer the hidden causes motivating this behavior. A key property in topic models is that they model $p(x)$ via a discrete hidden factor, z via $p(x|z)$ and $p(z)$. For instance, z may be the cluster of a document. In this case it leads to Gaussian and Dirichlet mixture models [14]. When z is a vector of topics associated with individual words, this leads to Latent Dirichlet Allocation [3]. Likewise, whenever z indicates a term in a hierarchy, it leads to structured and mixed-content annotations [19, 2, 4, 12].

1.1 Sparsity in Topic Models

One of the key obstacles in performing scalable inference is to draw $p(z|x)$ from the discrete state distribution associated with the data. A substantial improvement in this context was provided by [22] who exploited sparsity to decompose the collapsed sampler [9] for Latent Dirichlet Allocation. As a result the sampling cost can be reduced from $O(k)$, the total number of topics to $O(k_d + k_w)$, i.e. the number k_w of topics occurring for a particular word w and k_d for a particular document d. This insight led to an order of magnitude improvement for sampling topic models, thus making their implementation feasible at a large scale. In fact, the strategy is sufficiently robust that it can be extended to settings where the topic smoother depends on the words [15].

For small datasets the assumption $k_d + k_w \ll k$ is well satisfied. Unfortunately, as the number of documents grows, so does the number of topics in which a particular word occurs. In particular $k_w \to k$, since the probability of observing any particular topic for a given word is rarely nonzero: Assume that the probability of occurrence for a given topic for a word is bounded from below by δ. Then the probability of the topic occurring at least once in a collection of n documents is given by

$$1 - (1-\delta)^n \geq 1 - e^{-n\delta} \to 1 \text{ for } n \to \infty.$$

From this it follows that $k_w = O(k)$ for $n = O(\delta^{-1} \log k)$. In other words, for large numbers documents the efficiencies discussed in [22] vanish. This is troubling, since in many industrial settings n can be in the order of billions to trillions. Consequently, with increasing amounts of data, the *time to process individual documents* increases due to loss of sparsity, thus leading to a *superlinear* increase in runtime.

On the other hand, the topic-sparsity for a given document essentially remains unchanged, regardless of the total number of related documents that are available. This is due to the fact that the number of tokens per document is typically less than $O(k)$. For instance, microblogs contain only dozens of words, yet admit to thousands of topics.[1] This situation is exacerbated when it comes to hierarchical and structured topic models, since there the number of (sub)topics can grow considerably more rapidly. Hence the use of sparsity is crucial in designing efficient samplers.

1.2 Metropolis-Hastings-Walker Sampling

The present paper proposes a new decomposition of the collapsed conditional probability, in conjunction with a

[1]Obviously, this approach would not work to infer topics for Dostojevski's *War and Peace*. That said, a plain topic model is an unlikely candidate to represent very long documents.

KDD'14, August 24–27, 2014, New York, NY, USA.

ACM 978-1-4503-2956-9/14/08 ...$15.00.
http://dx.doi.org/10.1145/2623330.2623756.

Metropolis-Hastings [7] scheme and the use of the alias method, introduced by Walker [20, 13], to amortize dense updates for random variables. This method is highly versatile. It defers corrections to the model and avoids renormalization. This allows us to apply it to both flat and hierarchical models. Experimental evaluation demonstrates the efficacy of our approach, yielding orders of magnitude acceleration and a simplified algorithm.

While we introduce our algorithm in the context of topic models, it is entirely general and applies to a much richer class of models. At its heart lies the insight that in many inference problems the model parameters only change relatively slowly during sampling. For instance, the location of cluster centers, the definition of topics, or the shape of autoregressive functions, only change relatively slowly. Hence, if we could draw from a distribution over k outcomes k times, Walker's alias method would allow us to generate samples in amortized constant time. At the same time, the Metropolis Hastings algorithm allows us to use approximations of the correct probability distribution, provided that we compute ratios between successive states correctly. Our approach is to draw from the stale distribution in constant time and to accept the transition based on the ratio between successive states. This step takes constant time. Moreover, the proposal is independent of the current state. Once k samples have been drawn, we simply update the alias table. In honor of the constitutent algorithms we refer to our technique as the Metropolis Hastings Walker (MHW) sampler.

2. TOPIC MODELS

We begin with a brief introduction to topic models and the associated inference problems. This includes a short motivation of sampling schemes in the context collapsed samplers [9, 18] and of stochastic variational models [21]. It is followed by a description of extensions to hierarchical models.

2.1 Latent Dirichlet Allocation

In LDA [3] one assumes that documents are mixture distributions of language models associated with individual topics. That is, the documents are generated following the graphical model below:

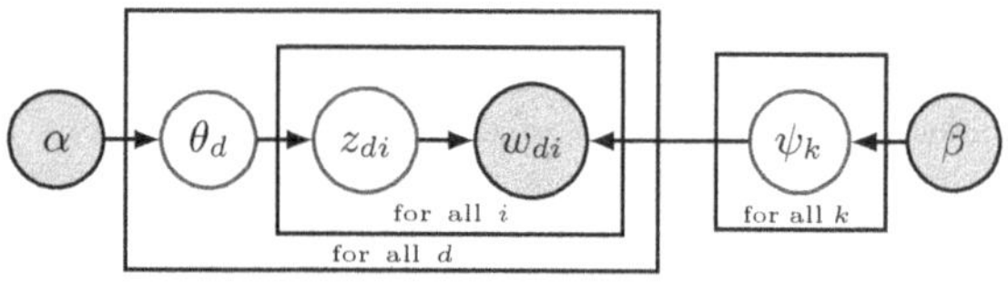

For each document d draw a topic distribution θ_d from a Dirichlet distribution with concentration parameter α

$$\theta_d \sim \text{Dir}(\alpha). \tag{1}$$

For each topic t draw a word distribution from a Dirichlet distribution with concentration parameter β

$$\psi_t \sim \text{Dir}(\beta). \tag{2}$$

For each word $i \in \{1 \dots n_d\}$ in document d draw a topic from the multinomial θ_d via

$$z_{di} \sim \text{Discrete}(\theta_d). \tag{3}$$

Draw a word from the multinomial $\psi_{z_{di}}$ via

$$w_{di} \sim \text{Discrete}(\psi_{z_{di}}). \tag{4}$$

The beauty of the Dirichlet-multinomial design is that the distributions are conjugate. This means that the multinomial distributions θ_d and ψ_k can be integrated out, thus allowing one to express $p(w, z|\alpha, \beta, n_d)$ in closed-form [9]. This yields a Gibbs sampler to draw $p(z_{di}|\text{rest})$ efficiently. The conditional probability is given by

$$p(z_{di}|\text{rest}) \propto \frac{(n_{td}^{-di} + \alpha_t)(n_{tw}^{-di} + \beta_w)}{n_t^{-di} + \bar{\beta}}. \tag{5}$$

Here the count variables n_{td}, n_{tw} and n_t denote the number of occurrences of a particular (topic,document) and (topic,word) pair, or of a particular topic respectively. Moreover, the superscript $\cdot^{-di}$ denotes said count when ignoring the pair (z_{di}, w_{di}). For instance, n_{tw}^{-di} is obtained when ignoring the (topic,word) combination at position (d, i). Finally, $\bar{\beta} := \sum_w \beta_w$ denotes the joint normalization.

At first glance, sampling from (5) appears to cost $O(k)$ time since we have k nonzero terms in a sum that needs to be normalized. [22] devised an ingenious strategy for exploiting sparsity by decomposing terms into

$$p(z_{di}|\text{rest}) \propto \beta_w \frac{\alpha_t}{n_t^{-di} + \bar{\beta}} + n_{td}^{-di} \frac{\beta_w}{n_t^{-di} + \bar{\beta}} + n_{tw}^{-di} \frac{n_{td}^{-di} + \alpha_t}{n_t^{-di} + \bar{\beta}}$$

As can be seen, for small collections of documents only the first term is dense, and more specifically, $\sum_t \alpha_t/(n_t^{-di} + \bar{\beta})$ can be computed from $\sum_t \alpha_t/(n_t + \bar{\beta})$ in $O(1)$ time. That is, whenever both n_{td} and n_{tw} are sparse, sampling from $p(z_{di}|\text{rest})$ can be accomplished efficiently. The use of packed index variables and a clever reordering of (topic,count) pairs further improve efficient sampling to $O(k_w + k_d)$.

Stochastic variational inference [11] requires an analogous sampling step. The main difference being that rather than using $\frac{n_{tw}+\beta_w}{n_t+\bar{\beta}}$ to capture $p(w|t)$ one uses a natural parameter η_{tw} associated with the conjugate variational distribution. Unfortunately this renders the model dense, unless rather careful precautions are undertaken [11] to separate residual dense and sparse components.

Instead, we devise a sampler to draw from $p(z_{di}|\text{rest})$ in amortized $O(k_d)$ time. We accomplish this by using

$$p(z_{di}|\text{rest}) \propto n_{td}^{-di} \frac{n_{tw}^{-di} + \beta_w}{n_t^{-di} + \bar{\beta}} + \frac{\alpha_t(n_{tw}^{-di} + \beta_w)}{n_t^{-di} + \bar{\beta}} \tag{6}$$

Here the first term is sparse in k_d and we can draw from it in $O(k_d)$ time. The second term is dense, regardless of the number of documents (this holds true for stochastic variational samplers, too). However, the 'language model' $p(w|t)$ does not change too drastically whenever we resample a single word. The number of words is huge, hence the amount of change per word is concomitantly small. This insight forms the basis for applying Metropolis-Hastings-Walker sampling.

2.2 Poisson Dirichlet Process

To illustrate the fact that the MHW sampler also works with models containing a dense generative part, we describe its application to the Poisson Dirichlet Process [1, 16]. The model is given by the following variant of the LDA model:

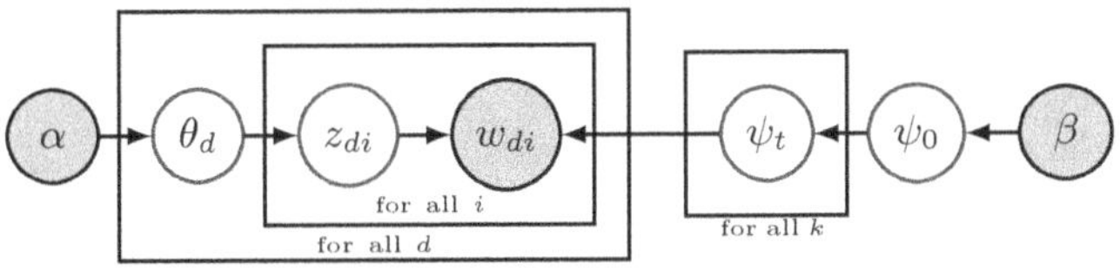

In a conventional topic model the language model is simply given by a multinomial draw from a Dirichlet distribution. This fails to exploit distribution information between topics, such as the fact that all topics have the same common underlying language. A means for addressing this problem is to add a level of hierarchy to model the distribution over ψ_t via $\prod_t p(\psi_t|\psi_0)p(\psi_0|\beta)$ rather than $\prod_t p(\psi_t|\beta)$. Such a model is depicted above.

The ingredients for a refined language model are a Pitman-Yor Topic Model (PYTM) [17] that is more appropriate to deal with natural languages. This is then combined with the Poisson Dirichlet Process (PDP) [16, 1] to capture the fact that the number of occurences of a word in a natural language corpus follows power-law. Within a corpus, the frequency of a word is approximately inversely proportional to its ranking in number of occurences. Each draw from a Poisson Dirichlet Process $\mathrm{PDP}(b, a, \psi_0)$ is a probability distribution. The base distribution ψ_0 defines the common underlying distribution shared across the generated distributions. Under the settings of Pitman-Yor Topic Model, each topic defines a distribution over words, and the base distribution defines the common underlying common language model shared by the topics. The concentration parameter b controls how likely a word is to occur again while being sampled from the generated distribution. The discount parameter a prevents a word to be sampled too often by imposing a penalty on its probability based on its frequency. The combined model described explicityly in [5]:

$$\theta_d \sim \mathrm{Dir}(\alpha) \qquad \psi_0 \sim \mathrm{Dir}(\beta)$$
$$z_{di} \sim \mathrm{Discrete}(\theta_d) \qquad \psi_t \sim \mathrm{PDP}(b, a, \psi_0)$$
$$w_{di} \sim \mathrm{Discrete}\left(\psi_{z_{di}}\right)$$

As can be seen, the document-specific part is identical to LDA whereas the language model is rather more sophisticated. Likewise, the collapsed inference scheme is analogous to a Chinese Restaurant Process [6, 5]. The technical difficulty arises from the fact that we are dealing with distributions over countable domains. Hence, we need to keep track of multiplicities, i.e. whether any given token is drawn from β_i or β_0. This will require the introduction of additional count variables in the collapsed inference algorithm.

Each topic is equivalent to a restaurant. Each token in the document is equivalent to a customer. Each type of word corresponds each type of dish served by the restaurant. The same results in [6] can be used to derive the conditional probability by introducing axillary variables:

- s_{tw} denotes the number of tables serving dish w in restaurant t. Here t is the equivalent of a topic.
- r_{di} indicates whether w_{di} opens a new table in the restaurant or not (to deal with multiplicities).
- m_{tw} denotes the number of times dish w has been served in restaurant t (analogously to n_{wk} in LDA).

The conditional probability is given by:

$$p(z_{di} = t, r_{di} = 0|\text{rest}) \propto \frac{\alpha_t + n_{dt}}{b_t + m_t} \frac{m_{tw} + 1 - s_{tw}}{m_{tw} + 1} \frac{S^{m_{tw}+1}_{s_{tw},a_t}}{S^{m_{tw}}_{s_{tw},a_t}} \quad (7)$$

if no additional 'table' is opened by word w_{di}. Otherwise

$$p(z_{di} = t, r_{di} = 1|\text{rest}) \quad (8)$$
$$\propto (\alpha_t + n_{dt}) \frac{b_t + a_t s_t}{b_t + m_t} \frac{s_{tw} + 1}{m_{tw} + 1} \frac{\gamma + s_{tw}}{\bar{\gamma} + s_t} \frac{S^{m_{tw}+1}_{s_{tw}+1,a_t}}{S^{m_{tw}}_{s_{tw},a_t}}$$

Here $S^N_{M,a}$ is the generalized Stirling number. It is given by

$$S^{N+1}_{M,a} = S^N_{M-1,a} + (N - Ma)S^N_{M,a} \text{ and } S^N_{M,a} = 0$$

for $M > N$, and $S^N_{0,a} = \delta_{N,0}$. A detailed analysis is given in [1]. Moreover we have $m_t = \sum_w m_{tw}$, and $s_t = \sum_t s_{tw}$.

Similar to the conditional probability expression in LDA, these two expressions can be written as a combination of a sparse term and a dense term, simply by splitting the factor $(\alpha_t + n_{dt})$ into its sparse component n_{dt} and its dense counterpart α_t. Hence we can apply the same strategy as before when sampling topics from LDA, albeit now using a twice as large space of state variables.

2.3 Hierarchical Dirichlet Process

To illustrate the efficacy and generality of our approach we discuss a third case where the *document* model itself is more sophisticated than a simple collapsed Dirichlet-multinomial. We demonstrate that there, too, inference can be performed efficiently. Consider the two-level topic model based on the Hierarchical Dirichlet Process [19] (HDP-LDA). In it, the topic distribution for each document θ_d is drawn from a Dirichlet process $\mathrm{DP}(b_1, \theta_0)$. In turn, θ_0 is drawn from a Dirichlet process $\mathrm{DP}(b_0, H(\cdot))$ governing the distribution over topics. In other words, we add an extra level of hierarchy on the document side (compared to the extra hierarchy on the language model used in the PDP).

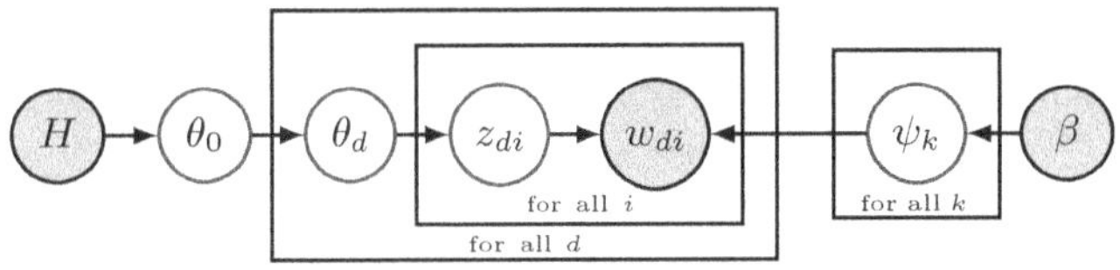

More formally, the joint distribution is as follows:

$$\theta_0 \sim \mathrm{DP}(b_0, H(\cdot)) \qquad \psi_t \sim \mathrm{Dir}(\beta)$$
$$\theta_d \sim \mathrm{DP}(b_1, \theta_0)$$
$$z_{di} \sim \mathrm{Discrete}(\theta_d)$$
$$w_{di} \sim \mathrm{Discrete}\left(\psi_{z_{di}}\right)$$

By construction, $\mathrm{DP}(b_0, H(\cdot))$ is a Dirichlet Process, equivalent to a Poisson Dirichlet Process $\mathrm{PDP}(b_0, a, H(\cdot))$ with the discount parameter a set to 0. The base distribution $H(.)$ is often assumed to be a uniform distribution in most cases.

At first, a base θ_0 is drawn from $\mathrm{DP}(b_0, H(\cdot))$. This governs how many topics there are in general, and what their overall prevalence is. The latter is then used in the next level of the hierarchy to draw a document-specific distribution θ_d that serves the same role as in LDA. The main difference is that unlike in LDA, we use θ_0 to infer which topics are more popular than others.

It is also possible to extend the model to more than two levels of hierarchy, such as the infinite mixture model [19]. Similar to Poisson Dirichlet Process, an equivalent Chinese Restaurant Franchise analogy [6, 19] exists for Hierarchical Dirichlet Process with multiple levels. In this analogy, each Dirichlet Process is mapped to a single Chinese Restaurant Process, and the hierarchical structure is constructed to identify the parent and children of each restaurant.

The general (collapsed) structure is as follows: let N_j be the total number of customers in restaurant j and n_{jt} be the number of customers in restaurant j served with dish t. When a new customer (a token) enters restaurant j with the corresponding Dirichlet Process $DP(b_j, H_j(\cdot))$, there are two types of seating arrangement for the customer:

- With probability $\frac{n_{jt}}{b_j+N_j}$ the customer is served with dish (topic) t and sits at an existing table.
- With probability $\frac{b_j}{b_j+N_j}$ the customer sits at a new table served with a new dish t drawn from $H_j(\cdot)$.

In the event that the customer sits at a new table, a phantom customer is sent upstream the hierarchy to the parent restaurant of j, denoted by j', with corresponding Dirichlet Process $DP(b_{j'}, H_{j'}(\cdot))$. The parent restaurant then decides the seating arrangement of the phantom customer under the same rules. This process repeats, until there is no more parent restaurant or any of phantom customer decides to sit in an existing table in any parent restaurant along the path.

We use the block Gibbs sampler given in [6] as it allows us to extend our approach for multi-level Hierarchical Dirichlet Process, and performs better than the samplers given in [19] and the collapsed Gibbs sampler given in [4], as measured in convergence speed, running time, and topic quality.

The key difference of [6] relative to [19] is that rather than keeping track of relative assignments of tables to each other (and the resulting multiplicities and infrequent block moves) it simply keeps track of the level within the hierarchy of restaurants at which an individual customer opens a new table. The advantage is that this allows us to factor out the relative assignment of customers to specific tables but rather only keep track of the dishes that they consume. The obvious downside being that a small number of customers can be blocked from moves if they opened a table at a high position of the hierarchy that other customers depend upon. Improving mixing in this context is subject to future work.

In the setting studied above we only have a two-level HDP: that of the parent DP tying all documents together and the DP within each document, governing its topic distribution. We use $z_{di} \in \mathbb{N}$ to denote the topic indicator of word i at position d and $u_{di} \in \{0, 1\}$ to indicate whether a new table is opened at the root level (i.e. $u_{di} = 1$). Moreover, define s_{td} to be the table counter for document d, i.e. the number of times a table serving topic t has been opened, and let s_t be the associated counter for the base DP, associated with tables opened at the parent level. Finally, let $s := \sum_t s_t$ be the total number of tables opened at the root level.

Clearly the situation where $s_t = 0$ and $u_{di} = 0$ is impossible since this would imply that we are opening a new table at document d while there is no matching table available at the root level. Hence for the collapsed sampler we only need to consider the following cases:

- A new root topic is generated. That is, we currently have s_t and need to set $u_{di} = 1$.
- A new table is added at document d. In this case we require that s_t, i.e. that the topic exists at the root level. Moreover, obviously it requires that $s_{td} = 0$ since we are adding the first table to serve dish t.
- No additional topic is introduced but we may be introducing an additional table.

This amounts to the following (unnormalized) conditional probabilities. See [6] for further details.

$$p(z_{di} = t, u_{di} = u|\text{rest}) \tag{9}$$
$$\propto \frac{\beta_w + m_{tw}}{\bar{\beta} + m_t} \begin{cases} \frac{b_0 b_1}{b_0+s} & \text{if } s_t = 0 \text{ and } u_{di} = 1 \\ \frac{b_1 s_t^2}{(s_t+1)(s+b_0)} & \text{if } s_t \neq 0 \text{ and } s_{td} = 0 \\ \frac{S^{n_{dt}+1}_{s_{dt}+1,0}}{S^{n_{dt}}_{s_{dt},0}} \frac{s_{dt}+1}{n_{dk}+1} & \text{if } s_t \neq 0 \text{ and } s_{td} \neq 0 \end{cases}$$

Expressions for the generalized form are analogous. Both forms contain a fraction with its numerator being the sum of a sparse term m_{tw} and a dense term β_w. Therefore, the conditional probability can be decomposed to a dense term multiplied by β_w, and a sparse term multiplied by m_{tw}. Applying the same methodology, the sampling complexity of a multi-level HDP can be reduced to $O(k_w)$.

3. METROPOLIS-HASTINGS-WALKER

We now introduce the key components for the MHW algorithm and how to use it in sampling topics. They consist of the alias method [20, 13] and a simplified version of the Metropolis-Hastings sampler [7].

3.1 Walker's Alias Method

Typically, when drawing from a distribution over l outcomes, it is accepted that one would need to perform $O(l)$ work to generate a sample. In fact, this is a lower bound, since we need to inspect each probability at least once before we can construct the sampler. However, what is commonly overlooked is that there exist algorithms that allow us to draw *subsequent samples from the same distribution* in $O(1)$ time. This means that drawing l samples from a distribution over l outcomes can be accomplished in $O(1)$ amortized time per draw. We make extensive use of this fact.

Denote by p_i with $i \in \{1 \ldots l\}$ the probabilities of a distribution over l outcomes from which we would like to sample. The algorithm works by decomposing a distribution over l events into l bins of equal probability by pairing at most two events per bin. Since it 'robs' from the probabilities $p_i > 1/l$ and adds to those with $p_i < 1/l$ it is also referred to as 'Robin Hood' method [13]. The algorithm proceeds as follows:

```
GenerateAlias(p, l)
Initialize L = H = ∅ and A = [].
for i = 1 to l do
  if p_i ≤ l^{-1} then
    L ← L ∪ {(i, p_i)}
  else
    H ← H ∪ {(i, p_i)}
  end if
end for
while L ≠ ∅ do
  Extract (i, p_i) from L and (h, p_h) from H
  A ← [A, (i, h, p_i)]
  if p_h − p_i > l^{-1} then
    H ← H ∪ {(h, p_h − p_i)}
  else
    L ← L ∪ {(h, p_h − p_i)}
  end if
end while
return A
```

This yields an array A containing triples (i, h, p_h) with $p_h < l^{-1}$. It runs in $O(l)$ time since at each step one event is removed from the list. And the probabilities remain unchanged, as can be seen by induction. All we need to do now is to draw a random element from A and flip a biased coin to accept h or i with probability lp_h and $1 - lp_h$ respectively.

```
SampleAlias(A, l)
bin = RandInt(l)
(i, h, p) = A[bin]
if lp > RandUnif(1) then
    return h
else
    return i
end if
```

Note that the alias method works since we are implicitly exploiting parallelism inherent in CPUs: as long as l does not exceed 2^{64} are guaranteed that even an information theoretically inefficient code will not require more than 64 bit, which can be generated in constant time.

3.2 Sampling with Proposal Distributions

Whenever we draw l identical samples from p it is clear that the above algorithm provides an $O(1)$ sampler. However, if p changes, it is difficult to apply the alias sampler directly. To address this, we use rejection sampling and Metropolis-Hastings procedures. Rejection sampling proceeds as follows:

```
Rejection(p, q, c)
repeat
    Draw i ~ q(i)
until p(i) >= cq(i)RandUnif(1)
return i
```

Here p is the distribution we would like to draw from, q is a reference distribution that makes sampling easy, and $c \geq 1$ is chosen such that $cq(i) \geq p(i)$ for all i. We then accept with probability $\frac{p(i)}{cq(i)}$. It is well known that the expected number of samples to draw via **Rejection**(p, q, c) is c, provided that a good bound c exists. In this case we have the following:

Lemma 1 *Given l distributions p_i and q over l outcomes satisfying $c_i q \geq p_i$, the expected amortized runtime complexity for drawing using **SampleAlias**(A, l) and rejecting using **Rejection**(p_i, q, c_i) is given by $O\left(\frac{1}{l}\sum_{i=1}^{l} c_i\right)$.*

PROOF. Preprocessing costs amortized $O(1)$ time. Each rejection sampler costs $O(c_i)$ work. Averaging over the draws proves the claim. □

In many cases, unfortunately, we do not know c_i, or computing c_i is essentially as costly as drawing from p_i itself. Moreover, in some cases c_i may be unreasonably large. In this situation we resort to Metropolis Hastings sampling [7] using a stationary proposal distribution. As in rejection sampling, we use a proposal distribution q and correct the effect of sampling from the 'wrong' distribution by a subsequent acceptance step. The main difference is that Metropolis Hastings can be considerably more efficient than Rejection sampling since it only requires that the ratios of probabilities are close rather than requiring knowledge of a uniform upper bound on the ratio. The drawback is that instead of drawing *iid* samples from p we end up with a *chain* of *dependent* samples from p, as governed by q.

For the purpose of the current method we only need to concern ourselves with stationary distributions p and q, i.e. $p(i) = p(i|j)$ and $q(i) = q(i|j)$, hence we only discuss this special case below. For a more general discussion see e.g. [8].

```
StationaryMetropolisHastings(p, q, n)
if no initial state exists then i ~ q(i)
for l = 1 to n do
    Draw j ~ q(j)
    if RandUnif(1) < min(1, p(j)q(i) / (p(i)q(j))) then
        i <- j
    end if
end for
return i
```

As a result, provided that p and q are sufficiently similar, the sampler accepts most of the time. This is the case, e.g. whenever we use a stale variant of p as the proposal q. Obviously, a necessary requirement is that $q(i) > 0$ whenever $p(i) > 0$, which holds, e.g. whenever we incorporate a smoother.

3.3 MHW Sampling

In combining both methods we arrive at, what we believe is a significant improvement over each component individually. It works as follows:

```
Initialize A <- GenerateAlias(p, l)
for i = 1 to N/n do
    Update q as needed
    Sample j ~ StationaryMetropolisHastings(p, A, n)
end for
```

Provided that the sampler mixes within n rounds of the MH-procedure, this generates draws from up-to-date versions of p. Note that a further improvement is possible whenever we can start with a more up-to-date draw from p, e.g. in the case of revisiting a document in a topic model. After burn-in the previous topic assignment for a given word is likely to be still pertinent for the current sampling pass.

Lemma 2 *If the Metropolis Hastings sampler over N outcomes using q instead of p mixes well in n steps, the amortized cost of drawing n samples from q is $O(n)$ per sample.*

This follows directly from the construction of the sampler and the fact that we can amortize generating the alias table. Note that by choosing a good starting point and after burn-in we can effectively set $n = 1$.

4. APPLICATIONS

We now have all components necessary for an accelerated sampler. The trick is to recycle old values for $p(w_{di}|z_{di})$ even when they change slightly and then to correct this via a Metropolis-Hastings scheme. Since the values change only slightly, we can therefore amortize the values efficiently. We begin by discussing this for the case of 'flat' topic models and extend it to hierarchical models subsequently.

4.1 Sampler for LDA

We now design a proposal distribution for (6). It involves computing the document-specific sparse term exactly and approximating the remainder with slightly stale data. Furthermore, to avoid the need to store a stale alias table A, we simply *draw* from the distribution and keep the samples. Once this supply is exhausted we compute a new table.

Alias table: Denote by

$$Q_w := \sum_t \alpha_t \frac{n_{tw} + \beta_w}{n_t + \bar{\beta}} \text{ and } q_w(t) := \frac{\alpha_t}{Q_w} \frac{n_{tw} + \beta_w}{n_t + \bar{\beta}}$$

the alias normalization and the associated probability distribution. Then we perform the following steps:

1. Generate the alias table A using q_w.
2. Draw k samples from q_w and store them in S_w.
3. Discard A and only retain Q_w and the array S_w.

Generating S_w and computing Q_w costs $O(k)$ time. In particular, storage of S_w requires at most $O(k \log_2 k)$ bits, thus it is much more compact than A. Note, however, that we need to store Q_w and $q_w(t)$.

Metropolis Hastings proposal: Denote by

$$P_{dw} := \sum_t n_{td}^{-di} \frac{n_{tw}^{-di} + \beta_w}{n_t^{-di} + \bar{\beta}} \text{ and } p_{dw}(t) := \frac{n_{td}^{-di}}{P_{dw}} \frac{n_{tw}^{-di} + \beta_w}{n_t^{-di} + \bar{\beta}}$$

the sparse document-dependent topic contribution. Computing it costs $O(k_d)$ time. This allows us to construct a proposal distribution

$$q(t) := \frac{P_{dw}}{P_{dw} + Q_w} p_{dw}(t) + \frac{Q_w}{P_{dw} + Q_w} q_w(t) \quad (10)$$

To perform an MH-step we then draw from $q(t)$ in $O(k_d)$ amortized time. The step from topic s to topic t is accepted with probability $\min(1, \pi)$ where

$$\pi = \frac{n_{td}^{-di} + \alpha_t}{n_{sd}^{-di} + \alpha_s} \cdot \frac{n_{tw}^{-di} + \beta_w}{n_{sw}^{-di} + \beta_w} \cdot \frac{n_s^{-di} + \bar{\beta}}{n_t^{-di} + \bar{\beta}} \cdot \frac{P_{dw} p_{dw}(s) + Q_w q_w(s)}{P_{dw} p_{dw}(t) + Q_w q_w(t)}$$

Note that the last fraction effectively removes the normalization in p_{dw} and q_w respectively, that is, we take ratios of unnormalized probabilities.

Complexity: To draw from q costs $O(k_d)$ time. This is so since computing P_{dw} has this time complexity, and so does the sampler for p_{dw}. Moreover, drawing from $q_w(t)$ is $O(1)$, hence it does not change the order of the algorithm. Note that repeated draws from q are only $O(1)$ since we can use the very same alias sampler also for draws from p_{dw}. Finally, evaluating π costs only $O(1)$ time. We have the following:

Lemma 3 *Drawing up to k steps in a Metropolis-Hastings proposal from $p(z_{di}|\text{rest})$ can be accomplished in $O(k_d)$ amortized time per sample and $O(k)$ space.*

4.2 Sampler for the Poisson Dirichlet Process

Following the same steps as above, the basic Poisson Dirichlet Process topic model can be decomposed by exploiting the sparsity of n_{dt}. The main difference to before is that we need to account for the auxiliary variable $r \in \{0, 1\}$ rather than just the topic indicator t. The alias table is:

$$q_w(t,r) := \begin{cases} \frac{\alpha_k}{b_t + m_{tw}} \frac{m_{tw} - s_{tw} + 1}{m_{tw} + 1} \frac{S^{m_{tw}+1}_{s_{tw}, a_t}}{S^{m_{tw}}_{s_{tw}, a_t}} & \text{if } r = 1 \\ \alpha_k \frac{b_t + a_t s_t}{b_t + m_t} \frac{s_{tw} + 1}{m_{tw} + 1} \frac{\beta + s_{tw}}{\bar{\beta} + s_t} \frac{S^{m_{tw}+1}_{s_{tw}+1, a_t}}{S^{m_{tw}}_{s_{tw}, a_t}} & \text{otherwise} \end{cases}$$

$$Q_w := \sum_{r,t} q_w(t,r)$$

Likewise, the sparse document-specific contribution is

$$p_{dw}(t,r) := n_{dt} \begin{cases} \frac{1}{b_t + m_t} \frac{m_{tw} - s_{tw} + 1}{m_{tw} + 1} \frac{S^{m_{tw}+1}_{s_{tw}, a_t}}{S^{m_{tw}}_{s_{tw}, a_t}} & \text{if } r = 1 \\ \frac{b_t + a_t s_{tw}}{b_t + m_{tw}} \frac{s_{tw} + 1}{m_{tw} + 1} \frac{\beta + s_{tw}}{\bar{\beta} + s_t} \frac{S^{m_{tw}+1}_{s_{tw}+1, a_t}}{S^{m_{tw}}_{s_{tw}, a_t}} & \text{otherwise} \end{cases}$$

$$P_{dw} := \sum_{r,t} p_{dw}(t,r)$$

As previously, computing $p_{dw}(t,r)$ only costs $O(k_d)$ time, which allows a proposal distribution very similar to the case in LDA to be constructed:

$$q(t,r) := \frac{P_{dw}}{P_{dw} + Q_w} p_{dw}(t,r) + \frac{Q_w}{P_{dw} + Q_w} q_w(t,r)$$

As before, we use a Metropolis-Hastings sampler, although this time for the state pair $(s,t) \rightarrow (s',t')$ and accept as before by using the ratio of current and stale probabilities (the latter given by q). As before in the context of LDA, the time complexity of this sampler is amortized $O(k_d)$.

4.3 Sampler for the HDP

Due to slight differences in the nature of the sparse term and the dense term, we demonstrate the efficacy of our approach for sparse language models here. That is, we show that whenever the document model is dense but the language model sparse, our strategy still applies. In other words, this sampler works at $O(k_w)$ cost which is beneficial for infrequent words.

For brevity, we only discuss the derivation for the two level HDP-LDA, given that the general multi-level HDP can be easily extended from the derivation. Recall (9). Now the alias table is now given by:

$$q_w(t,u) := p(z_{di} = t, u_{di} = u|\text{rest}) (\bar{\beta} + m_t) \beta_w$$

$$Q_w := \sum_{t,u} q_w(t,u)$$

and the exact term is given by

$$p_{dw}(t,u) := \gamma_w p(z_{di} = t, u_{di} = u|\text{rest})(\bar{\gamma} + m_t) m_{tw}$$

$$P_{dw} := \sum_{t,u} p_{dw}(t,u)$$

As before, we engineer the proposal distribution to be a combination of stale and fresh counts. It is given by

$$q(t,u) := \frac{P_{dw}}{P_{dw} + Q_w} p_{dw}(t,u) + \frac{Q_w}{P_{dw} + Q_w} q_w(t,u)$$

Subsequently, the state transition $(t,u) \rightarrow (t',u')$ is accepted using straightforward Metropolis-Hastings acceptance ratios. We omitted the subscript $w_{di} = w$ for brevity. The same argument as above shows that the time complexity of our sampler for drawing from HDP-LDA is amortized $O(k_w)$.

5. EXPERIMENTS

To demonstrate empirically the performance of the alias method we implemented the aforementioned samplers in both their base forms that have $O(k)$ time complexity, as well as our alias variants which have amortized $O(k_d)$ time complexity. In addition to this, we implemented the SparseLDA [22] algorithm with the full set of features including the sorted list containing a compact encoding of n_{tw} and n_{dt}, as well as dynamic $O(1)$ update of bucket values. Beyond the standard implementation provided in MalletLDA

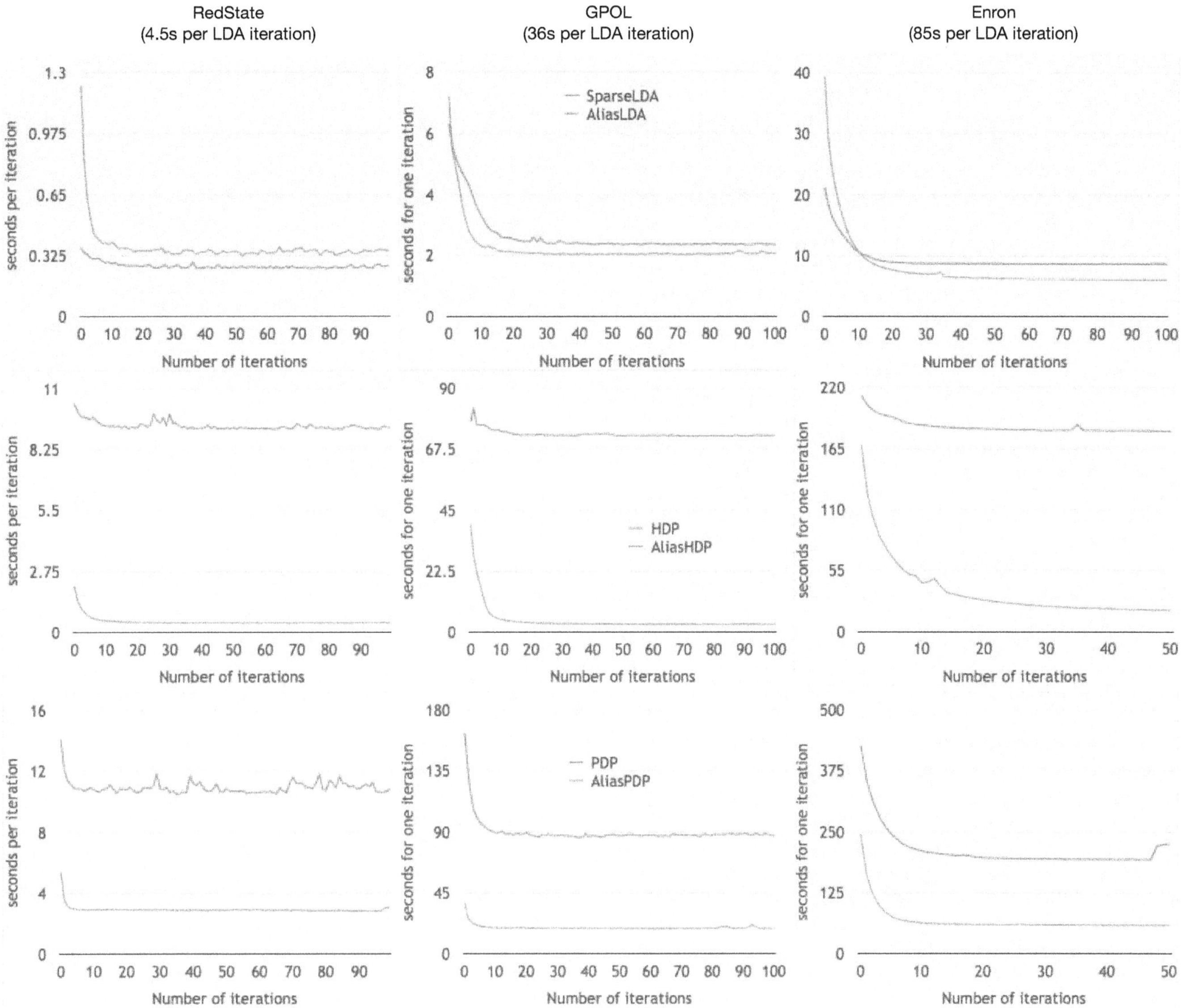

Figure 1: Runtime time comparison between LDA, HDP, PDP and their Alias sampled counterparts AliasLDA, AliasHDP and AliasPDP.

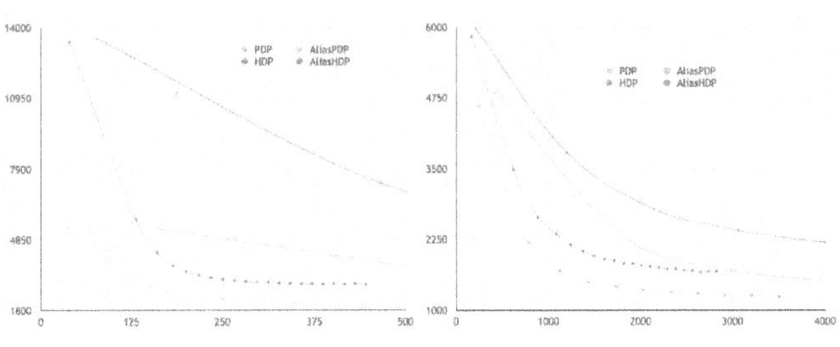

Figure 2: Perplexity as a function of runtime (in seconds) for PDP, AliasPDP, HDP, and AliasHDP on GPOL (left) and Enron (right).

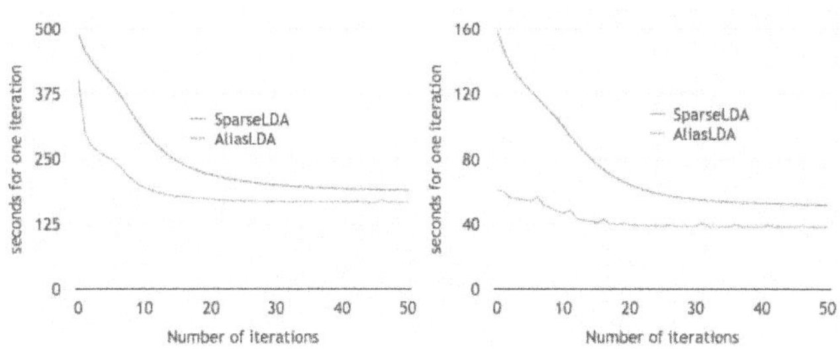

Figure 3: Runtimes of SparseLDA and AliasLDA on PubMedSmall (left) and NyTimes (right).

by [22], we made two major improvements: we accelerated the sorting algorithm for the compact list of encoded values to amortized $O(1)$; and we avoided hash maps which substantially improved the speed in general with small sacrifice of memory efficiency (we need an inverted list of the indices and an inverted list of the indices of the inverted lists).

In this section these implementations will be referred as **LDA** which is $O(k)$, **SparseLDA** which is $O(k_w + k_d)$,

AliasLDA which is $O(k_d)$, **PDP** at $O(k)$ [5], **AliasPDP** at $O(k_d)$, **HDP at** $O(k)$ [6], and **AliasHDP** at $O(k_w)$.

5.1 Environment and Datasets

All our implementations are written in `C++11` in a way that maximise runtime speed, compiled with `gcc 4.8` with `-O3` compiler optimisation in `amd64` architecture. All our experiments are conducted on a laptop with 12GB memory and an Intel i7-740QM processor with 1.73GHz clock rate, 4×256KB L2 Cache and 6MB L3 Cache. Furthermore, we only use one single sampling thread across all experiments. Therefore, only one CPU core is active throughout and only 256KB L2 cache is available. We further disabled Turbo Boost to ensure all experiment are run at exactly 1.73GHz clock rate. Ubuntu 13.10 64bit served as runtime.

We use 5 datasets with a variety in sizes, vocabulary length, and document lengths for evaluation, as shown in Table 1 . **RedState** dataset contains American political blogs crawled from redstate.com in year 2011. **GPOL** contains a subset of political news articles from Reuters RCV1 collection.[2] We also included the **Enron** Email Dataset,[3]. **NYTimes** contains articles published by New York Times between year 1987 and 2007. **PubMedSmall** is a subset of approximately 1% of the biomedical literature abstracts from PubMed. Stopwords are removed from all datasets. Furthermore, words occurring less than 10 times are removed from **NYTimes**, **Enron**, and **PubMedSmall**. **NYTimes**, **Enron**, and **PUBMED** datasets are available at [1].

5.2 Evaluation Metrics and Parameters

We evaluate the algorithms based on two metrics: the amount of time elapsed for one Gibbs sampling iteration and perplexity. The perplexity is evaluated after every 5 iterations, beginning with the first evaluation at the ending of the first Gibbs sampling iteration. We use the standard held-out method [10] to evaluate test perplexity, in which a small set of test documents originating from the same collection is set to query the model being trained. This produces an estimate of the document-topic mixtures $\tilde{\theta}_{dt}$ for each test document d. From there the perplexity is then evaluated as:

$$\pi(\mathbf{W}|\text{rest}) := \left[\sum_{d=1}^{D} N_d\right]^{-1} \sum_{d=1}^{D} \log p(w_d|\text{rest}) \text{ where}$$

$$p(w_d|\text{rest}) = \prod_{i=1}^{n_d} \sum_{t=1}^{k} p(w_i = w|z_{di} = t, \text{rest}) p(z_{di} = t|\text{rest})$$

Here we obtain the estimate of $p(w_i = w|z_{di} = t, \text{rest})$ from the model being trained. To avoid effects due to variation in the number of topics, we hardcoded $k = 1024$ for all experiments except one (GPOL) where we vary k and observe the effect on speed per iteration. We use fixed values for hyperparameters in all our models, setting $\alpha = \beta = 0.1$ for LDA, $a = 0.1$, $b = 10$, and $\gamma = 0.1$ for the PDP, and $b_0 = b_1 = 10$, $\gamma = 0.1$ for the HDP. For alias implementations, we fix the number of Metropolis-Hasting sampling steps at 2, as we observed a satisfactory acceptance rate (over 90%) at these settings. Only a negligible improvement in perplexity was observed by raising this value. Furthermore, we did not observe degraded topic quality even when Metropolis-Hasting sampling step was reduced to $n = 1$, and in all our experiments the perplexity almost perfectly converges at the same pace (i.e. along number of iterations) with the same algorithm without applying alias method (albeit with much less time per iteration).

[2]Reuters Vol. 1, English language, 1996-08-20 to 1997-08-19
[3]Source: www.cs.cmu.edu/˜enron

Dataset	V	L	D	T	L/V	L/D
RedState	12,272	321,699	2,045	231	26.21	157
GPOL	73,444	2,638,750	14,377	1,596	35.9	183
Enron	28,099	6,125,138	36,999	2,860	218	165
PubMedSmall	106,797	35,980,539	546,665	2,002	337	66
NYTimes	101,636	98,607,383	297,253	2,497	970	331

Table 1: Datasets and their statistics. V: vocabulary size; L: total number of training tokens, D: number of training documents; T: number of test documents. L/V is the average number occurrences of a word. L/D is the average document length.

5.3 Performance Summary

Figure 6 shows the overall performance of perplexity as a function of time elapsed when comparing SparseLDA vs AliasLDA on the four larger datasets. When k is fixed to 1024, substantial performance in perplexity over running time on all problems with the exception of the Enron dataset, most likely due to its uniquely small vocabulary size. The gap in performance is increased as the datasets become larger and more realistic in size. The gain in performance is noted in particular when the average document length is smaller since our sampler scales with $O(k_d)$ which is likely to be smaller for short documents.

Figure 2 gives the comparison between PDP, HDP and their aliased variants on GPOL and Enron. By the time AliasPDP and AliasHDP are converged, the straightforward sampler are still at their first few iterations.

5.4 Performance as a Function of Iterations

In the following we evaluate the performance in two separate parts: perplexity as a function of iterations and runtime vs. iterations. We first establish that the acceleration comes at no cost of degraded topic quality, as shown in Figure 6. The convergence speed and converged perplexity of AliasLDA, AliasPDP, and AliasHDP almost perfectly match the non-alias counterparts. This further shows that our choice of relatively small number of Metropolis-Hasting steps (2 per sample) is adequate.

The improved performance in running time of our alias implementations can be seen in all phases of sampling when compared to non-alias standard implementations (LDA, PDP, HDP). When compared to SparseLDA (Figure 3), the performance gain is salient during all phases on larger datasets (except for the early stage in Enron dataset), and the performance is very close on small datasets (0.35s per iteration on AliasLDA vs. 0.25s per iteration on SparseLDA). As the size of the data grows AliasLDA outperforms SparseLDA without degrading topic quality, reducing the amount of time for each Gibbs iteration on NYTimes corpus by around 12% to 38% overall, on Enron corpus by around 30% after 30 iterations, and on PubMedSmall corpus by 27%-60% throughout the first 50 iterations. Compared to SparseLDA, the time required for each Gibbs iteration with AliasLDA grows at a much slower rate, and the benefits of reduced sampling complexity is particularly clear when the average length of each document is small.

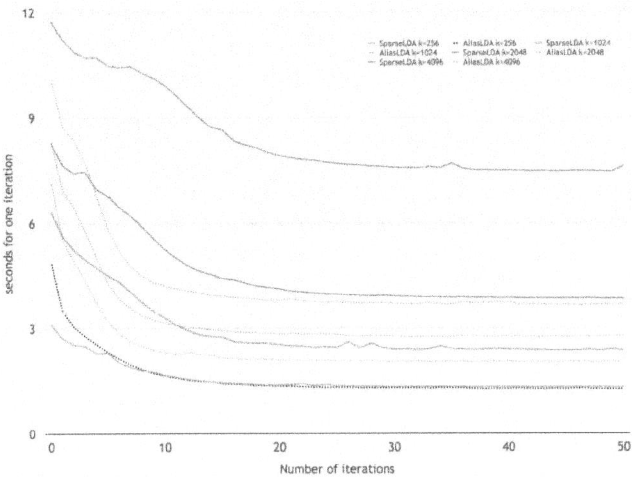

Figure 4: Comparison of SparseLDA and AliasLDA on GPOL when varying the number of topics for $k \in \{256, 1024, 2048, 4096\}$.

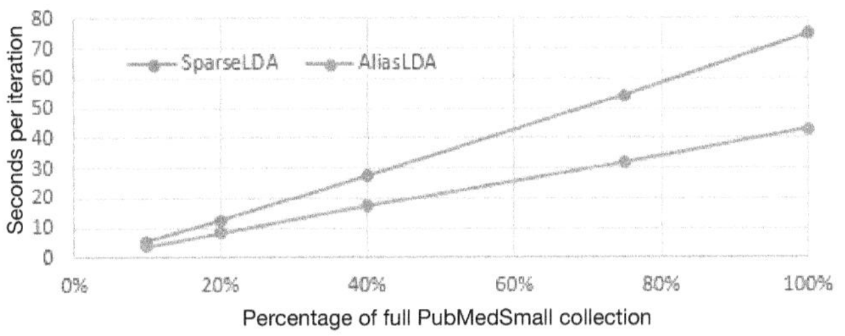

Figure 5: Average runtime per iteration when compared on $\{10\%, 20\%, 40\%, 75\%, 100\%\}$ of the PubMedSmall dataset for SparseLDA and AliasLDA.

The gap in performance is especially large for more sophisticated language modelsl such as PDP and HDP. The running time for each Gibbs iteration is reduced by 60% to 80% for PDP, and 80% to 95% for HDP, an order of magnitude on improvement.

5.5 Varying the number of topics

When the number of topics k increases, the running time for an iteration of AliasLDA increases at a much lower rate than SparseLDA, as seen from Figure 4 on dataset GPOL since k_d is almost constant. Even though the gap between SparseLDA and AliasLDA may seem insignificant at $k = 1024$, it becomes very pronounced at $k = 2048$ (45% improvement) and at $k = 4096$ (over 100%) This confirms the observation above that shorter documents benefits more from AliasLDA in the sense that the average documents length L/D relative to the number of topics k becomes "shorter" as k increases. This yields a more sparse n_{dt} and lower k_d for a document d on average.

5.6 Varying the corpus size

Figure 5 demonstrates how the gap in running time speed scales with growing number of documents in the same domain. We measure the average runtime for the first 50 Gibbs iterations on 10%, 20%, 40%, 75%, and 100% of PubMedSmall dataset. The speedup ratio for each subset is at 31%, 34%, 37%, 41%, 43% respectively. In other words, it increases with the amount of data, which conforms our intuition that adding new documents increases the density of n_{tw}, thus slowing down the sparse sampler much more than the alias sampler, since the latter only depends on k_d rather than $k_d + k_w$.

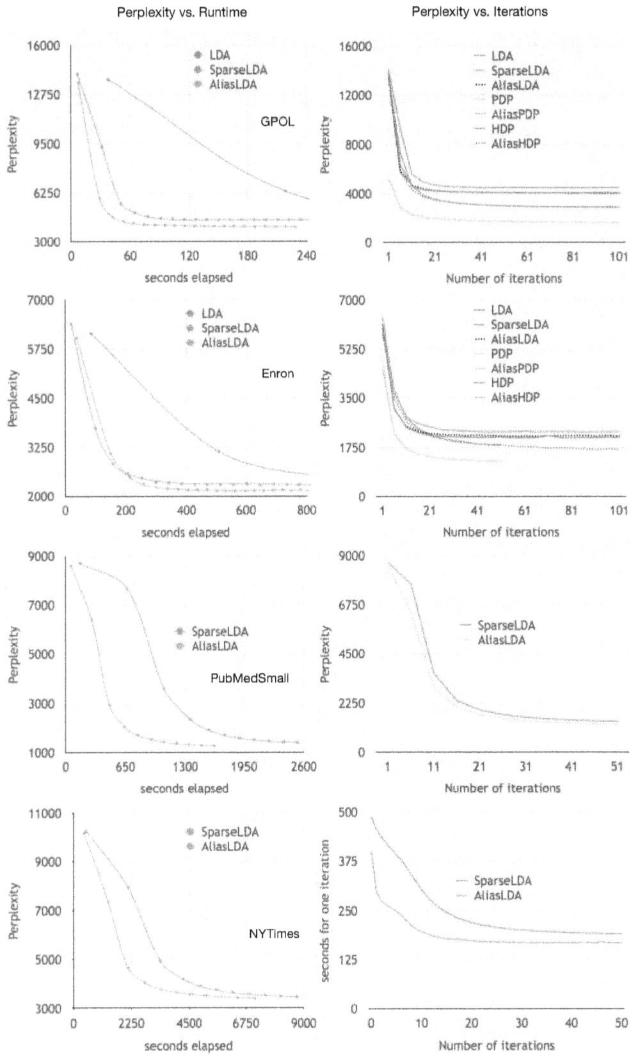

Figure 6: Perplexity as a function of runtime (left) and number of iterations (right) for LDA, SparseLDA, and LDA, PDP and HDP, both with and without using the Alias method. We see considerable acceleration at unchanged perplexity.

6. CONCLUSION

In this paper, we described an approach that effectively reduces sampling complexity of topic models from $O(k)$ to $O(k_d)$ in general, and from $O(k_w + k_d)$ (SparseLDA) to $O(k_d)$ (AliasLDA) for LDA topic model. Empirically, we showed that our approach scales better than existing state-of-the-art method when the number of topics and the number of documents become large. This enables many large scale applications, and many existing applications which require a scalable distributed approach. In many industrial applications where the number of tokens easily reaches billions, these properties are crucial and often desirable in designing a scalable and responsive service. We also demonstrated an order of magnitude improvement when our approach is applied to complex models such as PDP and HDP. With an order of magnitude gain in speed, PDP and HDP may become much more appealing to many applications for their superior convergence performance, and more sophisticated representation of topic distributions and language models.

For $k = 1024$ topics the number of tokens processed per second in our implementation is beyond 1 million for all datasets except one (NYTimes), of which contains substantially more lengthy documents. This is substantially faster than many known implementations when measured in number of tokens processed per computing second per core, such as YahooLDA [18], and GraphLab, given that we only utilise a single thread on a single laptop CPU core.

Acknowledgments: This work was supported in part by a resource grant from amazon.com, a Faculty Research Grant from Google, and Intel.

7. REFERENCES

[1] K. Bache and M. Lichman. UCI machine learning repository, 2013.

[2] D. Blei, T. Griffiths, and M. Jordan. The nested chinese restaurant process and Bayesian nonparametric inference of topic hierarchies. *Journal of the ACM*, 57(2):1–30, 2010.

[3] D. Blei, A. Ng, and M. Jordan. Latent Dirichlet allocation. *JMLR*, 3:993–1022, Jan. 2003.

[4] W. Buntine and M. Hutter. A bayesian review of the poisson-dirichlet process, 2010.

[5] C. Chen, W. Buntine, N. Ding, L. Xie, and L. Du. Differential topic models. In *IEEE Pattern Analysis and Machine Intelligence*, 2014.

[6] C. Chen, L. Du, and W. Buntine. Sampling table configurations for the hierarchical poisson-dirichlet process. In *ECML*, pages 296–311, 2011.

[7] J. Geweke and H. Tanizaki. Bayesian estimation of state-space model using the metropolis-hastings algorithm within gibbs sampling. *Computational Statistics and Data Analysis*, 37(2):151–170, 2001.

[8] W. R. Gilks, S. Richardson, and D. J. Spiegelhalter. *Markov Chain Monte Carlo in Practice*. 1995.

[9] T. Griffiths and M. Steyvers. Finding scientific topics. *PNAS*, 101:5228–5235, 2004.

[10] G. Heinrich. Parameter estimation for text analysis. Technical report, Fraunhofer IGD, 2004.

[11] M. Hoffman, D. M. Blei, C. Wang, and J. Paisley. Stochastic variational inference. In *ICML*, 2012.

[12] W. Li, D. Blei, and A. McCallum. Nonparametric bayes pachinko allocation. In *UAI*, 2007.

[13] G. Marsaglia, W. W. Tsang, and J. Wang. Fast generation of discrete random variables. *Journal of Statistical Software*, 11(3):1–8, 2004.

[14] R. M. Neal. Markov chain sampling methods for Dirichlet process mixture models. University of Toronto, Technical Report 9815, 1998.

[15] J. Petterson, A. Smola, T. Caetano, W. Buntine, and S. Narayanamurthy. Word features for latent dirichlet allocation. In *NIPS*, pages 1921–1929, 2010.

[16] J. Pitman and M. Yor. The two-parameter poisson-dirichlet distribution derived from a stable subordinator. *A. of Probability*, 25(2):855–900, 1997.

[17] I. Sato and H. Nakagawa. Topic models with power-law using Pitman-Yor process. In *KDD*, pages 673–682. ACM, 2010.

[18] A. J. Smola and S. Narayanamurthy. An architecture for parallel topic models. In *PVLDB*, 2010.

[19] Y. Teh, M. Jordan, M. Beal, and D. Blei. Hierarchical dirichlet processes. *JASA*, 101(576):1566–1581, 2006.

[20] A. J. Walker. An efficient method for generating discrete random variables with general distributions. *ACM TOMS*, 3(3):253–256, 1977.

[21] C. Wang, J. Paisley, and D. M. Blei. Online variational inference for the hierarchical Dirichlet process. In *Conference on Artificial Intelligence and Statistics*, 2011.

[22] L. Yao, D. Mimno, and A. McCallum. Efficient methods for topic model inference on streaming document collections. In *KDD'09*, 2009.

Dynamics of News Events and Social Media Reaction

Mikalai Tsytsarau
University of Trento
tsytsarau@disi.unitn.eu

Themis Palpanas
Paris Descartes University
themis@mi.parisdescartes.fr

Malu Castellanos
Hewlett Packard
malu.castellanos@hp.com

ABSTRACT

The analysis of social sentiment expressed on the Web is becoming increasingly relevant to a variety of applications, and it is important to understand the underlying mechanisms which drive the evolution of sentiments in one way or another, in order to be able to predict these changes in the future. In this paper, we study the dynamics of news events and their relation to changes of sentiment expressed on relevant topics. We propose a novel framework, which models the behavior of news and social media in response to events as a convolution between event's importance and media response function, specific to media and event type. This framework is suitable for detecting time and duration of events, as well as their impact and dynamics, from time series of publication volume. These data can greatly enhance events analysis; for instance, they can help distinguish important events from unimportant, or predict sentiment and stock market shifts. As an example of such application, we extracted news events for a variety of topics and then correlated this data with the corresponding sentiment time series, revealing the connection between sentiment shifts and event dynamics.

1. INTRODUCTION

The problem of monitoring the evolution of sentiment has been studied in the context of different research areas, from social studies to reputation management [13]. However, there is still a lack of understanding of what causes the crowd's sentiment to change. Some people change their attitude for personal reasons, some do so influenced by their connections, but most likely people change their opinion when a new evidence comes into their consideration.

By aggregating sentiments, expressed in multiple texts, and assessing the result with statistical measurements, we can capture certain changes, or shifts, in global sentiment, which cannot be attributed to random variation [12]. Understanding the reasons for these sentiment shifts provides insight about products, services and policies to companies and institutions. Thus, this problem has gained a lot of attention in academia and industry [16, 10, 4, 7].

In this paper, we propose studying the correlation of important shifts in sentiment to news events reported by different news sources. The objective of this paper is to exploit the current work on sentiment analysis and contradiction detection, and extend the state of the art by understanding news events dynamics and modeling relationships *between sentiment changes and news events*.

We observe that most news events are announced as atomic pieces of information and their impact is not readily intelligible from the text alone. To determine the importance and impact of news to people, it is crucial to consider the publication dynamics of the whole crowd, rather than only from news agencies or news media [10]. Analyzing the aggregated publication volume or user interest on a specific topic over time can help in understanding the event's importance and dynamics. Earlier detection of such events can be useful to publishers, content providers and search engines [9]. However, in certain cases social media can contribute to this volume all by themselves (without any external stimuli, such as a news event coming from a news agency) and also maintain a trending volume growth over long time periods. These effects distract the observed events dynamics and may even make them undetectable.

Our method addresses these problems by representing publication dynamics as the result of the interplay between the original news' importance and social response. More specifically, our modeling is based on the idea that news media (or social media) can be described by a special "response" function, which determines the resulting dynamics of news publication (or user interest) for an event. This opens up the possibility of recovering the original event sequence and its varying importance over the time dimension.

The response function can be seen as a likelihood of a "delayed" publication for an event: similar to a phone conversation, where a

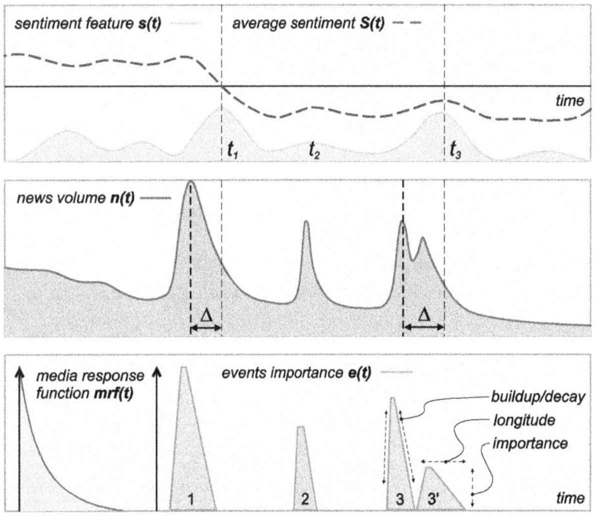

Figure 1: An example time series, with sentiment shifts (top) correlated to news volume (mid) and events importance (bottom).

KDD'14, August 24–27, 2014, New York, NY, USA.

http://dx.doi.org/10.1145/2623330.2623670.

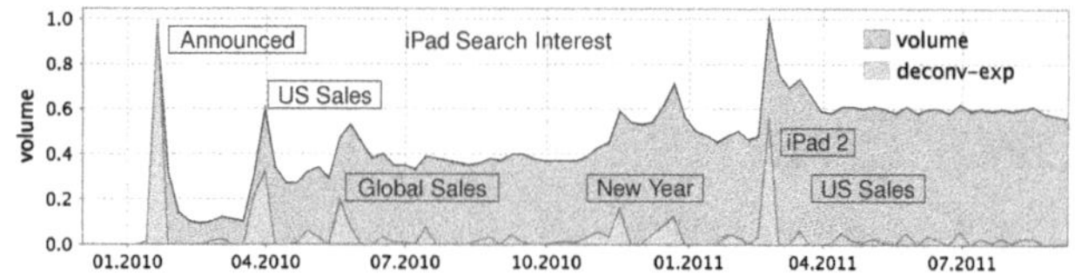

Figure 2: Some of the events identified by our system for "iPad".

delay in circuits creates the "echo" effect, news and social media tend to re-publish, cite, and discuss previous articles, extending this activity over time. In this case, the peak intensity of publications does not always coincide with the beginning of the event, or its peak importance. To tackle these problems and recover the original event importance, we employ deconvolution, which is a popular technique for improving audio or image quality [3].

Based on this method, we are able to accurately measure events importance and response dynamics, opening up the possibility to evaluate their impact on sentiment evolution. The results obtained by our study indicate the existence of different types of response dynamics in Twitter, and reveal their impact on sentiment changes.

1.1 Motivating Scenarios and Examples

We would like to make the reader more familiar with our goals by introducing the following use cases.

Example 1: Consider a *search interest* [9] time series extracted from Google for the topic "iPad", shown in Figure 2, blue. It features a growing number of search queries overlaid with a series of overlapping bursts of user interest, making it very hard to detect news events. The output time series (Figure 2, red), processed using our method, demonstrates a more vivid event separation and dynamics, making them easily detectable. Moreover, the output time series appears without the global trend, which is processed alongside the deconvolution. We note, that achieving the same effect is not possible by subtracting a moving average or by using linear regression, since the presence of peaks in time series biases the trend estimation.

Example 2: It is known, that response dynamics is often determined by events, and can be used to classify events by their impact and expectedness [2, 5]. For example, in the time series shown in Figure 3, we see that the death of Michael Jackson was so impacting to media, that their response lasted for over a year. On the contrary, the interest to Harry Potter movies has usually a two-month period of decay. Moreover, we observe that these events have different decay patterns (we further discuss this point later in the paper). Our method has been designed to detect and analyze different response dynamics, making suitable for cases like the above.

Example 3: Since its early announcement, Samsung's "Galaxy Tab" was regarded in social media as a very fine competitor to Apple's "iPad", receiving mostly positive sentiments. However, the attitude of people dramatically changed to negative at the moment when Samsung published the price for the device. By observing the media reaction to these and other impacting news, it becomes possible to predict changes in their opinion more rapidly, i.e., as soon as we are able to recognize the establishing trend dynamics.

$S(t)$	Raw sentiment time series	$\xi(t)$	Random variable
$s(t)$	Sentiment feature time series	$\rho()$	Correlation function
$e(t)$	Event importance time series	$\delta(t)$	Dirac (pulse) function
$n(t)$	News volume time series	$h(t)$	Heaviside (step) function
$x(t)$	Aggregated (total) news volume	Δ, δ	Lags between time series
$rf(t)$	Response function of a user	$\gamma(t)$	Importance decay function
$mrf(t)$	Response function of entire media	τ_0, α	Response decay parameters

Table 1: Notations used in this paper.

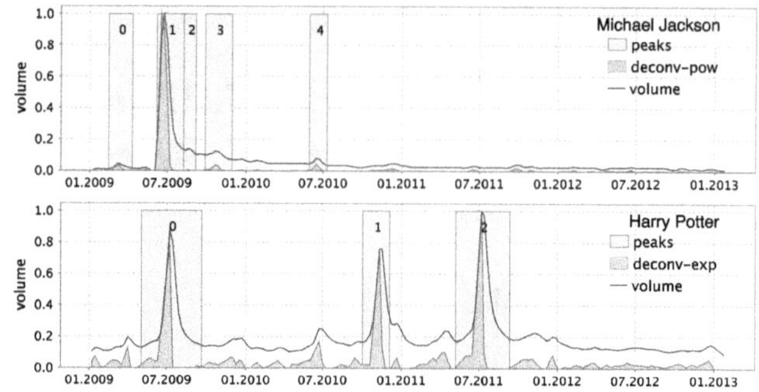

Figure 3: Dynamics of Google Search volume for different topics. Extracted event importance is shown as triangles (normalized).

1.2 Contributions

To the best of our knowledge, this is the first work that proposes a principled modeling of news dynamics in various media and news interaction with sentiments. Our main contributions are summarized as follows.

- We analyze the existing models of publication dynamics, and discuss their foundational principles.
- We model the dynamics of news volume as a convolution between events importance and media response function.
- We develop a method for news events extraction, based on deconvolution with automated parameter optimization.
- We assess several sentiment features for their correlation to news events, and the possibility of predicting their changes.

Since our framework relies on deconvolution, it can accommodate various response functions, suitable for different cases. We note that our method does not require describing the news publication dynamics using a differential equation. Moreover, it is possible to automatically learn media response functions from the data.

2. FORMALISM

We summarize the most important notations used in our paper in Table 1 and discuss them in Section 2.1. Following that, we introduce our problems in Section 2.2.

2.1 Definitions

We are given a time series of numeric values, $s(t)$, which is derived from raw sentiments $S(t)$ for a particular topic T and represents some sentiment feature or interestingness measure, e.g., contradiction level [15]. These time series are shown in Figure 1 (top), where $s(t)$ represents the contradiction level of raw sentiments $S(t)$. Along with the sentiment time series, we are given the news frequency time series represented by $n(t)$ (Figure 1, middle), and the corresponding correlation function $\rho(s,n)$, which takes both time series as input parameters and computes a real-valued correlation coefficient. We note that $\rho(s,n)$ can be a special function adapted for particular measures used to compute $s(t)$ and $n(t)$. For instance, $n(t)$ can be a rather bursty time series, where the notions of mean value and deviations from the mean make no apparent physical sense. Thus, it can be more effective in this case to consider a correlation measure based on derivatives, or on bursts alignment. Finally, we use the event importance time series $e(t)$ to model event dynamics, and response functions $rf(t)$ and $mrf(t)$ (represented in Figure 1, bottom) to model social and news media behavior. We describe these functions in more detail in Section 3.

2.2 Problems

We are given a collection of sentiment feature time series $s(t)$ and news volume time series $n(t)$ for various topics. For a particular topic T, we want to detect the most important sentiment shifts according to $s(t)$, and identify the news events, which have caused them, so that it will be possible to predict future sentiment changes on that topic upon observing and analyzing relevant news events. This general problem can be decomposed into a set of subproblems with the scopes of news-sentiment interaction and news-events interaction respectively.

News and sentiments interaction can be coarsely modeled by correlation. However, the problem of finding dependencies between sentiments and news is inherently complex, since sentiment shifts may be correlated not only with the news on the same topic, but also with several other (related) topics.

PROBLEM 1. *Given $s(t)$ for a topic T and a correlation measure $\rho(s,n)$, determine a list of topics T_i, whose news time series $n_i(t)$ correlate with $s(t)$. For each correlation pair, determine a time lag between the two series.*

After determining a substantial amount of news events, which caused sentiment changes, it may be possible to predict shifts in sentiment for related topics by extracting features of the recognized event and using them as input to a classifier model. Related topics can be determined by referring to the list of news time series, which are correlated with the given sentiment time series. The classifier model can be trained on a dataset of confirmed causality cases between news events and sentiment shifts. Alternatively, it can use automatically extracted correlation pairs. We note that this problem requires a deeper study with complex causality modeling, and we defer it to a future study. In this paper, our goal is to explore the event dynamics in different media, and establish the connection between events and sentiment shifts.

3. BACKGROUND AND RELATED WORK

There exist approaches that tackle specific aspects of our problem in various domains, yet, they cannot be combined to solve the problem that our approach solves. In this section, we provide a detailed evaluation of their properties and design principles, and use it to establish a theoretical and empirical background for our method.

To the best of our knowledge, there is currently no other system, or method, capable of automatically detecting impacting events and identifying properties of their dynamics from news publication volume. There exist only few news tracking methods which are able to recognize different event types, but neither of them provides numeric characteristics useful for event modeling and sentiment prediction purposes, such as a correct time framing and importance level of an event. Still, they are not capable of distinguishing adjacent events when their publications are highly overlapping. Finally, the existing dynamics models target only individual news propagation media (e.g., blogosphere, microblogging, youtube), and have not been generalized (or tested) on multiple domains.

3.1 Event Models

Lehmann et al. [5] study collective attention in Twitter and its propagation through user networks. They measure the aggregated volume before, during and after the event's peak by subtracting the baseline level of attention (computed using a sliding window). Based on the relationship between these three values, they define four classes of news events according to their expectedness and impact. Accordingly, events can be: a) *expected impacting*, where there is a growth of volume before an event (anticipation) and a decay afterwards (response); b) *expected non-impacting*, where the event's outcome is of a lesser concern than the event itself; c) *unexpected impacting*, featuring an instant appearance and a lengthy response; d) *unexpected non-impacting* or *transient*, where neither the event nor its outcome are important to the media;

Alternatively, Crane and Sornette [2] consider events as having internal (*endogenous*), or external (*exogenous*) origin, and being of either *critical*, or *sub-critical* importance to social media. We observe that *exogenous critical* and *exogenous sub-critical* event types in their classification coincide with *unexpected impacting* and *unexpected non-impacting* event types from [5]. In addition, the authors also introduce a concept of *endogenous* events, which is broadly similar to memes in social media.

While these classes capture events semantics on a very good level, a more detailed analysis of news dynamics requires reliable extraction of peak shapes and proper modeling of social media. The first requirement is important since publication volume often contains noise and (evolving) background level, which masks individual peaks. The second requirement is necessary to distinguish between the volume generated by endogenous factors (imitation) and that generated by exogenous factors (news importance). Therefore, we investigate the most recent models of news dynamics and their ability to correctly describe and predict news volume.

3.2 Meme Model

Memes in social media are the outbursts of publications on some topic, which can be assigned to the "endogenous critical" type of the above classification. Since they have no particular external driving force or impact on sentiment, we want to distinguish them from "expected impacting" events. The topic of news dynamics in social media (and memes in particular) was studied by Leskovec et al. [6], who propose a model of meme and news dynamics based on three assumptions for the interaction of news sources: *imitation*, *recency preference* and *concurrency*. The imitation (endogenous) hypothesis assumes that news sources are more likely to publish on events that have already seen large volume of publications. The recency hypothesis marks the tendency to publish more on recent events. Finally, the concurrency hypothesis states that news sources have a limited capacity and choose only one event at a time to report on. The authors express the imitation and recency preferences through the functions of a combined news volume, $f(x)$, and time passed since the beginning, $\gamma(t)$:

$$n(t) = \frac{dx}{dt} = c \cdot f(x)\gamma(t) \tag{1}$$

In the above equation, dx/dt represents the amount of publications at time t, and x represents the total amount integrated since the beginning. We note that whereas equation (1) is based on the assumptions given in [6], it is different to the equation studied in that paper, where $x + dx/dt$ were mistakenly used as $n(t)$[1].

Leskovec et al. demonstrate that in the simulated environment consisting of concurrent news sources, both time and volume components are necessary to generate the oscillating nature of news volume. However, repeating this experiment with the original meme time series revealed a substantial deviation between predicted and observed volumes, when the same assumptions (namely, global time and volume) were used. First, the global volume (accumulated since the beginning of the time series) is not useful to predict any but the very first peak. Second, the global time (either from the beginning of the time series or from the first peak) is both arbitrary (which peak is the first? when a time series begins?) and can not capture subsequent peaks. This said, we assume that the authors

[1] J. Leskovec. Personal communication, June 2013.

implied the global nature of their model with respect to parameters, while the time and the volume were local for every seeded event. Nevertheless, we believe that equation (1) intuitively captures some of the properties of news dynamics, and is therefore worth considering.

3.3 Stochastic Multiplicative Model

Asur et al. [1] propose a model for news dynamics, described by stochastic multiplicative process, driven by independent random variables (noise) and a time-decaying variable (recency). Based on this model, they predict a linear initial growth of publications volume, and a log-normal distribution of this volume over different time series. Both hypotheses are supported by an empirical evaluation on Twitter [1] and Digg [17] data. However, this model is not useful for prediction purposes, since it relies on a mixture of random variables (located at subsequent time intervals). Even though it is possible to infer values of these variables for past time intervals, the hypothesis that they are independently distributed forbids estimation of subsequent variables.

A closer look at this model reveals that it is formulated in a recursive manner, where the total volume accumulated by a time tick $t+dt$ is expressed through the volume at time t, i.i.d. random variable $\xi(t)$ and time-decaying component $\gamma(t)$:

$$x+dx = [1+\gamma(t)\xi(t)]x \tag{2}$$

To analyze the proposed dynamics, the above equation can be transformed into a more convenient form (remember though, that dx/dt, x and t remain discrete):

$$n(t) = \frac{dx}{dt} = \gamma(t)\xi(t)x \tag{3}$$

Now it can be clearly seen that the volume of news published at time t depends on the previously accumulated volume x, discounted by $\gamma(t)$, and on random variable $\xi(t)$. Although the dependency of (3) on random variables forbids its analytical derivation, we observe that it is very similar to (1), and can also be represented as the product of exponent and time factors, especially in the case when $\xi(t)$ are not i.i.d.

Another important observation in favor of the continuity of $\xi(t)$ is that these variables may represent an exogenous factor, the news importance $e(t)$, which pushes volume up and counteracts the decreasing trend of $\gamma(t)$. Comparing (1) and (3) under this perspective, it becomes evident that they are essentially the specific cases of a more general model, multiplying endogenous and exogenous factors. Our model differs from these two by considering a convolution between endogenous and exogenous factors.

3.4 Hawkes Poisson Process Model

A study of social system's dynamics by Crane and Sornette [2] comes the closest to our work with regard to a modeling based on user response. The authors study dynamics of book sales [8] and social content [2], based on a widespread model of hyperbolic (long-memory) user response function $rf(t) \sim 1/t^{1+\theta}, 0 < \theta < 1$. Taking the ensemble average of a Hawkes Poisson Process driven by this response function and a spontaneous rate $e(t)$, they express $n(t)$ conditional on itself and on an average branching ratio μ:

$$n(t) = e(t) + \mu \int_{-\infty}^{t} rf(t-\tau)n(\tau)d\tau \tag{4}$$

Correspondingly, equation (4) takes the form of the convolution between event importance $e(t)$ and a media response kernel $mrf(t)$, considered as the output of (4) in the case when $e(t) = \delta(t)$:

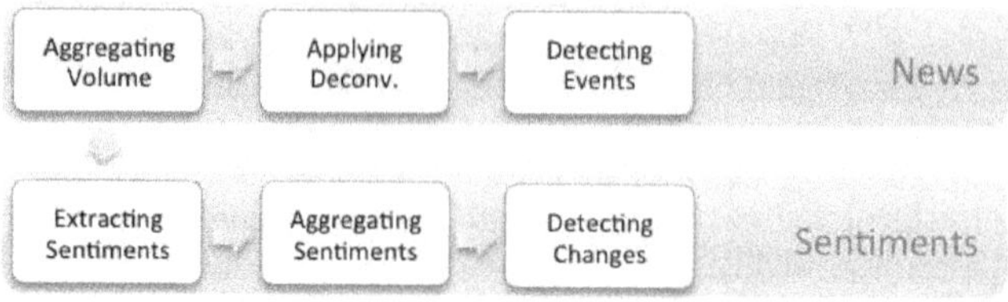

Figure 4: Interaction between key components of the system.

$$n(t) = \int_{-\infty}^{t} mrf(t-\tau)e(\tau)d\tau \tag{5}$$

Summarizing the above studies, we see that the imitation factor does not play as important role in news dynamics as in meme dynamics. Moreover, [1] and [5] observe that propagation of news through user networks is not epidemic, i.e., it rather depends on news importance than on numbers of followers of users who spread the news. Therefore, we consider publication likelihood being dependent more on recent volume than on past volume, deviating from the purely endogenous model. In addition, we consider that news events have continuity and varying importance, which also affect the publishing dynamics (exogenous assumption). These assumptions require a more complex modeling of news dynamics, but result in more accurate models, which we discuss in the following sections.

4. PROPOSED METHOD

Our task requires processing two different kinds of data, i.e., sentiments and news volume, which come from different sources and also at very different rates. In Figure 4, we show the overall architecture of our system by dividing its major components into two main layers: *News Layer* and *Sentiment Layer*.

In the *News* layer, we aggregate the volume of the news for a topic into a time series, which will be further analyzed to detect news events. To detect a news event and extract its features we perform a deconvolution of news volume time series (or its fragment).

The *Sentiments* layer aggregates sentiments over time for a specific topic, and detects interesting changes, which can be contradictions, outbursts of sentiments' volume, or other situations.

4.1 Detecting Impacting Events

As we already noted, not every kind of publications outbursts is caused by external news. For instance, "endogenous critical" and "expected impacting" events may produce a similar response in social media, yet only the latter one is relevant to our study. Moreover, not every kind of news dynamics has an impact on sentiment, so we want to distinguish them at a fine level of detail.

Following these observations, we introduce our model for social media and news dynamics. We start with the description of basic social media responses and our representation of event importance. Then, we introduce a novel method to extract important properties of events, which is based on deconvolution, and propose methods to estimate the parameters for this process.

4.1.1 Modeling News Dynamics

We model the observed news dynamics (frequency of publications) as a response of social media to external stimuli. We represent the output as a convolution of two functions: the news events importance sequence and the media response function:

$$n(t) = \int_{-\infty}^{+\infty} mrf(\tau)\cdot e(t-\tau)d\tau \tag{6}$$

where $mrf(t)$ is the media response function (in general, decaying), and $e(t)$ is the actual event sequence, which is unobserved. We depict these functions in Figure 1, bottom.

However, in order to recover the original event sequence, we need to perform a deconvolution of news frequency time series, for which we should know the exact shape of $mrf(t)$. To model the behavior of media, we propose using a family of normalized decaying functions, which have the aggregated volume equal to 1.0 and which are defined on $t > 0$ using the Heaviside step function $h(t)$. For instance, these functions can be *linear*, *hyperbolic* or *exponential*, as demonstrated in Figure 5 and formalized below.

$$\text{linear} \qquad mrf(t) = \left(\frac{2}{\tau_0} - \frac{2t}{\tau_0^2}\right) h(t)h(\tau_0 - t) \tag{7}$$

$$\text{hyperbolic} \qquad mrf(t) = h(t)\frac{\alpha-1}{\tau_0}\left(\frac{t+\tau_0}{\tau_0}\right)^{-\alpha} \tag{8}$$

$$\text{exponential} \qquad mrf(t) = \frac{1}{\tau_0}e^{-t/\tau_0}h(t) \tag{9}$$

We note, that linear response has the shortest effect and hyperbolic response has the longest effect on time series if we consider comparable values of decay time τ_0, which takes on a role similar to the half-life of radiation decay.

We consider decaying response functions, because news events become obsolete and cease being published very soon after their appearance. Another possible explanation for this phenomenon is the saturation of content providers: the likelihood (the temporal rate) of news publication in the absence of events activity is inversely dependent on the number of news, which have been previously published. Moreover, the shapes of response functions convey additional information regarding impact and expectability of events, and also reveal properties of the media.

Linear Response (7). In the case of a linear response, the probability of publishing on an event linearly decreases with time, and the media cease publishing after a finite cutoff time τ_0. Linear response is characterized by a constant rate of content generation, and results in nearly linear dynamics of news volume for spike event shapes. We are interested in evaluating it since this kind of dynamics was observed by [1] for event buildups.

Exponential Response (9). For the exponential response, the rate of decline is proportional to the current probability value at any moment, hence the decay is initially more rapid than the linear, but becomes less pronounced towards the end, with the probability reaching 0 in an infinite time.

Hyperbolic Response (8). In the case of hyperbolic (power law) response, the probability follows a more pronounced decay compared to exponential (the decay rate is usually quadratic to the current value). It decreases very rapidly when the time τ is small, but has a heavy tail afterwards. Here, parameters $\alpha > 1$ and $\tau_0 > 0$ control the sharpness of a response. The hyperbolic response is very interesting since its amplitude can reach infinity in a constant time (unlike the exponential) and in the case of $\alpha \approx 1$ its rate of decline is proportional to the square of its current value.

Symmetric and Asymmetric Responses. Aside from being impacting or non-impacting, events can be anticipated or unexpected. These properties of events manifest themselves through the observed response of the media. For instance, unexpected events will have no buildup of volume preceding the event (consider earthquakes), and expected non-impacting events will have abrupt decay of volume upon their end (consider football finals). Therefore,

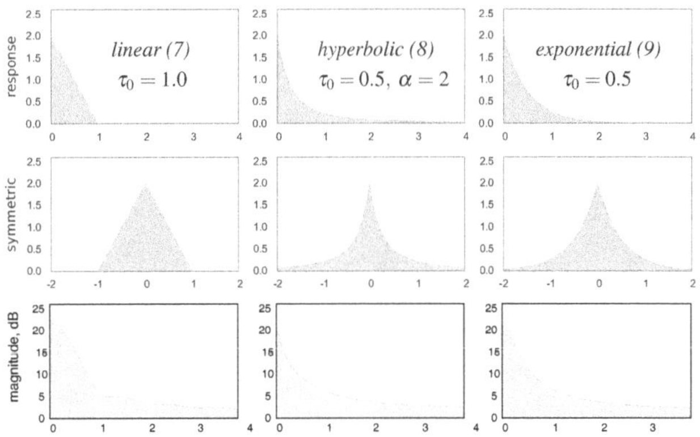

Figure 5: Media response functions and their frequency domain.

response functions for a particular event can be either *asymmetric* (Figure 5, top), featuring only buildup or only decay, or *symmetric*, featuring both sides, not necessarily of the same shape (Figure 5, middle). Both types are important to recognize, since they allow to reason about events semantics.

4.1.2 Modeling Events Importance

We model events by using a piecewise linear approximation of event importance $e(t)$. This model introduces a set of meaningful parameters, that can succinctly describe event importance, namely, *buildup and decay* rates, *longitude* of an event and its *maximum importance* level. We show the most basic shapes of event importance in Figure 1 (bottom) and describe them below. Accordingly, there are rectangular (Event 2) and triangular (Events 1 and 3) models, which can also merge to trapezoid-like shapes (Event 3').

The Rectangular model of $e(t)$ is suitable for long-duration events with roughly constant importance and coverage, like "Olympics". This model is represented using a step function with the constant height of n_0 and the longitude τ_e: $e(t) = n_0, 0 \le t \le \tau_e$.

The Triangular model adds the parameters of buildup a and decay b, when $e(t)$ is of varying importance to mass media during its period. Accordingly, we can represent it using a piecewise linear function, which originates at time $t = 0$, and reverses its direction at $t = t_0$: $e(t) = at, 0 \le t \le t_0$; $\quad e(t) = (a+b)t_0 - bt, t > t_0$.

We show the shapes of the resulting news functions in Figure 6. In this example, we used news events of three different longitudes (τ_e = 0.25, 0.5 and 1.0 day) and selected the parameters of response functions so that $n(t)$ would reach the same amplitude after 0.5 days for an event with a constant importance (as can be seen in the second event). We observe that a varying time length of events in this model results in varying sharpness of news frequency peaks. Correspondingly, short-time events have a shorter period of actuation and long-time events eventually result in the saturation of news media. In all cases, the period of relaxation of news media is mainly characterized by the shape of the corresponding media response function.

According to our model, the height of the event on the event sequence $e(t)$ indicates its importance, while the length describes its longitude. Events can be of constant importance, like those shown in Figure 6 (left side), or of varying importance, shown in Figure 6 (right side). In both cases, the time longitude as well as the maximum importance can be different for different events even for the same topic.

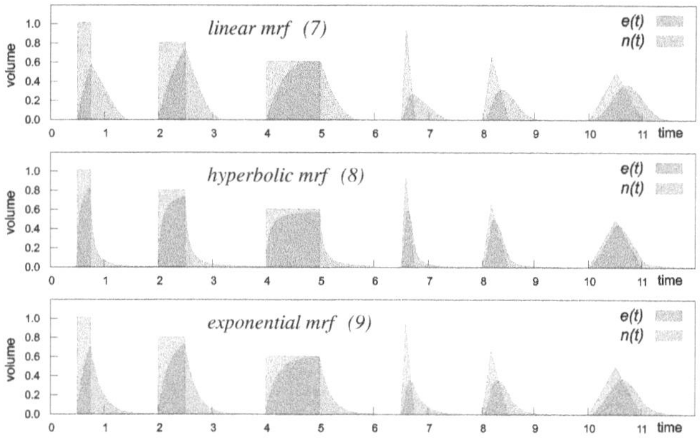

Figure 6: Convolution of rectangular and triangular event models.

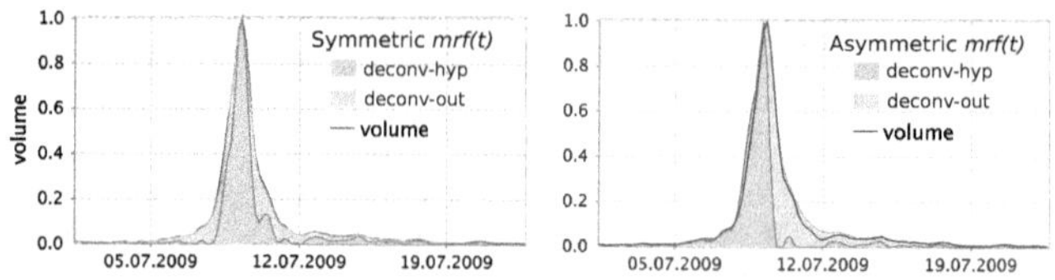

Figure 7: Symmetric (expected) and asymmetric (unexpected) response functions applied to "Solar Eclipse" event from Twitter.

4.1.3 News Deconvolution

Deconvolution is the opposite process to convolution [3]. With this procedure we are able to recreate the original event importance sequence, as shown in Figure 1, bottom. Moreover, deconvolution helps to detect and separate nearby, but distinct events, which may otherwise be considered as a single event due to their overlap.

However, deconvolution can be expressed in the functional form only for a limited number of response functions (e.g. exponential, linear), while our framework is designed to support any kind of finite integrable functions. Therefore, we take an approach to deconvolution, which relies on the frequency domain of the signals, as explained below.

The Convolution theorem states, that the Fourier transformation of a time-domain convolution of two series is equal to the multiplication of their Fourier transformations in the frequency domain:

$$\mathscr{F}\{n(t)\} = \mathscr{F}\{e(t) * mrf(t)\} = \mathscr{F}\{e(t)\} \cdot \mathscr{F}\{mrf(t)\} \qquad (10)$$

According to this equation, for every cyclic frequency ω, we can obtain Fourier coefficients $e(\omega)$ of the original series $e(t)$ by dividing Fourier coefficients of the observed series $n(t)$ by the corresponding coefficients of the response function $mrf(t)$. During this process, we can also remove global trends from the time series by lowering the values of low-frequency components. Finally, we obtain a time-domain representation of $e(t)$ by performing an inverse Fourier transformation:

$$e(t) = \mathscr{F}^{-1}\{e(\omega)\} = \mathscr{F}^{-1}\{n(\omega)/mrf(\omega)\} \qquad (11)$$

In this paper, we use the analytical Fourier representations of the three example response functions considered in our framework, although it is possible to use numerically-computed Fourier coefficients of *any arbitrary* decay function (symmetric or asymmetric).

Our method is also able to distinguish between symmetric and asymmetric $mrf(t)$, and use the appropriate one for deconvolution. For instance, let's consider the differences between the two models for the "Solar Eclipse" event from Twitter, illustrated in Figure 7. In the left part of the figure, we observe that the main event (shown in red) has a duration of one day, and was also discussed the day after (when photos were published). The symmetric deconvolution was able to extract these parameters and correctly match (green color) the observed volume of publications (blue color). For the asymmetric deconvolution, shown on the right, if we consider only the decay part of $mrf(t)$, we end up with the incorrect estimation of event's time and duration and also less correct prediction of the volume (green color, right side).

Deconvolution with small decay parameters is fail-safe and lossless as long as event shapes are not approximated or event importance is not becoming negative. However, only a high level of deconvolution helps to recover the original event importance, and to represent its dynamics using the desired model. Since higher than necessary deconvolution may result in smaller events becoming outcast by a "shade" from their preceding larger neighbors, we need to apply the largest possible, but still adequate level of deconvolution, using the parameter estimation as described below.

4.1.4 Parameters Estimation

A conventional method for estimating parameters of response functions relies on observing event decay shapes under the assumption that events are singular in time (i.e., they can be represented by Dirac's delta function). Parameter estimation in this case can be done by regression parameter fitting, following the peak detection and extraction of their slopes. First, we normalize the ascending or descending slopes of time series and then analyze them using either linear, power-law or exponential regression. Next, we take the average of the extracted parameters across the peaks, weighting them by regression error and level of importance.

Nevertheless, regression fitting can only be achieved for a few known response functions. In order to learn the parameters of *any* response function, we propose to optimize them over the fitness of our model for the entire time series (of news volume for a specific topic). A direct measure of fitness can be computed by averaging fitting errors of piecewise linear regression of event importance. However, this measure only improves with more powerful deconvolution, as more and more events obtain spike shapes, thus defeating our purpose. Therefore, we optimize the parameters using residual deconvolution errors, as follows.

First, we perform a deconvolution of $n(t)$ using a chosen response function with an initial set of parameters. Then, we approximate the resulting time series using a piecewise linear function, obtaining triangular $e(t)$. Following that, we repeat the process of deconvolution in the opposite way: convolving the approximated series with the same response function. Finally, the output is compared to the original time series, and the error of fitting is calculated. If the error of fitting improves by flipping to asymmetric response function, this type becomes chosen. The whole process repeats until the optimal parameters are identified. It is also possible to determine the best response function type for every peak and process the corresponding time interval individually. This choice can be based on the best fitness, or on the preferences of the given media and topic. In this paper, we apply deconvolution to the whole time series, to compare different response functions and the stability of their parameters, leaving per-peak processing for the future.

The proposed method is effective for identifying parameters for any event models and response functions. It is also efficient thanks to a concave error surface, where for small decay times the error is dominated by the event's model approximation, and for large decay times the error is caused by a longer than necessary response. Therefore, we apply gradient descent for estimating parameters.

4.2 Detecting Sentiment Shifts

In this paper, we are interested in sentiment measures that are sensitive to particular kinds of sentiment changes and that can also be correlated with events. Nevertheless, not many studies propose a suitable measure for opinion shifts, which can be analyzed coherently with the news time series in order to extract correlations. The particular methods which can be adopted to our problem are *sentiment volume* [10] and *contradiction level* [15], discussed below.

4.2.1 Sentiment Extraction

We extract texts for a particular topic using the Apache Lucene index, by querying it for documents that contain a given topic's keywords. Analyzed texts are first cleaned from markup, such as urls, user names, hashtags, and quotes in the case of tweets. Then, we use the SentiStrength algorithm [11, 10] to extract sentiment polarities of texts. Obtained sentiment labels S are scaled to be in the range [-1;1], and later aggregated as real values.

4.2.2 Sentiment Volume

Thelwall et al. [10] evaluate how twitter sentiment and its volume are changing before and after news events. By analyzing the peaks in sentiment, they show that the volume of negative sentiment is increasing just before an event, while there is an increase of positive sentiment at the event's peak intensity. Their results indicate that external events usually lead to changes in sentiment and, more importantly, increase the contradiction level. One more observation made by the same authors is that the changes in sentiment are particularly small, making it necessary to apply more sophisticated methods for shift detection and properly align these small fluctuations with the underlying news time series.

Sentiment Volume is defined as the amount, or the sum of sentiments of the same polarity, expressed within a specified time interval. It captures bursts of a particular opinion polarity, e.g., *positive*:

$$s(t) = \sum_{i=1}^{n} S_i^+(t), \quad \text{or} \quad s(t) = |S_i^+|(t) \tag{12}$$

4.2.3 Contradiction Level

Another suitable measure for sentiment shifts is the sentiment contradiction level [14, 15], which is based on the first statistical moments of sentiment values. The intuition behind this measure is that when the average sentiment value μ_S is close to zero, while the sentiment variance σ_S^2 is high, then the polarization of sentiments is high, indicating contradiction and diversity. Combining μ_S and σ_S^2 in a single formula, the authors propose the following measure for contradictions:

$$s(t) = \frac{\vartheta \cdot \sigma_S^2}{\vartheta + \mu_S^2} W(n) \tag{13}$$

where n is the number of sentiments, $\vartheta \neq 0$ is the normalizing constant, and W is a weight function that takes into account the significance of sentiment statistics involved in the calculation [15]. A distinct property of this measure is that it detects both changes of sentiment polarity as well as temporary shifts of sentiments.

4.3 Correlating News and Sentiments

We observe that different sentiment and news measures require different correlation methods $\rho(s,n,\delta)$, which also consider a time lag between the time series, δ. In the case of continuous time series, which usually deviate around their average values, we can use the Pearson cross-correlation coefficient, which is defined as the normalized covariance of two time series:

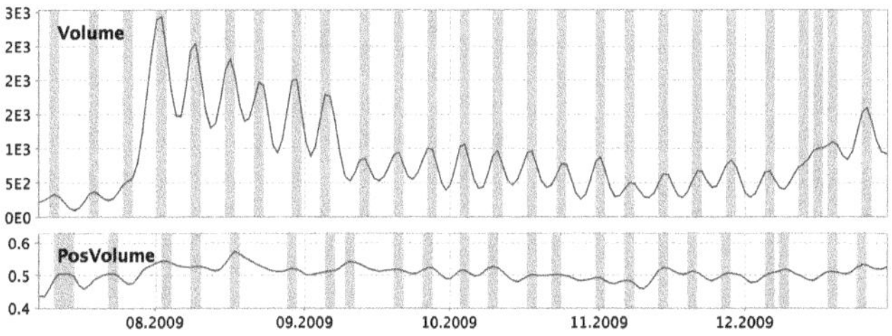

Figure 8: Correlated news and sentiment series from Twitter for movie "Hangover", where bursts are extracted using deconvolution.

$$\rho(s,n,\delta) = \frac{Cov[n(t), s(t+\delta)]}{\sigma_s \sigma_n} \tag{14}$$

However, Pearson correlation is intended to determine a linear dependency between variables, which is hardly observable for bursty time series such as unexpected events or sentiment contradiction. Such time series do not have a definite average level, around which the movement is happening. Instead, their values are outbursting from the minimum level at some points in time. This behavior requires a special correlation technique, which takes as input only the bursty points within a specified time interval. Let's assume that sets of bursts for sentiment and news are denoted as S_t and N_t respectively. Following this, any kind of binary similarity measure can be applied, for example *cosine similarity* ρ_C or *Jaccard coefficient* ρ_J:

$$\rho_C(s,n,\delta) = \frac{|S_{t+\delta} \cap N_t|}{||S_{t+\delta}||\,||N_t||}, \quad \rho_J(s,n,\delta) = \frac{|S_{t+\delta} \cap N_t|}{|S_{t+\delta} \cup N_t|} \tag{15}$$

In the above equations, intersecting bursts are determined according to some proximity region ξ, and in addition to counting the number of overlapping bursts, we can apply burst weighting, for example based on their magnitude.

While we can determine bursts of sentiments using simple methods, events require more robust methods, as can be seen in Figure 8, where a group of two (out of three) events in the right part of the time series are located on the monotonic slope of $n(t)$, and are not detectable by thresholds, or by derivative tracking. Remarkably, deconvolution can recover these and other "hidden" events and result in a more accurate correlation. It is also crucial to consider the level of event importance, obtained after the deconvolution, rather than the original news volume, as can be seen in Figure 2, where iPad 1 and iPad 2 announcements had different importance to people (red) but almost the same volume (blue) due to a trend. Thus, we select $n(t)$ peaks by their level of importance, that yields the highest correlation.

We also consider that sentiment changes may be preceded or followed by news events with some time lag. In order to align the two sequences, we have to determine this time lag, which is different for different topics and media. Here again, deconvolution helps identifying correct event timings and, therefore, time lags. It shifts peaks backwards in time to the extent determined by a response function and event dynamics. The optimal time lag Δ can be determined by maximizing the cross-correlation coefficient over a range of positive (reaction) and negative (anticipation) time lags δ:

$$\Delta = \underset{\delta}{\operatorname{argmax}} \left[\rho(s,n,\delta)\right] \tag{16}$$

An unconstrained optimization is inefficient, since it requires computing correlation for every parameter δ, whereas a heuristic optimization can produce wrong results, when news time sequence is a repetitive process. To overcome this, the absolute time lag must not exceed the first maximum of the news autocorrelation function.

5. EXPERIMENTAL EVALUATION

The main goal of our experimental evaluation is to study the properties of the real data and evaluate the proposed and existing models and their assumptions. We analyze the news dynamics and evaluate our models on several social media datasets with different characteristics. The agenda of our evaluation is the following:

- Compare accuracy to previous models;
- Evaluate the proposed response dynamics;
- Check the correlation of events and sentiments;

Our *Meme* dataset [6] consists of the top 100 meme time series[2] and approximately 500 peaks, that represent various events of endogenous nature, which circulated in the blogosphere in the period from August 2008 to May 2009. While some of the analyzed memes have a connection to real news events, the largest part of them are just sticky phrases gaining popularity from time to time. The analyzed time series have a granularity of aggregation of 4 hours and varying lengths (typically, one month).

For our *Twitter* dataset, we selected 30 topics[3], which featured the most prominent events for the period of half a year, from June 2009 till December 2009. The dataset contained approximately 7 million tweets in total and over 400 peaks during the events. We extracted time series of volume and sentiments using a 1 day aggregation. Twitter data has very different properties when compared to the output of blogs or news media. First, this platform has a distinct bias towards current events and temporal activity of users. So usually there is no accumulated interest, since any activity fades out to zero after a short time. Second, there are different types of dynamics present at the same time: *daily activity* and *trending activity*. Whereas the first one is largely driven by work schedules in different time zones, the second one demonstrates a more clear pattern of event interest and is our main subject.

To compare the accuracy of our models for different media, we perform news volume deconvolution using automatically extracted parameters (as described in Section 4.1.4), and then quantify the accuracy of fitting in a way that is comparable across different time series (and across different peak heights). Accordingly, errors in fitness are measured as RMSE for every peak, and then normalized by its height, so that the results can be averaged and compared across peaks.

5.1 Evaluation of Meme Dataset

Taking into account our findings in Section 3.2, we used dynamics equation (1) to predict the values of every peak by applying it on the volume and time accumulated since the peak's start time. Considering the linear form for the imitation factor expressed as $f(x) = a + bx$, and $\delta(t) = t^{-\alpha}$ ($\alpha > 1$), we have:

$$\begin{aligned} \frac{dx}{a+bx} &= ct^{-\alpha}dt \\ \frac{1}{b}\, ln\,|a+bx| &= \frac{c}{1-\alpha}t^{1-\alpha} + C \\ f(x) = a+bx &\sim exp(\frac{bc}{1-\alpha}t^{1-\alpha}) \\ n(t) = \frac{dx}{dt} &\sim exp(\frac{bc}{1-\alpha}t^{1-\alpha})t^{-\alpha} \end{aligned} \quad (17)$$

In Figure 9 (a) we demonstrate an example prediction of this model in the case when $\alpha = 3.3$ and $bc = 3.3$. We observe that the first peak's buildup and decay can be matched using these parameters only approximately, while the shapes of all the subsequent peaks cannot be matched at all.

[2]The complete meme dataset is available at: http://www.memetracker.org/

[3]The list of selected topics is available upon request.

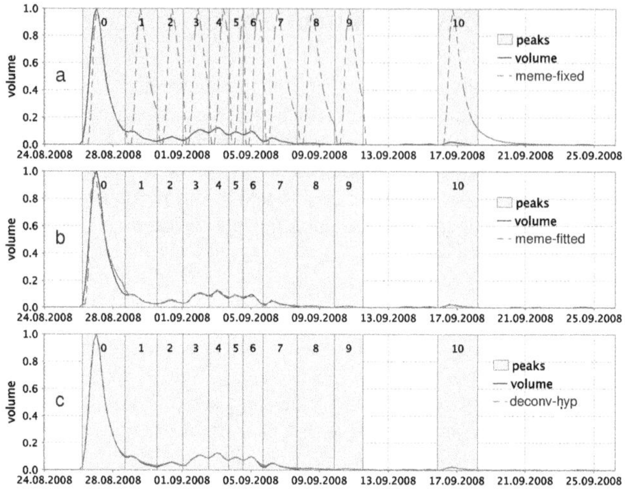

Figure 9: "No way, no how, no McCain!" meme from [6]. Peaks are approximated by meme model [6] using fixed (a) and fitted (b) parameters, and by deconvolution using fixed parameters (c).

Fitting equation (1) to individual peaks using *least squares* regression yields much better accuracy for small peaks (Figure 9 (b)), but does not match the sharpest peaks, where buildups and decays seem to require different model parameters. In the above experiment, fitting employed four parameters, which were independent among peaks and had different values for every peak. Two of these parameters are effectively stretching the model to accommodate real data: base level (a) indicates the volume accumulated before the peak, and scale (b) serves the purpose of fitting the peak's height, to counterweight the normalization effect caused by dividing on volume in equation (1). Normalizing the predicted volume over the top 100 time series (the concurrency factor) did not yield any improvement neither for fixed, nor for individually fitted peak parameters. This can either indicate that the time series evolve independently of each other, or that the top 100 time series are not sufficient to cover the whole publishing activity.

Overall, we observed an irregularity of meme model's parameters for different peaks of the same time series. In contrast, our deconvolution model uses a single set of parameters for the entire time series, which are automatically estimated by performing a peak slope regression (using a single or multiple peaks). Figure 9 (c) demonstrates the output of a hyperbolic deconvolution model, which fits the time series consistently across all peaks. The output in this case is the time series, constructed by performing an inverse process of convolution over the deconvolution-estimated time series of event importance.

5.1.1 Evaluation of Accuracy

First, we compare the observed error distributions between the meme and hyperbolic deconvolution models in Figure 10. A hyperbolic deconvolution model was chosen as the closest match to a meme model regarding the predicted shapes of peak slopes (refer to Equation 17). Moreover, our model used triangular $e(t)$ shapes, automatically extracted using a deconvolution with parameters $\tau = 0.8$ days and $\alpha = 2.0$, fixed for all time series. The deconvolution model reached an average RMSE of 0.11 with the standard deviation of 0.09. The meme model demonstrated an average RMSE of 0.22 with standard deviation of 0.09. Taking into account the artifacts of data aggregation, noise and deviation of peak starting times, the error level of 0.2 can still be considered as acceptable

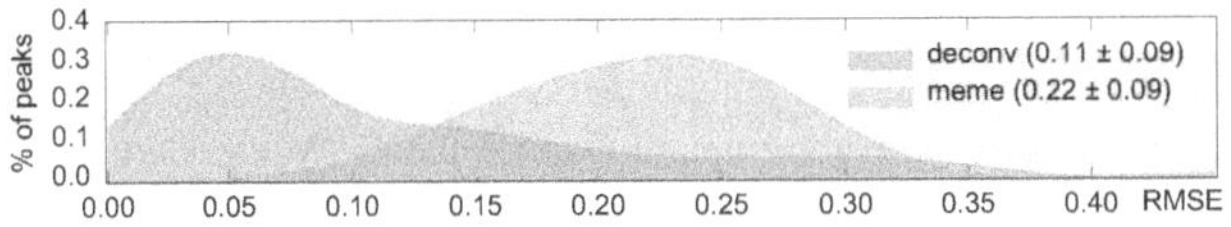

Figure 10: Accuracy of meme (fit) and deconv (fixed) models.

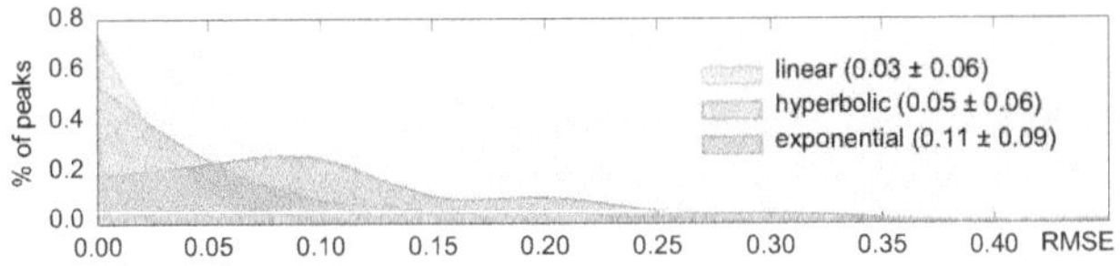

Figure 11: Deconvolution models accuracy for Meme dataset.

for the meme model. Nevertheless, it fitted more than half of the evaluated peaks with larger errors than our model, which used a single set of parameters for *all* time series.

We note that choosing smaller decay times results in smaller differences between event importance (deconvolved volume) and volume. On the other hand, this introduces more errors to the estimation of $e(t)$ shapes (performed by piecewise linear regression) and therefore results in larger errors for the output approximation. Choosing larger decay times, can also induce approximation errors due to the omission of smaller peaks from $e(t)$. Nevertheless, the output of our model is stable with respect to parameter variation (as demonstrated by our experiment in Figure 10, where fixed parameters still yield a good approximation quality). Thus, it is possible to perform deconvolution using the estimated parameters achieving nearly the same performance as when using the optimal parameters.

The performance of deconvolution models on meme dataset is depicted in Figure 11. We observe that the linear and hyperbolic deconvolution models reached the best accuracies with average errors of 0.03 and 0.05 respectively, and standard deviations of 0.06 (thus, the difference in performance is not significant). However, while the linear model had an average parameter τ of 0.5 (very small), the average parameters τ and α of the hyperbolic model were 0.36 and 2.8 respectively. A more careful evaluation of the estimated parameters reveals that the hyperbolic model has almost the same parameter τ of 0.36 ± 0.03 across all topics in the dataset, but quite different α of 2.8 ± 0.96. A similar pattern is observed for the triangular model, where a single decay parameter τ has values in the range 0.5 ± 0.3. The exponential model demonstrated an average RMSE of 0.11 with standard deviation of 0.09, almost the same to our previous experiment with fixed parameters, but in this case the estimated parameter τ was (on average) equal to 0.65, thus trying to approximate a usually much steeper hyperbolic response. From these observations we conclude that meme data is more likely to have a hyperbolic response pattern. But while the dominance of linear and hyperbolic response functions is clearly visible, their parameters are significantly different from peak to peak.

5.2 Evaluation of Twitter Dataset

We analyzed 30 time series from Twitter using $1d$ aggregations. The results of our evaluation, presented in Figure 12, demonstrate a good performance for the linear model, though the average parameter τ was 2.5 with a deviation of 0.9, indicating that a rather high fraction of peaks had small τ. Since in our dataset we usually have a small number of samples per peak (8-10), it is not possible to fully verify the hypothesis of the linear model. The obtained results only prove that most events have a fast rise and drop of importance around their peaks. The two other models (hyperbolic and exponential) have more powerful estimated decay parameters than the linear model but also larger errors ($\alpha = 2.4 \pm 0.5$, $\tau_h = 1.3 \pm 0.6$ and $\tau_e = 1.5 \pm 0.7$). Finally, we observe that both models encountered large variations of the error, probably indicating the existence of *different* kinds of response dynamics for topics or different response parameters for various events during the same time series.

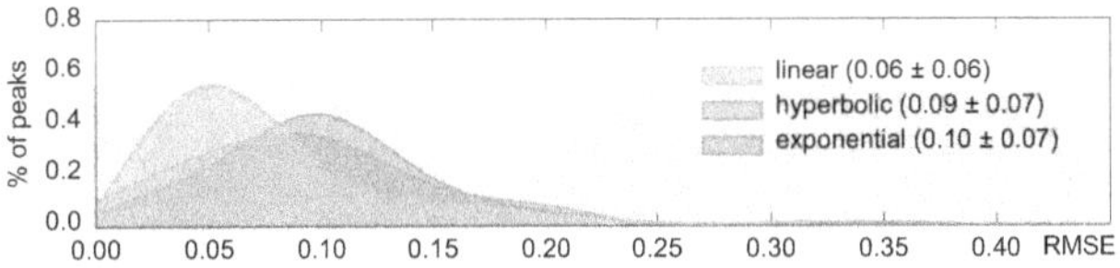

Figure 12: Deconvolution models accuracy for Twitter dataset.

5.3 News and Sentiments Correlation

In this section we evaluate correlation between sentiment shifts and events, where events are extracted with the help of deconvolution, and sentiment shifts are determined using the measures of positive and negative sentiment volumes $s^+(t)$ and $s^-(t)$, and sentiment contradiction level $C(t)$.

To evaluate the correlations, we picked 22 out of 30 selected topics in our Twitter dataset, which contained a sufficient number of events, and were suitable for computing bursts correlation. The results of our evaluation are summarized in Table 2, where for each time series and sentiment measure we present the values of Cosine similarity ρ_C and time lag Δ of the best correlation. Additionally, we report the best-fit response dynamics "Type", and the average number of overlapping bursts "Num". We do not report Jackard coefficient ρ_J, since for highly-overlapping sets it shows the same behavior as ρ_C.

We observe that negative sentiments demonstrate the highest overall correlation, followed by contradictions and positive sentiments. Taking a closer look at the data, we see that positive sentiments are usually preceding the expected events (correlated with a negative lag), whereas negative sentiments are observed after or during these events (positive lag). For instance, such behavior is observed in our table for events surrounding the movie sequels "Hangover", "Ice Age" and "Harry Potter", which had positive expectations before (during) the event, and negative sentiment afterwards. Anticipated events like "LCROSS", "Super Bowl" or "Leica" also have positive expectations, but in this time connected to events. Another group of anticipated events, like "CERN LHC", "Beer Summit", "Aquila Summit" and "Transformers" features negative expectations and positive outcomes. Interestingly, heavily promoted events like new camera announcement for "Leica" on 09.09.2009, or availability of "Google Wave", have initially positive sentiments, but then receive a mixture of controversial opinions during their peaking intervals. In addition, some of unexpected events, like "Iran Election", "Iraq", "Obama", "Gmail Blackout" seen a bump of negative sentiments after their appearance, while Michael Jackson death flipped initially controversial (negative and positive) sentiments to positive.

Overall, we observe that the particular types of sentiment changes are connected to the particular behavior of events, and the same is true for their news dynamics. While different topics and media can be better described with different response functions, unusual events can still occur in the course of time, affecting sentiments in their own way. Therefore, it makes sense to organize the dependency modeling component to operate at the level of events, rather than topics. This component still needs to monitor correlations for each topic, but this time filtering the events according to their type and particular characteristics, before trying to detect the relevant sentiment shifts in their proximity.

Topic Name	Type	Num	Contradiction		PosVolume		NegVolume	
Measures			ρ_C	*lag*	ρ_C	*lag*	ρ_C	*lag*
Hangover	lin	20	0.68	0.0	0.65	0.0	0.60	2.0
Ice Age	exp	22	0.58	0.6	0.66	-1.0	0.65	1.6
Harry Potter	exp	13	0.42	1.7	0.57	0.0	0.45	1.7
LCROSS	hyp	12	0.65	-0.9	0.73	-1.5	0.70	-1.4
CERN LHC	hyp	21	0.68	1.0	0.61	1.0	0.54	-1.4
NASA	hyp	6	0.67	-1.5	0.72	1.5	0.74	-1.5
Michael Jackson	hyp	14	0.54	-1.3	0.49	1.5	0.51	-1.1
Eclipse	hyp	6	0.67	-1.4	0.42	2.1	0.50	1.9
Swine Flu	exp	19	0.58	0.6	0.59	0.0	0.56	-0.5
Barack Obama	hyp	17	0.60	-1.6	0.55	0.0	0.47	0.6
Iran Election	hyp	17	0.51	-0.5	0.47	0.0	0.53	1.6
Iraq	hyp	22	0.61	-1.6	0.58	-1.6	0.74	0.6
Follow Friday	lin	20	0.83	-1.3	0.62	0.7	0.75	-1.4
"Aquila Summit"	exp	30	0.79	0.5	0.83	0.9	0.96	-0.5
"Beer Summit"	hyp	6	0.71	0.8	0.62	0.9	0.71	-0.8
Transformers	exp	16	0.56	-1.8	0.58	0.6	0.51	-1.9
Facebook	hyp	15	0.60	-1.2	0.50	0.8	0.56	-1.3
TwitterPeek	hyp	6	0.72	-1.3	0.72	0.0	0.77	0.0
Leica	hyp	22	0.70	0.0	0.60	-1.7	0.80	-0.5
Gmail	hyp	20	0.71	0.6	0.55	-1.9	0.67	0.6
Super Bowl	lin	20	0.71	0.0	0.53	-1.6	0.71	0.0
Google Wave	hyp	11	0.50	0.5	0.67	-1.0	0.51	0.5

Table 2: Correlation between sentiment shifts and events in Twitter.

6. CONCLUSIONS

Our evaluation of news dynamics and their impact on sentiments is the first systematic work in this direction, which employs a thorough and principled modeling of news distribution in various media and studies news interaction with sentiments. We develop a novel model of news event dynamics, which allows to capture meaningful and important characteristics of news events. Our model can accommodate various response functions, suitable for different cases, which should not necessarily be expressed as a differential equation, but can be learned from the data. The results obtained by applying our methods to different real datasets confirm their robustness and universality. Nevertheless, they also reveal that we need to address several more major challenges.

First, we observe that while different media have preferences for particular response dynamics, these are often determined by event types and topics. Thus, we need to extend our method of news volume deconvolution so that it will automatically determine the best model for every particular event and process the corresponding time interval individually. The choice of the suitable deconvolution model can be based on the (learned) preferences of the given media and topic, but should also take model fitness into account. Above all, this involves a refinement of the events importance model and development of a robust and precise deconvolution optimization strategy.

We also observe the existence of different parameters of response dynamics for various events even during the same topic time series. Each of these events has a different importance, and also a different impact on sentiments, suggesting that it is possible to predict sentiment changes. In order to do that, we need to take into account the type of response dynamics (*mrf*) in addition to the event's importance level, creating a more elaborate causality model. Still, predicting the types of these possible changes requires building a database of event and sentiment shift profiles, and constructing a classifier model based on these features. We aim at creating such a dataset as our next step towards the final solution.

Finally, we speculate that sentiment shifts may be caused by events on related topics, in addition to events on the same topic. This leads to the necessity for a more advanced correlation and causality modeling, in order to predict sentiment shifts across related topics.

7. REFERENCES

[1] S. Asur, B. A. Huberman, G. Szabó, and C. Wang. Trends in social media: Persistence and decay. In *ICWSM*, 2011.

[2] R. Crane and D. Sornette. Robust dynamic classes revealed by measuring the response function of a social system. *Proceedings of the National Academy of Sciences*, 105(41):15649–15653, 2008.

[3] K. Gaikovich. *Inverse problems in physical diagnostics*. Nova Science Publishers, 2004.

[4] X. Hu, L. Tang, J. Tang, and H. Liu. Exploiting social relations for sentiment analysis in microblogging. In *WSDM*, pages 537–546, New York, NY, USA, 2013. ACM.

[5] J. Lehmann, B. Gonçalves, J. J. Ramasco, and C. Cattuto. Dynamical classes of collective attention in twitter. In *WWW*, pages 251–260, 2012.

[6] J. Leskovec, L. Backstrom, and J. Kleinberg. Meme-tracking and the dynamics of the news cycle. In *KDD*, pages 497–506, New York, NY, USA, 2009. ACM.

[7] Y.-R. Lin, D. Margolin, B. Keegan, and D. Lazer. Voices of victory: A computational focus group framework for tracking opinion shift in real time. In *WWW PE Track*, 2013.

[8] D. Sornette, F. Deschâtres, T. Gilbert, and Y. Ageon. Endogenous versus exogenous shocks in complex networks: An empirical test using book sale rankings. *Phys. Rev. Lett.*, 93:228701, Nov 2004.

[9] I. Subasic and C. Castillo. Investigating query bursts in a web search engine. *Web Intelligence and Agent Systems*, 11(2):107–124, 2013.

[10] M. Thelwall, K. Buckley, and G. Paltoglou. Sentiment in twitter events. *JASIST*, 62(2):406–418, 2011.

[11] M. Thelwall, K. Buckley, G. Paltoglou, D. Cai, and A. Kappas. Sentiment in short strength detection informal text. *JASIST*, 61(12):2544–2558, 2010.

[12] M. Tsytsarau, S. Amer-Yahia, and T. Palpanas. Efficient sentiment correlation for large-scale demographics. In *SIGMOD*, pages 253–264, 2013.

[13] M. Tsytsarau and T. Palpanas. Survey on mining subjective data on the web. *Data Mining and Knowledge Discovery, Special Issue on 10 Years of Mining the Web*, pages 1–37, 2011. ISSN 1384-5810.

[14] M. Tsytsarau, T. Palpanas, and K. Denecke. Scalable discovery of contradictions on the web. In *WWW*, 2010.

[15] M. Tsytsarau, T. Palpanas, and K. Denecke. Scalable detection of sentiment-based contradictions. In *DiversiWeb Workshop, WWW 2011, Hyderabad, India*, 2011.

[16] A. Tumasjan, T. O. Sprenger, P. G. Sandner, and I. M. Welpe. Predicting elections with twitter: What 140 characters reveal about political sentiment. In W. W. Cohen and S. Gosling, editors, *ICWSM*. The AAAI Press, 2010.

[17] F. Wu and B. A. Huberman. Novelty and collective attention. *Proceedings of the National Academy of Sciences*, 104(45):17599–17601, 2007.

Differentially Private Network Data Release via Structural Inference

Qian Xiao
NGS
National University of Singapore, Singapore
xiaoqian@nus.edu.sg

Rui Chen
Dept. of Computer Science
Hong Kong Baptist University, Hong Kong
ruichen@hkbu.edu.hk

Kian-Lee Tan
NGS and School of Computing
National University of Singapore, Singapore
tankl@comp.nus.edu.sg

ABSTRACT

Information networks, such as social media and email networks, often contain sensitive information. Releasing such network data could seriously jeopardize individual privacy. Therefore, we need to sanitize network data before the release. In this paper, we present a novel data sanitization solution that infers a network's structure in a differentially private manner. We observe that, by estimating the connection probabilities between vertices instead of considering the observed edges directly, the noise scale enforced by differential privacy can be greatly reduced. Our proposed method infers the network structure by using a statistical *hierarchical random graph* (HRG) model. The guarantee of differential privacy is achieved by sampling possible HRG structures in the model space via Markov chain Monte Carlo (MCMC). We theoretically prove that the sensitivity of such inference is only $O(\log n)$, where n is the number of vertices in a network. This bound implies less noise to be injected than those of existing works. We experimentally evaluate our approach on four real-life network datasets and show that our solution effectively preserves essential network structural properties like degree distribution, shortest path length distribution and influential nodes.

Categories and Subject Descriptors

K.6.5 [**Management of Computing and Information Systems**]: Security and Protection

Keywords

Network data; differential privacy; structural inference

1. INTRODUCTION

Information networks are invaluable assets for exploratory data analysis in a wide range of real-life applications. For instance, online social networks (e.g., Facebook and Twitter) are studied by sociologists to understand human social relationships; co-author networks are explored to analyze the degree and patterns of collaboration between researchers; voting and election networks are used to expose different views in the community; trust networks like Epinions are great resources for personalized recommendations. However, many of such networks contain highly sensitive personal information, such as social contacts, personal opinions and private communication records. To respect the privacy of individual participants in the networks, network data cannot be released for public access and scientific studies without proper "sanitization".

Previously, a great deal of work has investigated *anonymization* techniques [27, 16, 8, 13, 28, 5] to ensure network data privacy. However, it has been shown that anonymization is susceptible to several newly discovered privacy attacks and might lead to further privacy breaches. Recently, *differential privacy* [9] has been proposed to solve such vulnerability. In this paper, we study the problem of releasing network data under this emerging privacy standard. Given a network dataset, our goal is to release its sanitized differentially private version to hide each participant's connections to others while preserving essential structural information to support data analysis.

To ensure differential privacy, the standard technique is to add Laplace noise to query answers. However, network data can be very sensitive to relatively small changes in the network structure. Direct perturbation in the data domain (e.g., adding noise to a subgraph counting query in order to obscure the presence or absence of an edge) normally incurs excessive noise, which makes it impossible to conduct any effective data mining on the sanitized data. An alternative solution is to first project the data to other domains (e.g., the graph spectral domain [25], which is analogous to the classical frequency domain, or some parametric model space that describes the observed network, such as dK-2 series [21, 24]). While this idea is appealing, the resultant data utility of the existing works in this line is still undesirable for many graph mining algorithms. For example, Wang et al. [25] propose to perturb the eigenvalues and eigenvectors of the corresponding adjacency matrix. This approach requires to impose noise of magnitude proportional to $O(\sqrt{n})$, where n is the number of vertices in the input network, and therefore massive noise has to be injected in large real-life network datasets. As another example, the works [21, 24] consider to approximate the original network by the dK-series. To achieve ϵ-differential privacy, the global sensitivity of this scheme is $O(n)$ even for dK-2 series, which also demands excessive noise to be added.

KDD'14, August 24–27, 2014, New York, NY, USA.

ACM 978-1-4503-2956-9/14/08 ...$15.00.
http://dx.doi.org/10.1145/2623330.2623642.

In this paper, we advocate a different approach that can offer better data utility. Broadly, we propose to encode a network's structural information in terms of *connection probabilities* between vertices, rather than the presence or absence of the observed edges. The fundamental advantage of adopting such a perspective is that we can capture the generally understandable and statistically meaningful properties of the network while "diluting" the impact of a single edge. In the context of differential privacy, this means that we can significantly lower the magnitude of noise added to mask the change of a single edge.

In essence, connection probabilities can be estimated by a set of edge-counting queries (i.e., a query that counts the number of edges between two given sets of vertices). Therefore, our problem can be converted to find a strategy that identifies a good set of edge-counting queries in order to truthfully represent a network's structure. This can be done in many possible ways. In particular, in this paper, we use a statistical *hierarchical random graph* (HRG) model [7] for this purpose. This HRG model carefully maps all participants of a network into a hierarchical structure (called a *dendrogram*) and records connection probabilities between any pair of vertices in the network. This allows us to draw a sample model from the model's space, which essentially consists of a set of good edge-counting queries. Moreover, the model itself is paired with a likelihood score, which makes it possible to observe the quality of released data.

Technically, we make the following contributions. Unlike existing studies, we propose to infer a network's structure via connection probabilities. We further identify that the HRG model can be used to encode a network in terms of a set of such connection probabilities. Generating a good HRG under differential privacy requires careful design. We do not directly perturb the best-fitting HRG of the input network (i.e., the HRG generated by the non-private algorithm), but rather, we infer the HRG by learning in the entire HRG model space and sampling an HRG by a Markov chain Monte Carlo (MCMC) method while satisfying differential privacy. Given a sampled HRG, we propose a carefully designed thresholding strategy coupled with the Erdős-Rényi model to calculate the noisy connection probabilities.

We adopt such a methodology for two reasons. First, relying on the best-fitting HRG itself will incur a high sensitivity. Changing even one edge in the network may result in a great number of changes in both the dendrogram's structure and the set of its associated connection probabilities. This is undesirable since it may alter many of the HRG's parameters in the worst case. In contrast, we design an MCMC method to iteratively learn a reasonably good HRG from the entire HRG space. By construction, with a single edge difference, only one probability in the HRG would be influenced. Second, it is non-trivial to sample a good HRG in our setting because it is computationally challenging to compute the scores of all possible HRGs even for a small network. It can be seen that there are a total of $(2n-3)!! \approx \sqrt{2}(2n)^{n-1}e^{-n}$ possible dendrograms for a network with n vertices. Hence, it is computationally infeasible to directly apply the exponential mechanism. We side-step this problem by using an MCMC method, which is in a similar spirit to the idea in [23]. However, our problem and challenges are quite different from those in [23]. Our goal is to publish the entire graph, *not* frequent subgraphs. A direct consequence is that we have to harness the large sensitivity in our problem, while it is always 1 in [23].

From the perspective of utility, we rigorously prove that the sensitivity of our proposed approach is $O(\log n)$ for fitting the dendrogram structure, which reaps the benefit of preserving good data utility in theory. We conduct extensive experiments on four real-life datasets to evaluate the effectiveness of our solution. We demonstrate that our approach significantly outperforms the state-of-the-art competitors [24, 25].

2. PRELIMINARIES

In this section, we briefly introduce the hierarchical random graph (HRG) model and differential privacy.

2.1 Hierarchical Random Graph

In this study, we follow the convention to model an input network dataset as a simple undirected graph $G = (V, E)$, where V is the set of vertices and $E \subseteq V \times V$ is the set of edges. Let $A \in \{0,1\}^{n\times n}$ be the adjacency matrix that represents a graph G, where $A_{i,j} = 1$ if there is an edge between vertices i and j in G and $A_{i,j} = 0$, otherwise.

The HRG model is based on the intuition that the connection probability between two vertices depends on their degree of relatedness, which can be modelled mathematically via statistical inference. Specifically, the HRG model represents a graph G in terms of its hierarchical structure and a set of connection probabilities [6, 7]. The hierarchical structure of G in an HRG is captured by a *dendrogram* T, which is a rooted binary tree with n leaf nodes corresponding to the n vertices of G. Each internal node r of T is associated with a probability p_r. For any two vertices i, j of G, their probability of being connected $p_{i,j} = p_r$, where r is their lowest common ancestor in T. Formally, an HRG is defined by a pair $(T, \{p_r\})$.

Let L_r and R_r be the left and right subtrees of r respectively, and n_{Lr} and n_{Rr} be the numbers of leaves in L_r and R_r respectively. Let e_r be the number of edges in G whose endpoints are leaves of each of the two subtrees of r in T. The *likelihood* of an HRG for a given graph G measures how plausible this HRG is to represent G, which can be calculated, by Bayes' theorem, as follows:

$$\mathcal{L}(T, \{p_r\}) = \prod_{r\in T} p_r^{e_r}(1-p_r)^{n_{Lr}n_{Rr}-e_r} \tag{1}$$

For a fixed dendrogram T, the maximum likelihood estimator of $p_r = \frac{e_r}{n_{Lr}\cdot n_{Rr}}$, which is the fraction of potential edges between the leaves of L_r and R_r that actually exist in G. In our scheme, we work with the logarithm of the likelihood (referred to as *log-likelihood* in the sequel):

$$\log \mathcal{L}(T, \{p_r\}) = -\sum_{r\in T} n_{Lr}n_{Rr}h(p_r) \tag{2}$$

where $h(p_r) = -p_r \log p_r - (1-p_r)\log(1-p_r)$ is the Gibbs-Shannon entropy function. Essentially, a dendrogram paired with a higher likelihood is a better representation of the network's structure than those with lower likelihoods. We denote $\log \mathcal{L}(T, \{p_r\})$ by $\log \mathcal{L}(T)$ from now on when no confusion arises.

EXAMPLE 1. *Figure 1(b) and (c) give an example of two possible dendrograms, T_1 and T_2, for an original graph in Figure 1(a). We first calculate the set of $\{p_r\}$ for each*

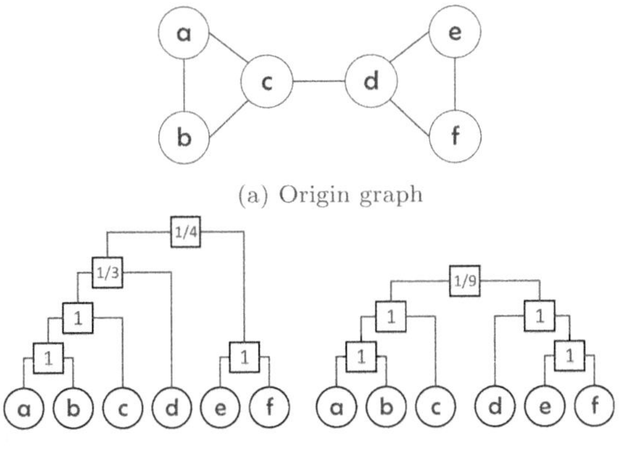

(a) Origin graph

(b) Dendrogram T_1 (c) Dendrogram T_2

Figure 1: An example of the HRG model in [7]

dendrogram. For example, to compute p_{r_2} associated with the root r_2 of T_2, we first obtain the two groups of leaf nodes in r_2's left and right subtrees, that is, $\{a, b, c\}$ and $\{d, e, f\}$. Since there is only one edge between these two sets of leaf nodes (i.e., the edge $\{c, d\}$), we have $e_{r_2} = 1$ and $p_{r_2} = 1/(3*3) = 1/9$. Similarly, we can calculate all $\{p_r\}$ and compute the likelihoods of the dendrogram T_1 and T_2. Specifically, $\mathcal{L}(T_1) = (1/3)(2/3)^2(1/4)^2(3/4)^6 \approx 0.00165$, and $\mathcal{L}(T_2) = (1/9)(8/9)^8 \approx 0.0433$. Since $\mathcal{L}(T_2)$ is much larger than $\mathcal{L}(T_1)$, T_2 is a more plausible hierarchy to describe the original graph. ∎

2.2 Differential Privacy

Differential privacy [9] has emerged as a prevalent privacy model to quantify the notion of "indistinguishability" of *neighboring* databases. The privacy guarantee of differential privacy in the context of network data depends on the interpretation of *neighboring* graphs. In this paper, we define two graphs $G_1 = (V_1, E_1)$ and $G_2 = (V_2, E_2)$ to be *neighbors* if $V_1 = V_2$, $E_1 \subset E_2$ and $|E_1|+1 = |E_2|$. Formally, ϵ-differential privacy for network data is defined below.

Definition 1 (ϵ-Differential privacy). *A randomized algorithm $\mathcal{A}$ is ϵ-differentially private if for any two neighboring graphs G_1 and G_2, and for any output $O \in Range(\mathcal{A})$,*

$$\Pr[\mathcal{A}(G_1) \in O] \leq e^{\epsilon} \times \Pr[\mathcal{A}(G_2) \in O]$$ ∎

Our definition of differential privacy is also known as *edge differential privacy* [12]. Intuitively, it hides the existence of *any* single edge from an adversary. The smaller ϵ is, the better the privacy protection is. Normally, ϵ is a small value (e.g., $\epsilon \leq 1$).

Differential privacy can be achieved by two standard mechanisms, the *Laplace mechanism* [9] and the *exponential mechanism* [18]. Both mechanisms are based on the concept of *global sensitivity* of a function f. For any two neighboring graphs G_1 and G_2, the global sensitivity of a function $f : G \to \mathbb{R}^d$ is defined as $\Delta f = \max_{G_1, G_2} \|f(G_1) - f(G_2)\|_1$.

The Laplace mechanism is mainly used for queries which return real values. It adds properly calibrated noise to the true answer to a query. More precisely, given a function f and the privacy parameter ϵ, the noise is drawn from a Laplace distribution with the probability density function $p(x|\lambda) = \frac{1}{2\lambda}e^{-|x|/\lambda}$, where $\lambda = \Delta f/\epsilon$.

Theorem 1 (Laplace mechanism [9]). *For any function $f : G \to \mathbb{R}^d$, the mechanism $\mathcal{A}$*

$$\mathcal{A}(G) = f(G) + \langle \texttt{Lap}_1(\frac{\Delta f}{\epsilon}), \ldots, \texttt{Lap}_d(\frac{\Delta f}{\epsilon}) \rangle$$

gives ϵ-differential privacy, where $\texttt{Lap}_i(\frac{\Delta f}{\epsilon})$ are i.i.d Laplace variables with scale parameter $\frac{\Delta f}{\epsilon}$. ∎

The exponential mechanism is mainly used for functions whose outputs are not real numbers. Its general idea is to sample an output O from the output space $\mathcal{O}$ according to a utility function u. It assigns exponentially greater probabilities of being selected to outputs of higher scores so that the final output would be close to the optimum with respect to u. Let the global sensitivity of u be $\Delta u = \max_{O, G_1, G_2} |u(G_1, O) - u(G_2, O)|$.

Theorem 2 (Exponential mechanism [18]). *Given a utility function $u : (G \times \mathcal{O}) \to \mathbb{R}$ for a graph G, the mechanism $\mathcal{A}$ that samples an output O with probability proportional to $\exp(\frac{\epsilon \cdot u(G,O)}{2\Delta u})$ satisfies ϵ-differential privacy.* ∎

3. STRUCTURAL INFERENCE UNDER DIFFERENTIAL PRIVACY

3.1 Overview

Before presenting the details, we first give an overview of our method. Our goal is to release a sanitized network $\widetilde{G}$ that matches the structural properties of the original network G as closely as possible while satisfying ϵ-differential privacy. Our general idea is to identify the hierarchical random graph (HRG) that best fits G and then generate $\widetilde{G}$ from the identified HRG.

Recall that an HRG consists of a dendrogram T and a set of associated probabilities $\{p_r\}$. This means that we need to not only identify a good fitting dendrogram but also calculate its associated probabilities. In this process, we face several major technical challenges: (1) How to find a good dendrogram from a factorial number of candidates while satisfying ϵ-differential privacy, and (2) how to calculate the probabilities that might be dominated by injected noise. We address the first challenge by designing a Markov chain Monte Carlo (MCMC) procedure, which samples a good dendrogram according to its likelihood. We cope with the second challenge by developing an effective thresholding strategy that is backed up by the Erdős-Rényi model. After generating a representative HRG for G, we generate $\widetilde{G}$ by placing edges according to $\{p_r\}$.

3.2 Algorithms

We now formally describe our solution (referred to as *HRG* in the sequel). Our solution is composed of three steps: (1) differentially privately sample a good dendrogram T_{sample} from the entire dendrogram space (Algorithm 1); (2) given the sampled dendrogram T_{sample}, compute the probabilities $\{p_r\}$ associated with T_{sample} (Algorithm 2); (3) generate the sanitized graph according to the identified HRG (Algorithm 3). We divide the total privacy parameter ϵ into 2 portions, ϵ_1 and ϵ_2, each being used in one of the first two

Algorithm 1: Differentially Private Dendrogram Fitting

Input : Input graph G, privacy parameter ϵ_1
Output: Sampled dendrogram T_{sample}

```
1 Initialize the Markov chain by choosing a random starting dendrogram T_0;
2 for each step i of the Markov chain do
3     Randomly pick an internal node r in T_{i-1};
4     Pick a neighboring dendrogram T' of T_{i-1} by randomly drawing a configuration of r's subtrees;
5     Accept the transition and set T_i = T' with probability min(1, exp(ε1/(2Δu)·log L(T')) / exp(ε1/(2Δu)·log L(T_{i-1})));
6 end
7 //when equilibrium is reached
8 return the sampled dendrogram T_sample = T_i;
```

steps. Note that the third step does not require any privacy parameter.

Differentially Private Dendrogram Fitting. Since, for an input graph G with n vertices, each of its dendrograms T is associated with a log-likelihood $\log \mathcal{L}(T)$, which measures its goodness of representing G, a straightforward attempt to achieve differential privacy is to employ the exponential mechanism. Let the utility function be $u(T) = \log \mathcal{L}(T)$. The exponential mechanism samples T with probability proportional to $\frac{\exp(\frac{\epsilon_1}{2\Delta u}\cdot u(T))}{\sum_{T'\in\mathcal{T}} \exp(\frac{\epsilon_1}{2\Delta u}\cdot u(T'))}$, where $\mathcal{T}$ is the entire output space (i.e., the set of all possible dendrograms of G). Unfortunately, this simple idea is computationally infeasible because it requires to enumerate a total of $|\mathcal{T}| = (2n-3)!! \approx \sqrt{2}(2n)^{n-1}e^{-n}$ possible dendrograms. In our solution, we overcome the issue by designing an MCMC process, which simulates the exponential mechanism by a sequence of *local* transitions in $\mathcal{T}$. Our differentially private dendrogram fitting algorithm is summarized in Algorithm 1.

Algorithm 1 is based on the Metropolis algorithm [2]. It starts by choosing an arbitrary dendrogram $T_0 \in \mathcal{T}$ as the initial state of the Markov chain (Line 1). It then iteratively performs the following procedure (Lines 2-6): randomly propose a neighboring dendrogram T' of the dendrogram T_{i-1} in the previous iteration and update the current state in the following way:

$$T_i = \begin{cases} T' & \text{with probability } \alpha \\ T_{i-1} & \text{with probability } 1-\alpha \end{cases}$$

where the acceptance ratio $\alpha = \min(1, \frac{\exp(\frac{\epsilon_1}{2\Delta u}\cdot\log\mathcal{L}(T'))}{\exp(\frac{\epsilon_1}{2\Delta u}\cdot\log\mathcal{L}(T_{i-1}))})$ and Δu is the global sensitivity of the utility function u. We show how to calculate Δu in Section 4.2.

To draw a neighbor T' of T_{i-1} uniformly at random, we first randomly choose an internal node r in T_{i-1} (other than the root) and then permute the three subtrees associated with r to generate two alternative configurations of r's subtrees, as illustrated in Figure 2. One of these two configurations is chosen to be the neighboring candidate T'. Let the state space of this Markov chain be $\mathcal{T}$. It is easy to verify that the transitions based on this permutation scheme are both *reversible* and *ergodic* (i.e., any pair of dendrograms

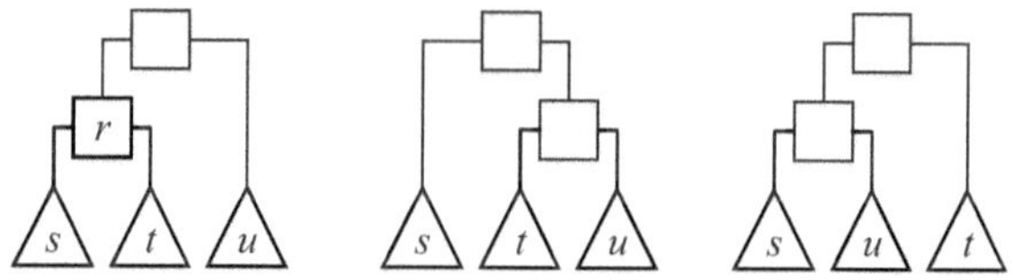

Figure 2: Three configurations of r's subtrees

can be connected by a finite sequence of such transitions). Hence, such an MCMC procedure has a unique stationary distribution after it converges to equilibrium. We run the above Markov chain until equilibrium is reached, which indicates that the desired distribution has already been reached. Therefore, the sampled dendrogram T_{sample} is indeed drawn from the stationary distribution (Line 8).

In practice, there are many approaches to diagnose MCMC convergence. Here we follow the method used in [6, 7]. Specifically, we use the heuristic of the average log-likelihood to judge whether the Markov chain has converged to the stationary distribution. We will elaborate more details of MCMC convergence time in Section 5.2. Additional discussion about the convergence and its mixing time can be found in [6, 7].

Noisy Probability Calculation. In the second step, we calculate the noisy probabilities associated with T_{sample}'s internal nodes. Recall that, for an internal node r, its associated probability $p_r = \frac{e_r}{n_{Lr}\cdot n_{Rr}}$ (see Section 2.1). It is easy to observe that the probabilities of the internal nodes rooted in smaller subtrees (i.e., in lower levels of T_{sample}) are generally more sensitive to Laplace noise injected. Indeed, according to our experiments, the direct application of the Laplace mechanism to these nodes' probabilities results in poor utility. To relieve such negative effects, we propose a carefully designed thresholding strategy coupled with the Erdős-Rényi model, which is presented in Algorithm 2.

The general idea is that if a probability p_r cannot be "reliably" estimated by applying the Laplace mechanism to $\frac{e_r}{n_{Lr}\cdot n_{Rr}}$, we employ the Erdős-Rényi model to approximate the probability. To measure the reliability of a noisy probability, we set up the sentinel λ_b. For an internal node r^* in T_{sample}, λ_b is set to $\frac{1}{\epsilon_2\cdot(n_{Lr^*}\cdot n_{Rr^*})}$ (Line 1), which measures the noise scale of the potential noisy probability $\widetilde{p_{r^*}}$. If λ_b is relatively large with respect to a threshold value τ_1 (that is, the probability cannot be reliably calculated by the Laplace mechanism), we model the subgraph induced by all leaf nodes of the subtree rooted at r^* as an Erdős-Rényi random graph. With this model, the connection probability of *any* pair of vertices in this subgraph is $\frac{e_c(r^*)}{(n_{Lr^*}+n_{Rr^*})(n_{Lr^*}+n_{Rr^*}-1)/2}$, which is later perturbed by the Laplace mechanism (Line 5). Otherwise, we can expect that $\frac{e_r}{n_{Lr}\cdot n_{Rr}}$ still gives a good estimation after adding noise. Hence we directly generate the noisy probability as $\min\{1, \frac{e_{r^*}+\text{Lap}(\frac{1}{\epsilon_2})}{n_{Lr^*}\cdot n_{Rr^*}}\}$ (Line 10) and perform the similar procedure on r^*'s children (Lines 11-14).

In Algorithm 2, we calculate the noisy probabilities in a top-down manner over T_{sample}. During this process, the approximated probabilities based on the Erdős-Rényi model also become less accurate due to added Laplace noise. Here, we would also like to guarantee the accuracy of the perturbed approximated probabilities. For this reason, we in-

Algorithm 2: `CalculateNoisyProb`$(G, T_{sample}, r^*, \epsilon_2)$

Input : Input graph G, sampled dendrogram T_{sample}, privacy parameter ϵ_2, internal node r^*
Output: A vector of noisy probabilities $\{\widetilde{p_r}\}$, where $r \in \{r^*$, all internal nodes below $r^*\}$

1 $\lambda_b = \frac{1}{\epsilon_2 \cdot (n_{L_{r^*}} \cdot n_{R_{r^*}})}$;
2 $\lambda_c = \frac{1}{\epsilon_2 \cdot ((n_{L_{r^*}} + n_{R_{r^*}})(n_{L_{r^*}} + n_{R_{r^*}} - 1)/2)}$;
3 **if** $\lambda_b \geq \tau_1$ and $\lambda_c \geq \tau_2$ **then**
4 $\quad e_c(r^*) \leftarrow$ number of edges in the subgraph induced by all leaf nodes of the subtree rooted at r^*;
5 $\quad \widetilde{p} = \min\{1, \frac{e_c(r^*) + \text{Lap}(\frac{1}{\epsilon_2})}{(n_{L_{r^*}} + n_{R_{r^*}})(n_{L_{r^*}} + n_{R_{r^*}} - 1)/2}\}$;
6 $\quad$ **for** each r in $\{r^*$, all internal nodes below $r^*\}$ **do**
7 $\quad\quad \widetilde{p_r} = \widetilde{p}$;
8 $\quad$ **end**
9 **else**
10 $\quad \widetilde{p}_{r^*} = \min\{1, \frac{e_{r^*} + \text{Lap}(\frac{1}{\epsilon_2})}{n_{L_{r^*}} \cdot n_{R_{r^*}}}\}$;
11 $\quad r_L \leftarrow r^*$'s left child;
12 $\quad r_R \leftarrow r^*$'s right child;
13 $\quad$ `CalculateNoisyProb`$(G, T_{sample}, r_L, \epsilon_2)$;
14 $\quad$ `CalculateNoisyProb`$(G, T_{sample}, r_R, \epsilon_2)$;
15 **end**

troduce another sentinel λ_c (Line 2), which is compared with a threshold value τ_2 to indicate whether the noise scale of the approximated probabilities is acceptable. In summary, we employ the Erdős-Rényi model when (1) the probability cannot be accurately estimated by $\frac{e_{r^*} + \text{Lap}(\frac{1}{\epsilon_2})}{n_{L_{r^*}} \cdot n_{R_{r^*}}}$ (guarded by λ_b), *and* (2) injecting noise to $\frac{e_c(r^*)}{(n_{L_{r^*}} + n_{R_{r^*}})(n_{L_{r^*}} + n_{R_{r^*}} - 1)/2}$ would not seriously affect its accuracy (guarded by λ_c). This explains our condition in Line 3. In this case, the probabilities of r^* and *all* internal nodes below r^* will be approximated by the Erdős-Rényi model (Lines 6-8). In our experiments, we observe that setting $\tau_1 = 0.05$ and $\tau_2 = 0.01$ gives good results over different real-life datasets. Note that the choices of these thresholds are *data-independent*: the tuning of τ_1 and τ_2 only relies on ϵ_2.

Sanitized Graph Generation. With the sampled dendrogram T_{sample} and the set of noisy probabilities $\{\widetilde{p_r}\}$, we generate the sanitized graph as follows (Algorithm 3). For each pair of vertices $i, j \in V$, we find their lowest common ancestor r in T_{sample} (Line 4), and then place an edge between them in $\widetilde{G}$ with probability $\widetilde{p_r}$ (Line 5).

4. PRIVACY ANALYSIS

In this section, we formally analyze the privacy guarantee of our algorithm *HRG*.

4.1 Privacy via Markov Chain Monte Carlo

We first show that the MCMC-based Algorithm 1 can satisfy differential privacy. Recall that the main purpose of applying the MCMC method is to draw a random sample from the desired distribution. Essentially, the standard exponential mechanism for achieving differential privacy is

Algorithm 3: Generate Sanitized Graph $\widetilde{G}$

Input : Input graph G, sampled dendrogram T_{sample}, privacy parameter ϵ_2
Output: Sanitized graph $\widetilde{G}$

1 $r_{root} \leftarrow$ root node of T_{sample};
2 `CalculateNoisyProb`$(G, T_{sample}, r_{root}, \epsilon_2)$;
3 **for** each pair of vertices $i, j \in V$ **do**
4 $\quad$ Find the lowest common ancestor r of i and j in T_{sample};
5 $\quad$ Place an edge in $\widetilde{G}$ between i and j with independent probability $\widetilde{p_r}$;
6 **end**
7 **return** sanitized graph $\widetilde{G}$;

also a method to sample an output $x \in \mathcal{X}$ in the target distribution with probability proportional to $\exp(\epsilon u(x)/2\Delta u)$, where $u(x)$ is the utility function and Δu is its sensitivity. Hence we see that, by matching the stationary distribution of MCMC with the target distribution required by the exponential mechanism, MCMC can be used to realize the exponential mechanism.

In our setting, we set the utility function $u(T)$ of a dendrogram T to be $\log \mathcal{L}(T)$, the *log-likelihood* of T, and the acceptance ratio of MCMC to be $\min(1, \frac{\exp(\frac{\epsilon_1}{2\Delta u} \cdot \log \mathcal{L}(T'))}{\exp(\frac{\epsilon_1}{2\Delta u} \cdot \log \mathcal{L}(T_{i-1}))})$. Therefore, when the Markov chain converges to the stationary distribution π, we indeed draw a sample T from π with the probability mass function:

$$Pr(T) = \frac{\exp(\frac{\epsilon_1}{2\Delta u} \cdot \log \mathcal{L}(T))}{\sum_{T' \in \mathcal{T}} \exp(\frac{\epsilon_1}{2\Delta u} \cdot \log \mathcal{L}(T'))}.$$

This is equivalent to the exponential mechanism which outputs T with probability proportional to $\exp(\frac{\epsilon_1}{2\Delta u} \cdot \log \mathcal{L}(T))$. Therefore, we can conclude that Algorithm 1 satisfies ϵ_1-differential privacy.

We refer interested readers to [23] in which the idea of applying MCMC to achieve the exponential mechanism was first proposed for more discussion about how MCMC's stationary distribution perfectly matches the required distribution under the exponential mechanism.

4.2 Sensitivity Analysis

We now formally analyze the global sensitivity Δu. In this section, we will first derive how the utility function u (i.e., $\log \mathcal{L}(T)$) varies in neighboring databases. After that, we will formulate Δu and show that Δu monotonically increases as n grows. Lastly, we prove that Δu is $O(\log n)$.

In this work, we consider each possible output to be a dendrogram T in the output space $\mathcal{T}$. From the definition of global sensitivity, we have the following.

DEFINITION 2 (GLOBAL SENSITIVITY Δu).

$$\Delta u = \max_{T \in \mathcal{T}, G, G'} |\log \mathcal{L}(T, G') - \log \mathcal{L}(T, G)|$$

where G and G' are neighboring graphs. ■

Intuitively, Δu is the maximum change in the log-likelihood of any dendrogram in the output space if one edge is missing. It is easy to observe that missing one edge will influence exactly one internal node's probability p_r in a dendrogram. Thus, we have:

LEMMA 1. $\Delta u = \max_{r\in\mathcal{T}} |(-n_{Lr}n_{Rr}h(p_r)) - (-n_{Lr}n_{Rr}h(p'_r))|$, *where* $p_r = \frac{e_r}{n_{Lr}n_{Rr}}$ *and* $p_r{}' = \frac{e_r-1}{n_{Lr}n_{Rr}}$. ■

We now analyze how Δu varies as parameters change. Let $N = n_{Lr}\cdot n_{Rr}$. It is easy to see that there are two independent variables in Δu, the number of all possible connections N and the number of the observed edges e_r.

THEOREM 3. *Δu monotonically increases as $n \to +\infty$, and*

$$\Delta u = \log N_{max} + \log(1 + \frac{1}{N_{max}-1})^{N_{max}-1},$$

where $N_{\max} = \frac{n^2}{4}$ when n is even and $N_{\max} = \frac{n^2-1}{4}$ when n is odd. ■

PROOF. To analyze Δu, we first fix N. Let $f(e) = h(p) - h(p')$ and $\Delta u = \max|f(e)|$. Figure 3(a) plots the entropy value $h(p)$ as p varies. Since $f(e)$ has the format of discrete derivative of $h(p)$, we can analyze the monotonicity of $f(e)$ by computing the second order derivative of $h(p)$. We have

$$h''(p) = -\frac{1}{1-p} - \frac{1}{p}$$

It can be observed that $h''(p) < 0$ for all p. Hence $h(p)$ is a concave function and $h'(p)$ (or the acceleration) monotonically decreases. Therefore, $f(e)$ monotonically decreases.

Since $\Delta u = \max|f(e)|$, we just need to derive the extreme values of $f(e)$. Note that $f(e) > 0$ when p is in [0,0.5] and $f(e) < 0$ when p is in (0.5,1]. Hence, $\Delta u = \max(-\min(N\cdot f(e)), \max(N\cdot f(e)))$. Due to the symmetric property of $h(p)$, we can get $\max(f(e)) = -\min(f(e))$. With the monotonic property of $f(e)$, we can derive the value of Δu when $e = 1$ or $e = N_{max}$. Next we fix $e = 1$ and vary N. Let $\Delta u = \max_{N\in[1,N_{max}]} |f(N)|$, where

$$\begin{aligned} f(N) &= 1\cdot\log\frac{1}{N} + (N-1)\cdot\log(1-\frac{1}{N}) - 0 \\ &= -\log N + (N-1)\cdot\log(1-\frac{1}{N}) \end{aligned}$$

The first order derivative of $f(N)$, $f'(N) = \log(1-\frac{1}{N}) < 0$. Hence $f(N)$ is a decreasing function. Since $f(N) \le 0$ for N in $[1, +\infty]$, we conclude that $\Delta u = -\min(f(N)) = -f(N_{\max})$. Hence,

$$\begin{aligned} \Delta u &= \log N_{max} - (N_{max}-1)\cdot\log\frac{N_{max}-1}{N_{max}} \\ &= \log N_{max} + (N_{max}-1)\log(1+\frac{1}{N_{max}-1}) \\ &= \log N_{max} + \log(1+\frac{1}{N_{max}-1})^{N_{max}-1} \end{aligned}$$

This completes the proof. □

Next we show that Δu is $O(\log n)$, where n is the number of vertices in the input network.

THEOREM 4. *The global sensitivity of a dendrogram's log-likelihood, Δu, is $O(\log n)$.* ■

PROOF. Based on Theorem 3, we first analyze the second term of Δu, that is, $\log(1+\frac{1}{N_{max}-1})^{N_{max}-1}$. Let $y = (1+\frac{1}{x})^x$. We have

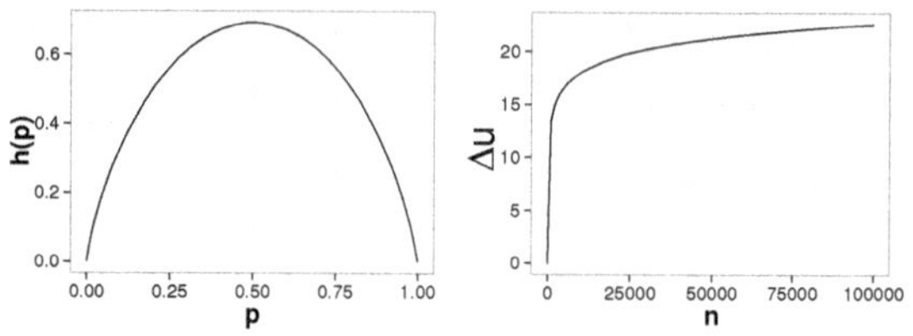

(a) (b)

Figure 3: Gibbs-Shannon entropy and plot of Δu

$$\begin{aligned} \left(1+\frac{1}{x}\right)^x &= 1 + \binom{x}{1}\frac{1}{x} + \binom{x}{2}\frac{1}{x^2} + \binom{x}{3}\frac{1}{x^3} + \cdots + \binom{x}{x}\frac{1}{x^x} \\ &= 1 + 1 + \sum_{k=2}^{n} \frac{1}{k!}\frac{x(x-1)\cdots(x-(k-1))}{x^k} \end{aligned}$$

Since, for each $k \in \{2, 3, ..., x\}$,

$$\frac{1}{k!}\frac{x(x-1)\cdots(x-(k-1))}{x^k} = \prod_{j=1}^{k-1}\left(1-\frac{j}{x}\right)$$

which increases with x, we learn that $y = (1+\frac{1}{x})^x$ also increases with x. As $x \to \infty$, we have $\lim_{x\to\infty}\left(1+\frac{1}{x}\right)^x = e$. Therefore we have:

$$\begin{aligned} \Delta u &= \log N_{max} + \log(1+\frac{1}{N_{max}-1})^{N_{max}-1} \\ &< \log N_{\max} + \log e \le \log\frac{n^2}{4} + 1 \\ &= O(\log n) \end{aligned}$$

This completes the proof. □

Figure 3(b) plots the value of Δu as n increases. We see that Δu increases slowly when n becomes larger. Thus we expect that applying the exponential mechanism in terms of MCMC in this setting would guarantee good data utility even for large-scale networks.

4.3 Privacy via Structural Inference

Finally, we prove that our solution *HRG* is ϵ-differentially private based on the *sequential composition* property.

THEOREM 5 (SEQUENTIAL COMPOSITION [17]). *Let each $\mathcal{A}_i$ provide ϵ_i-differential privacy. A sequence of $\mathcal{A}_i(D)$ over the database D provides $\sum\epsilon_i$-differential privacy.* ■

Taken with the above theorem, we can derive that our scheme ensures ϵ-differential privacy.

THEOREM 6. HRG *satisfies ϵ-differential privacy.* ■

PROOF. We use ϵ_1 in Algorithm 1 for sampling the dendrogram and ϵ_2 in Algorithm 2 for calculating the probabilities associated with the sampled dendrogram. From the analysis in above sections, we learn that Algorithm 1 is ϵ_1-differentially private. In Algorithm 2, we employ the Laplace mechanism to obtain the noisy answers to a set of *counting queries*. Since, by construction of a dendrogram, a single edge change will affect only one counting query by 1, Algorithm 2 is ϵ_2-differentially private. Since Algorithm 3 is based on the differentially private HRG generated by

Table 1: Network dataset statistics

Dataset	#Nodes	#Edges	Max Degree Pair
polblogs	1,224	16,715	(351, 277)
wiki-Vote	7,115	100,762	(1065, 773)
ca-HepPh	12,008	118,489	(491, 486)
ca-AstroPh	18,772	198,050	(504, 420)

Algorithm 1 and Algorithm 2, it does not consume any privacy budget. Hence, based on Theorem 5, we can conclude that our solution satisfies ϵ-differential privacy, where $\epsilon = \epsilon_1 + \epsilon_2$. □

5. EXPERIMENTAL EVALUATION

In this section, we experimentally study the equilibrium of our MCMC method and evaluate the utility of *HRG* over four real-life datasets, namely *polblogs*, *wiki-Vote*, *ca-HepPh* and *ca-AstroPh*[1]. *polblogs* is a network of hyperlinks between weblogs on US politics recorded in 2005. *wiki-Vote* is a social network containing Wikipedia voting information for adminship elections. An edge is created between two participants if one voted on or was voted by the other. *ca-HepPh* and *ca-AstroPh* are collaboration networks which cover scientific collaborations between authors submitted to High Energy Physics and Astro Physics categories, respectively. An edge is created if two authors co-authored a paper. The statistics of these datasets are given in Table 1. All datasets are pre-processed to be undirected without self-loops. All experiments were done on Intel Xeon E5607 servers with 2.27G CPU and 32GB RAM.

5.1 Experimental Settings

In our first set of experiments, we fix $\epsilon = 1.0$. Specifically, we assign $(\epsilon_1, \epsilon_2) = \{(0.1, 0.9), (0.5, 0.5), (0.9, 0.1)\}$ for sampling the dendrogram and computing noisy connection probabilities, respectively (see Figures 5-8). In the second set of experiments, we study the influence of different privacy parameters on data utility. Due to space constraint, we only report the results on *wiki-Vote* (Figures 9 and 10). We do observe similar trends on other datasets. In the figures, we denote our solution *HRG* with the legend *hrg*-ϵ_1-*e*-ϵ_2.

For comparison purposes, we implemented two state-of-the-art competitors, *spectral* [25] and *dk2* [24]. Since no systematic approach of choosing parameter values is provided in [25], we tune the parameters in *spectral* and report the best performance we obtain. More specifically, let k be the number of eigenvalues chosen in the scheme, ϵ_1 be the privacy budget for computing noisy eigenvalues and ϵ_2 for computing noisy eigenvectors. The literature [26] referred by Wang et al. in [25] suggests that k is usually in [2, 9]. Hence we vary k from 2 to 9 and report the best case. In the figures, *spectral* is denoted by the legend *spec*-k-ϵ_1-ϵ_2.

Due to the poor performance of *dk2* under ϵ-differential privacy, we compare with the scheme under a more relaxed privacy notion, that is, (ϵ, δ)-differential privacy. We follow the parameter settings in [24] and set $\delta = 0.01$. Unfortunately, even under (ϵ, δ)-differential privacy, we still need to use relatively large ϵ values (e.g., 200) to obtain comparable results. Moreover, the sensitivity in this case is data-dependent. It depends on the maximum degree pair in the networks (see Table 1). So we choose ϵ values proportional to the maximum degree pair in each network. The choice of parameters for *dk2* is denoted by the legend *dk2*-ϵ-δ.

From a privacy's perspective, *spectral* requires the number of edges in the input network to be known, whereas our scheme *HRG* and *dk2* do not require so. In addition, *dk2* is not able to remap the nodes to the observed network, so the experiments on influential node analysis is not applicable to *dk2*.

5.2 Log-likelihood and MCMC Equilibrium

In practice, we diagnose MCMC's convergence by tracing the *log-likelihood*, $\log \mathcal{L}(T)$, of the sampled dendrograms. The diagnostic takes down consecutive non-overlapping windows of the Markov chain (each window consists of 65536 MCMC steps in our experiments) and compares the means of $\log \mathcal{L}(T)$ within these windows. We use the difference of the means to judge whether the means of $\log \mathcal{L}(T)$ within the windows have stabilized. In our experiments, we continuously examine whether the difference falls into the range $[-0.05n, 0.05n]$ to check the equilibrium state, where n is the number of nodes in the network.

In Figure 4, we plot the trace of $\log \mathcal{L}(T)$ as a function of the number of MCMC steps, normalized by n. We observe that the Markov chains mix well over all datasets (i.e., $\log \mathcal{L}(T)$ becomes stable soon after the initial state), indicating the convergence to the stationary distributions. Even though the mixing time can be exponential in the worst case [19], we observe that, in practice, the Markov chain in *HRG* usually can converge within $1000n$ steps on networks of around ten thousand nodes. Figure 4 also shows that the integration of differential privacy actually speeds up the movement of the Markov chains and makes them mix even faster. Roughly, the running time of n MCMC steps in our experiments is 0.18s for *polblogs*, 4.1s for *wiki-Vote*, 9.5s for *ca-HepPh* and 22.9s for *ca-AstroPh*. More details about the mixing time can be found in [6].

Figure 4 also shows the comparison of the sampled dendrograms' $\log \mathcal{L}(T)$ in different parameter settings, including that of the dendrogram sampled in the non-private manner. We can observe that, for networks with around ten thousand vertices, $\log \mathcal{L}(T)$ of the dendrogram sampled under a relatively small privacy parameter (e.g., $\epsilon_1 = 0.5$) is still comparable with that under a relatively large privacy parameter (e.g., $\epsilon_1 = 0.9$). Hence, we expect that even assigning a relatively small ϵ_1 for sampling the dendrogram will not significantly harm the data utility of the released network. To validate this, we further conduct experiments with smaller ϵ_1, such as 0.2 and 0.4. The performance shown in Figures 9 and 10 confirm that our scheme preserves reasonably good data utility even under a stringent privacy parameter (see Section 5.3 for the explanation of the utility metrics in Figures 9 and 10).

5.3 Utility Analysis

To show the utility of the released networks, we compare their degree distributions, shortest path length distributions and influential node ranking with those of the original networks. Due to the randomness of our algorithm, we examine the variance of its performance by running the algorithm ten times on each network for each parameter setting. We observe that the variance in all cases is small.

[1]*polblogs* is available at `http://www-personal.umich.edu/~mejn/netdata/`; *wiki-Vote*, *ca-HepPh* and *ca-AstroPh* are available at `http://snap.stanford.edu/data/index.html`.

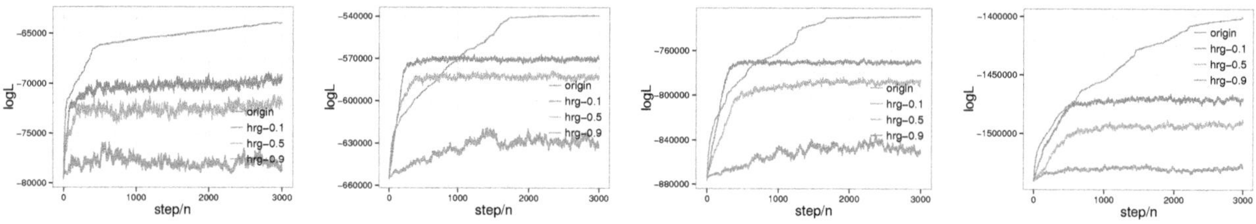

(a) *polblogs* (b) *wiki-Vote* (c) *ca-HepPh* (d) *ca-AstroPh*

Figure 4: Trace of log-likelihood as a function of the number of MCMC steps, normalized by n

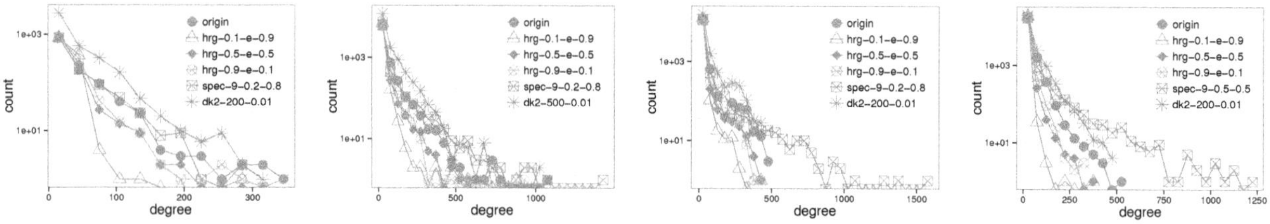

(a) *polblogs* (b) *wiki-Vote* (c) *ca-HepPh* (d) *ca-AstroPh*

Figure 5: Degree distribution

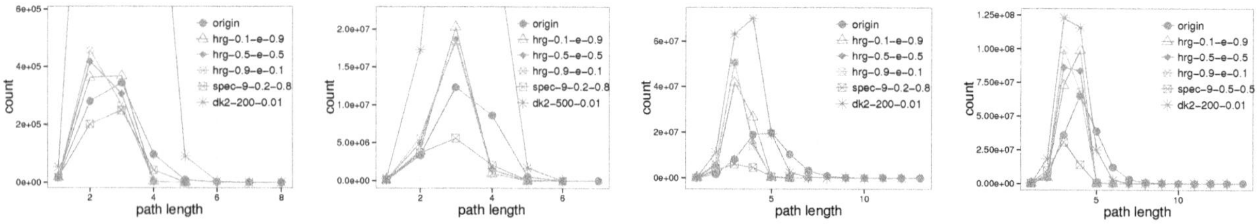

(a) *polblogs* (b) *wiki-Vote* (c) *ca-HepPh* (d) *ca-AstroPh*

Figure 6: Shortest path length distribution

Degree Distribution. Figure 5 shows the degree distributions of the released data under different sanitization schemes, with y-axis in log-scale. It can be seen that, in all cases, *HRG* preserves well the right-skewness of the original networks, meaning that it preserves good distance scale between "hubs" (i.e., nodes having high degrees) and the majority of low-degree nodes.

Shortest Path Length Distribution. Figure 6 depicts the shortest path length distribution of each network. We observe that, in general, the released networks preserve the shapes of the distributions with respect to those of the original networks. However, we also observe the increase of paths of small lengths (e.g., 1-3). We believe this is due to the extra edges added to the low levels of the sampled dendrogram, which corresponds to the local structures in a network. But this does not have a big influence on the network's global structure.

Influential Node Analysis. Identifying the most influential nodes in social networks is a key problem in social network analysis. In our experiments, we consider the *eigenvector centrality* (EVC) score as the measure to rank the nodes in networks. EVC scores correspond to the values of the first leading eigenvector of the graph's adjacency matrix (the one with the greatest eigenvalue). Intuitively, EVC measures the nodes' influence by virture of their positions in a network, that is, the sum of the geodesic distances from each node to all others. The eigenvector approach attempts to find the most central nodes (i.e., those with the smallest geodesic distance to others) in terms of the "global" or "overall" structure of the network. The first eigenvector usually captures the "global" aspects of distances among nodes, while the second and subsequent ones capture more specific and local structures.

In our experiments, we first test the percentage of common nodes in top-k most influential nodes of the original graphs and those of the sanitized graphs. We examine top 10, 20, 50 influential nodes as well as top 1% and 5% nodes in the networks. The results are presented in Figure 7. We see that *HRG* guarantees a consistent 25%-75% overlap of common nodes in all the cases.

We then calculate the mean absolute error of the top-k most influential nodes' EVC scores. Let the set of top-k nodes in the original graph be α and that of the sanitized graph be β. To show that nodes in β have similar centralities to those in α, we use the *mean absolute error* (MAE) to compare the EVC scores in β with those in α. Formally, the MAE value is formulated by: $MAE(\alpha, \beta) = \frac{1}{k}\sum_{i=1}^{k}\left|EVC(v_\alpha^i) - EVC(v_\beta^i)\right|$, where v_α^i and v_β^i are the top-i nodes in α and β, respectively. In Figure 8 , we observe that the MAE of *HRG* with $\epsilon_1 = 0.5$ and 0.9 is reasonably low (e.g., less than 25% in most cases). The overlaps in top-k nodes and the low MAE together indicate that *HRG* well preserves the hub nodes, which represent the global structure of the sanitized graph.

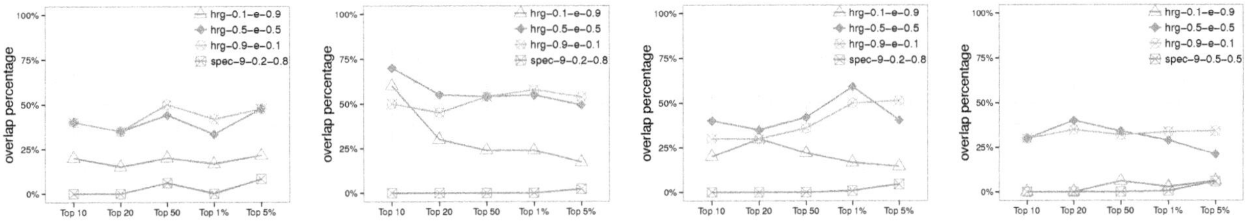

(a) *polblogs* (b) *wiki-Vote* (c) *ca-HepPh* (d) *ca-AstroPh*

Figure 7: Overlaps of top-k vertices

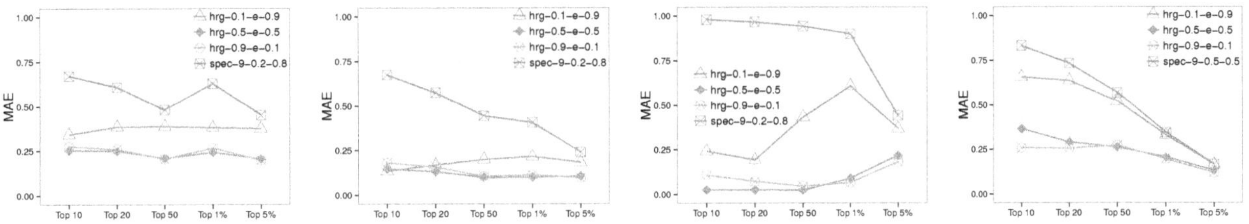

(a) *polblogs* (b) *wiki-Vote* (c) *ca-HepPh* (d) *ca-AstroPh*

Figure 8: Mean absolute error of top-k vertices

6. RELATED WORK

Early works on *privacy-preserving network data publishing* [16, 27, 28, 5] mainly focus on developing anonymization techniques for specific types of privacy attacks. Most of them employ privacy models derived from k-anonymity [22] by assuming different types of adversarial knowledge. Unfortunately, all these anonymization techniques are vulnerable to attackers with stronger background knowledge than assumed, which has stimulated the use of differential privacy for more rigorous privacy guarantees.

The recent research on applying differential privacy to network data roughly falls into two directions. The first direction aims to release certain differentially private data mining results, such as degree distributions, subgraph counts and frequent graph patterns [12, 14, 11, 23]. However, our problem is substantially more challenging than publishing certain network statistics or data mining results. Our goal is to publish the entire graph, which incurs a much larger global sensitivity. Note that the sensitivity in the problem setting of [23] is only 1. In contrast, our key technical contribution is to achieve a smaller sensitivity in releasing a graph (i.e., $O(\log n)$ as opposed to $O(n)$ and $O(\sqrt{n})$ of our state-of-the-art competitors [21, 24, 25]). In addition, some latest studies [4, 1, 15] attempt to answer graph queries under a more stringent instantiation of differential privacy known as *node differential privacy* [12]. In spite of the significant progress, it is still difficult to develop practical solutions under node differential privacy in our problem setting.

The second direction aims to publish a sanitized graph, which is also the objective of this paper. Most research in this direction [21, 20, 24] projects an input graph to dK-series and ensures differential privacy on dK-series statistics. These private statistics are then either fed into graph generators or used by MCMC to generate a fitting synthetic graph. While the general idea is appealing, the current techniques are still inadequate to provide desirable data utility for many graph mining tasks unless the privacy parameter is unreasonably large (e.g., $\epsilon \geq 100$), as demonstrated in Section 5. Wang et al. [25] propose to project a graph to the spectral domain and inject noise to the eigenvalues and eigenvectors. This approach successfully reduces the sensitivity to $O(\sqrt{n})$, which, unfortunately, is still not able to achieve good data utility. Comparing with all these studies based on the idea of projection, our approach takes an important step to achieve desirable data utility on real-life datasets in many practical settings. Gupta et al. [10] give an iterative database construction algorithm to generate synthetic graphs for answering cut queries. However, it requires an input graph to be dense, which is unlikely to be satisfiable on real-life network data and leaves finding an efficient algorithm as an open problem. Very recently, Chen et al. [3] propose a data-dependent solution by identifying and reconstructing the dense regions of a graph's adjacency matrix. Though it achieves reasonable utility on some datasets, its performance heavily relies on the fundamental assumption that most edge information must be captured by the dense regions of the adjacency matrix. In addition, this solution involves multiple ad-hoc parameters, which are difficult for a data publisher to tune.

7. CONCLUSION

In this paper, we address the privacy concerns in network data release by proposing a novel data sanitization method under differential privacy. Our solution is based on structural inference over the hierarchical random graph (HRG) model. Compared with the existing works, we theoretically prove that the sensitivity of our solution is much smaller, only logarithmic in the order of the network size(i.e., the number of vertices), implying a significant utility improvement. Extensive experiments on four real-life datasets confirm that our solution outperforms the state-of-the-art competitors.

8. REFERENCES

[1] J. Blocki, A. Blum, A. Datta, and O. Sheffet. Differentially private data analysis of social networks via restricted sensitivity. In *ITCS*, 2013.

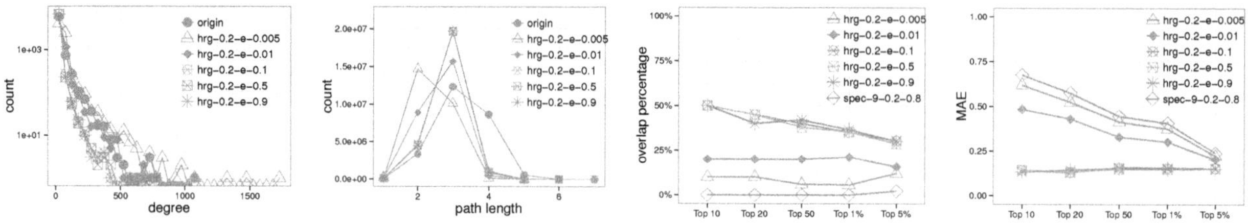

(a) Degree distribution (b) Shortest path length (c) Overlaps of top-k vertices (d) Mean absolute error

Figure 9: *wiki-Vote* with *hrg*-0.2

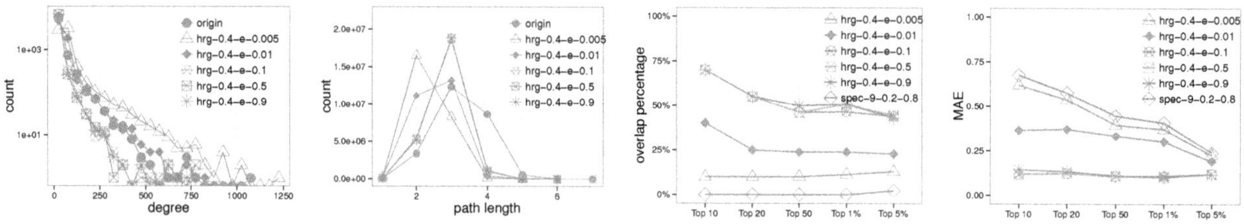

(a) Degree distribution (b) Shortest path length (c) Overlaps of top-k vertices (d) Mean absolute error

Figure 10: *wiki-Vote* with *hrg*-0.4

[2] S. Brooks, A. Gelman, G. L. Jones, and X.-L. Meng. *Handbook of Markov Chain Monte Carlo*. Chapman & Hall/CRC, 2011.

[3] R. Chen, B. C. M. Fung, P. S. Yu, and B. C. Desai. Correlated network data publication via differential privacy. *VLDBJ*, in press.

[4] S. Chen and S. Zhou. Recursive mechanism: towards node differential privacy and unrestricted joins. In *SIGMOD*, 2013.

[5] J. Cheng, A. W. C. Fu, and J. Liu. K-isomorphism: privacy preserving network publication against structural attacks. In *SIGMOD*, 2010.

[6] A. Clauset, C. Moore, and M. E. J. Newman. Structural inference of hierarchies in networks. In *ICML on Statistical Network Analysis*, 2007.

[7] A. Clauset, C. Moore, and M. E. J. Newman. Hierarchical structure and the prediction of missing links in networks. *Nature*, 453:98–101, 2008.

[8] G. Cormode, D. Srivastava, T. Yu, and Q. Zhang. Anonymizing bipartite graph data using safe groupings. *PVLDB*, 1(1):833–844, 2008.

[9] C. Dwork, F. McSherry, K. Nissim, and A. Smith. Calibrating noise to sensitivity in private data analysis. In *TCC*, 2006.

[10] A. Gupta, A. Roth, and J. Ullman. Iterative constructions and private data release. In *TCC*, 2012.

[11] M. Hardt and A. Roth. Beating randomized response on incoherent matrices. In *STOC*, 2012.

[12] M. Hay, C. Li, G. Miklau, and D. Jensen. Accurate estimation of the degree distribution of private networks. In *ICDM*, 2009.

[13] M. Hay, G. Miklau, D. Jensen, D. F. Towsley, and P. Weis. Resisting structural re-identification in anonymized social networks. *PVLDB*, 1(1):102–114, 2008.

[14] V. Karwa, S. Raskhodnikova, A. Smith, and G. Yaroslavtsev. Private analysis of graph structure. *PVLDB*, 4(11):1146–1157, 2011.

[15] S. P. Kasiviswanathan, K. Nissim, S. Raskhodnikova, and A. Smith. Analyzing graphs with node differential privacy. In *TCC*, 2013.

[16] K. Liu and E. Terzi. Towards identity anonymization on graphs. In *SIGMOD*, 2008.

[17] F. McSherry. Privacy integrated queries: an extensible platform for privacy-preserving data analysis. *Commun. ACM*, 53(9), 2010.

[18] F. McSherry and K. Talwar. Mechanism design via differential privacy. In *FOCS*, 2007.

[19] E. Mossel and E. Vigoda. Phylogenetic MCMC algorithms are misleading on mixtures of trees. *Science*, 309(5744):2207–2209, 2005.

[20] D. Proserpio, S. Goldberg, and F. McSherry. A workflow for differentially-private graph synthesis. In *WOSN*, 2012.

[21] A. Sala, X. Zhao, C. Wilson, H. Zheng, and B. Y. Zhao. Sharing graphs using differentially private graph models. In *IMC*, 2011.

[22] P. Samarati. Protecting respondents' identities in microdata release. *TKDE*, 13(6):1010–1027, 2001.

[23] E. Shen and T. Yu. Mining frequent graph patterns with differential privacy. In *SIGKDD*, 2013.

[24] Y. Wang and X. Wu. Preserving differential privacy in degree-correlation based graph generation. *TDP*, 6(2), 2013.

[25] Y. Wang, X. Wu, and L. Wu. Differential privacy preserving spectral graph analysis. In *PAKDD*, 2013.

[26] L. Wu, X. Ying, X. Wu, and Z.-H. Zhou. Line orthogonality in adjacency eigenspace with application to community partition. In *IJCAI*, 2011.

[27] B. Zhou and J. Pei. Preserving privacy in social networks against neighborhood attacks. In *ICDE*, 2008.

[28] L. Zou, L. Chen, and M. T. Ozsu. K-automorphism: a general framework for privacy preserving network publication. *PVLDB*, 2(1):946–957, 2009.

Exponential Random Graph Estimation under Differential Privacy

Wentian Lu
University of Massachusetts Amherst
wen@cs.umass.edu

Gerome Miklau
University of Massachusetts Amherst
miklau@cs.umass.edu

ABSTRACT

The effective analysis of social networks and graph-structured data is often limited by the privacy concerns of individuals whose data make up these networks. Differential privacy offers individuals a rigorous and appealing guarantee of privacy. But while differentially private algorithms for computing basic graph properties have been proposed, most graph *modeling* tasks common in the data mining community cannot yet be carried out privately.

In this work we propose algorithms for privately estimating the parameters of exponential random graph models (ERGMs). We break the estimation problem into two steps: computing private sufficient statistics, then using these to estimate the model parameters. We consider recent specifications of ERGMs and show that our perturbation method, the chain mechanism, offers provably less error than comparable methods. In addition, our redesigned estimation algorithm considers the noise distribution of the private statistics and offers better accuracy than directly performing parameter estimation on the statistics.

Categories and Subject Descriptors

H.2.7 [**Database Administration**]: Security, integrity, and protection; H.2.8 [**Database Management**]: Data Mining

Keywords

Differential privacy; Exponential random graph model

1. INTRODUCTION

The explosion in the collection of networked data has fueled researchers' interest in modeling networks and predicting their behavior. However, for important application areas such as disease transmission, network vulnerability assessment, and fraud detection (among others), networks contain sensitive information about individuals and their relationships. It is difficult for institutions to release network data and it remains difficult for reseachers to acquire data in many important application domains.

Recently, a rigorous privacy standard, *differential privacy* [8] was proposed that allows for formal bounds on the disclosure about individuals that may result from computations on sensitive data. Differential privacy provides each participant in a dataset with a strong guarantee and makes no assumptions about the prior knowledge of attackers.

Since its introduction, differentially private algorithms have been developed for a wide range of data mining and analysis tasks, for both tabular data and networked data. For networks, existing work has focused on algorithms for accurately releasing common graph statistics under differential privacy [12, 16, 25, 26, 28, 31]. However, graph statistics are only one aspect of social network analysis and are often most useful in conjunction with some paradigm for modeling structural features of graphs. Privately modeling graph data has only rarely been explored by researchers; we are aware only of work using the Kronecker model [19] under differential privacy [22].

In this work, we study the differentially private use of the classic exponential random graph model (ERGM) [21, 30, 27]. ERGMs are a powerful statistical modeling tool that allows analysts to analyze a network's social structure and formation process. In social science and related fields ERGMs have been successfully applied to many scenarios, such as co-sponsorship networks [5], friendship networks [11], and corporate and inter-organizational networks [21].

Our goal is to accurately support parameter estimation for ERGMs under differential privacy, focusing on a specific set of model parameters of recent interest to researchers: the *alternating statistics*. These sophisticated statistics represent more structural information than traditional star and triangle counts, and have been shown to lead to much better modeling results [30, 27, 13, 11].

Our adaptation of differential privacy to graphs protects relationships of individuals by limiting the influence on the output of any single relationship (edge) that is created or removed from the network.[1] A standard algorithm that implements this idea is the Laplace mechanism [8], which adds random noise to the output. The amount of noise required is related to the maximum difference in the output due to a single edge addition or removal for *any* possible network

KDD'14, August 24–27, 2014, New York, NY, USA.

ACM 978-1-4503-2956-9/14/08 ...$15.00.
http://dx.doi.org/10.1145/2623330.2623683 .

[1]This is one of the most common interpretations of differential privacy for graphs, called *edge* differential privacy [12]. *Node* differential privacy is stronger, but often hurts utility. Our results for edge-differential privacy can easily be extended to k-edge privacy to protect multiple edges.

(this is the *global sensitivity* of the function producing the output). For ERGM estimation, this requires calculating the exact change in the ERGM parameter estimates as a result of changing an edge. Unfortunately, the global sensitivity for most ERGM parameters is either hard to compute in general, or too high, so that using noise calibrated to the global sensitivity is not acceptable.

To overcome this obstacle, we decompose private ERGM estimation into two separate steps. We first privately compute the sufficient statistics for ERGM estimation (typically the model statistics required by model description) and then estimate the parameters using only these sufficient statistics. Since the estimation process uses only the differentially-private statistics, and there is no additional access to the original graph, the output of estimation is also differentially private. In practice, the estimation algorithm is executed either on the server side (data owner) or client side (the analyst). In either case, it does not violate the privacy condition to release both the statistics and the derived ERGM parameters.

Challenges arise in both steps of our approach. While prior work has proposed mechanisms for various graph statistics, common ERGM models use unique statistics, e.g., alternating graph statistics [30], which are a complex aggregation of a series of basic graph statistics. We propose new approaches for privately computing these statistics. The second parameter estimation step could be implemented using standard methods [29, 3] while treating the privately-computed statistics as if they were the true statistics. Instead, we propose a novel parameter estimation method based on Bayesian inference, which considers the noise distribution from which the private statistics are drawn and produces more accurate parameter estimates.

Contributions

- We propose a novel *chain mechanism* (in Section 3) that adds noise in proportion to a bound on the local (rather than global) sensitivity. Unlike global sensitivity, local sensitivity focuses only on changes to the current network. We use the chain mechanism to compute particular graph statistics (alternating k-triangle and alternating k-twopath) but it is a general technique that can be used more broadly. Compared with competing techniques that use local sensitivity, the chain mechanism is easier to deploy and more efficient.
- We provide a formal analysis of the error of the chain mechanism (in Section 3), showing that it provably outperforms prior work [16], offering lower error and a stronger privacy standard (ϵ-differential privacy, versus relaxed (ϵ, δ)-differential privacy).
- We describe a new Bayesian method for ERGM parameter estimation (in Section 4) that is designed for the noisy sufficient statistics produced by a differentially private algorithm. While it is possible to use a standard algorithm for estimation, our inference takes the unknown network as a hidden variable and can result in estimates with lower error.
- We study a set of ERGM models based on model terms consisting of alternating graph statistics [30] (in Section 5). Our experiments on both synthetic and real graphs show that our techniques significantly reduce noise over competing techniques, for fixed ϵ.

2. BACKGROUND

2.1 Exponential random graph model (ERGM)

A graph $G = (V, E)$ is defined as a set of nodes V and relationships $E : V \times V \rightarrow \{0, 1\}$. A common representation of a graph is as an adjacency matrix x, where $x_{ij} \in \{0, 1\}$ indicating whether there is an edge from node i to j. Let $f(\cdot)$ define a vector of graph statistics called the *model terms*; the concrete values of $f(x)$ are the *model statistics*. Formally, the ERGM with parameter vector θ defines a probability distribution over graphs in the space $\mathcal{X}$ (typically the set of all simple graphs with n vertices):

$$p(x|\theta) = \frac{\exp(\theta \cdot f(x))}{Z_\theta} \tag{1}$$

Z_θ is a normalizing constant to make $p(x)$ a true probability distribution, parameterized by θ. If x_0 is the observed graph and X represents the random variable defined by the distribution above, our goal is to tune the parameter vector θ, s.t. the expected value of $f(X)$ is equal to observed statistics, meaning $\mathbb{E}_\theta(f(X)) = f(x_0)$, which intuitively puts the observed graph in the "center" of space of possible graphs implied by the model. For example, the simplest ERGM uses the number of edges as the only model term. If m_0 is the total number of edges in x_0, the θ, which enables the expected number of edges of ERGM equal to m_0, is given by [24]:

$$\theta = \log \frac{m_0}{\binom{n}{2} - m_0} \tag{2}$$

Estimating θ. The optimal θ maximizes the likelihood of x_0 given θ [24], i.e., $\arg\max_\theta p(x_0|\theta)$. Unfortunately, most ERGMs do not have an analytical or closed-form estimate for the optimal θ. Thus, numerical solutions are proposed in the literature, such as Markov chain monte carlo maximum likelihood estimation [29] and Bayesian inference [3]. An interesting property of these inference methods is that the algorithm does not require access to the input graph itself, i.e., the sufficient statistics for the parameter estimation are just the model statistics. This feature enables us to decompose the private inference problem into two steps, allowing analysts to see only the sufficient statistics.

Alternating statistics. A model term is usually a counting query of a specific graph pattern. Common patterns include triangles, stars and loops [21]. Recent research has introduced alternating statistics for k-star, k-triangle and k-twopath, which can represent structural properties of a graph better than traditional star and triangle counts [30]. Many works have explored these statistics since they were proposed, and they are an active and promising form of ERGM [30, 27, 13, 11]. Our work is focused on these alternating statistics (defined precisely in Section 3) which have not been studied before under differential privacy. A wide variety of other model terms are used with ERGMs; our general approach is compatible with other terms but they are beyond the scope of this work.

2.2 Differential privacy

Differential privacy is traditionally defined over a tabular based database D consisting of records, each of which describes an individual. When querying the database, differential privacy protects individuals by restricting the impact on the output of any individual who opts into or out of the database. Two such databases that differ by one record are called *neighbors*.

Definition 2.1 (Differential Privacy[7]). Let D and D' be neighboring databases and $\mathcal{K}$ be any algorithm. For any subset of outputs $O \subseteq Range(\mathcal{K})$, the following holds:

$$\Pr[\mathcal{K}(D) \in O] \leq \exp(\epsilon) \times \Pr[\mathcal{K}(D') \in O] + \delta$$

If $\delta = 0$, $\mathcal{K}$ is standard ϵ-differentially private. Otherwise, $\mathcal{K}$ is relaxed (ϵ, δ)-differentially private.

The input privacy parameter ϵ (and δ if using the relaxed definition) are non-negative and are used to measure the degree of privacy protection. Smaller ϵ means better privacy as $\exp(\epsilon)$ is close to one.

In this paper, our database is a graph describing relationships among individuals. Our purpose is to protect relationships among individuals so we adapt differential privacy, following [12, 16, 26, 31, 28], by defining a neighboring graph as a graph that differs by one edge.

Global sensitivity and the Laplace mechanism

Differential privacy can be achieved by adding noise to the output of algorithms according to privacy parameters and query *sensitivity*. The global sensitivity of a query is the maximum possible difference in the output when evaluating the query on two neighboring graphs. E.g., the query asking for the maximum degree of a graph has global sensitivity 1, because adding or removing one edge changes any degree by at most 1. Let $Lap(b)$ be a Laplace random variable with mean 0 and scale b.

Definition 2.2 (Laplace mechanism [8]). Given query f on graph x, the following algorithm $\mathcal{K}(f, x)$ is ϵ-differentially private:

$$\mathcal{K}(f, x) = f(x) + Lap(\mathsf{GS}_f/\epsilon)$$

where global sensitivity

$$\mathsf{GS}_f = \max_{\forall x_1, x_2 \ neighbors} |f(x_1) - f(x_2)|$$

A basic property we rely on is that post-processing a noisy, differentially-private output using any algorithm that does not access the original data cannot alter the privacy guarantee [18]. Past research has shown that post-processing the noisy output can, however, have significant impact on utility. In addition, composition rules for differential privacy allow us to compute the ϵ privacy standard that results from the combined release of multiple query answers or releases. Precisely, if each release is ϵ_i-differential privacy, the combined is then $\sum_i \epsilon_i$-differential privacy.

In our perturbation step, we will use the composition rule to add noise to multiple model terms. In the parameter estimation step, we run post-processing.

Local sensitivity and its smooth bound

Some common graph analyses have high global sensitivity, requiring the Laplace mechanism to add enormous amounts of noise. For example, consider the simplest ERGM model above where θ is calculated by (2). On a graph where $m_0 = 0$ or a graph where $m_0 = \binom{n}{2}$, θ can change drastically with the addition or deletion of one edge. In other words, the global sensitivity is very high for this function. But the fact is that most real graphs are nothing like these extremes. Thus, by only focusing on the input graph's neighbors, the *local sensitivity* [25] can be much smaller.

Definition 2.3 (Local sensitivity[25]). Given query f and graph x, local sensitivity $\mathsf{LS}_f(x)$

$$\mathsf{LS}_f(x) = \max_{x, x' neighbors} |f(x) - f(x')|$$

However, one cannot achieve differential privacy by adding noise proportional to the local sensitivity because local sensitivity itself could disclose information. The authors of [25] proposed using a smooth upper bound on the local sensitivity, the *smooth sensitivity*. Intuitively, smooth sensitivity tries to "smooth" out the difference between local sensitivities of two neighbors, so that it is itself not sensitive. Let $d(x, x')$ be the distance between two graphs, i.e. the number of edges in which they differ:

Definition 2.4 (Smooth bound and smooth sensitivity[25]). Function $\mathsf{S}_f : \mathcal{X} \Rightarrow R$ defines a β-smooth bound of local sensitivity on query f if

$$\forall x \ : \ \mathsf{S}_f(x) \geq \mathsf{LS}_f(x)$$
$$\forall x, x' \text{ neighbors} \ : \ \mathsf{S}_f(x) \leq \exp(\beta)\mathsf{S}_f(x')$$

The β-smooth sensitivity of f is a β-smooth bound, and

$$\mathsf{SS}_{f,\beta}(x) = \max_{x'} \left\{ \mathsf{LS}_f(x') \cdot \exp\left(-\beta d(x, x')\right) \right\}$$

Calculating the smooth sensitivity for a function may be easy (in cases like the median of a list of numbers [25]) but could be quite difficult for other functions, requiring complex proofs and nontrivial algorithms [16]. Even though smooth sensitivity may provide tight bound for local sensitivity, we show that it is NP-hard for two alternating statistics commonly used in ERGMs.

3. PERTURBING MODEL STATISTICS

In this section we provide methods for privately computing alternating graph statistics. We show alternating k-star has a constant global sensitivity which allows the Laplace mechanism to be applied with relatively small error. However, alternating k-triangle and alternating k-twopath both have high global sensitivity. It is even hard to resort to smooth sensitivity, as calculating smooth sensitivity is NP-hard in both cases. To address this challenge, we propose the novel *chain mechanism* which allows us to efficiently bound the local sensitivity. We apply it to these two alternating statistics, but note that it is a technique that is widely applicable. We defer some proofs in this section to the Appendix.

3.1 Alternating graph statistics

Three alternating graph statistics, alternating k-star, alternating k-triangle and alternating k-twopath, are essentially complex aggregations of traditional k-star, k-triangle and k-twopath statistics. Instead of considering a vector of k terms, the alternating statistics aggregate over the terms but enforce alternating signs between each consecutive term, to weaken the correlation among different terms and effectively reduce the weight on higher terms near k.

Alternating k-star. The k-star is a counting query of a star pattern in the graph, where each star contains k edges, i.e., $S_k = \sum_i \binom{d_i}{k}$ where d_i is the degree of node i.

Definition 3.1 (Alternating k-star [30]). With parameter $\lambda \geq 1$, alternating k-star S is defined as

$$S(x;\lambda) = S_2 - \frac{S_3}{\lambda} + \ldots + (-1)^{n-1}\frac{S_{n-1}}{\lambda^{n-3}}$$

The λ parameter here is a good way to control the geometrical weights on all k-stars.

Alternating k-triangle. A k-triangle is a graph pattern in which k triangles share a common edge. The k-triangle query asks for the total number of k-triangles in the graph. Define the shared partner matrix C, where each entry (i,j) in C is the count of shared partners between nodes i and j, mathematically $C_{ij}(x) = \sum_l x_{il}x_{lj}$. Formally, k-triangle T_k is defined:

$$T_k = \sum_{i<j} x_{ij}\binom{C_{ij}}{k} \quad (k \geq 2), \quad \text{and } T_1 = \frac{1}{3}\sum_{i<j} x_{ij}C_{ij}$$

Alternating k-triangle is defined similarly as alternating k-star, using parameter λ:

Definition 3.2 (Alternating k-triangle [30]). With parameter $\lambda \geq 1$, alternating k-triangle T is:

$$T(x;\lambda) = 3T_1 - \frac{T_2}{\lambda} + \frac{T_3}{\lambda^2} - \ldots + \left(\frac{-1}{\lambda}\right)^{n-3} T_{n-2}$$

Alternating k-twopath. A k-twopath graph pattern is very similar to k-triangle, except it does not require the shared edge required by the k-triangle statistic. Using the shared partners matrix C above, the counting query for k-twopath U_k is:

$$U_k = \sum_{i<j}\binom{C_{ij}}{k} \quad (k \neq 2), \quad \text{and } U_2 = \frac{1}{2}\sum_{i<j}\binom{C_{ij}}{2}$$

And alternating k-twopath is:

Definition 3.3 (Alternating k-twopath [30]). With parameter $\lambda \geq 1$, alternating k-twopath U is

$$U(x;\lambda) = U_1 - \frac{2}{\lambda}U_2 + \sum_{k=3}^{n-2}\left(\frac{-1}{\lambda}\right)^{k-1} U_k$$

Alternating k-star S is the only statistic that can be readily solved using existing privacy mechanisms. Because the degree sequence is a sufficient statistic for S, one natural approach is to use the mechanism described by Hay et al [12] to compute a private degree sequence from x, and then use it to compute S by Eq. (3). But, in fact, it can be shown that the global sensitivity of S is at most 2λ. Thus, Laplace noise may be a better choice (λ is usually set to a small integer in practice). We make empirical comparisons between these methods in Section 5.

Lemma 3.4. *The global sensitivity of alternating k-star is at most 2λ.*

3.2 Chain mechanism

As the global sensitivity of alternating k-triangle and k-twopath could be as large as $O(n)$, we would like to use smooth sensitivity for perturbation. However, the following lemma shows the NP-hardness of finding the smooth sensitivity of these two statistics:

Lemma 3.5. *Computing the smooth sensitivity for both alternating k-triangle and alternating k-twopath is NP-hard.*

Inspired by the previous work [16], we should consider other techniques for bounding local sensitivity. There are two general conditions that must be satisfied if we are to use a bound on local sensitivity can be used safely (i.e., using the bound does not violate the privacy condition).

1. The bound is not smaller than the local sensitivity.
2. The bound itself is private.

In Definition 2.4 of the smooth bound, its first requirement is exactly our first condition and its second requirement satisfies the second condition here. However, the tightness of their second requirement results in the complexity of calculation of smooth sensitivity in some applications. To make the bound itself private, by relaxing the bound a bit, a simpler process can be applied. Before we introduce the chain mechanism, we define a random variable chain.

Definition 3.6. $Y_0, Y_1, \ldots, Y_n$ is a *random variable chain*, when the following condition is satisfied: for any $i \in [0, n-2]$, Y_i is conditionally independent of $Y_{i+2}, Y_{i+3}, \ldots Y_n$ given Y_{i+1}.

From conditional independence, an important property of random variable chain is the following:

$$\Pr(Y_i|Y_{i+1}, Y_{i+2}, \ldots, Y_n) = \Pr(Y_i|Y_{i+1})$$

Let $f(x)$ be the sensitive function/query. We use $\mathsf{LS}_{f,1}(x)$ to denote the local sensitivity of f, a function of the input graph x. More generally, we use $\mathsf{LS}_{f,i}(x)$ to denote the local sensitivity of function $\mathsf{LS}_{f,i-1}(x)$. We call $\mathsf{LS}_{f,0}(x)$, $\mathsf{LS}_{f,1}(x)$,$\mathsf{LS}_{f,2}(x)$,…,$\mathsf{LS}_{f,n}(x)$ *a local sensitivity chain of f*.

To satisfy condition one above, we bound the local sensitivity by adding random *positive* noise to $\mathsf{LS}_{f,1}(x)$ (recall Laplace noise is symmetric), so that we can calibrate the noise added to $f(x)$ according to that bound. The question is now how much noise should be added into $\mathsf{LS}_{f,1}(x)$, so that it is itself private, satisfying condition two above. It is actually decided by its global sensitivity $\mathsf{GS}(\mathsf{LS}_{f,1}(x))$. Moreover, if $\mathsf{GS}(\mathsf{LS}_{f,1}(x))$ is too large, we could repeat the step by adding noise to $\mathsf{LS}_{f,1}(x)$ calibrated to local sensitivity of $\mathsf{LS}_{f,1}(x)$, $\mathsf{LS}_{f,2}(x)$, and then safely bound $\mathsf{LS}_{f,2}(x)$ by its global sensitivity $\mathsf{GS}(\mathsf{LS}_{f,2}(x))$. We describe this general process as the *chain mechanism.* Let $Expn(b)$ be an exponential random variable with density function $p(y) = \frac{1}{b}\exp(\frac{-y}{b})$ for $y \geq 0$ and $p(y) = 0$ for $y < 0$.

Algorithm 1 Chain mechanism

Require: input graph x, query f, $\epsilon_0, \epsilon_1, \ldots, \epsilon_n$

```
y_n = LS_{f,n}(x) + Expn(GS(LS_{f,n})/ε_n)
for i in n − 1 to 1 do
    y_i = LS_{f,i}(x) + Expn(y_{i+1}/ε_i)
ỹ = f(x) + Lap(y_1/ε_0)
return ỹ, ..., y_n
```

Theorem 3.7. *Chain mechanism (Algorithm 1) is $\sum_i \epsilon_i$-differential privacy.*

In Algorithm 1, we refer to n as the size of the chain mechanism, i.e., the n-chain mechanism. Note that the chain mechanism does not specify how to distribute the privacy parameters ϵ_i among steps. An optimal distribution will require the knowledge of local sensitivity chain, which is sensitive information itself. A simple way is to distribute ϵ evenly, i.e., $\forall i\ \epsilon_i = \epsilon/(n+1)$.

Error analysis. We use mean squared error (MSE) as the measurement of error. MSE of $\tilde{y}$ in Algorithm 1 can be written as $\mathbb{E}[(\tilde{y} - f(x))^2] = \mathbb{V}[\tilde{y}] + (\mathbb{E}[\tilde{y}] - f(x))^2$. Since $\tilde{y}$ is always unbiased (Laplace noise in the last step with mean zero), $\text{MSE}(x) = \mathbb{V}[\tilde{y}]$. It is easy to see that $\tilde{y}, y_1, \ldots, y_n$ is actually a random variable chain. Specifically,

$$y_i - \mathsf{LS}_{f,i}(x) \sim Expn(y_{i+1}/\epsilon_i)\Big|y_{i+1},\ \forall i \in [1, n-1]$$

$$\tilde{y} - f(x) \sim Lap(y_1/\epsilon_0)\Big|y_1$$

Without knowing the true value of the local sensitivity chain, it is quite hard to compute the MSE. That is to say, we cannot compute the error of the chain mechanism like we do for the Laplace mechanism, since the noise in the latter is independent of input graph x. But, by exploring properties of the random variable chain, it is possible to utilize the following Lemma as a closed form calculation tool for the MSE of the chain mechanism. In fact, we generalize law of total expectation/variance [32] for random variable chains.

Lemma 3.8. *$Y_0, Y_1, \ldots, Y_n$ is a random variable chain. Write $\bigsqcup_{n,i} \mathbb{E}[\cdot]$ as a shortcut for $\mathbb{E}_{Y_n}[\mathbb{E}_{Y_{n-1}|Y_n}[\cdots \mathbb{E}_{Y_i|Y_{i+1}}[\cdot]]]$. Then*

$$\mathbb{E}[Y_0] = \bigsqcup_{n,0} \mathbb{E}[Y_0]$$

$$\mathbb{V}[Y_0] = \bigsqcup_{n,1} \mathbb{E}[\underset{Y_0|Y_1}{\mathbb{V}}[Y_0]] + \sum_{i=2}^{n-2}\left(\bigsqcup_{n,i} \mathbb{E}[\underset{Y_{i-1}|Y_i}{\mathbb{V}}[\bigsqcup_{i-2,0} \mathbb{E}[Y_0]]]\right) + \underset{Y_n}{\mathbb{V}}[\bigsqcup_{n-1,0} \mathbb{E}[Y_0]]$$

Theorem 3.9 (MSE of chain mechanism). *Given the output of an n-chain mechanism, $\tilde{y}, y_1, \ldots, y_n$, the mean squared error (MSE) is*

$$\text{MSE}_{f,n} = \bigsqcup_{n,1} \mathbb{E}[\underset{\tilde{y}|y_1}{\mathbb{V}}[\tilde{y}]]$$

Let $l_1, \ldots, l_n$ be the local sensitivity chain, with $l_i = \mathsf{LS}_{f,i}(x)$. Writing $\mathsf{GS}(\mathsf{LS}_{f,n}(x))$ as g_n, we have:

$$\text{MSE}_{f,1} = \frac{2}{\epsilon_1^2\epsilon_0^2}\left[g_1^2 + (l_1\epsilon_1 + g_1)^2\right] \tag{3}$$

$$\text{MSE}_{f,2} = \frac{2}{\epsilon_2^2\epsilon_1^2\epsilon_0^2}\left[2g_2^2 + (l_2\epsilon_2 + g_2)^2 + (l_2\epsilon_2 + l_1\epsilon_2\epsilon_1 + g_2)^2\right] \tag{4}$$

Theorem 3.9 is verified by applying Lemma 3.8 to Algorithm 1. The general MSE for any size n chain mechanism can be written as a lengthy closed-form equation, which we omit here. In experiments, $n = 2$ performs well for alternating statistics. In general, n should not be a very big number otherwise each part gets smaller ϵ_i, but users should also consider the difficulty of computing the local sensitivity chain, as well as the amount of global sensitivity at the tail (it should not be too large).

Comparison with RLSB [16]. Karwa et al. proposed a similar idea for bounding local sensitivity by adding specially generated noise [16]. We call their technique relaxed local sensitivity bounding (RLSB) because their bound does not strictly satisfy the first condition above for safely bounding local sensitivity. Consequently, only relaxed (ϵ, δ)-differential privacy is supported. More importantly, because they add too much noise to the local sensitivity, our work, which supports stronger privacy definition (ϵ-differential privacy), still offers better utility, as stated in Lemma 3.10.

Lemma 3.10. *Assuming ϵ is evenly distributed, for any function f, chain mechanism offers lower mean squared error than RLSB.*

3.3 Alternating k-triangle and k-twopath

Now we apply the chain mechanism to alternating k-triangle and alternating k-twopath. Let $\beta = 1 - 1/\lambda$. By binomial coefficients, we can rewrite alternating k-triangle $T(x;\lambda)$ as

$$T(x;\lambda) = \lambda \sum_{i<j} x_{ij}\left\{1 - \beta^{C_{ij}}\right\} \tag{5}$$

Lemma 3.11. *Set $C'_{iv} = C_{iv} - x_{ij}$ and $C'_{vj} = C_{vj} - x_{ij}$. Let N_{ij} be all shared partners of node i and j and $C_{max} = \max_{i<j} C_{ij}$. The local sensitivity of T is*

$$\mathsf{LS}_{T,1}(x) = \max_{i<j}\ \lambda\left\{1 - \beta^{C_{ij}}\right\} + \sum_{v \in N_{ij}}\left\{\beta^{C'_{iv}} + \beta^{C'_{vj}}\right\} \tag{6}$$

$$\leq \lambda + 2C_{max} \tag{7}$$

As C_{max} has global sensitivity 1, $\mathsf{LS}_{T,1}$ has global sensitivity at most 2. So we can construct a 1-chain mechanism using $\mathsf{LS}_{T,1} = \lambda + 2C_{max}$ to compute private alternating k-triangle.

For alternating k-twopath $U(x;\lambda)$, we can rewrite it as

$$U(x;\lambda) = \lambda \sum_{i<j}\left\{1 - \beta^{C_{ij}}\right\} \tag{8}$$

Lemma 3.12. *Let N_i be the set of neighbors of node i and d_{max} be the maximum degree. Set $C'_{iv} = C_{iv} - x_{ij}$ and $C'_{vj} = C_{vj} - x_{ij}$. We have local sensitivity*

$$\mathsf{LS}_{U,1}(x) = \max_{i<j}\left\{\sum_{v \in N_i, v \neq j} \beta^{C'_{vj}} + \sum_{v \in N_j, v \neq i} \beta^{C'_{iv}}\right\} \tag{9}$$

$$\leq 2d_{max} \tag{10}$$

$$\mathsf{LS}_{U,2}(x) \leq \frac{\max(4, 1 + C_{max})}{\lambda} \tag{11}$$

From Lemma 3.12 above, $2d_{max}$ has global sensitivity 2, since d_{max} will change by at most 1 by adding or removing an edge. $\frac{\max(4,1+C_{max})}{\lambda}$ has global sensitivity $1/\lambda$ for $C_{max} > 3$. Therefore, we can construct either a 1-chain or 2-chain mechanism. We will compare the resulting error empirically in Section 5.

4. ERGM PARAMETER ESTIMATION

The parameter estimation step in our workflow takes the private sufficient statistics $\tilde{y}$ from the previous perturbation step and finds the best parameter vector θ. As stated above, this step is essentially post-processing a differentially private output, so the output θ is also differentially private. In this section, we discuss different ways of estimating θ given $\tilde{y}$.

4.1 Standard estimation

Current estimation techniques [29, 3] provide a baseline solution for parameter estimation with private statistics. As these procedures essentially only need access to model statistics, our sufficient statistics in $\tilde{y}$ take the place of the true model terms. The semantics is now to search for θ that defines a probability distribution on graphs with expected model statistics equal to $\tilde{y}$. Intuitively, the utility of this method depends on the amount of noise added into y_0 and how θ reacts to those changes in y_0.

Prior to applying standard estimation, we post-process $\tilde{y}$ to cope with some of the difficulties of the perturbed model statistics. As the output of perturbed $\tilde{y}$ might not be *graphical* (i.e., no graph has statistics equal to $\tilde{y}$), standard estimation may fail to converge. We propose generating a graph that has the closest statistics to $\tilde{y}$ and use the statistics from that graph to replace $\tilde{y}$, in order to avoid non-converging situations and to potentially remove noise from $\tilde{y}$ simultaneously. We use simulated annealing for this purpose and, in practice, we often see big improvements in the accuracy of estimates.

4.2 Bayesian inference

Standard estimation is the direct way of post-processing $\tilde{y}$, but since we know the distribution of the noise added to $\tilde{y}$, we can "guess" the true values and incorporate them into the estimation algorithm. This idea naturally fits into *Bayesian inference* based post-processing. While based on earlier work [3] on Bayesian inference for non-private estimation, our method deals with the extra hidden variable of graph x in our setting. And later we will see, by introducing the unknown x, our method can utilize more information from private statistics, such as the local sensitivity chain from the chain mechanism. In particular, we search for θ given $\tilde{y}$, represented as the posterior distribution of ERGM parameter θ:

$$p(\theta|\tilde{y}) \propto p(\tilde{y}|\theta)p(\theta) = \sum_x p(\tilde{y}|x)p(x|\theta)p(\theta) = \sum_x p(\tilde{y}|x)q(x;\theta)p(\theta)/Z_\theta \quad (12)$$

where x is our guess about x_0, but the fact is that we need to summarize over all possible x to get to the posterior. In (12), $p(\tilde{y}|x)$ is the *privacy distribution*, defined by the differential privacy mechanism applied on sufficient statistics. $p(x|\theta)$ is the *ERGM distribution*, as shown in (1) and $q(x;\theta)$ represents the unnormalized distribution.

$$q(x;\theta) = \exp(\theta \cdot f(x)) \quad (13)$$

The probability distribution (12) is hard to calculate or even sample from directly due to summarization over all graphs and normalizing constant Z_θ. Using the exchange algorithm [23], we introduce extra variables x, θ' and x' to bypass the difficult terms (12). By carefully choosing the probability distribution of these new random variables, the posterior distribution is now augmented as shown in (14). The key is that the marginal posterior distribution for θ in (14) is equivalent to (12). Thus, if we are able to sample from the distribution in (14), the marginal posterior distribution for θ can be obtained by summarizing over all samples.

$$p(\theta, x, \theta', x'|\tilde{y}) \propto p(\tilde{y}|x)p(x|\theta)p(\theta)p(\theta'|\theta)p(x'|\theta') \quad (14)$$

θ' is sampled from *proposal distribution* $p(\theta'|\theta)$, where, for a given θ, a new θ' can be proposed according to $p(\theta'|\theta)$. A common choice is a multivariate normal distribution or a multivariate t distribution, with mean equal to θ. x, x' are sampled graphs under the ERGM with parameter θ and θ'.

Algorithm 2 ERGM parameter estimation with private model statistics

Require: $\tilde{y}$, initial θ, x

1: **for** i in 1 to T **do**
2: Sample $\theta' \sim p(\theta'|\theta)$
3: Sample $x' \sim p(x'|\theta')$
4: Replace θ with θ' and x with x', with probability $\min(1, H)$ //H by (15) below
5: **return** average of multiple samples of θ.

A MCMC based sampling process for (14) is shown in Algorithm 2. In particular, the initial input θ and x could be any parameters and any graph. In Line 3, we need a separated MCMC chain to sample $x' \sim p(x'|\theta')$. In such MCMC algorithms, at each iteration, we propose adding or removing edges in the current state of graph, calculate the new model statistics, compare the probability of new state x_{new} to that of old state x_{old}, and with probability $p(x_{new}|\theta')/p(x_{old}|\theta')$ the change is accepted. This process should be run long enough so that final sample x' is truly from $p(x'|\theta')$.

H in Line 4 is the ratio of accepting the exchange, computed by comparing the probability before and after exchange. That is, we exchange θ with θ' and x with x' in (14) and calculate the ratio. Then the complex terms are cancelled out and each remaining term is easy to compute.

$$H = \frac{p(\tilde{y}|x')p(x'|\theta')p(\theta')p(\theta|\theta')p(x|\theta)}{p(\tilde{y}|x)p(x|\theta)p(\theta)p(\theta'|\theta)p(x'|\theta')} = \frac{p(\tilde{y}|x')p(\theta')p(\theta|\theta')}{p(\tilde{y}|x)p(\theta)p(\theta'|\theta)} \quad (15)$$

In practice, Algorithm 2 usually results in low acceptance rates in the exchange step in Line 4 and thus long mixing times for the MCMC process. We now propose to separate that last step, isolating simultaneously updated θ and x into two different steps, as shown in Algorithm 3, which improves the acceptance rate significantly.

Algorithm 3 Improved ERGM parameter estimation with private model statistics

Require: $\tilde{y}$, initial θ, x

1: **for** i in 1 to T **do**
2: Sample $\theta' \sim p(\theta'|\theta)$
3: Sample $x' \sim p(x'|\theta')$
4: Exchange θ with θ', with probability $\min(1, H_1)$ //H_1 by (16) below
5: Replace x with x', with probability $\min(1, H_2)$ //H_2 by (17) below
6: **return** average of multiple samples of θ.

H_1 and H_2 in Algorithm 3 are defined as follows.

$$H_1 = \frac{p(\tilde{y}|x)p(x|\theta')p(\theta')p(\theta|\theta')p(x'|\theta)}{p(\tilde{y}|x)p(x|\theta)p(\theta)p(\theta'|\theta)p(x'|\theta')} = \frac{q(x;\theta')p(\theta')p(\theta|\theta')q(x';\theta)}{q(x;\theta)p(\theta)p(\theta'|\theta)q(x';\theta')} \quad (16)$$

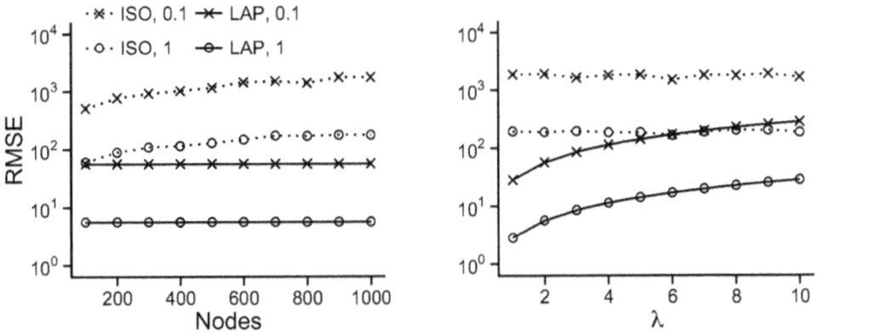

Figure 1: Perturbation error on alternating k-star on synthetic graphs. Left: $p = \log(n)/n$, varying size of graph n. Right: $n = 1000$, varying λ.

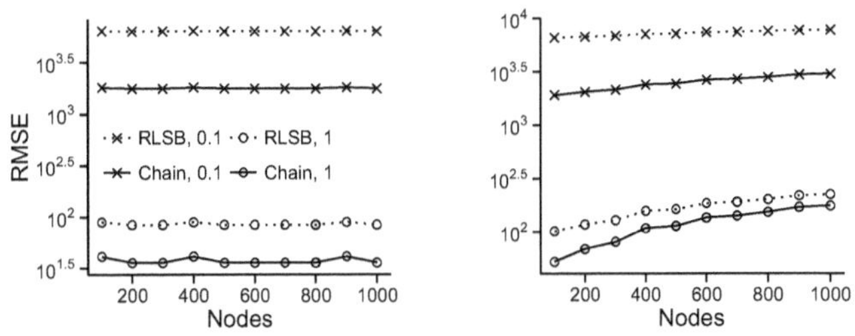

Figure 2: Perturbation error on alternating k-triangle. Left: $p = \log(n)/n$. Right: $p = 0.1$.

$$
\begin{aligned}
H_2 &= \frac{p(\tilde{y}|x')p(x'|\theta)p(\theta)p(\theta'|\theta)p(x|\theta')}{p(\tilde{y}|x)p(x|\theta)p(\theta)p(\theta'|\theta)p(x'|\theta')} \\
&= \frac{p(\tilde{y}|x')q(x';\theta)q(x;\theta')}{p(\tilde{y}|x)q(x;\theta)q(x';\theta')}
\end{aligned} \tag{17}
$$

The correctness of Algorithm 3 can be proved briefly in terms of a component-wise Metropolis-Hasting algorithm, with hybrid Gibbs updating steps. In each iteration, θ' and x' (Line 2 and 3) are drawn based on full conditional distribution, so the updating probability is always 1. In Line 4 and 5, we update θ and x with Hasting ratios. Although we may end up updating θ' and x' more times in a iteration, we still get to the detailed balance in MCMC [9].

When applying Algorithm 3 to real ERGM models, the key is correctly computing H_1 and H_2. Everything in H_1 is independent of the privacy mechanism used for the model terms. In H_2, the ratio of privacy distribution $\frac{p(\tilde{y}|x')}{p(\tilde{y}|x)}$ is mechanism dependent. Here, we illustrate the cases for both Laplace and Chain mechanism.

Example 4.1 (Laplace mechanism)**.** If the Laplace mechanism is applied on all model terms (f_i for i-th model term) independently, and $\tilde{y}$, ϵ and GS are the vectors of private statistics, privacy parameters and global sensitivities respectively, $p(\tilde{y}|x)$ is then:

$$
p(\tilde{y}|x) \propto \exp\left(-\sum_i |\tilde{y}_i - f_i(x)|\epsilon_i/\mathsf{GS}_i\right) \tag{18}
$$

Assume we use a symmetric proposal distribution for θ, i.e., $p(\theta'|\theta) = p(\theta|\theta')$. With Algorithm 3, ratio H_1 and H_2 can be written as (after taking logarithm)

$$
\log H_1 = \log\frac{p(\theta')}{p(\theta)} + (\theta - \theta')\cdot\big(f(x') - f(x)\big) \tag{19}
$$

$$
\begin{aligned}
\log H_2 = {} & (\theta - \theta')\cdot\big(f(x') - f(x)\big) + \\
& \sum_i \frac{\epsilon_i}{\mathsf{GS}_i}\big(|\tilde{y}_i - f_i(x)| - |\tilde{y}_i - f_i(x')|\big)
\end{aligned} \tag{20}
$$

Example 4.2 (Chain mechanism)**.** Assume a single model term (multiple model terms can be adjusted accordingly), and privacy parameter ϵ. In the process of MCMC, for current sampled graph x, we write $l_1, \ldots, l_n$ as the local sensitivity chain and y_{n+1} for the global sensitivity of l_n. The chain mechanism returns $\tilde{y}, y_1, \ldots, y_n$ for the observed graph. Based on Algorithm 1, $p(\tilde{y}|x)$ is then:

$$
\begin{aligned}
p(\tilde{y}|x) &= p(\tilde{y}|x, y_1)p(y_1|y_2, l_1)\ldots p(y_n|y_{n+1}, l_n) \\
&\propto \exp\left(\sum_{i\in[1,n]} \frac{l_i - y_i}{y_{i+1}/\epsilon_i} - \frac{|\tilde{y} - f(x)|}{y_1/\epsilon_0}\right)
\end{aligned} \tag{21}
$$

Calculation of $p(\tilde{y}|x)$ deals with not only the private version of local sensitivity chain $(y_1, \ldots, y_n)$, but also more statistics from the sampled graph in each iteration of MCMC $(l_1, \ldots, l_n)$. Recall in the standard estimation, none of them is incorporated in the process. In the next section, we empirically show that such extra information can benefit the estimation. As in the example above, assume a symmetric proposal distribution. With Algorithm 3, ratio H_1 is the same as (19). Before calculating H_2, we first check if all $l_i \le y_i$, otherwise $H_2 = 0$, because exponential noise in the chain mechanism is non-negative. If the check passes, H_2 is:

$$
\begin{aligned}
\log H_2 = {} & (\theta - \theta')\cdot\big(f(x') - f(x)\big) + \\
& \sum_{i\in[1,n]} \frac{l'_i - l_i}{y_{i+1}/\epsilon_i} + \frac{|\tilde{y} - f(x)| - |\tilde{y} - f(x')|}{y_1/\epsilon_0}
\end{aligned} \tag{22}
$$

Marginal maximum a posterior. In practice, instead of returning the mean of the marginal posterior (14), using a marginal maximum a posterior (MMAP) could give analysts better estimates. Formally, MMAP of θ is defined as $\operatorname{argmax}_\theta p(\theta|\tilde{y})$. A fast method we apply is reusing the samples of θ from Algorithm 3, and performing approximate MMAP estimation by histogram or density estimation. More sophisticated solutions require further expanding (14) before MCMC sampling [6, 15].

5. EVALUATION

Our evaluation has two goals. First we assess the perturbation error of our privacy mechanisms, particularly the Laplace mechanism on alternating k-star and the Chain mechanism on alternating k-triangle and k-twopath. Second, we evaluate the ERGM parameter estimation with private statistics using different approaches proposed in Section 4. All our experiments are run on Linux servers with Intel Xeon CPU and 8GB memory.

5.1 Perturbation error

Our datasets include synthetic and real graphs. Synthetic graphs are generated using a random graph model, $G(n,p)$, where parameters n and p control the size of graph and the probability of two nodes connecting respectively. We iterate n from 100 to 1000 with step 100. p is set to $\log(n)/n$ for relatively sparse graphs and then moved to 0.1 and higher by a step of 0.1. Though we only report the sparse case and $p = 0.1$, results for larger p agree with the conclusions. Error measurement is root mean square error (RMSE).

Alternating k-star As described in Section 3.1, we can apply the Laplace mechanism (LAP) directly or compute the degree distribution privately first, by isotonic regression

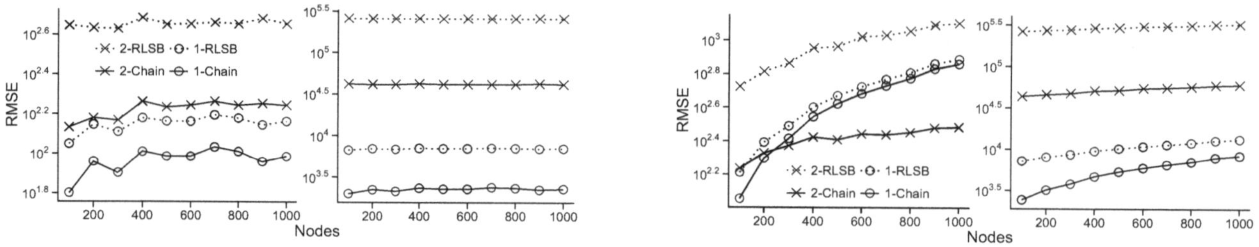

(1) $p = \log(n)/n, \epsilon = 1$ (2) $p = \log(n)/n, \epsilon = 0.1$ (3) $p = 0.1, \epsilon = 1$ (4) $p = 0.1, \epsilon = 0.1$

Figure 3: Perturbation error on alternating k-twopath.

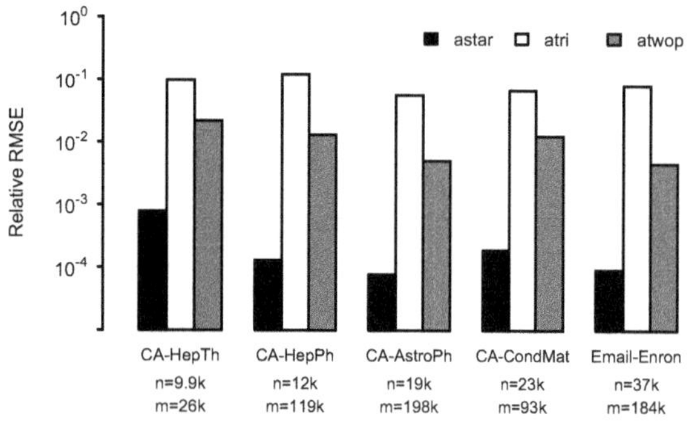

Figure 4: Perturbation error on real graphs

Network	nodes	edges	astar	atri	atwop
karate	34	78	194.0	88.7	411.7
dolphins	62	159	418.1	177.5	705.4
lesmis	77	254	756.4	426.5	1565.5
adjnoun	112	425	1292.9	452.2	3801.1
football	115	613	1992.4	922.4	3675.4

Table 1: Real networks for ERGM parameter estimation

Model	Model terms	Perturbation mech
M1	edges, astar	LAP, LAP
M2	edges, atri	LAP, 1-Chain
M3	edges, atwop	LAP, 1-Chain

Table 2: Model descriptions

(ISO) from [12] and use it as a sufficient statistic for alternating k-star. Figure 1 shows the error of the two methods by varying p and λ, with different settings of $\epsilon = 1, 0.1$, listed in the legend text. As we do not have analytical RMSE for the ISO case, it is calculated from 100 independent perturbations. We clearly see LAP significantly outperforms ISO, even when $\lambda = 10$ at both ϵ settings (and recall that the global sensitivity is 2λ). For the rest of this section, if not stated, we set $\lambda = 2$ as it is the value normally recommended [21] and usually plays a minor part in the workflow.

Alternating k-triangle The chain mechanism is applied to alternating k-triangle, with a size-one chain. We compare with RLSB [16], setting ϵ to 1 and 0.1 and fixing $\delta = 0.01$ for RLSB. Figure 2 shows that the Chain is constantly better, as stated by Lemma 3.10. Moreover, with smaller ϵ (meaning greater privacy protection), Chain can gain even more advantage over RLSB, not to mention that RLSB only offers relaxed differential privacy.

Alternating k-twopath We discussed in Section 3.3 how a 1-chain or 2-chain can be used for alternating k-twopath. Using RLSB's noise generation, we can bound local sensitivity with its global sensitivity (1-RLSB), or treating C_{max} as the deciding factor of local sensitivity and bounding it first (2-RLSB). We present results in Figure 3. As above, in all circumstances, Chain illustrates superior utility over RLSB and the difference is even more drastic in the 2-chain case. This is because RLSB adds more noise than necessary in each step of the local sensitivity chain, which accumulates in the final output. If the local sensitivity chain size is larger than 2, there will be an even greater difference. In Figure 3, with $\lambda = 2$, 1-chain generates less error than 2-chain on most cases, except on random graphs with $p = 0.1$ and $n > 300$. When increasing λ, 2-chain benefits from shrinked $\mathsf{LS}_{U.2}$. At small $\epsilon = 0.1$, with random graphs with $n = 1000$ and $p = 0.1$, 2-chain needs roughly $\lambda = 10$ to surpass 1-chain, which happens when Eq. (9) is much smaller than Eq. (10).

Real graphs For real graphs, we consider several collected networks from the SNAP collection[2] in order to figure out if our alternating statistics can be perturbed in a "meaningful" way, i.e., small relative noise that doesn't destroy the utility. Our metric is relative RMSE, which is RMSE divided by the true statistic. As shown in Figure 4, with $\epsilon = 0.1$, all three alternating statistics (with shortened names: astar, atri, atwop) are estimated with low relative error. In particular, error for alternating k-star is between 10^{-3} and 10^{-4}, alternating k-triangle at 10^{-1} and alternating k-twopath at 10^{-2}.

5.2 ERGM parameter estimation

For the evaluation of ERGM parameter estimation, we want to compare the algorithms in Section 4. In practice, the data owner will only perturb each statistic once and then release it to the analysts. As the perturbation is a randomized process, our goal is to understand how good our estimation algorithm is on *average*. So for each graph and each model description, we perturb the statistics $N = 50$ times and run the estimation algorithm on each perturbation, finally measuring their quality by RMSE with respect to estimates in the non-private case, $\sqrt{1/N \sum_{i \in [1,N]} (\hat{\theta}_i - \theta)^2}$, where θ is the "true" value, calculated from the non-private estimation algorithm from [14] or [3], $\hat{\theta}_i$ is θ from i-th perturbation.

As mentioned in [3], the estimation using the Bayesian technique has general scalability issues, where it becomes very slow for any graphs beyond a few hundred of nodes. Moreover such time cost also varies with the model terms,

[2] http://snap.stanford.edu

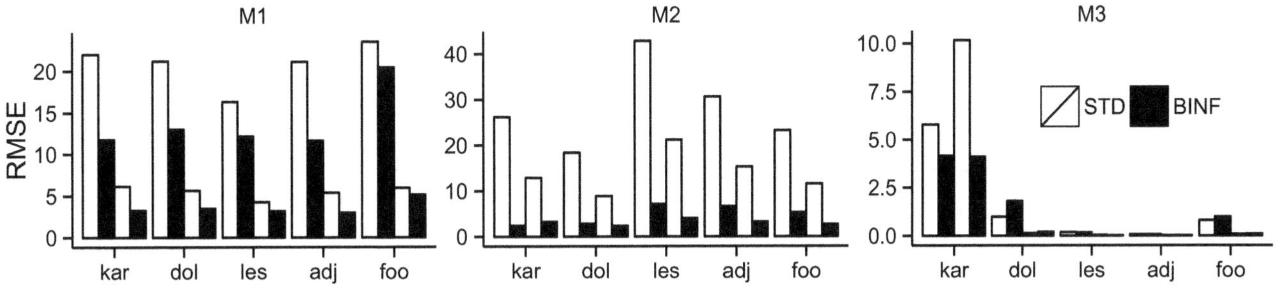

Figure 5: Parameter estimation with private statistics. Every four bars, from left to right, are $\theta_1, \theta_1, \theta_2, \theta_2$.

e.g., alternating k-twopath takes much more time than the other two alternating statistics, as calculation of the acceptance ratio in MCMC sampling of $x \sim p(x|\theta)$ is more complicated. Therefore, here we focus on smaller graphs, and this is the common practice for many ERGM works such as [3, 5, 21]. Our test networks[3] include karate, dolphins, lesmis, adjnoun and football. Detailed facts are listed in Table 1. We fix $\epsilon = 1$.

We experimented with three models, each of which corresponds to one of the alternating statistics, with the purpose of testing estimation by isolating other factors. We include the count of edges as a shared term in all models, as it is very common in ERGM applications. As shown in Table 2, each model contains two terms, with correspondingly two parameters, $\theta = (\theta_1, \theta_2)$. The estimation algorithms will be standard estimation (STD) and Bayesian inference (BINF). In all cases, the privacy budget is distributed evenly in a way such that each generation of noise uses same share of the overall ϵ. In Figure 5, each graph is represented with 4 bars, showing θ_1 of STD, θ_1 of BINF, θ_2 of STD, θ_2 of BINF. In M1 and M2, we see a significant improvement of θ from STD to BINF. Especially in M2, BINF limits all errors to around 5 or smaller where STD can go up to 40. We believe this is because BINF can utilize the extra information presented by the local sensitivity chain as shown in Example 4.2. In M3, we find BINF helps a lot on the bad case (karate graph) but not really on others as they already have low error in STD.

6. RELATED WORK

Differential privacy [8] has been actively studied in many sub-areas of computer science. Although the original focus was mainly on tabular data, the definition can be adapted to graph data [12] as well as other data models. Most research into differentially private analysis of graphs has focused on releasing graph statistics, e.g., degree sequence [12], triangle/star [16, 25], joint degree distribution/assortativity [26, 28] and clustering coefficient [31]. For modeling graphs privately, we are aware only of a private Kronecker graph modeling approach under differential privacy [22]. While our work relies on obtaining good private statistics, the ultimate goal is to allow ERGM modeling under differential privacy.

All of these works, including ours, protect relationships, i.e. they support edge-differential privacy. A stronger standard is to protect individuals, where neighbors are defined by changing a single node. Recently, researchers have developed some mechanisms for calculating private graph statistics under node differential privacy [17, 2, 4]. Our chain mechanism could be a good supporting algorithm when bounds on local sensitivity are required [17, 2].

Parameter estimation for ERGMs has also evolved from pseudo likelihood estimation (MPLE) [1], to Monte Carlo maximum likelihood (MC-MLE) [10] to recent stochastic approximation [29] and Bayesian inference [3]. These advances have helped ERGMs become central to social network analysis with many successful applications [21].

7. CONCLUSION AND FUTURE WORK

In this work, we consider the problem of estimating parameters for the exponential random graph model under differential privacy. Our solution decomposes the process into two steps: releasing private statistics first and running estimation second. Our local sensitivity-based chain mechanism can offer lower error than existing methods. The redesigned Bayesian parameter estimation is flexible and more accurate than standard methods. For future work, improving scalability is an important direction as well exploring alternative model terms.

8. ACKNOWLEDGMENTS

This material is based on work supported by the NSF through awards CNS-1012748 and IIS-0964094.

9. REFERENCES

[1] J. Besag. Spatial interaction and the statistical analysis of lattice systems. *Journal of the Royal Statistical Society. Series B (Methodological)*, 1974.

[2] J. Blocki, A. Blum, A. Datta, and O. Sheffet. Differentially private data analysis of social networks via restricted sensitivity. In *ITCS*, 2013.

[3] A. Caimo and N. Friel. Bayesian inference for exponential random graph models. *Social Networks*, 33(1):41–55, 2011.

[4] S. Chen and S. Zhou. Recursive mechanism: towards node differential privacy and unrestricted joins. In *SIGMOD*, 2013.

[5] S. J. Cranmer and B. A. Desmarais. Inferential network analysis with exponential random graph models. *Political Analysis*, 19(1):66–86, 2011.

[6] A. Doucet, S. J. Godsill, and C. P. Robert. Marginal maximum a posteriori estimation using markov chain monte carlo. *Statistics and Computing*, 2002.

[3] http://www-personal.umich.edu/~mejn/netdata/

[7] C. Dwork, K. Kenthapadi, F. McSherry, I. Mironov, and M. Naor. Our data, ourselves: Privacy via distributed noise generation. *EUROCRYPT*, 2006.

[8] C. Dwork, F. McSherry, K. Nissim, and A. Smith. Calibrating noise to sensitivity in private data analysis. *Theory of Cryptography*, 2006.

[9] D. Gamerman and H. F. Lopes. *Markov chain Monte Carlo: stochastic simulation for Bayesian inference*, volume 68. CRC Press, 2006.

[10] C. J. Geyer and E. A. Thompson. Constrained monte carlo maximum likelihood for dependent data. *Journal of the Royal Statistical Society.*, 1992.

[11] S. M. Goodreau, J. A. Kitts, and M. Morris. Birds of a feather, or friend of a friend? using exponential random graph models to investigate adolescent social networks*. *Demography*, 46(1):103–125, 2009.

[12] M. Hay, C. Li, G. Miklau, and D. Jensen. Accurate estimation of the degree distribution of private networks. In *ICDM*, 2009.

[13] D. Hunter. Curved exponential family models for social networks. *Social Networks*, 29(2):216–230, 2007.

[14] D. Hunter and M. Handcock. Inference in curved exponential family models for networks. *Journal of Computational and Graphical Statistics*, 2006.

[15] A. M. Johansen, A. Doucet, and M. Davy. Particle methods for maximum likelihood estimation in latent variable models. *Statistics and Computing*, 2008.

[16] V. Karwa, S. Raskhodnikova, A. Smith, and G. Yaroslavtsev. Private analysis of graph structure. In *VLDB*, 2011.

[17] S. P. Kasiviswanathan, K. Nissim, S. Raskhodnikova, and A. Smith. Analyzing graphs with node differential privacy. In *TCC*, 2013.

[18] D. Kifer and B.-R. Lin. An axiomatic view of statistical privacy and utility. *Journal of Privacy and Confidentiality*, 2012.

[19] J. Leskovec, D. Chakrabarti, J. Kleinberg, C. Faloutsos, and Z. Ghahramani. Kronecker graphs: An approach to modeling networks. *JMLR*, 2010.

[20] W. Lu and G. Miklau. Exponential random graph estimation under differential privacy. In *arXiv*, 2014.

[21] D. Lusher, J. Koskinen, and G. Robins. *Exponential Random Graph Models for Social Networks: Theory, Methods, and Applications*. Structural Analysis in the Social Sciences. Cambridge University Press, 2012.

[22] D. Mir and R. N. Wright. A differentially private estimator for the stochastic kronecker graph model. In *EDBT/ICDT Workshops*, 2012.

[23] I. Murray, Z. Ghahramani, and D. MacKay. Mcmc for doubly-intractable distributions. *arXiv*, 2012.

[24] M. Newman. *Networks: an introduction*. Oxford University Press, 2010.

[25] K. Nissim, S. Raskhodnikova, and A. Smith. Smooth sensitivity and sampling in private data analysis. In *STOC*, 2007.

[26] D. Proserpio, S. Goldberg, and F. McSherry. Calibrating data to sensitivity in private data analysis. In *VLDB*, 2014.

[27] G. Robins, T. Snijders, P. Wang, M. Handcock, and P. Pattison. Recent developments in exponential random graph p* models for social networks. *Social networks*, 2007.

[28] A. Sala, X. Zhao, C. Wilson, H. Zheng, and B. Zhao. Sharing graphs using differentially private graph models. In *SIGCOMM*, 2011.

[29] T. Snijders. Markov chain monte carlo estimation of exponential random graph models. *Journal of Social Structure*, 2002.

[30] T. A. Snijders, P. E. Pattison, G. L. Robins, and M. S. Handcock. New specifications for exponential random graph models. *Sociological methodology*, 2006.

[31] Y. Wang, X. Wu, J. Zhu, and Y. Xiang. On learning cluster coefficient of private networks. *Social network analysis and mining*, 2013.

[32] N. A. Weiss, P. T. Holmes, and M. Hardy. *A course in probability*. Pearson Addison Wesley, 2006.

APPENDIX

We provide other proofs in the full version of this paper [20].

Proof of Theorem 3.7. Let $\tilde{Y}, Y_1, \ldots, Y_n$ be the random variables representing output of chain mechanism. By the chain property of Y_i series (i.e., Y_i is conditionally independent of $Y_{i+2}, \ldots, Y_n$ given Y_{i+1}), we have:

$$\begin{aligned}&\Pr(\tilde{Y} = \tilde{y}, Y_1 = y_1, \ldots, Y_n = y_n)\\ =&\Pr(\tilde{Y} = \tilde{y} | Y_1 = y_1)\Pr(Y_1 = y_1 | Y_2 = y_2)\\ &\ldots \Pr(Y_{n-1} = y_{n-1} | Y_n = y_n)\Pr(Y_n = y_n)\end{aligned}$$

Now we want to prove for each combination of $y_1, \ldots, y_n$, the multiplicity of probabilities above satisfies differential privacy. More precisely, each $\Pr(Y_i = y_i | Y_{i+1} = y_{i+1})$ offers ϵ_i-differential privacy.

We start with $i = n$. Let $\Pr'(\cdot)$ represent the probability on neighbor x' and $g = \mathsf{GS}(\mathsf{LS}_{f,n}(x))$

$$\begin{aligned}\frac{\Pr(Y_n = y_n)}{\Pr'(Y_n = y_n)} &= \frac{\epsilon_n/g\ \exp(-(y_n - \mathsf{LS}_{f,n}(x)) * \epsilon_n/g)}{\epsilon_n/g\ \exp(-(y_n - \mathsf{LS}_{f,n}(x')) * \epsilon_n/g)}\\ &= \exp\left(\frac{(\mathsf{LS}_{f,n}(x) - \mathsf{LS}_{f,n}(x')) * \epsilon_n}{g}\right)\end{aligned}$$

Because $-g \leq \mathsf{LS}_{f,n}(x) - \mathsf{LS}_{f,n}(x') \leq g$, so

$$\exp(-\epsilon_n) \leq \frac{\Pr(Y_n = y_n)}{\Pr'(Y_n = y_n)} \leq \exp(\epsilon_n)$$

We move to $\Pr(Y_i = y_i | Y_{i+1} = y_{i+1})$ when $i < n$.

$$\begin{aligned}&\frac{\Pr(Y_i = y_i | Y_{i+1} = y_{i+1})}{\Pr'(Y_i = y_i | Y_{i+1} = y_{i+1})}\\ =&\frac{\epsilon_i/y_{i+1}\ \exp(-(y_i - \mathsf{LS}_{f,i}(x)) * \epsilon_i/y_{i+1})}{\epsilon_i/y_{i+1}\ \exp(-(y_i - \mathsf{LS}_{f,i}(x')) * \epsilon_i/y_{i+1})}\\ =&\exp\left(\frac{(\mathsf{LS}_{f,i}(x) - \mathsf{LS}_{f,i}(x')) * \epsilon_i}{y_{i+1}}\right)\end{aligned}$$

Because $-\mathsf{LS}_{f,i+1}(x) \leq \mathsf{LS}_{f,i}(x) - \mathsf{LS}_{f,i}(x') \leq \mathsf{LS}_{f,i+1}(x)$ and $y_{i+1} \geq \mathsf{LS}_{f,i+1}$ (due to positive exponential noise), we have:

$$\exp(-\epsilon_i) \leq \frac{\Pr(Y_i = y_i | Y_{i+1} = y_{i+1})}{\Pr'(Y_i = y_i | Y_{i+1} = y_{i+1})} \leq \exp(\epsilon_i)$$

Similarly, line 4 in Algorithm 1 is ϵ_0-differential private. Therefore, the whole algorithm is $\sum_i \epsilon_i$-differential private. □

Top-*k* Frequent Itemsets via Differentially Private FP-trees

Jaewoo Lee
Dept. of Computer Science / CERIAS
Purdue University
West Lafayette, IN USA
jaewoo@cs.purdue.edu

Chris Clifton
Dept. of Computer Science / CERIAS
Purdue University
West Lafayette, IN USA
clifton@cs.purdue.edu

ABSTRACT

Frequent itemset mining is a core data mining task and has been studied extensively. Although by their nature, frequent itemsets are aggregates over many individuals and would not seem to pose a privacy threat, an attacker with strong background information can learn private individual information from frequent itemsets. This has lead to differentially private frequent itemset mining, which protects privacy by giving inexact answers. We give an approach that first identifies top-k frequent itemsets, then uses them to construct a compact, differentially private FP-tree. Once the noisy FP-tree is built, the (privatized) support of all frequent itemsets can be derived from it without access to the original data. Experimental results show that the proposed algorithm gives substantially better results than prior approaches, especially for high levels of privacy.

Categories and Subject Descriptors

H.2.0 [**Information Systems**]: Database Management

General Terms

Algorithms, Security, Theory

Keywords

Frequent itemset, Differential privacy, FP-tree

1. INTRODUCTION

As volumes of personal data collected by many organizations increase, the problem of preserving privacy is increasingly important. In this paper, we investigate the problem of releasing top k frequent itemsets in a differentially private way. The problem of frequent itemset mining (FIM) has been extensively studied in the data mining community[2, 9] and it serves as an important building block for many exploratory data mining algorithms. Although frequent itemsets are inherently aggregated information common to many individuals, naïve release of frequent itemsets can reveal sensitive information about individuals in the dataset[3].

Differential privacy[7, 8] is a recent notion of privacy that guarantees the output of an algorithm is insensitive to the change of one individual's data. Differential privacy adds noise to the output (in our case, the frequent itemsets and their supports) such that the impact of any individual (transaction) on the outcome is small relative to the added noise - ensuring that even an adversary with extensive background knowledge cannot use the result to determine an individual's value. The main advantage of differential privacy is that it provides protection against a strong adversary without requiring a model of the adversary's knowledge, or defining what information is sensitive.

The main challenge in developing a differentially private FIM algorithm is that the sensitivity of an itemset query (the maximum impact a single individual can have on the set of frequent itemsets) is dependent on the dimensionality of itemsets in the dataset. Recently two works on differentially private FIM, PrivBasis[15] and SmartTruncation[19], were introduced. They reduce the dimensionality by projecting the data into a lower dimensional space and by truncating the transactions, respectively. While these methods guarantee differential privacy, they come at a substantial cost in the quality of the results.

In this paper, we propose a novel approach that integrates the low sensitivity of a threshold query set and the compactness of the FP-tree data structure[9]. The proposed algorithm uses a modified version of the general *sparse vector technique* introduced in [11, 10]. The sparse vector technique was originally used to release a small number of count queries whose count is greater than or equal to the given threshold. A variation of it appears in [17]. A big advantage of this technique is that information disclosure affecting differential privacy occurs only for count queries above the threshold; negative answers do not count against the "privacy budget". Intuitively, the itemsets whose supports are far above (below) the threshold remain frequent (infrequent) even after adding or removing one transaction. Only those itemsets whose supports are near the threshold can be switched from frequent to infrequent or vice versa by the change of single transaction. Based upon this observation, we modify the sparse vector technique to privately answer exponentially many threshold queries (with a constant number of non-null results) given a fixed threshold. The proposed algorithm is composed of two phases: (i) frequent itemset discovery and (ii) noisy support derivation. In the first phase, all frequent itemsets are identified. At

KDD'14, August 24–27, 2014, New York, NY, USA.
Copyright 2014 ACM 978-1-4503-2956-9/14/08 ...$15.00.
http://dx.doi.org/10.1145/2623330.2623723.

this stage, the algorithm does not know their supports, but only that their supports are above the threshold. Using this information, the second phase builds a differentially private FP-tree with privatized supports of the frequent itemsets. The proposed algorithm injects noise in the data structure at the intermediate (FP-tree) step. The final output (Frequent Itemsets, or any other output derivable from an FP-tree) can be further refined through an optional post-processing step.

The rest of this paper is organized as follows: In Section 2, related works are discussed. Section 3 defines the notations used throughout the paper and introduces the background knowledge about differential privacy. In Section 4, given the threshold, how the proposed algorithm identifies the set of frequent itemsets and derives their supports via differentially private FP-tree are described. In Section 5, the performance of the proposed algorithm is evaluated on a variety of datasets. Finally, Section 6 concludes our work.

2. RELATED WORKS

There has been concern for some time that data mining results could lead to privacy violations [13]. In [1], Aggarwal et al. claimed that in practice it is possible for an adversary to predict sensitive fields in records by using association rules learned from the dataset. Therefore, it is insufficient to simply hide sensitive values in the dataset. They introduced a technique for hiding minimal set of association rules to prevent disclosure of sensitive entries in the dataset. In order to hide sensitive association rules, the input dataset is anonymized so that sensitive rules cannot be learned.

Atzori et al. applied the concept of k-anonymity to the mining result instead of input dataset. To prevent inference on sensitive information, frequent patterns are distorted by changing their support values [3]. A collection of frequent patterns is called k anonymous if and only if the support of each pattern in the collection is greater than or equal to k.

The common problems from which both approaches described above suffer are difficulty on determining sensitive information and on modeling an adversary's background knowledge. Differential privacy, proposed in [8], has emerged as a promising solution for privacy protection and received considerable attention because of its privacy guarantee against an adversary with arbitrary background knowledge.

Bahaskar et al. studied the problem of differentially privately releasing top k frequent itemsets of length m [4]. Given the mining result of a non-private algorithm, it first selects top k itemsets to release using either the Laplace or exponential mechanism and then adds noise to each itemset's support value.

Li et al. proposed a method called *PrivBasis*[15], that finds top k frequent itemsets in a differentially private way. PrivBasis tries to reduce the search space by finding minimal sets of items in an initialization stage, that covers the top k frequent itemsets. Each such set is called a basis. The itemsets in transactional data are viewed as tabular data and projected onto each basis. The supports of all subsets of a basis are derived by using binary itemset support counting[5]. To find a basis set, PrivBasis employed the technique used in MaxClique[18]. However, basis finding based on frequent 2-itemsets may be very inaccurate and tends to generate many more bases than actually required.

Zeng et al. built a differentially private FIM algorithm[19] on apriori. Inspired by the observation that the sensitivity of

Symbol	Description
$D = \{t_1, \cdots, t_n\}$	A database of transactions
$\mathcal{I} = \{I_1, \cdots, I_p\}$	Set of items
ℓ-itemset	An itemset of length ℓ
$\mathsf{Lap}(\lambda)$	Laplace distribution with mean 0 and scale factor λ
$\sigma(X)$	Support of X, $\lvert\{t \in D \lvert X \subseteq t\}\rvert$
$\widehat{\sigma}(X)$	Noisy support of X, $\sigma(X) + \mathsf{Lap}(\cdot)$
τ	A user defined minimum support
$\mathcal{L}_i$	Set of large i-itemset
$\mathcal{C}_i$	Set of candidate i-itemset
$\mathcal{M}$	Set of maximal frequent itemsets
$v^{<t}$	Prefix of vector $\mathbf{v}$ of length $t-1$

Table 1: Notations

a counting query set used for support verification is dependent on the maximal length of transactions in the dataset, they introduced the idea of truncating transactions to reduce the amount of noise to inject. However, truncating transactions in their algorithm is heuristic and its performance is quite sensitive to parameter settings.

3. PRELIMINARIES

3.1 Notation

Let $\mathcal{I} = \{I_1, \cdots, I_p\}$ be a set of items. An ℓ-itemset $X = \{x_1, \cdots, x_\ell\}$ is a subset of $\mathcal{I}$ whose length is ℓ where $x_i \in \mathcal{I}(1 \leq i \leq \ell)$. The support of itemset X, denoted by $\sigma(X)$, is the number of transactions in D that includes X as a subset. An itemset X is frequent if and only if its support is greater than or equal to minimum support τ (i.e.,if $\sigma(X) \geq \tau$). We use $\widehat{Y}$ to denote the noisy version of Y, i.e., $\widehat{Y} = Y + \mathsf{Lap}(\lambda)$ where $\mathsf{Lap}(\lambda)$ is a random sample (i.i.d) drawn from a Laplace distribution whose scale factor is λ.

3.2 Differential Privacy

Two databases D_1 and D_2 are referred to as neighboring if one can be obtained by adding or removing one tuple from the other, i.e., $|(D_1 - D_2) \cup (D_2 - D_1)| = 1$. Informally, differential privacy ensures that any changes in the probability of any outcome due to a single change in the input database is bounded by a constant ratio.

DEFINITION 1 (ϵ-DIFFERENTIAL PRIVACY). *A randomized mechanism $\mathcal{K}$ is ϵ-differentially private if for all neighboring databases D_1 and D_2, $\forall S \subseteq Range(\mathcal{K})$*

$$P[\mathcal{K}(D_1) \in S] \leq \exp(\epsilon) P[\mathcal{K}(D_2) \in S]$$

One way to achieve differential privacy is to perturb the output with random noise. The magnitude of noise should be large enough to hide the change that can be made by one individual in the universe. This is captured by the concept of sensitivity [8].

DEFINITION 2 (SENSITIVITY). *The sensitivity of a query function q is defined as*

$$\Delta q = \max_{D_1, D_2} |q(D_1) - q(D_2)|$$

where D_1 and D_2 are neighboring databases.

It is known that Laplace mechanism achieves ϵ-differential privacy [7].

Definition 3 (Laplace mechanism). *Given a query function q, a mechanism $\mathcal{K}$ that adds a random noise drawn from $\mathsf{Lap}(\frac{\Delta q}{\epsilon})$ to the output value of q is referred to as Laplace mechanism.*

One nice property of differential privacy is that it is composable. The privacy guarantee provided by differential privacy gracefully degrades under sequential composition: any sequential composition of differentially private sub-routines, each of which satisfies ϵ_i-differential privacy, satisfies $\sum_i \epsilon_i$-differential privacy. This is useful when designing a differentially private algorithm since the entire algorithm will be ϵ-differentially private as long as the privacy budget allocated to each sub-routine sums to ϵ.

3.3 Sparse Vector Algorithm

The sparse vector algorithm was developed to release κ count queries that are above the given threshold τ. The algorithm starts by calculating the noisy threshold $\hat{\tau}$ using part of the privacy budget. Given a count query q, it calculates the noisy count and compares it with $\hat{\tau}$. Let $\mathcal{K}$ denote the algorithm and q be a count query.

$$\mathcal{K}(D) = \begin{cases} q(D) + \mathsf{Lap}(\frac{2\kappa}{\epsilon}) & \text{if } q(D) + \mathsf{Lap}(\frac{2\kappa}{\epsilon}) \geq \hat{\tau} \\ \perp & \text{otherwise} \end{cases}$$

The algorithm uses another half of the privacy budget to answer above threshold queries. Notice that the remaining privacy budget $\frac{\epsilon}{2}$ is divided into κ count queries. After answering κ count queries it halts. The nice property of this algorithm is that it only pays privacy budget for above threshold queries and all below threshold queries are answered without wasting the privacy budget. Hence, any number of below threshold queries can be answered without compromising privacy. In essence, although the noisy count is calculated for each query and it is compared to the noisy threshold $\hat{\tau}$, the algorithm does not release it but $\perp$ for all below threshold queries hence not paying the privacy budget. The privacy guarantee of above threshold queries is immediate since each query pays the budget of $\frac{\epsilon}{2\kappa}$. The privacy of below threshold queries comes from the fact that it is compared to the noisy threshold. The formal privacy proof appears in [10].

4. THE NOISYCUT ALGORITHM

We now describe each step of the proposed algorithm, called NoisyCut. The algorithm takes an integer k and output the top k most frequent itemsets. The algorithm first learns the support of the k^{th}most frequent itemset σ_k and uses it as a threshold. This can be done by running any non-private FIM algorithm. Since the only output of this stage is the σ_k, using only the noisy threshold $\hat{\tau} = \sigma_k + \mathsf{Lap}(\cdot)$ ensures differential privacy.

For each itemset in the itemset lattice, the algorithm tests if its noisy support is above the noisy threshold. If it is, the algorithm regards it as frequent. This can be viewed as cutting the itemset lattice into two groups, frequent $\mathcal{L}$ and infrequent $\mathcal{L}^{\complement}$, and hence the name of algorithm. We will show that this can be done with high accuracy and with small privacy budget while guaranteeing differential privacy. After identifying all frequent itemsets, to derive the support of each frequent itemset, the algorithm builds a noisy FP-tree. The supports of itemsets can be derived from the FP-tree

Algorithm 1 FindFreqItemsets

Input: Transactional database D, set of items $\mathcal{I}$, Top k, privacy budget ϵ_1

Output: a set of frequent itemsets $\mathcal{L}$

function FindFreqItemsets($D, \mathcal{I}, k, \epsilon_1$)
  $\hat{\tau} \leftarrow \sigma_k + \mathsf{Lap}\left(\frac{4}{\epsilon_1}\right)$
  $\mathcal{L}_1 \leftarrow$ GetFrequent($\mathcal{I}, \hat{\tau}, \frac{3\epsilon_1}{4}, \emptyset$)
  $\ell \leftarrow 2$, $\mathcal{L} \leftarrow \mathcal{L}_1$
  while $\mathcal{L}_{\ell-1} \neq \emptyset$ **and** $|\mathcal{L}| < k$ **do**
    $\mathcal{C}_\ell \leftarrow \{a \cup b \mid a, b \in \mathcal{L}_{i-1} \wedge a < b\}$
    $\mathcal{L}_\ell \leftarrow$ GetFrequent($\mathcal{C}_\ell, \hat{\tau}, \frac{3\epsilon_1}{4}, \mathcal{L}$)
    $\mathcal{L} \leftarrow \mathcal{L} \cup \mathcal{L}_\ell$, $\ell \leftarrow \ell + 1$
  return $\mathcal{L}$

function GetFrequent($\mathcal{C}, \hat{\tau}, \epsilon, L$)
  $S \leftarrow \emptyset$
  for each itemset $X \in \mathcal{C}$ **do**
    $\widehat{\sigma}(X) \leftarrow \sigma(X) + \mathsf{Lap}(\frac{1}{\epsilon})$
    if $\widehat{\sigma}(X) \geq \hat{\tau}$ **and** $|L \cup S| < k$ **then**
      $S \leftarrow S \cup \{X\}$
  return S

in a recursive manner. Generating noisy counts for frequent itemsets can also be done using the binary itemset support counting method proposed in [5].

The privacy budget ϵ is allocated between two phases. Let $\epsilon_1 = \xi\epsilon$ and $\epsilon_2 = (1-\xi)\epsilon$ be the privacy budget allocated to the first and second phase, respectively (i.e., $\epsilon = \epsilon_1 + \epsilon_2$), where $\xi \in (0,1)$ is the parameter that controls privacy budget allocation between two phases. The larger ξ is, the more accurately the proposed algorithm can find frequent itemsets in the first phase while it would increase the amount of noise added to the support of each itemset in the second phase. We empirically settled on $\xi = \frac{1}{3}$ and use this value in the experiments.

4.1 Discovering Frequent Itemsets

The algorithm for finding a set of frequent itemsets $\mathcal{L}$ is described in Algorithm 1. The algorithm is Apriori-based. The candidate $(\ell+1)$-itemsets are generated by joining two previously found frequent ℓ-itemsets that share a frequent $(\ell-1)$-itemset as a prefix. While the proposed algorithm follows the intuition of Apriori algorithm, the biggest difference is that Algorithm 1 finds frequent itemsets by asking a set of threshold queries, each of which asks if the noisy support of itemset in question is above the noisy threshold or not and receives a boolean answer.

This threshold query based approach has a significant advantage over the count query based one in terms of noise addition. Let's consider the case where count queries are used instead of threshold queries.

Definition 4 (ℓ-count query set). *Given a set of candidate ℓ-itemsets, $\mathcal{C}_\ell$, an ℓ-count query set CQ_ℓ is defined as*

$$\mathsf{CQ}_\ell = \langle q_1, \cdots, q_{|\mathcal{C}_\ell|} \rangle$$

where each query q_i asks for the count of ith itemset in $\mathcal{C}_\ell$.

At each iteration, the algorithm throws CQ_ℓ to the privacy mechanism to verify the supports of candidate itemsets.

Theorem 1. *The sensitivity of an ℓ-count query set $\Delta\mathsf{CQ}_\ell$ is the size of candidate set, $\mathcal{C}_\ell$.*

PROOF. Assume there is a transaction t that contributes to every $q_i (1 \leq i \leq n)$. Adding or removing t from D will change the answer of each q_i by one. Therefore, the global sensitivity of CQ_ℓ is the size of candidate set (i.e., $\Delta q = |\mathcal{C}|$). □

Since the sensitivity of a count query set is very high, a naïve application of the Laplace mechanism to the Apriori method will add unacceptable noise to each itemset.

DEFINITION 5 (ℓ-THRESHOLD QUERY SET). *An ℓ-threshold query set is a set of threshold queries for candidate ℓ-itemsets.*

$$\mathsf{TQ}_\ell = \langle q_1, \cdots, q_{|\mathcal{C}_\ell|} \rangle$$

where each q_i returns 1 if $\sigma(X) \geq \tau$, and 0 otherwise.

Privacy Analysis..

In a differentially private algorithm, all information disclosures must be performed in a differentially private way. Based on the sparse vector method, the noise in the result comes from the noise in the threshold, resulting in either near-frequent itemsets being treated as frequent, or vice-versa. This ensures that the effect of a single transaction on an itemset appearing in the result is low relative to the noise causing an itemset to appear in the result.

There would appear to be one issue: we don't ask if *all* itemsets are frequent, only candidates. However, the first round considers all possible items, and subsequent round *candidates* are generated from the (differentially private) output of the previous round without access to the database, satisfying differential privacy.

Given an integer $k > 0$, the algorithm starts from calculating the noisy threshold by adding noise to the support of the k^{th}most frequent itemset, $\sigma(k)$ (line 2). Observe that adding or removing a transaction can only change the support of the k^{th}most frequent itemset, $\sigma(k)$, by at most one. Hence, adding a random noise drawn from $\mathsf{Lap}\left(\frac{4}{\epsilon_1}\right)$ to $\sigma(k)$ satisfies $\frac{\epsilon_1}{4}$-differential privacy. Let $\hat{\tau}_1$ and $\hat{\tau}_2$ be the noisy thresholds for two neighboring database D_1 and D_2, respectively. For $\forall x \in \mathbb{R}$,

$$\mathrm{P}[\hat{\tau}_1 = x] \leq \exp\left(\frac{\epsilon_1}{4}\right) \mathrm{P}[\hat{\tau}_2 = x] \tag{1}$$

After computing $\hat{\tau}$, for each itemset $X \in \mathcal{C}$, the algorithm internally computes the noisy support $\widehat{\sigma}(X)$ by adding Laplacian random noise to its true support $\sigma(X)$. If the calculated noisy support is greater than or equal to the noisy threshold, the itemset is regarded frequent. Otherwise, it is regarded infrequent. Notice that in either case what is released by this phase of the algorithm is not the noisy support but *whether the itemset is frequent or not.* Let $\mathcal{C}$ be the set of all candidate itemsets and X_i be the i^{th}element in $\mathcal{C}$. We can model the set of answers the algorithm receives from the privacy mechanism as a vector $\mathbf{v} = \langle v_1, \cdots, v_t \rangle$ where $v_i = 1$ if $\widehat{\sigma}(X_i) \geq \hat{\tau}$, otherwise $v_i = 0$.

$$v_i = \begin{cases} 1 & \text{if } \widehat{\sigma}(X_i) \geq \hat{\tau} \\ 0 & \text{otherwise} \end{cases}$$

Therefore, to prove the privacy of Algorithm 1, it is sufficient to show that the privacy loss for all possible $\mathbf{v} \in \mathbb{Z}$ is bounded by $\exp(\epsilon)$ where $\mathbb{Z}$ is the set of all possible binary vectors. In Theorem 2, we prove that vector $\mathbf{v}$ released by the Algorithm 1 satisfies ϵ_1-differential privacy regardless of its length.

THEOREM 2. *Algorithm 1 is ϵ_1-differentially private.*

PROOF. Given any two neighboring databases D_1 and D_2, let V_1 and V_2 denote the output distribution on $\mathbf{v}$ when D_1 and D_2 are the input databases, respectively. We use $v^{<t}$ to denote $(t-1)$ previous answers from the mechanism (i.e., $v^{<t} = \langle v_1, \cdots, v_{t-1} \rangle$). Using the law of conditional probability, the privacy loss due to $\mathbf{v} = \langle v_1, \cdots, v_t \rangle$ for every $a_i \in \{0, 1\}$ is

$$\begin{aligned} \frac{V_1(\mathbf{v})}{V_2(\mathbf{v})} &= \frac{\prod_{i=1}^{t} V_1\left(v_i = a_i \mid v^{<i}\right)}{\prod_{i=1}^{t} V_2\left(v_i = a_i \mid v^{<i}\right)} \\ &= \prod_{i:a_i=1} \frac{V_1\left(v_i{=}1 \mid v^{<i}\right)}{V_2\left(v_i{=}1 \mid v^{<i}\right)} \cdot \prod_{j:a_j=0} \frac{V_1\left(v_j{=}0 \mid v^{<j}\right)}{V_2\left(v_j{=}0 \mid v^{<j}\right)} \end{aligned}$$

Once $v^{<i}$ is fixed, the conditional distributions of $\hat{\tau}$ and $\widehat{\sigma}(X)$ are just a Laplace distribution. Let $H_i^1(x)$ be the probability that the itemset X_i is frequent (*i.e.*, $v_i = 1$) in D_1 when the threshold is x.

$$\begin{aligned} H_i^1(x) &= \mathrm{P}\left[v_i = 1 \mid v^{<i}\right] = \mathrm{P}\left[\widehat{\sigma}_1(X_i) \geq x \mid v^{<i}\right] \\ &= \mathrm{P}\left[\mathsf{Lap}\left(\frac{4}{3\epsilon_1}\right) \geq x - \sigma_1(X_i) \,\middle|\, v^{<i}\right] \end{aligned}$$

Let $\lambda = \frac{4}{3\epsilon_1}$ and $f(y; \mu, \lambda) = \frac{1}{2\lambda} \exp\left(-\frac{|y-\mu|}{\lambda}\right)$.

$$H_i^1(x) = \int_x^\infty f\left(y; \sigma_1(X_i), \frac{4}{3\epsilon_1}\right) \mathrm{d}y$$

Recall that $\Delta\sigma = 1$. If we make a substitution $u = y + 1$, from $\mathrm{d}u = \mathrm{d}y$, the above yields

$$H_i^1(x) = \int_{x+1}^\infty f\left(u; \sigma_1(X_i){+}\Delta\sigma, \frac{4}{3\epsilon_1}\right) \mathrm{d}u \tag{2}$$

There are two possible cases:

- If $\sigma_2(X_i) = \sigma_1(X_i) + 1$, then equation (2) yields
$$H_i^1(x) = \int_{x+1}^\infty f\left(u; \sigma_2(X_i), \frac{4}{3\epsilon_1}\right) \mathrm{d}u = H_i^2(x+1)$$
- If $\sigma_2(X_i) = \sigma_1(X_i)$, then $H_i^1(x) = H_i^2(x)$.

Let the set of indices of answers for itemsets whose supports are the same in both D_1 and D_2 and for itemsets whose supports increase by one be $S = \{i | a_i{=}1 \wedge \sigma_1(X_i){=}\sigma_2(X_i)\}$ and $\bar{S} = \{i | a_i = 1 \wedge \sigma_2(X_i){=}\sigma_1(X_i){+}1\}$, respectively.

$$\begin{aligned} &\prod_{i:a_i=1} V_1\left(v_i{=}1 \mid v^{<i}\right) \\ &= \prod_{i \in S} V_1\left(v_i{=}1 \mid v^{<i}\right) \cdot \prod_{j \in \bar{S}} V_1\left(v_j{=}1 \mid v^{<j}\right) \\ &= A \cdot B \end{aligned} \tag{3}$$

where $A{=}\prod_{i \in S} V_1\left(v_i{=}1 | v^{<i}\right)$ and $B{=}\prod_{j \in \bar{S}} V_1\left(v_j{=}1 | v^{<j}\right)$.

$$\begin{aligned} A &= \int_{-\infty}^\infty \mathrm{P}[\hat{\tau}_1{=}x] \prod_{i \in S} H_i^1(x)\,\mathrm{d}x {=} \int_{-\infty}^\infty \mathrm{P}[\hat{\tau}_1{=}x] \prod_{i \in S} H_i^2(x)\,\mathrm{d}x \\ &\leq \exp\left(\frac{\epsilon_1}{4}\right) \int_{-\infty}^\infty \mathrm{P}[\hat{\tau}_2{=}x] \prod_{i \in S} H_i^2(x)\,\mathrm{d}x \\ &= \exp\left(\frac{\epsilon_1}{4}\right) \prod_{i \in S} V_2\left(v_i{=}1 \mid v^{<i}\right) \end{aligned} \tag{4}$$

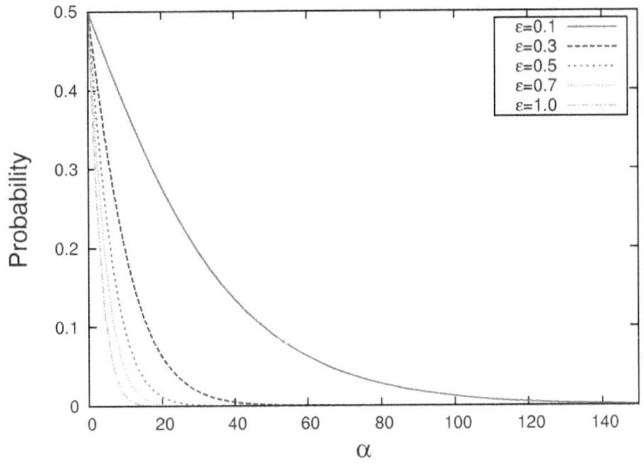

Figure 1: False negative probability

$$
\begin{aligned}
B &= \int_{-\infty}^{\infty} \mathrm{P}[\hat{\tau}_1{=}x] \prod_{j\in\bar{S}} H_j^1(x)\,\mathrm{d}x \\
&= \int_{-\infty}^{\infty} \mathrm{P}[\hat{\tau}_1{=}x] \prod_{j\in\bar{S}} H_j^2(x+1)\,\mathrm{d}x \\
&\le \exp\left(\frac{\epsilon_1}{4}\right) \int_{-\infty}^{\infty} \mathrm{P}[\hat{\tau}_2{=}x{+}1] \prod_{j\in\bar{S}} H_j^2(x+1)\,\mathrm{d}x \\
&= \exp\left(\frac{\epsilon_1}{4}\right) \int_{-\infty}^{\infty} \mathrm{P}[\hat{\tau}_2{=}x] \prod_{j\in\bar{S}} H_j^2(x)\,\mathrm{d}x \\
&= \exp\left(\frac{\epsilon_1}{4}\right) \prod_{j\in\bar{S}} V_2\left(v_j{=}1 \mid v^{<j}\right) \qquad (5)
\end{aligned}
$$

From (4) and (5), it is seen that

$$\prod_{i:a_i=1} V_1\left(v_i{=}1 \mid v^{<i}\right) \le \exp\left(\frac{\epsilon_1}{2}\right) \prod_{j:a_j=1} V_2\left(v_j{=}1 \mid v^{<j}\right)$$

By the same argument as in the preceding, we can prove

$$\prod_{i:a_i=0} V_1\left(v_i{=}0 \mid v^{<i}\right) \le \exp\left(\frac{\epsilon_1}{2}\right) \prod_{j:a_j=0} V_2\left(v_j{=}0 \mid v^{<j}\right)$$

Therefore, for all $\mathbf{v}$ of any length t, $\frac{V_1(\mathbf{v})}{V_2(\mathbf{v})} \le \exp(\epsilon_1)$. □

Utility Analysis..

As shown in Figure 1, the farther an itemset is from the threshold, the lower chance of being a false negative it has, which means that, except for itemsets that are close to the "borderline", the algorithm is highly likely to find all frequent itemsets.

THEOREM 3. *Given an itemset X whose support is $\tau+\alpha$, the probability that this itemset will become a false negative is* $\frac{1}{4}\exp\left(-\frac{\alpha\epsilon}{2}\right)\left(\frac{\alpha\epsilon}{2}+2\right)$.

PROOF. The mechanism will answer correctly if the following condition is satisfied:

$$\hat{\tau} - \tau - (\widehat{\sigma}(X) - \sigma(X)) < \alpha \qquad (6)$$

Observe that $\hat{\tau} - \tau$ and $\widehat{\sigma}(X) - \sigma(X)$ are two independent random variables whose distribution is $\mathsf{Lap}(\lambda = \frac{2}{\epsilon})$. Let V and W be random variables corresponding to $\hat{\tau} - \tau$ and $\widehat{\sigma}(X) - \sigma(X)$, respectively. Let $Z = V - W$ denote the difference between two random variables. Since Laplace distribution is symmetric, $Z{=}V{-}W{=}V{+}W$. To denote the probability density function of Z, we use the notation $f_Z(z)$.

$$
\begin{aligned}
f_Z(z) &= \int_{-\infty}^{\infty} f_V(x) f_W(x-z)\,\mathrm{d}x \\
&= \int_{-\infty}^{\infty} \frac{1}{4\lambda^2}\exp\left(-\frac{|x|}{\lambda}\right)\exp\left(-\frac{|x-z|}{\lambda}\right)\mathrm{d}x \\
&= \int_{-\infty}^{0} \frac{1}{4\lambda^2}\exp\left(\frac{x}{\lambda}\right)\exp\left(-\frac{|x-z|}{\lambda}\right)\mathrm{d}x \\
&\quad + \int_{0}^{\infty} \frac{1}{4\lambda^2}\exp\left(-\frac{x}{\lambda}\right)\exp\left(-\frac{|x-z|}{\lambda}\right)\mathrm{d}x \\
&= \frac{1}{4\lambda}\exp\left(-\frac{|z|}{\lambda}\right)\left(1-\frac{|z|}{\lambda}\right)
\end{aligned}
$$

The probability of not satisfying (6) is
$1-\int_{-\infty}^{\alpha} \frac{1}{4\lambda}\exp\left(-\frac{|z|}{\lambda}\right)\left(1+\frac{|z|}{\lambda}\right)\mathrm{d}z = \frac{1}{4}\exp\left(-\frac{\alpha}{\lambda}\right)\left(\frac{\alpha}{\lambda}+2\right)$ □

False positives may also occur (again, most likely if close to the top k), but are less critical as they may later be filtered by having a low (noisy) support.

4.2 Deriving Noisy Support

Given a set of frequent itemsets $\mathcal{L}$, it is easy to find the set of maximal frequent itemsets $\mathcal{M}$. This can be done on the fly by checking if the newly added frequent itemset is subsumed by any existing itemsets.

Algorithm 3 derives noisy supports of all itemsets in $\mathcal{L}$. The algorithm employs an FP-tree data structure and the FPGrowth algorithm [9]. As the algorithm follows the usual procedure of the FPGrowth algorithm, we only remark on the differences.

- A node v in the FP-tree has three fields: $v.item$, $v.count$ and $v.children$, where *item* denotes which item v represents, *count* is the number of transactions represented by the path from the root to v, and *children* is an array of v's child nodes.
- The original algorithm arranges items in a transaction in a decreasing order of their supports. However, since that information is not available to our algorithm, we sort them lexicographically.
- Before counting the support of each itemset, a node is created for each itemset $l \in 2^M$ where 2^M denotes the power set of M (line 3 in Algorithm 2). This is to ensure that the structure of FP-tree is not dependent on any particular database instance; the tree structure is completely determined by the output of the previous phase, $\mathcal{M}$, learned in a differentially private way.
- The count attribute of a newly created node in the FP-tree is initialized to $\mathsf{Lap}\left(\frac{|\mathcal{M}|}{\epsilon_2}\right)$. Note that, although it is omitted in the algorithm, every newly created node should be linked to the nodes with the same item via the side-link structure (line 8 in Algorithm 2).
- A transaction is mapped to a single path in the FP-tree and only increases the count of the last node on the path (line 17) by one. This means that adding or removing one transaction can only change the count of a node by at most one. Hence the sensitivity of releasing counts in the FP-tree is 1.

Algorithm 2 BuildFPTree

Input: set of dimensions for projection M
Output: FP-tree T

```
 1: function BuildFPTree(M, ε)
 2:     γ ← create a root node
 3:     for each itemset l ∈ 2^M do
 4:         v ← γ
 5:         for each item i ∈ l do
 6:             if ∄w s.t. w ∈ v.children ∧ w.item = i then
 7:                 create a new node w under v
 8:                 w.item ← i; w.count ← Lap(1/ε)
 9:             v ← w
10:     return γ

11: function UpdateCount(D, M, T)
12:     for each transaction t ∈ D do
13:         t ← t ∩ M; v ← T
14:         for each item i ∈ t do
15:             if v has a child w s.t. w.item = i then
16:                 v ← w
17:         v.count ← v.count + 1
```

- To get the correct count after building the FP-tree, starting from the leaf nodes going up toward the root node, the count of each node is added to its parent (line 7 in Algorithm 3). Observe that both actual occurrence count and noise are propagated to the parent.

Given an itemset X, its noisy support $\widehat{\sigma}(X)$ is an unbiased estimator of the true support and we measure the error of noisy support of X as its variance, i.e., $\mathsf{Error}(X) = \mathbb{E}\left[(\widehat{\sigma}(X) - \sigma(X))^2\right]$. If an itemset X is a subset of multiple maximal frequent itemsets, say $M_1, M_2, \cdots, M_m$, its support is counted by m FP-trees and they need to be aggregated in a way that minimize $\mathsf{Error}(X)$. To aggregate multiple noisy supports, each noisy support is weighted proportional to the inverse of its variance as in Lemma 1.

LEMMA 1. *Given m noisy supports, $\widehat{\sigma}_1(X), \cdots, \widehat{\sigma}_m(X)$, and their respective variances $v_1, \cdots, v_m$, the variance of weighted mean $\mathsf{Var}\left(\sum_{i=1}^{m} w_i\widehat{\sigma}_i(X)\right)$ is minimized by setting $w_i = \frac{1}{v_i} \Big/ \sum_{j=1}^{m} \frac{1}{v_j}$.*

While Algorithm 3 looks like a (non-noisy) query to the database, which would appear to violate differential privacy, the output is equivalent to constructing a tree from the (differentially private) set of maximal frequent itemsets, then filling in supports using a noisy count query for each node. The algorithm as written does this with a single pass through the database.

THEOREM 4. *Algorithm 3 achieves ϵ_2 differential privacy.*

PROOF. Given an input database D, the process of building the FP-tree can be viewed as a query function $g(D)$ which returns an FP-tree built upon D. An FP-tree is a set of nodes each of which contains the count of the corresponding itemset. Hence, using an arbitrary traversal order, it can be modeled as a vector $\mathbf{u}_D = (u_1, \cdots, u_i, \cdots, u_q)$ where $u_i (1 \le i \le q)$ represents a node count and q is the number of nodes in the tree. For the proof, it suffices to show that the function UPDATECOUNT satisfies differential privacy since this is the only place in the algorithm that requires access

Algorithm 3 GetNoisySupport

Input: database D, set of maximal frequent itemsets $\mathcal{M}$, privacy budget ϵ_2
Output: Top k frequent itemsets in $\mathcal{L}$ and their support

```
 1: function GetNoisySupport(D, 𝓜, ε2)
 2:     𝓛 ← φ
 3:     for each maximal itemset M ∈ 𝓜 do
 4:         T ← BuildFPTree(M, ε2/|𝓜|)
 5:         UpdateCount(D, M, T)
 6:         for each node v ∈ T do
 7:             v.count = v.count + Σ_{w∈v.children} w.count
 8:         FPGrowth(T, M, φ, 𝓛)
 9:     return top k itemsets and their supports in 𝓛

10: function FPGrowth(T, M, α, 𝓛)
11:     if T has a single path P then
12:         for each combination β ∈ P do
13:             𝓛(β ∪ α).count ← min. support of nodes in β
14:     else
15:         for each b_i ∈ M do
16:             β ← b_i ∪ α
17:             𝓛(β).count ← support of b_i
18:             construct β-conditional FP-tree T_β
19:             FPGrowth(T_β, M, β)
```

to D. Other steps, such as noise propagation and support derivation, can be done purely based on the output of the function. Notice that changing a transaction in D can only change the value of one entry by at most 1. This is because the algorithm is designed to update the count of only one node per transaction. Suppose the itemset X corresponding to u_i is removed from D. It will only decrease u_i by exactly 1 and other entries will remain the same. The resulting vector will be $\mathbf{u}_{D'} = (u_1, \cdots, u_{i-1}, u_i - 1, u_{i+1}, \cdots, u_q)$. Therefore, for all D and its neighboring database D',

$$\Delta g = \max_{D,D'} \left|g(D) - g(D')\right| = 1$$

According to the Laplace mechanism adding independent Laplace noise drawn from $\mathsf{Lap}\left(\frac{|\mathcal{M}|\Delta g}{\epsilon_2}\right)$ to each entry satisfies $\frac{\epsilon_2}{|\mathcal{M}|}$-differential privacy, and by the composition theorem of differential privacy [16] constructing $|\mathcal{M}|$ noisy FP-trees satisfies ϵ_2-differential privacy. □

Figure 2 gives an example of building a noisy version of an FP-tree. Let the input database be Figure 2(a) and, for simplicity, assume each transaction is lexicographically ordered after removing infrequent items. Given the minimum support τ=2, there are two maximal frequent itemsets, $M_1 = \{a, c, d\}$ and $M_2 = \{b, e\}$. The proposed algorithm will construct two FP-trees, one for M_1 and the other for M_2. We now explain how the algorithm constructs the noisy FP-tree for $M_1 = \{a, c, d\}$. First, the algorithm starts by creating a root node and inserts all the subsets of M_1 to the tree. I.e., it creates nodes corresponding to $\{a\}$, $\{c\}$, $\{d\}$, $\{a, c\}$, $\{a, d\}$, $\{c, d\}$ and $\{a, c, d\}$. The count of each newly created node is initialized with Laplace noise (line 8 in Algorithm 2). After creating nodes, the algorithm takes each transaction and filters out any item that does not appear in M_1. The item e is removed from the first transaction since it is not a part of M_1. The count of the node corresponding to

TID	Items
1	$\{a, c, d, e\}$
2	$\{a, c, d\}$
3	$\{b, d, e\}$
4	$\{a, c\}$
5	$\{b, e\}$

(a) Input database

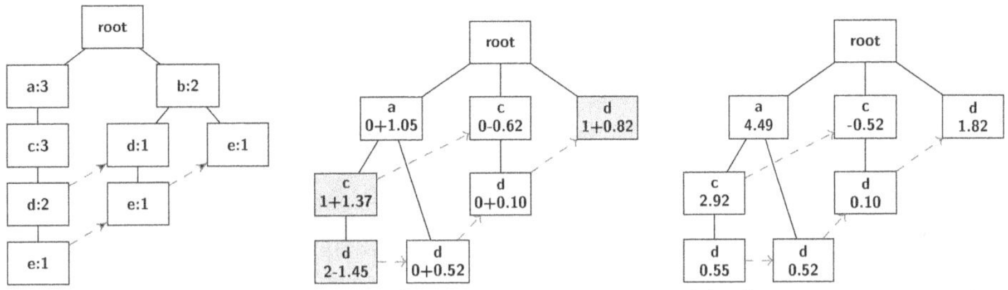

(b) original FP-tree (c) the tree built (d) after count propagation

Figure 2: Construction of noisy FP-tree

this filtered transaction is updated. Unlike the original FP-tree, only the count of the last node in the matching path is increased by 1 to reflect the occurrence of the transaction. In Figure 2(c), those nodes whose counts are updated to reflect the occurrence of transactions are marked as shaded. The first transaction causes to increase the count of node d, on the path $\langle(a : 1.05), (c : 1.37), (d : -1.45)\rangle$, by 1. The second transaction also increases the count of the same node since they become the same after the filtering step. The third transaction updates the count of node d on the first level. The fourth transaction results in $\langle(a : 1.05), (c : 2.37)\rangle$. The fifth transaction is ignored since it has no common item with M_1. All the items are removed from the transaction and the resulting transaction becomes an empty set. After building the tree, from the leaf toward the root, the count of each node is added to its parent. The FP-tree after the count propagation is shown in Figure 2(d).

4.3 Imposing Consistency

Given a node v in a non-perturbed FP-tree, according to the construction of the tree, the count of v cannot be smaller than the sum of counts of its children. Formally,

$$v.count \geq \sum_{w \in v.children} w.count \tag{7}$$

However, the constraint (7) may be violated in the noisy tree created by Algorithm 3 due to the noise injected to each node. The accuracy of randomized output can be improved though post-processing to impose consistency on the tree-like data structure [12, 6]. This is done without reference to the original data, only the already differentially-private structure, so the result is still differentially private.

In this section, we formulate the problem of imposing consistency on the noisy FP-tree as a *constrained least squares* problem and provide the formulation to find the solution. Let $\hat{x} = (\hat{x}_1, \cdots, \hat{x}_n)$ be an n-vector of noisy counts of nodes in an FP-tree, i.e., the i^{th}element of $\hat{x}_i$ corresponds to the noisy count of the i^{th}node v_i in the tree. Note that the ordering of nodes can be arbitrarily chosen. We impose consistency constraints on the noisy FP-tree by constructing a consistent vector $\bar{x}$ such that the distance between $\bar{x}$ and $\hat{x}$ is minimized. In other words, given a noisy FP-tree $\widehat{T}$, our algorithm tries to find another tree that is closest to $\widehat{T}$ while also satisfying the constraint.

Constraint (7) can be represented by a system of linear inequalities $C\bar{x} \leq \bar{x}$ where

$$C = (c_{ij}) = \begin{cases} 1 & \text{if } v_j \in v_i.children \\ 0 & \text{otherwise} \end{cases}$$

Let c_i^T denote the i^{th}row of C and W_i be the set of indices of v_i's children, i.e., $w_i = \{j \mid v_j \in v_i.children\}$. The $i^{\text{th}} c_i^T$ represents the constraint $\bar{x}_i \geq \sum_{j \in W_i} \bar{x}_j$. Hence, the problem can be formulated as follows:

$$\underset{\bar{x}}{\text{minimize}} \quad \|\bar{x} - \hat{x}\|_2 \qquad \text{subject to} \quad C\bar{x} \leq \bar{x} \tag{8}$$

We can reformulate the problem as a *least distance programming* (LDP) by substituting $\bar{x} - \hat{x}$ with $\bar{x}'$.

$$\underset{\bar{x}'}{\text{minimize}} \quad \|\bar{x}'\|_2 \qquad \text{subject to} \quad G\bar{x}' \geq g \tag{9}$$

where $G = I - C$ and $g = -G\hat{x}$.

THEOREM 5. *Let u be the solution to the* nonnegative least squares *problem*

$$\underset{u}{\textit{minimize}} \quad \|Eu - f\|_2 \qquad \textit{subject to} \quad u \geq 0$$

and $r = (r_1, \cdots, r_{n+1}) = Eu - f$ where

$$E = \begin{bmatrix} G^T \\ g^T \end{bmatrix}, f = [\overbrace{0, \cdots, 0}^{n}, 1]^T$$

. The unique solution to the problem (8) *is*

$$\bar{x} = (\bar{x}_1, \cdots \bar{x}_n), \quad \bar{x}_j = -r_j/r_{n+1} + \hat{x}_j$$

PROOF. See [14]. □

The impact of constraint enforcement on the accuracy is evaluated in Section 5.2.

5. EXPERIMENTAL RESULTS

In this section, we evaluate the performance of the proposed algorithm (NC) on a variety of datasets and compare it with two state-of-the-art algorithms: PrivBasis (PB) and SmartTruncation (ST). The datasets used in the experiments are described in Table 2. All experiments are conducted on an Intel Xeon 2.4GHz machine with 24GB of physical memory. To obtain an average performance estimate, each algorithm was run 10 times. PrivBasis finds top k frequent itemsets while SmartTruncation reports all frequent itemsets with respect to the given threshold. For comparison, the minimum support for SmartTruncation was set to the frequency of the k^{th}most frequent itemset. To compare the performance of algorithms, we employ F score and Relative error (RE) as measures of utility.

DEFINITION 6 (F SCORE). *Let $\mathcal{F}$ and $\hat{\mathcal{F}}$ be the set of correct and published frequent itemsets, respectively. The* F score *is defined as follows*

$$Fscore = 2 \times \frac{precision * recall}{precision + recall}$$

dataset	$\|D\|$	$\|\mathcal{I}\|$	max $\|t\|$	avg $\|t\|$
mushroom (MUS)	8,124	119	23	23
pumsb star (PUMSB)	49,046	2,088	63	50.5
retail (RETL)	88,162	16,470	76	10.3
kosarak (KOS)	990,002	41,270	2,498	8.1
aol (AOL)	647,377	2,290,685	48,070	34.9
BMS-POS (POS)	515,597	1,657	164	6.5
BMS-WebView1 (WV1)	59,602	497	267	2.5
BMS-WebView2 (WV2)	77,512	3,340	161	5.0

Table 2: Dataset description

where $precision = \frac{|\{\mathcal{F} \cap \hat{\mathcal{F}}\}|}{|\hat{\mathcal{F}}|}$ *and* $recall = \frac{|\{\mathcal{F} \cap \hat{\mathcal{F}}\}|}{|\mathcal{F}|}$

Notice that for top k FIM algorithms $|\mathcal{F}| = \left|\widehat{\mathcal{F}}\right| = k$, hence $precision = recall = Fscore = 1 - \text{FNR}$ where FNR, used in [15] for utility measure, is the fraction of false negatives in the released frequent itemsets.

DEFINITION 7 (RELATIVE ERROR). *The relative error of published frequent itemset $\hat{\mathcal{F}}$ is defined as*

$$RE = \text{median}_{X \in \hat{\mathcal{F}}} \frac{|\widehat{\sigma}(X) - \sigma(X)|}{\sigma(X)}$$

Before discussing the results, we note that the ST algorithm has maximal cardinality parameter ℓ that controls the trade-off between information loss and sensitivity reduction due to the transaction truncation. Its performance heavily relies on the proper setting of this parameter. However, there's no systematic way to set the parameter and the choice is merely heuristic. We fine-tuned this parameter until reasonable accuracy is obtained.

5.1 Comparison of Algorithms

Figure 3 shows the F scores of each algorithm by different values of ϵ. Observe that the proposed algorithm consistently outperforms both PB and ST algorithms and shows stable performance for different privacy budget and k. The F scores of PB and ST rapidly decrease at higher privacy levels (smaller ϵ). As the value of ϵ is decreased — higher privacy level is imposed—, the performance gap between the proposed algorithm and other two algorithms becomes more noticeable. Especially, in Figure 3(f) and 3(i) only the proposed algorithm shows a good performance when $\epsilon = 0.1$; both PB and ST have unacceptably low F scores.

One interesting observation is that PB shows better performance on POS dataset than ST while on the WV1 and WV2 dataset ST outperforms PB. One reason for this is that the maximal length of FIs in WV1 and WV2 dataset is 2, hence transaction truncation effectively reduces noise with relatively small cost of information loss. In contrast, PB tends to generate long and many bases because of abundance of frequent 2-itemsets. In addition, PB shows low performance when k is large. The best F scores of ST we were able to get for the PUMSB, retail and aol datasets were under 0.6 even after substantial parameter tuning. As shown in Figure 3, PB and ST algorithms are only useful when the low privacy level is required (large ϵ). Figure 4 describes the change of RE on different values of ϵ. Since ST algorithm doesn't report the support values of frequent itemsets, the RE of proposed algorithm is only compared with that of PB. The proposed algorithm shows similar or better performance on all tested datasets. Observe that in Figure 4(b) and 4(c) relative errors of PB are extremely high, which make the released FIs almost useless in practice.

5.2 Impact of Imposing Consistency

Figure 5 illustrates how optional consistency enforcement described in Section 4.3 affects performance. This experiment used the PUMSB dataset. As shown in Figure 5(a), imposing consistency on the FP-tree data structure not only produces consistent results but also improves utility. Although more improvement on accuracy is obtained when $k = 200$, this post-processing step increases processing time. The bigger FP-tree is, the longer it takes to find the consistent result. This is because that the size of constraint matrix is the number of nodes in the FP-tree, and solving least distance for a huge matrix is computationally expensive. Therefore, this post-processing step can be optionally executed when the consistency is essential to the problem or when there is enough computational power since the performance of the proposed algorithm without the optimization step is in general better than those of others. Although it is unfair to compare the processing time of each algorithm since the implementation of each algorithm is not written in the same language, we present it to show that the proposed algorithm is comparable to others.

6. CONCLUSION

We have proposed an algorithm for finding top-k frequent itemsets in a differentially private way. Our algorithm first discovers frequent itemsets (without their support values) using a small portion of the privacy budget. This enables the algorithm to use the remaining privacy budget to efficiently and effectively build a differentially private FP-tree. Once the tree is built, the supports of all frequent itemsets can be derived from the tree without access to the database.

We believe that the sparse vector mechanism demonstrated in this paper may also be applicable to other types of differentially private data mining, as it allows a potentially large amount of access to the data with the noise dependent only on the data that affects the output, rather than all data accessed.

Acknowledgment

This material is based upon work supported by the National Science Foundation under Grant No. CNS-1012208.

7. REFERENCES

[1] C. C. Aggarwal, J. Pei, and B. Zhang. On privacy preservation against adversarial data mining. In *KDD 2006*, pages 510–516, New York, NY, USA, 2006. ACM.

[2] R. Agrawal and R. Srikant. Fast algorithms for mining association rules in large databases. In *VLDB '94*, pages 487–499, San Francisco, CA, USA, 1994. Morgan Kaufmann Publishers Inc.

[3] M. Atzori, F. Bonchi, F. Giannotti, and D. Pedreschi. Anonymity preserving pattern discovery. *The VLDB Journal*, 17(4):703–727, July 2008.

[4] R. Bhaskar, S. Laxman, A. Smith, and A. Thakurta. Discovering frequent patterns in sensitive data. In

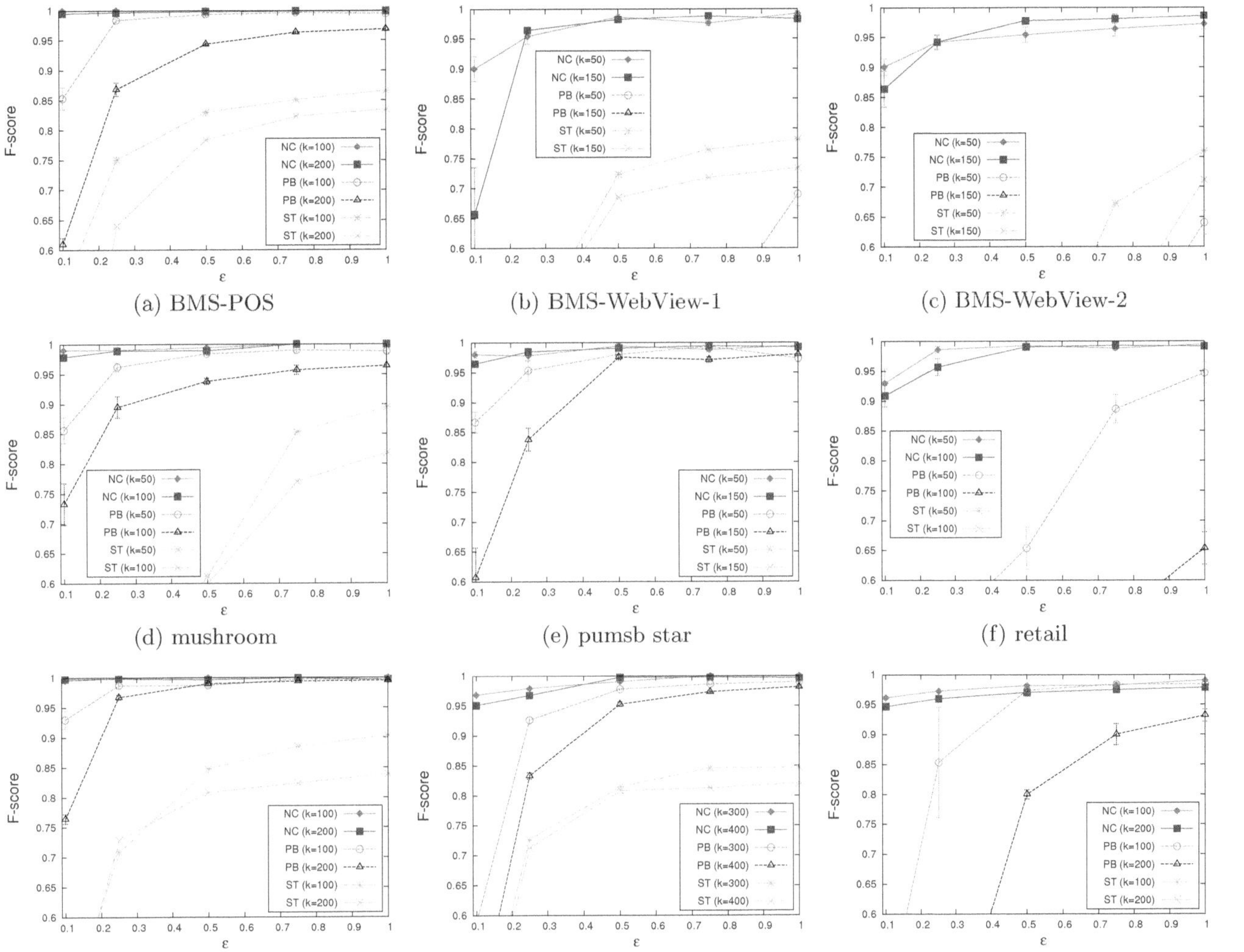

(a) BMS-POS (b) BMS-WebView-1 (c) BMS-WebView-2

(d) mushroom (e) pumsb star (f) retail

(g) kosarak (h) kosarak (i) aol

Figure 3: F score by varying ϵ

KDD 2010, pages 503–512, New York, NY, USA, 2010. ACM.

[5] J. Chen and K. Xiao. Bisc: A bitmap itemset support counting approach for efficient frequent itemset mining. *ACM Trans. Knowl. Discov. Data*, 4(3):12:1–12:37, Oct. 2010.

[6] B. Ding, M. Winslett, J. Han, and Z. Li. Differentially private data cubes: optimizing noise sources and consistency. In *SIGMOD 2011*, pages 217–228, New York, NY, USA, 2011. ACM.

[7] C. Dwork. Differential privacy. In *ICALP 2006*, pages 1–12, July 9-16 2006.

[8] C. Dwork, F. McSherry, K. Nissim, and A. Smith. Calibrating noise to sensitivity in private data analysis. In *TCC 2006*, pages 265–284. Springer, 2006.

[9] J. Han, J. Pei, and Y. Yin. Mining frequent patterns without candidate generation. *SIGMOD Rec.*, 29(2):1–12, May 2000.

[10] M. Hardt. *A Study of Privacy and Fairness in Sensitive Data Analysis*. PhD thesis, Princeton University, 2011.

[11] M. Hardt and G. N. Rothblum. A multiplicative weights mechanism for privacy-preserving data analysis. In *FOCS 2010*, pages 61–70, Washington, DC, USA, 2010. IEEE Computer Society.

[12] M. Hay, V. Rastogi, G. Miklau, and D. Suciu. Boosting the accuracy of differentially private histograms through consistency. *Proc. VLDB Endow.*, 3(1-2):1021–1032, Sept. 2010.

[13] M. Kantarcioğlu, J. Jin, and C. Clifton. When do data mining results violate privacy? In *KDD 2004*, pages 599–604, New York, NY, USA, 2004. ACM.

[14] C. L. Lawson and R. J. Hanson. *Solving least squares problems*. Classics in applied mathematics. SIAM, Philadelphia, PA, 3 edition, 1995.

[15] N. Li, W. Qardaji, D. Su, and J. Cao. Privbasis: frequent itemset mining with differential privacy. *Proc. VLDB Endow.*, 5(11):1340–1351, July 2012.

[16] F. D. McSherry. Privacy integrated queries: An extensible platform for privacy-preserving data analysis. In *SIGMOD 2009*, pages 19–30, New York, NY, USA, 2009. ACM.

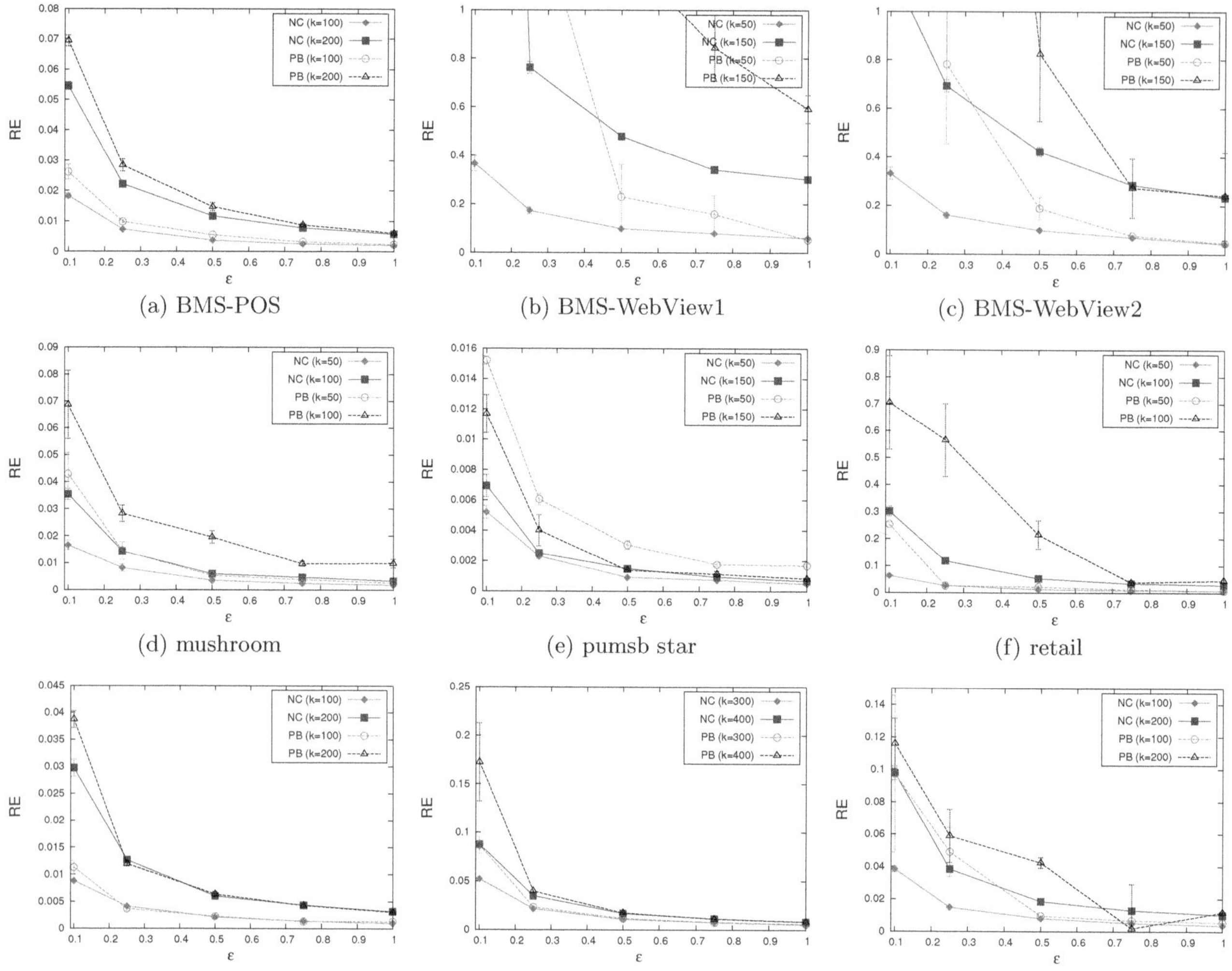

(a) BMS-POS (b) BMS-WebView1 (c) BMS-WebView2

(d) mushroom (e) pumsb star (f) retail

(g) kosarak (h) kosarak (i) aol

Figure 4: Relative error by varying ϵ

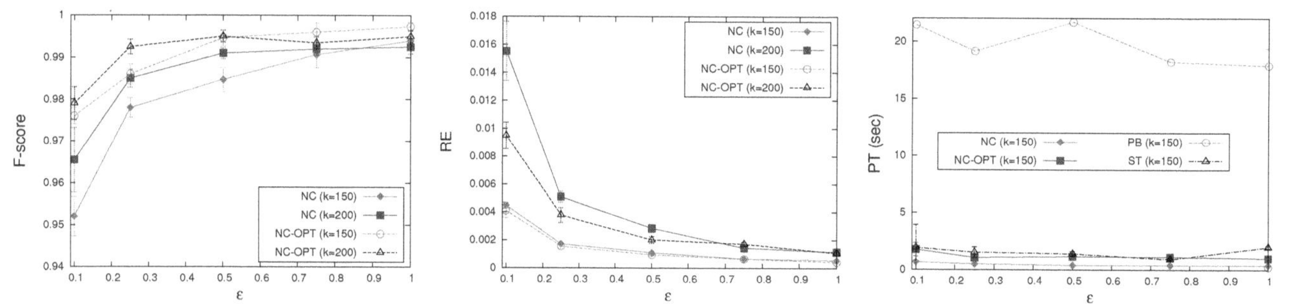

Figure 5: Effectiveness of consistency enforcement

[17] A. Roth and T. Roughgarden. Interactive privacy via the median mechanism. In *STOC 2010*, pages 765–774, New York, NY, USA, 2010. ACM.

[18] M. J. Zaki. Scalable algorithms for association mining. *IEEE Trans. on Knowl. and Data Eng.*, 12(3):372–390, May 2000.

[19] C. Zeng, J. F. Naughton, and J.-Y. Cai. On differentially private frequent itemset mining. *Proc. VLDB Endow.*, 6(1):25–36, Nov. 2012.

CatchSync : Catching Synchronized Behavior in Large Directed Graphs

Meng Jiang[123], Peng Cui[123], Alex Beutel[4], Christos Faloutsos[4], Shiqiang Yang[123]

[1]Tsinghua National Laboratory for Information Science and Technology
[2]Department of Computer Science and Technology, Tsinghua University, Beijing, China
[3]Beijing Key Laboratory of Networked Multimedia, Tsinghua University, China
[4]Computer Science Department, Carnegie Mellon University, PA, USA
jm06@mails.tsinghua.edu.cn, cuip@tsinghua.edu.cn, abeutel@cs.cmu.edu
christos@cs.cmu.edu, yangshq@tsinghua.edu.cn

ABSTRACT

Given a directed graph of millions of nodes, how can we automatically spot anomalous, suspicious nodes, judging only from their connectivity patterns? Suspicious graph patterns show up in many applications, from Twitter users who buy fake followers, manipulating the social network, to botnet members performing distributed denial of service attacks, disturbing the network traffic graph. We propose a fast and effective method, CATCHSYNC, which exploits two of the tell-tale signs left in graphs by fraudsters: (a) *synchronized* behavior: suspicious nodes have extremely similar behavior pattern, because they are often required to perform some task together (such as follow the same user); and (b) *rare* behavior: their connectivity patterns are very different from the majority. We introduce novel measures to quantify both concepts ("synchronicity" and "normality") and we propose a parameter-free algorithm that works on the resulting synchronicity-normality plots. Thanks to careful design, CATCHSYNC has the following desirable properties: (a) it is *scalable* to large datasets, being linear on the graph size; (b) it is *parameter free*; and (c) it is *side-information-oblivious*: it can operate using only the topology, without needing labeled data, nor timing information, etc., while still capable of using side information, if available. We applied CATCHSYNC on two large, real datasets *1-billion-edge* Twitter social graph and *3-billion-edge* Tencent Weibo social graph, and several synthetic ones; CATCHSYNC consistently outperforms existing competitors, both in detection accuracy by 36% on Twitter and 20% on Tencent Weibo, as well as in speed.

Categories and Subject Descriptors

H.3.5 [**Information Systems**]: Information Storage and Retrieval - On-line Information Services; J.4 [**Computer Applications**]: Social and Behavioral Sciences

Keywords

Zombie Follower; Anomalous Behavior; Outlier Detection

KDD'14, August 24–27, 2014, New York, NY, USA.
Copyright 2014 ACM 978-1-4503-2956-9/14/08 ...$15.00.
http://dx.doi.org/10.1145/2623330.2623632.

1. INTRODUCTION

Given a directed graph within millions of nodes, can we tell which nodes are suspicious just based on the graph structure? For many applications, fraudsters try to manipulate networks for personal gain. For example, in social networks, like Twitter's "who-follows-whom" graph, fraudsters are paid to make certain accounts seem more legitimate or famous through giving them many additional followers. The spammers deliver these purchases through either generating fake accounts or controlling real accounts through malware and using them to follow their "customers" [1, 2].

In this case, the attack is strictly manipulating the Twitter graph to give certain accounts undue credibility. Because the attack only requires adding edges to the graph, previous approaches for finding spam on Twitter that analyze users' tweets and profiles [4, 32, 9] will often miss this dubious behavior. Rather, we take a strictly graph mining approach, using exclusively the graph structure to find nodes that are suspicious because of their position in the graph.

By abstracting the attack to a graph mining problem, we find that it covers a wide variety of suspicious behavior found in the real world. For example, botnets often control hundreds of thousands of machines and use them to perform distributed denial of service (DDOS) attacks on websites, creating a similar pattern in the "who-visits-whom" web traffic graph. Online, on sites like Amazon or Yelp, spammers will create accounts to skew ratings for certain products or places, manipulating edges in the "who-rates-what" graph. On Facebook, Page owners will pay spammers to "Like" their page, distorting the "who-Likes-what" graph.

In this paper, we focus on the Twitter attack, looking for groups of accounts used to unfairly bolster the popularity of their customers. Figure 1a illustrates the scenario: it shows a set of suspicious followers and their followees. The followers, all 3 million of them, follow exactly 20 users from the same group of followees, creating a strange, rare connectivity structure. The side information, like the similarity of the login-names (@Buy_AB22, @Buy_BT27, @Buy_BT68), is an extra reason to suspect that they were created by a script.

Our main viewpoint: In more detail, suspicious nodes including suspicious followers and botnets exhibit behavior that is (a) *synchronized* (cause to occur at the same rate): they often connect to the very same 10, 100 or 500 targets and (b) *abnormal/rare*: their behavior pattern is very different from the majority of nodes. In this paper, we propose a fast and effective method, CATCHSYNC, to measure the two properties (*synchronicity* and the *normality*) of a group of nodes; we spot the suspicious nodes and efficiently catch

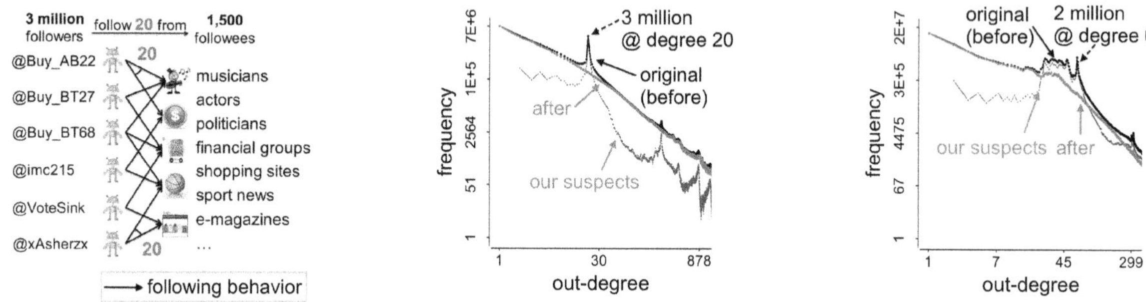

(a) Synchronized behavior (b) TWITTERSG (c) WEIBOSG

Figure 1: Suspicious followers and their footprints: (a) We spot synchronized behavior that millions of Twitter accounts follow the same group of followees. (b) Synchronized behavior causes spikes at out-degree distribution and the distribution becomes smoother after the removal of our suspects. (c) We have the same result on Tencent Weibo.

		Synchronized behaviors?	Parameter free?	No side information?
Proposed CATCHSYNC		√	√	√
Graph-based Anomaly Detection	AUTOPART [10]	×, edges across 2 of k node groups	√, but search for the best k	√
	OUTRANK [28]	×, high scoring nodes	√, but data dedicated threshold	√
	ODDBALL [6]	×, near-cliques or near-stars	√	√
	COPYCATCH [7]	√, temporally synchronized	×, seeds for propagation	×, timestamp
	NETPROBE [30]	×, fraudulent nodes	×, propagation matrix	×, committed frauds
Subgraph Mining	SPOKEN [33]	×, well-connected communities	×, eigenvector computation	√
	DSE [13]	×, d_G-dense subgraphs	×, density d_G	√
Spammer Detection	SPOT [32]	×, twitter spammers	√	×, text and URLs in tweets
	SYBILRANK [9]	×, social sybils	√, seeds for propagation	×, early non-Sybils

Table 1: Compare CATCHSYNC with existing approaches. It does not require any parameter or side information.

them in the synchronicity-normality plot. We study two real social graphs from Twitter and Tencent Weibo (denoted by TWITTERSG and WEIBOSG for abbreviation) and use them for evaluations. Note that both have millions of nodes and billions of edges.

Figure 1 gives an elaborate illustration on the effectiveness of CATCHSYNC. As we mentioned earlier, the distributions of the social network data have been seriously distorted by the volume of suspicious followers. Here we plot the out-degree distribution of TWITTERSG and WEIBOSG in log-log scale, which should have smooth, power-law-like distributions. However, several spikes appear, which are presumably caused by suspicious followers [8]. For example, as shown in Figure 1a, the 3 million followers on Twitter who connect to exactly 20 users create a spike at out-degree 20 on the distribution in Figure 1b. After removing the nodes that CATCHSYNC flags as suspicious (blue points), the distributions become much smoother and closer to a power law (red points).

Main contributions: In short, the proposed method CATCHSYNC has the following desirable properties:

- *Effectiveness*: it indeed spots groups of source-target groups, with suspicious behavior (see Section 5).
- *Scalability:* it is linear in the number of edges, and thus applicable to internet-scale graphs.
- *Parameter free:* the operator does not need to specify any parameters such as the density, the number of groups and the scale of each group.
- *Side information oblivious:* it needs no side information. It is solely based on topology, and it requires neither a training set, nor labeled nodes, nor node attributes, nor anything else, though it can incorporate the above for better performance.

Organization: We have the usual organization: Survey, problem definition, proposed method, experiments and conclusions.

2. RELATED WORK

There is a significant body on research related to our problem, which we categorize into four groups: graph-based anomaly detection, subgraph mining algorithms, social spammer detection. The majority of them are discussed in Table 1.

Graph-based Anomaly Detection: Many anomaly detection techniques have been developed [5, 34, 11, 23, 22] including discovering structural anomalies [29, 16],propagating beliefs for fake or fraudulent nodes [35, 12, 28]. AUTOPART [10] finds outlier edges across node groups; however, we need to detect suspicious nodes. ODDBALL [6] assumes near-cliques and stars are suspicious; however, these anomalies do not show up in directed graphs. NETPROBE [30] uses a list of committed frauds to blame all the fraudulent nodes on the graph; COPYCATCH [7] detects temporally bipartite cores that are ill-gotten "Likes" of Facebook; however, they require side information such as edge creation time. Note that our work is orthogonal to the above. We look for synchronized behavior, which forms strange subgraph structure.

Subgraph Mining Algorithms: A number of subgraph mining algorithms have been investigated [15], such as mining frequent subgraph patterns [39, 27, 40], mining dense subgraphs [25, 38, 13, 20] and finding quasi-cliques [31, 37]. In addition, some variants of community detection algorithms have been proposed to discover dense clusters [19] and well-connected communities [33]. These require typical parameters like density and number of clusters as input. Suspicious nodes can easily evade high density detection by reducing the number of targets and increasing the volume.

Social spammer detection: There are several recent works on detecting social spammers, for example, fake accounts on microblogging and social networks, mainly using the content-based features [4, 9, 21]. Perez *et al.* [32] proposed SPOT to catch suspicious Twitter profiles, by learning text and malicious URLs in tweets and scoring their suspiciousness. Our work is orthogonal to theirs when detecting the group attacks.

3. SYNCHRONIZED BEHAVIOR DETECTION

In this section, we first propose the problem of synchronized behavior detection and then present a fast and effective solution.

3.1 Problem Definition

Our goal is to find suspicious nodes on a directed graph and thus the problem is defined as:

Given: a directed graph of N nodes in the node set $\mathcal{U}$

Find: a set of suspicious source nodes (fake followers, botnets, etc.) $\mathcal{U}_{sync}$, and a set of suspicious target nodes (followees, target hosts, etc.) $\mathcal{V}_{sync}$ that the source nodes have *synchronized* and *abnormal* behaviors connecting to the target nodes. The word "synchronized" means that the source nodes have very similar behavior pattern, and "abnormal" means that their behavior pattern is very different from the majority of nodes. Table 2 gives a list of the symbols we use throughout the paper.

Symbol	Definition and Description
$\mathcal{U}$	The set of nodes
N=$\lvert\mathcal{U}\rvert$	The number of node
$\mathcal{I}(u)$	The set of node u's sources
$\mathcal{O}(u)$	The set of node u's targets
$d_i(u)$=$\lvert\mathcal{I}(u)\rvert$	In-degree of node u (number of sources)
$d_o(u)$=$\lvert\mathcal{O}(u)\rvert$	Out-degree of node u (number of targets)
$hub(u)$,$aut(u)$	"Hubness" and "authoritativeness" of u
$sync(u)$	"Synchronicity" of node u's targets
$norm(u)$	"Normality" of node u's targets
$\mathbf{p}(u)$	k-dimensional feature vector of node u
$c(u,v)$	Closeness of u and v in feature space

Table 2: Symbols and Definitions

3.2 Proposed Approach

In this section, we introduce our approach towards the above problem. First, we give a feature space for target nodes. Second, we show the definitions of synchronicity and normality that measure the nodes' behavior patterns. Then we provide a general theorem of the normal shape of the synchronicity-normality plot. Next, we detect the outliers on the plot, which are suspicious nodes with synchronize behavior on the graph.

3.2.1 Feature space

It has been established by past works that many data mining approaches on graphs benefit from exploiting the features from the nodes' behavior patterns, including (a) out-degree and in-degree, (b) HITS score (hubness and authoritativeness), (c) betweenness centrality, (e) node in-weight and out-weight, if the graph is weighted, (f) the score of the node in the i-th left or right singular vector, and many more. We denote k-dimensional feature vector of node u by $\mathbf{p}(u) \in \mathbb{R}^k$. We extract the feature vector from graph structure that somewhat reflects the node's behavior pattern. The features could be *any* from the above and the vector could have *any* dimensionality. In this paper, we choose the degree values and HITS score. We denote a set of u's source nodes by $\mathcal{I}(u)$ and a set of u's target nodes by $\mathcal{O}(u)$. The in-degree $d_i(u)$ of node u is the number of its sources, i.e. the size of $\mathcal{I}(u)$. The out-degree $d_o(u)$ of node u is the number of its targets, i.e. the size of $\mathcal{O}(u)$. Also we denote by $hub(u)$ the hubness of node u and by $aut(u)$ the authoritativeness of u, according to Kleinberg's famous work [24]. We choose these features for two reasons: they are fast to compute, as well as easy to plot. As our experiments show, they work well in pin-pointing suspicious nodes. Note that if the side information is available, it could be regarded as additional features that would be easily incorporated, and hopefully, the performance could be better.

Here we present some plots of the feature spaces. For a source node u, we plot a heat map of the 2-D feature space of out-degree $d_o(u)$ vs hubness $hub(u)$ in log-log scale, called "OutF-plot". Similarly, for a target node u, the heat map of the feature space of in-degree $d_i(u)$ vs authoritativeness $aut(u)$ in log-log scale is called "InF-plot". Table 3 summarizes the description of all the plots.

Plot	Description
OutF-plot	A heat map of source nodes in feature space: typically, out-degree vs hubness
InF-plot	A heat map of target nodes in feature space: typically, in-degree vs authoritativeness
SN-plot	A heat map of source nodes in synchronicity vs normality of their targets

Table 3: Plots and Descriptions

Specifically, Figure 2a and 2c are InF-plots of TWITTERSG and WEIBOSG. On TWITTERSG, we denote by *X* one of the suspicious followers we mentioned in Figure 1a and by *Y* an ordinary user whose out-degree is the same as *X*'s. We tag their targets (followees) in the Figure 2a and find out that *X*'s targets are coherent in the InF-plot, while *Y*'s targets are not. In other words, *X*'s target nodes have similar in-degree and authoritativeness, but *Y*'s targets are diverse in the feature space, ranging from top popular to ordinary users just like *Y*. Similar thing happens on WEIBOSG. Figure 2c shows that *X*'s targets are located at a micro-cluster which is away from the majority of followee nodes. They have large in-degree values from 1,000 to 100,000 but they are not as authoritative as the ones who are followed by *Y* and of the same in-degree.

3.2.2 Synchronicity and normality

We propose two novel concepts to investigate the behavior patterns of the source nodes: (a) "synchronicity" $sync(u)$ to qualify how synchronized the node u's targets are in the feature space (in-degree vs authoritativeness); and (b) "normality" $norm(u)$ to qualify how normal u's targets are relative to the rest of the data. These two measures consider the relative position of u's target nodes in the feature space. We denote by $c(v,v')$ the closeness (similarity) between two target nodes v and v' in the feature space (InF-plot). For fast computing the closeness of each pair of nodes, we divide the feature space into G grid cells and map each node to a specific grid cell. If two nodes are in the same grid cell, they have similar feature vectors, and they are close in the feature space. Thus, we have

$$c(v, v') = \begin{cases} 1 & \text{if nodes } v \text{ and } v' \text{ are in the same grid cell} \\ 0 & \text{otherwise} \end{cases}$$

Then we have the definition of synchronicity and normality.

Definition 1 Synchronicity and Normality
We define synchronicity of node u as the average closeness between each pair of u's targets (v,v')*:*

$$sync(u) = \frac{\sum_{(v,v')\in\mathcal{O}(u)\times\mathcal{O}(u)} c(v,v')}{d_o(u) \times d_o(u)} \quad (1)$$

We define normality of node u as the average closeness between

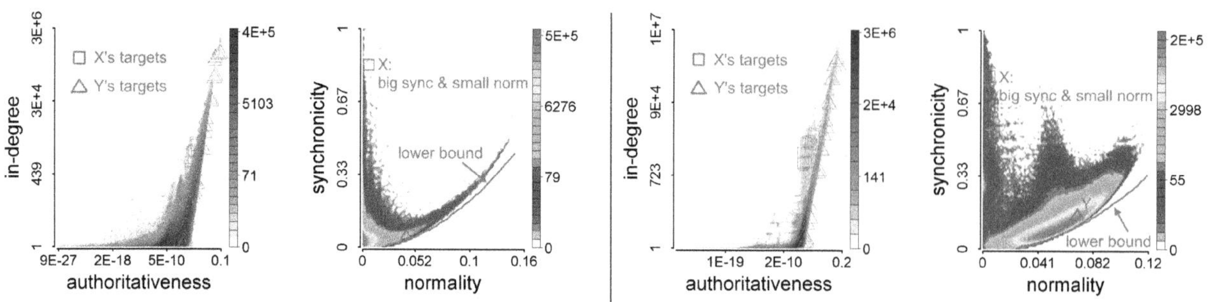

(a) InF-plot on TWITTERSG (b) SN-plot on TWITTERSG (c) InF-plot on WEIBOSG (d) SN-plot on WEIBOSG

Figure 2: Synchronicity-normality plot: the source nodes *X* have synchronized and abnormal behaviors that their targets are coherent in the InF-plots (a) and (c), while *Y*'s targets are not. *X* has big synchronicity and small normality in the SN-plots (b) and (d) while *Y* is near the parabolic, theoretical lower limit.

each pair of u's targets and other nodes (v,v'):

$$norm(u) = \frac{\sum_{(v,v')\in\mathcal{O}(u)\times\mathcal{U}} c(v,v')}{d_o(u)\times N} \quad (2)$$

Both values of synchronicity and normality range from 0 to 1. We know that a suspicious source node u has uncommonly large $sync(u)$ and abnormally small $norm(u)$. For a source node u, we name u's target nodes in the InF-plot as *foreground* points and name all the nodes in the plot as *background* points. We provide a theorem of the normal shape of SN-plot, which could be the basis for catching suspicious nodes

Theorem 1 *For any foreground/background distribution, there is a parabolic lower limit in the synchronicity-normality plot.*

PROOF. See appendix. It is based on Lagrange multipliers. The parabolic low limit is

$$s_{min} = (-Mn^2 + 2n - s_b)/(1 - Ms_b)$$

where M is the total number of grid cells, s_{min} is the minimum value of synchronicitiy of foreground points, s_b is the synchronicity of background points, and n is a given normality value. □

Figure 2b and 2d show the SN-plots of source nodes in TWITTERSG and WEIBOSG. Note that the source node *X* has synchronized and abnormal behavior and *Y* does not, as shown in Figure 2a and 2c. *X* has much bigger synchronicity and smaller normality than *Y*. The red parabola is the theoretical lower limit of synchronicity with a given normality, which has been given in the proof. *Y* is close to the parabola, while *X* is far away from the lower bound. The next step to find the suspicious nodes like *X* is to detect the outliers in the SN-plots.

3.2.3 Outliers in SN-plot

Here we introduce how to catch the outliers in the SN-plot based on Theorem 1. Informally, we want the nodes that are too far away from the lower limit. Formally, we denote by $r_{source}(u)$ the *residual score* of a source node u's synchronicity which indicates how suspicious it is. The set of suspicious source nodes $\mathcal{U}_{sync}$ includes the nodes whose suspiciousness is $\alpha = 3.0$ standard deviations away from the mean:

$$\mathcal{U}_{sync} \leftarrow \{u : r_{source}(u) > \mu[r_{source}] + \alpha \times \sigma[r_{source}]\} \quad (3)$$

Similarly, we denote by $r_{target}(v)$ the suspiciousness of a target node v, which is the proportion of v's sources that are reported in $\mathcal{U}_{sync}$. Then we could have the set of suspicious targets $\mathcal{V}_{sync}$:

$$\mathcal{V}_{sync} \leftarrow \{v : r_{target}(v) > \mu[r_{target}] + \alpha \times \sigma[r_{target}]\} \quad (4)$$

The default value of α is chosen according to Tax's classical outlier detection work in [36]. In the experimental section, we will validate that the performance of our method does not depend much on α.

4. CATCHSYNC ALGORITHM

In this section, we present the implementation of CATCHSYNC and analyze the complexity.

Implementation. The approach is outlined below in Algorithm 1. We first derive a feature space for target nodes. We then compute synchronicity and normality of the source nodes' behaviors, according to the relative positions of their target nodes in the feature space. Finally, we use a distance-based outlier detection method to detect the outliers in the synchronicity-normality plot.

Algorithm 1: CATCHSYNC: Catch suspicious nodes with synchronized behaviors in a large, directed graph.

Input: A directed graph of N nodes in the set $\mathcal{U}$.
Output: A set of source nodes $\mathcal{U}_{sync}$ who have synchronized and abnormal behaviors and a set of targets in $\mathcal{V}_{sync}$.
Step 1: plot a (2-D) feature space of target nodes.
foreach *node v as a target* **do**
  Compute in-degree $d_i(v)$ and authoritativeness $aut(v)$.
Give InF-plot $d_i(v)$ vs $aut(v)$ (see Figure 2a and 2c).
Step 2: plot synchronicity-normality of source nodes.
Divide the InF-plot into grids.
foreach *node u as a source* **do**
  Compute synchronicity $sync(u)$ and normality $norm(u)$ with Eq. (1) and (2).
Give SN-plot $sync(u)$ vs $norm(u)$ (see Figure 2b and 2d).
Step 3:
Adapt a distance-based method to report suspicious sources $\mathcal{U}_{sync}$ and targets $\mathcal{V}_{sync}$.

In detail, we choose 2-dimensional feature spaces and specifically out-degree vs hubness, for each source node, and in-degree vs authoritativeness, for each target node. The out-degree (in-degree) is the size of set of a source's targets (a target's sources). The hubness (authoritativeness) is the first left- (right-) singular vector of the graph's adjacency matrix. The algorithm to compute these values is omitted for saving space. When we divide the InF-plot into grids in Step 2, the length of each side of a grid is *log*2, that is, the grid lines at degree and HITS score are on powers of 2.

Complexity analysis. We now examine CATCHSYNC's complexity. We first compute degree and HITS score of each node. This process is linear in the number of edges E. Second, the process of computing synchronicity and normality is linear in the

	Nodes	Edges	Description	Suspicious/Labeled source nodes
TWITTERSG	41,652,230	1,468,365,182	Twitter social graph in July 2009 [26]	173 / 1,000
WEIBOSG	117,288,075	3,134,074,580	Tencent Weibo social graph in January 2011	237 / 1,000

Table 4: Real data: the real world graphs we study are complete social graphs with multimillion nodes and billion edges. We have used human labor to label a small piece of both of them for ground truth.

number of nodes N. We denote by G the number of grids that we divided the InF-plot into. Thus, the total time complexity is $\mathcal{O}(E+NG)$. CATCHSYNC is a scalable algorithm and able to process huge, directed graphs.

5. EXPERIMENTS

In this section we present an empirical evaluation of CATCHSYNC, demonstrating its effectiveness in spotting suspicious behavior. Although much of the research on anomaly detection frames the problem as a labelling task, in real world anomaly detection is a combination of machine learning, manual verification, and discovering new types of attacks as they arise. Here, we provide evidence that CATCHSYNC is effective at both the classic problem of labelling suspicious behavior, as well as surfacing new patterns of unusual group behavior:

- **Detection effectiveness:** We demonstrate CATCHSYNC's ability to accurately label suspicious behavior and remove anomalies through three techniques.
  (a) Injected attacks: We begin by testing the accuracy, precision, and recall on synthetic graphs with injected group attacks. We compare our algorithm against state-of-the-art methods and show that CATCHSYNC performs the best.
  (b) Labelling task: We also test our accuracy, precision, and recall on two real datasets, where we use the labeled data from random sampling of TWITTERSG and WEIBOSG as ground truth of suspicious and normal nodes.
  (c) Restore normal patterns: For all of these cases we show that removing the suspicious nodes restores the power law properties of the graph's edge degree, which when distorted is a common sign of spam, and remove anomalous patterns in the feature spaces (OutF-plots and InF-plots).
- **CATCHSYNC properties:** We test a number of properties of CATCHSYNC, including the robustness with respect to α, the speed and the scalability.
- **Discovery:** We demonstrate the effectiveness of CATCHSYNC as a discovery tool. We discuss a number of the unusual accounts caught and patterns detected in the TWITTERSG and WEIBOSG datasets.

5.1 Evaluation: Data and Ground Truth

We carry out experiments on synthetic and real datasets to evaluate the performance of CATCHSYNC. The synthetic datasets are described in Table 5, while the real datasets are in Table 4.

	# of Nodes	# of Injected sources	Camouflage
SYNTH-1M	1,034,100	31,000	-
SYNTH-2M	2,034,100	=16K	-
SYNTH-3M	3,034,100	+8K+4K	-
SYNTH-3M-RAND	3,034,100	+2K+1K	+10% Random
SYNTH-3M-POP	3,034,100		+50% Popular

Table 5: Synthetic data: we inject 5 different sizes of group attacks on random power law graphs of 1-3M nodes.

5.1.1 Synthetic data

Description. We generate random power-law graphs, following the Chung-Lu model [1] [14], and with a power-law exponent -1.5 since most real-world networks have been shown to have this value [17]. Next we inject groups of source and target nodes.

To demonstrate the effectiveness, we vary the following properties of the synthetic graphs:

- **Size of graph:** The random power-law graphs we generate contain approximately 1M, 2M, or 3M nodes, named as SYNTH-1M, SYNTH-2M and SYNTH-3M.
- **Size of injection:** We inject 5 source and target nodes groups of different sizes. The smallest group has 1,000 new sources, connecting to *20* of 100 new targets, because of the real case that the smallest number of fake followers a user can buy is often 1,000 [1]. The size of the injected group doubles one by one and thus the largest group has 16,000 sources and 1,600 targets. The total number of injected sources is 31,000.
- **Camouflage:** The injected source nodes may try to use "camouflage" to evade the detection, for example, the fake accounts can follow Barack Obama, Taylor Swift, or some random users, though they connect to tens or hundreds of customers. Inspired by this, we try two different techniques on SYNTH-3M: for each injected node, let it connect to (a) some "random", ordinary targets; (b) some from the top 100 "popular" targets. We also vary the weights of camouflage d_{camou}: (a) d_{camou} = 10%, 18 injected targets and 2 for camouflage; (b) d_{camou} = 50%, 10 injected ones and 10 for camouflage. Specifically, we denote by SYNTH-3M-RAND the injected graph with 10% random camouflage, and by SYNTH-3M-POP the graph with 50% popular camouflage.

With different settings of the above, we have the 5 synthetic datasets.

Evaluation. If we denote the injected nodes by positive samples, and the others by negative samples, we can record the true positive (TP), true negative (TN), false positive (FP), and false negative (FN) rates, which we use the standard definition [18] to calculate the three popular metrics: accuracy, precision and recall. High accuracy, precision and recall will be a better method.

5.1.2 Real data

Description. We also use our two real world datasets, TWITTERSG and WEIBOSG, both of which are complete graphs of popular online social networks with billions of edges. Thanks to the public download links [2], CATCHSYNC is reproducible. As the webpage says, due to Twitter's new Terms of Services, we academic researchers cannot access the side information like the tweet data. Fortunately, we can usually get the who-follows-whom data, or directed graphs from different applications. Then we can operate our side-information oblivious method CATCHSYNC.

WEIBOSG was crawled in January 2011 from Tencent Weibo, one of the biggest microblogging services in China. For each dataset

[1]Following the model, we assign out-degrees $d_o(u)$ and in-degrees $d_i(v)$ to each node u and v respectively; we then create edge (u, v) with probability proportional to $d_o(v)d_i(u)$.

[2]http://an.kaist.ac.kr/traces/WWW2010.html

Synthetic graph	SYNTH-1M	SYNTH-2M	SYNTH-3M	SYNTH-3M-RAND		SYNTH-3M-POP	
Camouflage (d_{camou})	None (0)	None (0)	None (0)	10%	50%	10%	50%
CATCHSYNC	**0.998**	**0.987**	**0.956**	**0.910**	**0.764**	**0.885**	**0.792**
ODDBALL	0.827	0.796	0.755	0.702	0.525	0.657	0.433
OUTRANK	0.805	0.777	0.725	0.678	0.516	0.694	0.392
SPOKEN	0.695	0.682	0.677	0.586	0.470	0.553	0.351

Table 6: CATCHSYNC consistently wins, despite of "camouflage": it reaches higher accuracy on detecting injected nodes.

CATCHSYNC only uses the graph structure, but we also have user id and name associated with the nodes, so that we can provide real links to check the users' profile information.

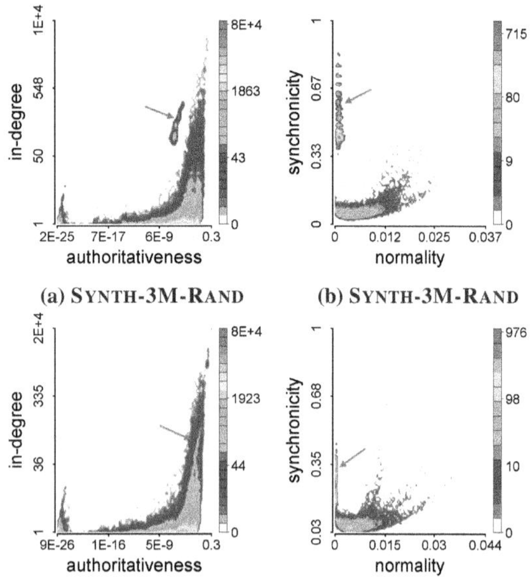

(a) SYNTH-3M-RAND (b) SYNTH-3M-RAND

(c) SYNTH-3M-POP (d) SYNTH-3M-POP

Figure 3: Our CATCHSYNC catches injections, despite of "camouflage": camouflage can hide the injected nodes in or put them close to dominating parts in (a) and (c), but SN-plots can catch them with big synchronicity and small normality in (b) and (d).

Evaluation. For WEIBOSG and TWITTERSG, we sample 1,000 nodes and conduct user study to label them as suspicious or normal accounts. Half of the nodes are randomly selected from the set U_{sync} and half are not. Although the average suspiciousness of samples is higher than that of the entire dataset, it is fair for all the algorithms in our experiments. The 5 volunteers are all 20 to 25-year-old college students who have been social network users for at least 3 years. They are provided URL links directed to the 1000 users' Twitter or Tencent Weibo pages, and read their tweets and profile information. A user is labeled as a suspicious one if the volunteer finds he or she matches too many of the following clues:

- **Disabled account:** It has been disabled by the services. For example, Weibo user @marra_xiao_bai had 9 followers and 36 followees in 2011. Twitter user @wYWvk0310 had 666 followers and 926 followees in 2010. But both of them have been disabled now.
- **Suspicious user name:** They have strange self-declared information that follows a narrow pattern such as Twitter names in the form of @"Buy_XX##" (@Buy_AB22, @Buy_BT47), Weibo names in the form of "a#####" (@a58444, @a70054).
- **Many followees but few or zero tweets:** It has hundreds of followees but it never posts a single tweet. Twitter user @P8igBg801 had 923 followees in 2010 and @AjaurNYj2 had 869 followees, but both of them post nothing.
- **Malicious tweet content:** The account posts duplicated tweets or malicious links for monetary purposes. For example, Twitter user @Buy_BT66 posts only 3 messages but all of them are about "bed flat for sale". Weibo account @aa52011 posts hundreds of similar messages about online games.

Finally, we give a user a "suspicious" label if 3 (more than a half) of the volunteers think it is suspicious. Our task here is to detect the users with the "suspicious" labels. Similarly with the evaluation method on synthetic data, we also use accuracy, precision and recall to evaluate the effectiveness. A good detection algorithm will have high values of accuracy, precision and recall.

5.2 Competing Algorithms

We carefully implement the following state-of-the-art methods as competing algorithms: (a) ODDBALL [6], looking for near-cliques and stars that are suspected as strange nodes in the graph; (b) OUTRANK [28], using random walk model across the similarity measure to give the outlierness of each node; (c) SPOKEN [33], using pairs of eigenvectors to find well-connected communities. When operating on the labeled real data, we implement a content-based spammer detection method SPOT [32], which learns the words and the number of malicious links in the accounts' tweets.

As mentioned before, our CATCHSYNC is orthogonal to the text-based methods like SPOT. Thus, we develop a hybrid method, CATCHSYNC+SPOT, that suspects the nodes detected by *either* CATCHSYNC *or* SPOT. It learns from both the graph structure and text-based features from tweets.

All the algorithms are implemented with JAVA, and all experiments are performed on a single machine with Intel Xeon CPU at 2.40GHz and 32GB RAM.

5.3 Detection Effectiveness on Synthetic Data

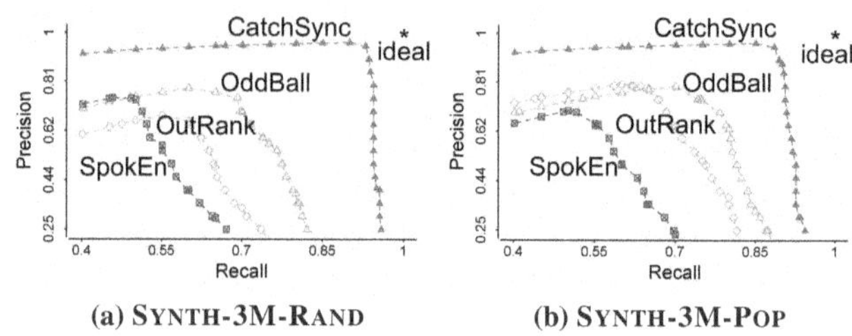

(a) SYNTH-3M-RAND (b) SYNTH-3M-POP

Figure 4: CATCHSYNC achieves higher precision and recall.

Injected group attacks shown in feature space and SN-plot. We plot the feature space (InF-plots) and SN-plots of two synthetic graphs with camouflage SYNTH-3M-RAND and SYNTH-3M-POP in Figure 3. When the weight of camouflage is small (d_{camou}=10% in SYNTH-3M-RAND), the InF-plot in Figure 3a shows the injected node groups as outliers from the majority. With the SN-plot in Figure 3c, CATCHSYNC can easily catch them since they fall along the synchronicity axis. When d_{camou} is as big as 50%, Figure 3c shows that the camouflage can hide the injected nodes in the dominating part. Our SN-plot in Figure 3c can catch them for their big synchronicity and small normality values.

Accuracy, precision and recall on injected node detection. Table 6 shows the accuracy on detecting the injected nodes from all the 5 synthetic datasets. When there is no "camouflage", CATCHSYNC reaches greater than 95% accuracy. When the nodes have camouflage, it can still outperforms the best of the other methods by 29.6% accuracy on SYNTH-3M-RAND and 27.5% accuracy on SYNTH-3M-POP. Figure 4 plots the precision-recall curves to test the performance of ranking the suspiciousness of nodes. Our method CATCHSYNC (the red filled triangle) can achieve both higher precision and higher recall.

Restoring the power law. The injected source nodes connect to 20 from the same set of targets. Due to this anomalous behavior pattern, the out-degree distribution has a spike at degree 20. Figure 5 plots the out-degree distributions before and after we operate CATCHSYNC on the synthetic graphs of different sizes. The spike on the distribution shrinks with the size of the graph increasing. No matter how big the spike is, our method can detect the injected nodes and we see if we remove them and their out-going edges, then the power-law degree distribution is restored.

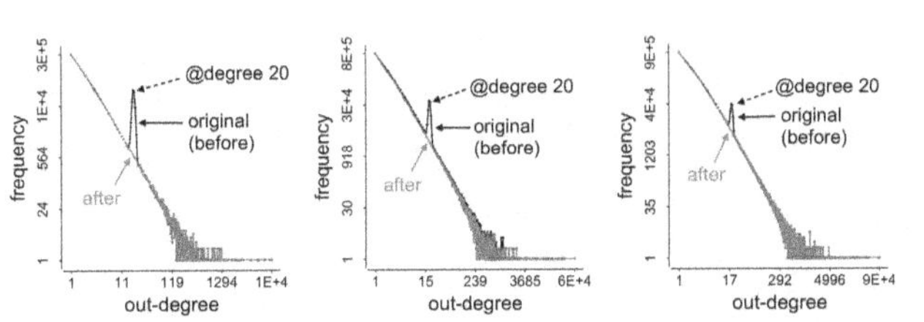

(a) SYNTH-1M (b) SYNTH-2M (c) SYNTH-3M

Figure 5: CATCHSYNC restores the power law: the degree distribution is recovered after the removal of suspicious nodes.

5.4 Detection Effectiveness on Real Data

Accuracy, precision and recall on real data. Table 7 shows the accuracy on detecting the labeled suspicious nodes from the two real social graphs. Also in Figure 6, we plot the precision-recall curves of CATCHSYNC, OUTRANK, SPOT and the hybrid algorithm CATCHSYNC+SPOT. We examine the results and give the following observations and explanations.

- **CATCHSYNC outperforms OUTRANK.** CATCHSYNC learns graph-based features of synchronized behavior that OUTRANK cannot capture using a random walk model with a data dedicated threshold.
- **CATCHSYNC outperforms SPOT.** CATCHSYNC learns graph-based features from the structural information, and SPOT learns text-based features from users' tweets. Since the main characteristics of the suspicious users are group attacks, CATCHSYNC has high accuracy, precision and recall than SPOT.

Actually, CATCHSYNC is *complementary* to SPOT: combining the flagged nodes, we get even better performance (purple line on Figure 6). The hybrid algorithm uses both of them to catch the different types of attackers. CATCHSYNC+SPOT consistently outperforms the competitors in detection accuracy by 36% on TWITTERSG and 20% on WEIBOSG. We suggest the social network applications to operate our CATCHSYNC on their who-follows-whom graphs, while they have used methods like SPOT that learns text-based features from their tweets and profiles.

Restoring the power law. While in the synthetic datasets the recovery of the power law followed directly from our high recall, this is not necessarily the case on real world data sets because we can only measure our accuracy on the subset of nodes we label.

	TWITTERSG	WEIBOSG
CATCHSYNC	0.751	0.694
OUTRANK	0.412	0.377
SPOT	0.597	0.653
CATCHSYNC+SPOT	**0.813**	**0.785**

Table 7: CATCHSYNC+SPOT outperforms each part: CATCHSYNC is better than OUTRANK at learning the structure, while SPOT learns the text; the combination wins the last.

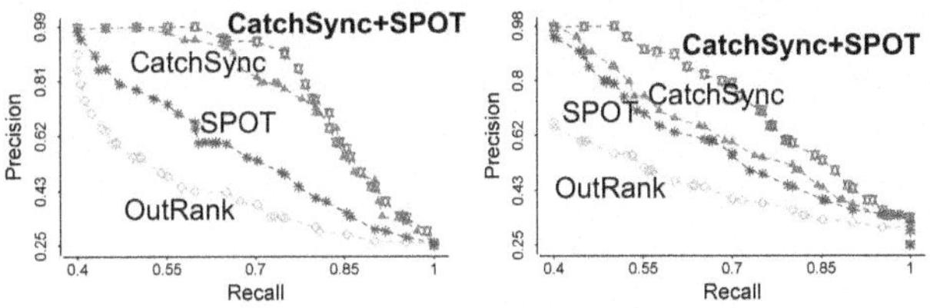

(a) TWITTERSG (b) WEIBOSG

Figure 6: CATCHSYNC+SPOT is the best at ranking the suspiciousness: it reaches the highest precision and recall.

Looking at the out-degree distribution of TWITTERSG in Figure 1b and WEIBOSG in Figure 1c, we see that removing the millions of caught suspicious nodes from the graph does leave only a smooth power law distribution on the remaining part of the graph. Because a power law distribution has been found to be typical of social networks and because the original distribution is not directly used in CATCHSYNC, this is strong evidence that our recall on the full datasets is high and that CATCHSYNC is effective.

Observations in the feature space. We provide interesting observations from the change of feature space before and after we operate CATCHSYNC on WEIBOSG. Figure 7a, 7b and 7c are OutF-plots arranged as an equation: all nodes *minus* suspicious nodes with synchronized behaviors *equals* normal nodes. Figure 7b shows the suspicious source nodes look synchronized and abnormal in the OutF-plot: they are coherent in red clusters or on blue stripes that deviate from the majority. The red clusters and blue stripes disappear in Figure 7c after we remove them from the graph. Figure 7d, 7e and 7f show a similar equation of InF-plots. Figure 7e shows that the suspicious targets are in a purple cluster in Figure 7f the cluster disappears after we remove them. The above observations provide evidence of the suspiciousness of the nodes who have synchronized behaviors. Our method CATCHSYNC can remove the strange patterns in the feature space.

5.5 CatchSync Properties

Robustness with respect to α. Within the synthetic data, we conduct experiments on the robustness to changes in α, the number of standard deviations from the mean for a node to be labelled as suspicious. In short, α=3.0 gives either the best result, or very close to it, and so do nearby values of α. In more detail, we test the sensitivity of precision and recall with respect to α, on the synthetic graphs of 3 different sizes. Figure 8 plots precision-recall curves: the ideal point is, of course, (1.0, 1.0); although α changes from 0.5 to 5.0, both precision and recall are still over 0.8. The performance of our algorithm is rather robust on α. We set $\alpha = 3.0$ as the default value for all of our other experiments. Note that approximately 99.7% of the observations fall within 3 standard deviations of the mean in the normal distribution. The suspicious nodes take the small percentage (0.3%) but still a big number since the graphs often contain millions of nodes, which makes this detection problem rather challenging.

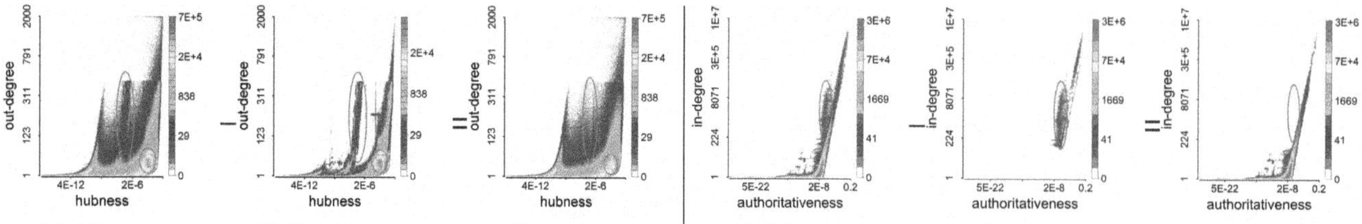

(a) All sources (b) Caught sources (c) Normal sources (d) All targets (e) Caught targets (f) Normal targets

Figure 7: Sources and targets caught by CATCHSYNC are outliers: (a,b,c) and (d,e,f) form two equations of OutF-/InF-plots. (a) minus (b) equals (c); (d) minus (e) equals (f), where (a,d) show all nodes, (b,e) show suspicious nodes and (c,f) show normal ones.

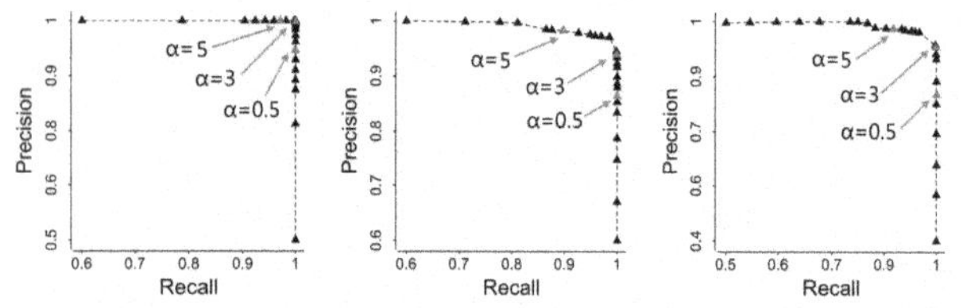

(a) SYNTH-1M (b) SYNTH-2M (c) SYNTH-3M

Figure 8: Robustness is perfect: the performance of CATCHSYNC is rather insensitive. We suggest $\alpha = 3.0$ as default.

Speed and scalability. We measure the run time on synthetic graphs with 1-3 million nodes. Figure 9 plots processor time vs graph size, showing that CATCHSYNC (the red filled triangles) scales linearly with the graph size and runs faster than alternatives. The measures, synchronicity and normality, could be computed very fast, taking only 10% time of the features (degree and HITS score), while the features can be previously chosen and calculated. Therefore, CATCHSYNC performs fast online for large graphs.

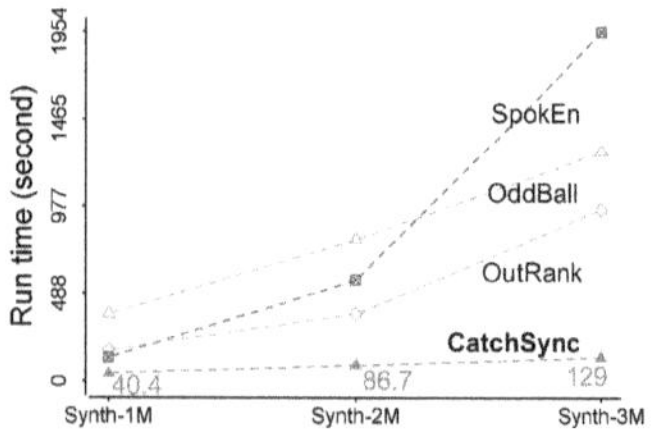

Figure 9: CATCHSYNC is fast and scalable: run time to detect injected nodes as the graph grows.

5.6 Discovery: A Case Study

As was mentioned earlier, detecting suspicious behavior is not merely a labeling problem. In the real world there are always new types of attacks that arise and distort the service being provided. While we have demonstrated that CATCHSYNC is successful at detecting classic spammy behavior, it also discovers more subtle types of suspicious behavior that a simpler labeling analysis would miss.

Looking online, it is easy to see that fraud on Twitter is much more complex than individual users posting tweets for money. In general users can get paid to tweet and the amount is based on how many followers they have [1, 2]. As a result, this has created marketplaces for buying Twitter followers, which besides providing politicians the appearance of popularity, also raises the value of the "Tweeter." Additionally there are marketplaces, e.g. buytwitteraccounts.org [2] and socialsellouts.com [3] to buy and sell Twitter accounts, again with the number of followers being the primary value. Because the market is complex, labeling accounts can be difficult with only a subtle red flags raising eyebrows. Here we examine closer some of the Twitter accounts we caught and we use side information to explain the range of suspicious behavior detected by CATCHSYNC.

Figure 10 shows a tiny subset (3 followers and 4 followees), from a large, suspicious group of 91K followers and about 700 followees), that was caught by CATCHSYNC. We see 3 accounts on the left that follow the 4 accounts on the right (and many others). Overall, each account, on its own, raises a few small suspicions, but our point is that, collectively, these accounts raise many more suspicions. Below we break down the types of accounts we find:

Dedicated Followers: Looking in Figure 10, we see on the left three followers: @AjaQwX1Z3, @AjaurNYj2 and @mastertwitlist. All three accounts have a slightly unusual name, few or no tweets, follow approximately 700 other accounts, and are surprisingly followed by approximately 400 accounts. Alone, each account may look slightly unusual but none of this evidence looks truly incriminating. As a group, however, the accounts are clearly suspicious because, along with them all having the same red flags, they all follow the same group of slightly unusual people.

Surprising Followees: On the right side of Figure 10 we see four of the accounts being followed. Within the group of followees, we find a few common patterns of obviously spam accounts, "SEO experts" tweeting suspicious content, and small business owners with an unusual number of followers. In the first case, @AaronMartirano is slightly suspicious with a most recent gibberish tweet (with words "auto follower", "follback") linking to an empty Blogger that had been labeled "*Unsafe*" by Twitter. Slightly different to the right we see @aaronseal, whose profile offers the GPS coordinates of a Bell Credit Union in Kansas and tweets to free Wordpress themes or asks users to "Like our Facebook Page" for a restaurant. Similarly we observe @biz2day, a self described "webmaster in the advertising and SEO business," who does not tweet "Unsafe" content, but links to other suspicious content like get-rich-quick schemes. For both @aaronseal and @biz2day, the consistent odd linking raises a red flag, and paired with the synchronized followers suggests that these are possibly purchased tweets and followers were bought to inflate the price. Last we see @HousingReporter a real estate agent with 164,700 followers - more than Massachusetts Senator and U.S. Presidential Hopeful Elizabeth Warren. A small red flag, but of course it is possible for a small business owner to want to appear more popular and thus buy followers.

In all of these cases it is of course impossible to know for sure how their followers were obtained or why they tweet the way they do. However, given that CATCHSYNC found these very different accounts based *only* on the graph structure, all of these other contextual red flags provide strong additional evidence that the followees caught are in fact very suspicious and that CATCHSYNC is effective at catching even subtle or hidden suspicious behavior.

6. CONCLUSION

We propose a novel method called CATCHSYNC that exploits

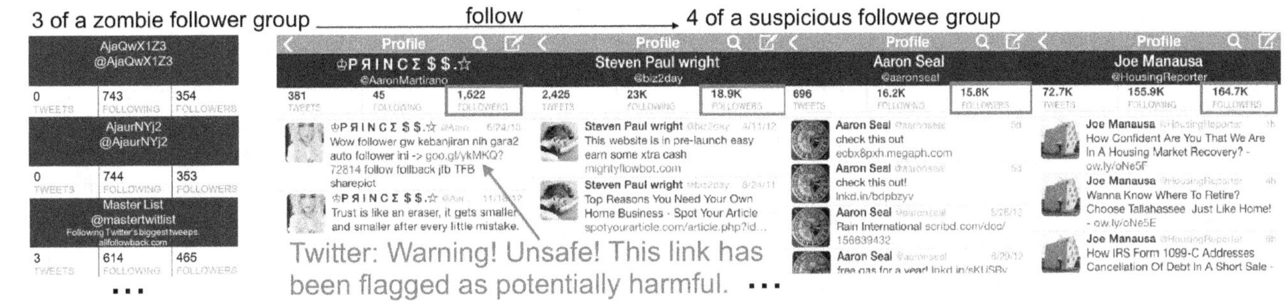

Figure 10: CATCHSYNC at work: using *only* structure information, we illustrate the biggest group that CATCHSYNC flagged (91,035 followers, 667 followees); we show 3 of the former and 4 of the latter. Side information *corroborates* our findings, raising several red flags: (a) the 3 shown followers have ~0 tweets, and near-identical counts of followers and followees, (b) the 4 shown followees mainly tweet urls, one of which is flagged by Twitter as unsafe.

two signs of artificial and non-organic behavior, synchronicity and normality, to automatically report and catch suspicious nodes on large directed graphs. CATCHSYNC has desirable properties:

- *Effectiveness*: it spots synchronized behavior and indeed catches suspicious source-target groups.
- *Scalability:* its complexity is linear in the number of edges.
- *Parameter free:* the operator can easily implement the algorithm without specifying any parameters such as the density, the number and scale of groups.
- *Side information oblivious:* it needs no side information. It is solely based on topology, and it requires neither labeled nodes nor node attributes, though it can incorporate them for better performance.

Experimental results using both real and synthetic datasets demonstrated that CATCHSYNC can catch the suspicious behavior patterns that previous approaches cannot capture.

7. ACKNOWLEDGEMENT

This work is supported by National Natural Science Foundation of China, No. 61370022, No. 61210008, and No. 61303075; International Science and Technology Cooperation Program of China, No. 2013DFG12870; National Program on Key Basic Research Project, No. 2011CB302206; NExT Research Center funded by MDA, Singapore, WBS:R-252-300-001-490. Thanks for the support of National Science Foundation, No. CNS-1314632; Army Research Laboratory under Cooperative Agreement Number W911NF-09-2-0053; U.S. Army Research Office (ARO) and Defense Advanced Research Projects Agency (DARPA), No. W911NF-11-C-0088; and the National Science Foundation Graduate Research Fellowship, Grant No. DGE-1252522.

Any opinions, findings and conclusions or recommendations expressed in this material are those of the author(s) and do not necessarily reflect the views of the National Science Foundation, DARPA, or other funding parties. The U.S. Government is authorized to reproduce and distribute reprints for Government purposes notwithstanding any copyright notation here on.

8. REFERENCES

[1] Buy Twitter Followers. http://www.buy-followers.org.

[2] Buy Twitter Accounts. http://buytwitteraccounts.org.

[3] Buy, Sell, and Trade Twitter accounts. http://socialsellouts.com.

[4] C. C. Aggarwal. *An introduction to social network data analytics*. Springer, 2011.

[5] C. C. Aggarwal and P. S. Yu. Outlier detection for high dimensional data. In *ACM Sigmod Record*, volume 30, pages 37–46, 2001.

[6] L. Akoglu, M. McGlohon, and C. Faloutsos. Oddball: Spotting anomalies in weighted graphs. In *AKDDM*, pages 410–421. 2010.

[7] A. Beutel, W. Xu, V. Guruswami, C. Palow, and C. Faloutsos. Copycatch: stopping group attacks by spotting lockstep behavior in social networks. In *WWW'13*, pages 119–130.

[8] A. Broder, R. Kumar, F. Maghoul, P. Raghavan, S. Rajagopalan, R. Stata, A. Tomkins, and J. Wiener. Graph structure in the web. *Computer networks*, 33(1), 2000.

[9] Q. Cao, M. Sirivianos, X. Yang, and T. Pregueiro. Aiding the detection of fake accounts in large scale social online services. In *NSDI'12*.

[10] D. Chakrabarti. Autopart: Parameter-free graph partitioning and outlier detection. In *PKDD'04*, pages 112–124.

[11] V. Chandola, A. Banerjee, and V. Kumar. Anomaly detection: A survey. *ACM Computing Surveys*, 41(3):15, 2009.

[12] D. H. Chau, S. Pandit, and C. Faloutsos. Detecting fraudulent personalities in networks of online auctioneers. In *PKDD'06*, pages 103–114.

[13] J. Chen and Y. Saad. Dense subgraph extraction with application to community detection. *TKDE*, 24(7):1216–1230, 2012.

[14] F. Chung and L. Lu. The average distances in random graphs with given expected degrees. *PNAS*, 99(25), 2002.

[15] D. J. Cook and L. B. Holder. *Mining graph data.* Wiley-Interscience, 2006.

[16] W. Eberle and L. Holder. Discovering structural anomalies in graph-based data. In *ICDM'07*, pages 393–398.

[17] M. Faloutsos, P. Faloutsos, and C. Faloutsos. On power-law relationships of the internet topology. *ACM SIGCOMM*, 29(4):251–262, 1999.

[18] T. Fawcett. An introduction to roc analysis. *PR letters*, 27(8):861–874, 2006.

[19] S. Fortunato. Community detection in graphs. *Physics Reports*, 486(3):75–174, 2010.

[20] C. Giatsidis, D. M. Thilikos, and M. Vazirgiannis. D-cores: measuring collaboration of directed graphs based on degeneracy. *KAIS*, 35(2):311–343, 2013.

[21] X. Hu, J. Tang, Y. Zhang, and H. Liu. Social spammer detection in microblogging. In *IJCAI'13*, pages 2633–2639.

[22] M. Jiang, P. Cui, A. Beutel, C. Faloutsos, and S. Yang. Detecting suspicious following behavior in multimillion-node social networks. In *WWW Companion*, pages 305–306, 2014.

[23] M. Jiang, P. Cui, A. Beutel, C. Faloutsos, and S. Yang. Inferring strange behavior from connectivity pattern in social

networks. In *Advances in Knowledge Discovery and Data Mining*, volume 8443, pages 126–138. 2014.

[24] J. M. Kleinberg. Authoritative sources in a hyperlinked environment. *JACM*, 46(5):604–632, 1999.

[25] R. Kumar, J. Novak, and A. Tomkins. Structure and evolution of online social networks. In *Link mining: models, algorithms, and applications*, pages 337–357. 2010.

[26] H. Kwak, C. Lee, H. Park, and S. Moon. What is twitter, a social network or a news media? In *WWW'10*, pages 591–600.

[27] C. Liu, X. Yan, H. Yu, J. Han, and S. Y. Philip. Mining behavior graphs for "backtrace" of noncrashing bugs. In *SDM'05*.

[28] H. Moonesinghe and P.-N. Tan. Outrank: a graph-based outlier detection framework using random walk. *International Journal on Artificial Intelligence Tools*, 17(01):19–36, 2008.

[29] C. C. Noble and D. J. Cook. Graph-based anomaly detection. In *KDD'03*, pages 631–636.

[30] S. Pandit, D. H. Chau, S. Wang, and C. Faloutsos. Netprobe: a fast and scalable system for fraud detection in online auction networks. In *WWW'07*, pages 201–210.

[31] J. Pei, D. Jiang, and A. Zhang. On mining cross-graph quasi-cliques. In *KDD'05*, pages 228–238.

[32] C. Perez, M. Lemercier, B. Birregah, and A. Corpel. Spot 1.0: Scoring suspicious profiles on twitter. In *ASONAM'11*, pages 377–381.

[33] B. A. Prakash, A. Sridharan, M. Seshadri, S. Machiraju, and C. Faloutsos. Eigenspokes: Surprising patterns and scalable community chipping in large graphs. In *AKDDM*, pages 435–448. 2010.

[34] S. Shekhar, C.-T. Lu, and P. Zhang. Detecting graph-based spatial outliers: algorithms and applications (a summary of results). In *KDD'01*, pages 371–376, 2001.

[35] J. Sun, H. Qu, D. Chakrabarti, and C. Faloutsos. Neighborhood formation and anomaly detection in bipartite graphs. In *ICDM'05*.

[36] D. M. Tax and R. P. Duin. Outlier detection using classifier instability. In *Advances in Pattern Recognition*. 1998.

[37] C. E. Tsourakakis, F. Bonchi, A. Gionis, F. Gullo, and M. A. Tsiarli. Denser than the densest subgraph: Extracting optimal quasi-cliques with quality guarantees. In *KDD'13*.

[38] X. Wang and I. Davidson. Active spectral clustering. In *ICDM'10*, pages 561–568.

[39] X. Yan and J. Han. Closegraph: mining closed frequent graph patterns. In *KDD'03*, pages 286–295.

[40] Z. Zou, J. Li, H. Gao, and S. Zhang. Mining frequent subgraph patterns from uncertain graph data. *TKDE*, 22(9):1203–1218, 2010.

APPENDIX

Here we provide the proof of Theorem 1.

PROOF. In order to find the lower limit of synchronicity when given a normality, we define the problem as follows.

Given G grids, f_g and b_g counts of points ($f_g \leq b_g$) from the foreground/background cloud in grid g ($g = 1, \ldots, G$), the normality n of $\vec{f}$, **find** values of $\vec{f}$ to *minimize* the synchronicity s.

Remind that (1) the synchronicity s is the synchronicity of foreground points, i.e., the dot product of (unit sum) foreground with the same foreground: $s = \sum_g \frac{f_g^2}{F^2}$; (2) the normality n is the dot product of (unit sum) foreground with (unit sum) background: $n = \sum_g \frac{f_g b_g}{FB}$.

Let $B(F)$ be the total counts: $\sum f_g = F$ and $\sum b_g = B$. Let $\hat{b}_g = b_g/B$ and similarly $\hat{f}_g = f_g/F$. Thus, the resulting vectors sum up to one ("probability vectors"). The problem definition is updated as follows.

Given a (probability) vector $\vec{\hat{b}}$ with M entries ($M \leq G$), **find** a (probability) vector $\vec{\hat{f}}$ with given normality $n = \vec{\hat{f}} \cdot \vec{\hat{b}} = \sum(\hat{f}_g * \hat{b}_g)$ and minimum synchronicity $s = \vec{\hat{f}} \cdot \vec{\hat{f}} = \sum \hat{f}_g^2$, and **report** both the optimal such vector $\vec{\hat{f}}_{opt}$, as well as the minimum synchronicity $s_{\min}$.

The method of Lagrange multipliers is a well-known strategy for finding the local minima (maxima) of a function subject to equality constraints. Here the Lagrange function is

$$\mathcal{F}(\hat{f}_g, \lambda, \mu) = (\sum_g \hat{f}_g^2) + \lambda(\sum_g \hat{f}_g - 1) + \mu(\sum_g (\hat{f}_g * \hat{b}_g) - n) \quad (5)$$

The gradients of the function are

$$\partial\mathcal{F}/\partial\hat{f}_g = 2\hat{f}_g + \lambda + \mu\hat{b}_g = 0 \quad g = 1, \ldots, M \quad (6)$$

and the two initial conditions are

$$\partial\mathcal{F}/\partial\lambda = \sum_g \hat{f}_g - 1 = 0 \quad (7)$$

$$\partial\mathcal{F}/\partial\mu = \sum_g (\hat{f}_g * \hat{b}_g) - n = 0 \quad (8)$$

From Eq 6 we have, after summing them all up:

$$2 + M\lambda + \mu = 0 \quad (9)$$

From Eq 6 we have, after multiplying each with $\hat{b}_g$ and summing them all up:

$$2 * n + \lambda + \mu s_b = 0 \quad (10)$$

where we call s_b the synchronicity of the background: $s_b = \sum_g \hat{b}_g^2 = \sum_g \frac{b_g^2}{B^2}$. Solving for μ we get

$$\mu = -2 - M\lambda \quad (11)$$

and substituting μ and for λ we get

$$\lambda = 2(s_b - n)/(1 - M * s_b) \quad (12)$$

We can substitute the values of μ and λ into Eq 6 and solve for each $\hat{f}_g$, or, even faster, we multiply each of Eq 6 with the corresponding $\hat{f}_g$ and we add, obtaining:

$$2 * s + \lambda + \mu n = 0 \quad (13)$$

which gives that the (optimal) s_{opt} satisfies

$$s_{opt} = 1/2(-\lambda - \mu n) \quad (14)$$

If the Hessian matrix is positive definite at a point, then the function is a *convex* function and it attains a local *minima* at the point. Here the Hessian is a diagonal matrix with "2" in the first M positions, and zeros everywhere else. So eventually the minimum synchronicity is

$$\boxed{s_{min} = (-Mn^2 + 2n - s_b)/(1 - Ms_b)} \quad (15)$$

That is, the minimum synchronicity s_{min} for a given normality n, is a quadratic function of n. □

Mobile App Recommendations with Security and Privacy Awareness

Hengshu Zhu[1] Hui Xiong[2*] Yong Ge[3] Enhong Chen[1*]

[1]University of Science and Technology of China, [2]Rutgers University, [3]UNC Charlotte

zhs@mail.ustc.edu.cn, hxiong@rutgers.edu, yong.ge@uncc.edu, cheneh@ustc.edu.cn

ABSTRACT

With the rapid prevalence of smart mobile devices, the number of mobile Apps available has exploded over the past few years. To facilitate the choice of mobile Apps, existing mobile App recommender systems typically recommend popular mobile Apps to mobile users. However, mobile Apps are highly varied and often poorly understood, particularly for their activities and functions related to privacy and security. Therefore, more and more mobile users are reluctant to adopt mobile Apps due to the risk of privacy invasion and other security concerns. To fill this crucial void, in this paper, we propose to develop a mobile App recommender system with privacy and security awareness. The design goal is to equip the recommender system with the functionality which allows to automatically detect and evaluate the security risk of mobile Apps. Then, the recommender system can provide App recommendations by considering both the Apps' popularity and the users' security preferences. Specifically, a mobile App can lead to security risk because insecure *data access permissions* have been implemented in this App. Therefore, we first develop the techniques to automatically detect the potential security risk for each mobile App by exploiting the requested permissions. Then, we propose a flexible approach based on *modern portfolio theory* for recommending Apps by striking a balance between the Apps' popularity and the users' security concerns, and build an *App hash tree* to efficiently recommend Apps. Finally, we evaluate our approach with extensive experiments on a large-scale data set collected from Google Play. The experimental results clearly validate the effectiveness of our approach.

Categories and Subject Descriptors

H.2.8.d [**Information Technology and Systems**]: Database Applications - Data Mining

Keywords

Mobile Apps, Recommender Systems, Security and Privacy

*Corresponding Author.

KDD'14, August 24–27, 2014, New York, NY, USA.
Copyright 2014 ACM 978-1-4503-2956-9/14/08 ...$15.00.
http://dx.doi.org/10.1145/2623330.2623705.

1. INTRODUCTION

Recent years have witnessed the rapid and increased prevalence of smart mobile devices, such as smart phones, a huge number of mobile Apps have been developed for mobile users. For example, as of the end of July 2013, the Google Play has had over 1 million Apps and there have been over 50 billion cumulative downloads, and these numbers are still growing dramatically. Due to the prospering mobile App industry, the functionalities of smart devices have been intensely extended to meet diversified user needs. However, mobile Apps are highly varied and often poorly understood, particularly for their activities and functions related to privacy and security. Indeed, to improve user experiences, more and more advanced mobile Apps are committed to provide intelligent and personalized services for users, such as location based services and social sharing services. These services usually involve access permissions of users' personal data, such as real-time locations and the contact lists.

However, such intelligent mobile Apps may result in the potential security and privacy risks for users. For instance, users may not expect their locations (e.g., home locations, workplaces) and other privacy information (e.g., contact lists, SMS records) to be spied by the third party Apps. In fact, as reported by NBC News [1], consumers have grown so concerned about privacy on their mobile phones. Many consumers have avoided downloading some mobile Apps, and many others have removed Apps which may have access to their personal data. Also, a recent survey from IDG News [2] reveals that 54% of U.S. mobile App users surveyed have decided not to install an App when they discovered how much personal information it would collect, and 30% of App users have uninstalled an App after learning about the personal information it collected. Therefore, the development of a mobile App recommender system with security and privacy awareness becomes critical for the healthy development of the mobile App industry.

In the literature, there are recent studies about security and privacy issues of mobile Apps, and mobile App recommendations. For example, some works are focused on malware code detection [6, 13], the security middleware development [7, 20], and the App access permission model development [5, 8]. However, these works either need to analyze the source code of each mobile App, or detect the system API calls during the App running. Indeed, these approaches are very hard to be implemented in practice, since it is not a trivial task to efficiently and accurately detect the malware

[1]http://www.nbcnews.com/
[2]http://www.idg.com/

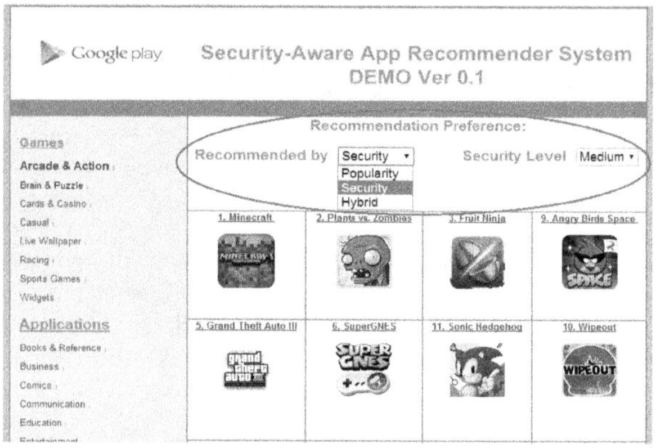

Figure 1: A demo system of mobile App recommendations with security and privacy awareness.

codes for each mobile App and users often do not want some security software to frequently scan their devices. Meanwhile, in the area of mobile App recommendation, some works studied the personalized App recommendation methods [17], the intelligent mobile App recommendations by exploiting enriched contextual information [10, 21], and the problem of App ranking fraud detection [22]. However, all these works only consider user preferences about the Apps' popularity (e.g., ratings, downloads), but not the security and privacy risks inherent in the mobile Apps.

To this end, in this paper, we propose to develop a mobile App recommender system with security and privacy awareness. The design goal is to equip the recommender system with the ability to automatically detect and evaluate the security and privacy risks of mobile Apps. Also, when applying this recommender system for App recommendations, it should be able to strike a balance between the Apps' popularity and the users' security preferences. Figure 1 shows the interface of our demo system for mobile App recommendations with security and privacy awareness. In this system, users can select different evaluation metrics, such as Popularity, Security, and Hybrid, to obtain App recommendations with respect to their preferred security levels. While we do not aim at developing personalized App recommender systems because the individual download statistics and App usage data are often not publicly available, our **non-personalized** App recommendations by considering both popularity and security are very important for mobile App services. For instance, both Apple and Google provide non-personalized top paid/free App recommendations based on the popularity information (e.g., overall download and rating) every day. However, they do not explore and consider the security preferences in their recommended top charts. Indeed, the developed system will be beneficial for the healthy development of the mobile App industry.

However, there are two critical challenge for developing an App recommender system with security and privacy awareness. Specifically, the first challenge is how to effectively identify the security risks of mobile Apps from the large-scale mobile App data. The second challenge is how to strike a balance between the Apps' popularity and the users' concerns about security and privacy. Indeed, our careful observation reveals that the potential security risks of mobile Apps are essentially caused by the *data access permissions* of each App, such as permissions requested for accessing real-time locations. Therefore, in this paper, we first propose to exploit the requested permissions for detecting the potential security risk of each mobile App. The proposed approach is based on random walk regularization with an *App-permission bipartite graph*, which can learn the security risk of mobile Apps automatically without relying on any predefined risk function. Furthermore, based on the *modern portfolio theory* [16], we develop a flexible optimization approach for recommending Apps by considering both Apps' popularity and users' concerns about security and privacy. Particularly, there are often many different security preferences of mobile users, and a huge number of Apps as candidates for recommendations. To enhance the performances of online App recommendations, we build an *App hash tree* to efficiently look up Apps. Finally, we evaluate our mobile App recommendation approach with extensive experiments on a large-scale real-world data set collected from Google Play, which contains 170,753 mobile Apps. The experimental results clearly validate the effectiveness and efficiency of our approach in terms of different evaluation metrics.

2. PROBLEM FORMULATION

In this section, we first introduce some preliminaries about the security/privacy problems of mobile Apps, and then introduce the framework of the proposed mobile App recommender system with security and privacy awareness.

Table 1: Examples of data access permissions.

Type	Permission ID	Description
String	`ACCESS_FINE_LOCATION`	Allows an application to access fine (e.g., GPS) location.
String	`READ_CONTACTS`	Allows an application to read the user's contacts data.
String	`READ_SMS`	Allows an application to read the user's SMS messages.
String	`READ_CALENDAR`	Allows an application to read the user's calendar data.
String	`READ_CALL_LOG`	Allows an application to read the user's call log.

2.1 Preliminaries

The most advanced mobile operating systems, such as Apple IOS, Google Android, and Microsoft Windows Phone, implement a sandbox which provides the security and privacy policy for the third-party mobile Apps. To be specific, these operating systems isolate Apps from each other and the resources, thus feature a permission system [7]. To access the personal data in users' mobile devices, the permission system will convey users to grant corresponding data access permissions explicitly (e.g., IOS) or implicitly (e.g., Android) for each mobile App. Actually, these data access permissions may enter some sensitive resources in mobile users' personal data, such as their locations or contact lists. For instance, Table 1 illustrates some examples of data access permissions in the Android system [1]. We can see that all these listed permissions contain potential security risks. For example, an App, which requests **`READ_CALENDAR`** and **`READ_SMS`** permissions, may access users' personal calendar and short messages. This may not be comfortable for a business man due to the risks of leaking confidential information.

Indeed, all these data access permissions can be categorized into different levels with respect to their potential security risks. For example, as defined by Android Developers [1], there are three different threat levels for managing data access permissions,

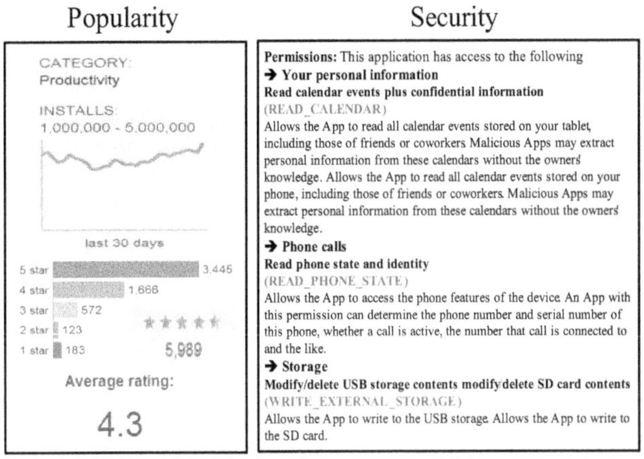

Figure 2: A motivating example.

- **Normal permissions** give an App access to isolated App level features, with the minimal risk to other applications, the system, or the user access (e.g., the permission to set screen wallpaper).
- **Dangerous permissions** give an App access to private user data or control over the device, with a potential risk that can negatively impact the user (e.g., the permission to have the user's current location).
- **Signature/System permissions** give an App access to the dangerous privileges, which need system signature certifications such as the ability to control the system process (e.g., the permission to delete Apps).

To provide better services to users and gain more downloads of Apps, mobile App developers try to request more and more data access permissions, which can help to implement the intelligent applications, such as social sharing services. However, these services may result in potential security and privacy risks. For example, Figure 2 shows an example of a mobile App in the Android market, which contains both popularity and security information. In this figure, we can observe that this App may request the permission of reading the users' calender (i.e., `READ_CALENDAR`), reading phone states (i.e., `READ_PHONE_STATE`) and external USB/SD card storage (i.e., `WRITE_EXTERNAL_STORAGE`). Although this is a quite popular App according to user ratings and the download information, it may still contain the potential risk of leaking user information. For instance, if this App is controlled by a Trojan, it could gather users' calender information and phone numbers, then upload the information into external USB disk or SD card (when connected) via the above permissions. However, to the best of our knowledge, this kind of security risks is not taken into account in most existing mobile App recommender systems. Indeed, they only focus on the Apps' popularity information (e.g., user ratings). Thus, we aim on developing a mobile App recommender system with security and privacy awareness.

2.2 The Recommendation Framework

Here, we first formally define the problem of mobile App recommendations with security and privacy awareness, and then show the recommendation framework.

DEFINITION 1 (PRO LEM STATEMENT). *Given a category label c, and a set of Apps $A = \{a\}$, each of which contains a set of data access permissions $\{p_i\}$, profile information (e.g., category, popularity), the goal of mobile App recommendation with security and privacy awareness is to build an optimal ranked list of Apps in category c based on both the Apps' popularity and users' security preferences.*

Indeed, the above problem statement raises two issues:

- How to mine the security risks of Apps and produce a ranked list $\Lambda^{(Risk)} = \{a|a \in c\}$ according to their **risk scores** $Risk(a)$, where a is ranked higher than a^* if and only if $Risk(a) > Risk(a^*)$.
- How to combine the risk based ranked list $\Lambda^{(Risk)}$ with the popularity based ranked list $\Lambda^{(Pop)}$ to produce final ranking so as to meet various expectations of users, who have different security and privacy concerns.

While it is appealing to provide mobile App recommendations with security and privacy awareness, it is a non-trivial task to effectively discover and evaluate the security risks of Apps, and produce desirable ranking of Apps by considering both Apps' popularity and users' security preferences. In addition, there are often many different security preferences of mobile users, and a huge number of Apps as candidates for recommendations. Thus, how to efficiently manage Apps for recommendation is also an open question. To that end, in this paper, we propose a novel recommendation framework to solve these problems.

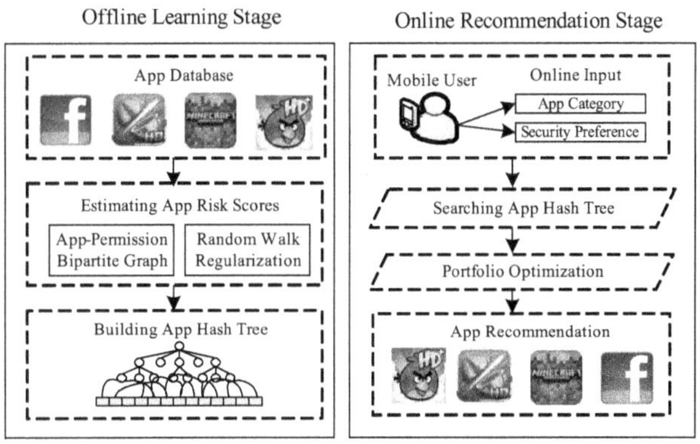

Figure 3: The recommendation framework.

Figure 3 shows the proposed recommendation framework, which consists of two stages. The *offline learning stage* automatically learns the risk scores for Apps by leveraging the random walk regularization with an *App-permission bipartite graph*, and forms an App hash tree from the App data set for efficiently managing Apps. The *online recommendation stage* matches the given mobile users' security preferences and App categories according to the App hash tree, ranks the candidate Apps with respect to both Apps' popularity and users' security preferences by leveraging the modern portfolio theory for recommendations.

3. ESTIMATING RISK SCORES FOR MOBILE APPS

Generally speaking, the risk score reflects the security level of an App. The smaller the score is, the more safe the App is. According to the above discussion, we can know the security risks are essentially caused by the data access permissions of Apps. Thus, an intuitive approach for measuring the risks of Apps is to directly check each of the dangerous permissions they request. However, there are many critical challenges along this line, which make the problem

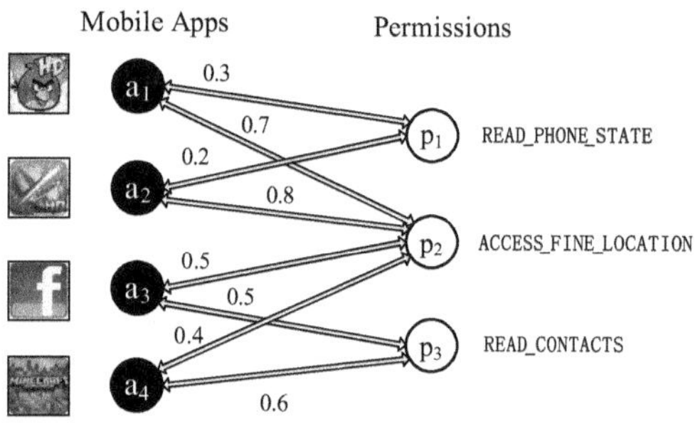

Figure 4: An example of the bipartite graph.

still under-addressed. First, it is hard to explicitly define a risk function with respect to different permissions for evaluating the potential risks of mobile Apps, since the permissions are often very ambiguous and poorly understood [5, 8]. For example, we observe that although some permissions are dangerous (e.g., location related permissions), they are commonly used in the Apps of some categories (e.g., navigation Apps). Second, the latent relationships between Apps and permissions should be taken into consideration, since similar Apps (permissions) should have similar risk scores. Finally, we should develop a scalable approach to refine risk scores, since rich external knowledge can be leveraged for evaluating potential risks of Apps. For example, some external risk reports, the state-of-the-art security models in relevant domains as well as the prior knowledge from domain experts can be leveraged for improving the performance of ranking App risks. To deal with the above challenges, in this paper, we propose a regularization approach based on a bipartite graph, which can learn the security risk of mobile Apps automatically without relying on any predefined risk function. Particularly, we develop an *App-permission bipartite graph* to build the connections between Apps and permissions, which is defined as follows.

DEFINITION (A - ERMISSION BI ARTITE GRA H). *The graph can be denoted as $G = \{V, E, W\}$. $V = \{V^a, V^p\}$ is the node set, where $V^a = \{a_1, \cdots, a_M\}$ denotes the set of Apps and $V^p = \{p_1, \cdots, p_N\}$ denotes the set of permissions. E is the edge set, where $e_{ij} \in E$ exists if and only if a_i re uests the permission p_j. W is the edge weight set, where each $w_{ij} \in W$ represents the weight of e_{ij} and denotes the probability that a_i will re uest p_j.*

Figure 4 shows an example of App-permission bipartite graph. Intuitively, the weight w_{ij} can be estimated by the permission records of all Apps in a_i's category. Specifically, we can compute the weight by

$$w_{ij} = \frac{f_{ij}}{\sum_{e_{ik} \in E} f_{ik}}, \tag{1}$$

where f_{ij} is the number of Apps in category c ($a_i \in c$) requesting permission p_j. Furthermore, we can denote each App a_j and permission p_j as vectors $\overrightarrow{a_i} = \{w_{i1}, \cdots, w_{iN}\}$ and $\overrightarrow{p_j} = \{w_{1j}, \cdots, w_{Mj}\}$, respectively. Accordingly, we define the latent similarity between Apps a_i and a_j by the Cosine distance,

$$s^a_{ij} = Cos(\overrightarrow{a_i}, \overrightarrow{a_j}) = \frac{\overrightarrow{a_i} \cdot \overrightarrow{a_j}}{||\overrightarrow{a_i}|| \cdot ||\overrightarrow{a_j}||}. \tag{2}$$

Similarly, we define the latent similarity between permissions p_i and p_j as $s^p_{ij} = Cos(\overrightarrow{p_i}, \overrightarrow{p_j})$.

To estimate App risk scores with the App-permission bipartite graph, we first define two scores $Risk(a_i)$ and $Risk(p_j)$ for node $a_i \in V^a$ and $p_j \in V^p$, respectively. Intuitively, $Risk(a_i)$ is the objective App risk score and $Risk(p)$ is the global permission risk score. Second, we develop a regularization framework by regularizing the smoothness of the above two scores over the bipartite graph. Specifically, if we denote $Risk(a_i)$ as R^a_i and $Risk(p_j)$ as R^p_j, we define a cost function as follows,

$$\begin{aligned} \mathcal{Q}(a,p) = \frac{\lambda}{2} \cdot \Big\{ \sum_i \Big\| R^a_i - \widetilde{R}^a_i \Big\|^2 + \sum_j \Big\| R^p_j - \widetilde{R}^p_j \Big\|^2 \Big\} + \\ \frac{\mu}{2} \cdot \Big\{ \sum_{i,j} s^a_{ij} \Big\| R^a_i - R^a_j \Big\|^2 + \sum_{i,j} s^p_{ij} \Big\| R^p_i - R^p_j \Big\|^2 \Big\} + \\ \frac{1}{2} \cdot \sum_{i,j} w_{ij} \Big\| R^a_i - R^p_j \Big\|^2, \end{aligned} \tag{3}$$

where λ and μ are the regularization parameters, $\widetilde{R}^a_i$ and $\widetilde{R}^p_j$ are the *prior risk scores* derived from *external knowledge*.

Intuitively, this cost function is formed by three parts. The first part controlled by λ defines the constraint that the two risk scores should fit prior knowledge. The second part controlled by μ defines the global consistency of the refined risk scores over the graph. Specifically, it satisfies that, if two Apps (permissions) have high latent similarity, their risk scores should be similar. The third part is the smoothness constraint between Apps and permissions, which guarantees that, if an App has high probability to request a specific permission, their risk scores should be similar. Therefore, the problem of estimating risk scores is converted to the optimization problem of finding optimal R^a_i and R^p_j to minimize the cost function $\mathcal{Q}$. In this paper, we exploit the classic gradient descent method to solve this problem. Specifically, we first assign values to $R^a_i = 1/M$ and $R^p_j = 1/N$ and iteratively update them by setting the following differentiated results to zero.

$$\begin{aligned} \frac{\partial \mathcal{Q}}{\partial a_i} = \lambda(R^a_i - \widetilde{R}^a_i) + \mu \sum_j s^a_{ij}(R^a_i - R^a_j) + \sum_j w_{ij}(R^a_i - R^p_j), \\ R^a_i = \frac{\lambda \widetilde{R}^a_i + \mu \sum_j s^a_{ij} R^a_j + \sum_j w_{ij} R^p_j}{\lambda + \mu \sum_j s^a_{ij} + \sum_j w_{ij}}. \end{aligned} \tag{4}$$

$$\begin{aligned} \frac{\partial \mathcal{Q}}{\partial p_j} = \lambda(R^p_j - \widetilde{R}^p_j) + \mu \sum_i s^p_{ij}(R^p_j - R^p_i) + \sum_i w_{ij}(R^p_j - R^a_i), \\ R^p_j = \frac{\lambda \widetilde{R}^p_j + \mu \sum_i s^p_{ij} R^p_i + \sum_i w_{ij} R^a_i}{\lambda + \mu \sum_i s^p_{ij} + \sum_i w_{ij}}. \end{aligned} \tag{5}$$

After each iteration, all the values of R^a_i and R^a_j will be normalized again, i.e., $\|R^a\|_1 = 1$ and $\|R^p\|_1 = 1$. Finally, we can obtain the optimal risk scores after the results converge.

How to assign prior risk scores $\widetilde{R}^a_i$ and $\widetilde{R}^p_j$ from external knowledge is an open question. In practice, some intuitive solutions include inviting domain experts for assigning risk scores, building a security classifier through external risk reports, or exploiting state-of-the-art security models in relevant domains. In this paper, as an attempt, we leverage the probabilistic approach PNB (Naive Bayes with information Priors) proposed in [14] for this task, which is based on the scoring scheme, and thus can be directly adopted by our regularization framework. Specifically, PNB aims to learn a Naive Bayes model with parameter θ that can best explain the generative process of permissions, i.e., $P(p_j|\theta)$. In this model, the parameter θ is assumed to follow the Beta prior $Beta(\theta; \alpha_0, \beta_0)$, and the probability can be estimated by

$$P(p_j|\theta) = \frac{\sum_i^M x_{i,j} + \alpha_0}{M + \alpha_0 + \beta_o}, \tag{6}$$

where M is the total number of Apps and $x_{i,j}$ is a binary function which is equal to 1 (i.e., a_i requests the permission p_j) or 0 (i.e., a_i does not request the permission p_j). Particularly, PNB also defines three categories of permissions with respect to their threat levels (i.e., similar as the preliminaries in Section 2), and each category has a specific $Beta(\theta; \alpha_0, \beta_0)$ as informative priors. Therfore, the risk scores of permission p_j and App a_i can be estimated by $\widetilde{R}^p_j = -\ln P(p_j|\theta)$ and $\widetilde{R}^a_i = -\ln P(p_1, \cdots, p_k|\theta)$, where each $p_k \in a_i$. Note that, both $\widetilde{R}^a_i$ and $\widetilde{R}^p_j$ are normalized before learning our regularization framework. Although PNB is a straightforward approach that cannot solve all the challenges mentioned before, its effectiveness on ranking risks of Apps has been well proved. Therefore, using PNB as prior knowledge in our regularization framework is appropriate.

4. RANKING FOR MOBILE APP RECOMMENDATION

Algorithm 1 Automatic Detection of Security Levels

Input: The set of Apps $A = \{a_i\}$; Parameter δ;
Output: The set of security levels Ψ;

Rank A in descending order according to $Risk(a)$;
$L = \emptyset$;
for each $i \in [1, |A|]$ **do**
  $A^* = L \cup \{A[i]\}$;
  calculate $CV(A^*)$ in terms of $Risk(a)$ $(a \in A^*)$;
  if $(CV(A^*) > \delta)$ **then**
    $\Psi \cup = L$; $L = \emptyset$ is a new level;
  else
    $L \cup = \{A[i]\}$;
  end if
end for
return Ψ

After computing the risk score for each mobile App, we can rank Apps in ascending order with respect to their risk scores for recommendations. Moreover, if some Apps have the same risk scores, they will be further ranked according to popularity scores (e.g., overall rating). However, for real-world App recommendation services, users may have difficulties to get clear perception about the risks of ranked Apps. A promising way to help users understand the different risks of Apps is to categorize the risks into discrete levels (e.g., Low, Medium, High). In fact, people often describe their perception about risk or security with such discrete levels. Therefore, in this paper, we further group Apps into different clusters, each of which has the same security level (e.g, Low or High). However, it is not easy to get an accurate and appropriate segmentation of Apps with respect to their risk scores due to the lack of appropriate benchmarks.

To solve the above problem, we develop a Coefficient of Variation (CV) based approach to automatically segment mobile Apps. The main idea of this approach is that two adjacent Apps in the globally ranked list are assigned with different security levels, if their risk scores have dramatic differences, which can be captured by the CV, i.e., $\frac{variance}{mean}$, of their risk scores. The detailed segmentation algorithm is shown in Algorithm 1. The parameter δ is a threshold used for determining the dramatic difference of CV. After segmentation, the Apps at lower security levels have higher security risk.

Now, we are able to recommend Apps for users. Specifically, given a specific security level L^* and a category c, we can treat all the Apps in category c with security $L \geq L^*$ as candidates. Intuitively, there are two types of ranking principles for recommending Apps.

- ***Security Principle***: We first rank App candidates in ascending order by their risk scores, and Apps have the same scores will be further ranked by popularity scores (e.g., overall rating).
- ***Popularity Principle***: We first rank App candidates in descending order by their popularity scores (e.g., overall rating), and Apps have the same popularity scores will be further ranked by risk scores.

Furthermore, we need to strike a balance between users' security preferences and Apps' popularity for recommendations. To achieve such a balance, we also propose a ***hybrid principle*** for App recommendations, which is based on the modern portfolio theory [16]. The portfolio theory is originally proposed in the field of finance, which focuses on the investment problem of financial market. For example, an investor often wants to select a portfolio of n stocks with a fixed investment budget, which will provide the maximum future return and the minimum risk. In our problem, the stocks can be regarded as Apps, the future return and risk can be regarded as popularity and security risk of Apps.

Specifically, an App portfolio Υ can be represented by a collection of n Apps with a corresponding weight w_i assigned to each App a, i.e.,

$$\Upsilon = \{(a_i, w_i)\}, \quad s.t. \sum_i w_i = 1. \tag{7}$$

Indeed, the weight w_i in finance is the percentage of the budget invested in the i-th stock. According to the discussion in [19], the weight w_i in our problem indicates how much attention the recommender system wants the target user to pay on the App a_i. Therefore, the weights can be used to determine the ranks of Apps; that is, Apps should be ranked by the descending order of their weights. Before obtaining the weights, we first define the future return of the App portfolio as $\mathbb{E}[\Upsilon]$, which can be computed by

$$\mathbb{E}[\Upsilon] = \sum_i^n w_i \cdot \Delta_i^{-1}, \tag{8}$$

where Δ_i is the rank of App a_i in the popularity based ranked list $\Lambda^{(Pop)}$. Also, we define the future risk of the App portfolio as $\mathbb{R}[\Upsilon]$, which can be computed by the following function [12],

$$\mathbb{R}[\Upsilon] = \sum_i^n (w_i^2 \nabla_i^{-1} + 2 \sum_{j=i+1}^n w_i w_j \nabla_i^{-1} \nabla_j^{-1} J_{ij}), \tag{9}$$

where ∇_i is the rank of App a_i in the risk based ranked list $\Lambda^{(Risk)}$, and J_{ij} is the risk correlation between Apps a_i and a_j. Here, we estimate J_{ij} according to the similarity of requested permissions. For any two Apps, the more common permissions are requested, the higher risk similarity they have. To this end, we compute J_{ij} using Jaccard coefficient between Apps a_i and a_j by,

$$J_{ij} = \frac{N_{ij}}{N_i + N_j - N_{ij}}, \tag{10}$$

where N_i is the number of permissions requested by App a_i, and N_{ij} is the number of common permissions requested by two Apps a_i and a_j.

In our problem, the objective is to learn a set of App weights $\mathbf{w}$ for maximizing the future return and minimizing

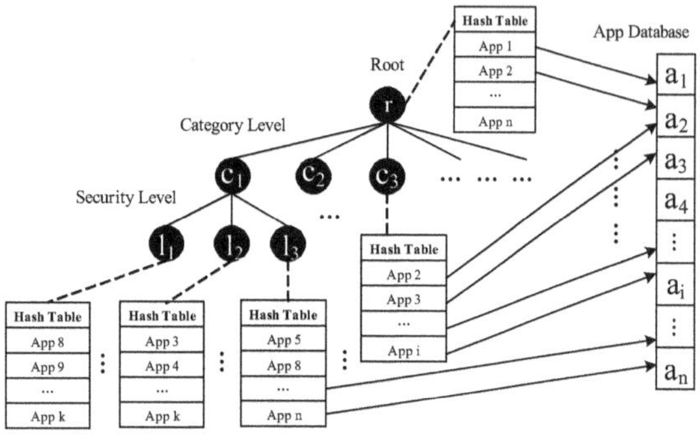

Figure 5: An example of the App hash tree.

the risk of the App portfolio Υ that consists of recommendation candidates (App candidates), i.e.,

$$\arg\max_{\mathbf{w}} \quad \mathbb{E}[\Upsilon] - b \cdot \mathbb{R}[\Upsilon], \tag{11}$$

where b is a specified risk preference parameter, which is defined as the given security level L^* in our experiments. The above optimization problem can be solved by the efficient frontier based approach introduced in [19]. Specifically, we can obtain the optimal weight $\mathbf{w}^*$ by

$$\mathbf{w}^* = \frac{\begin{vmatrix} 1 & \mathbf{1}^T\mathbf{\Sigma}^{-1}\mathbf{E} \\ E^* & \mathbf{E}^T\mathbf{\Sigma}^{-1}\mathbf{E} \end{vmatrix} \mathbf{\Sigma}^{-1}\mathbf{1} + \begin{vmatrix} \mathbf{1}^T\mathbf{\Sigma}^{-1}\mathbf{1} & 1 \\ \mathbf{E}^T\mathbf{\Sigma}^{-1}\mathbf{1} & E^* \end{vmatrix} \mathbf{\Sigma}^{-1}\mathbf{E}}{\begin{vmatrix} \mathbf{1}^T\mathbf{\Sigma}^{-1}\mathbf{1} & \mathbf{1}^T\mathbf{\Sigma}^{-1}\mathbf{E} \\ \mathbf{E}^T\mathbf{\Sigma}^{-1}\mathbf{1} & \mathbf{E}^T\mathbf{\Sigma}^{-1}\mathbf{E} \end{vmatrix}}, \tag{12}$$

where $\mathbf{\Sigma}_{ij} = \nabla_i^{-1}\nabla_j^{-1}J_{ij}$, $\mathbf{E} = (\Delta_1^{-1}, \cdots, \Delta_n^{-1})^T$, and E^* can be computed by

$$E^* = \frac{(xz - y^2)^2 - 2b(x\mathbf{E} - y\mathbf{1})^T\mathbf{\Sigma}^{-1}(z\mathbf{1} - y\mathbf{E})}{2b(x\mathbf{E} - y\mathbf{1})^T\mathbf{\Sigma}^{-1}(x\mathbf{E} - y\mathbf{1})}, \tag{13}$$

where $x = \mathbf{1}^T\mathbf{\Sigma}^{-1}\mathbf{1}$, $y = \mathbf{1}^T\mathbf{\Sigma}^{-1}\mathbf{E}$, and $z = \mathbf{E}^T\mathbf{\Sigma}^{-1}\mathbf{E}$.

After ranking Apps with respect to three different principles, the final challenge is how to organize and index such a large number of Apps with respect to their security levels and categories. Indeed, in an online App recommender system, it is necessary to quickly response users' requests and efficiently manage Apps in its back-end servers. To this end, we propose a data structure for App retrieval, namely *App hash tree*. Figure 5 illustrates an example of an App hash tree, which contains two hierarchies, namely a category level and a security level. For each node in the tree, it holds a hash table to store the index of corresponding Apps. For example, the node "*Root* $\rightarrow c_1 \rightarrow l_3$" may store the index of all Apps belong to category c_1 and security level l_3. Note that the App hash tree can be easily built with some basic tree search algorithms (e.g., *Breadth-First-Search* in our experiments). Actually, the ranking results of Apps in each node can be computed offline and pre-stored in the corresponding nodes of the App hash tree. Therefore, during the online recommendation, the system can quickly look up the ranked list for recommendations to users based on their specific security levels and App categories.

5. EXPERIMENTAL RESULTS

In this section, we empirically evaluate the **S**ecurity and **P**rivacy aware mobile **A**pp **R**ecommendation (SPAR) approach with a large-scale real-world data set.

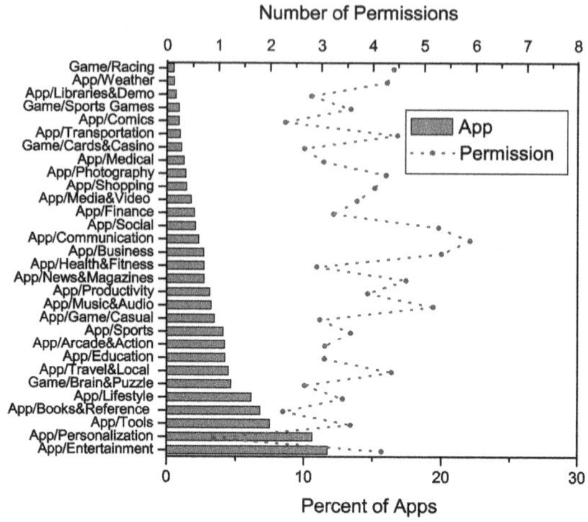

Figure 6: The percent of Apps and the average number of requested permissions by each App in different categories.

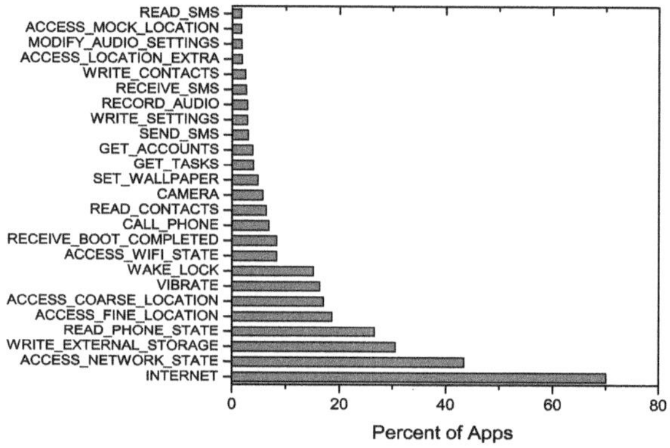

Figure 7: The top 25 most used permissions in our data set and the percent of Apps that request those permissions.

5.1 Experimental Data

The experimental data were collected from Google Play (Android Market) [4] in 2012. This real-world data set includes 170,753 Apps in 30 App categories, and the Apps have 173 unique data access permissions. Particularly, the data set includes more than 25% Apps available at the Android Market, which totally includes 675,000 Apps as of the end of September 2012 [3].

Figure 6 and Figure 7 illustrate some statistics of the data set. Specifically, Figure 6 shows the percent of Apps and the average number of requested permissions by each App in different categories. In this figure, we can observe that Apps in categories "Communication", "Business" and "Social" request more permissions. Figure 7 shows the top 25 most requested permissions and the percent of Apps that request those permissions. In this figure, we can find that most of the Apps request the network and location related permissions. To further study the relationship between permissions and Apps, we show the distributions of the number of Apps with respect to the number of requested permissions in Figure 8 (a). We can see that most of the Apps only request few permissions, which may indicate that not many Apps have security risks. Figure 8 (b) shows the distribution of the number of Apps with respect to the number of their ratings. We can find that the distribution roughly follows the

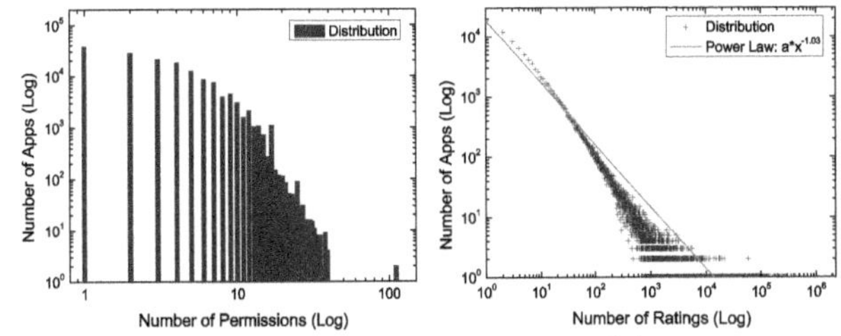

(a) (b)

Figure 8: The distribution of the number of Apps w.r.t (a) the number of requested access permissions, and (b) the number of their ratings.

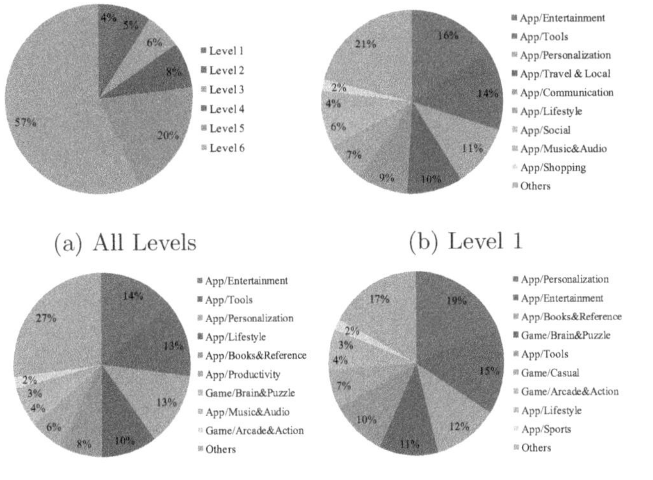

(a) All Levels (b) Level 1

(c) Level 3 (d) Level 6

Figure 9: The percent of (a) Apps and (b)-(d) App categories at different security levels.

power law. This indicates that only using App popularity for recommendation is not enough.

5.2 Evaluation of App Risk Scores

In this subsection, we evaluate the performances of estimating App risk scores and segmenting security levels.

5.2.1 App Security Levels

Specifically, we set the regularization parameters in Equation 3 as $\lambda = 0.5$ and $\mu = 1$, and the settings of PNB are similar as [14]. To segment Apps with respect to their risk scores, we empirically set $\delta = 0.01 \times CV(A)$ in Algorithm 1, where $CV(A)$ is the CV of all App risk scores.

Figure 9 (a) shows the percent of Apps with respect to 6 segmented security levels. We can see that level 6 (i.e., most secure) contains most Apps and the App numbers from level 1 to level 4 are relatively even, which indicate most Apps are secure while only a few Apps have security risks.

Figure 9 (b)-(d) show the percent of App categories at security levels 1, 3, and 6, respectively. In these figures, we can find that Apps with more permissions (e.g., Apps in categories "Tools", "Travel&Local", and "Communication") are more likely to have potential risks, and vice versa (e.g., Apps in categories "Personalization" and "Books&Reference"). Note that, since categories "Entertainment" and "Personalization" contain the largest portion of Apps in our data set, they always have high percent at all security levels.

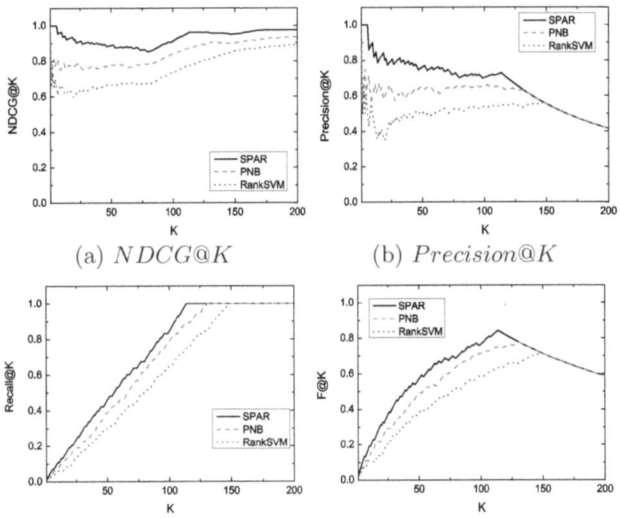

(a) $NDCG@K$ (b) $Precision@K$

(c) $Recall@K$ (d) $F@K$

Figure 10: The performance of each approach w.r.t different metrics based on user judgment.

5.2.2 Evaluation of Ranking App Risk

Evaluation Baselines. We adopt two state-of-the-art baselines to evaluate the performances of our SPAR approach in terms of ranking App risks. To the best of our knowledge, there is only one relevant recent study [14], which can be directly leveraged for ranking App risks. Therefore, we leverage the recommended approach in this work as the first baseline. **Naive Bayes with information Priors** (PNB) [14] aims to learn a Naive Bayes model with parameter θ that can best explain the generative process of permissions, i.e., $P(p_i|\theta)$. Therefore, the risk scores of App a_i can be estimated by $\widetilde{R}_i^a = -\ln P(p_1, \cdots, p_k|\theta)$, where each $p_k \in a_i$. Particularly, this baseline is also used for estimating the prior risk scores in our regularization framework. Moreover, we also use a popular learning-to-rank approach as the second baseline for ranking App risks. **RankSVM** [9] aims to rank App risk by the RankSVM model. Specifically, we manually labeled 200 secure Apps and 200 insecure Apps according to some previous studies [6, 14, 20] as training data. For each App, we used its category, developer, and permissions as features to learn the ranking model.

Evaluation Metrics. Specifically, we set up the evaluation as follows. First, we implemented our SPAR approach and other baselines on all the Apps in the data set. For each approach, we selected 100 top ranked mobile Apps (i.e., most insecure), and 100 bottom ranked mobile Apps (i.e., most secure) in the result. Then, we merged all the selected Apps into a pool which includes 496 unique mobile Apps in our data set. For each App, we invited three users who are familiar with Android Apps to manually label these Apps with score 2 (i.e., **Insecure**), 1 (i.e., **Not Sure**), and 0 (i.e., **Secure**). Each user gave a proper label by comprehensively considering their own experiences (i.e., they can download and try all these Apps), the App profile and the comments from other users. After user evaluation, each App a is assigned a judgement score $f(a) \in [0, 6]$. Moreover, we computed the Cohen's kappa coefficient [2] between each pair of evaluators to estimate the inter-evaluator agreement. The values of Cohen's kappa coefficient are between 0.67 to 0.72 in the user evaluation, which indicate the substantial agreement [11]. Finally, we further ranked the 496 Apps by each approach, and obtained three ranked lists of Apps. Thus, we can exploit the popular metric Normalized Discounted Cumulative Gain (NDCG) for determining the ranking performance of each approach. Specifically, the discounted cumulative gain given a cut-off rank K can be calculated by

$$DCG@K = \sum_{i=1}^{K} \frac{2^{Rel(a_i)} - 1}{\log_2(1+i)},$$

where $Rel(a_i) = f(a_i)$ is the relevance score. The $NDCG@K$ is the $DCG@K$ normalized by the $IDCG@K$, which is the $DCG@K$ value of the ideal ranking list of the returned results. In other words, we have

$$NDCG@K = \frac{DCG@K}{IDCG@K}.$$

$NDCG@K$ indicates how well the ranked order of the given Apps returned by an approach with a cut-off rank K. A larger $NDCG@K$ value indicates the better ranking performance. Particularly, if we treat the 83 commonly agreed insecure Apps (i.e., $f(a) = 6$) as the ground truth, we can evaluate each approach with the widely-used metrics, namely $Precision@K$, $Recall@K$, and $F@K$.

Overall Performances. Figure 10 shows the results of each approach with respect to four different evaluation metrics. In this figure, we can see that SPAR consistently outperforms other baselines and the improvement is more significant for smaller K. These results clearly validate the effectiveness of our regularization based approach. Particularly, the performances of PNB can be refined during the regularization on the bipartite graph. Also, SPAR and PNB outperform RankSVM, which indicates the straightforward learning-to-rank approach is not enough for estimating App risks. Indeed, the performances of learning-to-rank approaches mainly rely on the effectiveness of feature extraction. Based on the above observations, we can argue that SPAR is an appropriate approach for estimating App risks.

Case Study. This evaluation benchmark is based on some prior knowledge from other previous studies. As reported by Zhou *et al* [20], there are 13 Apps which may leak private information according to the TaintDroid system [6]. Here, we select 6 of them (i.e., *Horoscope, Layar, Trapster, Wertago, Astrid Task and DasTelefonbuch*), which are included in our data set, to evaluate SPAR and other baselines. Indeed, we study whether each approach can find these insecure Apps with high risk ranks, since a good approach should have the capability of capturing these suspicious Apps. Table 2 shows the top percentage position of each App in the ranked list returned by each approach. We can see that SPAR can rank those insecure Apps into higher positions than other baselines. Specially, all of these six Apps are categorized into low security levels (i.e., L_1 and L_2) by the segmentation approach, which also validates the effectiveness of our approach.

Table 2: The reported insecure mobile Apps.

	SPAR	PNB	RankSVM
Horoscope	**2.64%**	5.41%	7.13%
Layar	**5.34%**	7.21%	11.81%
Trapster	**6.21%**	9.34%	12.33%
Wertago	**2.72%**	4.89%	8.37%
Astrid Task	**8.09%**	11.29%	13.32%
DasTelefonbuch	**6.18%**	11.71%	14.38%

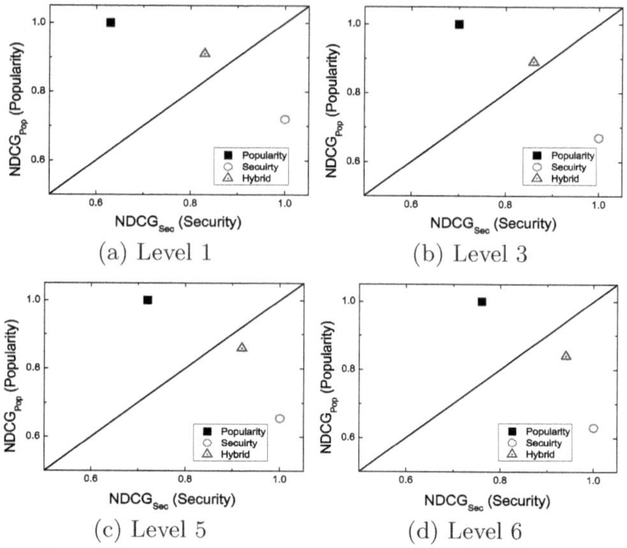

(a) Level 1 (b) Level 3 (c) Level 5 (d) Level 6

Figure 11: The recommendation performances of different ranking principles.

5.3 Evaluation of App Recommendation

Here, we evaluate the recommendation performances of our approach SPAR. Particularly, we use the average rating as the popularity score for each App and the parameter b in Equation 11 equals to the given security level in experiments.

5.3.1 Recommendation Performances

Since our App recommender system is non-personalized, there is no personal data could be used for evaluation. Also, there is no ground truth for us to evaluate which recommendation results really meet users' information needs. Thus, in this paper, we focus on evaluating our recommendation approach SPAR by checking whether it can strike a balance between App popularity and user's security preferences.

Specifically, there are three different ranking principles in our recommendation approach, i.e., popularity, security and hybrid principles. Given an App category and security level, each principle can generate a ranked App list as the recommendation result. Here, we propose to use two metrics $NDCG_{Pop}$ and $NDCG_{Sec}$ to evaluate the the performance of each recommendation result. Compared with traditional $NDCG$, the relevance scores of $NDCG_{Pop}$ and $NDCG_{Sec}$ are set to the popularity score and the reciprocal of risk score, respectively. Intuitively, if a recommendation result has higher $NDCG_{Pop}$ ($NDCG_{Sec}$), it has more emphasis on App popularity (App Security). Figure 11 shows the average recommendation performance across all App categories with respect to different ranking principles and security levels. From the results, we can observe that the hybrid principle can rank Apps with a trade-off between popularity and security, which means the recommended Apps are both popular and secure. Also, with the increase of security levels, the recommendation results have more emphasis on App security than popularity.

5.3.2 A Case Study

To further evaluate the recommendation performances of different ranking methods, we study five Apps in category "*App/Lifestyle*", which are "Weterago", "BeNaughty", "Moment Diary", "SimplyNoise" and "Bedside". Particularly,

Table 3: The case study of App recommendation.

	Recommendation
SEC	SimplyNoise,Moment Diary,Bedside,BeNaughty,Weterago
POP	Weterago,Bedside,Moment Diary,BeNaughty,SimplyNoise
H-1	Bedside,Moment Diary,Weterago,BeNaughty,SimplyNoise
H-3	Moment Diary,Bedside,BeNaughty,SimplyNoise
H-5	Moment Diary,SimplyNoise,Beside
H-6	SimplyNoise,Moment Diary

"Weterago" is one of the reported insecure Apps, and "SimplyNoise" is an App without requesting data access permissions. Table 3 shows the recommendation results, where SEC recommends most secure Apps based on risk scores with security level 1; POP is based on popularity scores (i.e., average ratings) with the security level 1; H-1, H-3, H-5 and H-6 denote the hybrid principle based recommendation with security levels 1, 3, 5 and 6, respectively. From these results, we can observe that the popularity-based method recommends insecure App "Weterago" in the first position, while it has the highest risk score. In contrast, if only using risk scores to recommend Apps, some unpopular Apps (e.g., SimplyNoise) will be ranked higher. Furthermore, we can observe that H-3, H-5, H-6 do not recommend all five Apps for users. The reason is that these methods only take Apps with security levels higher than the given levels as candidates. Finally, we can see that the App "Moment Diary" is ranked the highest by H-3, H-5, since the hybrid principle can reach some balance between popularity and security for App recommendation.

5.4 Efficiency and Scalability

Our approach consists of an offline stage and an online stage. In the offline stage, the computational cost mainly comes from two parts: the computation of regularization for estimating risk scores, and the computation for security level segmentation and building the App hash tree. To evaluate the efficiency and scalability of our approach, we test the running time of each part on different segmentation of the entire data set (i.e., 10%,..., 100%) to illustrate the scalability of our approach. All the tests were conducted on a 3.4GHZ×8-Core CPU, 8G main memory PC. Figure 12 shows the running time of each part with respect to different input data size. We can see that the computation times are almost linear with the size of input data. Thus, our approach is scalable in the offline stage.

In the online stage, given a security level and App category, the recommender system will return the ranked list of Apps to user according to different recommendation principles. Indeed, since the popularity scores (e.g., overall rating) and risk scores can be obtained in the offline stage, and the portfolio optimization for hybrid principle has a close-form solution (e.g., Equation 12), the computational cost in online stage is relatively low. In particular, as discussed in Section 4, the main ranking process can be conducted in advance and pre-stored in the App hash tree. In this case, the online recommendation process will be very fast.

6. RELATED WORK

Generally speaking, the related works of this study can be grouped into two categories.

The first category is about mobile App security. Indeed, many previous studies about security and privacy issues of mobile Apps have been reported. For example, Enck *et al.* [6] proposed a malware detection system named TaintDroid, which can provide efficient real-time analysis of other third party mobile Apps through the monitor of their data

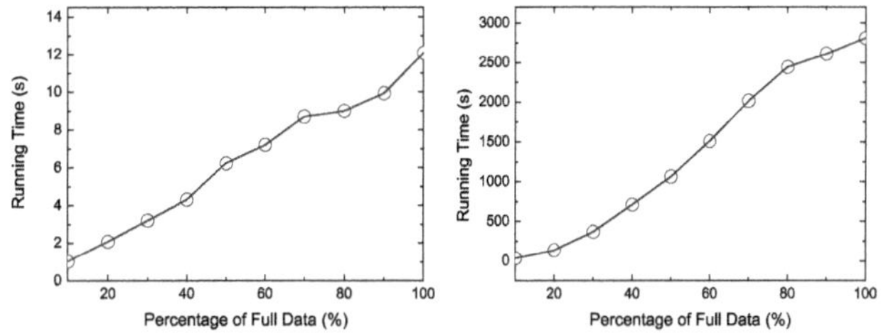

(a) (b)

Figure 12: The running time of (a) each iteration of regularization, and (b) security level segmentation and building the App hash tree.

access behavior. Luo *et al.* [13] discussed the problem of attacks on WebView in the Android system, analyzed the fundamental causes and proposed some potential solutions. To tame the information-stealing mobile Apps, Zhou *et al.* [20] proposed a new privacy model for Android system. Also, they developed a system named TISSA as security middleware to implement this model. Enck *et al.* [7] developed a rule-based certification model and system named Kirin, which can perform lightweight certification of mobile Apps at install time. Indeed, more and more advanced mobile Apps are committed to provide intelligent services for users by requesting various access permissions of users' personal data. To understand these data access permissions, Au *et al.* [5] surveyed the permission systems of several popular smart phone operating systems, such as Apple IOS, and Android. They also discussed the problem of permission over-declaration and proposed some insightful directions of relevant research. Similarly, Felt *et al.* [8] studied the permission requests of over 900 mobile Apps in Android system, and developed a tool named Stowaway to detect the over-privilege in compiled Android Apps.

However, these approaches are very hard to be implemented in practice, since it is not a trivial task to efficiently and accurately detect the malware codes for each mobile App and users often do not want some security software to frequently scan their devices. Recently, Peng *et al.* [14] proposed a novel approach with various probabilistic models for ranking Apps with respect to their risk scores. Although this approach is straightforward and not scalable for external knowledge, it is effective for estimating App risk. Therefore, we propose to leverage this approach for assigning prior risk scores in our regularization framework.

Another category is about mobile App recommendation, which aims to facilitate the choice of mobile users. For example, Yan *et al.* [17] developed a collaborative filtering based mobile App recommender system, namely Appjoy. Different from other mobile App recommender systems, the Appjoy is based on users' App usage records to build preference matrix but not explicit user ratings. However, sometimes the App usage records are very sparse. To solve this problem, Shi *et al.* [15] studied several recommendation models and proposed a content based collaborative filtering model named Eigenapp for recommending Apps in their Web site Getjar. Also, some researchers studied the problem of exploiting enriched contextual information for mobile App recommendation. For example, Yu *et al.* [18] proposed a novel personalized context-aware recommender system by analyzing mobile user's context logs. The proposed approach is based on Latent Dirichlet Allocation topic model and scalable for multiple contextual features. Furthermore, Zhu *et al.* [21] proposed a uniform framework for personalized context-aware recommendation, which can integrate both context independency and dependency assumptions. The framework can mine user's personal context-aware preferences for mobile App recommendation from the context logs of many mobile users. However, all the above recommendation approaches do not take consideration of the potential security/privacy risk of mobile Apps, which motivates our novel mobile App recommender system with security and privacy awareness.

7. CONCLUDING REMARKS

In this paper, we developed a mobile App recommender system with security and privacy awareness. Specifically, without relying on any predefined risk functions, we designed a scalable and automatic approach for estimating the security risks of Mobile Apps. An unique perspective of this approach is the creative use of external knowledge as prior scores and the regularization techniques in an App-permission bipartite graph. Moreover, to consider both Apps' popularity and users' security preferences for recommendations, we introduced a flexible App recommendation method based on the modern portfolio theory. Particularly, we also developed an App hash tree to efficiently look up Apps in recommendation. Finally, the experiments on a large-scale real-world data set clearly validated the effectiveness and efficiency of the proposed recommendation framework.

8. ACKNOWLEDGEMENTS

This work was supported in part by grants from National Science Foundation for Distinguished Young Scholars of China (Grant No. 61325010), Natural Science Foundation of China (NSFC, Grant No. 71329201), and National High Technology Research and Development Program of China (Grant No. SS2014AA012303). This work was also partially supported by grants from National Science Foundation (NSF, Grant No. CCF-1018151 and IIS-1256016), and UNC Charlotte Faculty Research Grants 2014-2015.

9. REFERENCES

[1] http://developer.android.com/.

[2] http://en.wikipedia.org/wiki/cohen's_kappa.

[3] http://en.wikipedia.org/wiki/google_play.

[4] https://play.google.com/apps.

[5] K. W. Y. Au, Y. F. Zhou, Z. Huang, P. Gill, and D. Lie. Short paper: a look at smartphone permission models. In *Proceedings of the 1st ACM workshop on Security and privacy in smartphones and mobile devices*, SPSM '11, pages 63–68, New York, NY, USA, 2011. ACM.

[6] W. Enck, P. Gilbert, B.-G. Chun, L. P. Cox, J. Jung, P. McDaniel, and A. N. Sheth. Taintdroid: an information-flow tracking system for realtime privacy monitoring on smartphones. In *Proceedings of the 9th USENIX conference on Operating systems design and implementation*, OSDI'10, pages 1–6, Berkeley, CA, USA, 2010. USENIX Association.

[7] W. Enck, M. Ongtang, and P. McDaniel. On lightweight mobile phone application certification. In *Proceedings of the 16th ACM conference on Computer and communications security*, CCS '09, pages 235–245, New York, NY, USA, 2009. ACM.

[8] A. P. Felt, E. Chin, S. Hanna, D. Song, and D. Wagner. Android permissions demystified. In *Proceedings of the 18th ACM conference on Computer and communications security*, CCS '11, pages 627–638, New York, NY, USA, 2011. ACM.

[9] T. Joachims. Optimizing search engines using clickthrough data. In *Proceedings of the Eighth ACM SIGKDD International Conference on Knowledge Discovery and Data Mining*, KDD '02, pages 133–142, New York, NY, USA, 2002. ACM.

[10] A. Karatzoglou, L. Baltrunas, K. Church, and M. Böhmer. Climbing the app wall: enabling mobile app discovery through context-aware recommendations. In *Proceedings of the 21st ACM international conference on Information and knowledge management*, CIKM '12, pages 2527–2530, New York, NY, USA, 2012. ACM.

[11] E.-P. Lim, V.-A. Nguyen, N. Jindal, B. Liu, and H. W. Lauw. Detecting product review spammers using rating behaviors. In *Proceedings of the 19th ACM international conference on Information and knowledge management*, CIKM '10, pages 939–948, New York, NY, USA, 2010. ACM.

[12] C. Luo, H. Xiong, W. Zhou, Y. Guo, and G. Deng. Enhancing investment decisions in p2p lending: An investor composition perspective. In *Proceedings of the 17th ACM SIGKDD International Conference on Knowledge Discovery and Data Mining*, KDD '11, pages 292–300, New York, NY, USA, 2011. ACM.

[13] T. Luo, H. Hao, W. Du, Y. Wang, and H. Yin. Attacks on webview in the android system. In *Proceedings of the 27th Annual Computer Security Applications Conference*, ACSAC '11, pages 343–352, New York, NY, USA, 2011. ACM.

[14] H. Peng, C. Gates, B. Sarma, N. Li, Y. Qi, R. Potharaju, C. Nita-Rotaru, and I. Molloy. Using probabilistic generative models for ranking risks of android apps. In *Proceedings of the 2012 ACM Conference on Computer and Communications Security*, CCS '12, pages 241–252, New York, NY, USA, 2012. ACM.

[15] K. Shi and K. Ali. Getjar mobile application recommendations with very sparse datasets. In *Proceedings of the 18th ACM SIGKDD international conference on Knowledge discovery and data mining*, KDD '12, pages 204–212, New York, NY, USA, 2012. ACM.

[16] J. Wang and J. Zhu. Portfolio theory of information retrieval. In *Proceedings of the 32Nd International ACM SIGIR Conference on Research and Development in Information Retrieval*, SIGIR '09, pages 115–122, New York, NY, USA, 2009. ACM.

[17] B. Yan and G. Chen. Appjoy: personalized mobile application discovery. In *Proceedings of the 9th international conference on Mobile systems, applications, and services*, MobiSys '11, pages 113–126, New York, NY, USA, 2011. ACM.

[18] K. Yu, B. Zhang, H. Zhu, H. Cao, and J. Tian. Towards personalized context-aware recommendation by mining context logs through topic models. In *Proceedings of the 16th Pacific-Asia conference on Advances in Knowledge Discovery and Data Mining - Volume Part I*, PAKDD'12, pages 431–443, Berlin, Heidelberg, 2012. Springer-Verlag.

[19] W. Zhang, J. Wang, B. Chen, and X. Zhao. To personalize or not: A risk management perspective. In *Proceedings of the 7th ACM Conference on Recommender Systems*, RecSys '13, pages 229–236, New York, NY, USA, 2013. ACM.

[20] Y. Zhou, X. Zhang, X. Jiang, and V. W. Freeh. Taming information-stealing smartphone applications (on android). In *Proceedings of the 4th international conference on Trust and trustworthy computing*, TRUST'11, pages 93–107, Berlin, Heidelberg, 2011. Springer-Verlag.

[21] H. Zhu, E. Chen, K. Yu, H. Cao, H. Xiong, and J. Tian. Mining personal context-aware preferences for mobile users. In *Proceedings of the IEEE 12th International Conference on Data Mining*, ICDM'12, pages 1212–1217, 2012.

[22] H. Zhu, H. Xiong, Y. Ge, and E. Chen. Ranking fraud detection for mobile apps: A holistic view. In *Proceedings of the 22Nd ACM International Conference on Conference on Information and Knowledge Management*, CIKM '13, pages 619–628, New York, NY, USA, 2013. ACM.

Author Index

www.ingramcontent.com/pod-product-compliance
Lightning Source LLC
LaVergne TN
LVHW080101011026
849160LV00013B/1006